McDougal Littell

MODERN WORLD HISTORY

PATTERNS OF INTERACTION

ANNOTATED TEACHER'S EDITION

ISBN 0-395-93830-9
Printed in the United States of America.
1 2 3 4 5 6 7 8 9–VJM–03 02 01 00 99 98

Table of Contents

Program Overview

Modern World History: Patterns of Interaction is a highly integrated program that provides teachers with a practical and motivational approach to teaching modern world history and to helping students think critically and reflectively. (For more information on each element, see pages T6–T32.)

Motivating and Captivating Students

History comes alive for students when they are actively involved in their own learning. Through interactive situations and lively encounters with people and ideas, students can begin to make personal connections to the past. *Modern World History: Patterns of Interaction* provides those lively encounters and personal connections—from a situation demanding personal involvement at the beginning of each chapter, to connections with people, both great and ordinary, from the past.

❶ Interact with History

In an interactive, imagined situation in each chapter, students encounter the difficult problems and decisions faced by real people of the past. As students put themselves in a key historical situation, they will analyze the issues, explore their options, and become decision-makers.

❷ History Makers

Focusing on people can make history human and fascinating. These short biographies allow students to see the great men and women of world history as individuals in both triumph and adversity.

❸ A Voice from the Past

Authentic primary sources scattered throughout the text resonate with the passions and sharp personal observations of people who lived through the historical periods discussed. These real voices from the past help students see that history is human and accessible.

HISTORY MAKERS

Mohandas K. Gandhi
1869–1948
From 1893 to 1914, Gandhi worked as a lawyer in South Africa, where he fought racial prejudice against Indians. Shortly after his arrival, Gandhi bought a first-class ticket and boarded a train. A white conductor ordered Gandhi to move to the third-class coach, reserved for Indians. But Gandhi refused. The conductor forced Gandhi off the train at the next station.

To honor Gandhi's act of resistance, South African president Nelson Mandela recognized him with a special freedom award in April 1997. Mandela declared,

Today we are righting a century-old wrong. This station, once one of the world's most notorious symbols of discrimination, intolerance, and oppression, today proclaims a message of dignity restored. . . . Gandhi's magnificent example of personal sacrifice and dedication in the face of oppression was one of his many legacies to our country and the world.

Interact *with* History

❶ World War II has been going on for several years—at great cost in lives to your side and the enemy's. You are an air force commander who has just received a report from military intelligence. The report identifies a city in enemy territory that is a major weapons manufacturing center. You and other officers know that by destroying the arms factories in the city, the war could be shortened. Thousands of lives could be saved. On the other hand, the bombing will kill hundreds, maybe thousands, of civilians living near the enemy factories. How do you weigh the lives that will be saved against the lives that will be lost?

Would you bomb this city?

One plane-load of bombs will wipe out a vital enemy weapons factory, along with hundreds of civilian homes around it.

Radar tells the pilot where to drop the bombs, but at 10,000 feet, he cannot see the casualties they will cause.

This is a bomb factory in the middle of a residential area.

This raid will probably shorten the war by at least two months.

EXAMINING *the* ISSUES

- Does shortening a war to save lives justify killing civilians?

- How are civilians sometimes as much a part of a war effort as soldiers?

- What percentage of lives saved would justify the deaths caused in the bombing?

As a class, discuss these questions. In your discussion, weigh the arguments for and against both choices.

As you read about World War II, think about the role that civilians play in a situation of total war. Think also about the hard moral choices that people often face in times of war.

440 Chapter 16

---

❸ **A VOICE FROM THE PAST**
We were raised on a mountain of lies. There was a fantastical difference between the things they told us and the things we saw. They published incredible statistics on agricultural production, and in the shops there was nothing to eat. On paper, we had freedom of expression, but anytime anyone said anything, members of the Communist Party told us to keep our mouths shut.
STEFAN GHENCEA, Romanian student

1 Hitler's Lightning War

TERMS & NAMES
- nonaggression pact
- blitzkrieg
- Charles de Gaulle
- Winston Churchill
- Battle of Britain
- Atlantic Charter

MAIN IDEA	WHY IT MATTERS NOW
Using the sudden, mass attack called the blitzkrieg, Germany overran much of Europe and North Africa.	Hitler's actions set off World War II. The results of the war still affect the politics and economics of today's world.

SETTING THE STAGE During the 1930s, Hitler played on the hopes and fears of the Western democracies. Each time the Nazi dictator grabbed new territory, he would declare an end to his demands. Peace seemed guaranteed—until Hitler started expanding again.

Germany Sparks a New War in Europe

After his moves into the Rhineland (March 1936), Austria (March 1938), and Czechoslovakia (September 1938 and March 1939), the Führer turned his eyes to Poland. On April 28, 1939, Hitler spoke before the Reichstag. He demanded that the Polish Corridor, along with its port city of Danzig, be returned to Germany. After World War I, the Allies had cut out the Polish Corridor from German territory to give Poland access to the sea.

This time, Great Britain and France decided to resist this threat of aggression. At this point, as was mentioned in Chapter 15, Soviet dictator Joseph Stalin signed a 10-year **nonaggression pact** with Hitler on August 23. After being excluded from the Munich Conference, Stalin was not eager to join with the West. Also, Hitler was promising him territory. In the public part of the pact, Germany and the Soviet Union promised not to attack each other. Secretly, however, they agreed that they would divide Poland between them. They also secretly agreed that the USSR could take over Finland and the Baltic countries (Lithuania, Latvia, and Estonia).

Germany's Lightning Attack on Poland The new nonaggression pact removed the threat to Germany of a Soviet attack from the east. Hitler then quickly moved ahead with plans to conquer Poland. His surprise attack took place at dawn on September 1, 1939. German warplanes invaded Polish airspace, raining bombs and terror on the Poles. At the same time, German tanks and troop trucks rumbled across the Polish border. The trucks carried more than 1.5 million soldiers into the assault. German aircraft and artillery then began a merciless bombing of Poland's capit[...] stun[...] Polis[...]

Fr[...] three[...] Hitle[...] y on September 3. But Poland fell [...] ary response. After his victory, [...] had a large German population.

Ein Volk, ein Reich, ein Führer!

A propaganda poster proclaims to the German nation: "One People, One Reich, One Führer!"

Background
Hitler hated communism, as Stalin despised fascism. Nonetheless, Hitler did not want to fight both the Allies *and* the Soviet Union. And Stalin wanted to keep his country out of a costly European war.

World War II **441**

Daily Life

The Cultural Revolution

The Cultural Revolution started in 1966, when Chihua Wen was eight years old. For the next decade, his world, and that of every other Chinese child, was turned inside out.

Wen's neighbors were well-known revolutionary writers and loyal members of the Communist Party. Their loyalty became meaningless, however, the night the Red Guards (shown above) stormed into their apartment. There was the sound of breaking glass and a child's scream. Then the teenaged Guards carried a sack of books out to the yard and set them on fire.

They returned to the apartment and emerged carrying two heavy sacks. As they raced off with the sacks in the back of the truck, Wen heard sounds of gagging. "No one ever saw the couple or their child again," he said. And Wen never forgot what he had seen.

---

5 Panama Canal

The Panama Canal is considered one of the world's greatest engineering accomplishments. Its completion changed the course of history by opening a worldwide trade route between the Atlantic and Pacific oceans. As shown in the 1914 map below, ships are raised and lowered a total of 170 feet during the 51-mile trip through the canal. It usually takes 15 to 20 hours.

The canal also had a lasting effect on other technologies. Ships are now built to dimensions that will allow them to pass through its locks.

This 1910 engraving shows the excavation of the Gaillard, or Culebra, Cut, at the narrowest part of the canal. Completion of this nine-mile cut took seven years because of frequent landslides. By the time the entire canal was finished, workers had dug up about 211 million cubic yards of earth.

The Gatun Locks include three levels of water-filled chambers that raise or lower ships 85 feet. Electric locomotives called mules help guide ships through the locks.

Canal Facts
- The canal took ten years to build (1904–1914) and cost $380 million.
- Thousands of workers died from diseases while building it.
- The trip from San Francisco to New York City via the Panama Canal is about 7,800 miles shorter than the trip around South America.
- The canal now handles more than 13,000 ships a year from around 70 nations carrying 168 million short tons of cargo.
- The United States now collects about $340 million a year in tolls.
- Panama will take control of the canal on December 31, 1999.

Connect to History
Identifying Problems What difficulties did workers face in constructing the canal?
SEE SKILLBUILDER HANDBOOK, PAGE 651

Connect to Today
Evaluating Decisions In the more than 80 years since it was built, do you think that the benefits of the Panama Canal to world trade have outweighed the costs in time, money, and human life? Explain your answer.

---

4 Main Idea and Why It Matters Now

By answering the old question, "Why does it matter now?" students begin to understand that historical events have influenced their own lives. Every section of *World History: Patterns of Interaction* clearly tells students the key concept of the section and explains why it matters.

5 Science & Technology

High-interest features such as Science & Technology involve students in learning how the Panama Canal was built, how the field of aviation developed, and other fascinating technological marvels. Students learn about the impact of science on history through the combination of pictures and words in these engaging and interactive features.

6 Daily Life

A sure way to get students motivated and involved is to show them how people really lived. The Daily Life features describe how people worked and played and provide some thought-provoking facts about their lives.

Finding Support for Reading and Understanding

Providing the resources for students to read critically and reflectively is a key aspect of *Modern World History: Patterns of Interaction*. Many resources help all students and every learning style:

- inner-column notes and questions
- graphics combining visual and verbal information
- assessment questions based on critical-thinking strategies
- visual summaries

1 Think Through History

These questions in the inner columns of the text help students both check their comprehension and think critically about historical events.

2 Vocabulary

Vocabulary notes define difficult words just when a reader might need help—at point of use.

3 Maps

Several hundred maps, developed with the latest computer technology, work together with the text to explain historical events and to help students explore their meanings

4 Visual Summary

A visual summary of the most important ideas and events ends each chapter. Some are cause-and-effect flow charts, others are time lines, still others are topical and thematic charts—all give visual learners and others another path to understanding.

---

1 THINK THROUGH HISTORY
A. Summarizing
How did Europe's colonial subjects help in the war effort?

2 **Vocabulary**
blockade: the forced closing off of a city or other area to traffic and communication through the use of ships or land forces.

English and French troops attacked Germany's four African possessions. They seized control of three.

Elsewhere in Asia and Africa, the British and French recruited subjects in their colonies for the struggle. Fighting troops as well as laborers came from India, South Africa, Senegal, Egypt, Algeria, and Indochina. Many fought and died on the battlefield. Others worked to keep the frontlines supplied. Some colonial subjects wanted nothing to do with their European rulers' conflicts. Others volunteered in the hope that service would lead to their independence. This was the view of Indian political leader Mohandas Gandhi, who supported Indian participation in the war. "If we would improve our status through the help and cooperation of the British," he wrote, "it was our duty to win their help by standing by them in their hour of need."

The United States Enters the War In 1917, the focus of the war shifted to the high seas. That year, the Germans intensified the submarine warfare that had raged in the Atlantic Ocean since shortly after the war began. By 1917, failed crops, as well as a British naval blockade, caused severe food shortages in Germany. Desperate to strike back, Germany decided to establish its own naval blockade around Britain. In January 1917, the Germans announced that their submarines would sink without warning any ship in the waters around Britain. This policy was called **unrestricted submarine warfare.**

The Germans had tried this policy before. On May 7, 1915, a German submarine, or U-boat, had sunk the British passenger ship *Lusitania.* The attack left 1,198 people dead, including 128 U.S. citizens. Germany claimed that the ship had been carrying ammunition—which turned out to be true. Nevertheless, the American public was outraged. President Woodrow Wilson sent a strong protest to Germany. After two further attacks, the Germans finally agreed to stop attacking neutral and passenger ships.

However, the Germans returned to unrestricted submarine warfare in 1917. They knew it might lead to war with the United States. They gambled that their naval

THINK THROUGH HISTORY
A. Summarizing
How did Europe's colonial subjects help in the war effort?

Vocabulary
blockade: the forced closing off of a city or other area to traffic and communication through the use of ships or land forces.

3 **The World at War, 1914–1918**

War rages in Southwest Asia as Arab nationalists battle their Turkish rulers.

Main fighting of the war occurs on Western and Eastern Fronts.

Japan declares war on Germany in 1914; seizes German colonies in China and the Pacific.

The United States enters the war on the side of the Allies in 1917.

Brazil is the only South American country to enter the war. It supports the Allies with warships and personnel.

The European colonies throughout Africa become a battlefield as the warring parties strike at one another's colonial possessions.

India provides about 1.3 million men to fight and labor alongside their British rulers throughout Europe.

Both countries fight on the side of the Allies and contribute many troops to the Gallipoli campaign of 1915, in Southwest Asia.

NORTH AMERICA · ATLANTIC OCEAN · PACIFIC OCEAN · SOUTH AMERICA · AFRICA · EUROPE · ASIA · SOUTHWEST ASIA · INDIA · JAPAN · AUSTRALIA · PACIFIC OCEAN

4,000 Miles
8,000 Kilometers

GEOGRAPHY SKILLBUILDER: Interpreting Maps
1. **Region** Which countries were aligned with the European Allies?
2. **Location** Outside of Europe, where was World War I fought?

374 Chapter 13

Visual Summary

4 **15 Years of Democratic Struggles**

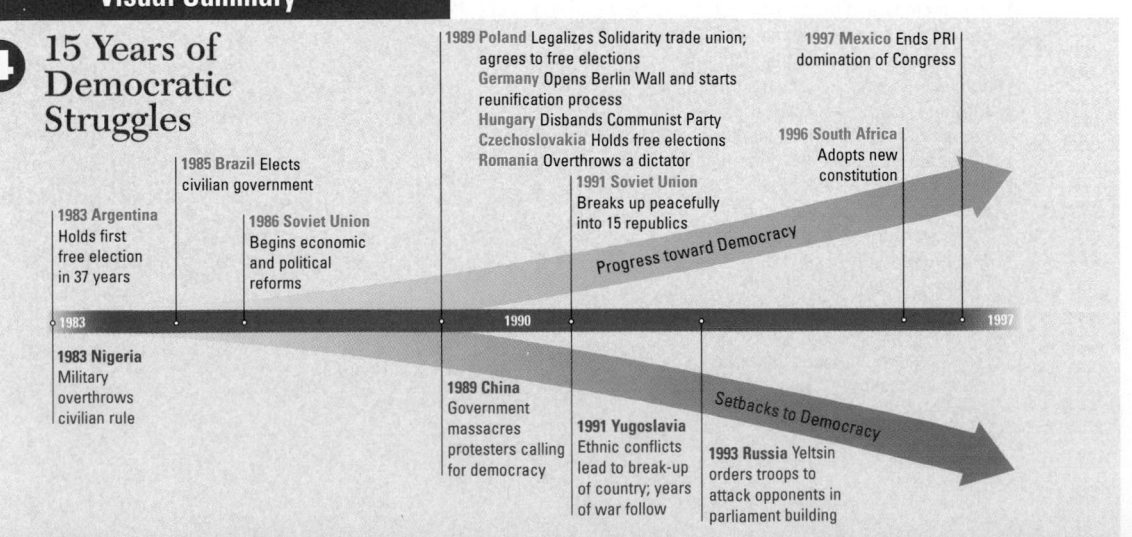

1983 Argentina Holds first free election in 37 years

1983 Nigeria Military overthrows civilian rule

1985 Brazil Elects civilian government

1986 Soviet Union Begins economic and political reforms

1989 China Government massacres protesters calling for democracy

1989 Poland Legalizes Solidarity trade union; agrees to free elections
Germany Opens Berlin Wall and starts reunification process
Hungary Disbands Communist Party
Czechoslovakia Holds free elections
Romania Overthrows a dictator

1991 Soviet Union Breaks up peacefully into 15 republics

1991 Yugoslavia Ethnic conflicts lead to break-up of country; years of war follow

1993 Russia Yeltsin orders troops to attack opponents in parliament building

1997 Mexico Ends PRI domination of Congress

1996 South Africa Adopts new constitution

Progress toward Democracy

Setbacks to Democracy

1983 · 1990 · 1997

blockade would starve Britain into defeat before the United States could mobilize. Ignoring warnings by President Wilson, German U-boats sank three American ships.

In February 1917, another German action pushed the United States closer to war. The British intercepted a telegram from Germany's foreign secretary, Arthur Zimmermann, to the German ambassador in Mexico. The message said that Germany would help Mexico "reconquer" the land it had lost to the United States if Mexico would ally itself with Germany. The British decoded the message and gave it to the U.S. government.

When the Zimmermann note was made public, Americans called for war against Germany. Even before news of the note, many Americans had sided with the Allies. A large part of the American population felt a bond with England. The two nations shared a common ancestry and language, as well as similar democratic institutions and legal systems. In addition, reports—some true and others not—of German war atrocities stirred anti-German sentiment in the United States. More important, America's economic ties with the Allies were far stronger than those with the Central Powers. America traded with Great Britain and France more than twice as much as with Germany.

The Zimmermann note simply proved to be the last straw. On April 2, 1917, President Wilson asked Congress to declare war. The United States entered the war on the side of the Allies.

Background
Land Mexico considered "lost" to the United States included New Mexico, Texas, and Arizona.

Vocabulary
atrocity: an act of extreme cruelty or violence.

War Affects the Home Front

By the time the United States joined the Allies, the war had been going on for nearly three years. In those three years, Europe had lost more men in battle than in all the wars of the previous three centuries. The war had claimed the lives of millions and had changed countless lives forever. The Great War, as the conflict came to be known, affected everyone. It touched not only the soldiers in the trenches, but civilians as well. It affected not just military institutions, but also political, economic, and social institutions.

Governments Wage Total War World War I soon became a **total war.** This meant that countries devoted all their resources to the war effort. In Britain, Germany, Austria, Russia, and France, the entire force of government was dedicated to winning the conflict.

In each country, the wartime government took control of the economy. Governments told factories what to produce and how much. Numerous facilities were converted to munitions factories. Nearly every able-bodied civilian was put to work. Unemployment in many European countries nearly disappeared. European governments even enlisted the help of foreign workers. For example, thousands of civilians were deported from German-occupied Belgium and France to work in Germany as farm and factory laborers. Britain and France recruited Chinese, West Indian, Algerian, and Egyptian laborers to work behind their lines at the front.

So many goods were in short supply that governments turned to **rationing.** Under this system, people could buy only small amounts of those items that were also needed for the war effort. Eventually, rationing covered a wide range of goods, from butter to shoe leather.

Governments also suppressed antiwar activity—sometimes forcibly. In addition, they censored news about the war. Many leaders feared

GlobalImpact

Influenza Epidemic
In the spring of 1918, a powerful new enemy emerged, threatening nations on each side of World War I. This "enemy" was a deadly strain of influenza. The Spanish flu, as it was popularly known, hit England and India in May. By the fall, it had spread through Europe, Russia, Asia, and to the United States.

The influenza epidemic killed soldiers and civilians alike. [...] at least 12 million people die [...] influenza. In Berlin, on a sing[...] in October, 1,500 people died [...] end, this global epidemic wa[...] destructive than the war itse[...] killing 20 million people worl[...]

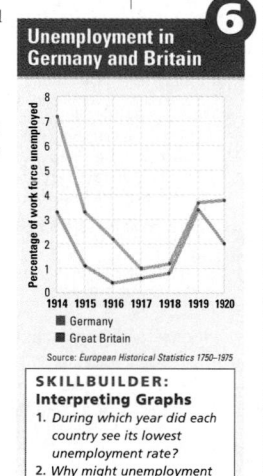

Unemployment in Germany and Britain

Percentage of work force unemployed

1914 1915 1916 1917 1918 1919 1920

■ Germany
■ Great Britain

Source: *European Historical Statistics 1750–1975*

SKILLBUILDER: Interpreting Graphs
1. *During which year did each country see its lowest unemployment rate?*
2. *Why might unemployment have been lowest during the war years?*

The Great War **375**

---

⑤ Background

Occasionally enhancing and extending the text, the background notes provide that little bit of additional information that helps readers comprehend.

⑥ Graphs

State-of-the-art graphs throughout the text present information and build critical-thinking skills through thought-provoking questions.

⑦ Section Assessments

Section and chapter assessments explicitly draw on various critical-thinking strategies to help students focus on the crucial process of becoming proficient thinkers. Among the strategies used are identifying and defining key concepts, using graphics to organize information, answering various critical-thinking questions, and analyzing and applying themes.

Background
Land Mexico considered "lost" to the United States included New Mexico, Texas, and Arizona.

---

⑦

Section ⑤ Assessment

1. TERMS & NAMES

Identify
- Pacific Rim
- King Mongkut
- Emilio Aguinaldo
- annexation
- Queen Liliuokalani

2. TAKING NOTES

Re-create on your paper the spider map below. In each circle, identify a Western power and the areas it controlled.

Western powers in Southeast Asia

3. DRAWING CONCLUSIONS

How did the reforms of the Siamese kings maintain Siam's independence?

THINK ABOUT
- what was happening to Siam's neighbors
- the results of the changes

4. THEME ACTIVITY

Empire Building Compose a series of letters to the editor expressing different views on the overthrow of the Hawaiian queen. Include both the Hawaiian and American views on this event.

Discovering Connections Across Time and Place

History becomes meaningful when students make connections between the past and the present, when they consider how historical events have influenced their lives, and when they discover some of the fascinating recurring patterns of history across the centuries. *Modern World History: Patterns of Interaction* provides many ways to make connections—both around the world and across time—from high-interest features like Global Impact and Something in Common to the sweeping themes of history.

❶ Chapter Openers

A two-page map giving the time and place of each chapter's content, along with images of people and events from the chapter and short anecdotes, offer a richly tempting introduction to the history to come. The connections among geography, history, and themes are firmly established.

❷ Previewing Themes

Themes emphasized throughout the text make the connections across time and place vividly real. The eight themes include Power and Authority, Religious and Ethical Systems, Revolution, Interaction with Environment, Economics, Cultural Interaction, Empire Building, and Science and Technology.

❸ Internet Connection

The McDougal Littell internet address leads students to a rich web site where they can learn more about the people and events featured in the chapter.

❹ Global Impact

These features, which occur in every unit, use pictures and words to help students see how certain major events or movements can have a great impact on history.

❺ Video

Eight videos developed especially for *Modern World History: Patterns of Interaction* portray the passions, conflicts, controversies, and triumphs of a developing world. By helping your students make connections across time and place, the videos make the patterns of history comprehensible.

PREVIEWING THE CHAPTER
Section **1** **PATTERNS OF CHANGE** **Democracy**
CASE STUDY: Latin American Democracies
Section **2** **Democratic Challenges in African Nations**
Section **3** **Gorbachev Moves Toward Democracy**
Section **4** **Collapse of the Soviet Union**
Section **5** **China Follows Its Own Path**

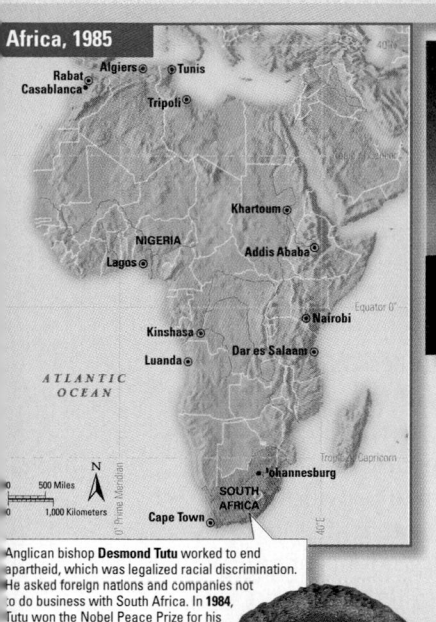

Africa, 1985

Rabat, Casablanca, Algiers, Tunis, Tripoli, Khartoum, NIGERIA, Lagos, Addis Ababa, Kinshasa, Nairobi, Luanda, Dar es Salaam, ATLANTIC OCEAN, Johannesburg, SOUTH AFRICA, Cape Town

Equator 0°
Tropic of Capricorn
0° Prime Meridian
500 Miles
1,000 Kilometers
40°E

Anglican bishop **Desmond Tutu** worked to end apartheid, which was legalized racial discrimination. He asked foreign nations and companies not to do business with South Africa. In **1984**, Tutu won the Nobel Peace Prize for his nonviolent methods.

In **1956**, the government of Brazil began to build a new capital city, **Brasília**, in the wilderness. Planners designed the city to look like a drawn bow and arrow from the air. Builders constructed many modern buildings, such as the bowl-shaped Chamber of Deputies and the twin towers that are home to congressional offices.

MEXICO, Mexico City, Gulf of Mexico, Havana, Tropic of Cancer, Caribbean Sea, ATLANTIC OCEAN, Bogotá, 0° Equator, Lima, BRAZIL, Salvador, La Paz, Brasília, Tropic of Capricorn, Rio de Janeiro, PACIFIC OCEAN, Buenos Aires, Montevideo, ARGENTINA, 40°W, 0, 500 Miles

6 Patterns of Change

Important sections called Patterns of Change provide case studies of large historical trends that caused great changes in people's ways of thinking and living. Focusing on one example of a large trend helps students see the patterns reflected in the lives of individuals not unlike themselves.

7 Something in Common

Weddings, sports, burials, healing arts, and entertainment are among the common threads that connect people across time and place. Special features in every unit use text and pictures to show students these common patterns.

8 Connect to History and Connect to Today

Each special feature in the text helps students make connections to the past and to the present.

SOMETHING IN COMMON *across cultures*

Wedding Rituals

In cultures throughout the world, people get married. They do so for a variety of reasons: to share life with a loved one, to raise a family, to gain social position, to gain independence, to carry on values and customs. In India, an elaborate wedding ritual has evolved within the Hindu tradition. That ritual expresses Hindus' deepest beliefs about the relationship between men and women, the importance of the family, and the role of the spiritual in the significant moments of life. Other cultures have different rituals with which they surround the wedding ceremony.

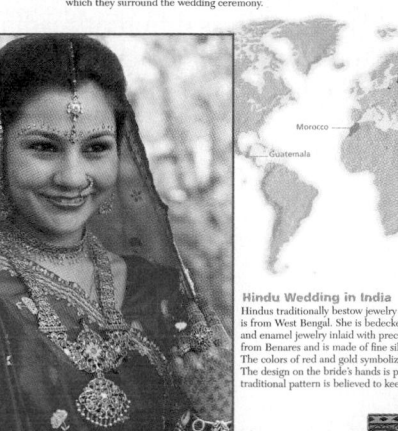

Russia, Morocco, Guatemala, India

Orthodox Wedding in Russia
The Church of the Transfiguration in St. Petersburg, Russia, is the site of this Russian Orthodox wedding ceremony. Crowns are held on the heads of the bride and groom, who hold candles. Orthodox churches make lavish use of gold and rich decoration to display religious works of art such as icons.

A Bridal Fair in Morocco
The bridal fair is part of the marriage ritual of some Berbers of Morocco. Marriageable young men and women attend the fair of Imilchil in the Atlas Mountains of North Africa in search of spouses. The women wear capes, headdresses, and veils as they survey the eligible prospects during the fair. Courtship, engagement, and marriage all take place during the three days of the fair. The couples shown are waiting to enter the wedding tent.

Wedding in Guatemala
The Indians shown to the left are of Mayan descent. They live in the highlands of Guatemala. Villagers in Guatemala combine suit jackets and Indian clothing in a wedding ceremony. The clothes worn by the Indians identify their home villages.

Hindu Wedding in India
Hindus traditionally bestow jewelry on brides. This bride is from West Bengal. She is bedecked with gold, silver, and enamel jewelry inlaid with precious stones. Her sari is from Benares and is made of fine silk and gold brocade. The colors of red and gold symbolize life and good luck. The design on the bride's hands is painted in henna. This traditional pattern is believed to keep away evil spirits.

A gold necklace called a thali is placed around the bride's...

In this Hindu wedding ritual, the bride is shrouded in a white sheet and tied...

8 Connect *to* History

Comparing What are some elements of the wedding ceremony that seem common from one culture to another?

SEE SKILLBUILDER HANDBOOK, PAGE 654.

Connect *to* Today

Researching Read about wedding rituals in other cultures, and then write a couple of paragraphs describing the ritual that most appeals to you.

Connect *to* History
Comparing What are some elements of the wedding ceremony that seem common from one culture to another?
SEE SKILLBUILDER HANDBOOK, PAGE 654.
Connect *to* Today
Researching Read about wedding rituals in other cultures, and then write a couple of paragraphs describing the ritual that most...

Teacher's Resource Materials

From block scheduling to teaching students acquiring English, teachers are structuring their history lessons to make them work in today's classrooms. *Modern World History: Patterns of Interaction* provides a full range of options to help you teach our shared heritage in ways that meet the needs of your students.

In-Depth Unit Resources

One book for each unit, organized by chapter, includes the following complete set of options for reinforcement, practice, enrichment, and extension:

- **Guided Reading** worksheets develop essential reading skills.

- **Skillbuilder Practice** worksheets supplement the Skillbuilder Handbook in the pupil edition.

- **Geography Application** worksheets provide practice in geography skills.

- **Primary Source** materials feature political cartoons, historical documents, diary entries, letters, and much more.

- **Literature Selection** pages let your students experience history through relevant works of literature.

- **History Maker** pages provide additional short biographies to augment those in each chapter.

- **Connections Across Time and Cultures** provide links between different eras by comparing similar events and developments in different times and places.

- **Science & Technology** worksheets develop, extend, and build upon the Science & Technology features in the Pupil's Edition.

Electronic Teacher Tools

Includes the print ancillaries on CD-ROM for convenience and easy access.

Lesson Plans

Provides a two-page lesson plan for each section of the Pupil's Edition. Each lesson plan incorporates print and electronic ancillaries and Internet references. Each plan provides customizing options for teaching less-proficient readers, for students acquiring English, for block scheduling, and for teaching thematically.

Planning for Block Schedules

Includes a pacing guide, chapter teaching models, organization charts, and suggestions for addressing multiple learning styles.

Outline Maps

Provides blackline masters for geography skills development.

Telescoping the Times: Chapter Summaries

Helps address different reading speeds, time constraints due to block scheduling, and the need to reteach. Also available in Spanish.

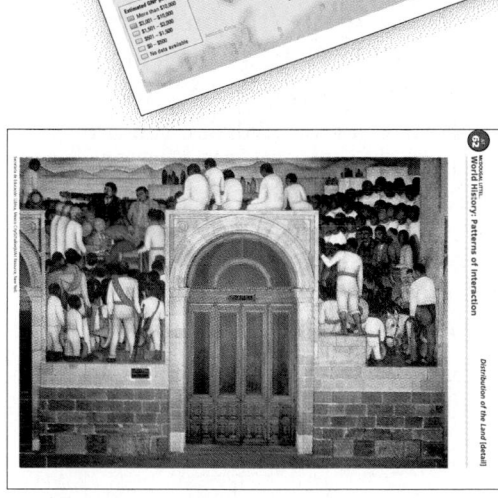

Case Studies

Provides 9 in-depth case studies of important issues in modern world history.

Access for Students Acquiring English: Spanish Translations

Provides strategies for teaching ESL students and Spanish translations of Chapter Summaries and of Guided Reading, Skillbuilder Practice, and Geography Application worksheets.

Writing for Social Studies

Offers support for writing research papers, historical narratives, essays, interviews, oral histories, book reviews, and short reports.

Test Generator

Includes all questions in the Section Quizzes and Chapter Tests, forms A and B—plus ten new test items for each chapter, leveled for basic and advanced students.

Warm-Up Transparencies

Five-minute warm-up activities help introduce each section of a chapter.

Formal Assessment

Includes the following:

- Section Quizzes
- Chapter Tests, Forms A and B
- Additional Test Questions
- ACT/SAT Test Practice
- Standards for Evaluating Writing

Alternative Assessment

Provides explanations and forms for a variety of assessment options, including cooperative learning, group discussion, role-playing, oral presentation, peer assessment, self-assessment, and portfolio assessment.

History from Visuals: Transparencies

Enliven lessons with three volumes of transparencies focusing on Critical Thinking, Geography, and World Art and Cultures.

Reading Study Guide

Provides access to history content and reading support for less proficient readers and students acquiring English. Also available in Spanish.

Video Series and Technology

Modern World History: Patterns of Interaction enables you to expand students' understanding by offering a wide array of technology, including an integrated video series.

VIDEOS

Patterns of Interaction

The eight-video *Patterns of Interaction* series relates to the *Global Impact* features in the text. These videos help students see how cultural interactions have shaped our world and how patterns in history continue to the present day. Each video is 10-12 minutes in length. The *Patterns of Interaction* Resource Book provides you with all the pre-teaching and post-teaching activities you need. Included in the series are:

Volume 1
- **Building Empires:**
  The Rise of the Persians and the Inca

- **Trade Connects the World:**
  Silk Roads and the Pacific Rim

Volume 2
- **The Spread of Epidemic Disease:**
  Bubonic Plague and Smallpox

- **The Geography of Food:**
  The Impact of Potatoes and Sugar

Volume 3
- **Struggling Toward Democracy:**
  Revolutions in Latin America and South Africa

- **Technology Transforms an Age:**
  The Industrial and Electronic Revolutions

Volume 4
- **Arming for War:**
  Modern and Medieval Weapons

- **Cultural Crossroads:**
  The United States and the World

AUDIOCASSETTES

Chapter Summaries on Audiocassette
Reinforce learning with recorded reading of each chapter summary. Available in English and Spanish.

SOFTWARE

Test Generator
Includes all questions in the formal assessment book, indexed by difficulty level. Available for Macintosh® and Windows®

McDougal Littell World History Curriculum Center

Visit **www.mlworldhistory.com** and click on the World History Curriculum Center for a wide range of information and activities you can put to immediate use. Handy point-and-click icons show the way to a world of possibilities:

- **World History Activities** integrate the Internet with sections of the textbook.

- **Professional Development Links** provide instant access to supplemental teaching and professional development resources.

- **Discussion Groups** encourage teacher-to-teacher exchanges on topics surrounding the teaching of world history.

- **The Diverse Classroom** focuses discussions on management techniques and teaching tools to maintain a successfully inclusive classroom.

Modern World History: Electronic Library of Primary Sources on CD-ROM

These primary source selections are correlated with every lesson in the text and include background information and reading comprehension questions.

Electronic Teacher Tools

Includes the print ancillaries on CD-ROM for convenience and easy access.

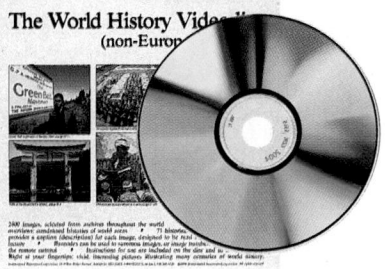

The World History Videodisc/

Enhance any lesson with still images, maps, and historical film footage. Also available on CD-ROM

Battles of the World on CD-ROM

Includes reenactments of main battles, a 4,000-year time line, a comprehensive war database, and analysis of military strategy.

Religions of the World on CD-ROM

Explore the beliefs and practices of the world's religions with over 1,000 photographs, maps, and illustrations.

The Western Civilization Videodisc

Enhance any lesson with still images, maps, and historical film footage.

Chapter Planning Guide

A convenient two-page planning guide can be found at the beginning of every chapter in the teacher's edition of *Modern World History: Patterns of Interaction.* The guide offers invaluable information and options to help you devise the most effective course of instruction.

1 Key Ideas

A chronological, section-by-section summary listing of the key ideas in each chapter. Each column of key ideas connects to the unifying theme for the whole chapter.

2 Copy Masters

A complete listing of reproducible materials for each section reveals the depth of resource material that is available.

3 Assessment

This column locates pages on which quizzes and tests are available for the section or chapter. Alternative assessment guidelines are also noted.

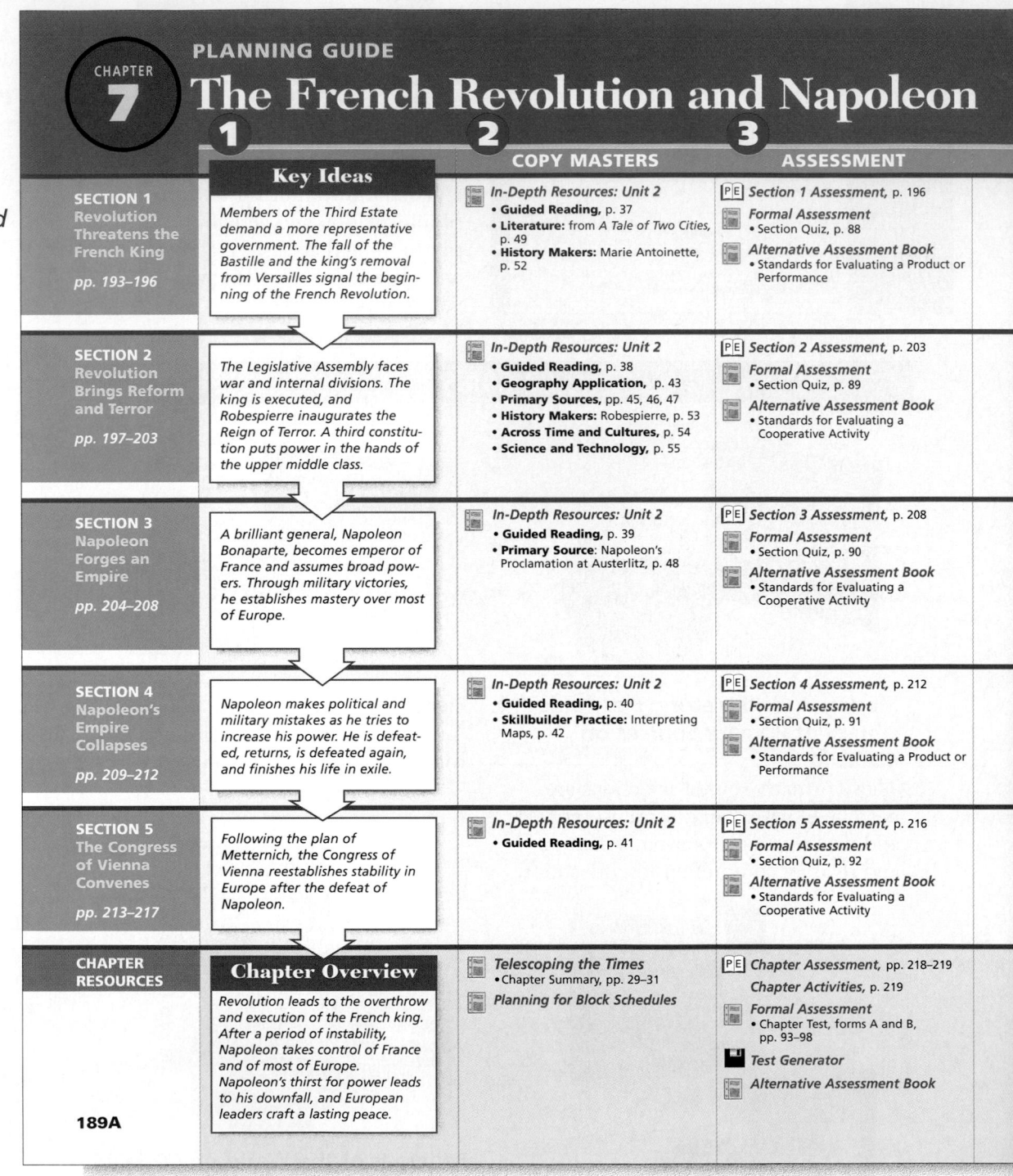

PLANNING GUIDE

CHAPTER **7**

The French Revolution and Napoleon

1 Key Ideas	**2 COPY MASTERS**	**3 ASSESSMENT**
SECTION 1 Revolution Threatens the French King pp. 193–196	Members of the Third Estate demand a more representative government. The fall of the Bastille and the king's removal from Versailles signal the beginning of the French Revolution.	*In-Depth Resources: Unit 2* • **Guided Reading,** p. 37 • **Literature:** from *A Tale of Two Cities,* p. 49 • **History Makers:** Marie Antoinette, p. 52	*Section 1 Assessment,* p. 196 *Formal Assessment* • Section Quiz, p. 88 *Alternative Assessment Book* • Standards for Evaluating a Product or Performance
SECTION 2 Revolution Brings Reform and Terror pp. 197–203	The Legislative Assembly faces war and internal divisions. The king is executed, and Robespierre inaugurates the Reign of Terror. A third constitution puts power in the hands of the upper middle class.	*In-Depth Resources: Unit 2* • **Guided Reading,** p. 38 • **Geography Application,** p. 43 • **Primary Sources,** pp. 45, 46, 47 • **History Makers:** Robespierre, p. 53 • **Across Time and Cultures,** p. 54 • **Science and Technology,** p. 55	*Section 2 Assessment,* p. 203 *Formal Assessment* • Section Quiz, p. 89 *Alternative Assessment Book* • Standards for Evaluating a Cooperative Activity
SECTION 3 Napoleon Forges an Empire pp. 204–208	A brilliant general, Napoleon Bonaparte, becomes emperor of France and assumes broad powers. Through military victories, he establishes mastery over most of Europe.	*In-Depth Resources: Unit 2* • **Guided Reading,** p. 39 • **Primary Source:** Napoleon's Proclamation at Austerlitz, p. 48	*Section 3 Assessment,* p. 208 *Formal Assessment* • Section Quiz, p. 90 *Alternative Assessment Book* • Standards for Evaluating a Cooperative Activity
SECTION 4 Napoleon's Empire Collapses pp. 209–212	Napoleon makes political and military mistakes as he tries to increase his power. He is defeated, returns, is defeated again, and finishes his life in exile.	*In-Depth Resources: Unit 2* • **Guided Reading,** p. 40 • **Skillbuilder Practice:** Interpreting Maps, p. 42	*Section 4 Assessment,* p. 212 *Formal Assessment* • Section Quiz, p. 91 *Alternative Assessment Book* • Standards for Evaluating a Product or Performance
SECTION 5 The Congress of Vienna Convenes pp. 213–217	Following the plan of Metternich, the Congress of Vienna reestablishes stability in Europe after the defeat of Napoleon.	*In-Depth Resources: Unit 2* • **Guided Reading,** p. 41	*Section 5 Assessment,* p. 216 *Formal Assessment* • Section Quiz, p. 92 *Alternative Assessment Book* • Standards for Evaluating a Cooperative Activity
CHAPTER RESOURCES 189A	**Chapter Overview** Revolution leads to the overthrow and execution of the French king. After a period of instability, Napoleon takes control of France and of most of Europe. Napoleon's thirst for power leads to his downfall, and European leaders craft a lasting peace.	*Telescoping the Times* • Chapter Summary, pp. 29–31 *Planning for Block Schedules*	*Chapter Assessment,* pp. 218–219 *Chapter Activities,* p. 219 *Formal Assessment* • Chapter Test, forms A and B, pp. 93–98 *Test Generator* *Alternative Assessment Book*

1789–1815

4

TECHNOLOGY

Warm-Up Transparency 7
Geography Transparencies
- G23 *Early Sites of the French Revolution, 1789*

World Art and Cultures Transparencies
- AT50 *Portrait of Marie Antoinette*

Electronic Library of Primary Sources
- from *Memoirs of Élisabeth Vigée-Lebrun*

INTERNET RESOURCES
www.mlworldhistory.com

Warm-Up Transparency 7
Critical Thinking Transparencies
- CT75 *Cause and Effect Graphic Organizer*

Electronic Library of Primary Sources
- from "Execution by Guillotine"

INTERNET RESOURCES
www.mlworldhistory.com

Warm-Up Transparency 7
World Art and Cultures Transparencies
- AT51 *Napoleon Crossing the St. Bernard Pass*

Electronic Library of Primary Sources
- from *The Letters of Napoleon I*

Battles of the World
- The Battle of Austerlitz

INTERNET RESOURCES
www.mlworldhistory.com

Warm-Up Transparency 7
Electronic Library of Primary Sources
- "The Battle of Waterloo: The Finale"

INTERNET RESOURCES
www.mlworldhistory.com

Warm-Up Transparency 7
Critical Thinking Transparencies
- CT23 *The French Revolution*

Electronic Library of Primary Sources
- from *Memoirs of Metternich*
- from "Frenchmen, Is This What You Want?"

INTERNET RESOURCES
www.mlworldhistory.com

Chapter Summaries on Audiocassette in English and Spanish

INTERNET RESOURCES
www.mlworldhistory.com

Block Scheduling (90 MINUTES)
5

Day 1
Section 1, pp. 193–196
Section Assessment, p. 196

Day 2
Section 2, pp. 197–203
COOPERATIVE ACTIVITY
Debating an Issue, p. 198
(Teacher's Edition)
Section Assessment, p. 203

Day 3
Section 3, pp. 204–208
COOPERATIVE ACTIVITY
Researching Napoleon
and Nelson, p. 207
(Teacher's Edition)
Section 4, pp. 209–212
Section Assessments,
pp. 208, 212

Day 4
Section 5, pp. 213–217
COOPERATIVE ACTIVITY
Investigating World
Peace Organizations,
p. 215 (Teacher's Edition)
Section Assessment, p. 217
Chapter Assessment,
pp. 218–219

Yearly Pacing *Chapter 7 Total:* 4 days *Yearly Total:* 85 days

Planning for Block Schedules

Customizing for Special Needs
6

Students Acquiring English

Access for Students Acquiring English
- **Guided Reading** for Sections 1–5 (Spanish), pp. 81–85
- **Chapter Summary** (Spanish), pp. 78–80
- **Skillbuilder Practice** Interpreting Maps (Spanish), p. 86
- **Geography Application** The French Revolution Under Siege (Spanish), p. 87

Chapter Summaries on Audiocassette in English and Spanish

Spanish Reading Study Guide pp. 73–84

Less Proficient Readers

In-Depth Resources: Unit 2
- **Guided Reading** for Sections 1–5, pp. 37–41
- **Skillbuilder Practice** Interpreting Maps, p. 42
- **Geography Application** The French Revolution Under Siege, p. 43

Telescoping the Times
- Chapter Summary, pp. 29–31

Reading Study Guide pp. 73–84

Chapter Summaries on Audiocassette

Gifted and Talented Students

In-Depth Resources: Unit 2
Primary Sources:
- from *A Declaration of the Rights of Man and of the Citizen, 1789*, p. 45
- "La Marseillaise," p. 46
- *from* The Execution of Louis XVI, p. 47
- Napoleon's Proclamation at Austerlitz, 1805, p. 48

History Makers
- Marie Antoinette, p. 52
- Maximilien Robespierre, p. 53

Connections to Literature READINGS FOR STUDENTS
7

In-Depth Resources: Unit 2
Literature: from *A Tale of Two Cities* by Charles Dickens, p. 48

Enrichment Reading
- Sherwood, Frances
Vindication
New York: Penguin, 1994
Mary Wollstonecraft, author of *A Vindication of the Rights of Woman*, is portrayed vividly in this fictionalized treatment of her life and times.

McDougal Littell
Literature Connections
- Dickens, Charles
A Tale of Two Cities
(with related readings)
A classic tale of the French Revolution, with themes of love and self-sacrifice, heroes and quests.

PE = Pupil's Edition	= Overhead Transparency	= Software	= Video
= Copy Master	= CD-ROM	= Audiocassette	= Internet

189B

Technology
4

Technology listed for each section ranges from a wealth of transparency choices to videos to CD-ROMs to the Internet.

Block Scheduling
5

This pacing guide for block scheduling also lists optional cooperative activities from the teacher's edition.

Customizing for Special Needs
6

Here are suggested resources for teaching students acquiring English, less proficient readers, and gifted and talented students. From worksheets and chapter summaries in Spanish to lists of primary-source material, these suggestions offer practical help for basic classroom needs.

Connections to Literature
7

Literature Connections from McDougal Littell are stand-alone books with related readings that offer in-depth literary supplements. A SourceBook provides student support materials for each selection. Other reading suggestions refer to ancillary materials or to outside sources.

Teacher's Edition Lesson Support

The *Modern World History: Patterns of Interaction* teacher's edition supports instruction from practical helps for dealing with maps and other graphics to abundant suggestions for classroom activities.

Side columns focus on core instruction with optional suggestions and teaching activities featured at the bottom of the pages.

1 **History from Visuals**

These notes provide a variety of learning strategies and extension activities to help students make the most of maps, charts, graphs, political cartoons, and key historical photographs.

2 **Key Ideas**

A listing of key ideas identifies the main points students need to understand in order to meet specific section objectives.

3 **More About . . .**

These terrific nuggets of information occur often to supplement the text.

1

History from Visuals

The Three Estates

Interpreting the Cartoon Ask students why the clergyman and the nobleman are standing on a stone rather than standing directly on the fallen man. *Possible Response: The stone represents the taxes and obligations that kept the members of the Third Estate subservient to the nobility and the clergy.*

Extension Activity Have students make lists of adjectives describing the feelings and attitudes of the people depicted in the cartoon.

SKILLBUILDER Answers
1. The Third Estate was oppressed because it paid 50% of its income in taxes to support the most privileged 2% of the French population.
2. They had no reason to desire change, since they already had privileges and wealth.

IN-DEPTH RESOURCES: UNIT 2
Literature: from *A Tale of Two Cities,* p. 49

OBJECTIVE 2 INSTRUCT

2 **The Forces of Change**

▶ **Key Ideas**
• New ideas about the power of the people take hold.
• Poor harvests, heavy taxes, and government debt cause instability in France.
• Louis XVI finally calls a meeting of the Estates-General to deal with the crisis.

3 **MORE ABOUT . . .**
Louis XVI
Louis XVI was a lethargic, somewhat fat, rather dull man who was more interested in hunting and tinkering with locks than in governing France. On the day the Bastille fell in Paris, the king wrote only *Rien* ("Nothing") in his diary—a reference to his lack of success in the hunt.

4

The Three Estates

■ **First Estate**
• made up of clergy of Roman Catholic Church
• scorned Enlightenment ideas

■ **Second Estate**
• made up of rich nobles
• held highest offices in government
• disagreed about Enlightenment ideas

■ **Third Estate**
• included bourgeoisie, urban lower class, and peasant farmers
• had no power to influence government
• embraced Enlightenment ideas

Population of France, 1787
98% (Third Estate)
less than 1% (First Estate)
2% (Second Estate)

Percent of Income Paid in Taxes
2% (First Estate)
0% (Second Estate)
50% (Third Estate)
0% 20% 40% 60% 80% 100%

SKILLBUILDER: Interpreting Charts and Political Cartoons
The Third Estate intensely resented the wealthy First and Second Estates.
1. How do the chart and the graphs help explain the political cartoon?
2. Why might the First and Second Estates be opposed to change?

The Forces of Change

In addition to the growing resentment of the lower classes, other factors were contributing to the revolutionary mood in France.

Enlightenment Ideas New views about power and authority in government were spreading among the Third Estate. The people began questioning long-standing notions about the structure of society and using words like *equality, liberty,* and *democracy.* The success of the American Revolution inspired them, and they discussed the radical ideas of Rousseau and Voltaire. Many shared the beliefs of the Comte d'Antraigues, a friend of Rousseau's:

> **A VOICE FROM THE PAST**
> The Third Estate is the People and the People is the foundation of the State; it is in fact the State itself; the other orders are merely political categories while by the *immutable laws of nature* the People is everything. Everything should be subordinated to it. . . . It is in the People that all national power resides and for the People that all states exist.
> **COMTE D'ANTRAIGUES,** quoted in *Citizens: A Chronicle of the French Revolution*

Economic Woes France's once prosperous economy was failing. The population was expanding rapidly, as were trade and production. However, the heavy burden of taxes made it impossible to conduct business profitably within France. The cost of living rose for everyone. In addition, bad weather in the 1780s caused widespread crop failures, resulting in a severe shortage of grain. The price of bread doubled in 1789, and many people faced starvation.

During this period, France's government sank deeply into debt. Extravagant spending by the king and queen was part of the problem. **Louis XVI,** who became king in 1774, inherited part of the debt from his predecessors. He also borrowed heavily in order to help the American revolutionaries in their war against Great Britain—France's chief rival—thereby nearly doubling the government's debt. When bankers, in 1786, refused to lend the government any more money, Louis faced serious problems.

A Weak Leader Strong leadership might have prevented the coming crisis, but Louis XVI was indecisive and allowed matters to drift. He paid little attention to his government advisers, preferring to spend his time hunting or tinkering with locks rather than attending to the details of governing.

Background
The ideas of Rousseau and Voltaire are also reflected in the United States Constitution.

194 Chapter 7

---

4 **TEACHING OPTIONS**

| EXPLORING PRIMARY SOURCES | CONNECTIONS ACROSS THE CURRICULUM |

A Voice from the Past The Comte d'Antraigues, whose statement about the Third Estate became one of the most popular axioms of the Revolution, was from an old aristocratic family. Believing that the feudal noble families should have more power, he initially supported change and even went as far as agreeing that the nobles should no longer be exempt from taxes. But when the people wanted to reduce all aristocrats to ordinary citizens, he became a counterrevolutionary and worked diligently against further changes. Ask students to research the lives of other French aristocrats, such as the Marquis de Lafayette.

Economics Taxes and debt are problems faced by most governments. In France at this time, most of the taxes were paid by the poorest people while wealthy nobles paid no taxes. Ask students to propose economic solutions to this situation. Then ask, What might be the political consequences of your solutions? What happens today when the U.S. government wants to raise taxes to pay off debts or to implement new programs?

194 Chapter 7

---

4 **Teaching Options**

Options at the bottom of pages offer a range of choices from connections to many subject areas to cooperative activities to strategies for multiple learning styles.

Vocabulary
deficit: debt.

THINK THROUGH HISTORY
A. Analyzing
Motives Why did
the Third Estate pro-
pose a change in the
Estates-General's
voting rules?
A. Possible Answer
to gain more power in
the meeting of the
Estates-General

Louis had married his wife, **Marie Antoinette,** when he was 15 and she was 14. Because Marie was a member of the royal family of Austria, France's long-time enemy, she became unpopular as soon as she set foot in France. As queen, Marie spent so much money on gowns, jewels, and gifts that she became known as Madame Deficit.

Rather than cutting expenses and increasing taxes, Louis put off dealing with the emergency until France faced bankruptcy. Then, when he tried to tax aristocrats, the Second Estate forced him to call a meeting of the **Estates-General**—an assembly of representatives from all three estates—to get approval for the tax reform. He had the meeting—the first in 175 years—on May 5, 1789, at Versailles.

Revolution Dawns

The clergy and the nobles had dominated the Estates-General throughout the Middle Ages and expected to do so in the 1789 meeting. Under the assembly's medieval rules, each estate's delegates met in a separate hall to vote, and each estate had one vote. The two privileged estates could always outvote the Third Estate.

The National Assembly The Third Estate delegates, mostly members of the bourgeoisie whose views had been shaped by the Enlightenment, were eager to make changes in the government. They insisted that all three estates meet together and that each delegate have a vote. This would give the advantage to the Third Estate, which had as many delegates as the other two estates combined.

Siding with the nobles, the king ordered the Estates-General to follow the medieval rules. The delegates of the Third Estate, however, became more and more determined to wield power. A leading spokesperson for their viewpoint was a clergyman sympathetic to their cause, the Abbé Sieyès (AB·AY syay·YEHS), who argued, "What is the Third Estate? Everything. What has it been up to now in the political order? Nothing. What does it demand? To become something herein." In a dramatic speech, he suggested that the Third Estate delegates name themselves the **National Assembly** and pass laws and reforms in the name of the French people.

HISTORY THROUGH ART: Fine Art

The gap between rich and poor in 18th-century France is clear in these portraits. David, painter of the Revolution, depicted a common woman (*left*) whose appearance displays none of the luxury of the French court (*right*).

Connect *to* History

Comparing What details of the women's expressions and clothing most clearly show the contrasts in lives?

SEE SKILLBUILDER HANDBOOK, PAGE 654.

Connect *to* Today

Contrasting How would you visually convey the gap between rich and poor in your country?

A Woman of the Revolution [La maraîchère]
(1795), Jacques Louis David

Marie Antoinette, Jacques Gautier d'Agoty

The French Revolution and Napoleon **195**

HISTORY MAKERS

Marie Antoinette
1755–1793

Marie Antoinette was a pretty, lighthearted, charming woman. However, she was unpopular with the French because of her spending and her involvement in controversial court affairs. She referred to Louis as "the poor man" and sometimes set the clock forward an hour to be rid of his presence.

Marie refused to wear the tight-fitting clothing styles of the day and introduced a loose cotton dress for women. The elderly, who viewed the dress as an undergarment, thought that Marie's clothing was scandalous. The French silk industry was equally angry.

In constant need of entertainment, Marie often spent her time playing cards. One year she lost the equivalent of $1.5 million by gambling in card games.

---

 5 **HISTORY MAKERS**
Marie Antoinette

Marie Antoinette was only a teenager when she came to France. Although her behavior made her many enemies, she did have some redeeming qualities. Ask students to investigate Marie Antoinette's life and to list some of her actions that might be considered foolish, as well as some that might be considered admirable.

📖 *IN-DEPTH RESOURCES: UNIT 2*
History Makers: Marie Antoinette, p. 52

🏛 *WORLD ART AND CULTURES TRANSPARENCIES*
Portrait of Marie Antoinette with Her Children

OBJECTIVE 3 INSTRUCT

Revolution Dawns

▶ *Key Ideas*
- Third Estate delegates in the Estates-General demand more rights.
- In the first deliberate act of revolution, the Third Estate delegates vote to establish the National Assembly.
- Peasants overthrow the Bastille on July 14, 1789, and the Revolution begins in earnest.

🏛 *GEOGRAPHY TRANSPARENCIES*
GT23 Early Sites of the French Revolution, 1789

💿 *ELECTRONIC LIBRARY OF PRIMARY SOURCES*
from *Memoirs of Élisabeth Vigée-Lebrun*

6

Connect *to* History			
Comparing		Woman of Revolution	Marie Antoinette
Suggest that students make a chart like the one here to compare the two portraits.	Clothing		
	Expression		
	Posture		

7

Connect *to* Today

Contrasting You may wish to suggest the following strategies for showing the gap between rich and poor today:

- Look for magazine images of homeless people, victims of floods or tornadoes, and richly dressed people in elegant homes.
- Check the Internet for census statistics showing percentages of people at various income levels. Check also for reports on wealth and poverty.

Teacher's Edition **195**

---

5 History Makers

Short features in the Pupil's Edition text are supplemented with additional information and suggested activities.

6 References to Resource Materials

Specific references identify where to find additional support for teaching each section.

Teacher's Edition Notes may also include:

- Cooperative Activities
- Customizing for Special Needs
- Multiple Learning Styles
- Exploring Primary Sources
- Connections Across the Curriculum
- Special Application Activities
- Skillbuilder Mini-Lessons
- Connections Across Time and Place
- Assessment Suggestions
- Critical Thinking Activities

 7 **Connect to History and Connect to Today**

These offer answers and strategies for responding to the questions and activities on the pupil's edition page.

Reading History

The best learners are active and engaged readers. Successful readers connect what they are reading with what they already know. These readers:
- build associations among ideas
- create visual images of what they are reading
- continually revise their interpretations as they gather more information.

Supporting Readers

Modern World History: Patterns of Interaction uses many strategies to help students become active and engaged readers.

Various Learning Styles We know that readers have different styles of understanding—some rely heavily on verbal input and discussion, some need visual supports, and some need to make notes and drawings or create graphic organizers as they learn. *Modern World History: Patterns of Interaction* addresses various learning styles and stimulates learning by posing problems, comparing and contrasting ideas, and presenting different points of view on issues.

Visual Information Many readers rely on visual information when reading unfamiliar material. Pictures make abstractions of time and space more real; photos and artifacts create a context for new ideas; maps help readers associate and compare ideas. In addition, charts of ideas and events in each chapter summarize and clarify information. A visual summary at the end of each chapter provides another way for remembering important ideas and events.

Inner-Column Notes Inner-column notes in *Modern World History: Patterns of Interaction* help students read the text. Vocabulary notes explain and define words and phrases. Background notes provide additional information about a person, idea, or event. Think Through History questions help students to read critically.

Personal Connections Personal stories and human connections can help to bring a subject such as history alive. *Modern World History: Patterns of Interaction* uses personal voices throughout to support student learning.

A VOICE FROM THE PAST
This great Nation will endure as it has endured, will revive and will prosper. . . . let me assert my firm belief that the only thing we have to fear is fear itself—nameless, unreasoning, unjustified terror which paralyzes needed efforts to convert retreat into advance.
FRANKLIN ROOSEVELT, *First Inaugural Address*

Students Acquiring English Second-language learners need to have information and ideas presented to them in multiple ways. Being able to "see" history helps make it real for them. *Modern World History: Patterns of Interaction* uses illustrations and visuals to present information to students in a variety of ways.

Evolving Forms of Reading

Students today need to be able to read in new ways.

Nonlinear Materials Today's students must:
- gather ideas from multiple sources—resource books, magazines, computerized databases, CD-ROMS, the Internet
- know how to evaluate these sources and make decisions about their content
- find their way through nonlinear materials, such as by deciding which area of a computer screen contains the information they want
- make decisions about what level of knowledge and elaboration they need.

Graphic Layouts Today's readers must deal with informational materials that come in various formats:
- multiple columns of text with many pictures, graphs, and maps
- single-column texts with large marginal areas used for illustrations, highlighted information, and thought-provoking ideas
- combination of layouts

Visual Summary

The Struggle for Independence

The time line shows the dates on which various countries in Asia and Africa achieved their independence after World War II. It also shows (in parentheses) the countries from which they achieved independence.

1945

1946
Philippines (United States)

1947
India, Pakistan (Great Britain)

1948
Israel (Great Britain)

1949
Indonesia (The Netherlands)

1955

1957
Federation of Malaya, Ghana (Great Britain)

1960
Zaire (Belgium)

1962
Algeria (France)

1963
Kenya (Great Britain)

1965
Singapore (Great Britain, Malaya)

1971
Bangladesh (Pakistan)

1975
Angola (Portugal)

526 Chapter 18

The Teacher's Role

Are your students prepared with strategies for reading and learning in the 21st century? Are they able to shift from one form of text presentation to another easily? Do they know how to construct meaning from multiple sources?

Strategies for Teachers You can help your students become active, engaged, and confident readers. Here are some strategies you might try:

• Ask students how they read.

• Do a "think aloud" as students begin to read a text. Ask them to tell you where they look on the page; when they look at the charts, maps, and pictures; and when they read the headings and titles.

• Introduce the text layout and features, and discuss students' options for reading.

• Show students that all material on a page does not have to be read in order.

• Have students experiment with reading the graphics first before reading the text on a page.

• Demonstrate how headings and subheadings can help readers find specific information.

• Use graphic organizers and reading guides to help students gain confidence.

Reading and discussing different types of written material and material expressing different points of view will help students learn to think critically about what they read.

GLOBAL IMPACT

THINK THROUGH HISTORY

VOCABULARY

BACKGROUND

POLITICAL, PHYSICAL, AND HISTORICAL MAPS

GRAPHS

SKILLBUILDER QUESTIONS

English and French troops attacked Germany's four Africa... control of three.

Elsewhere in Asia and Africa, the British and French recruited subjects in their colonies for the struggle. Fighting troops as well as laborers came from India, South Africa, Senegal, Egypt, Algeria, and Indochina. Many fought and died on the battlefield. Others worked to keep the frontlines supplied. Some colonial subjects wanted nothing to do with their Eur... that service would lead to th... leader Mohandas Gandhi, w... "If we would improve our status through the help and cooperation of the British," he wrote, "it was our duty to win their help by standing by them in their hour of need."

The United States Enters the War In 1917, the focus of the war shifted to the high seas. That year, the Germans intensified the submarine warfare that had raged in the Atlantic Ocean since shortly after the war began. By 1917, failed crops, as well as a British naval blockade, caused severe food shortages in Germany. Desperate to strike back, Germany decided to establish its own naval blockade around Britain. In January 1917, ...nced that their submarines would sink without warning any ship in the ...n. This policy was called **unrestricted submarine warfare.** ...d tried this policy before. On May 7, 1915, a German submarine, or ...e British passenger ship *Lusitania*. The attack left 1,198 people dead, ...itizens. Germany claimed that the ship had been carrying ammuni-...out to be true. Nevertheless, the American public was outraged. ...Wilson sent a strong protest to Germany. After two further attacks, the Germans finally agreed to stop attacking neutral and passenger ships.

However, the Germans returned to unrestricted submarine warfare in 1917. They knew it might lead to war with the United States. They gambled that their naval

THINK THROUGH HISTORY
A. Summarizing
How did Europe's colonial subjects help in the war effort?

Vocabulary
blockade: the forced closing off of a city or other area to traffic and communication through the use of ships or land forces.

blockade would starve Britain into defeat before the United States could mobilize. Ignoring warnings by President Wilson, German U-boats sank three American ships.

In February 1917, another German action pushed the United States closer to war. The British intercepted a telegram from Germany's foreign secretary, Arthur Zimmermann, to the German ambassador in Mexico. The message said that Germany would help Mexic... ...Mexico would... gave i...

When the Zimmermann note was made public, Americans called for war against Germany. Even before news of the note, many Americans had sided with the Allies. A large part of the American population felt a bond with England. The two nations shared a common ancestry and language, as well as similar democratic institutions and legal systems. In addition, reports—some true and others not—of German war atrocities stirred anti-German sentiment in the United States. More important, America's economic ties with the Allies were far stronger than those with the Central Powers. America traded with Great Britain and France more than twice as much as with Germany.

The Zimmermann note simply proved to be the last straw. On April 2, 1917, President Wilson asked Congress to declare war. The United States entered the war on the side of the Allies.

Background
Land Mexico considered "lost" to the United States included New Mexico, Texas, and Arizona.

Vocabulary
atrocity: an act of extreme cruelty or violence.

War Affects the Home Front

By the time the United States joined the Allies, the war had been going on for nearly three years. In those three years, Europe had lost more men in battle than in all the wars of the previous three centuries. The war had claimed the lives of millions and had changed countless lives forever. The Great War, as the conflict came to be known, affected everyone. It touched not only the soldiers in the trenches, but civilians as well. It affected not just military institutions, but also political, economic, and social institutions.

Governments Wage Total War World War I soon became a **total war.** This meant that countries devoted all their resources to the war effort. In Britain, Germany, Austria, Russia, and France, the entire force of government was dedicated to winning the conflict.

In each country, the wartime government took control of the economy. Governments told factories what to produce and how much. Numerous facilities were converted to munitions factories. Nearly every able-bodied civilian was put to work. Unemployment in many European countries nearly disappeared. European governments even enlisted the help of foreign workers. For example, thousands of civilians were deported from German-occupied Belgium and France to work in Germany as farm and factory laborers. Britain and France recruited Chinese, West Indian, Algerian, and Egyptian laborers to work behind their lines at the front.

So many goods were in short supply that governments turned to **rationing.** Under this system, people could buy only small amounts of those items that were also needed for the war effort. Eventually, rationing covered a wide range of goods, from butter to shoe leather.

Governments also suppressed antiwar activity—sometimes forcibly. In addition, they censored news about the war. Many leaders feared

GlobalImpact

Influenza Epidemic
In the spring of 1918, a powerful new enemy emerged, threatening nations on each side of World War I. This "enemy" was a deadly strain of influenza. The Spanish flu, as it was popularly known, hit England and India in May. By the fall, it had spread through Europe, Russia, Asia, and to the United States.

The influenza epidemic killed soldiers and civilians alike. In India, at least 12 million people died of influenza. In Berlin, on a single day in October, 1,500 people died. In the end, this global epidemic was more destructive than the war itself, killing 20 million people worldwide.

Unemployment in Germany and Britain

■ Germany
■ Great Britain
Source: *European Historical Statistics 1750–1975*

SKILLBUILDER: Interpreting Graphs
1. During which year did each country see its lowest unemployment rate?
2. Why might unemployment have been lowest during the war years?

The World at War, 1914–1918

War rages in Southwest Asia as Arab nationalists battle their Turkish rulers.

Main fighting of the war occurs on Western and Eastern Fronts.

Japan declares war on Germany in 1914; seizes German colonies in China and the Pacific.

The United States enters the war on the side of the Allies in 1917.

NORTH AMERICA

EUROPE

ASIA

ATLANTIC OCEAN

SOUTHWEST ASIA

JAPAN

INDIA

PACIFIC OCEAN

AFRICA

SOUTH AMERICA

The European colonies throughout Africa become a battlefield as the warring parties strike at one another's colonial possessions.

India provides about 1.3 million men to fight and labor alongside their British rulers throughout Europe.

AUSTRALIA

NEW ZEALAND

Both countries fight on the side of the Allies and contribute many troops to the Gallipoli campaign of 1915, in Southwest Asia.

GEOGRAPHY SKILLBUILDER: Interpreting Maps
1. **Region** Which countries were aligned with the European Allies?
2. **Location** Outside of Europe, where was World War I fought?

The Great War **375**

Block Schedules

Today block schedules provide new opportunities and challenges for teachers. *Modern World History: Patterns of Interaction* offers help for teaching in the block throughout both the pupil's edition and the teacher's edition. In addition, *Planning for Block Schedules,* found in the teacher's resource materials, includes a wealth of information and strategies.

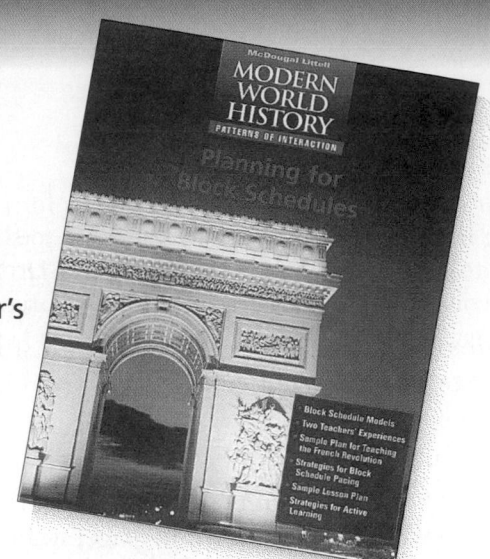

Block Scheduling Strategies

The longer class period in a block schedule provides an on-going opportunity for challenging classroom activities. *Modern World History: Patterns of Interaction* offers a variety of cooperative activities and strategies in both the pupil's edition and in the teacher's edition.

Pupil's Edition

- Each chapter begins with an **Interact with History** feature, which can be used as a collaborative activity.

- Each **Section Assessment** provides opportunities for collaborative learning, including a note-taking activity and frequent theme activities.

- **Chapter Assessments** include a variety of chapter activities including **Connect to Today**, a cooperative activity.

- **Unit Portfolio Projects** found on the unit time lines pages provide a variety of options for collaborative activities.

Teacher's Edition

- The **Planning Guide** includes a special section on block scheduling including suggestions for pacing and cooperative activities.

- **Technology Resources** listed in the Planning Guide lists many resources that are useful for cooperative activities.

- **Cooperative Activities** described on the teacher's edition pages offer abundant suggestions for a variety of activities. In addition, Skillbuilder Mini-Lessons, and many other activities presented on the teacher's edition pages help teachers find ideas to make their instruction active and engaging.

Pupil's Edition

2. CONNECT TO TODAY: Cooperative Learning

THEME REVOLUTION You read about the various causes that led to the Russian Revolution of 1917. Work with a team to create a mythical country that is on the brink of revolution today. Write a profile of the conditions in that country that are triggering widespread social unrest.

Use the Internet and other books to find out about more recent revolutions that have occurred in countries around the world. Look for common patterns that countries in political turmoil share. Use the following questions to help you brainstorm ideas for writing a profile of your mythical country.

- What type of government is currently in power?
- Who are the top political leaders, and what are they like?
- What grievances do the citizens have against the government?
- What is the gap between the rich and the poor?
- What revolutionary groups are forming? What are their goals and strategies?

Teachers' Edition

TEACHING OPTION **BLOCK SCHEDULING** **COOPERATIVE ACTIVITY: Making a Cold War Temperature Chart** **CLASS TIME 30 MINUTES**

Task: Students will develop a Cold War "thermometer" to track Cold War tensions.

Purpose: To explore the fluctuations in tensions over the course of the Cold War.

Activity: Have students brainstorm ways of tracking the rise and fall of Cold War tensions. You might suggest, for example, that they consider a scale such as ° C—degrees of crisis—and assign a number to each confrontation or avoidance of confrontation between the superpowers. Then have small groups each choose a Cold War incident, write a short description of their incident, and assign it a rating on the crisis scale. Finally, have the groups plot their individual incidents on a crisis temperature chart.

■ ***Building a Portfolio:*** Encourage students to include their crisis summaries and ratings in their portfolios.

ALTERNATIVE ASSESSMENT BOOK Standards for Evaluating a Cooperative Activity

Standards for Evaluation
Crisis summaries and ratings should . . .
- accurately depict a Cold War crisis
- realistically rank the seriousness of the confrontation
- be clear and succinct

Assessment Resources

Modern World History: Patterns of Interaction provides you with material that allows you to customize assessment to best fit the activities and structure of your particular classroom. With options for informal, formal, and alternative assessment, these resources furnish you with all the support you need.

Formal Assessment

- Asks, "What do you know?"
- Pencil-and-paper tests in standardized formats such as true-false and multiple choice
- Used to measure students' achievement against other students; report students' achievement; make instructional and grouping decisions

Informal Assessment

- Ongoing assessment
- Primarily based on recurring elements such as Think Through History inner-column questions and section assessments
- Done as students work their way through a chapter section by section

Types of Assessment

Alternative Assessment

- Asks, "What can you do?" and "How do you do it?"
- Implemented under 3 main headings:

  1. Process Assessment—observing students as they work

  2. Product and Performance Assessment—focusing on the end result of students' work

  3. Portfolio Assessment—reviewing and evaluating students' work together

Assessment Options for *Modern World History: Patterns of Interaction*

Assessment Type	Pupil's Edition	Teacher's Edition	Ancillaries
1. Informal	• Think Through History • Skillbuilder questions • Geography Skillbuilder • Section Assessment • Chapter Assessment		• *In-Depth Resources* Guided Reading, Skillbuilder Practice, and Geography Application
2. Formal			• *Formal Assessment* Section Quizzes, Chapter Tests (Forms A and B), and ACT/SAT Practice • Test Generator (software)
3. Alternative	• Chapter Activities • Skillbuilder Handbook exercises • Living History Portfolio Projects • Theme Activities	• Cooperative Activities • Skillbuilder Mini-Lessons • Suggested activities throughout the Teacher's Edition	• *In-Depth Resources* Primary Sources, Literature Selections • Alternative Assessment Book

Students' Learning Styles

It is probably no surprise to you that every student is unique. Each has not only an individual personality, interests, and abilities, but also a special way of learning. According to Harvard psychologist Howard Gardner, there are seven types of intelligences—linguistic, logical-mathematical, spatial or visual, kinesthetic, interpersonal, intrapersonal, and musical. Each student uses a unique combination of these intelligences, so one teaching method will not promote optimal learning for all students all the time. The following chart can help you recognize your individual students' learning styles so you can teach them most effectively.

Student Characteristics	Learning Style	Classroom Activities
Has good verbal and auditory skills, thinks in words, likes to read and write	Linguistic	Creative and expository writing, debates, speeches, oral reports, dramatic readings, storytelling
Thinks conceptually, abstractly, and logically	Logical-mathematical	Graphic organizers, charts, graphs, time lines, models, prediction exercises
Thinks in visual images, enjoys drawing, designing, and inventing	Spatial or visual	Drawings, maps, flow charts, murals, dioramas, collages, photography
Has good fine-motor coordination and body sense, communicates through body language	Kinesthetic	Demonstrations, role-playing, impersonations
Understands other people, communicates and socializes well	Interpersonal	Discussions, cooperative and collaborative projects, interviews, peer response
Prefers working alone, is intuitive, independent, and self-motivated	Intrapersonal	Response and dialogue journals, learning logs, written reports
Is sensitive to sound and rhythm, enjoys singing, playing, and listening and moving to music	Musical	Interpretive dances, rap songs, musical plays, rhyming games

The teacher's edition of *Modern World History: Patterns of Interaction* provides numerous teaching options that address these learning styles. Support materials for the program, including videos, transparencies, copy masters, and CD-ROMs, offer numerous opportunities to reach the special abilities of all your students.

Teaching Geography Through History

It is impossible to understand historical events without examining both where and when they occur. Geography is more than just the static setting for history, however. Just as the land shapes the people who inhabit it, their history continues to shape the land.

Each chapter in *Modern World History: Patterns of Interaction* begins with a two-page map that locates students firmly in time and place. Other maps within chapters help students visualize places and events they read about. Many of these maps contain several layers of information that provide a better understanding of how and why events in history occurred.

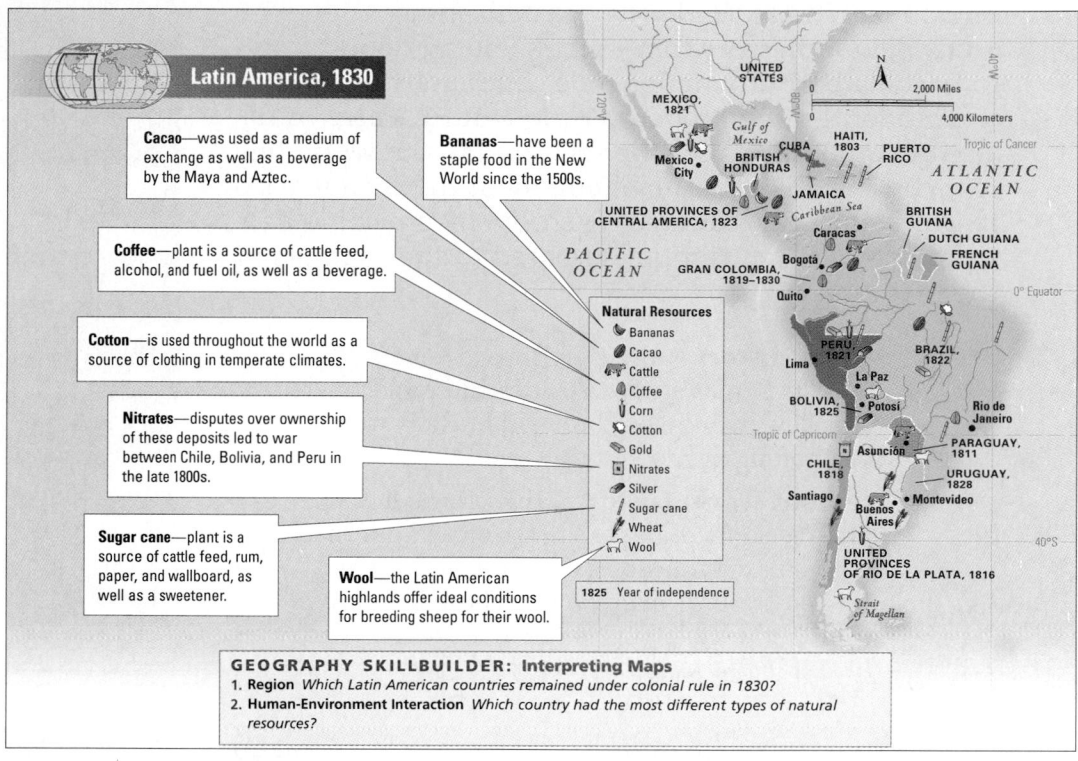

Latin America, 1830

Cacao—was used as a medium of exchange as well as a beverage by the Maya and Aztec.

Bananas—have been a staple food in the New World since the 1500s.

Coffee—plant is a source of cattle feed, alcohol, and fuel oil, as well as a beverage.

Cotton—is used throughout the world as a source of clothing in temperate climates.

Nitrates—disputes over ownership of these deposits led to war between Chile, Bolivia, and Peru in the late 1800s.

Sugar cane—plant is a source of cattle feed, rum, paper, and wallboard, as well as a sweetener.

Wool—the Latin American highlands offer ideal conditions for breeding sheep for their wool.

Natural Resources
- Bananas
- Cacao
- Cattle
- Coffee
- Corn
- Cotton
- Gold
- Nitrates
- Silver
- Sugar cane
- Wheat
- Wool

1825 Year of independence

GEOGRAPHY SKILLBUILDER: Interpreting Maps
1. **Region** Which Latin American countries remained under colonial rule in 1830?
2. **Human-Environment Interaction** Which country had the most different types of natural resources?

Nigeria, 1914

- Hausa-Fulani
- Igbo
- Yoruba
- British-imposed border

FRENCH WEST AFRICA

1851, British annex Lagos

NIGERIA

After 1884–85 Berlin Conference, Britain declares a protectorate over Niger Delta

The Royal Niger Company controls the palm-oil trade

CAMEROONS

Gulf of Guinea

Lake Chad

GEOGRAPHY SKILLBUILDER: Interpreting Maps
1. **Region** How many major culture regions are found within the colony of Nigeria? What sort of problems might result from combining or splitting groups of people?
2. **Movement** Why might the British want to be able to control the Niger River?

Five Themes

In *Modern World History: Patterns of Interaction*, the importance of the reciprocal relationship between history and geography is emphasized by a focus on five recurrent geographical themes:

- location • place • region • movement
- human/environment interaction

Maps in the Text

There are hundreds of maps in the pupil's edition that work together with the text to further explain historical events and their meaning. Maps can help clarify what is in the text or provide additional information that supplements the text. For example, the map above places students in a particular area of the world, while the map to the left pinpoints a particular area within the broader map above.

Skillbuilder Questions

Skillbuilder questions based on the five themes of geography accompany each map in the book, giving students a chance to develop their sensitivity to the themes, their awareness of geography in general, and their ability to interpret geographical information. To help you access this information easily, the front of the teacher's edition lists every map in the book.

Internet Resources

McDougal Littell's World History Web site—**www.mlworldhistory.com**—offers you an opportunity to become part of a nationwide community of teachers and students using *Modern World History: Patterns of Interaction*. With a user-friendly format, our world history curriculum center helps you meet the challenges of teaching in today's diverse classroom by providing access to a wide range of resources related to the chapters of the textbook.

World History Activities Engage your students in interactive activities and projects that allow them to explore world history topics in a thoroughly modern way.

General World History Links Our editors have gathered some of the best links on the Internet to help you extend lessons, expand your research, and boost your own creativity. These links are keyed to the table of contents for *Modern World History: Patterns of Interaction*.

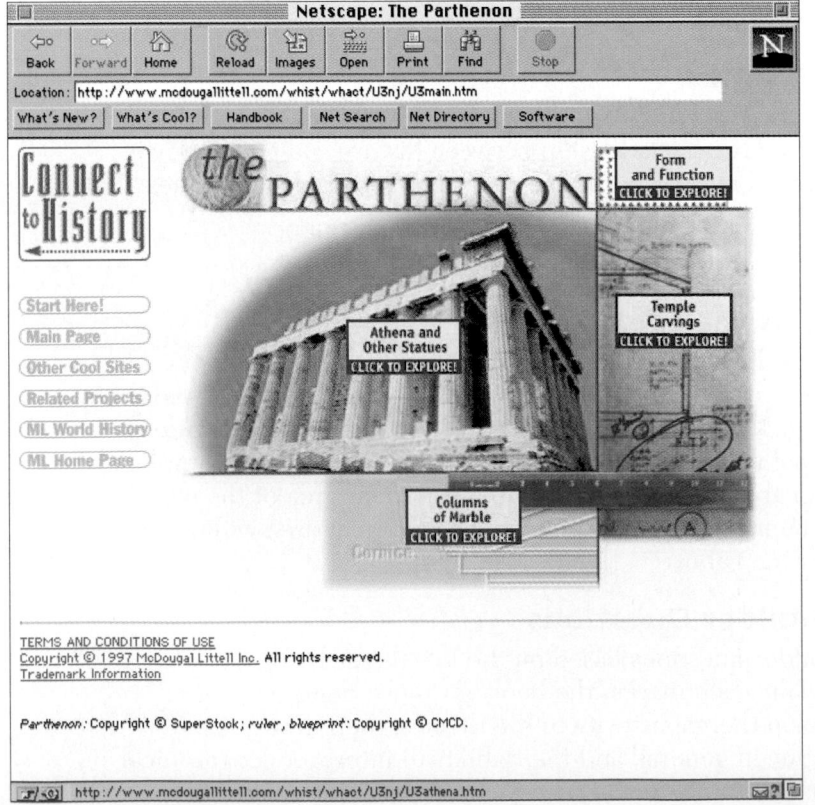

Professional Development Links This feature enables you to link to the homepages of professional social studies organizations around the globe.

Discussion Groups Exchange ideas, brainstorm, or network with your colleagues. Join the History Discussion Group to post or answer history- or program-related questions. Check out the Idea Exchange Discussion Group for more general teaching strategies and topics.

The Diverse Classroom Chat with educators, find links to a great variety of relevant Web sites, and read abstracts of articles from professional journals—all related to maintaining an inclusive classroom.

Monthly Special Feature Author profiles, web-site guests, and other special events are all part of this monthly feature.

Pacing Guide

The following pacing guide shows how the chapters in *Modern World History: Patterns of Interaction* can be adapted to fit your specific course needs. The Guide is based on 170 days of instruction during the school year. For **block schedules**, see ***Planning for Block Schedules*** in the teacher's resource materials.

	Modern World	1490 to 1919	Industrial Revolution to the Present	1900 to the Present
Prologue: Connection with Past Learnings: The Rise of Democratic Ideas	(days)	(days)	(days)	(days)
1. The Legacy of Ancient Greece and Rome	1	1	.5	.5
2. Judeo-Christian Tradition	1	1	.5	.5
3. Democratic Developments in England	1	1	.5	.5
4. The Enlightenment and Democratic Revolutions	1	1	.5	.5
Total Days for Prologue	**4**	**4**	**2**	**2**
UNIT 1 BEGINNINGS OF THE MODERN WORLD				
Chapter 1 European Renaissance and Reformation 1300–1600				
1. Italy: Birthplace of the Renaissance	2	2	.5	1
2. The Northern Renaissance	2	3	.5	1
3. Luther Starts the Reformation	2	3	.5	1
4. The Reformation Continues	1	3	.5	1
Chapter 2 The Muslim World Expands 1300–1700				
1. The Ottomans Build a Vast Empire	2	2	.5	1
2. Patterns of Change: Cultural Blending	2	3	1	1
3. The Mughals Establish an Empire in India	2	3	.5	1
Chapter 3 An Age of Exploration and Isolation 1400–1800				
1. Europeans Explore the East	2	2	.5	1
2. China Rejects European Outreach	2	3	.5	1
3. Japan Limits Western Contacts	2	3	.5	1
Chapter 4 The Atlantic World 1492–1800				
1. Spanish Conquests in the Americas	2	3	.5	1
2. Competing Claims in North America	1	3	.5	1
3. The Atlantic Slave Trade	2	3	1	1
4. The Columbian Exchange and Global Trade	2	3	.5	1
Total Days for Unit 1	**26**	**39**	**8**	**14**
UNIT 2 ABSOLUTISM TO REVOLUTION 1500–1900				
Chapter 5 Absolute Monarchs in Europe 1500–1800				
1. Spain's Empire and European Absolutism	2	3	.5	1
2. France's Ultimate Monarch	2	2	.5	1
3. Central European Monarchs Clash	1	2	.5	1
4. Russian Czars Increase Power	2	2	.5	1
5. Parliament Limits the English Monarchy	2	2	.5	1

For **block schedules**, see *Planning for Block Schedules* in the teacher's resource materials.

	Modern World	1490 to 1919	Industrial Revolution to the Present	1900 to the Present
Chapter 6 Enlightenment and Revolution 1550–1789	(days)	(days)	(days)	(days)
1. The Scientific Revolution	2	3	1	1
2. The Enlightenment in Europe	2	3	.5	1
3. The Spread of Enlightenment Ideas	2	2	.5	1
4. American Revolution: The Birth of a Republic	2	2	.5	1
Chapter 7 French Revolution and Napoleon 1789–1815				
1. Revolution Threatens the French King	2	2	.5	1
2. Revolution Brings Reform and Terror	2	2	.5	1
3. Napoleon Forges an Empire	2	2	.5	1
4. Napoleon's Empire Collapses	1	2	.5	1
5. The Congress of Vienna Convenes	2	3	.5	1
Chapter 8 Nationalist Revolutions Sweep The West 1789–1900				
1. Latin American Peoples Win Independence	2	3	.5	1
2. Revolutions Disrupt Europe	2	2	.5	1
3. Patterns of Change: Nationalism	2	3	1	1
4. Revolutions in the Arts	2	2	.5	1
Total Days for Unit 2	**34**	**42**	**10**	**18**
UNIT 3 INDUSTRIALISM AND THE RACE FOR EMPIRE 1700–1914				
Chapter 9 The Industrial Revolution 1700–1900				
1. The Beginnings of Industrialization	2	3	3	1
2. Patterns of Change: Industrialization	2	3	3	1
3. Industrialization Spreads	2	2	3	1
4. An Age of Reform	2	3	3	1
Chapter 10 An Age of Democracy and Progress 1815–1914				
1. Democratic Reform and Activism	2	3	3	2
2. Self-Rule for British Colonies	2	2	3	2
3. Expansion and Crisis in the United States	2	2	3	1
4. Nineteenth-Century Progress	2	2	3	1
Chapter 11 The Age of Imperialism 1850–1914				
1. Imperialists Divide Africa	2	2	3	1
2. Patterns of Change: Imperialism	2	3	3	2
3. Muslim Lands Fall to Imperialist Demands	2	2	2	1
4. British Imperialism in India	2	2	2	2
5. Western Powers Rule Southeast Asia	1	2	2	2

For **block schedules**, see *Planning for Block Schedules* in the teacher's resource materials.

	Modern World	1490 to 1919	Industrial Revolution to the Present	1900 to the Present
Chapter 12 Transformations Around the Globe 1800–1914	(days)	(days)	(days)	(days)
1. China Responds to Pressure from the West	2	2	3	2
2. Japan Modernizes	2	2	3	2
3. U.S. Economic Imperialism in Latin America	2	2	3	2
4. The Mexican Revolution	2	2	3	2
Total Days for Unit 3	**33**	**39**	**48**	**26**
UNIT 4 THE WORLD AT WAR 1900–1945				
Chapter 13 The Great War 1914–1918				
1. The Stage Is Set for War	2	3	3	4
2. War Consumes Europe	2	2	3	3
3. War Affects the World	2	2	3	3
4. A Flawed Peace	2	3	3	4
Chapter 14 Revolution and Nationalism 1900–1939				
1. Revolutions in Russia	2	2	3	3
2. Patterns of Change: Totalitarianism	2	2	3	4
3. Collapse of Chinese Imperial Rule	2	2	3	3
4. Nationalism in India and Southwest Asia	2	2	3	3
Chapter 15 Years of Crisis 1919–1939				
1. An Age of Uncertainty	2	1	3	3
2. A Global Depression	2	1	3	4
3. Fascism Rises in Europe	2	1	3	4
4. Aggressors on the March	2	1	3	3
Chapter 16 World War II 1939–1945				
1. Hitler's Lightning War	2	1	2	3
2. Japan Strikes in the Pacific	2	1	2	3
3. The Holocaust	1	1	2	3
4. The Allies are Victorious	2	1	3	3
5. The Devastation in Europe and Japan	2	1	3	3
Total Days for Unit 4	**33**	**27**	**48**	**56**
UNIT 5 PERSPECTIVES ON THE PRESENT 1945–PRESENT				
Chapter 17 Restructuring the Postwar World 1945–Present				
1. Two Superpowers Face Off	2	1	3	3
2. Communists Triumph in China	1	1	2	3
3. War in Korea and Vietnam	2	.5	2	3
4. Cold War Around the World	2	.5	2	3
5. The Cold War Thaws	2	1	3	4

For **block schedules**, see *Planning for Block Schedules* in the teacher's resource materials.

	Modern World	1490 to 1919	Industrial Revolution to the Present	1900 to the Present
Chapter 18 The Colonies Become New Nations 1945–Present	(days)	(days)	(days)	(days)
1. The Indian Subcontinent Gains Independence	2	1	3	3
2. Southeast Asian Nations Gain Independence	2	1	3	3
3. New Nations in Africa	2	1	3	3
4. Conflicts in the Middle East	2	1	3	3
Chapter 19 Struggles for Democracy 1945–Present				
1. Patterns of Change: Democracy	2	1	3	4
2. Democracy Challenges in African Nations	2	1	2	3
3. Gorbachev Moves Toward Democracy	2	.5	3	3
4. Collapse of the Soviet Union	1	.5	2	3
5. China Follows Its Own Path	2	1	2	3
Chapter 20 Global Interdependence 1960–Present				
1. Science and Technology Shape Human Outlook	2	1	3	3
2. Global Economic Development	2	1	3	4
3. Global Security Issues	2	1	3	4
4. Cultures Blend in a Global Age	2	1	3	3
Total Days for Unit 5	**34**	**16**	**48**	**58**
Epilogue: Unresolved Problems of the Modern World				
1. Technology Changes People's Lives	1	.5	1	1
2. Dangers to the Global Environment	1	.5	1	1
3. Feeding a Growing Population	1	.5	1	1
4. Economic Issues in the Developing World	1	.5	1	1
5. The Threat of Weapons and Terrorism	1	.5	1	1
6. Defending Human Rights and Freedoms	1	.5	1	1
Total Days for Epilogue	**6**	**3**	**6**	**6**

McDougal Littell

MODERN WORLD HISTORY

PATTERNS OF INTERACTION

Simón Bolívar, hero of the Latin American revolutionary wars

A woman in ceremonial head-dress, Kenya, Africa

A Japanese man

An 18th century self-portrait of Elisabeth Vigée-Lebrun

A farmer in Turkey

A woman in traditional dress, Rajasthan, India

Liliuokalani, Queen of Hawaii,
1841–1893

Vincent Van Gogh's portrait of
Alexander Reid

A young woman from Dali,
Yunnan Province, China

Roger B. Beck

Linda Black

Larry S. Krieger

Phillip C. Naylor

Dahia Ibo Shabaka

"The history of
civilizations, in fact,
is the history of
continual mutual
borrowings over many
centuries ..."

–Fernand Braudel

McDougal Littell
A HOUGHTON MIFFLIN COMPANY
Evanston, Illinois • Boston • Dallas

Senior Consultants

Roger B. Beck, Ph.D.

Roger B. Beck is a Professor of African History, World History, History of the Third World, and Social Studies Methods at Eastern Illinois University. He is also a Social Studies Student Teacher Supervisor at that university. Dr. Beck recently served as Associate Dean of the Graduate School and International Programs at Eastern Illinois University. In addition to his distinguished teaching career at high school, college, and graduate school levels, Dr. Beck is a contributing author to several books and has written numerous articles, reviews, and papers. He is also an active member of the National Council for the Social Studies, the World History Association, and the African Studies Association. Dr. Beck was a key contributor to the National Standards for World History.

Linda Black, B.A., M.Ed.

Linda Black teaches World History at Cypress Falls High School in Houston, Texas, and has had a distinguished career in education as a teacher of world history, American history, and Texas history. In 1993–1994, Mrs. Black was named an Outstanding Secondary Social Studies Teacher in the United States by the National Council for the Social Studies. In 1996, she was elected to the Board of Directors of the National Council for the Social Studies. As an active member of that Council, the Texas Council for the Social Studies, the Texas Humanities Alliance, and the World History Association, Mrs. Black frequently presents and directs workshops at the local, state, and national levels.

Larry S. Krieger, B.A., M.A., M.A.T.

Larry S. Krieger is the Social Studies Supervisor for Grades K-12 in Montgomery Township Public Schools in New Jersey. For 26 years he has taught world history in public schools. He has also introduced many innovative in-service programs, such as "Putting the Story Back in History," and has co-authored several successful history textbooks. Mr. Krieger earned his B.A. and M.A.T. from the University of North Carolina and his M.A. from Wake Forest University.

Phillip C. Naylor, Ph.D.

Phillip C. Naylor is an Associate Professor of History at Marquette University and teaches Modern European and non-Western history courses on both graduate and undergraduate levels. He is also the Director of the Western Civilization Program at Marquette University. He has co-authored and co-edited several books, including *State and Society in Algeria* and *Western Receptions/Perceptions: A Trans-Cultural Anthology*. In addition, Dr. Naylor is a contributing author to several history texts and study programs and has published numerous articles, papers, reviews, and CD-ROM projects. In 1996, Dr. Naylor received the Reverend John P. Raynor, S.J., Faculty Award for Teaching Excellence at Marquette University. In 1992, he received the Edward G. Roddy Teaching Award at Merrimack College.

Dahia Ibo Shabaka, B.A., M.A., Ed.S.

Dahia Ibo Shabaka is the Director of Social Studies and African-Centered Education in the Detroit Public Schools system. She has an extensive educational and scholarly background in the disciplines of history, political science, economics, law, and reading, and also in secondary education, curriculum development, and school administration and supervision. Ms. Shabaka has been a teacher, a curriculum coordinator, and a supervisor of Social Studies in the Detroit Secondary Schools. In 1991 she was named Social Studies Educator of the Year by the Michigan Council for the Social Studies. Ms. Shabaka is the recipient of a Fulbright Fellowship at the Hebrew University in Israel and has served as an executive board member of the National Social Studies Supervisors Association.

This text contains material that appeared originally in *World History: Perspectives on the Past* (D.C. Heath and Company) by Larry S. Krieger, Kenneth Neill, and Dr. Edward Reynolds.

Copyright © 1999 by McDougal Littell Inc. All rights reserved.

Address inquiries to Manager, Rights and Permissions, McDougal Littell Inc., P.O. Box 1667, Evanston, IL 60204
Acknowledgments begin on page 710.
ISBN 0-395-93829-5
Printed in the United States of America.
1 2 3 4 5 6 7 8 9–DWO–03 02 01 00 99 98

Consultants and Reviewers

Content Consultants

The content consultants reviewed the manuscript for historical depth and accuracy and for clarity of presentation.

Jerry Bentley
Department of History
University of Hawaii
Honolulu, Hawaii

Marc Brettler
Department of Near Eastern
  and Judaic Studies
Brandeis University
Waltham, Massachusetts

Steve Gosch
Department of History
University of Wisconsin at Eau Claire
Eau Claire, Wisconsin

Don Holsinger
Department of History
Seattle Pacific University
Seattle, Washington

Patrick Manning
World History Center
Department of History
Northeastern University
Boston, Massachusetts

Richard Saller
Department of History
University of Chicago
Chicago, Illinois

Wolfgang Schlauch
Department of History
Eastern Illinois University
Charleston, Illinois

Susan Schroeder
Department of History
Loyola University of Chicago
Chicago, Illinois

Scott Waugh
Department of History
University of California, Los Angeles
Los Angeles, California

Multicultural Advisory Board Consultants

The multicultural advisors reviewed the manuscript for appropriate historical content.

Pat A. Brown
Director of the Indianapolis
  Public Schools
  Office of African Centered
  Multicultural Education
Indianapolis Public Schools
Indianapolis, Indiana

Ogle B. Duff
Associate Professor of English
University of Pittsburgh
Pittsburgh, Pennsylvania

Mary Ellen Maddox
Black Education Commission
  Director
Los Angeles Unified School District
Los Angeles, California

Jon Reyhner
Associate Professor and Coordinator of
  the Bilingual Multicultural
  Education Program
Northern Arizona University
Flagstaff, Arizona

Ysidro Valenzuela
Fresno High School
Fresno, California

California Program Consultants

Wendell Brooks
Berkeley High School
Berkeley, California

Kevin Burgo
Banning High School
Wilmington, California

Nick Garcia
Salinas High School
Salinas, California

Roger Gold
Banning High School
Wilmington, California

Dennis Gregg
Washington High School
San Francisco, California

Bill Hanna
Social Science Department
Director, History-Social Science
  Project
San Jose State University
San Jose, California

Brian Irvine
Silver Creek High School
San Jose, California

Judith Mahnke
Wallenberg High School
San Francisco, California

Sharlynn Mar
Westmont High School
Campbell, California

Douglas E. Miller
Stanford Teaching Education Program
Palo Alto, California

James R. Mullen
Del Mar High School
San Jose, California

Karl Ochi
Washington High School
San Francisco, California

Ellen Oicles
Piedmont Hills High School
San Jose, California

Tim Paulson
Cerritos High School
Cerritos, California

Greg Raby
Bonita Vista High School
Chula Vista, California

Lauren Ream
Henry Gunn High School
Palo Alto, California

Ingrid Sayer
Washington High School
San Francisco, California

Bill Smiley
Leigh High School
San Jose, California

Claudia Udd
Del Mar High School
San Jose, California

Ysidro Valenzuela
Fresno High School
Fresno, California

Danny Villa
James Logan High School
Union City, California

Ruben Zepeda
Compliance Advisor, Language
  Acquisition and Curriculum
  Development
Los Angeles Unified School District
Los Angeles, California

Reviewers (continued)

Teacher Review Panels

The following educators provided ongoing review during the development of prototypes, the table of contents, and key components of the program.

California Teacher Panel

Anna Bolla
Lincoln High School
San Francisco, California

Bob Piercy
Wilson High School
Long Beach, California

Carolyn Keller
Fremont Senior High School
Oakland, California

Ernest Cervantes
East Bakersfield High School
Bakersfield, California

Jim Fletcher
Clairemont High School
San Diego, California

Jim Lloyd
Bullard High School
Fresno, California

Michael Denman
Grant High School
Van Nuys, California

Stefanie Raczka
Norco High School
Norco, California

Steve Rosenberg
Whitney High School
Artesia, California

Mike Cuckovich
Johnson High School
Sacramento, California

Midwest Teacher Panel

Bruce Bekemeyer
Marquette High School
Chesterfield, Missouri

Margaret Campbell
Central High School
St. Louis, Missouri

Nancy Coates
Belleville East High School
Belleville, Illinois

Kim Coil
Francis Howell North High School
St. Charles, Missouri

Gary Kasprovich
Granite City High School
Granite City, Illinois

Harry McCown
Hazelwood West High School
Hazelwood, Missouri

Joseph Naumann
McCluer North High School
Florissant, Missouri

Leonard Sullivan
Pattonville High School
Maryland Hts., Missouri

Carole Weeden
Fort Zumwalt South High School
St. Peters, Missouri

Rita Wylie
Parkway West Sr. High School
Ballwin, Missouri

Teacher Reviewers

Glenn Bird
Springville High School
Springville, Utah

Michael Cady
North High School
Phoenix, Arizona

William Canter
Guilford High School
Rockford, Illinois

Nancy Coates
Belleville East High School
Belleville, Illinois

Paul Fitzgerald
Estancia High School
Costa Mesa, California

Tom McDonald
Phoenix Union HSD
Phoenix, Arizona

Myras Osman
Homewood Flossmoor High School
Flossmoor, Illinois

Dorothy Schulze
Health Careers High School
Dallas, Texas

Student Board

The following students reviewed prototype materials for the textbook.

LaShaunda Allen
Weston High School
Greenville, MS

Brandy Andreas
Rayburn High School
Pasadena, TX

Adam Bishop
Jordan High School
Sandy, UT

Jennifer Bragg
Midlothian High School
Midlothian, VA

Nicole Fevry
Midwood High School
Brooklyn, NY

Phillip Gallegos
Hilltop High School
Chula Vista, CA

Matt Gave
Stevenson Senior High School
Sterling Heights, MI

Blair Hogan
Leesville Road High School
Raleigh, NC

Ngoc Hong
Watkins Mill Senior High School
Gaithersburg, MD

Iman Jalali
Glenbrook North High School
Northbrook, IL

Vivek Makhijani
Durfee High School
Fall River, MA

Todd McDavitt
Derby High School
Derby, KS

Teniqua Mitchell
Linden-McKinley High School
Columbus, OH

Cicely Nash
Edmond Memorial High School
Edmond, OK

Brian Nebrensky
Hillsboro High School
Hillsboro, OR

Jesse Neumyer
Cumberland Valley High School
Mechanicsburg, PA

Nora Patronas
Alba High School
Bayou La Batre, LA

Lindsey Petersen
Stoughton High School
Stoughton, WI

Nicholas Price
Central Lafourche Senior
High School
Mathews, LA

Ben Richey
Fort Vancouver High School
Vancouver, WA

Karen Ryan
Silver Creek High School
San Jose, CA

Matt Shaver
Weatherford High School
Weatherford, TX

Richie Spitler
Atlantic High School
Port Orange, FL

Jessie Stoneberg
Burnsville High School
Burnsville, MN

Kelly Swick
Ocean Township High School
Oakhurst, NJ

Jason Utzig
Kenmore East High School
Tonawanda, NY

Justin Woodly
North Cobb High School
Kennesaw, GA

Introduction

Beginnings of the Modern World

Unit 1
1300–1800

Industrialism and the Race for Empire

Unit 3
1700–1914

xii

Perspectives on the Present

xiv

Skillbuilder Handbook

The *Skillbuilder Handbook is at the back of the book on pages 648–672. Refer to it when you need help in answering Think Through History questions, doing the activities entitled Interact with History, or answering questions in Section Assessments and Chapter Assessments.*

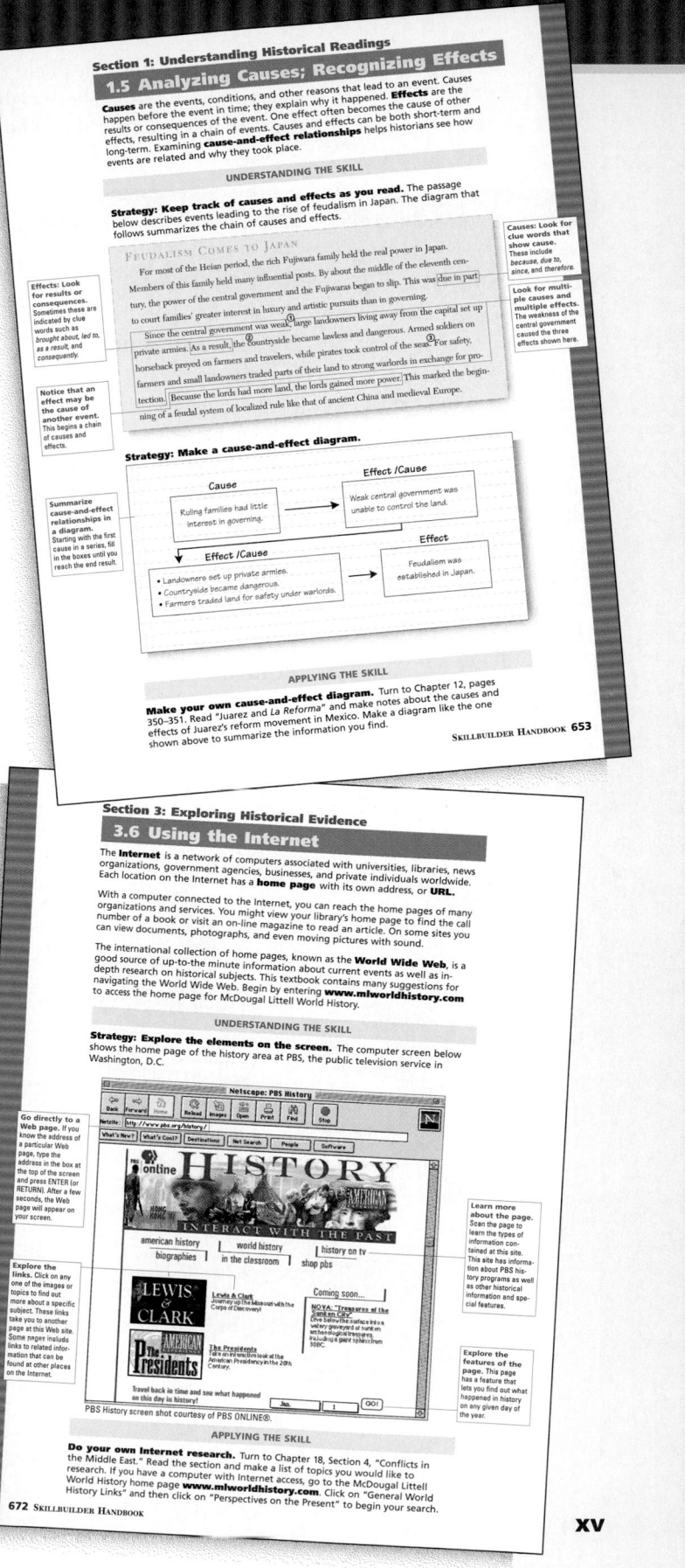

Patterns of Interaction Video Series

 VIDEO Each video in the series *Patterns of Interaction* relates to a **Global Impact** feature in the text. These eight exciting videos show how cultural interactions have shaped our world and how patterns in history continue to the present day.

VIDEO The Video Icon in the **Global Impact** feature provides you with a link to the *Patterns of Interaction* video series.

xvi

Major Features

Daily Life

different PERSPECTIVES

SCIENCE & TECHNOLOGY

HISTORY THROUGH ART

SOMETHING IN COMMON *across cultures*

Global Impact

*Links to VIDEO *Patterns of Interaction*

Features

xviii

CONNECT *to* TODAY

Unresolved*Problems*

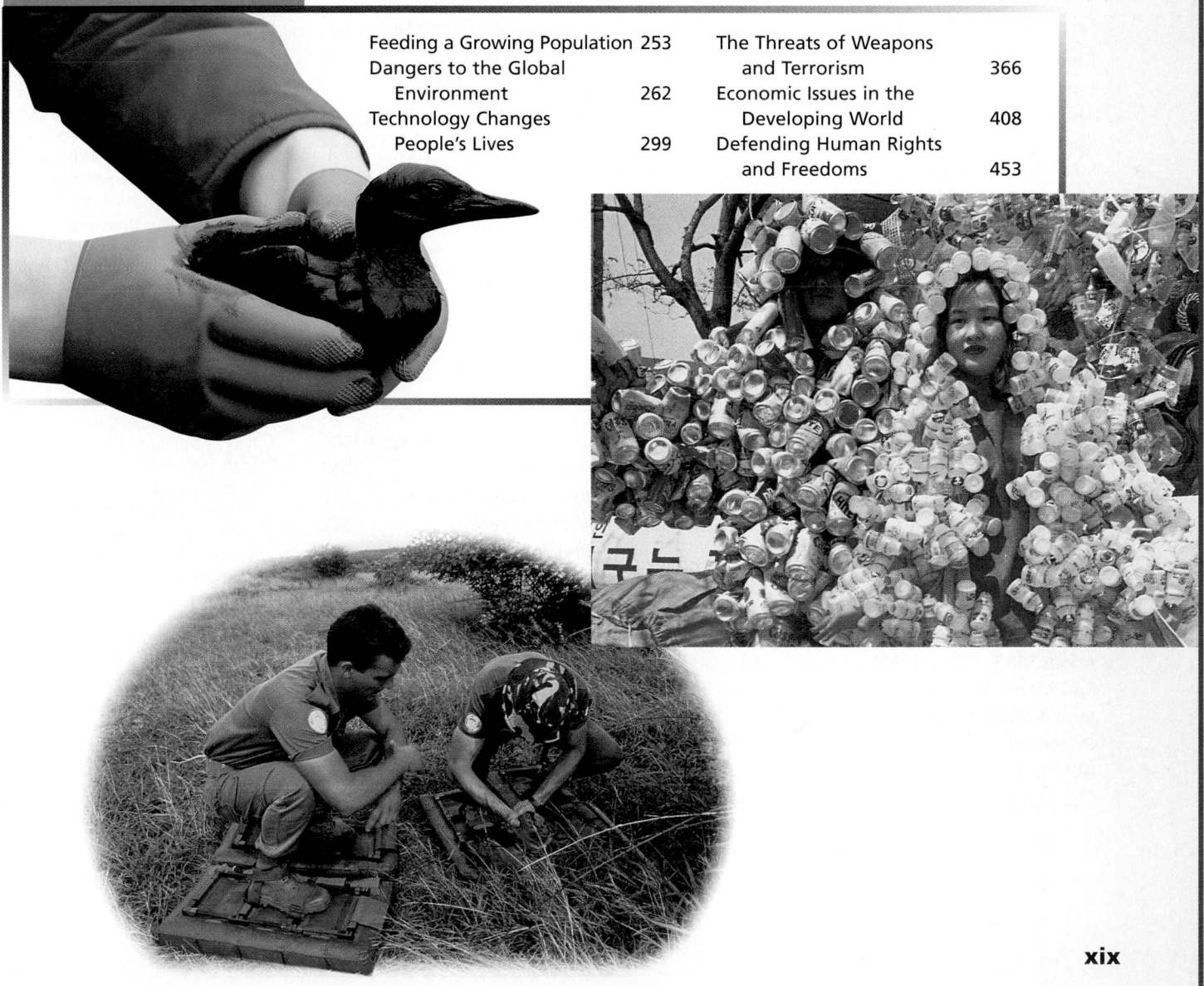

xix

Features

HISTORY MAKERS

HISTORY MAKERS

**Padre José Morelos
1765–1815**

Born into poverty, José Morelos did not begin to study for the priesthood until he was 25. In his parish work, he mainly served poor Indians and mestizos. In 1811, he joined Father Hidalgo, along with his parishioners. After Hidalgo's death, the skillful Morelos took command of the peasant army.

By 1813, his army controlled all of southern Mexico except for the largest cities. Morelos then called a Mexican congress to set up a democratic government. The supporters of Spain, however, finally caught up with the congress. As the rebels fled, Morelos stayed behind to fight. The Spanish finally captured and shot Morelos in 1815. Napoleon knew of this priest-revolutionary and said: "Give me three generals like him and I can conquer the world."

Historical and Political Maps

China, 1927–1938

Japanese attacks
Japanese territory, 1928
Japanese territory, 1933
Japanese territory, 1938
Long March, 1934–35
Communist bases

xxi

Charts, Graphs, and Time Lines

Charts

Graphs

Timelines

Infographics and Focus On

Infographics

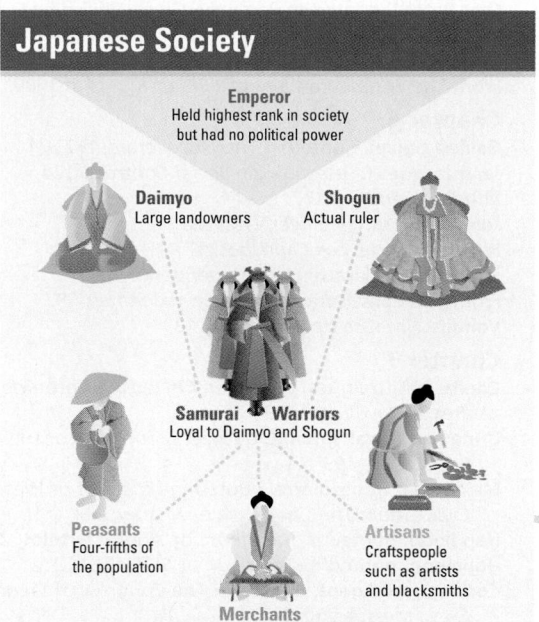

Japanese Society

Emperor
Held highest rank in society but had no political power

Daimyo
Large landowners

Shogun
Actual ruler

Samurai Warriors
Loyal to Daimyo and Shogun

Peasants
Four-fifths of the population

Artisans
Craftspeople such as artists and blacksmiths

Merchants
Low status but gradually gained influence

FOCUS ON

Primary Sources and Personal Voices

VOICE FROM THE PAST
For even though some of the Western methods are different from our own, and may even be an improvement, there is little about them that is new.

KANGXI, quoted in *Emperor of China: Self-Portrait of K'ang-hsi*

VOICE FROM THE PAST
We lie in the middle of Europe. We have at least three fronts on which we can be attacked. . . . So we are spurred forward on both sides to endeavors which perhaps we would not make otherwise.

OTTO VON BISMARCK, from an 1888 speech

VOICE FROM THE PAST
There is a new African in the world, and that new African is ready to fight his own battle.

KWAME NKRUMAH, 1957 speech

xxv

World History Themes

While historical events are unique, they often are driven by similar, repeated forces. In telling the history of our world, this book pays special attention to eight significant and recurring themes. These themes are presented to show that from America, to Africa, to Asia, people are more alike than they realize. Throughout history humans have confronted similar obstacles, have struggled to achieve similar goals, and continually have strived to better themselves and the world around them.

Power and Authority

History is often made by the people and institutions in power. As you read about the world's powerful people and governments, try to answer several key questions.

- Who holds the power?• How did that person or group get power?
- What system of government provides order in this society?
- How does the group or person in power keep or lose power?

Religious and Ethical Systems

Throughout history, humans around the world have been guided by, as much as anything else, their religious and ethical beliefs. As you examine the world's religious and ethical systems, pay attention to several important issues.

- What beliefs are held by a majority of people in a region?
- How do these major religious beliefs differ from one another?
- How do the various religious groups interact with one another?
- How do religious groups react toward nonmembers?

Revolution

Often in history, great change has been achieved only through force. As you read about the continuous overthrow of governments, institutions, and even ideas throughout history, examine several key questions.

- What long-term ideas or institutions are being overthrown?
- What caused people to make this radical change?
- What are the results of the change?

Interaction with Environment

Since the earliest of times, humans have had to deal with their surroundings in order to survive. As you read about our continuous interaction with the environment, keep in mind several important issues.

- How do humans adjust to the climate and terrain where they live?
- How have changes in the natural world forced people to change?
- What positive and negative changes have people made to their environment?

Economics

Economics has proven to be a powerful force in human history. From early times to the present, human cultures have been concerned with how to use their scarce resources to satisfy their needs. As you read about different groups, note several key issues regarding the role of economics in world history.

• What goods and services does a society produce?
• Who controls the wealth and resources of a society?
• How does a society obtain more goods and services?

Cultural Interaction

Today, people around the world share many things, from music, to food, to ideas. Human cultures actually have interacted with each other since ancient times. As you read about how different cultures have interacted, note several significant issues.

• How have cultures interacted (trade, migration, or conquest)?
• What items have cultures passed on to each other?
• What political, economic, and religious ideas have cultures shared?
• What positive and negative effects have resulted from cutural interaction?

Empire Building

Since the beginning of time, human cultures have shared a similar desire to grow more powerful—often by dominating other groups. As you read about empire building through the ages, keep in mind several key issues.

• What motivates groups to conquer other lands and people?
• How does one society gain control of others?
• How does a dominating society control and rule its subjects?

Science and Technology

All humans share an endless desire to know more about their world and to solve whatever problems they encounter. The development
of science and technology has played a key role in these quests. As you read about the role of science and technology in world history, try to answer several key questions.

• What tools and methods do people use to solve the various problems they face?
• How do people gain knowledge about their world? How do they use that knowledge?
• How do new discoveries and inventions change the way people live?

xxvii

Geography Themes

Geography is the study of the earth and its features. It is also an important part of human history. Since the beginning of time, all civilizations have had to control their surroundings in order to survive. In addition, geography has played a vital role in many historical events. Like history itself, geography reflects several key themes. These themes help us to understand the different ways in which geography has helped shape the story of world history.

Location

Location tells us where in the world a certain area is. Geographers describe location in two ways: *absolute* location and *relative* location. An area's absolute location is its point of latitude and longitude. Latitude is the distance in degrees north or south of the equator. Longitude is the degree distance east or west of an imaginary vertical line that runs through Greenwich, England, called the prime meridian. An area's relative location describes where it is in terms of other areas.

In absolute terms, the middle of Singapore lies at 1°20' north latitude and 103°50' east longitude. This information allows you to pinpoint Singapore on a map. In relative terms, Singapore is an island country on the southern tip of the Malay Peninsula near where the South China Sea and the Indian Ocean meet. How might Singapore's location on the sea have helped it develop into an economic power?

Human/Environment Interaction

Throughout history, humans have changed and have been changed by their environment. Because they live on an island, the people of Singapore have built a bridge in order to travel more easily to mainland Malaysia. In addition, Singapore residents have carved an inviting harbor out of parts of its coastline in order to accommodate the island's busy ocean traffic.

Singapore is one of the most densely populated countries in the world. Many of its nearly three million citizens live in the capital city, Singapore. The country's population density is about 12,000 persons per square mile. In contrast, the United States has a population density of 71 persons per square mile. What environmental challenges does this situation pose?

Singapore

0   5 Miles
0   10 Kilometers

1°25'N

Sembawang

Johor Strait

MALAYSIA

Kranji Reservoir

Woodlands

Punggol

Ubin

Tekong Besar

Seletar R.

Serangoon

Serangoon Harbor

Changi

SINGAPORE

Bedok Reservoir

Changi International Airport

Jurong

Bedok

City of Singapore

Ayer Chawan

Jurong Islands

Ayer Merbau

Sentosa

Bukum

Keppel Harbor

Singapore Strait

104°E

1°15'N

103°40'E

Selat Pandan

103°50'E

- ■ Urbanized area
- ☐ Other Singapore land
- — International border
- — Road

xxviii

Region

A region is any area that has common characteristics. These characteristics may include physical factors, such as landforms or climate. They also may include cultural aspects, such as language or religion. Singapore is part of a region known as Southeast Asia. The countries of this region share such characteristics as rich, fertile soil, as well as a strong influence of Buddhism and Islam.

Because regions share similar characteristics, they often share similar concerns. In 1967, Singapore joined with the other countries of Southeast Asia to form the Association of Southeast Asian Nations. This body was created to address the region's concerns. What concerns might Singapore have that are unique?

Place

Place, in geography, indicates what an area looks like in both physical and human terms. The physical setting of an area—its landforms, soil, climate, and resources—are aspects of place. So are the different cultures which inhabit an area.

The physical characteristics of Singapore include a hot, moist climate with numerous rain forests. In human terms, Singapore's population is mostly Chinese. How does Singapore's human characteristic tie it to other countries?

Movement

In geography, movement is the transfer of people, goods, and ideas from one place to another. In many ways, history is the story of movement. Since early times, people have migrated in search of better places to live. They have traded with distant peoples to obtain new goods. And they have spread a wealth of ideas from culture to culture.

Singapore, which is a prosperous center of trade and finance, attracts numerous people in search of greater wealth and new goods. What about Singapore's geography makes it the ideal place for the trading of goods?

xxix

Time

While history is the story of people, it is also the examination of when events occurred. Keeping track of the order of historical events will help you to better retain and understand the material. To help you remember the order and dates of important events in history, this book contains numerous time lines. Below is some instruction on how to read a time line, as well as a look at some terms associated with tracking time in history.

How to Read a Time Line

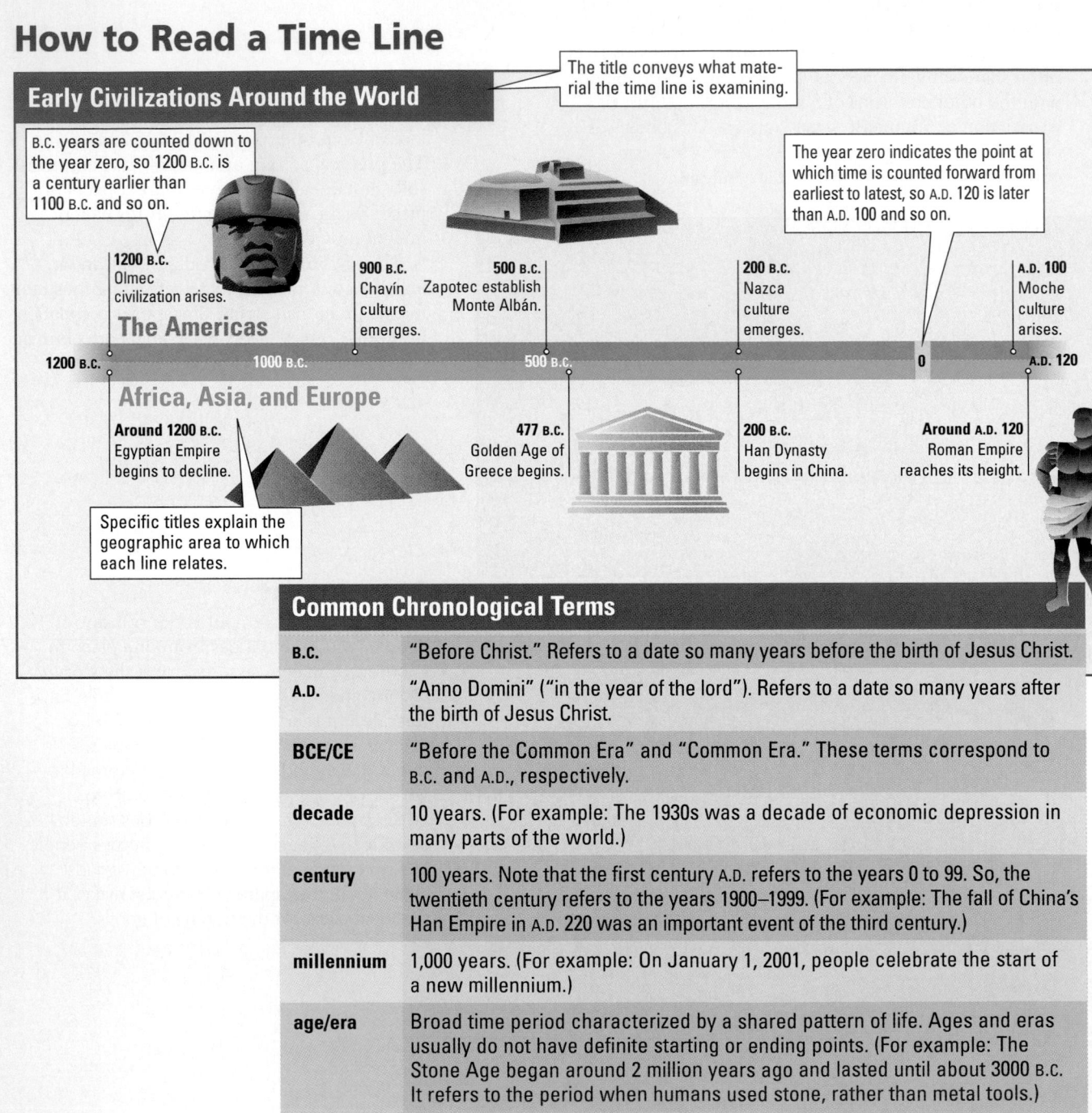

The title conveys what material the time line is examining.

Early Civilizations Around the World

B.C. years are counted down to the year zero, so 1200 B.C. is a century earlier than 1100 B.C. and so on.

The year zero indicates the point at which time is counted forward from earliest to latest, so A.D. 120 is later than A.D. 100 and so on.

The Americas

1200 B.C. Olmec civilization arises.

900 B.C. Chavín culture emerges.

500 B.C. Zapotec establish Monte Albán.

200 B.C. Nazca culture emerges.

A.D. 100 Moche culture arises.

1200 B.C. — 1000 B.C. — 500 B.C. — 0 — A.D. 120

Africa, Asia, and Europe

Around 1200 B.C. Egyptian Empire begins to decline.

477 B.C. Golden Age of Greece begins.

200 B.C. Han Dynasty begins in China.

Around A.D. 120 Roman Empire reaches its height.

Specific titles explain the geographic area to which each line relates.

Common Chronological Terms

B.C.	"Before Christ." Refers to a date so many years before the birth of Jesus Christ.
A.D.	"Anno Domini" ("in the year of the lord"). Refers to a date so many years after the birth of Jesus Christ.
BCE/CE	"Before the Common Era" and "Common Era." These terms correspond to B.C. and A.D., respectively.
decade	10 years. (For example: The 1930s was a decade of economic depression in many parts of the world.)
century	100 years. Note that the first century A.D. refers to the years 0 to 99. So, the twentieth century refers to the years 1900–1999. (For example: The fall of China's Han Empire in A.D. 220 was an important event of the third century.)
millennium	1,000 years. (For example: On January 1, 2001, people celebrate the start of a new millennium.)
age/era	Broad time period characterized by a shared pattern of life. Ages and eras usually do not have definite starting or ending points. (For example: The Stone Age began around 2 million years ago and lasted until about 3000 B.C. It refers to the period when humans used stone, rather than metal tools.)

You are about to examine not only thousands of years of history, but nearly every region of the globe. To help you visualize the faraway places you read about, this book contains numerous maps. Many of these maps contain several layers of information that provide a better understanding of how and why events in history occurred. Below is a look at how to read a map in order to obtain all of the rich information it offers.

How to Read a Map

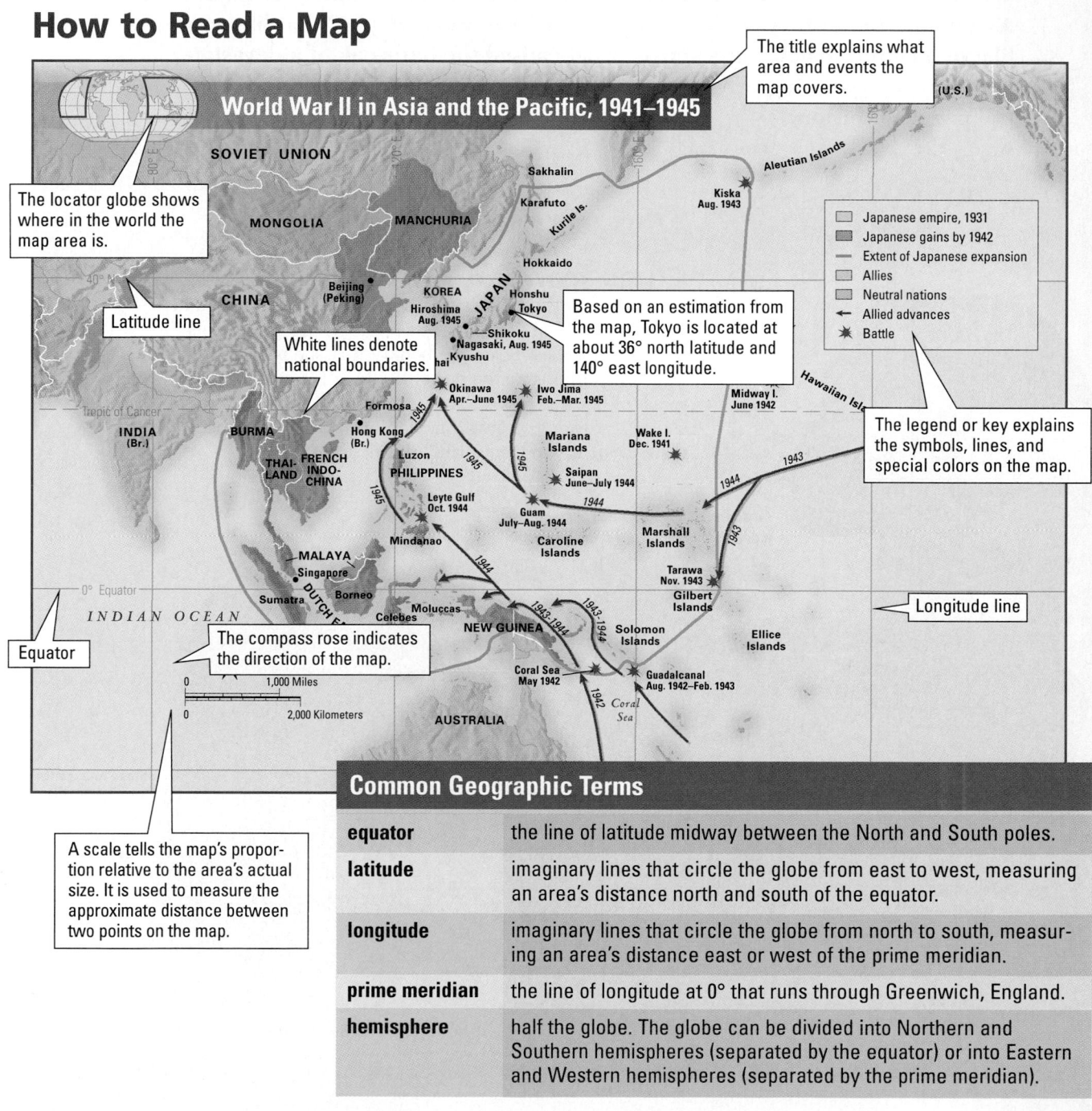

The title explains what area and events the map covers.

The locator globe shows where in the world the map area is.

Latitude line

White lines denote national boundaries.

Based on an estimation from the map, Tokyo is located at about 36° north latitude and 140° east longitude.

The legend or key explains the symbols, lines, and special colors on the map.

Longitude line

The compass rose indicates the direction of the map.

Equator

A scale tells the map's proportion relative to the area's actual size. It is used to measure the approximate distance between two points on the map.

World War II in Asia and the Pacific, 1941–1945

Japanese empire, 1931
Japanese gains by 1942
Extent of Japanese expansion
Allies
Neutral nations
Allied advances
Battle

Common Geographic Terms	
equator	the line of latitude midway between the North and South poles.
latitude	imaginary lines that circle the globe from east to west, measuring an area's distance north and south of the equator.
longitude	imaginary lines that circle the globe from north to south, measuring an area's distance east or west of the prime meridian.
prime meridian	the line of longitude at 0° that runs through Greenwich, England.
hemisphere	half the globe. The globe can be divided into Northern and Southern hemispheres (separated by the equator) or into Eastern and Western hemispheres (separated by the prime meridian).

xxxi

Do you like puzzles? If so, you are in luck. You are about to encounter the greatest puzzle there is: history. The study of history is much more than the recollection of dates and names. It is an attempt to answer a continuous and puzzling question: what really happened?

In their effort to solve this puzzle, historians and researchers use a variety of methods. From digging up artifacts, to uncovering eyewitness accounts, experts collect and analyze mountains of data in numerous ways. As a result, the history books you read more accurately depict what life was like in a culture 5,000 years ago, or what caused the outbreak of a devastating war. The following two pages examine some of the pieces used to solve the puzzle of history.

Clues from an Ancient Girl

In 1995, an anthropologist discovered the mummified and frozen remains of a teenage girl in the Andes Mountains of South America. Scientists believe that she is about 500 years old and was a member of the Inca Empire. Because much of her remains are well preserved, scientists hope she will provide them with new information about one of the Americas' most powerful ancient cultures.

An analysis of her stomach content may provide information about the Inca diet.

Her clothing, believed to belong to the upper class, should shed new light on how noble Inca women dressed.

Some of her DNA remains intact, which will help scientists determine whether she has any living descendants.

Modern Science

The ever-improving field of science has lent its hand in the search to learn more about the past. Using everything from microscopes to computers, researchers have shed new light on many historical mysteries. Here, a researcher uses computer technology to determine what the owner of a prehistoric human skull may have looked like.

Written Sources

Historians often look to written documents for insight into the past. There are various types of written sources. Documents written during the same time period as an event are known as *primary* sources. They include such things as diaries and newspapers. They also include drawings, such as the one shown here by Italian painter and inventor, Leonardo da Vinci. His rough sketch of a helicopter-type machine tells us that as early as the late 1400s, humans considered mechanical flight. Material written about an event later, such as books, are known as *secondary* sources. Some written sources began as oral tradition—legends, myths, and beliefs passed on by spoken word from generation to generation.

Digging Up History

Researchers have learned much about the past by discovering the remains of ancient societies. Spearheads like these, which date back to around 9,500 B.C., were found throughout North America. They tell us among other things that the early Americans were hunters. These spearheads were once considered to be the earliest evidence of humankind in the Americas. However, as an example of how history continues to change, scientists recently found evidence of human life in South America as early as 10,500 B.C.

xxxiii

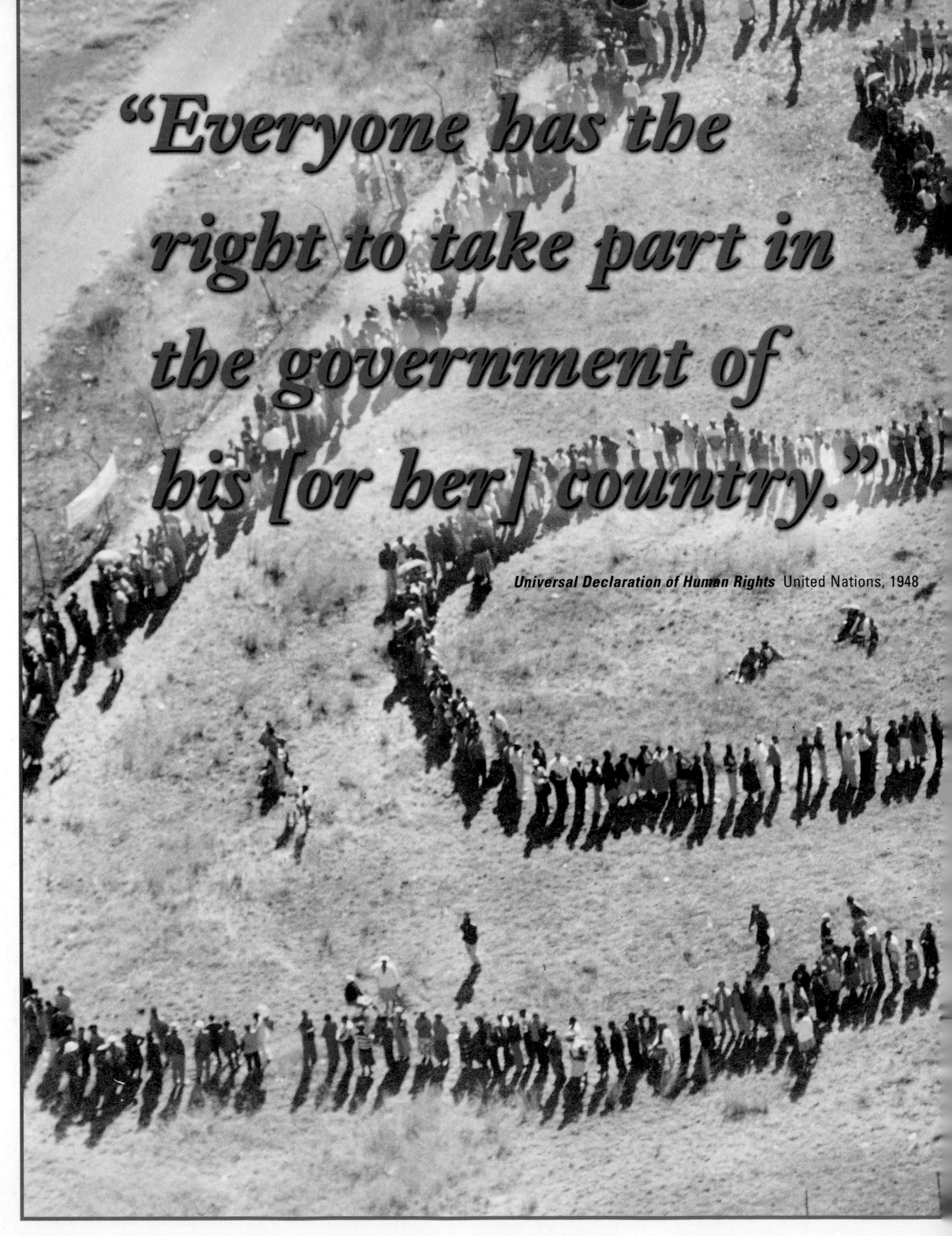

"*Everyone has the right to take part in the government of his [or her] country.*"

Universal Declaration of Human Rights United Nations, 1948

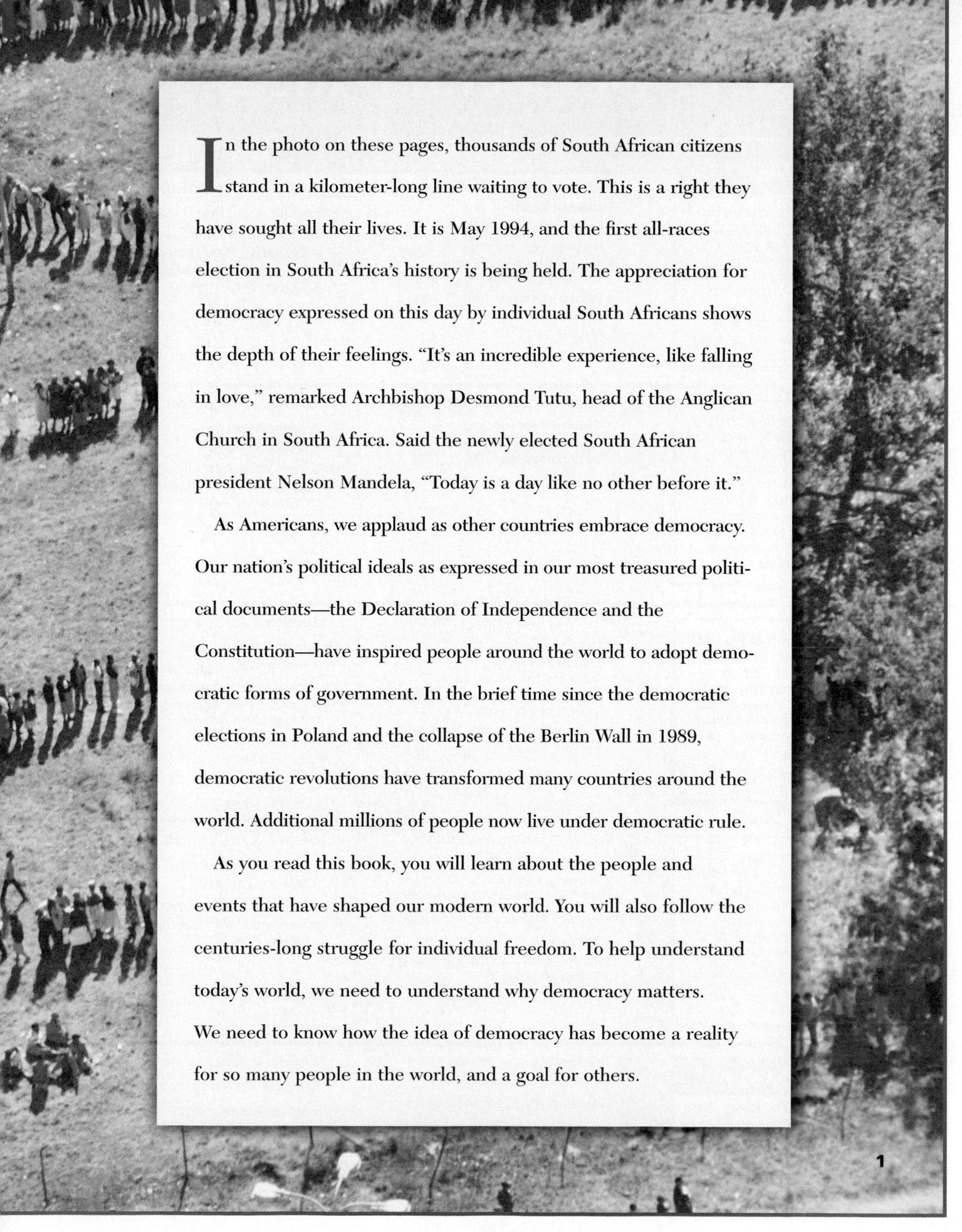

In the photo on these pages, thousands of South African citizens stand in a kilometer-long line waiting to vote. This is a right they have sought all their lives. It is May 1994, and the first all-races election in South Africa's history is being held. The appreciation for democracy expressed on this day by individual South Africans shows the depth of their feelings. "It's an incredible experience, like falling in love," remarked Archbishop Desmond Tutu, head of the Anglican Church in South Africa. Said the newly elected South African president Nelson Mandela, "Today is a day like no other before it."

As Americans, we applaud as other countries embrace democracy. Our nation's political ideals as expressed in our most treasured political documents—the Declaration of Independence and the Constitution—have inspired people around the world to adopt democratic forms of government. In the brief time since the democratic elections in Poland and the collapse of the Berlin Wall in 1989, democratic revolutions have transformed many countries around the world. Additional millions of people now live under democratic rule.

As you read this book, you will learn about the people and events that have shaped our modern world. You will also follow the centuries-long struggle for individual freedom. To help understand today's world, we need to understand why democracy matters. We need to know how the idea of democracy has become a reality for so many people in the world, and a goal for others.

1

The Rise of Democratic Ideas

	Key Ideas	**COPY MASTERS**	**ASSESSMENT**
SECTION 1 The Legacy of Ancient Greece and Rome pp. 5–9	Democratic ideas first develop in Greece in limited form around 500 B.C. The concept of a direct democracy is developed around 450 B.C. by the Greek ruler Pericles. Rome develops the idea of the republic and records fair, impartial laws, establishing the idea of a "government of laws, not of men."	*In-Depth Resources: Prologue* • **Guided Reading,** p. 1 • **Skillbuilder Practice:** Drawing Conclusions, p. 5 • **Geography Application:** The Roads of the Roman Empire, p. 6 • **Primary Source:** from *Politics*, p. 8 • **History Makers:** Justinian, p. 15	*Section 1 Assessment,* p. 9 *Formal Assessment* • Section Quiz, p. 5 *Alternative Assessment Book* • Standards for Evaluating a Cooperative Activity
SECTION 2 Judeo-Christian Tradition pp. 12–16	Judaism promotes the idea that people are responsible for making moral choices and for fighting against poverty and injustice. Christianity promotes the idea of equality, which is central to democracy. The Renaissance and the Reformation further the ideas of individualism and of challenging authoritarian institutions.	*In-Depth Resources: Prologue* • **Guided Reading,** p. 2 • **Primary Source:** The Ten Commandments, p. 9	*Section 2 Assessment,* p. 16 *Formal Assessment* • Section Quiz, p. 6 *Alternative Assessment Book* • Standards for Evaluating a Cooperative Activity
SECTION 3 Democratic Developments in England pp. 17–21	The Magna Carta limits the power of kings and promotes individual rights. The Parliament first develops in the late 13th century and grows stronger over the next four hundred years. As Parliament gains strength, England becomes a constitutional monarchy.	*In-Depth Resources: Prologue* • **Guided Reading,** p. 1 • **Primary Source:** From The Magna Carta, p. 10 • **Literature:** From *Here Be Dragons* by Sharon Kay Penman • **Connections Across Time and Cultures:** p. 17	*Section 3 Assessment,* p. 21 *Formal Assessment* • Section Quiz, p. 7 *Alternative Assessment Book* • Standards for Evaluating a Cooperative Activity
SECTION 4 The Enlightenment and Democratic Revolutions pp. 22–27	The ideas of Enlightenment thinkers Hobbes, Locke, Voltaire, Rousseau, and Montesquieu contribute to the rise of democratic ideals. They inspire the rise of democracy in America and France. The struggle for democracy continues today.	*In-Depth Resources: Prologue* • **Guided Reading,** p. 4 • **Primary Source:** From The Iroquois Constitution, p. 11 • **History Makers:** John Locke, p. 16 • **Literature:** From *1776*, p. 14 • **Connections Across Time and Cultures:** p. 17	*Section 4 Assessment,* p. 27 *Formal Assessment* • Section Quiz, p. 8 *Alternative Assessment Book* • Standards for Evaluating a Cooperative Activity
CHAPTER RESOURCES	**Chapter Overview** The rise of democratic ideas has taken thousands of years, beginning with the ancient Greeks and with the rise of Judaism and Christianity. Today, democratic institutions continue to grow and spread throughout the world.	*Telescoping the Times* • Prologue Summary, pp. 1–3 *Planning for Block Schedules* *Case Studies* • **Case Study 4**—Russia and Germany, p. 44 • **Case Study 8**—Argentina and South Africa, p. 100 • **Case Study 9**—Japan and Mexico, p. 114	*Prologue Assessment,* pp. 28–29 *Chapter Activities,* p. 29 *Formal Assessment* • Chapter Test, forms A and B, pp. 9–14 *Test Generator* *Alternative Assessment Book*

Warm-Up Transparency WTP

 World Art and Cultures Transparencies
- AT12 The Forum

 Electronic Library of Primary Sources
- "Wall Inscriptions from Pompeii," A.D. 79

 INTERNET RESOURCES
www.mlworldhistory.com

 Warm-Up Transparency WTP

 Electronic Library of Primary Sources
- from the *Book of Exodus* in the *Bible*, about 900s B.C.

 INTERNET RESOURCES
www.mlworldhistory.com

 Warm-Up Transparency WTP

 Electronic Library of Primary Sources
- "The Restoration of Charles II," 1660–1661

 INTERNET RESOURCES
www.mlworldhistory.com

 Warm-Up Transparency WTP

 World Art and Cultures Transparencies
- AT50 *Portrait of Marie Antoinette with Her Children*

 Electronic Library of Primary Sources
- "Destruction of the Berlin Wall," 1990

Block Scheduling (90 MINUTES)

Day 1
Section 1, pp. 5–9

 COOPERATIVE ACTIVITY
Comparing the governments of Sparta and Athens, p. 6 (Teacher's Edition)

Section Assessment, p. 9

Day 2
Section 2, pp. 12–16

 COOPERATIVE ACTIVITY
Mapping Paul's Travels, p. 14 (Teacher's Edition)

Section Assessment, p. 16

Day 3
Section 3, pp. 17–21

 COOPERATIVE ACTIVITY
A Skit about The Magna Carta, p. 18 (Teacher's Edition)

Section Assessment, p. 21

Day 4
Section 4, pp. 22–27

COOPERATIVE ACTIVITY
Learning about Leaders of the French Revolution, p. 26 (Teacher's Edition)

Section Assessment, p. 27

Chapter Assessment, pp. 28–29

Yearly Pacing *Chapter 1 Total:* 4 days *Yearly Total:* 85 days

 Planning for Block Schedules

Customizing for Special Needs

Students Acquiring English

 Access for Students Acquiring English
- **Guided Reading,** for Sections 1–4 (Spanish), pp. 12–15
- **Chapter Summary:** (Spanish), pp. 9–11
- **Skillbuilder Practice:** Drawing Conclusions (Spanish), p. 16
- **Geography Application:** The Roads of the Roman Empire (Spanish), p. 17

 Spanish Reading Study Guide
- pp. 5–13

 Chapter Summaries on Audiocassette in English and Spanish

Less Proficient Readers

 In-Depth Resources: Prologue
- **Guided Reading,** for Sections 1–4, pp. 1–4
- **Skillbuilder Practice:** Drawing Conclusions, p. 5
- **Geography Application:** The Roads of the Roman Empire, p. 6

 Telescoping the Times
- Prologue Summary, pp. 1–3

 Reading Study Guide
- pp. 5–13

 Chapter Summaries on Audiocassette

Gifted and Talented Students

 In-Depth Resources: Prologue

Primary Sources
- from *Politics*, p. 8
- The Ten Commandments, p. 9
- from The Magna Carta, p. 10
- from the Iroquois Constitution, p. 11

History Makers
- Justinian, p. 15
- John Locke, p. 16

Connections to Literature READINGS FOR STUDENTS

 In-Depth Resources: Prologue
Literature: from *Here Be Dragons* by Sharon Kay Penman; from *1776*, p. 14

Enrichment Reading
- **Roberts, Kenneth** *Oliver Wiswell* New York: Doubleday, 1940

This historically accurate story of the American Revolution is told from the viewpoint of a Tory.

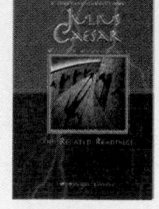

McDougal Littell *Literature Connections*

- **Shakespeare, William** *Julius Caesar* (with related readings)

This great play concerns events in ancient Rome as the republic comes to an end.

 = Pupil's Edition   = Overhead Transparency   = Software   = Video

= Copy Master   = CD-ROM   = Audiocassette   = Internet

Accessing Prior Knowledge

• Ask students to define democracy, discuss what they know about it, and relate experiences they have had participating in organizations or institutions that use democratic methods. Students might discuss experiences with school groups, community organizations, or within their families. Stress that in a democracy each individual has a say in how things are run.

Recognizing Sequencing

Have students read the captions on the spread.

• Ask them to create a time line showing the rise of democratic ideas and list the events depicted or described here on their time lines. Students can add to their time lines as they read the Prologue.

Geography Connection

Ask students to look at the map and read the captions.

• On which continent did democracy first arise? *Europe*

• Which civilizations and countries might have influenced each other to spread democratic ideas? *Greece might have influenced Rome. Accept other inferences students make that they back with reasons.*

PROLOGUE

The Rise of Democratic Ideas

PREVIEWING THEMES

Power and Authority
People long have recognized the need for government, or a system for exercising authority. For much of history, they lived under authoritarian rulers, such as kings. These absolute rulers gradually lost power with the rise of democratic ideas. People came to demand a role in governing themselves.

Revolution
In their Glorious Revolution, the English established the right to limit a ruler's power. This nonviolent revolution and the ideas developed in the Enlightenment sparked a rebellion of the American colonies against British rule. In turn, the American Revolution helped give rise to the French Revolution.

Cultural Interaction
Democracy developed in Greece and was adapted by the Romans. During the Renaissance, Reformation, and Enlightenment, questions concerning authority and individual rights were widely discussed throughout western Europe. From England, democratic ideas moved to its American colonies. The Declaration of Independence and the U.S. Constitution inspired democratic movements throughout the world.

UNITED STATES OF AMERICA

PACIFIC OCEAN

ATLANTIC OCEAN

George Washington addressed members of the **Constitutional Convention** who were meeting in Philadelphia in **1787** to draft a new plan for governing the United States. Below is a detail from the oil painting *Washington Addressing the Constitutional Convention* by Junius Brutus Stearns (1856).

Tropic of Cancer

INTERNET CONNECTION
Visit us at **www.mlworldhistory.com** to learn more about the rise of democratic ideas.

2

GEOGRAPHY THEMES

Place
Democratic ideas first arose in Greece. Greece is a mountainous country that, in ancient times, was divided into city-states. Each city-state was independent and had a fairly small population— about 20,000 people. Discuss with students how these factors might have helped contribute to the rise of democracy in ancient Greece. *Small size, isolation, and independence of political units might have made it easy for people to know and trust one another, which might spur democratic ideas.*

Movement
Tell students that this prologue is about how democratic ideas arose slowly over thousands of years and how these ideas have spread from civilization to civilization and region to region since ancient times. Ask students to look at the section titles near the top of page 3 and use the map to trace how they think different democratic ideas spread from one place to another in ancient times and in the modern world.

The **Roman Forum,** pictured here in a contemporary photo, was a government center and place of debate in ancient Rome for more than 600 years beginning in the **2nd century** B.C.

GREAT BRITAIN

GERMANY

FRANCE

ITALY

GREECE

AFRICA

Equator 0°

0° Prime Meridian

Arctic Circle

40°N

Tropic of Cancer

40°S

This ancient terracotta ballot box, discovered in the Agora in **Athens,** was used in the **5th century** B.C. by Athenian juries to cast verdicts at trials. Shown in detail are two of the ballots.

Some democratic traditions appeared in **West Africa** as early as the 9th century. Modern democracy in Africa did not begin until the **last half of the 20th century,** after a long period of European colonial rule. The photo to the right shows Hausa officials in contemporary West Africa. These men make decisions at several levels of government.

ADDITIONAL RESOURCES

Books for the Teacher

- Almond, Mark. *Revolution: 500 Years of Struggle for Change.* New York: De Agostini, 1996. Account of 27 revolutions.

- Aston, Margaret, ed. *The Panorama of the Renaissance.* New York: Abrams, 1996.

- Barber, James David. *The Book of Democracy.* Englewood Cliffs, New Jersey: Prentice Hall, 1995.

Books for the Student

- Hardy, W.G. *The Greek and Roman World.* Cambridge, MA: Schenkman, 1970.

- Shenkman, Richard. *Legends, Lies, and Cherished Myths of World History.* New York: Harper, 1993.

- Pierre, Michel. *The Renaissance.* Morristown: Silver Burdett, 1987.

- Swisher, Clarice. *The Glorious Revolution.* San Diego: Lucent, 1995. English Parliament gains supremacy over the monarchy.

Videos

- *Athenian Democracy.* Britannica, 1993. 800-554-9862.

- *Bill of Rights in Action.* Encyclopaedia Britannica, 800-554-9862. Connection of Bill of Rights to current issues.

- *The Age of Enlightenment.* Cambridge Social Studies, 1991. 800-468-4227.

Software

- *Ancient Greece.* CD-ROM. Educational Software Institute, 1994. 800-955-5570. Government, social rules, and daily life.

- *French Revolution.* CD-ROM. Educational Software Institute, 800-955-5570.

- *Renaissance and Reformation.* CD-ROM. Queue, 1994. 800-232-2224.

Washington Addressing the Constitutional Convention

Junius Brutus Stearns

Stearns (1810-1885) was a Vermont-born painter of portraits, scenes of everyday life, and recreated history. He is best-known for a sequence of five works chronicling the life of George Washington. This oil painting is one of that sequence. These paintings were the basis of a series of lithographs sold to a 19th-century public eager for patriotic scenes.

His paintings of Washington attempt to humanize America's great hero.

Washington played a vital role at the convention, more in his presence alone than in his actions as presiding officer. Many delegates were concerned about the power of the new federal government.

Confidence in Washington's judgment and the assumption that he would be the first president helped ease much of this concern.

Interpreting the Art. How does Stearns make Washington the main figure of the painting? How does the artist try to show the high regard in which Washington was held by the delegates to the constitutional convention?

This Interact with History feature encourages students to put themselves in the place of the young man in the picture, standing in front of Chinese Army tanks. He is pleading with the soldiers to not fire upon demonstrators who were calling for democracy in China. The feature helps students focus on how participating in or fighting for democracy affects people's lives.

Purpose

• to introduce students to the idea that people all over the world are interested in democracy

• to help students understand why democracy inspires people

• to prepare students to study the rise of democratic ideas and to help them make connections with the issues people have faced over time.

Teaching Strategy

Thinking Critically After students have reflected on this page, have them answer the key questions and explain their responses.

EXAMINING *the* ISSUES

Following are suggestions for addressing each bulleted question.

❶ Ask students to list personal freedoms that they have because they live in a democracy. Discuss how these freedoms affect the quality of their lives.

❷ Elicit a definition of the phrase *political oppression*. Ask students to discuss the relationship between political oppression and democracy.

❸ Ask students to list organizations or institutions in which democracy is the mode of government and those in which it is not. Encourage students to evaluate whether democracy could improve the way each undemocratic organization or institution runs.

Making Connections Have students discuss democratic institutions in which they participate now or might participate in the future.

Interact *with* History

The young man in the photo faced a line of tanks in Tiananmen Square in Beijing, China, on June 5, 1989. The tanks were poised to attack students who sparked a powerful pro-democracy movement in China that spring. Ultimately, the government sent troops into the square to crush the uprising. Hundreds were reportedly killed and thousands injured. This was neither the first nor the last time that people have rebelled against tyranny.

Why would people risk their lives for democracy?

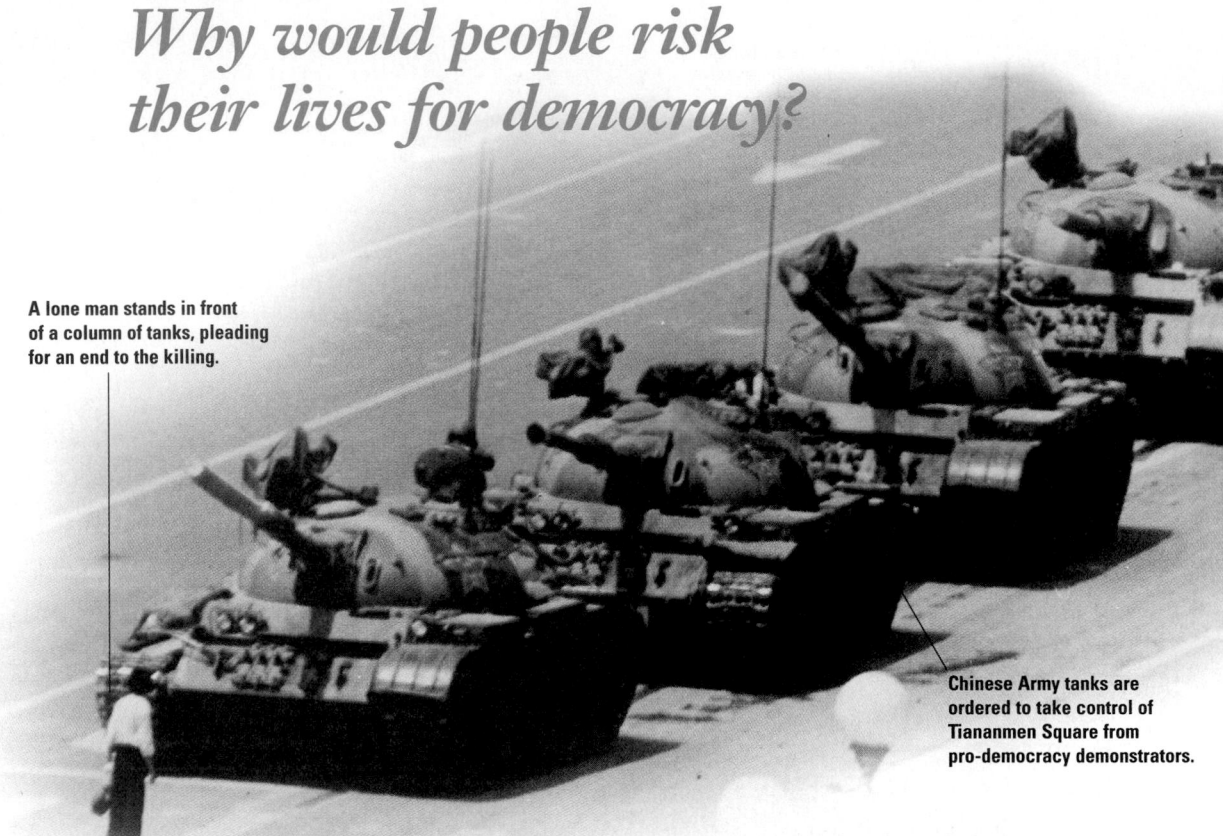

A lone man stands in front of a column of tanks, pleading for an end to the killing.

Chinese Army tanks are ordered to take control of Tiananmen Square from pro-democracy demonstrators.

EXAMINING *the* ISSUES

• How do the personal freedoms associated with democracy affect the quality of a person's life?

• Do people have an obligation to resist political oppression? Explain.

• How can people bring democracy into their lives?

Discuss these questions with your classmates. In your discussion, first think about what you value most in life, and why. Then imagine how people who are oppressed might feel and what they might do about these feelings.

As you read about the rise of democratic ideas in this prologue, think about how these ideas are expressed today.

Follow-Up

A feature on the chapter assessment will ask students to reevaluate their responses to the questions presented on this page. Remind students that their opinions may change as they learn more about the rise of democratic ideas.

The Legacy of Ancient Greece and Rome

TERMS & NAMES
- government
- democracy
- aristocracy
- citizen
- direct democracy
- monarchy
- natural laws
- republic
- senate

MAIN IDEA

The Greeks developed democracy, and the Romans added representative government and a written legal code.

WHY IT MATTERS NOW

Representation and a written law code are important features of democratic governments around the world.

SETTING THE STAGE Throughout history, people have recognized the need for a system for exercising authority, or a **government.** For the most part, they have lived under absolute rulers, such as chieftains, kings, or pharaohs, who have had total power. The idea that people can govern themselves—that is, the idea of **democracy**—evolved very slowly. It grew out of the contributions of many people over the course of thousands of years.

Athens Builds a Limited Democracy

Ancient Greek civilization claims the distinction of developing the first democracy. In fact, the word *democracy,* meaning "rule of the people," comes from the Greek words *demos,* meaning "people," and *kratos,* meaning "rule" or "authority."

Greek civilization began about 2000 B.C. The Greeks established cities in the small fertile valleys along Greece's rocky coast. Because of geographic isolation, each city-state had its own government. It was the basic political unit of ancient Greece.

Athens was the largest and most powerful city-state to emerge in Greece. It had a monarchy until 683 B.C. By then Athens had developed into an **aristocracy** (AR·uh·STAHK·ruh·see), or a state ruled by the noble class. Each year an assembly of citizens elected three nobles to rule the city-state. **Citizens** were adult male residents who were granted certain rights and responsibilities. After the nobles' year of service, they became part of a larger council of advisors.

The Reforms of Solon By 600 B.C., Athens was suffering severe economic problems. In order to pay their debts, poor farmers pledged part of their crops to wealthy landowners. They later pledged their land. Finally they sold themselves into slavery and were not able to leave the land. This situation caused a political and economic crisis.

In 594 B.C., Solon (SO·luhn), a respected statesman, tried to solve the problems of Athens. He passed a law outlawing slavery based on debt and canceled the farmers' debts. This simple act enabled Athens to avoid the devastation of revolution and civil war.

Solon continued his policies of political reform. He established four classes of citizenship based on wealth rather than heredity. Only citizens of the three higher classes were able to hold public office. Yet even the lowest class of citizens could vote in the assembly and, eventually, sit on juries. All free adult males were citizens. Solon also created a new Council of Four Hundred. This body prepared business for the already existing council.

Although these acts increased participation in government, Athens was still limited as a democracy. The aristrocracy was still dominant. Only citizens could participate in government, and only about one-

Background
A city-state included the city and its surrounding territory.

HISTORY MAKERS

**Solon
630?–560? B.C.**

Solon is known as one of the Seven Wise Men of Greece. He first gained public attention by urging the Athenians to go to war over possession of a nearby island. Athens listened to his advice and won the war. Solon became an Athenian hero.

Solon began a series of political reforms that greatly increased citizen participation in Athenian government. He said that he "stood with a strong shield before both parties [the common people and the powerful] and allowed neither to win an unfair victory." His reforms, unfortunately, did not please either the wealthy or the poor. He left Athens for ten years to travel. He died not long after his return. However, he spent that period warning people against rulers who would not uphold his reforms.

The Rise of Democratic Ideas **5**

OBJECTIVES

1. To identify the different political systems that developed in ancient Athens.

2. To trace changes in the Greek democracy and the flowering of Greek philosophy during the fifth century B.C.

3. To compare and contrast democracy in Athens with that under the Roman republic.

4. To describe the influence of Roman law on government.

CRITICAL THINKING

- Making inferences, p. 6
- Contrasting, p. 8
- Summarizing, p. 9
- Synthesizing, p. 9
- Analyzing themes, p. 9

FOCUS

5-Minute Warm-Up

Identifying Main Ideas
To examine the legacy of ancient Greece and Rome, have students answer these questions:

1. Read "Setting the Stage" on page 5. What has been the most common form of government in history?

2. What is democracy and did it evolve slowly or quickly?

 WARM-UP TRANSPARENCY WTP

OBJECTIVE ① INSTRUCT

Athens Builds a Limited Democracy

▶ *Key Ideas*
- At the beginning of its history, Athens is ruled by a king and later was ruled by an aristocracy.
- Solon introduces political reforms that give rights to more people in ancient Greece.
- Cleisthenes also works to make Athens more democratic.

 IN-DEPTH RESOURCES: PROLOGUE
Guided Reading, p. 1

 ACCESS FOR STUDENTS ACQUIRING ENGLISH
Guided Reading (Spanish), p. 12

SECTION 1 RESOURCES

PRINT RESOURCES

 IN-DEPTH RESOURCES: PROLOGUE
Guided Reading, p. 1
Skillbuilder Practice: Drawing Conclusions, p. 5
Geography Application: The Roads of the Roman Empire, p. 6
Primary Source: from *Politics,* p.8
History Makers: Justinian, p. 15

 ACCESS FOR STUDENTS ACQUIRING ENGLISH
Guided Reading (Spanish), p. 12
Skillbuilder Practice: (Spanish), p. 16
Geography Application: (Spanish), p. 17

 FORMAL ASSESSMENT
Section Quiz, p. 5
 ALTERNATIVE ASSESSMENT BOOK

TECHNOLOGY RESOURCES

WORLD ART AND CULTURES TRANSPARENCIES
AT00 The Forum

CD-ROM
Electronic Library of Primary Resources

Refer students to the quote about Solon as a shield. Ask students to draw political cartoons interpreting this quote and to discuss why people who treat all groups with fairness may have difficulty in politics. *Responses should relate to the conflicting demands of different groups, such as farmers, merchants, rich, and poor, especially when each group refuses to consider the needs of others.*

OBJECTIVE ② INSTRUCT

Changes in Greek Democracy

▶ **Key Ideas**
• In the fifth century B.C., Pericles introduces the idea of direct democracy in Athens.

• Philosophers, including Socrates, Plato, and Aristotle, use logic and reason to explore new ideas, creating an atmosphere conducive to democracy.

• The Greeks develop a number of ideas about and institutions for governing that are important in our government today.

CRITICAL THINKING ACTIVITY
CLASS TIME: 5 TO 10 MINUTES

Evaluating
Encourage students to discuss the benefits and drawbacks of a government making decisions democratically during a crisis such as a war. You might use a chart such as the one below as a discussion starter.

Democracy During a Crisis	
Benefits	**Drawbacks**
• Form of government remains stable	

---

tenth of the population were citizens. Athenian law denied citizenship to women, slaves, and foreign residents. Women generally were involved in rearing children, weaving clothing, preparing meals, and managing the household. Slaves formed about one-third of the Athenian population. They worked in mines, farmed fields, and did housework.

Solon introduced additional political reforms. These included a fairer code of laws and the right of citizens to bring charges against wrongdoers. His economic reforms benefited many. For example, by encouraging the export of grapes and olives, Solon started a profitable overseas trade and demand for these products. However, Solon stopped short of a complete program of land reform. This perhaps was because he knew that the nobility would not tolerate such an extreme measure.

The Reforms of Cleisthenes Conflicts continued between the landowners and the farming classes. Solon was succeeded by a series of powerful individuals who gained control of the government by appealing to the poor and the discontented for support. They gave land, voting rights, and citizenship to the masses in exchange for power.

Beginning in 508 B.C., the Athenian leader Cleisthenes (KLYS·thuh·NEEZ) introduced further reforms. He worked toward making Athens a full democracy by reorganizing the assembly. He wanted to break up the power of the nobility. He also increased the power of the assembly by allowing all citizens to submit laws for debate and passage. Cleisthenes then created the Council of Five Hundred. This body proposed laws and counseled the assembly. Council members were chosen by lot, or at random. These reforms allowed Athenian citizens to participate in a democracy. Because of his reforms, Cleisthenes is generally regarded as the founder of democracy in Athens.

Greek plays often dramatized themes important to democracy—leadership, justice, and duty. Pictured here is a modern British production of *The Oresteia*, written by Aeschylus in 458 B.C.

THINK THROUGH HISTORY
A. Summarizing
Why is Cleisthenes generally considered the founder of Athenian democracy?

Changes in Greek Democracy

In the 500s B.C., the Persian Empire was rapidly expanding northeast and southeast of Greece. In 490 B.C., Darius (duh·RY·uhs) the Great ordered a Persian fleet carrying 25,000 men to cross the Aegean Sea to invade Athens. The Greeks won this initial series of conflicts. Ten years later, Darius' son and successor, Xerxes (ZURK·seez), again tried to crush Greece. Eventually the Greek city-states fought side by side as allies and defeated the Persian forces in 479 B.C.

With the Persian threat ended, the Greek city-states felt a new sense of confidence and freedom. Athens, which played a major role in the Persian defeat, basked in the glory of the victory. After the war, Athens became the leader of an alliance of 140 city-states called the Delian League. The league drove the Persians from the territory surrounding Greece and ended the threat of future attacks. Soon after, Athens began to use its powerful navy to control other league members.

Pericles Strengthens Democracy The Athenians had maintained democracy during the Persian Wars by holding public debates about how to defend their city. After Persia's defeat, Athens continued to develop democracy. A wise and able statesman named Pericles led Athens for 32 years, from 461 to 429 B.C. The Age of Pericles became known as the Golden Age of Greece.

6 Prologue

 TEACHING OPTION / **BLOCK SCHEDULING**   **COOPERATIVE ACTIVITY: Comparing the Governments of Sparta and Athens**   **CLASS TIME 20 MINUTES**

Task: Student groups will research the government in either Sparta or Athens and work with members of another group to make a comparison chart.

Purpose: To compare and contrast the government in these two city-states.

Activity: Divide students into four groups. Assign one of the following topics to each group: role of

government in the lives of individuals in Sparta, or in Athens; responsibilities and privileges of citizens and noncitizens in Sparta, or in Athens. After completing their research, students should come together to make the chart. Allow paired groups to present their charts to the class.

 Building a Portfolio: Students should add the charts to their portfolio, along with an explanation of the assignment.

ALTERNATIVE ASSESSMENT BOOK
Standards for Evaluating a Cooperative Activity

Standards for Evaluation
Charts should . . .

• demonstrate students' understanding of their topics
• clearly convey differences and similarities
• show evidence of sound research

Pericles strengthened Greek democracy by increasing the number of paid public officials and by paying jurors. This allowed poorer citizens to participate in the government. Through greater citizen participation, Athens evolved into a **direct democracy.** This is a form of government in which citizens rule directly and not through representatives. In Athens more citizens were actively involved in government than in any other city-state. In a speech, Pericles expressed his great pride in Athenian democracy, when he said, "Our constitution is called a democracy because power is in the hands not of a minority but of the whole people."

Greece's Golden Age lasted for less than 50 years. Tensions grew between Athens and Sparta, a city-state known for its military values and strong army. The tensions between the two sparked the Peloponnesian War (431–404 B.C.). Sparta defeated Athens and disbanded the Delian League. Greece as a whole was weakened.

In the nearby kingdom of Macedonia, King Philip II also watched events in Greece—and dreamed of taking control of it. In 338 B.C., Philip invaded Greece and defeated the weakened city-states. The defeat led to the end of democracy in Greece. Philip, and then his son Alexander the Great, subjected the Greeks to rule by **monarchy,** or government controlled by one person.

Greek Philosophers Search for Truth During this time of questioning and uncertainty in Athens in the fourth century B.C., several great thinkers appeared. They used logic and reason to investigate the nature of the universe, human society, and morality. They were seeking the truth. The Greeks called such thinkers philosophers, meaning "lovers of wisdom." These Greek thinkers based their philosophy on the following assumptions: (1) The universe (land, sky, and sea) is put together in an orderly way and is subject to absolute and unchanging laws; and (2) people can understand these laws through logic and reason. The Greeks' respect for human intelligence and the power of reason had allowed the ideas of democracy to flourish.

The first of these great philosophers was Socrates (SAHK·ruh·TEEZ). He encouraged his students to examine their most closely held beliefs. He used a question-and-answer approach that became known as the Socratic method. Socrates' greatest pupil was Plato (PLAY·toh). In his famous work *The Republic,* Plato set forth his vision of a perfectly governed society. He wanted society governed not by the richest and most powerful but by the wisest:

> **A VOICE FROM THE PAST**
>
> Until philosophers are kings, or the kings and princes of this world have the spirit and power of philosophy, and political greatness and wisdom meet in one, and those commoner natures who pursue either to the exclusion of the other are compelled to stand aside, cities will never have rest from their evils, no, nor the human race.
>
> **PLATO,** *The Republic*

Plato's student Aristotle (AR·ih·STAHT·uhl) examined the nature of the world and of human belief, thought, and knowledge. In *Politics,* he stated, "Man is by nature a political animal; it is his nature to live in a state."

Legacy of Greece Greece set lasting standards in politics and philosophy. The Greeks did not rely on superstition or traditional explanations of the world. Instead, they used reason and intelligence to discover predictable patterns that they called **natural laws.** The Greeks did not wish to be subject to authoritarian rulers. So they developed direct democracy in order that citizens could actively participate in political decisions. The Greeks also were the first to think of three branches of government—a

SPOTLIGHT ON

The Igbo People

Western civilization did not have a monopoly on democratic government. The Igbo (IHG·boh) people—also called Ibo—of southern Nigeria in Africa practiced a form of democracy as early as the ninth century.

Igbo village government was made up of a council of elders and a village assembly. In the council, any adult male could take part in discussion, although the elders made the final decisions. In the assembly, everyone—young or old, rich or poor—had the right to speak. This practice encouraged a spirit of equality and competition among the Igbo.

SPOTLIGHT ON
The Igbo Tribe

Older people were accorded great respect in Igbo villages. The village council was traditionally made up of all the men in the village between the ages of 65 and 83. Men who were between the ages of 30 and 50 were considered "small boys;" only rarely were they involved in making important decisions for the village. Men did not retire from the village council until they were in their 80s. Even then, they served as advisers to the council. Encourage students to discuss whether the Igbo respect for elderly people could have helped strengthen their government.

MORE ABOUT . . .
Socrates, Plato, and Aristotle

These three philosophers laid some of the firmest foundations for Western education. The Socratic method is still used commonly in education. In the fields of law and medicine, for example, it is used to train students in analytical thinking. Plato opened an academy that lasted for about 900 years. Aristotle opened a rival school called the Lyceum, which served as a model for a later educational movement of the same name that began in New England in the early 1800s. The lyceums there were voluntary associations that brought in speakers to lecture and debate on current topics. The lyceums helped broaden school curricula and fostered the development of local museums and libraries.

IN-DEPTH RESOURCES: PROLOGUE
Primary Source: from Politics, p. 8

Gifted and Talented Students
Corresponding with Greek Philosophers
Have students read a section of at least one primary source by Socrates, Plato, or Aristotle (for example, Plato's discussion of the philosopher-king as ruler). Also have them read one secondary source about either Socractes, Plato, or Aristotle. After finishing the

sources, assign students to write a letter to the philosopher whose ideas they read.

In the letter, they should explain two qualities they admire about the person, two ideas they agree with, and two ideas they do not agree with or do not understand. After students have completed their letters, have

volunteers read their letters aloud and ask members of the class to respond to the students' ideas. Ask students how they think each of the philosophers would have responded to their analysis and questions.

Rome Develops a Republic

▶ **Key Ideas**

- Around 500 B.C., Rome develops a government called a republic.
- Expansion creates problems for the Roman republic, with alternating civil wars and rule by dictators.
- Rome ends democracy and becomes an empire in 27 B.C.

📄 **IN-DEPTH RESOURCES: PROLOGUE**
Geography Application: The Roads of the Roman Empire, p.6

 ELECTRONIC LIBRARY OF PRIMARY SOURCES
"Wall Inscriptions from Pompeii," A.D. 79

HISTORYMAKERS
Justinian

In his official writings about Justinian, court historian Procopius described the emperor as a serious, even-tempered ruler who worked from dawn to midnight. But in *The Secret History* (a book published after Justinian's death), Procopius portrayed Justinian as "deceitful, devious, false, hypocritical, two-faced, and cruel." Discuss with students why Procopius might have written such different opinions. Let students talk about how a ruler's personality may affect the way the ruler is viewed by history.

📄 **IN-DEPTH RESOURCES: PROLOGUE**
History Makers: Justinian, p. 15

Roman Law

▶ **Key Ideas**

- Rome develops a set of just laws that apply equally to people throughout the empire.
- Roman law furthers democratic traditions in Rome and in civilizations that follow.

Rome Develops a Republic

While the great civilization of Greece was in decline, a new civilization to the west was developing its power. From about 1000 to 500 B.C., the earliest Romans—the Latins—battled with Greeks and Etruscans for control of the Italian peninsula. The Romans were the victors. During the struggle, the Romans became familiar with and adapted elements of Greek civilization, including ideas about government.

From Kingdom to Republic Beginning in about 600 B.C., a series of kings ruled Rome. Then, in 509 B.C., a group of Roman aristocrats overthrew a harsh king. They set up a new government, calling it a republic. A **republic** is a form of government in which power rests with citizens who have the right to elect the leaders who make government decisions. It is an indirect democracy, in contrast to the direct democracy in which all citizens participate directly in the government. In Rome, as in Greece, citizenship with voting rights was granted only to free-born males.

In the early republic, two groups struggled for power. The patricians were aristocratic landowners who held most of the power. The plebeians were common farmers, artisans, and merchants. Over time, the plebeians forced the patricians to give them more power.

Republican Government Like the Athenians, the Romans established a government with separate branches. Two officials called consuls commanded the army and directed the government. Their term of office was only one year. The legislative branch was made up of a Senate and two assemblies. The **Senate** was the aristocratic branch of Rome's government. It controlled foreign and financial policies and advised the consuls. The two assemblies were more democratic, because they included other classes of citizens. In times of crisis, the republic also provided for a dictator, a leader who had absolute power to make laws and command the army. The dictator was limited to only a six-month term.

For hundreds of years after the founding of the republic, Rome expanded its territories through conquest and trade. By about 70 B.C., Rome's Mediterranean possessions stretched from Anatolia in the east to Spain in the west. But expansion created problems for the republic. For decades, Rome alternated between the chaos of civil war and the authoritarian rule of a series of dictators. Eventually the republic collapsed, and Augustus (aw·GUS·tus) became emperor in 27 B.C.

Roman Law

Rome had become a great power not only by conquering other lands but also by bringing the conquered peoples into its system. The Romans tried to create a system of laws that could be universally applied throughout the Roman Empire. Like the Greeks, they believed that laws should be based on principles of reason and justice and should protect citizens and their property. This idea applied to all people regardless of their nationality. It had a great influence on the development of democracy throughout the Western world.

Some of the most important principles of Roman law were the following:

- All citizens had the right to equal treatment under the law.
- A person was considered innocent until proven guilty.

HISTORY MAKERS

Justinian
482–565

By the time Justinian became emperor of the Roman Empire in the East in 527, the Western Roman Empire had fallen. During his reign, Justinian regained control of parts of the West and reunited them with the East as the Byzantine Empire.

To regulate this complex society, the emperor set up a panel of legal experts to comb through hundreds of years of Roman law and opinion. The panel's task was to create a single, uniform legal code for Justinian's "New Rome."

Justinian believed that "imperial majesty should not only be adorned with military might but also graced with laws, so that in times of peace and war alike the state may be governed aright." The Justinian Code has had a profound impact on the law of most Western countries.

Background
The Etruscans were an ancient people native to northern Italy.

THINK THROUGH HISTORY
B. Contrasting How does an indirect democracy differ from a direct democracy?

Background
Rome was never a true democracy, a government by and for all the people. In Rome, only upper-class or wealthy men had power. Women could not vote.

Written Laws The Romans set up the Twelve Tables (which were stone tablets), inscribed with the laws of Rome, in the town square of the Forum. Hammurabi, the Babylonian king, had his code of laws carved on a stone pillar. Although the laws of the United States are too numerous for public display, the four pages of the Constitution can be seen at the National Archives in Washington, D.C. Ask students to think of examples where written laws are displayed in public places today (for example, anti-nuisance laws in parks and no parking signs). Discuss reasons why a city, state, or national government chooses to display laws publicly.

Less Proficient Readers:
Taking Notes Pair a less proficient reader with a more proficient reader and ask them to read the information on pages 8 and 9. Direct the more proficient reader to show the less proficient reader how to take notes to remember the key ideas and facts of the section (for example, write an outline, make bulleted lists, or create a word web).

509 B.C. Romans establish a republic (representative government).

Rome

451 B.C. Roman law is collected in the Twelve Tables.

27 B.C. The Roman Republic is replaced by an empire.

A.D. 528 Emperor Justinian authorizes a panel to compile a written legal code, completed in 533.

600 B.C.   400 B.C.   200 B.C.   0   A.D. 200   A.D. 400   A.D. 600

Greece

508 B.C. Cleisthenes begins reorganizing the assembly to limit power of the nobles.

461 B.C. Pericles begins introducing direct democracy to Athens.

594 B.C. Solon begins reform of Greek laws by allowing all free adult males to attend the assembly.

- The burden of proof rested with the accuser rather than the accused.
- Any law that seemed unreasonable or grossly unfair could be set aside.

code: a systematically arranged and comprehensive collection of laws

A Written Legal Code Another characteristic of Roman government was its regard for written law. In 451 B.C., officials made a collection of Roman laws called the Twelve Tables. These tables assured that all citizens had a right to the protection of the law. Nearly 1,000 years later, in A.D. 528, Emperor Justinian ordered the compiling of all Roman laws since the earlier code. After its completion, this new code consisted of four works: *The Code,* containing nearly 5,000 Roman laws; *The Digest,* a summary of legal opinions; *The Institutes,* a textbook for law students; and *The Novellae,* laws passed after 534. The Code of Justinian later became a guide on legal matters throughout western Europe. Written laws helped establish the idea of "a government of laws, not of men," where even rulers and other powerful persons could sometimes be held accountable for their actions.

During the Roman Republic, citizens voted by dropping a stone tablet in a voting urn as depicted on this Roman coin from 137 B.C.

THINK THROUGH HISTORY
C. Summarizing
How did Rome influence the development of democracy in the western world?

Legacy of Rome Rome gave the world the idea of a republic. Legal and political terms that are common today, such as senate and dictator, originated in Rome. Rome also adopted from the Greeks the notion that an individual is a citizen in a state rather than the subject of a ruler. Perhaps Rome's greatest and most lasting legacy was its written legal code and the idea that this code should be applied equally and impartially to all citizens. Rome preserved and added to Greece's idea of democracy and passed on the early democratic tradition to civilizations that followed.

Section 1 Assessment

1. TERMS & NAMES
Identify
- government
- democracy
- aristocracy
- citizen
- direct democracy
- monarchy
- natural laws
- republic
- senate

2. TAKING NOTES
Using a diagram like the one below, list three contributions of Greece to democracy.

Democracy

Which contribution do you think had the greatest impact on the modern world?

3. SYNTHESIZING
Which characteristic of the government under the Roman Republic had the greatest impact on the democratic tradition?

THINK ABOUT
- the control of power by citizens
- the separation of government branches
- the regard for written law

4. ANALYZING THEMES
Power and Authority How do the steps Athens took reflect a turn toward democracy?

THINK ABOUT
- Solon's reforms
- Cleisthenes' reforms
- the Age of Pericles

The Rise of Democratic Ideas **9**

ANSWERS

1. TERMS & NAMES
government, p. 5
democracy, p. 5
aristocracy, p. 5
citizen, p. 5
direct democracy, p. 7
monarchy, p. 7
natural laws, p. 7

republic, p. 8
senate, p. 8

2. TAKING NOTES
Use of reason and intelligence to discover natural laws; development of direct democracy; three branches of government; paying jurors so that all people could participate in government

3. SYNTHESIZING
Possible Responses: Power resting with citizens, because the government does not have to depend on the whims of one person; separate branches of government, because power is balanced and justice is more likely to be preserved; regard for written law, because laws

are less likely to be arbitrary or to change on whim.

4. ANALYZING THEMES
Possible Responses: Over time, more and more people were given political power and had a direct voice in the running of the government.

Something in Common

OBJECTIVES

(1) To compare how legal judgments have been made at different times in different cultures.

(2) To demonstrate that law can be arbitrary and unfair in many of the systems that are not based on democracy.

FOCUS

To help students evaluate different ways of making legal judgments, have them answer these questions.

1. What makes one law fair and another law unfair?

2. What makes one judge fair and another judge unfair?

3. How do these evaluations compare with those made by people in other times and other places?

MORE ABOUT . . .

Ostracism

The practice of ostracism may have originated with the rule of Cleisthenes. For a person to be ostracized, he had to have at least 6,000 votes cast against him. Some people even think that Cleisthenes himself may have been subject to ostracism late in his career, but most historians consider the idea that Cleisthenes had been ostracized an invented story. Can students think of examples of ostracism today?

Making Legal Judgments

The rule of law is an essential feature of democracy. In a democracy, everyone, from the most powerful government official to the poorest citizen, must obey the law. While legal systems have existed in some form in most societies, only in democracies are laws made and enforced by the people themselves or by their representatives. For much of history, the law has often been nothing more than the wishes of an absolute ruler or a ruling elite and has been arbitrarily executed by them. In ancient Athens, however, nearly 2,500 years ago, citizens were first given the right to administer justice—by serving on juries.

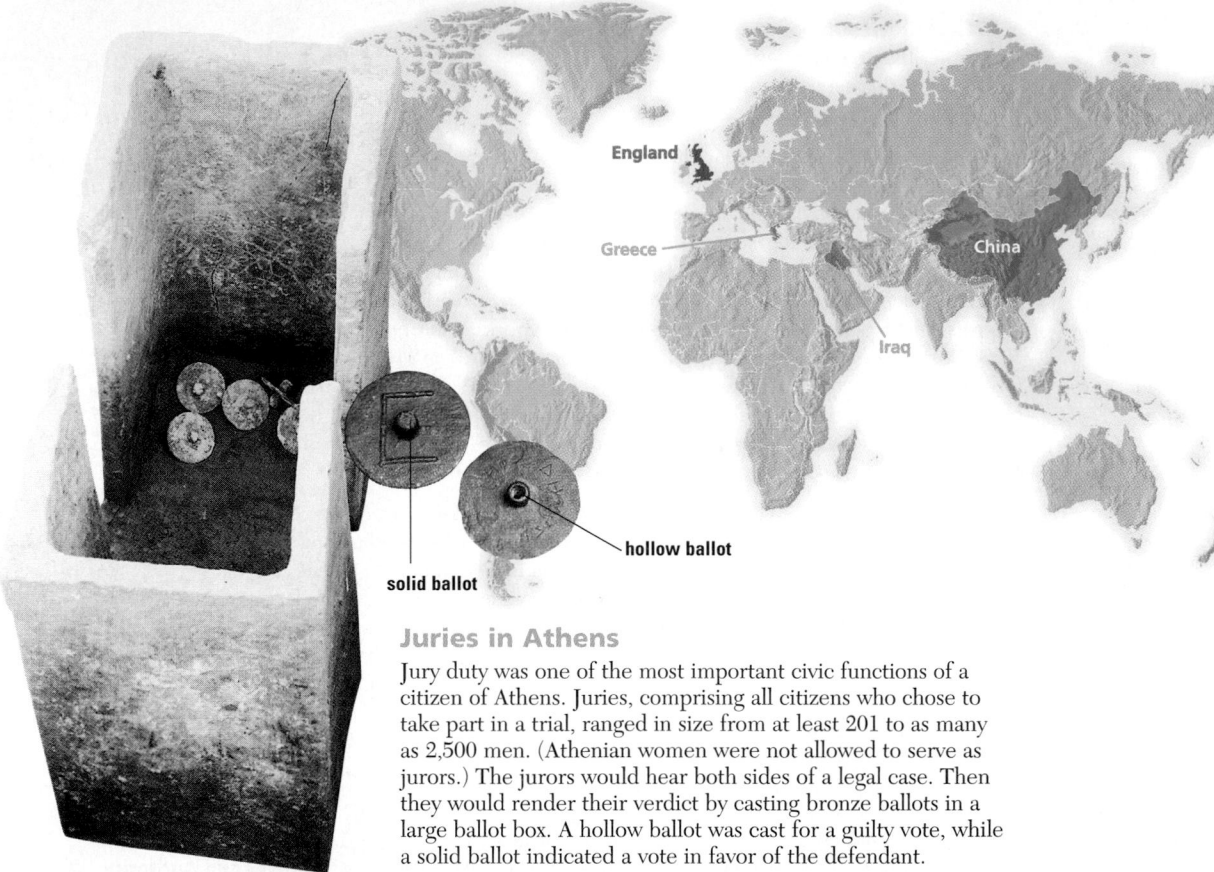

England

Greece

China

Iraq

hollow ballot

solid ballot

Juries in Athens

Jury duty was one of the most important civic functions of a citizen of Athens. Juries, comprising all citizens who chose to take part in a trial, ranged in size from at least 201 to as many as 2,500 men. (Athenian women were not allowed to serve as jurors.) The jurors would hear both sides of a legal case. Then they would render their verdict by casting bronze ballots in a large ballot box. A hollow ballot was cast for a guilty vote, while a solid ballot indicated a vote in favor of the defendant.

a closer look   ATHENIAN LAW

Each potential juror was given a bronze ticket inscribed with his name. After the tickets had been placed in a basket, jurors were randomly selected.

Citizens could vote to ostracize, or banish, a leader form Athens for ten years to prevent a person from gaining too much power. The person's name was inscribed on a pottery fragment called an *ostrakon*. This one bears the name of Pericles.

10 Prologue

TEACHING OPTION   BLOCK SCHEDULING   COOPERATIVE ACTIVITY: **Comparing Judgments**   CLASS TIME 30 MINUTES

Task: Students will hear a dispute and make a preliminary judgment from the point of view of an Athenian democracy, an Islamic court (oligarchy), a Chinese emperor (monarchy), and a trial by ordeal.

Materials Needed: The textbook and a written version of the dispute.

Activity: Divide the class into four teams, each representing one of the judicial systems described on these two pages. Each group should figure out a way to settle the following dispute in a way that would be characteristic of the judicial system they were assigned: A wealthy landowner has taken over the land of a poorer man. The poorer man asks for his land back.

As they make their judgments, students should answer the following questions about their judicial system: Who has the power to make a decision and what is the basis of that power? Which side in the dispute are they likely to favor and why? What is the judgment likely to be? Then discuss with students the answers they have written to the above questions and how they arrived at their preliminary judgment.

 ALTERNATE ASSESSMENT BOOK
Standards for Evaluating a Cooperative Activity

Islamic Court in Southwest Asia

Islamic law is based on the Qur'an, the Muslim holy book, and on the teachings of the prophet Muhammad. These teachings are believed to contain the general principles for all matters that need to be regulated. In this 14th-century illustration from the Abbasid period in southwest Asia, a *qadi*, or judge, administers the law. A *qadi* heard testimony from each party and then settled the dispute either by applying the letter of the law or by helping the parties reach agreement.

Imperial Decrees in China

Autocratic rulers like the 14th-century Ming emperor Hongwu, shown at the right, had unlimited power. They made laws through imperial decree, or pronouncement, and saw to their enforcement. Hongwu reportedly said, "In the morning I punish a few; by evening others commit the same crime. I punish these in the evening and by the next morning again there are violations. Although the corpses of the first have not been removed, already others follow their path."

Trial by Ordeal in England

Especially in the Middle Ages, guilt or innocence was sometimes determined through ordeal trials. The alleged evildoer was forced to undergo a physical ordeal, usually by fire or water. In this 17th-century illustration at the left, a woman is tried for witchcraft. It was believed that an innocent person would drown, but a witch would float. The judgment of witchcraft brought death by burning.

This stone relief from 336 B.C. shows **Democracy Crowning the People**, indicating the reverence Athenians had for democracy. The inscription below the image lists laws to guarantee democracy.

Connect *to* History

Comparing and Contrasting
What is similar and what is different among the ways legal judgments are made in the examples?

SEE SKILLBUILDER HANDBOOK PAGE 654

Connect *to* Today

Researching Read about the trial system in the United States today. Then write two paragraphs explaining which example on these pages is the forerunner of the U.S. system.

The Rise of Democratic Ideas **11**

Section 2 Overview

OBJECTIVES

1. To discuss the importance of Judaism's values.

2. To explain how Christianity spread and helped further democratic ideas.

3. To analyze the impact of the Renaissance and Reformation on democratic thinking.

SKILLBUILDER

- Interpreting Maps: location, region, p. 14

CRITICAL THINKING

- Drawing conclusions, pp. 12, 16
- Summarizing, p. 14
- Synthesizing, p. 16
- Analyzing themes, p. 16

FOCUS
5-Minute Warm-Up

Identifying Main Ideas
Answering these questions will help students focus on how the Judeo-Christian tradition helped further democratic ideas.

1. Turn to the time line on page 16. Which teachings from Judaism and Christianity reinforced democratic ideas?

2. Which philosophies of the Renaissance and the Reformation furthered the ideas of democracy?

🏛 ***WARM-UP TRANSPARENCY WTP***

OBJECTIVE ① INSTRUCT

Judaism

▶ ***Key Ideas***

- The Jewish religion emphasizes each person's worth and responsibility to make moral choices.

- Jewish law focuses on morality and ethics and urges people to oppose injustice and oppression.

📖 ***IN-DEPTH RESOURCES: PROLOGUE***
Guided Reading, p. 2

📖 ***ACCESS FOR STUDENTS ACQUIRING ENGLISH***
Guided Reading (Spanish), p. 13

TERMS & NAMES
- Judaism
- Ten Commandments
- prophet
- Christianity
- Roman Catholic Church
- Renaissance
- Reformation

② Judeo-Christian Tradition

MAIN IDEA	WHY IT MATTERS NOW
Judaism and Christianity taught individual worth, ethical standards, and the need to fight injustice.	These ideals continue to be important to democracy today.

SETTING THE STAGE Judaism and Christianity both began in a small corner of southwest Asia. Later, as they spread across the world, their ideas about the worth of individuals and the responsibility of individuals to the community had a strong impact on the development of democracy.

Judaism

Much of what we know about the early history of the Hebrews, later called the Jews, is contained in the first five books of the Hebrew Scriptures, the Torah. In the Torah, God chose Abraham to be the "father," or ancestor, of the Hebrew people. God commanded Abraham to move his people to Canaan, an area of ancient Palestine. This occurred around 2000 B.C.

In this engraving from the 19th century, Moses holds the Ten Commandments, which, according to Hebrew Scriptures, were given to him by God on Mount Sinai.

Created in God's Image Unlike the other groups around them, who were polytheists—people who believed in more than one god—the Hebrews were monotheists. They believed in one god. This God was perfect, all-knowing, all-powerful, and eternal. Earlier, people had generally thought that what the gods wanted from human beings was the performance of rituals and sacrifices in their honor. The Hebrews believed that it was God's wish for people to live moral lives. The religion of the Hebrews was called **Judaism.**

The Hebrew Scriptures (the Old Testament, to Christians) state that human beings are created in God's image. The Hebrews interpreted this to mean that each human being has a divine spark that gives him or her a dignity that can never be taken away. For the Greeks and Romans, the individual had dignity because of his or her ability to reason. For the Hebrews, each person had dignity simply by being a child of God.

The Hebrews believed that God had given human beings moral freedom—the capacity to choose between good and evil. Therefore, each person was responsible for the choices he or she made. These beliefs led to a new emphasis on the worth of the individual.

Jewish Law Teaches Morality Like the Greeks, the Romans, and other ancient peoples, the Jews had a written code of laws. The Bible

A. Possible Answers They believed in one god and thought that God wanted them to lead moral lives.

THINK THROUGH HISTORY
A. Drawing Conclusions What religious beliefs made the Hebrews different from other groups around them?

Background
The religion of the Hebrews was called Judaism after the Hebrew kingdom of Judah.

12 Prologue

SECTION 2 RESOURCES

PRINT RESOURCES

📖 ***IN-DEPTH RESOURCES: PROLOGUE***
Guided Reading, p. 2
Primary Source: The Ten Commandments, p. 9

📖 ***ACCESS FOR STUDENTS ACQUIRING ENGLISH***
Guided Reading, (Spanish), p. 13

📖 ***FORMAL ASSESSMENT***
Section Quiz, p. 6

📖 ***ALTERNATIVE ASSESSMENT BOOK***

TECHNOLOGY RESOURCES

💿 **CD-ROM**
Electronic Library of Primary Sources

🌐 **INTERNET** www.mlworldhistory.com

states that God gave this code to their leader Moses in about 1200 B.C., in the form of the **Ten Commandments** and other laws. Unlike the laws of other peoples, the Hebrews' code focused more on morality and ethics and less on political laws. The code included rules of social and religious behavior to which even rulers were subject. While the Hebrew code of justice was strict, it was softened by expressions of God's mercy.

A creative expansion of the religious thought of the Jews occurred with the emergence of prophets in the eighth century B.C. The **prophets** were leaders and teachers who were believed by the Jews to be messengers from God. The prophets attacked war, oppression, and greed in statements such as these from the Old Testament:

> **THE BIBLE**
> He has told you, O mortal, what is good; and what does the Lord require of you but to do justice, and to love kindness, and to walk humbly with your God?
> Micah, 6:8

The prophets strengthened the Jewish faith's social conscience, which has become part of the Western tradition. The Jews believed that it is the responsibility of every person to oppose injustice and oppression and that the community should assist the unfortunate. The prophets held out the hope that life on earth could be improved, that poverty and injustice need not exist, and that individuals are capable of living according to high moral standards.

Christianity

As Rome expanded, its power spread throughout the Mediterranean. It took control of Judea, homeland of the Jews, around 63 B.C. By A.D. 6, the Romans ruled Judea directly.

According to the New Testament, Jesus of Nazareth was born around 6 to 4 B.C. He was both a Jew and a Roman subject. He began his public ministry at the age of 30. His preaching contained many ideas from Jewish tradition, such as monotheism and the principles of the Ten Commandments. Jesus emphasized God's personal relationship to each human being.

But Jesus' ideas went beyond traditional morality. He stressed the importance of people's love for God, their neighbors, their enemies, and themselves. In the Sermon on the Mount, Jesus told the people, "I say unto you, Love your enemies, bless them that curse you, do good to them that hate you, and pray for them which despitefully use you, and persecute you." He also taught that God would eventually end wickedness in the world and would establish an eternal kingdom in which he would reign. People who sincerely repented their sins would find life after death in this kingdom.

About A.D. 29, Jesus visited Jerusalem. Because some referred to him as the "king of the Jews," the Roman governor considered him a political threat. They had him put to death by crucifixion. According to Jesus' followers, he rose from the dead three days later and ascended into heaven. His followers believed he was the Messiah, or savior. Jesus came to be referred to as Jesus Christ. *Christos* is a Greek word meaning "messiah" or "savior." The word **Christianity,** the name of the religion founded by Jesus, was derived from the name Christ.

The Teachings of Christianity In the first century after Jesus' death, his followers began to teach this new religion based on his message. Christianity spread slowly but steadily across the Roman Empire. One man, the apostle Paul, had enormous influence on Christianity's development.

Paul traveled from city to city around the eastern Mediterranean to preach. He

Vocabulary
apostle: one of the followers of Jesus who preached and spread his teaching.

The Rise of Democratic Ideas **13**

Spread of Christianity in the Roman World to A.D. 500

Interpreting the Map Ask students to notice the similarities between the spread of Christianity and the boundaries of the Roman Empire. Ask them to discuss why they think the spread of Christianity paralleled the boundaries of the empire so closely. *Possible Response: Missionaries used the roads and trade routes of the empire to travel to distant places.*

Extension Activity After students have studied the map, ask them to write one sentence that summarizes the information the map presents. *Possible Response: From 325 to 500, Christianity developed first in the major cities, and then spread outward, reaching every province of the Roman Empire.*

SKILLBUILDER Answers
1. Anatolia
2. Britain to the north, Egypt to the south, Spain to the west, and Armenia to the east.

MORE ABOUT . . .
Constantinople and the Spread of Christianity

Christianity spread quickly through the Roman Empire after the emperor Constantine looked positively on the religion. In A.D. 312, he was fighting his rivals for the imperial throne and prayed for divine help before going into battle. Constantine reported that he then saw a cross of light in the heavens bearing the inscription, "In this sign, conquer." He ordered artisans to put the Christian symbol of the cross on his soldiers' shields, and his troops were victorious in battle. Constantine gave credit for his success to the Christian God and put an end to the Roman persecution of Christians. In 380, Christianity was made the empire's official religion.

Spread of Christianity in the Roman World to A.D. 500

- Christian areas around 325
- Christian areas around 500
- Boundary of Roman Empire, 395

GEOGRAPHY SKILLBUILDER: Interpreting Maps
1. **Location** Where was Christianity most widespread in A.D. 325?
2. **Region** What was the extent (north to south, east to west) of Christianity's spread by A.D. 500?

stressed that Jesus was the son of God and that he had died for people's sins. Paul declared that Christianity was a universal religion. It should welcome all converts, Jew and non-Jew. He said, "There is neither Jew nor Greek, there is neither slave nor free, there is neither male nor female; for you are all one in Christ Jesus." He stressed the essential equality of all human beings, a belief central to democracy.

Rome Spreads Judeo-Christian Ideas In the beginning, the Roman Empire was hostile to the beliefs of Judaism and Christianity. Yet it was the empire that helped spread the ideas of these religions in two ways. The first way was indirect. After the Jews began to rebel against the Romans in the first century, they were exiled from their homeland in A.D. 70. This dispersal was called the *Diaspora*. The Jews then fled to many parts of the world. With them, they took their beliefs that all people had the right to be treated with justice and dignity.

The second way the empire spread Judeo-Christian ideas was more direct. Despite persecution of Christians over the years, Christianity became a powerful religion throughout the empire and beyond. By 380, it had become the official religion of the empire. Eventually it took root in Europe, the Near East, and northern Africa.

Islam

Another monotheistic religion that taught equality of all persons and individual worth also developed in southwest Asia, in the early 600s. Islam, as it was called, was based on the teachings of the prophet Muhammad. He emphasized the dignity of all human beings and the brotherhood of all people. A belief in the bond of community and the unity of all people led to a tolerance of different groups within the community. Muslims were required by their religion to offer charity and help to those in need. Under Muslim law, rulers had to obey the same laws as those they ruled.

B. Possible Answers They were spread by the Jews who took their beliefs with them in exile and by the Christians who wanted to convert others to their faith.
THINK THROUGH HISTORY
B. Summarizing How were Judeo-Christian ideas spread throughout the Roman Empire?

14 Prologue

Task: Students will research the life and travels of Paul and create three maps showing his three voyages.

Purpose: To learn about the mission of Paul and the cities he visited.

Activity: Paul made three separate voyages in his missionary work. Divide students into three groups and assign each group one of the three voyages to research. Each group will briefly describe the cities

that Paul visited, summarize his missionary activities in each city during a particular voyage, and draw a map showing his route among the cities. Each group can present their findings to the class, beginning with the first voyage.

Building a Portfolio: Students who include a copy of the report and map in their portfolio should write a brief description of their contribution.

ALTERNATIVE ASSESSMENT BOOK
Standards for Evaluating a Cooperative Activity

Standards for Evaluation
Maps and presentations should . . .

- demonstrate students' knowledge of Paul's mission and voyages
- show clearly his travel routes
- describe the cities he visited on each trip

The Legacy of Monotheistic Religions Several ideals crucial to the shaping of a democratic outlook emerged from the early monotheistic religions of southwest Asia. They include the following:

- the duty of the individual and the community to combat oppression
- the worth of the individual
- the equality of people before God

Renaissance and Reformation

By the Middle Ages, the **Roman Catholic Church,** one church that developed from Roman Christianity, had become the most powerful institution in Europe. It influenced all aspects of life—religious, social, and political. It was strongly authoritarian in structure.

Renaissance Revives Classical Ideas In the 1300s, a brilliant cultural movement arose in Italy. Over the next 300 years, it spread to the rest of Europe. This movement was called the **Renaissance,** from the French word for "rebirth." The Renaissance was marked by renewed interest in classical culture. This included the restoration of old monuments and works of art and the rediscovery of forgotten Greek and Latin manuscripts. Renaissance thinkers were interested in earthly life for its own sake. They rejected the medieval view that life was only a preparation for the afterlife.

Renaissance education was intended to prepare some men for public service rather than just for service to the Church. The latter had been the goal of medieval education. Scholars placed increasing value on subjects concerned with humankind and culture. Although Christianity remained a strong force in Europe, people began to be more critical of the Church.

During the Renaissance, individualism became deeply rooted in Western culture. It was expressed by artists, who sought to capture individual character. It was demonstrated by explorers, who ventured into uncharted seas, and by conquerors, who carved out vast empires in the Americas. It also was shown by merchant-capitalists, who amassed huge fortunes by taking great economic risks.

The Reformation Challenges Church Power The spirit of questioning that started during the Renaissance came to full bloom in the Reformation. The **Reformation** was a religious reform movement that began in the 16th century. Those who wanted to reform the Catholic Church were called Protestants, because they protested against the power and abuses of the Church. Reformers stressed the importance of a direct relationship with God.

The Reformation started in Germany. Martin Luther, a monk and teacher, criticized the Church's practice of selling pardons for sins. In 1521, Luther went even farther. He said that people could be saved only through faith in God. This contradicted the Church's position that salvation came through faith and good works. What began as a reform movement ended up as a new division of Christianity—Protestantism.

Because Protestantism encouraged people to make their own religious judgments, Protestants began to have differences

Vocabulary
individualism: belief in the importance of the individual and in the virtues of self-reliance and personal independence.

Vocabulary
pardon: cancellation of earthly punishment still due for a sin that has been forgiven.

GlobalImpact

Printing Press

The first European printing press with movable type is thought to have been invented in 1455, by Johannes Gutenberg of Germany. By 1500, presses were used in 13 European countries.

The printing press with movable type, shown below in a 16th-century French woodcut, made it possible to print books quickly and cheaply. This fueled Renaissance learning because scholars could read each other's works soon after they were written. The ideas of the Renaissance and, later, of the Enlightenment were spread through the printed word.

The spread of reading matter made literacy for large numbers of people suddenly possible. And an informed citizenry contributed to the rise of democracy. These informed citizens began to question authority. This ultimately spurred democratic revolutions in America and France in the late 1700s.

The Rise of Democratic Ideas **15**

OBJECTIVE ③ INSTRUCT

Renaissance and Reformation

▶ **Key Ideas**

- Beginning in the 14th century, the Renaissance places renewed focus on secular ideas and on individualism.
- The Reformation divides Christianity into Protestantism and Catholicism and furthers the spirit of questioning that had begun during the Renaissance.
- The Renaissance and the Reformation promote ideas that are important in the development of democracy.

MORE ABOUT . . .
The Middle Ages

During the Middle Ages, shared beliefs in the teachings of the Catholic Church bound people together. During an era of constant warfare and political turmoil, the Church was a stable force. The Church provided Christians with a sense of security and religious community. All Christians could follow the same path to salvation. The Church also created a system of justice to guide people's conduct. All Christians—kings and peasants alike—were subject to the laws of the Church. The Church also established courts to try people accused of violating their laws.

GlobalImpact
Printing Press

The printed word is still extremely important for the spread of ideas and information. Encourage students to list printed publications that currently allow the quick spread of information. Have them start another list of other technologies that also allow ideas to spread rapidly. Ask them to rank the technologies from most influential to least influential in bringing them new information.

TEACHING OPTIONS

MULTIPLE LEARNING STYLES

Visual Learners Encourage students to visit an art museum with a Renaissance collection or take out books that show photographs of great works of art from the Renaissance. Students should look at the subject of different paintings, the clothing, the interior and exterior decoration, and the symbols used. Based on the works they examine, students should draw conclusions about values of the Renaissance. Ask students to share what they learned with the class, showing pictures of the pieces of art they examined if possible.

EXPLORING PRIMARY SOURCES

King James Bible Written in 1611, the King James version of the Bible was one long-lasting product of the Renaissance and the Reformation. Ask students to find a copy of the King James Bible and read different passages from it. Have them compare this 17th-century translation with a modern translation. Let students discuss which translation seems more powerful, poetic, or inspiring to them.

A.D. 26 Jesus begins to teach the worth of each person before God and to remind people of the Jewish idea of caring for society's oppressed.

A.D. 29 Jesus' disciples start to spread the teachings of Christianity to non-Jews.

1521 Martin Luther starts the Reformation, which challenges authority and emphasizes individual responsibility for making choices.

| 1200 B.C. | | 100 | 700 | 900 | 1100 | | 1500 | 1600 |

1200 B.C. Moses begins to record Jewish law, which requires moral behavior for individuals in a community.

1300 Renaissance thinkers begin to teach the importance of the individual and the value of worldly pursuits.

1455 Johannes Gutenberg invents the printing press, which helps spread new ideas.

History from Visuals

The Rise of Democratic Ideas 1200 B.C.–A.D. 1600

Interpreting a Time Line Have students read the time line and summarize how Judaism and Christianity contributed to the rise of democratic ideas.

Extension Activity Ask students to compare the events on this time line with those on page 9. Ask for a class vote on which event or way of thinking students consider most important to the rise of democratic ideas.

SPOTLIGHT ON
The Peasants' Revolt

Martin Luther relied on the support of several German princes for protection from being tried by the powerful Catholic Church. Ask students to make a list of reasons why Luther might have withheld support from the peasants when they staged violent revolts. Encourage students to categorize their reasons as personal, political, social, or religious.

ASSESS & RETEACH

Section 2 Assessment
Have groups of three students take turns quizzing each other on the terms and names in question 1 and work together in making the chart in question 2.

Section Quiz
 FORMAL ASSESSMENT
Section Quiz, p. 6

Reteaching Activity
CLASS TIME: 15 MINUTES

To help students review the main ideas of this section, pair students and ask each pair to write a brief summary of the content of one heading. Let students post their summaries on a bulletin board.

CLOSE ACTIVITY

CLASS TIME: 15 MINUTES

Perceiving Effects
Go down the list of Terms & Names. For each one, have students discuss how it helped to hinder or further democracy.

---

of belief. They then established new churches in addition to the already-formed Lutheran Church. These included the Anglican, Presbyterian, and Calvinist churches. Catholics and Protestants differed on many issues. The Catholic Church claimed the right to interpret the Bible for all Christians. Protestants called on believers to read and interpret the Bible for themselves. The Catholic Church said that the only way to salvation was through the Church. Protestants said that the clergy had no special powers and that people could find individual paths to God. The Protestant emphasis on private judgment in religious matters—on a sense of conviction rather than a reliance on authority—further strengthened the importance of the individual.

Legacy of the Renaissance and Reformation The Reformation and the other changes that swept Europe during and after the Middle Ages greatly influenced the shaping of the modern world. By challenging the authority of monarchs and popes, the Reformation indirectly contributed to the growth of democracy. Also, by calling on believers to read and interpret the Bible for themselves, it introduced individuals to reading and exposed them to more than just religious ideas.

Both the Renaissance and the Reformation placed emphasis on the importance of the individual. This was an idea that would play a significant part in the democratic revolutions that followed and in the growth of political liberty in modern times.

SPOTLIGHT ON

The Peasants' Revolt
Luther questioned Church authority. Peasants in southern Germany went farther. In 1524, they questioned political and social authority. They wanted an end to serfdom, or being forced to serve a master. They stormed the castles of the nobles, forcing them, at least initially, to give in to the demands.

It was the largest mass uprising in the history of Germany. The peasants looked to Luther to support their rights, but Luther supported the nobles instead. As many as 100,000 peasants were killed during the rebellion.

C. Possible Answer Both emphasized the importance of the individual and challenged the rule of authoritarian leaders.
THINK THROUGH HISTORY
C. Synthesizing How did the Renaissance and the Reformation contribute to the growth of democracy?

Section 2 Assessment

1. TERMS & NAMES
Identify
- Judaism
- Ten Commandments
- prophet
- Christianity
- Roman Catholic Church
- Renaissance
- Reformation

2. TAKING NOTES
Using a chart like the one below, list one contribution to democracy associated with each of the following:

Category	Contribution
Judaism	
Christianity	
Renaissance	
Reformation	

3. DRAWING CONCLUSIONS
How did the Reformation promote the idea of individualism?

THINK ABOUT
- endorsing a direct relationship with God
- encouraging people to make their own religious judgments

4. ANALYZING THEMES
Cultural Interaction What ideas crucial to the shaping of democracy did Judaism and Christianity share?

THINK ABOUT
- the role of the individual
- a person's relationship to God
- a person's relationship to others

16 Prologue

A N S W E R S

1. TERMS & NAMES
Judaism, p. 12
Ten Commandments, p. 13
prophets, p. 13
Christianity, p. 14
Roman Catholic Church, p. 15
Renaissance, p. 15
Reformation, p. 15

2. TAKING NOTES
Possible Responses:
Judaism—emphasis on individual morality; Christianity—equality of believers; Renaissance—growth of individualism; Reformation—challenging of traditional authority.

3. DRAWING CONCLUSIONS
Possible Responses:
Individualism is the belief in the importance of the individual and of self-reliance. The Reformation promoted these ideas by asserting that people could have a direct relationship with God and that people should read the Bible and interpret it for themselves.

4. ANALYZING THEMES
Possible Responses: Both Judaism and Christianity respected the worth of the individual; both emphasized morality and each person's responsibility to make moral choices. Each of these ideas helped shape a democratic outlook.

3 Democratic Developments in England

TERMS & NAMES
- feudalism
- common law
- Magna Carta
- due process of law
- Parliament
- divine right
- Glorious Revolution
- constitutional monarchy
- bill of rights

MAIN IDEA

WHY IT MATTERS NOW

England began to develop democratic institutions that limited the power of the monarchy.

Democratic traditions developed in England have influenced many countries, including the United States.

SETTING THE STAGE In 1066, William, the Duke of Normandy in France, invaded England and claimed the English throne. It set in motion events that gradually led to the end of **feudalism**—the political and economic system of the Middles Ages—and to the development of democracy in England.

Medieval Reforms

One of William's descendants was Henry II, who ruled from 1154 to 1189. He controlled almost the entire western half of France, in addition to England. A man of great intelligence, wisdom, and vigor, Henry is considered one of the most gifted statesmen of the 12th century.

The Magna Carta (1215), pictured here, is the most celebrated document in English history because it guaranteed political rights for the first time.

Juries and Common Law One of Henry's greatest achievements was the development of the jury trial as a means of administering royal justice. Before then, people were tried in courts of feudal lords. In such courts, the accused would usually have to survive a duel or some physically painful or dangerous ordeal to be set free.

With Henry's innovation, a royal judge would visit each shire, or county, at least once a year. First, the judge would review the crime that had been committed. Then he would ask 12 men, often neighbors of the accused, to answer questions about the facts of the case. These people were known as a jury. Unlike our modern juries, they did not decide guilt or innocence. People came to prefer the jury trial over the feudal-court trial because they found it more just.

Legal decisions made by royal justices were used as precedents in new cases. Gradually, England was unified under a single legal system. This was called "common law" because it was common to the whole kingdom. Unlike Roman law, which expressed the will of a ruler or a lawmaker, **common law** reflected customs and principles established over time. Common law became the basis of the legal systems in many English-speaking countries, including the United States.

The Magna Carta When Henry II died, his son Richard the Lion-Hearted assumed the throne. He was followed by his brother John, an unpopular king. King John fought a costly and unsuccessful war with France. Not only did England lose many of its land holdings in France, but John also tried to raise taxes to pay for the war. This led to conflict between the English nobles and King John. In 1215 the angry nobles rebelled and forced John to grant guarantees of certain traditional political rights. They presented their demands to him in written form as the **Magna Carta** (Great Charter).

The Rise of Democratic Ideas **17**

Section 3 Overview

OBJECTIVES

1. To list medieval legal reforms in England that furthered democracy.

2. To explain how the English Parliament gained power between 1300 and 1650.

3. To discuss events that led to the establishment of a constitutional monarchy in England.

CRITICAL THINKING
- Drawing Conclusions, p. 18
- Analyzing Issues, p. 19
- Analyzing Causes, p. 20
- Summarizing, p. 21

FOCUS
5-Minute Warm-Up

▶ *Sequencing*

To help students understand the unfolding of democratic reforms and institutions in England, have them read the heads in the section, skim the text, and then answer the following questions.

1. Which developed first—juries or the Parliament?

2. Which was signed first—the Magna Carta or the English Bill of Rights?

📖 *WARM-UP TRANSPARENCY WTP*

OBJECTIVE ① INSTRUCT

Medieval Reforms

▶ *Key Ideas*
- Henry II develops a single legal system in England that includes juries and the beginnings of common law.
- At the demand of English nobles in 1215, King John signs the Magna Carta.
- The first English Parliament convenes in 1295.

📄 *IN-DEPTH RESOURCES: PROLOGUE*
Guided Reading, p. 3
Primary Source: from The Magna Carta, p. 10
Literature: from *Here Be Dragons*, p. 12

📄 *ACCESS FOR STUDENTS ACQUIRING ENGLISH*
Guided Reading, p. 14

SECTION 3 RESOURCES

PRINT RESOURCES

📄 *IN-DEPTH RESOURCES: PROLOGUE*
Guided Reading, p. 3
Primary Source: from The Magna Carta, p. 10
Literature: from *Here Be Dragons* by Sharon Kay Penman, p. 12
Connections Across Time and Cultures: p. 17

📄 *IACCESS FOR STUDENTS ACQUIRING ENGLISH*
Guided Reading, p. 14

📄 *FORMAL ASSESSMENT*
Section Quiz, p.7

📄 *ALTERNATIVE ASSESSMENT BOOK*

TECHNOLOGY RESOURCES

💿 **CD-ROM**
Electronic Library of Primary Sources

🌐 **INTERNET** www.mlworldhistory.com

The Magna Carta is celebrated as the source of traditional English respect for individual rights and liberties. Basically, it was a contract between the king and nobles of England. However, the Magna Carta contained certain important principles that limited the power of the English monarch over all his English subjects. Implied was the idea that monarchs had no right to rule in any way they pleased. They had to govern according to law.

The Magna Carta had 63 clauses. Two established basic legal rights for individuals. Clause 12 declared that taxes "shall be levied in our kingdom only by the common consent of our kingdom." This meant that the king could not demand taxes but rather had to ask for some form of popular consent.

Clause 39 declared, "No man shall be arrested or imprisoned . . . except by the legal judgment of his peers or by the law of the land." This meant that a person had the right to a jury trial and to the protection of the law. This right—to have the law work in known, orderly ways—is called **due process of law.** In other words, the king could not willfully, or arbitrarily, punish his subjects.

Over the centuries, the principles of the Magna Carta were extended to protect the liberties of all the English people. Clause 12, for example, was later interpreted to mean that the king could not levy taxes without the consent of **Parliament,** England's national legislature. The principle of "no taxation without representation" was a rallying cry, over five centuries later, of the American Revolution. Clause 39 was interpreted as forbidding the government from arresting people without grounds for suspicion.

Model Parliament Even before the Norman Conquest, Anglo-Saxon kings had discussed important issues with members of the nobility who acted as a council of advisors. This practice continued through the centuries. In 1295, King John's grandson, Edward I, needed money to pay for yet another war in France. He wanted wide support for the war. So he called together not only the lords but also lesser knights and some burgesses, or leading citizens of the towns. Edward explained his action by saying, "What affects all, by all should be approved." Historians refer to this famous gathering as the Model Parliament, because it established a standard for later Parliaments. The Model Parliament voted on taxes and helped Edward make reforms and consolidate laws.

By the mid-1300s, the knights and burgesses had gained an official role in the government. They had formed an assembly of their own—the House of Commons, which was the lower house of Parliament. Nobles and bishops met separately in the upper house, the House of Lords. Because the great majority of English people had no part in Parliament, it was not truly a democratic body. Even so, its existence limited the power of the monarch and established the principle of representation.

Parliament Grows Stronger

Over the next few centuries, Parliament's "power of the purse," or its right to approve certain expenses, gave it strong influence in governing. The House of Commons,

Vocabulary
contract: an agreement between two or more parties, especially one that is written and enforceable by law.

Vocabulary
tax: a contribution for the support of a government required of persons, groups, or businesses.

THINK THROUGH HISTORY
A. Drawing Conclusions How did the principle of rule by law, as implied in the Magna Carta, limit the power of the king?
A. Possible Answer It implied that monarchs could not rule as they pleased; they had to govern according to the law.

---

which controlled those purse strings, was gradually becoming the equal of the House of Lords. Parliament increasingly viewed itself as a partner with the monarch in governing. It voted on taxes, passed laws, and advised on royal policies.

Conflict With the Monarch The struggle to limit the power of the monarchy continued over the centuries. In the 1600s, monarchs on the European continent were asserting greater authority over lords than they had during the Middle Ages. These kings claimed not just the right to rule but the right to rule with absolute power. They claimed that a king's power came from God. This assertion was known as the theory of the **divine right** of kings. Advocates of divine right said that monarchs were chosen by God and responsible only to God. To challenge the authority of the monarch, therefore, was to challenge God.

Elizabeth I, the last Tudor monarch of England, died in 1603, without a child. She was succeeded by a new line of monarchs, the Stuarts, who were relatives from Scotland. The Stuarts were strong believers in divine right. King James of Scotland became James I, the first Stuart king. Because he came from Scotland and knew little of English laws and institutions, he clashed with Parliament over the traditional rights of the people.

Three issues caused conflict during James's reign. First, religious reformers known as Puritans were trying to change the Church of England, or Anglican Church, through legislation. They wanted to simplify, or purify, Church doctrines and ceremonies. They felt the Church of England was still too much like the Roman Catholic Church, which it had separated from, or left. The Puritans entered an ongoing battle with James, who was the official head of the Church.

Second, the king used the Star Chamber, a royal court of law, to administer justice. He ignored parliamentary courts, which used common law. The people began to accuse the king of tyranny.

Third, and perhaps most important, was the issue of money. Elizabeth had left James a large debt. In addition, he wanted even more money in order to have an extravagant court and to wage war. Parliament declined to grant him any additional funds. James then ignored Parliament and tried to raise money by other means.

Parliament Overthrows the King The troubles under James became explosions under his son, Charles I, who became king in 1625. Like James, Charles needed funds. He asked Parliament for money in 1628. In return for granting revenue from taxes, Parliament tried to further limit royal power. It sought to force Charles to accept the Petition of Right.

The Petition of Right went against theories of absolute monarchy. It is viewed as a landmark in constitutional history. It demanded an end to:
- taxing without Parliament's consent
- imprisoning citizens illegally
- housing troops in citizens' homes
- military government in peacetime

Charles agreed to sign the petition in order to get the funds he wanted. Later he ignored the commitments secured in the document.

Charles dismissed Parliament in 1629 and refused to convene it again for 11 years. But when the Scots invaded England in 1640, Charles was forced to call Parliament to get funds to defend the country. In a show of independence, Parliament refused to discuss money until Charles considered how he had wronged Parliament. Parliament passed laws to reduce the power of the monarchy, angering Charles. Grievances

The Rise of Democratic Ideas **19**

Vocabulary
tyranny: absolute power, especially when exercised harshly or unjustly.

THINK THROUGH HISTORY
B. Analyzing Issues
Explain the controversy between James I and Parliament.
B. Possible Answer
James believed in divine right—that he was responsible only to God. Parliament felt that this clashed with the traditional rights of the English people.

CONNECT *to* TODAY

Power of the Purse

Many of Parliament's struggles with the monarchy focused on money. Only Parliament could approve certain expenditures. The monarch had to convince Parliament that the proposed expenses were worthwhile.

Such struggles must seem familiar to the President of the United States and to Congress. The President proposes a yearly budget, which Congress either approves or amends. The tension between the two branches of government over the budget can reach crisis level.

At the end of 1995, President Clinton vetoed a budget amended by the House of Representatives. The House then cut off funds for operating the government, which shut down for several weeks. Both sides eventually agreed to a compromise.

CONNECT *to* TODAY

Power of the Purse

Point out to students that issues concerning finances are often pivotal for governments around the world. Encourage students to research recent governmental crises that have revolved around a nation's financial situation. Students might look into the downfall of the Suharto government of Indonesia in 1998, among others.

MORE ABOUT . . .
James's Conflicts with the Puritans

Among the demands for reform that the Puritans made of King James I was the request to set up a group of elders to help each bishop decide religious questions. James refused to make this change because he had control over the bishops and did not want to give up his power to a more democratic body. These were among the differences that led to problems between King James I and the English people.

CONNECTIONS ACROSS TIME AND PLACE

The English Parliament The Parliament of Great Britain is still composed of the House of Commons and the House of Lords, just as it was during the Middle Ages. However, the monarchy today no longer exercises real power. Ask students to research the structure of the modern-day British government and prepare an organization chart, showing the components of the government. Have students include captions explaining the function of each component of government.

MULTIPLE LEARNING STYLES

Kinesthetic Learners Have students use masking tape to make a time line on the floor that includes the dates covered in this section. Then have them make a set of cards with each card listing a king or other major political figure mentioned in the chapter. Each student should randomly select one of the cards, use the text to review what the political figure mentioned on the card did, and come up with a gesture or action that captures the figure's significance. Ask students to go stand in the correct place on the time line. One by one, the students should hold up their cards, say their figure's name, enact their performance, and explain it to the class.

Teacher's Edition **19**

Establishment of a Constitutional Monarchy

▶ *Key Ideas*
- Oliver Cromwell overthrows Charles I and establishes an unpopular military dictatorship.
- In 1660, the Parliament invites Charles II to restore the monarchy.
- Parliament maintains power and eventually offers the English throne to Prince William of Orange and his wife, Mary, daughter of Charles I.
- The English Bill of Rights of 1689 further limits the power of the monarch.

 ELECTRONIC LIBRARY OF PRIMARY SOURCES
"The Restoration of Charles II"

*Global*Impact
Prelude to the American Revolution

On April 18, 1689, New Englanders in the English North American colonies easily captured the hated royal governor, Sir Edmund Andros, and put him in jail. Although Andros was overthrown, England retained the power over the New England colonies. This power had been gained when England took back its royal charter in 1684. The king chose the governor of the colony, who could refuse to seat specific elected representatives in the colony's government. With the students, discuss how New Englanders might have reacted to the limitations England placed on their rights to govern themselves.

---

continued to grow. Eventually, in 1642, the English Civil War broke out. Royalists, who upheld the monarchy, were opposed by antiroyalists, who supported Parliament.

After several years of conflict, the antiroyalist forces, commanded by Puritan leader Oliver Cromwell, won control of the government. Charles was condemned as a "tyrant, murderer, and public enemy" and in 1649 was executed.

Establishment of Constitutional Monarchy

After Charles's execution, Oliver Cromwell established a republic called the Commonwealth of England. He spent the next several years crushing a series of uprisings against his rule. He was opposed both by supporters of monarchy and by more extreme Puritans. Cromwell became unhappy with Parliament's failure to enact his religious, social, and economic reforms. In 1653 he dissolved Parliament and created a government called the Protectorate. He named himself Lord Protector. In effect, Cromwell became a military dictator.

Cromwell's increasingly authoritarian rule was extremely unpopular. Most of the English were not unhappy at his death in 1658.

The Restoration Cromwell's son Richard succeeded him as Lord Protector. He was not a strong ruler, and the military dictatorship continued to be unpopular. Cromwell resigned in 1659. In 1660, a new Parliament restored the monarchy and invited Charles Stuart, the son of Charles I, to take the throne. This period was called the Restoration, because the monarchy was restored to the throne. Yet Parliament retained the powers it had gained through the struggles of the previous two decades. For example, the monarch could not tax without Parliament's consent.

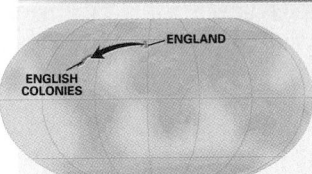
*Global*Impact

Prelude to the American Revolution

James II's unpopularity extended across the Atlantic Ocean to England's American colonies. In 1684, a royal court took away the charter of the Massachusetts Bay Colony. James II had decided to create a union of all colonies from New Jersey to New Hampshire.

James appointed Sir Edmund Andros as royal governor of the Dominion of New England. Andros abolished elective assemblies, declared town meetings illegal, and collected taxes that the people had never voted on.

When word of the Glorious Revolution reached America, the colonists overthrew Andros in their own version of the revolt. This action may have contributed to the colonists' belief that it was their right to overthrow an unjust king.

In addition, Parliament continued its attempts to limit the monarchy and to expand rights. In 1679 it passed the Habeas Corpus Amendment Act. *Habeas corpus* is a Latin term meaning "you are ordered to have the body." When someone is arrested, the police must produce the person in court. That person must be informed of what he or she is accused of having done. The court then decides if there is reason to hold the accused. Habeas corpus prevents authorities from detaining a person unjustly or wrongfully. (This right is still important in democracies today. It is mentioned in the U.S. Constitution.)

Glorious Revolution When Charles II died in 1685, his younger brother became King James II. James was a Roman Catholic and also a believer in the divine right of monarchs. The English people were afraid that he wanted to make Catholicism the official religion. They hoped that when James died, his Protestant daughter, Mary, would become queen. However, James's wife gave birth to a son in 1688. Because a male heir to the throne took precedence, or came before, a female, it seemed likely that Catholic rule would continue. This was unacceptable to most of the English people.

Parliament withdrew its support from James and offered the English throne to his Protestant daughter, Mary, and her husband, William of Orange, ruler of the Netherlands. William invaded England, and James fled to France. In 1689 William and Mary were crowned co-rulers of England. The **Glorious Revolution,** as it came to be called, is now seen as a turning point in English constitutional history. Parliament had established its right to limit the English monarch's power and to control succession to the throne. England was now a **constitutional monarchy,** where the powers of the ruler are restricted by the constitution and the laws of the country.

THINK THROUGH HISTORY
C. Analyzing Causes What caused Parliament to restore the monarchy?
C. Possible Answer The military dictatorship was extremely unpopular because it was authoritarian.

Gifted and Talented Students Researching Ask students to research the history of the writ of habeas corpus and how the idea has been expanded and used in different countries from ancient to modern times. Students can make a bulletin-board display to share what they learn.

U.S. Bill of Rights In 1791, the United States ratified a bill of rights in the form of ten amendments to the U.S. Constitution. Ask students to compare the English bill of rights with that of the United States and encourage students to discuss specifically how these sets of rights are similar and how they are different.

The Rise of Democratic Ideas, 1200–1700

1295 The Model Parliament, a more representative legislature, begins to meet.

1679 Parliament passes habeas corpus, a protection against unjust imprisonment.

1689 Parliament enacts the Bill of Rights, which further limits royal power.

1200   1400   1500   1600   1700

1215 King John signs the Magna Carta, guaranteeing certain basic political rights.

1628 King Charles I signs the Petition of Right, which states that the monarch must obey the law.

English Bill of Rights In 1689, the new monarchs, William and Mary, accepted from Parliament a **bill of rights,** or formal summary of the rights and liberties considered essential to the people. The English Bill of Rights limited the power of the monarchy and protected free speech in Parliament. The monarch was forbidden to suspend laws, to tax without the consent of Parliament, or to raise an army during peacetime without Parliament's approval. People were assured of their right to petition the king to seek remedies for their grievances against the government. Excessive bail and cruel and unusual punishment were forbidden. And foremost, the Bill of Rights declared:

A VOICE FROM THE PAST
. . . that for redress of all grievances, and for the amending, strengthening, and preserving of the laws, parliament ought to be held frequently.

English Bill of Rights

This 17th-century plate commemorates William and Mary's ascension to the English throne in 1689.

> **D. Possible Answers** England gave the world the guarantee of the rule of law, parliamentary government, individual liberties, and constitutional monarchy.
>
> **THINK THROUGH HISTORY**
> **D. Summarizing** What was England's legacy to democracy?

England's Legacy England's Glorious Revolution and the bill of rights that it produced had a great impact. English citizens were guaranteed the rule of law, parliamentary government, individual liberties, and a constitutional monarchy. This completed a process begun with the Magna Carta. The Bill of Rights also set an example for England's American colonists when they considered grievances against Britain nearly 100 years later. These precedents, along with the ideas of the Enlightenment, would give rise to democratic revolutions in America and France in the late 18th century.

Section ❸ Assessment

1. TERMS & NAMES
Identify
- feudalism
- common law
- Magna Carta
- due process of law
- Parliament
- divine right
- Glorious Revolution
- constitutional monarchy
- bill of rights

2. TAKING NOTES
Using a sequence graphic like the one below, show the main events that mark the development of constitutional monarchy in England.

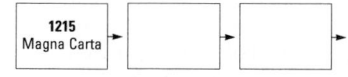

Which event do you think was the most important, and why do you think so?

3. SUMMARIZING
What were the main achievements of the Glorious Revolution?

THINK ABOUT
- William and Mary
- the role of Parliament
- English rights and liberties

4. THEME ACTIVITY
Power and Authority Think of yourself as an adviser to King John. Write him a letter in which you argue for or against accepting the Magna Carta. Tell the king the advantages and disadvantages of agreeing to the demands of the nobles.

The Rise of Democratic Ideas **21**

ANSWERS

1. TERMS & NAMES
feudalism, p. 17
common law, p. 17
Magna Carta, p. 17
due process of law, p. 18
Parliament, p. 18
divine right, p. 19
Glorious Revolution, p. 20

constitutional monarchy, p. 20
bill of right, p. 20

2. TAKING NOTES
Possible Responses: Events should include: Model Parliament, 1295; Execution of Charles I, 1649; Habeas Corpus Act, 1679; establishment of constitutional monarchy, 1689;

English bill of rights, 1689. Most important event: accept answers students support with clear reasons.

3. SUMMARIZING
Possible Responses: The establishment of Parliament's right to limit the power of English monarchs; the guarantee of rights

and liberties for English citizens.

4. THEME ACTIVITY
Responses should:
- list both advantages and disadvantages of the king's signing
- take a position on the monarch's signing of the Magna Carta

---

History from Visuals

The Rise of Democratic Ideas, 1200—1700
Interpreting a Time Line Ask students when the Model Parliament first met and when Parliament passed the habeas corpus act *1295; 1679.* Encourage students to summarize what happened in the approximately 400 years between these two events. *Possible Response: Parliament became an established body and grew in power.*

Extension Activity Encourage students to draw their own time line and fill in events that occurred between 1295 and 1679 that contributed to the establishment of Parliament and its growth in power.

ASSESS & RETEACH

Section 3 Assessment
After students have worked on the first three questions independently, have them work in pairs to check their answers and to complete the last section.

Section Quiz
FORMAL ASSESSMENT
Section Quiz, p. 7

Reteaching Activity
CLASS TIME: 15 MINUTES

Use the second assessment question to review the section. Have students make their own sequence graphics, adding as many boxes as they think are necessary to show the development of England's constitutional monarchy. Hold a class discussion about the event students think was the most important and why.

CLOSE ACTIVITY

CLASS TIME: 30 MINUTES

Clarifying
Divide the class into two teams. Direct each team to review the material in this section. Have the teams stand on opposite sides of the room, and ask them questions about democratic developments in England between 1200 and 1700. For each wrong answer, a team member sits down. The team with the most students still standing at the end wins.

Teacher's Edition **21**

OBJECTIVES

1. To compare ideas of the Enlightenment and discuss their influence.

2. To outline the origins of democracy in North America.

3. To trace the changes in government that occurred during the French Revolution.

4. To describe the continuing struggle for democracy in different parts of the world today.

CRITICAL THINKING

- Summarizing, p. 23
- Recognizing Effects, pp. 25, 26
- Forming and Supporting Opinions, p.27
- Comparing and Contrasting, p. 27

FOCUS
5-Minute Warm-Up

Perceiving Causes
To understand how Enlightenment thinkers put together previous ideas to further democratic thought, have students read the first paragraph under Enlightenment Ideas and answer the following questions.

1. What ancient Greek and Christian ideas did Enlightenment philosophers combine in their view of society?

2. How would these ideas clash with the idea of the divine right of kings?

 WARM-UP TRANSPARENCY WTP

OBJECTIVE ① INSTRUCT

Enlightenment Ideas

Key Ideas
- Enlightenment thinkers apply the scientific method to human affairs to discover natural laws that govern society.

- Hobbes develops the idea that people agree to submit to an absolute ruler to maintain order.

(continued on next page)

TERMS & NAMES
- Enlightenment
- social contract
- natural rights
- separation of powers
- American Revolution
- representative government
- federal system
- French Revolution
- United Nations

4 The Enlightenment and Democratic Revolutions

MAIN IDEA	WHY IT MATTERS NOW
Enlightenment ideas helped bring about the American and French revolutions.	These revolutions and the documents they produced have inspired other democratic movements.

SETTING THE STAGE The Renaissance continued to affect European thinking through the 17th century. Its emphasis on the individual and its desire to expand the limits of human ability were especially influential. At the same time, Europeans began to explore the limits of their physical world. They extended the boundaries of the known world in what the Europeans called the Age of Exploration. New ideas and discoveries had a great impact on Europeans' understanding of both themselves and the world.

Enlightenment Ideas

HISTORY MAKERS

John Locke
1632–1704
During Charles II's reign, John Locke fell under suspicion of treason. He fled England to the Netherlands. There he was befriended by Prince William of Orange and his wife, Mary. When they became the ruling monarchs of England, Locke also returned and became a court favorite.

In addition to his political writings, Locke published *An Essay Concerning Human Understanding* (1690). It describes how the mind learns about the world. Locke believed that at birth, the mind is a clean slate, a *tabula rasa*. As a person grows, he or she is affected by many experiences. People used reason, Locke asserted, to make sense of their experiences and to discover order in the universe.

In the 17th and 18th centuries, an intellectual movement called the **Enlightenment** developed. During this period, thinkers attempted to apply the principles of reason and the methods of science to all aspects of society. Enlightenment thinkers built upon the long history of Western thought.

The philosophers of ancient Greece had established the idea of natural laws that could be discovered by careful observation and reasoned inquiry. Christianity contributed the belief in the equality of souls. (This belief would later lead to the principle of equal rights in society.) During the Renaissance, thinkers had focused on worldly concerns. They criticized medieval philosophy for concentrating on questions that seemed unrelated to human conditions.

The Scientific Revolution of the 1500s and 1600s was an even more immediate source of Enlightenment thought. New ideas about society and government developed out of it. The Scientific Revolution caused thinkers to rely on their own reasoning instead of merely accepting traditional beliefs. Enlightenment thinkers praised both Isaac Newton's discovery of the mechanical laws that govern the universe and the scientific method that made such a discovery possible. They wanted to apply the scientific method, which relied on observation and testing of theories, to human affairs. They hoped that they could use reason to discover the natural laws that governed society just as scientists had used it to discover physical laws.

Hobbes and Locke The English philosopher Thomas Hobbes was influenced by the Scientific Revolution. In his masterpiece of political theory, *Leviathan* (1651), he gave his views on human nature. Hobbes believed that people were by nature selfish and ambitious. He thought the kind of government needed to control selfish ambitions was absolute monarchy. In a kind of **social contract,** people agreed to submit to an authoritarian ruler to prevent disorder.

John Locke, another early Enlightenment thinker, held a more positive view of human nature. His book *Two Treatises on Government* was published in 1690, the year after the Glorious Revolution. Locke

Background
The Age of Exploration was a period of more than 300 years during which European explorers sailed to Asia, Africa, and the Americas on voyages of discovery and exploration.

Vocabulary
Western thought: the intellectual activity of the culture that developed in Europe.

SECTION 4 RESOURCES

PRINT RESOURCES

 IN-DEPTH RESOURCES: PROLOGUE
Guided Reading, p. 4
Primary Source: from the Iroquois Constitution, p. 11
History Makers: John Locke, p. 16
Literature: from *1776,* p. 14
Connections Across Time and Cultures: p. 17

 ACCESS FOR STUDENTS ACQUIRING ENGLISH
Guided Reading (Spanish), p. 15

FORMAL ASSESSMENT
 Section Quiz, p. 8

TECHNOLOGY RESOURCES

 WORLD ART AND CULTURES TRANSPARENCIES
AT00 Portrait of Marie Antoinette with Her Children

 CD-ROM
Electronic Library of Primary Sources

 INTERNET www.mlworldhistory.com
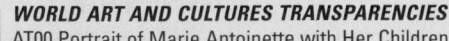

argued that the English people had been justified in overthrowing James II. The government had failed under James to perform its most fundamental duty—protecting the rights of the people. Locke said that all human beings had, by nature, the right to life, liberty, and property. In order to protect these **natural rights,** they formed governments. The people had an absolute right, he said, to rebel against a government that violated or failed to protect their rights.

Locke was indicating that a government's power comes from the people, not from God. Thus Locke provided a strong argument against the divine right of kings. Locke's ideas about self-government inspired people and became cornerstones of modern democratic thought.

Voltaire and Rousseau Other thinkers of the Enlightenment admired the democratic nature of English institutions. They themselves, however, lived under the rule of absolute monarchs. Voltaire was a brilliant 18th-century French writer and historian. He proposed tolerance, freedom of religion, and free speech. The French government and Christianity were frequent targets of his criticism.

Perhaps the most free-thinking of all Enlightenment philosophers was Jean-Jacques Rousseau. His most famous work was *The Social Contract* (1762). In it, Rousseau advocated democracy. Unlike Hobbes, he called the social contract an agreement among free individuals to create a government that would respond to the people's will:

> **A VOICE FROM THE PAST**
> The problem is to find a form of association which will defend and protect with the whole common force the person and goods of each associate, and in which each, while uniting himself with all, may still obey himself alone, and remain as free as before.
> JEAN-JACQUES ROUSSEAU, *The Social Contract*

For Rousseau, the only government that was legitimate came from the consent of the governed. The people, he hoped, would follow the dictates of their consciences to vote for, or choose, that which was best for the community as a whole.

Montesquieu Another French philosopher, Baron de Montesquieu, also recognized liberty as a natural right. In his book *The Spirit of the Laws* (1748), Montesquieu pointed out that any person or group in power will try to increase its power. Like Aristotle, Montesquieu searched for a way to keep government under control. He concluded that liberty could best be safeguarded by a **separation of powers,** that is,

THINK THROUGH HISTORY
A. Summarizing
What was John Locke's argument against the divine right of kings?
A. Possible Answer
Locke believed that a government's power comes from the people, not from God.

Vocabulary
legitimate: authentic, or genuine

Ideas of the Enlightenment

Right to life, liberty, and property

Social contract

Freedom of speech

Separation of powers

The Rise of Democratic Ideas **23**

OBJECTIVE ❶ INSTRUCT

(continued from page 22)
• Locke believes that the purpose of government is to protect people's natural rights.
• Voltaire and Rousseau promote democratic ideas, including the theory that legitimate government comes only with the people's consent.
• Montesquieu states that liberty is safeguarded by a separation of powers in government.

📖 **IN-DEPTH RESOURCES: PROLOGUE**
Guided Reading, p. 4

📖 **ACCESS FOR STUDENTS ACQUIRING ENGLISH**
Guided Reading (Spanish), p. 15

HISTORYMAKERS
John Locke

Locke was a strong advocate of religious freedom. He thought that no person held such complete wisdom or knowledge that he or she could dictate another person's beliefs. Encourage students to discuss Locke's idea that a person's mind is a clean slate at birth and to explain their reasons for agreeing or disagreeing with this statement.

📖 **IN-DEPTH RESOURCES: PROLOGUE**
History Makers: John Locke, p. 16

History from Visuals

Ideas of the Enlightenment
Interpreting the Diagram Have students follow the arrows from the center of the diagram and then list the Enlightenment ideas highlighted.

Extension Activity Ask students to reread the text on pages 22 and 23 and then have them write a paragraph promoting one of the Enlightenment ideas today.

TEACHING OPTIONS

CONNECTION ACROSS THE CURRICULUM

Science Encourage students to make a chart like the one on the right listing natural laws and major theories. For each scientific discipline, they should list one or more important natural laws or describe a major scientific theory important to that discipline.

Natural Laws and Scientific Theories	
Astronomy	
Biology	
Chemistry	
Geology	
Medicine	
Physics	

Literature Encourage students to read translations of Voltaire's works. Students may especially enjoy reading *Candide*. After students have read this or other writings of Voltaire, ask them to summarize the work and explain how it furthers ideas of the Enlightenment.

The Beginning of Democracy in America

▶ Key Ideas
- American colonists use the political ideas of the Enlightenment philosophers to protest British rule.
- Colonists fight the American Revolution and win independence from Britain.
- The United States adopts a constitution that is shaped by Enlightenment ideas.

 IN-DEPTH RESOURCES: PROLOGUE
Literature: from *1776*, p. 14

SPOTLIGHT On
The Iroquois Federation

The Iroquois Federation was formed in the late 1500s to unite the Mohawk, Oneida, Onondaga, Cayuga, and Seneca tribes. The Tuscarora joined in 1722. This federation lasted for more than 200 years.

 IN-DEPTH RESOURCES: PROLOGUE

Primary Source: from the Iroquois Constitution, p. 11

MORE ABOUT . . .
The Articles of Confederation

The purpose of the Articles of Confederation was to create a national government that would not interfere with the power of the states. There was only one branch of national government—the legislative branch. The legislature had no authority to raise taxes; it had to requisition funds from the states. It also could not regulate trade, which created serious financial problems for the United States. The nation did not even have a permanent place for Congress to meet.

---

by dividing government into three separate branches. These branches were (1) a legislature to make laws, (2) an executive to enforce them, and (3) courts to interpret them. This basic plan is used today by the United States and many other democratic countries.

The Beginning of Democracy in America

The ideas of the Enlightenment had a strong impact on Britain's North American colonies. By the mid-1700s, 13 British colonies had been established in North America. They were administered under the rule of the British government. To the north and west of Britain's colonies was New France, a French colony. In 1756, Britain and France went to war for control of North America. The war was called the French and Indian War. France and England were also fighting in Europe, where the conflict was known as the Seven Years' War.

Americans Protest British Policies The American colonists helped Britain defeat France in the French and Indian War. At war's end in 1763, the British Empire in North America stretched west to the Mississippi River. The war had been very costly, however, and further expenses lay ahead. Britain believed its colonies should pay some of the cost because they shared some of the benefits. To protect the newly acquired territory, the British needed to keep even more soldiers in America. To raise money, Britain sought to tax the colonists.

The colonists protested what they viewed as a violation of their rights as British citizens—there should be no taxation without representation. (The taxes were assessed by Parliament, but the colonists had no representation in Parliament.) The colonists also resented the British for preventing them from settling on land west of the Appalachian Mountains. They felt that the French and Indian War had been fought to allow westward expansion.

Americans Win Independence The Stamp Act of 1765 was the first in a series of measures by the British to tax the colonists. The colonists opposed each of these measures. Eventually, to protect their economic and political rights, the colonists united and began to arm themselves against what they called British oppression.

The **American Revolution,** the colonists' fight for independence from Great Britain, began with the Battle of Lexington and Concord on April 19, 1775. The Americans issued a Declaration of Independence on July 4, 1776. In it, they explained to King George III of England and to the world why they should be free of British rule. The ideas of the Enlightenment—especially Locke's ideas that governments are created by the people to protect their rights—strongly influenced the writers of the Declaration. After five more years of war, the British army surrendered in 1781. The Americans had their independence.

For several years, the new nation existed as a loose federation, or union, of states under the Articles of Confederation. Americans had wanted a weak central government. They feared that a strong government would lead to the kind of tyranny they had rebelled against. The government, however, was too weak. It could not collect taxes to pay war debt and finance the government. It did not have the power to make treaties and so commanded little respect from foreign countries.

Enlightenment Ideas Shape the Constitution In the summer of 1787, a group of Americans leaders met in Philadelphia. They had been chosen by their state legislatures to work out, or frame, a better plan of government. They wrote the Constitution of the United States. This document has served for more than two centuries as an inspiration and a model for new democracies around the world. Creating the Constitution was not an easy task, however. There was great debate over a very basic

SPOTLIGHT On
The Iroquois Federation

The Iroquois Federation was a loose organization of five, and later six, tribes from upper New York State. Clan and village chiefs from each tribe made up a common council. Each tribe had one vote. All decisions had to be unanimous.

The federation impressed the colonists with its efficient organization. Some people think that knowledge of the Iroquois Federation may have influenced an early plan for a colonial union—the Albany Plan of Union—proposed by Benjamin Franklin in 1854 or even the federal structure of the United States government. The Iroquois Federation split during the Revolutionary War. Some tribes supported the British, while others aided the Americans.

The Declaration of Independence and the U.S. Constitution Encourage students to photocopy the text of the Declaration of Independence and of the Constitution. (These can often be found in their entirety in American history textbooks.) Suggest that students work in small groups to search for Enlightenment ideas stated in these documents. Have students highlight passages they believe reflect such ideas and identify which Enlightenment philosopher or philosophers expounded or promoted these ideas. Let students share their findings in a class discussion.

Influence of the U.S. Constitution The Constitution of the United States serves as a model for many countries drafting a new constitution. Urge interested students to get translations of the constitutions of different nations and compare the wording, organization, and guaranteed rights to those of the U.S. Constitution. Ask them to present their comparisons in chart form.

question: Is it possible to establish a government that is strong and stable but not tyrannical? The answer that the framers reached was yes—such a government was possible if they created a system in which power and responsibility were shared in a balanced way.

First, the framers agreed to set up a **representative government,** one in which citizens elect representatives to make laws and policies for them. This was to ensure that the power to govern ultimately rested with the people, as advocated by Rousseau. Yet unlike Rousseau, they selected an indirect form of government over direct democracy. The Romans had also chosen an indirect democracy when they established a republic.

Second, the framers created a **federal system.** The powers of government were to be divided between the federal, or central, government and the states, or local, government. Third, within the federal government, the framers set up a separation of powers based on the writings of Montesquieu. Power was divided among the executive, legislative, and judicial branches. This provided a system of checks and balances to prevent any branch from having too much power.

The French Revolution

During the 18th century, the impulse toward democracy had also been stirring in France. Under Louis XIV, who reigned from 1638 to 1715, France experienced the excesses of absolute monarchy. Louis left unresolved problems and massive debts for his heirs. Unrest grew during the reigns of Louis XV and Louis XVI.

Causes of the Revolution Louis XVI came to the throne at the age of 19 in 1774. He was a well-intentioned but weak leader who was often dominated by his wife, Marie Antoinette. She was a spoiled and extravagant woman who often involved herself in matters of the royal court. She was unpopular with the French people. France's problems, however, went deeper than the monarchy. The clergy and the nobility enjoyed many privileges. Even though the monarchy was deeply in debt, only commoners paid taxes. Many historians say that the French Revolution was fought to balance the inequities, or injustices, in French society.

Throughout the 18th century, Enlightenment ideas caused people to rethink the structure of society. The French middle class and also some nobles were strongly impressed with ideas such as the social contract and freedom of speech. They were also inspired by the example of the American people throwing off an oppressive government in the 1770s. The peasants, too, were dissatisfied and restless. The year 1789 had been preceded by two years of poor harvests. The people were hungry and felt that neither the king nor the nobility cared.

Early Reforms of Revolution Louis XVI's government was about to go bankrupt in 1789. In desperation, Louis sought to raise taxes. He called into session the Estates-General. This representative assembly had not been summoned since 1614. The commoners in the Estates-General, however, felt their class was not fairly represented and protested. They left and formed the National Assembly. Eventually, members of other classes joined them. In the meantime, on July 14, 1789, the people of Paris stormed the Bastille, a much-hated prison in Paris that symbolized autocratic rule. Peasant uprisings then spread from Paris throughout the country. The fight to win democratic freedoms for the people, the **French Revolution,** had begun.

The National Assembly made many needed reforms. It adopted the Declaration of the Rights of Man and of the Citizen. This document was strongly influenced by Enlightenment ideas and the American Declaration of Independence. The declaration

**James Madison
1751–1836**

As a young man, James Madison was strongly influenced by the Enlightenment. When the Constitutional Convention was called, he spent a year preparing by reading the works of Locke, Montesquieu, Voltaire, and other Enlightenment philosophers.

Madison is known as the father of the Constitution. He designed the plan that included the three branches of government. He also helped to create the federal system. Madison kept careful records of the debates at the convention so that future Americans could know how the delegates made their decisions. Later, Madison served as the fourth president of the United States.

The Struggle for Democracy Continues

Key Ideas
- Most people in the world today consider democracy the preferred form of government.
- The United Nations sets world-wide standards for political, social, and economic rights.
- Many nations, including South Africa and the former republics of the Soviet Union, are struggling to set up democratic government and follow more democratic policies.

MORE ABOUT
The United Nations

Aside from the General Assembly, the United Nations has a number of branches and programs to help maintain international peace, foster economic cooperation and social equality, and develop and institute international law. The United Nations Children's Fund (UNICEF) is one such UN organization. UNICEF works to improve the general welfare of children around the world through programs in education, nutrition, and health. Another example is the World Court, which rules on issues brought by member nations.

History through Visuals

The Rise of Democratic Ideas 1690–1790
Interpreting a Time Line Ask students to compute how much time passed between the period when John Locke and Baron de Montesquieu each developed their ideas and when these ideas were first put into effect. *Locke— 86 years; Montesquieu—39 years*

(continued on next page)

Thousands of those suspected of not supporting the French Revolution were beheaded by the guillotine, shown here in a 19th-century engraving.

guaranteed the rights of "liberty, property, security, and resistance to oppression" to all people. The assembly also ended feudalism in France. It drafted a constitution that made France a limited monarchy. It reorganized the Catholic Church in France and redistributed its land. It reformed the court system. Believing its work to be over in 1791, it disbanded so that the new Legislative Assembly could take over.

French Republic Undone In France the new assembly was not accepted by the king, the aristocrats, or many Catholics. Other European countries who had absolute monarchs feared the spread of democratic ideas. They went to war with France, hoping to undo the new government. The new French republic was in a state of crisis. In 1792 the royal family was imprisoned. A new legislature, more radical in nature, took charge. A period historians call the Reign of Terror followed. Many people who were thought to be opponents of the revolution were killed for their beliefs. Included among them were the king and queen. Finally, in 1799, a military leader, Napoleon Bonaparte, assumed control of France and created a dictatorship.

It was not until the mid-1800s that democracy developed in France. The French Revolution illustrates why democracy sometimes fails. It is not enough to promise equality and freedom. Nor is it enough to have representative government. For democracy to work, a society must have rule by law, protections for both civil rights and civil liberties, tolerance of dissent, and acceptance of majority decisions by the minority.

The Struggle for Democracy Continues

It took centuries for the ideas of democracy to develop and take hold in the world. Today, most people view democracy as the preferred form of government. Even some authoritarian governments voice agreement with the idea of democracy. Generally, however, they do not follow through with democratic actions.

The United Nations Promotes Democracy Just before the end of World War II in 1945, a new international organization called the **United Nations** was established. Its goal was to work for world peace and the betterment of humanity. One of the branches of the UN, the General Assembly, is a kind of democracy. There, nations discuss their problems with the hope of settling them peacefully. Each nation has equal representation.

The UN's charter is based on the traditions of democracy. The UN's authority comes from the nations of the world. The charter reaffirms basic human rights, the need for justice and the rule of law, and the desire for social progress.

One of the UN's most important contributions is the Universal Declaration of Human Rights. It was adopted by the General Assembly in 1948. This document also draws on democratic ideas. It sets a worldwide standard for basic social, political, and

Background
The Assembly sold church lands to the highest bidders to raise money for the new government.

THINK THROUGH HISTORY
C. Recognizing Effects What factors brought an end to the French Republic?
C. Possible Answers The Assembly was not accepted by the king; other European countries went to war with France; a more radical legislature led to a military ruler.

 TEACHING OPTION BLOCK SCHEDULING **COOPERATIVE ACTIVITY: Learning About Leaders of the French Revolution**

Task: Students work in small groups to find out more about the leaders of the French Revolution.

Purpose: To gain insight into the personalities of the people who led the French Revolution.

Activity: Divide the class into groups of three or four. Have each group research the life of one of the leaders of the French Revolution, such as Georges-Jacques Danton, Jean-Paul Marat, Olympe de

Gouges, or Maximilien Robespierre. Students should work together to make a book or web site about their subject, including pictures of the person and significant events in his or her life. Encourage students to discuss the beliefs of each person and how these ideas relate to democracy. Let students display their books or post the addresses of their web sites.

Building a Portfolio: Students can add their book or a printout of their web site to their

portfolios, attaching an explanation of their role in its development.

Standards for Evaluation
Books or web sites should . . .

- give a concise, interesting biography of the subject
- include pictures of the subject
- provide an analysis of the subject's beliefs and an assessment of how these ideas relate to democracy

1748 Baron de Montesquieu suggests that a government's powers should be divided among three branches, which act as a check on one another.

1776 The American colonies declare independence from Britain, claiming the right to overthrow an unjust government.

1789 The French National Assembly issues the Declaration of the Rights of Man, stating that all persons are equal.

1690 · 1740 · 1750 · 1760 · 1770 · 1780 · 1790

1690 John Locke proposes that a government's power comes from the consent of the governed.

1787 The U.S. Constitution—creating a democratic, republican government based on the ideas of Locke and Montesquieu—is written.

History through Visuals
(continued from page 26)

Extension Activity Discuss why Montesquieu's and Locke's ideas were put into effect more quickly than those of earlier writers on democracy.

---

economic rights. Included are the right to life, liberty, and security. Also stated are the rights to equal protection under the law, free movement, and free association and assembly with other people. To these rights were added social and economic rights: the rights to work, to rest and leisure, and to education. The declaration's purpose is to serve as an international code of conduct.

Modern Struggles for Democracy In many places throughout the world today, the ideals of the UN's Universal Declaration of Human Rights have yet to be wholly achieved. Nations are struggling to move toward more democratic government. But it is not easy to establish democratic policies where dictatorship has been the rule. Still, beginnings have been made in a number of these countries.

For example, the breakup of the Soviet Union in the early 1990s enabled 15 new republics to assert their people's national identity and interests. Also, in South Africa, after many years of apartheid, or racial segregation, a democratic government in which all races are represented was established.

**THINK THROUGH HISTORY
D. Forming and Supporting Opinions** Why do you think people and nations continue to struggle toward more democratic government? Support your opinion with reasons.

There is no guarantee that democracy can be achieved in any particular time and place. There is also no guarantee that once achieved, democracy will not be lost if people are not constantly watchful. Yet, as you read the history of the modern world in the chapters that follow, you will see that the idea of democracy has survived dictators, wars, and oppression. It is an idea whose strength comes not just from leaders but from the people themselves.

GlobalImpact

Revolutions of 1989

Democratic revolutions swept Eastern Europe in 1989. Reforms in the Soviet Union opened the door for more freedoms throughout Communist-controlled Eastern Europe. In April 1989, Poland held its first free election since the Communists seized control during World War II.

Soon after, Hungary also launched a sweeping reform program. It then began to admit East Germans who claimed to be tourists but actually planned to escape to the West. Soon, demonstrations began in East Germany, leading to the tearing down of the hated Berlin Wall. Eventually the Communists fell from power, and East and West Germany voted to reunite.

Global Impact
Revolutions of 1989

Encourage students to find out more about the current governments of countries mentioned in the feature. They can discuss how democracy is doing in these countries and in others as well.

 ELECTRONIC LIBRARY OF PRIMARY SOURCES
"Destruction of the Berlin Wall"

 CASE STUDY 4—Russia and Germany: The Fall of Communism, p. 44

 CASE STUDY 8—Argentina and South Africa: Authoritarianism to Democracy, p. 100

CASE STUDY 9—Japan and Mexico: Pluralistic Politics and Economic Growth, p. 114

ASSESS & RETEACH

Section 4 Assessment
Divide the class into groups of four students. Within each group have one member answer each of the Assessment questions. Then have group members take turns presenting their answers to the group.

Section Quiz
 FORMAL ASSESSMENT
Section Quiz, p. 8

Reteaching Activity
CLASS TIME: 20 MINUTES

Making Inferences
Ask students how they think life today would be different had democracy never arisen.

Section 4 Assessment

1. TERMS & NAMES
Identify
• Enlightenment
• social contract
• natural rights
• separation of powers
• American Revolution
• representative government
• federal system
• French Revolution
• United Nations

2. TAKING NOTES
Make a bulleted chart like the one below, showing major ideas of the Enlightenment that helped to spark the American and French revolutions.

Enlightenment Ideas
•
•

Choose one and write a few sentences about its importance.

3. COMPARING AND CONTRASTING
In what ways was the French Revolution similar to and different from the American Revolution?

THINK ABOUT
• causes of the revolutions
• types of government established
• results

4. THEME ACTIVITIES
Imagine that you live in the time of the American Revolution or the French Revolution. You are planning to participate in a pro-democracy rally. Prepare a series of slogans describing your demands, to be displayed on posters for the demonstration. Write your slogans on 3-by-5-inch cards.

The Rise of Democratic Ideas **27**

CLOSE ACTIVITY

CLASS TIME: 20 MINUTES

Consolidating Time Lines
With the class, make a time line on the chalkboard that chronicles the rise of democratic ideas throughout history. The time line should begin in 1200 B.C. and end with the current year. Challenge students to add modern dates.

ANSWERS

1. TERMS & NAMES
Enlightenment, p. 22
social contract, p. 22
natural rights, p. 23
separation of powers, p. 24
American Revolution, p. 24
representative government, p. 25
federal system, p. 25
French Revolution, p. 25
United Nations, p. 26

2. TAKING NOTES
Possible Responses: social contract between government and people; people have rights to life, liberty, and property; religious freedom and freedom of speech; government should respond to will of people; legitimate government comes from consent of the governed; separation of powers.

3. COMPARING AND CONTRASTING
Possible Responses: Similar—desire for more freedoms and for a more responsive government were causes and republic was first government established; different—democracy prevailed with American Revolution but did not with French Revolution.

4. THEME ACTIVITIES
Slogans should be short, to the point, and do one of the following: address appropriate issues, list grievances, describe a democratic reform

TERMS & NAMES

1. aristocracy, p. 5
2. direct democracy, p. 7
3. monarchy, p. 7
4. republic, p. 8
5. due process of law, p. 18
6. divine right, p. 19
7. constitutional monarchy, p. 20
8. social contract, p. 22
9. representative government, p. 25
10. federal system, p. 25

REVIEW QUESTIONS

11. He increased the number of paid public officials, which allowed more poor people to participate in government, and he introduced direct democracy, in which citizens ruled directly.
12. In a direct democracy, all citizens participate directly in the decision-making of the government. In a republic, citizens elect leaders to make the decisions on their behalf.
13. All persons, even rulers and other powerful people, could be held accountable for their actions under the law.
14. Both the individual and the community were supposed to work to decrease oppression and injustice.
15. The emphasis on the importance of the individual played a part in the growth of political liberty.
16. Common law reflects the customs and principles of a country. Roman law represents the will of a ruler or lawmaker.
17. The rights guaranteed include the right to a jury trial and the protection of the law.
18. The monarch was forbidden to suspend laws, to tax without consent of Parliament, and to raise an army during peacetime without Parliament's approval.
19. The question was "Is it possible to establish a government that is strong and stable but not tyrannical?" The answer was yes, it was possible if they created a system in which power and responsibility were shared in a balanced way.
20. Democracy requires rule by law, protections for both civil rights and civil liberties, tolerance of dissent, and acceptance of majority decisions by the minority.

Visual Summary

The Rise of Democratic Ideas

1200 B.C.	Moses records Jewish law.
594 B.C.	Solon reforms Greek laws.
509 B.C.	Rome creates a republican (representative) government.
461 B.C.	Pericles introduces direct democracy to Athens
A.D. 26	Jesus teaches the worth of each person before God
528	Emperor Justinian authorizes a written legal code
1215	King John signs the Magna Carta
1295	The Model Parliament meets
1300	Renaissance thinkers teach the importance of the individual
1455	Gutenberg invents the printing press, with movable type, helping spread new ideas
1628	King Charles I signs the Petition of Right
1689	Parliament enacts the Bill of Rights
1690	John Locke writes about the consent of the governed.
1748	Baron de Montesquieu proposes the separation of government powers
1776	The American colonies declare independence from Britain
1787	The U.S. Constitution is written
1789	The French National Assembly issues the Declaration of the Rights of Man

TERMS & NAMES

Briefly explain the importance of each of the following to the rise of democratic ideas.

1. aristocracy
2. direct democracy
3. monarchy
4. republic
5. due process of law
6. divine right
7. constitutional monarchy
8. social contract
9. representative government
10. federal system

REVIEW QUESTIONS

SECTION 1 *(pages 5–9)*
The Legacy of Ancient Greece and Rome

11. What changes did Pericles introduce into Greek government to make it more democratic?
12. In what ways is a republic different from direct democracy?
13. What does the phrase "government of laws, not of men" mean?

SECTION 2 *(pages 12–16)*
Judeo-Christian Tradition

14. What did the Hebrew tradition teach about the responsibilities of the individual and community to combat injustice?
15. How did the Reformation contribute to the growth of democracy?

SECTION 3 *(pages 17–21)*
Democratic Developments in England

16. How does common law differ from Roman law?
17. Name two basic individual rights guaranteed in the Magna Carta.
18. In what three ways was the power of the English monarch limited by the English Bill of Rights?

SECTION 4 *(pages 22–27)*
The Enlightenment and Democratic Revolutions

19. What question did the framers of the American Constitution have to deal with, and what was the answer?
20. What is required in a society for democracy to work?

Interact *with* History

On page 4, you were asked to think about why people would risk death to have or preserve democracy. Imagine yourself as a television news reporter. Write at least five questions that you would ask the young man in the photo. Compare your questions with those of at least one other person in your class.

Interact *with* History

Students' questions may focus on individual freedoms, the rule of law, the value of justice, the emphasis on reason, or other features of democracy that have been discussed in the Prologue.

CRITICAL THINKING

1. LESSONS OF DEMOCRACY

THEME **CULTURAL INTERACTION** Name some examples from this chapter in which the positive impact of the ideas of democracy helped promote democracy in another part of the world.

2. DEMOCRATIC THINKERS

THEME **POWER AND AUTHORITY** Create a chart like the one below. For each philosopher, list his ideas about government and the book in which they are found.

Philosopher	Ideas About Government Power and Authority	Book
Hobbes		
Locke		
Rousseau		
Montesquieu		

3. FORMS OF DEMOCRACY

This chapter describes both direct and representative democracy. For what reasons would a nation in today's world choose representative democracy rather than direct democracy?

4. ANALYZING PRIMARY SOURCES

In the following selection from *Politics,* Aristotle presents his views on where the power of the state should reside. His conclusions reflect the idea that moderation is the best path to civic virtue. Read the paragraph and then answer the questions that follow:

> **A VOICE FROM THE PAST**
> Where ought the sovereign power of the state to reside? . . . The state aims to consist as far as possible of those who are alike and equal, a condition found chiefly among the middle section. . . . The middle class is also the steadiest element, the least eager for change. They neither covet, like the poor the possessions of others, nor do others covet theirs, as the poor covet those of the rich. . . . Tyranny often emerges from an over-enthusiastic democracy or from an oligarchy, but much more rarely from middle class constitutions . . .

- What is Aristotle arguing here?
- How closely does this model of an ideal state correspond to the reality of Athenian democracy?
- Do you agree with Aristotle? Support you opinion.

CHAPTER ACTIVITIES

1. LIVING HISTORY: Unit Portfolio Project

Your portfolio project focuses on the rise of democratic ideas. As documents, the U.S. Constitution and the Bill of Rights include many of the ideas of democracy that developed over the years. Use the information in this chapter and in Chapter 6, Section 4, to help you with one of the following ideas to add to your portfolio.

- Create a map that shows the countries where the ideas found in the U.S. Constitution originated.
- Working with a team, create a television public service announcement showing the democratic rights guaranteed in the U.S. Constitution. Videotape your announcement or present it to the class.
- Write a dialogue between James Madison and Thomas Jefferson on the topic of democratic ideas to be included in the U.S. Constitution.

2. CONNECT TO TODAY: Cooperative Learning

THEME **REVOLUTION** Democratic ideas continue to have enormous influence throughout the world. In the last 25 years of the 20th century, democratic changes have taken place in Mexico, Brazil, the former Soviet Union, and South Africa. Work with a team to create a chart comparing steps toward democracy in the countries above.

 Using the Internet or your library, research changes that took place in each of the countries listed.

- With the group decide on a set of categories you can use to compare the steps toward democracy in these nations. For example, you might want to compare changes in voting patterns in elections.
- Create a large poster chart comparing or contrasting the changes that took place.

3. INTERPRETING A TIME LINE

Look at the time line in the visual summary. Pick four events and tell why you think they are the most important events of the ones listed.

FOCUS ON **GRAPHS**

The percentage of registered voters who take part in elections in democracies varies widely, as shown on the graph to the right.

Compare the percentage of voters in the following countries.

- Which country had the highest voter turnout? Which had the lowest?
- Which countries had about 75 percent of the voters participate?

Connect to History
Based on the percentages, what can you conclude regarding the way people in South Africa and in the United States feel about the responsibilities of democracy?

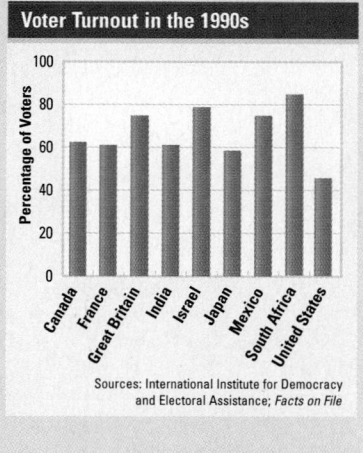

Voter Turnout in the 1990s

Sources: International Institute for Democracy and Electoral Assistance; *Facts on File*

The Rise of Democratic Ideas **29**

Marine Painting
Ludolf Backhuysen
(1631–1708)

Ludolf Backhuysen (also spelled Bakhuyzen) was a Dutch artist renowned for depicting the drama and movement of ships, whether in the harbor or on the high seas. In his time, he was the most popular marine painter in the Netherlands.

The Dutch ships shown here are the types of vessels used by many Europeans in exploration and trade in the late 17th century. The painting captures the perils to mariner and ship alike of long journeys over unfriendly seas to distant lands.

These voyages of exploration were made possible by advancements in ship design and navigational instruments. Sturdier ships and more accurate maps allowed sea captains and their crews to venture far from the sight of land toward previously uncharted territory.

The motives behind this era of worldwide exploration by the Europeans were many. A longing for riches was the principal motive. The wish to spread Christianity was another. The desire for adventure and the hope of fame also were powerful reasons. The Age of Exploration is often summed up as a mission for "glory, God, and gold."

By the end of this period, Portugal, Spain, the Netherlands, Britain, and France had spread European civilization to almost all areas of the globe.

UNIT 1 *Beginnings of the Modern World*
1300–1800

30

In this marine painting, Ludolf Bakhuyzen depicts a powerful Dutch fleet at sea. During this period, Europeans explored the world and interacted with the people of different lands for the first time.

31

Previewing the Unit

This unit covers the developments in the eastern and western hemispheres that result in connections through exploration and trade beginning in the late 1400s.

In the Americas, many diverse civilizations, including the Mayan, Aztec, and Incan, flourish prior to the arrival of the Europeans. These complex societies have common patterns of trade, religion, and social structure.

Europe is transformed from 1300 to 1650 by two powerful intellectual movements, the Renaissance and the Reformation. The Renaissance produces an outpouring of artistic creativity and a scientific revolution. The Reformation splits Christianity into Protestant and Catholic divisions.

In the area stretching from the Balkans to India, three potent Islamic empires emerge in the 1300s. The Ottomans of Turkey, the Safavids of Persia, and the Mughals of India thrive but eventually fall to both internal and external pressures.

The intellectual curiosity that produced the Renaissance and the new technology that resulted from the scientific revolution help lead Europeans to embark on voyages to explore the world.

The desire for profit and the hope of spreading Christianity send Europeans to the Far East. Goods and ideas are exchanged with the peoples of Asia. However, the Chinese and the Japanese eventually restrict European influence, preferring self-sufficiency.

The European exploration and colonization of the Americas begins with the voyages of Columbus. Interactions between Americans and Europeans leads to a global exchange of foods, animals, and ideas; the enrichment of Europe; and the devastation of Native American cultures.

Connecting Hemispheres

Teaching Strategies

Summarizing The ability to condense the pattern of events for a time period or a civilization is an important skill for students to employ as they work with the Unit Time Lines. Summarizing allows students to move from the level of individual events to that of the patterns at work in world history.

Cultural Interaction and Exploration You might ask students to examine the period between 1500 and 1600 to summarize patterns of contact among different civilizations. You might ask the class to group cultural interactions according to whether they occurred:

• within a continent (the Incan Empire reaches its height, Babur founds the Mughal Empire), or

• between continents (African slaves exported to the Americas, the Portuguese reach China, the circumnavigation of the globe by Magellan's crew, the conquest of the Aztecs and the Incas)

Cultural contact might also be summarized from the point of view of whether it was essentially peaceful or hostile in its intent. In fact, during the 1500s, a good deal of cultural interaction took place as a result of a desire to overcome another government or people, or to change others' religious beliefs.

The class might also discuss cultural interactions today and how the process may differ from that of the 1500s. The existence of the mass media and of modern transportation could be highlighted as important means of cultural interaction today.

Beginnings of the Modern World

| | 1300 | 1400 |

CHAPTER ① 1300–1600

European Renaissance and Reformation

1300 Italy Renaissance begins

1353 Italy Boccaccio finishes writing the *Decameron*

CHAPTER ② 1300–1700

The Muslim World Expands

1400s *Anatolia* ▶

1300 Anatolia Osman establishes Ottoman states

1361 Anatolia Ottoman Orkhan I captures Adrianople

CHAPTER ③ 1400–1800

An Age of Exploration and Isolation

1400s *China* ▶

1368 China Hong Wu founds Ming Dynasty

CHAPTER ④ 1492–1800

The Atlantic World

| | 1300 | 1400 |

CONNECTIONS ACROSS THE CURRICULUM

Geography You may want to use the *Geography Transparencies* (in full color) and the Geography Applications copymasters in the *In-Depth Resources* book to help students understand the physical settings of developments on the unit time line.

Geography Transparencies Map transparencies in Unit 1 depict developments such as "The Expansion of the Inca Empire, 1230–1525" or events such as "The Fall of Constantinople, 1453" (Chapter 2). The latter map details how the Turkish army found a small open gate in the walls of Constantinople and poured in to take the city.

You might show the map transparencies to the class as the Unit Time Line is discussed. (Teacher material accompanying the transparencies provides background and questions with answers.) You could also provide the map in advance to students who wish to present it as part of an oral report.

Geography Applications Discussion of the Unit Time Line may also provide an opportunity for students to work with the Geography Applications. Copymasters such as "Trade in Renaissance Europe" (Chapter 1) feature introductory text, followed by a map and one page of questions.

1455 _Germany_ Gutenberg Bible produced on printing press

1497 _Italy_ Leonardo da Vinci paints _The Last Supper_

1400 _India_ Timur the Lane devastates India

1453 _Anatolia_ Ottomans conquer Constantinople

1498 _Portugal_ Vasco da Gama sails to India

1420 _Portugal_ Prince Henry starts navigation school

1433 _China_ Last voyage of Zheng He

1494 _Spain_ Portugal Treaty of Tordesillas splits "New World"

1492 _Americas_ Columbus sails to Hispaniola

1508 _Italy_ Michelangelo begins painting Sistine Chapel

1517 _Germany_ Martin Luther begins Reformation

1534 _England_ Henry VIII breaks from Church

1501 _Persia_ Safavid Isma'il conquers Persia

1526 _India_ Babur founds Mughal Empire

1529 _Anatolia_ Suleiman the Magnificent rules Ottoman Empire

1514 _China_ First Portuguese ships reach China

1522 _Portugal_ Magellan's crew sails around world

1502 _Africa_ First slaves exported for work in the Americas

1521 _Mexico_ Cortés conquers Aztec

1532 _Peru_ Pizarro conquers Inca

1601 _England_ William Shakespeare writes _Hamlet_

1603 _England_ Queen Elizabeth I dies, ending Tudor rule

1631 _India_ Shah Jahan builds Taj Mahal

1658 _India_ Aurangzeb rules Mughal Empire

▲ **1500s _England_**

1603 _Japan_ Tokugawa Regime begins

1636 _China_ Manchus conquer Korea

1644 _China_ Manchus found Qing Dynasty

1607 _North America_ English settle Jamestown

1608 _Canada_ Champlain founds Quebec

1675 _North America_ Colonists and Indians clash in King Philip's War

1721 _Japan_ Edo (Tokyo) becomes world's largest city

1793 _China_ British seek trade concessions with Chinese

▼ **1675 _North America_**

1739 _North America_ South Carolina slaves lead Stono Rebellion

1754 _North America_ French and Indian War begins

TIME LINE 33

Living History
Unit 1 Portfolio Project

THEME Cultural Interaction

Your portfolio for Unit 1 will trace the ways cultures interact with one another and show the results of those influences. Types of interaction include conquest, trade, migration, and heritage. Results include the sharing of technology, religious concepts, political ideas, goods, crops, foods, diseases, and knowledge of all kinds.

Living History Project Choices

Each Chapter Assessment offers you choices of ways to show the cultural interaction in that chapter. Activities include the following:

Chapter ❶ magazine, letter, role-play, painting, interview

Chapter ❷ letter, political cartoon, inscription

Chapter ❸ letter, reply, editorial

Chapter ❹ description, collage, debate

Portfolio Project

Theme: Cultural Interaction The portfolio projects for Unit 1 ask students to consider the complex process of cultural interaction. The focus for the projects will be cultural exchanges as they occurred between 900 and 1800 on the continents of Europe, Asia, and the Americas. Some of the crucial aspects of this question that are dealt with in the projects include:

- the relationship between conquering and conquered peoples
- changes in daily life brought about by trade contacts among peoples
- the colonial experience from the point of view of colonizers and colonized
- the exchange of religious ideas between and among peoples
- the transfer of artistic influences from one people to another

Students Acquiring English
Students acquiring English (SAE) may have a unique perspective to offer on the implications of cultural interaction. Limitations of language may be overcome by assigning projects that call on students' art skills or that require a relatively controlled level of language.

Each chapter of this unit features at least one activity that offers students acquiring English the opportunity to display their understanding of cultural interaction.

You might encourage students acquiring English to discuss, to write about, or to depict in art their own experiences of cultural interaction.

The Western Civilization Videodisc

SECTION F: The Italian Renaissance, 1300–1550
Side One: Frame 22568

SECTION G: The Reformation, 1517–1600
Side One: Frame 25328

Universal Play Button

See Master Guide, page 112 for Section F, page 141 for Section G.

PLANNING GUIDE
European Renaissance and Reformation

	Key Ideas	COPY MASTERS	ASSESSMENT
SECTION 1 Italy: Birthplace of the Renaissance *pp. 37–42*	*The Renaissance, a period of intellectual and artistic creativity, flourishes in Italy, beginning about 1300. Versatile artists transform painting, sculpture, and literature.*	*In-Depth Resources: Unit 1* • **Guided Reading,** p. 18 • **Primary Sources:** from *The Courtier,* p. 25; from *The Prince,* p. 26 • **Literature:** from *The Agony and the Ecstasy,* p. 29 • **History Makers:** Niccolò Machiavelli, p. 32 • **Connections Across Time and Cultures:** p. 34	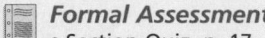 *Section 1 Assessment,* p. 42 *Formal Assessment* • Section Quiz, p. 17 *Alternative Assessment Book* • Standards for Evaluating a Cooperative Activity
SECTION 2 The Northern Renaissance *pp. 43–47*	*In the 1400s, Renaissance ideas spread to northern Europe, where German and Flemish masters create distinctive works of art. The books of northern Renaissance writers and philosophers become widely available because of the invention of the printing press.*	*In-Depth Resources: Unit 1* • **Guided Reading,** p. 19 • **Geography Application:** Trade in Renaissance Europe, p. 23	*Section 2 Assessment,* p. 47 *Formal Assessment* • Section Quiz, p. 18 *Alternative Assessment Book* • Standards for Evaluating a Cooperative Activity
SECTION 3 Luther Starts the Reformation *pp. 48–52*	*Martin Luther, a German monk, challenges the authority of the Catholic Church and triggers the Reformation—a movement for religious reform. The Reformation spreads to England when King Henry VIII breaks ties with the Catholic Church.*	*In-Depth Resources: Unit 1* • **Guided Reading,** p. 20 • **Skillbuilder Practice:** Synthesizing, p. 22 • **Primary Sources:** A Conference with Elizabeth I, p. 27; Report on the English Reformation, p. 28 • **History Makers:** Elizabeth I, p. 33	*Section 3 Assessment,* p. 52 *Formal Assessment* • Section Quiz, p. 19 *Alternative Assessment Book* • Standards for Evaluating a Cooperative Activity
SECTION 4 The Reformation Continues *pp. 53–57*	*John Calvin develops a system of Protestant theology that gains popularity among other European reformers. To stem the spread of Protestantism, the Catholic Church initiates its own reforms.*	*In-Depth Resources: Unit 1* • **Guided Reading,** p. 21	*Section 4 Assessment,* p. 56 *Formal Assessment* • Section Quiz, p. 20 *Alternative Assessment Book* • Standards for Evaluating a Cooperative Activity
CHAPTER RESOURCES	**Chapter Overview** *Two great European movements—the Renaissance and the Reformation—usher in dramatic cultural and social changes. The Renaissance marked the flowering of artistic creativity, while the Reformation led to new Christian beliefs.*	*Telescoping the Times* • Chapter Summary, pp. 5–7 *Planning for Block Schedules*	*Chapter Assessment,* pp. 58–59 *Chapter Activities,* p. 59 *Formal Assessment* • Chapter Test, forms A and B, pp. 21–26 *Test Generator* *Alternative Assessment Book*

1300–1600

TECHNOLOGY

 Warm-Up Transparency 1

 World Art and Cultures Transparencies
- AT36 Leonardo da Vinci's *The Last Supper*
- AT37 *Mona Lisa*

 Electronic Library of Primary Sources
- "The Art of Painting" from *Notebooks*

 INTERNET RESOURCES
www.mlworldhistory.com

 Warm-Up Transparency 1

 World Art and Cultures Transparencies
- AT38 Van Eyck's *Wedding Portrait*

 INTERNET RESOURCES
www.mlworldhistory.com

 Warm-Up Transparency 1

 Electronic Library of Primary Sources
- from the Ninety-Five Theses

 Religions of the World
- Christianity

 INTERNET RESOURCES
www.mlworldhistory.com

 Warm-Up Transparency 1

 Geography Transparencies
- GT17 Reformation: Lutheranism and Calvinism, 1500–1600

 Critical Thinking Transparencies
- CT17 Protestant and Catholic Reformations

 Electronic Library of Primary Sources
- "The St. Bartholomew's Day Massacre"
- "Luther: Giant of His Time and Ours"

 Religions of the World
- Christianity

Block Scheduling (90 MINUTES)

Day 1
Section 1, pp. 37–42
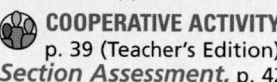 **COOPERATIVE ACTIVITY**
p. 39 (Teacher's Edition)
Section Assessment, p. 42

Day 2
Section 2, pp. 43–47
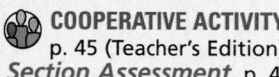 **COOPERATIVE ACTIVITY**
p. 45 (Teacher's Edition)
Section Assessment, p. 47

Day 3
Section 3, pp. 48–52
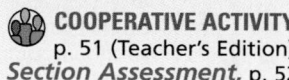 **COOPERATIVE ACTIVITY**
p. 51 (Teacher's Edition)
Section Assessment, p. 52

Day 4
Section 4, pp. 53–57
 COOPERATIVE ACTIVITY
p. 54 (Teacher's Edition)
Section Assessment, p. 56
Chapter Assessment,
pp. 58–59

Yearly Pacing *Chapter 1 Total:* 4 days *Yearly Total:* 85 days

 Planning for Block Schedules

Customizing for Special Needs

Students Acquiring English

 Access for Students Acquiring English
- **Guided Reading,** for Sections 1–4 (Spanish), pp. 22–25
- **Chapter Summary:** (Spanish), pp. 19–21
- **Skillbuilder Practice:** Synthesizing (Spanish), p. 26
- **Geography Application:** Trade in Renaissance Europe (Spanish), p. 27

 Spanish Reading Study Guide
- pp. 15–24

 Chapter Summaries on Audiocassette
in English and Spanish

Less Proficient Readers

 In-Depth Resources: Unit 1
- **Guided Reading,** for Sections 1–4, pp. 18–21
- **Skillbuilder Practice:** Synthesizing, p. 22
- **Geography Application:** Trade in Renaissance Europe, p. 23

 Telescoping the Times
- Chapter Summary, pp. 5–7

 Reading Study Guide
- pp. 15–24

 Chapter Summaries on Audiocassette

Gifted and Talented Students

 In-Depth Resources: Unit 1

Primary Sources
- from *The Courtier*, p. 25
- from *The Prince*, p. 26
- A Conference with Elizabeth, p. 27
- Report on the English Reformation, p. 28

History Makers
- Niccolò Machiavelli, p. 32
- Elizabeth I, p. 33

Connections to Literature READINGS FOR STUDENTS

 In-Depth Resources: Unit 1
Literature: from *The Agony and the Ecstasy,* p. 29

Enrichment Reading

- **Penman, Sharon Kay**
The Sunne in Splendour
New York: Penguin, 1984

A richly detailed story about Richard III involving fifteenth-century battle scenes, political intrigues, and family conflicts.

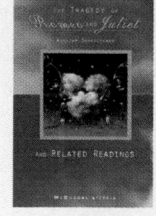

McDougal Littell
Literature Connections

- **Shakespeare, William**
The Tragedy of Romeo and Juliet
(with related readings)

Shakespeare's great Renaissance drama of love, conflict, and tragedy.

 = Pupil's Edition   = Overhead Transparency   ■ = Software   ▬ = Video

 = Copy Master   = CD-ROM   ▬ = Audiocassette   = Internet

European Renaissance and Reformation, 1300–1600

Accessing Prior Knowledge

- Ask students to read the captions accompanying each picture and to discuss what they already know about the people and situations.

Predicting and Making Inferences

- After students read about Anne Boleyn and the circumstances surrounding her marriage to King Henry VIII, ask them what they think might happen to her if she does not give birth to a male heir to the English throne.

- Ask students how they think Raphael felt about the culture of ancient Greece, based on the people he features in his painting.

Geography Connection

Ask students to note the distance between England and the Papal States.

- What geographic features isolate England from most of Europe?

- How might isolation and distance contribute to England's break with the Catholic Church in Rome?

CHAPTER **1**

European Renaissance and Reformation, 1300–1600

PREVIEWING THEMES

Cultural Interaction

Most medieval European art expressed either the values of Christianity or the code of chivalry. During the Renaissance, scholars and artists developed new cultural and artistic ideas based on the rediscovery of the literature of classical Greece and Rome.

Religious and Ethical Systems

For centuries, religious leaders had sought to reform the Catholic Church. They wanted to make it live up to its ideals. In the 1500s, Martin Luther began a reform movement called the Reformation. This led to the founding of Protestant churches.

Revolution

European scholars gained access to classical documents that they thought had been lost after the fall of Rome. This revolutionized their thinking. New ideas and values swept Europe. The invention of the printing press aided the spread of these revolutionary ideas. The printing press also spread ideas that called for a revolutionary rejection of the pope's authority.

INTERNET CONNECTION

Visit us at **www.mlworldhistory.com** to learn more about Renaissance artists, the Reformation, and related topics.

34

EUROPE, 1500

ATLANTIC OCEAN

IRELAN

By **1527**, King Henry VIII of England was sure that his queen was too old to bear a son. **Anne Boleyn** caught his eye. Anne was pretty and young enough to have children. When the pope refused to end Henry's first marriage, Henry started his own church. An English archbishop ended Henry's marriage and Anne became Henry's second wife.

Bay of Bisca

14°W   34°N   8°W

GEOGRAPHY THEMES

Location

Have the students note the boundaries of the Holy Roman Empire and the Papal States. Then have them turn to page 636 in the Atlas to examine modern European nations that now fall within these borders. Ask them to name five European countries that eventually arose from this vast region. *Italy, Germany, the Netherlands, Switzerland, Austria.* Have students speculate why the territory comprising the Holy Roman Empire eventually was carved up into smaller nations.

Human-Environment Interaction

Tell students that the map shows cities, falling within and around the area of the Papal States, that became thriving centers of trade. Ask students to speculate what role geography might have played in the economic development of these cities. *Many of the cities are located near or on a coastline, making them easily accessible to overseas trade.* Ask students to discuss why cities that are centers of trade are more likely to be exposed to new cultural ideas. Have them cite examples from historical periods they have previously studied.

ADDITIONAL RESOURCES

Books for the Teacher

• Aston, Margaret, ed. *The Panorama of the Renaissance.* New York: Abrams, 1996.

• Ozment, Steven E. *Protestants: The Birth of a Revolution.* New York: Doubleday, 1992. Shows the significance of becoming a Protestant during the Reformation.

Books for the Student

• Pierre, Michel. *The Renaissance.* Morristown: Silver Burdett, 1987.

• Romei, Francesca. *Leonardo da Vinci.* New York: Bedrick Books, 1995. Portrays the life of the artist, inventor, and scientist.

Videos

• *Printing Transforms Knowledge.* Society for Visual Education, 1986. 800-829-1900. Presents the impact of the printing press on education and the Reformation.

• *Exploring the Renaissance.* Knowledge Unlimited, 1994. 800-356-2303. Describes the revival in art, letters, and learning.

• *Martin Luther: Beginning of the Reformation.* Britannica, 1993. 800-554-9862.

• *Henry VIII.* Teacher's Discovery, 1996. 800-543-4180. Provides a lively look at the English king.

Software

• *Renaissance and Reformation.* CD-ROM. Queue, 1994. 800-232-2224. Presents the revival of classical learning and art, and the revolt against the Church.

Raphael's painting *School of Athens* was finished in **1508** in Rome. It shows the influence of Greek thought on the Renaissance. Under the center arch stand Plato and Aristotle. To their left, Socrates argues with several young men. Pythagoras draws a lesson on a slate and Ptolemy holds a globe. Other people in the crowd are Renaissance artists and philosophers.

In **1401**, the wool manufacturers of **Florence** decided to pay for new doors for the baptistery of the cathedral. They held a contest to choose the artist. The designs of **Lorenzo Ghiberti** won. Ghiberti labored on the bronze doors more than 20 years. Each door was divided into panels, showing Biblical scenes. This panel shows the Old Testament story of Jacob and Esau.

Map labels: North Sea, DENMARK, Baltic Sea, ENGLAND, PRUSSIA, London, Münster, Wittenberg, POLAND, Rhine, Elbe, Paris, Worms, HOLY ROMAN EMPIRE, Nantes, Loire, Danube, Augsberg, FRANCE, Zürich, Geneva, Trent, Milan, Mantua, Venice, VENICE, Avignon, Genoa, Florence, Pisa, Adriatic Sea, CORSICA, Genoa, PAPAL STATES, Rome, OTTOMAN EMPIRE, Tyrrhenian Sea, Naples, SARDINIA, KINGDOM OF NAPLES, Mediterranean Sea, Ottoman Sea

— Holy Roman Empire

0 ___ 200 Miles
0 ___ 400 Kilometers

N

35

HISTORY THROUGH ART

Gates of Paradise

Lorenzo Ghiberti

The city of Florence entered its golden age through Lorenzo Ghiberti's set of gleaming bronze doors. Each Biblical scene, such as the story of Jacob and Esau, creates the illusion of a grand theatrical stage. The background trees and buildings seem like props that stand far behind the people in the foreground. Yet the metal used for the sculpture is just about four inches deep. Ghiberti's use of perspective, realism, and detail is typical of Renaissance artists.

During the Renaissance, questions of religion were very much on the minds of Europeans. Italian artists created thousands of pictures of the Madonna, saints, and other Biblical figures. However, their portrayal of religious subjects differed from medieval artists. Ghiberti, for example, reveals the character of religious figures and shows the parts they play.

Ghiberti included two self-portraits in the doors. Perhaps this suggests how Ghiberti embodies such Renaissance values as pride in achievement, individuality, and creativity. Ghiberti's new doors were so magnificent that the artist Michelangelo later likened them to the gates of paradise.

Interpreting the Art: Why does Ghiberti's panel of Jacob and Esau seem so dramatic and lifelike?

This Interact with History feature motivates students by inviting them to role-play a historian who is examining a Renaissance work of art. As students look at Jan van Eyck's painting, they will gain first-hand experience in using a painting as a primary source.

Purpose

• to set the stage for studying the Renaissance

• to help students understand how some artists document history through their creative works

• to help students make connections with other paintings they will study in this chapter

Teaching Strategy

Thinking Critically After students have imagined themselves in the situation described on this page, have them answer the key question and support their responses.

EXAMINING *the* ISSUES

Following are suggestions for addressing each bulleted question.

1 Students may mention the role of religion and politics, views of men and women, and kinds of social relationships and customs.

2 Students may mention that people's clothing, their surroundings, and their poses can reveal personality traits and status.

3 Have students brainstorm a list of adjectives they would use to describe an object of beauty. Are these qualities mirrored in art forms?

Making Connections Ask students to discuss examples of modern art that reflect the values of today's society.

Follow Up

A feature on the chapter assessment will ask students to reevaluate their responses to the situation presented on this page.

Interact *with* History

You are a historian looking at primary sources from the Renaissance. One of them is this painting by Jan van Eyck.

Chancellor Rolin, a powerful government official in Burgundy (later part of France), asked the artist to paint this portrait. You are analyzing it to discover Rolin's values and how he wanted to be viewed by others. You can also use the art to learn about the times.

What do we learn from art?

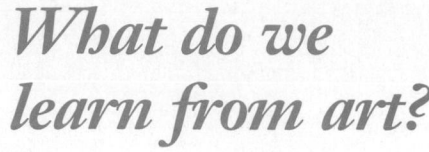

1 Van Eyck used a recently rediscovered technique called perspective, which makes distant objects look smaller than close ones. He also used oil paints, a new invention.

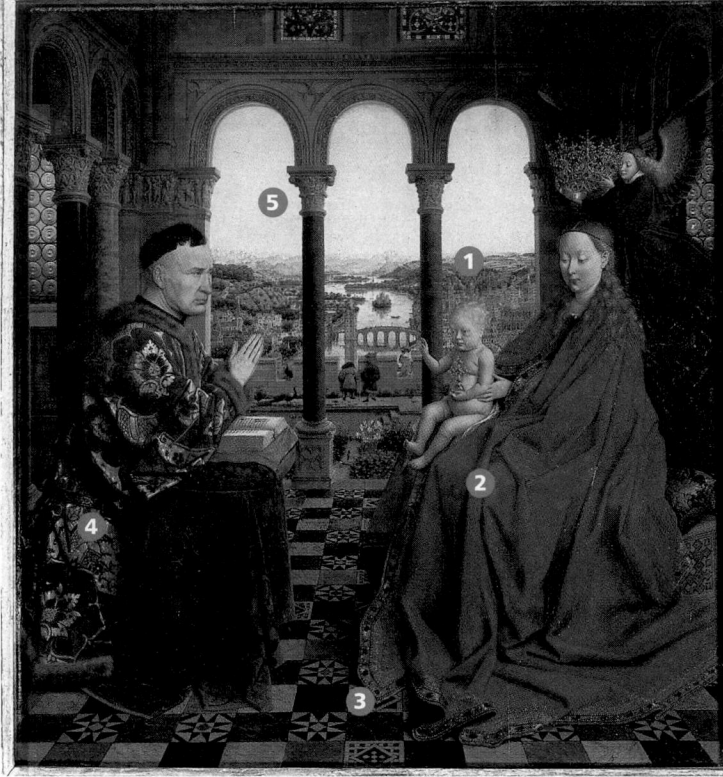

5 Renaissance artists were influenced by classical art. The columns and arches show classical influence.

2 This painting shows the infant Jesus and his mother Mary in 15th century Europe. By portraying biblical characters in their own time, Renaissance artists showed the importance of religion in their lives.

3 Van Eyck included many details simply for the sake of beauty. These include the fancy design on the floor, the folds of Mary's cloak, and the scenery outside the arches.

4 Renaissance artists portrayed the importance of individuals. Chancellor Rolin is kneeling to show respect, but he wears a fur-trimmed robe that shows his high status.

EXAMINING *the* ISSUES

• What does art tell us about the values and beliefs of the society that produced it?

• What does art show about how people of that society viewed themselves?

• How does art reflect a society's standards of beauty?

As a class, discuss these questions. In your discussion, review what you know about art in other places such as Egypt, India, China, and Benin.

As you read about the Renaissance, notice what the art of that time reveals about European society.

❶ Italy: Birthplace of the Renaissance

TERMS & NAMES
- Renaissance
- humanism
- secular
- patron
- perspective
- vernacular

MAIN IDEA	WHY IT MATTERS NOW
The European Renaissance, a rebirth of learning and the arts, began in Italy in the 1300s.	Renaissance ideas about classical studies, art, and literature still influence modern thought.

SETTING THE STAGE During the late Middle Ages, Europeans suffered from both war and plague. Those who survived wanted to enjoy life. As a result, they questioned the Church, which taught Christians to endure suffering to get a heavenly reward. They also questioned the structures of medieval society, which blocked social advancement. Educated people gradually began to reject medieval values and look to the classical past for ideas.

Italy's Advantages

The years 1300 to 1600 saw an explosion of creativity in Europe. Historians call this period the **Renaissance** (REHN·ih·SAHNS). The term means rebirth—in this case a rebirth of art and learning. The Renaissance began in northern Italy around 1300 and later spread north. One reason northern Europe lagged behind is that France and England were locked in the Hundred Years' War. Italy also had three advantages that fostered the Renaissance: thriving cities, a wealthy merchant class, and the classical heritage of Greece and Rome.

Urban Centers Overseas trade, spurred by the Crusades, had led to the growth of large city-states in northern Italy. The region also had many sizable towns. Thus, northern Italy was urban while the rest of Europe was still mostly rural. Since cities are often places where people exchange new ideas, they were an ideal breeding ground for an intellectual revolution.

The bubonic plague struck these cities hard, killing up to 60 percent of the population. This brought economic changes. Because there were fewer laborers, survivors could demand higher wages. In addition, the reduced population shrank opportunities for business expansion. Wealthy merchants began to pursue other interests, such as art.

Merchants and the Medici Milan, Florence, and other Italian city-states ran their own affairs. Each collected taxes and had its own army. Because city-states were relatively small, a high percentage of citizens could be intensely involved in political life. Merchants were the wealthiest, most powerful class, and they dominated politics. Unlike nobles, merchants did not inherit social rank. Success in business depended mostly on their own wits. As a result, many successful merchants believed they deserved power and wealth because of their individual merit. Individual achievement was to become an important Renaissance theme.

Florence came under the rule of one powerful family, the Medici (MEHD·ih·chee). They had made a fortune in trade and banking. Cosimo de' Medici was the wealthiest European of his time. In 1434, he won control of Florence's government. He did not seek political office for himself, but instead influenced members of the ruling council by giving them loans. For 30 years, he was virtually dictator of Florence.

Background
Florence lost up to 55,000 out of a population of 85,000.

A. Possible Answers Because if he were elected, he might lose his office; by staying behind the scenes, he could try to influence whoever held office.

THINK THROUGH HISTORY
A. Making Inferences Why do you suppose Cosimo de' Medici preferred to rule from behind the scenes rather than openly?

SPOTLIGHT ON

Other Renaissances
A Renaissance can be a rebirth of the arts and learning at any time in history. For example, the Tang (618–907) and Song (960–1279) dynasties in China oversaw a period of great artistic and technological advances.

Like the Italian Renaissance, the achievements of the Tang and the Song had roots in an earlier time—the Han Dynasty (202 B.C. to A.D. 220). After the Han collapsed, China experienced turmoil.

When order was restored, Chinese culture flourished. The Chinese invented gunpowder and printing. The most famous Chinese poets of all time wrote literary masterpieces. Breakthroughs were made in architecture, painting, and pottery. In many ways, the Tang and Song period was a true Renaissance.

European Renaissance and Reformation **37**

Section 1 Overview

OBJECTIVES

1. To explain the conditions in Italy that gave rise to the Renaissance.
2. To identify the values and ideas prized during the Renaissance.
3. To describe the artistic breakthrough and achievements of Renaissance artists.
4. To summarize influential literary works and techniques of key Renaissance writers.

CRITICAL THINKING
- Making inferences, p. 37
- Analyzing causes, p. 38
- Synthesizing, p. 39
- Clarifying, p. 40
- Supporting opinions, p. 42
- Analyzing themes, p. 42

FOCUS
5-Minute Warm-Up

▶ **Analyzing a Painting**
Have students answer these questions to explore the techniques of Renaissance art.

1. Read Perspective in Paintings on page 39, and study the diagram and painting. What optical illusion does the artist Raphael create in his painting?

2. Why does the use of perspective make the painting seem realistic?

 WARM-UP TRANSPARENCY 1

OBJECTIVE ❶ INSTRUCT

Italy's Advantages

▶ **Key Ideas**
- The Renaissance begins in northern Italy's urban centers around 1300.
- Italian merchants and bankers, such as the Medicis, support the arts.
- Renaissance scholars revive the study of Greek and Roman cultures.

IN-DEPTH RESOURCES: UNIT 1
Guided Reading, p. 18

ACCESS FOR STUDENTS ACQUIRING ENGLISH
Guided Reading (Spanish), p. 22

SECTION 1 RESOURCES

PRINT RESOURCES
 IN-DEPTH RESOURCES: UNIT 1
Guided Reading, p. 18
Primary Sources: *The Courtier*, p. 25; *The Prince*, p. 26
History Makers: Niccolò Machiavelli, p. 32
Literature: from *The Agony and the Ecstasy*, p. 29
Connections Across Time and Cultures, p. 34

 ACCESS FOR STUDENTS ACQUIRING ENGLISH
Guided Reading (Spanish), p. 22

FORMAL ASSESSMENT
Section Quiz, p. 17

TECHNOLOGY RESOURCES
WORLD ART AND CULTURES TRANSPARENCIES
AT36 Leonardo da Vinci's *The Last Supper*
AT37 *Mona Lisa*

CD-ROM
Electronic Library of Primary Sources

 INTERNET www.mlworldhistory.com

Teacher's Edition 37

HISTORY**MAKERS**

Medici Family
Giant banks with branches in many cities are nothing new. The Medici bank had branch offices not only throughout Italy but also in the major cities of Europe.

A rival family grew so jealous of the Medici that they plotted to kill Lorenzo (see bust below) and his brother Giuliano. As the Medici attended Mass, assassins murdered Giuliano at the altar. Drawing his sword, Lorenzo escaped to a small room and held off his attackers until help arrived. Then he had the killers brutally, publicly executed.

More positively, Lorenzo was a generous patron of the arts who collected many rare manuscripts. Eventually the Medici family made their library available to the public.

Cosimo de' Medici died in 1464, but his family retained control of Florence. His grandson, Lorenzo de' Medici, came into power in 1469. He became known as Lorenzo the Magnificent. Like his grandfather, Lorenzo ruled as a dictator yet kept up the appearance of having an elected government. Although the Medici did not foster true republican government, they aided the Renaissance by supporting the arts.

Classical Heritage Renaissance scholars looked down on the art and literature of the Middle Ages and wanted to return to the learning of the Greeks and Romans. One reason the Renaissance began in Italy is that artists and scholars drew inspiration from the ruins of Rome that surrounded them.

In the 1300s, scholars studied ancient Latin manuscripts, which had been preserved in monasteries. Then, when Constantinople fell to the Ottoman Turks in 1453, Byzantine scholars fled to Rome with ancient Greek manuscripts—which Italian scholars had assumed were lost forever.

Classical and Worldly Values

As scholars studied these Greek works, they became increasingly influenced by classical ideas. These ideas helped them to develop a new outlook on life, which had several characteristics.

Classics Lead to Humanism The study of classical texts led to **humanism,** which focused on human potential and achievements. Instead of trying to make classical texts agree with Christian teaching as medieval scholars had, humanists studied them to understand ancient Greek values. Humanists influenced artists and architects to carry on classical traditions. In addition, humanists popularized the study of subjects common to classical education, such as history, literature, and philosophy. These subjects are called the humanities.

Enjoyment of Worldly Pleasures In the Middle Ages, some religious people had proved their piety by wearing rough clothing and eating the plainest foods. However, humanists suggested that a person might enjoy life without offending God. In Renaissance Italy, the wealthy openly enjoyed material luxuries, fine music, and tasty foods.

Most people remained devout Catholics. However, the basic spirit of Renaissance society was **secular**—worldly and concerned with the here and now. Even church leaders became more worldly. They lived in beautiful mansions, threw lavish banquets, and wore expensive clothes.

Patrons of the Arts In addition to seeking pleasure, Renaissance popes beautified Rome by spending huge amounts of money for art. They became **patrons** of the arts by financially supporting artists. Renaissance merchants also were patrons of the arts. Wealthy families such as the Medici generously supported artists. By having their portraits painted or by donating public art to the city, the wealthy demonstrated their own importance.

The Renaissance Man Renaissance writers first introduced the idea that some people were artistic geniuses. Though genius was rare, all educated people were expected to create art. In fact, the ideal individual strove to master almost every area of study. A man who excelled in many fields was praised as a "universal man." Later ages called such people "Renaissance men."

A book called *The Courtier* (1528) by Baldassare Castiglione (KAHS·teel·YOH·nay) taught how to become such a person. A young man, said Castiglione, should be

38 Chapter 1

---

charming, witty, and well educated in the classics. He should dance, sing, play music, and write poetry. In addition, he should be a skilled rider, wrestler, and swordsman. Above all, he should have self-control:

This is a 19th-century engraving of the Renaissance writer Baldassare Castiglione.

The Renaissance Woman According to *The Courtier*, upper-class women also should know the classics and be charming. Yet they were not expected to seek fame. They were expected to inspire art but rarely to create it. Upper-class Renaissance women were far better educated than the women of the Middle Ages. However, most Renaissance women had less influence than medieval women had.

A few women, such as Isabella d'Este, did exercise power. Born into the ruling family of the city-state of Ferrara, she married the ruler of another city-state, Mantua. She brought many Renaissance artists to her court and acquired an art collection that was famous throughout Europe. She was also skilled in politics. When her husband was taken captive in war, she defended Mantua and won his release.

Renaissance Revolutionizes Art

Supported by patrons like Isabella d'Este, dozens of talented artists worked in northern Italy. As the Renaissance advanced, artistic styles changed. Medieval artists used religious subjects and tried to convey a spiritual ideal. Renaissance artists also often portrayed religious subjects, but they used a realistic style copied from classical models. Greek and Roman subjects also became popular.

Following the new emphasis on individuals, painters began to paint prominent citizens. These realistic portraits revealed what was distinctive about each person. In addition, artists such as the sculptor and painter Michelangelo (MY·kuhl·AN·juh·LOH) glorified the human body. (See page 40.)

New Techniques Donatello (DAHN·uh·TEHL·oh) made sculpture more realistic by carving natural postures and expressions that reveal personality. He revived a classical form by carving the statue *David.* It was the first European sculpture of a large, free-standing nude since ancient times. Renaissance artists, such as the painter Masaccio (muh·SAH·chee·oh), also rediscovered the technique of **perspective,** which indicates three dimensions.

Perspective in Paintings

Perspective is a technique that creates the appearance of three dimensions. Classical artists used perspective, but medieval artists abandoned the technique. In the 1400s, Italian artists rediscovered perspective. Since then, it has remained an important part of Western art.

Perspective is based on an optical illusion. As parallel lines stretch away from a viewer, they seem to draw together—until they meet at a spot on the horizon called the vanishing point.

Marriage of the Virgin (1504), Raphael

History Through Art

Renaissance Art

Renaissance artists and architects saw nature as the standard for balance and proportion. They imitated these qualities to add realism to their own work. Renaissance artists re-created lifelike depictions of people. Renaissance architects tried to make all parts of a building appear perfectly balanced in size and shape. Michelangelo displayed remarkable versatility as both an artist and architect.

MORE ABOUT . . .
The Sistine Chapel

To paint the ceiling of the Sistine Chapel, Michelangelo lay stretched on his back atop a high scaffold. The paint dripped into his eyes. During the day, he endured the heat of the sun beating upon the roof of the chapel. At night, he worked by candlelight. "I have been here a thousand years," Michelangelo wrote to his father. "I am more exhausted than any man ever was."

 IN-DEPTH RESOURCES: UNIT 1
Literature: from *The Agony and the Ecstasy* by Irving Stone, p. 29

MORE ABOUT . . .
David

Michelangelo considered himself a sculptor above all. He ranked sculpture as "the first of the arts." In this art form, he said, "each act, each limb, each bone is given life, and lo, man's body is raised breathing, alive, in wax or clay or stone." Michelangelo's *David* embodies these lofty qualities.

Michelangelo–Renaissance Artist

Like Leonardo da Vinci, Michelangelo Buonarroti was a true Renaissance man. He excelled at almost every area of study. Michelangelo was a painter, a sculptor, an architect, and a poet.

Michelangelo is most famous for the way he portrayed the human body in painting and sculpture. Influenced by classical art, he created figures that are forceful and show heroic grandeur and power. By doing this, he explored the Renaissance theme of human potential.

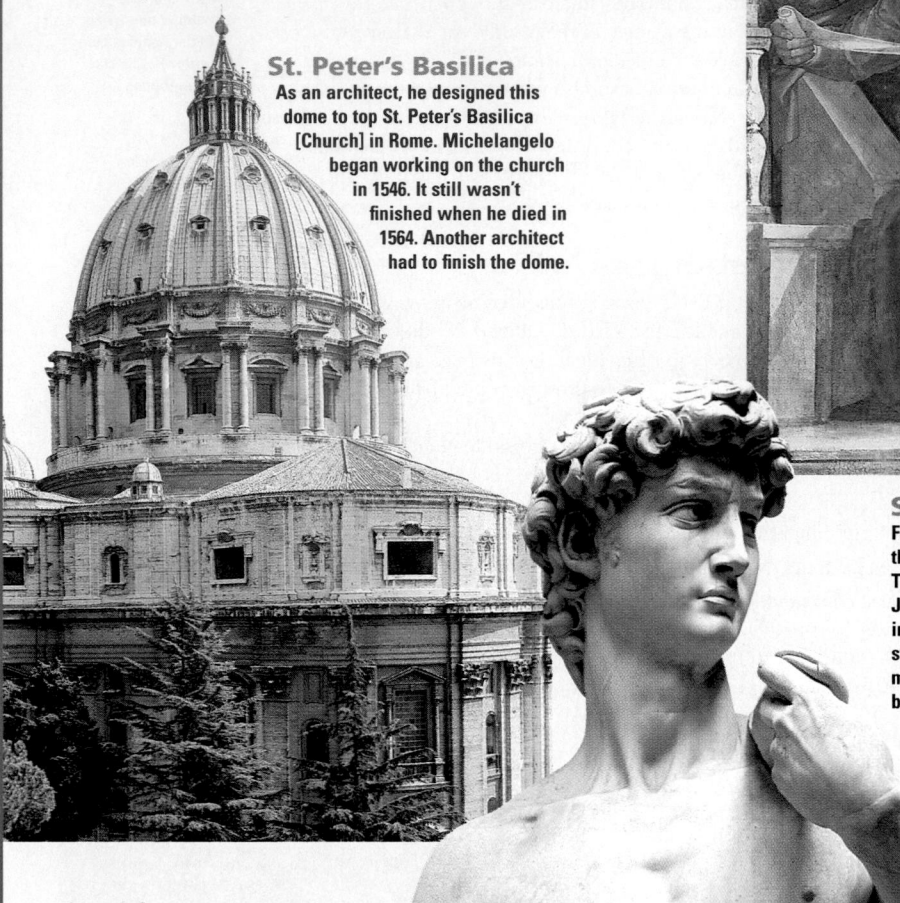

St. Peter's Basilica
As an architect, he designed this dome to top St. Peter's Basilica [Church] in Rome. Michelangelo began working on the church in 1546. It still wasn't finished when he died in 1564. Another architect had to finish the dome.

Sistine Chapel
From 1508 to 1512, Michelangelo painted the ceiling of the Sistine Chapel in Rome. This detail shows the Biblical prophet Joel. Many of the panels show classical influences, such as the two youths who stand behind Joel instead of angels. Like many Renaissance artists, Michelangelo blended Christian and Greek ideals.

David
Influenced by classical statues, Michelangelo sculpted *David* from 1501 to 1504. Michelangelo portrayed the Biblical hero in the moments just before battle. His posture is graceful, yet his figure also displays strength. The statue, which is 18 feet tall, towers over the viewer. This conveys a sense of power.

40 Chapter 1

Connect *to* History

Clarifying How does the work of Michelangelo show that he was influenced by Renaissance values? Explain.

 SEE SKILLBUILDER HANDBOOK, PAGE 650

Connect *to* Today

Researching Look through books on 20th century art to find artists who work in more than one medium, such as painting and sculpture. Share your findings with the class.

Connect *to* History

Clarifying
Possible Response:
Michelangelo's artwork glorifies the human body and reflects classical influence. He was a Renaissance man who excelled in many fields.

Connect *to* Today

Researching
Possible Responses: Other examples of versatile artists include Pablo Picasso, Marcel Duchamp, and Andy Warhol. Students should support their findings with illustrations of the artist's works.

Leonardo, Renaissance Man

Leonardo da Vinci (LAY·uh·NAHR·doh duh·VIHN·chee) was a painter, sculptor, inventor, and scientist. A true "Renaissance man," he was deeply interested in how things worked. He studied how a muscle moves or how veins are arranged in a leaf. He filled his notebooks with observations and sketches of new inventions, and he incorporated his findings in his art.

Among his many masterpieces, Leonardo painted one of the best-known portraits in the world, the Mona Lisa. The woman in the portrait seems so real that many writers have tried to explain the thoughts behind her slight smile. Leonardo also produced a famous religious painting, *The Last Supper.* It shows the personalities of Jesus' disciples through facial expressions.

Raphael Advances Realism

Raphael (RA·F·ee·uhl) was younger than Michelangelo and Leonardo. He learned from studying their works. One of Raphael's favorite subjects was the Madonna and child. Raphael often portrayed their expressions as gentle and calm.

In his greatest achievement, Raphael filled the walls of Pope Julius II's library with several paintings. One of these, *School of Athens* (page 34), conveys the classical influence of the Renaissance. It shows classical and Renaissance figures together. Listening to Greek philosophers are Raphael and Michelangelo, among others.

Women Painters Although Renaissance society generally restricted women's roles, a few Italian women became painters. Sofonisba Anguissola (ahng·GWEES·soh·lah) was the first woman artist to gain an international reputation. She is known for portraits of her sisters and of prominent people such as King Phillip II of Spain. Artemisia Gentileschi (JAYN·tee·LEHS·kee) trained with her painter father and helped with his work. In her own paintings, Gentileschi painted pictures of strong, heroic women.

Renaissance Writers Change Literature

Renaissance writers produced works that not only reflected their time but also used techniques that writers rely on today. Some followed the example of the medieval writer Dante. He wrote in the **vernacular,** his native language, instead of classical Latin. Dante's native language was Italian. In addition, Renaissance writers wrote either for self-expression or to portray the individuality of their subjects. In these ways, writers of the Renaissance began trends that modern writers still follow.

European Renaissance and Reformation **41**

Vocabulary
Madonna: a term for Mary, the mother of Jesus; it comes from a former Italian title for women, meaning "my lady."

Background
During most of the Middle Ages, educated Europeans wrote everything in Latin.

HISTORY MAKERS

Leonardo da Vinci 1452–1519	Raphael 1483–1520
Leonardo da Vinci's notebooks—and life—are mysterious in many ways. Some 3,500 pages closely covered with writings and drawings survive, but these may be only one-fourth of what Leonardo produced.	One of the artists influenced by Leonardo, Raphael began his career early. His father, Giovanni Santi, was a painter, and Raphael learned the basics of his art in his father's studio. At a young age, Raphael went to study with a painter named Perugino. He stayed there about ten years and then went to Florence.

Leonardo da Vinci's notebooks—and life—are mysterious in many ways. Some 3,500 pages closely covered with writings and drawings survive, but these may be only one-fourth of what Leonardo produced.

His writing is clear and easy to read—but only if you look at it in a mirror. He wrote backwards in "mirror-writing." No one knows why he took the time to do this.

Leonardo planned scholarly works that he never wrote, and he planned great feats of engineering that were never built. Only 17 of his paintings survive, and several of those were unfinished. The drawing above is the only self-portrait known to exist. And yet the work that Leonardo did produce is so amazing that his reputation as one of the world's geniuses is secure.

One of the artists influenced by Leonardo, Raphael began his career early. His father, Giovanni Santi, was a painter, and Raphael learned the basics of his art in his father's studio. At a young age, Raphael went to study with a painter named Perugino. He stayed there about ten years and then went to Florence.

In 1508, Raphael was asked by Pope Julius II to work for him in Rome. Raphael created a series of magnificent frescoes, paintings done on wet plaster, for the pope's private rooms in the Vatican.

Raphael, unlike many of his fellow artists, was easy to like. When he died on his 37th birthday after a short illness, many Romans—including the pope and his court—were stricken with grief and went into mourning.

Petrarch and Boccaccio Francesco Petrarch (PEE·trahrk) was one of the earliest and most influential humanists. He was also a great poet. Petrarch wrote both in Italian and in Latin. In Italian, he wrote sonnets—14-line poems. They were about a mysterious woman named Laura, who was his ideal. (Little is known of Laura except that she died of the plague in 1348.) In classical Latin, he wrote letters to his many important friends.

The Italian writer Boccaccio (boh·KAH·chee·oh) is best known for the *Decameron*, a series of realistic, sometimes off-color stories. The stories are supposedly told by a group of worldly young people waiting in a villa to avoid the plague sweeping through Florence. The humor of the *Decameron* is cutting. Boccaccio presents the follies of his characters—and all humans—with some sarcasm.

Machiavelli Advises Rulers *The Prince* (1513), by Niccolò Machiavelli (MAK·ee·uh·VEHL·ee), also examines the imperfect conduct of human beings. He does so in the form of a political guidebook. In *The Prince*, Machiavelli examines how a ruler can gain power and keep it in spite of his enemies. In answering this question, he began with the idea that most people are selfish, fickle, and corrupt. To succeed in such a wicked world, Machiavelli said, a prince must be strong as a lion and shrewd as a fox. He might have to trick his enemies and even his own people for the good of the state. In *The Prince*, Machiavelli was not concerned with what was morally right, but with what was politically effective:

A VOICE FROM THE PAST
Everyone admits how praiseworthy it is in a prince to keep faith, and to live with integrity and not with craft. Nevertheless our experience has been that those princes who have done great things have held good faith of little account, and have known how to circumvent the intellect of men by craft, and in the end have overcome those who have relied on their word.

NICCOLÒ MACHIAVELLI, *The Prince*

Niccolò Machiavelli, shown here with his hand on a book, was much more than just a cynical political thinker. He was also a patriot, a poet, and a historian.

Women Writers The women writers who gained fame in the Renaissance usually wrote about personal subjects, not politics. Yet, some of them had great influence. Vittoria Colonna exchanged sonnets with Michelangelo and helped Castiglione publish *The Courtier*. Her own poems are often very personal. For example, when her husband was away at war, she wrote to him, "Your uncertain enterprises do not hurt you; / but we who wait, mournfully grieving, / are wounded by doubt and fear."

Toward the end of the 15th century, Renaissance ideas began to spread north from Italy to countries such as France, Germany, and England. Northern artists and thinkers would adapt the Renaissance ideals in their own ways.

THINK THROUGH HISTORY
D. Supporting Opinions Do you think Machiavelli is right in his view that rulers must trick people and ignore morality? Explain.
D. Possible Answers Yes, because leaders sometimes have to hurt individuals to do what is best for a state; No, there is never a good reason to abandon one's morals.

Section 1 Assessment

1. TERMS & NAMES
Identify
• Renaissance
• humanism
• secular
• patron
• perspective
• vernacular

2. TAKING NOTES
Using a big-idea outline like the one below, record the main ideas from the section about the Italian Renaissance.
Renaissance
I. Italy's advantages
  A.
  B.
  C.
II. Classical and worldly values

3. SUPPORTING OPINIONS
Name three people from this section whom you regard as a "Renaissance man" or a "Renaissance woman." Explain your choices.
THINK ABOUT
• the idea of the "universal man"
• Castiglione's description of such a person
• which people from this section seem to match that description

4. ANALYZING THEMES
Revolution How did the Renaissance revolutionize European art and thought?
THINK ABOUT
• changes in ideas since medieval times
• changes in artistic techniques
• changes in artistic subjects

42 Chapter 1

ANSWERS

The Northern Renaissance

MAIN IDEA

In the 1400s, northern Europeans began to adapt the ideas of the Renaissance.

WHY IT MATTERS NOW

Renaissance ideas such as the importance of the individual are a strong part of modern thought.

SETTING THE STAGE The work of such artists as Leonardo da Vinci, Michelangelo, and Raphael showed the Renaissance spirit. All three artists demonstrated an interest in classical culture, a curiosity about the world, and a belief in human potential. These ideas impressed scholars and students who visited Italy. Merchants also carried these ideas when they traveled out of Italy. By the late 1400s, Renaissance ideas had spread to northern Europe—especially England, France, Germany, and Flanders.

Background
Flanders was a region in northern Europe. It included part of France and part of the Netherlands. The people of Flanders are the Flemish.

The Northern Renaissance Begins

By 1450 the population of northern Europe, which had been shattered by the bubonic plague, was beginning to recover. In addition, the destructive Hundred Years' War between France and England ended in 1453. Many cities grew rapidly. Urban merchants became wealthy enough to sponsor artists. This happened first in Flanders, which was rich from long-distance trade and the cloth industry. Then it happened in other countries.

As Section 1 explained, Italy was divided into city-states. In contrast, England and France were unified under strong monarchs. These rulers often sponsored the arts. For example, Francis I of France purchased Renaissance paintings. He also invited Leonardo da Vinci to retire in France, and hired Italian artists and architects to rebuild his castle at Fontainebleau (FAHN·tihn·BLOH). When completed, Fontainebleau became a showcase of the French Renaissance. Because of monarchs like Francis, royal courts played a major role in introducing Renaissance styles to northern Europe.

As Renaissance ideas spread out of Italy, they mingled with northern traditions. As a result, the northern Renaissance developed its own character. Many humanists there were more interested in religious ideas than in the secular themes popular in Italy. The Renaissance ideal of human dignity inspired some northern humanists to develop plans for social reform based on Christian values.

Albrecht Dürer painted *Adoration of the Trinity* after returning from studying in Italy.

Artistic Ideas Spread

In 1494, a French king claimed the throne of Naples in southern Italy and launched an invasion through northern Italy. As the war dragged on, many Italian artists and writers left for a safer life in northern Europe. With them, they brought the styles and techniques of the Renaissance. In addition, artists who studied in Italy also carried Renaissance ideas north.

A. Answer By making Italian artists flee north
THINK THROUGH HISTORY
A. Analyzing Causes How did the war in Italy spread the Renaissance?

Section 2 Overview

OBJECTIVES

1 To explain the origins and characteristics of the Northern Renaissance.

2 To trace the impact of the Renaissance on German and Flemish painters.

3 To profile key Northern Renaissance writers.

4 To explain how printing spread Renaissance ideas.

CRITICAL THINKING

• Analyzing causes, p. 43
• Contrasting, p. 44
• Making inferences, p. 45
• Summarizing, p. 46
• Recognizing effects, p. 47

FOCUS
5-Minute Warm-Up

▶ *Recognizing Effects*
Answering these questions will help students understand the enduring impact of Northern Renaissance writers.

1. Read the Connect to Today on page 46. Give examples of William Shakespeare's popularity among worldwide audiences today.

2. Name two Shakespearean plays that were recently made into Hollywood movies.

WARM-UP TRANSPARENCY 1

OBJECTIVE **1** INSTRUCT

The Northern Renaissance Begins

▶ *Key Ideas*
• England and France are unified under strong monarchs who often sponsor the arts.

• Renaissance ideas spreading from Italy mingle with northern European traditions.

• The Northern Renaissance develops distinctive features.

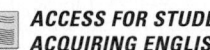

Artistic Ideas Spread

Key Ideas
- Artists studying in Italy bring Renaissance ideas to northern Europe.
- The realism of Dürer's paintings and engravings inspire other German artists.
- Flanders becomes the artistic center of northern Europe.
- Flemish painters Van Eyck and Bruegel focus on realistic details.

 IN-DEPTH RESOURCES: UNIT 1
Geography Application: Trade in Renaissance Europe, p. 23

MORE ABOUT . . .
Albert Dürer

Dürer also wrote books on geometry and artistic theory. He was the first person to publish scientific literature in German.

Daily *Life*
Flemish Peasant Life

Ask students to find a colored photograph of a modern wedding reception from a magazine or another source. Have them work in groups to compare the photograph with Bruegel's painting. Ask students to note how Bruegel directs the viewer's eye through the picture with color and action.

 WORLD ART AND CULTURES TRANSPARENCIES
AT38 Van Eyck's *Wedding Portrait*

German Painters Perhaps the most famous person to do this was the German artist Albrecht Dürer (DYUR-uhr). The son of a goldsmith, Dürer decided to become a painter. After serving an apprenticeship, he traveled to Italy to study in 1494.

After returning to Germany, Dürer produced woodcuts and engravings that became influential. Many of his prints portray religious subjects such as the one on page 43. Others portray classical myths. He also painted realistic landscapes and a self-portrait in which he portrayed himself as a Renaissance man. The popularity of Dürer's work helped to spread Renaissance styles. His work inspired other German artists.

Dürer's emphasis upon realism influenced the work of another German artist, Hans Holbein (HOHL-byn) the Younger. Holbein specialized in painting portraits that are almost photographic in detail. He enjoyed great success in England, where he painted portraits of King Henry VIII and other members of the royal family.

Flemish Painters As in Italy, wealthy merchant families in Flanders were attracted to the Renaissance emphasis on individualism and worldly pleasures. Their patronage helped to make Flanders the artistic center of northern Europe.

As in Italy, the Renaissance in Flanders was marked by an interest in realism. The first great Flemish Renaissance painter was Jan van Eyck (yahn van YK). Van Eyck lived from sometime in the late 1300s to 1441 and worked at the height of the Italian Renaissance.

Oil-based paints had recently been developed. Van Eyck used them to develop techniques that painters still use. Because oil paint does not dry quickly, it can be blended more easily than other paints. By applying layer upon layer of paint, van Eyck was able to create a variety of subtle colors in clothing and jewels. Oil painting became popular and spread to Italy.

Daily *Life*
Flemish Peasant Life

The Flemish painter Pieter Bruegel often portrayed peasants. Many of his paintings provide information about peasant life in the 1500s.

Peasant Wedding (1568), shown below, portrays a wedding feast in a rough but clean barn. The bride sits under the paper crown hanging on a piece of green cloth. Two young men who may be her brothers are pouring drinks and passing out plates.

Who, then, is the groom? Possibly the man sitting across the table from the bride and leaning back on a three-legged stool.

Children and at least one dog have come to the party. The couple to the right of the bride and the man on the far right with a sword are dressed more elegantly than the other guests. They may be wealthy townsfolk related to the groom.

B. Answer It spread from the North to Italy, instead of moving from Italy to the North.

THINK THROUGH HISTORY
B. Contrasting
How was the development and spread of oil painting different from many other Renaissance developments?

CONNECTIONS ACROSS THE CURRICULUM

Literature The American poet William Carlos Williams (1883–1963) found the paintings of Bruegel (also spelled *Brueghel*) a source of inspiration for his own work. Williams received, posthumously, the 1963 Pulitzer Prize in poetry for *Pictures from Brueghel, and Other Poems.* In this book, Williams wrote a series of poems—"word pictures"—that captured the images and mood of several of Bruegel's paintings.

Find the following paintings in art history books or the Internet.
- *The Wedding Dance in the Open Air*
- *Kermess*
- *Haymaking*
- *The Harvesters*
- *The Parable of the Blind*
- *The Fall of Icarus*
- *Children's Games*

Bring reproductions of these paintings to class, and have students read aloud the corresponding poems by Williams. Challenge students to write their own poems based on Bruegel's paintings.

In addition to new techniques, van Eyck's paintings display unusually realistic details and reveal the personality of their subjects. His work influenced later artists in northern Europe.

Flemish painting reached its peak after 1550 with the work of Pieter Bruegel (BROY-guhl) the Elder. Like van Eyck, Bruegel was interested in realistic details and individual people. He captured scenes from everyday peasant life such as weddings, dances, harvests, and the changing seasons. Bruegel also produced paintings that illustrated proverbs or taught a moral. Some of his paintings protested harsh Spanish rule over his country.

In all his work, Bruegel's rich colors, vivid details, and balanced use of space give a sense of life and feeling. He was also very skillful in portraying large numbers of people. Not only did Bruegel produce a large number of paintings, he inspired two sons and three grandsons to also became painters.

Northern Writers Try to Reform Society

Just as Italian art influenced northern European painters, so did Renaissance ideas influence the writers and philosophers of northern Europe. These writers adopted the ideal of humanism. However, some gave it a more religious slant. Because of this, some northern humanists are also called Christian humanists.

Christian Humanists The best known of the Christian humanists were Desiderius Erasmus (DEHZ·ih·DEER·ee·uhs ih·RAZ·muhs) of Holland and Thomas More of England. The two were close friends.

Born in Rotterdam, Erasmus received honors from princes, kings, and cardinals for his brilliant writings. In 1509, while he was a guest in More's house, Erasmus wrote his most famous work, *The Praise of Folly*. This book poked fun at greedy merchants, heartsick lovers, quarrelsome scholars, and pompous priests. Although some of Erasmus's most stinging barbs were aimed at the clergy, his work is strongly Christian. Erasmus believed in a Christianity of the heart, not one of ceremonies or rules. He thought that in order to improve society, all people should study the Bible.

Also concerned with society's flaws, Thomas More tried to show a better model. In 1516, he wrote the book *Utopia* about an imaginary land inhabited by a peace-loving people. In Greek, **Utopia** means "no place," but in English it has come to mean an ideal place because of More's book. In Utopia, greed, corruption, war, and crime had been weeded out. Because the Utopians weren't greedy, they had little use for money:

> ### A VOICE FROM THE PAST
> Gold and silver, of which money is made, are so treated . . . that no one values them more highly than their true nature deserves. Who does not see that they are far inferior to iron in usefulness since without iron mortals cannot live any more than without fire and water?
> **THOMAS MORE**, *Utopia*

The French humanist François Rabelais (RAB·eh·LAY) provided a contrast to Erasmus and More in several ways. They wrote in Latin, while Rabelais wrote his comic adventure *Gargantua and Pantagruel* in vernacular French. More secular than either Erasmus or More, Rabelais believed that human beings were basically good. They should live by their instincts rather than religious rules. As he told of the wild adventures of the giants Gargantua and Pantagruel, he poked fun at his society. Rabelais's humor was uproarious and earthy, although he made many serious points about the nature of humanity, education, and government.

William Shakespeare William Shakespeare wrote in Renaissance England. Many people regard him as the greatest playwright of all time. Shakespeare was born in

The Christian humanist Thomas More wrote about a nearly perfect society called Utopia. He did this to show his own society how to improve.

THINK THROUGH HISTORY
C. Making Inferences What point do you think More was making about his own society?
C. Possible Answers That they were too greedy or that they loved money too much.

European Renaissance and Reformation **45**

OBJECTIVE ③ INSTRUCT

Northern Writers Try to Reform Society

▶ *Key Ideas*
• Renaissance ideas influence northern European writers and philosophers.
• Christian humanist writers express their social and religious concerns.
• William Shakespeare's brilliant plays dramatize human nature.
• The Renaissance in England is also called the Elizabethan Age, named after Queen Elizabeth I.

CRITICAL THINKING ACTIVITY
CLASS TIME: 15 MINUTES

Summarizing
As students read, have them complete the chart below with details about the writers discussed in this section.

Writer	Nationality	Famous Work
Shakespeare	English	*Hamlet*

MORE ABOUT . . .
Utopia

The idea of a perfect society predates the publication of *Utopia* in 1516. Greek thinkers such as Plato and Plutarch described their own versions of such ideal places.

TEACHING OPTION | **BLOCK SCHEDULING** | **COOPERATIVE ACTIVITY: Planning a Utopian Community** | **CLASS TIME 30 MINUTES**

Task: Students will meet in small groups to design a utopian community. Groups will present oral reports, including visual aids, that describe their plans.

Purpose: To apply the ideas of Thomas More's *Utopia* to planning a community.

Activity: Have student groups address the following questions to help them plan their "perfect" communities: Are the community's values or beliefs similar to More's vision of a utopian society? What

laws or guidelines should be established that might promote a spirit of harmony? How will the community survive financially? What are families like?

📖 *Building a Portfolio:* Students might wish to place a written version of their plans in their portfolios.

📋 **ALTERNATIVE ASSESSMENT BOOK**
Standards for Evaluating a Cooperative Activity

Standards for Evaluation
Plans for a utopian community should . . .

• address key aspects of communities, such as laws, economics, values, and social organization
• provide specific details
• include clear, informative visual aids

Teacher's Edition **45**

Have student groups research a Shakespearean play that was made into a film. Ask each group to create a movie poster for a Shakespearean film festival.

MORE ABOUT . . .
Elizabethan Dramas

During Queen Elizabeth I's reign, new plays called Elizabethan dramas emerged. Along with devices borrowed from classical dramas, Elizabethan dramas included elements designed to entertain every member of the audience. For example, witches, battles, murders, ghosts, and bloody nights are the hallmarks of Shakespeare's *Macbeth*—a terror-filled tragedy guaranteed to captivate audiences. As a result, people of every social class enthusiastically attended the theater. Pickpockets and thieves loved the crowded theaters, too.

OBJECTIVE ④ INSTRUCT

Printing Spreads Renaissance Ideas

▶ *Key Ideas*
- Gutenberg invents the printing press and then prints a complete Bible.
- Faster bookmaking advances learning and increases literacy.
- More people read and interpret the Bible for themselves.

CONNECT *to* TODAY

William Shakespeare
Shakespeare's plays were very popular in London in the 1600s. They are popular today as well, but they appear in many places besides London. Shakespearean festivals are regularly held in such places as Stratford-upon-Avon, England; Stratford, Ontario, Canada; and Austin, Texas.

Even though he has been dead for almost 400 years, Shakespeare is one of Hollywood's favorite writers. In the 1990s, two film versions of *Hamlet* hit the theaters, as did a version of *Romeo and Juliet.* The poster below is from the 1990 version of *Hamlet,* starring Mel Gibson and Glenn Close.

1564 in Stratford-upon-Avon, a small town about 90 miles northwest of London. By 1592 he was living in London and writing poems and plays.

His works display a masterful command of the English language and a deep understanding of human beings. He revealed the souls of men and women through scenes of dramatic conflict. His most famous plays include the tragedies *Macbeth, King Lear, Hamlet, Romeo and Juliet,* and the comedy *A Midsummer Night's Dream.* Many of these plays frankly examine human flaws. However, Shakespeare also had one of his characters deliver a speech that expresses the Renaissance's high view of human nature:

A VOICE FROM THE PAST
What a piece of work is a man, how noble in reason, how infinite in faculties, in form and moving, how express and admirable in action, how like an angel in apprehension [understanding], how like a god! the beauty of the world; the paragon of animals.
WILLIAM SHAKESPEARE, *Hamlet*

Like many Renaissance writers, Shakespeare revered the classics and drew on them for inspiration and plots. One of his great tragedies, for example, tells the story of the assassination of Julius Caesar—the Roman general and statesman.

The Elizabethan Age The Renaissance in England is also called the Elizabethan Age, for Queen Elizabeth I. She reigned from 1558 to 1603. Elizabeth was well-educated and knew French, Italian, Latin, and Greek. In addition to running a kingdom (see page 52), she also wrote poetry. As queen, she patronized artists and writers. Poet Edmund Spenser dedicated his long poem *The Faerie Queene* (1590) to her with these words: "To the most high, mighty, and magnificent Empress, renowned for piety, virtue, and all gracious government, Elizabeth."

Printing Spreads Renaissance Ideas

One thing that helped spread Renaissance ideas throughout Europe was a new invention that adapted Chinese technology. The Chinese had invented block printing, in which a printer carved a word or letter on a wooden block, inked the block, and then used it to print on paper. Around 1045, Bi Sheng invented movable type, or a separate piece of type for each character in the language. However, since the Chinese writing system contained thousands of different characters, most Chinese printers found movable type impractical.

Gutenberg Invents the Printing Press During the 13th century, block-printed items reached Europe from China. European printers began to use block printing to create whole pages to bind into books. However, this process was too slow to satisfy the Renaissance demand for knowledge and books. Johann Gutenberg, a craftsman from Mainz, Germany, reinvented movable type around 1440. The method was practical for Europeans because their languages have a very small number of letters in their alphabets.

Gutenberg then invented the **printing press.** The printing press is a machine that presses paper against a tray full of inked movable type. Using this invention, Gutenberg printed a complete Bible, the **Gutenberg Bible,** in about 1455. It was the first full-size book printed with movable type.

THINK THROUGH HISTORY
D. Summarizing
State at least two ways in which Shakespeare's work showed Renaissance influences.
D. Possible Answers He wrote in vernacular English; he had a character express a high view of human nature; he wrote about classical subjects.

TEACHING OPTION · **BLOCK SCHEDULING** | **TECHNOLOGY APPLICATION ACTIVITY** | **CLASS TIME 20 MINUTES**

Task Students will explore the impact of the printing press by role-playing medieval bookmakers who copy books by hand.

Materials Needed Students should choose a book to use. They will also need a clock or watch with a minute hand.

Activity Have student pairs copy a paragraph

from a book by hand and jot down how long it takes. Next, ask them to roughly figure the amount of time it would take to copy the entire page. Tell them to multiply this amount by the total number of book pages. Their answer represents the estimated number of hours required to create a handwritten version of the book. Challenge student pairs to figure out how long it would take to reproduce a set of

these books for the entire class.

Conclusions Ask students to comment on how the invention of the printing press made bookmaking dramatically faster. Why did learning and new ideas spread quickly? Why did more people learn how to read?

History of Book Making

- 2700 B.C., Egyptians write books on papyrus scrolls.
- 1000 B.C., Chinese make books by writing on strips of bamboo.
- A.D. 300, Romans write on sheets of parchment (treated animal skin). These are sewn together into books.
- 800, Irish monks hand-write and hand-illustrate *The Book of Kells*.
- About 1455, Gutenberg prints the first complete book on a printing press—similar to the one shown at left.

Only 46 copies of the Gutenberg Bible still exist in the world. Because of this, each copy is considered priceless. A part of a page is shown above.

Printing Spreads Learning The printing press had a revolutionary impact on European society. It enabled a printer to produce hundreds of copies, all exactly alike, of a single work. For the first time, books were cheap enough that many people could buy them. Printing spread quickly to other cities in Europe. By 1500, presses in about 250 cities had printed between 9 and 10 million books.

New ideas spread more quickly than ever before. At first printers produced many religious works. Soon they began to provide books on other subjects such as travel guides and medical manuals. The availability of books encouraged people to learn to read and so caused a rise in literacy.

Writing in vernacular languages also increased because even people who could not afford a classical education could now buy books. Printers produced the Bible in the vernacular, which allowed more people to read it. People began to interpret the Bible for themselves and to become more critical of priests and their behavior. This eventually led to demands for religious reform.

THINK THROUGH HISTORY
E. Recognizing Effects What were the major effects of the invention of the printing press?
E. Answers Books became affordable; books were published on many subjects; new ideas spread; writing in vernacular languages increased; people formed their own opinions about religion.

The End of the Renaissance In both Italy and northern Europe, the Renaissance had stirred a burst of creative activity. Artists in both regions studied classical culture, praised individual achievement, and produced works using new techniques. During the 1600s, new ideas and artistic styles appeared. Nonetheless, Renaissance ideals continued to influence European thought. For example, the Renaissance belief in the dignity of the individual played a key role in the gradual rise of democratic ideas.

Section 2 Assessment

1. TERMS & NAMES

Identify
- Utopia
- printing press
- Gutenberg Bible

2. TAKING NOTES

On a time line like the one below, show important events in the Northern Renaissance.

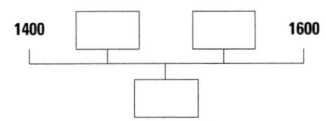

Which of the events do you think was most important? Explain.

3. RECOGNIZING EFFECTS

Choose one Northern Renaissance figure. Explain how he or she was influenced by Renaissance ideas.

THINK ABOUT
- the influence of humanism
- the use of new techniques
- the concept of the Renaissance man or woman

4. THEME ACTIVITY

Cultural Interaction Working in a small team, reproduce a map of Europe in 1500. On the map, use arrows, pictures, and captions to show the spread of Renaissance ideas and developments. Include not only the spread of ideas north from Italy, but also innovations that spread southward from northern Europe.

European Renaissance and Reformation **47**

MORE ABOUT . . .
History of Book Making . . .
The painting on the left shows a print shop during the Renaissance. Workers arranged metal letters according to the manuscript in front of them. Other workers then applied ink to the type that had been set. The printer (shown in the middle) used a press to transfer the print onto paper pages.

ASSESS & RETEACH

Section 2 Assessment
Divide the questions among groups of students and have them present their answers orally.

Section Quiz
FORMAL ASSESSMENT
Section Quiz, p. 18

Reteaching Activity
CLASS TIME: 10 MINUTES

Use students' time lines from item 2 in the section assessment to review the sequence of key events during the Northern Renaissance.

CLOSE ACTIVITY

CLASS TIME: 20 MINUTES

Summarizing
Divide students into four groups representing the following categories: German painting, Flemish painting, English literature, and technology. Have group members create a chart summarizing key innovations, changes, and achievements in these areas.

ANSWERS

1. TERMS AND NAMES
Utopia, p. 45
printing press, p. 46
Gutenberg Bible, p. 46

2. TAKING NOTES
Possible Responses: 1455—Gutenberg prints Bible on printing press; 1494—Dürer studies in Italy; 1509—Erasmus writes The *Praise of Folly*; 1516—More writes *Utopia*; 1592—Shakespeare writes plays in London. Most important: Shakespeare—his work is still influential; Gutenberg Bible—the printing press spread learning.

3. RECOGNIZING EFFECTS
Possible Responses: Dürer was influenced by realism and classical ideas; Van Eyck was influenced by realism and helped develop the oil painting; Breugel was interested in realistic details and peasant life; Erasmus and More combined humanist and Christian values in their calls for reform; Shakespeare was influenced by the classics and wrote in the vernacular; Queen Elizabeth was a monarch, a poet, a patron of the arts, and a linguist.

4. THEME ACTIVITY
Maps should accurately depict Europe's boundaries in 1500 and show the movement of Renaissance ideas.

Teacher's Edition **47**

① To analyze historical forces and religious issues that sparked the Reformation.

② To trace Martin Luther's role in the religious movement to reform the Catholic Church.

③ To analyze the impact of Luther's religious revolt.

④ To explain the spread of the Protestant faith to England during King Henry VIII's reign.

CRITICAL THINKING
- Analyzing causes, p.48
- Synthesizing, p. 49
- Drawing conclusions, p. 50
- Analyzing motives, p. 50
- Recognizing effects, p. 52
- Supporting opinions, p. 52
- Analyzing themes, p. 52

FOCUS
5-Minute Warm-Up

▶ *Perceiving Causes and Effects*
Answering these questions will help students analyze the events related to Henry VIII's reign.

1. Read the time line on page 51. How many times did Henry VIII marry?

2. How are the events shown for 1527 and 1529 connected?

 WARM-UP TRANSPARENCY 1

OBJECTIVE ① INSTRUCT

Causes of the Reformation

Key Ideas
- The spread of Renaissance ideas and claims of corruption among the clergy undermine the Catholic Church's authority.

- In the 1300s and 1400s, John Wycliffe and John Huss criticize church practices.

- In the late 1400s, Savonarola calls for church reform.

IN-DEPTH RESOURCES: UNIT 1
Guided Reading, p. 20

ACCESS FOR STUDENTS ACQUIRING ENGLISH
Guided Reading (Spanish), p. 24

---

3 Luther Starts the Reformation

TERMS & NAMES
- indulgence
- Reformation
- Lutheran
- Protestant
- Peace of Augsburg
- annul
- Anglican

MAIN IDEA
Martin Luther's protest over abuses in the Catholic Church led to the founding of Protestant churches.

WHY IT MATTERS NOW
Nearly one-fourth of the Christians in today's world are Protestants.

SETTING THE STAGE By the tenth century, the church in Rome had come to dominate religious life in northern and western Europe. However, the Roman Catholic Church had not won universal approval. Over the centuries, rulers, scholars, and members of the clergy criticized church practices. Even though church leaders made several important reforms during the Middle Ages, the problems lingered.

Causes of the Reformation

By 1500, additional forces weakened the Church. The Renaissance emphasis on the secular and the individual challenged Church authority. The printing press spread these secular ideas. In addition, rulers resented the popes' attempts to control them. In Germany—divided into many competing states—it was difficult for the pope or the emperor to impose central authority. Finally, northern merchants resented paying church taxes to Rome. Spurred by political and social forces, a new movement for religious reform began in Germany. It then swept much of Europe.

As this portrait shows, the friar Girolamo Savonarola was a serious-minded man. Disapproving of the worldly values of his time, he urged the people of Florence to give up their luxuries.

Problems in the Catholic Church Critics of the Church claimed that its leaders were corrupt. The popes who ruled during the Renaissance patronized the arts, spent extravagantly on personal pleasure, and fought wars. Pope Pius II admitted, "If the truth be confessed, the luxury and pomp of our courts is too great." Another pope, Alexander VI, publicly admitted that he had several children. These popes were too busy pursuing worldly affairs to have much time for spiritual duties.

The lower clergy had problems as well. Many priests and monks were so poorly educated that they could scarcely read, let alone teach people. Others broke their priestly vows by marrying, or by gambling or drinking to excess.

Early Calls for Reform Influenced by reformers, people had come to expect higher standards of conduct from priests and church leaders. In the late 1300s and early 1400s, John Wycliffe of England and John Huss of Bohemia had advocated church reform. They denied that the pope had the right to worldly power. They also taught that the Bible had more authority than Church leaders. In the 1500s, Christian humanists like Desiderius Erasmus and Thomas More added their voices to the chorus of criticism.

In the 1490s, an Italian friar named Girolamo Savonarola (jih·RAHL·uh·MOH SAV·uh·nuh·ROH·luh) came to Florence. He preached fiery sermons calling for reform. In 1497, the people of Florence responded to Savonarola by burning their worldly possessions, such as gambling equipment, in a giant bonfire. Only a year later, the Florentines turned against Savonarola, and he was executed for heresy.

THINK THROUGH HISTORY
A. Analyzing Causes How did political, social, and economic forces weaken the Church?
A. Answers Political—Rulers resented the popes' attempts to control them and Germany was not unified; Social—Printing press spread Renaissance ideas that challenged Church authority, Economic—Merchants resented paying Church taxes.

SECTION 3 RESOURCES

PRINT RESOURCES

 IN-DEPTH RESOURCES: UNIT 1
Guided Reading, p. 20
Skillbuilder Practice: Synthesizing, p. 22
Primary Sources: A Conference with Elizabeth I, p. 27; Report on the English Reformation, p. 28
History Makers: Elizabeth I, p. 33

 ACCESS FOR STUDENTS ACQUIRING ENGLISH
Guided Reading (Spanish), p. 24
Skillbuilder Practice: (Spanish), p. 26

 FORMAL ASSESSMENT
Section Quiz, p. 19

 ALTERNATIVE ASSESSMENT BOOK

TECHNOLOGY RESOURCES

 CD-ROM
Electronic Library of Primary Sources

INTERNET www.mlworldhistory.com

Luther Challenges the Church

Although some reformers died for their beliefs, their calls for change lived on. In addition, many Europeans were reading religious works for themselves and forming their own opinions about the Church. The atmosphere in Europe was ripe for reform by the early 1500s.

Martin Luther The son of a miner, Martin Luther became a monk in 1507. From 1512 until his death he taught scripture at the University of Wittenberg in the German state of Saxony. All he wanted was to be a good Christian, not to lead a religious revolution.

In 1517 Luther decided to take a public stand against the actions of a friar named Johann Tetzel. Tetzel was raising money to rebuild St. Peter's Cathedral in Rome. He did this by selling indulgences. An **indulgence** was a pardon. It released a sinner from performing the penalty—such as saying certain prayers—that a priest imposed for sins. Indulgences were not supposed to affect God's right to judge. Unfortunately, Tetzel gave people the impression that by buying indulgences, they could buy their way into heaven.

HISTORY MAKERS

Martin Luther
1483–1546

Martin Luther was sometimes unhappy as a child. Like many parents of that time, his father and mother were very strict. Luther later told stories of their beating him.

In one way, fear led Luther to become a monk. His father wanted him to go to law school, but at the age of 22, Luther was caught in a terrible thunderstorm. Lightning struck close to him. Convinced he would die, he cried out, "Saint Anne, help me! I will become a monk."

Even as a monk, Luther felt sinful, lost, and rejected by God. He confessed his sins regularly, fasted, and did penance. However, by studying the Bible, Luther came to the conclusion that faith alone was the key to salvation. Only then did he experience peace.

The 95 Theses Luther was troubled by Tetzel's tactics. He wrote 95 Theses, or formal statements, attacking the "pardon-merchants." On October 31, 1517, he posted his theses on the door of the castle church in Wittenberg and invited other scholars to debate him. Someone copied Luther's words and took them to a printer. Quickly, Luther's name became known all over Germany. His actions began the **Reformation,** a movement for religious reform. It led to the founding of Christian churches that did not accept the pope's authority.

Soon Luther went far beyond criticizing indulgences. He wanted a full reform of the Church. His teachings rested on three main ideas:

- People could win salvation only by faith in God's gift of forgiveness. The Church taught that faith and "good works" were needed for salvation.
- All Church teachings should be clearly based on the words of the Bible. The pope and church traditions were false authorities.
- All people with faith were equal. Therefore, people did not need priests to interpret the Bible for them.

Background
The door of the church served as a type of bulletin board for the University of Wittenberg. If scholars wanted to debate a subject, they would post their opinions on the door.

The Response to Luther

Luther himself was astonished at how rapidly his ideas spread and attracted followers. Many rulers and merchants had been unhappy with the Church for political and economic reasons. They saw Luther's protests as an excuse to throw off Church control.

The Pope's Threat Initially, the Church officials in Rome viewed Luther simply as a rebellious monk who needed to be punished by his superiors. However, as Luther's ideas became increasingly radical, the pope realized that the monk was a serious threat. In one angry reply to Church criticism, Luther actually suggested that Christians drive the pope from the Church by force.

In 1520, Pope Leo X issued a decree threatening Luther with excommunication unless he took back his statements. Luther did not take back a word. Instead, his students at Wittenberg gathered around a bonfire and cheered as he threw the pope's decree into the flames. Leo excommunicated Luther.

The Emperor's Opposition A devout Catholic, the Holy Roman emperor also opposed Luther's teaching. Although only 20 years old, Emperor Charles V controlled

THINK THROUGH HISTORY
B. Synthesizing
Review the list of Luther's teachings above. Which of these points help you to understand why he felt it was all right to defy the pope?
B. Possible Answers
He thought the pope was a false authority. He thought all Christians were equal, so the pope had no power to damn him.

OBJECTIVE ② INSTRUCT

Luther Challenges the Church

▶ **Key Ideas**
- Martin Luther, a German monk, protests the sale of indulgences.
- 1n 1517, Luther begins the Reformation when he posts the *95 Theses* attacking the sale of indulgences on a church door in Wittenberg.
- Luther teaches his views on the path to salvation and the interpretation of the Bible.

HISTORY MAKERS
Martin Luther

Remind students that Luther's goal was to become a good Christian, not to stage a religious revolt. Have students explore Luther as a revolutionary. In a class discussion, have students give examples of Luther's break with tradition, his defiance of authority, and his role as catalyst in launching a new era.

 ELECTRONIC LIBRARY OF PRIMARY SOURCES
from the *Ninety-Five Theses*

OBJECTIVE ③ INSTRUCT

The Response to Luther

▶ **Key Ideas**
- The pope excommunicates Luther.
- The Holy Roman emperor declares Luther a heretic and outlaw.
- German peasants revolt in 1524.
- The Holy Roman emperor wages war against the Protestant princes of Germany.

| TEACHING OPTION | BLOCK SCHEDULING | SKILLBUILDER MINI-LESSON: Synthesizing | CLASS TIME 15 MINUTES |

Explaining the Skill Synthesizing is the skill historians use in developing interpretations of the past. Like detective work, synthesizing involves putting together clues, facts, and ideas to form an overall picture of a historical event. Tell students that as they read they should try to bring together different kinds of information to arrive at a new understanding of the subject.

Applying the Skill: Think Through History To answer the question at the bottom of this page, suggest students use the following strategy: Have them reread the bulleted list of Luther's teachings and look for information to support the synthesis about the right to defy papal authority. Then ask students to use a cluster diagram showing how the synthesis was formed.

The pope is a false authority.

Synthesis: Defying the pope is all right.

The pope does not have the power to judge people's salvation.

Since all people of faith are equal, the pope is not a supreme authority.

 IN-DEPTH RESOURCES: UNIT 1
Skillbuilder Practice: Synthesizing, p. 22

Teacher's Edition **49**

Luther's Popular Ideas

- Personal interpretation of the Bible
- Religious freedom for Christians
- Independence from the Catholic Church

---

a vast empire, including Germany. He summoned Luther to the town of Worms in 1521 to stand trial. German princes and bishops crowded into the hall to witness the testimony. Told to recant, or take back his statements, Luther refused.

A VOICE FROM THE PAST
I am bound by the Scriptures I have quoted and my conscience is captive to the Word of God. I cannot and I will not retract anything, since it is neither safe nor right to go against conscience. I cannot do otherwise, here I stand, may God help me. Amen.

LUTHER, quoted in *The Protestant Reformation* by Lewis W. Spitz

A month after Luther made that speech, Charles issued an imperial order, the Edict of Worms. It declared Luther an outlaw and a heretic. According to this edict, no one in the empire was to give Luther food or shelter. All his books were to be burned. However, the ruler of the state where Luther lived disobeyed the emperor. For almost a year after the trial, Prince Frederick the Wise of Saxony sheltered Luther in one of his castles. While there, Luther translated the New Testament into German.

Luther returned to Wittenberg in 1522. There he discovered that many of his ideas were already being put into practice. Priests dressed in ordinary clothes and called themselves ministers. They led services in German instead of in Latin. Some ministers had married, because Luther taught that the clergy should be free to wed. Instead of continuing to seek reforms in the Catholic Church, Luther and his followers had become a separate religious group, called **Lutherans.**

The Peasants' Revolt Some people began to apply Luther's revolutionary ideas to society. In 1524, German peasants, excited by reformers' talk of Christian freedom, demanded an end to serfdom. Bands of angry peasants went about the countryside raiding monasteries, pillaging, and burning.

The revolt horrified Luther. He wrote a pamphlet urging the German princes to show the peasants no mercy. With brutal thoroughness, the princes' armies crushed the revolt. They massacred as many as 100,000 people. Feeling betrayed by Luther, many peasants rejected his religious leadership. However, through writings and lectures, Luther remained influential until the end of his life.

SPOTLIGHT On
Witch Hunts

Soon after the Reformation began, the number of people executed for being witches rose dramatically. From 1561 to 1670 in Germany, 3,229 people accused of witchcraft were burned at the stake, as the engraving above shows. Between 1559 and 1736 in England, almost 1,000 witches were put to death. Eighty percent of the people accused of witchcraft were women.

Some historians think that people felt so frightened by the ongoing religious conflicts they blamed them on witches. Other historians believe that religious reformers stirred up negative feelings about women that had long been part of Western culture. All agree that those executed for witchcraft were innocent victims.

Germany at War In contrast to the bitter peasants, many northern German princes supported Lutheranism. While some princes genuinely shared Luther's beliefs, others liked Luther's ideas for selfish reasons. They saw his teachings as a good excuse to seize Church property and to assert their independence from Charles V.

In 1529, German princes who remained loyal to the pope agreed to join forces against Luther's ideas. Princes who supported Luther signed a protest against that agreement. These protesting princes came to be known as Protestants. Eventually, the term **Protestant** was applied to Christians who belonged to non-Catholic churches.

Still determined that his subjects remain Catholic, Holy Roman Emperor Charles V went to war against the Protestant princes of Germany. Even though he defeated them in 1547, he failed to force them back into the Catholic Church.

Weary of fighting, Charles ordered all German princes, both Protestant and Catholic, to assemble in the city of Augsburg. At that meeting, the princes agreed that the religion of each German state was to be decided by its ruler. This famous religious settlement, signed in 1555, was known as the **Peace of Augsburg.**

England Becomes Protestant

The Catholic Church soon faced another great challenge to its authority. Unlike Luther, the man who broke England's ties to the Roman Catholic Church did so for political and personal, not religious, reasons.

Henry VIII Wants a Son When Henry became king of England, he was a devout Catholic. Political needs soon tested his religious loyalty. He needed a male heir. Henry's father had become king after a long civil war. Henry feared that a similar war would start if he died without a son as his heir. He and his wife, Catherine of Aragon, had one living child—a daughter, Mary—but no woman had ever successfully claimed the English throne.

By 1527, Henry was convinced that the 42-year-old Catherine would have no more children. He wanted to divorce her and take a younger queen. Church law did not allow divorce. However, the pope could **annul**, or set aside, Henry's marriage if he could find proof that it had never been legal in the first place. Excuses were frequently found to annul royal marriages if they produced no heirs. In 1527, King Henry asked the pope to annul his marriage, but the pope turned him down. The pope did not want to offend Catherine's powerful nephew, the Holy Roman Emperor Charles V.

The Reformation Parliament Henry solved his marriage problem himself. In 1529, he called Parliament into session and asked it to pass a set of laws that ended the pope's power in England. This Parliament is known as the Reformation Parliament.

In 1533, Henry secretly married Anne Boleyn (BULihn), who was in her twenties. Parliament legalized Henry's divorce from Catherine. In 1534, Henry's break with the pope was made complete when Parliament voted to approve the Act of Supremacy. This act made the English king, not the pope, the official head of England's Church.

Consequences of Henry's Changes Soon after making himself supreme head of the Church of England, Henry closed all English monasteries. He seized their wealth and lands. The monasteries had owned perhaps 20 percent of the land in England, so this act vastly increased royal power and enriched Henry's treasury.

Henry did not get the male heir he sought immediately. After Anne Boleyn gave birth to a girl, she fell out of Henry's favor. Eventually, he ordered her imprisoned in the Tower of London and later beheaded in 1536. Before his death, Henry married four more times. His third wife gave him a son named Edward.

Background
The pope had taken the losing side in a war against Emperor Charles V, who was now holding him prisoner. The pope did not dare annul Henry's marriage to Charles's aunt.

HISTORY MAKERS

Henry VIII
1491–1547

When Henry became king in 1509, he was young, strong, handsome, and intelligent. He loved sports, literature, music, and food. He also loved his Roman Catholic faith.

In 1521, he wrote a pamphlet attacking Martin Luther and his teachings. Impressed by Henry's loyalty, the pope gave him a special title, "Defender of the Faith."

Even Henry's religious actions were driven by political ambition. One of his motives for defending Catholicism was to keep up with his fellow European monarchs. Earlier popes had granted Spanish monarchs the title "Catholic Sovereigns" and French monarchs the title "Most Christian." Although Henry was proud of his papal honor, eventually his political needs drove him to break with the Church.

Henry VIII's Family Causes Religious Turmoil

1509 Henry VIII becomes king.

1516 Daughter Mary is born.

1527 Henry asks the pope to end his first marriage; the pope refuses.

1529 Henry breaks with pope; begins Protestant Anglican church.

1533 Henry marries Anne Boleyn; daughter Elizabeth is born.

1536 Anne Boleyn is beheaded.

1537 Henry's third wife has son, Edward. She dies from complications.

1540-1542 Henry divorces fourth wife and beheads fifth wife.

1547 Henry dies; his sixth wife outlives him; Edward VI begins six-year rule; Protestants are strong.

1553 Catholic Mary I begins rule and kills Protestants.

1558 Elizabeth I begins rule; she restores Protestant church.

1500 ——— 1560

European Renaissance and Reformation **51**

OBJECTIVE **4** INSTRUCT

England Becomes Protestant

▶ **Key Ideas**
- The pope refuses to annul King Henry VIII's marriage.
- Henry resolves the marriage problem by asking Parliament to end the pope's power in England.
- Parliament passes an act making the English king, not the pope, the head of the Church of England.
- Clashes over religious reform heighten when Henry's heirs take the throne.
- Henry's daughter Elizabeth I returns England to Protestantism during her reign.

HISTORY MAKERS
Henry VIII

At the time of Henry's break with Rome, most English people were devout Catholics. There was a small minority of dissenters—people who wanted to reform the church. However, Henry was careful to change nothing about the way people worshiped, which explains why there was not greater outcry about his actions.

History from Visuals

Henry VIII's Family Causes Religious Turmoil

Interpreting the Time Line
Ask students to notice how many years are represented on the time line. *60.* How many rulers of England are shown on the time line? *4.* How many years did Mary reign as queen? *5.*

Extension Ask students to create a diagram of a family tree, based on the time line, that shows Henry VIII's six wives and his children.

TEACHING OPTION | **BLOCK SCHEDULING** | COOPERATIVE ACTIVITY: **Reporting on the Wives of Henry VIII** | **CLASS TIME 30 MINUTES**

Task: Groups of students will create front pages of newspaper issues reporting on activities of different wives of Henry VIII.

Purpose: To learn more about the lives of Henry's six wives and to learn more daily life at court.

Activity: Divide the class into six groups and assign each group one of Henry's six wives. Students should choose an interesting date to highlight—for example, the wedding day, a childbirth announcement,

and the wife's execution or death. Students should then research the event. The front page may include news stories, interviews, and human-interest features. Different students in the group might serve as researchers, writers, editors, and layout designers.

📁 **Building a Portfolio:** Remind students to choose their strongest work for their portfolio.

📖 **ALTERNATE ASSESSMENT BOOK**
Standards for Evaluating a Cooperative Activity

Standards for Evaluation
Front pages should . . .

- contain attention-getting headlines
- present well-organized, engaging stories and features based on research
- show evidence of careful planning

After Henry's death in 1547, each of his three children eventually ruled. This created religious turmoil. Edward VI became king at age nine and ruled only six years. During his reign, the Protestants gained power. Edward's half-sister Mary ruled next. She was a Catholic who returned the English Church to the rule of the pope. Mary had many Protestants killed. England's next ruler was Anne Boleyn's daughter, Elizabeth.

Elizabeth Restores Protestantism Inheriting the throne in 1558, Elizabeth I returned her kingdom to Protestantism. In 1559, Parliament followed Elizabeth's request and set up a national church much like the one under Henry VIII. This was to be the only legal church in England. People were required to attend its services or pay a fine. Parliament declared that Elizabeth was head of the Church of England, or **Anglican** Church.

Elizabeth decided to establish a state church that moderate Catholics and moderate Protestants might both accept. As a concession to Protestants, priests in the Church of England were allowed to marry. They could deliver sermons in English, not Latin. As a concession to Catholics, the Church of England kept some of the trappings of the Catholic service such as rich robes and golden crucifixes. Under Elizabeth, the Book of Common Prayer was revised to be somewhat more acceptable to Catholics.

The Spanish Armada While Elizabeth was able to restore religious peace to her country, she soon faced the threat of invasion from the king of Catholic Spain. Philip II planned to attack England for several reasons. One reason was that Elizabeth had supported Protestant subjects who rebelled against him. In 1588, Philip assembled an invasion force of 130 ships, 8,000 sailors, and 19,000 soldiers. This force—known as the Spanish Armada—reached the southwest coast of England on July 29. However, bad weather and the English fleet defeated the Spanish completely.

Although Elizabeth's reign was triumphant, she had some difficulties. Money was one problem. In the late 1500s, the English began to think about building an American empire as a new source of income. (See Chapter 3.) While colonies strengthened England economically, they did not enrich the queen directly. The queen's constant need for money would carry over into the next reign and lead to bitter conflict between the monarch and Parliament. In the meantime, other countries experienced bloody religious conflicts.

HISTORY MAKERS

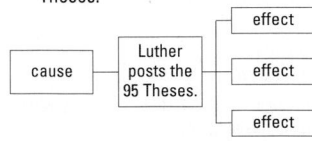

Elizabeth I
1533–1603
Elizabeth I was the third of Henry VIII's children to rule England. Like her father, Elizabeth had a fierce temper and a robust nature. Athletic as a girl, she showed amazing energy and strength into her sixties.

When the Spanish Armada threatened England, Elizabeth rode into the camp of soldiers preparing to defend their country. For this occasion, she wore her brightest red wig adorned with two white plumes that were easy for all to see above the soldier's long pikes.

From her horse, Elizabeth gave encouragement to her soldiers:

I know I have the body of a weak and feeble woman, but I have the heart and stomach of a king, and a king of England, too, and I think foul scorn [of] . . . any prince of Europe [who] should dare invade the borders of my realm.

THINK THROUGH HISTORY
E. Recognizing Effects How did Henry VIII and his three children cause religious turmoil in England?
E. Answer Under their rule, England switched back and forth from Catholic to Protestant to Catholic to Protestant again. Many people were persecuted and martyred, by both Henry and Mary.

Section **3** Assessment

1. TERMS & NAMES
Identify
• indulgence
• Reformation
• Lutheran
• Protestant
• Peace of Augsburg
• annul
• Anglican

52 Chapter 1

2. TAKING NOTES
Using a cause-and-effect graphic like the one below, show the main cause and several effects of Luther's action in posting the 95 Theses.

cause → Luther posts the 95 Theses. → effect / effect / effect

Which effect do you think had the most permanent impact? Explain.

3. SUPPORTING OPINIONS
Who do you think had a better reason to break with the Church, Luther or Henry VIII? Support your answer with details from the text.

THINK ABOUT
• why Luther criticized the Church
• what Henry asked the pope to do for him
• the Church's response to Luther
• the pope's response to Henry

4. ANALYZING THEMES
Revolution Which of Luther's ideas do you think might have motivated the peasants to revolt in 1524? Explain.

THINK ABOUT
• Luther's criticisms of the Church
• what change the peasants demanded
• the actions the peasants took

ANSWERS

1. TERMS AND NAMES
indulgence, p. 49
Reformation, p. 49
Lutheran, p. 50
Protestant, p. 50
Peace of Augsburg, p. 50
annul, p. 51
Anglican, p. 52

2. TAKING NOTES
Possible Responses: Cause: Tetzel sells indulgences under false pretenses. Effects: Luther protests; pope excommunicates Luther; Luther declared a heretic; Lutheran church begins; German peasants revolt; Charles V goes to war against Protestant princes of Germany. Impact: Lutheran church—led to permanent break between Catholics and Protestants.

3. DRAWING CONCLUSIONS
Possible Responses: Luther's reasons—legitimate complaints about indulgences and other Church problems; excommunication. Henry's reasons—his annulments denied; pope's political maneuvers.

4. ANALYZING THEMES
Possible Responses: The equality of all Christians spurred peasants to demand an end to serfdom. Peasants disrespected Church authority by raiding the monasteries.

The Reformation Continues

TERMS & NAMES
- predestination
- Calvinism
- theocracy
- Presbyterian
- Anabaptist
- Catholic Reformation
- Jesuits
- Council of Trent

MAIN IDEA

John Calvin and other Reformation leaders began new Protestant churches. The Catholic Church also made reforms.

WHY IT MATTERS NOW

Many Protestant churches began during this period, and many Catholic schools are the result of Catholic reforms.

SETTING THE STAGE Under the leadership of Elizabeth I, the Church of England remained similar to the Catholic Church in many of its doctrines and ceremonies. Meanwhile, other forms of Protestantism were developing elsewhere in Europe.

Calvin Begins Another Protestant Church

In 1521, the year Luther stood trial at Worms, John Calvin was a 12-year-old boy. Born in France, Calvin grew up to have as much influence on Protestants as Luther did. Calvin would give order to the new faith that Luther had begun.

Calvin and His Teachings In 1536, Calvin published a book called *Institutes of the Christian Religion.* This work expressed Calvin's ideas about God, salvation, and human nature. It also created a system of Protestant theology.

Calvin taught that men and women are sinful by nature. Taking Luther's idea that humans cannot earn salvation, Calvin went on to say that God chooses a very few people to save. Calvin called these few the "elect." He believed that God has known since the beginning of time who will be saved. This doctrine is called **predestination.** The religion based on Calvin's teachings is called **Calvinism.**

Calvin Runs Geneva Calvin believed that the ideal government was a **theocracy,** a government controlled by religious leaders. In 1541, Protestants in Geneva, Switzerland, asked Calvin to lead their city. When Calvin arrived there in the 1540s, Geneva was a self-governing city of about 20,000 people.

Calvin and his followers ran the city according to strict rules. Everyone attended religion class. No one wore bright clothing or played card games. Authorities would imprison, excommunicate, or banish those who broke such rules. Anyone who preached different doctrines might be burned at the stake. Yet, to many Protestants, Calvin's Geneva was a model city of highly moral citizens.

Calvinism Spreads One of the admiring visitors to Geneva was a preacher from Scotland named John Knox. When he returned home in 1559, Knox put Calvin's ideas to work in Scottish towns. Each community church was governed by a small group of laymen called elders or presbyters (PREHZ-buh-tuhrs). Followers of Knox became known as **Presbyterians.** In the 1560s, Protestant nobles led by Knox succeeded in making Calvinism Scotland's official religion. They also deposed their Catholic queen in favor of her infant son.

Elsewhere, Swiss, Dutch, and French reformers adopted the Calvinist form of church organization. One reason Calvin is considered so influential is that many Protestant churches today

Background

The deposed queen was Mary, Queen of Scots—Elizabeth I's cousin and heir. Many English Catholics wanted Mary to rule. Eventually, Elizabeth had Mary executed for taking part in plots against her.

HISTORY MAKERS

John Calvin
1509–1564

Unlike Luther, Calvin wrote little about his personal life. A quiet boy, he grew up to study law and philosophy at the University of Paris. Early in the 1530s, he came under the influence of French followers of Luther. When King Francis I ordered these Protestants arrested, Calvin fled. Eventually, he made his way to Geneva, Switzerland.

Calvin and his followers rigidly regulated morality in Geneva. Perhaps because of this, Calvinism is often described as strict and grim. However, Calvin taught that people should enjoy God's gifts. He wrote that it was not

> anywhere forbidden to laugh, or to enjoy food, or to add new possessions to old . . . or to be delighted with musical harmonies, or to drink wine.

European Renaissance and Reformation **53**

HISTORY MAKERS

John Calvin

(See page 53.)

Calvin did away with many religious ceremonies that Luther accepted and Catholics upheld. For example, Calvin forbade the clergy to wear rich, colorful garments. The following were not allowed in church: statues, incense, an altar, candles, chants, organ music, and stained-glass windows.

History from Visuals

Interpreting the Map Point out the complex color code and list of initials in the legend. Have students find an example of each religion on the map that is explained in the legend.

Extension Activity Have students make a chart of religious groups in Europe about 1560 with these headings: *Nation/Territory, Dominant Religion, Minority Religion.*

SKILLBUILDER Answers
1. Ireland, Portugal, Spain, France, the Netherlands, Swiss Confederation, Italian States, and Papal States remained mostly Catholic. Scotland, England, Norway, Sweden, Denmark, and the northern German States became mostly Protestant
2. Possible sites of future conflicts might include Ireland and the German States.

🏛 ***GEOGRAPHY TRANSPARENCIES***
GT17 Reformation: Lutheranism and Calvinism, 1500–1600

OBJECTIVE 2 INSTRUCT

Other Reformers

▶ **Key Ideas**
• New Protestant groups form over differences in beliefs
• Anabaptists believe that only adults should be baptized.
• Women play key roles in the early Reformation.

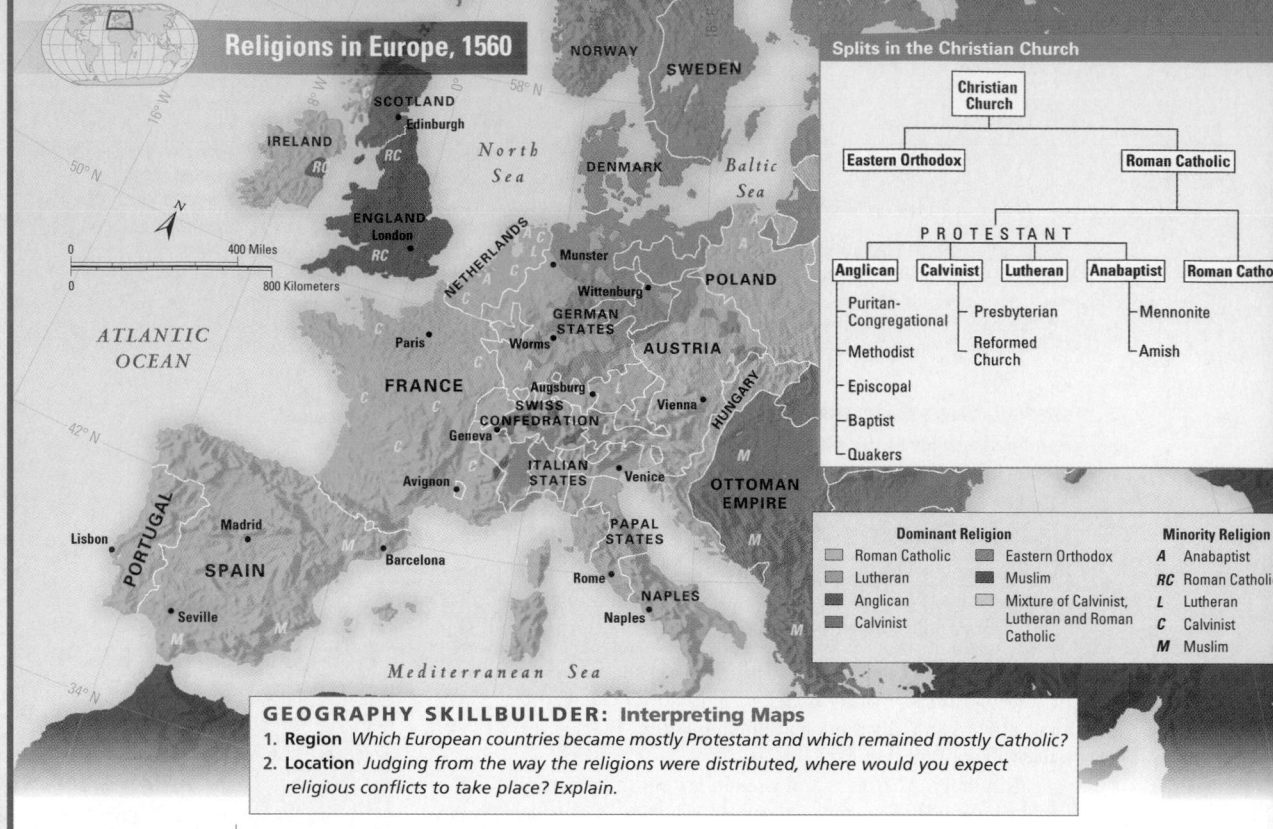

Religions in Europe, 1560

Splits in the Christian Church

GEOGRAPHY SKILLBUILDER: Interpreting Maps
1. **Region** *Which European countries became mostly Protestant and which remained mostly Catholic?*
2. **Location** *Judging from the way the religions were distributed, where would you expect religious conflicts to take place? Explain.*

Although Catholic, Marguerite of Navarre held unorthodox, mystical personal beliefs. She supported the call for reform in the Church.

trace their roots to Calvin. Over the years, however, many of them have softened Calvin's strict teachings.

In France, Calvin's followers were called Huguenots. Hatred between Catholics and Huguenots frequently led to violence. The worst outbreak of fury occurred in Paris on August 24, 1572—the Catholic feast of St. Bartholomew's Day. At dawn, Catholic mobs began hunting for Protestants and brutally murdering them. The massacres spread to other cities and lasted six months. Thousands, perhaps up to 12,000, Huguenots were killed.

Other Reformers

Protestants taught that the Bible is the source of all truth about religion and that all people should read it to discover those truths. As Christians began to interpret the Bible for themselves, new Protestant groups formed over differences in belief.

The Anabaptists One such group believed that only adults could decide to be baptized. They said that people who had been baptized as children should be rebaptized as adults. These believers were called **Anabaptists** from the Greek for "baptize again." Anabaptists also taught that church and state should be separate, and they refused to fight in wars. They shared their possessions. Viewing Anabaptists as radicals who threatened society, both Catholics and Protestants persecuted them. Yet, the Anabaptists survived and became the forerunners of the Mennonites and the Amish. Their teaching influenced the later Quakers and Baptists, who split from the Anglican church.

Women of the Reformation Many women played prominent roles in the Reformation, especially from 1519 to 1580. For example, Marguerite of Navarre, the sister of King Francis I, protected John Calvin from being

54 Chapter 1

THINK THROUGH HISTORY
A. Analyzing Causes How did Protestant teaching cause further divisions in the Christian church?
A. Answer By emphasizing that all Christians should interpret the Bible for themselves, the Protestants opened the door to many different sets of belief. This led to many different churches.

TEACHING OPTION 📦 **BLOCK SCHEDULING** — **COOPERATIVE ACTIVITY: Neighborhood Survey of Religious Groups** — **CLASS TIME 30 MINUTES**

Task: Student groups survey their neighborhood to find the different religions and Christian denominations located there.

Purpose: To explore the far-reaching impact that the establishment of Protestant denominations in the 16th century had on the United States

Activity: Divide students into groups and ask

them to check the local Yellow Pages or another phone directory for houses of worship located in their community. Have students create a three-column chart to classify the various faiths based on their relationship to religious groups formed during the Reformation. Students should use these headings: *Directly Related, Indirectly Related, Not Related.*

📁 ***Building a Portfolio:*** Remind students to make copies of their best work for their portfolio.

📖 ***ALTERNATIVE ASSESSMENT BOOK***
Standards for Evaluating a Cooperative Activity

Standards for Evaluation
Classification charts should . . .

• Be well-organized and easy-to-read
• Group information into correct categories
• Show evidence of research

executed for his beliefs while he lived in France. Other noblewomen played similar roles in protecting reformers.

Several wives of reformers also achieved fame. Katherina Zell, married to prominent reformer Matthew Zell of Strasbourg, once scolded a minister for speaking harshly of another. The minister responded by saying that she had "disturbed the peace." Katherina Zell answered his criticism sharply:

A VOICE FROM THE PAST
Do you call this disturbing the peace that instead of spending my time in frivolous amusements I have visited the plague infested and carried out the dead? I have visited those in prison and under sentence of death. Often for three days and three nights I have neither eaten nor slept. I have never mounted the pulpit, but I have done more than any minister in visiting those in misery.

KATHERINA ZELL, quoted in *Women of the Reformation*

Luther's wife Katherina von Bora played a more typical, behind-the-scenes role. However, her young life was unusual. Sent to a convent at about age 10, Katherina had taken the vows of a nun by 16. Inspired by Luther's teaching, she escaped from her convent. Some stories claim she escaped by hiding in an empty barrel that had contained smoked herring.

After marrying Luther, Katherina had six children. She managed the family finances, fed all who visited their house, and supported her husband's work. She submitted respectfully to Luther but also argued with him about woman's equal role in marriage. Their well-run household became a model for others to follow.

As Protestant religions became more firmly established, their organization became more formal. Male religious leaders narrowly limited women's activities to the home and discouraged them from being leaders.

THINK THROUGH HISTORY
B. Making Inferences Why was it easier for women to take part in the earlier stages of the Reformation than the later stages?
B. Possible Answers In the earlier stages, most churches did not have formal leaders who could tell women what to do. Once men began to have formal leadership roles, they did not want to share their authority with women.

The Catholic Reformation

While Protestant churches won many followers, millions remained true to Catholicism. Helping Catholics to remain loyal was a movement within the Catholic Church to reform itself. This movement is now known as the **Catholic Reformation.** One great Catholic reformer was Ignatius (ihg·NAY·shuhs) of Loyola.

Ignatius of Loyola Ignatius grew up in his father's castle in Loyola, Spain. The great turning point in his life came in 1521 when he was injured in a war. During his recovery, Ignatius thought about his past sins and about the life of Jesus. His daily devotions, he believed, cleansed his soul. In 1522, he began writing a book called *Spiritual Exercises* that laid out a day-by-day plan of meditation, prayer, and study. Ignatius compared spiritual and physical exercise:

A VOICE FROM THE PAST
Just as walking, traveling, and running are bodily exercises, preparing the soul to remove ill-ordered affections, and after their removal seeking and finding the will of God with respect to the ordering of one's own life and the salvation of one's soul, are Spiritual Exercises.

IGNATIUS OF LOYOLA, *Spiritual Exercises*

For the next 18 years, Ignatius gathered followers. In 1540, the pope made Ignatius's followers a religious order called the Society of Jesus. Members of the order were commonly called **Jesuits** (JEHZH·u·ihts).

The Jesuits concentrated on three activities. First, they founded superb schools throughout Europe. Jesuit teachers were rigorously trained in both classical studies and theology. The Jesuits' second mission was to convert non-Christians to Catholicism, so they sent out missionaries. Their third goal was to stop Protestantism from

GlobalImpact

Jesuit Missionaries

The work of Jesuit missionaries has had a lasting impact around the globe. By the time Ignatius died in 1556, about a thousand Jesuits were working in Europe, Africa, Asia, and the Americas. Two of the most famous Jesuit missionaries of the 1500s were Francis Xavier, who worked in India, and Matteo Ricci, who worked in China.

One reason the Jesuits had such a permanent impact is that they founded schools, colleges, and universities throughout the world. For example, the Jesuits today run about 45 high schools and 28 colleges and universities in the United States. Two of these are Boston College and Marquette University.

MORE ABOUT . . .
Katherina von Bora
Shortly after his marriage to Katherina von Bora, Luther told a friend that he was not in love. However after a few years of marriage, his feeling changed. He said that enduring love in marriage is God's greatest grace.

OBJECTIVE **3** INSTRUCT

The Catholic Reformation

▶ *Key Ideas*
• The Church launches reforms to strengthen and spread the Catholic religion.
• Ignatius of Loyola forms a Catholic religious order called the Society of Jesus, or the Jesuits.
• Two popes in the 1500s initiate reforms in the Catholic Church.
• A great council of church leaders meets in Trent to improve church governments and clarify beliefs.
• The Reformation leaves an enduring legacy.

 CRITICAL THINKING TRANSPARENCIES
CT17 The Protestant and Catholic Reformations

GlobalImpact
Jesuit Missionaries

The Jesuits were like a spiritual army, willing to go anywhere in the world in the service of the pope. Jesuit missionaries in Asia adapted their religious teachings to fit the culture of each country. Church officials criticized the missionaries for this approach. Matteo Ricci, for instance, was accused of allowing the Chinese reverence for their ancestors to become idolatry.

TEACHING OPTIONS

EXPLORING PRIMARY SOURCES

A Voice from the Past In a letter to the minister Ludwig Rabus, Katherina Zell wrote, "Ever since I was ten years old I have been a student and a sort of church mother, much given to attending sermons. I have loved and frequented the company of learned men, and I conversed much with them, not about dancing, masquerades and worldly pleasures but about the kingdom of God . . ." Based on this excerpt and *A Voice from the Past* on this page, have students make inferences about how Katherina Zell views her religious role and her relationship with men.

CUSTOMIZING FOR SPECIAL NEEDS

Gifted and Talented Students Divide students into small groups. Tell them to imagine that Ignatius of Loyola has asked them to write a pamphlet to recruit people into the Society of Jesus. Ask group members to brainstorm persuasive techniques, such as slogans and visuals, they would use to present this organization and its goals. Suggest that students come up with a catchy slogan, based on *A Voice from the Past* on this page, that might motivate people to join Ignatius' spiritual army. Display students' completed pamphlets in the classroom.

This Italian painting of the Council of Trent shows the large number of church leaders who met to discuss Catholic reforms.

spreading. The zeal of the Jesuits overcame the drift toward Protestantism in Poland and southern Germany.

Reforming Popes Two popes of the 1500s took the lead in reforming the Catholic Church. Paul III, who was pope from 1534 to 1549, took four important steps toward reform. First, he directed a council of cardinals to investigate indulgence selling and other abuses within the Church. Second, he approved the Jesuit order. Third, he used the Inquisition to seek out and punish heresy in papal territory. Fourth, and most important, he decided to call a great council of Church leaders to meet in Trent, in northern Italy. In 1545, at the **Council of Trent,** Catholic bishops and cardinals agreed on several doctrines:

- The church's interpretation of the Bible was final. Any Christian who substituted his or her own interpretation was a heretic.
- Christians need faith and good works for salvation. They were not saved by faith alone, as Luther argued.
- The Bible and Church tradition were equally powerful authorities for guiding Christian life.
- Indulgences were valid expressions of faith. (But the false selling of indulgences was banned.)

Another reforming pope, Paul IV, vigorously carried out the council's decrees. In 1559, he had officials draw up a list of books considered dangerous to the Catholic faith. This list was known as the Index of Forbidden Books. Catholic bishops throughout Europe were ordered to gather up the offensive books (including Protestant Bibles) and burn them in bonfires. In Venice alone, 10,000 books were burned in one day.

Legacy of the Reformation The Reformation had enduring effects. Protestant churches flourished, despite religious wars and persecutions. Because of the Reformation, religion no longer united Europe. As the Church's power declined, individual monarchs and states gained power. This paved the way for modern nation-states. In addition, the reformers' successful revolt against Church authority laid the groundwork for a rejection of Christian belief that occurred in Western culture in later centuries. Therefore, through its political and social effects, the Reformation helped to set the stage for the modern world.

Background
This Inquisition was called the Roman Inquisition. It generally was more moderate than the Spanish Inquisition.

Section 4 Assessment

1. TERMS & NAMES
Identify
- predestination
- Calvinism
- theocracy
- Presbyterian
- Anabaptist
- Catholic Reformation
- Jesuits
- Council of Trent

2. TAKING NOTES
Using a chart like the one below, compare the ideas of the reformers who came after Luther.

Reformers	Ideas
John Calvin	
Anabaptists	
Catholic Reformers	

3. EVALUATING DECISIONS
Which of the steps taken by Popes Paul III and Paul IV to reform the Catholic Church do you think were wise? Which were unwise? Explain.

THINK ABOUT
- the goals of the reforming popes
- whether the steps clearly addressed those goals
- possible effects of each step

4. THEME ACTIVITY

Religious and Ethical Systems In a group of three, hold a debate on whether Calvin was right to establish such a strict theocracy in Geneva. Debate such points as whether church leaders should be political rulers and whether government should try to control personal morality. One team member should support Calvin's policy, one should oppose it, and one should act as moderator.

56 Chapter 1

---

different PERSPECTIVES

different Perspectives

The Reformation

Martin Luther's criticisms of the Catholic church grew sharper over time. Some Catholics, in turn, responded with personal attacks on Luther. In recent times, historians have focused less on the theological and personal issues connected with the Reformation. Instead, many modern scholars analyze political, social, and economic conditions that contributed to the Reformation.

LETTER

Martin Luther

Although Luther began by criticizing the practice of selling indulgences, he soon began to attack the whole system of church government. In 1520, he sent the pope the following criticism of the Church leaders who served under him in Rome.

The Roman Church has become the most licentious [sinful] den of thieves. . . . They err who ascribe to thee the right of interpreting Scripture, for under cover of thy name they seek to set up their own wickedness in the Church, and, alas, through them Satan has already made much headway under thy predecessors. In short, believe none who exalt thee, believe those who humble thee.

ENGRAVING

Anonymous

In the early 1500s, an anonymous Catholic author published an engraving attacking Luther's "game of heresy." The following lines are part of a poem that appeared on the engraving.

I have in my simple way foreseen

What Luther's teaching promises
to bring:

Great rebellion and bloodletting,

Much hatred and strife.

The fear of God will vanish forever,

Together with the whole of Scripture,

And authority will everywhere
be despised.

HISTORIAN'S COMMENTARY

Steven Ozment

In 1992, historian Steven Ozment published *Protestants: The Birth of a Revolution.* Here he comments on some of the political aspects of the Reformation.

Beginning as a protest against arbitrary, self-aggrandizing, hierarchical authority in the person of the pope, the Reformation came to be closely identified in the minds of contemporaries with what we today might call states' rights or local control. To many townspeople and villagers, Luther seemed a godsend for their struggle to remain politically free and independent; they embraced his Reformation as a conserving political force, even though they knew it threatened to undo traditional religious beliefs and practices.

HISTORIAN'S COMMENTARY

G. R. Elton

In *Reformation Europe,* published in 1963, G. R. Elton notes the role of geography and trade in the spread of Reformation ideas.

Could the Reformation have spread so far and so fast if it had started anywhere but in Germany? At any rate, the fact that it had its beginnings in the middle of Europe made possible a very rapid radiation in all directions; the whole circle of countries surrounding the Empire came one after the other under its influence. Germany's position at the center of European trade also helped greatly. German merchants carried not only goods but Lutheran ideas and books to Venice and France; the north German Hanse [a trade league] transported the Reformation to the Scandinavian countries, parceled up with bales of cloth and cargoes of grain; trading links with Germany did much to encourage the growth of Lutheranism in the eastern lands.

Connect to History

Analyzing Causes How did politics and economics help spread the Reformation?

Comparing Compare Luther's attitude toward Church leaders with the Catholic attitudes toward him.

SEE SKILLBUILDER HANDBOOK, PAGES 653 and 654

Connect to Today

Comparing How do religious leaders spread their ideas today?

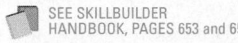 CD-ROM For another perspective on the Reformation, see the World History: Electronic Library of Primary Sources.

European Renaissance and Reformation **57**

different Perspectives

Why the Reformation Matters Now
As students discuss these perspectives on the Reformation, have them make a list evaluating the impact of the Reformation on modern life. Ask students to organize their list in a chart with the following headings: *Political Life, Economic Life, Family Life, Towns and Villages, Religious Tolerance.*

MORE ABOUT . . .
Protestants versus Catholics
The attacks on Protestants by Catholics and Catholics by Protestants were harsh, abusive, and cruel. Even such respected leaders as Martin Luther and Thomas More wrote books that criticize and insult one another.

ELECTRONIC LIBRARY OF PRIMARY SOURCES
• "The St. Bartholomew's Day Massacre"
• "Luther: Giant of His Time and Ours"

MORE ABOUT . . .
Attacks on Luther
Henry VIII of England also had unkind words for Martin Luther: "What serpent so venomous as he who calls the pope's authority tyrannous?" Though Henry himself later rejected the pope's authority, he never changed his opinion of Luther.

Connect to History | **Connect to Today**

Analyzing Causes
Possible Responses: Political motives helped spread the Reformation; many towns and villages turned Protestant in order to remain independent. Germany's strategic location at the center of European trade contributed to the spread of the Reformation. This economic advantage provided other benefits. Besides goods, German merchants carried Protestant ideas to Italy, France, Scandinavia and other places.

Comparing
Possible Responses: Luther and the anonymous Catholic writer accuse each other of wickedness, hurl insults, and attack each other's religious doctrines.

Comparing
Possible Responses: Students might mention books, magazines, revivals, television, and the Internet. Students also might note that Christian missionaries still work in countries around the world.

TERMS & NAMES

1. Renaissance, p. 37
2. humanism, p. 38
3. secular, p. 38
4. printing press, p. 46
5. indulgence, p. 49
6. Reformation, p. 49
7. Protestant, p. 50
8. Peace of Augsburg, p. 50
9. Catholic Reformation, p. 55
10. Council of Trent, p. 56

REVIEW QUESTIONS

Answers will vary.

11. Merchants' belief in individual merit would become a recurring theme in the Renaissance; merchants also were patrons of the arts.

12. Artists chose secular and classical subjects (as well as Christian subjects), painted prominent individuals, glorified the human body, and used new artistic techniques and a more realistic style.

13. Northern European rulers purchased Renaissance paintings and hired Italian artists and architects to work on important projects.

14. Dürer's prints portray both religious and classical subjects. He painted realistic landscapes and a self-portrait.

15. Humanists set out to improve society by writing works that criticized society or described the perfect society.

16. On a church door Luther posted his *95 Theses* criticizing the selling of indulgences.

17. The Holy Roman Emperor wanted to force the Protestant German princes to rejoin the Catholic church.

18. In 1534, Henry VIII assumed control of the English Church, so that he could obtain an annulment. After Mary I tried to restore Catholicism, Elizabeth I persuaded Parliament to set up the Anglican church.

19. Calvin taught that humans were sinful by nature, that God chooses a very few people to save, that God has known since the beginning of time who those few were, and that theocracy was the best government.

20. Jesuits founded schools throughout Europe, converted non-Christians to Catholicism, and helped stop the spread of Protestantism.

Chapter **1** Assessment

TERMS & NAMES

Briefly explain the importance of each of the following to European history from 1300 to 1600.

1. Renaissance
2. humanism
3. secular
4. printing press
5. indulgence
6. Reformation
7. Protestant
8. Peace of Augsburg
9. Catholic Reformation
10. Council of Trent

Interact *with* History

On page 36, you looked at a painting and discussed what you learned about Renaissance society from that painting. Now choose one other piece of art from the chapter. Explain what you learn about Renaissance or Reformation society from that piece of art.

REVIEW QUESTIONS

SECTION 1 *(pages 37–42)*
Italy: Birthplace of the Renaissance

11. How did the merchant class in northern Italy influence the Renaissance?
12. How did art change during the Renaissance?

SECTION 2 *(pages 43–47)*
The Northern Renaissance

13. How did northern European rulers encourage the spread of Renaissance ideas?
14. How does Albrecht Dürer's work reflect Renaissance ideas?
15. What did Christian humanists set out to do, and what method did they use?

SECTION 3 *(pages 48–52)*
Luther Starts the Reformation

16. What act by Martin Luther set off the Reformation?
17. Why did the Holy Roman Emperor go to war against Protestant German princes?
18. How did England establish a state church apart from the Catholic Church?

SECTION 4 *(pages 53–56)*
The Reformation Continues

19. What were the main teachings of John Calvin?
20. What role did the Jesuits play in the Catholic Reformation?

Visual Summary

European Renaissance and Reformation

Effect in Renaissance	Social Change	Effect in Reformation
• Art celebrates individual and personal expression.	• Growing emphasis on individual	• Individuals interpret Bible for themselves.
• Merchants sponsor artists and pay to beautify city.	• Growing prosperity of merchants	• German merchants resent flow of money to Church in Rome.
• Rulers sponsor artists and philosophers.	• Decline of feudalism and growing power of princes and kings	• Rulers defy pope and become Protestant.
• Political, social, and artistic theories spread.	• Printing press and spread of learning	• Luther's 95 Theses spread; Bible printed in vernacular languages, so more people have access.

Interact *with* History

Possible Responses: Students may cite some of these features: more concern for human rather than spiritual matters; emphasis on ordinary people in everyday situations; pride in individuality and creativity; admiration for classical culture; interest in realism; enjoyment of wordly pleasures; uniqueness of each individual, including Biblical figures.

CRITICAL THINKING

1. POWER OF THE WRITTEN WORD

THEME **REVOLUTION** Beginning in the 1300s, Europeans overturned many of the structures and ideas of the Middle Ages. How did the printing press contribute to this revolution? Explain.

2. REFORMING THE REFORMER

Choose one of the Protestant groups who came after Luther, such as Calvinists or Anabaptists. Do you think they thought Luther went too far in reforming Catholic Church practices or not far enough? Explain your answer by citing differences in their beliefs.

3. RENAISSANCE AND REFORMATION TODAY

Go back through the chapter and take note of Renaissance and Reformation developments that still influence modern life. Record your findings on a chart like the one shown.

Legacy of the Renaissance and Reformation in Modern Life	
Artistic	Political
Religious	Social

4. ANALYZING PRIMARY SOURCES

In the following excerpt from *The Prince*, Niccolò Machiavelli discusses what a ruler should do to win a good reputation among his subjects. Read the paragraph and answer the questions below it.

> **A VOICE FROM THE PAST**
> A prince must also show himself a lover of merit [excellence], give preferment [promotion] to the able, and honour those who excel in every art. Moreover he must encourage his citizens to follow their callings [professions] quietly, whether in commerce, or agriculture, or any other trade that men follow. . . . [The prince] should offer rewards to whoever does these things, and to whoever seeks in any way to improve his city or state.

- How was Machiavelli's description of a prince's duties influenced by Renaissance values?
- Do you agree with Machiavelli that a prince should do these things? Explain the effect you think such behavior would have on the prince's subjects.

CHAPTER ACTIVITIES

1. LIVING HISTORY: **Unit Portfolio Project**

THEME **CULTURAL INTERACTION** Your unit portfolio project focuses on the spread of ideas among cultures (see page 33). For Chapter 1, you might use one of the following ideas to add to your portfolio.

- Design the cover and prepare the table of contents for a 15th-century magazine devoted to Europe's classical heritage. The table of contents should include article titles and a brief summary of each article.
- As Francis I, write a letter to Leonardo da Vinci asking him to retire in France. Explain why you want Italian artists to come to your country.
- With a partner, role-play the reunion of two art students in 1500. One has returned from Italy; the other studied in Flanders. They should compare their techniques and views about art. Audiotape the role-play.

2. CONNECT TO TODAY: **Cooperative Learning**

THEME **RELIGIOUS AND ETHICAL SYSTEMS** During the late 20th century, both Protestants and Catholics made delayed responses to the Reformation. In the 1960s, the Catholic Church held a council called Vatican II to promote additional reforms. In 1997, several U.S. Protestant denominations signed a document agreeing to form closer ties with one another.

Work with a team to create a poster that explains one of these developments and how it is a response to the Reformation.

INTERNET Use the Internet, news magazines, encyclopedias, or books to research the topic. Look for specific information about what was decided during Vatican II or in the Protestant agreement.

- In your group, decide what are the most important points about Vatican II or the Protestant agreement. Discuss how these points either carry on or undo the work of the Reformation.
- Display your information on a poster. You may convey the information in either a written or an illustrated form, as long as it is clear and accurate.

3. INTERPRETING A TIME LINE

Revisit the Unit Time Line on pages 32–33. On the Chapter 1 time line, identify important writers of the period. Did they write before or after the invention of the printing press?

FOCUS ON ART

Look carefully at this drawing of a machine from the notebooks of Leonardo da Vinci. Notice the blade that curves around the center shaft and the round mechanism at the bottom of the shaft.

- What might happen if the shaft started to turn?
- What do you think Leonardo was trying to invent when he drew this machine?
- What modern machine does this drawing remind you of?

Connect to History A ruler paid Leonardo for some of his ideas for machines. How might a ruler use a machine like the one shown here?

European Renaissance and Reformation **59**

CHAPTER ACTIVITIES

1. LIVING HISTORY: UNIT PORTFOLIO PROJECT

Standards for Evaluation
A magazine format should meet the following criteria:

- Uses an effective visual on the cover.
- Describes how classical ideas influenced European ideas in both article titles and summaries.

A letter should meet the following criteria:

- Is written in the voice of Francis I.
- Uses persuasive language to lure da Vinci to France.
- Explains Francis I's goals in inviting Renaissance artists to his court.

A role-play should meet the following criteria:

- Demonstrates knowledge of how to write dialogue.
- Reveals a knowledge of artistic trends in both Italy and northern Europe in 1500.

2. CONNECT TO TODAY: COOPERATIVE LEARNING

Standards for Evaluation
A poster should meet the following criteria:

- Explains or illustrates specific points of either Vatican II or the Protestant agreement of 1997.
- Shows either that Vatican II carries on the work of the Reformation or that the Protestant agreement seeks to undo some of the divisions dating from the Reformation.

3. INTERPRETING A TIME LINE

Possible Response: Boccaccio wrote before the printing press was invented; Shakespeare wrote after its invention.

FOCUS ON ART

Possible Answers: If the shaft turned, the blade would begin to revolve. This might have been an early flying machine or propeller. It looks a little like a helicopter. A ruler could use this machine to attack his enemies from the air during war or to spy on them.

CRITICAL THINKING

1. POWER OF THE WRITTEN WORD
Possible Responses: The availability of books helped spread Renaissance philosophical, political, and social beliefs. These publications undermined medieval values and society.

2. REFORMING THE REFORMER
Possible Responses: The Calvinist view of predestination more extreme than Luther's doctrine of grace. The Anabaptists' ideas about adult baptism, separation of church and state, and pacifism were also more radical.

3. RENAISSANCE AND REFORMATION TODAY
Possible Responses: Artistic—use of perspective, oil painting, and realism; literature in vernacular languages. Political—Machiavelli's views on governing; loss of Church power. Religious—Protestant denominations; Bible in vernacular languages; Jesuit schools. Social—individualism; secular values.

4. ANALYZING PRIMARY SOURCES
Possible Responses: Suggests that a prince should be a patron of the arts. Agree—Encourages hard work, and patriotism. Disagree—interfering in people's private lives.

The Muslim World Expands

	Key Ideas	**COPY MASTERS**	**ASSESSMENT**
SECTION 1 **The Ottomans Build a Vast Empire** *pp. 63–67*	*Turkish religious warriors along the Byzantine frontier capture Constantinople and build an enduring empire. Their realm combines elements from many cultures and religions and eventually stretches from the Balkans to North Africa and Persia.*	*In-Depth Resources: Unit 1* • **Guided Reading,** p. 35 • **Skillbuilder Practice:** Following Chronological Order, p. 38 • **Primary Source:** Suleiman the Magnificent, p. 41 • **Literature:** from *The Bride of Suleiman,* p. 45 • **History Makers:** Suleiman, p. 48	PE *Section 1 Assessment,* p. 67 *Formal Assessment* • Section Quiz, p. 29 *Alternative Assessment Book* • Standards for Evaluating a Cooperative Activity
SECTION 2 **Patterns of Change: Cultural Blending** *pp. 68–70*	*Interactions among diverse people in the Islamic world give rise to a new cultural mix. The Safavids draw on Shi'i religious ideology, ancient Persian traditions, and Ottoman political ideas to forge a new Persian culture.*	*In-Depth Resources: Unit 1* • **Guided Reading,** p. 36	PE *Section 2 Assessment,* p. 70 *Formal Assessment* • Section Quiz, p. 30 *Alternative Assessment Book* • Standards for Evaluating a Cooperative Activity
SECTION 3 **The Mughals Establish an Empire in India** *pp. 71–77*	*The Mughals, Sunni Muslim Turks from Central Asia, conquer India and bring together Turks, Persians, and Indians in a vast empire.*	*In-Depth Resources: Unit 1* • **Guided Reading,** p. 37 • **Geography Application:** Europe Discovers the Riches of India, p. 39 • **Primary Sources:** Akbar, p. 43; Jahangir's Birthday, p. 44 • **History Makers:** Shah Jahan, p. 49 • **Connections Across Time and Cultures:** How To Treat the Conquered, p. 50	PE *Section 3 Assessment,* p. 77 *Formal Assessment* • Section Quiz, p. 31 *Alternative Assessment Book* • Standards for Evaluating a Cooperative Activity
CHAPTER RESOURCES	**Chapter Overview** *In the 14th century, three powerful Islamic empires emerge between India and the Balkans. The Ottomans of Turkey, the Safavids of Persia, and the Mughals of India successfully deal with ethnic, cultural, and religious diversity, but eventually fall prey to internal corruption and external pressure.*	*Telescoping the Times* • Chapter Summary, pp. 9–11 *Planning for Block Schedules*	PE *Chapter Assessment,* pp. 78–79 *Chapter Activities,* p. 79 *Formal Assessment* • Chapter Test, forms A and B, pp. 32–37 *Test Generator* *Alternative Assessment Book*

TECHNOLOGY

 Warm-Up Transparency 18

 Geography Transparencies
- GT18 The Fall of Constantinople, 1453

 World Art and Cultures Transparencies
- AT39 Ottoman miniature painting

 Electronic Library of Primary Sources
"Descriptions of the Turks and the Christians"
"The Fall of Constantinople"

 INTERNET RESOURCES
www.mlworldhistory.com

 Warm-Up Transparency 18

 Electronic Library of Primary Resources
"Report on Persia, Persians, and 'Abbas I'"

 INTERNET RESOURCES
www.mlworldhistory.com

 Warm-Up Transparency 18

Critical Thinking Transparencies
- CT18 Muslim Empires in Anatolia and India
- CT54 Visual Summary

World Art and Cultures Transparencies
- AT22 Great Mosque of Córdova
- AT30 Notre Dame Cathedral
- AT40 Mughal miniature painting

INTERNET RESOURCES
www.mlworldhistory.com

 Chapter Summaries on Audiocassette in English and Spanish

INTERNET RESOURCES
www.mlworldhistory.com

 ## Block Scheduling (90 MINUTES)

Day 1
Section 1, pp. 63–67

 COOPERATIVE ACTIVITY
Reporting on the Fall of Constantinople,
p. 64 (Teacher's Edition)

COOPERATIVE ACTIVITY
Writing Historical Dialogues, p. 69 (Teacher's Edition)

Section Assessments,
pp. 67, 70

Day 2
Section 3, pp. 71–77

 COOPERATIVE ACTIVITY
Debating the Decline of the Mughal Empire,
p. 75 (Teacher's Edition)

Section Assessment,
p. 77

Chapter Assessment,
pp. 78–79

Yearly Pacing *Chapter 2 Total:* 2 days *Yearly Total:* 85 days

 Planning for Block Schedules

Customizing for Special Needs

Students Acquiring English

 Access for Students Acquiring English
- **Guided Reading** for Sections 1–3 (Spanish), pp. 32–34
- **Chapter Summary** (Spanish), pp. 29–31
- **Skillbuilder Practice:** Following Chronological Order (Spanish), p. 35
- **Geography Application:** Europe Discovers the Riches of India (Spanish), p. 36

 Spanish Reading Study Guide
- pp. 25–32

 Chapter Summaries on Audiocassette
in English and Spanish

Less Proficient Readers

 In-Depth Resources: Unit 1
- **Guided Reading** for Sections 1–3, pp. 35–37
- **Skillbuilder Practice** Following Chronological Order, p. 38

Telescoping the Times
- Chapter Summary, pp. 9–11

Reading Study Guide
- pp. 25–32

Chapter Summaries on Audiocassette

Gifted and Talented Students

In-Depth Resources: Unit 1

Primary Sources
- Suleiman the Magnificent, p. 41
- Akbar, p. 43
- Jahangir's Birthday, p. 44

History Makers
- Suleiman, p. 48
- Shah Jahan, p. 49

Connections to Literature READINGS FOR STUDENTS

 In-Depth Resources: Unit 1
Literature: from *The Bride of Suleiman*, p. 45

Enrichment Reading

Beck, Brenda
Folktales of India
Chicago: U of Chicago P, 1987

Colorful stories of origins, families, and difficult choices.

Bon, Ottaviano
The Sultan's Seraglio
London: Sagi, 1966

An intimate portrait of life in the Ottoman Court in Istanbul from 1604–1607.

 = Pupil's Edition   = Overhead Transparency = Software = Video

= Copy Master = CD-ROM = Audiocassette   = Internet

The Muslim World Expands, 1300–1700

Accessing Prior Knowledge

- Ask students to read the captions accompanying each picture and to discuss what they already know about the people, the cultures, and the situations.

Predicting and Making Inferences

- After students look at Shah Jahan's picture and read about him, ask them to predict how his habits may have contributed to the fall of the Mughal Empire.

- Ask students what they can infer about the Ottomans from the painting of the attack on Constantinople.

Geography Connection

Ask students to note the borders of the three Islamic empires shown on the map.

- What geographic feature might have prevented the Mughal Empire from expanding farther east?

- What geographic features gave each empire access to trade routes?

CHAPTER 2
The Muslim World Expands, 1300–1700

PREVIEWING THEMES

Cultural Interaction
As powerful societies moved to expand their empires, Turkish, Mongol, Persian, and Arab ways of life came face to face. The result was a flowering of Islamic culture, which peaked in the 16th century.

Empire Building
Many conquerors emerged in the Muslim world between the 12th and 16th centuries; From their conquests arose three of the great empires of history—the Ottomans in Turkey, the Safavids in Iran, and the Mughals in India.

Power and Authority
The rulers of all three great Muslim empires of this era based their authority on the Islamic religion. Advanced technology and effective artillery supported this authority on the battlefield.

⬌ INTERNET CONNECTION

Visit us at **www.mlworldhistory.com** to learn more about the Ottoman, the Safavid, and the Mughal empires.

EMPIRE BUILDERS, 1700

EUROPE

Black Sea

Adrianople • • Constantinople (Istanbul)

Algiers • • Tunis

Mediterranean Sea

Damascus •

• Cairo

AFRIC

Constantinople was one of the most influential cities of the 15th-century world and seemed invulnerable. Its legend lasted far into the next century, however, when Italian Jacopo Palma Giovane recreated the clamor and chaos of its fall to the **Ottomans** in his painting *The First Attack on Constantinople by the Turks in 1453*. This 51-day Ottoman siege by 125 ships, 100,000 men, and cannons that launched half-ton boulders turned the city into a Muslim outpost.

60

GEOGRAPHY THEMES

Location
Have students note where each of the three empires covered in this chapter is located in relation to the others and to Europe, Asia, and Africa. Which empire had the most direct access to Europe? *Ottoman.* Which empire had the most direct access to Africa? *Ottoman.*

Which empire was most hemmed in by its neighbors? *Safavid.* Have them discuss how location may have affected the policies of each of the individual empires. How might geographical location have influenced the interactions among the three empires?

Region
Remind students that a region is an area that can be considered a unit because it exhibits common geographic, social, or political features. Despite the fact that this area was divided among three distinct empires at the beginning of the 18th century, it also

had general regional characteristics. Have students examine the map, the Previewing Themes box, and the captions, and suggest features that might make these three empires a region. *Religion, similar geography, lack of natural barriers.*

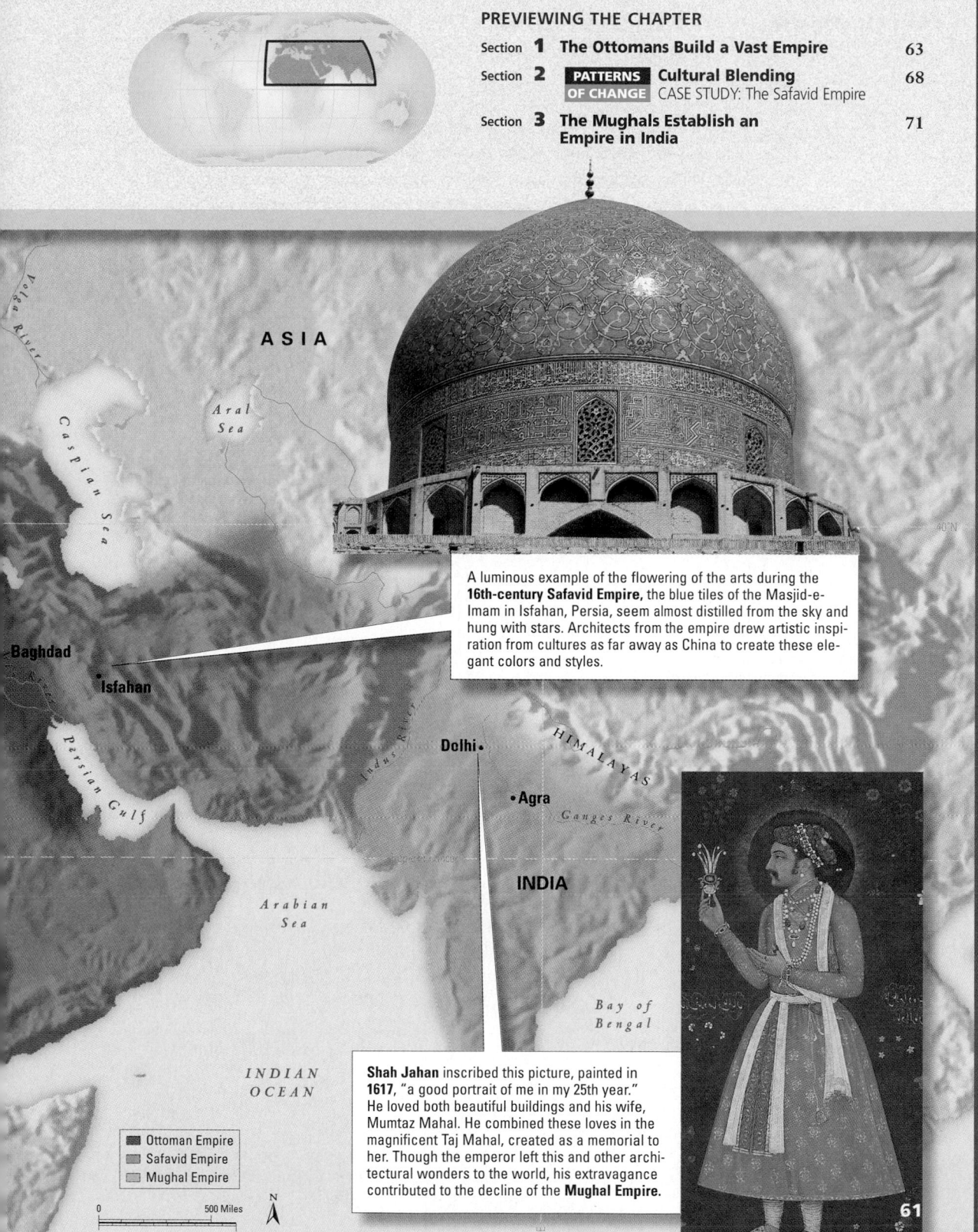

ASIA

A luminous example of the flowering of the arts during the **16th-century Safavid Empire,** the blue tiles of the Masjid-e-Imam in Isfahan, Persia, seem almost distilled from the sky and hung with stars. Architects from the empire drew artistic inspiration from cultures as far away as China to create these elegant colors and styles.

Baghdad

Isfahan

Delhi

Agra

INDIA

Arabian
Sea

Bay of
Bengal

INDIAN
OCEAN

Shah Jahan inscribed this picture, painted in **1617,** "a good portrait of me in my 25th year." He loved both beautiful buildings and his wife, Mumtaz Mahal. He combined these loves in the magnificent Taj Mahal, created as a memorial to her. Though the emperor left this and other architectural wonders to the world, his extravagance contributed to the decline of the **Mughal Empire.**

61

- Ottoman Empire
- Safavid Empire
- Mughal Empire

0   500 Miles
0   1,000 Kilometers

ADDITIONAL RESOURCES

Books for the Teacher

• Mansel, Philip. *Constantinople: City of the World's Desire, 1453-1924.* New York: St. Martin's, 1996.

• Wheatcroft, Andrew. *The Ottomans.* New York: Viking Penguin, 1994. Government, politics, and social customs in the Ottoman Empire.

• Richards, J. F. *The Mughal Empire.* New York: Cambridge UP, 1993. Political and economic history under the Mughals.

Books for the Student

• Irving, Clive. *Crossroads of Civilization: 3,000 Years of Persian History.* New York: Barnes & Noble, 1980. Dramatic history of Persia, 559 B.C.–A.D. 1941.

• Wigner, Annabel. *Elizabeth and Akbar: Portraits of Power.* New York: Dufour, 1987.

Videos

• *Ancient and Modern: The Fall and Rise of the Middle East.* Britannica, 1984. 800 554 9862. Probes the factors that retarded Ottoman growth.

• *The Ottoman Empire: 1280-1683.* Social Studies School Service, 1985. 800-421-4246. Profiles the Ottoman sultans and depicts their vast empire.

• *Suleyman the Magnificent.* Lucerne Media, 1990. 800-341-2293. Dramatizes the achievements of the Ottoman sultan.

HISTORY THROUGH ART

The First Attack on Constantinople by the Turks in 1453
Jacopo Palma Giovane

Jacopo Palma Giovane (1544–1628) was a leading artist in Venice in the early 17th century. He was an assistant to the renowned Renaissance painter Titian and completed that artist's Pietá, one of the greatest works of Italian art, after Titian's death.

Palma Giovane was known primarily for his depiction of historical subjects. In this portrayal of the siege of Constantinople by Turkish Muslims under the Ottoman ruler Mehmet II, he captures all the emotion and drama of the five-week conflict. The overall darkness of the painting conveys the confusion and desperation of a battle fought through a long night. The flaming reds of the Turks' tunics and weapons and the face of the soldier in the foreground seem to

be illuminated by the imminent Turkish victory.

Interpreting the Art Do you think this painting offers a realistic or an idealized view of the siege of Constantinople? What details or overall characteristics of the painting make you think so?

Interact *with* History

Interact *with* History

This Interact with History feature motivates students by inviting them to put themselves in the position of a 15th-century Ottoman sultan. Students will analyze the issues the conquerors of people with diverse customs faced, explore various options for dealing with the conquered people, and become decision makers.

Purpose

• to help students understand some of the issues that faced empire builders

• to provide an introduction to the concept of cultural blending

• to set the stage for the study of the growth of three Muslim empires

Teaching Strategy

Thinking Critically After students have imagined themselves in the situation described on this page, have them answer the key question and give reasons for their decisions.

EXAMINING *the* ISSUES

Following are suggestions for addressing each bulleted question.

1 Have students consider what it might feel like to be taken captive and forced to adopt a different way of life. How might they resist or show their dissatisfaction?

2 Have students think about how the United States has tried to integrate its own conquered people—Native Americans—into the society. How successful have these efforts been?

3 Ask students to brainstorm ways in which people of many customs and religions in the United States have learned to coexist. What similar strategies might the Ottomans have developed?

Making Connections Ask students to discuss the responsibilities of a conqueror to the people he conquers.

You are a 15th-century Ottoman sultan, the ruler of a growing empire. To increase your power and control over the area, you go to war against your neighbors. With a well-trained army and modern weapons, you conquer most of them easily. They do not share your religion and way of life, however, and if you allow them too much freedom, they might rebel. On the other hand, enslaving them and keeping them under strict control might sap your empire's resources.

How will you treat the people you conquer?

This Ottoman sultan sees conquered people as an asset to his empire and integrates them into his court.

The Ottomans force young Christian boys from conquered territories to become soldiers and convert to Islam. Many miss their old way of life terribly and resent serving as slaves to the sultan. Others see this as a way to improve their lives.

Once a slave himself, this man has been rewarded for his competence and good leadership. He kneels and swears allegiance to the sultan, who has appointed him leader of the elite military corps and adviser to the throne.

Military chiefs (left) and scholars (right) wear distinctive headgear to identify their rank. Drawn from all segments of Ottoman society, they are united in their loyal service to the sultan.

EXAMINING *the* ISSUES

• What problems might conquered people present for a conqueror?

• In what ways might a conqueror integrate those he conquers into the society?

• How might people of various religions and customs coexist without giving up their ways of life?

As a class, discuss the ways other empires, such as Rome or Egypt, treated their conquered peoples.

As you read, consider why the Ottomans developed their unique system of slavery. Do you think it was effective?

Follow Up

A feature on the chapter assessment will ask students to reevaluate their responses to the situation presented on this page.

1 The Ottomans Build a Vast Empire

TERMS & NAMES
- ghazi
- Osman
- Timur the Lame
- Mehmet II
- Suleiman the Lawgiver
- janissary
- *devshirme*

MAIN IDEA

The Ottomans established a Muslim empire that combined many cultures and lasted for more than 600 years.

WHY IT MATTERS NOW

Many modern societies—from Algeria to the Balkan countries—had their origins under Ottoman rule.

SETTING THE STAGE In 1300, the Byzantine Empire had begun to shrink, and the Mongols had destroyed the Turkish Seljuk sultanate, or kingdom, of Rum. Anatolia was inhabited mostly by the descendants of nomadic Turks. They were a militaristic people who had a long history of invading other countries. They were loyal to their own groups and were not united by a strong central power.

Turks Settle in Christian Byzantium

Vocabulary
emir: a prince or chief (derived from the Arabic *'amir,* meaning "commander").

Many Anatolian Turks saw themselves as **ghazis** (GAH·zees), or warriors for Islam. The ghazis were similar to the Christian knights in Europe during the Middle Ages. However, they formed military societies under the leadership of an emir and followed a strict Islamic code of conduct. They raided the territories of the "infidels," or people who didn't believe in Islam. These "infidels" lived on the frontiers of the Byzantine Empire.

Osman Establishes a State The most successful ghazi was **Osman.** People in the West called him Othman, however, and named his followers Ottomans. Osman built a small state in Anatolia between 1300 and 1326. His successors expanded it by buying land, forming alliances with other emirs, and conquering everyone they could.

The Ottomans' military success was largely based on the use of gunpowder. They replaced their archers on horseback with musket-carrying foot soldiers. They also were among the first people to use cannons as offensive weapons. Even heavily walled cities fell to an all-out attack by the Turks.

The second Ottoman leader, Orkhan I, felt strong enough to declare himself sultan, meaning "overlord" or "one with power." And in 1361, the Ottomans captured Adrianople (ay·dree·uh·NOH·puhl), the second most important city in the Byzantine Empire. A new Turkish Empire was on the rise.

The Ottomans acted kindly toward the people they conquered, however. They ruled through local officials appointed by the sultan and often improved the lives of the peasants. Most Muslims were required to serve in Turkish armies but did not have to pay a personal tax to the state. Non-Muslims did not have to serve in the army but had to pay the tax.

Timur the Lame Rebels Most of the conquered peoples seem to have adjusted to this somewhat lenient rule. The rise of the Ottoman Empire was briefly interrupted in the early 1400s, though, by a rebellious warrior and conqueror from Samarkand in central Asia. He was called Timur-i-Lang, or **Timur the Lame,** in his homeland. Europeans called him Tamerlane. Timur claimed to be descended

HISTORY MAKERS

Osman
1258–1326?

Osman I was just one of many ghazi princes who operated along the Byzantine frontier until 1301. At that time he gained sudden fame by defeating a 2,000-man Byzantine army with a much smaller force. This victory drew people eager for adventure, and enabled Osman to undertake larger conquests.

Osman's greatest success came in the last year of his life. That year his forces conquered the city of Bursa in northwest Turkey. Osman himself was too old and weak to lead the battle. Therefore, his son, Orkhan, commanded the troops. When Osman died, he probably had no idea that this conquest marked the birth of one of history's largest and longest-lived empires.

The Muslim World Expands **63**

SECTION 1 RESOURCES

PRINT RESOURCES

 IN-DEPTH RESOURCES: UNIT 1
Guided Reading, p. 35
Skillbuilder Practice: Following Chronological Order, p.38
Primary Source: Suleiman the Magnificent, p. 41
Literature: from *The Bride of Suleiman,* p. 45
History Makers: Suleiman, p. 48

 ACCESS FOR STUDENTS ACQUIRING ENGLISH
Guided Reading (Spanish), p. 32
Skillbuilder Practice, (Spanish), p. 35

 FORMAL ASSESSMENT
Section Quiz, p. 29

TECHNOLOGY RESOURCES

GEOGRAPHY TRANSPARENCIES
GT18 The Fall of Constantinople, 1453

WORLD ART AND CULTURES TRANSPARENCIES
AT39 Ottoman miniature painting

CD-ROM
Electronic Library of Primary Sources

INTERNET www.mlworldhistory.com

Section 1 Overview

OBJECTIVES

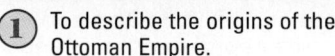 To describe the origins of the Ottoman Empire.

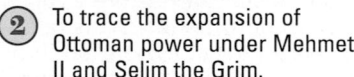 To trace the expansion of Ottoman power under Mehmet II and Selim the Grim.

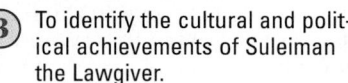 To identify the cultural and political achievements of Suleiman the Lawgiver.

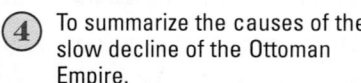 To summarize the causes of the slow decline of the Ottoman Empire.

SKILLBUILDERS
- Interpreting maps: region, movement, p. 65
- Interpreting charts, p. 66

CRITICAL THINKING
- Recognizing effects, p. 64
- Analyzing motives, p. 64
- Making inferences, p. 66
- Summarizing, p. 67
- Evaluating decisions, p. 67
- Analyzing themes, p. 67

FOCUS
5-Minute Warm-Up

▶ *Interpreting Maps*
To help students gain an appreciation of the extent of the Ottoman Empire, have them answer the following questions.

1. Look at the map on p. 65. What continents did the Ottoman Empire include?

2. What bodies of water might have facilitated the expansion of the empire?

 WARM-UP TRANSPARENCY 2

OBJECTIVE ① INSTRUCT

Turks Settle in Christian Byzantium

▶ *Key Ideas*
- Bands of Muslim warriors called ghazis carve out a state in Byzantine Anatolia.
- Timur the Lame crushes the Ottomans and slows the growth of the empire.

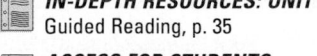 **IN-DEPTH RESOURCES: UNIT 1**
Guided Reading, p. 35

 ACCESS FOR STUDENTS ACQUIRING ENGLISH
Guided Reading (Spanish), p. 32

(See page 63.)

Osman and his followers adopted the white cap of the ghazis and wore it to set themselves apart from ordinary people. This headgear was later incorporated into the outfits of the Ottoman janissary corps. Why do you think the Ottomans retained this symbol of their ghazi roots?

OBJECTIVE **2** INSTRUCT

Powerful Sultans Spur Dramatic Expansion

▶ Key Ideas
- Led by Mehmet II, the Ottomans take Constantinople and end the Byzantine Empire.
- Selim the Grim expands the Ottoman Empire into North Africa.

 ELECTRONIC LIBRARY OF PRIMARY SOURCES
"Descriptions of the Turks and the Christians"

CRITICAL THINKING ACTIVITY
CLASS TIME: 10 MINUTES

Hypothesizing
Ask students to consider whether the Ottomans would have been able to build an empire if they had not taken Constantinople. Students might list reasons for both possible answers in a two-column chart before deciding.

Could Build an Empire	Could Not Build an Empire

---

from the Mongol conqueror, Genghis Khan. Although historians doubt the truth of this claim, Timur was certainly as ferocious as Genghis Khan. He was also physically impressive. Tall and with a large head, he had a dark, rosy complexion. This was set off by white hair, which he had had since he was a child.

Timur conquered both Russia and Persia. He also burned the powerful city of Baghdad in present-day Iraq to the ground. In 1398, he swept through northern India, leaving destruction and decaying corpses in his wake. He butchered the inhabitants of Delhi and made a pyramid of their skulls. Moving back west into Anatolia, he crushed the Ottoman forces at the Battle of Ankara in 1402. This defeat halted the expansion of their empire. Timur then took their sultan back to Samarkand in an iron cage. The sultan died in captivity. Timur himself died three years later on his way to conquer China. His body was returned to Samarkand, where he was buried in a magnificent tomb. That tomb remains a glorious sight today.

Timur the Lame's steely strength blazes from his eyes in this painting by an unknown 14th-century Italian artist.

Powerful Sultans Spur Dramatic Expansion

As soon as Timur moved out of Anatolia on the way to China, war broke out among the four sons of the Ottoman sultan. Mehmet I defeated his brothers and took the throne. His son, Murad II, restored the Ottoman military to its former power. Murad defeated the Venetians, invaded Hungary, and overcame an army of Italian crusaders in the Balkans. He was the first of four powerful sultans who kept the Ottoman Empire expanding through 1566.

Mehmet II Conquers Constantinople Murad's son **Mehmet II,** or Mehmet the Conqueror, achieved the most dramatic feat in Ottoman history. By the time Mehmet took power in 1451, the ancient city of Constantinople had shrunk from a population of a million to a mere 50,000. Although it controlled no territory outside its walls, it still dominated the Bosporus Strait. Controlling this waterway meant that it could choke off traffic between the Ottomans' territories in Asia and in the Balkans.

Mehmet II decided to face this situation head-on. "Give me Constantinople!" he thundered, shortly after taking power at age 21. He spent two years building a force of 125 ships and 100,000 foot soldiers. Then, in April 1453, he launched his attack. The Byzantine emperor in Constantinople sent desperate appeals to the Christian West, but only 700 volunteers from Italy responded.

Mehmet's forces began firing on the city walls with mighty cannons. One of these was a 26-foot gun that fired 1,200-pound boulders. Constantinople's 7,000 defenders could barely man all the walls. A chain across the Golden Horn between the Bosporus Strait and the Sea of Marmara kept the Turkish fleet out of the city's harbor. But beginning on the night of April 21, Mehmet's army advanced. They dragged 70 ships over a hill on greased runners from the Bosporus to the harbor. Constantinople was thus under attack from two sides. The city held out for five weeks, but the Turks finally found a break in the wall and gained entry to the city. The Muslim historian Oruc reported:

> **A VOICE FROM THE PAST**
> The ghazis, entering by force on every side, found a way in through the breaches in the fortress made by the guns. . . . Mounting on the tower they destroyed the infidels who were inside and entered the city. They looted and plundered. They seized their money and possessions and made their sons and daughters slaves. . . . They plundered for three days, and after three days plunder was forbidden.
>
> ORUC, quoted in *The Muslim Discovery of Europe*

THINK THROUGH HISTORY
A. Recognizing Effects What were Timur the Lame's accomplishments?
A. Answer He brought Russia, Persia, and India under his control and stopped the expansion of the Ottoman Empire.

THINK THROUGH HISTORY
B. Analyzing Motives Why was taking Constantinople so important to Mehmet II?
B. Answer It controlled many waterways that kept the Ottoman Empire divided.

Background
Conquerors did not usually limit the plundering of the cities they captured. Mehmet stopped the sacking of Constantinople after three days to protect the treasures he had won.

Task: Students will prepare a newscast documenting the fall of Constantinople.

Purpose: To experience the drama and significance of this historical event.

Activity: Working as a class, students will plan and present a multifaceted newscast, including segments such as a summary of the week's events,

reports of up-to-the-minute developments, debates between Turkish and Byzantine officials, human-interest stories, on-the-scene interviews, and editorial commentaries.

Small groups of students should each choose a segment of the newscast to work on. One group should take responsibility for organizing the individual segments into a finished newscast.

 ALTERNATIVE ASSESSMENT BOOK
Standards for Evaluating a Cooperative Activity

 GEOGRAPHY TRANSPARENCIES:
GT18 The Fall of Constantinople, 1453

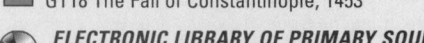 **ELECTRONIC LIBRARY OF PRIMARY SOURCES**
"The Fall of Constantinople"

Mehmet then proceeded to the Hagia Sophia on the Bosporus. This was the most important church in the Eastern Christian world. Reportedly, he found a soldier hacking at the marble floors. The church now belonged to the Muslim sultan. Therefore, Mehmet insisted that it be treated with respect. He had the soldier put to death. He then declared the Hagia Sophia a mosque. Muslim prayers were held there the first Friday the Ottomans occupied the city.

Mehmet the Conqueror, as he was now called, proved to be an able ruler as well as a magnificent warrior. He opened Constantinople to new citizens of many religions and backgrounds. Jews, Christians, and Muslims, Turks and non-Turks all flowed in. They helped rebuild the city that was now called Istanbul.

Background
Between the reigns of Mehmet II and Selim the Grim, Bayazid II oversaw the internal development and economic growth of the Ottoman Empire.

Selim the Grim Takes Islam's Holy Cities The next important sultan came to power in 1512. He did so by overthrowing his father and murdering his brothers. To protect his position, he also executed his nephews and all but one of his sons. It is small wonder that he is known as Selim the Grim. For all his brutality, Selim was an effective sultan and a great general. In 1514, he defeated the Safavids (suh·FAH·vihdz) of Persia at the Battle of Chaldiran. Then he swept south through Syria and Palestine and into North Africa. At the same time that Cortez was toppling the Aztec Empire in the Americas, Selim captured Mecca and Medina, the holiest cities of Islam. Finally he took Cairo, the intellectual center of the Muslim world. This conquest ended the Egyptian Mameluke Dynasty. The once-great civilization of Egypt had become just another province in the growing Ottoman Empire.

Suleiman the Lawgiver

Mehmet the Conqueror and Selim the Grim had achieved impressive military successes. However, the Ottoman Empire didn't reach its peak size and grandeur until the reign of Selim's son, Suleiman I (SOO·lay·mahn). Suleiman came to the throne in

MORE ABOUT . . .
Selim the Grim
Like many tyrants of his age, Selim was fond of literature and the arts and wrote poetry in three languages. But his troops knew him as *Yafuz*—"the Inflexible." He went through subordinate officers called viziers at such a clip that the phrase, "May you become the Sultan's vizier" came to be understood as a curse.

OBJECTIVE ③ INSTRUCT

Suleiman the Lawgiver

▶ *Key Ideas*
- Suleiman's conquests expand the empire to its greatest size.
- An efficient social structure incorporates Christian slaves in a policy known as *devshirme*.
- Ottoman achievements under Suleiman include liberal laws and architectural masterpieces.

History from Visuals

Ottoman Empire, 1451–1566
Interpreting the Map Point out that the box at the upper left explains the colors that show the size of the Ottoman Empire during a particular period of time. Which color shows the conquests of Selim the Grim (1512–1520)? *Orange.*

SKILLBUILDER Answers
1. 1521
2. Caucasus Mountains

Ottoman Empire, 1451–1566

Ottoman Empire, 1451
Acquisitions to 1481
Acquisitions to 1521
Acquisitions to 1566
★ Battles

AUSTRIA
Vienna 1529
HUNGARY
Mohács 1526
Danube R.
Belgrade
CRIMEA
Dniester R.
Black Sea
CAUCASUS
Caspian Sea
40° N
ITALY
Rome
Adriatic Sea
BALKANS
GOLDEN HORN
Bosporus
Istanbul (Constantinople)
Madrid
Naples
Taranto
SPAIN
Palermo
GREECE
Lepanto 1571
Athens
Chaldiran 1514
Tehran
Algiers
Tunis
ALGERIA
TUNISIA
Mediterranean Sea
Crete
Cyprus
SYRIA
Euphrates R.
Tigris R.
Baghdad
PERSIA
AFRICA
Tripoli
PALESTINE
Jerusalem
Damascus
MESOPOTAMIA
Cairo
EGYPT
ARABIA
Nile R.
Red Sea
Persian Gulf
SAHARA DESERT
Medina
Tripoli
TRIPOLI
Tropic of Cancer

0 500 Miles
0 1,000 Kilometers

GEOGRAPHY SKILLBUILDER:
Interpreting Maps
1. **Region** By what year did the Ottoman Empire reach its farthest westward extent?
2. **Movement** What landforms might have prevented the Ottomans from expanding farther east?

65

TEACHING OPTION **BLOCK SCHEDULING** **SKILLBUILDER MINI-LESSON: Following Chronological Order** **CLASS TIME 15 MINUTES**

Explaining the Skill Understanding the relationships between events—causes and effects, problems and solutions—depends on knowing how the events relate in time. Using dates provided in the text and clue words about time, such as *Then he swept south . . .* and *At the same time that Cortez . . .* found on this page, students can place events they read about in correct chronological order.

Applying the Skill Ask students to make a time line of events in the development of the Ottoman Empire from Osman's capture of Adrianople through Selim the Grim's defeat of the Safavids at the Battle of Chaldiran.

IN-DEPTH RESOURCES: UNIT 1
Skillbuilder Practice: Following Chronological Order, p. 38

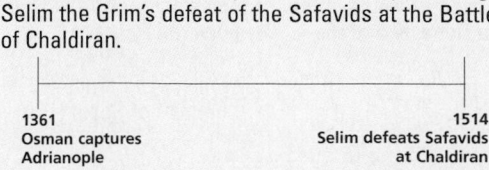

1361
Osman captures Adrianople

1514
Selim defeats Safavids at Chaldiran

1520 and ruled for 46 years. His own people called him **Suleiman the Lawgiver.** He was known in the West, though, as Suleiman the Magnificent. This title was a tribute to the splendor of his court and to his cultural achievements.

The Empire Reaches Its Limits Suleiman was above all a military leader. He conquered the important city of Belgrade in 1521. The next year, Turkish forces captured the island of Rhodes in the Mediterranean. With that conquest, the Ottomans dominated the whole eastern Mediterranean.

Applying their immense naval power, they captured Tripoli. They then continued conquering peoples along the North African coastline. Finally, they reached the Moroccan border. Although the Ottomans occupied only the coastal cities of Africa, they managed to control trade routes to the interior of the continent.

In 1525, Suleiman advanced into Hungary and Austria, throwing central Europe into a panic. Suleiman's armies then pushed to the outskirts of Vienna, Austria. But there the Ottoman expansion ended. When the 1529 siege of Vienna failed, Suleiman devoted himself to domestic affairs for two years. He then moved his forces east to deal with border uprisings with Safavid Persia. Reigning from Istanbul, Suleiman had waged war with central Europeans, North Africans, and central Asians. He had become the most powerful monarch on earth. Only Charles V, head of the Hapsburg Empire in Europe, came close to rivaling his power.

Highly Structured Social Organization Suleiman's massive Ottoman Empire required an efficient government structure and social organization. The empire was a complex military state. The Ottoman family—a dynasty that ruled for 600 years—held the power. Surrounding the family was the palace bureaucracy. It was staffed by the sultan's 20,000 personal slaves.

Among the sultan's slaves were the **janissaries.** This elite force of 30,000 was drawn from the peoples of conquered Christian territories as part of a policy called ***devshirme*** (dehv·SHEER·meh). Under the *devshirme* system, the sultan's army took boys from their families, educated them, converted them to Islam, and trained them as soldiers. Their superb discipline made them the heart of the Ottoman war machine. In fact, Christian families sometimes bribed officials to take their children into the janissary corps, because the brightest ones could rise to high government posts. The Ottomans also took non-Muslim girls from their families to become slaves to the wealthy.

In accordance with Islamic law, the Ottomans granted freedom of worship to other religious communities—particularly to Christians and Jews. They treated these communities as *millets*, or nations. They allowed each to follow its own religious laws and

Suleiman the Lawgiver's magnificent turban marked him as an influential man. But it was his outstanding contributions to Ottoman territory and culture that made his mark in history.

Organization of Ottoman Government

Sultan
Supreme military and political ruler

Imperial Council (Divan)
Advisers drawn from *devshirme*

Social / Military Administration
Local administrators/military
Landowners/tax collectors

Religious / Judicial Administration
Heads of individual religious *millets*
Muslim   Jewish   Christian

SKILLBUILDER: Interpreting Charts
1. *What was the relationship between the heads of the religious millets and the military leaders?*
2. *How does this organization show the incorporation of conquered peoples?*

66 Chapter 2

practices. The head of the *millets* reported to the sultan and his staff. This patchwork system kept conflict among people of the various religions to a minimum. But it may have sowed the seeds of modern ethnic conflicts in the area.

Cultural Achievements Binding the Ottoman Empire together in a workable social structure was surely Suleiman's crowning achievement. Suleiman was required to follow Islamic law, which covered most social matters. He did, however, simplify the system of taxation and reduce the government bureaucracy. These two changes bettered the daily life of almost every citizen. These reforms helped earn him the title of Lawgiver.

Suleiman had broad interests, which contributed to the cultural achievements of the empire. Even amid his many military campaigns, he found time to study poetry, history, geography, astronomy, mathematics, and architecture. He employed one of the world's finest architects, Sinan, who was probably from Albania. Sinan's masterpiece, the Mosque of Suleiman, is an immense complex topped with domes and half domes. It includes four schools, a college, a library, a bath, and a hospital.

Art and literature also flourished under Suleiman's rule. Both painters and poets looked to Persia and Arabia for models. The works that they produced used these foreign influences to express original Ottoman ideas in the Turkish style.

Despite Suleiman's magnificent social and cultural achievements and his splendid city of Istanbul, though, the Ottoman Empire was losing ground. Its decline had already begun.

Suleiman's artistic nature was reflected in everything he did, including his signature (above).

THINK THROUGH HISTORY
D. Summarizing
What were the major cultural achievements of Suleiman's reign?
D. Answer Legal reforms, architecture, art, literature.

The Empire Declines Slowly

Suleiman himself set the stage for this decline. Perhaps fearing for his position, he killed his ablest son and drove another into exile. His third son, the incompetent Selim II, inherited the throne. In 1571, Spain and Italy destroyed Selim's Turkish fleet at the Battle of Lepanto. This was a rare defeat for the Ottomans' superior sea power.

At the same time, corruption was eating away at the government. As each sultan grew older, his possible heirs began jockeying for power. It became customary for each new sultan to have his brothers strangled with the silk string of a bow. The sultan would then keep his sons prisoner in the harem, cutting them off from education or contact with the world. This practice produced a long line of weak, ignorant sultans who eventually brought ruin on the empire.

The great Ottoman Empire crumbled slowly. It continued to influence the world into the early 20th century. It was finally dissolved with the creation of the nation of Turkey after World War I. But throughout its long life, other Muslim empires were on the rise.

Section 1 Assessment

1. TERMS & NAMES
Identify
- ghazi
- Osman
- Timur the Lame
- Mehmet II
- Suleiman the Lawgiver
- janissary
- *devshirme*

2. TAKING NOTES
Using a chart like the one below, list the main rulers of the Ottoman Empire and their chief accomplishments.

Ottoman Ruler	Major Accomplishment

Rank these leaders in order of their impact on the Ottoman Empire.

3. EVALUATING DECISIONS
Do you think that the Ottomans were wise in staffing their military and government with slaves? Why or why not?

THINK ABOUT
- the loyalty of slaves to the sultan
- the training slaves received
- others who might have served in the government

4. ANALYZING THEMES
Empire Building Do you think that Suleiman's religious tolerance helped or hurt the Ottoman Empire? Explain.

THINK ABOUT
- Suleiman's treatment of non-Muslims
- the effect on the individual religious groups
- the long-term effect on the empire as a whole

The Muslim World Expands **67**

MORE ABOUT . . .
Sinan
Sinan was a janissary—a Christian boy taken from his home in Albania as a child and raised as a Muslim and a slave of the sultan. He was a military engineer until age 50 and did not begin his career as an architect until after he had retired from the military. In his retirement he designed 80 grand mosques and many prayer houses, bridges, palaces, and public baths.

OBJECTIVE 4 INSTRUCT

The Empire Declines Slowly

▶ *Key Idea*
- Internal problems and a series of weak sultans result in the slow decline of the Ottoman Empire.

ASSESS & RETEACH

Section 1 Assessment
Divide the class and have students debate question 3, using events from Ottoman history to support their arguments.

Section Quiz
FORMAL ASSESSMENT
Section Quiz, p. 29

Reteaching Activity
CLASS TIME: 10 MINUTES

Have students work in pairs to create a chart that answers the questions *who, what, where, when, why,* and *how* about the Ottoman Empire.

CLOSE ACTIVITY

CLASS TIME: 15 MINUTES

Perceiving Causes and Effects
Ask students to work together to construct a chart that summarizes the events and people that contributed to the expansion and decline of the Ottoman Empire.

ANSWERS

1. TERMS & NAMES
ghazi, p. 63
Osman, p. 63
Timur the Lame, p. 63
Mehmet II, p. 64
Suleiman the Lawgiver, p. 66
janissary, p. 66
devshirme, p. 66

2. TAKING NOTES
Possible Responses: Osman—establishes Ottoman state; Murad II—expands empire; Mehmet II—conquers Constantinople; Selim the Grim—defeats Safavids and captures Islamic holy cities; Suleiman I— unifies and expands empire; Selim II—loses Battle of Lepanto.

Students may cite Suleiman I as having the greatest impact.

3. EVALUATING DECISIONS
Possible Responses: Yes—Slaves received excellent education and training and had the chance to rise to high positions; they were loyal to the sultan. No—Slaves were forcibly taken from their homes and would be alert for opportunities to rebel or escape from the palace.

4. ANALYZING THEMES
Possible Responses: Helped—kept people of various religions happy; Hurt—did not encourage people to think of themselves as part of one Ottoman nation.

Teacher's Edition **67**

To explain how cultural blending results in new cultures.

② To summarize the rise and fall of the Safivids.

SKILLBUILDERS
• Interpreting charts, p. 68
• Interpreting maps: movement, location, p. 70

CRITICAL THINKING
• Summarizing, p. 68
• Making inferences, p. 69
• Comparing, p. 70
• Analyzing motives, p. 70

FOCUS
5-Minute Warm-Up

Interpreting Charts
To introduce students to the concept of cultural blending, have them answer these questions.

1. Look at the chart on page 68. What activities cause cultures to interact?

2. What generalizations can you draw about where and when cultural blending takes place?

 WARM-UP TRANSPARENCY 2

OBJECTIVE ① INSTRUCT

Patterns of Cultural Blending

Key Ideas
• Cultures interact as migration, trade, war, and spread of religions bring peoples into contact.
• Cultural blending is an important ongoing pattern in world history.

 IN-DEPTH RESOURCES: UNIT 1
Guided Reading, p. 36

 ACCESS FOR STUDENTS ACQUIRING ENGLISH
Guided Reading (Spanish), p. 33

 ELECTRONIC LIBRARY OF PRIMARY SOURCES
"Report on Persia, Persians, and 'Abbas I"

---

② Cultural Blending

PATTERNS OF CHANGE   CASE STUDY: The Safavid Empire

MAIN IDEA	WHY IT MATTERS NOW
Many world cultures incorporate influences from various peoples and traditions.	Modern Iran, which plays a key role in global politics, is descended from the culturally diverse Safavid Empire.

SETTING THE STAGE The Ottoman Empire provides a striking example of how inter-action among peoples can produce a blending of cultures. This mixture often com-bines the best of contributing cultures in new and exciting ways.

Patterns of Cultural Blending

As the 17th-century British poet John Donne observed, "No man is an island." But no group of people, or culture, is an island, either. Throughout history, peoples have min-gled and interacted, giving rise to new cultural blends.

Causes of Cultural Blending Cultural blending usually occurs in places where two or more cultures interact. This interaction most often is prompted by one or a combi-nation of the following four activities: migration, trade, conquest, and pursuit of reli-gious converts or religious freedom. Societies that are able to benefit from cultural blending are open to new ways and willing to adapt and change.

The blending that contributed to the culture of the Ottomans, for example, depended on all of these activities except migration. Surrounded by the peoples of Christian Byzantium, the Turks were motivated to win both territory for their empire and converts to their Muslim religion. Suleiman's interest in learning and culture prompted him to bring the best foreign artists and scholars to his court.

Cultural Blending Through History Similar patterns of blending have occurred throughout the world and across the ages. A few examples are shown below.

A. Answer
Migration, trade, con-quest, pursuit of reli-gious converts or religious freedom.
THINK THROUGH HISTORY
A. Summarizing
What four activities often contribute to cultural blending?

PATTERNS OF CHANGE: Cultural Blending

Location	Interacting Cultures	Reason for Interaction	Some Results of Interaction
India—1000 B.C.	Aryan and Dravidian Indian	Migration	Vedic culture, forerunner of Hinduism
East Africa—A.D. 700	Arab, African, Indian, Islamic, Christian	Trade, religious converts	New trade language, Swahili
Russia—A.D. 1000	Christian and Slavic	Religious converts	Eastern Christianity, Russian identity
Mexico—A.D. 1500	Spanish and Aztec Indian	Conquest	Mestizo culture, Mexican Catholicism
United States—A.D. 1900	European, Asian, Caribbean	Migration, religious freedom	Cultural diversity

SKILLBUILDER: Interpreting Charts
1. *What aspects of culture, such as language and religion, did these cultural blendings affect?*
2. *What evidence of cultural blending do you see in the United States today?*

SECTION 2 RESOURCES

PRINT RESOURCES

 IN-DEPTH RESOURCES: UNIT 1
Guided Reading, p. 36

 ACCESS FOR STUDENTS ACQUIRING ENGLISH
Guided Reading (Spanish), p. 33

 FORMAL ASSESSMENT
Section Quiz, p. 30

ALTERNATIVE ASSESSMENT BOOK

TECHNOLOGY RESOURCES

 CD-ROM
Electronic Library of Primary Sources

 INTERNET www.mlworldhistory.com

The Safavids Build a Shi'i Empire

Conquest and ongoing cultural interaction also fueled the development of another empire—the **Safavids.** Originally, the Safavids were members of an Islamic religious brotherhood. They were named after their founder, Safi al-Din, who died in 1334. Although the Safavids were of Iranian origin, they claimed that they were descended from the prophet Muhammad. In the 15th century, the Safavids aligned themselves with the Shi'i branch of Islam.

The Shi'i Safavids were persecuted on religious grounds by the Ottoman Sunni Muslims. This treatment was a departure from the Sunni's traditional religious tolerance. The Safavids were also squeezed geographically between the Ottomans and Uzbek tribespeople. (See the map on page 70.) To protect themselves from these potential enemies, the Safavids concentrated on building a powerful army.

Isma'il Conquers Persia The Safavid military became a force to reckon with. They wore unique red headgear with 12 folds, and so became known as the "redheads." In 1499, the leader of the redheads was a 14-year-old named **Isma'il** (is·MAH·eel). Despite his youth, he was a brilliant warrior. Within two years, he had seized most of what is now Iran. To celebrate his achievement, he took the ancient Persian title of shah, or king. He also established Shi'i Islam as the state religion:

> **A VOICE FROM THE PAST**
> [Isma'il] is loved and revered by his people as a god, and especially by his soldiers, many of whom enter into battle without armour, expecting their master . . . to watch over them in the fight. . . . The name of God is forgotten throughout Persia and only that of Isma'il is remembered.
> **A 16TH-CENTURY VENETIAN TRAVELER,** quoted in *Encyclopedia of Islam*

Despite the reverence of his people, however, Isma'il became a religious tyrant. Any citizen who did not convert to Shi'ism was put to death. Isma'il destroyed the Sunni population of Baghdad in his confrontation with the Ottomans. Their leader, Selim the Grim, later ordered the execution of all Shi'a in the Ottoman Empire. As many as 40,000 died. Their final faceoff was at the Battle of Chaldiran in 1514. But the confrontation between the cultures did not end then. In fact, it still continues today.

Isma'il's son Tahmasp took up the struggle. He expanded the Safavid Empire up to the Caucasus Mountains northeast of Turkey and brought Christians under Safavid rule. In adding this territory to the empire, Tahmasp laid the groundwork for the golden age of the Safavids.

Cultural Blending During the Reign of Shah Abbas This golden age came under **Shah Abbas,** or Abbas the Great. He took the throne in 1587. During his reign, he helped create a Safavid culture that drew from the best of the Ottoman, Persian, and Arab worlds.

Shah Abbas reformed both military and civilian aspects of life. He limited the power of the military redheads. He then created two new armies that would be loyal to him alone. One of these was an army of Persians. The other was a force like the Ottoman janissaries, which Abbas recruited from the Christian north. He equipped both of these armies with modern artillery. Abbas also reformed his government. He punished corruption severely and promoted only officials who proved their competence and loyalty.

Shah Abbas established relations with Europe. As a result, industry and art flourished. He also brought Chinese artisans to the

THINK THROUGH HISTORY
B. Making Inferences Which of Isma'il's traits do you think made him such a successful conqueror?
B. Possible Answers His expertise as a warrior; his singleminded devotion to Shi'i Islam; his ruthlessness.

GlobalImpact

First Persian Empire
The Safavid Empire was not the first empire to unite Persia. Centuries before, from about 550 to 350 B.C., the Persian Empire ruled many different people and a vast territory that stretched over 2000 miles.

To control such a huge empire, the Persians combined a strong military with tolerance and respect for people's customs and religions. The Persians also held their empire together by using an efficient administration of 20 provinces, each with its own governor, army leader, and inspector, who answered only to the king.

Thousands of years after the Persian Empire ended, the Safavids maintained control by using a type of government administration similar to the Persians.

 VIDEO *Building Empires: The Rise of the Persians and the Inca*

History from Visuals

Patterns of Change: Cultural Blending
(See page 68.)

Interpreting the Chart Make sure students understand that they should read across each row of the chart to learn about cultural blending in each of the five locations listed. What was the cause of cultural blending in Mexico?

Extension Activity Have students discuss how they would fill in the columns of the chart for the Ottoman Empire.

SKILLBUILDER Answers
1. Language, religion, cultural diversity.
2. Intermixing of customs, religions, languages, and races.

OBJECTIVE ① INSTRUCT

The Safavids Build a Shi'i Empire

▶ *Key Ideas*
- Isma'il conquers Persia in the name of Shi'i Islam.
- Shah Abbas brings Safavid culture to a peak of power and artistic achievement.
- Internal problems erode the Safavid dynasty.
- The Safavid legacy is a culture blended of Shi'ism and ancient Persian nationalism.

HISTORY MAKERS
Shah Abbas

Shah Abbas was a Shi'i Muslim but far more mild in his views than his predecessors. He welcomed Christians and foreigners at his court and ate and drank with the Spanish ambassador during the Muslim month of fasting. To help him forge an alliance with the Romans against the Ottomans, he even hinted that he might be ready to convert to Christianity.

Task: Students will write and present imaginary historical dialogues between foreigners and officials of the Safavid Empire.

Purpose: To understand the culture of the Safavids and their place in the world.

Activity: Have pairs of students create dialogues that might have occurred between emissaries from Europe or Turkey and officials in the Safavid Empire.

Student pairs should first select a particular issue to discuss and identify the participating speakers and their individual points of view. The pairs should then develop their dialogues. They should write out both parts of the exchange and, if possible, perform the dialogues for their classmates.

📓 **Building a Portfolio:** Students should highlight their contributions to the dialogues and add them to their portfolios.

📖 *ALTERNATIVE ASSESSMENT BOOK*
Standards for Evaluating a Cooperative Activity

Standards for Evaluation
Dialogues should . . .
- clearly identify the speakers
- attribute realistic positions to each speaker
- accurately reflect political and social issues
- be interesting and lively

Safavid Empire, 1683

Interpreting the Map Point out the topographical formations on the map. What landforms create the western and southern boundaries of the empire? *Caucasus Mountains and Persian Gulf*

Extension Activity Have students consider how geography may have contributed to the Safavids' poor relationship with the Ottomans. *They competed for territory along their shared border and were competing for trade with Europe and Asia.*

SKILLBUILDER Answers
1. Caspian Sea, Persian Gulf, Tigris River.
2. They were squeezed between the Ottoman and Mughal empires.

ASSESS & RETEACH

Section 2 Assessment
Have students work with partners to fill in the diagram for question 2.

Section Quiz

FORMAL ASSESSMENT
Section Quiz, p. 30

Reteaching Activity
CLASS TIME: 10 MINUTES

Have students create a new row for the chart on page 68 to include the Safavid Empire.

CLOSE ACTIVITY

CLASS TIME: 15 MINUTES

Evaluating
Have students conduct a debate about the effects of cultural blending on the Safavid Empire.

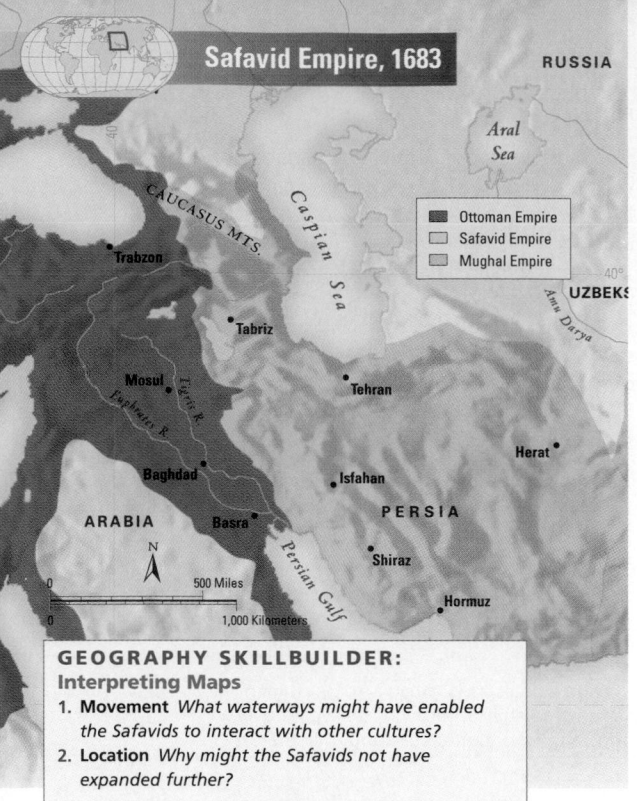

Safavid Empire, 1683

RUSSIA

Aral Sea

CAUCASUS MTS.

Caspian Sea

Amu Darya

UZBEKS

Trabzon

Tabriz

Tehran

40°

Mosul

Euphrates R.

Tigris R.

Herat

Baghdad

Isfahan

ARABIA

Basra

PERSIA

Shiraz

Persian Gulf

Hormuz

N

0   500 Miles

0   1,000 Kilometers

Legend:
- Ottoman Empire
- Safavid Empire
- Mughal Empire

GEOGRAPHY SKILLBUILDER:
Interpreting Maps
1. **Movement** *What waterways might have enabled the Safavids to interact with other cultures?*
2. **Location** *Why might the Safavids not have expanded further?*

Safavid Empire. This collaboration gave rise to gorgeous artwork. These decorations beautified the many mosques, palaces, and marketplaces of Abbas's rebuilt capital city of **Isfahan.**

The most important result of Western influence on the Safavids, however, may have been the demand for Persian carpets. This demand helped change carpet weaving from a local craft to a national industry.

The Dynasty Declines Quickly Shah Abbas unfortunately made the same mistake the Ottoman monarch Suleiman made. He killed or blinded his ablest sons. Abbas was succeeded by his incompetent grandson, Safi. This pampered young prince led the Safavids down the same road to decline that the Ottomans had taken, only more quickly.

By 1722, tribal armies from Afghanistan were taking over the eastern portions of the Safavid realm. Ottoman forces were attacking from the west. Some historians claim that these attacks marked the downfall of the Safavids.

In 1736, however, a ruler from a Sunni family—Nadir Shah Afshar—took command. He conquered all the way to India and created a new Persian empire. But Nadir Shah was a cruel man as well as an inspired military leader. One of his own troops assassinated him. With Nadir Shah's death in 1747, his empire also fell apart.

The Safavid Legacy Although the Safavid Empire died out as a political power, the culture that it produced endured. In this culture, the worldly and artistic features of Persian civilization mingled with the religious elements of Shi'ism. The Safavids also borrowed many ways from their enemies, the Ottomans. They based their government on the Ottoman model, welcomed foreigners into their empire, and created a slave army similar to the janissaries.

At the same time that the Safavids flourished, cultural blending and conquest led to the growth of a new empire in India, as you will learn in Section 3.

THINK THROUGH HISTORY
C. Comparing In what ways were Shah Abbas and Suleiman the Lawgiver similar?
C. Answer They both reformed civilian life and brought culture to their empires, adopting and adapting the best from around the world. Both also began the decline of their empires by killing their sons.

Section 2 Assessment

1. TERMS & NAMES
Identify
- Safavid
- Isma'il
- Shah Abbas
- Isfahan

2. TAKING NOTES
Using a cause-and-effect diagram like the one below, indicate the events that enabled the Safavids to build a powerful empire.

Events → Effect → Powerful Safavid Empire

3. ANALYZING MOTIVES
Within a century after the Safavids adopted Shi'i Islam, their leader, Isma'il, became a religious tyrant. Why might he have become so intolerant?

THINK ABOUT
- the persecution of Safavids by Ottoman Sunni Muslims
- the role of religion in Safavid life
- the geographic location of the Safavid Empire

4. THEME ACTIVITY
Cultural Interaction Write a letter from Shah Abbas to a Chinese artist persuading him to come teach and work in the Safavid Empire. In the letter, explain why the Safavids are interested in Chinese art and how they treat people from other cultures.

70 CHAPTER 2

ANSWERS

1. TERMS & NAMES
Safavid, p. 69
Isma'il, p. 69
Shah Abbas, p. 69
Isfahan, p. 70

2. TAKING NOTES
Possible Responses: Shi'ism becomes state religion; Isma'il builds a powerful army; Isma'il expands empire. Shah Abbas reforms military, society, and government; trade, industry, and art flourish.

3. ANALYZING MOTIVES
Possible Responses: Because the Sunni persecuted Shi'a, Isma'il wanted to strengthen Shi'ism and spread it throughout the empire. He may have believed that this was the only way to overcome Sunni opposition in Iran and from the Ottomans.

4. THEME ACTIVITY
Letters should indicate the cosmopolitan aspects of the empire under Shah Abbas and his interest in other cultures. They should stress the tolerance and respect that foreigners received in the Safavid Empire.

3 The Mughals Establish an Empire in India

TERMS & NAMES
- Mughal
- Babur
- Akbar
- Jahangir
- Nur Jahan
- Sikh
- Shah Jahan
- Taj Mahal
- Aurangzeb

MAIN IDEA

The Mughal Empire brought Turks, Persians, and Indians together in a vast empire.

WHY IT MATTERS NOW

The legacy of great art and deep social division left by the Mughal Empire still influences southern Asia.

SETTING THE STAGE In the late 15th century, India included lush lands studded with cities and temples. The Hindu lower classes labored in the service of their Muslim or Hindu masters. At the same time, nomadic warriors roamed the highlands to the northwest, eager for battle.

Early History of the Mughal Empire

The people who invaded India called themselves **Mughals,** which means "Mongols." The land they invaded had been through a long period of turmoil. The Gupta Empire crumbled in the 600s. First, Arabs invaded. Then, warlike Muslim tribes from central Asia carved northwestern India into many small kingdoms. Those kingdoms were ruled by leaders called Rajputs, or "sons of kings."

Ongoing Conflicts The 8th century began with a long, bloody clash between Hindus and Muslims in this fragmented land. For almost 300 years, though, the Hindus held off the Arab Muslims. They were able to advance only as far as the Indus River valley. Starting around the year 1000, however, well-trained Turkish armies swept into India. Led by Sultan Mahmud (muh·MOOD) of Ghazni, they devastated Indian cities and temples in 17 brutal campaigns. These attacks left the region weakened and vulnerable to other conquerors. Delhi eventually became the capital of a loose empire of Turkish warlords called the Delhi Sultanate. These sultans treated the Hindus as conquered people.

Between the 13th and 16th centuries, 33 different sultans ruled this divided territory from its seat in Delhi. In 1398, Timur the Lame destroyed Delhi so completely that, according to one witness, "for two whole months, not a bird moved in

Growth of the Mughal Empire, 1526–1707

Legend:
- Mughal Empire, 1526—Babur
- Added by 1605—Akbar
- Added by 1707—Aurangzeb

Kabul • KASHMIR • PUNJAB • Lahore • HIMALAYAS • Brahmaputra R. • Delhi • Agra • Ganges R. • Benares • Patna • BENGAL • Dacca • Calcutta • Tropic of Cancer • Arabian Sea • Surat • Bombay • DECCAN PLATEAU • Bay of Bengal • Madras • Calicut • Pondicherry • Cochin • CEYLON

N
0 300 Miles
0 600 Kilometers

71

GEOGRAPHY SKILLBUILDER:
Interpreting Maps
1. **Movement** During which time period was the most territory added to the Mughal Empire?
2. **Location** What landform might have prevented the empire from expanding farther east?

SECTION 3 RESOURCES

PRINT RESOURCES

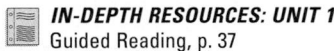 **IN-DEPTH RESOURCES: UNIT 1**
Guided Reading, p. 37
Geography Application: Europe Discovers India, p. 39
Primary Sources: Akbar, p. 43; Jahangir's Birthday, p. 44
History Makers: Shah Jahan, p. 49
Connections Across Time and Cultures, p. 50

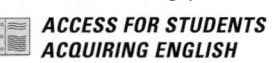 **ACCESS FOR STUDENTS ACQUIRING ENGLISH**
Guided Reading (Spanish), p. 34
Geography Application (Spanish), p. 36

FORMAL ASSESSMENT
Section Quiz, p. 31

TECHNOLOGY RESOURCES

WORLD ART AND CULTURES TRANSPARENCIES
AT40 Mughal miniature painting

CRITICAL THINKING TRANSPARENCIES
CT18 Muslim Empires in Anatolia and India
CT54 Visual Summary

 INTERNET www.mlworldhistory.com

Section 3 Overview

OBJECTIVES

(1) To describe the rise of the Mughal empire.

(2) To analyze the policies and achievements of Akbar.

(3) To list the triumphs and failures of Akbar's successors.

SKILLBUILDER

- Interpreting maps: movement, location, p. 71

CRITICAL THINKING

- Comparing, p. 72
- Analyzing causes, p. 74
- Making inferences, pp. 75, 76
- Recognizing effects, p. 77
- Comparing and contrasting, p. 77
- Analyzing themes, p. 77

FOCUS
5-Minute Warm-Up

▶ **Drawing Conclusions**
To spark students' interest in the Mughal Empire, have them answer these questions.

1. Look at the Daily Life feature on page 76. Name one gift the king rejected.
2. What evidence does this feature give about the wealth of the Mughal Empire?

WARM-UP TRANSPARENCY 2

OBJECTIVE (1) INSTRUCT

Early History of the Mughal Empire

▶ **Key Ideas**
- Centuries of bitter conflict mark Hindu-Muslim relations in India.
- Babur conquers India and founds the Mughal empire

IN-DEPTH RESOURCES: UNIT 1
Guided Reading, p. 37

ACCESS FOR STUDENTS ACQUIRING ENGLISH
Guided Reading (Spanish), p. 34

CRITICAL THINKING TRANSPARENCIES
CT18 Muslim Empires in Anatolia and India

Teacher's Edition 71

---

the city." Delhi eventually was rebuilt. But it was not until the 16th century that a leader arose who would unify the empire.

Babur Founds an Empire In 1494, an 11-year-old boy named **Babur** inherited a kingdom in the area that is now Uzbekistan and Tajikistan. It was only a tiny kingdom, and his elders soon took it away and drove him south. But the boy built up an army. In the years that followed, he swept down into India and laid the groundwork for the vast Mughal Empire.

Babur was a strong, sensitive leader. According to legend, he could leap a wall holding a man under each arm. But he also wrote poetry and loved art and gardens. He was a brilliant general as well. In 1526, for example, Babur led 12,000 troops to victory against an army of 100,000 commanded by a sultan of Delhi. Perhaps it was his sensitivity to his soldiers that made him such an effective leader:

> **A VOICE FROM THE PAST**
> Some in the army were very anxious and full of fear. Nothing recommends anxiety and fear. . . . Why? Because what God has fixed in eternity cannot be changed. But . . . it was no reproach to be afraid and anxious. . . . Why? Because those thus anxious and afraid were there with a two or three months' journey between them and their homes; our affair was with a foreign tribe and people; none knew their tongue, nor did they know ours.
>
> **BABUR**, *The Babur-Nama (Memoirs of Babur)*

A year later, Babur also defeated a massive Rajput army. After Babur's death, his incompetent son, Humayun, lost most of the territory Babur had gained. Babur's 13-year-old grandson took over the throne after Humayun's death.

The Golden Age of Akbar

Babur's grandson was called **Akbar,** which means "Great One." Akbar certainly lived up to his name by ruling India with wisdom and tolerance from 1556 to 1605.

A Liberal Ruler Akbar was a Muslim, and he firmly defended religious freedom. He proved his tolerance by marrying, among others, two Hindus, a Christian, and a Muslim. He allowed his wives to practice their religious rituals in the palace. He proved his tolerance again by abolishing both the tax on Hindu pilgrims and the hated *jizya*, or tax on non-Muslims. He even appointed a Spanish Jesuit to tutor his second son. Akbar was a genius at cultural blending.

Akbar governed through a bureaucracy of officials. Natives and foreigners, Hindus and Muslims, could all rise to high office. This approach contributed to the quality of his government. Akbar's chief finance minister, Todar Mal, for example, created a clever—and effective—taxation policy. He calculated the tax as a percent of the value of the peasants' crops, similar to the present-day U.S. graduated income tax. Because this tax was fair and affordable, the number of peasants who paid it increased. This payment brought in much needed money for the empire.

Akbar's land policies had more mixed results. He gave generous land grants to his bureaucrats. After they died, however, he reclaimed the lands and distributed them as he saw fit. On the positive side, this policy prevented the growth of feudal aristocracies. On the other hand, it did not encourage dedication and hard work by the Mughal officials. Their children would not inherit the land or benefit from their parents' work. So the officials apparently saw no point in devoting themselves to their property.

72 Chapter 2

A Military Conqueror For all his humanity, however, Akbar recognized military power as the root of his strength. He believed in war for its own sake. "A monarch should ever be intent on conquest," he said, "otherwise his neighbors rise in arms against him." Like the Safavids and the Ottomans, Akbar equipped his armies with heavy artillery. Cannons enabled him to crack into walled cities and extend his rule into much of the Deccan plateau. In a brilliant move, he appointed some Rajputs as officers. In this way he turned potential enemies into allies. This combination of military power and political wisdom enabled Akbar to unify a land of at least 100 million people—more than all of Europe put together.

A Flowering of Culture As Akbar extended the Mughal Empire, he welcomed influences from the many cultures it included. This cultural mingling affected art, education, politics, and the language as well. Persian was the language of Akbar's court and of high culture. The common people, however, spoke Hindi, a mixture of Persian and a local language. Hindi remains one of the most widely spoken languages in India today. Out of the Mughal armies, where soldiers of many backgrounds rubbed shoulders, came yet another new language. This language was Urdu, which means "from the soldier's camp." A blend of Arabic, Persian, and Hindi, Urdu is today the official language of Pakistan.

The arts flourished at the Mughal court, especially in the form of book illustrations. These small, highly detailed and colorful paintings were called miniatures. They were brought to a peak of perfection in the Safavid Empire. Babur's son, Humayun, brought two masters of this art to his court to teach it to the Mughals. Some of the most famous Mughal miniatures adorned the *Akbarnamah* ("Book of Akbar"), the story of the great emperor's campaigns and deeds. Indian art drew from Western traditions as well. After Akbar's time, for example, portraits of the Mughal emperors showed them wearing halos like Western saints.

Literature and Architecture Hindu literature also enjoyed a revival in Akbar's time. Akbar established a large library. The poet Tulsi Das, for example, was a contemporary of Akbar's. He retold the epic love story of Rama and Sita from the 4th-century B.C. Indian poem *Ramayana* (rah·MAH·yuh·nuh) in Hindi. This retelling, the *Ramcaritmanas,* is now even more popular than the original.

Akbar devoted himself to architecture, too. The style developed under his reign is still known as Akbar period architecture. Its massive, but graceful, structures are decorated with intricate stonework that depicts Hindu themes. The capital city of Fatehpur Sikri is one of the most important examples of this type of architecture. Akbar had this red-sandstone city built to thank a holy man who had predicted the birth of his first son. It included a great mosque, many palaces and other houses, as well as official and religious buildings. This magnificent city was abandoned after only 15 years because its water supply ran out. Ironically, the son whose birth it honored eventually rebelled against his father. He may even have plotted to cause his father's death.

Akbar's Successors

With Akbar's death in 1605, the Mughal court changed to deal with the changing times. The next three emperors were powerful men, and each left his mark on the Mughal Empire.

Headgear had symbolic importance in the society of Hindus in India. An important person's turban might include 50 yards of cloth wound around and held together with a jeweled pin such as this one.

The Muslim World Expands **73**

MORE ABOUT . . .
Akbar and Europe
Akbar's reign (1556–1605) almost exactly coincided with that of England's Elizabeth I (1558–1603). Although Akbar's empire was by far the wealthiest, he failed to develop his sea power. Elizabeth's destruction of the Spanish Armada, on the other hand, set the stage for the global dominance England would attain in the 18th century.

OBJECTIVE ③ INSTRUCT

Akbar's Successors

▶ **Key Ideas**
- Jahangir's queen, Nur Jahan, actually rules the Mughal Empire.
- Shah Jahan leaves a legacy of beautiful buildings, such as the Taj Mahal.
- Mughal extravagance impoverishes the people.
- Aurangzeb expands the empire but alienates his subjects.
- Poverty, corruption, and internal wars lead to the decline of the Mughal Empire.

📖 *IN-DEPTH RESOURCES: UNIT 1*
Primary Source: Jahangir's Birthday, p. 44

History Makers: Shah Jahan, p. 49

TEACHING OPTIONS

CUSTOMIZING FOR SPECIAL NEEDS

Less Proficient Readers
Identifying Main Ideas and
Supporting Details To help students understand Akbar's contributions to the Mughal Empire, have them complete a chart like the one here.

General Area	Akbar's Contribution
Military conquest	
Politics	
Religion	
Language	
Arts	
Literature	
Architecture	

CONNECTIONS ACROSS THE CURRICULUM

Art Encourage students to investigate Persian and Indian art, particularly miniatures and illuminated books. A good source is *Persian Miniatures* published by Mentor Books. What features characterize this art? *Its detail, delicacy, and rich colors.* Students may enjoy comparing this art to the works of the European masters of the period, such as Tintoretto, Titian, Rubens, and El Greco. What similarities and differences do they notice?

 WORLD ART AND CULTURES TRANSPARENCIES
AT40 Mughal miniature painting

Teacher's Edition **73**

Women Rulers

South Asia gave the world not only two women prime ministers, but also its first woman premier. She was Sirimavo Bandaranaike of Sri Lanka, an island off the southern tip of India. Bandaranaike was elected in 1960 and again (by a landslide) in 1970, ruling a total of 11 years. Ask students to speculate why women have been able to gain political power so often in this cultural region.

MORE ABOUT . . .
Nur Jahan

Legends surround Nur Jahan's life, perhaps reflecting her charismatic power. She was born, it is said, while her parents were in flight from Persia. They abandoned the child under a tree, but a cobra protected her, shading her from the hot sun with its hood until her remorseful parents returned. Nur Jahan married a Persian refugee in India, but he was hacked to bits in a quarrel with the governor of Bengal. Nur Jahan was then called to serve at court, where she caught the emperor's eye. Four years later, at the age of 34, she was married to him.

MORE ABOUT . . .
Mumtaz Mahal

According to tales, it was love at first sight between Prince Khurram, who later became Shah Jahan, and Mumtaz Mahal. On seeing her, he reportedly said, "Oh, that I were a glove upon that hand." After her marriage, Mumtaz Mahal traveled everywhere with her husband, even on military campaigns. She gave birth to four of his sons, including the next emperor, Aurangzeb, on the battlefield.

Women Rulers

Since World War II, India has seen the rise of several powerful women. Unlike Nur Jahan, however, they achieved power on their own—not through their husbands.

Indira Gandhi headed the Congress-I Party and dominated Indian politics for almost 30 years. She was elected prime minister in 1966 and again in 1980. Gandhi was assassinated in 1984 by Sikh terrorists.

In neighboring Pakistan, Benazir Bhutto (shown below), took charge of the Pakistan People's Party after her father was executed by his political enemies. She won election as her country's prime minister in 1988—the first woman to run a modern Muslim state. Pakistan's president unseated her, but she was reelected in 1993. In 1996, however, the president again ousted her from office. The supreme court ruled that her government was corrupt. Ironically, that was partially because her husband had made corrupt business deals.

Jahangir and Nur Jahan Akbar's son called himself **Jahangir** (juh·hahn·GEER)—"Grasper of the World." And he certainly did hold India in a powerful grasp. It was not his own hand in the iron glove, though, since Jahangir was an extremely weak ruler. For most of his reign, he left the affairs of state to his wife.

Jahangir's wife was the Persian princess **Nur Jahan.** She was a remarkably talented women with a variety of interests. Tiger hunting was among her favorite pastimes, and she rode horses with legendary skill. She composed poetry whenever the mood struck her. She also designed clothes that still influence Indian fashions. Above all, she was a brilliant politician who perfectly understood the use of power. As the real ruler of India from 1611 to 1622, she installed her father as prime minister in the Mughal court. She saw Jahangir's son Khusrau as her ticket to future power. But when Khusrau rebelled against his father, Nur Jahan ousted him. She then shifted her favor to another son, the future emperor, Shah Jahan.

This rejection of Khusrau affected more than the political future of the empire. It was also the basis of a long and bitter religious conflict. Both Nur Jahan and Jahangir rejected Akbar's religious tolerance and tried to promote only Islam in the Mughal state. When Khusrau rebelled against his father, he turned to the **Sikhs.** This was a nonviolent religious group whose doctrines blended Buddhism, Hinduism, and Sufism (Islamic mysticism). Their leader, Guru Arjun, sheltered Khusrau and defended him. In response, the Mughal rulers had Arjun arrested and tortured to death. The Sikhs thus became the target of the Mughals' particular hatred.

Shah Jahan Like his grandfather, **Shah Jahan** was a cultured man. He could not tolerate competition, however, and secured his throne by assassinating all his possible rivals. But he did have a great passion for two things: beautiful buildings and his wife Mumtaz Mahal (moom·TAHZ mah·HAHL). Nur Jahan had arranged this marriage between Jahangir's son and her niece for political reasons. Shah Jahan, however, fell genuinely in love with his Persian princess.

In 1631, Mumtaz Mahal died at age 38 giving birth to her 14th child. "Empire has no sweetness," the heartbroken Shah Jahan lamented, "life has no relish for me now." To enshrine his wife's memory, he ordered that a tomb be built "as beautiful as she was beautiful." Fine white marble and fabulous jewels were gathered from many parts of Asia. Some 20,000 workers labored for 22 years to build the famous tomb now known as the **Taj Mahal.** This memorial has been called one of the most beautiful buildings in the world. Its towering marble dome and slender towers look like lace and seem to change color as the sun moves across the sky. The inside of the building is as magnificent as the exterior. It is a glittering garden of thousands of carved marble flowers inlaid with tiny precious stones.

Shah Jahan also built the Red Fort at Delhi and completed the Peacock Throne, a priceless seat of gold encrusted with diamonds, rubies, emeralds, and pearls. The throne has a canopy that displays the figure of a peacock lined with blue sapphires. This magnificent throne was lost to the conqueror Nadir Shah in 1739.

The People Suffer But while Shah Jahan was building lovely things, his country was suffering. A Dutch merchant who was in India during a famine at that time reported that ". . . men abandoned towns and villages and wandered helplessly . . . eyes sunk deep in head, lips pale and covered with slime, the skin hard, the bones showing through. . . ." Farmers needed tools, roads, and ways of irrigating their crops and dealing with India's harsh environment. What they got instead were taxes and more taxes to support the building of monuments, their rulers' extravagant living, and war.

THINK THROUGH HISTORY
B. Analyzing Causes How did the Mughals' dislike of the Sikhs develop?
B. Answer They sheltered and defended Jahangir's son, who had rebelled against his father.

Background
While Shah Jahan was spending huge sums of money on the Taj Mahal, King Louis XIV of France was building his elaborate palace at Versailles. Both rulers heavily taxed their people to pay for their extravagance.

Task: Students will examine photographs of various buildings throughout the world.

Materials Needed: The feature about Versailles on page 141 of this text. Art transparencies AT22, AT30, and AT47 also provide images of world-famous architecture. Also see the book *Great Architecture of the World* edited by John Julius.

Activity: Have students choose a selection of buildings from a variety of times and places. Ask them to note their overall impression of each building and to identify the particular characteristics that contribute to that impression.

Conclusion: Ask students to write descriptive or expository paragraphs or poems capturing their responses to the buildings. Suggest that they

consider the similar impulses that motivated people to construct such monuments as well as the different forms the buildings took. Have students share their writing orally with the class.

 WORLD ART AND CULTURES TRANSPARENCIES
AT22, Great Mosque of Córdova; AT30, Notre Dame Cathedral; AT47, St. Basil's Cathedral

THINK THROUGH HISTORY
C. Making Inferences Do you think Shah Jahan's policies helped or harmed the Mughal Empire?
C. Possible Answer Helped—Left lasting legacy of architecture. Harmed—Did not improve the hard lives of his people.

All was not well in the royal court either. When Shah Jahan became ill in 1657, his four sons scrambled for the throne. The third son, **Aurangzeb** (AWR·uhng·zehb), moved first and most decisively. In a bitter civil war, he executed his older brother, who was his most serious rival. Then he arrested his father and put him in prison. When Shah Jahan died several years later, a mirror was found in his room, angled so that he could gaze from his cell at the reflection of the Taj Mahal. Aurangzeb, however, had his eyes on the empire.

Aurangzeb Aurangzeb ruled from 1658 to 1707. He was a master at military strategy and an aggressive empire builder. Although he expanded the Mughal holdings to their greatest size, the power of the empire weakened during his reign.

This loss of power was due largely to Aurangzeb's oppression of the people. He rigidly enforced Islamic laws, outlawing drinking, gambling, and other vices. He also appointed censors to police his subjects' morals and make sure they prayed at the appointed times. He also tried to erase all the gains Hindus had made under Akbar. For example, he brought back the hated tax on non-Muslims and dismissed Hindus from high positions in his government. He banned the construction of new temples and had Hindu monuments destroyed. Not surprisingly, these actions outraged the Hindus.

The Hindu Rajputs, whom Akbar had converted from potential enemies to allies, rebelled. Aurangzeb defeated them repeatedly, but never completely. In the southwest, militant Hindus called Marathas founded their own breakaway state. Aurangzeb captured their leader, but the Marathas turned to guerrilla warfare. Aurangzeb could never conquer them. Meanwhile, the Sikhs had transformed themselves into a militant brotherhood. They began to build a state in the Punjab, an area in northwest India.

Set in a formal garden and mirrored in a reflecting pool, the Taj Mahal draws tourists to Agra, southeast of New Delhi in India. It remains a monument to both love and the Mughal Empire.

MORE ABOUT . . .
Shah Jahan's Sons
Shah Jahan made no secret of his disdain for his younger son Aurangzeb and his great love for his elder son Dara Shikoh, a mystical and humane spirit like his great grandfather Akbar. Aurangzeb certainly was driven by grief, jealousy, and spite, and may have become such an aggressive empire builder to make up for the lack of his father's love. According to legend, after imprisoning his father and conquering his brother, Aurangzeb had Dara Shikoh's severed head delivered to his father in a box with the message: "Your son sends this [gift] to your majesty to let him see that he does not forget him."

MORE ABOUT . . .
Aurangzeb's Oppressive Policies
Aurangzeb ended all court luxuries, forbade parties that involved drinking, singing, and dancing, and put an end to the building of monuments. He also tore down all large-scale Hindu monuments erected before the Mughals established their empire in India. As a result, the only pre-Mughal architecture to be found in modern India is located in the southern sections that Aurangzeb never conquered.

TEACHING OPTION | **BLOCK SCHEDULING** | COOPERATIVE ACTIVITY: **Debating the Decline of the Mughal Empire** | **CLASS TIME 30 MINUTES**

Task: Students will stage a debate to determine which of Akbar's successors bore the greatest responsibility for the decline of the Mughal Empire.

Purpose: To explain the decline of the Mughal Empire.

Activity: Divide the class into groups of three. Each should choose Jahangir, Shah Jahan, or Aurangzeb. Students should research their emperors independently and write a formal indictment statement.

They should then meet with members of the other groups who prepared a case against the same emperor. Each large group should discuss the evidence, prepare a joint statement, and choose a spokesperson. The three spokespeople will then hold a debate.

 Building a Portfolio: Students could include their individual statements in their portfolios.

ALTERNATIVE ASSESSMENT BOOK
Standards for Evaluating a Cooperative Activity

Standards for Evaluation
Indictment statements should . . .
• include accurate and relevant facts about the emperor
• organize the evidence clearly
• display insight into the causes of Mughal decline

Teacher's Edition **75**

India, 1620
Mughal Society News

These news items present actual events and customs of the Mughal court as reported by various observers. One of these observers, Thomas Roe of the British East India Trading company, spent three years trying to negotiate a treaty with Jahangir, but finally went home with only a few minor trade agreements. One of his difficulties apparently was the uninspired gifts his English sponsors provided him to woo the emperor. Such gifts earned the monarch's forceful "thumbs down."

Have interested students do independent research into the Mughal court. Good sources include Waldemar Hansen's *The Peacock Throne* and Bamber Gascoigne's *The Great Moghuls.* Suggest that they collect interesting details and produce their own edition of *Mughal Society News* to share with the class.

Mughal Society News

Diet News

A person who does a good deed for the Mughal emperor may be rewarded with his weight in rupees (a unit of money). In fact, both the emperor's flute player and his astrologer recently received this generous prize. Sources said that the stout astrologer pocketed 200 rupees more than the musician.

The Doctor Is In

When a woman of the Mughal court gets sick, she must not be seen by a male doctor. The doctor first wraps his head in a cashmere shawl, which serves as a blindfold. He follows a servant into the women's quarters, where the patient lies hidden behind a curtain. If she needs to have a wound treated, the patient sticks her arm or leg out through the curtain. The doctor then examines the patient from his side of the curtain.

Woman of the Week

Naming Nur Jahan, the monarch's favorite queen "Woman of the Week" is a king-size understatement. Woman of the century is more like it. But people in the know go even further and call her "Light of the World"—and for good reason. In addition to being the true power behind Jahangir's throne, she excels in the arts, business, and sports.

Nur Jahan's bold, original designs for cloth, dresses with long trains, and even carpets dominate India's fashion scene. From her harem, Nur Jahan runs a bustling trade in indigo and cloth. She's also an accomplished huntress, and last week killed four tigers.

Nur Jahan is the power behind the throne and even designs the royal wardrobe.

The Shopping Corner

If you're trying to impress the emperor, bring him a unique gift. This is how he voted on recent offerings:

Thumbs Up	Thumbs Down
• walnut-sized ruby	• faded velvet
• portraits of English royal family	• mirror with loose frame
• unusual fish	• map showing a compressed view of India

Moving Day

Relocating the Mughal royal court requires as much effort as moving a small city. Simply transporting the royal tents requires 100 elephants, 500 camels, 400 carts, and 100 human bearers. When the procession stops for the night, it spans a length of 20 miles.

Connect *to* History

Making Inferences What can you conclude about the lives of women in the Mughal court?

SEE SKILLBUILDER
HANDBOOK, PAGE 663

Connect *to* Today

Women's Studies Using information from the "Connect to Today" feature on page 74 and the library or the Internet, research the public role of women in several Muslim cultures today. How has the role of women changed since Mughal times?

Connect *to* History

Possible Answer:
Women generally were protected from the outside world. They and their families apparently accumulated many possessions, since moving was such a major undertaking. One woman, Nur Jahan, was extraordinarily powerful, but this was probably due to her unique talents and position as queen.

Connect *to* Today

Women's Studies
Women's roles differ greatly in the Islamic world. In Turkey, for example, women enjoy almost full participation in public life. In Saudi Arabia, they are prohibited by law even from driving cars. In Afghanistan, the Taliban have virtually erased women from public life and stripped them of all rights. In some countries, such as Egypt and Algeria, for example, conservatives are struggling to erase the gains women have made.

Aurangzeb had to levy oppressive taxes to pay for the wars against these increasing numbers of enemies. He had done away with all taxes not authorized by Islamic law, so he doubled the taxes on Hindu merchants. This increased tax burden deepened the Hindus' bitterness and led to further rebellion. As a result, Aurangzeb needed to raise more money to increase his army. The more territory he conquered, the more desperate his situation became.

The Empire's Decline and Decay

By the end of Aurangzeb's reign, he had drained the empire of its resources. Most of his subjects felt little or no loyalty to him. According to a Dutch observer, "The condition of the common people in India is very miserable. . . . Their huts are low, built generally of mud . . . their bedding is scanty and thin . . . of little use when the weather is bitterly cold. . . . The nobles live in indescribable luxury and extravagance, caring only to indulge themselves whilst they can in every kind of pleasure." Over two million people died in a famine while Aurangzeb was away waging war.

As the power of the central state weakened, the power of local lords grew. After Aurangzeb's death, his sons fought a war of succession. Bahadur, who won the war, was over 60 when he gained the throne. This exhausted emperor did not last long. In fact, three emperors reigned in the 12 years after Aurengzeb died. By the end of this period, the Mughal emperor was nothing but a wealthy figurehead. He ruled not a united empire but a patchwork of independent states.

As the Mughal Empire was rising and falling and creating its cultural legacy, Western traders were slowly building their own power. The Portuguese were the first Europeans to reach India. In fact, they arrived just before Babur did. But they were ousted by the Dutch, who, in turn, gave way to the French and the English. The great Mughal emperors did not feel threatened by the European traders. Shah Jahan let the English build a fortified trading post at Madras. In 1661, Aurangzeb casually handed them the port of Bombay. Aurangzeb had no idea that he had given India's next conquerors their first foothold in a future empire.

THINK THROUGH HISTORY
D. Recognizing Effects How did Aurangzeb's personal qualities and political policies affect the Mughal Empire?
D. Answer He depleted the empire's resources and began the weakening of central power that led to its ruin.

Perhaps to offset their excessive spending, the Mughal rulers were weighed once a year. They donated their weight in gold and silver to the people. Here, Jahangir weighs Prince Khurran.

Section 3 Assessment

1. TERMS & NAMES

Identify
- Mughal
- Babur
- Akbar
- Jahangir
- Nur Jahan
- Sikh
- Shah Jahan
- Taj Mahal
- Aurangzeb

2. TAKING NOTES

Using a time line like the one below, indicate the effects each leader had on the Mughal Empire. Write positive effects above the line and negative effects below.

Effects on Mughal Empire

| Babur | Akbar | Jahangir/ Nur Jahan | Shah Jahan | Aurangzeb |

3. COMPARING AND CONTRASTING

In what ways was the golden age of Akbar similar to and different from the flowering of the Safavid Empire under Shah Abbas and of the Ottoman Empire under Suleiman I?

THINK ABOUT
- the rulers' cultural and military achievements
- their tolerance of other cultures
- their successors

4. ANALYZING THEMES

Power and Authority Do you think Shah Jahan made good use of his power and authority? Why or why not?

THINK ABOUT
- how Shah Jahan came to power
- the beautiful buildings he built
- conditions in India during his reign

The Muslim World Expands **77**

MORE ABOUT . . .
Europeans in India
Indian cloth was the great prize sought by European traders, who had only coarse linen and wool. Several types of cotton fabric are actually named for Indian cities—madras for Madras and calico for Calicut, now Calcutta.

IN-DEPTH RESOURCES: UNIT 1
Geography Application: Europe Discovers the Riches of India, p. 39

OBJECTIVE 4 INSTRUCT

The Empire's Decline and Decay

▶ *Key Ideas*
- The Mughal Empire breaks apart after Aurangzeb's death.
- The region attracts European empire builders.

ASSESS & RETEACH

Section 3 Assessment
Have pairs of students work on question 4.

Section Quiz
FORMAL ASSESSMENT
Section Quiz, p. 31

Reteaching Activity
CLASS TIME: 10 MINUTES

Have students compare their time lines in question 2 and make a combined class time line.

CRITICAL THINKING TRANSPARENCIES
CT54 Visual Summary

CLOSE ACTIVITY

CLASS TIME: 15 MINUTES

Comparing and Contrasting
Have students, as a class, create a Venn diagram in which they list the similarities and differences of the Ottoman, the Safavid, and the Mughal empires.

ANSWERS

1. TERMS & NAMES
Mughal, p. 71
Babur, p. 72
Akbar, p. 72
Jahangir, p. 74
Nur Jahan, p. 74
Sikh, p. 74
Shah Jahan, p. 74
Taj Mahal, p. 74
Aurangzeb, p. 75

2. TAKING NOTES
Possible Responses: Pos.— Babur expanded the empire; Akbar left a better government and a flowering of culture; Neg.—Jahangir and Nur Jahan sparked religious conflict with the Sikhs; Shah Jahan made life difficult for Hindus; Aurangzeb waged costly wars.

3. COMPARING AND CONTRASTING
Possible Responses: Similar— Governmental reform, cultural blending and flowering, military leadership; **Different**—Akbar didn't murder his sons.

4. ANALYZING THEMES
Possible Responses: Yes—Shah Jahan kept the empire together and built magnificent buildings that reflected the empire's glory; No—He turned his back on his suffering people while constructing beautiful buildings, living extravagantly, and pursuing war.

Chapter ② Assessment

TERMS & NAMES

1. Timur the Lame, p. 63
2. Mehmet II, p. 64
3. Suleiman the Lawgiver, p. 66
4. *devshirme*, p. 66
5. Isma'il, p. 69
6. Shah Abbas, p. 69
7. Babur, p. 72
8. Akbar, p. 72
9. Nur Jahan, p. 74
10. Aurangzeb, p. 75

REVIEW QUESTIONS

Answers will vary.

11. They used modern technology—muskets and cannons—to achieve military success and treated the conquered peoples humanely.

12. He opened Constantinople to Jews, Christians, and non-Turks.

13. Mecca and Medina were the holiest cities of Islam, and Cairo was its intellectual center. Capturing them gave the Ottomans almost total control of the Muslim world.

14. Male slaves could hold high posts in the government and join the janissaries; female slaves served the wealthy Ottoman families.

15. Positive—his military prowess and brilliance as a warrior; Negative—his religious intolerance in imposing Shi'ism as the state religion.

16. An army recruited from conquered people, like the janissaries; use of modern artillery; government reforms with rewards based on merit; support for the arts and learning.

17. The Safavids blended the literate, urban features of Persian civilization with the mystical elements of Shi'ism; they engaged in trade and cultural exchange with nations as far away as China.

18. The Mughals had to overcome Turkish warlords of the Delhi Sultanate and other warlike tribes from Central Asia led by Rajputs.

19. He married two Hindus, a Christian, and a Muslim; abolished taxes on non-Muslims; appointed a Spanish Jesuit to tutor his son; and allowed people of all faiths to compete for high office.

20. Nur Jahan and Jahangir persecuted Sikhs; Shah Jahan mistreated Hindus; Aurangzeb reversed Akbar's tolerant policies and levied oppressive taxes on Hindus.

TERMS & NAMES

Briefly explain the importance of each of the following to the Ottoman, Safavid, or Mughal empires.

1. Timur the Lame
2. Mehmet II
3. Suleiman the Lawgiver
4. *devshirme*
5. Isma'il
6. Shah Abbas
7. Babur
8. Akbar
9. Nur Jahan
10. Aurangzeb

Interact *with* History

On page 62, you considered how you might treat the people you conquered. Now that you have learned more about three Muslim empires, in what ways do you think you would change your policies? In what ways would you follow and differ from the Ottomans' example? Discuss your thoughts with a small group of classmates.

REVIEW QUESTIONS

SECTION 1 *(pages 63–67)*
The Ottomans Build a Vast Empire

11. Why were the Ottomans such successful conquerors?
12. How did Mehmet the Conqueror show his tolerance of other cultures?
13. Why was Selim the Grim's capture of Mecca, Medina, and Cairo so significant?
14. What role did slaves play in Ottoman society?

SECTION 2 *(pages 68–70)*
Cultural Blending
Case Study: The Safavid Empire

15. According to the 16th-century Voice from the Past on page 69, "The name of God is forgotten throughout Persia and only that of Isma'il is remembered." What deeds—both positive and negative—contributed to Isma'il's fame?
16. What ideas did Shah Abbas borrow from his enemies, the Ottomans?
17. In what other ways did the Safavids interweave foreign ideas into their culture?

SECTION 3 *(pages 71–77)*
The Mughals Establish an Empire in India

18. What opposition did the Mughals face when they invaded India?
19. In what ways did Akbar defend religious freedom during his reign?
20. How did Akbar's successors promote religious conflict in the empire?

Visual Summary

The Muslim World Expands

Ottoman Empire

| 1200 | 1400 | 1600 | 1800 |

- **1280–1326** Reign of Osman I
- **1361** Ottomans capture Adrianople
- **1451–1481** Reign of Mehmet II
- **1453** Turks take Constantinople
- **1520–1566** Reign of Suleiman I
- **1571** Defeat at Battle of Lepanto begins decline of Ottoman Empire

Safavid Empire

| 1200 | 1400 | 1600 | 1800 |

- **1501** Isma'il seizes Persia and declares himself shah
- **1508** Isma'il conquers Baghdad
- **1587–1629** Reign of Shah Abbas
- **1722** Afghans and Ottomans seize Safavid lands
- Safavid Empire collapses

Mughal Empire

| 1200 | 1400 | 1600 | 1800 |

- **1494** Babur begins his rise to power
- **1526** Babur seizes Delhi
- **1556–1605** Reign of Akbar
- **1628–1658** Reign of Shah Jahan
- **1658–1707** Reign of Aurangzeb
- **1719** Mughal Empire declines

78 Chapter 2

Interact *with* History

Possible Responses: Students might try to emulate the Ottomans' military success, tolerance, and cultural achievements. They will probably want to avoid the Ottoman rulers' violent elimination of competition for the throne and their practice of producing weak, uneducated successors.

CRITICAL THINKING

1. CONSTANTINOPLE'S LAST STAND

Why do you think that so few European countries helped defend Constantinople from the Ottomans? Consider the results of the Crusades in the Holy Roman Empire.

2. GROWTH OF AN EMPIRE

Conquest of new territories certainly contributed to **THEME EMPIRE BUILDING** the growth of the Muslim empires you read about. How might it have also hindered this growth?

3. MUSLIM MIRROR ON THE WALL

Using a Venn diagram like the one below, compare the personal traits and policies of Suleiman I and Akbar.

4. ANALYZING PRIMARY SOURCES

The Greek historian Kritovoulos was appointed a governor in the court of Mehmet II after his conquest of Constantinople. In the following quotation, Kritovoulos gives his view of Mehmet's actions. Read the paragraph and answer the questions below it.

> **A VOICE FROM THE PAST**
> When the Sultan [Mehmet] had captured the City of Constantinople, almost his very first care was to have the City repopulated. He also undertook the further care and repairs of it. He sent an order in the form of an imperial command to every part of his realm, that as many inhabitants as possible be transferred to the City, not only Christians but also his own people and many of the Hebrews.
> **KRITOVOULOS,** *History of Mehmet the Conqueror*

- Does the tone of this statement indicate that Kritovoulos thought Mehmet dealt fairly with Constantinople? Why or why not?
- Why do you think Mehmet wanted to open the city to Christians and Hebrews as well as Muslims? Support your answer with information from the chapter.

CHAPTER ACTIVITIES

1. LIVING HISTORY: Unit Portfolio Project

THEME CULTURAL INTERACTION Your unit portfolio project focuses on the cultural interaction that resulted from the expansion of the Muslim world (see page 33). For Chapter 2 you might use one of the following ideas to add to your portfolio.

- Expand your ideas for the Interact with History activity on the previous page into a speech to your people. Explain your policies and ask for your people's support.
- Draw a political cartoon showing that the Safavids borrowed ideas from their enemies, the Ottomans.
- Write an inscription for Akbar's tombstone, focusing on his religious tolerance and on the mix of cultures in his government bureaucracy.

2. CONNECT TO TODAY: Cooperative Learning

THEME POWER AND AUTHORITY The Muslim empires you have studied based their rule on the Islamic religion. Islam remains an important social and political force in modern Turkey, Iran, India, and Pakistan.

Work with a team to find out the status of Muslims in one of these countries today. Then collaborate with the other teams to create a summary chart of these modern Muslim countries.

 Using the Internet or other reference sources, determine the status of Muslims in your team's country.

- What role do Muslims play in the government?
- Do the country's leaders promote religious tolerance? Explain.
- What is the overall economic status of Muslims?

3. INTERPRETING A TIME LINE

Look at the time lines on the facing page. Which empire lasted longest? Which was the shortest lived?

FOCUS ON GRAPHS

Compare the territory and population of the following seven empires at their height.
- Which four empires had about the same territory?
- Which of those empires had the fewest people per square mile?

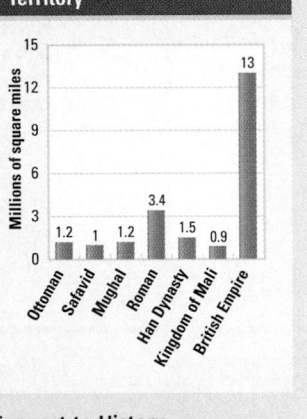

Connect to History
Why might the Safavid Empire have remained so relatively small?

The Muslim World Expands **79**

CHAPTER ACTIVITIES

1. LIVING HISTORY

Standards for Evaluation
A speech should meet the following criteria:

- Clearly states a general position and specific policies.
- Is brief and to the point.
- Elicits listener enthusiasm and support.

Standards for Evaluation
A political cartoon should meet the following criteria:

- Communicates a clear idea about the Safavids.
- Includes specific characters or images that represent the Safavids and the Ottomans.
- Uses well-chosen words, if necessary, to support the message.

Standards for Evaluation
A tombstone inscription should meet the following criteria:

- Reflects an understanding of Akbar's life and achievements.
- Uses strong, descriptive language.
- Follows standard epitaph style.

2. CONNECT TO TODAY

Standards for Evaluation
A chart should meet the following criteria:

- Presents the political, religious, and economic status of Muslims in the countries chosen.
- Organizes information in a clear, easy-to-follow graphic display.
- Includes verbal summaries as needed.

3. INTERPRETING A TIME LINE

Ottoman; Safavid

FOCUS ON GRAPHS

- Ottoman, Safavid, Mughal, Mali
- Kingdom of Mali

Connect to History *Possible Response:* It was squeezed between the Ottoman and Mughal empires and was unable to expand either its territory or its population.

Teacher's Edition 79

CRITICAL THINKING

1. CONSTANTINOPLE'S LAST STAND
Possible Responses: The failure of Christianity to overcome the Muslims during the Crusades was a bitter memory. In addition, the Ottomans had a powerful army.

2. GROWTH OF AN EMPIRE
Possible Responses: Overaggressive empire building, such as during Aurangzeb's reign led to overspending, rebellion, and the decline of the empire. Adding territory without tolerance for the conquered people could also be destructive.

3. MUSLIM MIRROR ON THE WALL
Possible Responses: Suleiman I—simplified tax system, Akbar—gave land grants to bureaucrats, created effective tax policy. Both—strong military leader; reformed bureaucracy; practiced religious tolerance; supported the arts, learning, and other cultures.

4. ANALYZING PRIMARY SOURCES
Possible Responses: The repeated use of the word *care* implies that he thought Mehmet was dealing very fairly and humanely with Constantinople and its people; Mehmet was tolerant of other religions and wished to take advantage of the skills of the local people.

CHAPTER 3
An Age of Exploration and Isolation

	Key Ideas	**COPY MASTERS**	**ASSESSMENT**

SECTION 1
Europeans Explore the East
pp. 83–88

The desire for profit and the hope of spreading Christianity motivate European exploration, and new technology makes it possible. The Portuguese dominate exploration until other Europeans, especially the Dutch, establish their own trading empires.

 In-Depth Resources: Unit 1
- **Guided Reading,** p. 51
- **Primary Sources:** Exploration of Cape Verde, p. 57; The Treaty of Tordesillas, p. 58
- **History Makers:** Vasco da Gama, p. 64
- **Science and Technology:** A Revolution in Cartography, p. 67

P E *Section 1 Assessment,* p. 88
Formal Assessment
- Section Quiz, p. 40

Alternative Assessment Book
- Standards for Evaluating a Cooperative Activity

SECTION 2
China Rejects European Outreach
pp. 89–93

After a series of successful voyages of exploration, China withdraws into isolation. Both the Ming and the Qing dynasties limit foreign trade and follow a policy of self-sufficiency.

 In-Depth Resources: Unit 1
- **Guided Reading,** p. 52
- **Skillbuilder Practice:** Interpreting Graphs, p. 54
- **Geography Application:** The Voyages of Zheng He, p. 55
- **Primary Source:** from *The Journals of Matteo Ricci,* p. 59
- **Literature:** from *The Dream of the Red Chamber,* p. 61

P E *Section 2 Assessment,* p. 93
Formal Assessment
- Section Quiz, p. 41

Alternative Assessment Book
- Standards for Evaluating a Cooperative Activity

SECTION 3
Japan Limits Western Contacts
pp. 94–97

After a period of severe disorder, the Tokugawa Shogunate unifies Japan. In the two centuries of peace and prosperity that follow, the Japanese close their country to foreign ideas by banning Christianity and severely restricting foreign trade.

 In-Depth Resources: Unit 1
- **Guided Reading,** p. 53
- **Literature:** Haiku, p. 63
- **History Makers:** Tokugawa Ieyasu, p. 65
- **Connections Across Time and Cultures:** Breakdown of Feudal Societies, p. 66

P E *Section 3 Assessment,* p. 97
Formal Assessment
- Section Quiz, p. 42

Alternative Assessment Book
- Standards for Evaluating a Product or Performance

CHAPTER RESOURCES

Chapter Overview

Seeking spices and converts, European nations lead successful voyages of exploration to the East. China and Japan both limit foreign contact after a brief period of acceptance.

 Telescoping the Times
- Chapter Summary, pp. 13–15

Planning for Block Schedules

P E *Chapter Assessment,* pp. 98–99
Chapter Activities, p. 99
Formal Assessment
- Chapter Test, forms A and B, pp. 43–48

Test Generator
Alternative Assessment Book

1400–1800

TECHNOLOGY

 Warm-Up Transparency 3

 World Art and Cultures Transparencies
- AT41 Portuguese Tower of Belém

 INTERNET RESOURCES
www.mlworldhistory.com

 Warm-Up Transparency 3

 Electronic Library of Primary Sources
- Letter to King George III

 INTERNET RESOURCES
www.mlworldhistory.com

 Warm-Up Transparency 3

 Geography Transparencies
- GT19 Tokugawa Ieyasu Unites Japan, 1603

 World Art and Cultures Transparencies
- AT42 Japanese screen painting

 Critical Thinking Transparencies
- CT19 The Impact of Exploration on East Asia
- CT40 Visual Summary

 Electronic Library of Primary Sources
- from *The Life and Letters of St. Francis Xavier*
- from the Act of Seclusion

 INTERNET RESOURCES
www.mlworldhistory.com

 Chapter Summaries on Audiocassette in English and Spanish

 INTERNET RESOURCES
www.mlworldhistory.com

Block Scheduling (90 MINUTES)

Day 1
Section 1, pp. 83–88

 COOPERATIVE ACTIVITY
Writing a Progress Report, p. 86 (Teacher's Edition)

Section Assessment, p. 88

Day 2
Section 2, pp. 89–93

 COOPERATIVE ACTIVITY
Panel Discussion, p. 90 (Teacher's Edition)

Section 3, pp. 94–97

Section Assessments, pp. 93, 97

Chapter Assessment, pp. 98–99

Yearly Pacing *Chapter 3 Total:* 2 days   *Yearly Total:* 85 days

 Planning for Block Schedules

Customizing for Special Needs

Students Acquiring English

 Access for Students Acquiring English
- **Guided Reading** for Sections 1–3 (Spanish), pp. 41–43
- **Chapter Summary** (Spanish), pp. 38–40
- **Skillbuilder Practice** Interpreting Graphs (Spanish) p. 44
- **Geography Application** The Voyages of Zheng He (Spanish), p. 45

 Spanish Reading Study Guide
- pp. 33–40

 Chapter Summaries on Audiocassette in English and Spanish

Less Proficient Readers

 In-Depth Resources: Unit 1
- **Guided Reading** for Sections 1–3, pp. 51–53
- **Skillbuilder Practice** Interpreting Graphs, p. 54
- **Geography Application** The Voyages of Zheng He, p. 55

Telescoping the Times
- Chapter Summary, pp. 13–15

 Reading Study Guide
- pp. 33–40

 Chapter Summaries on Audiocassette

Gifted and Talented Students

 In-Depth Resources: Unit 1

Primary Sources:
- Exploration of Cape Verde, p. 57
- The Treaty of Tordesillas, p. 58
- from *The Journals of Matteo Ricci,* p. 59

History Makers
- Vasco da Gama, p. 64
- Tokugawa Ieyasu, p. 65

Connections to Literature READINGS FOR STUDENTS

 In-Depth Resources: Unit 1
Literature: from *The Dream of the Red Chamber,* p. 61

Enrichment Reading

Spence, Jonathan D.
The Question of Hu
New York: Vintage, 1989

A suspenseful narrative of the 1722 travels of a Chinese Catholic and a Jesuit missionary to France.

Wood, Francis
Did Marco Polo Go to China?
New York: Westview, 1996

A readable presentation of the passionate debate concerning the authenticity of Marco Polo's travels.

 [P E] = Pupil's Edition   = Overhead Transparency   = Software   = Video

= Copy Master   = CD-ROM   = Audiocassette   = Internet

An Age of Exploration and Isolation, 1400–1800

Accessing Prior Knowledge

• Ask students to look at the pictures, read each related caption, and discuss what they know about previous interaction between the West and the East.

Predicting and Making Inferences

• After reading about Europeans' improving their navigational techniques, what can students predict about how these skills might be used?

• Ask students what they might infer about the possible response of the Japanese to Europeans, from looking at the print of the samurai warrior.

Geography Connection

Ask students to study the maps of Europe and Asia on these two pages.

• Which were the five major European countries that became involved in trade with the East? *Portugal, Spain, France, the Netherlands, England.*

• What geographic feature may have been a cause of Japan's isolation? *It was an island.*

CHAPTER
3

An Age of Exploration and Isolation, 1400–1800

PREVIEWING THEMES

Cultural Interaction
European exploration of Asia resulted in a meeting of different cultures. While this cultural interaction spurred the exchange of many goods and ideas, the people of Asia also resisted European influence.

Economics
The desire for wealth was a driving force behind European exploration of the East. Europeans sought control over the trade of popular goods from Asian countries; European merchants and sailors took to the seas in search of these lands.

Science & Technology
Europeans were able to explore faraway lands only after they improved their sailing technology. Innovations in shipbuilding and navigational techniques allowed Europeans to expand far beyond their borders.

INTERNET CONNECTION
Visit us at www.mlworldhistory.com to learn more about this age of exploration and isolation.

EUROPE AND ASIA, AROUND 1500

Norwegian Sea
North Sea
Baltic Sea
Moscow
ENGLAND
London • Amsterdam
NETHERLANDS Paris
FRANCE • EUROPE
OTTOMAN EMPIRE
SPAIN • Rome
Lisbon •
PORTUGAL *Mediterranean Sea*
Tripoli •
Arabian Sea
INDIAN OCEAN

By the **early 1400s, Europeans** were improving their navigational techniques in an effort to explore the lands beyond their shores. Here, for example, a French mapmaker uses an instrument to determine his position on the globe.

80

GEOGRAPHY THEMES

Location

Have students locate on the map Europe, Africa, South Asia (India), and East Asia (China and Japan). (Refer to the Atlas map on pages 630–631 to show students that the only water route to the east took ships around the tip of southern Africa.) Then have them use the distance scale to roughly estimate sailing distances from the port of Lisbon to the coasts of India, China, and Japan. *About 14,500 miles; 19,000; 19,500.* Make a chart of those distances on the chalkboard. You might also ask students to roughly estimate the distance if the journey to India could have been made overland. *About 6,000 miles.*

Movement

From the caption related to Japan, students should conclude that European explorers and traders were able to sail to Japan during this time period. First, ask students whether they think it was possible that a ship could sail from Europe to East Asia without making any stops. *Possible Response: No—the distance was too great; ships had to stop to find food and water for their crews.* Then, ask students how the lands between Europe and Japan might have been affected by European exploration and trade. Have them reread the first theme, cultural interaction, to help answer this question.

ADDITIONAL RESOURCES

Books for the Teacher

- Berry, Mary Elizabeth. *The Culture of Civil War in Kyoto.* Berkeley: U of California P, 1994.

- Boorstin, Daniel J. *The Discoverers.* New York: Random, 1983. European explorers.

- Levathes, Louise. *When China Ruled the Seas: The Treasure Fleet of the Dragon Throne, 1405–1433.* New York: Simon, 1994.

Books for the Student

- Hale, John R. *Age of Exploration.* Alexandria, Virginia: Time-Life Books, 1974.

- Reid, Struan. *Exploration by Sea.* New York: New Discovery Books, 1994. European trade empires.

Videos

- *Asia: 1600–1800.* Social Studies School Service, 1985. Asians respond to Western intrusions.

- *Forbidden City: The Great Within.* Cambridge Social Studies, 1995. 800-468-4227.

- *The Golden Age of Exploration.* Knowledge Unlimited, 1997. 800-356-2303.

Software

- *Exploration.* CD-ROM. Queue, 1997. 800-232-2224. Describes the voyages of the Portuguese, Columbus, and other explorers.

- *Stowaway!* CD-ROM. Social Studies School Service, 1994. 800-421-4246. Explore an 18th-century British warship.

Westerners were not the only ones to sail beyond their borders during the 1400s. In **1405**, the sailor, **Zheng He**, shown here, began exploring India, Persia, Arabia, and Africa for China. Unlike Europeans, however, the Chinese were uninterested in overseas exploration. After the voyages of Zheng He, China retreated into a 300-year period of isolationism in which it shunned the European explorers and traders who reached its shores.

Westerners had little luck making inroads into **Japan between 1600 and 1800.** Japan had a strong military tradition, reflected in this 18th century print of a samurai warrior. In addition, Japan's unified culture made it difficult for European traders to establish themselves there. Like the Chinese, the Japanese eventually closed their borders to outsiders and began a long period of isolationism.

— Holy Roman Empire

■ Ming Empire (1368–1644)

0   500 Miles

0   1,000 Kilometers

81

HISTORY THROUGH ART

Woodblock Print

The image of a samurai warrior is an 18th-century Japanese woodblock print. Woodblock print is the type of Japanese art best known to the Western world. It is the most famous art of the Tokugawa period (1603 to 1868). Because woodblock prints were inexpensively produced, they were popular among the common people. They depicted contemporary manners and customs, scenes of everyday life, beautiful women, kabuki actors, and rural landscapes. Woodblock prints are a valuable source of information about the lifestyle and social trends of the period. At first the prints were done in black and white. Later they were executed in brilliantly vibrant colors. Woodblock prints were a collaborative effort. An artist drew the design. A carver pasted the design on a block of wood and did the carving. A printer made the prints, and a publisher distributed them.

This print dramatically captures the samurai wearing the traditional short silk kimono and baggy trousers and carrying both the samurai's long and short sword.

Interpreting the Art Does this print seem effective in depicting the self-confidence and tenacity of a samurai warrior? In what ways?

Interact *with* History

Interact *with* History

Claiming new lands could bring glory and prestige to your country.

It is a gray and windy morning in 1430. You are standing on a dock in the European country of Portugal staring out at the dark and mysterious Atlantic Ocean. You, like most people at the time, have no idea what lies beyond the horizon. Now you may find out. You have been asked to go on a voyage of exploration.

You've heard all the terrifying stories of sea monsters and shipwrecks. You've heard the warnings that the currents along parts of western Africa are "so terrible that no ship having once passed . . . will ever be able to return." You also have heard that possible financial gain awaits those who help explore and claim new lands. Now, as the captain calls for you to come aboard, you must decide.

Would you go?

The large hold of your ship could carry back gold, jewels, and other valuable items found in distant lands.

Raging waves could destroy your ship and leave you at the mercy of the sea.

EXAMINING *the* ISSUES

- What possible rewards might come from exploring the seas for new lands?

- What are the risks involved in embarking on a voyage into the unknown?

Discuss these questions with your classmates. In your discussion, recall what you have learned about the lands beyond Europe and what they have to offer.

As you read about the age of exploration and isolation, see what goals prompted Europeans to explore and to what extent they achieved these goals.

1 Europeans Explore the East

TERMS & NAMES
- Bartolomeu Dias
- Prince Henry
- Vasco da Gama
- Treaty of Tordesillas
- Dutch East India Company

MAIN IDEA

Driven by the desire for wealth and Christian converts, Europeans began an age of exploration.

WHY IT MATTERS NOW

European exploration was an important step toward the global interaction that characterizes the world today.

SETTING THE STAGE By the early 1400s, Europeans were ready to venture beyond their borders. As Chapter 1 explained, the Renaissance encouraged, among other things, a new spirit of adventure and curiosity. This spirit of adventure—along with several other important factors—prompted Europeans to explore the world around them. This chapter and the next one describe how these explorations began a long process that would bring together the peoples of many different lands and permanently change the world.

This globe depicts the Europeans' view of the world around 1492. Europe and Africa, shown here, were the lands Europeans had explored most by that time.

Many Factors Encourage Exploration

Europeans had not been completely isolated from the rest of the world before the 1400s. Beginning around 1100, European crusaders battled Muslims for control of the Holy Lands in Southwest Asia. In 1275, the Italian trader Marco Polo reached the court of Kublai Khan in China. For the most part, however, Europeans had neither the interest nor the ability to explore foreign lands. That changed by the early 1400s. The desire to grow rich and to spread Christianity, coupled with advances in sailing technology, spurred an age of European exploration.

Europeans Seek Greater Wealth The desire for new sources of wealth was the main reason for European exploration. Through overseas exploration, merchants and traders hoped ultimately to benefit from what had become a profitable business in Europe: the trade of spices and other luxury goods from Asia. The people of Europe had been introduced to these items during the Crusades, the wars fought between Christians and Muslims from 1096 to 1270. After the Crusades ended, Europeans continued to demand such spices as nutmeg, ginger, cinnamon, and pepper—all of which added flavor to the bland foods of Europe. Because demand for these goods was greater than the supply, merchants could charge high prices and thus make great profits.

The Muslims and Italians controlled the trade of goods from East to West. Muslims sold Asian goods to Italian merchants, who controlled trade across the land routes of the Mediterranean region. The Italian merchants resold the items at increased prices to merchants throughout Europe. Other European traders did not like this arrangement. Paying such high prices to the Italians severely cut into their own profits. By the 1400s, European merchants—as well as the new monarchs of England, Spain, Portugal, and France—sought to bypass the Italian merchants. This meant finding a sea route directly to Asia.

The Spread of Christianity The desire to spread Christianity also fueled European exploration. Aside from leaving Europeans with a taste for spices, the Crusades left feelings of hostility between Christians and Muslims. European nations believed that they had a sacred duty not only to continue fighting

An Age of Exploration and Isolation **83**

A. Possible Answer The Italians controlled the trade and charged them high prices for the trade goods.

THINK THROUGH HISTORY
A. Analyzing Issues Why did many European merchants dislike the way goods were traded from East to West?

SECTION 1 RESOURCES

PRINT RESOURCES

 IN-DEPTH RESOURCES: UNIT 1
Guided Reading, p. 51
Primary Source: Exploration of Cape Verde, p. 57; The Treaty of Tordesillas, p. 58
History Makers: Vasco da Gama, p. 64
Science and Technology: A Revolution in Cartography, p. 67

 ACCESS FOR STUDENTS ACQUIRING ENGLISH
Guided Reading (Spanish), p. 41

 FORMAL ASSESSMENT
Section Quiz, p. 40

 ALTERNATIVE ASSESSMENT BOOK

TECHNOLOGY RESOURCES

 WORLD ART AND CULTURES TRANSPARENCIES
AT41 Portuguese Tower of Belém

 INTERNET www.mlworldhistory.com

Section 1 Overview

OBJECTIVES

1. To identify the factors that led to European exploration.
2. To describe how Portugal established a sea route to Asia.
3. To identify which nations set up trading empires in the East and where those nations dominated.

SKILLBUILDER
- Interpreting maps: place, region, p. 87

CRITICAL THINKING
- Analyzing issues, pp. 83, 86, 88
- Summarizing, p. 84
- Analyzing motives, p. 85
- Recognizing effects, pp. 87, 88
- Making inferences, p. 88
- Analyzing themes, p. 88

FOCUS
5-Minute Warm-Up

▶ *Interpreting Maps*
Answering the following questions will help students understand the impact of European exploration in the East.

1. Study the map on p. 87. Which European country sent out the first voyages of exploration to the East?

2. What European countries had established trading posts in the East by 1700?

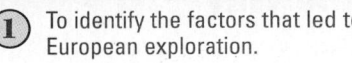 *WARM-UP TRANSPARENCY 3*

OBJECTIVE ① INSTRUCT

Many Factors Encourage Exploration

▶ *Key Ideas*
- Profit is the main motive for European exploration in the 1400s.
- Europeans also hope to spread Christianity to other lands.
- Technological advances make long-distance voyages possible.

 IN-DEPTH RESOURCES: UNIT 1
Guided Reading, p. 51

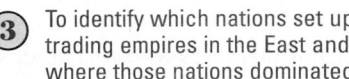 *ACCESS FOR STUDENTS ACQUIRING ENGLISH*
Guided Reading (Spanish), p. 41

Portugal Leads the Way

▶ *Key Ideas*
- Prince Henry pushes for voyages of exploration.
- Portuguese sailors establish a direct sea route to Asia.
- Columbus's voyage west across the Atlantic intensifies the rivalry between Spain and Portugal.

 IN-DEPTH RESOURCES: UNIT 1
Primary Source: Exploration of Cape Verde, p. 57

 WORLD ART AND CULTURES TRANSPARENCIES
AT41 Portuguese Tower of Belém

CRITICAL THINKING ACTIVITY
CLASS TIME: 15 MINUTES

Analyzing Causes
Have students use a graphic organizer to show the causes of European exploration. *Desire for profit; hope to spread Christianity; technological advances.*

Cause	
Cause	European exploration of the East
Cause	

Ask students which of these causes might have prompted wealthy individuals to finance voyages of exploration.

HISTORYMAKERS
Prince Henry

Briefly discuss Henry's personal characteristics and his devotion to his work. Then ask students to imagine that the king has invited Henry to travel to the Portuguese capital to attend a party celebrating the return of a ship from Africa. Have them write Henry's response either accepting the invitation or declining to go.

Muslims, but also to convert non-Christians throughout the world.

Europeans hoped to obtain popular goods directly from the peoples of Asia. They also hoped to Christianize them. **Bartolomeu Dias,** an early Portuguese explorer, explained his motives: "to serve God and His Majesty, to give light to those who were in darkness and to grow rich as all men desire to do."

Technological Advances While "God, glory, and gold" were the primary motives for exploration, advances in technology made the voyages of discovery possible. During the 1200s, it would have been nearly impossible for a European sea captain to cross 3,000 miles of ocean and return again. The main problem was that European ships could not sail against the wind. In the 1400s, shipbuilders designed a new vessel—the caravel. The caravel was sturdier than earlier vessels. In addition, its triangular sails allowed it to sail effectively against the wind.

Europeans also improved their navigational techniques. To better determine their location on the sea, sailors used the astrolabe, which the Muslims had perfected. The astrolabe was a brass circle with carefully adjusted rings marked off in degrees. Using the rings to sight the stars, a sea captain could tell how far north or south of the equator he was. Explorers were also able to more accurately track their direction by using a magnetic compass invented by the Chinese.

HISTORYMAKERS

**Prince Henry
1394–1460**

For his role in promoting Portuguese exploration, Prince Henry is often called Henry the Navigator. Historians paint Henry as a quiet and extremely driven man. So consumed was he by the quest to find new lands, that he reportedly shunned female companionship.

Throughout his life, Henry supposedly showed little emotion. It was said that no one ever saw him lose his temper. When angry with someone, Henry allegedly just waved them from his presence, uttering, "I commend you to God, may you be fortunate." While some considered him to be cold and distant, others insisted that the prince had a sensitive side. One writer claimed that upon learning of the death of a friend, Henry wept nonstop for several days.

Portugal Leads the Way

The leader in developing and applying these sailing innovations was Portugal. Located on the Atlantic Ocean at the southwest corner of Europe, Portugal first established trading outposts along the west coast of Africa. Eventually, Portuguese explorers pushed farther east into the Indian Ocean.

The Portuguese Explore Africa Portugal took the lead in overseas exploration in part due to strong government support. The nation's most enthusiastic supporter of exploration was **Prince Henry,** the son of Portugal's king. Henry's dreams of overseas exploration began in 1415 when he helped conquer the Muslim city of Ceuta in North Africa. There, he had his first glimpse of the dazzling wealth that lay beyond Europe. Throughout Ceuta, the Portuguese invaders found exotic stores filled with pepper, cinnamon, cloves, and other spices. In addition, they encountered large supplies of gold, silver, and jewels.

Henry returned to Portugal determined to reach the source of these treasures in the East. The prince also wished to spread the Christian faith. In 1419, Henry founded a navigation school on the southwestern coast of Portugal. Mapmakers, instrument makers, shipbuilders, scientists, and sea captains gathered there to perfect their trade.

Within several years, Portuguese ships began creeping down the western coast of Africa. By the time Henry died in 1460, the Portuguese had established a series of trading posts along the shores of Africa. There, they traded with Africans for such profitable items as gold and ivory. Eventually, they traded for African captives to be used as slaves. Having established their presence along Africa's western coast, Portuguese explorers plotted their next daring move. They would find a sea route to Asia.

Portuguese Sailors Reach Asia The Portuguese believed that to reach Asia by sea, they would have to sail around the southern tip of Africa. In 1487, Portuguese captain Bartolomeu Dias ventured

---

CONNECTIONS ACROSS TIME AND PLACE

The Caravel Ask students how they would have gone about designing a ship for the special needs of the long-distance explorer. The ship had to be large enough to carry cargo but agile enough to sail against the wind. The caravel's designers combined the features of two existing ships that offered those qualities. One was a kind of dhow called a *caravos,* a lateen-rigged vessel capable of hauling cargo of the size that explorers would need. Arabs had been sailing this type of dhow along the coasts of Egypt and Tunis since ancient times. The other model ship, known as a *caravela,* plied the waters of a river in northern Portugal. Designers liked this vessel's superb maneuverability.

MULTIPLE LEARNING STYLES

Linguistic Learners Tell students that in 1471, Portuguese explorers arrived at a region later known as the Gold Coast, or modern Ghana. Soon they controlled the West African trade in gold—one-tenth of the world's production. The riches of West Africa would help bankroll Portugal's exploration of the East. Invite students to theorize about how the first Portuguese, arriving at the Gold Coast, discovered that the region held such riches. Have them create and present a dialogue between a Portuguese sea captain and an African leader in which the European attempts to find out if there is gold in the area and then tries to establish a trading relationship.

The Tools of Exploration

Out on the open seas, winds easily blew ships off course. With only the sun, moon, and stars to guide them, few sailors willingly ventured beyond the sight of land. In order to travel to distant parts of the world, European inventors and sailors experimented with new tools for navigation and new designs for sailing ships.

The triangular sails allowed the caravel to sail effectively against the wind. With these sails the ship could tack (sail on a zigzag course) more directly into the wind than could a square-rigged ship.

Here, a naval officer uses a sextant, which replaced the astrolabe in measuring the height of the stars above the horizon.

The improved rudder allowed the caravel to turn more easily.

The large cargo area was capable of carrying the numerous supplies needed for long voyages.

This 16th century Italian compass (with its lid beside it) is typical of those taken by navigators on the great voyages of exploration. The compass was invented by the Chinese.

Connect *to* History

Analyzing Motives Why did inventors and sailors develop better tools for navigation?

SEE SKILLBUILDER HANDBOOK, PAGE 652

Connect *to* Today

Modern Sailing Investigate what types of navigational or other tools modern sailors use. Choose one tool and write a brief explanation of what it does. Be prepared to present your report to the class.

An Age of Exploration and Isolation **85**

Besides their sailing technology, Europeans developed another valuable aid to the expansion of trade—the shipboard cannon. Designers overcame great technical problems to be able to mount these powerful weapons all around a sailing ship's perimeter. Bristling with cannons, European warships defeated Muslim fleets in the Indian Ocean and controlled trade routes from Africa to the East Indies.

IN-DEPTH RESOURCES: UNIT 1
Science and Technology: A Revolution in Cartography, p. 67

MORE ABOUT . . .
The Sextant

The sextant incorporated a telescope, mirrors, and an arc of a circle calibrated in degrees. With this device, a mariner could read the angle of elevation above the horizon of the moon, the sun, or another star. With this information, the exact time of day, and published tables, the ship's latitude could be determined.

MORE ABOUT . . .
The Compass

The Italian compass shown here has a *T,* which stands for "north wind" but represents the direction north. The association of wind with direction is ancient. Before the invention of the magnetic compass, sailors throughout the world used familiar local winds to determine direction. (They also took note of where the sun rose and set.) Even after the compass came into use, the link between the wind and direction remained strong—and not just among Italian sailors. For example, Spanish mariners called compass directions *los vientos* ("the winds"). Portuguese sailors called their compass card, printed with the various compass directions, a *rosa dos ventos,* or "wind rose."

Connect *to* History

Analyzing Motives
Possible Responses: They might have been motivated by the basic need to improve the ability to navigate ships or by the desire to bring glory and wealth to their country; they might simply have delighted in the innovative and demanding task of improving navigational tools.

Connect *to* Today

Modern Sailing
You may wish to suggest to students the following strategies for investigating modern navigational tools and preparing a report on their findings:

• Check library resources and the Internet to locate information on modern maritime navigation.

• Obtain a visual of the navigational tool they select to be used with the explanatory paragraph.

Daily *Life*
A Rough Trip

Life aboard a ship during the age of exploration was no pleasure cruise. With no refrigeration system, foods such as fruits, vegetables, and meats quickly rotted. For nourishment, sailors often had to rely on a rock-hard, bland-tasting biscuit, known as hardtack.

In addition, swift and brutal punishment often awaited those who broke the ship's rules. The most common punishment was with the "cat-o'-nine-tails," a whip made of nine knotted cords (shown here). The sailor was tied down and repeatedly struck on his bare back.

---

farther down the coast of Africa until he reached the tip. As he arrived, a huge storm rose and battered his fleet for days. When the storm ended, Dias realized his ships had been blown around the tip to the other side of the continent. Dias explored the southeast coast of Africa and then considered sailing to India. However, his crew was exhausted and food supplies were low. As a result, the captain returned home.

With the southern tip of Africa finally rounded, the Portuguese continued pushing east. In 1498, the Portuguese explorer **Vasco da Gama** reached the port of Calicut, on the southwestern coast of India. Da Gama and his crew were amazed by the spices, as well as the rare silks and precious gems, that filled Calicut's shops. The Portuguese sailors filled their ships with such spices as pepper and cinnamon and returned to Portugal in 1499. The Portuguese gave da Gama a hero's welcome. His remarkable voyage of 27,000 miles had given Portugal a direct sea route to India.

Spanish Claims Before da Gama's historic voyage, as the Portuguese established trading posts along the west coast of Africa, Spain watched with increasing envy. The Spanish monarchs also desired a direct sea route to the treasures of Asia.

In 1492, an Italian sea captain, Christopher Columbus, convinced Spain to finance what was at that time a bold plan: finding a route to Asia by sailing west across the Atlantic Ocean. In October of that year, Columbus reached the shores of an island in the Caribbean. Columbus's voyage would open the way for European colonization of the American continents—a process that would forever change the world. The immediate impact of Columbus's voyage, however, was to increase tensions between Spain and Portugal.

Columbus thought that he had indeed reached Asia. Believing him to be right, Portugal suspected that Columbus had claimed for Spain lands that Portuguese sailors might have reached first. The rivalry between Spain and Portugal grew more tense. In 1493, Pope Alexander VI stepped in to keep peace between the two nations. He suggested an imaginary dividing line, drawn north to south, through the Atlantic Ocean. All lands to the west of the line, known as the Line of Demarcation, would be Spain's. All lands to the east of the line would belong to Portugal.

Portugal complained that the line gave too much to Spain. So it was moved farther west to include parts of modern-day Brazil for the Portuguese. In 1494, Spain and Portugal signed the **Treaty of Tordesillas,** in which they agreed to honor the line. The era of exploration and colonization was about to begin in earnest.

Trading Empires in the Indian Ocean

With da Gama's voyage, Europeans had finally opened direct sea trade with Asia. They also opened an era of violent conflict in the East. European nations scrambled to establish profitable trading outposts along the shores of South and Southeast Asia. And all the while they battled the region's inhabitants, as well as each other.

Portugal's Trading Empire In the years following da Gama's voyage, Portugal built a bustling trading empire throughout the Indian Ocean. As they moved into the region, they took control of the spice trade from Muslim merchants. In 1509, Portugal extended its control over the area when it defeated a Muslim fleet off the coast of India.

The following year, the Portuguese captured Goa, a port city on India's west coast. They made it the capital of their trading empire. They then sailed farther east to Indonesia, also known as the East Indies. In 1511, a Portuguese fleet attacked the city of Malacca on the west coast of the Malay peninsula. In capturing the town, the

---

Portuguese seized control of the Strait of Malacca. Seizing this waterway gave them control of the Moluccas. These were islands so rich in spices that they became known as the Spice Islands.

In convincing his crew to attack Malacca, Portuguese sea captain Afonso de Albuquerque stressed his country's intense desire to crush the Muslim-Italian domination over Asian trade:

A VOICE FROM THE PAST

. . . If we deprive them [Muslims] of this their ancient market there, there does not remain for them a single port in the whole of these parts, where they can carry on their trade in these things. . . . I hold it as very certain that if we take this trade of Malacca away out of their hands, Cairo and Mecca are entirely ruined, and to Venice will no spiceries . . . [be] . . . conveyed except that which her merchants go and buy in Portugal.

AFONSO DE ALBUQUERQUE, from *The Commentaries of the Great Afonso Dalboquerque*

Portugal did indeed break the old trade network from the East—much to the delight of European consumers. Portuguese merchants brought back goods from Asia at about a fifth of what they cost when purchased through the Arabs and Italians. As a result, more Europeans could afford these items.

In time, Portugal's success in Asia attracted the attention of other European nations. As early as 1521, a Spanish expedition led by Ferdinand Magellan arrived in the Philippines. Spain claimed the islands and began settling them in 1565. By the early 1600s, the rest of Europe had begun descending upon Asia. They were looking to establish their own trade empires in the East.

Other Nations Drive Out the Portuguese Beginning around 1600, the English and Dutch began to challenge Portugal's dominance over the Indian Ocean trade. The Dutch Republic is also known as the Netherlands. It is a small country situated along

Europeans in the East, 1700

GEOGRAPHY SKILLBUILDER: Interpreting Maps
1. **Place** Which Asian country had the most European trade outposts by 1700?
2. **Region** Where was the Dutch influence the greatest?

87

Logical-Mathematical Learners Remind students that as a result of Portugal's success in establishing a trading empire in the East, the cost to consumers of Asian goods fell to about a fifth of their former price. Have students make a chart listing a variety of fairly expensive consumer goods available today and showing both the retail price and one-fifth of the retail price. (They might find prices for such goods in newspaper advertisements or department store fliers.) Invite students to discuss what they think the effects might be today of such a radical drop in prices.

Economics Invite students to speculate about the economy of the East Indies before the appearance of Europeans. Tell them that in the 1500s, some 90 percent of Southeast Asians (including the people of the East Indies) made a living from agriculture. Most of them raised rice for local markets, but many had turned to commercial crops such as spices or sugar, which could be traded for manufactured goods, silk, and other luxuries. For Southeast Asia, this era was a golden age. Long-distance trade, even before the Europeans arrived, had increased wealth and introduced new products, cultures, and ideas.

the North Sea in northwestern Europe. Since the early 1500s, Spain had ruled this area. In 1581, the people of the region declared their independence from Spain and established the Dutch Republic.

In a short time, the Netherlands became a leading sea power. By 1600, the Dutch owned the largest fleet of ships in the world—20,000 vessels. Together, the English and Dutch broke Portuguese control of the Asian region. The two nations then battled one another for dominance of the area. Each nation had formed an East India Company to establish and direct trade throughout Asia. These companies had the power to mint money, make treaties, and even raise their own armies. The **Dutch East India Company** was richer and more powerful than England's company. As a result, the Dutch eventually drove out the English and established their dominance over the region.

European Trade Outposts In 1619, the Dutch established their trading headquarters at Batavia on the island of Java. From there they expanded west to conquer several nearby islands. In addition, the Dutch seized both the port of Malacca and the valuable Spice Islands from Portugal. Throughout the 1600s, the Netherlands increased its control over the Indian Ocean trade. With so many goods from the East traveling to the Netherlands, the nation's capital, Amsterdam, became a leading commercial center. By 1700, the Dutch ruled much of Indonesia and had trading posts in numerous Asian countries. They also controlled the Cape of Good Hope on the southern tip of Africa.

By this time, however, Britain and France had gained a foothold in the region. Having failed to gain control of the larger area, the English East India Company focused much of its energy on establishing outposts in India. There, the English built up a successful business trading fine cloth on the European market. In 1664, France also entered the Asia trade with its own East India Company. The company struggled at first, as it faced continual attacks by the Dutch. The French company finally established an outpost in India in the 1720s. However, it never showed a strong profit.

As the Europeans battled for a share of the profitable Indian Ocean trade, their influence in inland Southeast Asia remained relatively limited. European traders did gain control of numerous port cities throughout the region. However, their influence rarely spread beyond the ports into the countries' interiors. From 1500 to about 1800—when Europeans began to conquer much of the region—the peoples of Asia remained largely unaffected by European contact. As the next two sections explain, European traders who sailed farther east to seek riches in China and Japan had even less success in spreading Western culture.

CONNECT *to* TODAY

The Dutch in South Africa

Since colonizing the Cape of Good Hope, the Dutch have retained a powerful and controversial presence in South Africa. Dutch settlers, known as Boers, continually battled the British after Great Britain seized the region in 1806.

The Boers, who now call themselves Afrikaners, gained some control in 1924. They began restricting the rights of the nation's mostly nonwhite population. In 1948, the Afrikaners took control of the government. They established apartheid, a legal system of severe discrimination.

During the 1990s, the government began repealing its apartheid laws, as it finally agreed to share power with the Africans.

Section 1 Assessment

1. TERMS & NAMES

Identify
- Bartolomeu Dias
- Prince Henry
- Vasco da Gama
- Treaty of Tordesillas
- Dutch East India Company

2. TAKING NOTES

Trace the establishment of Portugal's trading empire in the Indian Ocean by supplying the significant event for each date shown on the time line below.

Write the lead paragraph for a news story about one of the time line events.

3. MAKING INFERENCES

What did the Treaty of Tordesillas reveal about Europeans' attitudes toward non-European lands and peoples?

THINK ABOUT
- the dispute between the Portuguese and Spanish
- how the treaty settled the dispute

4. ANALYZING THEMES

Science and Technology In what ways did Europeans owe some of their sailing technology to other peoples of the world?

THINK ABOUT
- the astrolabe
- the compass

88 Chapter 3

ANSWERS

2 China Rejects European Outreach

TERMS & NAMES
• Ming Dynasty
• Hongwu
• Yonglo
• Zheng He
• Manchus
• Qing Dynasty
• Kangxi

MAIN IDEA

Advances under the Ming and Qing dynasties left China self-contained and uninterested in European contact.

WHY IT MATTERS NOW

China's independence from the West continues today, even as it forges new economic ties with the outside world.

SETTING THE STAGE Europeans made healthy profits in the Indian Ocean trade. Looking for additional sources of wealth, they sought a trading relationship with China. By the time westerners arrived in the 1500s, China had driven out its Mongol rulers and had united under the Ming Dynasty.

The Ming Dynasty

By the time the first Portuguese ships dropped anchor off the Chinese coast in 1514, China had become the dominant power in the region under the rule of the **Ming Dynasty** (1368–1644). In recognition of China's power, vassal states from Korea to Southeast Asia paid their Ming overlords regular tribute, a payment by one nation to another to acknowledge its submission. China expected the Europeans to do the same. The Ming rulers would not allow outsiders from distant lands to threaten the peace and prosperity they had brought to China following the end of Mongol rule.

The Rise of the Ming **Hongwu,** the son of a peasant, commanded the rebel army that drove the Mongols out of China in 1368. That same year he became the first emperor of the Ming Dynasty. Hongwu continued to rule from the former Yuan capital of Nanjing in the south. He began reforms designed to restore agricultural lands devastated by war, erase all traces of the Mongol past, and promote China's power and prosperity. Hongwu's agricultural reforms increased rice production and improved irrigation. He also encouraged the introduction of fish farming and the growing of commercial crops, such as cotton and sugar cane.

The first Ming emperor used respected traditions and institutions to bring stability to China. For example, he encouraged a return to Confucian moral standards. He improved imperial administration by restoring the merit-based civil service examination system. Later in his rule, however, when problems began to develop, Hongwu became a ruthless tyrant. Suspecting plots against his rule everywhere, he conducted purges in which many thousands of government officials were killed.

Hongwu's death in 1398 led to a power struggle. His son **Yonglo** (yung·lu) emerged victorious from this struggle. Yonglo continued many of his father's policies, although he moved the royal court to Beijing. In addition, Yonglo had a far-ranging curiosity about the outside world. In 1405—before Europeans began to sail beyond their borders—he launched the first of seven voyages of exploration. All were led by a Chinese Muslim admiral named **Zheng He** (jung huh).

The Voyages of Zheng He Zheng He's expeditions were remarkable for their magnitude. Everything about them was large—distances traveled, size of the fleet, and measurements of the ships themselves. The earliest voyages were to Southeast Asia and India. Later expeditions roamed as far as Arabia and eastern Africa.

Vocabulary
vassal states: countries that recognize the overlordship, or domination, of another country.

Background
Confucianism stressed social order, harmony, and good government through education, strong family relationships, and respect for elders.

Vocabulary
purges: ways of ridding a nation, or political party, of people considered undesirable.

This blue and white porcelain vase, with its finely detailed pattern, is from the Ming Dynasty. Ming porcelain is considered to be one of the culture's most famous achievements.

An Age of Exploration and Isolation **89**

SKILLBUILDER
• Interpreting graphs, p. 92

CRITICAL THINKING
• Making inferences, pp. 90, 92
• Summarizing, p. 91
• Recognizing effects, p. 93
• Making decisions, p. 93

FOCUS
5-Minute Warm-Up

▶ *Making Inferences*
To help students understand something about Chinese history, have them answer the following questions.

1. Read the Spotlight On the Forbidden City on p. 90. Why was the palace complex called the Forbidden City?

2. What can you infer about the nature of China and of the emperor from this feature?

WARM-UP TRANSPARENCY 3

OBJECTIVE ① INSTRUCT

The Ming Dynasty

▶ *Key Ideas*
• The early Ming emperors stabilize China and help it prosper.
• The voyages of Zheng He showcase China's power and expand its tribute system.
• China officially limits trade with foreign merchants.
• Europeans help increase Chinese manufacturing and commerce and introduce Christianity.

IN-DEPTH RESOURCES: UNIT 1
Guided Reading, p. 52
Geography Application: The Voyages of Zheng He, p. 55
Primary Source: from *The Journals of Matteo Ricci*, p. 59

ACCESS FOR STUDENTS ACQUIRING ENGLISH
Guided Reading (Spanish), p. 42

CRITICAL THINKING ACTIVITY
CLASS TIME: 15 MINUTES

Hypothesizing

Ask students how history might have been different if the Chinese had continued to launch voyages like those of Zheng He for another hundred years. *Lead students to see that China's powerful fleet might well have clashed with European fleets seeking Indian Ocean trade.*

MORE ABOUT . . .
China's Trade Policies

Limits on trade did not begin with the arrival of Europeans. China had long restricted the access of Japan, Indonesia, and other neighboring lands, assigning specific ports through which they could trade. As a result, merchants turned to smuggling in order to meet the great demand for Chinese silks, porcelains, and other precious goods. Smuggling had a further effect—it encouraged the emergence of numerous Chinese and Japanese pirates, who preyed on the merchants' boats and made off with their illicit cargoes.

SPOTLIGHT ON
The Forbidden City

The palace complex contained living quarters, libraries, galleries, and audience halls for tribute ceremonies. Beautiful gardens of pines, cypresses, and rare flowers adorned the grounds. Ask students whether they would have enjoyed living in a place like this. Be sure that they weigh the pleasures of palace life against the limits of walled-in isolation.

Yonglo hoped to impress the world with the power and splendor of Ming China and also hoped to expand China's tribute system. Zheng He's voyages accomplished these goals. From about 40 to 300 ships sailed in each expedition. Among them were fighting ships, storage vessels, and huge "treasure" ships up to 440 feet long. The fleet's crews numbered over 27,000 on some voyages. They included sailors, soldiers, carpenters, interpreters, accountants, doctors, and religious leaders. Like some huge floating city, the fleet sailed from port to port along the Indian Ocean.

Everywhere Zheng He went, he distributed gifts, such as gold, silver, silk, and scented oils, to show Chinese superiority. As a result, more than 16 countries sent tribute to the Ming court. Many envoys traveled to China. Still, Chinese scholar-officials complained that these voyages wasted valuable resources. After the seventh voyage ended in 1433, there were no more. China withdrew into its self-sufficient isolation.

Ming Relations with Foreign Countries China's official trade policies in the 1500s reflected its isolation. To keep the influence of outsiders to a minimum, only the government was to conduct foreign trade, through three coastal ports. In reality, trade flourished up and down the coast. Profit-minded Chinese merchants smuggled cargoes of silk, porcelain, and other valuable goods out of the country into the eager hands of European merchants. Usually, Europeans paid for their purchases with silver—much of it from mines in the Americas.

Demand for Chinese goods had a ripple effect on the economy. Industries such as silk making and ceramics grew rapidly. Manufacturing and commerce increased. However, China did not become highly industrialized for two main reasons. First, the whole idea of commerce offended China's Confucian beliefs. Merchants, it was said, made their money "supporting foreigners and robbery." Second, Chinese economic policies traditionally favored agriculture. Taxes on agriculture stayed low. Taxes on manufacturing and trade skyrocketed.

Accompanying European traders into China were Christian missionaries. The missionaries brought Christianity as well as a variety of European inventions, including the clock and the prism. The first missionary to have an impact was an Italian Jesuit, Matteo Ricci. He gained special favor at the Ming court through his intelligence and his ability to speak and write Chinese. However, many educated Chinese opposed Christianity.

Vocabulary
envoys: government representatives sent to a foreign country.

THINK THROUGH HISTORY
A. Making Inferences What do you think the people of other countries thought about China when they were visited on one of Zheng He's voyages?
A. Possible Answer That China must be very powerful to send so many ships, men, and goods on such a voyage and, therefore, they should pay tribute.

SPOTLIGHT ON

The Forbidden City

A stunning monument to China's isolationism was an extravagant palace complex at the capital city, Beijing. It was built by emperor Yonglo between 1404 and 1420. The palace was known as the Forbidden City because all commoners and foreigners were forbidden to enter without special permission. Inside the complex's 35-foot-tall red walls, the emperors of China conducted the business of state and lived in luxury and isolation.

Only the emperor, his family, and his court lived in the palace—which contained 9,000 rooms. Maintaining such a splendid palace city was expensive. For example, every day some 6,000 cooks made meals for 10,000 to 15,000 people. In 1949, the palace complex was converted into a museum and opened to the public.

TEACHING OPTION | BLOCK SCHEDULING

COOPERATIVE ACTIVITY: Panel Discussion

CLASS TIME 30 MINUTES

Task: Students will take on the roles of Chinese officials and merchants and European traders and will discuss their concerns related to China's foreign trade.

Purpose: To examine issues surrounding China's trading relationship with foreign countries.

Activity: Have students brainstorm to create a list of issues associated with the China trade. Each group will then look at each problem from the perspective of a Chinese government official, a Chinese merchant, or a European trader and prepare a set of discussion points. One member of each group will join the panel to discuss the issues. Students not on the panel should take notes on the points made by other groups.

📁 **Building a Portfolio:** Students might wish to add their group's discussion points to their portfolios, along with a list of the main points presented by the other groups.

📖 **ALTERNATIVE ASSESSMENT BOOK**
Standards for Evaluating a Cooperative Activity

Standards for Evaluation
Discussion points should . . .

- clearly state issues related to China's foreign trade
- reflect one particular point of view
- be presented appropriately during the panel discussion

The Qing Dynasty

By 1600, the Ming had ruled for more than 200 years, and the dynasty was weakening. Its problems grew—ineffective rulers, corrupt officials, and a government out of money. Higher taxes and bad harvests pushed millions of peasants toward starvation. Civil strife and rebellion followed.

Beyond the northeast end of the Great Wall lay Manchuria. In 1644, the **Manchus** (MAN·chooz), the people of that region, invaded China. The Ming could not repel the invasion, and the dynasty collapsed. The Manchus took over Beijing, and the Manchu leader became China's new emperor. As the Mongols had done, the Manchus took a Chinese name for their dynasty, the **Qing** (chihng) **Dynasty.** They would rule China for more than 260 years and bring Taiwan, Chinese Central Asia, Mongolia, and Tibet into China.

China Under the Qing Dynasty Many Chinese resisted rule by the non-Chinese Manchus. Rebellions flared up periodically for decades. The Manchus forced Chinese men to wear their hair in a pigtail as a sign of submission to their rule. The Manchus, however, slowly earned the people's respect. They upheld China's traditional Confucian beliefs and social structures. They made the country's frontiers safe and restored China's prosperity. Two powerful Manchu rulers contributed greatly to the acceptance of the new dynasty.

The first, **Kangxi** (kahng·shee), became emperor in 1661 and ruled for some 60 years. Kangxi reduced government expenses and lowered taxes. A scholar and patron of the arts, Kangxi gained the support of Chinese intellectuals by offering them government positions. He also enjoyed the company of the Jesuits at court. They informed him of the latest developments in science, medicine, and mathematics in Europe.

Under Kangxi's grandson Qian-long (chyahn·lung), who ruled from 1736 to 1795, China reached its greatest size and prosperity. An industrious emperor like his grandfather, Qian-long often rose at dawn to work on the problems of the empire. Those problems included armed nomads on its borders, Christian missionaries, and European merchants.

Manchus Continue a Policy of Isolation To the Chinese, their country—the Middle Kingdom—had been the cultural center of the universe for two thousand years. If foreign states wished to trade with China, they would have to follow Chinese rules. These included trading only at special ports and paying tribute.

The Dutch, masters of the Indian Ocean trade by the time of Qian-long, accepted these restrictions. Their diplomats paid tribute to China's emperor through gifts and by performing the required "kowtow" ritual. This ritual involved their kneeling in front of the emperor and touching their heads to the ground nine times. As a result, the Chinese accepted the Dutch as trading partners. The Dutch returned home with traditional porcelains and silk, as well as China's highly prized new trade item—tea. By 1800, tea would make up 80 percent of shipments to Europe.

Great Britain also wanted to increase trade with China. However, the British did not like China's trade restrictions. In 1793, a British mission led by Lord George Macartney delivered a letter from King George III to Qian-long. The letter asked for a better trade arrangement, including Chinese acceptance of British manufactured goods. Macartney refused to kowtow to the emperor, although he reportedly bowed

THINK THROUGH HISTORY
B. Summarizing
How did the Manchus earn the respect of the Chinese?
B. Possible Answer They upheld China's traditional Confucian beliefs and social structures, secured the country's frontiers, and restored its prosperity.

Background
Tea was first known in China around 2700 B.C. as a medicine. It did not become a daily drink until the third century A.D.

HISTORY MAKERS

Kangxi
1654–1722

The emperor Kangxi had too much curiosity to remain isolated in the Forbidden City. To calm the Chinese in areas devastated by the Manchu conquest, Kangxi set out on a series of "tours."

On tours I learned about the common people's grievances by talking with them. . . . I asked peasants about their officials, looked at their houses, and discussed their crops.

In 1696, with Mongols threatening the northern border, Kangxi exhibited the kind of leadership unheard of in later Ming times. Instead of waiting in the palace for news from the front, he personally led 80,000 troops to victory over the Mongols.

An Age of Exploration and Isolation **91**

OBJECTIVE 2 INSTRUCT

The Qing Dynasty

▶ *Key Ideas*
- The Manchus bring security and prosperity back to China.
- Severe restrictions on foreign trade limit Europeans' access to China's goods.
- Korea maintains its strong political ties with China but experiences social changes.

HISTORY MAKERS
Kangxi

Tell students that people in southern China had fought fiercely against the Manchu invaders. When Kangxi toured their region, many resented the new, non-Chinese emperor. One of Kangxi's goals was to improve the Manchus' image. His ability to speak and write Chinese and his sincere admiration of Chinese culture helped him in this effort. (Point out the open book in the picture of Kangxi on this page.) Have students write an editorial that might have appeared in a southern Chinese newspaper the day after Kangxi left.

MORE ABOUT . . .
Kowtow

The price of trading with China included the kowtow as part of the tribute custom. The kowtow ritual, performed by anyone who came before the emperor, called for "three kneelings and nine prostrations." The term itself comes from a Chinese word meaning "head knockings." To show their sincerity, kowtowing Qing officials often knocked their heads so hard they bled. By kowtowing, foreign envoys acknowledged the superiority of China and its emperor, and this they found very difficult to do.

TEACHING OPTIONS

CUSTOMIZING FOR SPECIAL NEEDS

Less Proficient Readers Be sure students can explain the difference between the Mongols and the Manchus. Both peoples came from outside China's borders, and both conquered China. The Mongols originated on the vast grasslands north of China's Great Wall, while the Manchus came from a region to the northeast. The Mongols ruled for a little less than 100 years, from 1279 to 1368.

The Manchus ruled from 1644 to 1912, nearly 300 years, and were China's last dynasty. Students should also be able to explain that *Manchu* is the name of a people who formed the Qing dynasty. For clarification, you might write the following sentence on the chalkboard: *During the Qing dynasty, Manchu rulers fought several battles against Mongol groups who again threatened China.*

MULTIPLE LEARNING STYLES

Visual Learners The attempts by Europeans to loosen China's trade restrictions provide abundant subject matter for students who learn best through visual means. Ask students to draw a political cartoon on some aspect of the trade issue. One possible subject is the smuggling that took place along China's coast to avoid the official ports. A second is the idea that commerce

was offensive to traditional Confucian beliefs. Another is the Chinese requirement that Europeans give gifts to the emperor and perform the kowtow. The Emperor Qian-long–Lord George Macartney incident is an example. Remind students that political cartoons convey their message through humor.

Teacher's Edition 91

CONNECT *to* TODAY

North Korea: The Hermit Kingdom

Have students list some characteristics traditionally ascribed to hermits, such as being gruff, quiet, misunderstood, self-sufficient, and antisocial. Discuss how these characteristics might apply to a "hermit kingdom."

 OBJECTIVE 3 INSTRUCT

Daily Life in Ming and Qing China

▶ **Key Ideas**
- China remains largely a country of farmers.
- Women have important family responsibilities but suffer by being treated as socially inferior.
- The Chinese enjoy traditional cultural pursuits.

IN-DEPTH RESOURCES: UNIT 1
Literature: from *The Dream of the Red Chamber*, p. 61

History from Visuals

The Growth of Early Modern China

Interpreting Graphs What two fifty-year periods had the slowest rate of growth? *From 1650 to 1700 and from 1850 to 1900 (as indicated by the most gradual slope in the line).*

Extension Activity Ask students how the peace and prosperity of the 1600s and 1700s contributed to the population boom. *Possible Response: Fewer deaths occurred from warfare and starvation.*

SKILLBUILDER Answers
1. By about 250 percent.
2. A larger population means a growth in towns, where people live close together and exchange ideas and customs.

---

on one knee. Qian-long denied Britain's request. As Qian-long made clear in a letter to the British king, China was self-sufficient:

> **A VOICE FROM THE PAST**
> . . . There is nothing we lack, as your principal envoy and others have themselves observed. We have never set much store on strange or ingenious objects, nor do we need any more of your country's manufactures.
> **QIAN-LONG,** from a letter to King George III of Great Britain

In the 1800s, the British, Dutch, and others would attempt to chip away at China's trade restrictions until the empire itself began to crack, as Chapter 12 will describe.

THINK THROUGH HISTORY
C. Making Inferences Why do you think the kowtow ritual was so important to the Chinese emperor?
C. Possible Answer It reaffirmed for him the Chinese belief that their culture was vastly superior to others.

CONNECT *to* TODAY

North Korea: The Hermit Kingdom
In the 17th and 18th centuries, Korea's strict isolation from the outside world caused it to be described as "the hermit kingdom." In the 1990s, this description can still be applied to communist North Korea. Closed to outsiders, North Korea has very little contact with other nations, even South Korea. China is still its only real ally.

Korea Under the Manchus In 1636, even before they came to power in China, the Manchus conquered nearby Korea and made it a vassal state. As a member of the Chinese tribute system, Korea had long existed in China's shadow. Koreans organized their government according to Confucian principles. They adopted China's technology, its culture, and especially its policy of isolation.

When the Manchus established the Qing Dynasty, Korea's political relationship with China did not change. If anything, it grew stronger. Under the Manchus, Korea was China's "little brother." Below the surface, however, Korea did change. The Manchu invasion, combined with a Japanese attack in the 1590s, provoked strong feelings of nationalism in the Korean people. This sentiment was most evident in their art. Instead of traditional Chinese subjects, many artists chose to explore popular Korean themes. Painters, for example, depicted Korean wrestling matches. They painted Korean peasants tending their fields and landscapes of the Korean countryside.

Daily Life in Ming and Qing China

The Chinese devotion to agriculture began to pay off during the late Ming and early Qing dynasties. Greater rice production, along with the general peace and prosperity of the 1600s and 1700s, ushered in a better life for most Chinese. During this period, the population also doubled. It reached more than 300 million in 1800.

The Growth of Early Modern China

A Population Boom

This detail from Zhang Zeduan's painting, *Going Up-River at the Qing Ming Festival*, reflects the growth of urban life under the Ming and Qing.

SKILLBUILDER: Interpreting Graphs
1. By roughly what percentage did China's population increase between 1650 and 1900?
2. How might the growth of population, towns, and culture be related?

 SKILLBUILDER MINI-LESSON: Interpreting Graphs

CLASS TIME 20 MINUTES

Explaining the Skill Graphs offer illustrations of statistics and often make numerical information and relationships easier to grasp. Visual features such as color and size as well as labels and measurements on a graph all help clarify the information presented. Point out to students that the information in the graph is reinforced or supplemented by the inclusion of pictorial material.

Applying the Skill: The Growth of Early Modern China Have students study the line graph on this page, noting how the lines and dots are used to communicate information. Then ask,
1. What was the increase in population between 1650 and 1900? *More than 300 million.*

2. During what 100-year period did the greatest growth occur? What was the increase in that period? *1750–1850; about 200 million.*

3. About what year did the growth spurt begin to taper off? *Around 1850.*

4. What does the painting of an urban scene tell about China during this period? *Possible Answer: The cities were growing in population and becoming more crowded.*

 IN-DEPTH RESOURCES: UNIT 1
Skillbuilder Practice: Interpreting Graphs, p. 54

Family and the Role of Women Most Chinese families farmed the land. They farmed in much the same way as their ancestors had for thousands of years. During the Qing Dynasty, irrigation and the use of fertilizer increased. Farmers began to grow new crops. These crops, such as corn and sweet potatoes, had been brought by the Europeans from the Americas. With increased food production, nutrition and diet improved. Such changes encouraged families to expand, and a population explosion followed.

These expanded Chinese families favored sons over daughters. Only a son was allowed to carry on vital religious rituals. A son would raise his own family under his parents' roof, assuring aging parents of help with the farming. Because of this, females were not valued, and many female infants were killed as a result. Men dominated the household and their wives, but women did have some significant responsibilities. Besides working in the fields, they supervised the children's education and managed the family's finances. Although most women were forced to remain secluded in their homes, some found outside jobs as midwives or textile workers, for example.

Still, women generally suffered as a result of their inferior status in Chinese society. One glaring example was the continuation of the traditional practice of foot-binding. One-half to two-thirds of all Chinese women in this period may have undergone this painful procedure, which left them barely able to walk. The practice continued into the 20th century.

Cultural Developments The culture of early modern China was based mainly on traditional forms. It was a conservative reaction to changes in Chinese life. These changes included the Manchu conquest, the coming of the Europeans, and the population growth. The great masterpiece of traditional Chinese fiction was written during this period. *Dream of the Red Chamber* by Cao Zhan examines upper-class Manchu society in the 1700s. It has been praised for the sensitive portrayal of its female characters.

Most artists of the time painted in traditional styles, which valued technique over creativity. In pottery, technical skill as well as experimentation led to the production of high-quality ceramics, including porcelain.

Drama was a popular entertainment, especially in rural China, where literacy rates were low. Plays that presented Chinese history and portrayed cultural heroes served two purposes. They entertained people, and they also helped unify Chinese society by creating a kind of national culture.

While China was attempting to preserve its traditions and its isolation, another civilization that developed in relative seclusion—the Japanese—was in conflict. As you will learn in Section 3, it faced problems caused both by internal power struggles and by the arrival of foreigners.

Under the Ming and Qing, the arts, including painting, flourished. This detail, from one of two paintings entitled _Occupations of the Court Ladies_, shows society's privileged women relaxing.

Section 2 Assessment

1. TERMS & NAMES

Identify
• Ming Dynasty
• Hongwu
• Yonglo
• Zheng He
• Manchus
• Qing Dynasty
• Kangxi

2. TAKING NOTES

Complete a chart like the one below, listing five relevant facts about each emperor.

Emperor	Relevant Facts
Hongwu	
Yonglo	
Kangxi	
Qian-long	

Choose one emperor and write a one-paragraph biography using the information listed in the chart and text.

3. MAKING DECISIONS

When Qian-long expected Lord George Macartney to kowtow, what do you think Macartney should have done? Why?

THINK ABOUT
• cultural differences
• effect on trading
• the kowtow ritual
• political correctness

4. THEME ACTIVITY

Cultural Interaction Work in small groups to draw, paint, or sketch a mural of a Zheng He expedition. Include the figures, objects, maps, and symbols necessary to convey relevant information from the text. Use the pictures and maps in this chapter for additional ideas. Present the mural to your class.

Section 2 Assessment
Have students work individually on the questions. Then have them share with the class the charts they drew for question 2.

Section Quiz
FORMAL ASSESSMENT BOOK
Section quiz, p. 41

Reteaching Activity
CLASS TIME: 15 MINUTES

Use the Guided Reading Worksheet for Section 2 to review the key ideas of this section.

IN-DEPTH RESOURCES: UNIT 1
Guided Reading, p. 52

CLOSE ACTIVITY

CLASS TIME: 20 MINUTES

Role-Playing
Have interested students reenact the meeting of Lord George Macartney and Emperor Qian-long in 1793. Other students may then ask them about their actions and what each culture had expected of the other in such an interaction.

ANSWERS

1. TERMS & NAMES
Ming Dynasty, p. 89
Hongwu, p. 89
Yonglo, p. 89
Zheng He, p. 89
Manchus, p. 91
Qing Dynasty, p. 91
Kangxi, p. 91

2. TAKING NOTES
Possible Responses: Hongwu— defeated Mongols; ruled 1368–1398; first Ming emperor; encouraged agriculture, Confucian standards, administrative reforms; became brutal. Yonglo—1398, assumed throne; moved capital to Beijing; built Forbidden City; sponsored first Zheng He voyage; increased number of tributaries. Kangxi—ruled 1661–1722; first Manchu emperor; lowered taxes; defeated Mongols; patronized arts. Qian-long—ruled 1736–1795 at China's greatest size and prosperity; hard-working; dealt with border unrest and European missionaries and traders.

3. MAKING DECISIONS
Possible Responses: Kowtow to gain trade; bow to compromise; stand to show equality; refuse to see him to show disfavor.

4. THEME ACTIVITY
Cultural Interaction
Possible Responses: Murals may include maps; drawings of ships, crew, Zheng He, dignitaries paying tribute.

3 Japan Limits Western Contacts

TERMS & NAMES
- daimyo
- Oda Nobunaga
- Toyotomi Hideyoshi
- Tokugawa Shogunate
- kabuki
- haiku

MAIN IDEA	WHY IT MATTERS NOW
The Tokugawa regime unified Japan and began a 200-year period of isolation, autocracy, and economic growth.	Even now, Japan continues to limit and control dealings with foreigners, especially in the area of trade.

SETTING THE STAGE In the 1300s, the unity that had been achieved in Japan in the previous century broke down. Shoguns, or military leaders, in the north and south fought for power. Although these two rival courts came back together at the end of the century, a series of politically weak shoguns let control of the country slip from their grasp.

Strong Leaders Take Control

In 1467, civil war shattered Japan's feudal system. The country collapsed into chaos. Centralized rule ended. Power drained away from the shogun to territorial lords in hundreds of separate domains.

This samurai armor consists of leather and iron plates. It was made in 1714 for the Lord of Akita, a region in northwest Japan.

Local Lords Rule A violent era of disorder followed. This time in Japanese history, which lasted from 1467 to 1568, is known as the *Sengoku*, or "Warring States," period. Powerful samurai seized control of old feudal estates. They offered peasants and others protection in return for their loyalty. These warrior-chieftains, called **daimyo** (DYE·mee·OH), became lords in a new kind of Japanese feudalism. Under this system, security came from this group of powerful warlords. The emperor at Kyoto became a figurehead.

The new Japanese feudalism resembled European feudalism in many ways. The daimyo built fortified castles and created small armies of samurai on horses. Later they added foot soldiers with muskets (guns) to their ranks. Rival daimyo often fought each other for territory. This led to endless disorder throughout the land.

New Leaders Restore Order A number of ambitious daimyo hoped to gather enough power to take control of the entire country. One of them, the brutal and ambitious **Oda Nobunaga** (oh·dah noh·boo·nah·gah), defeated his rivals and seized the imperial capital Kyoto in 1568.

Following his own motto, "Rule the empire by force," Nobunaga sought to eliminate his remaining enemies. These included rival daimyo as well as wealthy Buddhist monasteries aligned with them. In 1575, Nobunaga's 3,000 musketeers crushed an enemy force of samurai cavalry. This was the first time firearms had been used effectively in battle in Japan. However, Nobunaga was not able to unify Japan. He committed seppuku, the ritual suicide of a samurai, in 1582, when one of his own generals turned on him.

Nobunaga's best general, **Toyotomi Hideyoshi** (toh·you·toh·mee hee·deh·yoh·shee), continued his fallen leader's mission. Hideyoshi set out to destroy the daimyos that remained hostile. By 1590, by combining brute force with shrewd political alliances, he controlled most of the country. Hideyoshi did not stop with Japan. With the idea of eventually conquering China, he invaded Korea in 1592 and began a long campaign against the Koreans and their Ming Chinese allies. When Hideyoshi died in 1598, his troops withdrew from Korea.

94 Chapter 3

Vocabulary
domains: the lands belonging to a single lord.

Vocabulary
figurehead: a person holding a position of seeming leadership but having no real power.

Vocabulary
musketeers: soldiers armed with muskets.

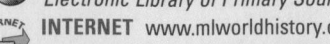

Tokugawa Shogunate Unites Japan

One of Hideyoshi's strongest daimyo allies, Tokugawa Ieyasu (toh·koo·gah·wah ee·yeh·yah·soo), completed the unification of Japan. In 1600, Ieyasu defeated his rivals at the Battle of Sekigahara. His victory earned him the loyalty of daimyo throughout Japan. Three years later, Ieyasu became the sole ruler, or shogun. He then moved Japan's capital to his power base at Edo, a small fishing village that would later become the city of Tokyo.

Japan was unified, but the daimyo still governed at the local level. To keep them from rebelling, Ieyasu required that they spend every other year in the capital. Even when they returned to their lands, they had to leave their families behind as hostages in Edo. Through this "alternate attendance policy" and other restrictions, Ieyasu tamed the daimyo. This was a major step toward restoring centralized government to Japan. As a result, the rule of law overcame the rule of the sword.

Ieyasu founded the **Tokugawa Shogunate,** which would continue until 1867. On his deathbed in 1616, Ieyasu advised his son and successor, Hidetada, "Take care of the people. Strive to be virtuous. Never neglect to protect the country." Most of the Tokugawa shoguns followed that advice, and their rule brought a welcome stability to Japan.

Tokugawa Society and Culture

Japan enjoyed more than two centuries of stability, prosperity, and isolation under the Tokugawa shoguns. The farming community produced more food, and the population rose. Still, the vast majority of peasants, weighed down by heavy taxes, led lives filled with misery. The people who prospered in Tokugawa society were the merchant class and the rich. However, everyone, rich and poor alike, benefited from a flowering of Japanese culture during this era.

Social History In Japan, as in China, Confucian values influenced ideas about society. According to Confucius, the ideal society depended on agriculture, not urban commerce. Farmers, not merchants, made ideal citizens. In the real world of Tokugawa Japan, however, peasant farmers bore the main tax burden and faced more difficulties than any other class. Many of them abandoned farm life and headed for the expanding towns and cities. There they mixed with samurai, artisans, and merchants—the other main classes of Tokugawa society.

By the mid-1700s, Japan began to shift from a rural to an urban society. Edo had grown by that time from a small town in 1600 to perhaps the largest city in the world. Its population was more than one million. The rise of large commercial centers increased employment opportunities for women. Women found jobs in entertainment, textile manufacturing, and publishing. Still, the typical Japanese woman led a sheltered and restricted life as a peasant wife. She worked in the fields, managed the household, cared for the children, and obeyed her husband without question.

Culture Under the Tokugawa Shogunate Traditional culture continued to thrive. Samurai attended ceremonial noh dramas based on tragic themes. They read tales of

Japanese Society

Emperor
Held highest rank in society but had no political power

Daimyo
Large landowners

Shogun
Actual ruler

Samurai Warriors
Loyal to Daimyo and Shogun

Peasants
Four-fifths of the population

Artisans
Craftspeople such as artists and blacksmiths

Merchants
Low status but gradually gained influence

ancient warriors and their courage in battle. In their homes, they hung paintings that showed scenes from classical literature.

Such traditional entertainment faced competition in the cities from new styles of drama, art, and literature. Townspeople attended **kabuki** theater. These were dramas in which actors in elaborate costumes, using music, dance, and mime, performed skits about modern urban life. The paintings they enjoyed were often woodblock prints showing sophisticated city life.

Townspeople read popular stories about self-made merchants or the hardships of life. This new type of urban fiction was created by the novelist Saikaku. The people also read **haiku** (HI-koo), poetry which does not express ideas, but presents images. For example, Matsuo Basho, the greatest of all the Japanese haiku poets, wrote just before his death in 1694:

Kabuki theater makes use of extravagant costumes, mask-like makeup, and exaggerated postures and gestures. This contemporary photo shows a dancer costumed as a lion.

A VOICE FROM THE PAST
On a journey, ailing—
My dreams roam about
Over a withered moor.
MATSUO BASHO, from *Matsuo Basho*

Tabi ni yande
Yume wa Kareno o
Kakemeguru
MATSUO BASHO, in Japanese

Contact Between Europe and Japan

Europeans began coming to Japan in the 16th century, during a time of severe disorder. At first, the Japanese were curious about these newcomers. They welcomed the traders and missionaries, who introduced fascinating new technologies and ideas. Within a century, the aggressive Europeans had worn out their welcome.

Portuguese Sailors and Technology Reach Japan The Japanese first encountered Europeans in 1543, when shipwrecked Portuguese sailors washed up on the shores of southern Japan. Portuguese merchants soon followed. They hoped to involve themselves in Japan's trade with China and Southeast Asia. The Portuguese brought clocks, eyeglasses, tobacco, firearms, and other unfamiliar items from Europe. Japanese merchants, eager to expand their markets, were happy to receive the newcomers and their goods.

The daimyo, too, welcomed the strangers. They were particularly interested in the Portuguese muskets and cannons. One warlord listened intently to a Japanese observer's description of a musket:

SPOTLIGHT ON

Introduction of Firearms
Europeans introduced firearms to Japan in the mid-1500s, when every daimyo sought an advantage over his rivals. Imagine the warlords' surprise when they first saw a lead pellet explode from a musket! Then imagine their eagerness to own firearms when they realized the musket's killing power.

Japanese gunsmiths set to work copying the European musket. Some 30 years later, they had mastered the technology. However, soldiers still had trouble firing the gun, and daimyos didn't know how to use their musketeers effectively. Nobunaga's victory in 1575 proved that those problems could be solved and led to daimyos arming their troops with muskets.

A VOICE FROM THE PAST
In their hands they carried something two or three feet long, straight on the outside with a passage inside, and made of a heavy substance. . . . This thing with one blow can smash a mountain of silver and a wall of iron. If one sought to do mischief in another man's domain and he was touched by it, he would lose his life instantly.
ANONYMOUS JAPANESE WRITER, quoted in *Sources of Japanese Tradition* (1958)

Firearms forever changed the time-honored tradition of the Japanese warrior, whose principal weapon had been the sword. Many samurai, who retained the sword as their principal weapon, would lose their lives to musket fire in future combat. The cannon also had a huge impact on Japan. Daimyo had to build fortified castles to withstand the destructive force of cannonballs. The castles attracted merchants, artisans, and others to surrounding lands. Many of these lands grew into the towns and cities of modern Japan.

Christian Missionaries in Japan In 1549, Christian missionaries began arriving in Japan. The Japanese accepted the missionaries in part because they associated them with the muskets and other

---

European goods that they wanted. The religious orders of Jesuits, Franciscans, and Dominicans came to convert the Japanese. Francis Xavier, a Jesuit, led the first mission to Japan and baptized about a hundred converts. Missionaries converted about 300,000 Japanese to Christianity by the year 1600.

The success of the missionaries upset Tokugawa Ieyasu. He found aspects of the Christian invasion troublesome. Missionaries, actively seeking converts, scorned traditional Japanese beliefs and sometimes involved themselves in local politics. At first, Ieyasu did not take any action. He feared driving off the Portuguese, English, Spanish, and Dutch traders who spurred Japan's economy. By 1612, however, the shogun had come to fear religious uprisings more. He banned Christianity and focused on ridding his country of all Christians.

Repression of Christianity continued off and on for the next two decades. In 1637, the issue came to a head. An uprising in southern Japan of some 30,000 peasants, led by dissatisfied samurai, shook the Tokugawa regime. Because so many of the rebels were Christian, the shogun decided that Christianity was at the root of the rebellion. After that, the shoguns ruthlessly persecuted Christians. All Japanese were forced to demonstrate faithfulness to some branch of Buddhism. These policies eventually eliminated Christianity in Japan.

The Closed Country Policy The persecution of Christians was part of an attempt to control foreign ideas. When Europeans first arrived, no central authority existed to contain them. The strong leaders who later took power did not like the introduction of European ideas and ways, but they valued European trade. As time passed, the Tokugawa shoguns realized that they could safely exclude both the missionaries and the merchants. By 1639, they had sealed Japan's borders and instituted a "closed country policy."

One port, Nagasaki, remained open to foreign traders. However, only Dutch and Chinese merchants were allowed into the port. Since the Tokugawa shoguns controlled Nagasaki, they now had a monopoly on foreign trade, which continued to be profitable.

For more than 200 years, Japan remained basically closed to Europeans. Japan would continue to develop as a self-sufficient country, free from European attempts to colonize or to establish their presence.

The Europeans had met with much resistance in their efforts to open the East to trade. Expansion to the West in the Americas, as you will learn in Chapter 4, would prove much more successful.

THINK THROUGH HISTORY
C. Comparing How was the treatment of Europeans different in Japan and China? How was it similar?
C. Possible Answers The Japanese were more receptive at first to European contact than the Chinese were; however, both countries eventually rebuffed European influences and entered an age of isolation.

Section ③ Assessment

1. TERMS & NAMES
Identify
- daimyo
- Oda Nobunaga
- Toyotomi Hideyoshi
- Tokugawa Shogunate
- kabuki
- haiku

2. TAKING NOTES
Japan was unified by a succession of daimyos. Using a chart like the one below, show the accomplishments of each.

Daimyo	Accomplishments
Nobunaga	
Hideyoshi	
Ieyasu	

3. FORMING AN OPINION
Do you think Japan's closed country policy effectively kept Western ideas and customs out of Japan?

THINK ABOUT
- the attitude toward European presence
- reaction to past restrictions on Christianity and trade
- the role of Nagasaki

4. THEME ACTIVITY
Cultural Interaction Reread about the role of women in China on page 93 and about the role of women in Japan on page 95. What are the similarities and the differences between the two? Create a Venn diagram to compare and contrast them.

An Age of Exploration and Isolation **97**

ANSWERS

1. TERMS & NAMES
daimyo, p. 94
Oda Nobunaga, p. 94
Toyotomi Hideyoshi, p. 94
Tokugawa Shogunate, p. 95
kabuki, p. 96
haiku, p. 96

2. TAKING NOTES
Possible Responses: Oda Nobunaga—1568, took Kyoto; defeated enemy daimyos; 1575, used firearms in battle. Hideyoshi—by 1590, claimed most of Japan; invaded Korea in 1592. Ieyasu—1600, defeated rival daimyos; 1603, took shogun title; moved capital to Edo; restricted daimyo power; rule of law.

3. FORMING AN OPINION
Possible Responses: Yes— European influence was confined to Nagasaki; large population uneducated; shoguns censored information. No— Nagasaki provided a port for European ideas as well as trade.

4. THEME ACTIVITY
Cultural Interaction
Possible Responses: China— female infanticide; footbinding; some jobs outside home. Both— subservient to husband; most work in fields; manage household and children. Japan—no female infanticide or footbinding; more job opportunities.

TERMS & NAMES

1. Bartolomeu Dias, p. 84
2. Vasco da Gama, p. 86
3. Treaty of Tordesillas, p. 86
4. Dutch East India Company, p. 88
5. Ming Dynasty, p. 89
6. Manchus, p. 91
7. Qing Dynasty, p. 91
8. Oda Nobunaga, p. 94
9. Toyotomi Hideyoshi, p. 94
10. Tokugawa Shogunate, p. 95

REVIEW QUESTIONS

11. Desire for new sources of wealth; desire to spread Christianity; technological advancements in sailing and navigation.

12. He encouraged exploration by establishing a navigation school for sailors to perfect their trade.

13. Dias showed that the southern tip of Africa could be circumnavigated; da Gama established a sea route from Europe to India.

14. The Dutch owned the largest fleet of ships in the world, and the Dutch East India Company was more powerful and better financed than other nations' trading companies.

15. Idea of commerce offended China's Confucian beliefs; economic policy gave priority to agriculture.

16. The clock and the prism.

17. Ineffective rulers, corrupt officials, government out of money, high taxes, bad harvests.

18. It was an era of disorder when powerful warrior-chieftains, called daimyo, seized control of old feudal estates and set up new type of feudalism and often fought each other for territory.

19. Confucian ideal—Japan was an agricultural society and the farmer was the ideal citizen. In reality—farmers were overburdened and over-taxed and often moved to the city for a better life.

20. Kabuki plays, popular stories, haiku, and woodblock prints.

TERMS & NAMES

Briefly explain the importance of the following to European exploration and the growth of China and Japan.

1. Bartolomeu Dias
2. Vasco da Gama
3. Treaty of Tordesillas
4. Dutch East India Company
5. Ming Dynasty
6. Manchus
7. Qing Dynasty
8. Oda Nobunaga
9. Toyotomi Hideyoshi
10. Tokugawa Shogunate

Interact *with* History

On page 82, you decided whether or not to go on a voyage of exploration. Now that you have read the chapter, reevaluate your decision. If you decided to go, did what you read reaffirm your decision? Why or why not? If you chose not to go, explain what your feelings are now. Discuss your answers within a small group.

REVIEW QUESTIONS

SECTION 1, *(pages 83–88)*
Europeans Explore the East

11. What factors helped spur European exploration?
12. What role did Portugal's Prince Henry play in overseas exploration?
13. What was the significance of Bartolomeu Dias's voyage? Vasco da Gama's?
14. Why were the Dutch so successful in establishing a trading empire in the Indian Ocean?

SECTION 2, *(pages 89–93)*
China Rejects European Outreach

15. Why didn't China undergo widespread industrialization?
16. Name two technological advancements the missionaries brought to China.
17. List five reasons why the Ming Dynasty fell to civil disorder.

SECTION 3, *(pages 94–97)*
Japan Limits Western Contacts

18. Why was the period between 1467 and 1568 called the Age of the Warring States?
19. What was the difference between the Confucian ideal of society and the real society of Japan?
20. Briefly describe the new drama, literature, and art found in Japanese cities.

Visual Summary

An Age of Exploration and Isolation

EXPLORATION

- In 1405, Zheng He of China launches voyages of exploration to Southeast Asia, India, Arabia, and eastern Africa.
- Beginning in the early 1500s, the Portuguese establish trading outposts throughout Asia and gain control of the spice trade.
- The Dutch drive out the Portuguese by the early 1600s and establish their own trading empire in the East.
- Europeans sail farther east to China and Japan in search of more trade; both nations ultimately reject European advances.

ISOLATION

- China abandons its voyages of exploration in 1433.
- Beginning in the 1500s, the Chinese severely restrict trade with foreigners.
- Japan outlaws Christianity in 1612 and drives out Christian missionaries.
- Beginning in the mid-1600s, the Japanese institute a "closed country policy" and remain isolated from Europe for 200 years.

Interact *with* History

Possible Responses: Students who originally wanted to go may now say that the rewards weren't great enough to go through all the hardships and give up that much time from their lives. Others may say that the opportunity to bring glory and prestige to their country and make some financial gain was worth the sacrifice.

CRITICAL THINKING

1. SAILING INNOVATIONS

THEME SCIENCE AND TECHNOLOGY Of all the technological advances that helped prompt European exploration, which do you think was the the most important? Why?

2. EMPERORS OF THE FORBIDDEN CITY

How might an emperor's attitude toward living in the Forbidden City affect his leadership? Consider how he might view his country, its people, and the outside world. Also think about the role of leaders and the values you think they should hold.

3. MISSIONARIES IN JAPAN

In a time line like the one below, trace the developments which led to Japan's expulsion of Christianity.

4. ANALYZING PRIMARY SOURCES

Emperor Kangxi invited Christian missionaries to his court, where they shared ideas about science, religion, government, and trade. In the following personal account, Kangxi reflects on what he has learned from the Europeans.

A VOICE FROM THE PAST
But I was careful not to refer to these Westerners as "Great Officials," and corrected Governor Liu Yin-shu when he referred to the Jesuits Regis and Fridelli . . . as if they were honored imperial commissioners. For even though some of the Western methods are different from our own, and may even be an improvement, there is little about them that is new. The principles of mathematics all derive from the Book of Changes, and the Western methods are Chinese in origin: this algebra—"A-erh-chu-pa-erh"—springs from an Eastern word. And though it was indeed the Westerners who showed us something our ancient calendar experts did not know—namely how to calculate the angles of the northern pole—this but shows the truth of what Chu Hsi arrived at through his investigation of things: the earth is like the yolk within an egg.

KANGXI, quoted in *Emperor of China: Self-portrait of K'ang-hsi*

- What do you think is Kangxi's attitude toward Westerners?
- Do you think Kangxi is a true scholar?

CHAPTER ACTIVITIES

1. LIVING HISTORY: Unit Portfolio Project

THEME CULTURAL INTERACTION Your Unit Portfolio project focuses on the ways in which different cultures interact (see page 33). For Chapter 3, you might use one of the following ideas to add to your portfolio.

- Imagine you are the Jesuit missionary, Matteo Ricci. Write a letter home describing your impressions of Chinese rule and culture.
- Draft a reply for King George III to the letter written by China's emperor, Qian-long, on page 92. Convince the emperor to open China by explaining the benefits of economic and cultural interaction.
- Imagine you are a Malaccan newspaper editor. Write an editorial about the arrival of Europeans, as well as their motives for being there.

2. CONNECT TO TODAY: Cooperative Learning

THEME ECONOMICS The primary force behind overseas exploration was economic, as Europeans sailed beyond their borders in search of new sources of wealth. Today the West retains strong economic ties with Asia. In recent years, maintaining those ties with China has been a hotly debated topic in the United States.

Work with a small team and prepare to debate another team over the issue of U.S. trade with China.

 Using the Internet, magazines, and other library sources, research the issues involved in the debate over U.S. trade with China.

- After being assigned one or the other position on the issue, work together to gather information that supports your side's position.
- In front of the class, debate a group that has taken the opposite position.

3. INTERPRETING A TIME LINE

Reexamine the unit time line on pages 32–33. Convert the Chapter 3 time line into a cartoon strip that conveys the same information.

FOCUS ON GEOGRAPHY

This map, produced by the German cartographer Henricus Martellus in about 1490, is believed to be the first world map to incorporate the discoveries made by Bartolomeu Dias.

- Where is Europe on the map?
- What is the continent in the lower left corner of the map?

Connect to History Obtain a modern-day world map and compare it with this one. How do you rate Martellus's assumptions of how the world to the east of Africa looked?

CHAPTER ACTIVITIES

1. LIVING HISTORY

Standards for Evaluation
Matteo Ricci's letters should meet the following criteria:

- Reflect the values of Matteo Ricci, a Jesuit priest.
- Present information about the Chinese culture and compare it with Western Christian culture.

Standards for Evaluation
King George's letters should meet the following criteria:

- Reflect the point of view of a European king.
- Respond to the points made in Qian-long's letter to the king.
- List the benefits that China would realize by opening up trade.
- Compare the cultures of China and England.

Standards for Evaluation
Editorials should meet the following criteria:

- Express clearly the opinions of the writer.
- List the negative effects of European incursion into the Malaccas.
- Tell readers why they should resist foreign influences.

2. CONNECT TO TODAY: COOPERATIVE LEARNING

Standards for Evaluation
Debate preparations should meet the following criteria:

- State each side's position clearly and persuasively.
- Give reasons to support one's stated argument.
- Be prepared to respond to the opposing side's arguments.

3. INTERPRETING A TIME LINE

Standards for Evaluation
A cartoon strip should meet the following criteria:

- Include the information on the time line.
- Have labels that are to the point.
- Be visually interesting and effective.

FOCUS ON GEOGRAPHY

- In the upper left corner.
- Africa.

Connect to History *Possible Responses:* Martellus's map seems to have the general outline of the land east of Africa, especially in the Near East. However, he is not correct on many details. For example, India appears to be an island, or there is a very large island off the coast of a much smaller India. Also all the islands in the Far East seem to be connected as one land mass.

CRITICAL THINKING

1. SAILING INNOVATIONS

Possible Responses: Caravel, because without its improved features, Europeans could not sail great distances; compass, because explorers had to know where they were when they lost sight of land.

2. EMPERORS OF THE FORBIDDEN CITY

Possible Responses: Emperors out of touch; may develop a lack of compassion; heightened contempt for foreigners; pleasure, greed, and court intrigue distract from leadership; corrupt officials may assume power.

3. MISSIONARIES IN JAPAN

Possible Responses: 1549, missionaries welcomed; 1600, some 300,000 Japanese converted; 1612, Christianity prohibited; 1637, about 30,000 peasants, mostly Christian, revolt; Christianity suppressed.

4. ANALYZING PRIMARY SOURCES

Possible Responses: Kangxi realizes he can learn from the West; he may believe that Chinese scholarship is superior; he may not show the Europeans full respect. Yes—Invites European ideas; draws on other knowledge; analyzes ideas. No—his prejudices may hinder judgment.

	Key Ideas	COPY MASTERS	ASSESSMENT
SECTION 1 Spanish Conquests in the Americas *pp. 103–108*	*Columbus lands in the Caribbean Islands, and Spain and Portugal begin the colonization of the Americas. The Spanish destroy the Aztec and Inca empires.*	*In-Depth Resources: Unit 1* • **Guided Reading,** p. 68 • **Primary Sources:** from *The Journal of Christopher Columbus*, p. 75; from *The Broken Spears*, p. 77 • **Literature:** from *The Feathered Serpent*, p. 79 • **History Makers:** Magellan, p. 82; Cortés, p. 83	PE *Section 1 Assessment*, p. 108 *Formal Assessment* • Section Quiz, p. 51 *Alternative Assessment Book* • Standards for Evaluating a Cooperative Activity
SECTION 2 Competing Claims in North America *pp. 110–114*	*European nations lay claim to large parts of North America, but England drives out the French and Dutch and creates thirteen colonies.*	*In-Depth Resources: Unit 1* • **Guided Reading,** p. 69 • **Skillbuilder Practice**: Contrasting, p. 72	PE *Section 2 Assessment*, p. 114 *Formal Assessment* • Section Quiz, p. 52 *Alternative Assessment Book* • Standards for Evaluating a Cooperative Activity
SECTION 3 The Atlantic Slave Trade *pp. 115–119*	*The slave trade decimates African social and family life, and millions of slaves are brought to the Americas to work in mines and on plantations.*	*In-Depth Resources: Unit 1* • **Guided Reading,** p. 70 • **Primary Source:** from *The Life of Olaudah Equiano*, p. 78	PE *Section 3 Assessment*, p. 119 *Formal Assessment* • Section Quiz, p. 53 *Alternative Assessment Book* • Standards for Evaluating a Cooperative Activity
SECTION 4 The Columbian Exchange and Global Trade *pp. 120–123*	*The colonization of the Americas leads to a global exchange of food, plants, animals, and diseases that enriches the European diet and economy and further shatters the native civilizations of the New World.*	*In-Depth Resources: Unit 1* • **Guided Reading,** p. 71 • **Geography Application:** The Potato Impacts the World, p. 73 • **Connections Across Time and Cultures:** Impact of the Columbian Exchange, p. 84	PE *Section 4 Assessment*, p. 123 *Formal Assessment* • Section Quiz, p. 54 *Alternative Assessment Book* • Standards for Evaluating a Product or Performance
CHAPTER RESOURCES	**Chapter Overview** *The European exploration and colonization of the Americas lead to an economic and cultural revolution in Europe and the devastation of Native American cultures in the New World.*	*Telescoping the Times* • Chapter Summary, pp. 17–20 *Planning for Block Schedules*	PE *Chapter Assessment*, pp. 124–125 *Chapter Activities*, p. 125 *Formal Assessment* • Chapter Test, forms A and B, pp. 55–60 *Test Generator* *Alternative Assessment Book*

TECHNOLOGY

 Warm-Up Transparency 4

 World Art and Cultures Transparencies
- AT43 *Meeting of Cortés and Montezuma*

 Electronic Library of Primary Sources
- "On the Destruction of the Indies"
- from *Letter to King Charles V of Spain*

 Patterns of Interaction:
The Spread of Epidemic Disease

 INTERNET RESOURCES
www.mlworldhistory.com

 Warm-Up Transparency 4

 Electronic Library of Primary Sources
- "The French Lose Quebec"

 INTERNET RESOURCES
www.mlworldhistory.com

 Warm-Up Transparency 4

 World Art and Cultures Transparencies
- AT44 Meynell's *Slaves Below the Deck of the Albanez*

 Critical Thinking Transparencies
- CT20 The Atlantic Slave Trade, 1451–1870

 Electronic Library of Primary Sources
- Letter to the King of Portugal

 INTERNET RESOURCES
www.mlworldhistory.com

 Warm-Up Transparency 4

 Geography Transparencies
- GT20 Spain's Colonies Provide Wealth, 1600–1790

 Critical Thinking Transparencies
- CT56 Visual Summary

 Electronic Library of Primary Sources
- "Concerning the Dearness of All Things and the Remedy Therefor"

 Patterns of Interaction
The Geography of Food

 Chapter Summaries on Audiocassette in English and Spanish

 INTERNET RESOURCES
www.mlworldhistory.com

 ## Block Scheduling (90 MINUTES)

Day 1
Section 1, pp. 103–108

 COOPERATIVE ACTIVITY
Displaying Explorers' Sailing Ships, p. 404 (Teacher's Edition)
Section Assessment, p. 108

Day 2
Section 2, pp. 110–114

 COOPERATIVE ACTIVITY
Planning a Journey, p. 113 (Teacher's Edition)
Section Assessment, p. 114

Day 3
Section 3, pp. 115–119

 COOPERATIVE ACTIVITY
Writing a Report, p. 116 (Teacher's Edition)
Section Assessment, p.119

Day 4
Section 4, pp. 120–123
Section Assessment, p. 123
Chapter Assessment, pp. 124–125

Yearly Pacing *Chapter 4 Total:* 4 days *Yearly Total:* 85 days

 Planning for Block Schedules

Customizing for Special Needs

Students Acquiring English

 Access for Students Acquiring English
- **Guided Reading,** for Sections 1–4 (Spanish), pp. 50–53
- **Chapter Summary:** (Spanish), pp. 47–49
- **Skillbuilder Practice:** Contrasting (Spanish), p. 54
- **Geography Application:** The Potato Impacts the World (Spanish), p. 55

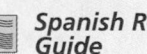 *Spanish Reading Study Guide*
- pp. 41–50

 Patterns of Interaction: Geography of Food (Spanish track)

 Chapter Summaries on Audiocassette in English and Spanish

Less Proficient Readers

 In-Depth Resources: Unit 1
- **Guided Reading,** for Sections 1–4, pp. 68–71
- **Skillbuilder Practice:** Contrasting, p. 72
- **Geography Application:** The Potato Impacts the World, p. 73

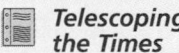 *Telescoping the Times*
- Chapter Summary, pp. 17–80

 Reading Study Guide
- pp. 41–50

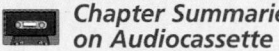 *Chapter Summaries on Audiocassette*

Gifted and Talented Students

 In-Depth Resources: Unit 1

Primary Sources:
- from *The Journal of Christopher Columbus,* p. 75
- from *The Broken Spears,* p. 77
- from *The Life of Olaudah Equiano,* p. 78

History Makers:
- Magellan, p. 82
- Cortés, p. 83

Connections to Literature READINGS FOR STUDENTS

 In-Depth Resources: Unit 1
Literature: from *The Feathered Serpent,* p. 79

Enrichment Reading

- **Cliff, Michelle**
Free Enterprise
New York: Plume, 1994

A gripping story about the slave trade.

- **Pate, Alexs**
The Amistad
New York: Penguin, 1997

The exciting tale of a slave revolt. This story was the basis of a major motion picture directed by Steven Spielberg.

 = Pupil's Edition   = Overhead Transparency   = Software   = Video

 = Copy Master   = CD-ROM   = Audiocassette   = Internet

The Atlantic World, 1492–1800

Accessing Prior Knowledge

- Ask students what they know about Columbus. Discuss with them any other early voyages to the Americas they might have heard of. Then ask them if they know about recent controversies over the impact of Columbus's voyage to the Americas.

Making Judgments

- Have students read each of the captions and then decide which of the three themes listed to the right (cultural interaction, economics, or empire building) seems to be the dominant theme expressed by each image and the caption that explains it.

Geography Connection

Ask students to look at the map on these two pages.

- What two main worlds were connected by the voyage of Columbus? *the Eastern and Western hemispheres, or Europe and Africa in the east and North and South America in the west*

CHAPTER 4

The Atlantic World, 1492–1800

PREVIEWING THEMES

Cultural Interaction
The voyages of Columbus prompted a worldwide exchange of everything from religious and political ideas to new foods and plants. In addition, they paved the way for the creation of new multicultural societies in the Americas.

Economics
The vast wealth to be had from colonizing the Americas sealed the fate of millions of Native Americans and Africans. Europeans forced them to toil in gold and silver mines, as well as on huge tobacco and sugar plantations.

Empire Building
Over the span of several centuries, Europeans conquered the Americas' native inhabitants. As a result, they built powerful American empires.

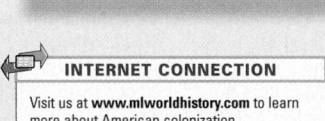

INTERNET CONNECTION

Visit us at **www.mlworldhistory.com** to learn more about American colonization.

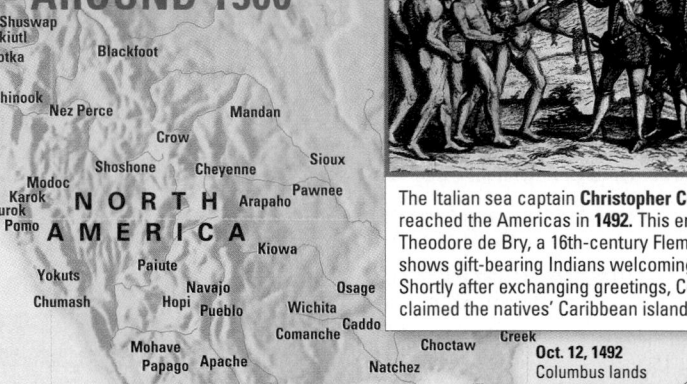

THE WESTERN WORLD AROUND 1500

Cree
Shuswap
Kwakiutl
Nootka
Blackfoot
Chinook
Nez Perce
Mandan
Crow
Shoshone
Cheyenne
Sioux
Modoc
Karok
Yurok
Pomo
Pawnee
Arapaho
NORTH AMERICA
Kiowa
Yokuts
Paiute
Navajo
Chumash
Hopi Pueblo
Wichita
Osage
Caddo
Comanche
Mohave
Papago Apache
Choctaw
Creek
Pima
Cochimi
Coahuiltec
Natchez
Timucua
Tarahumara
Tepehuan
Huichol
AZTEC EMPIRE
Cora
Huastec
Gulf of Mexico
Calusa
Ciboney
Island Arawak
Ciboney
Mixtec
Maya
Antigua
Zapotec
Lenca
Paya
Miskito
Caribbean Sea
Nicarao
Cuna
Guajibo
Warau
Guaymí
Choco
Chibcha
Gauhibo Yanomamo
Arawak
Paez
Carib
Tucano
Tri
Macu
Waiwai
Witoto
Yagua
Amazon
Hvero
Omagua
Munduruc
Tumbes
Chimú
Muchic
Cawahib
Cayap
Shipibo
Piro
Cara
INCA EMPIRE
Nambicuara
SOUTH AMERICA
Nazca
Aymara Mojos
Bororo
Guato
Sirionó

PACIFIC OCEAN

The Italian sea captain **Christopher Columbus** reached the Americas in **1492**. This engraving, by Theodore de Bry, a 16th-century Flemish engraver, shows gift-bearing Indians welcoming Columbus. Shortly after exchanging greetings, Columbus claimed the natives' Caribbean island for Spain.

Oct. 12, 1492 Columbus lands on San Salvador Island

In **1533**, the Spanish, led by **Francisco Pizarro**, conquered the mighty Inca Empire in Peru. This illustration by a Native American, Felipe Guamán Poma de Ayala, depicts the Indians' view of the conquering Spaniards.

100

GEOGRAPHY THEMES

Movement
Have students note and identify the four continents pictured on these pages. *North America, South America, Europe, and Africa.* Tell them that the movement of people—in large numbers and small—across vast areas of the globe has occurred throughout human history. Ask them which way the movement is going on these pages, and which forms of travel this movement would have taken. *From east to west; on the Atlantic Ocean and Caribbean Sea and on the lands of North and South America; forms of travel: ships, horses, by foot*

Human/Environment Interaction
Remind students that the presence of large numbers of people in a place causes major changes to the environment. Some of these changes have a positive impact and some have a negative impact. An example of a positive impact would be an increased food supply. An example of a negative impact might be pollution. Have them note the kind of natural environment the European explorers found when they came to the Americas and what kinds of changes they made to this environment.

ADDITIONAL RESOURCES

Books for the Teacher

- Dor-Ner, Zvi. *Columbus and the Age of Discovery.* New York: Morrow, 1991.

- Lewis, Bernard. *Cultures in Conflict.* New York: Oxford UP, 1995.

- Marks, Richard Lee. *Cortés: The Great Adventurer and the Fate of Aztec Mexico.* New York: Knopf, 1993.

- Sale, Kirkpatrick. *The Conquest of Paradise: Christopher Columbus and the Columbian Legacy.* New York: Knopf, 1990.

Books for the Student

- Baquedano, Elizabeth. *Aztec, Inca, & Maya.* New York: Knopf, 1993.

- Jones, Constance. *Africa, 1500-1900.* New York: Facts on File, 1993.

- Meltzer, Milton. *Columbus and the World Around Him.* New York: Watts, 1990.

- Platt, Richard. *Pirate.* New York: Knopf, 1994.

 Videos

- *Christopher Columbus: His Voyages and His Legacy.* Britannica, 1990. 800-554-9862.

- *Slavery in the Americas and the Triangular Trade.* Britannica, 1992. 800-554-9862.

Software

- *Explorers of the New World.* CD-ROM. Teacher's Discovery, 1995. 800–543–4180.

Soon after arriving in the Americas, **European colonists** forced **Africans** to supply their labor needs. This 19th-century print depicts enslaved Africans working on the British island of Antigua. For 300 years beginning around 1500, the demand for free labor in the Americas drained Africa of at least 9.5 million people.

Aug. 3, 1492 Columbus sails from Palos, Spain

Columbus's first voyage, 1492

Canary Islands

ATLANTIC OCEAN

EUROPE

London •
Paris •
Berlin •
Rome •
Madrid •

Black Sea

Caspian Sea

40°N

AFRICA

SONGHAI EMPIRE

Niger River

Timbuktu •

MALI

BENIN

membe
atehara
bira
vante

Tupinamba

Rotocudo

Mombasa •

Zanzibar

INDIAN OCEAN

Mozambique •

0° Prime Meridian

0°

101

HISTORY THROUGH ART

Pictures of the Conquest of Mexico

Felipe Guamán Poma de Ayala

Felipe Guamán Poma de Ayala was a native wise man of Peru. He painted scenes depicting the conquest of his native land by the Spanish in the 16th century. A codex, or manuscript volume, entitled *Nueva Cronica y Buen Gobierno,* was compiled by Poma de Ayala and completed in 1613. In many of the illustrations in this work the horse plays a key role. The use of the horse helped the Spanish conquerors to cover great distances in a short period of time. Horses also enabled the Spanish to defeat native armies even though the invaders were outnumbered.

Other native artists also depicted the Spanish conquests of the Americas and the role of the horse in these expeditions. For example, Tlaxcalan artists depicted Spanish soldiers on horseback in the highlands of Guatemala. Diego Duran's history of the conquest of Mexico also shows the horse playing a prominent role.

Interpreting the Art What does the Spanish soldier seem to stand for? Is this art likely to be a piece of propaganda? Why or why not?

Interact *with* History

This Interact with History feature motivates students by inviting them to choose between fighting on the side of the Aztecs or the Spanish. As they imagine themselves choosing sides, students will analyze the issues, explore their options, and become decision-makers.

Purpose

- to set the stage for the Spanish conquest of the Americas
- to help students understand some of the reasons for exploration and conquest
- to help students make connections with the people and events they will study in this chapter

Teaching Strategy

Thinking Critically After students have imagined themselves in the situation described on this page, have them answer the key questions and give reasons for their decisions.

EXAMINING *the* ISSUES

Following are suggestions for addressing each bulleted question.

1 Have students recall making a decision about joining a club or school group about which they knew little.

2 Ask students whether they would rather join a group of people like themselves, or one whose members are different.

3 Have students consider being in a position in which they are asked to take a side during an unpleasant conflict. What would they gain by choosing sides? By remaining neutral?

Making Connections Ask students to discuss the issue of choosing sides in situations involving conquest, such as the Roman, Assyrian, and Persian empires.

Interact *with* History

The year is 1520. You are a Native American living in central Mexico, and you are suddenly faced with a decision that may change your life forever. A group of white invaders, known as the Spanish, are engaged in fierce battle with the nearby Aztecs. You and many others have long hated the powerful Aztecs, who rule the land with a harsh and cruel hand. However, you are frightened of these newcomers who ride on large beasts and fire loud weapons.

Many of your friends are joining different sides of the fight. You can choose not to fight at all. However, if you do decide to fight, you must choose a side.

Which side would you choose?

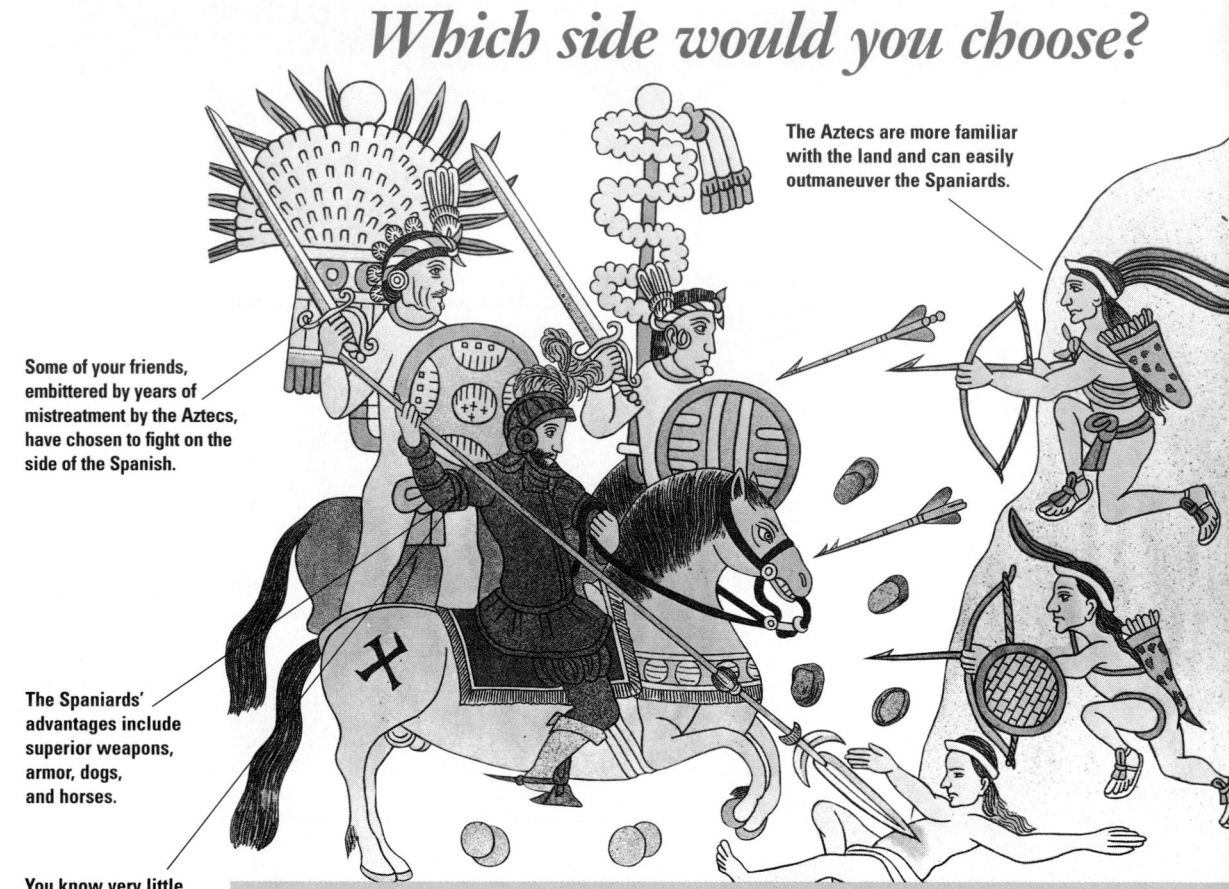

The Aztecs are more familiar with the land and can easily outmaneuver the Spaniards.

Some of your friends, embittered by years of mistreatment by the Aztecs, have chosen to fight on the side of the Spanish.

The Spaniards' advantages include superior weapons, armor, dogs, and horses.

You know very little about the invading Spanish and what they have in mind for you.

EXAMINING *the* ISSUES

- What risks are involved in supporting the invaders, whom you know almost nothing about?

- Does the fact that the Aztecs share a similar culture and heritage with you make a difference in your decision?

- What are the advantages and disadvantages of not fighting at all?

Discuss these questions with your classmates. In your discussion, examine whether invading armies throughout history have made life better or worse for people in the areas they conquer.

As you read about colonization in the Americas, see what course many natives took and learn the outcome of the battle between the Aztecs and Spanish.

102 Chapter 4

Follow Up

A feature on the chapter assessment will ask students to reevaluate their responses to the situation presented on this page.

1 Spanish Conquests in the Americas

TERMS & NAMES
- Christopher Columbus
- colony
- Hernando Cortés
- conquistadors
- Montezuma II
- Francisco Pizarro
- mestizo
- *encomienda*

MAIN IDEA

The voyages of Columbus prompted the Spanish to carve out the first European colonies in the Americas.

WHY IT MATTERS NOW

Throughout the Americas, Spanish culture, language, and descendants are the legacy of this period.

SETTING THE STAGE As you read in the previous chapter, competition for wealth in the East among European nations was fierce. This competition prompted sea captain **Christopher Columbus** to make a daring voyage for Spain in 1492. Instead of sailing east, Columbus sailed west across the Atlantic in search of an alternate trade route to Asia and its riches. Columbus never reached Asia. Instead he stepped onto an island in the Caribbean. That event set in motion a process that would bring together the peoples of Europe, Africa, and the Americas. And the world would change forever.

Columbus's Voyage Paves the Way

No one paid much attention as the *Nina, Pinta,* and *Santa Maria* slid out of a Spanish port around dawn on August 3, 1492. In a matter of months, however, Columbus's fleet would make history. It would reach the shores of what was to Europeans an astonishing new world.

First Encounters In the early hours of October 12, 1492, the long-awaited cry came. A lookout aboard the *Pinta* caught sight of a shoreline in the distance. *"Tierra! Tierra!"* he shouted. "Land! Land!" By dawn, Columbus and his crew were ashore. Thinking he had successfully reached the East Indies, Columbus called the surprised inhabitants who greeted him, *los indios.* The term translated into "Indian," a word mistakenly applied to all the native peoples of the Americas. In his memoirs, Columbus recounted his first meeting with the native peoples:

THINK THROUGH HISTORY
A. Clarifying
Why did Columbus refer to Native Americans as Indians?
B. Possible Answer Because he thought he had reached the East Indies.

A VOICE FROM THE PAST
I presented them with some red caps, and strings of glass beads to wear upon the neck, and many other trifles of small value, wherewith they were much delighted, and became wonderfully attached to us. Afterwards they came swimming to the boats where we were, bringing parrots, balls of cotton thread, javelins, and many other things which they exchanged for the articles we gave them . . . in fact they accepted anything and gave what they had with the utmost good will.
CHRISTOPHER COLUMBUS, *Journal of Columbus*

This portrait of Christopher Columbus was painted by the Spanish artist Pedro Berruguete, who lived at the same time. It is believed to be the most accurate depiction of the Italian sea captain.

Columbus, however, had miscalculated where he was. He had not reached the East Indies. Scholars believe he landed instead on an island in the Bahamas in the Caribbean Sea. The natives there were not Indians, but a group who called themselves the Taino. Nonetheless, Columbus claimed the island for Spain. He named it San Salvador, or "Holy Savior."

Columbus, like other explorers, was interested in gold. Finding none on San Salvador, he explored other islands throughout the Caribbean, staking his claim to each one. "It was my wish to bypass no island without taking possession," he wrote.

In early 1493, Columbus returned to Spain. The reports he relayed about his journey delighted the Spanish monarchs. Spain's rulers, who had funded his first voyage, agreed

---

SECTION 1 RESOURCES

PRINT RESOURCES

IN-DEPTH RESOURCES: UNIT 1
Guided Reading, p. 68
Primary Sources: from *The Journal of Christopher Columbus,* p. 75; from *The Broken Spears,* p. 77
Literature: from *The Feathered Serpent,* p. 79
History Makers: Magellan, p. 82; Cortés, p. 83

ACCESS FOR STUDENTS ACQUIRING ENGLISH
Guided Reading (Spanish), p. 50

FORMAL ASSESSMENT
Section Quiz, p. 51

TECHNOLOGY RESOURCES

WORLD ART AND CULTURES TRANSPARENCIES
AT43 *Meeting of Cortés and Montezuma*

CD-ROM
Electronic Library of Primary Sources

VIDEO *Patterns of Interaction: The Spread of Epidemic Disease*

INTERNET www.mlworldhistory.com

Section 1 Overview

OBJECTIVES

1. To describe the Spanish conquest of the Americas beginning with Columbus.
2. To describe the conquest of the Aztec and Inca by the Spanish.
3. To identify the effects of Spanish colonization on the Americas.

SKILLBUILDERS

- Interpreting maps: movement, region, p. 104
- Interpreting graphs, p. 106

CRITICAL THINKING

- Clarifying, p. 103
- Making inferences, p. 105
- Analyzing issues, p. 106
- Contrasting, pp. 107, 109
- Analyzing causes, p. 108
- Recognizing bias, p. 108

FOCUS
5-Minute Warm-Up

Interpreting Maps
To help students understand the European exploration of the Americas, have them answer these questions.

1. Look at the map on page 104. Who besides the Spanish made voyages to South America?
2. Which country explored the coast of California?

WARM-UP TRANSPARENCY 4

OBJECTIVE 1 INSTRUCT

Columbus's Voyage Paves the Way

▶ **Key Ideas**
- Columbus lands on San Salvador and claims it for Spain.
- Explorer Pedro Cabral claims Brazil for Portugal.
- Portuguese explorer Ferdinand Magellan leads a crew that is the first to circumnavigate the globe.

IN-DEPTH RESOURCES: UNIT 1
Guided Reading, p. 68

ACCESS FOR STUDENTS ACQUIRING ENGLISH
Guided Reading (Spanish), p. 50

European Exploration of the Americas, 1492–1682

Interpreting the Map Have students trace with a finger the route of one explorer at a time.

Extension Activity Have students speculate on why the English and French explorers stayed much farther north than the Spanish. *Students may suggest that since the Spanish had already laid claim to parts of South America and the islands, the other countries wanted to claim their own lands as far away as possible.*

SKILLBUILDER Answers
1. Four
2. The Spanish and Portuguese explored South and Central America; the French, Dutch, and English explored North America.

MORE ABOUT . . .
What Columbus Found

In the West Indies, Columbus and his crew discovered a new way to get a good night's sleep. The native people slept in hanging beds called *hamacas*. The crew made and strung their own *hammocks* on board ship, above the wet deck and the rats.

 IN-DEPTH RESOURCES: UNIT 1
Primary Source: from *The Journal of Christopher Columbus*, p. 75

MORE ABOUT . . .
Magellan

Although Balboa was the first European to see the Pacific Ocean, Magellan named it. After sailing through the stormy Atlantic, Magellan rounded the tip of South America and sailed into a quiet sea, which he named *Pacific*, meaning "peaceful."

 IN-DEPTH RESOURCES: UNIT 1
History Makers: Magellan, p. 82

European Exploration of the Americas, 1492–1682

Explorers' Routes
- Spanish
- Portuguese
- French
- English
- Dutch

GEOGRAPHY SKILLBUILDER: Interpreting Maps
1. **Movement** *How many different voyages did Columbus make to the Americas?*
2. **Region** *Which general region did the Spanish and Portuguese explore? Where did the English, Dutch, and French explore?*

to finance three more trips. Columbus embarked on his second voyage to the Americas in September of 1493. He journeyed no longer as an explorer, but as an empire builder. He commanded a fleet of some 17 ships and several hundred armed soldiers. He also brought 1,000 settlers. The Spanish intended to transform the islands of the Caribbean into **colonies,** or lands that are controlled by another nation.

Columbus and his followers began a process of colonization that would reach nearly every corner of the Americas. Over the next two centuries, other European explorers began sailing across the Atlantic in search of unclaimed lands.

Other Explorers Take to the Seas In 1500, Portuguese explorer Pedro Álvares Cabral reached the shores of modern-day Brazil and claimed the land for his country. A year later, Amerigo Vespucci (vehs·POO·chee), an Italian in the service of Spain, also traveled along the eastern coast of South America. Upon his return to Europe, he claimed that the newly discovered land was not part of Asia, but a "new" world. In 1507, a German mapmaker named the new continent America in honor of Vespucci. Eventually, America became the name for both continents in the Western Hemisphere.

In 1519, Portuguese explorer Ferdinand Magellan led the boldest exploration yet. Several years earlier, Spanish explorer Vasco Núñez de Balboa had marched through modern-day Panama and become the first European to gaze upon the Pacific Ocean. Soon after, Magellan convinced the king of Spain to fund his voyage into the newly discovered ocean.

With about 230 men and five ships, Magellan sailed around the southern end of South America and into the mysterious waters of the Pacific. The fleet sailed for months without seeing land. Food supplies soon ran out. "We were eating biscuits

---

Task: Students will research sailing ships of the Spanish era of exploration, as well as life on board such ships, and create a classroom display.

Purpose: To learn about ship design of 500 years ago and what life was like aboard these ships.

Activity: Small groups will read and research to find out about the ships; draw pictures or make

mockups of the ships; and read about the sailing conditions of the time. Help students design a space in the classroom for the mockups or graphics of these ships, as well as the information to accompany them. Re-creations of the *Niña* and the *Pinta* are now on display in Corpus Christi, Texas.

 Building a Portfolio: If this report is among their best work, students should add it to their portfolios.

 ALTERNATIVE ASSESSMENT BOOK
Standards for Evaluating a Cooperative Activity

Standards for Evaluation
The display should . . .

- present clear graphic examples.
- provide detailed written descriptions.
- show evidence of research using a variety of sources.

THINK THROUGH HISTORY
B. Making
Inferences What
was the significance
of Magellan's voyage?
B. Possible Answer
It proved once and
for all that the world
was round.

that were no longer biscuits but crumbs full of weevils [beetles]," one crew member wrote. "We also often ate sawdust."

After exploring the island of Guam, Magellan and his crew eventually reached the Philippines. Unfortunately, Magellan became involved in a local war there and was killed. His crew, greatly reduced by disease and starvation, continued sailing west toward home. Out of Magellan's original crew, only 18 men and one ship arrived back in Spain in 1522—nearly three years after they had left. They were the first persons to circumnavigate, or sail around, the world.

Spain Builds an American Empire

In 1519, as Magellan embarked on his historic voyage, a Spaniard named **Hernando Cortés** landed on the shores of Mexico. After colonizing several Caribbean islands, the Spanish had turned their attention to the American mainland. Cortés marched inward, looking to claim new lands for Spain. Cortés and the many other Spanish explorers who followed him were known as **conquistadors** (conquerors). Lured by rumors of vast lands filled with gold and silver, conquistadors carved out colonies in regions that would become Mexico, South America, and the United States. The Spanish were the first European settlers in the Americas. As a result of their colonization, the Spanish greatly enriched their empire and left a mark on the cultures of North and South America that exists today.

Cortés Conquers the Aztecs

Soon after landing in Mexico, Cortés learned of the vast and wealthy Aztec Empire in the region's interior. After marching for weeks through difficult mountain passes, Cortés and his force of roughly 600 men finally reached the magnificent Aztec capital of Tenochtitlan (teh-NAWCH-tee-TLAHN). The Aztec emperor, **Montezuma II,** was convinced at first that Cortés was an armor-clad god. He agreed to give the Spanish explorer a share of the empire's existing gold supply. The conquistador was not satisfied. Cortés, who admitted that he and his comrades had a "disease of the heart that only gold can cure," forced the Aztecs to mine more gold and silver. In the spring of 1520, the Aztecs rebelled against the Spanish intruders and drove out Cortés's forces.

The Spaniards, however, struck back. Despite being greatly outnumbered, Cortés and his men conquered the Aztecs in 1521. Several factors played a key role in the

HISTORY MAKERS

**Hernando Cortés
1485–1547**

To look at Hernando Cortés, it may have been difficult to guess he was a daring conquistador. According to one description, Cortés stood only about five feet, four inches tall and had a "deep chest, no belly to speak of, and was bow-legged. He was fairly thin."

But what Spain's first conquistador may have lacked in physical strength, he more than made up for in determination, courage, and ruthlessness. Upon arriving in Mexico, for example, Cortés reportedly burned his ships to keep his men from turning back. The Aztecs also experienced Cortés's toughness when they refused to surrender after months of fierce fighting. In response, Cortés ordered that the Aztec capital, Tenochtitlan, be destroyed.

**Montezuma II
1480?–1520**

While Cortés was a feared leader, Montezuma was a much beloved ruler who showed particular talent as an orator. "When he spoke," commented one historian, "he drew the sympathy of others by his subtle phrases and seduced them by his profound reasoning."

His words, however, would ultimately fail him. During a speech in which he tried to convince his subjects to make peace with the Spanish, the crowd denounced him as a traitor. "What is that which is being said by that scoundrel of a Montezuma . . ." shouted Montezuma's own cousin, Cuauhtémoc. ". . . We must give him the punishment which we give to a wicked man." And with that, the crowd stoned to death the Aztec ruler.

OBJECTIVE ② INSTRUCT

Spain Builds an American Empire

▶ **Key Ideas**
• Cortés explores Mexico and conquers the Aztec Empire.
• Pizarro explores Peru and conquers the Inca Empire.
• Disease and slavery decimate the native populations of Central and South America.

HISTORY MAKERS
Cortés and Montezuma II

When Cortés and Montezuma first faced each other, they displayed many similarities. About the same age, both were in equally good physical shape. Each dressed in the mode of his culture—Montezuma in quetzal feathers and Cortés in armor. Finally, both were accompanied by attendants whose duty was to serve their masters. Have students write a diary entry for each man giving his impressions of their first meeting.

 IN-DEPTH RESOURCES: UNIT 1
History Makers: Cortés, p. 83
Primary Source: from *The Broken Spears,* p. 77
Literature: from *The Feathered Serpent,* p. 79

 WORLD ART AND CULTURES TRANSPARENCIES
AT43 *Meeting of Cortés and Montezuma*

 ELECTRONIC LIBRARY OF PRIMARY SOURCES
from *Letter to King Charles V of Spain*

MORE ABOUT . . .
Cultural Differences

A major difference between the Spanish and Aztec was their cleanliness. Most Europeans were filthy; they rarely bathed. The Aztec capital, by contrast, was washed and swept daily, and the people took daily baths. The Aztecs found it necessary to hold flowers to their noses when near the Spanish.

TEACHING OPTIONS | MULTIPLE LEARNING STYLES | MULTIPLE LEARNING STYLES

Interpersonal Learners Have students work in pairs to construct a debate between Montezuma and Cortés. Each pair may decide which issues they wish to debate and then set up opposing arguments. Subjects may include

religion, way of life, dress, warfare, the definition of civilization, what each thinks of the other's culture, and so forth. Have volunteer pairs present their debate to the rest of the class.

Linguistic Learners Have students imagine they are news reporters or editorial columnists for newspapers in Spain, Portugal, and Italy during the era of exploration. Have those playing the reporters write news stories about the discoveries that are

taking place and the events that follow such discoveries. Ask those playing editorial columnists to write commentary on the discoveries, giving their opinions about the explorations, the people, the consequences, and so forth.

stunning victory. First, the Spanish had the advantage of superior weaponry. Aztec arrows were no match for the Spaniards' rifles and cannons.

Second, Cortés was able to enlist the help of various native groups. With the aid of a native woman translator named Malinche, Cortés learned that some natives resented the Aztecs. They hated their harsh practices, including human sacrifice. Through Malinche, Cortés convinced these natives to fight on his side.

Finally, and most important, the natives could do little to stop the invisible warrior that marched alongside the Spaniards—disease. Measles, mumps, smallpox, and typhus were just some of the diseases Europeans had brought with them to the Americas. Native Americans had never been exposed to these diseases. Thus, they had developed no natural immunity to them. As a result, they died by the hundreds of thousands. By the time Cortés launched his counterattack, the Aztec population had been greatly reduced by smallpox and measles. In time, European disease would truly devastate the natives of central Mexico.

Pizarro Subdues the Inca In 1532, another conquistador, **Francisco Pizarro,** marched an even smaller force into South America. He conquered the mighty Inca Empire. Pizarro and his army of about 200 met the Inca ruler, Atahualpa (Aн·tuh·WAHL·puh), near the city of Cajamarca. Atahualpa, who commanded a force of about 30,000, brought several thousand mostly unarmed men for the meeting. The Spaniards crushed the Inca force and kidnapped Atahualpa.

Atahualpa offered to fill a room once with gold and twice with silver in exchange for his release. However, after receiving the ransom, the Spanish strangled the Inca king. Demoralized by their leader's death, the remaining Inca force retreated from Cajamarca. Pizarro then marched on the Inca capital, Cuzco. He captured it without a struggle.

As Cortés and Pizarro conquered the once mighty civilizations of the Americas, fellow conquistadors defeated other native peoples. Spanish explorers also conquered the Maya in Yucatan and Guatemala. By the middle of the 16th century, Spain had created a wide-reaching American empire. It included New Spain (Mexico and parts of Guatemala), as well as other lands in Central and South America and the Caribbean.

Spain's Pattern of Conquest In building their new American empire, the Spaniards drew from techniques used during the *reconquista* of Spain. When conquering the Muslims, the Spanish lived among them and imposed upon them their Spanish culture. The Spanish settlers to the Americas, known as *peninsulares*, were mostly men. As a result, marriage between Spanish settlers and native women was common. These marriages created a large **mestizo**—or mixed Spanish and Native American—population. Their descendants live today in Mexico, other Latin American countries, and the United States.

Although the Spanish conquerors lived among and intermarried with the native people, they also oppressed them. In their effort to exploit the land for its precious resources, the Spanish forced Native Americans to labor within a system known as **encomienda.** Under this system, natives farmed, ranched, or mined for Spanish landlords. These landlords had received the rights to the natives' labor from Spanish authorities. The holders of *encomiendas* promised the Spanish rulers that they would act fairly and respect the workers. However, many abused the natives and worked many laborers to death, especially inside dangerous mines. The Spanish employed the same system in the Caribbean.

Background
In 1494, the Treaty of Tordesillas between Spain and Portugal gave the Portuguese the rights to Brazil.

The Portuguese in Brazil One area of South America that remained outside of Spanish control was Brazil. In 1500, Cabral claimed the land for Portugal. During the 1530s, colonists began settling Brazil's coastal region. Finding little gold or silver, the settlers began growing sugar. Clearing out huge swaths of forest land, the Portuguese built giant sugar plantations. The demand for sugar in Europe was great, and the colony soon enriched Portugal. In time, the colonists pushed further west into Brazil. They settled even more land for the production of sugar.

Along the way, the Portuguese—like the Spanish—conquered Native Americans and inflicted thousands of them with disease. Also like the Spanish, the Portuguese enslaved a great number of the land's original inhabitants.

Spain Expands Its Influence

Spain's American colonies helped make it the richest, most powerful nation in the world during much of the 16th century. Ships filled with treasures from the Americas continually sailed into Spanish harbors. This newfound wealth helped usher in a golden age of art and culture in Spain. (See Chapter 5.)

Throughout the 16th century, Spain also increased its military might. To protect its treasure-filled ships, Spain built a powerful navy. The Spanish also strengthened their other military forces, creating a skillful and determined army. For a century and a half, Spain's army never lost a battle. Meanwhile, Spain enlarged its American empire by settling in parts of what is now the United States.

Conquistadors Push North Dreams of new conquests prompted Spain to back a series of expeditions into the southwestern United States. The Spanish actually had settled in parts of the United States before they even dreamed of building an empire on the American mainland. In 1513, Spanish explorer Juan Ponce de León wandered through modern-day Florida and claimed it for Spain.

By 1540, after building an empire that stretched from Mexico to Peru, the Spanish once again looked to the land that is now the United States. That year, Francisco Vásquez de Coronado led an expedition throughout much of present-day Arizona, New Mexico, Texas, Oklahoma, and Kansas. He was searching for another wealthy empire to conquer. Coronado found little gold amidst the dry deserts of the Southwest. As a result, the Spanish monarchy assigned mostly priests to explore and colonize the future United States.

Catholic priests had accompanied conquistadors from the very beginning of American colonization. The conquistadors had come in search of wealth. The priests who accompanied them had come in search of converts. In the winter of 1609–1610, Pedro de Peralta, governor of Spain's northern holdings—called New Mexico—led settlers to a tributary on the upper Rio Grande. Together they built a capital called Santa Fe, or "Holy Faith." In the next two decades, a string of Christian missions arose among the Pueblo, the native inhabitants of the region. Scattered missions, forts, and small ranches dotted the lands of New Mexico. These became the headquarters for advancing the Catholic religion.

Opposition to Spanish Rule Spanish priests worked to spread Christianity in the Americas. They also pushed for better treatment of Native Americans. Priests spoke out against the cruel treatment of natives. In particular, they criticized the harsh

In this 19th-century illustration, Coronado leads his army back to Mexico after failing to find wealth in the southwest United States. During his return, Coronado fell from his horse and had to travel part of the way on a stretcher.

D. Possible Answer New Mexico offered little in the way of wealth, so the Spanish were more concerned there with spreading the Catholic religion.
THINK THROUGH HISTORY
D. Contrasting How did Spain's colony in New Mexico differ from its colonies in New Spain?

OBJECTIVE 3 INSTRUCT

Spain Expands Its Influence

▶ *Key Ideas*
• The Spanish advance into North America.
• Spanish missionaries follow the soldiers and establish Catholic missions.
• Native American peoples resist Spanish colonization in a variety of ways.

CRITICAL THINKING ACTIVITY
CLASS TIME: 15 MINUTES

Making a Chart To help students understand how and why Spain expanded its influence, have them fill in the chart below. Next to each category have them list a relevant fact, example, or cause.

Category	Fact, Example, Cause
navy	to protect its treasure-filled ships, Spain built a strong navy
army	
gold	
southwestern United States	
religion	

TEACHING OPTIONS
MULTIPLE LEARNING STYLES

Visual Learners Have students imagine they are Aztec and Inca artists at the time of the conquest of the Americas. Have students draw editorial cartoons that examine the explorers and their actions from the point of view of the Native Americans who already live in the Americas. The cartoons may have a caption or they may be just drawings. They may be funny or angry or exhibit any feeling at all, as long as each expresses an opinion of some kind. Encourage students to display their cartoons in the classroom.

CONNECTIONS ACROSS THE CURRICULUM

Science If Coronado and his men had had a modern-day understanding of plate tectonics, they might have altered their route and indeed have found gold in the United States. Today's geologists have learned that many gold deposits are found at the present or former boundaries of the earth's slowly moving plates. The reason for this is not fully understood. But a look at a gold distribution map shows clearly that major sources of gold lie along the Sierra Mountains in the western United States and along the Sierra Madre and Andes ranges in Mexico and South America, just where the Aztec and Inca lived.

Teacher's Edition **107**

pattern of labor that emerged under the *encomienda* system. "There is nothing more detestable or cruel," Dominican monk Bartolomé de Las Casas wrote, "than the tyranny which the Spaniards use toward the Indians for the getting of pearl [riches]."

Largely in response to the writings of Las Casas and others, the Spanish government abolished the *encomienda* system in 1542. To meet the colonies' desperate need for labor, Las Casas suggested the use of Africans. "The labor of one . . . [African] . . . [is] more valuable than that of four Indians," Las Casas declared. The priest later changed his view and denounced African slavery. However, many others promoted it. The Spanish, as well as the other nations that colonized the Americas, would soon enslave Africans to meet their growing labor needs.

Native Resistance Opposition to the Spanish method of colonization came not only from Spanish priests, but from the natives themselves. Resistance to Spain's attempt at domination began shortly after the Spanish arrived in the Caribbean. In November of 1493, Columbus encountered resistance in his attempt to conquer the present-day island of St. Croix. Before finally surrendering, the inhabitants defended themselves by firing poison arrows. Efforts to control the Taino on Hispaniola were even more difficult. After several rebellions, the Taino submitted to Columbus for several years. They revolted yet again in 1495.

As late as the end of the 17th century, natives in New Mexico fought against Spanish rule. While there were no silver mines to work in the region, the natives there still felt the weight of Spanish force. In converting the natives to Christianity, Spanish priests and soldiers often burned their sacred objects and prohibited many native rituals. The Spanish also forced natives to work for them and sometimes abused them physically. Native Americans who practiced their own religion were beaten.

In 1680, Popé, a Pueblo ruler, led a well-organized uprising against the Spanish. The rebellion involved some 17,000 warriors from villages all over New Mexico. The native fighters drove the Spanish back into New Spain. For the next 12 years—until the Spanish regained control of the area— the southwest region of the future United States once again belonged to its original inhabitants. By this time, however, the rulers of Spain had far greater concerns. Nearly 80 years before Popé ran the Spanish out of New Mexico, the other nations of Europe had begun to establish their own colonies in the Americas.

This European drawing of the 1600s depicts Indians taking revenge on a Spanish colonist— by pouring gold down his throat.

THINK THROUGH HISTORY
E. Analyzing Causes Why did the natives of New Mexico revolt against Spanish settlers?
E. Possible Answer Spanish attempts to destroy their culture and repressive measures, including beatings.

Section 1 Assessment

1. TERMS & NAMES
Identify
- Christopher Columbus
- colony
- Hernando Cortés
- conquistadors
- Montezuma II
- Francisco Pizarro
- mestizo
- *encomienda*

2. TAKING NOTES
Using a diagram like the one below, trace the major events in the establishment of Spain's empire in the Americas beginning with Columbus's arrival.

Columbus arrives in Americas

3. RECOGNIZING BIAS
Reread "A Voice from the Past" on page 103. How might Columbus's view of the Taino Indians have led the Spanish to think they could take advantage of and impose their will on the natives?

THINK ABOUT
- the Taino's desire for Spanish items even of "small value"
- the Taino's willingness to give whatever they had to the Spanish
- the Taino's appearance as a peaceful people

4. THEME ACTIVITY
Empire Building Working in small groups, debate the merits of Spain's colonization of the Americas. Have one half of the group take the position of conquistadors, and the other take the position of Native Americans.

THINK ABOUT
- how colonization of the Americas affected Spain
- what effect colonization had on the Native Americans

ANSWERS

1. TERMS & NAMES
Christopher Columbus, p. 103
colony, p. 104
Hernando Cortés, p.105
conquistadors, p. 105
Montezuma II, p. 105
Francisco Pizarro, p. 106
mestizo, p. 106
encomienda, p. 106

2. TAKING NOTES
Possible Steps: Columbus arrives in the Americas; Cortés defeats the Aztecs; Pizarro conquers the Inca; conquistadors colonize the southwest United States.

3. RECOGNIZING BIAS
Possible Answers: The Spanish may have taken the Taino's generosity and naïvete about the worth of material goods as an invitation to take whatever they wanted; the Spanish also may have assumed that the natives' gentleness meant they could be subdued.

4. THEME ACTIVITY
Possible Responses:
Conquistadors: colonization good—increased Spain's wealth and power; introduced natives to Christianity; spread Spanish culture. Native Americans: colonization bad—brought disease and warfare; led to enslavement; suppressed native culture.

The Legacy of Columbus

In the years and centuries since his historic journeys, people still debate the legacy of Christopher Columbus's voyages. Some argue they were the heroic first steps in the creation of great and democratic societies. Others claim they were the beginnings of an era of widespread cruelty and bloodshed.

HISTORIAN'S COMMENTARY
Samuel Eliot Morison

Morison, a strong supporter of Columbus, laments that the sea captain died without realizing the true greatness of his deeds.

One only wishes that the Admiral might have been afforded the sense of fulfillment that would have come from foreseeing all that flowed from his discoveries; that would have turned all the sorrows of his last years to joy. The whole history of the Americas stems from the Four Voyages of Columbus; and as the Greek city-states looked back to the deathless gods as their founders, so today a score of independent nations and dominions unite in homage to Christopher, the stout-hearted son of Genoa, who carried Christian civilization across the Ocean Sea.

ESSAY
Alphonse Lamartine

Lamartine, a French writer and politician, praises Columbus for bringing the virtues of civil society to the Americas.

All of the characteristics of a truly great man are united in Columbus. Genius, labor, patience, obscurity of origin, overcome by energy of will; mild but persisting firmness . . . fearlessness of death in civil strife; confidence in the destiny—not of an individual but of the human race. . . . He was worthy to represent the ancient world before that unknown continent on which he was the first to set foot, and carry to these men of a new race all the virtues, without any of the vices, of the elder hemisphere. So great was his influence on the destiny of the earth, that none more than he ever deserved the name of Civilizer.

EYEWITNESS ACCOUNT
Bartolomé de Las Casas

Las Casas was an early Spanish missionary who watched fellow Spaniards unleash attack dogs on Native Americans. He predicted that Columbus's legacy would be one of disaster for America's original inhabitants.

. . . Their other frightening weapon after the horses: twenty hunting greyhounds. They were unleashed and fell on the Indians at the cry of *Tómalo!* ["Get them!"] Within an hour they had preyed on one hundred of them. As the Indians were used to going completely naked, it is easy to imagine what the fierce greyhounds did, urged to bite naked bodies and skin much more delicate than that of the wild boars they were used to. . . . This tactic, begun here and invented by the devil, spread throughout these Indies and will end when there is no more land nor people to subjugate and destroy in this part of the world.

ESSAY
Suzan Shown Harjo

Harjo, a Native American, disputes the so-called benefits that resulted from Columbus's voyages and the European colonization of the Americas that followed.

"We will be asked to buy into the thinking that . . . genocide and ecocide are offset by the benefits of horses, cut-glass beads, pickup trucks, and microwave ovens."

Connect *to* History

Contrasting What opposing ideas are presented on this page?

SEE SKILLBUILDER HANDBOOK, PAGE 654

Connect *to* Today

Supporting an Opinion
Find several opinions about Columbus in 1992—the 500th anniversary of his discovery of America. Choose the opinion you agree with most and write a brief paper explaining why.

 CD-ROM For another perspective on the legacy of Columbus, see World History: Electronic Library of Primary Sources.

The Atlantic World **109**

---

110 Chapter 4

Section 2 Overview

OBJECTIVES

① To identify the French, English, and Dutch colonial activities in North America.

② To summarize competing claims in North America.

③ To describe the Native American response to the land claims made by European nations.

SKILLBUILDER

• Interpreting maps: region, place, p. 113

CRITICAL THINKING

• Summarizing, p. 111
• Contrasting, pp. 111, 112
• Analyzing issues, p. 113
• Identifying problems, p. 114
• Making inferences, p. 114
• Analyzing themes, p. 114

FOCUS
5-Minute Warm-Up

▶ *Summarizing*
To understand the sufferings endured by the English colonists at Jamestown, have students answer these questions.

1. Read "A Voice from the Past" on page 111. What seems to be killing the colonists?

2. What are the prospects of the colonists at this point?

 WARM-UP TRANSPARENCY 4

OBJECTIVE ① INSTRUCT

European Nations Settle North America

▶ *Key Ideas*
• The French colonize the St. Lawrence and Mississippi river valleys and begin the fur trade.

• The English settle at Jamestown and seek religious freedom in Massachusetts.

• The Dutch encourage a diverse population in New Netherland.

📋 *IN-DEPTH RESOURCES: UNIT 1*
Guided Reading, p. 69

📋 *ACCESS FOR STUDENTS ACQUIRING ENGLISH*
Guided Reading (Spanish), p. 51

---

2 Competing Claims in North America

MAIN IDEA
Several European nations fought for control of North America, and England eventually emerged victorious.

WHY IT MATTERS NOW
The English settlers in North America left a legacy of law and government that guides the United States today.

SETTING THE STAGE Spain's successful colonization efforts in the Americas did not go unnoticed. Other European nations soon became interested in obtaining their own valuable colonies across the Atlantic. The Treaty of Tordesillas had divided the newly discovered lands between Spain and Portugal. However, other European countries ignored the treaty. They set out to build their own empires in the Americas.

European Nations Settle North America

Magellan's voyage showed that ships could reach Asia by way of the Pacific Ocean. Spain claimed the route around the southern tip of South America. Other European countries hoped to find an easier and more direct route to the Pacific. If it existed, a northwest route through North America to Asia would become a highly profitable trade route. Not finding the route, the French, English, and Dutch instead established colonies in North America.

CONNECT to TODAY

Cajun Culture

French culture still thrives in Louisiana due in large part to the influence of people known as Cajuns. Cajuns are the descendants of French colonists who in 1604 settled the region known as Acadia in eastern Canada. Battles with the British led thousands of Acadians to move to French settlements in Louisiana, where their legacy lives on.

Today, more than 1 million Louisianans speak French. In addition, Cajun food, such as a spicy thick soup called gumbo, is popular not only in the Bayou region but also throughout the United States. Also popular around the nation are the fast-paced sounds of Cajun zydeco music.

Explorers Establish New France Just as Columbus had before them, the early French explorers sailed west with dreams of reaching the East Indies. One such explorer was Giovanni da Verrazzano (VEHR·uh·ZAH·noh), an Italian in the service of France. In 1524, he sailed to North America in search of a possible sea route to the Pacific. While he did not find the route, Verrazzano did discover what is today New York Harbor. Ten years later, the Frenchman Jacques Cartier (kahr·TYAY) reached a gulf off the eastern coast of Canada that led to a broad river. Cartier named the river the St. Lawrence. He followed it inward until he reached a large island dominated by a hill. He named the island Mont Royal, which later became known as Montreal. In 1608, another French explorer, Samuel de Champlain, sailed up the St. Lawrence. He laid claim to a region he called Quebec. The settlement grew. It eventually became the base of France's colonial empire in North America, known as **New France.**

After establishing Quebec, the French penetrated the heart of the North American continent. In 1673, French priest Jacques Marquette and trader Louis Joliet explored the Great Lakes and the upper Mississippi River. Nearly 10 years later, Sieur de La Salle explored the lower Mississippi. He claimed the entire river valley for France. He named it Louisiana in honor of the French king, Louis XIV. By the early 1700s, New France covered much of what is now the midwest United States and eastern Canada. (See the map on page 113.)

A Trading Empire France's North American empire was immense. But it was sparsely populated. By 1760, the European population of New France had grown to only about 65,000. A large number of French colonists had no desire to build towns or raise families. These settlers included Catholic priests who sought to convert

---

SECTION 2 RESOURCES

PRINT RESOURCES

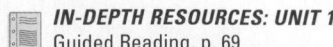 *IN-DEPTH RESOURCES: UNIT 1*
Guided Reading, p. 69
Skillbuilder Practice: Contrasting, p. 72

ACCESS FOR STUDENTS ACQUIRING ENGLISH
Guided Reading (Spanish), p. 51
Skillbuilder Practice: (Spanish), p. 54

 FORMAL ASSESSMENT
Section Quiz, p. 52

 ALTERNATIVE ASSESSMENT BOOK

TECHNOLOGY RESOURCES

 CD-ROM
Electronic Library of Primary Sources

 INTERNET www.mlworldhistory.com

Native Americans. They also included young, single men engaged in what had become New France's main economic activity: fur trade.

By the late 1500s, one of the hottest fashion trends in Europe was hats made of beaver skin. Beavers were almost extinct in Europe but plentiful in North America. This led to a thriving trade in furs. Unlike the English, the French were less interested in occupying territories than they were in making money off the land.

The English Settle at Jamestown The explorations of the Spanish and French fired the imagination of the English. In 1606, a company of London investors obtained from King James a charter to found a colony in North America. In 1607, the company's three ships—and more than 100 settlers—pushed out of an English harbor. Four months later, the North American shore rose along the horizon. After reaching the coast of Virginia, the vessels slipped into a broad coastal river. They sailed inland until they reached a small peninsula. There, the colonists climbed off their ships and claimed the land as theirs. They named the settlement **Jamestown** in honor of their king.

The colony's start was disastrous. The settlers were more interested in finding gold than planting crops. They soon fell victim to their harsh surroundings. During the first few years, seven out of every ten people died of hunger, disease, or fighting with the Native Americans. After several months in this hostile environment, one settler described the terrible situation:

The first English colonists arrive at Jamestown in 1607, as depicted in this 19th-century engraving.

A VOICE FROM THE PAST
Thus we lived for the space of five months in this miserable distress . . . our men night and day groaning in every corner of the fort, most pitiful to hear. If there were any conscience in men, it would make their hearts to bleed to hear the pitiful murmuring and outcries of our sick men for relief, every night and day for the space of six weeks: some departing out of the World, many times three or four in a night; in the morning their bodies trailed out of their cabins like dogs, to be buried.
A JAMESTOWN COLONIST, quoted in *A New World*

Despite their nightmarish start, the colonists eventually gained a foothold in their new land. Jamestown became England's first permanent settlement in North America. The colony's outlook improved greatly after farmers there discovered tobacco. High demand in England for tobacco turned it into a profitable cash crop, or a crop grown primarily for sale. The colony, however, continued to struggle financially. Jamestown's investors finally let King James take over the colony. As a royal colony, Jamestown slowly grew and prospered.

Puritans Create a "New England" In 1620, as the colonists at Jamestown were struggling to survive, a group known as **Pilgrims** founded a second English colony, Plymouth, in Massachusetts. Persecuted for their religious beliefs in England, these colonists sought religious freedom. Eight years later, a group known as **Puritans** also sought religious freedom from England's Anglican Church. They established a larger colony at nearby Massachusetts Bay.

The Puritans wanted to build a model community that would set an example for other Christians to follow. Although the colony experienced early difficulties, it gradually took hold. This was due in large part to the numerous families in the colony, unlike the mostly single, male population in Jamestown. Family life created a sense of order among the settlers. It also ensured that the population would reproduce itself.

The Dutch Found New Netherland Following the English and French into North America were the Dutch. The Dutch had established the Dutch East India Company in 1602 to compete for trade in the Indian Ocean. Several years later, they turned

MORE ABOUT . . .
The Dutch

When the English took over New Netherland, the English language quickly outpaced Dutch. Today, however, there are many familiar words borrowed from Dutch in the English language, including *cooky, boss, crib,* and *spook.*

OBJECTIVE ② INSTRUCT

The Fight for North America

▶ Key Ideas

- The English drive the Dutch from New Netherland and rename the colony New York.
- The Seven Years' War in Europe spills over into conflicts between French and English colonists in North America.
- The English defeat the French and rule eastern North America.

SPOTLIGHT ON
Pirates

Blackbeard was finally trapped by a British navy crew in 1718 in an inlet of Okracoke Island, off North Carolina. It is said of Blackbeard's last battle that he fought with a pistol in one hand and a cutlass in the other, before dying with more than 25 wounds in his body. Ask students to find more information about Blackbeard's last battle and bring copies of the accounts they find to class. Volunteers might read their accounts to the class.

---

their attention to the Americas. In 1609, Henry Hudson, an Englishman in the service of the Netherlands, sailed west. He was searching for a northwest sea route to Asia. Hudson did not find a route. He did, however, explore three waterways near present-day New York that were later named for him—the Hudson River, Hudson Bay, and Hudson Strait.

The Dutch claimed the region along these waterways. They established a fur trade with the Iroquois Indians. They also built trading posts along the Hudson River at Fort Orange (now Albany) and on Manhattan Island, at the mouth of the river. Dutch merchants quickly formed the Dutch West India Company. In 1621, the Dutch government granted the company permission to colonize the region and expand the thriving fur trade. The Dutch holdings in North America became known as **New Netherland.**

Although the Dutch company profited from its fur trade, it was slow to attract Dutch colonists. To encourage settlers to come and stay, the colony opened its doors to a variety of peoples. Gradually, more Dutch, as well as Germans, French, Scandinavians, and other Europeans settled the area. The colony's population was so ethnically diverse that one visitor called it a great "confusion of tongues." The Dutch reputation for religious tolerance also drew people of many faiths, including Protestants, Catholics, Muslims, and Jews.

Colonizing the Caribbean During the 1600s, the nations of Europe also colonized the Caribbean. The French seized control of several Caribbean islands, including present-day Haiti, Guadeloupe, and Martinique. The English settled Barbados and Jamaica. In 1634, the Dutch captured what are now the Netherlands Antilles and Aruba from Spain.

On these islands, the Europeans built huge tobacco and sugar plantations. These products, although profitable, demanded a large and steady supply of free labor. Enslaved Africans eventually would supply this labor.

The Fight for North America

As they expanded their settlements in North America, the nations of France, England, and the Netherlands battled each other for colonial supremacy. After years of skirmishes and war, the English gained control of much of the continent.

The English Oust the Dutch To the English, New Netherland had become a "Dutch wedge" separating its northern and southern colonies. In 1664, the English king, Charles II, granted his brother, the Duke of York, permission to drive out the Dutch. When the duke's fleet arrived at New Netherland, the Dutch surrendered without firing a shot. The Duke of York claimed the colony for England and renamed it New York.

With the Dutch gone, the English continued to colonize the Atlantic coast of North America. By 1750, about 1.3 million English settlers lived in 13 colonies stretching from New Hampshire to Georgia.

England Battles France The English soon became hungry for more land to suit their growing colonial population. So they pushed further west into the continent. By doing so, however, they collided with France's North American holdings. France and England, long-time enemies, had brought their dislike for one another with them to North America. As their colonies expanded, they began to interfere with each other. It seemed that a major conflict was on the horizon.

That conflict began in 1754. That year a dispute over land claims in the Ohio Valley led to a war between the British and French on the North American continent. The conflict became known as

SPOTLIGHT ON
Pirates

The battle for colonial supremacy occurred not only on land, but also on the sea. Acting on behalf of their government, privately owned armed ships, known as privateers, attacked merchant ships of enemy nations and sank or robbed them.

Also patrolling the high seas were pirates. Unlike privateers, pirates were not licensed by any country. They attacked ships for their gold and did not care what nation the vessels represented. Pirates were ruthless men who did not hesitate to kill for treasure.

One of the most well-known pirates was Edward B. Teach, whose prominent beard earned him the nickname Blackbeard (above). According to one account, Blackbeard attempted to frighten his victims by sticking "lighted matches under his hat, which appeared on both sides of his face and eyes, naturally fierce and wild. . . ."

THINK THROUGH HISTORY
C. Contrasting
How were the Dutch and French colonies different from the English colonies in North America?
C. Possible Answer
The English colonies were more populated; while the Dutch and French colonies were established mainly for commercial reasons. New England was begun for religious reasons.

Background
In 1707, England united with Scotland to become the United Kingdom of Great Britain.

| TEACHING OPTION | BLOCK SCHEDULING | SKILLBUILDER MINI-LESSON: Contrasting | CLASS TIME 15 MINUTES |

Explaining the Skill Finding the differences between ideas, institutions, behaviors, or events helps students understand historical events more clearly. Often, one concept is easier to grasp if its features can be contrasted with similar features of something else. For example, understanding the rules of rugby might be made easier by contrasting them with the rules of soccer or football.

Applying the Skill: Think Through History Question To answer the Think Through History question on this page, students will first need to review pages 110–112. Have them take note of the green subheads on these pages. Then ask the following questions.

1. What sort of empire was France's North American territory? *a trading empire*

2. Who founded New England, and what was their main reason for settling there? *Puritans; religious freedom*

3. Which colony had the most diversity of people and languages? Who founded it? *New Netherland; the Dutch*

📖 ***IN-DEPTH RESOURCES: UNIT 1***
Skillbuilder Practice: Contrasting, p. 72

Europeans in N. America, 1754

Holdings after 1763

Legend (Holdings after 1763):
- English
- French
- Russian
- Spanish

Legend (Europeans in N. America, 1754):
- Disputed
- English
- French
- Spanish

GEOGRAPHY SKILLBUILDER: Interpreting Maps
1. **Region** *Which nation claimed the largest area of the present-day United States in 1754?*
2. **Place** *How did Britain's North American empire change after 1763?*

History from Visuals

Europeans in N. America, 1754
Holdings after 1763
Interpreting the Map Have students examine the map legend to see which colors are used for the various European claims and how these colored areas shift, grow, or shrink from the first map to the second.

Extension Activity Ask students to read the map to see which national group that has claims in the map of 1754 has lost them by 1763, and which national group that has no claims in 1754 has entered the picture by 1763. *the French; the Russians*

SKILLBUILDER Answers
1. France
2. It increased greatly as the British seized most of the French territory and took control of nearly the entire eastern half of the continent.

 ELECTRONIC LIBRARY OF PRIMARY SOURCES
"The French Lose Quebec"

Background
The name French and Indian War was the colonists' name for the war. The French and many Indians were allied against the British and the colonists.

the **French and Indian War.** The war became part of a larger conflict known as the Seven Years' War. Britain and France—along with their Europian allies—also battled for territorial and colonial supremacy in Europe and the West Indies.

In North America, the British colonists, with the help of the British Army, defeated the French in 1763. The French surrendered most of their colonial holdings on the continent. As a result of the French and Indian War, the British seized control of nearly the entire eastern half of North America.

Native American Reaction

D. Possible Answer
Because both groups benefited from their cooperation in the fur trade: the Indians did the trapping and then traded the furs to the French and Dutch for numerous desired goods.

THINK THROUGH HISTORY
D. Analyzing Issues
Why were the Dutch and French able to coexist in relative peace with the Native Americans?

As in Mexico and South America, the arrival of Europeans in the present-day United States had a great impact on Native Americans. European colonization brought mostly disaster for the lands' original inhabitants, as many fell to disease and warfare.

A Strained Relationship French and Dutch settlers developed a mostly cooperative relationship with the Native Americans. This was due mainly to the mutual benefits of the fur trade. Native Americans did most of the trapping and then traded the furs to the French for such items as guns, hatchets, mirrors, and beads. The Dutch also cooperated with Native Americans in an effort to establish a fur-trading enterprise.

The groups, however, did not live together in complete harmony. Dutch settlers engaged in fighting with various Native American groups over land claims and trading rights. In 1643, for example, the Dutch and Wappinger tribe fought a bloody battle in which hundreds died. For the most part, however, the French and Dutch colonists lived together peacefully with their North American hosts.

The same could not be said of the English. Early relations between English settlers and Native Americans were cooperative. However, they quickly worsened—mostly over

The Atlantic World **113**

OBJECTIVE 3 INSTRUCT

Native American Reaction

▶ *Key Ideas*
- French and Dutch fur traders cooperate, at least at first, with the Native American peoples.
- English colonization sparks conflict with Native Americans over land and religion.
- Metacom engages the English in King Philip's war and is defeated.
- European diseases decimate the Native American populations.

TEACHING OPTION | **BLOCK SCHEDULING** | **COOPERATIVE ACTIVITY: Planning a Journey** | **CLASS TIME 15 MINUTES**

Task: Students will plan a list of items to take with them on a journey during which they will have to depend only on what is in their backpack.

Purpose: To imagine the planning a sailor had to put into preparing for an ocean voyage and deciding what to take.

Activity: Have students work in groups to figure out what items they might take in a large backpack

for a one-week trip in the wilderness. Have them imagine, just for the purposes of the activity, that they will not be able to replace anything or eat off the land. They may replace water in a canteen from freshwater sources, but that is all. Have one group work on a list for clothing, another on food, another on necessities such as matches, medical supplies, shelter materials, and so forth. Remind them that everything they choose to take has to fit in a large

backpack or duffel bag, which they will have to carry everywhere. Students may discuss with one another the decisions they are making and why. When the lists are complete, display them in the classroom for comment and discussion.

 ALTERNATIVE ASSESSMENT BOOK
Standards for Evaluating a Cooperative Activity

Teacher's Edition **113**

Comparing and Contrasting
Ask students why they think the Dutch and French at first had better relationships with Native Americans than did the English. Have them put their ideas in a chart like the one here.

Nation	Relationship with Native Americans	Reason
Dutch		
French		
English		

ASSESS & RETEACH

Section 2 Assessment
Have students list the pages in the section on which answers to each question can be found.

Section Quiz
FORMAL ASSESSMENT
Section Quiz, p. 52

Reteaching Activity
CLASS TIME: 15 MINUTES

Review the students' charts for the Taking Notes activity in the section assessment. The reasons they have listed for establishment of the settlement should form the persuasive letter they write.

CLOSE ACTIVITY

CLASS TIME: 15 MINUTES

Summarizing the Section
Have students make a chart that lists the English, French, and Dutch colonies in North America, their locations, the reasons for the settlements, and the valuable products and crops of the colonies.

King Philip's War was one of the bloodiest battles fought between English colonists and Native Americans. About 600 colonists and 3,000 Indians were killed during the fighting.

the issues of land and religion. Unlike the French and Dutch, the English sought to populate their colonies in North America. This meant pushing the natives off their land. The English colonists seized more and more land for their swelling population—and to grow more tobacco. As a result, tensions between the two groups rose.

Misunderstandings over religion also heightened tensions. The English settlers, particularly the Puritans, considered Native Americans heathens—people without a faith. Over time, many Puritans viewed Native Americans as agents of the devil and as a threat to their godly society. For their part, Native Americans developed a similarly hard view toward the white invaders.

Settlers and Native Americans Battle The hostility between the English settlers and Native Americans led to warfare. As early as 1622, the Powhatan tribe attacked colonial villages around Jamestown and killed about 350 settlers. The colonists eventually struck back and massacred hundreds of Powhatan.

One of the bloodiest battles colonists and Native Americans waged was known as King Philip's War. It began in 1675 when the Native American ruler **Metacom** (also known as King Philip) led an attack on 52 colonial villages throughout Massachusetts. In the months that followed, both sides massacred hundreds of victims. After a year of fierce fighting, the colonists defeated the natives. Throughout the 17th century, many more smaller skirmishes erupted throughout North America. While the Native Americans fought fiercely, they were no match for the colonists' rifles and cannons.

Natives Fall to Disease More destructive than the Europeans' weapons were their diseases. Like the Spanish in Central and South America, the Europeans who settled North America brought with them several diseases. And just as had happened in Mexico and Peru, the diseases devastated the native population in North America.

In 1616, for example, an epidemic of smallpox ravaged Native Americans living along the New England coast. The population of one tribe, the Massachusett, dropped from 24,000 to 750 by 1631. Thousands of other natives throughout the region also perished. "They died on heapes, as they lay in their houses," observed one eyewitness. From South Carolina to Missouri, nearly whole tribes fell to smallpox, measles, and other diseases.

Throughout the Americas, the loss of native life due to disease was incredible. One of the effects of this loss was a severe shortage of labor in the colonies. In order to meet their growing labor needs, European colonists from South America to North America soon turned to another group: Africans, whom they would enslave by the millions.

THINK THROUGH HISTORY
E. Identifying Problems Why did the issues of land and religion cause such strife between the Native Americans and English settlers?
E. Possible Answer The settlers continually wanted more land for their growing population as well as their crops; they also viewed the natives as godless devils.

Background
To celebrate their victory over Metacom, the Puritans cut off his head and displayed it at Plymouth for many years.

Section 2 Assessment

1. TERMS & NAMES
Identify
• New France
• Jamestown
• Pilgrims
• Puritans
• New Netherland
• French and Indian War
• Metacom

2. TAKING NOTES
Copy this chart and fill in the location of each settlement and the main reasons for its establishment.

Name of Settlement	General Location	Reasons for Establishment
New France		
New Netherland		
Massachusetts Bay		

Write a letter convincing someone to settle in one of the settlements.

3. MAKING INFERENCES
What may have been one reason the English eventually beat the French in North America?
THINK ABOUT
• how England's colonies differed from those of the French
• English and French colonial populations on the eve of the French and Indian War

4. ANALYZING THEMES
Cultural Interaction
Imagine that you have been asked to settle a dispute between a group of English colonists and Native Americans. Summarize each side's grievances and offer possible solutions.

114 Chapter 4

ANSWERS

1. TERMS & NAMES
New France, p. 110
Jamestown, p. 111
Pilgrims, p.111
Puritans, p. 111
New Netherland, p. 112
French and Indian War, p. 113
Metacom, p. 114

2. TAKING NOTES
New France: eastern Canada and much of midwest United States/Christian missionary and fur trading post; New Netherland: upper east coast of United States/ fur trading post; Massachusetts Bay: upper east coast of United States/religious refuge

3. MAKING INFERENCES
Possible Response: The English, unlike the French and Dutch, populated their colonies in North America, so that by the eve of the French and Indian War, England's colonial population was more than 1 million, while France's was only 65,000.

4. ANALYZING THEMES
Possible Responses: Colonists' grievances—need more land for growing population and farming, Native Americans are heathens; Native Americans' grievances— colonists are pushing them off their land. Possible solutions— share the land by establishing boundary lines.

3 The Atlantic Slave Trade

TERMS & NAMES
• Atlantic slave trade
• triangular trade
• middle passage

MAIN IDEA

To meet their growing labor needs, Europeans enslaved millions of Africans in forced labor in the Americas.

WHY IT MATTERS NOW

Descendants of enslaved Africans represent a significant part of the Americas' population today.

SETTING THE STAGE Sugar plantations and tobacco farms required a large supply of workers to make them profitable for their owners. European owners had planned to use Native Americans as a source of cheap labor. But millions of Native Americans died from disease and warfare. Therefore, the Europeans in Brazil, the Caribbean, and the southern colonies of North America soon turned to Africa for workers.

The Evolution of African Slavery

Beginning around 1500, European colonists began enslaving Africans in the Americas in order to meet their great demand for large numbers of people to work as cheap labor.

Slavery in Africa As it had in other parts of the world, slavery had existed in Africa for many years. In most regions, however, it was a relatively minor institution. The spread of Islam into Africa during the seventh century, however, ushered in an increase in slavery and the slave trade. African rulers justified enslavement with the Muslim belief that non-Muslim prisoners of war could be bought and sold as slaves. As a result, between 650 and 1600, black as well as white Muslims transported as many as 4.8 million Africans—mostly prisoners of war and criminals—to the Muslim lands of Southwest Asia. Once there, these enslaved Africans worked primarily as domestic servants.

In most African and Muslim societies, slaves had some legal rights and opportunity for social mobility. In the Muslim world, slaves even occupied positions of influence and power. Some served as generals in the army. Others bought large estates and even owned slaves of their own. In African societies, slaves could escape their bondage in numerous ways, including marrying into the family they served. Furthermore, slavery in Africa was not hereditary. Thus the sons and daughters of slaves were considered free.

The Desire for Africans The first Europeans to explore Africa were the Portuguese during the 1400s. Initially, Portuguese traders were more interested in trading for gold than for captured Africans. That changed, however, with the colonization of the Americas. At first, European colonists in the Americas forced Native Americans to work their profitable mines and plantations. As natives began dying by the millions from disease, Europeans became desperate for new workers.

To resupply their labor force, colonists in the Americas soon looked to Africa. Europeans saw several advantages in using Africans. First, many Africans had been exposed to various European diseases and had built up some immunity to them. Second, many Africans had experience in farming and thus could be taught large-scale plantation work. Third, Africans—strangers to the Americas—had little knowledge of

---

A. Possible Answer In Muslim society, slaves had legal rights and opportunities for social mobility; in Africa, slaves could escape their bondage in numerous ways, and slavery was not hereditary.

THINK THROUGH HISTORY
A. Summarizing What were some characteristics of Muslim and African slavery?

SPOTLIGHT ON

Slavery

The enslavement of human beings by others is believed to be as old as civilization itself. Slavery probably began with the development of farming about 10,000 years ago. Farming gave people the need to force prisoners of war to work for them.

Slavery has existed in numerous societies around the world. People were enslaved in civilizations from Egypt to China to India, as well as among Indians in America, and in Greece and Rome.

Race was not always a factor in slavery. Often, slaves were captured prisoners of war, or people of a different nationality or religion. In ancient Rome, for example, both owners and slaves were white.

However, the slavery that developed in the Americas was based largely on race. Europeans viewed black people as naturally inferior. Because of this, slavery in the Americas was hereditary— children of slaves were also slaves.

The Atlantic World **115**

Section 3 Overview

OBJECTIVES

1. To summarize the evolution of the slave trade in Africa and the New World.
2. To describe the triangular trade and the middle passage.
3. To describe the life of slaves in the colonies.
4. To identify the consequences of the Atlantic slave trade.

SKILLBUILDER
• Interpreting maps: movement, region, p. 117

CRITICAL THINKING
• Summarizing, pp. 115, 119
• Analyzing motives, p. 116
• Analyzing issues, p. 117
• Recognizing effects, p. 119
• Contrasting, p. 119

FOCUS
5-Minute Warm-Up

▶ **Making Inferences**
Have students answer the following questions to help them understand the slave trade.

1. Look at the map on page 117. Which two areas of the world imported the fewest slaves?
2. From what region of Africa did most of the slaves come?

WARM-UP TRANSPARENCY 4

OBJECTIVE ① INSTRUCT

The Evolution of African Slavery

▶ **Key Ideas**
• Europeans join the developing African slave trade.
• Spain and Portugal import slaves to the Americas, followed by Holland, France, and England.
• Although many Africans profit from the slave trade, some rulers oppose it.

IN-DEPTH RESOURCES: UNIT 1
Guided Reading, p. 70

ACCESS FOR STUDENTS ACQUIRING ENGLISH
Guided Reading (Spanish), p. 52

SECTION 3 RESOURCES

PRINT RESOURCES

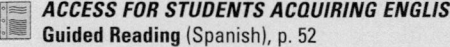 *IN-DEPTH RESOURCES: UNIT 1*
Guided Reading, p. 70
Primary Source: from *The Life of Olaudah Equiano*, p. 78

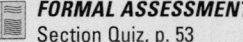 *ACCESS FOR STUDENTS ACQUIRING ENGLISH*
Guided Reading (Spanish), p. 52

FORMAL ASSESSMENT
Section Quiz, p. 53

ALTERNATIVE ASSESSMENT BOOK

TECHNOLOGY RESOURCES

 WORLD ART AND CULTURES TRANSPARENCIES
AT44 Meynell's *Slaves Below the Deck of the* Albanez

 CRITICAL THINKING TRANSPARENCIES
CT20 The Atlantic Slave Trade, 1451–1870

CD-ROM
Electronic Library of Primary Sources

INTERNET www.mlworldhistory.com

the land and had no familiar tribes in which to hide. As a result, they were less likely to try to escape.

In time, the buying and selling of Africans for work in the Americas—known as the **Atlantic slave trade**—became a massive enterprise. Between 1500 and 1600, nearly 300,000 Africans were transported to the Americas. During the next century, that number climbed to almost 1.5 million. By the time the Atlantic slave trade ended around 1870, Europeans had imported about 9.5 million Africans to the Americas.

Spain and Portugal Lead the Way The Spanish took an early lead in importing Africans to the Americas. As early as 1511, a small number of Africans were working in the copper mines on Hispaniola. In time, Spain moved on from the Caribbean and began to colonize the American mainland. As a result, the Spanish imported and enslaved thousands more Africans. By 1650, nearly 300,000 Africans labored throughout Spanish America on plantations and in gold and silver mines.

By this time, however, the Portuguese had surpassed the Spanish in the importation of Africans to the Americas. During the 1600s, Brazil dominated the European sugar market. As the colony's sugar industry grew, so too did European colonists' demand for slaves. During the 17th century, more than 40 percent of all Africans brought to the Americas went to Brazil. By the time the slave trade ended, Brazil had received more than 3.6 million Africans. That was nearly 10 times the number of Africans who would arrive in North America.

The development of sugar, shown here in its cane form, helped spur the growth of slavery in the Americas.

Slavery Spreads Throughout the Americas As the other European nations established colonies in the Americas, their demand for cheap labor grew. Thus, they also began to import and enslave large numbers of Africans. A majority of these slaves labored on sugar, tobacco, and coffee plantations in the Dutch, French, and English colonies in the Caribbean.

As England's presence in the Americas grew, it came to dominate the Atlantic slave trade. From 1690 until the nation abolished the slave trade in 1807, England was the leading carrier of enslaved Africans. By the time the slave trade ended, the English had transported nearly 1.7 million Africans to their colonies in the West Indies.

A much smaller number of enslaved Africans eventually arrived in what is now the United States. In all, nearly 400,000 Africans were imported to Britain's North American colonies. Once in North America, however, the slave population steadily grew. By 1830, roughly 2 million slaves toiled in the United States.

African Cooperation and Resistance Many African rulers and merchants played a willing role in the Atlantic slave trade. Those African leaders who had been selling Africans as slaves to Muslims and other African rulers saw little difference in selling them to Westerners. Most European traders, rather than travel inland, waited in ports along the western and eastern coasts of Africa. African merchants, with the help of local rulers, captured Africans to be enslaved. They then delivered them to the Europeans in exchange for gold, guns, and other goods.

As the slave trade grew, some African rulers voiced their opposition to the practice. One such ruler was King Nzinga Mbemba of Congo in west-central Africa. Mbemba, also known as Affonso, had originally participated in the slave trade. However, he soon realized its devastating effect on African societies. In 1526, he wrote a letter to the king of Portugal in which he protested the taking of Africans for enslavement:

> **A VOICE FROM THE PAST**
> And we cannot reckon how great the damage is, since . . . merchants are taking every day our natives, sons of the land and the sons of our noblemen and vassals and our relatives, because the thieves and men of bad conscience grab them . . . they grab them and get them to be sold; and so great, Sir, is the corruption . . . that our country is being completely depopulated, and Your Highness should not agree with this nor accept it. . . . *it is our will that in these Kingdoms there should not be any trade of slaves nor outlet for them.*
> **KING AFFONSO,** quoted in *African Civilization Revisited*

116 Chapter 4

THINK THROUGH HISTORY
C. Analyzing Issues
Why did many African rulers participate in the Atlantic slave trade?
C. Possible Answer
It was profitable, and they saw little difference between trading African slaves to Muslims and other Africans and Westerners.

Despite Affonso's plea, the slave trade continued and steadily grew. Lured by its profits, many African rulers continued to participate. As for African merchants, they simply developed new trade routes to avoid rulers who refused to cooperate.

A Forced Journey

After being captured, African men and women were shipped to the Americas as part of a profitable trade network. Along the way, millions of captured Africans endured a dehumanizing voyage across the Atlantic. Many died on the way.

The Triangular Trade Africans transported to the Americas were part of a transatlantic trading network known as the **triangular trade.** Over one trade route, Europeans transported manufactured goods to the west coast of Africa. There, traders exchanged these goods for captured Africans. The Africans were then transported across the Atlantic Ocean and sold in the West Indies. Merchants then bought sugar, coffee, and tobacco in the West Indies and sailed back to Europe to sell these products.

On another triangular route, merchants carried rum and other goods from the New England colonies to Africa. There they exchanged their merchandise for Africans. The traders then transported the Africans to the West Indies and sold them for sugar and molasses. They then sold these goods to rum producers in New England.

Various other transatlantic routes existed. In fact, the "triangular" trade encompassed a network of trade routes crisscrossing the Northern and Southern colonies, the West Indies, England, Europe, and Africa. The network carried a variety of traded goods. These included furs, fruit, tar, and tobacco, as well as millions of African people.

The Middle Passage The voyage that brought captured Africans to the West Indies and later to North and South America was known as the **middle passage.** It was so named because it was considered the middle leg of the transatlantic trade triangle.

Triangle Trade System, 1451–1870

GREAT BRITAIN
London
Paris
EUROPE

NORTH AMERICA
New York
Charleston

Manufactures
Cotton, Tobacco
Rum

CARIBBEAN REGION
JAMAICA
MEXICO

Sugar, Molasses, Cotton
Sugar, Molasses, Slaves
Rum
Slaves, Gold
Manufactures, Guns
Slaves, Ivory, Gum

PACIFIC OCEAN

SOUTH AMERICA
Rio de Janeiro
Tobacco

ATLANTIC OCEAN

AFRICA

KONGO
Luanda
Benguela
Mozambique

INDIAN OCEAN

Slaves

40°N
Tropic of Cancer
0° Equator
Tropic of Capricorn
40°S

Primary slave trade routes
Other trade routes

N

0   2,000 Miles
0   4,000 Kilometers

Africans Enslaved in the Americas, 1451–1870

Total Number Imported: 9.5 Million*

40% Caribbean Islands (Dutch, French, British)
4% British North America
2% Europe, Asia
16% Spanish America and Spanish Caribbean
38% Portuguese Brazil

* Estimated   Source: *The Atlantic Slave Trade: A Census*

GEOGRAPHY SKILLBUILDER: Interpreting Maps
1. **Movement** What items were transported to Africa and traded for captured Africans?
2. **Region** According to the graph, what region of the Americas imported the most Africans? Which imported the second most?

The Atlantic World **117**

OBJECTIVE **2** INSTRUCT

A Forced Journey

▶ **Key Ideas**
• African slaves become part of a triangular trade involving Europe, Africa, and the Americas.
• Millions of slaves endure the middle passage across the Atlantic.
• Over one fifth of African passengers die during the middle passage, some by suicide.

CRITICAL THINKING TRANSPARENCIES
CT20 The Atlantic Slave Trade, 1451–1870

History from Visuals

Triangle Trade System, 1451–1870

Interpreting the Map Have students read both the map and the circle graph and compare and contrast the different kinds of information to be found in each. For example, the map shows the routes and products and human cargo of the triangular trade, while the graph gives the percentages of the slave population taken to each area of the world.

Extension Activity Have students point to the route on the map of the middle passage. They might point to a number of spots, because the middle passage was the voyage across the ocean. The route was different, depending on where enslaved Africans were sent.

SKILLBUILDER Answers
1. Tobacco, rum, manufactured goods, guns
2. The Caribbean was first, Brazil was second.

Task Students will look at an art transparency to examine the horrors of life aboard a slave ship. They should note the close quarters of the enslaved Africans as well as other discomforts of the voyage.

Materials Needed Use copies of Art Transparency AT44, *Slaves Below the Deck of the Albanez.* You might also use the drawing of the interior of a slave ship on page 118.

Activity Mention to students that the British had outlawed slavery in 1807. A British patrol captured the slave ship *Albanez* in 1846. A British naval officer painted the scene on the slave ship; it shows conditions that were found on many such ships. Have the class help you make a list of the horrible conditions aboard a slave ship.

Conclusion Ask students which conditions aboard a slave ship they would have found the most intolerable. What would they have done in those circumstances? How might they have attempted to improve conditions?

 WORLD ART AND CULTURES TRANSPARENCIES
AT44, *Slaves Below the Deck of the Albanez*

OBJECTIVE 3 INSTRUCT

Slavery in the Americas

Key Ideas
• Upon reaching the Americas, Africans are sold for work in mines or on plantations.
• Slaves resist slavery through sabotage, uprisings, escape, and preserving their cultural heritage.

MORE ABOUT . . .
Slave Resistance

In addition to other forms of resistance, slaves also found ways to supplement their meager food rations. Some took their masters' pigs, buried the pigs' hides, and then pretended they were eating possum, which was available to slaveowners and slaves alike. Others stole chickens and scattered the feathers to make it look as though a fox had been in the hen house. When slaves raided the potato fields, they released pigs into the fields and blamed the destruction on them.

This design of a British slave ship offers a glimpse of what life was like for enslaved Africans during their trip to the Americas.

Sickening cruelty characterized this journey. In the bustling ports along the African coasts, European traders packed Africans into the dark holds of large ships. On board a slave ship, Africans fell victim to whippings and beatings from merchants, as well as diseases that swept through the vessel. The smell of blood, sweat, and excrement filled the hold. African captives often lived in their own vomit and waste. One African, Olaudah Equiano, recalled the inhumane conditions on his trip from West Africa to the West Indies at age 11 in 1756:

A VOICE FROM THE PAST
I was soon put down under the decks, and there I received such a salutation [greeting] in my nostrils as I never experienced in my life; so that, with the loathsomeness of the stench, and crying together, I became so sick and low that I was not able to eat . . . but soon, to my grief, two of the white men offered me eatables; and on my refusing to eat, one of them held me fast by the hands, and laid me across . . . the windlass, and tied my feet, while the other flogged me severely.

OLAUDAH EQUIANO, quoted in *Eyewitness: The Negro in American History*

Olaudah Equiano

Numerous Africans died aboard the slave ships from disease or from cruel treatment by merchants. Many others committed suicide by plunging into the ocean rather than be enslaved. Scholars estimate that roughly 20 percent of the Africans aboard each slave ship perished during the brutal trip to the Americas.

Background
After working for some time in the West Indies, Equiano was freed. He eventually went to England, where he crusaded against slavery.

Slavery in the Americas

Africans who survived their ocean voyage entered a difficult life of bondage in the Americas. Forced to work in a strange land, enslaved Africans coped in a variety of ways. Many embraced their African culture, while others rebelled against their enslavers.

A Harsh Life Upon arriving in the Americas, captured Africans usually were auctioned off to the highest bidder. A British minister who visited a slave market in Brazil commented on the process: "When a customer comes in, they [the slaves] are turned before him; such as he wishes are handled by the purchaser in different parts, exactly as I have seen butchers feeling a calf."

After being sold, slaves worked in mines or fields or as domestic servants. Whatever their task, slaves lived a grueling existence. Many lived on little food in small, dreary huts. They worked long days and often suffered whippings and beatings. In much of the Americas, slavery was a lifelong condition, as well as a hereditary one. This meant that the sons and daughters of slaves were born into a lifetime of bondage.

Resistance and Rebellion To cope with the horrors of slavery, Africans developed a way of life based strongly on their cultural heritage. They kept alive such things as their musical traditions as well as the stories of their ancestors.

Enslaved Africans also found ways to resist their bondage. They made themselves less productive by breaking hoes, uprooting plants, and working slowly. This resistance hurt their owners' profit. Although they were unfamiliar with the land, thousands of slaves also ran away.

Some slaves pushed their resistance to open revolt. As early as 1522, about 20 slaves on Hispaniola attacked and killed several Spanish colonists. Larger revolts

118 Chapter 4

---

occurred throughout Spanish settlements during the 16th century. In Colombia, for example, enslaved Africans destroyed the town of Santa Marta in 1530.

Occasional uprisings also occurred throughout Brazil, the West Indies, and North America. In 1739, a group of slaves in South Carolina led an uprising known as the Stono Rebellion. They killed several colonists and then engaged the local militia in battle. Many slaves died during the fighting. Those who were captured were executed. Despite the ultimate failure of slave revolts, uprisings continued into the 1800s.

Consequences of the Atlantic Slave Trade

The Atlantic slave trade had a profound impact on both Africa and the Americas. In Africa, numerous cultures lost generations of their fittest members—their young and able—to European traders and plantation owners. In addition, countless African families were torn apart. Many of them were never reunited. The slave trade devastated African societies in another way: by introducing guns into the continent. More effective than spears, guns were in great demand by African rulers seeking to conquer new territory. Firearms, which African chiefs and kings traded for potential slaves, helped spread war and conflict throughout Africa.

While they were unwilling participants in the growth of the colonies, African slaves contributed greatly to the economic and cultural development of the Americas. Their greatest contribution was their labor. Without their back-breaking work, colonies such as those on Haiti and Barbados may not have survived. In addition to their muscle, enslaved Africans also brought their expertise, especially in agriculture. Africans from the Upper Guinea region in West Africa, for example, brought their rice-growing techniques to South Carolina. There, they helped make that colony a profitable rice producer. Africans also brought with them their culture. Aspects of their culture—including art, music, and food—continue to influence American societies.

The influx of so many Africans to the Americas also has left its mark on the very population itself. From the United States to Brazil, many of the nations of the Western Hemisphere today have substantial African-American populations. Furthermore, many Latin American countries—where intermarriage between slaves and colonists was much more common than in North America—have sizable mixed-race populations.

As the next section explains, Africans were not the only cargo transported across the Atlantic during the colonization of the Americas. The settlement of the Americas brought many different items from Europe, Asia, and Africa to North and South America. It also introduced items from the Americas to the rest of the world.

CONNECT to TODAY

Gullah
One legacy of African slaves lives in the quick-paced words of Gullah. Gullah is a combination of English and colonial speech and the languages from several West African societies. Nearly 6,000 African words have been identified in Gullah. The American descendants of slaves still speak Gullah on the Sea Islands of South Carolina and Georgia and on the mainland nearby.

Gullah speakers live in relatively isolated communities. Over the years they have contributed words to the language spoken in the United States. The words include goober (peanut), juke (as in jukebox), and voodoo (witchcraft).

Section 3 Assessment

1. TERMS & NAMES
Identify
• Atlantic slave trade
• triangular trade
• middle passage

2. TAKING NOTES
Using a diagram like the one below, list the ways in which the Atlantic slave trade affected both Africa and the Americas.

Consequences of the Slave Trade

In Africa	In the Americas
1.	1.
2.	2.
3.	3.

3. CONTRASTING
How was slavery in the Americas different from slavery in Africa and Muslim lands?

THINK ABOUT
• the length of bondage
• the children of slaves
• opportunities for slaves within each society
• racial basis

4. THEME ACTIVITY
Cultural Interaction
Reread the excerpt from King Affonso's letter on page 116. Imagine you are an African ruler. Write your own letter to a European leader in which you try to convince him or her to stop participating in the slave trade. Include in your letter the various aspects of slavery and the slave trade you learned about in this section.

The Atlantic World **119**

ANSWERS

1. TERMS & NAMES
Atlantic slave trade, p. 116
triangular trade, p. 117
middle passage, p. 117

2. TAKING NOTES
Possible Responses: Impact on Africa—loss of significant population; increase in civil war and strife through the introduction of guns; families torn apart; cultures lost. Impact on the Americas—significant labor supply; expertise in farming techniques; introduction of African culture; mixed races.

3. CONTRASTING
Possible Responses: In most African societies, slaves could escape their bondage, while in the Americas, most slaves worked for life; unlike in most African societies, slavery in the Americas was hereditary; unlike in most African and Muslim societies, slaves in the Americas lacked legal rights and social mobility.

4. ANALYZING THEMES
Standards for Evaluation
A persuasive letter should . . .
• present a thoughtful, logical argument supported by facts.
• show an understanding of the injustices of the slave trade.
• be well written and engaging.

To explain the Columbian Exchange.

② To identify aspects of the Commercial Revolution.

CRITICAL THINKING

- Making inferences, pp. 120, 122, 123
- Forming opinions, p. 121
- Summarizing, p. 123
- Analyzing themes, p. 123

FOCUS
5-Minute Warm-Up

▶ **Interpreting Maps**
Have students answer these questions to help them understand the Columbian Exchange.

1. Look at the map on page 121. What animal traveled from the Americas to Europe?

2. What insect was taken to the Americas?

 WARM-UP TRANSPARENCY 4

OBJECTIVE ① INSTRUCT

The Columbian Exchange

▶ **Key Idea**
- Colonization of the Americas sets up a global exchange.

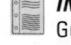 **IN-DEPTH RESOURCES: UNIT 1**
Guided Reading, p. 71

 ACCESS FOR STUDENTS ACQUIRING ENGLISH
Guided Reading (Spanish), p. 53

OBJECTIVE ② INSTRUCT

A Commercial Revolution

▶ **Key Ideas**
- Colonial trade promotes an economic revolution in Europe.
- Joint-stock companies invest in overseas colonies.
- Mercantilism demands a favorable balance of trade.
- The Commercial Revolution promotes city growth and gives rise to a middle class.

---

4 # The Columbian Exchange and Global Trade

TERMS & NAMES
- Columbian Exchange
- Commercial Revolution
- capitalism
- joint-stock company
- mercantilism
- favorable balance of trade

MAIN IDEA	WHY IT MATTERS NOW
The colonization of the Americas introduced new and different items into the Eastern and Western hemispheres.	This global exchange of goods permanently changed Europe, Asia, Africa, and the Americas.

SETTING THE STAGE The colonization of the Americas dramatically changed the world. It prompted both voluntary and forced migration of millions of people. It also led to the establishment of new and powerful societies. European settlement of the Americas also changed the world in less noticeable but equally important ways. It led to the exchange of new items that greatly affected the lives of people throughout the world.

The Columbian Exchange

The global transfer of foods, plants, and animals during the colonization of the Americas was known as the **Columbian Exchange**. Ships from the Americas brought back a wide array of items that Europeans, Asians, and Africans had never before seen. They included such plants as tomatoes, squash, pineapples, tobacco, and cacao beans (for chocolate).

Perhaps the most important items to travel from the Americas to the rest of the world were corn and potatoes. Corn and potatoes were inexpensive to grow and highly nutritious. Over time, both crops became an important and steady part of diets throughout the world. These foods helped people live healthier and longer lives. Thus they played a significant role in boosting the world's population. The planting of the first white potato in Ireland and the first sweet potato in China probably changed more lives than the deeds of 100 kings.

Traffic across the Atlantic did not flow in just one direction, however. Europeans introduced various livestock animals into the Americas. These included horses, cattle, and pigs. Foods from Africa (including some that originated in Asia) migrated west in European ships. They included bananas, black-eyed peas, and yams.

Some aspects of the Columbian Exchange had a tragic impact on many Native Americans. Disease was just as much a part of the Columbian Exchange as goods and food. The diseases Europeans brought with them, which included smallpox and measles, led to the death of millions of Native Americans.

In this Spanish illustration, a medicine man tends to an Aztec with smallpox.

A Commercial Revolution

The establishment of colonial empires in the Americas influenced the nations of Europe in still other ways. New wealth from the Americas was coupled with a dramatic growth in overseas trade. These together prompted a wave of new business and trade practices in Europe during the 16th and 17th centuries. These practices—many of which served as the root of today's financial dealings—dramatically changed the economic atmosphere of Europe. Together they became known as the **Commercial Revolution.**

THINK THROUGH HISTORY
A. Making Inferences
Why is the Columbian Exchange considered a significant event?
A. Possible Answer It greatly improved diets and lifestyles in Europe and Asia and helped prompt an increase in the world's population; it also led to the death of millions of Native Americans by way of disease.

SECTION 4 RESOURCES

PRINT RESOURCES

 IN-DEPTH RESOURCES: UNIT 1
Guided Reading, p. 71
Geography Application: The Potato Impacts the World, p. 73
Connections Across Time and Cultures: Impact of the Columbian Exchange, p. 84

 ACCESS FOR STUDENTS ACQUIRING ENGLISH
Guided Reading (Spanish), p. 53
Geography Application (Spanish), p. 55

 FORMAL ASSESSMENT
Section Quiz, p. 54

TECHNOLOGY RESOURCES

 GEOGRAPHY TRANSPARENCIES
GT20 Spain's Colonies Provide Wealth, 1600–1790

 CRITICAL THINKING TRANSPARENCIES
CT56 Visual Summary

CD-ROM
Electronic Library of Primary Sources

VIDEO Patterns of Interaction: The Geography of Food

 INTERNET www.mlworldhistory.com

The Columbian Exchange

Few events transformed the world like the Columbian Exchange. This global transfer of plants, animals, disease, and especially food, brought together the Eastern and Western hemispheres and touched, in some way, nearly all the peoples of the world.

Frightening Foods

Several foods from the Americas that we now take for granted at first amazed and terrified Europeans.

Early on, people thought the tomato was harmful to eat. "If I should eat this fruit," explained one Italian man, "it would be injurious and harmful to me." One German official warned that the tomato "should not be taken internally."

In 1619, officials in Burgundy, France, banned the potato, explaining that "too frequent use of them caused the leprosy." In 1774, starving peasants in Prussia refused to eat the spud.

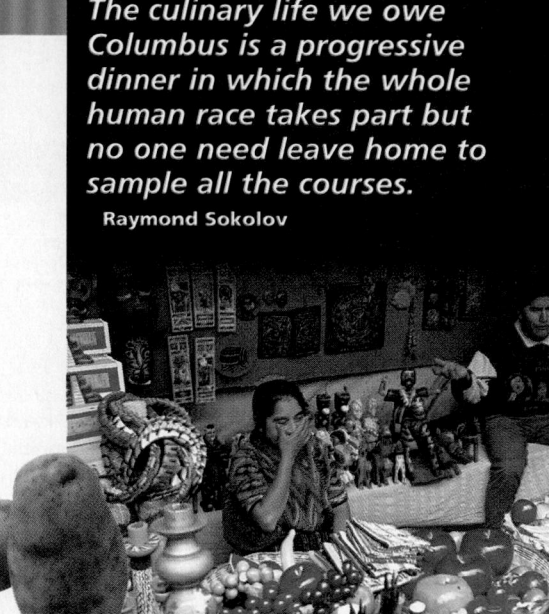

The culinary life we owe Columbus is a progressive dinner in which the whole human race takes part but no one need leave home to sample all the courses.
Raymond Sokolov

The Columbian Exchange

AMERICAS TO EUROPE, AFRICA, AND ASIA

NORTH AMERICA

Cassava — Peanut — Potato — Tomato — Corn

Avocado — Peppers

Sweet Potato

Beans — Vanilla

Cacao Bean

Squash — Pineapple

Turkey

Quinine

Tobacco — Pumpkin

ATLANTIC OCEAN

Citrus Fruits — Grape — Banana — Sugar Cane

EUROPE, AFRICA, AND ASIA TO AMERICAS

Onion

Olive — Turnip — Coffee Bean — Peach, Pear

EUROPE

Disease
• Smallpox
• Influenza
• Typhus
Livestock • Measles
• Cattle • Malaria
• Sheep • Diphtheria
• Pig • Whooping
• Horse   Cough

Honeybee

Grains
• Wheat
• Rice
• Barley
• Oats

AFRICA

Patterns of Interaction

Think about your favorite foods. Chances are that at least one originated in a distant land. Throughout history, the introduction of new foods into a region has dramatically changed lives—for better and worse. Dependence on the potato, for example, led to a famine in Ireland. This prompted a massive migration of Irish people to other countries. In the Americas, the introduction of sugar led to riches for some and enslavement for many others.

VIDEO *The Geography of Food: The Impact of Potatoes and Sugar*

Connect *to* History

Forming Opinions What were the most beneficial and harmful aspects of the Columbian Exchange? Why?

SEE SKILLBUILDER HANDBOOK, PAGE 662

Connect *to* Today

Researching Find out what are the major items exchanged or traded between the United States and either Asia, Africa, or Europe. Report your findings to the class.

The Atlantic World **121**

Connect *to* History

Forming Opinions
Possible Responses:
Beneficial—the introduction of corn and potatoes into Europe, because they improved diets and helped people live longer; harmful—diseases from Europe, because they killed millions of Native Americans.

Connect *to* Today

Researching
Suggest that students use various resources to find the information required about trade between the United States and Asia, Africa, or Europe. For example, students might consult magazines (by means of the *Readers' Guide to Periodical*

Literature), newspapers, current encyclopedias (in book, CD-ROM, and on-line form), almanacs (such as *Information Please*), the *Statistical Abstract of the United States,* as well as the Internet.

Three Worlds Meet, 1492–1700
Interpreting the Time Line

Help students to understand the time line by showing them that it uses three colors, each of which stands for a different group: orange for Europeans, blue for Africans, and purple for Americans. Point out that each event is keyed to a particular color and group.

Extension Activity Ask students to make a list of additional events from the chapter they might add to the time line for each of the three colors (groups).

MORE ABOUT . . .
Spanish Gold

Spain may have been too rich for its own good. Other nations and individuals began to attack Spanish ships and holdings to get some of the gold for themselves and to keep Spain from getting too powerful. In Spain, meanwhile, the lust for gold blinded many people to the need for skilled work, farming, manufacturing, and trade.

 ELECTRONIC LIBRARY OF PRIMARY SOURCES
"Concerning the Dearness of All Things and the Remedy Therefor"

 GEOGRAPHY TRANSPARENCIES
GT20 Spain's Colonies Provide Wealth, 1600–1790

Three Worlds Meet, 1492–1700

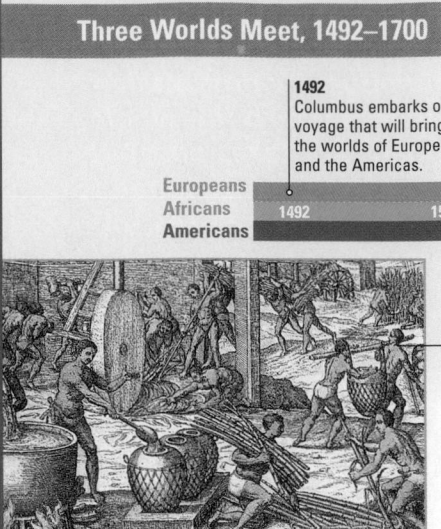

Europeans
Africans
Americans

| 1492 | 1510 | 1530 |

1492
Columbus embarks on a voyage that will bring together the worlds of Europe, Africa, and the Americas.

1521
The Aztec Empire in Mexico is conquered by Hernando Cortés.

1511
Africans begin working as slaves in the Americas.

1533
The Inca Empire in South America falls to Francisco Pizarro.

The Rise of Capitalism One aspect of the European Commercial Revolution was the growth of **capitalism.** Capitalism is an economic system based on private ownership and the investment of wealth for profit. No longer were governments the sole owners of great wealth. Due to overseas colonization and trade, numerous merchants had obtained great wealth. These merchants continued to invest their money in trade and overseas exploration. Profits from these investments enabled merchants and traders to reinvest even more money in other enterprises. As a result, businesses across Europe grew and flourished.

The increase in economic activity in Europe led to an overall increase in many nations' money supply. This in turn brought on inflation, or the steady rise in the price of goods. Inflation occurs when people have more money to spend and thus demand more goods and services. Because the supply of goods is less than the demand requires, the goods become both scarce and more valuable. Prices, then, rise. At this time in Europe, the costs of many goods rose. Spain, for example, endured a crushing bout of inflation during the 1600s, as boatloads of gold and silver from the Americas greatly increased the nation's money supply.

Joint-Stock Companies Another business venture developed during this period was the **joint-stock company.** The joint-stock company worked much like the modern-day corporation. It involved a number of people pooling their wealth for a common purpose.

In Europe during the 1500s and 1600s, that common purpose was American colonization. It took large amounts of money to establish overseas colonies. Moreover, while profits may have been great, so were risks. Many ships, for instance, never completed the long and dangerous ocean voyage. Because joint-stock companies involved numerous investors, the individual members paid only a fraction of the total colonization cost. If the colony failed, investors lost only their small share. If the colony thrived, the investors shared in the profits. It was a joint-stock company that was responsible for establishing Jamestown, England's first North American colony.

The Growth of Mercantilism During this time, the nations of Europe adopted a new economic policy known as **mercantilism.** The theory of mercantilism held that a country's power depended mainly on its wealth. It was wealth, after all, that allowed nations to build strong navies and purchase vital goods. As a result, the goal of every nation became the attainment of as much wealth as possible.

According to the theory of mercantilism, a nation could increase its wealth and power in two ways. First, it could obtain as much gold and silver as possible. Second, it could establish a **favorable balance of trade,** in which it sold more goods than it bought. A nation's ultimate goal under mercantilism was to become self-sufficient, not

Vocabulary
invest: to spend time, money, or effort for future advantage or benefit.

THINK THROUGH HISTORY
B. Making Inferences Why would a joint-stock company be popular with investors in overseas colonies?
B. Possible Answer Because they paid only a fraction of the total colonization cost.

122 Chapter 4

CUSTOMIZING FOR SPECIAL NEEDS

Less Proficient Readers: Vocabulary Activity Pair a less proficient reader with a more proficient reader and ask them to help each other learn the key terms in this section. One strategy they might use to remember a term's meaning is to "interview" the term, playing the part of journalists investigating the who, what, where, when, how, and why of a situation.

An example interview question is, "Who are you?" For *capitalism,* the answer might be, "I am an economic system based on private ownership and the investment of wealth for profit." For the *joint-stock company,* students might ask, "What do you want?" The answer might be, "I want to pool the wealth of a number of different people for a common purpose, such as colonization of the Americas."

Have students apply this strategy to other key terms in the section: *Columbian Exchange; Commercial Revolution; mercantilism;* and *favorable balance of trade.*

1607
Colonists found Jamestown, first permanent English settlement in North America.

1628
Puritans establish the Massachusetts Bay Colony in North America.

1700
The number of enslaved Africans imported to the Americas reaches almost 1.5 million. It will climb to nearly 6 million by the end of the century.

| 1610 | 1630 | 1670 | 1690 |

1650
The number of Africans toiling in Spanish America reaches 300,000.

1675
Native Americans battle colonists in King Philip's War.

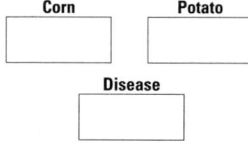

MORE ABOUT . . .
Colonies
Colonies were considered, at least partially, a dumping ground for Europeans who did not fit in at home. British poet John Donne told the Virginia Company, a joint-stock company, in 1622, "[Jamestown] shall redeem many a wretch from the jaws of death, from the hands of the executioner . . . . It shall sweep your streets and wash your doors from idle persons and the children of idle persons, and employ them."

dependent on other countries for goods. An English author of the time wrote about the new economic idea of mercantilism:

A VOICE FROM THE PAST
Although a Kingdom may be enriched by gifts received, or by purchases taken from some other Nations. . . . these are things uncertain and of small consideration when they happen. The ordinary means therefore to increase our wealth and treasure is by Foreign Trade, wherein we must ever observe this rule: to sell more to strangers yearly than we consume of theirs in value.
THOMAS MUN, quoted in *World Civilizations*

 THINK THROUGH HISTORY
C. Summarizing
What role did colonies play in the policy of mercantilism?
C. Possible Answer
They provided gold and silver, as well as raw materials, and were a market for the home country to sell its goods.

Mercantilism went hand in hand with colonization, for colonies played a vital role in this new economic practice. Aside from providing silver and gold, colonies provided raw materials that could not be found in the home country, such as wood or furs. In addition to playing the role of supplier, the colonies under mercantilism also provided a market. The home country could sell its goods to their colonies.

Changes in European Society The economic changes that swept through much of Europe during the age of American colonization also led to changes in European society. The Commercial Revolution spurred the growth of towns and the rise of the merchant class. Merchants—because they controlled great wealth—rose in status.

The changes in European society, however, only went so far. While towns and cities grew in size, much of Europe's population continued to live in rural areas. And although merchants and traders enjoyed a period of social mobility, a majority of Europeans remained poor. More than anything else, the Commercial Revolution increased the wealth of European nations. Also, as Chapter 5 will describe, the new economic practices helped to expand the power of European rulers.

ASSESS & RETEACH

Section 4 Assessment
Have students take turns leading the class. They should ask individual classmates to answer the questions in the Assessment and have other students determine whether the answers are correct.

Section Quiz
FORMAL ASSESSMENT
Section Quiz, p. 54

Reteaching Activity
CLASS TIME: 15 MINUTES

Have students make a two-column chart listing the various items that passed from west to east and from east to west in the Columbian Exchange.

CRITICAL THINKING TRANSPARENCIES
CT41 Visual Summary

CLOSE ACTIVITY

CLASS TIME: 20 MINUTES

Arranging Events in Sequential Order
Assign one student to each event on the time line on pages 122–123. Tell students to arrange themselves in the sequential order of the time line and then have each student summarize the significance of the event he or she represents.

Section 4 Assessment

1. TERMS & NAMES
Identify
• Columbian Exchange
• Commercial Revolution
• capitalism
• joint-stock company
• mercantilism
• favorable balance of trade

2. TAKING NOTES
For each Columbian Exchange item or aspect below, write where it originated and explain its significance.

| Corn | Potato |

| Disease |

Write an explanation of one of the items to someone who has never encountered it.

3. MAKING INFERENCES
Why were colonies considered so important to the nations of Europe?

THINK ABOUT
• the philosophy of mercantilism
• the notion of a favorable balance of trade

4. ANALYZING THEMES
Economics Do you think the economic changes in Europe during the era of American colonization qualify as a revolution? Why or why not?

THINK ABOUT
• the legacy of the new business and trade practices
• how the economic changes affected European society as a whole

The Atlantic World **123**

ANSWERS

1. TERMS & NAMES
Columbian Exchange, p. 120
Commercial Revolution, p. 120
capitalism, p. 122
joint-stock company, p. 122
mercantilism, p. 122
favorable balance of trade, p. 122

2. TAKING NOTES
Corn: the Americas; nutritious basis of many diets
Potato: the Americas; became staple throughout the world
Disease: Europe; killed millions of Native Americans

3. MAKING INFERENCES
Possible Responses: The mercantilistic philosophy of Europe drove nations to acquire colonies to obtain wealth. Colonies provided precious metals, raw materials, and markets for European goods, allowing European nations to establish a favorable balance of trade with their colonies.

4. ANALYZING THEMES
Possible Responses: Yes—many of the new practices, including capitalism and joint-stock companies, served as the root of today's economy. No—Europe's population remained mostly rural, and many Europeans remained poor.

TERMS & NAMES

1. conquistadors, p. 105
2. Montezuma II, p. 105
3. *encomienda*, p. 106
4. Jamestown, p. 111
5. French and Indian War, p. 113
6. Atlantic slave trade, p. 116
7. triangular trade, p. 117
8. Columbian Exchange, p. 120
9. Commercial Revolution, p. 120
10. mercantilism, p. 122

REVIEW QUESTIONS

Answers may vary.

11. To seek an alternative trade route to Asia.

12. To enrich Spain, to colonize the land, and to convert Native Americans to Christianity.

13. Because the Spanish abused the natives and tried to destroy their culture.

14. Sugar and tobacco.

15. The English took control of nearly the entire eastern half of the United States.

16. Slaves were experienced at farming, they had built up some immunity to disease, they were unfamiliar with the land and could not blend in with the white population, so were less likely to escape.

17. Slaves were crammed into the dark bottom of the boat, where they lived among their own waste and suffered from disease, beatings, and poor food.

18. African slaves resisted by preserving their cultural heritage, sabotaging work efforts, running away, and forming armed rebellions.

19. Corn and potatoes were inexpensive and nutritious and thus improved diets throughout Europe and Asia.

20. Mercantilism held that a country's true power was measured by its wealth, which came by obtaining as much gold and silver as possible and by establishing a favorable balance of trade.

TERMS & NAMES

Briefly explain the importance of each of the following in the European colonization of the Americas.

1. conquistadors
2. Montezuma II
3. *encomienda*
4. Jamestown
5. French and Indian War
6. Atlantic slave trade
7. triangular trade
8. Columbian Exchange
9. Commercial Revolution
10. mercantilism

Interact *with* History

On page 102 you examined the choices some Native Americans faced during the invasion by Spanish conquistadors. Now that you have read the chapter, rethink the choice you made. If you chose to side with the Spaniards, would you now change your mind? Why or why not? If you decided to fight with the Aztecs, what are your feelings now? Discuss your opinions with a small group.

REVIEW QUESTIONS

SECTION 1 *(pages 103–109)*
Spanish Conquests in the Americas

11. Why did Columbus set sail on the Atlantic?
12. List three goals of the Spanish in the Americas.
13. Why did Popé lead a rebellion against the Spanish?

SECTION 2 *(pages 110–114)*
Competing Claims in North America

14. What did the Europeans mostly grow in their Caribbean colonies?
15. What was the result of the French and Indian War?

SECTION 3 *(pages 115–119)*
The Atlantic Slave Trade

16. What factors led European colonists to use Africans to resupply their labor force?
17. Describe the conditions on board a slave ship.
18. Name several ways in which enslaved Africans resisted their position in the Americas.

SECTION 4 *(pages 120–123)*
The Columbian Exchange and Global Trade

19. Why was the introduction of corn and potatoes to Europe and Asia so significant?
20. Explain the economic policy of mercantilism.

Visual Summary

The Atlantic World

Europeans
- Beginning around 1500, the Spanish and Portuguese colonize Central and South America and establish prosperous overseas empires.
- Throughout the 1600s and 1700s, the English, French, and Dutch battle for control of North America, with the English emerging victorious.
- Over time, Europeans take control of nearly all of the Americas and create new societies.

GLOBAL INTERACTION

Africans
- Beginning around 1500, millions of Africans are taken from their homeland and forced to labor as slaves for Europeans in the Americas.
- Numerous Africans perish during the brutal ocean voyage to the Americas, known as the middle passage.
- Africans eventually become an important part of the Americas, as they populate the various regions and lend aspects of their culture to American societies.

Native Americans
- Between 1520 and 1533, the once mighty Aztec and Inca empires fall to the invading Spanish.
- Throughout the Americas, the native population is devastated by European conquests and diseases.
- In Central and South America, many Spanish settlers and Native Americans intermarry, creating a large mestizo population that thrives today.

Interact *with* History

Possible Responses: Students who originally chose to side with the Spaniards may now say that the Spaniards were cruel and unjust in their treatment of Native Americans. Others may say their decision to fight for the Aztecs was unwise, because they were defeated by the Spanish.

CRITICAL THINKING

1. THE TOOLS OF CONQUEST

THEME **EMPIRE BUILDING** In conquering much of the Americas, Europeans were aided by several things. What were they? Which do you consider to be the most important? Why?

2. EXPLORERS OF THE WEST

Copy the chart below on your paper. For each explorer named, write which nation sponsored him and the regions he explored.

Explorer	Nation	Regions
Pedro Álvares Cabral		
Ferdinand Magellan		
Francisco Vásquez de Coronado		
Jacques Cartier		
Samuel de Champlain		
Henry Hudson		

3. A HISTORIC VOYAGE

It has been said that Columbus's voyage began a process that changed the world forever. Explain the meaning of this statement. In your explanation, consider all the peoples and places American colonization impacted and what effects it had on them.

4. ANALYZING PRIMARY SOURCES

In 1630, a Puritan minister, John Cotton, delivered a sermon to fellow Puritans as they embarked on their journey to America. In it, Cotton tried to reassure the future colonists that they could legitimately claim a new land.

A VOICE FROM THE PAST
Where there is a vacant place, there is liberty for . . . [Christians] . . . to come and inhabit, though they neither buy it nor ask their leaves. . . . Indeed, no nation is to drive out another without special commission from Heaven . . . unless the natives do unjustly wrong them, and will not recompense the wrongs done in a peaceable fort [way]. And then they may right themselves by lawful war and subdue the country unto themselves.

JOHN COTTON, quoted in *The Annals of America*

- What do you think Native Americans might have said about Cotton's statement that America was a "vacant place"?
- How might the last part of Cotton's statement have helped the Puritans to justify taking land from the Native Americans?
- How is this passage an example of a biased statement?

CHAPTER ACTIVITIES

1. LIVING HISTORY: Unit Portfolio Project

THEME **CULTURAL INTERACTION** Your unit portfolio project focuses on showing how different cultures have interacted in history. (See page 33.) For Chapter 4, you might use one of the following ideas to add to your portfolio:

- Draw a political cartoon that contrasts the Europeans' and Native Americans' view of American colonization.
- Write a newspaper editorial explaining how Africans helped create the societies that grew in the Americas.
- Imagine you are a Native American entering an English colony for the first time. Write a journal entry describing your encounter with the culture.

2. CONNECT TO TODAY: Cooperative Learning

THEME **ECONOMICS** The Columbian Exchange marked the beginning of worldwide trade. The plants, foods, and animals that traveled across hemispheres during the Columbian Exchange are now just some of the many foods and items that are traded around the globe today.

Work with a team to chart the global trade of a chosen food or item.

INTERNET Using the Internet, magazines, or books, track the movement of the item from its country of origin to its various destinations around the world.

- Determine how much of the item the various countries import. Compare the cost of the item in these countries.
- Compare your team's item with those of the other teams to determine which is the most popular.

3. INTERPRETING A TIME LINE

Revisit the time line on pages 32–33. Examine the Chapter 4 time line. Which two events do you think had the most lasting effects on the Americas? Explain why.

FOCUS ON ART

This Aztec drawing depicts natives attacking several Spaniards, who after killing Indian nobles, took refuge in a nearby palace.

- How does the image depict the clash of cultures in the Americas?
- What is the drawing's point of view regarding the Aztec warriors? The Spanish?

Connect to History Of the factors that enabled the Spanish to defeat the Aztecs, which one is visible in this drawing?

UNIT 2

Absolutism to Revolution

1500-1900

Detail of* From Porfirio's Dictatorship to the Revolution, *by David Alfáro Siqueiros

This dramatic section from a mural by Mexican artist David Alfáro Siqueiros shows the power and determination of a people united to fight for a political cause. Mexico, like many countries from the 1700s to 1900s, suffered through a series of revolutions in its transformation from a monarchy to a democracy.

The revolution depicted in this mural was an uprising of peasants, farmers, and military and political leaders in 1910 against President Porfirio Díaz. Although Díaz had tried to improve Mexico's economy, he had ruthlessly suppressed all opposition. Under his rule, foreign investors and a few Mexican elite became wealthy, while the peasants and other workers sank deeper into poverty. The revolt, led by Francisco Madero, ousted Díaz, who went into exile in France.

David Alfáro Siqueiros (1898–1974) used the history of Mexico as inspiration for his vivid murals. After his experiences fighting in the Spanish Civil War in the 1930s, Siqueiros identified with the poor and powerless in his own country. His murals often satirize the lifestyles of the wealthy classes while portraying revolutionaries as strong and fearless. The mural *From Porfirio's Dictatorship to the Revolution* can be seen today in the National Museum of History in Mexico City.

UNIT 2

Absolutism to Revolution

1500–1900

126

This scene is from a mural entitled *From Porfirio's Dictatorship to the Revolution*, by the Mexican artist David Alfaro Siqueiros. During this time, revolution swept the globe as people from Europe to Latin America overthrew old institutions.

127

Previewing the Unit

This unit covers the struggles of people in Europe and the New World to build their own nations and to create new forms of government that more clearly reflect the will of the governed.

From 1500 to 1800 marks the era of absolute monarchs in Europe. Although in some countries monarchs have vast power and wealth, toward the end of the 1500s, the force of constitutional law is already limiting royal power in such nations as England and the Netherlands.

The Enlightenment ushers in a new era of discovery and inquiry. Philosophers believe that human reason can create a more humane and just government, religion, and society. These ideas influence the American Revolution and the resulting creation of a democratic federal government.

Revolution sweeps through France, overthrowing the monarchy. Instead of creating a democracy, however, France embraces Napoleon, who attempts to conquer most of Europe. After his downfall, Europe enjoys a brief period of peace and stability.

The forces of nationalism spur Germany, Italy, and several Latin American nations to forge their own political identities in the 1800s. Although Latin American nations throw off colonial rule, they struggle to build stable governments and to ensure prosperity for their people.

Teaching Strategies

Synthesizing One way to help students synthesize the material in Unit 2 is to present the *Patterns of Interaction* video *Struggling Toward Democracy: Revolutions in Latin America and South Africa* as you begin the unit. In each unit, one 12-minute video focuses on a major theme of one of the unit chapters. In Unit 2, the video focuses on Chapter 8, which also develops the unit theme: Revolution.

Synthesizing Through Video The videos for each unit seek to synthesize the elements of a historical pattern, underscoring those elements that hold true over time—at times, over thousands of years. The Unit 2 video shows how ideas can spark revolutions. The case studies that illustrate the power of ideas are the democratic revolutions in 19th-century Venezuela and 20th-century South Africa. You might also point out the revolutionary thinkers in the Unit Time Line (Montesquieu, Voltaire, Diderot) and recall their impact on the revolutions in Europe and Latin America.

Patterns of Interaction The *Patterns of Interaction Resource Book* provides you with an overview of each video, previewing classroom activities (including vocabulary previews) and post-viewing activities that include text and visual primary sources and map activities.

UNIT 2
Time Line
Absolutism to Revolution

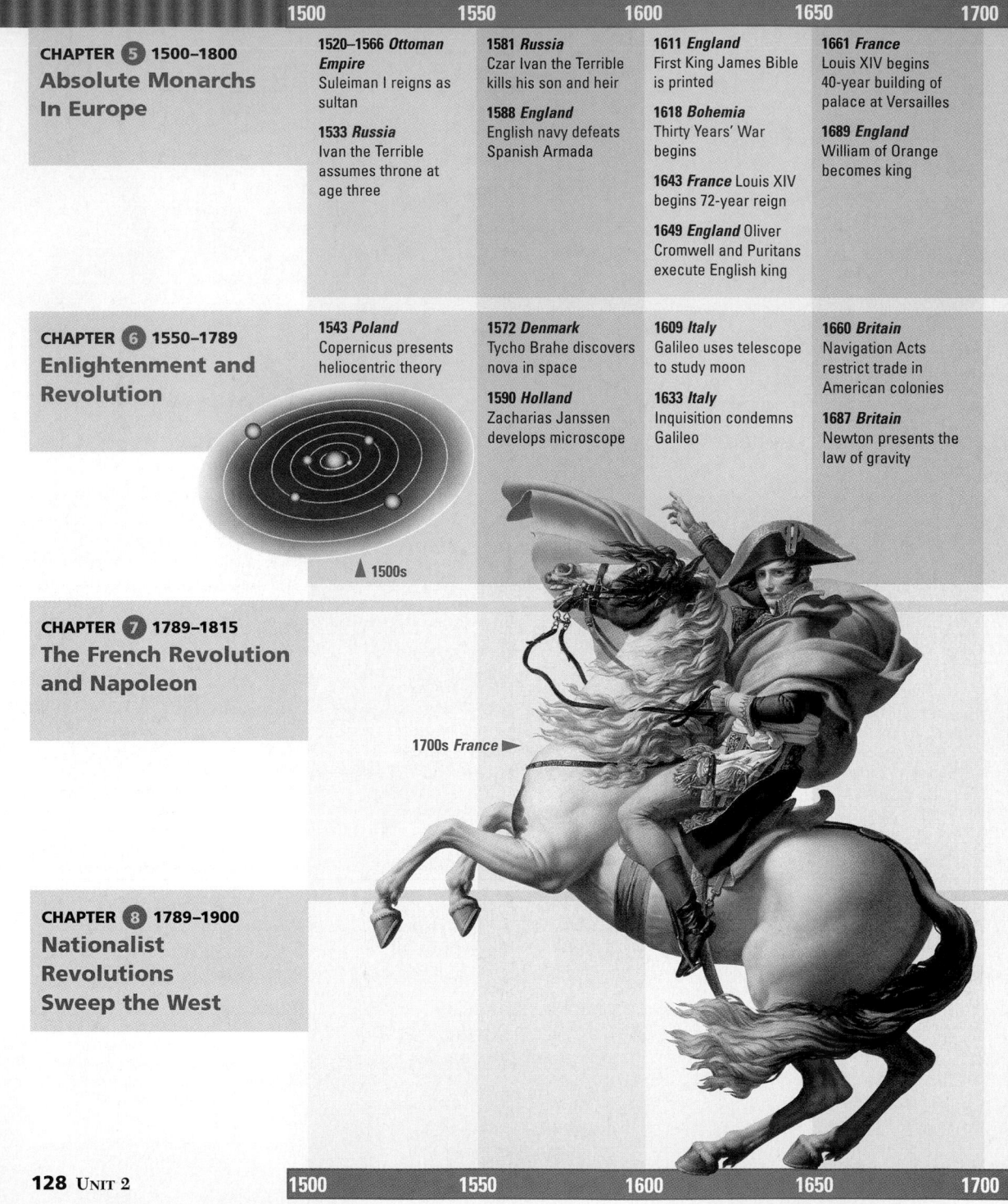

	1500	1550	1600	1650	1700

CHAPTER 5 1500–1800
Absolute Monarchs In Europe

1520–1566 Ottoman Empire Suleiman I reigns as sultan

1533 Russia Ivan the Terrible assumes throne at age three

1581 Russia Czar Ivan the Terrible kills his son and heir

1588 England English navy defeats Spanish Armada

1611 England First King James Bible is printed

1618 Bohemia Thirty Years' War begins

1643 France Louis XIV begins 72-year reign

1649 England Oliver Cromwell and Puritans execute English king

1661 France Louis XIV begins 40-year building of palace at Versailles

1689 England William of Orange becomes king

CHAPTER 6 1550–1789
Enlightenment and Revolution

1543 Poland Copernicus presents heliocentric theory

1590 Holland Zacharias Janssen develops microscope

1572 Denmark Tycho Brahe discovers nova in space

1609 Italy Galileo uses telescope to study moon

1633 Italy Inquisition condemns Galileo

1660 Britain Navigation Acts restrict trade in American colonies

1687 Britain Newton presents the law of gravity

▲ 1500s

CHAPTER 7 1789–1815
The French Revolution and Napoleon

1700s *France* ▶

CHAPTER 8 1789–1900
Nationalist Revolutions Sweep the West

	1500	1550	1600	1650	1700

CONNECTIONS ACROSS THE CURRICULUM

Literature Literature dealing with history offers the advantage of evoking the sights, sounds, thoughts, and personalities associated with historical events. Such literature possesses an immediacy that ordinary historical narrative usually cannot create. You may wish to focus on certain events or

personalities in the Unit Time Line by asking students to read the selections in the *In-Depth Resources* books that accompany the program.

Literary selections for Unit 2 cover the following topics:
• **Chapter 5** The court of Louis XIV
• **Chapter 6** Galileo's trial for heresy

• **Chapter 7** Robespierre's Reign of Terror
• **Chapter 8** Toussaint L'Ouverture and the Haitian revolution.

***See* In-Depth Resources:
Unit 2** Students might read the Unit 2 literary selections outside of class for a later in-class discussion or for written analysis. Since the selections are

relatively short, the class might read the texts aloud in class. (The text for Chapter 6 is taken from the play *The Recantation of Galileo Galilei* by Eric Bentley and might be rehearsed and presented by students to the rest of the class.) A discussion of historical setting and character could then follow.

Timeline

1700	1750	1800	1850	1900

1703 Russia
Peter the Great orders St. Petersburg to be built

1740 Austria
Maria Theresa inherits throne

1756 Prussia
Frederick the Great starts Seven Years' War

◀ 1700s *Prussia*

1740 Britain
Samuel Richardson publishes novel *Pamela*

1748 France
Montesquieu publishes *Spirit of the Laws*

1759 France
Voltaire writes *Candide*

1751 France Diderot begins publishing *Encyclopedia*

1762 Russia
Catherine the Great becomes empress

1776 America Colonies declare independence from Britain

1788 United States
Constitution ratified

1789 France
French Revolution begins

1793 France
King Louis XVI executed by guillotine

1793-1794 France
Robespierre conducts Reign of Terror

1804 France Napoleon becomes emperor

1805-1812 France
Napoleon conquers most countries in Europe

1815 France Napoleon defeated at Waterloo

1815 Austria Congress of Vienna restores old European boundaries

1804 Haiti gains independence from France

1821 Mexico declares independence

1830 Greece wins full independence

1848 Europe Revolutions sweep Europe

1861 Russia
Alexander II frees the serfs

1870 Italy
Italy is unified

1871 Germany Franco-Prussian War ends; Germany is unified

◀ 1800s *Greece*

1700	1750	1800	1850	1900

Living History
Unit 2 Portfolio Project

THEME Revolution

Your portfolio for Unit 2 will compare and contrast the different kinds of revolutions that take place during this time period. While some groups overthrow governments, others overthrow long-held ideas about science, economy, religion, and even art. You can compare and contrast the causes of these revolutions, how they occur, and their results.

Living History Project Choices
Each Chapter Assessment offers you choices of ways to show the revolutionary changes that take place in that chapter. Activities include the following:

Chapter 5 poster, editorial, HistoryMaker

Chapter 6 magazine cover, news report, song lyrics

Chapter 7 interviews, cartoons, dialogue

Chapter 8 newspaper report, speech, how-to book

Portfolio Project

Theme: Revolution The portfolio projects for Unit 2 stress the theme of reform and radical political and social changes that overturned established orders in Europe between 1600 and 1900. The transformations that students will be asked to focus on include:

- the English Civil War and the Glorious Revolution in Great Britain
- Peter the Great's efforts at westernizing Russia
- the American and French Revolutions and
- the revolutions in Europe and Latin America during the 19th century

Students will be asked to show their understanding of underlying social and political causes, the ideals, and the outcomes of these upheavals. And they may choose among oral, written, and spoken formats to do so.

Projects for Interpersonal Learners
Certain students learn best when working in groups, where they can share ideas and insights. These interpersonal learners tend to organize, communicate, and socialize well. To accommodate the learning styles of such students, many of the projects suggested in the units can be turned into group activities.

Of course, certain project suggestions are already intended for groups. For example, in Unit 2, the interview projects in Chapters 7 and 8 will be performed by more than one student.

Nonetheless, you might decide to designate the projects for an entire unit as group projects. Creating posters, song lyrics, newspaper editorials, History Maker biographies, or magazine covers need not be individual tasks.

The Western Civilization Videodisc

SECTION H: The Beginnings of the Nation–State, 1600–1715

Side One: Frame 28153

SECTION I: The Enlightenment, French Revolution, and Napoleon, 1715–1815

Side One: Frame 30803

Universal Play Button

See Master Guide, page 166 for Section H, page 189 for Section I.

Absolute Monarchs in Europe

	Key Ideas	COPY MASTERS	ASSESSMENT

SECTION 1
Spain's Empire and European Absolutism

pp. 133–137

In the 1500s, Philip II of Spain becomes the strongest ruler in Europe, helping establish absolute monarchy. But in time Spain weakens, and the Netherlands breaks away from Spanish rule.

In-Depth Resources: Unit 2
• **Guided Reading,** p. 1

PE *Section 1 Assessment,* p. 137

Formal Assessment
• Section Quiz, p. 63

Alternative Assessment Book
• Standards for Evaluating a Cooperative Activity

SECTION 2
France's Ultimate Monarch

pp. 138–145

Religious wars plague France in the 1500s. With the rise of Louis XIV, France becomes Europe's most powerful nation. Louis's rule extends French power and prestige, but he leads the country into crippling wars.

In-Depth Resources: Unit 2
• **Guided Reading,** p. 2
• **Primary Source:** Louis XIV's Advice to His Son, p. 9
• **Literature:** from *The Cat and the King,* p. 13

PE *Section 2 Assessment,* p. 143

Formal Assessment
• Section Quiz, p. 64

Alternative Assessment Book
• Standards for Evaluating a Cooperative Activity

SECTION 3
Central European Monarchs Clash

pp. 146–150

Central Europe also becomes the scene of devastating wars. The most destructive conflict, the Thirty Years' War, severely weakens the Holy Roman Empire. Afterward, Austria and Prussia struggle for power.

In-Depth Resources: Unit 2
• **Guided Reading,** p. 3
• **Geography Application:** Old Empires and New Powers, p. 7
• **History Makers:** Maria Theresa, p. 16

PE *Section 3 Assessment,* p. 150

Formal Assessment
• Section Quiz, p. 65

Alternative Assessment Book
• Standards for Evaluating a Cooperative Activity

SECTION 4
Russian Czars Increase Power

pp. 151–155

Russian rulers begin to dominate the nobility in the 16th and 17th centuries. Under Peter the Great, Russia opens up to the West and becomes a key European power.

In-Depth Resources: Unit 2
• **Guided Reading,** p. 4
• **Skillbuilder Practice:** Evaluating Decisions, p. 6
• **Primary Source:** Peter the Great's Reforms, p. 10

PE *Section 4 Assessment,* p. 155

Formal Assessment
• Section Quiz, p. 66

Alternative Assessment Book
• Standards for Evaluating a Cooperative Activity

SECTION 5
Parliament Limits the English Monarchy

pp. 156–159

English kings battle Parliament for power in the 1600s, leading to civil war. Parliament wins, and a Puritan government is formed. The monarchy is later restored, but its power is limited by law.

In-Depth Resources: Unit 2
• **Guided Reading,** p. 5
• **Primary Sources:** from *Diary of Samuel Pepys,* p. 11; from the English Bill of Rights, p. 12
• **History Makers:** Wm. of Orange, p. 17
• **Connections Across Time and Cultures,** p. 18

PE *Section 5 Assessment,* p. 159

Formal Assessment
• Section Quiz, p. 67

Alternative Assessment Book
• Standards for Evaluating a Cooperative Activity

CHAPTER RESOURCES

Chapter Overview

From 1500 to 1800, absolute monarchs rule in Europe. In countries such as Spain and France, rulers wield great power and build major monuments to their rule. In countries such as England and the Netherlands, constitutional law limits royal power.

Telescoping the Times
• Chapter Summary, pp. 21–23

Planning for Block Schedules

PE *Chapter Assessment,* pp. 160–161

Chapter Activities, p. 161

Formal Assessment
• Chapter Test, forms A and B, pp. 68–73

 Test Generator

Alternative Assessment Book

1500–1800

TECHNOLOGY

 Warm-Up Transparency 5
 Geography Transparencies
• GT21 Hapsburg Europe, 1560
 World Art and Cultures Transparencies
• AT45 St. George Civic Guard Company
 Electronic Library of Primary Sources
• "Defeat of the Spanish Armada"
 INTERNET RESOURCES
www.mlworldhistory.com

 Warm-Up Transparency 5
 Electronic Library of Primary Sources
• "Two Views of Versailles"
INTERNET RESOURCES
www.mlworldhistory.com

Warm-Up Transparency 5
Critical Thinking Transparencies
• CT74 Compare and Contrast
Electronic Library of Primary Sources
• from *Essay on Forms of Government*
INTERNET RESOURCES
www.mlworldhistory.com

Warm-Up Transparency 5
World Art and Cultures Transparencies
• AT46 Peter I the Great
• AT47 Saint Basil's Cathedral
Critical Thinking Transparencies
• CT21 The Age of Absolute Monarchs
Electronic Library of Primary Sources
• from Letters of Peter the Great

Warm-Up Transparency 5
Critical Thinking Transparencies
• CT57 Visual Summary
Electronic Library of Primary Sources
• "The Restoration of Charles II"
INTERNET RESOURCES
www.mlworldhistory.com

 Chapter Summaries on Audiocassette in English and Spanish
 INTERNET RESOURCES
www.mlworldhistory.com

Block Scheduling (90 MINUTES)

Day 1
Section 1, pp. 133–137
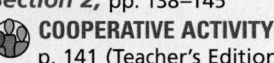 **COOPERATIVE ACTIVITY**
p. 135 (Teacher's Edition)
Section Assessment, p. 137

Day 2
Section 2, pp. 138–145
COOPERATIVE ACTIVITY
p. 141 (Teacher's Edition)

Section 3, pp. 146–150
 COOPERATIVE ACTIVITY
p. 147 (Teacher's Edition)
Section Assessments,
pp. 145, 150

Day 3
Section 4, pp. 151–155
COOPERATIVE ACTIVITY
p. 153 (Teacher's Edition)
Section Assessment, p. 155

Day 4
Section 5, pp. 156–159
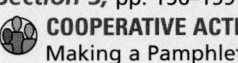 **COOPERATIVE ACTIVITY**
Making a Pamphlet,
p. 157 (Teacher's Edition)
Section Assessment, p. 159
Chapter Assessment,
pp. 160–161

Yearly Pacing *Chapter 5 Total:* 4 days *Yearly Total:* 85 days

 Planning for Block Schedules

Customizing for Special Needs

Students Acquiring English

 Access for Students Acquiring English
• **Guided Reading** for Sections 1–5 (Spanish), pp. 60–64
• **Chapter Summary** (Spanish), pp. 57–59
• **Skillbuilder Practice** Evaluating Decisions (Spanish), p. 65
• **Geography Application** Old Empires and New Powers (Spanish), p. 66
 Chapter Summaries on Audiocassette in English and Spanish
 Spanish Reading Study Guide
• pp. 51–62

Less Proficient Readers

 In-Depth Resources: Unit 2
• **Guided Reading** for Sections 1–5, pp. 1–5
• **Skillbuilder Practice** Evaluating Decisions, p. 6
• **Geography Application** Old Empires and New Powers, p. 7
 Telescoping the Times
• Chapter Summary, pp. 21–23
 Reading Study Guide
• pp. 51–62
 Chapter Summaries on Audiocassette

Gifted and Talented Students

 In-Depth Resources: Unit 2
Primary Sources:
• Louis XIV's Advice to His Son, p. 9
• Peter the Great's Reforms, p. 10
• from *Diary of Samuel Pepys,* p. 11
• from the English Bill of Rights, p. 12
History Makers
• Maria Theresa, p. 16
• William of Orange, p. 17

Connections to Literature READINGS FOR STUDENTS

 In-Depth Resources: Unit 2
Literature: from *The Cat and the King,* p. 13

Enrichment Reading

• **Babel, Isaac**
"The King," *Collected Stories*
New York: Penguin, 1994

Gangsters, helpless police, and regular raids enliven this story of Moldavanka aristocrats at a wedding ceremony in Odessa.

• **Sutcliff, Rosemary**
Bonnie Dundee
New York: Dutton, 1984

In this story a rebellious teenager rejects his family's beliefs in 17th century Scotland and sides with the king's cavalry.

 PE = Pupil's Edition   = Copy Master   = Overhead Transparency = CD-ROM = Software = Audiocassette   = Video = Internet

Absolute Monarchs in Europe, 1500–1800

Predicting and Making Inferences

• How do students think government in England might change after Cromwell's rule?

• Have students look at the pictures and captions and consider what they reveal about European life at the time.

Interpreting Maps

• Ask students to look at the map and identify the major European powers of the time. (Point out that this chapter covers events in Europe over a period of several centuries.)

• Which major powers occupy land in the Holy Roman Empire?

• Which countries do Bourbon rulers control?

Geography Connection

Have students compare this map with the map of modern Europe on page 636 in the Atlas.

• Which countries now occupy the lands once controlled by the Hapsburgs?

• What challenges might governing an ethnically diverse population pose for a ruler?

CHAPTER 5

Absolute Monarchs in Europe, 1500–1800

PREVIEWING THEMES

Power and Authority
Because of the Reformation and the Age of Exploration, Europe experienced religious, economic, and political turmoil. To deal with these crises, European rulers increased their power. They claimed God gave them the authority to do so.

Revolution
When the Spanish king tried to wipe out Protestantism, the Spanish Netherlands revolted. When English kings tried to increase their power at the expense of Parliament, they lost their thrones. England had two revolutions—one bloody and one bloodless.

Economics
When Spain imported tons of silver from the Americas, it experienced severe inflation. Spain spent much money to buy goods from the Spanish Netherlands, which had a thriving commercial empire. France used the practice of mercantilism to improve its economy.

INTERNET CONNECTION

Visit us at **www.mlworldhistory.com** to learn more about European monarchs.

EUROPE, 1650

Oliver Cromwell overthrew the English king in **1649** and set up a republican government. However, he eventually seized as much power as any monarch. He waged war, doubled the late king's budget, and regulated the economy. He also banned newspapers, hired spies to keep track of his enemies, and executed his opponents.

SCOTLAND
IRELAND
North Sea
ENGLAND
London
UNITED NETHERLANDS
Amsterdam
Utrecht
Paris
Nantes
FRANCE
SWITZERLAND
SAVOY
MILA
GENO
TUSCAN
Bay of Biscay
PORTUGAL
Lisbon
Madrid
SPAIN
CORSIC
Genoa
MINORCA
Gr. Br.
SARDINI
Austria
Gibraltar
Mediterranean Sea

☐ French Bourbon lands
☐ Spanish Bourbon lands
☐ Austrian Hapsburg lands
☐ Prussian lands
☐ British Stuart lands
☐ Russian lands
— Boundary of Holy Roman Empire

0   100 Miles
0   200 Kilometers

130

GEOGRAPHY THEMES

Region

Tell students that the idea of region is important to the events covered in this chapter. Ask them what major powers occupy the region of Europe. *France, England, Austria, Spain, the Holy Roman Empire, and Prussia.* Why might this region become a center of conflict between powers with territorial ambitions? *Because no single power dominates it.* Why might Peter the Great's desire to establish a major seaport at St. Petersburg cause Sweden concern? *Possible response: Because it might help Russia compete with Sweden for economic and military dominance of the Baltic region.*

Location

Ask students to locate Russia on this map. Point out that this country is not part of western Europe and that it is separated from Europe by a great distance. Discuss with students the possible benefits and drawbacks of Russia's location in relation to western Europe.

How might Russia's location affect its development? *Possible responses: Benefits—Russia might be less likely to go to war with or be invaded by western European countries. Drawbacks—Russia might be less able to exchange goods and ideas with western European countries. Distance could slow Russia's development.*

ADDITIONAL RESOURCES

Books for the Teacher

• Duffy, James P. *Czars: Russia's Rulers for More Than One Thousand Years.* New York: Facts on File, 1995.

• Wolf, John B. *Louis XIV.* New York: Norton, 1968.

Books for the Student

• Miller, John. *Bourbon and Stuart: Kings and Kingship in France and England in the Seventeenth Century.* New York: Watts, 1987.

• Swisher, Clarice. *The Glorious Revolution.* San Diego: Lucent, 1995. English Parliament gains supremacy over the monarchy.

• Taylor, Laurence. *The Seventeenth Century.* Morristown: Silver Burdett, 1984. Daily life in Europe through illustrations.

Videos

• *Europe: State and Power—1453–1700.* Social Studies School Service, 1985. 800-421-4246.

• *The Rise of National Monarchies: 15th to 16th Centuries.* Cambridge Social Studies, 1991. 800-468-4227.

• *The Spanish Armada.* Ambrose Video, 1997. 800-526-4663.

 ### Software

• *The Baroque.* CD-ROM. Society for Visual Education, 1994. 800-829-1900.

• *Thirty Years' War.* Educational Software Institute, 1995. 800-955-5570.

In **1703**, **Peter the Great** ordered the city of **St. Petersburg** to be built upon a swamp. Instead of sinking into the mud, St. Petersburg quickly grew into one of the most beautiful cities in Europe. The palace below was built by a later Russian monarch, Catherine the Great.

The Spanish painter **Diego Velázquez** painted this portrait of his enslaved servant, Juan de Pareja, in **1650**. Velázquez taught Pareja to be a painter and granted him his freedom, also in **1650**. The painting is notable for the human dignity it gives to its subject.

131

HISTORY THROUGH ART

Juan de Pareja

Diego Velázquez

When *Juan de Pareja* was displayed beside works of other great artists of Velázquez's day, it struck the artists that "everything else seemed like painting but this alone like truth."

In contrast to the smooth, unified finish that typified paintings of the period, the surface of Velázquez's portrait shows variations that produce convincing optical effects. In depicting Pareja's costume, for example, Velázquez played warm tones off cool tones by varying the thickness of the gray paint applied over the medium-light-brown ground. To suggest that the bodice and cloak consist of a coarser material than the sleeve, he applied brushstrokes more close-ly together and gently rubbed the surface, thereby reflecting more light. The result of such techniques is to heighten the sense of Pareja's presence.

Interpreting the Art Compare this portrait with Hyacinthe Rigaud's portrait of Louis XIV on page 144. How might Velázquez have depicted the king differently?

Interact *with* History

This Interact with History feature motivates students by inviting them to put themselves in a key historical situation—an absolute monarch's demonstration of power. As students imagine themselves designing their own palace, they will analyze the issues, explore their options, and become decision-makers.

Purpose

- to set the stage for studying the era of absolute monarchy in Europe
- to help students understand how monarchs in Europe held and exercised power during this era
- to help students make connection with people and events they will study in this chapter

Teaching Strategy

Thinking Critically After students have imagined themselves in the situation described on this page, have them answer the key questions and give reasons for their decision.

EXAMINING *the* ISSUES

Here are suggestions for addressing each bulleted question.

1 In considering this question, student monarchs should weigh the threat to their rule against the need to convince others of their power. Which concern takes priority?

2 Ask students to think about what qualities in a ruler might impress people and ensure their loyalty and support.

3 Have students recall buildings or other structures that impressed them, and ask them to consider the reasons for their reaction.

Making Connections Have students consider ways that rulers in other periods they have studied used palaces and other large-scale building projects to project a sense of their power.

Interact *with* History

You are the monarch of a European nation. After a long struggle—during which your life was in danger—you have come into power. Now that you have the throne, you want to make sure that no one ever threatens you again. In addition, you want everyone to believe that you are the greatest ruler in all of Europe. You decide to build a palace that will impress both your subjects and visitors to your kingdom.

How will you design your palace?

The workers in this painting are building a 2,000-room palace for Louis XIV of France. The royal court will live there.

Instead of defensive walls and moats, elegant gardens and lawns will surround the palace. This is to impress visitors, especially rival monarchs and statesmen.

In the foreground, workers move champagne-colored stones for the palace walls. The king chose these stones for their beauty.

The Building of Versailles, Adam François van der Meulen, 1632-1690, The Royal Collection © Her Majesty Queen Elizabeth II

EXAMINING *the* ISSUES

- What will be your palace's main function: as a fortress, the seat of government, housing for the court, or a place to entertain visitors?

- What qualities do you want people to associate with your rule: military strength, wealth, political power, cultural brilliance?

- How can a palace demonstrate the qualities that you have decided are important? What features should the palace have?

As a class, discuss these questions. You may want to refer back to other royal building projects that you have studied. Some examples are the hanging gardens in Babylon, the castles in feudal Europe, and Great Zimbabwe in Africa.

As you read about absolute monarchs in Europe, notice their building projects. Especially note the projects of Philip II of Spain, Louis XIV of France, and Peter the Great of Russia.

Follow Up

A feature on the chapter assessment will ask students to reevaluate their responses to the situation presented on this page.

1 Spain's Empire and European Absolutism

TERMS & NAMES
- Philip II
- absolute monarch
- divine right

MAIN IDEA

During a time of religious and economic instability, Philip II ruled Spain with a strong hand.

WHY IT MATTERS NOW

When faced with crises, many heads of government take on additional economic or political powers.

SETTING THE STAGE From 1520 to 1566, Suleiman I exercised great power as sultan of the Ottoman Empire. A European monarch of the same period—Charles V—came close to matching Suleiman's power. As the Hapsburg king, Charles inherited Spain, Spain's American colonies, parts of Italy, and lands in Austria and the Netherlands. As the elected Holy Roman emperor, he ruled much of Germany. It was the first time since Charlemagne that a European ruler controlled so much territory.

Spain's Powerful Empire

A devout Catholic, Charles not only fought Muslims but also opposed Lutherans. In 1555, he unwillingly agreed to the Peace of Augsburg. It allowed German princes to choose the religion for their territory. The following year, Charles V divided his immense empire and retired to a monastery. To his brother Ferdinand, he left Austria and the Holy Roman Empire. His son, **Philip II,** inherited Spain, the Spanish Netherlands, and the American colonies.

Philip II's Empire Philip was shy, serious, and—like his father— deeply religious. However, he could be aggressive for the sake of his empire. In 1580, the king of Portugal died without an heir. Because Philip was the king's nephew, he seized the Portuguese kingdom. Counting Portuguese strongholds in Africa, India, and the East Indies, he now had an empire that circled the globe.

Philip's empire provided him with incredible wealth. By 1600, American mines had supplied Spain with an estimated 339,000 pounds of gold. Between 1550 and 1650, roughly 16,000 tons of silver bullion were unloaded from Spanish galleons. The king of Spain claimed between a fourth and a fifth of every shipload of treasure as his royal share. With this wealth, Spain was able to support a large standing army of 50,000 soldiers.

Vocabulary
bullion: gold or silver in the form of solid bars.

Defender of Catholicism When Philip took power, Europe was experiencing religious wars, caused by the Reformation. However, religious conflict was not new to Spain. The Reconquista—the campaign to drive Muslims from Spain—had been completed only 64 years before. In addition, Philip's great-grandparents Isabella and Ferdinand had used the Inquisition to investigate suspected heretics.

Philip saw himself as part of this tradition. He believed it was his duty to defend Catholicism against the Muslims of the Ottoman Empire and the Protestants of Europe. In 1571 the pope called on all Catholic princes to take up arms against the mounting power of the Ottoman Empire. Philip responded like a true crusader. Two hundred and fifty Spanish and Venetian ships defeated a large Ottoman fleet in

HISTORY MAKERS

Philip II of Spain
1527–1598

The most powerful ruler in Europe, Philip was also the hardest working. He demanded reports, reports, and more reports from his advisers. Then, in his tiny office, he would agonize over decisions. Often he could not bring himself to choose one policy over another. Then the government of Spain would grind to a halt.

Yet Philip would not allow anyone to help him. When his father was still emperor, he told Philip not to trust his advisers completely. Perhaps Philip followed his father's advice too closely. Deeply suspicious, he trusted no one for long. As his own court historian wrote, "His smile and his dagger were very close."

Absolute Monarchs in Europe **133**

Section 1 Overview
OBJECTIVES

(1) To describe Spanish power under Philip II.

(2) To explain weaknesses in the Spanish Empire.

(3) To describe the birth of the Netherlands.

(4) To explain the origins of absolute monarchy.

CRITICAL THINKING
- Making inferences, p. 134
- Identifying problems, p. 135
- Drawing conclusions, p. 137

FOCUS
5-Minute Warm-Up

▶ *Perceiving Causes*
To help students understand absolute rule, have them answer these questions.

1. Read History Makers on page 133. Name two qualities of Philip II that hindered him from ruling effectively.

2. Why might the government have stopped functioning when Philip could not make a decision?

📖 *WARM-UP TRANSPARENCY 5*

OBJECTIVE (1) INSTRUCT

Spain's Powerful Empire

▶ *Key Ideas*
- In 1556 Philip II becomes king of Spain, the wealthiest, most powerful nation in Europe.
- Philip defends Roman Catholicism against Protantism and Islam.
- Spanish riches help stimulate a golden age in the arts.

📑 *IN-DEPTH RESOURCES: UNIT 2*
Guided Reading, p. 1

📑 *ACCESS FOR STUDENTS ACQUIRING ENGLISH*
Guided Reading (Spanish), p. 60

📖 *GEOGRAPHY TRANSPARENCIES*
GT21 Hapsburg Europe, 1560

SECTION 1 RESOURCES

PRINT RESOURCES

📑 *IN-DEPTH RESOURCES: UNIT 2*
Guided Reading, p. 1

📑 *ACCESS FOR STUDENTS ACQUIRING ENGLISH*
Guided Reading (Spanish), p. 60

📑 *FORMAL ASSESSMENT*
Section Quiz, p. 65

📑 *ALTERNATIVE ASSESSMENT BOOK*

TECHNOLOGY RESOURCES

📖 *GEOGRAPHY TRANSPARENCIES*
GT21 Hapsburg Europe, 1560

📖 *WORLD ART AND CULTURES TRANSPARENCIES*
AT45 Banquet of the Officers of St. George Civic Guard Company

💿 **CD-ROM**
Electronic Library of Primary Sources

🌐 **INTERNET** www.mlworldhistory.com

Philip II was a man of simple tastes who enjoyed outdoor activities and rural life. Reportedly, he and his wife, Queen Anne, even enjoyed sheep shearing as a form of entertainment. Have students consider why a man of Philip's power and influence might enjoy simple pleasures. For more on Philip, students might visit **www.mlworldhistory.com** or consult *Philip of Spain* by Henry Kamen.

SPOTLIGHT ON
The Defeat of the Spanish Armada

English artillery made the difference in the sea battle with Spain. More efficient guns and better gunners allowed England to fire ten rounds to every one fired by Spain. England also sent unmanned ships packed with explosives into the Spanish fleet. Such tactics were unconventional at the time. Ask students why England might have used them.

 ELECTRONIC LIBRARY OF PRIMARY SOURCES
"Defeat of the Spanish Armada"

OBJECTIVE ② INSTRUCT

Problems Weaken the Spanish Empire

Key Ideas
- Inflation and an unequal tax structure unbalance the Spanish economy.
- Spain spends much of its money overseas, further harming the economy.
- The Dutch revolt and break away from Spain to form a new nation.

SPOTLIGHT ON

The Defeat of the Spanish Armada

The Spanish Navy reigned supreme on the Atlantic until 1588. That year, the Spanish Armada—the naval fleet assembled to invade England—went down to defeat.

After a series of raids on his treasure ships, King Philip II of Spain dispatched about 130 ships. They carried 19,000 soldiers to the English Channel in the summer of 1588. England, however, was ready. English warships outmaneuvered the Spanish vessels and bombarded the Armada with their heavier long-range cannons. (See picture above.) Stormy weather further damaged the Armada.

The defeat of the Armada was a significant event. It dealt a crippling blow to Spain's dominance on the high seas. It also opened the way for the rest of Europe to venture into the Americas.

---

a fierce battle near Lepanto. In 1588, Philip launched the Spanish Armada in an attempt to punish Protestant England. However, his fleet was defeated.

Although this setback weakened Spain seriously, its wealth gave it the appearance of strength for a while longer. Philip's gray granite palace, the Escorial, had massive walls and huge gates that demonstrated his power. The Escorial also reflected Philip's faith. Within its walls stood a monastery as well as a palace.

Golden Age of Spanish Art Spain's great wealth did more than support navies and build palaces. It also allowed monarchs and nobles to become patrons of artists. During the 16th and 17th centuries, Spain experienced a golden age in the arts. The works of two great painters show both the faith and the pride of Spain during this period.

Born in Crete, El Greco (GREHK-oh) spent much of his adult life in Spain. His real name was Domenikos Theotokopoulos, but Spaniards called him El Greco, meaning "the Greek." El Greco's art often puzzled the people of his time. He chose brilliant, sometimes clashing colors, distorted the human figure, and expressed emotion symbolically in his paintings. Although unusual, El Greco's techniques showed the deep Catholic faith of Spain. He painted saints and martyrs as huge, long-limbed figures that have a supernatural air.

The paintings of Diego Velázquez (vuh·LAHS·kehs), on the other hand, showed the pride of Spain's monarchy. Velázquez, who painted 50 years after El Greco, was the court painter to Philip IV of Spain. He is best known for his portraits of the royal family and scenes of court life. Like El Greco, he was noted for using rich colors. (See his painting of Juan de Pareja on page 131.)

Don Quixote The publication of *Don Quixote de la Mancha* in 1605 is often called the birth of the modern European novel. In this book, Miguel de Cervantes (suhr·VAN·teez) wrote about a poor Spanish nobleman. This nobleman went a little crazy after reading too many books about heroic knights. Hoping to "right every manner of wrong," Don Quixote rode forth in a rusty suit of armor, mounted on a feeble nag. At one point he mistook some windmills for giants:

> **A VOICE FROM THE PAST**
> He rushed with [his horse's] utmost speed upon the first windmill he could come at, and, running his lance into the sail, the wind whirled about with such swiftness, that the rapidity of such motion presently broke the lance into shivers, and hurled away both knight and horse along with it, till down he fell, rolling a good way off into the field.
>
> **MIGUEL DE CERVANTES**, *Don Quixote de la Mancha*

Some critics believe that Cervantes was mocking chivalry, the knightly code of the Middle Ages. Others maintain that the book is about an idealistic person who longs for the romantic past because he is frustrated with his materialistic world.

Problems Weaken the Spanish Empire

Certainly, the age in which Cervantes wrote was a materialistic one. The gold and silver coming from the Americas made Spain temporarily wealthy. However, such treasure helped to cause long-term economic problems.

THINK THROUGH HISTORY
A. Making Inferences What did Philip want his palace to demonstrate about his monarchy?
A. Possible Answer That he was a strong and religious king.

A Voice from the Past By Cervantes's time the art of writing dialogue had been perfected. Cervantes, who had failed as a playwright, succeeded in giving the dialogue in *Don Quixote* the tones and rhythms of real speech. Especially vivid are the conversations between Sancho (Don Quixote's squire) and his wife. (Refer, for example, to Volume 1, Chapter 52 and Volume 2, Chapter 5.) Students might enjoy giving dramatic readings of such passages.

Unlike dialogue, landscapes described in literature before the 1800s tend to be artificial and trite. The Spain of *Don Quixote* (see Volume 1, Chapter 25 and Volume 2, Chapter 14) teems with "gay-colored birds" greeting the dawn, "liquid pearls," laughing springs, murmuring brooks, and luxuriant green meadows. "My goodness," exclaimed the 20th-century writer Vladimir Nabokov, "to think of the wild, bitter, sun-stunned, frozen, parched, tawny, brown pinedark

mountains of Spain and then to read of those dew pearls and birdies! It is as if [a visitor to] the sagebrush plateaus of our own West, or the mountains . . . with their aspens and pines and granite and gulches and bogs and glaciers and grim peaks . . . would describe all this in terms of a New England rock garden, with imported shrubs trimmed like poodles and a rubber hose painted a mimetic green."

Inflation and Taxes One of these problems was severe inflation, which had two causes. First, Spain's population had been growing. As more people demanded food and other goods, merchants were able to raise prices. Second, as silver bullion flooded the market, its value dropped. It took increased amounts of silver to buy things.

Spain's economic decline also had other causes. When Spain expelled the Jews and Moors (Muslims) around 1500, it lost many valuable artisans and businesspeople. In addition, Spain's nobles did not have to pay taxes. The tax burden fell on the lower classes. That burden prevented them from accumulating enough wealth to start their own businesses. Therefore, Spain never developed a middle class.

Making Spain's Enemies Rich Guilds that had emerged in the Middle Ages still dominated business in Spain. Such guilds used old-fashioned methods. This made Spanish cloth and manufactured goods more expensive than those made elsewhere. As a result, Spaniards bought much of what they needed from France, England, and the Netherlands. Spain's great wealth flowed into the pockets of foreigners, who were mostly Spain's enemies.

To finance their wars, Spanish kings borrowed money from German and Italian bankers. When shiploads of silver came in, the money was sent abroad to repay debts. The economy was so feeble that Philip had to declare the Spanish state bankrupt three times.

The Dutch Revolt In the Spanish Netherlands, Philip had to maintain an army to keep his subjects under control. The Dutch had little in common with their Spanish rulers. While Spain was Catholic, the Netherlands had many Calvinist congregations. Also, Spain had a sluggish economy, while the Dutch were involved in trade and had a prosperous middle class.

Philip raised taxes in the Netherlands and took steps to crush Protestantism. In response, in 1566, angry Protestant mobs swept through Catholic churches. They destroyed religious paintings and statues. Philip then sent an army under the Spanish duke of Alva to punish them. On a single day in 1568, the duke executed 1,500 Protestants and suspected rebels.

In the struggle against the Spanish, William of Orange emerged as a great leader. William's motives for fighting the Spaniards were political, not religious. He wanted to free the Netherlands from Spain. At first, William lost battle after battle. Then, in 1574, when the Spaniards had the city of Leiden under seige, the Dutch took a desperate step. Their lands were called the Low Countries, because much of the land was actually below sea level. Only great dikes kept the seawater from flooding over the fields. The Dutch opened the floodgates, flooding the land with water. The floods drove the Spanish troops from their camp outside Leiden.

Finally, in 1579, the seven northern provinces of the Netherlands, which were largely Protestant, united and declared their independence from Spain. They became the United Provinces of the Netherlands. The ten southern provinces (present-day Belgium) were Catholic and remained under Spanish control.

The Independent Dutch Prosper

The United Provinces of the Netherlands was different from other European states of the time. For one thing, religious toleration was practiced there. In addition, the United Provinces was not a kingdom but a republic. Each province had an elected governor, whose power depended on the support of merchants and landholders.

Global**Impact**

Tulip Mania

Tulips came to Europe from Turkey around 1550. People went wild over the flowers' delicate beauty and exotic colors and began to buy rare varieties.

The supply of tulips could not meet the demand, and prices began to rise. One man even traded his mansion for three bulbs! Soon people were spending all their savings on bulbs and taking out loans to buy more.

Tulip mania reached a peak between 1633 and 1637. Then people began to doubt whether prices could continue to rise. In fact, tulip prices sank rapidly. Many Dutch families lost property and were left with bulbs that were nearly worthless.

Even so, tulips remained popular in the Netherlands—which is one of the world's biggest exporters of tulip bulbs today.

Jan Vermeer

Vermeer's work was barely recognized during his life, and he struggled with financial difficulties. A number of his paintings were given to local bakers and grocers in exchange for food. Some of the food, such as loaves of bread and jugs of milk, made its way into his paintings.

OBJECTIVE 4 INSTRUCT

Absolutism in Europe

▶ *Key Ideas*
• Absolute monarchs try to ensure that all power stays in their hands.
• They believe that God gives them the right to rule.
• Both the centralization of state authority and crises in Europe fuel the growth of absolute rule.

CRITICAL THINKING ACTIVITY

CLASS TIME: 10 MINUTES

Synthesizing

On the chalkboard write the heading *Reasons for Absolutism* and circle it. Then invite students to help you make a cluster diagram showing major reasons for the rise of absolute monarchs. The diagram might look like this:

This painting by Rembrandt is called *The Syndics*. A syndic was a city official. Such art shows that city leaders and the middle class played a major role in Dutch society.

Dutch Trading Empire The stability of the government allowed the Dutch people to concentrate on economic growth. The merchants of Amsterdam bought surplus grain in Poland and crammed it into their warehouses. When they heard about poor harvests in southern Europe, they shipped the grain south while prices were highest. Western Europe was also short of timber, a fact that Dutch merchants were quick to use for their benefit. They shipped Scandinavian lumber to Spain, France, Italy, and England, all in ships owned by Dutch capitalists. The Dutch had the largest fleet of ships in the world—perhaps 4,800 ships in 1636. Gradually, the Dutch replaced the Italians as the bankers of Europe. One reason for this is that the trade routes of the Atlantic became more important than those of the Mediterranean.

Dutch Art During the 1600s, the Netherlands became what Florence had been during the 1400s. It boasted not only the best banks but also many of the best artists in Europe. As in Florence, wealthy merchants sponsored many of these artists.

The greatest Dutch artist of the period was Rembrandt van Rijn (REHM·BRANT vahn RYN). Rembrandt painted portraits of wealthy middle-class merchants. He also produced group portraits. In *The Syndics* (shown above), he portrayed a group of city officials. Rembrandt showed the individuality of each man by capturing his distinctive facial expression and posture. Rembrandt also used sharp contrasts of light and shadow to draw attention to his focus.

Another artist fascinated with the effects of light was Jan Vermeer (YAHN vuhr·MEER). Like many other Dutch artists, he chose domestic, indoor settings for his portraits. He often painted women doing such familiar activities as pouring milk from a jug or reading a letter. Unlike Rembrandt, who was famous in his time, Vermeer did not become widely admired until the late 19th century. The work of both Rembrandt and Vermeer reveals how important merchants, civic leaders, and the middle class in general were in 17th-century Netherlands.

Absolutism in Europe

Even though Philip II lost his Dutch possessions, he was a forceful ruler in many ways. He tried to control every aspect of his empire's affairs. During the next few centuries, many European monarchs would also claim the authority to rule without limits.

Background
The large fleet helped the Dutch East India Company to dominate the Asian spice trade and the Indian Ocean trade. This added to Dutch prosperity.

Economics Unlike the Netherlands in the 16th and 17th centuries, Spain never developed much of a middle class. Encourage students to investigate why. They might consider these obstacles: (1) the expulsion of Jews and Moors, (2) the government's failure to invest in productive ventures, (3) high government spending and taxation, (4) the Spanish public's generally negative attitude toward moneymaking, (5) limited opportunities for advancement outside the nobility and the church, and (6) severe inflation. Have students compare these factors with those that helped the Dutch middle class flourish.

Visual Learners Invite interested students to find paintings by Dutch or Spanish artists of the 16th and 17th centuries, including Ribera, Zurbarán, and Velázquez of Spain and Honthorst, Hals, Rembrandt, Vermeer, Kalf, and Ruisdael of the independent Netherlands. Ask students to bring examples to class and to discuss how similarities and differences in the cultures of the two countries are expressed in the artworks. Encourage students to read about the artists and their cultures to inform their analysis.

THINK THROUGH HISTORY
C. Drawing Conclusions How was Philip II typical of an absolute monarch?
C. Possible Answers He involved himself in every aspect of government, he trusted no one but himself, he built an imposing palace to impress people, he tried to force his subjects to accept his religion, he raised taxes.

The Theory of Absolutism These rulers wanted to be **absolute monarchs,** kings or queens who believed that all power within their state's boundaries rested in their hands. Their goal was to control every aspect of society. Absolute monarchs believed in **divine right,** the idea that God created the monarchy and that the monarch acted as God's representative on earth. An absolute monarch answered only to God, not to his or her subjects.

These ideas were not new to the 16th century. Absolute rulers from ancient times included Darius in Persia, Shi Huangdi in China, and the Roman Caesars. After the decline of the Roman Empire, however, European monarchs had been weak. The feudal nobility, the Church, and other rulers had limited the power that any one monarch could wield.

Growing Power of Europe's Monarchs As Europe emerged from the Middle Ages, monarchs grew increasingly powerful. The decline of feudalism, the rise of cities, and the growth of national kingdoms all helped to centralize authority. In addition, the growing middle class usually backed monarchs, because they promised a peaceful, supportive climate for business. Monarchs used the wealth of colonies to pay for their ambitions. Church authority also broke down during the late Middle Ages and the Reformation. That opened the way for monarchs to assume even greater control. In 1576, Jean Bodin, an influential French writer, defined absolute rule:

> **A VOICE FROM THE PAST**
> The first characteristic of the sovereign prince is the power to make general and special laws, but—and this qualification is important—without the consent of superiors, equals, or inferiors. If the prince requires the consent of superiors, then he is a subject himself; if that of equals, he shares his authority with others; if that of his subjects, senate or people, he is not sovereign.
>
> **JEAN BODIN,** *Six Books on the State*

Crises Lead to Absolutism The 17th century was a period of great upheaval in Europe. Religious and territorial conflicts between states led to almost continuous warfare. This caused governments to build huge armies and to levy even heavier taxes on an already suffering population. These pressures in turn would bring on widespread unrest. Sometimes peasants revolted. In response to these crises, monarchs tried to impose order by increasing their own power. As absolute rulers, they regulated everything from religious worship to social gatherings. To seem more powerful, they increased the size of their courts. They created new government bureaucracies to control their countries' economic life. Their goal was to free themselves from the limitations imposed by the nobility and by representative bodies such as Parliament. Only with such freedom could they rule absolutely, as did the most famous monarch of his time, Louis XIV of France.

Section ❶ Assessment

1. TERMS & NAMES

Identify
• Philip II
• absolute monarch
• divine right

2. TAKING NOTES

On a chart like the one shown, list the conditions that allowed European monarchs to gain power. Then list the ways they exercised their increased power.

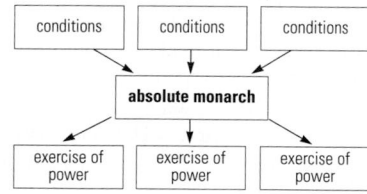

```
  conditions    conditions    conditions
        \           |           /
          absolute monarch
        /           |           \
 exercise of   exercise of   exercise of
   power         power         power
```

3. DRAWING CONCLUSIONS

What does the art described in this section reveal about the cultures of Spain and the Netherlands?

THINK ABOUT
• what the art of Velázquez and El Greco reveals about Spain
• what the art of Rembrandt and Vermeer reveals about the Netherlands

4. THEME ACTIVITY

Economics With a partner, create an illustrated poster contrasting the economies of Spain and the Netherlands around 1600. Compare such characteristics as

• sources of wealth
• existence of a middle class
• trends such as inflation or high taxes
• who controlled financial services

Absolute Monarchs in Europe **137**

MORE ABOUT . . .
Divine Right
The idea that God or the gods provide the basis for absolute rule has been seen in many cultures. The Chinese called this notion the Mandate of Heaven. The Aztecs, Inca, and Maya also believed that their rulers were representatives of the gods on earth.

ASSESS & RETEACH

Section 1 Assessment
Have students work in pairs or small groups to answer the questions. As they share answers, have them point to information in the text that supports their answers.

Section Quiz
 FORMAL ASSESSMENT
Section Quiz, p. 63

Reteaching Activity
CLASS TIME: 10 MINUTES

Use Guided Reading Worksheet 1 to review the main ideas of the section.

 IN-DEPTH RESOURCES: UNIT 2
Guided Reading, p. 1

CLOSE ACTIVITY

CLASS TIME: 10 MINUTES

Summarizing
Use the Concept Web transparency to help students list problems that weakened the Spanish Empire. Include details that exemplify each weakness.

 CRITICAL THINKING TRANSPARENCIES
CT78 Concept Web

ANSWERS

1. TERMS & NAMES
Philip II, p. 133
absolute monarch, p. 137
divine right, p. 137

2. TAKING NOTES
Possible Responses:
Conditions—decline of feudalism, rise of cities, growth of national kingdoms, growth of middle class, wealth of colonies, breakdown of Church authority, economic and religious crises, revolts.

Exercise of power—regulated worship, social gatherings, and economy; increased size of court; created new government bureaucracies; reduced power of nobles and representative bodies.

3. DRAWING CONCLUSIONS
Possible Responses:
Velázquez showed pride of Spanish monarchs; El Greco showed Catholic faith in Spain; Rembrandt and Vermeer showed the importance of merchants, civic leaders, and the middle class in the Netherlands.

4. THEME ACTIVITY
Standards for Evaluation
A poster should:
• compare the economies of Spain and the Netherlands
• convey that the Netherlands had the stronger economy
• combine written and visual materials

OBJECTIVES

1. To describe religious and political conflicts in France.
2. To explain Louis XIV's policies.
3. To characterize the style of the French royal court.
4. To identify causes and effects of French wars.

SKILLBUILDER

- Interpreting charts, p. 143

CRITICAL THINKING

- Recognizing effects, pp. 138, 140, 142
- Making inferences, pp. 139, 141
- Supporting opinions, p. 143
- Analyzing themes, p. 143

FOCUS

5-Minute Warm-Up

▶ **Making Inferences**
Answering these questions will help students understand the power of Louis XIV.

1. Read the paragraphs under "Louis Controls the Nobility" on page 141. What did the most privileged nobles at Louis's court hope to receive?
2. How did Louis treat nobles who failed to come to court to flatter him?

📖 **WARM-UP TRANSPARENCY 5**

OBJECTIVE 1 INSTRUCT

Religious Wars Create a Crisis

▶ **Key Ideas**
- In the late 1500s, French Protestants and Catholics fight eight civil wars.
- King Henry IV tries to end the conflict by guaranteeing religious tolerance.
- After Henry's death, Cardinal Richelieu becomes the power behind the throne.
- French thinkers embrace skepticism as a world view.

📘 **IN-DEPTH RESOURCES: UNIT 2**
Guided Reading, p. 2

📘 **ACCESS FOR STUDENTS ACQUIRING ENGLISH**
Guided Reading (Spanish), p. 61

2 France's Ultimate Monarch

TERMS & NAMES
- Edict of Nantes
- Cardinal Richelieu
- skepticism
- Louis XIV
- intendant
- Jean Baptiste Colbert
- War of the Spanish Succession

MAIN IDEA

After a century of war and riots, France was ruled by Louis XIV, the most powerful monarch of his time.

WHY IT MATTERS NOW

Louis used his power to build a great palace and sponsor art that is part of France's cultural legacy.

SETTING THE STAGE In 1559, King Henry II of France died, leaving four young sons. Three of them ruled, one after the other, but all proved incompetent. The real power behind the throne during this period was their mother, Catherine de Médicis. Catherine tried to preserve royal authority, but growing conflicts between Catholics and Huguenots—French Protestants—rocked the country.

Religious Wars Create a Crisis

Between 1562 and 1598, Huguenots and Catholics fought eight religious wars. Chaos spread through France. For example, in 1572 the St. Bartholomew's Day Massacre in Paris sparked a six-week, nationwide slaughter of Huguenots.

Henry of Navarre The massacre occurred when many Huguenot nobles were in Paris. They were attending the marriage of Catherine's daughter to a Huguenot prince, Henry of Navarre. Most of these nobles died, but Henry survived. Descended from the popular medieval king Louis IX, Henry was robust, athletic, and handsome. In 1589, when both Catherine and her last son died, Prince Henry inherited the throne. He became Henry IV, the first king of the Bourbon dynasty in France. As king, he showed himself to be decisive, fearless in battle, and a clever politician.

Many Catholics, including the people of Paris, opposed Henry. For the sake of his war-weary country, Henry chose to give up Protestantism and become a Catholic. Explaining his conversion, Henry declared, "Paris is well worth a Mass."

In 1598, Henry took another step toward healing France's wounds. He declared that the Huguenots could live in peace in France and set up their own houses of worship in some cities. This declaration of religious toleration was called the **Edict of Nantes.**

Phillipe de Champaigne painted many portraits of the powerful Cardinal Richelieu. This triple portrait shows his front view and two profiles.

Aided by an adviser who enacted wise financial policies, Henry devoted his reign to rebuilding France and its prosperity. He restored the French monarchy to a strong position. After a generation of war, most French people welcomed peace. Some people, however, hated Henry for his religious compromises. In 1610, a fanatic leaped into the royal carriage and stabbed Henry to death.

Louis XIII and Cardinal Richelieu
After Henry IV's death, his son Louis XIII reigned. Louis was a weak king, but in 1624 he appointed a strong minister who made up for all of Louis's weaknesses.

Cardinal Richelieu (RIHSH·uh·LOO) became, in effect, the ruler of France. For

Background
Catherine was descended from the Renaissance de' Medici family. She spelled her name the French way.

Background
The Bourbon dynasty took its name from a French town.

THINK THROUGH HISTORY
A. Recognizing Effects What were the effects of Henry's conversion to Catholicism and of the Edict of Nantes?
A. Possible Answers They restored peace to France by ending religious wars, but they prompted a fanatic to assassinate Henry.

SECTION 2 RESOURCES

PRINT RESOURCES

📘 **IN-DEPTH RESOURCES: UNIT 2**
Guided Reading, p. 2
Primary Source: Louis XIV's Advice to His Son, p. 9
Literature: from *The Cat and the King*, p. 13

📘 **ACCESS FOR STUDENTS ACQUIRING ENGLISH**
Guided Reading (Spanish), p. 61

📘 **FORMAL ASSESSMENT**
Section Quiz, p. 64

📘 **ALTERNATIVE ASSESSMENT BOOK**

TECHNOLOGY RESOURCES

💿 **CD-ROM**
Electronic Library of Primary Sources

🌐 **INTERNET** www.mlworldhistory.com

several years, he had been a hard-working leader of the Catholic church in France. Although he tried sincerely to lead according to moral principles, he was also ambitious and enjoyed exercising authority. As Louis XIII's minister, he was able to pursue his ambitions in the political arena.

This lean-faced, hawk-nosed cardinal took two steps to increase the power of the Bourbon monarchy. First, he moved against Huguenots. He believed that Protestantism often served as an excuse for political conspiracies against the Catholic king. Although Richelieu did not end the Huguenots' right to worship, he forbade Protestant cities from having walls. He did not want them to be able to defy the king and then withdraw behind strong defenses.

Second, he sought to weaken the nobles' power. Richelieu ordered nobles to take down their fortified castles. He increased the power of government agents who came from the middle class. This action ended the need for the king to use noble officials.

Richelieu also wanted to make France the strongest state in Europe. The greatest obstacle to this, he believed, was the Hapsburg rulers whose lands surrounded France. Hapsburgs ruled Spain, Austria, the Netherlands, and parts of Germany. To limit Hapsburg power, Richelieu involved France in the Thirty Years' War.

Writers Express Skepticism As France regained political power, a new French intellectual movement developed. French thinkers had witnessed the religious wars with horror. What they saw turned them toward **skepticism,** the idea that nothing can ever be known for certain. These thinkers expressed an attitude of doubt toward churches that claimed to have the only correct set of doctrines. To doubt old ideas, skeptics thought, was the first step toward finding truth.

Michel de Montaigne lived during the worst years of the French religious wars. After the death of a dear friend, Montaigne retired to his library and thought deeply about life's meaning. To communicate his ideas, Montaigne developed a new form of literature, the essay. An essay is a brief work that expresses a person's thoughts and opinions.

In one essay, Montaigne pointed out that whenever a new belief arose, it replaced an old belief that people once accepted as truth. In the same way, he went on, the new belief would also probably be replaced by some different idea in the future. For these reasons, Montaigne believed that humans could never have absolute knowledge of what is true. To remind himself of this, he had the beams of his study painted with the sentence "All that is certain is that nothing is certain."

Another French writer of the time, René Descartes, was a brilliant thinker. In his *Meditations of First Philosophy,* Descartes examined the skeptical argument that one could never be certain of anything. Descartes used his observations and his reason to answer such arguments. In doing so, he created a philosophy that influenced modern thinkers and helped to develop the scientific method. Because of this, he became an important figure in the Enlightenment. (See Chapter 6.)

Louis XIV Rules Absolutely

The efforts of Henry IV and Richelieu to strengthen the French monarchy paved the way for the most powerful ruler in French history—**Louis XIV.** In Louis's view, he and the state were one and the same. He reportedly boasted, *"L'état, c'est moi,"* meaning "I am the state." Although Louis XIV became the strongest king of his time, when he began his reign he was only a five-year-old boy.

Louis, the Boy King When Louis became king in 1643, the true ruler of France was Richelieu's successor, Cardinal Mazarin (MAZ·uh·RAN). Mazarin's greatest triumph

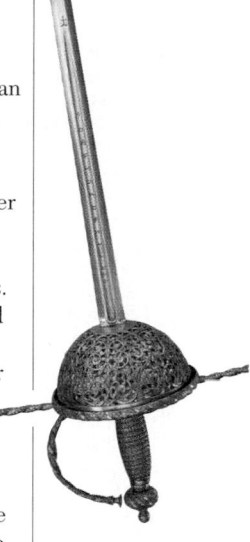

Absolute Monarchs in Europe **139**

SPOTLIGHT ON

The Three Musketeers
The uneasy relationship between Louis XIII and Cardinal Richelieu provides the background for a lively work of historical fiction—*The Three Musketeers.*

It was written by Alexandre Dumas *père* (the father) in 1844. The novel is based on actual events involving the intrigues at Louis XIII's royal court. The main characters, the musketeers, are members of Louis's guard. They often become involved in sword fights, using weapons like the one shown below. From this novel comes the famous slogan "All for one and one for all." Hollywood has produced at least six film versions of this classic, a sign of its lasting popularity.

Louis XIV

Despite his royal standing, Louis was neglected as a child. Once he nearly drowned in a pond because no one was watching him. As king he worked hard and paid great attention to the smallest details of government. Have students read more about Louis and his life. Helpful resources include online documents at **www.mlworldhistory.com** and *The Sun King* by Nancy Mitford.

MORE ABOUT . . .
Cardinal Mazarin

Born in Italy, Mazarin first came to France on a diplomatic mission for the pope. Taking Richelieu as a model, he eventually became first minister of France, instructing the young Louis XIV in statecraft. Mazarin's enemies forced him out of power twice, but the royal family brought him back each time.

OBJECTIVE ③ INSTRUCT

Louis's Grand Style

▶ **Key Ideas**
- Louis XIV surrounds himself with luxury.
- He brings nobles to his court and makes them wait on him.
- He builds a lavish palace at Versailles and becomes a great patron of the arts.

 IN-DEPTH RESOURCES: UNIT 2
Literature: from *The Cat and the King*, p. 13

 ELECTRONIC LIBRARY OF PRIMARY SOURCES
"Two Views of Versailles"

HISTORY MAKERS

Louis XIV
1638–1715

Although Louis XIV stood only 5 feet 5 inches tall, his erect and dignified posture made him appear much taller. (It also helped that he wore high-heeled shoes.)

Louis had very strong likes and dislikes. He hated cities and loved to travel through France's countryside. The people who traveled with him were at his mercy, however, for he allowed no stopping except for his own comfort.

Louis liked to be informed of every detail in his government. He explained to his son the secrets of his success:

Two things without doubt were absolutely necessary: very hard work on my part, and a wise choice of persons capable of seconding it.

It is small wonder that the vain Louis XIV liked to be called the Sun King. He believed that, as with the sun, all power radiated from him.

---

came in 1648, with the ending of the Thirty Years' War. The peace treaty made France the most powerful country in Europe.

Many people in France, particularly the nobles, hated Mazarin because he increased taxes and strengthened the central government. From 1648 to 1653, violent anti-Mazarin riots tore France apart. At times, the nobles who led the riots threatened the young king's life. Even after the violence was over, Louis never forgot his fear or his anger at the nobility. He determined to become so strong that they could never threaten him again.

In the end, the rebellion failed for three reasons. Its leaders distrusted one another even more than they distrusted Mazarin. In addition, the government used violent repression. Finally, peasants and townspeople grew weary of disorder and fighting. For many years afterward, the people of France accepted the oppressive laws of an absolute king. They were convinced that the alternative—rebellion—was even worse.

Louis Takes Control When Cardinal Mazarin died in 1661, the 23-year-old Louis took control of the government himself. A courtier remembered coming into the king's apartments that morning with the chancellor and hearing Louis announce, "The scene has changed. In the government of my realm . . . I shall have other principles than those of the late cardinal. You know my wishes, gentlemen; it now remains for you to execute them."

Louis weakened the power of the nobles by excluding them from his councils. In contrast, he increased the power of the government agents called **intendants,** who collected taxes and administered justice. To keep power under central control, he made sure that local officials communicated regularly with him.

Economic Growth Louis devoted himself to helping France attain economic, political, and cultural brilliance. No one assisted him more in achieving these goals than his minister of finance, **Jean Baptiste Colbert** (kawl·BEHR). Colbert believed in the theory of mercantilism. To prevent wealth from leaving the country, Colbert tried to make France self-sufficient. He wanted it to be able to manufacture everything it needed instead of relying on imports.

To expand manufacturing, Colbert gave government funds and tax benefits to French companies. To protect France's industries, he placed a high tariff on goods from other countries. Colbert also recognized the importance of colonies, which provided raw materials and a market for manufactured goods. The French government encouraged people to migrate to France's colony in Canada. There the fur trade added to French commerce.

After Colbert's death, Louis announced a policy that slowed France's economic progress. In 1685 he cancelled the Edict of Nantes, which protected the religious freedom of Huguenots. In response, thousands of Huguenot artisans and business people fled the country. Louis's policy thus robbed France of many skilled workers.

Louis's Grand Style

In his personal finances, Louis spent a fortune to surround himself with luxury. For example, each meal was a feast. An observer claimed that the king once devoured four plates of soup, a whole pheasant, a partridge in garlic sauce, two slices of ham, a salad, a plate of pastries, fruit, and hard-boiled eggs in a single sitting! Nearly 500 cooks, waiters, and other servants worked to satisfy his tastes.

THINK THROUGH HISTORY
C. Recognizing Effects What effects did the years of riots have on Louis XIV? on his subjects?
C. Answer Louis increased his power so no one could ever threaten him again; the subjects allowed him to do so because they hoped a strong leader would prevent future turmoil.

Vocabulary
mercantilism: the economic theory that nations should protect their home industries and export more than they import.

Huguenots After Louis XIV revoked the Edict of Nantes, many Huguenots immigrated to England, Prussia, the Netherlands, and North America, where their skills in commerce and industry helped develop the economy. Huguenot merchants and financiers helped make Amsterdam the financial and trading center of the 17th-century world. Huguenot winemakers who settled in the Dutch colony around what is now Cape Town, South Africa, established a flourishing wine industry there. Many Huguenots who settled in America were artisans. Invite students to find out more about the Huguenots' contributions to other lands.

Economics *Mercantilism,* a term used by the Scottish economist Adam Smith, refers to a popular economic theory during the age of absolute monarchs. A principal goal of mercantilism was to increase state power at the expense of other nations. Mercantilists believed that this was done by increasing exports and reducing imports, by holding large stores of gold and silver, and by exploiting the resources of colonies. Encourage students to research mercantilism and find out why this theory eventually lost favor.

Louis Controls the Nobility Every morning, the chief valet woke Louis at 7:30. Outside the curtains of Louis's canopy bed stood at least 100 of the most privileged nobles at court. They were waiting to help the great king dress. Only four would be allowed the honor of handing Louis his slippers or holding his sleeves for him.

Meanwhile, outside the bedchamber, lesser nobles waited in the palace halls and hoped Louis would notice them. A kingly nod, a glance of approval, a kind word— these marks of royal attention determined whether a noble succeeded or failed. A duke recorded how Louis turned against nobles who did not come to court to flatter him:

THINK THROUGH HISTORY
D. Making Inferences How did Louis's treatment of the nobles reflect his belief in his absolute authority?

A VOICE FROM THE PAST
He looked to the right and to the left, not only upon rising but upon going to bed, at his meals, in passing through his apartments, or his gardens. . . . He marked well all absentees from the Court, found out the reason of their absence, and never lost an opportunity of acting toward them as the occasion might seem to justify. . . . When their names were in any way mentioned, "I do not know them," the King would reply haughtily.

DUKE OF SAINT-SIMON, *Memoirs of Louis XIV and the Regency*

Having the nobles at the palace increased royal authority in two ways. It made the nobility totally dependent on Louis. It also took them from their homes, thereby giving more power to the intendants. Louis required hundreds of nobles to live with him at the splendid palace he built at Versailles, 11 miles southwest of Paris.

The Splendor of Versailles Everything about the Versailles palace was immense. It faced a huge royal courtyard dominated by a statue of Louis XIV. The palace itself stretched for a distance of about 500 yards.

The Palace at Versailles

- cost—an estimated $2 billion in 1994 dollars
- 36,000 laborers and 6,000 horses worked on the palace

- two wings—each 150 yards long
- main building—about 500 yards long
- about 2,000 rooms

This photograph shows the gardens of Versailles as they appear today. Versailles was built with
- 15,000 acres of gardens, lawns, and woods
- 1,400 fountains

It took so much water to run all the fountains at the same time that it was only done on special occasions. On other days, when the king walked in the garden, servants would turn on fountains just before he reached them. To conserve water, the servants would turn them off after he walked away.

Molière

Molière's comedies ridicule human folly, poking fun at misers, hypocrites, and snobs. Targets of his barbed humor sometimes took offense. His greatest play, *Tartuffe,* so angered some Parisians that they called for him to be burned at the stake. Louis XIV protected him, however, and supported his work.

OBJECTIVE 4 INSTRUCT

Louis Fights Disastrous Wars

Key Ideas

- Louis XIV builds up a huge army and wages war to expand French territory and influence.
- Other European nations join forces to equal French power.
- France gains but eventually weakens from constant war.

CRITICAL THINKING ACTIVITY

CLASS TIME: 10 MINUTES

Summarizing

Help students recall facts about Louis's wars by filling in a chart like the one below.

Wars	Results
Spanish Netherlands	France gained 12 towns
Dutch Netherlands	France gained several towns and the Franche-Comté region
Spanish Succession	Louis's grandson allowed to remain king of Spain; France lost N. American territories

---

In fact, the palace was so long that food from the kitchens was often cold by the time servants reached Louis's chambers.

Because of its great size, Versailles was like a small royal city. Its rich decoration and furnishings clearly showed Louis's wealth and power to everyone who came to the palace. The elaborate ceremonies there impressed the king's subjects and aroused the admiration and envy of all other European monarchs.

Patronage of the Arts Versailles was a center of the arts during Louis's reign. Louis made opera and ballet more popular. He even danced the title role in the ballet *The Sun King.* One of his favorite writers was Molière (mohl·YAIR), who wrote some of the funniest plays in French literature. Molière's comedies include *Tartuffe,* which mocks religious hypocrisy. *The Would-be Gentleman* mocks the newly rich, and *The Imaginary Invalid* mocks hypochondriacs.

Not since Augustus of Rome had there been a monarch who aided the arts as much as Louis. Under Louis, the chief purpose of art was no longer to glorify God, as it had been in the Middle Ages. Nor was its purpose to glorify human potential, as it had been in the Renaissance. Now the purpose of art was to glorify the king and promote values that supported Louis's absolute rule.

Louis Fights Disastrous Wars

Under Louis, France was the most powerful country in Europe. In 1660, France had about 20 million people. This was four times as many as England and 10 times as many as the Dutch republic. The French army, numbering 100,000 in peacetime and 400,000 in wartime, was far ahead of other states' armies in size, training, and weaponry.

Attempts to Expand France's Boundaries In 1667, just six years after Mazarin's death, Louis invaded the Spanish Netherlands. Through this campaign, he gained 12 towns. Encouraged by his success, he personally led an army into the Dutch Netherlands in 1672. The Dutch saved their country by opening the dikes and flooding the countryside. This was the same tactic they had used in their revolt against Spain a century earlier. The war ended in 1678 with the Treaty of Nijmegen. France gained several towns and a region called Franche-Comté.

Louis decided to fight additional wars, but his luck had run out. By the end of the 1680s, a European-wide alliance had formed to stop France. By joining together, weaker countries could match France's strength. This defensive strategy was meant to achieve a balance of power, in which no single country or group of countries could dominate others.

In 1689, the Dutch prince William of Orange became the king of England. He joined the League of Augsburg, which consisted of the Hapsburg emperor, the kings of Sweden and Spain, and the leaders of several smaller European states. Joined together, these countries equaled France's strength.

The painting below shows the Siege of Namur, which took place during Louis XIV's war with the League of Augsburg.

Background
Louis adopted the title *Sun King* for himself. He decorated Versailles with suns and statues of Apollo, the Greek god of the sun.

THINK THROUGH HISTORY
E. Recognizing Effects How did Louis's wars against weaker countries backfire?
E. Possible Answer He motivated his enemies to band together and thereby become strong enough to rival France.

CONNECTIONS ACROSS TIME AND PLACE

MULTIPLE LEARNING STYLES

Balance of Power In international relations, the matching of power against power is called balance of power. This policy has figured importantly in world politics since the days of absolute monarchs. Until the 20th century, the political world consisted of several separate balance-of-power systems, including the European, American, Chinese, and Indian. Beginning with alliances formed in World War I, most nations became integrated into a single balance-of-power system. Invite students to find out how the quest for a balance of power has played out over the years. Have them draw parallels between old and new alliances.

Interpersonal Learners Ask students to hold a mock press conference between reporters and two kings: Louis XIV and William of Orange. Have two students play the kings' roles, and have the rest act as reporter-interviewers. Questions should concern the European wars of the late 1600s and the reasons for those wars. The kings should faithfully represent views that would correspond to royal and national interests at the time. If desired, students can switch roles at various points in the press conference.

France at this time had been weakened by a series of poor harvests. That, added to the constant warfare, brought great suffering to the French people. So, too, did new taxes, which Louis imposed to finance his wars.

War of the Spanish Succession Tired of hardship, the French people longed for peace. What they got was another war. In 1700, the childless king of Spain, Charles II, died after promising his throne to Louis XIV's 17-year-old grandson, Philip of Anjou. The two greatest powers in Europe, enemies for so long, were now both ruled by Bourbons.

Other countries felt threatened by this increase in the Bourbon dynasty's power. In 1701, England, Austria, the Dutch republic, Portugal, and several German and Italian states joined together against France and Spain. The long struggle that followed is known as the **War of the Spanish Succession.**

The costly war dragged on until 1713. The Treaty of Utrecht was signed in that year. Under its terms, Louis's grandson was allowed to remain king of Spain so long as the thrones of France and Spain were not united.

The big winner in the war was Great Britain. From Spain, Britain took Gibraltar, a fortress that controlled the entrance to the Mediterranean. Spain also granted a British company an *asiento*—permission to send enslaved Africans to Spain's American colonies. This increased Britain's involvement in trading enslaved Africans. In addition, France gave Britain the North American territories of Nova Scotia, Newfoundland, and the Hudson Bay. The Austrian Hapsburgs took the Spanish Netherlands and other Spanish lands in Italy. Prussia and Savoy were recognized as kingdoms.

Louis's Death and Legacy Louis's last years were more sad than glorious. Realizing that his wars had ruined France, he regretted the suffering he had brought to his people. He died in bed in 1715. News of his death prompted rejoicing throughout France. The people had had enough of the Sun King.

Louis left a mixed legacy to his country. France was certainly a power to be reckoned with in Europe. But the staggering debts and resentment over the royal abuse of power would plague Louis XIV's heirs. Eventually, this resentment led to revolution. In the meantime, Louis's enemies in Prussia and Austria had been experimenting with their own forms of absolute monarchy, as you will learn in Section 3.

Background
Louis XIV lived so long that he outlived his son and two grandsons. His great-grandson succeeded him as Louis XV.

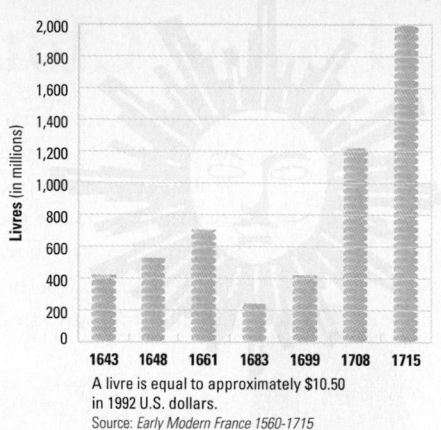

Debt of the Royal Family, 1643–1715

Livres (in millions)

Year	
1643	400
1648	400
1661	700
1683	250
1699	450
1708	1,200
1715	2,000

A livre is equal to approximately $10.50 in 1992 U.S. dollars.
Source: *Early Modern France 1560-1715*

SKILLBUILDER: Interpreting Charts
1. *How many times greater was the royal debt in 1715 than in 1643?*
2. *What was the royal debt of 1715 equal to in 1992 dollars?*

Section ② Assessment

1. TERMS & NAMES
Identify
• Edict of Nantes
• Cardinal Richelieu
• skepticism
• Louis XIV
• intendant
• Jean Baptiste Colbert
• War of the Spanish Succession

2. TAKING NOTES
On a time line like the one shown, list the major events of Louis XIV's reign.

1643   1715

Identify which events on your time line strengthened the French monarchy and which weakened it.

3. SUPPORTING OPINIONS
Many historians think of Louis XIV as the perfect example of an absolute monarch. Do you agree? Explain why or why not.

THINK ABOUT
• the description of an absolute monarch at the end of Section 1
• the ways in which Louis XIV fits that description
• any ways in which Louis XIV does not fit the description

4. ANALYZING THEMES
Economics How did the policies of Colbert and Louis XIV affect the French economy? Explain both positive and negative effects.

THINK ABOUT
• Colbert's attempts to make France self-sufficient
• what happened when Louis cancelled the Edict of Nantes
• the cost of Versailles and wars

Absolute Monarchs in Europe **143**

History from Visuals

Debt of the Royal Family, 1643–1715
Interpreting the Graph Point out that the graph gives amounts of livres in millions. So 1,200 means 1.2 billion livres.

Extension Activity Have students determine the equivalent in 1992 U.S. dollars of the royal debt in 1708. *about $12.6 billion*

SKILLBUILDER Answers
1. Five times greater
2. About $21 billion

ASSESS & RETEACH

Section 2 Assessment
Have pairs of students work together to quiz each other on terms and names.

Section Quiz
FORMAL ASSESSMENT
Section Quiz, p. 64

Reteaching Activity
CLASS TIME: 10 MINUTES

To help students review the section, have them make a time line of the key events described.

CLOSE ACTIVITY

CLASS TIME: 10 MINUTES

Evaluating
Have groups of students debate the value of Louis's reign, with one side giving a positive view and the other a negative view. Groups should consider conditions in France before his reign, achievements and failures while he was in power, and the legacy of his rule.

ANSWERS

1. TERMS & NAMES
Edict of Nantes, p. 138
Cardinal Richelieu, p. 138
skepticism, p. 139
Louis XIV, p. 139
intendant, p. 140
Jean Baptiste Colbert, p. 140
War of the Spanish Succession, p. 143

2. TAKING NOTES
Possible Responses: 1643 L. becomes king; 1648–1653 Riots disrupt F.; 1661 L. starts rule; 1667 L. invades Sp. Neth.; 1672 L. invades D. Neth.; 1685 L. voids Edict of Nantes; 1701–1713 L. fights War of Sp. Suc; 1715 L. dies. Strengthen— 1661, 1667, 1672; weaken— 1648–1653, 1685, 1701–1713, 1715.

3. SUPPORTING OPINIONS
Possible Responses: Yes—regulated worship by voiding Edict of Nantes, weakened nobility by using intendants and making nobles live at court, built palace to show power, used mercantilist policies to control economy.

4. ANALYZING THEMES
Possible Responses: C.'s mercantilism helped economy by building up and protecting French industries. L. helped economy by using C.'s policies but hurt it by voiding Edict of Nantes, which drove out Huguenots, and by taxing and spending to fund building and wars.

Teacher's Edition **143**

OBJECTIVES

 To show how clothing is used as a symbol of power.

 To compare ways clothing has served this purpose in various cultures at various times.

FOCUS

Ask students to think about the clothing they or their friends and family wear.

- Have them consider the ways in which clothing makes an impression and the kind of impression it makes.

- Ask how they might dress differently if they were or wanted to be a powerful person, such as a king or queen.

MORE ABOUT . . .

The Crown and Scepter

The royal crown probably has its origins in the wreaths worn by athletes and heroes in ancient Greek and Roman times, and in the special helmets worn by warrior chiefs. The first jeweled crowns consisted of a string of precious stones tied in back, but they soon evolved into more elaborate creations. The scepter derives from the staff, a symbol of power and authority since ancient times.

Power Clothes

Traditionally, rulers have used clothing to show their status as monarchs. Past rulers frequently wore symbols that only rulers were allowed to wear. In addition, they often chose clothing that indicated wealth or military strength. For example, in one portrait Louis XIV of France wears the uniform of a Roman general to show his military might. As you study the following pictures, notice whether the rulers conveyed power through royal symbols, wealth, or military strength.

France

Egypt

Thailand

Hawaii

Louis XIV, France, 1701
This portrait of Louis by Hyacinthe Rigaud conveyed the image of a strong monarch to Europeans of the 1700s. The high heels made Louis look taller and therefore more powerful. The gold flower embroidered on his robe is the fleur-de-lis (FLUR·duh·LEE), the royal symbol of French kings. The inside of the robe is lined with ermine, a type of fur that only nobles wore. The sword, scepter, and crown are additional symbols of royal power.

Ostrich plumes were very expensive, so usually only royalty or the nobility wore them. This plumed hat belonged to Louis.

a **closer look** LOUIS XIV

144 Chapter 5

CUSTOMIZING FOR SPECIAL NEEDS

Gifted and Talented Students Fashion became a major symbol of wealth and power in Europe in the 16th century. During the centuries of absolute monarchs, European capitals became centers of fashion extravagance. In part, this was the result of colonial expansion, which led to the importation of new and luxurious fabrics and dyes, as well as the acquisition of gold and silver to pay for them. Increasingly, merchants and other middle-class Europeans found that they were able to afford fine clothing.

At the same time, noble families tried to maintain their distinction from other social classes by restricting others from dressing luxuriously. Suggest that interested students research clothing styles worn by European nobles during the age of absolute monarchs. Have them report to the class on fashion trends of the 16th through 19th centuries and where and why those styles were popular.

Queen Hatshepsut, Egypt, 1490 B.C.

Although a woman, Hatshepsut ruled as pharaoh. This red granite statue shows her wearing two symbols of royal power—the false beard and the headdress with the asp (snake), both worn only by pharaohs.

High Chief Boki and his wife, Liliha; Hawaii, about 1824

In Hawaii, only male chiefs of high rank could wear feather garments, such as the cloak and helmets shown here. The red and yellow feathers came from birds native to the islands. Each cloak required about a half million feathers to produce.

King Bhumibol Adulyadej, Thailand, 1990

Just as Louis XIV liked to dress as a Roman general, many modern rulers portray themselves as military leaders. Here King Bhumibol Adulyadej prays while wearing a white military uniform and rows of medals.

Connect to History

Clarifying Which of the rulers on this page wear clothing that displays wealth? military power? symbols that only rulers were allowed to wear?

SEE SKILLBUILDER HANDBOOK, PAGE 650

Connect to Today

Clarifying In today's world, many books and articles tell businesspeople how to dress to convey a sense of power. Find at least one of these books or articles and read to discover the main points of advice. List the main points and share them with the class.

This is a copy of a diamond cross that Louis XIV had. The stones in the middle are set in the design of a dove. The dove's beak is a ruby.

This bust shows the elaborate wigs that French monarchs and nobles wore.

Absolute Monarchs in Europe **145**

INSTRUCT

Power Clothes

▶ *Key Ideas*
- European monarchs like Louis XIV wear luxurious clothing that symbolizes their wealth and power.
- Cultures in different times and places develop their own symbols of power, including feathered garments.
- Rulers throughout history adopt military costumes to emphasize state power and their own leadership qualities.

MORE ABOUT . . .
Feather Work

The use of feathered clothing as a symbol of power was also common in the ancient Americas. The Maya, Aztecs, and Inca all created dramatic garments, headdresses, and blankets from the feathers of tropical birds. As in Hawaii, these items were restricted to the highest classes.

MORE ABOUT . . .
Wigs

The wearing of wigs dates back as far as ancient Egypt, but it was during the 16th and 17th centuries that the use of wigs became popular in Europe. France's Louis XIII began wearing one in 1624, and the first wig makers' guild was formed in 1665. In general, men wore wigs more than women.

Connect to History

Clarifying
Possible Responses: Wealth—Louis XIV, High Chief Boki; military power—Louis XIV, King Bhumibol; royal symbols—Louis XIV, Queen Hatshepsut, High Chief Boki

Connect to Today

Clarifying
Students might find sources at the local public library by searching under such terms as *clothing and dress* or *business etiquette* or *businesswomen—clothing,* or they might use one of the following:
- *Dressing Up: How to Look and Feel Absolutely Perfect for Any Social*

Occasion by Marisa Berenson, 1984
- *The Professional Image: The Total Program for Marketing Yourself Visually* by Susan Bixler, 1984
- "Image," *Forbes,* June 16, 1997
- "The New Corporate Uniforms," *Fortune,* Nov. 13, 1995

Teacher's Edition   145

Section 3 Overview

OBJECTIVES

 To describe the Thirty Years' War.

 To explain the growth of central European kingdoms.

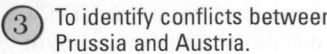 To identify conflicts between Prussia and Austria.

SKILLBUILDER

• Interpreting maps: place, region, p. 147

CRITICAL THINKING

• Analyzing motives, p. 146
• Drawing conclusions, p. 147
• Contrasting, p. 148
• Clarifying, p. 149
• Making inferences, p. 150
• Recognizing effects, p. 150

FOCUS

5-Minute Warm-Up

▶ **Making Inferences**
Have students answer these questions to examine the relative merits of two absolute rulers in central Europe.

1. Read History Makers on page 149. Describe one domestic policy of each ruler.

2. What character trait of each ruler might have motivated each policy?

 WARM-UP TRANSPARENCY 5

OBJECTIVE ① INSTRUCT

The Thirty Years' War

Key Ideas
• In 1618, Protestant and Catholic states in Germany go to war.
• The Thirty Years' War causes great destruction.
• The Peace of Westphalia ends the war in 1648, with major effects on central European states and their allies.

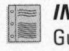 **IN-DEPTH RESOURCES: UNIT 2**
Guided Reading, p. 3

 ACCESS FOR STUDENTS ACQUIRING ENGLISH
Guided Reading (Spanish), p. 62

146 Chapter 5

---

3 Central European Monarchs Clash

MAIN IDEA	WHY IT MATTERS NOW
After a period of turmoil, absolute monarchs ruled Austria and the Germanic state of Prussia.	Prussia built a strong military tradition in Germany that contributed in part to world wars in the 20th century.

SETTING THE STAGE For a brief while, it appeared that the German rulers had settled their religious differences through the Peace of Augsburg (1555). They had agreed that the faith of each prince would determine the religion of his subjects. Churches in Germany could be either Lutheran or Catholic, but not Calvinist.

The Thirty Years' War

The peace was short-lived—soon to be replaced by a long war. After the Peace of Augsburg, the Catholic and Lutheran princes of Germany watched each other suspiciously. Each religion tried to gain followers. In addition, both sides felt threatened by Calvinism, which was spreading in Germany and gaining many followers. As tension mounted, the Lutherans joined together in the Protestant Union in 1608. The following year, the Catholic princes formed the Catholic League. Now, only a spark would set off a war.

Bohemian Protestants Revolt That spark came in 1618. The future Holy Roman emperor, Ferdinand II, was head of the Hapsburg family. As such, he ruled the Czech kingdom of Bohemia. The Protestants in Bohemia did not trust Ferdinand, who was a foreigner and a Catholic. When he closed some Protestant churches, the Protestants revolted. Ferdinand sent an army into Bohemia to crush the revolt. Several German Protestant princes took this chance to challenge their Catholic emperor.

This engraving shows the siege of the German city of Magdeburg in 1631. The city was destroyed during the Thirty Years' War.

Thus began the **Thirty Years' War**—a conflict over religion, over territory, and for power among European ruling families. Historians think of it as having two main phases: the phase of Hapsburg triumphs and the phase of Hapsburg defeats.

Hapsburg Triumphs The Thirty Years' War lasted from 1618 to 1648. During the first 12 years, Hapsburg armies from Austria and Spain crushed the troops hired by the Protestant princes. They succeeded in putting down the Czech uprising. They also defeated the German Protestants who had supported the Czechs.

Ferdinand II paid his army of 125,000 men by allowing them to plunder, or rob, German villages. This huge army destroyed everything in

A. Possible Answer
To punish Protestants who aided the Czech uprising.

THINK THROUGH HISTORY
A. Analyzing Motives Why did Ferdinand attack northern Germany?

146 Chapter 5

SECTION 3 RESOURCES

PRINT RESOURCES

 IN-DEPTH RESOURCES: UNIT 2
Guided Reading, p. 3
Geography Application: Old Empires and New Powers, p. 7
History Makers: Maria Theresa, p. 16

 ACCESS FOR STUDENTS ACQUIRING ENGLISH
Guided Reading (Spanish), p. 62
Geography Application (Spanish), p. 66

 FORMAL ASSESSMENT
Section Quiz, p. 65

 ALTERNATIVE ASSESSMENT BOOK

TECHNOLOGY RESOURCES

 CD-ROM
Electronic Library of Primary Sources

 INTERNET www.mlworldhistory.com

its path. The mayor of Magdeburg in northern Germany described the horrible destruction of his city:

A VOICE FROM THE PAST

In this frenzied rage, the great and splendid city that had stood like a fair princess in the land was now . . . given over to the flames, and thousands of innocent men, women, and children, in the midst of a horrible din of heartrending shrieks and cries, were tortured and put to death in so cruel and shameful a manner that no words would suffice to describe it nor no tears to bewail it.

OTTO VON GUERICKE, quoted in *Readings in European History*

Hapsburg Defeats The Protestant Gustavus Adolphus of Sweden and his disciplined army of 13,000 shifted the tide of war in 1630. They drove the Hapsburg armies out of northern Germany. However, Gustavus Adolphus was killed in battle in 1632.

Cardinal Richelieu and Cardinal Mazarin of France dominated the remaining years of the war. Although Catholic, these two cardinals feared the Hapsburgs more than the Protestants. They did not want other European rulers to have as much power as the French king. Therefore, in 1635, Richelieu sent French troops to join the German and Swedish Protestants in their struggle against the Hapsburg armies.

Peace of Westphalia The war did great damage to Germany. Its population dropped from 20 million to about 16 million. Both trade and agriculture were disrupted, and Germany's economy was ruined. Germany had a long, difficult recovery from this devastation. That is a major reason that it did not become a unified state until the 1800s.

The Peace of Westphalia (1648) ended the war and had important consequences. First, it weakened the Hapsburg states of Spain and Austria. Second, it strengthened France by awarding it German territory. Third, it made German princes independent of the Holy Roman emperor. Fourth, it ended religious wars in Europe. Fifth, it introduced a new method of peace negotiation. In that method, still used today, all participants meet to settle the problems of a war and decide the terms of peace.

Europe After the Thirty Years' War, 1648

Population Losses During the War

Up to 15% | 33–66%
15–33% | Over 66%
The Holy Roman Empire

GEOGRAPHY SKILLBUILDER: Interpreting Maps
1. **Place** Name at least five modern European countries that existed at the end of the Thirty Years' War.
2. **Region** Refer to the inset map. Which regions lost the most population in the Thirty Years' War?

The Hapsburgs, a royal German family, were one of the chief ruling dynasties of Europe from the 16th century to the 20th. Hapsburgs ruled Austria continuously from 1282 to 1918. They also ruled Hungary, Bohemia, Spain, and other lands. The Holy Roman Empire was under Hapsburg control from the mid-1400s until its disintegration in 1806.

OBJECTIVE 2 INSTRUCT

Central Europe Differs from the West

▶ *Key Ideas*
- The formation of states in central Europe occurs more slowly than in western Europe.
- Central European nobles hold down serfs and block the development of strong kings.
- The Holy Roman Empire loses strength after the Thirty Years' War, but Austria remains a powerful force in central Europe.

CRITICAL THINKING ACTIVITY

CLASS TIME: 10 MINUTES

Perceiving Causes and Effects
Have students fill in a chart like the one below, listing actions and effects that helped central European nobles maintain power.

Nobles' Power
Action: kept control over serfs
Effect: increased wealth
Action:
Effect:

Beginning of Modern States The treaty thus abandoned the idea of a Catholic empire that would rule most of Europe. It recognized Europe as a group of independent states that could negotiate for themselves. Each independent state was seen as essentially equal to the others. This marked the beginning of the modern state system and was the most important result of the Thirty Years' War.

Central Europe Differs from the West

The formation of strong states occurred more slowly in central Europe. The major powers of this region were the kingdom of Poland, the Holy Roman Empire, and the Ottoman Empire. None of them was well-organized in the mid-1600s.

Economic Contrasts One reason for this is that the economy of central Europe developed differently from that of western Europe. During the late Middle Ages, serfs in western Europe slowly won freedom and moved to towns. There, they joined middle-class townspeople, who gained economic power because of the commercial revolution and the development of capitalism. In turn, western European monarchs taxed the towns. They used the tax money to raise armies and reduce the influence of the nobility.

By contrast, the landowning aristocracy in central Europe passed laws restricting the ability of serfs to gain freedom and move to cities. These nobles wanted to keep the serfs on the land, where they could produce large harvests. The nobles could then sell the surplus crops to western European cities at great profit. To increase productivity, the aristocracy increased their control over their serfs. By 1700, Polish landowners could demand that their serfs work as much as six days a week. This left the serfs only one day a week to grow their own food.

Several Weak Empires The landowning nobles in central Europe not only held down the serfs but also blocked the development of strong kings. For example, the Polish nobility elected the Polish king and sharply limited his power. They allowed the king little income, no law courts, and no standing army.

The two empires of central Europe were also weak. Although Suleiman the Magnificent had conquered Hungary and threatened Vienna in 1529, the Ottoman Empire could not take its European conquest any farther. From then on the Ottoman Empire declined from its peak of power.

In addition, the Holy Roman Empire was seriously weakened by the Thirty Years' War. No longer able to command the obedience of the German states, the Holy Roman Empire had no real power. These old, weakened empires and kingdoms left a power vacuum in central Europe. In the late 1600s, two German-speaking families decided to try to fill this vacuum by becoming absolute rulers themselves.

Austria Grows Stronger One of these families was the Hapsburgs of Austria. Even after the terrible losses in the Thirty Years' War, Austria remained the most powerful and important state within the Holy Roman Empire. The Austrian Hapsburgs took several steps to become absolute monarchs. First, during the Thirty Years' War, they reconquered Bohemia. The Hapsburgs wiped out Protestantism there and created a new Czech nobility that pledged loyalty to them. Second, after the war, the Hapsburg ruler centralized the government and created a standing army. Third, by 1699, the Hapsburgs had retaken Hungary from the Ottomans.

In 1711, Charles VI became the Hapsburg ruler. Charles's empire was a difficult one to rule. Within its borders lived a diverse assortment of people—Czechs, Hungarians, Italians, Croatians, and Germans. Only the fact that one Hapsburg ruler wore the Austrian, Hungarian, and Bohemian crowns kept the empire together.

This is the imperial crest of the Hapsburgs. It shows a double-headed eagle with a crown.

148 Chapter 5

Background
Western Europe included such countries as England, France, and the Netherlands.

THINK THROUGH HISTORY
C. Contrasting How did the economies of central and western Europe differ?
C. Answer Western Europe developed capitalism and towns, while central Europe remained more feudal.

Background
Bohemia was a kingdom. The Czechs were the people who lived there.

TEACHING OPTION **BLOCK SCHEDULING**

GEOGRAPHY APPLICATION ACTIVITY

CLASS TIME 20 MINUTES

Task: Students will list what they know about central Europe after the Thirty Years' War, determine what else they want to know, then complete a worksheet and note what they learned.

Materials Needed: Use the textbook and the Geography Application worksheet for Chapter 5.

Activity: On the board, write the following subject headings: *Declining Powers* (Poland, Ottoman Empire, Holy Roman Empire) and *Rising Powers* (Austria, Prussia). Have students help you list under the headings what they know, based on textbook pages 148–149, about the situation in central Europe. Then have groups of students list questions they have about these subjects. Next they should study and complete the worksheet, also noting answers they find to their own questions.

Conclusion: Under the headings on the board, have students help you list what they learned from the worksheet. Discuss questions still unanswered.

IN-DEPTH RESOURCES: UNIT 2
Geography Application: Old Empires and New Powers, p. 7

Maria Theresa Inherits the Austrian Throne How could the Hapsburgs make sure that they continued to rule all those lands? Charles VI spent his entire reign working out an answer to this problem. By endless arm-twisting, he persuaded other leaders of Europe to sign an agreement that declared they would recognize Charles's eldest daughter as the heir to all his Hapsburg territories. That heir was a young woman named **Maria Theresa.** In theory, this agreement guaranteed Maria Theresa a peaceful reign. Instead, she faced years of war. Her main enemy was Prussia, a new state to the north of Austria.

Prussia and Austria Clash

Like Austria, Prussia rose to power in the late 1600s. Like the Hapsburgs of Austria, Prussia's ruling family, the Hohenzollerns, also had ambitions. Those ambitions threatened to upset central Europe's delicate balance of power.

The Rise of Prussia and Frederick the Great The Hohenzollerns built up their state from a number of small holdings—beginning with the German states of Brandenburg and Prussia. In 1640, a 20-year-old Hohenzollern named Frederick William inherited the title of elector of Brandenburg. After seeing the destruction of the Thirty Years' War, Frederick William, later known as the Great Elector, decided that having a strong army was the only way to ensure safety.

To protect their lands, the Great Elector and his descendants moved toward absolute monarchy. They created a standing army—the best in Europe. They built it to a force of 80,000 men. To pay for the army, they introduced permanent taxation. Beginning with the Great Elector's son, they called themselves kings. They also weakened the representative assemblies of their territories.

Prussia's landowning nobility, the Junkers (YUNG-kuhrz), resisted the king's growing power. However, in the early 1700s, King Frederick William I bought their cooperation. He gave the Junkers the exclusive right to be officers in his army. Prussia became a rigidly controlled, military society.

Frederick William worried that his son, Frederick, was not military enough to rule. The prince loved music, philosophy, and poetry. In 1730, when he and a friend tried to run away, they were caught. To punish Frederick, the king ordered him to witness his friend's beheading. Despite such bitter memories, Frederick II, known as **Frederick the Great,** followed his father's military policies when it came to

HISTORY MAKERS

Maria Theresa
1717–1780

An able ruler, Maria Theresa also devoted herself to her family. Unlike many monarchs, she married for love. She gave birth to 16 children, 10 of whom reached adulthood.

Maria Theresa continued to advise her children even after they were grown. Perhaps her most famous child was Marie Antoinette, wife of Louis XVI of France. Maria Theresa often scolded Marie for spending too much money and making the French people angry.

As empress, Maria Theresa decreased the power of the nobility. Very religious, she cared more for the peasants' well-being than most rulers. She limited the amount of labor that nobles could force peasants to do. She argued: "The peasantry must be able to sustain itself."

Frederick the Great
1712–1786

Although they reigned during the same time, Frederick the Great and Maria Theresa were very different. Where Maria was religious, Frederick was practical and atheistic. Maria Theresa had a happy home life; Frederick married a woman whom he never cared for and neglected. Maria Theresa had a huge family; Frederick died without a son to succeed him.

An aggressor in foreign affairs, Frederick once wrote that "the fundamental role of governments is the principle of extending their territories." With regard to domestic affairs, he encouraged religious toleration and legal reform. Frederick earned the title "the Great" by achieving his goals for Prussia, in both domestic and foreign affairs.

Absolute Monarchs in Europe **149**

power. However, he also softened some of his father's laws, because he believed that a ruler should be like a father to his people:

A VOICE FROM THE PAST
A prince . . . is only the first servant of the state, who is obliged to act with probity [honesty] and prudence. . . . As the sovereign is properly the head of a family of citizens, the father of his people, he ought on all occasions to be the last refuge of the unfortunate.

FREDERICK II, *Essay on Forms of Government*

CONNECT *to* TODAY

Quebec Separatists
In North America, the Seven Years' War was called the French and Indian War. As a result of this war, the British took over France's American colonies. Today Canada has a large French-speaking population, many of whom believe that they should be independent from Canada. A demonstration for independence is shown above.

In 1995, Quebec voters narrowly rejected a vote for independence. Before the vote was taken, Jacques Parizeau, then Quebec's premier and leader of the secessionist movement, said, "We, the people of Quebec, through our National Assembly, proclaim: Quebec is a sovereign [independent] country." Although the vote did not make Parizeau's declaration come true, separation continues to be an important issue in Quebec.

War of the Austrian Succession In 1740, Maria Theresa succeeded her father, just five months after Frederick II became king of Prussia. Frederick wanted the Austrian land of Silesia, which bordered Prussia. Silesia produced iron ore, textiles, and food products. Frederick assumed that because Maria Theresa was a woman, she would not be forceful enough to defend her lands. In 1740, he sent his army to occupy Silesia, beginning the War of the Austrian Succession.

Even though Maria Theresa had recently given birth, she journeyed to Hungary. There she held her infant in her arms as she asked the Hungarian nobles for aid. Even though the nobles resented their Hapsburg rulers, they pledged to give Maria Theresa an army. Great Britain also joined Austria to fight its longtime enemy France, which was Prussia's ally. Although Maria Theresa did stop Prussia's aggression, she lost Silesia at the Treaty of Aix-la-Chapelle in 1748.

The Seven Years' War Maria Theresa decided that the French kings were no longer Austria's chief enemies. She made an alliance with them. The result was a diplomatic revolution. When Frederick heard of her actions, he signed a treaty with Britain—Austria's former ally. Now, Austria, France, Russia, and others were allied against Britain and Prussia. Not only had Austria and Prussia switched allies, but for the first time Russia was playing a role in European affairs.

In 1756, Frederick attacked Saxony, an Austrian ally. Soon every great European power was involved in the war. Fought in Europe, India, and North America, the war lasted until 1763. It was called the **Seven Years' War.** The war did not change the territorial situation in Europe.

It was a different story on other continents. Both France and Britain had colonies in North America and the West Indies. Both were competing economically in India. The British emerged as the real victors in the Seven Years' War. France lost its colonies in North America, and Britain gained sole economic domination of India. This set the stage for further British expansion in India in the 1800s, as you will see in Chapter 11.

THINK THROUGH HISTORY
E. Making Inferences Why would iron ore, agriculture, and textiles be helpful acquisitions for Frederick the Great?
E. Possible Answer Frederick needed to feed and clothe his troops and supply them with weapons. Also, by gaining these resources through conquest, he freed more of his own citizens to be in the army.

Section ❸ Assessment

1. TERMS & NAMES
Identify
• Thirty Years' War
• Maria Theresa
• Frederick the Great
• Seven Years' War

2. TAKING NOTES
On a chart like the one shown, compare Maria Theresa and Frederick the Great.

Points of Comparison	Maria Theresa	Frederick the Great
years of reign		
foreign policy		
success in war		
their policies as monarchs		

3. RECOGNIZING EFFECTS
Name several ways that the Peace of Westphalia laid the foundations of modern Europe.

THINK ABOUT
• religious effects
• diplomatic effects
• political effects

4. THEME ACTIVITY
Power and Authority Write an outline for a lecture on "How to Increase Royal Power and Become an Absolute Monarch." In your outline, jot down examples that support your main points. The examples should be of Hapsburg and Hohenzollern actions that increased the power of those ruling families.

150 Chapter 5

ANSWERS

4 Russian Czars Increase Power

TERMS & NAMES
• Ivan the Terrible
• boyars
• Peter the Great
• westernization

MAIN IDEA

Peter the Great made many changes in Russia to try to make it more like western Europe.

WHY IT MATTERS NOW

Many Russians today debate whether to model themselves on the West or to focus on traditional Russian culture.

SETTING THE STAGE Ivan III of Moscow, who ruled Russia from 1462 to 1505, accomplished several things. First, he conquered much of the territory around Moscow. Second, he liberated Russia from the Mongols. Third, he began to centralize the Russian government. This laid the foundation for the absolute monarchy that would come later.

From Ivan to the Romanovs

Ivan III was succeeded by his son, Vasily, who ruled for 28 years. Vasily continued his father's work of adding territory to the growing Russian state. He also increased the power of the central government, a trend that would continue under his son, Ivan IV.

The First Czar Ivan IV, called **Ivan the Terrible,** came to the throne in 1533 when he was only three years old. His young life was disrupted by struggles for power among Russia's landowning nobles, known as **boyars.** The boyars fought to control young Ivan. When he was 16, Ivan seized power and had himself crowned czar. This title meant "caesar," and Ivan was the first Russian ruler to use it officially. He also married the beautiful Anastasia, related to an old boyar family, the Romanovs.

The years from 1547 to 1560 are often called Ivan's "good period." He won great victories, added lands to Russia, gave Russia a code of laws, and ruled justly.

Rule by Terror Ivan's "bad period" began in 1560 after Anastasia died. Accusing the boyars of poisoning his wife, Ivan turned against them. He organized his own police force, whose chief duty was to hunt down and murder people Ivan considered traitors. The members of this police force dressed in black and rode black horses.

Using these secret police, Ivan executed many boyars, their families, and the peasants who worked their lands. Thousands of people died. Ivan seized the boyars'

Background
Prince Kurbsky was an adviser to Ivan and also won many battles for him. When Ivan turned against him, Kurbsky fled to Lithuania.

estates and gave them to a new class of nobles, who had to remain loyal to him or lose their land. One noble, Prince Kurbsky, described the suffering Ivan caused him:

A VOICE FROM THE PAST
In front of your army have I marched—and marched again; and no dishonor have I brought upon you, but only brilliant victories. . . . But to you, O czar, was all this as naught; rather do you show us your intolerable wrath and bitterest hatred, and furthermore, burning stoves [a means of torture].
PRINCE ANDREW KURBSKY, letter to Czar Ivan IV

This portrait of Ivan IV is painted in the style of Russian icons. Perhaps this style was chosen to encourage deep respect for Ivan—who believed in his divine right to rule.

Absolute Monarchs in Europe **151**

(continued from page 151)

- Russia enters the Time of Troubles after Ivan's death, but Romanov rulers restore order.

 IN-DEPTH RESOURCES: UNIT 2
Guided Reading, p. 4

 ACCESS FOR STUDENTS ACQUIRING ENGLISH
Guided Reading (Spanish), p. 63

 WORLD ART AND CULTURES TRANSPARENCIES
AT47 Saint Basil's Cathedral

OBJECTIVE **2** INSTRUCT

Peter the Great Takes the Throne

▶ **Key Ideas**
- In 1696 Peter the Great becomes sole ruler of Russia.
- Russia is still a land of nobles and serfs, isolated and backward.
- Peter visits western Europe to study its customs and technology.

HISTORY MAKERS
Peter the Great

Peter avoided the pomp and splendor of earlier czars. He also had a tremendous temper. He was known to beat his officials with a stick. Have students find out how Peter's oldest son died. *He was sentenced to death for opposing Peter's reforms, but he died in prison before the execution.*

 WORLD ART AND CULTURES TRANSPARENCIES
AT46 Peter I the Great Interrogating the Czarevich at Peterhof

 ELECTRONIC LIBRARY OF PRIMARY SOURCES
from Letters of Peter the Great and His Son Alexis

Eventually, Ivan committed an act that was both a personal tragedy and a national disaster. In 1581, during a violent quarrel, he killed his oldest son and heir. When Ivan died three years later, only his weak second son was left to rule.

Rise of the Romanovs Ivan's son proved to be physically and mentally incapable of ruling. After he died without an heir, Russia experienced a period of turmoil known as the Time of Troubles. Boyars struggled for power and heirs of czars died under mysterious conditions. Several imposters tried to claim the throne.

Finally, in 1613, representatives from many Russian cities met to choose the next czar. Their choice was Michael Romanov, grandnephew of Ivan the Terrible's wife Anastasia. Thus began the Romanov dynasty, which ruled Russia for 300 years (1613–1917).

Peter the Great Takes the Throne

Over time, the Romanovs restored order to Russia. They strengthened government by passing a law code and putting down a revolt. This paved the way for the absolute rule of Czar Peter I. At first, Peter shared the throne with a feeble-minded half-brother. However, in 1696, Peter became sole ruler of Russia. He is known to history as **Peter the Great,** because he was one of Russia's greatest reformers. He also continued the trend of increasing the czar's power.

Russia's Differences from Europe When Peter I came to power, Russia was still a land of boyars and serfs. Serfdom in Russia lasted much longer than it did in western Europe. Serfdom continued in Russia into the mid-1800s. When a Russian landowner sold a piece of land, he sold the serfs with it. Landowners could give serfs away as presents or to pay debts. It was also against the law for serfs to run away from their owners.

Most boyars knew little of western Europe. In the Middle Ages, Russia had looked to Constantinople, not to Rome, for leadership. Then Mongol rule had cut Russia off from the Renaissance and the Age of Exploration. Geographic barriers also isolated Russia. Its only seaport, Archangel, was choked with ice much of the year. The few travelers who reached Moscow were usually Dutch or German, and they had to stay in a separate part of the city.

Religious differences widened the gap between western Europe and Russia. The Russians had adopted the Eastern Orthodox branch of Christianity. Western Europeans were mostly Catholics or Protestants, and the Russians viewed them as heretics and avoided them.

Peter Visits the West In the 1680s, people in the German quarter of Moscow were accustomed to seeing the young Peter striding through their neighborhood on his long legs. (Peter was more than six and a half feet tall.) He was fascinated by the modern tools and machines in the foreigners' shops. Above all, he had a passion for ships and the sea. The young czar believed that Russia's future depended on having a warm-water port. Only then could Russia compete with the more modern states of western Europe.

Peter was 24 years old when he became sole ruler of Russia. In 1697, just one year later, he embarked on the "Grand Embassy," a long visit to western Europe. Peter's goal was to learn about European customs and industrial techniques. With him were 200 servants and 55 boyars. Never before had a czar traveled among Western "heretics."

On his journey, Peter insisted on keeping his identity a secret. He went to the Netherlands in the plain clothes of an ordinary worker

Peter the Great
1672–1725

Peter the Great had the mind of a genius, the body of a giant, and the ferocious temper of a bear. One could not help but look up to Peter, who stood about 6 feet 8 inches tall. He was so strong that he was known to take a heavy silver plate and roll it up as if it were a piece of paper.

Peter had a good, if crude, sense of humor and loved to make practical jokes. But heaven help the person who crossed his path. If someone annoyed him, he would take his massive fist and knock the offender unconscious. If he were angrier, he would have the person's nostrils torn out with iron pincers.

Although Peter saw himself as a father to his people, he was cruel to his own family. When his oldest son opposed him, he had him imprisoned and killed.

THINK THROUGH HISTORY
A. Recognizing Effects What were the long-term effects of Ivan's murder of his oldest son?
A. Answer First Russia was ruled by a weak czar, then it experienced turmoil as several struggled to gain power, and finally the Romanov dynasty was established.

THINK THROUGH HISTORY
B. Summarizing Restate the main reasons that Russia was culturally different from western Europe.
B. Answers It had a feudal rather than a commercial economy; it had been influenced by Constantinople and the Mongols; it followed a different form of Christianity.

 TEACHING OPTION **BLOCK SCHEDULING** **SKILLBUILDER MINI-LESSON: Evaluating Decisions** **CLASS TIME 15 MINUTES**

Explaining the Skill Historians evaluate decisions of the past partly by looking at the short-term and long-term consequences of those decisions. Students might evaluate their own decisions similarly. They might at first be glad they took an after-school job because of the extra spending money it brings. But that decision might not seem as good after their grades slip because they have less time to study.

Applying the Skill: Evaluating Peter's Decision to Westernize Russia Have students read about Peter's steps to westernize Russia on pages 153 and 155. Then ask these questions:
1. What were some key short-term effects of the decision to westernize Russia? *Possible responses: The Russian army was trained in western tactics; and St. Petersburg was built.*
2. What were some key long-term effects? *Possible response: Russia could compete militarily and*

commercially with western Europe.
3. Was the decision to westernize a good one? Why or why not? *Possible responses: Yes, because it helped make Russia a great European power; no, because westernizing the military required imposing heavy taxes, and building St. Petersburg cost many lives.*

 IN-DEPTH RESOURCES: UNIT 2
Skillbuilder Practice: Evaluating Decisions, p. 6

and labored as a ship's carpenter for four months. However, a Russian giant in a Dutch seaport attracted attention. Word of his identity soon spread. Yet if a fellow worker addressed him as "Your Majesty" or "Sire," he would not answer. After all, he was just plain "Carpenter Peter." Peter also visited England and Austria before returning home.

Peter Rules Absolutely

Inspired by his trip to the West, Peter resolved that Russia would compete with Europe on both military and commercial terms. Peter's goal of **westernization,** of using western Europe as a model for change, was not an end in itself. Peter saw it as a way to make Russia stronger.

THINK THROUGH HISTORY
C. Recognizing Bias Judging from this remark, what was Peter's view of his people?
C. Possible Answers That they were backward and stubborn; that they were wrong and he was right.

Peter's Reforms Although Peter believed Russia needed to change, he knew that many of his people disagreed. As he said to one official, "For you know yourself that, though a thing be good and necessary, our people will not do it unless forced to." To force change upon his state, Peter increased his powers as an absolute ruler.

Peter brought the Russian Orthodox church under state control. He abolished the office of patriarch, head of the church. He set up a group called the Holy Synod to run the church—under his direction.

Like Ivan the Terrible, Peter reduced the power of the great landowners. He recruited able men from lower-ranking families. He then promoted them to positions of authority and rewarded them with grants of land. Because these men owed everything to the czar, they were loyal to him alone.

To modernize his army, Peter hired European officers, who drilled his soldiers in European tactics with European weapons. Being a soldier became a lifetime job. By the time of Peter's death, the Russian army numbered 200,000 men. To pay for this huge army, Peter imposed heavy taxes.

CONNECT to TODAY

Russia: East vs. West
Peter's reforms sparked the beginning of a debate in Russia that continues today—whether to westernize or to focus on Russian culture. The breakup of the Soviet Union in 1991 has led to developments in both directions.

Many ethnic groups have established individual republics or are striving to do so. On the other hand, Russia and other former Soviet countries are experimenting with democracy and a market economy. These are distinctly Western traditions.

Because Russia straddles two continents—Asia and Europe—the tension between East and West will probably be an enduring part of its culture.

OBJECTIVE ③ INSTRUCT

Peter Rules Absolutely

▶ **Key Ideas**
- Peter decides to westernize Russia so it can compete with western Europe.
- He places religion under state control, limits nobles' power, and modernizes the army.
- He gains territory on the Baltic Sea and builds the warm-water seaport St. Petersburg to gain easier access to the West.

📖 *IN-DEPTH RESOURCES: UNIT 2*
Primary Source: Peter the Great's Reforms, p. 10

🖥 *CRITICAL THINKING TRANSPARENCIES*
CT21 The Age of Absolute Monarchs, 1500–1800

CONNECT to TODAY
Russia: East vs. West

Have students find out about nationalist sentiments in Russia since the fall of communism. What issues are involved? Which way does Russia seem to be going: toward the West or back to its traditions?

History from Visuals

The Expansion of Russia, 1500–1800

Interpreting the Map Point out that the colored areas on the map correspond to periods of Russian expansion identified in the key. By what year had Russia gained land on the Arctic Ocean? *1505.* To what major body of water did Ivan IV, who ruled from 1533 to 1584, gain access? *Caspian Sea.*

(continued on next page)

The Expansion of Russia, 1500–1800

1462	Acquisitions to 1682
Acquisitions to 1505	Acquisitions to 1725
Acquisitions to 1584	Acquisitions to 1796

ARCTIC OCEAN
Arctic Circle
FINLAND
SWEDEN
St. Petersburg
Novgorod
RUSSIA
Baltic Sea
Volga R.
Moscow
Ob R.
Yenisei R.
Lena R.
Yakutsk
Okhotsk
Tomsk
Sea of Okhotsk
Warsaw
Kiev
POLAND
Ural R.
Irkutsk
Amur R.
Nerchinsk
AUSTRIA
Azov
Dniester R.
Caspian Sea
MONGOLIA
MANCHURIA
PACIFIC OCEAN
Constantinople
Black Sea
40° N
OTTOMAN EMPIRE
Mediterranean Sea
N
0   1,000 Miles
0   2,000 Kilometers
Tropic of Cancer

GEOGRAPHY SKILLBUILDER: Interpreting Maps
1. **Location** Locate the territories that Peter added to Russia during his reign, from 1682 to 1725. What bodies of water did Russia gain access to because of these acquisitions?
2. **Region** Who added a larger amount of territory to Russia—Ivan III, who ruled from 1462 to 1505, or Peter the Great?

TEACHING OPTION **BLOCK SCHEDULING** **COOPERATIVE ACTIVITY: Reporting on Modernization** **CLASS TIME 30 MINUTES**

Task: Students will research other countries that have struggled with issues of modernization and give an oral report on their findings.

Purpose: To become more aware of the tensions and difficulties involved in modern nation building.

Activity: Begin by asking students what, based on their reading about Peter the Great, they think modernization means. *Students might say that it*

means adopting the latest technique, technology, or style or simply bringing society up to date. Point out that modernization generally involves moving away from traditional values toward impersonal, practical ones, such as gathering scientific knowledge and applying it to technology so that goods and services can be produced more efficiently.

Have groups of students give an oral report on one of these modernizing countries: Japan during the Meiji

period, Turkey under Atatürk, or Iran under Reza Shah Pahlavi. Students should describe how modernization affected the country's political system, economy, customs and social structure, environment, and arts.

📖 *ALTERNATIVE ASSESSMENT BOOK*
Standards for Evaluating a Cooperative Activity

Extension Activity Ask students to name the five settlements on the map that were established in the territory Peter gained east of the Ob River. *Tomsk, Irkutsk, Nerchinsk, Yakutsk, Okhotsk.* Have students find out how Russians won and settled this region.

SKILLBUILDER Answers
1. Baltic Sea; Sea of Okhotsk, Pacific Ocean
2. Peter the Great

Daily *Life*
Russia, 1700

Peter introduced Western dress, customs, and usages to Russia often by force and against strong opposition. Yet by the end of his reign, members of the civil service, military, aristocracy, and to some extent even the middle class were clean-shaven and wore Western dress. Other Western innovations also won wide acceptance with time.

MORE ABOUT . . .
Personal Appearance

The shaving of beards came to symbolize Peter's reign. He actually shaved some boyars and officials himself. Traditionalists objected to shaving because they thought it impaired the image of God in men and made men look like cats, dogs, or monkeys. Peter also prohibited Russians from wearing the traditional long coat. In some cases, he cut the bottoms off nobles' coats.

MORE ABOUT . . .
Moscow

When Peter transferred the capital from Moscow to St. Petersburg, Moscow suffered not only a loss of status but also a "brain drain." Nobles were forced to move to St. Petersburg, and many merchants and artisans also moved. Population growth and new building slowed for a time, but later in Peter's reign, the city began to recover. Peter himself spurred new economic growth in Moscow by setting up new industries—such as a textile mill for making sailcloth—which encouraged private entrepreneurs to follow suit.

Daily *Life*: Russia, 1700

New Russian News

Your Money or Your Beard

About a year ago, as part of his attempt to westernize Russia, Peter the Great decided that the Russian custom of wearing beards showed too much Mongol influence. Our modernizing czar offered most men a hard choice: shave their beards, or plunk down money to keep their whiskers. Those who paid the beard tax received a token (shown below) to prove that they had the right to have hairy faces.

Peter's beard tax ranged from a sixth of a kopeck for a peasant to one hundred rubles a year for a wealthy merchant. The rich had to pay 60,000 times as much as the poor!

Now that the policy has been in effect for a year, the results are in. Most peasants and merchants and all priests and monks chose to pay rather than shave. All soldiers, officers, and court officials are clean-shaven for a good reason: Peter didn't give them a choice.

Winter Happenings: Moscow

It takes more than sub-zero temperatures to keep hardy Russians home. While some people brave the frigid air to sell their wares or to shop, others find delight at the fair.

Yesterday's outdoor market featured the rock-hard frozen carcasses of cows, sheep, pigs, and chickens piled into pyramidlike heaps. On hand-pulled sleds, shoppers carted home their purchases of meat, butter, eggs, and fish.

This winter scene shows bustling activity in Ivan the Great Square in Moscow.

Clowns, magicians, jugglers, and musicians entertained at the outdoor fair. For the athletic, there was an ice-skating rink, as well as a 35-foot ice hill to delight sledders. Dizzy visitors swung back and forth in boats suspended from a wooden frame.

Happy New Year!

Forward-looking Russians are celebrating the new year with festivities in January—instead of waiting until September, as their grandparents would have done. Just last month, Peter the Great decreed that Russia would adopt the calendar used by western Europe. He ushered in the calendar change with a fireworks display and a week of public feasting.

Build It Today, Move in Tomorrow

Need a new house or a replacement part for your current dwelling? Check out the carpenter's market at the end of any major street. There you'll find logs cut in a variety of lengths and widths and marked for easy assembly. In addition, ready-made beams, roof shingles, and door and window frames are also offered for sale.

With a little help from your friends, you can move into your new house in almost no time at all. Some tips for keeping that new house cozy in the winter:

- Buy windows with double glass.
- Keep ceilings low.
- Stuff the spaces between the logs with moss.
- Make a steep roof so that snow will slide off.

154 Chapter 5

Connect *to* History

Synthesizing How have Russians adapted to their cold climate? Discuss transportation, housing, and activities.

📁 SEE SKILLBUILDER
HANDBOOK, PAGE 665

Connect *to* Today

Researching At the library, research the records of the winter Olympics for the last 20 years to learn what events Russians (or Soviets) participated in and how many they won. What winter sports do modern Russians like and excel at?

Connect *to* History

Synthesizing
Possible Response: They have used sleds, built houses that withstand the cold and snow, and engaged in ice skating and other sports appropriate to cold-weather conditions.

Connect *to* Today

Researching
For records on the winter Olympics, suggest that students consult the sports section of a world almanac or the latest edition of *The Information Please Sports Almanac,* which is available in both book and on-line formats.

Westernizing Russia As part of his attempts to westernize Russia, Peter

- introduced potatoes, which became a staple of the Russian diet
- started Russia's first newspaper and edited its first issue himself
- raised women's status by having them attend social gatherings
- ordered the nobles to give up their traditional clothes for Western fashions

Peter also believed education was a key to Russia's progress. In his journal, Peter (referring to himself as "the Czar") described his efforts to advance learning:

A VOICE FROM THE PAST
A school of marine [navigation] was opened, and schools for the other arts and sciences began to be introduced gradually. . . . At the same time the Czar permitted his subjects to leave the country in order to study the sciences in foreign lands. This was forbidden in former times under pain of death, but now not only was permission given for it but many were forced to undertake it.

CZAR PETER I, quoted in *Peter the Great*, edited by L. Jay Oliva

A New Capital To promote education and growth, Peter wanted a seaport that would make it easier to travel to the West. Therefore, Peter fought Sweden to gain a piece of the Baltic coast. After 21 long years of war, Russia finally won the "window on the sea" that Peter wanted.

Actually, Peter had secured that window many years before Sweden officially surrendered it. In 1703 he began building a new city on Swedish lands occupied by Russian troops. Although the swampy site was unhealthful, it seemed ideal to Peter. Ships could sail down the Neva River into the Baltic Sea and on to western Europe. Peter called the city St. Petersburg, after his patron saint.

To build a city on a desolate swamp was no easy matter. Every summer, the army forced thousands of luckless serfs to leave home and work at St. Petersburg. An estimated 25,000 to 100,000 people died from the terrible working conditions and widespread diseases. When St. Petersburg was finished, Peter ordered many Russian nobles to leave the comforts of Moscow and settle in his new capital.

For better or for worse, Peter the Great had tried to reform the culture and government of Russia. To an amazing extent he had succeeded. By the time of his death in 1725, Russia was a power to be reckoned with in Europe. Meanwhile, another great European power, England, had been developing a form of government that limited the power of absolute monarchs, as you will see in Section 5.

This 1753 painting shows a view of St. Petersburg from the water. The ships indicate that it did become a booming port, as Peter had wanted.

D. Possible Answer He ordered peasants to work there, and he ordered nobles to move there.

THINK THROUGH HISTORY
D. Synthesizing Which of Peter's actions in the building of St. Petersburg demonstrate his power as an absolute monarch?

Section ④ Assessment

1. TERMS & NAMES
Identify
- Ivan the Terrible
- boyars
- Peter the Great
- westernization

2. TAKING NOTES
On a cluster diagram like the one shown, list the important events of Peter the Great's reign.

Peter the Great

3. SUPPORTING OPINIONS
Do you think Ivan the Terrible or Peter the Great was more of an absolute monarch? Explain the standards by which you made your decision.

THINK ABOUT
- ways that each increased the power of the Russian czar
- long term effects of each one's rule

4. ANALYZING THEMES
Power and Authority Which of Peter the Great's actions reveal that he saw himself as the highest authority in Russia? Explain.

THINK ABOUT
- steps he took to reduce the authority of others
- actions that overturned traditional sources of authority in Russia

Absolute Monarchs in Europe **155**

MORE ABOUT . . .
St. Petersburg
St. Petersburg was the first planned city in Russia. Peter insisted that the streets be broad, straight, paved with stone, and lined with houses built flush with the streets to form a continuous façade that would impress on-lookers. Houses were required to conform to standard patterns—one for each social class—drawn up by official architects. By Peter's death, more than 1,000 experts from western Europe, including architects, sculptors, painters, and gardeners —along with con-scripted Russian peasants and Swedish prisoners of war—had made St. Petersburg one of the wonders of Europe.

ASSESS & RETEACH

Section 4 Assessment
Suggest that students jot down important points that they want to include in each response before they write their final responses.

Section Quiz
FORMAL ASSESSMENT
Section Quiz, p. 66

Reteaching Activity
CLASS TIME: 10 MINUTES

Have pairs of students work together to answer item 3. Each partner should address a different point to think about. Then partners should pool their information to write a final answer.

CLOSE ACTIVITY

CLASS TIME: 15 MINUTES

Summarizing
Ask students to identify the reforms Peter the Great made to westernize Russia. List the reforms on the board. Then call on students to explain each reform and its significance.

ANSWERS

1. TERMS & NAMES
Ivan the Terrible, p. 151
boyars, p. 151
Peter the Great, p. 152
westernization, p. 153

2. TAKING NOTES
Possible Responses: Visited western Europe; took control of church; reduced power of landowners; modernized army; tried to westernize Russia; fought Sweden for Baltic land; had St. Petersburg built

3. SUPPORTING OPINIONS
Possible Responses: Ivan—Took title *czar,* which means "caesar"; expanded Russia; gave law code; organized his own police force; persecuted boyars; created new class of nobles. Aimed to increase and protect his own power more than to improve Russia. **Peter—** Took control of church; reduced power of landowners; strengthened army; imposed heavy taxes; forced nobles to move to St. Petersburg. Made reforms whether people wanted them or not.

4. ANALYZING THEMES
Possible Responses: Showed he saw himself above church by taking control of it; showed he saw himself above nobility by weakening it and forcing it to westernize; showed he saw himself above tradition by forcing Western customs on Russia.

Teacher's Edition **155**

Section 5 Overview

OBJECTIVES

(1) To identify conflicts between English rulers and Parliament.

(2) To explain the causes and results of the English Civil War.

(3) To describe the Restoration and Glorious Revolution.

(4) To explain political changes under William and Mary.

SKILLBUILDER

- Interpreting maps: movement, place, p. 157

CRITICAL THINKING

- Making inferences, p. 157
- Comparing, p. 157
- Contrasting, p. 159
- Evaluating decisions, p. 159

FOCUS

5-Minute Warm-Up

▶ *Predicting*

To examine the conflict between English rulers and Parliament, have students answer these questions.

1. Read Setting the Stage on page 156. What power of the English Parliament helped keep English rulers from becoming absolute monarchs?

2. How might Parliament have used its financial power to stop an English ruler from seizing absolute power?

 WARM-UP TRANSPARENCY 5

OBJECTIVE **(1)** INSTRUCT

Monarchs Clash with Parliament

▶ *Key Ideas*

- English kings clash with Parliament over money and power.
- Charles I dissolves Parliament when it opposes him.

IN-DEPTH RESOURCES: UNIT 2
Guided Reading, p. 5
Connections Across Time and Cultures: The Absolute Power of Rulers, p. 18

ACCESS FOR STUDENTS ACQUIRING ENGLISH
Guided Reading (Spanish), p. 64

TERMS & NAMES
- Charles I
- English Civil War
- Oliver Cromwell
- Restoration
- habeas corpus
- Glorious Revolution
- constitutional monarchy
- cabinet

MAIN IDEA	WHY IT MATTERS NOW
Absolute rulers in England were overthrown, and Parliament gained power.	Many of the government reforms of this period contributed to the democratic tradition of the United States.

SETTING THE STAGE During her reign, Queen Elizabeth I of England had frequent conflicts with Parliament. Many of the arguments were over money, because the treasury did not have enough funds to pay the queen's expenses. By the time Elizabeth died in 1603, she left a huge debt for her successor to deal with. Parliament's financial power was one obstacle to English rulers' becoming absolute monarchs.

Monarchs Clash with Parliament

Elizabeth had no child, and her nearest relative was her cousin, James Stuart. Already king of Scotland, James Stuart became King James I of England in 1603. Although England and Scotland were not united until 1707, they now shared a ruler.

Background
James was the son of Mary, Queen of Scots—whom Elizabeth had executed for plotting against her.

James's Problems James inherited the unsettled issues of Elizabeth's reign. The key question was how much power Parliament would have in governing. James believed he had absolute authority to rule. He said in a speech, "Kings are justly called gods, for that they exercise a manner or resemblance of divine power upon earth."

Elizabeth had also believed in her divine right to rule, but she was more tactful than James. She flattered Parliament to get her way. James thought it was beneath him to try to win Parliament's favor. His worst struggles with Parliament were over money. Parliament was reluctant to pay for James's expensive court and foreign wars.

In addition, James offended the Puritan members of Parliament. Because James was a Calvinist, the Puritans hoped he would enact reforms to purify the English church of Catholic practices. However, James resented being told what to do. Except for agreeing to a new translation of the Bible, he refused to make Puritan reforms.

Charles I Fights Parliament In 1625, James I died. **Charles I,** his son, took the throne. Charles always needed money—in part because he was at war with both Spain and France. Several times when Parliament refused to give him funds, he dissolved it.

By 1628, Charles was forced to call Parliament again. This time it refused to grant him any money until he signed a document that is known as the Petition of Right. In this petition, the king agreed to four points:

- He would not imprison subjects without due cause.
- He would not levy taxes without Parliament's consent.
- He would not house soldiers in private homes.
- He would not impose martial law in peacetime.

After agreeing to the petition, Charles ignored it. Even so, the petition was important. It set forth the idea that the law was higher

---

SECTION 5 RESOURCES

PRINT RESOURCES

 IN-DEPTH RESOURCES: UNIT 2
Guided Reading, p. 5
Primary Source: from *Diary of Samuel Pepys,* p. 11; from the English Bill of Rights, p. 12
History Makers: William of Orange, p. 17
Connections Across Time and Cultures: The Absolute Power of Rulers, p. 18

 ACCESS FOR STUDENTS ACQUIRING ENGLISH
Guided Reading (Spanish), p. 64

 FORMAL ASSESSMENT
Section Quiz, p. 67

TECHNOLOGY RESOURCES

🏛 ***CRITICAL THINKING TRANSPARENCIES***
CT57 Visual Summary

💿 **CD-ROM**
Electronic Library of Primary Sources

🌐 **INTERNET** www.mlworldhistory.com

THINK THROUGH HISTORY
A. Making Inferences Explain how the Petition of Right contradicted the idea of absolute monarchy.
A. Possible Answer An absolute sovereign was supposed to be above everyone; the Petition of Right said that the law and Parliament could limit the power of the English monarch.

than the king. This contradicted theories of absolute monarchy. In 1629, Charles dissolved Parliament and refused to call it back into session. To get money, he imposed all kinds of fees and fines on the English people. His popularity decreased year by year.

English Civil War

Charles offended Puritans by upholding church ritual and a formal prayer book. In addition, in 1637, Charles tried to force the Presbyterian Scots to accept a version of the Anglican prayer book. He wanted both his kingdoms to follow one religion. The Scots rebelled, assembled a huge army, and threatened to invade England. To meet this danger, Charles needed money—money he could get only by calling Parliament into session. This gave Parliament a chance to oppose him.

War Topples a King During the autumn of 1641, Parliament passed laws to limit royal power. Furious, Charles tried to arrest Parliament's leaders in January 1642, but they escaped. Equally furious, a mob of Londoners raged outside the palace. Charles fled London and raised an army in the north of England, where people were loyal to him.

From 1642 to 1649, supporters and opponents of King Charles fought the **English Civil War.** Those who remained loyal to Charles were called Royalists or Cavaliers. On the other side were Puritan supporters of Parliament. Because these men wore their hair short over their ears, Cavaliers mockingly called them Roundheads.

At first neither side could gain a lasting advantage. However, by 1644 the Puritans found a general who could win—**Oliver Cromwell.** In 1646, Cromwell's New Model Army defeated the Cavaliers. By the following year, the Puritans held the king prisoner.

In 1649, Cromwell and the Puritans brought Charles to trial for treason. They found him guilty and sentenced him to death. The execution of Charles was revolutionary. Kings had often been overthrown, killed in battle, or put to death in secret. Never before had a reigning monarch faced a public trial and execution.

The English Civil War from 1642 to 1645

December 1642
December 1643
December 1644
December 1645

■ Areas controlled by Puritans
■ Areas controlled by Royalists
★ Battle

GEOGRAPHY SKILLBUILDER: Interpreting Maps
1. **Movement** *Explain which side gained and which side lost territory during each year from 1643 to 1645.*
2. **Place** *Which side maintained control of the capital city of London? Why would this be important?*

Cromwell's Rule Cromwell now held the reins of power. In 1649, he abolished the monarchy and the House of Lords. He established a commonwealth—a republican form of government. In 1653, Cromwell sent the remaining members of Parliament home. Cromwell's associate John Lambert drafted a constitution, the first written constitution of any modern European state. However, Cromwell eventually tore up the document and ruled as a military dictator.

B. Possible Answer He abolished the legislative body, which might interfere with him, and he set himself above the law.

Absolute Monarchs in Europe **157**

Restoration and Revolution

▶ *Key Ideas*

• After Cromwell's death, disillusionment with Puritan rule leads to the restoration of the monarchy under Charles II.

• James II takes the throne next but is deposed for his pro-Catholic bias and contempt for Parliament.

• William and Mary take power in the Glorious Revolution.

 ELECTRONIC LIBRARY OF PRIMARY SOURCES
"The Restoration of Charles II"

SPOTLIGHT*On*
The London Fire

The Great Fire, which lasted four days and damaged four-fifths of the city, was the second disaster to strike London in two years. In the period 1664–1665 an outbreak of the plague had killed 75,000 Londoners. "Essentially," observes one scholar, " the plague was a disease of the badly housed poor." Indeed, it had always thrived in the filthy, rickety, and overcrowded inner city. The only cure for it was to raze the entire area. This the fire effectively did, making it possible for London to be redesigned along more open and orderly lines. After the fire the city was rebuilt mainly with brick, rather than timbered, structures.

Invite students to read more about historic London and to bring pictures of the city to class. They might begin by reading the larger excerpt of Samuel Pepys's account in the Teacher's Resources. They might also consult John Russell's *London,* an acclaimed pictorial history of the city.

 IN-DEPTH RESOURCES: UNIT 2
Primary Source: from *Diary of Samuel Pepys,* p. 11

Cromwell almost immediately had to put down a rebellion in Ireland. Henry VIII and his children had brought that country under English rule. In 1649 Cromwell landed on Irish shores with an army and crushed the uprising. The lands and homes of the Irish were taken from them and given to English soldiers. Fighting, plague, and famine killed an estimated 616,000 Irish.

Puritan Morality In England, Cromwell and the Puritans sought to reform society. They made laws that promoted Puritan morality and abolished activities they found sinful, such as going to the theater. In a speech, Cromwell explained his reasons for this:

> **A VOICE FROM THE PAST**
> I did hint to you my thoughts about the reformation of manners; and those abuses that are in this nation through disorder . . . should be much in your hearts. . . . I am confident our liberty and prosperity depends upon—reformation. To make it a shame to see men to be bold in sin and profaneness—and God will bless you. You will be a blessing to the nation.
> **OLIVER CROMWELL,** speech of September 17, 1656

Although a strict Puritan, Cromwell favored religious toleration for all Christians except Catholics. He even welcomed back Jews, who had been expelled from England in 1290.

Restoration and Revolution

Oliver Cromwell ruled until his death in 1658. Shortly afterward, the government he had established collapsed, and a new Parliament was selected. The English people were sick of military rule. In 1659, Parliament voted to ask the older son of Charles I to rule England.

Charles II Reigns When Prince Charles entered London in 1660, crowds shouted joyfully and bells rang. On this note of celebration, the reign of Charles II began. Because he restored the monarchy, the period of his rule is called the **Restoration.**

Charles also restored the theater, sporting events, and dancing, which the Puritans had banned. Theater, especially comedy, and the other arts flourished during the Restoration. For the first time, women appeared on the English stage to play female roles.

During Charles II's reign, Parliament passed an important guarantee of freedom, **habeas corpus.** This 1679 law gave every prisoner the right to obtain a writ or document ordering that the prisoner be brought before a judge. The judge would decide whether the prisoner should be tried or set free. Because of the Habeas Corpus Act, a monarch could not put someone in jail simply for opposing the ruler. Also, prisoners could not be held indefinitely without trials.

In addition, Parliament debated who should inherit Charles's throne. Because Charles had no legitimate child, his heir was his brother James, who was Catholic. A group called the Whigs opposed James, and a group called the Tories supported him. These two groups were the ancestors of England's first political parties.

Background
Habeas corpus comes from Latin words meaning "to have the body."

SPOTLIGHT *On*
The London Fire

A disastrous fire broke out in London on September 2, 1666. It began in the house of the king's baker, near London Bridge. The flames, stirred by a strong east wind, leaped from building to building. People desperately tried to escape. The Thames River was crawling with boats filled with survivors and their belongings.

Samuel Pepys, a public official, wrote an eyewitness account of the fire in his diary:

> It made me weep to see it. The churches, houses, and all on fire and flaming at once; and a horrid noise the flames made, and the cracking of houses at their ruin.

In the end, the fire destroyed St. Paul's Cathedral, 87 parish churches, and around 13,000 houses. It was the worst fire in London's history.

Literature The 17th-century English author John Milton wrote what are considered some of the greatest poems in the language, including *Paradise Lost.* But from 1641 to 1660 he focused on writing prose works in defense of religious and civil liberties. In "Areopagitica" Milton wrote what is now regarded as the classic statement against censorship. He also argued that power rests always with the people, who delegate it to a ruler but may, if it is abused, take it back and depose or even execute the tyrant. Have students find examples of Milton's poetry or prose to read and discuss in class.

Irish Troubles Point out to students that present-day conflicts between Protestants and Catholics in Northern Ireland stem from events of the 1600s. England promoted Protestant emigration to Ireland, particularly to the north, and Irish Catholics steadily lost power and influence. The decisive blow to Catholics came in 1690, when the English army of King William of Orange defeated Irish forces loyal to the deposed Catholic king of England, James II. Today, a group known as the Orange Order, named after William, continues to uphold the Protestant domination of Northern Ireland.

James II and the Glorious Revolution In 1685, Charles II died, and James II became king. James soon offended his subjects by flaunting his Catholicism. Violating English law, he appointed several Catholics to high office. When Parliament protested, James dissolved it. In 1688, James's second wife gave birth to a son. English Protestants became terrified at the prospect of a line of Catholic kings.

James had an older daughter, Mary, who was Protestant. She was also the wife of William of Orange, a prince of the Netherlands. Seven members of Parliament invited William and Mary to overthrow James for the sake of Protestantism. When William led his army to London in 1688, James fled to France. This bloodless overthrow of King James II is called the **Glorious Revolution.**

THINK THROUGH HISTORY
C. Contrasting How was the overthrow of James II different from the overthrow of Charles I?
C. Possible Answers It was basically peaceful; there was no execution of the king; the monarchy was not abolished.

Political Changes

At their coronation, William and Mary vowed "to govern the people of this kingdom of England . . . according to the statutes in Parliament agreed on and the laws and customs of the same." By doing so, William and Mary recognized Parliament as their partner in governing. England had become not an absolute monarchy but a **constitutional monarchy,** where laws limited the ruler's power.

Bill of Rights To make clear the limits of royal power, Parliament drafted a Bill of Rights in 1689. This document listed many things that a ruler could not do:

- No suspending of Parliament's laws
- No levying of taxes without a specific grant from Parliament
- No interfering with freedom of speech in Parliament
- No penalty for a citizen who petitions the king about grievances

William and Mary officially consented to these and other limits on their royal power.

Cabinet System Develops After 1688, no British monarch could rule without consent of Parliament. At the same time, Parliament could not rule without the consent of the monarch. If the two disagreed, government came to a standstill.

Background
Although the power of Parliament increased, England was still not democratic. Parliament represented the upper classes, not the majority of the English people.

During the 1700s, this potential problem was remedied by the development of a group of government ministers called the **cabinet**. These ministers acted in the ruler's name but in reality represented the major party of Parliament. Therefore, they became the link between the monarch and the majority in Parliament.

Over time, the cabinet became the center of power and policymaking. Under the cabinet system, the leader of the majority party in Parliament heads the cabinet and is called the prime minister. This system of English government continues today.

CONNECT to TODAY

U.S. Democracy
The United States adopted many of the government reforms and institutions that the English developed during this period. These include the following:

- the right to obtain habeas corpus—a document that prevents authorities from holding a person in jail without being charged

- a Bill of Rights, guaranteeing such rights as freedom of speech and freedom of worship

- a strong legislature and strong executive, which act as checks on each other

- a cabinet, made up of heads of executive departments, such as the Department of State

- two dominant political parties

Section ⑤ Assessment

1. TERMS & NAMES
Identify
- Charles I
- English Civil War
- Oliver Cromwell
- Restoration
- habeas corpus
- Glorious Revolution
- constitutional monarchy
- cabinet

2. TAKING NOTES
On a chart like the one shown, list the causes of each monarch's conflicts with Parliament.

Monarch	Conflicts with Parliament
James I	
Charles I	
James II	

What patterns do you see in the causes of these conflicts?

3. EVALUATING DECISIONS
In your opinion, which decisions of Charles I made his conflict with Parliament worse? Explain.

THINK ABOUT
- decisions that lost him the support of Parliament
- decisions that lost him the support of his people

4. THEME ACTIVITY
Revolution Using a dictionary, encyclopedia, or your textbook for reference, write a definition of revolution. Then write a paragraph explaining how the English Civil War and the Glorious Revolution are examples of revolution.

Absolute Monarchs in Europe **159**

OBJECTIVE **4** INSTRUCT

Political Changes
▶ *Key Ideas*
- William and Mary agree to govern with Parliament in a constitutional monarchy.
- Parliament drafts a Bill of Rights, limiting royal power.
- The cabinet, set up as a link between Parliament and the monarchy, becomes the center of power.

 IN-DEPTH RESOURCES: UNIT 2
History Makers: William of Orange, p. 17
Primary Source: from the English Bill of Rights, p. 12

CONNECT to TODAY
U.S. Democracy

Have students find out how the U.S. and British governments differ in their legislative and executive branches.

ASSESS & RETEACH

Section 5 Assessment
Have pairs of students help each other with key terms by making word cards with definitions on the back. Students can take turns quizzing each other.

Section Quiz
 FORMAL ASSESSMENT
Section Quiz, p. 67

Reteaching Activity
CLASS TIME: 10 MINUTES

Have pairs of students list statements summarizing the Royalist and Parliamentary positions, with each partner taking a different side. Partners should then present their positions to each other.

 CRITICAL THINKING TRANSPARENCIES
CT57 Visual Summary

CLOSE ACTIVITY

CLASS TIME: 15 MINUTES

Recognizing Sequences
Have small groups of students create time lines that show the main events covered in the section. Invite students to display their time lines and discuss how events in England in the 1600s led to the growth of constitutional rule.

ANSWERS

1. TERMS & NAMES
Charles I, p. 156
English Civil War, p. 157
Oliver Cromwell, p. 157
Restoration, p. 158
habeas corpus, p. 158
Glorious Revolution, p. 159
constitutional monarchy, p. 159
cabinet, p. 159

2. TAKING NOTES
Possible Responses: **James I**—Believed in divine right to rule; wanted large funds to pay for court and wars; did not make Puritan reforms. **Charles I**—Wanted funds to finance wars; tried to force all subjects to be Anglican; resisted Parliament's attempts to restrict his power.

James II—Offended Protestants by flaunting his Catholicism; named Catholics to high office.

3. EVALUATING DECISIONS
Possible Responses: Alienated Parliament by dissolving it, ignoring Petition of Right, and trying to arrest Parliamentary leaders; alienated his subjects by imposing

fines and fees on them and trying to force them all to be Anglican, thus encouraging them to support Parliament's struggle against him.

4. THEME ACTIVITY
Responses should
- clearly define revolution and explain how the examples fit the definition.

Teacher's Edition **159**

TERMS & NAMES

1. absolute monarch, p. 137
2. divine right, p. 137
3. Louis XIV, p. 139
4. War of the Spanish Succession, p. 143
5. Thirty Years' War, p. 146
6. Seven Years' War, p. 150
7. Peter the Great, p. 152
8. English Civil War, p. 157
9. Glorious Revolution, p. 159
10. constitutional monarchy, p. 159

REVIEW QUESTIONS

11. He fought the Muslim Ottoman Empire, he sent the Spanish Armada to punish Protestant England; he tried to destroy Protestantism in the Netherlands.

12. A prince should not share power because if he has to get the consent of someone else, he becomes that person's subject, not ruler.

13. He relied on non-noble intendants (government agents), and he forced nobles to live at Versailles, where they were dependent on him.

14. He ran up huge debts; he fought unpopular wars and imposed taxes to finance them.

15. It weakened Spain and Austria, it strengthened France, it made German princes independent of the Holy Roman emperor, it ended religious wars in Europe, it introduced a new method of negotiating peace, and it began the modern state system, in which all states are independent and equal.

16. They were battling over territory.

17. Russian serfdom was firmly implanted; people knew little of ideas from the Renaissance and Age of Exploration; Russians had adopted Eastern Orthodox Christianity.

18. Westernization to enable Russia to compete militarily and commercially with western Europe.

19. Cavaliers (Royalists) and Roundheads (Puritans) fought from 1642 to 1649, provoked by conflicts between the king and Parliament over religion, money, and the extent of the king's power. The Roundheads won and beheaded Charles I.

20. Parliament often refused to grant monarchs funds; it forced Charles I to sign the Petition of Right; Parliament leaders invited William and Mary to rule, but only as the partners of Parliament; Parliament drafted a Bill of Rights.

Absolute Monarchs in Europe

Long-Term Causes

- decline of feudalism
- rise of cities and growth of middle class
- growth of national kingdoms
- loss of Church authority

Immediate Causes

- religious and territorial conflicts
- buildup of armies
- need for increased taxes
- revolts by peasants or nobles

European Monarchs Claim Divine Right to Rule Absolutely

Immediate Effects

- regulation of religion and society
- larger courts
- huge building projects
- new government bureaucracies
- loss of power by nobility and legislatures

Long-Term Effects

- revolution in France
- western European influence on Russia
- English political reforms that influence U.S. democracy

TERMS & NAMES

Briefly explain the importance of each of the following during the age of absolute monarchs in Europe.

1. absolute monarch
2. divine right
3. Louis XIV
4. War of the Spanish Succession
5. Thirty Years' War
6. Seven Years' War
7. Peter the Great
8. English Civil War
9. Glorious Revolution
10. constitutional monarchy

REVIEW QUESTIONS

SECTION 1 *(pages 133–137)*

Spain's Empire and European Absolutism

11. Name three actions that demonstrate that Philip II of Spain saw himself as a defender of Catholicism.

12. According to French writer Jean Bodin, should a prince share power with anyone else? Explain why or why not.

SECTION 2 *(pages 138–145)*

France's Ultimate Monarch

13. Name two ways that Louis XIV controlled the French nobility.

14. In what ways did Louis XIV cause suffering to the French people?

SECTION 3 *(pages 146–150)*

Central European Monarchs Clash

15. What were six results of the Peace of Westphalia?

16. What was the reason that Maria Theresa and Frederick the Great fought two wars against each other?

SECTION 4 *(pages 151–155)*

Russia Czars Increase Power

17. List three differences between Russia and western Europe.

18. What were Peter the Great's goals for Russia?

SECTION 5 *(pages 156–159)*

Parliament Limits the English Monarchy

19. Describe the causes, participants, and outcome of the English Civil War.

20. List at least three ways that Parliament tried to limit the power of the English monarchy.

Interact *with* History

On page 132, you made decisions about what type of palace you would build if you were a monarch. Now that you have read the chapter, would you say that your palace was more like the one built by Philip II of Spain or the one built by Louis XIV of France? Explain.

Interact *with* History

Standards for Evaluation

A response should meet these criteria:

- Shows knowledge of they key features of the Escorial and Versailles.
- Explains how the features of one palace more closely reflect the qualities the student wanted to demonstrate.

CRITICAL THINKING

1. IMPROVING THE ECONOMY

THEME ECONOMICS Of all the monarchs that you studied in this chapter, which one do you think helped his or her country's economy the most? Explain your answer by citing evidence from the chapter.

2. MONARCHS RULE ABSOLUTELY

Create a chart like the one shown. In the left-hand column of your chart, list actions that absolute monarchs often took to increase their power. Then for each action, name at least one monarch who actually did that. Use at least five different monarchs in your chart as examples.

Actions of absolute monarchs	Example of a monarch who did this

3. LAND GRABBERS

Many of the monarchs that you studied in this chapter tried to increase their countries' territory. Why might an absolute monarch want to gain territory? Explain what benefits these monarchs hoped to gain.

4. ANALYZING PRIMARY SOURCES

After the Glorious Revolution of 1688, Parliament passed the Bill of Rights in 1689. The following is an excerpt from that document. Read it and then answer the questions that follow.

A VOICE FROM THE PAST

That the pretended power of suspending [canceling] of laws or the execution [carrying out] of laws by regal authority without consent of Parliament is illegal; . . .

That it is the right of the subjects to petition [make requests of] the king, and all commitments [imprisonments] and prosecutions for such petitioning are illegal;

That the raising or keeping a standing army within the kingdom in time of peace, unless it be with consent of Parliament, is against the law; . . .

That election of members of Parliament ought to be free [not restricted].

Bill of Rights

- In what ways did Parliament limit the power of the monarch?
- How did the Parliament try to protect itself?

CHAPTER ACTIVITIES

1. LIVING HISTORY: Unit Portfolio Project

THEME REVOLUTION Your unit portfolio project focuses on showing the causes and results of various revolutions (see page 129). For Chapter 5, you might use one of the following ideas to add to your portfolio.

- Peter the Great tried to revolutionize Russian culture and society. Create an educational poster that Peter could have used to explain one practice he wanted his people to give up and what he wanted them to replace it with.
- Write an editorial stating whether you think the English Civil War or the Glorious Revolution was more revolutionary. To support your opinion, examine both short-term and long-term effects.
- Write a HistoryMaker, like the ones you've read throughout this textbook, focusing on Oliver Cromwell as a leader of a revolution.

2. CONNECT TO TODAY: Cooperative Learning

THEME POWER AND AUTHORITY One of the ideas that came out of this time period is that Parliament should prevent the English monarch from exercising too much power. In the United States, the legislative body also limits the power of the head of government. At the same time, in the United States the head of government—or chief executive—also limits the power of the legislature. Create a diagram that shows how these two branches of government limit each other's power.

- Use the Internet, the library, or other sources to research the various branches of the U.S. national government.
- Identify the legislative and executive branches of government and the powers of each. Especially note how each branch acts to limit the power of the other.
- Display this information on a diagram. Some of the diagrams in this textbook might provide ideas for how to use visual elements such as arrows to demonstrate relationships.

3. INTERPRETING A TIME LINE

Revisit the unit time line on pages 128–129. Use the Chapter 5 time line to find out when Louis XIV began his reign. What happened in England shortly after Louis took the throne? How might that have affected his views on monarchy?

FOCUS ON GEOGRAPHY

On the map, notice which modern European nations are still ruled by royal monarchs.

- Of the countries that you studied in this chapter, which have monarchs today?

Connect to History
- Which of those countries was a republic during the period of this chapter?
- Did the countries whose rulers exercised the most power retain the monarchy? Explain.

Modern European Monarchs

Nations with monarchs today

NORWAY, SWEDEN, DENMARK, UNITED KINGDOM, NETHERLANDS, BELGIUM, LUXEMBOURG, LIECHTENSTEIN, MONACO, SPAIN, ANDORRA

ATLANTIC OCEAN

500 Miles / 1,000 Kilometers

CHAPTER 6
Enlightenment and Revolution

	Key Ideas	COPY MASTERS	ASSESSMENT
SECTION 1 **The Scientific Revolution** *pp. 165–170*	*The Scientific Revolution begins as scientists replace old ideas with new theories. New approaches to science include using observation and experiments to develop theories. In astronomy, scientists challenge the earth-centered model of the universe.*	*In-Depth Resources: Unit 2* • **Guided Reading,** p. 19 • **Skillbuilder Practice:** Clarifiying, p. 23 • **Geography Application:** Three Theories of the Solar System, p. 24 • **Primary Source:** from *Starry Messenger,* p. 26 • **Literature:** from *The Recantation of Galileo Galilei,* p. 31 • **History Makers:** Copernicus, p. 34	*Section 1 Assessment,* p. 170 *Formal Assessment* • Section Quiz, p. 76 *Alternative Assessment Book* • Standards for Evaluating a Cooperative Activity
SECTION 2 **The Enlightenment in Europe** *pp. 171–177*	*Enlightenment philosophers admire scientists' use of reason to understand the natural world. These philosophers promote the use of reason to understand government, religion, education, and economics. They advocate government reform and social improvement.*	*In-Depth Resources: Unit 2* • **Guided Reading,** p. 20 • **Primary Sources:** from *The Social Contract,* p. 27; from *Two Treatises on Government,* p. 28; from *A Vindication of the Rights of Woman,* p. 29 • **History Makers:** Baron de Montesquieu, p. 35	*Section 2 Assessment,* p. 176 *Formal Assessment* • Section Quiz, p. 77 *Alternative Assessment Book* • Standards for Evaluating a Cooperative Activity
SECTION 3 **The Spread of Enlightenment Ideas** *pp. 178–182*	*Enlightenment ideas circulate in pamphlets and formal discussions. The new ideals of order and reason are reflected in the arts and music. European monarchs make limited reforms based on Enlightenment ideas.*	*In-Depth Resources: Unit 2* • **Guided Reading,** p. 21 • **Connections Across Time and Cultures:** The Search for Truth and Reason, p. 36	*Section 3 Assessment,* p. 182 *Formal Assessment* • Section Quiz, p. 78 *Alternative Assessment Book* • Standards for Evaluating a Cooperative Activity
SECTION 4 **American Revolution: The Birth of a Republic** *pp. 183–187*	*Colonists resist the laws and taxes imposed by the British. Colonial leaders use Enlightenment ideas to justify independence from Britain, and, after winning the Revolution, create a federal government.*	*In-Depth Resources: Unit 2* • **Guided Reading,** p. 22 • **Primary Source:** from The Declaration of Independence, p. 30	*Section 4 Assessment,* p. 187 *Formal Assessment* • Section Quiz, p. 79 *Alternative Assessment Book* • Standards for Evaluating a Cooperative Activity
CHAPTER RESOURCES	**Chapter Overview** *In Europe, scientists question old ideas and use reason to make discoveries about the natural world. Philosophers support the use of reason to reform government, religion, and society. Enlightenment ideas are used to create a federal government in the newly created United States.*	*Telescoping the Times* • Chapter Summary, pp. 25–27 *Planning for Block Schedules*	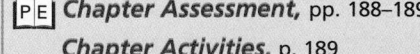 *Chapter Assessment,* pp. 188–189 *Chapter Activities,* p. 189 *Formal Assessment* • Chapter Test, forms A and B, pp. 80–85 *Test Generator* *Alternative Assessment Book*

TECHNOLOGY

 Warm-Up Transparency 6

 Geography Transparencies
• GT22 Maps of the World, 1492–1761

 World Art and Cultures Transparencies
• AT48 Vermeer's *The Astronomer*

 Electronic Library of Primary Sources
• "Of Studies"

 INTERNET RESOURCES
www.mlworldhistory.com

 Warm-Up Transparency 6

 Electronic Library of Primary Sources
• from *The Persian Letters*
• from *Gulliver's Travels*

 INTERNET RESOURCES
www.mlworldhistory.com

 Warm-Up Transparency 6

 World Art and Cultures Transparencies
• AT49 Goya's *The Pottery Vendor* (cartoon for a tapestry)

 Critical Thinking Transparencies
• CT22 The Spread of Enlightenment Ideas

 Electronic Library of Primary Sources
• Letter to Catherine the Great

 INTERNET RESOURCES
www.mlworldhistory.com

 Warm-Up Transparency 6

 Critical Thinking Transparencies
• CT58 Visual Summary

 Electronic Library of Primary Sources
• Conflicting Accounts of the Battles at Lexington and Concord

 INTERNET RESOURCES
www.mlworldhistory.com

 Chapter Summaries on Audiocassette in English and Spanish

INTERNET RESOURCES
www.mlworldhistory.com

Block Scheduling (90 MINUTES)

Day 1
Section 1, pp. 165–170
 COOPERATIVE ACTIVITY
p. 168 (Teacher's Edition)
Section Assessment, p. 170

Day 2
Section 2, pp. 171–177
 COOPERATIVE ACTIVITY
p. 173 (Teacher's Edition)

Section Assessment, p. 176

Day 3
Section 3, pp. 178–182
 COOPERATIVE ACTIVITY
p. 181 (Teacher's Edition)
Section Assessment, p.182

Day 4
Section 4, pp. 183–187
 COOPERATIVE ACTIVITY
p. 186 (Teacher's Edition)
Section Assessment, p. 187
Chapter Assessment, pp. 188–189

Yearly Pacing *Chapter 6 Total:* 4 days *Yearly Total:* 85 days

 Planning for Block Schedules

Customizing for Special Needs

Students Acquiring English

 Access for Students Acquiring English
• **Guided Reading** for Sections 1–4 (Spanish), pp. 71–74
• **Chapter Summary** (Spanish), pp. 68–70
• **Skillbuilder Practice** Clarifying (Spanish), p. 75
• **Geography Application** Three Theories of the Solar System (Spanish), pp. 76–77

 Spanish Reading Study Guide
• pp. 63–72

 Chapter Summaries on Audiocassette in English and Spanish

Less Proficient Readers

 In-Depth Resources: Unit 2
• **Guided Reading** for Sections 1–4, pp. 19–22
• **Skillbuilder Practice** Clarifying, p. 23
• **Geography Application** Three Theories of the Solar System, p. 24

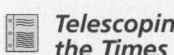 *Telescoping the Times*
• Chapter Summary, pp. 25–27

 Reading Study Guide
• pp. 63–72

 Chapter Summaries on Audiocassette

Gifted and Talented Students

 In-Depth Resources: Unit 2
Primary Sources:
• from *Starry Messenger*, p. 26
• from *The Social Contract*, p. 27
• from *Two Treatises on Government*, p. 28
• from *A Vindication of the Rights of Woman*, p. 29
• from The Declaration of Independence, p. 30

History Makers
• Copernicus, p. 34
• Baron de Montesquieu, p. 35

Connections to Literature READINGS FOR STUDENTS

 In-Depth Resources: Unit 2
Literature: from *The Recantation of Galileo Galilei*, p. 31

Enrichment Reading
• **Fast, Howard**
Citizen Tom Paine
New York: Duell, 1943

In this historical novel, the hot temper, feisty character, and extensive travels of Tom Paine are brought to life.

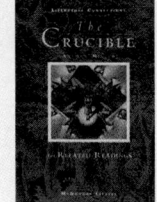

McDougal Littell
Literature Connections

• **Miller, Arthur**
The Crucible
(with related readings)

Injustice and hysteria take center stage in this historical drama about witchcraft accusations in Puritan New England.

 = Pupil's Edition   = Overhead Transparency   = Software   = Video

= Copy Master = CD-ROM = Audiocassette   = Internet

Enlightenment and Revolution, 1550–1789

CHAPTER
6 Enlightenment and Revolution, 1550–1789

Introducing the Chapter

Accessing Prior Knowledge

• Ask students to read the captions that accompany the pictures and discuss what they already know about the people and the situations.

Making Inferences and Drawing Conclusions

• After reading about Catherine the Great and about Rembrandt's painting, ask students to infer whether life in Europe was changing or staying the same during the Enlightenment. How can students tell?

• After reading about Patrick Henry, ask students to draw conclusions about the changes Henry is demanding.

Geography Connection

Ask students to study the maps and to use the map key to answer the questions.

• In which cities and countries were the centers of Enlightenment located?

• On which two continents are the centers of Enlightenment located?

PREVIEWING THEMES

Revolution

Between the 16th and 18th centuries, a series of revolutions helped usher in the modern era in Western history. First was a revolution in understanding, called the Scientific Revolution. Second was a revolution of ideas, called the Enlightenment. Third was a revolution in action—the American Revolution.

Science and Technology

The Scientific Revolution began when some astronomers questioned the old understanding of how the universe operates—one that was deeply tied to people's religious beliefs. By shattering this view, the astronomers opened a new universe of scientific discovery.

Power and Authority

Like their counterparts in science, the political thinkers of the Enlightenment challenged established ideas about power and authority. A ruler does not own authority by divine right, the thinkers said. Rather, a ruler receives authority by the consent of the people. Such ideas led to the political upheaval of the American Revolution.

INTERNET CONNECTION

Visit us at **www.mlworldhistory.com** to learn more about the Scientific Revolution, the Enlightenment, and the American Revolution.

CENTERS OF ENLIGHTENMENT, 1750

  Enlightenment centers

0 _____ 300 Miles
0 _____ 600 Kilometers

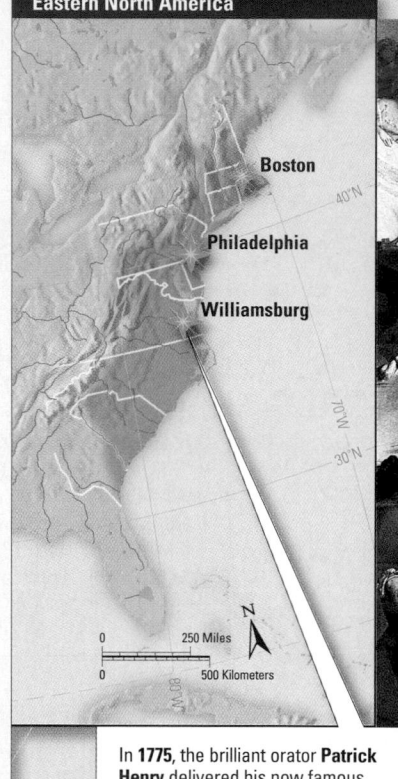

Eastern North America

Boston

Philadelphia

Williamsburg

0 ___ 250 Miles
0 ___ 500 Kilometers

SPAIN

ATLANTIC OCEAN

In **1775**, the brilliant orator **Patrick Henry** delivered his now famous speech to the Second Virginia Convention. In this speech he declared, "Give me liberty, or give me death!" In this 19th-century painting by artist Peter Rothermel, Henry speaks before the Virginia House of Burgesses. He repeatedly spoke against British laws that restricted the colonists' rights.

162

GEOGRAPHY THEMES

Location

Ask students to note the centers of Enlightenment in Europe. Then ask how students can tell that most of the Enlightenment ideas came from western Europe and not from Russia or Poland? *Most of the centers are in this area.* Next, have students use the scale to calculate the distance between Geneva and Milan, *(about 200 miles);* Paris and Warsaw, *(about 1050 miles);* and London and Austria, *(about 775 miles).* Point out that most of the centers of Enlightenment are close together in western Europe. Ask students how this might have affected the spread of ideas.

Movement

Ask students to look at the map of eastern North America. Remind students that in the 18th century, this region was the site of the British colonies. How can students tell from the map that the colonies were influenced by Europe?

How might Enlightenment ideas have spread to North America? Ask students to predict whether these ideas will strengthen or weaken ties between Europe and the colonies. Tell students to check their predictions as they read this chapter.

ADDITIONAL RESOURCES

Books for the Teacher

- A!mond, Mark. *Revolution: 500 Years of Struggle for Change.* New York: De Agostini, 1996. Account of 27 revolutions and movements.

- Durant, Will, and Ariel Durant. *The Age of Reason Begins.* New York: Simon, 1965. History of Enlightenment from 1558 to 1648.

- Shapin, Steven. *The Scientific Revolution.* Chicago: U of Chicago P, 1996.

Books for the Student

- Christianson, Gale E. *Isaac Newton and the Scientific Revolution.* New York: Oxford UP, 1996.

- Wilson, Ellen Judy, and Peter Hanns Reill. *Encyclopedia of the Enlightenment.* New York: Facts on File, 1996.

Videos

- *The Age of Enlightenment.* Cambridge Social Studies, 1991. 800-468-4227.

- *The Age of Reason: Europe After the Renaissance.* Knowledge Unlimited, 1995. 800-356-2303.

- *Galileo and the Universe.* BFA Educational, 1972. 800-221-1274.

Software

- *The Scientific Revolution.* CD-ROM. Society for Visual Education, 1994. 800-829-1900.

In **1762**, a former German princess succeeded her husband, Czar Peter III, and became Empress Catherine II of Russia. The brilliant empress ruled Russia for 34 years, vastly expanded Russian territory, and tried to create reforms. For her accomplishments, she is known to history as **Catherine the Great.**

The Guild of Surgeons-Anatomists of Amsterdam asked Rembrandt van Rijn to paint *Anatomy Lesson of Dr. Tulp* in **1632**. The corpse was that of a criminal. By the mid-1500s, European doctors had begun to dissect bodies for the first time to directly observe human anatomy. This contributed to a revolution in medical knowledge.

HISTORY THROUGH ART

Anatomy Lesson of Dr. Tulp

Rembrandt van Rijn

At age 26, Rembrandt was hired to paint a group portrait of the annual anatomy demonstration performed by the chief surgeon of Amsterdam for the city's guild of surgeons. The painting made Rembrandt the most popular portraitist in Amsterdam.

Until this time, group portraits usually focused on the heads of the subjects, which were arranged in a row. The *Anatomy Lesson* departs from this style in several ways. The heads of the surgeons form a pyramid, not a line. Rembrandt's use of light places emphasis on the anatomy lesson and not on the surgeons. Each surgeon's face bears a different expression. Rembrandt seems to have caught a moment in time, much as a photographer does.

The subject of Rembrandt's painting reflects the changes in science that were sweeping through western Europe at the time. Instead of relying on ancient ideas to understand the natural world, scientists were observing, performing experiments, and using their own reason to figure things out.

Interpreting the Art What are the surgeons trying to learn from Dr. Tulp? Where do the individual surgeons and the doctor seem to be looking? How has Rembrandt caught a moment in time?

Interact *with* History

This Interact with History feature motivates students by inviting them to put themselves in the place of a key historical figure—Galileo Galilei. As they imagine themselves having to choose between death and denying ideas they know are right, students will analyze the issues, explore their options, and become decision makers.

Purpose

• to prepare students for studying the Scientific Revolution and the Enlightenment

• to help students understand the intellectual climate in which the Scientific Revolution began

• to help students connect with the events and historical figures they will study in this chapter

EXAMINING *the* ISSUES

Following are suggestions for addressing each bulleted question.

1 Do students think this idea would have disappeared if Galileo had been killed? Who else had this idea?

2 Students may mention nuclear weapons as an example of dangerous knowledge. Does modern scientific knowledge seem mostly harmful or helpful?

3 Have students think of countries or periods in history when people have been persecuted for their beliefs.

Follow Up

A feature on the chapter assessment will ask students to reevaluate their responses to the situation presented on this page.

I t is the year 1633, and the Italian scientist Galileo Galilei faces a life-or-death dilemma. The Roman Inquisition, a court of the Catholic Church, has condemned him for holding an idea—that the earth revolves around the sun. The court has asked Galileo to publicly deny this idea. If he agrees, the court will show leniency. If he refuses, Galileo will likely face torture or a painful death.

The idea that the earth revolves around the sun had been put forth almost a century before by the Polish astronomer Copernicus. Galileo is firmly convinced that Copernicus was right. Galileo has been looking through a telescope at the planets and stars. What he has seen with his own eyes is proof enough of Copernicus's theory.

The church has denounced Copernicus's theory as dangerous to the faith. The idea that the earth is the center of the universe is part of church teachings. Church leaders have warned Galileo to stop defending the new theory. But Galileo has written a book that explains why Copernicus's ideas make sense. Now he is on trial.

Put yourself in the place of Galileo as he weighs the choice the Inquisition has given him.

Galileo tries to defend himself before the Inquisition. The court, however, demands that he recant.

Would you deny an idea you know to be true?

EXAMINING *the* ISSUES

• By silencing Galileo, the church wanted to suppress an idea. Do you think this was an effective strategy? Can an idea have a life of its own?

• Are there any cases in which an idea is too dangerous to be openly discussed or taught?

• Galileo faced persecution for teaching new ideas. Could this happen today?

Meet in small groups and discuss these questions. As you share ideas, recall other times in history when people expressed ideas that were different from accepted ones.

As you read this chapter, watch for the effects revolutionary ideas have on others.

① The Scientific Revolution

TERMS & NAMES
- Scientific Revolution
- Nicolaus Copernicus
- heliocentric theory
- Johannes Kepler
- Galileo Galilei
- scientific method
- Francis Bacon
- René Descartes
- Isaac Newton

MAIN IDEA

In the mid-1500s, scientists began to question accepted beliefs and make new theories based on experimentation.

WHY IT MATTERS NOW

Scientists' questioning led to the development of the scientific method still in use today.

SETTING THE STAGE The Renaissance inspired a spirit of curiosity in many fields. Scholars began to question ideas that had been accepted for hundreds of years. During the Reformation, religious leaders challenged accepted ways of thinking about God and salvation. While the Reformation was taking place, another revolution in European thought was also occurring. It challenged how people viewed their place in the universe.

The Roots of Modern Science

Before 1500, scholars generally decided what was true or false by referring to an ancient Greek or Roman author or to the Bible. Whatever Aristotle said about the material world was true unless the Bible said otherwise. Few European scholars questioned the scientific ideas of the ancient thinkers or the church by carefully observing nature for themselves.

The Medieval View During the Middle Ages, most scholars believed that the earth was an unmoving object located at the center of the universe. According to that belief, the moon, the sun, and the planets all moved in perfectly circular paths around the earth. Beyond the planets lay a sphere of fixed stars, with heaven still farther beyond. Common sense seemed to support this view. After all, the sun appeared to be moving around the earth as it rose in the morning and set in the evening.

This earth-centered view of the universe, called the geocentric theory, was supported by more than just common sense. The idea came from Aristotle, the Greek philosopher of the fourth century B.C. The Greek astronomer Ptolemy expanded the theory in the second century A.D. In addition, Christianity taught that God had deliberately placed earth at the center of the universe. Earth was thus a special place on which the great drama of life took place.

This drawing from an astrology text of 1531 shows the signs of the zodiac moving around the earth. It is based on Ptolemy's system, with the earth at the center.

A New Way of Thinking Beginning in the mid-1500s, a few scholars published works that challenged the ideas of the ancient thinkers and the church. As these scholars replaced old assumptions with new theories, they launched a change in European thought that historians call the Scientific Revolution. The **Scientific Revolution** was a new way of thinking about the natural world. That way was based upon careful observation and a willingness to question accepted beliefs.

A combination of discoveries and circumstances led to the Scientific Revolution and helped spread its impact. By the late Middle Ages, European scholars had translated many works by Muslim scholars. These scholars had compiled a storehouse of ancient and current scientific knowledge. Based on this knowledge, medieval universities added scientific courses in astronomy, physics, and mathematics.

During the Renaissance, scholars uncovered many classical manuscripts. They found that the ancient authorities often did not agree with each other. Moreover,

THINK THROUGH HISTORY
A. Analyzing Issues
Why did most people believe the geocentric theory?
A. Answer It was supported by common sense, the learned authority of Aristotle and Ptolemy, and church teachings.

Enlightenment and Revolution **165**

SECTION 1 RESOURCES

PRINT RESOURCES

IN-DEPTH RESOURCES: UNIT 2
Guided Reading, p. 19
Skillbuilder Practice: Clarifying, p. 23
Geography Application: Theories of the Solar System, p. 24
Primary Source: from *Starry Messenger*, p. 26
Literature: from *The Recantation of Galileo Galilei*, p. 31
History Makers: Copernicus, p. 34

ACCESS FOR STUDENTS ACQUIRING ENGLISH
Guided Reading (Spanish), p. 71
Skillbuilder Practice: (Spanish), p. 75
Geography Application: (Spanish), pp. 76–77

FORMAL ASSESSMENT
Section Quiz, p. 76

TECHNOLOGY RESOURCES

GEOGRAPHY TRANSPARENCIES
GT22 Maps of the World, 1492–1761

WORLD ART AND CULTURES TRANSPARENCIES
AT48 Vermeer's *The Astronomer*

CD-ROM
Electronic Library of Primary Sources

Section 1 Overview

OBJECTIVES

① To list circumstances that led to the Scientific Revolution.

② To summarize the development of the heliocentric theory and explain why it led to conflict.

③ To describe the scientific method and show how Bacon and Descartes advanced this approach.

④ To explain Newton's law of gravity.

⑤ To describe the importance of the scientific method in different fields.

CRITICAL THINKING

- Analyzing issues, p. 165
- Clarifying, pp. 166, 169
- Recognizing effects, p. 166
- Contrasting, p. 168
- Drawing conclusions, p. 170

FOCUS

5-Minute Warm-Up

▶ **Identifying Key Concepts**
To examine Enlightenment ideas, have students answer these questions.

1. Study the Changing Idea chart on page 168. What were the old methods used to understand the physical world?

2. What new methods replaced the old methods?

WARM-UP TRANSPARENCY 6

OBJECTIVE ① INSTRUCT

The Roots of Modern Science

▶ **Key Ideas**
- Medieval scholars have a geocentric view of the universe.
- Exploration and new discoveries challenge old ways of thinking about the world and lead to the Scientific Revolution.

IN-DEPTH RESOURCES: UNIT 2
Guided Reading, p. 19

ACCESS FOR STUDENTS ACQUIRING ENGLISH
Guided Reading (Spanish), 71

(continued on next page)

Teacher's Edition **165**

(continued from page 165)

 GEOGRAPHY TRANSPARENCIES
GT22 Maps of the World, 1492–1761

OBJECTIVE **2** INSTRUCT

A Revolutionary Model of the Universe

▶ *Key Ideas*
- Scientists develop the heliocentric theory through observation and mathematics.
- Galileo's observations and his laws of motion support the heliocentric theory.
- Galileo's ideas conflict with religious teaching and authority, and lead to his arrest.

 IN-DEPTH RESOURCES: UNIT 2
Geography Application: Three Theories of the Solar System, p. 24
History Makers: Copernicus, p. 34

 WORLD ART AND CULTURES TRANSPARENCIES
AT48 Vermeer's *The Astronomer*

CRITICAL THINKING ACTIVITY
CLASS TIME: 15 MINUTES

Sequence
To help students understand the development of the heliocentric theory, have them create a flow chart like the one below. After each scientist's name, students should write his contribution to the theory.

Copernicus
↓
Tycho Brahe
↓
Johannes Kepler
↓
Galileo

European explorers traveled to Africa, Asia, and the Americas. Such lands were inhabited by peoples and animals previously unknown in Europe. These discoveries opened Europeans to the possibility that there were new truths to be found. The invention of the printing press during this period helped spread challenging ideas—both old and new—more widely among Europe's thinkers.

The age of European exploration also fueled a great deal of scientific research, especially in astronomy and mathematics. Navigators needed better instruments and geographic measurements, for example, to determine their location in the open sea. As scientists began to look more closely at the world around them, they made observations that did not match the ancient beliefs. They found they had reached the limit of the classical world's knowledge. Yet, they still needed to know more.

A Revolutionary Model of the Universe

The first major challenge to accepted scientific thinking came in the field of astronomy. The Scientific Revolution started when a small group of scholars began to question the geocentric theory.

This model shows how Copernicus saw the planets revolving around the sun—in perfect circles.

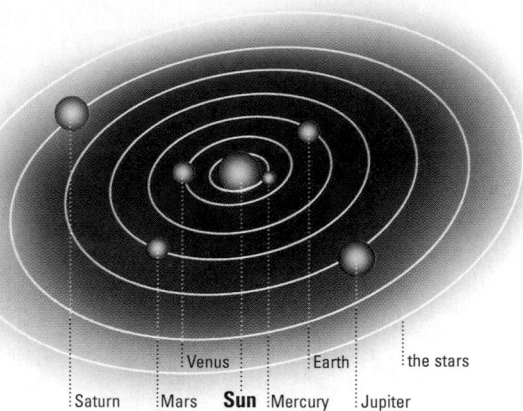

Saturn | Mars | **Sun** | Mercury | Jupiter
Venus | Earth | the stars

The Heliocentric Theory Although backed by authority and common sense, the geocentric theory did not accurately explain the movements of the sun, moon, and planets. This problem troubled a Polish cleric and astronomer named **Nicolaus Copernicus** (koh·PUR·nuh·kuhs). In the early 1500s, Copernicus became interested in an old Greek idea that the sun stood at the center of the universe. After studying planetary movements for more than 25 years, Copernicus reasoned that indeed, the stars, the earth, and the other planets revolved around the sun.

Copernicus's **heliocentric,** or sun-centered, **theory** still did not completely explain why the planets orbited the way they did. He also knew that most scholars and clergy would reject his theory because it contradicted their religious views. Fearing ridicule or persecution, Copernicus did not publish his findings until 1543, the last year of his life. He received a copy of his book, *On the Revolutions of the Heavenly Bodies,* on his deathbed.

While revolutionary, Copernicus's book caused little stir at first. Over the next century and a half, other scientists built on the foundations he had laid. A Danish astronomer, Tycho Brahe (TEE·koh brah), carefully recorded the movements of the planets for many years. Brahe produced mountains of accurate data based on his observations. However, it was left to his followers to make mathematical sense of them.

After Brahe's death in 1601, his assistant, a brilliant mathematician named **Johannes Kepler,** continued his work. After studying Brahe's data, Kepler concluded that certain mathematical laws govern planetary motion. One of these laws showed that the planets revolve around the sun in elliptical orbits instead of circles, as was previously thought. Kepler's laws showed that Copernicus's basic ideas were true. They demonstrated mathematically that the planets revolve around the sun.

Galileo's Discoveries In 1581, a 17-year-old Italian student named **Galileo Galilei** sat in a cathedral closely watching a chandelier swing on its chain. Aristotle had said that a pendulum swings at a slower rhythm as it approaches its resting place. Using his beating pulse, Galileo carefully timed the chandelier's swings. Aristotle's idea was wrong. Instead, each swing of the pendulum took exactly the same amount of time. Galileo had discovered the law of the pendulum.

THINK THROUGH HISTORY
B. Clarifying How did Copernicus arrive at the heliocentric theory?
B. Answer He studied planetary movements for 25 years and reasoned from these observations.

THINK THROUGH HISTORY
C. Recognizing Effects How did Kepler's findings support the heliocentric theory?
C. Answer They supported the theory mathematically.

Explaining the Skill: To clarify concepts in their reading material, students should define unfamiliar terms in the material and restate the content in their own words. This process can help reinforce students' understanding of the concepts.

Applying the Skill: To understand how the heliocentric model developed, students will need to understand some key terms. Ask students to use a dictionary and the Glossary on page 673 to define the following terms: *geocentric theory, heliocentric theory, revolved, orbited, elliptical orbit.*

Next, have students reread the passage titled "The Heliocentric Theory" on page 166. Then have students work in pairs to write questions about the main ideas of the passage. One possible question might be "How did the heliocentric theory develop?"

Suggest students use the Think Through History questions in the margin, as well as their own questions, and write their own answers to them. Partners should answer the questions in their own words and use their answers to write a summary of the passage. Encourage students to read their summaries aloud.

 IN-DEPTH RESOURCES: UNIT 2
Skillbuilder Practice: Clarifying , p. 23

Galileo used this telescope to observe the moon. He saw that the moon's surface is rough, not smooth as others thought.

In another study, Galileo found that a falling object accelerates at a fixed and predictable rate. Galileo also tested Aristotle's theory that heavy objects fall faster than lighter ones. According to legend, he dropped stones of different weights from the Leaning Tower of Pisa. He then calculated how fast each fell. Contrary to Aristotle's assumption, the objects fell at the same speed.

Later, Galileo learned that a Dutch lens maker had built an instrument that could enlarge far-off objects. Without seeing this device, Galileo successfully built his own telescope. After making some improvements, Galileo used his telescope to study the heavens in 1609.

Then in 1610, he published a little book called *Starry Messenger*, which described his astonishing observations. Galileo announced that Jupiter had four moons and that the sun had dark spots. He also noted that the earth's moon had a rough and uneven surface. His description of the moon's surface shattered Aristotle's theory that the moon and stars were made of a pure and perfect substance. Galileo's observations, as well as his laws of motion, also clearly supported the theories of Copernicus.

Conflict with the Church Galileo's findings frightened both Catholic and Protestant leaders because they went against church teaching and authority. If people believed the church could be wrong about this, they could question other church teachings as well.

In 1616, the Catholic Church warned Galileo not to defend the ideas of Copernicus. Although Galileo remained publicly silent, he continued his studies. Then, in 1632, he published *Dialogue Concerning the Two Chief World Systems*. This book presented the ideas of both Copernicus and Ptolemy, but it clearly showed that Galileo supported the Copernican theory. The pope angrily summoned Galileo to Rome to stand trial before the Inquisition.

Galileo stood before the court in 1633. Under the threat of torture, he knelt before the cardinals and read aloud a signed confession. In it, he agreed that the ideas of Copernicus were false.

> **A VOICE FROM THE PAST**
> With sincere heart and unpretended faith I abjure, curse, and detest the aforesaid errors and heresies [of Copernicus] and also every other error . . . contrary to the Holy Church, and I swear that in the future I will never again say or assert . . . anything that might cause a similar suspicion toward me.
>
> **GALILEO GALILEI,** quoted in *The Discoverers*

Galileo was never again a free man. He lived under house arrest and died in 1642 at his villa near Florence. However, his books and ideas still spread all over Europe.

The Scientific Method

The revolution in scientific thinking that Copernicus, Kepler, and Galileo began eventually developed into a new approach to science called the scientific method. The **scientific method** is a logical procedure for gathering and testing ideas. It begins with a problem or question arising from an observation. Scientists next form a hypothesis, or unproved assumption. The hypothesis is then tested in an experiment or on the basis of data. In the final step, scientists analyze and interpret their data to reach a new conclusion. That conclusion either confirms or disproves the hypothesis.

The scientific method did not develop overnight. The work of two important thinkers of the 1600s, Francis Bacon and René Descartes, helped to advance the new approach.

Francis Bacon, an English politician and writer, had a passionate interest in science. He believed that by better understanding the world, scientists would generate practical knowledge that would improve people's lives. In his writings, Bacon attacked medieval

CONNECT to TODAY

The Vatican Clears Galileo

In 1992, Pope John Paul II officially acknowledged that Galileo was correct in asserting that the earth revolves around the sun. His pronouncement came after a 13-year study of Galileo's case by a Vatican science panel.

The panel concluded that church leaders were clearly wrong to condemn Galileo but that they had acted in good faith. They were working within the knowledge of their time, the panel said. Therefore, they could not see how Galileo's discoveries could go along with their interpretation of the Bible.

Enlightenment and Revolution **167**

Major Steps in the Scientific Revolution

Interpreting the Chart Have students read the time line. Then ask students how they can tell that the scientific revolution was spreading by the 1600s. *Answer: Important scientific events are more frequent after 1600.*

Extension Activity Tell students to connect early events on the time line with later scientific developments. For example, the invention of the microscope in 1590 probably led to the observation of bacteria in 1674.

OBJECTIVE 4 INSTRUCT

Newton Explains the Law of Gravity

▶ **Key Ideas**
• Newton's law of gravity explains how the same physical laws govern motion on the earth and in the heavens.

MORE ABOUT . . .
Newton's Law of Gravity

What does an apple have to do with gravity? According to George Stukeley, Newton's biographer and close friend, Newton was sitting in the shade of an apple tree when an apple fell nearby. Newton was in a thoughtful mood and began to wonder why apples always fall to the ground. Why don't they fall sideways or up? Newton reasoned that the earth must have a power that draws objects to it. This was the beginning of the law of gravity.

Nicolaus Copernicus began the Scientific Revolution with his heliocentric theory.

Major Steps in the Scientific Revolution

1543 Copernicus publishes heliocentric theory.
Vesalius publishes human anatomy textbook.

1572 Brahe discovers nova, or bright new star, which contradicts Aristotle's idea that universe is unchanging.

1590 Janssen invents microscope.

1609 Kepler publishes first two laws of planetary motion.

1610 Galileo publishes *Starry Messenger*.

1620 Bacon's book *Novum Organum (New Instrument)* encourages experimental method.

1520 ... 1570 ... 1620

This microscope dates from the 17th century.

scholars for relying too heavily on the conclusions of Aristotle and other ancient thinkers. He also criticized the way in which both Aristotle and medieval scholars arrived at their conclusions. They had reasoned from abstract theories. Instead, he urged scientists to experiment. Scientists, he wrote, should observe the world and gather information about it first. Then they should draw conclusions from that information. This approach is called empiricism, or the experimental method.

In France, **René Descartes** (day-KAHRT) also took a keen interest in science. He developed analytical geometry, which linked algebra and geometry. This provided an important new tool for scientific research.

Like Bacon, Descartes believed that scientists needed to reject old assumptions and teachings. As a mathematician, however, his approach to gaining knowledge differed from Bacon's. Rather than using experimentation, Descartes relied on mathematics and logic. He believed that everything should be doubted until proved by reason. The only thing he knew for certain was that he existed—because, as he wrote, "I think, therefore I am." From this starting point, he followed a train of strict reasoning to arrive at other basic truths.

Modern scientific methods are based on the ideas of Bacon and Descartes. Scientists have shown that observation and experimentation, together with general laws that can be expressed mathematically, can lead people to a better understanding of the natural world.

THINK THROUGH HISTORY
D. Contrasting How did Descartes's approach to science differ from Bacon's?
D. Answer Descartes emphasized mathematical reasoning; Bacon, experimentation.

Changing Idea: Scientific Method

Old Science
Scholars generally relied on ancient authorities, church teachings, common sense, and reasoning to explain the physical world.

New Science
In time, scholars began to use observation, experimentation, and scientific reasoning to gather knowledge and draw conclusions about the physical world.

Newton Explains the Law of Gravity

By the mid-1600s, the accomplishments of Copernicus, Kepler, and Galileo had shattered the old views of astronomy and physics. Later, the great English scientist **Isaac Newton** helped to bring together their breakthroughs under a single theory of motion.

Newton studied mathematics and physics at Cambridge University. By the time he was 24, Newton was certain that all physical objects were affected equally by the same forces. Kepler had worked out laws for a planet's motion around the sun. Galileo had studied the motion of pendulums. Newton's great discovery was that the same force ruled the motions of the planets, the pendulum, and all matter on earth and in space.

168 Chapter 6

COOPERATIVE ACTIVITY: Technology Interviews

CLASS TIME 30 MINUTES

Task: Partners will conduct interviews to find out how people of different generations have reacted to technological developments. Partners will present the results of their interviews.

Purpose: To learn how people feel about new ideas.

Activity: Tell partners to interview three people from three different generations to find out how they reacted to technological developments such as space travel, television, computers, and other recent developments. Partners should make a list of interview questions that ask people to recall an important development, how they learned about it, how they and others reacted to it, and how the new development affected their lives. Suggest students interview parents, grandparents, other relatives, neighbors, and friends. Have partners take notes during the interviews and use the notes as a basis for presenting the results of their interviews. Remind partners to include in their presentations background information about each interview subject, such as age, occupation, and whether the person is a friend or relative.

 ALTERNATIVE ASSESSMENT BOOK
Standards for Evaluating a Cooperative Activity

1628 Harvey reveals how human heart functions.

1637 Descartes's book *Discourse on Method* sets forth his scientific method of reasoning from the basis of doubt.

1662 Boyle discovers mathematical relationship between the pressure and volume of gases, known as Boyle's law.

1674 Leeuwenhoek observes bacteria through microscope.

1714 Fahrenheit invents mercury thermometer.

1620 • • • • 1670 • • 1720

1633 Galileo faces Inquisition for support of Copernicus's theory.

1643 Torricelli invents barometer.

1660 England establishes Royal Society to support scientific study.

1666 France establishes Academy of Sciences.

1687 Newton publishes law of gravity.

Isaac Newton's law of gravity explained how the same physical laws governed motion both on the earth and in the heavens.

He disproved the idea of Aristotle that one set of physical laws governed earth and another set governed the rest of the universe.

The key idea that linked motion in the heavens with motion on the earth was the law of universal gravitation. According to this law, every object in the universe attracts every other object. The degree of attraction depends on the mass of the objects and the distance between them.

In 1687, Newton published his ideas in a work called *Mathematical Principles of Natural Philosophy*—one of the most important scientific books ever written. The universe he described was like a giant clock. Its parts all worked together perfectly in ways that could be expressed mathematically. Newton believed that God was the creator of this orderly universe, the clockmaker who had set everything in motion.

The Scientific Revolution Spreads

After astronomers explored the secrets of the universe, other scientists began to study the secrets of nature on earth. Careful observation and the use of the scientific method eventually became important in many different fields.

Scientific Instruments Scientists developed new tools and instruments to make the precise observations that the scientific method demanded. The first microscope was invented by a Dutch maker of eyeglasses, Zacharias Janssen (YAHN·suhn), in 1590. In the 1670s, a Dutch drapery merchant and amateur scientist named Anton van Leeuwenhoek (LAY·vuhn·HUK) used a microscope to observe bacteria swimming in tooth scrapings. He also saw red blood cells for the first time. His examination of grubs, maggots, and other such organisms showed that they did not come to life spontaneously, as was previously thought. Rather, they were immature insects.

In 1643, one of Galileo's students, Evangelista Torricelli (TAWR·uh·CHEHL·ee), developed the first mercury barometer, a tool for measuring atmospheric pressure and predicting weather. In 1714, the Dutch physicist Gabriel Fahrenheit (FAR·uhn·HYT) made the first thermometer to use mercury in glass. Fahrenheit's thermometer showed water freezing at 32°. A Swedish astronomer, Anders Celsius (SEHL·see·uhs), created another scale for the mercury thermometer in 1742. Celsius's scale showed freezing at 0°.

Medicine and the Human Body During the Middle Ages, European doctors had accepted as fact the writings of an ancient Greek physician named Galen. However, Galen had never dissected the body of a human being. Instead, he had studied the anatomy of pigs and other animals. Galen assumed that human anatomy was much the same. Galen's assumptions were proved wrong by Andreas Vesalius, a Flemish physician. Vesalius dissected human corpses (despite disapproval of this practice) and published his observations. His book, *On the Fabric of the Human Body* (1543), was filled with detailed drawings of human organs, bones, and muscle.

Enlightenment and Revolution **169**

An English doctor named William Harvey continued Vesalius's work in anatomy. In 1628, he published *On the Motion of the Heart and Blood in Animals,* which showed that the heart acted as a pump to circulate blood throughout the body. He also described the function of blood vessels.

In the late 1700s, British physician Edward Jenner introduced a vaccine to prevent smallpox. Inoculation using live smallpox germs had been practiced in Asia for centuries. While beneficial, this technique was also dangerous. Jenner discovered that inoculation with germs from a cattle disease called cowpox gave permanent protection from smallpox for humans. Because cowpox was a much milder disease, the risks for this form of inoculation were much lower. Jenner used cowpox to produce the world's first vaccination.

Vocabulary
inoculation: injecting a germ into a person's body so as to create an immunity to the disease.

Discoveries in Chemistry Robert Boyle pioneered the use of the scientific method in chemistry. He is considered the founder of modern chemistry. In a book called *The Sceptical Chymist* (1661), Boyle challenged Aristotle's idea that the physical world consisted of four elements—earth, air, fire, and water. Instead, Boyle proposed that matter was made up of smaller primary particles that joined together in different ways. Boyle's most famous contribution to chemistry is Boyle's law. This law explains how the volume, temperature, and pressure of gas affect each other.

Another chemist, Joseph Priestley, separated one pure gas from air in 1774. He noticed how good he felt after breathing this special air and watched how alert two mice were while breathing it. Wrote Priestley, "Who can tell but that, in time, this pure air may become a fashionable article of luxury? Hitherto only two mice and I have had the privilege of breathing it." Meanwhile, in France, Antoine Lavoisier (lah·vwah·ZYAY) was performing similar experiments. In 1779, Lavoisier named the newly discovered gas oxygen.

Other scholars and philosophers applied a scientific approach to other areas of life. Believing themselves to be orderly, rational, and industrious, they thought of themselves as enlightened. They would become the leaders of a new intellectual and social movement called the Enlightenment.

Section ❶ Assessment

1. TERMS & NAMES

Identify
- Scientific Revolution
- Nicolaus Copernicus
- heliocentric theory
- Johannes Kepler
- Galileo Galilei
- scientific method
- Francis Bacon
- René Descartes
- Isaac Newton

2. TAKING NOTES

Use a web diagram such as the one below to show the events and circumstances that led to the Scientific Revolution.

Causes of the
Scientific Revolution

3. DRAWING CONCLUSIONS

"If I have seen farther than others," said Newton, "it is because I have stood on the shoulders of giants." Who were the giants to whom Newton was referring? Could this be said of any scientific accomplishment? Explain.

4. THEME ACTIVITY

Science & Technology Working in groups of three or four, create a Scientific Revolution Discovery Board. Use these categories: Astronomy, Science, Medicine, Chemistry, Biology. Include important people, ideas, accomplishments.

170 Chapter 6

ANSWERS

The Enlightenment in Europe

TERMS & NAMES
- Enlightenment
- social contract
- John Locke
- natural rights
- philosophe
- Voltaire
- Montesquieu
- separation of powers
- Jean Jacques Rousseau
- Mary Wollstonecraft

MAIN IDEA

A revolution in intellectual activity changed Europeans' view of government and society.

WHY IT MATTERS NOW

Freedoms and some forms of government in many countries today are a result of Enlightenment thinking.

SETTING THE STAGE The influence of the Scientific Revolution soon spread beyond the world of science. Philosophers admired Newton because he had used reason to explain the laws governing nature. People began to look for laws governing human behavior as well. They hoped to apply reason and the scientific method to all aspects of society—government, religion, economics, and education. In this way, the ideas of the Scientific Revolution paved the way for a new movement called the **Enlightenment,** or the Age of Reason. This movement reached its height in the mid-1700s.

Two Views on Government

The Enlightenment started from some key ideas put forth by two English political thinkers of the 1600s, Thomas Hobbes and John Locke. Both men experienced the political turmoil of England early in that century. However, they came to very different conclusions about government and human nature.

Hobbes's Social Contract Thomas Hobbes expressed his views in a work called *Leviathan* (1651). The horrors of the English Civil War convinced him that all humans were naturally selfish and wicked. Without governments to keep order, Hobbes said, there would be "war of every man against every man." In this state of nature, as Hobbes called it, life would be "solitary, poor, nasty, brutish, and short."

Hobbes argued that to escape such a bleak life, people gave up their rights to a strong ruler. In exchange, they gained law and order. Hobbes called this agreement, by which people created government, the **social contract.** Because people acted in their own self-interest, Hobbes said, the ruler needed total power to keep citizens under control. The best government was one that had the awesome power of a leviathan (sea monster). In Hobbes's view, such a government was an absolute monarchy, which could impose order and demand obedience.

Locke's Natural Rights The philosopher **John Locke** held a different, more positive, view of human nature. He believed that people could learn from experience and improve themselves. As reasonable beings, they had the natural ability to govern their own affairs and to look after the welfare of society. Locke criticized absolute monarchy and favored the idea of self-government.

According to Locke, all people are born free and equal, with three **natural rights**— life, liberty, and property. The purpose of government, said Locke, is to protect these rights. If a government fails to do so, citizens have a right to overthrow it. Locke

This engraving depicts the beheading of Charles I. Hobbes developed his political ideas out of the violent events in England in the early 1600s.

Enlightenment and Revolution **171**

A. Possible Answer People enter into a social contract with a strong ruler to gain safety and security.

B. Possible Answer Hobbes believed that humans were naturally selfish and wicked; Locke's view was more positive— humans were reasonable, could learn and grow, and had natural rights.

THINK THROUGH HISTORY
A. Clarifying According to Hobbes, why would people want to live under the rule of an absolute monarch?

THINK THROUGH HISTORY
B. Contrasting How does Locke's view of human nature differ from that of Hobbes?

SECTION 2 RESOURCES

PRINT RESOURCES

📖 **IN-DEPTH RESOURCES: UNIT 2**
Guided Reading, p. 20
Primary Source: from *The Social Contract,* p. 27; from *Two Treatises on Government,* p. 28; from *A Vindication of the Rights of Women,* p. 29
History Makers: Baron de Montesquieu, p. 35

📖 **ACCESS FOR STUDENTS ACQUIRING ENGLISH**
Guided Reading (Spanish), p. 72

📄 **FORMAL ASSESSMENT**
Section Quiz, p. 77

📄 **ALTERNATIVE ASSESSMENT BOOK**

TECHNOLOGY RESOURCES
💿 **CD-ROM**
Electronic Library of Primary Sources
🌐 **INTERNET** www.mworldhistory.com

Section 2 Overview

OBJECTIVES

① To explain Hobbes's and Locke's views on government.

② To list important Enlightenment philosophers and concepts.

③ To describe women's contributions to the Enlightenment.

④ To explain the impact of the Enlightenment on Western civilization.

SKILLBUILDER
- Interpreting charts, p. 174

CRITICAL THINKING
- Clarifying, pp. 171, 174, 177
- Contrasting, p. 171
- Comparing, p. 172
- Analyzing issues, p. 173
- Summarizing, p. 174
- Drawing conclusions, p. 175
- Synthesizing, p. 176
- Analyzing themes, p. 176

FOCUS
5-Minute Warm-Up

Drawing Conclusions
To understand Enlightenment ideas about government, have students answer these questions.

1. Study the Changing Idea chart on page 172. According to the old idea, where does a monarch's power come from?

2. According to the new idea, where should a government's power come from?

📖 **WARM-UP TRANSPARENCY 6**

OBJECTIVE ① INSTRUCT

Two Views on Government

▶ **Key Ideas**
- Hobbes believes that people need a strong government to keep order.
- Locke believes that people have a natural ability to govern themselves.

(continued on next page)

OBJECTIVE 1 INSTRUCT

(continued from page 171)

- Locke's ideas about government are the foundation of modern democracy.

 IN-DEPTH RESOURCES: UNIT 2
Guided Reading, p. 20
Primary Source: from *Two Treatises on Government,* p. 28

ACCESS FOR STUDENTS ACQUIRING ENGLISH
Guided Reading (Spanish), p. 72

OBJECTIVE 2 INSTRUCT

The Philosophes Advocate Reason

▶ *Key Ideas*

- The five important philosophical concepts are reason, nature, happiness, progress, and liberty.
- Voltaire fights intolerance through his writing.
- Montesquieu believes a government's power should be divided into different branches.
- Rousseau believes governments should be formed through the agreement of free individuals.
- Beccaria's ideas about the justice system promote criminal justice.

 ELECTRONIC LIBRARY OF PRIMARY SOURCES
from *The Persian Letters*

HISTORY MAKERS
Voltaire

Voltaire is credited with having made the following famous statement: "I disapprove of what you say, but I will defend to the death your right to say it." What does this statement indicate about Voltaire's views on free speech? How is it similar to beliefs about free speech in the United States?

Changing Idea: The Right to Govern

Old Idea
A monarch's rule is justified by divine right.

New Idea
A government's power comes from the consent of the governed.

---

published his ideas in 1690, two years after the Glorious Revolution. His book, *Two Treatises on Government,* served to justify the overthrow of James II.

Locke's theory had a deep influence on modern political thinking. His statement that a government's power comes from the consent of the people is the foundation of modern democracy. The ideas of government by popular consent and the right to rebel against unjust rulers helped inspire struggles for liberty in Europe and the Americas.

HISTORY MAKERS

Voltaire
1694–1778

Voltaire corresponded with several European monarchs and nobles. Among them was the Prussian king Frederick II. At the king's invitation, Voltaire spent three years at Frederick's palace. At first, the two men seemed like ideal companions. Both were witty. Both cared nothing for appearances and dressed in shabby, rumpled clothes. Each friend paid the other elegant compliments.

Before long, however, the king and the philosophe got on each other's nerves. Voltaire disliked editing Frederick's mediocre poetry. Frederick suspected Voltaire of some shady business dealings. Eventually, Voltaire tried to sneak away, but Prussian soldiers captured him and made him spend the night in jail.

After returning to France, Voltaire described the Prussian king as "a nasty monkey, perfidious friend, [and] wretched poet." Frederick returned the abuse, calling Voltaire a "miser, dirty rogue, [and] coward."

The Philosophes Advocate Reason

The Enlightenment reached its height in France in the mid-1700s. Paris became the meeting place for people who wanted to discuss politics and ideas. The social critics of this period in France were known as **philosophes** (FIHL·uh·SAHFS), the French word for philosophers. The philosophes believed that people could apply reason to all aspects of life—just as Isaac Newton had applied reason to science. Five important concepts formed the core of their philosophy:

1. **Reason** Enlightened thinkers believed truth could be discovered through reason or logical thinking. Reason, they said, was the absence of intolerance, bigotry, or prejudice in one's thinking.

2. **Nature** The philosophes referred to nature frequently. To them, what was natural was also good and reasonable. They believed that there were natural laws of economics and politics just as there were natural laws of motion.

3. **Happiness** A person who lived by nature's laws would find happiness, the philosophes said. They were impatient with the medieval notion that people should accept misery in this world to find joy in the hereafter. The philosophes wanted well-being on earth, and they believed it was possible.

4. **Progress** The philosophes were the first Europeans to believe in progress for society. Now that people used a scientific approach, they believed, society and humankind could be perfected.

5. **Liberty** The philosophes envied the liberties that the English people had won in their Glorious Revolution and Bill of Rights. In France, there were many restrictions on speech, religion, trade, and personal travel. Through reason, the philosophes believed, society could be set free.

Voltaire Combats Intolerance Probably the most brilliant and influential of the philosophes was François Marie Arouet. Using the pen name **Voltaire,** he published more than 70 books of political essays, philosophy, history, fiction, and drama.

Voltaire often used satire against his opponents. He made frequent targets of the clergy, the aristocracy, and the government. His sharp tongue made him enemies at the French court, and twice he was sent to prison. After his second jail term, Voltaire was exiled to England for two years. There, Voltaire came to admire the English government much more than his own. After he returned to Paris,

C. Possible Answer
Nature good and reasonable, betterment and progress possible, believed in human liberty.

THINK THROUGH HISTORY
C. Comparing How were the philosophes' views similar to Locke's?

Vocabulary
satire: irony, sarcasm, or wit used to attack folly, vice, or stupidity.

MULTIPLE LEARNING STYLES

Kinesthetic Learners: Role-Playing Students who process knowledge best through hands-on activities may benefit from using role-play to understand the philosophes' concepts. Have students work in groups of five. Each group member should choose one of the five philosophical

concepts described on page 172. After group members have reviewed the concepts, have them discuss and describe them by role-playing philosophes. Encourage the philosophes to ask each other questions about the concepts. Suggest groups perform their discussions for the class.

CUSTOMIZING FOR SPECIAL NEEDS

Gifted and Talented Students: Montesquieu Biography After students have read the information about Montesquieu on page 173, distribute the biography of Montesquieu from the Teacher's Resources. Have students read the biography and then work in pairs to answer the questions. After all pairs have finished, have them discuss

their answers as a group. Suggest students also discuss the new information they learned about Montesquieu from the biography. Then ask volunteers to present the questions and their answers to the rest of the class.

 IN-DEPTH RESOURCES: UNIT 2
History Makers: *Baron de Montesquieu,* p. 35

much of his work mocked the laws and customs of France. He even dared to raise doubts about the Christian religion. The French king and France's Catholic bishops were outraged. In 1734, fearing another unpleasant jail term, Voltaire fled Paris.

Although he made powerful enemies, Voltaire never stopped fighting for tolerance, reason, freedom of religious belief, and freedom of speech. He used his quill pen as if it were a deadly weapon in a thinker's war against humanity's worst enemies—intolerance, prejudice, and superstition. Such attitudes were, he said, *l'infâme*—infamous or evil things. He often ended his letters with a fighting slogan, *"Écrasez l'infâme!"* (ay·crah·ZAY lahn·FAM). The phrase meant "Crush the evil thing!"

Montesquieu and the Separation of Powers Another influential French writer, the Baron de **Montesquieu** (MAHN·tuh·SKYOO), devoted himself to the study of political liberty. An aristocrat and lawyer, Montesquieu studied the history of ancient Rome. He concluded that Rome's collapse was directly related to its loss of political liberties.

Like Voltaire, Montesquieu believed that Britain was the best-governed country of his own day. Here was a government, he thought, in which power was balanced among three groups of officials. The British king and his ministers held executive power. They carried out the laws of the state. The members of Parliament held legislative, or lawmaking, power. The judges of the English courts held judicial power. They interpreted the laws to see how each applied to a specific case. Montesquieu called this division of power among different branches **separation of powers.**

THINK THROUGH HISTORY
D. Analyzing Issues What advantages did Montesquieu see in the separation of powers?
D. Answer It would keep any individual or group from gaining total power; each branch would check the power of the other two.

Montesquieu oversimplified the British system (it did not actually separate powers this way). His idea, however, became a part of his most famous book, *On the Spirit of Laws* (1748). In his book, Montesquieu proposed that separation of powers would keep any individual or group from gaining total control of the government. "Power," he wrote, "should be a check to power." Each branch of government would serve as a check on the other two. This idea later would be called "checks and balances."

"Power should be a check to power."
Baron de Montesquieu

Montesquieu's book was admired by political leaders in the British colonies of North America. His ideas about separation of powers and checks and balances became the basis for the United States Constitution.

Changing Idea: Government Powers

Old Idea
Monarch rules with absolute authority.

New Idea
Separation of government powers among executive, legislative, and judicial branches.

Rousseau: Champion of Freedom A third great philosophe, **Jean Jacques Rousseau** (roo·SOH), was passionately committed to individual freedom. The son of a poor Swiss watchmaker, Rousseau worked as an engraver, music teacher, tutor, and secretary. Eventually, Rousseau made his way to Paris and won recognition as a writer of essays. There he met and befriended other philosophes, although he felt out of place in the circles of Paris high society in which they traveled.

A strange, brilliant, and controversial figure, Rousseau strongly disagreed with other Enlightenment thinkers on many matters. Most philosophes believed that reason, science, and art would improve life for all people. Rousseau, however, argued that civilization corrupted people's natural goodness. "Man is born free, and everywhere he is in chains," he wrote. In the earliest times, according to Rousseau, people had lived as free and equal individuals in a primitive "state of nature." As people became civilized, however, the strongest among them forced everyone else to obey unjust laws. Thus, freedom and equality were destroyed.

"Man is born free, and everywhere he is in chains."
Jean Jacques Rousseau

Enlightenment and Revolution **173**

MORE ABOUT . . .
Voltaire's Early Years
Voltaire, born in Paris, was the son of a lawyer. He received an excellent education but chose not to follow his father into law. Instead, he ended his schooling at age 16 and devoted himself to literary pursuits. He joined a group of irreverent young aristocrats and began to write witty political verses. As a young man, Voltaire got himself into a certain amount of trouble with his writing, but he also managed to meet like-minded people. Through acquaintances with philosophers, artists, and thinkers, and also through his own desire to learn and understand the world, Voltaire became a great thinker.

MORE ABOUT . . .
Jean Jacques Rousseau
All through his life, Rousseau was plagued by feelings of guilt, depression, and inferiority. His attempts to form friendships often failed, and he spent his life as an outsider in society. These difficulties may have been the result of a very unhappy childhood. Rousseau's mother died giving birth to him. His father made him feel guilty for this and was either warm and affectionate or very cold and rejecting toward his son. When Rousseau was ten years old, his father abandoned him. As an adult, Rousseau realized he was more comfortable opposing society that trying to fit into it.

TEACHING OPTION | **BLOCK SCHEDULING** | **COOPERATIVE ACTIVITY: Enlightenment Philosophers** | **CLASS TIME 45 MINUTES**

Task: Groups will write reports about Enlightenment philosophers.

Purpose: To understand the ideas of the Enlightenment philosophers.

Activity: Divide the class into five groups and assign each group one of the following philosophers: Hobbes, Locke, Voltaire, Montesquieu, Rousseau. Group members should work together to research and write reports about their philosopher. Each group's report should explain who the man was, his ideas about government, and how he agreed or disagreed with the ideas of one of the other philosophers. Each group should choose one member to present its report to the class.

📁 **Building a Portfolio:** Remind students to place their best work in their portfolios.

📖 **ALTERNATIVE ASSESSMENT BOOK** Standards for Evaluating a Cooperative Activity

Standards for Evaluation
Reports should . . .

• clearly state the philosophers' ideas
• show evidence of research and group effort
• explain how the philosophers agreed and disagreed

Teacher's Edition **173**

Rousseau believed that the only good government was one that was freely formed by the people and guided by the "general will" of society—a direct democracy. Under such a government, people agree to give up some of their freedom in favor of the common good. In 1762, he explained his political philosophy in a book called *The Social Contract*.

> **A VOICE FROM THE PAST**
> The heart of the idea of the social contract may be stated simply: Each of us places his person and authority under the supreme direction of the general will, and the group receives each individual as an indivisible part of the whole. . . .
> In order that the social contract may not be a mere empty formula, everyone must understand that any individual who refuses to obey the general will must be forced by his fellows to do so. This is a way of saying that it may be necessary to force a man to be free; freedom in this case being obedience to the will of all.
>
> **JEAN JACQUES ROUSSEAU,** *The Social Contract*

Rousseau's view of the social contract differed greatly from that of Hobbes. For Hobbes, the social contract was an agreement between a society and its government. For Rousseau, it was an agreement among free individuals to create a society and a government.

Like Locke, Rousseau argued that legitimate government came from the consent of the governed. However, Rousseau believed in a much broader democracy than Locke had stood for. He argued that all people were equal and that titles of nobility should be abolished. Rousseau's ideas inspired many of the leaders of the French Revolution who overthrew the monarchy in 1789.

Beccaria Promotes Criminal Justice An Italian philosophe named Cesare Bonesana Beccaria (BAYK·uh·REE·ah) turned his thoughts to the justice system. He believed that laws existed to preserve social order, not to avenge crimes. In his celebrated book *On Crimes and Punishments* (1764), Beccaria railed against common abuses of justice. They included torturing of witnesses and suspects, irregular proceedings in trials, and punishments that were arbitrary or cruel. He argued that a person accused of a crime should receive a speedy trial, and that torture should never be used. Moreover, he said, the degree of punishment should be based on the seriousness of the crime. He also believed that capital punishment should be abolished.

Major Ideas of the Enlightenment

Idea	Thinker	Impact
Natural rights—life, liberty, property	Locke	Fundamental to U.S. Declaration of Independence
Separation of powers	Montesquieu	France, United States, Latin American nations use separation of powers in new constitutions.
Freedom of thought and expression	Voltaire	Guaranteed in U.S. Bill of Rights and French Declaration of the Rights of Man and Citizen; European monarchs reduce or eliminate censorship
Abolishment of torture	Beccaria	Guaranteed in U.S. Bill of Rights; torture outlawed or reduced in nations of Europe and the Americas
Religious freedom	Voltaire	Guaranteed in U.S. Bill of Rights and French Declaration of the Rights of Man and Citizen; European monarchs reduce persecution
Women's equality	Wollstonecraft	Women's rights groups form in Europe and North America.

SKILLBUILDER: Interpreting Charts
1. *What important documents reflect the influence of Enlightenment ideas?*
2. *In your opinion, which are the two most important Enlightenment ideas? Support your answer with reasons.*

Beccaria based his ideas about justice on the principle that governments should seek the greatest good for the greatest number of people. His ideas influenced criminal law reformers in Europe and North America.

Women and the Enlightenment

The philosophes challenged many assumptions about government and society. But they often took a traditional view toward women. Rousseau, for example, developed many progressive ideas about education. However, he believed that a girl's education should mainly teach her how to be a helpful wife and mother. Other male social critics scolded women for reading novels because they thought it encouraged idleness and wickedness. Still, some male writers argued for more education for women and for women's equality in marriage.

Women writers also tried to improve the status of women. In 1694, the English writer Mary Astell published *A Serious Proposal to the Ladies.* Her book addressed the lack of educational opportunities for women. In later writings, she used Enlightenment arguments about government to criticize the unequal relationship between men and women in marriage. She wrote, "If absolute sovereignty be not necessary in a state, how comes it to be so in a family? . . . If all men are born free, how is it that all women are born slaves?"

During the 1700s, other women picked up these themes. Among the most persuasive was **Mary Wollstonecraft,** who published an essay called *A Vindication of the Rights of Woman* in 1792. In the essay, she disagreed with Rousseau that women's education should be secondary to men's. Rather, she argued that women, like men, need education to become virtuous and useful. Even if they are to be mothers, education will make them better mothers. Wollstonecraft also believed that women not only should be able to be nurses but also should be able to become doctors. She also argued for women's right to participate in politics.

Women made important contributions to the Enlightenment in other ways. In Paris and other European cities, wealthy women helped spread Enlightenment ideas through social gatherings called salons. (The importance of salons is discussed later in this chapter.)

One woman fortunate enough to receive education in the sciences was Emilie du Châtelet (shah·tlay). Du Châtelet was an aristocrat trained as a mathematician and physicist. By translating Newton's work from Latin into French, she helped stimulate interest in science in France.

Impact of the Enlightenment

Over a span of a few decades, Enlightenment writers challenged long-held ideas about society. They examined such principles as the divine right of monarchs, the union of church and state, and unequal social classes. They held these beliefs up to the light of reason and found them unreasonable.

The philosophes mainly lived in the world of ideas. They formed and popularized new theories. Although they encouraged European monarchs to make reforms, they were not active revolutionaries. However, their theories eventually inspired the American and French revolutions and other revolutionary movements in the 1800s. Enlightenment thinking produced three other long-term effects that helped shape Western civilization.

THINK THROUGH HISTORY
G. Drawing Conclusions Why do you think the issue of education was important to both Astell and Wollstonecraft?
G. Possible Answer Education was closed to women; education could help women improve themselves and their situation; education was key to exercising the same rights as men.

HISTORY MAKERS

Mary Wollstonecraft 1759–1797

In *A Vindication of the Rights of Woman,* Mary Wollstonecraft argued that women deserved the same rights as men. "Let women share the rights and she will emulate [imitate] the virtues of men; for she must grow more perfect when emancipated," she wrote. The key to gaining equality and freedom, she argued, was better education.

Wollstonecraft herself received little formal education. She and her two sisters taught themselves by studying books at home. With her sisters, she briefly ran a school. These experiences shaped her thoughts about education.

After joining a London publisher, Wollstonecraft met many leading radicals of the day. One of them was her future husband, the writer Richard Godwin. She died at age 38, after giving birth to their daughter, Mary. This child, whose married name was Mary Wollstonecraft Shelley, went on to write the classic novel *Frankenstein.*

Enlightenment and Revolution **175**

Daily *Life*

Attitudes Toward Children

Before the mid-1700s, people commonly believed that children were naturally sinful. Parents raised their children with a harsh hand and treated them like miniature adults.

During the Enlightenment, such attitudes changed. People believed children should be better educated and could be allowed to mature into adulthood. Parents lessened the use of corporal punishment and increased play time.

By 1780, there was a new market for rocking horses, jigsaw puzzles, and baby clothes. In Britain, the first Mother Goose book of nursery rhymes appeared. Books like *The Newtonian System of the Universe Digested for Young Minds* by Tom Telescope appeared in print. Children even began to get discount tickets to museums and curiosity shows.

Belief in Progress The first effect was a belief in progress. Pioneers such as Galileo and Newton had discovered the key for unlocking the mysteries of nature in the 1500s and 1600s. With the door thus opened, the growth of scientific knowledge seemed to quicken in the 1700s. Scientists made key new discoveries in chemistry, physics, biology, and mechanics. The successes of the Scientific Revolution gave people the confidence that human reason could solve social problems. Philosophes and reformers urged an end to the practice of slavery. They also argued for more social equality and improvements in education. Through reason, a better society was possible.

A More Secular Outlook A second outcome was the rise of a more secular, or worldly, outlook. During the Enlightenment, people began to openly question their religious beliefs and the teachings of the church. Before the Scientific Revolution, people accepted the mysteries of the universe as the mysteries of God. One by one, scientists discovered that these mysteries could be explained mathematically. Newton himself was a deeply religious man, and he sought to reveal God's majesty through his work. However, his findings caused some people to change the way they thought about God.

Voltaire and other critics attacked some of the beliefs and practices of organized Christianity. They wanted to rid religious faith of superstition and fear and promote tolerance of all religions.

Importance of the Individual Faith in science and in progress produced a third outcome—the rise of individualism. As people began to turn away from the church and royalty for guidance, they looked to themselves instead.

The philosophes encouraged people to use their own ability to reason in order to judge what is right or wrong. They also emphasized the importance of the individual in society. Government, they argued, was formed by individuals to promote their welfare. The British thinker Adam Smith extended the emphasis on the individual to economic thinking. He believed that individuals acting in their own self-interest created economic progress. Smith's theory is discussed in detail in Chapter 9.

During the Enlightenment, reason took center stage. The greatest minds of Europe followed each other's work with interest and often met to discuss their ideas. Some of the kings and queens of Europe were also very interested. As you will learn in Section 3, they sought to apply some of the philosophes' ideas to create progress in their countries.

Section **2** Assessment

1. TERMS & NAMES
Identify
- Enlightenment
- social contract
- John Locke
- natural rights
- philosophe
- Voltaire
- Montesquieu
- separation of powers
- Jean Jacques Rousseau
- Mary Wollstonecraft

2. TAKING NOTES
In a chart like the one below, list the important ideas of Hobbes, Locke, Voltaire, Montesquieu, Rousseau, Beccaria, and Wollstonecraft.

Thinker	Key Idea

Choose one of these thinkers and write a paragraph on how his or her ideas are influential today.

3. SYNTHESIZING
For each of the statements below, identify who said it and explain what it means. Then say how each viewpoint reflects Enlightenment ideas.
- "Power should be a check to power."
- "Man is born free, and everywhere he is in chains."
- "Let women share the rights and she will emulate the virtues of men."

4. ANALYZING THEMES
Power and Authority
Compare the views of Hobbes, Locke, and Rousseau on government. How do their differing ideas reflect their understanding of human behavior?

THINK ABOUT
- how each philosopher viewed the "state of nature"
- what each considered the source of a government's authority

176 Chapter 6

ANSWERS

TERMS & NAMES
- Enlightenment, p. 171
- social contract, p. 171
- John Locke, p. 171
- natural rights, p. 171
- philosophe, p. 172
- Voltaire, p. 172
- Montesquieu, p. 173
- separation of powers, p. 173
- Jean Jacques Rousseau, p. 173
- Mary Wollstonecraft, p. 175

2. TAKING NOTES
Possible Responses: Hobbes—social contract; Locke—consent of the governed; Voltaire—tolerance; Montesquieu—separation of powers; Rousseau—government by general will; Beccaria—abolition of torture; Wollstonecraft—access to education for women.

3. FORMING OPINIONS
Possible Responses: "Power"—Montesquieu; each branch of government should limit power of other branches; "Man"—Rousseau; civilization corrupted the state of nature; "Let women"—Wollstonecraft; give women equal rights and they will display men's goodness.

4. ANALYZING THEMES
Possible Responses: Hobbes—humans are naturally selfish and wicked; governments keep order. Locke—humans naturally able to govern themselves; favored self-government. Rousseau—people are naturally good; society corrupts them; power comes from the general will.

European Values

Writers and artists of the Enlightenment often used satire to comment on European values. Using wit and humor, they ridiculed ideas and customs for the purpose of improving society. Satire allowed artists to explore human faults and failings in a way that is powerful but not preachy. In the two literary excerpts and the drawing below, notice how the writer or artist makes his point.

LITERATURE
Voltaire

Voltaire wrote *Candide* (1759) to attack a philosophy called Optimism, which held that all is right with the world. The hero of the story, a young man named Candide, encounters the most awful disasters and human evils as he travels far and wide. In this passage, Candide has met a slave in Surinam, a Dutch colony in South America. The slave explains why he is missing a leg and a hand.

"When we're working at the sugar mill and catch our finger in the grinding-wheel, they cut off our hand. When we try to run away, they cut off a leg. I have been in both of these situations. This is the price you pay for the sugar you eat in Europe. . . .

"The Dutch fetishes [i.e., missionaries] who converted me [to Christianity] tell me every Sunday that we are all the sons of Adam, Whites and Blacks alike. I'm no genealogist, but if these preachers are right, we are all cousins born of first cousins. Well, you will grant me that you can't treat a relative much worse than this."

ENGRAVING
Francisco Goya

The Spanish artist Francisco Goya issued a series of 80 engravings called *Los Caprichos* (*Caprices*) in 1797. In them, he criticized a range of "human errors and evils" and also satirized Spanish politics and society. In the image shown here, titled "Out Hunting for Teeth," Goya attacks superstition. He wrote this caption for the image:

The teeth of a man who has been hung are indispensable for casting a spell. Without this ingredient, nothing succeeds. A pity that people believe such nonsense.

LITERATURE
Jonathan Swift

The narrator of *Gulliver's Travels* (1726), an English doctor named Lemuel Gulliver, takes four disastrous voyages that leave him stranded in strange lands. In the following passage, Gulliver tries to win points with the king of Brobdingnag—a land of giants—by offering to show him how to make guns and cannons. The reaction of the king, who is above such things, shows how Swift felt about the inhuman side of the human race.

[I told the king that] a proper quantity of this powder [gunpowder] rammed into a hollow tube of brass or iron . . . would drive a ball of iron or lead with such violence and speed, as nothing was able to sustain its force. That, the largest balls thus discharged, would not only destroy whole ranks of an army at once; but batter the strongest walls to the ground; sink down ships with a thousand men in each, to the bottom of the sea; and when linked together by a chain, would cut through masts and rigging; divide hundreds of bodies in the middle, and lay all waste before them. . . .

The king was struck with horror at the description I had given of those terrible engines. . . . He was amazed how so impotent and grovelling an insect as I (these were his expressions) could entertain such inhuman ideas, and in so familiar a manner as to appear wholly unmoved at all the scenes of blood and desolation, which I had painted as the common effects of those destructive machines; whereof, he said, some evil genius, enemy to mankind, must have been the first contriver [inventor].

Connect *to* History

Clarifying Write a statement that summarizes the main point each writer and artist is making. What techniques do they use to reinforce their messages?

SEE SKILLBUILDER
HANDBOOK, PAGE 650

Connect *to* Today

Writing Both Voltaire and Swift used a fictional travel narrative as a type of satire. Imagine you are an alien visitor to your school or community. Write a letter or a narrative that describes how the people you see think and behave.

 CD-ROM For another perspective on the Enlightenment, see World History: Electronic Library of Primary Sources.

Enlightenment and Revolution **177**

Satire
Satire is a style of writing or visual expression that uses humor to ridicule the practices of a society or institution. Many Enlightenment writers, such as Voltaire and Jonathan Swift, used satire to show readers the foolishness of certain ideas or conditions. Instead of openly criticizing society or government, these writers expressed their opinions through the words and actions of story characters. For example, in Voltaire's *Candide,* the optimistic title character continues to believe that all is for the best even though he is confronted with endless examples of evil and stupidity in the world. Voltaire's point is that Optimism lacks reason and anyone who follows the philosophy of the Optimists is also lacking in reason.

 ELECTRONIC LIBRARY OF PRIMARY SOURCES
from *Gulliver's Travels*

Connect *to* History

Clarifying
Possible Responses: Voltaire's main point is that Christian missionaries are hypocritical in their treatment of slaves. He shows this by contrasting the brutality of slavery with the missionaries' empty words about all men being sons of Adam. Swift uses humor to assert his belief that war and the instruments of war are inhuman and that people have become immune to the horrors of war. Goya creates an image more repulsive than humorous to show that he believes superstition is ridiculous and pathetic. All three men use humor and exaggeration to make their points.

Connect *to* Today

Writing
To help students get started, brainstorm a list of everyday situations that an alien visitor might think are strange. These could include going to a noisy cafeteria to eat lunch, responding to school bells, and playing sports in gym. Encourage students to use humor and exaggeration in their letters and narratives.

To explain how Enlightenment ideas spread throughout Europe.

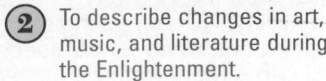 To describe changes in art, music, and literature during the Enlightenment.

 To show how Enlightenment ideas reformed monarchies in Prussia, Austria, and Russia.

CRITICAL THINKING
- Making inferences, p. 179
- Contrasting, p. 179
- Analyzing issues, p. 180
- Analyzing motives, p. 181
- Synthesizing, p. 182
- Drawing conclusions, p. 182

FOCUS

5-Minute Warm-Up

Identifying Key Concepts
To help students understand how the Enlightenment changed monarchies, have them answer these questions.

1. Study the Changing Idea chart on page 181. Which ruler expected citizens to serve the monarch?

2. What were the new ideas about monarchs?

 WARM-UP TRANSPARENCY 6

OBJECTIVE ① INSTRUCT

A World of Ideas

Key Ideas
- Philosophers, writers, artists, scientists, and others gather regularly to discuss new ideas.

- Diderot creates an encyclopedia containing current ideas about science, art, and government.

- Enlightenment ideas spread to intellectuals and the middle class throughout Europe.

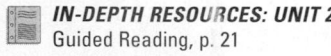 *IN-DEPTH RESOURCES: UNIT 2*
Guided Reading, p. 21

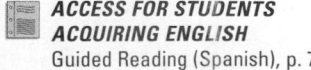 *ACCESS FOR STUDENTS ACQUIRING ENGLISH*
Guided Reading (Spanish), p. 73

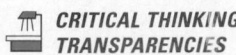 *CRITICAL THINKING TRANSPARENCIES*
CT22 The Spread of Enlightenment Ideas

---

3 # The Spread of Enlightenment Ideas

TERMS & NAMES
- salon
- baroque
- neoclassical
- enlightened despot
- Catherine the Great

MAIN IDEA
Enlightenment ideas spread through the Western world and profoundly influenced the arts and government.

WHY IT MATTERS NOW
An "enlightened" problem-solving approach to government and society prevails in modern civilization today.

SETTING THE STAGE The philosophes' views often got them in trouble. In France it was illegal to criticize either the Catholic Church or the government. Many philosophes landed in jail or were exiled. Voltaire, for example, experienced both punishments. Nevertheless, Enlightenment ideas spread throughout Europe.

A World of Ideas

In the 1700s, Paris was the cultural and intellectual capital of Europe. Young people from around Europe—and also from the Americas—came to study, philosophize, and enjoy fine culture. The brightest minds of the age gathered there. From their circles radiated the ideas of the Enlightenment.

The Paris Salons The buzz of Enlightenment ideas was most intense in the mansions of several wealthy women of Paris. There, in their large drawing rooms, these hostesses held regular social gatherings called **salons.** At these events, philosophers, writers, artists, scientists, and other great intellects met to discuss ideas and enjoy artistic performances.

The most influential of the salon hostesses in Voltaire's time was Marie-Thérèse Geoffrin (zhuh-frehn). Self-educated and from the well-to-do middle class, Madame Geoffrin was friends with both philosophes and heads of state. She corresponded with the king of Sweden and Catherine the Great of Russia.

Diderot's *Encyclopedia* Madame Geoffrin also helped finance the project of a leading philosophe named Denis Diderot (DEE-duh-ROH). Diderot imagined a large set of books to which all the leading scholars of Europe would contribute articles and essays. This *Encyclopedia*, as he called it, would bring together all the most current and enlightened thinking about science, technology, art, government, and more. Diderot began publishing the first volumes in 1751.

This painting by Anicet Charles Lemonnier shows a salon in the home of Madame Geoffrin (inset, and seated third from right). The guests are listening to an actor reading aloud from a new play.

SECTION 3 RESOURCES

PRINT RESOURCES

 IN-DEPTH RESOURCES: UNIT 2
Guided Reading, p. 21
Connections Across Time and Cultures: The Search for Truth and Reason, p. 36

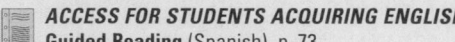 *ACCESS FOR STUDENTS ACQUIRING ENGLISH*
Guided Reading (Spanish), p. 73

 FORMAL ASSESSMENT
Section Quiz, p. 78

ALTERNATIVE ASSESSMENT BOOK

TECHNOLOGY RESOURCES

 WORLD ART AND CULTURES TRANSPARENCIES
AT49 Goya's *The Pottery Vendor* (cartoon for a tapestry)

 CRITICAL THINKING TRANSPARENCIES
CT22 The Spread of Enlightenment Ideas

 CD-ROM
Electronic Library of Primary Sources

 INTERNET www.mlworldhistory.com

The Enlightenment views expressed in the articles soon angered both the French government and the Catholic Church. Their censors banned the work. They said it undermined royal authority, encouraged a spirit of revolt, and fostered "moral corruption, irreligion, and unbelief." Fearing arrest, some leading philosophes withdrew from the project and urged Diderot to quit. Diderot pressed on, however, and finally won permission to continue publishing the *Encyclopedia*. New volumes came out regularly under his editorship until 1772.

New Ideas Circulate The salons and the *Encyclopedia* helped spread Enlightenment ideas to educated people all over Europe. The enlightened thinkers of Europe considered themselves part of an intellectual community. They shared their ideas through books, personal letters, visits back and forth, and magazine articles. As one writer of the day described the flurry of communication, "Never have new ideas had such rapid circulation at such long distance."

Enlightenment ideas also eventually reached middle-class people through newspapers, pamphlets, and even political songs. Enlightenment ideas about government and equality attracted the attention of a growing literate middle class. This group had money but limited status and political power. With their money, middle-class people could afford to buy many books and support the work of artists. Through its purchasing power, this group had growing influence over European culture in the 1700s.

This detail of *Seated Woman with Book*, by French artist Jean-Baptiste Chardin, shows a middle-class woman whose interests include reading. In the 1700s, the middle class had more leisure time for such pursuits.

Art and Literature in the Age of Reason

The Enlightenment ideals of order and reason were reflected in the arts—music, literature, painting, and architecture. European art of the 1600s and early 1700s had been dominated by the style called **baroque**—a grand, ornate style. Monarchs had built elaborate palaces such as Versailles (see page 141). Musicians like the German composer Johann Sebastian Bach and the English composer George Frederick Handel had written dramatic organ and choral music. Artists had created paintings rich in color, detail, and ornate imagery.

Under the influence of the Enlightenment, styles began to change. The arts began to reflect the new emphasis on order and balance. Artists and architects worked in a simple and elegant style that borrowed ideas and themes from classical Greece and Rome. The style of the late 1700s is therefore called **neoclassical** ("new classical"). In music, the style of this period is called classical.

Classical Music Three composers in Vienna, Austria, rank among the greatest figures of the classical period in music. They were Franz Joseph Haydn, Wolfgang Amadeus Mozart, and Ludwig van Beethoven.

Haydn was particularly important in developing new musical forms, such as the sonata and symphony. Mozart was a gifted child who began composing music at the age of five and gave concerts throughout Europe as a youth. At 12, he wrote his first opera. Mozart's great operas—*The Marriage of Figaro, Don Giovanni,* and *The Magic Flute*—set a new standard for elegance and originality. Although he lived only to age 35, he wrote more than 600 musical works.

Beethoven showed enormous range in his work. He wrote beautiful piano music, string quartets, and stirring symphonies. Beethoven's earlier works were in the same classical style as Mozart's. However, his later compositions began new trends, which carried music into the Age of Romanticism.

Popularity of the Novel Writers in the 18th century also developed new styles and forms of literature. A number of European authors began writing novels—lengthy works of prose fiction. These books were popular with a wide middle-class audience,

Enlightenment and Revolution **179**

History Through Art

William Hogarth

Hogarth was one of the first artists to use painting as a form of political commentary. He admired the English satirical writers who were his contemporaries, and he attempted to bring satire into the visual arts. His paintings made fun of contemporary customs and manners and, like a novel, seem to include plot, characters, and layers of details. As he said, "I have endeavored to treat my subjects as a dramatic writer; my picture is my stage, and men and women my players." Hogarth liked to create series of paintings that followed the actions of one or more characters. Typically, these characters are shown encountering different evils of society. Hogarth's paintings were very popular with the English middle class.

MORE ABOUT . . .
English Painters

Before Hogarth, England had great architects but no great painters. Most painters in England had come over from the European continent. Hogarth's efforts to establish English artists included founding an academy for painters and organizing the first public exhibition of paintings by contemporary English painters.

 WORLD ART AND CULTURES TRANSPARENCIES

AT49 Goya's *The Pottery Vendor* (cartoon for a tapestry)

Art in the Age of Enlightenment

The Enlightenment influenced many European painters of the middle and late 1700s. Increasingly, artists looked for inspiration in the material world—in nature and human nature. Some artists showed an Enlightenment interest in science and social issues in their work. Others emphasized a new sensitivity toward individuals.

The Individual

The French painter Elisabeth-Louise Vigée-Le Brun was one of the most celebrated portrait artists of the late 1700s. She was the favorite painter of Queen Marie Antoinette of France. Her portraits bring out the personalities of her subjects. Her own energy, success, and independence also reflected the Enlightenment spirit. These qualities shine through this detail of a self-portrait with her daughter.

Politics and Society

The English artist William Hogarth often used satire in his paintings. In the painting above, *Canvassing for Votes— The Election*, he comments on political corruption. While the candidate flirts with the ladies on the balcony, his supporters offer a man money for his vote. Hogarth's detailed, realistic style and moralistic topics were meant—like the popular novels of his day—to appeal to a wide middle-class audience.

The Promise of Science

The English artist Joseph Wright of Derby was fascinated by science and its impact on people's lives. The painting below, *Philosopher Giving a Lecture on the Orrery*, shows children and adults gazing into a miniature planetarium. The way Wright uses light in this picture makes a point about how science can educate and enlighten people.

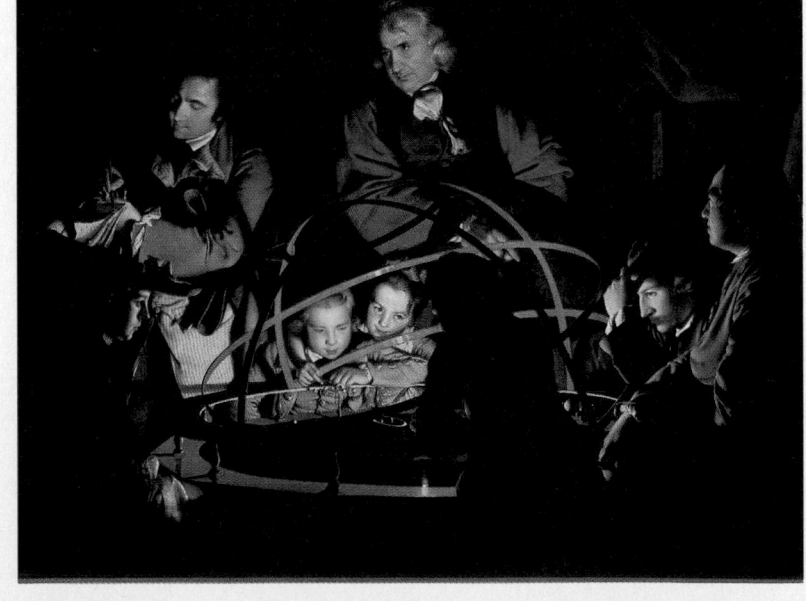

Connect to History

Analyzing Issues Imagine you are a philosophe who moonlights as an art critic. For each of these paintings, write a brief statement about how it reflects Enlightenment ideas.

 SEE SKILLBUILDER HANDBOOK, PAGE 659

Connect to Today

Updating a Picture Choose one of the paintings on this page and think about how you might change it to depict politics, science, or people today. You might describe the modern version in words or using a sketch or other kind of artwork.

Connect to History

Analyzing Issues Possible Responses:
Vigée-Le Brun's portrait is simple, not ornate. It shows the mother and child in a natural embrace. By emphasizing the individuality of her subjects, Vigée-Le Brun pays tribute to their humanity.

Hogarth uses satire to point out the corrupt nature of politics. He makes fun of politicians by portraying them as dishonest. Joseph Wright highlights the achievements of science and the human ability to reason in his painting.

Connect to Today

Updating a Picture
To help students get started, discuss the following questions: What are some recent technological developments and how do people view them—with amazement, fear, boredom, or excitement? What other roles in

society do women who are mothers have today? Are politics today corrupt? You might suggest students look at images in contemporary magazines to get more ideas.

who liked the entertaining stories written in everyday language. Writers—including many women—turned out a flood of popular novels in the 1700s.

English novelists such as Samuel Richardson and Henry Fielding developed many of the features of the modern novel. Their works had carefully crafted plots, used suspense and climax, and explored their characters' thoughts and feelings. Richardson's *Pamela* is often considered the first true English novel. It told the story of a young servant girl who refused the advances of her master. In Fielding's comic masterpiece *Tom Jones*, the hero of the book is an orphan who has been kicked out of his adopted home. He travels all over England and overcomes numerous obstacles to win the hand of his lady.

A third popular English novelist was Daniel Defoe, author of the adventure *Robinson Crusoe*. Crusoe is a sailor stranded on a tropical island. Through his wits and the help of a native he calls Friday, Crusoe learns how to survive on the island and is eventually rescued.

Enlightenment and Monarchy

From the salons, artists' studios, and concert halls of Europe, the Enlightenment spirit also swept through Europe's royal courts. Many philosophes, including Voltaire, believed that the best form of government was a monarchy in which the ruler respected the people's rights. The philosophes tried to convince monarchs to rule justly. Some monarchs embraced the new ideas and made reforms that reflected the Enlightenment spirit. They became known as **enlightened despots.** *Despot* means absolute ruler.

THINK THROUGH HISTORY
C. Analyzing Motives Why did the enlightened despots undertake reforms?
C. Possible Answers Intrigued by Enlightenment ideas, convinced by philosophes, wanted to make their countries stronger and own rule more effective.

The enlightened despots supported the philosophes' ideas. But they also had no intention of giving up any power. The changes they made were motivated by two desires: they wanted to make their countries stronger and their own rule more effective. The foremost of Europe's enlightened despots were Frederick II of Prussia, Holy Roman Emperor Joseph II of Austria, and Catherine the Great of Russia.

Frederick the Great Frederick II, the king of Prussia from 1740 to 1786, once wrote to Voltaire: "I must enlighten my people, cultivate their manners and morals, and make them as happy as human beings can be, or as happy as the means at my disposal permit." Frederick indeed committed himself to reforming Prussia. He granted many religious freedoms, reduced censorship, and improved education. He also reformed the justice system and abolished the use of torture. However, Frederick's changes only went so far. For example, he believed that serfdom was wrong, but he did nothing to end it. This was because he needed the support of wealthy landowners. As a result, he never challenged the power of the Junkers or tried to change the existing social order.

Perhaps Frederick's most important contribution was his attitude toward being king. He called himself "the first servant of the state." From the beginning of his reign, he made it clear that his goal was to serve and strengthen his country. This attitude was clearly one that appealed to the philosophes.

Changing Idea: Relationship Between Ruler and State

Old Idea
The state and its citizens exist to serve the monarch—as Louis XIV reportedly said, "I am the state."

New Idea
The monarch exists to serve the state and support citizens' welfare—as Frederick the Great said, a ruler is only "the first servant of the state."

Joseph II The most radical royal reformer was Joseph II of Austria. The son and successor of Maria Theresa, Joseph II ruled Austria from 1780 to 1790. He introduced legal reforms and freedom of the press. He also supported freedom of worship—even for Protestants, Orthodox Christians, and Jews. In his most radical reform, Joseph abolished serfdom and ordered that peasants be paid for their labor with cash. Not

Enlightenment and Revolution **181**

OBJECTIVE **3** INSTRUCT

Enlightenment and Monarchy

▶ *Key Ideas*
• Frederick II of Prussia announces that his goal is to serve and strengthen his country.
• In Austria, Joseph II's radical reforms include freedom of worship and the end of serfdom.
• Catherine II of Russia makes limited reforms, which she later revokes.
• Catherine vastly enlarges the Russian Empire and wins a warm-weather port for her country.

CRITICAL THINKING ACTIVITY
CLASS TIME: 20 MINUTES

Comparing and Contrasting
Ask students which enlightened despot made the most sincere effort to reform his or her country. Then ask which one made the least effort. Remind students to use facts from the text to support their opinions.

MORE ABOUT . . .
Joseph II

In 1765, Joseph was appointed co-regent by his mother, Maria Theresa. He had very little power and could do almost nothing without his mother's approval. While in this position, he created a list of radical reforms, including mandatory military service for young nobles, religious toleration, an end to government spying on private affairs, limiting the power of nobles, and using the army for public works projects. Almost all of Joseph's proposed reforms conflicted with his mother's more conservative style. It was not until her death in 1780 that Joseph could implement his reforms.

TEACHING OPTION   BLOCK SCHEDULING   COOPERATIVE ACTIVITY: Researching Enlightenment Arts   CLASS TIME 40 MINUTES

Task: Student groups will develop oral reports about architecture and the arts during the Enlightenment.

Purpose: To help students recognize the Enlightenment's impact on culture.

Activity: Divide the class into five groups and assign each group one of the following topics:

painting and sculpture, architecture, music, literature, drama. Groups should conduct research to learn how their art form changed during the Enlightenment and who were the most important figures associated with it. (Students can begin their research using their textbooks and then move on to general and topical encyclopedias and other books.) Each group will develop and present an oral report that includes

examples of the art form. These can include pictures, books, audio recordings, videos, and other items. The literature and drama groups may wish to read aloud a short excerpt from a novel or a play.

ALTERNATIVE ASSESSMENT BOOK
Standards for Evaluating a Cooperative Activity

182 Chapter 6

HISTORY MAKERS

**Catherine the Great
1729–1796**

Catherine was the daughter of a minor German prince. At age 15, she was summoned to the distant Russian court at St. Petersburg. She was to marry the Grand Duke Peter, heir to the Russian throne.

The marriage between Catherine and Peter was a disaster. Peter was mentally unstable. His chief pleasure was playing with toy soldiers. More than once he tormented his own dogs.

Catherine soon saw that Peter's weakness gave her a chance to seize power. She made important friends among Russia's army officers, and she became known as the most intelligent and best-informed person at court. In 1762, only months after her husband became czar as Peter III, Catherine had him arrested and confined. Soon afterward, Peter conveniently died, probably by murder.

surprisingly, the nobles firmly resisted this change. Like many of Joseph's reforms, it was undone after his death.

Catherine the Great The ruler most admired by the philosophes was Catherine II, known as **Catherine the Great.** She ruled Russia from 1762 to 1796. The well-educated empress read the works of philosophes, and she exchanged many letters with Voltaire. She ruled with absolute authority, but she also took steps to modernize and reform Russia.

In 1767, Catherine formed a commission to review Russia's laws. She presented it with a brilliant proposal for reforms based on the ideas of Montesquieu and Beccaria. Among other changes, she recommended allowing religious toleration and abolishing torture and capital punishment. Her commission, however, accomplished none of these lofty goals.

Catherine eventually put in place limited reforms, but she did little to improve the life of the Russian peasants. Her thinking about enlightened ideas changed after a massive uprising of serfs in 1773. With great brutality, Catherine's army crushed the rebellion. Catherine had previously favored an end to serfdom. However, the revolt convinced her that she needed the nobles' support to keep her throne. Therefore, she gave the nobles absolute power over the serfs. As a result, Russian serfs lost their last traces of freedom.

Catherine Expands Russia Peter the Great had fought for years to win a port on the Baltic Sea. Likewise, Catherine sought access to the Black Sea. In two wars with the Ottoman Turks, her armies finally won control of the northern shore of the Black Sea. Russia also gained the right to send ships through Ottoman-controlled straits leading from the Black Sea to the Mediterranean Sea.

Catherine also expanded her empire westward into Poland. In Poland, the king was relatively weak, and independent nobles held the most power. The three neighboring powers—Russia, Prussia, and Austria—each tried to assert their influence over the country. In 1772, these land-hungry neighbors each took a piece of Poland in what is called the First Partition of Poland. In further partitions in 1793 and 1795, they grabbed up the rest of Poland's territory. With these partitions, Poland disappeared from the map of Europe. It did not reappear as an independent country until after World War I.

By the end of her remarkable reign, Catherine had vastly enlarged the Russian empire. Meanwhile, as Russia was becoming an international power, another great power, Britain, faced a challenge in its 13 American colonies. Inspired by Enlightenment ideas, colonial leaders decided to cast off British rule and found an independent republic.

D. Possible Answer It accurately describes two sides of her rule—she tried to make reforms, but she also ruled with absolute authority; it's not very accurate, since she was ultimately more despotic than enlightened.

**THINK THROUGH HISTORY
D. Synthesizing**
How accurately does the term *enlightened despot* describe Catherine the Great? Explain.

Section ③ Assessment

1. TERMS & NAMES
Identify
• salon
• baroque
• neoclassical
• enlightened despot
• Catherine the Great

2. TAKING NOTES
Copy the concept web shown below and add to it examples that illustrate the concepts.

Write two generalizations about the spread of Enlightenment ideas.

3. DRAWING CONCLUSIONS
What advantages do you think salons had over earlier forms of communication in spreading new ideas? Justify your response with specific references to the text.

THINK ABOUT
• who hosted the salons and where they were held
• who was invited to the salons
• church and state influence on publishing and education

4. THEME ACTIVITY
Power and Authority
Imagine you are a public relations consultant for Frederick the Great, Joseph II, or Catherine the Great. The monarch you represent wants to be named "Most Enlightened Despot of the 1700s." Write a press release or design a poster or flyer that presents reasons why your client should be given this honor.

182 Chapter 6

ANSWERS

American Revolution: The Birth of a Republic

TERMS & NAMES
- Declaration of Independence
- Thomas Jefferson
- checks and balances
- federal system
- Bill of Rights

MAIN IDEA

Enlightenment ideas helped spur the American colonies to create a new nation.

WHY IT MATTERS NOW

The revolution created a republic, the United States of America, that became a model for many nations of the world.

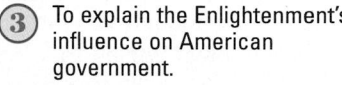

Section 4 Overview

OBJECTIVES

1. To describe the American colonies in the late 1700s.
2. To list events that led to the American Revolution.
3. To explain the Enlightenment's influence on American government.

SKILLBUILDERS

- Interpreting maps: region, human-environment interaction, p. 185
- Interpreting charts, p. 186

CRITICAL THINKING

- Recognizing effects, p. 183
- Analyzing causes, p. 184
- Comparing, p. 184
- Making inferences, p. 186
- Analyzing issues, p. 187
- Analyzing themes, p. 187

SETTING THE STAGE Philosophes such as Voltaire considered England's government the most progressive in Europe. England's ruler was no despot, not even an enlightened one. His power had been limited by law. The Glorious Revolution of 1688 had given England a constitutional monarchy. However, while the English monarch's power was being limited at home, the power of the English nation was spreading overseas.

Britain and Its American Colonies

When George III became king of Great Britain in 1760, his Atlantic coastal colonies were growing by leaps and bounds. Their combined population went from about 250,000 in 1700 to 2,150,000 in 1770, an eightfold increase. Economically, the colonies thrived on trade with the nations of Europe.

Along with increasing population and prosperity, a new sense of identity was growing in the colonists' minds. By the mid-1700s, colonists had been living in America for nearly 150 years. Each of the 13 colonies had its own government, and people were used to a great degree of independence. Colonists saw themselves less as British and more as Virginians or Pennsylvanians. However, they were still British subjects and were expected to obey British law.

In the 1660s, Parliament had passed trade laws called the Navigation Acts. These laws prevented colonists from selling their most valuable products to any country except Britain. In addition, colonists had to pay high taxes on imported French and Dutch goods. However, colonists found ways to get around these laws. Some merchants smuggled in goods to avoid paying British taxes. Smugglers could sneak in and out of the many small harbors all along the lengthy Atlantic coastline. British customs agents found it difficult to enforce the Navigation Acts.

For many years, Britain felt no need to tighten its hold on the colonies. Despite the smuggling, Britain's mercantilist policies had made colonial trade very profitable. Britain bought American raw materials for low prices and sold manufactured goods to the colonists. And despite British trade restrictions, colonial merchants also thrived. However, after the French and Indian War ended in 1763, Britain toughened its trade laws. These changes sparked growing anger in the colonies.

Americans Win Independence

In 1760, when George III took the throne, most Americans had no thoughts of either revolution or independence. They still thought of themselves as loyal subjects of the British king. Yet by 1776, many Americans were willing to risk their lives to break free of Britain.

During the French and Indian War, Great Britain had run up a huge debt in the war against France. Because American colonists benefited from Britain's victory, Britain expected the colonists to help pay the costs of the war. In 1765, Parliament passed the Stamp Act. According

Enlightenment and Revolution **183**

THINK THROUGH HISTORY
A. Recognizing Effects How did some colonists respond to the Navigation Acts?
A. Answer Smuggling.

Background
The French and Indian War was the part of the Seven Years' War fought in North America.

Many educated colonists were influenced by Enlightenment thought. This French snuff box pictures (left to right) Voltaire, Rousseau, and colonial statesman Benjamin Franklin.

FOCUS

5-Minute Warm-Up

▶ Making Inferences
To help students understand how Enlightenment ideas influenced American colonists, have them answer these questions.

1. Study the History Makers feature on page 184. What is one way Thomas Jefferson contributed to American independence?

2. Name two Enlightenment ideas that Jefferson supported.

WARM-UP TRANSPARENCY 6

OBJECTIVE ① INSTRUCT

Britain and Its American Colonies

▶ Key Idea
- British tax and trade laws regulate the colonists' import and export of goods.

IN-DEPTH RESOURCES: UNIT 2
Guided Reading, p. 22

ACCESS FOR STUDENTS ACQUIRING ENGLISH
Guided Reading (Spanish), p. 74

(See page 183.)

Americans Win Independence

▶ Key Ideas

- England angers the colonists by expecting them to pay the costs of the French and Indian War.
- Colonists protest England's harsh taxes and begin to organize for war.
- Colonial leaders use Enlightenment ideas to justify independence and to write the Declaration of Independence.
- Americans are victorious because they were motivated to fight, among other reasons.

💿 **ELECTRONIC LIBRARY OF PRIMARY SOURCES**
Conflicting Accounts of the Battles at Lexington and Concord

HISTORY MAKERS
Thomas Jefferson

In his lifetime, Jefferson held many different government positions, including governor, congressman, minister to France, secretary of state, vice-president, and president. In retirement, he pursued his interests in music, architecture, and scientific experiments. He also studied religion, philosophy, law, and education. How do Jefferson's ideas, interests, and career reflect the spirit of the Enlightenment? Encourage students to use the list of important Enlightenment concepts on page 172 to think about and answer this question.

---

to this law, colonists had to pay a tax to have an official stamp put on wills, deeds, newspapers, and other printed material.

American colonists were outraged. They had never paid taxes directly to the British government before. Colonial lawyers argued that the stamp tax violated colonists' natural rights. In Britain, citizens consented to taxes through their representatives in Parliament. Because the colonists had no such representatives, Parliament could not tax them. The colonists demonstrated their defiance of this tax with angry protests and a boycott of British manufactured goods. The boycott proved so effective that Parliament gave up and repealed the Stamp Act in 1766.

Growing Hostility Leads to War Over the next decade, further events steadily led to war. Some colonial leaders, such as Boston's Samuel Adams, favored independence from Britain. They encouraged conflict with British authorities. At the same time, George III and his ministers made enemies of many moderate colonists by their harsh stands. In 1773, to protest an import tax on tea, Adams organized a raid against three British ships in Boston Harbor. The raiders dumped 342 chests of tea into the water. George III, infuriated by the "Boston Tea Party," as it was called, ordered the British navy to close the port of Boston. British troops occupied the city.

In September 1774, representatives from every colony except Georgia gathered in Philadelphia to form the First Continental Congress. This group protested the treatment of Boston. When the king paid little attention to their complaints, all 13 colonies decided to form the Second Continental Congress to debate their next move.

On April 19, 1775, British soldiers and American militiamen exchanged gunfire on the village green in Lexington, Massachusetts. The fighting spread to nearby Concord. When news of the fighting reached the Second Continental Congress, its members voted to raise an army under the command of a Virginian named George Washington. The American Revolution had begun.

Enlightenment Ideas Influence American Colonists Although a war had begun, the American colonists still debated their attachment to Great Britain. Many colonists wanted to remain part of Britain. A growing number, however, favored independence. They heard the persuasive arguments of colonial leaders such as Patrick Henry, John Adams, and Benjamin Franklin. These leaders used Enlightenment ideas to justify independence. The colonists had asked for the same political rights as people in Britain, they said, but the king had stubbornly refused. Therefore, the colonists were justified in rebelling against a tyrant who had broken the social contract.

In July 1776, the Second Continental Congress issued the **Declaration of Independence.** This document, written by **Thomas Jefferson,** was firmly based on the ideas of John Locke and the Enlightenment. The Declaration reflected these ideas in its eloquent argument for natural rights.

> ### A VOICE FROM THE PAST
> We hold these Truths to be self-evident, that all Men are created equal, that they are endowed by their Creator with certain unalienable Rights, that among these are Life, Liberty, and the Pursuit of Happiness; that to secure these Rights, Governments are instituted among Men, deriving their just Powers from the Consent of the Governed.
> Declaration of Independence

Since Locke had asserted that people had the right to rebel against an unjust ruler, the Declaration of Independence included a long list

Thomas Jefferson
1743–1826
The author of the Declaration of Independence, Thomas Jefferson of Virginia was a true figure of the Enlightenment. As a writer and statesman, he supported free speech, religious freedom, and other civil liberties. At the same time, he was also a slave owner.

Outside of politics, Jefferson was accomplished in many fields, including law, science, agriculture, and languages. He invented many practical devices, including an improved type of plow. One of the great architects of early America, he designed his magnificent home, Monticello. He also designed the Virginia state capitol building in Richmond and many buildings for the University of Virginia.

Of all his many achievements, Jefferson wanted to be most remembered for three: author of the Declaration of Independence, author of the Statute of Virginia for Religious Freedom, and founder of the University of Virginia.

THINK THROUGH HISTORY
B. Analyzing Causes How did the French and Indian War lead to the Stamp Act?

Vocabulary
boycott: refusal to buy goods produced in a certain place or by a certain group.

B. Answer Britain passed the act to help pay the costs of the war.

C. Possible Answer Jefferson wrote "Life, Liberty, and the Pursuit of Happiness"; Locke explained the natural rights as life, liberty, and property.
THINK THROUGH HISTORY
C. Comparing How do Jefferson's "unalienable rights" compare with the natural rights expressed by Locke?

CUSTOMIZING FOR SPECIAL NEEDS

Less Proficient Readers: Paired Reading Have partners read the first part of the passage titled "Americans Win Independence," beginning on page 183. After both have finished, one partner should retell what was read while the other partner listens. Neither partner should look at the text.

The partner who is listening should not interrupt the retelling. After the retelling, the partner who was listening should correct any ideas that were not summarized correctly and add any important information that was left out. Partners can alternate the retelling and listening roles as they read this and other passages.

EXPLORING PRIMARY SOURCES

A Voice from the Past Read aloud the excerpt from the Declaration of Independence. Then work with students to paraphrase it. *We believe the following ideas are true and do not need to be proven: all people are created equal, they are given by God certain rights that can never be taken away, and among these rights are the right to life, to freedom, and to seek*

happiness; to protect these rights, governments are established among people; these governments get their lawful power from the people they govern. Is the Declaration of Independence a social contract?

 IN-DEPTH RESOURCES: UNIT 2 Primary Source: from *The Declaration of Independence*, p. 30

of George III's abuses. The document ended by breaking the ties between the colonies and Britain. The colonies, the Declaration said, "are absolved from all allegiance to the British crown."

Success for the Colonists When war was first declared, the odds seemed heavily weighted against the Americans. Washington's ragtag, poorly trained army faced the well-trained forces of the most powerful country in the world. In the end, however, the Americans won their war for independence.

Several reasons explain their success. First, the Americans' motivation for fighting was much stronger than that of the British, since their army was defending their homeland. Second, the overconfident British generals made several mistakes. Third, time itself was on the side of the Americans. The British could win battle after battle, as they did, and still lose the war. Fighting an overseas war, 3,000 miles from London, was terribly expensive. After a few years, tax-weary British citizens clamored for peace.

Finally, the Americans did not fight alone. Louis XVI of France had little sympathy for the ideals of the American Revolution, but he was eager to weaken France's rival, Britain. French entry into the war in 1778 was decisive. In 1781, combined forces of about 9,500 Americans and 7,800 French trapped a British army commanded by Lord Cornwallis near Yorktown, Virginia. Unable to escape, Cornwallis surrendered. The Americans were victorious.

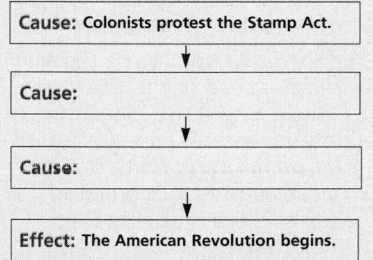

North America, 1783

ALASKA

UNCLAIMED

Hudson Bay

PACIFIC OCEAN

CANADA

Quebec

Boston

New York

UNITED STATES

LOUISIANA TERRITORY

ATLANTIC OCEAN

Charleston

FLORIDA

New Orleans

BAHAMAS

PUERTO RICO

NEW SPAIN

Gulf of Mexico

Tropic of Cancer

CUBA

JAMAICA

Mexico City

HONDURAS

HISPANIOLA

Caribbean Sea

SOUTH AMERICA

0 500 Miles

0 1,000 Kilometers

- ▨ British territory
- ☐ French territory
- ▨ Russian territory
- ▨ Spanish territory
- ▨ Claimed by U.S. and Great Britain
- ▨ Claimed by U.S. and Spain

GEOGRAPHY SKILLBUILDER: Interpreting Maps
1. **Region** *What feature formed the western border of the United States?*
2. **Human-Environment Interaction** *What European countries had claims on the North American continent in 1783?*

Changing Idea: Colonial Attachment to Britain

Old Idea
American colonists considered themselves as subjects of the British king.

New Idea
After a long train of perceived abuses by the king, the colonists asserted their right to declare independence.

Americans Create a Republic

Shortly after declaring their independence, the 13 individual states recognized the need for a national government. As victory became certain, in 1781 all 13 states ratified a constitution. This plan of government was known as the Articles of Confederation. The Articles established the United States as a republic—a government in which citizens rule through elected representatives.

The Articles Create a Weak National Government To protect their authority, the 13 states created a loose confederation in which they held most of the power. Thus, the Articles of Confederation deliberately created a weak national government.

Enlightenment and Revolution **185**

History from Visuals

North America, 1783
Interpreting the Map Have students use the map key to identify which European country claimed the largest area of land on the map and which claimed the smallest. *Answers: Largest—Spain, Smallest—France*

Extension Activity Assign pairs of students one of the territories on the map. Tell partners to use an encyclopedia to learn more about this territory in 1783. Have partners share what they learned with the class.

SKILLBUILDER Answers
1. Mississippi River.
2. Spain, Russia, England, France.

CRITICAL THINKING ACTIVITY
CLASS TIME: 15 MINUTES

Analyzing Causes
To help students understand the events that led to the American Revolution, have them complete a chart like the one below.

Cause: Colonists protest the Stamp Act.

↓

Cause:

↓

Cause:

↓

Effect: The American Revolution begins.

OBJECTIVE 3 INSTRUCT

Americans Create a Republic

▶ **Key Ideas**
- To protect their authority, the 13 states create a weak national government, which fails.
- Congressional delegates create a new system of government based on Enlightenment ideas.
- The new government system is made up of three separate branches.

(continued on next page)

TEACHING OPTION **BLOCK SCHEDULING**

MAKING NEW LAWS

CLASS TIME 20 MINUTES

Task: Students will work in small groups to write a list of American laws concerning taxes, trade, and government.

Materials Needed: Textbooks, writing instruments, paper.

Activity: Ask students to name some of the British laws and actions that angered the colonists.

Students might mention that the British imposed unfair taxes, restricted trade, and did not provide representation of the colonies in Parliament. Discuss with students how laws created by colonial leaders might have been different from British laws. Next, have groups of students write a list of three or four laws that the newly independent Americans might have written. These laws should concern taxes,

trade, and government. To help students get started, write this law on the board: "Americans may sell goods at the market price to all countries."

Conclusion: Ask groups to share their laws and explain their reasoning. Invite volunteers to write their laws on the board.

Teacher's Edition **185**

(continued from page 185)

• The Bill of Rights is created to further protect the rights of individual citizens.

MORE ABOUT . . .
The Colonies

Enlightenment ideas spread through the colonies in books and pamphlets. Literacy rates in the colonies were high among white males. While only one-third of males in England could read, in some colonies, over 50 percent of the males could read. Literacy rates in New England were particularly high because the Puritans who settled there advocated public education so that everyone, women included, could read the Bible.

History from Visuals

U.S. Constitution: An Enlightenment Document

Interpreting the Chart Explain that the purpose of the chart is to show where the ideas of Enlightenment thinkers are found in the Constitution. Point out the boldfaced names and bulleted phrases and tell students that these elements will help them read the chart. Next, ask students this question: From whose idea stems the freedom of speech and religion? *Voltaire's idea.*

Extension Activity Divide the class into five groups and assign each group a row from the chart. Have groups make a poster that uses words and images to display the Enlightenment idea and the way it is reflected in the Constitution. Display posters.

SKILLBUILDER Answers
1. Montesquieu's
2. Free speech, religious toleration, rights of accused, no torture

---

There were no executive or judicial branches. Instead, the Articles established only one body of government, the Congress. Each state, regardless of size, had one vote in Congress. Congress could declare war, enter into treaties, and coin money. It had no power, however, to collect taxes or regulate trade. Passing new laws was difficult because laws needed the approval of 9 of the 13 states.

These limits on the national government soon produced many problems. Although the new national government needed money in order to operate, it could only request contributions from the states. Angry Revolutionary War veterans bitterly complained that Congress still owed them back pay. Meanwhile, several states issued their own money. Some states even put tariffs on goods from neighboring states.

The nation's growing financial problems sparked a violent protest in Massachusetts. Debt-ridden farmers, led by a war veteran named Daniel Shays, demanded that the state lower taxes and issue paper money so that they could repay their debts. When the state refused, the rebels attacked several courthouses. Massachusetts authorities quickly crushed Shays's Rebellion.

A New Constitution Concerned leaders such as George Washington and James Madison believed that Shays's Rebellion underscored the need for a strong national government. In February 1787, Congress approved a Constitutional Convention to revise the Articles of Confederation. The Constitutional Convention held its first session on May 25, 1787. The 55 delegates were experienced statesmen who were familiar with the political theories of Locke, Montesquieu, and Rousseau.

Although the delegates shared basic ideas on government, they sometimes disagreed on how to put them into practice. For almost four months the delegates argued over important questions. Who should be represented in Congress? How many votes should each state have? The delegates' deliberations produced not only compromises but also new approaches to governing. Using the political ideas of the Enlightenment, the delegates created a new system of government.

The Federal System Like Montesquieu, the delegates distrusted a powerful central government controlled by one person or group. They therefore established three separate branches—legislative, executive, and judicial. This provided a built-in system of **checks**

THINK THROUGH HISTORY
D. Making Inferences What was the fundamental cause of the nation's problems under the Articles of Confederation?
D. Answer Weak federal government.

U.S. Constitution: An Enlightenment Document

Enlightenment Idea	U.S. Constitution
Locke A government's power comes from the consent of the people	• Preamble begins "We the People of the United States" to establish legitimacy • Creates representative government • Limits government powers
Montesquieu Separation of powers	• Federal system of government • Powers divided among three branches • System of checks and balances
Rousseau Direct democracy	• Public election of president and Congress
Voltaire Free speech, religious toleration	• Bill of Rights provides for freedom of speech and religion
Beccaria Accused have rights, no torture	• Bill of Rights protects rights of accused and prohibits cruel and unusual punishment

SKILLBUILDER: Interpreting Charts
1. *From whose idea stems the system of checks and balances?*
2. *Which of the Enlightenment ideas are reflected in the Bill of Rights?*

Task: Student pairs will find an article that reflects Enlightenment ideas and develop oral reports that explain how the article and ideas are connected.

Purpose: To recognize the influence of Enlightenment ideas today.

Activity: Brainstorm with students a list of Enlightenment thinkers' ideas. These should include separation of powers, elections and direct democracy,

freedom of speech and religion, protection of the accused, prohibition of torture, importance of reason and scientific inquiry, and a government's power comes from the consent of the governed.

Have partners look in local, regional, or national newspapers and magazines to find an article that reflects one or more of these ideas. For example, partners might use an article about a political election to show the idea of direct democracy and

the power of government coming from the governed. Have partners cut out or copy their article.

Each pair should prepare and present an oral report that describes what the article is about, tells which Enlightenment ideas and thinkers the article reflects, and explains how it does this.

 ALTERNATIVE ASSESSMENT BOOK
Standards for Evaluating a Cooperative Activity

and balances, with each branch checking the actions of the other two. For example, the president received the power to veto legislation passed by Congress. However, the Congress could override a presidential veto with the approval of two-thirds of its members.

Although the Constitution created a strong central government, it did not eliminate local governments. Instead, the Constitution set up a **federal system** in which power was divided between national and state governments.

The delegates agreed with Locke and Rousseau that governments draw their authority from the consent of the governed. The Constitution's preamble sums up this principle:

> **A VOICE FROM THE PAST**
> We the People of the United States, in order to form a more perfect Union, establish Justice, insure domestic Tranquillity, provide for the common defense, promote the general Welfare, and secure the Blessings of Liberty to ourselves and our Posterity, do ordain and establish this Constitution for the United States of America.
> **CONSTITUTION OF THE UNITED STATES OF AMERICA**

E. Possible Answer
Federalists believed the Constitution reflected balance between federal and state powers; Antifederalists thought federal government too powerful, wanted Bill of Rights to protect individual freedoms.

THINK THROUGH HISTORY
E. Analyzing Issues
Explain the controversy over ratifying the Constitution. What did each side believe?

The Bill of Rights The delegates signed the new Constitution on September 17, 1787. In order to become law, however, the Constitution required approval by conventions in at least 9 of the 13 states. These conventions were marked by sharp debate. Supporters of the Constitution, called the Federalists, argued that the new government would provide a better balance between national and state powers. Their opponents, the Antifederalists, feared that the Constitution gave the central government too much power. They also wanted a bill of rights to protect the rights of individual citizens.

In order to gain support, the Federalists promised to add a bill of rights to the Constitution. This promise cleared the way for approval. Congress formally added to the Constitution the ten amendments known as the **Bill of Rights.** These amendments protected such basic rights as freedom of speech, press, assembly, and religion. Many of these rights had been advocated by Voltaire, Rousseau, and Locke.

The Constitution and Bill of Rights marked a turning point in people's ideas about government. Both documents put Enlightenment ideas into practice. They expressed an optimistic view that reason and reform could prevail and that progress was inevitable. Such optimism swept across the Atlantic. However, the monarchies and the privileged classes didn't give up power and position easily. As Chapter 7 explains, the struggle to attain the principles of the Enlightenment continued in France.

GlobalImpact

The French Revolution
The American Revolution inspired the growing number of French people who were seeking reform in their own country. They saw the new government of the United States as a step toward realizing the ideals of the Enlightenment. They hoped the next step would be reform in France.

The Declaration of Independence was widely circulated and admired in France. French officers like the Marquis de Lafayette, who fought for American independence, returned to France with stories of the war. Such personal accounts intrigued many a reader.

When the French bishop Charles-Maurice de Talleyrand wrote about this time period years later, he would say, "We talked of nothing but America."

GlobalImpact
The French Revolution

In 1789, a French writer made this comment about the newly formed United States: "This vast continent which the seas surround will soon change Europe and the universe." What does this writer believe about the United States? What kind of change might the writer be talking about? Would kings and commoners have viewed this change in the same way? Explain.

ASSESS & RETEACH

Section 4 Assessment
Have pairs of students quiz each other on the list of terms and names. Then have them work together to answer the questions.

Section Quiz
FORMAL ASSESSMENT
Section Quiz, p. 79

Reteaching Activity
CLASS TIME: 30 MINUTES

Work with students to use the small and large heads in this section to make up questions about the section contents. For example, you can make up the following question from the first head in the section: "What was the relationship between Britain and its American Colonies?" List the questions on the board and have students copy them. Then have pairs of students work together to answer the questions. Go over students' answers.

CRITICAL THINKING TRANSPARENCIES
CT58 Visual Summary

Section ❹ Assessment

1. TERMS & NAMES
Identify
• Declaration of Independence
• Thomas Jefferson
• checks and balances
• federal system
• Bill of Rights

2. TAKING NOTES
Create a chart like the one below. On the left, list problems faced by the Americans as colonists and in shaping their republic. On the right, record their actions and decisions to solve those problems.

Problem	Solution

Which of the solutions that you recorded represented a compromise?

3. ANALYZING ISSUES
How does the opening statement from the Declaration of Independence (page 184) reflect enlightened thinking?

4. ANALYZING THEMES
Revolution Do you think the American Revolution would have happened if there had not been an Age of Enlightenment? Explain.

THINK ABOUT
• John Locke's impact on government
• other British colonies
• Enlightenment ideas

Enlightenment and Revolution **187**

CLOSE ACTIVITY

CLASS TIME: 20 MINUTES

Making a Comic Strip
Have small groups of students work together to create a simple comic strip depicting one of the events in this section. Comic strips should be one to three cells and include dialogue or captions to explain what is happening in the pictures. Subjects for comic strips include American hostility toward the British, the drafting of important documents, and congressional debates about government. Encourage groups to share their work.

ANSWERS

1. TERMS & NAMES
• Declaration of Independence, p. 184
• Thomas Jefferson, p. 184
• checks and balances, pp. 186–187
• federal system, p. 187
• Bill of Rights, p. 187

2. TAKING NOTES
Possible Responses: Navigation Acts/smuggling; Stamp Act/boycott; import tax on tea/Boston Tea Party; weaknesses of Articles of Confederation/Constitutional Convention; distrust of central government/federal system.

3. ANALYZING ISSUES
Possible Response: It reflects the supremacy of reason, and shows a belief in human progress. It also includes the ideas that humans have natural rights, and that a government gets its power from the consent of the governed.

4. ANALYZING THEMES
Possible Responses: No; during Enlightenment, the average person started to question his or her happiness, which led to questioning authority. Yes; the people who came to America were self-reliant and individualistic; they were more open to change and revolution.

TERMS & NAMES

1. heliocentric theory, p. 166
2. Galileo Galilei, p. 166
3. Isaac Newton, p. 168
4. social contract, p. 171
5. natural rights, p. 171
6. separation of powers, p. 173
7. salon, p. 178
8. enlightened despot, p. 181
9. Declaration of Independence, p. 184
10. federal system, p. 187

REVIEW QUESTIONS

Answers may vary on some questions.

11. Center; earth revolved around the sun; Copernicus's theory.

12. (1) Identify a problem based on an observation, (2) form a hypothesis, (3) test the hypothesis, (4) analyze and interpret the results to reach a conclusion.

13. Telescope, to enlarge distant objects; microscope, to enlarge minute objects; thermometer, to measure temperature; barometer, to measure atmospheric pressure.

14. Hobbes thought that all people were naturally selfish and that governments were created to protect people from their own selfishness. He believed that an absolute monarchy was best. Locke thought that people had the natural ability to reason, govern their own affairs, and look after society. He believed that governments should be formed to protect these natural rights. Locke promoted self-government.

15. Loss of political liberties led to the fall of Rome; Montesquieu admired the separation of power.

16. Science offered new explanations of mysteries of nature; more people questioned religious teaching and authority.

17. The arts reflected order and balance; artists and architects borrowed ideas from classical Rome and Greece; the novel developed.

18. Greater religious toleration, reduced censorship, reduced torture, various other reforms; many reforms were limited or temporary, and all the enlightened despots failed to improve life of peasants.

19. There were no executive or judicial branches; Congress had no power to collect taxes or regulate trade; new laws were difficult to pass because nine of the 13 states needed to approve them.

TERMS & NAMES

Briefly explain the importance of each of the following to the Scientific Revolution, the Enlightenment, or the American Revolution (1550–1789).

1. heliocentric theory
2. Galileo Galilei
3. Isaac Newton
4. social contract
5. natural rights
6. separation of powers
7. salon
8. enlightened despot
9. Declaration of Independence
10. federal system

Interact with History

On page 164, you put yourself in the dilemma of Galileo. As you have read, Galileo did recant, but the idea he supported eventually became widely accepted. Think about the decisions of both Galileo and the church. Did the choices they made advance their goals? Discuss your opinions with a small group.

REVIEW QUESTIONS

SECTION 1 (pages 165–170)
The Scientific Revolution

11. According to Ptolemy, what was earth's position in the universe? How did Copernicus's view differ? Which did Kepler's observations support?

12. What are four steps in the scientific method?

13. List four new instruments that came into use during the Scientific Revolution. Identify the purpose of each one.

SECTION 2 (pages 171–177)
The Enlightenment in Europe

14. How did the ideas of Hobbes and Locke differ?

15. What did Montesquieu believe led to the fall of Rome? What did he admire about the government of Britain?

16. How did the Enlightenment lead to a more secular outlook?

SECTION 3 (pages 178–182)
The Spread of Enlightenment Ideas

17. Name three developments in the arts during the Enlightenment.

18. What sorts of reforms did the enlightened despots make? In what respects did their reforms fail?

SECTION 4 (pages 183–187)
American Revolution: The Birth of a Republic

19. Why did the Articles of Confederation result in a weak national government?

20. How did the writers of the U.S. Constitution put into practice the idea of separation of powers? A system of checks and balances?

Visual Summary

Enlightenment and Revolution, 1550–1789

Scientific Revolution

- Heliocentric theory challenges geocentric theory.
- Mathematics and observation support heliocentric theory.
- Scientific method develops.
- Scientists make discoveries in many fields.

A new way of thinking about the world develops—based on observation and a willingness to question assumptions.

Enlightenment

- People try to apply the scientific approach to all aspects of society.
- Political scientists propose new ideas about government.
- Philosophes advocate the use of reason to discover truths.
- Philosophes address social issues through reason.

Enlightenment writers challenge many accepted ideas about government and society.

Spread of Enlightenment Ideas

- Enlightenment ideas appeal to thinkers and artists across Europe.
- Salons help spread Enlightenment thinking.
- Ideas spread to literate middle class.
- Enlightened despots attempt reforms.

Enlightenment ideas sweep through European society and also to colonial America.

American Revolution

- Enlightenment ideas influence colonists.
- Britain taxes colonies after French and Indian War.
- Colonists denounce taxation without representation.
- War begins in Lexington and Concord.

Colonists declare independence, defeat Britain, and establish republic.

20. Separation of powers: created three separate branches of government—executive, legislative, and judicial; checks and balances: gave each of the three branches some control over the others.

Interact with History

Possible Responses: Students who originally refused to publicly deny the ideas about the universe may now say that Galileo's ideas would have had followers whether he lived or died. They may also believe that Galileo was right to recant his ideas instead of dying for them because the ideas were already circulating widely. Nothing Galileo did could have changed this. Others may say that Galileo should have stood up for what he believed in, regardless of the consequences.

CRITICAL THINKING

1. ROLE OF TECHNOLOGY

What role did new technology play in the Scientific Revolution?

2. THE U.S. CONSTITUTION

THEME POWER AND AUTHORITY What was the source of the Constitution's authority? How did this reflect Enlightenment ideas?

3. REVOLUTIONARY IDEAS

Create a two-column table like the one below. In the left column, list important new ideas that arose during the Scientific Revolution and Enlightenment. In the right column, briefly explain why the idea was revolutionary.

New Idea	Why Revolutionary

4. ANALYZING PRIMARY SOURCES

One of Voltaire's most passionate causes was religious toleration. The following excerpt comes from his *Treatise on Toleration* (1763). Voltaire wrote the essay in response to the case of a French Protestant who was falsely accused of murdering his Catholic son. The man was tortured and executed by French authorities. Read the passage and answer the questions that follow.

> **A VOICE FROM THE PAST**
> No great . . . eloquence is needed to prove that Christians should tolerate one another. I go even further and declare that we must look upon all men as our brothers. . . . Are we not all the children of one father and creatures of the same God? . . .
>
> This little globe, nothing more than a point, rolls in space like so many other globes; we are lost in this immensity. Man, some five feet tall, is surely a very small part of the universe. One of these imperceptible [virtually invisible] beings says to some of his neighbors in Arabia or Africa: "Listen to me, for the God of all these worlds has enlightened me: there are nine hundred million little ants like us on earth, but only my anthill is beloved of God; he will hold all others in horror through all eternity; only mine will be blessed, the others will be eternally wretched.

- Summarize the main point conveyed in this passage. How does Voltaire illustrate his point?
- Do you think Voltaire is directing his message to one religion in particular or to all organized religions? Explain your response.

CHAPTER ACTIVITIES

1. LIVING HISTORY: Unit Portfolio Project

THEME REVOLUTION Your unit portfolio project focuses on showing the similarities and differences among revolutions (see page 129). For Chapter 6, you might use one of the following ideas to add to your portfolio:

- Design the cover for a special magazine issue that spotlights the most revolutionary thinker of the Scientific Revolution or Enlightenment. Indicate the focus of the articles that might appear inside the magazine by writing the table of contents page.
- Present a live or taped news report covering a major event of the American Revolution or early republic.
- Write song lyrics for a Revolutionary War ballad or march that explain why the Americans are fighting for independence.

2. CONNECT TO TODAY: Cooperative Learning

THEME SCIENCE AND TECHNOLOGY The Scientific Revolution produced ideas that profoundly changed how people viewed the natural world. In today's world, scientific discoveries have become commonplace. Yet often they are as revolutionary as those of the 16th century.

Work with a team to create a visual presentation highlighting a recent breakthrough in science or medicine. Focus on how the new knowledge changed what scientists previously thought about the topic.

Use the Internet or magazines to research the topic. Look for information that will help you to understand the nature of the discovery and to explain why it is significant.

- Write two brief sentences that summarize the difference in scientific understanding before and after the breakthrough. For an example of such a summary, look at the box on the bottom of page 168.
- Use text, charts, and other illustrations to explain the discovery's impact.

3. INTERPRETING A TIME LINE

Revisit the unit time line on pages 128–129. What events in Chapters 7 and 8 were probably influenced by the Enlightenment? Why?

FOCUS ON FINE ART

The Spanish artist Francisco Goya produced this engraving, titled "The Sleep of Reason Produces Monsters," in 1797. Here is his caption: Imagination abandoned by reason produces impossible monsters; united with her, she is the mother of the arts and the source of their wonders.

- What do you think the monsters represent?
- What is the artist saying will happen when a person lets his or her reason go to sleep?

Connect to History How does the engraving reflect the ideas of Enlightenment thinkers?

Enlightenment and Revolution **189**

	Key Ideas	**COPY MASTERS**	**ASSESSMENT**
SECTION 1 **Revolution Threatens the French King** *pp. 193–196*	*Members of the Third Estate demand a more representative government. The fall of the Bastille and the king's removal from Versailles signal the beginning of the French Revolution.*	*In-Depth Resources: Unit 2* • **Guided Reading,** p. 37 • **Literature:** from *A Tale of Two Cities,* p. 49 • **History Makers:** Marie Antoinette, p. 52	PE *Section 1 Assessment,* p. 196 *Formal Assessment* • Section Quiz, p. 88 *Alternative Assessment Book* • Standards for Evaluating a Product or Performance
SECTION 2 **Revolution Brings Reform and Terror** *pp. 197–203*	*The Legislative Assembly faces war and internal divisions. The king is executed, and Robespierre inaugurates the Reign of Terror. A third constitution puts power in the hands of the upper middle class.*	*In-Depth Resources: Unit 2* • **Guided Reading,** p. 38 • **Geography Application,** p. 43 • **Primary Sources,** pp. 45, 46, 47 • **History Makers:** Robespierre, p. 53 • **Across Time and Cultures,** p. 54 • **Science and Technology,** p. 55	PE *Section 2 Assessment,* p. 203 *Formal Assessment* • Section Quiz, p. 89 *Alternative Assessment Book* • Standards for Evaluating a Cooperative Activity
SECTION 3 **Napoleon Forges an Empire** *pp. 204–208*	*A brilliant general, Napoleon Bonaparte, becomes emperor of France and assumes broad powers. Through military victories, he establishes mastery over most of Europe.*	*In-Depth Resources: Unit 2* • **Guided Reading,** p. 39 • **Primary Source**: Napoleon's Proclamation at Austerlitz, p. 48	PE *Section 3 Assessment,* p. 208 *Formal Assessment* • Section Quiz, p. 90 *Alternative Assessment Book* • Standards for Evaluating a Cooperative Activity
SECTION 4 **Napoleon's Empire Collapses** *pp. 209–212*	*Napoleon makes political and military mistakes as he tries to increase his power. He is defeated, returns, is defeated again, and finishes his life in exile.*	*In-Depth Resources: Unit 2* • **Guided Reading,** p. 40 • **Skillbuilder Practice:** Interpreting Maps, p. 42	PE *Section 4 Assessment,* p. 212 *Formal Assessment* • Section Quiz, p. 91 *Alternative Assessment Book* • Standards for Evaluating a Product or Performance
SECTION 5 **The Congress of Vienna Convenes** *pp. 213–217*	*Following the plan of Metternich, the Congress of Vienna reestablishes stability in Europe after the defeat of Napoleon.*	*In-Depth Resources: Unit 2* • **Guided Reading,** p. 41	PE *Section 5 Assessment,* p. 216 *Formal Assessment* • Section Quiz, p. 92 *Alternative Assessment Book* • Standards for Evaluating a Cooperative Activity
CHAPTER RESOURCES	**Chapter Overview** *Revolution leads to the overthrow and execution of the French king. After a period of instability, Napoleon takes control of France and of most of Europe. Napoleon's thirst for power leads to his downfall, and European leaders craft a lasting peace.*	*Telescoping the Times* • Chapter Summary, pp. 29–31 *Planning for Block Schedules*	*Chapter Assessment,* pp. 218–219 *Chapter Activities,* p. 219 *Formal Assessment* • Chapter Test, forms A and B, pp. 93–98 *Test Generator* *Alternative Assessment Book*

1789–1815

TECHNOLOGY

 Warm-Up Transparency 7

 Geography Transparencies
- G23 Early Sites of the French Revolution, 1789

 World Art and Cultures Transparencies
- AT50 *Portrait of Marie Antoinette*

 Electronic Library of Primary Sources
- from *Memoirs of Élisabeth Vigée-Lebrun*

 INTERNET RESOURCES
www.mlworldhistory.com

 Warm-Up Transparency 7

 Critical Thinking Transparencies
- CT75 Cause and Effect Graphic Organizer

 Electronic Library of Primary Sources
- from "Execution by Guillotine"

 INTERNET RESOURCES
www.mlworldhistory.com

 Warm-Up Transparency 7

 World Art and Cultures Transparencies
- AT51 *Napoleon Crossing the St. Bernard Pass*

 Electronic Library of Primary Sources
- from *The Letters of Napoleon I*

 Battles of the World
- The Battle of Austerlitz

 INTERNET RESOURCES
www.mlworldhistory.com

 Warm-Up Transparency 7

 Electronic Library of Primary Sources
- "The Battle of Waterloo: The Finale"

 INTERNET RESOURCES
www.mlworldhistory.com

 Warm-Up Transparency 7

 Critical Thinking Transparencies
- CT23 The French Revolution

 Electronic Library of Primary Sources
- from *Memoirs of Metternich*
- from "Frenchmen, Is This What You Want?"

 INTERNET RESOURCES
www.mlworldhistory.com

 Chapter Summaries on Audiocassette in English and Spanish

 INTERNET RESOURCES
www.mlworldhistory.com

Block Scheduling (90 MINUTES)

Day 1
Section 1, pp. 193–196
Section Assessment, p. 196

Day 2
Section 2, pp. 197–203

 COOPERATIVE ACTIVITY
Debating an Issue, p. 198 (Teacher's Edition)

Section Assessment, p. 203

Day 3
Section 3, pp. 204–208

 COOPERATIVE ACTIVITY
Researching Napoleon and Nelson, p. 207 (Teacher's Edition)

Section 4, pp. 209–212
Section Assessments, pp. 208, 212

Day 4
Section 5, pp. 213–217

COOPERATIVE ACTIVITY
Investigating World Peace Organizations, p. 215 (Teacher's Edition)

Section Assessment, p. 217
Chapter Assessment, pp. 218–219

Yearly Pacing *Chapter 7 Total:* 4 days *Yearly Total:* 85 days

 Planning for Block Schedules

Customizing for Special Needs

Students Acquiring English

 Access for Students Acquiring English
- **Guided Reading** for Sections 1–5 (Spanish), pp. 81–85
- **Chapter Summary** (Spanish), pp. 78–80
- **Skillbuilder Practice** Interpreting Maps (Spanish), p. 86
- **Geography Application** The French Revolution Under Siege (Spanish), p. 87

 Chapter Summaries on Audiocassette in English and Spanish

 Spanish Reading Study Guide pp. 73–84

Less Proficient Readers

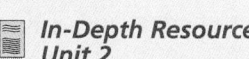 *In-Depth Resources: Unit 2*
- **Guided Reading** for Sections 1–5, pp. 37–41
- **Skillbuilder Practice** Interpreting Maps, p. 42
- **Geography Application** The French Revolution Under Siege, p. 43

 Telescoping the Times
- Chapter Summary, pp. 29–31

 Reading Study Guide pp. 73–84

 Chapter Summaries on Audiocassette

Gifted and Talented Students

 In-Depth Resources: Unit 2

Primary Sources:
- from *A Declaration of the Rights of Man and of the Citizen, 1789,* p. 45
- "La Marseillaise," p. 46
- *from* The Execution of Louis XVI, p. 47
- Napoleon's Proclamation at Austerlitz, 1805, p. 48

History Makers
- Marie Antoinette, p. 52
- Maximilien Robespierre, p. 53

Connections to Literature   READINGS FOR STUDENTS

 In-Depth Resources: Unit 2
Literature: from *A Tale of Two Cities* by Charles Dickens, p. 48

Enrichment Reading
- **Sherwood, Frances** *Vindication* New York: Penguin, 1994

Mary Wollstonecraft, author of *A Vindication of the Rights of Woman,* is portrayed vividly in this fictionalized treatment of her life and times.

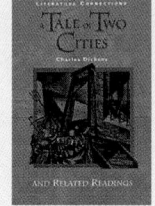

McDougal Littell *Literature Connections*
- Dickens, Charles *A Tale of Two Cities* (with related readings)

A classic tale of the French Revolution, with themes of love and self-sacrifice, heroes and quests.

 PE = Pupil's Edition   = Overhead Transparency   = Software   = Video

= Copy Master   = CD-ROM   = Audiocassette   = Internet

CHAPTER 7 OVERVIEW

The French Revolution and Napoleon, 1789–1815

Accessing Prior Knowledge

- Ask students to read the captions accompanying each picture and to discuss what they already know about the people and the situations.

Predicting and Making Inferences

- After reading about Marie Antoinette's taste for fine clothes, ask students what they predict will happen to her.
- Ask students what they can tell about Napoleon's character from the painting of him astride his white horse.

Geography Connection

Ask students to study the border area of France and Spain.

- What is the geography of this area like?
- Could the geography protect Spain from its more powerful neighbor?

CHAPTER 7
The French Revolution and Napoleon, 1789–1815

PREVIEWING THEMES

Power and Authority

With absolute rulers dominating Europe, Enlightenment thinkers began questioning why so few held so much power. The French Revolution was an attempt to put power in the hands of the many. Power changed hands several times in this short period of history.

Revolution

The success of the American Revolution inspired the French, some of whom even participated in it. The French people were deeply affected by the colonists' overthrow of the British and, in turn, revolted against their own repressive rulers.

Economics

The gap between the rich and the poor widened when France's economy weakened. Hungry peasants and city dwellers were outraged by what they felt was unjust treatment. The economy of France became a major cause of the Revolution.

> **INTERNET CONNECTION**
>
> Visit us at **www.mlworldhistory.com** to learn more about the French Revolution, Napoleon, and related topics.

EUROPE, 1789

At Versailles, **Queen Marie Antoinette** spent so much money on clothes that in **1785** her enemies falsely accused her of buying a necklace with 647 diamonds. The rumor increased her unpopularity.

ATLANTIC OCEAN

— Holy Roman Empire

0 ——— 200 Miles
0 ——— 400 Kilometers

In Paris, a mob stormed the **Bastille,** the fortress looming in the background, and seized the weapons stored there. This **1789** event ignited the French Revolution.

SPAIN

◉ **Madrid**

. Cádiz
. Gibraltar

190

GEOGRAPHY THEMES

Location

Ask students to note the political boundaries in Europe just before the French Revolution. Then have them turn to page 636 in the Atlas to examine Europe today. Ask them to name three European countries that did not exist in 1789. *Possibilities include Belgium,* *Greece, Germany, Italy, Czech Republic, Slovakia, Bosnia-Herzegovina, Croatia, and Albania.* Have students speculate about reasons for political changes in Europe over time.

Place

Tell students that geography played a key role in the political and military events discussed in this chapter. Ask them to examine this map and the one on page 637, to note the mountains between France and Italy, and to speculate about the difficulties involved in moving an army across the Alps. Explain that Napoleon's ability to conduct military campaigns despite physical barriers was one source of his success as a general. You might also ask students why Napoleon may have ridden a mule.

ADDITIONAL RESOURCES

Books for the Teacher
- Jones, R. Ben. *Napoleon: Man and Myth.* New York: Holmes, 1978.
- Kennedy, Emmet. *A Cultural History of the French Revolution.* New Haven: Yale UP, 1989.
- Schama, Simon. *Citizens: A Chronicle of the French Revolution.* New York: Knopf, 1989.

Books for the Student
- Robiquet, Jean. *Daily Life in the French Revolution.* Trans. James Kirkup. New York: Macmillan, 1965.
- Shenkman, Richard. *Legends, Lies, and Cherished Myths of World History.* New York: Harper, 1993.

Videos
- *The French Revolution.* Social Studies School Service, 800-421-4246.
- *Marie Antoinette: The Tragic Queen.* Arts and Entertainment, 1996.
- *Napoleon Bonaparte.* Films for the Humanities, 1988.
- *A Tale of Two Cities.* Social Studies School Service, 800-421-4246. British production (1958) starring Dirk Bogarde. With curriculum unit.

Software
- *French Revolution.* CD-ROM. Educational Software Institute, 800-955-5570.
- *Napoleonic Era.* CD-ROM. Educational Software Institute, 800-955-5570. Napoleon from different points of view.

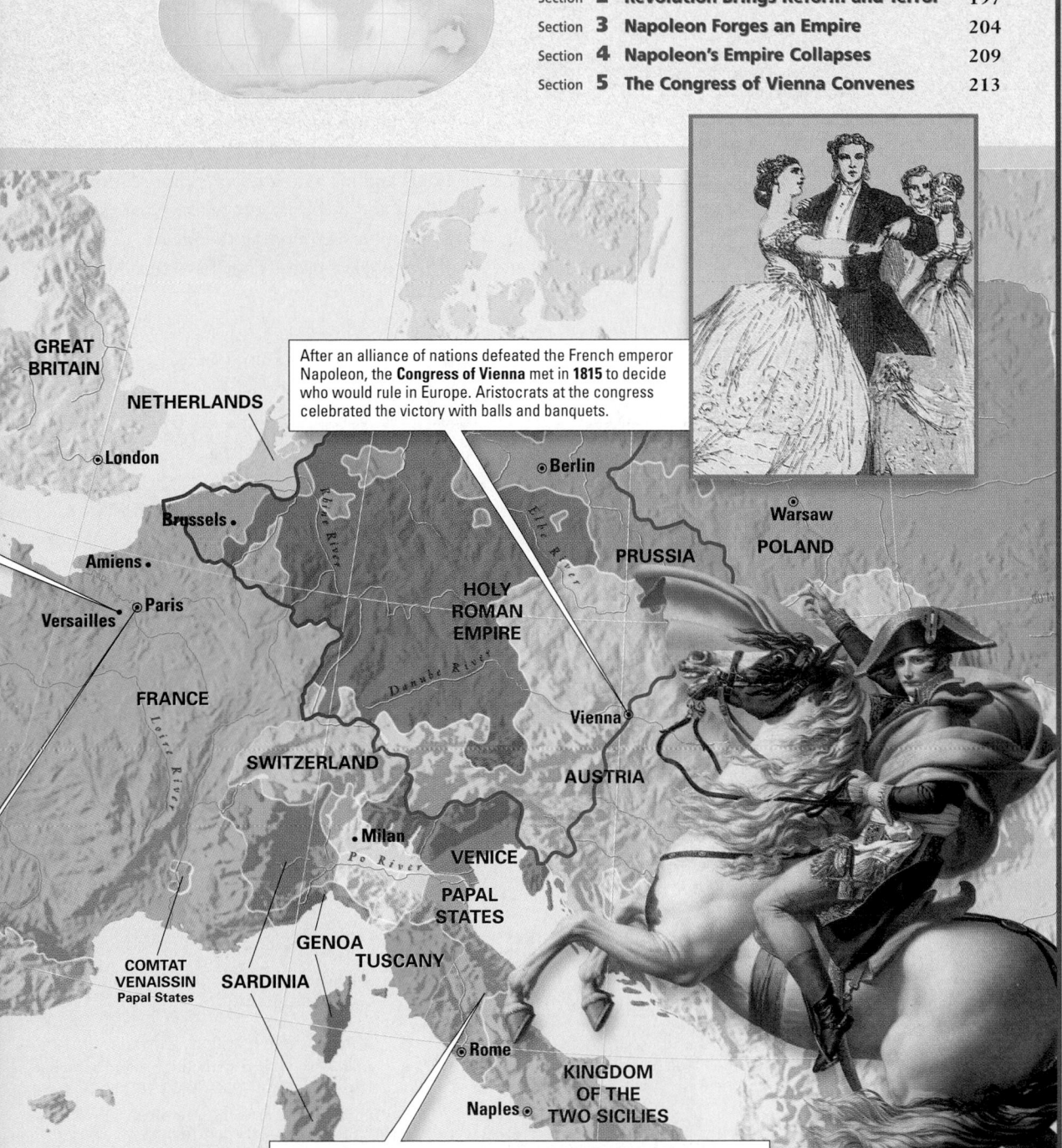

After an alliance of nations defeated the French emperor Napoleon, the **Congress of Vienna** met in **1815** to decide who would rule in Europe. Aristocrats at the congress celebrated the victory with balls and banquets.

Napoleon led a French army into Italy and defeated France's enemy, Austria, in **1796**. This detail of *Napoleon Crossing the St. Bernard Pass* by Jacques Louis David presents a heroic Napoleon astride a magnificent stallion. Actually, Napoleon crossed the Alps on a mule, not a horse.

HISTORY THROUGH ART

Napoleon Crossing the St. Bernard Pass
Jacques-Louis David

The detail from *Napoleon Crossing the St. Bernard Pass* shows a young Napoleon on his way to military glory in Italy in 1796–1797. In the painting, Napoleon faces out from the foreground with the soaring Alps in the background.

The painter, Jacques-Louis David, was the most famous French artist of his time. He won fame for his huge paintings on classical themes, and he became a leading figure of Neoclassicism, a revival of classical forms stressing order and simplicity of style.

An ardent supporter of the Revolution and of Robespierre, David became a Deputy and voted for the execution of Louis XVI.

After the execution of Robespierre, David was arrested and spent time in prison. Later he became attached to Napoleon and painted a series of pictures glorifying the exploits of the Emperor.

Interpreting the Art In what ways does this painting glorify Napoleon? Do you consider this a piece of propaganda? Why or why not?

Interact *with* History

This Interact with History feature motivates students by inviting them to put themselves in a key historical situation—the French Revolution. As they imagine themselves confronted with an angry mob, students will analyze the issues, explore their options, and become decision makers.

Purpose

- to set the stage for studying the French Revolution
- to help students understand some of the forces that can fuel a revolution
- to help students make connections with the people and events they will study in this chapter

Teaching Strategy

Thinking Critically After students have imagined themselves in the situation described on this page, have them answer the key question and give reasons for their decision.

EXAMINING *the* ISSUES

Following are suggestions for addressing each bulleted question.

1 Have students describe riots they know about or have seen. What motivated people to riot?

2 Students may mention racial tensions, poverty, or a sense of being treated unfairly as causes of violence.

3 Have students brainstorm what problems a group of laborers and farmers (peasants) bent on revolution might face.

Making Connections Ask students to discuss the role of ordinary people in the American Revolution and in the English Civil War.

Follow Up

A feature on the chapter assessment will ask students to reevaluate their responses to the situation presented on this page.

Interact *with* History

The mob waves the severed heads of palace guards on poles.

City people shout demands for bread and equality.

Angry peasants carry shovels, rakes, and any other weapons they can find.

Some women carry branches that symbolize the liberty tree.

192 Chapter 7

You are returning home from a bakery that is out of bread—again. You have no food to take to your starving children. You are desperate.

Suddenly you turn a corner and come upon the king's palace. King Louis and his wife are living there in luxury while your children and most of your fellow citizens are starving. You see a mob surrounding the palace, demanding food and relief from heavy taxes. They have turned violent.

Would you join the mob?

EXAMINING *the* ISSUES

- How could such a situation develop in one of the most advanced countries in the world?

- What could make people angry enough to behead others and then carry their heads on poles?

- How successful could a revolution of peasants be?

Discuss these questions with your classmates. In your discussion, remember what you've learned about other revolutionary conflicts, such as the American Revolution and the English Civil War.

As you read about the French Revolution in this chapter, see how events turn out for the peasants.

❶ Revolution Threatens the French King

TERMS & NAMES
- Old Regime
- estate
- Louis XVI
- Marie Antoinette
- Estates-General
- National Assembly
- Tennis Court Oath
- Great Fear

MAIN IDEA

Economic and social inequalities in the Old Regime helped cause the French Revolution.

WHY IT MATTERS NOW

Throughout history, economic and social inequalities have at times led peoples to revolt against their governments.

SETTING THE STAGE In the 1700s, France was considered the most advanced country of Europe. It was the center of the Enlightenment. It had a large population and a prosperous foreign trade. France's culture was widely praised and emulated by the rest of the world. However, the appearance of success was deceiving. There was great unrest in France, caused by high prices, high taxes, and disturbing questions raised by the Enlightenment ideas of Rousseau and Voltaire.

The Old Regime

In the 1770s, the system of feudalism left over from the Middle Ages—called the **Old Regime**—remained in place. The people of France were still divided into three large social classes, or **estates.**

The Privileged Estates Two of the estates had privileges, including access to high offices and exemptions from paying taxes, that were not granted to the members of the third.

The Roman Catholic Church, whose clergy formed the First Estate, owned 10 percent of the land in France. It provided education and relief services to the poor and contributed about 2 percent of its income to the government.

The Second Estate was made up of rich nobles, much of whose wealth was in land. Although they made up only 2 percent of the population, the nobles owned 20 percent of the land and paid almost no taxes. The majority of the clergy and the nobility scorned Enlightenment ideas as radical notions that threatened their status and power as privileged persons.

The Third Estate About 98 percent of the people belonged to the Third Estate. The three groups that made up this estate differed greatly in their economic conditions.

The first group—the bourgeoisie (BUR·zhwah·ZEE)—were merchants and artisans. They were well-educated and believed strongly in the Enlightenment ideals of liberty and equality. Although some of the bourgeoisie were as rich as nobles, they paid high taxes and lacked privileges like the other members of the Third Estate. Many felt that their wealth entitled them to a greater degree of social status and political power.

The workers of France's cities—cooks, servants, and others—formed the second group within the Third Estate, a group poorer than the bourgeoisie. Paid low wages and frequently out of work, they often went hungry. If the cost of bread rose, mobs of these workers might attack carts of grain and bread to steal what they needed.

Peasants formed the largest group within the Third Estate—more than 80 percent of France's 26 million people. Peasants paid about half their income in dues to nobles, tithes to the church, and taxes to the king's agents. They even paid taxes on such basic staples as salt. Peasants joined the urban poor in resenting the clergy and the nobles for their privileges and special treatment. The heavily taxed and discontented Third Estate was eager for change.

Vocabulary
bourgeoisie: the middle class. (The term derives from the walled cities, or *bourgs*, in which the middle class began to develop in the 1200s.)

This medallion bears the image of King Louis XVI of France.

The French Revolution and Napoleon **193**

FOCUS
5-Minute Warm-Up

▶ **Perceiving Causes**
To help students understand revolution, have them answer these questions.

1. Look at the two paintings on page 195. What is the most striking difference between the two women?

2. How do poor people sometimes feel about wealthy people?

🖳 *WARM-UP TRANSPARENCY 7*

OBJECTIVE ① INSTRUCT

The Old Regime

▶ **Key Ideas**
- The clergy of the Roman Catholic Church form the First Estate.
- The Second Estate consists of rich nobles, who own 20 percent of the land and pay no taxes.
- The other 98 percent of the people make up the Third Estate. They are heavily taxed and discontented.

📖 *IN-DEPTH RESOURCES: UNIT 2*
Guided Reading, p. 37

📖 *ACCESS FOR STUDENTS ACQUIRING ENGLISH*
Guided Reading (Spanish), p. 81

Teacher's Edition **193**

The Three Estates

Interpreting the Cartoon Ask students why the clergyman and the nobleman are standing on a stone rather than standing directly on the fallen man. *Possible Response: The stone represents the taxes and obligations that kept the members of the Third Estate subservient to the nobility and the clergy.*

Extension Activity Have students make lists of adjectives describing the feelings and attitudes of the people depicted in the cartoon.

SKILLBUILDER Answers

1. The Third Estate was oppressed because it paid 50% of its income in taxes to support the most privileged 2% of the French population.
2. They had no reason to desire change, since they already had privileges and wealth.

IN-DEPTH RESOURCES: UNIT 2
Literature: from *A Tale of Two Cities*, p. 49

OBJECTIVE 2 INSTRUCT

The Forces of Change

▶ *Key Ideas*
- New ideas about the power of the people take hold.
- Poor harvests, heavy taxes, and government debt cause instability in France.
- Louis XVI finally calls a meeting of the Estates-General to deal with the crisis.

MORE ABOUT . . .
Louis XVI

Louis XVI was a lethargic, somewhat fat, rather dull man who was more interested in hunting and tinkering with locks than in governing France. On the day the Bastille fell in Paris, the king wrote only *Rien* ("Nothing") in his diary—a reference to his lack of success in the hunt.

The Three Estates

- **First Estate**
  - made up of clergy of Roman Catholic Church
  - scorned Enlightenment ideas

- **Second Estate**
  - made up of rich nobles
  - held highest offices in government
  - disagreed about Enlightenment ideas

- **Third Estate**
  - included bourgeoisie, urban lower class, and peasant farmers
  - had no power to influence government
  - embraced Enlightenment ideas

Population of France, 1787
- 98% (Third Estate)
- less than 1% (First Estate)
- 2% (Second Estate)

Percent of Income Paid in Taxes
- 2% (First Estate)
- 0% (Second Estate)
- 50% (Third Estate)

0% 20% 40% 60% 80% 100%

SKILLBUILDER: Interpreting Charts and Political Cartoons
The Third Estate intensely resented the wealthy First and Second Estates.
1. *How do the chart and the graphs help explain the political cartoon?*
2. *Why might the First and Second Estates be opposed to change?*

The Forces of Change

In addition to the growing resentment of the lower classes, other factors were contributing to the revolutionary mood in France.

Enlightenment Ideas New views about power and authority in government were spreading among the Third Estate. The people began questioning long-standing notions about the structure of society and using words like *equality*, *liberty*, and *democracy*. The success of the American Revolution inspired them, and they discussed the radical ideas of Rousseau and Voltaire. Many shared the beliefs of the Comte d'Antraigues, a friend of Rousseau's:

Background
The ideas of Rousseau and Voltaire are also reflected in the United States Constitution.

> **A VOICE FROM THE PAST**
> The Third Estate is the People and the People is the foundation of the State; it is in fact the State itself; the other orders are merely political categories while by the *immutable laws of nature* the People is everything. Everything should be subordinated to it. . . . It is in the People that all national power resides and for the People that all states exist.
>
> **COMTE D'ANTRAIGUES,** quoted in *Citizens: A Chronicle of the French Revolution*

Economic Woes France's once prosperous economy was failing. The population was expanding rapidly, as were trade and production. However, the heavy burden of taxes made it impossible to conduct business profitably within France. The cost of living rose for everyone. In addition, bad weather in the 1780s caused widespread crop failures, resulting in a severe shortage of grain. The price of bread doubled in 1789, and many people faced starvation.

During this period, France's government sank deeply into debt. Extravagant spending by the king and queen was part of the problem. **Louis XVI,** who became king in 1774, inherited part of the debt from his predecessors. He also borrowed heavily in order to help the American revolutionaries in their war against Great Britain—France's chief rival—thereby nearly doubling the government's debt. When bankers, in 1786, refused to lend the government any more money, Louis faced serious problems.

A Weak Leader Strong leadership might have prevented the coming crisis, but Louis XVI was indecisive and allowed matters to drift. He paid little attention to his government advisers, preferring to spend his time hunting or tinkering with locks rather than attending to the details of governing.

194 Chapter 7

TEACHING OPTIONS | **EXPLORING PRIMARY SOURCES**

A Voice from the Past The Comte d'Antraigues, whose statement about the Third Estate became one of the most popular axioms of the Revolution, was from an old aristocratic family. Believing that the feudal noble families should have more power, he initially supported change and even went as far as agreeing that the nobles should no longer be exempt from taxes. But when the people wanted to reduce all aristocrats to ordinary citizens, he became a counterrevolutionary and worked diligently against further changes. Ask students to research the lives of other French aristocrats, such as the Marquis de Lafayette.

CONNECTIONS ACROSS THE CURRICULUM

Economics Taxes and debt are problems faced by most governments. In France at this time, most of the taxes were paid by the poorest people while wealthy nobles paid no taxes. Ask students to propose economic solutions to this situation. Then ask, What might be the political consequences of your solutions? What happens today when the U.S. government wants to raise taxes to pay off debts or to implement new programs?

Vocabulary
deficit: debt.

Louis had married his wife, **Marie Antoinette,** when he was 15 and she was 14. Because Marie was a member of the royal family of Austria, France's long-time enemy, she became unpopular as soon as she set foot in France. As queen, Marie spent so much money on gowns, jewels, and gifts that she became known as Madame Deficit.

Rather than cutting expenses and increasing taxes, Louis put off dealing with the emergency until France faced bankruptcy. Then, when he tried to tax aristocrats, the Second Estate forced him to call a meeting of the **Estates-General**—an assembly of representatives from all three estates—to get approval for the tax reform. He had the meeting—the first in 175 years—on May 5, 1789, at Versailles.

Revolution Dawns

The clergy and the nobles had dominated the Estates-General throughout the Middle Ages and expected to do so in the 1789 meeting. Under the assembly's medieval rules, each estate's delegates met in a separate hall to vote, and each estate had one vote. The two privileged estates could always outvote the Third Estate.

THINK THROUGH HISTORY
A. Analyzing Motives Why did the Third Estate propose a change in the Estates-General's voting rules?
A. Possible Answer To gain more power in the meeting of the Estates-General

The National Assembly The Third Estate delegates, mostly members of the bourgeoisie whose views had been shaped by the Enlightenment, were eager to make changes in the government. They insisted that all three estates meet together and that each delegate have a vote. This would give the advantage to the Third Estate, which had as many delegates as the other two estates combined.

Siding with the nobles, the king ordered the Estates-General to follow the medieval rules. The delegates of the Third Estate, however, became more and more determined to wield power. A leading spokesperson for their viewpoint was a clergyman sympathetic to their cause, the Abbé Sieyès (AB·AY syay·YEHS), who argued, "What is the Third Estate? Everything. What has it been up to now in the political order? Nothing. What does it demand? To become something herein." In a dramatic speech, he suggested that the Third Estate delegates name themselves the **National Assembly** and pass laws and reforms in the name of the French people.

HISTORY MAKERS

Marie Antoinette
1755–1793

Marie Antoinette was a pretty, lighthearted, charming woman. However, she was unpopular with the French because of her spending and her involvement in controversial court affairs. She referred to Louis as "the poor man" and sometimes set the clock forward an hour to be rid of his presence.

Marie refused to wear the tight-fitting clothing styles of the day and introduced a loose cotton dress for women. The elderly, who viewed the dress as an undergarment, thought that Marie's clothing was scandalous. The French silk industry was equally angry.

In constant need of entertainment, Marie often spent her time playing cards. One year she lost the equivalent of $1.5 million by gambling in card games.

HISTORY THROUGH ART: Fine Art

A Woman of the Revolution [*La maraîchère*] (1795), Jacques Louis David

The gap between rich and poor in 18th-century France is clear in these portraits. David, painter of the Revolution, depicted a common woman (*left*) whose appearance displays none of the luxury of the French court (*right*).

Connect *to* **History**

Comparing What details of the women's expressions and clothing most clearly show the contrasts in lives?

SEE SKILLBUILDER HANDBOOK, PAGE 654.

Connect *to* **Today**

Contrasting How would you visually convey the gap between rich and poor in your country?

Marie Antoinette, Jacques Gautier d'Agoty

The French Revolution and Napoleon **195**

Connect *to* **History**		
Comparing Suggest that students make a chart like the one here to compare the two portraits.		

After a long night of excited debate, the delegates of the Third Estate agreed to Sieyès's idea by an overwhelming majority. On June 17, 1789, they voted to establish the National Assembly, in effect proclaiming the end of absolute monarchy and the beginning of representative government. This vote was the first deliberate act of revolution.

Three days later, the Third Estate delegates found themselves locked out of their meeting room. They broke down a door to an indoor tennis court, pledging to stay until they had drawn up a new constitution. Their pledge was called the **Tennis Court Oath.**

Storming the Bastille In response, Louis tried to make peace with the Third Estate by yielding to the National Assembly's demands. He ordered the nobles and the clergy to join the Third Estate in the National Assembly. At the same time, sensing trouble, the king stationed his mercenary army of Swiss guards in Paris, since he no longer trusted the loyalty of the French soldiers.

In Paris, rumors flew that foreign troops were coming to massacre French citizens. People gathered weapons in order to defend Paris against the king's foreign troops. On July 14, a mob tried to get gunpowder from the Bastille, a Paris prison. The angry crowd overwhelmed the king's soldiers, and the Bastille fell into the control of the citizens. The fall of the Bastille became a great symbolic act of revolution to the French people. Ever since, July 14 has been a French national holiday, similar to the U.S. Fourth of July.

Vocabulary
mercenary army: a group of soldiers who will work for any country or employer that will pay them.

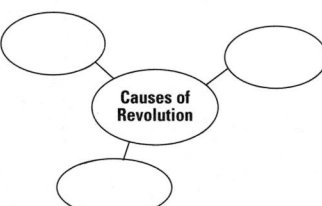

Daily *Life*

The Women's March
When the women of Paris marched 12 miles in the rain to the luxurious palace at Versailles, they were infuriated. They deeply resented the extravagances of Louis and Marie Antoinette at a time when their own children were starving.

After forcing the king and queen out of the palace, the women followed Louis's family and entourage of almost 60,000 persons to Paris—another 12-mile march.

During their return, they sang that they were bringing "the baker, the baker's wife, and the baker's lad" to Paris. (They expected the "baker" to provide bread to alleviate the terrible hunger in the city.) Revolutionary leaders would later honor the women as heroes of the Revolution.

A Great Fear Sweeps France

Before long, rebellion spread from Paris into the countryside. From one village to the next, wild rumors circulated that the nobles were hiring outlaws to terrorize the peasants.

A wave of senseless panic called the **Great Fear** rolled through France. When the peasants met no enemy bandits, they became outlaws themselves. Waving pitchforks and torches, they broke into nobles' manor houses, tore up the old legal papers that bound them to pay feudal dues, and in some cases burned the manor houses as well.

In October 1789, approximately 6,000 Parisian women rioted over the rising price of bread. Their anger quickly turned against the king and queen. Seizing knives and axes, the women and a great many men marched on Versailles. They broke into the palace and killed two guards. The women demanded that Louis and Marie Antoinette come to Paris. Finally, the king agreed to take his wife and children to Paris.

Three hours later the king, his family, and servants left Versailles, never again to see their magnificent palace. Their exit signaled the change of power and radical reforms about to overtake France.

THINK THROUGH HISTORY
B. Recognizing Effects How did the women's march mark a turning point in the relationship between the king and the people?
B. Possible Answer The king had to bow to the will of the people.

Section **1** Assessment

1. TERMS & NAMES

Identify
• Old Regime
• estate
• Louis XVI
• Marie Antoinette
• Estates-General
• National Assembly
• Tennis Court Oath
• Great Fear

2. TAKING NOTES

Use a web diagram like the one below to show the causes of the French Revolution.

Causes of Revolution

3. FORMING OPINIONS

Do you think that changes in the French government were inevitable?

THINK ABOUT
• the leadership of Louis XVI
• the French national debt
• Enlightenment ideas
• other world revolutions

4. ANALYZING THEMES

Economics How were the economic conditions in France similar to or different from those in England and the American colonies before their revolutions?

THINK ABOUT
• France's three estates
• the role of taxation
• France's national debt
• conditions in England before the Civil War
• conditions in the colonies before the American Revolution

A N S W E R S

1. TERMS & NAMES
Old Regime, p. 193
estate, p. 193
Louis XVI, p. 194
Marie Antoinette, p. 195
Estates-General, p. 195
National Assembly, p. 195
Tennis Court Oath, p. 196
Great Fear, p. 196

2. TAKING NOTES
Possible Responses:
• heavy taxes
• desire for privileges
• poor harvest and high bread prices
• gap between rich and poor
• poor leadership
• government debt
• Enlightenment ideas

3. FORMING OPINIONS
Possible Responses: Some students may say that changes were inevitable because conditions were bad and new ideas were powerful. Others may say that the situation in France could have been solved with better leadership, better communication, and a sharing of privileges and power.

4. ANALYZING THEMES
Possible Responses:
Similarities—unfair taxes and class system. Differences— Most American colonists were better off financially than French peasants; the colonists were not laboring to support a feudal nobility.

TERMS & NAMES
• Declaration of the Rights of Man
• Legislative Assembly
• émigrés
• sans-culottes
• guillotine
• Maximilien Robespierre
• Committee of Public Safety
• Reign of Terror

MAIN IDEA

The revolutionary government of France made reforms but also used terror and violence to retain power.

WHY IT MATTERS NOW

Some governments that lack the support of a majority of their people still use terrorism to control their citizens.

SETTING THE STAGE Peasants were not the only members of French society to feel the Great Fear; nobles and clergymen were equally afraid. Throughout France, bands of angry peasants struck out against members of the upper classes. In the summer of 1789, a few months before the women's march to Versailles, some nobles and clergymen in the National Assembly responded to the uprisings in an emotional late-night meeting.

The Assembly Reforms France

Throughout the night of August 4, 1789, noblemen made grand speeches, declaring their love of liberty and equality. Although motivated more by fear than by idealism, they joined other members of the National Assembly in sweeping away the feudal privileges of the First Estate and the Second Estate, thus making commoners and peasants equal to the nobles and the clergy. By morning, the Old Regime was dead.

The Rights of Man Three weeks later, on August 27, the National Assembly adopted a statement of revolutionary ideals called "A Declaration of the Rights of Man and of the Citizen," commonly known as the **Declaration of the Rights of Man.** Reflecting the influence of Enlightenment ideas and of the Declaration of Independence, the document stated that "men are born and remain free and equal in rights" and that "the aim of all political association is the preservation of the natural . . . rights of man. These rights are liberty, property, security, and resistance to oppression." Other articles of the famous document guaranteed citizens equal justice, freedom of speech, and freedom of religion. As the French people embraced the principles of the declaration, the expression "Liberty, Equality, Fraternity" became the slogan of the Revolution.

However, the Declaration of the Rights of Man did not apply to women. When Olympe de Gouges (aw·LAMP duh GOOZH) wrote a declaration of the rights of women, not only were her ideas rejected, but she eventually lost her head as an enemy of the Revolution.

A State-Controlled Church During 1790, many of the National Assembly's reforms focused on the relationship between church and state. The assembly took over church lands and declared that church officials and priests were to be elected by property owners and paid as state officials. Thus, the Catholic Church lost both its lands and its political independence. The reasons for the assembly's actions were economic. The delegates hesitated to further tax the bourgeoisie, who were strong supporters of the Revolution. However, the delegates were willing to sell church lands to help pay off France's large debt.

THINK THROUGH HISTORY
A. Synthesizing
How did the slogan "Liberty, Equality, Fraternity" sum up the goals of the Revolution?
A. Possible Answer
It conveyed the desire for freedom from old class structures, equal rights for all citizens, and unity among the French people.

HISTORY MAKERS

Olympe de Gouges
1748–1793

Olympe de Gouges was a playwright and journalist whose feminist writings reached a large audience. In 1791 this strong supporter of democracy demanded the same rights for French women that French men were demanding for themselves. In her "Declaration of the Rights of Woman and the Female Citizen," she challenged the oppression of male authority and the notion of male-female inequality:

Male and female citizens, being equal in the eyes of the law, must be equally admitted to all honors, positions, and public employment according to their capacity and without other distinctions besides those of their virtues and talents.

SECTION 2 RESOURCES

PRINT RESOURCES

 IN-DEPTH RESOURCES: UNIT 2
Guided Reading, p. 38
Geography Application: The Revolution Under Siege, p. 43
Primary Source: from Declaration, p. 45; "La Marseillaise," p. 46; from The Execution of Louis XVI, p. 47
History Makers: Maximilien Robespierre, p. 53
Connections Across Time and Cultures, p. 54
Science and Technology, p. 55

 ACCESS FOR STUDENTS ACQUIRING ENGLISH
Guided Reading (Spanish), p. 82
Geography Application: (Spanish), p. 87

 FORMAL ASSESSMENT
Section Quiz, p. 89

TECHNOLOGY RESOURCES

 CRITICAL THINKING TRANSPARENCIES
CT75 Cause-and-Effect Graphic Organizer

CD-ROM
Electronic Library of Primary Sources

INTERNET www.mlworldhistory.com

Section 2 Overview
OBJECTIVES

① To explain the provisions of the Declaration of the Rights of Man.

② To summarize the positions of the three factions that tried to govern France.

③ To explain how the war with Austria and the execution of the king affected the Revolution.

④ To describe the events of the Reign of Terror.

⑤ To explain what happened after the Terror came to an end.

SKILLBUILDER
• Interpreting charts, p. 198

CRITICAL THINKING
• Synthesizing, pp. 197, 201
• Identifying problems, p. 198
• Recognizing causes, pp. 200, 203
• Summarizing, p. 202

FOCUS
5-Minute Warm-Up

▶ *Recognizing Facts and Details*
To understand one means of controlling people, have students answer these questions.

1. Read about the guillotine on page 201. How did condemned persons die?

2. Why were some spectators displeased with the guillotine?

 WARM-UP TRANSPARENCY 7

OBJECTIVE ① INSTRUCT

The Assembly Reforms France

▶ *Key Ideas*
• The National Assembly sweeps away the privileges of the nobility and the clergy.

• The state takes control of the Catholic Church, alarming devout peasants.

• Louis XVI is caught as he tries to flee from France.

 IN-DEPTH RESOURCES: UNIT 2
Guided Reading, p. 38
Primary Source: from A Declaration of the Rights of Man and of the Citizen, 1789, p. 45

 ACCESS FOR STUDENTS ACQUIRING ENGLISH
Guided Reading (Spanish), p. 82

Conflicting Goals Cause Divisions

▶ **Key Ideas**
• A new constitution ends the absolute monarchy.
• The Legislative Assembly is given the power to create laws.
• Old problems remain, and the government splits into three factions.

The Legislative Assembly
Interpreting the Chart Point out to students that, as an aid to understanding, the columns can be read both across and down.

Extension Activity Ask students to do some reading about the French Revolution and to write a short biography of a member of each of the three groups—radicals, moderates, and conservatives.

SKILLBUILDER Answers
1. The three groups in the assembly mirrored the three estates of French society.
2. The radicals might be likened to liberals in the United States. The moderates and conservatives were like the same groups in the United States today, except that people in the United States do not support any kind of monarchy.

The assembly's actions alarmed millions of devout French peasants, who rallied to the support of their parish priests. Many French peasants, like their priests, were conservative Catholics. Although the assembly's move to make the church a part of the state was in accord with Enlightenment philosophy, it offended such Catholics, who believed that the pope should rule over a church independent of the state.

These changes in the church drove a wedge between the peasants and the bourgeoisie. From this time on, the peasants often opposed further revolutionary changes.

Louis Tries to Escape As the National Assembly restructured the relationship between church and state, Louis XVI pondered his fate as a monarch. Some of the king's advisers warned Louis that he and his family were in danger. Many supporters of the monarchy thought France unsafe and left the country. Then, in June 1791, Louis and his family tried to escape from France to the Austrian Netherlands. As they neared the French border, however, a postmaster recognized the king from his portrait on some paper money. The royal family was returned to Paris under guard. By his attempted escape, Louis XVI had increased the influence of his radical enemies and sealed his own doom.

Conflicting Goals Cause Divisions

For two years, the National Assembly argued over a new constitution for France. By 1791, the delegates had made significant changes in France's government and society.

A Limited Monarchy The National Assembly created a limited constitutional monarchy. The new constitution stripped the king of much of his authority and gave the Legislative Assembly the power to create French law. Although the king and his ministers would still hold the executive power to enforce laws, France's assemblymen would be the lawmakers in the country.

In September 1791, the National Assembly completed its new constitution, which Louis reluctantly approved, and then handed over its power to a new assembly—the **Legislative Assembly.** This assembly had the power to create laws and to approve or prevent any war the king declared on other nations.

Factions Split France Despite the new government, old problems, such as food shortages and government debt, remained. Angry cries for more liberty, more equality, and more bread soon caused the Revolution's leaders to turn against one another. The Legislative Assembly split into three general groups, each of which sat in a different part of the meeting hall. (The three divisions are summarized below.)

THINK THROUGH HISTORY
B. Identifying Problems What problems were not solved by the new government?
B. Answer Food shortages and government debt

The Legislative Assembly

Radicals	Moderates	Conservatives
• sat on the left side of the hall; were called left-wing and said to be on the left	• sat in the center of the hall and were called centrists	• sat on the right side of the hall; were called right-wing and said to be on the right
• opposed the king and the idea of a monarchy	• wanted some changes in government, but not as many as the radicals	• upheld the idea of a limited monarchy
• wanted sweeping changes in government and proposed that common people have full power in a republic		• wanted few changes in government

SKILLBUILDER: Interpreting Charts
1. *What do the divisions in the Legislative Assembly say about the differences in French society?*
2. *What similarities and differences do you see between the political factions in the Legislative Assembly and those in the U.S. government today?*

Task: Students will take on the roles of present-day radicals, moderates, and conservatives and debate a current controversial issue after preparing position statements in keeping with their roles.

Purpose: To immerse students in varying political philosophies.

Activity: Have students brainstorm a list of current controversial issues in such areas as education, welfare, taxes, and the environment. Then divide the class into groups of three. Have each group choose an issue and its members take on the roles of a radical, a moderate, and a conservative. Each group's members will debate the issue.

Building a Portfolio: Students should attach an explanation of the assignment to their statements.

ALTERNATIVE ASSESSMENT BOOK Standards for Evaluating a Cooperative Activity

Standards for Evaluation
Position statements should . . .
• clearly state the issues
• express clear positions and support them with facts and examples
• address opposing viewpoints

Although these groups disagreed, there were groups in France that were far more extreme. **Émigrés** (EHM·ih·GRAYZ)—nobles and others who had fled France during the peasant uprisings—were on the extreme right. They hoped to undo the Revolution and restore the Old Regime.

On the extreme left, the most radical group was the **sans-culottes** (SANZ kyoo·LAHTS), "those without knee breeches." Unlike the upper classes, who wore fancy knee-length pants, sans-culottes wore regular trousers. They were Parisian wage-earners and small shopkeepers who wanted a greater voice in government, lower food prices, and an end to food shortages. Although they did not have a role in the assembly, they soon discovered other ways to exert their power as a group, especially by influencing one of the political clubs that developed later.

War and Extreme Measures

In 1792, the French were faced not only with reforms at home but also with a disastrous foreign war. Monarchs and nobles in many European countries feared the changes that were taking place in France. They worried that peasant revolts similar to the ones in France could break out in their own countries.

War with Austria French radicals hoped to spread their revolution to all the peoples of Europe. When Austria and Prussia proposed that France put Louis back on the throne, the Legislative Assembly responded by declaring war on Austria in April 1792. Prussia later joined Austria in the war against the French. By going to war with France, the European leaders believed, they would be helping Louis XVI to regain his position as an absolute monarch, as well as preserving their own positions as monarchs.

The war began badly for the poorly equipped French forces. By the summer of 1792, enemy armies were advancing toward Paris. On July 25, the Prussian commander threatened to destroy Paris if the revolutionaries harmed any member of the royal family. This rash statement infuriated the Parisians. On August 10, about 20,000 men and women invaded the Tuileries, the royal palace where Louis and his family were staying. The king's Swiss guard of 900 men fought desperately to defend Louis. The mob brutally massacred them and imprisoned Louis, Marie Antoinette, and their children in a stone tower. A witness in the palace recalled the scene:

In June 1792, rioters invaded the Tuileries—Louis's palace in Paris. They shouted at Louis and waved swords in his face for hours before being persuaded to leave peacefully.

A VOICE FROM THE PAST
I ran from place to place, and finding the apartments and staircases already strewed with dead bodies, I . . . ran away to the Dauphin's garden gate where some Marseillais [citizen soldiers from Marseille], who had just butchered several of the Swiss, were stripping them. One of them came up to me with a bloody sword in his hand, saying, "Hello, citizen! Without arms! Here, take this and help us to kill." But luckily . . . I managed to make my escape. Some of the Swiss who were persued took refuge in an adjoining stable. I concealed myself in the same place. They were soon cut to pieces close to me. . . .
UNNAMED ROYAL SERVANT, quoted in *The Days of the French Revolution*

France's war with Austria and Prussia also affected daily life in Paris. During the summer of 1792, Parisians learned that French troops were failing to hold back the approaching Prussian forces. Just as bands of volunteer soldiers were preparing to leave Paris and reinforce the French soldiers in the field, they heard rumors that the royalists imprisoned in Paris would seize control of the city in their absence. Angry

The French Revolution and Napoleon **199**

Teacher's Edition **199**

THINK THROUGH HISTORY
C. Recognizing Causes What did the September massacres show about the mood of the people?
C. Possible Answer The people were impatient and fearful. They were willing to act violently.

citizens responded by taking the law into their own hands. For several days in early September, Parisians raided the prisons and murdered over 1,000 prisoners. Many royalists, nobles, and clergymen fell victim to the angry mobs in these so-called September massacres.

Faced with the threat of the Parisian radicals, the members of the Legislative Assembly gave up the idea of a limited monarchy. They set aside the Constitution of 1791, declared the king deposed, and dissolved their assembly, calling for the election of a new legislature.

The new governing body, elected in September, called itself the National Convention. Just as the new government took office, France had a stroke of luck. A French army won a battle against the Austrians and Prussians. For the moment, France was out of danger from abroad.

In this engraving, titled *Execution of Louis XVI*, a revolutionary presents Louis's head to the crowd after the king's execution in Paris.

Radicals Execute the King During the frenzied summer of 1792, the leaders of the mobs on the streets had more real power than any government assembly. Although the mobs were made up of the poor, their leaders came from the bourgeoisie.

Both men and women of the middle class joined political clubs. The most radical club in 1792 was the Jacobin (JAK·uh·bihn) Club, where violent speech-making was the order of the day. The Jacobins wanted to remove the king and establish a republic.

One of the prominent radical leaders was Jean Paul Marat (mah·RAH). During the Revolution, he edited a radical newspaper. His fiery editorials called for "five or six hundred heads cut off" to rid France of the enemies of the Revolution. Georges Danton (zhawrzh dahn·TAWN), a revolutionary leader who was devoted to the rights of Paris's poor people, joined the club as a talented speaker.

The National Convention, meeting in Paris on September 21, quickly abolished the monarchy and declared France a republic. Adult male citizens were granted the right to vote and hold office. Despite the important part they had already played in the Revolution, women were not given the right to vote. The delegates reduced Louis XVI's role from that of a king to that of a common citizen and prisoner. Then, guided by radical Jacobins, they tried Louis for treason and found him guilty. By a very close vote, they sentenced him to death. On January 21, 1793, the ex-king walked with calm dignity up the steps of the scaffold to be beheaded by a machine called the **guillotine** (GIHL·uh·TEEN). Thousands died by the guillotine during the French Revolution.

France's Citizen Army The new republic's first problem was the continuing war with Austria and Prussia. Early in 1793, Great Britain, Holland, and Spain joined Prussia and Austria in an alliance known as the First Coalition. Forced to contend with so many enemies, France suffered a string of defeats.

The Jacobin leaders took extreme steps to meet the new danger. In February 1793, the National Convention decreed a draft into the army of 300,000 French citizens between the ages of 18 and 40. By 1794, the army had grown to 800,000 and included women.

Vocabulary
coalition: a temporary alliance between groups for some specific purpose.

Task Students will examine a map to explore how much threat the French Revolution was under from external and internal enemies. They should note the central location of Paris, the fact of enemies on all sides, and the scattered internal enemies.

Materials Needed Use copies of the Geography Application worksheet for Chapter 7 or make a transparency of the map from that worksheet.

Activity Have the class help you make a list of the enemies of the Revolution. Then trace on the worksheet the locations of those enemies. If you are using a transparency, have individual students point out various locations. Have pairs of students collaborate to answer the questions from the worksheet.

Conclusion Ask students to comment on how seriously Paris was in danger at this time. What do they think might have happened if Paris had fallen? Why do they think the Reign of Terror happened in France at about this time?

IN-DEPTH RESOURCES: UNIT 2
Geography Application: The French Revolution Under Siege, p. 43

The Guillotine

If you think the guillotine was a cruel form of capital punishment, think again. Dr. Joseph Ignace Guillotin proposed a machine that satisfied many needs—it was efficient, humane, and democratic. A physician and member of the National Assembly, Guillotin claimed that those executed with the device "wouldn't even feel the slightest pain."

Prior to the guillotine's introduction in 1792, many French criminals had suffered through horrible punishments in public places. Although public punishments continued to attract large crowds, not all spectators were pleased with the new machine. Some witnesses felt that death by the guillotine occurred much too quickly to be enjoyed by an audience.

Some doctors believed that a victim's head retained its hearing and eyesight for up to 15 minutes after the blade's deadly blow. All remains were eventually gathered and buried in simple graves.

Earlier Forms of Punishment

Criminals in 17th- and 18th-century France sometimes faced one or more of the following fatal penalties:

- Burning
- Strangulation
- Being broken on a wheel
- Hanging
- Dismemberment
- Beheading
- Being pulled apart by horses

Once the executioner cranked the blade to the top, a mechanism released it. The sharp weighted blade fell, severing the victim's head from his or her body.

Woman knitters, or *tricoteuses,* were regular spectators at executions and knitted stockings for soldiers as they sat near the base of the scaffold.

Beheading by Class

More than 2,100 people were executed during the last 132 days of the Reign of Terror. The pie graph below displays the breakdown of beheadings by class.

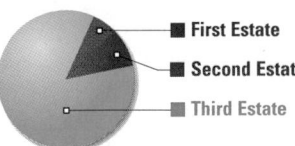

- ■ First Estate
- ■ Second Estate
- ■ Third Estate

Before each execution, bound victims traveled from the prison to the scaffold in horse-drawn carts during a 1½ hour procession through city streets.

Connect *to* History

Synthesizing In what ways was the guillotine an efficient means of execution?

SEE SKILLBUILDER
HANDBOOK, PAGE 665.

Connect *to* Today

Comparing France continued to use the guillotine until the late 1970s. Compare this instrument of capital punishment with the ones used in the United States today, and present your findings in an oral report. Speculate on what the goals of capital punishment are and whether they have been achieved—in the French Revolution or in today's world.

INTERNET CONNECTION

Visit us at **www.mlworldhistory.com** to learn more about the French Revolution and Napoleon.

Although prerevolutionary France is often depicted as backward and strangled by the aristocracy and the church, many historians feel that this picture is wrong. They point to the springing up of new enterprises involving mechanization. Textile dyeing, silk production, sugar refining, textile manufacturing, and mining were all being revolutionized by increasingly sophisticated industrial technology.

IN-DEPTH RESOURCES: UNIT 2
Science and Technology: Science Helps Create the Metric System, p. 55

MORE ABOUT . . .
The Guillotine

One reason for the development of the guillotine was the desire to apply capital punishment equally to all social classes. The guillotine, it was felt, would give even common prisoners the kind of dignified execution previously reserved for the upper classes.

ELECTRONIC LIBRARY OF PRIMARY SOURCES
from "Execution by Guillotine"

INTERNET
Click *World History* at
www.mlworldhistory.com

Connect *to* History

Analyzing
Possible Answer: The guillotine was fast, allowing many executions in a short time. Elaborate rituals, complicated machinery, and lengthy waits for the victims to die were not involved.

Connect *to* Today

Comparing
Between 1987 and 1997 executions in the United States were carried out by hanging, electrocution, lethal injection, and firing squad. Students may speculate that the goals of capital punishment are to deter criminal behavior and to remove extreme criminals from society. Public executions during the French Revolution helped keep restless armed mobs from attacking the government. Executions were a way to show the Parisian mobs that the state was working for their benefit.

The Terror Grips France

> **Key Ideas**
> • Maximilien Robespierre gains control of the revolutionary government.
> • Robespierre and his supporters try to wipe out every trace of the French nobility.
> • Robespierre institutes the Reign of Terror, a time of thousands of arbitrary executions.

MORE ABOUT . . .
Robespierre
Robespierre believed passionately that only persons of absolute virtue should be political leaders. He believed in freedom for Jews and slaves, in the abolition of the death penalty, and in absolute loyalty to the state. Convinced that true patriots should devote themselves wholeheartedly to an existence of unselfish work and moral regularity, he had no private life. It is ironic that this believer in virtue should have presided over one of the most brutal periods in French history.

 IN-DEPTH RESOURCES: UNIT 2
History Makers: Maximilien Robespierre, p. 53

On this late-18th-century French inkwell, the liberty cap worn by revolutionaries crushes a clergyman of the Old Regime.

The Terror Grips France

Foreign armies were not the only enemies of the French republic. The Jacobins had thousands of enemies within France itself—peasants who were horrified by the beheading of the king, priests who would not accept government control, and rival leaders who were stirring up rebellion in the provinces. How to contain and control these enemies became a central issue.

Robespierre Assumes Control As dozens of leaders struggled for power, **Maximilien Robespierre** (ROHBZ·peer) slowly gathered control into his own hands. Robespierre and his supporters set out to build a "republic of virtue." They tried to wipe out every trace of France's past monarchy and nobility. Many families named Leroy ("king"), for instance, changed their names to something less political. No household item was too small to escape the influence of Robespierre—even the kings, queens, and jacks in decks of cards were changed to figures that represented revolutionary ideals.

Firm believers in reason, the radicals changed the calendar to be more scientific. They divided the year into 12 months of 30 days and renamed each month. The new calendar had no Sundays because the radicals considered religion old-fashioned and dangerous. They even closed all churches in Paris, and towns all over France soon did the same.

In the summer of 1793, Robespierre became the leader of the **Committee of Public Safety.** As head of the committee, he decided who should be considered enemies of the republic. The committee often had people tried in the morning and guillotined the same afternoon. From July 1793 to July 1794, Robespierre governed France nearly as a dictator, and the period of his rule became known as the **Reign of Terror.** In his speeches, Robespierre justified the Reign of Terror, explaining that it enabled French citizens to remain true to the ideals of the Revolution. In this speech excerpt, Robespierre makes a connection between virtue and terror:

> ### A VOICE FROM THE PAST
> The first maxim of our politics ought to be to lead the people by means of reason and the enemies of the people by terror. If the basis of popular government in time of peace is virtue, the basis of popular government in time of revolution is both virtue and terror: virtue without which terror is murderous, terror without which virtue is powerless. Terror is nothing else than swift, severe, indomitable justice; it flows, then, from virtue.
> **MAXIMILIEN ROBESPIERRE,** quoted in *Problems of Western Civilization: The Challenge of History*

The most famous victim of the Terror was the widowed queen, Marie Antoinette. Calm and dignified, she rode in the death cart past jeering crowds. On the scaffold, she accidentally stepped on her executioner's foot. "Monsieur," she apologized, "I beg your pardon. I did not do it on purpose." Those were her last words.

The "enemies of the republic" who troubled Robespierre the most were fellow revolutionaries who challenged his leadership. In October 1793, revolutionary courts pronounced death sentences on many of the leaders who had first helped set up the republic. Their only crime was that they were less radical than Robespierre.

By the beginning of 1794, even Georges Danton found himself in danger. (Marat had already been stabbed to death by a young woman.) Danton's friends in the

THINK THROUGH HISTORY
D. Summarizing
How did Robespierre justify his use of terror?
D. Possible Answer
By saying that terror was the same thing as justice

Gifted and Talented Students
Drawing Conclusions Ask students to read the biography of Robespierre in the Teacher's Resource materials and to answer the questions that accompany it. Then have them do some additional research to explore the possible discrepancy between Robespierre's

belief in virtue and freedom from tyranny and his involvement in the arbitrary judgments and hasty executions of the Reign of Terror. Ask them to draw a conclusion about Robespierre's actions.

State Opposition to Religion
The closing of churches and elimination of Sundays from the calendar during the French Revolution demonstrate the strength of the radicals' opposition to religion. A similar situation occurred in Russia in 1917, when the Bolsheviks, led by Lenin, gained power. Basing his

ideas on the Communist Manifesto of Karl Marx, Lenin banned religion and closed the churches. In both France and Russia, people began to practice religion again when the antireligious governments fell.

National Convention, afraid to defend him, joined in condemning him to death. On the scaffold, he told the executioner, "Don't forget to show my head to the people. It's well worth seeing."

Besides leading political figures, thousands of unknown people were sent to death on the flimsiest of charges. A revolutionary court sentenced an 18-year-old youth to die by the guillotine for sawing down a tree that had been planted as a symbol of liberty. A tavern keeper was executed because he sold sour wine "to the defenders of the country."

During the Terror, approximately 3,000 people were executed in Paris. Some historians believe that as many as 40,000 were killed all together. About 85 percent were peasants or members of the urban poor or middle class—common people for whose benefit the Revolution had supposedly been carried out.

End of the Terror

By July 1794, the members of the National Convention knew that none of them were safe from Robespierre. To save themselves, they turned on him. A group of conspirators demanded his arrest, shouting, "Down with the tyrant!" The next day the Revolution's last powerful leader went to the guillotine. The Reign of Terror, the radical phase of the French Revolution, ended when Maximilien Robespierre lost his head on July 28, 1794.

French public opinion shifted dramatically to the right after Robespierre's death. People of all classes had grown weary of the Terror. They were also tired of the skyrocketing prices of bread, salt, and other necessities of life after the Terror.

In 1795, moderate leaders in the National Convention drafted a new plan of government. The third since 1789, the new constitution placed power firmly in the hands of the upper middle class and called for a two-house legislature and an executive body of five men, known as the Directory. The five directors were moderates, not revolutionary idealists. Some of them freely enriched themselves at the public's expense. Despite their corruption, however, they gave their troubled country a period of order.

The Directory also found the right general to command France's armies. This supremely talented young man was named Napoleon Bonaparte.

Vocabulary
conspirators: people involved in a secret plot.

Section 2 Assessment

1. TERMS & NAMES
Identify
• Declaration of the Rights of Man
• Legislative Assembly
• émigrés
• sans-culottes
• guillotine
• Maximilien Robespierre
• Committee of Public Safety
• Reign of Terror

2. TAKING NOTES
Recreate the cause-and-effect graphic below on your paper. Fill in the main events that occurred after the creation of the Constitution of 1791.

Assembly creates a constitution.

3. RECOGNIZING CAUSES
After the French rejected the king's absolute control, they struggled to create a more democratic government. However, in 1793, Robespierre became a dictator. What caused this to happen?

THINK ABOUT
• the political climate prior to Robespierre's rule
• the need for a leader
• Robespierre's personality

4. THEME ACTIVITY
Revolution Create a revolutionaries' "Wall of Fame." Working in small teams, write short biographies of revolutionary figures mentioned in this section (including pictures if possible). Then add biographies of other revolutionary figures—from England and the Americas—mentioned in the unit.

Section 3 Overview

OBJECTIVES

1. To explain how Napoleon Bonaparte came to power in France.

2. To summarize the steps Napoleon took to restore order to France.

3. To describe the extent and weaknesses of Napoleon's empire.

SKILLBUILDERS

- Interpreting charts, p. 205
- Interpreting maps: region, location, p. 208

CRITICAL THINKING

- Analyzing causes, p. 205
- Analyzing motives, p. 206
- Recognizing effects, p. 207
- Evaluating, p. 207
- Forming an opinion, p. 208
- Analyzing themes, p. 208

FOCUS

5-Minute Warm-Up

> **Summarizing**
> Have students answer these questions to explore the influence of a hero on society.
> 1. Read History Makers on page 204. How did Napoleon reward his troops?
> 2. How did they feel about him?
>
> 📖 **WARM-UP TRANSPARENCY 7**

OBJECTIVE ① INSTRUCT

Napoleon Grasps the Power

> **Key Ideas**
> - Napoleon wins key battles to save the French republic.
> - Napoleon seizes political control from the Directory.
> - Napoleon's successes in battle and diplomacy lead to peace in Europe.
>
> 📄 **IN-DEPTH RESOURCES: UNIT 2**
> Guided Reading, p. 39
>
> 📄 **ACCESS FOR STUDENTS ACQUIRING ENGLISH**
> Guided Reading (Spanish), p. 83

TERMS & NAMES
- Napoleon Bonaparte
- coup d'état
- plebiscite
- lycée
- concordat
- Napoleonic Code
- Battle of Trafalgar

③ Napoleon Forges an Empire

MAIN IDEA	WHY IT MATTERS NOW
A military genius, Napoleon Bonaparte, seized power in France and made himself emperor.	In times of political turmoil, military dictators often seize control of nations, as in Haiti in 1991.

SETTING THE STAGE Napoleon was a short man (five feet three inches tall) who cast a long shadow over the history of modern times. He would come to be recognized as one of the world's greatest military geniuses, along with Alexander the Great of Macedonia, Hannibal of Carthage, and Julius Caesar of Rome. In only four years (1795–1799), Napoleon rose from relative obscurity to become master of France.

Napoleon Grasps the Power

Napoleon Bonaparte was born in 1769 on the Mediterranean island of Corsica. When he was nine years old, his parents sent him to a military school in northern France. In 1785, at the age of 16, he finished school and became a lieutenant in the artillery. When the Revolution broke out, Napoleon joined the army of the new government.

Hero of the Hour In October 1795, fate handed the young officer a chance for glory. When royalist rebels marched on the National Convention, a government official told Napoleon to defend the delegates. Napoleon and his gunners greeted the thousands of royalists with a cannonade. Within minutes, the attackers fled in panic and confusion. Napoleon Bonaparte became the hero of the hour and was hailed throughout Paris as the savior of the French republic.

In 1796, the Directory appointed Napoleon to lead a French army against the forces of Austria and the Kingdom of Sardinia. Crossing the Alps, the young general swept into Italy and won a series of remarkable victories, which crushed the Austrian troops' threat to France. Next, in an attempt to protect French trade interests and to disrupt British trade with India, Napoleon led an expedition to Egypt. Unfortunately, his luck did not hold. His army was pinned down in Egypt, and his naval forces were defeated by the British admiral Horatio Nelson. However, he managed to keep the reports of his defeat out of the press, so that by 1799 the words "the general" could mean only one man to the French—Napoleon.

Coup d'État By 1799, the Directory had lost control of the political situation and the confidence of the French people. Only the directors' control of the army kept them in power. Upon Napoleon's return from Egypt, the Abbé Sieyès urged him to seize political power. Napoleon and Josephine, his lovely socialite wife, set a plan in motion. Napoleon met with influential persons to discuss his role in the Directory, while Josephine used her connections with the wealthy directors to influence their decisions. The action began on November 9, 1799, when Napoleon was put in charge of the military. It ended the next day when his troops drove out the members of one chamber of the

Vocabulary
cannonade: a bombardment with heavy artillery fire.

HISTORY MAKERS

Napoleon Bonaparte 1769–1821

Napoleon Bonaparte had a magnetism that attracted the admiration of his men. His speeches were designed to inspire his troops to valorous feats. In one speech, he told soldiers, "If the victory is for a moment uncertain, you shall see your Emperor place himself on the front line."

Bonaparte was generous in his rewards to the troops. Many received the Legion of Honor—a medal for bravery. Sometimes Napoleon would take the medal from his own chest to present it to a soldier. (He kept a few spares in his pocket for these occasions.) A cavalry commander, Auguste de Colbert, wrote, "He awakened in my soul the desire for glory."

SECTION 3 RESOURCES

PRINT RESOURCES

📄 **IN-DEPTH RESOURCES: UNIT 2**
Guided Reading, p. 39
Primary Source: Napoleon's Proclamation at Austerlitz, 1805, p. 48

📄 **ACCESS FOR STUDENTS ACQUIRING ENGLISH**
Guided Reading (Spanish), p. 83

📄 **FORMAL ASSESSMENT**
Section Quiz, p. 90

📄 **ALTERNATIVE ASSESSMENT BOOK**

TECHNOLOGY RESOURCES

🏛 **WORLD ART AND CULTURES TRANSPARENCIES**
AT51 *Napoleon Crossing the St. Bernard Pass*

💿 **CD-ROM** *Electronic Library of Primary Sources*
Battles of the World: The Battle of Austerlitz

🌐 **INTERNET** www.mlworldhistory.com

THINK THROUGH HISTORY
A. Analyzing
Causes For what
reasons was
Napoleon able to
become a dictator?
A. Possible Answer
General political
chaos created a need
for a strong leader,
and Napoleon had
control of the army.

national legislature. The legislature voted to dissolve the Directory. In its place, the legislature established a group of three consuls, one of whom was Napoleon. Napoleon quickly assumed dictatorial powers as the first consul of the French republic. A sudden seizure of power like Napoleon's is known as a coup—from the French phrase **coup d'état** (KOO day·TAH), or "blow of state."

At the time of Napoleon's coup, France was still at war. In 1799, British diplomats assembled the Second Coalition of anti-French powers—Britain, Austria, and Russia— with the goal of driving Napoleon from power. Once again, Napoleon rode from Paris at the head of his troops. Eventually, as a result of war and diplomacy, all three nations signed peace agreements with France. By 1802, Europe was at peace for the first time in ten years. Napoleon was free to focus his energies on restoring order in France.

Napoleon Rules France

At first, Napoleon pretended to be the constitutionally chosen leader of a free repub-lic. In 1800, a **plebiscite** (PLEHB·ih·SYT), or vote of the people, was held to approve a new constitution, the fourth in eight years. Desperate for strong leadership, the people voted overwhelmingly in favor of the constitution, which gave all real power to Napoleon as first consul.

Restoring Order at Home Under Napoleon, France would have order and stability. He did not try to return the nation to the days of Louis XVI; instead, he kept many of the changes that had come with the Revolution. He supported laws that would both strengthen the central government and achieve some of the goals of the Revolution, such as a stable economy and more equality in taxation.

The first order of business was to get the economy on a solid footing. Napoleon set up an efficient tax-collection system and established a national bank. In addition to assuring the government a steady supply of tax money, these actions promoted sound financial management and better control of the economy.

Napoleon also needed to reduce government corruption and improve the delivery of government services. He dismissed corrupt officials and, in order to provide his government with trained officials, set up **lycées,** or government-run public schools. The students at the lycées included children of ordinary citizens as well as children of

Napoleon Brings Order After the Revolution

	The Economy	Government & Society	Religion
Goals of the Revolution	• Equal taxation • Lower inflation	• Less government corruption • Equal opportunity in government	• Less powerful Catholic Church • Religious tolerance
Napoleon's Actions	• Set up fairer tax code • Set up national bank • Stabilized currency • Gave state loans to businesses	• Appointed officials by merit • Fired corrupt officials • Created lycées • Created code of laws	• Recognized Catholicism as "faith of Frenchmen" • Signed concordat with pope • Retained seized church lands
Results	• Equal taxation • Stable economy	• Honest, competent officials • Equal opportunity in government • Public education	• Religious tolerance • Government control of church lands • Government recognition of church influence

SKILLBUILDER: Interpreting Charts
Napoleon's changes brought France closer to achieving the Revolution's goals.
1. Which goals of the Revolution did Napoleon achieve?
2. If you had been a member of the bourgeoisie in Napoleon's France, would you have been satisfied with the results of Napoleon's actions? Why or why not?

Napoleon Rules France

▶ **Key Ideas**
• Napoleon gains power; voters approve a fourth constitution.
• Napoleon gives France order and stability.
• The Napoleonic Code establishes a uniform set of laws for France.
• Napoleon crowns himself as emperor of France.

CRITICAL THINKING ACTIVITY
CLASS TIME: 15 MINUTES

Perceiving Cause and Effect Relationships
To help students understand Napoleon's accomplishments, have them make two-column charts in which they list his actions and the benefits of the actions.

Action	Benefit

History from Visuals

Napoleon Brings Order After the Revolution

Interpreting the Chart Show students how to read the chart in multiple ways: read each column to compare Napoleon's actions with the goals of the Revolution, and read each row to get a full overview.

Extension Activity Ask students to think of topics for additional columns they might add to the chart. *Possible Responses: education, land reform, aristocracy*

SKILLBUILDER Answers
1. He provided equal taxation, equal oppor-tunity in government, honest officials, reli-gious tolerance, and state control of church lands
2. Probable answer is *yes,* because the country became stable. Some students may answer *no,* because the bourgeoisie received no special privileges.

Economics Much of France's stability under Napoleon came from economic reforms. Discuss with students the practical meanings of these economic terms used in describing Napoleon's policies: *national bank, low inflation,* and *stable currency.*

A *national bank* system allows a central government to regulate banking activities. It eliminates problems that arise when private banks operate independently,

perhaps even issuing their own currencies. When a country has a national bank, people feel more secure about their bank deposits, so that their confidence in the government increases.

Inflation is a general rise in the level of prices. Increases in the prices of food, clothing, and housing are caused by decreases in the value of money. During extreme inflation, for example, a loaf of bread

might cost hundreds of dollars. Low inflation can lead to prosperity and political stability.

A *stabilized currency* results from a national banking system, low inflation, and other factors. Currency that does not change in value quickly and that is backed by a central government contributes to national stability and peace.

Napoleon Creates an Empire

Key Ideas

- Napoleon tries to expand his empire in the Americas but fails in Saint Domingue.
- The United States buys the Louisiana Territory from Napoleon.
- Napoleon conquers much of Europe, but his navy is defeated in the Battle of Trafalgar.

 ELECTRONIC LIBRARY OF PRIMARY SOURCES
from *The Letters of Napoleon I*

MORE ABOUT . . .
Napoleon Bonaparte

Napoleon is popularly supposed to have wanted to rule the world to compensate for being short. Historians disagree about his height, however. After his autopsy, his height was reported as five feet two inches, but that figure was based on an old French system of measure. In modern terms, he may have been a little over five feet six inches tall.

 IN-DEPTH RESOURCES: UNIT 2
Primary Source: Napoleon's Proclamation at Austerlitz, 1805, p. 48

 WORLD ART AND CULTURES TRANSPARENCIES
AT51 *Napoleon Crossing the St. Bernard Pass*

 Battles of the World
The Battle of Austerlitz

---

the wealthy. The trained candidates could then be appointed to public office on the basis of merit rather than family connections.

Both the clergy and the peasants wanted to restore the position of the church in France. Napoleon signed a **concordat** (agreement) with Pope Pius VII, spelling out a new relationship between church and state. The government recognized the influence of the church but rejected church control in national affairs. Specifically the French government would appoint bishops, but the bishops would appoint parish priests. The concordat gained Napoleon the support of the organized church as well as the majority of the French people.

Napoleon thought that his greatest work was his comprehensive system of laws, known as the **Napoleonic Code.** Although the code gave the country a uniform set of laws and eliminated many injustices, it actually limited liberty and promoted order and authority over individual rights. The code took away some rights that women had won during the Revolution, such as the right to sell their property. Freedom of speech and of the press, also established during the Revolution, were restricted rather than expanded. The new laws also restored slavery in the French colonies of the Caribbean, which the revolutionary government had abolished.

The emperor Napoleon appears almost godlike in this 1806 portrait by Jean Auguste Dominique Ingres, entitled *Napoleon on His Imperial Throne.*

Napoleon Crowned as Emperor In 1804, Napoleon decided to make himself emperor, and the French voters supported him. On December 2, 1804, dressed in a splendid robe of purple velvet, Napoleon walked down the long aisle of Notre Dame Cathedral in Paris. The pope waited for him with a glittering crown. As thousands watched, the new emperor took the crown from the pope and placed it on his own head. With this arrogant gesture, Napoleon signaled that he was more powerful than the church, which had traditionally crowned the rulers of France.

THINK THROUGH HISTORY
B. Analyzing Motives Why would Napoleon crown himself?
B. Possible Answer To show that he was not under the control of anyone

Napoleon Creates an Empire

Napoleon was not content simply to be master of France. He wanted to control the rest of Europe and to reassert French power in the New World. He envisioned his western empire to include Louisiana, Florida, French Guiana, and the French West Indies. He knew that the key to this area was the sugar-producing French colony of Saint Domingue on the island of Hispaniola.

New World Territories In 1789, when the ideas of the Revolution had reached the planters in Saint Domingue, they had demanded that the National Assembly give them the same privileges as the people of France. Eventually, the slaves in the colony had demanded their freedom. A civil war had erupted, and slaves under the leadership of Toussaint L'Ouverture had seized control of the productive colony. In 1801, Napoleon decided to regain French control of the war-torn island and restore its productive sugar industry. Although he sent 23,000 soldiers to accomplish the task, the former slaves proved to be difficult to defeat, and thousands of soldiers died of yellow fever.

When the expedition to Saint Domingue was unsuccessful and the U.S. government showed interest in buying the port of New Orleans, Napoleon recognized an opportunity to make some money and cut his losses in the Americas. He offered to sell all of the Louisiana Territory to the United States, and in 1803 President

206 Chapter 7

CONNECTIONS ACROSS TIME AND PLACE

Disease and History The French expedition to Saint Domingue was unsuccessful largely because so many soldiers died of yellow fever. This was not the only time that disease affected Napoleon's armies. The campaign in Russia, Napoleon's first major defeat, was severely handicapped by an outbreak of typhus fever that at one point affected over 80,000 of Napoleon's men.

Diseases have long had a powerful effect on the course of history. One historian has argued that a severe type of malaria played a role in the fall of Rome because it caused the birthrate to fall steeply and produced chronic weakness and ill health—a general slackness of spirit. Hundreds of years later, smallpox decimated the Native American population

of Mexico and aided the Spanish conquest. In the early 20th century, the control of yellow fever made the construction of the Panama Canal possible. Interested students may wish to investigate other instances of the impact of disease on history.

Jefferson's administration agreed to purchase the land for $15 million. Napoleon was delighted. He saw a twofold benefit to the sale: he would gain money to finance operations in Europe, and he would further punish his British enemies. He exulted,"The sale assures forever the power of the United States, and I have given England a rival who, sooner or later, will humble her pride."

Conquering Europe Napoleon abandoned his imperial ambitions in the New World and turned his attention to Europe. He had already annexed the Austrian Netherlands and parts of Italy to France and set up a puppet government in Switzerland. Now he looked to expand his influence further. Fearful of his ambitions, Britain persuaded Russia, Austria, and Sweden to join in a third coalition against France.

Napoleon met this challenge with his usual boldness. He rallied the troops and rode out to defeat the Third Coalition, exclaiming, "My army is formidable. . . . Once we had an Army of the Rhine, an Army of Italy, an Army of Holland; there has never been a French Army—but now it exists, and we shall soon see it in action." In a series of brilliant battles, Napoleon crushed the opposition. (See the map on page 208.) The commanders of the enemy armies could never predict his next move and took heavy losses. After the Battle of Austerlitz, Napoleon issued a proclamation expressing his pride in his troops:

A VOICE FROM THE PAST
Soldiers! I am pleased with you. On the day of Austerlitz, you justified everything that I was expecting of your intrepidity. . . . In less than four hours, an army of 100,000 men, commanded by the emperors of Russia and Austria, was cut up and dispersed. . . . 120 pieces of artillery, 20 generals, and more than 30,000 men taken prisoner—such are the results of this day which will forever be famous. . . . My nation will be overjoyed to see you again. And it will be enough for you to say, "I was at Austerlitz," to hear the reply: "There is a brave man!"

NAPOLEON, quoted in *Napoleon* by André Castelot

Eventually, the rulers of Austria, Prussia, and Russia all signed peace treaties with Napoleon, whose proud and patriotic army had enabled him to build the largest European empire since the Romans'. The only major enemy left undefeated was Britain, whose power lay in its navy. In 1805, Napoleon tried to remove the threat of that navy.

The Battle of Trafalgar In his war against the Third Coalition, Napoleon lost only one major battle, the **Battle of Trafalgar** (truh·FAL·guhr)—but that naval defeat was more important than all of Napoleon's victories on land. The battle took place in 1805 off the southern coast of Spain. The commander of the British fleet, Horatio Nelson—the admiral who had defeated Napoleon's fleet near Egypt in 1799— outmaneuvered the larger French-Spanish fleet, showing as much brilliance in warfare at sea as Napoleon had in warfare on land. (See map inset on page 208.) During the furious battle, Nelson was mortally wounded by a French sharpshooter. As he lay dying aboard his flagship, Nelson heard the welcome news of British victory. "Now I am satisfied," murmured the admiral. "Thank God, I have done my duty."

The destruction of the French fleet had two major results. First, it assured the supremacy of the British navy for the next hundred years. Second, it forced Napoleon to give up his plans of invading Britain. He had to look for another way to control his powerful enemy across the English Channel. Eventually, Napoleon's extravagant efforts to crush Britain would lead to his own undoing.

The French Empire During the first decade of the 1800s, Napoleon's victories had given him mastery over most of Europe. By 1812, the only major European countries free from Napoleon's control were Britain, the Ottoman Empire, Portugal, and Sweden.

As the map on page 208 shows, Napoleon controlled numerous supposedly independent lands in addition to those that were formally part of the French Empire. These included

The French Revolution and Napoleon **207**

History from Visuals

French Empire and Battles, 1805–1812

Interpreting the Map Tell students to read the map key carefully to help them identify the territory of the French Empire and the nations controlled by Napoleon.

Extension Activity Have students read more about the tactics employed by the British in the Battle of Trafalgar.

SKILLBUILDER Answers
1. From the North Sea in the north to central Italy in the south, from Illyria in the east to the Atlantic Ocean in the west
2. Near the Strait of Gibraltar. Nelson divided the French fleet, enabling his forces to attack smaller groups of ships.

ASSESS & RETEACH

Section 3 Assessment

Have pairs of students take turns quizzing each other on the questions. Then have them start a time line of Napoleon's career.

Section Quiz

📖 **FORMAL ASSESSMENT**
Section Quiz, p. 90

Reteaching Activity

CLASS TIME: 15 MINUTES

Go over the key terms to help students understand the events in this section.

CLOSE ACTIVITY

CLASS TIME: 20 MINUTES

Analyzing Events

Using the map on page 208 in the text, write the names of countries in Europe on 3x5 file cards. Students draw a card and then arrange themselves in the front of the room as one of the countries at the height of Napoleon's empire. Students representing adjacent countries should stand next to each other and should face other countries appropriately. Each student will talk about who they are, where they are, and how they responded to Napoleon as their conqueror or ally.

French Empire and Battles, 1805–1812

Legend:
- French Empire
- Controlled by Napoleon
- ★ Major battle

The Battle of Trafalgar, Oct. 21, 1805
- British fleet
- French and Spanish fleet
- British thrust

By dividing Villeneuve's formation, Admiral Nelson captured nearly two-thirds of the enemy fleet.

GEOGRAPHY SKILLBUILDER: Interpreting Maps
1. **Region** What was the extent (north to south, east to west) of Napoleon's empire in 1812?
2. **Location** Where was the Battle of Trafalgar fought? What tactic did Nelson use, and why was it successful?

Spain, the Grand Duchy of Warsaw, and a number of German kingdoms in central Europe. The rulers of these countries were Napoleon's puppets; some, in fact, were his brothers and in-laws. Furthermore, the powerful countries of Russia, Prussia, and Austria were loosely attached to Napoleon's empire through alliances. Not totally under Napoleon's control, they were easily manipulated by threats of military action.

Ironically, Napoleon's power and military threats actually made the conquered peoples more conscious of their loyalty to their own nations. The French empire was huge but unstable. Napoleon was able to maintain it at its greatest extent for only five years (1807–1812). Then it quickly fell to pieces. Its sudden collapse was caused in part by Napoleon himself.

Section ③ Assessment

1. TERMS & NAMES
Identify
- Napoleon Bonaparte
- coup d'état
- plebiscite
- lycée
- concordat
- Napoleonic Code
- Battle of Trafalgar

2. TAKING NOTES
Create a time line showing events leading to the crowning of Napoleon as emperor of France.

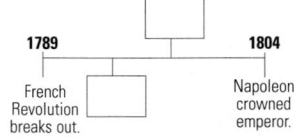

1789 — French Revolution breaks out.   1804 — Napoleon crowned emperor.

Which of these events did Napoleon cause?

3. FORMING AN OPINION
There is an old question: "Do the times make the man, or does the man make the times?" In your opinion, was Napoleon the creator of or the creation of his times?

THINK ABOUT
- the government after the Terror
- Napoleon's defense of France
- Napoleon's popularity

4. ANALYZING THEMES
Power and Authority To keep his empire together, Napoleon had to deal with forces both inside and outside the French Empire. In your judgment, which area was more crucial to control?

THINK ABOUT
- the length of the period of civil unrest in France
- the power and activities of the other European nations

ANSWERS

1. TERMS & NAMES
Napoleon Bonaparte, p. 204
coup d'état, p.205
plebiscite, p. 205
lycée, p. 205
concordat, p. 206
Napoleonic Code, p. 206
Battle of Trafalgar, p. 207

2. TAKING NOTES
1795—Napoleon defeats royalist rebels; 1796 to 1799—Napoleon wins many victories; 1799—Napoleon seizes power from the Directory; 1800—New constitution gives Napoleon all real power.

3. FORMING AN OPINION
Possible Responses: Some students will say that Napoleon became powerful because of his military abilities and the political chaos after the Terror. Others may think that Napoleon's strong personality would have dominated no matter the circumstances.

4. ANALYZING THEMES
Possible Responses: Some students will argue that internal unrest was most important, because division and chaos at home would have made military success impossible. Others may say that victory against external enemies would have led to union within France.

4 Napoleon's Empire Collapses

TERMS & NAMES
- blockade
- Continental System
- guerrilla
- Peninsular War
- scorched-earth policy
- Waterloo
- Hundred Days

MAIN IDEA

Napoleon's conquests aroused nationalistic feelings across Europe and contributed to his downfall.

WHY IT MATTERS NOW

In the 1990s, nationalistic feelings contributed to the breakup of nations such as Yugoslavia.

SETTING THE STAGE Napoleon worried that his vast empire would fall apart unless he had an heir whose right to succeed him was undisputed, so he decided that he needed a son. Consequently, he divorced Josephine, who had failed to bear him a child, and formed an alliance with the Austrian royal family by marrying Marie Louise, the grand-niece of Marie Antoinette. In 1811, Marie Louise gave birth to a son, Napoleon II, whom his father named king of Rome.

Napoleon's Three Costly Mistakes

Napoleon's own personality proved to be the greatest danger to the future of his empire. "I love power," he once said, "as a musician loves his violin." It was the drive for power that had raised Napoleon to great heights, and the same love of power led to his doom. In his efforts to extend the French Empire and crush Britain, Napoleon made three disastrous misjudgments.

The Continental System In November 1806, Napoleon signed a decree ordering a **blockade**—a forcible closing of ports—to prevent all trade and communication between Great Britain and other European nations. Napoleon called this policy the **Continental System** because it was supposed to make continental Europe more self-sufficient. It was also intended to destroy Britain's commercial and industrial economy.

Unfortunately for Napoleon, his blockade was not nearly tight enough. Aided by the British, smugglers managed to bring cargo from Britain into Europe. At times, Napoleon's allies disregarded his order—in fact, Napoleon's own brother Louis, whom Napoleon had made king of Holland, defied the policy. For these reasons, the blockade weakened British trade but did not destroy it.

In addition, Britain responded with its own blockade. The British navy stopped neutral ships bound for the continent and forced them to sail to a British port to be searched and taxed. Because the British had a stronger navy, they were better able than the French to make their blockade work.

American ships were among those stopped by the British navy. Angered, the U.S. Congress declared war on Britain in 1812. The War of 1812 ended in a draw, however, and was only a minor inconvenience to Britain in its struggle with Napoleon.

In effect, the Continental System hurt Napoleon more than it hurt his enemies. It weakened the economies of France and the other lands under Napoleon's control more than it damaged Britain.

The Peninsular War In 1808, Napoleon made a second costly mistake. Because Portugal was ignoring the Continental System, he sent an army through Spain to invade Portugal. When Spanish towns rioted in protest, Napoleon deposed the Spanish king and put his brother Joseph on the throne. This move outraged the Spanish people and enflamed their nationalistic feelings, since they remained fiercely loyal to their former monarch.

Background
England's navy had been the strongest in Europe ever since its defeat of the Spanish Armada in 1588.

A STOPPAGE to a STRIDE over the GLOBE.

"Little Johnny Bull"—Great Britain—waves a sword at Napoleon as the emperor straddles the globe.

The French Revolution and Napoleon **209**

SECTION 4 RESOURCES

PRINT RESOURCES

 IN-DEPTH RESOURCES: UNIT 2
Guided Reading, p. 40
Skillbuilder Practice: Interpreting Maps, p. 42

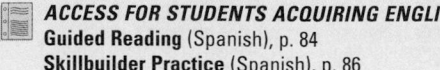 *ACCESS FOR STUDENTS ACQUIRING ENGLISH*
Guided Reading (Spanish), p. 84
Skillbuilder Practice (Spanish), p. 86

 FORMAL ASSESSMENT
Section Quiz, p. 91

 ALTERNATIVE ASSESSMENT BOOK

TECHNOLOGY RESOURCES

 CD-ROM
Electronic Library of Primary Sources

 INTERNET www.mlworldhistory.com

Section 4 Overview

OBJECTIVES

(1) To explain Napoleon's tactical and political mistakes.

(2) To summarize Napoleon's defeat, comeback, and final downfall.

SKILLBUILDER
- Interpreting maps and graphs, p. 211

CRITICAL THINKING
- Recognizing effects, p. 210
- Analyzing motives, p. 212

FOCUS

5-Minute Warm-Up

▶ *Interpreting a Political Cartoon*

To help students understand Napoleon's power, have them answer these questions.

1. What words describe Napoleon in the cartoon on page 209?

2. What words describe Britain in the cartoon?

 WARM-UP TRANSPARENCY 7

OBJECTIVE (1) INSTRUCT

Napoleon's Three Costly Mistakes

▶ *Key Ideas*
- In a policy known as the Continental System, Napoleon unsuccessfully attempts to cut off trade between Great Britain and other European nations.
- The Peninsular War in Spain inflames Spanish nationalism and weakens France.
- The French invasion of Russia fails, with terrible loss of life.

 IN-DEPTH RESOURCES: UNIT 2
Guided Reading, p. 40

 ACCESS FOR STUDENTS ACQUIRING ENGLISH
Guided Reading (Spanish), p. 84

In addition, Spain was a devoutly Catholic nation with a long history of persecuting those who deviated from the faith. Because the French Revolution had weakened the Catholic Church in France, many Spanish Catholics feared that their French conquerors would undermine the church in Spain. In fact, the French did attack church power by outlawing the Spanish Inquisition, which was still prosecuting people accused of heresy.

GlobalImpact

Latin American Revolutions

Class conflict had begun in Spain's American colonies long before the Peninsular War. *Peninsulares,* colonists who had been born in Spain, dominated colonial society. Creoles, those born in the colonies themselves, were denied power.

When Napoleon forced the Spanish king to abdicate, Creole leaders in the colonies saw the collapse of the Spanish government as an opportunity to take over colonial governments and gain independence from Spain.

Among the leaders who worked for independence were Simón Bolívar of Venezuela and José de San Martín of Argentina. Both Venezuela and Argentina had to struggle long and hard to defeat the Spanish, but they did prevail.

For five years (1808–1813), bands of Spanish peasant fighters, known as **guerrillas,** struck at French armies in Spain. The guerrillas were not an army that Napoleon could defeat in open battle; they were ordinary people who ambushed French troops and then fled into hiding. The British added to the French troubles in Spain by sending troops to aid the rebels. Napoleon lost about 300,000 men during this **Peninsular War** (so called because Spain lies on the Iberian Peninsula). These losses weakened the French Empire.

In Spain and elsewhere, nationalism, or loyalty to one's own country, was becoming a powerful weapon against Napoleon. People who had at first welcomed the French as their liberators now felt abused by a foreign conqueror. Like the Spanish guerrillas, Germans and Italians and other conquered peoples turned against the French.

The Invasion of Russia In 1812, Napoleon's thirst for power led to his most disastrous mistake of all. Even though Alexander I had become Napoleon's ally, the Russian czar refused to stop selling grain to Britain. In addition, the French and Russian rulers suspected each other of having competing designs on Poland. Because of this breakdown in their alliance, Napoleon decided to invade Russia.

In June 1812, Napoleon and his Grand Army marched into Russia. Many of his troops were not French. They had been drafted from all over Europe, and they felt little loyalty to Napoleon.

As Napoleon's army entered Russia, Alexander pulled back his troops, refusing to be lured into an unequal battle. As the Russians retreated toward Moscow, they practiced a **scorched-earth policy,** burning grain fields and slaughtering livestock so as to leave nothing that the enemy could eat. Desperate soldiers deserted the French army to search for scraps of food.

On September 7, 1812, the two armies finally clashed in the Battle of Borodino. During the morning, the advantage swung back and forth between the Russians and the French. After several more hours of indecisive fighting, the Russians retreated—giving Napoleon a narrow victory that allowed him to take Moscow.

When Napoleon finally entered Moscow on September 14, he soon found it in flames. Rather than surrender Russia's "holy city" to the French, Alexander had set fire to it. Napoleon stayed in the ruined city for five weeks, expecting the czar to make a peace offer, but no offer ever came. By then, it was the middle of October, too late to advance farther and perhaps too late even to retreat.

Grimly, Napoleon ordered his starving army to turn back. As the snows began to fall in early November, Russian raiders mercilessly attacked Napoleon's ragged, retreating army. One French sergeant recorded, "Many of the survivors were walking barefoot, using pieces of wood as canes, but their feet were frozen so hard that the sound they made on the road was like that of wooden clogs."

As the soldiers staggered through the snow, many dropped in their tracks from wounds, exhaustion, hunger, and cold. The temperature fell to about 30 degrees below zero, so cold that birds fell dead from the sky. Finally, in the middle of December, the last survivors straggled out of Russia. Of his Grand Army, Napoleon had only 10,000 soldiers who were left fit to fight.

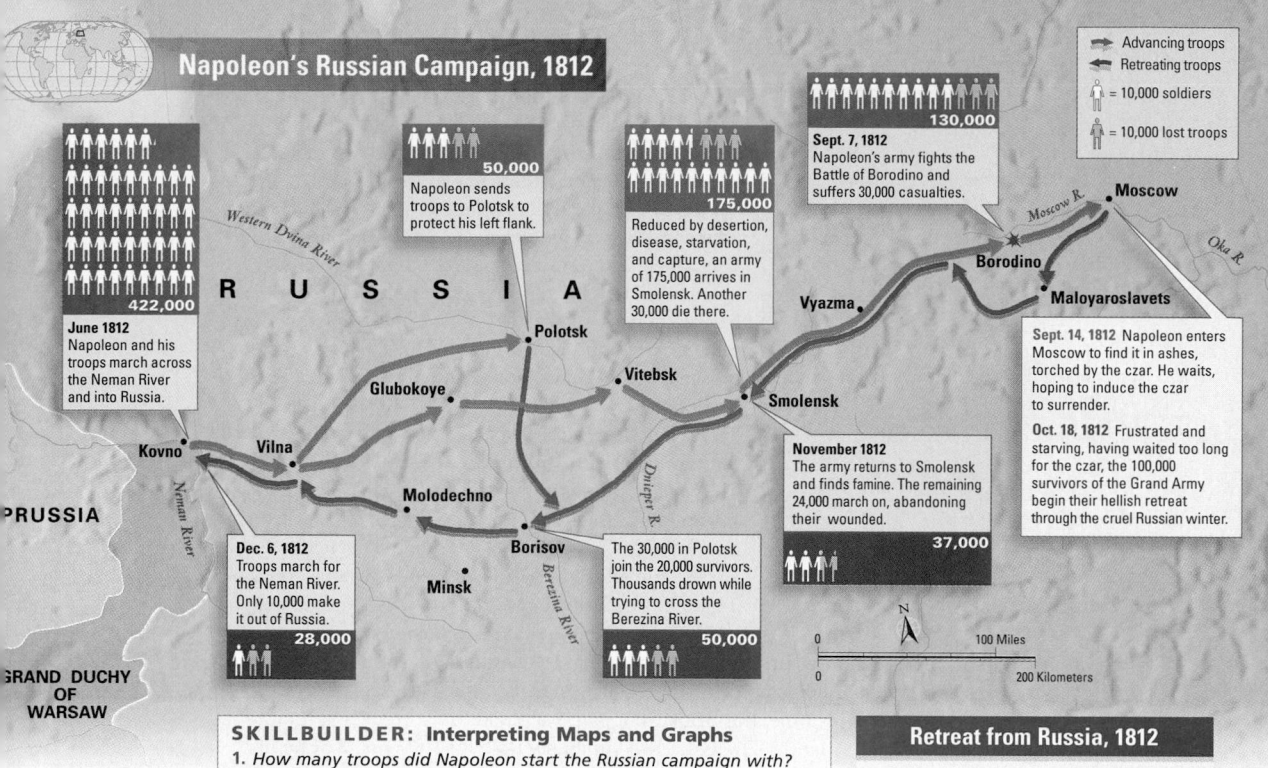

Napoleon's Russian Campaign, 1812

Advancing troops
Retreating troops
= 10,000 soldiers
= 10,000 lost troops

130,000
Sept. 7, 1812 Napoleon's army fights the Battle of Borodino and suffers 30,000 casualties.

50,000
Napoleon sends troops to Polotsk to protect his left flank.

175,000
Reduced by desertion, disease, starvation, and capture, an army of 175,000 arrives in Smolensk. Another 30,000 die there.

422,000
June 1812 Napoleon and his troops march across the Neman River and into Russia.

Sept. 14, 1812 Napoleon enters Moscow to find it in ashes, torched by the czar. He waits, hoping to induce the czar to surrender.

Oct. 18, 1812 Frustrated and starving, having waited too long for the czar, the 100,000 survivors of the Grand Army begin their hellish retreat through the cruel Russian winter.

November 1812 The army returns to Smolensk and finds famine. The remaining 24,000 march on, abandoning their wounded.

37,000

Dec. 6, 1812 Troops march for the Neman River. Only 10,000 make it out of Russia.

28,000

The 30,000 in Polotsk join the 20,000 survivors. Thousands drown while trying to cross the Berezina River.

50,000

RUSSIA — Polotsk, Vitebsk, Glubokoye, Vilna, Kovno, Molodechno, Borisov, Minsk, Smolensk, Vyazma, Borodino, Maloyaroslavets, Moscow. Western Dvina River, Neman River, Dnieper R., Berezina River, Moscow R., Oka R. PRUSSIA, GRAND DUCHY OF WARSAW.

N

100 Miles / 200 Kilometers

Source: Chart by Charles Joseph Minard, 1861

SKILLBUILDER: Interpreting Maps and Graphs
1. How many troops did Napoleon start the Russian campaign with? How many survived?
2. Review the graph on the right. Why was Napoleon's decision to stay in Moscow until mid-October a tactical blunder?

Napoleon's Downfall

Napoleon's enemies were quick to take advantage of his weakness. Britain, Russia, Prussia, and Sweden joined forces against him in the Fourth Coalition. Napoleon had hoped that his marriage to Marie Louise would keep at least Austria on his side, but Austria also joined the coalition. All of the main powers of Europe were now at war with France.

The Coalition Defeats Napoleon In only a few months, Napoleon managed to raise another army. He faced his enemies outside the German city of Leipzig (LYP·sihg) in October 1813. At this crucial point, Napoleon's army no longer consisted of trained veterans. In the Battle of Leipzig, the allies cut his inexperienced army to pieces.

Napoleon's empire crumbled quickly. By January 1814, armies of Austrians, Russians, and Prussians were pushing steadily toward Paris. In March, the Russian czar and the Prussian king led their troops in a triumphant parade through the French capital. Napoleon wanted to fight on, but his generals refused.

In April 1814, the defeated emperor gave up his throne and accepted the terms of surrender drawn up by Alexander I. The victors gave Napoleon a small pension and exiled, or banished, him to Elba, a tiny island off the Italian coast. Although the allies expected no further trouble from Napoleon, they were wrong. Napoleon was a man of action who, at age 45, would find it difficult to retire.

A Comeback Fails As Napoleon arrived on Elba, a Bourbon king arrived in Paris to rule France—Louis XVIII, brother of the guillotined king. (Louis XVI's son and heir had died in prison in 1795.) However, the new king quickly became unpopular among

Background
Royalists had called Louis XVI's son Louis XVII after his father was guillotined.

Retreat from Russia, 1812

Temperature (Degrees Fahrenheit): 35, 25, 15, 5, -5, -15, -25, -35
Moscow, Oct. 18 · Nov. 9 · Smolensk, Nov. 14 · Borisov, Nov. 28 · Dec. 1 · Molodechno, Dec. 6

The French Revolution and Napoleon **211**

This portrait by Paul Delaroche, entitled *Napoleon I After His Abdication,* shows Napoleon's depression after he abdicated his throne.

his subjects—especially the peasants, who suspected him of wanting to undo the Revolution's land reforms.

The news that the French king was in trouble was all the incentive Napoleon needed to try to regain power. He escaped from Elba and, on March 1, 1815, landed in France. In a proclamation, he urged the French to rally to his cause. "Victory will march at full speed," he said. "You will be the liberators of your country." Thousands of French people welcomed Napoleon back. The ranks of his army swelled with volunteers as it approached Paris. Within days, Napoleon was again emperor of France. Louis XVIII fled to the border.

In response, the European allies quickly marshaled their armies. The British army, led by the Duke of Wellington, prepared for battle near the village of **Waterloo** in Belgium. On June 15, 1815, Napoleon attacked. The British army defended its ground all day. Late in the afternoon, the Prussian army arrived. Together, the British and the Prussian forces attacked the French. Two days later, Napoleon's exhausted troops gave way, and the British and Prussian forces chased them from the field.

This defeat ended Napoleon's last bid for power, called the **Hundred Days.** Taking no chances this time, the British shipped Napoleon to St. Helena, a remote island in the South Atlantic. There, he lived in lonely exile for six years, writing his memoirs. He died in 1821 of a stomach ailment, perhaps cancer. Shortly before his death, he attempted to justify all he had done during his life:

Background
Napoleon was emperor for 10 years; he was exiled to Elba for 1 year; he ruled again for 100 days; then he was exiled to St. Helena for 6 years.

A VOICE FROM THE PAST
Such work as mine is not done twice in a century. . . . I have saved the Revolution as it lay dying. I have cleansed it of its crimes, and have held it up to the people shining with fame. I have inspired France and Europe with new ideas that will never be forgotten.
NAPOLEON, quoted in *Napoleon at St. Helena*

Without doubt, Napoleon was a military genius and a brilliant administrator. Yet all his victories must be measured against the millions of lives that were lost in his wars. Of his many achievements, only his law code and some of his reforms in France's government proved lasting—and they were not won on the battlefield. A later French statesman and writer, Alexis de Tocqueville, summed up Napoleon's character by saying, "He was as great as a man can be without virtue." Napoleon's defeat opened the door for the freed European countries to establish a new order.

Section 4 Assessment

1. TERMS & NAMES
Identify
• blockade
• Continental System
• guerrilla
• Peninsular War
• scorched-earth policy
• Waterloo
• Hundred Days

2. TAKING NOTES
Create a two-column chart like the one below, listing Napoleon's three disastrous mistakes and the effects that each one had on his empire.

Napoleon's Mistakes	Effect on Empire

Which mistake was most serious? Why?

3. ANALYZING MOTIVES
What were the main reasons people in other European countries resisted Napoleon?

THINK ABOUT
• why some of his own allies refused to abide by the Continental System
• why the Spanish fought a guerrilla war for several years
• why the Russians destroyed their own crops and cities

4. THEME ACTIVITY
Power and Authority Using information from Sections 3 and 4, create a chart, sketch, or drawing to show what positive and negative effects Napoleon's rule had on France. Then judge Napoleon's use of power, showing your judgment in a visual way. Be prepared to defend your opinion.

212 Chapter 7

ANSWERS

1. TERMS & NAMES
blockade, p. 209
Continental System, p. 209
guerrilla, p. 210
Peninsular War, p. 210
scorched-earth policy, p. 210
Waterloo, p. 212
Hundred Days, p. 212

2. TAKING NOTES
Possible Responses: Mistakes—Continental System, Peninsular War, Russian invasion. Effects—weakening of France, great loss of life and prestige, loss of much of army

3. ANALYZING MOTIVES
Possible Responses: Nationalistic feelings caused resistance to French control; invaded countries did not support Napoleon's drive for power; Russians did not want French rulers.

4. THEME ACTIVITY
Possible Responses: Positive effects might be the Napoleonic Code, stable economy, fairer taxation, and religious tolerance. Negative effects might be the economic disruptions caused by continual warfare, great loss of life, and resistance fueled by nationalism.

5 The Congress of Vienna Convenes

TERMS & NAMES
- Congress of Vienna
- Klemens von Metternich
- balance of power
- legitimacy
- Holy Alliance
- Concert of Europe

MAIN IDEA

After exiling Napoleon, European leaders at the Congress of Vienna tried to restore order and reestablish peace.

WHY IT MATTERS NOW

International bodies such as the United Nations play an active role in trying to maintain world peace and stability today.

SETTING THE STAGE European heads of government were looking to establish long-lasting peace and stability on the continent after the defeat of Napoleon. They had a goal of a new European order—one of collective security and stability for the entire continent. A series of meetings in Vienna, known as the **Congress of Vienna,** were called to set up policies to achieve this goal. Originally, the Congress of Vienna was scheduled to last for four weeks. Instead, it went on for eight months.

Metternich Restores Stability

Most of the decisions made in Vienna during the winter of 1814–1815 were made in secret among representatives of the five "great powers." The rulers of three of these countries—King Frederick William III of Prussia, Czar Alexander I of Russia, and Emperor Francis I of Austria—were themselves in Vienna. Britain and France were represented by their foreign ministers. However, none of these men were as influential as the foreign minister of Austria, Prince **Klemens von Metternich** (MEHT-uhr-nihk).

Metternich distrusted the democratic ideals of the French Revolution. Like most other European aristocrats, he maintained that Napoleon's expansionist dictatorship had been a natural outcome of experiments with democracy. Metternich wanted to keep things as they were and remarked, "The first and greatest concern for the immense majority of every nation is the stability of laws—never their change."

Metternich had three goals at the Congress of Vienna. First, he wanted to prevent future French aggression by surrounding France with strong countries. Second, he wanted to restore a **balance of power,** so that no country would be a threat to others. Third, he wanted to restore Europe's royal families to the thrones they had held before Napoleon's conquests.

The Containment of France The congress made the weaker countries around France stronger:

- The former Austrian Netherlands and Dutch Republic were united to form the Kingdom of the Netherlands.

- A group of 39 German states were loosely joined as the newly created German Confederation, dominated by Austria.

- Switzerland was recognized as an independent nation.

- The Kingdom of Sardinia in Italy was strengthened by the addition of Genoa.

These changes allowed the countries of Europe to contain France and prevent it from overpowering weaker nations. (See the map on page 216.)

The French Revolution and Napoleon **213**

THINK THROUGH HISTORY
A. Analyzing Motives Why would aristocrats be against democracy?
A. Possible Answer They would lose power under a democratic government.

HISTORY MAKERS

Klemens von Metternich
1773–1859

Klemens von Metternich was a tall, handsome man whose charm worked equally well on his fellow diplomats and on the elegant ladies of Vienna. He spoke five languages fluently and thought of himself as a European, not as a citizen of any single country. "Europe has for a long time held for me the significance of a fatherland," he once said.

Early in his career, Metternich linked himself to the Hapsburgs, the rulers of Austria. In 1809, he became Austria's foreign minister, and he held that office for the next 39 years. Because of his immense influence on European politics, these years are often called the Age of Metternich.

Section 5 Overview
OBJECTIVES

1. To explain the importance of the decisions made at the Congress of Vienna.

2. To show how the ideas of the French Revolution continued to influence people throughout Europe.

SKILLBUILDER
- Interpreting maps: region, p. 216

CRITICAL THINKING
- Analyzing motives, p. 213
- Identifying effects, p. 215
- Summarizing, p. 216
- Evaluating, p. 216
- Analyzing themes, p. 216

FOCUS
5-Minute Warm-Up

▶ **Identifying Main Ideas**
To explore the work of peace organizations, have students answer these questions.

1. Read Connect to Today on page 215. What is the purpose of the United Nations?

2. What did the major powers agree to do after World War II?

 WARM-UP TRANSPARENCY 7

OBJECTIVE ① INSTRUCT

Metternich Restores Stability

▶ **Key Ideas**
- Metternich influences European rulers to restore stability to Europe.
- France is kept intact, and a balance of power is established in Europe.
- Under the principle of legitimacy, rulers deposed by Napoleon are restored to power.
- The Congress of Vienna makes fair settlements and produces a lasting peace.

📖 *IN-DEPTH RESOURCES: UNIT 2*
Guided Reading, p. 41

📖 *ACCESS FOR STUDENTS ACQUIRING ENGLISH*
Guided Reading (Spanish), p. 85

SECTION 5 RESOURCES

PRINT RESOURCES

 IN-DEPTH RESOURCES: UNIT 2
Guided Reading, p. 41

 ACCESS FOR STUDENTS ACQUIRING ENGLISH
Guided Reading (Spanish), p. 85

📖 *FORMAL ASSESSMENT*
Section Quiz, p. 92

 ALTERNATIVE ASSESSMENT BOOK

TECHNOLOGY RESOURCES

 CRITICAL THINKING TRANSPARENCIES
CT23 The French Revolution to the Congress of Vienna
CT59 Visual Summary

 CD-ROM
Electronic Library of Primary Sources

 INTERNET www.mlworldhistory.com

During the Congress of Vienna, diplomats exchanged secrets and made deals during the endless rounds of parties. Much of the congress's work was accomplished by means of such "diplomacy through entertainment."

Balance of Power Although the leaders of Europe wanted to weaken France, they did not want to go too far. If they severely punished France, they might encourage the French to take revenge. If they broke up France, then another country might become so strong that it would threaten them all. Thus, the victorious powers were surprisingly easy on the defeated nation. Although the French were required to give up all the territories Napoleon had taken, France remained intact, with roughly the same boundaries it had had in 1790. France also kept some of its overseas possessions, its army, and an independent government. As a result, France remained a major but diminished European power, and no country in Europe could easily overpower another.

Legitimacy The great powers affirmed the principle of **legitimacy**—agreeing that as many as possible of the rulers whom Napoleon had driven from their thrones should be restored to power. In France, the brother of Louis XVI returned to power as King Louis XVIII. He wisely adopted a constitution and ruled as a constitutional monarch. The congress also restored the Bourbon rulers of Spain and the Kingdom of the Two Sicilies. Hapsburg princes came back to rule several states in northern Italy. Many (though not all) of the former rulers of the German states of central Europe also regained their thrones. The participants in the Congress of Vienna believed that the return of the former monarchs would stabilize political relations among the nations.

The Congress of Vienna was a political triumph in many ways. Because its settlements were fair enough for no country to be left bearing a grudge, it did not sow the seeds of future wars. In that sense, it was more successful than many other peace meetings in history. For the first time, the nations of an entire continent were cooperating to control political affairs. On June 13, 1815, four days after the signing of the document that ended the congress, an observer wrote down his impressions:

Background
Most rulers in Europe at this time gained legitimacy by inheriting a throne.

> **A VOICE FROM THE PAST**
> It is contended that, on the whole, the Congress in its eight months of meetings has performed a tremendous task and never has a congress achieved more meaningful or grander results. . . . The majority of people now are saying: "The minister of foreign affairs [Metternich] has reaped honor from his work, from the conception and execution of the idea of the Congress of Vienna, and from the meeting of the sovereigns in consequence thereof."
>
> **CONFIDENTIAL AGENT,** quoted in *The Congress of Vienna: An Eyewitness Account*

How lasting was the peace? Until 1853, none of the five great powers waged war on one another, and some were at peace until the First World War in 1914. By agreeing to come to one another's aid in case of threats to peace, the European nations had assured that there would be a balance of power on the continent and that no nation would be able to expand at the expense of others. The Congress of Vienna had created an age of peace in Europe.

Political Changes Beyond Vienna

Background
Conservatives wanted the political situation to return to what it had been before the French Revolution.

The Congress of Vienna was a victory for conservatives. Kings and princes were restored in country after country, in keeping with Metternich's goals. Nevertheless, there were important differences from one country to another. Louis XVIII's decision to rule France as a constitutional monarch meant that both Britain and France now had constitutional monarchies. Generally speaking, however, the governments in eastern Europe were more conservative than these. The rulers of Russia, Prussia, and Austria were absolute monarchs.

Conservative Europe The rulers of Europe were very jittery about the legacy of the French Revolution, especially the threatening revolutionary ideals of liberty, equality, and fraternity. Late in 1815, Czar Alexander, Emperor Francis I of Austria, and King Frederick William III of Prussia entered a league called the **Holy Alliance.** That agreement loosely bound them together. Finally, a series of alliances devised by Metternich, called the **Concert of Europe,** assured that nations would help one another if any revolutions broke out.

Across Europe, conservatives held firm control of the governments, but they could not contain the ideas that had emerged during the French Revolution. France after 1815 was deeply divided politically. Conservatives were happy with the monarchy of Louis XVIII and were determined to make it last. Liberals wanted the king to share more power with the Chamber of Deputies and to grant the middle class the right to vote. Many people in the lower class remained committed to the ideals of liberty, equality, and fraternity even though women and many poor men could not vote. In other countries as well, like Austria, Prussia, and the small German states, there was an explosive mixture of ideas and factions that would contribute directly to revolutions in 1830 and again in 1848.

Despite their efforts to undo the French Revolution, the leaders at the Congress of Vienna could not turn back the clock. The Revolution had given Europe its first experiment in democratic government. Although the experiment had failed, it had set new political ideas in motion. The major political divisions of the early 1800s had their roots in the French Revolution.

THINK THROUGH HISTORY
B. Identifying Effects What seeds of democracy had been sown by the French Revolution?
B. Possible Answers Sharing of power, social equality, freedom of speech and religion, fair taxation, voting rights

Revolution in Latin America The actions of the Congress of Vienna had consequences beyond Europe. When the congress restored Ferdinand VII to the Spanish throne, the reasons for the Spanish colonial revolts against Napoleon's puppet king, Joseph Bonaparte, should have disappeared. However, clashes among conservatives, liberals, and radicals erupted quickly.

In the colonies, the royalist *peninsulares* wanted to restore their power and control over the land, and the liberal Creoles saw their chance to retain and expand the powers they had seized. Revolts against the king broke out in many parts of Spanish America, with only Mexico remaining loyal to Ferdinand. In 1820, a liberalist revolt in Spain prompted the Spanish king to tighten control over both Spain and its American colonies. This action angered the Mexicans, who rose in revolt and successfully threw off Spain's control. A liberalist revolt in Portugal at about the same time created an opportunity for Brazilians to declare independence as well.

Long-Term Legacy The Congress of Vienna left a legacy that would influence world politics for the next 100 years. The continent-wide efforts to establish and maintain a balance of power diminished the size and the power of France, while the power of Britain and Prussia increased. Nationalism began to grow in Italy, Germany, Greece, and other areas that the congress had put under foreign control. Eventually, the nationalistic feelings would explode into revolutions, and new nations would be

CONNECT *to* TODAY

Congress of Vienna—United Nations

The work of the Congress of Vienna and the Concert of Europe was intended to keep the world safe from war. The modern equivalent is the United Nations, an international organization established in 1945 and continuing today, whose purpose is to promote world peace.

Like the Congress of Vienna, the United Nations was formed by major powers after a war (World War II). They agreed to cooperate to reduce tensions and bring greater harmony to international relations. Although not always successful, both the Concert of Europe and the United Nations used diplomacy to keep peace.

OBJECTIVE ② INSTRUCT

Political Changes Beyond Vienna

▶ *Key Ideas*
- The situation in Europe after the Congress of Vienna represents a victory for conservatives.
- A series of alliances, called the Concert of Europe, allows nations to help one another in case of internal revolutions.
- Latin American colonies revolt against Spanish rule.
- Nationalism grows, and democratic ideas begin to take hold in European nations.

CONNECT *to* TODAY

Congress of Vienna—United Nations

Ask students to check national newspapers for one week and to clip all articles referring to the United Nations. Have students share the articles and make a list of current UN activities.

TEACHING OPTION — BLOCK SCHEDULING — **COOPERATIVE ACTIVITY: Investigating World Peace Organizations** — CLASS TIME 30 MINUTES

Task: Pairs of students will choose peace organizations—such as the Congress of Vienna, the United Nations, NATO, and Amnesty International—to research. Then each pair will meet with another pair to exchange information and to develop a comparison of the organizations they chose.

Purpose: To learn more about historical efforts to establish peacekeeping organizations in the world.

Activity: Ask each pair of students to choose an organization dedicated to peace among nations and to research the activities and successes of the organization. Students should pay close attention to the purpose of the organization and to the ways in which the organization makes decisions. After the pair exchanges information with another pair of students, the four students should make a chart

comparing the two organizations and presenting conclusions about the positive and negative aspects of each.

 ALTERNATIVE ASSESSMENT BOOK
Standards for Evaluating a Cooperative Activity

The French Empire, 1810

Europe, 1817

French Empire
Countries controlled by Napoleon
Countries allied with Napoleon
Countries at war with Napoleon

Small German states
Boundary of the German Confederation

GEOGRAPHY SKILLBUILDER: Interpreting Maps
1. **Region** *What parts of Napoleon's French Empire did France lose as a result of the Congress of Vienna agreements?*
2. **Region** *In what sense did the territorial changes of 1815 reflect a restoration of order and balance?*

formed. European colonies also responded to the power shift. Spanish colonies took advantage of the events in Europe to declare their independence and break away from their European rulers.

On the other hand, ideas about the basis of power and authority had changed permanently as a result of the French Revolution. Old ideas about who should control governments were discarded. More and more, the principles of democracy were seen as the best way for equity and justice to prevail for all people. Europeans challenged old economic patterns of taxation and property ownership and began to adopt more equal treatment for all. The French Revolution changed the "business as usual" attitude that had dominated Europe for centuries. A new era had begun.

C. Answer Colonies wanted independence, and ideas about power and authority changed forever.

THINK THROUGH HISTORY
C. Summarizing How did the French Revolution affect not only Europe but also other areas of the world?

Section 5 Assessment

1. TERMS & NAMES
Identify
• Congress of Vienna
• Klemens von Metternich
• balance of power
• legitimacy
• Holy Alliance
• Concert of Europe

2. TAKING NOTES
Think about the ways in which the three main goals of Metternich's plan at the Congress of Vienna solved a political problem. Fill in the chart below.

Metternich's Plan	
Problem	Solution

What was the overall effect of Metternich's plan on France?

3. EVALUATING
From France's point of view, were the decisions made at the Congress of Vienna fair?

THINK ABOUT
• Metternich's three goals
• France's loss of territory
• the fears of the rest of Europe

4. ANALYZING THEMES
Power and Authority Why do you think liberals and conservatives differed over who should have power?

THINK ABOUT
• Old Regime privileges
• attitudes toward change
• Enlightenment ideas

216 Chapter 7

ANSWERS

1. TERMS & NAMES
Congress of Vienna, p. 213
Klemens von Metternich, p. 213
balance of power, p. 213
legitimacy, p. 214
Holy Alliance, p. 215
Concert of Europe, p. 215

2. TAKING NOTES
Possible Responses: Problems—French aggression, power struggles between countries, lack of legitimate leaders. Solutions—surrounding France with strong countries, creating a balance of power so that no country can dominate others, restoring royal families to their thrones.

3. EVALUATING
Possible Responses: Students may say that the French would have considered the decisions fair because as a defeated country, France could have had its territory divided among the victors. Instead, its original borders were left intact. Others may say that France lost all that it had gained.

4. ANALYZING THEMES
Possible Responses: Students may say that liberals, mostly of the Third Estate, wanted a more representative government and more power for the common people. Conservatives feared the common people and wanted to preserve royalty and privilege, viewing change as dangerous and frightening.

The French Revolution

Even today, historians have a wide variety of opinions about what caused the French Revolution and whether it was a good thing. The following excerpts, dating from the 1790s to 1859, show a variety of opinions about the Revolution.

SPEECH
Maximilien Robespierre

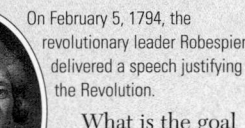

On February 5, 1794, the revolutionary leader Robespierre delivered a speech justifying the Revolution.

What is the goal for which we strive? A peaceful enjoyment of liberty and equality, the rule of that eternal justice whose laws are engraved, not upon marble or stone, but in the hearts of all men.

We wish an order of things where all low and cruel passions are enchained by the laws, all beneficent and generous feelings aroused; . . . where the citizen is subject to the magistrate, the magistrate to the people, the people to justice; where the nation safeguards the welfare of each individual, and each individual proudly enjoys the prosperity and glory of his fatherland.

LETTER

Thomas Paine

In 1790, Paine—a strong supporter of the American Revolution—defended the French Revolution against its critics.

It is no longer the paltry cause of kings or of this or of that individual, that calls France and her armies into action. It is the great cause of all. It is the establishment of a new era, that shall blot despotism from the earth, and fix, on the lasting principles of peace and citizenship, the great Republic of Man.

The scene that now opens itself to France extends far beyond the boundaries of her own dominions. Every nation is becoming her ally, and every court has become her enemy. It is now the cause of all nations, against the cause of all courts.

LITERATURE
Charles Dickens

In 1859, the English writer Dickens wrote *A Tale of Two Cities,* a novel about the French Revolution for which he did much research. In the following scene, Charles Darnay—an aristocrat who gave up his title because he hated the injustices done to the people—has returned to France and been put on trial.

His judges sat upon the bench in feathered hats; but the rough red cap and tricolored cockade was the headdress otherwise prevailing. Looking at the jury and the turbulent audience, he might have thought that the usual order of things was reversed, and that the felons were trying the honest men. The lowest, cruelest, and worst populace of a city, never without its quantity of low, cruel, and bad, were the directing spirits of the scene. . . .

Charles Evrémonde, called Darnay, was accused by the public prosecutor as an emigrant, whose life was forfeit to the Republic, under the decree which banished all emigrants on pain of Death. It was nothing that the decree bore date since his return to France. There he was, and there was the decree; he had been taken in France, and his head was demanded.

"Take off his head!" cried the audience. "An enemy to the Republic!"

ESSAY
Edmund Burke

A British statesman, Burke was one of the earliest and most severe critics of the French Revolution. In October 1793, he expressed this opinion.

> *"The Jacobin Revolution is carried on by men of no rank, of no consideration, of wild, savage minds, full of levity, arrogance, and presumption, without morals."*

Connect *to* History

Summarizing In your own words, summarize the attitude toward the French Revolution expressed in each of these excerpts.

 SEE SKILLBUILDER HANDBOOK, PAGE 650.

Connect *to* Today

Research Find a modern view of the French Revolution and bring it to class. It may be a historian's analysis or an artistic portrayal, such as a novel or film.

 CD-ROM For another perspective on the French Revolution, see World History Electronic Library of Primary Sources.

Why the French Revolution Matters Now
As students discuss these perspectives on the French Revolution, you might have them consider the broader picture: why does the Revolution matter?

The French Revolution matters because it left a lasting political legacy that has affected people all around the world. The political legacy includes the following beliefs, some of which are contradictory:

• Political revolution can remake society for the better.
• Nationalism is a positive force for change.
• People should have civil liberties and equality before the law.
• Social position and wealth should depend on individual achievement, not inherited status.
• Democratic ideals and activism lead to war, class conflict, and savage dictatorship.
• The old ways were better because government was firm, society was orderly, and common people were respectful of authority.

The power of these beliefs has led to revolutions around the world. In the 1990s, conflicts in Bosnia, Zaire, Chechnya, and Palestine were fueled by several of them.

ELECTRONIC LIBRARY OF PRIMARY SOURCES
from "Frenchmen, Is This What You Want?"

Connect *to* History

Analyzing Possible Responses:
Robespierre—The Revolution is justified because it will lead to a benevolent and just government under which individuals will enjoy peace and prosperity. Dickens—The Revolution gave power to the lowest and cruelest members of the populace, leading to rampant injustice and mob rule. Burke—The men of the Revolution are unprincipled savages. Paine—The great cause of eliminating despotism justifies revolution.

Connect *to* Today

Research
Students may wish to use one of the following:

• One of the film versions of *A Tale of Two Cities*

• The music from *Les Misérables,* a musical version of Victor Hugo's book about social conflicts in France after Napoleon's death

• *Guillotine, Its Legend and Lore* by Daniel Gerould. New York: Blast, 1990

• "The Great Revolution," *National Geographic Magazine,* July 1989

Teacher's Edition 217

TERMS & NAMES

1. estate, p. 193
2. Great Fear, p. 196
3. Declaration of the Rights of Man, p. 197
4. guillotine, p. 200
5. Maximilien Robespierre, p. 202
6. coup d'état, p. 205
7. Napoleonic Code, p. 206
8. Continental System, p. 209
9. Waterloo, p. 212
10. Congress of Vienna, p. 213

REVIEW QUESTIONS

Answers will vary.

11. They were heavily taxed and had no political voice, no access to political office, and not enough to eat.

12. The Bastille symbolized the repression of the Old Regime.

13. Equal justice, freedom of speech, freedom of religion

14. It was an effort to wipe out those who wanted a return to the old ways. Members of Robespierre's government turned against him, and with his death, the Terror ended.

15. Napoleon established a code of laws, set up a fairer tax code, stabilized the economy, fired corrupt officials, gave equal opportunity in government, set up public schools, and reduced the power of the church while supporting religious tolerance.

16. He conquered much of Europe and put his relatives in charge of several nations.

17. Scorched-earth policy and the weather

18. In 1814, Napoleon's army had been weakened by losses in Russia and Spain, and enemy forces were too numerous. In 1815, the allies again had greater numbers of troops.

19. To prevent French aggression, to restore a balance of power in Europe, and to restore royal families to thrones held before Napoleon's conquests

20. The balance of power worked; mutual-aid agreements among nations helped ensure stability.

The French Revolution and Napoleon

Long-Term Causes

- Enlightenment ideas—liberty and equality
- Example furnished by the American Revolution
- Social and economic injustices of the Old Regime

Immediate Causes

- Economic crisis—famine and government debt
- Weak leadership
- Discontent of the Third Estate

Revolution
- Fall of the Bastille
- National Assembly
- Declaration of the Rights of Man and a new constitution

Immediate Effects

- End of the Old Regime
- Execution of monarchs
- War with the First Coalition
- Reign of Terror
- Rise of Napoleon

Long-Term Effects

- Conservative reaction
- Decline in French power
- Spread of Enlightenment ideas
- Growth of nationalism
- Rise of international organizations (Congress of Vienna)
- Revolutions in Latin America

TERMS & NAMES

Briefly explain the importance of each of the following during the French Revolution or the rise and fall of Napoleon's rule.

1. estate
2. Great Fear
3. Declaration of the Rights of Man
4. guillotine
5. Maximilien Robespierre
6. coup d'état
7. Napoleonic Code
8. Continental System
9. Waterloo
10. Congress of Vienna

REVIEW QUESTIONS

SECTION 1 *(pages 193–196)*
Revolution Threatens the French King

11. Why were the members of the Third Estate dissatisfied with their way of life under the Old Regime?

12. Why was the fall of the Bastille important to the French people?

SECTION 2 *(pages 197–203)*
Revolution Brings Reform and Terror

13. Name three political reforms that resulted from the French Revolution.

14. What was the Reign of Terror, and how did it end?

SECTION 3 *(pages 204–208)*
Napoleon Forges an Empire

15. Summarize Napoleon's reforms in France.

16. What steps did Napoleon take to create an empire in Europe?

SECTION 4 *(pages 209–211)*
Napoleon's Empire Collapses

17. What factors led to Napoleon's defeat in Russia?

18. Summarize the reasons that the European allies were able to defeat Napoleon in 1814 and again in 1815.

SECTION 5 *(pages 213–217)*
The Congress of Vienna Convenes

19. What were Metternich's three goals at the Congress of Vienna?

20. How did the Congress of Vienna assure peace in Europe for the next 38 years?

Interact *with* History

On page 192, you looked at a French mob's actions before completely knowing why they occurred. Now that you've read the chapter, reevaluate your decision about joining the mob. Were the mob's actions justified? effective? Would you have advised different actions? Discuss your opinions with a small group.

Interact *with* History

Possible Responses: Students who originally wanted to join the mob may now say that the mob's actions led to terror and many unjust executions and that the peasants did not really benefit from their revolutionary actions. Others may say that the actions of the peasants were essential to starting and maintaining the momentum of the Revolution.

CRITICAL THINKING

1. CONGRESS OF VIENNA

THEME POWER AND AUTHORITY How did the Congress of Vienna affect power and authority in European countries after Napoleon's defeat? Consider both who held power in the countries and the power of the countries themselves.

2. NAPOLEON'S CAREER

Below is a chart of dates and events in Napoleon's career. Copy the chart on your paper. For each event, draw an arrow up or down to show whether Napoleon gained or lost power because of it.

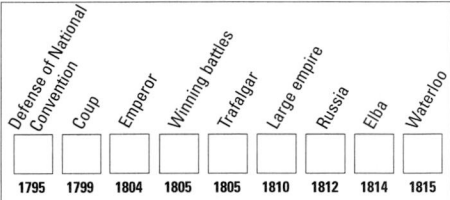

Defense of National Convention	Coup	Emperor	Winning battles	Trafalgar	Large empire	Russia	Elba	Waterloo
1795	1799	1804	1805	1805	1810	1812	1814	1815

3. EFFECTS OF REVOLUTION

There is a saying: "Revolutions devour their own children." What evidence from this chapter supports that statement? Why might revolutions generally be dangerous to their participants?

4. ANALYZING PRIMARY SOURCES

The following quotation from the South American liberator Simón Bolívar shows what he thought would happen if Napoleon came to the New World after his defeat at Waterloo. Read the paragraph and answer the questions below it.

> **A VOICE FROM THE PAST**
> If South America is struck by the thunderbolt of Bonaparte's arrival, misfortune will ever be ours if our country accords him a friendly reception. His thirst for conquest is insatiable [cannot be satisfied]; he has mowed down the flower of European youth . . . in order to carry out his ambitious projects. The same designs will bring him to the New World.

- What was Bolívar's judgment of Napoleon? What words convey it to you?
- Do you agree with Bolívar, or do you think Napoleon had less selfish motives for his actions? Support your opinion with details from the text.

CHAPTER ACTIVITIES

1. LIVING HISTORY: Unit Portfolio Project

THEME REVOLUTION Your unit portfolio project focuses on showing the similarities and differences among revolutions (see page 129). For Chapter 7, you might use one of the following ideas to add to your portfolio:

- Ask classmates to role-play French people from different estates as you interview them about their feelings toward the Revolution. Tape-record your interviews and add a commentary to create an "objective" newscast.
- Draw cartoons that compare and contrast a member of France's Third Estate with an American colonist.
- Write a dialogue between King George III of England and King Louis XVI of France, in which they discuss their problems with rebelling subjects.

2. CONNECT TO TODAY: Cooperative Learning

THEME ECONOMICS One major cause of the French Revolution was the extreme contrast between the lives of the few rich and the many poor in France. Some people feel that the gap between the rich and poor in the United States is similar today.

Work with a team to create a graph showing the distribution of wealth in the United States today.

INTERNET Use the Internet or magazines to research the topic. Look for statistics that answer such questions as, What percentages of the population own various proportions of the country's wealth? What percentage of individuals live at or below the poverty line? How much is the wealthiest person in the United States worth?

- Look for parallel statistics. Figure out how to present them visually. You may use any type of graphic as long as it is labeled clearly.
- Make comparisons between the distribution of wealth in France before the Revolution and the distribution of wealth in the United States today.

3. INTERPRETING A TIME LINE

Revisit the unit time line on page 129. Which three events entered for the period 1780–1815 do you think were most significant? Why?

FOCUS ON **GEOGRAPHY**

Notice the locations of Britain and France in this map.

- How far away from France is Britain?
- What geographical barrier protected Britain from becoming part of Napoleon's empire?

Connect to History What would Napoleon have needed to do to overcome that geographical barrier? Did he? What happened?

Great Britain and France, 1810

North Sea

GREAT BRITAIN

London

ATLANTIC OCEAN

English Channel

Brussels

Amiens

Paris

Versailles

0 100 Miles

0 200 Kilometers

FRENCH EMPIRE

Mediterranean Sea

CHAPTER ACTIVITIES

1. LIVING HISTORY

Standards for Evaluation
An interview and commentary should meet the following criteria:

- Presents members of all three estates.
- Shows an understanding of each estate.
- Clearly defines the roles.
- Provides clear commentary and draws thoughtful conclusions about the Revolution.

Standards for Evaluation
A cartoon should meet the following criteria:

- Clearly identifies the member of the Third Estate and the American colonist.
- Makes a point about similarities or differences in their conditions or beliefs.
- Has labels that are clear and to the point.

Standards for Evaluation
A dialogue between George II and Louis XVI should meet the following criteria:

- Clearly identifies each person.
- Contains speeches focused on rebelling subjects.
- Indicates similarities and differences in the two rebellions.
- Shows distinct personality differences in the two figures.

2. CONNECT TO TODAY

About 20 percent of Americans own more than 80 percent of the country's wealth. In 1994, about 15 percent of American families lived below the poverty line. The wealthiest person in the United States in 1996 was Bill Gates, with $18.5 billion.

3. INTERPRETING A TIME LINE

Student answers should provide clear reasons and support for choosing three events as most significant.

FOCUS ON **GEOGRAPHY**

- Only about 25 miles at the countries' nearest points
- The English Channel

Connect to History *Possible Responses:* Napoleon needed a large navy in order to attack Britain. He did have a navy, but its defeat by the British navy at the Battle of Trafalgar ended his hope of invading Britain.

CRITICAL THINKING

1. CONGRESS OF VIENNA
Possible Response: It restored power within the countries to those who had held it before—the royalty and aristocracy. It also made the countries more equal in power, so that no one could dominate.

2. NAPOLEON'S CAREER
1795—gained; 1799—gained; 1804—gained; Winning battles—gained; Trafalgar—lost; Large empire—gained; Russia—lost; Elba—lost; Waterloo—lost

3. EFFECTS OF REVOLUTION
Possible Responses: After beginning with high ideals of equality and justice, the French Revolution degenerated into mob rule, savagery, and injustice. Many revolutionaries were guillotined in the Reign of Terror. Revolutionary leaders usually aren't good at governing after the revolution is over.

4. ANALYZING PRIMARY SOURCES
Possible Responses: Bolívar saw Napoleon as power hungry and willing to sacrifice young soldiers to his ambitions. Some students may agree, citing Napoleon's efforts to conquer Britain and Russia through force, not diplomacy. Others may cite Napoleon's reforms in France as evidence of his good character.

PLANNING GUIDE
Nationalist Revolutions Sweep the West

	Key Ideas	**COPY MASTERS**	**ASSESSMENT**
SECTION 1 Latin American Peoples Win Independence *pp. 223–228*	*A slave revolt in Haiti leads to independence from French rule. Freedom from colonial rule is achieved throughout Latin America, but independence does not bring unity and prosperity as some liberators had hoped.*	*In-Depth Resources: Unit 2* • **Guided Reading,** p. 56 • **Skillbuilder Practice:** Hypothesizing, p. 60 • **Primary Source:** from Proclamation of 1813, p. 63 • **Literature:** from *All Souls' Rising,* p. 67 • **History Makers:** Simón Bolívar, p. 70	P E *Section 1 Assessment,* p. 228 *Formal Assessment* • Section Quiz, p. 101 *Alternative Assessment Book* • Standards for Evaluating a Product or Performance
SECTION 2 Revolutions Disrupt Europe *pp. 229–232*	*The forces of nationalism bring revolutions in Europe. With the exception of Greece, most revolutions fail, and by mid-century most of Europe returns to authoritarian rule.*	*In-Depth Resources: Unit 2* • **Guided Reading,** p. 57 • **Primary Source:** Letter to Thomas Moore, p. 64	P E *Section 2 Assessment,* p. 232 *Formal Assessment* • Section Quiz, p. 102 *Alternative Assessment Book* • Standards for Evaluating a Cooperative Activity
SECTION 3 Patterns of Change Nationalism Case Studies: Italy and Germany *pp. 233–238*	*The idea of nationalism eventually causes the breakup of the Austrian, Russian, and Ottoman empires. Italy is united through the efforts of Mazzini, Garibaldi, and Cavour. Prussian prime minister Otto von Bismarck succeeds in uniting and strengthening Germany.*	*In-Depth Resources: Unit 2* • **Guided Reading,** p. 58 • **Geography Application:** Languages Fuel Nationalism, p. 61 • **Primary Sources:** Proclamation of 1860, p. 65; Nationalist Speech by Otto von Bismarck, p. 66 • **Connections Across Time and Cultures:** Bonds that Create a Nation-State, p. 72	P E *Section 3 Assessment,* p. 238 *Formal Assessment* • Section Quiz, p. 103 *Alternative Assessment Book* • Standards for Evaluating a Cooperative Activity
SECTION 4 Revolutions in the Arts *pp. 239–243*	*During the first half of the 1800s, the Romantic movement in art, literature, and music arises in reaction to the rationalism of the Enlightenment. By mid-century, writers and artists shift to Realism in response to the harsh realities of the Industrial Age.*	*In-Depth Resources: Unit 2* • **Guided Reading,** p. 59 • **History Makers:** Beethoven, p. 71	P E *Section 4 Assessment,* p. 243 *Formal Assessment* • Section Quiz, p. 104 *Alternative Assessment Book* • Standards for Evaluating a Cooperative Activity
CHAPTER RESOURCES	**Chapter Overview** *During the first half of the century, Romantic idealism and nationalism spark revolutions in Latin America and Europe. Latin Americans succeed in throwing off colonial rule. However, revolutions throughout Europe fail to achieve their goals.*	*Telescoping the Times* • Chapter Summary, pp. 33–35 *Planning for Block Schedules*	P E *Chapter Assessment,* pp. 244–245 *Chapter Activities,* p. 245 *Formal Assessment* • Chapter Test, forms A and B, pp. 105–110 💾 *Test Generator* *Alternative Assessment Book*

TECHNOLOGY

Warm-Up Transparency 8

World Art and Cultures Transparencies
- AT52 *Father Miguel Hidalgo Crowns Mexico and Breaks Chains Binding Her to Spain*

Electronic Library of Primary Sources
- from Address to the Second National Congress of Venezuela, 1819

Patterns of Interaction:
Struggling Toward Democracy

INTERNET RESOURCES
www.mlworldhistory.com

Warm-Up Transparency 8

INTERNET RESOURCES
www.mlworldhistory.com

Warm-Up Transparency 8

Geography Transparencies
- GT24 Ethnic Groups of Austria-Hungary, 1867

Critical Thinking Transparencies
- CT24 The Unification of Germany and Italy

Electronic Library of Primary Sources
- from "Duties of Country"

INTERNET RESOURCES
www.mlworldhistory.com

Warm-Up Transparency 8

World Art and Cultures Transparencies
- AT53 *Couturiere*

Critical Thinking Transparencies
- CT60 Visual Summary

Electronic Library of Primary Sources
- "Kubla Khan"
- from *Frankenstein*

INTERNET RESOURCES
www.mlworldhistory.com

Chapter Summaries on Audiocassette in English and Spanish

INTERNET RESOURCES
www.mlworldhistory.com

 Block Scheduling (90 MINUTES)

Day 1
Section 1, pp. 223–228
Section Assessment, p. 228

Day 2
Section 2, pp. 229–232
 COOPERATIVE ACTIVITY
Creating Political Cartoons, p. 231 (Teacher's Edition)
Section Assessment, p. 232

Day 3
Section 3, pp. 233–238
 COOPERATIVE ACTIVITY
Interviewing Garibaldi, p. 236 (Teacher's Edition)
Section Assessment, p. 238

Day 4
Section 4, pp. 239–243
 COOPERATIVE ACTIVITY
Presenting a Romantic Composer, p. 241 (Teacher's Edition)
Section Assessment, p. 243
Chapter Assessment, pp. 244–245

Yearly Pacing *Chapter 8 Total:* 4 days *Yearly Total:* 85 days

Planning for Block Schedules

Customizing for Special Needs

Students Acquiring English

Access for Students Acquiring English
- **Guided Reading** for Sections 1–4 (Spanish), pp. 92–95
- **Chapter Summary** (Spanish), pp. 89–91
- **Skillbuilder Practice** Hypothesizing (Spanish),p. 96
- **Geography Application** Languages Fuel Nationalism (Spanish), p. 97

Chapter Summaries on Audiocassette in English and Spanish

Patterns of Interaction Struggling Toward Democracy (Spanish track)

Spanish Reading Study Guide
- pp. 85–94

Less Proficient Readers

In-Depth Resources: Unit 2
- **Guided Reading** for Sections 1–4, pp. 56–59
- **Skillbuilder Practice** Hypothesizing, p. 60
- **Geography Application** Languages Fuel Nationalism, p. 61

Telescoping the Times
- Chapter Summary, pp. 33–35

Reading Study Guide
- pp. 85–94

Chapter Summaries on Audiocassette

Gifted and Talented Students

In-Depth Resources: Unit 2

Primary Sources:
- from Proclamation of 1813, p. 63
- Letter to Thomas Moore, p. 64
- Proclamation of 1860, p. 65
- Nationalist Speech by Otto von Bismarck, p. 66

History Makers
- Simón Bolívar, p. 70
- Beethoven, p. 71

Connections to Literature READINGS FOR STUDENTS

In-Depth Resources: Unit 2
- Literature: from *All Souls Rising,* p. 67

Enrichment Reading
- **Emil, Ludwig**
Bolívar: The Life of an Idealist
New York: Alliance, 1942

A lively story of Bolívar's childhood and later successes, this book features swords, battles, and cheering mobs.

McDougal Littell
The Language of Literature
Grade 10
Guy de Maupassant, "Two Friends," p. 567

Nationalist Revolutions Sweep the West, 1789–1900

Accessing Prior Knowledge

• Ask students to look at the picture of the Arc de Triomphe and read the caption that accompanies it. What other monuments and symbols of military conquest and victory have they seen or read about in earlier chapters?

Making Judgments

• Have students read each of the captions and then decide which of the three themes listed to the left (revolution, power and authority, cultural interaction) seems to be the dominant theme expressed by the image and the caption that explains it.

Geography Connection

Ask students to look at the map on page 221.

• Why might the location of France have made governments throughout Europe apprehensive after the French Revolution of 1789? *France has a fairly central location and shares borders with a number of countries that might have feared revolution.*

Nationalist Revolutions Sweep the West, 1789–1900

PREVIEWING THEMES

Revolution
The 19th century was a time of revolutions around the Western world, as people under foreign rule established their own nation-states. The 1800s was also a time of revolutionary changes in literature, music, and art.

Power and Authority
In country after country, governments controlled by aristocrats came crashing down. In their place, revolutionaries set up republics and nation-states. With mixed success at first, members of the middle class increased their influence in government.

Cultural Interaction
The ideas of nationalism and democracy swept out over Europe from France, finally reaching across the Atlantic to the Americas. Likewise, the ideas of the Romantic movement and later the Realist movement revolutionized art, music, and literature.

INTERNET CONNECTION

Visit us at **www.mlworldhistory.com** to learn more about nationalism, romanticism, realism, and related topics.

REGIONS OF NATIONALIST REVOLUTIONS, 1789–1900

Central and South America

In 1810, **Padre Miguel Hidalgo** issued his *Grito de Dolores* (Cry of Dolores). In it, he called for the poor of **Mexico** to revolt against Spanish rule. In this 20th-century mural by Mexican artist Juan O'Gorman, Mexicans of *all* classes revolt—which was not the case. O'Gorman also slips in his own politics: He inserts a communist symbol (the sickle) next to the religious banner.

220

GEOGRAPHY THEMES

Region

Remind students that regions have certain characteristics in common. Ask students why Havana, Port au Prince, and Santo Domingo might be considered as part of the same region. *They are all located in the Caribbean.* Ask students to identify other regions shown on the map on these two pages and to name a common characteristic of each. *Students might identify North America, Central America, South America, and Europe.* Ask students to identify the region in which they live. Then have them list characteristics of the region, including topography, climate, and so forth.

Movement

In this chapter students will study revolutions in Mexico, Central America, South America, and the Caribbean. Ask students to recall what they learned about European conquests in these regions in Chapter 4. Have them discuss how European revolutionary ideas might have arrived in these regions. Have them discuss the Spanish conquest of the Americas in terms of the movement of people and ideas across the ocean. Have them summarize the Spanish colonization of North, Central, and South America.

ADDITIONAL RESOURCES

Books for the Teacher

- Friedrich, Otto. *Blood and Iron: From Bismarck to Hitler, the Von Moltke Family's Impact on German History.* New York: HarperCollins, 1995.

- Tenenbaum, Barbara A., ed. *Encyclopedia of Latin American History and Culture.* New York: Scribner's, 1996.

Books for the Student

- Stefoff, Rebecca. *Independence and Revolution in Mexico, 1810–1940.* New York: Facts on File, 1993.

- Vinke, Herman. *Giuseppe Garibaldi.* New York: Chelsea House, 1987.

▭▭▭ Videos

- *The Age of Revolutions: 1776–1848.* Social Studies School Service, 1985. 800–421–4246.

- *Bismarck: Germany from Blood and Iron.* Social Studies School Service, 1976. 800–421–4246.

- *Simón Bolívar.* Society for Visual Education, 1994. 800–829–1900.

◉ Software

- *The 1848 Revolutions.* CD-ROM. Educational Software Institute, 1995. 800–955–5570.

- *Nineteenth-Century Nationalism.* CD-ROM. Society for Visual Education, 1994. 800–829–1900.

- *Romanticism.* CD-ROM. Society for Visual Education, 1994. 800–829–1900.

In **November 1860**, colorful Italian revolutionary **Giuseppe Garibaldi** met on a bridge in **Naples** with **Victor Emmanuel**, the king of Piedmont-Sardinia. To assure Italy's unity, Garibaldi made a grand gesture. During the Naples meeting, he handed over his southern conquests to Victor Emmanuel. By Garibaldi's generous act, north and south were joined. The Kingdom of Italy was born. This 19th-century fresco recalls the event.

In 1806, **Napoleon** began construction of the **Arc de Triomphe** in **Paris**. It was not completed until 1836—15 years after the emperor died. The heroic sculptures celebrate the victories of Napoleon's armies. Even today, the Arc de Triomphe is the largest triumphal arch in the world. It is also one of the symbols of France's capital city.

221

HISTORY THROUGH ART

20th-Century Mural
Juan O'Gorman

Juan O'Gorman (1905–1982) was an architect as well as a painter. The detail from the mural on page 220 shows Miguel Hidalgo, a priest, leading Mexicans in a rebellion against Spanish rule. The painter's father, Cecil Crawford O'Gorman, was also a well-known artist. Juan O'Gorman graduated from the school of architecture at the National University of Mexico in Mexico City in 1927. He began designing houses in the International Style of the architect Le Corbusier. For a time he was head of the Department of Building Construction for Mexico City. He was also a professor of architecture at the National Polytechnic Institute.

Some of O'Gorman's major art works included mosaic designs on public buildings, murals, and frescoes. Some of his most important public murals were done at the Mexico City airport. The murals, which were anti-Fascist and anti-Church, were destroyed in 1939 during a rightward turn of the Mexican government. This mural does not display an anti-clerical bias. Indeed, a priest (Miguel Hidalgo) is shown in a heroic pose in the forefront leading the people in revolt.

Interpreting the Art Have students explain why Hidalgo seems to be the hero in this mural. How does the artist make him look heroic?

This Interact with History feature motivates students by inviting them to put themselves in the position of an artist who is designing a national symbol. As they imagine themselves choosing a design, students will analyze the issues, explore their options, and become decision makers.

Purpose

- to set the stage for studying the spread of revolutions through the West during the 19th century
- to help students understand some of the causes and effects of revolution
- to help students make connections with the people and events they will study in this chapter

Teaching Strategy

Thinking Critically After students have imagined themselves in the situation described on this page, have them answer the key question and give reasons for their decision.

EXAMINING *the* ISSUES

Following are suggestions for addressing each bulleted question.

1 Ask students to think of some of the symbols that represent our country. What ideals do these symbols represent?

2 Point out that symbols can be borrowed from other cultures. For example, the eagle was a symbol of ancient Rome.

3 Ask students what elements of the American flag represent its past.

4 Ask students to look at the words on a dollar bill and on a quarter. How do they represent our ideals?

Making Connections Ask students to discuss the role of ordinary people in the American and French revolutions.

Interact *with* History

You are an artist in a nation that has just freed itself from foreign rule. The new government is asking you to design a symbol that will show what your country stands for. It's up to you to design the symbol that best suits the spirit of your people. Will your symbol be peaceful or warlike, dignified or joyful? Or will it be a combination of these and other qualities?

UNITED STATES
The olive branch and arrows symbolize a desire for peace but a readiness for war. The Latin phrase *E pluribus unum* means "Out of many, one," expressing unity in diversity.

Your country is free. What kind of national symbol will you design?

AUSTRIA
The hammer and sickle symbolize agriculture and industry. The broken chains celebrate Austria's liberation from Germany at the end of World War II.

BOTSWANA
Industry and livestock are connected by water, the key to the country's prosperity. *Pula* in the Setswana language means "rain," "water," "wealth."

PERU
The country's wealth is shown by the vicuña (with its silky fur), the quinine tree (which helps to cure malaria), and a horn of plenty.

URUGUAY
The shield features symbols of justice, strength, freedom, and prosperity.

222 Chapter 8

EXAMINING *the* ISSUES

- What values and goals of your new country do you want to show?
- What symbols will you use?
- Will your symbol represent your country's past or future? Its land? Its goals?
- Will your design have words that also express values?

As a class, discuss these questions. During the discussion, think of the role played by symbols in expressing a country's view of itself and the world.

As you read about the rise of new nations in Latin America and Europe, think of how artists encourage national pride.

Follow Up

A feature on the chapter assessment will ask students to reevaluate their responses to the situation presented on this page.

Latin American Peoples Win Independence

TERMS & NAMES
- *peninsulares*
- creoles
- mulattos
- Simón Bolívar
- José de San Martín
- Miguel Hidalgo
- José Morelos

MAIN IDEA

Spurred by discontent and Enlightenment ideas, peoples in Latin America fought colonial rule.

WHY IT MATTERS NOW

Sixteen of today's Latin American nations gained their independence at this time.

SETTING THE STAGE By the late 1700s, the Americas, already troubled by Enlightenment ideas, were electrified by the news of the French Revolution. The French ideals of liberty, equality, and fraternity inspired many Latin Americans to rise up against their French, Spanish, and Portuguese masters.

Revolution in Haiti

The French colony called Saint Domingue was the first Latin American territory to free itself from European rule. Saint Domingue, now known as Haiti, occupied the western third of the island of Hispaniola in the Caribbean Sea.

Background
About 35,000 Europeans stood at the top of the social ladder in Haiti in the late 1700s. They were mainly French.

HISPANIOLA
HAITI
Caribbean Sea

Nearly 500,000 enslaved Africans—the vast majority of Saint Domingue's population—lived at the bottom of the social system. Most slaves worked on plantations, and they outnumbered their masters dramatically. White masters thus used brutal methods to terrorize slaves and keep them powerless.

The Fight for Freedom The slaves soon showed that, in fact, they were not powerless. In August 1791, an African priest named Boukman raised a call for revolution. Within a few days, 100,000 slaves rose in revolt. A leader soon emerged, Toussaint L'Ouverture (too·SAN loo·vair·TOOR), an ex-slave. Toussaint was untrained in the military and in diplomacy. Even so, he rose to become a skilled general and diplomat. It is said that he got the name L'Ouverture ("opening" in French) because he was so skilled at finding openings in the enemy lines. By 1801, Toussaint had moved into Spanish Santo Domingo (the eastern two-thirds of Hispaniola). He took control of the territory and freed the slaves.

In January 1802, 16,000 French troops landed in Saint-Domingue to depose Toussaint. In May, Toussaint agreed to halt the revolution if the French would end slavery. Despite the agreement, the French soon accused him of planning another uprising. They seized him and sent him to a prison in the French Alps. In that cold mountain jail, he died 10 months later, in April 1803.

Background
By 1600, almost the entire Arawak population had disappeared because of European conquest, warfare, disease, or slavery.

Haiti's Independence Toussaint's general, Jean-Jacques Dessalines (zhahn·ZHAHK day·sah·LEEN), took up the fight for freedom where Toussaint had left off. On January 1, 1804, General Dessalines declared the colony an independent country. It was the first black colony to free itself from European control. He called the country Haiti, which meant "mountainous land" in the language of the native Arawak inhabitants of the island.

This statue, called *The Unknown Maroon of Saint Domingue,* stands in front of Haiti's National Palace. *Maroon* was a name for runaway slaves. Using a shell as a trumpet, the maroon is sounding the call to freedom.

SECTION 1 RESOURCES

PRINT RESOURCES

IN-DEPTH RESOURCES: UNIT 2
Guided Reading, p. 56
Skillbuilder Practice: Hypothesizing, p. 60
Primary Source: from Proclamation of 1813, p. 63
Literature: from *All Souls' Rising,* p. 67
History Makers: Simón Bolívar, p. 70

ACCESS FOR STUDENTS ACQUIRING ENGLISH
Guided Reading (Spanish), p. 92
Skillbuilder Practice (Spanish), p. 96

FORMAL ASSESSMENT
Section Quiz, p. 101

TECHNOLOGY RESOURCES

WORLD ART AND CULTURES TRANSPARENCIES
AT52 *Father Miguel Hidalgo*

CD-ROM
Electronic Library of Primary Sources

VIDEO *Patterns of Interaction: Struggling Toward Democracy*

INTERNET www.mlworldhistory.com

Section 1 Overview

OBJECTIVES

1. To describe how Haiti achieved independence.
2. To identify influences in Latin America's independence struggle.
3. To describe how Bolívar and San Martín ended Spanish rule.
4. To explain the role that Native Americans and mestizos played in achieving independence.
5. To show how Brazil's liberation differed from other countries'.
6. To show the negative effects of independence.

SKILLBUILDERS
- Interpreting charts, p. 224
- Interpreting maps: region, p. 228

CRITICAL THINKING
- Recognizing effects, p. 224
- Summarizing, p. 225
- Making inferences, pp. 226, 227
- Comparing, p. 226
- Forming and supporting opinions, p. 228
- Analyzing themes, p. 228

FOCUS
5-Minute Warm-Up

▶ *Interpreting Maps*
To help students understand the changes in Latin America, have them answer these questions.

1. Look at the map on page 228. On which coast did most of the battles take place?
2. Which countries retained colonies in Latin America, and where were they located?

WARM-UP TRANSPARENCY 8

OBJECTIVE 1 INSTRUCT

Revolution in Haiti

▶ *Key Idea*
- Haiti becomes the first black colony to gain independence.

IN-DEPTH RESOURCES: UNIT 2
Guided Reading, p. 56

ACCESS FOR STUDENTS ACQUIRING ENGLISH
Guided Reading (Spanish), p. 92

Latin America Sweeps to Freedom

▶ **Key Ideas**

- Society in Latin America is based on class, with a small number of peninsulares holding most of the power, while large numbers of Native Americans are the most oppressed.

- The well-educated creole class leads the fight for independence in Latin America.

- Napoleon puts his brother on the Spanish throne, sparking rebellion in Latin America.

History from Visuals

The Divisions in Spanish Colonial Society in 1789

Interpreting the Chart Point out to students that the category "Europeans" in the chart is made up of two groups: peninsulares and creoles.

Extension Activity Ask students to add up the numbers on the chart to arrive at the total population of Spanish colonial society. *13,945,000.* Have them identify the number of peninsulares in colonial society *(15,000)* and then discuss how such a comparatively small number of people could exercise power over so many.

SKILLBUILDER Answers

1. Indians and Europeans, or Indians and Creoles.
2. Peninsulares were an extremely small portion of the population (0.1%) but held all the real power in the colonies.

Latin America Sweeps to Freedom

Latin American colonial society was sharply divided into classes based on birth. At the top of Spanish American society were the *peninsulares* (pay-neen-soo-LAH-rayz), men who had been born in Spain. Only peninsulares could hold high office in Spanish colonial government. In this way, Spain kept the loyalty of its colonial leaders. **Creoles**, Spaniards born in Latin America, ranked after the *peninsulares*. Creoles could not hold high-level political office. But they could rise as officers in Spanish colonial armies. Together these two minority groups controlled wealth and power in the Spanish colonies.

Below the *peninsulares* and creoles came the mestizos (persons of mixed European and Indian ancestry). Next were the **mulattos** (persons of mixed European and African ancestry) and Africans. At the bottom of the social ladder stood Indians. Unlike enslaved Africans, Indians were of little economic value to the Spaniards. As a result, they were more severely oppressed than any other group.

This 18th-century painting shows a lower-class mestizo family in Mexico. Like many of the poor, this is a family of vendors. They are setting up their stand for market day.

Background
The *peninsulares* got their name because they came from the Iberian Peninsula, where Spain is located.

THINK THROUGH HISTORY
A. Recognizing Effects How might creole officers serving in colonial armies become a threat to Spanish rule?
A. Possible Answer Since they received training in war, creoles might use it against the Spanish in a revolution.

Creoles Spearhead Independence Even though they could not hold high public office, creoles were the least oppressed of those born in Latin America. They were also the best educated. In fact, many wealthy young creoles traveled to Europe for their education. In Europe, they read about and adopted Enlightenment ideas. When they returned to Latin America, they brought ideas of revolution with them.

The Divisions in Spanish Colonial Society in 1789

Mestizos (7.3%) 1,030,000
Mulattos (7.6%) 1,070,000
Africans (6.4%) 900,000
Peninsulares (0.1%) 15,000
EUROPEANS
Creoles (22.8%) 3,070,000
Indians (55.8%) 7,860,000

SKILLBUILDER:
Interpreting Charts

1. *Which two groups made up the vast majority of the population in Spanish America?*
2. *Looking at the chart, what was one possible reason that creoles felt resentful of the privileges of the peninsulares?*

Creoles not only held revolutionary ideas. They also felt that Spain had inflicted serious injustices on them. A creole aristocrat wrote this complaint to the king of Spain:

A VOICE FROM THE PAST
[T]he Viceroys here and their retainers . . . mock, humiliate and oppress us. . . . The more distinguished the unhappy Americans are, the more they suffer. . . . Their honor and reputations are attacked, insulting them by depriving them of any honorific office of consequence.

MARQUÉS DE SAN JORGE, quoted in *Americas: The Changing Face of Latin America and the Caribbean*

Spanish royal officials suppressed actions and ideas that might fuel creole discontent. For example, Colombian patriot Antonio Nariño published a translation of the French *Declaration of the Rights of Man*. He was quickly sentenced to exile in Africa.

Background
Of the 170 Spanish viceroys (colonial governors) between 1492 and 1810, 166 were *peninsulares;* only four were creoles.

TEACHING OPTIONS

CUSTOMIZING FOR SPECIAL NEEDS

Gifted and Talented Students
Toussaint L'Ouverture was an extraordinary historical figure and revolutionary leader. The grandson of an African king, born a slave in Saint Domingue, he was a complex and mysterious man. Ask students to read a biography of Toussaint and then write a brief report on him, focusing on his leadership of the revolution. As an alternative to a biography, you might have students read the Literature selection for this section from *All Souls' Rising* by Madison Smartt Bell, a novel about Toussaint L'Ouverture and the revolution in Haiti.

📖 **IN-DEPTH RESOURCES: UNIT 2**
Literature: from *All Souls' Rising*, p. 67

MULTIPLE LEARNING STYLES

Logical-Mathematical Learners To help students visualize the social classes of colonial Latin America, ask them to complete a Venn diagram like the one to the right and then use the figures from the chart on this page to indicate on the diagram the percentage of population each group represents.

Native American 55.8
Mestizo 7.3
European/ 22.9 Creoles/Peninsulares
Mulatto 7.6
African 6.4

Events in Europe Trigger Latin American Revolutions Napoleon's conquest of Spain in 1808 finally triggered revolts in the Spanish colonies. After he had removed Spain's King Ferdinand VII, Napoleon made his brother Joseph king of Spain. Many creoles might have supported a Spanish king. However, they felt no loyalty to a king imposed by the French. Creoles argued that when the real king was removed, power shifted to the people.

In 1810, rebellion broke out in several parts of Latin America. In 1814, with the defeat of Napoleon, King Ferdinand VII returned to Spain. But the creoles had already begun their drive for independence. And they would continue until victory.

The *Libertadores* End Spanish Rule

The South American wars of independence produced two brilliant generals. Their leadership largely achieved victory for the rebels. One was **Simón Bolívar** (see·MAWN boh·LEE·vahr), a wealthy Venezuelan creole. Called *Libertador* (Liberator), Bolívar was at the same time romantic and practical, a writer and a fighter.

The other great liberator was **José de San Martín** (hoh·SAY day san mahr·TEEN). Unlike the dashing Bolívar, San Martín was a simple, modest man. But he too displayed great courage in battle. Though born in Argentina, he spent much of his youth in Spain as a career military officer. San Martín believed in strict military discipline. However, he also showed concern for the well-being of his troops.

Bolívar's Route to Victory Simón Bolívar's native Venezuela declared its independence from Spain in 1811. But the struggle for independence had only begun. Bolívar's volunteer army of revolutionaries suffered numerous defeats. Twice he had to go into exile. A turning point came in August 1819. Bolívar led over 2,000 soldiers on a daring march through the Andes into what is now Colombia. (See the 1830 map on page 608.) Coming from this direction, Bolívar took the Spanish army in Bogotá completely by surprise. There he won a decisive victory.

By 1821, Bolívar had won Venezuela's independence. He then marched south into Ecuador. In Ecuador, Bolívar would finally meet with José de San Martín. Together they would decide the future of the Latin American revolutionary movement.

San Martín Triumphs and Withdraws San Martín's Argentina had declared its independence in 1816. However, Spanish forces in nearby Chile and Peru still posed a threat. In 1817, San Martín led his army on a grueling march across the Andes to Chile. He was joined there by forces led by Bernardo O'Higgins, son of a former viceroy of Peru. With O'Higgins's help, San Martín finally freed Chile.

Next, in 1821 San Martín took his army north by sea to Lima, Peru. His plan was to drive out the remaining Spanish forces there. However, he needed a much larger force to accomplish this. This was the problem that faced both San Martín and Bolívar as they met at Guayaquil, Ecuador, in 1822.

No one knows how the two men reached an agreement. But San Martín left his army for Bolívar to command. Soon after, San Martín sailed for Europe. He died, almost forgotten, on French soil in 1850.

With unified revolutionary forces, Bolívar's army went on to defeat the Spanish at the Battle of Ayacucho (Peru) on December 9, 1824. In this last major battle of the war for independence, the Spanish colonies in Latin America won their freedom.

Educated in Spain from the age of six, José de San Martín returned to Latin America as a man in his early 30s. Fighting for 10 years, he became the liberator of Argentina, Chile, and Peru.

Nationalist Revolutions Sweep the West **225**

Bolívar was an inspiration to later revolutionaries throughout Latin America. For example, he inspired the Cubans who rose up against Spain in their struggle for independence in 1895, as well as a later revolution in Cuba led by Fidel Castro. Even rebellions as recent as the 20th century were, in part, inspired by the example of Simón Bolívar. Often these revolutions were influenced by a variety of sources, including Marxist doctrine as well as Bolívar's example.

Viewing the Video

Show *Struggling Toward Democracy: Revolutions in Latin America and South Africa* to examine how oppressed peoples in different times and places have fought for self-rule.

- The first segment of the video investigates the South American independence movement championed by "the Liberator," Simón Bolívar.
- The second segment chronicles a more recent struggle for equality: South Africa's anti-apartheid movement, led by Nelson Mandela.

Using the Teacher's Resource Book as a guide, discuss the meaning of the word "democracy"; compare the revolutions described in the video with recent struggles for democracy; and enrich the lesson with primary-source and visual-literacy activities included in the resource book.

 PATTERNS OF INTERACTION
Struggling Toward Democracy: Revolutions in Latin America and South Africa
Videocassette: Tape 3

Ideas and Revolution

Revolutions are as much a matter of ideas as they are of weapons. And Simón Bolívar, the hero of Latin American independence, was both a thinker and a fighter. Through his education, readings, travels, and friendships, Bolívar was able to combine Enlightenment political ideas, ideas from Greece and Rome, and his own original thinking. The result was a system of democratic ideas that would help spark revolutions throughout Latin America.

Enlightenment Ideas to Latin America: 1789–1810

Bolívar's 1807 return from Europe by way of the United States allowed him to study the American system of Government.

In 1810, Bolívar went to London to seek support for the revolution in Latin America. At the same time, he studied British institutions of government.

By 1800, the writings of Enlightenment authors were widely read throughout the Spanish American colonies.

"I will not rest until I have broken the chains that bind us to the will of Spain."
Bolívar, after watching the crowning of Napoleon

Besides being a military leader, Bolívar was also a superb speaker and statesman. He is shown here presenting his plans for a new government.

After winning independence in 1819, Simón Bolívar organized the Republic of Venezuela and wrote the Constitution of Bolivia. Like many successful revolutionaries, Simón Bolívar became disillusioned with Latin America's chaos after independence. Before his death in 1830, he commented bitterly: "Those who worked for South American independence have plowed the sea."

Bolívar admired Napoleon. But later, he was disappointed by Napoleon's betrayal of democracy.

Patterns of Interaction

The Latin American independence movement is just one example of how the Enlightenment spread democratic ideals throughout the world. In countries facing oppressive conditions, a leader frequently emerges to establish a popular government. Even today, as can be seen in South Africa, democratic ideals inspire people to struggle for political independence and to overthrow oppressive governments.

 VIDEO *Struggling Toward Democracy: Revolutions in Latin America and South Africa*

Connect *to* History

Making Inferences How is Enlightenment thought reflected in Bolívar's ideas on Latin American independence and government?
SEE SKILLBUILDER HANDBOOK, PAGE 663

Connect *to* Today

Comparing What recent events in today's world could be compared to Simón Bolívar's movement for Latin American independence?

226 Chapter 8

Connect *to* History

Making Inferences
Possible Answer: The thinkers of the Enlightenment undermined the institutions of monarchy and a titled aristocracy by advocating ideals of equality, democracy, and individual rights. Bolívar, as the heir of these thinkers, translated their ideas into practice by fighting for political independence and democracy in Latin America.

Connect *to* Today

Comparing
Possible Answer: Some students might mention the independence achieved by the former republics of the Soviet Union when it dissolved in 1991, as well as the autonomy gained by former Soviet satellites in Eastern Europe. Other students might cite groups around the world, such as the Basques in Spain, that are fighting for greater autonomy.

Mexico Ends Spanish Rule

In most Latin American countries, creoles led the revolutionary movements. In Mexico, ethnic and racial groups mixed more freely. There Indians and mestizos played the leading role.

A Cry for Freedom In 1810, Padre **Miguel Hidalgo** (mee·GEHL ee·THAHL·goh), a priest in the small village of Dolores, took the first step toward independence. Hidalgo was a poor but well-educated man. He firmly believed in Enlightenment ideals. On September 16, 1810, he rang the bells of his village church. When the peasants gathered in the church, he issued a call for rebellion against the Spanish. Today, that call is known as the *grito de Dolores* (the cry of Dolores).

The very next day, Hidalgo's Indian and mestizo followers began a march toward Mexico City. This unruly army soon numbered 60,000 men. The Spanish army and creoles were alarmed by this uprising of the lower classes. In reaction, they joined forces against Hidalgo's army. Hidalgo was defeated in 1811. The rebels then rallied around another strong leader, Padre **José María Morelos** (moh·RAY·lohs). Morelos led the revolution for four years. However, in 1815, he was defeated by a creole officer, Agustín de Iturbide (ah·goos·TEEN day ee·toor·BEE·day).

Mexico's Independence Events in Mexico took yet another turn in 1820 when a revolution in Spain put a liberal group in power there. Mexico's creoles feared the loss of their privileges. So they united in support of Mexico's independence from Spain. Ironically, Agustín de Iturbide—the man who had defeated Padre Morelos—made peace with the last rebel leader. He proclaimed independence in 1821.

Before the Mexican revolution, Central America had been governed from Mexico. In 1821, several Central American states declared their independence from Spain and thus from Mexico as well. Iturbide, however, refused to recognize those declarations.

Iturbide (who had declared himself emperor) was finally overthrown in 1823. Central America then pulled together. The region declared its absolute independence from Mexico. It took the name the United Provinces of Central America.

Brazil's Royal Liberator

With no violent upheavals or bloody atrocities, Brazil's quest for independence was unique in this period of Latin American history. In fact, a member of the Portuguese royal family actually played a key role in freeing Brazil from Portugal.

The Portuguese Royal Family in Brazil In 1807, Napoleon's armies swarmed across the Pyrenees mountains to invade both Spain and Portugal. Napoleon's aim was to close the ports of these countries to British shipping. As French troops approached Lisbon, the Portuguese capital, Prince John (later King John VI) and the royal family boarded ships to escape capture. They also took their court and royal treasury with them. The royal family then sailed to Portugal's largest colony, Brazil. For 14 years, Brazil was the center of the Portuguese empire. During that time, Brazilians had developed a sense of their own uniqueness. Many of them could not imagine their country becoming a colony again. However, after Napoleon's defeat in 1815, the Portuguese government wanted exactly that.

By 1822, creoles demanded Brazil's independence from Portugal. Eight thousand Brazilians signed a petition asking Dom Pedro, King John's son, to rule. He agreed.

HISTORY MAKERS

Padre José Morelos
1765–1815

Born into poverty, José Morelos did not begin to study for the priesthood until he was 25. In his parish work, he mainly served poor Indians and mestizos. In 1811, he joined Father Hidalgo, along with his parishioners. After Hidalgo's death, the skillful Morelos took command of the peasant army.

By 1813, his army controlled all of southern Mexico except for the largest cities. Morelos then called a Mexican congress to set up a democratic government. The supporters of Spain, however, finally caught up with the congress. As the rebels fled, Morelos stayed behind to fight. The Spanish finally captured and shot Morelos in 1815. Napoleon knew of this priest-revolutionary and said: "Give me three generals like him and I can conquer the world."

Nationalist Revolutions Sweep the West **227**

Latin America, 1800
Latin America, 1830
Interpreting the Maps Point out to students that the best way to understand the differences between the two maps is to look at the different elements contained in each map key.

Extension Activity Have students compare the map of 1830 with the map in their Atlas on page 640 in order to see what countries have remained the same and what political boundaries and names have changed since 1830.

SKILLBUILDER Answers
1. Spain and Portugal
2. Mexico, United Provinces of Central America, Gran Colombia, Bolivia, Peru, Chile, Paraguay, Uruguay, United Provinces of La Plata

---

OBJECTIVE **6** **INSTRUCT**

Independence Brings Disunity

Key Idea
• Destruction caused by the wars for independence leaves Latin America poor and disunited.

ASSESS & RETEACH

Section 1 Assessment
Have students work in pairs to answer the questions.

Section Quiz

FORMAL ASSESSMENT
Section Quiz, p. 101

Reteaching Activity
CLASS TIME: 10 MINUTES

Use the Guided Reading worksheet for Section 1 to review the main ideas of the section.

IN-DEPTH RESOURCES: UNIT 2
Guided Reading, p. 56

CLOSE ACTIVITY

CLASS TIME: 15 MINUTES

Creating a Time Line
On the board, draw a time line with a beginning date of 1791 and an ending date of 1841. Ask the class to add important dates from this section.

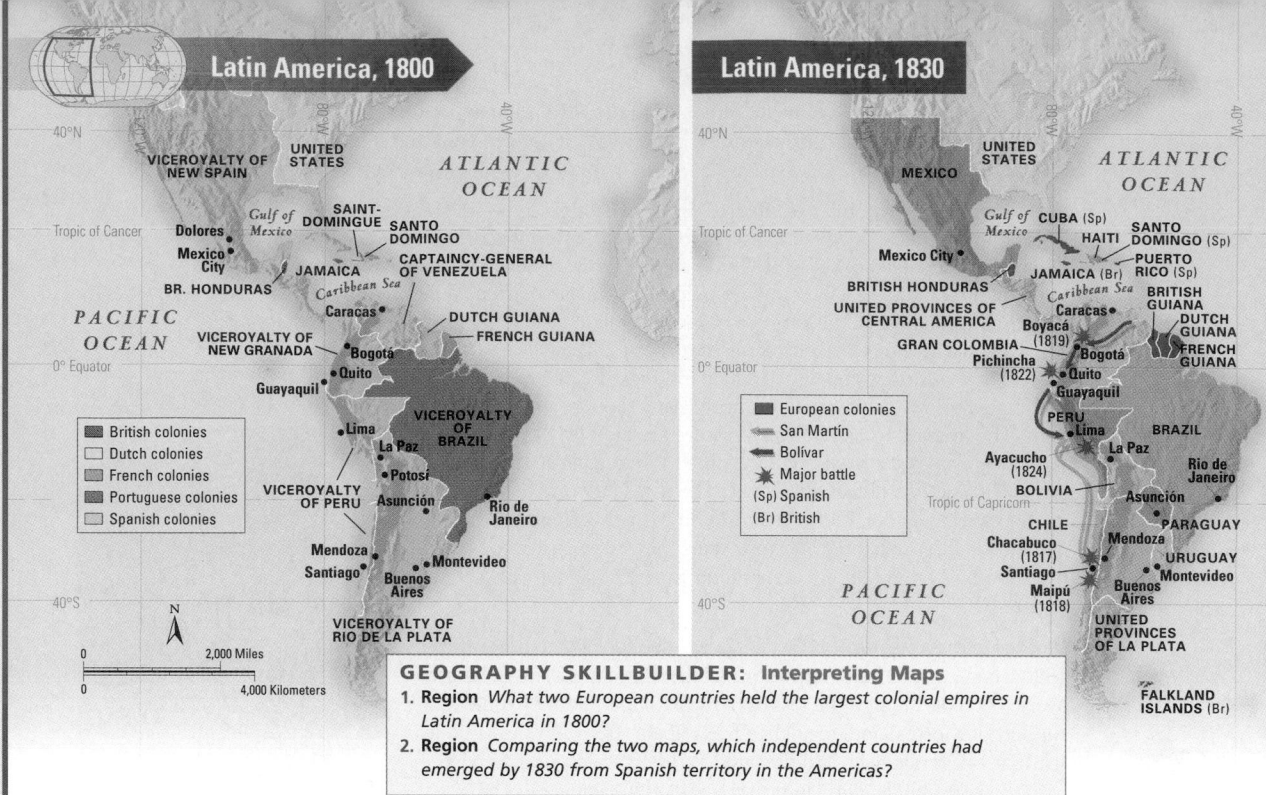

Latin America, 1800

Latin America, 1830

British colonies
Dutch colonies
French colonies
Portuguese colonies
Spanish colonies

European colonies
San Martín
Bolívar
Major battle
(Sp) Spanish
(Br) British

GEOGRAPHY SKILLBUILDER: Interpreting Maps
1. **Region** What two European countries held the largest colonial empires in Latin America in 1800?
2. **Region** Comparing the two maps, which independent countries had emerged by 1830 from Spanish territory in the Americas?

On September 7, 1822, he officially declared Brazil's independence. Brazil had won its independence through a bloodless revolution.

Independence Brings Disunity

Throughout Latin America, independence actually brought an increase in poverty. The wars had disrupted trade and devastated cities and countryside. After all the destruction, the dream of a united Latin America quickly fell apart. In South America, Bolívar's united Gran Colombia divided into Colombia, Ecuador, and Venezuela in early 1830. And by 1841, the United Provinces of Central America had split into the republics of El Salvador, Nicaragua, Costa Rica, Guatemala, and Honduras.

Meanwhile, the ideas of the French Revolution and the aftermath of the Napoleonic Wars were causing upheaval in Europe, as you will learn in Section 2.

Section 1 Assessment

1. TERMS & NAMES

Identify
• *peninsulares*
• creoles
• mulattos
• Simón Bolívar
• José de San Martín
• Miguel Hidalgo
• José Morelos

2. TAKING NOTES

Using a chart like the one below, compare independence movements in Latin America.

Where?	Who rebelled?	Why?	What happened?
Haiti			
Spanish South America			
Mexico			
Brazil			

3. FORMING AND SUPPORTING OPINIONS

Think about the background of many creole revolutionaries. What do you think might have been their tendencies as government leaders: toward democracy or authoritarianism? Explain your answer.

THINK ABOUT
• their education
• their professions
• their economic interests

4. ANALYZING THEMES

Power and Authority
Consider the following statement: "Through its policies, Spain gave up its right to rule in South America." Do you agree or disagree? Explain. Did Spain ever have the right to rule?

THINK ABOUT
• Spanish colonial society
• why independence movements arose
• who gained the power that Spain lost

ANSWERS

1. TERMS & NAMES
peninsulares, p. 224
creoles, p. 224
mulattos, p. 224
Simón Bolívar, p. 225
José de San Martín, p. 225
Miguel Hidalgo, p. 227
José Morelos, p. 227

2. TAKING NOTES
Possible Responses: Haiti—slaves; freedom; independence. Spanish South America—creoles; freedom; independence. Mexico—Native Americans and mestizos/creoles; slavery; independence. Brazil—creoles and royal family; end colonial rule; independence.

3. FORMING AND SUPPORTING OPINIONS
Possible Responses:
Democracy—With their education, skills, and economic interests, creoles might become democratic leaders.

Authoritarianism—As military officers, creoles might use

weapons instead of elections to resolve political disputes.

4. ANALYZING THEMES
Possible Responses: Agree—Spain oppressed people in Latin America, so Spain deserved to lose its colonies. Disagree—Spain ruled its colonies by accepted European standards.

2 Revolutions Disrupt Europe

TERMS & NAMES
- conservatives
- liberals
- radicals
- nationalism
- nation-state
- the Balkans
- Louis-Napoleon
- Alexander II

MAIN IDEA

Liberal and nationalist uprisings challenged the old conservative order of Europe.

WHY IT MATTERS NOW

The system of nation-states established in Europe during this period continues today.

SETTING THE STAGE As revolutions shook the colonies in Latin America, Europe was also undergoing dramatic changes. Under the leadership of Austrian Prince Metternich, the Congress of Vienna tried to restore the old monarchies and territorial divisions that had existed before the French Revolution. On an international level, this attempt to turn back history succeeded. For the next century, Europeans seldom turned to war to solve their differences. Within these countries, however, the effort failed. Revolutions erupted across Europe between 1815 and 1848.

Nationalism Changes Europe

In the first half of the 1800s, three forces struggled for supremacy in European societies. **Conservatives**—usually wealthy property owners and nobility—argued for protecting the traditional monarchies of Europe. In certain cases, as in France, conservatives approved of constitutional monarchies. **Liberals**—mostly middle-class business leaders and merchants—wanted to give more power to elected parliaments, but only to parliaments in which the educated and the landowners could vote. **Radicals** favored drastic change to extend democracy to the people as a whole. They believed that governments should practice the ideals of the French Revolution. This was still a radical idea, even 30 years after the Revolution.

The Idea of the Nation-State As conservatives, liberals, and radicals debated issues of government, a new movement called nationalism was emerging. This movement would blur the lines that separated these political theories. **Nationalism** is the belief that one's greatest loyalty should not be to a king or an empire but to a nation of people who share a common culture and history. When the nation also had its own independent government, it became a **nation-state.**

Modern nationalism and the nation-state grew out of the French Revolution. Revolutionary leaders stressed the equality of all French people. The idea of equality fostered a sense of national pride in the French. That pride, in turn, helped French citizens' armies win stunning victories for the Revolution.

Nationalism Sparks Revolts in the Balkans The first people to win self-rule during this period were the Greeks. For centuries, Greece had been part of the Ottoman Empire. The Ottomans controlled most of **the Balkans.** That region includes all or part of present-day Greece, Albania, Bulgaria, Romania, and Turkey, and the former Yugoslavia. Greeks, however, had kept alive the memory of their ancient history and culture. Spurred on by the nationalist spirit, Greeks demanded that their

Carved on Napoleon's Arc de Triomphe, a fierce goddess of war leads French revolutionary volunteers into battle.

Background
In 1815, only France, England, and Spain could be called nation-states. Ethnic unrest would soon change that.

Background
Serbs revolted against the Ottomans in 1804 and 1815, winning self-rule within the Ottoman Empire in 1829. Full independence for Serbia came in 1878.

Section 2 Overview

OBJECTIVES

1. To define nationalism and describe how the nationalist spirit affected the Balkans.

2. To describe how revolutions and reforms affected Europe, especially France and Russia.

CRITICAL THINKING
- Summarizing, p. 231
- Analyzing issues, p. 232
- Drawing conclusions, p. 232

FOCUS
5-Minute Warm-Up

Clarifying
To help students better understand the impact of emancipation, have them answer these questions.

1. Look at the Spotlight on Emancipation on p. 232. Who is pictured in the photograph accompanying the feature?

2. Did emancipation free the serfs from working the land?

WARM-UP TRANSPARENCY 8

OBJECTIVE 1 INSTRUCT

Nationalism Changes Europe

Key Ideas
- Conservatives, liberals, and radicals struggle for power in European nations.
- Nationalism and the idea of a nation-state begin to emerge.
- In the Balkans, the spirit of nationalism sparks a revolt against the Ottoman Empire, which results in full independence for Greece.

IN-DEPTH RESOURCES: UNIT 2
Guided Reading, p. 57
Primary Source: Letter to Thomas Moore, p. 64

ACCESS FOR STUDENTS ACQUIRING ENGLISH
Guided Reading (Spanish), p. 93

SECTION 2 RESOURCES

PRINT RESOURCES

IN-DEPTH RESOURCES: UNIT 2
Guided Reading, p. 57
Primary Source: Letter to Thomas Moore, p. 64

ACCESS FOR STUDENTS ACQUIRING ENGLISH
Guided Reading (Spanish), p. 93

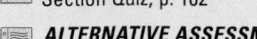
FORMAL ASSESSMENT
Section Quiz, p. 102

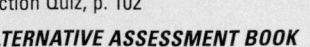
ALTERNATIVE ASSESSMENT BOOK

TECHNOLOGY RESOURCES

INTERNET www.mlworldhistory.com

CONNECT *to* TODAY
Greeks and Turks on Cyprus

Ask students to consult either the *Reader's Guide to Periodical Literature* or the Internet to find recent information about the political situation on Cyprus.

The Tide of Reform in Western Europe

▶ Key Ideas

- In the 1830s and again in 1848, revolutions sweep Europe.
- In 1848 France establishes a republic, but within four years Louis-Napoleon becomes emperor.
- The weakness of Russia's industrial system is exposed by its defeat in the Crimean War.
- In 1861, the liberal Czar Alexander II frees the serfs, but his successor tightens czarist control.

CRITICAL THINKING ACTIVITY
CLASS TIME: 15 MINUTES

Summarizing
To help students understand the reforms and revolutions that occurred during the first half of the 1800s, have them complete a chart like the one below.

Revolutions/Reforms		
Nation	**Date**	**Outcome**
Belgium	1830	Independence from Dutch control
Italy		
Poland		

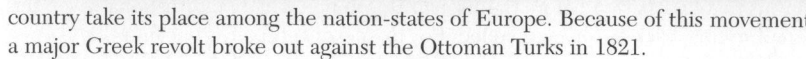

This 1839 lithograph shows Greeks in blue coats battling Ottoman Turks during the war for Greek independence.

country take its place among the nation-states of Europe. Because of this movement, a major Greek revolt broke out against the Ottoman Turks in 1821.

The most powerful governments opposed revolution in all its forms. However, the cause of Greek independence was popular with people around the world. Russians, for example, felt a connection to Greek Orthodox Christians, who were ruled by the Muslim Ottomans. Educated Europeans and Americans loved and respected ancient Greek culture, which they spent years studying in school. In his poetry, British romantic poet Lord Byron compared modern Greek nationalists to the ancient Spartans:

> **A VOICE FROM THE PAST**
> The sword, the banner, and the field,
> Glory and Greece, around us see!
> The Spartan, borne upon his shield,
> Was not more free.
>
> **LORD BYRON,** from the poem "On this day I complete my thirty-sixth year"

Lord Byron wears the uniform of a Greek freedom fighter.

In 1823, Byron made a large personal gift of £4,000 to the Greek fleet. After that, he went to Greece. There, he volunteered as a soldier for the Greek cause. He soon commanded a group of Greek soldiers. Unfortunately, he would not live to see the victory of the cause he fought for. In February of 1824, a cold Greek rain drenched the poet. Soon afterward, he caught a fever. He died from his illness in April.

Eventually, with growing popular sympathy for Greece, the powerful nations of Europe took the side of the Greeks. In 1827, a combined British, French, and Russian fleet destroyed the Ottoman fleet at the Battle of Navarino. By 1830, Britain, France, and Russia signed a treaty recognizing the full independence of Greece.

CONNECT *to* TODAY

Greeks and Turks on Cyprus
The hostility between Greeks and Turks continues to this day—with the island nation of Cyprus as its focal point. In 1974, Turkish troops invaded this island off the coast of Turkey with its majority Greek population. The Turks justified their invasion by saying that they were defending the rights of the minority of Turkish Cypriots. They captured the northern third of the island and declared the region an independent state.

The United Nations later established a "green line" on Cyprus—separating the Turkish north and the Greek south. However, the arrangement satisfies no one today. The Greek Cypriot government accuses the Turks of illegally seizing its territory. The Turks, in turn, maintain that they have the right to defend Turkish Cypriots from harm. The situation currently remains deadlocked.

The Tide of Reform in Western Europe

By the 1830s, the return to the old order—carefully arranged at the Congress of Vienna—was breaking down. Liberals and nationalists throughout Europe were openly revolting against conservative governments. In most cases, the liberal middle class—teachers, lawyers, and businesspeople—led the struggle for constitutional government and the formation of nation-states.

Waves of Failed Revolutions Revolutionary zeal swept across Europe. Nationalist riots broke out against Dutch rule in the Belgian city of Brussels. In November 1830, Belgians finally declared their independence from Dutch control. In Italy, nationalists

---

EXPLORING PRIMARY SOURCES

A Voice From the Past: Byron's career was a strange mixture of idealism and cynicism. Some of his poems portray a type of character who came to be known as the Byronic hero—idealistic, moody, proud, and defiant. Other poems by Byron are wonderfully funny and satirical. His letters show the same mix of idealism and satirical humor. You might read to students the primary source for this section, Byron's Letter to Thomas Moore, which he addressed to his friend from Greece. Ask students to write a sentence or two in which they describe Byron's mood in his letter as he faces military life.

 IN-DEPTH RESOURCES: UNIT 2
Primary Source: Byron's Letter to Thomas Moore, p. 64

CUSTOMIZING FOR SPECIAL NEEDS

Less Proficient Readers: Analyzing Poetry Help students understand the passage from the poem by Lord Byron by explaining that the first line refers to a field of battle, with soldiers wielding their swords and carrying their banners, just as the ancient Greek warriors did. You may direct them to the painting shown on this page depicting a battle between Greeks and Turks. Explain that in ancient Sparta, a warrior who had fallen in battle was carried home on his shield. Then pair up a less proficient reader with a more proficient reader and have them address any other obstacles that the poem might present to comprehension.

worked to unite the many separate states on the Italian peninsula. Some were independent. Others were ruled by Austria, others by the pope. Eventually, Prime Minister Metternich sent Austrian troops to restore order in Italy. The Poles living under the rule of Russia staged a revolt in Warsaw late in 1830. Russian armies took an entire year to crush the Polish uprising. By the mid-1830s, it seemed as if the old order had reestablished itself. But with the political instability of the period, that impression did not last long.

In 1848, ethnic uprisings erupted throughout Europe. In Budapest, nationalist leader Louis Kossuth called for a parliament and self-government for Hungary. In Prague, Czech liberals demanded Bohemian independence. An unruly mob in Vienna itself clashed with police. That forced Metternich to resign and set off liberal uprisings throughout the German states.

But European politics continued to seesaw. Many of these liberal gains were lost to conservatives within a year. In one country after another, the revolutionaries failed to unite themselves or their nation. And conservatives regained their nerve and their power. By 1849, Europe had practically returned to the conservatism that had controlled governments before 1848.

Reform and Revolution in France Radicals participated in many of the 1848 revolts. Only in France, however, was the radical demand for democratic government the main goal of revolution. In 1830, France's King Charles X tried to stage a return to absolute monarchy. The attempt sparked riots that forced Charles to flee to Great Britain. He was replaced by Louis-Philippe, who had long supported liberal reforms in France. One French noble looked down on Louis. The aristocrat thought the king had "the manners of a citizen and the plainness of dress and demeanor very suitable to an American president, but unbecoming a descendant of Louis XIV [the Sun King]."

However, in 1848, after a lengthy reign of almost 18 years, Louis-Philippe fell from popular favor. Once again, a Paris mob overturned a monarchy and established a republic. Alphonse de Lamartine (lah·mahr·TEEN), one of France's leading poets, led the temporary government. After the victory of the Revolution of 1848, Lamartine proclaimed: "We are making together the most sublime of poems."

Far from being inspiring, the new republican government began to fall apart almost immediately. The radicals soon split into factions. One side, led by Lamartine, wanted only political reform. The other, led by Louis Blanc, also wanted social and economic reform. The differences set off bloody battles in Parisian streets. The violence turned French citizens away from the radicals. As a result, a moderate constitution was drawn up later in 1848. It called for a parliament and a strong president to be elected by the people.

France Accepts a Strong Ruler In December 1848, Louis-Napoleon Bonaparte, the nephew of Napoleon Bonaparte, won the presidential election. Four years later, **Louis-Napoleon** took the title of Emperor Napoleon III, which a large majority of French voters surprisingly accepted. The French were weary of instability and welcomed a strong ruler who would bring peace to France.

As France's emperor, Louis-Napoleon built railroads, encouraged industrialization, and promoted an ambitious program of public works. Gradually, because of Louis-Napoleon's policies, unemployment decreased in France, and the country experienced real prosperity.

This color engraving of the time shows Parisian revolutionaries fighting and dying behind the barricades in the Revolution of 1848.

A. Possible Answer
Absolute monarchy (Charles X) to liberal monarchy (Louis-Philippe) to radical republic (1848 revolution) to constitutional government (Louis-Napoleon Bonaparte) to monarchy (Emperor Napoleon III).

THINK THROUGH HISTORY
A. Summarizing
How would you outline the political swings occurring in France between 1830 and 1852?

SPOTLIGHT ON
Emancipation

Ask students to read about Alexander's and Lincoln's motives for their proclamations of emancipation. What did each hope to achieve by emancipation?

MORE ABOUT . . .
The Crimean War

It was during the Crimean War that Florence Nightingale first gained fame and the Red Cross gained prominence. The war also inspired the British poet Alfred Lord Tennyson to write the poem "The Charge of the Light Brigade," romanticizing British bravery during a battle of that war.

ASSESS & RETEACH

Section 2 Assessment
Have students work individually to answer the questions. Then have them check their answers with a partner.

Section Quiz
 FORMAL ASSESSMENT
Section Quiz, p. 102

Reteaching Activity
CLASS TIME: 10 MINUTES

To help students remember the major uprisings in Europe in the first half of the 1800s, review the charts they have made for item 2 in the section assessment.

CLOSE ACTIVITY

CLASS TIME: 15 MINUTES

Comparing
Most of the revolutions that swept Europe during the first part of the century were led by the liberal middle class. Only in France were the revolutions led by radicals. Ask pairs of students to write a paragraph comparing the goals of the revolutions of 1830 and 1848 in France with the goals of revolutions elsewhere in Europe.

232 Chapter 8

SPOTLIGHT ON

Emancipation

On March 3, 1861, Czar Alexander II issued the Edict of Emancipation, freeing 20 million serfs with the stroke of a pen. Alexander, in fact, signed his edict one day before Abraham Lincoln became president of the United States. Less than two years later, President Lincoln issued the Emancipation Proclamation, freeing slaves in the United States. Lincoln's proclamation, like Alexander's edict, was issued on his authority alone.

Nonetheless, emancipation did not entirely fulfill the hopes of Russian serfs or former slaves in the United States. The peasant communities, like the one pictured above, still bound many Russian serfs to the land, while others earned poor livings as laborers in the cities. And Lincoln did not free all slaves—only those living under the Confederacy.

Reform in Russia Unlike France, Russia in the 1800s had yet to make its leap into the modern industrialized world. Under Russia's feudal system, serfs were bound to the nobles whose land they worked. And nobles enjoyed almost unlimited power over them. By the 1820s, many Russians believed that serfdom must end. In their eyes, the system was morally wrong. It also prevented the empire from advancing economically. The czars, however, were reluctant to free the serfs. Freeing them would anger the landowners, whose support the czars needed.

Defeat Brings Change Eventually, Russia's lack of development became obvious to Russians and to the whole world. In 1853, Czar Nicholas I threatened to take over part of the Ottoman Empire in the Crimean War. However, Russia's industries and transportation system failed to provide adequate supplies for the country's troops. As a result, in 1856, Russia lost the war against the combined forces of France, Great Britain, Sardinia, and the Ottoman Empire. This was a humiliating defeat for the czar.

After the war, Nicholas's son, **Alexander II**, decided to move Russia toward modernization and social change. Through his reforms, Alexander and his advisers believed that Russia would compete with western Europe for world power.

Reform and Reaction The first and boldest of Alexander's reforms was a decree freeing the serfs in 1861. The abolition of serfdom, however, went only halfway. Peasant communities—rather than individual peasants—received about half the farmland in the country. Nobles kept the other half. The government paid the nobles for their land. Each peasant community, on the other hand, had 49 years to pay the government for the land it had received. So, while the serfs were legally free, the debt still tied them to the land.

Political and social reforms ground to a halt when terrorists assassinated Alexander II in 1881. His successor, Alexander III, tightened czarist control on the country. Alexander III and his ministers, however, encouraged industrial development to expand Russia's power. A major force behind Russia's drive toward industrial expansion was nationalism. Nationalism also stirred other ethnic groups. During the 1800s, such groups were uniting into nations and building industries to survive among other nation-states.

Background
In December 1825, when Nicholas became czar, a group of army officers (the "Decembrists") demanded liberal reforms. Nicholas crushed the Decembrists and then ruled with an iron fist.

B. Possible Answer
The czars needed to reform Russia to bring its power up to the level of Western European powers. Nonetheless, czarist power rested on authoritarianism, as well as on the support of landowners who wanted to keep the feudal system.

THINK THROUGH HISTORY
B. Analyzing Issues
Why were czars torn between social and economic reforms in their country?

Section 2 Assessment

1. TERMS & NAMES
Identify
• conservatives
• liberals
• radicals
• nationalism
• nation-state
• the Balkans
• Louis-Napoleon
• Alexander II

2. TAKING NOTES
Using a chart like the one below, list the major uprisings that challenged the old order of Europe in the first half of the 1800s. Group them under the year they occurred.

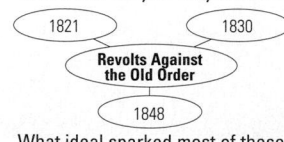

What ideal sparked most of these revolts? Explain.

3. DRAWING CONCLUSIONS
Why do you think some liberals might disapprove of the way Louis-Napoleon ruled France after the uprisings of 1848?

THINK ABOUT
• who the liberals were and what they believed in
• conditions in France in 1848
• Louis-Napoleon's actions and policies

4. THEME ACTIVITY
Cultural Interaction Imagine that you are a conservative, liberal, or radical in 1848. You have just heard that revolts have broken out in Europe. Write a letter to a friend, stating your political position and expressing your feelings about the uprisings. Then, express your thoughts about the future of Europe.

232 Chapter 8

ANSWERS

1. TERMS & NAMES
conservatives, p. 229
liberals, p. 229
radicals, p. 229
nationalism, p. 229
nation-state, p. 229
the Balkans, p. 229
Louis-Napoleon, p. 231
Alexander II, p. 232

2. TAKING NOTES
Possible Responses: 1821—Greece rebels against Ottoman Turks. 1830—Belgians declare independence from the Dutch; Italians try to unite; Poles rebel against Russia; French throw out Charles X. 1848—Hungarians call for self-government; Czechs demand independence for Bohemia; liberals revolt in the German states; French demand democratic government.
Nationalism—People wanted to establish their own nation-states.

3. DRAWING CONCLUSIONS
Possible Responses: Liberals wanted to give power to parliaments, but Louis-Napoleon declared himself sole ruler.

4. THEME ACTIVITY
Writers may express enthusiasm, caution, disgust, or other emotion, depending on their political position. They should also make predictions about Europe's future.

③ Nationalism

PATTERNS OF CHANGE

CASE STUDIES: Italy and Germany

TERMS & NAMES
- Camillo di Cavour
- Giuseppe Garibaldi
- Red Shirts
- Otto von Bismarck
- realpolitik
- kaiser

MAIN IDEA	WHY IT MATTERS NOW
The force of nationalism contributed to the formation of two new nations and a new political order in Europe.	Nationalism is the basis of world politics today and has often caused conflicts and wars.

SETTING THE STAGE Nationalism was the most powerful ideal of the 1800s. Its influence stretched throughout Europe. Nationalism shaped countries. It also upset the balance of power set up at the Congress of Vienna in 1815, and affected the lives of millions.

The Ideal of Nationalism

Nationalism during the 1800s fueled efforts to build nation-states. Nationalists were not loyal to kings, but to their *people*—to those who shared common bonds. These bonds might include a common history, culture, world-view, or language. Nationalists believed that people of a single "nationality," or ancestry, should unite under a single government. People would then identify with their government to create a united nation-state.

Romantic nationalists preached that a nation, like a person, has the right to independence. Independence would allow a nation's identity to develop.

As nationalists saw it, a number of links bound a people together as a nation. Some—though not all—had to exist before a nation-state would evolve and survive. The chart below summarizes those nationalist links.

Background
Nationalists often spoke of a "national character." Thus, they saw the French as "civilized"; the Germans as "scientific"; the English as "practical."

PATTERNS OF CHANGE: Nationalism

Bonds That Create a Nation-State

Nationality	• A belief in a common ethnic ancestry—a belief that may or may not be true
Language	• Different dialects (forms) of one language; one dialect chosen as the "national language"
Culture	• A shared way of life (food, dress, behavior, ideals)
History	• A common past; common experiences
Religion	• A religion shared by all or most of the people
Territory	• A certain territory that belongs to the ethnic group; its "land"
Nation-State	• Defends the nation's territory and its way of life • Represents the nation to the rest of the world • Embodies the people and its ideals

SKILLBUILDER: Interpreting Charts
1. *Besides food, dress, behavior, and ideals, what are two other elements that could fall under the category of "culture"?*
2. *Which factors listed in the upper part of the chart are absolutely necessary to form a nation-state?*

SECTION 3 RESOURCES

PRINT RESOURCES

IN-DEPTH RESOURCES: UNIT 2
Guided Reading, p. 58
Geography Application: Languages Fuel Nationalism, p. 61
Primary Sources: Proclamation of 1860, p. 65; Nationalist speech by Otto von Bismarck, p. 66
Connections Across Time and Cultures, p. 72

ACCESS FOR STUDENTS ACQUIRING ENGLISH
Guided Reading (Spanish), p. 94
Geography Application (Spanish), p. 97

FORMAL ASSESSMENT
Section Quiz, p. 103

TECHNOLOGY RESOURCES
GEOGRAPHY TRANSPARENCIES
GT24 Ethnic Groups of Austria-Hungary, 1867
CRITICAL THINKING TRANSPARENCIES
CT24 The Unification of Germany and Italy
CD-ROM
Electronic Library of Primary Sources
INTERNET www.mlworldhistory.com

Section 3 Overview

OBJECTIVES

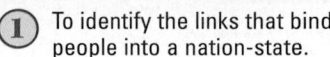
① To identify the links that bind people into a nation-state.

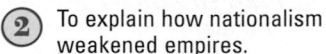
② To explain how nationalism weakened empires.

③ To summarize how Cavour unified Italy.

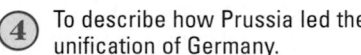
④ To describe how Prussia led the unification of Germany.

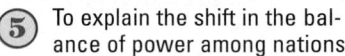
⑤ To explain the shift in the balance of power among nations.

SKILLBUILDER
- Interpreting charts, p. 233
- Interpreting maps: region, p. 235
- Interpreting maps: location, region, p. 237

CRITICAL THINKING
- Making inferences, p. 234
- Analyzing causes, p. 236
- Drawing conclusions, p. 237
- Analyzing issues, p. 238
- Analyzing themes, p. 238

FOCUS
5-Minute Warm-Up

Summarizing
Have students answer the following questions to understand the concept of nationalism.

1. Read the first paragraph under "The Ideal of Nationalism" on p. 233. What are some of the common bonds that unite people into a nation?

2. How did nationalists believe that people who share a common bond should be united?

 WARM-UP TRANSPARENCY 8

OBJECTIVE ① INSTRUCT

The Ideal of Nationalism

Key Idea
- Nationalists believe in uniting people who share a common history and culture.

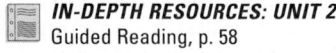
IN-DEPTH RESOURCES: UNIT 2
Guided Reading, p. 58

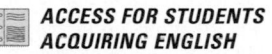
ACCESS FOR STUDENTS ACQUIRING ENGLISH
Guided Reading (Spanish), p. 94

Teacher's Edition 233

Interpreting the Chart Point out that two elements are represented in the chart: bonds that create a nation-state and the functions of a nation-state.

Extension Activity Ask students to explain how each of these bonds is represented in the United States.

SKILLBUILDER Answers
1. Art and architecture; literature; holidays; ways of working; sports and games.
2. *Possible Responses:* Language, history and territory.

OBJECTIVE ② INSTRUCT

Nationalism Shakes Aging Empires

▶ **Key Ideas**
• The Austro-Hungarian Empire is weakened by various nationalist groups and finally dismantled at the end of World War I.
• The Russian czar's attempts to unify diverse cultures fail, and the empire finally collapses with the Bolshevik Revolution.
• Despite efforts at reform, the Ottoman Empire collapses at the end of World War I.

 IN-DEPTH RESOURCES: UNIT 2
Geography Application: Languages Fuel Nationalism, p. 61
Connections Across Time and Cultures: Bonds that Create a Nation-State, p. 72

 GEOGRAPHY TRANSPARENCIES
GT24 Ethnic Groups of Austria-Hungary, 1867

Nationalism Shakes Aging Empires

Three aging empires—the Austro-Hungarian Empire of the Hapsburgs, the Russian Empire of the Romanovs, and the Ottoman Empire of the Turks—were a jumble of ethnic groups. After all, territory and peoples had for centuries been pawns in a political chess game for these empires. Land and ethnic groups moved back and forth, depending on victories or defeats in war and on royal marriages. When nationalism emerged in the 19th century, ethnic unrest threatened and eventually toppled these empires.

A Force for Disunity or Unity? Nationalist movements were capable of tearing apart long-established empires. They could also create new, unified nation-states. Those who wanted to restore the old order from before the French Revolution saw nationalism as a force for disunity. The kingdoms and empires of the old order often ruled over a variety of ethnic groups. Conservatives of the old order reasoned that if each ethnic group wanted its own state, empires would split and crumble.

Gradually, however, rulers began to see that nationalism could also unify masses of people. The rulers of Europe had seen how the nationalist spirit inspired French citizen armies to conquer the armies of other European powers. Authoritarian rulers soon began to use nationalist feelings for their own purposes. They built nation-states in areas where they remained firmly in control. Nationalism worked as a force for disunity, shaking centuries-old empires. But it also worked as a force for unity. It gave rise to the nation-state that is basic to our world today.

The Breakup of the Austro-Hungarian Empire The Austro-Hungarian Empire brought together Hungarians, Germans, Czechs, Slovaks, Croats, Poles, Serbs, Slavs, and Italians. In 1866, Prussia defeated Austria in the Austro-Prussian War. With its victory, Prussia gained control of the new North German Federation. Then, pressured by the Hungarians, Emperor Francis Joseph of Austria split his empire in half, declaring Austria and Hungary independent states—with himself as ruler of both.

Nevertheless, nationalist disputes continued to plague the empire for more than 40 years. Finally, after World War I, Austria-Hungary crumbled into separate nation-states.

In 1903, Ottoman troops moved against rebellious subjects in Salonika, Greece. A drawing of the period illustrates the event.

The Russian Empire Crumbles Nationalism also helped break up the 400-year-old empire of the czars in Russia. In addition to the Russians themselves, the czar ruled over 22 million Ukrainians, 8 million Poles, and smaller numbers of Lithuanians, Latvians, Estonians, Finns, Jews, Romanians, Georgians, Armenians, and Turks. Each group had its own culture.

The ruling Romanov dynasty of Russia was determined to maintain iron control over this diversity. However, their severe policy of Russification—imposing Russian culture on all the ethnic groups in the empire—strengthened nationalist feelings. The rise in nationalism then helped to disunify Russia. The weakened czarist empire finally could not withstand the double shock of World War I and the communist revolution. The last Romanov czar fell to Bolshevik revolutionaries in 1917.

The Ottoman Empire Weakens The Ottomans controlled Greeks, Slavs, Arabs, Bulgarians, and Armenians, in addition to the ruling Turks. In 1856, under pressure from the British and the French, the Ottomans issued reforms to grant equal citizenship to all the people under their rule. That measure, however, angered conservative Turks, who wanted no change in the situation, and caused tensions in the empire. For example, in response to nationalism in Armenia, the Ottomans carried out massacres and deportations of Armenians in 1894 to 1896 and in 1915. Like Austria-Hungary, the Ottoman Empire broke apart soon after World War I.

234 PATTERNS OF CHANGE

Background
In 1867, the Czechs demanded self-rule in the empire, like the Austrians and Hungarians. Ethnic groups in Hungary demanded their own states.

THINK THROUGH HISTORY
A. Making Inferences Why would a policy like Russification tend to produce results that are the opposite of those intended?
A. Possible Answer Trying to force a culture or language on a group of people will probably create resentment. As a reaction, the group will probably take even greater pride in its own language and culture.

Nationalism and Disunity
Today nationalism continues to be a force for disunity. After the Soviet Union collapsed in 1991, forces of nationalism, contained by the Soviet government, once again appeared. Countries and regions demanded independent governments. Some countries, such as Czechoslovakia, separated peacefully into two independent states. In other countries or regions once part of the Soviet Union, nationalism caused violent upheavals. Ask students to read about the former Yugoslavia or about Chechnya and write a brief report explaining how nationalism is a force in these areas.

Biology The Hapsburg royal family, who ruled the Austro-Hungarian Empire until its fall in 1918, was one of the oldest and most famous royal families of Europe. The Hapsburgs increased their power and influence through judicious marriages to members of other royal houses. Have students research the Hapsburg royal family and write a brief report describing the genetic effects of Hapsburg intermarriages, especially the famous Hapsburg chin. The report should also give some background on genetic theory to explain how physical traits can be magnified in intermarriage.

Cavour Unites Italy

While nationalism destroyed empires, it also built nations. Italy was one of the countries to form from the territory of crumbling empires. After the Congress of Vienna in 1815, Austria ruled the Italian provinces of Venetia and Lombardy in the north, and several small states. In the south, the Spanish Bourbon family ruled the Kingdom of the Two Sicilies.

Nevertheless, between 1815 and 1848, increasing numbers of Italians were no longer content to live under foreign rulers. Amid growing discontent, two leaders appeared—one was idealistic, the other practical. They had different personalities and pursued different goals. But each contributed to the unification of Italy.

The Movement for Unity Begins
In 1832, an idealistic 26-year-old Italian named Giuseppe Mazzini (maht·TSEE·nee) organized a nationalist group called Young Italy. No one older than 40 was allowed to join.

During the violent year of 1848, revolts broke out in eight states on the Italian peninsula. Mazzini briefly headed a republican government at Rome. He believed that nation-states were the best hope for social justice, democracy, and peace in Europe. However, the 1848 rebellions failed in Italy as they did elsewhere in Europe. The former rulers of the Italian states drove Mazzini and other nationalist leaders into exile.

Sardinia Leads Italian Unification After 1848, Italian nationalists looked to the Kingdom of Piedmont-Sardinia for leadership. Piedmont-Sardinia was the largest and most powerful of the Italian states. The kingdom had also adopted a liberal constitution in 1848. So, to the Italian middle classes, unification under Piedmont-Sardinia seemed a sensible alternative to Mazzini's democratic idealism.

In 1852, Sardinia's King Victor Emmanuel II named Count **Camillo di Cavour** (kuh·VOOR) as his prime minister. Cavour was a wealthy, middle-aged aristocrat, who worked tirelessly to expand Piedmont-Sardinia's power. With careful diplomacy and well-chosen alliances, he achieved that expansion. Almost as a coincidence, he also achieved the unification of Italy. Mazzini distrusted Cavour. He believed correctly that Cavour wanted to strengthen Sardinia's power, not to unite Italy.

At first, Cavour's major goal was to get control of northern Italy for Sardinia. He carefully went about achieving this territorial goal through diplomacy and cunning. Cavour realized that the greatest roadblock to annexing northern Italy was Austria. To help him expel the Austrians from the north, Cavour found an ally in France. In 1858, the French emperor Napoleon III agreed to help drive Austria out of the northern provinces of Lombardy and Venetia. Cavour soon after provoked a war with Austria. A combined French-Sardinian army won two quick victories against Austria. Sardinia succeeded in taking over all of northern Italy, except Venetia, from the Austrians.

The Unification of Italy, 1858–1870

Kingdom of Sardinia, 1858
Added to Sardinia, 1859–1860
Added to Italy, 1866
Added to Italy, 1870
Kingdom of Italy
Papal States

200 Miles

400 Kilometers

GEOGRAPHY SKILLBUILDER: Interpreting Maps
1. **Region** During what time period was the greatest amount of territory unified in Italy?
2. **Region** What territory did the Italians actually lose during their process of unification?

OBJECTIVE **3** INSTRUCT

Cavour Unites Italy

▶ **Key Ideas**
- Mazzini attempts to unite Italy and free it from foreign rulers.
- Sardinia's prime minister, Cavour, wins most of northern Italy from the Austrians.
- Cavour arranges to unite Italy under the Sardinian king.
- Following unification, Italy suffers severe political and economic problems.

ELECTRONIC LIBRARY OF PRIMARY SOURCES
from "Duties of Country"

CRITICAL THINKING ACTIVITY
CLASS TIME: 15 MINUTES

Evaluating Decisions
Ask students to consider the differences between northern and southern Italy. Would it have been better to create two separate nations? Have them make up a chart in which they list the advantages and disadvantages of two separate nations.

History from Visuals

The Unification of Italy, 1858–1870

Interpreting the Map Have students identify which areas were added to the Kingdom of Sardinia and which areas were added to Italy later.

Extension Activity Ask students to read about one or more regions of Italy shown on this map—such as Lombardy and Tuscany—and write a report of two paragraphs describing its major cities, agricultural produce, brief history, and any other distinguishing characteristics.

SKILLBUILDER Answers
1. 1859–1860.
2. The provinces of Savoy and Nice.

Less Proficient Readers
Making a Summary To help students understand the three aging empires and their collapse, ask them to fill out a chart like the one to the right. You might then discuss which of the groups in each empire established its own independent state.

Empire	Culture Groups	When Collapsed
Austro-Hungarian	Hungarians, Germans, Czechs, Slovaks, Croats, Poles . . .	End of World War I
Russian		
Ottoman		

Gifted and Talented Students
Researching Mazzini Giuseppe Mazzini was a dreamer and visionary who believed that the formation of nation-states across Europe would bring peace and justice. Mazzini wrote about his vision. Have students:
- Locate some of Mazzini's writings. (You might suggest students consult one of

the following: Bolton King's *The Life of Mazzini,* Gwilym O. Griffith's *Mazzini: Prophet of Modern Europe,* or E. E. Y. Hales's *Mazzini and the Secret Societies.*)
- Choose one or more passages from Mazzini's writings.
- Read the passages aloud for the class.

For his contribution as a fighter for independence in Italy and in Latin America, Garibaldi was given the title "Hero of Two Worlds." Ask students to read about Garibaldi's campaigns in Latin America.

 IN-DEPTH RESOURCES: UNIT 2
Primary Source: Proclamation of 1860, p. 65

MORE ABOUT . . .
Vatican City

Since 1929, Vatican City has been an independent country, the smallest in the world. It is about the size of a city park, with a population of about 1,000, and is contained entirely within the city of Rome. The pope is its absolute ruler. Like any country, it has its own mail and telephone systems. It has a diplomatic corps—its ambassadors are known as legates. Although it has no army or navy, it does have the Swiss Guard, a military unit whose job is to protect the pope and his residence.

OBJECTIVE ④ INSTRUCT

The Rise of Prussia

▶ **Key Ideas**
• King William I of Prussia appoints Bismarck as prime minister.
• Bismarck goes to war to win two provinces from Denmark.
• The Prussians defeat the Austrians and gain control of a North German Confederation.
• Prussia defeats France, making Prussia the dominant force in Europe.

 CRITICAL THINKING TRANSPARENCIES
CT24 The Unification of Germany and Italy

HISTORY**MAKERS**

Giuseppe Garibaldi
1807–1882
Giuseppe Garibaldi might have been a character out of a romantic novel. Fisherman, trader, naval commander, guerrilla fighter, poet, rancher, teacher, idealistic revolutionary in Europe and South America— Garibaldi captured the imagination of Europe. The red shirts of his soldiers helped spread his fame, but they started out simply as the cheapest way to clothe his soldiers.

The independence of Italy was Garibaldi's great dream. The French writer Alexandre Dumas wrote of him: "Once mention the word independence, or that of Italy, and he becomes a volcano in eruption."

Garibaldi's bravery attracted the attention of U.S. President Abraham Lincoln. In 1861, Lincoln offered him a command in the Civil War. Garibaldi declined for two reasons: he felt Lincoln did not condemn slavery strongly enough, and he told Lincoln that he wanted to command the entire Union Army!

Cavour Looks South As Cavour was uniting the north of Italy, he began to consider the possibility of controlling the south. He secretly started helping nationalist rebels in southern Italy. In May 1860, a small army of Italian nationalists led by a bold and romantic soldier, **Giuseppe Garibaldi** (GAR·uh·BAWL·dee), captured Sicily. In battle, Garibaldi always wore a bright red shirt, as did his followers. As a result, they became known as the **Red Shirts.**

From Sicily, Garibaldi crossed to the Italian mainland and marched north. Volunteers flocked to his banner. In an election, voters gave Garibaldi permission to unite the southern areas he conquered with the Kingdom of Piedmont-Sardinia. Cavour arranged for King Victor Emmanuel II to meet Garibaldi in Naples. "The Red One" willingly agreed to step aside and let the Sardinian king rule.

Challenges After Unification In 1866, the Austrian province of Venetia, which included the city of Venice, became part of Italy. In 1870, Italian forces took over the last part of a territory known as the Papal States. The Roman Catholic popes had governed the territory as both its spiritual and earthly rulers. With this victory, the city of Rome came under Italian control. Soon after, Rome became the capital of the united Kingdom of Italy. The pope, however, would continue to govern a section of Rome known as Vatican City.

Despite unification, Italy suffered from many unsolved problems. Centuries of separation had bred fierce rivalries among the different Italian provinces. The greatest tension arose between the industrialized north and the agricultural south. The people of these two regions had very different ways of life, and they scarcely understood each other's versions of the Italian language. In the Italian parliament, disorganized parties with vague policies constantly squabbled. As a result, prime ministers and cabinets changed frequently.

In addition to its political instability, Italy also faced severe economic problems. Bloody peasant revolts broke out in the south. At the same time, strikes and riots troubled the northern cities. Meanwhile, the Italian government could not deal with the country's economic problems. As a result, Italy entered the 20th century as a poor country.

CASE STUDY: Germany

The Rise of Prussia

Like Italy, Germany also achieved national unity in the mid-1800s. Since 1815, 39 German states had formed a loose grouping called the German Confederation. The two largest states, the Austro-Hungarian Empire and Prussia, dominated the confederation.

Prussia enjoyed several advantages that would eventually help it forge a strong German state. First of all, unlike the Austro-Hungarian Empire, Prussia had a mainly German population. As a result, nationalism actually unified Prussia, while ethnic groups in Austria-Hungary tore it apart. Moreover, Prussia's army was by far the most powerful in central Europe. Finally, Prussia industrialized more quickly than other German states.

Prussia Leads German Unification Like many other European powers, Prussia experienced the disorder of the revolutions of 1848. In that year, Berlin rioters forced the frightened and unstable Prussian king, Friedrich Wilhelm IV, to call a constitutional convention. The convention then drew up a liberal constitution for the kingdom.

In 1861, Wilhelm I succeeded Friedrich Wilhelm to the throne. The strong-minded Wilhelm first moved to reform the army and double the already powerful Prussian

THINK THROUGH HISTORY
B. Analyzing Causes Besides their old rivalries, what is another reason why the Italian provinces might have a hard time cooperating?
B. Possible Answers The provinces had no experience in working together. In fact, some had been independent and were used to acting alone.

 TEACHING OPTION **BLOCK SCHEDULING**   COOPERATIVE ACTIVITY: Interviewing Garibaldi   CLASS TIME 20 MINUTES

Task: Groups of two to three students will research the life of Giuseppe Garibaldi and present an interview with Garibaldi.

Purpose: To explore the character of Garibaldi and learn more about his contribution to Italian unification.

Activity: Students will work together to read more about the life of Garibaldi and choose several interesting incidents from his life and campaigns in Italy. Students will make notes for an interview with Garibaldi, in which one or two students take the role of interviewer and another takes the role of Garibaldi. The interview will focus on one or two incidents in

his life. The interview will elicit not only a narrative of the incidents, but Garibaldi's ideas and feelings about his role as fighter for Italian unification. Students will present the interview for the class.

 ALTERNATIVE ASSESSMENT BOOK
Standards for Evaluating a Cooperative Activity

military. However, his liberal parliament refused him the money for his reforms.

Wilhelm saw the parliament's refusal as a major challenge to his authority. He was supported in his view by the Junkers (YUNG·kuhrz), members of Prussia's wealthy landowning class. The Junkers were strongly conservative and opposed liberal ideas. For that reason, Wilhelm drew all his ministers and army officers from the Junker class. In 1862, to help solve his problem with parliament, Wilhelm chose a conservative Junker named **Otto von Bismarck** as his prime minister. Bismarck was a master of what came to be known as **realpolitik.** This German term means "the politics of reality." The word described tough power politics with no room for idealism. With realpolitik as his style, Bismarck would become one of the commanding figures of German history.

Unable to persuade parliament to grant Wilhelm's desires, Bismarck took a dramatic step. With the king's approval, he declared that he would rule without the consent of parliament and without a legal budget. Those actions were in direct violation of the constitution. In his first speech as prime minister, he defiantly told members of the Prussian parliament, "The great questions of the day will not be settled by speeches or by majority decisions—that was the great mistake of 1848 and 1849—but by blood and iron."

Germany Expands Though he was devoted to country and king, Bismarck was also ambitious. One contemporary described him as a man "who is striving after supreme power, including military power." By working to expand Prussia, he could satisfy both his patriotism and his desire for power. In 1864, Bismarck took the first step toward molding an empire. He formed an alliance between Prussia and Austria. They then went to war against Denmark to win two border provinces, Schleswig and Holstein.

A quick victory increased national pride among Prussians. It also won new respect from other Germans and lent support for Prussia as head of a unified Germany. After the victory, Prussia governed Schleswig, while Austria controlled Holstein. Bismarck suspected that this arrangement would soon lead to friction between the two powers. And such tensions would suit his plans perfectly.

Bismarck Eliminates Austria To disable his powerful rival, Bismarck purposely stirred up border conflicts with Austria over Schleswig and Holstein. The tensions provoked Austria into declaring war on Prussia in 1866. This conflict became known as the Seven Weeks' War. As the name suggests, the war was over quickly. The Prussians used their superior training and equipment to win a smashing victory. They humiliated Austria. The Austrians lost the region of Venetia, which was given to Italy. They also had to accept Prussian annexation of yet more German territory.

With its victory in the Seven Weeks' War, Prussia took control of northern Germany. For the first time, the eastern and western parts of the Prussian kingdom were joined. In 1867, the remaining states of the north joined a North German Confederation, which Prussia dominated completely.

THINK THROUGH HISTORY
C. Drawing Conclusions Bismarck succeeded in ignoring both the parliament and constitution of Prussia. How do you think his success would affect Prussian government?
C. Possible Answer The parliament and constitution would grow weaker. The king and prime minister would grow stronger.

Background Many Germans looked on Austria as their natural leader. Vienna had been capital of the Holy Roman Empire and was a center of German music, art, and literature.

The Unification of Germany, 1865 – 1871

Legend:
- Prussia, 1865
- Annexed by Prussia, 1866
- Joined Prussia in North German Confederation, 1867
- South German States (joined Prussia to form German Empire, 1871)
- Conquered from France, 1871
- German Empire, 1871

0 — 200 Miles
0 — 400 Kilometers

GEOGRAPHY SKILLBUILDER:
Interpreting Maps
1. **Location** *What was unusual about the territory of Prussia as it existed in 1865?*
2. **Regions** *After 1865, what year saw the biggest expansion of Prussian territory?*

History from Visuals

The Unification of Germany, 1865–1871

Interpreting the Map Have students notice the dates in which territory was added to Prussia. Point out that the German Empire was built in just six years.

Extension Activity Ask students to compare this map with a map of Germany in their Atlas on page 636. Have them describe what territory is still controlled by Germany and what territory has been lost. *Lost: East Prussia, most of West Prussia*

SKILLBUILDER Answers
1. It was actually cut in two—with Hanover dividing Westphalia from the rest of Prussia.
2. 1871.

MORE ABOUT . . .
Otto von Bismarck

Bismarck focused single-mindedly on his goal and used anything at hand to achieve his purposes. As an acquaintance of his observed, "He listens only to himself, and if once in a while he hears someone else it is only something that suits his purpose; then he picks up a phrase and drops everything else. This can all be attributed to the fundamental trait of his character: concentrated energy." For his unshakable determination and his "blood and iron" policies, Bismarck earned the title the Iron Chancellor.

MORE ABOUT . . .
The Seven Weeks' War

Although the Austrians outnumbered the Prussian troops, the brilliant Prussian general Helmuth von Moltke made use of a new invention, the railroad, to move troops quickly and efficiently to the front. The Prussians used other new inventions, the telegraph and the rapid-fire "needle gun," to win a quick and decisive victory over the Austrians.

TEACHING OPTIONS

MULTIPLE LEARNING STYLES

Visual Learners Many images can be associated with the rise of Prussia: the distinctive Prussian military uniform; the stern portrait of Bismarck; Bismarck's idea of "blood and iron"; trains carrying Prussian troops; the siege of Paris and the suffering of the Parisians; the crowning of King William I as emperor.

Ask students to prepare a collage of images that depict the rise of Prussia and the establishment of Germany's Second Reich. Encourage students both to photocopy images and to use their imaginations in drawing their own images. Display the collages in class.

CUSTOMIZING FOR SPECIAL NEEDS

Gifted and Talented Students People disagree on the character of Bismarck. Ask students to work in pairs to complete the following:
• Research Bismarck using sources such as biographies, comments from historians, and primary sources such as letters. (The primary source for this section is a Bismarck speech.)

• Use the research materials to prepare a debate, with one student viewing Bismarck as a hero, and the other viewing Bismarck as a villain.
• Present the debate before the class.

 IN-DEPTH RESOURCES: UNIT 2
Primary Sources: Nationalist Speech by Otto von Bismarck, p. 66

Teacher's Edition **237**

Bismarck grew up on a country estate and spent several years there as an adult. In his later years, Bismarck often spoke of the time he spent on his estate, living the life of a country gentleman, as one of the happiest and most peaceful of his life and wondered why he had left such a pleasant life for the uncertainties of politics. Ask students to read more about the life of Bismarck and report some interesting personal anecdotes about him.

ASSESS & RETEACH

Section 3 Assessment
Have students work in small groups to discuss the questions and review one another's responses.

Section Quiz
FORMAL ASSESSMENT
Section Quiz, p. 103

Reteaching Activity
CLASS TIME: 10 MINUTES

To help students understand the development of nation-states in Europe, have them review the events they have listed on the time line. Then have them choose one event and write one paragraph explaining its importance.

CLOSE ACTIVITY

CLASS TIME: 10 MINUTES

Forming and Supporting Opinions
Cavour and Bismarck both used cunning and deceit, and deliberately provoked war, in order to unite a people of common background and culture under a single government. Ask students to write several paragraphs explaining whether or not they believe these two men were justified in their actions. Have volunteers read their paragraphs to the class.

HISTORY MAKERS

Otto von Bismarck
1815–1898
Germans have still not decided how to judge Otto von Bismarck. To some Germans, he was the greatest and noblest of Germany's statesmen. They say he almost single-handedly unified the nation and raised it to greatness. To others, he was a devious politician who abused his powers and led Germany into dictatorship.

Bismarck's complex personality has also fascinated historians. By 1895, 650 books had already been written about his life. His speeches, letters, and his memoirs do not help to simplify him. They show him to be both cunning and deeply religious. At one moment, he could declare "It is the destiny of the weak to be devoured by the strong." At another moment he could claim "We Germans shall never wage aggressive war, ambitious war, a war of conquest."

The Franco-Prussian War By 1867, a few southern German states remained independent of Prussia. The majority of southern Germans were Catholics. So, many in the region resisted domination by a Protestant Prussia. However, Bismarck felt he could win the support of southerners if they faced a threat from outside. He reasoned that a war with France would rally the south.

Bismarck was an expert at manufacturing "incidents" to gain his ends. And he was successful with France. He published an altered version of a diplomatic telegram he had received. The telegram gave a false description of a meeting between Wilhelm I and the French ambassador. In the description, Wilhelm seemed to insult the French. Reacting to the insult, France declared war on Prussia on July 19, 1870.

At once, the Prussian army poured into northern France. In September 1870, the Prussian army surrounded the main French force at Sedan. Among the 80,000 French prisoners taken was Napoleon III himself—a beaten and broken man. Only Paris held out against the Germans. For four months, Parisians withstood a German siege. Finally, hunger forced them to surrender.

The Franco-Prussian War was the final stage in German unification. Now the nationalistic fever also seized people in southern Germany. They finally accepted Prussian leadership.

On January 18, 1871, at the captured French palace of Versailles, King Wilhelm I of Prussia was crowned **kaiser** (KY·zuhr), or emperor. Germans called their empire the Second Reich. (The Holy Roman Empire was the first.) Bismarck had achieved Prussian dominance over Germany and Europe "by blood and iron," as he had set out to do.

The Balance of Power Shifts

The 1815 Congress of Vienna established five Great Powers in Europe—Britain, France, Austria, Prussia, and Russia. The wars of the mid-1800s greatly strengthened one of the Great Powers, as Prussia became Germany. In 1815, the Great Powers were nearly equal in strength. By 1871, however, Britain and Germany were clearly the most powerful—both militarily and economically. Austria, Russia, and Italy lagged far behind. France struggled along somewhere in the middle. The European balance of power had broken down. This shift also found expression in the art of the period. In fact, during that century, artists, composers, and writers pointed to paths that European society should follow.

Background
Food became so scarce during the siege of Paris that people ate sawdust, leather, and rats. Parisians even slaughtered animals in the zoo for food.

Section ③ Assessment

1. TERMS & NAMES
Identify
• Camillo di Cavour
• Giuseppe Garibaldi
• Red Shirts
• Otto von Bismarck
• realpolitik
• kaiser

2. TAKING NOTES
On your own paper, make a time line like the one below. On it, show the development of independent nation-states in Europe.

Congress of
Vienna 1815

1800 1820 1840 1860 1880 1900

3. ANALYZING ISSUES
Look at the quotation from Bismarck's "blood and iron" speech (page 617). How would you say his approach to settling political issues differed from the approach of liberals?

THINK ABOUT
• the goals of liberals
• the meaning of the phrase "blood and iron"
• Bismarck's goals and how he attained them

4. ANALYZING THEMES
Revolution How might Cavour and Garibaldi have criticized each other as contributors to Italian unity?

THINK ABOUT
• the personalities of the two men
• methods used by Cavour and Garibaldi to win Italian unity

ANSWERS

1. TERMS & NAMES
Camillo di Cavour, p. 235
Giuseppe Garibaldi, p. 236
Red Shirts, p. 236
Otto von Bismarck, p. 237
realpolitik, p. 237
kaiser, p. 238

2. TAKING NOTES
Possible Responses: Greece wins independence from Ottomans, 1830; revolts throughout Europe, 1848; Victor Emmanuel II declared king of Italy, 1861; Seven Weeks' War between Prussia and Austria, 1866; Franco-Prussian War, 1870; William I crowned kaiser of new German Empire, 1871.

3. ANALYZING ISSUES
Possible Answers: Liberals wanted government by elected parliaments—issues would be settled by majority decisions. Bismarck preferred to settle issues by "blood and iron"—the blood of soldiers and the iron of weapons (or military equipment).

4. ANALYZING THEMES
Possible Answers: Cavour might have criticized Garibaldi for being an impractical idealist who was unable to lead a unified country. Garibaldi might have criticized Cavour for being a cold-hearted opportunist who was more interested in power than in a unified Italy.

Revolutions in the Arts

MAIN IDEA	WHY IT MATTERS NOW
Artistic and intellectual movements both reflected and fueled changes in Europe during the 1800s.	Romanticism and realism continue to dominate the novels, dramas, and films produced today.

SETTING THE STAGE European countries passed through severe political troubles during the 1800s. At the same time, two separate artistic and intellectual movements divided the century in half. Thinkers and artists focused on ideas of freedom, the rights of individuals, and an idealistic view of history during the first half of the century. After the great revolutions of 1848, political focus shifted to men who practiced realpolitik. Similarly, intellectuals and artists expressed a "realistic" view of the world. In their view of the world, the rich pursued their selfish interests while ordinary people struggled and suffered.

The Romantic Movement

At the beginning of the 19th century, the Enlightenment idea of reason gradually gave way to another major movement: romanticism. **Romanticism** was a movement in art and ideas. It showed deep interest both in nature and in the thoughts and feelings of the individual. In many ways, romantic thinkers and writers reacted against the ideals of the Enlightenment. Romantics rejected the rigidly ordered world of the middle-class. They turned from reason to emotion, from society to nature. Nationalism also fired the romantic imagination. For example, a fighter for freedom in Greece, Lord Byron also ranked as one of the leading romantic poets of the time.

The Ideas of Romanticism Emotion, sometimes wild emotion, was a key element of romanticism. Nevertheless, romanticism went beyond feelings. Romantics expressed a wide range of ideas and attitudes. In general, romantic thinkers and artists

- emphasized inner feelings, emotions, imagination
- focused on the mysterious and the supernatural; also, on the odd, exotic, and grotesque or horrifying
- loved the beauties of untamed nature
- idealized the past as a simpler and nobler time
- glorified heroes and heroic actions
- cherished folk traditions, music, and stories
- valued the common people and the individual
- promoted radical change and democracy

Not all romantics gave the same emphasis to these features. The brothers Jakob and Wilhelm Grimm, for example, concentrated on history and the sense of national pride it fostered. During the first half of the 19th century, they collected German fairy tales. They also created a dictionary and grammar of the German language. Both the tales and the dictionary of the Grimm brothers celebrated the spirit of

Though created in the early 20th century, this watercolor of British artist Arthur Rackham is full of romantic fantasy. It illustrates the tale "The Old Woman in the Wood" by Jakob and Wilhelm Grimm.

A. Possible Answer Romantics idealized the past as a simpler nobler time; glorified heroes and their actions; cherished folk traditions, music, and stories.

THINK THROUGH HISTORY
A. Analyzing Causes Which ideas of romanticism would encourage nationalism?

Background
The Grimm brothers also collected tales from other countries: England, Scotland, Ireland, Spain, the Netherlands, Scandinavia, and Serbia.

Nationalist Revolutions Sweep the West **239**

SECTION 4 RESOURCES

PRINT RESOURCES

IN-DEPTH RESOURCES: UNIT 2
Guided Reading, p. 59
History Makers: Beethoven, p. 71

ACCESS FOR STUDENTS ACQUIRING ENGLISH
Guided Reading (Spanish), p. 95

FORMAL ASSESSMENT
Section Quiz, p. 104

ALTERNATIVE ASSESSMENT BOOK

TECHNOLOGY RESOURCES

WORLD ART AND CULTURES TRANSPARENCIES
AT53 *Couturiere*

CRITICAL THINKING TRANSPARENCIES
CT60 *Visual Summary*

CD-ROM
Electronic Library of Primary Sources

INTERNET www.mlworldhistory.com

Section 4 Overview

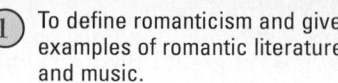

OBJECTIVES

① To define romanticism and give examples of romantic literature and music.

② To explain the shift to realism and give examples of realistic art and literature.

CRITICAL THINKING

- Analyzing causes, pp. 239, 243
- Summarizing, p. 240
- Synthesizing, p. 242
- Comparing, p. 242
- Analyzing causes, p. 243

FOCUS

5-Minute Warm-Up

▶ **Clarifying**
Have students answer these questions to help them understand something about a great romantic composer.

1. Read the History Makers on Beethoven on p. 241. What handicaps did Beethoven fight against?

2. How did Beethoven's handicaps affect his work?

 WARM-UP TRANSPARENCY 8

OBJECTIVE ① INSTRUCT

The Romantic Movement

▶ **Key Ideas**
- Romanticism includes a number of key elements.
- Some romantic writers emphasize emotion, love of nature, history, and individualism, while others focus on the mysterious, the exotic, and the horrifying.
- Romantic composers, the greatest of whom is Beethoven, flourish in the 19th century.

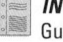 *IN-DEPTH RESOURCES: UNIT 2*
Guided Reading, p. 59

 ACCESS FOR STUDENTS ACQUIRING ENGLISH
Guided Reading (Spanish), p. 95

being German. And they celebrated the German spirit long before Germans had united into a single country.

Other writers and artists focused on strong individuals. They glorified real or mythical rebels and leaders, such as Napoleon or the legendary King Arthur. Still others celebrated the beauty and mystery of unspoiled nature. For example, one of France's leading romantic novelists, Amandine Aurore Dupin (better known as George Sand), lovingly described the French countryside and country life. British writer Emily Brontë set her powerful romantic novel, *Wuthering Heights,* in the windswept moors of northern England. The British poet William Blake believed he could "see a World in a Grain of Sand/And a Heaven in a Wild Flower." In painting, English romantic artist Joseph Turner captured the raging of the sea. Another English artist, John Constable, celebrated the peaceful English countryside. Whatever their particular emphasis, romantic writers and artists affected all the arts.

Romanticism in Literature Germany produced one of the earliest and greatest romantic writers. In 1774, Johann Wolfgang von Goethe (YO·hahn VUHLF·gahng fuhn GER·tuh) published *The Sorrows of Young Werther.* Goethe's novel told of a sensitive young man whose hopeless love for a virtuous married woman drives him to suicide.

Victor Hugo led the French romantics. Hugo's huge output of poems, plays, and novels expressed romanticism's revolutionary spirit. His works also reflect the romantic fascination with history and support for the individual. His novels *Les Misérables* and *The Hunchback of Notre Dame* both show the struggles of individuals against a hostile society.

The British romantic poets William Wordsworth and Samuel Taylor Coleridge both honored nature as the source of truth and beauty. To Wordsworth, nature was richly alive. Coleridge, on the other hand, put the accent on horror and the supernatural in his poem "The Rime of the Ancient Mariner." Later English romantic poets, such as Byron, Shelley, and Keats, wrote poems celebrating rebellious heroes, passionate love, and the mystery and beauty of nature. Like many romantics, many of these British poets lived stormy lives and died young. Byron, for example, died at the age of 36, while Shelley died at 29.

The Gothic Novel The Gothic horror story was a form that became hugely popular. These novels often took place in medieval Gothic castles. They were also filled with fearful, violent, sometimes supernatural events. Mary Shelley, wife of the poet Percy Shelley, wrote one of the earliest and most successful Gothic horror novels, *Frankenstein.* The novel told the story of a monster created from the body parts of dead human beings. The following passage shows Mary Shelley's romantic imagination at work. She describes how the idea for the monster took shape. After an evening telling ghost stories with her husband and Lord Byron, the following vision appeared to her:

A VOICE FROM THE PAST
Night waned upon this talk, and even the witching hour had gone by, before we retired to rest. When I placed my head on my pillow, I did not sleep, nor could I be said to think. My imagination, unbidden, possessed and guided me. . . . I saw—with shut eyes, but acute mental vision—I saw the pale student of [unholy] arts kneeling beside the thing he had put together. I saw the hideous phantasm of a man stretched out, and then, on the working of some powerful engine, show signs of life, and stir with an uneasy, half-vital motion.

MARY SHELLEY, Introduction to *Frankenstein*

Romantic Composers Emphasize Emotion Emotion dominated the music produced by romantic composers. Romantic composers moved away from the tightly controlled, formal compositions of the Enlightenment period. Instead, they celebrated heroism and villainy, tragedy and joy, with a new power of expression.

One of romanticism's first composers rose to become its greatest: Ludwig van Beethoven (LOOD-vihg vahn BAY-toh-vuhn). In his early years, Beethoven wrote the classical music of the Enlightenment. But in later years, he turned to romantic compositions. His Ninth Symphony soars, celebrating freedom, dignity, and triumph.

While they never matched Beethoven's greatness, later romantic composers also appealed to the hearts and souls of their listeners. Robert Schumann's compositions sparkle with merriment. Like many romantic composers, Felix Mendelssohn drew on literature, such as Shakespeare's *A Midsummer Night's Dream*, as the inspiration for his music. Polish composer and concert pianist Frederic Chopin (SHOH-pan) was popular both with other musicians and with the public. Chopin's compositions, such as his first and second piano concertos, contain melodies that are still familiar today.

Romanticism made music a popular art form. As music became part of middle-class life, musicians and composers became popular heroes of romanticism. Composer and pianist Franz Liszt (lihst), for example, achieved earnings and popularity equal to that of today's rock stars.

The Shift to Realism

By the middle of the 19th century, rapid industrialization had a deep effect on everyday life in Europe. And this change began to make the dreams of the romantics seem pointless. In literature and the visual arts, **realism** tried to show life as it is, not as it should be. Realist painting reflected the increasing political importance of the working class in the 1850s. The growing class of industrial workers lived grim lives in dirty, crowded cities. Along with paintings, novels proved especially suited to describing workers' suffering. The interest in science and the scientific method during this period encouraged this "realistic" approach to art and literature. Science operated through objective observation and the reporting of facts. That new invention, the camera, also recorded objective and precise images. In the same way, realist authors observed and reported as precisely and objectively as they could.

Writers Study Society Realism in literature flourished in France with writers such as Honoré de Balzac and Emile Zola. Balzac wrote a massive series of almost one hundred novels entitled *The Human Comedy.* These stories detail the lives of over 2,000 people from all levels of French society following the Revolution. They also describe in detail the brutal struggle for wealth and power among France's business class. Zola's explosive novels scandalized France at the end of the 1800s. He exposed the miseries of French workers in small shops, factories, and coal mines. His revelations shocked readers. His work spurred reforms of labor laws and working conditions in France.

The famous English realist novelist, Charles Dickens, created unforgettable characters and scenes. Many were humorous, but others showed the despair of London's

Nationalist Revolutions Sweep the West **241**

HISTORY MAKERS

Ludwig van Beethoven 1770–1827
A genius of European music, Beethoven suffered the most tragic disability a composer can endure. At the age of 30, he began to go deaf. His deafness grew worse for 19 years. By 1819, it was total.

At first, Beethoven's handicap barely affected his career. His composing and concerts went on as before. By 1802, however, he knew that his hearing would only worsen. He suffered then from bouts of depression. The depressions would bring him to the brink of suicide. Nonetheless, he would rebound:

> . . . It seemed unthinkable for me to leave the world forever before I had produced all that I felt called upon to produce. . . .

After 1819, Beethoven's friends had to write their questions to him in notebooks. He continued to compose, however, and left many "sketchbooks" of musical ideas he would never hear.

HISTORY MAKERS
Ludwig van Beethoven

As the son of an alcoholic father, Beethoven had a difficult childhood. As an adult, he was irritable, odd, and hard to get along with. Ask students to read more about the personal life of Beethoven and relate some interesting anecdotes to the class.

 IN-DEPTH RESOURCES: UNIT 2
History Makers: Beethoven, p. 71

MORE ABOUT . . .
Romanticism

Romanticism was a movement based on emotional sensitivity and expression. The romantics' emotionalism often led to what many people considered scandalous behavior. The poet Percy Shelley ran away with Mary Godwin while he was still married to another woman. (They were later married after Shelley's wife died.) The poet Lord Byron, the writer Goethe, and the composer Liszt all had numerous love affairs. Despite Liszt's popularity, England's Queen Victoria and Prince Albert refused to attend his concert in London because of his scandalous reputation.

OBJECTIVE 2 INSTRUCT

The Shift to Realism

▶ *Key Ideas*
- With industrialization and a new interest in the scientific method, a realistic approach to art and literature emerges.
- Photography, first invented by Daguerre, becomes the art of the new industrial age.
- French and English realistic writers expose the misery of the working poor.

TEACHING OPTION **BLOCK SCHEDULING** **COOPERATIVE ACTIVITY: Presenting a Romantic Composer** **CLASS TIME 20 MINUTES**

Task: Students will research one of the romantic composers and give a presentation about his work.

Purpose: To learn more about romanticism in music.

Activity: Groups of students will research a romantic composer and prepare a brief biographical report. Students will also obtain recordings of some of the composer's works and research some background on the musical pieces. The groups will then give a presentation that includes playing one or two selections from the composer's work in class. The presentation will also include a biographical sketch, along with a picture of the composer, and an explanation of how the music reflects romantic ideas.

 Building a Portfolio: If students choose to include this work in their portfolio, have them include a note indicating the part they played in the presentation.

ALTERNATIVE ASSESSMENT BOOK
Standards for Evaluating a Cooperative Activity

Standards for Evaluation
Presentations should . . .
- include a concise biographical sketch
- include appropriate musical selections
- show how the music embodies romanticism

Teacher's Edition **241**

History Through Art

Artistic Movements

Romanticism included a wide variety of artistic styles. Some artists focused almost entirely on painting historical scenes. Others focused on landscape paintings with broad panoramas. In France, a small group of painters known as the Barbizon School (named for the village of Barbizon in the French forest of Fountainebleau) concentrated on painting small sections of a landscape—a field, a meadow, even a single tree.

 WORLD ART AND CULTURES TRANSPARENCIES
AT53 *Couturiere*

MORE ABOUT . . .

Realism

Many of Courbet's great realist paintings portray rural society as he had seen it in his birthplace of Ornans in provincial France. Courbet tried to show the people and events of rural society realistically, rather than sentimentally or satirically. He showed peasants as possessing an inherent dignity and worth, and this offended conservative elements in French society.

MORE ABOUT . . .

Impressionism

The term *impressionism* was coined in 1874 when Claude Monet exhibited a painting entitled *Impression: Sunrise.* A hostile art critic, unused to the unfinished, sketchy look of this new style of art, dismissed the entire art show as "impressionist." The term, which came to be applied to a whole group of artists, was intended as an insulting, derogatory name, but it soon became an expression of admiration.

Artistic Movements

In the 19th century, as always, artistic movements reflected the social conditions of the time. During the first half of the century, common people began to fight for political power. During that same period, romanticism was the dominant artistic style. By mid-century, political realism had taken over. At the same time, art began to celebrate working, sweating, everyday people. But the romantic ideal did not die. By the end of the century, a new movement called impressionism portrayed the life of middle-class people as a beautiful dream.

Realism

Realist artists reacted against the dreams of the romantics. These artists believed that their art should portray people as they really were, not as they should be. *The Winnowers,* by Gustave Courbet, the most famous realist, shows the world of everyday work. The winnowers are removing hulls from newly harvested grain. Courbet does not romanticize the work. He records it.

Romanticism

Romantic landscape artists idealized nature. Some emphasized the harmony between humans and nature. Others showed nature's power and mystery, as in this painting, *Moonrise Over the Sea,* by German artist Caspar David Friedrich. Still other romantic artists focused on heroes and scenes from history, legend, or literature.

Impressionism

Impressionists aimed at capturing their immediate "impression" of a brief moment. They used bright colors and loose brushwork to catch the fleeting light that sparkles and shimmers. As a result, *Poppies at Argenteuil* by Claude Monet shows less attention to exact "realistic" detail than does *The Winnowers.* It also does not express the sense of serene mystery of *Moonrise Over the Sea.*

Connect *to* History

Synthesizing Artists choose specific elements for their paintings to create the world they want to show. Compare the settings, use of color and light, sharpness of line, and atmosphere of these paintings.

 SEE SKILLBUILDER HANDBOOK, PAGE 665

Connect *to* Today

Comparing Look for examples of modern art in books and magazines. Show examples of paintings where artists still use techniques that could be called romantic or realist or impressionist.

Connect *to* History	Connect *to* Today

Synthesizing

Suggest that students make a chart like the one here to compare the three paintings.

	Moonrise Over the Sea	The Winnowers	Poppies at Argenteuil
setting			
color and light			
sharpness of line			
atmosphere			

Comparing

Students will show examples of modern art that reflect techniques and points of view that are recognizably similar to those of romantic, realist, and impressionist artists of the 19th century.

working poor. In this passage, Dickens describes the gloom of working-class life:

A VOICE FROM THE PAST

It was a Sunday evening in London, gloomy, close, and stale. . . . Melancholy streets, in a penitential garb of soot, steeped the souls of the people who were condemned to look at them out of windows, in dire despondency. . . . No pictures, no unfamiliar animals, no rare plants or flowers. . . . Nothing for the spent toiler to do, but to compare the monotony of his seventh day with the monotony of his six days, think what a weary life he led, and make the best of it.

CHARLES DICKENS, *Little Dorrit*

Vocabulary
despondency: lack of hope

THINK THROUGH HISTORY
C. Analyzing Causes Why do you think a description of London like Dickens's might lead to social change?

Background
Daguerre's photo process required about 20–30 minutes exposure time—a big advance over a previous method that took eight hours.

C. Possible Answer
His dark description might make people think of how social conditions could be changed to bring some hope and prosperity to British workers.

Photographers Capture the Passing Moment As realist painters and writers detailed the lives of actual people, photographers could record an instant in time with scientific precision. The first practical photographs were called daguerreotypes (duh·GEHR·uh·TYPS). They were named after their French inventor, Louis Daguerre. Daguerre was an artist who created scenery for theaters. To improve the realism of his scenery, Daguerre developed his photographic invention. The images produced in his daguerrotypes were startlingly real and won him worldwide fame.

Daguerreotype prints were made on metal. However, the British inventor William Talbot invented a light-sensitive paper that he used to produce photographic negatives. The advantage of paper was that many prints could be made from one negative. The Talbot process also allowed photos to be reproduced in books and newspapers. Mass distribution gained a wide audience for the realism of photography. With its scientific, mechanical, and mass-produced features, photography was the art of the new industrial age.

"Ships at Low Tide," an early photograph taken in 1844 by William Talbot.

Impressionists React Against Realism Beginning in the 1860s, a group of painters in Paris reacted against the realistic style. Instead of showing life "as it really is," they tried giving their impression of a subject or a moment in time. For this reason, this style of art came to be known as impressionism. Fascinated by light, impressionist artists used pure, shimmering colors to capture a moment seen at a glance.

Artists like Edouard Manet (mah·NAY), Claude Monet (moh·NAY), Edgar Degas (duh·GAH), and Pierre-Auguste Renoir (ruhn·WHAR) also found new subjects for their art. Unlike the realists, impressionists showed a more positive view of the new urban society in Western Europe. Instead of abused workers, they showed shop clerks and dock workers enjoying themselves in dance halls and cafés. They painted performers in the theater and circuses. And they glorified the delights of the life of the rising middle class.

Section 4 Assessment

1. TERMS & NAMES
Identify
• romanticism
• realism
• impressionism

2. TAKING NOTES
Using a chart like the one below, contrast romanticism, realism, and impressionism. For each movement, provide a brief description, the social conditions that each reflects, and representative artists.

Movement	Description	Social Conditions	Artists
Romanticism			
Realism			
Impressionism			

3. ANALYZING CAUSES
How might a realist novel bring about changes in society? Describe the steps by which this might happen.
THINK ABOUT
• the conditions described in realist novels
• who reads realist novels
• how political change takes place

4. THEME ACTIVITY
Revolution Listen to a symphony or concerto by Beethoven. Imagine that you are a music critic who has previously heard only formal classical compositions. Write a review of Beethoven's piece. Make the theme of your review the revolutionary quality of Beethoven's music—which you may admire or dislike.

Nationalist Revolutions Sweep the West **243**

TERMS & NAMES

1. creoles, p. 224
2. Simón Bolívar, p. 225
3. conservatives, p. 229
4. liberals, p. 229
5. nationalism, p. 229
6. Camillo di Cavour, p. 235
7. Otto von Bismarck, p. 237
8. realpolitik, p.237
9. romanticism, p. 239
10. realism, p. 241

REVIEW QUESTIONS

Answers will vary.

11. They resented that the peninsulares held nearly all high government offices. Their loyalty to Spain evaporated when Napoleon set his brother on the Spanish throne.

12. Iturbide began by opposing the Mexican revolution but wound up as the leader who proclaimed Mexico's independence. He tried to keep control of Central America, but when he fell from power after two years, Central America declared its independence from Mexico.

13. Dom Pedro, the ruler of Brazil, was the son of the king of Portugal; in 1822, he officially declared Brazil's independence from Portugal.

14. Both Europeans and Americans respected ancient Greek culture and so felt a sympathy for the Greeks of their own time. Russians felt a kinship with Greek Orthodox Christians.

15. Not very successful, because by 1849, Europe had practically returned to its pre-1848 status.

16. Disunity—It broke up centuries-old empires into nation-states; Unity—It inspired people with the same history, culture, and language to form nation-states.

17. He used careful diplomacy and well-chosen alliances, as well as cunning.

18. He provoked Austria and France into separate wars, reasoning that the two wars would unite the German people behind Prussia.

19. The Romantic Movement emphasized heroic actions, promoted radical change, favored democracy, was concerned with common people. Many nationalists shared these ideals.

20. Workers in the Industrial Age often lived grim lives in dirty, crowded cities.

Chapter 8 Assessment

TERMS & NAMES

Briefly explain the importance of each of the following to the revolutions in Latin America or Europe.

1. creoles
2. Simón Bolívar
3. conservatives
4. liberals
5. nationalism
6. Camillo di Cavour
7. Otto von Bismarck
8. realpolitik
9. romanticism
10. realism

Interact with History

On page 222, you were asked to create a symbol for your newly independent country. Show your symbol to the class. Explain the elements of your design and what they are intended to express. With your classmates' comments in mind, what might you change in your design?

REVIEW QUESTIONS

SECTION 1 (pages 223–228)
Latin American Peoples Win Independence

11. What caused the creoles in South America to rebel against Spain?

12. What role did Agustín de Iturbide play in the independence of Mexico and of the countries of Central America?

13. Who was Dom Pedro, and what role did he play in Brazil's move to independence?

SECTION 2 (pages 229–232)
Revolutions Disrupt Europe

14. Why did so many people in Europe and North America support the revolution of Greek nationalists against the Ottoman Empire?

15. How successful were the revolts of 1848? Explain.

SECTION 3 (pages 233–238)
Nationalism
Case Studies: Italy and Germany

16. How did nationalism in the 1800s work as a force both for disunity and for unity?

17. What approaches did Camillo di Cavour use to try to acquire more territory for Piedmont-Sardinia?

18. What strategy did Otto von Bismarck use to try to make Prussia the leader of a united Germany?

SECTION 4 (pages 239–243)
Revolutions in the Arts

19. Name two ideas or attitudes of the Romantic movement that reflected the ideals of nationalism.

20. What new conditions caused a change in the arts from romanticism to realism?

Visual Summary

Nationalist Revolutions Sweep the West

Milestones of the 1800s

Politics

1804 Haiti gains independence from France
1814 The Congress of Vienna begins
1821 Bolívar wins Venezuela's independence from Spain
1824 Bolívar completes the liberation of Latin America
1830 Greece wins full independence; revolts break out in France, Belgium, and Poland
1848 Revolutions sweep Europe
1861 Alexander II frees the serfs in Russia
1870 Italy is unified
1871 The Franco-Prussian War ends; Germany is unified

Arts

1804 Beethoven completes his First Symphony
1812 The Brothers Grimm publish a collection of fairy tales
1818 Mary Shelley's *Frankenstein* is published
1824 Lord Byron dies in Greece; Beethoven completes the Ninth Symphony—his last
1831 Victor Hugo publishes *The Hunchback of Notre Dame*
1836 Charles Dickens becomes an overnight success with his novel *Pickwick Papers*
1839 Louis Daguerre reveals his photographic process
1849 Gustave Courbet's early paintings receive public recognition
1867 Claude Monet begins painting in the impressionist style

244 Chapter 8

Interact with History

Possible Responses: Students may now revise their symbols to reflect the comments they hear from the class. For example, students might suggest a different animal to represent the fictional country or offer advice on colors or symbols. Ask students to display their new designs in the classroom.

CRITICAL THINKING

1. GARIBALDI'S CHOICE

THEME POWER AND AUTHORITY Giuseppe Garibaldi stepped aside to let Victor Emmanuel II rule areas that Garibaldi had conquered in southern Italy. Why do you think he made that choice?

2. NATIONALISM

Using a chart like the one below, describe the nationalist movement in each of the following countries and the results of those movements.

Country	Nationalism and its Results
Mexico	
Greece	
Italy	
Germany	

3. THE MEANS TO VICTORY

In the 1800s, revolutionaries often fought with inferior weapons and scarce supplies. How do you think nationalism might help revolutionaries overcome the disadvantages of old weapons and poor supplies to win a war for national independence? Explain.

4. ANALYZING PRIMARY SOURCES

In a speech to the German parliament in 1888, Otto von Bismarck called for further expansion of the army. In the following quote from that speech, "the Iron Chancellor" explains why Germany must always be prepared for war.

A VOICE FROM THE PAST

When I say that we must strive continually to be ready for all emergencies, I advance the proposition that, on account of our geographical position, we must make greater efforts than other powers would be obliged to make in view of the same ends. We lie in the middle of Europe. We have at least three fronts on which we can be attacked. France has only an eastern boundary; Russia only its western, exposed to assault. . . . So we are spurred forward on both sides to endeavors which perhaps we would not make otherwise.

OTTO VON BISMARCK, speech to the German parliament on February 6, 1888.

- According to Bismarck, what key factor makes Germany a potential target for invasion? Why?
- Do you think Bismarck might have been overstating the threat to Germany? Explain.

CHAPTER ACTIVITIES

1. LIVING HISTORY: Unit Portfolio Project

THEME REVOLUTION Your unit portfolio project focuses on showing the similarities and differences among revolutions (see page 129). For Chapter 8, you might use one of the following ideas to add to your portfolio.

- Ask classmates to role-play bystanders present at Padre Hidalgo's *grito de Dolores*. Ask them to express their feelings about what they have witnessed. Audiotape their comments and use them to write a newspaper report about Mexicans' reactions to the event.
- Write a speech that might have been delivered to a rally somewhere in Europe. Urge the country's leaders to help the Greeks in their struggle for independence from the Ottoman Empire.
- Create a "How-to Booklet for Nationalists," based on the strategies used either by Cavour or by Bismarck.

2. CONNECT TO TODAY: Research Project

THEME CULTURAL INTERACTION Romanticism and realism in the arts reflected social and political conditions. In various forms, these two artistic movements still exist today. Create a chart comparing romantic and realistic aspects of modern films.

INTERNET Use the Internet, newspapers, magazines, or your own personal experience to search for romantic and realistic portrayals of social and political conditions in movies today.

- For your chart, make two lists—one for examples of modern films that are romantic and one for films that are realistic. Include still shots from movies that support your findings.
- In your search, consider movies from at least three countries.

3. INTERPRETING A TIME LINE

Revisit the unit time line on pages 508–509. If you were shown only the period from 1820 to 1848, what fate would you predict for Europe's old order? Why?

FOCUS ON POLITICAL CARTOONS

The 19th-century French cartoonist Charles Philipon was testing a law to see how far away an artist could get from the true features of Louis-Philippe before being condemned to prison and a fine. Since the French word *poire* ("pear") also means "fool,"

- how does the cartoonist show King Louis-Philippe developing as a monarch?
- what do you think was the legal fate of the cartoonist?

Connect to History What right was Charles Philipon standing up for by drawing his cartoon and testing the law?

LES POIRES,

Vendues pour payer les 6,000 fr. d'amende du journal le *Charivari*.

(CHEZ AUBERT, GALERIE VÉRO-BODAT.)

CHAPTER ACTIVITIES

1. LIVING HISTORY

Standards for Evaluation

Role-playing and news reports should meet the following criteria:

- Role-playing presentations should express personal feelings about the event and present descriptions by individuals about what they have seen.
- Audiotapes of the event should contain different sound effects.
- Reports of the event should be written in journalism style—who, what, where, when, why, how.

Standards for Evaluation

Speeches should meet the following criteria:

- Contain factual information about the Greek independence struggle.
- Present persuasive arguments to move listeners to the speaker's point of view.
- Conclude with a call to action.

Standards for Evaluation

How-to booklets should meet the following criteria:

- Present clearly the ideas of either Cavour or Bismarck.
- Explain how the ideas of each can be used in a nationalist struggle.
- Use graphics to illustrate main points.

2. CONNECT TO TODAY

Standards for Evaluation

Charts should meet the following criteria:

- Distinguish visually the romantic and realistic films.
- Include information that compares and contrasts the two forms.
- Present stills from specific films to illustrate main points.

3. INTERPRETING A TIME LINE

Students might answer that events at this time suggest that the old order was about to expire.

FOCUS ON POLITICAL CARTOONS

- The cartoonist shows the king becoming more foolish as time goes on.
- He ended up in prison.

Connect to History He was standing up for the right of free speech and expression, even if such expression insulted a monarch.

CRITICAL THINKING

1. GARIBALDI'S CHOICE
Possible Response: Garibaldi probably realized that with his experience and prestige as king of Piedmont-Sardinia, Victor Emmanuel stood a better chance of keeping Italy together.

2. NATIONALISM
Possible Responses: Mexico—a popular revolt led to independence from Spain; Greece—a revolt with international support freed the country from Ottoman control; Italy—a 30-year struggle joined Italy's territories into a unified country; Germany—Under Bismarck's leadership, Prussia unified the German states.

3. THE MEANS TO VICTORY
Soldiers inspired by the ideal of nationalism might overcome unfavorable odds by force of will. The revolutionary armies of France are examples of the power of the nationalist ideal.

4. ANALYZING PRIMARY SOURCES
Possible Response: Geography: Germany's location at the center of Europe would allow invaders to attack on three fronts. He may have exaggerated: Bismarck's power rested on his army, so expanding the army increased his power.

Canton, China, about 1800

In this painting, the artist has included a wealth of detail that captures the era of Western expansion into Asia and Africa. On the left side of the painting, the flags of five European nations and the United States fly over the Canton harbor. The white, neoclassical architecture of the foreign warehouses and offices stands in stark contrast to the houses and river boats of the Chinese.

Canton (now called Guangzhou) was founded on the Pearl River sometime between 1111 and 771 B.C. The area's mild climate and abundant rainfall made it a major agricultural region. Canton was divided into sections by a series of high walls, parts of which can be seen in this painting. They were demolished in the 1920s. The painting also shows several types of Chinese sampans and junks—river boats that serve as homes and floating businesses to many Chinese families.

As a major trading center, Canton was a prime target for foreigners seeking to open China to Western trade. In the mid 1800s, British and French forces defeated Chinese forces in two Opium Wars. As part of the peace settlement, the city had to open its gates to Western businesses and trade. In response, Chinese patriots in Canton formed secret societies whose goal was to purge China of all foreign influence.

246

The flags of numerous nations fly along the harbor in Canton, China, in this scene painted by an unknown Chinese artist. By the late 1800s, the nations of Europe had built far-reaching empires that included much of Africa and parts of Asia.

Previewing the Unit

This unit describes the effects of the Industrial Revolution on Western nations and the nations' race to divide Asia and Africa among themselves. Colonial rule brings more hardships than benefits to native peoples, who eventually rebel against Western rulers.

During the 1800s, Britain, the United States, and some European countries undergo great changes as a result of the Industrial Revolution. The widening gap between rich and poor prompts a series of social and political reforms.

Nations in Western Europe and North America, along with Australia and New Zealand, adopt democratic institutions, but some of these nations also suppress their native populations. Changes in the arts and sciences transform people's daily lives and create a mass culture.

With their superior technology and weapons, Western nations compete to acquire territory in Africa, Asia, and the South Pacific. The colonies are rich in natural resources and markets for Western goods. Native resistance movements rebel against colonial rule.

Countries around the world must adapt to contact with Western nations. China falls under foreign domination, but Japan and Korea respond by modernizing their countries. Although Latin American nations free themselves from colonialism, they remain economically and politically unstable.

247

Teaching Strategies

Formulating Historical Questions

You may wish to encourage students to formulate questions concerning the events, patterns, and personalities featured in the Unit Time Lines. Such questions would deal with the causes of events, the reasons that made them so important, or the motivations for the actions of certain historical figures.

Using Historical Questioning

You might encourage students to develop questions to help them determine the factors that underlie events and personalities. For example, with a statement such as **"1893 Vietnam** France takes over Indochina," students might ask questions such as:

• How did the French go about taking control of Vietnam?

• Why did the French want territory in Southeast Asia?

• What were the reactions of the Vietnamese to attempts at a takeover?

• What were the long-term effects of French control on Vietnam and the Vietnamese?

• How did French control in Vietnam affect other European and Asian countries?

The results of this questioning process not only will bring students to a fuller understanding of the French takeover in Vietnam but also will help them to develop an essential skill for historical inquiry.

UNIT 3 Time Line

Industrialism and the Race for Empire

	1800	1815	1830	1845	1860

CHAPTER ⑨ 1700–1900

The Industrial Revolution

1700–1815

1701 *Britain* Jethro Tull invents seed drill

1733 *Britain* John Kay invents flying shuttle

1764 *Britain* James Hargreaves invents spinning jenny

1776 *Britain* Adam Smith publishes *The Wealth of Nations*

1793 *U.S.* Eli Whitney invents cotton gin

1807 *U.S.* Robert Fulton launches steamboat, the *Clermont*

1811 *Britain* Luddites attack factories

1813 *U.S.* Lowell textile factories open

1830 *Britain* Rail line between Liverpool and Manchester opened

1848 *Germany* Marx and Engels publish *The Communist Manifesto*

1850 *Britain* Population of city of Manchester reaches 300,000

CHAPTER ⑩ 1815–1914

An Age of Democracy and Progress

1800s *United States* ▶

1832 *Britain* First Reform Bill passes

1837 *Britain* Victoria becomes queen

1838 *Britain* Chartist movement presents demands on People's Charter

1840 *New Zealand* Maoris sign treaty to accept British rule

1845 *Ireland* Great potato famine begins

1847 *Mexico* U.S. wins Mexican-American War

1848 *U.S.* Woman suffragists hold Seneca Falls Convention

1859 *Britain* Charles Darwin presents theory of evolution

CHAPTER ⑪ 1850–1914

The Age of Imperialism

1800s *India* ▶

1853 *Ottoman Empire* Crimean War with Russia breaks out

1857 *India* Sepoy Mutiny

CHAPTER ⑫ 1800–1914

Transformations Around the Globe

1823 *U.S.* President Monroe issues Monroe Doctrine

1833 *Mexico* Santa Anna becomes president

1839 *China* China and Britain fight first Opium War

1840s *Mexico* Benito Juárez begins liberal reform movement

1848 *U.S.* Treaty of Guadalupe Hidalgo adds California and other southwestern states to U.S.

1853 *China* Taiping rebels capture Nanjing and declare it new capital

1854 *Japan* Treaty of Kanagawa gives U.S. access to two ports

248 UNIT 3

1800	1815	1830	1845	1860

MULTIPLE LEARNING STYLES

Kinesthetic Learners You may point out to students that many of the elements featured in the Unit 3 time line concern science and technology. Those two factors actually played a major role in the empire building occurring around the world during the 19th and early 20th centuries.

Have students create their own time lines that focus on the progress of science and technology. Stress to students that they need not follow the format of the Unit Time Lines. Show them other formats in their textbook or other books.

CONNECTIONS ACROSS TIME AND PLACE

Women in the 19th Century You might ask interested students to do research and write a play scene dramatizing an event in the life of a woman or group of women appearing in the Unit 3 time line (Queen Victoria, woman suffragists, Empress Cixi). The scene should show an understanding of

the women's characters and of the importance of the event in their lives.

If you judge that the rest of the class might benefit from a scene (for example, if it provides insights into the woman and her life), you might ask if some students wish to present a reading of the scene in class.

1863 France
Martin brothers develop open-hearth steel furnace

1866 Sweden
Alfred Nobel invents dynamite

1875 Britain
Labor unions win right to strike

1886 U.S.
Forerunner of AFL labor union forms

1896 U.S.
Henry Ford builds his first automobile

◄ **1800s Germany**

1860s France Louis Pasteur develops process of pasteurization

1865 U.S.
Civil War ends

1867 Canada
Dominion of Canada is formed

1871 France
Paris Commune takes control of Paris

1875 France
Third Republic begins

1879 U.S.
Thomas Edison invents light bulb

1894 France
Captain Alfred Dreyfus found guilty of espionage

1901 Britain
Queen Victoria dies

1903 Britain
Emmeline Pankhurst forms Women's Social and Political Union

1908 U.S.
Henry Ford introduces the Model T

1869 Egypt
Suez Canal completed

1871 Congo
Stanley finds Dr. Livingstone in central Africa

1884-85 Germany
Berlin Conference divides Africa among European nations

1885 India
Formation of the Indian National Congress

1893 Vietnam France takes over Indochina

1898 Hawaii
U.S. annexes Hawaii

1898 Philippines
U.S. acquires Philippine Islands

1889 Ethiopia Menelik II leads Ethiopia

1902 South Africa Boer War ends

1905 East Africa
Maji Maji rebellion

1907 Persia Russia and Britain divide Persia into spheres of influence

1908 Persia
Oil discovered

1861 China Empress Cixi begins reign

1867 Japan Meiji era begins a period of modernization

1867 Mexico Juárez reelected president after France defeated

1868 Cuba Ten-year struggle for independence from Spain begins

1876 Mexico
Porfirio Díaz comes to power

1894 Korea Sino-Japanese War begins

1898 Cuba Spanish-American War begins

1900 China Boxer Rebellion protests foreign influence in China

1904 Manchuria
Russo-Japanese War for possession of Manchuria

1910 Korea
Japan annexes Korea

1910 Mexico Mexican Revolution begins

1912 China
Qing Dynasty falls; Sun Yixian elected president

1914 Panama
Panama Canal opens

◄ **1800s Japan**

TIME LINE **249**

Living History
Unit 3 Portfolio Project

THEME Empire Building

Your portfolio for Unit 3 will follow the growth of nations as they build empires and dominate other cultures. You will record not only the effects on the empire-building nations, but also the effects of their colonizing on the lands and peoples whom they take over.

Living History Project Choices
Each Chapter Assessment offers you choices of ways to show the building of empires in that chapter. Activities include the following:

Chapter 9 debate, letter, poster

Chapter 10 handbill, editorial, political cartoon

Chapter 11 script, diary, display

Chapter 12 debate, advertisement, action figure

Portfolio Projects

Empire Building Portfolio projects suggested for Unit 3 deal with the military, economic, social, and political aspects of empire building—from the point of view of both the colonizers and the colonized. Some features of the aspects of empire building covered in the projects include:

- the role of industrialization in enabling a nation to expand its territory and power
- the treatment of colonized peoples
- human rights in colonized territories
- how some nations try to deal with increasing foreign influence
- the problems caused by foreign economic competition from a powerful industrialized nation
- the vestiges of colonialist influence today.

Projects for Linguistic Learners
Portfolio projects for Unit 6 offer numerous possibilities for those students who learn best through verbal media (either oral or written). Those who excel in the spoken word may wish to participate in such debates as the one in Chapter 11 about the U.S. colonization of the Philippines.

Students who best display their knowledge in written form may decide to write a letter to the editor about the influx of cheap foreign products in an unindustrialized country or compose an editorial for a 19th-century New Zealand newspaper concerning Maori land rights.

 The Western Civilization Videodisc

SECTION J: Industrial, Political and Social Revolutions, 1815–1850

Side One: Frame 33458

SECTION K: Colonialism, Nationalism and Militarism, 1850–1914

Side One: Frame 36067

Universal Play Button

See Master Guide, page 217 for Section J, page 240 for Section K.

The Industrial Revolution

	Key Ideas	COPY MASTERS	ASSESSMENT
SECTION 1 The Beginnings of Industrialization *pp. 253–257*	*In Britain, changes in agriculture lay the foundations for the Industrial Revolution. Other factors—including ample resources, an expanding economy, and political stability—provide the conditions for the rapid growth of industry.*	**In-Depth Resources: Unit 3** • **Guided Reading,** p. 1 • **Primary Source:** from "The Opening of the Liverpool to Manchester Railway," p. 8 • **History Makers:** James Watt, p. 15	P E *Section 1 Assessment,* p. 257 *Formal Assessment* • Section Quiz, p. 113 *Alternative Assessment Book* • Standards for Evaluating a Product or Performance
SECTION 2 Patterns of Change: Industrialization Case Study: Manchester *pp. 258–262*	*Industrialization transforms British society: cities grow, work patterns change, and a middle class emerges. The city of Manchester becomes a notable example of the benefits and drawbacks of the new industrial age.*	**In-Depth Resources: Unit 3** • **Guided Reading,** p. 2 • **Geography Application:** British Population Moves to the Cities, p. 6 • **Primary Source:** Testimony on Child Labor in Britain, p. 9 • **Literature:** from *Mary Barton,* p. 12	P E *Section 2 Assessment,* p. 262 *Formal Assessment* • Section Quiz, p. 114 *Alternative Assessment Book* • Standards for Evaluating a Cooperative Activity
SECTION 3 Industrialization Spreads *pp. 263–266*	*Industrial technologies travel from Britain to America, causing an industrial boom in the United States. Industrialization also spreads to continental Europe and contributes to the rise of imperialism.*	**In-Depth Resources: Unit 3** • **Guided Reading,** p. 3 • **Primary Source:** "Life in a New England Factory," from *Voice of Industry,* p. 10	P E *Section 3 Assessment,* p. 266 *Formal Assessment* • Section Quiz, p. 115 *Alternative Assessment Book* • Standards for Evaluating a Cooperative Activity
SECTION 4 An Age of Reform *pp. 267–273*	*Industrialization provokes positive and negative reactions in society. Some philosophers extol the virtues of free market capitalism, while others promote socialism, unionization, and a variety of reform movements designed to blunt the harsh effects of industrialism.*	**In-Depth Resources: Unit 3** • **Guided Reading,** p. 4 • **Skillbuilder Practice:** Developing Historical Perspective, p. 5 • **Primary Source:** from *The Wealth of Nations,* p. 11 • **History Makers:** Saint-Simon, p. 16 • **Connections Across Time and Cultures:** Enlightenment Ideals in an Industrial Age, p. 17	P E *Section 4 Assessment,* p. 272 *Formal Assessment* • Section Quiz, p. 116 *Alternative Assessment Book* • Standards for Evaluating a Cooperative Activity
CHAPTER RESOURCES	**Chapter Overview** *During the 1800s, Britain, the United States, and some European countries undergo a rapid process of industrialization. The Industrial Revolution creates great wealth but also great social and economic inequality, prompting a backlash of reform.*	*Telescoping the Times* • Chapter Summary, pp. 37–39 *Planning for Block Schedules*	P E *Chapter Assessment,* pp. 274–275 *Chapter Activities,* p. 275 *Formal Assessment* • Chapter Test, forms A and B, pp. 117–122 💾 *Test Generator* *Alternative Assessment Book*

TECHNOLOGY

 Warm-Up Transparency 9

 Patterns of Interaction:
Technology Transforms an Age

 INTERNET RESOURCES
www.mlworldhistory.com

 Warm-Up Transparency 9

 Geography Transparencies
• G25 The Industrial Revolution in Great Britain, 1850

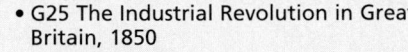 *World Art and Cultures Transparencies*
• AT54 *Arkwright's Cotton Mill at Comford, Derbyshire, England*

 Electronic Library of Primary Sources
• from "Child Labor in the Mines"
• "The Sentencing of the Luddites"

 Warm-Up Transparency 9

 World Art and Cultures Transparencies
• AT55 Monet's *Saint Lazare Train Station, the Normandy Train*

 Electronic Library of Primary Sources
• from *A New England Girlhood*

 INTERNET RESOURCES
www.mlworldhistory.com

 Warm-Up Transparency 9

 Critical Thinking Transparencies
• CT61 Visual Summary
• CT25 Industrialists and Reformers

 Electronic Library of Primary Sources
• from *The Communist Manifesto*
• from "How I Served My Apprenticeship"

 INTERNET RESOURCES
www.mlworldhistory.com

 Chapter Summaries on Audiocassette in English and Spanish

 INTERNET RESOURCES
www.mlworldhistory.com

 Block Scheduling (90 MINUTES)

Day 1
Section 1, pp. 253–257
Section Assessment, p. 257
Day 2
Section 2, pp. 258–262
 COOPERATIVE ACTIVITY
Debating the Effects of Industrialization, p. 260 (Teacher's Edition)

Section Assessment, p. 258
Day 3
Section 3, pp. 263–266
 COOPERATIVE ACTIVITY
Planning an Industrial Fair, p. 265 (Teacher's Edition)

Section Assessment, p. 266

Day 4
Section 4, pp. 267–273
 COOPERATIVE ACTIVITY
Playing an Identity Game, p. 271 (Teacher's Edition)

Section Assessment, p. 272

Chapter Assessment, pp. 274–275

Yearly Pacing *Chapter 9 Total:* 4 days *Yearly Total:* 85 days

 Planning for Block Schedules

Customizing for Special Needs

Students Acquiring English

 Access for Students Acquiring English
• **Guided Reading** for Sections 1–4 (Spanish), pp. 102–105
• **Chapter Summary** (Spanish), pp. 99–101
• **Skillbuilder Practice** (Spanish), p. 106
• **Geography Application** (Spanish), p. 107

 Spanish Reading Study Guide pp. 95–104

 Chapter Summaries on Audiocassette in English and Spanish

 Patterns of Interaction: Technology Transforms an Age (Spanish track)

Less Proficient Readers

 In-Depth Resources: Unit 3
• **Guided Reading** for Sections 1–4, pp. 1–4
• **Skillbuilder Practice** Developing Historical Perspective, p. 5
• **Geography Application** British Population Moves to the Cities, p. 6

 Telescoping the Times
• Chapter Summary, pp. 37–39

 Reading Study Guide
• pp. 95–104

 Chapter Summaries on Audiocassette

Gifted and Talented Students

 In-Depth Resources: Unit 3

Primary Sources:
• from "The Opening of the Liverpool to Manchester Railway," p. 8
• Testimony on Child Labor in Britain, p. 9
• "Life in a New England Factory," from *Voice of Industry*, p. 10
• from *The Wealth of Nations*, p. 11

History Makers
• James Watt, p. 15
• Saint-Simon, p. 16

Connections to Literature READINGS FOR STUDENTS

 In-Depth Resources: Unit 3
Literature: from *Mary Barton*, p. 12

Enrichment Reading
• **Forrest, Anthony**
The Pandora Secret
New York: Hill, 1982

In 1804, inventor Robert Fulton leaves France to continue his work on a "plunging" boat for the British Admiralty. This exciting story of the first submarine is rich in period detail.

• **Moore, Ruth Nulton**
In Search of Liberty
Scottdale, PA: Herald, 1983

This memorable story traces the path of a Liberty penny through 200 years of American history.

 = Pupil's Edition   = Overhead Transparency   = Software   = Video

 = Copy Master   = CD-ROM   = Audiocassette   = Internet

The Industrial Revolution, 1700–1900

Accessing Prior Knowledge

- Ask students what they know about railroads. Ask them if any of their family members have ever worked in a factory.

Making Inferences and Predicting

- After students have surveyed the captions and pictures on these two pages, ask them what they think working conditions were like for people at this time.

- After students have looked at the pictures and captions on page 251, ask them to predict what workers might do in response to difficult working conditions.

Geography Connection

Ask students to look at the map of the United States on page 250.

- In what region of the United States were there no railroads? *The West.*

- In what direction were the railroads likely to expand? *Westward.*

The Industrial Revolution, 1700–1900

PREVIEWING THEMES

Science & Technology
From the spinning jenny to the locomotive train, there was an explosion of inventions and technological advances. These improvements paved the way for the Industrial Revolution.

Empire Building
The global power balance shifted after the Industrial Revolution. This shift occurred because industrialized nations dominated the rest of the world.

Economics
The Industrial Revolution transformed economic systems. In part, this was because nations dramatically changed the way they produced and distributed goods.

INTERNET CONNECTION
Visit us at **www.mlworldhistory.com** to learn more about the Industrial Revolution.

EUROPE AND THE U.S. IN THE 1800s

— U.S. Railroads 1840

Hudson Bay

CANADA

0 — 1,000 Miles
0 — 2,000 Kilometers

New York
Washington D.C.
St Louis

UNITED STATES OF AMERICA

New Orleans

Gulf of Mexico

PACIFIC OCEAN

Caribbean Sea

Locomotives began to crisscross the eastern **United States** in the **1840s.** At that time, train tracks started to connect some American cities. Railroads enabled raw materials and finished goods to move back and forth between mines, factories, cities, and ports.

250

GEOGRAPHY THEMES

Movement

Ask students to reread the captions on the map to identify examples of the movement of goods and ideas during the Industrial Revolution. One means of transporting goods is shown—the locomotive. Other means of transportation were developed during the 19th century, often making use of steam engines. Ask students to speculate about how the development of new means of transportation might have expedited movement of people and products during the 1800s. Further, you might ask students to speculate about the effect this increased efficiency might have had on the pace of life in the 19th century.

Human/Environment Interaction

Point out to students that industrialization brought about changes in the way people interacted with their environment. Have students discuss what some of those changes were and how the environment and human life were affected as a result. Mention that industrialization consumed large quantities of resources that had to be extracted from the earth, extended transportation networks (such as shipping routes and railroads), and produced pollution. Many of these changes harmed the environment and eventually became problems for human life as well.

ADDITIONAL RESOURCES

Books for the Teacher

- Burchell, Samuel C. *Age of Progress.* New York: Time-Life, 1966.

- Stearns, Peter N., and John H. Hinshaw. *The ABC-CLIO World History Companion to the Industrial Revolution.* Santa Barbara, Calif.: ABC-CLIO, 1996.

Books for the Student

- Addy, John. *Coal and Iron Community in the Industrial Revolution.* White Plains, N.Y.: Longman, 1978.

- Bland, Celia. *The Mechanical Age: The Industrial Revolution in England.* New York: Facts on File, 1995.

- Macaulay, David. *Mill.* Boston: Houghton, 1983.

- Tann, Jennifer. *Children at Work.* London: Batsford, 1981. Child labor in Great Britain, late 1700s to 1900.

Videos

- *Coal, Blood, and Iron.* Coronet/ MTI, 1991. 800-321-3106. Coal sets the Industrial Revolution ablaze.

- *The Luddites.* Social Studies School Service, 1992. 800-421-4246. Violent resistance to new technology.

Software

- *The Industrial Revolution.* CD-ROM. Society for Visual Education, 1994. 800-829-1900.

As industrialization swept across the countries of Western Europe in the **19th century,** workers began to organize. They did so in order to defend their interests against those of the factory owners. Here workers in **Germany** meet before a strike in order to plan their strategy.

British workers are shown here laboring in terrible smoke and heat. They are "drawing the retorts"—that is, releasing heat from the furnaces. The place shown is the Great Gas Light Establishment in Brick Lane in **London** in the early **1800s.**

251

HISTORY THROUGH ART

Great Gas Light Establishment, Brick Lane, London

This scene shows British workers laboring in difficult conditions to produce coke oven gas, or coal gas, which was made by roasting coal. As the coal turned into coke, various gases were released. Coke oven gas was used for illumination in England. The conditions shown in this picture bring to mind the English poet William Blake's description of England's "dark satanic mills," or factories, in his poem *Milton* (1809).

Blake's was one of many critical voices raised in England in the late 18th and early 19th centuries against the dire consequences of the Industrial Revolution. Blake and William Wordsworth, among other writers of the time, worried about the impact of
industrialization on the English landscape, rural villages, and the lives of workers in factories.

Interpreting the Art What other scenes or images does this painting suggest? Does this illustration suggest an inferno? Might this scene be a proletarian version of the scenes of hell that are frequently depicted in Western art?

Interact *with* History

This Interact with History feature motivates students by inviting them to speculate about what they would do to change their situation in a dangerous factory setting. As they imagine themselves confronting these conditions, students will analyze the issues, explore their options, and become decision makers.

Purpose

• to set the stage for studying the Industrial Revolution

• to help students understand some of the causes and effects of the Industrial Revolution

• to help students make connections with the people and events they will study in this chapter

Teaching Strategy

Thinking Critically After students have imagined themselves in the situation described on this page, have them answer the key question and give reasons for their decision.

EXAMINING *the* ISSUES

Following are suggestions for addressing each bulleted question.

① Ask students if they have ever had a job and, if so, what it was about the job that they liked least.

② Have students speculate about the reasons for the conditions described here and how they might be changed.

③ Have students brainstorm solutions to the problem of getting out of a bad situation.

Making Connections Ask students to summarize the characteristics of revolution that they have learned about from their study of the American and French revolutions. Tell them to think about the ways in which the Industrial Revolution is similar to and different from those earlier revolutions.

Interact *with* History

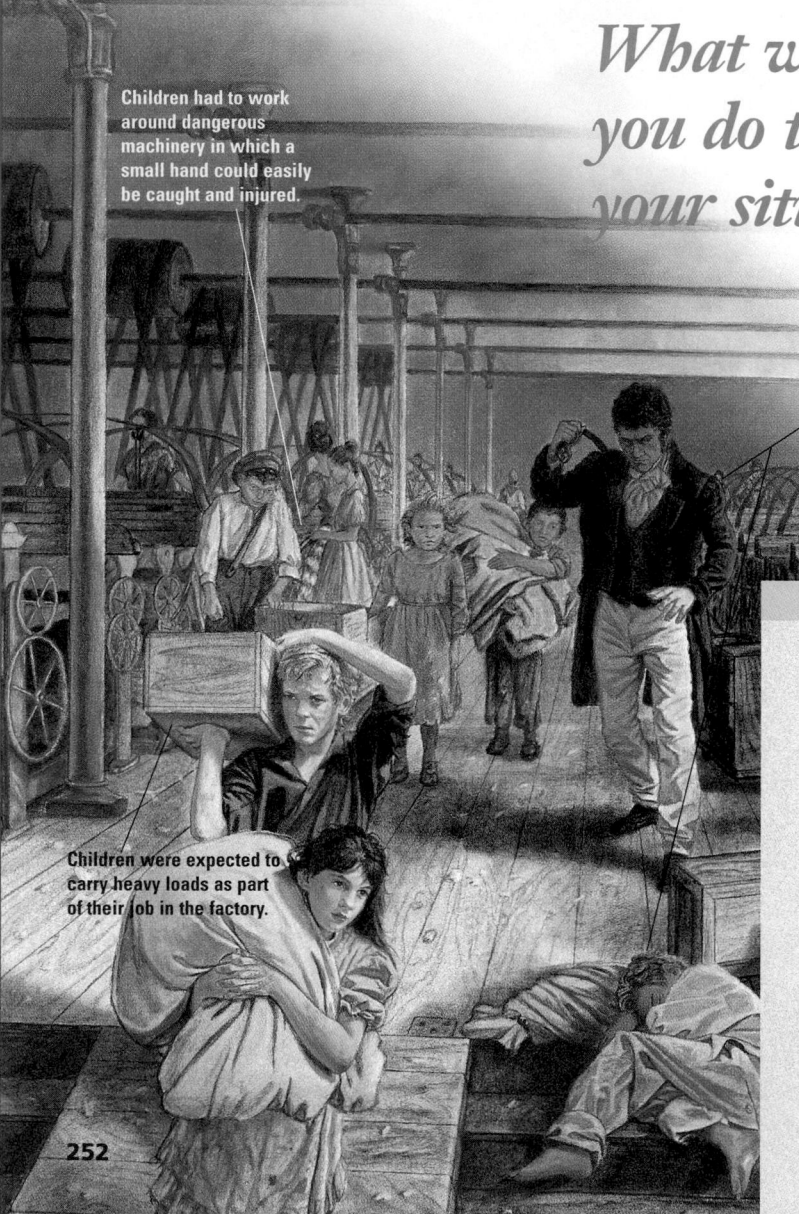

You are a 15-year-old living in England where the Industrial Revolution has spurred the growth of thousands of factories. Cheap labor is in great demand. Like millions of other teenagers, you do not go to school. Instead you work in a factory six days a week, 14 hours a day. The small pay you receive is needed to help support your family. You trudge to work before dawn every day and work until after sundown. The dangerous machines injure your fellow workers. Minding the machines is exhausting, dirty, and dangerous. Inside the factory the air is foul, and it is so dark it is hard to see.

What would you do to change your situation?

Children had to work around dangerous machinery in which a small hand could easily be caught and injured.

Adult overseers sometimes whipped exhausted children in order to keep them awake during their long, 14-hour days.

Children were expected to carry heavy loads as part of their job in the factory.

252

EXAMINING *the* ISSUES

• What factory conditions concern you the most?

• Would you attempt to change conditions in the factory?

• Would you join a union, go to school, or run away?

In small groups, discuss these questions; then share your conclusions with your class. In your discussions, think about how children live in pre-industrial and industrial societies all over the world.

As you read about the changes caused by industrialization, note how reform movements eventually improve conditions for all laborers, including children.

Follow Up

A feature on the chapter assessment will ask students to reevaluate their responses to the situation presented on this page.

① The Beginnings of Industrialization

TERMS & NAMES
- Industrial Revolution
- enclosure
- crop rotation
- industrialization
- factors of production
- factory
- entrepreneur

MAIN IDEA

The Industrial Revolution started in England and soon spread elsewhere.

WHY IT MATTERS NOW

The changes that began in Britain paved the way for modern industrial societies.

SETTING THE STAGE In the United States, France, and Latin America, political revolutions brought in new governments. A different type of revolution now transformed the way people did work. The **Industrial Revolution** refers to the greatly increased output of machine-made goods that began in England during the 18th century. Before the Industrial Revolution, people wove textiles by hand. Beginning in the middle 1700s, machines did this and other jobs as well. The Industrial Revolution started in England and soon spread to Continental Europe and North America.

The Industrial Revolution Begins

By 1700, small farms covered England's landscape. Wealthy landowners, however, bought up much of the land that village farmers had once worked. Beginning in the early 1700s, large landowners dramatically improved farming methods. These agricultural changes amounted to an agricultural revolution. They eventually paved the way for the Industrial Revolution.

The Agricultural Revolution After buying up the land of village farmers, wealthy landowners enclosed their land with fences or hedges. The increase in their landholdings enabled them to cultivate larger fields, using new seeding and harvesting methods. Within these larger fields, called **enclosures,** landowners experimented to discover more productive farming methods to boost crop yields. The enclosure movement had two important results. First, landowners experimented with new agricultural methods. Second, large landowners forced small farmers to become tenant farmers or to give up farming and move to the cities.

Jethro Tull was one of the first of these scientific farmers. He saw that the usual way of sowing seed by scattering it across the ground was wasteful. Many of the seeds failed to take root. He solved this problem with an invention called the seed drill in about 1701. The seed drill allowed farmers to sow seeds in well-spaced rows at specific depths. A larger share of the seed germinated, boosting crop yields.

Crop Rotation The process of **crop rotation** proved to be one of the best developments of the scientific farmers. The process improved upon older methods of crop rotation, such as the medieval three-field system. One year, for example, a farmer might plant a field with wheat, which exhausted soil nutrients. The next year he planted a root crop, such as turnips, to restore nutrients. This might be followed in turn by barley, then clover.

Livestock breeders improved their methods, too. In the 1700s, for example, Robert Bakewell increased his mutton output by allowing only his best sheep to breed. Other farmers followed Bakewell's lead. Between 1700 and 1786 the average weight for lambs climbed from 18 to 50 pounds.

A. Possible Answer
Enclosure resulted in experiments with new agricultural methods, and it caused many small farmers to move to the cities. Crop rotation produced increased yields.

THINK THROUGH HISTORY
A. Recognizing Effects What were some of the effects of enclosure and crop rotation?

Unresolved*Problems*

Feeding a Growing Population
Charles Townsend was a landowner in England. He encouraged the use of a four-crop rotation system using turnips, grain, and clover. These crops were used to feed humans and animals. The technique was so successful that Townsend gained the nickname "Turnip."

Changes in farming practices resulted in more and cheaper food. For example, in 1700 each English farmer produced enough food for 1.7 people. By 1800 that farmer could produce enough food for 2.5 people.

See Epilogue, p. 595.

The Industrial Revolution **253**

SECTION 1 RESOURCES

PRINT RESOURCES

IN-DEPTH RESOURCES: UNIT 3
Guided Reading, p. 1
Primary Source: from "The Opening of the Liverpool to Manchester Railway," p. 8
History Makers: James Watt, p. 15

ACCESS FOR STUDENTS ACQUIRING ENGLISH
Guided Reading (Spanish), p. 102

FORMAL ASSESSMENT
Section Quiz, p. 113

ALTERNATIVE ASSESSMENT BOOK

TECHNOLOGY RESOURCES

VIDEO *Patterns of Interaction: Technology Transforms An Age*

INTERNET www.mlworldhistory.com

Section 1 Overview

OBJECTIVES

① To explain the beginnings of industrialization in Britain.

② To describe key inventions that furthered the Industrial Revolution.

SKILLBUILDER
- Interpreting graphs, p. 256

CRITICAL THINKING
- Recognizing effects, pp. 253, 254
- Making inferences, pp. 254, 257
- Synthesizing, pp. 255, 257
- Hypothesizing, p. 255
- Summarizing, p. 256

FOCUS

5-Minute Warm-Up

▶ *Clarifying*
To help students understand the range of inventions in this period, have them answer the following questions.

1. Read "Spotlight on Inventions in America" on page 257. Of the four bulleted inventions mentioned in the feature, which represented revolutions in communications?

2. Which of the four represented a revolution in agriculture? Which a revolution in manufacturing?

WARM-UP TRANSPARENCY 9

OBJECTIVE ① INSTRUCT

The Industrial Revolution Begins

▶ *Key Ideas*
- Improvements in farming methods in the 1700s boost crop yields and lead to enclosed lands.
- Many small farmers lose their land, move to the city, and become urban workers.
- Britain possesses ideal conditions for the growth of industry.

IN-DEPTH RESOURCES: UNIT 3
Guided Reading, p. 1

ACCESS FOR STUDENTS ACQUIRING ENGLISH
Guided Reading (Spanish), p. 102

MORE ABOUT . . .
The Business of War

Warfare in the early 1800s actually helped promote British business. Although British trade with Europe declined during the Napoleonic Wars, British victories gained the country new colonies and new markets. The British navy ruled the seas, making shipping safe for British merchants. French troops even marched into Russia wearing English-made overcoats!

Viewing the Video

Show *Technology Transforms an Age: The Industrial and Electronic Revolutions* to explore the global impact of inventions in the past and today.

• The first segment of the video traces the origins of the Industrial Revolution and its effect on global relations.

• The second segment investigates how technology is creating opportunities for the worldwide exchange of information and ideas.

Using the *Teacher's Resource Book* as a guide, discuss how technology affects students' lives; compare the innovations explored in the video with other inventions in history; and enrich the lesson with primary-source and visual-literacy activities included in the resource book.

PATTERNS OF INTERACTION
Technology Transforms an Age: The Industrial and Electronic Revolutions
Videocassette: Tape 3

These improvements in farming that began in the early 1700s made up an agricultural revolution. As food supplies increased and living conditions improved, England's population mushroomed. An increasing population boosted the demand for food and goods. As farmers lost their land to large enclosed farms, many became factory workers.

Britain's Advantages Why did the Industrial Revolution begin in England? In addition to a large population of workers, the small island country had extensive natural resources. And **industrialization**—the process of developing machine production of goods—required such resources. These natural resources included 1) water power and coal to fuel the new machines; 2) iron ore to construct machines, tools, and buildings; 3) rivers for inland transportation; 4) harbors from which its merchant ships set sail.

Economic Strength and Political Stability In addition to its natural resources, Britain had an expanding economy to support industrialization. Businesspeople invested in the manufacture of new inventions. Britain's highly developed banking system also contributed to the country's industrialization. People were encouraged by the availability of bank loans to invest in new machinery and expand their operations. Growing overseas trade, economic prosperity, and a climate of progress contributed to the increased demand for goods.

Britain's political stability gave the country a tremendous advantage over its neighbors. Though Britain took part in many wars during the 1700s, none of these struggles occurred on British soil. Furthermore, their military and political successes gave the British a positive attitude. Parliament also passed laws that protected business and helped expansion. Other countries had some of these advantages. However, Britain had all the **factors of production.** These were the resources needed to produce goods and services that the Industrial Revolution required. They included land, labor, and capital (or wealth).

GlobalImpact : Revolutions in Technology

Technology in the Textile Industry

The Industrial Revolution that began in Britain was spurred by a revolution in technology. This is most obvious in the textile industry where inventions in the late 1700s transformed the manufacture of cloth. These developments, in turn, had an impact on the rest of the world. For example, England's cotton came from plantations in the American South, where cotton production skyrocketed from 1790 to 1810 in response to demand from the textile mills of England.

John Kay's flying shuttle speedily carried threads of yarn back and forth when the weaver pulled a handle. The flying shuttle greatly increased the productivity of weavers.

James Hargreaves's spinning jenny dramatically increased the output of spinners. It helped them to keep pace with the weavers.

254 Chapter 9

TEACHING OPTION **BLOCK SCHEDULING**

VIDEO ACTIVITY

CLASS TIME 20 MINUTES

Task: Students will use the Global Impact video to increase their understanding of the importance of the steam engine in the development of industrialization and transportation.

Materials Needed: Have students view the video for the Global Impact, *TechnologyTransforms an Age: The Industrial and Electronic Revolutions.*

More information about the steam engine is also available on pages 256–257 of the text.

Activity: Using information from the video and their own prior knowledge, groups of students will brainstorm a list of some of the specific machines that were powered by steam engines.

Conclusion: Have the groups of students compare their lists with one another. What else besides steam might be used to power factory machines? How else might boats be powered? What about locomotives?

 VIDEO
Technology Transforms an Age: The Industrial and Electronic Revolutions

Inventions Spur Technological Advances

In an explosion of creativity, inventions now revolutionized industry. Britain's textile industry clothed the world in wool, linen, and cotton. This industry was the first to be transformed. Cloth merchants boosted their profits by speeding up the process by which spinners and weavers made cloth.

Major Inventions in the Textile Industry By 1800, several major inventions had modernized the cotton industry. One invention led to another. In 1733, a machinist named John Kay made a shuttle that sped back and forth on wheels. This flying shuttle, a boat-shaped piece of wood to which yarn was attached, doubled the work a weaver could do in a day.

Because spinners could not keep up with these speedy weavers, a cash prize attracted contestants to produce a better spinning machine. Around 1764, a textile worker named James Hargreaves invented a spinning wheel he named after his daughter. Hargreaves's spinning jenny allowed one spinner to work eight threads at a time.

At first, textile workers operated the flying shuttle and the spinning jenny by hand. Richard Arkwright invented the water frame in 1769. The machine used the water-power from rapid streams to drive spinning wheels.

In 1779, Samuel Crompton combined features of the spinning jenny and the water frame to produce the spinning mule. The spinning mule made thread that was stronger, finer, and more consistent than earlier spinning machines. Run by water-power, Edmund Cartwright's power loom sped up weaving after its invention in 1787.

The water frame, the spinning mule, and the power loom were bulky and expensive machines. They took the work of spinning and weaving out of the house. Wealthy textile merchants set up the machines in large buildings called **factories.** At first,

Background
The spinning mule was so named because, just as a mule is the off-spring of a horse and donkey, this machine was the offspring of two inventions.

The first factories were built to house spinning and weaving machines in the textile industry and to keep the processes secret. Such factories were built close to rivers and streams, which provided a source of energy.

All work, even cotton spinning, is noble; work is alone noble.
—Scottish writer Thomas Carlyle in 1843

Patterns of Interaction

Inventions in the textile industry started in Britain and brought about the Industrial Revolution. This revolution soon spread to other countries in Europe and the United States. The process of industrialization is still spreading around the world, especially in Third World countries. A similar technological revolution is occurring in today's world of electronics. The telephone, television, and (more recently) the computer and the Internet are transforming the spread of information around the world.

VIDEO *Technology Transforms An Age: The Industrial and Electronic Revolutions*

Connect *to* History

Synthesizing Technological innovation and industrialization took place in the textile industry during the Industrial Revolution. How might these forces have provided a model for other industries?
SEE SKILLBUILDER HANDBOOK, PAGE 665

Connect *to* Today

Hypothesizing How might the textile industry be affected by new technology, including the computer?

The Industrial Revolution **255**

Inventions Spur Technological Advances

OBJECTIVE ② INSTRUCT

▶ *Key Ideas*
- Key inventions revolutionize industry during the 1700s and 1800s.
- The textile industry is the first to benefit, with the invention of machines to produce cotton cloth.
- Transportation expands with the invention of the steam engine and the construction of canals, roads, and railroads.

IN-DEPTH RESOURCES: UNIT 3
History Maker: James Watt, p. 15
Primary Source: from "The Opening of the Liverpool to Manchester Railway," p. 8

CRITICAL THINKING ACTIVITY
CLASS TIME: 15 MINUTES

Summarizing
Have students make a chart like the one below and list major inventions or improvements in each category.

Textiles	Transport
Flying shuttle	Steam engine

Connect *to* History

Synthesizing Possible Answer:
Many of the techniques of production and processes of standardization were applicable to other industries as the Industrial Revolution developed. This can be seen, for example, in the improvements in transportation, in which the steam engine was adapted to a number of different methods of transportation, including boats and railroads.

Connect *to* Today

Hypothesizing
Computer technology will probably streamline the textile industry and reduce the number of jobs for unskilled workers. Students may wish to do some research to find out about the latest techniques and technologies used in the textile industry, much of which is now automated.

THINK THROUGH HISTORY
D. Summarizing
What were the major inventions in the textile industry?
D. Possible Answer
Flying shuttle; spinning jenny; water frame; spinning mule; factory.

MORE ABOUT . . .
The Cotton Gin

Eli Whitney's cotton gin made Southern planters rich, but not the inventor. The gin was easy to make and therefore easy to pirate. Whitney later pioneered the concept of interchangeable parts, building muskets from machine-made components.

History from Visuals

British Cotton Consumption
Interpreting the Graph Point out to students that the years increase by increments of ten, or decades, across the bottom of the chart. Also mention that the scale on the left increases by increments of 100,000 metric tons.

Extension Activity Have students speculate about why cotton consumption might have fallen off between 1860 and 1870. *One possible cause might be the American Civil War, which affected both cotton production and cotton consumption.*

SKILLBUILDER Answers
1. 1850–1860.
2. 1810–1820 and 1860–1870.

MORE ABOUT . . .
Roads

In the late 1700s, British roads were worse than they had been 1,500 years earlier under Roman rule. Rain and mud often made roads impassable. Men were known to drown in potholes. In one region, an inland lighthouse was built to guide travelers over treacherous roads.

---

the new factories needed waterpower, so they were built near sources of water such as rivers and streams:

A VOICE FROM THE PAST
. . . A great number of streams . . . furnish water-power adequate to turn many hundred mills: they afford the element of water, indispensable for scouring, bleaching, printing, dyeing, and other processes of manufacture: and when collected in their larger channels, or employed to feed canals, they supply a superior inland navigation, so important for the transit of raw materials and merchandise.

EDWARD BAINS, *The History of Cotton Manufacture in Great Britain* (1835)

British Cotton Consumption

New inventions led to a big increase in the production and consumption of textiles, including cotton. The consumption of cotton rose dramatically in Britain during the 1800s. The following chart shows the increase in cotton consumption as measured in thousands of metric tons for each decade of the century.

Source: Historical Statistics of the United States

SKILLBUILDER: Interpreting Graphs
1. In what decade did the steepest increase in cotton consumption in Britain take place?
2. In what two decades did the consumption of cotton level off or slightly decrease?

England's cotton came from plantations in the American South in the 1790s. Removing seeds from the raw cotton by hand was hard work. In 1793, an American inventor named Eli Whitney invented a machine to speed the chore. His cotton gin multiplied the amount of cotton that could be cleaned. American cotton production skyrocketed from 1.5 million pounds in 1790 to 85 million pounds in 1810.

Improvements in Transportation Progress in the textile industry spurred other industrial improvements. The first such development, the steam engine, stemmed from the search for a cheap, convenient source of power. The earliest steam engine was used in mining as early as 1705. But this early model gobbled great quantities of fuel, making it expensive to run.

James Watt, a mathematical instrument maker at the University of Glasgow in Scotland, thought about the problem for two years. In 1765, Watt figured out a way to make the steam engine work faster and more efficiently while burning less fuel. In 1774, Watt joined with a businessman named Matthew Boulton. This **entrepreneur** (AHN·truh·pruh·NUR)—a person who organizes, manages, and takes on the risks of a business—paid Watt a salary and encouraged him to build better engines.

Water Transportation Steam could also be used to propel boats. An American inventor named Robert Fulton ordered a steam engine from Boulton and Watt. After its first successful trip in 1807, Fulton's steamboat, the *Clermont*, ferried passengers up and down New York's Hudson River.

In England, water transportation improved with the creation of a network of canals, or human-made waterways. By the mid-1800s, 4,250 miles of inland channels slashed the cost of transporting raw materials.

Road Transportation British roads improved, too, thanks largely to the efforts of John McAdam, a Scottish engineer. Working in the early 1800s, McAdam equipped roadbeds with a layer of large stones for drainage. On top, he placed a carefully smoothed layer of crushed rock. Even in rainy weather heavy wagons could travel over the new "macadam" roads without sinking in mud.

Private investors formed companies that built roads and then operated them for profit. People called the new roads turnpikes because travelers had to stop at tollgates (turnstiles or turnpikes) to pay a toll before traveling farther.

The Railway Age Begins Steam-driven machinery propelled English factories in the late 1700s. A steam engine on wheels—the railroad locomotive—drove English industry after 1820.

256 Chapter 9

Modern Industry Have students recall the factors that helped Britain establish itself as the world's first industrial power. Then have students do research on economies that have prospered in the modern age. In 1997, the Geneva World Economic Forum listed the world's most competitive economies. Singapore topped the list. It was followed in order by Hong Kong, the United States, Canada, New Zealand, Switzerland, and Great Britain. Have students compare the reasons for economic success then and now. Have they changed?

Science The steam engine as developed by James Watt helped to revolutionize industry and transportation. Ask pairs or small groups of students to research the invention to determine the scientific principles on which it operated. Invite them to draw a diagram to illustrate those principles, and to discuss their findings in class. Or they might research Robert Fulton's steamboat the *Clermont,* which was powered by steam. They might consult encyclopedia articles on James Watt or Robert Fulton, as well as biographies. Articles and books on the invention of the steam engine will also prove useful.

In 1804, an English engineer named Richard Trevithick won a bet of several thousand dollars. He did this by hauling ten tons of iron over nearly ten miles of track in a steam-driven locomotive. Other British engineers soon built improved versions of Trevithick's locomotive. One of these early railroad engineers was George Stephenson. He had gained a solid reputation by building some 20 engines for mine operators in northern England. In 1821, Stephenson began work on the world's first railroad line. It was to run 27 miles from the Yorkshire coalfields to the port of Stockton on the North Sea. In 1825, the railroad opened. It used four locomotives that Stephenson had designed and built.

The Liverpool-Manchester Railroad News of this success quickly spread throughout Britain. The entrepreneurs of northern England wanted a railroad line to connect the port of Liverpool with the inland city of Manchester. The track was laid. In 1829 trials were held to choose the best locomotive for use on the new line. Five engines entered the competition. None could compare with the *Rocket*, designed by Stephenson and his son. Smoke poured from its tall smokestack and its two pistons pumped to and fro as they drove the front wheels. The *Rocket* hauled a 13-ton load at an unheard-of speed—more than 24 miles per hour. The Liverpool-Manchester Railway opened officially in 1830. It was an immediate success.

Railroads Revolutionize Life in Britain
First, railroads spurred industrial growth by giving manufacturers a cheap way to transport materials and finished products. Second, the railroad boom created hundreds of thousands of new jobs for both railroad workers and miners. These miners provided iron for the tracks and coal for the steam engines. Third, the railroads boosted England's agricultural and fishing industries, which could transport their products to distant cities. Finally, by making travel easier, railroads encouraged country people to take distant city jobs. Also, railroads lured city dwellers to resorts in the countryside. Like a locomotive racing across the country, the Industrial Revolution brought rapid and unsettling changes to people's lives.

E. Possible Answer Canals cut the cost of transporting materials; improved roads fostered the movement of heavy wagons; railroads linked manufacturing cities with raw materials.

THINK THROUGH HISTORY
E. Synthesizing How did improvements in transportation promote industrialization in Britain?

SPOTLIGHT ON

Inventions in America
Across the Atlantic in the United States, American inventors worked at making railroad travel more comfortable. They invented, for example, adjustable upholstered seats that converted into couches so that everyone could travel first class.

American inventors also revolutionized agriculture, manufacturing, and communications:

- Cyrus McCormick's reaper, invented in 1831, boosted American wheat production.

- In 1837, a New England painter named Samuel F. B. Morse first sent electrical signals over a telegraph.

- In 1851, I. M. Singer improved the sewing machine by inventing a foot treadle.

- Scottish-born inventor Alexander Graham Bell patented the telephone in 1876.

SPOTLIGHT ON
Inventions in America
Have students research one of the inventions listed here. Then have them explain basic facts about the invention and its inventor's life.

ASSESS & RETEACH

Section 1 Assessment
Have students work individually to answer the questions. Then invite students to read the letters they wrote for item 4 in class.

Section Quiz
FORMAL ASSESSMENT
Section Quiz, p. 113

Reteaching Activity
CLASS TIME: 10 MINUTES

Use the Guided Reading worksheet for Section 1 to review the main ideas of the section.

IN-DEPTH RESOURCES: UNIT 3
Guided Reading, p. 1

CLOSE ACTIVITY

CLASS TIME: 10 MINUTES

Making a Cause-Effect Diagram
Have students create a diagram or chart that shows the causes and effects of the agricultural revolution and Industrial Revolution. Then have students compare their charts.

	Causes	Effects
Agricultural Revolution		
Industrial Revolution		

Section ① Assessment

1. TERMS & NAMES
Identify
- Industrial Revolution
- enclosure
- crop rotation
- industrialization
- factors of production
- factory
- entrepreneur

2. TAKING NOTES
Create a two-column chart like the one below that lists four natural resources needed for industrialization and how each is used.

Natural Resource	Use
1. coal	
2.	
3.	
4.	

3. MAKING INFERENCES
What effect did entrepreneurs have upon the Industrial Revolution?

THINK ABOUT
- new technological developments
- business opportunities
- increase in prosperity

4. THEME ACTIVITY

Science and Technology
Write a letter as a British government official during the Industrial Revolution. Write to a government official in a non-industrial nation about how the railroad has changed Britain.

The Industrial Revolution **257**

ANSWERS

1. TERMS & NAMES
Industrial Revolution, p. 253

enclosure, p. 253

crop rotation, p. 253

industrialization, p. 254

factors of production, p. 254

factory, p. 255

entrepreneur, p. 256

2. TAKING NOTES
Coal—fuel new machines; iron ore—construct new machines, tools, buildings; rivers—inland transportation; good harbors—docking stations for merchant ships.

3. MAKING INFERENCES
Possible Responses:
Entrepreneurs helped to promote the Industrial Revolution, because they were willing to risk their capital by investing it in new inventions and enterprises.

4. THEME ACTIVITY
Standards for Evaluation
An effective letter should . . .
- introduce several changes in British society
- be written in a thoughtful, coherent, and engaging manner
- give a clear sense of place and time

Section 2 Overview

OBJECTIVES

① To describe the social and economic effects of industrialization.

② To show how Manchester exemplified the new industrial city.

SKILLBUILDERS
- Interpreting charts, p. 260
- Interpreting graphs, p. 261

CRITICAL THINKING
- Drawing conclusions, pp. 259, 261
- Summarizing, p. 259
- Analyzing issues, p. 262
- Analyzing themes, p. 262

FOCUS

5-Minute Warm-Up

▶ **Evaluating**
To better understand the life of a child laborer, have students answer these questions.

1. Look at the feature on the day in the life of a child laborer on page 262. How long was William Cooper's work day?

2. What hours did Cooper's sister work?

 WARM-UP TRANSPARENCY 9

OBJECTIVE ① INSTRUCT

Industrialization Changes Ways of Life

▶ **Key Ideas**
- Industrialization leads to economic growth and urbanization.
- Industry generates wealth for some but hardship for others.
- As divisions between rich and poor grow, class tensions escalate.

 IN-DEPTH RESOURCES: UNIT 3
Guided Reading, p. 2

 ACCESS FOR STUDENTS ACQUIRING ENGLISH
Guided Reading (Spanish), p. 103

 ② Industrialization

PATTERNS OF CHANGE CASE STUDY: Manchester

MAIN IDEA	**WHY IT MATTERS NOW**
The factory system changed the way people lived and worked, introducing a variety of problems.	The difficult process of industrialization is being repeated in many less-developed countries today.

SETTING THE STAGE The Industrial Revolution eventually led to a better quality of life for most people. Yet the change to machine production also caused immense human suffering. In Britain, the Industrial Revolution proved to be a mixed blessing.

Industrialization Changes Ways of Life

The pace of industrialization quickened in Britain. By the 1800s more people could afford to heat their homes with coal from Wales and to dine on Scottish beef. They wore better clothing, too, woven on power looms in England's industrial cities. These cities soon swelled with workers. However, other people suffered from industrialization.

Growth of Industrial Cities For centuries, most Europeans had lived in rural areas. After 1800, the balance shifted toward cities. The growth of the factory system—manufacturing goods in a central location—brought waves of jobseekers to cities and towns. Between 1800 and 1850, the number of European cities boasting more than 100,000 inhabitants rose from 22 to 47. Most of Europe's urban areas at least doubled in population. This period was one of **urbanization**—city building and the movement of people to cities. Some cities, such as Glasgow and Berlin, tripled or even quadrupled in size.

Factories developed in clusters because entrepreneurs built them near sources of energy. Major new industrial centers sprang up between the coal-rich area of southern Wales and the Clyde River valley in Scotland. The biggest of these centers developed in England.

Britain's capital, London, was the country's most important city. Containing twice as many people as its closest rival (Paris), London became Europe's largest city. It had a population of about 1 million people by 1800. During the 1800s London's population exploded, providing a vast labor pool and market for new industry.

Newer cities challenged London's industrial leadership. Birmingham and Sheffield became iron-smelting centers. Leeds and Manchester dominated textile manufacturing. Along with the port of Liverpool, Manchester formed the center of Britain's bustling cotton industry. During the 1800s, Manchester experienced rapid growth. In 1760, the population of this market town was around 45,000. By 1850, it had swelled to 300,000 people.

As cities grew all over Europe, people crowded into tenements and row houses such as these in London.

Living Conditions No plans, no sanitary codes, and no building codes controlled the growth of England's cities. They lacked adequate housing, education, and police protection for the people who poured in from the countryside seeking jobs. Most of the unpaved streets had no drains and collected heaps of garbage. Workers lived in dark, dirty shelters, whole families crowding into one bedroom.

SECTION 2 RESOURCES

PRINT RESOURCES

 IN-DEPTH RESOURCES: UNIT 3
Guided Reading, p. 2
Geography Application: British Population Moves to the Cities, p. 6
Primary Source: Testimony on Child Labor in Britain, p. 9
Literature: from *Mary Barton*, p. 12

 ACCESS FOR STUDENTS ACQUIRING ENGLISH
Guided Reading (Spanish), p. 103
Geography Application (Spanish), p. 107

 FORMAL ASSESSMENT
Section Quiz, p. 114

TECHNOLOGY RESOURCES

 GEOGRAPHY TRANSPARENCIES
GT25 The Industrial Revolution in Great Britain, 1850

 WORLD ART AND CULTURES TRANSPARENCIES
AT54 *Arkwright's Cotton Mill*

 CD-ROM
Electronic Library of Primary Sources

 INTERNET www.mlworldhistory.com

Vocabulary
cholera: a deadly disease caused by bacteria that usually occur in contaminated drinking water.

Not surprisingly, sickness was widespread. Cholera epidemics regularly swept through the slums of Great Britain's industrial cities. In 1842, a British government study showed an average life span to be 17 years for working-class people in one large city, compared with 38 years in a nearby rural area.

Elizabeth Gaskell's *Mary Barton* (1848) is a work of fiction. Nonetheless, its realistic description of the dank cellar dwelling place of one family in a Manchester slum presents a startlingly accurate portrayal of urban life at the time:

A VOICE FROM THE PAST
You went down one step even from the foul area into the cellar in which a family of human beings lived. It was very dark inside. The window-panes many of them were broken and stuffed with rags . . . . the smell was so fetid [foul] as almost to knock the two men down . . . . they began to penetrate the thick darkness of the place, and to see three or four little children rolling on the damp, nay wet brick floor, through which the stagnant, filthy moisture of the street oozed up. . . .
ELIZABETH GASKELL, *Mary Barton*

Working Conditions Factory owners wanted to keep their machines running for as many hours a day as possible. As a result, the average worker spent 14 hours a day at the job, 6 days a week. Instead of changing with the seasons, the work was the same week after week, year after year. Workers had to keep up with the machines.

Industry also posed new dangers in work. Factories were seldom well-lit or clean. Machines injured workers in countless ways. A boiler might explode or a drive belt might catch the worker's arm. And there was no government program to provide aid in case of injury. The most dangerous conditions of all were found in the coal mines. Frequent accidents, damp conditions, and the constant breathing of coal dust made the average miner's life span ten years shorter than that of other workers.

Class Tensions Not everyone in the new cities lived miserably. Well-to-do merchants and factory owners built fancy homes in the suburbs. In addition, a new class began to emerge.

Though poverty gripped Britain's working classes, the Industrial Revolution created enormous amounts of money in the country. Most of this wealth lined the pockets of factory owners, shippers, and merchants. These wealthy people made up a growing **middle class**—a social class of skilled workers, professionals, businesspeople, and wealthy farmers.

The new middle class transformed the social structure of Great Britain. In the past, landowners and aristocrats occupied the top position in British society. With most of the wealth, they wielded the power. Now some factory owners, merchants, and investment bankers grew wealthier than the landowners and aristocrats.

Yet important social distinctions divided the two wealthy classes. Landowners looked down on those who had made their fortunes in the "vulgar" business world. Not until late in the 1800s were rich entrepreneurs considered the social equals of the lords of the countryside.

Gradually, a larger middle class—neither rich nor poor—emerged. This group included an upper middle class of government employees, doctors, lawyers, and managers of factories, mines, and shops. A lower middle class consisted of factory overseers and such skilled workers as toolmakers, mechanical drafters, and printers. These people enjoyed a comfortable standard of living.

During the years 1800 to 1850, however, poor workers saw little improvement in their own living and working conditions. Frustrated workers watched their livelihoods disappear as machines replaced them. In response, they smashed the machines they thought were putting them out of work. One group of such workers was called the Luddites. They were named after Ned Ludd. Ludd, probably a mythical English

THINK THROUGH HISTORY
A. Drawing Conclusions What was the impact of living and working conditions on workers?
A. Possible Answer Health was undermined; work was dangerous and could result in injuries.

B. Possible Answer An upper class made up of landowners and aristrocrats; an upper middle class made up of managers, merchants, government employees, doctors, lawyers; a lower middle class of factory overseers and skilled workers; working class.
THINK THROUGH HISTORY
B. Summarizing Describe the social classes in Britain.

Elizabeth Gaskell (1810–1865) was a British writer whose novels such as *Mary Barton* (1848) and *North and South* (1855) show a sympathy for the working class. *Cranford* (1853) deals with the life of a peaceful English village.

PATTERNS OF CHANGE 259

MORE ABOUT . . .
Urban Growth

In the 1700s, Britain was primarily a rural country. By 1851, however, more of the British people lived in cities than in the countryside. In 1901, the ratio of urban to rural population was 3 to 1. The population of London at that time was 4.5 million.

 IN-DEPTH RESOURCES: UNIT 3
Geography Application: British Population Moves to the Cities, p. 6

 GEOGRAPHY TRANSPARENCIES
GT25 The Industrial Revolution in Great Britain, 1850

 WORLD ART AND CULTURES TRANSPARENCIES
AT54 *Arkwright's Cotton Mill at Comford, Derbyshire, England*

MORE ABOUT . . .
Cholera

Polluted water was a major problem in British cities in the 1800s. In London, most drinking water came straight from the Thames River, which was filthy with sewage and industrial waste. In 1849, a cholera epidemic killed 400 Londoners a day.

TEACHING OPTIONS | **CONNECTIONS ACROSS THE CURRICULUM** | **MULTIPLE LEARNING STYLES**

Literature Elizabeth Gaskell's *Mary Barton* was an example of a literary style known as realism, which came into fashion during the 1800s. You might want to give students a copy of the literature selection from *Mary Barton*, which can be found in the Teacher's Resources for this chapter. Ask students to find works by Gaskell, Charles Dickens, William Makepeace Thackeray, or other realist writers of the time. Invite them to discuss the works and read passages in class.

 IN-DEPTH RESOURCES: UNIT 3
Literature: from *Mary Barton*, p. 12

Visual Learners: Creating a Political Cartoon Suggest that students create a political cartoon that highlights a condition or problem associated with the Industrial Revolution in Great Britain. Some problems they might choose to illustrate include the pollution of the air, the hierarchy of social classes, the dangerous conditions in the factories, and the crowded conditions in tenements. Cartoons should combine drawings and text. Remind students that political cartoons convey a message in humorous and thought-provoking ways.

Teacher's Edition 259

MORE ABOUT . . .
Luddites

The Luddites were angry not only about losing their jobs but also about the life changes forced on them by industrialization. Instead of working at home alongside their families, textile workers now had to labor under dehumanizing factory conditions. The term *Luddites* is still sometimes used to refer to people opposed to modern technology.

ELECTRONIC LIBRARY OF PRIMARY SOURCES
"The Sentencing of the Luddites"

History from Visuals

Patterns of Change: Industrialization

Interpreting the Chart Have students read the headings on the chart. Point out that the left column lists general areas or categories affected by industrialization and the right column provides specific examples. Ask students to try to come up with other categories that might be added to the chart. *Possible Responses: Rural areas, families, careers and occupations.*

Extension Activity Have students add one other specific example to each category on the chart, based on their reading of the text. *Possible Response: Size of Cities—New cities challenging London for influence.*

SKILLBUILDER Answers

1. The workers suffered the most; the middle class benefited the most.
2. Advantages: Industrialization made a new middle class prosperous; it created jobs and wealth, as well as better housing and healthier diets.
   Disadvantages: It contributed to harsh living and working conditions; it exploited workers.

---

laborer, was said to have destroyed weaving machinery around 1779. The Luddites attacked whole factories in northern England beginning in 1811, destroying labor-saving machinery. Outside the factories, mob disorder took the form of riots, mainly because of the poor living and working conditions of the workers.

Positive Effects of the Industrial Revolution Despite the problems that followed industrialization, the Industrial Revolution eventually had a number of positive effects. It created jobs for workers. It contributed to the wealth of the nation. It fostered technological progress and invention. It greatly increased the production of goods and raised the standard of living. Perhaps most important, it provided the hope of improvement in people's lives.

The Industrial Revolution produced a number of other benefits as well. These included healthier diets; better housing; and cheaper, mass-produced clothing. Because the Industrial Revolution created a demand for engineers as well as clerical and professional workers, it expanded educational opportunities.

The middle and upper classes prospered immediately from the Industrial Revolution. For the workers it took longer, but their lives gradually improved during the 1800s. Labor eventually won higher wages, shorter hours, and better working conditions.

PATTERNS OF CHANGE: Industrialization

Effects of Industrialization

Size of Cities	• Growth of factories, bringing job seekers to cities • Urban areas doubling, tripling, or quadrupling in size • Factories developing near sources of energy • Many new industrial cities specializing in certain industries
Living Conditions	• No sanitary codes or building controls • Lack of adequate housing, education, and police protection • Lack of running water and indoor plumbing • Frequent epidemics sweeping through slums • Eventually, better housing, healthier diets, and cheaper clothing
Working Conditions	• Industrialization creating new jobs for workers • Workers trying to keep pace with machines • Factories dirty and unsanitary • Workers running dangerous machines for long hours in unsafe conditions • Harsh and severe factory discipline • Eventually, higher wages, shorter hours, and better working conditions
Emerging Social Classes	• Growing middle class of factory owners, shippers, and merchants • Upper class of landowners and aristocrats resentful of rich middle class • Lower middle class of factory overseers and skilled workers • Workers overworked and underpaid • In general, a rising standard of living, with some groups excluded

SKILLBUILDER: Interpreting Charts
1. *Which social class benefited most and which suffered most from industrialization?*
2. *What were some of the advantages and disadvantages of industrialization?*

The long-term effects of the Industrial Revolution are still evident. Most people today in the industrialized countries can afford consumer goods that would have been considered luxuries fifty or a hundred years ago. Further, their living and working conditions are much improved over those of workers in the 19th century.

As the Industrial Revolution in Manchester demonstrated, economic success can unleash a variety of problems. Even today, the economic pressures of industrialization frequently lead to the overuse of natural resources and the abuse of the environment. The profits derived from industrialization, however, permit thoughtful governments to invest in urban improvements.

Task: Students will prepare position statements and debate the merits of the Industrial Revolution.

Purpose: To consider the economic, social, political, and environmental effects of industrialization.

Activity: Divide students into groups and assign each group a position in favor of or opposed to industrialization. Have groups research their position

and gather evidence that supports it. Have students prepare position statements. Have opposing groups debate.

 Building a Portfolio: Students may add their position statements to their portfolio, along with an explanation of the assignment.

ALTERNATIVE ASSESSMENT BOOK
Standards for Evaluating a Cooperative Activity

Standards for Evaluation
Position statements should . . .

• clearly state the issue being debated
• take a distinct position supported by facts and examples
• address opposing viewpoints directly and reasonably

The Mills of Manchester

Manchester's unique advantages made it a leading example of the new industrial city. This northern English town had ready access to water power. It also had available labor from the nearby countryside and an outlet to the sea at Liverpool.

"From this filthy sewer pure gold flows," wrote Alexis de Tocqueville (ah·lehk·SEE duh TOHK·vihl), the French writer, after he visited Manchester in 1835. Indeed, the industrial giant showed the best and worst of the Industrial Revolution. Manchester's rapid, unplanned growth made it a filthy sewer for the poor people who worked there. But gold certainly flowed toward the mill owners and the new middle class. Eventually, although not immediately, the working class saw their standard of living rise as well.

Manchester's businesspeople took pride in mastering each detail of the manufacturing process, working many hours and risking their own money. For their efforts, they pocketed high profits and erected gracious homes on the outskirts of town.

To provide the mill owners with their high profits, workers labored under terrible conditions. Children as young as six joined their parents in the factories. There, for six days a week, they toiled from 6 A.M. to 7 or 8 P.M., with only a half an hour for lunch and an hour for dinner. To keep the children awake, mill supervisors beat them. Tiny hands repaired broken threads in Manchester's spinning machines, replaced thread in the bobbins, or swept up cotton fluff. The dangerous machinery injured many children. The fluff filled their lungs and made them cough.

Until the first Factory Act passed in 1819, the British government exerted little control over child labor in Manchester and other factory cities. The act restricted working age and hours. For years after the act passed, young children still did heavy, dangerous work in Manchester's factories.

Putting so much industry into one place polluted the natural environment. The coal that powered factories and warmed houses blackened the air. Textile dyes and

C. Possible Answer Factory owners profited by being able to pay children low wages; families also benefited from the wages children earned.
THINK THROUGH HISTORY
C. Drawing Conclusions Whose interests did child labor serve?

An English engraving of 1876 shows a bird's-eye view of the city of Manchester during the Industrial Revolution.

Manchester's Growth

- 1801: 93,400
- 1831: 232,800
- 1871: 476,000

(y-axis: Population)

SKILLBUILDER: Interpreting Graphs
1. How many people did the city of Manchester gain between 1801 and 1831? How many did it gain between 1831 and 1871?
2. What does the engraving show were the effects of such rapid growth?

261

TEACHING OPTION

CONNECTIONS ACROSS TIME AND PLACE

Pollution Have students research the problem of environmental pollution during the Industrial Revolution and today. Have them discuss the issue, considering questions such as the following: Is pollution better or worse now? What new pollution dangers exist now that did not exist in the 1800s? During this discussion, have students fill in information on a chart like the one here.

Pollution: Then & Now	
Then	Now
Coal smoke	Car exhaust
Dyes & sewage in water	Chemicals in water

The Day of a Child Laborer, William Cooper

William Cooper began working in a textile factory at the age of ten. He had a sister who worked upstairs in the same factory. In 1832, Cooper was called to testify before a parliamentary committee about the conditions among child laborers in the textile industry. The following sketch of his day is based upon his testimony.

5 A.M.—The workday began. Cooper and his sister rose as early as 4:00 or 4:30 in the morning in order to get to the factory for the start of their workday at 5:00. Children usually grabbed their breakfast on the run.

12 noon—The children were given a 40-minute break for lunch. This was the only break they received during the whole course of the day.

3 P.M.—The children often became drowsy during the afternoon or evening hours. In order to keep them awake, adult overseers sometimes whipped the children.

6 P.M.—There was no break allowed for an evening meal. Children ate on the run. From 12:40 until 9:00 at night, the children worked without a break.

9 P.M.—William Cooper's day ended after an exhausting 16-hour shift at work.

11 P.M.—Cooper's sister worked another two hours even though she had to be back at work at 5:00 the next morning.

Unresolved *Problems*

Dangers to the Global Environment

After London experienced major cholera and typhus epidemics early in the 19th century, a sewer system was built to empty sewage into the Thames River. However, in the middle of the century, an environmental disaster occurred.

During the summer of 1858, sewage in the Thames turned the water murky brown. It smelled so bad that life on the riverfront was unbearable. Carloads of decaying fish from the polluted river added to the stink. The odor was so bad that Parliament order the window drapes to be soaked in lime chloride to make working in the rooms possible.

Finally, Parliament agreed on a plan to create a modern sewer system. That system discharged the sewage into the Thames beyond the city limits so that the sewage ended up in the North Sea.

See Epilogue, p. 591.

other wastes poisoned Manchester's Irwell River. The following description of the river was written by an eyewitness observer in 1862:

A VOICE FROM THE PAST
Steam boilers discharge into it their seething contents, and drains and sewers their fetid impurities; till at length it rolls on—here between tall dingy walls, there under precipices of red sandstone—considerably less a river than a flood of liquid manure.

HUGH MILLER, "Old Red Sandstone"

Manchester produced consumer goods and created wealth on a grand scale. Yet this unplanned industrial city also stood as a reminder of industrialization's dark side. In the 1800s, the industrialization that began in Great Britain spread to the United States and to continental Europe, as you will learn in Section 3.

Section 2 Assessment

1. TERMS & NAMES
Identify
• urbanization
• middle class

2. TAKING NOTES
Create a pyramid like the one below listing the social classes in industrial England. List the types of laborers and professionals included in each group.

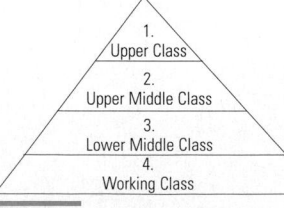

1. Upper Class
2. Upper Middle Class
3. Lower Middle Class
4. Working Class

3. ANALYZING ISSUES
How did industrialization contribute to city growth?

THINK ABOUT
• growth of industry
• creation of jobs
• the economic advantages of centralization

4. ANALYZING THEMES
Economics How might a factory owner have justified the harsh conditions in his factory?

THINK ABOUT
• class distinctions
• the spread of factories
• financial gains

262 CHAPTER 9

---

3 Industrialization Spreads

TERMS & NAMES
• corporation

MAIN IDEA

The industrialization that began in Great Britain spread to other parts of the world.

WHY IT MATTERS NOW

The Industrial Revolution set the stage for the growth of modern cities.

SETTING THE STAGE Britain's favorable location, geography, financial systems, political stability, and natural resources sparked its industrialization. British power-driven machinery began to mass-produce textiles and other goods at the end of the 1700s. Paying low wages to many workers, British merchants built the world's first factories. When these factories prospered, wealthy business leaders invented more labor-saving machines. They also built more factories, and eventually industrialized the country. The Industrial Revolution that began in Britain soon spread to other countries. They had similar conditions that made them ripe for industrialization.

Industrial Development in the United States

The United States possessed the same resources that allowed Britain to mechanize its industries and develop large-scale factories. America also had rushing rivers, rich deposits of coal and iron ore, and a supply of immigrant laborers. During the War of 1812, Britain blockaded the United States in an attempt to keep it from engaging in international trade. This blockade forced the young country to use its own resources to develop independent industries. Those industries would manufacture the goods the United States could no longer import.

Industrialization in the United States As in Britain, industrialization in the United States began in the textile industry. Eager to keep the secrets of industrialization to itself, Britain had forbidden engineers, mechanics, and toolmakers to leave the country. In 1789, however, a young British mill worker named Samuel Slater emigrated to the United States. There Slater built a spinning machine from memory and a partial design. The following year, Moses Brown opened the first factory in the United States to house Slater's machines in Pawtucket, Rhode Island. But the Pawtucket factory mass-produced only one part of finished cloth, the thread.

In 1813, Francis Cabot Lowell and four other investors revolutionized the American textile industry. They mechanized every stage in the manufacture of cloth. Their weaving factory in Waltham, Massachusetts, earned the partners enough money to fund a larger operation in another Massachusetts town. When Francis Lowell died, the remaining partners named the town after him. By the late 1820s, Lowell, Massachusetts, had become a booming manufacturing center and a model for other such towns.

Thousands of workers, mostly young single women, flocked from their rural homes to work as mill girls in factory towns like Lowell. To ensure proper behavior, the young women were watched closely inside and outside the factory. The mill girls toiled over 12 hours a day, six days a week, for

Background
The War of 1812 began over British interference with America's merchant ships. It ended in a draw between Britain and the United States.

These Massachusetts women of the mid-19th century are shown holding shuttles that were used during weaving.

263

SECTION 3 RESOURCES

PRINT RESOURCES

 IN-DEPTH RESOURCES: UNIT 3
Guided Reading, p. 3
Primary Source: "Life in a New England Factory," p. 10

 ACCESS FOR STUDENTS ACQUIRING ENGLISH
Guided Reading (Spanish), p. 104

FORMAL ASSESSMENT
Section Quiz, p. 115

ALTERNATIVE ASSESSMENT BOOK

TECHNOLOGY RESOURCES

 WORLD ART AND CULTURES TRANSPARENCIES
AT55 Monet's *Saint Lazare Train Station, the Normandy Train*

 CD-ROM
Electronic Library of Primary Sources

INTERNET www.mlworldhistory.com

Section 3 Overview

OBJECTIVES

① To describe industrial growth in the United States.

② To explain the spread of industry in Europe.

③ To identify the effects of industrialization on the rest of the world.

SKILLBUILDER
• Interpreting maps: region, movement, p. 264

CRITICAL THINKING
• Forming and supporting opinions, p. 264
• Analyzing causes, p. 265
• Clarifying, p. 266
• Recognizing bias, p. 266

FOCUS
5-Minute Warm-Up

▶ *Interpreting Maps*
Answering the following questions will help students understand the role of the railroads in the growth of the United States.

1. Look at the map on page 264. What was the total mileage of railroad track in 1840?

2. What was the total mileage in 1890?

🏛 *WARM-UP TRANSPARENCY 9*

OBJECTIVE ① INSTRUCT

Industrial Development in the United States

▶ *Key Ideas*
• Like Britain, the United States offers conditions favorable to the growth of industry.
• British machinery spawns an American textile industry.
• American industry expands rapidly in the late 1800s, fueled by the growth of railroads.

 IN-DEPTH RESOURCES: UNIT 3
Guided Reading, p. 3
Primary Source: "Life in a New England Factory," from *Voice of Industry*, p. 10

 ACCESS FOR STUDENTS ACQUIRING ENGLISH
Guided Reading (Spanish), p. 104

Early Railroads

The first trains, in the early 1800s, were drawn by horses; some even used sails to move by wind power. Early trains had no brakes, so passengers had to get out and pull the train to the stop. The trains also had no lights, so they couldn't travel at night. Single tracks meant that trains often had to wait on sidings for hours until other trains had passed.

WORLD ART AND CULTURES TRANSPARENCIES
AT55 Monet's *Saint Lazare Train Station, the Normandy Train*

History from Visuals

The Growth of the United States

Interpreting the Map Have students look at the two maps in order to figure out the increase in total trackage between 1840 and 1890. *205,334 miles.*

Extension Activity Ask students to name at least three states that were formed from the western part of the continent between 1840 and 1890. *Possible Responses: Texas, New Mexico, Arizona, California, Wyoming, Montana, Oregon.*

SKILLBUILDER Answers
1. East; Midwest.
2. East to West.

---

decent wages. For some young women, the mill job meant a welcome alternative to becoming a servant, often the only other job open to them:

A VOICE FROM THE PAST
Country girls were naturally independent, and the feeling that at this new work the few hours they had of everyday leisure were entirely their own was a satisfaction to them. They preferred it to going out as "hired help." It was like a young man's pleasure in entering upon business for himself. Girls had never tried that experiment before, and they liked it.
LUCY LARCOM, *A New England Girlhood*

Textiles led the way, but clothing manufacture and shoemaking also underwent mechanization. Especially in the Northeast, skilled workers and farmers had formerly worked at home. Now they labored in factories in towns and cities such as Waltham, Lowell, and Lawrence, Massachusetts.

Later Expansion of U.S. Industry There was a great deal of industrial growth in the Northeast in the early 1800s. Nonetheless, the United States remained primarily an agricultural nation until the Civil War ended in 1865. During the last third of the 1800s, however, the country experienced a technological boom. As in Britain, a number of causes contributed to this boom. These included a wealth of natural resources, among them oil, coal, and iron; a burst of inventions, such as the electric light bulb and the telephone; and a swelling urban population that consumed the new manufactured goods.

Also as in Britain, railroads played a major role in America's industrialization. Cities like Chicago and Minneapolis expanded rapidly during the late 1800s. This was due to their location along the nation's expanding railroad lines. Chicago's stockyards and Minneapolis's grain industries prospered by selling their products to the rest of the country.

Indeed, the railroads themselves proved to be a profitable business. By the end of the 1800s, a limited number of large, powerful companies controlled over two-thirds of the nation's railroad tracks. Businesses of all kinds began to merge as the railroads had. Smaller companies joined together to form a larger one.

Building large businesses like railroads required a great deal of money. To raise the money, entrepreneurs sold shares of stock. People who bought stock became

THINK THROUGH HISTORY
A. Forming and Supporting Opinions
Why did Lucy Larcom think mill work benefited young women?
A. Possible Answer Larcom believed that mill work offered women more free time and suited the independence of their country upbringing. She called mill work an "experiment" that girls liked.

Vocabulary
stock: a share in certain rights of ownership of a business.

The Growth of the United States

Railroad System, 1840

Total trackage: 2,818 miles

Railroad System, 1890

Total trackage: 208,152 miles

SKILLBUILDER: Interpreting Maps
1. **Region** *In what part of the country were the first railroads built?*
   By 1890, what other part of the country was densely covered by railroad tracks?
2. **Movement** *In what direction did the railroads help people move across the country?*

EXPLORING PRIMARY SOURCES

A Voice from the Past Lucy Larcom took up factory work as a young woman. She was well educated, and while working in the Lowell mills, she founded a literary journal. Eventually she became a teacher and journalist. Ask students what they think Lucy Larcom's attitude is toward factory work. *She says that she liked the life of working in the factory and preferred it to working as a servant.* Ask students how they think Lucy Larcom's life differed from that of most factory workers. *Possible Response: She managed to make a better life for herself.*

ELECTRONIC LIBRARY OF PRIMARY SOURCES
from *A New England Girlhood*

MULTIPLE LEARNING STYLES

Logical Mathematical Learners: Making a Graph Tell students that the number of miles of railroad track in the United States increased dramatically during the second half of the 1800s. Write the following years and figures on the board: 1840—3,000 miles; 1865—35,000 miles; 1890—200,000 miles. Have students do research to see if they can find railroad-track totals for other years during the period 1840–1890. Ask them to make a graph that shows these figures. Then ask students to speculate about the impact of this growth of railroads on the nation. How might the railroads have helped to unify the country?

part-owners of these businesses called corporations. A **corporation** is a business owned by stockholders who share in its profits but are not personally responsible for its debts. In the late 1800s large corporations such as Standard Oil (founded by John D. Rockefeller) and the Carnegie Steel Company (founded by Andrew Carnegie) sprang up. They sought to control every aspect of their own industries in order to make big profits.

Big business—the giants that controlled entire industries—also made big profits by cutting the cost of producing goods. While workers earned small wages for long hours at hard labor, stockholders earned high profits and corporate leaders made fortunes.

Industrialization Reaches Continental Europe

European businesses yearned to adopt the "British miracle," the result of Britain's profitable new methods of manufacturing goods. Yet the troubles sparked by the French Revolution and the Napoleonic wars had halted trade, interrupted communication, and caused inflation in some parts of the continent. European countries were absorbed in the French Revolution and the Napoleonic wars between 1789 and 1815. They watched the gap widen between themselves and Britain. Nonetheless, industrialization eventually reached continental Europe.

Beginnings in Belgium Belgium led Europe in adopting Britain's new technology. Belgium had rich deposits of iron and coal as well as fine waterways for transportation.

Samuel Slater had smuggled to the United States the design of a spinning machine. Like him, British skilled workers played a key role in carrying industrialization to Belgium. A Lancashire carpenter named William Cockerill made his way to Belgium in 1799. He carried secret plans for building spinning machinery. Cockerill's son John eventually built an enormous industrial enterprise in eastern Belgium. It produced machinery, steam engines, and railway locomotives. Carrying the latest British advances, more British workers came to work with Cockerill. Several then founded their own companies in Europe.

German workers labor in a steel mill in this 1875 painting by Adolph von Menzel.

Germany Industrializes Germany was a politically divided empire. Economic isolation and scattered resources hampered countrywide industrialization in the early 1800s. Instead, pockets of industrialization appeared, as in the coal-rich Ruhr Valley of west-central Germany. Beginning around 1835, Germany began to copy the British model. Germany imported British equipment and engineers. German manufacturers also sent their children to England to learn industrial management.

Most important, Germany built railroads that linked its growing manufacturing cities, such as Frankfurt, with the Ruhr Valley's coal and iron deposits. In 1858, a German economist wrote, "Railroads and machine shops, coal mines and iron foundries, spinneries and rolling mills seem to spring up out of the ground, and smokestacks sprout from the earth like mushrooms."

Germany's economic strength spurred its ability to develop as a military power. By the late 19th century, Germany had become both an industrial and a military giant.

Expansion Throughout Europe In the rest of Europe, as in Germany, industrialization during the early 1800s proceeded by region rather than by country. Even in countries where agriculture dominated, pockets of industrialization arose. For example, Bohemia developed its spinning industry. Spain's Catalonia processed more cotton than Belgium. Northern Italy mechanized its textile production, specializing in silk spinning. Serf labor ran factories in regions around Moscow and St. Petersburg.

In France, continual industrial growth occurred only after 1850, when the central government constructed railroads. These railroads created a thriving national market for new French products.

The Industrial Revolution **265**

THINK THROUGH HISTORY
B. Analyzing Causes What factors slowed industrialization in Germany?
B. Answer Germany was politically divided, economically isolated, and its resources were scattered.

OBJECTIVE **2** INSTRUCT

Industrialization Reaches Continental Europe

▶ *Key Ideas*
• At first, war and unrest in Europe delay the growth of industry.
• Belgium is the first country in Europe to industrialize, followed by Germany.
• Other parts of Europe begin to develop industry in the mid-1800s, though progress is slow in some areas.

CRITICAL THINKING ACTIVITY
CLASS TIME: 15 MINUTES

Making a Web
Have students fill out a web like the one below with factors that impeded the growth of industry in continental Europe.

French Revolution and wars — Obstacles to Industrial Growth — political disunity in Germany — social structure — geographic problems

TEACHING OPTION | BLOCK SCHEDULING — COOPERATIVE ACTIVITY: **Planning an Industrial Fair** — CLASS TIME 30 MINUTES

Task: Students will plan an industrial fair that compares the products of today with those on display at London's Great Exhibition of 1851.

Purpose: To compare and contrast industrial technologies of the 1800s with those of the present.

Activity: Tell students that London hosted the Great Exhibition in 1851 to showcase industry throughout the world. Have students research this exhibition. Then ask groups to plan another exhibition that places modern products and technologies alongside those of the 1800s. Have them write a description of the exhibits.

Building a Portfolio: Students may wish to add a description of their contribution to this project, along with a summary, to their portfolio.

ALTERNATIVE ASSESSMENT BOOK Standards for Evaluating a Cooperative Activity

Standards for Evaluation Summaries should . . .

• explain why the group's featured technologies or products were chosen
• make connections between the Industrial Revolution and the industries of today

Teacher's Edition **265**

<table>
<tr>
<td>

OBJECTIVE 3 INSTRUCT

Worldwide Impact of Industrialization

▶ **Key Ideas**
- The Industrial Revolution widens the gap between more-developed and less-developed nations.
- Industrialized countries exploit overseas colonies for resources and markets.
- Over time, standards of living rise in the industrial nations.

---

*Global*Impact

Industrialism Spreads to Egypt

Egypt was one of the few countries outside Europe and the United States to attempt industrialization in the 1800s. Others included Japan and Mexico, both in the late 1800s. Have students research these three cases and report on how they compared.

ASSESS & RETEACH

Section 3 Assessment
Have pairs of students work on the questions and share their answers with another pair of students.

Section Quiz
📋 ***FORMAL ASSESSMENT***
Section Quiz, p. 115

Reteaching Activity
CLASS TIME: 15 MINUTES

To help students understand the effects of industrialization, review the diagrams they have made for item 2 in the section assessment.

CLOSE ACTIVITY

CLASS TIME: 15 MINUTES

Writing an Editorial
Have students imagine that they are newspaper editors in the late 1800s. Ask them to write an editorial explaining the connection between industrialization and imperialism and to express an opinion on the issue. Tell them to support their view with evidence.

266   Chapter 9

</td>
<td>

For a variety of reasons, many European countries did not industrialize. In some nations, the social structure delayed the adoption of new methods of production. The accidents of geography held back others. In Austria-Hungary and Spain, transportation posed great obstacles. Austria-Hungary's mountains defeated railroad builders. Spain lacked both good roads and waterways for canals.

Worldwide Impact of Industrialization

The Industrial Revolution shifted the world balance of power. It promoted competition between industrialized nations and increased poverty in less developed nations.

*Global*Impact

Industrialism Spreads to Egypt

When an Ottoman officer named Muhammad Ali (1769–1849) took power in Egypt, the new ruler sought to propel his country into the industrialized world. Muhammad Ali reformed Egypt's government and improved communications. He also established cotton mills, a glass factory, and a sugar refinery.

To earn the money required to purchase European goods and services, Muhammad Ali also advanced the development of commercial agriculture. During his rule, landlords forced peasants to become tenant farmers and grow cash crops for European markets. The modernizing and industrializing of Egypt was often done at the expense of the peasants.

Rise of Global Inequality Industrialization widened the gap between industrialized and non-industrialized countries, even while it strengthened their economic ties. To keep factories running and workers fed, industrialized countries required a steady supply of raw materials from less developed lands. In turn, industrialized countries viewed poor countries as markets for their manufactured products. A large inequality developed between the industrialized West and the rest of the world.

Britain led in exploiting its overseas colonies for resources and markets. Soon other European countries, the United States, Russia, and Japan followed Britain's lead, seizing colonies for their economic resources. Imperialism, the policy of extending one country's rule over many other lands, gave even more power and wealth to these already wealthy nations. Imperialism was born out of the cycle of industrialization, the development of new markets around the world, and the need for resources to supply the factories of Europe. (See Chapter 11.)

Transformation of Society Between 1700 and 1900, revolutions in agriculture, production, transportation, and communication changed the lives of people in Western Europe and the United States. Industrialization gave Europe tremendous economic power. Much of Europe was gaining the capability to produce many goods faster and more cheaply. In contrast, the economies of Asia and Africa were still based on agriculture and small workshops.

The industrialization that took place in the 1700s and 1800s revolutionized every aspect of society, from daily life to life expectancy. Despite the hardships early urban workers suffered, population, health, and wealth eventually rose dramatically in all industrialized countries. The development of a middle class created great opportunities for education and democratic participation. Greater democratic participation, in turn, fueled a powerful movement for social reform.

THINK THROUGH HISTORY
C. Clarifying Why did imperialism grow out of industrialization?
C. Possible Answer Industrialized countries depended on less-developed lands for raw materials and as markets for manufactured goods. They seized colonies for their resources and markets.

<table>
<tr><td colspan="4" align="center">Section **3** Assessment</td></tr>
<tr>
<td>**1. TERMS & NAMES**
Identify
• corporation</td>
<td>**2. TAKING NOTES**
Using a web diagram like the one below, show the effects of industrialization on the world.

</td>
<td>**3. RECOGNIZING BIAS**
Go back to the quote from Lucy Larcom on page 644. Do you think her feelings about working in the mill are typical? Why or why not?

THINK ABOUT
• her experiences in a mill
• her possible bias</td>
<td>**4. THEME ACTIVITY**
Empire Building Draw a political cartoon that could have been used by the British government. It should show their sense of their own superiority over non-industrialized nations that they planned to colonize.</td>
</tr>
</table>

266 Chapter 9

</td>
</tr>
</table>

ANSWERS

1. TERMS & NAMES
corporation, p. 265

2. TAKING NOTES
Strengthened economic ties between countries; widened gap between industrialized and non-industrialized countries; promoted colonization

3. RECOGNIZING BIAS
Students who answer yes will note that she seems to be

speaking as a young woman from New England who chose to work in the mill and was pleased with the experience. Students who answer no may point out that since she recorded her thoughts and experiences in a memoir or journal, she may have been more independent than most young women.

4. THEME ACTIVITY
Standards for Evaluation
An effective cartoon should meet the following criteria:
• shows a British point of view
• demonstrates knowledge of industrialization
• includes a variety of detail that enriches the cartoon

4 An Age of Reforms

TERMS & NAMES
- laissez faire
- Adam Smith
- capitalism
- utilitarianism
- socialism
- Karl Marx
- communism
- union
- collective bargaining
- strike

MAIN IDEA

The Industrial Revolution led to economic, social, and political reforms.

WHY IT MATTERS NOW

Many modern social welfare programs developed during this period.

SETTING THE STAGE In industrialized countries in the 1800s, many business leaders believed that progress opened a gap between rich and poor. These leaders cautioned governments to stay out of business and economic affairs. Reformers, however, felt that governments should play an active role in bettering conditions for the poor.

The Philosophers of Industrialization

The term **laissez faire** (LEHS·ay·FAIR) refers to the economic policy of letting owners of industry and business set working conditions without interference. That policy favors a free market unregulated by the government. The term comes from a French phrase that means "let do," and by extension, "let people do as they please."

Laissez-faire Economics Laissez faire stemmed from French economic philosophers of the 18th-century Enlightenment. They criticized the idea that nations grow wealthy by placing heavy tariffs on foreign goods. In fact, they argued, government regulations only interfered with the production of wealth. These philosophers believed that if the government allowed free trade—the flow of commerce in the world market without government regulation—the economy would prosper.

Adam Smith, a professor at the University of Glasgow, Scotland, defended the idea of a free economy, or free markets, in his 1776 book *The Wealth of Nations.* According to Smith, economic liberty guaranteed economic progress. Smith claimed that government need not interfere in the economy.

The Ideas of Malthus and Ricardo Economists Thomas Malthus and David Ricardo supported Smith's basic ideas. Like Smith, they believed that natural laws governed economic life. Their important ideas were the foundation of laissez-faire capitalism. **Capitalism** is an economic system in which money is invested in business ventures with the goal of making a profit. These ideas helped bring about the Industrial Revolution.

In *An Essay on the Principle of Population,* written in 1798, Thomas Malthus argued that population tended to increase more rapidly than the food supply. Without wars and epidemics to kill off the extra people, most were destined to be poor and miserable. The predictions of Malthus seemed to be coming true in the 1840s.

David Ricardo, a wealthy stockbroker, took Malthus's theory one step further in his book, *Principles of Political Economy and Taxation* (1817). Like Malthus, Ricardo believed that a permanent underclass would always be poor. In a market system, if there are many workers and abundant resources, then labor and resources are cheap. If there

Background
Ricardo stated the "iron law of wages." He argued that because of population growth wages would be just high enough to keep workers from starving.

HISTORY MAKERS

Adam Smith
1723–1790

In his book *The Wealth of Nations,* Smith argued that if individuals freely followed their own self-interest, the world would be an orderly and progressive place. After all, sellers made money by producing things that other people wanted to buy. Buyers spent money for the things they wanted most. In such a marketplace, Smith thought, social harmony would result without any government direction, "as if by an invisible hand." Smith's ideas were central to the development of capitalism.

Smith applied an invisible hand of his own. When the economist died, people discovered that he had secretly donated large chunks of his income to charities.

The Industrial Revolution **267**

SECTION 4 RESOURCES

PRINT RESOURCES

 IN-DEPTH RESOURCES: UNIT 3
Guided Reading, p. 4
Skillbuilder Practice: Developing Historical Perspective, p. 5
Primary Source: from *The Wealth of Nations,* p. 11
History Makers: Saint-Simon, p. 16
Connections Across Time and Cultures: Enlightenment Ideals in an Industrial Age, p. 17

 ACCESS FOR STUDENTS ACQUIRING ENGLISH
Guided Reading (Spanish), p. 105
Skillbuilder Practice (Spanish), p. 106

 FORMAL ASSESSMENT
Section Quiz, p. 116

TECHNOLOGY RESOURCES

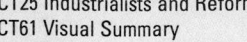 **CRITICAL THINKING TRANSPARENCIES**
CT25 Industrialists and Reformers
CT61 Visual Summary

CD-ROM
Electronic Library of Primary Sources

INTERNET www.mlworldhistory.com

Section 4 Overview

OBJECTIVES

1. To identify ideas and thinkers that supported industrialization.

2. To explain the origins and main concepts of socialism.

3. To examine unionization and legislative reform.

4. To describe other reform movements of the 1800s.

SKILLBUILDER
- Interpreting charts, p. 270

CRITICAL THINKING
- Making inferences, pp. 268, 272
- Clarifying, p. 268
- Summarizing, pp. 269, 271
- Identifying problems, p. 272
- Analyzing themes, p. 272
- Contrasting, p. 273

FOCUS

5-Minute Warm-Up

Making Inferences
To help students understand the origins of capitalism, have them answer the following questions.

1. Read the History Maker on Adam Smith on page 267. What was Smith's attitude toward government intervention in business?

2. Does Smith's economic theory assume an optimistic or pessimistic view of human nature?

 WARM-UP TRANSPARENCY 9

OBJECTIVE ① INSTRUCT

The Philosophers of Industrialization

▶ *Key Ideas*
- Laissez-faire thinkers support a free market and oppose government regulation.
- Economists Adam Smith, Thomas Malthus, and David Ricardo argue that natural law governs economic life.

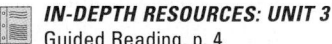 **IN-DEPTH RESOURCES: UNIT 3**
Guided Reading, p. 4

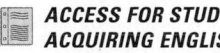 **ACCESS FOR STUDENTS ACQUIRING ENGLISH**
Guided Reading (Spanish), p. 105

(See page 267.)

Smith opposed government interference in business on principle, including efforts to help business. For example, he opposed the mercantilist policy of supporting industry through tariffs and other restrictions on competition. Ask students how trying to help business might be as harmful as trying to restrict it.

 IN-DEPTH RESOURCES: UNIT 3
Primary Source: from *The Wealth of Nations,* p. 11
Connections Across Time and Cultures: Enlightenment Ideals in an Industrial Age, p. 17

OBJECTIVE **2** INSTRUCT

Rise of Socialism

▶ *Key Ideas*
• Some thinkers oppose laissez-faire policies and favor government efforts to improve people's lives.
• Utilitarian thinkers Jeremy Bentham and John Stuart Mill argue that government should promote the general welfare.
• Socialists and Marxists propose state controls to achieve social and economic equality.

 IN-DEPTH RESOURCES: UNIT 3
History Maker: Saint-Simon, p. 16

---

are few workers and scarce resources, then they are expensive. Ricardo believed that wages would be forced down as population increased.

Laissez-faire thinkers such as Smith, Malthus, and Ricardo opposed government efforts to help poor workers. They thought that creating minimum wage laws and better working conditions would upset the free market system, lower profits, and undermine the production of wealth in society.

Rise of Socialism

In contrast to laissez-faire philosophy, which advised governments to leave business alone, other theorists believed that governments should intervene. These thinkers believed that wealthy people or the government must take action to improve people's lives. The French writer Alexis de Tocqueville gave a warning:

A VOICE FROM THE PAST
Consider what is happening among the working classes. . . . Do you not see spreading among them, little by little, opinions and ideas that aim not to overturn such and such a ministry, or such laws, or such a government, but society itself, to shake it to the foundations upon which it now rests?
ALEXIS DE TOCQUEVILLE, 1848 speech

Jeremy Bentham's skeleton, dressed in Bentham's clothes and topped off by a wax head, is preserved in a wooden cabinet at University College, London.

268 Chapter 9

Utilitarianism Modifying the ideas of Adam Smith, an English philosopher named Jeremy Bentham introduced the philosophy of **utilitarianism.** Bentham wrote his most influential works in the late 1700s. He argued that people should judge ideas, institutions, and actions on the basis of their utility, or usefulness. He argued that the government should try to promote the greatest good for the greatest number of people. A government policy was only useful if it promoted this goal. Bentham argued that in general the individual should be free to pursue his or her own advantage without interference from the state.

John Stuart Mill, a philosopher and economist, led the utilitarian movement in the 1800s. Mill came to question unregulated capitalism. He believed it was wrong that workers should lead deprived lives that sometimes bordered on starvation. Mill wished to help ordinary working people with policies that would lead to a more equal division of profits. He also favored a cooperative system of agriculture and women's rights, including the right to vote. Mill called for the government to do away with great differences in wealth. Utilitarians also pushed for reforms in the legal and prison systems and in education.

Utopian Ideas Other reformers took an even more active approach. Shocked by the misery and poverty of the working class, a British factory owner named Robert Owen improved working conditions for his employees. Near his cotton mill in New Lanark, Scotland, Owen built houses, which he rented at low rates. He prohibited children under ten from working in the mills and provided free schooling.

Then, in 1824, he traveled to the United States. He founded a cooperative community in New Harmony, Indiana, in 1825. He intended this community to be a utopia, or perfect living place. New Harmony only lasted three years. However, it inspired the founding of other communities.

Socialism and Marxism French reformers such as Charles Fourier (FUR·ee·AY), Saint-Simon (san see·MOHN), and others sought to offset the effects of industrialization with a new kind of economic system called socialism. In **socialism,** the factors of production are owned by the public and operate for the welfare of all. Socialism grew out of an optimistic view of human nature, a belief in progress, and a concern for social justice.

THINK THROUGH HISTORY
A. Making Inferences
Economics came to be called the "dismal [gloomy] science," in part because of the ideas of Malthus and Ricardo. Why might their ideas have earned this phrase?
A. Possible Answer
Malthus's ideas about overpopulation, wars, and epidemics, and Ricardo's "iron law of wages" were pessimistic concepts.

THINK THROUGH HISTORY
B. Clarifying How did Mill want to change the economic system?
B. Possible Answer He wanted to equalize the distribution of wealth and give the poor a break; he favored a cooperative system of agriculture.

Background
The word *utopia* comes from the name for an imaginary island in a book of the same name written by Sir Thomas More. It means "no place" in Greek. More's *Utopia* (1516) is a political essay that discusses life under an ideal government.

CONNECTIONS ACROSS TIME AND PLACE

Socialism Have students do research to find out about countries that have adopted socialist or Marxist forms of government since these ideas first appeared in the 1800s. You might direct students to the democratic socialist countries of Scandinavia or to such communist or formerly communist

countries as Russia, China, Vietnam, and the nations of eastern Europe. Have students choose one of these countries and report to the class on the way socialism was implemented and what happened as a result. Ask students if any countries in the world today still practice socialism.

CUSTOMIZING FOR SPECIAL NEEDS

Gifted and Talented Students: Utopian Communities Invite students to find out more about utopian communities, either in Britain or the United States. Have students report to the class on a particular community or group of communities and the principles

that inspired them. For example, they might examine New Harmony, Indiana, or Brook Farm, near Boston. Encourage students to show pictures or a diagram of the community, if possible. Have students explain what happened to the community, and why.

Socialists argued that the government should actively plan the economy rather than depending on free-market capitalism to do the job. They argued that government control of factories, mines, railroads, and other key industries would abolish poverty and promote equality. Public ownership, they believed, would help the workers, who were at the mercy of greedy employers.

The Communist Manifesto The writings of a German journalist named **Karl Marx** introduced the world to a radical type of socialism called Marxism. Marx and Friedrich Engels, a German whose father owned a textile mill in Manchester, outlined their ideas in a 23-page pamphlet called *The Communist Manifesto*. In their manifesto, Marx and Engels argued that human societies have always been divided into warring classes. In their own time, these were the middle-class "haves" or employers, called the bourgeoisie (BUR·zhwah·ZEE), and the "have-nots" or workers, called the proletariat (PROH·lih·TAIR·ee·iht). While the wealthy controlled the means of producing goods, the poor performed backbreaking labor under terrible conditions. This situation resulted in conflict:

A VOICE FROM THE PAST
Freeman and slave, patrician and plebeian, lord and serf, guild-master and journeyman, in a word, oppressor and oppressed, stood in constant opposition to one another, carried on an uninterrupted, now hidden, now open fight, a fight that each time ended, either in a revolutionary reconstitution of society at large, or in the common ruin of the contending classes.

KARL MARX AND FRIEDRICH ENGELS, *The Communist Manifesto* (1848)

According to Marx and Engels, the Industrial Revolution had enriched the wealthy and impoverished the poor. The two writers predicted that the workers would overthrow the owners: "The proletarians have nothing to lose but their chains. They have a world to win. Workingmen of all countries, unite."

The Future According to Marx Marx believed that the capitalist system, which produced the Industrial Revolution, would eventually destroy itself in the following way. Factories would drive small artisans out of business, leaving a small number of manufacturers to control all the wealth. The large proletariat would revolt, seize the factories and mills from the capitalists, and produce what society needed. Workers, sharing in the profits, would bring about economic equality for all people. The workers would control the government in a "dictatorship of the proletariat." After a period of cooperative living and education, the state or government would wither away as a classless society developed.

Marx called this final phase pure communism. Marx described **communism** as a form of complete socialism in which the means of production—all land, mines, factories, railroads, and businesses—would be owned by the people. Private property would in effect cease to exist. All goods and services would be shared equally.

Published in 1848, *The Communist Manifesto* produced few short-term results. Though widespread revolts shook Europe during 1848 and 1849, Europe's leaders eventually put down the uprisings. Only after the turn of the century did the fiery Marxist pamphlet produce explosive results. In the 1900s, Marxism inspired revolutionaries such as Russia's Lenin, China's Mao Zedong, Vietnam's Ho Chi Minh, and Cuba's Fidel Castro. These revolutionary leaders adapted Marx's beliefs and arguments to their own specific situations and needs.

In their pamphlet, Marx and Engels condemned the inequalities of early industrial economies. Yet several of Marx's and Engels's predictions have since proved wrong.

HISTORY MAKERS

Karl Marx
1818–1883
Karl Marx studied philosophy at the University of Berlin before he turned to journalism and economics. In 1849, Marx joined the flood of radicals who fled continental Europe for England. He had declared in *The Communist Manifesto* that "the working men have no country."

Marx's theories of socialism and the inevitable revolt of the working class made him very little money. He earned a meager living as a journalist. His wealthy coauthor and fellow German, Friedrich Engels, gave Marx financial aid.

THINK THROUGH HISTORY
C. Summarizing
What were the ideas of Marx and Engels concerning relations between the owners and the working class?
C. Possible Answer Marx and Engels believed the working class and the owners were natural enemies.

HISTORY MAKERS
Karl Marx

Though a revolutionary, Marx disliked crowds and avoided demonstrations. He was said to be arrogant in debate and uncomfortable before mass audiences. He remained poor almost on principle, yet accepted the financial support of his friend Friedrich Engels. Suggest to students that they read more about Marx and discuss his life in class.

 ELECTRONIC LIBRARY OF PRIMARY SOURCES
from *The Communist Manifesto*

MORE ABOUT . . .
Revolutionary Upheaval

The most successful workers' revolt of the 1800s occurred in Paris in 1871. Calling for an end to unfair wages and working conditions, workers seized Paris and set up a people's government, called the Paris Commune. Although Marx supported this revolt, the workers were not communist-inspired. The Commune lasted just two months, then was crushed by French troops.

Explaining the Skill Using historical perspective means evaluating a time in history based on the conditions that existed then instead of judging by what we know now. For example, given Marxism's record of totalitarianism and economic failure in the 20th century, some students might initially wonder why people believed that the theories of Karl Marx could improve their lives. However, knowing about the difficult conditions experienced by many workers during the Industrial Revolution can help students realize Marxism's appeal at the time.

Applying the Skill: *A Voice from the Past*
Ask students to reread "A Voice from the Past," then ask them the following questions:

1. What was the relationship between different social classes, according to Marx and Engels?

2. What was the end result of their relationship?

3. Do the terms *oppressor* and *oppressed* seem to adequately define all social relationships today?

 IN-DEPTH RESOURCES: UNIT 3
Skillbuilder Practice: Developing Historical Perspective, p. 5

Capitalism vs. Marxism

Interpreting the Chart Have students read the title and headings and explain what the chart compares. *Ideas of capitalism and Marxism.* Point out that the chart is a list of ideas that do not necessarily match up from one column to the other.

Extension Activity Ask students how capitalism and Marxism differ in their idea of progress. *In capitalism, progress occurs when people pursue their self-interest. In Marxism, it occurs when the state is destroyed and a classless society emerges.*

SKILLBUILDER Answers

1. Intense class struggle; workers exploited by employers; labor of workers creates profit.

2. Answers will vary. Students might mention the breakup of the Soviet Union and economic reform in China as signs of the decline of Marxist ideas. Capitalist societies, on the other hand, seem to be prospering.

OBJECTIVE 3 INSTRUCT

Unionization and Legislative Reform

▶ **Key Ideas**

• Workers organize unions to raise wages and improve conditions.

• Unions eventually become established and legal.

• Reform laws are passed in Britain and the United States to limit child labor and set work hours.

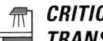 **CRITICAL THINKING TRANSPARENCIES**
CT25 Industrialists and Reformers

Capitalism vs. Marxism

Capitalist Ideas	Marxist Ideas
• Progress results when individuals follow their own self-interest.	• All great movements in history are the result of an economic class struggle.
• Businesses follow their own self-interest when they compete with one another for the consumer's money.	• The "haves" take advantage of the "have-nots."
• Each producer tries to provide goods and services that are better and less expensive than those of competitors.	• The Industrial Revolution intensified the class struggle.
• Consumers compete with one another to purchase the best goods at the lowest prices.	• Workers are exploited by employers.
• Market economy aims to produce the best products and the lowest prices.	• The labor of workers creates profit for employers.
Adam Smith • Government should not interfere in the economy.	• The capitalist system will eventually destroy itself. The state will wither away as a classless society develops. **Karl Marx**

SKILLBUILDER: Interpreting Charts

1. *Which ideas of Marxism seem to be a direct reaction to the Industrial Revolution?*
2. *Which system of ideas seems dominant in the world today? Support your opinion.*

They believed that economic forces alone dominated society. Time has shown, however, that religion, nationalism, ethnic loyalties, and a desire for democratic reforms may be as strong influences on history as economic forces. In addition, the gap between the rich and poor within the industrialized countries failed to widen in the way that Marx and Engels predicted, mostly because of the following types of reform.

Unionization and Legislative Reform

Factory workers faced long hours, dirty and dangerous working conditions, and the threat of being laid off. By the 1800s, working people became more active in politics. To press for reforms, workers joined together in voluntary associations called **unions.**

The Union Movement A union spoke for all the workers in a particular trade. Unions engaged in **collective bargaining**—negotiations between workers and their employers. They bargained for better working conditions and higher pay. If factory owners refused these demands, union members could **strike,** or refuse to work.

Skilled workers led the way in forming unions because their special skills gave them extra bargaining power. Management would have trouble replacing such skilled workers as carpenters, printers, and spinners. Thus the earliest unions helped the lower middle class more than they helped the poorest workers.

The union movement underwent slow, painful growth in both Great Britain and the United States. For years, the British government denied workers the right to form unions. The government saw unions as a threat to social order and stability. Indeed, the Combination Acts of 1799 and 1800 outlawed unions and strikes. Bravely ignoring the threat of jail or job loss, factory workers joined unions anyway. Parliament finally repealed the Combination Acts in 1824. After 1825, the British government unhappily tolerated unions.

British unions had shared goals of raising wages and improving working conditions. By 1875, British trade unions had won the right to strike and picket peacefully. They had also built up a membership of about 1 million people.

In the United States, skilled workers had belonged to unions since the early 1800s. In 1886, several unions joined together to form the organization that would become the

---

Linguistic Learners: Internet Research Invite students to use the Internet to research issues of labor organizing or legislative reform in the late 1800s. Students might find out about a particular union or labor struggle. A fruitful subject of investigation might be the Homestead steel strike of 1892, in which Andrew Carnegie and Henry Clay Frick used Pinkerton guards to end a strike. Have students share the results of their research in a short report or class discussion.

 INTERNET
Click on *World History* at
www.mlworldhistory.com

Students Acquiring English Vocabulary Study Pair less fluent English speakers with more fluent speakers and have them work with the key terms for this section. Encourage students to quiz each other on the meaning of the terms. More fluent students might also explain the meaning of terms based on word parts. For example, *utilitarianism, socialism,* and *communism* all combine root words with the suffix *-ism.* In this context, *-ism* is added to designate a doctrine, theory, or system of principles related to the root word. Thus, *socialism* means "the belief that the wealth of a country should be shared equally among all its citizens."

American Federation of Labor (AFL). A series of successful strikes won AFL members higher wages and shorter hours.

Reform Laws In both Great Britain and the United States, new laws reformed some of the worst abuses of industrialization. In 1832, for example, Parliament set up a committee to investigate child labor. As a result of this committee's findings, Parliament passed the Factory Act of 1833. The new law made it illegal to hire children under 9 years old. Children from the ages of 9 to 12 could not work more than 8 hours a day. Young people from 13 to 17 could not work more than 12 hours. In 1842 the Mines Act prevented women and children from working underground.

In 1847, the Parliament passed a bill that helped working women as well as their children. The Ten Hours Act of 1847 limited the workday to ten hours for women and children who worked in factories.

Reformers in the United States also passed legislation to protect child workers. In 1904, a group of progressive reformers organized the National Child Labor Committee to end child labor. Arguing that child labor lowered wages for all workers, labor union members joined the reformers. Together these groups pressured national and state politicians to ban child labor and set maximum working hours. The Supreme Court in 1919 had objected to a federal child labor law. However, it did allow individual states to legally limit the working hours of women and, later, of men.

This print shows an attack on the workhouse, a prison in which limited sentences at manual labor are served. The attack took place in Stockport, England, during demonstrations by workers in the 1830s. The workers are shown distributing bread from the workhouse.

THINK THROUGH HISTORY
D. Summarizing
What were some of the important reform bills passed in Britain during this period?
D. Possible Answer
Factory Act of 1833; Mines Act of 1842; Ten Hours Act of 1847.

Other Reform Movements

Almost from the beginning, reform movements sprang up in response to the negative impact of industrialization. These reforms included improving the workplace and extending the right to vote to working-class men. The same impulse toward reform, along with the ideals of the French Revolution, also helped to end slavery and promote new rights for women and children.

Abolition of Slavery William Wilberforce, a highly religious man, was a member of Parliament who led the fight for abolition—the end of the slave trade and slavery in the British Empire. Parliament passed a bill to end the slave trade in the British West Indies in 1807. After he retired from Parliament in 1825, Wilberforce continued his fight to free the slaves. Britain finally abolished slavery in its empire in 1833.

British antislavery activists had mixed motives. Some were morally against slavery, such as the abolitionist William Wilberforce. Others viewed slave labor as an economic threat. Furthermore, a new class of industrialists developed who supported cheap labor rather than slave labor. They soon gained power in Parliament.

In the United States the movement to fulfill the promise of the Declaration of Independence by ending slavery grew in the early 1800s. The enslavement of African people finally ended in the United States when the Union won the Civil War in 1865.

With the end of the U.S. Civil War, enslavement persisted in the Americas only in Puerto Rico, Cuba, and Brazil. In Puerto Rico, slavery was ended in 1873. Spain finally abolished slavery in its Cuban colony in 1886. Not until 1888 did Brazil's huge enslaved population win freedom.

THINK THROUGH HISTORY
E. Summarizing
What were some of the motives of British abolitionists?
E. Possible Answer
Religious beliefs; economic self-interest of competing workers; economic self-interest of those interested in hiring cheap labor rather than using slave labor.

The Industrial Revolution **271**

OBJECTIVE ④ INSTRUCT

Other Reform Movements

▶ *Key Ideas*
• Industrialization spurs the growth of various reform movements.
• The abolition movement helps to end slavery by the late 1800s.
• Women fight for their rights, while education and prison reform make strides.

CRITICAL THINKING ACTIVITY
CLASS TIME: 10 MINUTES

Making Connections
Have students explain connections between industrialization and reform movements by filling in the chart below.

Reform	Link to Industrialization
Abolition	
Women's rights	
Education	

| TEACHING OPTION | BLOCK SCHEDULING | **COOPERATIVE ACTIVITY: Playing an Identity Game** | CLASS TIME 15 MINUTES |

Task: Students will play a guessing game—something like the television show *What's My Line?*—in which they try to guess the identity of other students posing as historical figures.

Purpose: To reinforce and further students' knowledge of key thinkers from the early Industrial Age.

Activity: Tell students that they are going to play a guessing game in which they try to identify important thinkers from the 1800s. Have pairs of students choose one of the people discussed in this section (such as Smith, Malthus, Ricardo, Bentham, Marx, and so forth) and do further research on that person's life and ideas. Then have them write a sentence or two describing the person but don't give

away his or her identity in any obvious way. To play the game, students should say their sentences to the class. The class can then ask up to five questions to try to determine the identity of the person being portrayed.

 ALTERNATIVE ASSESSMENT BOOK
Standards for Evaluating a Cooperative Activity

Teacher's Edition **271**

HISTORY MAKERS

Jane Addams
1860–1935

After graduating from college, Jane Addams wondered what to do with her life.

I gradually became convinced that it would be a good thing to rent a house in a part of the city where many primitive and actual needs are found, in which young women who had been given over too exclusively to study, might . . . learn of life from life itself.

Addams and her friend Ellen Starr set up Hull House in a working-class district in Chicago. Eventually the facilities included a nursery, a gym, a kitchen, and a boarding house for working women. Hull House not only served the immigrant population of the neighborhood, it also trained social workers.

Women Fight for Change The Industrial Revolution proved a mixed blessing for women. On the one hand, factory work offered higher wages than work done at home. Women spinners in Manchester, for example, earned much more money than women who stayed home to spin cotton thread. On the other hand, women factory workers usually made only one-third as much money as men.

Women led reform movements to address this and other pressing social issues. During the mid-1800s, for example, women formed unions in the trades where they dominated. In Britain, some women served as safety inspectors in factories where other women worked. In the United States, college-educated women like Jane Addams ran settlement houses. These community centers served the poor residents of slum neighborhoods.

In both the United States and Britain, women who had rallied for the abolition of slavery began to wonder why their own rights should be denied on the basis of gender. The movement for women's rights began in the United States as early as 1848. Women activists around the world joined to found the International Council for Women in 1888. Delegates and observers from 27 countries attended the council's 1899 meeting.

Reforms Spread to Many Areas of Life In the United States and Western Europe, reformers tried to correct the problems troubling the newly industrialized nations. Public education and prison reform ranked high on the reformers' lists.

One of the most prominent U.S. reformers, Horace Mann of Massachusetts, favored free public education for all children. Mann, who spent his own childhood working at hard labor, warned, "If we do not prepare children to become good citizens . . . if we do not enrich their minds with knowledge, then our republic must go down to destruction." By the 1850s many states were starting to establish a system of public schools. In Western Europe, free public schooling became available in the late 1800s.

In 1831, French writer Alexis de Tocqueville had contrasted the brutal conditions in American prisons to the "extended liberty" of American society. Reformers took on the challenge of prison reform, emphasizing the goal of restoring prisoners to useful lives.

During the 1800s, democracy grew in the industrialized countries even as foreign expansion increased. The industrialized western democracies faced new challenges both at home and abroad. You will learn about these challenges in Chapter 10.

THINK THROUGH HISTORY
F. Making Inferences Why might women abolitionists have headed the movement for women's rights?
F. Possible Answer Their work to gain rights for African Americans may have led them to try to gain equal rights for themselves.

Section ④ Assessment

1. TERMS & NAMES
Identify
• laissez faire
• Adam Smith
• capitalism
• utilitarianism
• socialism
• Karl Marx
• communism
• union
• collective bargaining
• strike

2. TAKING NOTES
Compare capitalism with Marxism using a Venn diagram such as the one below.

Capitalism only

Both

Marxism only

Write a paragraph comparing and contrasting capitalism and Marxism.

3. IDENTIFYING PROBLEMS
What were the main problems faced by the unions during the 1800s? How did the unions overcome these problems?

THINK ABOUT
• government restrictions
• labor reforms
• skilled workers vs. unskilled workers

4. ANALYZING THEMES
Economics According to Marx and Engels, economic forces alone dominate society. How important do you think such forces are? Support your opinion using evidence from this and previous chapters.

THINK ABOUT
• other forces, like ethnic loyalties, desire for democracy
• causes of the Industrial Revolution
• the class structure

272 Chapter 9

ANSWERS

Industrialization

Industrialization eventually lifted the standard of living for many people in Europe and North America in the 1800s. Yet the process also brought suffering to countless workers who crowded into filthy cities to toil for starvation wages. The following excerpts reveal a variety of perspectives on this major historical event.

TESTIMONY
Ellison Jack

An 11-year-old girl who worked in the mines testified before a Parliamentary commission on child labor in 1842.

I have been working below three years on my father's account; he takes me down at two in the morning, and I come up at one and two next afternoon. I go to bed at six at night to be ready for work next morning. . . . I have to bear my burthen [burden] up four traps, or ladders, before I get to the main road which leads to the pit bottom. My task is four or five tubs. . . . I fill five tubs in twenty journeys.

I have had the strap [beating] when I did not do my bidding. Am very glad when my task is wrought, as it sore fatigues.

LETTER

Mary Paul

Mary Paul worked in a textile factory in Lowell, Massachusetts. In an 1846 letter to her father in New Hampshire, the 16-year-old expressed her satisfaction with her situation at Lowell.

I am at work in a spinning room tending four sides of warp which is one girl's work. The overseer tells me that he never had a girl get along better than I do. . . . I have a very good boarding place, have enough to eat. . . . The girls are all kind and obliging. . . . I think that the factory is the best place for me and if any girl wants employment, I advise them to come to Lowell.

BOOK
Andrew Carnegie

In his autobiography, published in 1920, the multimillionaire industrialist views with optimism the growth of American industry.

America is soon to change from being the dearest steel manufacturing country to the cheapest. Already the shipyards of Belfast are our customers. This is but the beginning. Under present conditions America can produce steel as cheaply as any other land, notwithstanding its higher-priced labor. There is no other labor so cheap as the dearest in the mechanical field, provided it is free, contented, zealous, and reaping reward as it renders service. And here America leads.

One great advantage which America will have in competing in the markets of the world is that her manufacturers will have the best home market. Upon this they can depend for a return upon capital, and the surplus product can be exported with advantage, even when the prices received for it do no more than cover actual cost, provided the exports be charged with their proportion of all expenses. The nation that has the best home market, especially if products are standardized, as ours are, can soon outsell the foreign producer.

BOOK
Friedrich Engels

Friedrich Engels, who managed a textile factory in Manchester, England, spent his nights wandering the city's slums.

Nobody troubles about the poor as they struggle helplessly in the whirlpool of modern industrial life. The working man may be lucky enough to find employment, if by his labor he can enrich some member of the middle classes. But his wages are so low that they hardly keep body and soul together. If he cannot find work, he can steal, unless he is afraid of the police; or he can go hungry and then the police will see to it that he will die of hunger in such a way as not to disturb the equanimity of the middle classes.

Connect *to* History

Contrasting Contrast two different points of view on the Industrial Revolution. Why do you think the viewpoints differ?

 SEE SKILLBUILDER HANDBOOK, PAGE 654

Connect *to* Today

Researching Find a modern view of industrialization in an editorial cartoon, a poem, an excerpt from a novel, or a photograph. Bring it to class and explain its point of view.

 CD-ROM For another perspective on the Industrial Revolution, see World History: Electronic Library of Primary Sources.

---

different **Perspectives**

Industrialization: Before and After

As students discuss these perspectives, have them consider how life is different today as a result of the Industrial Revolution.

A list of effects might include some of the following points:

- The world has become more interconnected through the development of rapid transport and systems of communications, allowing a global exchange of people, information, and goods.
- Mass-produced goods—clothes, computers, cars, paper clips—have helped raise standards of living, but many traditional craft skills have been lost.
- Many people enjoy good diets, which may include exotic foods from around the world, but others still suffer hunger, in part because food production geared for mass markets may ignore local needs.
- Cities have developed to an extraordinary degree and offer great advantages, but they are often overcrowded, polluted, and dangerous.
- Many people enjoy good jobs at good pay, but others still work at menial labor or suffer stress or physical harm from poor work conditions.

 ELECTRONIC LIBRARY OF PRIMARY SOURCES
from "How I Served My Apprenticeship" by Andrew Carnegie

Connect *to* History

Contrasting
Possible Response: The views of Ellison Jack and Mary Paul differ because their work conditions differed. Jack labored under miserable conditions, while Paul seemed to have had her basic needs met. Working in a mill represented a positive alternative to a less interesting life.

Connect *to* Today

Researching
Students might find a photograph of wage laborers in a factory along the United States-Mexico border or an article about the benefits enjoyed by high-tech workers in the computer industry. Perspectives on industrialization might vary from highly positive to highly negative.

Chapter ⑨ Assessment

TERMS & NAMES

1. Industrial Revolution, p. 253
2. enclosure, p. 253
3. factory, p. 255
4. urbanization, p. 258
5. middle class, p. 259
6. corporation, p. 265
7. laissez faire, p. 267
8. socialism, p. 268
9. Karl Marx, p. 269
10. collective bargaining, p. 270

REVIEW QUESTIONS

Answers will vary.

11. Water power and coal; iron ore; rivers; good harbors

12. Forced small farmers to give up farming; caused forced migration to cities; some farmers became tenant farmers

13. Possible Responses: steam engine, locomotive, factory, spinning jenny, flying shuttle. Student descriptions of impact will vary.

14. No sanitary codes; lack of adequate housing, education, police protection, running water, indoor plumbing; frequent epidemics

15. Some participants in Industrial Revolution became wealthier than landowners and threatened their power; spurred even more class divisions, resulting in upper class, upper middle class, lower middle class, working class.

16. Dyes and wastes poisoned the river; coal polluted the air.

17. Political turmoil caused by the French Revolution slowed trade, interrupted communication, and caused inflation.

18. Industrialized countries needed more natural resources from less developed countries for factories; industrialized countries also needed to develop new markets around the world; these needs fostered inequality.

19. Bourgeoisie ("haves," employers), proletariat ("have-nots," workers)

20. *Possible responses:* formed unions, served as safety inspectors, rallied for abolition of slavery, founded the International Council for Women

TERMS & NAMES

Briefly explain the importance of each of the following to industrialization.

1. Industrial Revolution
2. enclosure
3. factory
4. urbanization
5. middle class
6. corporation
7. laissez faire
8. socialism
9. Karl Marx
10. collective bargaining

Interact *with* History

On page 252, you looked at working conditions in an English factory in the 19th century before reading about the Industrial Revolution. Now that you've read the chapter, rethink your decision about what you would do to change your situation. What factory working conditions would you like to see change? What benefits might a union bring? What disadvantages might result if workers organize? Discuss your opinions with a small group.

REVIEW QUESTIONS

SECTION 1 *(pages 253–257)*
The Beginnings of Industrialization

11. What were the four natural resources needed for British industrialization?

12. How did the enclosure movement change agriculture in England?

13. Name two inventions that were created during the Industrial Revolution. Describe their impact.

SECTION 2 *(pages 258–262)*
Patterns of Change: Industrialization

14. Describe the living conditions in Britain during industrialization.

15. How did the new middle class transform the social structure of Great Britain during industrialization?

16. How did industrialization affect Manchester's natural environment?

SECTION 3 *(pages 263–266)*
Industrialization Spreads

17. Why were other European countries slower to industrialize than Britain?

18. What helps to explain the rise of global inequality during the Industrial Revolution?

SECTION 4 *(pages 267–272)*
An Age of Reforms

19. What were the two warring classes that Marx and Engels outlined in *The Communist Manifesto*?

20. Name two ways women fought for change during the Industrial Revolution.

Visual Summary

The Industrial Revolution

Economic Effects

- New inventions and development of factories
- Rapidly growing industry in the 1800s
- Increased production and higher demand for raw materials
- Growth of worldwide trade
- Population explosion and a large labor force
- Exploitation of mineral resources
- Highly developed banking and investment system
- Advances in transportation, agriculture, and communication

Social Effects

- Long hours worked by children in factories
- Increase in population of cities
- Poor city planning
- Loss of family stability
- Expansion of middle class
- Harsh conditions for laborers
- Workers' progress vs. laissez-faire economic attitudes
- Improved standard of living
- Creation of new jobs
- Encouragement of technological progress

Political Effects

- Child labor laws to end abuses
- Reformers urging equal distribution of wealth
- Trade unions
- Social reform movements, such as utilitarianism, utopianism, socialism, and Marxism
- Reform bills in Parliament

274 Chapter 9

Interact *with* History

Possible Responses: Students may mention changing conditions such as poor lighting and bad air in the factories. Others might mention the bargaining power that a union could bring to bear upon the fight to improve working conditions. Still others may say that if workers organized, then individual productivity might decline.

CRITICAL THINKING

1. INDUSTRIAL REVOLUTION BRINGS CHANGE

How significant were the changes the Industrial Revolution brought to the world? How enduring were they? Explain your conclusion. Think about economic, social, and political changes.

2. TECHNOLOGICAL ADVANCES

THEME SCIENCE & TECHNOLOGY Create a chart like the one below that lists some of the major technological advances and their effects on industrial society.

Technological Advance	Effect(s)

3. MILITARY POWER

How did the Industrial Revolution help to increase Germany's military power?

4. ANALYZING PRIMARY SOURCES

The following quotation comes from Charles Dickens's *Hard Times,* first published in book form in 1854. In *Hard Times,* as well as in several of his other novels, Dickens exposes such evils of industrialization as child labor, polluted cities, and corrupt factory owners. The following excerpt begins the chapter "No Way Out." Read the paragraph and answer the questions that follow.

A VOICE FROM THE PAST

The Fairy Palaces burst into illumination before pale morning showed the monstrous serpents of smoke trailing themselves over Coketown. A clattering of clogs upon the pavement, a rapid ringing of bells, and all the melancholy mad elephants, polished and oiled up for the day's monotony, were at their heavy exercise again.

- What is Dickens's opinion of the factory town? What words give you that impression?

- Why do you think Dickens called the chapter "No Way Out"?

CHAPTER ACTIVITIES

1. LIVING HISTORY: Unit Portfolio Project

THEME EMPIRE BUILDING Your unit portfolio project focuses on how different nations built empires (see page 249). For Chapter 9, you might use one of the following ideas to add to your portfolio:

- Would a non-industrialized or an industrialized nation more likely be an empire builder in the 19th and 20th centuries? Stage a debate to discuss this question. Videotape the session.

- You are an artisan in a non-industrialized nation threatened by a flood of cheap European goods into your marketplace. Write a letter to the editor of a local paper describing your situation, with any suggestions for improvement.

- Work with a partner to create British posters advertising their manufactured goods in overseas, less-developed markets.

2. CONNECT TO TODAY: Cooperative Learning

THEME ECONOMICS You read about harsh child labor practices during the Industrial Revolution. Today, child labor still exists in many developing nations, with many of the same unsanitary, unsafe, and grueling conditions. Work with a team to find out what the various child labor situations are in different places.

 Using the Internet or your library, research organizations that are fighting child labor.

- Write a letter, or in some other manner voice your concern and support to these organizations.

3. INTERPRETING A TIME LINE

Revisit the unit time line on pages 248–249. Look at events for Chapter 9. Write two more entries that could be added to the time line from Chapter 9. Support your answer with evidence from the text.

FOCUS ON GRAPHS

The graph to the right shows population growth in four European cities from 1700 to 1900, that is, before and after the Industrial Revolution.

- Which city had the smallest population in 1700? How many people had it gained by 1900?

- Which city gained the most people in this period? How many people did it gain between 1700 and 1900?

Connect to History
Why did cities grow so rapidly in this period? What lured people to the cities?

The Growth of Cities, 1700-1900

10,000 / 1.2 Million — Birmingham — 1700 1900
60,000 / 2.4 Million — Berlin — 1700 1900
500,000 / 3.3 Million — Paris — 1700 1900
110,000 / 1.6 Million — Vienna — 1700 1900

0 — 400 Miles
0 — 800 Kilometers

An Age of Democracy and Progress

	Key Ideas	**COPY MASTERS**	**ASSESSMENT**
SECTION 1 Democratic Reform and Activism pp. 279–283	*After considerable struggle, Great Britain evolves into a constitutional monarchy, while in France the Third Republic emerges as a parliamentary democracy. Women in both nations fail to obtain the right to vote.*	*In-Depth Resources: Unit 3* • **Guided Reading,** p. 18 • **Primary Source:** from *Five Years of My Life, 1894–1899,* p. 25 • **History Makers:** Emmeline Pankhurst, p. 34	P E *Section 1 Assessment,* p. 283 *Formal Assessment* • Section Quiz, p. 125 *Alternative Assessment Book* • Standards for Evaluating a Cooperative Activity
SECTION 2 Self-Rule for British Colonies pp. 284–288	*The British colonies of Canada, Australia, and New Zealand become democratic states within the British empire. In Ireland the struggle for home rule fails. Ireland splits into an independent country and a British province.*	*In-Depth Resources: Unit 3* • **Guided Reading,** p. 19 • **Geography Application:** The British Settle Australia and New Zealand, p. 23 • **Primary Source:** Irish Petition to Emigrate, p. 26 • **Literature:** "Easter 1916," p. 29	P E *Section 2 Assessment,* p. 288 *Formal Assessment* • Section Quiz, p. 126 *Alternative Assessment Book* • Standards for Evaluating a Product or Performance
SECTION 3 Expansion and Crisis in the United States pp. 289–292	*The United States expands to the Pacific Ocean. The Civil War ends slavery, preserves the Union, and speeds the industrial development of the North. After the war, the country experiences an unprecedented economic boom.*	*In-Depth Resources: Unit 3* • **Guided Reading,** p. 20 • **Primary Source:** Railroad Poster, p. 27	P E *Section 3 Assessment,* p. 292 *Formal Assessment* • Section Quiz, p. 127 *Alternative Assessment Book* • Standards for Evaluating a Cooperative Activity
SECTION 4 Nineteenth Century Progress pp. 293–299	*Key inventions, new theories in physics and biology, and medical advances transform daily life for many people. New technologies and growing democratic institutions create a mass culture in the United States.*	*In-Depth Resources: Unit 3* • **Guided Reading,** p. 21 • **Skillbuilder Practice:** Analyzing Issues, p. 22 • **Primary Source:** Orville Wright's Diary, p. 28 • **Literature:** from *The Origin,* p. 31 • **History Makers:** Marie and Pierre Curie, p. 35 • **Connections Across Time and Cultures:** Breakthroughs in Science and Technology, p. 36	P E *Section 4 Assessment,* p. 299 *Formal Assessment* • Section Quiz, p. 128 *Alternative Assessment Book* • Standards for Evaluating a Product or Performance
CHAPTER RESOURCES	**Chapter Overview** *Democratic institutions evolve in western Europe, North America, Australia, and New Zealand, although native people are suppressed. Industrialization and democracy spur revolutionary changes in the arts and sciences, transforming people's daily lives.*	*Telescoping the Times* • Chapter Summary, pp. 41–43 *Planning for Block Schedules*	P E *Chapter Assessment,* pp. 300–301 *Chapter Activities,* p. 301 *Formal Assessment* • Chapter Test, forms A and B, pp. 129–134 💾 Test Generator *Alternative Assessment Book*

TECHNOLOGY

Warm-Up Transparency 10

World Art and Cultures Transparencies
• AT56 *The Lady of Shalott*

 Electronic Library of Primary Sources
• from *Prisons and Prisoners*

INTERNET RESOURCES
www.mlworldhistory.com

Warm-Up Transparency 10

Geography Transparencies
• GT26 Canada: Growth of the Dominion, 1867–Present

World Art and Cultures Transparencies
• AT57 Maori pigment container

Electronic Library of Primary Sources
• "The Irish Potato Famine"

Patterns of Interaction:
The Geography of Food

INTERNET RESOURCES
www.mlworldhistory.com

Warm-Up Transparency 10

Electronic Library of Primary Sources
• from *A Message to Congress on Indian Policy*

INTERNET RESOURCES
www.mlworldhistory.com

Warm-Up Transparency 10

Critical Thinking Transparencies
• CT26 Movers and Shakers, 1815–1914
• CT62 Visual Summary

Electronic Library of Primary Sources
• from *Journal of the Voyage of HMS Beagle*

INTERNET RESOURCES
www.mlworldhistory.com

Chapter Summaries on Audiocassette in English and Spanish

INTERNET RESOURCES
www.mlworldhistory.com

 Block Scheduling (90 MINUTES)

Day 1
Section 1, pp. 279–283

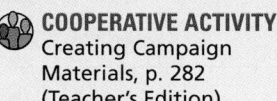 **COOPERATIVE ACTIVITY**
Creating Campaign Materials, p. 282
(Teacher's Edition)

Section Assessment, p. 283

Day 2
Section 2, pp. 284–288
Section Assessment, p. 288

Day 3
Section 3, pp. 289–292

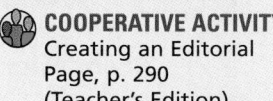 **COOPERATIVE ACTIVITY**
Creating an Editorial Page, p. 290
(Teacher's Edition)

Section Assessment, p. 292

Day 4
Section 4, pp. 293–299
Section Assessment, p. 299
Chapter Assessment, pp. 300–301

Yearly Pacing *Chapter 10 Total:* 4 days *Yearly Total:* 85 days

 Planning for Block Schedules

Customizing for Special Needs

Students Acquiring English

 Access for Students Acquiring English
• **Guided Reading** for Sections 1–4 (Spanish), pp. 112–115
• **Chapter Summary** (Spanish), pp. 109–111
• **Skillbuilder Practice** Analyzing Issues (Spanish), p. 116
• **Geography Application** The British Settle Australia and New Zealand (Spanish), p. 117

 Spanish Reading Study Guide
• pp. 105–114

 • **Patterns of Interaction** *The Geography of Food* (Spanish track)

Less Proficient Readers

 In-Depth Resources: Unit 3
• **Guided Reading** for Sections 1–4, pp. 18–21
• **Skillbuilder Practice** Analyzing Issues, p. 22
• *Geography* **Application** The British Settle Australia and New Zealand, p. 23

 Telescoping the Times
• Chapter Summary, pp. 41–43

 Reading Study Guide
• pp. 105–114

 Chapter Summaries on Audiocassette in English and Spanish

Gifted and Talented Students

In-Depth Resources: Unit 3

Primary Sources:
• from *Five Years of My Life, 1894–1899,* p. 25
• Irish Petition to Emigrate, p. 26
• Railroad Poster, p. 27
• Orville Wright's Diary, p. 28

History Makers
• Emmeline Pankhurst, p. 34
• Marie and Pierre Curie, p. 35

Connections to Literature READINGS FOR STUDENTS

 In-Depth Resources: Unit 3
Literature: "Easter, 1916," p. 29; from *The Origin,* p. 31

• **McDougal Littell**
The Language of Literature, Grade 10
R. K. Narayan, "Like the Sun," p. 608
Rabindranath Tagore, "The Cabulwallah," p. 622
Isaac Bashevis Singer, "The Son from America," p. 761
Linda Pastan, "Grudnow," p. 768

Santha Rama Rau, "By Any Other Name," p. 772

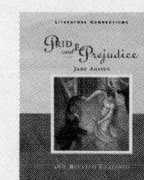

McDougal Littell
Literature Connections

• **Austin, Jane**
Pride and Prejudice
(with related readings)
This gentle and witty satire of courtship and marriage in 18th-century England is one of Jane Austin's best-loved novels.

 = Pupil's Edition   = Overhead Transparency = Software   = Video

= Copy Master = CD-ROM = Audiocassette   = Internet

An Age of Democracy and Progress, 1815–1914

Accessing Prior Knowledge

Have students look over these two pages.

- Ask them to name two or three facts they already know about each topic portrayed in the images.

Making Predictions

Point out to students that each picture represents a process of momentous change.

- What is likely to happen as European immigrants encounter native cultures in Australia?

- As people become wealthier through industrial progress, how might this influence Western European democracies?

Geography Connection

Ask students to notice how few countries are democratic at this time and how far-flung the democracies are.

- What problems might Great Britain have in keeping control of its overseas colonies?

- Would the United States have similar problems in governing its western territories?

CHAPTER
10

An Age of Democracy and Progress, 1815–1914

PREVIEWING THEMES

Empire Building
During the 1800s, Great Britain gradually allowed three of its colonies—Canada, Australia, and New Zealand—greater self-rule. At the same time, Britain maintained tight control over Ireland.

Economics
In western Europe and the United States, a growing middle class both demanded and benefited from democratic reforms. During the 1800s, U.S. economic growth and territorial expansion made the nation one of the leading industrial countries of the world.

Science & Technology
Breakthroughs in science and technology transformed daily life during the 19th century. From the electric light bulb to the automobile, emerging products speeded up the pace of life, shrank distances, and expanded the hours available for work or play.

WESTERN DEMOCRACIES, 1900

CANADA

UNITED STATES OF AMERICA

PACIFIC OCEAN

ATLANTIC OCEAN

Kansas pioneers, by George Melville Stone, depicts Americans making the westward journey across the **Great Plains** by Conestoga wagon. The Great Plains became part of the United States with the Louisiana Purchase of **1803**. During the 1800s, thousands of Americans migrated west.

INTERNET CONNECTION

Visit us at **www.mlworldhistory.com** to learn more about Western democracies in the 19th century.

NEW ZEALAND

← Australia 1,300 miles

GEOGRAPHY THEMES

Movement

In this chapter, three major migrations are discussed: the movement of British convicts and citizens to Australia; the movement of white, African American, and Asian settlers across the western United States; and the immigration of thousands of Irish to the United States.

As students read the chapter, encourage them to think about the following: Over what period of time did each migration occur? What effects did these migrations have on each country?

Ask students if any of these movements affected their own families in the past or the families of anyone they know.

Human-Environment Interaction

As Europeans moved to new and "undeveloped" lands, they greatly changed the environment. Point out to students that in the countries where they settled, Europeans used the land in vastly different ways than did most native peoples. They mined, cleared forest land, dammed or diverted waterways, and altered the shape of the landscape to meet their needs for manufacturing, farming, and building cities.

Encourage students to find photographs or paintings of what their area looked like before and after settlers came to the region.

ADDITIONAL RESOURCES

Books for the Teacher

- Meltzer, Milton, ed. *Voices from the Civil War.* New York: Crowell, 1989. A documentary history of the war.

- Schroeder, Paul W. *The Transformation of European Politics, 1763–1848.* New York: Oxford UP, 1994.

Books for the Student

- Chamberlin, E. R. *The Nineteenth Century.* Morristown, NJ: Silver Burdett, 1984. Everyday life in Europe in the 1800s.

- Drabble, Margaret. *For Queen and Country: Britain in the Victorian Age.* New York: Seabury, 1978. The lives of ordinary British citizens.

Videos

- *The Glory of Europe—1900: Hey Day Fever.* Ambrose Video, 1977. 800-526-4663. Europe as the most dominant force in the world.

- *The Mechanical Paradise.* Ambrose Video, 1980. 800-526-4663. Engineers and inventors: 1870–1914.

Software

- *Impressionism and Its Sources.* CD-ROM. Queue. 800-232-2224.

- *The Victorian Era.* CD-ROM. Society for Visual Education, 1994. 800-829-1900. The growth of British industry, social and parliamentary reform, and women's changing role.

IRELAND

GREAT BRITAIN

FRANCE

In Paris, the 984-foot-tall **Eiffel Tower** opened in **1889**. Bridge engineer Gustave Eiffel designed the tower to mark the hundredth anniversary of the French Revolution. It also served as a fitting monument to the age of industrial progress. The Eiffel Tower was the world's tallest structure until 1930.

This engraving shows British convicts being ferried to a prison ship in an English port. Beginning in **1788**, the British government sent many such convicts to its penal colony in **Australia**. Australia received British prisoners until the mid-1800s.

INDIAN OCEAN

AUSTRALIA

New Zealand 1,300 miles

0   400 Miles

0   800 Kilometers

N

277

HISTORY THROUGH ART

Kansas Pioneers and British Convicts Bound for Australia

The United States and Australia were both settled by immigrants, but people left their homeland for widely different reasons. Immigrants to the U.S. wanted a better life. In contrast, British immigrants to Australia were shipped halfway around the world by a government glad to get rid of them.

The composition of the two pictures reflects the different conditions of these immigrant groups. The Kansas pioneers stride confidently toward their new home. The two men in the foreground dominate even the oxen and covered wagon behind them. In contrast, the prison ship completely dwarfs the human cargo being ferried to meet it. This is undoubtedly how many prisoners felt on first viewing the ship.

Interpreting the Art What is the mood of each picture? *Kansas pioneers—optimistic, light; British convicts—dark, brooding, somber.* How does each artist view the people in these pictures? *Possible answers: Kansas pioneers—the pioneers all seem strong, unafraid, willing to encounter the unknown. No one is leading or driving them. British convicts—they are anonymous, huddled together, and completely under someone else's control.*

Interact *with* History

Interact *with* History

You live in a glorious age. Trains and telegraphs are not even 50 years old—and so much remains to be discovered! You're something of a tinkerer yourself. Maybe you can perfect a gas-powered engine and invent the car. Or maybe you can invent a device to use electricity to light up a room! But wait—if people could move five times faster, would they *really* be happier? What are the dangers of playing with strange new forces such as electricity and X-rays? Considering all the possible consequences . . .

Automobiles provide a new level of mobility and freedom. The cost of early cars has meant that few can afford them. What will happen if the price comes down?

1906 Ford 6 Cylinder Touring Car
Price $2,500

6 cylinders—40 h. p. 4 to 50 miles per hour on high gear. *Perfected* magneto ignition—mechanical oiler, 114 inch wheel base, luxurious body for 5 passengers, weight 2000 pounds.

1906 Ford Runabout, as advanced as our touring car in design and even more surprising in price—will be fully illustrated and described in our next advertisement.

Both these Cars on exhibition at the New York Automobile Show.

Ford Motor Company
Detroit, Mich.

What would you invent?

The invention of the electric light can turn night into day. What will people do with the extra daylight hours?

24172 **Magneto Bell Telephone.** Loudest talking, clearest tone and best constructed magneto phone on the market. As no batteries are required with this phone, the current being generated by means of a powerful generator in the telephone box, a large part of the expense of maintenance is eliminated. Suitable for use for exchange or private lines of any length. This instrument cannot be excelled in general excellence, nor inappearance. The boxes being of highly polished hardwood, and metal parts of nickel, plated or oxidized. Full directions for putting up the phone and constructing lines accompany each instrument. Prices quoted below are for phone complete and do not include any materials for line construction. Weight, each phone, 15 lbs. Price, per phone............................$18.00
Price, per pair, complete for two stations......35.00
For quotations of wire, insulators, etc., see No. 24218

With telephones, people can speak directly to one another from within their own homes. Will they ever get used to the wires running from their homes and along their roads?

EXAMINING *the* ISSUES

- What were the drawbacks of living in a time before telephones, cars, electric lights, radios, and so on?

- What might have been better about life before the "progress" of the 19th century—and for whom?

- How might inventions affect social life: the closeness of families, the gap between rich and poor, the power of different social groups?

Break into groups and have each group choose one truly beneficial invention of the past two centuries. Debate one another's choices and see if you can find some costs, as well as benefits, of each invention.

As you read this chapter, consider how invention and democracy were intertwined in the 19th century. How did each promote the other? Think about the Industrial Revolution and its consequences. Also consider more recent inventions, such as compact disc players and the Internet.

1 Democratic Reform and Activism

TERMS & NAMES
- suffrage
- Chartist movement
- Queen Victoria
- Third Republic
- Dreyfus affair
- anti-Semitism
- Zionism

MAIN IDEA	WHY IT MATTERS NOW
Spurred by the demands of ordinary people, Great Britain and France underwent democratic reforms.	During this period, Britain and France were transformed into the democracies they are today.

SETTING THE STAGE Urbanization and industrialization brought sweeping changes to Western nations. People looking for solutions to the problems created by these developments began to demand reforms. They wanted to improve conditions for workers and the poor. Many people also began to call for political reforms. They demanded that ordinary people be given a greater voice in government.

Britain Adopts Democratic Reforms

As Chapter 21 explained, Britain became a constitutional monarchy in the late 1600s. And it remains so today. Under this system of government, the monarch serves as the head of state, but Parliament holds the real power. The British Parliament consists of a House of Lords and a House of Commons. Members of the House of Lords either inherit their seats or are appointed. Members of the House of Commons are elected by the British people.

In the early 1800s, the British government was not a true democracy. Only about 6 percent of the population had the right to elect the members of the House of Commons. Voting was limited to men who owned a substantial amount of land. Women could not vote at all. As a result, the upper classes ran the government.

During the 1800s, however, democracy gradually expanded in Great Britain. The ideas of liberalism that were popular in France and other countries spread among Britain's growing middle and working classes. These groups demanded a greater share of the power held by the aristocratic landowners. Yet unlike the French, the British achieved reforms without the bitter bloodshed of revolution.

The Reform Bill of 1832 The first group to demand a greater voice in politics was the wealthy middle class—factory owners, bankers, merchants. Beginning in 1830, protests took place around England in favor of a bill in Parliament that would extend **suffrage,** or the right to vote. The Revolution of 1830 in France frightened parliamentary leaders. They feared that revolutionary violence would spread to Britain. Thus, Parliament passed the Reform Bill of 1832. This law eased the property requirements so that well-to-do men in the middle class could vote.

The Reform Bill also modernized the districts for electing members of Parliament. Many of the old districts were areas owned by aristocrats and actually contained few people. In contrast, cities such as Manchester and Sheffield had no representatives in Parliament. The Reform Bill eliminated the so-called "rotten boroughs," or empty districts, and gave the thriving new industrial cities more representation.

Workers Demand Suffrage Although the Reform Bill increased the number of British voters, only about one in five men were now eligible to

The House of Commons 1833 by Sir George Hayter shows this assembly a year after the important Reform Bill.

A. Possible Answers Gave vote to middle class, gave representation to cities, reduced power base of aristocracy by eliminating "rotten boroughs," created momentum to reform.

THINK THROUGH HISTORY
A. Clarifying How did the Reform Bill increase democracy in Great Britain?

Section 1 Overview

OBJECTIVES

1. To describe the evolution of British democracy.
2. To explain the origins and goals of the women's suffrage movement.
3. To trace the development of democratic institutions in France.

SKILLBUILDER
- Interpreting charts, p. 280

CRITICAL THINKING
- Clarifying, pp. 279, 282
- Making inferences, p. 280
- Synthesizing, p. 281
- Analyzing Issues, p. 283

FOCUS
5-Minute Warm-Up

▶ *Making Generalizations*
Answering the following questions will help students to understand social roles in the Victorian Age.

1. Read "Victorian Manners" on page 281. What must a gentleman never do?
2. If a young lady decides to take a walk and to visit a gentleman, what must she do?

📖 *WARM-UP TRANSPARENCY 10*

OBJECTIVE 1 INSTRUCT

Britain Adopts Democratic Reforms

▶ *Key Ideas*
- Parliament extends voting rights to the British middle class.
- Further reform bills extend voting rights to most adult male citizens.
- During Queen Victoria's reign, the monarchy becomes largely ceremonial.

📑 *IN-DEPTH RESOURCES: UNIT 3*
Guided Reading, p. 18

📑 *ACCESS FOR STUDENTS ACQUIRING ENGLISH*
Guided Reading (Spanish), p. 112

SECTION 1 RESOURCES

PRINT RESOURCES

📑 *IN-DEPTH RESOURCES: UNIT 3*
Guided Reading, p. 18
Primary Source: from *Five Years of My Life, 1894–1899*, p. 25
History Makers: Emmeline Pankhurst, p. 34

📑 *ACCESS FOR STUDENTS ACQUIRING ENGLISH*
Guided Reading (Spanish), p. 112

📑 *FORMAL ASSESSMENT*
Section Quiz, p. 125

📑 *ALTERNATIVE ASSESSMENT BOOK*

TECHNOLOGY RESOURCES

🏛 *WORLD ART AND CULTURES TRANSPARENCIES*
AT56 *The Lady of Shalott*

💿 **CD-ROM**
Electronic Library of Primary Sources

🌐 **INTERNET** www.mlworldhistory.com

Growth of Voting in Britain

Interpreting the Chart Point out that each circle contains more information than the previous one because each reform bill added new groups to the voters' rolls. Which group was added in 1832? *middle-class men.* In 1867? *working-class men.* In 1884? *rural men.*

Extension Activity Ask students how a bill to raise working-class wages might have fared in Parliament— based on who was allowed to vote— if the bill had been introduced in 1832, 1867, and 1918. *It would have been defeated in 1832, may have gotten more votes in 1867, and had a chance of passing in 1918.*

SKILLBUILDER Answers
1. 7 percent
2. 21 percent

HISTORY MAKERS
Queen Victoria

The image of Victoria as a sour-faced conservative comes mainly from her later years. As a young queen she was lively and even frivolous. Ask students to compare Queen Victoria to Elizabeth I and Elizabeth II, other important English queens.

OBJECTIVE ② INSTRUCT

Women Demand the Vote

Key Ideas
• Activist women agitate for the right to vote.
• Gradually women use more drastic political tactics to obtain their goals.

 ELECTRONIC LIBRARY OF PRIMARY SOURCES
from *Prisons and Prisoners*

Growth of Voting in Britain

Before 1832	1832	1867, 1884	1918
5% / 95%	2% / 5% / 93%	7% / 21% / 72%	26% / 28% / 46%

Percentage of population over age 20
■ had right to vote
■ gained right to vote
■ could not vote

Reform Bill granted vote to middle-class men.

Reforms granted vote to working-class men in 1867 and to rural men in 1884.

Reforms granted vote to women over 30.

Source: R.L. Leonard, *Elections in Britain*

> **SKILLBUILDER: Interpreting Charts**
> 1. What percentage of the adults in Britain could vote in 1832?
> 2. By how much did the percentage of voters increase after the reforms of 1867 and 1884?

The modern Parliament building was completed in 1867.

vote. The passage of the bill, however, encouraged reformers. Among the workers and other groups who still could not vote, a popular movement arose to press for more rights. It was called the **Chartist movement** because the group first presented its demands to Parliament on a petition called The People's Charter of 1838.

The People's Charter called for suffrage for all men and annual Parliamentary elections. It also proposed to reform Parliament in other ways. In Britain at the time, eligible men voted openly by voice. Since their vote was not secret, they could feel pressure to vote in a certain way. Moreover, members of Parliament had to own land and received no salary, so they needed to be independently wealthy. The Chartists wanted to make Parliament more responsive to the interests of the lower classes. To achieve this, they demanded a secret ballot, an end to the property requirements for serving in Parliament, and pay for members of Parliament.

Parliament rejected the Chartists' demands. However, their protests convinced many people that workers had sound complaints. Over the years, workers continued to press for political reform, and Parliament eventually responded. It gave the vote to working-class men in 1867 and to male rural workers in 1884. After 1884, therefore, most adult males in Britain had the right to vote. By the early 1900s, all the demands of the Chartists, except for annual elections, became law.

The Victorian Age The figure who presided over all this historic change was **Queen Victoria.** Victoria came to the throne in 1837 at the age of 18. She was queen for 64 years, one of the longest reigns in history. During the Victorian Age, the British empire reached the height of its wealth and power. Victoria was popular with her subjects, and she performed her duties wisely and capably. However, she was forced to accept a new, virtually powerless role for the British monarchy.

The kings who preceded Victoria in the 1700s and 1800s had exercised great influence over Parliament. The spread of democracy in the 1800s shifted political power almost completely to Parliament, and especially to the elected House of Commons. Now the government was completely run by the prime minister and the cabinet. Thus, ever since Queen Victoria, British monarchs have been mainly symbolic rulers with no political power.

Women Demand the Vote

By 1890, several industrial countries had universal male suffrage (the right of all men to vote). No country, however, allowed women to vote. As more men gained suffrage, more women demanded the same.

HISTORY MAKERS

Queen Victoria 1819–1901

Three years after her coronation, Queen Victoria fell in love with her cousin Albert, a German prince. She proposed to him and they were married in 1840. Together they had nine children. The strait-laced Prince Albert established a tone of polite propriety at court, and the royal couple presented a picture of loving family life that became a British ideal.

After Albert died in 1861, the Queen wore black silk for the rest of her life in mourning. She once said of Albert, "Without him everything loses its interest."

280 Chapter 10

B. Possible Answers Allowed people to vote their conscience, made voters less subject to intimidation, reduced power of bribery.

THINK THROUGH HISTORY
B. Making Inferences Why do you think the Chartists demanded a secret ballot rather than public voting?

C. Possible Answers Resisting change might have led to overthrow of monarchy, so accepting change helped preserve the British monarchy; wanted to avoid violence or revolution; calls for reform gained momentum and reform may have seemed inevitable.

THINK THROUGH HISTORY
C. Making Inferences Why might Queen Victoria have accepted a powerless new role for the British monarchy? Think about other monarchies in Europe in the 1800s.

TEACHING OPTIONS   CONNECTIONS ACROSS THE CURRICULUM

Mathematics Different types of graphs have different uses. Discuss what a pie chart reveals especially well—that is, changes in portions of a whole. The pie charts show clearly which groups increased over time and by how much.

Then encourage students to translate the information in the three pie charts into a single line graph that shows the growth of the total voting population in England—from the 7 percent of 1832, to the 28 percent of 1867, 1884, to the 74 percent of 1918. Explain to students that a line graph is particularly good for showing the direction of trends (up or down) over time.

CUSTOMIZING FOR SPECIAL NEEDS

Less Proficient Readers To help students gain a clear overview of the expansion of suffrage, have them create a time line showing when universal male suffrage was achieved in the United States, Australia, France, Britain, and New Zealand and when women gained the right to vote in each country.

Have them obtain what information they can from the text and use encyclopedias to supply dates for this chart as needed.

	Brit	Aus	NZ	US	France
M	1884	1851	1853	1865	1848
F	1918	1902	1893	1920	1945

Victorian Ladies' News

Mind Your Tea and Cakes

Taking afternoon tea at about 5:00 P.M. has become as English as London fog, but tea drinkers should be careful to buy supplies only from reputable sources. Some so-called tea merchants add coloring to convert blackthorn leaves into something that looks like tea. In London, several factories dye recycled tea leaves for dishonest merchants to sell as new tea.

Be careful, too, about those cakes you serve with your tea. To get the brightest colors to decorate cakes, some dishonest bakers use dangerous chemicals: copper and zinc to get gold and silver; iron for blue and lead for red; and even arsenic for green.

Cholera Comes from Bad Water

London: This fall, Dr. John Snow published a revised edition of his 1849 pamphlet entitled "On the Mode of Communication of Cholera." In his pamphlet, Dr. Snow uses case examples to show that contaminated drinking water caused the cholera epidemics that killed thousands of poor Londoners in 1831–1832, 1848–1849, and 1854. Dr. Snow's critics scorn his theory, maintaining that cholera spreads from the air that surrounds rubbish heaps.

CHOLERA.

THE DUDLEY BOARD OF HEALTH,
HEREBY GIVE NOTICE, THAT IN CONSEQUENCE OF THE

Church-yards at Dudley

Being so full, no one who has died of the CHOLERA will be permitted to be buried after **SUNDAY** next, (To-morrow) in either of the Burial Grounds of *St. Thomas's*, or *St. Edmund's*, in this Town.

All Persons who die from CHOLERA, must for the future be buried in the Church-yard at Netherton.

BOARD of HEALTH, DUDLEY.
September 1st, 1832.

Riding the Rails

If you want to travel quickly and cheaply, you can't beat the new and improved British railways. Regular trains will speed you to your destination at 20 miles an hour; on express routes, you'll whiz along at nearly 40. Here are some tips for happier traveling:

- Bring your own candles if you intend to read at night.
- Prepare to rent a metal foot warmer if you're taking a winter journey.
- Bring your own food or prepare to brave the crowds at station restaurants.
- For long journeys, tote a chamber pot in a basket.

London's Paddington Station bustles with passengers in this painting.

Victorian Manners

The proper gentleman

- lets a lady walk or ride along the wall
- never speaks to a lady unless she speaks to him first
- precedes a lady walking upstairs and follows one walking downstairs
- takes the backward-facing seat in a carriage and gets out first to help a lady dismount
- never smokes in a lady's presence

The proper lady

- never walks alone or never walks unchaperoned if she is unmarried and under 30
- does not go alone to make a social call on a man
- never wears pearls or diamonds in the morning
- never dances more than three dances with the same partner

Connect *to* History

Synthesizing List examples from this page to demonstrate that popular culture in Victorian England admired both tradition and change.

SEE SKILLBUILDER HANDBOOK, PAGE 665

Connect *to* Today

Researching Using the library or Internet, research some aspect of American culture that shows an example of either tradition or dramatic change. As possible subjects, consider transportation, communications, entertainment, or fashion.

An Age of Democracy and Progress **281**

Organization and Resistance During the 1800s, women in both Great Britain and the United States worked to gain the right to vote. In the United States, women such as Lucretia Mott and Elizabeth Cady Stanton organized a campaign for women's rights as early as 1848. From a convention in Seneca Falls, New York, they issued a declaration of women's rights modeled on the Declaration of Independence. "We hold these truths to be self-evident," the declaration stated, "that all men and women are created equal."

A VOICE FROM THE PAST
The history of mankind is a history of repeated injuries and usurpations on the part of man toward woman, having in direct object the establishment of an absolute tyranny over her. To prove this, let facts be submitted to a candid world.

He has never permitted her to exercise her inalienable right to the elective franchise.

He has compelled her to submit to laws in the formation of which she has no voice.

THE SENECA FALLS CONVENTION, "Declaration of Sentiments"

British women, too, organized reform societies and protested unfair laws and customs. As women became more vocal, however, resistance to their demands grew. Many people, both men and women, thought that women's suffrage was too radical a break with tradition. Some claimed that women lacked the ability to take part in politics.

Militant Protests After decades of peaceful efforts to win the right to vote, some women took more drastic steps. In Britain, Emmeline Pankhurst formed the Women's Social and Political Union (WSPU) in 1903. The WSPU became the most militant organization for women's rights. Besides peaceful demonstrations and parades, its members heckled government speakers, cut telegraph wires, and committed arson. Their goal was to draw attention to the cause of women's suffrage.

Emmeline Pankhurst, her daughters Christabel and Sylvia, and other WSPU members were arrested and imprisoned many times. When they were jailed, the Pankhursts led hunger strikes to keep their cause in the public eye. British officials force-fed Sylvia and other activists to keep them alive. One WSPU member, Emily Davison, did give her life for the women's movement. As a protest, she threw herself in front of the king's horse at the English Derby.

Though the women's suffrage movement commanded wide attention between 1880 and 1914, its successes were gradual. Women did not win the right to vote in national elections in Great Britain and the United States until after World War I.

Democracy in France

While Great Britain moved toward true democracy in the late 1800s, democracy finally took permanent hold in France. However, France's road to democracy was rocky.

The Third Republic In the aftermath of the Franco-Prussian War, France went through a series of crises. After being released by Prussia, Napoleon III spent his last years in exile in Britain. France's National Assembly met to decide on a new government.

Meanwhile, in March 1871, a radical government called the Paris Commune took control of Paris. In May, troops loyal to the National Assembly marched into the city. Parisian workers threw up barricades in the streets and fought the army block by block. After a week of fighting, the army stamped out the Communards, as supporters of the Commune were called. About 20,000 Parisians were massacred, and much of the city burned.

Not until 1875 could the National Assembly agree on a new government. Eventually, the members voted to set up a republic. In the words of a leading French politician, it was "the system of government that divides us least." The **Third Republic,** as this new system was called, lasted over 60 years. However, France remained bitterly divided. A dozen political parties competed for power. Between 1871 and 1914, France averaged a change of government every ten months.

The Dreyfus Affair During the 1880s and 1890s, the unsteady Third Republic was threatened by monarchists, aristocrats, clergy, and army leaders. These groups wanted to return France to a monarchy or to have military rule. A controversy known as the **Dreyfus affair** became a battleground for these opposing forces. Widespread feelings of **anti-Semitism,** or prejudice against Jews, also played a role in this scandal.

In 1894, Captain Alfred Dreyfus, one of the few Jewish officers in the French army, was accused of selling military secrets to Germany. A court found him guilty, based on false evidence, and sentenced him to life in prison. In a few years, new evidence showed that Dreyfus had been framed by other army officers.

Public opinion was sharply divided over the scandal. Many army leaders, nationalists, leaders in the clergy, and anti-Jewish groups refused to let the case be reopened. They feared sudden action would cast doubt on the honor of the army. Dreyfus's defenders insisted that justice was more important and that he should be freed. In 1898, the writer Émile Zola published an open letter titled *J'accuse!* (I Accuse) in a popular French newspaper. In the letter, Zola denounced the army for covering up a scandal. Zola was given a year in prison for his views, but his letter gave strength to Dreyfus's cause. Eventually, the French government officially declared his innocence.

The Rise of Zionism The Dreyfus case showed the strength of anti-Semitism in France and other parts of Western Europe. However, persecution of Jews was even more severe in Eastern Europe. Russian officials, for example, permitted and even encouraged pogroms (puh·GRAHMS)—organized campaigns of violence against Jewish communities. From the late 1880s on, thousands of Jews fled Eastern Europe. Many headed for the United States.

For many Jews, the long history of exile and persecution convinced them that they should work for a separate homeland in Palestine. In the 1890s, a movement known as **Zionism** developed to pursue this goal. Its leader was Theodor Herzl (HEHRT·suhl), a writer in Vienna. It took many years, however, before the state of Israel was established, making the dream a reality.

E. Possible Answer Dreyfus, a Jewish army officer, was framed for spying. Army refused to reopen case; its stand was supported by nationalists, clergy, anti-Jewish groups. Others wanted to clear Dreyfus's name and expose the abuse of power by the military.

THINK THROUGH HISTORY
E. Analyzing Issues Explain the controversy over the Dreyfus affair.

Background Zion is another name for Israel, the Jewish homeland.

Communards lie massacred in this painting titled *A Street in Paris in May 1871, or the Commune* by Maximilien Luce.

ASSESS & RETEACH

Section 1 Assessment
Have students work through the assessment questions independently, and then trade papers with a partner and critique the responses.

Section Quiz
FORMAL ASSESSMENT Section Quiz, p. 125

Reteaching Activity
CLASS TIME: 20 MINUTES

Hand out copies of the compare and contrast graphic organizer and ask students to work in small groups to compare and contrast democracy in France and England.

CRITICAL THINKING TRANSPARENCIES
CT74 Compare and Contrast

CLOSE ACTIVITY

CLASS TIME: 20 MINUTES

Recognizing Effects
Have students list at least three trends in the era they have just read about and describe the results of each trend. *Possible Response: more groups demanding a voice in government; power of monarchy declining; anti-Semitism rising in Europe.*

Section 1 Assessment

1. TERMS & NAMES
Identify
- suffrage
- Chartist movement
- Queen Victoria
- Third Republic
- Dreyfus affair
- anti-Semitism
- Zionism

2. TAKING NOTES
List and evaluate five significant events from this section, using a table like the one shown. Next to each event, put a "+" if it expanded democracy, a "–" if it negatively affected democracy, and a "0" if it had a mixed impact.

Event	Evaluation

3. ANALYZING ISSUES
Look again at the excerpt from the Seneca Falls "Declaration of Sentiments" on page 662. Why do you think the members of the Seneca Falls Convention chose to model their demands on the Declaration of Independence? (It may be helpful to locate the similar section in a copy of the Declaration of Independence and compare the two passages.)

4. THEME ACTIVITY
Economics Among the Chartists' demands was pay for members of Parliament. Often when a U.S. legislature raises the pay for its own members, it creates controversy. Imagine such a raise is being considered. Write a "letter to the editor" that supports or criticizes the raise. Be sure to refer to the historical reasons for giving pay to legislators.

An Age of Democracy and Progress **283**

A N S W E R S

1. TERMS & NAMES
suffrage, p. 279
Chartist movement, p. 280
Queen Victoria, p. 280
Third Republic, p. 283
Dreyfus affair, p. 283
anti-Semitism, p. 283
Zionism, p. 283

2. TAKING NOTES
Possible Answers: Tables might include Reform Bill of 1832, Chartist movement, expansion of male suffrage in Britain in 1867, Seneca Falls declaration, Paris Commune, Third Republic, Dreyfus affair.

3. ANALYZING ISSUES
Possible Responses: To show that their demands for rights were as legitimate as the colonists' demands for rights from Great Britain; to emphasize the injustice of womens' unequal status by comparing the tyranny of men to that of King George.

4. THEME ACTIVITY
Possible Responses: Letters to the editor should refer to the Chartists' demands for pay, have a logical organization, and present a well-reasoned argument.

OBJECTIVES

① To describe how Canada achieved self-rule.

② To explain how Australia and New Zealand became Western democracies.

③ To describe the British domination of Ireland.

SKILLBUILDER

- Interpreting maps: place, region, p. 286
- Interpreting graphs, p. 287

CRITICAL THINKING

- Clarifying, p. 284
- Recognizing effects, p. 285
- Contrasting, p. 286
- Evaluating decisions, p. 288
- Comparing, p. 288
- Analyzing themes, p. 288

FOCUS

5-Minute Warm-Up

▶ **Key Ideas**

Help students understand the settlement of Australia and New Zealand by having them answer the following questions.

- Study the map on page 286. Which part of Australia most resembles Great Britain?

- Why would the settlers initially have avoided the northern and central parts of Australia?

 WARM-UP TRANSPARENCY 10

OBJECTIVE ① INSTRUCT

Canada Struggles for Self-Rule

▶ **Key Ideas**

- Conflict between French and English settlers leads to a partition of Canada.

- The Dominion of Canada is formed, and Canada expands to the Pacific.

 IN-DEPTH RESOURCES: UNIT 3
Guided Reading, p. 19

 ACCESS FOR STUDENTS ACQUIRING ENGLISH
Guided Reading (Spanish), p. 113

---

② Self-Rule for British Colonies

TERMS & NAMES
- dominion
- Maori
- Aborigine
- penal colony
- home rule

MAIN IDEA	WHY IT MATTERS NOW
Britain allowed self-rule in Canada, Australia, and New Zealand but delayed independence for Ireland.	Canada, Australia, and New Zealand are strong democracies today, while Ireland is divided and troubled.

SETTING THE STAGE By 1800, Great Britain had colonies around the world. These included small outposts in Africa and Asia. In these areas, the British managed trade with the local peoples, but they had little influence over the population at large. In the colonies of Canada, Australia, and New Zealand, on the other hand, European colonists had overrun and replaced the native populations. As Britain industrialized and prospered in the 1800s, so did these colonies. Like the United States, which had already broken away from British rule, some of these colonies were becoming strong enough to stand on their own.

Canada Struggles for Self-Rule

Canada was originally home to many Native American peoples, including the Algonquin, Huron, Cree, Blackfoot, and Inuit. The first European country to colonize Canada was France. Great Britain took possession of the country in 1763, following the French and Indian War. The thousands of French who remained there lived mostly in the lower St. Lawrence Valley. Many English-speaking colonists arrived in Canada after it came under British rule. Some came from Great Britain, and others were Americans who had stayed loyal to Britain after the American Revolution. They settled separately from the French—mostly along the Atlantic seaboard and north of the Great Lakes.

The earliest French colonists had included many fur trappers and missionaries. They tended to live among the Native Americans rather than displace them. Some French intermarried with Native Americans. As more French and British settlers arrived, they took over much of eastern and southern Canada. Native groups in the north and west, however, remained largely undisturbed until later in the 1800s.

French and English Canada Religious and cultural differences between the mostly Roman Catholic French and the mainly Protestant English-speaking colonists caused conflict in Canada. Both groups also pressed Britain for a greater voice in governing their own affairs. In 1791 the British Parliament tried to resolve both issues by creating two new Canadian provinces. Upper Canada (now Ontario) had an English-speaking majority. Lower Canada (now Quebec) had a French-speaking majority. Each province had its own elected assembly with limited powers.

The Durham Report The division of Upper and Lower Canada eased colonial tensions only temporarily. In both colonies, the royal governor and a small group of wealthy British held most of the power. During the early 1800s, the people in both colonies, led by middle-class professionals, began to demand political and economic reforms. In Lower Canada, these demands were also fueled by French resentment toward British rule. In the late 1830s, rebellions broke out in both

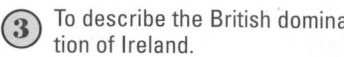

SPOTLIGHT ON

Canadian Mounties

One of the most recognized symbols of Canada, the Royal Canadian Mounted Police, began its existence in the 1870s to patrol Canada's western frontier. One of its first tasks was to drive out whiskey smugglers from the United States.

The Mounties' main purpose was to prevent bloodshed as white settlers moved into traditional Native American lands in the west. Although it was meant to be a temporary force, the Mounties became Canada's national police force.

THINK THROUGH HISTORY
A. Clarifying Why did Britain create Upper Canada and Lower Canada? Who lived in each colony?
A. Answer Created to resolve conflicts between French and English and give each group greater voice in own affairs; Upper Canada mainly English-speaking; Lower Canada mainly French

284 Chapter 10

SECTION 2 RESOURCES

PRINT RESOURCES

 IN-DEPTH RESOURCES: UNIT 3
Guided Reading, p. 19
Geography Application: The British Settle Australia and New Zealand, p. 23
Primary Source: Irish Petition to Emigrate, p. 26
Literature: "Easter 1916," p. 29

 ACCESS FOR STUDENTS ACQUIRING ENGLISH
Guided Reading (Spanish), p. 113
Geography Application: (Spanish), p. 117

FORMAL ASSESSMENT
Section Quiz, p. 126

TECHNOLOGY RESOURCES

 GEOGRAPHY TRANSPARENCIES
GT26 Canada: Growth of the Dominion, 1867–Present

 WORLD ART AND CULTURES TRANSPARENCIES
AT57 Maori pigment container

CD-ROM
Electronic Library of Primary Sources

VIDEO *Patterns of Interaction: The Geography of Food*

 INTERNET www.mlworldhistory.com

Upper and Lower Canada. The British Parliament remembered the events that had led to the American Revolution. So, it sent a reform-minded statesman, Lord Durham, to investigate Canadians' demands for self-rule.

Durham's report, issued in 1839, urged two major reforms. First, Upper and Lower Canada should be reunited as the Province of Canada, and British immigration should be encouraged. In this way, Durham said, the French would slowly become part of the dominant English culture. Second, colonists in the provinces of Canada should be allowed to govern themselves in domestic matters. Parliament should regulate only in matters of foreign policy. Within ten years, both proposals had been carried out.

The Dominion of Canada By the mid-1800s, many Canadians believed that Canada needed a central government. A central government would be better able to protect the interests of Canadians against the United States, whose territory now extended from the Atlantic to the Pacific oceans. In 1867, Nova Scotia and New Brunswick joined with the Province of Canada to form the Dominion of Canada. As a **dominion,** Canada was self-governing in domestic affairs but remained part of the British Empire.

Canada's Westward Expansion Canada's first prime minister, John MacDonald, quickly expanded Canada westward by purchasing lands and persuading frontier territories to join the Canadian union. Canada stretched to the Pacific Ocean by 1871. MacDonald also began the construction of a transcontinental railroad to unite distant parts of the dominion. It was completed in 1885.

The dominion government also took other steps to strengthen Canada. It encouraged foreign investment to develop Canada's rich supply of natural resources. It also encouraged immigration to provide a labor force for Canada's farms and factories.

Australia and New Zealand

The British sea captain James Cook claimed New Zealand in 1769 and Australia in 1770 for Great Britain. Both lands were already inhabited. On New Zealand, Cook was greeted by the **Maoris,** a Polynesian people who had settled on New Zealand's two main islands around A.D. 800. Maori culture was based on farming, hunting, and fishing. Although the Maoris had driven away Dutch explorers in the 1640s, they made peace with Cook. As British colonization began, however, they stood ready to defend their land.

When Cook reached Australia, he considered the land uninhabited. In fact, Australia was sparsely populated by **Aborigines,** as Europeans later called the native peoples. These nomadic peoples fished, hunted, and gathered food. As they did not practice warfare among themselves, they at first raised little resistance to the flood of British immigrants who settled their country.

Britain's Penal Colony Britain began colonizing Australia in 1788—not with ordinary settlers, but with convicted criminals. The prisons in England were severely overcrowded. To solve this problem, the British government established a penal colony in Australia. A **penal colony** is a place where convicts were sent to serve their sentences as an alternative to prison. (Before the American Revolution, the British had sent a few convicts to the colony of Georgia.) After their release, these people could buy land and settle as free men and women.

An Age of Democracy and Progress **285**

CONNECT *to* TODAY

The Nunavut Territory

While Canada expanded westward in the 1870s, it also gained vast lands in the Arctic north. Most of the inhabitants of this sparsely populated region were Inuit. This native people had developed a way of life in the harsh Arctic climate over a period of thousands of years.

During the 20th century, the northern region became important to Canada for its rich natural resources and as a location for military bases. At the same time, the Inuit wanted more control over the resources of their native lands and a greater voice in their own affairs.

In the early 1990s, the Inuit and the Canadian government agreed to create a new self-governing territory called Nunavut in 1999. The name is an Inuit word meaning "Our Land." Nunavut includes the eastern two-thirds of the Northwest Territories—an area of land one-fifth the size of Canada.

Australia and New Zealand to 1850

Climate Regions
- Desert
- Grassland
- Mediterranean
- Rainforest
- Savanna
- Woodlands
- Densest Aborigine or Maori populations, around 1770

GEOGRAPHY SKILLBUILDER: Interpreting Maps
1. **Place** What is the site of the first British settlement on Australia?
2. **Region** What regions of Australia and New Zealand were most densely inhabited by native peoples?

Free Settlers Arrive In time, the former convicts in both Australia and New Zealand were joined by other British settlers who came of their own free will. In the early 1800s, an Australian settler named John MacArthur experimented with breeds of sheep until he found one that produced high quality wool and thrived in the country's warm dry weather. Although sheep are not native to Australia, the raising and export of wool became its biggest business. Australians say that their country "rode to prosperity on the back of a sheep."

To encourage immigration, the government offered settlers cheap land. It used the money from land sales to lure laborers from Britain by paying the costs of the long voyage. The population grew steadily in the early 1800s and then skyrocketed after a gold rush in 1851.

The scattered settlements on Australia's east coast grew into separate colonies. Meanwhile, a few pioneers pushed westward across the vast dry interior and established outposts in western Australia. In the 1860s, settlers finally pressured the British to stop sending convicts to Australia.

Settling New Zealand European settlement of New Zealand grew more slowly. This was because the British did not claim ownership of New Zealand, as it did Australia. Rather, it recognized the land rights of the Maoris. Among the first British settlers in New Zealand were convicts who had escaped from Australia. In 1814, missionary groups began arriving from Australia seeking to convert the Maoris to Christianity.

The arrival of more foreigners stirred conflicts between the Maoris and the European settlers over land. Responding to the settlers' pleas, the British decided to annex New Zealand in 1838 and appointed a governor to negotiate with the Maoris. In a treaty signed in 1840, the Maoris accepted British rule in exchange for recognition of their land rights. Britain quickly established colonies around New Zealand. Many colonists successfully turned to producing wool and other agricultural products for export.

Self-Government Like many Canadians, the colonists of Australia and New Zealand wanted to rule themselves, yet remain in the British Empire. During the 1850s, the colonies in both Australia and New Zealand became self-governing and created parliamentary forms of government. In 1901, the Australian colonies were united under a federal constitution as the Commonwealth of Australia. During the early 1900s, both Australia and New Zealand became dominions.

The people of Australia and New Zealand pioneered a number of political reforms. For example, the secret ballot, sometimes called the Australian ballot, was first used in Australia in the 1850s. In 1893, New Zealand became the first nation in the world to give full voting rights to women. These rights were granted only to white women of European descent.

This photo from the early 20th century shows a Maori man with traditional dress and face markings.

Status of Native Peoples Native peoples and other non-Europeans were generally excluded from democracy and prosperity. As in the Americas, diseases brought by the Europeans killed a great number of both Aborigines and Maoris. As Australian settlement grew, the colonists displaced or killed many Aborigines. Sheep ranchers in particular took possession of vast tracts of land for grazing. Both the loss of open land and the spread of diseases contributed to the destruction of the Aborigines' way of life.

In New Zealand, tensions between settlers and Maoris continued to grow after it became a British colony. Between 1845 and 1872, the colonial government fought the Maoris in a series of wars. Reduced by disease and outgunned by British weapons, the Maoris were finally driven into a remote part of the country.

The Irish Fight for Home Rule

English expansion into Ireland had begun in the 1100s, when the pope granted control of Ireland to the English king. English knights invaded Ireland, and many settled there to form a new aristocracy. The Irish, who had their own ancestry, culture, and language, bitterly resented the English presence.

This resentment grew stronger after English King Henry VIII tried to tighten England's hold on Ireland. In hopes of planting a pro-English population in Ireland, Henry VIII and some later English leaders (including Elizabeth I and Oliver Cromwell) encouraged English and Scottish subjects to move there. Large numbers did, mostly to the north. Religious differences between the native Irish, who were Catholic, and these Protestant settlers caused conflicts.

Laws imposed in the 1500s and 1600s limited the rights of Catholics. For example, Catholics could no longer hold public office. They had to pay taxes to support the Church of Ireland, which was Protestant. In addition, English was made Ireland's official language.

Background
The act that joined Ireland to Britain created the United Kingdom of Great Britain and Ireland. The 1707 Act of Union had created Great Britain out of England, Scotland, and Wales.

Many Irish hated British rule. However, the British government was determined to preserve its control over Ireland. It formally joined Ireland to Britain in 1801. Though a setback for Irish nationalism, this move did give Ireland representation in the British Parliament. One brilliant Irish leader, Daniel O'Connell, persuaded Parliament to pass the Catholic Emancipation Act in 1829. This law restored many rights to Catholics.

Background
Before the famine, the average Irish adult ate an estimated 9 to 14 pounds of potatoes a day.

The Great Famine In the 1840s, Ireland experienced one of the worst famines of modern history. For many years, Irish peasants had depended on potatoes as virtually their sole source of food. From 1845 to 1848, a plant fungus ruined nearly all of Ireland's potato crop. Out of a population of 8 million, about a million people died from starvation and disease over the next few years. A traveler described what he saw on a journey through Ireland in 1847:

A VOICE FROM THE PAST
We entered a cabin. Stretched in one dark corner, scarcely visible, from the smoke and rags that covered them, were three children huddled together, lying there *because they were too weak to rise*, pale and ghastly, their little limbs—on removing a portion of the filthy covering—perfectly emaciated, eyes sunk, voice gone, and evidently in the last stage of actual starvation.
WILLIAM BENNETT, quoted in *The Peoples of Ireland*

The Great Famine, 1845–1851

Fate of the Irish during the famine

- 70% remained in Ireland, though millions more Irish emigrated after 1851
- 12% died
- 18% emigrated

Where they emigrated to (1851)

- Australia, 2.5%
- Canada, 11.5%
- Britain, 36%
- United States, 50%

Sources: R.F. Foster, *Modern Ireland, 1600–1972*; D. Fitzpatrick, *Irish Emigration, 1804–1921*

SKILLBUILDER: Interpreting Graphs
1. What percentage of Ireland's population died during the great famine?
2. Which country received the most Irish emigrants?

An Age of Democracy and Progress **287**

OBJECTIVE 3 INSTRUCT

The Irish Fight for Home Rule

▶ **Key Ideas**
- Irish Catholics struggle against British rule and Protestants.
- The great famine spurs Irish emigration.
- Ireland divides into a southern state and a northern province.

 ELECTRONIC LIBRARY OF PRIMARY SOURCES
"The Irish Potato Famine"

IN-DEPTH RESOURCES: UNIT 3
Primary Source: Irish Petition to Emigrate, p. 26

MORE ABOUT . . .
The Great Famine

The *Geography of Food* video investigates why Irish peasants came to depend so heavily on potatoes and how the Great Famine affected Irish history and world history.

PATTERNS OF INTERACTION
The Geography of Food: The Impact of Potatoes and Sugar
Videocassette: Tape 2

History from Visuals

The Great Famine, 1845–1851
Interpreting the Graphs Have students study both pie graphs. Ask them how the smaller pie graph is related to the larger one. *The smaller graph represents the 18 percent of the population who emigrated and gives a breakdown of where they went.*

Extension Activity Ask students to calculate the number of Irish who emigrated and the number who went to each country, based on a population of 8 million people. *18% = 1.44 million; Aus = 36,000; Can = 165,600; Brit = 518,400; U.S. = 720,000*

SKILLBUILDER Answers
1. 12 percent
2. United States

TEACHING OPTION | **BLOCK SCHEDULING** | ANALYZING CAUSES AND EFFECTS | **CLASS TIME 20 MINUTES**

Task Students will view the video on the Irish potato famine and analyze the causes and effects of the famine.

Materials Needed The video *The Geography of Food: The Impact of Potatoes and Sugar;* copies of the Cause and Effect graphic organizer.

Activity Have students view the video, taking notes as they can. Then ask students to work in small groups to create a cause and effect chart showing the contributing factors that led to the famine and the effects of the famine on Irish and U.S. history.

Conclusion: Discuss with students how a single disaster such as the potato famine can have multiple

causes, both human and natural, and multiple effects. How would Irish history have been different if the famine had been dealt with at the outset? What would have been the effect on Irish immigration to the United States?

 CRITICAL THINKING TRANSPARENCIES
CT75 Cause and Effect

Teacher's Edition **287**

CONNECT to TODAY

"Troubles" in Northern Ireland

The best known militant group in Northern Ireland is the Irish Republican Army (IRA). Their roots go back to another underground army, The Irish Volunteers, and to the Fenians—a group founded in the wake of the potato famine to drive the British out of Ireland by force. In a sense, the potato famine still reverberates in Ireland and Great Britain.

 IN-DEPTH RESOURCES: UNIT 3
Literature: "Easter 1916," p. 29

ASSESS & RETEACH

Section 2 Assessment

Have students work through the assessment questions in small groups. Remind them to check the chapter opener to help them respond to the question related to themes.

Section Quiz

 FORMAL ASSESSMENT
Section Quiz, p. 126

Reteaching Activity

CLASS TIME: 15 MINUTES

Have students create a chart listing the Inuit, Aborigines, and Maori. Ask them to fill in the chart by listing the native country, one or two distinguishing characteristics, and the current situation of each group.

CLOSE ACTIVITY

CLASS TIME: 20 MINUTES

Identifying Problems and Solutions

Divide the class into three groups, each representing Canada, Australia, and Ireland. Have each group describe their problems in obtaining self-rule, the solutions they proposed, and the results.

During the famine years, about a million-and-a-half people fled from Ireland. Most went to the United States; others went to Britain, Canada, and Australia. At home, in Ireland, the British government enforced the demands of the English landowners that the Irish peasants pay their rent. Many Irish lost their land and fell hopelessly in debt, while large landowners profited from higher food prices. This situation fueled even greater Irish resentment toward their British overlords.

Demands for Home Rule During the second half of the 1800s, opposition to British rule over Ireland took two forms. Some people wanted Ireland to be completely independent. A greater number of Irish preferred **home rule**—local control over internal matters only. The British refused, however, to consider home rule for many decades.

One reason for Britain's opposition to home rule was concern for Ireland's Protestants. Protestants made up a minority of the population. Most lived in the northern part of Ireland, known as Ulster. Irish Protestants feared being dominated by Catholics. Finally, in 1914, Parliament enacted a home rule bill for southern Ireland. But during World War I, Irish independence was put on hold.

Rebellion and Division Frustrated over the delay, a small group of Irish nationalists rebelled in Dublin in Easter week, 1916. British troops quickly put down the Easter Rising and executed its leaders. Their fate, however, aroused wider nationalist support.

After World War I ended, the Irish nationalists won a major victory in the elections for the British Parliament. To protest delays in home rule, the nationalist members decided not to attend Parliament. Instead, they formed an underground Irish government and led a series of violent attacks against British officials in Ireland. The attacks sparked war between the nationalists and the British government.

In 1921, Britain tried to end the violence by dividing Ireland and granting home rule to southern Ireland. Ulster, or Northern Ireland, remained a part of Great Britain. The south became a dominion called the Irish Free State. However, many Irish nationalists, led by Eamon De Valera, continued to seek total independence from Britain. In 1949, the Irish Free State declared itself the independent Republic of Ireland. The future of Northern Ireland remained an issue. Violence between Catholics and Protestants there continued off and on for decades. Then, in 1998, all parties involved in the conflict agreed to resolve the situation in Northern Ireland peacefully.

CONNECT to TODAY

The Irish Republican Army

The Irish Republican Army (IRA) was formed in 1919. It was the military arm of the Sinn Fein—an Irish nationalist party. Its original goal was to make British rule of Ireland ineffective and to drive the British out of Ireland.

In 1949 the Republic of Ireland was established. The IRA began to work for unification of Northern Ireland and the Republic of Ireland. However, Protestants in Northern Ireland do not want unification. They wish to remain a part of the United Kingdom.

Beginning in the 1970s, both the IRA and Protestant groups turned to terrorism to achieve their goals. Bombings, ambushes, and assassinations in both Ireland and Britain killed thousands before a peace agreement on Northern Ireland was reached in 1998.

This poster urges Protestant Northern Ireland to reject home rule. The militant tone foreshadows the political troubles that continued in Northern Ireland for decades.

D. Possible Answers *Yes*—it allowed the majority in each part to have its way; *No*—it has led to continuing violence and bloodshed.

THINK THROUGH HISTORY
D. Evaluating Decisions Was Britain's policy in dividing Ireland successful? Why or why not?

Section ② Assessment

1. TERMS & NAMES

Identify
- dominion
- Maori
- Aborigine
- penal colony
- home rule

2. TAKING NOTES

Using a chart like the one below, compare progress toward self-rule by recording significant political events in Canada, Australia, New Zealand, and Ireland during the period.

Country	Political Events
Canada	
Australia	
New Zealand	
Ireland	

3. COMPARING

How was Great Britain's policy towards Canada beginning in the late 1700s similar to its policy towards Ireland in the 1900s?

THINK ABOUT
- the creation of Upper and Lower Canada
- the division of Ireland into Northern Ireland and the Irish Free State

4. ANALYZING THEMES

Empire Building At various times, England encouraged emigration to each of the colonies covered in this section. What effects did this policy have on these areas?

THINK ABOUT
- cultural divisions in Canada
- native peoples in Canada, Australia, and New Zealand
- political divisions in Ireland

ANSWERS

1. TERMS & NAMES
dominion, p. 285
Maori, p. 285
Aborigine, p. 285
penal colony, p. 285
home rule, p. 288

2. TAKING NOTES
Possible Responses: (Canada) Given responsibility for own affairs, mid-1800s; dominion status, 1867. (Australia) Self-governing, set up legislature, 1850s; male suffrage, secret ballot, 1850s; dominion, early 1900s. (New Zealand) Self-governing, set up legislature, 1850s; women gain suffrage, 1893; dominion, early 1900s. (Ireland) Joins Britain, gains representation in Parliament, 1801; home rule bill passes, but does not take effect, 1914; southern Ireland becomes dominion, 1921, and becomes independent, 1949.

3. COMPARING
Possible Responses: In both, Britain created political divisions to resolve conflicts.

4. ANALYZING THEMES
Possible Responses: In Canada, Australia, and New Zealand, the British displaced the native populations (in Canada, conflicts with French caused creation of Upper and Lower Canada); religious differences became political division between northern and southern Ireland.

Expansion and Crisis in the United States

TERMS & NAMES
- manifest destiny
- Abraham Lincoln
- secede
- U.S. Civil War
- Emancipation Proclamation
- segregation

MAIN IDEA

WHY IT MATTERS NOW

The United States expanded across North America and fought a bloody civil war.

The 20th-century movements to ensure civil rights for African Americans and Hispanics are a legacy of this period.

SETTING THE STAGE The United States had won its independence from Britain in 1783. At the end of the Revolutionary War, the Mississippi River marked the western boundary of the new republic. As the original United States filled with settlers, land-hungry newcomers pushed beyond the Mississippi, looking for opportunity. The government helped them by acquiring new territory for settlement.

Americans Move Westward

Piece by piece, the United States added new territory. In 1803, President Thomas Jefferson bought the Louisiana Territory from France. The Louisiana Purchase nearly doubled the size of the new republic and extended its boundary to the Rocky Mountains. In 1819, Spain gave up Florida to the United States. In 1846, a treaty with Great Britain gave the United States part of the Oregon Territory. In the north, the nation now stretched from the Atlantic Ocean to the Pacific Ocean.

War with Mexico Meanwhile, the United States had entered a war with Mexico over Texas. When Mexico had gained its independence from Spain in 1821, it included the lands west of the Louisiana Purchase—from Texas to California. Many American settlers moved into these areas, with Mexico's acceptance. Some settlers were unhappy with Mexico's rule.

The largest number of American settlers were in the Mexican territory of Texas. In 1836, Texans revolted against Mexican rule. For nine-and-a-half years, Texas was an independent country. Then, in 1845, the United States annexed Texas. Mexico responded angrily to what it believed was an act of aggression.

Between May 1846 and September 1847, war flared between the two countries. In bitter fighting, U.S. troops captured Mexico City and forced Mexico to surrender. As part of the settlement of the Mexican-American War, Mexico ceded, or gave up possession of, territory to the United States. The Mexican Cession included California and a huge amount of territory in the Southwest. A few years later, in 1853, the Gadsden Purchase from Mexico brought the lower continental United States to its present boundaries.

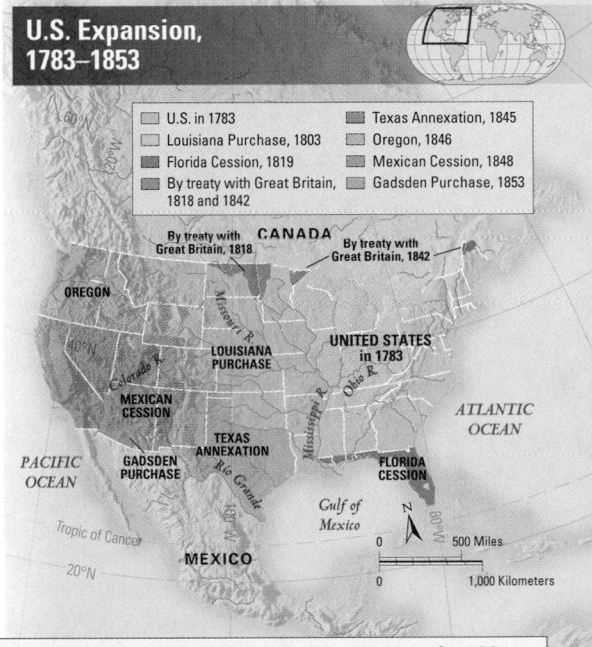

U.S. Expansion, 1783–1853

- ☐ U.S. in 1783
- ☐ Louisiana Purchase, 1803
- ■ Florida Cession, 1819
- ■ By treaty with Great Britain, 1818 and 1842
- ■ Texas Annexation, 1845
- ☐ Oregon, 1846
- ■ Mexican Cession, 1848
- ■ Gadsden Purchase, 1853

GEOGRAPHY SKILLBUILDER: Interpreting Maps
1. **Movement** *What was the first territory to be added to the United States after 1783?*
2. **Region** *What present-day states were part of the Mexican Cession?*

An Age of Democracy and Progress **289**

SECTION 3 RESOURCES

PRINT RESOURCES

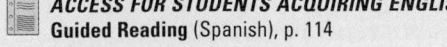 *IN-DEPTH RESOURCES: UNIT 3*
Guided Reading, p. 20
Primary Source: Railroad Poster, p. 27

 ACCESS FOR STUDENTS ACQUIRING ENGLISH
Guided Reading (Spanish), p. 114

 FORMAL ASSESSMENT
Section Quiz, p. 127

 ALTERNATIVE ASSESSMENT BOOK

TECHNOLOGY RESOURCES

CD-ROM
Electronic Library of Primary Sources

INTERNET www.mlworldhistory.com

Section 3 Overview

OBJECTIVES

(1) To trace U. S. expansion to the Pacific.

(2) To describe the effect of the Civil War on the United States.

(3) To explain the economic expansion after the Civil War.

SKILLBUILDER
- Interpreting maps: movement, region, page 289
- Interpreting maps: place, human-environment interaction, p. 291

CRITICAL THINKING
- Contrasting, p. 290
- Analyzing issues, p. 291
- Recognizing effects, p. 292
- Distinguishing fact from opinion, p. 292
- Analyzing themes, p. 292

FOCUS

5-Minute Warm-Up

▶ *Making Inferences*
By answering the following questions, students will better understand the motive for U.S. westward expansion.

- Read the first paragraph under "Manifest Destiny" on page 290. What was manifest destiny?
- How did government leaders use the concept?

 WARM-UP TRANSPARENCY 10

OBJECTIVE (1) INSTRUCT

Americans Move Westward

▶ *Key Ideas*
- The United States acquires more territory from Mexico.
- Manifest destiny justifies westward expansion.

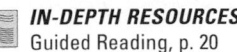 *IN-DEPTH RESOURCES: UNIT 3*
Guided Reading, p. 20

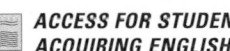 *ACCESS FOR STUDENTS ACQUIRING ENGLISH*
Guided Reading (Spanish), p. 114

U.S. Expansion, 1783–1853
(See page 289.)

Interpreting the Map Ask students what each color represents. *a U.S. land acquisition.* By how much did the U.S. grow during this period? *tripled in size*

Extension Activity Ask students whether any obvious cultural differences survive among the regions shown here. *Blue and purple areas show distinct Hispanic influences.*

SKILLBUILDER Answers
1. Louisiana Territory
2. California, Nevada, Utah, parts of Arizona, New Mexico, Colorado, and Wyoming

---

MORE ABOUT . . .
Manifest Destiny

It was newspaper editor John L. O'Sullivan who wrote that the United States had a "manifest destiny to overspread . . . the continent which Providence has given us for the development of the great experiment of liberty and . . . self-government entrusted to us."

 ELECTRONIC LIBRARY OF PRIMARY SOURCES
from A Message to Congress on Indian Policy

OBJECTIVE ② INSTRUCT

Civil War Tests Democracy

Key Ideas
• A civil war pits industrial North against agricultural South.
• The Emancipation Proclamation bans slavery in Confederate states.
• After the Civil War, Southern state laws limit freedom and opportunity for African Americans.

Manifest Destiny Many Americans eagerly supported their country's westward expansion. These people believed in **manifest destiny**—the idea that the United States had the right and duty to rule North America from the Atlantic Ocean to the Pacific Ocean. Government leaders used manifest destiny as a way of justifying any action that helped white settlers occupy new land. This included evicting Native Americans from their tribal lands.

The Indian Removal Act of 1830 made such actions official policy. This law enabled the federal government to force Native Americans living in the East to move to the West. Georgia's Cherokee tribe successfully challenged the law before the Supreme Court. However, federal and state officials found ways to sidestep this ruling. Like many other Native American tribes, the Cherokees had to move. They traveled 800 miles to Oklahoma, mostly on foot, on a journey later called the Trail of Tears. About a quarter of the Cherokees died on the trip. A survivor recalled how the journey began:

> **A VOICE FROM THE PAST**
> The day was bright and beautiful, but a gloomy thoughtfulness was depicted in the lineaments of every face. . . . At this very moment a low sound of distant thunder fell on my ear . . . and sent forth a murmur, I almost thought a voice of divine indignation for the wrong of my poor and unhappy countrymen, driven by brutal power from all they loved and cherished in the land of their fathers.
> **WILLIAM SHOREY COODEY,** quoted in *The Trail of Tears*

When the Cherokees reached their destination, they ended up on land far inferior to that which they had been forced to leave. Nor did the trail end there. As whites moved west during the second half of the 19th century, the government continued to push Native Americans off their land to make room for the new settlers. Eventually, the government demanded that Native Americans abandon most of their lands and move to reservations.

Civil War Tests Democracy

America's westward expansion raised questions about what laws and customs should be followed in the West. Ever since the nation's early days, the northern and southern parts of the United States had followed different ways of life. Each section wanted to extend its own way of life to the new territories and states in the West.

North and South The North had a diversified economy with both farms and industry. For both its factories and farms, the North depended on free workers. The South's economy, on the other hand, was based on just a few cash crops, mainly cotton. Southern planters relied on slave labor.

The economic differences between the two regions led to a conflict over slavery. Many Northerners considered slavery morally wrong. They wanted to outlaw slavery in the new western states. Some wanted to abolish slavery altogether. Most white Southerners believed slavery was necessary for their economy. They wanted laws to protect slavery in the West so that they could continue to raise cotton on the fertile soil there.

The disagreement over slavery fueled a debate about the rights of the individual states against those of the federal government. Southern politicians argued that the states had freely joined the Union, and so they could freely leave. Most Northerners felt that the Constitution of the United States had established the Union once and for all—it could not be broken.

Civil War Breaks Out Conflict between the North and South reached a climax in 1860, when **Abraham Lincoln** was elected President. Southerners fiercely opposed Lincoln, who had promised to stop the spread of slavery. One by one, Southern states began to **secede,** or withdraw, from the Union. These states came together as the Confederate States of America.

Vocabulary
manifest: clearly apparent or obvious.

THINK THROUGH HISTORY
A. Contrasting
What were the main economic differences between the Northern and Southern states?
A. Answer North had diversified economy with farms and industry, depended on free workers; South's economy relied on few cash crops and slave labor.

Task Students will create a newspaper editorial page focusing on manifest destiny.

Purpose To examine a key doctrine in American history from various perspectives.

Activity Groups of students will create part of an editorial page on manifest destiny. Students will write editorials or letters to the editor from various points

of view—Native Americans, Mexicans, Canadians, recent European immigrants, and so on. Each group will support or attack the doctrine.

 Building a Portfolio Students may want to include their part of the editorial page in their portfolios.

ALTERNATIVE ASSESSMENT BOOK
Standards for Evaluating a Cooperative Activity

Standards for Evaluation
Letters or essays should . . .

• identify each writer and cultural or ethnic group
• present a strong argument for or against manifest destiny, with supporting details
• use historically appropriate examples

Civil War in the United States, 1861–1865

Legend:
- United States
- Confederate States
- → Union advances
- ★ Major battle

Map labels:
VT., N.H., MASS., Boston, NEW YORK, CONN., R.I., New York, NEW JERSEY, Philadelphia, Baltimore, DEL, Washington, Richmond, IOWA, Chicago, ILLINOIS, INDIANA, OHIO, PENNSYLVANIA, Gettysburg, 1863, Antietam, 1862, Bull Run, 1861, W.VA. 1861-65, VIRGINIA, St. Louis, MISSOURI, KENTUCKY, NORTH CAROLINA, Goldsboro, ATLANTIC OCEAN, Memphis, TENNESSEE, Chattanooga, 1863, SOUTH CAROLINA, Shiloh, 1862, ARKANSAS, Atlanta, 1864, Ft. Sumter, 1861 (Charleston), MISSISSIPPI, ALABAMA, GEORGIA, Savannah, LOUISIANA, Vicksburg, 1863, New Orleans, FLORIDA, Gulf of Mexico

0 — 250 Miles
0 — 400 Kilometers

Civil War Casualties (in thousands)
- Union
- Confederacy

Like many other cities in the South, Richmond, Virginia, lay in ruins after the Civil War.

GEOGRAPHY SKILLBUILDER: Interpreting Maps

1. **Place** *Where and when was the northernmost battle fought in the war?*
2. **Human-Environment Interaction** *Which side do you think suffered the most devastation? Why?*

On April 12, 1861, Confederate forces fired on Fort Sumter, a federal fort in Charleston, South Carolina. Lincoln ordered the army to bring the rebel states back into the Union. The **U.S. Civil War** had begun. Four years of fighting followed, most of it in the South. Although the South had superior military leadership, the North had a larger population, better transportation, greater resources, and more factories to turn out weapons and supplies. These advantages proved too much for the South to overcome. In April 1865, the South surrendered. The United States had survived the toughest test of its democracy.

Abolition of Slavery From the beginning of the war, Lincoln declared that it was being fought to save the Union and not to end slavery. Lincoln eventually decided that ending slavery would help to save the Union. In late 1862, he issued the **Emancipation Proclamation,** declaring that all slaves in the Confederate states were free.

At first, the proclamation freed no slaves, because the Confederate states did not accept it as law. As Union armies advanced into the South, however, they freed slaves in the lands they conquered. The Emancipation Proclamation also showed people in Europe that the war was being fought against slavery. The proclamation made many Europeans, especially the British, less sympathetic to the South. They did not send the money and supplies that the South had hoped they would.

In the aftermath of the war, the U.S. Congress passed the Thirteenth Amendment to the Constitution, which forever abolished slavery in all parts of the United States. Soon after, the Fourteenth and Fifteenth Amendments extended the rights of citizenship to all Americans, black or white, and guaranteed former slaves the right to vote.

THINK THROUGH HISTORY
B. Analyzing Issues Did the Emancipation Proclamation reflect a change in Lincoln's main goal for the war?
B. Answer No, he believed that ending slavery would help him achieve his primary goal—preserving the Union.

HISTORY MAKERS

Abraham Lincoln
1809–1865

Lincoln passionately believed in preserving the Union. His upbringing might help explain why. The son of rural, illiterate parents, he educated himself. After working as rail splitter, boatman, storekeeper, and surveyor, he taught himself to be a lawyer. This led to careers in law and politics—and eventually to the White House.

In Europe, people were more or less fixed in the level of society into which they had been born. Yet the United States had been founded on the belief that all men were created equal. Therefore, Lincoln was free to achieve whatever he could. Small wonder that he fought to preserve the democracy he described as the "last best hope of earth."

An Age of Democracy and Progress **291**

Postwar Economic Expansion

▶ **Key Ideas**
• After the Civil War, an economic boom is fueled by immigration, railroads, and the opening of the West.

 IN-DEPTH RESOURCES: UNIT 3
Primary Source: Railroad Poster, p. 27

Global**Impact**
Settling the West

About 40,000 Chinese workers helped build the transcontinental railroad. These workers achieved astounding feats, such as digging tunnels through solid rock. After the railroad was finished, many Chinese settled in San Francisco in what came to be known as Chinatown.

ASSESS & RETEACH

Section 3 Assessment
Have students write their response to each question then share their papers in small groups.

Section Quiz
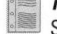 **FORMAL ASSESSMENT**
Section Quiz, p. 127

Reteaching Activity
CLASS TIME: 15 MINUTES

Ask students to create a time line of the events in this section and discuss how each event relates to U.S. history.

CLOSE ACTIVITY

CLASS TIME:

Hypothesizing
Ask students to suppose they are preparing a miniseries on U.S. history titled: *Before the Civil War, The Civil War,* and *After the Civil War.* Have students write a brief, informative, and dramatic blurb giving background information for each of the three parts.

Reconstruction From 1865 to 1877, Union troops occupied the South and enforced the constitutional protections. This period is called Reconstruction. After federal troops left the South, white Southerners passed laws that limited African Americans' rights and made it difficult for them to vote. Such laws also encouraged **segregation,** or separation, of blacks and whites in the South. African Americans continued to face discrimination in Northern states as well. Decades passed before African Americans made significant progress towards equality with other citizens.

Postwar Economic Expansion

While the South struggled to rebuild its shattered economy, the United States as a whole experienced a period of industrial expansion unmatched in history. The need for mass production and distribution of goods during the Civil War greatly speeded America's industrialization. By 1914, the United States was a leading industrial power in the world.

Immigration Industrialization could not have occurred so rapidly without the tremendous contribution of immigrants. During the 1870s, immigrants arrived at a rate of nearly 2,000 a day. By 1914, more than 20 million people had moved to the United States from Europe and Asia. Many settled in the growing industrial cities of the Northeast and Midwest. Others staked their claims in the open spaces of the West, lured by government offers of free land.

The Railroads As settlers moved west, so did the nation's rail system. In 1862, Congress had authorized money to build a transcontinental railroad. For seven years, Chinese and Irish immigrants, Mexican Americans, African Americans, and others did the backbreaking labor. They dug tunnels, built bridges, and hammered down the heavy steel tracks and wooden ties. When the transcontinental railroad was completed in 1869, railroads linked California with the Midwest and Eastern United States.

By 1900, nearly 200,000 miles of track spiderwebbed the nation. This massive system linked farm to city and boosted trade and industry. For one thing, the railroads bought huge quantities of steel. Also, trains brought materials such as coal and iron ore to factories and moved the finished goods quickly to market. They carried corn, wheat, and cattle from the Great Plains to processing plants in St. Louis, Chicago, and Minneapolis. These developments helped to make the United States a world leader in the great explosion of technological progress that marked the late nineteenth century.

Global**Impact**
Settling the West

The settling of the American West affected people in many parts of the world. Most of those drawn to the "Wild West" were American-born. However, many Europeans and Asians also arrived in search of work and land.

U.S. railroad companies, who owned much land in the West, sent agents to Europe to recruit people to buy and settle their land. Facing wars, overpopulation, and economic problems, many Europeans jumped at the offer. German and Scandinavian farmers, for example, settled widely in the upper Midwest.

The railroads also hired many immigrants as laborers—including thousands of Chinese. The Chinese sought opportunity in the United States for many of the same reasons Europeans did. Desperate families scraped together money to send one son to America. Once they arrived, however, the Chinese faced not only backbreaking labor but much discrimination.

Foreign Settlers in the West*, 1900
Top Five Countries of Origin
(in thousands)

Germany
Sweden
Britain
Norway
Ireland

*States and territories west of the Mississippi River
Source: U.S. Census Bureau

C. Possible Answer
Drew people to West, including many immigrants; by carrying raw materials to factories and finished goods to market, it boosted agriculture and industry; helped steel industry

THINK THROUGH HISTORY
C. Recognizing Effects How did railroads affect the growth of the United States?

Section **3** Assessment

1. TERMS & NAMES
Identify
• manifest destiny
• Abraham Lincoln
• secede
• U.S Civil War
• Emancipation Proclamation
• segregation

2. TAKING NOTES
Following the example below, create a time line showing the major events of the United States in the 19th century.

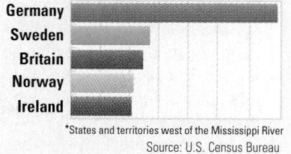

Indicate which events contributed to U.S. expansion and which events involved a war or other crisis. Label your time line "Expansion and Crisis in the United States."

3. DISTINGUISHING FACT FROM OPINION

Reread the quotation from William Shorey Coodey on page 288. What facts are conveyed in his statement? What opinions—judgment, beliefs, or feelings—does he express about the Trail of Tears? How does he use his description of events to help justify his opinions?

4. ANALYZING THEMES

Economics Imagine that circumstances had forced the North to surrender to the South in the Civil War. Therefore, two countries shared the region now occupied by the United States. What economic effects might this have had on the North? the South? the region as a whole?

THINK ABOUT
• the issue of slavery
• the impact of the Civil War
• postwar economic expansion of the United States

A N S W E R S

1. TERMS & NAMES
manifest destiny, p. 290
Abraham Lincoln, p. 290
secede, p. 290
U.S Civil War, p. 291
Emancipation Proclamation, p. 291
segregation, p. 292

2. TAKING NOTES
1803 Louisiana Purchase; 1819

Florida Cession; 1830 Trail of Tears; 1836 Texas independence; 1845 Texas Annexation; 1846–47 Mexican-American War; 1848 Mexican Cession; 1853 Gadsen Purchase; 1861–65 Civil War; 1862 Emancipation Proclamation; 1865–77 Reconstruction; 1869 Transcontinental railroad completed

3. DISTINGUISHING FACT FROM OPINION
Possible Response: Facts: elements of weather, people present, eviction taking place. Opinions: description of thunder as "divine indignation" at the wrong done to "my poor and unhappy countrymen" and at the "brutal power" of the whites.

4. ANALYZING THEMES
Possible Response: If the North had surrendered, it probably wouldn't have developed as much industrially, slowing settlement of the West. The South would have remained agricultural, and the economy of the country as a whole probably would not have grown as fast.

4 Nineteenth-Century Progress

TERMS & NAMES
- assembly line
- mass culture
- Charles Darwin
- theory of evolution
- radioactivity
- psychology

MAIN IDEA

Breakthroughs in science and technology transformed daily life and entertainment.

WHY IT MATTERS NOW

Electric lights, telephones, cars, and many other conveniences of modern life were invented during this period.

SETTING THE STAGE The Industrial Revolution happened because of inventions like the spinning jenny and the steam engine. In turn, the demands of growing industries spurred even greater advances in technology. By the late 1800s, advances in both industry and technology were occurring faster than ever before. In industrialized countries, economic growth produced many social changes. At the same time, a surge of scientific discovery pushed the frontiers of knowledge forward.

Inventions Change Ways of Life

In the early 1800s, coal and steam drove the machines of industry. By the late 1800s, new kinds of energy were coming into use. One was gasoline, which powered a new type of engine called an internal combustion engine. Small, light, and efficient, this engine would eventually make the automobile possible. Another kind of energy was the mysterious force called electricity. In the 1870s, the electric generator was developed, which produced a current that could power machines. This invention made it possible to bring the magic of electricity into daily life.

Edison the Inventor If electricity seemed like magic to people in the 19th century, Thomas Edison was perhaps the century's greatest magician. Over his career, Edison patented more than 1,000 inventions, including the light bulb and the phonograph.

Early in his career, Edison started a research laboratory in Menlo Park, New Jersey. Most of his important inventions were developed there, with help from the researchers he employed. Indeed, the idea of a laboratory for industrial research and development may have been Edison's most important invention.

Bell and Marconi Revolutionize Communication Other inventors helped harness electricity to transmit sounds over great distances. Alexander Graham Bell was a teacher of deaf students who invented the telephone in his spare time. He displayed his device at the Philadelphia Exposition of 1876. The emperor of Brazil used it to speak to his aide in another room. When he heard the reply he exclaimed, "My word! It speaks Portuguese!"

The Italian inventor Guglielmo Marconi used theoretical discoveries about electromagnetic waves to create the first radio in 1895. This device was important because it sent messages (using Morse Code) through the air, without the use of wires. Primitive radios soon became standard equipment for ships at sea. Not until later could radios transmit human voices.

Ford Sparks the Automobile Industry In the 1880s, German inventors used a gasoline engine to power a vehicle—the automobile.

An Age of Inventions

Light Bulb
Edison and his team invented the first practical electric light bulb in 1879. Within a few years, Edison had perfected a longer-lasting bulb and begun installing electric lighting in New York City.

Telephone
Alexander Graham Bell demonstrated the first telephone in 1876. It quickly became an essential of modern life. By 1900, there were nearly 2 million telephones in the United States. By 1912, there were 8.7 million.

An Age of Democracy and Progress **293**

Section 4 Overview

OBJECTIVES

1. To describe inventions of the late 19th century and their impact on daily life.

2. To explain the rise of mass culture.

3. To list 19th century advances in medicine and science.

4. To describe the emergence of the social sciences.

CRITICAL THINKING

- Making inferences, p. 294
- Recognizing effects, p. 295
- Analyzing causes, pp. 294, 297
- Clarifying, pp. 298, 299
- Comparing and contrasting, p. 299

FOCUS

5-Minute Warm-Up

▶ *Recognizing Effects*
Answering the following questions will help students understand the impact of 19th-century inventions.

1. Read "An Age of Inventions" on pages 293 and 294. Between 1910 and 1912, how many more people acquired telephones?

2. What invention enabled companies to make products more efficiently?

 WARM-UP TRANSPARENCY 10

OBJECTIVE 1 INSTRUCT

Inventions Change Ways of Life

▶ *Key Ideas*
- Inventions in electronics, communication technology, manufacturing methods, and aircraft usher in a new industrial age.

IN-DEPTH RESOURCES: UNIT 3
Guided Reading, p. 21

Primary Source: Orville Wright's Diary, p. 28

ACCESS FOR STUDENTS ACQUIRING ENGLISH
Guided Reading (Spanish), p. 115

SECTION 4 RESOURCES

PRINT RESOURCES

IN-DEPTH RESOURCES: UNIT 3
Guided Reading, p. 21
Skillbuilder Practice: Analyzing Issues, p. 22
Primary Source: Orville Wright's Diary, p. 28
Literature: from *The Origin*, p. 31
History Makers: Marie and Pierre Curie, p. 35
Connections Across Time and Cultures, p. 36

ACCESS FOR STUDENTS ACQUIRING ENGLISH
Guided Reading (Spanish), p. 115
Skillbuilder Practice: (Spanish), p. 116

FORMAL ASSESSMENT
Section Quiz, p. 128

TECHNOLOGY RESOURCES

CRITICAL THINKING TRANSPARENCIES
CT26 Movers and Shakers, 1815–1914
CT62 Visual Summary

CD-ROM
Electronic Library of Primary Sources

INTERNET www.mlworldhistory.com

Teacher's Edition **293**

An Age of Inventions

Automobile Assembly Line
Ford's major innovation was to improve efficiency in his factory. By introducing the assembly line, he reduced the time it took to build a car from 12.5 to 1.5 worker-hours.

Airplane
Through trial and error, the Wright brothers designed wings that provided lift and balance in flight. Their design is based on principles that are still used in every aircraft.

French artist Henri de Toulouse-Lautrec designed this bicycle poster in 1896.

Automobile technology developed quickly, but since early cars were built by hand, they were expensive to buy and repair.

An American mechanic named Henry Ford decided to make cars that were affordable for most people. "The way to make automobiles is to make them all alike," he said, "just as one pin is like another when it comes from the pin factory." To build his cars alike, Ford used standardized, interchangeable parts. He also built them on an **assembly line**—a line of workers who each put a single piece on unfinished cars as they passed on a moving belt.

Assembly line workers could put together an entire Model T Ford in less than two hours. When Ford introduced this plain, black, reliable car in 1908, it sold for $850. As his production costs fell, Ford lowered the price. Eventually it dropped to less than $300—well within the reach of the middle class. Other factories adopted Ford's ideas. By 1914, more than 600,000 cars were traveling around on the world's roads.

The Wright Brothers Fly Two bicycle mechanics from Dayton, Ohio, named Wilbur and Orville Wright solved the age-old riddle of flight. On December 17, 1903, they flew a gasoline-powered flying machine at Kitty Hawk, North Carolina. The longest flight that day lasted only 59 seconds, but it was enough to begin a whole new industry—aircraft manufacture.

The Rise of Mass Culture

In earlier periods, art, music, and most theater had been largely the concern of the wealthy. This group had the money, leisure time, and education to enjoy high culture. It was not until about 1900 that people could speak of **mass culture**—the appeal of art, writing, music, and other forms of entertainment to a much larger audience.

Changes Produce Mass Culture There were several causes for the rise of mass culture around the turn of the century. First, the spread of public education increased literacy in both Europe and North America. This, in turn, provided a mass market for books, newspapers, and magazines. Improvements in communications made it possible to meet the broad demand for information and entertainment. For example, new high-speed presses duplicated thousands of pages in a few hours. They made publications cheaper and easier to produce. The invention of the phonograph and records brought music directly into people's homes.

Working folks now had more time for leisure pursuits. By 1900, most industrial countries had limited the working day to ten hours. Most people worked Monday through Friday and a half-day on Saturday. This five-and-a-half day work week created the "weekend," a special time for relaxation. More leisure time in evenings and on weekends allowed workers to take part in activities that their grandparents never had time to enjoy.

Music Halls and Vaudeville A popular leisure activity was a trip to the local music hall. On a typical evening, a music hall might offer a dozen or more different acts. It might feature singers, dancers, comedians, jugglers, magicians, acrobats, and even trained parakeets. In the United States, musical variety shows were called vaudeville.

294 Chapter 10

Vaudeville acts traveled from town to town, appearing at theaters with names such as the Gaiety, the Grand, and the Orpheum.

Movies Are Born During the 1880s, several inventors worked at trying to record and project moving images. One successful design came from France. Another came from Thomas Edison's laboratory. The earliest motion pictures caused a sensation only because of their novelty. They were black and white, lasted less than a minute, and had no plot. One of Edison's first films, for example, showed nothing but a man sneezing.

By the early 1900s, filmmakers were producing the first feature films (see Something in Common, page 296). Movies quickly became big business. By 1910, five million Americans attended some 10,000 theaters each day to watch silent movies. The European movie industry experienced similar growth.

Sports Entertain Millions With new time at their disposal, ordinary people began to enjoy all kinds of sports and outdoor activities. For every person who played sports, even more enjoyed watching them. Spectator sports now became entertainment for many. In the United States, football and baseball soared in popularity. In Europe, the first professional soccer clubs formed and drew big crowds—120,000 fans turned out to watch a 1913 match in England. Favorite English sports such as cricket spread to the British colonies of Australia, India, and South Africa.

As a result of the growing interest in sports, the international Olympic Games began in 1896. They revived the ancient Greek tradition of holding an athletic competition among countries every four years. Fittingly, the first modern Olympics took place in Athens.

Fans pack a stadium to watch an English soccer championship in 1911.

New Ideas in Medicine and Science

Earlier centuries had established the scientific method as a road to knowledge. Now this method brought powerful new insights into nature as well as many practical results.

The Germ Theory of Disease An important breakthrough in the history of medicine was the germ theory of disease. It was developed by French chemist Louis Pasteur in the mid-1800s. While examining the fermentation process of alcohol, Pasteur discovered that it was caused by microscopic organisms he called bacteria. He also learned that heat killed bacteria. This led him to develop the process of *pasteurization* to kill germs in liquids such as milk. Soon, it became clear to Pasteur and others that bacteria also caused diseases.

A British surgeon named Joseph Lister read about Pasteur's work. He thought germs might explain why half of all surgical patients died of infections. In 1865, he ordered that his surgical wards be kept spotlessly clean. He insisted that wounds be washed in antiseptics, or germ-killing liquids. As a result, 85 percent of Lister's patients survived. Soon, other hospitals began to follow Lister's standards of cleanliness.

Public officials, too, began to understand that cleanliness helped prevent the spread of disease. Cities built plumbing and sewer systems and took other steps to improve public health. Meanwhile, medical researchers developed vaccines or cures for such deadly diseases as typhus, typhoid fever, diphtheria, and yellow fever. These advances helped people live longer, healthier lives.

C. Possible Answer Created better understanding of how infectious disease spreads, led to pasteurization, improved survival rates for surgery, led to installation of city sanitation, led to development of vaccines or cures for some deadly infectious diseases.

THINK THROUGH HISTORY
C. Recognizing Effects What impact did the germ theory of disease have on public health?

An Age of Democracy and Progress **295**

Mass Entertainment

In 1903, an American filmmaker named Edwin S. Porter presented the first feature film, *The Great Train Robbery*. Audiences packed theaters on both sides of the Atlantic to see it. Movies soon became one of the most popular forms of mass entertainment around the world. Today, billions of people still flock to movie theaters, despite newer forms of entertainment such as television and videos. One reason that going to the movies remains popular is the pleasure of shared experience—seeing a movie, a play, a circus, or sporting event as part of a large audience.

American Movies

Edwin S. Porter's *The Great Train Robbery* did something no other motion picture had done—it told a story! The silent, 12-minute action film portrayed a sensational robbery (shown in these stills) and the capture of bandits by a sheriff's posse. Films such as *The Great Train Robbery* launched a new art form. Movies made possible a new kind of visual storytelling, whose realistic images were a hit with a mass audience.

a closer look MOVIE STARS

296 Chapter 10

"Little Mary" Pickford, as she was affectionately known, is best remembered for portraying sweet, innocent roles.

Francis X. Bushman was a popular leading man. He is shown here in *Ben Hur* (1926).

Russian Circus

The Russian circus began when an English showman sent a troupe of stunt horse riders to Empress Catherine the Great in the 1790s. Russia has been famous for the popularity and quality of its circuses ever since. Most Russian circuses, like this one with animal trainer Vyacheslav Zolkin, feature trained bears. Russian circuses usually use a single ring so that audiences can sit close to the performers.

Chinese Opera

The performing arts have a long history in China. Characters in Chinese drama, such as this troupe from the Beijing Opera, wear elaborate silk costumes and stylized facial makeup or masks. The character of the actors is expressed in part through the symbolic use of color. This scene is from *The Story of the White Snake*, a tragic love story about a white snake that is transformed into a human being and marries a young man.

Camel Races in India

Seasonal festivals provide entertainment in rural areas throughout the world. Thousands of people from all over India, as well as foreign tourists, flock to the town of Pushkar in November for its annual fair. Although the main business is camel trading, the Pushkar fair is enlivened with dramas, food stalls, magic shows—and the races. Shown here is a camel rider racing at these annual festivities. These races are as eagerly anticipated as the Kentucky Derby is in the United States.

Theda Bara, the silent screen's "vamp," became an overnight sensation after her first starring role in 1915.

Connect *to* History

Analyzing Causes How does each type of entertainment reflect its country's culture?

SEE SKILLBUILDER HANDBOOK, PAGE 653

Connect *to* Today

Making a Chart List at least three other forms of entertainment that you enjoy during your leisure. Combine them in a class chart. Identify which ones are individual experiences and which are pop culture events.

INTERNET CONNECTION

Visit us at www.mlworldhistory.com to learn more about popular entertainment.

An Age of Democracy and Progress **297**

HISTORY MAKERS

**Charles Darwin
1809–1882**

The key event in Charles Darwin's life was his five-year journey as a naturalist aboard the *H.M.S. Beagle.* The ship was on an expedition to survey the western and southern coast of South America and some Pacific islands. Darwin kept notebooks of the plants and animals he saw in various environments. After he came home, he used the data in these notebooks to develop his theory of evolution.

Darwin's Theory of Evolution No scientific idea of modern times aroused more controversy than the work of English biologist **Charles Darwin.** The cause of the controversy was Darwin's answer to the question that faced biologists: How can we explain the tremendous variety of plants and animals on earth? A widely accepted answer in the 1800s was the idea of special creation. According to this view, every kind of plant and animal had been created by God at the beginning of the world and had remained the same since then.

Darwin challenged the idea of special creation. Based on his research, he developed a theory that all forms of life, including human beings, evolved from earlier living forms that had existed millions of years ago.

In 1859, Darwin published his thinking in a book titled *The Origin of Species by Means of Natural Selection.* According to the idea of natural selection, populations tend to grow faster than the food supply and so must compete for food. The members of a species that survive are those that are fittest, or best adapted to their environment. These surviving members of a species produce offspring that share their advantages. Gradually, over many generations, the species may change. In this way, new species evolve. Darwin's idea of change through natural selection came to be called the **theory of evolution.**

The Origin of Species caused great excitement among scientists. At the same time, Darwin's ideas roused a storm of debate outside the scientific community. Many people believed that the idea of evolution directly contradicted the account of creation in the Bible.

Even today, well over 100 years after *The Origin of Species* was first published, Darwin's ideas are controversial.

Mendel and Genetics Although Darwin said that living things passed on their variations from one generation to the next, he did not know how they did so. In the 1850s and 1860s, an Austrian monk named Gregor Mendel discovered that there is a pattern to the way that certain traits are inherited. Although his work was not widely known until 1900, Mendel's work began the science of genetics. Later, biologists discovered genes, the units of living matter that carry traits from parents to offspring.

This photograph shows Marie Curie in her laboratory.

Advances in Chemistry and Physics In 1803, the British chemist John Dalton theorized that all matter is made of tiny particles called atoms. Dalton showed that elements contain only one kind of atom, which has a specific weight. Compounds, on the other hand, contain more than one kind of atom.

In 1869, Dmitri Mendeleev (MEHN·duh·LAY·uhf), a Russian chemist, organized a chart on which all the known elements were arranged in order of weight, from lightest to heaviest. He left gaps where he predicted that new elements would be discovered. Later, his predictions proved correct. Mendeleev's chart, called the Periodic Table, is still used by scientists today.

A husband and wife team working in Paris discovered two of the missing elements. Marie and Pierre Curie found that a mineral called pitchblende released a powerful form of energy. In 1898, Marie Curie gave this energy the name **radioactivity.** The Curies discovered two new elements that they named radium and polonium. Both were highly radioactive. In 1903, the Curies shared the Nobel Prize for physics for their work on radioactivity. In 1911, Marie won the Nobel Prize for chemistry for the discovery of radium and polonium.

Physicists around 1900 tried to unravel the secrets of the atom. Earlier scientists believed that the atom was the smallest particle that existed. A British physicist named Ernest Rutherford suggested that atoms were made up of yet smaller particles. Each atom, he said, had a nucleus surrounded by one or more particles called electrons. Soon other physicists such as Max Planck, Neils Bohr, and Albert Einstein were studying the structure and energy of atoms. Their discoveries, discussed in Chapter 15, were fully as revolutionary as Newton's or Darwin's ideas.

The Social Sciences

The scientific theories of the 1800s prompted scholars to study human society and behavior in a scientific way. Interest in these fields grew enormously during that century, as global expeditions produced a flood of new discoveries about ancient civilizations and world cultures. This interest led to the development of modern social sciences such as archaeology, anthropology, and sociology.

An important new social science was **psychology,** the study of the human mind and behavior. The Russian biologist Ivan Pavlov broke new ground in psychology with a famous experiment in the early 1900s. Ordinarily, a dog's mouth waters at the smell of food. Pavlov began ringing a bell each time he gave food to a dog. Eventually, the dog learned to associate the bell with food. Each time the bell rang, the dog salivated, even if no food was present.

Pavlov concluded that an animal's reflexes could be changed, or conditioned, through training. He also applied these findings to humans. He believed that human actions were often unconscious reactions to experiences and could be changed by training.

Another pioneer in psychology, the Austrian doctor Sigmund Freud, also believed that the unconscious mind drives how people think and act. In Freud's view, unconscious forces such as suppressed memories, desires, and impulses help shape behavior. He created a type of therapy called psychoanalysis to help people deal with the psychological conflicts created by these forces.

As Chapter 15 explains, Freud's theories became very influential. However, his idea that the mind was beyond conscious control also shocked many people. The ideas of Freud and Pavlov challenged the fundamental idea of the Enlightenment—that reason was supreme. The new ideas about psychology began to shake the 19th-century faith that humans could perfect themselves and society through reason.

Unresolved Problems

Technology Changes People's Lives

In the mid-1800s, science and technology began to work together to improve life. Scientific discoveries were applied to industrial and commercial problems. Technological changes altered the location and methods of work, play, and even warfare.

Many of the inventions that modernized life grew out of earlier discoveries. For example, a German watchmaker created the first form of electric light in 1854. But in 1880, Thomas Edison perfected a practical electric light.

Introduction of electric lights dramatically changed the lives of people. The day was extended, streets became safer, and new leisure time activities developed.

See Epilogue, p. 587.

Section 4 Assessment

1. TERMS & NAMES
Identify
• assembly line
• mass culture
• Charles Darwin
• theory of evolution
• radioactivity
• psychology

2. TAKING NOTES
Using a web diagram like the one below, connect the inventors, scientists, and thinkers with the invention, discovery, or new idea for which they were responsible.

People and Progress

Which breakthrough do you think helped people the most? Why?

3. COMPARING AND CONTRASTING
How is the mass culture that rose at the end of the 19th century similar to mass culture today? How is it different? Explain your response.

THINK ABOUT
• the role of technology
• increase in leisure time
• new forms of entertainment

4. THEME ACTIVITY
Science and Technology
Choose one of the inventions, discoveries, or new ideas that occurred in this period and plan a museum exhibit of that breakthrough. Decide how to display the invention or discovery. Write a description of it, who was responsible for it, and how it has affected peoples' lives.

An Age of Democracy and Progress **299**

ANSWERS

Chapter 10 Assessment

TERMS & NAMES

1. suffrage, p. 279
2. anti-Semitism, p. 283
3. dominion, p. 285
4. penal colony, p. 285
5. home rule, p. 288
6. manifest destiny, p. 290
7. Emancipation Proclamation, p. 291
8. segregation, p. 292
9. assembly line, p. 294
10. theory of evolution, p. 298

REVIEW QUESTIONS

Answers will vary.

11. Reform Bill of 1832, expansion of suffrage in 1867 and 1884, secret ballot, pay members of Parliament and an end to property requirement for serving in Parliament.

12. Its members carried out peaceful demonstrations and parades, heckled government speakers, cut telegraph wires, and committed arson.

13. Cultural and religious differences between English- and French-speaking Canadians.

14. It was not open to ordinary settlers but was used instead as a penal colony.

15. Britain was concerned about the Protestants in Northern Ireland, a small minority who wanted British protection.

16. Louisiana Purchase (from France), Florida Cession (from Spain), Texas Annexation, treaties with Britain, Mexican Cession, Gadsden Purchase (from Mexico).

17. Economic differences: North had a diversified economy with both farms and industry; South depended on a few cash crops, mainly cotton. Slavery issue: Southerners depended on slavery to protect their economy, while Northerners considered slavery morally wrong.

18. The members of a species that are best adapted to their environment will survive. Many people believed that evolution directly contradicted the account of creation in the Bible.

19. (a) genetics (b) showed that each element contains only one kind of atom (c) Periodic Table of elements (d) discovered radioactivity and two new elements (e) suggested atoms were made

Visual Summary

Democracy   Progress

1815

1825

1832 First Reform Bill in Britain

1835

1845

1848 Seneca Falls Convention

1850s Mendel experiments with genetics

1855

1859 Darwin's *Origin of Species*

1861 Outbreak of U.S. Civil War

1860s Medical advances of Pasteur and Lister

1862 Emancipation Proclamation

1865

1867 Suffrage extended to working-class men in Britain

1869 Transcontinental railroad completed in United States

Dominion of Canada formed

Mendeleev's Periodic Table of Elements

1871 Paris Commune

1875

1876 Bell patents telephone

1875 Third Republic in France

1879 Edison develops light bulb

1880s Internal combustion engine perfected

1884 Suffrage extended to male rural workers in Britain

1885

1895 Marconi invents radio

1893 Women gain voting rights in New Zealand

1896 First modern Olympic Games

1895

1894 Dreyfus affair begins

1898 Curies discover radioactivity

1896 Zionist movement founded

1903 First airplane flight by Wright brothers

1903 WSPU founded

1905

The Great Train Robbery released

1908 Ford introduces Model T

1915

up of smaller elements

20. After conditioning a dog's reflexes, Pavlov concluded that human actions were not always determined consciously. Freud worked to understand how suppressed memories, desires, and impulses help shape behavior and created psychoanalysis to help people deal with psychological problems.

TERMS & NAMES

Briefly explain the importance of each of the following to the reforms, crises, or advances of Western nations from 1815 to 1914.

1. suffrage
2. anti-Semitism
3. dominion
4. penal colony
5. home rule
6. manifest destiny
7. Emancipation Proclamation
8. segregation
9. assembly line
10. theory of evolution

REVIEW QUESTIONS

SECTION 1 *(pages 279–283)*
Democratic Reform and Activism

11. What political reforms had the effect of expanding democracy for men in Britain?

12. How did the Women's Social and Political Union call attention to its cause?

SECTION 2 *(pages 284–288)*
Self-Rule for British Colonies

13. What cultural conflict caused problems for Canada?

14. How did Australia's early history differ from that of other British colonies?

15. Why did the British government pass a home rule bill for Southern Ireland only?

SECTION 3 *(pages 289–292)*
Expansion and Crisis in the United States

16. In what different ways did the United States gain territory in the 1800s?

17. How did the North and South differ economically? Why was the issue of slavery so divisive?

SECTION 4 *(pages 293–299)*
Nineteenth-Century Progress

18. What was Darwin's principle of natural selection? Why did many people oppose his theory of evolution?

19. What contributions did each of the following scientists make?
(a) Mendel (b) Dalton (c) Mendeleev (d) Marie Curie (e) Rutherford

20. How did Pavlov and Freud contribute to the study of psychology?

1906 Ford 6 Cylinder Touring Car
Price $2,500

6 cylinders—40 h. p. 4 to 50 miles per hour on high gear. *Perfected* magneto ignition—mechanical oiler, 114 inch wheel base, luxurious body for 5 passengers, weight 2000 pounds.

1906 Ford Runabout, as advanced as our touring car in design and even more surprising in price—will be fully illustrated and described in our next advertisement.

Both these Cars on exhibition at the New York Automobile Show.

Ford Motor Company
Detroit, Mich.

Interact *with* History

On page 278, you considered the benefits and drawbacks of technological progress. Now consider the inventions you read about in this chapter. Write a paragraph explaining which you think was most significant. State the reasons for your choice. Consider

• Which affected the most people?
• Which changed daily life the most?
• Which changed industry the most?
• Which produced the greatest benefit with the fewest drawbacks?

Share your paragraph with the class.

Interact *with* History

Possible Responses: Students should be able to explain why they believe their invention had the greatest impact on people, how it changed daily life and industry, and what its benefits and drawbacks were. Be sure they consider carefully the trade-offs between benefits and costs. Remind students that many inventions have had benefits and drawbacks that were not known at the time the item was developed.

CRITICAL THINKING

1. ASSEMBLY LINE WORK

THEME ECONOMICS Using the quotation from Henry Ford on page 294, explain how his attitude on making goods might have differed from those of a traditional craftsperson. From a worker's point of view, what would be the advantages and disadvantages of an assembly line?

2. AN ERA OF CHANGE

Create a web diagram of the major political, economic, social and cultural, and scientific and technological changes of the 1800s and early 1900s.

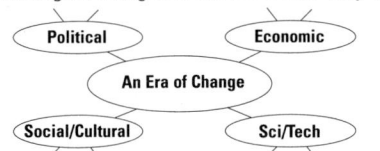

3. SOCIAL DARWINISM

Charles Darwin did not fully agree with the Social Darwinists. How do natural selection and economic competition differ?

4. ANALYZING PRIMARY SOURCES

On January 11, 1898, Major Esterhazy, the army officer who had actually committed the crimes of which Alfred Dreyfus was accused, was judged innocent by a court martial, or military court. Two days later, Émile Zola published an open letter about the Dreyfus affair. Part of that letter appears below.

> **A VOICE FROM THE PAST**
> It is only now that the Affair is beginning, because only now are men assuming clear positions: on the one hand, the guilty, who do not wish justice to be done; on the other, the followers of justice, who will give their lives so that justice may triumph.
> I accuse the War Office of having carried on in the press an abominable campaign in order to screen their mistake and mislead the public.
> I accuse the first Court Martial of having violated the law by condemning an accused man on the basis of a secret document and I accuse the second Court Martial of having, in obedience to orders, screened that illegal act by knowingly acquitting a guilty man.
> As to the men I accuse, I do not know them. I have never seen them, I have no resentment or hatred toward them. I have but one passion—that of light.

- Of what crimes did Zola accuse the French War Office and the Courts Martial?
- What did Zola claim to be his motive for making these accusations?

CHAPTER ACTIVITIES

1. LIVING HISTORY: Unit Portfolio Project

THEME EMPIRE BUILDING Your unit portfolio project focuses on the effects of empire building on all the lands and peoples involved (see page 249). For Chapter 10 you might use one of the following ideas to add to your portfolio.

- Design and produce a handbill that might have been distributed by English-speaking Canadians demanding a representative government.
- Write an editorial that might have appeared in a newspaper in 19th-century New Zealand. In the editorial, address the issue of British settlers' taking land from the Maori, and the Maori response.
- Draw a political cartoon that reflects how Britain treated Ireland during the Great Famine.

2. CONNECT TO TODAY: Cooperative Learning

THEME SCIENCE AND TECHNOLOGY Breakthroughs in science, technology, and medicine transformed daily life in the 1800s. Many of those inventions and discoveries still affect us today. Work with a partner to make a collage of 19th-century breakthroughs as they are reflected in modern life.

- Begin by noting all the inventions and discoveries presented in the chapter. Then brainstorm ways that they might be represented visually.
- In magazines or newspapers, look for the pictures you need. If you cannot find a particular picture, try drawing it.
- Determine a creative way to identify the pictures and link them with the 19th-century breakthroughs.

3. INTERPRETING A TIME LINE

Revisit the time line on pages 248–249, and study the segment for Chapter 10. Which event do you think was the most significant? Why?

FOCUS ON POLITICAL CARTOONS

This 1852 English cartoon titled "A Court for King Cholera" depicts a poor section of the city. Notice the children playing with a dead rat and the woman picking through the rubbish heap. At the time, some health experts believed that the epidemic disease cholera spread from the air around rubbish heaps.

- What does the artist say about the unhealthy living conditions of the poor?
- Do you think the artist is sympathetic to the urban poor? Why or why not?

Connect to History What changes took place in the 19th century that helped eliminate the spread of diseases like cholera in Western cities?

An Age of Democracy and Progress **301**

CHAPTER ACTIVITIES

1. LIVING HISTORY: UNIT PORTFOLIO PROJECT

Standards for Evaluation
Handbills should meet the following criteria:

- Present a strong point of view.
- Contain a slogan to catch people's attention.
- Give specific data about the problem.
- Tell how to join the struggle.

Standards for Evaluation
Editorials should meet the following criteria:

- Express a strong point of view supported by facts.
- Present the Maori side of the issue.
- Recommend a course of action.

Standards for Evaluation
Political cartoons should meet the following criteria:

- Show a definite point of view.
- Illustrate one aspect of Britain's treatment of Ireland.

2. CONNECT TO TODAY: COOPERATIVE LEARNING

Standards for Evaluation
Collages should meet the following criteria:

- Present a range of inventions and discoveries.
- Include labels or other descriptions.
- Show the value of the inventions.

3. INTERPRETING A TIME LINE

Students should give reasons for their choices and be able to discuss the significance of the event they choose.

FOCUS ON POLITICAL CARTOONS

- The artist shows how crowded and unsanitary conditions were
- Sympathetic: artist has compassion for people living in such conditions; Unsympathetic: artist shows that people create such conditions themselves

Connect to History Germ theory of disease; discovery by Dr. John Snow that cholera spread by contaminated drinking water; building of urban plumbing and sewage systems

Teacher's Edition **301**

CRITICAL THINKING

1. ASSEMBLY LINE WORK
Possible Responses: Political: Ford: pride in efficiency vs. pride in work. Advantages: steady job, efficient use of time/energy, specialization. Disadvantages: repetition, impersonality.

2. AN ERA OF CHANGE
Possible Responses: Political: British democratic reforms, British monarchy, suffrage campaigns, Third Republic, self-rule for Canada, Australia, and New Zealand, U.S. territorial expansion, secession, and civil war. *Economic:* abolition of slavery in U.S., postwar expansion, transcontinental railroad, assembly line. *Social/Cultural:* colonization of Australia/New Zealand, Zionism, manifest destiny, settlement of the U.S. West, U.S. immigration, mass culture, Social Darwinism. *Sci/Tech:* light bulb, phonograph, telephone, radio, internal combustion engine, airplane, motion pictures, germ theory, pasteurization, theory of evolution, genetics, atomic theory.

3. SOCIAL DARWINISM
Possible Responses: Nature of adaptation, element of luck in entrepreneurship, inherited wealth.

4. ANALYZING PRIMARY SOURCES
- War Office: lied to public about case; Courts Martial: condemned innocent man; acquitted guilty man.
- His passion for "light," or truth and justice

	Key Ideas	**COPY MASTERS**	**ASSESSMENT**
SECTION 1 **Imperialists Divide Africa** *pp. 305–309*	*Western European nations race to divide Africa among themselves. They draw territorial boundaries without regard to Africans' ethnic, linguistic, and cultural divisions.*	*In-Depth Resources: Unit 3* • **Guided Reading,** p. 37 • **Geography Application:** David Livingstone Explores Southern Africa, p. 43 • **Primary Source:** British Contract with an African King, p. 45 • **Literature:** "The Burial," p. 49	P E *Section 1 Assessment,* p. 309 *Formal Assessment* • Section Quiz, p. 137 *Alternative Assessment Book* • Standards for Evaluating a Cooperative Activity
SECTION 2 **Imperialism Case Study: Nigeria** *pp. 310–316*	*Europeans use colonies, protectorates, spheres of influence, economic imperialism, and different patterns of management to control African colonies. African resistance movements emerge in response.*	*In-Depth Resources: Unit 3* • **Guided Reading,** p. 38 • **Primary Source:** Letter from Menelik II, p. 46 • **Literature:** from *Things Fall Apart,* p. 50 • **History Makers:** Menelik II, p. 52 • **Connections Across Time and Cultures:** Two Periods of Colonization and Imperialism, p. 54	P E *Section 2 Assessment,* p. 315 *Formal Assessment* • Section Quiz, p. 138 *Alternative Assessment Book* • Standards for Evaluating a Cooperative Activity
SECTION 3 **Muslim Lands Fall to Imperialist Demands** *pp. 317–320*	*After the death of Suleiman I, European nations divide the Ottoman Empire. A combined British-French-Ottoman force defeats the Russians in the Crimean War, and the British seize the Suez Canal.*	*In-Depth Resources: Unit 3* • **Guided Reading,** p. 39	P E *Section 3 Assessment,* p. 320 *Formal Assessment* • Section Quiz, p. 139 *Alternative Assessment Book* • Standards for Evaluating a Cooperative Activity
SECTION 4 **British Imperialism in India** *pp. 321–325*	*Britain gradually attains control over India, establishing the Raj. British rule gives rise to nationalist feelings and to resistance movements.*	*In-Depth Resources: Unit 3* • **Guided Reading,** p. 40 • **Skillbuilder Practice:** Analyzing Assumptions and Biases, p. 42 • **Primary Source:** Letter Opposing the English, p. 47	P E *Section 4 Assessment,* p. 325 *Formal Assessment* • Section Quiz, p. 140 *Alternative Assessment Book* • Standards for Evaluating a Cooperative Activity
SECTION 5 **Western Powers Rule Southeast Asia** *pp. 326–329*	*Western imperialists, including the United States, claim lands in the South Pacific, Southeast Asia, and Hawaiian Islands. Only Siam remains independent.*	*In-Depth Resources: Unit 3* • **Guided Reading,** p. 41 • **Primary Source:** In Favor of Imperialism, p. 48 • **History Makers:** Mongkut, p. 53	P E *Section 5 Assessment,* p. 329 *Formal Assessment* • Section Quiz, p. 141 *Alternative Assessment Book* • Standards for Evaluating a Cooperative Activity
CHAPTER RESOURCES	**Chapter Overview** *Western imperialists, with superior arms and technology, establish colonies in Asia and Africa. The Europeans export finished goods to the colonies and import raw materials and cash crops. Colonial rule provokes native resistance movements.*	*Telescoping the Times* • Chapter Summary, pp. 45–47 *Planning for Block Schedules* *Case Studies* • **Case Study 1**—India and Britain: Colonialism and Imperialism, p. 2	P E *Chapter Assessment,* pp. 330–331 *Chapter Activities,* p. 331 *Formal Assessment* • Chapter Test, forms A and B, pp. 142–147 ■ *Test Generator* *Alternative Assessment Book*

TECHNOLOGY

Warm-Up Transparency 11

Electronic Library of Primary Sources
- "The Boer War: The Suffering of the Civilian Population"
- "Stanley finds Livingstone"
- "Private Company Rule in the Congo"

INTERNET RESOURCES
www.mlworldhistory.com

Warm-Up Transparency 11

Electronic Library of Primary Sources
- from "Africa at the Center"

INTERNET RESOURCES
www.mlworldhistory.com

Warm-Up Transparency 11

World Art and Cultures Transparencies
- AT58 *Reception at the Court of Sultan Selim III*

INTERNET RESOURCES
www.mlworldhistory.com

Warm-Up Transparency 11

Geography Transparencies
- GT27 *India Under British Rule, 1805–1886*

World Art and Cultures Transparencies
- AT59 *Raja Ram Singh in Procession*

Electronic Library of Primary Sources
- "The Rise of the Color Bar"

INTERNET RESOURCES
www.mlworldhistory.com

Warm-Up Transparency 11

Critical Thinking Transparencies
- CT27 Comparing Imperialist Styles
- CT63 Visual Summary

Electronic Library of Primary Sources
- from *Hawaii's Story by Hawaii's Queen*

INTERNET RESOURCES
www.mlworldhistory.com

Chapter Summaries on Audiocassette in English and Spanish

INTERNET RESOURCES
www.mlworldhistory.com

Block Scheduling (90 MINUTES)

Day 1
Section 1, pp. 305-309

 COOPERATIVE ACTIVITY
Teacher's Edition, p. 308

Section Assessment, p. 309

Day 2
Section 2, pp. 310–316

 COOPERATIVE ACTIVITY
Teacher's Edition, p. 314

Section Assessment, p. 315

Day 3
Section 3, pp. 317–320

 COOPERATIVE ACTIVITY
Teacher's Edition, p. 318

Day 4
Section 4, pp. 321–325

 COOPERATIVE ACTIVITY
Teacher's Edition, p. 322

Section Assessment, p. 325

Day 5
Section 5, pp. 326–329

 COOPERATIVE ACTIVITY
Teacher's Edition, p. 328

Section Assessment, p. 329

Chapter Assessment,
pp. 330–331

Yearly Pacing *Chapter 11 Total:* 5 days *Yearly Total:* 85 days

Planning for Block Schedules

Customizing for Special Needs

Students Acquiring English

Access for Students Acquiring English
- **Guided Reading** for Sections 1–5 (Spanish), pp. 122–126
- **Chapter Summary** (Spanish), pp. 119–121
- **Skillbuilder Practice** Analyzing Assumptions and Biases (Spanish), p. 127
- **Geography Application** David Livingstone Explores Southern Africa (Spanish), p. 128

Spanish Reading Study Guide
- pp. 115–126

Chapter Summaries on Audiocassette in English and Spanish

Less Proficient Readers

In-Depth Resources: Unit 3
- **Guided Reading** for Sections 1–5, pp. 37–41
- **Skillbuilder Practice** Analyzing Assumptions and Biases, p. 42
- **Geography Application** David Livingstone Explores Southern Africa, p. 43

Telescoping the Times
- Chapter Summary, pp. 45–47

Reading Study Guide pp. 115–126

Chapter Summaries on Audiocassette

Gifted and Talented Students

In-Depth Resources: Unit 3

Primary Sources:
- British Contract with an African King, p. 45
- Letter from Menelik II, p. 46
- Letter Opposing the British, p. 47
- In Favor of Imperialism, p. 48

History Makers
- Menelik II, p. 52
- Mongkut, p. 53

Connections to Literature READINGS FOR STUDENTS

In-Depth Resources: Unit 3
Literature: "The Burial," p. 49; from *Things Fall Apart,* p. 50

- **McDougal Littell** *Language of Literature,* Grade 10
Doris Lessing, "No Witchcraft for Sale," p. 744

McDougal Littell *Literature Connections*

- Achebe, Chinua *Things Fall Apart* (with related readings)

In this classic story, the traditional ways of an Ibo village in Nigeria are challenged by new European ways.

 = Pupil's Edition   = Overhead Transparency   = Software   = Video

= Copy Master   = CD-ROM = Audiocassette   = Internet

The Age of Imperialism, 1850–1914

Making Predictions

Ask students to study the map on these two pages. Then ask them the following question.

- What predictions can you make about why European nations would want to acquire territory in Africa, Asia, and Australia? *Possible responses: wealth, prestige, Christian missionary work, manifest destiny, exporting unwanted population*

Making Inferences

Have students compare the size of the European countries with the size of the territories they acquired. What can students infer about the political organization and the military strength of the peoples in the occupied territories? *Most of the areas were probably politically chaotic or weak*

Geography Connection

- What nation held the most territory on all four continents (including North America)? *Great Britain*

- Africa was divided up among how many European nations? *Seven—Great Britain, France, Belgium, Germany, Italy, Portugal, and Spain*

CHAPTER 11

The Age of Imperialism, 1850–1914

PREVIEWING THEMES

Empire Building

The Industrial Revolution gave European nations the necessary technology to dominate other peoples. During the 1800s, the European powers competed with one another to claim parts of Africa, Southeast Asia, India, and the Pacific. Toward the end of the century, the United States established its own overseas colonies in the Pacific.

Economics

The imperialists regarded their colonies as captive markets as well as sources of raw materials and trade goods. The colonizers demanded production of cash crops at the expense of the peasants' own subsistence agriculture. In tropical areas, plantation agriculture increased the need for laborers and spurred immigration.

Power and Authority

Colonizers were divided on the best method of rule. Britain and the United States ruled indirectly, using local leaders and institutions where possible. The French and others ruled the colonies directly from a central authority. Often the two methods were blended.

INTERNET CONNECTION

Visit us at **www.mlworldhistory.com** to learn more about imperialism.

302

EUROPEAN COLONIES, 1850–1914

Territory Controlled By:
- Belgium
- France
- German Empire
- Great Britain
- Italy
- The Netherlands
- Portugal
- Russian Empire
- Spain
- United States
- Independent States

0   500 Miles
0   1,000 Kilometers

N

ATLANTIC OCEAN

This sculptured brass weight was used by the **Asante** people of Africa. The elaborate nature of the weight may indicate that trade was especially important to the Asante. The British traded with the Asante on the west coast of **Africa**, also known as the Gold Coast.

GEOGRAPHY THEMES

Place

A major attraction of the colonies for the imperialist powers was not only their wealth of natural resources but their strategic location in terms of controlling both land and waterway trading routes. Ask students to study the map on pages 302 and 303 and the map key indicating which European nations controlled which lands. Ask students what strategic advantages each colony gave its European ruler. Which country appears to dominate much of the seafaring routes? Have students predict how England, smallest of the European nations, came to control so much colonial territory. Remind students of the importance of naval power in this era and the need to control vital waterways.

Movement

Advances in naval technology made possible relatively quick trips between the homeland and the colonies. Europeans could dispatch colonial administrators and armies to these lands and bring back mineral and agricultural wealth. Have students trace with their fingers the possible routes taken by imperialists to African, Southwest Asian, and Southeast Asian colonies. Remind students that along with the imperialist forces came Western technologies, languages, religions, and customs.

Queen Victoria of **England** ruled during most of the Age of Imperialism. During her reign, the saying, "The sun never sets on the British Empire" was true of the colonial holdings of Britain.

Ethiopian ruler **Menelik II** defeated the Italians at the Battle of Adowa in **1896**. The Ethiopians' defeat of the Italians was one of the few successful resistances to the European imperialists.

PACIFIC OCEAN

Arctic Circle

40°N

Tropic of Cancer

Equator 0°

INDIAN OCEAN

Tropic of Capricorn

303

ADDITIONAL RESOURCES

Books for the Teacher

• Copland, Ian. *The Burden of Empire.* Melbourne, Australia: Oxford UP, 1990. Study of imperialism and colonialism.

• Wesseling, H. L. *Divide and Rule: The Partition of Africa, 1880-1914.* New York: Praeger, 1996.

Books for the Student

• Bayly, C. A. *Indian Society and the Making of the British Empire.* New York: Cambridge UP, 1988. Examines the British East India Company's rise in the period of Mughal decline.

• Rowell, Trevor. *The Scramble for Africa.* London: Batsford, 1987.

 Videos

• *The Bible and the Gun/The Magnificent African Cake.* Knowledge Unlimited, 1984. 800-356-2303. Explores the effect of missionaries, slave trade, and imperialism.

• *The Lure of Empire: America Debates Imperialism.* Coronet/ MTI, 1974. 800-321-3106. Examines American annexation of the Philippines.

• *Zulus at War.* Ambrose Video, 1995. 800-526-4663. Depicts battles between Zulus and the British.

Software

• *Imperialism.* CD-ROM. Crystal Productions, 1994. 800-255-8629. Provides case studies, including the British in India and multiple powers in Africa.

HISTORY THROUGH ART

Ashanti Brass Weight

The brass weight shown on page 302 was made by the Ashanti (also spelled Asante) people. These weights were generally used to measure quantities of minerals, such as gold. Like many African peoples, the Ashanti used highly stylized forms and abstract designs in their art (see the Ashanti textile patterns on page 312).

The Ashanti lived on the west coast of Africa in an area so mineral rich that the Europeans dubbed it the Gold Coast. At the time the Europeans came, the Ashanti were among the most highly organized peoples in Africa. The British referred to them as a "nation" because of their bureaucratic government system.

Interpreting the Art What physical characteristics did the artist give the human figure in this picture?

Possible answers: "Corn row" hairstyle, face that looks like a combination of human and animal (perhaps leopard or lion) features, stylized body, an object in either hand. The figure dominates the animal being ridden. What does this suggest about the importance of the person? *Because the object was used for measurement, the person could represent a local authority or someone with authority in commercial matters.*

Interact *with* History

This Interact with History feature motivates students by asking them to evaluate the potential impact of imperialism. As they consider the question posed, they will analyze the issues, explore their options, and evaluate the impact of Western culture on Africa, Australia, and Asia.

Purpose

• to introduce students to the study of European colonization of foreign lands.

• to help students understand the benefits and problems of imperialism.

• to help students connect to the people and events they will encounter in this chapter.

Teaching Strategy

Thinking Critically Ask students what they remember from past chapters about what happens when a more technologically advanced people encounters a less developed people.

EXAMINING *the* ISSUES

Following are suggestions for answering each bulleted question.

1 Under what conditions might advanced technology be helpful? harmful?

2 Ask students how they would feel if someone from another land tried to force an alien culture on them.

3 Have students consider the rights of the original inhabitants and of those whose technology is used to develop the resources.

4 What does "too much power" mean? Is *any* power over others acceptable? Why or why not?

Making Connections Ask students if they were ever playing a game or working on a project that was taken over by someone else. How did they feel? What could they do if the person were older or stronger?

The 19th-century Europeans have access to steam engines and medical advances. They have the technical know-how to develop the resources of the land they control. They want to develop these resources to make themselves great profits. Many believe that they also have both the right and the responsibility to develop the lands and cultures of less advanced areas of the world.

You wonder about the Europeans' thinking. What rights and responsibilities do they really have? How much should they try to change other peoples and other cultures?

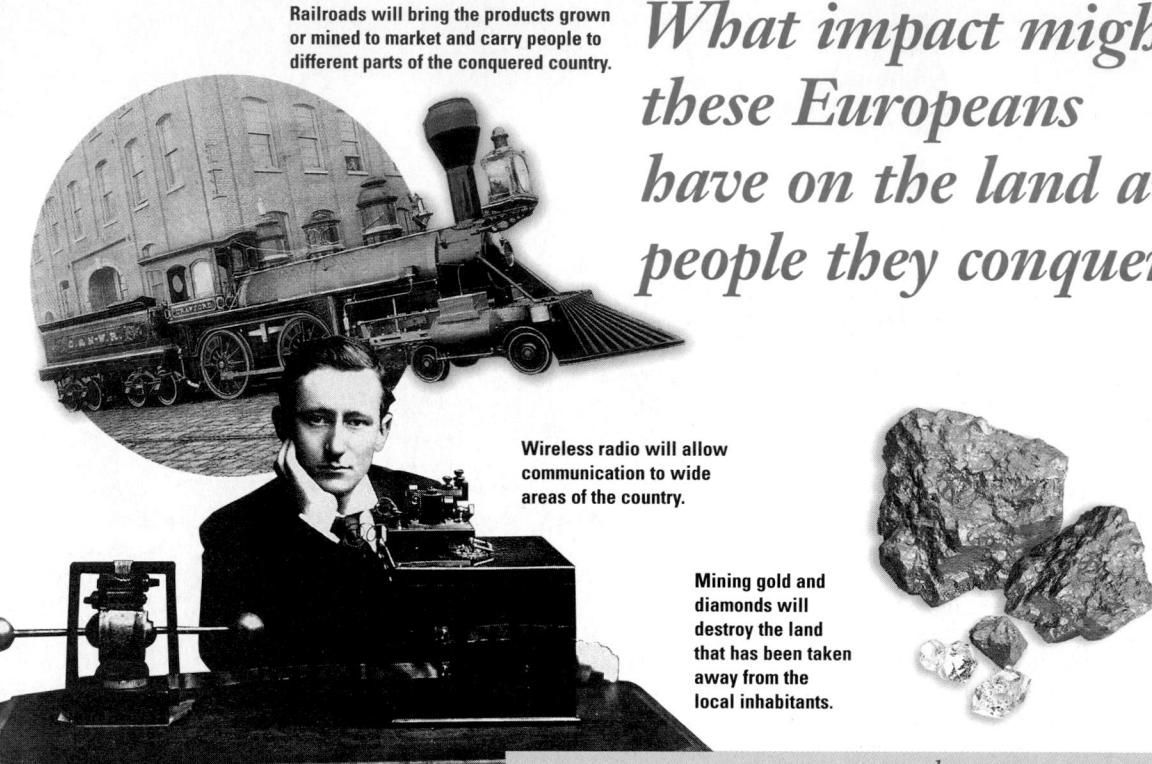

Railroads will bring the products grown or mined to market and carry people to different parts of the conquered country.

What impact might these Europeans have on the land and people they conquer?

Wireless radio will allow communication to wide areas of the country.

Mining gold and diamonds will destroy the land that has been taken away from the local inhabitants.

Local rule might be eliminated or replaced with rule by European monarchs and their representatives.

304 Chapter 11

EXAMINING *the* ISSUES

• Does a technologically advanced nation have a responsibility to share its advances with less developed areas?

• Is it acceptable to impose your culture on another culture group?

• Who should benefit from the resources of a place?

• Is there such a thing as having too much power over others?

Discuss these questions with your classmates. In your discussion, remember what you have already learned about conquests and cultural changes.

As you read about imperialists in this chapter, look for their effects on both the colonizers and the colonized.

Follow-Up

A feature on the chapter assessment will ask students to reevaluate their responses to the question posed on this page.

1 Imperialists Divide Africa

TERMS & NAMES
- imperialism
- racism
- Social Darwinism
- Berlin Conference 1884–85
- Shaka
- Boer
- Great Trek
- Boer War

MAIN IDEA

Ignoring the claims of African ethnic groups, kingdoms, and city-states, Europeans established colonial claims.

WHY IT MATTERS NOW

African nations continue to feel the effects of the colonial presence of 100 years ago.

SETTING THE STAGE Industrialization stirred ambitions in many European nations. They wanted more resources to fuel their industrial production. They competed for new markets for their goods. They looked to Africa and Asia as sources of the raw materials and as markets for cloth, plows, guns, and other industrial products.

Africa Before Imperialism

In the mid-1800s, on the eve of the European domination of Africa, African peoples were divided into hundreds of ethnic and linguistic groups. Most continued to follow traditional beliefs, while others converted to Islam or Christianity. These groups spoke more than 1,000 different languages. Politically, they ranged from large empires that united many ethnic groups to independent villages. The largest empire in West Africa at its peak had a population of about 10 million people.

Although Europeans had established contacts with Africans as early as the 1450s, they actually controlled very little land. Powerful African armies were able to keep the Europeans out of most of Africa for 400 years. As late as 1880, Europeans controlled only 10 percent of the continent's land, mainly on the coast.

Furthermore, European travel into the interior on a large-scale basis was virtually impossible. Europeans could not navigate African rivers that had so many rapids and cataracts and drastically changing flows. Until the introduction of steam-powered riverboats, Europeans would not be able to conduct major expeditions into the interior of Africa.

THINK THROUGH HISTORY
A. Analyzing Causes Why did the Europeans control such a small portion of Africa in the 1800s?
A. Answer African armies and traders kept them out and the rivers were impassable, making it difficult to get inland.

Finally, large networks of Africans conducted trade. These trade networks kept Europeans from controlling the sources of trade items such as gold and ivory. These trade networks were specialized. The Chokwe, for example, devoted themselves to collecting ivory and beeswax in the Angola highlands. Others such as the Yao carried their goods to merchants on the coast.

This highly valued ivory mask is one of four taken from the King of Benin in 1897. It was worn with several others on the belt of a ceremonial costume of the king.

Nations Compete for Overseas Empires

Those Europeans who did penetrate the interior of Africa tended to be explorers, missionaries, or humanitarians who opposed the slave trade. Europeans and Americans learned about Africa through travel books and newspapers. These publications competed for readers by hiring reporters to search the globe for stories of adventure, mystery, or excitement.

The Congo Sparks Interest In the late 1860s, David Livingstone, a minister from Scotland, traveled with a group of Africans deep into central Africa. They were searching for the source of the Nile. When several years passed with no word from him or his party, many people feared he was dead. An American newspaper hired reporter Henry Stanley to find Livingstone. In 1871, he found Dr. Livingstone on the shores of Lake Tanganyika. Stanley's account of the meeting made headlines around the world.

The Age of Imperialism **305**

SECTION 1 RESOURCES

PRINT RESOURCES

IN-DEPTH RESOURCES: UNIT 3
Guided Reading, p. 37
Geography Application: David Livingstone Explores Southern Africa, p. 43
Primary Source: British Contract with an African King, p. 45
Literature: "The Burial," p. 49

ACCESS FOR STUDENTS ACQUIRING ENGLISH
Guided Reading (Spanish), p. 122
Geography Application (Spanish), p. 128

FORMAL ASSESSMENT
Section Quiz, p. 137

ALTERNATIVE ASSESSMENT BOOK

TECHNOLOGY RESOURCES

CD-ROM
Electronic Library of Primary Sources

INTERNET www.mlworldhistory.com

Section 1 Overview

OBJECTIVES

1. To describe Africa before European domination.
2. To summarize the motives of European colonizers.
3. To identify factors allowing the Europeans to control Africa.
4. To identify the three groups that clashed in South Africa.

SKILLBUILDERS
- Interpreting charts, p. 307
- Interpreting maps: region, p. 308

CRITICAL THINKING
- Analyzing causes, p. 305
- Making inferences, pp. 306, 309
- Analyzing issues, p. 307
- Recognizing effects, p. 308
- Contrasting, p. 309

FOCUS
5-Minute Warm-Up

Interpreting Maps
Answering the following questions will help students understand the division of Africa.

- Look at the map on page 308. Which country holds the most territory in North Africa?
- What two strategic waterways are held by Spain and Britain?

WARM-UP TRANSPARENCY 11

OBJECTIVE 1 INSTRUCT

Africa Before Imperialism

▶ *Key Ideas*
- Many ethnic groups but few Europeans rule in Africa.

IN-DEPTH RESOURCES: UNIT 3
Guided Reading, p. 37

ACCESS FOR STUDENTS ACQUIRING ENGLISH
Guided Reading (Spanish), p. 122

OBJECTIVE 2 INSTRUCT

Nations Compete for Overseas Empires

▶ *Key Ideas*
- Europeans learn about Africa from explorers.

(continued on next page)

(continued from page 305)

- Henry Stanley claims the Congo River Valley for Belgium.
- Greed, nationalism, racism, and philanthropy motivate European colonialism.
- Superior arms, the steam engine, medicines, and African rivalries help Europeans dominate Africa.

 ELECTRONIC LIBRARY OF PRIMARY SOURCES
"The Boer War: The Suffering of the Civilian Population"
"Stanley Finds Livingstone"
"Private Company Rule in the Congo"

MORE ABOUT . . .
Collecting Wild Rubber

Rubber production under Belgium rule was one of the worst exploitations of Africans in the history of African colonialism. Armed soldiers drove people into the forest to collect wild rubber. Those who refused were killed, and their left hands taken as trophies to show the commissioner. The hands were then counted to determine that the soldiers had not wasted cartridges. European outrage over this practice forced the Belgians to stop.

MORE ABOUT . . .
Cecil Rhodes

Cecil Rhodes first went to South Africa as a young man to improve his health. He built an immense fortune in the diamond fields of southern Africa. He gave a portion of this fortune in his will to Oxford and Cambridge universities to establish scholarships for promising English-speaking students throughout the world. President Clinton studied at Oxford as a Rhodes scholar.

"Dr. Livingstone, I presume?" was the greeting of American reporter Henry Stanley in their famous meeting in 1871 at Lake Tanganyika. This picture is from a drawing based on Dr. Livingstone's own material.

In 1879, Stanley returned to Africa, and in 1882 he signed treaties with local chiefs of the Congo River valley. The treaties gave King Leopold II of Belgium personal control of these lands.

Leopold claimed that his primary motive in establishing the colony was to abolish the slave trade. However, he licensed companies that brutally exploited Africans, by forcing them to collect sap from rubber plants. The time required to do this interfered with the care of their own food crops. So severe were the forced labor, excessive taxation, and abuses of the native Congolese that humanitarians from around the world demanded changes. In 1908, the Belgian government took over the colony. The Belgian Congo, as the colony later became known, was 80 times larger than Belgium. Leopold's seizure of the Congo alarmed France. Earlier, in 1882, the French had approved a treaty that gave France the north bank of the Congo River. Soon Britain, Germany, Italy, Portugal, and Spain were also claiming parts of Africa.

Motives Driving Imperialism Economic, political, and social forces accelerated the drive to take over land in all parts of the globe. The takeover of a country or territory by a stronger nation with the intent of dominating the political, economic, and social life of the people of that nation is called **imperialism.** The Industrial Revolution provided European countries with a need to add lands to their control. As European nations industrialized, they searched for new markets and raw materials to improve their economies.

The race for colonies grew out of a strong sense of national pride as well as from economic competition. Europeans viewed an empire as a measure of national greatness. "All great nations in the fullness of their strength have desired to set their mark upon barbarian lands," wrote the German historian Heinrich von Treitschke, "and those who fail to participate in this great rivalry will play a pitiable role in time to come." As the competition for colonies intensified, each country was determined to plant its flag on as much of the world as possible.

Because of their advanced technology, many Europeans basically believed that they were better than other peoples. This belief was **racism,** the idea that one race is superior to others. The attitude was a reflection of a social theory of the time, called **Social Darwinism.** In this theory, Charles Darwin's ideas about evolution and "survival of the fittest" were applied to social change. Those who were fittest for survival enjoyed wealth and success and were considered superior to others. According to the theory, non-Europeans were considered to be on a lower scale of cultural and physical development because they did not have the technology that Europeans had. Europeans believed that they had the right and the duty to bring the results of their progress to other countries. Cecil Rhodes, a successful businessman and one of the major supporters of British expansion, clearly stated this position:

A VOICE FROM THE PAST
I contend that we [Britons] are the finest race in the world, and the more of the world we inhabit, the better it is for the human race. . . . It is our duty to seize every opportunity of acquiring more territory and we should keep this one idea steadily before our eyes that more territory simply means more of the Anglo-Saxon race, more of the best, the most human, most honourable race the world possesses.
CECIL RHODES, *Confession of Faith* 1877

B. Possible Answer British superiority to all other groups.

THINK THROUGH HISTORY
B. Making Inferences What attitude about the British does Rhodes's statement display?

TEACHING OPTIONS

CONNECTIONS ACROSS TIME AND PLACE

Civil Wars Point out that many current conflicts among African nations have their roots in the colonial era. In the 1800s and early 1900s, the European imperialists drew national boundaries with little thought about how they might affect native people. Natural enemies were forced together, and cultural families were split. After the colonial era ended following World War II, many emerging African nations fought prolonged, painful civil wars, as ethnic groups sought to regain their traditional lands or force enemies out. Interested students can read about such struggles in Nigeria, the Sudan, the former Belgian Congo, and Angola.

EXPLORING PRIMARY SOURCES

A Voice from the Past Ask students to identify phrases in the excerpt that suggest Cecil Rhodes held racist as well as nationalistic views. What did he mean by the statement "Britons are the first race in the world" and "the best, the most human, most honourable race the world possesses"? *Most students will recognize that he meant "first" as the primary, or most* significant, race. He also thought the Britons were superior to all other colonizers.

Have interested students read more about the life of this colorful Englishman. Tell them that Rhodes's life is a prime example of the positive and negative aspects of European imperialism.

The push for expansion also came from missionaries who worked to Christianize the peoples of Asia, Africa, and the Pacific Islands. Many missionaries believed that European rule was the best way to end evil practices such as the slave trade. They also wanted to "civilize," that is, to "westernize," the peoples of the foreign land.

Forces Enabling Imperialism External and internal forces contributed to the Europeans' conquest of Africa. The overwhelming advantage was the Europeans' technological superiority. The Maxim gun, invented in 1889, was the world's first automatic machine gun. European countries quickly acquired the Maxim, while the resisting Africans were forced to rely on outdated weapons.

European countries also had the means to control their empire. The invention of the steam engine allowed Europeans to easily travel upstream to establish bases of control deep in the African continent. Railroads, cables, and steamers allowed close communications within a colony and between the colony and its controlling nation. All these made control easier.

Even with superior arms and steam engines to transport them, Europeans might still have stayed confined to the coast. Europeans were highly susceptible to malaria. One discovery changed that—the drug quinine. Regular doses of quinine protected Europeans from attacks of this disease caused by mosquitoes.

Internal factors also made the European sweep through Africa easier. Africans' huge variety of languages and cultures discouraged unity among them. Wars fought between ethnic groups over land, water, and trade rights also prevented a unified stand. Europeans soon learned to play rival groups against each other. Finally, Africans fought at a tremendous disadvantage because they did not have the weapons and technology the Europeans had.

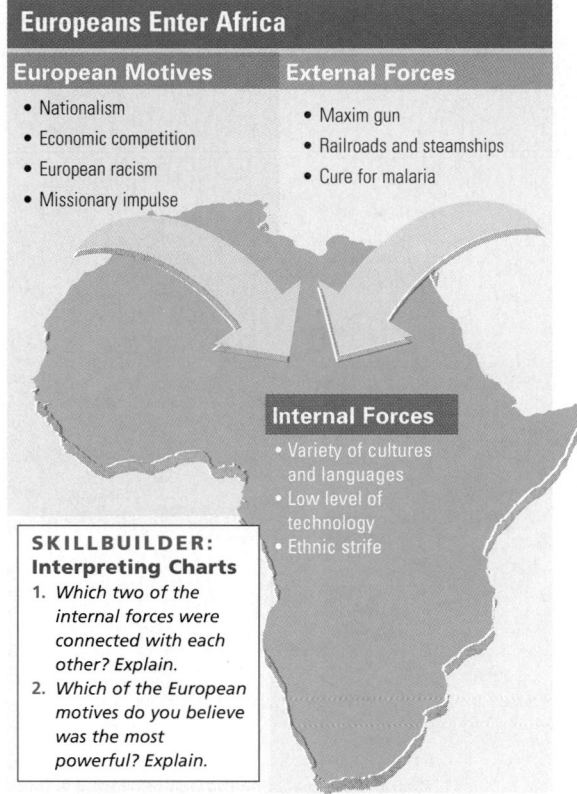

Europeans Enter Africa

European Motives	External Forces
• Nationalism	• Maxim gun
• Economic competition	• Railroads and steamships
• European racism	• Cure for malaria
• Missionary impulse	

Internal Forces
• Variety of cultures and languages
• Low level of technology
• Ethnic strife

SKILLBUILDER: Interpreting Charts
1. *Which two of the internal forces were connected with each other? Explain.*
2. *Which of the European motives do you believe was the most powerful? Explain.*

African Lands Become European Colonies

The scramble for African territory began in earnest about 1880. At that time, the French began to expand from the West African coast toward western Sudan. The discoveries of diamonds in 1867 and gold in 1886 in South Africa increased European interest in colonizing the land. No European power wanted to be left out of the race.

Berlin Conference Divides Africa The competition was so fierce that European countries feared war among themselves. To prevent fighting, 14 European nations met at the **Berlin Conference** in **1884–85** to lay down rules for the division of Africa. They agreed that any European country could claim land in Africa by notifying other nations of their claims and showing they could control the area. The European nations

The Age of Imperialism **307**

Imperialism in Africa, 1913

Interpreting the Map Which imperial powers that claimed African land in 1878 had lost their colonies by 1914? Who took over these colonies? *Land held by the Ottoman Empire was acquired by France, Italy, and Britain. Boer colonies were absorbed into the Union of South Africa (modern-day South Africa), dominated by the British.*

Extension Activity Ask students to list the lands each nation claimed. Who had the most African lands? *France and Britain.* Which country had the fewest? *Belgium.* What was the largest European landholding in Africa? *French West Africa and Algeria*

 IN-DEPTH RESOURCES: UNIT 3
Primary Source: British Contract with an African King, p. 45
Literature: "The Burial," p. 49

SKILLBUILDER Answers
1. About 10%; about 96%
2. France and Britain; 35.6%; 32.3%

Imperialism in Africa, 1913

Imperialism in Africa, 1878

Political Divisions in Africa, 1913

- Independent states (3.4%)
- Italian (5.2%)
- Portuguese (6.8%)
- Belgian (7.9%)
- German (7.9%)
- French (35.6%)
- Spanish (.06%)
- Britain (32.3%)

Legend:
- Belgian
- Britain
- French
- German
- Italian
- Portuguese
- Spanish
- Independent states
- Boer
- Ottoman

GEOGRAPHY SKILLBUILDER: Interpreting Maps and Charts
1. **Region** *About what percentage of Africa was colonized by Europeans in 1878? How much by 1913?*
2. **Region** *According to the map of 1913, which two imperial powers held the most land? According to the chart, what percentage of land in Africa was held by the two powers?*

---

divided the rest of the continent with little thought to how African ethnic or linguistic groups were distributed. No African ruler attended these meetings, yet the conference sealed Africa's fate. By 1914, only Liberia and Ethiopia remained free from European control.

Demand for Product Shapes Colonies When European countries began colonizing, many believed that Africans would soon be buying European goods in great quantities. They were wrong; European goods were not bought. However, European businesses still needed raw materials from Africa. Businesses eventually developed cash-crop plantations to grow peanuts, palm oil, cocoa, and rubber. These products displaced the food crops grown by farmers to feed their families.

The major source of great wealth in Africa proved to be the continent's rich mineral resources. The Belgian Congo contained untold wealth in copper and tin. Even these riches seemed small compared to the gold and diamonds in South Africa.

THINK THROUGH HISTORY
D. Recognizing Effects What sort of problems might result from combining or splitting groups of people?
D. Answer Some might fight each other and some might fight to get back with those they were separated from.

308 Chapter 11

Task: Students will research, write, and perform brief 5- to 10-minute skits dramatizing a central episode in the history of South Africa.

Purpose: To help students understand history from different points of view.

Activity: Students work in three groups: Zulus, Boers, and British. Each group writes and performs a short skit that dramatizes an episode central to the history of the group they represent. Examples might include a war council among the Zulu whether to fight the British, a day on the Boers' Great Trek, or the discovery of gold in South Africa.

 Building a Portfolio Students may want to include a copy of the script in their portfolios.

ALTERNATIVE ASSESSMENT BOOK
Standards for Evaluating a Cooperative Activity

Standards for Evaluation
The script and presentation should . . .

- show careful research of the incident
- demonstrate knowledge of each group
- accurately present historical information

Three Groups Clash over South Africa

The history of South Africa is a history of Africans, Dutch, and British clashing over land and resources. Although the African lands seemed empty to the Europeans, there were huge areas claimed by various ethnic groups. The local control of these lands, especially in the east, had been in dispute for about 100 years.

Zulu Expansion From the late 1700s to the late 1800s, a series of local wars shook southern Africa. Around 1816, a Zulu chief, **Shaka,** used highly disciplined warriors and good military organization to create a large centralized state. Shaka's successors, however, were unable to keep the kingdom intact against the superior arms of the British invaders. The Zulu land became a part of British-controlled land in 1887.

Boers and British Settle in the Cape The Dutch first came to the Cape of Good Hope in 1652 to establish a way station for their ships sailing between the Dutch East Indies and home. Dutch settlers known as **Boers** (Dutch for "farmers") gradually took over native Africans' land and established large farms. When the British took over the Cape Colony in the 1800s, the two groups of settlers clashed over British policy regarding land and slaves.

In the 1830s, to escape the British, several thousand Boers began to move north. This movement has become known as the **Great Trek.** The Boers soon found themselves fighting fiercely with Zulu and other African groups whose land they were taking.

The Boer War Diamonds and gold were discovered in southern Africa in the 1860s and 1880s. Suddenly, "outsiders" from all parts of the world rushed in to make their fortunes. The Boers tried to keep the outsiders from gaining political rights. An attempt to start a rebellion against the Boers failed. The Boers blamed the British. In 1899, the Boers took up arms against the British.

In many ways the **Boer War** between the British and the Boers was the first modern "total" war. The Boers launched commando raids and used guerrilla tactics against the British. The British countered by burning Boer farms and imprisoning women and children in disease-ridden concentration camps. Britain won the war. In 1902, the Boer republics were joined into a self-governing Union of South Africa, controlled by the British.

The establishing of colonies signaled a change in the way of life of the Africans. The Europeans made efforts to change the political, social, and economic lives of the peoples they conquered. You will learn about these changes in Section 2.

D. Answer It was between two European nations not between Europeans and Africans.

THINK THROUGH HISTORY
E. Contrasting How was the struggle for land in the Boer War different from other takeovers in Africa?

Global Impact

Americans in the Boer War

Americans as well as nationals from other countries volunteered to fight in the Boer War (1899–1902). Although they joined both sides, most fought for the Boers. They believed the Boers were fighting for freedom against British tyrants.

One group of 46 Irish Americans from Chicago and Massachusetts caused an international scandal when they deserted their Red Cross unit and took up arms for the Boers.

Some Irish who fought for the Boers became leaders in the Irish rebellion when they returned home. John MacBride, a leader of a Boer unit that included many Irish Americans, later took part in the 1916 Easter Rising in Dublin. He was executed by the British.

Section 1 Assessment

1. TERMS & NAMES

Identify
• imperialism
• racism
• Social Darwinism
• Berlin Conference 1884–85
• Shaka
• Boer
• Great Trek
• Boer War

2. TAKING NOTES

Copy the spider map below and fill in the four motives that caused the growth of imperialism during the late 1800s.

How did Europeans use Social Darwinism to justify empire-building?

3. MAKING INFERENCES

What can you infer about the Europeans' attitude toward Africans from the Berlin Conference?

THINK ABOUT
• who attended the conference
• the outcome of the conference

4. THEME ACTIVITY

Empire Building Create a time line that includes events that occurred in South Africa between 1800 and 1914. What motives caused most of these events?

The Age of Imperialism **309**

---

❷ Imperialism

PATTERNS OF CHANGE

CASE STUDY: Nigeria

MAIN IDEA	WHY IT MATTERS NOW
Europeans embarked on a new phase of empire-building that affected both Africa and the rest of the world.	Many former colonies have political problems that are the result of colonial rule.

SETTING THE STAGE The Berlin Conference of 1884–85 was a Europeans' conference, and the Boer War was a Europeans' war. Europeans argued and fought among themselves over the lands of Africa. In carving up Africa, the European countries paid little or no attention to historical political divisions such as kingdoms or caliphates, or to ethnic and language groupings. Uppermost in the minds of the Europeans was the ability to control the land, its people, and their resources.

Colonial Control Takes Many Forms

The imperialism of the 18th and 19th centuries was conducted differently than the empire-building of the 15th and 16th centuries. In the earlier period, imperial powers often did not penetrate far into the conquered areas in Asia and Africa. Nor did they always have a substantial influence on the lives of the people. During this new period of imperialism, the Europeans demanded more influence over the economic, political, and social lives of the people. They were determined to shape the economies of the lands to benefit European economies. They also wanted the people to adopt European customs.

Forms of Colonial Control Each European nation had certain policies and goals for establishing colonies. To establish control of an area, Europeans used different techniques. Over time, four forms of colonial control emerged: colony, protectorate, sphere of influence, and economic imperialism. In practice, gaining control of an area might involve the use of several of these forms.

PATTERNS OF CHANGE: Imperialism

Forms of Imperialism	Characteristics	Example
Colony	A country or a region governed internally by a foreign power	Somaliland in East Africa was a French colony.
Protectorate	A country or territory with its own internal government but under the control of an outside power	Britain established a protectorate over the Niger River delta.
Sphere of Influence	An area in which an outside power claims exclusive investment or trading privileges	Liberia was under the sphere of influence of the United States.
Economic Imperialism	Independent but less developed nations controlled by private business interests rather than by other governments	The Dole Fruit company controlled pineapple trade in Hawaii.

SKILLBUILDER: Interpreting Charts
1. *Which two forms are guided by interests in business or trade?*
2. *What is the difference between a protectorate and a colony?*

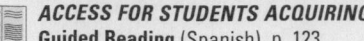

Patterns of Imperialist Management

In addition to the external form of control preferred by the colonizing country, European rulers also needed to develop methods of day-to-day management of the colony. Two basic methods of internal management emerged. Britain and other nations such as the United States in its Pacific Island colonies preferred indirect control. France and most other European nations wielded a more direct control. Later, when colonies gained independence, the management method used had an influence on the type of government chosen in the new nation.

Indirect Control Indirect control relied on existing political rulers. In some areas, the British asked a local ruler to accept British authority to rule. These local officials handled much of the daily management of the colony. In addition, each colony had a legislative council that included colonial officials as well as local merchants and professionals nominated by the colonial governor.

The assumption was that the councils would train local leaders in the British method of government and that a time would come when the local population would govern itself. This happened earlier in the British colonies of South Africa and Canada. In the 1890s, the United States began to colonize. It chose the indirect method of control for its colonies.

Direct Control The French and other European powers preferred a more direct control of their colonies. They viewed the Africans as children unable to handle the complex business of running a country. Based on this attitude, the Europeans developed a policy called **paternalism.** Using that policy, Europeans governed people in a fatherly way by providing for their needs but not giving them rights. To accomplish this, the Europeans brought in their own bureaucrats and did not train local people in European methods of governing.

The French also supported a policy of **assimilation.** That policy was based on the idea that in time, the local populations would become absorbed into French culture. To aid in the transition, all local schools, courts, and businesses were patterned after French institutions. In practice, the French abandoned the ideal of assimilation for all but a few places and settled for a policy of "association." They recognized African institutions and culture but regarded them as inferior to French culture. Other European nations used this style of rule but made changes to suit their European culture.

Management Methods

Indirect Control	Direct Control
• Local government officials were used	• Foreign officials brought in to rule
• Limited self-rule	• No self-rule
• Goal: to develop future leaders	• Goal: assimilation
• Government institutions are based on European styles but may have local rules	• Government institutions are based only on European styles
Examples • British colonies such as Nigeria, India, Burma • U.S. colonies on Pacific Islands	Examples • French colonies such as Somaliland, Vietnam • German colonies such as Tanganyika • Portuguese colonies such as Angola

SKILLBUILDER: Interpreting Charts
1. *In which management method are the people less empowered to rule themselves? Explain.*
2. *In what ways are the two management methods different?*

History Through Art

Textiles

In Africa, as in some other parts of the world with long-established traditions, garments provide a great deal of information about the person who wears them. For example, only the Ashanti king is allowed to wear certain silk kente patterns. On days when people come before him with disputes or petitions, he may choose to wear a particular pattern, such as the "Liar's Cloth," to convey a subtle message to those pleading their case that they should be truthful.

MORE ABOUT . . .
Uses of Textiles

- Men's and women's roles in society can be indicated by the parts they play in the manufacture of textiles. For example, women spin, weave, stamp, dye, and embroider many cloths. However, kente cloth is woven only by men.

- Making and selling textiles is one way women can gain some economic independence, which makes a difference in the social freedom women are allowed in their society.

- Political statements are often made by the wearers of certain adinkra prints or tie-dyed patterns. Sometimes the name or the picture of a leader is included.

African Weaving

When Europeans began colonizing Africa, they found a variety of cultures, many with distinctive textiles. Just as the colonizers learned to identify peoples from the textiles they wore, so historians also learn from these fabrics. For example, the materials used in the fabrics reveal clues about the environment of the weavers. The designs and patterns often used traditional symbols or myths of the culture. When and how the fabrics were used also provide information about the culture's celebrations and social roles. Many of these fabrics, such as the ones below, continue to be produced in modern times.

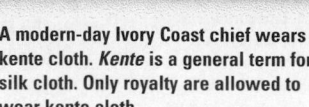

A modern-day Ivory Coast chief wears kente cloth. *Kente* is a general term for silk cloth. Only royalty are allowed to wear kente cloth.

Adinkra Cloth
Gyaman people of the Ivory Coast produced this hand-printed and embroidered cloth. Stamp patterns were made from a gourd and dipped in a dye made of bark paste. The cloth was stamped with symbols. The name of each symbol represented a proverb, an event, or a human, animal, or plant. The symbol shown (rams' horns) is a sign of strength and humility.

Kuba Cloth
Made by Kuba people of Congo, this cloth was made of raffia, a palm-leaf fiber. The cloth design was based on traditional geometric styles. The cloth was worn at ceremonial events, was used as currency, and may have been offered for part of a dowry.

Kente Cloth
This cloth was produced by the Asante people of Ghana. The word *kente* is not used by the Asante. It comes from a Fante (another society) word for basket. The Asante called the cloth *asasia*. Asasia production was a monopoly of the king of the Asante.

Connect *to* History

Contrasting Each of these textiles reflects a specific group. Identify characteristics that make the textiles different from each other.

 SEE SKILLBUILDER HANDBOOK, PAGE 654

Connect *to* Today

Comparing To show their roots, some African Americans wear clothing with a kente cloth pattern. What other ethnic groups have specific clothing that connects them to their roots?

Connect *to* History

Contrasting Suggest to students that they consider what the cloth is made from, how it is made, and how it is decorated. The kente cloth is made from silk yarn, the adinkra from cotton, and the kuba cloth from raffia. The kente is woven in strips, which requires a completely different loom than the wider adinkra or the kuba cloth. The kente design emerges in the weaving and in the way the strips are sewn together. The adinkra pattern is stamped on the cloth, and the edges are embroidered. The kuba cloth starts out as a one-color cloth, which is then embroidered, and the edges of the embroidery are cut to create a pile or velvet effect.

Connect *to* Today

Comparing Most ethnic groups have some type of clothing or pattern that connects them to their roots. Students might mention Scottish or Irish tartans that identify the ancestral clans of these groups. The tartans are traditionally worn as kilts. Although many East Indians and Pakistanis now wear Western dress for everyday use, they wear saris or other traditional costumes for weddings and festivals. Many Native Americans wear patterns to identify their clans or family groups. Special headdresses, such as an Islamic woman's head covering or a male Sikh's turban, are related to religious affiliation as well as to place of origin.

A British Colony

A close look at Britain's rule of Nigeria illustrates the forms of imperialism used by European powers to gain control of an area, and also shows management methods used to continue the control of the economic and political life of the area.

In 1807, Britain outlawed slavery. The British freed some slaves on the West African coast, who then assisted the British in overpowering other groups. To get a group's land, the British persuaded that group's enemies to help fight them. The winning African groups might then be open to British control.

Later, the Royal Niger Company gained control of the palm-oil trade along the Niger River. In 1884–85, the Berlin Conference gave Britain a protectorate in lands along the Niger River. In 1914, the British claimed the entire area of Nigeria as a colony. But in this new age of imperialism, it was necessary to not only claim the territory but also to govern the people living there.

Nigeria is one of the most culturally diverse areas in Africa. About 250 different ethnic groups lived there. The three largest groups were the Hausa-Fulani in the north, the Yoruba in the southwest, and the Igbo in the southeast. The groups in the area claimed by Britain were different from each other in many ways including language, culture, and religion. The Hausa-Fulani people of the north were Muslim and were accustomed to a strong central government. The Igbo and Yoruba peoples relied on local chiefs or governing councils for control. The Hausa-Fulani and Yoruba were traditional enemies.

Britain did not have enough troops to govern such a wide and complex area. So it turned to indirect rule of the land. The British relied on local administrations and chiefs to keep order, avoid rebellion, and collect taxes.

Ruling indirectly through local officials functioned well in northern Nigeria. There the traditional government was most like the British style of government. The process did not work as well in eastern or southwestern Nigeria, where the chiefdoms and councils had trouble with British indirect rule. One reason was that the British appointed chiefs where there had been no chiefs before. Then the British restricted their powers. This left the chiefs with little real status and led to problems governing the area.

African Resistance

Across Africa, European attempts to colonize the lands were met with resistance. The contest between African states and European powers was never equal due to the Europeans' superior arms. Sometimes African societies tried to form alliances with

---

THINK THROUGH HISTORY
B. Summarizing
Which forms of imperialistic control did Britain use in Nigeria?
B. Answer Protectorate, colony, and economic imperialism (Royal Niger Company)

THINK THROUGH HISTORY
C. Analyzing Motives Why was using local governments to control a colony a logical solution for the British?
C. Possible Answers Britain did not have enough troops to directly control the land. Also it might have reduced hostility by the local groups by having local government.

Nigeria, 1914

Hausa-Fulani
Igbo
Yoruba
— British-imposed border

0   250 Miles
0   500 Kilometers

FRENCH WEST AFRICA

Niger R.

Lake Chad

1851, British annex Lagos

NIGERIA

Benue R.

After 1884–85 Berlin Conference, Britain declares a protectorate over Niger Delta

Lagos

Niger R.

The Royal Niger Company controls the palm-oil trade

CAMEROONS

Gulf of Guinea

GEOGRAPHY SKILLBUILDER: Interpreting Maps
1. **Region** How many major culture regions are found within the colony of Nigeria? What sort of problems might result from combining or splitting groups of people?
2. **Movement** Why might the British want to be able to control the Niger River?

---

the Europeans. They hoped the agreement would allow them to remain independent. In some cases the Europeans did help defeat the rivals, but they then turned on their African allies. Other times Africans resisted the Europeans with whatever forces they could raise. With the single exception of Ethiopia, all these attempts at resistance ultimately failed. Edward Morel, a British journalist who lived for a time in the Congo, made an observation about the Africans' fate:

A VOICE FROM THE PAST

Nor is violent physical opposition to abuse and injustice henceforth possible for the African in any part of Africa. His chances of effective resistance have been steadily dwindling with the increasing perfectibility in the killing power of modern armament.

Thus the African is really helpless against the material gods of the white man, as embodied in the trinity of imperialism, capitalistic exploitation, and militarism.

EDWARD MOREL, *The Black Man's Burden*

THINK THROUGH HISTORY
D. Clarifying What does Morel believe is the fate of Africa?
D. Answer Africans are unable to resist the power of white men.

Unsuccessful Movements The unsuccessful resistance attempts included active resistance and religious movements. Algeria's almost 50-year resistance to French rule was one outstanding example of active resistance. In West Africa, Samori Touré led resistance against the French for 16 years.

Africans in German East Africa put their faith in a spiritual defense. African villagers resisted the Germans' insistence that they plant cotton, a cash crop for export, rather than attend to their own food crops. In 1905, the belief suddenly arose that a magic water (*maji-maji*) sprinkled on their bodies would turn the Germans' bullets into water. The uprising became known as the Maji Maji rebellion. When resistance fighters armed with spears and protected by the magic water attacked a German machine-gun post, they were mowed down by the thousands. Officially, Germans recorded 26,000 resisters dead. But almost twice that number perished in the famine that followed.

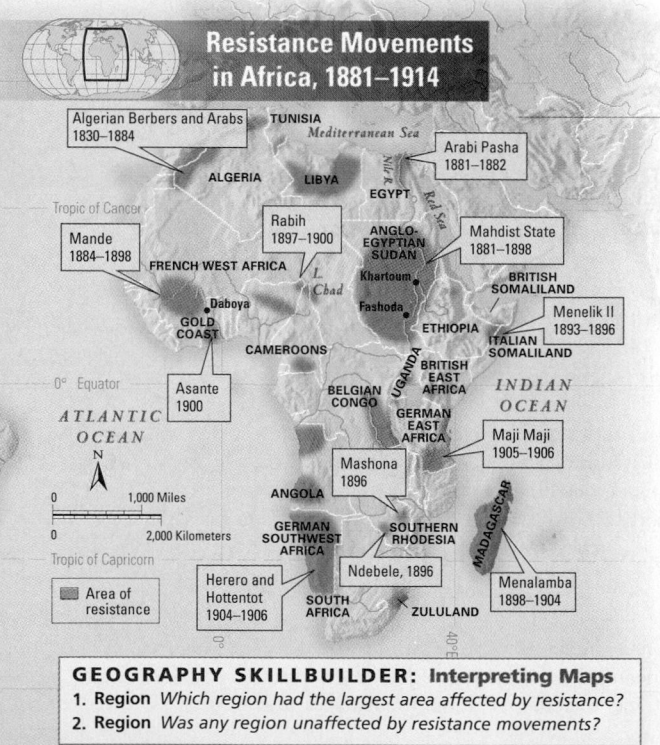

Resistance Movements in Africa, 1881–1914

Algerian Berbers and Arabs 1830–1884
TUNISIA
Mediterranean Sea
Arabi Pasha 1881–1882
ALGERIA
LIBYA
EGYPT
Rabih 1897–1900
Mande 1884–1898
FRENCH WEST AFRICA
L. Chad
ANGLO-EGYPTIAN SUDAN
Mahdist State 1881–1898
Khartoum
BRITISH SOMALILAND
Daboya
GOLD COAST
Fashoda
ETHIOPIA
Menelik II 1893–1896
CAMEROONS
ITALIAN SOMALILAND
BRITISH EAST AFRICA
UGANDA
Asante 1900
BELGIAN CONGO
GERMAN EAST AFRICA
INDIAN OCEAN
ATLANTIC OCEAN
Maji Maji 1905–1906
N
Mashona 1896
0 1,000 Miles
ANGOLA
0 2,000 Kilometers
GERMAN SOUTHWEST AFRICA
SOUTHERN RHODESIA
MADAGASCAR
Tropic of Capricorn
Ndebele, 1896
Menalamba 1898–1904
Herero and Hottentot 1904–1906
SOUTH AFRICA
ZULULAND
Area of resistance

GEOGRAPHY SKILLBUILDER: Interpreting Maps
1. **Region** Which region had the largest area affected by resistance?
2. **Region** Was any region unaffected by resistance movements?

314 CHAPTER 11

Ethiopia: A Successful Resistance
Ethiopia was the only African nation to successfully resist the Europeans. Its victory was due to one man—**Menelik II.** He became emperor of Ethiopia in 1889. He successfully played Italians, French, and British against each other, all of whom were striving to bring Ethiopia into their spheres of influence. In the meantime he built up a large arsenal of modern weapons purchased from France and Russia. About to sign a treaty with Italy, Menelik discovered differences between the wording of the treaty in Amharic—the Ethiopian language —and in Italian. Menelik believed he was giving up a tiny portion of Ethiopia. However, the Italians claimed all of Ethiopia as a protectorate. Meanwhile, Italian forces were advancing into northern Ethiopia. Menelik declared war. In 1896, in one of the greatest battles in the history of Africa—the Battle of Adowa—Ethiopian forces successfully defeated the Italians and maintained their nation's independence.

THINK THROUGH HISTORY
E. Analyzing Causes Why would the French and Russians sell arms to Ethiopia?
E. Possible Answer To prevent Britain from taking over Ethiopia.

Impact of Colonial Rule

European colonial rule forever altered Africans' lives. For the most part, the effects were negative, but in some cases the Europeans brought benefits.

On the positive side, colonialism reduced local warfare. Now, under the control of the European military, raids between rival tribes were reduced. Humanitarian efforts in some colonies improved sanitation and brought hospitals and schools. As a result, life spans increased and literacy rates improved. Also positive was the economic expansion. African products came to be valued on the international market. To aid the economic growth, African colonies gained railroads, dams, and telephone and telegraph lines. But for the most part, these only benefited European business interests, not Africans' lives.

On the negative side, Africans lost control of their land and their independence. Many died of new diseases such as smallpox. They also lost thousands of their people in resisting the Europeans. Famines resulted from the change to cash crops in place of subsistence agriculture.

Africans also suffered from a breakdown of their traditional cultures. Traditional authority figures were replaced. Homes and property were transferred with little regard to their importance to the people. Men were forced to leave villages to find ways to support themselves and their families. They had to work in mines, on European-owned farms, or on government projects such as railroad building. Contempt for the traditional culture and admiration of European life undermined stable societies and caused identity problems for Africans.

The most troublesome political legacy from the colonial period was the dividing of the African continent. Long-term rival chiefdoms were sometimes united, while at other times, kinship groups were split between colonies. The artificial boundaries that combined or unnaturally divided groups created problems that plagued African colonies during European occupation. These boundaries continue to create problems for the nations that evolved from the former colonies.

The patterns of behavior of imperialist powers were similar, no matter where their colonies were located. Dealing with local traditions and peoples continued to cause problems in other areas of the world dominated by Europeans. Resistance to the European imperialists also continued, as you will see in Section 3.

THINK THROUGH HISTORY
F. Recognizing Effects Why might the problems caused by artificial boundaries continue after the Europeans left?

F. Possible Answer The European military would not be there to prevent rival groups from attacking each other.

Section 2 Assessment

1. TERMS & NAMES

Identify
- paternalism
- assimilation
- Menelik II

2. TAKING NOTES

Re-create the chart below on your paper. Fill in the information on how Europeans controlled and managed other areas of the world.

European Imperialism	
Forms of Control	
Management Methods	

3. FORMING OPINIONS

Do you think Europeans could have conquered Africa if the Industrial Revolution had never occurred? Explain your answer.

THINK ABOUT
- the limited role of Europeans in Africa until the late 1800s
- what inventions changed Europeans' ability to enter Africa

4. THEME ACTIVITY

Power and Authority With a small group of students, divide into two teams, one representing the Europeans and one representing the Africans. Debate the following statement: "The negative effects of imperialism outweighed its positive results."

ANSWERS

1. TERMS & NAMES
paternalism, p. 311
assimilation, p. 311
Menelik II, p. 314

2. TAKING NOTES
Possible Responses: Forms of Control—colony, protectorate, sphere of influence, economic imperialism; Management Methods—direct control, indirect control

3. FORMING OPINIONS
Possible Response: Inventions from the Industrial Revolution enabled Europeans to conquer Africa. They reached the interior using steamboats and railroads. Telegraphs and telephones gave them rapid communications. New weapons and quinine to treat malaria enabled European armies to defeat all other armies.

4. THEME ACTIVITY
Standards for Evaluation

Arguments should meet the following criteria:
- State the positive or negative effects of colonialism
- Use reasons and specific examples
- Summarize the argument in a closing statement

---

different PERSPECTIVES

Views of Imperialism

European imperialism extended to the continents beyond Africa. As imperialism spread, the colonizer and the colonized viewed the experience of imperialism in very different ways. Some Europeans were outspoken about the superiority they felt toward the peoples they conquered. Others thought imperialism was very wrong. Even the conquered had mixed feelings about their encounter with the Europeans.

ESSAY
J. A. Hobson
A journalist and essayist, Hobson was an outspoken critic of imperialism. His 1902 book, *Imperialism*, made a great impression on his fellow Britons.

For Europe to rule Asia by force for purposes of gain, and to justify that rule by the pretence that she is civilizing Asia and raising her to a higher level of spiritual life, will be adjudged by history, perhaps, to be the crowning wrong and folly of Imperialism. What Asia has to give, her priceless stores of wisdom garnered from her experience of ages, we refuse to take; the much or little which we could give we spoil by the brutal manner of our giving. This is what Imperialism has done, and is doing, for Asia.

POLITICAL CARTOON
Devilfish in Egyptian Waters
Notice that Egypt is not yet one of the areas controlled by the British.

THE DEVILFISH IN EGYPTIAN WATERS.

SPEECH
Jules Ferry
In a speech before the French National Assembly on July 28,1883, Jules Ferry summarized reasons for supporting French imperialism.

Nations are great in our times only by means of the activities which they develop; it is not simply 'by the peaceful shining forth of institutions . . .' that they are great at this hour. . . . Something else is needed for France: . . . that she must also be a great country exercising all of her rightful influence over the destiny of Europe, that she ought to propagate this influence throughout the world and carry everywhere that she can her language, her customs, her flag, her arms, and her genius.

SPEECH
Dadabhai Naoroji
Dadabhai Naoroji was the first Indian elected to the British Parliament. He was also a part of the founding of the Indian National Congress. In 1871, he delivered a speech answering a question about the impact of Great Britain on India. In the speech he listed positives and negatives about the rule of the British. The conclusion of the speech is printed below.

To sum up the whole, the British rule has been — morally, a great blessing; politically peace and order on one hand, blunders on the other, materially, impoverishment. . . . The natives call the British system "Sakar ki Churi," the knife of sugar. That is to say there is no oppression, it is all smooth and sweet, but it is the knife, notwithstanding. I mention this that you should know these feelings. Our great misfortune is that you do not know our wants. When you will know our real wishes, I have not the least doubt that you would do justice. The genius and spirit of the British people is fair play and justice.

Connect *to* History

Analyzing Effects For each excerpt, list the positive and negative effects of imperialism mentioned by the speaker.

 SEE SKILLBUILDER HANDBOOK, PAGE 653

Connect *to* Today

Research List the countries controlled by England as shown in the political cartoon. Research to find out what year each of them became independent. Make a chart showing the countries in order by the year they were freed from colonial status. Next to each one also write its current name.

CD-ROM For another perspective on imperialism, see *World History: Electronic Library of Primary Sources*

Muslim Lands Fall to Imperialist Demands

MAIN IDEA

European nations expanded their empires by seizing territories from Muslim states.

WHY IT MATTERS NOW

Political events in this vital resource area are still influenced by actions from the imperialistic period.

SETTING THE STAGE The European powers who carved up Africa among themselves also looked elsewhere to see what other lands they could control. The Muslim lands that rimmed the Mediterranean had largely been claimed as a result of Arab and Ottoman conquests. Now the Muslim power in those areas was weakening. Europeans competed with each other to gain control of this strategically important area.

Ottoman Empire Loses Power

The Ottoman Empire at its peak stretched from Hungary in the north, through Greece, around the Black Sea, south through Syria, and across Egypt all the way west to the borders of Morocco. But during the empire's last 300 years, it steadily declined in power. The declining empire had difficulties trying to fit into the modern world. However, the Ottomans made attempts to change before they finally were unable to hold back the European imperialist powers.

Reforms Fail When Suleiman I, the last great Ottoman sultan, died in 1566, he was followed by a succession of weak sultans. The ruling party broke up into a number of quarreling, often corrupt factions. Along with weakening power came other problems. Corruption and theft had caused financial losses. Coinage was devalued, causing inflation. Unemployed ex-soldiers and students caused trouble. Once a leader in scientific, mechanical, and administrative achievements, the Ottoman Empire fell further and further behind Europe.

When Selim III came into power in 1789, he attempted to modernize the army. The older janissary corps resisted his efforts. Selim III was overthrown and reform movements were temporar-

Ottoman Empire, 1699–1914

(to Austria 1699, 1878) AUSTRIA
(to Russia 1783) RUSSIA
FRANCE
HUNGARY
ROMANIA CRIMEA
(to Russia 1803, 1829)
ITALY BULGARIA *Black Sea*
SERBIA Istanbul
ALBANIA
SPAIN BALKANS
(independent 1817, 1913) GREECE ANATOLIA
Caspian Sea
ALGERIA TUNISIA AZERBAIJAN (independent 1730)
(to France 1830) (to France 1881) *Mediterranean Sea* Cyprus (to Britain 1878)
MOROCCO (to France 1912) PERSIA
TRIPOLI (to Italy 1912)
EGYPT (partially independent 1841)
Persian Gulf
ARABIA
Red Sea
Mecca
Tropic of Cancer

☐ Ottoman Empire at its greatest extent in 1699
☐ Ottoman Empire in 1914
← Territory becomes part of

N
0   1,000 Miles
0   2,000 Kilometers

GEOGRAPHY SKILLBUILDER: Interpreting Maps
1. **Region** *Approximately how much of the Ottoman Empire was lost by 1914?*
2. **Region** *How many European nations claimed parts of the Ottoman Empire? Which areas became independent?*

ily abandoned. Meanwhile, nationalist feelings began to stir among the Ottoman's subject peoples. In 1830, Greece gained its independence, and Serbia gained self-rule. The Ottomans' weakness was becoming apparent to European powers, who were expanding their territories. They began to look for ways to take the lands away from the Ottomans.

The Age of Imperialism **317**

SECTION 3 RESOURCES

PRINT RESOURCES

  IN-DEPTH RESOURCES: UNIT 3
Guided Reading, p. 39

ACCESS FOR STUDENTS ACQUIRING ENGLISH
Guided Reading (Spanish), p. 124

FORMAL ASSESSMENT
Section Quiz, p. 139

ALTERNATIVE ASSESSMENT BOOK

TECHNOLOGY RESOURCES

 WORLD ART AND CULTURES TRANSPARENCIES
AT58 *Reception at the Court of Sultan Selim III*

 INTERNET www.mlworldhistory.com

Section 3 Overview

OBJECTIVES

① To summarize the decline of the Ottoman Empire.

② To describe the Crimean War and the division of the Ottoman Empire.

SKILLBUILDERS
- Interpreting maps: region, p. 317
- Interpreting graphs and maps: place, location, p. 319

CRITICAL THINKING
- Analyzing causes, p. 318
- Recognizing effects, p. 319
- Clarifying, p. 320
- Comparing/contrasting, p. 320
- Analyzing themes, p. 320

FOCUS
5-Minute Warm-Up

▶ ***Recognizing Effects***
Answering the following questions will help students understand the decline of the Ottoman Empire.

1. Study the map on page 317. At its height, what were the furthest boundaries of the Ottoman Empire to the east, west, north, and south?

2. By 1914, what were the only major cities still within the empire?

 WARM-UP TRANSPARENCY 11

OBJECTIVE ① INSTRUCT

Ottoman Empire Loses Power

▶ *Key Ideas*
- The great Suleiman I is succeeded by a series of weak rulers.
- Selim III's reforms give rise to nationalist feelings.
- Europeans seize the opportunity to divide the empire.

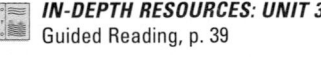 ***IN-DEPTH RESOURCES: UNIT 3***
Guided Reading, p. 39

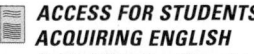 ***ACCESS FOR STUDENTS ACQUIRING ENGLISH***
Guided Reading (Spanish), p. 124

Ottoman Empire, 1699-1914
(See page 317.)

Interpreting the Map Which countries acquired land from the Ottomans? *Austria, Russia, France, Italy, Britain, independent Azerbaijan, and partially independent Egypt*

Extension Activity Ask students to compare this map with the map on page 308. Have them list which parts of the African Ottoman Empire were taken by which European nations. *Egypt/ Suez = Britain; Libya = Italy; Algeria, Tunisia = France*

SKILLBUILDER Answers
1. About two-thirds
2. Five European nations; Azerbaijan, Egypt, Balkans

 OBJECTIVE **2** INSTRUCT

Europeans Grab Territory

▶ **Key Ideas**
- The Ottomans control access to the Atlantic and Mediterranean sea trade.
- The Ottomans, British, and French defeat the Russians in the Crimean War.
- Egypt loses control of the Suez Canal to Britain.
- Although Persia attempts to modernize, Russia and Britain take control.

WORLD ART AND CULTURES TRANSPARENCIES
AT58 *Reception at the Court of Sultan Selim III*

MORE ABOUT . . .
Florence Nightingale
Although born into a wealthy British family, Florence Nightingale rejected marriage and a carefree
(continued on next page)

This 1897 lithograph shows the British forces at the Battle of Balaklava in the Crimean War. This battle was the inspiration for a famous poem by Alfred, Lord Tennyson, "The Charge of the Light Brigade."

Europeans Grab Territory

Geopolitics—an interest in or taking of land for its strategic location or products—played an important role in the fate of the Ottoman Empire. World powers were attracted to its strategic location. The Ottomans controlled access to the Mediterranean and the Atlantic sea trade. Merchants in landlocked countries that lay beyond the Black Sea had to go through Ottoman lands. Russia, for example, desperately wanted passage for its grain exports across the Black Sea and into the Mediterranean Sea. This desire strongly influenced Russia's relations with the Ottoman Empire. Russia attempted to win Ottoman favor, formed alliances with Ottoman enemies, and finally waged war against the Ottomans. Discovery of oil in Persia and the Arabian Peninsula around 1900 focused even more attention on the area.

Russia and the Crimean War Each generation of Russian czars launched a war on the Ottomans to try to gain land on the Black Sea. In 1853, war broke out between the Russians and the Ottomans. The war was called the **Crimean War,** after a peninsula in the Black Sea where most of the war was fought. Britain and France wanted to prevent the Russians from gaining control of additional Ottoman lands. So they entered the war on the side of the Ottoman Empire. The combined forces of the Ottomans, Britain, and France defeated Russia. The Crimean War was the first war in which women, led by Florence Nightingale, established their position as army nurses. It was also the first war to be covered by newspaper correspondents.

The Crimean War revealed the Ottoman Empire's military weakness. Despite the help of Britain and France, the Ottoman Empire continued to lose lands. The Russians came to the aid of Slavic people in the Balkans who rebelled against the Ottomans. The Ottomans lost control of Romania, Montenegro, Cyprus, Bosnia, Herzegovina, and an area that became Bulgaria. The Ottomans lost land in Africa, too. By the beginning of World War I, the Ottoman Empire was reduced to a small portion of its former size.

Observing the slow decline of the Ottoman Empire, some Muslim leaders decided that their countries would either have to adjust to the modern world or be consumed by it. Egypt and Persia both initiated political and social reforms, in part to block European domination of their lands.

Egypt Tries Reform Modernization came to Egypt as a result of the interest in the area created by the French Revolution. Egypt's strategic location at the head of the Red Sea appeared valuable to France and Britain. After Napoleon failed to win Egypt, a new leader emerged: Muhammad Ali. The Ottomans sent him to govern

A. Answer If the Ottoman Empire could not keep the Europeans out, they worried they would not be able to keep the Europeans out of their lands either.

THINK THROUGH HISTORY
A. Analyzing Causes Why would the decline of the Ottoman Empire make other Muslim countries try to change?

 TEACHING OPTION | BLOCK SCHEDULING

COOPERATIVE ACTIVITY: Debating Issues

CLASS TIME 30 MINUTES

Task: Students will debate the statement: "All countries should have equal access to strategic waterways such as the Suez Canal."

Purpose: To help students understand the history of the Suez Canal from different points of view.

Activity: Students form two groups to debate this question. They should research the history of the

Suez Canal, paying particular attention to the issues of nations' access in the late 1850s to vital waterways, the strategic importance of the canal, the relationships of the nations who use the canal, and the rights of the nation that must oversee and maintain the canal. Each group should designate members as researchers, presenters, coaches, time keepers, and producers of graphic aids. The class can decide which team presents the best case.

 Building a Portfolio: Students may want to write a brief description of this assignment to add to their portfolios.

ALTERNATIVE ASSESSMENT BOOK
Standards for Evaluating a Cooperative Activity

Egypt, but he soon broke away from Ottoman control. In 1841, he fought a series of battles in which he gained control of Syria and Arabia. Through the combined efforts of European powers, he and his heirs were recognized as hereditary rulers of Egypt.

THINK THOUGH HISTORY
B. Recognizing Effects What two effects did raising cotton have on Egyptian agriculture?
B. Answer Brought Egyptians into the international market, reduced production of food crops.

Muhammad Ali began a series of reforms in the military and in the economy. He personally directed a shift of Egyptian agriculture to a plantation cash crop—cotton. This brought Egypt into the international marketplace, but at a cost to the peasants. They lost the use of lands they traditionally farmed. They were forced to grow cash crops in place of food crops.

Muhammad Ali's efforts to modernize Egypt were continued by his grandson, Isma'il. Isma'il supported the construction of the **Suez Canal.** The canal was a man-made waterway that cut through the Isthmus of Suez. It connected the Red Sea to the Mediterranean. It was built mainly with French money and Egyptian labor. The Suez Canal was opened in 1869 with a huge international celebration. However, Isma'il's modernization efforts, such as irrigation projects and communication networks, were enormously expensive. Egypt soon found that it could not pay its European bankers even the interest on its $450 million debt. The British insisted on overseeing financial control of the canal, and in 1882 the British occupied Egypt.

British control of the Suez Canal remained an important part of British imperial policy. The canal was viewed as the "Lifeline of the Empire" because it allowed the British quicker access to its colonies in Asia and Africa. A British imperialist, Joseph Chamberlain, presented a speech to Parliament. In it he supported the continued control of the canal:

> **A VOICE FROM THE PAST**
> I approve of the continued occupation of Egypt; and for the same reasons I have urged upon this Government, . . . the necessity for using every legitimate opportunity to extend our influence and control in that great African continent which is now being opened up to civilization and to commerce. . . .
> **JOSEPH CHAMBERLAIN,** in a speech, January 22, 1894

Persia Pressured to Change Elsewhere in southwest Asia, Russia and Britain competed to exploit Persia commercially and to bring that country under their own spheres of influence. Russia was especially interested in gaining access to the Persian Gulf and the Indian Ocean. Twice Persia gave up territories to Russia after military defeats in 1813 and 1828. Britain was interested in using Afghanistan as a buffer between India and Russia.

Suez Canal

Time saved: 2 weeks

Miles saved: 4,000

TONNAGE SHIPPED

Source: *The Suez Canal*, Charles W. Hallberg

EGYPT

Mediterranean Sea

Suez Canal

Nile R.

Red Sea

SINAI

0   100 Miles
0   200 Kilometers

SKILLBUILDER: Interpreting Graphs and Maps
1. **Place** Approximately how long is the Suez Canal?
2. **Location** The map on the left indicates that 4,000 miles were cut off the trip and 2 weeks' time was saved. How many miles were saved per day?
3. Approximately how much tonnage was shipped in 1880?

The Age of Imperialism **319**

MORE ABOUT . . .
Florence Nightingale
(continued from page 318)

life to tend to the sick and suffering. She was superintendent of a women's hospital in London when the secretary of war asked her to take charge of nursing British wounded in the Crimean War. She saved many lives on the battlefield.

MORE ABOUT . . .
Muhammad Ali

Muhammad Ali's main goal was to turn Egypt into one vast plantation to benefit his family. He changed the tax system to divert benefits from former rulers and for a time held a monopoly over agricultural trade. As a result, his family became extremely wealthy and accumulated large landholdings.

History from Visuals

Suez Canal

Interpreting the Graph and Maps Once a ship is through the canal, how many more miles must it travel to get to the main body of the Red Sea? *About another 200 miles.* What was the increase in tonnage shipped between 1872 and 1876? *About 1.5 million tons (1.5 to 3.0 million)*

Extension Activity Have students consult an encyclopedia or almanac to determine current traffic through the Suez Canal.

SKILLBUILDER Answers
1. About 100 miles
2. About 286 miles per day
3. About 4.2 million tons

Less Proficient Readers Pair less proficient readers with more able readers and ask them to read the text titled "Europeans Grab Territory" on pages 318–320. Then have the more proficient reader help the less able reader create a chart listing the motives of the Russians, British, and Persians and the actions each group took. Their completed chart might look like the one on the right.

	Motives	Actions
Russia	Wanted access to Persian Gulf and Indian Ocean	Took territories from Persia by force
Britain	Wanted Afghanistan as a barrier between Russia and India	Took Afghanistan by force
Persia	Wanted to raise capital to develop resources	Sold concessions to Europeans

In 1857, Persia resisted British demands but was forced to give up all claims to Afghanistan. Britain's interest in Persia increased greatly after the discovery of oil there in 1908.

Persia lacked the capital to develop its own resources. To raise money and to gain economic prestige, the Persian ruler began granting concessions to Western businesses. Businesses bought the right to operate in a certain area or develop a certain product. For example, a British corporation, the Anglo-Persian Oil Company, began to develop Persia's rich oil fields in the early 1900s.

Tension arose between the often corrupt rulers, who wanted to sell concessions to Europeans, and the people. The people were often backed by religious leaders who feared change or disliked Western influence in their nation. In 1891, Nasir al-Din attempted to sell the rights to export and distribute Persian tobacco to a British company. This action outraged Sayyid Jamal al-Din al-Afghani, a modernist leader, who helped set up a tobacco boycott by the heavy-smoking Persians. In the following quote, he expresses his contempt for the Persian ruler:

Background
Britain needed oil for its ships, which now ran on oil rather than coal. Thus, they needed greater supplies of petroleum.

CONNECT to TODAY

Tobacco and Politics
Tobacco production is a huge industry in the world. It is estimated that about 7 million metric tons of tobacco are consumed each year. (That is about 6 trillion cigarettes per year.)

In some countries, production of tobacco is a major part of the economy. Taxes on tobacco products generate much revenue in countries across the world. Since the tobacco industry creates huge profits, it often has an impact on the politics of a country as well.

Health concerns about tobacco consumption have also found their way into politics. Worldwide, countries are looking at government control of tobacco products as a way to deal with health problems.

Since the 1980s the World Health Organization has promoted a World No-Tobacco Day, which occurs on May 31 each year.

A VOICE FROM THE PAST
. . . He has sold to the foes of our Faith the greater part of the Persian lands and the profits derived from them, for example . . . tobacco, with the chief centers of its cultivation, the lands on which it is grown and the warehouses, carriers, and sellers, wherever these are found. . . .
In short, this criminal has offered the provinces of Persia to auction among the Powers, and is selling the realms of Islam and the abodes of Muhammad and his household to foreigners.

SAYYID JAMAL-AL-DIN AL-AFGHANI, in a letter to Hasan Shirazi, April 1891

THINK THROUGH HISTORY
C. Clarifying Why did al-Afghani condemn the actions of the Persian ruler?
C. Possible Answer He sold out the land and the profits from them to foreigners.

The tobacco boycott worked. Riots broke out and the ruler was compelled to cancel the concession. As unrest continued in Persia, the government was unable to control the situation. In 1906, a group of revolutionaries forced the ruler to establish a constitution. In 1907, Russia and Britain took over the country and divided it into spheres of influence.

In the Muslim lands, the European imperialists gained control by using economic imperialism and creating spheres of influence. Although some governments made attempts at modernization, in most cases it was too little too late. In other areas of the globe, imperialists provided the modernization. India, for example, became a colony that experienced massive change as a result of the occupation of the imperialist British. You will learn about India in Section 4.

Section 3 Assessment

1. TERMS & NAMES
Identify
• geopolitics
• Crimean War
• Suez Canal

2. TAKING NOTES
Re-create the diagram below and fill in at least three details that support the main idea.

Muslim states failed to keep European imperialists out of their lands.		
Detail	Detail	Detail

What imperialistic forms of control did the Europeans use to govern these lands?

3. COMPARING AND CONTRASTING
How were the reactions of African and Muslim rulers to imperialism similar? How were they different?

THINK ABOUT
• African and Muslim patterns of resistance
• African and Muslim efforts toward modernization

4. ANALYZING THEMES
Economics Why did European imperialist powers want to take over Ottoman Empire lands?

THINK ABOUT
• the location of the Ottoman Empire
• its special resources
• European ambitions

ANSWERS

1. TERMS & NAMES
geopolitics, p. 308
Crimean War, p. 308
Suez Canal, p. 309

2. TAKING NOTES
Possible Responses: Ottoman Empire tries to reform but fails; Egyptian leaders cannot complete modernization; Persia falls to economic imperialism. The Europeans used economic imperialism and spheres of influence to govern these lands.

3. COMPARING AND CONTRASTING
Possible Responses: Both African and Muslim rulers resisted Europeans. Muslims tried to modernize to resist Western imperialism, while many Africans simply signed away their lands. Menelik II was the only African ruler to remain independent.

4. ANALYZING THEMES
The Ottoman Empire ruled much of North Africa, the Middle East, and Eastern Europe. It controlled key overland trade routes and sea trade on the Mediterranean and on the Atlantic Ocean and Black Sea. It also contained many important natural resources, such as oil. European nations wanted to control trade and to obtain greater wealth.

MAIN IDEA

As the Mughal Empire declined, Britain seized Indian territory until it controlled almost the whole subcontinent.

WHY IT MATTERS NOW

India, the second most populated nation in the world, has its political roots in this colony.

SETTING THE STAGE British economic interest in India began in the 1600s, when the British East India Company set up trading posts at Bombay, Madras, and Calcutta. At first, India's ruling Mughal Dynasty kept European traders under control. By 1707, however, the Mughal Empire was collapsing. Dozens of small states, each headed by a ruler or maharajah, broke away from Mughal control.

British Expand Control Over India

The East India Company quickly took advantage of the growing weakness of the Mughals. In 1757, Robert Clive led company troops in a decisive victory over Indian forces at the Battle of Plassey. From that time on, the East India Company was the leading power in India. The area controlled by the company grew over time. Eventually, it governed directly or indirectly an area that included modern Bangladesh, most of southern India, and nearly all the territory along the Ganges River in the north.

East India Company Dominates Officially, the British government regulated the East India Company's efforts both in London and in India. Until the beginning of the 19th century, the company ruled India with little interference from the British government. The company even had its own army, led by British officers and staffed by **sepoys,** or Indian soldiers. The governor of Bombay, Mountstuart Elphinstone, referred to the sepoy army as "a delicate and dangerous machine, which a little mismanagement may easily turn against us."

"Jewel in the Crown" Produces Trade Products At first, India was treasured by the British more for its potential than its actual profit. The Industrial Revolution had turned Britain into the world's workshop, and India was a major supplier of raw materials for that workshop. Its 300 million people were also a large potential market for British-made goods. It is not surprising, then, that the British considered India the brightest **"jewel in the crown"** — the most valuable of all of Britain's colonies.

The British set up restrictions that prevented the Indian economy from operating on its own. British policies called for India to produce raw materials for British manufacturing and to buy British finished goods. In addition,

Tea from the Lipton plantation in Darjeeling is loaded onto an elephant for transport to Calcutta.

The Age of Imperialism **321**

FOCUS
5-Minute Warm-Up

▶ *Identifying Main Ideas*
To help students understand nationalism in India, have them answer these questions.

• Read History Makers on page 325. After seeing his sister-in-law killed, what decision did Ram Mohun Roy make?

• How did his decision affect the Indian nationalist movements?

WARM-UP TRANSPARENCY 11

OBJECTIVE ① INSTRUCT

British Expand Control Over India

▶ *Key Ideas*
• The East India Company seizes control of most of India.

• Britain considers India its primary colony.

• India benefits and suffers under British colonial rule.

IN-DEPTH RESOURCES: UNIT 3
Guided Reading, p. 40

ACCESS FOR STUDENTS ACQUIRING ENGLISH
Guided Reading (Spanish), p. 125

CASE STUDY—India and Britain: Colonialism and Imperialism, p. 2

Western-held Territories in Asia, 1910

Interpreting the Map Which of the Indian exports listed on the map is the largest amount? The most valuable? *largest—oil seeds; most valuable—cotton*

Extension Activity Based on information provided by the map, ask students to list what features made India the "jewel in the crown" for Great Britain. Have them consider not only resources but also India's strategic location between the Far East, Western Asia, Africa, and the Pacific Islands. What problems might Great Britain have faced trying to trade in the Far East if it had not held India?

SKILLBUILDER Answers
1. Britain
2. India has access to trade with Southeast Asia, East Asia, and Africa.

MORE ABOUT . . .
British Economic Impact on Indian Classes

British economic policies affected Indian classes unequally, although they were supposed to improve the lot of poor farmers. In fact, the only classes to benefit from British rule were the zamindars, or landowners, who leased land to tenant farmers, and the entrepreneurs of Calcutta, who served as agents and bankers to the British. The farmers themselves, called cultivators, remained as poor as ever throughout the period of British rule.

Western-held Territories in Asia, 1910

India's Exports

- jute—765,000 tons in 1909
- wheat—1.3 million tons in 1914
- oilseeds—1.5 million tons in 1913
- tea—192 million pounds in 1900
- cotton—valued at 410 million rupees* in 1913
- hides and skins—valued at 160 million rupees in 1913

*A rupee is the Indian currency.

GEOGRAPHY SKILLBUILDER: Interpreting Maps
1. **Region** *Which nation in 1900 held the most land in colonies?*
2. **Location** *How is the location of India a great advantage for trade?*

Indian competition with British finished goods was prohibited. For example, India's own handloom textile industry was almost put out of business by imported British textiles. Cheap cloth and ready-made clothes from England flooded the Indian market and drove out local producers.

India became economically valuable only after the British established a railroad network. Railroads transported raw products from the interior to the ports and manufactured goods back again. The majority of the raw materials were agricultural products produced on plantations. Plantation crops included tea, indigo, coffee, cotton, and jute. Another crop was opium. The British shipped opium to China and exchanged it for tea, which they then sold in England.

Trading these crops was closely tied to international events. For example, the Crimean War in the 1850s cut off the supply of Russian jute to Scottish jute mills. This boosted the export of raw jute from Bengal, a province in India. Likewise, cotton production in India increased when the Civil War in the United States cut off supplies of cotton for British textile mills.

Impact of Colonialism India both benefited from and was oppressed by British colonialism. On the positive side, the laying of the world's third largest railroad network was a major British achievement. When completed, the railroads enabled India to develop a modern economy and brought unity to the connected regions. Along with the railroads, a modern road network, telephone and telegraph lines, dams, bridges, and irrigation canals enabled India to modernize. Sanitation and public health improved. Schools and colleges were founded, and literacy increased. Also, British troops cleared central India of bandits and put an end to local warfare among competing local rulers.

Vocabulary
jute: a fiber used for sacks and cord.

THINK THROUGH HISTORY
A. Summarizing On which continents are Indian goods being traded?
A. Answer
Asia and Europe.

322 Chapter 11

Task: Students will research and write a report on the Indian handloom industry.

Purpose: To help students understand the impact of foreign rule on India.

Activity: Students work in small groups, each group researching a separate topic of the Indian handloom industry: its history, types of textiles

produced, fame in Europe, words added to English (such as *calico* or *chintz*), effect of British competition, return to the handloom as a political statement, comparison with African textiles, and the handloom industry in India today. Each group should write a brief report on its topic, using graphic aids.

 Building a Portfolio: Students adding this report to their portfolios should explain the assignment.

ALTERNATIVE ASSESSMENT BOOK
Standards for Evaluating a Cooperative Activity

Standards for Evaluation
Reports should . . .

- show information from various sources
- make effective use of visual aids
- demonstrate students' knowledge of the subject

On the negative side, the British held much of the political and economic power. The British restricted Indian-owned industries such as cotton textiles. The emphasis on cash crops resulted in a loss of self-sufficiency for many villagers. The conversion to cash crops reduced food production, causing famines in the late 1800s. The British officially adopted a hands-off policy regarding Indian religious and social customs. Even so, the increased presence of missionaries and the outspoken racist attitude of most British officials threatened Indian traditional life.

Indians Rebel

By 1850, the British controlled most of the Indian subcontinent. However, there were many pockets of discontent. Many Indians believed that in addition to controlling their land the British were trying to convert them to Christianity. The Indian people also resented the constant racism that the British expressed toward them.

Sepoy Rebellion As economic problems increased for Indians, so did their feelings of resentment and nationalism. In 1857, gossip spread among the sepoys, the Indian soldiers, that the cartridges of their new Enfield rifles were sealed with beef and pork fat. To use the cartridges, soldiers had to

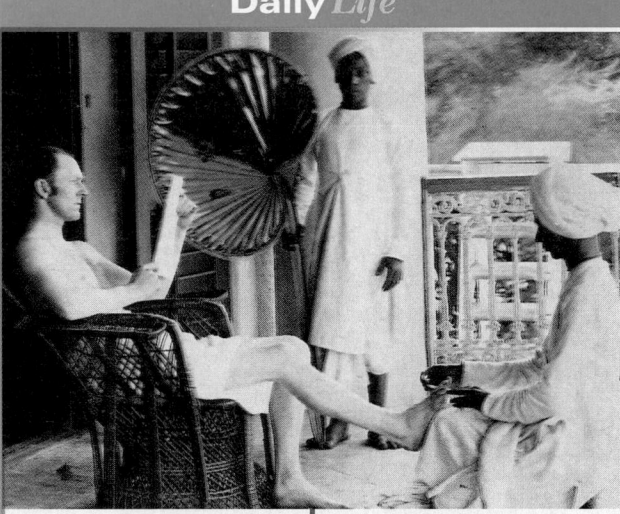

Daily *Life*

British Army
Social class determined the way of life for the British Army in India. Upper-class men served as officers. Lower-class British served at lesser rank and did not advance past the rank of sergeant. Only men with the rank of sergeant and above were allowed to bring their wives to India.

Each English officer's wife attempted to re-create England in the home setting. Like a general, she directed an army of 20 to 30 servants.

Officers and enlisted men spent much of each day involved in sports such as cricket, polo, and rugby. Athletics were encouraged to keep the men from "drink and idleness." The upper-class officers also spent time socializing at fancy-dress dances, concerts, and after-polo events.

Indian Servants
Caste determined Indian occupations. Jobs were strictly divided by caste. Castes were divided into four broad categories called varna. Indian civil servants were of the third varna. House and personal servants were of the fourth varna.

Even within the varna, jobs were strictly regulated, which is why such large servant staffs were required. For example, in the picture above, although both were of the same varna, the person washing the man's feet was of a different caste than the person doing the fanning.

The social life of the servants centered around religious festivals and ceremonies marking important life passages. These included a child's first haircut, religious initiation, engagement, marriage, or childbirth.

bite off the seal. Both Hindus, who consider the cow sacred, and Muslims, who do not eat pork, were outraged by the news.

A garrison commander was shocked when 85 of the 90 sepoys refused to accept the cartridges. The British handled the crisis badly. The soldiers who had disobeyed were jailed. The next day, on May 10, 1857, the sepoys rebelled. They marched to Delhi, where they were joined by Indian soldiers stationed there. They captured the city of Delhi. From Delhi, the rebellion spread to northern and central India.

Some historians have called this outbreak the **Sepoy Mutiny.** The uprising spread over much of northern India. Fierce fighting took place. Both British and sepoys tried to slaughter each other's armies. The East India Company took more than a year to regain control of the country. The British government sent troops to help them.

The Indians could not unite against the British due to weak leadership and serious splits between Hindus and Muslims. Hindus did not want the Muslim Mughal Empire restored. Indeed, many Hindus preferred British rule to Muslim rule. Most

The Age of Imperialism **323**

B. Possible Answer
Yes, he predicted problems with sepoy armies if they were not handled correctly. The mutiny was proof of this.

THINK THROUGH HISTORY
B. Recognizing Effects Look back at Elphinstone's comment on page 701. Did the Sepoy Mutiny prove him correct? Explain your answer.

OBJECTIVE ② INSTRUCT

Indians Rebel

▶ *Key Ideas*
• Indians object to the racist attitudes of the British rulers.
• The Sepoy Mutiny turns into widespread rebellion.
• The British government takes direct control of India.

IN-DEPTH RESOURCES: UNIT 3
Primary Source: Letter Opposing the English, p. 47

ELECTRONIC LIBRARY OF PRIMARY SOURCES
"The Rise of the Color Bar"

Daily *Life*
British Army and Indian Servants

Ask students how the daily lives of British army officers differed from the lives of their Indian servants. How were they the same? *Students may point to the British dominance and their enjoyment of greater leisure time. Some students might note that both groups socialized only with their "own kind."*

MORE ABOUT . . .
The Sepoy Mutiny

Hindu and Muslim soldiers jumped to the conclusion that sealing the cartridges with animal fat was a deliberate move by the British to force them to convert to Christianity.

They reasoned that the religious pollution from touching the fat would be so damaging that they would be expelled from their religious groups. With nowhere else to go, the soldiers would have to convert to Christianity. Although the manufacturers of the cartridges sought to correct this mistaken idea, the Indians' distrust of the British deepened.

TEACHING OPTIONS

CONNECTIONS ACROSS THE CURRICULUM

Literature To find out more about the lives of the British and Indians under the Raj, students might wish to read stories and novels about this period in history. For a sympathetic British point of view, they can read the fiction of Rudyard Kipling. For stories from the Indian perspective, they can read Prem Chand (*The Gift of a Cow,* Bloomington, IN: Indiana UP, 1968) or the work of

Rabindranath Tagore (*The Crescent Moon,* New York: Macmillan, 1922). For a picture of Indian village life little changed from life under the Raj, they can read books by R.K. Narayan (*The Grandmother's Tale and Other Stories,* New York: Viking, 1994; *A Tiger for Malgudi,* New York: Viking, 1983).

MULTIPLE LEARNING STYLES

Visual Learners The new art of photography was popular during the time of British rule in India. Refer students to collections of photographs of British India by both European and Indian photographers (such as *The Last Empire: Photography in British India 1855-1911.* Millerton, NY: Aperture, 1976; *Princely India* by Raja Deen Dayal, New York: Knopf, 1980; and *Through Indian*

Eyes by Judith Mara Gutman, New York: Oxford UP, 1982). Ask students to analyze the photographs for information about the social attitudes of the British and the Indians. Each student should write a few paragraphs on a photograph of his or her choice taken in India between 1850 and 1914.

Teacher's Edition **323**

The term "Raj" is a Hindi word meaning *rule* or *sovereignty*. It has been used to refer both to British rule of India and to the viceroy of India, who was appointed by the British government for five or six years. By 1910, the Raj was one of the most powerful rulers in the world. He governed 300 million subjects and had one of the finest armies of the time.

The wives of the different Rajs, called first ladies, faced many challenges in moving to India. Unused to the hot climate, many suffered ill health. Also, with so many servants to attend to every need, the first ladies were hard pressed to fill their time. Yet, unlike their busy viceroy husbands, these women often caught glimpses of the appalling poverty of India. Many returned to England changed forever by their experiences.

 GEOGRAPHY TRANSPARENCIES
GT27 India Under British Rule, 1805–1886

 WORLD ART AND CULTURES TRANSPARENCIES
AT59 *Raja Ram Singh in Procession*

This English engraving shows the British troops defending the Royal Residency at Lucknow against a sepoy attack on July 30, 1857.

of the princes and maharajahs who had made alliances with the East India Company did not take part in the rebellion. The Sikhs, a religious group that had been hostile to the Mughals, also remained loyal to the British. Indeed, from then on, the bearded and turbaned Sikhs became the mainstay of Britain's army in India.

Turning Point The mutiny marked a turning point in Indian history. As a result of the mutiny, in 1858, the British government took direct command of India. The part of India that was under direct British rule was called the Raj. The term **Raj** referred to British rule over India from 1757 until 1947. India was divided into 11 provinces and some 250 districts. Sometimes a handful of officials were the only British among the million or so people in a district. A cabinet minister in London directed policy, and a British governor-general in India carried out the government's orders. After 1877, this official held the title of viceroy. To reward the many princes who had remained loyal to Britain, the British promised to respect all treaties the East India Company had made with them. They also promised that the Indian states that were still free would remain independent. Unofficially, however, Britain won greater and greater control of those states.

The Sepoy Mutiny fueled the racist attitudes of the English. The English attitude is illustrated in the following quote by Lord Kitchener, British commander in chief of the army in India:

> **A VOICE FROM THE PAST**
> It is this consciousness of the inherent superiority of the European which has won for us India. However well educated and clever a native may be, and however brave he may prove himself, I believe that no rank we can bestow on him would cause him to be considered an equal of the British officer.
>
> **LORD KITCHENER,** quoted in K. M. Panikkar, *Asia and Western Dominance*

The mutiny increased distrust between the British and the Indians. A political pamphlet suggested that both Hindus and Muslims "are being ruined under the tyranny and oppression of the . . . treacherous English."

C. Possible Answers More of India was under British control; greater distrust between Indians and the British.

THINK THROUGH HISTORY
C. Recognizing Effects In what ways did the Sepoy Mutiny change the political climate of India?

Explaining the Skill: An "assumption" is a belief or an idea taken for granted to be true. People can make assumptions based on evidence or simply on personal opinion. "Bias" is a prejudiced point of view. Biased historical accounts tend to be one-sided and to reflect the personal prejudices of the writer. To help students detect assumptions and biases, instruct them to look for language that conveys a positive or negative

slant on the subject. Are these views backed by facts?

Applying the Skill: Read "A Voice from the Past" on this page. To analyze Kitchener's assumptions and biases, use a chart like the one to the right.

 IN-DEPTH RESOURCES: UNIT 3
Skillbuilder Practice: Analyzing Assumptions and Biases, p. 42

Assumptions:	The European is inherently superior. A native can never be equal.
Biases:	Natives cannot be trusted with positions of authority, no matter how clever or well educated. Europeans must always remain in control.

Indian Nationalist Movements Begin

In the early 1800s, some Indians began demanding more modernization and a greater role in governing themselves. Ram Mohun Roy, a modern-thinking, well-educated Indian, began a campaign to move India away from traditional practices and ideas. Sometimes called the "Father of Modern India," Ram Mohun Roy called for an end to widow suicide, which he believed was a murderous act. He saw child marriages and the rigid caste separation as parts of religious life that needed to be changed to bring India into a more modern frame of mind. He believed that if the practices were not changed, India would continue to be controlled by outsiders. Roy's writings inspired other Indian reformers to call for adoption of Western ways. Roy also founded a social reform movement that worked for change in India.

Background
Hindu tradition called *suttee* called for a widow to be burned alive on the funeral pyre of her husband.

Besides modernization and westernization, nationalist feelings started to surface in India. Indians resented a system that made them second-class citizens in their own country. Even Indians with a European education faced discrimination. They were barred from top posts in the Indian Civil Service. Those who managed to get middle-level jobs were paid less than Europeans. A British engineer on the East India Railway, for example, made nearly 20 times as much money as an Indian engineer.

A spirit of Indian nationalism led to the founding of two nationalist groups, the Indian National Congress in 1885 and the Muslim League in 1906. At first, such groups concentrated on specific concerns for Indians. Gradually their demands broadened. By the early 1900s, they were calling for self-government.

D. Possible Answer Because these groups often were hostile to each other, it would make control of the areas easier.

THINK THROUGH HISTORY
D. Analyzing Motives Why would the British think that dividing the Hindus and Muslims into separate sections would be good?

The nationalists were further inflamed in 1905 by the partition of Bengal. The province, which had a population of 85 million, was too large for administrative purposes. So the British divided it into a Hindu section and a Muslim section. Acts of terrorism broke out. The province was on the edge of open rebellion. In 1911, yielding to the pressure, the British took back the order and divided the province in a different way.

Conflict over the control of India continued to develop between the Indians and the British in the following years. Elsewhere in Southeast Asia, the same struggles for control of land took place between local groups and the major European powers that dominated them. You will learn about them in Section 5.

HISTORY MAKERS

Ram Mohun Roy
1772–1833

An extremely bright student, Ram Mohun Roy learned Persian, Sanskrit, and Arabic as a child. He spent many hours studying the religions of the world to understand people. He also studied the social and political ideas of the American and French revolutions.

Roy watched his sister-in-law burned alive on the funeral pyre of her husband. After that, he resolved to end practices that rooted India to the past. He challenged traditional Hindu culture and called for modernization of Hindu society.

The Hindu reform society he organized, Brahmo Samaj, shaped the thinking of the 19th-century Indian reformers. The society was the forerunner of the Indian nationalist movements.

Section 4 Assessment

1. TERMS & NAMES

Identify
• sepoy
• "jewel in the crown"
• Sepoy Mutiny
• Raj

2. TAKING NOTES

Re-create on your paper the cause-and-effect diagram below and fill in the effects of the three causes listed.

Cause	Effect
1. Decline of the Mughal Empire	
2. Colonial policies	
3. Sepoy Mutiny	

Which of the effects you listed later became causes?

3. ANALYZING

How did imperialism contribute to unity and the growth of nationalism in India?

THINK ABOUT
• the benefits of imperialism
• the negative effects of imperialism

4. ANALYZING THEMES

Empire Building How did economic imperialism lead to India's becoming a British colony?

THINK ABOUT
• the role of the British East India Company
• the Sepoy Mutiny

The Age of Imperialism **325**

OBJECTIVE 3 INSTRUCT

Indian Nationalist Movements Begin

▶ *Key Ideas*
• Indians begin to demand a greater role in government.
• Ram Mohun Roy speaks out against social injustices.
• Nationalists form the Indian National Congress and the Muslim League.
• A public outcry forces Britain to redraw its partition of Bengal.

HISTORY MAKERS
Ram Mohun Roy

Ask students if they think Ram Mohun Roy was a courageous man. Why or why not?

ASSESS & RETEACH

Section 4 Assessment
Suggest that students write down important points they want to include in each answer before they begin.

 FORMAL ASSESSMENT BOOK
Section Quiz, p. 140

Reteaching Activity
CLASS TIME: 15 MINUTES

Hand out copies of the concept web graphic organizer. Ask students to work in groups to fill in the diagram, using the following sentence as a main idea: "The Indian population never fully accepted British rule."

 CRITICAL THINKING TRANSPARENCIES
CT78 Concept Web

CLOSE ACTIVITY

CLASS TIME: 25 MINUTES

Evaluating
Tell students they are part of a panel evaluating the British occupation of India. Ask them to rate Britain in the following categories: technological assistance; improvements in health and social welfare; respect for native culture; economic fairness; attitudes toward native peoples; uses of military force. Students must give reasons for their ratings.

ANSWERS

1. TERMS & NAMES
sepoy, p. 321
"jewel in the crown," p. 321
Sepoy Mutiny, p. 323
Raj, p. 324

2. TAKING NOTES
1. Effect—East India Company expanded its colonial territory.
2. Effect—Created resentment and nationalist feelings among Indians. 3. Effect—Built support for nationalist groups. Each effect became the cause of the next effect.

3. ANALYZING
Possible Responses: Positive effects of imperialism—railroads, roads, telephones, telegraph, unified rule; improved communications and unified many Indians. Negative effects—racism, economic hardships; contributed to the growth of nationalism and a desire for self-rule.

4. ANALYZING THEMES
The British East India Company had its own private army to maintain control of its territory in India. When the Sepoy Munity occurred, the company was unable to regain control. The British government stepped in, seized control, and claimed India as a colony of the crown.

Teacher's Edition **325**

OBJECTIVES

1. To summarize the acquisition of European colonies in Southeast Asia.

2. To describe how Siam remained independent.

3. To summarize U.S. acquisition of the Philippines and Hawaii.

CRITICAL THINKING

• Comparing, p. 326
• Analyzing motives, p. 327
• Recognizing effects, p. 327
• Drawing conclusions, p. 329

FOCUS

5-Minute Warm-Up

▶ **Making Inferences**
By answering these questions, students will understand more about the development of Southeast Asia.

1. Study the picture on page 326. What U.S. city does Singapore remind you of?

2. What influences from European rule does the picture show?

 WARM-UP TRANSPARENCY 11

OBJECTIVE ① INSTRUCT

Western Rivalries for Pacific Rim Lands

▶ **Key Ideas**
• European powers race to claim a part of Southeast Asia for themselves.

• The Dutch East India Company, which controls Indonesia, creates a rigid social hierarchy.

• The British encourage large-scale immigration of the Chinese to Malaysia.

• The French try to impose their culture on their colonies.

📖 **IN-DEPTH RESOURCES: UNIT 3**
Guided Reading, p. 41

📖 **ACCESS FOR STUDENTS ACQUIRING ENGLISH**
Guided Reading (Spanish), p. 126

TERMS & NAMES
• Pacific Rim
• King Mongkut
• Emilio Aguinaldo
• annexation
• Queen Liliuokalani

5 Western Powers Rule Southeast Asia

MAIN IDEA	WHY IT MATTERS NOW
Demand for Asian products drove Western imperialists to seek possession of Southeast Asian lands.	Southeast Asian independence struggles in the 20th century have their roots in this period of imperialism.

SETTING THE STAGE Just as the European powers rushed to divide Africa, they also competed to carve up the lands of Southeast Asia. These lands form part of the **Pacific Rim,** the countries that border the Pacific Ocean. Western nations desired the Pacific Rim lands for their strategic location along the sea route to China. Westerners also recognized the value of the Pacific colonies as sources of tropical agriculture, minerals, and oil.

Western Rivalries for Pacific Rim Lands

Early in the 19th century, the Dutch East India Company established control over most of the 3,000-mile-long chain of Indonesian islands. As the European powers began to appreciate the value of the area, they challenged each other for their own parts of the prize. The British established a major trading port at Singapore. The French took over Indochina on the Southeast Asian mainland. The Germans claimed New Guinea and the Marshall and Solomon islands.

Plantation Products Spur Competition The lands of Southeast Asia were perfect for plantation agriculture. The major focus was on sugar cane, coffee, cocoa, rubber, coconuts, bananas, and pineapple. As these products became more important in the world trade markets, European powers raced each other to claim lands.

Dutch Expand Control The Dutch East India Company, chartered in 1602, actively sought lands in Southeast Asia. It seized Melaka from the Portuguese and fought the British and Javanese for control of Java. The discovery of oil and tin on the islands and the desire for more rubber plantations prompted the Dutch to gradually expand their control over Sumatra, Borneo, Celebes, the Moluccas, and Bali. Finally the company ruled the whole island chain of Indonesia, then called the Dutch East Indies.

Management of plantations and trade brought a large Dutch population to the islands. In contrast to the British, who lived temporarily in India but retired in Britain, the Dutch thought of Indonesia as their home. They created a rigid social class system. The Dutch were on top, wealthy and educated Indonesians came next, and plantation workers resided at the bottom. The Dutch also forced farmers to plant one-fifth of their land in specified export crops.

British Take the Malayan Peninsula To compete with the Dutch, the British sought a trading base that would

Traditional-style boats anchor in modern Singapore harbor. High-rise buildings of the 20th century mark Singapore as a major city. Today Singapore is a successful trading nation on the Pacific Rim.

A. Answer Both were trading companies that practiced economic imperialism

THINK THROUGH HISTORY
A. Comparing How was the Dutch East India Company like the British East India Company?

SECTION 5 RESOURCES

PRINT RESOURCES

 IN-DEPTH RESOURCES: UNIT 3
Guided Reading, p. 41
Primary Source: In Favor of Imperialism, p. 48
History Makers: Mongkut, p. 53

 ACCESS FOR STUDENTS ACQUIRING ENGLISH
Guided Reading (Spanish), p. 126

 FORMAL ASSESSMENT
Section Quiz, p. 141

ALTERNATIVE ASSESSMENT BOOK

TECHNOLOGY RESOURCES

🎞 **CRITICAL THINKING TRANSPARENCIES**
CT27 Comparing Imperialist Styles 1850–1900
CT63 Visual Summary

💿 **CD-ROM**
Electronic Library of Primary Sources

 INTERNET www.mlworldhistory.com

serve as a stop for its ships that traveled the India-China sea routes. They found the ideal location—a large, sheltered harbor—on Singapore, an island just off the tip of the Malay Peninsula. The opening of the Suez Canal and the increased demand for tin and rubber combined to make Singapore one of the world's busiest ports.

Britain also gained colonies in Malaysia and in Burma (modern Myanmar). Malaysia had large deposits of tin and became the world's leading rubber exporter. Upper Burma provided teak, while central Burma exported oil. Needing workers to mine the tin and tap the rubber trees, Britain encouraged Chinese to immigrate to Malaysia. Chinese flocked to the area, and some of them became highly successful in business. As a result of such immigration, the Malays soon became a minority in their own country. Conflict between the resident Chinese and the native Malays remains unresolved today.

THINK THROUGH HISTORY
B. Analyzing Motives Why do you think so many Chinese would move to Malaysia?
B. Possible Answer They were probably in search of jobs due to overcrowding, famine, or political unrest.

French Control Indochina The French had been active in Southeast Asia since the turn of the century. They even helped the Nguyen (nuh·WIN) dynasty rise to power in Vietnam. In the 1840s, during the rule of an anti-Christian Vietnamese emperor, seven French missionaries were killed. Church leaders and capitalists who wanted a larger share of the overseas market demanded military intervention. Emperor Napoleon III ordered the French army to invade southern Vietnam. Later, the French added Laos, Cambodia, and northern Vietnam to the territory. The combined states would eventually be called French Indochina. In 1867, a governor of a Vietnamese state told how overpowering the French were:

A VOICE FROM THE PAST

Now, the French are come, with their powerful weapons of war to cause dissension among us. We are weak against them; our commanders and our soldiers have been vanquished. Each battle adds to our misery. . . . The French have immense warships, filled with soldiers and armed with huge cannons. No one can resist them. They go where they want, the strongest ramparts fall before them.

PHAN THANH GIAN, in a letter to his administrators

The French colonists tried to impose their culture on the Indochinese. Using direct colonial management, the French themselves filled all important positions in the government bureaucracy. They did not encourage local industry. Rice became a major export crop. Four times as much land was devoted to rice production. However, the peasants' consumption of rice decreased because rice was shipped out of the region. Anger over this reduction set the stage for Vietnamese resistance against the French.

C. Possible Answer Economies grew, education and health improved, areas unified but lost local leaders, migration resulted in cultural change.

Colonial Impact In Southeast Asia, colonization brought mixed results. Economies grew based on cash crops or goods such as tin and rubber that could be sold on the world market. Roads, harbors, and rail systems linked areas and improved communication and transportation. These improvements were more for the benefit of European business than the local population. However, education, health, and sanitation did improve. Political changes included unification of areas at the cost of weaker local leaders and governments.

THINK THROUGH HISTORY
C. Recognizing Effects What changes took place in Southeast Asia as a result of colonial control?

Unlike other colonial areas, millions of people from other areas of Asia and the world migrated to work on plantations and in the mines in Southeast Asia. This migration changed the cultural and racial makeup of the area. Southeast Asia became a melting pot of Hindus, Muslims, Christians, and Buddhists. The resulting cultural changes often led to racial and religious clashes that are still seen today.

The Age of Imperialism **327**

GlobalImpact

Migrating Rubber Plants
The rubber tree is native to the South American tropics. South American Indians first realized its potential and used the sap to make balls and "waterproof" shoes.

At first rubber sap was only a curiosity in Europe. Then American, Scottish, and British inventors discovered ways of processing it. In 1876, an English botanist collected seeds from wild trees in the Amazon rainforest and planted them in Kew Gardens in London. Later, young trees grown from those seeds were taken to Ceylon and the Malay Peninsula to start rubber plantations there.

The invention of automobiles created a huge demand for rubber. Rubber plantations soon mushroomed in Southeast Asia, Africa, and Central and South America.

GlobalImpact
Migrating Rubber Plants

What advantages might plantation rubber have over wild rubber? *Students' answers might include uniformity of the product, a greater area where it is grown, easier to harvest and market.*

MORE ABOUT . . .
Phan Thanh Gian

When Phan Thanh Gian saw the power of the French warships and cannons, he knew his nation was hopelessly outmatched. He told his countrymen: "It would be as senseless for you to wish to defeat your enemies by force of arms as for a young fawn to attack a tiger." To avoid further bloodshed, he ordered the mandarins and war commanders to surrender without fighting.

Grief-stricken at delivering his country into French hands, Phan committed suicide. He left behind a letter to his district administrators and to the emperor, explaining why he took his own life.

TEACHING OPTIONS

CONNECTIONS ACROSS THE CURRICULUM

Science: Southeast Asian Crops Have students research why Southeast Asian lands are suitable for plantation economy. Students should describe the soil, climate, growing seasons, and agricultural traditions of the area. They can find information in books on Southeast Asia and on world farming methods.

They might prepare a booklet of plants most suitable for cash crops. The booklet could include illustrations of the plants, their places of origin, climate and soil conditions required, and product uses in the world market.

CONNECTIONS ACROSS THE CURRICULUM

Mathematics: Population Percentages Have students research the percentage of Chinese and Indians in Singapore and Malaysia, according to the latest census information they can find. Ask them to create a graph illustrating the percentage of total population each group represents. Students will find up-to-date information in the *Statesman's Yearbook* and the *Britannica Book of the Year.* Have students who are good in math help those who are less proficient. Caution students that when comparing countries, they should try to get statistics from the same census year for each country.

Teacher's Edition **327**

Siam Maintains Independence

While its neighbors on all sides fell under the control of imperialists, Siam (present-day Thailand) maintained its independence throughout the colonial period. Siam lay between British-controlled Burma and French Indochina. (See map on page 702.) France and Britain each aimed to prevent the other from gaining control of Siam. Knowing this, Siamese kings skillfully promoted Siam as a neutral zone between the two powers.

Siam modernized itself under the guidance of **King Mongkut** and his son Chulalongkorn. In a royal proclamation, King Chulalongkorn showed his understanding of the importance of progress:

A VOICE FROM THE PAST
As the times and the course of things in our country have changed, it is essential to promote the advancement of all our academic and technical knowledge and to prevent it from succumbing [giving in] to competition from the outside. In order to achieve this, it is imperative to make haste in education so that knowledge and ability will increase.

KING CHULALONGKORN, "Royal Proclamation in Education"

To accomplish the changes, Siam started schools, reformed the legal system, and reorganized the government. The government built its own railroads and telegraph systems and ended slavery. Because the changes came from their own government, the Siamese people escaped the social turmoil, racist treatment, and economic exploitation that occurred in countries controlled by foreigners.

U.S. Acquires Pacific Islands

Because they fought for their independence from Britain, most Americans disliked the idea of colonizing other nations. However, two groups of Americans were outspoken in their support of imperialism. One group of ambitious empire-builders felt the United States should fulfill its destiny as a world power, colonizing like the Europeans. The other group, business interests, welcomed the opening of new markets and trade possibilities. Beginning in 1898, the United States began to acquire territory and to establish trading posts in the Pacific.

The Philippines Change Hands The United States acquired the Philippine Islands, Puerto Rico, and Guam as a result of the Spanish-American War in 1898. Gaining the Philippines touched off a debate in the United States over imperialism. President McKinley's views swayed many to his side. He told a group of Methodist ministers that he had concluded "that there was nothing left for us to do but to take them all [the Philippine Islands], and to educate Filipinos, and uplift and Christianize them."

Filipino nationalists who had already been fighting with the Spanish were not happy to trade one colonizer for another. **Emilio Aguinaldo** (eh·MEE·lyoh AH·gee·NAHL·doh), leader of the Filipino nationalists, claimed that the United States had promised immediate independence after the Spanish-American War ended. The nationalists declared independence and the establishment of the Philippine Republic.

The United States immediately plunged into a fierce struggle with the Filipino nationalists and defeated them in 1902. The United States promised the Philippine people that it would prepare them for self-rule. To achieve this goal, the United States provided many benefits to the islands. It built roads, railroads, and hospitals, and set up school systems. However, American businesses exploited the Philippines

Background
Siam was named Thailand in 1939.

The progressive Siamese king Mongkut ruled from 1851 to 1868. During his reign he modernized his land and prevented the British and French from taking over.

Vocabulary
Filipino: an inhabitant of the Philippine Islands

---

economically. As with other Southeast Asian areas, businessmen encouraged growing cash crops such as sugar at the expense of basic food crops.

Hawaii Becomes a Republic U.S. interest in Hawaii began around the 1790s when Hawaii was a port on the way to China and East India. Beginning about the 1820s, sugar trade began to change the Hawaiian economy. Americans established sugar-cane plantations and became so successful that they imported laborers from China, Japan, and Portugal. By the mid-19th century, American sugar plantations accounted for 75 percent of Hawaii's wealth. At the same time, American sugar planters also gained great political power in Hawaii.

Then in 1890, the McKinley Tariff Act passed by the U.S. government set off a crisis in the islands. The act eliminated the tariffs on all sugar entering the United States. Now, sugar from Hawaii was no longer cheaper than sugar produced elsewhere. That change cut into the sugar producers' profits. Some U.S. business leaders pushed for **annexation** of Hawaii, or the adding of the territory to the United States. Making Hawaii a part of the United States meant that Hawaiian sugar could be sold for greater profits because American producers got an extra two cents a pound from the U.S. government.

About the same time, the new Hawaiian ruler, **Queen Liliuo-kalani** (luh·LEE·uh·oh·kuh·LAH·nee), took the throne. In 1893, she called for a new constitution that would increase her power. It would also restore the political power of Hawaiians at the expense of wealthy planters. To prevent this from happening, a group of American businessmen hatched a plot to overthrow the Hawaiian monarchy. In 1893, Queen Liliuokalani was removed from power.

Background
President McKinley, who had strong imperialist feelings, came to office in 1897 and encouraged annexation of Hawaii.

In 1894, Sanford B. Dole, a wealthy plantation owner, was named president of the new Republic of Hawaii. The president of the new republic asked the United States to annex it. Acting on the findings of a commission sent to the islands, President Cleveland refused. However, about five years later, in 1898, the Republic of Hawaii was annexed by the United States.

The period of imperialism was a time of great power and domination of others by mostly European powers. As the 19th century closed, the lands of the world were all claimed. The European powers now faced each other with competing claims. Their battles with each other would become the focus of the 20th century.

HISTORY MAKERS

**Queen Liliuokalani
1838–1917**

Liliuokalani was Hawaii's only queen and the last monarch of Hawaii. At the death of her younger brother, she became next in line for the throne. In 1891, she took that throne after the death of her older brother.

Liliuokalani bitterly regretted her brother's loss of power to American planters. She worked to regain power for the Hawaiian monarchy. As queen she refused to renew a treaty signed by her brother that would have given commercial privileges to foreign businessmen. It was a decision that would cost her the crown.

In 1895, she was forced to give up power. However, she continued to oppose the annexation of Hawaii by the United States as a part of the Oni pa'a (Stand Firm) movement.

Section 5 Assessment

1. TERMS & NAMES
Identify
• Pacific Rim
• King Mongkut
• Emilio Aguinaldo
• annexation
• Queen Liliuokalani

2. TAKING NOTES
Re-create on your paper the spider map below. In each circle, identify a Western power and the areas it controlled.

Western powers in Southeast Asia

3. DRAWING CONCLUSIONS
How did the reforms of the Siamese kings maintain Siam's independence?

THINK ABOUT
• what was happening to Siam's neighbors
• the results of the changes

4. THEME ACTIVITY
Empire Building Compose a series of letters to the editor expressing different views on the overthrow of the Hawaiian queen. Include both the Hawaiian and American views on this event.

The Age of Imperialism **329**

HISTORY MAKERS
Queen Liliuokalani

The queen received a modern education and toured the Western world before taking the throne. A talented musician, she is best known for her song "Aloha Oe," the national song of farewell in Hawaii. She worked diligently to preserve Hawaiian culture.

ASSESS & RETEACH

Section 5 Assessment
Have students list the pages in the section on which the answers to the questions can be found.

 FORMAL ASSESSMENT BOOK
Section Quiz, p. 141

Reteaching Activity
CLASS TIME: 20 MINUTES

Hand out copies of the primary source for this section. Ask volunteers to read sections of the speech. List what the speaker wanted the United States to do. Then have students identify which of these goals the country accomplished, as described in this section.

 IN-DEPTH RESOURCES: UNIT 3
Primary Source: In Favor of Imperialism, p. 48

 CRITICAL THINKING TRANSPARENCIES
CT63 Visual Summary

CLOSE ACTIVITY

CLASS TIME: 25 MINUTES

Categorizing
Work with the class to complete a chart that lists the countries of Southeast Asia studied, the Western nation(s) that controlled each one, the country's chief products, and the positive and negative results of colonization.

ANSWERS

1. TERMS & NAMES
Pacific Rim, p. 326
King Mongkut, p. 328
Emilio Aguinaldo, p. 328
annexation, p. 329
Queen Liliuokalani, p. 329

2. TAKING NOTES
Dutch-Indonesia; British-Malayan Peninsula; French-Indochina; United States-Hawaii/Philippines

3. DRAWING CONCLUSIONS
Possible Responses: Siam's neighbors were dominated or taken over by European nations. Siam was able to stay independent because it modernized and could compete with Europeans. There was little social turmoil in Siam, and the king was able to stay in power and resist European demands.

4. THEME ACTIVITY
Standards for Evaluation: The letters should meet the following criteria:
• Reflect accurate information about the topic.
• Present at least two viewpoints with supporting details.
• Be free from errors in spelling and grammar.

Chapter 11 Assessment

TERMS & NAMES

1. imperialism, p. 306
2. racism, p. 306
3. Berlin Conference 1884–1885, p. 307
4. paternalism, p. 311
5. Menelik II, 314
6. geopolitics, 318
7. Suez Canal, p. 319
8. "jewel in the crown," p. 321
9. Raj, p. 324
10. Queen Liliuokalani, p. 329

REVIEW QUESTIONS

Answers will vary.

11. The four motives were nationalism, economic competition, racism, and missionary impulse.

12. During the Boer War, many Africans lost their lives, had their crops destroyed, and their lands burned. The survivors were placed under European rule.

13. The most common forms of imperial rule were colonies, protectorates, spheres of influence, and economic imperialism.

14. Ethiopia resisted European rule largely because of the leadership of Emperor Menelik II. He played the Italians, the French, and the British against each other; bought a large arsenal of modern weapons from France and Russia; discovered flaws in a treaty with the Italians; and defeated the Italian troops.

15. The location of the lands made them attractive for trading purposes, as did the resources found on the lands.

16. The Muslim leaders tried reforms, modernization, and resistance; none of these methods worked.

17. The British used India as a market for manufactured goods, which drove native industries out of business. The British also diverted land to grow cash crops instead of food crops. India's natural resources, instead of being used to develop native industries, were exported to Great Britain.

18. The Sepoy Mutiny began when the sepoys heard a rumor that their new cartridges were sealed with beef and pork fat. The soldiers had to bite off the seal to use the cartridge. This offended both the Muslims, who did not eat pork, and the Hindus, who considered the cow sacred. The Sepoys viewed this incident as a British attempt to force their religion and culture on the Indians.

TERMS & NAMES

Briefly explain the importance of each of the following to the imperialism of 1850–1914.

1. imperialism
2. racism
3. Berlin Conference 1884–1885
4. paternalism
5. Menelik II
6. geopolitics
7. Suez Canal
8. "jewel in the crown"
9. Raj
10. Queen Liliuokalani

Interact *with* History

Make a chart showing the advantages and disadvantages to a local person living in a place that became a European colony. Next make a similar chart for a European living in a foreign place. How do they compare? Discuss with members of your class a way to decide whether the advantages outweigh the disadvantages for each group.

REVIEW QUESTIONS

SECTION 1 (pages 305–309)
Imperialists Divide Africa

11. What motives caused the nations of Europe to engage in imperialist activities?

12. What effect did the Boer War have on Africans?

SECTION 2 (pages 310–316)
Patterns of Change: Imperialism
Case Study: Nigeria

13. What are the forms of imperial rule?

14. How did Ethiopia resist European rule so successfully?

SECTION 3 (pages 317–320)
Muslim Lands Fall to Imperialist Demands

15. Why did the European nations have an interest in controlling the Muslim lands?

16. What methods did the Muslim leaders use to try to prevent European imperialism?

SECTION 4 (pages 321–325)
British Imperialism in India

17. How was the economy of India transformed by the British?

18. What caused the Sepoy Mutiny?

SECTION 5 (pages 326–329)
Western Powers Rule Southeast Asia

19. How did Siam manage to remain independent when others countries in the area were colonized?

20. Describe the attitudes held by Americans about colonizing other lands.

Visual Summary

The New Imperialism, 1850–1914

CAUSES

Nationalism
To gain power, European nations compete for colonies and trade.

Economic Competition
Demand for raw materials and new markets spurs a search for colonies.

Missionary Spirit
Europeans believe they must spread their Christian teachings to the world.

IMPERIALISM
Europeans exerted influence over the economic, political, and social lives of people they colonized.

EFFECTS

Colonization
Europeans control land and people in areas of Africa, Asia, and Latin America.

Colonial Economics
Europeans control trade in the colonies and set up dependent cash-crop economies.

Christianization
Christianity is spread to Africa, India, and Asia.

330 Chapter 11

19. The King of Siam played Britain and France against each other to make Siam a buffer zone between them. He and his descendants made great efforts to modernize Siam.

20. Some Americans wanted to join the Europeans in imperialist activities. Others thought imperialism violated the ideals of democracy.

Interact *with* History

Possible Responses: *Local person: Advantages:* Modern technology, education, medical care, and unified control of area. *Disadvantages:* Racism, economic imperialism, loss of freedom and control of land and culture. *European: Advantages:* New opportunities for wealth, travel, advancement. *Disadvantages:* Distance from family, strange climate and people, new diseases, potentially hostile population

CRITICAL THINKING

1. SUEZ CANAL

THEME **ECONOMICS** Why did the British view the Suez Canal as the lifeline of their empire?

2. RESISTANCE TO IMPERIALISM

Re-create on your paper the diagram below. For each geographic area, tell how the local people resisted the demands of the Europeans.

Africa	Muslim Lands	India	Southeast Asia

3. ECONOMIC EFFECTS OF IMPERIALISM ON COLONIES

How did imperialism alter the economic life of the lands Europeans colonized?

4. ANALYZING PRIMARY SOURCES

The following quotation is from Kwaku Dua III, king of the Asante people. He was being pressured by the British government to allow his kingdom to become a protectorate of Britain. Read the quotation and answer the questions below it.

> **A VOICE FROM THE PAST**
> The suggestion that Ashanti [Asante] in its present state should come and enjoy the protection of Her Majesty the Queen and Empress of India, I may say this is a matter of serious consideration, and which I am happy to say we have arrived at the conclusion, that my kingdom of Ashanti will never commit itself to any such conclusion, that Ashanti must remain independent as of old, at the same time to remain friendly with all white men. I do not write this with a boastful spirit, but in the clear sense of its meaning. Ashanti is an independent kingdom.
> **KWAKU DUA III** to Frederic M. Hodgson, December 27, 1889

- Briefly, what is Kwaku Dua III's answer to the queen?
- Why do you think Kwaku Dua III responded that he wanted to remain friendly to white men?
- What aspects of the response would lead you to believe that Kwaku Dua III did not feel inferior to the Queen of England?

CHAPTER ACTIVITIES

1. LIVING HISTORY: Unit Portfolio Project

THEME **EMPIRE BUILDING** Your unit portfolio project focuses on empire-building in lands around the globe by Western powers during the late 1800s and early 1900s (see page 249). For Chapter 11, you might use one of the following ideas to add to your portfolio:

- Imagine that it is 1899 and you are hosting a debate on the United States' takeover of the Philippine Islands. Your guests will be William McKinley and Emilio Aguinaldo. Prepare a script that includes at least five questions you will ask each of them and their possible responses.

- Write a series of diary entries or a poem from the point of view of a person in a land colonized by Europeans. Write a brief opening describing where you live and from what country the colonizers have come.

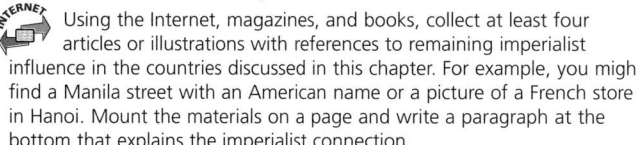 Using the Internet, magazines, and books, collect at least four articles or illustrations with references to remaining imperialist influence in the countries discussed in this chapter. For example, you might find a Manila street with an American name or a picture of a French store in Hanoi. Mount the materials on a page and write a paragraph at the bottom that explains the imperialist connection.

2. CONNECT TO TODAY: Cooperative Learning

THEME **POWER AND AUTHORITY** Problems that continue to plague Africa today often have their roots in imperialism. Divide into small groups and choose one of the following countries: Somalia, Republic of South Africa, Angola, Democratic Republic of Congo (Zaire), Nigeria, and Chad. Research the country's history from colonialism to the present. Prepare a report on the history of the colony, including how imperialism has continued to affect life there.

3. INTERPRETING A TIME LINE

Revisit the unit time line on pages 248–249. Look at the Chapter 11 section. Name two events that occurred in Europe between 1850 and 1914 that demonstrated the growth of nationalism, which was one of the forces driving imperialism.

FOCUS ON GEOGRAPHY

Where the Sun Never Set
"The sun never sets on the British Empire" was a saying about the British Empire at the peak of its power.

- From the map below, what does this saying mean?
- Which British colony is also a continent?

Connect to History
Explain how such a small nation as Britain could gain such a large empire.

The Age of Imperialism **331**

CHAPTER ACTIVITIES

1. LIVING HISTORY

Standards for Evaluation
Scripts should meet these criteria:

- Present questions that require President McKinley to justify his actions.
- Present questions that allow Emilio Aguinaldo to discuss international law and human rights issues.
- Show responses that plausibly represent the stand of each man.

Standards for Evaluation
Diary entries or poems should meet the following criteria:

- Identify the person writing and his or her country.
- Present details about the effects of colonialism.
- Express strong feelings about colonialism and its effects.

Standards for Evaluation
Graphic examples and written paragraphs should meet the following criteria:

- Present clear images of remaining colonial influences.
- Clearly explain the imperialist connection between the past and present.

2. CONNECT TO TODAY: COOPERATIVE LEARNING

Standards for Evaluation
Reports should meet the following criteria:

- Accurately describe colonial and post-colonial conditions.
- Show the long-term effects of colonialism on the country.

3. INTERPRETING A TIME LINE

The Crimean War occurred because Russia wanted to gain lands from the Ottoman Empire. The Berlin Conference 1884–1885 reflected the intense rivalry for overseas colonies that nationalism inspired.

FOCUS ON GEOGRAPHY

- Because Britain had colonies around the world, the sun would always be shining on one of the colonies as the earth revolved.
- Australia

Connect to History: *Possible response:* Britain possessed a superior navy, a private imperialist arm in the British East India Company, the latest technology, and an unshakable belief that it was destined to spread British culture throughout the world.

CRITICAL THINKING

1. SUEZ CANAL
Without the Suez Canal, the British would have had to travel around the west coast of Africa to reach many of their colonies.

2. RESISTANCE TO IMPERIALISM
Africa—armed resistance all over the continent; Muslim Lands—attempts at modernization and reform; India—armed rebellion and formation of nationalist parties; Southeast Asia—armed resistance in some areas, modernization in others

3. ECONOMIC EFFECTS OF IMPERIALISM ON COLONIES
Production patterns of the colonies changed from subsistence crops to cash crops that would sell on the world market. Colonies had to buy European finished goods, which reduced production of local goods. Transportation and communication systems benefited Europeans, not the colonials.

4. ANALYZING PRIMARY SOURCES
- He refused her offer.
- He probably knew he could not completely resist the British and was trying to be diplomatic.
- He addressed the queen as an equal and stressed his country's independence.

Transformations Around the Globe

	Key Ideas	COPY MASTERS	ASSESSMENT
SECTION 1 China Responds to Pressure from the West *pp. 335–339*	*China clings to its ancient traditions and self-sufficiency, but eventually succumbs to both external pressure from Western powers and internal population and governmental pressures.*	*In-Depth Resources: Unit 3* • **Guided Reading**, p. 55 • **Geography Application:** The Opium Wars, p. 60. • **Primary Source:** from Letter to Queen Victoria, p. 62 • **History Makers:** Cixi, p. 69	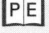 *Section 1 Assessment*, p. 339 *Formal Assessment* • Section Quiz, p. 150 *Alternative Assessment Book* • Standards for Evaluating a Cooperative Activity
SECTION 2 Japan Modernizes *pp. 340–343*	*Japan also faces pressures from Western nations, but, unlike China, it begins to modernize rapidly. It also emulates the Western imperialistic model and annexes Korea.*	*In-Depth Resources: Unit 3* • **Guided Reading**, p. 56 • **Primary Source:** from The Autobiography of Yukichi Fukuzawa, p. 63	*Section 2 Assessment*, p. 343 *Formal Assessment* • Section Quiz, p. 151 *Alternative Assessment Book* • Standards for Evaluating a Cooperative Activity
SECTION 3 U.S. Economic Imperialism in Latin America *pp. 344–348*	*With its colonial legacy and political instability, Latin America remains economically underdeveloped after independence. In the late 1800s, the United States begins to exert great economic and political influence in Latin America.*	*In-Depth Resources: Unit 3* • **Guided Reading**, p. 57 • **Primary Source:** Building the Panama Canal, p. 64 • **Connections Across Time and Cultures:** Responses to Western Pressure, p. 71 • **Science and Technology:** Technology Revolutionizes Communications, p. 72	*Section 3 Assessment*, p. 347 *Formal Assessment* • Section Quiz, p. 152 *Alternative Assessment Book* • Standards for Evaluating a Product or Performance
SECTION 4 The Mexican Revolution *pp. 349–353*	*After territorial struggles with the United States, Mexico fights to achieve independence from Spain. It remains politically unstable, however, under the rule of military dictators. In the early 1900s, economic and political inequality incite the Mexican people to rebel.*	*In-Depth Resources: Unit 3* • **Guided Reading**, p. 58 • **Skillbuilder Practice:** Identifying Problems, p. 59 • **Primary Source:** from The Plan of Ayala, p. 65 • **Literature:** from Tom Mix and Pancho Villa, p. 66 • **History Makers:** Porfirio Díaz, p. 70	*Section 4 Assessment*, p. 353 *Formal Assessment* • Section Quiz, p. 153 *Alternative Assessment Book* • Standards for Evaluating a Cooperative Activity
CHAPTER RESOURCES	**Chapter Overview** *Countries in East Asia and Latin America respond to Western imperialism in different ways. China and Japan try to modernize. Latin America becomes dependent on exports and foreign investments. Mexico fights for independence and political stability.*	*Telescoping the Times* • Chapter Summary, pp. 49–51 *Planning for Block Schedules* *Case Studies* • **Case Study 9**—Japan and Mexico: Pluralistic Politics and Economic Growth, p. 114	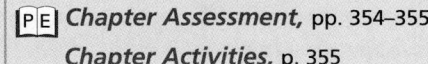 *Chapter Assessment*, pp. 354–355 *Chapter Activities*, p. 355 *Formal Assessment* • Chapter Test, forms A and B, pp. 154–159 *Test Generator* *Alternative Assessment Book*

TECHNOLOGY

 Warm-Up Transparency 12

 World Art and Cultures Transparencies
- AT60 Sorting of Cocoons (Chinese book illustration)

 Electronic Library of Primary Sources
- from *Two Years in the Forbidden City*

 INTERNET RESOURCES
www.mlworldhistory.com

 Warm-Up Transparency 12

 Geography Transparencies
- GT28 Japanese Imperialism, 1875–1910

 World Art and Cultures Transparencies
- AT61 *Japanese Girl in Western Dress*

 Electronic Library of Primary Sources
- from *Fifty Years of New Japan*

 INTERNET RESOURCES
www.mlworldhistory.com

 Warm-Up Transparency 12

 Critical Thinking Transparencies
- CT28 Patterns of Resistance, 1830–1914

 Electronic Library of Primary Sources
- from *The Rough Riders*

 INTERNET RESOURCES
www.mlworldhistory.com

 Warm-Up Transparency 12

 Critical Thinking Transparencies
- CT64 Visual Summary

 World Art and Cultures Transparencies
- AT62 *Distribution of the Land*

 Electronic Library of Primary Sources
- "Alamo Massacre"

 INTERNET RESOURCES
www.mlworldhistory.com

 Chapter Summaries on Audiocassette in English and Spanish

 INTERNET RESOURCES
www.mlworldhistory.com

Block Scheduling (90 MINUTES)

Day 1
Section 1, pp. 335–339
 COOPERATIVE ACTIVITY Debating Reform, p. 338 (Teacher's Edition)
Section Assessment, p. 339

Day 2
Section 2, pp. 340–343
 COOPERATIVE ACTIVITY Creating an Itinerary, p. 342 (Teacher's Edition)
Section Assessment, p. 343

Day 3
Section 3, pp. 344–348
Section Assessment, p. 348

Day 4
Section 4, pp. 349–353
 COOPERATIVE ACTIVITY Making a Mural, p. 352 (Teacher's Edition)
Section Assessment, p. 353
Chapter Assessment, pp. 354–355

Yearly Pacing *Chapter 12 Total:* 4 days *Yearly Total:* 85 days

 Planning for Block Schedules

Customizing for Special Needs

Students Acquiring English

 Access for Students Acquiring English
- **Guided Reading** for Sections 1–4 (Spanish), pp. 133–136
- **Chapter Summary** (Spanish), pp. 130–132
- **Skillbuilder Practice** Identifying Problems (Spanish), p. 137
- **Geography Application** The Opium Wars (Spanish), p. 138

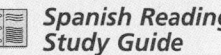 *Spanish Reading Study Guide*
- pp. 127–136

 Chapter Summaries on Audiocassette in English and Spanish

Less Proficient Readers

 In-Depth Resources: Unit 3
- **Guided Reading** for Sections 1–4, pp. 55–58
- **Skillbuilder Practice** Identifying Problems, p. 59
- **Geography Application** The Opium Wars, p. 60

 Telescoping the Times
- Chapter Summary, pp. 49–51

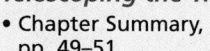 *Reading Study Guide*
- pp. 127–136

 Chapter Summaries on Audiocassette

Gifted and Talented Students

 In-Depth Resources: Unit 3

Primary Sources:
- from Letter to Queen Victoria, p. 62
- from *The Autobiography of Yukichi Fukuzawa*, p. 63
- Building the Panama Canal, p. 64
- from The Plan of Ayala, p. 65

History Makers
- Cixi, p. 69
- Porfirio Díaz, p. 70

Connections to Literature READINGS FOR STUDENTS

 In-Depth Resources: Unit 3
Literature: from *Tom Mix and Pancho Villa*, p. 66

Enrichment Reading
- **Paterson, Katherine** *Rebels of the Heavenly Kingdom* New York: Lodestar Books, 1983

In this story a Chinese peasant boy is kidnapped by bandits during the Taiping Rebellion.

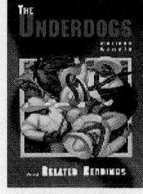

McDougal Littell *Literature Connections*

- **Azuela, Mariano** *The Underdogs* (with related readings)

Set during the aftermath of the Mexican Revolution in 1910, this is the story of Demetrio Macias, who has a ranch near the chaos and corruption of the revolutionary struggle.

 = Pupil's Edition   = Overhead Transparency   = Software   = Video

= Copy Master = CD-ROM   = Audiocassette   = Internet

Transformations Around the Globe, 1800–1914

Predicting

- From reading the section titles and looking at the images and captions, what kinds of global transformations do students expect to learn about in the chapter?

Accessing Prior Knowledge

- Ask students to recall what they have already learned about the history of China's and Japan's relationships with the outside world.

- What can students say about Latin American countries' struggles for independence from colonial rule?

Geography Connection

Have students study the map.

- Which countries are highlighted?

- Which two countries might find themselves in conflict over Korea?

CHAPTER
12 Transformations Around the Globe, 1800–1914

PREVIEWING THEMES

Empire Building

During the 19th and early 20th centuries, many Western nations sought influence over other countries. Great Britain, additional European countries, and the United States tried to dominate various nations both politically and economically.

Cultural Interaction

Imperialism brought new religions, philosophies, and technological innovations to East Asia and Latin America. Chinese, Japanese, and Latin American people resisted some Western ideas and adapted others.

Revolution

As the world took the first steps toward becoming a global community, political and social unrest were common. Both China and Japan struggled to deal with foreign influence and modernize their governments. Mexicans staged a revolution that brought political and economic reforms.

INTERNET CONNECTION

Visit us at **www.mlworldhistory.com** to learn more about worldwide changes during the 19th and early 20th centuries.

A WORLD IN TURMOIL, 1850–1914

Rebel Mexican girls called *soldaderas* armed themselves with rifles and bullets to fight in their country's civil war in the early **1900s.** *Soldaderas* such as this one followed the troops of revolutionary leader Victoriano Huerta.

Hudson Bay

CANADA

UNITED STATES OF AMERICA

Gulf of Mexico

MEXICO

DOMINICAN REPUBLIC
HAITI
PUERTO RICO
CUBA
JAMAICA
Caribbean Sea

BRITISH HONDURAS
GUATEMALA
EL SALVADOR
HONDURAS
COSTA RICA
PANAMA
NICARAGUA

VENEZUELA
COLOMBIA
FRENCH GUIANA
DUTCH GUIANA
BRITISH GUIANA
ECUADOR

PERU
BRAZIL
BOLIVIA
PARAGUAY

PACIFIC OCEAN

Tropic of Capricorn

0 1,000 Miles
0 2,000 Kilometers
N

CHILE
URUGUAY
ARGENTINA

ATLANTIC OCEAN

332

GEOGRAPHY THEMES

Region

Ask students to locate China, Mongolia, Manchuria, Korea, and Japan on the map. Point out that this region—the Far East—had maintained very little contact with the West before the 1800s. Ask students why this might have been so. *distance and differences in cultures*

Then have students locate Mexico, Central America, and South America. Ask them to suggest why this region is often called Latin America. *The first European colonists spoke either Spanish or Portuguese—languages that are closely related to Latin.* Encourage students to discuss similarities and differences between the Far East and Latin America.

Human/Environment Interaction

Ask students to use this map and the map on page 345 to identify some of the main resources of China, Japan, Mexico, and Latin America. Encourage them to consider geographic resources, such as good ports, navigable rivers, and oceans.

Tell students that political instability led to violent conflict in many of the countries they will study in this chapter. Ask what effects war might have had on the land and its resources. Have them discuss how these changes might have affected the economies of these countries.

ADDITIONAL RESOURCES

Books for the Teacher

- Spence, Jonathan D. *The Search for Modern China.* New York: Norton, 1990.

- Burns, E. Bradford. *Latin America: A Concise Interpretive History.* Englewood Cliffs, N.J.: Prentice, 1994.

Books for the Student

- Blumberg, Rhoda. *Commodore Perry in the Land of the Shogun.* New York: Lothrop, 1985. The United States pressures Japan to open its markets.

- Brown, Charles H. *Agents of Manifest Destiny: The Lives and Times of the Filibusters.* Chapel Hill: U North Carolina P, 1980. Expanding U.S. interests in Latin America.

Videos

- *The Battle of Tsushima—1905 A.D.* Ambrose Video, 1995. 800-526-4663. Japanese victory over Russia changes the balance of power in Asia.

- *China: The Mandate of Heaven.* Social Studies School Service, 1991. 800-421-4246. Chinese civilization—core values and cross-cultural influences.

- *Pancho Villa.* Society for Visual Education, 1994. 800-829-1900.

Software

- *History and Culture of Mexico.* CD-ROM. Queue, 1997. 800-232-2224.

As the **20th century** dawned, thousands of Chinese peasants and workers joined an organization called the Society of Harmonious Fists. They protested their country's dealings with foreigners. Popularly known as the **Boxers**, protesters were punished by being made to wear wooden collars in public, as shown here. They could not lie down or reach their mouths while wearing the collars.

When **U.S. Commodore Perry** steamed into Edo Bay in **Japan** with four ships in **1853,** the Japanese couldn't ignore them. The belching smoke and exaggerated features of this ship painted by a Japanese artist show his country's fear and mistrust of foreigners. Ironically, Japan quickly realized the necessity of dealing with the West and soon became a rival power.

333

HISTORY THROUGH ART

Caricature

Caricature is a way of representing something in words or pictures in which its distinctive features are exaggerated. For this reason, caricatures are generally humorous or even grotesque. They are often used to comment on political and social situations.

This painting by a 19th-century Japanese artist from Tokyo is a caricature of a foreign trading ship. It humorously reflects the national negative attitudes toward and fear of foreigners—especially Westerners. This "black ship," as the Japanese called these foreign vessels, is made to look like a menacing monster, with its dark smoke and glaring eyes. Oddly, the artist gave the ship several Japanese touches as well, such as the pedestal lamp and the deckhouse shaped like a pagoda.

Accounts brought back from Japanese travelers who visited the West eventually helped give the people a more realistic view of the foreigners and whetted Japanese curiosity about the outside world.

Interpreting the Art In what ways do you think caricature is an effective way of presenting ideas? In what ways might it be misleading or biased?

Interact *with* History

This Interact with History feature motivates students by inviting them to put themselves in the position of a member of the Chinese local government in the 19th century. Students will analyze the pros and cons of trading with foreign nations and become decision makers.

Purpose

• to set the stage for studying China's dealings with the West

• to help students understand the issues that emerging nations face

• to clarify the reasons that nations become imperialistic

Teaching Strategy

Thinking Critically After students have imagined themselves in the situation described on this page, have them answer the key question and give reasons for their decision.

EXAMINING *the* ISSUES

Following are suggestions for addressing each bulleted question.

1 Encourage students to name imported items that are available in the United States today, such as Japanese electronics. Ask them to think about the benefits and drawbacks of these items to the United States.

2 Invite pairs of students to role-play a situation in which one has an item the other wants. Have them negotiate a trade that is mutually satisfactory.

3 Have students use what they've learned in earlier chapters to describe negative and positive interactions between countries.

Interact *with* History

Life is good for you as a member of the local government in 19th-century China, but it could be even better. People from the West are eager to trade with your country. China, however, produces all that its people need, and government officials discourage contact with foreigners. Many foreign products, such as ceramics, are inferior to Chinese goods. The foreigners, however, do offer items that can improve your life, including rifles, cameras, and small sticks called matches that can be scraped against a rock to start a fire. You are curious about these inventions. But you wonder why the foreigners are so eager to trade with China and what they hope to gain.

Would you trade with the foreigners?

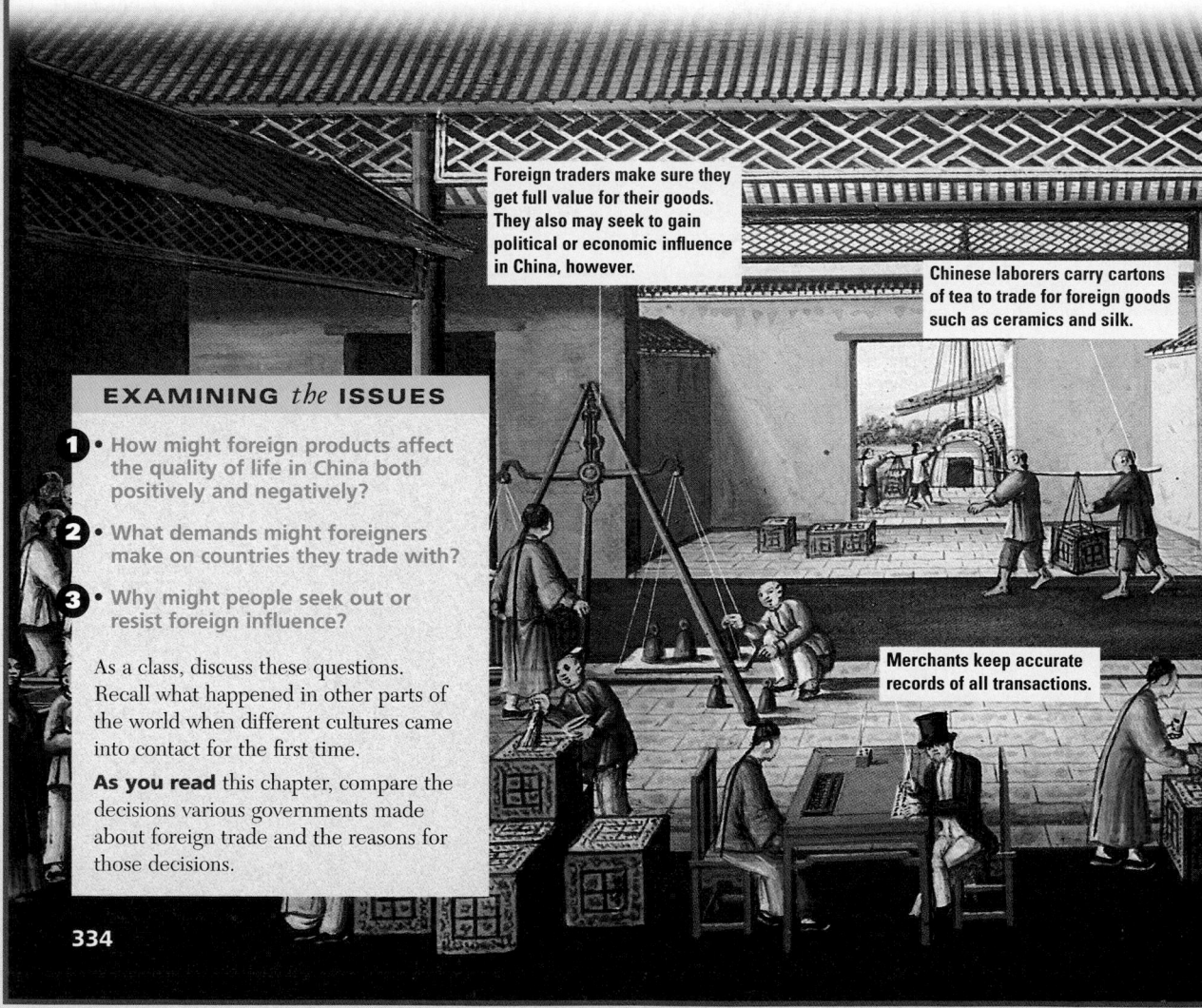

Foreign traders make sure they get full value for their goods. They also may seek to gain political or economic influence in China, however.

Chinese laborers carry cartons of tea to trade for foreign goods such as ceramics and silk.

EXAMINING *the* ISSUES

1 • How might foreign products affect the quality of life in China both positively and negatively?

2 • What demands might foreigners make on countries they trade with?

3 • Why might people seek out or resist foreign influence?

As a class, discuss these questions. Recall what happened in other parts of the world when different cultures came into contact for the first time.

As you read this chapter, compare the decisions various governments made about foreign trade and the reasons for those decisions.

Merchants keep accurate records of all transactions.

334

Follow Up

A feature on the chapter assessment will ask students to reevaluate their responses to the situation presented on this page.

1 China Responds to Pressure from the West

TERMS & NAMES
- Opium War
- extraterritorial rights
- Taiping Rebellion
- sphere of influence
- Open Door Policy
- Boxer Rebellion

MAIN IDEA

Western economic pressure forced China to open to foreign trade and influence.

WHY IT MATTERS NOW

China has become an increasingly important member of the global community.

SETTING THE STAGE In the late 18th century, China had more people than any other empire in the world. Under the Manchus of the Qing Dynasty, the empire was stable and secure. The people lived by traditions that were thousands of years old.

China Resists Foreign Influence

Out of pride in their ancient culture, the Chinese looked down on all foreigners. In 1793, however, the Qing emperor agreed to receive an ambassador from England. The Englishman brought gifts of the West's most advanced technology—clocks, globes, musical instruments, and even a hot-air balloon. The emperor was not impressed. In a letter to England's King George III, he stated that the Chinese already had everything they needed. They were not interested in the "strange objects" and gadgets that the West was offering them.

China Remains Self-Sufficient The basis of Qing China's wealth was its healthy agricultural economy. During the 11th century, China had acquired a quick-growing strain of rice from Southeast Asia. By the time of the Qing Dynasty, the rice was being grown throughout the southern part of the country. Around the same time—the 17th and 18th centuries—Spanish and Portuguese traders brought maize, sweet potatoes, and peanuts from the Americas. These crops helped China increase the productivity of its land and more effectively feed its 300 million people. Better nutrition, in turn, led to a population boom.

China also had extensive mining and manufacturing industries. Rich salt, tin, silver, and iron mines produced great quantities of ore. The mines provided work for tens of thousands of people. The Chinese also produced beautiful silks, high-quality cottons, and fine porcelain. The Chinese people were essentially self-sufficient.

This 18th-century painted fan depicts Guangzhou in southern China as a cosmopolitan port, flying the flags of its many foreign traders. The rest of China, however, remained firmly isolated until the mid-19th century.

335

SECTION 1 RESOURCES

PRINT RESOURCES

IN-DEPTH RESOURCES: UNIT 3
Guided Reading, p. 55
Geography Application: The Opium Wars, p. 60
Primary Source: from Letter to Queen Victoria, p. 62
History Makers: Cixi, p. 69

ACCESS FOR STUDENTS ACQUIRING ENGLISH
Guided Reading (Spanish), p. 133
Geography Application, (Spanish), p. 138

FORMAL ASSESSMENT
Section Quiz, p. 150

TECHNOLOGY RESOURCES

WORLD ART AND CULTURES TRANSPARENCIES
AT60 Sorting of Cocoons (Chinese book illustration)

CD-ROM
Electronic Library of Primary Sources

INTERNET www.mlworldhistory.com

Section 1 Overview

OBJECTIVES

(1) To explain China's resistance to foreigners in the 1800s.

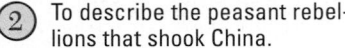
(2) To describe the peasant rebellions that shook China.

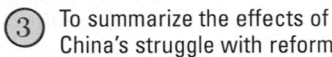
(3) To summarize the effects of China's struggle with reform.

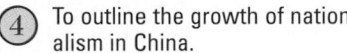
(4) To outline the growth of nationalism in China.

SKILLBUILDER

- Interpreting maps: human-environment interaction, location, p. 338

CRITICAL THINKING

- Analyzing issues, p. 336
- Recognizing effects, p. 337
- Making inferences, p. 338
- Analyzing causes, p. 339

FOCUS

5-Minute Warm-Up

Interpreting Maps
To help students understand the importance of China to foreign nations, have them answer the following questions.

1. Look at the map on page 338. Which nations had colonies in China between 1850 and 1911?

2. In what parts of China were the foreign spheres of influence and the colonies located?

 WARM-UP TRANSPARENCY 12

OBJECTIVE ① **INSTRUCT**

China Resists Foreign Influence

▶ *Key Ideas*
- In the early 1800s, China has little interest in trading with Western nations.
- The British import large amounts of tea from China and smuggle opium into the country.
- War breaks out when the British refuse to stop trading opium.

IN-DEPTH RESOURCES: UNIT 3
Guided Reading, p. 55

ACCESS FOR STUDENTS ACQUIRING ENGLISH
Guided Reading (Spanish), p. 133

Teacher's Edition **335**

MORE ABOUT . . .
Opium Addiction

Opium addiction was a problem in 19th-century Britain as well as in China. Some doctors prescribed opium to calm the nerves, and it helped people relax after long hours in unhealthy and dangerous factories. In China, opium addiction spread rapidly among bored government employees and soldiers. Historians blame the drug for a decline in China's standard of living and for the deterioration of public services, which eventually led to massive peasant uprisings during the mid-1800s.

 IN-DEPTH RESOURCES: UNIT 3
Geography Application: The Opium Wars, p. 60

CRITICAL THINKING ACTIVITY
CLASS TIME: 15 MINUTES

Identifying Main Ideas
Have students identify the main actions in the conflict between Britain and China over the opium trade. Suggest that they use a two-column chart like the one below to list each country's moves.

China	Britain
Sells large amounts of tea to Britain	Smuggles opium into China

CONNECT to TODAY
Hong Kong

Encourage students to research the political and economic issues that have arisen in Hong Kong since the island returned to Chinese control in 1997.

The Tea-Opium Connection Because of their self-sufficiency, the Chinese had little interest in trading with the West. For decades, the only place they would allow foreigners to do business was at the southern port of Guangzhou (gwahng·joh). And the balance of trade at Guangzhou was clearly in China's favor. This means that China earned much more for its exports than it spent on imports. The British imported millions of pounds of tea from China every year and exported goods worth much less. They made up for the difference in silver. This imbalance drained Britain's silver supply.

European merchants were determined to find a product the Chinese would buy in large quantities. Eventually they found one—opium. Opium is a habit-forming narcotic made from the poppy plant. Chinese doctors had been using it to relieve pain for hundreds of years. In the late 18th century, however, British merchants smuggled opium into China for nonmedical use. It took a few decades for opium smoking to catch on, but by 1835, as many as 12 million Chinese people were addicted to the drug.

War Breaks Out This growing supply of opium caused great social, moral, and monetary problems for the country. The Qing emperor was angry. In 1839, one of the emperor's highest advisers wrote a letter to England's Queen Victoria about the problem:

A VOICE FROM THE PAST
By what right do they [British merchants] . . . use the poisonous drug [opium] to injure the Chinese people? . . . I have heard that the smoking of opium is very strictly forbidden by your country; that is because the harm caused by opium is clearly understood. Since it is not permitted to do harm to your own country, then even less should you let it be passed on to the harm of other countries.

LIN ZEXU, quoted in *China's Response to the West*

CONNECT to TODAY

Hong Kong

The Treaty of Nanjing gave the island of Hong Kong to the British. After another conflict in 1899, China leased that territory and parts of the mainland to Britain for 99 years. On July 1, 1997, Hong Kong returned to Chinese control.

Although the name *Hong Kong* means "fragrant harbor," this bustling economic center is one of the most crowded places on earth. About 15,000 people occupy each square mile.

Nearly all the residents of Hong Kong are Chinese. Most of them are emigrants from Communist mainland China. The major cities, Hong Kong City and Kowloon, are bustling centers of banking, manufacturing, tourism, and trade. High-rise buildings and gaudy neon signs rub shoulders with open-air markets and traditional shops on the cities' winding, narrow streets.

There has been almost a century of exposure to capitalism and British rule in Hong Kong. Integration of the former colony into Chinese society probably will be difficult for everyone.

336

The pleas went unanswered, and Britain refused to stop trading opium. The result was an open clash between the British and the Chinese—the **Opium War** of 1839. The battles took place mostly at sea. China's outdated ships were no match for Britain's steam-powered gunboats and sophisticated cannons. As a result, the Chinese suffered a humiliating defeat. In 1842, they signed a peace treaty, the Treaty of Nanjing.

This treaty gave Britain the island of Hong Kong. After signing another treaty in 1844, U.S. and other foreign citizens also gained **extraterritorial rights.** These rights provided exemption from Chinese law at four Chinese ports besides Guangzhou. Many Chinese greatly resented these privileges and the foreigners among them. And a bustling trade in opium continued.

THINK THROUGH HISTORY
A. Analyzing Issues
What conflicting British and Chinese positions led to the Opium War?
A. Possible Answer
The British desire to trade with China and shift the balance of trade in its own favor; the Chinese resentment of the harm opium caused its citizens.

EXPLORING PRIMARY SOURCES

A Voice from the Past Have students read excerpt from Lin Zexu's letter to Queen Victoria in the Teacher's Resources. Ask them to analyze Lin Zexu's argument against the British smuggling of opium, discussing its strengths and weaknesses. Then have students work in small groups to write their own letters to try to persuade the queen to intervene against the British opium smugglers. Have the groups read their letters aloud and let the class vote on the most persuasive letter.

 IN-DEPTH RESOURCES: UNIT 3
Primary Source: from Letter to Queen Victoria, p. 62

CONNECTIONS ACROSS TIME AND PLACE

Macao Near the southern Chinese port of Guangzhou and just across the Pearl River estuary from Hong Kong is the Portuguese colony of Macao. This colony, established in 1513, was the center of the international trading community in China until Hong Kong surpassed it in the mid-19th century. In 1997, Macao was returned to Chinese jurisdiction. Encourage students to conduct research to discover the reasons Hong Kong and Macao were returned to China and the subsequent economic, political, and cultural issues that have arisen in both places.

Internal Problems Increase

Foreigners were not the greatest of China's problems in the mid-19th century, however. Its own population provided an overwhelming challenge. That population had grown to 430 million by 1850—a 30-percent gain in only 60 years. Yet food production had barely increased. As a result, hunger was widespread, even in good years. In the frequent bad years, the Huang He (Yellow River) broke through its dikes and flooded vast farming areas. Millions starved.

The Chinese government itself was riddled with corruption and could do little to ease its people's suffering. Dikes that might have held back the river had fallen into disrepair. Public granaries were empty. Talented people who were unable or unwilling to bribe state examiners often were denied government jobs. The people became discouraged, and opium addiction rose steadily. As their problems mounted, the Chinese actively began to rebel against the Qing Dynasty.

The Taiping Rebellion The rebellion that was to become China's largest was led by Hong Xiuquan (hung·shee·oo·choo·ahn). The Treaty of Nanjing had granted Christian missionaries increased privileges in China. The missionaries greatly influenced this sensitive young man. Hong had mystical visions and wanted to save the world, beginning with China. He dreamed of a "Heavenly Kingdom of Great Peace." In this kingdom, all Chinese people would share China's vast wealth and no one would live in poverty. Hong's revolt was called the **Taiping Rebellion,** from the Chinese expression *taiping,* meaning "great peace."

Beginning in the late 1840s, Hong organized an army made up mainly of peasants—both men and women—from southern China. By 1853, 1 million people had joined his rebel forces. That year, Hong captured the city of Nanjing and declared it his capital. The Taiping government controlled large areas of southeastern China.

Over the next ten years, however, the Qing regained control of the country. Imperial troops, local militias, and British and French forces all fought against the Taiping. By 1864, they crushed the 14-year rebellion. But China paid a terrible price. Huge, hungry armies had destroyed fertile farmland in their search for food. At least 20 million—and possibly twice that many—people died.

China Wrestles with Reform

The Taiping Rebellion and other smaller uprisings put tremendous internal pressure on the Chinese government. And, despite the Treaty of Nanjing, external pressure from foreign powers was increasing. At the Qing court, stormy debates raged about how best to deal with these pressures. Some government leaders called for reforms patterned on Western ways. Others insisted on honoring Chinese traditions. The Chinese Empire was conservative overall, though. Clinging to traditional ways and resisting change started at the top.

The Dowager Empress Cixi Resists Change During the last half of the 19th century, there was only one person at the top in the Qing imperial palace. The Dowager Empress Cixi (tsoo·shee) ruled China, with only one brief gap, from 1861 until 1908.

Although she was committed to traditional values, the Dowager Empress did support certain reforms. In the 1860s, for example, she backed the self-strengthening movement. That program aimed to update China's educational system, diplomatic service,

THINK THROUGH HISTORY
B. Recognizing Effects What were the results of the Taiping Rebellion?
B. Possible Answer Little change in the status of the people and massive death and destruction.

Background
The Dowager Empress Cixi first served as ruler for two emperors who took the throne as children. When she gained the throne herself she was known as "dowager," or endowed empress.

HISTORY MAKERS

**Hong Xiuquan
1814–1864**

Hong Xiuquan came from a rural family. As a young man, he tried to move up in Chinese society by seeking a government post. However, he kept failing the civil service exam. In his early twenties, Hong had a dream that ordered him to fight evil. From then on, he worked to overthrow the "evil" Qing dynasty and the same Qing system that he had tried so hard to enter. To destroy evil, Hong and his rebel followers destroyed Qing artworks and outlawed such Qing symbols as the pigtail.

Hong slowly developed his own personal vision of Christianity. That vision led him to forbid opium, tobacco, alcohol, and gambling. Under Hong, men and women were treated as equals. Women, for example, could fight for Hong's cause just as men could. However, men and women were divided into separate divisions, and even husbands and wives were not allowed contact.

After winning Nanjing, Hong withdrew into his mystical visions. After years of bloody feuding among his lieutenants, Hong's Taiping government fell. After that defeat, thousands of his followers burned themselves to death rather than surrender to the emperor.

Transformations Around the Globe **337**

OBJECTIVE **2** INSTRUCT

Internal Problems Increase

► *Key Ideas*
• Poverty and political corruption create problems for China in the mid-1800s.
• The 14-year Taiping Rebellion expresses the Chinese people's discontent with the Qing government.

HISTORY MAKERS
Hong Xiuquan

Hong Xiuquan first had contact with Protestant missionaries in the 1830s and undertook further Biblical study ten years later. Although Hong's original inspiration for his rebellion came from the Western teachings of Christianity, Western governments failed to support his uprising against the Qing. Encourage students to speculate why the British might not have supported the Taiping government.

OBJECTIVE **3** INSTRUCT

China Wrestles with Reform

► *Key Ideas*
• The Chinese government resists modernization, but the self-strengthening movement produces some changes.
• Western nations and Japan gain spheres of influence in China.
• The United States promotes the Open Door Policy to assure trading rights for all nations and to protect China from colonization.

🏛 *WORLD ART AND CULTURES TRANSPARENCIES*
AT60 Sorting of Cocoons (Chinese book illustration)

TEACHING OPTIONS   **CUSTOMIZING FOR SPECIAL NEEDS**   **CUSTOMIZING FOR SPECIAL NEEDS**

Gifted and Talented Students
Evaluating The ideas that fueled the Taiping Rebellion were a mix of ancient ideals and modern practical methods. For example, the rebels worked the land and shared resources collectively. Men and women also were treated as equals both at home and in the workplace.

Encourage students to do additional research on the ideology behind this massive uprising, using encyclopedias and books such as Jean Chesneaux's *China from the Opium Wars to the 1911 Revolution.* Have students present their information in a creative format, such as a mural, a web site, or a skit.

Less Proficient Readers
Identifying Topic Sentences
Remind students that a topic sentence carries the main idea of a paragraph. Point out that the topic sentence can appear anywhere in the paragraph. Have students work in pairs to identify the topic sentences in the seven full paragraphs on this page,

recording their positions in a chart like this one.

¶ No.	Beginning of ¶	Middle of ¶	End of ¶
1			
2			
3			
4			
5			
6			
7			

Foreign Influence in China, 1850–1911

Interpreting the Map Ask students which nations had both colonies and spheres of influence in China. *Britain, France, and Japan*

Extension Activity The United States did not have a colony or a sphere of influence in China during this period. Have students research the history of U.S. dealings with China.

SKILLBUILDER Answers
1. Britain, France, Germany, Japan, Russia
2. Britain; the Yangtze River

OBJECTIVE 4 INSTRUCT

Chinese Nationalism Grows

Key Ideas
- Dowager Empress Cixi and others prevent changes to China's traditional government.
- Chinese frustration with the government and foreigner privilege erupt into the Boxer Rebellion.
- After the defeat of the Boxers, the Qing Dynasty begins to work toward reform.

 IN-DEPTH RESOURCES: UNIT 3
History Makers: Cixi, p. 69

 ELECTRONIC LIBRARY OF PRIMARY SOURCES
from *Two Years in the Forbidden City*

MORE ABOUT . . .
The Boxer Rebellion

Many women fought in the Boxer Rebellion in their own companies. Young single women from ages 12 to 18 were known as the Red Lanterns. Married women belonged to the Blue or the Black Lanterns. Widows fought in the Green Lanterns. Boxer women who did not fight formed a group called the Cooking-Pan Lanterns to help feed others.

Foreign Influence in China, 1850–1911

Spheres of influence
- British
- French
- German
- Japanese
- Russian

Foreign colonies
- British
- French
- Japanese

— Qing Empire, 1850
— China, 1911

GEOGRAPHY SKILLBUILDER: Interpreting Maps
1. **Human-Environment Interaction** *Which countries had spheres of influence in China?*
2. **Location** *What foreign power shown on the map had access to inland China? What geographic feature made this possible?*

---

and military. Under this program, China set up arsenals to manufacture steam-powered gunboats, rifles, and ammunition. By 1875, these ammunition supply and storage facilities were among the largest in the world.

The self-strengthening movement had mixed results, however. The ability to produce its own warships and ammunition was undoubtedly good for China's morale. But the Chinese hired foreigners to run many of its arsenals. These outsiders often didn't feel comfortable working with Chinese resources. So they imported both raw materials and factory machinery from abroad. This practice contributed to both an imbalance in trade for China and a lack of quality control. In addition, the movement lacked support from the Chinese people as a whole.

Other Nations Step In China's weak military technology and its economic and political problems were not a secret from the rest of the world. Throughout the late 19th century, many foreign nations took advantage of this weakness and attacked China. Treaty negotiations after each conflict gave the West increasing control over China's economy. As shown in the map, many of Europe's main political powers and Japan gained a strong foothold in China. This foothold, or **sphere of influence,** was a region in which the foreign nation controlled trade and investment.

The United States was a long-time trading partner with China. Americans worried that other nations would soon divide China into formal colonies and shut out American traders. To prevent this occurrence, in 1899 the United States declared the **Open Door Policy.** This policy proposed that China's "doors" be open to merchants of all nations. Britain and the other European nations agreed. The policy thus protected both American trading rights in China and China's freedom from colonization. But the country was still at the mercy of foreign powers.

Chinese Nationalism Grows

Humiliated by their loss of power, many Chinese pressed for strong reforms. Among them was China's young emperor, Guangxu (gwahng·shoo). In June 1898, Guangxu's aunt, the Dowager Empress Cixi, was relaxing at the summer palace. Assuming that he had her support, Guangxu introduced measures to modernize China. These measures called for overhauling China's educational system, strengthening the economy, modernizing the military, and streamlining the government. Guangxu asked progressive, creative advisers to help carry out his programs.

Most Qing officials saw these innovations as threats to their power. They reacted with alarm. In September 1899, they called the Dowager Empress back to the imperial court. Guangxu realized too late that he had misjudged her. Striking with the same speed as her nephew, the Dowager Empress Cixi placed him under arrest at the

THINK THROUGH HISTORY
C. Making Inferences What importance did spheres of influence have for China and for the nations involved?
C. Answer They weakened China's control over its economy and gave foreign nations the ability to exploit Chinese resources.

TEACHING OPTION | **BLOCK SCHEDULING** | **COOPERATIVE ACTIVITY: Debating Reform** | **CLASS TIME 30 MINUTES**

Task: Student groups will research the conflict between the Dowager Empress Cixi and Guangxu and then conduct a debate on reform in China.

Purpose: To help students understand China's struggle for reform.

Activity: Divide the class into groups of four. Within each group, two students should research the reforms Guangxu made and why these reforms were necessary. The other pair should research the Dowager Empress Cixi's reaction to Guangxu's reforms and why she felt as she did. Groups can use their textbooks and library materials for their research.

After group members have finished their research, have them stage a debate between Guangxu and the empress. Two at a time, group members should take turns role-playing the figures and debating the need for reform. Remind students to be specific in their arguments and rebuttals. Encourage volunteers to conduct the debate for the class.

Finally, discuss with students what they learned about reform in China from their research.

 ALTERNATIVE ASSESSMENT BOOK
Standards for Evaluating a Cooperative Activity

palace. She then took back her own power. She reversed his reforms and executed a number of the movement's leaders. Guangxu's Hundred Days of Reform ended without a single long-term change. The Chinese people's frustration with their situation did change, however. It grew.

The Boxer Rebellion This widespread frustration finally erupted. Poor peasants and workers particularly resented the special privileges granted to foreigners. They also resented Chinese Christians, who were protected by foreign missionaries. To demonstrate their discontent, they formed a secret organization called the Society of Harmonious Fists. They soon came to be known as the Boxers. Their campaign against the Dowager Empress's rule and foreigner privilege was called the **Boxer Rebellion.**

In the spring of 1900, the Boxers descended on Beijing. Shouting "Death to the foreign devils," the Boxers surrounded the European section of the city. They kept it under siege for several months. The Dowager Empress expressed support for the Boxers but did not back her words with military aid. In August, a multinational force of 20,000 troops marched toward Beijing. Soldiers from Britain, France, Germany, Austria, Italy, Russia, Japan, and the United States quickly defeated the Boxers.

Despite the failure of the Boxer Rebellion, a strong sense of nationalism had emerged in China. The Chinese people realized that their country must resist more foreign intervention. Most important, however, the government must become responsive to their needs.

The Beginnings of Reform At this point, even the Qing court realized that China needed to make profound changes to survive. In 1905, the Dowager Empress sent a select group of Chinese officials on a world tour to study the operation of different governments. The group traveled to Japan, the United States, Britain, France, Germany, Russia, and Italy. On its return in the spring of 1906, the officials recommended that China restructure its government. They based their suggestions on the constitutional monarchy of Japan. The empress accepted this recommendation and began making reforms. Although she convened a national assembly within a year, change was slow. In 1908, the court announced that it would establish a full constitutional government by 1917.

Unfortunately, however, the turmoil in China did not end with these progressive steps. Unrest would continue for the next four decades as the Chinese faced internal and external threats. But as wholeheartedly as China had struggled to remain isolated from the outside world, its neighbor Japan responded to Western influence in a much different way.

THINK THROUGH HISTORY
D. Analyzing Causes Why did the Boxer Rebellion fail?
D. Answers Multinational troops overpowered the rebels and the Dowager Empress Cixi wanted it to fail.

Boxer rebels like this one drawn by a 20th-century artist were driven by a fierce hatred of foreigners. They used their fists, swords, and guns in an unsuccessful attempt to oust the "foreign devils" from China.

MORE ABOUT . . .
Reform in China

In the early 1900s, women in China began questioning their traditional roles as wives and mothers. Exposed to Western fashions and Western ideas, many unwrapped the binding that crippled their feet and kept them close to home. Some pursued their education either in China or in Japan. These "nontraditional" women pledged loyalty to each other and gained support from men who promised to start a new social trend and marry women with the still unfashionable "large" feet. Some women even joined the Revolutionary Alliance and worked along with men toward political reform in China.

ASSESS & RETEACH

Section 1 Assessment
Have students work individually to complete question 1 and then work as a class to answer questions 2 and 3.

Section Quiz
FORMAL ASSESSMENT
Section Quiz, p. 150

Reteaching Activity
CLASS TIME: 15 MINUTES

Have students review the visual material—maps and illustrations—on pages 333, 334, 335, 338, and 339. Ask volunteers to explain how each image reflects the issues that China faced as it entered the 20th century.

CLOSE ACTIVITY

CLASS TIME: 20 MINUTES

Perceiving Causes and Effects
Write the main events and concepts covered in this section on pieces of paper. Have students choose a piece of paper and make sure they understand the importance of the issue. Then have them arrange themselves in a cause-and-effect chain that clarifies the relationship among the concepts and events.

Section 1 Assessment

1. TERMS & NAMES
Identify
- Opium War
- extraterritorial rights
- Taiping Rebellion
- sphere of influence
- Open Door Policy
- Boxer Rebellion

2. TAKING NOTES
In a flow chart like the one below, list the major events in China's dealings with foreign nations between 1830 and 1900. Include both policies and actual confrontations.

3. RECOGNIZING EFFECTS
Do you think the opium trade was finally more harmful or beneficial to China? Explain.

THINK ABOUT
- the effects of the Opium War
- other Chinese responses to foreign influence
- the aftermath of the Boxer Rebellion

4. THEME ACTIVITY
Cultural Interaction Under the long rule of the Dowager Empress Cixi, China fiercely resisted foreign influence. As a class or in a small group, role-play a debate among the Dowager Empress's advisers. Some should argue for continued isolation, and others for openness to foreign influence and trade.

Transformations Around the Globe **339**

ANSWERS

1. TERMS & NAMES
Opium War, p. 336
extraterritorial rights, p. 336
Taiping Rebellion, p. 337
sphere of influence, p. 338
Open Door Policy, p. 338
Boxer Rebellion, p. 339

2. TAKING NOTES
Possible Responses: Opium War (1839); Treaty of Nanjing (1842); Taiping Rebellion (1850–1864); Open Door Policy (1899); Boxer Rebellion (1900).

3. ANALYZING EFFECTS
Possible Responses: Harmful— It had a negative effect on the people's health and triggered numerous wars and uprisings. Beneficial—It ultimately forced the Chinese government to face the discontent of the people and begin to reform.

4. THEME ACTIVITY
Possible Responses: Arguments for continued isolation should point out China's pride in its own culture and fear of foreign domination. Arguments for increased contact with foreign nations should stress the development that would make China a player on the world stage.

OBJECTIVES

① To describe why Japan ended its isolation and how it began modernizing.

② To trace the growth of Japanese imperialism in wars with China and Russia and in its policies toward Korea.

SKILLBUILDERS

- Interpreting charts, p. 341
- Interpreting political cartoons, p. 343

CRITICAL THINKING

- Recognizing effects, p. 341
- Making inferences, p. 342
- Clarifying, p. 343
- Forming an opinion, p. 343
- Analyzing themes, p. 343

FOCUS

5-Minute Warm-Up

▶ **Interpreting Charts**

To help students compare China's and Japan's responses to Western influence, have them answer these questions.

1. Look at the Venn diagram on page 341. Which country borrows Western ideas and ways?

2. Which country remains committed to traditional values?

 WARM-UP TRANSPARENCY 12

OBJECTIVE ① INSTRUCT

Japan Ends Its Isolation

▶ **Key Ideas**

- Japan opens its ports to trade in 1854.
- The Japanese modernize quickly.

 IN-DEPTH RESOURCES: UNIT 3
Guided Reading, p. 56

ACCESS FOR STUDENTS ACQUIRING ENGLISH
Guided Reading (Spanish), p. 134

---

2 Japan Modernizes

MAIN IDEA	WHY IT MATTERS NOW
Japan followed the model of Western powers by industrializing and expanding its foreign influence.	Japan's continued development of its own way of life has made it a leading world power.

SETTING THE STAGE In the early 17th century, Japan had shut itself off from almost all contact with other nations. Under the rule of the Tokugawa shoguns, the society was tightly ordered. The shogun parceled out land to the lords. The peasants worked for and lived under the protection of their lord and his samurai. This rigid system kept Japan free of civil war. Peace and relative prosperity reigned for two centuries.

Daily *Life*

Japanese Women

Japan not only restricted its citizens' contact with the outside world but it also severely confined its own women. The supreme duty of a woman was to honor the men in her life. Her restrictive dress and footwear helped ensure that she did not stray far from her place in the home.

As a child, she was expected to be obedient to her father, and as a wife, to her husband. Even as a widow, she was expected to submit to her son or sons.

In Japan today, increasing numbers of women work outside the home, most of them as "office ladies" or "OLs." These secretarial workers have no opportunity to advance, and are arguably no better off than their grandmothers were.

The number of women managers is increasing today, however, and Japanese women are becoming more vocal about playing an active role in their society.

Japan Ends Its Isolation

The Japanese had almost no contact with the industrialized world during this time of isolation. They continued, however, to trade with China and with Dutch traders from Indonesia. They also had diplomatic contact with Korea. However, trade was growing in importance, both inside and outside Japan.

Facing the Demand for Foreign Trade In the early 19th century, Westerners began trying to convince the Japanese to open their ports to trade. British, French, Russian, and American officials occasionally anchored off the Japanese coast. Like China, however, Japan repeatedly refused to receive them. Then, in 1853, U.S. Commodore Matthew Perry took four ships into what is now Tokyo Harbor. The Japanese were astounded by these massive black iron ships that were powered by steam. They were also shocked by the cannons and rifles. These weapons could have wiped out hundreds of the fiercest samurai in a matter of seconds. The Tokugawa shogun realized he had no choice but to receive the letter Perry had brought from U.S. President Millard Fillmore:

A VOICE FROM THE PAST

It seems to be wise from time to time to make new laws. . . . If your Imperial Majesty were so far to change the ancient laws as to allow a free trade between the two countries [the U.S. and Japan], it would be extremely beneficial to both. . . . Our steamships, in crossing the great ocean, burn a great deal of coal, and it is not convenient to bring it all the way from America. We wish that our steamships and other vessels should be allowed to stop in Japan and supply themselves with coal, provisions, and water. They will pay for them, in money, or anything else your Imperial Majesty's subjects may prefer.

MILLARD FILLMORE, quoted in *Millard Fillmore Papers*

Polite as President Fillmore's letter was, Perry delivered it with a threat. He would come back with a larger fleet in a year to receive Japan's reply. That reply was the **Treaty of Kanagawa,** which was signed in 1854. Under the terms of the treaty, Japan opened two ports at which American ships could take on supplies. The treaty

---

SECTION 2 RESOURCES

PRINT RESOURCES

 IN-DEPTH RESOURCES: UNIT 3
Guided Reading, p. 56
Primary Source: from *The Autobiography of Yukichi Fukuzawa,* p. 63

 ACCESS FOR STUDENTS ACQUIRING ENGLISH
Guided Reading (Spanish), p. 134

 FORMAL ASSESSMENT
Section Quiz, p. 151

ALTERNATIVE ASSESSMENT BOOK

TECHNOLOGY RESOURCES

 GEOGRAPHY TRANSPARENCIES
GT28 *Japanese Imperialism, 1875–1910*

 WORLD ART AND CULTURES TRANSPARENCIES
AT61 *Japanese Girl in Western Dress*

 CD-ROM
Electronic Library of Primary Sources

  INTERNET www.mlworldhistory.com

THINK THROUGH HISTORY
A. Recognizing Effects How did the Treaty of Kanagawa affect Japan?
A. Answer It opened the country to foreign trade, first with the United States and then with other countries.

also allowed the United States to set up an embassy in Japan. Once the United States had a foot in Japan's door, other Western powers soon followed. By 1860, Japan, like China, had granted foreigners permission to trade at treaty ports. It had also extended extraterritorial rights to many foreign nations.

Reform and Modernization Under the Meiji Reign The Japanese, however, were angry that the shogun had given in to the foreigners' demands. They feared that he was losing control over the country. The people rallied around Japan's young emperor, Mutsuhito (moot·soo·HEE·toh), who appealed to Japan's strong sense of pride and nationalism. In 1867, the Tokugawa shogun stepped down. He thus ended the military dictatorships that had lasted since the 12th century. Mutsuhito established a new government. He chose the name *Meiji* for his reign, which means "enlightened rule." Only 15 when he took over, Mutsuhito reigned for 45 years. This period of Japanese history—from 1867 to 1912—is called the **Meiji era.**

As part of this new enlightenment, the Meiji emperor realized that the best way to oppose Western imperialism was to adopt new ways. The feudal lords, for example, realized that private ownership of land prevented the entire country from benefiting from it. In one of the first acts of the Meiji era, they gave their land to the emperor.

Another way the Meiji government attempted to modernize Japan was by sending its statesmen to Europe and North America to study foreign ways. The Japanese chose what they believed to be the best Western civilization had to offer and adapted it to their own country. They admired Germany's strong centralized government, for example. And they used its constitution as a model for their own. As in Germany, a small group of men held political power in Japan. They were determined to build a mighty nation.

The Japanese also admired the discipline of the German army and the skill of the British navy. They attempted to imitate these European powers as they modernized their military. Japan adopted the American system of universal public education and required that all Japanese children attend school. Their teachers often included foreign experts. Students could go abroad to study as well.

China and Japan Confront the West

The Dowager Empress Cixi (1862–1908)

China
- Remains committed to traditional values
- Loses numerous territorial conflicts
- Grants other nations spheres of influence within China
- Finally accepts necessity for reform

Both
- Have well-established traditional values
- Initially resist change
- Oppose Western imperialism

Japan
- Considers modernization to be necessary
- Borrows and adapts Western ways
- Strengthens its economic and military power
- Becomes an empire builder

The Meiji Emperor Mutsuhito (1867–1912)

SKILLBUILDER: Interpreting Charts
1. *According to this Venn diagram, in what ways did China and Japan deal differently with Western influence?*
2. *What similar responses did both countries share despite the different paths they followed?*

Transformations Around the Globe **341**

Daily *Life*
Japanese Women
(See page 340.)

The Meiji era saw an increase in women's political awareness. For instance, women began lobbying for the vote as early as 1876. Have students compare the status of women in 19th-century Japan with that of women in other places they have learned about.

 WORLD ART AND CULTURES TRANSPARENCIES
AT61 *Japanese Girl in Western Dress*

MORE ABOUT . . .
Mutsuhito

In Japan, as in China, the emperor was revered as a god. Therefore, details about Mutsuhito's personal life were considered sacred and were never recorded. The political advisers who worked closely with Mutsuhito, however, described him as modest, reserved, and a wise, disciplined ruler.

History from Visuals

China and Japan Confront the West

Interpreting the Chart Make sure students understand that a Venn diagram is a visual representation of similarities and differences. Ask them to construct another way of presenting the same information.

Extension Activity Encourage interested students to find out more about the military defeats China suffered in contrast to Japan's military victories. Suggest that they research, for example, the Second Opium War, the Russian takeover of Manchuria, and the Sino-French War.

SKILLBULDER Answers
1. China remained isolated from the West as long as it could. Japan quickly adopted Western ways and became a rival power.
2. Hatred of Western imperialism and initial resistance to change

---

TEACHING OPTIONS

CUSTOMIZING FOR SPECIAL NEEDS

Students Acquiring English
The two phrases "discard old traditions" and "adopt new ways" are crucial to students' understanding of this section. To make sure these concepts are clear, you may wish to demonstrate the words *discard* and *adopt* by using body language illustrating casting away and

gathering in. Ask students to suggest simple synonyms, such as *throw away* and *take on*. Make sure students understand the word *traditions* by asking them to give examples of traditions from their own cultures. Ask them what old traditions the Japanese discarded and what new ways they adopted.

MULTIPLE LEARNING STYLES

Visual Learners Encourage students to visually summarize the Western concepts and ways that the Japanese people adopted. Suggest that they make a two-column chart. In one column they should list each nation the Japanese borrowed from, and in the other, the specific concept or tradition they adopted.

Nation	What Japan Adopted
Germany	government and constitution
Great Britain	
United States	

Teacher's Edition **341**

The emperor also energetically supported following the Western path of industrialization. By the early 20th century, the Japanese economy had become as modern as any in the world. The country built its first railroad line in 1872. The track connected Tokyo, the nation's capital, with the port of Yokohama, 20 miles to the south. By 1914, Japan had more than 7,000 miles of rails. Coal production grew from half a million tons in 1875 to more than 21 million tons in 1913. Meanwhile, large, state-supported companies built thousands of factories. Traditional Japanese industries, such as tea processing and silk production, expanded to give the country unique products to trade. Developing modern industries, such as shipbuilding and weapons production, made Japan competitive with the West.

Japanese Imperialism Grows

Japan's race to modernize paid off. By 1890, the country had several dozen warships and 500,000 well-trained, well-armed soldiers. It had become the strongest military power in Asia.

Japan had gained military, political, and economic strength. It then sought to eliminate the extraterritorial rights of foreigners. The Japanese foreign minister assured foreigners that they could rely on fair treatment in Japan. This was because its constitution and legal codes were similar to those of European nations, he explained. His reasoning was convincing, and in 1894, Britain and the other foreign powers abolished the extraterritorial rights of their citizens living in Japan. Japan's feeling of strength and equality with the Western nations rose.

As Japan's sense of power grew, the nation also became more imperialistic. Like many European nations, Japan saw empire building as a way of protecting its security and meeting economic needs. As in Europe, national pride also played a large part in this policy. The Japanese were determined to show the world that they were a powerful nation.

Japan Attacks China The Japanese first turned their sights to their Asian neighbors. Japan's neighbor, Korea, is not far from southern Japan (see the map on page 718). In 1876, Japan forced Korea to open three ports to Japanese trade. But China also considered Korea to be important as both a trading partner and a military outpost. Recognizing their similar interests in Korea, Japan and China signed a hands-off agreement. In 1885, both countries pledged that they would not send their armies into Korea.

 GlobalImpact

Changing Image of the East
The Japanese victory over the Russians in 1905 exploded a strong Western myth. Many Westerners believed that white people were a superior race. The overwhelming success of European colonialism and imperialism in the Americas, Africa, and Asia had reinforced this belief. But the Japanese had shown Europeans that people of other races were their equals in modern warfare.

Unfortunately, Japan's military victory led to a different form of Western racism. Influenced by the ideas of Germany's emperor Wilhelm II, the West imagined the Japanese uniting with the Chinese and conquering Europe. The resulting racist Western fear of what it called the "yellow peril" influenced world politics for many decades.

In June 1894, however, China broke that agreement. Rebellions had broken out against Korea's king. He asked China for military help in putting them down. Chinese troops marched into Korea. Japan protested and sent its troops to Korea to fight the Chinese. The Sino-Japanese War had begun. Within a few months, Japan had driven the Chinese out of Korea, had destroyed the Chinese navy, and had begun taking over Manchuria. In 1895, China and Japan signed a peace treaty. This treaty gave Japan its first colonies—Taiwan and the Pescadores Islands.

Russo-Japanese War Most Western nations had expected China to win the showdown with Japan fairly easily. The Japanese victory surprised them. It also changed the world's balance of power. Russia and Japan emerged as the major powers—and enemies—in East Asia.

Russia and Japan soon went to war over Manchuria. This was a region north of Korea that was under Chinese rule. In 1903, Japan offered to recognize Russia's rights in Manchuria if the Russians would agree to stay out of Korea. But the Russians refused. So, in February 1904, Japan launched a surprise attack. It struck at the

342 Chapter 12

Russian navy, which was anchored off the coast of Manchuria. In the resulting **Russo-Japanese War,** Japan drove Russian troops out of Korea. Japan won brutal land battles and captured most of Russia's Pacific fleet. It also destroyed Russia's Baltic fleet, which had sailed all the way around Africa to participate in the war.

In 1905, Japan and Russia began peace negotiations. U.S. president Theodore Roosevelt helped draft the treaty, which the two nations signed on a ship off Portsmouth, New Hampshire. This agreement, the Treaty of Portsmouth, gave Japan the captured territories. It also forced Russia to withdraw from Manchuria and to stay out of Korea.

Korea Under Japanese Occupation After defeating Russia, Japan attacked Korea with a vengeance. In 1905, it made Korea a protectorate. Japan sent in "advisers," who grabbed more and more power from the Korean government. The Korean king was unable to rally international support for his regime. In 1907, he gave up control of the country. Within two years the Korean Imperial Army was disbanded. In 1910, Japan officially imposed **annexation** in Korea, or brought that country under Japan's control.

The Japanese were harsh rulers. For the next 35 years, they forbade public protest. They shut down Korean newspapers and took over Korean schools. There they replaced the study of Korean language and history with that of Japan. They took land away from Korean farmers and gave it to Japanese settlers. They encouraged Japanese businessmen to start industries in Korea, but forbade Koreans from going into business in their own country. Resentment of the Japanese led to nonviolent protests and to a growing Korean nationalist movement. The Japanese did modernize Korean factories and transportation and communications systems, however. Despite this technological progress, Japan's repressive rule in Korea was an example of imperialism at its worst.

The rest of the world clearly saw the brutal results of Japan's imperialism in Korea. Nevertheless, the United States and other European countries moved ahead with their own imperialistic aims, as you will learn in Section 3.

Vocabulary
protectorate: a country under the partial control and protection of another nation.

THINK THROUGH HISTORY
C. Clarifying How did Japan treat the Koreans after it annexed the country?
C. Answer Harshly and brutally.

L'HOMME DU JOUR : LE MIKADO

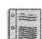

SKILLBUILDER:
Interpreting Political Cartoons
1. *In this cartoon of the Russo-Japanese War, which animal represents Russia and which represents Japan?*
2. *Whom do you think the Japanese and the Russians are crushing?*

Section **2** Assessment

1. TERMS & NAMES
Identify
• Treaty of Kanagawa
• Meiji era
• Russo-Japanese War
• annexation

2. TAKING NOTES
In a chart like the one below, list the steps that Japan took toward modernization and the events that contributed to its growth as an imperialistic power.

Modernization	Imperialism

Do you think that Japan could have become an imperialistic power if it had not modernized? Why or why not?

3. FORMING AN OPINION
In your view, was Japan's aggressive imperialism justified? Support your answer with examples from the text.

THINK ABOUT
• reasons for Japan's early isolation
• what Japan could gain from imperialism
• Japan's treatment of conquered peoples

4. ANALYZING THEMES
Empire Building What influences do you think were most important in provoking Japan to build its empire?

THINK ABOUT
• Japan's size and geographical features
• Japan's relations with China and Russia
• the interest of countries such as Britain and the United States in Japan

Transformations Around the Globe **343**

ANSWERS

1. TERMS & NAMES
Treaty of Kanagawa, p. 340
Meiji era, p. 341
Russo-Japanese War, p. 343
annexation, p. 343

2. TAKING NOTES
Possible Responses: Modernization—claimed feudal lands for government; studied Western ways; industrialized. Imperialism—abolished extraterritorial rights; forced Korean ports to open; fought Sino-Japanese and Russo-Japanese wars; annexed Korea.

3. FORMING AN OPINION
Possible Responses: Justified— Japan had to expand to compete in the global economy. Not justified—Japan didn't have to rule Korea as harshly as it did.

4. ANALYZING THEMES
Possible Responses: Because Japan is a small island, it was vulnerable to invaders. Having huge empire builders as neighbors forced Japan to expand in self-defense. The Japanese feared they might lose control of their country to the Western powers that traded at its ports.

Teacher's Edition **343**

① To explain how Latin America's colonial legacy and political instability shaped its history after independence.

② To document how foreign powers influenced the growth of Latin American economies.

③ To describe U.S. intervention in Latin America.

SKILLBUILDER

• Interpreting maps: region, human-environment interaction, p. 345

CRITICAL THINKING

• Identifying problems, pp. 345, 348
• Analyzing motives, p. 346
• Making inferences, p. 347
• Forming opinions, p. 347
• Evaluating decisions, p. 348

FOCUS

5-Minute Warm-Up

▶ **Interpreting Maps**
To help students understand the reasons for U.S. imperialism in Latin America, have them answer these questions.

1. Look at the map on page 345. What countries were included in Latin America in 1830?

2. What Latin American natural resources might the United States want?

 WARM-UP TRANSPARENCY 12

OBJECTIVE ① INSTRUCT

Latin America After Independence

▶ **Key Ideas**
• After independence, most Latin Americans remain poverty-stricken.

• Political power in Latin America is restricted to a few wealthy people, who support military dictators called caudillos.

 IN-DEPTH RESOURCES: UNIT 3
Guided Reading, p. 57

 ACCESS FOR STUDENTS ACQUIRING ENGLISH
Guided Reading (Spanish), p. 135

---

3 U.S. Economic Imperialism in Latin America

TERMS & NAMES
• caudillo
• Monroe Doctrine
• José Martí
• Spanish-American War
• Panama Canal
• Roosevelt Corollary

MAIN IDEA	WHY IT MATTERS NOW
The United States put increasing economic and political pressure on Latin America during the 19th century.	This policy set the stage for 20th-century relations between Latin America and the United States.

SETTING THE STAGE Latin America's long struggle to gain independence from colonial domination between the late 18th and the mid-19th centuries left the new nations in shambles. Weeds choked off farm fields. Cities and towns collapsed. The new nations faced a struggle for recovery as difficult as their struggle for independence had been.

Latin America After Independence

Political independence meant little for most citizens of the new Latin American nations. The majority remained poor, illiterate laborers caught up in a cycle of poverty.

Colonial Legacy During colonial times, most Latin Americans worked for large landowners. The employers paid their workers with vouchers that could be used only at their own supply stores. Since wages were low and prices were high, workers went into debt. Their debt accumulated and passed from one generation to the next. These "free" workers were almost like slaves in a system known as peonage.

The landowners, on the other hand, only got wealthier after independence. Many new Latin American governments took over the lands owned by native peoples and by the Catholic Church. They then put those lands up for sale. Wealthy landowners were the only people able to afford to buy them, and they snapped them up. But as one Argentinean newspaper reported, "Their greed for land does not equal their ability to use it intelligently." The unequal distribution of land and its poor use combined to prevent social and economic development in Latin America.

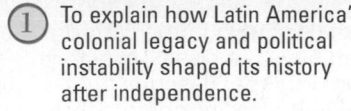

The land—and its rich resources—was and is Latin America's major asset. The peasants worked all of their lives in the fields and remained poor and propertyless, as many still are today.

Political Instability Political instability also was a widespread problem in 19th-century Latin America. Many Latin American army leaders had gained fame and power during their long struggle for independence. They often continued to assert their power. They controlled the new nations as dictators, or **caudillos.** By 1830, nearly all the countries of Latin America were ruled by caudillos. One typical caudillo was Juan Vicente Gómez. He was a ruthless man who ruled Venezuela for nearly 30 years after seizing power in 1908. "All Venezuela is my cattle ranch," he once boasted.

There were some exceptions, however. Reform-minded presidents, such as Argentina's Domingo Sarmiento, made strong commitments to improving education. During Sarmiento's presidency, between 1868 and 1874, the number of students in Argentina doubled. But such reformers usually didn't stay in office long. Eventually a caudillo would return to power, forcing the reformer out at the point of a bayonet or gun.

The caudillos found little opposition. The upper classes usually supported them because they opposed giving power to the lower classes. In addition, Latin Americans had gained little experience with democracy under European colonial rule. So the dictatorship of a caudillo did not seem unusual to them. But even when caudillos

344 Chapter 12

SECTION 3 RESOURCES

PRINT RESOURCES

 IN-DEPTH RESOURCES: UNIT 3
Guided Reading, p. 57
Primary Source: Building the Panama Canal, p. 64
Connections Across Time and Cultures: Responses to Western Pressure, p. 71
Science and Technology: Technology Revolutionizes Communications, p. 72

 ACCESS FOR STUDENTS ACQUIRING ENGLISH
Guided Reading (Spanish), p. 135

 FORMAL ASSESSMENT
Section Quiz, p. 152

 ALTERNATIVE ASSESSMENT BOOK

TECHNOLOGY RESOURCES

 CRITICAL THINKING TRANSPARENCIES
CT28 Patterns of Resistance, 1830–1914

 CD-ROM
Electronic Library of Primary Sources

 INTERNET www.mlworldhistory.com

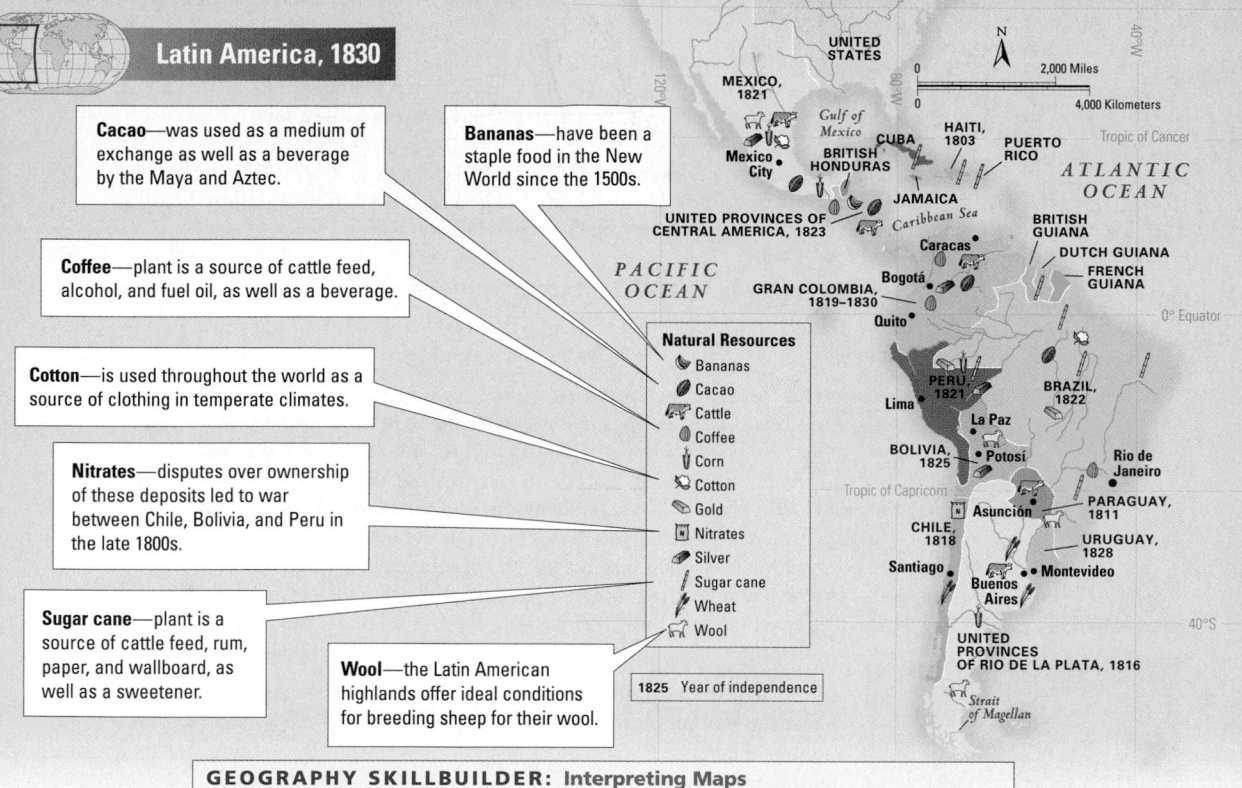

Latin America, 1830

Cacao—was used as a medium of exchange as well as a beverage by the Maya and Aztec.

Bananas—have been a staple food in the New World since the 1500s.

Coffee—plant is a source of cattle feed, alcohol, and fuel oil, as well as a beverage.

Cotton—is used throughout the world as a source of clothing in temperate climates.

Nitrates—disputes over ownership of these deposits led to war between Chile, Bolivia, and Peru in the late 1800s.

Sugar cane—plant is a source of cattle feed, rum, paper, and wallboard, as well as a sweetener.

Wool—the Latin American highlands offer ideal conditions for breeding sheep for their wool.

Natural Resources
- Bananas
- Cacao
- Cattle
- Coffee
- Corn
- Cotton
- Gold
- Nitrates
- Silver
- Sugar cane
- Wheat
- Wool

1825 Year of independence

GEOGRAPHY SKILLBUILDER: Interpreting Maps
1. **Region** *Which Latin American countries remained under colonial rule in 1830?*
2. **Human-Environment Interaction** *Which country had the most different types of natural resources?*

THINK THROUGH HISTORY
A. Identifying Problems What difficulties did lower-class Latin Americans continue to face after independence?
A. Possible Answer Poverty, lack of voice in government, lack of education.

weren't in power, most Latin Americans still lacked a voice in the government. Voting rights—and so, political power—were restricted to the relatively few members of the upper and middle classes who owned property or could read.

Economies Grow Under Foreign Influence

When colonial rule ended in Latin America in the early 1800s, the new nations were no longer restricted to trading with colonial powers. Britain and, later, the United States became Latin America's main trading partners.

Old Products and New Markets No matter with whom the new Latin American nations were trading, their economies continued to depend on exports. As during the colonial era, each country concentrated on one or two products. With advances in technology, however, Latin America's exports grew. The development of the steamship and the building of railroads in the 19th century, for example, greatly increased Latin American trade. Toward the end of the century, the invention of refrigeration helped increase Latin America's exports. The sale of beef, fruits and vegetables, and other perishable goods soared.

But foreign nations benefited far more from the increased trade than Latin America did. In exchange for their exports, Latin Americans imported European and North American manufactured goods. They therefore had little reason to develop their own manufacturing industries. And as long as Latin America remained unindustrialized, it could not play a leading role on the world stage.

Outside Investment and Interference Furthermore, Latin American countries used little of their export income to build roads, schools, or hospitals. Nor did they

Transformations Around the Globe **345**

Caudillos ruled Latin America with a combination of bribery, patronage, and force. Although the constitutions of many Latin American nations were patterned after the U.S. Constitution, the documents were seldom upheld. As one of Latin America's greatest liberators, Simón Bolívar, put it, "Treaties are scraps of paper; constitutions, printed matter; elections, battles; freedom, anarchy; and life, a torment."

History from Visuals

Latin America, 1830
Interpreting the Map
Encourage students to study the map key and identify the resources and products associated with each country. Suggest that interested students research the resources not included in the call-out boxes and report their findings to the class.

Extension Activity Ask students to use the map to make a time line of Latin American independence to share with the class. Point out that in some parts of Latin America, the struggle for independence went on for decades. Discuss how this long struggle for independence might have affected the development of Latin American economies.

SKILLBUILDER Answers
1. British Honduras; Jamaica; Cuba; Puerto Rico; French, Dutch, and British Guiana
2. Mexico

OBJECTIVE 2 INSTRUCT

Economies Grow Under Foreign Influence

▶ *Key Ideas*
- Latin America focuses on trade.
- Latin American countries' reliance on exports keeps them in debt.

Peonage and Sharecropping The peonage system that held Latin American farmers in a cycle of poverty was similar in many ways to the sharecropping system in the southern United States. Encourage interested students to do additional research on peonage and to check American history textbooks or the encyclopedia for information about

the sharecropping system in the southern United States after the Civil War.

Then have students construct a Venn diagram comparing the two systems. Suggest that they answer questions such as these for each system: Who owned the land? How were the farmers paid?

What caused them to go into debt? Have students share their completed diagrams with the class.

Peonage in Latin America — Both — Sharecropping in U.S.

Teacher's Edition **345**

OBJECTIVE ③ INSTRUCT

The United States and Latin America

▶ **Key Ideas**
- The United States issues the Monroe Doctrine to prevent recolonization of Latin America.
- The United States joins Cuba's fight for independence from Spain.
- The United States builds the Panama Canal.
- The Roosevelt Corollary gives the United States the right to police Latin American nations.

MORE ABOUT . . .

European Interference in Latin America

European powers interfered many times in Latin America during the 19th century before the United States enforced the Monroe Doctrine: Britain—the Argentinian Falkland Islands (1833); France—Mexico and Uruguay (several times between the 1830s and the 1860s); and Spain—the Chincha Islands (1862–1866).

IN-DEPTH RESOURCES: UNIT 3
Connections Across Time and Cultures: Responses to Western Pressure, p. 71

HISTORYMAKERS
José Martí

José Martí was a much-admired poet and essayist as well as a revolutionary. One of Martí's poems was set to music in 1961, and the song "Guantanamera" was made famous by U.S. folksinger Pete Seeger. Play a recording of this song for the class and ask students who speak or have studied Spanish to translate it.

---

fund programs that would help them be self-sufficient. Instead, they often borrowed money—at high interest rates—to develop facilities for their export industries. Countries such as Britain, France, the United States, and Germany were willing lenders. The Latin American countries often were unable to pay back their loans, however. In response, foreign lenders either threatened to collect the debt by force or to take over the facility it had funded. Foreigners thus gained control of many industries in Latin America. Thus began a new age of economic colonialism.

The United States and Latin America

Long before the United States had a real economic interest in Latin America, it was aware that its security depended on that of its southern neighbors.

The Monroe Doctrine Most of the Latin American colonies had gained their independence by the early 1800s. But their position was not secure. Many Latin Americans feared that European countries would try to reconquer the new republics. The United States, a young nation itself, feared this too. In 1823, therefore, President James Monroe issued what came to be called the **Monroe Doctrine.** This document stated that "the American continents . . . are henceforth not to be considered as subjects for future colonization by any European powers." Britain was Latin America's largest trading partner. It agreed to back the Monroe Doctrine with its powerful navy. Until 1898, though, the United States did little to enforce the Monroe Doctrine. Cuba provided a real testing ground.

Cuba Declares Independence Cuba was one of Spain's last colonies in the Americas. In 1868, Cuba declared its independence and fought a ten-year war against Spain. In 1878, with the island in ruins, the Cubans gave up the fight.

But some Cubans continued to seek independence. In 1895, **José Martí,** a writer who had been exiled, returned to fight for Cuban independence. Martí was killed early in the war, but the Cubans battled on.

By that time, the United States had developed substantial business holdings in Cuba. Therefore it had an economic stake in the fate of the country. In addition, the Spanish had forced many Cuban civilians into concentration camps. Americans objected to the Spanish brutality. In 1898, the United States joined the Cuban war for independence. This conflict, which came to be known as the **Spanish-American War,** lasted only six weeks. Years of fighting had exhausted the Spanish soldiers, and they gave up easily.

In 1901, Cuba became an independent nation, at least in name. But the Cubans resented U.S. intervention, the military government the United States had installed, and its preventing Cuba from becoming truly independent. The split that began to develop between the United States and Cuba continues to keep those close neighbors miles apart a century later.

After its defeat in the Spanish-American War, Spain turned over the last of its colonies. Puerto Rico, Guam, and the Philippines became U.S. territories. Having become the dominant imperial power in Latin America, the United States next set its sights on Panama.

The Panama Canal Connects the Oceans Latin Americans were beginning to regard the United States as the political and economic "Colossus of the North." It was also a huge country geographically. By the 1870s, the transcontinental railroad connected its east and west coasts. Land travel was long and difficult, however. And sea travel involved a trip around the tip of South America. This was a

HISTORYMAKER

**José Martí
1853–1895**

José Martí was only 15 in 1868 when he first began speaking out for Cuban independence. In 1871, the Spanish colonial government punished Martí's open opposition with exile to Spain.

With only a brief return to his homeland in 1878, Martí remained in exile for about 20 years. He lived most of his life in New York City. There he continued his career as a writer and a revolutionary. "Life on earth is a hand-to-hand combat . . . between the law of love and the law of hate," he proclaimed.

While in New York, Martí helped raise an army to fight for Cuban independence. He died on the battlefield only a month after the war began. But Martí's cry for freedom echoes in his essays and poems and in folk songs that are still sung throughout the world.

THINK THROUGH HISTORY
B. Analyzing Motives Why did the United States join the Cuban war for independence?
B. Possible Answers To protect its economic interests in Cuba and to protest Spain's brutal treatment of Cuban civilians.

TEACHING OPTIONS

CONNECTIONS ACROSS THE CURRICULUM

Science and Engineering The building of the Panama Canal was one of the greatest feats of modern engineering. Panama was not the only site considered for the canal, however. The United States had also considered building the canal across Nicaragua. Ask students to look at topographical maps of Central America and identify the pros and cons of each site. Have them discuss why Panama ultimately was chosen.

Have students make a diorama, model, or poster illustrating the building of the Panama Canal. Encourage them to include labels describing technological difficulties workers encountered and how they were overcome.

CONNECTIONS ACROSS THE CURRICULUM

Literature Not all Americans supported the imperialistic policies of the United States in the late 1800s and early 1900s. One eloquent and outspoken critic was German-American journalist, writer, and politician Carl Schurz.

Ask interested students to read selections from Schurz's autobiography

Autobiography of Carl Schurz or from biographies such as *Carl Schurz: Reformer* by Claude Moore Fuess and *Defender of Human Rights: Carl Schurz* by James P. Terzian. Have them present to the class a short report on Schurz's life, beliefs, and social contributions.

journey of about 13,000 miles. If a canal could be dug across a narrow section of Central America, the coast-to-coast journey would be cut in half. The United States had been thinking about such a project since the early 19th century. In the 1880s, a French company tried—but failed—to build a canal across Panama.

Despite the French failure, Americans remained enthusiastic about the canal. And no one was more enthusiastic than President Theodore Roosevelt, who led the nation from 1901 to 1909. In 1903, Panama was a province of Colombia. Roosevelt offered that country $10 million plus a yearly payment for the right to build a canal. When the Colombian government demanded more money, the United States responded by encouraging a revolution in Panama. The Panamanians had been trying to break away from Colombia for almost a century. In 1903, with help from the U.S. navy, they won their country's independence. In gratitude, Panama gave the United States a ten-mile-wide zone in which to build a canal.

For the next ten years, American engineers battled floods, heat, and disease-carrying insects to build the massive waterway. The United States began a campaign to destroy the mosquitoes that carried yellow fever and malaria, and the rats that carried bubonic plague. The effort to control these diseases was eventually successful. But thousands of workers died during construction of the canal. The **Panama Canal** finally opened in 1914. Ships from both hemispheres soon began to use it. Latin America had become a crossroads of world trade. And the United States controlled the tollgate.

Roosevelt Corollary The building of the Panama Canal was only one way that the United States expanded its influence in Latin America in the early 20th century. Its presence in Cuba and large investments in many Central and South American countries strengthened its foothold. To protect those economic interests, in 1904, President Roosevelt issued a corollary, or extension, to the Monroe Doctrine. The **Roosevelt Corollary** gave the United States the right to be "an international police power" in the Western Hemisphere.

The United States used the Roosevelt Corollary many times in the following years to justify American intervention in Latin America. The troops occupied some countries for decades. Many Latin Americans protested this intervention by the United States. But they were powerless to stop their giant neighbor to the north.

The U.S. government turned a deaf ear to these protests. It could not ignore the rumblings of revolution just over its border with Mexico, however. You will learn about this revolution in Section 4.

In the view of this political cartoonist, the Roosevelt Corollary gave the U.S. president so much power, the Caribbean became his wading pool.

THE BIG STICK IN THE CARIBBEAN SEA
From the *Herald* (New York)

Section 3 Assessment

1. TERMS & NAMES
Identify
• caudillo
• Monroe Doctrine
• José Martí
• Spanish-American War
• Panama Canal
• Roosevelt Corollary

2. TAKING NOTES
Using a time line like the one below, list the major events of U.S. involvement in Latin America.

1823   1898 1903 1904   1914

Which event do you think was most beneficial to Latin America? Why?

3. FORMING OPINIONS
Do you think that U.S. imperialism was more beneficial or harmful to Latin American people? Explain.

THINK ABOUT
• the benefits provided by U.S.-owned companies
• the harmful effects of foreign economic and political influence

4. THEME ACTIVITY
Revolution It is 1898 and you have been fighting for the independence of your country, Cuba, for three years. The United States has just joined the war against Spain. Design a political poster that shows your feelings about U.S. participation in this war.

Transformations Around the Globe **347**

The Roosevelt Corollary stated in part, "In the Western Hemisphere the adherence of the United States to the Monroe Doctrine may force the United States, however reluctantly, . . . to the exercise of an international police power." In the first half of the 20th century, the United States used this corollary to justify sending troops into Haiti, Nicaragua, the Dominican Republic, Mexico, Cuba, Honduras, Guatemala, and Costa Rica.

 ELECTRONIC LIBRARY OF PRIMARY SOURCES
from *The Rough Riders*

ANSWERS

1. TERMS & NAMES
caudillo, p. 344
Monroe Doctrine, p. 346
José Martí, p. 346
Spanish-American War, p. 346
Panama Canal, p. 347
Roosevelt Corollary, p. 347

2. TAKING NOTES
1823—Monroe Doctrine; 1898—Spanish-American War; 1903—Panamanian rebellion; 1904—Roosevelt Corollary; 1914—Panama Canal opened.
Answers will vary.

3. FORMING OPINIONS
Possible Responses:
Beneficial—The jobs and export income that U.S.-owned companies generated helped poor farmers and working people. Harmful—Foreign intervention prevented Latin American countries from becoming truly independent.

4. THEME ACTIVITY
Posters should include images and text that either support or condemn U.S. intervention in the Cuban war for independence.

The Panama Canal includes an intricate system of locks that raises and lowers ships to the level of the various waterways along the route. The lock mechanisms are so delicate that even the wake from a ship can damage them. Therefore, most large boats are helped through the locks by tugboats and locomotives that run alongside the canal.

 IN-DEPTH RESOURCES: UNIT 3
Primary Source: Building the Panama Canal, p. 64
Science and Technology: Technology Revolutionizes Communications, p. 72

CRITICAL THINKING ACTIVITY
CLASS TIME: 15 MINUTES

Interpreting Maps
Ask students to use the elevation chart along the top of the map to identify which part of the canal went through the land with the highest elevation. *the Culebra Cut.* What other interesting facts about this part of the canal can they learn from the map and the captions? *It is also the narrowest part.* Why do they think this is so?

Panama Canal

The Panama Canal is considered one of the world's greatest engineering accomplishments. Its completion changed the course of history by opening a worldwide trade route between the Atlantic and Pacific oceans. As shown in the 1914 map below, ships are raised and lowered a total of 170 feet during the 51-mile trip through the canal. It usually takes 15 to 20 hours.

The canal also had a lasting effect on other technologies. Ships are now built to dimensions that will allow them to pass through its locks.

This 1910 engraving shows the excavation of the Gaillard, or Culebra, Cut, at the narrowest part of the canal. Completion of this nine-mile cut took seven years because of frequent landslides. By the time the entire canal was finished, workers had dug up about 211 million cubic yards of earth.

The Gatun Locks include three levels of water-filled chambers that raise or lower ships 85 feet. Electric locomotives called mules help guide ships through the locks.

Canal Facts

- The canal took ten years to build (1904–1914) and cost $380 million.
- Thousands of workers died from diseases while building it.
- The trip from San Francisco to New York City via the Panama Canal is about 7,800 miles shorter than the trip around South America.
- The canal now handles more than 13,000 ships a year from around 70 nations carrying 168 million short tons of cargo.
- The United States now collects about $340 million a year in tolls.
- Panama will take control of the canal on December 31, 1999.

Connect *to* History

Identifying Problems What difficulties did workers face in constructing the canal?
 SEE SKILLBUILDER HANDBOOK, PAGE 651

Connect *to* Today

Evaluating Decisions In the more than 80 years since it was built, do you think that the benefits of the Panama Canal to world trade have outweighed the costs in time, money, and human life? Explain your answer.

Connect *to* History

Identifying Problems
Possible Answers: The workers faced diseases such as malaria, yellow fever, and bubonic plague. As they excavated huge amounts of earth, landslides often occurred, which could bury them alive.

Connect *to* Today

Evaluating Decisions
Possible Answers: Yes—The canal is one of the world's major trade routes, and the United States collects nearly its cost each year in tolls. No—The money and time could have been better spent in helping Latin American countries develop their economies and become more self-sufficient.

4 The Mexican Revolution

TERMS & NAMES
- Antonio López de Santa Anna
- Benito Juárez
- *La Reforma*
- Porfirio Díaz
- Francisco Madero
- Francisco "Pancho" Villa
- Emiliano Zapata

MAIN IDEA

Political, economic, and social inequalities in Mexico triggered a period of revolution and reform.

WHY IT MATTERS NOW

Mexico has moved toward political democracy and is a strong economic force in the Americas.

SETTING THE STAGE The legacy of Spanish colonialism and long-term political instability that plagued the newly emerging Latin American nations in the 19th century caused problems for Mexico as well. Only Mexico, however, shared a border with the United States. The "Colossus of the North" wanted to extend its territory to the Pacific Ocean. But most of the lands in the American Southwest belonged to Mexico.

Santa Anna and the Mexican War

During the early 19th century, no one dominated Mexican political life more than **Antonio López de Santa Anna.** Santa Anna played a leading role in Mexico's fight for independence from Spain in 1821. In 1829, he fought against Spain again, as it tried to reconquer Mexico. In 1833, Santa Anna became Mexico's president.

One of Latin America's most powerful caudillos, Santa Anna was a clever politician. He would support a measure one year and oppose it the next if he thought that would keep him in power. His policy apparently worked. Between 1833 and 1855, Santa Anna was Mexico's president four times. He gave up the presidency twice, however, to serve Mexico in a more urgent cause—retaining the territory of Texas.

The Texas Revolt In the 1820s, Mexico encouraged American citizens to move to the Mexican territory of Texas to help populate the country. Thousands of English-speaking colonists, or Anglos, did. In return for inexpensive land, they pledged to follow the laws of Mexico. As the Anglo population grew, though, tensions developed between the colonists and Mexico over several issues, including slavery and religion. As a result, many Texas colonists wanted greater self-government. But when Mexico refused to grant this, Stephen Austin encouraged a revolt against Mexico in 1835.

Santa Anna led Mexican forces north to try to hold the rebellious territory. He won a few early battles, including a bitter fight at the Alamo. The colonists captured him at the Battle of San Jacinto, however. They then took him to Washington as a prisoner. President Jackson released Santa Anna after he promised to respect the independence of Texas. When he returned to Mexico in 1836, Santa Anna was quickly ousted from power.

War and the Fall of Santa Anna Santa Anna regained power, though, and fought against the United States again. In 1845, the United States annexed Texas.

Mexicans and Americans fought in a blazing, bloody battle at the Alamo, from February 23 to March 6, 1836. Santa Anna's forces had one of their few victories in the attempt to hold the Texas territory.

Transformations Around the Globe **349**

SECTION 4 RESOURCES

PRINT RESOURCES

IN-DEPTH RESOURCES: UNIT 3
Guided Reading, p. 58
Skillbuilder Practice: Identifying Problems, p. 59
Primary Source: from The Plan of Ayala, p. 65
Literature: from *Tom Mix and Pancho Villa*, p. 66
History Makers: Porfirio Díaz, p. 70

ACCESS FOR STUDENTS ACQUIRING ENGLISH
Guided Reading (Spanish), p. 136
Skillbuilder Practice (Spanish), p. 137

FORMAL ASSESSMENT
Section Quiz, p. 153

TECHNOLOGY RESOURCES

WORLD ART AND CULTURES TRANSPARENCIES
AT62 Distribution of the Land

CRITICAL THINKING TRANSPARENCIES
CT64 Visual Summary

CD-ROM
Electronic Library of Primary Sources

INTERNET www.mlworldhistory.com

Section 4 Overview

OBJECTIVES

1. To describe the role Antonio López de Santa Anna played in the history of Mexico.

2. To list the goals of and obstacles to Benito Juárez's reform movement.

3. To describe the 25-year rule of caudillo Porfirio Díaz.

4. To explain the causes and results of the Mexican Revolution.

SKILLBUILDER
- Interpreting charts, p. 353

CRITICAL THINKING
- Contrasting, p. 350
- Identifying problems, p. 350
- Making inferences, p. 351
- Comparing, p. 351
- Recognizing effects, p. 352
- Summarizing, p. 353
- Analyzing issues, p. 353
- Analyzing themes, p. 353

FOCUS
5-Minute Warm-Up

▶ *Making Inferences*
To introduce students to the issues faced by the Mexican people in the 19th century, have them answer these questions.

1. Look at the History Through Art feature on page 351. Which Mexican leader is portrayed in the bottom painting?

2. Which painting seems more optimistic?

WARM-UP TRANSPARENCY 12

OBJECTIVE 1 INSTRUCT

Santa Anna and the Mexican War

▶ *Key Ideas*
- Antonio López de Santa Anna dominates Mexican political life between 1833 and 1855.
- The United States gains vast Western territories from Mexico.

IN-DEPTH RESOURCES: UNIT 3
Guided Reading, p. 58

ACCESS FOR STUDENTS ACQUIRING ENGLISH
Guided Reading (Spanish), p. 136

ELECTRONIC LIBRARY OF PRIMARY SOURCES
"Alamo Massacre"

Outraged Mexicans considered this a U.S. act of aggression. In a dispute over the border, the United States invaded Mexico. Santa Anna's army fought valiantly. But U.S. troops defeated them after two years of war. In 1848, the two nations signed the Treaty of Guadalupe Hidalgo. The United States received the northern third of what was then Mexico, including California and the American Southwest. Santa Anna went into exile. He returned as dictator one final time, however, in 1853. After his final fall, in 1855, he remained in exile for almost 20 years. When he returned to Mexico in 1874, he was poor, blind, powerless, and essentially forgotten.

Juárez and *La Reforma*

During the mid-19th century, as Santa Anna's power rose and fell, a liberal reformer, **Benito Juárez,** strongly influenced the politics of Mexico. Juárez was Santa Anna's complete opposite in background as well as in goals. Santa Anna came from a well-off Creole family. Juárez was a poor, orphaned Zapotec Indian. While Santa Anna put his own personal power first, Juárez worked primarily to serve his country.

Benito Juárez Rises to Power Ancestry and racial background were important elements of political power and economic success in 19th-century Mexico. For that reason, the rise of Benito Juárez was clearly due to his personal leadership qualities. Juárez was raised on a small farm in the Mexican state of Oaxaca. When he was 12, he moved to the city of Oaxaca. He started going to school at age 15, and in 1829, he entered a newly opened state-run university. He received his law degree in 1831.

He then returned to the city of Oaxaca, where he opened a law office. Most of his clients were poor people who could not otherwise have afforded legal assistance. Juárez gained a reputation for honesty, integrity, hard work, and good judgment. He was elected to the city legislature and then rose steadily in power. Beginning in 1847, he served as governor of the state of Oaxaca.

Juárez Works for Reform Throughout the late 1840s and early 1850s, Juárez worked to start a liberal reform movement. He called this movement **La Reforma.** Redistribution of land, separation of church and state, and increased educational opportunities were among its goals. In 1853, however, Santa Anna returned to power for the last time. He sent Juárez and other liberals into exile.

Just two years later, rebellion against Santa Anna brought down his government. Benito Juárez and other liberal leaders returned to Mexico to deal with their country's tremendous problems. As in other Latin American nations, rich landowners kept most other Mexicans in a cycle of debt and poverty. Liberal leader Ponciano Arriaga described how these circumstances led to great problems for both poor farmers and the government:

> **A VOICE FROM THE PAST**
> There are Mexican landowners who occupy . . . an extent of land greater than the areas of some of our sovereign states, greater even than that of one of several European states. In this vast area, much of which lies idle, deserted, abandoned . . . live four or five million Mexicans who know no other industry than agriculture, yet are without land or the means to work it, and who cannot emigrate in the hope of bettering their fortunes. . . . How can a hungry, naked, miserable people practice popular government? How can we proclaim the equal rights of men and leave the majority of the nation in [this condition]?
> **PONCIANO ARRIAGA,** speech to the Constitutional Convention, 1856–1857

The French Invade Mexico Not surprisingly, Arriaga's ideas and those of the other liberals in government threatened most conservative upper-class Mexicans. To express their dissatisfaction, these conservative rebels fought against the liberal government. The civil war lasted for three years before the government defeated the rebels. Juárez took over the presidency in 1858. He was officially elected president in 1861.

The end of the civil war did not end Mexico's troubles, though. The country was deeply in debt. Exiled conservatives plotted with some Europeans to reconquer Mexico. In 1862, France was ruled by Napoleon III, who sent a large army to Mexico. Within 18 months, France had taken over the country. Napoleon appointed Austrian archduke Maximilian to rule Mexico as emperor. Juárez and other Mexicans fought against French rule. After five years under siege, the French decided that the struggle was too costly. They ordered the army to withdraw from Mexico in 1867. Maximilian was captured and executed.

Juárez was reelected Mexico's president in 1867. He returned to the reforms he had proposed more than ten years earlier. He began rebuilding the country, which had been shattered during decades of war. He promoted trade with foreign countries, the opening of new roads, the building of railroads, and the establishment of a telegraph service. He set up a national education system, separate from that run by the Catholic Church. In 1872, Juárez died of a heart attack. But after half a century of civil strife and chaos, he left his country a legacy of relative peace, progress, and reform.

HISTORY THROUGH ART: Political Art

A century after Mexico's long struggle for independence, artist José Clemente Orozco made many paintings dealing with the burdens that prevent people from being free, happy, and creative. Here he depicts the starving, suffering masses protesting their oppression by those in power *(right)*. Benito Juárez emerges as a product of and symbol of hope for his people *(below)*.

Fresco detail at University of Guadalajara (1936–1939), José Clemente Orozco

Fresco detail at Hospicio Cabañas (1948), José Clemente Orozco

Connect *to* History

Making Inferences What conclusions can you draw about Orozco's feeling for his people from these two murals?

 SEE SKILLBUILDER HANDBOOK, PAGE 663

Connect *to* Today

Comparing What modern countries or peoples face problems similar to those of the 19th-century Mexico that Orozco portrayed?

Transformations Around the Globe **351**

CRITICAL THINKING ACTIVITY
CLASS TIME: 10 MINUTES

Making Generalizations
Ask students to list the political changes that took place in Mexico from 1833 to 1872. Then have them note the general trends that they see. Students can add to their lists as they read the rest of the section and see if those trends continued to 1928.

MORE ABOUT . . .
José Clemente Orozco

Orozco was a rare combination of philosopher and painter. He used his paintings to express ideas rather than stories or anecdotes. He tried neither to condemn nor to eulogize, but only to present events realistically and to represent their true meaning. He said, "No artist has or ever has had, political convictions of any sort. Those who profess them are not artists."

Connect *to* History

Making Inferences
Possible Answer: Orozco seems to feel proud of his people and to admire Juárez. In the top painting, he portrays the starving masses as fighters who do not submit to oppression. His portrait of Juárez glorifies and shows respect for this leader.

Connect *to* Today

Comparing
People all over the world continue to live in poverty and to suffer under oppressive regimes. You might bring in a sampling of recent newspapers or news magazines or suggest students investigate news sources on the Internet. Encourage students to find information about various parts of the world, including Africa, the Middle East, Latin America, Asia, eastern Europe, and the former Soviet Union. Also have them document problems minority groups face in the United States, Canada, and western European countries.

Porfirio Díaz and "Order and Progress"

Juárez's era of reform didn't last long, however. In the mid-1870s, a new caudillo, **Porfirio Díaz,** came to power. Like Juárez, Díaz was an Indian from Oaxaca. He rose through the army and became a noted general in the fight against the French. In 1876, Díaz took control of Mexico by ousting the president. He had the support of the military, whose power had been reduced during and after the Juárez years. Indians and small landholders also supported him, because they thought he would work for land reforms.

During the Díaz years, elections became meaningless. Díaz offered land, power, or political favors to anyone who supported him. He terrorized many who didn't support him, ordering them to be beaten or put in jail. As a political slogan, Díaz adapted a rallying cry from the Juárez era. Juárez's "Liberty, Order, and Progress" became merely "Order and Progress." With this motto and his strong-arm methods, Díaz remained in power for almost 25 years—until 1910.

Order and progress did come to Mexico under Díaz, in spite of his methods. Railroads expanded, banks were built, the currency stabilized, and foreign investment grew. Mexico seemed to be a stable, prospering country. But appearances were deceiving. The wealthy owned more and more land, which they didn't put to good use. As a result, food costs rose steadily. Most Mexicans remained poor farmers and workers, and they continued to grow poorer.

HISTORY MAKERS

**Francisco "Pancho" Villa
1877?–1923**

Pancho Villa was famous in Mexico, but infamous in the United States. In 1916, the United States permitted revolutionary politician Venustiano Carranza to use U.S. trains to transport troops who were fighting Villa in northern Mexico. In retaliation, Villa raided the town of Columbus, New Mexico, and killed 16 Americans traveling on a train in northern Mexico.

President Wilson was furious and ordered the U.S. Army to capture Villa. Villa hid out in the desert country he knew so well. The Americans never did find him.

Meanwhile, the Mexican government considered the American pursuit of Villa to be an invasion of its country. The United States and Mexico might well have gone to war over Villa. However, the United States entered World War I in 1917, forcing the withdrawal of its troops from Mexico.

Revolution and Civil War

In the early 1900s, Mexicans from many walks of life began to protest Díaz's harsh rule. Idealistic liberals hungered for liberty. Farm laborers hungered for land. Workers hungered for fairer wages and better working conditions. Even some of Díaz's hand-picked political allies spoke out for reform. A variety of political parties began to form. Among the most powerful was a party led by Francisco Madero.

Madero Begins the Revolution Born into one of Mexico's ten richest families, **Francisco Madero** was educated in the United States and France. He believed in democracy and wanted to strengthen its hold in Mexico. Madero announced his candidacy for president of Mexico early in 1910. Soon afterward, Díaz had him arrested. From exile in the United States, Madero called for an armed revolution against Díaz.

The Mexican Revolution began slowly. Leaders arose in different parts of Mexico and gathered their own armies. In the north, cowboy **Francisco "Pancho" Villa** became immensely popular. He had a bold Robin-Hood policy of taking money from the rich and giving it to the poor. South of Mexico City, another strong, popular leader, **Emiliano Zapata,** raised a powerful revolutionary army. Like Villa, Zapata came from a poor family. He was determined to see that land was returned to peasants and small farmers. He wanted the laws reformed to protect their rights. *"Tierra y Libertad* [Land and Liberty]" was his battle cry. Villa, Zapata, and other armed revolutionaries won important victories against Díaz's army. By the spring of 1911, Díaz agreed to step down. He called for new elections.

Mexican Leaders Struggle for Power Madero was elected president in November 1911. But he had a difficult time holding on to power. He resigned and was murdered shortly afterward. The military leader General Victoriano Huerta then took over the presidency.

**THINK THROUGH HISTORY
C. Recognizing Effects** What effects did Díaz's rule have on Mexico?
C. Possible Answers Some economic and industrial progress, but increasing poverty for most citizens.

Huerta was unpopular with many people, including Villa and Zapata. These revolutionary leaders allied themselves with another politician who also wanted to overthrow Huerta. His name was Venustiano Carranza. Their three armies advanced, seizing the Mexican countryside from Huerta's forces and approaching the capital, Mexico City. They overthrew Huerta only 15 months after he took power.

Carranza took over the government. He then turned his army on his former revolutionary allies. Both Villa and Zapata continued to fight. In 1919, however, Carranza lured Zapata into a trap and murdered him. With Zapata's death, the civil war also came to an end. More than a million Mexicans had lost their lives.

The New Mexican Constitution Carranza began a revision of Mexico's constitution. It was adopted in 1917. A revolutionary document, that constitution is still in effect today. As shown in the chart below, it promoted education, land reforms, and workers' rights. Carranza didn't support the final version of the constitution, however, and in 1920, he was overthrown by his former general, Alvaro Obregón.

Reforms of Mexican Constitution of 1917

Land	Religion	Labor	Social Issues
• Breakup of large estates • Restrictions on foreign ownership of land • Government control of resources (oil)	• State takeover of land owned by the Church	• Minimum wage for workers • Right to strike • Institution of labor unions	• Equal pay for equal work • Limited legal rights for women (spending money and bringing lawsuits)

SKILLBUILDER: Interpreting Charts
1. Which reforms do you think landowners resented?
2. Which reforms benefited workers?

Although Obregón seized power violently, he did not remain a dictator. Instead, he supported the reforms the constitution called for. He also promoted public education. Mexican public schools taught a common language—Spanish—and stressed nationalism. In this way, his policies helped unite the various regions and peoples of the country. Nevertheless, Obregón was assassinated in 1928.

The next year, a new political party that attempted to address the interests of all sectors of the society arose. Although the Institutional Revolutionary Party (PRI) did not tolerate opposition, it initiated an ongoing period of peace and political stability in Mexico. While Mexico was struggling toward peace, however, the rest of the world was on the brink of war.

Section 4 Assessment

1. TERMS & NAMES
Identify
• Antonio López de Santa Anna
• Benito Juárez
• *La Reforma*
• Porfirio Díaz
• Francisco Madero
• Francisco "Pancho" Villa
• Emiliano Zapata

2. TAKING NOTES
In a chart like the one below, list the major accomplishment of each Mexican leader.

Leader	Major Accomplishment

Which leader do you think benefited his country most? Why?

3. ANALYZING ISSUES
Why did Juárez have trouble putting his liberal program *La Reforma* into action?

THINK ABOUT
• the types of reforms Juárez wanted
• how those reforms would affect Mexicans of the upper and lower classes
• the political climate of the country

4. ANALYZING THEMES
Revolution Juárez's motto for change in Mexico was "Liberty, Order, and Progress." Díaz's slogan was "Order and Progress." What did this difference in goals mean for the country?

THINK ABOUT
• Juárez's accomplishments
• Díaz's accomplishments
• the value of order and progress without liberty

Transformations Around the Globe **353**

TERMS & NAMES

1. Opium War, p. 336
2. Taiping Rebellion, p. 337
3. Boxer Rebellion, p. 339
4. Meiji era, p. 341
5. Russo-Japanese War, p. 343
6. Monroe Doctrine, p. 346
7. Spanish-American War, p. 346
8. Antonio López de Santa Anna, p. 349
9. Benito Juárez, p. 350
10. Francisco "Pancho" Villa, p. 352

REVIEW QUESTIONS

Answers will vary.

11. It had extensive natural resources and industries and was essentially self-sufficient.

12. Population explosion, famine, and government corruption, which led to great suffering for the Chinese people.

13. It triggered the Boxer Rebellion and led to a revived sense of Chinese nationalism.

14. The signing of the Treaty of Kanagawa, Japan's granting foreigners permission to trade at treaty ports, and the extension of extraterritorial rights to foreign nations. Because of these actions, the Japanese feared they were losing control of their country and were inspired to westernize in order to maintain control.

15. Invasion of Korea and annexation of Taiwan and the Pescadores Islands in the Sino-Japanese War; defeat of Russia, occupation of Korea following the Russo-Japanese War.

16. Colonialism left many Latin American countries politically and economically unstable and ripe for takeover by the military caudillos. The caudillos were able to maintain power because the upper classes supported them and the people were used to absolute rule.

17. These policies led to ongoing imperialism in Latin America, which kept these countries dependent and unable to deal with their internal problems.

18. The canal provided a short route between the Atlantic and Pacific and between the east and west coasts of the United States. It made worldwide trade easier and made Latin American products more accessible.

19. After accepting Mexico's invitation to move to Texas, colonists ignored Mexican laws and worked to gain independence from Mexico.

Chapter 12 Assessment

TERMS & NAMES

Briefly explain the importance of each of the following to the changes in global power between 1800 and 1914.

1. Opium War
2. Taiping Rebellion
3. Boxer Rebellion
4. Meiji era
5. Russo-Japanese War
6. Monroe Doctrine
7. Spanish-American War
8. Antonio López de Santa Anna
9. Benito Juárez
10. Francisco "Pancho" Villa

Interact with History

On page 334, you considered whether or not you would urge your country to trade with foreigners. Now that you've learned how several countries dealt with foreign influence and what the results were, would you change your recommendation? Discuss your ideas in a small group.

REVIEW QUESTIONS

SECTION 1 *(pages 335–339)*
China Responds to Pressure from the West

11. Why was China traditionally not interested in trading with the West?

12. What conditions during the Qing Dynasty gave rise to the Taiping Rebellion?

13. Although Guangxu's Hundred Days of Reform failed, what changes did it finally set in motion?

SECTION 2 *(pages 340–343)*
Japan Modernizes

14. What events caused Japan to end its isolation and begin to westernize?

15. What were the results of Japan's growing imperialism at the end of the 19th century?

SECTION 3 *(pages 344–348)*
U.S. Economic Imperialism in Latin America

16. How were Latin American caudillos able to achieve power and hold on to it?

17. What effects did the Monroe Doctrine and the Roosevelt Corollary have on Latin America?

18. Why was the United States so intent on building the Panama Canal?

SECTION 4 *(pages 349–353)*
The Mexican Revolution

19. What were the major causes of tension between the Mexicans and the American colonists who settled in Texas?

20. What roles did Francisco "Pancho" Villa and Emiliano Zapata play in the Mexican Revolution?

Visual Summary

Transformations Around the Globe

China
- Fails to prevent Britain from pursuing illegal opium trade in 1839 **Opium War**
- Deals with internal unrest during almost two decades of Hong Xiuquan's **Taiping Rebellion**
- Attempts to build self-sufficiency during 1860s in **self-strengthening movement**
- Violently opposes foreigners in 1900 **Boxer Rebellion**
- Begins to establish **constitutional government** in 1908

Japan
- Signs 1854 **Treaty of Kanagawa,** opening Japanese ports to foreign trade
- Modernizes based on Western models during **Meiji era** (1867–1912)
- Fights 1894 **Sino-Japanese War** seeking control of Korea
- Wages 1904 **Russo-Japanese War** seeking control of Manchuria
- Annexes **Korea** in 1910

Foreign Influence

Latin America
- Depends on **exports** to fuel economy
- Receives much **foreign investment**
- Gains U.S. military support in 1898 **Spanish-American War**
- Becomes crossroads of world trade when U.S. completes **Panama Canal** in 1914

Mexico
- Fights to hold **Texas territory** from U.S. colonialism (1835–1845)
- Tries to establish a national identity in the early 1850s under Benito Juárez's **La Reforma**
- Overcomes **French occupation** in 1867
- Stages the **Mexican Revolution** in 1910

354 Chapter 12

20. Both men were leaders of the revolution; they fought to aid and protect poor peasants and small farmers.

Interact with History

Possible Responses: Students who originally opted to trade with the foreigners might cite Japan's experience as support for their decision. Those who chose to remain isolated might offer the difficulties Latin American countries and Mexico faced as support. Students might speculate what would have happened if China had refused to trade with the West.

CRITICAL THINKING

1. BYPASSING THE EMPRESS

Do you think that Emperor Guangxu would have been able to put his reforms into practice if the Dowager Empress Cixi had not intervened? Why or why not? Think about China's government, its attitude toward foreign influence, and Guangxu's power.

2. THE SWORD VS. THE PEN

THEME **REVOLUTION** Consider what you have learned in this and other chapters about Latin American colonial history and about how countries undergo change. What are the pros and cons of both military strategies and peaceful political means of improving a country's economic, social, and political conditions?

3. CHARTING SANTA ANNA'S CAREER

On a time line like the one below, indicate the major events of Santa Anna's military and political career in Mexico. Why do you think he was able to remain in power for so long?

Fights for independence
from Spain

1820s

4. ANALYZING PRIMARY SOURCES

In 1877, the Meiji era of modernization in Japan had been underway for about a decade. The following excerpt from an article in one of Japan's major newspapers, the *Tokyo Times,* comments on the changes that had taken place. Read the selection and answer the questions that follow.

A VOICE FROM THE PAST
In the second and third years of Meiji, the demand for foreign goods remarkably increased. Those who formerly looked upon them with contempt changed their minds and even dressed in foreign clothes. Our males adopted the European style. They put on fine tall hats instead of wearing large [queues] on their heads, and took to carrying sticks after discarding their swords. They dressed in coats of the English fashion and trousers of the American. They would only eat from tables and nothing would satisfy them but French cookery.

- Do you think this newswriter sees the adoption of foreign ways as a good or a bad thing for Japan? What specific words in the article make you feel that way?
- What dangers might a nation face when its people uncritically take on the behaviors and ways of life of another culture?

CHAPTER ACTIVITIES

1. LIVING HISTORY: Unit Portfolio Project

THEME **EMPIRE BUILDING** Your unit portfolio project focuses on empire building and colonialism. For Chapter 12, you might use one of the ideas suggested below:

- Stage a debate between a conservative member of the Dowager Empress Cixi's court and an official in Emperor Mutsuhito's Meiji government. Each should defend the leader's position on dealing with foreign intervention.
- Create a poster that dramatically illustrates one of the challenges that Mexico faced from the 1840s to the 1920s.
- Design an action figure based on one of the reformers or leaders you studied in this chapter. Draw a picture of the figure or construct a simple model. Then write a paragraph describing the reformer.

2. CONNECT TO TODAY: Cooperative Learning

THEME **CULTURAL INTERACTION** On May 5, 1862, badly outnumbered Mexican forces defeated the French at the Battle of Puebla. Mexicans still celebrate their country's triumph on the holiday Cinco de Mayo.

Working with a team, honor Cinco de Mayo by presenting a report to the class about some aspect of Mexican culture.

Use the Internet, books, interviews, and other resources to gather information about topics such as Mexican customs and traditions, music, dance, holidays, food, or art.

- Collect pictures or samples, or decide how you will demonstrate your Mexican custom to make it come alive for the class.
- Consider staging a cultural fair and inviting other students, administrators, parents, and community members to participate.

3. INTERPRETING A TIME LINE

Study the unit time line on pages 248–249. Which events on the Chapter 12 segment were the result of U.S. imperialism? of European imperialism? of Japanese imperialism?

FOCUS ON **GEOGRAPHY**

The United States wanted the Panama Canal so badly that it both supported a revolution and suffered the deaths of thousands of workers to get it built.

- How many miles did the canal cut from a trip between San Francisco and New Orleans?
- Would a trip from Rio de Janeiro to Valparaíso be shorter via the Panama Canal or the Strait of Magellan?

Connect to History How might the canal have forced Latin American countries to change?

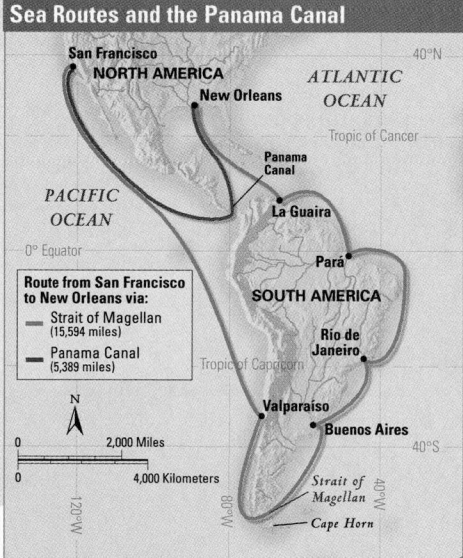

Sea Routes and the Panama Canal

40°N
San Francisco
NORTH AMERICA
New Orleans
ATLANTIC OCEAN
Tropic of Cancer
Panama Canal
PACIFIC OCEAN
La Guaira
0° Equator
Pará
SOUTH AMERICA
Rio de Janeiro
Tropic of Capricorn

Route from San Francisco to New Orleans via:
— Strait of Magellan (15,594 miles)
— Panama Canal (5,389 miles)

Valparaíso
Buenos Aires
40°S
0   2,000 Miles
0   4,000 Kilometers
Strait of Magellan
Cape Horn
120°W   80°W

---

1. LIVING HISTORY

Standards for Evaluation
A debate should meet the following criteria:

- Includes historically correct information about China and Japan.
- Presents persuasive arguments and counter arguments.
- Shows an understanding of each government's point of view.

Standards for Evaluation
An advertisement should meet the following criteria:

- Presents a product produced in Latin America.
- Includes a visual representation of the product.
- Persuasively describes the features of the product.

Standards for Evaluation
An action figure design should meet the following criteria:

- Is based on a leader or reformer from this chapter.
- Shows an effort to accurately portray the historical figure.
- Includes a paragraph describing the reformer and his actions.

2. CONNECT TO TODAY

Standards for Evaluation
A report should meet the following criteria:

- Uses information from a number of sources.
- Gives in-depth information about an aspect of Mexican culture.
- Shows evidence of teamwork.

3. INTERPRETING A TIME LINE

U.S. imperialism—Monroe Doctrine, Treaty of Guadalupe Hidalgo, Treaty of Kanagawa, Panama Canal; European imperialism—Opium War, Spanish-American War, Boxer Rebellion; Japanese imperialism—Sino-Japanese War, Russo-Japanese War, Japan annexes Korea

FOCUS ON **GEOGRAPHY**

- Over 10,000 miles
- Strait of Magellan

Connect to History *Possible Response:* It might have encouraged them to grow more crops for export rather than to feed their own population and to build roads, railroads, and ships to get their products to markets accessible to the canal.

CRITICAL THINKING

1. BYPASSING THE EMPRESS
Possible Responses: Yes—Guangxu had gathered talented advisers and other support. No—The Qing government was too strongly opposed to reform and too powerful.

2. THE SWORD VS. THE PEN
Possible Responses: Military strategies enable leader to seize control of the country and enact his policies, but can cause great suffering for the people. Peaceful political means take longer and are more difficult to achieve than military takeover, but may allow the people more voice in their country.

3. CHARTING SANTA ANNA'S CAREER
Possible Responses: 1833—becomes Mexico's president; 1835—fights to hold Texas; 1836—loses Mexican presidency; 1845—loses Texas to U.S.; 1853—returns as dictator; 1855—exiled

4. ANALYZING PRIMARY SOURCES
Possible Responses: Phrases such as "they would only eat from" and "nothing would satisfy them but" suggest that he thinks these new practices are absurd; when the people of a nation adopt another culture's ways, they run the risk of losing their national pride and identity.

The World at War
1900–1945

The Menin Road *by Paul Nash*

Nash, a World War I British combat soldier who saw the horrifying human carnage on the Western Front firsthand, found it "utterly indescribable." Instead of depicting this slaughter directly, he implied it by showing the war's savage effects on the landscape.

The Menin Road shows a shell-battered countryside extending into the distance, suggesting endless destruction. The lonely pairs of soldiers in the middle ground seem lost in the chaotic and menacing space.

Nash set the scene in a forward section of the Ypres Salient, a section of Allied-held Belgium projecting into German-held territory. The Salient posed special dangers, exposing Allied soldiers to shellfire from three—and sometimes four—sides. The Menin Road, the main route to the Allied front line, was shelled day and night.

Mud compounded the danger. Rain turned the naturally soggy ground into a soupy morass one could drown in. During one of the bitterest military campaigns in history, the Passchendaele offensive of 1917, tens of thousands of men slogged, hid, fought, died, or disappeared in this treacherous mud.

"How difficult it is," wrote Nash as he was beginning *The Menin Road*, to "brood on those wastes of Flanders, the torments, the cruelty & terror of this war. Well it is on these I brood for it seems the only justification of what I do now—if I can rob the war of the last shred of glory, the last shine of glamour." Nash became one of the most celebrated British artists of the 1900s.

UNIT
4
The World
at War
1900–1945

356

This painting, entitled *The Menin Road*, depicts the desolate, bombed-out landscape of World War I through the eyes of artist Paul Nash. Sadly, the war was merely the opening act of a half-century of global violence and bloodshed.

357

Previewing the Unit

This unit covers a period of unprecedented violence and social upheaval—from World War I, to revolution and civil war in Russia and China, to global economic depression and the rise of fascism, to World War II.

Rivalries among European powers lead to a system of military alliances that, sparked by a political assassination, draws Europe and other regions into World War I. The victors dictate harsh peace terms, leaving hard feelings that set the stage for World War II.

World War I helps ignite the Russian Revolutions of 1917, which replace czarist rule with the first communist government, under Lenin. Stalin completes the transformation of the Soviet Union into a totalitarian state. After the fall of the Qing Dynasty in China, nationalists and Communists vie for power. Nationalist movements rise in India and Southwest Asia.

New ideas in science, technology, and the arts emerge in the postwar period. The Great Depression of the 1930s brings new political crises. In response to aggression by Fascist Italy and Nazi Germany, Britain and France pursue a policy of appeasement, while the United States follows a path of isolationism.

The expansionism of Germany and Japan leads to World War II. After initial defeats in Europe and the Pacific, the Allies win the war. The victory costs millions of lives and leaves Europe and Japan economically and socially devastated.

UNIT 4 Time Line
The World at War

Teaching Strategies

Summary Charts Events relevant to a unit sometimes fall outside the range of the Unit Time Line. Also, there may be a large number of important events occurring within the range of a time line, and some events may have had to be omitted due to space limitations. In those cases, summary charts condense such information as an overview.

Because of the large number of events related to World Wars I and II, you will find three summary charts in the time line for Unit 4 *(1915–1919, 1935–1939, 1940–1945)*. You may wish to call students' attention to these charts and point out their usefulness both for synthesizing the major events of these time periods and for review.

UNIT 4 Time Line — *The World at War*

	1905	1910	1915	1920	1925

CHAPTER 13 1914–1918
The Great War

1914 *The Balkans* Austria-Hungary's Archduke Franz Ferdinand and his wife are assassinated

1914 *Europe* World War I begins; Russia, France, and Britain against Germany and Austria-Hungary

1915–1919

1915 *Southwest Asia* Allies and Central Powers clash at Gallipoli in the Ottoman Empire

1916 *France* French suffer massive losses at the Battles of Verdun and Somme

1917 *U.S.* U.S. enters the war on the side of the Allies

1918 *Russia* Russia withdraws from the war and signs a peace treaty with Germany

1918 *Europe* The Allies defeat the Central Powers, ending World War I

1919 *France* The Allies and Germany sign the Treaty of Versailles

CHAPTER 14 1900–1939
Revolution and Nationalism

1905 *Russia* Workers revolt in St. Petersburg

1912 *China* Qing Dynasty topples

1917 *Russia* Russian Revolution ushers in a communist government

1918-20 *Russia* Civil war between Bolshevik Red Army and White Army

1919 *India* Gandhi becomes leader of the independence movement

1921 *China* Communist party forms

1922 *Russia* Union of Soviet Socialist Republics (USSR) is formed

1923 *Turkey* Kemal becomes president of the Turkish republic

CHAPTER 15 1919–1939
Years of Crisis

1919 *Germany* Weimar Republic is set up as democratic government

1920 *U.S.* First radio station broadcasts in Pittsburgh

1922 *Italy* Benito Mussolini comes to power

1923 *Germany* Hitler writes *Mein Kampf* while in jail

CHAPTER 16 1939–1945
World War II

◀ *1930s Germany*

	1905	1910	1915	1920	1925

CONNECTIONS ACROSS TIME AND PLACE

Weapons of War The video for Unit 4, *Arming for War: Modern and Medieval Weapons,* reviews the close relationship that has existed between technological advance and military supremacy. You may wish to discuss examples of this pattern in the video, asking students for additional examples both from history and from today's world. One of the themes developed in the video concerns the constant search for the "ultimate weapon." You might ask students to discuss examples of weapons that were considered "ultimate" in their time. They might also speculate about what the next ultimate weapon might be.

CUSTOMIZING FOR SPECIAL NEEDS

Gifted and Talented Students The first half of the 20th century produced numerous strong leaders who helped shape events in their time. The biographies appearing in *In-Depth Resources: Unit 4* provide accounts of the lives of eight leaders in war, government, diplomacy, and science. You might ask some of your more gifted students to use one of these biographies as a basis for doing further research. They might present the results of their study as a written or oral report with visuals, as a bulletin board, or as a brief dramatic scene highlighting a crucial moment in the person's life.

1915 *Germany* ▶

1925 **1930** **1935** **1940** **1945**

1925 *China*
Sun Yixian dies;
Jiang Jieshi heads
Kuomintang

1928 *U.S.S.R.*
Stalin becomes
dictator

1930 *China*
Civil war between
Nationalists and
Communists erupts

1930 *India*
Gandhi organizes
the Salt March

1934 *China*
Mao Zedong leads the
Long March

1937 *China*
Japan invades China;
Chinese civil war
suspended

1930s *India* ▶

Living History
Unit 4 Portfolio Project

THEME Science and Technology

Your portfolio for Unit 4 will record
some of the many innovations in
science and technology that occur
during and between the First and
Second World Wars. From military
technology to civilian scientific
gains, the rate of technical and
scientific growth in this period was
incredibly fast.

Living History Project Choices
Each Chapter Assessment offers
you choices of ways to show the
advances in science and technology
in that chapter. Activities include
the following:

Chapter 13 historical fiction,
report, display diagram

Chapter 14 travel poster, science
fiction story, diagrams

Chapter 15 artistic work,
demonstration speech

Chapter 16 invention card, fictional
account, questions, time
line

1927 *U.S.*
Charles Lindbergh
flies solo from
New York to Paris

1929 *U.S.*
Stock market crashes

1931 *China*
Japan invades
Manchuria

1933 *Germany*
Adolf Hitler appointed
chancellor

1935–1939

1935 *Ethiopia*
Italy attacks Ethiopia

1936 *Spain* Civil war erupts

1937 *China* Japan invades China

1938 *Germany* Nazis destroy
Jewish businesses on
Kristallnacht

1938 *Austria* Germany annexes
Austria

1939 *Czechoslovakia* Germany
seizes Czechoslovakia

1939 *Soviet Union* Nazi-Soviet
nonaggression pact signed

1939 *Central Europe*
Germany invades Poland;
World War II begins

1940–1945

1940 *France, Britain*
France surrenders;
Battle of Britain begins

1941 *Eastern Europe*
Germany invades
Soviet Union

1941 *U.S.* Japan bombs
Pearl Harbor; U.S. declares
war on Japan

1943 *Soviet Union* Germans
surrender at Stalingrad

1944 *France* Allies invade
Europe on D-Day

1945 *Germany*
Germany surrenders to Allies

1945 *Japan*
U.S. drops atomic bombs;
Japan surrenders

1925 **1930** **1935** **1940** **1945**

TIME LINE **359**

Portfolio Project

Science and Technology The projects suggested for Unit 4 deal
with the rapid rate of technological
innovation from the beginning of
the 20th century to the end of
World War II.

Students are asked to consider
both military and civilian advances
during this period, as well as the
uses of technology by totalitarian
states.

The wide-ranging topics suggested
for the Portfolio Project in the unit
reflect the multifaceted developments in science and technology
that occurred during the first half
of the 20th century. The projects
should convey a sense of the
rapidity with which these developments took place.

Visual Learners At least one suggested project per chapter will
appeal to the visual learners in
your classroom. These include:

• a technology display

• a poster about the Trans-Siberian
Railway

• diagrams about oil-drilling techniques in Southwest Asia

• an artwork done in the style of
an architect or artist, and

• a science and technology time
line for World War II

The variety of media and formats
suggested for these projects is
designed to appeal to visual learners of differing interests and
graphic talents. You may wish to
guide students into considering
projects that best utilize their
visual skills.

The Western Civilization Videodisc

SECTION L: World War I and the Russian
Revolution, 1914–1920

Side One:
Frame 38728

SECTION M: Between the Wars, 1920–1939

Side One:
Frame 41521

SECTION N: World War II, 1939–1945

Side One:
Frame 44138

Universal Play
Button

See Master Guide, page 273 for Section L, page
291 for Section M, page 313 for Section N.

The Great War

	Key Ideas	COPY MASTERS	ASSESSMENT
SECTION 1 **The Stage Is Set for War** *pp. 363–366*	*Nationalism unifies countries in Europe but also leads to commercial and territorial rivalries. Bismarck forms the Triple Alliance, while Britain joins with France and Russia to form the Triple Entente. An assassination causes war to break out.*	*In-Depth Resources: Unit 4* • **Guided Reading,** p. 1 • **Skillbuilder Practice:** Summarizing, p. 5 • **Primary Source:** The Murder of Archduke Franz Ferdinand, p. 8 • **History Makers:** Wilhelm II, p. 15	*Section 1 Assessment,* p. 366 *Formal Assessment* • Section Quiz, p. 162 *Alternative Assessment Book* • Standards for Evaluating a Product or Performance
SECTION 2 **War Consumes Europe** *pp. 367–372*	*European nations take up frontlines divided between the Central Powers and the Allies. Despite major battles and terrible casualties, neither side advances.*	*In-Depth Resources: Unit 4* • **Guided Reading,** p. 2 • **Geography Application:** The Battle of the Somme, p. 6 • **Primary Source:** Poison Gas, p. 9 • **Literature:** from *All Quiet on the Western Front,* p. 12; "The Soldier" and "Dulce et Decorum Est," p. 14 • **Science and Technology:** Industrial Technology Creates Poison Gas, p. 18	*Section 2 Assessment,* p. 371 *Formal Assessment* • Section Quiz, p. 163 *Alternative Assessment Book* • Standards for Evaluating a Cooperative Activity
SECTION 3 **War Affects the World** *pp. 373–379*	*The Allies expand the war beyond Europe. The U.S. enters the conflict. Citizens undergo rationing, and many women go to work in factories. Fresh American troops give the Allies an edge. The Kaiser abdicates, and an armistice is signed.*	*In-Depth Resources: Unit 4* • **Guided Reading,** p. 3 • **Primary Source:** *The Zimmerman Note,* p. 10	*Section 3 Assessment,* p. 377 *Formal Assessment* • Section Quiz, p. 164 *Alternative Assessment Book* • Standards for Evaluating a Cooperative Activity
SECTION 4 **A Flawed Peace** *pp. 380–383*	*The Treaty of Versailles ignores Wilson's Fourteen Points, creates new nations in Europe, and is rejected by the U.S. Senate. The war leaves millions dead and wounded and costs hundreds of billions of dollars.*	*In-Depth Resources: Unit 4* • **Guided Reading,** p. 4 • **Primary Source:** Signing the Treaty of Versailles, p. 11 • **History Makers:** Georges Clemenceau, p. 16 • **Connections Across Time and Cultures:** Planning for Peace: Vienna and Versailles, p. 17	*Section 4 Assessment,* p. 383 *Formal Assessment* • Section Quiz, p. 165 *Alternative Assessment Book* • Standards for Evaluating a Cooperative Activity
CHAPTER RESOURCES	**Chapter Overview** *With a political assassination, a complex system of alliances draws Europe into war. Some colonial subjects support the Allies, while others remain uninvolved. The Treaty of Versailles does little to build a lasting peace.*	*Telescoping the Times* • Chapter Summary, pp. 53–55 *Planning for Block Schedules*	*Chapter Assessment,* pp. 384–385 *Chapter Activities,* p. 385 *Formal Assessment* • Chapter Test, forms A and B, pp. 166–171 *Test Generator* *Alternative Assessment Book*

1914–1918

TECHNOLOGY

 Warm-Up Transparency 13

 Electronic Library of Primary Sources
• "Death Comes to Sarajevo"

 INTERNET RESOURCES
www.mlworldhistory.com

 Warm-Up Transparency 13

 World Art and Cultures Transparencies
• AT63 *The Fate of the Animals*
• AT64 *L'Assault*

 Electronic Library of Primary Sources
"The German Army Marches through Brussels"

 INTERNET RESOURCES
www.mlworldhistory.com

 Warm-Up Transparency 13

 Battles of the World
• The Battle of Kaiserschlacht

 Electronic Library of Primary Sources
• "A Suffolk Farmhand at Gallipoli"

INTERNET RESOURCES
www.mlworldhistory.com

 Warm-Up Transparency 13

 Geography Transparencies
• GT29 Danzig and the Polish Corridor

Critical Thinking Transparencies
• CT29 The Human and Financial Costs of World War I
• CT65 Visual Summary

Electronic LIbrary of Primary Sources
• The Fourteen Points

INTERNET RESOURCES
www.mlworldhistory.com

 Chapter Summaries on Audiocassette in English and Spanish

 INTERNET RESOURCES
www.mlworldhistory.com

Block Scheduling (90 MINUTES)

Day 1
Section 1, pp. 363–366
Section Assessment, p. 366
Day 2
Section 2, pp. 367–372
 COOPERATIVE ACTIVITY
Understanding Life in the Trenches, p. 369 (Teacher's Edition)

Section Assessment, p. 371
Day 3
Section 3, pp. 373–379
 COOPERATIVE ACTIVITY
p. 376 (Teacher's Edition)
Section Assessment, p. 377

Day 4
Section 4, pp. 380–383
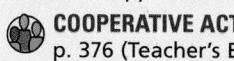 **COOPERATIVE ACTIVITY**
p. 381 (Teacher's Edition)
Section Assessment, p. 383
Chapter Assessment, pp. 384–385

Yearly Pacing *Chapter 13 Total:* 4 days **Yearly Total:** 85 days

 Planning for Block Schedules

Customizing for Special Needs

Students Acquiring English

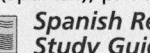 *Access for Students Acquiring English*
• **Guided Reading** for Sections 1–4 (Spanish), pp. 143–146
• **Chapter Summary** (Spanish), pp. 140–142
• **Skillbuilder Practice** Summarizing (Spanish), p. 147
• **Geography Application** The Battle of the Somme (Spanish), p. 148

 Spanish Reading Study Guide
• pp. 137–146

 Chapter Summaries on Audiocassette in English and Spanish

Less Proficient Readers

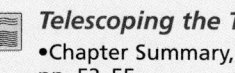 *In-Depth Resources: Unit 4*
• **Guided Reading** for Sections 1–4, pp. 1–4
• **Skillbuilder Practice** Summarizing, p. 5
• **Geography Application** The Battle of the Somme, p. 6

 Telescoping the Times
•Chapter Summary, pp. 53–55

Reading Study Guide
• pp. 137–146

Chapter Summaries on Audiocassette

Gifted and Talented Students

 In-Depth Resources: Unit 4

Primary Sources:
• The Murder of Archduke Franz Ferdinand, p. 8
• Poison Gas, p. 9
• *The Zimmermann Note*, p. 10
• Signing the Treaty of Versailles, p. 11

History Makers
• Wilhelm II, p. 15
• Georges Clemenceau, p. 16

Connections to Literature   READINGS FOR STUDENTS

 In-Depth Resources: Unit 4
Literature: from *All Quiet on the Western Front*, p. 12; "The Soldier" and "Dulce et Decorum Est," p. 14

Enrichment Reading

Cummings, E. E.
The Enormous Room
New York: Norton, 1994
The author's experience in the ambulance corps in France during World War I.

Japrisot, Sebastien
A Very Long Engagement
New York: Plume, 1994

This story about five French soldiers in 1917 is part history and part mystery as the fiancée of one soldier later tries to learn how he died.

 PE = Pupil's Edition   = Overhead Transparency   = Software   = Video

= Copy Master   = CD-ROM   = Audiocassette   = Internet

359B

The Great War, 1914–1918

Accessing Prior Knowledge

- Ask students what other kinds of posters they have seen that encourage people to join a branch of a country's military. What inducements do such posters use?

- Have students note the time frame of the chapter. Perhaps family members can tell them of ancestors who fought in the war or who lived through it on the home front.

Making Predictions

- Ask students to study the war photo on page 361. How might the new weapon shown in the photo have affected the way the war was fought? What might happen if both sides had the same types of weapons?

Geography Connection

Ask students to look at the map on these two pages.

- What neutral country interrupted the line of the Western Front? *Switzerland*

- With what border did the line marking the furthest advance of the Central Powers in the east coincide? *Austria-Hungary and Russia*

CHAPTER
13 *The Great War, 1914–1918*

PREVIEWING THEMES

Science & Technology

Advances in weaponry, from improvements to the machine gun and airplane, to the invention of the tank, led to mass devastation during World War I.

Economics

The war greatly affected many European economies. The warring governments—desperate for resources—converted many industries to munitions factories. They also took greater control of the production of goods. In addition, they put thousands of unemployed people to work.

Power and Authority

The quest among European nations for greater power played a role in causing World War I. By the turn of the 20th century, the nations of Europe—driven by intense feelings of superiority—competed with each other on many fronts. They also built large armies to display their might.

INTERNET CONNECTION

Visit us at **www.mlworldhistory.com** to learn more about World War I.

EUROPE, 1914

0   250 Miles
0   500 Kilometers

☐ Central Powers
☐ Allied Powers
☐ Neutral Nations
▬ Furthest Central Power Advancement

North Sea

NORWA

DENMAR

GREAT BRITAIN

London

NETHERLANDS

Battle of Marne
Sept. 1914

Battle of Somme
July 1916

BELGIUM

Paris

LUXEMBOUR

Battle of Verdun
Feb. 1916

FRANCE

SWITZERLAND

ITAL

Ro

ATLANTIC OCEAN

360

This **1914** British poster was one of many used by the warring nations to recruit soldiers for battle. Here, the British government presents an image of **Lord Kitchener,** a hero of the Boer War of 1899–1902, to stir British patriotism. This poster inspired the 1917 United States recruiting poster captioned, "I Want You for the U.S. Army." In that poster Uncle Sam strikes a similar pose.

GEOGRAPHY THEMES

Location

Have students examine the map on this page and on page 361 to see the locations of the continents and countries where World War I took place. Tell students that the fighting took place mostly on the continent of Europe but that other areas were also involved because of ties with an opposing country. Ask students to examine the map here to find names of countries that may be unfamiliar to them (*Bosnia and Herzegovina*), and point out that one of the effects a war has is to rearrange boundaries and rename nations. You might ask students what they know about current unrest in Bosnia.

Movement

Tell students that in this chapter they will read about many battles between opposing armies. Have them consider the vast machinery involved in moving large numbers of soldiers, equipment, weapons, animals, and support systems from one place to another in a short time, and the effects this kind of movement has on the land, the environment, and the people who already live in these areas. Remind students that armies had to seek out tank drivers among people who were wealthy enough to own cars and therefore knew how to drive.

ADDITIONAL RESOURCES

Books for the Teacher

- Dadrian, Vahakn N. *The History of the Armenian Genocide.* Providence, R.I.: Berghahn Books, 1995.

- Tuchman, Barbara. *The Guns of August.* New York: Macmillan, 1962.

Books for the Student

- Masefield, John. *John Masefield's Letters from the Front, 1915–1917.* New York: Watts, 1985.

- Vansittart, Peter. *Voices from the Great War.* New York: Watts, 1984.

▄▄▄ Videos

- *The Great War: 1918.* PBS Video, 1989. 800–344–3337. The ordeal of war through the letters and diaries of U.S. soldiers.

- *The Politics of Peacemaking.* Coronet/MTI, 1983. 800–321–3106. Self-interest leads to a failed treaty ending World War I.

- *The Shot That Started the Great War.* Ambrose Video, 1997. 800–526–4663. The murder of Archduke Franz Ferdinand triggers a chain of events.

💿 Software

- *The Causes of World War I.* CD-ROM. Society for Visual Education, 1994. 800–829–1900. Political, economic, and social factors leading to the Great War.

A German machine-gun team engages the enemy along the **Western Front.** The invention of new weapons and the improvement of others led to the killing of people on a scale the world had never before seen. The terrible destruction throughout Europe prompted one French soldier to write, "Humanity is mad! It must be mad to do what it is doing! . . . Hell cannot be so terrible."

This painting by John Christen Johansen depicts the signing of the **Treaty of Versailles** in **1919.** The treaty, failing to resolve many issues that caused the war, left many nations unsatisfied. Particularly bitter was Germany, which was forced to accept full responsibility for the war. "We are required to admit that we alone are war guilty," declared a senior German delegate. "Such an admission on my lips would be a lie."

361

HISTORY THROUGH ART

World War I Recruiting Posters

All of the combatant powers in the Great War used posters as a means to recruit soldiers for the war. In the United States, the government set up the nation's first propaganda agency, the Committee on Public Information, to directly popularize the war. The head of the CPI was a former muckraking journalist named George Creel. He mobilized the nation's artists and advertising people, who created thousands of paintings, cartoons, sculptures, and posters promoting the war.

James Montgomery Flagg's *I Want You,* with its portrayal of Uncle Sam, became the most famous recruiting poster in American history, but there were many others. Some World War I government posters scared Americans into buying Liberty Bonds by portraying the Germans as bloodthirsty barbarians. Some wartime posters encouraged Americans to help the war effort by saving resources such as food.

Interpreting the Art How does this poster make its appeal to potential recruits? To what feelings does it appeal? How might it make a young man feel guilty?

This Interact with History feature motivates students by inviting them to decide whether or not they would come to the support of an ally even if it meant unleashing a destructive war. As they imagine the dilemma, students will analyze the issues, explore their options, and become decision makers.

Purpose

- to set the stage for studying World War I
- to help students understand some of the causes and effects of World War I
- to help students make connections with the people and events they will study in this chapter

Teaching Strategy

Thinking Critically After students have imagined themselves in the situation, have them answer the key question and give reasons for their decision.

EXAMINING *the* ISSUES

Following are suggestions for addressing each bulleted question.

1 Can students think of situations in today's world in which one nation has been asked to support another in a conflict?

2 What might happen if countries did not support other countries in their wars?

3 What might happen if countries that went to war were able to involve lots of other countries in their conflict?

Making Connections Ask students to think about the impact of extensive and destructive wars (such as the Hundred Years' War or the Napoleonic wars) on societies.

Follow Up

A feature on the chapter assessment will ask students to reevaluate their response to the situation presented on this page.

Interact *with* History

It is the summer of 1914 in Europe and tensions are high. The continent has been divided into two rival camps. The countries in each camp have pledged to fight along-side one another in case of war. Suddenly the unthinkable happens. The leader of a country you are allied with is assassinated. The dead leader's country blames a rival nation and declares war. The country calls on you to keep your word and join the war on its side.

As a member of your country's government, you are called to an emergency meeting to discuss your nation's response. On one hand, you have promised to support your ally. However, if you declare war, it probably will set off a chain reaction of war declarations throughout the two camps. As a result, all of Europe could find itself locked in a large, destructive war.

The leader of an allied nation is murdered. His country declares war and asks for your support.

If all nations keep their pledges to go to war, it will force millions of Europeans to fight and die.

Would you support your ally?

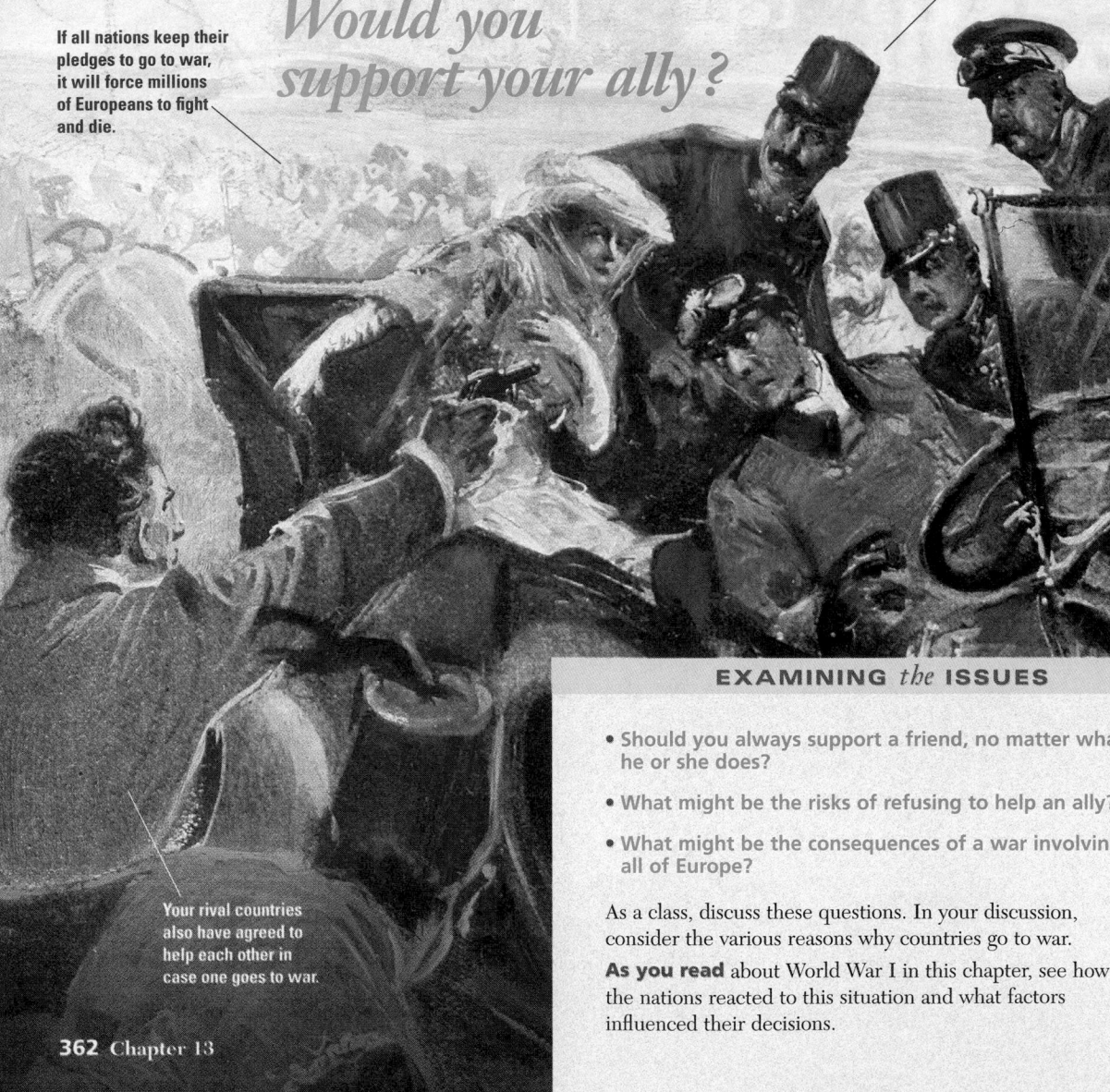

Your rival countries also have agreed to help each other in case one goes to war.

362 Chapter 13

EXAMINING *the* ISSUES

- Should you always support a friend, no matter what he or she does?

- What might be the risks of refusing to help an ally?

- What might be the consequences of a war involving all of Europe?

As a class, discuss these questions. In your discussion, consider the various reasons why countries go to war.

As you read about World War I in this chapter, see how the nations reacted to this situation and what factors influenced their decisions.

The Stage Is Set for War

TERMS & NAMES
- militarism
- Triple Alliance
- Kaiser Wilhelm II
- Triple Entente

MAIN IDEA

In Europe, military buildup, nationalistic feelings, and rival alliances set the stage for a continental war.

WHY IT MATTERS NOW

Ethnic conflict in the Balkan region, which helped start the war, continued to erupt in that area in the 1990s.

SETTING THE STAGE At the turn of the 20th century, the nations of Europe had been at peace with one another for nearly 30 years. An entire generation had grown up ignorant of the horrors of war. Some Europeans believed that progress had made war a thing of the past. Yet in little more than a decade, a massive war would engulf Europe and spread across the globe.

An Uneasy Peace Grips Europe

Efforts to outlaw war and achieve a permanent peace had been gaining momentum in Europe since the middle of the 19th century. By 1900, hundreds of peace organizations were active. In addition, peace congresses convened regularly between 1843 and 1907. However, below this surface of peace and goodwill, several forces were at work that would help propel Europe into war.

The Steady Rise of Nationalism One such force was nationalism, or a deep devotion to one's nation. Nationalism can serve as a unifying force within a country. However, it also can cause intense competition between nations, with each seeking to overpower the other. By the turn of the 20th century, a fierce rivalry indeed had developed among Europe's Great Powers. Those nations were Germany, Austria-Hungary, Great Britain, Russia, Italy, and France.

This increasing rivalry among European nations stemmed from several sources. Competition for materials and markets was one. Great Britain, home of the Industrial Revolution, had long been Europe's leader in industry, finance, and shipping. After 1850, however, other nations began to challenge Britain's power. One such nation was Germany. Germany's many new industries made its economy the fastest-growing one on the continent. As a result, Germany competed with Great Britain for industrial dominance.

Nationalistic rivalries also grew out of territorial disputes. France, for example, had never gotten over the loss of Alsace-Lorraine to Germany in the Franco-Prussian War (1870). Austria-Hungary and Russia both tried to dominate in the Balkans, a region in southeast Europe. Within the Balkans, the intense nationalism of Serbs, Bulgarians, Romanians, and other ethnic groups led to demands for independence.

Imperialism Another force that helped set the stage for war in Europe was imperialism. As Chapter 27 explained, the nations of Europe competed fiercely for colonies in Africa and Asia. The quest for colonies sometimes pushed European nations to the brink of war. In 1905 and again in 1911, Germany and France nearly fought over who would control Morocco, in northern Africa. With most of Europe supporting France, Germany eventually backed down. As European countries continued to compete for overseas empires, their sense of rivalry and mistrust of one another deepened.

THINK THROUGH HISTORY
A. Analyzing Issues What helped fuel nationalistic rivalries among the countries of Europe?
A. Possible Answer Economic competition, territorial disputes, and independence demands.

German chancellor Otto von Bismarck led his nation to victory over France in the Franco-Prussian War in 1870. The war, which earned Germany some French territory, increased tensions between the two nations.

The Great War **363**

SECTION 1 RESOURCES

PRINT RESOURCES

IN-DEPTH RESOURCES: UNIT 4
Guided Reading, p. 1
Skillbuilder Practice: Summarizing, p. 5
Primary Source: The Murder of Archduke Franz Ferdinand, p. 8
History Makers: Wilhelm II, p. 15

ACCESS FOR STUDENTS ACQUIRING ENGLISH
Guided Reading (Spanish), p. 143
Skillbuilder Practice: (Spanish), p. 147

FORMAL ASSESSMENT
Section Quiz, p. 162

ALTERNATIVE ASSESSMENT BOOK

TECHNOLOGY RESOURCES

 CD-ROM
Electronic Library of Primary Sources

 INTERNET www.mlworldhistory.com

Section 1 Overview
OBJECTIVES

(1) To identify the political and military forces that took root in Europe in the late 1800s.

(2) To list the countries that composed the Triple Alliance and the Triple Entente.

(3) To summarize the events that set World War I in motion.

SKILLBUILDER
- Interpreting maps: region, location, p. 365

CRITICAL THINKING
- Analyzing issues, pp. 363, 366
- Summarizing, p. 365
- Analyzing themes, p. 366

FOCUS
5-Minute Warm-Up

▶ *Interpreting Maps*
To help students understand the situation in Europe on the eve of World War I, have them answer the following questions.

1. Look at the map on page 365. Which landlocked country in the middle of Western Europe was neutral?

2. Which two countries on the North Sea were neutral?

WARM-UP TRANSPARENCY 13

OBJECTIVE (1) INSTRUCT

An Uneasy Peace Grips Europe

▶ *Key Ideas*
- Nationalism unifies countries in Europe but also leads to commercial and territorial rivalries.
- Competition among European nations over colonial holdings in Asia and Africa fuels rivalry.
- The arms race leads to a concentration on large armies and the ability to mobilize quickly for war.

IN-DEPTH RESOURCES: UNIT 4
Guided Reading, p. 1

ACCESS FOR STUDENTS ACQUIRING ENGLISH
Guided Reading (Spanish), p. 143

The Growth of Militarism Beginning in the 1890s, increasing nationalism led to a dangerous European arms race. The nations of Europe believed that to be truly great, they needed to have a powerful military. By 1914, all the Great Powers except Britain had large standing armies. In addition, military experts stressed the importance of being able to quickly mobilize, or organize and move troops in case of a war. Generals in each country developed highly detailed plans for such a mobilization.

The policy of glorifying military power and keeping an army prepared for war was known as **militarism.** Having a large and strong standing army made citizens feel patriotic. However, it also frightened some people. As early as 1895, Frédéric Passy, a peace activist and future Nobel Peace Prize winner, expressed a concern that many shared:

A VOICE FROM THE PAST
The entire able-bodied population are preparing to massacre one another; though no one, it is true, wants to attack, and everybody protests his love of peace and determination to maintain it, yet the whole world feels that it only requires some unforeseen incident, some unpreventable accident, for the spark to fall in a flash . . . and blow all Europe sky-high.

FRÉDÉRIC PASSY, quoted in *Nobel: The Man and His Prizes*

HISTORYMAKERS

**Kaiser Wilhelm II
1859–1941**

Wilhelm II was related to the leaders of two nations he eventually would engage in war. Wilhelm, George V of Great Britain, and Nicholas II of Russia were all cousins.

The Kaiser thought a great deal of himself and his place in history. Once, when a doctor told him he had a small cold, Wilhelm reportedly responded, "No, it is a big cold. Everything about me must be big."

The Kaiser also could be sly and deceitful. After he forced the popular Bismarck to resign, Wilhelm pretended to be upset. "I feel as sorrowful as though I had lost my grandfather all over again," he announced publicly. Most people, however, including Bismarck, were not fooled. In his retirement, the former chancellor grumbled that Wilhelm "thinks he knows better than anyone. He recognizes no authority but himself."

Tangled Alliances

The growing international rivalries had led to the creation of several military alliances among the Great Powers as early as the 1870s. This alliance system had been designed to keep peace in Europe. But it would instead help push the continent into war.

Bismarck Forges Early Pacts Between 1864 and 1871, Prussia's blood-and-iron chancellor, Otto von Bismarck, freely used war to unify Germany. After 1871, however, Bismarck declared Germany to be a "satisfied power." He then turned his energies to maintaining peace in Europe.

Bismarck saw France as the greatest threat to peace. He believed that France still wanted revenge for its defeat in the Franco-Prussian War. Bismarck's first goal, therefore, was to isolate France. "As long as it is without allies," Bismarck stressed, "France poses no danger to us." In 1879, Bismarck formed the Dual Alliance between Germany and Austria-Hungary. Three years later, Italy joined the two countries, forming the **Triple Alliance**. In 1887, Bismarck took yet another possible ally away from France by making a treaty with Russia.

Bismarck knew that his network of alliances was unstable. Two of Germany's allies, Russia and Austria, were themselves bitter rivals for the Balkans. The slightest shift in diplomatic winds could blow apart the fragile web of treaties.

Shifting Alliances Threaten Peace In 1890, Germany's foreign policy changed dramatically. That year, **Kaiser Wilhelm II**—who two years earlier had become ruler of Germany—forced Bismarck to resign. A proud and stubborn man, Wilhelm II did not wish to share power with anyone. Besides wanting to assert his own power, the new Kaiser was eager to show the world just how mighty Germany had become. The army was his greatest pride. "I and the army were born for one another," Wilhelm declared shortly after taking power.

Wilhelm set Germany on a new course. He let his nation's treaty with Russia lapse in 1890. Russia responded by forming a defensive military alliance with France in 1891. Such an alliance had been Bismarck's greatest fear. A war with either Russia or France would

Vocabulary
impulsive: inclined to act on a sudden feeling rather than thought.

make Germany the enemy of both. Germany would then be forced to fight a two-front war, or a war on both its eastern and western borders.

Next, the impulsive Kaiser, envious of Britain's large empire and mighty navy, decided to challenge Britain. During the 1890s, Germany built its own small colonial empire. At the same time, Wilhelm started a tremendous shipbuilding program in an effort to make the German navy equal to Britain's.

Alarmed, Great Britain began to enlarge its own fleet. In 1904, Britain formed an entente, or alliance, with France. In 1907, Britain made another entente, this time with both France and Russia. The **Triple Entente,** as it was called, did not bind Britain to fight with France and Russia. However, it did almost certainly ensure that Britain would not fight against them.

By 1907, two rival camps existed in Europe. On one side was the Triple Alliance—Germany, Austria-Hungary, and Italy. On the other side was the Triple Entente—Great Britain, France, and Russia. A dispute between two rival powers could draw the entire continent into war.

**THINK THROUGH HISTORY
B. Summarizing**
Which countries made up the Triple Alliance? the Triple Entente?
B. Answers Triple Alliance: Germany, Austria-Hungary, Italy. Triple Entente: Great Britain, France, Russia

Crisis in the Balkans

Nowhere was that dispute more likely to occur than on the Balkan Peninsula. This mountainous peninsula in the southeastern corner of Europe was home to an assortment of ethnic groups. With a long history of nationalist uprisings and ethnic clashes, the Balkans were known as the "powder keg" of Europe.

Europe's Powder Keg By the early 1900s, the Ottoman Empire—which included the Balkan region—was in rapid decline. While some Balkan groups struggled to free themselves from Ottoman rule, others already had succeeded in breaking away from their Turkish rulers. These peoples had formed new nations, including Bulgaria, Greece, Montenegro, Romania, and Serbia.

Nationalism was a powerful force in these countries. Each group longed to extend its borders. Serbia, for example, had a large Slavic population. Serbia hoped to absorb all the Slavs on the Balkan Peninsula. On this issue of Serbian nationalism, Russia and Austria-Hungary were in direct conflict. Russia, itself a mostly Slavic nation, supported Serbian nationalism. Austria, which feared rebellion among its small Slavic population, felt threatened by Serbia's growth. In addition, both Russia and Austria-Hungary had hoped to fill the power vacuum created by the Ottoman decline in the Balkans.

In 1908, Austria annexed, or took over, Bosnia and Herzegovina.

Europe on the Eve of World War I, 1914

Triple Alliance
Triple Entente
Non-aligned nations
The Balkans

St. Petersburg · GREAT BRITAIN · North Sea · DENMARK · Baltic Sea · London · NETH. · RUSSIA · BELGIUM · Berlin · GERMANY · Paris · LUX. · ALSACE-LORRAINE · Vienna · AUSTRIA-HUNGARY · FRANCE · SWITZ. · ROMANIA · SPAIN · BOSNIA AND HERZEGOVINA · Sarajevo · SERBIA · Black Sea · CORSICA (France) · ITALY · MONTENEGRO · BULGARIA · Constantinople · Rome · ALBANIA · SARDINIA (Italy) · OTTOMAN EMPIRE · SICILY (Italy) · GREECE

0 400 Miles
0 800 Kilometers

**GEOGRAPHY SKILLBUILDER:
Interpreting Maps**
1. **Region** What countries made up the Balkans?
2. **Location** Based on the map, which alliance might have an advantage if war erupted? Why?

SPOTLIGHT ON

The Armenian Massacre
One Balkan group that suffered greatly for its independence efforts was the Armenians. By the 1880s, the roughly 2.5 million Christian Armenians in the Ottoman Empire had begun to demand their freedom. As a result, relations between the group and its Turkish rulers grew strained.

Throughout the 1890s, Turkish troops killed tens of thousands of Armenians. When World War I erupted in 1914, the Armenians pledged their support to the Turks' enemies. In response, the Turkish government deported nearly 2 million Armenians. Along the way, more than 600,000 died of starvation or were killed by Turkish soldiers.

The Great War **365**

Unresolved Problems

The Threats of Weapons and Terrorism

The assassination of Archduke Franz Ferdinand was an act of terrorism. Terrorism is the use of violence or force against a person or property to gain a political or social objective. Acts of terrorism can include kidnappings, bombings, hijackings and other acts.

In the 20th century, the use of terrorism expanded greatly. Groups representing a variety of political views chose to use terrorism to try to achieve their goals. Modern terrorists often target innocent civilians, making ithe terrorism even more frightening.

Technological advances, such as automatic weapons and easily transported bombs, make the activity even more deadly. Mass media coverage expands the impact of the violent acts to all areas of the globe.
See Epilogue, p. 602.

These were two Balkan areas with large Slavic populations. Serbian leaders, who had sought to rule these provinces, were outraged. The possibility of war arose. Russia offered Serbia full support, but the offer meant little. Russia was totally unprepared for war. When Germany stood firmly behind Austria, Russia and Serbia had to back down.

By 1914, tensions in the Balkan region were once again on the rise. Serbia had emerged victorious from several local conflicts. As a result, the nation had gained additional territory and a new confidence. It was more eager than ever to take Bosnia and Herzegovina away from Austria. In response, Austria-Hungary vowed to crush any Serbian effort to undermine its authority in the Balkans.

A Shot Rings Throughout Europe Into this poisoned atmosphere of mutual dislike and mistrust stepped the heir to the Austro-Hungarian throne, Archduke Franz Ferdinand, and his wife, Sophie. On June 28, 1914, the couple paid a state visit to Sarajevo, the capital of Bosnia. It was to be their last. The royal pair were shot at point-blank range as they rode through the streets of Sarajevo in an open car. The killer was Gavrilo Princip, a 19-year-old member of the Black Hand. The Black Hand was a secret society committed to ridding Bosnia of Austrian rule.

Because the assassin was a Serbian, Austria decided to use the murders as an excuse to punish Serbia. An angry Kaiser Wilhelm II urged Austria to be aggressive, and he offered Germany's unconditional support. In effect this gave Austria license to do what it wanted with Serbia.

On July 23, Austria presented Serbia with an ultimatum. An ultimatum is a list of demands that if not met, will lead to serious consequences. The ultimatum was deliberately harsh. Demands included an end to all anti-Austrian activity. In addition, Serbian leaders would have had to allow Austrian officials into their country to conduct an investigation into the assassinations. Serbia knew that refusing the ultimatum would lead to war against the more powerful Austria. Therefore, Serbian leaders agreed to most of Austria's demands. They offered to have several others settled by an international conference.

Austria, however, was in no mood to negotiate. The nation's leaders, it seemed, had already settled on war. On July 28, Austria rejected Serbia's offer and declared war. That same day, Serbia's ally, Russia, took action. Russian leaders ordered the mobilization of troops toward the Austrian border.

Leaders all over Europe suddenly took alarm. The fragile European stability seemed about to collapse. The British foreign minister, the Italian government, and even Kaiser Wilhelm himself urged Austria and Russia to negotiate. But it was too late. The machinery of war had been set in motion.

Section 1 Assessment

1. TERMS & NAMES
Identify
- militarism
- Triple Alliance
- Kaiser Wilhelm II
- Triple Entente

2. TAKING NOTES
Create a time line of major events that led to World War I.

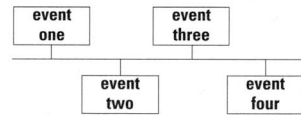

Write the lead paragraph of a news story about one event.

3. ANALYZING ISSUES
Why might the "machinery of war," set in motion by the assassination of Archduke Franz Ferdinand, have been difficult to stop?

THINK ABOUT
- nationalism
- militarism
- the alliance system

4. ANALYZING THEMES
Power & Authority With another student, play the roles of Bismarck and Kaiser Wilhelm. In front of the class, debate each other over Germany's foreign policy goals.

THINK ABOUT
- the extent of Germany's "satisfaction" as a world power
- keeping Russia as an ally
- peace in Europe

366 Chapter 13

ANSWERS

1. TERMS & NAMES
militarism, p. 364

Triple Alliance, p. 364

Kaiser Wilhelm II, p. 364

Triple Entente, p. 365

2. TAKING NOTES
Possible Responses: 1882 Triple Alliance formed; 1890 German foreign policy changed; 1890s European arms race; 1907 Triple Entente formed; 1908 Austria annexed Bosnia and Herzegovina; 1914 Archduke Franz Ferdinand and wife killed.

3. ANALYZING ISSUES
Possible Responses: Intense nationalism prompted nations to compete for superiority in all areas; militarism had led to the establishment of large armies, as well as to the glorification of military might; the alliance system required its members to support one another in case of war.

4. ANALYZING THEMES
Students should state clearly and correctly each man's position regarding the mentioned topics.

TERMS & NAMES
- Schlieffen Plan
- Central Powers
- Allies
- Western Front
- trench warfare
- Eastern Front

Section 2 Overview

OBJECTIVES

① To describe the reaction to Austria's declaration of war.

② To summarize the military events on the Western Front.

③ To explain the progression of the war on the Eastern Front.

SKILLBUILDER
- Interpreting maps: location, p. 368

CRITICAL THINKING
- Making inferences, p. 367
- Recognizing effects, p. 369
- Synthesizing, p. 371
- Comparing and contrasting, p. 371
- Clarifying, p. 372

MAIN IDEA

One European nation after another was drawn into a large and industrialized war that resulted in many casualties.

WHY IT MATTERS NOW

Much of the technology of modern warfare, such as fighter planes and tanks, was introduced in World War I.

SETTING THE STAGE The assassination of Archduke Franz Ferdinand on June 28, 1914, was the spark that ignited a giant blaze. This single terrorist act set off a chain reaction within the alliance system that would result in the largest war Europe—and the world—had ever seen.

The Alliance System Collapses

By 1914, Europe was divided into two rival camps. One alliance, the Triple Entente, included Great Britain, France, and Russia. The other, known as the Triple Alliance, included Germany, Austria-Hungary, and Italy.

Austria-Hungary's declaration of war against Serbia set off a chain reaction within the alliance system. The countries of Europe followed through on their numerous and complex pledges to support one another. As a result, nearly all the nations of Europe soon were drawn into the war.

A Chain Reaction In response to Austria's declaration of war, Russia, Serbia's ally, began moving its army toward the Russian-Austrian border. Expecting Germany to join Austria, Russia also mobilized along the German border. Czar Nicholas II of Russia told the Kaiser that the maneuvers were just a precaution. Yet to Germany, Russia's mobilization amounted to a declaration of war. On August 1, the German government declared war on Russia.

Russia looked to its ally France for help. Germany, however, did not even wait for France to react. Two days after declaring war on Russia, Germany also declared war on France. Much of Europe was now locked in battle.

The Schlieffen Plan Germany quickly put its military plan into effect. The plan was named after its designer, General Alfred Graf von Schlieffen (SHLEE-fuhn). In the event of a two-front war, Schlieffen had called for attacking France and then Russia. The general had reasoned that Russia—with its lack of railroads— would have difficulty mobilizing its troops. Under the **Schlieffen Plan,** a large part of the German army would race west, to defeat France, and then return to fight Russia in the east.

Speed was vital to the German plan. The French had troops all along their border with Germany. Thus, the Germans knew that breaking through would be slow work. There was another route, however: France's northern border with Belgium was unprotected.

Germany demanded that its troops be allowed to pass through Belgium on their way to France. Belgium, a neutral country, refused. Germany then invaded Belgium. This brought Great Britain into the conflict. The British had close

A. Possible Answer Because the plan called for Germany to defeat France and then return its troops to the east before Russia fully mobilized.

THINK THROUGH HISTORY
A. Making Inferences Why was speed so important to the Schlieffen Plan?

This war poster shows a German soldier dragging off a woman during the invasion of Belgium. The image was intended to stir public outrage over the attack.

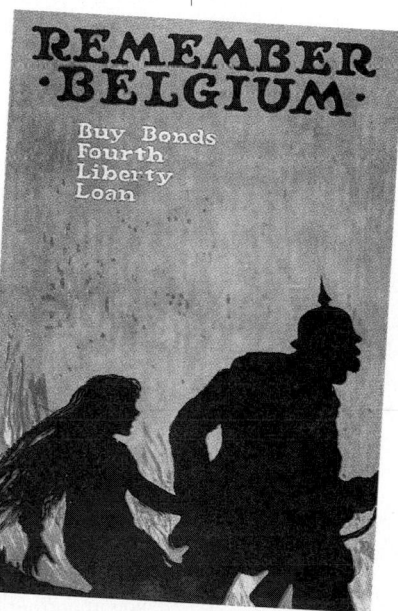

REMEMBER BELGIUM

Buy Bonds
Fourth
Liberty
Loan

The Great War **367**

FOCUS

5-Minute Warm-Up

▶ **Making Inferences**
Have students answer the following questions to help them understand trench warfare.

1. Look at the photograph on page 369. Why would it have been difficult to keep clothes and body clean and dry?

2. What long-term effect would living in such an environment have on people?

🗄 **WARM-UP TRANSPARENCY 13**

OBJECTIVE ① INSTRUCT

The Alliance System Collapses

▶ **Key Ideas**
- A complex system of alliances and special interests draws continental Europe into war.

- European nations take up frontlines divided between the Central Powers and the Allies.

📋 **IN-DEPTH RESOURCES: UNIT 4**
Guided Reading, p. 2

📋 **ACCESS FOR STUDENTS ACQUIRING ENGLISH**
Guided Reading (Spanish), p. 144

💿 **ELECTRONIC LIBRARY OF PRIMARY SOURCES**
"The German Army Marches Through Brussels"

SECTION 2 RESOURCES

PRINT RESOURCES

📋 **IN-DEPTH RESOURCES: UNIT 4**
Guided Reading, p. 2
Geography Application: The Battle of the Somme, p. 6
Primary Source: Poison Gas, p. 9
Literature: from *All Quiet on the Western Front,* p. 12; "The Soldier" and "Dulce et Decorum Est," p. 14
Science and Technology, p. 18

📋 **ACCESS FOR STUDENTS ACQUIRING ENGLISH**
Guided Reading (Spanish), p. 144
Geography Application Spanish, p. 148

📋 **FORMAL ASSESSMENT**
Section Quiz, p. 163

TECHNOLOGY RESOURCES

🖥 **WORLD ART AND CULTURES TRANSPARENCIES**
AT63 *The Fate of the Animals*
AT64 *L'Assault*

💿 **CD-ROM**
Electronic Library of Primary Sources

🌐 **INTERNET** www.mlworldhistory.com

World War I in Europe, 1914–1918

Interpreting the Map Have students examine the map and note the countries in northern Europe that remained neutral. *Norway, Sweden, and Denmark* Also have them note the large country in the west of Europe that remained neutral. *Spain*

Extension Activity Ask students why they think Germany violated Belgium's neutrality but not that of the Netherlands or Switzerland. *Students may suggest that the Netherlands does not border France, and although Switzerland does, the German strategy was to attack France and move quickly to the capital—Paris—which is directly west of Belgium.*

SKILLBUILDER Answers
1. France
2. They were between the Allies. Thus they had to fight a two-front war and could not concentrate all their resources on one front.

OBJECTIVE ② INSTRUCT

A Bloody Stalemate Along the Western Front

Key Ideas
- The Allied victory at the Marne breaks the back of the Schlieffen Plan.
- Trench warfare and the failure to capture new ground make life on the Western Front an ongoing horror.
- Despite major battles and horrific casualties, neither side advances.

IN-DEPTH RESOURCES: UNIT 4
Geography Application: The Battle of the Somme, p. 6
Primary Source: Poison Gas, p. 9
Literature: from *All Quiet on the Western Front*, p. 12; "The Soldier" and "Dulce et Decorum Est," p. 14

WORLD ART AND CULTURES TRANSPARENCIES
AT63 *The Fate of the Animals*

World War I in Europe, 1914–1918

Map legend:
- Allied countries
- Central Powers
- Neutral countries
- Central Powers advances
- Allied advances
- Farthest Central Powers advance
- Farthest Allied advance
- Central powers victory
- Allied victory
- Armistice Line, Nov. 1918

GEOGRAPHY SKILLBUILDER: Interpreting Maps
1. **Location** In which country was almost all of the war in the West fought?
2. **Location** What geographic disadvantage did Germany and Austria-Hungary face in fighting the war? How might this have affected their war strategy?

ties with Belgium, one of their nearest neighbors on the continent. Outraged over the violation of Belgian neutrality, Britain declared war on Germany on August 4.

European Nations Take Sides By mid-August 1914, the battle lines were clearly drawn. On one side were Germany and Austria-Hungary. They were known as the **Central Powers,** because of their location in the heart of Europe. Bulgaria and the Ottoman Empire would later join the Central Powers in the hopes of regaining lost territories.

On the other side were Great Britain, France, and Russia. Together, they were known as the Allied Powers or the **Allies.** Japan joined the Allies within weeks. Italy, which at first was neutral, joined the Allies nine months into the war. Italy claimed that its membership in the Triple Alliance had been a defensive strategy. The Italians felt that the Germans had made an unprovoked attack on Belgium. Therefore, the Italians argued, they were not obligated to stand by their old ally.

In the late summer of 1914, millions of soldiers marched happily off to battle, convinced that the war would be short. Only a few people foresaw the horror ahead. One of them was Britain's foreign minister, Sir Edward Grey. Staring out over London at nightfall, Grey said sadly to a friend, "The lamps are going out all over Europe. We shall not see them lit again in our lifetime."

Background
Before the war, the Central Powers were part of the Triple Alliance, and the Allies were known as the Triple Entente.

A Bloody Stalemate Along the Western Front

It did not take long for Sir Edward Grey's prediction to ring true. As the summer of 1914 turned to fall, Germany's lightning-quick strike instead turned into a long and bloody stalemate, or deadlock, along the battlefields of France. This deadlocked region in northern France became known as the **Western Front.**

368 Chapter 13

MULTIPLE LEARNING STYLES

Logical-Mathematical Learners The Allied victory in the first Battle of the Marne was due in part to the reinforcement of the Allied lines by troops transported by taxicabs to the battle. Ask students, if 600 taxis were used, each one carrying 5 passengers, how many trips did each taxi make to get 6,000 troops to the front? *Each of the 600 taxis made two trips, carrying five soldiers each time.* Have students speculate on other ways the troops could have been quickly transported to the front. Have them calculate how many troops were to be transported. How far? In how many trips?

MULTIPLE LEARNING STYLES

Visual Learners Have students use the map here to aid their understanding of the actions and strategies of the opposing armies throughout the chapter. Help them become familiar with cardinal directions on the map, so that they can comfortably say, "The arrow shows that the Germans moved west across Belgium and into France" and so forth.

Also ask students questions that require their using the map key, such as "Who won the Battle of Tannenberg in August 1914?" or "Who won the Battle of Kovel in June 1916?" Then you might have students trace over the map in order to reinforce their understanding of the geography of the war.

The Conflict Grinds to a Halt Early on, Germany's Schlieffen Plan worked brilliantly. By the end of August, the Germans had overrun Belgium and swept into France. By September 3, German units were on the edge of Paris. A major German victory appeared just days away. The French military then came into possession of intelligence that told them the exact direction the German army was about to take.

On September 5, the Allies attacked the Germans northeast of Paris, in the valley of the Marne River. Every available soldier was hurled into the struggle. When reinforcements were needed, more than 600 taxicabs rushed soldiers from Paris to the front. After four days of fighting, the German generals gave the order to retreat. "It was an inspiring thought," a British officer later wrote, "that the time had now come to chase the German." By September 13, the Germans had been driven back nearly 60 miles.

Although it was only the first major clash on the Western Front, the First Battle of the Marne was perhaps the single most important event of the war. The defeat of the Germans left the Schlieffen Plan in ruins. A quick victory in the west no longer seemed possible. In the east, Russian forces had already invaded Germany. Germany was going to have to fight a long war on two fronts. Realizing this, the German high command sent thousands of troops from France to aid its forces in the east. Meanwhile, the war on the Western Front settled into a stalemate.

War in the Trenches By early 1915, opposing armies on the Western Front had dug miles of parallel trenches to protect themselves from enemy fire. This set the stage for what became known as **trench warfare.** In this type of warfare, soldiers fought each other from trenches. And armies traded huge losses for pitifully small land gains.

Life in the trenches was pure misery. "The men slept in mud, washed in mud, ate mud, and dreamed mud," wrote one soldier. The trenches swarmed with rats. Fresh food was nonexistent. Sleep was nearly impossible.

The space between the opposing trenches won the grim name "no man's land." When the officers ordered an attack, their men went "over the top" of their trenches into this bombed-out landscape. There, they usually met murderous rounds of machine-gun fire. Staying put in the trench, however, did not ensure one's safety. Artillery fire brought death right into the trenches. "Shells of all calibers kept raining on our sector," wrote one French soldier. "The trenches disappeared, filled with earth

Along the Western Front, soldiers battled one another from trenches dug out of the earth. Here, a British soldier peers out of the trench at "no man's land."

MORE ABOUT . . .
The Battle of the Marne
Finding important information by chance is not just a plot element of war and spy movies. An unfortunate German officer who drove away from his general's camp on the evening of September 1, 1914, took a wrong turn that led him into a French patrol, who killed him. When his bloodstained belongings were examined by the French, they were found to contain a map that showed two important things: the exact location of the German troops and the direction of advancement planned for the next day.

MORE ABOUT . . .
Trench Warfare
When a soldier went "over the top" of the trenches, he was expected to carry the following equipment: a rifle, a bayonet, grenades, 170 rounds of ammunition, a gas mask, a shovel and wire cutters, a full water bottle and food rations, extra clothing and medical supplies, and a portable cooking stove with fuel. Carrying all of this, he had to fight the enemy, assuming he lived while crossing "no man's land." The average kit bag weighed more than 66 pounds.

TEACHING OPTION | **BLOCK SCHEDULING** | COOPERATIVE ACTIVITY: **Understanding Life in the Trenches** | CLASS TIME 30 MINUTES

Task: Students will learn what soldiers did in the trenches, both when they were fighting and when they were not, and create a classroom display.

Purpose: To understand the mix of boredom and terror that made up life in the trenches.

Activity: Have students find a variety of sources that describe daily life in the trenches: diaries and letters written by soldiers in the war; photographs of trenches,

and narrative descriptions. For the display, some students may draw the design of a trench. Others may prepare short quotes from primary sources describing the weather, rats, bombardment, loneliness, and so forth. Encourage students to mount their writings and illustrations on a large poster display board.

📁 **Building a Portfolio:** Students should add their part of the display to their portfolio.

📖 **ALTERNATIVE ASSESSMENT BOOK**
Standards for Evaluating a Cooperative Activity

Standards for Evaluation
The display should . . .
• present clear graphic examples
• provide detailed written descriptions
• show evidence of research

370 Chapter 13

MORE ABOUT . . .

A Voice from the Past

Valentine Fleming was a member of Parliament and a major in the army. His two sons—Peter, a travel writer, and Ian, the author of the James Bond spy novels—were children during World War I. Fleming ended his letter, "It's going to be a *long* war in spite of the fact that on both sides every single man wants it stopped *at once*." He was killed in 1917, fighting on the Western Front.

MORE ABOUT . . .

Tanks

The first tanks were made in Britain and grew out of a design to put machine guns on motorcycles. When Britain shipped the first of the new vehicles to France, it labeled them "water tanks" to keep the weapon secret. The name stuck. The first tank drivers were from the upper class, because they were the only ones wealthy enough to have cars and therefore know how to drive.

OBJECTIVE 3 INSTRUCT

The Battle on the Eastern Front

▶ Key Ideas

- While Germany gains the upper hand over Russian troops, the Austrian army pushes Russia out of Austria-Hungary.
- Without modern technology, the Russian army hangs on through the sheer strength of its numbers.

The New Weapons of War

Poison Gas
Soldiers wore masks to protect themselves from a horrible new weapon—poison gas. Gas was introduced by the Germans but used by both sides. While some gases caused blinding or severe blisters, others caused death by choking.

Machine Gun
The machine gun, which fires ammunition automatically, was much improved by the time of World War I. As a result, it saw wide use in combat. Because the gun could wipe out waves of attackers and make it difficult for forces to advance, it helped create a stalemate.

Tank
The tank was an armored combat vehicle that moved on chain tracks. It was introduced by the British in 1916 at the Battle of the Somme. The early tanks were slow and clumsy. They eventually improved, and thus aided the Allies in their war effort.

. . . the air was unbreathable. Our blinded, wounded, crawling, and shouting soldiers kept falling on top of us and died splashing us with blood. It was living hell."

The Western Front had become a "terrain of death." It stretched nearly 500 miles from the North Sea to the Swiss border. A British officer described it in a letter:

> **A VOICE FROM THE PAST**
> Imagine a broad belt, ten miles or so in width, stretching from the Channel to the German frontier near Basle, which is positively littered with the bodies of men and scarified with their rude graves; in which farms, villages and cottages are shapeless heaps of blackened masonry; in which fields, roads and trees are pitted and torn and twisted by shells and disfigured by dead horses, cattle, sheep and goats, scattered in every attitude of repulsive distortion and dismemberment.
> **VALENTINE FLEMING,** quoted in *The First World War*

Military strategists were at a loss. New tools of war—machine guns, poison gas, armored tanks, larger artillery—had not delivered the fast-moving war they had expected. All this new technology did was kill huge numbers of people more effectively.

The slaughter reached a peak in 1916. In February, the Germans launched a massive attack against the French near Verdun. Each side lost more than 300,000 men.

In July of 1916, the British army tried to relieve the pressure on the French. British forces attacked the Germans northwest of Verdun, in the valley of the Somme River. In the first day of battle alone, more than 20,000 British soldiers were killed. By the time the Battle of the Somme ended in November, each side had suffered over half a million casualties.

What did the warring sides gain? Near Verdun, the Germans advanced about four miles. In the Somme valley, the British gained about five miles.

Background
In war, a casualty is anyone killed, injured, captured, or considered missing in action.

The Battle on the Eastern Front

Even as the war on the Western Front claimed thousands of lives, both sides were sending millions more men to fight on the **Eastern Front.** This area was a stretch of battlefield along the German and Russian border. Here, Russians and Serbs battled Germans, Austrians, and Turks. The war in the east was a more mobile war than that in the west. Here too, however, slaughter and stalemate were common.

Central Powers Gain the Advantage At the very beginning of the war, Russian forces had launched an attack into both Austria and Germany. At the end of August 1914, Germany counterattacked near the town of Tannenberg. During the four-day battle that followed, the Germans crushed the invading Russian army and drove it into full retreat. Germany regained East Prussia and seized numerous guns and horses from the enemy. More than 30,000 Russian soldiers were killed.

370 Chapter 13

Task Students will examine an art transparency to learn the horrors of combat as experienced by the soldiers in World War I. Students should note the look on the face of the soldier in the forefront of the assault.

Materials Needed Use copies of Art Transparency AT64, *L'Assault.* You might also reread

the paragraph in the text on page 370 that describes the Battle of Verdun.

Activity Have students help you make up a factual list of the impact of the battle. Such a list might include the number of troops engaged in the conflict, the number of dead, the number of wounded, the length of the battle, and so forth.

Conclusion Ask students which conditions in battle would have bothered them most. Would it have been the conditions in the trenches? the launching of an assault, when the troops had to storm over the top of the trenches and into "no man's land"?

📽 ***WORLD ART AND CULTURES TRANSPARENCIES***
AT64 *L'Assault*

Airplane
World War I signaled the first time in history that planes were used in a combat role. At first, nations used planes for taking photographs of enemy lines. Soon, both sides used them to drop bombs. Guns soon were attached to the planes, and pilots fought each other in the air.

Submarine
In 1914, the Germans introduced the submarine as an effective warship. German submarines, known as U-boats, eventually waged unrestricted warfare on Allied ships. The submarine's primary weapon was the torpedo, a self-propelled underwater missile.

Russia fared somewhat better against the Austrians. Russian forces defeated the Austrians twice in September 1914, driving them deep into Austria. Not until December of that year did the Austrian army—with German assistance—manage to turn the tide. In a 17-day battle near Limanowa, Austria defeated the Russians and drove them eastward. Two weeks later, the Austrian army pushed the Russians out of Austria-Hungary.

Russia's War Effort Weakens By 1916, Russia's war effort was near collapse. Unlike the nations of western Europe, Russia had yet to become industrialized. As a result, the Russian army was continually short on food, guns, ammunition, clothes, boots, and blankets. Moreover, the Allies were unable to ship supplies to Russia's ports. In the north, a German naval fleet blocked the Baltic Sea. In the south, the Ottomans still controlled the straits leading from the Mediterranean to the Black Sea.

The Russian army had only one asset—its numbers. Throughout the war the Russian army suffered enormous battlefield losses. More than 2 million Russian soldiers were killed, wounded, or captured in 1915 alone. And yet the army continually rebuilt its ranks from the country's enormous population. For more than three years, the battered Russian army managed to tie up hundreds of thousands of German troops in the east. Thus, Germany could not hurl its full fighting force at the west.

Germany and her allies, however, were concerned with more than just the Eastern or Western Fronts. As the war raged on, fighting spread beyond Europe to Africa, as well as to Southwest and Southeast Asia. In the years after it began, the massive European conflict indeed became a world war.

THINK THROUGH HISTORY
C. Synthesizing
Why was Russia's involvement in the war so important to the other Allies?
C. Possible Answer
Russia's huge army tied up German troops in the east and kept them from fighting in the west.

Section 2 Assessment

1. TERMS & NAMES
Identify
• Schlieffen Plan
• Central Powers
• Allies
• Western Front
• trench warfare
• Eastern Front

2. TAKING NOTES
Using a chart like the one below, write the immediate reason why each nation declared war on the other.

War Declaration	Reason for Declaration
Germany on Russia	
Germany on France	
Britain on Germany	

3. COMPARING AND CONTRASTING
How was war on the Western Front and Eastern Front different? How was it the same?

THINK ABOUT
• trench warfare
• which nations fought on each front
• war casualties

4. THEME ACTIVITY
Science & Technology
Draw a political cartoon showing the effects of the new technology on warfare. Include a caption that expresses the point of the cartoon.

The Great War **371**

The German air force ruled the skies at first. The average air combat time of a new flyer in the British Royal Air Force was 17 hours. When the Allies began to fly Sopwith Camels, they were able to threaten German dominance of the air war. The Sopwiths were so named because they carried guns in a hump behind the engine.

 IN-DEPTH RESOURCES: UNIT 4
Science and Technology: Industrial Technology Creates Poison Gas, p. 18

MORE ABOUT . . .
Pilots

The parachute had been invented by World War I. German pilots carried them, but American pilots did not. The U.S. War Department felt that a pilot would be more likely to try to bring his injured plane to safety if he could not immediately bail out when he was hit.

Aviation

World War I introduced plane warfare. And with it came daring dogfights and legendary pilots. Two such pilots were America's Eddie Rickenbacker and Germany's Baron Manfred von Richthofen, better known as the Red Baron. In a larger sense, however, the war ushered in an era of great progress in the field of aviation. In the warring nations' quest to dominate the skies, they produced thousands of planes and continually worked to improve engine designs. After the war, these nations converted their war planes to commercial use. They also began designing larger, stronger planes for civilian transport. The age of air travel had begun.

By 1926, passenger airlines were operating in Europe, Africa, Australia, and North and South America. Built in 1928, the Ford Tri-motor model, shown below, was one of the better-known American passenger planes of the time.

On the eve of World War I, planes were still considered a novelty. Here, an early plane races an automobile at a track in Columbus, Ohio, in 1914. The finish was so close that no one knew who won.

Designers of the early passenger planes made sure to devote plenty of space for luggage.

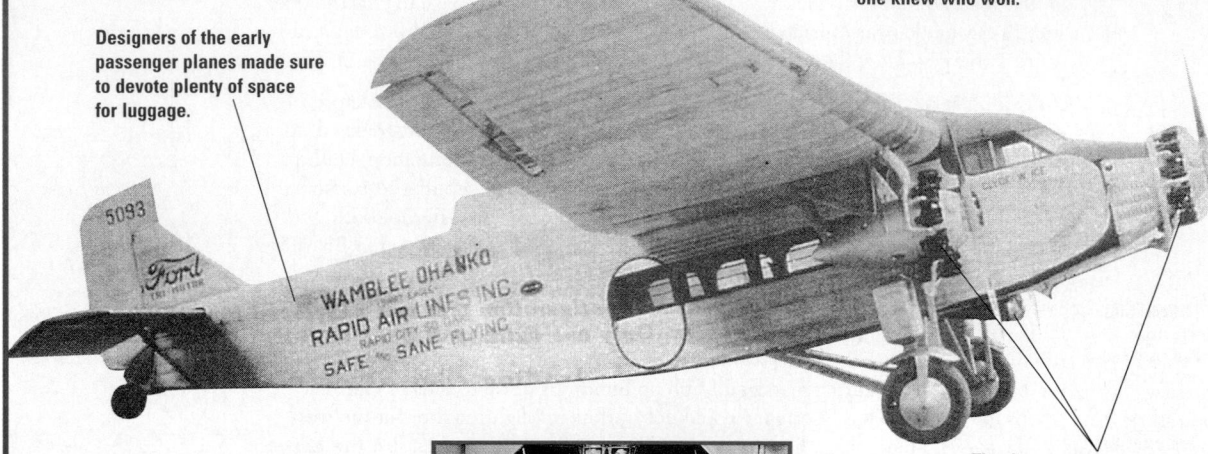

The three-motor system gave the plane greater power. It became the prototype for many later models.

The Tri-motor carried about 10 passengers. Temperature control, however, was still many years away. Passengers often bundled up in coats to keep warm.

Annual Ridership

Riders (in billions)

- 1930: Less than 3 million*
- 1960: 100 million*
- 1990s: 1.25 billion*

*estimated
Source: *The World Book Encyclopedia*

Connect *to* History

Clarifying What role did World War I play in the advancement of aviation technology?

SEE SKILLBUILDER HANDBOOK, PAGE 650.

Connect *to* Today

Investigating Find out about any one of today's more advanced aircraft, such as the Concorde, or the latest military jet or commercial airplane. Write a brief report about the craft's most advanced and interesting features. Present your report to the class.

Connect *to* History

Clarifying
Possible Answer: The desire to win battles in the air led countries to build many planes and develop new designs. These were turned to commercial uses after the war.

Connect *to* Today

Investigating
Have students discuss the different kinds of planes in which they have flown. For example, do they fly only in the big jets, or have some flown in planes with propellors? Have any students flown in gliders or been taken up with friends or relatives who fly their own small planes? Which kinds of plane travel do students prefer? Are there any they dislike?

3 War Affects the World

TERMS & NAMES
- unrestricted submarine warfare
- total war
- rationing
- propaganda
- armistice

MAIN IDEA

World War I spread to several continents and required the full resources of many governments.

WHY IT MATTERS NOW

The war propelled the United States to a new position of international power, which it retains today.

TERMS & NAMES
- unrestricted submarine warfare
- total war
- rationing
- propaganda
- armistice

SETTING THE STAGE By early 1915, it was apparent to all the warring nations that swift victory had eluded them. As war on both European fronts promised to be a grim, drawn-out affair, all the Great Powers looked for new allies to tip the balance. They also sought new war fronts on which to achieve victory.

A Truly Global Conflict

Geographical widening of the war actually had begun soon after the conflict started. The Ottoman Turks and later Bulgaria allied themselves with Germany and the Central Powers. Then Japan entered the war on the Allies' side. That widened the conflict further. By early 1915, the only major neutral power left besides the United States was Italy. And Italy joined the Allies in April. None of these alliances gave an advantage to either side. But they did give military leaders more war zones in which to try to secure victory.

Fighting Rages Beyond Europe As the war dragged on, the Allies desperately searched for a way to end the stalemate. A promising strategy seemed to be to attack a region in the Ottoman Empire known as the Dardanelles. This narrow sea strait was the gateway to the Ottoman capital, Constantinople. By securing the Dardanelles, the Allies believed that they could take Constantinople, defeat the Turks, and establish a supply line to Russia. They might even be able to mount an offensive into the Austrian heartland by way of the Danube River.

The effort to take the Dardanelles strait began in February 1915. It was known as the Gallipoli campaign. British, Australian, New Zealand, and French troops made repeated assaults on the Gallipoli Peninsula on the western side of the strait. Turkish troops, some commanded by German officers, vigorously defended the region. By May, Gallipoli had turned into another bloody stalemate. Both sides dug trenches, from which they battled for the rest of the year. In December, the Allies gave up the campaign and began to evacuate. They had suffered about 250,000 casualties.

Despite the Allies' failure at Gallipoli, they remained determined to topple the Ottoman Empire. In Southwest Asia, the British helped Arab nationalists rise up against their Turkish rulers. Particularly devoted to the Arab cause was a British soldier named T. E. Lawrence. Better known as Lawrence of Arabia, he helped lead daring guerrilla raids against the Turks. With the help of the Arabs, Allied armies took control of Baghdad, Jerusalem, and Damascus.

In various parts of Asia and Africa, Germany's colonial possessions came under assault. The Japanese quickly overran German outposts in China. They also captured Germany's Pacific island colonies.

Background
Although the Ottoman Empire had greatly declined by World War I, it still ruled Arab lands in Southwest Asia.

Map labels: Black Sea, Bosporus, Constantinople, Sea of Marmara, Gallipoli Peninsula, GREECE, OTTOMAN EMPIRE, Dardanelles, Aegean Sea, 100 Miles, 200 Kilometers

Arab fighters patrol the desert on camels. The rider in front is believed to be T. E. Lawrence.

373

Section 3 Overview

OBJECTIVES

1. To describe the escalation of World War I.
2. To identify how governments established wartime economies.
3. To summarize how the Allies pushed to victory.

SKILLBUILDERS
- Interpreting maps: region, location, p. 374
- Interpreting graphs, p. 375

CRITICAL THINKING
- Summarizing, pp. 374, 376
- Comparing, p. 377
- Analyzing issues, p. 377
- Analyzing themes, p. 377
- Analyzing motives, p. 379

FOCUS
5-Minute Warm-Up

▶ *Interpreting Maps*
Have students answer the following questions to help them understand the global nature of World War I.

1. Look at the map on page 374. Which colony provided the most soldiers to fight alongside their rulers?

2. Which country that provided troops was farthest away from Europe?

 WARM-UP TRANSPARENCY 13

OBJECTIVE 1 INSTRUCT

A Truly Global Conflict

▶ *Key Ideas*
- The Allies expand the war, suffering grievous losses.
- Germany's attacks on passenger ships and a German plot bring the U.S. into the conflict.

 IN-DEPTH RESOURCES: UNIT 4
Guided Reading, p. 3
Primary Source: *The Zimmermann Note*, p. 10

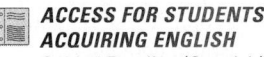 **ACCESS FOR STUDENTS ACQUIRING ENGLISH**
Guided Reading (Spanish), p. 145

 ELECTRONIC LIBRARY OF PRIMARY SOURCES
"A Suffolk Farmhand at Gallipoli"

English and French troops attacked Germany's four African possessions. They seized control of three.

Elsewhere in Asia and Africa, the British and French recruited subjects in their colonies for the struggle. Fighting troops as well as laborers came from India, South Africa, Senegal, Egypt, Algeria, and Indochina. Many fought and died on the battlefield. Others worked to keep the frontlines supplied. Some colonial subjects wanted nothing to do with their European rulers' conflicts. Others volunteered in the hope that service would lead to their independence. This was the view of Indian political leader Mohandas Gandhi, who supported Indian participation in the war. "If we would improve our status through the help and cooperation of the British," he wrote, "it was our duty to win their help by standing by them in their hour of need."

The United States Enters the War In 1917, the focus of the war shifted to the high seas. That year, the Germans intensified the submarine warfare that had raged in the Atlantic Ocean since shortly after the war began. By 1917, failed crops, as well as a British naval blockade, caused severe food shortages in Germany. Desperate to strike back, Germany decided to establish its own naval blockade around Britain. In January 1917, the Germans announced that their submarines would sink without warning any ship in the waters around Britain. This policy was called **unrestricted submarine warfare.**

The Germans had tried this policy before. On May 7, 1915, a German submarine, or U-boat, had sunk the British passenger ship *Lusitania.* The attack left 1,198 people dead, including 128 U.S. citizens. Germany claimed that the ship had been carrying ammunition—which turned out to be true. Nevertheless, the American public was outraged. President Woodrow Wilson sent a strong protest to Germany. After two further attacks, the Germans finally agreed to stop attacking neutral and passenger ships.

However, the Germans returned to unrestricted submarine warfare in 1917. They knew it might lead to war with the United States. They gambled that their naval

A. Possible Answer Some fought as soldiers, while others worked as laborers keeping the frontlines supplied.

THINK THROUGH HISTORY

A. Summarizing How did Europe's colonial subjects help in the war effort?

Vocabulary

blockade: the forced closing off of a city or other area to traffic and communication through the use of ships or land forces.

The World at War, 1914–1918

War rages in Southwest Asia as Arab nationalists battle their Turkish rulers.

Main fighting of the war occurs on Western and Eastern Fronts.

Japan declares war on Germany in 1914; seizes German colonies in China and the Pacific.

The United States enters the war on the side of the Allies in 1917.

India provides about 1.3 million men to fight and labor alongside their British rulers throughout Europe.

Brazil is the only South American country to enter the war. It supports the Allies with warships and personnel.

The European colonies throughout Africa become a battlefield as the warring parties strike at one another's colonial possessions.

Both countries fight on the side of the Allies and contribute many troops to the Gallipoli campaign of 1915, in Southwest Asia.

NORTH AMERICA · SOUTH AMERICA · EUROPE · ASIA · JAPAN · SOUTHWEST ASIA · INDIA · AFRICA · AUSTRALIA · NEW ZEALAND · ATLANTIC OCEAN · PACIFIC OCEAN

4,000 Miles / 8,000 Kilometers

GEOGRAPHY SKILLBUILDER: Interpreting Maps
1. **Region** *Which countries were aligned with the European Allies?*
2. **Location** *Outside of Europe, where was World War I fought?*

374 Chapter 13

blockade would starve Britain into defeat before the United States could mobilize. Ignoring warnings by President Wilson, German U-boats sank three American ships.

In February 1917, another German action pushed the United States closer to war. The British intercepted a telegram from Germany's foreign secretary, Arthur Zimmermann, to the German ambassador in Mexico. The message said that Germany would help Mexico "reconquer" the land it had lost to the United States if Mexico would ally itself with Germany. The British decoded the message and gave it to the U.S. government.

When the Zimmermann note was made public, Americans called for war against Germany. Even before news of the note, many Americans had sided with the Allies. A large part of the American population felt a bond with England. The two nations shared a common ancestry and language, as well as similar democratic institutions and legal systems. In addition, reports—some true and others not—of German war atrocities stirred anti-German sentiment in the United States. More important, America's economic ties with the Allies were far stronger than those with the Central Powers. America traded with Great Britain and France more than twice as much as with Germany.

The Zimmermann note simply proved to be the last straw. On April 2, 1917, President Wilson asked Congress to declare war. The United States entered the war on the side of the Allies.

War Affects the Home Front

By the time the United States joined the Allies, the war had been going on for nearly three years. In those three years, Europe had lost more men in battle than in all the wars of the previous three centuries. The war had claimed the lives of millions and had changed countless lives forever. The Great War, as the conflict came to be known, affected everyone. It touched not only the soldiers in the trenches, but civilians as well. It affected not just military institutions, but also political, economic, and social institutions.

Governments Wage Total War World War I soon became a **total war.** This meant that countries devoted all their resources to the war effort. In Britain, Germany, Austria, Russia, and France, the entire force of government was dedicated to winning the conflict.

In each country, the wartime government took control of the economy. Governments told factories what to produce and how much. Numerous facilities were converted to munitions factories. Nearly every able-bodied civilian was put to work. Unemployment in many European countries nearly disappeared. European governments even enlisted the help of foreign workers. For example, thousands of civilians were deported from German-occupied Belgium and France to work in Germany as farm and factory laborers. Britain and France recruited Chinese, West Indian, Algerian, and Egyptian laborers to work behind their lines at the front.

So many goods were in short supply that governments turned to **rationing.** Under this system, people could buy only small amounts of those items that were also needed for the war effort. Eventually, rationing covered a wide range of goods, from butter to shoe leather.

Governments also suppressed antiwar activity—sometimes forcibly. In addition, they censored news about the war. Many leaders feared

Background
Land Mexico considered "lost" to the United States included New Mexico, Texas, and Arizona.

Vocabulary
atrocity: an act of extreme cruelty or violence.

GlobalImpact

Influenza Epidemic

In the spring of 1918, a powerful new enemy emerged, threatening nations on each side of World War I. This "enemy" was a deadly strain of influenza. The Spanish flu, as it was popularly known, hit England and India in May. By the fall, it had spread through Europe, Russia, Asia, and to the United States.

The influenza epidemic killed soldiers and civilians alike. In India, at least 12 million people died of influenza. In Berlin, on a single day in October, 1,500 people died. In the end, this global epidemic was more destructive than the war itself, killing 20 million people worldwide.

Unemployment in Germany and Britain

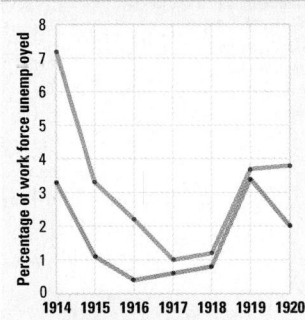

Source: *European Historical Statistics 1750–1975*

SKILLBUILDER:
Interpreting Graphs
1. *During which year did each country see its lowest unemployment rate?*
2. *Why might unemployment have been lowest during the war years?*

The Great War **375**

GlobalImpact
Influenza Epidemic

Many epidemiologists now believe that the influenza epidemic started in army camps in the United States. Ask students to find out more about the epidemic and report their findings to the class.

OBJECTIVE ② INSTRUCT

War Affects the Home Front

▶ **Key Ideas**
• World War I becomes a total war, and governments take control of national economies.
• In the U.S. and Europe, citizens undergo rationing of goods.
• With millions of men at the front, many women go to work in factories and elsewhere.

History from Visuals

Unemployment in Germany and Britain
Interpreting a Graph Help students read the graph by pointing out to them that the unemployment rate in Great Britain in 1914 was about 3.5 percent and in Germany in the same year about 7.25 percent.

Extension Activity Ask students what happened to the unemployment rate at the end of the war. *After dipping during war, the unemployment rate climbed back up at the end of the war.*

SKILLBUILDER Answers
1. Great Britain, 1916; Germany, 1917
2. As part of a total war effort, governments sought to increase production, which meant hiring more workers.

TEACHING OPTIONS

CONNECTIONS ACROSS THE CURRICULUM

Science Antibiotics would not have helped against the virus that causes influenza, because a virus is not a biological agent. Antibiotics work against bacterial infections. However, a growing problem today is that antibiotics are becoming less effective against bacteria, which have developed resistance to

them. Just as any organism tries to adapt in order to survive, bacteria have become stronger than the antibiotics used to kill them. Scientists are working hard to develop new antibiotics that will work against these new strains of bacteria.

CUSTOMIZING FOR SPECIAL NEEDS

Gifted and Talented Students Researching the Influenza Epidemic Influenza was not a new disease in 1918, but it was targeting the young and healthy, including hundreds of thousands of soldiers in the trenches. Drinking fountains were blowtorched every hour, telephones were sterilized with alcohol, and people wore gauze

masks. But the flu moved through the countryside and towns despite such precautions. Have students research the flu epidemic of 1918 in order to list some of the treatments that were suggested at the time. *These included chewing snuff, chewing tobacco, removing the patient's tonsils, extracting teeth, and sprinkling sulfur in shoes.*

Teacher's Edition **375**

The Allies Win the War

In total war all citizens were called on to help in the war effort. Thus women were offered new employment opportunities. Pictured here are women workers at a French munitions factory.

that honest reporting of the war would turn people against it. Governments also used **propaganda**—one-sided information designed to persuade—to keep up morale and support for the war. One of the main instruments of propaganda was the war poster. In nations throughout Europe, striking, colorful posters urged support for the war by painting the enemy as monsters and allies as heroes. (See poster on page 365.)

The War's Impact on Women Total war meant that governments turned to help from women as never before. Thousands of women replaced men in factories, offices, and shops. Women built tanks and munitions, plowed fields, paved streets, and ran hospitals. They also kept troops supplied with food, clothing, and weapons. Although most women left the work force when the war ended, they changed many people's views of what women were capable of doing.

The Allies Win the War

With the United States finally in the war, the balance, it seemed, was about to tip in the Allies' favor. Before that happened, however, events in Russia gave Germany a victory on the Eastern Front.

Russia Withdraws from the War By March 1917, civil unrest in Russia—due in part to war-related shortages of food and fuel—had brought the czar's government to the brink of collapse. Czar Nicholas, faced with the prospect of revolution, abdicated his throne on March 15. In his place a provisional government was established. The new government pledged to continue fighting the war. However, by 1917, nearly 5.5 million Russian soldiers had been wounded, killed, or taken prisoner. The war-weary Russian army refused to fight any longer.

Eight months later, a second revolution shook Russia (see Chapter 14). In November 1917, Communist leader Vladimir Ilyich Lenin seized power. Lenin insisted on ending his country's involvement in the war. One of his first acts was to offer Germany a truce. In March 1918, Germany and Russia signed the Treaty of Brest-Litovsk, which ended the war between them.

The treaty was extremely hard on Russia. It required the Russian government to surrender lands to Germany that now include Finland, Poland, Ukraine, Estonia, Latvia, and Lithuania. (See map on page 380.) Even though the treaty became invalid after the war, these nations still gained their independence.

A Failed Final Push Russia's withdrawal from the war at last allowed Germany to send nearly all its forces to the Western Front. In March 1918, the Germans mounted one final, massive attack on the Allies in France. More than 6,000 German cannons opened the offensive with the largest artillery attack of the entire war.

As in the opening weeks of the war, the German forces crushed everything in their path. By late May 1918, the Germans had again reached the Marne River. Paris was less than 40 miles away. Victory seemed within reach.

By this time, however, the German military had weakened. The effort to reach the Marne had exhausted men and supplies alike. Sensing this weakness, the Allies—with the aid of nearly 140,000 fresh American troops—launched a counterattack. Marshal Ferdinand Foch, the French commander of the Allied forces, used Americans to fill the gaps in his ranks. The U.S. soldiers were inexperienced but courageous and eager to

1914

June 1914
Archduke
Ferdinand and
his wife are
assassinated.

July 1914
Austria-
Hungary
declares war
on Serbia.

July–August 1914
Russia, France, and
Britain go to war
against Germany
and Austria-Hungary.

1916

1916
Combatants
suffer devas-
tating losses
at battles of
Verdun and
the Somme.

1917

1917
United
States enters
the war.

1918

March 1918
Russia withdraws
from the war.

July 1918
Allies defeat Germany
at Second Battle of
the Marne.

November 1918
Warring nations
sign armistice
ending the war.

British and German soldiers help one another during a break in the fighting.

fight. A British nurse, Vera Brittain, later recalled her joy in seeing the American reinforcements:

A VOICE FROM THE PAST

They were swinging rapidly toward Camiers, and though the sight of soldiers marching was now too familiar to arouse curiosity, an unusual quality of bold vigor in their swift stride caused me to stare at them with puzzled interest. They looked larger than ordinary men; their tall, straight figures were in vivid contrast to the undersized armies of pale recruits to which we had grown accustomed. . . . Then I heard an excited exclamation from a group of Sisters behind me. "Look! Look! Here are the Americans!"

VERA BRITTAIN, *Testament of Youth*

THINK THROUGH HISTORY
C. Comparing How was the Second Battle of the Marne similar to the first?
C. Possible Answer Both times, the Allies defeated the Germans just as they seemed poised for victory.

In July 1918, the Allies and Germans clashed at the Second Battle of the Marne. Leading the Allied attack were some 350 tanks that rumbled slowly forward, smashing through the German lines. With the arrival of 2 million more American troops, the Allied forces began to advance steadily toward Germany.

Soon, the Central Powers began to crumble. First the Bulgarians and then the Ottoman Turks surrendered. In October, a revolution in Austria-Hungary brought that empire to an end. In Germany, soldiers mutinied, and the public turned on the Kaiser.

On November 9, 1918, Kaiser Wilhelm II was forced to step down. Germany declared itself a republic. A representative of the new German government met with Marshal Foch. In a railway car in a forest near Paris, the two signed an **armistice,** or an agreement to stop fighting. On November 11, World War I came to an end.

After four years of slaughter and destruction, the time had come to forge a peace settlement. Leaders of the victorious nations gathered outside Paris to work out the terms of peace. While these leaders had come with high hopes, the peace settlement they crafted left many feeling bitter and betrayed.

Section 3 Assessment

1. TERMS & NAMES

Identify
• unrestricted submarine warfare
• total war
• rationing
• propaganda
• armistice

2. TAKING NOTES

Using a chart like the one below, list the reasons why the United States entered World War I.

Reasons for U.S. Entry
1.
2.
3.
4.

3. ANALYZING ISSUES

In what ways was World War I truly a global conflict?

THINK ABOUT
• where the war was fought
• who participated in the war effort

4. ANALYZING THEMES

Economics How did the concept of total war affect the warring nations' economies?

THINK ABOUT
• the governments' new role in their economies
• the scarcity of food and other products
• the role of women
• unemployment rates during the war years

The Great War **377**

MORE ABOUT . . .
A Voice from the Past
Vera Brittain lost her fiancé, her brother, and two close friends in the war, not unusual for families in Britain and France, to say nothing of Germany. Her book *Testament of Youth* is well worth reading for an account of the war from an observer on two fronts—at home and as a nurse on the frontlines.

ASSESS & RETEACH

Section 3 Assessment
Have the class divide into two groups to answer the questions, then have one group compare its answers with those of the other.

Section Quiz
FORMAL ASSESSMENT
Section Quiz, p. 164

Reteaching Activity
CLASS TIME: 10 MINUTES

Have students make a list of factors that brought the U.S. into the war and then a second list telling how the war affected people on the home front.

CLOSE ACTIVITY

CLASS TIME: 10 MINUTES
Role-Playing
Have a pair of students play the roles of President Wilson and German foreign secretary Zimmermann. Have them stage a press conference in which they defend their differing views of the telegram sent by the foreign secretary to the German ambassador in Mexico. Other students will play reporters and ask questions of the two.

ANSWERS

1. TERMS & NAMES
unrestricted submarine warfare, p. 374

total war, p. 375

rationing, p. 375

propaganda, p. 376

armistice, p. 377

2. TAKING NOTES
Germans sink *Lusitania,* a British ship carrying some American passengers; Germany returns to unrestricted submarine warfare, sinking U.S. ships; Zimmermann note decoded—German note urging Mexico to take up arms against U.S.; strong feelings of sympathy for the Allies

3. ANALYZING ISSUES
Possible Responses: The war was fought in numerous places outside Europe: Africa, Southwest Asia, China, and the Pacific. People from many nations participated in the war effort, including colonial subjects throughout Africa and Asia.

4. ANALYZING THEMES
Possible Responses:
Governments took greater control of economies, telling factories what and how much to produce; civilian factories were turned into munitions factories; rationing was common; women became a significant part of the work force; more people were put to work.

Honoring War Heroes

Throughout history, people around the world have shared in a somber, healing ritual: honoring their country's soldiers killed in battle. In many nations, people come together to honor those citizens who have fought and died for their country. After World War I, France built a ceremonial grave to honor all of its soldiers killed in the great conflict. From early times to today, other nations have paid their respects to their dead soldiers with medals, monuments, and parades.

Tomb of the Unknown Soldier
A woman pays her quiet respects at the Tomb of the Unknown Soldier in Paris. On top of the memorial rests an eternal flame in honor of France's dead soldiers. Each year on Armistice Day, the president of France lays a wreath at the site. Following World War I, similar memorials to unknown dead soldiers were created in the United States, Great Britain, Belgium, and Italy.

a closer look WORLD WAR I MONUMENTS

This German war memorial was built in 1926 and placed in the courtyard of the Technical University in Berlin.

378 Chapter 13

The Wall

A man pays tribute at the Vietnam Veterans Memorial in Washington, D.C. The monument, known as the Wall, is a memorial to the men and women who fought and died in the Vietnam War in the 1960s and 1970s. The monument consists of two adjoining black granite walls inscribed with the names of all Americans who either died in the war or were listed as missing in action.

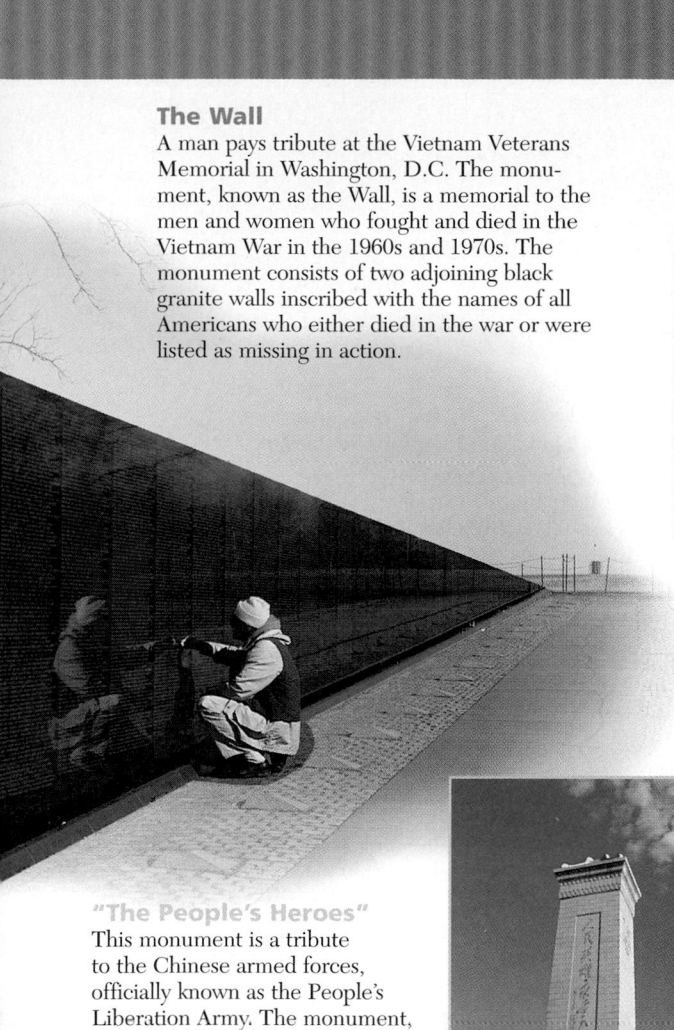

"The People's Heroes"

This monument is a tribute to the Chinese armed forces, officially known as the People's Liberation Army. The monument, which sits in Beijing, is called the Memorial to the People's Heroes. It is a tribute to the soldiers, past and present, who have taken part in the struggle to forge a Communist China, which began around 1946.

Trajan's Column

The Romans relied greatly on their powerful military to oversee a huge empire. Consequently, they glorified war and soldiers with numerous statues and monuments. Shown here is a detail from Trajan's Column, in Rome. The 100-foot-high column was dedicated in A.D. 113 to the emperor Trajan after he conquered Dacia. The column is a continuous spiral carving of soldiers and battle scenes.

Great Britain built its own Tomb of the Unknown Warrior in London to honor those who lost their lives in World War I.

Connect *to* History

Analyzing Motives Why do you think nations honor their dead soldiers?

SEE SKILLBUILDER HANDBOOK, PAGE 652

Connect *to* Today

Designing Working with one or more students, design a memorial to your country's dead soldiers. Include any words or images that you feel convey your message. Present the memorial to the class.

The Great War **379**

CRITICAL THINKING ACTIVITY
CLASS TIME: 10 MINUTES

Making a Chart
To help students recognize that there are different kinds of memorials, have them make a chart listing the various monuments described on these two pages.

Kind of Monument	Specific Example

MORE ABOUT . . .
Trajan's Column

Trajan's Column stands in Trajan's Forum in Rome. There is a spiral staircase inside the column that leads to the top. According to some sources the ashes of Trajan were sealed inside the column, but they have never been found.

Connect *to* History

Analyzing Motives
Possible Answer: Nations honor their dead for a variety of reasons, including to recognize soldiers' valor in combat, honor their families, encourage the young in martial virtues, and ensure that soldiers' valiant deeds will be remembered.

Connect *to* Today

Designing
Students might work in a variety of mediums to design their memorial. For example, they might draw a design, model one in clay or popsicle sticks, or copy examples of memorials they admire from books and other sources.

① To list the main points of the Treaty of Versailles.

② To describe the effects of World War I on Western society.

SKILLBUILDERS

• Interpreting charts, p. 381
• Interpreting maps: region, location, p. 382

CRITICAL THINKING

• Summarizing, p. 380
• Contrasting, p. 381
• Analyzing issues, p. 382
• Making inferences, p. 383
• Forming opinions, p. 383

FOCUS

5-Minute Warm-Up

▶ **Making Inferences**
To help students understand the importance of individuals in history, have them answer the following questions.

1. Read the History Makers on page 380. Why might Clemenceau have been more concerned with revenge and punishment than was Wilson?

2. What does Lloyd George's comment about the two men seem to imply about them?

 WARM-UP TRANSPARENCY 13

OBJECTIVE ① INSTRUCT

The Allies Meet at Versailles

▶ **Key Ideas**
• Wilson submits 14 points.
• The Treaty of Versailles punishes Germany and makes new nations.
• A League of Nations is created but given little power.

 IN-DEPTH RESOURCES: UNIT 4
Guided Reading, p. 4

 ACCESS FOR STUDENTS ACQUIRING ENGLISH
Guided Reading (Spanish), p. 146

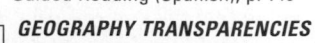 *GEOGRAPHY TRANSPARENCIES*
GT29 Danzig and the Polish Corridor, 1919

 ELECTRONIC LIBRARY OF PRIMARY SOURCES
The Fourteen Points

TERMS & NAMES
• Woodrow Wilson
• Georges Clemenceau
• David Lloyd George
• Fourteen Points
• self-determination
• Treaty of Versailles
• League of Nations

4 A Flawed Peace

MAIN IDEA	WHY IT MATTERS NOW
After winning the war, the Allies dictated a harsh peace settlement that left many nations feeling betrayed.	Hard feelings left by the peace settlement helped cause World War II.

SETTING THE STAGE World War I was over. The killing had stopped. The terms of peace, however, still had to be worked out. On January 18, 1919, a conference to establish those terms began at the Palace of Versailles, outside Paris. For one year this conference would be the scene of vigorous, often bitter debate. The Allied powers struggled to solve their conflicting aims in various peace treaties.

The Allies Meet at Versailles

Attending the talks, known as the Paris Peace Conference, were delegates representing 32 countries. However, the meeting's major decisions were hammered out by a group known as the Big Four: **Woodrow Wilson** of the United States, **Georges Clemenceau** of France, **David Lloyd George** of Great Britain, and Vittorio Orlando of Italy. Russia, in the grip of civil war, was not represented. Neither were Germany and its allies.

Wilson's Plan for Peace In January 1918, while the war was still raging, President Wilson had drawn up a series of proposals. Known as the **Fourteen Points,** they outlined a plan for achieving a just and lasting peace. The first five points included an end to secret treaties, freedom of the seas, free trade, and reduced national armies and navies. The fifth goal was the adjustment of colonial claims with fairness toward colonial peoples. The sixth through thirteenth points were specific suggestions for changing borders and creating new nations. The guiding idea behind these points was **self-determination.** This meant allowing people to decide for themselves under what government they wished to live.

Finally, the fourteenth point proposed a "general association of nations" that would protect "great and small states alike." This reflected Wilson's hope for an organization that could peacefully negotiate solutions to world conflicts.

HISTORY MAKERS

Georges Clemenceau
1841–1929

Woodrow Wilson
1856–1924

The most hostile relationship at the Paris Peace Conference was that between two allies: Wilson and Clemenceau. These two highly intelligent and committed leaders brought very different visions of peace to the negotiating table.

Woodrow Wilson was the son of a Presbyterian minister. He had been a history scholar, professor, and president of Princeton University before becoming president. A morally upright man, he was guided by a deep inner religious faith.

Clemenceau, by contrast, had been a physician, journalist, and sometime playwright before becoming premier of France.

In Paris, the two men clashed. Wilson's idealism, as embodied in the Fourteen Points, stood in stark contrast to Clemenceau's desire to punish Germany.

The stubborn personalities of the two men made reaching agreement even harder. Lloyd George of Britain summed it up nicely when he was asked how he did at the Paris Peace Conference. "Not badly," he replied, "considering I was seated between Jesus Christ and Napoleon."

A. Possible Answer
An end to secret treaties, freedom of the seas, free trade, reduced national armies and navies, and the adjustment of colonial claims with fairness toward colonial people.

THINK THROUGH HISTORY
A. Summarizing
What were Wilson's general goals for the postwar world?

SECTION 4 RESOURCES

PRINT RESOURCES

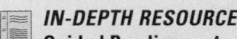 *IN-DEPTH RESOURCES: UNIT 4*
Guided Reading, p. 4
Primary Source: Signing the Treaty of Versailles, p. 11
History Makers: Georges Clemenceau, p. 16

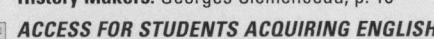 *ACCESS FOR STUDENTS ACQUIRING ENGLISH*
Guided Reading (Spanish), p. 146

 FORMAL ASSESSMENT
Section Quiz, p. 165

ALTERNATIVE ASSESSMENT BOOK

TECHNOLOGY RESOURCES

 GEOGRAPHY TRANSPARENCIES
GT29 Danzig and the Polish Corridor, 1919

 CRITICAL THINKING TRANSPARENCIES
CT29 The Human and Financial Costs of World War I
CT65 Visual Summary

 CD-ROM
Electronic Library of Primary Sources

 INTERNET www.mlworldhistory.com

The Allies Dictate a Harsh Peace As the Paris Peace Conference opened, Britain and France showed little sign of agreeing to Wilson's vision of peace. Both nations were concerned with national security. They also wanted to strip Germany of its war-making power. The French, in particular, were determined to punish Germany. France was where much of the fighting had occurred. The nation had lost more than a million soldiers and had seen large amounts of its land destroyed. Clemenceau wanted Germany to pay for the suffering the war had caused.

The differences between French, British, and U.S. aims led to heated arguments among the nations' leaders. Finally a compromise was reached. The **Treaty of Versailles** between Germany and the Allied powers was signed on June 28, 1919—five years to the day after Franz Ferdinand's assassination in Sarajevo.

Adopting Wilson's fourteenth point, the treaty created a **League of Nations.** The league was to be an international association whose goal would be to keep peace among nations. The five Allied powers—the United States, Great Britain, France, Italy, and Japan—were to be permanent members of the league's Executive Council. Its General Assembly would consist of representatives of 32 Allied and neutral nations. Germany was deliberately excluded. Also left out was Russia. Russia's early withdrawal from the war and its revolutionary leadership had made it an outcast in the eyes of the other Allies.

The treaty also punished Germany. The defeated nation lost substantial territory and had severe restrictions placed on its military operations. As punishing as these provisions were, the harshest was Article 231. It was also known as the "war guilt" clause. It placed sole responsibility for the war on Germany's shoulders. As a result, Germany had to pay reparations to the Allies.

All of Germany's territories in Africa and the Pacific were declared mandates, or territories to be administered by the League of Nations. Under the peace agreement, the Allies would govern the mandates until they were judged ready for independence.

The Treaty of Versailles: Major Provisions

League of Nations	Territorial Losses	Military Restrictions	War Guilt
• International peace organization; membership to include Allied war powers and 32 Allied and neutral nations • Germany and Russia excluded	• Germany returns Alsace-Lorraine to France, French border extended to the west bank of the Rhine River • Germany surrenders all of its overseas colonies in Africa and the Pacific	• Limits set on the size of the German army • Germany prohibited from importing or manufacturing weapons or war materiel • Germany forbidden to build or buy submarines or have an air force	• Sole responsibility for the war placed on Germany's shoulders • Germany forced to pay the Allies $33 billion in reparations over 30 years

SKILLBUILDER: Interpreting Charts
1. *In what ways did the treaty punish Germany?*
2. *What two provinces were returned to France as a result of the treaty?*

The Creation of New Nations The Versailles treaty with Germany was just one of five treaties negotiated by the Allies. The Western powers signed separate peace treaties in 1919 and 1920 with each of the other defeated nations: Austria, Hungary, Bulgaria, and the Ottoman Empire.

These treaties, too, led to huge land losses for the Central Powers. Several new countries were created out of the Austro-Hungarian Empire. Austria, Hungary, Czechoslovakia, and Yugoslavia were all recognized as independent nations.

The Great War **381**

THINK THROUGH HISTORY
B. Contrasting
How did Britain and France's aims at Versailles differ from Wilson's?
B. Possible Answer Britain and France were concerned mainly with punishing Germany and stripping it of its war-making power, while Wilson was more concerned with achieving a just peace.

Vocabulary
reparations: money paid by a defeated nation to compensate for damage or injury during a war.

HISTORY MAKERS
Georges Clemenceau and Woodrow Wilson

(See page 380.)

Georges Clemenceau's desire to see that Germany could never again threaten France was a primary motivation at Versailles. He even made a symbolic point at the signing of the document: he insisted it take place in the Hall of Mirrors, where in 1871 Wilhelm I had been proclaimed emperor of Germany.

 IN-DEPTH RESOURCES: UNIT 4
History Makers: Georges Clemenceau, p. 16

History from Visuals

The Treaty of Versailles: Major Provisions

Interpreting the Chart Have students examine the chart to see how the provisions are grouped. For example, ask them which column shows provisions limiting Germany as a colonial power and which column provisions limiting her military power.

Extension Activity Ask students to imagine how ordinary Germans might have felt about the treaty. Then have them write a paragraph describing their thoughts and feelings.

SKILLBUILDER Answers
1. It excluded Germany from the League of Nations, seized its territory, restricted the size and activities of its military, forced it to accept full responsibility for the war, and required it to pay war reparations.
2. Alsace and Lorraine

 IN-DEPTH RESOURCES: UNIT 4
Primary Sources: Signing the Treaty of Versailles, p. 11
Connections Across Time and Cultures: Planning for Peace: Vienna and Versailles, p. 17

TEACHING OPTION **BLOCK SCHEDULING** **COOPERATIVE ACTIVITY: Debating the Provisions of the Versailles Treaty** **CLASS TIME 20 MINUTES**

Task: Students will learn about the various debates engaged in by the three major representatives at Versailles and divide into pairs to debate the issues.

Purpose: To understand how ending a war can be as political and divisive as beginning one.

Activity: Have students find a variety of sources about the deliberations at Versailles. Be sure they collect at least one direct quote from each of the three main participants—Wilson, Clemenceau, and Lloyd George. Students might consult a dictionary of quotations, encyclopedia articles, biographies, and books about the war for quotes. When they understand the differences of opinion, have them break into pairs, each member representing the position of one of the participants. Students may debate more than one opponent as well as different sides of the issue. As each pair completes a debate, have the class determine who made the best argument.

 ALTERNATIVE ASSESSMENT BOOK
Standards for Evaluating a Cooperative Activity

Teacher's Edition **381**

Europe Before World War I
Europe After World War I

Interpreting the Maps Have students examine the maps to see the major changes that occurred from the beginning of the war to the end. Have them note the new nations that were created in the former Austro-Hungarian Empire and in the northern and north-western portions of Russia. Also have them note that on this map color has no political meaning but simply distinguishes one country from another.

Extension Activity Have students note the change in the status of Great Britain by the end of the war. *Ireland had become independent.* Have students do some research to find out when and how Ireland achieved its independence.

SKILLBUILDER Answers
1. Austria-Hungary
2. Russia's

MORE ABOUT . . .
The Aftermath

When the German diplomats were called to Versailles to sign the treaty, they were in a terrible position. Britain was blockading Germany, and without regular food deliveries, Germans were close to starvation. The blockade would only be ended if Germany signed the treaty. This situation, added to the provisions of the treaty, increased the Germans' resentment.

Europe Before World War I

Europe After World War I

GEOGRAPHY SKILLBUILDER: Interpreting Maps
1. **Region** *Which Central Powers nation appears to have lost the most territory?*
2. **Location** *On which nation's former lands were most of the new countries created?*

The Ottoman Turks were forced to give up almost all of their former empire. They retained only the territory that is today the country of Turkey. The Allies carved up the lands that the Ottomans lost in Southwest Asia into mandates rather than independent nations. Palestine, Iraq, and Transjordan came under British control; Syria and Lebanon went to France.

Russia, alienated by the Allies, suffered land losses as well. Romania and Poland both gained Russian territory. Finland, Estonia, Latvia, and Lithuania, formerly part of Russia, became independent nations.

"A Peace Built on Quicksand" In the end, the Treaty of Versailles did little to build a lasting peace. For one thing, the United States—considered after the war to be the dominant nation in the world—ultimately rejected the treaty. Many Americans objected to the settlement and especially to President Wilson's League of Nations. Americans believed that the United States' best hope for peace was to stay out of European affairs. The United States worked out a separate treaty with Germany and its allies several years later.

In addition, the treaty with Germany—in particular the war-guilt clause—left a legacy of bitterness and hatred in the hearts of the German people. Other countries felt cheated and betrayed as well by the peace settlements. Throughout Africa and Asia, people in the mandated territories were angry at the way the Allies disregarded their desire for independence. The European powers, it seemed to them, merely talked about the principle of national self-determination. European colonialism, disguised as the mandate system, continued in Asia and Africa.

Some Allied powers, too, were embittered by the outcome. Both Japan and Italy, which had entered the war to gain territory, had gained less than they wanted.

Lacking the support of the United States, and later other world powers, the League of Nations was in no position to take action on these complaints. The settlements at

C. Possible Answer Germany was embittered by the war-guilt clause, the peoples of Africa and Asia saw the mandate system as a continuation of European colonialism, Japan and Italy had gained less land than they wanted

THINK THROUGH HISTORY
C. Analyzing Issues What complaints did various countries voice about the Treaty of Versailles?

CUSTOMIZING FOR SPECIAL NEEDS

Gifted and Talented Students: Researching War Poetry Have students find collections of poetry written during World War I, particularly by those who fought. Poets they might investigate include the following: Siegfried Sassoon, Wilfred Owen, Robert Graves, and Alan Seeger. What images did these poets use to describe their experiences? What feelings did they have about the war and the people who led them into the war? Which poets died in the war? Students may copy out a selection of their favorite poems and mount them in a display, along with biographical information about each poet.

CUSTOMIZING FOR SPECIAL NEEDS

Students Acquiring English: Developing Vocabulary Have students work with some of the words in this section that denote or describe feelings and emotions. On this page, for example, are *bitterness, hatred, cheated, betrayed, angry,* etc. Have them define each word and give an example of how someone with that feeling would act. Then have students make lists of related words, such as *bitterness, embittered, bitterly; betrayed, betrayal, traitor;* and so forth, and use each in a sentence. Finally, students might draw pictures of faces showing these emotions or list actions that could result from these feelings.

Versailles represented, as one observer noted, "a peace built on quicksand." Indeed, that quicksand eventually would give way. In a little more than two decades, the treaties' legacy of bitterness would help plunge the world into another catastrophic war.

The Legacy of the War

World War I was, in many ways, a new kind of war. It involved the use of new technologies. It ushered in the notion of war on a grand and global scale. It also left behind a landscape of death and destruction such as was never before seen.

The War's Extreme Cost Both sides in World War I paid a tremendous price in terms of human life. About 8.5 million soldiers died as a result of the war. Another 21 million more were wounded. In addition, the war led to the death of countless civilians by way of starvation, disease, and slaughter. Taken together, these figures spelled tragedy—an entire generation of Europeans wiped out.

The war also had a devastating economic impact on Europe. The great conflict drained the treasuries of Europe. One account put the total cost of the war at $338 billion—a staggering amount for that time. The war also destroyed acres of farmland, as well as homes, villages, and towns.

A Lost Generation The enormous suffering and apparent pointlessness of the Great War left a deep mark on Western society as well. A sense of disillusionment settled over the survivors. The insecurity and despair that many people experienced are reflected in the art and literature of the time. In a poem written in 1919, the Russian poet Anna Akhmatova captured these feelings:

> **A VOICE FROM THE PAST**
> Why is our century worse than any other?
> Is it that in the stupor of fear and grief
> It has plunged its fingers in the blackest ulcer,
> Yet cannot bring relief?
>
> Westward the sun is dropping,
> And the roofs of towns are shining in its light.
> Already death is chalking doors with crosses
> And calling the ravens and the ravens are in flight.
>
> **ANNA AKHMATOVA**, from *You Will Hear Thunder*, translated by D. M. Thomas

The Great War shook European society to its foundations. While the war would continue to haunt future generations, its more immediate impact was to help ignite one of the most significant events of the 20th century. In Chapter 14, you will learn about that event: the Russian Revolution.

Section 4 Assessment

1. TERMS & NAMES

Identify
- Woodrow Wilson
- Georges Clemenceau
- David Lloyd George
- Fourteen Points
- self-determination
- Treaty of Versailles
- League of Nations

2. TAKING NOTES

Using a web diagram like the one below, show the effects of World War I.

Effects of WWI

Which effect do you think was most significant? Why?

3. FORMING OPINIONS

Do you think the peace settlements at Versailles were fair? Why or why not? Consider the warring and nonwarring nations affected.

THINK ABOUT
- Germany's punishment
- the creation of new nations
- the mandate system

4. THEME ACTIVITY

Power and Authority In small groups, create a list of 8-10 interview questions a reporter might ask Wilson, Clemenceau, or Lloyd George about the Paris Peace Conference. Ask about such topics as:

- Wilson's Fourteen Points
- the handling of Germany and Russia
- the numerous demands from different nations and groups

The Great War **383**

TERMS & NAMES

1. Triple Alliance, p. 364
2. Triple Entente, p. 365
3. Central Powers, p. 368
4. Allies, p. 368
5. trench warfare, p. 369
6. total war, p. 375
7. armistice, p. 377
8. Fourteen Points, p. 380
9. Treaty of Versailles, p. 381
10. League of Nations, p. 381

REVIEW QUESTIONS

Answers will vary.

11. Nationalism and imperialism intensified rivalries between nations, while militarism led countries to increase the size of their armies.

12. The Balkans, which are home to many ethnic groups, had a long history of nationalist uprising and ethnic clashes.

13. Germany's defeat there meant that it had to abandon the Schlieffen Plan and fight a two-front war.

14. The Western Front extended across northern France from the North Sea to the Swiss border. The Eastern Front stretched along the German and Russian border.

15. Military stalemate, huge losses on both sides, miserable living conditions, and little territorial gain.

16. The campaign was an attempt to conquer the Dardanelles and Constantinople and eventually establish a supply line to Russia.

17. Unrestricted submarine warfare, the Zimmermann note, a common bond with and sympathy toward the Allies.

18. Governments devoted all their resources to winning the war. They took control of the economy, converted many industries to munitions factories, put numerous citizens to work, used propaganda and censorship, and instituted a policy of rationing.

19. The League of Nations was created to keep peace among nations by settling world conflicts through negotiation.

20. The mandate system was a means by which the Allied countries governed former Central Powers' colonies and territories until they were deemed ready for independence. These groups wanted independence, and they saw the mandate system as just another form of colonialism.

Visual Summary

The Great War

Long-Term Causes

- Nationalism spurs competition among European nations.
- Imperialism deepens national rivalries.
- Militarism leads to large standing armies.
- The alliance system divides Europe into two rival camps.

Immediate Causes

- The assassination of Archduke Franz Ferdinand in June 1914 prompts Austria to declare war on Serbia.
- The alliance system requires nations to support their allies. European countries declare war on one another.

WORLD WAR I

Immediate Effects

- A generation of Europeans are killed or wounded.
- Dynasties fall in Germany, Austria-Hungary, and Russia.
- New countries are created.
- The League of Nations is established to help promote peace.

Long-Term Effects

- Many nations feel bitter and betrayed by the peace settlements.
- Problems that helped cause the war—nationalism, competition—remain.

TERMS & NAMES

Briefly explain the importance of each of the following regarding World War I.

1. Triple Alliance
2. Triple Entente
3. Central Powers
4. Allies
5. trench warfare
6. total war
7. armistice
8. Fourteen Points
9. Treaty of Versailles
10. League of Nations

REVIEW QUESTIONS

SECTION 1 *(pages 363–366)*
The Stage Is Set for War

11. How did nationalism, imperialism, and militarism help set the stage for World War I?

12. Why were the Balkans known as "the powder keg of Europe"?

SECTION 2 *(pages 367–371)*
War Consumes Europe

13. Why was the first Battle of the Marne considered so significant?

14. Where was the Western Front? the Eastern Front?

15. What were the characteristics of trench warfare?

SECTION 3 *(pages 373–377)*
War Affects the World

16. What was the purpose of the Gallipoli campaign?

17. What factors prompted the United States to enter the war?

18. In what ways was World War I a total war?

SECTION 4 *(pages 380–383)*
A Flawed Peace

19. What was the purpose of the League of Nations?

20. What was the mandate system, and why did it leave many groups feeling betrayed?

Interact *with* History

On page 362, you examined whether you would keep your word and follow your ally into war. Now that you have read the chapter, reevaluate your decision.

If you chose to support your ally, do you still feel it was the right thing to do? Why or why not?

If you decided to break your pledge and stay out of war, what are your feelings now? Discuss your opinions with a small group.

Interact *with* History

Possible Responses: Students who originally wanted to support an ally might feel that the carnage of the war exposed their position as foolish, or they might feel that such loyalty is necessary in international affairs. Those who decided to stay out of the war may feel that the massive number of deaths justified their decision.

CRITICAL THINKING

1. ALLIED LEADERS

THEME POWER AND AUTHORITY Often, it is the people in power who determine events and make history. How did the Treaty of Versailles reflect the different personalities and agendas of the men in power at the end of World War I?

2. THE ALLIANCE SYSTEM

Trace the formation of the two major alliance systems that dominated Europe on the eve of World War I by providing the event that corresponds with each date on the chart.

3. A HOLLOW VICTORY

Winston Churchill, Great Britain's prime minister in the 1940s and 1950s, was under-secretary of the British navy during World War I. He said that the Allied victory in World War I had been "bought so dear [high in price] as to be indistinguishable from defeat." What did he mean by this statement? Use examples from the text to support your answer.

4. ANALYZING PRIMARY SOURCES

The following quotation is from an editorial in the German newspaper *Vossische Zeitung* on May 18, 1915. It is in response to President Wilson's protest to the German government after the sinking of the British passenger ship *Lusitania*. The writer believes that Americans were aboard the ship to deter a possible attack against the ship—and its war cargo.

A VOICE FROM THE PAST
The responsibility for the death of so many American citizens, which is deeply regretted by everyone in Germany, in a large measure falls upon the American government. It could not admit that Americans were being used as shields for English contraband [smuggled goods]. In this regard America had permitted herself to be misused in a disgraceful manner by England. And now, instead of calling England to account, she sends a note to the German government.

- Why does the writer hold the American government responsible for the deaths of the Americans on board?
- How does this paragraph reinforce the idea that history can be based on different points of view?

CHAPTER ACTIVITIES

1. LIVING HISTORY: Unit Portfolio Project

THEME SCIENCE AND TECHNOLOGY Your unit portfolio project focuses on how science and technology have influenced history. (See page 359.) For Chapter 13, you might use one of the following ideas to add to your portfolio:

- Write a piece of historical fiction describing a World War I airplane battle.
- After doing further research, write a brief report describing what life was like aboard a German U-boat.
- Using images from magazines and books, create a display to show how technology affects warfare.

2. CONNECT TO TODAY: Cooperative Learning

THEME ECONOMICS While World War I was extremely costly, staying prepared for the possibility of war today is also expensive.

Work with a small team to present the military and defense budgets of several of the world's nations.

 Use the Internet and other resources to research the topic. Have each group member be responsible for one country.

- Examine how much money each country spends on military and defense, as well as what percentage of the overall budget it represents.
- Combine your research on a large chart and present it to the class.
- Discuss whether the amounts spent for military and defense are justified.

3. INTERPRETING A TIME LINE

Revisit the unit time line on pages 358–359. Examine the Chapter 13 time line. For each event, draw an image or symbol that represents that event.

FOCUS ON GRAPHS

This graph provides the total number of troops mobilized, as well as the number of military deaths each major nation suffered in World War I.

- Which nation suffered the most deaths? Which one suffered the least?
- Which nations had more than a million soldiers killed?

Connect to History

Based on the number of troops each side mobilized, what may be one reason the Allies won?

World War I Battlefield Deaths

Total Number of Troops Mobilized

Allied Powers: 42 million

Central Powers: 23 million

Battlefield Deaths of Major Combatants

- USA 116,000
- Ottoman Empire 325,000
- Italy 650,000
- *British Empire 908,000
- Austria-Hungary 1.2 million
- France 1.3 million
- Russia 1.7 million
- Germany 1.8 million

*Includes troops from Britain, Canada, Australia, New Zealand, India, and South Africa
Source: *Encyclopaedia Britannica*

The Great War **385**

---

1. LIVING HISTORY

Standards for Evaluation
A historical fiction selection should meet the following criteria:

- Shows evidence of research into the air war.
- Identifies one pilot from each side.
- Presents the feelings and political beliefs of the opposing pilots.
- Describes the action of the battle, including who won and who lost.

Standards for Evaluation
A report should meet the following criteria:

- Shows evidence of research into U-boat life during World War I.
- Presents a picture of the daily chores carried out by a U-boat crew.
- Includes feelings of the crew members about being inside such a device over a long period of time.

Standards for Evaluation
A display should meet the following criteria:

- Shows evidence of library research.
- Arranges the graphic material to show cause-and-effect relationships between technology and weaponry.
- Gives examples of war technology that is no longer used or that has been replaced by new technology.

2. CONNECT TO TODAY

Research on military budgets should:

- Give examples for each of the countries considered.
- Arrange the budget into areas of spending—weapons, personnel, etc.
- Show comparison-and-contrast graphs among budgets in order to make points about spending.

3. INTERPRETING A TIME LINE

Students' images or symbols should capture something essential about the events they are meant to describe.

FOCUS ON GRAPHS

- Germany suffered the most deaths, the U.S. the fewest.
- Germany, Russia, France, Austria-Hungary

Connect to History *Possible Responses:*
The Allies had over 42 million troops versus 23 million for the Central Powers. The Allies had a decided advantage in the number of troops they could put in the field.

CRITICAL THINKING

1. ALLIED LEADERS

League of Nations provision reflected Wilson's desire for lasting peace. Harsh terms reflected European leaders' desires to punish Germany.

2. THE ALLIANCE SYSTEM

1879—Germany and Austria-Hungary form the Dual Alliance; 1882—Italy joins Germany and Austria-Hungary, forming the Triple Alliance; 1887—Germany and Russia forge a treaty; 1890—Germany lets the treaty with Russia lapse; 1891— Russia and France form a military alliance; 1907—Britain signs an entente with Russia and France, forming the Triple Entente.

3. A HOLLOW VICTORY

Churchill was referring to the fact that while the Allies won, victory had come at a terrible price: an entire generation of Europeans was lost; many European countries' treasuries were drained; farmland, towns, and villages were destroyed; and millions of citizens were left feeling disillusioned and bitter.

4. ANALYZING PRIMARY SOURCES

Possible Responses: The writer believes that the American government knew—or should have known—the ship carried war cargo. Wilson viewed the sinking of the *Lusitania* as an attack on innocent American lives. The Germans saw the *Lusitania* as a legitimate war target.

CHAPTER 14
Revolution and Nationalism

	Key Ideas	COPY MASTERS	ASSESSMENT	
SECTION 1 Revolutions in Russia pp. 389–394	The Russian Revolutions of 1917 end czarist rule and usher in the first communist government. Lenin seizes power and launches major economic and political reforms.	*In-Depth Resources: Unit 4* • **Guided Reading,** p. 19 • **Skillbuilder Practice:** Analyzing Causes, p. 23 • **Primary Source:** from Bloody Sunday, p. 26 • **History Makers:** Vladimir Lenin, p. 34	*Section 1 Assessment,* p. 394 *Formal Assessment* • Section Quiz, p. 174 *Alternative Assessment Book* • Standards for Evaluating a Cooperative Activity	
SECTION 2 Totalitarianism Case Study: Stalinist Russia pp. 395–400	After Lenin's death, Stalin transforms the Soviet Union into a totalitarian state. He revolutionizes the economy and uses terror, propaganda, and censorship to maintain power.	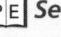 *In-Depth Resources: Unit 4* • **Guided Reading,** p. 20 • **Primary Source:** The Need for Progress, p. 27 • **Literature:** from *Darkness at Noon*, p. 30; from *1984*, p. 32	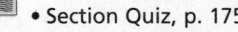 *Section 2 Assessment,* p. 400 *Formal Assessment* • Section Quiz, p. 175 *Alternative Assessment Book* • Standards for Evaluating a Cooperative Activity	
SECTION 3 Collapse of Chinese Imperial Rule pp. 401–404	In 1912, Chinese nationalists overthrow the Qing dynasty and establish a new republic. Civil war erupts as Nationalists and Communists vie for control of China.	*In-Depth Resources: Unit 4* • **Guided Reading,** p. 21 • **Primary Source:** from *The Peasants of Hunan*, p. 28 • **Geography Application:** Nationalists Battle Warlords and Communists, p. 24 • **History Makers:** Jiang Jieshi, p. 35	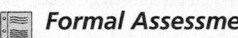 *Section 3 Assessment,* p. 404 *Formal Assessment* • Section Quiz, p. 176 *Alternative Assessment Book* • Standards for Evaluating a Cooperative Activity	
SECTION 4 Nationalism in India and Southwest Asia pp. 405–409	World War I heightens nationalist activity and independence movements to overthrow colonial power. Gandhi uses nonviolent tactics to free India from British rule. Turkey, Persia, and Arabia also seek self-rule.	*In-Depth Resources: Unit 4* • **Guided Reading,** p. 22 • **Primary Source:** from *Hind Swaraj*, p. 29	*Section 4 Assessment,* p. 409 *Formal Assessment* • Section Quiz, p. 177 *Alternative Assessment Book* • Standards for Evaluating a Cooperative Activity	
CHAPTER RESOURCES	**Chapter Overview** Social unrest in Russia erupts in revolution. Under Stalin, the USSR becomes a totalitarian state. After the Qing dynasty falls, Chinese Nationalists and Communists clash. World War II fuels nationalism in India and Southwest Asia.	*Telescoping the Times* • Chapter Summary, pp. 57–59 *Planning for Block Schedules* *Case Studies* • **Case Study 1**—India and Britain: Colonialism and Imperialism, p. 2	*Chapter Assessment,* pp. 410–411 *Chapter Activities,* p. 411 *Formal Assessment* • Chapter Test, forms A and B, pp. 178–183 Test Generator *Alternative Assessment Book*	

TECHNOLOGY

  Warm-Up Transparency 14

 World Art and Cultures Transparencies
• AT65 *Friendship of the People*

 Electronic Library of Primary Sources
from *Ten Days That Shook the World*
INTERNET RESOURCES
www.mlworldhistory.com

 Warm-Up Transparency 14

 Geography Transparencies
• GT30 European Totalitarianism by 1938

 Electronic Library of Primary Sources
• from *1984*

 INTERNET RESOURCES
www.mlworldhistory.com

 Warm-Up Transparency 14

 Electronic Library of Primary Sources
• from *Autobiography of a Chinese Girl*

 INTERNET RESOURCES
www.mlworldhistory.com

 Warm-Up Transparency 14

 World Art and Cultures Transparencies
• AT66 *Persian Musicians*

 Critical Thinking Transparencies
• CT30 Time Machine: Revolution and Nationalism
• CT66 Visual Summary

 Electronic Library of Primary Sources
• from "Nonviolence"

 INTERNET RESOURCES
www.mlworldhistory.com

 Chapter Summaries on Audiocassette in English and Spanish

 INTERNET RESOURCES
www.mlworldhistory.com

Block Scheduling (90 MINUTES)

Day 1
Section 1, pp. 389–394
 COOPERATIVE ACTIVITY
p. 392 (Teacher's Edition)
Section Assessment, p. 394

Day 2
Section 2, pp. 395–400
 COOPERATIVE ACTIVITY
p. 396 (Teacher's Edition)

Section Assessment, p. 400

Day 3
Section 3, pp. 401–404
COOPERATIVE ACTIVITY
 Commemorating the Long March, p. 403 (Teacher's Edition)
Section Assessment, p. 404

Day 4
Section 4, pp. 405–409
 COOPERATIVE ACTIVITY
Investigating Examples of Nonviolent Protests, p. 407 (Teacher's Edition)
Section Assessment, p. 409
Chapter Assessment, pp. 410–411

Yearly Pacing *Chapter 14 Total:* 4 days *Yearly Total:* 85 days

 Planning for Block Schedules

Customizing for Special Needs

Students Acquiring English

 Access for Students Acquiring English
• **Guided Reading** for Sections 1–4 (Spanish), pp. 153–156
• **Chapter Summary** (Spanish), pp. 150–152
• **Skillbuilder Practice:** Analyzing Causes (Spanish), p. 157
• **Geography Application** Nationalists Battle Warlords and Communists (Spanish), p. 158

 Spanish Reading Study Guide
• pp. 147–156

 Chapter Summaries on Audiocassette in English and Spanish

Less Proficient Readers

 In-Depth Resources: Unit 4
• **Guided Reading** for Sections 1–4, pp. 19–22
• **Skillbuilder Practice:** Analyzing Causes, p. 23
• **Geography Application:** Nationalists Battle Warlords and Communists, p. 24

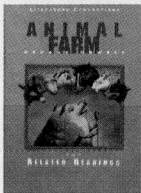 *Telescoping the Times*
• Chapter Summary, pp. 57–59

Reading Study Guide
• pp. 147–156

Chapter Summaries on Audiocassette

Gifted and Talented Students

 In-Depth Resources: Unit 4
Primary Sources:
• from *Bloody Sunday*, p. 26
• The Need for Progress, p. 27
• from *The Peasants of Hunan*, p. 28
• from *Hind Swaraj*, p. 29

History Makers:
• Vladimir Lenin, p. 34
• Jiang Jieshi, p. 35

Connections to Literature READINGS FOR STUDENTS

 In-Depth Resources: Unit 4
Literature: from *Darkness at Noon*, p. 30; from *1984*, p. 32

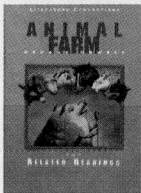 **McDougal Littell**
Literature Connections
Orwell, George
Animal Farm
(with related readings)
Satirizing the events of the Russian Revolution, this novel uses animals to comment on human society and nature.

 McDougal Littell
Literature Connections
Orwell, George
1984
(with related readings)
This novel presents a chilling vision of a future totalitarian society where the government can control individual thought and even reality itself.

 = Pupil's Edition   = Overhead Transparency   = Software   = Video

= Copy Master   = CD-ROM   = Audiocassette   = Internet

Revolution and Nationalism, 1900–1939

Accessing Prior Knowledge

- Ask students to read the captions accompanying each picture and to discuss what they already know about Russia, Turkey, and China.

Predicting and Making Inferences

- Have students examine the poster of an unveiled woman leading Mustafa Kemal on horseback. Then ask them to speculate on the political and social status of Turkish women during Kemal's presidency.

- Ask students what they can tell about the political and social unrest in Russia during the early 1900s from the painting on page 387.

Geography Connection

Ask students to study the political boundaries of the Soviet Union.

- What countries run along the Soviet Union's southern border?

- How might geography influence the relationship between the Soviet Union and these neighboring countries?

CHAPTER
14

Revolution and Nationalism, 1900–1939

PREVIEWING THEMES

Revolution
Widespread social unrest in China and Russia during the late 1800s and early 1900s eventually erupted in revolutions. Both countries overthrew autocratic dynasties that had ruled for centuries.

Science & Technology
After World War I, leaders in Russia, China, and Turkey launched new programs to modernize their countries. Advances in technology boosted industrial production. These countries were then able to resist foreign control and to compete in world affairs.

Economics
The gap between rich and poor, especially in Russia and China, was enormous. Growing resentment against economic injustice became a major cause of revolutionary activity.

INTERNET CONNECTION
Visit us at **www.mlworldhistory.com** to learn more about the revolutions in Russia and China, Gandhi's strategy of nonviolent resistance, and related topics.

SOVIET UNION, 1939

ARCTIC OCEAN

Norweigian Sea

Baltic Sea

• Leningrad (St. Petersburg)

RUSSIA

North Sea

• Moscow • Kazan

• Rostov

Aral Sea

Black Sea

Caspian Sea

TURKEY

PERSIA/IRAN

Persian Gulf

Red Sea

SAUDI ARABIA

Arabia Sea

ATLANTIC OCEAN

386

In **1923**, **Mustafa Kemal**, as president of the new **Republic of Turkey**, favored greater freedom for women. He scorned the Turkish social custom requiring women to wear veils in public. "What is the sense in this behavior?" Kemal asked. "It makes the nation look ridiculous." In this poster, an unveiled woman leads Kemal on horseback.

INDIAN OCEAN

GEOGRAPHY THEMES

Location

Point out that the former Soviet Union was by far the largest country in the world. This vast nation spread across two continents, Europe and Asia. The Soviet Union covered an area of about 8.6 million square miles—roughly two and one half times the size of the United States and almost one-sixth of the Earth's total land surface.

The Soviet Union stretches so far from west to east that it is crossed by eleven standard time zones. Ask students to name the labeled regions that line the Soviet Union's southern border in 1939. *Turkey, Iran, Xinjiang, Outer Mongolia, Manchuria*

Place

Much of the former Soviet Union has long, cold winters because of its northerly location and great distance from the warming effect of the oceans. In addition, the area is cut off from the flow of warm southern air by the large chains of mountains that rim its southern border from the Black Sea to the Pacific Ocean. In fact, the coldest temperatures in the world, besides Antarctica, have been recorded in north central Siberia. Winter temperatures are commonly as low as –60°F (–51°C).

Ask students to discuss why throughout much of Russian history criminals and political prisoners were sent to Siberia.

ADDITIONAL RESOURCES

Books for the Teacher

• Pipes, Richard. *A Concise History of the Russian Revolution.* New York: Knopf, 1995.

• Leone, Bruno. *Nationalism: Opposing Viewpoints.* St. Paul: Greenhaven, 1986.

Books for the Student

• Faber, Doris. *Mahatma Gandhi.* New York: Messner, 1986.

• Vail, John J. *Peace, Land, Bread! A History of the Russian Revolution.* New York: Facts on File, 1995.

▄▄▄ Videos

• *Gandhi.* Cambridge Social Studies, 1990. 800-468-4227.

• *The Incredible March.* Ambrose Video, 1997. 800-526-4663.

• *Doctor Zhivago.* Dir. David Lean. MGM/UA Home Videos, 1965.

◎ Software

• *The Russian Revolution.* CD-ROM. Society for Visual Education, 1994. 800-829-1900. Overview of the causes, events, and aftermath of the 1917 revolution.

• *Seeds of Discord (1933–1936).* CD-ROM. AIMS, 1986. 800-367-2467. World political and social changes, including struggles in India and China.

In January **1905**, about 200,000 workers and their families marched to the czar's royal palace in **St. Petersburg.** The marchers demanded reforms. Soldiers fired on the unarmed crowd. An eyewitness described the slaughter, known as "Bloody Sunday": "With shouts and cries, the procession scattered, and the dead and wounded lay upon the snow."

SIBERIA

• Tomsk • Krasnoyarsk

msk

Chita

OUTER MONGOLIA

MANCHURIA

XINJIANG

INNER MONGOLIA

Vladivostok

Sea of Okhotsk

PACIFIC OCEAN

Sea of Japan

40°N

CHINA

Yellow Sea

INDIA

In 1911, revolutionaries staged uprisings throughout **China** to overthrow the Qing Dynasty. In February **1912**, they forced **Puyi**, the six-year-old emperor, to give up his throne. Puyi took his place in history as China's last emperor.

Bay of Bengal

South China Sea

Philippine Sea

Tropic of Cancer

0 500 Miles
0 1,000 Kilometers

387

HISTORY THROUGH ART

Shooting of the Workers at the Winter Palace in Petersburg, January 1905

N. Vladimirov

The Russian artist N. Vladimirov captures a compelling image from Bloody Sunday—unarmed workers as the victims of senseless violence. Presenting history as an art form has a long tradition. Paintings, like photos, are visual sources that can provide information and opinions about issues or events.

As paintings are artists' interpretations of events and photos show actual events, are photos more historically reliable? Compare Vladimirov's painting of Bloody Sunday to photos of public demonstrations. A close-up of someone being clubbed can give a very different impression than a view of the entire crowd. Publishing the close-up, rather than the broader perspective, affects what people think of the event. Similarly, Vladimirov's choice of painting a close-up view of the victims, rather than the palace guards,

also influences the way people might view this famous event in Russia's past. Both historical paintings and photos are interpretive pictures that typically convey a negative or positive view of an event, person, or group.

Interpreting the Art: What is your emotional response to the painting? In what ways is the painting like a visual editorial?

Interact *with* History

Purpose

This Interact with History feature motivates students by inviting them to put themselves in a fictional historical setting—a country on the brink of revolution. As students imagine that they are at the center of revolutionary activity, they will analyze the issues surrounding the use of violence and nonviolence to bring about change.

Purpose

• to set the stage for studying revolutionary activity in Russia, China, and India

• to help students understand revolutionary tactics and their impact

• to help students make connections between people and events in the chapter

Teaching Strategy

Thinking Critically After students have imagined themselves in the situation described on this page, have them answer the key questions and give reasons to support their opinion.

EXAMINING *the* ISSUES

Following are suggestions for addressing each bulleted question.

1 Students might cite instances of people using violence in self-defense.

2 Have students describe religious beliefs, such as "turning the other cheek."

3 Have students discuss why nonviolent groups might be perceived as either weak or intimidating.

4 Have students brainstorm possible outcomes resulting from the use of violence in revolutions.

Making Connections Ask students to discuss what they know about Dr. Martin Luther King's nonviolent protests.

Interact *with* History

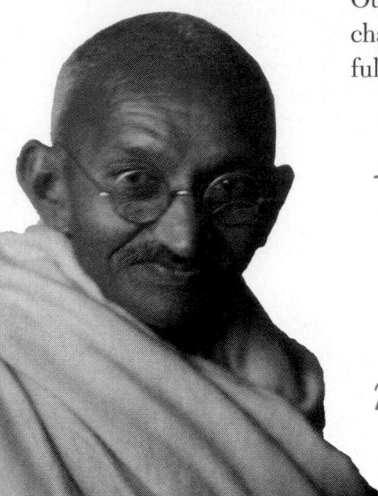

In 1920, Mohandas K. Gandhi became the leader of the independence movement to free India of British rule.

You are living in a country in which the government benefits a small, wealthy class and ignores the demands of the vast majority. Thousands of poor peasants and workers have few rights.

The government has failed to tackle economic, social, and political problems. Various revolutionary groups are all clamoring for change. Some groups call for a violent overthrow of the government. Others believe in battling injustice and achieving change through nonviolent methods, such as peaceful strikes and protests.

In the late 1920s, Communist leader Mao Zedong believed revolution would solve China's problems.

How do you resist oppressive rule— with violent or nonviolent action?

"[Nonviolent] resistance . . . is superior to the force of arms . . . One who is free from hatred requires no sword."

"A revolution is not a dinner party . . . A revolution is an insurrection, an act of violence by which one class overthrows another."

EXAMINING *the* ISSUES

• What situations might provoke some people to take violent steps to achieve change?

• What strengths would a person need to remain nonviolent in the face of violent attacks?

• How might armed and powerful opponents respond to groups committed to nonviolent action?

• Which strategy—violence or nonviolence—would prove more successful and bring more long-lasting consequences? Why?

As a class, discuss these questions. In your discussion, consider what you have learned about the strategies revolutionaries used to accomplish change in other countries, such as France, the United States, Brazil, Mexico, Haiti, and so on.

As you read about the revolutions in Russia and China and the independence movement in India, see which strategy was used and rate its effectiveness for achieving change.

388 Chapter 14

Follow Up

A feature on the chapter assessment will ask students to reevaluate their response to the situation presented on this page.

1 Revolutions in Russia

TERMS & NAMES
- pogrom
- Trans-Siberian Railway
- Bolsheviks
- V. I. Lenin
- Duma
- Rasputin
- provisional government
- soviet

MAIN IDEA	WHY IT MATTERS NOW
Long-term social unrest in Russia erupted in revolution, ushering in the first Communist government.	The Communist Party controlled the Soviet Union until the country's breakup in 1991.

SETTING THE STAGE The Russian Revolution was like a firecracker with a very long fuse. The explosion came in 1917. Yet the fuse had been burning for nearly a century. The cruel, oppressive rule of most 19th-century czars caused widespread social unrest for decades. Anger over social inequalities and the ruthless treatment of peasants grew. The czars' unfair governing sparked many violent reactions. Army officers revolted in 1825. Hundreds of peasants rioted. Secret revolutionary groups formed and plotted to overthrow the government. In 1881, student revolutionaries were angry over the slow pace of political change. They assassinated the reform-minded czar, Alexander II. Russia was heading toward a full-scale revolution.

Alexander III Upholds the Autocracy

In 1881, Alexander III succeeded his father, Alexander II, to the throne and halted all reforms in Russia. Like his grandfather, Nicholas I, Alexander III clung to the principles of autocracy, a government in which he had total power. Alexander III was determined to strengthen "autocracy, orthodoxy, and nationality." Anyone who questioned the absolute authority of the czar, worshiped outside the Russian Orthodox Church, or spoke a language other than Russian was tagged as dangerous.

To wipe out revolutionaries, Alexander III used harsh measures. He imposed strict censorship codes on published materials and written documents, including private letters. His secret police carefully watched both secondary schools and universities. Teachers had to send detailed reports on every student. Political prisoners were exiled to Siberia, a region of eastern and central Russia.

To establish a uniform Russian culture, Alexander III oppressed other national groups within Russia. He made Russian the official language of the empire and forbade the use of minority languages, such as Polish, in schools. Alexander made Jews the target of persecution. He subjected them to new laws that encouraged prejudice. Jews could not buy land or live among other Russians. Universities set strict quotas for Jewish students. A wave of **pogroms**—organized violence against Jews—broke out in many parts of Russia. Police and soldiers stood by and watched Russian citizens loot and destroy Jewish homes, stores, and synagogues.

Alexander III turned Russia into a police state, teeming with spies and informers.

THINK THROUGH HISTORY
A. Summarizing
What methods did Alexander III use to maintain his authority over the Russian people?
A. Possible Answers Censorship, secret police, religious persecution, discrimination against minorities

Nicholas II Resists Change

When Nicholas II became czar in 1894, he announced, "The principle of autocracy will be maintained by me as firmly and unswervingly as by my lamented father [Alexander III]." Nicholas stubbornly refused to surrender any of his power. His trust in the tradition of Russian autocracy blinded him to the changing conditions of his times. Yet the sweeping forces of change would override his pledge to preserve the czarist rule of Russia's past.

Revolution and Nationalism **389**

Section 1 Overview

OBJECTIVES

1. To describe the autocratic methods of Alexander III.
2. To explain the economic changes under Nicholas II.
3. To summarize crises that paved the way for revolution.
4. To describe the March Revolution and end of czarist rule.
5. To summarize the Bolshevik Revolution and its outcome.
6. To explain Lenin's reforms.

SKILLBUILDERS
- Interpreting charts, p. 392
- Interpreting maps: region, p. 393

CRITICAL THINKING
- Summarizing, p. 389
- Analyzing causes, p. 390
- Making inferences, pp. 372, 374
- Identifying problems, p. 393
- Evaluating decisions, p. 394
- Analyzing themes, p. 394

FOCUS
5-Minute Warm-Up

▶ **Making Inferences**
To acquaint students with a key Russian figure, have them answer these questions.

1. Read the History Makers on page 391. How did Rasputin die?
2. Why was Rasputin considered mysterious and dangerous?

WARM-UP TRANSPARENCY 14

OBJECTIVE ① INSTRUCT

Alexander III Upholds the Autocracy

▶ **Key Ideas**
- Alexander III rejects reform.
- Alexander oppresses minorities.

IN-DEPTH RESOURCES: UNIT 4
Guided Reading, p. 19

ACCESS FOR STUDENTS ACQUIRING ENGLISH
Guided Reading (Spanish), p. 153

SECTION 1 RESOURCES

PRINT RESOURCES

IN-DEPTH RESOURCES: UNIT 4
Guided Reading, p. 19
Skillbuilder Practice: Analyzing Causes, p. 23
Primary Source: from Bloody Sunday, p. 26
History Makers: Vladimir Lenin, p. 34

ACCESS FOR STUDENTS ACQUIRING ENGLISH
Guided Reading (Spanish), p. 153
Skillbuilder Practice: (Spanish), p. 157

FORMAL ASSESSMENT
Section Quiz, p. 174

ALTERNATIVE ASSESSMENT BOOK

TECHNOLOGY RESOURCES

WORLD ART AND CULTURES TRANSPARENCIES
AT65 *Friendship of the People*

CD-ROM
Electronic Library of Primary Sources

INTERNET www.mlworldhistory.com

Teacher's Edition **389**

Nicholas II Resists Change

(See page 389.)

▶ **Key Ideas**

- Nicholas II vows to maintain autocratic rule.
- The rapid buildup of Russian industry helps the country prosper.
- Worker exploitation spurs the growth of revolutionary movements.

SPOTLIGHT On

The Trans-Siberian Railway

The Trans-Siberian Railway crossed huge forests, immense bogs, and open steppes. Railroad workers constructed dozens of tunnels through mountains and countless bridges over rivers. Have students research the difficulties in building the Trans-Siberian Railway.

Crises at Home and Abroad

▶ **Key Ideas**

- Russia's defeat in the Russo-Japanese War sparks unrest.
- Russia's first parliament is formed after the Revolution of 1905.
- Russia faces defeats and food shortages during World War I.

 IN-DEPTH RESOURCES: UNIT 4
Primary Source: from Bloody Sunday, p. 26

SPOTLIGHT On

The Trans-Siberian Railway

The Trans-Siberian Railway ran about 5,800 miles across the vast area of Siberia, from Moscow to the city of Vladivostok on the Sea of Japan. Like the transcontinental railroad in the United States (built from 1863 to 1869), the Trans-Siberian Railway was constructed over difficult terrain and completed in sections.

To celebrate the opening of the Trans-Siberian Railway, Czar Nicholas II had the jewelry firm of Fabergé create a golden Easter egg (shown below) for Czarina Alexandra. The inscription on the silver band encircling the egg reads, "Great Siberian Railway, 1900." Hidden inside the egg is a wonderful surprise—a miniature replica of a train studded with precious gems. The tiny engine is actually a wind-up toy that can pull the cars attached to it.

Economic Growth and Its Impact At the beginning of Nicholas II's reign, Russia lagged behind the industrial nations of western Europe. In the 1890s, Sergey Witte (VYEET·tyih), the czar's most capable minister, launched a program to move the country forward. Through higher taxes and foreign investments, Witte helped finance the buildup of Russian industries. The number of factories more than doubled between 1863 and 1900. Witte's steps also boosted the growth of heavy industry, particularly steel. By around 1900, Russia had become the world's fourth-ranking producer of steel. Only the United States, Germany, and Great Britain produced more steel.

Witte also pushed for the building of the great **Trans-Siberian Railway**—the world's longest continuous rail line. With the help of British and French investors, work began in 1891. The Trans-Siberian Railway was completed in 1904. It connected European Russia in the west with Russian ports on the Pacific Ocean in the east.

The Revolutionary Movement Grows Rapid industrialization also stirred discontent among the people of Russia. The growth of factories brought new problems. Among these problems were grueling working conditions, miserably low wages, and child labor. Trade unions were outlawed. Still, exploited laborers who worked in factories and built the railway lines organized strikes. Workers were unhappy with their low standard of living and lack of political power. The gap between rich and poor was enormous.

Amid the widespread unrest of workers and other members of Russian society, various revolutionary movements began to grow. They also competed for power. The group that would eventually succeed in establishing a new government in Russia followed the views of Karl Marx. These revolutionaries believed that the industrial class of workers would overthrow the czar. The industrial class would then form "a dictatorship of the proletariat." In such a state, the workers would rule.

In 1903, Russian Marxists split into two groups over revolutionary tactics. The Mensheviks (MEHN·shuh·vihks) wanted a broad base of popular support for the revolution. The **Bolsheviks** (BOHL·shuh·vihks) supported a small number of committed revolutionaries willing to sacrifice everything for radical change.

The major leader of the Bolsheviks was Vladimir Ilyich Ulyanov (ool·YAH·nuhf). He adopted the name of **Lenin.** He had an engaging personality and was an excellent organizer. He was also ruthless. These traits would ultimately help him gain command of the Bolsheviks. In the early 1900s, Lenin fled to western Europe to avoid arrest by the czarist regime. He maintained contact with other Bolsheviks. Lenin then waited until he could safely return to Russia.

Crises at Home and Abroad

The revolutionaries would not have to wait long to realize their visions. Between 1904 and 1917, Russia faced a series of crises. These events showed the czar's weakness and paved the way for revolution.

The Russo-Japanese War In the late 1800s, Russia and Japan were imperialist powers. They both competed for control of Korea and Manchuria. The two nations signed a series of agreements over the territories, but Russia broke them. In retaliation, Japan attacked the Russians at Port Arthur, Manchuria, in February 1904.

Though Russian soldiers and sailors went confidently to war, the Japanese defeated them. News of repeated losses sparked unrest at home and led to revolt in the midst of the war.

390 Chapter 14

Vocabulary
minister: person in charge of an area of government, such as finance.

B. Possible Answer Exploitation of factory workers and the huge gap between the rich and poor caused discontent.

THINK THROUGH HISTORY
B. Analyzing Causes Why did industrialization in Russia lead to unrest?

Background
Karl Marx, a 19th-century German philosopher, argued that the workers of the world would one day overthrow the ruling class and share equally in society's wealth.

Explaining the Skill Analyzing causes is the skill historians use to investigate *why* events in the past happened. Historical events, such as social unrest and revolutionary movements, often stem from a number of reasons, or multiple causes. Analyzing causes helps historians see how a series of events are related.

Applying the Skill: *Think Through History Question* To answer the question, suggest that students use the following strategy. Ask them to reread the first two paragraphs under the subheading "The Revolutionary Movement Grows." Then have them create a multiple-causes chart to analyze conditions related to industrialization that created social unrest

Causes

| Exploitation of factory workers |
| • grueling working conditions |
| • miserably low wages |
| • child labor |

| Huge gap between rich and poor |
| • low standard of living among factory workers |

Outcome

| Social unrest |
| • labor strikes |
| • revolutionary activity |

IN-DEPTH RESOURCES: UNIT 4
Skillbuilder Practice: Analyzing Causes, p. 23

Bloody Sunday: The Revolution of 1905 On January 22, 1905, about 200,000 workers and their families approached the czar's Winter Palace in St. Petersburg. They carried a petition asking for better working conditions, more personal freedom, and an elected national legislature. Nicholas II was not at the palace. His generals and police chiefs were. They ordered the soldiers to fire on the crowd. Between 500 and 1,000 unarmed people were killed. Russians quickly named the event "Bloody Sunday." Lenin called the incident a "dress rehearsal" for the later revolution that would usher in a Communist regime.

Bloody Sunday provoked a wave of strikes and violence that spread across the country. Though Nicholas still opposed reform, in October 1905 he reluctantly promised more freedom. He approved the creation of the **Duma** (DOO·muh)—Russia's first parliament. The first Duma met in May 1906. Its leaders were moderates who wanted Russia to become a constitutional monarchy similar to Britain. Hesitant to share his power, the czar dissolved the Duma after ten weeks. Other Dumas would meet later. Yet none would have real power to make sweeping reforms.

World War I: The Final Blow In 1914, Nicholas II made the fateful decision to drag Russia into World War I. Russia, though, was unprepared to handle the military and economic costs. Russia's weak generals and poorly equipped troops were no match for the German army. Before a year had passed, more than 4 million Russian soldiers had been killed, wounded, or taken prisoner. German machine guns mowed down advancing Russians by the thousands. Defeat followed defeat. As in the Russo-Japanese War, Russia's involvement in World War I revealed the weaknesses of czarist rule and military leadership.

In 1915, Nicholas moved his headquarters to the war front. From there, he hoped to rally his discouraged troops to victory. His wife, Czarina Alexandra, ran the government while he was away. She ignored the czar's chief advisers. Instead, she continued to fall under the influence of the mysterious **Rasputin** (ras·PYOO·tihn)—a self-described "holy man." He claimed to have magical healing powers.

Alexis, Nicholas and Alexandra's son, suffered from hemophilia, a life-threatening disease. Rasputin seemed to ease the boy's symptoms. To show her gratitude, Alexandra allowed Rasputin to make key political decisions. He opposed reform measures and obtained powerful positions for his friends. He spread corruption throughout the royal court. In 1916, a group of nobles murdered Rasputin. They feared his increasing role in government affairs.

Meanwhile, the war was destroying the morale of Russian troops. Soldiers mutinied, deserted, or ignored orders. On the homefront, food and fuel supplies were dwindling. Prices were wildly inflated. People from all classes were clamoring for change and an end to the war. Neither Nicholas nor Alexandra proved capable of tackling these enormous problems.

The March Revolution

In March 1917, women textile workers in Petrograd led a citywide strike. Soon afterward, riots flared up over shortages of bread and fuel. Nearly 200,000 workers swarmed the streets. At first the soldiers obeyed orders to shoot the rioters but later sided with them. The soldiers fired at their commanding officers and joined the rebellion. Large crowds gathered, shouting "Down with the autocracy!" and "Down with the war!"

Revolution and Nationalism **391**

Vocabulary
constitutional monarchy: a form of government in which a single ruler heads the state and shares authority with elected lawmakers.

Background
Hemophilia is a rare blood disease in which blood fails to clot. A deep cut may cause uncontrollable bleeding.

Background
St. Petersburg was renamed Petrograd in 1914 because the original name seemed too German. In 1924, the name was changed to Leningrad. In 1991, the name St. Petersburg was restored.

HISTORY MAKERS

**Rasputin
1872–1916**
Born a peasant in Siberia, Rasputin became a religious teacher, although he was never ordained as a priest. The sinister monk seemed to cast a hypnotic spell on people, especially Czarina Alexandra and her ailing son. Rasputin's reputation for having mysterious powers followed him to his grave.

In December 1916, a small group of young aristocrats plotted his assassination because he was reportedly taking control of the government. They lured him to a mansion and fed him poisoned cakes. The poison apparently had no effect on Rasputin's extraordinary strength. The conspirators then shot him several times. Assuming he was finally dead, they threw him in the Neva River. When his body was discovered three days later, doctors confirmed the cause of his death—drowning.

Rasputin's death threw the czarina into shock. His prediction haunted her: "If I die or you desert me, in six months you will lose your son and your throne."

CONNECT to TODAY

DNA Solves the Mystery of Anastasia

For about 65 years after the execution of Czar Nicholas II and his family, a woman named Anna Anderson claimed that she was the Grand Duchess Anastasia, the czar's sole surviving daughter (circled above). According to Anna, she managed to escape her assassins.

Anna's regal manners and detailed knowledge about the Romanov family convinced many that she was telling the truth. Others believed she was a fraud seeking personal gain. Anna held fast to her story until her death in 1984.

In 1993, scientists finally solved the 75-year-old mystery. Prince Philip of Britain is a living descendant of Czarina Alexandra. Scientists compared his DNA to Anna Anderson's. The DNA proved that Anna was not a blood relative of the Romanovs. Instead, she carried the DNA of Polish peasants.

The Czar Steps Down The local protest exploded into a general uprising—the March Revolution. It forced Czar Nicholas II to abdicate his throne. A year later revolutionaries executed Nicholas and his family. The czarist rule of the Romanovs, which spanned over three centuries, had finally collapsed. The March Revolution succeeded in bringing down the czar. Yet it failed to set up a strong government to replace his regime.

Leaders of the Duma established a **provisional government**, or temporary government. It was eventually headed by Alexander Kerensky. His decision to continue fighting the war cost him the support of both soldiers and civilians. As the war dragged on, conditions inside Russia worsened. Angry peasants demanded land. City workers grew more radical. Social revolutionaries, competing for power, formed soviets. **Soviets** were local councils consisting of workers, peasants, and soldiers. In many cities, especially Petrograd, the soviets had more influence than the provisional government.

Lenin Returns to Russia The Germans launched their own "secret weapon" that would erode the provisional government's authority. They arranged Lenin's return to Russia after many years of exile. The Germans believed that Lenin and his Bolshevik supporters would stir unrest in Russia and hurt the Russian war effort. Traveling in a sealed railway boxcar, Lenin reached Petrograd in April 1917.

The Bolshevik Revolution

Lenin and the Bolsheviks recognized their opportunity to seize power. They soon gained control of the Petrograd soviet, as well as the soviets in other major Russian cities. By the fall of 1917, people in the cities were rallying to the call, "All power to the soviets." Lenin's slogan—"Peace, Land, and Bread"—was gaining widespread appeal. Lenin decided to take action.

The Provisional Government Topples In November 1917, without warning, Bolshevik Red Guards made up of armed factory workers stormed the Winter Palace in Petrograd. They took over government offices and arrested the leaders of the provisional government. The Bolshevik Revolution was over in a matter of hours. Kerensky and his colleagues disappeared almost as quickly as the czarist regime they had replaced.

Causes and Effects of Two Russian Revolutions

Causes	Russian Revolutions of 1917	Effects
• Widespread discontent among all classes of Russian society	• Abdication of Czar Nicholas	• Civil war (1918–1920)
• Agitation from revolutionaries	• Failure of provisional government	• Czar and his family killed—end of czarist rule
• Weak leadership of Czar Nicholas II	• Growing power of soviets	• Peace with Germany under Treaty of Brest-Litovsk (1918)
• Defeat in Russo-Japanese War (1905)	• Lenin's return to Russia	• Bolshevik control of government
• Bloody Sunday (1905)	• Bolshevik takeover under Lenin	• Russian economy in ruins
• Losses in World War I		
• Strikes and riots		

SKILLBUILDER: Interpreting Charts
1. *Based on the chart, form a generalization about why the Russian Revolutions occurred.*
2. *What similarities exist between the causes of the Revolution and the effects?*

Russian Revolution and Civil War, 1905–1922

Map Key:
- Western boundaries of Russia, 1905–1917
- ★ Bolshevik uprisings, 1917–1918
- Bolshevik territory, Oct. 1919
- Territories lost (Treaty of Brest-Litovsk, 1918)
- White Russian and Allied attacks, 1918–1920
- Bolshevik counterattacks, 1918–1920
- ★ Major civil war battle areas, 1918–1920
- Boundaries of Russia, 1922

Romanov family executed, 1918

Ukraine lost in Treaty of Brest-Litovsk; regained in 1922

GEOGRAPHY SKILLBUILDER: Interpreting Maps

1. **Region** What was the extent (north to south, east to west) of the Bolshevik territory in 1919?
2. **Region** What European countries were no longer within Russian boundaries by 1922 because of the Brest-Litovsk treaty?

Bolsheviks in Power

Lenin's next step was tackling the problems he inherited from czarist rule. Within days after the Bolshevik takeover, Lenin ordered that all farmland be distributed among the peasants. Lenin and the Bolsheviks gave control of factories to the workers. The Bolshevik government also signed a truce with Germany to stop all fighting on the eastern war front and began peace talks.

In March 1918, Russia and Germany signed the Treaty of Brest-Litovsk. The price of peace was costly. Russia surrendered a large chunk of its territory to Germany and its allies. The humiliating terms of this treaty triggered widespread anger among many Russians. They objected to the Bolsheviks and their policies.

D. Possible Answer Russia's involvement in World War I, social unrest, political opponents, civil war, famine

THINK THROUGH HISTORY
D. Identifying Problems What problems did Lenin and the Bolsheviks face after the revolution?

Civil War Rages in Russia

Still recovering from their painful losses of land to Germany, the Bolsheviks now faced a new challenge—stamping out their enemies at home. Their opponents formed the White Army. The revolutionary leader Leon Trotsky, who helped negotiate the Treaty of Brest-Litovsk, expertly commanded the Bolshevik Red Army. From 1918 to 1920, civil war raged in Russia. Several Western nations, including the United States, sent military aid and forces to Russia to help the White Army.

Russia's civil war proved far more deadly than the earlier revolutions. Around 15 million Russians died in the three-year struggle and in the famine that followed. The destruction and loss of life from fighting, hunger, and a worldwide flu epidemic left Russia in chaos.

In the end the Red Army triumphed and finally crushed all opposition to Bolshevik rule. The victory showed that the Bolsheviks were able both to seize power and to maintain it. Yet in the aftermath of the civil war, Lenin and the Bolsheviks faced overwhelming problems.

During the Bolshevik Revolution of 1917, these Petrograd workers seized an armored car from the provisional government's forces.

Revolution and Nationalism **393**

Teacher's Edition **393**

Lenin Restores Order

War and revolution destroyed the Russian economy. Trade was at a standstill. Industrial production dropped and many skilled workers fled to other countries. Lenin, who helped mastermind the Bolshevik Revolution, shifted his role. He turned to reviving the economy and restructuring the government.

HISTORY MAKERS

V. I. Lenin
1870–1924

A brilliant student, Lenin enrolled in law school as a young man but was expelled for taking part in a student protest meeting. In 1887, when he was 17, his brother, Alexander, was hanged for plotting to kill the czar. Legend has it that this event turned Lenin into a revolutionary.

Though Alexander's execution influenced Lenin, Lenin already harbored feelings against the government. By the early 1900s, he planned to overthrow the czar. After 1917, Russians revered him as the "Father of the Revolution."

Following Lenin's death in 1924, the government placed his tomb in Red Square in Moscow. His preserved body, encased in a bulletproof, glass-topped coffin, is still on display. Many Russians, though, favor moving Lenin's corpse away from public view.

New Economic Policy In March 1921, Lenin launched the New Economic Policy (NEP). Under the NEP, he temporarily put aside his plan for a state-controlled economy. Instead, he resorted to a small-scale version of capitalism. The reforms under the NEP allowed peasants to sell their surplus crops instead of turning them over to the government. Individuals could buy and sell goods for profit. The government kept control of major industries, banks, and means of communication. However, it did let some small factories, businesses, and farms operate under private ownership. Lenin also tried to encourage foreign investment.

Political Reforms The many different nationalities within Russia had always posed an obstacle to national unity. Lenin began political reform by organizing Russia into several self-governing republics under the central government. In 1922, the country was named the Union of Soviet Socialist Republics (USSR), in honor of the councils that helped launch the Bolshevik Revolution. Each republic was controlled from the new capital—Moscow.

The Bolsheviks also renamed their party the Communist Party. The name came from the writings of Karl Marx. He had used the word *communism* to describe the classless society that would exist after workers had seized power. In 1924, the Communists created a constitution based on socialist and democratic principles. In reality, the Communist Party held all the power. Lenin had established a dictatorship of the Communist Party, not "a dictatorship of the proletariat," as Marx had promoted.

Thanks partly to the new policies and to the peace that followed the civil war, the USSR slowly recovered. By 1928, the country's farms and factories were producing as much as they had before World War I.

Lenin did not live to see this recovery. He had several strokes and spent the last 18 months of his life as a semi-invalid. His death in 1924 opened a power struggle for control of the party and the country. You will learn about the outcome of this struggle in Section 2.

THINK THROUGH HISTORY
E. Making Inferences How did the formation of the USSR benefit both the Communist Party and the many nationalities in Russia?
E. Possible Answer Self-governing republics represented major nationalities; Communist Party controlled the republics.

Section 1 Assessment

1. TERMS & NAMES

Identify
- pogrom
- Trans-Siberian Railway
- Bolsheviks
- V. I. Lenin
- Duma
- Rasputin
- provisional government
- soviet

2. TAKING NOTES

Create a time line like the one below to show significant events during the last phases of czarist rule and the beginning of Communist rule.

```
1891        1917        1922

   1894        1921
```

Write a paragraph explaining one of these events in more detail.

3. EVALUATING DECISIONS

What do you think were Czar Nicholas II's worst errors in judgment during his rule? Why?

THINK ABOUT
- the czar's military decisions
- the political outcome of "Bloody Sunday"

4. ANALYZING THEMES

Revolution Why was Lenin's leadership crucial to the success of the Russian Revolution?

THINK ABOUT
- Lenin's personal traits
- his slogan—"Peace, Land, and Bread"
- his role in organizing the Bolsheviks
- his role after the Revolution

394 Chapter 14

ANSWERS

1. TERMS & NAMES
pogrom, p. 389
Trans-Siberian Railway, p. 390
Bolsheviks, p. 390
V. I. Lenin, p. 390
Duma, p. 391
Rasputin, p. 391
provisional government, p. 392
soviet, p. 392

2. TAKING NOTES
Possible Responses: 1891—Construction of the Trans-Siberian Railway begins. 1894—Nicholas II becomes the last Russian czar. 1917—Russian Revolution ends czarist rule. 1921—Lenin launches New Economic Policy. 1922—Union of Soviet Socialist Republics formed.

2. EVALUATING DECISIONS
Possible Responses: Involvement in the Russo-Japanese War, the czar's refusal to share power with the Duma, Russia's entry into World War I, and the czar's change of headquarters to the war front all paved the way to revolution and the end of czarist rule.

4. ANALYZING THEMES
Possible Responses: Lenin was able to win and maintain power because of his energetic, disciplined leadership; his awareness of the demands of various groups in Russian society; his careful planning; and his ability to tackle difficult problems and crises.

❷ Totalitarianism

PATTERNS OF CHANGE CASE STUDY: Stalinist Russia

TERMS & NAMES
- Joseph Stalin
- totalitarianism
- command economy
- collective farm
- kulak
- Great Purge
- socialist realism

MAIN IDEA	WHY IT MATTERS NOW
After Lenin died, Stalin seized power and transformed the Soviet Union into a totalitarian state.	More recent dictators have used Stalin's tactics for seizing total control over individuals and the state.

SETTING THE STAGE Leon Trotsky and Joseph Stalin were among Lenin's revolutionary supporters. They both helped create the Soviet state. After Lenin died, these two men became bitter rivals for control of the Communist Party. The outcome of this struggle would determine the future course of the Soviet Union. Stalin, Lenin's successor, would aim at dramatically transforming the government and controlling every aspect of citizens' lives.

Stalin Becomes Dictator

Joseph Stalin was a quiet man who rarely received much public notice. During his early days as a Bolshevik, he changed his name from Dzhugashivili (joo·guhsh·VEEL·yih) to Stalin, which means "man of steel" in Russian. The name fit well. Stalin was cold, hard, and impersonal. Lenin, unsure of his successor, began to distrust Stalin. Lenin believed that Stalin was a dangerous man. Shortly before Lenin died, he wrote, "Comrade Stalin has concentrated enormous power in his hands, and I am not sure that he always knows how to use that power with sufficient caution."

From 1922 to 1927, Stalin began his ruthless climb to the head of the government. In 1922, as general secretary of the Communist Party, he worked behind the scenes. He shrewdly moved his followers into strategic government offices. By 1924, he had placed many of his supporters in key positions. By 1928, Stalin was in total command of the Communist Party. Trotsky, forced into exile in 1929, was no longer a threat. Stalin now stood poised to wield absolute power as a dictator.

Background
While in exile, Trotsky published articles and books criticizing Stalin's regime. In 1940, Stalin's agents murdered Trotsky in Mexico.

Stalin Builds a Totalitarian State

Lenin and Trotsky promoted a worldwide Communist revolution. Stalin, however, focused on Russian development. He coined the phrase "socialism in one country" to describe his aims of perfecting a Communist state in Russia. To realize his vision, Stalin would transform the Soviet Union into a totalitarian state.

The term **totalitarianism** describes a government that takes total, centralized state control over every aspect of public and private life. Totalitarian leaders, such as Stalin, appear to provide a sense of security and to give a direction for the future.

Totalitarianism challenges the highest values prized by Western democracies—reason, freedom, human dignity, and the worth of the individual. As the chart on the next page shows, all totalitarian states share basic characteristics.

HISTORY MAKERS

Joseph Stalin
1879–1953

Stalin was born in bitter poverty in Georgia, a region in southern Russia. Unlike the well-educated and cultured Lenin, Stalin was rough and crude.

Despite having millions of Russians killed, Stalin tried to create a myth that he was the country's father and savior. Stalin glorified himself as the symbol of the nation. He encouraged people to think of him as "The Greatest Genius of All Times and Peoples."

Many towns, factories, and streets in the Soviet Union were named for Stalin. A new metal was called Stalinite. An orchid was named Stalinchid. Children standing before their desks every morning said, "Thank Comrade Stalin for this happy life."

PATTERNS OF CHANGE 395

Section 2 Overview

OBJECTIVES

① To explain how Stalin gained control of the Communist Party.

② To describe Stalin's goal of transforming the Soviet Union into a totalitarian state.

③ To summarize Stalin's state-controlled economic programs.

④ To explain the methods of control used in totalitarian states.

⑤ To describe Soviet daily life.

SKILLBUILDERS
- Interpreting charts, p. 396
- Interpreting graphs, p. 397

CRITICAL THINKING
- Summarizing, p. 397
- Making inferences, p. 398
- Analyzing issues, p. 399
- Comparing, p. 399
- Evaluating, p. 400
- Synthesizing, p. 400

FOCUS
5-Minute Warm-Up

▶ ***Interpreting Art***
Answering these questions will help students understand life in the Soviet Union under Stalin.

1. Look at the posters of Soviet workers on page 399. What is most striking about them?

2. What are the slogans written on these posters?

 WARM-UP TRANSPARENCY 14

OBJECTIVE ① INSTRUCT

Stalin Becomes Dictator

▶ *Key Ideas*
- Stalin wants to succeed Lenin.
- Stalin ruthlessly climbs to the head of the Soviet government.

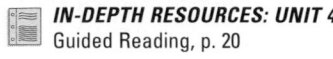 ***IN-DEPTH RESOURCES: UNIT 4***
Guided Reading, p. 20

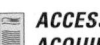 ***ACCESS FOR STUDENTS ACQUIRING ENGLISH***
Guided Reading (Spanish), p. 154

Stalin Builds a Totalitarian State

(See page 395.)

▶ *Key Ideas*
- Stalin transforms the Soviet Union into a totalitarian state.
- Totalitarian governments take control over all aspects of life.
- Several totalitarian states emerge during the 20th century.

HISTORY MAKERS
Joseph Stalin

(See page 395.)

President Harry Truman described Stalin as "a little bit of a squirt." Ask students to research other anecdotes about Stalin.

History from Visuals

Patterns of Change: Totalitarianism

Interpreting the Chart
Emphasize that the key traits apply to all totalitarian states, not just the Soviet Union.

Extension Activity Have students cite examples of technology that a totalitarian state today might use to spread propaganda.

SKILLBUILDER Answers
1. Through propaganda and force
2. No individual freedoms, great personal sacrifice, limited privacy

Stalin Seizes Control of the Economy

▶ *Key Ideas*
- Stalin launches Five-Year Plans and ushers in an agricultural revolution.

PATTERNS OF CHANGE: Totalitarianism

Key Traits	Description
Dictatorship and One-Party Rule	• Exercises absolute authority • Dominates the government
Dynamic Leader	• Helps unite people toward meeting shared goals or realizing a common vision • Encourages people to devote their unconditional loyalty and uncritical support to the regime • Becomes a symbol of the government
Ideology (set of beliefs)	• Justifies government actions • Glorifies the aims of the state
State Control Over All Sectors of Society	• business • labor • housing • education • family life • youth groups • religion • the arts
State Control Over the Individual	• Demands total obedience to authority and personal sacrifice for the good of the state • Denies basic liberties
Dependence on Modern Technology	• Relies on mass communication, such as radios, newsreels, and loudspeakers, to spread propaganda • Builds up advanced military weapons
Organized Violence	• Uses force, such as police terror, to crush all opposition • Targets certain groups, such as national minorities and political opponents, as enemies

SKILLBUILDER: Interpreting Charts
1. *Based on the chart, how are individuals in a totalitarian state molded into obedient citizens?*
2. *How would your life change if you lived in a totalitarian state?*

Other totalitarian governments besides the Soviet Union emerged in the twentieth century. In the 1920s and 1930s, two other European dictators—Hitler in Germany and Mussolini in Italy—were shaping their visions of a totalitarian state. After Communists formed the People's Republic of China in 1949, Mao Zedong used tactics similar to Stalin's to establish totalitarian control. The North Korean dictator Kim Il Sung ruled over a totalitarian Communist state from 1948 to 1994.

By 1928 Stalin began taking great strides to build a totalitarian state. He had achieved personal power and was ready to begin overhauling the economy.

CASE STUDY: Stalinist Russia

Stalin Seizes Control of the Economy

While Lenin's New Economic Policy (NEP) was a mixture of free enterprise and state control, Stalin's economic policies involved total state control. His plans called for a **command economy**—a system in which the government made all economic decisions. Under this system, political leaders identify the country's economic needs and determine how to fulfill them. To modernize the Soviet state, Stalin ushered in revolutions in industry and agriculture.

An Industrial Revolution In 1928, Stalin outlined the first of several Five-Year Plans for the development of the Soviet Union's economy. The government would take drastic steps to promote rapid industrial growth and to strengthen national defense. Stalin announced, "We are fifty or a hundred years behind the advanced countries. We must make good this distance in ten years. Either we do it or we shall be crushed."

The Five-Year Plans set impossibly high quotas, or numerical goals, to increase the output of steel, coal, oil, and electricity. To reach these targets, the government limited production of consumer goods. As a result, people faced severe shortages of housing, food, clothing, and other necessary goods.

The number of tractors in the Soviet Union increased from 25,000 in 1927 to 483,000 in 1938.

Task: Student groups will use the chart on this page to help them create a fictional totalitarian state.

Purpose: To explore the characteristics and costs of totalitarianism.

Activity: Have small groups brainstorm examples for each key trait of totalitarianism listed on the Patterns of Change chart. They should invent a

name for the totalitarian state, identify its location, make up a name for the dictator, and list the effects on individual lives. Ask groups to make charts of their profiles of fictional totalitarian regimes.

 Building a Portfolio If the chart is among their best work, students should add it to their portfolio.

ALTERNATIVE ASSESSMENT BOOK
Standards for Evaluating a Cooperative Activity

Standards for Evaluation
Charts should . . .

- include specific examples of each key trait of totalitarianism
- demonstrate a clear understanding of the principles underlying totalitarian regimes
- show how individual lives would be affected

Under Stalin's totalitarian regime, the government controlled every aspect of the worker's life. Officials chose the workers, assigned them jobs, and determined their working hours. Workers needed the police's permission to move. The secret police were ready to imprison or execute those who did not contribute to the Soviet economy. These forceful means of making the Soviet Union a modern industrial nation took a great toll on people's personal lives. Many families and marriages broke up.

Stalin's grim methods, however, also produced fantastic economic results. Although most of the targets of the first Five-Year Plan fell short, the Soviets made impressive gains. A second plan, launched in 1933, proved equally successful. From 1928 to 1937, industrial production increased more than 25 percent.

An Agricultural Revolution Stalin's agricultural revolution was also successful—and far more brutal—than his industrial revolution. In 1928, the government began to seize over 25 million privately owned farms in the USSR. It combined them into large, government-owned farms, called **collective farms**. Hundreds of families worked on these farms, producing food for the state. The government expected that the modern machinery on the collective farms would boost food production and reduce the number of workers.

Peasants resisted fiercely. Many killed livestock and destroyed crops in protest. Stalin used terror and violence to force peasants to work on collective farms. Soviet secret police herded them onto collective farms at the point of a bayonet. Between 5 million and 10 million peasants died as a direct result of Stalin's agricultural revolution. Millions more were shipped to Siberia.

Resistance was especially strong among **kulaks**, a class of wealthy peasants. The Soviet government decided to eliminate them. Thousands were executed or sent to work camps.

By 1938, more than 90 percent of all peasants lived on collective farms. Agricultural production was on the upswing. That year the country produced almost twice the wheat than it had in 1928 before collective farming.

Weapons of Totalitarianism

To dominate an entire nation, Stalin, like other totalitarian leaders, devised methods of control and persuasion.

Police Terror Dictators of totalitarian states use terror and violence to force obedience and to crush opposition. Stalin began building his totalitarian state by destroying his enemies—real and imagined. Stalin's secret police used tanks and armored cars to stop riots. They monitored telephone lines, read mail, and planted informers everywhere. Even children told authorities about disloyal remarks they heard at home. The secret police arrested and executed millions of so-called traitors.

In 1934, Stalin turned against members of the Communist Party. He launched the **Great Purge**—a campaign of terror. It was directed at eliminating anyone who threatened his power. Thousands of old Bolsheviks who helped stage the Revolution in 1917 stood trial. They were executed for "crimes against the Soviet state."

The state had the authority to punish even the most minor acts. The police arrested the director of the Moscow Zoo because his monkeys got tuberculosis. The police

PATTERNS OF CHANGE 397

Sidebar (left margin)

Background
Many peasants had only recently won their own land. For centuries, they had struggled against the nobles. Now they were forced to submit to yet another landlord—the Soviet government.

THINK THROUGH HISTORY
A. Summarizing
What methods did Stalin use to bring agriculture under state control?
A. Possible Answer
Establishment of collective farms; use of terror and violence; destruction of the kulaks

Vocabulary
purge: a systematic effort to eliminate a targeted group of people.

The Buildup of the Soviet Economy

INDUSTRY

- Coal Production
- Steel Production

AGRICULTURE

- Livestock

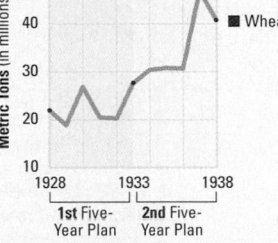

- Wheat

Source: *European Historical Statistics*

SKILLBUILDER: Interpreting Graphs
1. *How many more metric tons of coal were produced in 1938 than in 1928?*
2. *What do the graphs show about the contrast between the progress of industry and livestock production under Stalin's first Five-Year Plan?*

Sidebar (right)

Rulers of the society depicted in *1984* make widespread use of propaganda. Even a new language—Newspeak—is adopted that will serve the propaganda needs of the state. Ask students to read the appendix to *1984*, which contains a description of Newspeak, and to explain some Newspeak words to the class.

 IN-DEPTH RESOURCES: UNIT 4
Literature: from *1984*, p. 32

 ELECTRONIC LIBRARY OF PRIMARY SOURCES
from *1984*

MORE ABOUT . . .
Artists, Writers, and Propaganda

Art and literature became tools of propaganda, as Stalin ordered intellectuals to become "engineers of human minds." Writers and artists who could successfully create works of propaganda were generously rewarded, often living better than the highest members of government.

MORE ABOUT . . .
Religious Persecution

Under Stalin's totalitarian regime, the chapel of the Iberian Virgin, one of Moscow's most revered religious sites, was destroyed. Religious Soviet citizens were horrified. The gold-domed Church of Christ the Savior, built to commemorate Russia's victory over Napoleon, was blown up to make way for a towering building, the Palace of the Soviets. The Palace, however, was never built.

SPOTLIGHT ON

1984

George Orwell wrote the chilling novel *1984* in response to the threat of two totalitarian regimes. They were Communist Russia under Stalin and Nazi Germany under Adolf Hitler. The novel depicts a frightening world in which personal freedom and privacy have vanished. The sinister slogan "Big Brother Is Watching You" appears everywhere. Even citizens' homes have television cameras that constantly survey their behavior.

Orwell intended his novel, published in 1949, as a warning, not as a prophecy. He sounded an alarm about a world that a totalitarian state could create through modern technology. For millions of people in the Soviet Union and Nazi Germany, the world of totalitarianism was not fiction. It was terrifying fact.

---

themselves were not above suspicion, especially if they did not meet their quotas of "criminals" arrested. Every family came to fear the knock on the door in the early hours of the morning. Such a surprise visit from the secret police usually meant the arrest of a family member.

When the Great Purge ended in 1939, Stalin had gained total control of both the Soviet government and the Communist Party. Historians estimate that Stalin was responsible for the deaths of 8 million to 13 million people.

Indoctrination and Propaganda Totalitarian states rely on indoctrination—instruction in the government's set of beliefs—to mold people's minds. Party leaders in the Soviet Union lectured workers and peasants on the ideals of communism. They also stressed the importance of sacrifice and hard work to build the Communist state. State-supported youth groups served as training grounds for future party members.

Totalitarian states also spread propaganda. Propaganda is biased or incomplete information used to sway people to accept certain beliefs or actions. Soviet newspapers and radio broadcasts glorified the achievements of communism, Stalin, and his economic programs.

Under Stalin, art also became a method of propaganda. In 1930, an editorial in the Communist Party newspaper *Pravda* explained the purpose of art: "Literature, the cinema, the arts are levers in the hands of the proletariat which must be used to show the masses positive models of initiative and heroic labor." **Socialist realism** was an artistic style that praised Soviet life and Communist values. It became a vehicle to rally the workers. Yevgeny Yevtushenko, a Russian poet, described this form of artistic expression:

A VOICE FROM THE PAST
Blankly smiling workers and collective farmers looked out from the covers of books. Almost every novel and short story had a happy ending. Painters more and more often took as their subjects state banquets, weddings, solemn public meetings, and parades.
Poets visited factories and construction sites but wrote more about machines than about the men who worked them. If machines could read, they might have found such poems interesting. Human beings did not.
YEVGENY YEVTUSHENKO, *A Precocious Autobiography*

Censorship Many Soviet writers, composers, and other artists also fell victim to official censorship. Stalin would not tolerate individual creativity that threatened the conformity and obedience required of citizens in a totalitarian state. The government also controlled all newspapers, motion pictures, radio, and other sources of information.

Religious Persecution Communists aimed to replace religious teachings with the ideals of communism. Under Stalin, the government and the League of the Militant Godless, an officially sponsored group of atheists, spread propaganda attacking religion. "Museums of atheism" displayed exhibits to show that religious beliefs were mere superstitions. Yet many people in the Soviet Union still clung to their faiths.

The Russian Orthodox Church was the main target of persecution. Other religious groups, including Roman Catholics and Jews, also suffered greatly under Stalin's totalitarian rule. The police destroyed magnificent churches and synagogues. Many religious leaders of all faiths were killed or sent to labor camps.

THINK THROUGH HISTORY
B. Making Inferences What forms of art did Stalin encourage?
B. Possible Answer Literature, films, and paintings that served a political purpose—glorifying the goals of the communist state

Vocabulary
atheists: people who do not think there is a god.

Propaganda Through Art

Low-cost printing techniques made socialist realism posters an important form of propaganda in the Soviet Union. People might not listen to the radio or go to propaganda films. However, if they left their houses, they could not avoid viewing the posters plastered on buildings and walls in every town.

Images of energetic laborers, such as the special groups called "shock brigades," urged Soviets to work harder. Portraits glorifying Stalin were also popular subjects of Soviet posters.

The slogan on the above poster reads, "Day Laborers and Young Communists—Join the Tractor Shock Brigades for Spring Sowing."

The slogan on this poster reads, "Young Communists [are] the Shock Brigade of the Five-Year Plan."

This profile of Stalin is imposed on a shadowy image of Lenin. Miniature portraits of other Communist leaders trail off in the background.

Connect *to* History

Analyzing Issues What messages do you think these posters communicate?

SEE SKILLBUILDER HANDBOOK, PAGE 659

Connect *to* Today

Comparing How do the Soviet posters portraying workers resemble the billboards that modern-day advertisers use to sell products? Support your answer with examples.

Revolution and Nationalism **399**

Connect *to* History

Analyzing Issues
Possible Responses: The two posters on the top half of the page convey the dedication and great effort of Soviet workers and their dazzling machinery. The poster on the bottom of the page glorifies the brilliant leadership of Stalin as he follows in Lenin's footsteps.

Connect *to* Today

Comparing
Possible Responses: Like modern-day billboards, the posters rely on catchy slogans and striking but unrealistic images to sway people's emotions.

Daily Life Under Stalin

▶ **Key Ideas**
- Soviet women contribute to the prosperity of Stalin's state-controlled economy but also make great sacrifices.
- Soviet state-controlled education indoctrinates citizens and offers them technical training and opportunities for a better life.

ASSESS & RETEACH

Section 2 Assessment

Have students work individually to answer the questions. Then have them check their answers with a partner.

 FORMAL ASSESSMENT
Section Quiz, p. 154

Reteaching Activity
CLASS TIME: 15 MINUTES

For each key trait of totalitarianism described in the chart on page 396, have students cite at least one example from Stalinist Russia.

 GEOGRAPHY TRANSPARENCIES
GT30 European Totalitarianism by 1938

CLOSE ACTIVITY

CLASS TIME: 15 MINUTES

Role-Playing
Write down the following "cast of characters" from Stalinist Russia on 3" × 5" file cards: a member of the secret police, an artist, a journalist, a kulak, a former Bolshevik, a Russian Orthodox priest, a woman doctor, and a college student. Have interested students draw a card. Other students will interview the Soviet characters about how their lives have changed since Stalin came to power.

Daily Life Under Stalin

Stalin's totalitarian rule revolutionized Soviet society. Women's roles greatly expanded. People became better educated and mastered new technical skills. The dramatic changes in people's lives had a downside, though. As servants of a totalitarian state, they would make great sacrifices in exchange for progress.

This Soviet woman worked in a textile factory during Stalin's regime.

Soviet Women With the Bolshevik Revolution of 1917, women won equal rights. After Stalin became dictator, women helped the state-controlled economy prosper. Under his Five-Year Plans, they had no choice but to join the labor force in increasing numbers. Young women performed the same jobs as men. Millions of women worked in factories and built dams and roads.

Given new educational opportunities, women prepared for careers in engineering and science. Medicine, in particular, attracted many women. By 1950, they made up 75 percent of Soviet doctors.

Soviet women paid a heavy price for their rising status in society. Besides their full-time jobs, they were responsible for housework and child care. Motherhood was also considered a patriotic duty in totalitarian regimes. Soviet women were expected to provide the state with future generations of loyal, obedient citizens.

Education Under Stalin, the government controlled all education—from nursery schools through the universities. Schoolchildren learned the virtues of the Communist Party. College professors and students who questioned the Communist Party's interpretations of history or science risked losing their jobs or faced imprisonment.

Education was not merely indoctrination. Stalin's economic plans created a high demand for many skilled workers. University and technical training became the key to a better life. As one young man explained, "If a person does not want to become a collective farmer or just a cleaning woman, the only means you have to get something is through education."

By the mid-1930s, Stalin had forcibly transformed the Soviet Union into a totalitarian regime, as well as an industrial and a political power. He stood unopposed as dictator and maintained his authority over the Communist Party. Stalin also ushered in a period of total social control and rule by terror. His network of laws and regulations guided every aspect of individual behavior.

Like Russia, China would fall under the influence of Karl Marx's theories and Communist beliefs. The dynamic leader Mao Zedong would pave the way for transforming China into a totalitarian Communist state, as you will read in Section 3.

THINK THROUGH HISTORY
C. Evaluating What were the pros and cons of women's new roles in Soviet society under Stalin?
C. Possible Answer
Pros—more job and educational opportunities. Cons—motherhood considered a patriotic duty; limited freedom as a worker.

Section **2** Assessment

1. TERMS & NAMES

Identify
- Joseph Stalin
- totalitarianism
- command economy
- collective farm
- kulak
- Great Purge
- socialist realism

2. TAKING NOTES

Create a chart like the one below listing the weapons of totalitarianism. Cite examples from Stalinist Russia for each method shown.

Weapons	Examples
Police Terror	
Propaganda	
Censorship	
Religious Persecution	

Which method do you think was most influential in maintaining Stalin's totalitarian rule? Why?

3. SYNTHESIZING

What kind of person would be considered an ideal citizen under Stalin's totalitarian regime? Support your answer with reasons.

THINK ABOUT
- the chart explaining the key traits of totalitarianism
- personal qualities that are prized under totalitarianism
- people who were persecuted or punished under Stalin

4. THEME ACTIVITY

Economics Role-play an industrial worker in a steel mill, a peasant on a collective farm, or a student at a technical school. Write a secret journal entry describing what your life is like under Stalin's economic plans.

ANSWERS

1. TERMS & NAMES
Identify
Joseph Stalin, p. 395
totalitarianism, p. 395
command economy, p. 396
collective farm, p. 397
kulak, p. 397
Great Purge, p. 397
socialist realism, p. 398

2. TAKING NOTES
Possible Responses: Police Terror—Great Purge, execution of kulaks. Propaganda—socialist realism, training of youth. Censorship—government-controlled media. Religious Persecution—destruction of buildings, elimination of leadership.

3. SYNTHESIZING
Possible Responses: An ideal citizen in Stalinist Russia would be extremely loyal, obedient, uncritical, hard-working, and productive. He or she would embrace Communist beliefs, denounce religion, and willingly make sacrifices for the good of the state.

4. THEME ACTIVITY
Possible Responses: A journal entry might mention the role of the secret police, Stalin's rigid demands under his Five-Year Plans, government control over their jobs and education, and the barrage of propaganda.

TERMS & NAMES
• Kuomintang
• Sun Yixian
• Mao Zedong
• May Fourth Movement
• Long March

3 Collapse of Chinese Imperial Rule

MAIN IDEA

After the fall of the Qing dynasty, nationalist and Communist movements struggled for power.

WHY IT MATTERS NOW

The seeds of China's late-20th-century political thought, communism, were planted at this time.

SETTING THE STAGE In the early 1900s, China was ripe for revolution. China had faced years of humiliation at the hands of outsiders. Foreign countries controlled China's trade and economic resources. Many Chinese believed that modernization and nationalism held the country's keys for survival. They wanted to build up the army and navy, to construct modern factories, and to reform education. Yet others feared change. They believed that China's greatness lay in its traditional ways.

Nationalists Overthrow Qing Dynasty

Among the groups pushing for modernization and nationalization was the **Kuomintang** (KWOH·mihn·TANG), or the Nationalist Party. Its first great leader, **Sun Yixian** (soon yee·shyahn), was a physician who had spent many years in the United States. In 1912, Sun's Revolutionary Alliance, a forerunner of the Kuomintang, succeeded in overthrowing the last emperor of the Qing dynasty. The Qing had ruled China since 1644.

Shaky Start for the New Republic In 1912, Sun became president of the new Republic of China. He held the post for just six weeks. Sun hoped to establish a modern government based on the "Three Principles of the People": (1) nationalism—an end to foreign control, (2) people's rights—democracy, and (3) people's livelihood—economic security for all Chinese. Sun Yixian considered nationalism vital. He said, "The Chinese people . . . do not have national spirit. Therefore even though we have four hundred million people gathered together in one China, in reality, they are just a heap of loose sand." Despite his lasting influence as a revolutionary leader, Sun lacked the authority and the military support to secure national unity.

Sun turned over the presidency to Yuan Shikai (yoo·ahn shee·ky), a powerful general. Yuan quickly betrayed the democratic ideals of the revolution. By 1913, he was ruling as a military dictator. His actions sparked local revolts. Even Yuan's own generals refused to fight the rebels. After Yuan died in 1916, chaos reigned. China remained divided and Sun's Kuomintang powerless. Civil war broke out as one rival group battled another. Sun tried to reorganize his Kuomintang. Real authority, though, fell into the hands of provincial warlords. They ruled territories as large as their armies could conquer.

As always during times of unrest, the Chinese peasants suffered most. Warlord armies terrorized the countryside. They pillaged and looted everywhere. Roads and bridges fell into disrepair, and crops were destroyed. Famine took the lives of millions. This was the situation in China as World War I was being waged in Europe.

Vocabulary
warlord: powerful military leader.

HISTORY MAKERS

Sun Yixian
1866–1925

A traditional Chinese proverb says that knowing what to do is easier than doing it. Sun Yixian disagreed. "Knowledge is difficult," he said. "Action is easy."

Sun led an action-filled life. He traveled, organized, and plotted tirelessly to bring down the Qing dynasty. Aware of Sun's activity and influence, Qing officials tracked him down in London. They kidnapped him and held him prisoner. They planned to ship him back to China, where he faced probable execution.

Sun would meet his death, he said, by "first having my ankles crushed in a vise and broken by a hammer, my eyelids cut off, and finally being chopped up into small fragments so that none could claim my mortal remains." Sun's British friends helped him escape his captors. The episode made him world-famous as a leader of the revolution in China. Sun Yixian is still known as the "father of modern China."

Revolution and Nationalism **401**

Section 3 Overview

OBJECTIVES

1. To explain the problems facing the Republic of China after the overthrow of the Qing dynasty.

2. To trace the rise of the Communist Party in China.

3. To summarize key events of the civil war between Chinese Communists and Nationalists.

SKILLBUILDERS

• Interpreting maps: region, movement, p. 404

CRITICAL THINKING

• Identifying problems, p. 402
• Contrasting, p. 403
• Recognizing effects, p. 404
• Analyzing themes, p. 404

FOCUS

5-Minute Warm-Up

▶ **Recognizing Facts and Details**
Have students answer these questions to help them gain insight into the leadership of a famous Chinese revolutionary.

• Read the History Makers on page 401. How did Sun Yixian describe his probable execution?

• Who helped Sun escape?

WARM-UP TRANSPARENCY 14

OBJECTIVE ① INSTRUCT

Nationalists Overthrow Qing Dynasty

Key Ideas
• Nationalists establish the new Republic of China.

• Sun fails to secure national unity.

• Under the Treaty of Versailles, the Allies give Japan territories previously held by Germany.

• The Treaty of Versailles triggers nationwide protests.

IN-DEPTH RESOURCES: UNIT 4
Guided Reading, p. 21

ACCESS FOR STUDENTS ACQUIRING ENGLISH
Guided Reading (Spanish), p. 155

SECTION 3 RESOURCES

PRINT RESOURCES

IN-DEPTH RESOURCES: UNIT 4
Guided Reading, p. 21
Primary Source: from The Peasants of Hunan, p. 28
Geography Application: Nationalists Battle Warlords and Communists, p. 24
History Makers: Jiang Jieshi, p. 35

ACCESS FOR STUDENTS ACQUIRING ENGLISH
Guided Reading (Spanish), p. 155
Geography Application (Spanish), p. 158

FORMAL ASSESSMENT
Section Quiz, p. 176

ALTERNATIVE ASSESSMENT BOOK

TECHNOLOGY RESOURCES

CD-ROM
Electronic Library of Primary Sources

INTERNET www.mlworldhistory.com

(See page 401.)

According to his contemporaries, Sun possessed a magnetic personality and a tolerance for others. His experiences as a student in British and American schools left him with a clear understanding of Western ideals. Ask students to discuss how Sun's familiarity with the Western democracies might have influenced his "Three Principles of the People."

OBJECTIVE **2** INSTRUCT

The Communist Party in China

Key Ideas

- Western democracies' refusal to aid Sun Yixian prompts him to seek the Soviet Union's support.
- Kuomintang leader Jiang Jieshi turns against the Chinese Communists and becomes president of the Nationalist Republic of China in 1928.
- Peasants throw their support to the Chinese Communists led by Mao Zedong.

IN-DEPTH RESOURCES: UNIT 4
Primary Source: from *The Peasants of Hunan*, p. 28
History Maker: Jiang Jieshi, p. 35

CRITICAL THINKING ACTIVITY
CLASS TIME: 15 MINUTES

Understanding Sequential Order

To help students track the sequence of events in China, have them create a time line explaining the dates shown below.

```
1920        1923        1927
|-----------|-----------|
      1921        1925
```

World War I Spells More Problems In 1917, the government in Beijing, hoping for an Allied victory, declared war against Germany. For China's participation, some leaders mistakenly believed that the thankful Allies would return control of China to the Chinese. Under the Treaty of Versailles, however, the Allied leaders gave Japan the territories and privileges that had previously belonged to Germany.

The May Fourth Movement When news of the Treaty of Versailles reached China, outrage swept the country. On May 4, 1919, over 3,000 angry students gathered in the center of Beijing. "Down with the European imperialists!" they shouted. "Boycott Japan!" **Mao Zedong** (MOW dzuh·dahng), a young schoolteacher who had studied at Beijing University, supported the student protesters. He would later become China's greatest revolutionary leader, sometimes called "The Great Helmsman."

Student protesters gathered at Tiananmen Square in summer 1919.

The demonstrations spread to other cities and exploded into a national movement. It was called the **May Fourth Movement.** Workers, manufacturers, shopkeepers, and professionals joined the cause. Though not officially a revolution, these demonstrations showed the Chinese people's commitment to the goal of establishing a strong, modern nation. Sun Yixian and members of the Kuomintang also shared the aims of the movement. But they could not strengthen central rule on their own. Many young Chinese intellectuals turned against Sun Yixian's beliefs in Western democracy in favor of Lenin's brand of Soviet communism.

Vocabulary
helmsman: person who steers a ship.

THINK THROUGH HISTORY
A. Identifying Problems What problems did the new Republic of China face?
A. Possible Answer Weak leadership, civil war, terror of warlord armies, famine, outcome of World War I, nationwide protests

The Communist Party in China

In 1920, small groups of young intellectuals were meeting in Shanghai and Beijing University to discuss Marx's revolutionary beliefs. They viewed the Soviet Union under Lenin as a model for political and economic change. In 1921, a group met in Shanghai to organize the Chinese Communist Party. Mao Zedong was among its founders.

Lenin Befriends China While the Communist Party was forming, Sun Yixian and his Nationalist Party set up a government in south China. Like the Communists, Sun became disillusioned with the Western democracies that refused to support his struggling government. Sun decided to ally the Kuomintang with the newly formed Communist Party. Sun used Lenin's blueprint for organizing his party along Bolshevik lines. Sun hoped to unite all the revolutionary groups for common action.

After Western governments failed to aid Sun, he accepted an offer from the Soviets. Lenin preached worldwide revolution. He seized the opportunity to help China's Nationalist government. In 1923, Lenin began sending military advisers and equipment to the Nationalists in return for allowing the Chinese Communists to join the Kuomintang. Several Chinese Nationalist leaders traveled to Moscow for military training.

This portrait of Mao Zedong was taken around 1919, when he was a young revolutionary.

Nationalists and Communists Clash After Sun Yixian died in 1925, Jiang Jieshi (Jee·ahng jee·shee), formerly called Chiang Kai-shek, headed the Kuomintang. Jiang was the son of a middle-class merchant. Many of Jiang's followers were bankers and

Background
Jiang was Sun's brother-in-law and military assistant.

TEACHING OPTION

CONNECTIONS ACROSS TIME AND PLACE

Tiananmen Square When the Communists came into power in 1949, they designated the fourth of May as National Youth Day, in honor of the May Fourth Movement of 1919. The 70th anniversary of the May Fourth Movement sparked a new wave of protests. In April 1989, university students in China once again began staging demonstrations at Tiananmen Square. Protesters demanded democracy

and political change. On May 29, they constructed a replica of the Statue of Liberty, which they dubbed the "Goddess of Democracy."

China's premier Li Peng took military action. On June 3, 1989, troops in armored tanks entered the square and fired on the crowd. Soldiers killed hundreds of protesters. Government officials ordered the arrest of

others, some of whom were executed. Television audiences from the world's democratic countries watched broadcasts of these shocking events. Though the protest was crushed, one student said, "Maybe we'll fail today. Maybe we'll fail tomorrow. But someday we'll succeed. It's a historical inevitability." By 1990, the Chinese government started making economic reforms.

businesspeople. Like Jiang, they feared the Communists' goal of creating a socialist economy modeled after the Soviet Union's.

At first, Jiang put aside his differences with the Communists. Together Jiang's Nationalist forces and the Communists successfully fought the warlords. Soon afterward, though, he turned against the Communists.

In April 1927, Nationalist troops and armed gangs moved into Shanghai. They killed many Communist leaders and trade union members in the city streets. Similar killings took place in other cities. The Nationalists nearly wiped out the Chinese Communist Party. Its few survivors went into hiding.

In 1928, Jiang became president of the Nationalist Republic of China. Great Britain and the United States both formally recognized the new government. The Soviet Union, as a result of the Shanghai massacre, did not. Jiang's treachery also had long-term effects. The Communists' deep-seated rage over the massacre erupted in a civil war that would last until 1949.

Peasants Align Themselves with the Communists Jiang had promised democracy and political rights to all Chinese. Yet his government became steadily less democratic and more corrupt. It launched programs to modernize and develop the cities. However, Jiang did nothing to improve the life of China's rural peasants. As a result, many peasants threw their support to the Chinese Communist Party. To enlist the support of the peasants, Mao divided land that the Communists won among the local farmers.

Communist leader Mao Zedong had survived Jiang's bloody rampage by fleeing to the countryside. He had already begun to develop his own brand of communism. Lenin had shown that a Marxist revolution could take place in a largely rural country, but he had based his organization in Russia's cities. Mao envisioned a different setting. He believed he could bring revolution to a rural country where the peasants could be the true revolutionaries. He argued his point passionately in 1927:

THINK THROUGH HISTORY
B. Contrasting How did Mao's vision of revolution differ from Lenin's?
B. Possible Answer Mao believed that peasants could stage a revolution in a rural country. Lenin's supporters were based in cities.

> **A VOICE FROM THE PAST**
> The force of the peasantry is like that of the raging winds and driving rain. It is rapidly increasing in violence. No force can stand in its way. The peasantry will tear apart all nets which bind it and hasten along the road to liberation. They will bury beneath them all forces of imperialism, militarism, corrupt officialdom, village bosses and evil gentry.
> **MAO ZEDONG,** quoted in *A History of World Societies*

Civil War Rages in China

By 1930, Nationalists and Communists were fighting a bloody civil war. Mao and other Communist leaders established themselves in the hills of south-central China. Mao referred to this tactic of taking his revolution to the countryside as "swimming in the peasant sea." He recruited the peasants to join his Red Army. He then trained them in guerrilla warfare. Nationalists attacked the Communists repeatedly but failed to drive them out.

The Long March In 1933, Jiang gathered an army of at least 700,000 men. Jiang's army then surrounded the Communists' mountain stronghold. Outnumbered nearly six to one,

Along with the Red Army, Mao (riding on horseback) and his wife He Zizhan (wearing a round hat) made the grueling Long March to safety in western China.

MORE ABOUT . . .
The Life of Chinese Peasants
American author Pearl S. Buck wrote extensively about life in China, where she grew up. Her most famous book, *The Good Earth,* winner of the 1932 Pulitzer Prize, tells the story of the Chinese peasant Wang Lung. The book gives a sympathetic account of the hardships suffered by Chinese peasants before Communist rule.

 ELECTRONIC LIBRARY OF PRIMARY SOURCES
from *Autobiography of a Chinese Girl*

OBJECTIVE ③ INSTRUCT

Civil War Rages in China

▶ *Key Ideas*
• Jiang's army surrounds the Communists' stronghold, forcing them to flee.
• Fleeing Communist forces make a 6,000-mile-long journey called the Long March.
• Japan's invasion of Manchuria in 1931 and of China in 1937 forces both Nationalists and Communists to fight the Japanese.

MORE ABOUT . . .
Mao's Guerrilla Tactics
From his mountain hideout, Mao waged guerrilla war against Jiang's armies. He outlined his strategy:
1. Retreat when the enemy advances.
2. Harass when the enemy encamps.
3. Attack when the enemy hesitates.
4. Pursue when the enemy retreats.
Such tactics were possible only with the support of the peasants in the area where the guerrillas were fighting.

TEACHING OPTION | **BLOCK SCHEDULING** | COOPERATIVE ACTIVITY: Commemorating the Long March | **CLASS TIME 30 MINUTES**

Task: Groups of students will design a memorial paying tribute to the thousands of Chinese people who lost their lives during the Long March. They will create a model or replica of the memorial to present to the class.

Purpose: To broaden students' understanding of a historical event.

Activity: Divide students into groups and have them research the overwhelming obstacles that

Mao's followers faced during the Long March. Have them discuss feelings or ideas that they think a memorial of this epic journey should communicate. Ask students to brainstorm possible designs and then draw a rough sketch. Group members should also consider the construction materials they might use and inscriptions they might include.

📁 **Building a Portfolio** If the visual display is among their best, they should add it to their portfolio.

Standards for Evaluation
Visual displays should . . .

• illustrate the design of the memorial
• include meaningful inscriptions
• show evidence of research

China, 1927–1938

GEOGRAPHY SKILLBUILDER: Interpreting Maps
1. **Movement** What was the course of the Long March, in terms of direction, beginning in Riujan and ending near Yan'an?
2. **Region** What geographic barriers did Mao's forces face during the Long March?

Communist Party leaders realized that they faced defeat. In 1934, the Communist forces fled. They began a hazardous, 6,000-mile-long journey called the **Long March**. Over the next year, the Communists kept only a step ahead of Jiang's forces.

Mao's Red Army crossed many rivers and climbed over mountain ranges. They fought several major battles and faced minor skirmishes almost every day. They also crossed miles of swampland. They had to sleep sitting up, leaning back-to-back in pairs, to keep from sinking into the mud and drowning.

The chase lasted more than a year. About 100,000 people began the march. From 10,000 to 30,000 reached safety in northwestern China, beyond the reach of Jiang's forces.

Mao and the other Communist survivors settled in caves in northwestern China. Despite the discouraging turn of events, they quickly gained new followers. Meanwhile, as civil war between Nationalists and Communists raged, Japan invaded China.

Japan's Invasion Suspends the Civil War In 1931, as Chinese fought Chinese, the Japanese watched the power struggles with rising interest. Japanese forces took advantage of China's weakening situation. They invaded Manchuria, an industrialized province in the northeast part of China. This attack signaled the onset of World War II in Asia.

In 1937, the Japanese launched an all-out invasion of China. Massive bombings of villages and cities killed thousands of Chinese. The destruction of farms caused many more to die of starvation. By 1938, Japan held control of a large part of China.

The Japanese threat forced an uneasy truce between Jiang's and Mao's forces. The civil war gradually ground to a halt as Nationalists and Communists temporarily united to fight the Japanese. Jiang further agreed to promote changes outlined in Sun Yixian's "Three Principles of the People"—nationalism, democracy, and people's livelihood. As you will learn in Section 4, similar principles were also serving as a guiding force in India and Southwest Asia.

THINK THROUGH HISTORY
C. Recognizing Effects What were the results of the Long March?
C. Possible Answer Although at least two-thirds of the original marchers did not complete the journey, more Chinese people joined the Communists.

Background
The truce between Communists and Nationalists lasted throughout World War II.

Section ❸ Assessment

1. TERMS & NAMES
Identify
• Kuomintang
• Sun Yixian
• Mao Zedong
• May Fourth Movement
• Long March

2. TAKING NOTES
Make a chart like the one below to compare and contrast Jiang Jieshi and Mao Zedong.

	Jiang	Mao
Party		
Key Supporters		
Reforms		
Military Actions		

3. RECOGNIZING EFFECTS
What influence did foreign nations have on China from 1912 to 1938? Support your answer with details from the text.

THINK ABOUT
• the outcome of the Treaty of Versailles
• the role of the Soviet Union
• the temporary truce during the Chinese civil war

4. ANALYZING THEMES
Revolution What caused the Communist revolutionary movement in China to gain strength?

THINK ABOUT
• Jiang's government and policies
• the Soviet Union's influence
• the conditions of rural peasants
• Mao's role and achievements

ANSWERS

1. TERMS & NAMES
Kuomintang, p. 401
Sun Yixian, p. 401
Mao Zedong, p. 402
May Fourth Movement, p. 402
Long March, p. 404

2. TAKING NOTES
Possible Responses: Party:

(Jiang) Nationalist; (Mao) Communist. Supporters: (Jiang) bankers and business people; (Mao) peasants. Reforms: (Jiang) Launched programs to modernize cities; (Mao) Divided land among local farmers. Military Actions: (Jiang) Defeated warlords; (Mao) Established Red Army.

3. RECOGNIZING EFFECTS
Possible Responses: Treaty of Versailles triggered the May Fourth Movement. Western democracies refused to support Sun's government, but the Soviet Union did. Great Britain and United States recognized the Nationalist Republic of China. Japan's invasion of China united

Jiang's and Mao's forces.

4. ANALYZING THEMES
Possible Responses: Failures of the Kuomintang; corruption in Jiang's government; Soviet Union's involvement in Chinese affairs; poverty of peasants; Mao's strong leadership.

4 Nationalism in India and Southwest Asia

TERMS & NAMES
- Mohandas K. Gandhi
- civil disobedience
- Mustafa Kemal

MAIN IDEA	**WHY IT MATTERS NOW**
Nationalism triggered independence movements to overthrow colonial power.	These independent nations—India, Turkey, Iran, and Saudi Arabia—are key players on the world stage today.

SETTING THE STAGE The end of World War I stirred nationalist activity in India, Turkey, and some Southwest Asian countries. The British Empire, which controlled India, began to show signs of cracking.

Indian Nationalism Grows

Indian nationalism had been growing since the mid-1800s. Many upper-class Indians who attended British schools learned European views of nationalism and democracy. They began to apply these political ideas to their own country. Well-educated Indians began to resent the two centuries of British rule.

Two groups formed to rid India of foreign rule: the Indian National Congress, or Congress Party, in 1885, and the Muslim League in 1906. Though deep divisions existed between Hindus and Muslims, they found common ground. They shared the heritage of British rule and an understanding of democratic ideals. These two groups both worked toward the goal of national independence.

This Indian soldier fought for the British in World War I.

World War I Heightens Nationalist Activity Until World War I, the vast majority of Indians had little interest in nationalism. The situation changed as over a million Indians enlisted in the British army. In return for their service, the British government promised reforms that would eventually lead to self-government. Indian leaders bided their time. They expected to make gains once the war was over.

Later in the war, Indian demands led to the declaration in Parliament favoring the "increasing association of Indians in every branch of the administration, and the gradual development of self-governing institutions." To many Indians, these political reforms signaled that Indians would gain a greater voice in government and ultimately achieve their goal of self-rule.

In 1918, Indian troops returned home from the war. They expected Britain to fulfill its promise. Instead, they found themselves once again treated as second-class citizens. Radical nationalists carried out acts of violence to show their hatred of British rule. To curb dissent, in 1919 the British passed the Rowlatt Act. This law allowed the government to jail protesters without trial for as long as two years. To Western-educated Indians, denial of a trial by jury violated their individual rights. Violent protests against the act flared in the Punjab, the Indian province with the greatest number of World War I veterans.

Background
Unlike Europeans, Asians, including Indians, viewed World War I as a civil war among the feuding nations of Europe.

Vocabulary
dissent: difference of opinion.

Revolution and Nationalism **405**

Section 4 Overview

OBJECTIVES

1. To trace the events that fueled nationalist activity in India.

2. To summarize how Gandhi used nonviolent tactics to free India from British rule.

3. To explain how Indian self-rule heightened conflicts between Muslims and Hindus.

4. To describe nationalist activity and the rise of independence movements in Southwest Asia.

SKILLBUILDER
- Interpreting maps: location, region, p. 409

CRITICAL THINKING
- Recognizing effects, p. 406
- Making inferences, p. 407
- Comparing, p. 408
- Hypothesizing, p. 409

FOCUS

5-Minute Warm-Up

▶ **Perceiving Causes**
To help students understand Gandhi's tactics, have them answer these questions.

1. Look at the History Makers on page 406. Why was Gandhi forced off the train in South Africa?

2. Why did South African president Nelson Mandela recognize Gandhi with a special freedom award?

WARM-UP TRANSPARENCY 14

OBJECTIVE ① INSTRUCT

Indian Nationalism Grows

▶ **Key Ideas**
- After World War I, Indian nationalists defy British rule.
- In 1919, British troops fire on Hindu and Muslim protesters meeting in the city of Amritsar.

IN-DEPTH RESOURCES: UNIT 4
Guided Reading, p. 22

ACCESS FOR STUDENTS ACQUIRING ENGLISH
Guided Reading (Spanish), p. 156

SECTION 4 RESOURCES

PRINT RESOURCES

IN-DEPTH RESOURCES: UNIT 4
Guided Reading, p. 22
Primary Source: from *Hind Swaraj*, p. 29

ACCESS FOR STUDENTS ACQUIRING ENGLISH
Guided Reading (Spanish), p. 156

FORMAL ASSESSMENT
Section Quiz, p. 177

ALTERNATIVE ASSESSMENT BOOK

TECHNOLOGY RESOURCES

WORLD ART AND CULTURES TRANSPARENCIES
AT66 *Persian Musicians*

CRITICAL THINKING TRANSPARENCIES
CT30 Time Machine: Revolution and Nationalism
CT66 Visual Summary

CD-ROM
Electronic Library of Primary Sources

INTERNET www.mlworldhistory.com

Teacher's Edition **405**

OBJECTIVE **2** INSTRUCT

Gandhi's Principles of Nonviolence

▶ *Key Ideas*
- Gandhi develops nonviolent tactics to battle injustice.
- Gandhi's successful campaign of civil disobedience weakens the British government's authority and economic power.
- Gandhi gains worldwide support for his independence movement following the Salt March in 1930.

HISTORY MAKERS
Mohandas K. Gandhi

Besides being denied first-class seating on trains, Indians faced other humiliations in South Africa. Outraged at such injustices, Gandhi organized and led hunger strikes, public demonstrations, and marches. Though Gandhi and his followers landed in jail for these defiant acts, his persistence finally paid off. By the summer of 1914, many of the discriminatory laws against Indians in South Africa were repealed. Ask students to discuss how South Africa was a training ground for Gandhi's future role as the leader of the Indian independence movement.

 IN-DEPTH RESOURCES: UNIT 4
Primary Source: from *Hind Swaraj*, p. 29

 ELECTRONIC LIBRARY OF PRIMARY SOURCES
from "Nonviolence"

Amritsar Massacre To protest the Rowlatt Act, around 10,000 Hindus and Muslims flocked to Amritsar, the capital city of the Punjab, in the spring of 1919. At a huge festival, they intended to fast and pray and to listen to political speeches. A small group of nationalists were also on the scene. The demonstration, especially the alliance of Hindus and Muslims, alarmed the British.

Most people at the gathering were unaware that the British government had banned public meetings. However, General Reginald Dyer, the British commander at Amritsar, believed they were openly defying the ban. He ordered his troops to fire on the crowd without warning. The shooting lasted ten minutes. British troops killed nearly 400 Indians and wounded about 1200.

News of the slaughter sparked an explosion of anger across India. Almost overnight, millions of Indians changed from loyal British subjects into revolutionaries and nationalists. These Indians demanded independence.

Background The Punjab is located in northwest India.

HISTORY MAKERS

**Mohandas K. Gandhi
1869–1948**

From 1893 to 1914, Gandhi worked as a lawyer in South Africa, where he fought racial prejudice against Indians. Shortly after his arrival, Gandhi bought a first-class ticket and boarded a train. A white conductor ordered Gandhi to move to the third-class coach, reserved for Indians. But Gandhi refused. The conductor forced Gandhi off the train at the next station.

To honor Gandhi's act of resistance, South African president Nelson Mandela recognized him with a special freedom award in April 1997. Mandela declared,

Today we are righting a century-old wrong. This station, once one of the world's most notorious symbols of discrimination, intolerance, and oppression, today proclaims a message of dignity restored. . . . Gandhi's magnificent example of personal sacrifice and dedication in the face of oppression was one of his many legacies to our country and the world.

Gandhi's Principles of Nonviolence

The massacre at Amritsar set the stage for **Mohandas K. Gandhi** (GAHN·dee) to emerge as the leader of the independence movement. He began to form his social and political ideas during the mid-1880s before he attended law school in England. Gandhi's new strategy for battling injustice evolved from his deeply religious approach to political activity. His teachings blended ideas from all of the major world religions, including Hinduism, Islam, and Christianity. The Indian poet Rabindranath Tagore described him as "this great soul in a beggar's garb." Gandhi attracted millions of followers. Soon they were calling him the Mahatma (muh·HAHT·muh), meaning "Great Soul."

When the British failed to punish the officers responsible for the killings at the Amritsar massacre, Gandhi urged the Indian National Congress to follow a policy of noncooperation with the British government:

A VOICE FROM THE PAST
This is in essence the principle of nonviolent noncooperation. It follows therefore that it must have its root in love. Its object should not be to punish the opponent or to inflict injury upon him. Even while noncooperating with him, we must make him feel that in us he has a friend and we should try to reach his heart by rendering him humanitarian service wherever possible.

MOHANDAS K. GANDHI, quoted in *Gandhi the Man*

**THINK THROUGH HISTORY
A. Recognizing Effects** What changes resulted from the Amritsar massacre?
A. Possible Answer Spirit of nationalism grew more intense; Gandhi became leader of the independence movement.

Civil Disobedience Gandhi developed the principle of satyagraha (SUH·tyah·grah·ha), or "truth-force." In English, satyagraha is called passive resistance or **civil disobedience**—the deliberate and public refusal to obey an unjust law. Gandhi wrote, "Complete civil disobedience is a rebellion without the element of violence . . . One *perfect* civil resister is enough to win the battle of Right and Wrong." In 1920, under Gandhi's influence, the Congress Party endorsed civil disobedience and nonviolence as the means to achieve independence.

Gandhi launched his campaign of civil disobedience to weaken the British government's authority and economic power. He called on Indians to refuse to do the following: buy British goods, attend government schools, pay British taxes, and vote in elections. Gandhi staged a successful boycott of British cloth, a source of wealth for the

Vocabulary
boycott: a refusal to buy.

CONNECTIONS ACROSS TIME AND PLACE

Civil Disobedience Henry David Thoreau's views on moral conduct and nonviolent resistance helped shape Gandhi's philosophical beliefs. In 1844, Thoreau spent a night in jail for refusing to pay a poll tax used to finance the U.S. government's war with Mexico. In 1847, Thoreau published an essay, now titled "Civil Disobedience," inspired by this experience. He defended his actions on ethical grounds. "Unjust laws exist," he wrote, "but shall we obey them?" Thoreau suggested that a "peaceable revolution" could be staged if enough people refused to pay taxes.

Thoreau later willfully violated the law by his active involvement in the underground railroad. Other civil resisters brought enslaved African Americans to Thoreau's cabin in Walden Pond and hid them in the woods. In the dark of night, Thoreau escorted the runaway slaves to another safe house. Through the years, Thoreau and other citizens of Concord, Massachusetts, helped many of these fugitives secure their freedom.

Encourage interested students to read Thoreau's essay "Civil Disobedience" and point out ideas that are reflected in Gandhi's principles of nonviolence.

Background
The spinning wheel is the symbol on the Indian flag.

British. He urged all Indians to weave their own cloth. Gandhi himself devoted two hours each day to spinning his own yarn on a simple handwheel. He wore only home-spun cloth and encouraged Indians to follow his example. As a result of the boycott, the sale of British cloth in India dropped sharply.

Throughout 1920, the British arrested thousands of Indians who had participated in strikes and demonstrations. Gandhi's weapon of civil disobedience took an economic toll on the British. They struggled to keep trains running, factories operating, and overcrowded jails from bursting. Despite Gandhi's pleas for nonviolence, protests often led to riots. In 1922, rioters attacked a police station and set several officers on fire.

The Slow March to Independence In 1930, Gandhi organized a demonstration to defy the hated Salt Acts. According to these British laws, Indians could buy salt from no other source but the government. They also had to pay sales tax on salt. To show their opposition, Gandhi and his followers walked about 240 miles to the seacoast. There they began to make their own salt by collecting seawater and letting it evaporate. This peaceful protest was called the Salt March.

Soon afterward, some demonstrators planned a march to a site where the British government processed salt. They intended to shut this saltworks down. Police officers with steel-tipped clubs attacked the demonstrators. An American journalist was an eyewitness to the event. He described the "sickening whacks of clubs on unprotected skulls" and people "writhing in pain with fractured skulls or broken shoulders." Still the people continued to march peacefully, refusing to defend themselves against their attackers. Newspapers across the globe carried the journalist's story, which won worldwide support for Gandhi's independence movement.

Gandhi (standing in the center with his head bowed) led Indians in the Salt March. The demonstrators protested the British government's control of salt sales.

More demonstrations took place throughout India. Eventually, about 60,000 people, including Gandhi, were arrested.

THINK THROUGH HISTORY
B. Making Inferences How did the Salt March represent Gandhi's methods for change?
B. Possible Answer The protest against British rule was based on noncooperation and civil disobedience.

Great Britain Grants India Self-Rule

Gandhi and his followers gradually reaped the rewards of their civil disobedience campaigns and gained greater political power for the Indian people. In 1935, the British Parliament passed the Government of India Act. It provided local self-government and limited democratic elections.

With this act, India began moving toward full independence from Great Britain. However, the Government of India Act also fueled mounting tensions between Muslims and Hindus. These two groups had conflicting visions of India's future as an independent nation. Indian Muslims, outnumbered by Hindus, feared that Hindus would control India if it won independence. In Chapter 17, you will read about the outcome of India's bid for independence.

Revolution and Nationalism **407**

MORE ABOUT . . .
Gandhi's Views
Gandhi's emphasis on the traditional values of village life and on handicrafts made it clear to the majority of Indians that he understood and sympathized with their problems. Gandhi realized that any feeling of Indian nationalism had to begin with the village. Gandhi sought to make the spinning wheel a symbol of contact between the masses of poor people and their middle-class leaders.

MORE ABOUT . . .
The Impact of the Salt March
Dr. Martin Luther King, Jr., wrote his doctoral thesis on the life and teachings of Gandhi. The Salt March was one of King's models for the sit-ins in Birmingham, Alabama. In 1963, King led a massive civil rights campaign there for African-American voter registration and desegregation in housing and education. Like Gandhi, King was often jailed, believing it was honorable to be imprisoned for a just cause.

OBJECTIVE ③ INSTRUCT

Great Britain Grants India Self-Rule

▶ *Key Ideas*
• In 1935, India gains the right to establish local self-government and to hold limited democratic elections.
• As India moves toward complete independence, tensions mount between Muslims and Hindus.

CASE STUDY 1—India and Britain: Colonialism and Imperialism, p. 2

TEACHING OPTION **BLOCK SCHEDULING** **COOPERATIVE ACTIVITY: Investigating Examples of Nonviolent Protests** **CLASS TIME 30 MINUTES**

Task: Pairs of students will choose and research a movement or organization that uses nonviolent protests to advocate a cause. Examples include Earth First!, Greenpeace, and other environmental, animal rights, and political activist movements. Then each pair will meet with another pair to exchange information and to draw comparisons among the movements or organizations they chose.

Purpose: To learn more about the legacy of Gandhi's nonviolent tactics for battling injustice.

Activity: Ask each pair of students to find an organization or movement that is dedicated to the principles of nonviolence as a strategy for effecting change. Students should focus on the goals of the organization or movement and the methods it uses to achieve those goals. Have students cite specific examples of nonviolent tactics, such as marches,

demonstrations, boycotts, advertising campaigns, and acts of civil disobedience. After the two sets of partners exchange information with one another, the four students should make a Venn diagram comparing the goals and the nonviolent strategies of each organization or movement.

ALTERNATIVE ASSESSMENT BOOK
Standards for Evaluating a Cooperative Activity

Teacher's Edition **407**

Nationalism Spreads to Southwest Asia

▶ Key Ideas

- Mustafa Kemal leads Turkish nationalists in overthrowing the last Ottoman sultan and helps establish a new republic.
- After a nationalist revolt in Persia, Reza Shah seizes power and in 1935 renames the country Iran.
- Ibn Saud unifies Arabia and in 1932 renames the new kingdom Saudi Arabia.
- High demand for oil transforms the economy of Southwest Asia.

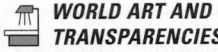 **WORLD ART AND CULTURES TRANSPARENCIES**
AT66 *Persian Musicians*

HISTORYMAKERS
Mustafa Kemal

In 1928, Kemal introduced the Latin alphabet, replacing the Arabic letters. He wanted people to forget their history under the Ottomans and to return to the roots of their ancient Turkish language. After his reform, Turkish authors and poets began following the models of Western literature.

CRITICAL THINKING ACTIVITY
CLASS TIME: 15 MINUTES

To help students analyze the similarities and differences among three nationalist leaders in Southwest Asia, have them copy the diagram below and fill it in.

UnresolvedProblems

Economic Issues in the Developing World

Attempts at modernization can bring unexpected difficulties. For example, in Persia, the leader Shah Pahlavi wanted to improve health care. To do this, he had a very modern hospital constructed. The hospital had the most up-to-date equipment and doctors trained in Vienna and New York. However, the hospital was a failure. The failure was caused by the lack of trained nurses and orderlies to carry out doctors' orders and technicians to service the modern equipment. Furthermore, the local population had little understanding of the ideas of sanitation and did not follow doctors' directions correctly.

In another action by the Shah, an 870-mile railroad was constructed that bypassed all but two major cities and did not connect with any neighboring country.
See Epilogue, p. 599.

Nationalism Spreads to Southwest Asia

Just as the people of India fought to have their own nation after World War I, the people of Southwest Asia also launched independence movements during this time. Each group in Southwest Asia chose a different path toward nation building.

The breakup of the Ottoman Empire and growing Western interest in Southwest Asia spurred the rise of nationalism in this region.

Turkey Becomes a Republic By the end of World War I, Turkey was all that remained of the Ottoman Empire. It included the old Turkish homeland of Anatolia and a small strip of land around Istanbul.

In 1919, Greek soldiers dealt a death blow to the Ottoman Empire. They invaded Turkey and threatened to conquer it. The Turkish sultan, weak and corrupt, was powerless to stop them. In 1922, a brilliant commander, **Mustafa Kemal** (keh·MAHL), led Turkish nationalists in overthrowing the last Ottoman sultan. A young woman who played a major role in the revolution described her strong nationalistic feelings: "I suddenly ceased to exist as an individual. I worked, wrote and lived as a unit of that magnificent national madness."

In 1923, Kemal became the president of the new Republic of Turkey, the first republic in Southwest Asia. He ushered in many sweeping reforms to achieve his goal of transforming Turkey into a modern nation. Kemal separated the laws of Islam from the laws of the nation. He abolished religious courts and created a new legal system based on European law. Under Kemal, women gained more freedom. He granted women the right to vote and to hold public office. Kemal also launched government-funded programs to industrialize Turkey and to spur economic growth.

Persia Becomes Iran Before World War I, both Great Britain and Russia had established spheres of influence in the ancient country of Persia. After the war, when Russia was still reeling from the Bolshevik Revolution, the British tried to take over all of Persia. This maneuver triggered a nationalist revolt in Persia. In 1921, a Persian army officer seized power. In 1925 he deposed the ruling shah.

Persia's new leader, Reza Shah Pahlavi (PAL·uh·vee), like Kemal in Turkey, set out to modernize his country. He established public schools, built roads and railroads, promoted industrial growth, and extended women's rights. Unlike Kemal, Reza Shah kept all power in his own hands. In 1935, he changed the name of his country from Persia to Iran.

Saudi Arabia Keeps Islamic Traditions While Turkey broke with many Islamic traditions, another new country held strictly to Islamic law. In 1902, Abd al-Aziz Ibn Saud (sah·OOD), a member of a once-powerful Arabian family, began a successful campaign to unify Arabia. In 1932, he renamed the new kingdom Saudi Arabia after his family.

Ibn Saud carried on Arab and Islamic traditions. Loyalty to the Saudi government was based on custom, religion, and family ties. Alcoholic drinks were illegal. Like Kemal and Reza Shah, Ibn Saud brought some modern technology, such as telephones and radios, to his country. However, modernization in Saudi Arabia was limited to religiously acceptable areas.

Oil Resources Spur Economic Development While nationalism steadily emerged as a major force in Southwest Asia, the region's economy was also taking a new direction. The rising demand for petroleum products in industrialized countries brought new oil explorations to Southwest Asia. During the 1920s and 1930s, European and American companies discovered huge oil deposits in Iran, Iraq, Saudi Arabia, and

Background
The Ottoman Empire had ruled in Southwest Asia for about 500 years.

THINK THROUGH HISTORY
C. Comparing How were Kemal's leadership and Reza Shah's leadership similar?

Less Proficient Readers: Clarifying In reading pages 405–409, less proficient readers might use the SQ3R study method, as follows:

1. Survey the pages by skimming for headings and topic sentences.
2. Jot down any questions about the text, such as what role nationalism

played in India, Turkey, Iran, and Saudi Arabia.
3. Read the pages and look for answers to these questions.
4. Recite or record any answers that are found.
5. Review the information to answer any questions that remain.

Science The word *petroleum* means "rock oil." Wells are drilled into oil-bearing rock to release the oil. The pressure of the natural gas helps bring the oil to the surface. Unless the drilling is carefully controlled, the high pressure causes wasteful oil gushers. Even with modern technology, only about 40 percent of the oil is pumped out of a given well.

When petroleum is refined, it is separated into many byproducts, such as gasoline for automobiles and kerosene and fuel oil for heating. Other petroleum products are used as lubricants. Both natural gas and petroleum are used as raw materials in making such substances as plastics, fertilizers, medicines, and dyes.

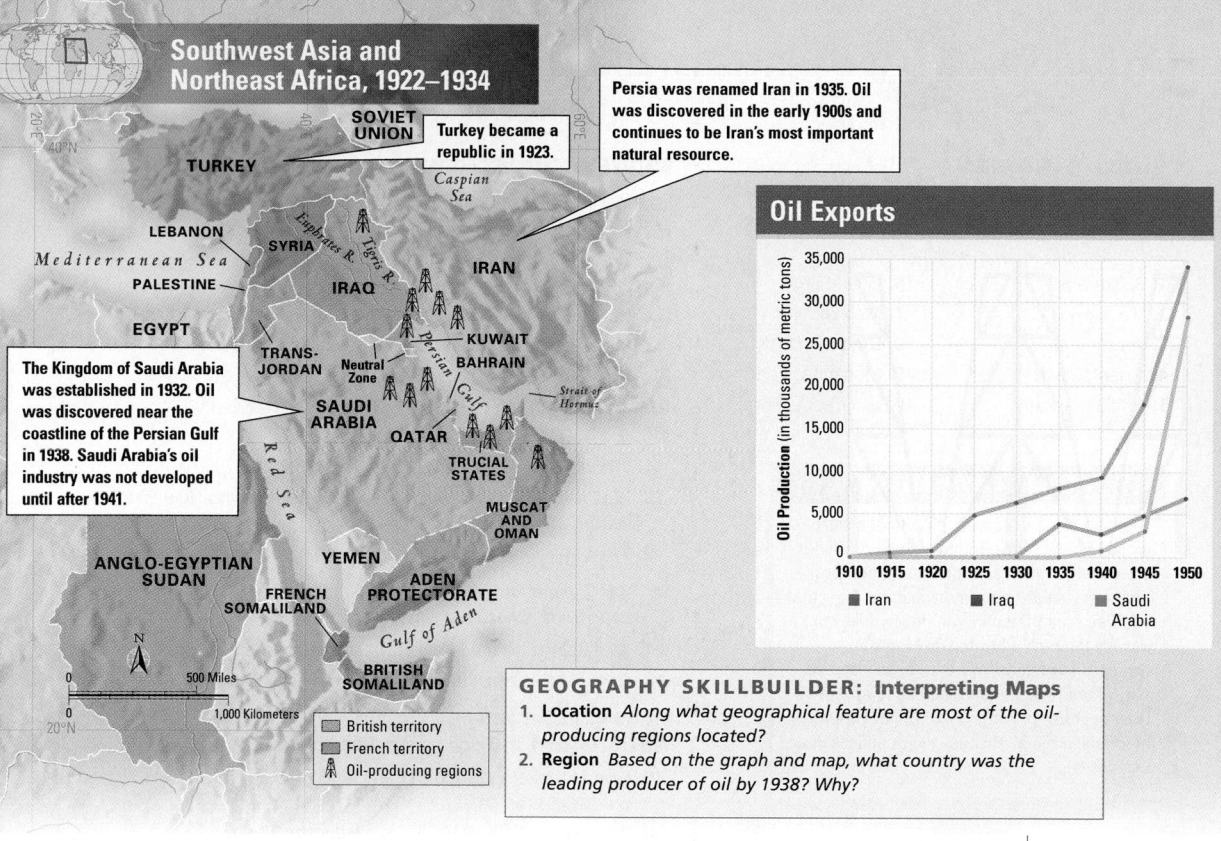

Southwest Asia and Northeast Africa, 1922–1934

Turkey became a republic in 1923.

Persia was renamed Iran in 1935. Oil was discovered in the early 1900s and continues to be Iran's most important natural resource.

SOVIET UNION
TURKEY
Caspian Sea
LEBANON
SYRIA
Mediterranean Sea
PALESTINE
IRAQ
IRAN
EGYPT
TRANS-JORDAN
Neutral Zone
KUWAIT
BAHRAIN
Persian Gulf
SAUDI ARABIA
QATAR
TRUCIAL STATES
Strait of Hormuz
Red Sea
MUSCAT AND OMAN
ANGLO-EGYPTIAN SUDAN
YEMEN
FRENCH SOMALILAND
ADEN PROTECTORATE
Gulf of Aden
BRITISH SOMALILAND

The Kingdom of Saudi Arabia was established in 1932. Oil was discovered near the coastline of the Persian Gulf in 1938. Saudi Arabia's oil industry was not developed until after 1941.

0   500 Miles
0   1,000 Kilometers

- British territory
- French territory
- Oil-producing regions

Oil Exports

Oil Production (in thousands of metric tons)

35,000 · 30,000 · 25,000 · 20,000 · 15,000 · 10,000 · 5,000

1910 1915 1920 1925 1930 1935 1940 1945 1950

- Iran
- Iraq
- Saudi Arabia

GEOGRAPHY SKILLBUILDER: Interpreting Maps

1. **Location** Along what geographical feature are most of the oil-producing regions located?
2. **Region** Based on the graph and map, what country was the leading producer of oil by 1938? Why?

Kuwait. Foreign businesses invested huge sums of money to develop these oil fields. Geologists later learned that the land around the Persian Gulf has nearly two-thirds of the world's known supply of oil.

This important resource led to rapid and dramatic economic changes and development. Saudi Arabia, for example, would soon become a nation of wealthy oil exporters. Yet oil proved to be a mixed blessing for Southwest Asia. Though oil brought huge profits, it also encouraged Western nations to try to dominate this region. Meanwhile, Western nations were about to face a more immediate crisis as power-hungry leaders seized control in Italy and Germany.

Section 4 Assessment

1. TERMS & NAMES

Identify
- Mohandas K. Gandhi
- civil disobedience
- Mustafa Kemal

2. TAKING NOTES

Create a web diagram like the one below. Show the different forms of nationalism that developed in the Asian countries shown.

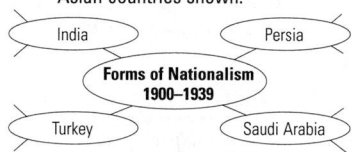

India — Persia
Forms of Nationalism 1900–1939
Turkey — Saudi Arabia

In which of these countries did World War I trigger nationalist movements?

3. HYPOTHESIZING

What do you think a nation might gain and lose by modernizing?

THINK ABOUT
- what positive changes occurred in Turkey and Iran
- why modernization was limited in Saudi Arabia
- why Kemal set rules for clothing
- why Gandhi wore only homespun cloth

4. THEME ACTIVITY

Science and Technology
Work in small groups to research products and consumer goods made from petroleum. Create an illustrated list of items that were in great demand in industrialized countries during the 1930s.

Revolution and Nationalism **409**

ANSWERS

1. TERMS & NAMES
Mohandas K. Gandhi, p. 406
civil disobedience, p. 406
Mustafa Kemal, p. 408

2. TAKING NOTES
Possible Responses: India—Nationalists use nonviolent methods to work for independence from British rule. Turkey—Nationalists overthrow last Ottoman sultan; Kemal seeks Western-style modernization. Persia—Nationalists free Persia from British and Russian rule; Reza Shah changes country's name to Iran. Saudi Arabia—Ibn Saud unifies the nation and creates a state based on Islamic law.

3. HYPOTHESIZING
Possible Responses: Gains—increased economic and political power; greater acceptance and respect from Western nations; equal rights for women. Losses—a unique sense of cultural identity; traditional values and ways of life.

4. THEME ACTIVITY
Possible Responses: Lists should include various plastic products, cosmetics, cleaning products, lubricants, and fuels. Remind students to confine their choice of products to those in demand in the 1930s.

TERMS & NAMES

1. Bolsheviks, p. 390
2. V. I. Lenin, p. 390
3. soviet , p. 392
4. Joseph Stalin, p. 395
5. totalitarianism, p. 395
6. Great Purge, p. 397
7. Mao Zedong, p. 402
8. Long March, p. 404
9. Mohandas K. Gandhi, p. 406
10. civil disobedience, p. 406

REVIEW QUESTIONS

Answers may vary on some questions.

11. Rasputin apparently eased the symptoms of the Romanovs' hemophiliac son. To show their gratitude, the Romanovs allowed Rasputin to make key political decisions.

12. Recurring defeats in battle, the death of many soldiers, the sinking morale of the troops, bread and food shortages led to strikes and riots that forced Nicholas II to abdicate.

13. Causes—opposition in Russia to Communist rule under the Bolsheviks'; desire by Western nations to bring down Bolsheviks. Outcomes—Bolsheviks won, but country faced political chaos; economic crises.

14. Dictatorship and one-party rule; dynamic leader; rigid ideology; state control over all sectors of society; state control over the individual; dependence on modern technology; organized violence to enforce dictator's rule.

15. Stalin's Five-Year Plans—total government control over the economy. NEP—mixture of government control with some free enterprise and some private ownership.

16. Freedom of religion, freedom of speech, artistic freedom, political freedom, freedom to choose professions and locale.

17. Student demonstrations protesting the Treaty of Versailles led to a national movement that included workers, manufacturers, shopkeepers, professionals, Sun Yixian, and members of the Kuomintang.

18. Japan took advantage of China's weakened situation by invading Manchuria.

19. Gandhi called on Indians to refuse to attend government schools or to pay British taxes; staged a successful boycott of British goods, particularly cloth; staged the Salt March and gained international support for his cause.

TERMS & NAMES
Briefly explain the importance of each of the following in Russia, China, or India.

1. Bolsheviks
2. V. I. Lenin
3. soviet
4. Joseph Stalin
5. totalitarianism
6. Great Purge
7. Mao Zedong
8. Long March
9. Mohandas K. Gandhi
10. civil disobedience

Interact *with* History

On page 388, you played the role of a citizen whose country was brimming with revolutionary activity. You evaluated two tactics for change—violence and nonviolence. Now that you have read the chapter, how would you assess the pros and cons of Mao's and Gandhi's strategies? What role did violence play in the Russian and Chinese revolutions? How successful were Gandhi's nonviolent methods in India? Discuss your opinions in a small group.

REVIEW QUESTIONS

SECTION 1 *(pages 389–394)*
Revolutions in Russia

11. How did Rasputin gain political influence over the Romanov family and Russian political affairs?

12. How did World War I lead to the downfall of Czar Nicholas II?

13. Explain the causes of Russia's civil war and its outcome.

SECTION 2 *(pages 395–400)*
PATTERNS OF CHANGE: Totalitarianism
CASE STUDY: Stalinist Russia

14. What are the key traits of totalitarianism?

15. How did Stalin's Five-Year Plans differ from Lenin's New Economic Policy?

16. What individual freedoms are denied in a totalitarian state?

SECTION 3 *(pages 401–404)*
Collapse of Chinese Imperial Rule

17. Briefly describe the May Fourth Movement and its supporters.

18. How did the Japanese react to the civil war in China?

SECTION 4 *(pages 405–409)*
Nationalism in India and Southwest Asia

19. Give examples of Gandhi's campaign of civil disobedience against the British government.

20. What steps did Kemal take to modernize Turkey?

Visual Summary

Revolutionary Leaders: 1900–1939

	Lenin	Stalin	Sun Yixian	Mao Zedong	Gandhi	Kemal
Country	Russia	Russia	China	China	India	Turkey
Political Career	late 1890s–1924	early 1900s–1953	late 1890s–1925	early 1900s–1976	late 1800s–1948	early 1900s–1938
Key Role	Bolshevik revolutionary and first ruler of Communist Russia	Dictator	First president of the new Republic of China	Leader of the Chinese Communist Party	Leader of the Indian independence movement	First president of the new Republic of Turkey
Popular Name	"Father of the Revolution"	"Man of Steel"	"Father of Modern China"	"The Great Helmsman"	"Great Soul"	"Father of the Turks"
Goal	To promote a worldwide Communist revolution led by workers	To perfect a Communist state in Russia through totalitarian rule	To establish a modern government based on nationalism, democracy, and economic security	To stage a Communist revolution in China led by peasants	To achieve Indian self-rule through campaigns of civil disobedience	To transform Turkey into a modern nation

20. Kemal abolished religious courts and created a new legal system based on European law; granted women more freedom; launched government-funded programs to industrialize Turkey.

Interact *with* History

Possible Responses: Students who originally advocated violent action may now side with Gandhi's strategy of passive, or nonviolent, resistance, based on the success of his boycotts and demonstrations. Using the aftermath of the Bolshevik Revolution as an example, students may also conclude that violence breeds violence.

CRITICAL THINKING

1. THE SHIFTING ROLES OF WOMEN

Compare and contrast how women's roles changed under Stalin in Russia and Kemal in Turkey.

2. THE SOVIET ECONOMY UNDER STALIN

THEME ECONOMICS Cite evidence that Stalin might have used to disprove this claim: Economic systems that allow private ownership and encourage competition are the most productive.

3. MASSACRES IN RUSSIA AND ASIA

Copy the following chart on your paper to analyze the similarities among the events shown. Fill in the chart and write a paragraph that compares the events.

	Description	Political Outcome
Bloody Sunday (Russia, 1905)		
Amritsar Massacre (India, 1919)		
Shanghai Massacre (China, 1927)		

4. ANALYZING PRIMARY SOURCES

The following quotation from Mohandas K. Gandhi, written in 1922, describes his views of industrialization in India. Read the passage and answer the questions below it.

> **A VOICE FROM THE PAST**
> India does not need to be industrialized in the modern sense of the term. It has 7,500,000 villages scattered over a vast area 1,900 miles long, 1,500 broad. The people are rooted to the soil, and the vast majority are living a hand-to-mouth existence. . . . Agriculture does not need revolutionary changes. The Indian peasant requires a supplementary industry. The most natural is the introduction of the spinning wheel.
> **MOHANDAS K. GANDHI,** *Letter to Sir Daniel Hamilton*

- What picture does Gandhi present of India and its people?
- Gandhi believed that the spinning wheel would make Indians less dependent on the British economy. Based on what you have learned in this chapter, what was the economic impact of the widespread use of the spinning wheel?

CHAPTER ACTIVITIES

1. LIVING HISTORY: Unit Portfolio Project

THEME SCIENCE AND TECHNOLOGY Your unit portfolio project focuses on showing the impact of science and technology during the early 1900s. For Chapter 14, you might use one of these ideas to add to your portfolio.

- After reading more about the Trans-Siberian Railway, create a travel poster for a tourist agency that features interesting facts about the train and its routes.
- Write a science fiction story about a totalitarian state that uses modern technology to spread propaganda and control people. Refer to the section on Stalinist Russia for ideas.
- Draw diagrams that show the technology and methods used to drill oil in Southwest Asia during the 1920s and 1930s. Use encyclopedias or books to research the topic.

2. CONNECT TO TODAY: Cooperative Learning

THEME REVOLUTION You read about the various causes that led to the Russian Revolution of 1917. Work with a team to create a mythical country that is on the brink of revolution today. Write a profile of the conditions in that country that are triggering widespread social unrest.

INTERNET Use the Internet and other books to find out about more recent revolutions that have occurred in countries around the world. Look for common patterns that countries in political turmoil share. Use the following questions to help you brainstorm ideas for writing a profile of your mythical country.

- What type of government is currently in power?
- Who are the top political leaders, and what are they like?
- What grievances do the citizens have against the government?
- What is the gap between the rich and the poor?
- What revolutionary groups are forming? What are their goals and strategies?

FOCUS ON TIME LINES

The time line below highlights key events discussed in this chapter that fall roughly within the time span of World War I. As you study the time line, note the relationships among events that occurred in Russia, China, and India.

- What two events occurred in 1917?

Connect to History

- Explain the role that the end of World War I played in the following two events: the May Fourth Movement in China and the Amritsar Massacre in India. Support your answer with information from the text.
- How did the Russian Revolutions of 1917 trigger the Treaty of Brest-Litovsk?

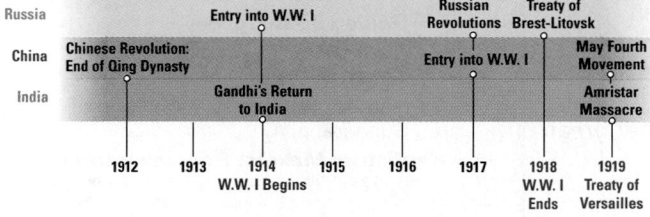

Revolution and Nationalism **411**

CHAPTER ACTIVITIES

1. LIVING HISTORY: UNIT PORTFOLIO PROJECT

Standards for Evaluation
A travel poster should meet the following criteria:

- Displays eye-catching graphics.
- Contains anecdotal and historical details about the railway.
- Includes information about stops along the train route.

Standards for Evaluation
A science fiction story should meet the following criteria:

- Re-creates aspects of Stalinist Russia in a futuristic setting.
- Contains a well-constructed plot and interesting characters.
- Features the role of propaganda in a totalitarian state.

Standards for Evaluation
Diagrams of oil-drilling methods and technology should meet the following criteria:

- Be clear and easy to follow.
- Contain well-organized graphic representations.
- Include informative labels for the diagrams.

2. CONNECT TO TODAY: COOPERATIVE LEARNING

Standards for Evaluation
A profile of a mythical country should meet the following criteria:

- Identifies revolutionary groups and their aims.
- Contains information about the oppressive life of ordinary people.
- Analyzes the weaknesses of the political leaders and government in power.
- Shows evidence of research.

FOCUS ON TIME LINES

- Russian Revolution and China's entry into World War I.

Connect to History *Possible Responses:*
- China—Anger over the Treaty of Versailles sparked a student protest that grew into May Fourth Movement. India—End of World War I heightened nationalist activity. The British government failed to keep its promises regarding Indian self-government, then passed the Rowlett Act in 1919 to curb dissent. In protest, demonstrators flocked to Amritsar, where hundreds were gunned down.
- Severe military losses in World War I were one of the causes of the Russian Revolutions. The Bolsheviks fulfilled their promise to obtain peace by signing the Treaty of Brest-Litovsk with the Germans, thus ending Russia's role in the war.

CRITICAL THINKING

1. THE SHIFTING ROLES OF WOMEN

Possible Responses: Under both—equal rights. Under Stalin—new educational and job opportunities but limited freedom. Under Kemal—could vote and hold public office.

2. THE SOVIET ECONOMY UNDER STALIN

Possible Responses: Stalin might cite statistics pointing to the enormous increase in industrial and agricultural production under his state-controlled Five-Year Plans.

3. MASSACRES IN RUSSIA AND ASIA

Possible Responses: Bloody Sunday—The killing of unarmed protesters sparked the Revolution of 1905 and led to the establishment of Russia's first parliament. Amritsar Massacre—The killing of unarmed protesters led to the emergence of Gandhi as the leader of India's independence movement. Shanghai Massacre—The killing of many Communists led to Mao's emergence as a revolutionary leader.

4. ANALYZING PRIMARY SOURCES

Possible Responses: It is largely a rural nation whose people could be self-sufficient. The spinning wheel was key to Gandhi's boycott of British cloth.

	Key Ideas	COPY MASTERS	ASSESSMENT
SECTION 1 An Age of Uncertainty *pp. 415–420*	*New ideas in science, the arts, and technology develop in the postwar period and change the way people look at the world and live their lives.*	*In-Depth Resources: Unit 4* • **Guided Reading,** p. 37 • **Primary Source:** from An Interview with Charles Lindbergh, p. 44 • **Literature:** from *This Side of Paradise,* p. 48 • **History Makers:** Sigmund Freud, p. 51	P E *Section 1 Assessment,* p. 420 *Formal Assessment* • Section Quiz, p. 186 *Alternative Assessment Book* • Standards for Evaluating a Cooperative Activity
SECTION 2 A Global Depression *pp. 421–426*	*An economic depression begins in the United States in 1929. It spreads throughout the world and lasts for a decade.*	*In-Depth Resources: Unit 4* • **Guided Reading,** p. 38 • **Skillbuilder Practice:** Identifying Problems, p 41 • **Primary Source:** German Inflation, p. 45	P E *Section 2 Assessment,* p. 426 *Formal Assessment* • Section Quiz, p. 187 *Alternative Assessment Book* • Standards for Evaluating a Cooperative Activity
SECTION 3 Fascism Rises in Europe *pp. 427–430*	*In response to political turmoil and economic crises, many countries in Europe, including Italy and Germany, turn to Fascist dictators.*	*In-Depth Resources: Unit 4* • **Guided Reading,** p. 39 • **Primary Source:** Kristallnacht, p. 46 • **Literature:** Poems by Bertolt Brecht, p. 49 • **Connections Across Time and Cultures:** Absolutism and Fascism, p. 53	P E *Section 3 Assessment,* p. 430 *Formal Assessment* • Section Quiz, p. 188 *Alternative Assessment Book* • Standards for Evaluating a Product or Performance
SECTION 4 Aggressors on the March *pp. 431–435*	*Germany, Italy, and Japan conquer other countries. The League of Nations and the rest of the world do nothing to stop them, and the specter of another great war haunts Europe.*	*In-Depth Resources: Unit 4* • **Guided Reading,** p. 40 • **Geography Application:** Spain During the 1930s, p. 42 • **Primary Source:** The Bombing of Guernica, p. 47 • **History Makers:** Francisco Franco, p. 52	P E *Section 4 Assessment,* p. 435 *Formal Assessment* • Section Quiz, p. 189 *Alternative Assessment Book* • Standards for Evaluating a Cooperative Activity
CHAPTER RESOURCES	Chapter Overview *The 1920s see great changes in technology, science, and the arts. The Great Depression of the 1930s causes worldwide crisis. In response to aggression by Fascist Italy and Nazi Germany, Britain and France pursue appeasement; the United States, isolationism.*	*Telescoping the Times* • Chapter Summary, pp. 61–63 *Planning for Block Schedules*	P E *Chapter Assessment,* pp. 436–437 *Chapter Activities,* p. 437 *Formal Assessment* • Chapter Test, forms A and B, pp. 190–195 *Test Generator* *Alternative Assessment Book*

TECHNOLOGY

 Warm-Up Transparency 15

 World Art and Cultures Transparencies
- AT67 *The Twittering Machine*
- AT68 *Electric Prisms*

 Electronic Library of Primary Sources
- "The Death of God"

 INTERNET RESOURCES
www.mlworldhistory.com

 Warm-Up Transparency 15

 Electronic Library of Primary Sources
- "Famine in Russia"

 INTERNET RESOURCES
www.mlworldhistory.com

 Warm-Up Transparency 15

 World Art and Cultures Transparencies
- AT69 *Pillars of Society*

 Critical Thinking Transparencies
- CT31 Economic Crisis: Between Two Fires

 Electronic Library of Primary Sources
- from Memos on the Aims of Germany and Japan

 INTERNET RESOURCES
www.mlworldhistory.com

 Warm-Up Transparency 15

 Geography Transparencies
- GT31 Expansion of Nazi Germany, 1933–1939

 Critical Thinking Transparencies
- CT67 Visual Summary

 Electronic Library of Primary Sources
- from Speech in the House of Commons

 INTERNET RESOURCES
www.mlworldhistory.com

 Chapter Summaries on Audiocassette in English and Spanish

 INTERNET RESOURCES
www.mlworldhistory.com

 ## Block Scheduling (90 MINUTES)

Day 1
Section 1, pp. 415–420

 COOPERATIVE ACTIVITY
Pick a Person of the Decade, p. 417 (Teacher's Edition)

Section Assessment, p. 420

Day 2
Section 2, pp. 421–426

 COOPERATIVE ACTIVITY
Creating a Political Cartoon, p. 425 (Teacher's Edition)

Section Assessment, p. 426

Day 3
Section 3, pp. 427–430
Section Assessment, p. 430

Day 4
Section 4, pp. 431–435

 COOPERATIVE ACTIVITY
Headlining the News, p. 432 (Teacher's Edition)

Section Assessment, p. 435
Chapter Assessment, pp. 436–437

Yearly Pacing *Chapter 15 Total:* 4 days *Yearly Total:* 85 days

 Planning for Block Schedules

Customizing for Special Needs

Students Acquiring English

 Access for Students Acquiring English
- **Guided Reading** for Sections 1–4 (Spanish), pp. 163–166
- **Chapter Summary** (Spanish), pp. 160–162
- **Skillbuilder Practice** Identifying Problems (Spanish), p. 167
- **Geography Application** Spain During the 1930s (Spanish), p. 168

 Spanish Reading Study Guide
- pp. 157–166

 Chapter Summaries on Audiocassette in English and Spanish

Less Proficient Readers

 In-Depth Resources: Unit 4
- **Guided Reading** for Sections 1–4, pp. 37–40
- **Skillbuilder Practice** Identifying Problems, p. 41
- **Geography Application** Spain During the 1930s, p. 42

 Telescoping the Times
- Chapter Summary, pp. 61–63

 Reading Study Guide
- pp. 157–166

 Chapter Summaries on Audiocassette

Gifted and Talented Students

 In-Depth Resources: Unit 4

Primary Sources:
- from An Interview with Charles Lindbergh, p. 44
- German Inflation, p. 45
- Kristallnacht, p. 46
- The Bombing of Guernica, p. 47

History Makers
- Sigmund Freud, p. 51
- Francisco Franco, p. 52

Connections to Literature READINGS FOR STUDENTS

 In-Depth Resources: Unit 4
Literature: from *This Side of Paradise,* p. 48; poems by Bertolt Brecht, p. 49

Enrichment Reading
- **Peck, Robert**
Arly
New York: Walker, 1989
The Great Depression doesn't much affect Arly's family because they are already poor field workers. The first schoolteacher in the community has a great impact on Arly's life.

- **Uhlman, Fred**
Reunion
New York: Penguin, 1978
A brief, improbable friendship is shared by two boys in the Germany of 1932. One boy is the son of a Jewish doctor; the other is the son of a German aristocrat.

 PE = Pupil's Edition   = Overhead Transparency   = Software   = Video

= Copy Master   = CD-ROM   = Audiocassette   = Internet

Years of Crisis, 1919–1939

Accessing Prior Knowledge

- Ask students to read the captions for each of the three pictures and discuss what they already know about Charles Lindbergh and his airplane, the *Spirit of St. Louis,* about the Great Depression, and about the Nazi party.

Drawing Conclusions and Analyzing

- Have students contrast Dorothea Lange's photograph from the Great Depression with the Nazi rally in Nuremberg. Ask them what the mood of each photograph seems to be. Explain how these different feelings are conveyed.

- Ask students to discuss what the people in each picture might be doing. Have them generate a list of questions these pictures raise.

Geography Connection

Ask students to look at the map and inset on these two pages.

- What countries would play major roles in Europe in the period 1919–1939? *Great Britain, Germany, France, Spain, Italy, and the Soviet Union.*

- What island nation in Asia was an aggressor during this time? *Japan.*

CHAPTER 15 — Years of Crisis, 1919–1939

PREVIEWING THEMES

Science and Technology
The decades of the 1920s and 1930s saw great changes in technology. Transportation was revolutionized by the spread of the automobile and the use of the airplane. Mass communication through radio, telephone, and motion pictures made the world seem smaller.

Economics
Despite signs of prosperity, the world economy of the 1920s suffered from serious flaws. It was too dependent on the economic well-being of the United States. The American stock market crashed in 1929, and the world was plunged into the worst economic depression in history.

Power and Authority
New, and yet untested, democracies rose in Europe from the ashes of World War I. However, the political and economic crises of the post-war period proved fatal for these governments. Many people turned to authoritarian leaders for answers. A new, dangerous form of national-ism—fascism—took hold in Italy and Germany. That fas-cism led the world to the brink of war in 1939.

INTERNET CONNECTION
Visit us at **www.mlworldhistory.com** to learn more about the world between the wars.

412

THE WORLD BETWEEN THE WARS, 1919–1939

Hudson Bay

0   500 Miles
0   1,000 Kilometers

N

UNITED STATES OF AMERICA

ATLANTIC OCEAN

120°W

Charles Lindbergh flew solo across the Atlantic from New York to Paris in the *Spirit of St. Louis* in **1927**. The flight sym-bolized the technological advances in the period following World War I.

The Great Depression of the 1930s started in the United States and quickly spread world-wide. It caused unemployment and hardship for millions. Despair is evident in this photo of a jobless man waiting with others for free food in 1933. The photo, taken by photogra-pher Dorothea Lange, is titled *White Angel Breadline, San Francisco.*

GEOGRAPHY THEMES

Movement

Ask students to locate roughly where Lindbergh started his historic 33½-hour solo flight across the Atlantic *(New York)* and where he landed *(Paris, France).* Have them use the scale to find the distance from New York to Paris. Then discuss with them the particular challenges of flying over an ocean rather than over land. *Possible Responses: Could not refuel over the ocean; scarcity of visual landmarks. Also, there was no place to land in an emergency. If a plane did go down, it would be difficult if not impossible to find.*

Human/Environment Interaction

Tell students that in addition to examin-ing the advances in aviation that changed the way humans think about spatial distances and the size of the world, they will also look at how devel-opments in radio and motion pictures have altered the way people communi-cate with one another across the conti-nents. Have students speculate about how the world was connected by trans-portation and communication during the 1920s and 1930s and how the develop-ment of television, computers, and satellites has changed the way we per-ceive the size of our planet and interact with peoples around the world.

Nazis marched, flags held high, in a rally in Nuremberg, Germany, in **1933**. These brown-shirted storm-troopers were militant followers of Adolf Hitler. He used them to force his will on the German nation.

East Asia

SOVIET UNION

MANCHURIA

CHINA

KOREA

JAPAN

Sea of Japan

Yellow Sea

Japan invaded Manchuria in **1931**.

SOVIET UNION

GREAT BRITAIN

GERMANY

FRANCE

ITALY

SPAIN

Black Sea

Caspian Sea

0° Equator

ADDITIONAL RESOURCES

Books for the Teacher

- Garraty, John Arthur. *The Great Depression.* San Diego: Harcourt, 1986. Causes and consequences.

- Guérin, Daniel. *The Brown Plague: Travels in Late Weimar and Early Nazi Germany.* Durham, NC: Duke UP, 1994. First-person account of the rise of Hitler and the Nazis.

Books for the Student

- Banyard, Peter. *Rise of Dictators, 1919–1939.* New York: Watts, 1986. The rise of Hitler, Mussolini, and Franco.

- Burg, David F. *The Great Depression: An Eyewitness History.* New York: Facts on File, 1996.

Videos

- *Heil Hitler: Confessions of a Hitler Youth.* Ambrose Video, 1991. 800-526-4663. The Third Reich, as viewed through the eyes of a man who joined Hitler's cause at age ten.

- *The World at War: Japan.* Coronet/MTI, 1989. 800-321-3106. Japan's road to war.

- *The World in Conflict: 1929–1945.* Social Studies School Service, 1985. 800-421-4246. Global depression and the rise of fascism.

Software

- *The Causes of World War II.* CD-ROM. Society for Visual Education, 1994. 800-829-1900.

HISTORY THROUGH ART

The Photojournalism of Dorothea Lange

The photo titled *White Angel Breadline, San Francisco,* was taken during the Great Depression in 1933 by American photographer Dorothea Lange (1895–1965). Some have considered it to be one of the most important photographs of the 20th century. This stark, haunting photo of a group of men in a bread line epitomizes in a single image the conflict between dignity and desperation that many people felt during the Great Depression.

Lange's concern for people, her appreciation of the ordinary, and the striking empathy she showed for her subjects made her unique among photographers of her day. Of her work as a photographer, Lange said, "You put your camera around your neck along with putting on your shoes, and there it is, an appendage of the body that shares your life with you. The camera is an instrument that teaches people how to see without a camera."

Many of Lange's photographs of the Great Depression were taken for the Farm Security Administration under a federal government-sponsored photography project to document conditions in the United States during that period.

Interpreting the Photograph What does this photograph tell you about life during the Great Depression? Why do you think only men are waiting in the bread line for food?

Interact *with* History

Interact *with* History

This Interact with History feature motivates students by asking them to imagine themselves in a perilous time in history—in Germany in the early 1930s. As they imagine themselves confronted with choosing a leader for their country, students will analyze the issues, explore their options, and become decision makers.

Purpose

- to set the stage for studying the years of crisis, 1919–1939.
- to help students understand some of the critical issues confronting nations, leaders, and citizens.
- to help students make connections with the various people and events that they will study in this chapter.

Teaching Strategy

Thinking Critically After students have imagined themselves in the situation described on this page, have them answer the key question and give reasons for their decision.

EXAMINING *the* ISSUES

Following are suggestions for addressing each bulleted question.

❶ Have students explain how the first candidate appeals to German patriotism and bitterness over the Versailles Treaty.

❷ Ask students how they think the crowd will react to the second candidate's statement that there are no simple or quick solutions to Germany's problems and economic recovery will be slow.

❸ Ask students why the strong leadership promised by the first candidate might seem particularly attractive during the Great Depression.

Making Connections Ask students to discuss the issue of choosing leaders in a period of crisis. What qualities are required of an effective leader at such a time?

On a spring evening in the early 1930s during the Great Depression, you are one of thousands of Germans gathered at an outdoor stadium in Munich. You are unemployed; your country is suffering. Like everyone else, you have come to this mass meeting to hear two politicians campaigning for office. Huge speakers blare out patriotic music, while you and the rest of the crowd wait impatiently for the speeches to begin.

Before long you will have to cast your ballot.

First candidate's platform:

- Remember Germany's long and glorious past.
- Our present leadership is indecisive; we need a strong, effective leader.
- Rebuild the army to protect against enemies.
- Regain the lands taken unfairly from us.
- Make sacrifices to return to economic health.
- Put the welfare of the state above all, and our country will be a great power again.

Which candidate will you choose?

Second candidate's platform:

- There are no simple or quick solutions to problems.
- Put people back to work, but economic recovery will be slow.
- Provide for the poor, elderly, and sick.
- Avoid reckless military spending.
- Act responsibly to safeguard democracy.
- Be a good neighbor country; honor our debts and treaty commitments.

EXAMINING *the* ISSUES

❶ • What strategy does each candidate have for solving the nation's problems?

❷ • How does each candidate view the role of the citizen in meeting the challenges facing the nation?

❸ • Which candidate makes the strongest appeal to the listener's emotions?

As a class, discuss these questions. In your discussion, remember what you have read about the defeated nations' bitterness toward the Versailles Treaty following World War I. How might this influence which candidate voters favor?

As you read this chapter, see how dictators were voted into power as people lost faith in democratic government in the 1920s and 1930s. Examine the factors that influenced political decisions in this troubled time.

414

Follow Up

A question on the chapter assessment will send students back to issues highlighted on this page. Remind students that their opinions may change as they learn more about the solutions offered by democratic leaders and dictators of the period.

1 An Age of Uncertainty

TERMS & NAMES
- Albert Einstein
- theory of relativity
- Sigmund Freud
- existentialism
- Friedrich Nietzsche
- surrealism
- jazz
- Charles Lindbergh

MAIN IDEA

The postwar period was one of loss and uncertainty but also one of invention, creativity, and new ideas.

WHY IT MATTERS NOW

Postwar trends in physics, psychiatry, art, literature, communication, music, and transportation still affect our lives.

SETTING THE STAGE The horrors of World War I shattered the Enlightenment belief that progress would continue and reason would prevail. New ideas and patterns of life developed in the 1920s that changed the way people looked at the world.

Science Challenges Old Ideas

The ideas of two remarkable thinkers became widely known during this "age of uncertainty." They were Albert Einstein and Sigmund Freud. Both had an enormous impact on the 20th century. Einstein and Freud challenged some of the most deeply rooted ideas that people held about themselves and their world. They were part of a scientific revolution as important as that brought about centuries earlier by Copernicus and Galileo.

Impact of Einstein's Theory of Relativity A German-born physicist, **Albert Einstein,** offered startling new ideas on space, time, energy, and matter. He began by tackling a problem that baffled physicists. Scientists had found that light travels at exactly the same speed no matter what direction it moves in relation to earth. Earth moves through space, yet its movement did not affect the speed at which light seemed to travel. This finding seemed to break the laws of motion and gravity discovered by Isaac Newton.

In 1905, Einstein theorized that while the speed of light is constant, other things that seem constant, such as space and time, are not. Space and time can change when measured relative to an object moving near the speed of light—about 186,000 miles per second. Since relative motion is the key to Einstein's idea, it is called the **theory of relativity.** Einstein's ideas had implications not only for science but for how people viewed the world. Now uncertainty and relativity replaced Newton's comforting belief of a world operating according to absolute laws of motion and gravity.

Influence of Freudian Psychology The ideas of **Sigmund Freud,** an Austrian physician, were as revolutionary as Einstein's. Freud treated patients with psychological problems. From his experiences, he constructed a theory about the human mind. He believed that much of human behavior is irrational, or beyond reason. He called the irrational part of the mind the unconscious. In the unconscious, a number of drives existed, especially pleasure-seeking drives, of which the conscious mind was unaware. Freud's theories, first published in *The Interpretation of Dreams* (1900), met with opposition, especially his ideas about the unconscious. His ideas weakened faith in reason. All the same, by the 1920s, Freud's theories had developed widespread influence.

A. Possible Answers They changed the way people thought about the world; they weakened faith in absolute truths and reason.

THINK THROUGH HISTORY
A. Recognizing Effects Why were the ideas of Einstein and Freud revolutionary?

HISTORY MAKERS

Albert Einstein
1879–1955

Albert Einstein was the greatest scientific genius since Isaac Newton. He was thought to be a slow learner as a child because he did not talk at the same age as other children. Later in life, he recalled that at age two or three he wanted to speak in sentences. But he did not want to say sentences aloud until he was sure he had them right.

As a child, Einstein was quiet, serious, and solitary. He was also a daydreamer who did not impress his teachers. In this, he was unlike many geniuses who showed exceptional ability at an early age.

However, it was at this time that Einstein developed a desire to stay with a question until it was answered. He later called this his "flight from wonder."

Years of Crisis **415**

SECTION 1 RESOURCES

PRINT RESOURCES

 IN-DEPTH RESOURCES: UNIT 4
Guided Reading, p. 37
Primary Source: from An Interview with Lindbergh, p. 44
Literature: from *This Side of Paradise,* p. 48
History Makers: Sigmund Freud, p. 51

 ACCESS FOR STUDENTS ACQUIRING ENGLISH
Guided Reading (Spanish), p. 163

 FORMAL ASSESSMENT
Section Quiz, p. 186

 ALTERNATIVE ASSESSMENT BOOK

TECHNOLOGY RESOURCES

 WORLD ART AND CULTURES TRANSPARENCIES
AT67 *The Twittering Machine*
AT68 *Electric Prisms*

CD-ROM
Electronic Library of Primary Sources

 INTERNET www.mlworldhistory.com

Section 1 Overview

OBJECTIVES

1. To explain how the scientific ideas of Einstein, Freud, and others challenged old beliefs.

2. To describe how the brutality of war led philosophers to question accepted ideas.

3. To summarize new styles in art, architecture, and music.

4. To show how new ideas and ways of life led to a new kind of individual freedom in the 1920s.

5. To explain how technological advances changed daily life.

CRITICAL THINKING

- Recognizing effects, pp. 415, 420
- Making inferences, p. 417
- Summarizing, p. 418
- Analyzing causes, p. 419
- Forming an opinion, p. 420

FOCUS

5-Minute Warm-Up

▶ **Making Inferences**
To help students understand the age of uncertainty, have them answer the following questions.

1. Read "Daily Life in 1927" on page 419. Who were newsmakers that year?

2. Which public figure was the world's newest hero?

 WARM-UP TRANSPARENCY 15

OBJECTIVE 1 INSTRUCT

Science Challenges Old Ideas

▶ **Key Ideas**
- Albert Einstein and Sigmund Freud are two important thinkers of the 20th century.
- Einstein's theory of relativity overturns accepted laws of motion and gravity.
- Freud's theories about human behavior weaken faith in reason.

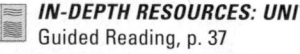 **IN-DEPTH RESOURCES: UNIT 4**
Guided Reading, p. 37

ACCESS FOR STUDENTS ACQUIRING ENGLISH
Guided Reading (Spanish), p. 163

Teacher's Edition 415

By treating matter and energy as exchangeable in his famous equation $E=MC^2$ (energy equals mass times the velocity of light squared), Einstein laid the basis for controlling the release of energy from the atom. His theories led to the development of nuclear energy. Ask students to research and report on the events in Einstein's life that led to the recognition of his genius.

OBJECTIVE ② INSTRUCT

Literature in an Age of Doubt

▶ **Key Ideas**
- Disillusionment over the brutality of World War I causes such writers and thinkers as T. S. Eliot, Jean Paul Sartre, and Friedrich Nietzsche to question traditional religious beliefs.
- Freud's theories on the unconscious influence the novels of James Joyce and others.

 IN-DEPTH RESOURCES: UNIT 4
History Makers: Sigmund Freud, p. 51

 ELECTRONIC LIBRARY OF PRIMARY SOURCES
"The Death of God"

SPOTLIGHT ON
The Lost Generation

F. Scott Fitzgerald was only 24 years old when he wrote *This Side of Paradise,* his novel of the lost generation. Ask students to prepare biographical sketches of Fitzgerald and his wife Zelda. They might consider how the lives of this famous couple reflect both the desperation and the frantic gaiety of the expatriate artists.

 IN-DEPTH RESOURCES: UNIT 4
Literature: from *This Side of Paradise,* p. 48

Literature in an Age of Doubt

The brutality of World War I caused philosophers and writers to question accepted ideas about reason and progress. Disillusioned by the war, many people also feared the future and expressed doubts about traditional religious beliefs. Some artists and writers expressed their anxieties by creating unsettling visions of the present and the future.

In 1922, T. S. Eliot, an American poet living in England, wrote that Western society had lost its spiritual values. He described the postwar world as a barren "waste land," drained of hope and faith. In 1924, the Irish poet William Butler Yeats conveyed a sense of dark times ahead in the poem "The Second Coming": "Things fall apart; the centre cannot hold; / Mere anarchy is loosed upon the world . . ."

SPOTLIGHT ON
The Lost Generation
During the 1920s, many American writers, musicians, and painters left the United States to live in Europe. Among them were writers Ernest Hemingway, John Dos Passos, and F. Scott Fitzgerald.

These expatriates, people who left their native country to live elsewhere, often settled in Paris. They gathered at the home of American writer Gertrude Stein. There they mixed with Europe's leading artists and intellectuals.

Stein called these expatriates the "Lost Generation." She remarked, "All of you young people who served in the war [World War I], you are the lost generation."

In his first major novel, *The Sun Also Rises* (1926), Hemingway captured the desperation of the young expatriate crowd. They moved frantically from one European city to another, trying to find meaning in life. Life empty of meaning is the theme of Fitzgerald's *The Great Gatsby* (1925).

Thinkers React to Uncertainties In their search for meaning in an uncertain world, some thinkers turned to the philosophy known as **existentialism.** Leaders of this movement included the philosophers Jean Paul Sartre (SAHR·truh) of France and Karl Jaspers of Germany. Existentialists believed that there is no universal meaning to life. Each person gives his or her own meaning to life through choices made and actions taken. The existentialists would have their greatest influence after World War II.

The existentialists had been influenced by the German philosopher **Friedrich Nietzsche** (NEE·chuh). In the 1880s, Nietzsche wrote that Western society had put too much stress on such ideas as reason, democracy, and progress. This stifled actions based on emotion and instinct. As a result, individuality and creativity suffered. Nietzsche urged a return to the ancient heroic values of pride, assertiveness, and strength. He wrote that through willpower and courage, some humans could become supermen. They could rise above and control the common herd. His ideas attracted growing attention in the 20th century and had a great impact on politics in Italy and Germany in the 1920s and 1930s.

Writers Reflect Society's Concerns New attitudes also appeared in literature. The French poet Paul Valéry spoke for many writers of the 1920s when he described how he felt restless and uneasy:

A VOICE FROM THE PAST
We think of what has disappeared, and we are almost destroyed by what has been destroyed; we do not know what will be born, and we fear the future. . . . Doubt and disorder are in us and with us. There is no thinking man, however shrewd or learned he may be, who can hope to dominate this anxiety, to escape from this impression of darkness.
PAUL VALÉRY, *Variété*

The horror of war made a deep impression on many writers. The Czech-born author Franz Kafka wrote eerie novels like *The Trial* (1925) and *The Castle* (1926). His books featured people crushed in threatening situations they could neither understand nor escape. He started writing before the war, but much of his work was published after his death in 1924. It struck a chord among readers in the uneasy postwar years.

Many novels showed the influence of Freud's theories on the unconscious. The Irish-born author James Joyce caused a stir with his stream-of-consciousness novel *Ulysses* (1922). This lengthy book focused on a single day in the lives of three Dubliners. Joyce broke with normal sentence structure and vocabulary, trying to mirror the workings of the human mind.

Vocabulary
stream of consciousness: a literary technique a writer uses to present a character's thoughts and feelings as they develop.

A Voice from the Past Paul Valéry, who lived from 1871 to 1945, is considered one of the greatest French poets of the 20th century. His major works include the long poem *The Young Fate* (1917) and the lyrics collected in *Charms* (1922). He composed little poetry of consequence after 1922 but wrote numerous essays on a remarkably wide variety of subjects. These included the arts, mathematics, language, philosophy, education, politics, and the sciences. At his death, Valéry was given a full state funeral. Ask students how they think the experiences of the Great War contributed to the uncertainty and pessimism expressed in Valéry's quote.

Gifted and Talented Students Some of the concepts discussed by the Austrian physician Sigmund Freud in his revolutionary study of the mind and its workings were the *id, ego, superego, unconscious,* and *repression.* Have gifted and talented students use an introductory psychology textbook or some other reference work to find the meanings of these important terms. After the students have made a list of the terms and their meanings, have them write a short essay discussing the roles these ideas played in the development of Freud's psychological theories.

Rebellion in the Arts

Although many of the new directions in painting, architecture, and music began in the prewar period, they evolved after the war.

Painters Break Away from Tradition Artists rebelled against earlier realistic styles of painting. They wanted to depict the inner world of emotion and imagination rather than show realistic representations of objects. Expressionist painters like Paul Klee and Wassily Kandinsky used bold colors and distorted or exaggerated shapes and forms.

Inspired by traditional African art, Georges Braque of France and Pablo Picasso of Spain founded Cubism in 1907. Cubism transformed natural shapes into geometric forms. Objects were broken down into different parts with sharp angles and edges. Often several views were depicted at the same time.

The Dada movement (1916–1924) was as much a protest as an art movement. Its message was that established values had been made meaningless by the savagery of World War I. The term *Dada,* French for "hobbyhorse," was reportedly picked at random. Sounding like a nonsense word, it fit the spirit of the movement. Dadaist works were meant to be absurd, nonsensical, and meaningless.

Surrealism followed Dada. Inspired by Freud's ideas, **surrealism** was an art movement that sought to link the world of dreams with real life. The term *surreal* means "beyond or above reality." Surrealists tried to call on the unconscious part of their minds. Their paintings frequently had a dream-like quality and depicted objects in unrealistic ways.

The Persistence of Memory, a surrealist work by Spanish artist Salvador Dali, 1931, shows watches melting in a desert landscape. Insects feed on the clockwork.

Architects Move in New Directions An architectural revolution occurred when architects rejected traditional building styles for completely new forms. Instead of highly ornamented structures, they constructed buildings in which the design reflected the building's function or use. The American architect Frank Lloyd Wright pioneered this new style, known as functionalism. He designed houses featuring clean, low lines and open interiors that blended with the surrounding landscape. Walter Gropius led the functionalist movement in Germany. After the war, he started an art and design school in Weimar called the Bauhaus.

Composers Try New Styles In both classical and popular music, composers moved away from traditional styles. In his ballet masterpiece, *The Rite of Spring,* the Russian composer Igor Stravinsky used irregular rhythms and dissonances, or harsh combinations of sound. The audience booed and walked out of its opening performance. The Austrian composer Arnold Schoenberg rejected traditional harmonies and musical scales. He created his own 12-tone scale in which the notes were unrelated except as mathematical patterns.

A new popular musical style called **jazz** came out of the United States. It was developed by musicians, mainly African Americans, in New Orleans, Memphis, and Chicago. It swept the United States and Europe. The lively, loose beat of jazz seemed to capture the new freedom of the age. Uninhibited, energetic jazz dances, such as the Charleston and the Black Bottom, at first shocked respectable society before becoming widely accepted.

Years of Crisis **417**

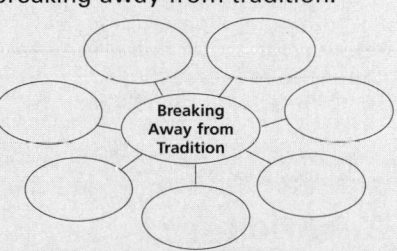

Society Becomes More Open

▶ **Key Ideas**
- In the 1920s, young people are willing to break with the past and experiment with different values.
- Women take on new roles.

MORE ABOUT . . .
Women's Fashions in the 1920s

In the 1920s, women not only shortened their skirts, but shed their petticoats, long cotton stockings, and constricting corsets. The plumply rounded Gibson girl (shown on this page) was replaced by the flapper, with her slim, almost boyish figure. Flappers wore bright lipsticks and other cosmetics that earlier had been considered unacceptable for ladies.

American illustrator John Held, Jr., created the image of the flapper in cartoons he created for such magazines as *Harper's Bazaar, Vanity Fair, Life,* and *The New Yorker.* The flapper with her short hair and skirt, dangling cigarette, beads, and heavy makeup became a symbol for the rebelliousness of young people in the 1920s.

Technology Changes Life

▶ **Key Ideas**
- After World War I ends, the war's technological advances are used to improve transportation and communication.
- The automobile affects where people live and work and increases leisure travel.
- International air travel increases.
- Radio and movies provide new outlets for entertainment.

Society Becomes More Open

World War I had disrupted traditional social patterns. New ideas and ways of life led to a new kind of individual freedom during the 1920s. Young people especially were willing to break with the past and experiment with values that often differed from those of their parents. Their pleasure-seeking defiance of accepted conventions was the first "youth rebellion" of the 20th century.

The independent spirit of the times showed clearly in the changes women were making in their lives. The war had allowed women to take on new roles. Their work in the war effort was decisive in helping them win the right to vote. After the war, women's suffrage became law in many countries, including the United States, Britain, Germany, Sweden, and Austria.

Women abandoned restrictive clothing and hairstyles. They wore shorter, looser garments and had their hair "bobbed," or cut short. They also wore makeup, drove cars, and drank and smoked in public. Although most women still followed traditional paths of marriage and family, a growing number spoke out for greater freedom in their lives. Wives should not be second-class members of the family, feminists argued, but equal partners with their husbands. Margaret Sanger and Emma Goldman risked arrest by speaking in favor of birth control. As women sought new careers, the numbers of women in medicine, education, journalism, and other professions increased.

Technology Changes Life

World War I quickened the pace of invention. During the war, scientists developed new drugs and medical treatments that helped millions of people in the postwar years. The war's technological advances were put to use to improve transportation and communication after the war.

The Automobile Alters Society The automobile benefited from a host of wartime innovations and improvements—electric starters, air-filled tires, and more powerful engines. Cars no longer looked like boxes on wheels. They were sleek and brightly polished, complete with headlights and chrome-plated bumpers. In prewar Britain, autos were owned exclusively by the rich. British factories produced 34,000 autos in 1913. After the war, prices dropped, and the middle class could afford cars. In 1923 the number of autos built in Britain had almost tripled. By 1937, the British were producing 511,000 autos a year.

Increased auto use by the average family led to lifestyle changes. More people traveled for pleasure. In Europe and the United States, new businesses, from motor hotels to vacation campgrounds, opened to serve the mobile tourist. The auto also affected where people lived and worked. People moved to suburbs and commuted to work.

Airplanes Transform Travel The war also brought spectacular improvements in aircraft. By 1918, planes could fly hundreds of miles. In the postwar era, daring fliers carried the first airmail letters. Wartime aviators became stunt pilots, flying to country fairs to perform aerial acrobatics and take people for their first plane rides.

International air travel became an objective after the war. In 1919, two British pilots made the first successful flight across the Atlantic, from Newfoundland to Ireland. The next major crossing came in 1927, when an American pilot named **Charles Lindbergh** captured world attention with a 33-hour solo flight from New York to Paris. Most of the world's major passenger airlines were established during the

Pre-World War I "Gibson girls"

From "Gibson girl" to "Flapper," the restrictive clothing styles of the pre-war period depicted in the early 20th-century illustration gave way to the comfortable, casual fashions shown in the 1920s photograph.

Background
"Gibson girl" referred to the idealized type of young woman drawn by illustrator Charles Dana Gibson in the pre-World War I period.

THINK THROUGH HISTORY
C. Summarizing
How did the changes of the post-war years affect women?
C. Answer Women won the right to vote, changed style of dress, sought new careers.

The Automobile Help students investigate the many ways the automobile has transformed all aspects of social life. Make a diagram like the one to the right on the chalkboard. Have students work in small groups to complete the diagram, detailing the effects on work, personal life, and travel caused by the automobile. This might include listing businesses that were no longer important, like blacksmithing and harness making, and new businesses, such as auto repair and service stations. Students can also investigate and list the ways the automobile changed dating patterns, where people lived and worked, how they dressed, and how the physical landscape changed through road building.

Cause:
Automobile Changes Society

| 1. Effect: Work Changes Details: | 2. Effect: Life Changes Details: | 3. Effect: Travel Changes Details: |

People in the News

Duke Ellington at Cotton Club

NEW YORK CITY, December 4: Featuring jazz pianist and composer Edward Kennedy "Duke" Ellington, Ellington's band opened today at Harlem's Cotton Club for what looks like a long run. Sources say Ellington's nickname Duke comes from the bandleader's expensive taste.

Parisians Greet Lindy

PARIS, May 21: Nearly 100,000 Parisians rushed onto the tarmac at Le Bourget Airport this evening. They ran to greet the world's newest hero—Charles Lindbergh. Lindbergh had just touched down safely at 10:24 P.M. in the *Spirit of St. Louis*, after completing the first solo flight across the Atlantic.

Looking pale and worn out, Lindbergh smiled and said, "Well, I made it." He had just flown 33 hours and 39 minutes nonstop from New York to Paris. His flight has great implications for the future of air travel.

Babe Ruth Slugs Sixtieth Homer

NEW YORK CITY, September 30: Today George Herman "Babe" Ruth thrilled 10,000 fans in Yankee Stadium, swatting his sixtieth home run of the season. He broke his own 1921 record of 59. After hitting the pitch down the right field foul line into the stands, he said, "That's sixty home runs, count 'em. Sixty."

The fast-living, hard-hitting Babe delights the press. They employ many colorful nicknames to refer to him. Among them are the Bambino, the Sultan of Swat, the Mammoth of Maul, and the Colossus of Clout.

Helen Wills Captures Wimbledon Title

WIMBLEDON, England, July 2: Helen Wills won the women's singles title at the All-England Tennis matches here today. She captured the famous tennis trophy for the United States for the first time in 20 years, beating Ella de Alvarez of Spain.

"Little Miss Poker Face," as she is called, is an intense competitor. She took the American Open title at age 17 in 1923 and repeated in 1924 and 1925. Wills also won gold medals in singles and doubles competition at the 1924 Olympics in Paris.

Connect *to* History

Analyzing Causes What factors contributed to the phenomenon of popular public heroes such as Charles Lindbergh, Babe Ruth, and Helen Wills?

Connect *to* Today

Researching Using the library or the Internet, compare a recent sporting or popular event to one from the 1920s in terms of audience and effect. Be sure to indicate how today's mass media create popular heroes and fans.

Years of Crisis **419**

People in the News

The multi-talented Duke Ellington led a jazz band, composed music, and played piano. Born in Washington, D.C., Ellington began playing piano at age 7 and made his professional debut at 17. Ellington did have a long run at the Cotton Club. His band was the house band at this famous Harlem nightclub from 1927 to 1932. Considered one of jazz's greatest composers, Ellington's reputation grew through the many recordings of his compositions, like "Mood Indigo" and "Sophisticated Lady."

MORE ABOUT . . .
Charles Lindbergh

Nicknamed "Lucky Lindy" and "Lone Eagle" by the press, Lindbergh won international fame and became the object of hero worship following his solo, nonstop flight across the Atlantic. He had been a stunt flyer at county fairs and an airmail pilot before competing for the $25,000 prize offered for the first nonstop New York–Paris flight. Several pilots had been killed or injured seeking the prize, which had been offered since 1919.

IN-DEPTH RESOURCES: UNIT 4
Primary Source: from An Interview with Charles Lindbergh, p. 44

MORE ABOUT . . .
Babe Ruth

Babe Ruth was the first great home-run hitter in baseball. His batting skills, coupled with his colorful personality, made him a crowd favorite wherever he went. Babe Ruth started in major-league baseball as a pitcher with the Boston Red Sox and was later an outfielder for the New York Yankees. He hit 714 homers during his career, a record until Henry Aaron hit his 715th home run in 1974. Ruth was one of many larger-than-life celebrities in professional sports in the 1920s and 1930s. Others were Ty Cobb of the Detroit Tigers; Gertrude Ederle, the first woman to swim the English Channel; and heavyweight prizefighters Jack Dempsey and Gene Tunney.

Connect *to* History

Analyzing Causes
Possible Response: Students might suggest that several factors contributed to the enormous popularity of such public figures as Lindbergh, Ruth, and Wills. They might point out that people in an age of uncertainty were looking for heroes. Certainly the increasing popularity of radio and movies with their newsreels made people more aware than ever before of sporting events and the feats of such men and women as Lindbergh, Ruth, and Wills.

Connect *to* Today

Researching
Have students make a chart comparing similar events in the two eras.

	1920s	Today
Advance Publicity		
Type of Media Coverage		
Size of Audience		
Impact of Event		

Daily *Life*
How Technology Revolutionized Life

The spread of technological innovations in the postwar period changed the way people lived. Autos removed dependence on public transportation. They made travel to work and travel for recreation more convenient and less time-consuming.

The telephone instantly connected family and friends, and buyers and sellers. Radio brought entertainment into the home. The whole family could share listening to sports, comedy, drama, music, and the news.

The drudgery of housework was lightened by labor-saving appliances, including refrigerators, vacuum cleaners, irons, toasters, and washing machines. Convenience foods, such as packaged cereals and quick-frozen vegetables, saved time in the kitchen. The United States was far more advanced than most nations in the use of these technological breakthroughs.

1920s. At first only the rich were able to afford air travel. Still, everyone enjoyed the exploits of the aviation pioneers, including Amelia Earhart. She was an American who, in 1932, became the first woman to fly solo across the Atlantic.

Radio Reaches Millions Guglielmo Marconi conducted his first successful experiments with radio in 1895. However, the real push for radio development came during World War I. The advantages of wireless communication in battle were so great that all countries gave radio research a high priority. Armies developed a wide range of radio equipment that would also have uses in peacetime.

In 1920, the world's first commercial radio station—KDKA in Pittsburgh, Pennsylvania—began broadcasting. Almost overnight, radio mania swept the United States. Soon every major city had stations broadcasting news, plays, and even live sporting events. In many European nations, unlike the United States, radio broadcasting was controlled by the government. In Great Britain, radio was a public monopoly run solely by the British Broadcasting Company, or BBC. Like Americans, however, Europeans eagerly listened to a variety of radio broadcasts. Soon most families owned a radio.

Movies Revolutionize Popular Entertainment In the 1920s, motion pictures were a major industry. Many countries, from Cuba to Japan, produced movies. In Europe, film was a serious art form. Directors like Sergei Eisenstein in Russia and Fritz Lang in Germany created films that explored psychological or political themes. However, in the Los Angeles suburb of Hollywood, where 90 percent of all films were made, movies were entertainment.

From Hollywood in the 1920s came the zany, slapstick comedies of Mack Sennett and his Keystone Kops, and dramas that starred Mary Pickford or Rudolph Valentino. But the king of the silent screen was the English-born Charlie Chaplin, a comic genius best known for his portrayal of the lonely little tramp bewildered by life. In the late 1920s, the addition of sound transformed movies. By the mid-1930s, nearly 90 million Americans escaped from the hardships of life by attending movies each week.

The advances in transportation and communication that followed the war had brought the world in closer touch. Countries had become more interdependent economically. Global prosperity came to depend on the economic well-being of all major nations, especially the United States.

D. Possible Answers Autos were mass produced; airlines carried mail and passengers; most families owned a radio.

THINK THROUGH HISTORY
D. Recognizing Effects What were the results of the peacetime adaptations of the technology of war?

In *Modern Times* (1936) Charlie Chaplin captured the discomfort many felt about the increasing automation of life.

Section ❶ Assessment

1. TERMS & NAMES
Identify
• Albert Einstein
• theory of relativity
• Sigmund Freud
• existentialism
• Friedrich Nietzsche
• surrealism
• jazz
• Charles Lindbergh

2. TAKING NOTES
Draw a chart like the one below. For each category shown, name two people you read about who contributed to that field.

FIELD	CONTRIBUTORS
philosophy literature art architecture music	

Write one or two sentences about their beliefs or contributions.

3. FORMING AN OPINION
In your opinion, whose ideas had a bigger impact on the world—Einstein's or Freud's? Give reasons to support your position.

THINK ABOUT
• the state of knowledge before their contributions
• the field in which they worked
• how life would be different without their contributions

4. THEME ACTIVITY
Science and Technology As a class, hold a media event. In small groups, choose a topic from the scientific and technological contributions of the 1920s. Collect pictures, audio tapes, biographies, or literature that represent the people or ideas you have chosen. Present your topic to the class and use your collection to help create a multimedia effect.

ANSWERS

2 A Global Depression

TERMS & NAMES
- coalition government
- Weimar Republic
- Great Depression
- Franklin D. Roosevelt
- New Deal

MAIN IDEA

An economic depression in the United States spread throughout the world and lasted for a decade.

WHY IT MATTERS NOW

Many social and economic programs introduced worldwide to combat the Great Depression are still operating.

SETTING THE STAGE By the late 1920s, European nations were rebuilding war-torn economies. They were aided by loans from the more prosperous United States. In the United States, Americans seemed confident that the country would continue on the road to even greater economic prosperity. One sign of this was the booming stock market. Yet the American economy had serious weaknesses that were soon to bring about the most severe economic downturn the world had yet known.

Europe After the War

In both human suffering and economic terms, the cost of World War I was immense. The Great War left every major European country nearly bankrupt. Only the United States and Japan came out of the war in better financial shape than before. Neither had been a wartime battlefield. In fact, both had expanded their trade during the war. In addition, Europe's domination in world affairs had declined since the war. The long and brutal fight had drained the continent's resources.

New Democracies Are Unstable

War's end saw the sudden rise of new democracies. From 1914 to 1918, Europe's last absolute rulers had been overthrown. The dynasties of the Hohenzollerns in Germany, the Hapsburgs in Austria-Hungary, the Romanovs in Russia, and the Ottomans in Turkey all ended. The first of the new governments was formed in Russia in 1917. The Provisional Government, as it was called, hoped to establish constitutional and democratic rule. However, within months it had fallen to a Communist dictatorship. Even so, for the first time, most European nations had democratic governments.

Many citizens of the new democracies had little experience with representative government. For generations, kings and emperors had ruled Germany and the new nations formed from Austria-Hungary. Even in France and Italy, whose parliaments had existed before World War I, the large number of political parties made effective government difficult. Some countries had a dozen or more political groups. In these countries, it was almost impossible for one party to win enough support to govern effectively. When no single party won a majority, a **coalition government,** or temporary alliance of several parties, was needed to form a parliamentary majority. Because the parties disagreed on so many policies, coalitions seldom lasted very long. France,

THINK THROUGH HISTORY
A. Drawing Conclusions How did World War I change the balance of economic power in the world?
A. Possible Answers Europe's resources had been drained by World War I. Japan and the U.S. were economically strong.

Demonstrators flee gunfire in the streets of Petrograd in 1917 as the Russian Provisional Government tries to fight off Bolshevik (Communist) revolutionaries.

Years of Crisis **421**

SECTION 2 RESOURCES

PRINT RESOURCES

IN-DEPTH RESOURCES: UNIT 4
Guided Reading, p. 38
Skillbuilder Practice: Identifying Problems, p. 41
Primary Source: German Inflation, p. 45

ACCESS FOR STUDENTS ACQUIRING ENGLISH
Guided Reading (Spanish), p. 164
Skillbuilder Practice: (Spanish), p. 167

FORMAL ASSESSMENT
Section Quiz, p. 187

ALTERNATIVE ASSESSMENT BOOK

TECHNOLOGY RESOURCES

CD-ROM
Electronic Library of Primary Sources

INTERNET www.mlworldhistory.com

Section 2 Overview

OBJECTIVES

(1) To describe the impact of World War I on postwar Europe.

(2) To summarize the causes of the Great Depression.

(3) To explain how the United States and Europe reacted to the Depression.

SKILLBUILDER
- Interpreting graphs, pp. 423, 425

CRITICAL THINKING
- Drawing conclusions, p. 421
- Identifying problems, pp. 422, 423
- Synthesizing, p. 425
- Analyzing causes, p. 426
- Analyzing themes, p. 426

FOCUS
5-Minute Warm-Up

Summarizing
Having students answer the following will help them understand the Great Depression.

1. Read "Daily Life" on page 424. What kind of aid did the unemployed need?

2. What groups provided relief to the unemployed?

WARM-UP TRANSPARENCY 15

OBJECTIVE (1) INSTRUCT

Europe After the War

▶ *Key Ideas*
- The new European democracies formed after the war are weak.
- Frequent changes in government make it hard for democracies to develop strong leadership.
- Many Germans blame the democratic Weimar government for their country's problems.
- Dawes Plan helps Germany curb inflation and build its economy.

ELECTRONIC LIBRARY OF PRIMARY SOURCES
"Famine in Russia"

(continued on next page)

Teacher's Edition **421**

OBJECTIVE ① INSTRUCT

(continued from page 421)

- The Kellogg-Briand peace pact raises hopes for world peace.

IN-DEPTH RESOURCES: UNIT 4
Guided Reading, p. 38

ACCESS FOR STUDENTS ACQUIRING ENGLISH
Guided Reading (Spanish), p. 164

MORE ABOUT . . .
The Weimar Republic

At the time they signed the Versailles Treaty, the men who became the leaders of the Weimar government recognized that the agreement would cause grave problems for Germany. German Prime Minister Philipp Scheidemann remarked, "What hand would not wither that binds itself and us in these fetters?" Yet the members of the Social Democratic and Catholic Center parties, who later became the leaders of the Weimar government, felt they had no choice but to sign the agreement. The German people never forgave them.

MORE ABOUT . . .
Germany's Money Problems

The German government's printing of large amounts of currency to keep it afloat after the war caused prices in Germany to rise more than 1 trillion percent from August 1922 to November 1923. Economists typically define severe inflation as an annual inflation rate of 10 percent or higher. In 1923, $1 in United States currency was worth over 4 trillion German marks.

IN-DEPTH RESOURCES: UNIT 4
Primary Source: German Inflation, p. 45

"Money to burn"—this German woman uses millions of marks made worthless by inflation as heating fuel in the early 1920s.

for example, endured some 40 changes of government from 1919 to 1939.

Frequent changes in government made it hard for democratic countries to develop strong leadership and move toward long-term goals. In peaceful times, a country could get by with weak leadership. However, the weaknesses of a coalition government became a major problem in times of crisis. Voters in several countries were then willing to sacrifice democracy for strong, totalitarian leadership.

Weimar Republic Is Weak Germany's new democratic government was set up in 1919. Known as the **Weimar** (WY·MAHR) **Republic,** it was named after the city where the national assembly met. The Weimar Republic had serious weaknesses from the start. First, Germany lacked a strong democratic tradition. Furthermore, postwar Germany had several major political parties and many minor ones. Worst of all, millions of Germans blamed the Weimar government, not their wartime leaders, for the country's defeat and postwar humiliation. It was, after all, the Weimar government that had signed the Treaty of Versailles.

Inflation Causes Crisis in Germany Germany also faced enormous economic problems that began during the war. Unlike Britain and France, Germany did not greatly increase its wartime taxes. To pay the expenses of the war, the Germans simply printed money. After Germany's defeat, this paper money steadily lost its value. Burdened with heavy reparations payments to the Allies and with other economic problems, Germany printed even more money. The result was the value of the mark, as Germany's currency was called, fell sharply. Severe inflation set in. Germans needed more and more money to buy even the most basic goods. For example, in Berlin a loaf of bread cost less than a mark in 1918, more than 160 marks in 1922, and some 200 billion marks by late 1923. People took wheelbarrows full of money to buy food. The mark had become worthless.

Consequently, people with fixed incomes saw their life savings become worthless. The money people had saved to buy a house now barely covered the cost of a table. Many Germans also questioned the value of their new democratic government.

Attempts at Economic Stability Germany recovered from the 1923 inflation largely thanks to the work of an international committee. The committee was headed by Charles Dawes, an American banker. The Dawes Plan provided for a $200 million loan from American banks to stabilize German currency and strengthen its economy. The plan also set a more realistic schedule for Germany's reparations payments.

Put into effect in 1924, the Dawes Plan helped slow inflation. As the German economy began to recover, it attracted more loans and investments from the United States. By 1929, German factories were producing as much as they had before the war.

Efforts at a Lasting Peace As prosperity returned, Germany's foreign minister, Gustav Stresemann (STRAY·zuh·MAHN), and France's foreign minister, Aristide Briand (bree·AHND), tried to improve relations between their countries. In 1925, they met in Locarno, Switzerland, with officials from Belgium, Italy, and Britain. They signed a treaty promising that France and Germany would never again make war against each other. Germany also agreed to respect the existing borders of France and Belgium. It then was admitted to the League of Nations.

422 Chapter 15

B. Possible Answers lack of democratic tradition, too many political parties, new government bore the blame for defeat.

THINK THROUGH HISTORY
B. Identifying Problems What political problems did the Weimar Republic face?

Background
Germany's reparations payments for damages caused during World War I totaled $33 billion.

TEACHING OPTION

CONNECTIONS ACROSS THE CURRICULUM

Economics Crushed by huge war expenses and heavy payments to the Allies, Germany was in the midst of disastrous *hyperinflation* in the early 1920s. From 1918 to 1923, the value of the Germany currency, the *mark,* had fallen sharply and rapidly. By mid-1923, the printing presses at Germany's mints were turning out 400 quadrillion (400,000,000,000,000,000) marks a day!

Hyperinflation is rapid, very high inflation. Left unchecked, it can destroy a nation's economy, because money loses nearly all its value. Hyperinflation occurs when a government spends much more money than it receives in taxes and other revenues. To raise more money, the government simply prints more, further weakening the value of its currency. As money growth increases, inflation rises, driving prices up. The

government is forced to keep printing even more money to pay for its expenditures. A downward spiral begins as the process repeats itself. Have students trace the steps that led to hyperinflation in Germany and then research and report to the class on how the Dawes Plan helped stabilize the currency and break the cycle of rising prices.

In 1928, the hopes raised by the "spirit of Locarno" led to the Kellogg-Briand peace pact. Frank Kellogg, the U.S. Secretary of State, arranged this agreement with France's Briand. Almost every country in the world, including the Soviet Union, signed. They pledged "to renounce war as an instrument of national policy."

Unfortunately, the treaty had no means to enforce its provisions. The League of Nations, the obvious choice as enforcer, had no armed forces. The refusal of the United States to join the League also weakened it. Nonetheless, the peace agreements seemed a good start. In addition, Europeans were enjoying an economic boom based largely on massive American investment.

The Great Depression

In the late 1920s, the world economy was like a delicately balanced house of cards. The key card that held up the rest was American economic prosperity. If the United States economy weakened, the whole world's economic system might collapse. In 1929, it did.

A Flawed U.S. Economy Despite prosperity, three weaknesses in the U.S. economy caused serious problems. These were uneven distribution of wealth, overproduction by business and agriculture, and lessening demand for consumer goods.

By 1929, American factories were turning out nearly half of the world's industrial goods. The rising productivity led to enormous profits. However, this new wealth was not evenly distributed. The richest 5 percent of the population received 33 percent of all personal income in 1929. Yet 60 percent of all American families earned less than $2,000 a year. Thus, most families were too poor to buy the goods being produced. Unable to sell all their goods, store owners eventually cut back their orders from factories. Factories in turn reduced production and laid off workers. A downward economic spiral began. As more workers lost their jobs, families bought even fewer goods. In turn, factories made further cuts in production and laid off more workers.

During the 1920s, overproduction affected American farmers as well. Scientific farming methods and new farm machinery had dramatically increased crop yields. American farmers were producing more food. Meanwhile they faced new competition from farmers in Australia, Latin America, and Europe. As a result, a worldwide surplus of agricultural products drove prices and profits down.

Unable to sell their crops at a profit, many farmers could not pay off the bank loans that kept them in business. Their unpaid debts weakened banks and forced some to close. The danger signs of overproduction by factories and farms should have warned people against gambling on the stock market. Yet no one heeded the warning.

The Stock Market Crashes In 1929, Wall Street, in New York City, was the financial capital of the world. Banks and investment companies lined its sidewalks. At Wall Street's New York Stock Exchange, optimism about the booming U.S. economy showed in soaring prices for stocks. To get in on the boom, many middle-income people began buying stocks on margin. This meant that they paid a small percentage of a stock's price as a down payment and borrowed the rest from a stockbroker. The

Stock Prices, 1925–1933

Graph-Source: *Historical Statistics of the United States*

SKILLBUILDER: Interpreting Graphs
1. *What year did stock prices fall lowest before beginning to rise again?*
2. *What was the average stock price in 1929? in 1932?*

Years of Crisis **423**

system worked well as long as stock prices were rising. However, if they fell, investors had no money to pay off the loan.

In September 1929, some investors began to feel that stock prices were unnaturally high. They started selling their stocks, believing the rates would soon go down. By Thursday, October 24, the gradual lowering of stock prices had became an all-out slide downward. A panic resulted. Everyone wanted to sell stocks, and no one wanted to buy. Prices sank quickly. The wild shouting of 1,000 brokers and their assistants at the Stock Exchange became what one observer called a "weird roar." Prices plunged to a new low on Tuesday, October 29. A record 16 million stocks were sold. Then the market collapsed.

In the stock market crash, billions of dollars in "paper wealth" simply vanished. People could not pay the money they owed on margin purchases. Stocks they had bought at high prices were now worthless. Within months of the crash, unemployment rates began to rise as industrial production, prices, and wages declined. A long business slump, or depression, followed. The **Great Depression,** as it came to be called, touched every corner of the American economy. By 1932, factory production had been cut in half. Thousands of businesses failed, and banks closed. Around 9 million people lost the money in their savings accounts when banks had no money to pay them. Many farmers lost their lands when they could not make mortgage payments. By 1933 one-fourth of all American workers had no jobs.

A Global Depression The collapse of the American economy sent shock waves around the world. Worried American bankers demanded repayment of their overseas loans, and American investors withdrew their money from Europe. The American market for European goods dropped sharply as the U.S. Congress placed high tariffs on imported goods so that American dollars would stay in the United States and support American workers. The government was trying to force Americans to buy American goods. This policy backfired. Conditions worsened for the United States. Many countries who depended on exporting goods to the United States also suffered. Moreover, when the United States raised tariffs, it set off a chain reaction. Other nations imposed their own higher tariffs. World trade dropped

Background
The day of the stock market crash, Tuesday, October 29, 1929, is called "Black Tuesday."

Vocabulary
tariffs: taxes charged by a government on imported or exported goods.

424 Chapter 15

Unemployment, 1928–1938

Unemployment, 1928–1938

Hitler comes to power

Roosevelt begins New Deal

Stock market crashes

30
25
20
15
10
5
0

Percent of Work Force

1928 1930 1932 1934 1936 1938

■ Great Britain ■ Germany ■ United States

Sources: *European Historical Statistics: 1750–1970;*
Historical Statistics of the United States: Colonial Times to 1970.

SKILLBUILDER:
Interpreting Graphs
1. *What nation had the highest rate of unemployment? How high did it reach?*
2. *When did unemployment begin to decrease in the United States? Germany? Great Britain?*

THINK THROUGH HISTORY
D. Synthesizing
What problems did the collapse of the American economy cause in other countries?
D. Possible Answers Their economies slumped, trade dropped, unemployment soared, and a financial panic started.

Background
Scandinavia, in northern Europe, includes Sweden, Norway, and Denmark. Finland and Iceland are often also included in the region.

by 65 percent. This contributed further to the economic downturn. Unemployment rates soared.

Because of war debts and dependence on American loans and investments, Germany and Austria were particularly hard hit. In 1931, Austria's largest bank failed. This started a financial panic in central European countries and sent their economies plunging.

In Asia, the Japanese economy also slumped. Japanese farmers suffered greatly during the Depression. In the rice-growing areas of the northeast, crop failures in 1931 led to famine. Starving families ate tree bark and the roots of wild plants. City workers suffered, too, as the value of exports fell by half between 1929 and 1931. As many as 3 million workers lost their jobs, forcing many to go back to their rural villages.

The economic crisis fell heavily in Latin America as well. Many of its nations were tied to the global economy by trade in such cash crops or raw materials as sugar, beef, copper, and tin. During the 1920s, world prices and market demand for these products were already dropping. As European and U.S. demand for Latin American products dried up in the 1930s, prices for these goods collapsed. At the same time, the cost of imported goods rose, pushed up by high tariffs. Latin American nations that had borrowed heavily from other nations could not repay their debts. The worldwide crisis spread rapidly.

The World Responds to the Crisis

The Depression confronted democracies with a serious challenge to their economic and political systems. Each country met the crisis in its own way.

Britain Takes Steps to Improve Its Economy Because its economy depended on foreign trade, the Depression hit Britain severely. To meet the emergency, British voters elected a multi-party coalition known as the National Government. This government's policies were designed to rescue the nation from economic calamity. It passed high protective tariffs, increased taxes, and regulated the currency. It also lowered interest rates to encourage industrial growth. These measures brought about a slow but steady recovery. By 1937, unemployment had been cut in half, and production had risen above 1929 levels. Britain avoided political extremes and preserved democracy.

France Responds to Economic Crisis Unlike Britain, France had a more self-sufficient economy. In 1930, it was still heavily agricultural and less dependent on foreign trade. Thus, France was somewhat cushioned against the Depression. Nevertheless, by 1935, one million French workers were unemployed.

The economic crisis contributed to political instability. In 1933, five coalition governments formed and fell. Many political leaders were frightened by the growth of anti-democratic forces both in France and in other parts of Europe. So in 1936, moderates, Socialists, and Communists formed a coalition. The Popular Front, as it was called, passed a series of reforms to help the workers. These reforms included pay increases, holidays with pay, and a 40-hour work week. Unfortunately, price increases quickly offset wage gains. Unemployment remained high. Yet France also preserved democratic government.

Socialist Governments Find Solutions The Socialist governments in the Scandinavian countries of Denmark, Sweden, and Norway also met the challenge of economic crisis successfully. They built their recovery programs on an existing

Years of Crisis **425**

tradition of cooperative community action. In Sweden the government sponsored massive public works projects that kept people employed and producing. All the Scandinavian countries raised pensions for the elderly and increased unemployment insurance, subsidies for housing, and other welfare benefits. To pay for these benefits, the governments taxed all citizens. Under this program, both private and cooperative businesses prospered. Democracy remained intact.

Recovery in the United States In 1932, in the first presidential election after the Depression had begun, U.S. voters elected **Franklin D. Roosevelt.** His confident manner appealed to millions of Americans who felt bewildered by the Depression. On March 4, 1933, the new president sought to restore Americans' faith in their nation.

Governments responded to widespread unemployment by creating jobs. Here is a group of young men employed by the U.S. Civilian Conservation Corps.

A VOICE FROM THE PAST
This great Nation will endure as it has endured, will revive and will prosper. . . . let me assert my firm belief that the only thing we have to fear is fear itself—nameless, unreasoning, unjustified terror which paralyzes needed efforts to convert retreat into advance.

FRANKLIN ROOSEVELT, First Inaugural Address

Roosevelt immediately began a program of reform that he called the **New Deal.** Large public works projects helped to provide jobs for the unemployed. New government agencies gave financial help to businesses and farms. Large amounts of public money were spent on welfare and relief programs. Roosevelt and his advisers believed that government spending would create jobs and start a recovery. Regulations were imposed to reform the stock market and the banking system. Despite these efforts, recovery was slow.

The New Deal did eventually reform the American economic system. Roosevelt's leadership preserved the country's faith in its democratic political system. It also established him as a leader of democracy in a world threatened by ruthless dictators, as you will read about in Section 3.

Section 2 Assessment

1. TERMS & NAMES
- coalition government
- Weimar Republic
- Great Depression
- Franklin D. Roosevelt
- New Deal

2. TAKING NOTES
Using a web diagram like the one below, show the effects of the Great Depression in the United States.

The Great Depression

3. ANALYZING CAUSES
The collapse of the American economy had a devastating effect on the world. List one cause for each of the following effects: American market for European goods dropped; unemployment rates soared; European banks and businesses closed.

THINK ABOUT
- economic conditions in the United States
- the interdependence of the economies of the world

4. ANALYZING THEMES
Economics What actions did the United States, Britain, France, and the Scandinavian countries take to try to recover from the Great Depression? Give specific examples for each country.

THINK ABOUT
- Roosevelt and the New Deal
- coalition governments in Britain and France
- traditional community cooperative action in Scandinavia

ANSWERS

1. TERMS & NAMES
coalition government, p. 421
Weimar Republic, p. 422
Great Depression, p. 424
Franklin D. Roosevelt, p. 426
New Deal, p. 426

2. TAKING NOTES
Possible Responses:
Businesses failed, banks closed, savings were lost, farms were foreclosed, unemployment rose.

3. ANALYZING CAUSES
Possible Responses: High U.S. tariffs; drop in world trade; demand for repayment of American loans and withdrawal of American investment money.

4. ANALYZING THEMES
Possible Responses: United States—New Deal supported public works, financial aid to businesses and farms, money for welfare and relief programs; regulated stock market and banks.

Britain—National Government passed tariffs; increased taxes; regulated currency; decreased interest rates. France—Popular Front enacted worker reforms. Scandinavia—public works projects; raised pensions, unemployment insurance, housing subsidies, welfare benefits.

3 Fascism Rises in Europe

TERMS & NAMES
- fascism
- Benito Mussolini
- Adolf Hitler
- Nazism
- *Mein Kampf*
- *lebensraum*

MAIN IDEA

In response to political turmoil and economic crises, Italy and Germany turned to totalitarian dictators.

WHY IT MATTERS NOW

These dictators changed the course of history, and the world is still recovering from their abuse of power.

SETTING THE STAGE Many democracies, including the United States, Britain, and France, remained strong despite the economic crisis caused by the Great Depression. However, millions of people lost faith in democratic government. In response, they turned to an extreme system of government called fascism.

Fascist Beliefs and Policies

Background
The term *fascism* was intended to recall memories of ancient Rome. In Latin, *fasces* is the word for a bundle of wooden rods tied around an ax handle—a symbol of authority for Roman officials.

This new, militant political movement called **fascism** (FASH·IHZ·uhm) emphasized loyalty to the state and obedience to its leader. Fascists promised to revive the economy, punish those responsible for hard times, and restore national pride. Their message attracted many people who felt frustrated and angered by the peace treaties that followed World War I and by the Great Depression.

Unlike communism, fascism had no clearly defined theory or program. Nevertheless, most Fascists shared several ideas. They preached an extreme form of nationalism, or loyalty to one's country. Fascists believed that nations must struggle—peaceful states were doomed to be conquered. They pledged loyalty to an authoritarian leader who guided the state. In each nation, Fascists wore uniforms of a certain color, used special salutes, and held mass rallies.

In some ways, fascism was similar to communism. Both systems were ruled by dictators who allowed only their political party (one-party rule). Both denied individual rights. In both, the state was supreme. Neither practiced any kind of democracy. However, unlike Communists, Fascists did not seek a classless society. Rather, they believed that each class had its place and function. Communism claimed to be a dictatorship of the working class. In most cases, fascist parties were made up of aristocrats and industrialists, war veterans, and the lower middle class. Also, Fascists were nationalists, and Communists were internationalists, hoping to unite workers worldwide.

Mussolini Comes to Power in Italy

A. Possible Answers Italians felt betrayed by the Paris Peace Conference, faced rising inflation and unemployment and social unrest.

THINK THROUGH HISTORY
A. Analyzing Causes What factors led to the rise of fascism in Italy?

Fascism's rise in Italy was fueled by bitter disappointment over the failure to win large territorial gains at the 1919 Paris Peace Conference. Rising inflation and unemployment also contributed to widespread social unrest. Italy's upper and middle classes feared a Communist revolution, as in Russia. To growing numbers of Italians, their democratic government seemed helpless to deal with the country's problems. They wanted a leader who would take action.

The Rise of Mussolini A newspaper editor and politician named **Benito Mussolini** boldly promised to rescue Italy by reviving its

HISTORY MAKERS

Benito Mussolini
1883–1945

Mussolini was a dazzling orator. Because he was of modest height, he usually chose a location for his speeches where he towered above the crowds—often a balcony high above a public square. He then roused audiences with his emotional speeches and theatrical gestures and body movements.

Vowing to lead Italy "back to her ways of ancient greatness," Mussolini peppered his speeches with aggressive words such as "war" and "power."

Mussolini wanted to win support for an overseas empire in Africa and a militaristic state at home. So he often used settings and symbols from the period of Italy's glory—the Roman Empire.

Years of Crisis **427**

Section 3 Overview

OBJECTIVES

1. To summarize Fascist beliefs and policies.
2. To describe Mussolini's rise to power.
3. To explain how Hitler and the Nazis gained control of Germany.
4. To describe the shift from democratic governments to dictatorships in eastern Europe.

CRITICAL THINKING
- Analyzing causes, p. 427
- Summarizing, p. 429
- Making inferences, p. 429
- Drawing conclusions, p. 430

FOCUS
5-Minute Warm-Up

Making Inferences
Answering these questions will help students understand more about one of the key figures in the 20th century.

1. Read History Makers on Adolf Hitler on p. 428. Why did Hitler believe making speeches was so important?
2. What kind of person do you think the foreign diplomat believed Hitler to be after hearing him speak?

 WARM-UP TRANSPARENCY 15

OBJECTIVE ① INSTRUCT

Fascist Beliefs and Policies

Key Ideas
- Fascism is a political movement that stresses extreme loyalty to the state and its leader.
- Support for Fascists comes from aristocrats, industrialists, veterans, and the lower middle class.

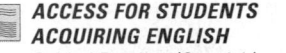 **IN-DEPTH RESOURCES: UNIT 4**
Guided Reading, p. 39
Connections Across Time and Cultures: Absolutism and Fascism, p. 53

ACCESS FOR STUDENTS ACQUIRING ENGLISH
Guided Reading (Spanish), p. 165

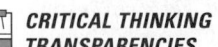 **CRITICAL THINKING TRANSPARENCIES**
CT31 Economic Crisis: Between Two Fires

SECTION 3 RESOURCES

PRINT RESOURCES

 IN-DEPTH RESOURCES: UNIT 4
Guided Reading, p. 39
Primary Source: Kristallnacht, p. 46
Literature: Poems by Bertolt Brecht, p. 49
Connections Across Time and Cultures: p. 53

 ACCESS FOR STUDENTS ACQUIRING ENGLISH
Guided Reading (Spanish), p. 165

 FORMAL ASSESSMENT
Section Quiz, p. 188

TECHNOLOGY RESOURCES

 WORLD ART AND CULTURES TRANSPARENCIES
AT69 *Pillars of Society*

 CRITICAL THINKING TRANSPARENCIES
CT31 Economic Crisis: Between Two Fires

 CD-ROM
Electronic Library of Primary Sources

 INTERNET www.mlworldhistory.com

Mussolini Comes to Power in Italy

(See page 427.)

▶ **Key Ideas**

- In Italy, fascism gains followers because of disappointment over the 1919 Paris Peace Conference, inflation, and unemployment.
- Benito Mussolini gains supporters because he is seen as a strong leader.
- In October 1922, after Fascists march on Rome, Mussolini takes charge of Italy's government.

HISTORY MAKERS
Benito Mussolini

(See page 427.)

Have students research Mussolini's rise to power and write a paper describing the way he used symbols of ancient Rome and other propaganda techniques to persuade Italians to support fascism.

Hitler Takes Control in Germany

▶ **Key Ideas**

- The German brand of fascism is called Nazism.
- Adolf Hitler's skills as an organizer and speaker help him become head of the Nazi party.
- Hitler's book, *Mein Kampf,* sets forth his anti-Semitic beliefs and his plans for conquest.
- Germany's economic problems and fear of the Communist party help Hitler take power legally.
- Hitler uses his power to turn Germany into a totalitarian state.

 IN-DEPTH RESOURCES: UNIT 4
Primary Source: Kristallnacht, p. 46
Literature: Poems by Bertolt Brecht, p. 49

---

economy and rebuilding its armed forces. He vowed to give Italy strong leadership. Mussolini had founded the Fascist Party in 1919. At first, he failed to win widespread support. As economic conditions worsened, however, his popularity rapidly increased. Finally, Mussolini publicly criticized Italy's government. Groups of Fascists wearing black shirts attacked Communists and Socialists on the streets. This campaign of terror weakened his opponents. Because Mussolini played on the fear of a workers' revolt, he began to win support from the middle classes, the aristocracy, and industrial leaders.

In October 1922, about 30,000 Fascists marched on Rome. They demanded that King Victor Emmanuel III put Mussolini in charge of the government. The king decided that Mussolini was the best hope for his dynasty to survive, so he let Mussolini form a government. Thus, after widespread violence and a threat of armed uprising, Mussolini took power "legally." At the time, a foreign diplomat described him as "an actor, a dangerous rascal, and possibly slightly off his head."

Il Duce's Leadership Mussolini was now Il Duce (ihl DOO·chay), or the leader. He abolished democracy and outlawed all political parties except the Fascists. Secret police jailed his opponents. Government censors forced radio stations and publications to broadcast or publish only Fascist doctrines. Mussolini outlawed strikes. He sought to control the economy by allying the Fascists with the industrialists and large landowners. Under his leadership, Italy became the model for Fascists in other countries. However, Mussolini never had the total control achieved by Joseph Stalin in the Soviet Union or Adolf Hitler in Germany.

Hitler Takes Control in Germany

When Mussolini became dictator of Italy in the mid-1920s, **Adolf Hitler** was a little-known political leader whose early life had been marked by disappointment. Born in a small town in Austria in 1889, he dropped out of high school and failed as an artist. When World War I broke out, Hitler found a new beginning. He would fight to defend Germany and crush its opponents. He volunteered for the German army and was twice awarded the Iron Cross, a medal for bravery.

The Rise of the Nazis At the end of the war, Hitler settled in Munich. In early 1920, he joined a tiny right-wing political group. This group shared his belief that Germany had to overturn the Treaty of Versailles and combat communism. The group later named itself the National Socialist German Workers' Party, called Nazi for short. Its policies, supported by people in the middle and lower middle classes, formed the German brand of fascism known as **Nazism.** The party adopted the swastika, or hooked cross, as its symbol. The Nazis also set up a private militia called the storm troopers or Brownshirts.

Within a short time, Hitler's success as an organizer and speaker led him to be chosen *der Führer* (duhr FYUR·uhr), or the leader, of the

HISTORY MAKERS

Adolf Hitler
1889–1945

Like Mussolini, Hitler could manipulate huge audiences with his fiery oratory. Making speeches was crucial to Hitler. He believed: "All great world-shaking events have been brought about . . . by the spoken word!"

Because he appeared awkward and unimposing, Hitler rehearsed his speeches. Usually he began a speech in a normal voice. Suddenly, he spoke louder as his anger grew. His voice rose to a screech, and his hands flailed the air. Then he would stop, smooth his hair, and look quite calm.

In the 1930s, a foreign diplomat described Hitler: ". . . he was all violence . . . with a fierce energy ready at no provocation to pull down the universe. . . . [His] face was the face of a lunatic."

428 Chapter 15

The swastika, which means "well-being" in Sanskrit, was an ancient good-luck symbol. Forms of it had been used by Hindus, Buddhists, early Christians, and Native Americans.

"Heil Hitler!" Hitler Youth members salute their Führer at a rally in the 1930s. Hitler skillfully used mass rallies to generate enthusiasm.

Gifted and Talented Students
Drawing Conclusions Radically different viewpoints of Nazism were expressed in two highly successful motion pictures of the era. The propaganda film *The Triumph of the Will* (1934) was a documentary made about a Nazi party rally in Nuremberg by a young German female director, Leni Riefenstahl. The comedy *The Great Dictator* (1940) was a satire of Adolf Hitler directed in the United States by actor Charlie Chaplin. Students should view the films and then write a comparison of the political viewpoints in each.

Linguistic Learners Have students read the following Hitler quotations. ". . .I, as leader and representative of the German nation, assure the world that now that the Saar issue has been solved, I will make no other territorial request. . . ." "All depends on me . . . because of my political talents. Probably no one will ever again have the confidence of the whole German people as I have . . . [or] more authority. . . ." ". . . [I] would not tolerate a small second-rate country treating the mighty thousand-year-old Reich as something inferior . . .[I] would face any war, even a world war, for this." Then have each student write a paragraph describing what the quotes tell us about Hitler and where he was leading Germany.

Nazi party. These skills also helped make the Nazis a growing political force. Inspired by Mussolini's march on Rome, Hitler and the Nazis plotted to seize power in Munich in 1923. The attempt failed, and Hitler was arrested. He was tried for treason, but sympathetic judges sentenced him to only five years in prison. He served less than nine months.

While in jail, Hitler wrote **Mein Kampf** *(My Struggle)*. This book set forth his beliefs and his goals for Germany. It became the blueprint, or plan of action, for the Nazis. Hitler asserted that the Germans, especially those who were blond and blue-eyed—whom he incorrectly called "Aryans"—were a "master race." He declared that non-Aryan "races"—such as Jews, Slavs, and Gypsies—were inferior or subhuman. He called the Versailles Treaty an outrage and vowed to regain the lands taken from Germany. Hitler also declared that Germany was overcrowded and needed more **lebensraum,** or living space. He promised to get that space by conquering eastern Europe and Russia.

After leaving prison in 1924, Hitler revived the Nazi party. Most Germans ignored him and his angry message until the Depression ended the nation's brief postwar recovery. When American loans stopped, the German economy collapsed. Factories ground to a halt and banks closed. Nearly six million people, about 30 percent of Germany's work force, were unemployed in 1932. Civil unrest broke out. Frightened and confused, Germans now turned to Hitler, hoping for security and firm leadership.

Hitler Becomes Chancellor The Nazis had become the largest political party by 1932. Conservative leaders mistakenly believed they could control Hitler and use him for their purposes. In January 1933, they advised President Paul von Hindenburg to name Hitler chancellor. Only Hitler, they said, could stand up to the strong Communist party in Germany. Thus Hitler came to power legally. Soon after, General Erich Ludendorff, a former Hitler ally, wrote to Hindenburg:

> **A VOICE FROM THE PAST**
> By naming Hitler as *Reichschancellor,* you have delivered up our holy Fatherland to one of the greatest [rabblerousers] of all time. I solemnly [predict] that this accursed man will plunge our Reich into the abyss and bring our nation into inconceivable misery.
> **ERICH LUDENDORFF,** from a letter to President Hindenburg, February 1, 1933

Once in office, Hitler acted quickly to strengthen his position. He called for new elections, hoping to win a parliamentary majority. Six days before the election, a fire destroyed the Reichstag building where parliament met. The Nazis blamed the Communists. By stirring up fear of the Communists, the Nazis and their allies won a slim majority.

With majority control, Hitler demanded dictatorial, or absolute, power for four years. Only one deputy dared to speak against the resulting Enabling Act. Hitler used his new power to turn Germany into a totalitarian state. He banned all other political parties and had opponents arrested. Meanwhile, an elite, black-uniformed unit called the SS *(Schutzstaffel,* or protection squad) was created. It was loyal only to Hitler. In 1934, the SS arrested and murdered hundreds of Hitler's enemies. This brutal action and the terror applied by the Gestapo, the Nazi secret police, shocked most Germans into total obedience.

The Nazis quickly took command of the economy. New laws banned strikes, dissolved independent labor unions, and gave the government authority over business and labor. Hitler put millions of Germans to work. They constructed factories, built highways, manufactured weapons, and served in the military. As a result, unemployment dropped from about 6 to 1.5 million in 1936.

The Führer Is Supreme Hitler wanted more than just economic and political power—he wanted control over every aspect of German life. To shape public opinion and to win

Years of Crisis **429**

GlobaImpact

Fascism to Argentina
Juan Perón served as Argentina's president from 1946 to 1955 and again in 1973 and 1974. The two years he spent in Europe before World War II greatly influenced his strong-man rule.

A career army officer, Perón went to Italy in 1939 for military training. He then served at the Argentine embassy in Rome. A visit to Berlin gave Perón a chance to see Nazi Germany. The ability of Hitler and Mussolini to manipulate their citizens impressed Perón.

When Perón himself gained power, he patterned his military dictatorship on that of the European Fascists. Like them, he restrained his opponents through press censorship and suppression of civil rights. But he never achieved the same total control as his fascist role models.

Other Countries Fall to Dictators

▶ **Key Ideas**
- In Hungary and Poland, the new democratic governments formed after World War I fall to dictators.
- In Yugoslavia, Albania, Bulgaria, and Romania, kings suspend constitutions and turn to strongman rule.
- By 1935, Czechoslovakia is the only democracy in eastern Europe.
- Eastern Europeans turn to dictatorship because they see authoritarian rule as the only way to prevent instability.

 ELECTRONIC LIBRARY OF PRIMARY SOURCES
from *Memos on the Aims of Germany and Japan*

ASSESS & RETEACH

Section 3 Assessment
Students might work in pairs to respond to the questions. Then have them share with the class their diagrams for item 2.

Section Quiz
 FORMAL ASSESSMENT
Section Quiz, p. 188

Reteaching Activity
CLASS TIME: 10 MINUTES

Use the Guided Reading Worksheet for Section 3 to help review the main ideas of the section.

 IN-DEPTH RESOURCES: UNIT 4
Guided Reading, p. 39

CLOSE ACTIVITY

CLASS TIME: 20 MINUTES

Role-Playing
Assign students the roles of Italian citizens or German citizens. After researching the causes of the rise of fascism and ideas of Benito Mussolini and Adolf Hitler, have individual students present the views of individual citizens toward these two leaders.

---

praise for his leadership, Hitler turned the press, radio, literature, painting, and film into propaganda tools. Books that did not conform to Nazi beliefs were burned in huge bonfires. Churches were forbidden to criticize the Nazis or the government. Schoolchildren had to join the Hitler Youth (for boys) or the League of German Girls. Hitler was greatly influenced by Social Darwinism. He believed that a continuous struggle brought victory to the strong. He twisted the philosophy of Friedrich Nietzsche to support his use of brute force to maintain power and his glorification of war.

Hitler Makes War on the Jews Hatred of Jews, or anti-Semitism, was a key part of Nazi ideology. Although Jews were less than one percent of the population, the Nazis used them as scapegoats for all Germany's troubles since the war. This led to a wave of anti-Semitism across Germany. Beginning in 1933, the Nazis passed laws depriving Jews of most of their rights. Violence against Jews mounted. On the night of November 9, 1938, Nazi mobs attacked Jews in their homes and on the streets and destroyed thousands of Jewish-owned buildings. This rampage, called *Kristallnacht* (Night of the Broken Glass), signaled the real start of the process of eliminating the Jews from German life. (See Chapter 16.)

Background
The term *anti-Semitism* is derived from the fact that the earliest Jews were Semites (people who spoke a Semitic language).

SPOTLIGHT ON

The 1936 Olympics
The 1936 Summer Olympics were held in Berlin, Nazi Germany's capital. Hitler built a new $30 million stadium for the Games. To hide from the world his persecution of Jews, he took down all anti-Semitic signs in Berlin.

Prior to the Olympics' opening, Hitler announced that the Games would show the world Aryan superiority and the inferiority of Jews and blacks. Hitler's plan failed, however, in part because of the successes of African-American runner Jesse Owens. A sprinter and long jumper, Owens won four gold medals.

When Owens or other black athletes won medals, Hitler left the reviewing stand. He did not want to be seen congratulating them.

Other Countries Fall to Dictators

While Fascists took power in Italy and Germany, the nations formed in eastern Europe after World War I also were falling to dictators. The parliamentary governments that had been set up in these countries rarely lasted. In Hungary in 1919, after a brief Communist regime, military forces and wealthy landowners joined to make Admiral Miklós Horthy the first European postwar dictator. In Poland, Marshal Joseph Pilsudski (pihl·SOOT·skee) seized power in 1926. In Yugoslavia, Albania, Bulgaria, and Romania, kings turned to strong-man rule. They suspended constitutions and silenced foes. In 1935, one democracy, Czechoslovakia, remained in eastern Europe.

Elsewhere in Europe, only in nations with strong democratic traditions—Britain, France, and the Scandinavian countries—did democracy survive. With no democratic experience and severe economic problems, many Europeans saw dictatorship as the only way to prevent instability. Although all of these dictatorships restricted civil rights, none asserted control with the brutality of the Russian Communists or the Nazis.

By the mid-1930s, the powerful nations of the world were split into two antagonistic camps—democratic and totalitarian. And to gain their ends, the Fascist dictatorships had indicated a willingness to use military aggression.

Section **3** Assessment

1. TERMS & NAMES
Identify
- fascism
- Benito Mussolini
- Adolf Hitler
- Nazism
- *Mein Kampf*
- *lebensraum*

2. TAKING NOTES
Draw a chart like the one below. Compare Mussolini and Hitler by completing the chart.

	Hitler	Mussolini
Method of taking power		
Style of leadership		
Handling of economic crisis		
Goals		

Were the two more alike or different? Explain why.

3. DRAWING CONCLUSIONS
Why did a movement like fascism and leaders like Mussolini and Hitler come to power during a period of crisis?

THINK ABOUT
- what problems Italy and Germany faced
- political traditions in each country
- the state of the world at the time

4. THEME ACTIVITY
Power and Authority
Imagine you live in Italy and it is 1933, ten years since Benito Mussolini became dictator. In Germany, President Paul von Hindenburg is considering appointing Adolf Hitler, a Fascist like Mussolini, chancellor of Germany. What would you advise Hindenburg to do? Write him a letter telling him what has happened in your country under a fascist dictatorship.

430 Chapter 15

ANSWERS

1. TERMS & NAMES
fascism, p. 427
Benito Mussolini, p. 427
Adolf Hitler, p. 428
Nazism, p. 428
Mein Kampf, p. 429
lebensraum, p. 429

2. TAKING NOTES
Possible Responses: Hitler—appointed chancellor, then became dictator; revived economy; sought to regain lost lands and take over more. Mussolini—appointed by king then became dictator; took control of economy; wanted Italy to return to its ancient greatness.

3. DRAWING CONCLUSIONS
Possible Responses: During periods of crisis, people often turn to doctrines or leaders who promise to take charge and solve the country's problems. These doctrines or leaders often offer simple solutions to complex problems and blame outsiders, or scapegoats, for the problems.

4. THEME ACTIVITY
Possible Responses: Opposition letters: under Mussolini democracy abolished; all parties except Fascists outlawed; opponents imprisoned; radio and publications censored; strikes banned. Support letters: order restored, economy revived, and national pride awakened.

TERMS & NAMES
• appeasement
• Axis Powers
• Francisco Franco
• isolationism
• Third Reich
• Munich Conference

MAIN IDEA

As Germany, Italy, and Japan conquered other countries, the rest of the world did nothing to stop them.

WHY IT MATTERS NOW

Many nations today take a more active and collective role in world affairs, as in the United Nations.

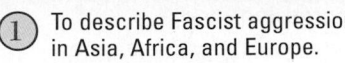
Section 4 Overview

OBJECTIVES

① To describe Fascist aggression in Asia, Africa, and Europe.

② To summarize why British and French appeasement and American isolationism fail to stop Fascist aggression.

③ To explain why the Soviet Union and Germany sign a peace pact.

SKILLBUILDERS
• Interpreting maps: location, movement, p. 433

CRITICAL THINKING
• Comparing, p. 431
• Making inferences, p. 432
• Analyzing visuals, p. 434
• Summarizing, p. 434
• Recognizing effects, p. 435
• Drawing conclusions, p. 435
• Analyzing themes, p. 435

SETTING THE STAGE By the mid-1930s, Germany and Italy seemed bent on military conquest. The major democracies—Britain, France, and the United States—were distracted by economic problems at home and longed to remain at peace. The Soviet Union was not committed to either camp. With the world moving toward war, many people pinned their hopes for peace on the League of Nations.

World Drifts Toward War

As fascism spread in Europe, a powerful nation in Asia moved toward a similar system. Following a period of reform and progress in the 1920s, Japan fell under military rule.

Democracy Struggles in Japan During the 1920s, the Japanese government became more democratic. In 1922, Japan signed an international treaty agreeing to respect China's borders. In 1928, it signed the Kellogg-Briand Pact renouncing war. Japan's parliamentary system had several weaknesses, however. Its constitution put strict limits on the powers of the prime minister and the cabinet. Most importantly, civilian leaders had little control over the armed forces. Military leaders reported only to the emperor.

Militarists Take Control of Japan As long as Japan remained prosperous, the civilian government kept power. When the Great Depression struck in 1930, the government was blamed. Military leaders gained support and soon won control of the country. Unlike the Fascists in Europe, the militarists did not try to establish a new system of government. They wanted to restore traditional control of the government to the military. Instead of a forceful leader like Mussolini or Hitler, the militarists made the emperor the symbol of state power.

Keeping Emperor Hirohito as head of state won popular support for the army leaders who ruled in his name. Like Hitler and Mussolini, Japan's militarists were extreme nationalists. They wanted to solve the country's economic problems by foreign expansion. They planned a Pacific empire that included a conquered China. The empire would provide Japan with raw materials and markets for its goods. It would also give Japan room for its rising population.

Japan Invades Manchuria Japanese businesses had invested heavily in China's northeast province, Manchuria. It was an area rich in iron and coal. In 1931, the Japanese army seized Manchuria, despite objections from the Japanese parliament. The army then set up a puppet government. Japanese engineers and technicians began arriving in large numbers to build mines and factories.

Victorious Japanese troops march through the streets after occupying Manchuria in 1931.

A. Possible Answers Both were extremely nationalistic, wanted to solve economic problems by expanding. European fascists wanted a new government; Japanese wanted to return to traditional military control.

Background
The control of the government by the military had centuries-old roots in Japanese history. The shoguns had been military leaders.

THINK THROUGH HISTORY
A. Comparing
Compare the militarists in Japan with the European Fascists.

FOCUS
5-Minute Warm-Up

▶ *Interpreting a Time line*
To help students understand aggression in the 1930s, have them answer these questions.

1. Look at the time line on page 432. Who committed the first act of aggression and when?

2. Which country committed more aggressive acts?

 WARM-UP TRANSPARENCY 15

OBJECTIVE ① **INSTRUCT**

World Drifts Toward War

▶ *Key Ideas*
• In the 1930s, military leaders take control of Japan, seize Manchuria, and invade China.
• Mussolini invades Ethiopia.
• Hitler rebuilds armed forces and moves troops into Rhineland.

(continued on next page)

Years of Crisis **431**

SECTION 4 RESOURCES

PRINT RESOURCES

 IN-DEPTH RESOURCES: UNIT 4
Guided Reading, p. 40
Geography Application: Spain During the 1930s, p. 42
Primary Source: The Bombing of Guernica, p. 47
History Makers: Francisco Franco, p. 52

ACCESS FOR STUDENTS ACQUIRING ENGLISH
Guided Reading (Spanish), p. 166
Geography Application: (Spanish), p. 168

 FORMAL ASSESSMENT
Section Quiz, p. 189

ALTERNATIVE ASSESSMENT BOOK

TECHNOLOGY RESOURCES

GEOGRAPHY TRANSPARENCIES
GT31 Expansion of Nazi Germany, 1933–1939

CRITICAL THINKING TRANSPARENCIES
CT67 Visual Summary

CD-ROM
Electronic Library of Primary Sources

INTERNET www.mlworldhistory.com

Teacher's Edition **431**

(continued from page 431)

- League of Nations fails to stop aggression.
- Germany, Italy, and Japan become allies as the Axis Powers.
- Civil War in Spain leads to a Fascist dictatorship.

 IN-DEPTH RESOURCES: UNIT 4
Guided Reading, p. 40
Geography Application: Spain During the 1930s, p. 42

ACCESS FOR STUDENTS ACQUIRING ENGLISH
Guided Reading (Spanish), p. 166

MORE ABOUT . . .
Ethiopia and the League of Nations

After Italy attacked Ethiopia, the League of Nations called for an embargo restricting loans to and imports from Italy. However, Britain and France feared angering Mussolini, and they refused to place an embargo on oil. Even more important, Britain refused to stop Italian troops and arms from moving through the British-controlled Suez Canal. This inaction fatally weakened the League.

HISTORY MAKERS
Haile Selassie

Discuss Selassie's warning to League members. Ask students why Selassie says: "It is us today. It will be you tomorrow." Have students speculate on how the failure of League members to act affected Mussolini. Have students brainstorm alternate courses of action in Ethiopia and consider what impact they might have had on Italy.

The Japanese attack on Manchuria was the first direct challenge to the League of Nations. In the early 1930s, the League's members included all major democracies except the United States. Also members were the three countries that posed the greatest threat to peace—Germany, Japan, and Italy. When Japan seized Manchuria, many League members vigorously protested. The League condemned Japanese aggression, but it had no power to enforce its decisions. Japan ignored the protests and withdrew from the League in 1933.

Japan Invades China Four years later, a border incident touched off a full-scale war between Japan and China. On July 7, 1937, the Japanese and the Chinese exchanged shots at a railroad bridge near Beijing. Japanese forces then swept into northern China. Despite having a million soldiers, China's army led by Jiang Jieshi was no match for the better equipped and trained Japanese.

Beijing and other northern cities as well as the capital, Nanjing (formerly Nanking), fell to the Japanese in 1937. Japanese troops killed tens of thousands of captured soldiers and civilians in what was called "the rape" of Nanjing. Forced to retreat, Jiang Jieshi set up a new capital at Chongqing. At the same time, Chinese Communist guerrillas led by Mao Zedong continued to fight in the conquered area.

Mussolini Attacks Ethiopia The League's failure to stop the Japanese encouraged Mussolini to plan aggression of his own. Mussolini dreamed of building a colonial empire in Africa like that of Britain and France. He bitterly complained that Britain and France had left only "a collection of deserts" from which to choose.

Ethiopia was one of Africa's four remaining independent nations. The Ethiopians had successfully resisted an Italian attempt at conquest during the 1890s. To avenge that defeat, Mussolini ordered a massive invasion of Ethiopia in October 1935. The spears and swords of the Ethiopians were no match for Italian airplanes, tanks, guns, and poison gas. In May 1936, Mussolini told a cheering crowd that "Italy has at last her empire . . . a Fascist empire."

The Ethiopian emperor Haile Selassie urgently appealed to the League for help. Although the League condemned the attack, its members did nothing. Britain continued to let Italian troops and supplies pass through the British-controlled Suez Canal on their way to Ethiopia. By giving in to Mussolini in Africa, Britain and France hoped to keep peace in Europe.

Hitler Defies Versailles Treaty Hitler had long pledged to undo the Versailles Treaty. Among its provisions, the treaty limited the size of Germany's army. In March 1935, the Führer announced that Germany would not obey these restrictions. In fact, Germany had already begun rebuilding its armed forces. The League issued only a mild condemnation. Banners throughout Germany announced, "Today Germany! Tomorrow the World!"

HISTORY MAKERS

HAILE SELASSIE
1892–1975
Haile Selassie, the emperor of Ethiopia, belonged to a dynasty that traced its roots back to King Solomon and the Queen of Sheba. When he became emperor in 1930, he was hailed as the 111th descendant of Solomon and Sheba to rule.

Five years after he took the throne, his country was invaded by Italy. Selassie was forced into exile. On June 30, 1936, he appeared before the League of Nations to plead for its help.

He warned League members that if they failed to impose military sanctions on Italy, "God and history will remember your judgment. . . . It is us today. It will be you tomorrow." The League did not heed his warning.

Aggression in Europe and Asia, 1930–1939

September 1931 Japan invades Manchuria.

October 1935 Italy attacks Ethiopia.

March 1938 Germany annexes Austria.

September 1938 Germany takes Sudetenland.

1930 — 1935 — 1939

March 1936 Germany occupies Rhineland.

July 1937 Japan invades China.

March 1939 Germany seizes Czechoslovakia.

April 1939 Italy conquers Albania

Task: Student groups choose a headline and then write a news article, Internet news piece, or a short news spot for a television or radio news show.

Purpose: To understand the events of the 1930s that led to World War II.

Activity: Before dividing students into small groups, prepare a series of headlines, using the subsections of Section 4 as guides. For example, headlines might include Militarists Take Control of Japan, Civil War Erupts in Spain, and so on. Write each headline on a slip of paper and have each group draw from a hat. Another option would be to allow each group to write its own headline. Then ask the group to prepare a newspaper article, short skit for a television news show, radio broadcast, or Internet news blurb explaining the headline. Have students present their news pieces for the class.

 Building a Portfolio: Students may want to put articles or scripts in their portfolios.

ALTERNATIVE ASSESSMENT BOOK
Standards for Evaluating a Cooperative Activity

Standards for Evaluation
News articles should . . .

- clearly explain the *who, what, when, where,* and if possible, the *why* or *how* of this event
- show an understanding of its significance
- be accurate and factual
- be appropriate in tone and content

The League's failure to stop Germany from rearming convinced Hitler to take even greater risks. The treaty had forbidden German troops to enter a 30-mile-wide zone on either side of the Rhine River. Known as the Rhineland, it formed a buffer zone between Germany and France. It was also an important industrial area. On March 7, 1936, German troops moved into the Rhineland. Stunned, the French were unwilling to risk war. The British urged **appeasement,** giving in to an aggressor to keep peace.

Hitler later admitted that he would have backed down if the French and British had challenged him. The German reoccupation of the Rhineland marked a turning point in the march toward war. First, it strengthened Hitler's power and prestige within Germany. Cautious generals who had urged restraint now agreed to follow him. Second, the balance of power changed in Germany's favor. France and Belgium were now open to attack from German troops. Finally, the weak response by France and Britain encouraged Hitler to speed up his military and territorial expansion.

Hitler's growing strength convinced Mussolini that he should seek an alliance with Germany. In October 1936, the two dictators reached an agreement that became known as the Rome-Berlin Axis. A month later, Germany also made an agreement with Japan. Germany, Italy, and Japan came to be called the **Axis Powers.**

Civil War Erupts in Spain Hitler and Mussolini again tested the will of the democracies of Europe in the Spanish civil war. Spain had been a monarchy until 1931, when a republic was declared. The government, run by liberals and socialists, held office amid many crises. In July 1936, army leaders, favoring a Fascist-style government, joined General **Francisco Franco** in a revolt. Thus began a civil war that dragged on for three years.

Hitler and Mussolini sent troops, tanks, and airplanes to help Franco's forces, which were called the Nationalists. The armed forces of

Vocabulary
axis: a straight line around which an object rotates. Hitler and Mussolini expected their alliance to become the axis around which Europe would rotate.

GERMANY
SUDETENLAND
CZECHOSLOVAKIA
AUSTRIA
0   200 Miles
0   400 Kilometers

MEMEL
North Sea
Baltic Sea
E. PRUSSIA (GER.)
UNITED KINGDOM
SOVIET UNION
GERMANY
POLAND
SUDETENLAND
CZECHOSLOVAKIA
RHINELAND
ATLANTIC OCEAN
AUSTRIA
FRANCE
Black Sea
40°N
ITALY
SPAIN (Civil War, 1936–1939)
N
ALBANIA
Mediterranean Sea
0   500 Miles
0   1,000 Kilometers

Aggression in Europe, Africa and Asia, 1930–1939

■ Italy
■ Italian colony
■ Taken by Italy
■ Germany
□ Taken by Germany
□ Japan
□ Taken by Japan

SOVIET UNION
MANCHURIA
N
0   3,000 Miles
0   6,000 Kilometers
Sea of Japan
40°N
CHINA
KOREA
JAPAN
Mediterranean Sea
LIBYA
Tropic of Cancer
PACIFIC OCEAN
ERITREA
Bay of Bengal
ETHIOPIA
SOMALIA
INDIAN OCEAN
0° Equator
ATLANTIC OCEAN

GEOGRAPHY SKILLBUILDER: Interpreting Maps
1. **Location** What countries were aggressors in this period?
2. **Movement** Aggression occurred on what three continents?

CRITICAL THINKING ACTIVITY
CLASS TIME: 20 MINUTES

Recognizing Effects
To help students recognize the effects of each of these peace-treaty violations on relations between Germany, Italy, France, and Britain, have them make a simple cause and effect diagram.

1936: Demilitarized Rhineland occupied by German forces	→	Effect
1938: Austria united with Germany	→	Effect
1938 Sudetenland taken from Czechoslovakia.	→	Effect

MORE ABOUT . . .
Francisco Franco
After the Nationalist victory in the Spanish Civil War, General Francisco Franco declared himself military chief. He ruled Spain until his death in 1975. Initially his reign was quite harsh. He executed 200,000 Spaniards between 1939 and 1943. He sympathized with the Axis Powers but did not enter World War II.

IN-DEPTH RESOURCES: UNIT 4
History Makers: Francisco Franco, p. 52
Primary Source: The Bombing of Guernica, p. 47

Learning from Visuals

Aggression in Europe, Africa and Asia, 1930–1939
Interpreting the Map Ask students to explain what the areas in purple *(lands attacked or claimed by Italy)*, pink *(by Germany)*, and gold *(by Japan)* represent.

Extension Have students use the map to name the continents where each Axis Power claimed territory by 1939. *Japan: Asia; Italy: Africa and Europe; Germany: Europe.* Ask them why Poland might be a next step for German aggression. *Polish Corridor forms a wedge between Germany and its territory in East Prussia.*

SKILLBUILDER Answers
1. Italy, Germany, Japan.
2. Europe, Africa, and Asia

TEACHING OPTIONS

CONNECTIONS ACROSS TIME AND PLACE

Totalitarian Rule A totalitarian government is one that is controlled by a single political group. It suppresses all opposition, often through violent means. It controls all aspects of people's lives, including education, production of goods and services, culture, and travel, both within the country and abroad. A totalitarian state also exercises total control of the media, particularly newspapers, radio, and television.

Both Nazi Germany under Adolf Hitler and the Soviet Union under Joseph Stalin are examples of totalitarian states. Have students name modern-day dictators such as Saddam Hussein and Fidel Castro and decide whether their rule can be described as totalitarian.

CONNECTIONS ACROSS THE CURRICULUM

Literature Students interested in seeing an insider's perspective on the Spanish Civil War can read the American writer Ernest Hemingway's novel *For Whom the Bell Tolls* (1940). Hemingway was in Spain during the war as a newspaper correspondent. The Englishman George Orwell, best known for his novels *1984* and *Animal Farm*, wrote a nonfiction work, *Homage to Catalonia* (1938), about his experiences as a soldier. It describes his disillusionment with the Loyalists during the war. Students might contrast the idealism of Hemingway's hero with Orwell's view of war.

Western Democracies Fail to Halt Aggression

▶ Key Issues

- In the 1930s, the United States follows an isolationist foreign policy in an effort to keep out of war.
- Germany annexes Austria and takes the Sudetenland from Czechoslovakia.
- Following a policy of appeasement, France and Britain let Hitler have the Sudetenland.
- Appeasement policy convinces Hitler that Britain and France will not stop his seizure of Czechoslovakia.
- Germany and the Soviet Union sign a nonaggression pact.

 GEOGRAPHY TRANSPARENCIES
GT31 Expansion of Nazi Germany, 1933–1939

 ELECTRONIC LIBRARY OF PRIMARY SOURCES
from Speech in the House of Commons

MORE ABOUT . . .
U.S. Isolationism

Many factors contributed to American isolationism. These included fear of war, hatred of profiteers whom many believed had dragged America into World War I, and distrust of presidential power.

MORE ABOUT . . .
Anschluss

Many years before the Anschluss, Hitler had built a strong base of support in Austria. The country had its own Nazi party, which campaigned for union until it was banned in 1934. Working in secret, Austria's Nazi party formed close ties with Germany's Nazi government. After Hitler invaded Austria in March 1938, Austrian Hitler Youth helped to make Austria a solidly pro-Nazi nation almost overnight.

HISTORY THROUGH ART: Fine Art

Connect *to* History

Analyzing Visuals How does Picasso's use of image and color depict the horrors of the Spanish Civil War?

SEE SKILLBUILDER HANDBOOK, PAGE 667

Connect *to* Today

Research Research the civil war in Bosnia. Collect different types of visuals that show the horror of that war. Describe your selections.

The Spanish artist Pablo Picasso painted *Guernica* shortly after Nazi planes destroyed the ancient Basque city of Guernica in 1937. The air attacks killed a thousand people, one out of every eight residents. At left, a mother cries over her dead child. In the center, a horse screams and a soldier lies dead. At right, a woman falls from a burning house. The canvas is huge—11 feet high and 25 feet long.

the Republicans, as supporters of Spain's elected government were known, received little help from abroad. The Western democracies remained neutral. Only the Soviet Union sent equipment and advisers. An International Brigade of volunteers fought on the Republican side but had little chance against a professional army. Early in 1939, Republican resistance collapsed. Franco became Spain's Fascist dictator.

Western Democracies Fail to Halt Aggression

Instead of taking a stand against Fascist aggression in the 1930s, Britain and France repeatedly made concessions, hoping to keep peace. Both nations were dealing with serious economic problems as a result of the Great Depression. In addition, the horrors of World War I had created a deep desire to avoid war. Allowing Hitler and Mussolini small territorial gains seemed a small price to pay for peace.

United States Follows an Isolationist Policy Many Americans resisted accepting the nation's new position as a world leader. **Isolationism**—the belief that political ties to other countries should be avoided—won wide support. Isolationists argued that entry into World War I had been a costly error. They were determined to prevent a repeat of this mistake. Beginning in 1935, Congress passed three Neutrality Acts. These laws banned loans and the sale of arms to nations at war. The isolationists believed this action would keep the United States out of another foreign war.

The German Reich Expands On November 5, 1937, Hitler announced to his advisers his plans to absorb Austria and Czechoslovakia into the **Third Reich** (ryk), or German Empire. The Germans would then expand into Poland and Russia. Hitler's first target was Austria. The Treaty of Versailles prohibited Anschluss (AHN·shlus), or a union between Austria and Germany. However, many Austrians supported unity with Germany. In March 1938, Hitler sent his army into Austria and annexed it. France and Britain ignored their pledge to protect Austrian independence.

Hitler next turned to Czechoslovakia. After World War I, Czechoslovakia had developed into a prosperous democracy with a strong army and a defense treaty with France. About 3 million German-speaking people lived in the western border regions of Czechoslovakia called the Sudetenland. (See map, page 433.) This heavily fortified area formed the Czechs' main defense against Germany. The Anschluss raised pro-Nazi feelings among Sudeten Germans. In September 1938, Hitler demanded that the Sudetenland be given to Germany. The Czechs refused and asked France for help.

THINK THROUGH HISTORY

C. Summarizing What foreign countries were involved in the Spanish Civil War?

C. Answer Germany and Italy on the side of Franco; the Soviet Union in support of the Spanish government.

Background According to Hitler, there were three great German empires. They were the Holy Roman Empire; the German Empire of 1871–1918; and the Third Reich, ruled by the Nazis. The Third Reich, Hitler believed, would last 1,000 years.

Connect *to* History

Analyzing Visuals
The only explanation Picasso ever gave of this famous painting was this: "The horse represents the people and the bull brutality and darkness." Ask students to pick out the following symbols and speculate about their meaning 1) a woman falling from a burning house, 2) a horse screaming as it falls to the ground, 3) a soldier lying dead holding a broken sword, 4) a mother crying over her dead child, 5) a woman watching from a window. Note how the images are distorted and in some cases disembodied. What is the effect of these disjointed images? Have students discuss reasons why Picasso might have chosen blacks and grays for this painting. What might these colors suggest about his view of war?

Connect *to* Today

Research
Suggest the following strategies for researching the civil war in Bosnia.

- Look for newspaper or magazine photos depicting the devastation caused.
- Check library resources or the Internet for artistic images, such as political cartoons or paintings.

Britain and France Again Choose Appeasement France and Britain were preparing for war when Mussolini proposed a meeting of Germany, France, Britain, and Italy in Munich, Germany. The **Munich Conference** was held on September 29, 1938. The Czechs were not invited. British Prime Minister Neville Chamberlain believed that he could preserve peace by giving in to Hitler's demand. The next morning, a tense world learned that the crisis was over. Britain and France agreed that Hitler could take the Sudetenland. In exchange, Hitler pledged to respect Czechoslovakia's new borders.

Chamberlain's policy of appeasement seemed to have prevented war. When he returned to London, Chamberlain told cheering crowds, "I believe it is peace for our time." Winston Churchill, then a member of the British Parliament, strongly disagreed. He opposed the appeasement policy and gloomily warned of its consequences.

A VOICE FROM THE PAST

We are in the presence of a disaster of the first magnitude. . . . we have sustained a defeat without a war. . . . And do not suppose that this is the end. . . . This is only the first sip, the first foretaste of a bitter cup which will be proffered to us year by year unless, by a supreme recovery of moral health and martial vigor, we arise again and take our stand for freedom as in the olden time.

WINSTON CHURCHILL, speech before the House of Commons, October 5, 1938

Less than six months after the Munich meeting, Hitler's troops took Czechoslovakia. Soon after, Mussolini seized nearby Albania. Then Hitler demanded that Poland return the former German port of Danzig. The Poles refused and turned to Britain and France for aid. Both countries said they would guarantee Polish independence. But appeasement had convinced Hitler that neither nation would risk war.

Nazis and Soviets Sign Nonaggression Pact Britain and France asked the Soviet Union to join them in stopping Hitler's aggression. Negotiations proceeded slowly. The two democracies distrusted the Communist government, and Stalin resented having been left out of the Munich Conference. As the Soviet leader talked with Britain and France, he also bargained with Hitler. The two dictators reached an agreement. Once bitter enemies, fascist Germany and communist Russia now publicly committed never to attack one another. On August 23, 1939, a nonaggression pact was signed. As the Axis Powers moved unchecked at the end of the decade, the whole world waited to see what would happen next. War appeared inevitable.

THINK THROUGH HISTORY
D. Recognizing Effects What were the effects of isolationism and appeasement?
D. Answer Aggressor nations continued their aggressions unchecked.

CONNECT *to* TODAY

Aggression in the Persian Gulf
After World War II, the Munich Conference of 1938 became a symbol for surrender. Leaders of democracies vowed never again to appease a ruthless dictator. U.S. President George Bush used Munich as an example when responding to aggression in the Persian Gulf in 1990.

When troops of Iraqi dictator Saddam Hussein invaded nearby Kuwait, the United States responded to Kuwait's call for help by forming a coalition of forces to fight the Persian Gulf War. In explaining why, Bush noted how Britain's Neville Chamberlain failed to help Czechoslovakia after Hitler claimed the Sudetenland. Bush said:

The world cannot turn a blind eye to aggression. You know the tragic consequences when nations, confronted with aggression, choose to tell themselves it is no concern of theirs, "just a quarrel [as Chamberlain said] in a faraway country between people of whom we know nothing."

Section 4 Assessment

1. TERMS & NAMES

Identify
- appeasement
- Axis Powers
- Francisco Franco
- isolationism
- Third Reich
- Munich Conference

2. TAKING NOTES

Trace the movement of Japan from democratic reform in the 1920s to military aggression in the 1930s by supplying the events following the dates shown on the time line below.

```
1922      1930      1936
   1928      1931      1937
```

What event was the most significant? Why?

3. DRAWING CONCLUSIONS

Review Germany's aggressive actions after Hitler defied the Versailles Treaty by rebuilding Germany's armed forces. At what point do you think Hitler concluded that he could take any territory without being stopped? Why?

THINK ABOUT
- Hitler's goals
- responses of the democracies to his statements and actions
- the role of the League of Nations

4. ANALYZING THEMES

Power and Authority After World War I, many Americans became isolationists. Do you recommend that America practice isolationism today? Why or why not?

THINK ABOUT
- America's role as world leader
- the global economy
- America's domestic problems
- the economic and political goals of other countries

Years of Crisis **435**

ANSWERS

1. TERMS & NAMES
appeasement, p. 433
Axis Powers, p. 433
Francisco Franco, p. 433
isolationism, p. 434
Third Reich, p. 434
Munich Conference, p. 435

2. TAKING NOTES
Possible Responses:
1922—Signs treaty agreeing to respect China's borders; 1928— Signs Kellogg-Briand Pact renouncing war; 1930—Great Depression puts military in control; 1931—Invades Manchuria; 1936—Allies with Germany; 1937—Invades China

3. DRAWING CONCLUSIONS
Possible Responses: After Hitler renounced Versailles Treaty—nothing happened; after seizing Rhineland—Britain urged appeasement; after taking Austria—France and Britain ignored pledge to protect Austria; after Munich Conference—Britain and France let Germany take Sudetenland.

4. ANALYZING THEMES
Possible Responses: Yes— world leadership costs in money and respect; global economy costs in jobs and social services; cannot solve other countries' problems. No—power and prestige as a world leader; need to compete in a global economy; benefits from maintaining order.

Teacher's Edition 435

TERMS & NAMES

1. Albert Einstein, p. 415
2. Sigmund Freud, p. 415
3. Weimar Republic, p. 422
4. New Deal, p. 426
5. fascism, p. 427
6. Benito Mussolini, p. 427
7. Adolf Hitler, p. 428
8. appeasement, p. 433
9. Francisco Franco, p. 433
10. Munich Conference, p. 435

REVIEW QUESTIONS

Answers will vary.

11. They created a revolution in science and the study of human behavior, disturbing many people and leading them to question their own beliefs.

12. *Possible Responses:* Passenger airlines, improved autos, radio broadcasting widespread, and movies a major industry.

13. Lacked democratic heritage; lacked strong ruling party (had several major parties); criticized for loss of war; humiliation of the Versailles Treaty.

14. Provided for $200 million U.S. loan and better German reparation repayment schedule; increased U.S. investment and industrial production; slowed inflation.

15. Investors bought on margin; investors sold, hoping to reinvest with lower rates; falling prices caused panic selling; stocks lost value.

16. Dissatisfaction with Paris Peace Conference; unemployment; fear of communist revolution; democratic government unable to solve problems.

17. Germans were master race and other "races" inferior; Treaty of Versailles was intolerable and Hitler would reclaim territory; takeover of eastern Europe and Russia would give Germany more *lebensraum*.

18. Through foreign expansion; a Pacific empire on Chinese mainland yielding raw materials; increased living space.

19. The military was convinced Hitler had the power to succeed; with France and Belgium open to attack, the balance of power favored Germany; Hitler pursued military and territorial expansion.

20. From 1936 to 1939 Franco and his Fascist army fought the Spanish Republicans; Franco's forces won, and Franco became the military dictator of Spain.

Visual Summary

The Great Depression

Long-Term Causes
- World economies are connected.
- Some countries have huge war debts from World War I.
- Europe relies on American loans and investments.
- Prosperity is built on borrowed money.
- Wealth is unequally distributed.

Immediate Causes
- U.S. stock market crashes.
- Banks demand repayment of loans.
- Farms fail and factories close.
- Americans reduce foreign trade to protect economy.
- Americans stop loans to foreign countries.
- American banking system collapses.

Worldwide Economic Depression

Immediate Effects
- Millions become unemployed worldwide.
- Businesses go bankrupt.
- Governments take emergency measures to protect economies.
- Citizens lose faith in capitalism and democracy.
- Nations turn toward authoritarian leaders.

Long-Term Effects
- Nazis take control in Germany.
- Fascists come to power in other countries.
- Democracies try social welfare programs.
- Japan expands in East Asia.
- World War II breaks out.

TERMS & NAMES

Briefly explain the importance of each of the following during the years 1919 to 1939.

1. Albert Einstein
2. Sigmund Freud
3. Weimar Republic
4. New Deal
5. fascism
6. Benito Mussolini
7. Adolf Hitler
8. appeasement
9. Francisco Franco
10. Munich Conference

REVIEW QUESTIONS

SECTION 1 *(pages 415–420)*
An Age of Uncertainty

11. What effect did Einstein's theory of relativity and Freud's theory of the unconscious have on the public?

12. What advances were made in transportation and communication in the 1920s and 1930s?

SECTION 2 *(pages 421–426)*
A Global Depression

13. List three reasons the Weimar Republic was considered weak.

14. What was the Dawes Plan? How did it affect the German economy?

15. What caused the stock market crash of 1929?

SECTION 3 *(pages 427–430)*
Fascism Rises in Europe

16. List three political and economic reasons the Italians turned to Mussolini.

17. List three of Hitler's beliefs and goals presented in *Mein Kampf*.

SECTION 4 *(pages 431–435)*
Aggressors on the March

18. Explain how Japan planned to solve its economic problems.

19. Why was Germany's reoccupation of the Rhineland a significant turning point toward war?

20. Briefly describe the Spanish Civil War. Include when it occurred, who fought, and who won.

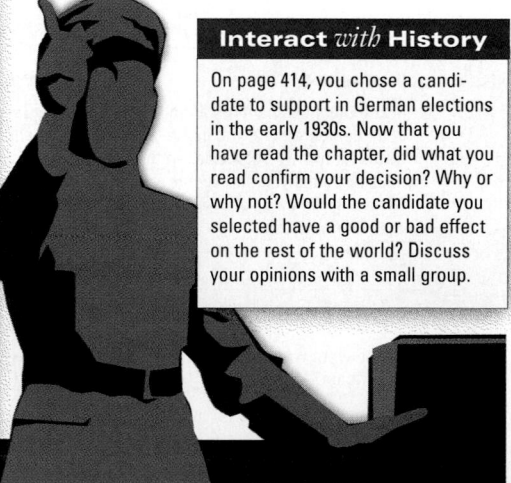

Interact *with* History

On page 414, you chose a candidate to support in German elections in the early 1930s. Now that you have read the chapter, did what you read confirm your decision? Why or why not? Would the candidate you selected have a good or bad effect on the rest of the world? Discuss your opinions with a small group.

Interact *with* History

Possible Responses: Students who selected candidate one may say they made the right choice because their candidate was like Hitler, who made Germany strong again. Or they may rethink their choice, saying that Hitler's kind of nationalistic leadership imposed totalitarian rule to achieve its aims. Those who chose number two may support or reject their choice based on whether they approved of the direction Germany took under Hitler.

CRITICAL THINKING

1. THE STOCK MARKET CRASH

THEME ECONOMICS Your text says that the economy in 1929 was "like a delicately balanced house of cards." Use a sequence graphic like the one below to identify the events that led to the stock market collapse.

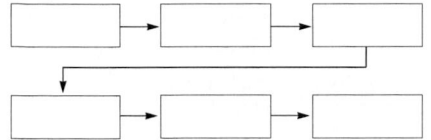

2. SUPPORT FOR FASCISM

Millions of people were attracted to fascist principles and leaders following World War I. What conditions made them give their support to these authoritarian doctrines? What were the advantages and disadvantages of being under fascist rule?

3. THE LEAGUE OF NATIONS

What weaknesses made the League of Nations an ineffective force for peace in the 1920s and 1930s? Give specific examples to prove your point.

4. ANALYZING PRIMARY SOURCES

In 1938, France, Britain, Italy, and Germany met to discuss Hitler's demand for the Sudetenland. Columbia Broadcasting System transmitted the following live report on radios around the world.

A VOICE FROM THE PAST

Prague—6:30 p.m.   September 29
WILLIAM SHIRER: It took the Big Four just five hours and twenty-five minutes here in Munich today to dispel the clouds of war and come to an agreement over the partition of Czechoslovakia. There is to be no European war. . . the price of that peace is, roughly, the ceding by Czechoslovakia of the Sudeten territory to Herr Hitler's Germany. The German Führer gets what he wanted, only he has to wait a little longer for it. . . .

His waiting ten short days has saved Europe from a world war. . . most of the peoples of Europe are happy that they won't have to be marching off to war on Saturday. Probably only the Czechs. . . are not too happy. But there seems very little that they can do about it in face of all the might and power represented here. . .

WILLIAM SHIRER, quoted in *The Strenuous Decade*

• Summarize the news Shirer is reporting.

• What do you think is Shirer's opinion about it? Give specific examples to support your opinion.

CHAPTER ACTIVITIES

1. LIVING HISTORY: Unit Portfolio Project

THEME SCIENCE AND TECHNOLOGY Your unit portfolio project focuses on the impact of scientific and technological innovation on history. For chapter 15, you might select one of the following ideas to add to your portfolio.

• Study the style of an architect, artist, author, or musician in this chapter. Compose or create your own work imitating this person's style. For example, design a functional building like Wright or a cubist painting like Picasso.

• Give a demonstration speech on an invention, tool, or other device from this time period. While showing the class how it works, explain its social, political, or economic effects.

• With a small group, invent a weapon to be used for peaceful purposes by the League of Nations, and rewrite history. Choose an incident of aggression that you read about and write a fictional account headlined *League's New Weapon Halts Fascists*. Read your version of history to the class.

2. CONNECT TO TODAY: Cooperative Learning

THEME POWER AND AUTHORITY After World War I, authoritarian leaders came to power in many countries during times of crisis. Could a Hitler or Mussolini come to power now in any country? Work with a small group. Select a country to research.

 Using the Internet and library sources, investigate your chosen country's political and economic condition today. Review its history.

• Use information from your research to prepare a scenario, or situation, where a dictator could take power in that country. Present your results.

3. INTERPRETING A TIME LINE

Review the unit time line on page 358. Which three events most seriously defied the peace treaties of this time period? In a short paragraph, explain why. Share your paragraph with another student.

FOCUS ON CHARTS

Comparing Fascism/Nazism and Communism Fascism/Nazism and Communism are two different totalitarian political systems with some common characteristics.

	Fascism/Nazism	Communism
Basic principles	Authoritarian; action-oriented; charismatic leader; state more important than individual	Marxist-Leninist ideas; dictatorship of proletariat; state more important than individual
Political	Nationalist; racist (Nazism); one-party rule; supreme leader	Internationalist; one-party rule; supreme leader
Social	Supported by middle class, industrialists, and military	Supported by workers and peasants
Cultural	Censorship; indoctrination; secret police	Censorship; indoctrination; secret police
Economic	Private property control by state corporations or state	Collective ownership; centralized state planning
Examples	Italy, Spain, Germany	U.S.S.R.

• What characteristics do they have in common? How do they differ?

Years of Crisis **437**

---

1. LIVING HISTORY

Standards for Evaluation
Works of art or architectural designs should meet the following criteria:

• Contain elements of the person's style.
• Show evidence of research

Standards for Evaluation
Demonstration speeches should meet the following criteria:

• Clearly explain the origin and function of the item.
• Discuss the effects of the item on society.

Standards for Evaluation
Student versions of history should meet the following criteria:

• Describe the weapon invented.
• Explain how its use changed history.

2. CONNECT TO TODAY: COOPERATIVE LEARNING

Standards for Evaluation
Takeover scenarios should meet the following criteria:

• Describe the weaknesses and problems in the country.
• Explain how they provide an opportunity for fascist takeover.
• Show how the dictator acquired power.

3. INTERPRETING A TIME LINE

Possible Response: Japan's invasion of Manchuria in 1931, Italy's invasion of Ethiopia in 1935, and Germany's annexation of Austria in 1938. These actions showed the aggressors' willingness to disregard existing treaties and to use force to acquire territory.

FOCUS ON CHARTS

Possible Answers: Common characteristics: state more important than individual, one-party rule, supreme leader, censorship, indoctrination, and secret police. Differences: Fascism/Nazism—authoritarian; action-oriented; charismatic leader; nationalist, racist; supported by middle class, industrialists, and military; private property control led by state or state corporations. Communism—Marxist-Leninist ideas, dictatorship of proletariat; internationalist; supported by workers and peasants; collective ownership; and centralized state planning.

CRITICAL THINKING

1. THE STOCK MARKET CRASH

Possible Responses: Stock prices high, investors sold stocks, prices fell, panic resulted, prices plunged further, market crashed.

2. SUPPORT FOR FASCISM

Possible Responses: People were frustrated and angry over problems; wanted strong leaders to restore national pride and provide security and jobs. Advantages—strong leadership, end to social unrest, government put people back to work. Disadvantages—only one political party, no democracy, rights limited, censorship.

3. THE LEAGUE OF NATIONS

Possible Responses: No armed forces to stop aggression. Weakened by the United States not being a member. When it condemned an aggressor, it could not speak for all the world's powers.

4. ANALYZING PRIMARY SOURCES

Possible Responses: Shirer is reporting on the meeting of Germany, France, Britain, and Italy in Munich that allowed Germany to take the Sudetenland from Czechoslovakia. Shirer seems to support the agreement, believing it has saved the world from war. He also appears to sympathize with the Czechs but says they are powerless to resist.

	Key Ideas	COPY MASTERS	ASSESSMENT	
SECTION 1 Hitler's Lightning War *pp. 441–446*	*Hitler launches a surprise attack on Poland, overruns much of Europe, and invades Russia. Britain survives to fight on alone, aided by arms from the United States.*	*In-Depth Resources: Unit 4* • **Guided Reading,** p. 54 • **Primary Source:** from *Berlin Diary,* p. 62 • **History Makers:** Charles de Gaulle, p. 69 Winston Churchill, p. 70	PE *Section 1 Assessment,* p. 446 *Formal Assessment* • Section Quiz, p. 198 *Alternative Assessment Book* • Standards for Evaluating a Cooperative Activity	
SECTION 2 Japan Strikes in the Pacific *pp. 447–450*	*Japan's attack on Pearl Harbor draws the United States into the war. Initial Japanese victories in the Pacific are overturned as U.S. naval forces fight back, gaining the offensive.*	*In-Depth Resources: Unit 4* • **Guided Reading,** p. 55 • **Geography Application:** The Fall of Singapore, p. 60	PE *Section 2 Assessment,* p. 450 *Formal Assessment* • Section Quiz, p. 199 *Alternative Assessment Book* • Standards for Evaluating a Cooperative Activity	
SECTION 3 The Holocaust *pp. 451–454*	*Nazi persecution of Jews throughout Germany and the conquered nations leads to Hitler's "Final Solution," the mass extermination of 6 million of Europe's Jews.*	*In-Depth Resources: Unit 4* • **Guided Reading,** p. 56 • **Primary Sources:** from *The Diary of a Young Girl,* p. 64 • **Literature:** from *Night,* p. 66	PE *Section 3 Assessment,* p. 454 *Formal Assessment* • Section Quiz, p. 200 *Alternative Assessment Book* • Standards for Evaluating a Cooperative Activity	
SECTION 4 The Allies Are Victorious *pp. 455–461*	*The Allies invade Europe as the Soviet Union drives the Germans westward, leading to Germany's final defeat. Japan surrenders following an atomic bomb attack by the United States.*	*In-Depth Resources: Unit 4* • **Guided Reading,** p. 57 • **Skillbuilder Practice:** Following Chronological Order, p. 59 • **Primary Sources:** from *Farewell to Manzanar,* p. 63 from *Hiroshima,* p. 65	PE *Section 4 Assessment,* p. 461 *Formal Assessment* • Section Quiz, p. 201 *Alternative Assessment Book* • Standards for Evaluating a Cooperative Activity	
SECTION 5 The Devastation of Europe and Japan *pp. 462–465*	*A ravaged Europe struggles to survive as the United States occupies Japan and begins to bring political change and stability.*	*In-Depth Resources: Unit 4* • **Guided Reading,** p. 58	PE *Section 5 Assessment,* p. 465 *Formal Assessment* • Section Quiz, p. 202 *Alternative Assessment Book* • Standards for Evaluating a Cooperative Activity	
CHAPTER RESOURCES	Chapter Overview *The expansionist designs of Germany and Japan lead to worldwide conflict. After initial defeats in Europe and the Pacific, the Allies are victorious but at the cost of millions of lives and the economic and political devastation of Europe and Japan.*	*Telescoping the Times* • Chapter Summary, pp. 65–67 *Planning for Block Schedules* *Case Studies* • **Case Study 1**—Japan and Mexico: Pluralistic Politics and Economic Growth, p. 114	PE *Chapter Assessment,* pp. 466–467 *Chapter Activities,* p. 467 *Formal Assessment* • Chapter Test, forms A and B, pp. 203–208 *Test Generator* *Alternative Assessment Book*	

TECHNOLOGY

 Warm-Up Transparency 16

 Geography Transparencies
• GT32 The Battle of Britain, 1940–1941

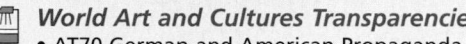 *World Art and Cultures Transparencies*
• AT70 German and American Propaganda

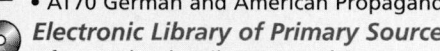 *Electronic Library of Primary Sources*
• from "Blood, Toil, Tears, and Sweat"

 INTERNET RESOURCES
www.mlworldhistory.com

 Warm-Up Transparency 16

 Electronic Library of Primary Sources
• from "Japanese Attack Sinks HMS Repulse"

 INTERNET RESOURCES
www.mlworldhistory.com

 Warm-Up Transparency 16

 Electronic Library of Primary Sources
• from Affadavit Given at Nuremberg

 INTERNET RESOURCES
www.mlworldhistory.com

 Warm-Up Transparency 16

 Battles of the World
• The Battle of Stalingrad

 Electronic Library of Primary Sources
• from Testimony Before the Special Senate Committee on Atomic Energy

 Patterns of Interaction: Arming for War

 Warm-Up Transparency 16

World Art and Cultures Transparencies
• AT71 *Liberation*

Critical Thinking Transparencies
• CT32 The Causes and Effects of World War II
• CT68 Visual Summary

 INTERNET RESOURCES
www.mlworldhistory.com

 Chapter Summaries on Audiocassette in English and Spanish

 INTERNET RESOURCES
www.mlworldhistory.com

Block Scheduling (90 MINUTES)

Day 1
Section 1, pp. 441–446
 COOPERATIVE ACTIVITY Teacher's Edition, p. 443
Section Assessment, p. 446

Day 2
Section 2, pp. 447–450
 COOPERATIVE ACTIVITY Teacher's Edition, p. 449

Section 3, p. 451–454
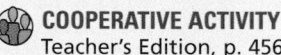 **COOPERATIVE ACTIVITY** Teacher's Edition, p. 453
Section Assessments, pp. 450, 454

Day 3
Section 4, pp. 455–461
COOPERATIVE ACTIVITY Teacher's Edition, p. 456

Section Assessment, p. 461
Day 4
Section 5, pp. 462–465
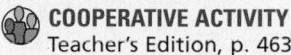 **COOPERATIVE ACTIVITY** Teacher's Edition, p. 463
Section Assessment, p. 465
Chapter Assessment, pp. 466–467

Yearly Pacing *Chapter 16 Total:* 4 days *Yearly Total:* 85 days

Planning for Block Schedules

Customizing for Special Needs

Students Acquiring English

 Access for Students Acquiring English
• **Guided Reading** for Sections 1–5 (Spanish), pp. 173–177
• **Chapter Summary** (Spanish), pp. 170–172
• **Skillbuilder Practice** Following Chronological Order (Spanish), p. 178
• **Geography Application** The Fall of Singapore (Spanish), pp. 179–180

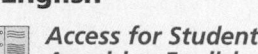 *Spanish Reading Study Guide*
• pp. 167–178

 Chapter Summaries on Audiocassette

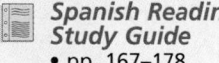 *Patterns of Interaction: Arming for War* (Spanish track)

Less Proficient Readers

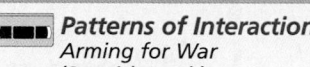 *In-Depth Resources: Unit 4*
• **Guided Reading** for Sections 1–5, pp. 54–58
• **Skillbuilder Practice** Following Chronological Order, p. 59
• **Geography Application** The Fall of Singapore, p. 60

 Telescoping the Times
• Chapter Summary, pp. 65–67

 Reading Study Guide
• pp. 167–178

 Chapter Summaries on Audiocassette

Gifted and Talented Students

In-Depth Resources: Unit 4
Primary Sources:
• from *Berlin Diary,* p. 62
• from *The Diary of a Young Girl,* p. 64
• from *Farewell to Manzanar,* p. 63
• from *Hiroshima,* p. 65

History Makers
• Charles de Gaulle, p. 69
• Winston Churchill, p. 70

Connections to Literature READINGS FOR STUDENTS

 In-Depth Resources: Unit 4
Literature: from *Night,* p. 66

McDougal Littell
The Language of Literature, Grade 10
Elie Wiesel, from *Night,* p. 308
Elie Wiesel, from "Nobel Prize Acceptance Speech," p. 314
Jeanne and James Houston, from *Farewell to Manzanar,* p. 330

McDougal Littell
Literature Connections
Houston, Jeanne Wakatsuki
Houston, James
Farewell to Manzanar
(with related readings)

Here is the true story of a Japanese-American confinement in California's Manzanar internment camp during World War II. Ms. Houston's fierce pride and determination shine through this story.

 PE = Pupil's Edition   = Overhead Transparency   = Software   = Video

= Copy Master   = CD-ROM   = Audiocassette   = Internet

World War II, 1939–1945

Accessing Prior Knowledge

• Have students look at the pictures on these two pages and ask them what they know about World War II. Have they seen stories set during the war in movies or on television? Do they know of any relatives who fought in the war?

Making Inferences

• After students have surveyed the captions and pictures on these pages, ask them what they think it would have been like to have served in the armed forces during this period. What would it have been like to face danger and death? What would it have been like to be away from home, fighting across the ocean?

Geography Connection

Ask students to look at the map on these two pages.

• How might the different locations of the war in Europe and the war in the Pacific have affected tactics and weapons in each area? *In the Pacific aircraft carriers were likely to have been very important, while in Europe tanks were of great use because they could move across wide expanses of land (something they could not do in the Pacific war).*

CHAPTER 16 World War II, 1939–1945

PREVIEWING THEMES

Science and Technology

Far-reaching developments in science and technology changed the course of World War II. Important improvements in aircraft, tanks, and submarines had occurred since World War I. The invention of radar, aircraft carriers, and especially the atomic bomb changed how war was fought.

Empire Building

Germany, Italy, and Japan tried to build empires. They began expanding their own territories by conquering other nations and dominating them politically and economically.

Economics

Fighting the Nazi terror weakened the economies of Great Britain, the Soviet Union, and most other European allies. When the United States entered the war, its economy actually grew sharply after years of depression. With the strength of its economy, the United States strengthened the Allied effort with its resources and products.

INTERNET CONNECTION

Visit us at **www.mlworldhistory.com** to learn more about World War II.

THE BATTLES OF WORLD WAR II, 1939–1945

Leningrad (Sept. 1941–Jan. 1944)

Warsaw (Aug. 1944–Jan. 1945)
Minsk (June–Aug. 1944)
Kursk (July 1943)

Britain (July 1940–May 1941)
Normandy (June 1944)
Paris (Aug. 1944)
Berlin (Apr.–May 1945)
Battle of the Bulge (Dec. 1944)
Stalingrad (Nov. 1942–Feb. 1943)

Anzio (Jan.–Mar. 1944)
Sicily (July 1943)
Monte Cassino (May 1944)
Tunis (May 1943)
Tobruk (Nov. 1942)

El Alamein (Oct.–Nov. 1942)

In **1939**, construction began on Nazi concentration camps to kill Jews and members of other groups. Prisoners were to die by hard labor, poor nutrition, and disease. Impatient with the pace of the killing, Adolf Hitler later had death camps built. In the camps, millions were killed by poison gas. Survivors of Hitler's **Holocaust** lived to tell the horrors of Nazi brutality.

ATLANTIC OCEAN

☐ Major Allied powers
■ Major Axis powers
✳ Major battle
☢ Nuclear explosion

0   1,000 Miles
0   2,000 Kilometers

N

438

GEOGRAPHY THEMES

Location

Ask students to note the major battles of World War II and identify the areas in which the conflicts occurred. Have students contrast the fighting in Europe with the fighting in the Pacific and ask how the conflicts differ. *Europe was a land war; the Pacific was a sea war.*

Ask students to speculate on the difficulties of fighting a war on two fronts. Discuss with students the different climates that soldiers in these two locations would have encountered. Ask students where they would have preferred to fight—in Europe or in the Pacific. Ask them to explain their choice.

Movement

Point out to students that movement was an important aspect of World War II. The ability to move troops and supplies easily and quickly was crucial to the success of the combatants. Ask students to speculate on what other kinds of movement might be involved in a worldwide conflict. *They may suggest*

the movement of people who are trying to escape the fighting. Ask students in what direction American troops moved to defeat Japan. *westward—from east to west.* Ask students in what direction Allied troops moved to defeat Germany. *British and American troops moved eastward; Russian troops moved westward.*

ADDITIONAL RESOURCES

Books for the Teacher

- Miller, Nathan. *War at Sea: A Naval History of World War II.* New York: Scribner's, 1995.

- Shirer, William Lawrence. *The Rise and Fall of the Third Reich: A History of Nazi Germany.* New York: Simon, 1959.

- Toland, John. *The Rising Sun: The Decline and Fall of the Japanese Empire, 1939-1945.* New York: Random, 1970.

- Weinberg, Gerhard L. *A World at Arms: A Global History of World War II.* New York: Cambridge UP, 1994.

Books for the Student

- Sherrow, Victoria. *Hiroshima.* New York: New Discovery, 1994.

- Wigoder, Geoffrey. *The Holocaust.* Danbury, CT: Grolier, 1997.

- Winston, Keith. *Letters of a World War II G.I.* New York: Watts, 1995.

Videos

- *The Atomic Bomb—1945* A.D. Ambrose Video, 1995. 800-526-4663.

- *Hitler.* Cambridge Social Studies, 1990. 800-468-4227.

- *We Must Never Forget: The Story of the Holocaust.* Society for Visual Education, 1994. 800-829-1900.

Software

- *World War II: 1931-1945.* CD-ROM. Lucerne, 1995. 800-341-2293. Describes events, personalities, and issues related to the war.

On **June 6, 1944,** the Allies launched the greatest naval and land campaign in history against Nazi forces in **Normandy**. Supreme Commander U.S. General Dwight David Eisenhower led the attack against the Nazis with massive air and ground forces. Despite huge losses, the Allies' invasion of Europe spelled the beginning of the end of Adolf Hitler's regime.

Hiroshima (Aug. 6, 1945)

Nagasaki (Aug. 9, 1945)

✳ **Okinawa** (Mar.–June 1945)

✳ **Iwo Jima** (Feb.–March 1945)

✳ **Midway** (June 1942)

Philippine Sea (June 1944)

✳ **Wake Island** (Dec. 1941)

✳ **Pearl Harbor** (Dec. 1941)

✳ **Saipan** (June–July 1944)

✳ **Guam** (July–Aug. 1944)

PACIFIC OCEAN

Bataan ✳ (Jan.–Feb. 1944)

✳ **Leyte Gulf** (Oct. 1944)

✳ **Singapore** (Feb. 1942)

0° Equator

✳ **Hollandia** (Apr. 1944)

Guadalcanal (Aug. 1942–Feb. 1943)

INDIAN OCEAN

On **April 9, 1942,** the Bataan Peninsula in the Philippines fell to Japan. After their victory, the Japanese led 70,000 American and Filipino prisoners of war on a 60-mile forced march north—the **Bataan Death March**. The prisoners marched under a blazing sun. They were also starved and brutally beaten. Prisoners who showed signs of weakening were often buried alive.

HISTORY THROUGH ART

Photography

Photography is both a means of recording important events and an art form. Photographs can both capture dramatic moments in history and preserve them for posterity. The three pictures on these pages capture important events in the history of the Second World War. The Bataan Death March represented a low point in American fortunes early in World War II.

The photograph shows captured American soldiers being marched off to captivity after their defense of Corregidor, the rock fortress of Manila Bay. The D-Day landing on June 6, 1944, marked a dramatic turning point in World War II. The photograph shows troops leaving a landing craft and wading toward a beach in Normandy. The photograph of the prisoner in a concentration camp illustrates the brutality of the Nazi regime. The picture shows an emaciated

survivor drinking from a metal bowl in front of a barracks in Buchenwald.

Interpreting the Art What do these photographs seem to suggest about World War II? What emotions might troops experience while storming a beach? How might captives on a forced march feel? How would a prisoner in a concentration camp feel at the moment of liberation?

Interact *with* History

This Interact with History feature motivates students by inviting them to decide on whether or not to bomb a city during World War II. As they imagine themselves making this difficult decision, students will analyze the issues, explore their options, and become decision makers.

Purpose

• to set the stage for studying World War II

• to help students understand some of the causes and effects of World War II

• to help students make connections with the people and events they will study in this chapter

Teaching Strategy

Thinking Critically After students have imagined themselves in the situation described on this page, have them answer the key questions and give reasons for their decision.

EXAMINING *the* ISSUES

Following are suggestions for addressing each bulleted question.

❶ Ask students to suggest arguments for and against shortening a war by taking civilian lives. Does shortening a war by two months justify such actions? Would killing civilians be justified if it shortened a war? Is taking the lives of civilians ever justified?

❷ Have students give examples of civilian contributions to a war effort, such as making weapons in factories.

❸ Ask students what information a commander would need in order to weigh arguments for lives saved against the percentage of lives lost.

Making Connections Ask students to think about the impact of extensive and destructive wars (such as World War I) on societies and people.

Interact *with* History

World War II has been going on for several years—at great cost in lives to your side and the enemy's. You are an air force commander who has just received a report from military intelligence. The report identifies a city in enemy territory that is a major weapons manufacturing center. You and other officers know that by destroying the arms factories in the city, the war could be shortened. Thousands of lives could be saved. On the other hand, the bombing will kill hundreds, maybe thousands, of civilians living near the enemy factories. How do you weigh the lives that will be saved against the lives that will be lost?

Would you bomb this city?

One plane-load of bombs will wipe out a vital enemy weapons factory, along with hundreds of civilian homes around it.

Radar tells the pilot where to drop the bombs, but at 10,000 feet, he cannot see the casualties they will cause.

This is a bomb factory in the middle of a residential area.

This raid will probably shorten the war by at least two months.

EXAMINING *the* ISSUES

• Does shortening a war to save lives justify killing civilians?

• How are civilians sometimes as much a part of a war effort as soldiers?

• What percentage of lives saved would justify the deaths caused in the bombing?

As a class, discuss these questions. In your discussion, weigh the arguments for and against both choices.

As you read about World War II, think about the role that civilians play in a situation of total war. Think also about the hard moral choices that people often face in times of war.

440 Chapter 16

Follow Up

A feature on the chapter assessment will ask students to reevaluate their response to the situation presented on this page.

1 Hitler's Lightning War

TERMS & NAMES
- nonaggression pact
- blitzkrieg
- Charles de Gaulle
- Winston Churchill
- Battle of Britain
- Atlantic Charter

MAIN IDEA

Using the sudden, mass attack called the blitzkrieg, Germany overran much of Europe and North Africa.

WHY IT MATTERS NOW

Hitler's actions set off World War II. The results of the war still affect the politics and economics of today's world.

SETTING THE STAGE During the 1930s, Hitler played on the hopes and fears of the Western democracies. Each time the Nazi dictator grabbed new territory, he would declare an end to his demands. Peace seemed guaranteed—until Hitler started expanding again.

Germany Sparks a New War in Europe

After his moves into the Rhineland (March 1936), Austria (March 1938), and Czechoslovakia (September 1938 and March 1939), the Führer turned his eyes to Poland. On April 28, 1939, Hitler spoke before the Reichstag. He demanded that the Polish Corridor, along with its port city of Danzig, be returned to Germany. After World War I, the Allies had cut out the Polish Corridor from German territory to give Poland access to the sea.

This time, Great Britain and France decided to resist this threat of aggression. At this point, as was mentioned in Chapter 15, Soviet dictator Joseph Stalin signed a 10-year **nonaggression pact** with Hitler on August 23. After being excluded from the Munich Conference, Stalin was not eager to join with the West. Also, Hitler was promising him territory. In the public part of the pact, Germany and the Soviet Union promised not to attack each other. Secretly, however, they agreed that they would divide Poland between them. They also secretly agreed that the USSR could take over Finland and the Baltic countries (Lithuania, Latvia, and Estonia).

Background
Hitler hated communism, as Stalin despised fascism. Nonetheless, Hitler did not want to fight both the Allies *and* the Soviet Union. And Stalin wanted to keep his country out of a costly European war.

Germany's Lightning Attack on Poland The new nonaggression pact removed the threat to Germany of a Soviet attack from the east. Hitler then quickly moved ahead with plans to conquer Poland. His surprise attack took place at dawn on September 1, 1939. German warplanes invaded Polish airspace, raining bombs and terror on the Poles. At the same time, German tanks and troop trucks rumbled across the Polish border. The trucks carried more than 1.5 million soldiers into the assault. German aircraft and artillery then began a merciless bombing of Poland's capital, Warsaw. The city crumbled under the assault. A stunned world looked on. No one yet realized that the Polish invasion had unleashed World War II.

France and Great Britain declared war on Germany on September 3. But Poland fell three weeks before those nations could make any military response. After his victory, Hitler annexed the western half of Poland. That region had a large German population.

Ein Volk, ein Reich, ein Führer!

A propaganda poster proclaims to the German nation: "One People, One Reich, One Führer!"

World War II **441**

World War II: German Advances, 1939–1941

Interpreting the Map Point out to students that the Germans advanced on all fronts and in all directions in these years.

Extension Activity Have students identify one country in each direction of the map into which the Germans advanced. *North—Denmark, Norway, etc.; South—Austria, Yugoslavia, etc.; East—Poland, Soviet Union, etc.; West—Belgium, France, etc.*

SKILLBUILDER Answers
1. Austria, Yugoslavia, Bulgaria, Greece, Romania, Czechoslovakia, Hungary, Poland, Lithuania, Latvia, Estonia, Finland, Norway, Denmark, France, Belgium, the Netherlands.
2. It was centrally located and could strike out in all directions.

MORE ABOUT . . .
Blitzkrieg

The blitzkrieg strategy was developed by General Heinz Guderian, who presented his idea of lightning attacks as early as 1937. Guderian also introduced the idea of the panzer, or "armor," divisions—fast-moving, self-contained forces consisting of two regiments of tanks supported by one infantry and one artillery regiment.

MORE ABOUT . . .
The Maginot Line

Built in the 1930s, the Maginot Line extended along an 87-mile front in northeastern France. Fronted by tank traps, barbed wire, and guns encased in concrete walls ten feet thick, the line was a series of underground forts placed at three- to five-mile intervals. Troops lived underground on three-month tours, manning the observation posts and gun emplacements and enjoying such amenities as sun lamps. But the line was not built for mobile warfare and was useless against the swift, German forces.

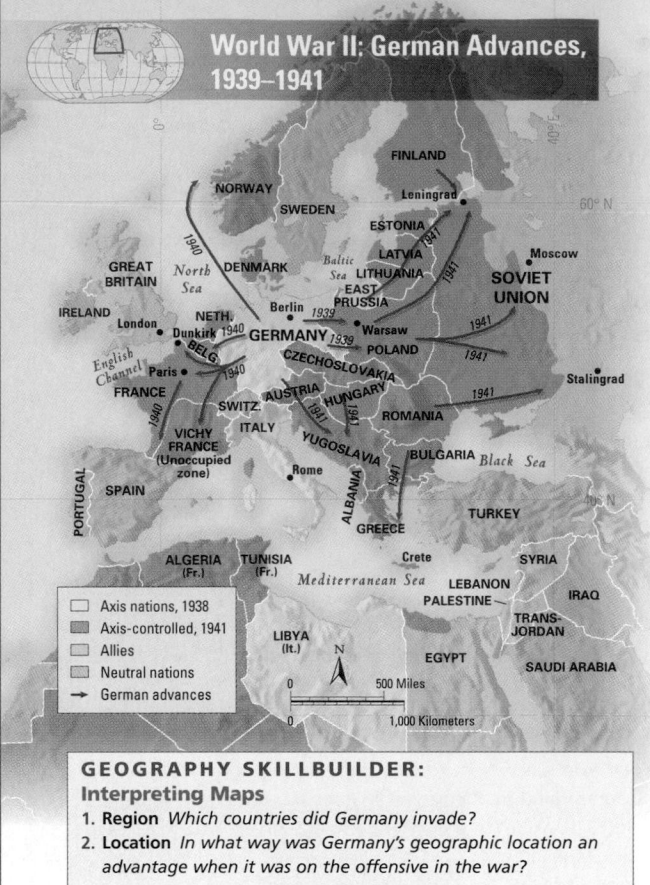

World War II: German Advances, 1939–1941

GEOGRAPHY SKILLBUILDER:
Interpreting Maps
1. **Region** *Which countries did Germany invade?*
2. **Location** *In what way was Germany's geographic location an advantage when it was on the offensive in the war?*

The German invasion of Poland was the first test of Germany's newest military strategy—the **blitzkrieg** (BLIHTS·kreeg), or "lightning war." It involved using fast-moving airplanes and tanks, followed by massive infantry forces, to take the enemy by surprise. Then, blitzkrieg forces swiftly crushed all opposition with overwhelming force. In the case of Poland, the strategy worked.

The Soviets Make Their Move On September 17, after his secret agreement with Hitler, Stalin sent Soviet troops to occupy the eastern half of Poland. Stalin then began annexing the regions in the second part of the agreement. Lithuania, Latvia, and Estonia fell without a struggle, but Finland resisted.

In November 1939, Stalin sent nearly 1 million Soviet troops into Finland. He thought that his soldiers would win a quick victory. So, Stalin did not worry about the Finnish winter. This was a crucial mistake. The Finns were outnumbered and outgunned, but they fiercely defended their country. In the freezing weather, they attacked on swift skis. Meanwhile, the Soviets struggled through deep snow, crippled by frostbite. Despite their losses, the Soviet invaders finally won through sheer force of numbers. By March 1940, Stalin had forced the Finns to accept his surrender terms.

The Phony War For almost seven months after the fall of Poland, there was a strange calm in the land fighting in Europe. After their declaration of war, the French and British had mobilized their armies. They stationed their troops along the Maginot (MAZH·uh·NOH) Line, a system of fortifications along France's border with Germany. There they waited for Germans to attack—but nothing happened. With little to do, the bored Allied soldiers stared eastward toward the enemy. Equally bored, German soldiers stared back from their Siegfried Line a few miles away. Germans jokingly called it the *sitzkrieg*, or "sitting war." Some newspapers referred to it simply as "the phony war."

Suddenly, on April 9, 1940, the phony war ended. Hitler launched a surprise invasion of Denmark and Norway. He planned to build bases along the Norwegian and Danish coasts to strike at Great Britain. In just four hours after the attack, Denmark fell. Two months later, Norway surrendered as well.

The Battle for France and Great Britain

After conquering Denmark and Norway, Hitler began a sweep through Holland, Belgium, and Luxembourg. This was part of a strategy to strike at France. Keeping the Allies' attention on those countries, Hitler then sent an even larger force of tanks and troop trucks to slice through the Ardennes (ahr·DEHN). This was a heavily wooded area in northeastern France and Luxembourg. Moving through the forest, the

THINK THROUGH HISTORY
A. Analyzing Motives What would you say were the political reasons behind Stalin's actions in Europe at the beginning of World War II?
A. Possible Answer Stalin aimed at expanding the Soviet Union's territory and power, while keeping his country out of the war. He seemed ready to make an agreement with anybody, even Hitler, to achieve those goals.

TEACHING OPTION

CONNECTIONS ACROSS THE CURRICULUM

Government Germany annexed conquered nations as part of the Third Reich and governed through military commanders. Belgium, the Netherlands, Luxembourg, Norway, and Denmark were occupied by German troops. All the occupied territories were exploited for their material and human resources in order to supply the German war effort.

In France the situation was different. France was divided into two governments. German troops occupied the western coast line and the northern two-thirds of France, which was governed by the German military. The southern third of the nation was "unoccupied" France, headed by a puppet government. Under the leadership of the much admired and respected World War I hero, Marshal Henri Pétain, southern France

was relatively independent until 1942, when German troops took over the entire country.

Have students speculate on Germany's purpose in setting up two different governments in France. What would be the advantage to Germany in allowing southern France to be relatively free? How might the citizens of France have dealt with the occupation?

Germans "squeezed between" the Maginot Line. From there, they moved across France and reached France's northern coast in 10 days.

France Battles Back When the Germans reached the French coast, they swung north again and joined forces with German troops in Belgium. By May 26, 1940, the Germans had trapped the Allied forces around the northern French city of Lille (leel). With a German victory inevitable, Belgium surrendered. Outnumbered, outgunned, and pounded from the air, the Allies escaped to the beaches of Dunkirk, a French port city on the English Channel. They were trapped with their backs to the sea.

In one of the most heroic acts of the war, Great Britain set out to rescue the army. It sent a fleet of some 850 ships across the English Channel to Dunkirk. Along with Royal Navy ships, civilian craft—yachts, lifeboats, motorboats, paddle steamers, and fishing boats—joined the rescue effort. From May 26 to June 4, this amateur armada, under heavy fire from German bombers, sailed back and forth from Britain to Dunkirk. The boats carried an incredible 338,000 battle-weary soldiers to safety.

France Falls Following Dunkirk, France seemed doomed to defeat. On June 10, sensing a quick victory, Italy's Benito Mussolini joined forces with Hitler and declared war on both Great Britain and France. Italy then attacked France from the south. By June 14, Paris had fallen to the Germans. Nazi troops marched triumphantly down the city's main boulevard.

Two days later, seeing defeat approaching, the French parliament asked Marshal Henri Pétain (pay·TAN), an aging hero from World War I, to become prime minister. On June 22, 1940, France surrendered. The Germans took control of the northern part of the country. They left the southern part to a puppet government headed by Pétain. The headquarters of this government was in the city of Vichy (VEESH·ee).

After France fell, a French general named **Charles de Gaulle** (duh GOHL) fled to London. There, he set up a government-in-exile committed to reconquering France. On June 18, 1940, he delivered a broadcast from England. He called on the people of France to resist:

> **A VOICE FROM THE PAST**
> It is the bounden [obligatory] duty of all Frenchmen who still bear arms to continue the struggle. For them to lay down their arms, to evacuate any position of military importance, or agree to hand over any part of French territory, however small, to enemy control would be a crime against our country. . . .
> **GENERAL CHARLES DE GAULLE**, quoted in *Charles de Gaulle: A Biography*

De Gaulle went on to organize the Free French military forces that battled the Nazis until France was liberated in 1944.

Germany Attacks Great Britain With the fall of France, Great Britain stood alone against the Nazis. **Winston Churchill,** the new British prime minister, had already declared that his nation would never give in. In a speech, he said, "We shall fight on the beaches, we shall fight on the landing grounds, we shall fight in the fields and in the streets . . . we shall never surrender."

Background
Hitler demanded that the surrender take place in the same railroad car where the French had dictated terms to the Germans in World War I.

Hundreds of British soldiers crowd aboard ship during the mass evacuation at Dunkirk.

World War II **443**

Winston Churchill was an inspiring and encouraging presence to embattled Londoners during the "Blitz." In September of 1940, Buckingham Palace was bombed, and officials wanted to keep it quiet. "Stupid fools," Churchill said. "Spread the news at once! Let the humble people of London know that the King and Queen are sharing their perils with them!"

IN-DEPTH RESOURCES: UNIT 4
History Makers: Winston Churchill, p. 70

ELECTRONIC LIBRARY OF PRIMARY SOURCES
from "Blood, Toil, Tears, and Sweat"

MORE ABOUT . . .
The Battle of Britain

As the bombings grew worse, a group found shelter in an old railway tunnel and were discovered by a police officer who reported: "The first thing I heard was a great hollow hubbub, a sort of soughing and wailing, as if there were animals down there moaning and crying. And then this terrible stench hit me. It was worse than dead bodies. . . . I stopped. Ahead of me I could see faces peering towards me lit by candles and lanterns. It was like a painting of hell."

GEOGRAPHY TRANSPARENCIES
GT32 The Battle of Britain, 1940–1941

OBJECTIVE 3 INSTRUCT

The Eastern Front and the Mediterranean

▶ Key Ideas
- German forces gain victories in North Africa.
- In preparation for the attack on the Soviet Union, Hitler invades and secures the Balkans.
- Sweeping into the Soviet Union, German forces become bogged down near Moscow.

Winston Churchill
1874–1965

Probably the greatest weapon the British had as they stood alone against Hitler's Germany was the nation's prime minister—Winston Churchill. "Big Winnie," Londoners boasted, "was the lad for us. . . ."

Although as a youngster Churchill had a speech defect, he grew to become one of the greatest orators of all time. He used all his gifts as a speaker to rally the people behind the effort to crush Germany. He declared that Britain would

. . . wage war, by sea, land, and air, with all our might and with all the strength that God can give us . . . against monstrous tyranny.

Hitler now turned his mind to an invasion of Great Britain. His plan—*Operation Sea Lion*—was first to knock out the Royal Air Force (RAF) and then to land 250,000 soldiers on England's shores. In the summer of 1940, the Luftwaffe (LOOFT·vahf·uh), Germany's air force, began bombing Great Britain. Badly outnumbered, the RAF had 2,900 planes to the Luftwaffe's 4,500. At first, the Germans targeted British airfields and aircraft factories. Then, on September 7, 1940, they began focusing on the cities, especially London—to break British morale. Bombs exploded daily in city streets. They killed civilians and set buildings ablaze. However, despite the destruction and loss of life, the British fought on.

With the pressure off the airfields, the RAF hit back hard. Two secret weapons helped turn the tide in their favor. One was an electronic tracking system known as radar. Developed in the late 1930s, radar could tell the number, speed, and direction of incoming warplanes. The other was a German code-making machine named Enigma. A complete Enigma machine was smuggled to Great Britain in 1938. With Enigma in their possession, the British had German secret messages open to them. With information gathered by these devices, RAF fliers could quickly get to their airplanes and inflict deadly harm on the enemy.

To avoid the RAF's attacks, the Germans gave up daylight raids in October 1940 in favor of night bombing. At sunset, the wail of sirens filled the air as Londoners flocked to the subways. There they spent the night in air-raid shelters. Some rode out the blasts at home in basements or in smaller air-raid shelters.

The **Battle of Britain** continued until May 10, 1941. Stunned by British resistance, Hitler decided to call off his attacks. Instead, he focused his attention on Eastern Europe and the Mediterranean. The Battle of Britain had ended. And, from it, the Allies had learned a crucial lesson: Hitler's advances could be blocked.

The Eastern Front and the Mediterranean

The stubborn resistance of the British in the Battle of Britain caused a shift in Hitler's strategy in Europe. Although the resistance surprised Hitler, it did not defeat him. He would deal with Great Britain later. Instead, he turned his attention east to the Balkans and the Mediterranean area—and to the ultimate prize, the Soviet Union.

Germany and Italy Attack North Africa Germany's first objective in the Mediterranean region was North Africa—mainly because of Hitler's partner Mussolini. Despite Italy's alliance with Germany, the country had remained neutral at the beginning of the war. With Hitler's conquest of France, however, Mussolini knew he had to take action. Otherwise, Italy would not share in Germany's victories. "I need a few thousand dead," he told a member of his staff. After declaring war on France and Great Britain, Italy became Germany's most important Axis ally. Then, Mussolini moved into France along with the Nazis.

Mussolini took his next step in September 1940. While the Battle of Britain was raging, he ordered Italy's North African army to move east from Libya. His goal was to seize British-controlled Egypt. Egypt's Suez Canal was key to reaching the oil fields of the Middle East. Within a week, Italian troops had pushed 60 miles inside Egypt, forcing British units back. Then both sides dug in and waited.

Great Britain Strikes Back Finally, in December, the British decided to strike back. The result was a disaster for the Italians. By February 1941, the British had swept 500 miles across North Africa. They had taken 130,000 Italian prisoners.

444 Chapter 16

Background
Luftwaffe in German means "air weapon."

Vocabulary
morale: state of mind.

C. Possible Answers A few thousand Italian dead would have meant that Mussolini was serious about committing Italy to the war. A few thousand enemy dead would prove Italy's military effectiveness to Hitler.

THINK THROUGH HISTORY
B. Drawing Conclusions How could "a few thousand dead" have helped Mussolini's position in the Axis powers?

Background
The Middle East is an area that includes the countries of Southwest Asia and northeast Africa.

CUSTOMIZING FOR SPECIAL NEEDS

Less Proficient Readers: Making a Chart
Pair a less proficient reader with a more proficient student and have them create a flow chart tracing events in the Mediterranean and on the Eastern Front leading to the siege of Moscow. The chart might look like this.

Then have students display their charts on a wall in the classroom. You might have pairs of students compare the charts they have made and discuss similarities and differences.

Hitler had to step in to save his Axis partner. In February 1941, he sent General Erwin Rommel, later known as the "Desert Fox," to Libya. His mission was to command a newly formed tank corps, the Afrika Korps. Determined to take control of Egypt and the Suez Canal, Rommel attacked the British at Agheila (uh·GAY·luh) on March 24. Caught by surprise, British forces retreated 500 miles west to Tobruk.

However, by mid-January 1942, after fierce fighting for Tobruk, the British drove Rommel back to where he had started. By June, the tide of battle turned again. Rommel regrouped, pushed the British back across the desert, and seized Tobruk. This was a shattering loss for the Allies. Rommel later wrote, "To every man of us, Tobruk was a symbol of British resistance, and we were now going to finish with it for good."

The War in the Balkans While Rommel campaigned in North Africa, Hitler was active in the Balkans. As early as the summer of 1940, Hitler had begun planning to attack his ally, the USSR, by the following spring. The Balkan countries of southeastern Europe were key to Hitler's invasion plan. Hitler wanted to build bases in southeastern Europe for the attack on the Soviet Union. He also wanted to make sure that the British did not interfere.

To prepare for his invasion, Hitler moved to expand his influence in the Balkans. In the face of overwhelming German strength, Bulgaria, Romania, and Hungary cooperated by joining the Axis powers in early 1941. Yugoslavia and Greece, which had pro-British governments, resisted. On Sunday, April 6, 1941, Hitler invaded both countries. Yugoslavia fell in 11 days. Greece surrendered in 17. In Athens, the Nazis celebrated their victory by raising swastikas on the Acropolis.

Hitler Invades the Soviet Union With the Balkans firmly in control, Hitler could move ahead with his plan to invade the Soviet Union. He called that plan *Operation Barbarossa.* Early on Sunday morning, June 22, 1941, the roar of German tanks and aircraft announced the beginning of the blitzkrieg invasion. The Soviet Union was not prepared for this attack. With its 5 million men, the Red Army was the largest in the world. But it was neither well equipped nor well trained.

The invasion rolled on week after week until the Germans had pushed 500 miles inside the Soviet Union. As the Russians retreated, they burned and destroyed everything in the enemy's path. Russians had used this same strategy against Napoleon.

By September 8, Germans had surrounded Leningrad and isolated the city from the rest of the world. If necessary, Hitler would starve the city's 2.5 million inhabitants. German bombs destroyed warehouses where food was stored. Desperately hungry, people began eating cattle and horse feed, as well as cats and dogs and, finally, crows and rats. More than 1 million people died in Leningrad that terrible winter. Yet the city refused to fall.

Seeing that Leningrad would not surrender, Hitler looked to Moscow, the capital and heart of the Soviet Union. A Nazi drive on the capital began on October 2, 1941.

CRITICAL THINKING ACTIVITY
CLASS TIME: 15 MINUTES
Making a Chart
Have students analyze the effects of Germany's campaigns in the Mediterranean and the Soviet Union by making a chart like the one below.

	Effects
North Africa	
Balkans	
Soviet Union	

MORE ABOUT . . .
The Siege of Leningrad
During the siege, as the composer Dmitri Shostakovich worked on his Seventh, or "Leningrad," Symphony, he also broadcast appeals to the people to resist the invaders. "When I walk through the city," he said, "a feeling of deep conviction grows within me that Leningrad will always stand, grand and beautiful, on the banks of the Neva. . . ." Authorities moved Shostakovich to a safer city, where he finished the symphony. The score was put on microfilm and flown out of the Soviet Union to the West. Years later, the composer wrote that the work was not about the German siege of the city but about the suffering of Leningrad under the terrible Stalinist purges of the 1930s.

A Soviet photo taken in 1942 shows the horrors of the war in the Soviet Union. Civilians in the Crimea search over a barren field for their dead loved ones.

445

TEACHING OPTION
CONNECTIONS ACROSS TIME AND PLACE

Invading Russia Sweden's King Charles XII was one of the great rivals of the Russian czar Peter the Great. Russia and Sweden engaged in the Great Northern War between 1700–1721. In 1708, Charles XII attempted a march on Moscow from the north. As Russian forces retreated, they destroyed provisions while the Swedes struggled through a bitter winter and finally withdrew. In 1812, Napoleon Bonaparte ignored the lesson of the Swedish disaster and

marched into Russia, where his army suffered the same fate as that of the Swedes. For a graphic depiction of the fate that befell Napoleon's armies in Russia, see the map and graphs on page 211 of this text.

Exactly 129 years to the month after Napoleon's invasion, Hitler's forces swept into the Soviet Union. Soviet authorities directed that if retreat was

necessary, the enemy should find only a scorched earth. The head of the Soviet Information Bureau proclaimed, "The bloodsoaked murderers won't find anything. They won't be able to find enough wood to build a fire to thaw their frozen hands. They won't be able to find enough food to keep them alive." His prediction was accurate as German forces stalled near Moscow and faced the Russian winter of 1941.

The United States Aids Its Allies

▶ **Key Ideas**
- The United States gives aid to Britain through the Lend-Lease Act of 1941.
- Roosevelt and Churchill issue the Atlantic Charter declaring free trade among nations and the right of people to choose their own governments.
- The United States draws closer to war when a German submarine attacks a U.S. destroyer.

By December, the Germans had advanced to the outskirts of Moscow. Soviet General Georgi Zhukov (ZHOO·kuhf) counterattacked. He had 100 fresh Siberian divisions and the harsh Soviet winter on his side.

As temperatures fell, the Germans, in summer uniforms, retreated. Their fuel and oil froze. Tanks, trucks, and weapons became useless. Ignoring Napoleon's winter defeat 130 years before, the Führer sent his generals a stunning order: "No retreat!" German troops dug in about 125 miles west of the capital. They held the line against the Soviets until March 1943. Nonetheless, Moscow had been saved and had cost the Germans 500,000 lives.

U.S. industry achieved amazing rates of speed when it began to produce for the war effort. This ship, for example, was produced in a U.S. shipyard in only 10 days.

The United States Aids Its Allies

As disturbing as these events were to Americans, bitter memories of World War I convinced most people in the United States that their country should not get involved. Between 1935 and 1937, Congress passed a series of Neutrality Acts. The laws made it illegal to sell arms or lend money to nations at war. But President Roosevelt knew that if the Allies fell, the United States would be drawn into the war. In September 1939, he persuaded Congress to allow the Allies to buy American arms. According to his plan, they would pay cash and then carry the goods on their own ships.

Under the Lend-Lease Act, passed in March 1941, the president could lend or lease arms and other supplies to any country vital to the United States. By the summer of 1941, the U.S. Navy was escorting British ships carrying U.S. arms. In response, Hitler ordered his submarines to sink any cargo ships they met.

Although the United States had not yet entered the war, Roosevelt and Churchill met secretly on a battleship off Newfoundland on August 9. The two leaders issued a joint declaration called the **Atlantic Charter.** It upheld free trade among nations and the right of people to choose their own government. The charter later served as the Allies' peace plan at the end of World War II.

On September 4, a German U-boat suddenly fired on a U.S. destroyer in the Atlantic. Roosevelt ordered navy commanders to respond. They were to shoot German submarines on sight. The United States was now involved in an undeclared naval war with Hitler. To almost everyone's surprise, however, the attack that actually drew the United States into the war did not come from Germany. It came from Japan.

THINK THROUGH HISTORY
C. Making Inferences What does the fact that German armies were not prepared for the Russian winter indicate about Hitler's expectations for the campaign in the Soviet Union?
D. Possible Answer Hitler expected a quick victory in the Soviet Union and did not think that his fighting men would still be in combat by winter.

Background
Newfoundland is a province of Canada.

Section ① Assessment

1. TERMS & NAMES
Identify
- nonaggression pact
- blitzkrieg
- Charles de Gaulle
- Winston Churchill
- Battle of Britain
- Atlantic Charter

2. TAKING NOTES
Create a chart like the one below. Identify the effects of each of these early events of World War II.

Cause	Effect
First blitzkrieg	
Allies stranded at Dunkirk	
British radar detects German aircraft	
Lend-Lease Act	

3. MAKING INFERENCES
Great Britain and the Soviet city of Leningrad each fought off a German invasion. Other countries gave in to the Germans without much resistance. What factors do you think a country's leaders consider when deciding whether to surrender or to fight?

THINK ABOUT
- the country's ability to fight
- the costs of resisting
- the costs of surrendering

4. THEME ACTIVITY
Economics In groups of 3 or 4, prepare a dramatic scene for a play or film that focuses on an economic problem that might have been suffered by Europeans during World War II.

ANSWERS

1. TERMS & NAMES
nonaggression pact, p. 441
blitzkrieg, p. 442
Charles de Gaulle, p. 443
Winston Churchill, p. 443
Battle of Britain, p. 444
Atlantic Charter, p. 446

2. TAKING NOTES
Possible Answers: Blitzkrieg: the fall of Poland; Dunkirk: 338,000 soldiers saved, British forces leave Western Europe; Radar: the British able to hold off German occupation; Lend-Lease Act: U.S. supplied Allies with war goods, U.S. decision to favor the Allies.

3. MAKING INFERENCES
Possible Answers: Ability to Fight: army large enough to fight the enemy, sufficient weapons; Costs of Resisting: Major civilian and military deaths, destruction of property, economic chaos; Costs of Surrendering: Enemy control of the government, repression of the population.

4. THEME ACTIVITY
Standards for Evaluation
An effective scene should . . .
- give a sense of time and place
- focus on a war-related economic problem
- convey the human dimension of the economic problem
- show evidence of teamwork

TERMS & NAMES
• Isoroku Yamamoto
• Pearl Harbor
• Battle of Midway
• Douglas MacArthur
• Battle of Guadalcanal

2 Japan Strikes in the Pacific

MAIN IDEA

Carving out an empire, Japan attacked Pearl Harbor in Hawaii and brought the United States into World War II.

WHY IT MATTERS NOW

World War II established the role of the United States as a leading player in international affairs.

SETTING THE STAGE Like Hitler, Japan's military leaders also had dreams of empire. Japan was overcrowded and faced shortages of raw materials. To solve these problems—and to encourage nationalism—the Japanese began a program of empire building that would lead to war.

Japan Seeks a Pacific Empire

Japan's expansion began in 1931. In that year, Japanese troops took over Manchuria in northeastern China. Six years later, Japanese armies swept into the heartland of China. They expected quick victory. Chinese resistance, however, caused the war to drag on. This caused a strain on Japan's economy. To increase their resources, Japanese leaders looked toward the rich European colonies of Southeast Asia.

The Surprise Attack on Pearl Harbor By August 1940, Americans had cracked a Japanese secret code. They were well aware of Japanese plans for Southeast Asia. If Japan conquered European colonies there, it could also threaten the American-controlled Philippine Islands and Guam. To stop the Japanese advance, the U.S. government sent aid to strengthen Chinese resistance. And when the Japanese overran French Indochina in July 1941, Roosevelt cut off oil shipments to Japan.

> **Background**
> French Indochina was an area now made up by Vietnam, Cambodia, and Laos.

Despite an oil shortage, the Japanese continued their conquests. They hoped to catch the United States by surprise. So they planned massive attacks in Southeast Asia and in the Pacific—both at the same time. Japan's greatest naval strategist, Admiral **Isoroku Yamamoto** (ih·soh·ROO·koo YAH·muh·MOH·toh), also argued that the U.S. fleet in Hawaii was "a dagger pointed at our throat" and must be destroyed.

Early in the morning of December 7, 1941, American sailors at **Pearl Harbor** in Hawaii awoke to the roar of explosives. A Japanese attack was underway! The United States had known from a coded Japanese message that an attack might come. But they did not know when or where it would occur. Within two hours, the Japanese had sunk or damaged 18 ships, including 8 battleships—nearly the whole U.S. Pacific fleet. Some 2,400 Americans were killed—with more than 1,000 wounded. News of the attack stunned the American people. The next day, Congress declared war on Japan. In his speech to Congress, President Roosevelt described December 7 as "a date which will live in infamy."

The *U.S.S. West Virginia* in flames after taking a direct hit during the Japanese attack on Pearl Harbor.

World War II **447**

Section 2 Overview

OBJECTIVES

(1) To explain how Japanese expansionism led to war with the Allies in Asia.

(2) To explain the importance of the Allies' strategy in turning the tide of war against Japan.

SKILLBUILDER
• Interpreting maps: movement, p. 448

CRITICAL THINKING
• Analyzing motives, p. 449
• Identifying problems, p. 450
• Analyzing causes, p. 450
• Evaluating decisions, p. 450
• Analyzing themes, p. 450

FOCUS
5-Minute Warm-Up

▶ *Clarifying*
To help students understand the suffering of soldiers, have them answer these questions.

1. Look at A Voice from the Past on page 450. What were some of the horrors faced by soldiers on Guadalcanal?

2. Why might soldiers have described it as "hell"?

WARM-UP TRANSPARENCY 16

OBJECTIVE (1) INSTRUCT

Japan Seeks a Pacific Empire

▶ *Key Ideas*
• Japan attacks the U.S. fleet at Pearl Harbor, and the United States declares war.
• Victories in the Pacific and Asia give Japan a vast empire.

IN-DEPTH RESOURCES: UNIT 4
Guided Reading, p. 55
Geography Application: The Fall of Singapore, p. 60

ELECTRONIC LIBRARY OF PRIMARY SOURCES
from "Japanese Attack Sinks HMS *Repulse*"

ACCESS FOR STUDENTS ACQUIRING ENGLISH
Guided Reading (Spanish), p. 174

The Tide of Japanese Victories The Japanese had planned a series of strikes at the United States in the Pacific. After the bombing at Pearl Harbor, the Japanese seized Guam and Wake Island in the western Pacific. They then launched an attack on the Philippines. In January 1942, the Japanese marched into the Philippine capital of Manila. They overwhelmed American and Filipino defenders on the Bataan Peninsula (buh·TAN) in April—and in May, on the island of Corregidor.

The Japanese also hit the British, seizing Hong Kong and invading Malaya. By February 1942, the Japanese had reached Singapore. After a fierce pounding, the colony surrendered. By March, the Japanese had conquered the resource-rich Dutch East Indies (now Indonesia), including the islands of Java, Sumatra, Borneo, and Celebes (SEHL-uh-BEEZ). After Malaya, the Japanese took Burma, between China and India. China received supplies by way of the Burma Road. The Japanese could now close off the road. Now they might force the Chinese to surrender.

By the time Burma fell, Japan had conquered more than 1 million square miles of land with about 150 million people. Before these conquests, the Japanese had tried to win the support of Asians with the anticolonialist idea of "Asia for the Asians." After victory, however, the Japanese quickly made it clear that they had come as conquerors.

Native peoples often received the same brutal treatment as the 150,000 prisoners of war. On what is called the Bataan Death March, the Japanese subjected prisoners to terrible cruelties. One American soldier reported:

> ### A VOICE FROM THE PAST
> I was questioned by a Japanese officer who found out that I had been in a Philippine Scout Battalion. The [Japanese] hated the Scouts. . . . Anyway, they took me outside and I was forced to watch as they buried six of my Scouts alive. They made the men dig their own graves, and then had them kneel down in a pit. The guards hit them over the head with shovels to stun them and piled earth on top.
> **LIEUTENANT JOHN SPAINHOWER,** quoted in *War Diary 1939–1945*

Background
According to the centuries-old warrior code called *Bushido,* a Japanese soldier must commit suicide, or hari-kari, rather than surrender. So Japanese soldiers had contempt for Allied prisoners of war.

World War II in Asia and the Pacific, 1941–1945

Legend:
- Japanese empire, 1931
- Japanese gains by 1942
- Extent of Japanese expansion
- Allies
- Neutral nations
- Allied advances
- Battle

GEOGRAPHY SKILLBUILDER:
Interpreting Maps
1. **Movement** What Japanese conquest came closest to the territory of the United States?
2. **Movement** From what two general directions did Allied forces move in on Japan?

448

CONNECTIONS ACROSS TIME AND PLACE

Remembering Pearl Harbor The bombing of Pearl Harbor rallied Americans around the cry, "Remember Pearl Harbor!" There was even a popular song that made use of the phrase.

Some three-quarters of the United States' military planes were destroyed at Pearl Harbor and 18 warships were sunk or damaged. However, within weeks many of the ships, with the exception of the

Arizona, Utah, and *Oklahoma,* were repaired and at sea. But not all of the U.S. fleet was at Pearl Harbor. Most importantly, three aircraft carriers escaped the Japanese surprise attack.

During the remainder of the the war in the Pacific, U.S. naval forces sank all of the Japanese ships involved in the attack on Pearl Harbor. In August 1945, an atomic bomb leveled the city of Nagasaki,

which manufactured special torpedoes. And the battleship *West Virginia* was among those gathered in Tokyo Bay when the Japanese signed the surrender on September 2, 1945. Have students do some research on American and Japanese battle fleets, including numbers of ships, kinds of ships, battle tactics, and so forth, and present their findings to the class.

The Allies Strike Back

After a string of victories, the Japanese seemed unbeatable. Nonetheless, the Allies—mainly Americans and Australians—were anxious to strike back in the Pacific. In April 1942, the United States wanted revenge for Pearl Harbor. So the United States sent 16 B-25 bombers under the command of Lieutenant Colonel James H. Doolittle to bomb Tokyo and other major Japanese cities. The bombs did little damage. The attack, however, made an important psychological point: the Japanese could be attacked.

The Allies Turn the Tide of War Doolittle's raid on Japan raised American morale and shook the confidence of some Japanese. As one Japanese citizen described it, "We started to doubt that we were invincible." In addition, Japan had won a vast empire that was becoming difficult to defend and control.

Slowly, the Allies began to turn the tide of war. Early in May 1942, an American fleet with Australian support intercepted a Japanese strike force. The force had been about to attack Port Moresby. The city housed a critical Allied air base in southeastern New Guinea (GIHN-ee). From this base, the Japanese could have easily invaded Australia.

In the battle that followed—the Battle of the Coral Sea—both fleets fought using a new kind of naval warfare. The opposing ships did not fire a single shot. In fact, they often could not see one other. Instead, airplanes taking off from huge aircraft carriers did all the fighting. In the end, the battle was something of a draw. The Allies lost more ships than the Japanese, who claimed victory. But the Allies had stopped Japan's southward expansion for the first time.

The Battle of Midway Japan next targeted Midway Island, west of Hawaii. The island was home to a key American airfield. However, by June 1942, yet another Japanese code had been broken. As a result, the new commander in chief of the U.S. Pacific Fleet, Admiral Chester Nimitz, knew that a force of over 150 ships was heading toward Midway. The Japanese fleet was the largest naval force ever assembled. It could also boast the world's largest battleship, carrying Admiral Yamamoto himself. Yamamoto hoped not only to seize Midway but also to finish off the U.S. Pacific fleet. He hoped the American force would come from Pearl Harbor to defend the island.

Nimitz was outnumbered four to one in ships and planes. Even so, he was preparing an ambush for the Japanese at Midway. On June 3, with American forces hidden beyond the horizon, Nimitz allowed the enemy to launch the first strike. As Japanese planes roared over Midway Island, American carrier planes swooped in to attack Japanese ships. Many Japanese planes were still on the decks of the ships. The strategy was a success. American pilots destroyed 322 Japanese planes, all four aircraft carriers, and one support ship. Yamamoto ordered his crippled fleet to withdraw. By June 6, 1942, the battle was over. One Japanese official commented, "The Americans had avenged Pearl Harbor." The **Battle of Midway** had also turned the tide of war in the Pacific against the Japanese.

The Allies Go on the Offensive With morale high after their Midway victory, the Allies took the offensive. The Pacific war was one of vast distances. Japanese troops had dug in on hundreds of islands across the ocean. General **Douglas MacArthur** was

World War II **449**

As happened in other battles of the Pacific war, U.S. Marines destroy a cave connected to a Japanese fort on the island of Iwo Jima.

Vocabulary
invincible: unconquerable.

A. Possible Answers Midway Island had an important U.S. air base, so defending the island would be vital to the Americans. Midway was located just west of Hawaii, so the Americans would probably do as much as they could to keep the Japanese away from this important American territory.

THINK THROUGH HISTORY
A. Analyzing Motives What reasons might Admiral Yamamoto have had for thinking the Americans would send their entire Pacific fleet to defend Midway Island?

OBJECTIVE 2 INSTRUCT

The Allies Strike Back

▶ **Key Ideas**
• Allied bombing of Tokyo shows the Japanese are vulnerable.
• The Allies win significant naval battles by striking with planes from aircraft carriers.
• The Allied strategy of island hopping brings them closer to Japan.

CRITICAL THINKING ACTIVITY
CLASS TIME: 15 MINUTES

Analyzing Effects
Using two subheads on this page, have students analyze the impact of the Allies' strategy in the Pacific on the course of the war by making a chart like this listing Allied actions and their results.

	Actions	Results
Turning the Tide of War		
Going on the Offensive		

MORE ABOUT . . .
Admiral Yamamoto

Although Yamamoto argued for a surprise strike at Pearl Harbor, he had few illusions about the final outcome of the war. In a brief period of study at Harvard and as a naval attaché in Washington, D.C., for two years, Yamamoto was aware of the industrial potential of the United States. In 1940, he advised that Japan could not beat the United States and should not fight it. When the war opened, Yamamoto predicted the future: "In the first six to twelve months of a war with the United States and Britain, I will run wild and win victory after victory. After that, I have no expectation of success."

TEACHING OPTION | **BLOCK SCHEDULING** | **COOPERATIVE ACTIVITY: Charting a Battle Strategy** | **CLASS TIME 30 MINUTES**

Task: Student groups will chart the Allied battle strategy in the Pacific.

Purpose: To explain how the Allied battle strategy in the Pacific turned the tide of war against Japan.

Activity: Student groups will each review a major battle in the Allied offensive against Japan. In their description of the battle, they will identify the opposing forces, the tactics of the battle, and the outcome. They will present their work in a chart of the battle. Groups should then combine their separate battle charts into a class chart and discuss the overall Allied strategy, explaining how it turned the tide of war against Japan.

📁 ***Building a Portfolio*** If the chart is among their best work, students should add it to their portfolio.

📋 **ALTERNATIVE ASSESSMENT BOOK**
Standards for Evaluating a Cooperative Activity

Standards for Evaluation
Charts should . . .

• clearly describe the Allied battle strategy
• explain how Japan was defeated
• be visually interesting

Flamboyant and supremely confident of his abilities, MacArthur had a talent for publicizing himself, which brought him admirers as well as detractors. Generals George Marshall and Dwight Eisenhower did not like him, and even President Roosevelt resented MacArthur's popularity. Have students read more about MacArthur and identify characteristics that might gain him loyal supporters and qualities that might earn him criticism.

ASSESS & RETEACH

Section 2 Assessment

After students have finished the section assessment, have them find places in the text that answer the questions and compare their answers to those in the text.

Section Quiz

FORMAL ASSESSMENT
Section quiz, p. 199

Reteaching Activity

CLASS TIME: 10 MINUTES

To help students understand the war in the Pacific between 1941 and 1943, review the charts they have made for item 2 in the section assessment.

CLOSE ACTIVITY

CLASS TIME: 15 MINUTES

Role-Playing

Have two students role-play Admiral Yamamoto and Admiral Nimitz and stage a conversation between the two as they explain what they hoped to accomplish at the Battle of Midway and how they hoped to achieve their goals. Have the other students in the class act as newspaper reporters and ask the two admirals questions about their battle plans and strategies.

---

commander of the Allied land forces in the Pacific. He believed that storming each island would be a long, costly effort. Instead, he wanted to "island-hop" past Japanese strongpoints. He would then seize islands that were not well defended but were closer to Japan. After taking the islands, MacArthur would use air power to cut supply lines and starve enemy troops. "Hit 'em where they ain't, let 'em die on the vine," MacArthur declared.

MacArthur's first target soon presented itself. The U.S. government had learned that the Japanese were building a huge air base on the island of Guadalcanal in the Solomon Islands. The Allies had to strike fast before the base was completed and became another Japanese strongpoint. At dawn on August 7, 1942, about 19,000 U.S. Marines, with Australian support, landed on Guadalcanal and a few nearby islands. Caught unprepared, the Japanese at Guadalcanal radioed, "Enemy forces overwhelming. We will defend our posts to the death."

The marines had easily taken the Japanese airfield. But the battle for control of the island turned into a savage struggle as both sides poured in fresh troops. In February 1943, after six months of fighting on land and at sea, the **Battle of Guadalcanal** finally ended. After losing 23,000 men out of 36,000, the Japanese abandoned the island they came to call "the Island of Death."

To war correspondent Ralph Martin and the soldiers who fought there, Guadalcanal was simply "hell":

A VOICE FROM THE PAST

Hell was furry red spiders as big as your fist, giant lizards as long as your leg, leeches falling from trees to suck blood, armies of white ants with bites of fire, scurrying scorpions inflaming any flesh they touched, enormous rats and bats everywhere, and rivers with waiting crocodiles. Hell was the sour, foul smell of the squishy jungle, humidity that rotted a body within hours. . . . Hell was an enemy . . . so fanatic that it used its own dead as booby traps.

RALPH G. MARTIN, quoted in *The GI War*

As Japan worked to establish a new order in Southeast Asia and the Pacific, the Nazis moved ahead with Hitler's plan for a new order in Europe. Hitler's goal was not only the conquest of Europe. He also aimed at enslaving Europe's people and forcing them to work for Germany's prosperity. In particular, the Führer had plans for dealing with those he considered unfit for the Third Reich. You will learn about Hitler's plans in Section 3.

HISTORY MAKERS

Douglas MacArthur
1880–1964
Son of a Civil War army officer, Douglas MacArthur said that his first memory was the "sound of bugles." MacArthur yearned, even at an early age, for a life of action and adventure. With a strong will and his mother's encouragement, he grew to become one of the most brilliant military strategists of World War II.

MacArthur believed that destiny had called him to perform great deeds. He once boasted, "All Germany cannot fabricate the shell that will kill me." The general had his critics, but he also inspired deep loyalty among his men. One remarked, "His first thought was always for the soldier."

THINK THROUGH HISTORY
B. Identifying Problems If the vast distances of the Pacific caused problems for the Allies, how might they have also caused problems for the Japanese?
B. Possible Answer Supplying their outposts over great distances and keeping the Allies out of thousands of square miles of ocean would probably be problems for the Japanese.

THINK THROUGH HISTORY
C. Analyzing Causes What reasons could have made the Japanese fight until they lost 23,000 out of 36,000 defending the island of Guadalcanal?
C. Possible Answers The military importance of the airfield; bravery; honor; blind obedience; a belief in country over an individual human life.

Section 2 Assessment

1. TERMS & NAMES

Identify
• Isoroku Yamamoto
• Pearl Harbor
• Battle of Midway
• Douglas MacArthur
• Battle of Guadalcanal

2. TAKING NOTES

Create a chart like the one below. List four major events of the war in the Pacific between 1941 and 1943.

| Event 1: |
| Event 2: |
| Event 3: |
| Event 4: |

Which event was most important in turning the tide of the war in the Pacific against the Japanese? Why?

3. EVALUATING DECISIONS

Judging from the effects of the attack on Pearl Harbor, do you think Yamamoto made a wise decision in bombing Pearl Harbor? Why or why not?

THINK ABOUT
• Yamamoto's goals in the bombing
• U.S. involvement in World War II
• the effects of the bombing

4. ANALYZING THEMES

Empire Building What do you think Yamamoto's biggest problems were in building the Japanese empire in the Pacific?

THINK ABOUT
• geographical problems
• European/American interests in the Pacific
• psychological factors

ANSWERS

1. TERMS & NAMES
Isoroku Yamamoto, p. 447
Pearl Harbor, p. 447
Battle of Midway, p. 449
Douglas MacArthur, p. 449
Battle of Guadalcanal, p. 450

2. TAKING NOTES
Possible Answers: Japan bombs Pearl Harbor; United States bombs Tokyo; Battle of Midway; Battle of Guadalcanal.

3. EVALUATING DECISIONS
Wise: If the Japanese did not destroy the U.S. Pacific fleet, it would have been used against them. Unwise: If the Japanese did not bomb Pearl Harbor, the United States may never have entered the war.

4. ANALYZING THEMES
Possible Answers: Geography: the Pacific region is so huge that it would be difficult to build an empire. European/American Interests: The United States and certain European countries had military posts in the Pacific. Psychological Factors: After the bombing of Tokyo, Yamamoto had to deal with shaken Japanese confidence.

TERMS & NAMES
- Aryans
- Holocaust
- *Kristallnacht*
- ghettos
- "Final Solution"
- genocide

MAIN IDEA

During the Holocaust, Hitler's Nazis killed 6 million Jews and 5 million other "non-Aryans."

WHY IT MATTERS NOW

The violence against Jews during the Holocaust led to the founding of Israel after World War II.

Background
Hitler misused the term *Aryan* to mean "Germanic." In fact, the term refers to the Indo-European peoples.

SETTING THE STAGE As part of their new order for Europe, Nazis proclaimed that **Aryans,** or Germanic peoples, were a "master race." They claimed that Jews and other non-Aryan peoples were inferior. This racist message would eventually lead to the **Holocaust**—the mass slaughter of civilians, especially Jews.

The Holocaust Begins

Nazi propaganda started as an ugly campaign of anti-Semitism. It eventually flared into persecution across Germany. Hitler knowingly tapped into a hatred for Jews that had deep roots in European history. For generations, many Germans, along with other Europeans, had targeted Jews as the cause of their failures. The Nazis even blamed Jews for Germany's defeat in World War I and for its economic problems after that war.

THINK THROUGH HISTORY
A. Analyzing Motives Why might the people of a country want to blame a minority group for most of its problems?
A. Possible Answers A minority group may be different culturally, and some people are afraid of differences; targeting a minority for blame takes responsibility away from a country and its leaders, so the majority can feel better about itself.

In 1933, the Nazis made persecution a government policy. They first passed laws forbidding Jews to hold public office. Then, in 1935, the Nuremberg Laws deprived Jews of their rights to German citizenship, jobs, and property. To make it easier for the Nazis to identify them, Jews had to wear a bright yellow star attached to their clothing.

Kristallnacht: **"Night of Broken Glass"**
Worse was yet to come. Early in November 1938, 17-year-old Herschel Grynszpan (GRIHN·shpahn), a Jewish youth from Germany, was visiting an uncle in Paris. While Grynszpan was there, he received a postcard. It said that after living in Germany for 27 years, his father had been deported to his native Poland. On November 7, wishing to avenge his father's deportation, Grynszpan shot an employee of the German Embassy in Paris.

When Nazi leaders heard the news, they launched a violent attack on the Jewish community. On November 9, Nazi storm troopers attacked Jewish homes, businesses, and synagogues across Germany and murdered around 100 Jews. An American in Leipzig wrote, "Jewish shop windows by the hundreds were systematically . . . smashed. . . . The main streets of the city were a positive litter of shattered plate glass." It is for this reason that the night of November 9 became known as *Kristallnacht* (Krih·STAHL·NAHKT), or "Night of Broken Glass."

Hitler's special troops helped spread the message of the government's anti-Semitic policy. The sign these troops are putting up reads, "Germans! Protect yourselves! Don't buy in Jewish stores!"

SECTION 3 RESOURCES

PRINT RESOURCES

IN-DEPTH RESOURCES: UNIT 4
Guided Reading, p. 56
Primary Source: from *The Diary of a Young Girl,* p. 64
Literature: from *Night,* p. 66

ACCESS FOR STUDENTS ACQUIRING ENGLISH
Guided Reading (Spanish), p. 175

FORMAL ASSESSMENT
Section Quiz, p. 200

ALTERNATIVE ASSESSMENT BOOK

TECHNOLOGY RESOURCES

CD-ROM
Electronic Library of Primary Sources

INTERNET www.mlworldhistory.com

Section 3 Overview

OBJECTIVES

(1) To trace the course of the Nazis' persecution of Jews.

(2) To describe the results of the Nazis' "Final Solution."

CRITICAL THINKING
- Analyzing motives, pp. 451, 454
- Analyzing causes, p. 452
- Making inferences, p. 454

FOCUS
5-Minute Warm-Up

▶ **Making Inferences**
Have students answer the following questions to help them understand the situation of the Jews in Nazi Germany.

1. Read A Voice from the Past on page 452. What happened to the Libau family's possessions?

2. What do the Nazis threaten to do to the Libau family when they return?

🏛 *WARM-UP TRANSPARENCY 16*

OBJECTIVE (1) INSTRUCT

The Holocaust Begins

▶ **Key Ideas**
- Nazi Germany embarks on a policy of persecution of Jews and others deemed inferior.
- Nazis force thousands of Jews to emigrate.
- Nazis isolate Jews in conquered territories by forcing them into ghettos.
- Nazis begin the final step in their program of genocide.

📄 *IN-DEPTH RESOURCES, UNIT 4*
Guided Reading, p. 56

📄 *ACCESS FOR STUDENTS ACQUIRING ENGLISH*
Guided Reading (Spanish), p. 175

💿 *ELECTRONIC LIBRARY OF PRIMARY SOURCES*
from *Affadavit Given at Nuremberg*

Creating a Summary
Have students use a chart like the one below to summarize the steps the Nazis took against Jews that resulted in the "Final Solution."

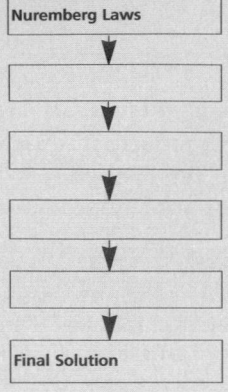

Nuremberg Laws

↓

↓

↓

↓

Final Solution

MORE ABOUT . . .
Refugees

France's Vichy government appeared to be indifferent to the fate of Jewish refugees, most of whom the Nazis had forcibly moved to unoccupied France and whom the French detained. One writer reported that when Marshal Henri Pétain was questioned about persecuting Jews, he replied ". . . as for free-masons, I hate them, as for communists I am afraid of them, as for the Jews it is not my fault." The majority of Jewish refugees in Vichy France were housed in camps of window-less barracks surrounded by barbed wire. When in 1941, foreign reporters were allowed to visit some of the camps, one reporter wrote: ". . . these people have been detained for reasons they, in many instances, do not under-stand and . . . they are without the slightest information about what is to be their future . . . ."

Most of the refugees were kept in the camps until 1942 when the Nazis began transporting them to camps in Eastern Europe.

Young M.I. Libau was only 14 years old when Nazis attacked his family's home. Libau described what the Nazis did:

A VOICE FROM THE PAST
All the things for which my parents had worked for eighteen long years were destroyed in less than ten minutes. Piles of valuable glasses, expensive furniture, linens—in short, everything was destroyed. . . . The Nazis left us, yelling, "Don't try to leave this house! We'll soon be back again and take you to a concentration camp to be shot."

M.I. LIBAU, quoted in *Never to Forget: The Jews of the Holocaust*

Kristallnacht marked a major step-up in the Nazi policy of Jewish persecution. The future for Jews in Germany looked grim.

The Flood of Refugees After Kristallnacht, some Jews realized that violence against them was bound to increase. By the end of 1939, a number of Jews in Germany had fled for safety to other countries. Many of them, however, remained in Germany. Later, there would be millions more in territories conquered by Hitler. At first, Hitler favored emigration as a solution to what he called "the Jewish problem." The Nazis sped up the process. They forced Jews who did not want to leave into emigrating.

Getting other countries to continue admitting Germany's Jews became a problem. France had admitted 25,000 Jewish refugees and wanted no more. The British, who had accepted 80,000 Jews, worried about fueling anti-Semitism if that number increased. Some 40,000 Jews found homes in Latin America, but that region had closed its doors by the end of 1938. The United States took in around 100,000 refugees (including German scientist Albert Einstein). Many Americans, however, wanted U.S. doors closed. Germany's foreign minister observed: "We all want to get rid of our Jews. The difficulty is that no country wishes to receive them."

This pile of shoes taken from Nazi victims represents the murder of thousands of Jews. The inset shows the living inmates at Auschwitz trying to salvage shoes left by the dead.

Isolating the Jews Hitler found that he could not get rid of Jews through emigration. So he put another part of his plan into effect. Hitler ordered Jews in all countries under his control to be moved into certain cities in Poland. In those cities, they were herded into dismal, overcrowded **ghettos,** or segregated Jewish areas. The Nazis then sealed off the ghettos with barbed wire and stone walls. They wanted the Jews inside to starve or die from disease. One survivor wrote, "One sees people dying, lying with arms and legs outstretched in the middle of the road. Their legs are bloated, often frostbitten, and their faces distorted with pain."

Even under these horrible conditions, the Jews hung on. Some formed resistance organizations within the ghettos. They smuggled in food and other needed items. In the midst of chaos, Jews also struggled to keep their traditions. Ghetto theaters produced plays and concerts. Teachers taught lessons in secret schools. Scholars kept records so that one day people would find out the truth.

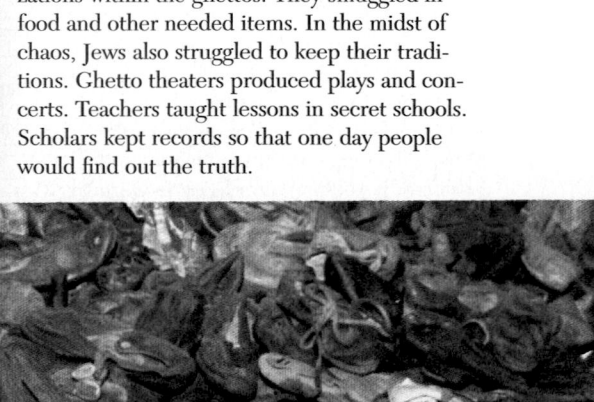

B. Possible Answers Poland was a weak, con-quered country, so Hitler could do what-ever he wanted there; Hitler considered the Polish subhuman, so he may have felt that he could do whatever he wanted in their country.

THINK THROUGH HISTORY
B. Analyzing Causes Why might Hitler have chosen Poland to put his ghetto policy for "the Jewish problem" into effect?

452

Task Students will read a primary source and a literature excerpt to examine the horrors of the Holocaust as experienced by two young people during World War II. Students should note that both Anne Frank and Elie Wiesel were teenagers.

Materials Needed Use the Primary Source (Anne Frank) and the Literature selection (Elie Wiesel) for this section from the Teacher's Resources.

Activity Have students compare the experiences of the two young people that are recorded in these excerpts. Have students make up a list of the similarities and differences between their experiences.

Conclusion Ask students to discuss the role of hope in the different lives of these two young people. Why might hope have been easier for Anne Frank to hold on to than for Elie Wiesel?

IN-DEPTH RESOURCES: UNIT 4
Primary Source: from *The Diary of a Young Girl* by Anne Frank, p. 64

Literature: from *Night* by Elie Wiesel, p. 66

452 Chapter 16

Hitler's "Final Solution"

Hitler soon grew impatient waiting for Jews to die from starvation or disease in the ghettos. He decided to take more direct action. His plan was called the **"Final Solution."** It was actually a program of **genocide,** the systematic killing of an entire people.

Hitler believed that his plan of conquest depended on the purity of the Aryan race. To protect racial purity, the Nazis not only had to eliminate the Jews, but also other races, nationalities, or groups they viewed as inferior—as "subhumans." They included gypsies, Poles, Russians, homosexuals, the insane, the disabled, and the incurably ill. But the Nazis focused especially on the Jews.

The Mass Killings Begin After Hitler invaded Poland in 1939, it was still not clear that the Führer meant to eliminate Jews totally. As Nazi armies swept across Eastern Europe, Hitler sent SS units from town to town to hunt Jews down. The SS (Hitler's elite security force) and some thousands of collaborators rounded up Jews—men, women, young children, and even babies—and took them to isolated spots. They then shot their prisoners in pits that became the prisoners' grave.

Jews in communities not reached by the killing squads were rounded up and taken to concentration camps, or slave-labor prisons. These camps were located mainly in Germany and Poland. Later, Nazis built camps in other countries they occupied. (See the map on page 467.) Hitler hoped that the horrible conditions in the camps would speed the total elimination of the Jews.

The prisoners worked seven days a week as slaves for the SS or for German businesses. Guards severely beat or killed their prisoners for not working fast enough. With meals of thin soup, a scrap of bread, and potato peelings, most prisoners lost 50 pounds the first month. "Hunger was so intense," recalled one survivor, "that if a bit of soup spilled over, prisoners would . . . dig their spoons into the mud and stuff the mess into their mouths."

The Final Stage: Mass Extermination The "Final Solution" officially reached its final stage in early 1942. At that time, the Nazis built extermination camps equipped with gas chambers for mass murder. The Nazis built the first six death camps in Poland. The first, Chelmno, actually began operating in late 1941. (See the map on

Vocabulary
collaborators: people who assist an occupying enemy force.

Background
Nazis also slaughtered 5 million Poles, Soviets, and others they considered as "undesirables."

UnresolvedProblems

Defending Human Rights and Freedoms

After the horrible crimes of the Final Solution were revealed at the end of World War II, nations of the world resolved to work for the protection of human rights for people in every nation. The Universal Declaration of Human Rights was adopted by the United Nations General Assembly in 1948. The declaration identifies the basic political, economic, and social rights and freedoms of every person.

In that same year, the UN drew up an agreement that made genocide an international war crime. The United States approved the Genocide Convention in 1986.
See Epilogue, p. 606.

Slave workers in the Buchenwald concentration camp in Germany. They were among the lucky to have survived to the end of the war. The prisoner highlighted with a circle is Nobel Prize winning author Elie Wiesel. (See "A Voice from the Past," page 454.)

453

OBJECTIVE 2 INSTRUCT

Hitler's "Final Solution"

▶ **Key Ideas**
• The Nazis unleash killing squads and ship Jews and others to concentration camps.
• The "Final Solution" results in the death of six million Jews.

SPOTLIGHT ON
Nazi Medicine

Tell students that the terrible experiments carried out by many German doctors served no real medical purpose and were nothing more than torture under the name of medicine. Ask students why they think doctors who are supposed to follow a code of ethics would engage in such practices.

MORE ABOUT . . .
The "Final Solution"

The program for the "Final Solution" was spelled out in January 1942 by Reinhard Heydrich at a conference of Nazi senior civil servants. In his speech Heydrich, who was head of the SS intelligence service, stated clearly the fate of Jews. "The Reichsführer SS has forbidden any further emigration of Jews. The Jews remaining in the Reich and all European Jews in our present and future spheres of influence will be evacuated to the East for the final solution. . . ."

| TEACHING OPTION | BLOCK SCHEDULING | COOPERATIVE ACTIVITY: Investigating the German Wartime Economy | CLASS TIME 30 MINUTES |

Task: Student groups will research aspects of the German wartime economy and present reports on it to the class.

Purpose: To understand how Germany financed its massive war effort.

Activity: Student groups will research aspects of Germany's wartime economy such as its banking system, its use of slave labor as a work force, the relationship between business and the government,

its gold supplies, the distribution of goods and services, whether or not there was a black market. Have each group choose an aspect of Germany's economy and research how it functioned. Students should present their reports to the class and speculate on whether Germany's economy could sustain a lengthy war.

Building a Portfolio If the report is among their best work, students should add it to their portfolio.

ALTERNATIVE ASSESSMENT BOOK
Standards for Evaluating a Cooperative Activity

Standards for Evaluation
Reports should . . .
• convey how the German economy functioned
• show evidence of thorough research
• be clear and understandable

Teacher's Edition 453

In 1941, Hitler's government required all Jews in German-controlled territories to wear a yellow Star of David when appearing in public places.

Jews Killed under Nazi Rule*			
	Original Jewish Population	**Jews Killed**	**Percent Surviving**
Poland	3,300,000	3,000,000	10%
Soviet Union	2,850,000	1,252,000	56%
Hungary	650,000	450,000	30%
Romania	600,000	300,000	50%
Germany/Austria	240,000	200,000	10%

*Estimates

page 467.) The huge gas chambers in the camps could kill as many as 6,000 human beings in a day.

When prisoners arrived at the largest of the death camps, Auschwitz (OUSH·vihts), they paraded before a committee of SS doctors. With a wave of the hand, these doctors separated the strong (mostly men) from the weak, who would die that day. Those chosen to die (mostly women, young children, the elderly, and the sick) were told to undress for a shower. They were led into a chamber with fake showerheads, and the doors closed. The prisoners were then poisoned with cyanide gas that poured from the showerheads. Later, the Nazis installed crematoriums, or ovens, to burn the bodies.

SPOTLIGHT *ON*

Jewish Resistance

The 700 members of the Jewish Fighting Organization in the Warsaw ghetto were among the Jews who resisted the horrors of Nazism. In April 1943, most of these young people lost their lives battling Nazi tanks and troops who were destroying the ghetto.

Even in the death camps, Jews rose up against the Nazis. In August 1943 at Treblinka, Poland, a small group of Jews revolted. Breaking into the armory, they stole guns and grenades. They then attacked guards and set fire to the gas chambers. Most of these brave fighters died. They had paid the highest price possible to combat Nazi atrocities.

The Survivors Six million Jews died in the death camps and in Nazi massacres. Fewer than 4 million European Jews survived the horrors of the Holocaust. Many had help from non-Jewish people who were against the Nazis' treatment of Jews. Swedish businessman Raoul Wallenberg and Protestant religious thinker Dietrich Bonhoeffer are just two examples of Christians who risked their lives to oppose Hitler's policies. These people risked their lives by hiding Jews or by helping them escape to neutral countries such as Switzerland or Sweden.

Those who survived the camps were changed forever by what they had seen. For Elie Wiesel, 15 years old when he entered Auschwitz, the light had gone out:

A VOICE FROM THE PAST
Never shall I forget the little faces of the children, whose bodies I saw turned into wreaths of smoke beneath a silent blue sky. Never shall I forget those flames which consumed my faith forever. . . . Never shall I forget those moments which murdered my God and my soul and turned my dreams to dust. . . . Never.

ELIE WIESEL, quoted in *Night*

Section ③ Assessment

1. TERMS & NAMES
Identify
• Aryans
• Holocaust
• *Kristallnacht*
• ghettos
• "Final Solution"
• genocide

2. TAKING NOTES
Using a web diagram like the one below, give examples of Nazi persecutions.

Nazi persecutions

3. MAKING INFERENCES
Why do you think German soldiers and the German people went along with the Nazi policy of persecution of the Jews?

THINK ABOUT
• Nazi treatment of those who disagreed
• Nazi propaganda
• the political and social conditions in Germany at the time

4. THEME ACTIVITY
Science and Technology In groups of three or four students, discuss the ethical dilemmas of German scientists, engineers, and doctors asked to organize and participate in the Holocaust.
How might they have opposed Hitler's policy? In public? In secret? What might have been the consequences of public opposition?

454 Chapter 16

ANSWERS

The Allies Are Victorious

TERMS & NAMES
- Erwin Rommel
- Bernard Montgomery
- Dwight D. Eisenhower
- Battle of Stalingrad
- D-Day
- Battle of the Bulge
- kamikaze

MAIN IDEA

Led by the United States, Great Britain, and the Soviet Union, the Allies scored key victories and won the war.

WHY IT MATTERS NOW

The Allies' victory in World War II set up conditions for both the Cold War and today's post-Cold War world.

SETTING THE STAGE As 1941 came to an end, Hitler said, "Let's hope 1942 brings me as much good fortune as 1941." Despite the Führer's hopes, Germany's victories slowed considerably during 1942. The United States had entered the war, boosting the Allies' morale and strength.

The Allies Plan for Victory

On December 22, 1941, just after Pearl Harbor, Winston Churchill and President Roosevelt met at the White House to develop a joint war policy. Stalin had asked his allies to relieve German pressure on his armies in the east. He wanted them to open a second front in the west. The second front would split the Germans' strength by forcing them to fight major battles in two regions instead of one. Churchill agreed with Stalin's strategy: The Allies would weaken Germany on two fronts before dealing a deathblow. At first, Roosevelt was torn, but ultimately he agreed.

The Tide Turns on Two Fronts

Churchill urged that Britain and the United States strike first at North Africa and southern Europe. The strategy angered Stalin. He wanted the Allies to open the second front in France. In the meantime, the Soviet Union would have to hold out on its own against the Germans—with the help of some supplies from its partners. Nevertheless, late in 1942, the Allies began to turn the tide of war both in the Mediterranean and on the Eastern Front.

The North African Campaign German forces had been advancing and retreating across the North African desert since early 1941. Finally, General **Erwin Rommel** took the key port city of Tobruk in June 1942. With Tobruk's fall, London sent General **Bernard Montgomery**—"Monty" to his men—to take control of British forces in North Africa. By this time, the Germans had advanced to an Egyptian village called El Alamein (AL-uh-MAYN), west of Alexandria. They were dug in so well that British forces could not go around them. So, Montgomery had to launch the Battle of El Alamein with a massive attack from the front. On the night of October 23, the roar of more than 1,700 British guns took the Axis soldiers totally by surprise. They fought back fiercely, but by November 3, Rommel's army had been beaten. He and his forces retreated westward.

As Rommel retreated west, the Allies launched *Operation Torch*. On November 8, an Allied force of more than 107,000 troops—mostly Americans—landed in Morocco and Algeria. This force was led by American General **Dwight D. Eisenhower.** Caught between the two armies, the Desert Fox's Afrika Korps was finally smashed in May 1943.

Background
Montgomery, like Rommel himself, used dummy regiments built from timber and canvas. They were intended to fool the enemy into thinking that forces were stationed where, in fact, they were not.

HISTORY MAKERS

General Erwin Rommel
1891–1944

On July 20, 1944, a plot to assassinate Hitler by a group of German officers failed. Under torture, one conspirator accused war hero General Erwin Rommel of involvement in the plot. The news shook and enraged Hitler, since Rommel had always been devoted to him.

Was Rommel actually involved? Evidence indicates that he was ready to bypass Hitler and personally negotiate for peace with the Allies. However, many believe that he knew nothing of the plot. Hitler believed that he did. He offered Rommel a choice—a public trial or suicide and a state funeral. On October 14, 1944, Rommel took poison and died.

World War II **455**

SECTION 4 RESOURCES

PRINT RESOURCES

IN-DEPTH RESOURCES: UNIT 4
Guided Reading, p. 57
Skillbuilder Practice: Following Chronological Order, p. 59
Primary Sources: from *Farewell to Manzanar,* p. 63;
from *Hiroshima,* p. 65

ACCESS FOR STUDENTS ACQUIRING ENGLISH
Guided Reading (Spanish), p. 176
Skillbuilder Practice: (Spanish), p. 178

FORMAL ASSESSMENT
Section Quiz, p. 201

ALTERNATIVE ASSESSMENT BOOK

TECHNOLOGY RESOURCES

CD-ROM
Battles of the World
Electronic Library of Primary Sources

VIDEO *Patterns of Interaction: Arming for War*

INTERNET www.mlworldhistory.com

Section 4 Overview

OBJECTIVES

1. To describe the Allied plan for victory.
2. To show the Allied strategy on two fronts.
3. To explain how civilians on the Allied home fronts contributed to the war effort.
4. To summarize events that led to the surrender of Germany.
5. To explain the importance of the atom bomb in the Allied victory over Japan.

SKILLBUILDER

- Interpreting maps: region, movement, p. 456
- Interpreting maps: human-environment interaction, movement, p. 458

CRITICAL THINKING

- Making inferences, pp. 456, 460
- Analyzing motives, p. 457
- Forming an opinion, p. 461
- Summarizing, p. 461
- Analyzing themes, p. 461

FOCUS

5-Minute Warm-Up

▶ **Interpreting Maps**

Have students answer the following questions to help them understand the D-day invasion.

1. Look at the map on page 458. Which landing area was isolated from the rest?

2. Approximately how many miles is it from Sword Beach in the east to Utah Beach in the west?

WARM-UP TRANSPARENCY 16

OBJECTIVE 1 INSTRUCT

The Allies Plan for Victory

▶ **Key Idea**
- With the U.S. in the war, the Allies open a second front.

IN-DEPTH RESOURCES: UNIT 4
Guided Reading, p. 57

ACCESS FOR STUDENTS ACQUIRING ENGLISH
Guided Reading (Spanish), p. 176

The Tide Turns on Two Fronts

(See page 455.)

▶ **Key Ideas**
• The Allied invasion of North Africa smashes Rommel's forces.
• The Soviets defeat Germans at Stalingrad and push the German army westward.
• The Allies attack in southern Europe and push through Italy.

HISTORY MAKERS
General Erwin Rommel

(See page 455.)

Controversy has surrounded the possible role of Rommel in the plot to kill Hitler. He once confided to those he trusted that he believed the war could not be won and that Hitler should be replaced. And he had heard talk from other generals of killing Hitler. On the day of his death, he told his wife the charges were not true. Ask students to research the plot and form an opinion about whether Rommel was involved.

History from Visuals

World War II: Allied Advances, 1942–1945

Interpreting the Map Have students look at the map key to distinguish Axis, Allied, and neutral nations.

Extension Activity Have students note where most of the neutral countries outside of Europe are located on this map and then make a list of them. *Southwest Asia—Turkey, Saudi Arabia*

SKILLBUILDER Answers
1. Ireland, Spain, Portugal, Sweden, Switzerland
2. Germany

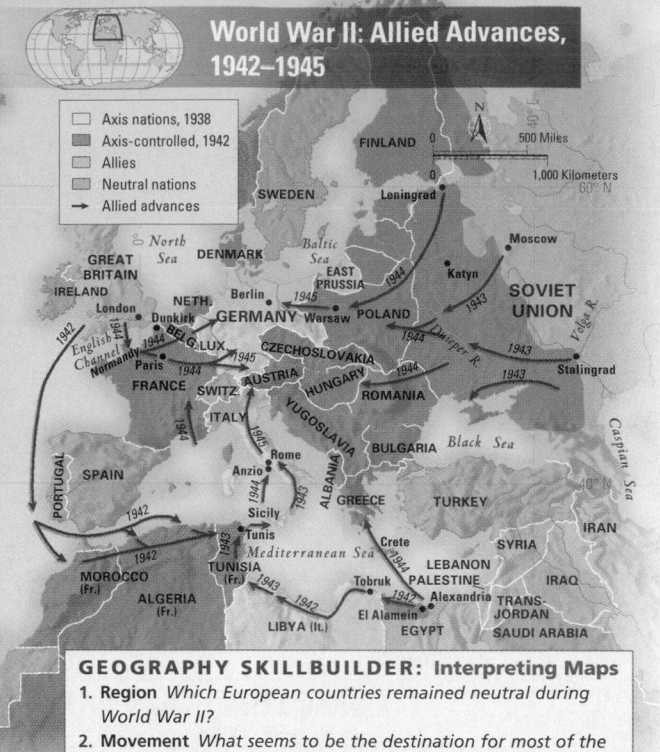

World War II: Allied Advances, 1942–1945

Map key:
- ☐ Axis nations, 1938
- ■ Axis-controlled, 1942
- ☐ Allies
- ☐ Neutral nations
- → Allied advances

GEOGRAPHY SKILLBUILDER: Interpreting Maps
1. **Region** Which European countries remained neutral during World War II?
2. **Movement** What seems to be the destination for most of the Allied advances that took place in Europe during 1943–1944?

These dazed, freezing, and starved German prisoners were actually lucky to be alive. About 240,000 Germans died during the battle for the city of Stalingrad.

Turning Point at Stalingrad As Rommel suffered defeats in North Africa, German armies also met their match in the Soviet Union. They had stalled at Leningrad and Moscow. Germans suffered heavy losses in battle because of the Russian winter. When the summer of 1942 arrived, German tanks were again ready to roll. Hitler sent his Sixth Army south to seize the rich oil fields in the Caucasus Mountains. The army was also to capture Stalingrad (now Volgograd) on the Volga River. With its 500,000 people, Stalingrad was a major industrial center.

The **Battle of Stalingrad** began on August 23, 1942. The Luftwaffe went on nightly bombing raids that set much of the city ablaze and reduced the rest to rubble. The situation looked desperate. Nonetheless, Stalin had already told his commanders to defend the city named after him at all costs. "Not one step backward," he ordered.

By early November 1942, Germans controlled 90 percent of the ruined city. Stalingrad was an "enormous cloud of burning, blinding smoke," as one German officer wrote. Then, another Russian winter set in. On November 19, Soviet troops outside the city launched a counterattack. Closing in around Stalingrad, they trapped the Germans inside and cut off their supplies. Hitler's commander, General Friedrich von Paulus, begged him to order a retreat. But Hitler refused, saying the city was "to be held at all costs."

On February 2, 1943, some 90,000 frostbitten, half-starved German troops surrendered to the Soviets. These pitiful survivors were all that remained of an army of 330,000. Stalingrad's defense had cost the Soviets over 1 million soldiers. The city they defended was 99 percent destroyed. After Stalingrad, however, the Germans were on the defensive, with the Soviets pushing them steadily westward.

The Invasion of Italy As the Battle of Stalingrad raged, Stalin continued to urge the British and the Americans to invade France. In January 1943, Roosevelt and Churchill met at Casablanca, Morocco, and decided to attack Italy first. On July 10, 1943, Allied forces of 180,000 soldiers landed on Sicily and captured it from Italian and German troops by August.

A. Possible Answers The army fighting on its own soil would know the territory better than the invading army; it would have the support of the local population, which the invaders would not; it would have the additional energy that comes with defending one's own home.

THINK THROUGH HISTORY
A. Making Inferences What advantages might a weaker army fighting on its home soil have over a stronger invading army?

| TEACHING OPTION | BLOCK SCHEDULING | COOPERATIVE ACTIVITY: Writing Letters About the Allied Invasion | CLASS TIME 30 MINUTES |

Task: Students will represent the Allied leaders (Churchill, Stalin, and Roosevelt) and write letters to one another expressing their points of view about the invasion of Europe and a two-front war.

Purpose: To help students understand the conflict among the Allied leaders.

Activity: Students will work in three groups, each representing one of the Allied leaders and discuss plans for a war on two fronts. Students should then collaborate to write their letters.

📁 **Building a Portfolio** If the letter is among their best work, students should add it to their portfolio.

📄 **ALTERNATIVE ASSESSMENT BOOK**
Standards for Evaluating a Cooperative Activity

Standards for Evaluation
Letters should . . .

• clearly convey the views of the three leaders
• show an understanding of the views of the other leaders
• show an understanding of the advantages and disadvantages of waging a war on two fronts

The conquest of Sicily toppled Mussolini from power. On July 25, King Victor Emmanuel III fired the dictator and had him arrested. On September 3, Italy surrendered. But the Germans seized control of northern Italy and put Mussolini back in charge. Finally, the Germans retreated northward, and the victorious Allies entered Rome on June 4. Fighting in Italy, however, continued until Germany fell in May 1945. On April 28, 1945, as the Germans were retreating from northern Italy, the Italian resistance ambushed some trucks. Inside one of them, resistance fighters found Mussolini disguised as a German soldier. The following day, he was shot, and his body was hanged in the Milan town square.

Life on Allied Home Fronts

Wherever Allied forces fought, people on the home fronts rallied to support them. In war-torn countries like the Soviet Union or Great Britain, civilians lost their lives and endured extreme hardships. Except for a few of its territories, such as Hawaii, the United States did not suffer invasion or bombing. Nonetheless, Americans at home made a crucial contribution to the Allied war effort. Americans produced the weapons and equipment that would help win the war.

Mobilizing for Total War Defeating the Axis powers required mobilizing for total war. In the United States, factories converted their peacetime operations to wartime production and made everything from machine guns to boots. Automobile factories produced tanks. A U.S. typewriter company made armor-piercing shells. By 1944, almost 18 million U.S. workers—many of them women—were working in war industries.

With factories turning out products for the war, a shortage of consumer goods hit the United States. From meat and sugar to tires and gasoline, from nylon stockings to laundry soap, the American government rationed scarce items. Setting the speed limit at 35 miles per hour also helped to save on gasoline and rubber. In European countries directly affected by the war, rationing was even more drastic.

To inspire their people to greater efforts, Allied governments conducted highly effective propaganda campaigns. In the Soviet Union, a Moscow youngster collected enough scrap metal to produce 14,000 artillery shells. Another Russian family, the Shirmanovs, used their life savings to buy a tank for the Red Army. In the United States, youngsters saved their pennies and bought government war stamps and bonds to help finance the war.

Japanese Americans Imprisoned Government propaganda also had a negative effect. After Pearl Harbor, a wave of prejudice arose in the United States against the 127,000 Japanese Americans. Most lived in Hawaii and on the West Coast. The bombing of Pearl Harbor frightened Americans. This fear, encouraged by government propaganda, was turned against Japanese Americans. They were suddenly seen as "the enemy." On February 19, 1942, President Roosevelt set up a program of internment and loss of property, since Japanese Americans were considered a threat to the country.

In March, the military began rounding up "aliens" and shipping them to relocation camps. Two-thirds of those interned were Nisei, or Japanese Americans who were native-born American citizens. The camps were restricted military areas located away

Armed soldiers stand guard over Japanese Americans in an internment camp. In one camp, some of the occupants used horse stalls as living quarters. In other camps, hastily constructed barracks housed people considered "enemy aliens."

Background
As the Allies advanced, the Italian resistance aided them by blowing up bridges, roads, and rail lines; cutting telephone lines; and ambushing German trucks.

Vocabulary
rationed: distributed in limited amounts.

B. Possible Answer It would be easier to get Americans' support to fight the Japanese if they believed they were

Vocabulary
internment: detention.

MORE ABOUT . . .
The Battle of Stalingrad
(See page 456.)

With most of the city in rubble from bombing and shelling, the Soviets defended Stalingrad street by street and house by house in what one writer has called the fiercest of all city battles of World War II. As German soldiers advanced, the Soviets moved back, setting mines and booby traps everywhere they could. In one instance, a sailor armed with only a Molotov cocktail died throwing himself under an advancing tank, which exploded. In another instance, a Soviet died beside a German tank upon which he had written a message in his own blood: "I die, but my country and the Party will win."

 BATTLES OF THE WORLD
The Battle of Stalingrad

OBJECTIVE 3 INSTRUCT

Life on Allied Home Fronts

▶ *Key Ideas*
• Civilians mobilize on the home front to support the war effort.
• In the United States, fear of the Japanese results in the internment of thousands of Japanese Americans.

MORE ABOUT . . .
The Home Front
While many women in England were collecting pots and pans for scrap metal, in the United States war bond rallies were held across the nation. Film stars and other celebrities often appeared at these rallies and were very effective in helping to raise 36 billion dollars, the total amount of bonds sold during the war.

TEACHING OPTIONS

CONNECTIONS ACROSS TIME AND PLACE

Japanese Internment In 1988, President Ronald Reagan signed legislation admitting that the United States was wrong in incarcerating Japanese Americans during the war. The legislation apologized for "wartime hysteria" and authorized payments of $20,000 to survivors of the camps. For many of the people, the compensation came too late.

Other groups protested that if reparations were to be paid to Japanese Americans, then compensation should be offered to African Americans for slavery, to Native Americans for their dispossession from the land, and to other groups as well.

 IN-DEPTH RESOURCES: UNIT 4
Primary Source: from *Farewell to Manzanar*, p. 63

CUSTOMIZING FOR SPECIAL NEEDS

Gifted and Talented Students: Creating Posters Tell the students that posters were one of the ways in which governments encouraged people to rally around the war effort. Posters were also used to spread propaganda. Have students research some World War II posters. If possible, have them bring books of poster art to class to

show examples of war posters. Then have students create posters of their own. Their posters might encourage civilians to greater efforts, denounce the enemy, or show support for the armed services. Provide a wall or other area in the class where students can display the posters they have made.

Teacher's Edition **457**

Allied Victory in Europe

▶ **Key Ideas**
- Allies invade Normandy and push on toward Germany.
- As Soviet forces invade from the East, Hitler commits suicide and Germany surrenders.

HISTORY MAKERS
General Dwight Eisenhower

Eisenhower once told the poet Carl Sandburg, "When they [soldiers] called me Uncle Ike or . . . just plain Ike, I knew everything was going well." Ask students to identify characteristics Eisenhower had that inspired loyalty.

History from Visuals

The D-Day Invasion, June 6, 1944

Interpreting the Map Have students note the broad front along which Allied forces landed. Have them consider the advantages and disadvantages of invading along such a broad front.

Extension Activity Have students do some research on the various beaches on which the Allied forces landed in the D-Day invasion. They might investigate which beach was invaded by Canadian forces. *Juno Beach*

SKILLBUILDER Answers
1. Flooding.
2. Troops parachuted into France would have moved into the interior more quickly than soldiers who fought their way in from the coast.

---

from the coast. With such a location, it was thought that the Nisei could not participate in an invasion. From 1941 until 1946, the United States imprisoned some 31,275 people it wrongly considered "enemy aliens (foreigners)." Most of those prisoners were American citizens of Japanese descent.

HISTORY MAKERS

General Dwight Eisenhower
1890–1969
In his career, U.S. General Dwight Eisenhower had shown an uncommon ability to work with all kinds of people—even competitive Allies. His Chief of Staff said of Eisenhower, "The sun rises and sets on him for me." He was also wildly popular with the troops, who affectionately called him "Uncle Ike."

So, it was not a surprise when in December 1943, U.S. Army Chief of Staff George Marshall named Eisenhower as supreme commander of the Allied forces in Europe. The new commander's "people skills" enabled him to join American and British forces together to put a permanent end to Nazi aggression.

Allied Victory in Europe

While the Allies were dealing with issues on the home front, they were preparing to push toward victory in Europe. By the end of 1942, the war had begun to turn in favor of the Allies. By 1943, the Allies began secretly building a force in Great Britain. Their plan was to attack the Germans across the English Channel.

The D-Day Invasion By May 1944, the invasion force was ready. Thousands of planes, ships, tanks, landing craft, and 3.5 million troops awaited orders to attack. American General Dwight D. Eisenhower, the commander of this enormous force, planned to strike on the coast of Normandy, in northwestern France. The Germans knew that an attack was coming. But they did not know where it would be launched. To keep Hitler guessing, the Allies set up a huge dummy army with its own headquarters and equipment. They ordered the make-believe army to attack at the French seaport of Calais (ka·LAY).

Code-named *Operation Overlord*, the invasion of Normandy was the greatest land and sea attack in history. The day chosen for the invasion to begin—called **D-Day**—was June 6, 1944.

At dawn on June 6, British, American, French, and Canadian troops fought their way onto a 60-mile stretch of beach in Normandy. The Germans had dug in with machine guns, rocket launchers, and cannons. They protected themselves behind concrete walls three feet thick. Among the Americans alone, 3,000 soldiers died on the beach that day. Captain Joseph Dawson said, "The beach was a total chaos, with men's bodies everywhere, with wounded men crying both in the water and on the shingle [coarse gravel]."

Despite heavy casualties, the Allies held the beachheads. A month later, more than 1 million additional troops had landed. On July 25, the Allies punched a hole in the German defenses near Saint-Lô (san·LOH), and General George Patton's Third Army raced through.

Background
The name *D-Day* came from the words *designated + day*.

Vocabulary
beachheads: enemy shoreline captured just before invading forces move inland.

The D-Day Invasion, June 6, 1944

GEOGRAPHY SKILLBUILDER: Interpreting Maps
1. **Human–Environment Interaction** *What environmental problem might have been encountered by 1st Army soldiers landing at Utah Beach?*
2. **Movement** *Looking at the map, what might have been the Allied strategy behind parachuting troops into France?*

CONNECTIONS ACROSS TIME AND PLACE

The Parachute World War II was the first war in which parachutes were used extensively for a variety of purposes, including landing troops and supplies in isolated or otherwise inaccessible places. On the night before D-Day, some 10,000 American paratroopers were scattered behind the Normandy beaches. The result, writes historian David Howarth, was a "gigantic . . . game of hide-and-seek" in which

"the Americans knew what was happening, but few of them knew where they were; the Germans knew where they were, but none of them knew what was happening."

After World War II, parachuting, or skydiving, emerged as a popular sport. Early parachuting competitions were limited to accuracy in landing.

Later, as skydivers learned to control their bodies in free fall, they added style events that involved performing aerobatic maneuvers before opening their parachutes. In the most popular form of competition, teams of skydivers form geometric patterns, racing to make as many patterns as they can. Today, teams from more than 30 countries participate in world skydiving championships.

Soon, the Germans were retreating. On August 25, the Allies marched triumphantly into Paris. By September, they had liberated France, Belgium, Luxembourg, and much of the Netherlands. They then set their sights on Germany.

The Battle of the Bulge As Allied forces moved toward Germany from the west, the Soviet army was advancing toward Germany from the east. Hitler now faced a war on two fronts. In a desperate gamble, the Führer decided to counterattack in the west. The Führer hoped a victory would split American and British forces and break up Allied supply lines. Explaining the reasoning behind his plan, Hitler said, "This battle is to decide whether we shall live or die. . . . All resistance must be broken in a wave of terror."

On December 16, German tanks broke through weak American defenses along an 85-mile front in the Ardennes. The push into the Allied lines gave the campaign its name—the **Battle of the Bulge.** Although caught off guard, the Allies eventually pushed the Germans back and won. The Nazis could do little but retreat, since Hitler had lost men that he could no longer replace.

Germany's Unconditional Surrender After the Battle of the Bulge, the war in Europe neared its end. In late March 1945, the Allies rolled across the Rhine River into Germany. By the middle of April, a noose was closing around Berlin. Three million Allied soldiers approached Berlin from the southwest. Six million Soviet troops approached from the east—some of them just 40 miles from the capital. By April 25, 1945, the Soviets had surrounded the capital, as their artillery pounded the city.

While Soviet shells burst over Berlin, Hitler prepared for his end in an underground headquarters beneath the crumbling city. On April 29, he married his long-time companion, Eva Braun. He also wrote his final address to the German people. In it, he blamed Jews for starting the war and his generals for losing it. "I myself and my wife choose to die in order to escape the disgrace of . . . capitulation," he said. "I die with a happy heart aware of the immeasurable deeds of our soldiers at the front." Two days later, Hitler shot himself after taking poison. His new wife simply swallowed poison. The bodies were then carried outside and burned.

On May 7, 1945, General Eisenhower accepted the unconditional surrender of the Third Reich from the German military. President Roosevelt, however, did not live to witness the long-awaited victory. He had died suddenly on April 12, as Allied armies were advancing toward Berlin. Roosevelt's successor, Harry Truman, received the news of the Nazi surrender. On May 8, the surrender was officially signed in Berlin. The United States and other Allied powers celebrated V-E Day—Victory in Europe Day. The war in Europe had ended at last.

Vocabulary
capitulation: surrender.

Victory in the Pacific

Although the war in Europe was over, the Allies were still fighting the Japanese in the Pacific. With the Allied victory at Guadalcanal, however, the Japanese advances in the Pacific had been stopped. For the rest of the war, the Japanese retreated before the counterattack of the Allied powers.

The Japanese Retreat By the fall of 1944, the Allies were moving in on Japan. In October, Allied forces landed on the island of Leyte (LAY-tee) in the Philippines. General MacArthur, who had been forced to surrender the islands in February 1942, waded ashore. He then declared, "People of the Philippines, I have returned."

Actually, the takeover would not be quite that easy. The Japanese had decided to destroy the American fleet. The Allies could not then resupply their ground troops. To

---

SPOTLIGHT ON

Dresden

On the night of February 13, 1945, 800 British and American bombers launched a massive air attack on Dresden, a German city southeast of Berlin. During the bombing, some 4,000 tons of explosives were dropped, creating raging firestorms. One author described the city as a "furnace fueled by people," as its citizens—mostly women, children, and the elderly—burned to death. Estimates of those killed vary from 35,000 to 135,000.

The firestorm reduced Dresden to rubble, accomplishing no important military goals but killing many civilians. Dresden has come to symbolize the strategy of "total war": massive attacks on both military and civilian targets to break a country's fighting spirit.

World War II **459**

The Atomic Bomb

The plane that dropped the atom bomb on Hiroshima was called the *Enola Gay* and was piloted by Colonel Paul W. Tibbets, Jr. He described what he saw after releasing the bomb: ". . . down below [the mushroom cloud] the thing reminded me more of a boiling pot of tar than any other description I can give. It was black and boiling underneath with a steam haze on top of it. . . . We had seen the city when we went in, and there was nothing to see when we came back. It was covered by this boiling, black-looking mass."

 IN-DEPTH RESOURCES: UNIT 4
Primary Source: from *Hiroshima*, p. 65

 ELECTRONIC LIBRARY OF PRIMARY SOURCES
from Testimony Before the Special Senate Committee on Atomic Energy

Viewing the Video

Show *Arming for War: Modern and Medieval Weapons* to demonstrate that arms races have existed throughout history.

- The first segment of the video chronicles nations' quests for new and more effective weapons during World War I and World War II.

- The second segment shows students that arms races took place in medieval times as well, when the longbow and other weapons changed military history. Using the Teacher's Resource Book as a guide, have students consider how new or enhanced weapons can change warfare; discuss the costs and benefits of weapons development; and enrich the lesson with primary-source and visual-literacy activities included in the resource book.

 PATTERNS OF INTERACTION
Arming for War: Modern and Medieval Weapons
Videocassette: Tape 4

The Atomic Bomb

On the eve of World War II, scientists in Germany succeeded in splitting the nucleus of a uranium atom, releasing a huge amount of energy. Albert Einstein wrote to President Franklin Roosevelt and warned him that Nazi Germany might be working to develop atomic weapons. Roosevelt responded by giving his approval for an American program, later code-named the Manhattan Project, to develop an atomic bomb. Roosevelt's decision set off a race to assure that the United States would be the first to develop the bomb.

On the morning of August 6, 1945, the B-29 bomber *Enola Gay*, flown by commander Colonel Paul W. Tibbets, Jr., took off from Tinian Island in the Mariana Islands. At precisely 8:16 A.M., the atomic bomb exploded above Hiroshima, a city on the Japanese island of Honshu.

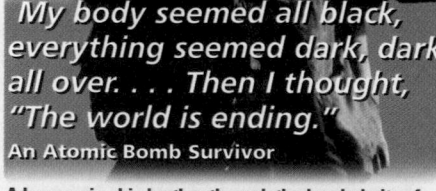

My body seemed all black, everything seemed dark, dark all over. . . . Then I thought, "The world is ending."
An Atomic Bomb Survivor

A boy carries his brother through the leveled city of Nagasaki. This is one of a series of photos taken by Japanese photographer Yosuke Yamahata soon after the atomic bomb devastated the city on August 9, 1945.

Hiroshima: Day of Fire

Effects of the bombing

Ground temperatures	7,000°F
Hurricane force winds	980 miles per hour
Energy released	20,000 tons of TNT
Buildings destroyed	62,000 buildings
Killed immediately	70,000 people
Dead by the end of 1945	140,000 people
Total deaths related to A-bomb	200,000 people

The overwhelming destructive power of the Hiroshima bomb, and of the bomb dropped on Nagasaki three days later, changed the nature of war forever. Nuclear destruction also led to questions about the ethics of scientists and politicians who chose to use the bomb.

Patterns of Interaction

Just as in World War I, the conflicts of World War II spurred the development of ever more powerful weapons. Mightier tanks, more elusive submarines, faster fighter planes—all emerged from this period. From ancient times to the present day, the pattern remains the same: Every new weapon causes other countries to develop others of similar or greater force. This pattern results in a deadly race for an ultimate weapon: for example, the atomic bomb.

 VIDEO *Arming for War: Modern and Medieval Weapons*

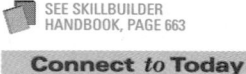 **Connect** *to* **History**

Making Inferences What advantages did the United States have over Germany in the race to develop the atomic bomb?

SEE SKILLBUILDER HANDBOOK, PAGE 663

Connect *to* **Today**

Contrast If you had to design a memorial to the victims of the Hiroshima and Nagasaki bombings, what symbol would you use? Make a sketch of your memorial.

Nagasaki citizens trudge through the still smoldering ruins of their city in another photo by Yosuke Yamahata.

460

Connect *to* **History**

Making Inferences
Possible Answer:
The U.S. mainland was insulated from the war. No bombs were being dropped on the country, so that scientists and technicians were able to pursue their research with less disruption than the Germans had. Also, scientists such as Einstein had fled Germany to work in the United States.

Connect *to* **Today**

Contrast
You might wish to set aside a special area in the classroom where the students can display their sketches of memorials to the victims of Hiroshima and Nagasaki. Ask students to explain why they chose the symbols that they did to use in their memorials.

carry out this strategy, the Japanese had to risk almost their entire fleet. They gambled everything on October 23, in the Battle of Leyte Gulf. Within three days, the Japanese navy had lost disastrously—eliminating it as a fighting force in the war. Now, only the Japanese army and the feared kamikaze stood between the Allies and Japan. The **kamikaze** were Japanese suicide pilots. They would sink Allied ships by crash-diving into them in their bomb-filled planes.

In March 1945, after a month of bitter fighting and heavy losses, American Marines took Iwo Jima (EE-wuh JEE-muh), an island 660 miles from Tokyo. On April 1, U.S. troops moved to the island of Okinawa, only about 350 miles from southern Japan. The Japanese put up a desperate fight. Nevertheless, on June 22, the bloodiest land battle of the war ended. The Japanese lost 110,000 troops, and the Americans, 12,500.

The Atomic Bomb Brings Japanese Surrender After Okinawa, the next stop had to be Japan. President Truman's advisers had informed him that an invasion of the Japanese homeland might cost the Allies half a million lives. Truman had to make a decision whether to use a powerful new weapon called the atomic bomb, or A-bomb. The A-bomb would bring the war to the quickest possible end. It had been developed by the top-secret Manhattan Project, headed by General Leslie Groves and chief scientist Robert J. Oppenheimer. The Manhattan Project became a major spending item in U.S. military budgets. Truman only learned of the new bomb's existence when he became president.

The first atomic bomb was exploded in a desert in New Mexico on July 16, 1945. President Truman then warned the Japanese. He told them that unless they surrendered, they could expect a "rain of ruin from the air." The Japanese did not reply. So, on August 6, 1945, the United States dropped an atomic bomb on Hiroshima, a Japanese city of 365,000 people. Almost 73,000 people died in the attack. Three days later, on August 9, a second bomb was dropped on Nagasaki, a city of 200,000. It killed about 37,500 people. Radiation killed many more. A Japanese journalist described the horror in Hiroshima:

A VOICE FROM THE PAST
Within a few seconds the thousands of people in the streets and the gardens in the center of the town were scorched by a wave of searing heat. Many were killed instantly, others lay writhing in agony from the intolerable pain of their burns. Everything standing upright in the way of the blast, walls, houses, factories, and other buildings, was annihilated.

JAPANESE JOURNALIST, quoted in *The American Heritage Picture History of World War II*

The Japanese surrendered to General Douglas MacArthur on September 2. The surrender took place aboard the United States battleship *Missouri* in Tokyo Bay. With Japan's surrender, the war had ended. Now, countries faced the task of rebuilding a war-torn world.

 Section 4 Assessment

1. TERMS & NAMES
Identify
- Erwin Rommel
- Bernard Montgomery
- Dwight Eisenhower
- Battle of Stalingrad
- D-Day
- Battle of the Bulge
- kamikaze

2. TAKING NOTES
Create a chart like the one below, listing outcomes of the following World War II battles.

Battle	Outcome
Battle of El Alamein	
Battle of Stalingrad	
D-Day Invasion	
Battle of the Bulge	

Which battle do you think was most important in turning the war in favor of the Allies? Why?

3. SUMMARIZING
Based on what you have read in this section, how do governments gather support for a war effort on the home front?

THINK ABOUT
- the economy
- forms of propaganda
- individual participation in the war effort

4. ANALYZING THEMES
Science and Technology Do you think President Truman made the correct decision by ordering the atomic bomb dropped on Hiroshima and Nagasaki? Why or why not?

THINK ABOUT
- the likely consequences if the atomic bomb had not been dropped
- the destruction caused by the atomic bomb
- World War II after the dropping of the atomic bomb

World War II **461**

Section 5 Overview
OBJECTIVES

1. To describe the devastation of Europe following the war.

2. To identify some of the political consequences of the Allied victory in postwar Europe.

3. To show how defeat affected political and civic life in Japan.

4. To give examples of ways in which Japan changed under United States' occupation.

SKILLBUILDER
• Interpreting charts, p. 465

CRITICAL THINKING
• Identifying problems, p. 463
• Making inferences, p. 464
• Analyzing causes, p. 465

FOCUS
5-Minute Warm-Up

Clarifying

Have students answer these questions to help them understand the human costs of war.

1. Look at the chart on page 465. What was the approximate number of military killed in the war? How many civilians were killed in the war?

2. How many people, both military and civilian, were killed on both sides in the war?

 WARM-UP TRANSPARENCY 16

OBJECTIVE ① INSTRUCT

Europe in Ruins

Key Ideas
• Many European cities lie in ruins.
• Misery in Europe continues for years after the war.

IN-DEPTH RESOURCES: UNIT 4
Guided Reading, p. 58

ACCESS FOR STUDENTS ACQUIRING ENGLISH
Guided Reading (Spanish), p. 177

WORLD ART AND CULTURES TRANSPARENCIES
AT71 Liberation

CRITICAL THINKING TRANSPARENCIES
CT32 The Causes and Effects of World War II

5 The Devastation of Europe and Japan

MAIN IDEA	WHY IT MATTERS NOW
World War II cost millions of human lives and billions of dollars in damages. It left Europe and Japan in ruins.	The United States survived World War II undamaged, allowing it to become a world leader.

SETTING THE STAGE Allied victory in the war had been achieved at a high price. World War II had caused more death and destruction than any other conflict in history. It left 60 million dead, 50 million uprooted from their homes, and property damage that ran into billions of U.S. dollars.

Europe in Ruins

By the end of World War II, Europe lay in ruins. Close to 40 million Europeans had died—two-thirds of them civilians. Constant bombing and shelling had reduced hundreds of cities to rubble. The ground war had destroyed much of the countryside. Displaced persons from many nations were struggling to get home.

A Harvest of Destruction A few of the great cities of Europe—Paris, Rome, Brussels—remained undamaged by war. Many, however, had suffered terrible destruction. The Blitz left blackened ruins in London. Over five years, 60,595 London civilians had died in the German bombings. Eastern Europe and Germany were far worse off. Warsaw, the capital of Poland, was almost wiped from the face of the earth. In 1939, Warsaw had a population of 1,289,000 people. When the Soviets entered the city in January 1945, only 153,000 people remained. In Berlin, 25,000 tons of Allied bombs had demolished 95 percent of the central city. One U.S. officer stationed in Berlin reported, "Wherever we looked we saw desolation. It was like a city of the dead."

Background
Two-thirds of the deaths in the war occurred in Europe, making the war there far bloodier than in Asia.

Winston Churchill looks at Nazi firebomb damage to the British House of Commons.

After the bombings, many civilians stayed where they were and tried to get on with their lives. Some lived in partially destroyed homes or apartments. Others huddled in caves and cellars beneath the rubble. They had no water, no electricity, and very little food. Hunger was a constant companion. With factories destroyed or damaged, most people had no earnings to buy the food that was available.

Although many remained in the cities, a large number of city dwellers fled. They joined the army of displaced persons wandering Europe following the war. These displaced persons included the survivors of concentration camps, prisoners of war, and refugees fleeing the Soviet army. Millions found themselves in the wrong country when the postwar treaties changed national borders. They jammed the roads trying to get home, hoping to find their families or to find a safe place.

SECTION 5 RESOURCES

PRINT RESOURCES

IN-DEPTH RESOURCES: UNIT 4
Guided Reading, p. 58

ACCESS FOR STUDENTS ACQUIRING ENGLISH
Guided Reading (Spanish), p. 177

FORMAL ASSESSMENT
Section Quiz, p. 202

ALTERNATIVE ASSESSMENT BOOK

TECHNOLOGY RESOURCES

WORLD ART AND CULTURES TRANSPARENCIES
AT71 Liberation

CRITICAL THINKING TRANSPARENCIES
CT32 The Causes and Effects of World War II
CT68 Visual Summary

INTERNET www.mlworldhistory.com

Simon Weisenthal described the search made by survivors of the Holocaust:

A VOICE FROM THE PAST
Across Europe a wild tide of frantic survivors was flowing. . . . Many of them didn't really know where to go. . . . And yet the survivors continued their pilgrimage of despair, sleeping on highways or in railroad stations, waiting for another train, another horse-drawn cart to come along, always driven to hope. "Perhaps someone is still alive. . . ." Someone might tell where to find a wife, a mother, children, a brother—or whether they were dead. . . . The desire to find one's people was stronger than hunger, thirst, fatigue.
SIMON WEISENTHAL, quoted in *Never to Forget: The Jews of the Holocaust*

Misery Continues After the War Although the war had ended, misery in Europe continued for years. Europe lay ravaged by the fighting. Agriculture was disrupted. Most able-bodied men had served in the military and the women had worked in war production. Few remained to plant the fields. With the transportation system destroyed, the meager harvests often did not reach the cities. Thousands died as famine and disease spread through the bombed-out cities. In August 1945, 4,000 citizens of Berlin died every day. To get a few potatoes, people would barter any valuable items they had left. The first post-war winter brought more suffering as people went without shoes and coats.

Postwar Governments and Politics

Despairing Europeans often blamed their leaders for the war and its aftermath. Once the Germans had lost, some prewar governments—like those in Belgium, Holland, Denmark, and Norway—returned quickly. In countries like Germany, Italy, and France, however, a return to the old leadership was not so simple. Hitler's Nazi government had brought Germany to ruins. Mussolini had led Italy to defeat. The Vichy government had collaborated with the Nazis. Much of the old leadership was in disgrace. Besides, in Italy and France, many resistance fighters were Communists.

After the war, the Communist Party promised change, and millions were ready to listen. In both France and Italy, Communist Party membership skyrocketed. The Communists made huge gains in the first postwar elections. Anxious to speed up a political takeover, the Communists staged a series of violent strikes. Alarmed French and Italians reacted by voting for anti-Communist parties. Communist membership and influence then began to decline. And they declined even more so as the economies of France and Italy began to recover.

An Attempt at Justice: The Nuremberg Trials While nations were struggling to recover politically and economically, they also were trying to deal with Germany's guilt in the Holocaust. To make sure that such crimes would never happen again, the Allies put Nazis on trial. In 1946, an International Military Tribunal representing 23 nations put Nazi war criminals on trial in Nuremberg, Germany. In the first of the **Nuremberg Trials**, 22 Nazi leaders were charged with waging a war of aggression. They were also accused of violating the laws of war and of committing "crimes against humanity"—the murder of 11 million people.

Führer Adolf Hitler, SS chief Heinrich Himmler, and Minister of Propaganda Joseph Goebbels had escaped trial by committing suicide. However, Marshall Hermann Göring, Deputy Führer Rudolf Hess, and other high ranking Nazi leaders had to face the charges.

Of the 22 defendants, 12 were sentenced to death. Göring cheated the executioner by killing himself. The rest were hanged on October 16, 1946. Hans Frank, the "Slayer of Poles," was the only convicted Nazi to express remorse: "A thousand years will pass," he said, "and still this guilt of Germany

CONNECT *to* TODAY

Genocide in Rwanda
Genocide is a crime that human beings have committed against one another throughout history. In April 1994, the president of the East African nation of Rwanda died in a suspicious plane crash. The president was a member of the Hutu tribe. In Rwanda, the Hutu and Tutsi tribes have long hated and fought each other.

After the president's death, about 1 million Tutsis were slaughtered by the majority Hutus. In the end, Tutsi rebels ended the worst of the genocide.

The United Nations has set up an international war crimes tribunal to judge the worst acts of genocide. Yet, many criminals are still at large, and ethnic conflict in Rwanda continues.

The Effects of Defeat in Japan

▶ **Key Ideas**
- U.S. forces occupy Japan under the leadership of General Douglas MacArthur.
- MacArthur begins the process of democratization by drawing up a new constitution.

CRITICAL THINKING ACTIVITY
CLASS TIME: 10 MINUTES

Forming an Opinion
Have students use a chart to list the steps MacArthur took to change Japan's government and economy and the results of those steps and draw a conclusion about the effects of U.S. occupation.

Steps	Results
Conclusion	

U.S. Occupation Brings Deep Changes

▶ **Key Ideas**
- The power of Japan's emperor as a supreme leader is reduced.
- A new constitution makes Japan a democratic nation.

📰 **CASE STUDY**—Japan and Mexico: Pluralistic Politics and Economic Growth, p. 114

---

will not have been erased." The bodies of those executed were burned at the concentration camp of Dachau (DAHK·ow). They were cremated in the same ovens that had burned so many of their victims.

The Effects of Defeat in Japan

The defeat suffered by Japan in World War II left the country in ruins. Two million lives had been lost in the war. The country's major cities had been largely destroyed by Allied bombing raids, including the capital, Tokyo. The atomic bomb had left Hiroshima and Nagasaki as blackened wastelands. The Allies had stripped Japan of its colonial empire. They even took away areas that had belonged to the Japanese for centuries.

The United States Occupies Japan Even after these disasters, some Japanese military leaders wanted to continue the fight. In a radio broadcast on August 15, 1945, Emperor Hirohito urged the Japanese people to lay down their arms and work together to rebuild Japan. "Should we continue to fight," he declared, "it would only result in an ultimate collapse . . . of the Japanese nation." Two weeks after that broadcast, General Douglas MacArthur, now supreme commander for the Allied powers, accepted the Japanese surrender. He took charge of the U.S. occupation.

Emperor Hirohito and U.S. General Douglas MacArthur look distant and uncomfortable as they pose for a photo. The photo was taken in the American Embassy in Tokyo on September 27, 1945.

Demilitarization in Japan MacArthur was determined to be fair and not to plant the seeds for a future war. Nevertheless, to ensure that fighting would end, he began a process of **demilitarization**—disbanding the Japanese armed forces. He achieved this quickly, leaving the Japanese with only a small police force. MacArthur also began bringing war criminals to trial. Out of 25 surviving defendants, former Premier Hideki Tojo and six others were condemned to hang.

The general then turned his attention to democratization—the process of creating a government elected by the people. In February 1946, MacArthur and his American political advisers drew up a new constitution. It changed the empire into a parliamentary democracy like that of Great Britain. The Japanese accepted the constitution. It went into effect on May 3, 1947.

MacArthur was not told to revive the Japanese economy. However, he was instructed to broaden land ownership and increase the participation of workers and farmers in the new democracy. Absentee landlords with huge estates had to sell land to tenant farmers at reasonable prices. Workers could now create independent labor unions. Still bitter over Pearl Harbor, Americans did not provide much aid for rebuilding Japan. The United States did send 2 billion dollars in emergency relief. This was a small amount, however, considering the task that lay ahead.

U.S. Occupation Brings Deep Changes

The new constitution was the most important achievement of the occupation. It brought deep changes to Japanese society. In 1945, the Japanese had agreed to surrender. They insisted, however, that "the supreme power of the emperor not be compromised." The Allies agreed, but now things had changed. A long Japanese tradition had viewed the emperor as a god. He was also an absolute ruler whose divine will was law. The emperor now had to declare that he was not a god. That admission was as

B. Possible Answer The reduced military influence of military leaders and increased economic power among the Japanese people might result in a wider sharing of power in Japan.

THINK THROUGH HISTORY
B. Making Inferences How would demilitarization and a revived economy help Japan achieve democracy?

CONNECTIONS ACROSS TIME AND PLACE

Demilitarization One of MacArthur's first acts as head of the U.S. occupation forces was to free about 500 political prisoners and fire 5,000 government people who were known to be "thought police." He also purged the government of those known to be war criminals and dismissed all senior military officials and anyone else who had been actively involved in

promoting aggression since 1931. MacArthur's success as a military leader gave him the authority to impose demilitarization upon the Japanese.

By the time MacArthur was through, a little less than half of 1 percent of the population was barred from public office; in Germany 2.5 percent of the

population was not allowed to take part in public life or hold positions of influence. MacArthur's policies in Japan transformed the nation from a militaristic power to one that since that time has rejected a standing army and resisted attempts over the years to build up a military force.

Costs of World War II: Allies and Axis

	Direct War Costs	Military Killed/Missing	Civilians Killed
United States	$288.0 billion*	292,131	—
Great Britain	$117.0 billion	271,311	60,595
France	$111.3 billion	205,707**	173,260***
USSR	$93.0 billion	13,600,000	7,720,000
Germany	$212.3 billion	3,300,000	2,893,000†
Japan	$41.3 billion	1,140,429	953,000

*In 1994 dollars.
**Before surrender to Nazis.
***Includes 65,000 murdered Jews.
†Includes about 170,000 murdered Jews and 56,000 foreign civilians in Germany.

SKILLBUILDER: Interpreting Charts
1. *Which of the nations listed in the chart suffered the greatest human costs?*
2. *How does U.S. spending on the war compare with the spending of Germany and Japan?*

C. Possible Answer
The Japanese were to have a constitutional monarch, just like the British. The American system had no place for monarchs.

THINK THROUGH HISTORY
C. Analyzing Causes Why did the Americans choose the British system of government for the Japanese, instead of the American system?

shocking to the Japanese as defeat. His power was also dramatically reduced as he became a constitutional monarch. Like the ruler of Great Britain, the emperor became largely a figurehead—a symbol of Japan.

The new constitution guaranteed that real political power in Japan rested with the people. The people elected a two-house parliament, called the Diet. All citizens over the age of 20, including women, had the right to vote. The government was led by a prime minister chosen by a majority of the Diet. A constitutional bill of rights protected basic freedoms. One more key provision—Article 9—stated that the Japanese could no longer make war. They could only fight if attacked.

In September 1951, the United States and 48 other nations signed a formal peace treaty with Japan. The treaty officially ended the war. With no armed forces, the Japanese also agreed to continuing U.S. military protection for their country. Six months later, the U.S. occupation of Japan was over. Relieved of the burden of paying for the occupation, Japan's economy recovered more quickly. With the official end of the war, the United States and Japan became allies.

In the postwar world, however, enemies not only became allies. Allies also became enemies. World War II had changed the political landscape of Europe. It weakened some nations and strengthened others. The Soviet Union and the United States had come out of the war as allies. Nevertheless, once the fighting was over, the differences in their postwar goals emerged. These differences stirred up conflicts that would shape the modern world for decades.

Section 5 Assessment

1. TERMS & NAMES
Identify
• Nuremberg Trials
• demilitarization

2. TAKING NOTES
Using a Venn diagram like the one below, compare and contrast the aftermath of World War II in Europe and Japan.

3. ANALYZING CAUSES
Why do you think that many Europeans favored communism directly following World War II?

THINK ABOUT
• World War II destruction
• pre-World War II governments
• economic concerns

4. THEME ACTIVITY
Economics Draw a political cartoon from a Japanese absentee landlord's or industrialist's point of view on MacArthur's postwar economic reforms. Remember that MacArthur is an American making important changes in a country that is not his own.

World War II **465**

History from Visuals

Costs of World War II: Allies and Axis

Interpreting the Chart Point out to students that these charts help them compare the war costs of individual nations to the total cost of the war.

Extension Activity Ask students what other column they might add to the first chart. *Possible answer: a column on the number of refugees created by the war.*

SKILLBUILDER Answers
1. USSR
2. The United States spent more than Germany and Japan combined.

ASSESS & RETEACH

Section 5 Assessment
Have students answer the questions individually and then meet in small groups to discuss their answers.

Section Quiz
 FORMAL ASSESSMENT
Section quiz, p. 202

Reteaching Activity
CLASS TIME: 15 MINUTES

Have students identify the political and economic differences in postwar Japan and Europe and compare and contrast them.

 CRITICAL THINKING TRANSPARENCIES
CT68 Visual Summary

CLOSE ACTIVITY

CLASS TIME: 15 MINUTES

Identifying Problems
Ask students to make a chart listing the problems MacArthur faced in Japan and his solutions to the problems.

Problem	Solution

ANSWERS

1. TERMS & NAMES
Nuremberg Trials, p. 463
demilitarization, p. 464

2. TAKING NOTES
Possible Answers:
Europe only: Displaced persons looking for families; famine; rise of communism
Japan only: Japanese emperor

no longer a god; Japanese people humiliated; radiation poisoning from the atomic bomb
Both: Destruction of land and property; natural resources depleted; heavy loss of life; major cities in shambles

3. ANALYZING CAUSES
Possible Answers: People lost

faith in leaders of the past who had participated in starting or conducting the war; communism promised food and prosperity to people who had none.

4. THEME ACTIVITY
Standards for Evaluation
An effective cartoon should meet the following criteria:

• show a basic understanding of Japanese economics in the post-World War II period
• be convincingly presented from the point of view of a Japanese landlord or industrialist whose life is being changed by foreign influence
• include a variety of detail that enriches the cartoon

TERMS & NAMES

1. blitzkrieg, p. 442
2. Atlantic Charter, p. 446
3. Isoroku Yamamoto, p. 447
4. Battle of Midway, p. 449
5. Holocaust, p. 451
6. "Final Solution," p. 453
7. genocide, p. 453
8. D-Day, p. 458
9. Nuremberg Trials, p. 463
10. demilitarization, 464

REVIEW QUESTIONS

Answers may vary for some questions.

11. The German attack on Poland on September 1, 1939.

12. The Suez Canal was the key to getting to the oil fields of Southwest Asia.

13. To destroy the United States fleet.

14. By appealing to their hatred of European colonization, the idea of "Asia for the Asians."

15. *Kristallnacht,* forced emigration, relocation to ghettos in Poland.

16. genocide; concentration camps; death camps; gas chambers.

17. Governments needed to send food and other supplies to armies. Industry began producing war-related products, causing a shortage of consumer goods.

18. *Operation Overlord* was the largest sea, air, and land battle in history. It began on the beaches of Normandy, France, on June 6, 1944. It is also called the D-Day invasion.

19. Many homes and cities were destroyed; so people often had to go searching for a place to live; food was scarce in many areas; people often went in search of lost family members; postwar treaties sometimes forced people to move.

20. Democratization and demilitarization.

Visual Summary

Events of World War II

Europe		Pacific
Aug. 1939 Nonaggression pact between Germany and the Soviet Union	**1939**	
Sept. 1939 Germany invades Poland; World War II begins		
May 1940 Evacuation of British forces at Dunkirk		
Jun. 1940 France surrenders; the Battle of Britain begins	**1940**	
Jun. 1941 Germany invades the Soviet Union	**1941**	**Dec. 1941** Japanese attack Pearl Harbor; U.S. declares war on Japan
		Apr. 1942 Allies surrender in Philippines; Bataan Death March begins
Aug. 1942 Hitler orders attack on Stalingrad	**1942**	**May 1942** Allies turn back Japanese fleet in Battle of the Coral Sea
Nov. 1942 Allies land in North Africa		**Jun. 1942** Allies defeat Japan in Battle of Midway
Feb. 1943 Germans surrender at Stalingrad	**1943**	**Feb. 1943** Japanese abandon the island of Guadalcanal
Jun. 1944 Allies invade Europe on D-Day	**1944**	**Oct. 1944** Allies defeat Japan in Battle of Leyte
Dec. 1944 Battle of the Bulge begins		**Mar. 1945** Allies capture Iwo Jima
		Jun. 1945 Allies capture Okinawa
May 1945 Germany surrenders	**1945**	**Aug. 1945** Atomic bombs dropped on Hiroshima and Nagasaki
		Sep. 1945 Japan surrenders

TERMS & NAMES

Briefly explain the importance of each of the following during and after World War II.

1. blitzkrieg
2. Atlantic Charter
3. Isoroku Yamamoto
4. Battle of Midway
5. Holocaust
6. Final Solution
7. genocide
8. D-Day
9. Nuremberg Trials
10. demilitarization

REVIEW QUESTIONS

SECTION 1 *(pages 441–446)*
Hitler's Lightning War

11. What event finally unleashed World War II?

12. Why was capturing Egypt's Suez Canal so important to the Axis powers?

SECTION 2 *(pages 447–450)*
Japan Strikes in the Pacific

13. What was Yamamoto's objective at Pearl Harbor?

14. How did Japan try to win support from other Asian countries?

SECTION 3 *(pages 451–454)*
The Holocaust

15. Name two tactics that Hitler used to rid Germany of Jews before creating his "Final Solution."

16. What tactics did Hitler use during the "Final Solution"?

SECTION 4 *(pages 455–461)*
The Allies Are Victorious

17. Why were items rationed during the war?

18. What was *Operation Overlord?*

SECTION 5 *(pages 462–465)*
The Devastation of Europe and Japan

19. Why did Europeans leave their homes following the war?

20. What were two of the most important steps that MacArthur took in Japan following the war?

Interact *with* History

On page 440, you had to decide whether to bomb the civilian population in an enemy city to shorten a war. Now that you have read the chapter, what bombing incidents in World War II seem to reflect a decision to bomb civilians to speed victory? Remember to consider bombings carried out by both sides in the war.

Interact *with* History

Possible Responses: Students might mention the German Luftwaffe's bombing of Great Britain or the Allied bombing of Dresden. Students should consider whether the policy of bombing civilian populations was effective in winning victory.

CRITICAL THINKING

1. WAR LEADERS

Consider the personalities, tactics, and policies of Hitler, Rommel, MacArthur, and Churchill. What qualities do you think make a successful leader in war? Explain your answer.

2. WORLD WAR II BATTLES

Below is a list of World War II battles/conflicts. Copy the chart on your paper and specify for each whether the Axis powers or the Allied powers gained an advantage over their enemies.

Battle/Conflict	Allied or Axis Powers?
Battle of Britain	
War in the Balkans	
Pearl Harbor	
Battle of the Coral Sea	
Battle of Midway	
Battle of Stalingrad	

3. WAR GOALS

THEME EMPIRE BUILDING Compare and contrast Japan's and Germany's goals in World War II.

4. ANALYZING PRIMARY SOURCES

The following quotation comes from the August 29, 1945 edition of *The Christian Century*, a prominent Protestant journal. In this passage, the writer raises questions about the American use of the atomic bomb on the Japanese.

A VOICE FROM THE PAST
Perhaps it was inevitable that the bomb would ultimately be employed to bring Japan to the point of surrender. . . . But there was no military advantage in hurling the bomb upon Japan without warning. The least we might have done was to announce to our foe that we possessed the atomic bomb; that its destructive power was beyond anything known in warfare; and that its terrible effectiveness had been experimentally demonstrated in this country. . . . If she [Japan] doubted the good faith of our representations, it would have been a simple matter to select a demonstration target in the enemy's own country at a place where the loss of human life would be at a minimum. If, despite such warning, Japan had still held out, we would have been in a far less questionable position had we then dropped the bombs on Hiroshima and Nagasaki.

- Does *The Christian Century* oppose all use of the atomic bomb as a weapon of war? Explain.
- What advantages might the alternative proposed by *The Christian Century* have had in ending World War II?

CHAPTER ACTIVITIES

1. LIVING HISTORY: Unit Portfolio Project

THEME SCIENCE AND TECHNOLOGY Your unit portfolio project focuses on how science and technology influence history. For Chapter 16, you might use one of the following ideas to add to your portfolio:

- Do research and create a set of science and technology cards for important inventions developed or perfected during World War II. Include the following categories on your cards: *Name of Invention, Country, Year, Use in the War, Use Today.*
- Write a list of five questions that you would ask Robert Oppenheimer if you were on a committee deciding whether to develop an atomic bomb.
- Do research and create a science and technology time line for 1935–1945. Include major events of the war and five scientific and technological developments.

2. CONNECT TO TODAY: Cooperative Learning

THEME ECONOMICS During World War II, many nations, including the United States, converted their consumer-goods factories to produce vital products for the war effort. Today many of those factories still exist but are back to producing consumer goods.

Work with a team to prepare a short "company history."

Using the Internet, library, magazines, or Chamber of Commerce, do research on a consumer-goods company. (A consumer-goods company makes products for personal use or enjoyment—for example, cars, radios, clothing.) Look for a company that was around before 1945. (Several of today's important car and appliance manufacturers, as well as manufacturers of steel, tires, detergents, etc., existed before 1945.)

As you come up with ideas, try to find answers to questions such as: What products did the company make before World War II? During the war? After? What were working conditions like during the war? After the war? In a two- to three-page paper, write your company history. Include copies of any articles, photographs, or pictures that you find about the company.

3. INTERPRETING A TIME LINE

Revisit the unit time line on pages 358–359. Which two leaders do you think had the largest impact on events between 1939 and 1945? Why?

FOCUS ON GEOGRAPHY

Notice the locations in Europe of German death camps and labor camps.

- Which country had the most labor camps?
- Which country had the most death camps?

Connect to History
In what year did most of the death camps begin to operate? Why?

Legend:
- Labor camp
- Death camp
- 1942 Date founded
- Border, 1933

LATVIA — Jungernhof 1942
Baltic Sea
EAST PRUSSIA — Stutthof, 1939
Neuengamme, 1940
Bergen-Belsen 1943
Ravensbrück, 1936
Sachsenhausen, 1936
NETH.
Vught, 1943
GERMANY
Chelmnitz 1941 — Treblinka 1942 — Sobibor 1942
BELG.
Mittelbau-Dora, 1943
Buchenwald 1937
POLAND
Gross-Rosen 1941 — Majdanek 1942
Theresienstadt 1941
LUX.
Natzweiler 1941
Flossenbürg 1938
CZECH.
Auschwitz 1940
Plasow 1942 — Belzec 1942
FRANCE
Dachau 1933
Mauthausen, 1941
SWITZ.
AUSTRIA
Jasenovac, 1941
Jadovno, 1941
YUGOSLAVIA — Sajmiste, 1941
0 200 Miles
0 400 Kilometers
Adriatic Sea

---

1. LIVING HISTORY

Standards for Evaluation
Science and Technology cards should meet the following criteria:

- Divide information categories between two sides of each card.
- Present information clearly and succinctly.
- Include graphic information where possible for clarification.

Standards for Evaluation
Questions should meet these criteria:

- Show an understanding of Oppenheimer's work.
- Show an understanding of what such a weapon might be capable of doing.
- Present questions that reflect attitudes from different areas of public and governmental life at that time.

Standards for Evaluation
Time lines should meet the following requirements:

- Present information starting with 1935 on the left and ending with 1945 on the right.
- Show causal connections between science and technology leading to events of the war, or vice versa.
- Be arranged and lettered clearly.

2. CONNECT TO TODAY

Standards for Evaluation
Company histories should meet the following criteria:

- Explain the team's choice of company.
- Present clearly the progression of products from the company's founding to its wartime production.
- Include anecdotes from people who worked for the company during the war.
- Provide team opinions about the social or moral effects of the company's wartime work.

3. INTERPRETING A TIME LINE

Student answers should provide clear reasons and support for choosing two leaders as having had the greatest impact between 1939 and 1945.

FOCUS ON GEOGRAPHY

- Germany
- Poland

Connect to History In 1942. The death camps were part of the last stage of Hitler's "Final Solution" and construction on them did not begin until late 1941.

CRITICAL THINKING

1. WAR LEADERS
Possible Answers: An ability to unite large groups of people in a common cause; an ability to convince masses of people that the cause the leader represents is noble; a powerful or attractive personality; intelligence and flexibility, an ability to see many different angles of a situation.

2. WORLD WAR II BATTLES
Allied powers, Axis powers, Axis powers, a draw, Allied powers, Allied powers.

3. WAR GOALS
Answers may vary.
Japan: Wanted Europeans/Americans out of Asia, needed space for populations.
Germany: Wanted Germany to be ethnically pure, wanted to make up for losses suffered in World War I.
Both: Wanted to expand their territory, their wealth, their resources.

4. ANALYZING PRIMARY SOURCES
Possible Answers: No, *The Christian Century* does not seem to oppose all use of the bomb.
The strategy proposed by *The Christian Century* might have resulted in far fewer deaths and a far lower toll of physical destruction.

UNIT 5

Perspectives on the Present

1945–present

South Africa, April 1994

The long line of voters in this picture is remarkable for the fact that these South Africans are voting in their own country for the first time—and helping elect a black president, Nelson Mandela. The revolution that occurred in South Africa in the early 1990s is part of the ongoing worldwide struggle for democracy that began at the end of World War II. Many nations in Asia, Africa, Latin America, and Eastern Europe are emerging from decades of oppression and are striving to create their own forms of government and to ensure economic security for their people.

Because South Africa's racist policies were so repressive, many people feared that change would come only after armed conflict, as had happened in Angola and Zimbabwe. Instead, the white-controlled government and the black-controlled African National Congress worked together to open the political process to all South Africans.

The call for all races to work together for the future of South Africa was eloquently voiced by President Mandela in his 1994 inauguration speech:

". . . The time for the healing of wounds has come. The moment to bridge the chasms that divide us has come. The time to build is upon us . . . We understand it still that there is no easy road to freedom. We know it well that none of us acting alone can achieve success. We must therefore act together as a unified people, for national reconciliation, for nation building, for the birth of a new world. . . ."

468

Black South Africans wait to vote during the nation's first "all-races" election in April 1994. While the present era has been one of struggle and strife, it also has produced events that show people's continuing desire to achieve democracy and justice.

469

This unit describes the momentous political, social, and economic changes occurring around the globe after World War II.

With much of Europe and parts of Asia in ruins after World War II, the United States and the Soviet Union emerge as rival superpowers. Their political and military confrontations dominate world affairs for the next 40 years.

The end of World War II also heralds the end of colonialism, as native peoples in Africa, Asia, and the South Pacific demand independence. Although some European nations try to hold onto their colonies, others help native populations prepare for independent rule.

The 1980s and 1990s witness a dramatic shift toward democracy in many areas around the world. The Soviet Union dissolves into 15 separate republics, while military dictatorships fall in Latin America. Nigeria and South Africa pursue democratic goals, and China reforms its economy.

Advances in science, communications, and technology improve life for many people and help create a global economy. Nations around the world must adjust to new patterns of work, ensure the rights of their diverse populations, protect their environments, and achieve peaceful relations with their neighbors.

UNIT 5 Time Line

Perspectives on the Present

Teaching Strategies

Making Generalizations You might ask students to study the time line for Unit 5 to form generalizations about events highlighted there. Ask students to group some time-line events into categories from which they can try to detect general patterns. Categories might include:

- War and Revolution
- Decolonization
- Assassinations
- China
- South Africa
- The Middle East
- India and Pakistan

Generalization Charts You might ask students to create charts with three or four categories and events grouped under them in chronological order. Stress that events may fall into more than one category.

After the charts have been completed, students will examine the events within each category and create one generalization for each of them.

Numerous generalizations can be drawn from the events under these categories—for example, pace of decolonization, the development of the apartheid policy in South Africa, the evolution of China from the postwar era to the present, and many others. Students should be prepared to explain to the rest of the class the process by which they drew their general statements from the information listed in their charts.

	1945	1955	1965	1975
CHAPTER 17 1945–PRESENT **Restructuring the Postwar World**	**1945** *Yalta* Allied leaders meet to plan postwar world **1946** *Soviet Union, U.S.* Cold War begins **1946** *China* Civil war between Nationalists and Communists resumes **1950–53** *Korea* Korean War between North and South Korea **1953** *Iran* U.S. restores ousted shah to power	**1958** *China* Mao Zedong begins Great Leap Forward **1959** *Cuba* Fidel Castro overthrows Batista **1960** *Soviet Union* Soviets catch U.S. spy plane in U-2 incident **1961** *Cuba* Castro routs U.S.-supported invasion of Bay of Pigs	**1965** *Vietnam* U.S. sends troops to Vietnam **1966** *China* Red Guards begin Cultural Revolution in China **1969** *Vietnam* Nixon begins withdrawal of U.S. troops from Vietnam	
CHAPTER 18 1945–PRESENT **The Colonies Become New Nations**	**1946** *Philippines* Philippines gains independence from U.S. **1947** *India* Independent India becomes partitioned into India and Pakistan **1948** *Middle East* Israel becomes a nation **1948** *India* Gandhi is assassinated	**1957** *Ghana* Ghana achieves independence from Great Britain **1962** *Algeria* Algeria achieves independence from France **1964** *Kenya* Jomo Kenyatta becomes president	**1965** *Malaysia* Singapore becomes independent **1967** *Indonesia* Suharto becomes president **1971** *East Pakistan* East Pakistan becomes independent Bangladesh **1973** *Middle East* Arab forces attack Israel in the Yom Kippur War	
CHAPTER 19 1945–PRESENT **Struggles for Democracy**	**1946** *Argentina* Juan Perón is elected president and becomes a dictator **1948** *South Africa* National Party sets up apartheid	**1960** *South Africa* Police kill 69 demonstrators in Sharpeville Massacre **1964** *Brazil* A military government seizes power	**1966** *China* Mao Zedong launches Cultural Revolution **1967** *Nigeria* Biafra secedes and civil war erupts	
CHAPTER 20 1960–PRESENT **Global Interdependence**				

◀ 1990s *Afghanistan*

	1945	1955	1965	1975

470 Unit 5

CONNECTIONS ACROSS TIME AND PLACE

Revolutions You might ask students to do research to compare the revolutions mentioned in the time line that occurred from the 1940s to the 1960s with any that are ongoing at the present time.

Students might choose two revolutions (one past and one present) to compare and contrast the objectives, ideologies, and strategies behind each. Ask them to draw conclusions about how revolutions have changed or remained the same in the past 50 or so years.

MULTIPLE LEARNING STYLES

Visual Learners The three photographs included in the time line for Unit 5 are all images drawn from the 1990s. Ask students to go to books, magazines, and the Internet to find five additional images that they feel are characteristic of the 1990s.

After they have chosen their images, they may make a photocopy of the time line and add their new images of the 1990s. They should be prepared to explain to the rest of the class why they made their photo selections.

1979 *Iran* Shah flees Iran; Muslims take over government

1979 *Nicaragua* U.S. and Soviets support Marxist rebels

1979 *Afghanistan* Soviets invade Afghanistan

1981 *Iran* Islamic revolutionaries free U.S. hostages

► 1950s *China*

1979 *Middle East* Camp David Accords signed by Egypt's Sadat and Israel's Begin ends war between Egypt and Israel

1981 *Egypt* Anwar Sadat is assassinated

1984 *India* Indira Gandhi is assassinated

1987 *Middle East* Palestinians begin intifada

1993 *Israel* Israel grants Palestinians self-rule in Gaza Strip and West Bank

1995 *Israel* Prime Minister Yitzhak Rabin is assassinated

1997 *Congo* Laurent Kabila becomes president of Democratic Republic of the Congo

Living History
Unit 5 Portfolio Project

THEME Economics

Your portfolio for Unit 5 will show the economic changes within and among nations from World War II to the present. You will trace the growing global interdependence of the economies of all nations of the world.

Living History Project Choices
Each Chapter Assessment offers you choices of ways to show how the economies of the nations grew or shrank and became tied to the economies of others. Activities include the following:

Chapter 17 newscast, poster, skit

Chapter 18 list, chart, magazine article

Chapter 19 action list, poster, interview

Chapter 20 poem or song, map graph or chart

1978 *China* Deng Xiaoping begins Four Modernizations

1982 *Argentina* Britain defeats Argentina in war over Falkland Islands

1989 *Germany* Berlin Wall is knocked down

1989 *China* Student demonstrators killed in Tiananmen Square

1991 *Soviet Union* Soviet Union breaks up into 15 republics

1992 *Bosnia-Herzegovina* Serbs begin war against Muslims and Croats

1994 *South Africa* First all-race election; Nelson Mandela becomes president

1997 *Mexico* Single-party control of Mexican congress ends.

1997 *Hong Kong* Britain returns Hong Kong to China

▲ 1990s *South Africa*

1975 *Space* U.S. *Apollo* docks with Soviet *Soyuz* spacecraft

1975 *Finland* Helsinki Accords on Human Rights established

1986 *Space* Soviet space station *Mir* established in space

1991 *Middle East* Iraq takes over Kuwait, provoking Persian Gulf War

1992 *Brazil* Earth Summit Environmental Conference held in Rio de Janeiro

1995 *China* International Conference on Women held in Beijing

1995 *Worldwide* World Trade Organization established

Portfolio Project

Interaction with Environment The projects suggested for Unit 5 deal with the theme of both economic and environmental interdependence around the globe. Several projects deal with the contrasting characteristics of communism and capitalism—a major element of world events in the 20th century. They may also examine the growth of multinational corporations, the impact of economic conditions on immigration, or the effect of the global economy on the world's ecology.

Logical-Mathematical Learners At least one portfolio project suggestion per chapter in Unit 5 emphasizes the logical skills of listing, categorizing, and contrasting. In Chapter 19, for example, students are asked to create an action list for turning a communist country into a free-market economy. Logical-mathematical learners may want to select these projects to use their skills for organizing information and reducing it to its essentials.

The Western Civilization Videodisc

SECTION O: The Postwar Era: The New Global Civilization, 1945–1990s

Side One: Frame 46958

Universal Play Button

See Master Guide, page 335 for Section O.

PLANNING GUIDE

Restructuring the Postwar World

	Key Ideas	COPY MASTERS	ASSESSMENT
SECTION 1 Two Superpowers Face Off *pp. 475–481*	The Soviet Union builds a buffer zone in Eastern Europe, and the United States aids its Western European allies as it struggles to block Communist expansion.	*In-Depth Resources: Unit 5* • **Guided Reading,** p. 1 • **Literature:** from *The Nuclear Age,* p. 13 • **Connections Across Time and Cultures:** Restoring the Peace, p. 18 • **Science and Technology:** Super Spy Plane, p. 19	*Section 1 Assessment,* p. 480 *Formal Assessment* • Section Quiz, p. 211 *Alternative Assessment Book* • Standards for Evaluating a Cooperative Activity
SECTION 2 Communists Triumph in China *pp. 482–485*	China splits into two nations—one Communist and one not. Mao Zedong expands the Communist state and launches ambitious, but often disastrous, programs to transform its society.	*In-Depth Resources: Unit 5* • **Guided Reading,** p. 2 • **Skillbuilder Practice:** Interpreting Charts, p. 6 • **Primary Source:** from *No Tears for Mao,* p. 9	*Section 2 Assessment,* p. 485 *Formal Assessment* • Section Quiz, p. 212 *Alternative Assessment Book* • Standards for Evaluating a Cooperative Activity
SECTION 3 War in Korea and Vietnam *pp. 486–490*	The United States fights bloody wars to prevent Communist takeovers in Korea and Vietnam, but Korea remains split into Communist and non-Communist nations and Vietnam becomes Communist.	*In-Depth Resources: Unit 5* • **Guided Reading,** p. 3 • **Primary Source:** from *When Heaven and Earth Changed Places,* p. 10 • **History Makers:** Ho Chi Minh, p. 16	*Section 3 Assessment,* p. 490 *Formal Assessment* • Section Quiz, p. 213 *Alternative Assessment Book* • Standards for Evaluating a Cooperative Activity
SECTION 4 Cold War Around the World *pp. 491–495*	The United States and the Soviet Union compete for influence throughout the developing world by supporting rival factions in Latin America, Asia, and Africa.	*In-Depth Resources: Unit 5* • **Guided Reading,** p. 4 • **Geography Application:** The Cuban Missile Crisis, p. 7 • **Primary Source:** The Cuban Missile Crisis (Speech by John F. Kennedy), p. 11 • **History Makers:** Ruholla Khomeini, p. 17	*Section 4 Assessment,* p. 495 *Formal Assessment* • Section Quiz, p. 214 *Alternative Assessment Book* • Standards for Evaluating a Cooperative Activity
SECTION 5 The Cold War Thaws *pp. 496–499*	The Cold War begins to thaw as Khrushchev denounces Stalinism and U.S. leaders adopt a foreign policy of lessened tensions.	*In-Depth Resources: Unit 5* • **Guided Reading,** p. 5 • **Primary Source:** Political Cartoon, p. 12	*Section 5 Assessment,* p. 499 *Formal Assessment* • Section Quiz, p. 215 *Alternative Assessment Book* • Standards for Evaluating a Cooperative Activity
CHAPTER RESOURCES	**Chapter Overview** After World War II, the Soviet Union and the United States emerge as rivals. This rivalry is mainly diplomatic and strategic, but also leads both to become involved in military actions around the world. The rivalry dominates world politics for four decades.	*Telescoping the Times* • Chapter Summary, pp. 69–71 *Planning for Block Schedules* *Case Studies* • Case Study 3—The Soviet Union and China: Two World Powers, p. 30	*Chapter Assessment,* pp. 500–501 *Chapter Activities,* p. 501 *Formal Assessment* • Chapter Test, forms A and B, pp. 216–221 *Test Generator* *Alternative Assessment Book*

TECHNOLOGY

 Warm-Up Transparency 17

 Geography Transparencies
• GT33 The Berlin Airlift, 1948–1949

 INTERNET RESOURCES
www.mlworldhistory.com

 Warm-Up Transparency 17

 World Art and Cultures Transparencies
• AT72 *Spring Walk to the Chi-Ch'ang Park*

 INTERNET RESOURCES
www.mlworldhistory.com

 Warm-Up Transparency 17

 World Art and Cultures Transparencies
• AT73 *Laying a Road*

 Battles of the World
• Tet Offensive

 Electronic Library of Primary Sources
• from *Peace Without Conquest*

 INTERNET RESOURCES
www.mlworldhistory.com

 Warm-Up Transparency 17

 Critical Thinking Transparencies
• CT33 Global Superpowers Face Off

 Electronic Library of Primary Sources
• from *444 Days: The Hostages Remember*

 Warm-Up Transparency 17

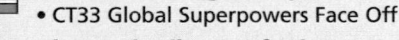 *Critical Thinking Transparencies*
• CT69 Visual Summary

 Electronic Library of Primary Sources
• Speech on Stalin by Nikita Khrushchev
• from *A Student's Diary*

 INTERNET RESOURCES
www.mlworldhistory.com

 Chapter Summaries on Audiocassette in English and Spanish

 INTERNET RESOURCES
www.mlworldhistory.com

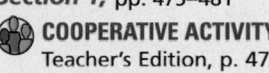 Block Scheduling (90 MINUTES)

Day 1
Section 1, pp. 475–481
 COOPERATIVE ACTIVITY
Teacher's Edition, p. 479
Section Assessment, p. 480

Day 2
Section 2, pp. 482–485
 COOPERATIVE ACTIVITY
Teacher's Edition, p. 484
Section Assessment, p. 485

Day 3
Section 3, pp. 486–490
 COOPERATIVE ACTIVITY
Teacher's Edition, p. 488
Section Assessment, p. 490

Day 4
Section 4, pp. 491–495
 COOPERATIVE ACTIVITY
Teacher's Edition, p. 493
Section Assessment, p. 490

Day 5
Section 5, pp. 496–499
 COOPERATIVE ACTIVITY
Teacher's Edition, p. 498
Section Assessment, p. 499
Chapter Assessment,
pp. 500–501

Yearly Pacing *Chapter 17 Total:* 5 days *Yearly Total:* 85 days

 Planning for Block Schedules

Customizing for Special Needs

Students Acquiring English

 Access for Students Acquiring English
• **Guided Reading** for Sections 1–5 (Spanish), pp. 184–188
• **Chapter Summary** (Spanish), pp. 181–183
• **Skillbuilder Practice :** Interpreting Charts (Spanish), p. 189
• **Geography Application** The Cuban Missile Crisis (Spanish), p. 190

 Spanish Reading Study Guide
• pp. 179–190

 Chapter Summaries on Audiocassette in English and Spanish

Less Proficient Readers

 In-Depth Resources: Unit 5
• **Guided Reading** for Sections 1–5, pp. 1–5
• **Skillbuilder Practice:** Interpreting Charts, p. 6
• **Geography Application:** The Cuban Missile Crisis, p. 7

 Telescoping the Times
• Chapter Summary, pp. 69–71

 Reading Study Guide
• pp. 179–190

 Chapter Summaries on Audiocassette

Gifted and Talented Students

 In-Depth Resources: Unit 5
Primary Sources:
• from *No Tears for Mao,* p. 9
• from *When Heaven and Earth Changed Places,* p. 10
• The Cuban Missile Crisis (Speech by John F. Kennedy), p. 11
• Political Cartoon p. 12

History Makers:
• Ho Chi Minh, p. 16
• Ruholla Khomeini, p. 17

Connections to Literature READINGS FOR STUDENTS

 In-Depth Resources: Unit 5
Literature: from *The Nuclear Age,* p. 13

Enrichment Reading

McDougal Littell
The Language of Literature, Grade 10
Le Ly Hayslip, from *When Heaven and Earth Changed Places,* p. 140
Tim O'Brien, "On the Rainy River," p. 266
Nguyen Thi Vinh, "Thoughts of Hanoi, p. 754

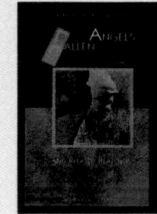

McDougal Littell
Literature Connections

• Myers, William Dean
Fallen Angels
(with related readings)

In this novel a small group of men come of age during the Vietnam War. Their experiences range from numbingly routine to traumatic and heartbreaking.

 = Pupil's Edition   = Overhead Transparency   = Software   = Video

= Copy Master   = CD-ROM   = Audiocassette   = Internet

Restructuring the Postwar World, 1945–present

Accessing Prior Knowledge

- Ask students what they already know about the Cold War.

Making Inferences

- After students look at the cartoon and caption about the U.S.-Soviet arms race, ask why they think these countries were hostile to each other.

- What can students infer from the images and captions about the effects of the U.S.-Soviet hostility on the rest of the world?

Geography Connection

Ask students to look at the colored areas of the map.

- Which countries make up the major Communist powers?

- What boundary line divides Europe into Communist and non-Communist areas?

CHAPTER 17

Restructuring the Postwar World, 1945–present

PREVIEWING THEMES

Economics

After World War II, two conflicting economic systems—capitalism and communism—competed for influence and power. The major players in this struggle, the United States and the Soviet Union, each tried to win other nations to its side.

Revolution

In Asia, Latin America, and Eastern Europe, people revolted against repressive governments or rule by foreign powers. These revolutions often became the arenas for conflicts between the United States and the Soviet Union.

Empire Building

The United States and the Soviet Union used military, economic, and humanitarian aid to extend their control over other countries. They also sought to prevent the other superpower from gaining influence.

INTERNET CONNECTION

Visit us at **www.mlworldhistory.com** to learn more about the Cold War and the wars in Korea and Vietnam.

COLD WAR ENEMIES, 1946

UNITED STATES

Beginning in the **late 1940s**, the **United States** and the **Soviet Union** faced off in a deadly arms race. Luckily for the world, each side merely stockpiled its weapons, afraid to make the first move.

ATLANTIC OCEAN

During the **late 1970s**, **Nicaragua** became the arena for a U.S. stand against communism. These Communist Nicaraguan rebels fought to end the dictatorship of their country's U.S.-supported regime. But they also supported leftist rebels in El Salvador. In response, the United States backed anti-Communist guerrillas in Nicaragua called Contras.

472

GEOGRAPHY THEMES

Place

Tell students that geography played an important role in the development of U.S. and Soviet Cold War strategies. Point out the huge landmass of the Soviet Union and the two oceans that surround the United States. Have them discuss how these factors may have influenced the countries' policies. *The oceans offered the United States natural defense and motivated its leaders to build air and sea power. In contrast, the Soviet Union was vulnerable to land invasion, which led Soviet leaders to build massive armies.*

Location

Ask students to note the caption arrows pointing at Nicaragua and Vietnam. What aspects of their location might have made these countries Cold War hot spots? As they read the chapter, students should verify their predictions and consider why other countries were drawn into Cold War struggles.

Vietnam, located next to China, could have served either as a wall to contain Communism or a funnel through which it would spread. Nicaragua, as part of North America, represented a stronghold against communism that was essential to the United States.

ADDITIONAL RESOURCES

Books for the Teacher

- Kutler, Stanley, ed. *Encyclopedia of the Vietnam War.* New York: Scribner's, 1996.

- Walker, Martin. *The Cold War: A History.* New York: Holt & Co., 1994.

Books for the Student

- Arms, Thomas S. *Encyclopedia of the Cold War.* New York: Facts on File, 1994.

- Denenberg, Barry. *Voices from Vietnam.* New York: Scholastic, 1995.

- Dudman, John. *The Division of Berlin.* Vero Beach, FL: Rourke, 1988.

▆▆▆ Videos

- *Berlin Airlift.* Britannica, 1990. 800-554-9862.

- *From Bay of Pigs to the Brink.* Films for the Humanities & Sciences, 1993. 800-257-5126.

- *Vietnam: A Case Study for Critical Thinking.* Society for Visual Education, 1987. 800-829-1900.

Software

- *Decisions, Decisions: The Cold War.* CD-ROM or Diskette. Tom Snyder Productions, 1996. 800-342-0236.

- *Seven Days in August: The Cold War's Defining Moment.* Social Studies School Service, 1995. 800-421-4246. Day-by-day look at the week in 1961 when the Berlin Wall went up.

SOVIET UNION

Iron Curtain

CHINA

PACIFIC OCEAN

Tropic of Cancer

Chinese youths waved banners and carried flowers and models of ICBM missiles to celebrate Soviet Premier Nikita Khrushchev's visit to **Beijing.** Despite this enthusiastic welcome, the two Communist giants split in **1959.**

Major Communist powers
Major Non-Communist power
Iron Curtain

0   1,000 Miles
0   2,000 Kilometers

0° Equator

Tropic of Capricorn

In **1975,** in the wake of the Vietnam War, this South Vietnamese man fled from his homeland with his family. The war devastated **Vietnam.** It also led to massive popular protests in the United States against U.S. military support for South Vietnam.

473

HISTORY THROUGH ART

South Vietnamese "Convoy of Tears"

This photograph was taken in March 1975, after the South Vietnamese government abandoned the central highlands and as many as 1.5 million people joined what came to be known as a "convoy of tears" in flight from their inland homes to the coast. An estimated 30,000 to 40,000 people died on this 15-day march, harrassed all the way by North Vietnamese army troops.

A Vietnamese participant described this tragic episode in a tragic war:

> The evacuees . . . included soldiers, children, very old people. . . . Refugees moving on foot were hit by Communist machine guns, falling down on the road. The blood flowed on the road like a tiny stream. The sound of roaring artillery and small arms, the screams of seriously wounded people at death's door, and children, created a voice out of hell.

Interpreting the Photograph How do you think the photographer of this scene felt? Do you think that photographers are justified in merely recording such human suffering rather than doing what they can to help? Why or why not?

Interact *with* History

This Interact with History feature motivates students by inviting them to imagine themselves the leader of the United States or the Soviet Union after World War II. As they consider their country's goals in the struggle between superpowers and the importance of a developing nation in achieving those goals, they will identify the issues, weigh their options, and become decision makers.

Purpose

- to set the stage for studying the Cold War
- to help students realize how the Cold War influenced world events
- to enable students to experience the issues that face powerful world leaders

Teaching Strategy

Thinking Critically After students have imagined themselves in the situation described on this page, have them answer the key question and give reasons for their decision.

EXAMINING *the* ISSUES

Following are suggestions for addressing each bulleted item.

❶ Ask students when they have been so angry at or afraid of someone that they would do anything to oppose the person, even if it meant hurting someone else.

❷ Have students consider how leaders of rival school social or academic groups enlist and mobilize their followers.

❸ Students may say that such countries might have to sacrifice either their ideals or their economic security.

Making Connections Ask students to discuss what they know about conflicts in countries such as Cuba, Nicaragua, El Salvador, and Guatemala.

Follow Up

A feature on the chapter assessment will ask students to reevaluate their responses to the situation presented on this page.

World War II has ended and two superpowers—the United States and the Soviet Union—dominate the world. You are the leader of one of those superpowers. Civil war has broken out in a developing country that supplies you with essential raw materials.

For that reason, it is important for you to help restore peace. The ruler of that country is a brutal dictator who makes life miserable for his people. Rebels are fighting to topple him, but they are backed by your superpower enemy.

Would you support the country's ruler or the rebels?

Rebel forces are skilled at guerrilla warfare. With weapons supplied by your superpower enemy and their knowledge of the land, they are powerful military opponents.

The developing country has rich natural resources that both superpowers need.

Life is difficult for the country's people. They suffer even more as the civil war continues.

474

EXAMINING *the* ISSUES

- What is most important to you—aiding the people of the developing nation or preventing your enemy from gaining influence there?

- How might competing superpowers use weaker countries in their competition?

- How might being caught in a struggle between superpowers affect a developing nation?

As a class, discuss the effects of the conflict between superpowers on the rest of the world. Think about the experiences of Latin American and other countries under colonialism and how those lessons might be useful.

As you read about how the two superpowers divided up the world, notice the part weaker countries played in their conflict.

Two Superpowers Face Off

TERMS & NAMES
- United Nations
- iron curtain
- containment
- Truman Doctrine
- Marshall Plan
- Cold War
- NATO
- Warsaw Pact
- brinkmanship
- U-2 incident

MAIN IDEA

The conflicting aims between the United States and the Soviet Union led to global competition.

WHY IT MATTERS NOW

The conflicts between these two superpowers played a major role in reshaping the modern world.

SETTING THE STAGE During World War II, the United States and the Soviet Union joined forces to fight against the Germans. The Soviet army marched west. The Americans marched east to meet them in a defeated Germany. When the Allied soldiers met at the Elbe River, they embraced each other warmly. Their leaders, however, regarded each other much more coolly.

Former Allies Diverge

Even before World War II ended, the U.S. alliance with the Soviet Union had begun to unravel. The United States was upset that Joseph Stalin, the Soviet Union's leader, had signed a nonaggression pact with Adolf Hitler, Germany's leader, in 1939. Later, Stalin blamed the Allies for delaying their invasion of German-occupied Europe until 1944. Driven by these and other conflicts, the two allies began to pursue opposing goals.

A Joint Postwar Plan In February 1945, the war was not yet over. But the leaders of the three Allied nations—the United States, Britain, and the Soviet Union—met in the Soviet Black Sea resort city of Yalta. There, they agreed to divide Germany into zones of occupation controlled by the Allied military forces. Germany also would have to pay the Soviet Union to compensate for its loss of life and property. Stalin promised that Eastern Europeans would have free elections. Skeptical Winston Churchill recognized this as an empty promise. And he predicted that Stalin would keep his pledge only if the Eastern Europeans followed "a policy friendly to Russia." In return, Stalin agreed to join the war against Japan, an ally of Germany.

Creation of the United Nations In June 1945, the United States and the Soviet Union temporarily set aside their differences. They joined 48 other countries in forming the **United Nations.** This international organization was intended to protect the members against aggression. It was to be based in New York. The 50 nations that signed the UN charter pledged "to save succeeding generations from the scourge of war."

The charter for the new peacekeeping organization established a large body called the General Assembly. This was like an international town meeting. Each UN member nation could cast its vote on a broad range of issues, including membership. An 11-member body called the Security Council had the real power to investigate and settle disputes, though. The five permanent members of the Security Council were Britain, China,

SPOTLIGHT ON

Yalta Conference

When the leaders of the United States, the Soviet Union, and Great Britain met at Yalta, their goals were noble ones:

- to promote world peace
- to provide emergency relief
- to help form interim governments based on the will of the people.

Prime Minister Winston Churchill (left) was optimistic about "the broad sunlight of victorious peace."

But "victorious peace" meant very different things to Stalin (right) and Roosevelt (center). The Soviet leader wanted a strong Communist state and protection against renewed invasion from the West. The ailing U.S. president wanted a democratic world led by his country. And those conflicting views made continuing peace impossible.

475

SECTION 1 RESOURCES

PRINT RESOURCES

IN-DEPTH RESOURCES: UNIT 5
Guided Reading, p. 1
Literature: from *The Nuclear Age,* p. 13
Connections Across Time and Cultures, p. 18
Science and Technology: Super Spy Plane, p. 19

ACCESS FOR STUDENTS ACQUIRING ENGLISH
Guided Reading (Spanish), p. 184

FORMAL ASSESSMENT
Section Quiz, p. 211

TECHNOLOGY RESOURCES

GEOGRAPHY TRANSPARENCIES
GT33 The Berlin Airlift, 1948–1949

INTERNET www.mlworldhistory.com

Section 1 Overview

OBJECTIVES

① To explain the U.S.-Soviet post-war split.

② To trace how the Soviets came to dominate Eastern Europe.

③ To describe U. S. containment of Communist expansion.

④ To define the Cold War.

SKILLBUILDERS

- Interpreting charts, pp. 476, 478
- Interpreting maps: location, place, p. 477

CRITICAL THINKING

- Summarizing, p. 476
- Analyzing causes, p. 477
- Making inferences, pp. 478, 481
- Analyzing issues, p. 479
- Recognizing effects, p. 480
- Analyzing motives, p. 480
- Comparing, p. 481

FOCUS

5-Minute Warm-Up

▶ *Clarifying*
To help students understand the players in the Cold War, have them answer these questions.

1. Look at the chart on page 476. Which country wanted to reunite Germany?

2. Which country wanted to control Eastern Europe?

WARM-UP TRANSPARENCY 17

OBJECTIVE ① INSTRUCT

Former Allies Diverge

▶ *Key Ideas*
- Britain, the Soviet Union, and the United States partition Germany after the war.
- Fifty countries form the United Nations to promote peace.
- The United States and the Soviet Union pursue conflicting goals in Europe.

IN-DEPTH RESOURCES: UNIT 5
Guided Reading, p. 1

ACCESS FOR STUDENTS ACQUIRING ENGLISH
Guided Reading (Spanish), p. 184

France, the United States, and the Soviet Union. Each could veto any Security Council action. This provision was intended to prevent any members of the Council from voting as a bloc to override the others.

France, the United States, and the Soviet Union. Each could veto any Security Council action. This provision was intended to prevent any members of the Council from voting as a bloc to override the others.

Differing U.S. and Soviet Goals Despite their agreement at Yalta and their mutual presence on the UN Security Council, the United States and the Soviet Union split sharply after the war ended. The war had affected these two superpowers very differently. The United States, the world's richest and most powerful country at that time, suffered 400,000 deaths. Its cities and factories remained intact, however. The Soviet Union experienced at least 50 times as many fatalities. One in four Soviets was wounded or killed. In addition, many Soviet cities were demolished. These contrasting situations, as well as striking political and economic differences, affected the two countries' postwar goals. As the following chart shows, their aims in postwar Europe were contradictory.

Superpower Aims in Europe	
United States	**Soviet Union**
• Encourage democracy in other countries to help prevent the rise of Communist governments	• Encourage communism in other countries as part of a worldwide workers' revolution
• Gain access to raw materials and markets to fuel booming industries	• Rebuild its war-ravaged economy using Eastern Europe's industrial equipment and raw materials
• Rebuild European governments to promote stability and create new markets for American goods	• Control Eastern Europe to protect Soviet borders and balance the U.S. influence in Western Europe
• Reunite Germany to stabilize it and increase the security of Europe	• Keep Germany divided to prevent its waging war again

> **SKILLBUILDER: Interpreting Charts**
> 1. *Which Soviet aims involved self-protection?*
> 2. *Which U.S. and Soviet aims in Europe conflicted?*

The Soviet Union Corrals Eastern Europe

With the end of World War II, a major goal of the Soviet Union was to shield itself from another invasion from the west. Even before the devastation of World War II, centuries of history had taught the Soviets to fear invasion. Because it lacked natural western borders, Russia fell victim to each of its neighbors in turn. In the 17th century, the Poles captured the Kremlin. During the next century, the Swedes attacked. Napoleon overran Moscow in 1812. The Germans invaded Russia during World War I.

Soviets Build a Wall of Satellite Nations As the war drew to a close, the Soviet Union pushed the Nazis back across Eastern Europe. By the end of the war, Soviet troops occupied a strip of countries along the Soviet Union's own western border. The Soviet Union regarded these countries as a necessary buffer, or wall of protection. Stalin ignored the agreement made in Yalta to allow free elections in Eastern Europe. He installed or secured Communist governments in Albania, Bulgaria, Hungary, Czechoslovakia, Romania, Poland, and Yugoslavia.

The Soviet leader's American partner at Yalta, President Franklin D. Roosevelt, had died on April 12, 1945. Roosevelt's successor, President Harry S. Truman, was a tougher adversary for Stalin. To the new president, Stalin's reluctance to allow free elections in Poland and other Eastern European nations represented a clear violation of those countries' rights. Truman, Stalin, and Churchill met at Potsdam, Germany, in July 1945. There, President Truman pressed Stalin to permit free elections in Eastern Europe. The Soviet leader refused. In a speech in early 1946, Stalin declared that

---

THINK THROUGH HISTORY
A. Summarizing Why did the United States and the Soviet Union split after the war?
A. Answer Their basic aims were in conflict: the U.S. was interested in promoting the economic recovery and growth of Western Europe, and the Soviet Union was interested in protecting itself and spreading communism.

The Cold War World, 1949

Communist countries
Non-Communist countries

Iron curtain

North Sea

Baltic Sea

NORWAY
SWEDEN
FINLAND
DENMARK
GREAT BRITAIN
IRELAND
NETH.
BELG.
LUX.
E. GER.
WEST GERMANY
POLAND
CZECHOSLOVAKIA
FRANCE
SWITZ.
AUSTRIA
HUNGARY
ITALY
YUGOSLAVIA
ROMANIA
BULGARIA
ALBANIA
GREECE
TURKEY
SPAIN
PORTUGAL

SOVIET UNION

ATLANTIC OCEAN

Mediterranean Sea

Black Sea

Caspian Sea

Aral Sea

0   500 Miles
0   1,000 Kilometers

DENMARK
POLAND
NETH.
British Zone
Berlin
EAST GERMANY
WEST GERMANY
French Zone
CZECHOSLOVAKIA
FRANCE
American Zone
AUSTRIA
SWITZ.
ITALY

Iron curtain

0   200 Miles
0   400 Kilometers

50° N

GEOGRAPHY SKILLBUILDER: Interpreting Maps
1. **Location** In which part of Germany was Berlin located?
2. **Place** Which countries separated the Soviet Union from Western Europe?

communism and capitalism could not exist in the same world. He said that war between the United States and the Soviet Union was certain.

The Iron Curtain Divides East and West Europe now lay divided between East and West. Germany's postwar fate, which had been decided at Yalta, left the country split into two sections. The Soviets controlled the eastern part, including half of Germany's capital, Berlin. Under a Communist government, East Germany was named the German Democratic Republic. The western zones became the Federal Republic of Germany in 1949. Winston Churchill described the division of Europe:

A VOICE FROM THE PAST
From Stettin in the Baltic to Trieste in the Adriatic, an iron curtain has descended across the continent. Behind that line lie all the capitals of the ancient states of Central and Eastern Europe. . . . All these famous cities and the populations around them lie in the Soviet sphere and all are subject in one form or another, not only to Soviet influence but to a very high and increasing measure of control from Moscow.
WINSTON CHURCHILL, "Iron Curtain" speech, March 5, 1946

THINK THROUGH HISTORY
B. Analyzing Causes What events led to the division of Europe?
B. Answer Soviets surrounding themselves with an "iron curtain" of Communist satellites and refusing to allow free elections.

Churchill's phrase **"iron curtain"** came to represent Europe's division between a mostly democratic Western Europe and a Communist Eastern Europe. From behind the iron curtain, Stalin termed Churchill's words a "call to war."

United States Counters Soviet Expansion
Soviet-American relations continued to worsen in 1946 and 1947. An increasingly worried United States sought to offset the growing Soviet threat in Eastern Europe. President Truman declared that it was time to stop "babying the Soviets." He adopted a foreign policy called **containment**. Containment was a policy directed at blocking Soviet influence and preventing the expansion of communism. Containment policies included creating alliances and helping weak countries resist Soviet advances.

Restructuring the Postwar World **477**

History from Visuals

The Cold War World, 1949
Interpreting the Map To make sure students know how to read the map key, ask how many countries besides the Soviet Union were Communist? *Eight.* Which country did the iron curtain divide? *Germany.*

Extension Activity Ask students to determine which of those countries currently have Communist governments. *As of 1998, none of the countries were Communist.*

SKILLBUILDER Answers
1. East Germany.
2. Poland, Czechoslovakia, Hungary, Romania, Yugoslavia, Bulgaria, Albania, East Germany.

OBJECTIVE 3 INSTRUCT

United States Counters Soviet Expansion

▶ *Key Ideas*
- The U.S. pledges to support nations that resist communism.
- The U.S. Marshall Plan pours money into Western Europe.
- A U.S. and British airlift of supplies breaks a Soviet blockade of West Berlin.

 GEOGRAPHY TRANSPARENCIES
GT33 The Berlin Airlift, 1948–1949

CRITICAL THINKING ACTIVITY
CLASS TIME: 15 MINUTES

Evaluating
Have students rate the effectiveness of the Marshall Plan and the Berlin airlift in preventing the spread of communism on a scale that they devise. Ask them to explain their ratings.

TEACHING OPTIONS | **CONNECTIONS ACROSS THE CURRICULUM** | **EXPLORING PRIMARY SOURCES**

Literature The Cold War affected not only politics, but literature as well. Both espionage novels and science fiction took on new dimensions as writers reflected the realities of the Cold War. Spy novels such as John le Carré's *The Spy Who Came In from the Cold,* for example, include agents with double agendas and sophisticated technology.

Science fiction works such as Ray Bradbury's *The Martian Chronicles* and Jack Finney's *The Body Snatchers* explore what the world might be like if Cold War trends in nuclear weapons and pervasive fear continued. Have students read one of these books and write a report that addresses how realistic it seems in today's world.

A Voice from the Past Winston Churchill was not only a participant in, but was also an eloquent commentator on, his eventful times. His speeches were particularly stirring and are among the most memorable in the English language.

Read Churchill's first speech as Prime Minister (May 1940) on the CD-ROM that

accompanies this text, or have students read selections from his collected speeches, *End of the Beginning: War Speeches,* or from his six-volume masterpiece, *The Second World War.*

Teacher's Edition **477**

The Truman Doctrine In a speech asking Congress for foreign aid for Turkey and Greece, President Truman contrasted democracy with communism:

> ### A VOICE FROM THE PAST
> One way of life is based upon the will of the majority, and is distinguished by free institutions . . . free elections . . . and freedom from political oppression. The second way of life is based upon the will of a minority forcibly imposed upon the majority. It relies upon terror and oppression . . . fixed elections, and the suppression of personal freedoms. I believe it must be the policy of the United States to support free people who are resisting attempted subjugation by armed minorities or by outside pressures.
> **HARRY S. TRUMAN,** speech to Congress, March 12, 1947

Truman's support for countries that rejected communism was called the **Truman Doctrine.** It caused great controversy. Some opponents objected to American interference in other nations' affairs. Others argued that the United States lacked the resources to carry on a global crusade against communism. Still others pointed out that some U.S. support would go to dictators. Congress, however, immediately authorized over $400 million in aid to Turkey and Greece.

The Marshall Plan Much of Western Europe lay in ruins after the war. Europe's problems included record-breaking cold and snow, postwar unemployment, lack of food, and economic turmoil. In June 1947, U.S. Secretary of State George Marshall proposed that America give aid to any European country that needed it. This assistance program, called the **Marshall Plan,** would provide food, machines, and other materials. As Congress debated the $12.5 billion program in February 1948, the Communists seized power in Czechoslovakia. Congress immediately approved the Marshall Plan. The plan achieved spectacular success in Western Europe and in Yugoslavia.

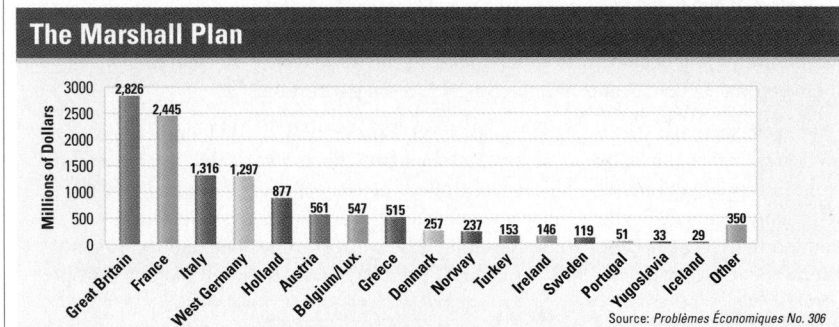

The Marshall Plan

[Bar chart titled "The Marshall Plan", y-axis "Millions of Dollars": Great Britain 2,826; France 2,445; Italy 1,316; West Germany 1,297; Holland 877; Austria 561; Belgium/Lux. 547; Greece 515; Denmark 257; Norway 237; Turkey 153; Ireland 146; Sweden 119; Portugal 51; Yugoslavia 33; Iceland 29; Other 350. Source: *Problèmes Économiques No. 306*]

> **SKILLBUILDER: Interpreting Charts**
> 1. *Which country received the most aid from the United States?*
> 2. *Why do you think Great Britain and France received so much aid?*

The Berlin Airlift While Europe began rebuilding, the United States and its allies clashed with the Soviet Union over Germany. The Soviets meant to keep their former enemy weak and divided. In 1948, France, Britain, and the United States decided to withdraw their forces from Germany. They would allow their three occupation zones to form one nation. The Soviet Union responded by holding West Berlin hostage.

Although Berlin lay well within the Soviet occupation zone of Germany, it too had been divided into four zones. The Soviet Union cut off highway, water, and rail traffic into Berlin's western zones. Since no supplies could get in, the city faced starvation. Stalin gambled that the threat would frighten Western countries. He hoped it would force them to surrender West Berlin or give up their idea of reunifying Germany.

The Soviet leader lost his gamble. To break the blockade, American and British officials flew food and supplies into West Berlin. For nearly 11 months, planes took

OBJECTIVE 4 INSTRUCT

The Cold War and a Divided World

▶ **Key Ideas**
• The United States and the Soviet Union each organize a military alliance.
• Both superpowers acquire nuclear and thermonuclear weapons.
• The two superpowers compete for control of the skies.

📖 **IN-DEPTH RESOURCES: UNIT 5**
Literature: from *The Nuclear Age*, p. 13

THINK THROUGH HISTORY
D. Analyzing Issues What Soviet actions were the Truman Doctrine, the Marshall Plan, and the Berlin airlift responses to?
D. Answer The aggressive spread of communism and the Soviet blockade of West Berlin.

off and landed every three minutes. In 277,000 flights, pilots brought in 2.3 million tons of supplies—food, fuel, medicine, and even Christmas presents. The Soviet Union, admitting defeat, lifted the Berlin blockade in May 1949.

The Cold War and a Divided World

These increasing conflicts were the beginnings of the **Cold War.** This was a state of diplomatic hostility that developed between the two superpowers. Beginning in 1949, the superpowers used spying, propaganda, diplomacy, and secret operations in their dealings with each other. Much of the world allied with one side or the other. In fact, until the Soviet Union finally broke up in 1991, the Cold War dictated not only U.S. and Soviet foreign policy. It influenced world alliances as well.

Rival Alliances The Berlin blockade heightened Western Europe's fears of Soviet aggression. As a result, in 1949, ten Western European nations joined with the United States and Canada to form a defensive military alliance. This alliance was called the North Atlantic Treaty Organization (**NATO).** These nations promised to meet an attack on any NATO member with armed force. For the United States, NATO membership marked the country's first peacetime military commitment.

The Soviet Union viewed NATO as a threat. In response, the Soviets developed an alliance system in 1955 as part of their own containment policy. It was known as the **Warsaw Pact.** This alliance included the Soviet Union, Poland, East Germany, Czechoslovakia, Hungary, Romania, Bulgaria, and Albania.

In the 1950s, the United States also organized several other alliances to fight the threat of communism. In 1955 SEATO—Southeast Asia Treaty Organization—was formed to stabilize that area after open military aggression occurred in Korea and Indochina.

Nuclear Threat As these alliances were forming, the Cold War threatened to heat up enough to destroy the world. The United States already had atomic bombs. As early as 1949, the Soviet Union exploded its own atomic weapon. The superpowers had both become nuclear powers.

President Truman was determined to develop an even more deadly weapon before the Soviets did. He authorized work on a thermonuclear weapon in January 1950. This

Background
The East Germans built a wall in 1961 to separate East and West Berlin. This Berlin Wall symbolized the division of the world into rival camps.

Children in West Berlin in 1948 welcome planes that landed every few minutes with supplies to break the Soviet blockade of the city.

CRITICAL THINKING ACTIVITY
CLASS TIME: 15 MINUTES

Debating
Suggest that students debate whether or not a thermonuclear war could be won.

MORE ABOUT . . .
NATO
In 1949, when NATO was formed, the Soviet Union had 30 military divisions stationed in Eastern Europe. The Western European nations had deployed a combined total of about 18 divisions. Even so, Americans were not unanimous in their support for NATO. Influential Republicans such as Senator Robert Taft attacked the treaty because he thought the United States should return to its prewar tradition of isolation from global affairs. Hard lobbying by Truman and members of his cabinet turned the tide, however. The final vote was 83–13 in favor of joining the alliance.

Restructuring the Postwar World **479**

Task: Students will write memos to President Truman advising him on nuclear policy.

Purpose: To explore the complexities of nuclear issues in the Cold War era.

Activity: Divide the class into small groups. Each group will act as a consultant to President Truman as he faces a decision about developing a thermonuclear weapon. Suggest that each group first analyze

positive and negative consequences of developing the hydrogen bomb. The groups should then construct an argument supporting their recommendation. Have them write a memo urging the president either to authorize or to abandon development of the H-bomb.

📁 **Building a Portfolio:** Suggest that students include their discussion notes and memos in their portfolios.

Standards for Evaluation
Memos should . . .
• make a clear recommendation
• support the recommendation with logical reasons
• respond to possible opposing arguments
• reflect an accurate understanding of the issues

ASSESS & RETEACH

Section 1 Assessment
Suggest that students review the political cartoon on page 472 and the chart on page 476 before completing question 4.

Section Quiz
FORMAL ASSESSMENT
Section Quiz, p. 211

Reteaching Activity
CLASS TIME: 10 MINUTES

Use the chart on page 476 to review the basis for the U.S.-Soviet split after World War II.

CLOSE ACTIVITY

CLASS TIME: 10 MINUTES

Identifying Main Ideas
Have students work in small groups and write a series of eight to ten newspaper headlines that summarizes the main events of this section.

---

hydrogen or H-bomb would be thousands of times more powerful than the A-bomb. Its power came from the fusion, or joining together, of atoms, rather than from the splitting of atoms, as in the A-bomb. In November 1952, the United States successfully tested the first H-bomb. By August of the following year, the Soviets had exploded their own thermonuclear weapon.

Dwight D. Eisenhower became the U.S. president in 1953. He appointed the firmly anti-Communist John Foster Dulles as his secretary of state. If the Soviet Union or its supporters attacked U.S. interests, Dulles threatened, the United States would "retaliate instantly, by means and at places of our own choosing." This willingness to go to the brink, or edge, of war became known as **brinkmanship.**

Brinkmanship required a reliable source of nuclear weapons and airplanes to deliver them. So the United States strengthened its air force and began producing stockpiles of nuclear weapons. In response, the Soviet Union made its own collection of nuclear bombs. This arms race would go on for four decades.

The Cold War in the Skies The Cold War also affected the science and education programs of the two countries. In August 1957, the Soviets announced the development of a rocket that could travel great distances. This was a true intercontinental ballistic missile, or ICBM. On October 4, the Soviets used an ICBM to push the first unmanned satellite above the earth's atmosphere.

The launching of this Soviet satellite, *Sputnik I*, made Americans feel as if they had fallen behind in science and technology. In response, the U.S. government poured huge amounts of money into education, especially in science, mathematics, and foreign languages. Within months, by January 1958, the United States had successfully launched its own satellite.

In 1960, the skies provided the arena for an even more serious showdown between the superpowers. Five years earlier, President Eisenhower proposed an "open skies" policy. This policy stated that the United States and the Soviet Union could fly freely over each other's territory to guard against surprise nuclear attacks. The Soviet Union rejected Eisenhower's proposal. In response, the U.S. Central Intelligence Agency (CIA) authorized secret high-altitude spy flights over Soviet territory in planes called U-2s. In May 1960, a Soviet pilot brought down a U-2 plane, and its pilot, Francis Gary Powers, was captured. The Soviets sentenced him to ten years in prison but released him after 19 months. This **U-2 incident** brought mistrust and tensions between the superpowers to a new height.

While Soviet Communists were squaring off against the United States, Communists in China were fighting an internal battle for control of that country.

The Cold War took to the skies as the United States and the Soviet Union raced to produce ICBMs. Missiles like this one were capable of inflicting destruction from great distances.

Section 1 Assessment

1. TERMS & NAMES
Identify
• United Nations
• iron curtain
• containment
• Truman Doctrine
• Marshall Plan
• Cold War
• NATO
• Warsaw Pact
• brinkmanship
• U-2 incident

2. TAKING NOTES
Using a web diagram like the one below, list the causes of the Cold War between the United States and the Soviet Union.

Cold War

Which cause was a direct result of World War II? Explain.

3. ANALYZING MOTIVES
What were Stalin's objectives in supporting Communist governments in Eastern Europe?

THINK ABOUT
• the effects of World War II
• the location of the Soviet Union
• U.S. aims in Europe

4. THEME ACTIVITY
Economics Draw a cartoon that shows either capitalism from the Soviet point of view or communism from the U.S. point of view.

480 Chapter 17

ANSWERS

1. TERMS & NAMES
United Nations, p. 475
iron curtain, p. 477
containment, p. 477
Truman Doctrine, p. 478
Marshall Plan, p. 478
Cold War, p. 479
NATO, p. 479
Warsaw Pact, p. 479
brinkmanship, p. 480

U-2 incident, p. 480

2. TAKING NOTES
Incompatible political and economic philosophies; conflicting aims in Europe; desire for world domination; Soviet defiance of Yalta agreement; Berlin blockade. *Possible Responses:* Conflicting aims in Europe,

Soviet defiance of Yalta agreement, Berlin blockade.

3. ANALYZING MOTIVES
To protect borders; to counteract U.S. influence in Europe; to have access to raw materials to help rebuild war-ravaged country; to keep Germany from rebuilding and attacking Russia again.

4. THEME ACTIVITY
Standards for Evaluation
An effective cartoon should meet the following criteria:
• Shows differences between capitalism and communism
• Shows a distinct point of view
• Is clear and consistent

The Space Race

Beginning in the late 1950s, the United States and the Soviet Union competed for influence not only among the nations of the world, but in the skies as well. Once the superpowers had ICBMs to deliver nuclear warheads and aircraft for spying missions, they both began to develop technology that could be used to explore—and ultimately control—space.

The Soviet Union launched *Sputnik,* the first successful artificial space satellite, on October 4, 1957. As it circled the earth every 96 minutes, Premier Nikita Khrushchev boasted that his country would soon be "turning out long-range missiles like sausages." Unable to let this challenge go unanswered, the United States began beefing up its own space program. Its first attempts failed, however, and became known as "Stayputnik" or "Flopnik."

In a major technological triumph, the United States put human beings on the moon on July 20, 1969. In this historic "giant leap for mankind," astronaut Buzz Aldrin plants the U.S. flag and leaves his footprints on the lunar surface.

United States

1961 First American in space (Alan Shepard)	**1969** First manned lunar landing	**1977** *Voyager 2* launched to Jupiter, Saturn, Uranus, and Neptune	**1997** *Mars Pathfinder* explores surface of Mars
1962 First American orbits the earth (John Glenn, Jr.)	**1976** *Viking 1* lands on Mars	**1981** Space shuttle *Columbia* launched	**1992** *Mars Observer* launched

1960 — 1970 — 1980 — 1990

1975 U.S. and Soviet Union launch first joint space mission

1995 U.S. shuttle *Discovery* links up with Soviet Space Station *Mir*

1960 — 1970 — 1980 — 1990

1970 *Venera 7* lands on Venus

1971 First manned space station *(Salyut 1)*

1988 Cosmonauts spend 366 days on space station *Mir*

1963 First woman in space (Valentina Tereshkova)

1997 Two spacecraft land on Mars

1961 First human orbits the earth (Yuri Gagarin)

1959 *Luna 2* probe reaches the moon

Soviet Union

This view of the Soviet spacecraft *Soyuz* taken from the window of the U.S. *Apollo* in 1975 shows the curve of the earth beneath them. It symbolizes the superpowers' realization that they would have to coexist in space as well as on earth.

Connect *to* History

Comparing Which destinations in space did both the United States and the Soviet Union explore?

SEE SKILLBUILDER HANDBOOK, PAGE 654

Connect *to* Today

Making Inferences What role might space continue to play in achieving world peace?

Restructuring the Postwar World **481**

The space race developed out of the Cold War superpowers' search for military dominance. In reality, however, the skies have provided an opportunity for the United States and the Soviet Union, and now Russia, to learn to cooperate and peacefully coexist.

CRITICAL THINKING ACTIVITY
CLASS TIME: 15 MINUTES

Evaluating
Inform students that the U.S. *Mars Surveyor* is slated to land a spacecraft on Mars every 26 months until 2003. The cost to the American public will be approximately $100 million a year. Discuss whether students think this expenditure is justified. Why or why not?

MORE ABOUT . . .
Current Space Exploration
U.S. astronauts and Russian cosmonauts work together on the Russian space station *Mir.* They took a joint six-hour space walk in September 1997 to repair damage to the space station's exterior. Meanwhile, the United States landed the *Pathfinder* spacecraft on Mars on July 4, 1997. A robot explored the planet's surface and sent images back to earth that were seen by millions of people. The *Pathfinder* mission discovered that Mars may have once had water and supported primitive life.

IN-DEPTH RESOURCES: UNIT 5
Science & Technology: Super Spy Plane, p. 19

Connect *to* History

Comparing
Both countries have sent missions to explore the moon, Venus, and Mars.

Connect *to* Today

Making Inferences
The United States and Russia continue to cooperate in the exploration of space. The two countries are using space flights to test new metals and industrial materials, to learn more about the structure of the universe, and to research topics such as people's responses to aging and disease. Such joint research projects for peaceful purposes cannot help but contribute to world peace.

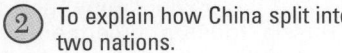
① To analyze the civil war between the Nationalists and the Communists in China.

② To explain how China split into two nations.

③ To describe how Mao's Marxist regime transformed China.

SKILLBUILDER
• Interpreting charts, p. 483

CRITICAL THINKING
• Recognizing effects, p. 483
• Analyzing issues, p. 484
• Making inferences, p. 485
• Identifying problems, p. 485
• Analyzing themes, p. 485

FOCUS
5-Minute Warm-Up

▶ *Interpreting Charts*
To help students understand the political climate in China after World War II, have them answer these questions.

1. Look at the chart on page 483. Which side did the Soviet Union support?

2. Which side had a weak military organization?

 WARM-UP TRANSPARENCY 17

OBJECTIVE ① INSTRUCT

Civil War in China

Key Ideas
• Mao Zedong's Communist guerrillas battle Jiang Jieshi's Nationalists after World War II.

• Despite massive U.S. support, the Communists defeat the unpopular Nationalists.

 IN-DEPTH RESOURCES: UNIT 5
Guided Reading, p. 2
Primary Source: from *No Tears for Mao*, p. 9

 ACCESS FOR STUDENTS ACQUIRING ENGLISH
Guided Reading (Spanish), p. 185

WORLD ART AND CULTURES TRANSPARENCIES
AT72 *Spring Walk to the Chi-Ch'ang Park*

TERMS & NAMES
• Mao Zedong
• Jiang Jieshi
• commune
• Red Guards
• Cultural Revolution

② Communists Triumph in China

MAIN IDEA	WHY IT MATTERS NOW
After World War II, Chinese Communists defeated Nationalist forces and two separate Chinas emerged.	China remains a Communist country and a major player on the world stage.

SETTING THE STAGE In World War II, China fought on the side of the victorious Allies. During the war, however, Japan's occupation armies devastated China's major cities. China's civilian death toll alone was in the millions. This vast country suffered casualties second only to those of the Soviet Union.

Civil War in China

When the Japanese invaded China in 1937, a bitter civil war was raging between the Nationalists and the Communists. During World War II, the political opponents temporarily united to fight the Japanese. With the war's end, however, they resumed their fight for control of the country.

Internal Struggles Under their leader, **Mao Zedong** (mow dzuh-dahng), the Communists held a stronghold in northwestern China. From there, they mobilized Chinese peasants for guerrilla war against the Japanese in the northeast. Thanks to their efforts to teach literacy and improve food production, the Communists won the peasants' loyalty. By 1945, Mao's Red Army controlled much of northern China.

Meanwhile, the Nationalist forces under **Jiang Jieshi** (jee-ahng jee-shee), whose name was formerly spelled Chiang Kai-shek, dominated southwestern China. Protected from the Japanese by rugged mountain ranges, Jiang gathered an army of 2.5 million men. Between 1942 and 1945, the United States sent the Nationalist army at least $1.5 billion in aid to fight the Japanese. Instead of benefiting the army, however, these supplies and money often ended up in the hands of a few corrupt officers. In addition, Jiang's army actually fought few battles against the Japanese. Instead, the Nationalist army saved its strength for the coming battle against Mao's Red Army. As soon as the Japanese surrendered, the Nationalists and Communists resumed their civil war.

Background
The Japanese had controlled Manchuria in northeast China since 1905. In 1937, they launched an all-out attack.

Background
The English spelling of Chinese words has been changed to make the pronunciation as close to Chinese as possible and to standardize it throughout the world.

Chinese peasants performed the backbreaking labor that supported the country. After World War II, the Communists worked hard to win their support.

Involvement of the United States That renewed civil war lasted from 1946 to 1949. At first, the Nationalists enjoyed a considerable advantage. Their army outnumbered the Communists' army by as much as three to one. And the United States provided nearly $2 billion more in aid.

The Nationalist forces, however, did little to win popular support. With China's economy collapsing, thousands of Nationalist soldiers deserted to the Communists. In spring 1949, China's major cities fell to the Red forces one by one. Mao's troops were well trained in guerrilla warfare. But they were also enthusiastic about his promised return of land to the peasants. The remnants of Jiang's shattered army fled south. In October 1949, Mao Zedong gained control of the country. He proclaimed it the

482

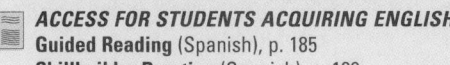
SECTION 2 RESOURCES

PRINT RESOURCES

 IN-DEPTH RESOURCES: UNIT 5
Guided Reading, p. 2
Skillbuilder Practice: Interpreting Charts, p. 6
Primary Source: from *No Tears for Mao*, p. 9

ACCESS FOR STUDENTS ACQUIRING ENGLISH
Guided Reading (Spanish), p. 185
Skillbuilder Practice (Spanish), p. 189

FORMAL ASSESSMENT
Section Quiz, p. 212

TECHNOLOGY RESOURCES

 WORLD ART AND CULTURES TRANSPARENCIES
AT72 *Spring Walk to the Chi-Ch'ang Park*

 INTERNET www.mlworldhistory.com

Chinese Political Opponents—1945

Nationalists		Communists
Jiang Jieshi	**LEADER**	Mao Zedong
Southern China	**AREA RULED**	Northern China
United States	**FOREIGN SUPPORT**	Soviet Union
Defeat of Communists	**DOMESTIC POLICY**	National liberation
Weak due to inflation and failing economy	**PUBLIC SUPPORT**	Strong due to promised land reform
Ineffective, corrupt leadership and poor morale	**MILITARY ORGANIZATION**	Experienced, motivated guerrilla army

SKILLBUILDER: Interpreting Charts
1. *Which party's domestic policy appealed more to Chinese peasants?*
2. *Which aspect of the Communist approach do you think was most responsible for Mao's victory?*

THINK THROUGH HISTORY
A. Recognizing Effects How did the outcome of the Chinese civil war contribute to Cold War tensions?
A. Possible Answer The victory of the Chinese Communists reinforced U.S. belief that the Communists were poised to take over the world.

People's Republic of China. Jiang and other Nationalist leaders retreated to the island of Taiwan, which westerners called Formosa.

Mao Zedong's victory fueled U.S. anti-Communist feelings. Those feelings only grew after the Chinese and Soviets signed a treaty of friendship in February 1950. Many people in the United States viewed the takeover of China as another step in a Communist campaign to conquer the world.

Two Chinas and the Cold War

China had split into two nations. One was the island of Taiwan, or Nationalist China, with an area of 13,000 square miles. The mainland, or People's Republic of China, had an area of more than 3.5 million square miles. The existence of two Chinas, and the conflicting international loyalties they inspired, intensified the Cold War.

The Superpowers React After Jiang Jieshi fled to Taiwan, the United States helped him set up a Nationalist government on that small island. They called it the Republic of China. The Soviets gave financial, military, and technical aid to the Communist People's Republic of China. In addition, the Chinese and the Soviets pledged to come to each other's defense if either country were attacked.

The United States responded by attempting to enlarge its own sphere of influence in Asia. For example, the United States limited the Soviet Union's occupation of Japan to only the few small islands it had gained at the Yalta talks. The two superpowers divided up Korea into a Soviet-supported Communist north and a U.S.-supported south.

Communist China Continues to Expand In the early years of Mao's reign, Chinese troops expanded into southern, or Inner, Mongolia, Tibet, and India. Northern, or Outer, Mongolia, which bordered the Soviet Union, remained in the Soviet sphere. After declaring Inner Mongolia an "Autonomous Area," China challenged that autonomy. It took control of the country.

In a brutal assault in 1950 and 1951, China also took control of Tibet. This was another so-called Autonomous Area. The Chinese promised autonomy to Tibetans, who followed the religious leader, the Dalai Lama. When China's control over Tibet tightened in the late 1950s, however, the Dalai Lama fled to India. Tibetans responded by rioting.

Vocabulary
autonomous: self-governing.

Restructuring the Postwar World **483**

History from Visuals

Chinese Political Opponents—1945

Interpreting the Chart Make sure students understand that the middle column identifies the topic of each row. Ask which rows help explain why the Nationalists lost to the Communists. *The last three.*

Extension Activity Have students examine a map and contrast the topography, cities, and resources of northern and southern China. Which area seems to be more developed and economically important? *Southern China.* Ask them to discuss how Mao triumphed given his weaker geographic position.

SKILLBUILDER ANSWERS
1. Communists.
2. Possible Responses: Military organization or public support.

OBJECTIVE 2 INSTRUCT

Two Chinas and the Cold War

▶ *Key Ideas*
• China splits into a tiny island nation aided by the United States and a huge mainland nation aided by the Soviet Union.
• Communist China expands into Mongolia and Tibet.

CRITICAL THINKING ACTIVITY
CLASS TIME: 10 MINUTES

Comparing and Contrasting
To help students understand the two Chinas, have them complete a Venn diagram such as this.

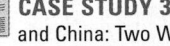

Nationalists U.S.-supported | Both Dictatorship | Communists Soviet-supported

CASE STUDY 3—The Soviet Union and China: Two World Powers, p. 30

TEACHING OPTION

SKILLBUILDER MINI-LESSON: Interpreting Charts

CLASS TIME 20 MINUTES

Explaining the Skill Charts offer a visual presentation of information that clarifies the relationships between ideas and makes them easier to grasp. In a chart, information is grouped into categories. Reading down the columns and across the rows of a chart offers a quick summary of the information in a particular category. It also makes the comparison and contrast between entries immediately clear.

Applying the Skill: Chinese Political Opponents—1945 Have students identify the titles of the rows and columns of this chart. *Rows— Leader, Area ruled, Foreign support, Domestic policy, Public support, Military organization; Columns— Nationalists, Communists.*

1. Based on the information in the chart, which characteristics did the Nationalists and Communists share? *None.*

2. Which category indicates that the conflict in China was part of the Cold War? *Foreign support.*

3. Which category indicates that the Nationalists and the Communists were directly opposed? *Domestic policy.*

 IN-DEPTH RESOURCES: UNIT 5
Skillbuilder Practice: Interpreting Charts, p. 6

Teacher's Edition **483**

Transformation and Revolution

Key Ideas
- Mao Zedong heads both the government and the Communist Party of China.
- Mao redistributes land to peasant collectives and nationalizes China's industries.
- Mao creates huge agricultural communes.
- China splits with the Soviet Union and retreats from Mao's extreme policies.
- In retaliation, Mao launches the Cultural Revolution, which leads to widespread chaos.

HISTORY MAKERS
Mao Zedong

In 1972, when President Nixon told Mao Zedong that his teachings had transformed China and affected the whole world, Mao replied, "All I have done is change Beijing and a few of its suburbs." Considering the size of China's population (a quarter of the world's total), however, Mao may have been the most influential leader of the 20th century. Suggest that students discuss how they would judge the influence of world leaders and create a standard for comparing them.

MORE ABOUT . . .
"The Great Leap Forward"

Mao thought the agricultural communes could make their own steel in "backyard steel furnaces." Though hundreds of these installations were built, they were a dismal failure. Workers sometimes melted down their household implements to make it seem as if they were producing steel. As one critic noted, knives were melted down to make steel which could then be used to make knives.

India welcomed the Dalai Lama and other Tibetan refugees after Tibet's failed revolt in 1959. As a result, resentment between India and China grew. In 1962, when India trespassed across the two countries' unclear border into China's territory, Mao unleashed his forces. China held its border, but resentment continued.

Transformation and Revolution

For decades China had been either at war with or occupied by Japan. Mao and the Communists moved rapidly to strengthen their rule over China's 550 million people. The Communists claimed to have a new "Mandate of Heaven." And they aimed to restore China as a powerful nation.

Transformation Under Mao Zedong After taking power, the Chinese Communists began to tighten their hold on the country. The party's 4.5 million members made up just one percent of the Chinese population. But they were a highly disciplined group. Like the Soviets, the Chinese Communists set up two parallel organizations. These were the Communist party and the national government. Until 1959, Mao ruled as both chairman of the Communist party and head of state.

Mao's Marxist Socialism Mao determined to reshape China's economy based on Marxist socialism. Eighty percent of the population still lived in rural areas. But most Chinese farmers owned no land. Instead, ten percent of the rural population controlled 70 percent of the farmland. Under the Agrarian Reform Law of 1950, Mao seized the holdings of these landlords. He then divided them among the peasants. His forces killed more than a million landlords who resisted this policy.

To further his socialist principles, between 1953 and 1957, Mao's government forced the peasants to join collective farms. These farms each consisted of 200 to 300 households. The Chinese Communists also eagerly embraced Marxist ideas about women and the family. They made women fully equal in the home and in the workplace. They also instituted state-sponsored child care.

Mao's changes also transformed industry and business. Gradually, the government nationalized all private companies, or brought them under government ownership. In 1953, Mao launched a Soviet-style five-year plan that set high production targets for industry. The plan succeeded. By 1957, China's output of coal, cement, and electricity had doubled. Steel production had quadrupled.

Mao's Communes To expand the success of the first five-year plan in industry, Chinese leaders planned another ambitious program. Early in 1958, Mao proclaimed the "Great Leap Forward." This plan called for still larger collective farms, or **communes.** By the end of 1958, the government had created about 26,000 communes. The average commune sprawled over 15,000 acres and supported over 25,000 people.

In the strictly controlled life of the communes, peasants organized into "production battalions." Under the leadership of company and squad leaders, they worked the land together. They ate in communal dining rooms, slept in communal dormitories, and raised children in communal nurseries. And they owned nothing. The peasants had no incentive to work hard when only the state profited from their labor. Most of them hated living in the huge, impersonal communes.

The Great Leap Forward proved to be a great leap backward for China. Poor planning and inefficient "backyard" industries hampered growth. Worst of all, crop failures between 1958 and 1961 unleashed a famine that killed approximately 20 million people. The government officially discontinued the program in 1961.

HISTORY MAKERS

Mao Zedong
1893–1976

Born to a poor, but increasingly wealthy peasant family, Mao embraced Marxist socialism as a young man. Though he began as an urban labor organizer, Mao quickly realized the revolutionary potential of China's peasants. In a 1927 report, Mao predicted:

The force of the peasantry is like that of the raging winds and driving rain. . . . They will bury beneath them all forces of imperialism, militarism, corrupt officialdom, village bosses and evil gentry.

Mao's first attempt to lead the peasants in revolt failed in 1927. But during the Japanese occupation, Mao and his followers won the widespread support of the peasants by reducing rents and promising to redistribute land.

THINK THROUGH HISTORY
B. Analyzing Issues
What aspects of Marxist socialism did Mao try to bring to China?
B. Answer
Collective ownership of land, communal living, government control of industry.

Task: Students will create an edition of a news magazine covering the Communist takeover of China.

Purpose: To explore the significance of Mao's victory from several different perspectives.

Activity: Provide a copy of several issues of *Time* or *Newsweek* for students to use as models. On the board, list magazine components such as a factual

local news report, an analysis of the event's effects on the world, a human-interest story, an editorial, a letter to the editor, and a cartoon. Have each group choose one of these components to develop. Suggest that logical-mathematical learners include charts and graphs in their presentations.

 Building a Portfolio: Encourage students to include their news stories in their portfolios.

ALTERNATIVE ASSESSMENT BOOK
Standards for Evaluating a Cooperative Activity

Standards for Evaluation
News magazines should . . .

- include historically accurate information
- present various viewpoints on the Communist victory
- exhibit lively journalistic style

New Policies and Mao's Response China was facing external problems as well as internal ones in the late 1950s. The spirit of cooperation that had bound the Soviet Union and China began to fade. Each sought to lead the worldwide Communist movement. They also shared the longest border in the world. And they faced numerous territorial disputes. In 1960, the Soviets halted economic aid to China.

After the failure of the Great Leap Forward and the split with the Soviet Union, Mao reduced his role in the government. Other leaders moved away from Mao's strict socialist ideas. Under the new leaders, for example, farm families could live in their own homes. They also could sell crops they grew on small private plots. Factory workers could compete for wage increases, bonuses, and promotions.

Mao disapproved of China's new economic policies, believing that they weakened the Communist goal of social equality. Determined to revive the revolution, Mao launched a new campaign in 1966. He urged China's young people to "learn revolution by making revolution." Millions of high school and college students responded to Mao's call. They left their classrooms and formed militia units called **Red Guards.**

The Cultural Revolution The Red Guards led a major uprising known as the **Cultural Revolution.** The goal of the Cultural Revolution was to establish a society of peasants and workers in which all were equal. The new hero was the peasant who worked with his hands. The life of the mind—intellectual and artistic activity—was considered useless and dangerous. To help stamp out this threat, the Red Guards shut down colleges and schools. They lashed out at professors, government officials, factory managers, and even their own parents. They targeted anyone who seemed to have special privileges or who resisted the regime. Exiled intellectuals had to "purify" themselves by doing hard labor in remote villages. Thousands of people were executed or died in jail.

The resulting widespread chaos closed down factories and threatened farm production. Civil war seemed possible. By 1976, even Mao admitted that the Cultural Revolution had to stop. With Mao's approval, the army dissolved the Red Guards. Zhou Enlai (joh ehn·leye), one of the founders of the Chinese Communist party and premier since 1949, began to restore order.

While China was struggling to become stable, the Cold War continued to rage. Between the 1950s and the 1970s, two full-scale wars broke out—in Korea and in Vietnam.

C. Possible Answer The social upheaval it caused brought about economic chaos and threatened civil war.
THINK THROUGH HISTORY
C. Making Inferences Why did the Cultural Revolution fail?

Daily *Life*

The Cultural Revolution

The Cultural Revolution started in 1966, when Chihua Wen was eight years old. For the next decade, his world, and that of every other Chinese child, was turned inside out.

Wen's neighbors were well-known revolutionary writers and loyal members of the Communist Party. Their loyalty became meaningless, however, the night the Red Guards (shown above) stormed into their apartment. There was the sound of breaking glass and a child's scream. Then the teenaged Guards carried a sack of books out to the yard and set them on fire.

They returned to the apartment and emerged carrying two heavy sacks. As they raced off with the sacks in the back of the truck, Wen heard sounds of gagging. "No one ever saw the couple or their child again," he said. And Wen never forgot what he had seen.

Section ② Assessment

1. TERMS & NAMES

Identify
• Mao Zedong
• Jiang Jieshi
• commune
• Red Guards
• Cultural Revolution

2. TAKING NOTES

Using a chart like the one below, summarize the reforms Mao Zedong proposed for China.

Mao Zedong's Reforms

Aspect of Life	Reform
Agriculture	
Industry	
Family	

Create a propaganda poster supporting one of these reforms.

3. IDENTIFYING PROBLEMS

What circumstances prevented Mao's Great Leap Forward from bringing economic prosperity to China?

THINK ABOUT
• Mao's strict socialism
• life in a commune
• environmental problems

4. ANALYZING THEMES

Revolution What policies or actions enabled the Communists to defeat the Nationalists in their long civil war?

THINK ABOUT
• the goals of each group
• the leaders of the Communists and the Nationalists
• foreign support

Restructuring the Postwar World **485**

ANSWERS

1. TERMS & NAMES
Mao Zedong, p. 482
Jiang Jieshi, p. 482
commune, p. 484
Red Guards, p. 485
Cultural Revolution, p. 485

2. TAKING NOTES
Agriculture—divided land among peasants, established collective farms, established communes; Industry—nationalized private companies, set high production goals; Family—supported women workers, sponsored childcare.

3. IDENTIFYING PROBLEMS
Possible Responses: Lack of privacy and personal life in the communes, lack of incentives for working hard, poor planning, crop failure.

4. ANALYZING THEMES
Possible Responses: Won peasant loyalty; trained troops in guerrilla techniques; promised land reform.

OBJECTIVES

 To trace the course and consequences of the Korean War.

 To summarize the causes and events of the Vietnam War and to describe its aftermath.

SKILLBUILDER

- Interpreting maps: movement, p. 487; human-environment interaction, movement, p. 489

CRITICAL THINKING

- Recognizing effects, pp. 487, 490
- Making inferences, p. 488
- Forming opinions, p. 490

FOCUS

5-Minute Warm-Up

Making Generalizations
Have students answer these questions to prepare them to study the wars in Korea and Vietnam.

1. Look at the maps on pages 487 and 489. What similarities do you notice about Korea and Vietnam?

2. Which country shares a border with the Soviet Union?

 WARM-UP TRANSPARENCY 17

OBJECTIVE 1 INSTRUCT

War in Korea

Key Ideas

- Communist North Korea invades South Korea but is driven back by UN peacekeeping forces.
- China and the United States pour troops into the war but neither North nor South Korea is victorious.
- South Korea's free-market economy booms after the war, while Communist North Korea's economy declines.

 IN-DEPTH RESOURCES: UNIT 5
Guided Reading, p. 3

 ACCESS FOR STUDENTS ACQUIRING ENGLISH
Guided Reading (Spanish), p. 186

---

3 **War in Korea and Vietnam**

TERMS & NAMES
- 38th parallel
- Douglas MacArthur
- Ho Chi Minh
- domino theory
- Ngo Dinh Diem
- Vietcong
- Vietnamization
- Khmer Rouge

MAIN IDEA	WHY IT MATTERS NOW
In Asia, the Cold War flared into actual wars supported mainly by the superpowers.	Today, Vietnam is a Communist country and Korea is split into Communist and non-Communist nations.

SETTING THE STAGE When World War II ended, Korea became a divided nation. North of the **38th parallel,** a line that crosses Korea at 38 degrees north latitude, Japanese troops surrendered to the Soviets. South of this line, the Japanese surrendered to the Americans. As in Germany, two nations developed. One was the Communist industrial north. The other was the non-Communist rural south.

War in Korea

By 1949, both the United States and the Soviet Union had withdrawn most of their troops from Korea. The Soviets gambled that the United States would not defend South Korea. So they supplied North Korea with tanks, airplanes, and money in an attempt to take over the peninsula.

Standoff at the 38th Parallel On June 25, 1950, the North Koreans swept across the 38th parallel in a surprise attack on South Korea. Within days, North Korean troops had penetrated deep into the south.

President Truman was convinced that the North Korean aggressors were repeating what Hitler, Mussolini, and the Japanese had done in the 1930s. His policy of containment was being put to the test. And Truman resolved to help South Korea resist Communist influence.

South Korea also asked the United Nations to intervene. When the matter came to a vote in the Security Council, the Soviets were absent. They had boycotted the council to protest the seating of Nationalist China (Taiwan) rather than mainland China. The Soviet Union thus forfeited its chance to veto the UN's plan of action. This plan was to send an international force to Korea to stop the invasion. A total of 15 nations, including Britain and Canada, participated under the leadership of General **Douglas MacArthur.**

Meanwhile, the North Koreans continued to advance. By September 1950, they controlled the entire Korean peninsula except for a tiny area around Pusan in the far southeast. That month, however, MacArthur launched a surprise attack. Troops moving north from Pusan met up with forces that had made an amphibious landing at Inchon. Caught in this pincer action, about half of the North Koreans surrendered. The rest retreated.

The Fighting Continues The UN army pursued the retreating North Korean troops across the 38th parallel into North Korea. By late November, UN troops had pushed the North Koreans almost to the Yalu River at the border with China. These troops were mostly from the United States.

U.S. infantry troops fire heavy mortar shells at Communist strongholds in North Korea in 1950.

Vocabulary
boycotted: refused to take part in.

SECTION 3 RESOURCES

PRINT RESOURCES

 IN-DEPTH RESOURCES: UNIT 5
Guided Reading, p. 3
Primary Source: from *When Heaven and Earth Changed Places*, p. 10
History Makers: Ho Chi Minh, p. 16

 ACCESS FOR STUDENTS ACQUIRING ENGLISH
Guided Reading (Spanish), p. 186

 FORMAL ASSESSMENT
Section Quiz, p. 213

TECHNOLOGY RESOURCES

 WORLD ART AND CULTURES TRANSPARENCIES
AT73 *Laying a Road*

 CD-ROM
Electronic Library of Primary Sources
Battles of the World

 INTERNET www.mlworldhistory.com

Then, in October 1950, the Chinese felt threatened by the American fleet off their coast. They sent 300,000 troops to aid North Korea. The fight between North and South Korea had grown into a war between the Chinese and the Americans.

Greatly outnumbering the UN forces, the Chinese drove them southward. By early January 1951, they had pushed all UN and South Korean troops out of North Korea. The Chinese then moved south. They finally captured the South Korean capital, Seoul.

"We face an entirely new war," declared General MacArthur. And he called for a nuclear attack against Chinese cities. President Truman disagreed, viewing MacArthur's proposals as reckless. "We are trying to prevent a world war, not start one," the president explained. MacArthur tried to go over the president's head by taking his case to Congress and to the press. In response, Truman fired him.

Over the next two years, UN forces continued to fight to drive the North Koreans back to the 38th parallel. By 1952, UN troops had recaptured Seoul and regained control of South Korea. Finally, in July 1953, the UN forces and North Korea signed a cease-fire agreement. After three years of fighting, the border between the two Koreas was set near the 38th parallel. This was almost where it had been before the war started. But approximately 5 million soldiers and civilians had died.

THINK THROUGH HISTORY
A. Recognizing Effects What effects did the Korean war have on the Korean people and nation?
A. Answer About 5 million Koreans and foreign soldiers died and neither North nor South Korea had gained any territory.

Aftermath and Legacy of the War After the war, Korea remained divided into two countries. In North Korea, the Communist dictator Kim Il Sung established collective farms, developed heavy industry, and built up the country's military power. At Kim's death in 1994, his son Kim Jong Il ascended to power. Under Kim Jong Il's rule, Communist North Korea developed nuclear weapons. Although the country is well-armed, it has serious economic problems. It continues to struggle with shortages of energy and food.

On the other hand, South Korea prospered, thanks to massive aid from the United States and other countries. In the 1960s, South Korea concentrated on developing its industry and boosting foreign trade. A succession of dictatorships ruled the rapidly developing country. With the 1987 adoption of a democratic constitution, however, South Korea established free elections. During the 1980s and early 1990s, South Korea claimed one of the highest economic growth rates in the world.

Political differences keep the two Koreas apart, despite periodic discussions of reuniting the country. In a show of force in 1996, for example, North Korea sent troops into the demilitarized zone that separates the two nations. And the United States still maintains 37,000 troops in South Korea. In 1997, however, South Korea joined several other countries in sending food to North Korea. Although talks continue, the Communist North Koreans remain firmly opposed to reunification.

Restructuring the Postwar World **487**

War in Korea, 1950-1953

GEOGRAPHY SKILLBUILDER:
Interpreting Maps
1. **Movement** *What was the northernmost Korean city UN troops had reached by November 1950?*
2. **Movement** *Did North or South Korean forces advance further into the other's territory?*

Map legend:
- Farthest North Korean advance, September 1950
- Farthest UN advance, November 1950
- Farthest Chinese and North Korean advance, January 1951
- Armistice line, 1953

War in Vietnam

▶ Key Ideas
- Ho Chi Minh leads Vietnam in a revolt against the French.
- Vietnam is split into the Communist North and the U.S.-supported South.
- The United States fails to prevent a Communist takeover. After the U.S. withdrawal, North Vietnam overruns the south.
- The Communist Khmer Rouge take over Cambodia.
- Vietnam recovers slowly from the war's aftermath and begins to seek foreign investment.

 IN-DEPTH RESOURCES: UNIT 5
Primary Source: from *When Heaven and Earth Changed Places*, p. 10

CRITICAL THINKING ACTIVITY
CLASS TIME : 15 MINUTES

Sequencing Events
Suggest that students create a time line to help them trace the development of events in the Vietnam War.

1954	1963	1969
French defeated at Dien Bien Phu	Diem assassinated	U.S. troop withdrawal begins

---

HISTORYMAKERS
Ho Chi Minh

In 1945, Ho sent two telegrams to President Truman seeking a seat on a British-American-Russian-Chinese Advisory Commission on the Far East which would decide the fate of Indochina. Truman ignored him. Have students discuss why they think the United States refused to deal with Ho.

 IN-DEPTH RESOURCES: UNIT 5
History Makers: Ho Chi Minh, p. 16

War in Vietnam

Like America's involvement in the Korean War, its involvement in Vietnam stemmed from its Cold War policy of containment. Beginning after World War II, many Americans and their leaders had one foreign policy goal. They were committed to halting the spread of communism.

By the 1950s, the United States had begun providing financial aid, advisers, and finally, half a million soldiers to a former French colony, Vietnam. America's aim was to keep Southeast Asia from embracing communism as China had done.

The Road to War In the early 1900s, France controlled most of resource-rich Southeast Asia. Nationalist independence movements, however, had begun to develop in the part of French Indochina that is now Vietnam. A young Vietnamese nationalist, **Ho Chi Minh,** turned to the Communists for help in his struggle. During the 1930s, Ho's Indochinese Communist party led revolts and strikes against the French. The French responded by jailing Vietnamese protesters. They also sentenced Ho, the party's leader, to death. Ho fled his death sentence but continued to inspire Vietnam's growing nationalist movement from exile. Ho returned to Vietnam in 1941, a year after the Japanese seized control of his country. He and other nationalists founded the Vietminh (Independence) League.

The Japanese left Vietnam in 1945, after their defeat in World War II. Ho Chi Minh believed that independence would surely follow. France, however, intended to regain its former colony.

War Breaks Out Vietnamese Nationalists and Communists joined to fight the French armies. While the French held most of the major cities, they remained powerless in the countryside. There the Vietminh had widespread peasant support. The Vietminh used hit-and-run tactics to confine the French to the cities.

The French people began to doubt that maintaining their colony in Vietnam was worth the lives and money the struggle cost. In 1954, the French suffered a major military defeat at Dien Bien Phu. They surrendered to Ho.

The United States had supported the French in Vietnam. With the defeat of the French, the United States saw a rising threat to the rest of Asia. U.S. President Eisenhower described this threat in terms of the **domino theory.** The Southeast Asian nations were like a row of dominos, he said. The fall of one to communism would lead to the fall of its neighbors. This theory became a major justification for U.S. foreign policy during the Cold War era.

After France's defeat, an international peace conference met in Geneva to discuss the future of Indochina. Based on these talks, Vietnam was divided at 17° north latitude. North of that line, Ho Chi Minh's Communist forces governed. To the south, the United States and France set up an anti-Communist government under the leadership of **Ngo Dinh Diem** (NOH dihn D'YEM).

Vietnam—A Divided Country Diem, an unpopular leader, ruled the south as a dictator. In contrast, Ho Chi Minh began a popular program of land redistribution in the north. The United States sensed that an election might lead to victory for the Communists. So it supported Diem's cancellation of the elections.

Vietnamese opposition to Diem's corrupt government grew. Communist guerrillas, called **Vietcong,** began to gain strength in the south. While some of the Vietcong were trained soldiers from North Vietnam, most were South Vietnamese who hated Diem. Gradually, the Vietcong won control of large areas of the countryside.

HISTORYMAKERS

Ho Chi Minh
1890–1969

When he was young, the poor Vietnamese Nguyen That (uhng-wihn thaht) Thanh worked as a cook on a French steamship. In visiting American cities where the boat docked, such as Boston and New York, he learned about both American culture and ideals.

He later took a new name—Ho Chi Minh, meaning "He who enlightens." But he held onto those American ideals. Though a Communist, in announcing Vietnam's independence from France in 1945, he declared, "All men are created equal."

His people revered him and fondly called him Uncle Ho. However, Ho Chi Minh did not put his democratic ideals into practice. From 1954 to 1969, he ruled North Vietnam by crushing all opposition.

THINK THROUGH HISTORY
B. Making Inferences What actions might the United States have justified by the domino theory?
B. Possible Answer Intervention in any situation that might result in a gain of Communist territory or power.

Task: Students will create scripts for movie scenes about the Vietnam War.

Purpose: To develop an understanding of the political and personal realities of the Vietnam War.

Activity: Small groups of students will brainstorm a scene for a movie about the Vietnam War and will create a script for the scene. Remind students that

their scripts should include both descriptive passages, stage directions, and realistic dialogue to advance the plot.

 Building a Portfolio: Encourage students to include their scripts in their portfolios.

ALTERNATIVE ASSESSMENT BOOK
Standards for Evaluating a Cooperative Activity

Standards for Evaluation
Scripts should . . .

- demonstrate an understanding of the Vietnam War
- provide historical context, vivid description, and realistic dialogue
- focus on a single dramatic situation and several well-defined characters

In 1963, backed by the United States, a group of South Vietnamese generals planned a coup. Meeting almost no resistance, they overthrew and assassinated Diem. The new leaders, however, were no more popular than Diem had been. A takeover by the Communist Vietcong with the backing of North Vietnam seemed inevitable.

The United States Gets Involved
Faced with this possibility, the United States decided to escalate, or increase, its involvement. Americans had been serving as advisers to the South Vietnamese since the late 1950s. But their numbers steadily grew. The United States also sent increasing numbers of planes, tanks, and other military equipment to South Vietnam.

In August 1964, U.S. President Lyndon Johnson told Congress that North Vietnamese patrol boats had attacked two American destroyers in the Gulf of Tonkin. As a result, Congress authorized the president to send American troops into Vietnam. By late 1965, more than 185,000 American soldiers were fighting on Vietnamese soil, although war had not officially been declared. American planes had also begun to bomb North Vietnam. By 1968, more than half a million American soldiers were in combat there.

The United States boasted the best-equipped, most advanced army in the world. Yet the Americans faced two major difficulties. First, they were fighting a guerrilla war in unfamiliar jungle terrain. Second, the South Vietnamese government they were defending was becoming steadily more unpopular. At the same time, popular support for the Vietcong grew. Ho Chi Minh also strongly supported the Vietcong with troops and munitions, as did the Soviet Union and China.

Unable to win a decisive victory on the ground, the United States turned to air power. American forces bombed millions of acres of farmland and forest in an attempt to destroy enemy hideouts. This bombing strengthened peasants' opposition to the South Vietnamese government.

The United States Withdraws During the late 1960s, the war grew increasingly unpopular in the United States. Dissatisfied youth began to protest the tremendous loss of life in an unpopular conflict on the other side of the world. Bowing to intense public pressure, President Richard Nixon began withdrawing U.S. troops from Vietnam in 1969. Nixon's plan was called **Vietnamization.** It allowed for U.S. troops to gradually pull out, while the South Vietnamese increased their combat role. Nixon wanted to pursue Vietnamization while preserving the South Vietnamese government. So he authorized a massive bombing campaign against North Vietnamese bases and supply routes. The president also authorized bombings in neighboring Laos and Cambodia to wipe out Vietcong hiding places.

Restructuring the Postwar World **489**

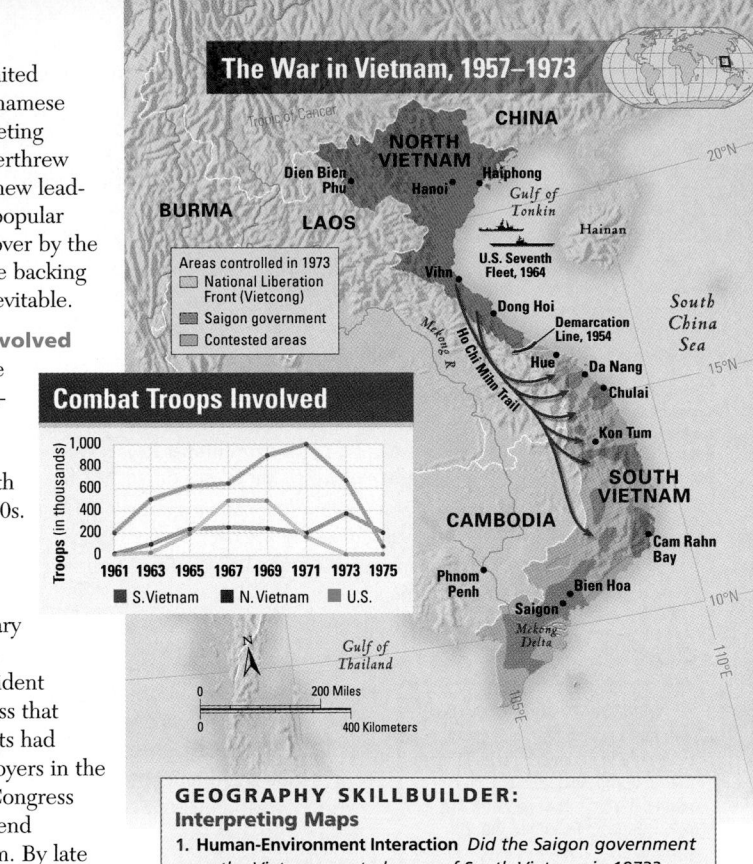

The War in Vietnam, 1957–1973

Areas controlled in 1973
- National Liberation Front (Vietcong)
- Saigon government
- Contested areas

CHINA, NORTH VIETNAM, BURMA, LAOS, Dien Bien Phu, Hanoi, Haiphong, Gulf of Tonkin, Hainan, Vinh, U.S. Seventh Fleet, 1964, Dong Hoi, Demarcation Line, 1954, South China Sea, Hue, Da Nang, Chulai, Kon Tum, SOUTH VIETNAM, CAMBODIA, Cam Rahn Bay, Phnom Penh, Bien Hoa, Saigon, Mekong Delta, Gulf of Thailand, Mekong R., Ho Chi Minh Trail

0   200 Miles
0   400 Kilometers

Combat Troops Involved

Troops (in thousands): 1,000 / 800 / 600 / 400 / 200 / 0
1961 1963 1965 1967 1969 1971 1973 1975
■ S. Vietnam   ■ N. Vietnam   ■ U.S.

GEOGRAPHY SKILLBUILDER:
Interpreting Maps
1. **Human-Environment Interaction** Did the Saigon government or the Vietcong control more of South Vietnam in 1973?
2. **Movement** Which country committed the most troops to the war in Vietnam?

The skulls of Cambodian citizens form a haunting memorial to the brutality of the Khmer Rouge during the 1970s.

CONNECT *to* TODAY

Capitalism in Vietnam
Vietnam is now a Communist country. But its economy is modeled more on that of the Soviets' Cold War enemy, the United States. In 1997, a travel magazine claimed that Hanoi, the capital of Vietnam, "jumps with vitality, its streets and shops jammed with locals and handfuls of Western tourists and businesspeople."

Along Hanoi's shaded boulevards, billboards advertise American and Japanese copiers, motorcycles, video recorders, and soft drinks. On the streets, enterprising Vietnamese businesspeople offer more traditional services. These include bicycle repair, a haircut, a shave, or a tasty snack.

Under continued popular protest and political pressure at home, President Nixon kept withdrawing U.S. troops. The last forces left in 1973. The North Vietnamese overran South Vietnam two years later because the South Vietnamese could not fend off the North Vietnamese on their own. The Communists renamed Saigon, the former capital of the South, Ho Chi Minh City to honor their dead leader. But more than 1.5 million Vietnamese and 58,000 Americans had also died during the war.

Ongoing Turmoil in Cambodia The end of the war did not put an end to bloodshed and chaos in Southeast Asia, however. Cambodia (also known as Kampuchea) had suffered U.S. bombing during the war. And it remained unstable for years. In 1975, Communist rebels known as the **Khmer Rouge** set up a brutal Communist government under the leadership of Pol Pot. In a ruthless attempt to transform Cambodia into a rural society, Pol Pot's followers slaughtered 2 million people. This was almost one quarter of the nation's population. A Vietnamese invasion in 1978 overthrew the Khmer Rouge. The Vietnamese finally withdrew in 1989. In 1993, under the supervision of UN peacekeepers, Cambodia adopted a democratic constitution and held a free election. Pol Pot was captured and detained in 1997 for the war crimes he had committed.

Postwar Vietnam After 1975, the victorious North Vietnamese imposed strict controls over the South. Officials sent thousands of people to "reeducation camps" for training in Communist thought. They nationalized industries and strictly controlled businesses.

Communist oppression also caused 1.5 million people to flee from Vietnam. Most refugees escaped in dangerously overcrowded ships. More than 200,000 of these "boat people" died at sea. The survivors often spent long months in crowded refugee camps scattered across Southeast Asia. About 70,000 Vietnamese refugees eventually settled in the United States or in Canada.

Though Communists still govern Vietnam, the country now welcomes foreign investment. Much of that investment comes from Vietnam's old enemy, the United States. America lifted its trade embargo against Vietnam in 1994 and is moving toward official recognition of the country.

While the Cold War superpowers were struggling for power in the Korean and Vietnam wars, they also were using economic and diplomatic means to bring other countries under their control.

Section 3 Assessment

1. TERMS & NAMES
Identify
• 38th parallel
• Douglas MacArthur
• Ho Chi Minh
• domino theory
• Ngo Dinh Diem
• Vietcong
• Vietnamization
• Khmer Rouge

2. TAKING NOTES
Using a Venn diagram like the one below, compare and contrast the causes and effects of the wars in Vietnam and Korea.

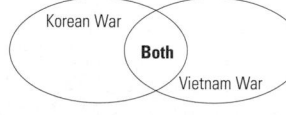
Korean War / Both / Vietnam War

Do you think the similarities or the differences between the two wars are more striking? Why?

3. FORMING OPINIONS
Do you think U.S. involvement in Vietnam was justified? Why or why not?

THINK ABOUT
• the U.S. policy of containment
• the domino theory
• U.S. public opinion

4. THEME ACTIVITY
Empire Building Create a propaganda poster for either the United States or the Soviet Union supporting its involvement in Asia.

ANSWERS

1. TERMS & NAMES
38th parallel, p. 486
Douglas MacArthur, p. 486
Ho Chi Minh, p. 488
domino theory, p. 488
Ngo Dinh Diem, p. 488
Vietcong, p. 488
Vietnamization, p. 489
Khmer Rouge, p. 490

2. TAKING NOTES
Korean War—neither side gained an advantage; Vietnam War—Soviet-supported North Vietnamese won; Both—American and Soviet involvement stemmed from Cold War; land was destroyed; millions of people died.

3. FORMING OPINIONS
Not justified—It was a civil war that did not involve the United States; war is not justified under any circumstances; Justified—It was the responsibility of a nation founded on democratic ideals to support democracy in other countries, especially those in danger of becoming Communist.

4. THEME ACTIVITY
Standards for Evaluation
An effective poster should meet the following criteria:
• Demonstrates understanding of U.S. or Soviet goals in Asia
• Uses slogans and pictures to convey the message
• Is clear and easy to understand

Cold War Around the World

TERMS & NAMES
- **Third World**
- **nonaligned nations**
- **Fidel Castro**
- **Anastasio Somoza**
- **Daniel Ortega**
- **Shah Mohammed Reza Pahlavi**
- **Ayatollah Ruholla Khomeini**

MAIN IDEA

The Cold War superpowers supported opposing sides in Latin American and Middle Eastern conflicts.

WHY IT MATTERS NOW

Many of these areas today are troubled by political, economic, and military conflict and crisis.

SETTING THE STAGE Vietnam was just one of many countries that attempted to shake off colonial rule after World War II. Local battles for independence provided yet another arena for competition between the Cold War superpowers.

Confrontations over Developing Nations

Following World War II, the world's nations were grouped politically into three "worlds." The First World was the United States and its allies. The Second World included the Soviet Union and its allies. The **Third World** consisted of developing nations, often newly independent, who were not aligned with either superpower.

These Third World countries in Latin America, Asia, and Africa experienced terrible poverty and political instability. This was largely due to a long history of imperialism. They also suffered from ethnic conflicts and lack of technology and education. Each desperately needed a political and economic system around which to build its society. Soviet-style communism and U.S.-style free-market democracy were the countries' main choices.

Cold War Strategies The United States, the Soviet Union, and, in some cases, China, used a variety of techniques to gain influence in the Third World. These competing superpowers sponsored or backed wars of revolution, liberation, or counterrevolution. The U.S. and Soviet spy agencies—the CIA and the KGB—engaged in a variety of covert, or secret, activities. These activities ranged from spying to assassination attempts. The United States also provided military aid, built schools, set up programs to combat poverty, and sent volunteer workers to developing nations in Latin America, Asia, and Africa. The Soviets offered military and technical assistance, mainly to India and Egypt.

Association of Nonaligned Nations Other developing nations also had pressing needs for assistance. They became important players in the Cold War competition between the United States, the Soviet Union, and also China.

Not all Third World countries wished to play such a role, however. India, for example, vowed to remain neutral in the Cold War. Indonesia, a populous island nation in Southeast Asia, also struggled to stay uninvolved. In 1955, Indonesia hosted the leaders of Asian and African countries in the Bandung Conference. They met to form what they called a "third force" of such independent countries, or **nonaligned nations.**

Nations such as India and Indonesia remained neutral. But other countries took sides with the superpowers or played the competing sides off against each other.

Background

In the 1970s, the three worlds were redefined in economic terms. The small but prosperous First World was at the top of a pyramid and the large, poverty-stricken Third World was at the bottom.

A. Possible Answers

Advantages—control over their own politics and economies; ability to accept help from either side; Disadvantages—lack of economic and military support from the strong superpowers, if needed.

THINK THROUGH HISTORY
A. Making Inferences What advantages and disadvantages might being nonaligned have offered a developing nation?

The flour provided by U.S. aid helped keep these Colombian children alive. They also learned to make the flour sacks into clothing in a school run by missionaries.

491

Section 4 Overview

OBJECTIVES

1. To explain how the Cold War affected developing nations.

2. To describe superpower confrontations in Latin America after World War II.

3. To identify Cold War conflicts in the Middle East.

SKILLBUILDER
- Interpreting maps: location, region, p. 493

CRITICAL THINKING
- Making inferences, p. 491
- Contrasting, p. 492
- Analyzing motives, pp. 493, 494
- Comparing, p. 495
- Analyzing themes, p. 495

FOCUS
5-Minute Warm-Up

▶ *Analyzing Events*
To give students an appreciation of the worldwide scope of the Cold War, have them answer these questions.

1. Look at the map on page 493. Which countries did the Communists take over?

2. In which Central and South American countries did the United States prevent Communist takeovers?

WARM-UP TRANSPARENCY 17

OBJECTIVE ① INSTRUCT

Confrontations over Developing Nations

▶ *Key Ideas*
- The superpowers compete for influence among developing nations through covert activities, military force, and economic aid.
- A few nations cling to neutrality.

IN-DEPTH RESOURCES : UNIT 5
Guided Reading, p. 4

ACCESS FOR STUDENTS ACQUIRING ENGLISH
Guided Reading (Spanish), p. 187

Postwar Face-off in Latin America

Key Ideas
- Castro leads a successful Communist revolution in Cuba.
- A face-off over missile sites in Cuba brings the U.S. and the Soviet Union to the brink of nuclear war.
- Communist Sandinistas and U.S.-backed Contras fight a ten-year civil war in Nicaragua.

 IN-DEPTH RESOURCES : UNIT 5
Primary Source: The Cuban Missile Crisis (Speech by John F. Kennedy), p. 11

CRITICAL THINKING ACTIVITY
CLASS TIME: 10 MINUTES

Identifying Main Ideas
As students read this section, have them organize the information they gather about Cold War confrontations in a chart like this.

	Cuba	Nicaragua	Iran	Afghanistan
Leader	Fidel Castro			
Conflict				
Dates				
Superpower involved				
Outcome				

HISTORY MAKERS
Fidel Castro

Since 1959, when he overthrew the Batista regime, Castro has withstood numerous attempts to topple his regime through assassination, invasion, and economic pressure to become the world's longest-surviving Communist ruler.

Postwar Face-off in Latin America

Long before World War II, American businesses dominated Latin American politics. They backed leaders who often oppressed their people but who protected U.S. interests. After the war, a lingering gap between the rich and the poor led Latin American nations to seek aid from both superpowers. Communism and nationalistic feelings inspired revolutionary movements in parts of Latin America. These revolutionary movements found enthusiastic Soviet support. In response, the United States provided military support and economic assistance to anti-Communist dictators.

For example, in 1970 Salvador Allende, an admitted Marxist, was freely elected the president of Chile. The United States government feared the expansion of communism in the area. Through the CIA, it helped forces opposed to Allende topple his government in 1973. His replacement, Augusto Pinochet, was a military dictator who used brutal tactics to maintain order in the country. Since he was not a communist, he had United States support and remained in power. Cold war struggles in other areas of Latin America occupied the United States from the 1950s through the 1990s.

Cuban Revolution Throughout the 1950s, U.S. support maintained Cuba's unpopular dictator, Fulgencio Batista. Cuban resentment led to a popular revolution, which overthrew Batista in January 1959. A young lawyer named **Fidel Castro** led that revolution.

At first, many people praised Castro for bringing reforms to Cuba and improving the economy, literacy, health care, and conditions for women. Yet Castro was a harsh dictator. He suspended elections, jailed or executed his opponents, and strangled the press with tight government controls.

When Castro nationalized the Cuban economy, he took over U.S.-owned sugar mills and refineries. In response, President Eisenhower ordered an embargo on all trade with Cuba. As relations with the United States deteriorated, Castro turned to the Soviets for the economic and military aid he needed.

In April 1961, the United States offered support to a group of anti-Castro Cuban exiles living in Florida. These exiles attempted to retake Cuba by invading at a remote beach called the Bay of Pigs. Castro easily turned back the invaders. This victory embarrassed the United States.

The Cuban Missile Crisis The failed Bay of Pigs invasion convinced the Soviet leader, Nikita Khrushchev, that the United States would not resist Soviet expansion in Latin America. Consequently, in July 1962, Khrushchev secretly began to build 42 missile sites in Cuba. In October, an American spy plane discovered the sites. The U.S. President, John F. Kennedy, declared that missiles so close to the U.S. mainland were a threat. He demanded that the Soviets remove the missiles. Kennedy also announced a quarantine, or blockade, of Cuba to prevent the Soviets installing more missiles. Castro protested his country's being used as a tool in the Cold War:

A VOICE FROM THE PAST
Cuba did not and does not intend to be in the middle of a conflict between the East and the West. Our problem is above all one of national sovereignty. Cuba does not mean to get involved in the Cold War.
FIDEL CASTRO, quoted in an interview October 27, 1962

Nevertheless, Cuba was deeply involved. Kennedy's demand for the removal of Soviet

HISTORY MAKERS

Fidel Castro
1927–

The son of a wealthy Spanish-Cuban farmer, Fidel Castro became involved in politics while enrolled at the University of Havana. He first attempted to overthrow the Cuban dictator, Batista, in 1953. He was imprisoned, but vowed not to give up the struggle for independence:

Personally, I am not interested in power nor do I envisage assuming it at any time. All that I will do is to make sure that the sacrifices of so many compatriots should not be in vain. . . .

Despite this declaration, Castro became a staunch Soviet ally and has been dictator of Cuba for over 30 years.

THINK THROUGH HISTORY
B. Contrasting
What differing U.S. and Soviet aims led to the Cuban missile crisis?
B. Answer U.S.—desire to protect itself and prevent the spread of communism; Soviet—desire to support its Communist ally.

EXPLORING PRIMARY SOURCES

A Voice from the Past The same day that Castro insisted on Cuba's desire to stay out of the Cold War, he wrote a letter to Khrushchev asking the Soviet leader to launch a nuclear strike against the United States. He had no idea that Kennedy and Khrushchev were carrying on secret negotiations.

Have interested students read sources such as A.I. Gribkov's *Operation ANADYR: U.S. and Soviet Generals Recount the Cuban Missile Crisis,* and Dino A. Brugioni's *Eyeball to Eyeball: The Inside Story of the Cuban Missile Crisis* to learn more about this period.

CUSTOMIZING FOR SPECIAL NEEDS

Less Proficient Readers: Recognizing Sequences Pair less proficient readers with more able students. Suggest that each pair create a storyboard that presents the drama of the Cuban missile crisis. Instruct students to work together to decide which events to include in their storyboard and in which order they

should be presented. Then have them plan the pictures and words they will use in each panel and produce the storyboard. Have the pairs present their storyboards to the class.

 IN-DEPTH RESOURCES : UNIT 5
Geography Application: The Cuban Missile Crisis, p. 7

missiles put the United States and the Soviet Union on a collision course. U.S. troops assembled in Florida, ready to invade Cuba. People around the world began to fear that this standoff would lead to World War III and a nuclear disaster. Fortunately, Khrushchev agreed to remove the missiles in return for a U.S. promise not to invade Cuba.

The resolution of the Cuban missile crisis left Castro completely dependent on Soviet support. In exchange for this support, Castro backed Communist revolutions in Latin America and Africa. Approximately 36,000 Cubans fought in Angola's war against colonialism in the 1970s. Soviet aid to Cuba, however, ended abruptly with the breakup of the Soviet Union in 1991. This loss dealt a crippling blow to the Cuban economy. The country still suffers a scarcity of vital supplies. But the aging Castro refuses to adopt economic reforms or to give up power. An equally stubborn United States refuses to lift its trade embargo.

C. Answer Because the Sandinistas were supporting socialist rebels in El Salvador.

THINK THROUGH HISTORY
C. Analyzing Motives Why did the U.S. switch its support from the Sandinistas to the Contras?

Civil War in Nicaragua Just as the United States had supported the unpopular Batista in Cuba, it had funded the Nicaraguan dictatorship of **Anastasio Somoza** and his family since 1933. In 1979, Communist Sandinista rebels toppled the dictatorship of Somoza's son. Both the United States and the Soviet Union initially gave aid to the Sandinistas and their leader, **Daniel Ortega** (awr·TAY·guh).

The Sandinistas, however, had aided other socialist rebels in nearby El Salvador. To help the El Salvadoran government fight those rebels, the United States supported Nicaraguan anti-Communist rebel forces. These rebels were called Contras or *contrarevolucionarios*.

The civil war in Nicaragua lasted over a decade and seriously weakened the country's economy. Finally, in 1990, President Ortega agreed to hold free elections. He was defeated by Violeta Chamorro. In 1997, José Lacayo was elected president.

MORE ABOUT . . .
The Cuban Missile Crisis
One week into the Cuban missile crisis, Khrushchev sent Kennedy a personal message offering a deal. "You can be certain," Khrushchev wrote, "that we are quite sane and understand clearly that if we attack you, you will retaliate. But we will match you blow for blow. . . . Why, then, should we court disaster. . . ? Only a lunatic or suicide would do that. . . ."

 CRITICAL THINKING TRANSPARENCIES
CT33 Global Superpowers Face Off

MORE ABOUT . . .
The Sandinistas
The Sandinistas took their name from Augusto Cesar Sandino, a Nicaraguan guerrilla leader of the 1920s. Sandino fought the U.S. marines who occupied Nicaragua from 1912 to 1933. The marines withdrew but only after installing the Somoza family in power. Somoza guards captured and killed Sandino in 1934.

History from Visuals

Cold War Hot Spots, 1948–1975
Interpreting the Map Ask students to identify the five countries taken over by Communists that are not on the same continent as the Soviet Union and China. *Angola, Congo, Mozambique, Cuba, and Nicaragua. What happened in each of the countries colored gold?* *The United States and its allies prevented Communist takeovers.*

Extension Activity Have students do research to determine if the Communist countries shown were allied with the Soviet Union, with China, or were not allied with either Communist power. *Yugoslavia and North Korea were not allied with either power; Albania was allied with China; the other countries were allied with the Soviet Union.*

SKILLBUILDER ANSWERS
1. North America, Australia.
2. About 1/3.

Cold War Hot Spots, 1948–1975

The United States helps Greece defeat Communist-led rebels (1946–1949) and gives economic and military aid to Turkey (1947–1950).

The Soviets down U.S. U-2 pilot Francis Gary Powers in 1960.

Communists gain control after bloody wars in Korea (1950–1953) and Vietnam (1957–1975) supported by China and the Soviet Union.

The United States and the Soviet Union bring the world to the brink of nuclear war during the Cuban missile crisis in 1962.

The Soviet Union aids anticolonial struggles in Congo (1960) and Mozambique (1971) and, with help from Cuba, in Angola (1974).

Britain helps Indonesian government repress an uprising by Communists in 1965.

The United States prevents Communist takeovers in Guatemala (1954), Bolivia (1956), and Chile (1973).

Communist expansion
Communist expansion prevented by U.S. and allies

GEOGRAPHY SKILLBUILDER: Interpreting Maps
1. **Location** On what continents identified on the map did Cold War conflicts *not* occur?
2. **Region** About what fraction of the globe did Communists control by 1975?

TEACHING OPTION **BLOCK SCHEDULING** **COOPERATIVE ACTIVITY: Making a Cold War Temperature Chart** **CLASS TIME 30 MINUTES**

Task: Students will develop a Cold War "thermometer" to track Cold War tensions.

Purpose: To explore the fluctuations in tensions over the course of the Cold War.

Activity: Have students brainstorm ways of tracking the rise and fall of Cold War tensions. You might suggest, for example, that they consider a scale such as ° C—degrees of crisis—and assign a number to each confrontation or avoidance of confrontation between the superpowers. Then have small groups each choose a Cold War incident, write a short description of their incident, and assign it a rating on the crisis scale. Finally, have the groups plot their individual incidents on a crisis temperature chart.

 Building a Portfolio: Encourage students to include their crisis summaries and ratings in their portfolios.

ALTERNATIVE ASSESSMENT BOOK
Standards for Evaluating a Cooperative Activity

Standards for Evaluation
Crisis summaries and ratings should . . .
• accurately depict a Cold War crisis
• realistically rank the seriousness of the confrontation
• be clear and succinct

Confrontations in the Middle East

▶ **Key Ideas**
- Oil wealth feeds a secular culture in Iran.
- Ayatollah Khomeini leads a religious revolt against the U.S.-backed secular government.
- Khomeini promotes an Islamic state and pursues radical anti-U.S. policies.
- The Soviet Union invades Afghanistan.

 IN-DEPTH RESOURCES : UNIT 5
History Makers: Ruholla Khomeini, p. 17

MORE ABOUT . . .
American Hostages in Iran

Taking diplomats hostage was so unprecedented that no one dreamed how long the Iranian crisis would endure. One of the hostages recalled that he refused to take off his jacket or tie after he was blindfolded and strapped to a chair on the first day because he was due at a dinner party that night. At the time, his most pressing worry was notifying his "very chic Iranian hostess" that he was not going to be able to attend her party.

 ELECTRONIC LIBRARY OF PRIMARY SOURCES
from *444 Days: The Hostages Remember*

Confrontations in the Middle East

As the map on the previous page shows, Cold War confrontations continued to erupt around the globe. (For more information about African conflicts, see Chapter 18.) With its rich supplies of oil, the Middle East lured both the United States and the Soviet Union.

Religious and Secular Values Clash in Iran Throughout the Middle East, wealth from the oil industry fueled a growing conflict between traditional Islamic values and modern Western materialism. In no country did the clash between cultures erupt more dramatically than in the former Persia, or Iran.

After World War II, Iran's leader, **Shah Mohammed Reza Pahlavi** (PAH·luh·vee), embraced Western governments and wealthy Western oil companies. Angry Iranian nationalists resented these foreign alliances. They united under the leadership of Prime Minister Muhammad Mossaddeq (moh·sah·DEHK). They seized and nationalized a British-owned oil company and, in 1953, forced the shah to flee. Fearing that Mossaddeq might turn to the Soviets for support, the United States had him arrested. It then restored the shah to power.

The United States Supports Secular Rule With U.S. support, the shah westernized his country. By the end of the 1950s, Iran's capital, Tehran, featured gleaming skyscrapers, foreign banks, and modern factories. Millions of Iranians, however, still lived in extreme poverty. And the shah's secret police brutally punished anyone who dared to oppose him. The shah also tried to weaken the political influence of religion in the country by limiting the role of Islamic legal and academic experts. Iran's conservative Muslim leaders, known as ayatollahs (eye·uh·TOH·luhz), bitterly opposed this move. They also opposed what they saw as socially and morally corrupting Western influences. They wanted Iran to become a republic ruled strictly by Islamic law.

The leader of this religious opposition, **Ayatollah Ruholla Khomeini** (koh·MAY·nee), was living in exile. Spurred by his tape-recorded messages, Iranian

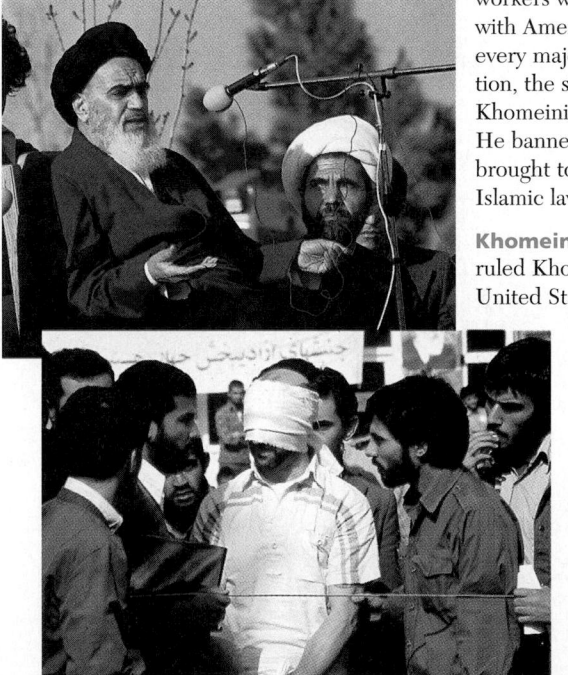

Ayatollah Khomeini (top) supported the taking of U.S. hostages in Tehran in 1979. During their 14-month captivity, the hostages were blindfolded and paraded through the city streets (bottom).

workers went on strike. "Death to the shah!" and "Down with America!" they vowed. In late 1978, riots erupted in every major city in Iran. Faced with overwhelming opposition, the shah fled Iran in January 1979. A triumphant Khomeini returned from exile to establish an Islamic state. He banned the Western influences that the shah had brought to Iran and reinstated traditional Muslim values. Islamic law became the legal code for the country.

Khomeini's Anti-U.S. Policies Adherence to Islam ruled Khomeini's domestic policies. But hatred of the United States was at the heart of his politics. The Americans had long supported the shah. Their admitting him into the United States for medical treatment in 1979, however, was the final insult. That year, with the ayatollah's blessing, a group of young Islamic revolutionaries seized the U.S. embassy in Tehran. They took more than 60 Americans hostage. They also demanded the return of the shah to face trial. Most of the U.S. hostages remained prisoners for 444 days before they were released on January 20, 1981.

THINK THROUGH HISTORY
D. Analyzing Motives Why did the United States support the Shah of Iran?
D. Answer To maintain the Shah's alliance with the West and prevent the Soviets from gaining influence in Iran.

Logical/Mathematical Learners
Suggest that students create a cause-and-effect graphic to help them understand the sequence of events in the Iranian crisis. They can use a format like this.

> Shah Pahlavi welcomes Western oil companies.
> ↓
> Iranian nationalists are angered.
> ↓
> Mossaddeq seizes British oil company.

📽 *CRITICAL THINKING TRANSPARENCIES*
CT61 Cause and Effect

Worldwide ideological movements In the 1970s, the same time that Islamic fundamentalism was on the rise in Iran under the leadership of Ayatollah Khomeini, Christian fundamentalism was on the rise in the United States.

Similarly, in the 1960s, when U.S. youth were protesting the Vietnam War and authority in general, similar protest movements were sweeping countries from China to France. Encourage students to discuss this phenomenon of worldwide ideological movements. Do they think that these developments are merely coincidental or do they see a broader explanation?

Khomeini also encouraged Muslim fundamentalists, or strict believers, in other countries to overthrow their secular governments. Intended to be a means of unifying Muslims, this policy only heightened tensions between Iran and its neighbor, Iraq. While the Iranians were Shi'a, the Iraqis belonged to the rival Sunni Muslim sect. In addition, a military leader, Saddam Hussein (hoo-SAYN), governed Iraq as a secular state.

War broke out between the two countries in 1980. For eight years, Muslim killed Muslim in a territorial struggle. Caught in the middle, the United States secretly sold weapons to Iran in an effort to get their hostages released. A million Iranians and Iraqis died before a UN ceasefire ended the hostilities in 1988.

The Superpowers Face Off in Afghanistan Iran was not the only country in the Middle East in which Cold War tensions erupted. For several years following World War II, Afghanistan maintained its independence from both the neighboring Soviet Union and the United States. In the 1950s, however, Soviet influence in the country began to increase. In the late 1970s, a Muslim revolt threatened to topple Afghanistan's Communist regime. This revolt triggered a Soviet invasion in December 1979.

The Soviets expected to prop up the Afghan Communists quickly and withdraw. Instead, just as the United States had gotten mired in Vietnam in the 1960s, the Soviets found themselves stuck in Afghanistan. And like the Vietcong in Vietnam, determined Afghan rebel forces outmaneuvered and overpowered a military superpower. Soviet helicopter rocket attacks secured the cities. They failed to dislodge the rebels, called *mujahideen*, from their mountain strongholds, however. Supplied with American weapons, the *mujahideen* fought on.

The United States had armed the rebels because they considered the Soviet invasion a threat to the rich Middle Eastern oil supplies. U.S. President Jimmy Carter sternly warned the Soviets that any attempt to gain control of the Persian Gulf would be "repelled by any means necessary, including military force." No threat developed, though. Therefore, the United States limited its response to an embargo of grain shipments to the Soviet Union. It also boycotted the 1980 summer Olympic games in Moscow.

In the 1980s, a new Soviet regime acknowledged the war's devastating costs to both Afghanistan and the Soviet Union. After a ten-year occupation—as long as U.S. involvement in Vietnam—President Mikhail Gorbachev ordered his forces to withdraw. The last Soviet troops left Afghanistan in February 1989. By then, internal unrest and economic problems were tearing the Soviet Union itself apart.

SPOTLIGHT ON

Boycott of 1980 Olympics

Sixty-two nations, including Japan, West Germany, and Canada, joined the U.S. boycott of the 1980 Moscow Olympics. In sympathy, 16 of the 81 teams who did participate refused to carry their national flags in the opening ceremony.

U.S. athletes had trained for years to compete in the Olympics. They received Congressional Olympic medals as a consolation for their dashed hopes and disappointment.

Disappointed athletes and other critics suggested that future games should be played in a neutral location. This move would help separate international sports competition from politics.

Section 4 Assessment

1. TERMS & NAMES
Identify
• Third World
• nonaligned nations
• Fidel Castro
• Anastasio Somoza
• Daniel Ortega
• Shah Mohammed Reza Pahlavi
• Ayatollah Ruholla Khomeini

2. TAKING NOTES
Using a flow chart like the one below, fill in the main events of U.S. involvement in Cuba.

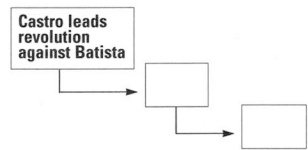
Castro leads revolution against Batista

Write a newspaper headline for one of the events you listed.

3. COMPARING
What similarities do you see among U.S. actions in Nicaragua, Cuba, and Iran?

THINK ABOUT
• the type of leader the United States supported in each country
• U.S. interests in these countries

4. ANALYZING THEMES
Economics Today, Cuba suffers a severe shortage of vital supplies, largely due to the U.S. trade embargo that has lasted for almost 40 years. Do you think the United States should lift that embargo? Why or why not?

THINK ABOUT
• Castro's leadership
• prior U.S. conflicts with Cuba
• human suffering

Restructuring the Postwar World **495**

ANSWERS

1. TERMS & NAMES
Third World, p. 491
nonaligned nations, p. 491
Fidel Castro, p. 492
Anastasio Somoza, p. 493
Daniel Ortega, p. 493
Shah Mohammed Reza Pahlavi, p. 494
Ayatollah Ruholla Khomeini, p. 494

2. TAKING NOTES
Castro nationalizes U.S.-owned sugar mills; Eisenhower orders embargo on trade; Castro turns to Soviets for aid; Bay of Pigs invasion; Cuban missile crisis.

3. COMPARING
The United States supported dictatorial leaders who were overthrown by popular uprisings. It intervened in all three countries to protect its own interests—a takeover by Communist Sandinistas in Nicaragua and by Castro in Cuba, and loss of vital oil supplies from Iran.

4. ANALYZING THEMES
Lift embargo—Cuba is no longer receiving aid from the Soviets; all Cubans—not only those who agree with Castro—are suffering; Retain embargo—Castro is still a threat to U.S. security; eventually embargo may cause the fall of the Communist regime.

OBJECTIVES

1. To analyze Soviet domination of Eastern Europe and the Soviet Union–China split.

2. To trace the origins of détente and its effects on the Cold War.

3. To describe the renewal of Cold War tensions in the 1980s.

CRITICAL THINKING

- Recognizing effects, p. 496
- Recognizing bias, p. 498
- Analyzing causes, p. 499
- Contrasting, p. 499
- Evaluating decisions, p. 499

FOCUS
5-Minute Warm-Up

Interpreting Political Cartoons

To give students a concise idea of the next stages in the Cold War, ask the following questions.

1. Look at the political cartoon on page 498. Which two nations are represented?

2. What does the bomb stand for? What are the two nations trying to do?

 WARM-UP TRANSPARENCY 17

OBJECTIVE 1 INSTRUCT

The Soviets Dominate Eastern Europe

Key Ideas

- Khrushchev removes Stalinist influences from the Soviet Union but puts down a revolt in Hungary.

- Brezhnev imposes repressive measures in the Soviet Union and crushes Czechoslovakian reforms.

- China's defiance leads to a split with the Soviet Union.

 IN-DEPTH RESOURCES
Guided Reading, p. 5
Primary Source: Political Cartoon, p. 12

 ACCESS FOR STUDENTS ACQUIRING ENGLISH
Guided Reading (Spanish), p. 188

---

5 The Cold War Thaws

TERMS & NAMES
- Nikita Khrushchev
- destalinization
- Leonid Brezhnev
- John F. Kennedy
- Lyndon Johnson
- détente
- Richard M. Nixon
- SALT
- Ronald Reagan
- Star Wars

MAIN IDEA

The Cold War began to thaw as the superpowers entered an era of uneasy diplomacy.

WHY IT MATTERS NOW

The United States and the countries of the former Soviet Union continue to cooperate and maintain a cautious peace.

SETTING THE STAGE In the postwar years, the Soviet Union kept a firm grip on its satellite countries in Eastern Europe. These countries were Poland, Czechoslovakia, Hungary, Romania, Yugoslavia, Bulgaria, Albania, and East Germany. It did not allow them to direct and develop their own economies. Instead, it insisted that they develop industries to meet Soviet needs. These policies greatly hampered Eastern Europe's economic recovery.

The Soviets Dominate Eastern Europe

After Stalin died, a new, more moderate group of Soviet leaders came to power. These new leaders allowed their satellite countries a taste of independence, as long as they remained firmly Communist and allied with the Soviet Union. During the 1950s and 1960s, however, growing protest movements in Eastern Europe threatened the Soviet Union's grip over the region. Increasing tensions with Communist China also diverted Soviet attention and forces.

Destalinization and Rumblings of Protest Joseph Stalin died on March 5, 1953. Shortly after his death, a loyal member of the Communist party named **Nikita Khrushchev** became the dominant Soviet leader. The shrewd, tough Khrushchev publicly denounced Stalin for jailing and killing loyal Soviet citizens. His speech signaled the beginning of a policy called **destalinization,** or purging the country of Stalin's memory. Workers destroyed monuments of the former dictator and reburied his body outside the Kremlin wall. Khrushchev also called for "peaceful competition" with the capitalist states.

A toppled statue of Stalin lies in Moscow, a stark symbol of Khrushchev's policy of destalinization.

This new Soviet outlook did not change life in the satellite countries, however. Their resentment occasionally turned into active protest. In October 1956, for example, the Hungarian army joined with protesters to overthrow Hungary's Soviet-controlled government. Storming through the capital, Budapest, angry mobs waved Hungarian flags with the Communist hammer-and-sickle emblem cut out. "From the youngest child to the oldest man," one protester declared, "no one wants communism."

A popular and liberal Hungarian Communist leader named Imre Nagy (IHM·ray nahj) formed a new government. Nagy promised free elections and demanded that Soviet troops leave Hungary. In response, in early November, Soviet tanks rolled into Budapest. They were backed by infantry units. Thousands of Hungarian freedom fighters armed themselves with pistols and bottles. The Soviets overpowered them, however. The invaders replaced the Hungarian government with pro-Soviet leaders and eventually executed Nagy.

THINK THROUGH HISTORY
A. Recognizing Effects What effects did destalinization have on Soviet satellite countries?
A. Answer None. Their resentment and protest against Soviet rule continued.

SECTION 5 RESOURCES

PRINT RESOURCES

 IN-DEPTH RESOURCES: UNIT 5
Guided Reading, p. 5
Primary Source: Political Cartoon, p. 12

 ACCESS FOR STUDENTS ACQUIRING ENGLISH
Guided Reading (Spanish), p. 188

 FORMAL ASSESSMENT
Section Quiz, p. 215

 ALTERNATIVE ASSESSMENT BOOK

TECHNOLOGY RESOURCES

 CRITICAL THINKING TRANSPARENCIES
CT69 Visual Summary

 CD-ROM
Electronic Library of Primary Sources

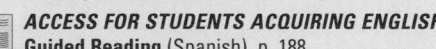 **INTERNET** www.mlworldhistory.com

The Victim

HUNGARY

Faces of Protest

Soviet tanks move into Prague in 1968 to stamp out Czech reforms.

The Survivor

CZECHOSLOVAKIA

Imre Nagy (1896–1958)

Of peasant background, Imre Nagy was captured by the Soviets during World War I and recruited into their army. He became a Communist and lived in Moscow until 1944, when he returned to Soviet-occupied Hungary.

Although he held several posts in his country's Communist government, his loyalty remained with the peasants. Because of his independent approach, he fell in and out of favor with the Soviet regime. He led the anti-Soviet revolt in October 1956.

The Soviets forcefully put down the uprising and deported Nagy. They then brought him back to Hungary, where they tried and executed him. He remained in disgrace until the Hungarian Supreme Court cleared his name in 1989.

Alexander Dubček (1921–1992)

Alexander Dubček was the son of a member of the Czech Communist Party and moved rapidly up through the Communist ranks in Czechoslovakia.

In response to the spirit of change in the 1960s, Dubček instituted broad reforms in the 1968 Prague Spring. Not surprisingly, Soviet officials reacted negatively. Tanks rolled into Prague to suppress a feared revolt.

The Soviets expelled Dubček from the Communist Party in 1970. He survived, though. He regained political prominence in 1989, when the Communists agreed to share power in a coalition government. When the new nation of Slovakia was formed in 1992, Dubček became head of its Social Democratic Party.

Brezhnev and the Revolt in Czechoslovakia Despite this show of force in Hungary, Khrushchev lost prestige in his country as a result of the Cuban missile crisis. In 1964, Communist party leaders voted to remove him from power. His replacement, **Leonid Brezhnev,** quickly adopted repressive domestic policies. The Communist party strictly enforced laws to limit such basic human rights as freedom of speech and worship. Government censors carefully controlled what writers could publish. And Brezhnev clamped down on those who dared to protest his government's policies. For example, the secret police arrested many dissidents, including Aleksandr Solzhenitsyn, winner of the 1970 Nobel Prize for literature. They then expelled him from the Soviet Union.

Brezhnev made it clear that he would not tolerate dissent in Eastern Europe either. His policy was put to the test in early 1968. At that time, Czech Communist leader Alexander Dubček (DOOB-chehk) loosened controls on censorship to offer his country socialism with "a human face." This period of reform, when Czechoslovakia's capital bloomed with new ideas, became known as Prague Spring.

Prague Spring, however, did not survive the summer. On August 20, armed forces from the Warsaw Pact nations invaded Czechoslovakia. Brezhnev justified this invasion by claiming the Soviet right to prevent its satellites from rejecting communism.

Split with China While many of the Soviet satellite countries resisted Communist rule, China seemed firmly committed to communism. In fact, to cement the ties between their Communist powers, Mao and Stalin had signed a 30-year treaty of friendship in 1950. Their spirit of cooperation, however, ran out before the treaty did.

Restructuring the Postwar World **497**

HISTORY MAKERS
Faces of Protest: Imre Nagy and Alexander Dubček

Imre Nagy and Alexander Dubček were both unlikely heroes. Nagy seemed to be more of an idealistic bookworm than a man of action. Although some people suspected him of being a Soviet agent, he not only agreed to lead the Hungarian uprising, but defended his country's bid for independence with his life. A Hungarian supporter said, "If his life was a question mark, his death was an answer."

In contrast, Dubček struck many observers as a colorless bureaucrat. He played by Communist rules and rose steadily through the ranks. He revealed his reformist colors, however, in 1967, when he rallied the support of political and economic reformers. He granted greater freedom of expression to the press and, in 1968, proposed a full-blown reform program— "Czechoslovakia's Road to Socialism"—designed to democratize the country.

MORE ABOUT . . .
The Brezhnev Doctrine

Leonid Brezhnev's claim that the Soviet Union had a right to prevent its satellite countries from rejecting Communism came to be known as the Brezhnev Doctrine. This policy was invoked as late as 1979 to justify the Soviet invasion of Afghanistan.

 ELECTRONIC LIBRARY OF PRIMARY SOURCES
Speech on Stalin by Nikita Khrushchev
From *A Student's Diary*

Foreign Intervention Policies
Although the United States and the Soviet Union occupied opposite ends of the political spectrum during the Cold War, both developed policy statements that enabled them to occupy other countries.

Have students compare the provisions of the U.S. Monroe Doctrine (page 346) and Truman Doctrine (page 478) and the

Soviet Brezhnev Doctrine (page 497). Suggest that they make a compare-and-contrast chart summarizing each doctrine and indicating what actions the doctrine has been used to justify.

Students Acquiring English Vocabulary Activity To help students pronounce the foreign names on these pages, ask any native speakers of Russian, Hungarian, or Czech in the class to say the names aloud so everyone can hear the accent.

Remind students that in the pronunciation guides provided in parentheses, a

space separates words, a dot separates syllables, and capital letters indicate stress. Then pair native with nonnative English speakers and have them pronounce Imre Nagy and Alexander Dubček.

From Brinkmanship to Détente

▶ *Key Ideas*
- Repeated crises force U.S. and Soviet leaders to seek alternatives to the policy of brinkmanship.
- The U. S. seeks to lessen tensions and avoid confrontations with the Soviet Union.
- President Nixon opens talks with both China and the Soviet Union.

CRITICAL THINKING ACTIVITY
CLASS TIME: 15 MINUTES

Perceiving Causes and Effects
To help students understand the reasons behind and results of détente, have them complete a cause-and-effect diagram as they read.

CRITICAL THINKING TRANSPARENCIES
CT75 Cause and Effect

History from Visuals

Cartoon

Interpreting the Cartoon Make sure students understand that this cartoon depicts the world as a bomb with a lit fuse. Which item in the cartoon represents détente? *The scissors.*

Extension Activity Ask students to discuss ways they might represent the policy of brinkmanship visually. Then have them work in pairs to create a political cartoon about this Cold War strategy.

The Soviets assumed that the Chinese would follow Soviet leadership in world affairs. As the Chinese grew more confident, however, they came to resent being Moscow's junior partner. They began to spread their own brand of communism in Africa and other parts of Asia. In 1959, Khrushchev punished the Chinese for their independence by refusing to share nuclear secrets with them. The following year, the Soviets ended technical economic aid to China. This split eventually grew so wide that fighting broke out along the long Chinese-Soviet border. After repeated incidents, the two neighbors today maintain a fragile peace.

From Brinkmanship to Détente

In the 1970s, the United States and the Soviet Union finally backed away from the aggressive policies of brinkmanship they had followed during the early postwar years. The superpowers slowly moved toward a period of lowered tensions.

Brinkmanship Breaks Down The brinkmanship policy that the United States followed during the Eisenhower, Kennedy, and Johnson administrations resulted in one terrifying crisis after another. Though these crises erupted all over the world, they were united by a common fear. Nuclear war seemed possible.

In 1960, the U-2 incident prevented a meeting between the United States and the Soviet Union to discuss the buildup of arms on both sides. Then, during the presidency of **John F. Kennedy** in the early 1960s, the Cuban missile crisis made the superpowers' use of nuclear weapons a very real possibility. (See pages 492–493.) The crisis ended when the Soviet ships turned back to avoid a confrontation at sea. "We're eyeball to eyeball," the relieved U.S. Secretary of State Dean Rusk said, "and I think the other fellow just blinked." President Kennedy's Secretary of Defense, Robert McNamara, however, admitted just how close the world had come to disaster:

> **A VOICE FROM THE PAST**
> In the face of an air attack [on Cuba] and in the face of the probability of a ground attack, it was certainly possible, and I would say probable, that a Cuban sergeant or Soviet officer in a missile silo, without authority from Moscow, would have launched one or more of those intermediate-range missiles, equipped with a nuclear warhead, against one or more of the cities on the East Coast of the United States.
> **ROBERT McNAMARA,** quoted in *Inside the Cold War*

Tensions remained high, and after the assassination of President Kennedy in 1963, **Lyndon Johnson** assumed the U.S. presidency. Committed to stopping the spread of communism, President Johnson escalated U.S. involvement in the war in Vietnam.

The United States Embraces Détente Widespread popular protests wracked the United States during the Vietnam War. And the turmoil did not end with U.S. withdrawal. As it tried to heal its internal wounds, the United States began backing away from its policy of direct confrontation with the Soviet Union. **Détente,** a policy of lessened Cold War tensions, finally replaced brinkmanship during the administration of President **Richard M. Nixon.**

President Nixon's move toward détente grew out of a philosophy known as realpolitik. This term comes from the German word meaning "realistic politics." In practice, realpolitik meant dealing with other nations in a practical and flexible manner. While the United States continued to contain the spread of communism, the two superpowers agreed to pursue détente and to reduce tensions.

Nixon's new policy represented a dramatic personal reversal as well as a political shift for the

In a spirit of cooperation and détente, the U.S. and the Soviet Union try to prevent their conflicts from destroying the world.

(C) J.G. SZABO - ROTHCO CARTOONS   86-6E43

498 Chapter 17

Vocabulary
détente: a French word meaning "a loosening"

THINK THROUGH HISTORY
B. Recognizing Bias Do you think that Robert McNamara's view of the Soviet threat in Cuba was justified or was due to a biased U.S. fear of the Soviet Union? Explain.
B. Possible Answers
Justified—The Soviets had installed missiles in Cuba with the intent to use them against the United States. *Biased*—The Soviets intended their missiles only to be a threat. They knew that using them might start a nuclear war that would destroy the world.

Task: Students will write statements and stage a ceremony to honor heroes of the Cold War.

Purpose: To evaluate Cold War issues and personalities.

Activity: Working in small groups, students will choose a Cold War hero, such as Imre Nagy, and write a testimonial statement honoring that person's

contributions to history. Encourage the groups to create visual materials, such as plaques, posters, and collages to accompany their statements. Then have the class stage an awards ceremony in which a volunteer from each group makes a presentation.

Building a Portfolio: Students should consider including testimonial statements in their portfolios.

ALTERNATIVE ASSESSMENT BOOK
Standards for Evaluating a Cooperative Activity

Standards for Evaluation
Testimonial statements should . . .
- identify the hero
- indicate the person's involvement with the Cold War
- convey the person's personality and achievements

498 Chapter 17

THINK THROUGH HISTORY
C. Analyzing Causes Why did the United States begin pursuing a policy of détente?
C. Possible Answer Internal turmoil following the Vietnam War and a realization that it would have to deal realistically and flexibly with not only the Soviet Union, but with China as well; fear of nuclear war.

country. His rise in politics in the 1950s was largely due to his strong anti-Communist position. Twenty years later, he became the first American president after World War II to visit Communist China. The visit made sense in a world in which three—rather than just two—superpowers eyed each other suspiciously. "We want the Chinese with us when we sit down and negotiate with the Russians," Nixon explained.

Nixon Visits the Communist Superpowers Three months after visiting Beijing in February 1972, President Nixon made history again by becoming the first American president to visit the Soviet Union. After a series of meetings called the Strategic Arms Limitation Talks (**SALT**), Nixon and Brezhnev signed the SALT I Treaty. This five-year agreement limited to 1972 levels the number of intercontinental ballistic and submarine-launched missiles each country could have. In 1975, 33 nations joined the United States and the Soviet Union in signing a commitment to détente and cooperation, the Helsinki Accords.

Détente Cools

Under Presidents Nixon and Gerald Ford, the United States gradually improved relations with China and the Soviet Union. In the late 1970s, however, President Jimmy Carter's concern over harsh treatment of Soviet protesters threatened to prevent a second round of SALT negotiations. In June 1979, Carter and Brezhnev finally signed the SALT II agreement. When the Soviets invaded Afghanistan in December of that year, however, the U.S. Congress refused to ratify SALT II. Tensions continued to mount as increasing numbers of European and Asian countries began building nuclear arsenals.

THINK THROUGH HISTORY
D. Contrasting In what ways did Presidents Nixon's and Reagan's policies toward the Soviet Union differ?
D. Answer Nixon pursued a policy of détente, or easing of tensions. Reagan brought tensions to a new height.

Ronald Reagan Abandons Détente The fiercely anti-Communist U.S. president **Ronald Reagan** took office in 1981. He continued his country's retreat from détente. In 1983, he announced a program—the Strategic Defense Initiative (SDI)—to protect America against enemy missiles. The program, called **Star Wars** after a popular movie, was never put into effect. It remained a symbol of U.S. anti-Communist sentiment, however.

Tensions increased as U.S. activities such as arming Nicaragua's Contras pushed the two countries even farther from détente. A transfer of power in the Soviet Union in 1985, however, brought a new policy toward the United States and the beginnings of a final thaw in the Cold War.

The Cold War between the two superpowers ebbed and flowed. Meanwhile, as you will learn in the next chapter, developing countries continued their own struggles for independence from colonialism.

U.S. President Jimmy Carter and Soviet Premier Leonid Brezhnev optimistically mark the signing of the SALT II treaty in Vienna, Austria, in 1979. Carter, however, remained concerned over Soviet violations of its citizens' human rights.

Section ⑤ Assessment

1. TERMS & NAMES
Identify
- Nikita Khrushchev
- destalinization
- Leonid Brezhnev
- John F. Kennedy
- Lyndon Johnson
- détente
- Richard M. Nixon
- SALT
- Ronald Reagan
- Star Wars

2. TAKING NOTES
In a chart like the one below, indicate each U.S. president's contribution to Cold War tensions by writing his name in the correct column.

Tensions Increased	Tensions Decreased
Eisenhower	

Write a paragraph summarizing the policies and actions of one of these presidents.

3. EVALUATING DECISIONS
Do you think it was a wise political move for Nixon to visit Communist China and the Soviet Union? Why or why not?

THINK ABOUT
- the Cuban missile crisis
- realpolitik
- public sentiment after the Vietnam War

4. THEME ACTIVITY
Revolution Write a poem or song lyrics expressing a Hungarian or Czech citizen's protest against Communist rule.

Restructuring the Postwar World **499**

ANSWERS

1. TERMS & NAMES
Nikita Khrushchev, p. 496
destalinization, p. 496
Leonid Brezhnev, p. 497
John F. Kennedy, p. 498
Lyndon Johnson, p. 498
détente, p. 498
Richard M. Nixon, p. 498
SALT, p. 499
Ronald Reagan, 499

Star Wars, 499

2. TAKING NOTES
Increased—Eisenhower, Kennedy, Johnson, Carter, Reagan; Decreased—Nixon, Ford

3. EVALUATING DECISIONS
Wise—Nuclear war threatened the world and any efforts made

to weaken the threat were good; Communist China was becoming a power that could not be ignored. Unwise—By meeting with officials in China and the Soviet Union, Nixon was condoning communism and undermining efforts to contain it.

4. THEME ACTIVITY
Standards for Evaluation
Effective poems or lyrics should meet the following criteria:
- Indicates reasons for revolting against the Communist regime
- Gives an idea of life under communism
- Uses rhythm and repetition to reinforce the message

OBJECTIVE ③ INSTRUCT

Détente Cools

▶ **Key Idea**
- As U.S.-Soviet tensions increase, U.S. presidents Carter and Reagan back away from détente.

MORE ABOUT . . .
Nixon in China
Mao met the U.S. president on February 21, 1972. Mao liked Nixon and his assessment of the man widely known as "Tricky Dick" might have surprised many Americans: "He speaks forthrightly," said Mao, "no beating around the bush, not like the leftists, who say one thing and mean another."

ASSESS & RETEACH

Section 5 Assessment
Have students answer questions 1, 2, and 3 independently. Ask them to work in small groups to create poems or song lyrics for question 4.

Section Quiz
 FORMAL ASSESSMENT
Section Quiz, p. 215

Reteaching Activity
CLASS TIME: 10 MINUTES
Divide the class in half. Have one group portray the United States and the other group the Soviet Union. Ask the groups to plan and act out three skits—one depicting brinkmanship, one depicting détente, and the third depicting U.S.-Soviet relations under President Reagan.

 CRITICAL THINKING TRANSPARENCIES
CT69 Visual Summary

CLOSE ACTIVITY

CLASS TIME: 15 MINUTES
Summarizing and Sequencing Events
Divide the class into six groups. Have each group create a poster about a key Cold War event—the Hungarian revolt, Prague Spring, the Cuban missile crisis, President Nixon's visit to China, the Soviet invasion of Afghanistan, and the signing of the SALT I Treaty. Have the groups consult and present their posters to the class.

Teacher's Edition **499**

Chapter 17 Assessment

TERMS & NAMES

1. containment, p. 477
2. Cold War, p. 479
3. Mao Zedong, p. 482
4. Cultural Revolution, p. 485
5. 38th parallel, p. 486
6. Vietnamization, p. 489
7. Fidel Castro, p. 492
8. Nikita Khrushchev, p. 496
9. détente, p. 498
10. SALT, p. 499

REVIEW QUESTIONS

Answers will vary.

11. They believed the United States should not interfere with other nations' affairs, that it lacked resources to carry out a worldwide war on communism, and that economic aid might support dictators.

12. It proved that it would go to the brink itself by building up a nuclear arsenal and competing aggressively in the arms race.

13. The United States supported the Nationalists in their fight against the Communists. The Soviet Union supported the Communists.

14. Both programs failed to create the powerful socialist nation Mao envisioned and actually weakened it.

15. Five million people died, and North and South Korea remained divided at the 38th parallel, as before the war.

16. Unfamiliar jungle terrain and guerrilla warfare and lack of popular support for the South Vietnamese government they were bolstering.

17. They needed financial aid and investment to help them industrialize as well as a political and economic system on which to model their governments.

18. It secretly built 42 missile sites in Cuba.

19. It did not allow the East Europeans to run their own economies or give them enough money to repair war damages. It also promoted industries necessary to the Soviets, not to the satellite countries.

20. Dealing with nations in a realistic manner, which meant giving up long-held fear and hatred of communism. Pursuit of this policy helped ease Cold War tensions.

Chapter 17 Assessment

TERMS & NAMES

Briefly explain the importance of each of the following in reconstructing the postwar world since 1945.

1. containment
2. Cold War
3. Mao Zedong
4. Cultural Revolution
5. 38th parallel
6. Vietnamization
7. Fidel Castro
8. Nikita Khrushchev
9. détente
10. SALT

Interact *with* History

On page 474, you considered what action you would take in a civil war in a developing country that both the United States and the Soviet Union were interested in. Now that you have learned more about the Cold War, would your decision change? Discuss your ideas with a small group.

Visual Summary

REVIEW QUESTIONS

SECTION 1 (pages 475–480)
Two Superpowers Face Off

11. Why did some Americans oppose the Truman Doctrine?

12. How did the Soviet Union respond to the U.S. policy of brinkmanship?

SECTION 2 (pages 482–485)
Communists Triumph in China

13. Which sides did the superpowers support in the Chinese internal struggle for control of the country?

14. What were the results of Mao Zedong's Great Leap Forward and Cultural Revolution?

SECTION 3 (pages 486–490)
War in Korea and Vietnam

15. What effects did the Korean War have on Korea's land and people?

16. What major difficulties did the U.S. Army face in fighting the war in Vietnam?

SECTION 4 (pages 491–495)
Cold War Around the World

17. Why did developing nations often align themselves with one or the other superpower?

18. How did the Soviet Union respond to the U.S.-supported Bay of Pigs invasion?

SECTION 5 (pages 496–499)
The Cold War Thaws

19. In what ways did Soviet actions hamper Eastern Europe's economic recovery after World War II?

20. What policies characterized realpolitik and how did they affect the course of the Cold War?

Cold War, 1946–1980

United States

- 1946 Institutes containment policy to block Soviet influence
- 1948 Gives massive foreign aid to Europe under Marshall Plan
- 1952 Tests first H-bomb
- 1953 Adopts brinkmanship policy, which escalates Cold War
- 1965 Sends troops to Vietnam

- 1948 U.S. and Britain break Soviet blockade of Berlin with airlift
- 1950 Communist North Korea attacks South Korea
- 1960 U-2 incident reignites tension between superpowers
- 1962 U.S. blockades Cuba in response to buildup of Soviet missiles
- 1972 Nixon and Brezhnev sign SALT I treaty
- 1980 U.S. boycotts Moscow Summer Olympics to protest invasion of Afghanistan

- 1950 Signs friendship treaty with China
- 1953 Tests first H-bomb
- 1957 Launches Sputnik, starting space race
- 1956 Puts down revolt in Hungary and later executes Imre Nagy
- 1968 Violently brings Prague Spring to an end
- 1979 Invades Afghanistan

Soviet Union

Interact *with* History

Possible Responses: Students who originally wanted to help the rebels may now say that their support by an enemy superpower made them enemies of our vital interests. Others who supported the dictator may now say that his brutality made it difficult for him to ever win the support of the people.

CRITICAL THINKING

1. COLD WAR MANEUVERS

Using a web like the one below, indicate various tactics the Soviet Union and the United States used during the Cold War.

Cold War Tactics

2. RECOGNIZING THE ENEMY

American cartoonist Walt Kelly once said, "We have met the enemy, and he is us." In what sense do you think this saying applies to the Cold War superpowers? In what specific ways were the United States and the Soviet Union more similar than they were different?

3. FROM WORLD WAR TO COLD WAR

THEME EMPIRE BUILDING The Soviet Union emerged from World War II economically and physically devastated. How do you think the development of the Cold War would have proceeded if the United States had been in that position?

4. ANALYZING PRIMARY SOURCES

The following poem by Ho Chi Minh was broadcast over Hanoi Radio on January 1, 1968. Read the poem and answer the questions that follow.

> **A VOICE FROM THE PAST**
> This Spring far outshines the previous Springs,
> Of victories throughout the land come happy tidings.
> South and North, rushing heroically together, shall
> smite the American invaders!
> Go Forward!
> Total victory shall be ours.
> **HO CHI MINH**, quoted in *America and Vietnam*

- In Ho's opinion, who was the enemy in the Vietnam War?
- What purpose might the North Vietnamese have had in broadcasting this poem?

CHAPTER ACTIVITIES

1. LIVING HISTORY: Unit Portfolio Project

THEME ECONOMICS Your unit portfolio project focuses on the ways economic factors influence history. For Chapter 17, you might use one of the following ideas to add to your portfolio.

- Ask classmates to think about what life would be like for peasants in a Communist satellite country. Then stage an interview in which you ask them to discuss their feelings about communism and capitalism. Audiotape your interviews and add a commentary to create an "objective" newscast.
- Create a poster to teach elementary school students about the differences between capitalism and communism.
- Working in a small group, develop and perform a five- to ten-minute skit that pokes fun at communism or capitalism.

2. CONNECT TO TODAY: Cooperative Learning

THEME REVOLUTION During the Cold War, the superpowers played a part in many revolutions or upheavals in developing nations. This unrest continues today as countries struggle to develop suitable political and economic systems.

Working with a team, create an oral presentation about a current political struggle or revolution.

Using the Internet or magazines, research a current political conflict. Investigate the beliefs, programs, tactics, and popular support of the rival factions. Determine which side is in power and what the outcome of the struggle appears to be.

- Collect photographs, charts, artifacts, or other visual aids to illustrate the issues involved in the struggle.
- If possible, interview people from that country who have immigrated to the United States and include their viewpoints in your presentation.

3. INTERPRETING A TIME LINE

Look back at the unit time line on pages 470–471. Which two events during the Cold War do you think had the greatest impact on the U.S. decision to pursue a policy of détente?

FOCUS ON **GEOGRAPHY**

Cold War tensions between the United States and the Soviet Union were fed by the fear of nuclear war.

- What does this map projection suggest about the distance between the countries?
- Which country had more ICBM bases?

Connect to History
How did the United States and the Soviet Union avoid a nuclear confrontation?

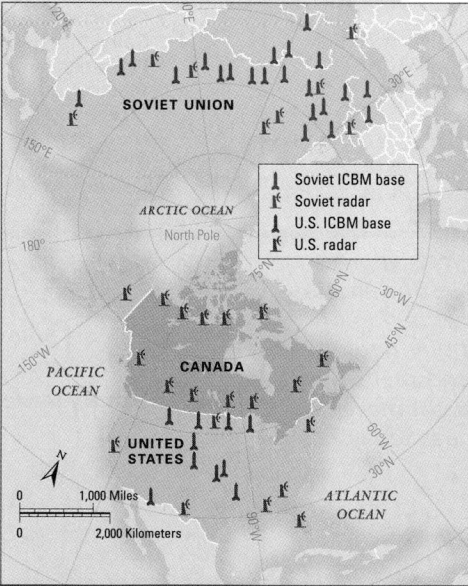

SOVIET UNION
ARCTIC OCEAN
North Pole
CANADA
PACIFIC OCEAN
UNITED STATES
ATLANTIC OCEAN

Soviet ICBM base
Soviet radar
U.S. ICBM base
U.S. radar

0 1,000 Miles
0 2,000 Kilometers

	Key Ideas	COPY MASTERS	ASSESSMENT

SECTION 1
The Indian Subcontinent Gains Independence

pp. 505–511

At the end of World War II, South Asians demand independence. Britain partitions the Indian subcontinent into two new nations, India and Pakistan; a part of Pakistan later becomes Bangladesh. Britain also frees Ceylon.

 In-Depth Resources: Unit 5
• **Guided Reading,** p. 20
• **Primary Source:** from "First Servant of the Indian People," p. 27

 Section 1 Assessment, p. 511

Formal Assessment
• Section Quiz, p. 224

Alternative Assessment Book
• Standards for Evaluating a Cooperative Activity

SECTION 2
Southeast Asian Nations Gain Independence

pp. 512–515

Some of the Southeast Asian colonies that become independent after World War II prosper, while others suffer under authoritarian regimes.

 In-Depth Resources: Unit 5
• **Guided Reading,** p. 21
• **Primary Source:** Call to Boycott Presidential Election, p. 28
• **Literature:** from *The Year of Living Dangerously,* p. 31

 Section 2 Assessment, p. 515

Formal Assessment
• Section Quiz, p. 225

Alternative Assessment Book
• Standards for Evaluating a Cooperative Activity

SECTION 3
New Nations in Africa

pp. 516–520

Colonizers differ in their willingness to grant independence to their African colonies and in the amount of help they give their colonies in preparing to become modern nations.

 In-Depth Resources: Unit 5
• **Guided Reading,** p. 22
• **Skillbuilder Practice:** Evaluating Decisions, p. 24
• **Geography Application:** The Congo Gains Independence, p. 25
• **Primary Source:** Farewell Without Tears, p. 29
• **Literature:** Négritude poems, p. 32
• **History Makers:** Jomo Kenyatta, p. 34
• **Connections Across Time and Cultures:** p. 36

Section 3 Assessment, p. 520

Formal Assessment
• Section Quiz, p. 226

Alternative Assessment Book
• Standards for Evaluating a Product or Performance

SECTION 4
Conflicts in the Middle East

pp. 521–525

The division of Palestine and the creation of the new nation of Israel after World War II result in conflict between Israeli and Palestinian nationalist movements that continues today.

In-Depth Resources: Unit 5
• **Guided Reading,** p. 23
• **Primary Source:** The Balfour Declaration, p. 30
• **History Makers:** Golda Meir, p. 35

Section 4 Assessment, p. 525

Formal Assessment
• Section Quiz, p. 227

Alternative Assessment Book
• Standards for Evaluating a Cooperative Activity

CHAPTER RESOURCES

Chapter Overview

After World War II, imperialist powers rethink the cost of colonies as they demand their independence. The imperialists differ in the speed with which they relinquish control and in the amount of preparation for independence they provide.

 Telescoping the Times
• Chapter Summary, pp. 73–75

 Planning for Block Schedules

Case Studies
• **Case Study 1**—India and Britain: Colonialism and Imperialism, p. 2
• **Case Study 2**—Ghana and South Africa: Political Problems of Two African Nations, p. 16
• **Case Study 5**—Israel and Syria: Nationalism and Religion, p. 58

 Chapter Assessment, pp. 526–527

Chapter Activities, p. 527

Formal Assessment
• Chapter Test, forms A and B, pp. 228–233

Test Generator

Alternative Assessment Book

TECHNOLOGY

Warm-Up Transparency 18

World Art and Cultures Transparencies
• AT74 *Vene, Vidi, Vici*

Electronic Library of Primary Sources
• from Radio Address from New Delhi

INTERNET RESOURCES
www.mlworldhistory.com

Warm-Up Transparency 18

Geography Transparencies
• GT34 Indonesia and Malaysia, 1945–1976

Electronic Library of Primary Sources
• "The Fall of President Marcos"

INTERNET RESOURCES
www.mlworldhistory.com

Warm-Up Transparency 18

INTERNET RESOURCES
www.mlworldhistory.com

Warm-Up Transparency 18
Critical Thinking Transparencies
• CT34 Time Machine: The Middle East Conflict
• CT70 Visual Summary
World Art and Cultures Transparencies
• AT76 *After the Storm*
Electronic Library of Primary Sources
• "Enough of Blood and Tears"

INTERNET RESOURCES
www.mlworldhistory.com

Chapter Summaries on Audiocassette in English and Spanish

INTERNET RESOURCES
www.mlworldhistory.com

Block Scheduling (90 MINUTES)

Day 1
Section 1, pp. 505–511

COOPERATIVE ACTIVITY
Writing Indian Political Statements, p. 506 (Teacher's Edition)
Section Assessment, p. 509

Day 2
Section 2, pp. 512–515
COOPERATIVE ACTIVITY
Creating a Brochure, p. 514 (Teacher's Edition)
Section Assessment, p. 515

Day 3
Section 3, pp. 516–520
Section Assessment, p. 520

Day 4
Section 4, pp. 521–525
COOPERATIVE ACTIVITY
Researching West Bank Settlements, p. 523 (Teacher's Edition)
Section Assessment, p. 525
Chapter Assessment, pp. 526–527

Yearly Pacing *Chapter 18 Total:* 4 days *Yearly Total:* 85 days

 Planning for Block Schedules

Customizing for Special Needs

Students Acquiring English

 Access for Students Acquiring English
• **Guided Reading** for Sections 1–4 (Spanish), pp. 195–198
• **Chapter Summary** (Spanish), pp. 192–194
• **Skillbuilder Practice** Evaluating Decisions (Spanish), p. 199
• **Geography Application** The Congo Gains Independence (Spanish), p. 200

 Spanish Reading Study Guide
• pp. 191–200

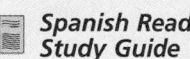 *Chapter Summaries on Audiocassette* in English and Spanish

Less Proficient Readers

 In-Depth Resources: Unit 5
• **Guided Reading** for Sections 1–4, pp. 20–23
• **Skillbuilder Practice** Evaluating Decisions, p. 24
• **Geography Application** The Congo Gains Independence, p. 25

 Telescoping the Times
• Chapter Summary, pp. 73–75

 Reading Study Guide
• pp. 191–200

 Chapter Summaries on Audiocassette

Gifted and Talented Students

 In-Depth Resources: Unit 5

Primary Sources
• from "First Servant of the Indian People," p. 27
• Call to Boycott Presidential Election, p. 28
• Farewell Without Tears, p. 29
• The Balfour Declaration, p. 30

History Makers
• Jomo Kenyatta, p. 34
• Golda Meir, p. 35

Connections to Literature READINGS FOR STUDENTS

 In-Depth Resources: Unit 5
Literature: from *The Year of Living Dangerously,* p. 31; Négritude poems, p. 32

Enrichment Reading

• **Head, Bessie**
"Snapshots of a Wedding," *African Short Stories*
Oxford, Heinmann, 1987
A bridegroom is forced to choose between two loves: a traditional girl who would tie him to the past and a modern girl who would take him into an exciting, unknown future.

McDougal Littell
The Language of Literature, Grade 10

Anita Desai, "Games at Twilight," p. 545
Abioseh Nicol, "As the Night the Day," p. 638

 = Pupil's Edition   = Overhead Transparency   = Software   = Video

 = Copy Master   = CD-ROM   = Audiocassette   = Internet

The Colonies Become New Nations, 1945–Present

Accessing Prior Knowledge

- Have students look at the flags displayed in two of the four photographs on this spread. Ask students what a flag represents in the life of a nation. Discuss with them the symbolism of a national flag.

Making Inferences and Predicting

- After students have surveyed the captions and pictures on these pages, ask them what conditions might motivate people to fight for their independence.

- Ask students to predict the possible outcomes of a nationalistic struggle for independence.

Geography Connection

Ask students to look at the map on these two pages.

- On what continents did the struggles for independence that are pictured in the photographs take place? *Africa and Asia.*

- Which of the pictured struggles for independence took place closest to the equator? *Kenya.*

CHAPTER 18

The Colonies Become New Nations, 1945–Present

PREVIEWING THEMES

Economics

The emergence of new nations from European- and U.S.-ruled colonies brought a change in the ownership of vital resources and markets. In many cases, new nations formed trade alliances with their former rulers. Most new nations struggled to build up local industries.

Power and Authority

Systems of government shifted for one billion people when colonies in Asia and Africa gained their freedom. A challenge for many of the new nations was how to unify diverse factions. Authoritarian rule and military coups were common.

Revolution

Independence movements swept Africa and Asia as World War II ended. Revolutionaries overthrew existing political and economic systems to create new nations. The revolutionary leaders had difficulty maintaining common goals after independence.

INTERNET CONNECTION

Visit us at **www.mlworldhistory.com** to learn more about India, Southeast Asia, Africa, and the Middle East.

INDEPENDENCE, 1945–PRESENT

British rule in **Palestine** ended on **May 14, 1948.** A British Royal Marine lowered the Union Jack (the British flag) for the last time in Haifa as British troops prepared to board ship and sail home. Britain's withdrawal led to the creation of the state of Israel, sparking conflict between Arabs and Jews in the region.

Algiers

Mediterranean Sea

Jerusalem

MIDDLE EAST

PALESTINE

AFRICA

Nairobi

ATLANTIC OCEAN

502

40°W

Jomo Kenyatta was sworn in as prime minister of Kenya on **December 12, 1963,** in the capital of Nairobi. When Kenya gained its independence, Kenyatta became the nation's first prime minister (1963–64). Then, when, the country became a republic, he became its first president (1964–78).

GEOGRAPHY THEMES

Place

Tell students that geography played a significant role in the emergence of new nations discussed in this chapter. The natural resources of a colony significantly affected how willing the colonizers were to give up the land. In Kenya, Algeria, and Indonesia, coloniz-ers who had lived there for generations were reluctant to leave. In many places, diverse populations, thrown together by arbitrary boundaries established by the colonizers, made up the new nations. These nations had to create unity among the diverse peoples. Mistakes were made, and old ethnic hostilities sometimes persisted.

Movement

The birth of the new nations was often accompanied by huge migrations of people as Europeans returned to their homelands and ethnic groups sought a more harmonious grouping. The worst of these migrations accompanied the partition of the Indian subcontinent and resulted in the deaths of thousands. Ideas were also on the move as many of the new nations entered the modern world for the first time. New communi-cation technologies broke down barri-ers between countries and continents and between cities and villages.

ADDITIONAL RESOURCES

Books for the Teacher

- Davidson, Basil. *The Black Man's Burden: Africa and the Curse of the Nation State.* New York: Random, 1993.

- Tessler, Mark A. *A History of the Israeli-Palestinian Conflict.* Bloomington, IN: Indiana UP, 1994.

Books for the Student

- Baynham, Simon. *Africa from 1945.* New York: Watts, 1987.

- De Lee, Nigel. *Rise of the Asian Superpowers from 1945.* New York: Watts, 1987.

▭▭▭ Videos

- *The Arab World.* Society for Visual Education, 1988. 800-829-1900.

- *Ghana.* Altschul Group, 1994. 800-323-9084.

- *India Unveiled: Emergence of the State.* Britannica, 1986. 800-554-9862.

- *Raising the Bamboo Curtain: Vietnam, Burma, and Cambodia.* Cambridge Social Studies, 1995. 800-468-4227.

◉ Software

- *Decisions, Decisions: Building a Nation.* CD-ROM or diskette. Tom Snyder Productions, 1996. 800-342-0236.

- *Twentieth-Century Nationalism.* CD-ROM. Society for Visual Education, 1994. 800-829-1900.

Jawaharlal Nehru addressed a massive crowd at Delhi's Red Fort on **August 15, 1947,** as India gained independence. Partition of the British colony into mostly Hindu India and mostly Muslim Pakistan forced millions to move.

ASIA

Delhi

INDIA

Arabian Sea

Bay of Bengal

South China Sea

Manila

SOUTHEAST ASIA

0° Equator

PACIFIC OCEAN

Tropic of Cancer

Philippine Sea

INDIAN OCEAN

In her campaign to become president of the Philippines in **1986, Corazón Aquino** used her hand to form the letter *L* (for *laban*, or "struggle"), the symbol of her campaign.

N

0 — 2,000 Miles

0 — 4,000 Kilometers

Tropic of Capricorn

AUSTRALIA

503

HISTORY THROUGH ART

Photography

Photography is both a means of recording important events and an art form. Photographs can capture dramatic moments in history and preserve them for posterity. Three of the pictures on these pages show important moments in the history of new nations as they achieve their independence. The British Royal Marine symbolizes a whole empire as he lowers the British flag and prepares to depart from the former British mandate of Palestine. Nehru, who is to become India's first prime minister, addresses a huge crowd on the eve of independence. Jomo Kenyatta jubilantly takes office as Kenya's prime minister when the country gains its independence from Great Britain. All of these pictures capture symbolic moments as British rule is withdrawn from former colonies and protectorates.

Interpreting the Photographs What do these photographs seem to suggest about the end of British rule? What emotions might people in the newly independent nations experience? What emotions and thoughts might they have about their former colonial masters?

Interact *with* History

Independence has come to a former British colony, which has been divided into the new nations of India and Pakistan. Serious conflict occurs among the various factions within each country. The Hindu majority in India attacks Muslims, and the Muslim majority in Pakistan attacks Hindus. Some Hindus in Pakistan are choosing to stay in their homeland; others are choosing to flee to India to join the Hindu majority there. Either alternative involves risk.

You are a Hindu whose homeland is Pakistan. Trains are leaving that will carry you through hostile territory to a new homeland, where you will no longer be in a minority. What will you do? Will you leave your homeland behind in order to move to a new land to live among people who share your religious beliefs? Or will you stay where you are and take your chances?

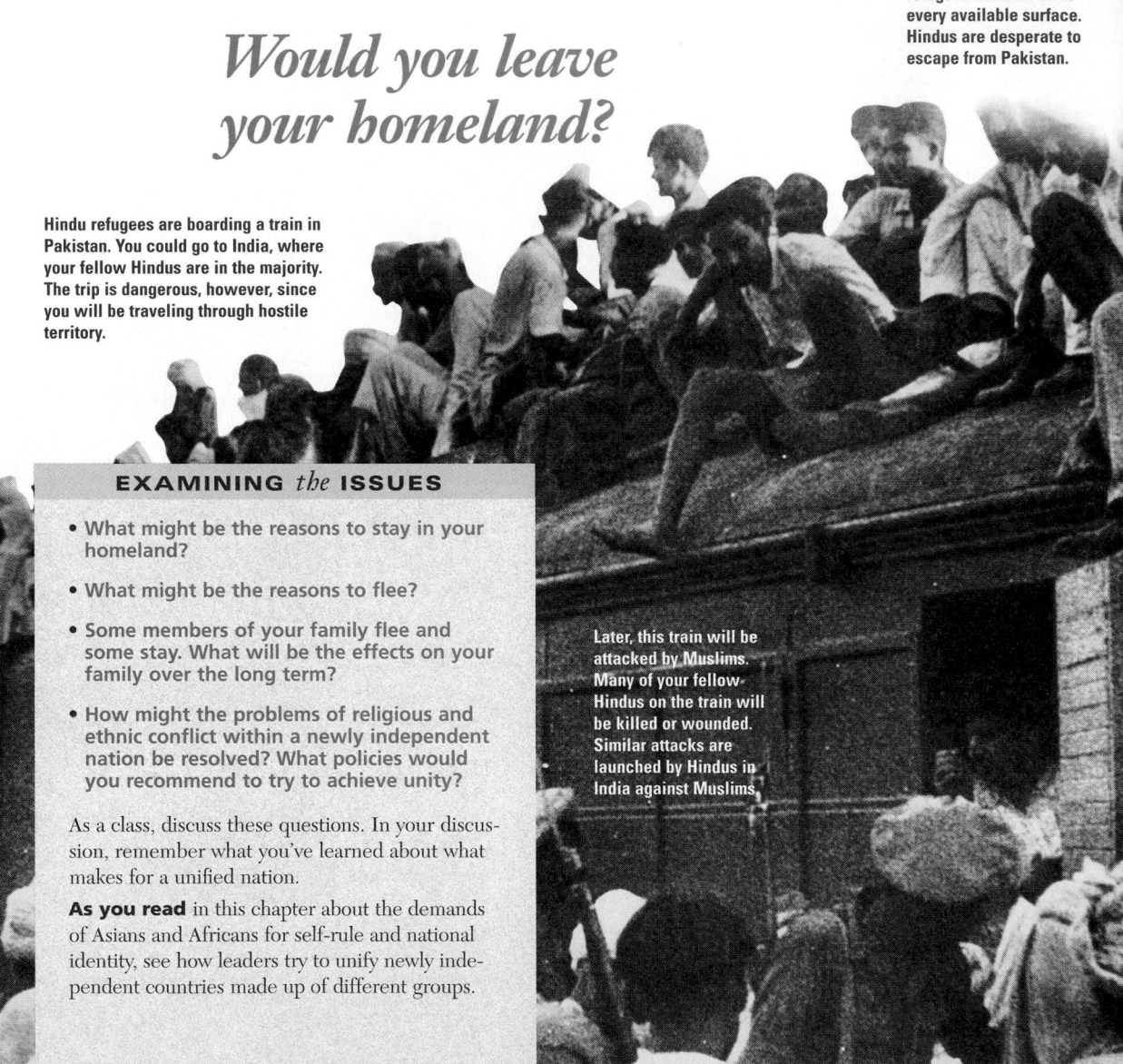

After the passenger cars have been filled, refugees clamber on to every available surface. Hindus are desperate to escape from Pakistan.

Would you leave your homeland?

Hindu refugees are boarding a train in Pakistan. You could go to India, where your fellow Hindus are in the majority. The trip is dangerous, however, since you will be traveling through hostile territory.

Later, this train will be attacked by Muslims. Many of your fellow-Hindus on the train will be killed or wounded. Similar attacks are launched by Hindus in India against Muslims.

EXAMINING *the* ISSUES

- What might be the reasons to stay in your homeland?

- What might be the reasons to flee?

- Some members of your family flee and some stay. What will be the effects on your family over the long term?

- How might the problems of religious and ethnic conflict within a newly independent nation be resolved? What policies would you recommend to try to achieve unity?

As a class, discuss these questions. In your discussion, remember what you've learned about what makes for a unified nation.

As you read in this chapter about the demands of Asians and Africans for self-rule and national identity, see how leaders try to unify newly independent countries made up of different groups.

1 The Indian Subcontinent Gains Independence

TERMS & NAMES
- Congress Party
- Muslim League
- Muhammad Ali Jinnah
- Lord Mountbatten
- partition
- Jawaharlal Nehru
- Indira Gandhi
- Rajiv Gandhi
- Benazir Bhutto

MAIN IDEA	WHY IT MATTERS NOW
New nations emerged from the British colony of India.	India today is the largest democracy in the world.

SETTING THE STAGE Britain had ruled India for many years. During this time, some Indians had been pressing for self-rule. In 1939, India was stunned when Britain committed India's armed forces to World War II without first consulting the colony's elected representatives. Indian nationalists felt humiliated. In 1942, the Congress Party launched a "Quit India" campaign. It was intended to drive Great Britain out of India. The end of World War II, in 1945, brought changes to the Indian subcontinent as dramatic as those anywhere in the world.

A Movement Toward Independence

The story was similar throughout the colonial world. When World War II broke out, Africans and Asians answered their colonial rulers' cries for help. These Africans and Asians fought on distant battlefields. They also guarded strategic bases and resources at home. The war brought soldiers from widely separated colonies into contact with one another. Soldiers from the colonies shared their frustrations, dreams for independence, and strategies for achieving it.

"Asia for Asians" During World War II, the Japanese "Asia for Asians" campaign helped to generate nationalism throughout the region. It also sparked independence movements in the various countries Japan occupied in Southeast Asia. The Japanese defeat of European forces was a sign to the nationalists that the Europeans were not as strong as they had thought them to be. Asian nationalists came to realize that their colonial masters were not unbeatable. Sometimes the Europeans suffered defeat at the hands of others—such as the Japanese—who were nonwhite and non-Western, like the nationalists.

THINK THROUGH HISTORY
A. Recognizing Effects What was the effect on Asians of Japanese victories over Europeans?
A. Answer It made Asian nationalists realize the Europeans were vulnerable.

The Colonial Response Britain was recovering from the enormous costs of the war. It began to rethink the expense of maintaining and governing distant colonies. The new government in Britain also called into question the very basis of imperialism. Was it acceptable to take by force the land and resources of another nation in order to enrich the imperial nation?

Independence Brings Partition to India

In 1919, the British massacred unarmed Indians at Amritsar. (See Chapter 14.) This incident, more than any other single event, had marked the beginning of the end of British rule in India. The incident had caused millions of Indians to become strong nationalists overnight. A year later, in 1920, Mohandas Gandhi launched his first nonviolent

This photo shows British soldiers held in a Japanese prisoner-of-war camp at the end of World War II.

The Colonies Become New Nations **505**

SECTION 1 RESOURCES

PRINT RESOURCES

IN-DEPTH RESOURCES: UNIT 5
Guided Reading, p. 20
Primary Source: from "First Servant of the Indian People" by Jawaharlal Nehru, p. 27

ACCESS FOR STUDENTS ACQUIRING ENGLISH
Guided Reading (Spanish), p. 195

FORMAL ASSESSMENT
Section Quiz, p. 224

ALTERNATIVE ASSESSMENT BOOK

TECHNOLOGY RESOURCES

WORLD ART AND CULTURES TRANSPARENCIES
AT74 *Vene, Vidi, Vici*

CD-ROM
Electronic Library of Primary Sources

INTERNET www.mlworldhistory.com

Section 1 Overview

OBJECTIVES

1. To summarize the effect of World War II on the colonies.

2. To describe the events that led to the partition of India.

3. To summarize the leadership of Nehru and his descendants.

4. To summarize the politics of Pakistan and Sri Lanka.

SKILLBUILDERS
- Interpreting maps: location, p. 507

CRITICAL THINKING
- Recognizing effects, p. 505
- Making inferences, p. 506
- Analyzing causes, p. 507
- Clarifying, p. 509
- Synthesizing, p. 509
- Analyzing themes p. 509

FOCUS
5-Minute Warm-Up

Making Inferences
To help students understand the changes that swept former colonies, have them answer the following questions.

1. Read Daily Life on page 508. What might Gandhi have thought of Narayanan's election?

2. Why might Narayanan's election suggest that the caste system will be reformed?

WARM-UP TRANSPARENCY 18

OBJECTIVE 1 INSTRUCT

A Movement Toward Independence

▶ *Key Ideas*
- Soldiers from the colonies fight in World War II.
- People in the colonies realize their rulers are not unbeatable.
- Britain begins to rethink the cost of maintaining its colonies.

IN-DEPTH RESOURCES: UNIT 5
Guided Reading, p. 20

ACCESS FOR STUDENTS ACQUIRING ENGLISH
Guided Reading (Spanish), p. 195

Teacher's Edition **505**

Independence Brings Partition to India

(See page 505.)

▶ **Key Ideas**
• Jinnah proposes partition of India along religious lines.
• Britain supports partition.
• Mass migrations and killings precede independence.

HISTORYMAKERS
Muhammad Ali Jinnah

Have students read the text on page 509 about the breakup of Pakistan. Then have them analyze Jinnah's statement about the distinct culture of Muslims. Ask students how they account for the seeming conflict between Jinnah's view and the subsequent split.

MORE ABOUT . . .
Partition and Religion

A major difference between the two new nations of Pakistan and India was the role religion played in the state. Pakistan established Islam as the official national religion. India's constitution declared India a secular nation with no official religion. The difference influenced each nation's legal system and policies on the family. Pakistan's court system and its marriage and divorce laws, for example, must all be in accordance with Islamic law. India allows Hindus and Muslims to choose to be governed by their own religious codes.

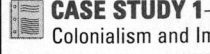 **CASE STUDY 1**—India and Britain: Colonialism and Imperialism, p. 2

---

campaign for Indian independence. Gandhi was admired as the Mahatma, or "Great Soul," of the Indian independence movement.

HISTORY MAKERS

**Muhammad Ali Jinnah
1876–1948**

Muhammad Ali Jinnah was born in Karachi, India, which is now part of Pakistan. His Muslim family was wealthy and sent him to England to study. He became a brilliant lawyer and a leader in India's movement for independence.

As the leader of the Muslim League, Jinnah argued for a separate state for Muslims. Called the "great leader," Jinnah was the founder of Pakistan and its first governor-general. He described the Indian Muslims as "a nation with [a] distinct culture and civilization, . . . our own distinctive outlook on . . . life."

The Congress Party and the Muslim League The Indian National Congress, or the **Congress Party,** was a national political party. It claimed to represent all of India. India in the 1940s had approximately 350 million Hindus and about 100 million Muslims. Most members of the Congress Party were Hindus, but the party at times had many Muslim members. A Muslim even served as one of its presidents, from 1940 to 1945.

The **Muslim League** was an organization founded in 1906 in India to protect Muslim interests. The league was concerned that the mainly Hindu Congress Party would look out primarily for Hindu interests. The leader of the Muslim League, **Muhammad Ali Jinnah** (mu·HAM·ihd ah·LEE JIHN·uh), had once been a member of the Congress Party. However, he later insisted that only the league spoke for Muslims. He said that all Muslims ought to resign from the Congress Party. The Muslim League stated that it would never accept Indian independence if it meant rule by the Hindu-dominated Congress Party. Jinnah stated, "The only thing the Muslim has in common with the Hindu is his slavery to the British." The British encouraged the division between Hindus and Muslims in the belief that it would strengthen their authority.

The Muslim League first officially proposed the partition of India into separate Hindu and Muslim nations at its Lahore conference in 1940. Most Muslims lived in the northwest and northeast areas of the subcontinent. Gandhi was deeply hurt. He strongly opposed the two-nation theory on political, cultural, and even moral grounds.

Partition into India and Pakistan When World War II ended, the British government changed from the Conservative Party's Winston Churchill to the Labour Party's Clement Atlee. The stage was set for the British transfer of power. However, the problem persisted of who should receive that power once it was transferred.

Rioting of Hindus and Muslims against one another broke out in Calcutta, East Bengal, Bihar, and Bombay. In August 1946, four days of rioting in Calcutta left more than 5,000 people dead and more than 15,000 hurt. Gandhi walked through the worst areas there. He did his best to reduce the violence between Hindus and Muslims. **Lord Louis Mountbatten** was the last viceroy of India. He feared that the Hindus and Muslims of India would never be able to live together in peace. He began to accept the idea that **partition,** or the dividing up, of India into two nations—mostly Hindu India and mostly Muslim Pakistan—was unavoidable.

The British House of Commons passed an act on July 16, 1947, that granted the two nations independence in one month's time. In that short period, more than 500 independent native princes had to decide which nation they would join—India or Pakistan. The administration of the courts, the military, the railways, and the police— the whole of the civil service—had to be divided down to the last paper clip. Most difficult of all, millions of Hindus, Muslims, and Sikhs would shortly find themselves minorities in a hostile nation. These people had to decide where to go.

During the summer of 1947, 10 million people were on the move in the Indian subcontinent. Whole trainloads of refugees were massacred. Muslims killed Sikhs who were moving into India. Hindus and Sikhs killed Muslims who were headed into Pakistan. In all, an estimated 1 million died. "What is there to celebrate?" Gandhi mourned. "I see nothing but rivers of blood." Gandhi personally went to Delhi to plead for fair treatment of Muslim refugees. While he was there, he himself became

Vocabulary
viceroy: a person who governs on behalf of a king.

B. Possible Answer
He was hurt that his dream of a unified India was not to be, and he mourned the many lost lives.
**THINK THROUGH HISTORY
B. Making Inferences** Why did Gandhi mourn as India achieved independence?

Task: Students will write political statements representing different views on the partition of India.

Purpose: To help students understand different perspectives on an issue.

Activity: Divide the class into four groups representing the Indian National Congress, the Muslim League, the British government, and

followers of Gandhi. Have each group research and write a political statement on the partition of India that might have been written by a leader or significant member of the group represented.

 Building a Portfolio: Students can attach an explanation of the assignment to their statements.

ALTERNATIVE ASSESSMENT BOOK
Standards for Evaluating a Cooperative Activity

Standards for Evaluation
Statements should . . .

• use specific details to back up a point of view
• accurately represent the opinions of the group represented
• demonstrate writing skills

a victim. He was shot on January 30, 1948, by a Hindu extremist who thought Gandhi too protective of Muslims.

Modern India

At the stroke of midnight on August 15, 1947, India would become free. It would also become the world's largest democracy. As the hour approached, **Jawaharlal Nehru** (jah·WAH·hahr·lahl NAY·roo), independent India's first prime minister, addressed the Constituent Assembly:

A VOICE FROM THE PAST
Long years ago, we made a tryst [appointment] with destiny, and now the time comes when we shall redeem our pledge, not wholly or in full measure, but very substantially. At the stroke of the midnight hour, when the world sleeps, India will wake to life and freedom.
JAWAHARLAL NEHRU

Nehru Leads India For the first 17 years after independence, India had one prime minister—Jawaharlal Nehru. He had been one of Gandhi's most devoted followers. Educated in Britain, Nehru won popularity among all groups in India. He emphasized democracy, unity, and economic modernization.

Nehru assumed several large challenges along with the office of prime minister. One such challenge was a dispute over the territory of Kashmir. Although its ruler was Hindu, Kashmir had a large Muslim population. The state bordered both India and Pakistan. Pakistan invaded the area shortly after independence, causing Kashmir's ruler to align Kashmir with India. War between India and Pakistan in Kashmir continued until the United Nations arranged a cease-fire in 1949. The cease-fire left a third of Kashmir under Pakistani control and the rest under Indian control. Later, in 1962, China seized part of Kashmir. In 1972, Indian and Pakistani forces fought there again. In that year, a new truce line was set up between the Indian and Pakistani areas of Kashmir. Today, tensions continue to flare along the cease-fire line established by the UN in 1949.

Nehru used his leadership to move India forward. He led other newly independent nations of the world in forming an alliance of countries that were neutral in the dispute between the United States and the Soviet Union. On the home front, Nehru called for a reorganization of the states by language. He also pushed for industrialization and sponsored social reforms. He tried to elevate the status of the lower castes and expand the rights of women.

The Nehru Family Rules Nehru's death in 1964 left the Congress Party with no leader strong enough to hold together its many factions. Then, in 1966, Nehru's daughter, **Indira Gandhi,** was chosen prime minister.

The Indian Subcontinent, 1947

Mostly Muslim
Mostly Hindu
Mostly Sikhs
Mostly Buddhist

GEOGRAPHY SKILLBUILDER: Interpreting Maps
1. **Location** What Muslim country, divided into two portions, bordered India on the east and the west?
2. **Location** What Buddhist countries bordered India to the north and the south?

The Colonies Become New Nations **507**

After a short spell out of office, she was reelected in 1980. Under Gandhi's leadership, the country substantially increased its production of food grains.

Gandhi soon faced a threat from Sikh extremists, who were agitating for an independent state. Sikh terrorists took refuge in the Golden Temple at Amritsar, the most important Sikh religious center. From there, they ventured out to commit many acts of violence. In June 1984, Indian army troops overran the Golden Temple. They killed about 500 Sikhs and destroyed sacred property. In retaliation, Indira Gandhi was gunned down four months later by two of her Sikh bodyguards. This act set off another murderous frenzy, causing the deaths of thousands of Sikhs.

Gandhi was succeeded by her son, **Rajiv** (rah·jeev) **Gandhi,** in 1984. He immediately called for a new election. He won by the largest majority of any of the Nehru-Gandhi family. His party lost the leadership in 1989, however, because it was accused of corruption. In 1991, while campaigning near Madras, Rajiv was killed by a bomb. It was carried by a female terrorist from Sri Lanka who opposed Gandhi's policies.

Social Issues Challenge India India faces challenges today. Its steadily climbing population is expected to top 1 billion early in the next century. The caste system continues to undermine social equality. India still faces the threat of religious fanaticism. Many separatist movements exist throughout the country. On the plus side, Indian industry has continued to develop. New oil and coal resources have been discovered. Scientific and technical education have expanded.

A Turbulent History

Ali Bhutto

1977 Ali Bhutto
Prime Minister Ali Bhutto of Pakistan is deposed in a coup led by General Zia. Bhutto is later hanged for having ordered the assassination of a political opponent.

General Zia

1988 General Zia
General Zia, president of Pakistan, dies in a mysterious plane crash.

Pakistan

1950   1960   1970   1980   1991

India

1948 Mohandas Gandhi
Gandhi is shot to death by a Hindu extremist. The assassin opposes Gandhi's efforts to achieve equal treatment for all Indians, including Muslims.

1984 Indira Gandhi
Indira Gandhi is machine-gunned by two of her Sikh bodyguards. Her murder is in retaliation for an attack she ordered on a Sikh temple.

1991 Rajiv Gandhi
Rajiv Gandhi is killed by a bomb while campaigning. The bomb is carried by a woman who belongs to a group of Tamil separatists.

Rajiv Gandhi

Mohandas Gandhi

Indira Gandhi

508 Chapter 18

Pakistan and Sri Lanka

Pakistan gained its independence in 1947, and Ceylon, an island country southeast of India, in 1948. After independence, both countries suffered from religious and ethnic fighting. In 1972 Ceylon changed its name to Sri Lanka (sree LAHNG·kuh).

Civil War in Pakistan Pakistan began as a divided nation. Its east and west regions were separated by more than 1,000 miles of Indian territory. One region lay to the northeast of India, the other to the northwest. In culture, language, history, geography, economics, and ethnic background, the two regions were very different. Only the Islamic religion united them. East Pakistan had a larger population than the West. It felt neglected by the government in West Pakistan. Rebellion broke out in April 1971. In December 1971, the Indian army lent its support to East Pakistan. The army of West Pakistan, which had occupied East Pakistan, withdrew. A new nation, Bangladesh, was formed from East Pakistan.

Muhammad Ali Jinnah, the first governor-general of Pakistan, died shortly after independence. This left the nation without strong leadership. Pakistan went through a series of military coups, the first in 1958. Ali Bhutto took over leadership of the country following the civil war. A military coup in 1977 led by General Zia removed Bhutto, who was later executed for crimes allegedly committed while in office. After Zia's death, Bhutto's daughter, **Benazir Bhutto,** was twice elected prime minister. After months of disorder, she was removed from office in 1996. Nawaz Sharif became prime minister after the 1997 elections.

Pictured here is the emblem of the Liberation Tigers of Tamil Eelam, a militant group based in Sri Lanka. The group has fought for the independence of Tamils.

Sri Lanka Split by Factions Sri Lanka's recent history has also been one of turmoil. Three-quarters of Sri Lanka's 16 million people are Buddhists. A fifth are Tamils, a Hindu people of southern India and northern Sri Lanka. A militant group of Tamils have called for a separate Tamil nation. Since 1981, when Tamil militants began strong-armed resistance, thousands of lives have been lost. In an effort to end the violence, Rajiv Gandhi and the Sri Lankan president tried to reach an accord in 1983. The agreement called for Indian troops to enter Sri Lanka and help disarm Tamil rebels. This effort was not successful, and the Indian troops left in 1990. A civil war between Tamils and other Sri Lankans continues today.

Section 1 Assessment

1. TERMS & NAMES
Identify
- Congress Party
- Muslim League
- Muhammad Ali Jinnah
- Lord Mountbatten
- partition
- Jawaharlal Nehru
- Indira Gandhi
- Rajiv Gandhi
- Benazir Bhutto

2. TAKING NOTES
Create a time line of prominent Indian prime ministers from independence in 1947 through 1989, using a form like the one below.

```
 first              third
   |                  |
   +--------+---------+
            |
         second
```

Note one important accomplishment of each prime minister.

3. SYNTHESIZING
Do you think that India's political and economic success is crucial to the future of democracy in Asia? Why?

THINK ABOUT
- India's influence in Asia
- religious and ethnic differences and conflicts
- social implications of economic failure

4. ANALYZING THEMES
Power and Authority
What were some of the problems shared by leaders of India and Pakistan?

THINK ABOUT
- the factions within these countries
- their thoughts about independence
- how their problems were resolved

The Colonies Become New Nations **509**

OBJECTIVE 4 INSTRUCT

Pakistan and Sri Lanka

▶ *Key Ideas*
- Civil war breaks out in Pakistan, and East Pakistan becomes Bangladesh.
- Sri Lanka copes with Tamil rebels.

ASSESS & RETEACH

Section 1 Assessment
Divide the questions among groups of students and have them present their answers orally.

Section Quiz

 FORMAL ASSESSMENT
Section Quiz, p. 224

Reteaching Activity
CLASS TIME: 10 MINUTES

Use the Guided Reading worksheet for Section 1 to review the main ideas of the section.

 IN-DEPTH RESOURCES: UNIT 5
Guided Reading, p. 20

CLOSE ACTIVITY

CLASS TIME: 10 MINUTES

Making a Chart
Work with the class to create a chart listing the countries of South Asia, their date of independence, former colonizer, prominent leaders, and major events. The chart might look like this:

	India	Pak.	Bang.	S.L.
Date	1947	1947	1971	1948
Colonizer				
Leaders				
Events				

Teacher's Edition **509**

SOMETHING IN COMMON

OBJECTIVES

① To explain how people around the world celebrate the marriage ceremony.

② To describe specific wedding rituals of different cultures.

FOCUS

Ask students if they have ever attended a wedding ceremony. Were they ever in the wedding party as a flower girl or ring bearer? Do they have an older brother or sister or another relative who has recently gotten married?

INSTRUCT

Wedding Rituals

▶ *Key Ideas*
• Rituals such as weddings celebrate the important occasions of people's lives.
• Although wedding rituals differ from one culture to another, they have many characteristics in common.
• Wedding rituals strengthen the bond between the bride and the groom as well as among members of the community.

Wedding Rituals

In cultures throughout the world, people get married. They do so for a variety of reasons: to share life with a loved one, to raise a family, to gain social position, to gain independence, to carry on values and customs. In India, an elaborate wedding ritual has evolved within the Hindu tradition. That ritual expresses Hindus' deepest beliefs about the relationship between men and women, the importance of the family, and the role of the spiritual in the significant moments of life. Other cultures have different rituals with which they surround the wedding ceremony.

Hindu Wedding in India

Hindus traditionally bestow jewelry on brides. This bride is from West Bengal. She is bedecked with gold, silver, and enamel jewelry inlaid with precious stones. Her sari is from Benares and is made of fine silk and gold brocade. The colors of red and gold symbolize life and good luck. The design on the bride's hands is painted in henna. This traditional pattern is believed to keep away evil spirits.

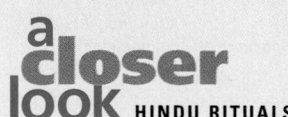
a closer look HINDU RITUALS

510 Chapter 18

A gold necklace called a thali is placed around the bride's neck. This necklace contains a medallion with the three symbols of the Hindu trinity—a conch shell, a trident, and a ring.

TEACHING OPTIONS

CUSTOMIZING FOR SPECIAL NEEDS

Gifted and Talented Students
Some students might wish to look at other ceremonies, such as death rites, to see how they are observed within different religions and cultures. What elements are the same? What features are different? How do funerals and burial or cremation rites communicate the values and belief systems of the people who conduct them? You might have students compare and contrast the wedding rituals and the death rites within a particular culture, such as Morocco or Guatemala. Or you might have students compare either wedding rituals or death rites across cultures.

CONNECTIONS ACROSS TIME AND PLACE

Religious Observances in Russia For many years, the Communist government discouraged religious observances in the Soviet Union. Church attendance dwindled, and many beautiful old structures were neglected. The dissolution of the Soviet Union did lead to a greater tolerance of religion, particularly of the Russian Orthodox Church, an important force in Russia for centuries. Recently, the Orthodox Church has campaigned to be recognized as the official church in Russia. This campaign has been strongly opposed by those who believe that all religions should have equal standing in the eyes of the state.

Orthodox Wedding in Russia
The Church of the Transfiguration in St. Petersburg, Russia, is the site of this Russian Orthodox wedding ceremony. Crowns are placed on the heads of the bride and groom, who hold candles. Orthodox churches make lavish use of gold and rich decoration to display religious works of art such as icons.

A Bridal Fair in Morocco
The bridal fair is part of the marriage ritual of some Berbers of Morocco. Marriageable young men and women attend the fair of Imilchil in the Atlas Mountains of North Africa in search of spouses. The women wear capes, headdresses, and veils as they survey the eligible prospects during the fair. Court- ship, engagement, and marriage all take place during the three days of the fair. The couples shown are waiting to enter the wedding tent.

Wedding in Guatemala
The Indians shown to the left are of Mayan descent. They live in the highlands of Guatemala. Villagers in Guatemala combine suit jackets and Indian clothing in a wedding ceremony. The clothes worn by the Indians identify their home villages.

Connect to History

Comparing What are some ele- ments of the wedding ceremony that seem common from one cul- ture to another?

 SEE SKILLBUILDER HANDBOOK, PAGE 654.

Connect to Today

Researching Read about wed- ding rituals in other cultures, and then write a couple of paragraphs describing the ritual that most appeals to you.

In this Hindu wedding ritual, the bride is shrouded in a white sheet and tied to the groom. The couple takes seven steps around the sacred fire, a symbol of purification, to seal the marriage.

The Colonies Become New Nations **511**

Section 2 Overview

OBJECTIVES

① To summarize events that led to the Philippines' independence and to describe the political rule of Marcos and his overthrow.

② To summarize problems facing Burma, Malaysia, and Singapore.

③ To summarize Indonesia's fight for independence from the Dutch.

SKILLBUILDERS

• Interpreting maps: region, p. 513
• Interpreting graphs, p. 515

CRITICAL THINKING

• Making inferences, pp. 512, 514, 515
• Contrasting, p. 515

FOCUS
5-Minute Warm-Up

Summarizing

Have students answer the following questions to help them understand the impact that one person can have on history.

1. Read History Makers on page 514. What kind of government is Aung San Suu Kyi struggling to establish in Burma?

2. How does the military government of Burma view her?

 WARM-UP TRANSPARENCY 18

OBJECTIVE ① INSTRUCT

The United States and the Philippines

▶ **Key Ideas**
• The Philippines gains independence from the United States.
• The continued presence of U.S. military bases in the Philippines causes conflict.
• Ferdinand Marcos imposes authoritarian rule and is eventually forced out of office.

IN-DEPTH RESOURCES: UNIT 5
Guided Reading, p. 21

ACCESS FOR STUDENTS ACQUIRING ENGLISH
Guided Reading (Spanish), p. 196

2 Southeast Asian Nations Gain Independence

TERMS & NAMES
• Ferdinand Marcos
• Corazón Aquino
• Aung San
• Aung San Suu Kyi
• Sukarno
• Suharto

MAIN IDEA
The European colonies in Southeast Asia became independent countries in the postwar period.

WHY IT MATTERS NOW
The power and influence of the Pacific Rim nations are likely to expand during the next century.

SETTING THE STAGE At the end of World War II, colonized people all over the world agitated for independence. As it had in India, Britain gave up control of its Southeast Asian colonies; it gave up Burma quickly and Malaysia after some delay. Some imperialists, the Dutch among them, were reluctant to give up their Southeast Asian possessions. They waged bitter and losing battles to retain control. The United States gave up its Asian colony in the Philippines soon after World War II.

The United States and the Philippines

The Philippines became the first of the world's colonies to achieve independence following World War II. The United States granted the Philippines independence in 1946, on the anniversary of its own Declaration of Independence, the Fourth of July.

The Philippines Achieves Independence The Filipinos' immediate goals were to rebuild the economy and to restore the capital of Manila. The city had been badly damaged in World War II. The United States had promised the Philippines $600 million in war damages. However, the U.S. government insisted that Filipinos approve the Bell Act in order to get the money. This act would establish free trade between the United States and the Philippines for eight years, to be followed by gradually increasing tariffs. Filipinos were worried that American businesses would exploit the resources and environment of the Philippines. In spite of this concern, Filipinos approved the Bell Act and received their money.

The United States wanted to maintain its military presence in the Philippines. With the onset of the Cold War (see Chapter 17), the United States needed to be able to protect its interests in Asia. Both China and the Soviet Union were opponents of the United States at the time. Both were Pacific powers with bases close to allies of the United States as well as to raw materials and resources vital to U.S. interests. Therefore, the United States demanded a 99-year lease on its military and naval bases in the Philippines. The bases—Clark Air Force Base and Subic Bay Naval Base near Manila—proved to be critical to the United States later, in the staging of the Korean and Vietnam wars.

These military bases also became the single greatest source of conflict between the United States and the Philippines. Many Filipinos regarded the bases as proof of American imperialism. Later agreements shortened the terms of the lease, and the United States gave up both bases in 1991.

Vocabulary
Filipino: an inhabitant of the Philippines.

Ships of the U.S. Navy docked at Subic Bay in the Philippines from 1901 to 1991.

A. Possible Answer To protect its vital economic and political interests. The Philippines were centrally located and therefore within striking distance of many potential hot spots in the region.

THINK THROUGH HISTORY
A. Making Inferences Why might the United States have been interested in maintaining military bases in the Philippines?

SECTION 2 RESOURCES

PRINT RESOURCES

IN-DEPTH RESOURCES: UNIT 5
Guided Reading, p. 21
Primary Source: Call to Boycott Presidential Election, p. 28
Literature: from *The Year of Living Dangerously*, p. 31

ACCESS FOR STUDENTS ACQUIRING ENGLISH
Guided Reading (Spanish), p. 196

FORMAL ASSESSMENT
Section Quiz, p. 225

ALTERNATIVE ASSESSMENT BOOK

TECHNOLOGY RESOURCES

GEOGRAPHY TRANSPARENCIES
GT34 Indonesia and Malaysia, 1945–1976

CD-ROM
Electronic Library of Primary Sources

INTERNET www.mlworldhistory.com

Southeast Asia, 1945–1975

BHUTAN
CHINA
INDIA
BURMA 1948
BANGLADESH
20° N
Hanoi
NORTH VIETNAM 1954
LAOS 1953
Vientiane
Rangoon
THAILAND
Bangkok
CAMBODIA 1953
Phnom Penh
SOUTH VIETNAM 1954
Saigon
INDIAN OCEAN
South China Sea
PHILIPPINES 1946
Manila
PACIFIC OCEAN

Former French colony
Former British colony
Former Dutch colony
Former U.S. colony
Continuously independent
1945 Date of independence

BRUNEI (Br.)
MALAYSIA 1957
Kuala Lumpur
Singapore 1965
BORNEO
0° Equator
I N D O N E S I A 1949
Jakarta

N

0   500 Miles
0   1,000 Kilometers

100°E   120°E   140°E

GEOGRAPHY SKILLBUILDER: Interpreting Maps
1. **Region** *Which former Dutch colony is made up of a series of islands spread out from the Indian Ocean to the Pacific Ocean?*
2. **Region** *From what European country did the most colonies shown above gain their independence?*

After World War II, the Philippine government was still almost completely dependent on the United States economically and politically. The Philippine government looked for ways to lessen this dependency. It welcomed Japanese investments. It also broadened its contacts with Southeast Asian neighbors and with nonaligned nations.

The Marcos Regime and Corazón Aquino **Ferdinand Marcos** was elected president of the Philippines in 1965. The country suffered under his rule from 1966 to 1986. Marcos imposed an authoritarian regime and stole millions of dollars from the public treasury. Although the constitution limited Marcos to eight years in office, he got around this restriction by imposing martial law from 1972 to 1981. Two years later, his chief opponent, Benigno Aquino, Jr., was shot when he returned from the United States to the Philippines, lured by the promise of coming elections.

In the elections of 1986, Marcos ran against Aquino's widow, **Corazón Aquino**. Aquino won decisively, but Marcos refused to acknowledge her victory. When he declared himself the official winner, a public outcry resulted. He was forced into exile in Hawaii, where he later died. In 1995, the Philippines succeeded in recovering $475 million Marcos had stolen from his country and deposited in Swiss banks.

During Aquino's presidency, the Philippine government ratified a new constitution. It also negotiated successfully with the United States to end the lease on the U.S. military bases. In 1992, Fidel V. Ramos succeeded Aquino as president. Ramos is restricted by the constitution to a single six-year term. The single-term limit is intended to prevent the abuse of power that occurred during Marcos's 20-year rule.

Background
Before the Philippines belonged to the United States, it was a Spanish colony. This is why many Filipinos, who are mostly Asian, have Spanish names.

The Colonies Become New Nations **513**

British Colonies Gain Independence

▶ **Key Ideas**
- Burma leaves the British Commonwealth and is later renamed Myanmar.
- Malaysia and Singapore split.
- The city-state of Singapore, dominated by ethnic Chinese, prospers.

MORE ABOUT . . .
Aung San Suu Kyi

Aung San Suu Kyi originally returned to Burma only for a short while, to care for her terminally ill mother. She left her son and husband behind. While under house arrest, she was able to give speeches at her gate to crowds that numbered as many as 5,000 people. She was released from house arrest in 1995 but was forbidden to make speeches.

HISTORYMAKERS
Aung San Suu Kyi

Why did Aung San Suu Kyi not take the government's offer to free her? *Students might respond that her having won the Nobel Prize gave her an even greater opportunity than before to be politically effective. She might also have been especially determined to aid Burma because of her father's political assassination.*

HISTORYMAKERS

Aung San Suu Kyi
1945–

Aung San Suu Kyi won the Nobel Peace Prize in 1991 for her efforts to establish democracy in Burma. She could not accept the award in person, however, because she was still under house arrest. The Nobel Prize committee said that in awarding her the peace prize, it intended

. . . to show its support for the many people throughout the world who are striving to attain democracy, human rights, and ethnic conciliation by peaceful means. Suu Kyi's struggle is one of the most extraordinary examples of civil courage in Asia in recent decades.

The military government had offered to free her if she would leave the country. However, she refused, insisting she would not leave until a civilian government was restored to Burma and all political prisoners were freed.

British Colonies Gain Independence

Britain's timetable for giving its colonies independence depended on local circumstances. Burma had been pressing for independence from Britain for decades. It became a sovereign republic in 1948 and chose not to join the British Commonwealth. In 1989, Burma was officially named Myanmar (myahn·MAH), its name in the Burmese language.

Burma Experiences Turmoil In the postwar years, Burma suffered one political upheaval after another. Its people struggled between repressive military governments and pro-democracy forces. When the Japanese occupied Burma during World War II, they had declared Burma a sovereign state. In fact, the Japanese were in control. Their demands for forced labor were particularly unpopular. The Burmese nationalists' army, led by **Aung San** (owng sahn), at first cooperated with the Japanese in order to drive the British out of Burma. Then the army linked up with British forces to defeat the Japanese. They succeeded in driving out the Japanese and were about to become independent. Then Aung San and most of his cabinet were gunned down on orders of Burmese political rivals.

Conflict among Communists and ethnic minorities disrupted the nation. In 1962, General Ne Win set up a repressive military government, with the goal of making Burma a socialist state. Although Ne Win stepped down in 1988, the military continued to rule Burma repressively. Also in 1988, **Aung San Suu Kyi** (owng sahn soo chee), the daughter of Aung San, returned to Burma after many years abroad. She became active in the newly formed National League for Democracy. For her pro-democracy activities, she was placed under house arrest for six years by the government. In the 1990 election—the country's first multiparty election in 30 years—the National League for Democracy won 80 percent of the seats. The military government refused to recognize the election, and it kept Aung San Suu Kyi under house arrest. She was finally released in 1995 though still kept under surveillance.

Malaysia and Singapore During World War II, the Japanese conquered the Malay Peninsula, formerly ruled by the British. The British returned to the peninsula after the Japanese defeat in 1945. They tried, unsuccessfully, to organize Malaya into one state. They also struggled to put down a Communist uprising. Ethnic groups resisted British efforts to unite their colonies on the peninsula and in the northern part of the island of Borneo. Malays were a slight majority on the peninsula, while Chinese were the largest group in Singapore. In 1957, the Federation of Malaya was created from Singapore, Malaya, Sarawak, and Sabah. The two regions—on the Malay Peninsula and on northern Borneo—were separated by 400 miles of ocean. In 1965, Singapore separated from the federation and became an independent city-state. The Federation of Malaysia—consisting of Malaya, Sarawak, and Sabah—was created. A coalition of many ethnic groups maintained steady economic progress in Malaysia.

Singapore, extremely prosperous, was one of the busiest ports in the world. Lee Kuan Yew ruled Singapore as prime minister from 1959 to 1990. Under his guidance, Singapore emerged as a banking center as well as a trade center. It had a standard of living far higher than any of its Southeast Asian neighbors. In early 1997, the Geneva World Economic Forum listed the world's most competitive economies. Singapore topped the list. It was followed, in order, by Hong Kong, the United States, Canada, New Zealand, Switzerland, and Great Britain.

Vocabulary
repressive government: a government that puts down opposition by force.

Vocabulary
house arrest: confinement to one's quarters, or house, rather than to prison.

B. Possible Answer
They are capitalist economies.

THINK THROUGH HISTORY
B. Making Inferences What do these competitive economies all have in common?

Task: Students will create a brochure promoting Singapore.

Purpose: To provide students with an opportunity to learn about one Southeast Asian nation in depth.

Activity: Have students form groups of four. Ask each group to research a different aspect of Singapore, such as the standard of living, business opportunities, cultural life, or government, and then

create a section of a brochure promoting the city-state. Before beginning, the class should decide on the intended audience. Each group should name a researcher, a writer-editor, a designer-illustrator, and a producer, who will meet with like members from the other groups to coordinate their efforts.

📁 ***Building a Portfolio:*** Students adding a brochure to their portfolio should attach an explanation of the assignment.

 ALTERNATIVE ASSESSMENT BOOK
Standards for Evaluating a Cooperative Activity

Standards for Evaluation
Brochures should . . .

- be tailored to the intended audience
- show evidence of careful research
- demonstrate good writing and visual skills

THINK THROUGH HISTORY
C. Contrasting How did the British and the Dutch differ in their attitudes toward their colonies?

Indonesia Gains Independence from the Dutch

The Japanese occupation of Indonesia during World War II destroyed the Dutch colonial order. Waiting in the wings to lead Indonesia was **Sukarno** (soo·KAHR·noh), known only by his one name. He was a leader of the Indonesian independence movement. In August 1945, two days after the Japanese surrendered, Sukarno proclaimed Indonesia's independence and named himself president. The Dutch, however, backed up initially by the British and the United States, attempted to regain control of Indonesia.

The Dutch in Indonesia Unlike British colonialists, who served their term in India and then returned to England, the pre-war Dutch looked upon the East Indies as their permanent home. To keep it that way, the Dutch resisted native Indonesians' attempts to enter the civil service or to acquire higher education. After the war, Indonesians were unwilling to return to their condition of servitude under the Dutch. They therefore put together a successful guerrilla army. After losing the support of the United Nations and the United States, the Dutch agreed to grant Indonesia its independence in 1949.

A Variety of People, Islands, and Religions The new Indonesia became the world's fourth most populous nation. It consisted of more than 13,600 islands, with 300 different ethnic groups, 250 languages, and most of the world's major religions. It contained the world's largest Islamic population. Sukarno, who took the official title of "life-time president," attempted to guide this diverse nation in a parliamentary democracy. Unfortunately, this attempt failed.

In 1965, a group of junior army officers attempted a coup, which was suppressed by a general named **Suharto** (suh·HAHR·toh). He then seized power for himself. He blamed the coup on Indonesian Communists. In the bloodbath that followed, 500,000 to 1 million Indonesians were killed. These included most of the known Communists, Chinese who may or may not have been Communists, and any others who were on a local "hit" list.

Suharto, officially named president in 1967, turned Indonesia into a police state and imposed frequent periods of martial law. Outside observers heavily criticized him for his annexation of East Timor in 1976 and for human rights violations there. Bribery and corruption became commonplace. Only the rich enjoyed prosperity. Political and economic conditions worsened in the late 1990s. In 1998 protesters forced Suharto, Asia's longest ruling dictator, to resign.

Vocabulary
coup: the sudden overthrow of a government by a small group of people.

Comparing Economies

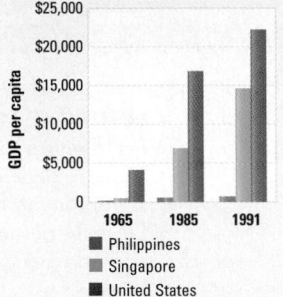

Gross Domestic Product is the dollar value of all goods and services produced within a country during one year. In this graph, the GDP is divided by the number of productive workers in each country. This results in the GDP per capita, or per person.

- ■ Philippines
- ■ Singapore
- ■ United States

Sources: *World Statistics in Brief* (1978) and *World Statistics Pocketbook* (1995), published by the United Nations.

SKILLBUILDER:
Interpreting Graphs
1. Which country had the highest GDP per capita in both 1965 and 1991? Which had the lowest?
2. Which country showed the biggest increase in GDP per capita from 1985 to 1991?

Section ❷ Assessment

1. TERMS & NAMES
Identify
- Ferdinand Marcos
- Corazón Aquino
- Aung San
- Aung San Suu Kyi
- Sukarno
- Suharto

2. TAKING NOTES
Using a chart like the one below, summarize the major challenges the countries faced following independence.

Nation	Colonizer	Challenges Following Independence
The Philippines		
Burma		
Indonesia		

3. MAKING INFERENCES
Why do you think that the United States demanded a 99-year lease on military and naval bases in the Philippines?
THINK ABOUT
- U.S. economic interests in the Philippines
- geographical location
- reasons for military presence

4. THEME ACTIVITY
Power and Authority
Write a two-paragraph essay contrasting a peaceful transfer of authority from a colonial power to a newly independent nation with a transfer that was violent.

The Colonies Become New Nations **515**

TERMS & NAMES
• **Negritude movement**
• **Kwame Nkrumah**
• **Jomo Kenyatta**
• **Mau Mau**
• **Mobutu Sese Seko**
• **FLN**
• **Ahmed Ben Bella**

3 New Nations in Africa

MAIN IDEA
After World War II, African leaders threw off colonial rule and created independent countries.

WHY IT MATTERS NOW
Today, many of those independent countries are engaged in building political and economic stability.

SETTING THE STAGE Like the Asian countries, the countries of Africa were unwilling to return to colonial domination after World War II. The problem of building strong, independent nations in Africa, however, was complicated by the way in which European imperialists had divided up the continent, plundered its resources, and left the countries unprepared to deal with independence. The colonialists had imposed borders having little to do with the areas where ethnic groups actually lived. While borders separated culturally similar people, they also enclosed traditional enemies.

Background to Independence

Between the two world wars, an educated middle class had begun to emerge in African cities. Young men went abroad for college and graduate studies. They listened to American jazz musicians and read literature of the Harlem Renaissance. They were influenced by African Americans such as W.E.B. Du Bois as well as by such older Africans as Blaise Diagne, who organized Pan-African (all-African) congresses in 1919 and 1921.

French-speaking Africans and West Indians began to express their growing sense of black consciousness and pride in traditional Africa. They formed the **Negritude movement**—a movement to celebrate African culture, heritage, and values. This movement viewed the black experience as unique. One of the movement's leaders, Leopold Senghor (lay·aw·PAWLD san·GAWR), later became the first president of Senegal.

African soldiers in World War II fought alongside Europeans to "defend freedom." This experience made them unwilling to accept colonial domination when they returned home. The postwar world changed the thinking of Europeans too. They began to question the cost of maintaining their colonies abroad.

Leopold Senghor was a politician and poet. In his poetry, he reaffirmed African traditions and the need for Africa to separate from Europe.

British Colonies Seek Independence

After World War II, many European countries were ready to transfer government to the African people. For the Europeans, the question was when and how to do that.

Ghana Leads the Way to Independence The British colony of the Gold Coast became the first African colony south of the Sahara to achieve independence. Following World War II, the British in the Gold Coast began making preparations. For example, they allowed more Africans to be nominated to the Legislative Council. However, the Africans wanted elected, not nominated, representatives, and they wanted "Freedom Now!" The leader of their largely nonviolent protests was **Kwame Nkrumah** (KWAH·mee uhn·KROO·muh). He was a former teacher who had spent several years studying in the United States. In the 1940s, he worked to liberate the Gold Coast from

516 Chapter 18

A. Possible Answer
After World War II, British colonies in Africa were unwilling to be dominated by Britain; Britain began to question the cost of maintaining colonies abroad and coping with rebellion.

THINK THROUGH HISTORY
A. Analyzing Motives Why might the British have been willing to grant the Gold Coast colony its independence?

the British. Nkrumah organized strikes and boycotts and was often imprisoned by the British government. Ultimately, however, his efforts were successful.

On receiving its independence in 1957, the Gold Coast took the name Ghana. This name honored a famous West African kingdom of the past. Ghana became the first nation governed by black Africans to join the British Commonwealth. During the independence celebrations, Nkrumah addressed the crowds:

> **A VOICE FROM THE PAST**
> There is a new African in the world, and that new African is ready to fight his own battle. . . . It is the only way in which we can show the world we are masters of our own destiny.
>
> **KWAME NKRUMAH**, 1957 speech

Nkrumah became Ghana's first prime minister and later its president-for-life. Nkrumah pushed through expensive development plans and economic projects—new roads, new schools, and expanded health facilities. These costly projects soon crippled the country. His programs for industrialization, health and welfare, and expanded educational facilities showed good intentions. However, the expense of the programs undermined the economy and strengthened his opposition.

In addition, Nkrumah was often criticized for spending too much time on Pan-African efforts and neglecting economic problems in his own country. In his dream of a "United States of Africa," Nkrumah was influenced by the thinking of Marcus Garvey. Garvey was a Jamaican-born black man who in the 1920s called for forcing all Europeans out of Africa and creating a black empire there. Nkrumah, influenced by Garvey (among others), wanted to create an Africa ruled by Africans. Nkrumah helped develop the Pan-African Congress held in Manchester, England, in 1945. Later, in 1958, he hosted the first Pan-African meeting held in Africa. This led to the formation of the Organization of African Unity (OAU) in 1963.

In 1966, while Nkrumah was in China, the army and police in Ghana seized power. Since then, the country has shifted back and forth between civilian and military rule. At the same time, it has struggled for economic stability. Jerry Rawlings, an Air Force pilot, seized power in 1979 and again in 1981, and still rules Ghana today.

Kenya and the Mau Mau Rebellion British settlers had taken over prize farmland in the northern highlands of Kenya. They fiercely resisted independence for Kenya. They were forced to accept black self-government as a result of two developments. One was the strong leadership of Kenyan nationalist **Jomo Kenyatta,** a Kikuyu educated in London. The second was the rise of the **Mau Mau** (MOW mow). This was a secret society made up mostly of Kikuyu farmers forced out of the highlands by the British.

The Mau Mau's aim was primarily to frighten the white farmers into leaving the highlands rather than to engage in outright war. Kenyatta had no connection to the Mau Mau. However, he refused to condemn the organization and was imprisoned by the British for a time for this refusal. By the time the British granted Kenya independence in 1963, more than 10,000 black Kenyans and 100 white Kenyans had been killed.

Kenyatta became president of the new nation. He worked hard to unite the various ethnic and language groups in the country. Nairobi, the capital, grew into a major business center of East Africa. When Kenyatta died in 1978, his successor, Daniel arap Moi, was less successful in governing the country. Moi faced more and more opposition to his one-party rule. Under him, university strikes and protests resulted in the deaths of some students. These demonstrations put pressure on Moi to make the country more democratic.

The Colonies Become New Nations **517**

HISTORY MAKERS

Kwame Nkrumah
1909–1972

Kwame Nkrumah studied at Lincoln University in Pennsylvania from 1935 to 1939. After graduating from Lincoln, he went on to earn a master's degree from the University of Pennsylvania.

Nkrumah studied socialism, especially the writings of Marx and Lenin, and nationalism, especially the thinking of Marcus Garvey. He became president of the African Students' Organization of the United States and Canada.

Nkrumah returned to the Gold Coast in 1947. He helped to stage strikes and riots against the government. He said at the time, "We prefer self-government with danger to servitude in tranquility."

Africa, 1955, and Africa, 1975

Interpreting the Maps What countries were created out of 1955 French West Africa? *Senegal, Mauritania, Mali, Niger, Upper Volta, Guinea, Ivory Coast.*

Extension Activity Have students use an almanac or other reference book to determine the present status of the colonies shown on the 1975 map.

SKILLBUILDER Answers
1. Libya, Egypt, Ethiopia, South Africa, Liberia.
2. 1960s.

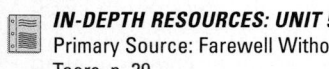

OBJECTIVE ③ INSTRUCT

The Congo Gains Independence

Key Ideas
- Belgium leaves the Congo unprepared for independence.
- The first prime minister, Patrice Lumumba, is overthrown and murdered.
- Mobutu Sese Seko rules as a dictator for 32 years.
- Laurent Kabila overthrows Mobutu.

IN-DEPTH RESOURCES: UNIT 5
Primary Source: Farewell Without Tears, p. 29

MORE ABOUT . . .
Ethnic Conflict in the Congo
Within days after the forces of Laurent Kabila took over, rumors began to surface about wholesale massacres in the Congo of Hutu refugees from Rwanda. Kabila was supported by Rwanda, and his army included large numbers of Tutsis. The refugees are ethnic Hutus who fled Rwanda in 1994 after a Tutsi-led government came to power, ending a three-month-long campaign of genocide of Tutsis by Hutus.

Africa, 1955

Africa, 1975

GEOGRAPHY SKILLBUILDER: Interpreting Maps
1. **Location** *Which countries in Africa were already independent in 1955?*
2. **Location** *In what decade did most of the African nations gain their independence?*

In the early 1990s, Kenya's economy suffered a severe reversal. Adding to the nation's woes were corruption in Moi's government and ethnic conflicts that killed hundreds and left thousands homeless.

The Congo Gains Independence

Of all the European possessions in Africa, probably the most exploited was the Belgian Congo. Belgium had ruthlessly plundered the colony's rich resources of rubber and copper. It had employed a system of forced labor. While draining wealth from the colony, Belgium had provided no social services. It also had made no attempt to prepare the people for independence.

Independence Brings Change Belgium's granting of independence in 1960 to the Congo (known as Zaire [zah·IHR] from 1965 to 1997) resulted in upheaval. Patrice Lumumba became the nation's first prime minister. He ruled a divided country. In the mineral-rich southeastern province of Katanga, a local leader named Moise Tshombe (MOH·zee CHUHM·bee) declared that region's independence. This was a serious threat, especially since copper from Katanga's mines was the nation's primary export.

Intervention by outside forces added to the problems. Tshombe was backed by Belgian mining interests. Lumumba, with Communist connections, first appealed to the United Nations for help in putting down Tshombe's rebellion. He then turned to the Soviet Union for aid. At this point, a coup led by an army officer, Colonel Joseph Mobutu, later known as **Mobutu Sese Seko** (moh·BOO·too SAY·say SAY·koh), overthrew Lumumba and turned him over to his enemy, Tshombe. Lumumba was murdered while in Tshombe's custody. Tshombe himself ruled briefly until he was overthrown by Mobutu, who seized power in a bloodless coup in 1965.

TEACHING OPTION **BLOCK SCHEDULING** | **GEOGRAPHY APPLICATION ACTIVITY** | **CLASS TIME 20 MINUTES**

Task Students will examine the map from the Geography Application for this section in order to explore the movement of various groups in the Congo during the years 1960–1965.

Materials Needed Use copies of the Geography Application worksheet for Chapter 18 or make a transparency of the map from that worksheet.

Activity Have the class help you make a list of the participants in the Congo crisis and of the movement of troops during the rebellions of 1960–1965. If you are using a transparency, have individual students point out various points of the rebel advance, railways, centers of rebellion, sites of intervention by Belgian paratroops, and so forth.

Conclusion Ask students to comment on the political situation in the Congo at this time. What must it have been like living in a time of political and social chaos? Why might people have been willing to turn to a dictator?

 IN-DEPTH RESOURCES: UNIT 5
Geography Application: The Congo Gains Independence, p. 25

Mobutu Comes to Power For 32 years, Mobutu ruled the country that he renamed Zaire. He used a combination of force, one-party rule, and gifts to supporters. Zaire had the mineral wealth and natural resources to make it one of the richest countries in Africa. It was reduced under Mobutu's rule to one of the continent's poorest. Mobutu and his associates were accused of looting the country of billions of dollars. They opened secret bank accounts abroad and bought real estate in Europe, Africa, and Brazil.

Mobutu successfully withstood several armed rebellions and ethnic clashes. He was finally overthrown in 1997 by Laurent Kabila after a seven-month-long civil war. On becoming president, Kabila banned all political parties. However, he promised a transition to democracy and free elections by April 1999.

Algeria Fights for Its Independence

In 1945, about 1 million French colonists and about 9 million Arab and Berber Muslims were living in the North African country of Algeria, France's principal overseas colony. Some of the colonists had lived there for generations. They were unwilling to give up their land without a fight. France claimed to offer full citizenship rights to its colonial subjects—a policy called assimilation. In reality, assimilation was hard to achieve. The colonists refused to share political power.

The Struggle The post–World War II conflict in Algeria began in 1945 when French troops fired on Algerian nationalists who were demonstrating in the town of Setif. Before peace was restored, thousands of Muslims and about 100 Europeans were killed. Subsequent French reforms did not satisfy the Algerian nationalists.

In 1954, the Algerian National Liberation Front, or **FLN**, announced its intention to fight for independence. The FLN would use guerrilla tactics at home and diplomatic tactics internationally. The French sent over half a million troops into Algeria to fight the FLN. Both sides committed atrocities. European settlers in Algeria began calling for the World War II hero Charles de Gaulle to return as president of France and restore order in the French colony.

De Gaulle Takes Control De Gaulle returned to power in 1958. He soon concluded that Algeria could not be held by force. Fearful that the rebellion might spread, France let go of most of its other possessions in Africa.

In 1962, a referendum setting out the conditions for Algerian independence in cooperation with France passed with overwhelming majorities in Algeria and France. As France planned the transfer of power after the cease-fire in March 1962, 750,000 French settlers fled Algeria. Independence came in July 1962.

Ahmed Ben Bella, a leader of the FLN who had been imprisoned by the French, was named first prime minister (1962–1963) and first president (1963–1965). Ben Bella reestablished national order, began land reforms, and developed new plans for education. In 1965, he was overthrown by his chief of staff.

From 1965 until 1988, Algerians tried to modernize and industrialize. Their efforts were undermined when oil prices plunged in 1985–1986. Unemployment and the unfulfilled promises of the revolution contributed to an Islamic revival. Riots in 1988 against the secular government left hundreds dead. The chief Islamic party, the Islamic Salvation Front (FIS), won local and parliamentary elections in 1990 and 1991. However, the ruling government and army refused to accept the election results. Eventually, a civil war broke out between Islamic militants and the government—a war that continues, on and off, to this day. Efforts to restore democratic government included presidential elections

The Colonies Become New Nations **519**

THINK THROUGH HISTORY
C. Clarifying Why did French colonists fight so hard to hold on to their land in Algeria?
C. Possible Answer They had lived there for so long, in some cases for generations, that they thought of it as home.

CONNECT *to* **TODAY**

Zaire Again Becomes the Congo

The march of Congo rebels in 1996–1997 from the eastern provinces of Zaire to the capital city of Kinshasa to overthrow Mobutu (pictured above) took only seven months. The rebels met little opposition as they crossed the country. The *New York Times* called the Zaire government "a house that had been eaten by termites. The rebels came along and pushed it over." That is, the corruption of Mobutu's rule had undermined his support among the people.

Laurent Kabila overthrew Mobutu and had himself sworn in as president of the country on May 29, 1997. The name of the country was changed from Zaire to the Congo. Mobutu died in September 1997.

CONNECT *to* **TODAY**
Zaire Again Becomes the Congo

Why did the Congo rebels overthrow Mobutu so easily? Have students write a paragraph supporting their answer to this question. *Possible answers might include reference to Mobutu's long rule and to dissatisfaction over his personal wealth, which was amassed at the Congo's expense.*

OBJECTIVE ④ INSTRUCT

Algeria Fights for Its Independence

▶ *Key Ideas*
- French colonists are unwilling to give up land in Algeria.
- Continuous fighting between French troops and Algerian nationalists prompts the return of Charles de Gaulle to power.
- A referendum for Algerian independence passes overwhelmingly in both countries.
- Conflict arises between Islamic militants and the secular government.

TEACHING OPTIONS

CONNECTIONS ACROSS THE CURRICULUM

Writing Have students assume arbitrarily assigned roles of French colonists and native Algerians. Then have them write a letter to their imagined families explaining why they decided either to stay or to leave Algeria. To receive their assignments, students might draw out of a box a slip of paper marked "French Staying," "French Leaving," "Algerian Staying," or "Algerian Leaving." Before writing their letters, students of like roles might meet to discuss reasons why they would make such a decision.

CONNECTIONS ACROSS TIME AND PLACE

Islamic Resurgence A reassertion of Islamic cultural values has been evident since the 1970s. This can be seen in a range of activities, from strict observance of Islamic dress to political takeovers and acts of terrorism. Instances of Islamic resurgence have been seen in Libya, Pakistan, Iran, Egypt, and Afghanistan, as well as in Algeria. Some observers attribute the Islamic resurgence to the religious community's disappointment over events such as the 1967 Arab-Israeli war, Malay-Chinese rioting in 1969, and Bangladesh's break from Pakistan in 1971.

Angola Gains Its Independence

▶ **Key Ideas**
- Portugal fails to prepare Angola for independence.
- Rebel groups fight for control.
- Portugal leaves without handing over power to anyone.
- The United States helps engineer a cease-fire among warring groups.

GlobalImpact
Cold War Reaches Angola

Was Angola better off or worse off for drawing the attention of world powers? Write a sentence or two to support your view. Some students will feel foreign powers helped to move Angola toward independence; others will feel that foreign intervention prolonged the chaos and disorder.

ASSESS & RETEACH

Section 3 Assessment
Assign pairs of students to help each other answer the questions. Then ask selected pairs to share their answers with the rest of the class.

Section Quiz
 FORMAL ASSESSMENT
Section Quiz, p. 226

Reteaching Activity
CLASS TIME: 15 MINUTES

Use the map on page 518 to review the main ideas of the section.

CLOSE ACTIVITY

CLASS TIME: 20 MINUTES

Role Playing
Assign students the roles of various leaders they have read about in this section: Leopold Senghor, Kwame Nkrumah, Jomo Kenyatta, Mobutu Sese Seko, and Ahmed Ben Bella. Have them discuss their views of European colonial rule, independence movements, and other issues. Have the rest of the class, as audience members listening to the discussion, ask questions of the leaders.

---

in 1995 and parliamentary elections in 1997. However, these efforts excluded the FIS. Recently, there have been calls from the FIS for a truce and a national peace conference to end the violence that has claimed the lives of thousands of people.

Angola Gains Its Independence

The Portuguese had been the first Europeans to enter Africa, 400 years ago, and they were the last to leave. Portugal was unwilling to give up any of its colonies. It made no preparations for helping its colony of Angola emerge into the modern world. At the end of World War II, Angola had no education or health facilities and little commerce.

GlobalImpact

Cold War Reaches Angola
Picture the plight of Angola, which had suffered already from the neglect of its colonizer, Portugal. While it struggled to become a nation, Angola became a battleground in the Cold War between the United States and the Soviet Union.

From 1945 until 1991, these two countries competed with one another for economic, political, and cultural dominance around the globe. This rivalry affected their relations with nations around the world. In Africa, even U.S. friendship with Mobutu, the dictator of Zaire, was tied into the Cold War. By urging Mobutu to aid the opposition to the MPLA in Angola, the United States used him as a check against Soviet influence in Angola.

The Movement Towards Independence Still, some Angolans gained an education. Accounts of other African countries that had become independent inspired them. In the 1960s, three revolutionary groups emerged. Foreign powers supported each group.

To put down the rebels in Angola, Portugal sent in 50,000 troops. The cost of the conflict amounted to almost half of Portugal's national budget. Discontent over the colonial wars built up among the Portuguese troops until the Portuguese dictatorship in Lisbon was toppled by the military.

Civil War Follows Independence The Portuguese withdrew from Angola in 1975 without formally handing over power to anyone. The lack of preparation for independence in Angola was complicated by the Communist seizure of power. The MPLA (Popular Movement for the Liberation of Angola) took control of the capital, Luanda. The Communist MPLA declared itself the rightful government. This led to a prolonged civil war among various rebel groups. Each group received help from outside sources. The MPLA was assisted by some 50,000 Cuban troops and by the Soviet Union. The FNLA (National Front for the Liberation of Angola), which eventually faded away, was backed by Zaire and the United States. The major opposition to the MPLA was UNITA (National Union for the Total Independence of Angola), which was assisted by South Africa and the United States.

In 1988, the United States, with a nod from the Soviet Union, pressed for a settlement among the MPLA, UNITA, South Africa, and Cuba and for the evacuation of Cuban troops. A shaky cease-fire went into effect in June 1989. The different groups continued to feel ill at ease with one another. However, in 1995, they began discussions about representation of each group in the government.

Trouble in the Middle East also prompted intervention by the United States and other powers. These efforts, too, met with mixed results, as you will learn in Section 4.

Section 3 Assessment

1. TERMS & NAMES

Identify
- Negritude movement
- Kwame Nkrumah
- Jomo Kenyatta
- Mau Mau
- Mobutu Sese Seko
- FLN
- Ahmed Ben Bella

2. TAKING NOTES
Copy the chart below on your paper. Next to each country, list an idea, an event, or a leader important to that country's history.

Ghana	
Kenya	
Zaire	
Algeria	
Angola	

3. ANALYZING MOTIVES
Why do you think that non-African nations supported certain factions that claimed power in the newly independent nations of Africa?

THINK ABOUT
- economic interests of the non-African nations
- Lumumba's request for Soviet aid in the Congo
- U.S. support of the FNLA
- the Cold War

4. ANALYZING THEMES
Revolution Why do you think revolution swept so many African nations following their independence from European rule after World War II?

THINK ABOUT
- how World War II influenced Africans
- the conditions preceding independence
- economic interests of European powers and newly independent nations

---

ANSWERS

1. TERMS & NAMES
Negritude movement, p. 516
Kwame Nkrumah, p. 516
Jomo Kenyatta, p. 517
Mau Mau, p. 517
Mobutu Sese Seko, p. 518
FLN, p. 519
Ahmed Ben Bella, p. 519

2. TAKING NOTES
Possible Responses: Ghana—took its name from African kingdom of the past; Kenya—Nairobi became a major business center; Zaire—renamed the Congo; Algeria—Ben Bella was prime minister and president; Angola—fought Portuguese for independence.

3. ANALYZING MOTIVES
Possible Responses: The factions may have promised non-African nations economic opportunities, such as trading or business privileges, in return for support; the non-African nations may have wanted to preserve economic interests they already had in the region.

4. ANALYZING THEMES
Possible Responses: There were many different religious and ethnic groups with competing interests; Europeans, Americans, and Soviets supported different groups; World War II had given Africans a new confidence.

4 Conflicts in the Middle East

TERMS & NAMES
- Balfour Declaration
- Suez Crisis
- Six-Day War
- Anwar Sadat
- Golda Meir
- Menachem Begin
- Camp David Accords
- Hosni Mubarak
- PLO

MAIN IDEA

Division of Palestine after World War II made the Middle East a hotbed of competing nationalist movements.

WHY IT MATTERS NOW

The conflict in the Middle East threatens the stability of the region today.

SETTING THE STAGE The division of Palestine after World War II set off bitter disputes in the Middle East. Some of the problems faced by the new nation of Israel were similar to those experienced by new nations in Africa and Asia. These included the writing of a new constitution, the merging of diverse peoples, and involvement in territorial disputes with neighbors. Palestinians who did not remain in Israel faced a disruptive life as refugees.

Palestine and Israel

The conflict between Jews and Arabs (including Palestinians) over a Palestinian homeland is one that has its roots in ancient history. To Jews, their claim to the land goes back 3,000 years, when Jewish kings ruled from Jerusalem. To Palestinians (both Muslim and Christian), the land has belonged to them since the Jews were driven out around A.D. 135. To Arabs, the land has belonged to them since their conquest of the area in the 7th century. Mixed in with the intertwined history of Jews and Arabs in the region have been more modern events. These include the persecution of Jews in Europe, the rising value of oil in the Middle East, and global politics that have influenced decisions half a world away.

Zionists—people who favored a Jewish national homeland in Palestine—had begun to settle in Palestine in the late 19th and early 20th century. At the time, the region was still part of the Ottoman Empire, ruled by Islamic Turks. Zionists at first made up only about 10 percent of the population. After the defeat of the Ottomans in World War I, the League of Nations asked Britain to oversee Palestine until it was ready for independence.

The Early Stages Palestinians feared that the increasing numbers of Jewish immigrants would result in hardships for them. Jews asked that a Jewish nation be carved out of the territory. Engaged in fighting World War I, Britain did not want to lose the support of either side. In a letter from the British foreign secretary to a Zionist supporter, Britain seemed to make promises to both sides.

A. Answer As long as the civil and religious rights of the non-Jews in Palestine were respected.

THINK THROUGH HISTORY
A. Clarifying Balfour approved the establishment of a home for Jews in Palestine with what qualification?

A VOICE FROM THE PAST

His Majesty's Government view with favour the establishment in Palestine of a national home for the Jewish people, and will use their best endeavours to facilitate the achievement of this object, it being clearly understood that nothing shall be done which may prejudice the civil and religious rights of existing non-Jewish communities in Palestine, or the rights and political status enjoyed by Jews in any other country.

ARTHUR JAMES BALFOUR, in a letter to Lord Rothschild, November 2, 1917

Britain found the terms of the **Balfour Declaration** to be unworkable because the two sides could not live together. Therefore, Britain called for partition of the country. Meanwhile, Nazi Germany's persecution of Jews spurred immigration to Palestine.

Dear Lord Rothschild,
I have much pleasure in conveying to you, on behalf of His Majesty's Government, the following declaration of sympathy with Jewish Zionist aspirations which has been submitted to, and approved by, the Cabinet.

His Majesty's Government view with favour the establishment in Palestine of a national home for the Jewish people, and will use their best endeavours to facilitate the achievement of this object, it being clearly understood that nothing shall be done which may prejudice the civil and religious rights of existing non-Jewish communities in Palestine, or the rights and political status enjoyed by Jews in any other country.

I should be grateful if you would bring this declaration to the knowledge of the Zionist Federation.

The Balfour Declaration is contained in this letter written by Sir Arthur Balfour (pictured above), the British foreign secretary. The letter was addressed to Lord Rothschild, head of the English branch of a banking family and a Zionist leader.

The Colonies Become New Nations **521**

Section 4 Overview

OBJECTIVES

① To describe the events that led to the formation of the new nation of Israel.

② To list the outbreaks of war between Israel and Arab states.

③ To identify the Camp David Accords.

④ To describe the Palestinian struggle for independence.

SKILLBUILDER
- Interpreting maps: location, region, p. 523

CRITICAL THINKING
- Clarifying, p. 521
- Summarizing, pp. 522, 523
- Recognizing effects, p. 523
- Synthesizing, p. 524
- Forming an opinion, p. 525
- Analyzing issues, p. 525

FOCUS

5-Minute Warm-Up

▶ *Interpreting Maps*
Have students answer these questions to help them understand events in the Middle East.

1. Look at the map on page 523. What bodies of water separate the Sinai Peninsula from Egypt?

2. What bodies of water separate the West Bank from Jordan?

WARM-UP TRANSPARENCY 18

OBJECTIVE ① INSTRUCT

Palestine and Israel

▶ *Key Ideas*
- During WWI, Britain makes promises to Jews and Arabs.
- Germany's persecution of Jews spurs immigration to Palestine.
- Jews accept the UN partition of Palestine, Muslims reject it, and Israel declares its independence.

IN-DEPTH RESOURCES: UNIT 5
Guided Reading, p. 23

ACCESS FOR STUDENTS ACQUIRING ENGLISH
Guided Reading (Spanish), p. 198

SECTION 4 RESOURCES

PRINT RESOURCES

IN-DEPTH RESOURCES: UNIT 5
Guided Reading, p. 23
Primary Source: The Balfour Declaration, p. 30
History Makers: Golda Meir, p. 35

ACCESS FOR STUDENTS ACQUIRING ENGLISH
Guided Reading (Spanish), p. 198

FORMAL ASSESSMENT
Section Quiz, p. 227

ALTERNATIVE ASSESSMENT BOOK

TECHNOLOGY RESOURCES

WORLD ART AND CULTURES TRANSPARENCIES
AT76 *After the Storm*

CRITICAL THINKING TRANSPARENCIES
CT34 Time Machine: The Middle East Conflict
CT70 Visual Summary

CD-ROM
Electronic Library of Primary Sources

INTERNET www.mlworldhistory.com

Israel and the Arab States in Conflict

▶ **Key Ideas**

- Israel's Arab neighbors greet the new nation with hostility.
- Full-scale war breaks out four times.
- Israel seizes control of old Jerusalem and other buffer areas, offering citizenship to Palestinians living in Jerusalem.

 CRITICAL THINKING TRANSPARENCIES
CT34 Time Machine: The Middle East Conflict

HISTORYMAKERS
Golda Meir

Have students compare Golda Meir's achievements with those of similarly qualified women of her generation in the United States. Ask how they would explain the differences. *Students might state that reform movements have generally held progressive views of women; also, the small and young nation of Israel could not afford to waste good leadership. Others might say that perhaps Meir was an exception.*

 IN-DEPTH RESOURCES: UNIT 5
History Makers: Golda Meir, p. 35

 CASE STUDY 5—Israel and Syria: Nationalism and Religion, p. 58

Israel Becomes a State Britain failed in its many attempts to work out a satisfactory compromise. At the end of World War II, a weary Britain referred the Palestine issue to the United Nations. The UN recommendations, accepted by the General Assembly in 1947, called for a partition of Palestine into a Palestinian state and a Jewish state. Jerusalem was to be an international city owned by neither side.

All of the Islamic countries voted against partition, and the Palestinians rejected it outright. They objected that the UN did not have the right to partition a country without considering the wishes of the majority of its people. However, the Jews welcomed the proposal. The terms of the partition were very favorable to them, giving them 55 percent of the area even though Jews made up only 34 percent of the population. Certain nations, such as the United States and many in Europe, felt sympathy for the Jews because of the Holocaust. Such nations supported the concept of giving Jews their own nation. Finally, the date was set for the formation of Israel—May 14, 1948. On that date, David Ben Gurion, long-time leader of the Jews residing in Palestine, announced the creation of an independent Israel.

Israel and the Arab States in Conflict

The new nation of Israel got a hostile greeting from its neighbors. The day after it proclaimed itself a state, six Arab states—Egypt, Iraq, Jordan, Lebanon, Saudi Arabia, and Syria—invaded Israel. The first of many Arab-Israeli wars, this one ended within months in a victory for Israel. Israel depended on strong American support in this conflict, as well as in most of its other wars. Full-scale war broke out again in 1956, 1967, and 1973.

The Palestinian state that the UN had set aside for Palestinians never came into being. Israel seized half the land in the 1948–1949 fighting. Egypt took control of the Gaza Strip, and Jordan annexed the West Bank. (See map on page 521.) While the fighting raged, thousands of Palestinians fled, migrating from the areas under Jewish control. They settled in UN-sponsored refugee camps that ringed the borders of their former homeland.

The 1956 Suez Crisis The second Arab-Israeli war followed Egypt's seizure of the Suez Canal in 1956. This seizure was ordered by Egyptian president Gamal Abdel Nasser, who had led the military coup that overthrew King Farouk in 1952. French and British business interests had continued to control the canal after the coup.

In 1956, angered by the loss of U.S. and British financial support for the building of the Aswan Dam, Nasser sent his troops to take the canal. Outraged, the British and the French made an agreement with Israel. With air support provided by their European allies, the Israelis marched on the Suez Canal and quickly defeated the Egyptians. However, pressure from the rest of the world's community, including the United States and the Soviet Union, forced Israel and its European allies to withdraw from Egypt. This left Egypt in charge of the canal and thus ended the **Suez Crisis.**

The 1967 Six-Day War Tensions between Israel and the Arab states began to build again in the years following the resolution of the Suez Crisis. By early 1967, Nasser and his Arab allies, equipped with Soviet tanks and aircraft, felt ready to confront Israel. Nasser announced, "We are eager for battle in order to force the enemy to awake from his dreams, and meet Arab reality face to face." He moved to close off the Gulf of Aqaba, Israel's outlet to the Red Sea. Convinced that the Arabs were about to attack, the Israelis attacked airfields in Egypt, Iran,

**Golda Meir
1898–1978**

Golda Meir, one of the signers of Israel's declaration of independence, was born in Kiev, Russia, and emigrated with her family to Milwaukee, Wisconsin, when she was eight.

In those days, she was known as Goldie Mabovitch. The Mabovitch home was a gathering place for discussions among Zionists. Golda listened excitedly to the talk about Jews working for a Jewish state.

In 1921, after becoming a teacher, Golda and her husband, Morris Myerson, moved to Palestine, where they joined a kibbutz, a collective farm. In 1956, Golda Myerson began using a Hebraic form of her married name, Meir. She served Israel as ambassador to the Soviet Union, minister of labor, foreign minister, and finally prime minister.

522 Chapter 18

THINK THROUGH HISTORY
B. Summarizing
What recommendations did the UN make for Palestine?
B. Possible Answer
The UN recommended the partition of Palestine into a Palestinian state and a Jewish state, with Jerusalem as an international city.

Background
The 1952 overthrow led by Nasser marked the first time that Egypt had been ruled by native Egyptians since the 6th century B.C.

A Voice from the Past Ask students if they think that Jews and non-Jews living in Palestine might have understood the Balfour Declaration (page 521) differently. How might the Jews have interpreted it? How might Muslims and Christians already living there have understood the document?

Could the declaration have been worded differently and still have achieved its purpose of appeasing both sides?

 IN-DEPTH RESOURCES: UNIT 5
Primary Source: The Balfour Declaration, p. 30

Less Proficient Readers Pair less proficient readers with more skilled readers and have them read the text on pages 522–523. Then have them draw a time line of events, beginning with the birth of the new state of Israel. Their time line might look like this:

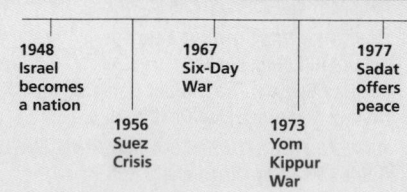

1948 Israel becomes a nation	1956 Suez Crisis	1967 Six-Day War	1973 Yom Kippur War	1977 Sadat offers peace

Jordan, and Syria. Safe from air attack, Israeli ground forces struck like lightning on three fronts. The war was over in six days. Israel lost 800 troops in the fighting, while Arab losses exceeded 15,000.

As a consequence of the **Six-Day War,** Israel occupied militarily the old city of Jerusalem, the Sinai Peninsula, the Golan Heights, and the West Bank. This was done to provide a buffer zone and improve security. Palestinians who lived in Jerusalem were given the choice of Israeli or Jordanian citizenship. Most chose the latter. Palestinians who lived in the other areas were not offered Israeli citizenship and became stateless.

The 1973 War A fourth Arab-Israeli conflict erupted in October 1973. Nasser's successor, Egyptian president **Anwar Sadat** (AHN·wahr suh·DAT), planned a joint Arab attack on the date of Yom Kippur, the holiest of Jewish holidays. This time the Israelis were caught by surprise. Arab forces inflicted heavy casualties and recaptured some of the territory lost in 1967. The Israelis, under their prime minister, **Golda Meir** (MY·uhr), launched a counterattack and regained most of the lost territory. An uneasy truce was agreed to after several weeks of fighting, ending the October war.

THINK THROUGH HISTORY
C. Recognizing
Effects What were
some of the effects
of the Arab-Israeli
conflicts?
C. Possible Answer
Some territory
changed hands;
hostilities continued;
instability threatened
the region.

Trading Land for Peace

Since no peace treaty ended the Yom Kippur War, many people feared that another war could start. Four years later, however, in November 1977, Anwar Sadat stunned the world by offering peace to Israel. No Arab country up to this point had recognized Israel's right to exist. In a dramatic gesture, he flew to Jerusalem and told the Knesset, the Israeli parliament, "We used to reject you. . . . Yet, today we agree to live with you in permanent peace and justice." Sadat emphasized that in exchange for peace, Israel would have to recognize the rights of Palestinians. Further, it would have to withdraw from territory seized in 1967 from Egypt, Jordan, and Syria.

D. Answer It was
the first signed agree-
ment between Israel
and an Arab country.
THINK THROUGH HISTORY
D. Summarizing
What was the signifi-
cance of the Camp
David Accords?

President Jimmy Carter recognized that Sadat had created a historic opportunity for peace. In 1978, Carter invited Sadat and Israeli prime minister **Menachem Begin** (mehn·AHK·hehm BAY·gihn) to Camp David, the presidential retreat in rural Maryland. Isolated from the press and from domestic political pressures, Sadat and Begin discussed the issues dividing their two countries. After 13 days of negotiations, Carter triumphantly announced that Egypt recognized Israel as a legitimate state. In exchange, Israel agreed to return the Sinai Peninsula to Egypt. Signed in 1979, the **Camp David Accords,** the first signed agreement between Israel and an Arab country, ended 30 years of hostilities between Egypt and Israel.

While world leaders praised Sadat, his peace initiative enraged many Arab countries. In 1981, a group of Muslim extremists assassinated him. Egypt's new leader, **Hosni Mubarak** (HAHS·nee moo·BAHR·uhk), maintained peace with Israel.

The Colonies Become New Nations **523**

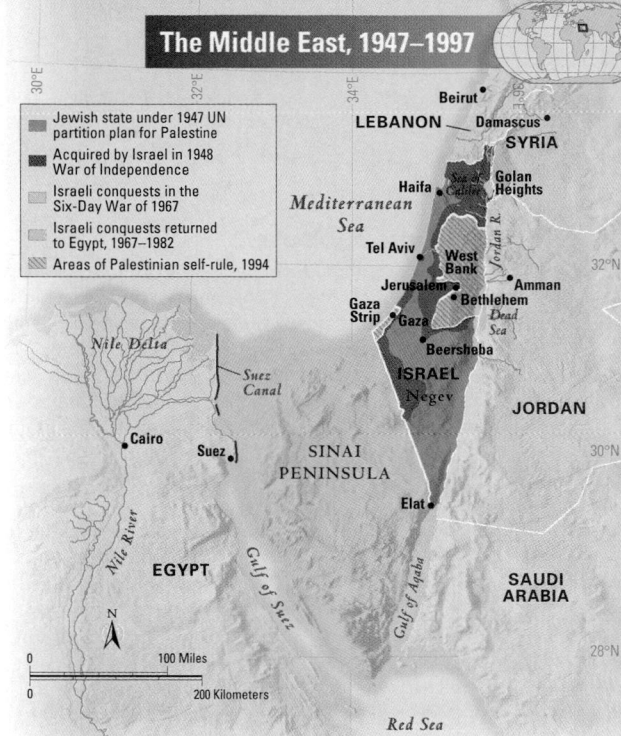

Jewish state under 1947 UN partition plan for Palestine
Acquired by Israel in 1948 War of Independence
Israeli conquests in the Six-Day War of 1967
Israeli conquests returned to Egypt, 1967–1982
Areas of Palestinian self-rule, 1994

LEBANON
Beirut
Damascus
SYRIA
Haifa
Golan Heights
Mediterranean Sea
Tel Aviv
West Bank
Amman
Jerusalem
Bethlehem
Gaza Strip
Gaza
Dead Sea
Beersheba
ISRAEL
Negev
JORDAN
Nile Delta
Suez Canal
Cairo
Suez
SINAI PENINSULA
Elat
EGYPT
Nile River
Gulf of Suez
Gulf of Aqaba
SAUDI ARABIA
Red Sea

0 100 Miles
0 200 Kilometers

GEOGRAPHY SKILLBUILDER: Interpreting Maps
1. **Location** What was the southernmost point in Israel in 1947 and what might have been its strategic value?
2. **Region** What country lies due north of Israel? east? northeast?

History from Visuals

The Middle East, 1947–1997
Interpreting the Map What access do Jews and Palestinians have to the Mediterranean? to the Red Sea? *Jews have seaports on the Mediterranean, and Palestinians have access to it from the Gaza Strip; Jews can reach the Red Sea through the Gulf of Aqaba; Palestinians have no access.*

Extension Activity Compare this map with maps showing the vegetation and resources of the area.

SKILLBUILDER Answers
1. Elat; it gave Israel access, by way of the Gulf of Aqaba, to the Red Sea.
2. Lebanon; Jordan; Syria.

OBJECTIVE **3** INSTRUCT

Trading Land for Peace

▶ *Key Ideas*
• Egypt and Israel sign the Camp David Accords, the first peace treaty between an Arab country and Israel.
• Egypt recognizes the state of Israel, and Israel returns the Sinai Peninsula to Egypt.

MORE ABOUT . . .
Camp David Accords
Some of the most successful peace talks have been held outside of the Middle East, in neutral territory, often in secrecy. This has allowed negotiators to work undistracted by the day-to-day business of running a government. It has also shielded negotiators from groups at home who oppose peace efforts. This was the case at Camp David, in rural Maryland, where Begin of Israel and Sadat of Egypt reached an agreement.

TEACHING OPTION | BLOCK SCHEDULING | COOPERATIVE ACTIVITY: **Researching West Bank Settlements** | CLASS TIME 30 MINUTES

Task: Students will research various positions on the issue of Israeli settlements on the West Bank.

Purpose: To encourage students to recognize that most issues have many sides to them.

Activity: Ask students to form groups of three or four. Have them do research, using the Internet, newspapers, and current magazines, on the issue of Israeli settlements on the West Bank and their effect on the Palestinian population and the prospects for peace in the region. Have each group research the various positions on the issue and list the arguments for each position.

Building a Portfolio Students may add the list to their portfolio.

ALTERNATIVE ASSESSMENT BOOK
Standards for Evaluating a Cooperative Activity

Standards for Evaluation
Lists should . . .

• clearly convey various sides of the issue
• list an equal number of arguments for all sides
• be fair and impartial

Teacher's Edition **523**

Kibbutz Childcare

Children on a kibbutz typically live in special children's houses. That means they eat, sleep, learn, and play with children of similar ages. They go to their family home each day, when school and work are over, to visit with their parents and do their homework. Parents and children eat in separate dining rooms, then the parents go to the children's houses to tuck their children into bed.

MORE ABOUT . . .

Jews Abroad

The surge in immigration to Israel resulted in sudden and drastic changes in Jewish communities elsewhere. For example, the number of Jews in Bulgaria shrank from 45,000 in 1948 to 7,700 in 1951. Almost all Libyan, Yemenite, and Iraqi Jews moved to Israel. Two-thirds of all Polish Jews immigrated to Israel, as did one-third of the Jews in Romania.

Daily *Life* : Israel, 1951

Israeli Independent News

A tractor driver carries a rifle slung across his back as he works to develop the land on his kibbutz.

Life on a Kibbutz

On this communal farm, women work right along with men in the fields. Children receive care from trained teachers and nurses. One young girl being raised on a kibbutz wrote her American friend about the freedom and responsibility of kibbutz life: "Among us the children's opinion is very important. We decide when and how to work and when to do a project. I study six hours a day and I work one and a half hours. I am also taking lessons in music and crafts."

Population Doubles in Three Years

Israel's Jewish population has doubled from 700,000 in May 1948 to 1,400,000 on the country's third birthday, thanks to a huge influx of immigrants. The new Israelis hail from 70 different countries, including Poland, Romania, Germany, Italy, Austria, Bulgaria, Libya, and Iraq. At a cost of about $1,600 per immigrant, the Jewish Agency sees to all the immigrants' needs when they first arrive, from housing to health care.

(Bar chart: Population (in thousands) with scale 0, 300, 600, 900, 1200, 1500. 1948 bar ≈ 700; 1951 bar ≈ 1400.)

Tent cities have sprung up throughout Israel to house new immigrants. Within ten years, these temporary shelters will be replaced by permanent housing.

Temporary Housing Springs Up

Near the large towns and farming areas that offer employment, transit camps called *ma'abarot* offer shelter and food for Israel's refugees. Workers quickly raise tents and canvas huts to house the refugees. Then they build wooden huts to hold kindergartens, nurseries, clinics, and employment centers. Workers can erect a *ma'abarot* within a few weeks. These camps provide welcome shelter for hundreds of thousands of needy immigrants.

From Culture to Agriculture

Many of Israel's eager immigrants are former lawyers, professors, or physicians. They find themselves drawn to the hard work of clearing Israel's swamps and making her deserts bloom. At one collective farm, the professors who work as farmers could probably open their own college. Now, instead of teaching math, philosophy, or psychology, they eagerly pore over the latest publications on scientific farming from the U.S. Department of Agriculture.

Connect *to* History

Synthesizing From the articles in the newsletter, what problems did new immigrants to Israel face in 1951?

 SEE SKILLBUILDER HANDBOOK, PAGE 665.

Connect *to* Today

Researching In the library or on the Internet, research a facet of life in modern-day Israel. You might choose the kibbutzim, Palestinian-Israeli relations, or the current status of Jerusalem.

Connect *to* History

Synthesizing

Students should mention the difficulties in creating a unified population— all speaking Hebrew—out of the great variety of immigrants who flooded Israel immediately after it was created. Students may also point out that many immigrants changed occupations when they arrived in Israel, requiring them to learn new skills and in some cases to alter their image of who they were. The sudden influx of immigrants required Israel to set up temporary camps in which facilities were at a minimum.

Connect *to* Today

Researching

Suggest to students that they use indexes such as the *Readers' Guide to Periodical Literature* and library computer databases such as the Periodical Abstracts. If students have access to the Internet, they may also look at newspaper and media sites such as CNN or *The New York Times*.

The Palestinians Demand Independence

Peace agreements between Israelis and Palestinians were harder to achieve. Unwilling to give up territories they had seized for security, the Israelis began to build settlements on the West Bank and the Gaza Strip.

The Intifada Palestinians living in Israel resented Israeli rule. As their anger mounted, they turned increasingly to the Palestine Liberation Organization, or **PLO,** led by Yasir Arafat (YAH·sur AR·uh·FAT). During the 1970s and 1980s, the military wing of the PLO conducted a campaign of armed struggle against Israel. Israel turned to strong measures, bombing suspected bases in Palestinian towns. In 1982, the Israeli army invaded Lebanon in an attempt to destroy strongholds in Palestinian villages. The Israelis soon became involved in Lebanon's civil war and were forced to withdraw.

In 1987, Palestinians began to express their frustrations in a widespread campaign of civil disobedience called the intifada, or "uprising." The intifada took the form of boycotts, demonstrations, attacks on Israeli soldiers, and rock throwing by unarmed teenagers. The intifada continued into the 1990s, with little progress made towards a solution. However, the civil disobedience affected world opinion, which, in turn, put pressure on Israel. Finally, in October 1991, Israeli and Palestinian delegates met for the first time in a series of peace talks.

The Declaration of Principles The status of the Israeli-occupied territories proved to be a bitterly divisive issue. In 1993, however, secret talks held in Oslo, Norway, produced a surprise agreement. In a document called the Declaration of Principles, Israel, under the leadership of Prime Minister Yitzhak Rabin (YIHTS·hahk rah·BEEN), agreed to grant the Palestinians self-rule in the Gaza Strip and the West Bank, beginning with the town of Jericho. Rabin and Arafat signed the agreement on the South Lawn of the White House on September 13, 1993.

The difficulty of making an agreement work was demonstrated by the assassination of Rabin in 1995. He was killed by a right-wing Jewish extremist who opposed concessions to the Palestinians. Rabin was succeeded as prime minister by Benjamin Netanyahu (neh·tan·YAH·hoo), who had opposed the plan. Still, Netanyahu made efforts to keep to the agreement. In January 1997, he met with Arafat to work out plans for a partial Israeli withdrawal from Hebron, on the West Bank. The U.S. secretary of state, Madeleine Albright, traveled to the region in September 1997, but peace continued to be difficult to achieve.

E. Possible Answer
Most students will probably see that both sides have legitimate claims to the land and have reasonable arguments on their side.

THINK THROUGH HISTORY
E. Forming an Opinion Political commentators have said that the Arab-Israeli conflict represents the struggle not of right against wrong, but of right against right. Do you agree or disagree? Explain.

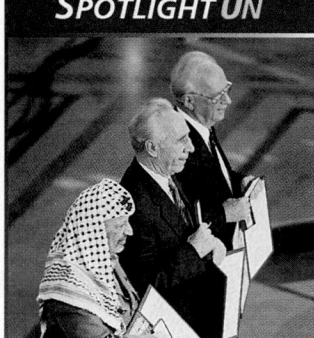

Section 4 Assessment

1. TERMS & NAMES

Identify
- Balfour Declaration
- Suez Crisis
- Six-Day War
- Anwar Sadat
- Golda Meir
- Menachem Begin
- Camp David Accords
- Hosni Mubarak
- PLO

2. TAKING NOTES

Draw a cause-and-effect graphic and fill in some important political and military events that occurred following the Suez Crisis.

Write a paragraph explaining which event is most important.

3. ANALYZING ISSUES

Explain the conflict between Jews and Arabs over a Palestinian homeland. What does each side believe? What other factors influence this issue?

THINK ABOUT
- the Balfour Declaration
- the ancient history of the Middle East
- the economics of oil

4. THEME ACTIVITY

Power and Authority In groups of three or four, come up with a list of ten interview questions for Gamal Abdel Nasser, Anwar Sadat, Yasir Arafat, or Yitzhak Rabin.

The Colonies Become New Nations **525**

TERMS & NAMES

1. partition, p. 506
2. Jawaharlal Nehru, p. 507
3. Indira Gandhi, p. 507
4. Ferdinand Marcos, p. 513
5. Corazón Aquino, p. 513
6. Negritude movement, p. 516
7. FLN, p. 519
8. Balfour Declaration, p. 521
9. Anwar Sadat, p. 523
10. PLO, p. 525

REVIEW QUESTIONS

Answers to some questions may vary.

11. The massacre of unarmed Indians at Amritsar.

12. India and Pakistan.

13. One-fifth of Sri Lanka's people are Tamils, a Hindu people; some want to set up a separate Tamil nation. Most Sri Lankans are Buddhists, and they oppose the Tamils.

14. The United States got free trading rights; the Filipinos felt U.S. businesses might exploit the Philippines' natural resources and environment.

15. A leader of the Indonesian independence movement, and Indonesia's first president.

16. Some Ghanians felt he spent too much money on programs that the country could not afford and too much time on Pan-African efforts, neglecting Ghana's own problems.

17. Belgium had not prepared the country for independence; the province of Katanga tried to secede.

18. French colonists refused to share political power with the Africans.

19. When Egypt seized the Suez Canal in 1956, Israelis, supported by the British and the French, marched in and took the canal; they later withdrew because of world pressure, and Egypt regained control of the canal.

20. Most of the world responded favorably; some Arabs were angered by Sadat's peace initiative.

Visual Summary

The Struggle for Independence

The time line shows the dates on which various countries in Asia and Africa achieved their independence after World War II. It also shows (in parentheses) the countries from which they achieved independence.

1945	
	1946 Philippines (United States)
	1947 India, Pakistan (Great Britain)
	1948 Israel (Great Britain)
	1949 Indonesia (The Netherlands)
1955	
	1957 Federation of Malaya, Ghana (Great Britain)
	1960 Zaire (Belgium)
	1962 Algeria (France)
	1963 Kenya (Great Britain)
1965	**1965** Singapore (Great Britain, Malaya)
	1971 Bangladesh (Pakistan)
1975	**1975** Angola (Portugal)

526 Chapter 18

TERMS & NAMES

Briefly explain the importance of each of the following to colonies becoming new nations after World War II.

1. partition
2. Jawaharlal Nehru
3. Indira Gandhi
4. Ferdinand Marcos
5. Corazón Aquino
6. Negritude movement
7. FLN
8. Balfour Declaration
9. Anwar Sadat
10. PLO

REVIEW QUESTIONS

SECTION 1 *(pages 505–509)*
The Indian Subcontinent Gains Independence

11. What incident marked the beginning of the end of British rule in India?
12. What two nations emerged from the British colony of India in 1947?
13. Briefly explain the reason for the civil disorder in Sri Lanka.

SECTION 2 *(pages 512–515)*
Southeast Asian Nations Gain Independence

14. What were some concerns the Filipinos had regarding the Bell Act?
15. Who was Sukarno?

SECTION 3 *(pages 516–520)*
New Nations in Africa

16. Why were Kwame Nkrumah's politics criticized?
17. Name two problems Zaire faced in gaining independence.
18. Why was the policy of assimilation in Algeria hard to achieve?

SECTION 4 *(pages 521–525)*
Conflicts in the Middle East

19. What was the Suez Crisis?
20. What was the reaction to the Camp David Accords?

Interact *with* History

On page 504, you decided whether to flee your country to take a chance in a new country. Now that you've read the chapter, do you think the separation into different countries of ethnically and religiously similar people was good or bad? List positives and negatives of such splits.

Interact *with* History

Possible Responses: Students who think the separation of ethnically and religiously similar people into different countries was good might cite evidence of the continuing inability of such people to live with people different from them in today's world. Others might cite examples of secular nations in which people of different backgrounds live together peaceably.

CRITICAL THINKING

1. CHALLENGES OF INDEPENDENCE

Using a web diagram like the one below, show some of the challenges that newly independent nations have faced.

Challenges for Newly Independent Nations

Which challenge is the hardest to overcome? Why?

2. REVOLUTIONARY METHODS

THEME REVOLUTION Following independence, many former colonies went through revolutions. They often experienced assassination, rigged elections, and massacres. Keep in mind what you learned about revolutions in this chapter and that revolutions are meant to bring about change. Do you think there should be a limit to the methods revolutionaries employ? Explain your opinion.

3. THE BRITISH COMMONWEALTH

Some new nations, such as Ghana, agreed to become part of the British Commonwealth. Other nations, such as Myanmar (formerly Burma), chose not to join. What factors affected a former colony's decision to join or not to join the British Commonwealth?

4. ANALYZING PRIMARY SOURCES

The following passage comes from an article titled "Reunited Jerusalem Faces Its Problems," published in December 1968. Read the passage and answer the questions below it.

> **A VOICE FROM THE PAST**
> Jerusalem nurtured Judaism, Christianity, and Islam, whose adherents have slaughtered each other in its twisted streets throughout centuries of nominal civilization. It has been burned and pillaged, wrecked and razed, always to grow again from its own rubble. Today it remains poor, lovely, and troubled, infinitely greater as a symbol than as a city.
> **KENNETH MACLEISH,** *National Geographic*

• What is the writer trying to point out here?

• What do you think the writer means by "infinitely greater as a symbol than as a city"?

CHAPTER ACTIVITIES

1. LIVING HISTORY: Unit Portfolio Project

THEME ECONOMICS Your unit portfolio project focuses on how economic factors influence history (see page 471). For Chapter 18, you might use one of the following ideas to add to your portfolio:

• List the top four economic issues that newly independent nations face. Read them to your class. Be prepared to answer why you put them in the order you did.

• Choose a country discussed in this chapter and create a chart of major economic events in that country.

• Write a magazine article explaining why the Middle East is historically a hotspot for competing nationalist movements. Be sure to include major economic factors.

2. CONNECT TO TODAY: Cooperative Learning

THEME POWER AND AUTHORITY Following World War II, many newly independent countries were shaped by strong leaders like Indira Gandhi, Anwar Sadat, Jomo Kenyatta, and Suharto. Their actions and policies have continued to affect their countries even up to the present. Work with a team to write a letter to one historical leader mentioned in this chapter.

 Using the Internet or magazines, research current developments in your chosen leader's country.

• Using the library, research the policies of the historic leader you have chosen.

• Write a letter to the historical leader to bring him or her up to date as to the impact that leader's actions and policies have had on the course of development in his or her country.

3. INTERPRETING A TIME LINE

Revisit the unit time line on pages 470–471. Which two events from Chapter 18 do you think were most significant? Explain why.

FOCUS ON GRAPHS

India's population continues to grow very rapidly. Despite the growing population, some headway has been made against poverty, as the graphs below show.

• What percentage of the population was poor in 1951? What percentage was poor in 1994?

• Were there more people living in poverty in India in 1994 or in 1951? Did the percentage of people living in poverty increase or decrease from 1951 to 1994?

Connect to History
What social and economic developments might have contributed to the lower percentage of those living in poverty in India?

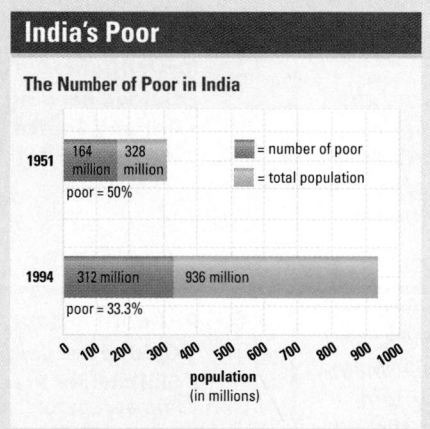

India's Poor

The Number of Poor in India

1951 164 million 328 million poor = 50%

1994 312 million 936 million poor = 33.3%

= number of poor
= total population

population
(in millions)

The Colonies Become New Nations **527**

CHAPTER ACTIVITIES

1. LIVING HISTORY

Standards for Evaluation
Lists of economic issues should meet the following criteria:

• Use information from the text.
• Show an understanding of basic economic theory.
• Indicate a ranking of issues from most important to least important.
• Include a brief summary of the thinking behind the choices.

Standards for Evaluation
Charts should meet the following criteria:

• Show a graphic arrangement that focuses on the major events.
• Organize information logically.
• Contain clear headings and sub-headings.

Standards for Evaluation
Magazine articles should meet the following criteria:

• Be well organized and well developed.
• Contain internal heads to show main ideas.
• Provide explanations for main ideas given.

2. CONNECT TO TODAY

Standards for Evaluation
Letters should meet the following criteria:

• Show an understanding of the importance of the leader chosen.
• Indicate research into the modern history of the country.
• List the effects the leader's policies have had on the country.
• Contain personal opinions about the effects of such policies.

3. INTERPRETING A TIME LINE

Student answers should provide clear reasons and support for choosing two events as most significant.

FOCUS ON GRAPHS

• 50% in 1951; 33.3% in 1993–94.
• In 1993–94; decrease.

Connect to History *Possible Responses:*
Industry in India has developed; new resources, such as oil and coal, have been discovered; scientific and technical education has been expanded.

CRITICAL THINKING

1. CHALLENGES OF INDEPENDENCE

Possible Responses: constant threat of revolution; former colonizers' continued meddling; developing profitable trade relationships with former colonizers; civil wars; random boundaries.

2. REVOLUTIONARY METHODS

Students who think there should be a limit may point out that regardless of whether revolutionaries are fighting for a good or a bad cause, they should go about it peacefully, like Gandhi. Students who think there should be no limit may point out that sometimes it is necessary to use all possible force to get rid of an existing government that is evil.

3. THE BRITISH COMMONWEALTH

Possible Responses: how the colony had been treated by the British during colonization and the struggle for independence; how self-sufficient the economy was; how influenced leaders were by British customs.

4. ANALYZING PRIMARY SOURCES

Possible Responses: Religious groups continue to fight for their rights in the city of Jerusalem. It is not the physical city that is important, but the religious symbolism of the city.

	Key Ideas	COPY MASTERS	ASSESSMENT
SECTION 1 Democracy Case Study: Latin American Democracies *pp. 531–535*	*Democracy requires key institutions and practices to ensure popular participation. After World War II, Latin American countries struggle to create stable democratic systems.*	*In-Depth Resources: Unit 5* • **Guided Reading,** p. 37 • **Geography Application:** Democracy in Central and South America, p. 43 • **Literature:** from *Brazil,* p. 49 • **History Makers:** Juan and Eva Perón, p. 52	P E *Section 1 Assessment,* p. 535 *Formal Assessment* • Section Quiz, p. 236 *Alternative Assessment Book* • Standards for Evaluating a Cooperative Activity
SECTION 2 Democratic Challenges in African Nations *pp. 536–540*	*African nations work to build democracy. While Nigeria suffers setbacks, South Africa casts off white rule and lays the foundations for a democratic, multiracial government.*	*In-Depth Resources: Unit 5* • **Guided Reading,** p. 38 • **Primary Sources:** from *Kaffir Boy,* p. 45; Mandela's Inaugural Address, p. 46 • **History Makers:** Nelson Mandela, p. 53	P E *Section 2 Assessment,* p. 540 *Formal Assessment* • Section Quiz, p. 237 *Alternative Assessment Book* • Standards for Evaluating a Cooperative Activity
SECTION 3 Gorbachev Moves Toward Democracy *pp. 541–545*	*Under Mikhail Gorbachev, the Soviet Union undertakes major reforms to open up the Communist system. Soviet bloc countries in Eastern Europe go a step further and throw off Communist rule completely.*	*In-Depth Resources: Unit 5* • **Guided Reading,** p. 39 • **Primary Source:** Political Cartoon, p. 47	P E *Section 3 Assessment,* p. 545 *Formal Assessment* • Section Quiz, p. 238 *Alternative Assessment Book* • Standards for Evaluating a Cooperative Activity
SECTION 4 Collapse of the Soviet Union *pp. 546–550*	*Reforms lead to unrest and the breakup of the Soviet Union. Yugoslavia, Poland, and Czechoslovakia face problems after becoming free of communism.*	*In-Depth Resources: Unit 5* • **Guided Reading,** p. 40 • **Primary Source:** The Road to Marjača, p. 48	P E *Section 4 Assessment,* p. 550 *Formal Assessment* • Section Quiz, p. 239 *Alternative Assessment Book* • Standards for Evaluating a Cooperative Activity
SECTION 5 China Follows Its Own Path *pp. 551–555*	*China opens up to the West and implements reforms while maintaining its Communist system. Questions remain about the prospects for democracy in China, even as China regains Hong Kong.*	*In-Depth Resources: Unit 5* • **Guided Reading,** p. 41 • **Skillbuilder Practice:** Analyzing Primary Sources, p. 42	P E *Section 5 Assessment,* p. 555 *Formal Assessment* • Section Quiz, p. 240 *Alternative Assessment Book* • Standards for Evaluating a Cooperative Activity
CHAPTER RESOURCES	**Chapter Overview** *The establishment of democracy can be a long, difficult process, as events in Latin America, Africa, the former Soviet bloc, and China show. Democracy appears to be on the rise worldwide as people recognize their common economic and political goals.*	*Telescoping the Times* • Chapter Summary, pp. 77–79 *Planning for Block Schedules* *Case Studies* • **Case Study 2**—Ghana and South Africa: Political Problems of Two African Nations, p. 16 • **Case Study 4**—Russia and Germany: The Fall of Communism, p. 44	P E *Chapter Assessment,* pp. 556–557 *Chapter Activities,* p. 557 *Formal Assessment* • Chapter Test, forms A and B, pp. 241–246 **Test Generator** *Alternative Assessment Book*

TECHNOLOGY

Warm-Up Transparency 19
World Art and Cultures Transparencies
• AT76 *The Family*

INTERNET RESOURCES
www.mlworldhistory.com

Warm-Up Transparency 19
World Art and Cultures Transparencies
• AT77 Multiple-Mask Headdress
Electronic Library of Primary Sources
• from "Masakhane—Let Us Build Together"
Patterns of Interaction:
Struggling Toward Democracy
INTERNET RESOURCES
www.mlworldhistory.com

Warm-Up Transparency 19
Geography Transparencies
• GT35 Germany, Post World War I–Present
World Art and Cultures Transparencies
• AT78 *Burning Rods*
Electronic Library of Primary Sources
• "Destruction of the Berlin Wall"
INTERNET RESOURCES
www.mlworldhistory.com

Warm-Up Transparency 19
Electronic Library of Primary Sources
• "Will I Ever Go Home Again?"
INTERNET RESOURCES
www.mlworldhistory.com

Warm-Up Transparency 19
Critical Thinking Transparencies
• CT35 Democratic Struggles Around the Globe
• CT71 Visual Summary
Electronic Library of Primary Sources
• "The Massacre in Tiananmen Square"

Chapter Summaries on Audiocassette in English and Spanish
INTERNET RESOURCES
www.mlworldhistory.com

Block Scheduling (90 MINUTES)

Day 1
Section 1, pp. 531–535
 COOPERATIVE ACTIVITY
Teacher's Edition, p. 534
Section Assessment, p. 535

Day 2
Section 2, pp. 536–540
COOPERATIVE ACTIVITY
Teacher's Edition, p. 539

Section Assessment, p. 540
Day 3
Section 3, pp. 541–545
COOPERATIVE ACTIVITY
Teacher's Edition, p. 543
Section Assessment, p. 545
Day 4
Section 4, pp. 546–550

COOPERATIVE ACTIVITY
Teacher's Edition, p. 549
Section Assessment, p. 550
Day 5
Section 5, pp. 551–555
COOPERATIVE ACTIVITY
Teacher's Edition, p. 552
Section Assessment, p. 555
Chapter Assessment, pp. 556–557

Yearly Pacing *Chapter 19 Total:* 5 days *Yearly Total:* 85 days

Planning for Block Schedules

Customizing for Special Needs

Students Acquiring English

Access for Students Acquiring English
• **Guided Reading** for Sections 1–5 (Spanish), pp. 205–209
• **Chapter Summary** (Spanish), pp. 202–204
• **Skillbuilder Practice** Analyzing Primary Sources (Spanish), p. 210
• **Geography Application** Democracy in South America (Spanish), p. 211

Spanish Reading Study Guide
• pp. 201–212

Patterns of Interaction:
Struggling Toward Democracy
(Spanish track)

Less Proficient Readers

In-Depth Resources: Unit 5
• **Guided Reading** for Sections 1–5, pp. 37–41
• **Skillbuilder Practice** Analyzing Primary Sources, p. 42
• **Geography Application** Democracy in Central and South America, p. 43

Telescoping the Times
• Chapter Summary, pp. 77–79

Reading Study Guide
• pp. 201–212

Chapter Summaries on Audiocassette
in English and Spanish

Gifted and Talented Students

In-Depth Resources: Unit 5
Primary Sources:
• from *Kaffir Boy*, p. 45
• Mandela's Inaugural Address, p. 46
• Political Cartoon, p. 47
• The Road to Marjača, p. 48

History Makers:
• Juan and Eva Perón, p. 52
• Nelson Mandela, p. 53

Connections to Literature READINGS FOR STUDENTS

In-Depth Resources: Unit 8
Literature: from *Brazil*, p. 49

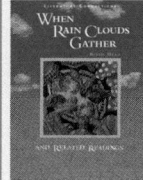
McDougal Littell
Literature Connections
• **Head, Bessie**
When Rain Clouds Gather
(with related readings)
Makhosja flees South Africa in the mid-1960s into Botswana. There he struggles against the bitterness within him as Botswana approaches independence.

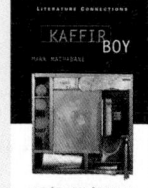
McDougal Littell
Literature Connections
• **Mathabane, Mark**
Kaffir Boy
(with related readings)
In this powerful memoir, Mathabane shows how the strength of the human spirit endures even in the face of a crushing system like apartheid.

 = Pupil's Edition   = Overhead Transparency   = Software   = Video
= Copy Master   = CD-ROM = Audiocassette   = Internet

Struggles for Democracy, 1945–Present

Accessing Prior Knowledge

- Have students discuss why Germany was divided and why the Berlin Wall was constructed.

- Ask students what factors in the colonial history of South Africa set the stage for a civil rights movement among its nonwhite citizens.

- Ask students what factors in Brazil's history might have led the government to build a new capital city.

Making Inferences

- Ask students what they can infer about Desmond Tutu from the caption and the photograph.

- Have students consider what the construction of Brasília says about the Brazilian view of government.

Geography Connection

Ask students to study the maps of Europe and Africa.

- Refer to the map of Europe on page 477. In which part of divided Germany was Berlin located?

- Refer to the map of Africa on page 308. Which European country controlled the two areas highlighted in the map of Africa on page 529?

Struggles for Democracy, 1945–Present

PREVIEWING THEMES

Economics
Gorbachev in the Soviet Union and Deng Xiaoping in China allowed reforms that moved their Communist economies toward capitalism. Many nations—such as Brazil and Poland—discovered that economic stability is important for democratic progress.

Revolution
In 1989, democratic revolutions overthrew Communist governments in the Soviet Union and most of Eastern Europe. In China, the Communist government and the army put down a student protest calling for democracy.

Cultural Interaction
Democratic reforms spread from one Eastern European country to another, causing Communist governments to fall like dominoes. In addition, Chinese students brought democratic ideas from the West back to China and tried to change Chinese culture.

INTERNET CONNECTION
Visit us at **www.mlworldhistory.com** to learn more about democratic movements in the 20th century.

EUROPE, AFRICA, SOUTH AMERICA

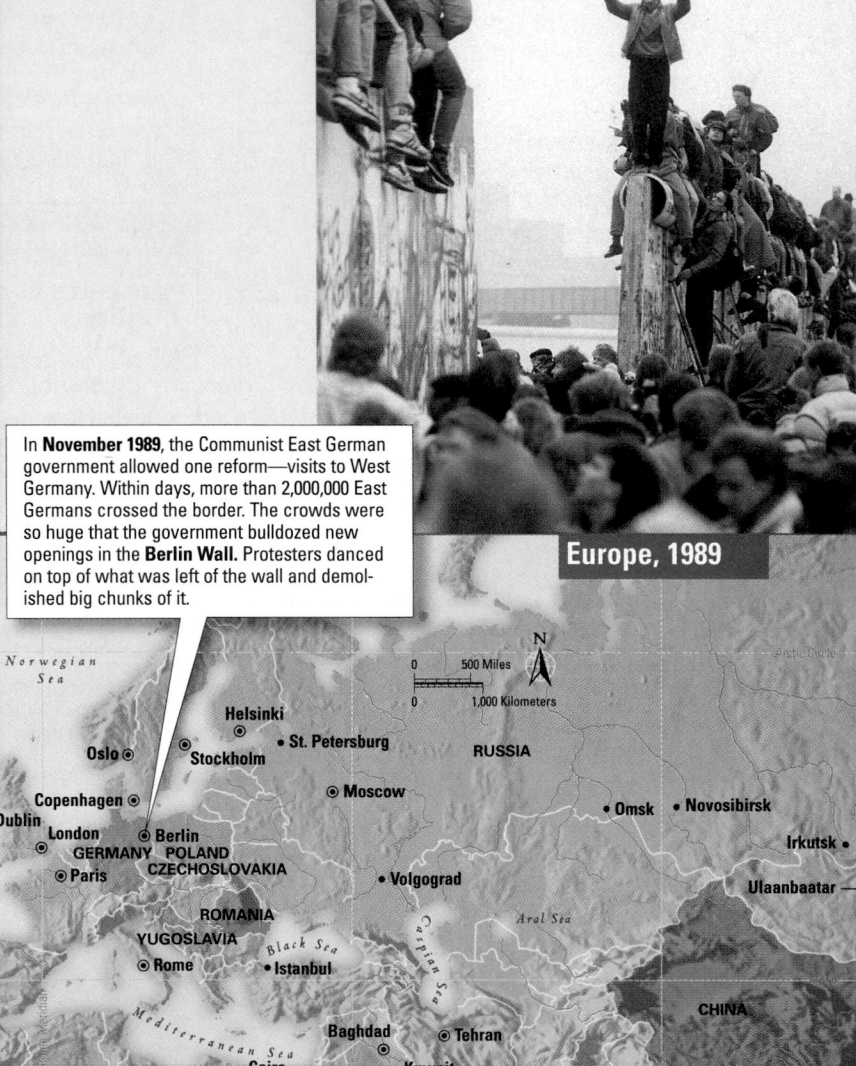

In **November 1989**, the Communist East German government allowed one reform—visits to West Germany. Within days, more than 2,000,000 East Germans crossed the border. The crowds were so huge that the government bulldozed new openings in the **Berlin Wall.** Protesters danced on top of what was left of the wall and demolished big chunks of it.

Europe, 1989

Norwegian Sea — Helsinki • St. Petersburg — RUSSIA — Oslo • Stockholm — • Moscow — • Omsk • Novosibirsk — Copenhagen • Dublin • London • Berlin GERMANY POLAND CZECHOSLOVAKIA • Paris — Irkutsk • — • Volgograd — Ulaanbaatar — *Aral Sea* — ROMANIA YUGOSLAVIA *Black Sea* • Rome • Istanbul — *Caspian Sea* — CHINA — *Mediterranean Sea* Baghdad • Tehran — Cairo Kuwait

0 500 Miles
0 1,000 Kilometers

528

GEOGRAPHY THEMES

Place
Point out to students that in 1985 South Africa was the only white-ruled nation left in the southern part of Africa. In the preceding decades, many former colonial governments had given way to black-controlled administrations. In addition, apartheid in South Africa was coming under increasing criticism from the international community. South Africa was more and more isolated from its neighboring states, Europe, and the United States.

Ask students to think about what effect these facts may have had on people in South Africa.

Location
Have students speculate on why Brasília was built in the Brazilian interior. What advantages and disadvantages would this location give the government? Tell students that the Brazilian government wanted the city to be a showcase of architectural design.

On the European map, point out that Germany, which is located in Western Europe, borders the former Soviet satellites. Ask students to consider what impact a reunified Germany might have on Europe in terms of trade and political alliances. Remind them that for decades after World War II, West Germany had the strongest economy in Europe.

Africa, 1985

Algiers · Rabat · Casablanca · Tunis · Tripoli · Khartoum · NIGERIA · Lagos · Addis Ababa · Kinshasa · Nairobi · Luanda · Dar es Salaam · Johannesburg · SOUTH AFRICA · Cape Town

ATLANTIC OCEAN

0 — 500 Miles
0 — 1,000 Kilometers

Anglican bishop **Desmond Tutu** worked to end apartheid, which was legalized racial discrimination. He asked foreign nations and companies not to do business with South Africa. In **1984**, Tutu won the Nobel Peace Prize for his nonviolent methods.

In **1956**, the government of Brazil began to build a new capital city, **Brasília**, in the wilderness. Planners designed the city to look like a drawn bow and arrow from the air. Builders constructed many modern buildings, such as the bowl-shaped Chamber of Deputies and the twin towers that are home to congressional offices.

South America, 1956

Gulf of Mexico · MEXICO · Mexico City · Havana · Caribbean Sea · ATLANTIC OCEAN · Bogotá · Lima · BRAZIL · Brasília · Salvador · La Paz · Rio de Janeiro · PACIFIC OCEAN · Buenos Aires · Montevideo · ARGENTINA

Tropic of Cancer · Equator · Tropic of Capricorn

0 — 500 Miles
0 — 1,000 Kilometers

529

ADDITIONAL RESOURCES

Books for the Teacher

• Berry, Ian. *Living Apart: South Africa Under Apartheid.* London: Phaidon, 1996.

• Brown, Archie. *The Gorbachev Factor.* New York: Oxford UP, 1996.

• Miles, James A. R. *The Legacy of Tiananmen: China in Disarray.* Ann Arbor, MI: Michigan UP, 1996.

• Winn, Peter. *Americas: The Changing Face of Latin America and the Caribbean.* New York: Pantheon, 1992.

Books for the Student

• Baynham, Simon. *Africa from 1945.* New York: Watts, 1987.

• Kort, Michael. *China Under Communism.* Brookfield, CT: Millbrook, 1994.

• Symynkywicz, Jeffrey B. *1989: The Year the World Changed.* Parsippany, NJ: Dillon, 1996.

Videos

• *Project HIP-HOP South Africa,* Cambridge Educational, 800–468–4227.

• *The Revolution in Eastern Europe.* Society for Visual Education, 800–829–1900. Students discuss changes in their countries.

Software

• *The Last Days of Apartheid.* CD-ROM. Society for Visual Education, 800–829–1900.

HISTORY THROUGH ART

Brasília, Brazil

Brasília was completed in 1960, a city of light surrounded by barren wilderness. In building the city, President Juscelino Kubitschek fulfilled a constitutional decree that the capital be placed in the interior of the country. Designed by Brazilian architect Lúcio Costa, the city plan emphasizes efficiency, order, and simplicity. Oscar Niemeyer, architect of the UN headquarters, designed all the government buildings. The twin towers (shown in the picture above) open onto the circle of Three Powers Square. The square contains the legislative, judicial, and executive buildings. Brasília has sectors for hotels, residences, the military, government, leisure activities, conventions and education. The city boasts a population of nearly 2 million people—half of them under the age of 25.

Interpreting the Art What comparisons can you make between Brasília and Washington, D.C.? *Both are designed as seats of national government; both have separate buildings for the executive, judicial, and legislative branches; and both showcase national talent in architecture and the arts.*

Interact *with* History

This Interact with History feature motivates students by inviting them to think about the foundations of democracy. As they imagine talking with a foreign student, they will consider the factors that make democracy possible and the ways in which living in a democracy affects their lives.

Purpose

• to prepare students to study democratic processes in other countries

• to help students analyze the foundations of democracy

• to help students connect to the people and events they will study in this chapter

Teaching Strategy

Thinking Critically Have students read the page. Then have them answer the key questions and give reasons for their answers.

EXAMINING *the* ISSUES

Following are suggestions for addressing each bulleted question.

❶ What rights and institutions did the framers of the U.S. Constitution consider necessary to ensure democratic rule?

❷ Ask students to think about ways their parents or other people they know participate in democracy.

❸ Have students consider the importance of literacy, economic security, and cultural unity in establishing a successful democracy.

Making Connections If students were drafting a constitution, what rights and guarantees would they rank first, second, and third? Have them explain their answers.

Follow Up

A feature on the chapter assessment will ask students to reevaluate their responses to the situation presented on this page.

On the news, you watch stories about protesters who demand more democratic freedom in their countries. Such demonstrations are taking place all over the world. Many times, students lead the protests. These students have learned about democracy through watching television or by attending school in the West.

At school, you meet a foreign exchange student who comes from a country that is controlled by a non-democratic government. At lunch, this student asks you to explain what democracy is and how it works. What would you say?

What makes democracy work?

In Beijing, China, in 1989, students gather in a public square to call for more democracy. For example, they want freedom of speech and the press.

For inspiration, they erect a statue that looks like the Statue of Liberty.

They demand an end to corrupt, authoritarian government.

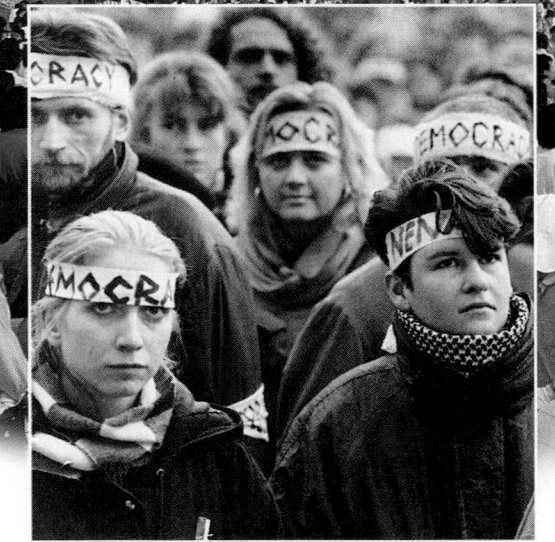

Students in Czechoslovakia demonstrate in memory of the pro-democracy protests in China. They wear headbands that say "democracy." They also demand more non-Communist representatives in their own government.

EXAMINING *the* ISSUES

• What rights and institutions are necessary for a government to be democratic?

• How do citizens participate in a democracy? How can participation be encouraged?

• What obstacles can prevent a democracy from succeeding?

Discuss these questions in class and list important points on the board. For your discussion, consider what you know about democracy in ancient Greece and in the United States.

As you read this chapter, think about the challenges many countries face in trying to develop democratic systems.

❶ Democracy

PATTERNS OF CHANGE

CASE STUDY: Latin American Democracies

TERMS & NAMES
- Brasília
- land reform
- standard of living
- recession
- PRI

MAIN IDEA	**WHY IT MATTERS NOW**
Democracy is not easy to achieve. In Latin America, economic problems and authoritarian rule delayed democracy.	By the mid-1990s, almost all Latin American nations had democratic governments.

Background
Indirect democracy is also called representative democracy.

SETTING THE STAGE By definition, democracy is government by the people. Direct democracy, in which all citizens meet to pass laws, is not practical for nations. Therefore, democratic nations such as the United States developed indirect democracy, in which citizens elect representatives to make laws for them.

Making Democracy Work

Democracy is more than a form of government. It is also a way of life and an ideal goal. A democratic way of life includes practices such as free and open elections. The chart on this page lists four basic practices and ideal conditions that help those practices to succeed. Many nations follow these democratic practices to a large degree. However, none does so perfectly. Establishing democracy is a process that takes years.

Even in the United States, the establishment of democracy has taken time. Although the principle of equality is part of the Constitution, many Americans have struggled for equal rights. To cite one example, women did not receive the right to vote until 1920—132 years after the Constitution went into effect. Under the best of circumstances, democracy is always a "work in progress."

Democratic institutions may not ensure stable, civilian government if other conditions are not present. In general, the participation of a nation's citizens in government is essential to democracy. If citizens don't vote or don't contribute to public discussions of important issues, democracy suffers. Education and literacy—the ability to

PATTERNS OF CHANGE: Making Democracy Work

Common Practices	Conditions That Foster Those Practices
Free elections	• Having more than one political party • Universal suffrage — all adult citizens can vote
Citizen participation	• High levels of education and literacy • Economic security • Freedoms of speech, press, and assembly
Majority rule, minority rights	• All citizens equal before the law • Shared national identity • Protection of such individual rights as freedom of religion • Representatives elected by citizens to carry out their will
Constitutional government	• Clear body of traditions and laws on which government is based • Widespread education about how government works • National acceptance of majority decisions • Shared belief that no one is above the law

SKILLBUILDER: Interpreting Charts
1. *Which of those conditions that foster democratic practices refer to political institutions?*
2. *Identify the conditions that increase citizen participation and explain why they would do so.*

Section 1 Overview

OBJECTIVES

① To identify key building blocks of democracy.

② To describe Brazil's efforts to build democracy.

③ To analyze the struggle for democracy in Mexico.

④ To describe key events in postwar Argentina.

SKILLBUILDER
- Interpreting charts, p. 531
- Interpreting graphs, p. 533

CRITICAL THINKING
- Making inferences, p. 532
- Analyzing motives, p. 532
- Analyzing problems, p. 533
- Recognizing effects, p. 534
- Analyzing causes, p. 535
- Comparing and contrasting, p. 535
- Analyzing themes, p. 535

FOCUS
5-Minute Warm-Up

Making Inferences
To help students realize the economic challenges facing Brazil, have them answer the following questions.

1. Read the Daily Life feature on page 532. How did Carolina Maria de Jesus support herself and her children?

2. According to the feature, are favelas disappearing?

 WARM-UP TRANSPARENCY 19

OBJECTIVE ① INSTRUCT

Making Democracy Work

▶ *Key Ideas*
- Stable democracies require key institutions and practices.

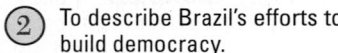 **IN-DEPTH RESOURCES: UNIT 5**
Guided Reading, p. 37
Geography Application: Democracy in Central and South America, p. 43

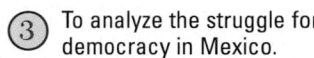 **ACCESS FOR STUDENTS ACQUIRING ENGLISH**
Guided Reading (Spanish), p. 205

read and write—give citizens the tools they need to make political decisions. Also, a stable economy with a strong middle class and opportunities for advancement helps democracy. It does so by giving citizens a stake in the future of their nation.

Other factors advance democracy. First, a firm belief in the rights of the individual promotes the fair and equal treatment of citizens. Second, rule by law helps prevent leaders from abusing power without fear of punishment. Third, a sense of national identity—the idea that members of a society have a shared culture—helps encourage citizens to work together for the good of the nation.

The struggle to establish democracy continued in the 1990s as many nations abandoned authoritarian rule for democratic institutions. Several Latin American countries, such as Brazil, Mexico, and Argentina, were among those making democratic progress.

CASE STUDY: Brazil

From Dictators to Democracy

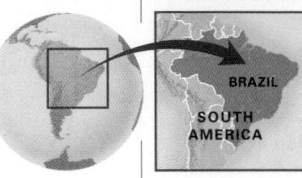

Many Latin American nations won their independence in the early 1800s. However, three centuries of colonial rule left problems. This included powerful militaries, one-crop economies, and sharp class divisions. These patterns persisted in the modern era. One reason is that Europe and the United States dominated the region economically and politically. In addition, many Latin American leaders seemed more interested in personal power than in democracy.

Like much of Latin America, Brazil struggled to establish democracy. After gaining independence from Portugal in 1822, Brazil became a monarchy. This lasted until 1889, when Brazilians established a republican government—which a wealthy elite actually controlled. Then, in the 1930s, Getulio Vargas became dictator of Brazil. Vargas suppressed political opposition. At the same time, however, he promoted economic growth and helped turn Brazil into a modern industrial nation.

Kubitschek's Ambitious Program After Vargas, three popularly elected presidents tried to steer Brazil toward democracy. Juscelino Kubitschek (zhoo·suh·LEE·nuh KOO·bih·chehk), who governed from 1956 to 1961, continued to develop Brazil's economy. Promising "fifty years of progress in five," Kubitschek encouraged foreign investment to help pay for elaborate development projects. He built a new capital city, **Brasília** (bruh·ZIHL·yuh), in the country's interior. Kubitschek's dream proved expensive. The nation's foreign debt soared and inflation shot up. This caused hardship for most Brazilians.

Kubitschek's successors proposed reforms to lessen economic and social problems. Conservatives resisted this strongly. They especially opposed the plan for **land reform**—breaking up large estates and distributing that land to peasants. In 1964, with the blessing of wealthy Brazilians, the army seized power in a military coup.

Military Dictators For two decades, military dictators ruled Brazil. Emphasizing economic growth at all costs, the generals opened the country to foreign investment. They began huge development projects in the Amazon jungle. The economy boomed, in what many described as Brazil's "economic miracle."

The boom had a downside, though. The government froze wages and cut back on social programs. This caused a decline in the **standard of living**—or quality of life, which is judged by the amount of goods people have. When Brazilians protested, the government imposed censorship. It also jailed and tortured government critics. Nevertheless, opposition to military rule continued to grow.

Brazilian Economy, 1955-1990

Foreign Debt (in billions of U.S. dollars)

140, 120, 100, 80, 60, 40, 20, 0

1955 1960 1965 1970 1975 1980 1985 1990

Source: The Brazilian Economy: Growth and Development

Inflation Rate

250%, 200%, 150%, 100%, 50%, 0%

1477%

1955 1960 1965 1970 1975 1980 1985 1990

SKILLBUILDER: Interpreting Graphs
1. *How much did Brazil's foreign debt increase from 1955 to 1990?*
2. *Of the years shown on the bar graph, which was the worst year for inflation?*
3. *Did Brazil's economy get better or worse from 1955 to 1990? Explain.*

Background
Before the change to direct elections, the president was chosen by members of the congress and state legislatures.

THINK THROUGH HISTORY
C. Analyzing Problems In your opinion, what is the worst problem Sarney faced? Explain.
C. Possible Answers The foreign debt because it put Brazil under the power of other nations; inflation because no one could get ahead.

The Road to Democracy By the early 1980s, a **recession**—or slowdown in the economy—gripped Brazil. At that point, the generals decided to open up the political system. They allowed direct elections of local, state, and national officials.

In 1985, a new civilian president, José Sarney (zhoh·ZAY SAHR·nay), took office. Although he was elected indirectly, a 1985 constitutional amendment declared that all future presidents would be elected directly by the people. Sarney inherited a country in crisis:

A VOICE FROM THE PAST
I . . . became the holder of the largest foreign debt on the face of the earth, as well as the greatest internal debt. My inheritance included the deepest recession in our history, the highest rate of unemployment, an unprecedented climate of violence, potential political disintegration and the highest rate of inflation ever recorded in our country's history—250 percent a year, with the prospect of reaching 1,000 percent.
JOSÉ SARNEY, "Brazil: A President's Story"

Though well-intentioned, Sarney failed to solve the country's problems and lost support. The next elected president fared even worse. He resigned because of corruption charges. In 1994, Brazilians elected Fernando Henrique Cardoso, who achieved some success in tackling the nation's economic and political problems. Although Brazil faced many challenges, during the 1990s it continued on the path of democracy. It maintained an elected civilian government.

CASE STUDY: Mexico

One Dominant Party

Unlike Brazil, Mexico enjoyed relative political stability for most of the 20th century. Following the Mexican Revolution, the government passed the Constitution of 1917. It outlined a democracy and promised reforms. This document helped prevent direct military involvement in politics—which has been a common problem in many Latin American countries.

Beginnings of One-Party Domination From 1920 to 1934, Mexico elected several generals as president. However, these men did not rule as military dictators. They did create a ruling party—the National Revolutionary Party, which has dominated Mexico under various names ever since.

From 1934 to 1940, President Lázaro Cárdenas (KAHR·day·nahs) tried to improve life for peasants and workers. He carried out land reform and promoted labor rights.

SPOTLIGHT ON

Liberation Theology
At a 1968 conference, Roman Catholic leaders of Latin America—including several prominent Brazilians—started a movement known as liberation theology. These leaders taught that the Church must become a church of the poor. It must work to ease poverty by becoming involved in political affairs and crying out against injustice.

One of the most outspoken advocates of liberation theology was Archbishop Oscar Romero of El Salvador, shown below. In 1980, a right-wing assassin murdered the Archbishop for speaking out against government oppression of poor Salvadorans.

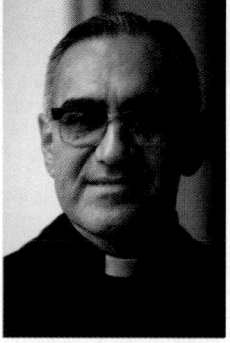

PATTERNS OF CHANGE 533

History from Visuals

Brazilian Economy, 1955–1990

Interpreting the Graphs Tell students that bar and line graphs show changes in quantities over time. Ask them to notice how the rise in Brazil's inflation rate generally parallels the rise in foreign debt. Ask them to look at the debt/inflation figures for each year listed. In what 5-year period did the debt go up and the inflation rate go down? *1965–1970.*

Extension Activity Ask students to reread A Voice from the Past on page 533. Sarney was concerned about the 250 percent inflation rate. According to the graph, had the inflation rate risen by 1990? *Yes, to 1477 percent.* What effect did this have on Sarney's political career?

SKILLBUILDER Answers
1. About $120 billion.
2. 1990, when inflation was 1477 percent.
3. It got worse. Both prices and foreign debt increased, making it harder for people to buy necessities and for the government to raise money.

SPOTLIGHT ON
Liberation Theology

Catholics have been deeply divided over liberation theology. Supporters say the Church should serve the poor, but opponents say the Church should stay out of politics. Ask students, if a country's government is corrupt, should the Church remain neutral? Why or why not?

OBJECTIVE 3 INSTRUCT

Mexico: One Dominant Party

▶ **Key Ideas**
• Despite economic and political crises, Mexico maintains democratic rule.

TEACHING OPTIONS

CONNECTIONS ACROSS THE CURRICULUM

Economics Brazil has experienced severe inflation. Tell students that inflation exists when prices rise and the value of money declines. A 10 percent inflation rate, for example, means that an item that cost $100 a year ago, now costs $110 ($100 × .10 = $10; $100 + $10 = $110). Have students suppose that in 1979, a Brazilian middle-class family could live comfortably on the equivalent of $25,000 U.S. dollars. In 1980, when the inflation rate was 115 percent, how much would the family have to earn to maintain the same standard of living? *$53,750.* If they earned $25,000 in 1989, how much would they have to earn in 1990? *$394,250.* What might be the political implications of such conditions?

CONNECTIONS ACROSS TIME AND PLACE

Nationalist Leaders Lázaro Cárdenas was one of a number of nationalist leaders in Latin America who advocated economic development and independence from foreign control during the 1930s and 1940s. Others include Getúlio Vargas in Brazil, Rómulo Gallegos in Venezuela, Juan Perón in Argentina, José Figueres Ferrer in Costa Rica, and Víctor Raúl Haya de la Torre in Peru. Have interested students research the life of Lázaro Cárdenas or read the biography of Juan and Eva Perón, who are featured on page 535.

 IN-DEPTH RESOURCES: UNIT 5
History Makers: Juan and Eva Perón, p. 52

Teacher's Edition 533

He nationalized the Mexican oil industry, kicking out foreign oil companies and creating a state-run oil industry. After Cárdenas, however, a series of more conservative presidents turned away from reform. For the most part, they worked to develop the economy for the benefit of wealthy Mexicans.

The Party Becomes the PRI In 1946, the main political party changed its name to the Institutional Revolutionary Party, or **PRI.** In the half-century that followed, the PRI became the main force for political stability in Mexico.

Although stable, the government was an imperfect democracy. The PRI controlled the congress and won every presidential election. The government allowed opposition parties to compete, but fraud and corruption spoiled elections and blocked opposition gains.

Even as the Mexican economy rapidly developed, Mexico continued to suffer severe economic problems. Lacking land and jobs, millions of Mexicans struggled for survival. In addition, a huge foreign debt forced the government to spend money on interest payments instead of helping the Mexican people. Two episodes highlighted Mexico's growing difficulties. In the late 1960s, students and workers began calling for economic and political change. On October 2, 1968, protesters gathered at the site of an ancient Aztec market in Mexico City. A reporter recalled what happened next:

> ### A VOICE FROM THE PAST
> Suddenly one helicopter flew low over the crowd and dropped a flare. Immediately hundreds of soldiers hidden among the Aztec ruins of the square opened fire with automatic weapons. . . . Students who fled . . . were chased and beaten and some were murdered. . . . That night, army vehicles carried away the bodies, while firetrucks washed away the blood.
> **ALAN RIDING,** *Distant Neighbors*

The massacre in the Aztec ruins claimed several hundred lives.

A second critical episode occurred during the early 1980s. By that time huge new oil and natural gas reserves had been discovered in Mexico. The economy had become dependent on oil and gas exports. In 1981, however, world oil prices fell sharply, cutting Mexico's oil and gas revenues in half. Mexico went into an economic decline.

SPOTLIGHT ON

Chiapas Revolt

In January 1994, a rebel army burst out of the jungle and seized several towns in the state of Chiapas. The rebels, one of whom is shown above, called themselves Zapatistas—after the revolutionary hero Emiliano Zapata. Demanding greater democracy, the Zapatistas especially wanted to improve life for Maya Indians, who were among the poorest Mexicans. The Zapatistas demanded better housing, health clinics, and schools.

Although the revolt had little chance of military success, the Mexican president appointed a peace negotiator to discuss the rebels' demands. Negotiations continued for months. Mexico's move toward multi-party rule in 1997 might perhaps provide a way for groups like the Zapatistas to influence the government legally.

Economic and Political Crises The rest of the 1980s and 1990s saw Mexico facing various crises. In 1988, opposition parties seriously challenged the PRI in national elections. The PRI candidate, Carlos Salinas de Gortari, won the presidency—some argued by fraud. Even so, opposition parties won seats in congress and began to force a gradual opening of the political system.

During his presidency, Salinas signed NAFTA, the North American Free Trade Agreement. NAFTA removed trade barriers between Mexico, the United States, and Canada. In early 1994, just as the agreement was going into effect, peasant rebels in the southern Mexican state of Chiapas (chee·AH·pahs) staged a major uprising. Shortly afterward, a gunman assassinated the PRI presidential candidate.

The PRI Loses Control After these events, Mexicans felt more concerned than ever about the prospects for democratic stability. Nevertheless, the elections of 1994 went ahead as planned. The new PRI candidate, Ernesto Zedillo (zuh·DEE·yoh), won in what appeared to be a fair ballot. At the same time, opposition parties continued to challenge the PRI.

In 1997, two opposition parties each won a large number of congressional seats—denying the PRI control of congress for the first time in its history. At last, Mexico seemed to be on its way to multi-party, democratic rule.

Argentina Casts Off Repression

SOUTH AMERICA

ARGENTINA

Mexico and Brazil were not the only Latin American countries where democracy had made progress. By the late 1990s, all of Latin America—except Cuba—was under democratic rule. One notable example of democratic progress was Argentina.

Perón Rules Argentina The second largest country in South America, Argentina had struggled to establish democracy. Argentina was a major exporter of grain and beef. It was also an industrial nation with a large working class. In 1946, Argentine workers supported an army officer, Juan Perón, who won the presidency and then established a dictatorship.

Perón did not rule alone. He received critical support from his wife, Eva—known as "Evita" to the millions of Argentines who idolized her. Together, the Peróns created a welfare state. The state offered social programs with broad popular appeal but limited freedoms. After Eva's death in 1952, Perón's popularity declined and his enemies—the military and the Catholic Church—moved against him. In 1955, the military ousted Perón and drove him into exile.

Repression in Argentina For the next three decades, the military essentially controlled Argentine politics. Perón returned to power once more, in 1973, but ruled for only a year before dying in office. By the mid-1970s, Argentina was in chaos. The economy was in ruins and radical terrorism was on the rise.

In 1976, the generals seized power again. They established a brutal dictatorship and hunted down political opponents. For several years, torture and murder were everyday events. By the early 1980s, several thousand Argentines had simply disappeared—kidnapped by their own government. The government killed at least 10,000 people. Critics charged that some of the victims were pushed out of airplanes over the ocean.

Moving Toward Democracy In 1982, the military government went to war with Britain over the nearby Falkland Islands and suffered a humiliating defeat. Thoroughly disgraced, the generals agreed to step down. In 1983, Argentines elected Raúl Alfonsín (ahl-fohn-SEEN) president in the country's first truly free election in 40 years.

During the 1980s, Alfonsín worked to rebuild democracy and the economy. The next president continued that process. By the late 1990s, democracy seemed established in Argentina, though economic problems continued. In Section 2 you will read how ethnic and racial conflicts slowed democratic progress in parts of Africa.

Vocabulary
welfare state: a government that tries to provide for all its citizens' needs—such as health, education, and employment.

In 1950, President Juan Perón and his wife Eva greet a crowd of hundreds of thousands. The Peróns are standing on the balcony of the government house.

THINK THROUGH HISTORY
E. Analyzing Causes What finally caused military rule to end in Argentina?
E. Answer The military government lost a humiliating war and had to turn the government over to civilians.

Section 1 Assessment

1. TERMS & NAMES
Identify
• Brasília
• land reform
• standard of living
• recession
• PRI

2. TAKING NOTES
On a chart like the one below, record the steps that Brazil, Mexico, and Argentina have taken toward establishing democracy.

Nation	Steps toward democracy
Brazil	
Mexico	
Argentina	

3. COMPARING AND CONTRASTING
Compare and contrast the roles of the military in the governments of Brazil, Mexico, and Argentina.

THINK ABOUT
• their relationship to civilian governments
• whether they hindered or advanced democracy

4. ANALYZING THEMES
Economics How does the state of a nation's economy affect its democratic progress?

THINK ABOUT
• how economic conditions affect citizens' support for the government
• how economic conditions affect the government's ability to provide for its citizens

PATTERNS OF CHANGE **535**

OBJECTIVE 4 INSTRUCT

Argentina Casts Off Repression

▶ *Key Ideas*
• Juan Perón creates a welfare state with limited freedoms.
• The military takes over and establishes a brutal dictatorship.
• After the generals step down, Argentina moves toward a true democracy.

ASSESS & RETEACH

Section 1 Assessment
Have students work in pairs to answer the questions and then share their answers with other pairs of students.

Section Quiz
 FORMAL ASSESSMENT
Section Quiz, p. 236

Reteaching Activity
CLASS TIME: 15 MINUTES
Have students review the section by writing at least three statements about each country's quest for democracy.

CLOSE ACTIVITY

CLASS TIME: 20 MINUTES

Creating a Time Line
Have students work in small groups to create time lines of events in Brazil, Mexico, and Argentina in the postwar period. Students should use information from the section and note instances in which similar events occurred in more than one country. Discuss with them the similarities and differences among the three countries.

ANSWERS

1. TERMS & NAMES
Brasília, p. 532
land reform, p. 532
standard of living, p. 532
recession, p. 533
PRI, p. 534

2. TAKING NOTES
Possible Responses:
Brazil—direct elections, civilian government, attempts to mend

economy; Mexico—democratic constitution, some land reform, gradual opening of political system to opposition; Argentina—civilian government, free elections, economic reforms

3. COMPARING AND CONTRASTING
Possible Responses: In Brazil and Argentina, the military over-

threw civilian governments. Eventually they were forced to give up power and allow free elections. In Mexico, the military has never directly controlled the government.

4. ANALYZING THEMES
Possible Responses: Citizens are more likely to take part in political processes if they have

economic security. Also, they are more likely to have a stake in their country's future if they have a chance of economic improvement. If a government faces economic problems, such as high foreign debt, it has less money to spend on its people and may therefore lose public support.

Teacher's Edition **535**

① To explain the legacy of colonialism in Africa.

② To show how ethnic divisions in Nigeria led to war.

③ To describe events in Nigeria since 1970.

④ To explain the history of white rule in South Africa.

⑤ To describe South Africa's shift toward democracy.

SKILLBUILDER

• Interpreting maps: region, location, p. 537

CRITICAL THINKING

• Recognizing effects, pp. 536, 538
• Clarifying, p. 538
• Making inferences, p. 539
• Analyzing causes, p. 539
• Drawing conclusions, p. 540
• Identifying problems, p. 540

FOCUS
5-Minute Warm-Up

Interpreting Maps
Answering the following questions will help students understand the divisions in Nigeria.

1. Study the map on page 537. Into how many regions is Nigeria divided?

2. What Nigerian cities provide access to the Atlantic Ocean?

 WARM-UP TRANSPARENCY 19

OBJECTIVE ① INSTRUCT

Colonial Rule Hampers Democracy

▶ *Key Ideas*
• Colonial rule fails to prepare Africans for democracy.
• African countries face ethnic divisions, weak economies, and political corruption.

 IN-DEPTH RESOURCES: UNIT 5
Guided Reading, p. 38

 ACCESS FOR STUDENTS ACQUIRING ENGLISH
Guided Reading (Spanish), p. 206

---

2 Democratic Challenges in African Nations

TERMS & NAMES
• federal system
• martial law
• dissident
• apartheid
• Nelson Mandela

MAIN IDEA	WHY IT MATTERS NOW
As the recent histories of Nigeria and South Africa show, ethnic and racial conflicts can hinder democracy.	As Nigeria struggled with democracy, in 1996 South Africa adopted a bill of rights that promotes racial equality.

SETTING THE STAGE Beginning in the late 1950s, dozens of European colonies in Africa gained their independence and became nations. As in Latin America, the establishment of democracy in Africa proved difficult. In many cases, the newly independent nations faced a host of problems that slowed their progress toward democracy.

Colonial Rule Hampers Democracy

The main reason for Africa's difficulties was the negative impact of colonial rule. European powers did little to prepare their African colonies for independence. In fact, the lingering effects of colonialism undermined efforts to build stable, democratic states.

European Policies Cause Problems When the Europeans established colonial boundaries, they ignored ethnic or cultural divisions. Borders often divided peoples of the same background or threw different—often rival—groups together. Because of this, a sense of national identity was almost impossible to develop. After independence, the old colonial boundaries became the borders of the newly independent states. As a result, ethnic and cultural conflicts remained, and even increased.

Other problems had an economic basis. European powers had viewed colonies as sources of wealth for the home country. They had no desire to develop the colonies for the benefit of the Africans who lived there. The colonial powers encouraged the export of one or two cash crops—such as coffee or rubber—rather than the production of a range of products to serve local needs. Europeans developed plantations and mines but few factories. Manufactured goods were imported from European countries. They also built few roads, bridges, or communications systems—all necessary for economic development. These policies left new African nations with unbalanced economies and a small middle class. Such economic problems lessened their chances to create democratic stability.

European rule also disrupted African family and community life. In some cases,

This photo shows the 1957 ceremony marking Ghana's independence from Britain. At the ceremony were Britain's Duchess of Kent and Ghana's new President Kwame Nkrumah.

colonial powers moved Africans far from their families and villages to work in mines or on plantations. In addition, colonial governments did little to educate the majority of African people. As a result, most newly independent nations lacked a skilled, literate work force that could take on the task of building a new nation.

Short-Lived Democracies When Britain and France gave up their colonies, they left new democratic governments in place. Soon problems threatened those governments. Rival ethnic groups often fought each other for power. Strong militaries, left over from colonial rule, became a tool for ambitious leaders. In many cases, a military dictatorship quickly replaced democracy. Since independence, the struggle between democracy and authoritarian rule has torn apart many African nations.

THINK THROUGH HISTORY
A. Recognizing Effects What were the main negative effects of the economic policies of European colonizers?
A. Answer The economy was dependent on one or two products, goods had to be imported to meet local needs, and no structures were built to support industry.

Background
Many colonies had strong militaries because the colonizers created them to control the local people.

PRINT RESOURCES

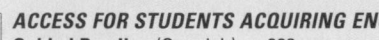 *IN-DEPTH RESOURCES: UNIT 5*
Guided Reading, p. 38
Primary Sources: from *Kaffir Boy*, p. 45; Mandela's Inaugural Address, p. 46
History Makers: Nelson Mandela, p. 53

ACCESS FOR STUDENTS ACQUIRING ENGLISH
Guided Reading (Spanish), p. 206

FORMAL ASSESSMENT
Section Quiz, p. 237

TECHNOLOGY RESOURCES

 WORLD ART AND CULTURES TRANSPARENCIES
AT77 Multiple-Mask Headdress

 CD-ROM
Electronic Library of Primary Sources

 VIDEO *Patterns of Interaction: Struggling Toward Democracy*

 INTERNET www.mlworldhistory.com

Nigeria Erupts in Civil War

Background
In 1995, Nigeria's estimated population was about 95 million. More than 250 ethnic groups live in the country.

Nigeria provides a good example of the political struggles that have shaken Africa. Nigeria, a former British colony, won its independence peacefully in 1960. Nigeria is Africa's most populous country and one of its richest. Because of that, Nigeria seemed to have good prospects for democratic stability. The country was ethnically divided, however. This soon created problems that led to war.

A Land of Many Peoples Three major ethnic groups and many smaller ones live within Nigeria's borders. In the north are the Hausa-Fulani, who are Muslim. In the south are the Yoruba and the Igbo (also called Ibo), who are mostly either Christians or animists. The Yoruba, a farming people with a tradition of kings, live to the west. The Igbo, a farming people who have a democratic tradition, live to the east.

After independence, Nigeria adopted a **federal system.** In a federal system, power is shared between state governments and a central authority, much like in the United States. The Nigerians set up three states, one for each region and ethnic group, with a corresponding political party in each.

War with Biafra Although one group dominated each state, the states also had other ethnic minorities. In the Western Region—the Yoruba homeland—non-Yoruba minorities began to resent Yoruba control. In 1963, they tried to break away and form their own region. This led to fighting. In January 1966, a group of army officers, most of them Igbo, seized power in the capital city of Lagos. These officers abolished the regional governments and declared **martial law,** or temporary military rule.

The Hausa-Fulani, who had long distrusted the Igbo, launched an attack from the north. They persecuted and killed many Igbo. The survivors fled east to their homeland. In 1967, the Eastern Region seceded from Nigeria, declaring itself the new nation of Biafra (bee·AF·ruh).

During the civil war in Nigeria, Biafra was so desperate for troops that it enlisted boys younger than 18 in its army.

Africa, 1967

Regions of Nigeria, 1967

- Eastern Region
- Midwestern Region
- Western Region
- Northern Region

GEOGRAPHY SKILLBUILDER: Interpreting Maps
1. **Region** *Describe the Eastern Region, which seceded as Biafra. Describe its size and location compared to the rest of Nigeria.*
2. **Location** *In which region is Nigeria's capital city of Lagos?*

Struggles for Democracy **537**

Nigeria's Struggle for Democracy

Key Ideas

- The military governs Nigeria after the war, developing an oil-based economy.
- Democracy returns briefly to Nigeria, but the military again takes over.
- Under military rule, political rights are severely limited.

SPOTLIGHT On
Silencing Dissidents

Have students use periodicals or the Internet to research the case of Ken Saro-Wiwa and other jailed activists in Nigeria. What were the issues in the case, and what were Saro-Wiwa's objectives as a protester?

South Africa Under White Rule

Key Ideas

- South Africa's rulers create a segregated society.
- After independence, South Africa's white rulers impose apartheid, an even more rigid system of segregation.
- Black South African protests lead to violence and a state of emergency.

 IN-DEPTH RESOURCES: UNIT 5
Primary Source: from *Kaffir Boy*, p. 45

The Nigerian government then went to war to reunite the country. The Nigerian civil war lasted three years. The Igbo fought heroically but were badly outnumbered and outgunned. In 1970, Biafra surrendered. Nigeria was reunited, but the war took a tremendous toll. Although exact numbers are unknown, perhaps several million Igbo died, most from starvation.

Nigeria's Struggle for Democracy

After the war, Nigerians returned to the process of nation-building. "When the war ended," noted one officer, "it was like a referee blowing a whistle in a football game. People just put down their guns and went back to the business of living." The Nigerian government did not punish the Igbo. It used federal money to rebuild the Igbo region.

Federal Government Restored The military governed Nigeria for most of the 1970s. During this time, Nigerian leaders tried to create a more stable federal system, with a strong central government and 19 regional units. The government also tried to build a more modern economy, based on oil income. Nigeria became the world's seventh largest oil producer. For a time, it grew wealthy from oil money.

In 1979, the military handed power back to civilian rulers. Nigerians were cheered by the return to democracy. Some people, like businessman Godfrey Amachree, however, remained concerned about ethnic divisions in the nation:

SPOTLIGHT On

Silencing Dissidents

On November 10, 1995, Nigeria hanged nine political prisoners—all critics of the military government. Many around the world believed the nine were convicted on false charges just to silence them.

One of the nine was Ken Saro-Wiwa, a noted writer and activist. Saro-Wiwa had protested oil drilling in his native province. He charged oil companies and the government with destroying the environment.

Although Saro-Wiwa died, his protest lived on. Shortly before his death, Saro-Wiwa smuggled several manuscripts out of prison. In one, he wrote:

Injustice stalks the land like a tiger on the prowl. To be at the mercy of buffoons [fools] is the ultimate insult. To find the instruments of state power reducing you to dust is the injury.

A VOICE FROM THE PAST
We've got such great potential in this country if we can truly pull together as one people, one nation. But there are these deep divisions that have torn us apart before. I can only hope we've learned our lesson. Have we? I don't know. I'd only be guessing. It all depends on whether we're ready to start thinking in terms of nation instead of tribe.
GODFREY AMACHREE, from *The Africans* by David Lamb

Nigerian democracy was short-lived. In 1983, the military overthrew the civilian government, charging it with corruption. A new military regime, dominated by the Hausa-Fulani, took charge. It carried out a policy of discrimination against other ethnic groups.

Continued Military Rule Since then, the military has continued to govern Nigeria, while promising to bring back civilian rule. The army held elections in 1993, which resulted in the victory of popular leader Moshood Abiola. However, officers declared the results not valid and handed power to a new dictator, General Sani Abacha.

General Abacha banned political activity and jailed Abiola and numerous other **dissidents,** or opponents of government policy. Although Nigeria's military rulers vowed to move Nigeria gradually toward democracy, they continued to cling to power. Clearly, Nigeria had a long way to go before it became truly democratic.

South Africa Under White Rule

In South Africa, racial conflict was the result of colonial rule. From its beginnings under Dutch and British control, South Africa was racially divided. A small white minority ruled a large black majority. In 1910, South Africa gained self-rule as a dominion of the British Empire. In 1931 it became an independent member of the British Commonwealth. Although South Africa had a constitutional government, the constitution gave whites power and denied the black majority its rights.

Apartheid Segregates Society In 1948, the National Party came to power in South Africa. This party promoted Afrikaner, or Dutch South African, nationalism. It also

THINK THROUGH HISTORY
B. Recognizing Effects What was the effect of the war on the Igbo?
B. Answers They were forced to rejoin Nigeria; millions died.

THINK THROUGH HISTORY
C. Clarifying Review the chart on page 529. Which element of a democratic way of life was Godfrey Amachree discussing?
C. Answer The need for national identity.

Background
South Africa's population is 75.2 percent black, 13.6 percent white, 8.6 percent mixed race, and 2.6 percent Asian.

538 Chapter 19

CONNECTIONS ACROSS TIME AND PLACE

Civil Rights Struggles Point out that South Africa and the United States have both experienced civil rights struggles. Ask students to construct a chart to compare and contrast the civil rights struggles of the two countries in the following areas: time frames of the civil rights movements, major racial policies established by white rulers, key civil rights organizations and leaders, a few of the key protest events (sit-ins, demonstrations, killings, and so on), important civil rights legislation passed or racial policies eliminated, and current situations in each country.

CONNECTIONS ACROSS THE CURRICULUM

Geography Have students create a cultural and political map of South Africa as it is today. The map should include the names of ethnic groups, the 11 languages they speak, and where they reside. Students can use a different color to represent each ethnic group, constructing a key to explain the colors.

Ask students to include a 3 × 5 card for each group, giving a brief description of the geography of the area in which the group lives (for example, "semiarid, poor soil, few wild animals"). Display the finished map in class, and have students discuss the difficulties of governing such a diverse population.

instituted a policy of **apartheid,** a complete separation of the races. The minority government banned social contacts between whites and blacks. It established segregated schools, hospitals, and neighborhoods. It provided the best facilities for whites.

In 1959, the minority government set up reserves, called homelands, for the country's major black groups. Blacks were forbidden to live in white areas unless they worked as servants or laborers for whites. The homelands policy was totally unbalanced. Although blacks made up 75 percent of the population, the government set aside only 13 percent of the land for them. Whites kept the best lands.

Blacks Protest Black South Africans resisted the controls imposed by the white minority. In 1912, they formed the African National Congress (ANC) to fight for their rights. The ANC organized strikes and boycotts to protest racist policies. During one demonstration in 1960, police killed 69 people—an incident known as the Sharpeville Massacre. Afterward, the government banned the ANC and imprisoned many of its members. One was ANC leader **Nelson Mandela** (man·DEHL·uh).

The troubles continued. In 1976, riots over school policies broke out in the black township of Soweto, leaving 600 students dead. In 1977, police beat popular protest leader Steve Biko to death while he was in custody. This sparked an international outcry. As protests mounted, the government declared a state of emergency in 1986.

South Africa Moves Toward Democracy

By the late 1980s, South Africa was under enormous pressure to change. For years, a black South African bishop, Desmond Tutu, had led an economic campaign against apartheid. He asked foreign nations not to do business with South Africa. In response, many nations of the world imposed trade restrictions. They also isolated South Africa in other ways. For example, since the 1960s, South Africa had not been allowed to take part in the Olympic Games.

The First Steps In 1989, white South Africans elected a new president, F. W. de Klerk. His goal was to transform South Africa and end its isolation. In February 1990, he legalized the ANC and also released Nelson Mandela from prison.

These dramatic actions marked the beginning of a new era in South Africa. Over the next 18 months, the South African Parliament repealed apartheid laws that had segregated public facilities and restricted land ownership by blacks. World leaders welcomed these changes and began to ease restrictions on South Africa.

Although some legal barriers had fallen, others would remain until a new constitution was in place. First, the country needed to form a multiracial government. After lengthy negotiations, President de Klerk agreed to hold South Africa's first universal elections, in which people of all races could vote, in April 1994.

Majority Rule Among the candidates for president were F. W. de Klerk and Nelson Mandela. During the campaign, the Inkatha Freedom Party—a rival party

Global Impact

International Boycott

South Africa's racial policies and violent actions made it an outcast among nations. In 1974, the United Nations forbade South Africa's delegates to attend UN sessions. In 1976, the UN urged its members to stop trading with South Africa and competing against its athletes.

One year later, the UN banned all military sales to the country. In the mid-1980s, many countries imposed trade restrictions on South Africa. For example, in 1985 the U.S. government banned the importing of Krugerrand gold coins, which had been a popular investment item. Eventually, international pressure helped convince South Africa's government that it must end apartheid.

South Africa adopted this flag in 1994.

South Africa 1948–1998

1948	1958	1968	1978	1988	1998
1948 National Party in power; passed apartheid laws	**1959** Black homelands established		**1976** 600 black students killed during Soweto protest	**1989** F.W. de Klerk elected president	**1996** New constitution adopted
		1960 Sharpeville Massacre, 69 protesters killed	**1977** Steven Biko killed in police custody	**1990** ANC legalized and Mandela released	
		1962 Nelson Mandela jailed		**1994** ANC won 62.7% of the vote; Mandela elected president	

539

Nelson Mandela and F. W. de Klerk

Both Mandela and de Klerk were called traitors by some members of their own parties. Some whites believed that black rule would destroy South Africa, while some members of the ANC wanted to rid South Africa of all whites. Moderate voices won out, and both races are working together to help the nation.

 IN-DEPTH RESOURCES: UNIT 5
Primary Source: Mandela's Inaugural Address, p. 46

 ELECTRONIC LIBRARY OF PRIMARY SOURCES
from "Masakhane—Let Us Build Together"

ASSESS & RETEACH

Section 2 Assessment
Have students answer the questions and then discuss their answers to items 3 and 4 in class.

Section Quiz
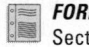 **FORMAL ASSESSMENT**
Section Quiz, p. 237

Reteaching Activity
CLASS TIME: 20 MINUTES

Have students make a time line (similar to the one on page 539) showing important events in Nigeria's struggle for democracy. Discuss with students why Nigeria has had a difficult time achieving self-government.

CLOSE ACTIVITY

CLASS TIME: 20 MINUTES

Comparing
Have students make a Venn diagram to compare the struggles for democracy in Nigeria and South Africa. Students should think of ways in which the experiences of the two countries are similar and different, then write these items in the appropriate parts of the diagram.

HISTORYMAKERS

Nelson Mandela
1918–

Nelson Mandela has said that he first grew interested in politics when he heard elders in his village describe how freely his people lived before whites came. Inspired to help his people regain that freedom, Mandela trained as a lawyer and became a top official in the ANC. Convinced that apartheid would never end peacefully, he joined the armed struggle against white rule. For this, he was imprisoned for 27 years.

After his presidential victory, Mandela looked to the future,

We must . . . build a better life for all South Africans. This means creating jobs, building houses, providing education, and bringing peace and security for all.

As president, he continued to work to heal his country.

F.W. de Klerk
1936–

Like Mandela, Frederik W. de Klerk also trained as a lawyer. Born to an Afrikaner family with close links to the National Party, de Klerk was elected to Parliament in 1972.

A firm party loyalist, de Klerk backed apartheid but was also open to reform. Friends say that his flexibility on racial issues stemmed from his relatively liberal religious background. De Klerk explained his willingness to negotiate with black leaders by saying, "Dialogue is God's style."

In 1993, de Klerk and Mandela were jointly awarded the Nobel Peace Prize for their efforts to bring democracy to South Africa. The next year, de Klerk ran for president against Mandela. Coming in second, de Klerk became vice president. The photograph above shows them after one of their campaign debates.

to the ANC—threatened to disrupt the process. Nevertheless, the vote went smoothly. South Africans of all races peacefully waited at the polls in lines that sometimes stretched for up to a kilometer, which is .62 mile. (See pages 468–469.) To no one's surprise, the ANC won 62.7 percent of the vote. They won 252 of 400 seats in the National Assembly (the larger of the two houses in Parliament). Mandela was elected president. In his inaugural address, he looked to the future: "We must therefore act together as a united people, for national reconciliation. . . . Let there be justice for all. Let there be peace for all."

A New Constitution In 1996, after much debate, South African lawmakers passed a new, more democratic constitution. It guaranteed equal rights for all citizens. The constitution included a bill of rights modeled on the U.S. Bill of Rights, but with important differences. The South African document expressly forbids discrimination and protects the rights of minorities and children. It also guarantees the right to travel freely—a right denied blacks in the past. It proclaims social and economic rights, including the right to adequate housing, education, and health care.

As they passed the constitution, South African leaders realized that these sweeping promises would be difficult to fulfill. Many South African blacks wanted instant results. Even so, the political changes that South Africa had achieved gave other peoples around the world great hope for the future of democracy. In Section 3, you will read how democratic ideas changed the Communist Soviet Union.

THINK THROUGH HISTORY
F. Drawing Conclusions How did the memory of apartheid influence the writing of the new bill of rights?
F. Possible Answer The bill of rights guarantees freedoms and rights denied to blacks under apartheid.

Section ❷ Assessment

1. TERMS & NAMES
Identify
- federal system
- martial law
- dissident
- apartheid
- Nelson Mandela

2. TAKING NOTES
Compare political events in Nigeria and South Africa using a Venn diagram like the one below.

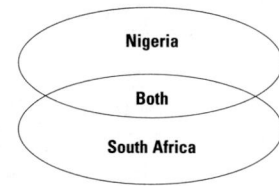

Nigeria

Both

South Africa

Which is more democratic?

3. IDENTIFYING PROBLEMS
What do you think is the main problem that Nigeria must overcome before it can establish a democratic government?

THINK ABOUT
- the problems that led to the civil war
- the actions of the current military government

4. THEME ACTIVITY
Revolution Working in small teams, write biographies of South African leaders who were instrumental in the revolutionary overturn of apartheid. Include pictures if possible. Use these biographies to create or expand a revolutionaries' "Wall of Fame."

ANSWERS

1. TERMS & NAMES
federal system, p. 537
martial law, p. 537
dissident, p. 538
apartheid, p. 539
Nelson Mandela, p. 539

2. TAKING NOTES
Possible Responses:
Nigeria—civil war when Biafra seceded, reunification of country, continued military rule. Both—former British colonies, conflict among ethnic or racial groups, jailed (and killed) political dissidents. South Africa—passage of apartheid, international protest and boycott, first universal elections, majority rule, first black president, new constitution and bill of rights. South Africa is more democratic.

3. IDENTIFYING PROBLEMS
Possible Responses: The different ethnic groups must learn to accept one another, to prevent future conflicts. The military must give up power and allow civilians to rule.

4. THEME ACTIVITY
Standards for Evaluation
Biographies should meet the following criteria:
- Describe important events in a person's life.
- Explain how the person helped overturn apartheid.

3 Gorbachev Moves Toward Democracy

TERMS & NAMES
- Politburo
- Mikhail Gorbachev
- glasnost
- perestroika
- Solidarity
- Lech Walesa
- reunification

MAIN IDEA

Soviet leader Mikhail Gorbachev promoted democratic reforms, which inspired many Eastern Europeans.

WHY IT MATTERS NOW

In the 1990s, most Eastern European nations overthrew communist governments. Germany reunified.

SETTING THE STAGE After World War II, the Soviet Union and the United States engaged in a Cold War. Each tried to increase its worldwide influence. The Soviet Union extended its power over much of Eastern Europe. By the 1960s, it appeared that communism was permanently established in the region.

Gorbachev's Reforms

Background
Like Nigeria, the Soviet Union jailed dissidents. Aleksandr Solzhenitsyn, a dissident writer who wrote about the Soviet prison system, lived in exile from 1974 to 1994.

During the 1960s and 1970s, the Soviet Union's Communist leadership kept tight control over the Soviet people. Leonid Brezhnev and the **Politburo**—the ruling committee of the Communist Party—crushed all political disagreement. Censors decided what writers could publish. The Communist Party restricted such basic rights as freedom of speech and worship.

After Brezhnev's death in 1982, the aging leadership of the Soviet Union tried to hold on to power. Time was against them, however. Each of Brezhnev's two successors died after only about a year in office. Who would succeed them?

A Younger Leader To answer that question, the Politburo debated between two men. One was a conservative named Victor Grishin. The other was **Mikhail Gorbachev** (mih·KYL gawr·buh·CHAWF). Gorbachev's supporters praised his youth, energy, and political skills. With their backing, Gorbachev became the party's new general secretary. In choosing him, Politburo members signalled their support for mild reform in the Soviet Union. They did not realize they were unleashing a second Russian Revolution.

THINK THROUGH HISTORY
A. Making Inferences How might Gorbachev's young age have made him more open to reform?
A. Possible Answer Because he had not had to conform to Stalin's policies as older leaders had.

The Soviet people welcomed Gorbachev's election. At 54, he was the youngest Soviet leader since Stalin. Gorbachev was only a child during Stalin's ruthless purge of independent-minded party members. Unlike other Soviet leaders, Gorbachev had not needed to blindly follow Stalin's policies. He could pursue new ideas.

Glasnost Promotes Openness Past Soviet leaders had created a totalitarian state. It rewarded silence and discouraged individuals from acting on their own. As a result, Soviet society rarely changed. Gorbachev realized that economic and social reforms could not occur without a free flow of ideas and information. In 1985, he announced a policy known as **glasnost** (GLAHS·nuhst), or openness. He encouraged Soviet citizens to discuss ways to improve their society.

Glasnost brought remarkable changes. The government allowed churches to open. It released dissidents from prison and allowed the publication of books by previously banned authors. Reporters actively investigated social problems and openly criticized government officials.

HISTORY MAKERS

Mikhail Gorbachev
1931–

Mikhail Gorbachev's background shaped the role he would play in history. Both of his grandfathers were arrested during Stalin's purges. Both were eventually freed. However, one died at an early age, perhaps because of the torture he had suffered. Gorbachev never forgot his grandfathers' stories.

After working on a state farm, Gorbachev studied law in Moscow and joined the Communist Party. As an official in a farming region, Gorbachev learned much about the Soviet system and its problems.

He advanced quickly in the party. When he became general secretary in 1985, he was the youngest Politburo member and a man who wanted to bring change. He succeeded. Although he pursued reform to save the Soviet Union, ultimately he triggered its breakup.

Struggles for Democracy **541**

Section 3 Overview

OBJECTIVES

1. To list Soviet reforms under Mikhail Gorbachev.
2. To explain reforms in Poland and Hungary.
3. To summarize changes in East Germany.
4. To describe democratic change in Czechoslovakia and Romania.

CRITICAL THINKING
- Making inferences, pp. 541, 542
- Analyzing causes, p. 543
- Clarifying, p. 544
- Contrasting, p. 545
- Synthesizing, p. 545

FOCUS
5-Minute Warm-Up

▶ *Perceiving Cause and Effect*
To help students learn how changes in the Soviet bloc occurred, have them answer the following questions.

1. Read History Makers on page 543. How did Walesa attract world attention to the workers' struggles?
2. What immediate effect did this attention have on the Polish government?

 WARM-UP TRANSPARENCY 19

OBJECTIVE 1 INSTRUCT

Gorbachev's Reforms

▶ *Key Ideas*
- Mikhail Gorbachev gains power in the Soviet Union in 1985.
- He promotes reforms to revive the Soviet system.

IN-DEPTH RESOURCES: UNIT 5
Guided Reading, p. 39
Primary Source: Political Cartoon, p. 47

ACCESS FOR STUDENTS ACQUIRING ENGLISH
Guided Reading (Spanish), p. 207

SECTION 3 RESOURCES

PRINT RESOURCES

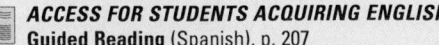 *IN-DEPTH RESOURCES: UNIT 5*
Guided Reading, p. 39
Primary Source: Political Cartoon, p. 47

 ACCESS FOR STUDENTS ACQUIRING ENGLISH
Guided Reading (Spanish), p. 207

 FORMAL ASSESSMENT
Section Quiz, p. 238

ALTERNATIVE ASSESSMENT BOOK

TECHNOLOGY RESOURCES

 GEOGRAPHY TRANSPARENCIES
GT35 Germany, Post World War I—Present

 WORLD ART AND CULTURES TRANSPARENCIES
AT78 *Burning Rods*

CD-ROM
Electronic Library of Primary Sources

INTERNET www.mlworldhistory.com

Gorbachev brought a new sense of energy and style to official life in the Soviet Union. He even walked through crowds, shaking hands like an American politician, a custom unheard of in Soviet politics. Ask students why his gesture might have had such a powerful impact on the Soviet public.

MORE ABOUT . . .
Soviet-U.S. Relations

At first, U.S. officials distrusted Gorbachev and his reforms and argued that the United States, rather than helping, should continue its tough policies toward the Soviet Union. When Gorbachev allowed Eastern Europe to break away from Soviet control, however, the attitude of U.S. officials toward the Soviet leader became more positive.

OBJECTIVE ② INSTRUCT

Reforms in Poland and Hungary

▶ *Key Ideas*
• Poland and Hungary are among the first Eastern European nations to embrace reform.
• Poland's Solidarity trade union forces change and wins elections.
• Hungary also deposes its Communist regime.

This political cartoon contrasts the old Soviet closed-door system with Gorbachev's new policy. The sign over the open doorway reads "Glasnost," which means openness.

Perestroika Reforms the Economy The new openness allowed Soviet citizens to complain publicly about economic problems. Angry consumers protested that they had to stand in long lines to buy food, soap, and other basics. Gorbachev blamed these problems on the Soviet Union's inefficient system of central planning. Under central planning, party officials told farm and factory managers how much to produce. They also told them what wages to pay, and what prices to charge. Because individuals could not increase their pay by producing more, they had little motive to improve efficiency.

In 1985, Gorbachev introduced the idea of **perestroika** (PEHR-ih-STROY-kuh), or economic restructuring. In 1986, he made changes to revive the Soviet economy. Local managers gained greater authority over their farms and factories, and people were allowed to open small private businesses. Gorbachev's goal was not to throw out communism, but to make the system more efficient and productive.

Democratization Opens the Political System Gorbachev also knew that for the economy to thrive, the Communist Party would have to loosen its grip on Soviet society and politics. In 1987, he unveiled a third new policy called democratization. This would be a gradual opening of the political system.

The plan called for the election of a new legislative body. In the past, voters had merely approved candidates who were hand-picked by the Communist Party. Now, voters could choose from a list of candidates for each office. The election produced many surprises. In several places, voters chose lesser-known candidates over powerful party bosses. Voters also elected a number of outspoken reformers.

Foreign Policy Soviet foreign policy also changed. Gorbachev realized that the troubled Soviet economy could no longer afford the costly arms race. He announced a "new thinking" in foreign affairs that stressed diplomacy over force. Therefore, arms control became one of Gorbachev's top priorities. In December 1987, he and President Reagan signed the Intermediate-Range Nuclear Forces (INF) Treaty. This treaty banned nuclear missiles with ranges of 300 to 3,400 miles.

Gorbachev's new thinking led him to urge Eastern European leaders to open up their economic and political systems. The aging Communist rulers of Eastern Europe resisted reform. However, powerful forces for democracy were building in those countries. In the past, the threat of Soviet intervention had kept those forces in check. Now, Gorbachev was saying that the Soviet Union would not oppose reform. "Each people determines the future of its own country and chooses its own form of society," he announced. "There must be no interference from outside, no matter what the pretext."

Reforms in Poland and Hungary

Poland and Hungary were among the first countries in Eastern Europe to embrace the spirit of change. In fact, the Polish struggle for democracy had begun before Gorbachev's rise to power. In 1978, a Polish archbishop became Pope John Paul II and lent his support to the anti-communist movement. In 1980, workers at the Gdansk shipyard went on strike, demanding government recognition of their union, **Solidarity.** When millions of Poles supported the action, the government gave in to the union's demands. Union leader **Lech Walesa** (lehk vah-WEHN-sah) became a national hero.

THINK THROUGH HISTORY
B. Making Inferences Why would it be inefficient for the central government to decide what should be produced all over the country?
B. Possible Answer Because they would not understand local conditions, needs, or problems.

Background
In 1972, President Nixon and Soviet leader Brezhnev had signed the Strategic Arms Limitation Treaty (SALT), which limited the number of nuclear missiles the superpowers could build.

Background
These striking workers took a great risk. Communist governments often sent the army to attack such protesters.

CUSTOMIZING FOR SPECIAL NEEDS | MULTIPLE LEARNING STYLES

Gifted and Talented Students: Discussing Opposing Views
Ask students to consider the following quotations about Gorbachev and his reforms: "Part of his genius is to make what was unthinkable yesterday seem sensible today and inevitable tomorrow" (Strobe Talbott, American journalist).

"Western observers think that glasnost fell from the sky. It's not from the sky. . . . It was society that prepared this glasnost" (Soviet dissident writer). Have students form a panel to discuss the implications of these comments. Ask, Where does change originate—From dynamic leaders or from society?

Visual Learners: Design a Poster Invite students to create posters that urge Soviet citizens to support Gorbachev's reforms. Posters may focus on specific reforms, such as glasnost or perestroika, or on the whole reform movement.

Encourage students to find examples of political poster art to serve as models for their designs. Display the posters and have students discuss their different designs and approaches.

Solidarity Defeats Communists The next year, however, the Polish government banned Solidarity again and declared martial law. The Communist Party quickly discovered that military rule could not revive Poland's failing economy. In the 1980s, industrial production declined, while foreign debt rose to more than $40 billion. Frustrated shoppers endured long lines, shortages, and rising prices.

Public discontent deepened as the economic crisis worsened. In August 1988, defiant workers walked off their jobs. They demanded raises and the legalization of Solidarity. Faced with Poland's worst labor unrest since 1980, the military leader, General Jaruzelski (YAH·roo·ZEHL·skee), agreed to hold talks with Solidarity leaders. In April 1989, Jaruzelski legalized Solidarity and agreed to hold Poland's first free election since the Communists took power.

In elections during 1989 and 1990, Polish voters voted against Communists and overwhelmingly chose Solidarity candidates. They elected Lech Walesa president. For the first time, the people of a nation had turned a Communist regime out of office peacefully.

Hungarian Communists Disband Inspired by the changes in Poland, Hungarian leaders also launched a sweeping reform program. To stimulate economic growth, reformers encouraged private enterprise and allowed a small stock market to operate. A new constitution permitted a multiparty system with free parliamentary elections.

Vocabulary
deposed: removed
from power

The pace of change grew faster when radical reformers took over a Communist Party congress in October 1989. The radicals deposed the party's leaders and then dissolved the party itself. Here was another first: a European Communist Party had voted itself out of existence. A year later, in national elections, the nation's voters put a non-Communist government in power.

In 1994, a socialist party—largely made up of former Communists—won a majority of seats in Hungary's parliament. The socialist party and a democratic party formed a coalition, or alliance, to rule. The following year, the government sought to improve the economy by raising taxes and cutting back on government services.

Communism Falls in East Germany

THINK THROUGH HISTORY
**C. Analyzing
Causes** How did the fall of communism in Hungary contribute to turmoil in East Germany?
C. Answer The non-Communist government of Hungary gave East Germans more freedom by allowing them to use Hungary as an escape route to Austria and West Germany.

While Poland and Hungary were moving toward reform, conservative leaders in East Germany stubbornly refused to accept change. East Germany's 77-year-old party boss Erich Honecker dismissed reforms as unnecessary. Then in 1989, Hungary allowed vacationing East German tourists to cross the border into Austria. From there they could travel to West Germany. Thousands of East Germans took this new escape route.

Fall of the Berlin Wall In response, the East German government closed its borders entirely. By October 1989, huge demonstrations had broken out in cities across East Germany. The protesters demanded the right to travel freely—and later added the demand for free elections. At one point, Honecker tried to regain control by ordering the police to break up a demonstration in Leipzig. The police refused. Honecker lost his authority with the party and resigned on October 18.

The new East German leader, Egon Krenz, boldly gambled that he could restore stability by allowing people to leave East Germany. On November 9, 1989, he opened the Berlin Wall. Thousands of East Germans poured into West Berlin. The long-divided city of Berlin erupted in joyous celebration. Once-feared border guards smiled as huge crowds climbed on top of the wall to celebrate. The jubilant Berliners danced and chanted, "The wall is gone! The wall is gone!" (See photograph on page 528.)

HISTORY MAKERS

**Lech Walesa
1943–**

When Lech Walesa was 18 months old, his father died. Before dying, he predicted that his wife would be proud of Lech someday.

At 24, Walesa began to work at the shipyard in Gdansk, Poland. Three years later, he took up the struggle for free trade unions after seeing police shoot protesters.

During the 1980 strike, Walesa and others locked themselves inside the shipyard. This attracted the attention of the world to their demands for a legally recognized union and the right to strike.

The government granted these demands but later outlawed Solidarity and jailed Walesa and other leaders. After his release, Walesa fulfilled his father's prediction. He won both the Nobel Prize and his country's presidency.

HISTORY MAKERS
Lech Walesa

Walesa won the Nobel Peace Prize in 1983 but sent his wife to the award ceremony in Norway because he feared that the Polish government would not let him return if he left. Have students find out more about Walesa's background and values and discuss his commitment to reform.

OBJECTIVE 3 INSTRUCT

Communism Falls in East Germany

▶ *Key Ideas*
• Protests break out in East Germany despite official repression.
• The Berlin Wall falls and Germany is reunified.
• Germany faces many challenges in integrating the peoples and economies of the former East and West Germanies.

 GEOGRAPHY TRANSPARENCIES
GT35 Germany, Post World War I–Present

 ELECTRONIC LIBRARY OF PRIMARY SOURCES
"Destruction of the Berlin Wall"

 WORLD ART AND CULTURES TRANSPARENCIES
AT78 *Burning Rods*

CRITICAL THINKING ACTIVITY
CLASS TIME: 15 MINUTES

Analyzing Cause and Effect
Hand out copies of the Cause and Effect graphic organizer. Have students list the steps that led to the reunification of Germany. Why do they think that after nearly 50 years of division, the reunification happened so quickly?

 CRITICAL THINKING TRANSPARENCIES
CT75 Cause and Effect

TEACHING OPTION **BLOCK SCHEDULING**   **COOPERATIVE ACTIVITY: Creating a Storyboard**   **CLASS TIME 20 MINUTES**

Task: Students will create storyboards that dramatize events related to the collapse of communism in the Soviet bloc.

Purpose: To better understand the significance of events during this period.

Activity: Have groups of students create storyboards dramatizing events, such as the fall of the Berlin Wall, that illustrate the collapse of communism in the Soviet bloc. Point out that their stories may be purely factual or may contain fictional characters and events, as long as they accurately portray the historical incidents of the time. Students will need to conduct some research. Ask each group to share its creation with the class.

 Building a Portfolio: Students may want to include a photocopy of their storyboard in their portfolio.

 ALTERNATIVE ASSESSMENT BOOK
Standards for Evaluating a Cooperative Activity

Standards for Evaluation
Storyboards should . . .

• dramatize specific events of the period
• present strong characters and good story lines

Teacher's Edition **543**

Point out that the neo-Nazi movement exists not only in Germany but in other countries, including the United States. Suggest that students use the Internet and other sources to find out more about this movement and governments' efforts to deal with it. The Southern Poverty Law Center in Montgomery, Alabama, publishes a special report on neo-Nazis and other militant groups.

OBJECTIVE ③ INSTRUCT

Democracy Spreads

▶ **Key Ideas**
- Inspired by events in neighboring countries, Czechs also end Communist rule.
- In Romania, the dictator Nicolae Ceausescu is killed and free elections are held.

MORE ABOUT . . .
Vaclav Havel
(See page 545.)

Havel was a key figure in the reform period of 1968, known as the Prague Spring, and a staunch advocate of human rights. He was often arrested for his political views and spent four years in prison. After becoming president, he urged Czechs to think of politics as "the art of the impossible, . . . the art of making both ourselves and the world better."

Krenz's dramatic gamble to save communism did not work. When the public discovered evidence of widespread corruption among party leaders, Krenz and other top officials were forced to resign in disgrace. By the end of 1989, the East German Communist Party had ceased to exist.

Fighting Neo-Nazis
The new, united Germany faced the problem of increasing violence. After communism fell, refugees flooded into Germany from the poorer countries of Eastern Europe. This immigration angered many Germans, who accused foreigners of stealing jobs by working for cheap wages.

Thousands of angry young people joined neo-Nazi groups, which began to carry out violent actions against foreigners. In May 1993, five Turkish immigrants died when their house was set on fire.

Attacks such as this revived ugly memories of Nazi violence in the 1930s. By the 1990s, however, Germany had deep democratic roots. Millions of Germans spoke out against racism and antiforeign violence and held candlelight vigils to declare, "Never again!" One such vigil is shown below.

Germany Is Reunified With the fall of Communism in East Germany, many Germans began to speak of **reunification**—the merging of the two Germanys. However, the movement for reunification worried many people. They feared that a united Germany would once again try to dominate Europe.

West German Chancellor Helmut Kohl assured world leaders that Germans had learned from the past. They were now committed to democracy and human rights. Kohl's assurances helped persuade other European nations to accept German reunification. Forty-five years after its crushing defeat in World War II, Germany was officially reunited on October 3, 1990.

Germany's Challenges The newly united Germany faced serious problems. More than 40 years of Communist rule had left eastern Germany in ruins. Its railroads, highways, and telephone system had not been modernized since World War II. Many East German industries produced shoddy goods that could not compete in the global market.

Rebuilding eastern Germany's bankrupt economy was going to be a difficult, costly process. To pay these costs, Kohl raised taxes. As taxpayers tightened their belts, workers in eastern Germany faced a second problem—unemployment. Inefficient factories closed, depriving millions of workers of their jobs.

In spite of these difficulties, German voters returned the ruling coalition of political parties to power in late 1994. Kohl was re-elected chancellor. In early 1995 he met with industry leaders to discuss how to create jobs. In the mid-1990s Germany's economy slowly began to improve.

Reunification forced Germany to rethink its role in international affairs. As central Europe's largest country, Germany had important global responsibilities. For example, in 1993, German troops joined the UN peacekeeping mission in Somalia. As Germany's global responsibilities grew, German leaders began to argue that the country deserved a permanent seat on the UN Security Council. The Security Council is a group of 15 nations with the authority to decide UN actions.

Democracy Spreads

Changes in the Soviet Union, Poland, and Hungary had helped inspire reforms in East Germany. In the same way, changes in East Germany affected other Eastern European countries, including Czechoslovakia and Romania. In those countries, however, repressive governments delayed the movement toward democracy.

Czechoslovakia Reforms While huge crowds were demanding democracy in East Germany, neighboring Czechoslovakia remained quiet. Vivid memories of the violent crackdown against the reforms of 1968 made the Czechs cautious. A conservative

THINK THROUGH HISTORY
D. Clarifying Why would Europeans fear the reunification of Germany?
D. Possible Answer A reunified Germany would be larger and stronger than the two separate Germanys— and could once again be a military threat as Nazi Germany had been.

TEACHING OPTIONS

MULTIPLE LEARNING STYLES

Kinesthetic Learners: Creating a Board Game Have students create a board game based on the fall of communism in Europe and the Soviet Union. The game might have "spokes" that radiate from a central point, with each spoke representing a different country and with players attempting to

move along the spokes to "freedom." The obstacles (such as "Leaders jailed" or "Coup attempted") and aids (such as "Military refuses to fire" or "Citizens take over communications") along each spoke might reflect specific events in the country's history. Have students explain their game to the class.

CONNECTIONS ACROSS THE CURRICULUM

Literature Tell students that Vaclav Havel was one of a number of dissident writers in the Soviet Union and Eastern Europe who continued to do their work despite censorship and official repression. In some countries, government censorship of these writers was so strong that it was against the law to read their works aloud in a public place

or even to own copies of their stories, novels, or poems.

Have students find out more about such dissident writers as Havel, Aleksandr Solzhenitsyn, Andrei Sinyavsky, and Milan Kundera. Ask students to create a "Hall of Fame" featuring short biographies of these writers and lists of their major works.

government led by Milos Jakes resisted all change. In October 1989, the police arrested several dissidents. Among these was the Czech playwright Vaclav Havel (VAH·tslahv HAH·vehl), a popular critic of the government.

On October 28, 1989, 10,000 people gathered in Wenceslas Square in the center of Prague. They demanded democracy and freedom. Hundreds were arrested. Three weeks later, 25,000 students inspired by the fall of the Berlin Wall gathered in Prague to demand reform. Following orders from the government, the police brutally attacked the demonstrators and injured hundreds.

The government crackdown angered the Czech people. On each of the next eight days, huge crowds gathered in Wenceslas Square. They demanded an end to Communist rule. On November 24, 500,000 protesters crowded into downtown Prague. Within hours, Milos Jakes and his entire Politburo resigned. One month later, a new parliament elected Vaclav Havel president of Czechoslovakia.

Overthrow in Romania By late 1989, only Romania seemed unmoved by the calls of reform. Romania's ruthless Communist dictator Nicolae Ceausescu (chow·SHES·koo) maintained a firm grip on power. His secret police enforced his orders brutally. Nevertheless, Romanians were aware of the reforms in other countries. They began a protest movement of their own. One student explained their anger at the government:

A VOICE FROM THE PAST
We were raised on a mountain of lies. There was a fantastical difference between the things they told us and the things we saw. They published incredible statistics on agricultural production, and in the shops there was nothing to eat. On paper, we had freedom of expression, but anytime anyone said anything, members of the Communist Party told us to keep our mouths shut.

STEFAN GHENCEA, Romanian student

In December, Ceausescu ordered the army to fire on demonstrators in the city of Timisoara (tee·mee·SHWAH·rah). The army killed and wounded scores of people. The massacre in Timisoara ignited a popular uprising against Ceausescu. Within days, the army joined the people. They fought to defeat the secret police and overthrow their ruler. Shocked by the sudden collapse of his power, Ceausescu and his wife attempted to flee. They were captured, however, then hastily tried and executed on Christmas Day, 1989.

Romania held general elections in 1990 and in 1992. The government also made economic reforms to introduce elements of capitalism. At the same time, the slow pace of Gorbachev's economic reforms began to cause unrest in the Soviet Union.

SPOTLIGHT ON
Television's Influence
Television played a key role in the movements for democracy. Mikhail Gorbachev used television to spread news of reform programs and bolster his image. In East Germany, people viewed Western programs and saw the contrast between affluence in the West and their own lower standard of living.

In Romania the role of television was more direct. Revolutionaries captured the state television station in Bucharest and broadcast their own views of the struggle. They used television to coordinate revolutionary actions in different parts of the country. When Nicolae Ceausescu and his wife were tried and executed, television carried the news throughout the country—along with pictures of their dead bodies. Ceausescu is shown below.

Section 3 Assessment

1. TERMS & NAMES
Identify
• Politburo
• Mikhail Gorbachev
• glasnost
• perestroika
• Solidarity
• Lech Walesa
• reunification

2. TAKING NOTES
Use a time line like the one below to record significant events in the Soviet Union and Eastern Europe.

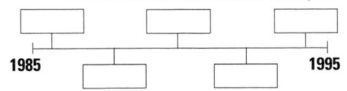
1985   1995

During which year did most of Eastern Europe turn toward democracy?

3. SYNTHESIZING
Explain how Gorbachev's reforms helped to move the Soviet Union closer toward democracy.

THINK ABOUT
• the democratic practices and conditions listed on the chart on page 531
• how Gorbachev's policies promoted those practices and conditions

4. THEME ACTIVITY
Cultural Interaction With a partner, create a cause-and-effect diagram to show how democratic reform spread through Eastern Europe. The diagram should show the order in which reform happened and which countries influenced others. You may want to look through this textbook for model diagrams.

Struggles for Democracy **545**

546 Chapter 19

Section 4 Overview

OBJECTIVES

(1) To describe the collapse of the Soviet Union.

(2) To identify problems facing the Russian government.

(3) To summarize the conflict in the former Yugoslavia.

(4) To explain problems in Poland and Czechoslovakia.

SKILLBUILDER

• Interpreting maps: place, region, p. 547

• Interpreting maps: region, location, p. 549

CRITICAL THINKING

• Analyzing motives, p. 547
• Evaluating decisions, p. 548
• Identifying problems, p. 549
• Contrasting, p. 550
• Analyzing causes, p. 550
• Analyzing themes, p. 550

FOCUS

5-Minute Warm-Up

▶ *Making Inferences*

Students will understand more about the former Soviet Union by answering the following questions.

1. Study the map on page 547. Where are all the new republics located in relation to Russia?

2. Having been invaded several times, why might Russia have wanted to annex these countries?

 WARM-UP TRANSPARENCY 19

OBJECTIVE (1) INSTRUCT

Unrest in the Soviet Union

Key Ideas
• Soviet republics break away, and the Soviet Union dissolves.

📖 *IN-DEPTH RESOURCES: UNIT 5* Guided Reading, p. 40

📖 *ACCESS FOR STUDENTS ACQUIRING ENGLISH* Guided Reading (Spanish), p. 208

4 Collapse of the Soviet Union

MAIN IDEA

In the early 1990s, the Soviet Union, Yugoslavia, and Czechoslovakia all broke apart.

WHY IT MATTERS NOW

Many of the new nations created after those breakups continue to struggle to establish democracy.

SETTING THE STAGE The reforms of the late 1980s brought high hopes to the people of the Soviet Union and Eastern Europe. For the first time in decades, they were free to make choices about the economic and political systems governing their lives. They soon discovered that increased freedom sometimes challenges the social order.

Unrest in the Soviet Union

HISTORY MAKERS

Boris Yeltsin
1931–

Boris Yeltsin was raised in poverty. For 10 years, his family lived in a single room and slept on the floor next to their goat for warmth.

As a youth, Yeltsin earned good grades but behaved badly. Mikhail Gorbachev named him party boss and mayor of Moscow in 1985. Yeltsin's outspokenness got him into trouble. At one meeting, he launched into a bitter speech criticizing conservatives for working against perestroika. Gorbachev fired him for the sake of party unity.

Yeltsin made a dramatic comeback and won a seat in parliament in 1989. Parliament elected him president of Russia in 1990, and voters re-elected him in 1991. But his health—heart problems—raised doubts about how long he could remain in power.

As Eastern Europe gained freedom from Soviet control, various nationalities in the Soviet Union began to call for their own freedom. More than 100 ethnic groups lived in the Soviet Union. Russians were the largest, most powerful group. However, non-Russians formed a majority in the 14 Soviet republics other than Russia.

Ethnic tensions brewed beneath the surface of Soviet society. As reforms loosened central controls, unrest spread across the country. Nationalist groups in Georgia, Ukraine, and Moldavia (now Moldova) demanded self-rule. The Muslim peoples of Soviet Central Asia called for religious freedom.

Lithuania Defies Gorbachev The first challenge came from the Baltic nations of Lithuania, Estonia, and Latvia. These republics had been independent states between the two world wars—until the Soviets annexed them in 1940. Fifty years later, in March 1990, Lithuania declared its independence. To try to force it back into the Soviet Union, Gorbachev ordered a blockade of the republic.

Although Gorbachev was reluctant to use stronger measures, he feared that Lithuania's example might encourage other republics to secede. In January 1991 Soviet troops attacked unarmed civilians in Lithuania's capital. The army killed 14 and wounded more than 150.

Yeltsin Denounces Gorbachev The bloody assault in Lithuania and the lack of real economic progress in the Soviet Union damaged Gorbachev's popularity. More and more people looked for leadership to **Boris Yeltsin.** He was a member of parliament and the former mayor of Moscow. Yeltsin criticized the crackdown in Lithuania and the slow pace of reforms. In June 1991, voters overwhelmingly chose Yeltsin to become the Russian Republic's first directly elected president.

Yeltsin and Gorbachev were now on a collision course. In spite of their rivalry, they faced a common enemy in the old guard of Communist officials. Hard-liners—conservatives who opposed reform—were furious at Gorbachev. They were angry that he had given up the Soviet Union's role as the dominant force in Eastern Europe. They also feared losing their power and privileges. These officials vowed to overthrow Gorbachev and undo his reforms.

546 Chapter 19

Background
About three-fourths of the Soviet population were Slavic peoples such as Russians or Ukrainians. Turkic peoples, such as Uzbeks or Azerbaijani, were the second largest group. Most of these were Muslim. Other groups included Georgians and Armenians.

Background
As part of government reform, Gorbachev became president of the Soviet Union—a new office modeled on the U.S. presidency. Each of the 15 republics was also allowed to have a president. For example, Yeltsin was the president of Russia.

SECTION 4 RESOURCES

PRINT RESOURCES

📖 *IN-DEPTH RESOURCES: UNIT 5*
Guided Reading, p. 40
Primary Source: The Road to Marjača, p. 48

📖 *ACCESS FOR STUDENTS ACQUIRING ENGLISH*
Guided Reading (Spanish), p. 208

📖 *FORMAL ASSESSMENT*
Section Quiz, p. 239

📖 *ALTERNATIVE ASSESSMENT BOOK*

TECHNOLOGY RESOURCES

💿 **CD-ROM**
Electronic Library of Primary Sources

🌐 **INTERNET** www.mlworldhistory.com

The Breakup of the Soviet Union, 1991

Distribution of Territory, 1991

Other Republics (23.3%)

Russian Republic (76.7%)

ARCTIC OCEAN

RUSSIA

Ob R.

Irtysh R.

Yenisey R.

Lena R.

Amur R.

Sea of Okhotsk

PACIFIC OCEAN

Tallinn — ESTONIA
LATVIA
Riga
Moscow
Vilnius — Minsk — BELARUS
LITHUANIA
Kiev
UKRAINE
Chisinau
MOLDOVA
GEORGIA
Black Sea
Tbilisi
Volga R.
Caspian Sea
ARMENIA — Baku
Yerevan
AZERBAIJAN
TURKMENISTAN
Ashgabat
UZBEKISTAN
Tashkent
Dushanbe
TAJIKISTAN
Bishkek
KYRGYZSTAN
Almaty
KAZAKHSTAN
Aral Sea
Lake Balkhash
Lake Baikal
Sea of Japan
Mediterranean Sea
Baltic Sea
JSSIA

Arctic Circle

N

0   1,000 Miles
0   2,000 Kilometers

— Border of the Soviet Union

GEOGRAPHY SKILLBUILDER: Interpreting Maps

1. **Place** Name the 15 republics of the former Soviet Union.
2. **Region** Which republic received the largest percentage of the former Soviet Union's territory?

The August Coup On August 18, 1991, the hard-liners detained Gorbachev at his vacation home on the Black Sea. They demanded his resignation as Soviet president. Early the next day, hundreds of tanks and armored vehicles rolled into Moscow. The hard-liners—who called themselves the State Committee—assumed that a show of force would ensure obedience. However, the Soviet people had lost their fear of the party. They were willing to defend their freedoms. Protesters gathered at the Russian parliament building, where Yeltsin had his office.

Around midday, Yeltsin emerged and climbed atop one of the tanks. As his supporters cheered, Yeltsin declared, "We proclaim all decisions and decrees of this committee to be illegal. . . . We appeal to the citizens of Russia to . . . demand a return of the country to normal constitutional developments."

On August 20, the State Committee ordered troops to attack the parliament, but they refused. Their refusal turned the tide. On August 21, the military withdrew its forces from Moscow. That night, Gorbachev returned to Moscow.

End of the Soviet Union The coup attempt sparked anger against the Communist party. Gorbachev resigned as general secretary of the party. The Soviet parliament voted to stop all party activities. Having first seized power in 1917 in a coup that succeeded, the all-powerful Communist Party now collapsed because of a coup that failed.

The coup also played a decisive role in accelerating the breakup of the Soviet Union. Estonia and Latvia quickly declared their independence. Other republics soon followed. Although Gorbachev pleaded for unity, no one was listening. By early December, all 15 republics had declared independence.

THINK THROUGH HISTORY
A. Analyzing Motives Why do you think the Soviet troops refused the order to attack the parliament?
A. Possible Answers They were inspired by Yeltsin's courage, they were sick of Communist rule, or they were unwilling to gun down civilians.

Crowds of citizens surround the tanks in Moscow during the August coup attempt. The soldiers' refusal to fight doomed the coup.

Struggles for Democracy **547**

Global Impact
Cuba

Ask students why Cuba came to rely so heavily on Soviet aid. Then ask them to use current periodicals or the Internet to find out what Cuba is doing to cope with its economic problems and what success it is having.

OBJECTIVE ② INSTRUCT

The Yeltsin Era

▶ *Key Ideas*
- Boris Yeltsin takes charge of Russia.
- Yeltsin uses "shock therapy" to move Russia toward capitalism.
- Opposition grows to Yeltsin's economic policies and the war in Chechnya.

 IN-DEPTH RESOURCES: UNIT 5
Primary Source: The Road to Marjača, p. 48

OBJECTIVE ③ INSTRUCT

Yugoslavia Falls Apart

▶ *Key Ideas*
- Yugoslavia, a patchwork quilt of ethnic groups, falls apart in the 1980s.
- War engulfs the region, especially in Bosnia, where Serbs, Croats, and Muslims fight for control.
- A peace agreement is signed in 1995, but unrest continues.

Global Impact
Cuba

The Soviet collapse harmed Cuba. Since becoming a Communist state in the early 1960s, Cuba had depended on Soviet assistance. By the late 1980s, Cuba relied on the Soviet Union for more than three-fourths of its imports and all of its oil.

As reform swept the Soviet Union and Eastern Europe, Cuba's leader, Fidel Castro, criticized the reformers. He also vowed that Cuba would remain Communist.

After the August Coup of 1991, Soviet support of Cuba's economy came to an abrupt end. Cut off from Soviet aid and deeply affected by an American trade embargo, Cuba went into severe economic decline. During the 1990s, Cuba struggled to form new trade relationships and mend its tattered economy.

Yeltsin met with the leaders of other republics to chart a new course. They agreed to form the Commonwealth of Independent States, or **CIS**, a loose federation of former Soviet territories. Only the Baltic republics and Georgia refused to join.

The formation of the CIS meant the death of the Soviet Union. On Christmas Day 1991, Gorbachev announced his resignation as president of the Soviet Union, a country that by then had ceased to exist. Although Gorbachev had failed to hold the Soviet Union together, he will be remembered as the man who launched one of the most dramatic revolutions of the 20th century.

The Yeltsin Era

As president of the large Russian Republic, Boris Yeltsin was now the most powerful figure in the CIS. He would face many problems—an ailing economy, tough political opposition, and an unpopular war.

Yeltsin Faces Problems One of Yeltsin's goals was to reform the Russian economy. He adopted a bold plan known as **"shock therapy,"** an abrupt shift to free-market economics. To eliminate government involvement in the economy, Yeltsin lowered trade barriers, removed price controls, and ended subsidies to state-owned industries.

Initially, the plan produced more shock than therapy. Prices soared; from 1992 to 1994, the inflation rate averaged 800 percent. Many factories dependent on government money had to cut production or shut down entirely. This forced thousands of people out of work. By 1993, most Russians were suffering severe economic hardship:

> **A VOICE FROM THE PAST**
> A visitor to Moscow cannot escape the feeling of a society in collapse. Child beggars accost foreigners on the street. . . . Children ask why they should stay in school when educated professionals do not make enough money to survive. . . . A garment worker complains that now her wages do not cover even the food bills, while fear of growing crime makes her dread leaving home.
> **DAVID M. KOTZ,** "The Cure That Could Kill"

Economic problems fueled a political crisis. In October 1993, legislators opposed to Yeltsin's policies shut themselves inside the parliament building. Yeltsin ordered troops to bombard the building, forcing hundreds of rebel legislators to surrender. Many were killed. Opponents accused Yeltsin of acting like a dictator.

Chechnya Rebels Yeltsin's troubles included war in Chechnya (CHEHCH·nee·uh), a largely Muslim area in southwestern Russia. In 1991, Chechnya declared its independence, but Yeltsin denied the region's right to secede. In 1994, he ordered 40,000 Russian troops into the breakaway republic. Russian forces pounded the capital city of Grozny (GROHZ·nee) and reduced it to rubble. News of the death and destruction in Chechnya sparked anger throughout Russia. With an election coming, Yeltsin sought to end the war. In August 1996, the two sides signed a peace treaty.

In the presidential elections of mid-1996, Yeltsin faced stiff opposition from former Communists and right-wing nationalists. Although Yeltsin won the election, his future remained unclear. So did the future of Russian democracy.

Yugoslavia Falls Apart

Ethnic conflict also plagued Yugoslavia. This country, formed after World War I, had six major groups of people—Serbs, Croats, Muslims, Slovenes, Macedonians, and Montenegrins. Ethnic and religious differences dating back centuries caused these groups to view each other with suspicion. After World War II, Yugoslavia became a federation of six republics. Each republic had a mixed population.

Background
Georgia did join the CIS later, in 1993, but the Baltic states remained separate.

Vocabulary
subsidies: government funds given to support industries.

THINK THROUGH HISTORY
B. Evaluating Decisions Compare Yeltsin's action here to his actions during the August Coup. Which actions were more supportive of democracy?
B. Possible Answer He was more supportive of democracy during the August coup because he defied a military takeover. Here he used the military to stay in power.

548 Chapter 19

TEACHING OPTIONS

EXPLORING PRIMARY SOURCES

A Voice from the Past Ask students to reread the quotation from David M. Kotz on this page. What details does the writer provide to show that Russia was "a society in collapse"? Tell students that despite the picture of poverty the writer paints, a whole class of Russians became wealthy during this same time. If readers did not know this fact, what impression of Moscow would they get from Kotz's article? Would they think the shift from communism to capitalism had been a mistake? Contrast Kotz's picture of Moscow in 1993 to the picture today. What did he fail to see about economic changes in Russia at that time that might have changed his description?

CONNECTIONS ACROSS TIME AND PLACE

Emerging Republics Ask five or six interested students to role-play a delegation from former Soviet republics who are approaching the United Nations for aid. Students will decide which of the former Soviet republics they will represent and should talk about conditions under former Soviet rule, the problems their country faces today, and the kind of aid the country needs from the United Nations. Each student should also draw or photocopy a picture of the country's flag and national symbol. Students should end their presentations with an evaluation of the Soviet legacy in their countries with regard to language, culture, government, and economics.

Slovenia and Croatia Protest Josip Tito, who led Yugoslavia from 1945 to 1980, held the country together. After Tito's death, however, long-simmering ethnic resentments boiled over. Serbian leader Slobodan Milosevic (mee·LOH·sheh·vihch) asserted Serbian leadership over Yugoslavia. Two republics—Slovenia and Croatia—then declared independence. In June 1991, the Serbian-led Yugoslav army invaded both republics.

The Slovenes quickly repelled the Serbs, but the war in Croatia proved far bloodier. Unlike Slovenia, Croatia had a large Serbian minority, which resented Croatian control. Centuries of Serb-Croat hatred exploded in an all-out war. The fighting claimed thousands of lives and left cities in ruins. By the time the United Nations arranged a cease-fire in January 1992, Serbian forces occupied about 30 percent of Croatia.

The Bosnian Nightmare In February 1992, Bosnia-Herzegovina joined Slovenia and Croatia in declaring independence. (In April, Serbia and Montenegro formed a new Yugoslavia. See the map below.) Bosnia's ethnically mixed population included Muslims (44 percent), Serbs (31 percent), and Croats (17 percent). While Bosnia's Muslims and Croats backed independence, Bosnian Serbs strongly opposed it. Supported by Serbia, the Bosnian Serbs launched a brutal war in March 1992. As many as 200,000 people died over the next three years, while 2 million people—more than half of Bosnia's population—fled their homes.

During the war, the Serbs used murder and other forms of brutality against Bosnian Muslims living in Serb-held lands. Called **ethnic cleansing**, this policy was intended to rid Bosnia of its Muslim population. By 1995, the Serbs controlled 70 percent of Bosnia.

International Response Although Serbia's brutality outraged other nations, they remained anxious to stay out of the fighting. To relieve suffering, a multinational force of 25,000 UN troops was sent to Bosnia to keep peace and to distribute food and medical supplies. UN and U.S.-sponsored negotiations dragged on for several years. In December 1995, the leaders of the three factions involved in the war signed a peace treaty. In September 1996, Bosnians elected a three-person presidency—one leader from each ethnic group. However, the nation continued to experience unrest.

THINK THROUGH HISTORY
C. Identifying Problems Why did Bosnia's mixed population cause a problem after Bosnia declared independence?
C. Answer Bosnia's Serbs did not want to lose their ties to Serbia, while Croats and Muslims did.

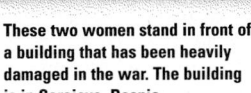
These two women stand in front of a building that has been heavily damaged in the war. The building is in Sarajevo, Bosnia.

Former Yugoslavia, 1989–1997

AUSTRIA
HUNGARY
Drava River
Ljubljana
SLOVENIA
Zagreb
CROATIA
ROMANIA
Sava River
Danube River
BOSNIA-HERZEGOVINA
Belgrade
Sarajevo
SERBIA
Adriatic Sea
YUGOSLAVIA
MONTENEGRO
Podgorica
Skopje
ITALY
MACEDONIA
ALBANIA

0 ——— 100 Miles
0 ——— 200 Kilometers

— Yugoslavia, 1989
▨ Yugoslavia, 1997

GEOGRAPHY SKILLBUILDER: Interpreting Maps
1. **Region** Which nations now make up what used to be Yugoslavia in 1989?
2. **Location** Where is Serbia located relative to the republics that declared independence from Yugoslavia?

549

MORE ABOUT . . .
Ethnic Differences
Most Serbs are Orthodox Christians, unlike the Croats, who are mostly Roman Catholic, and the Muslims, who follow Islam. In the past, the Serbs have been dominated by Croats and Muslims. Muslim Turks ruled Serbia for 400 years. During World War II, Croats joined forces with the Nazis in persecuting Serbs.

IN-DEPTH RESOURCES: UNIT 5
Primary Source: The Road to Marjača, p. 48

ELECTRONIC LIBRARY OF PRIMARY SOURCES
"Will I Ever Go Home Again?"

History from Visuals

Former Yugoslavia, 1989–1997
Interpreting the Map Have students look at the map and its key. Ask what they show. *The former Yugoslavia and current republics.* Have students identify the countries surrounding the former Yugoslavia. *Austria, Hungary, Romania, Albania.*

Extension Activity Have students turn to the Atlas, page 637, and study the geography of this region. Ask them to describe the terrain of the republics. What effect would the terrain have on war in this region? *Mountainous terrain would make it difficult for any side to obtain a quick victory. Armed conflicts would be likely to drag on for years.*

SKILLBUILDER Answers
1. Slovenia, Croatia, Bosnia-Herzegovina, Yugoslavia, Macedonia.
2. It occupies most of the eastern part of the former Yugoslavia, with Croatia, Bosnia-Herzegovina, and Slovenia to the west of it and Macedonia to the south of it.

TEACHING OPTION
BLOCK SCHEDULING
COOPERATIVE ACTIVITY: Preparing a Newscast
CLASS TIME 20 MINUTES

Task: Students will create a newscast dealing with the troubles in Bosnia, providing background and current information about the conflict.

Purpose: To develop in-depth knowledge about this issue.

Activity: Divide students into small groups. Each group will create a portion of a newscast on the Bosnian conflict. Each group chooses a topic for research, such as ethnic and geographic issues,

political history of Yugoslavia, course of the war, international aid and peace efforts, or recent events. Each group will write a 5-minute news report on their topic. Groups will combine their stories in a finished news report, using photos, maps, and other visual aids.

Building a Portfolio: Students may wish to include a copy of their group's report in their portfolio, with a summary of their contribution to the project.

ALTERNATIVE ASSESSMENT BOOK
Standards for Evaluating a Cooperative Activity

Standards for Evaluation
News reports should . . .
• provide accurate information about their topics
• be clearly and concisely written
• contain appropriate visual aids

Teacher's Edition 549

OBJECTIVE 4 INSTRUCT

Eastern Europe Faces Problems

▶ **Key Ideas**
- Poland's economy suffers, and the Poles vote Lech Walesa out of office.
- Czechoslovakia's economy also falters, and the country splits into the Czech Republic and Slovakia.

SPOTLIGHT ON
Rising Crime Rates in Poland

Ask students how economic chaos could be a cause of rising crime rates.

ASSESS & RETEACH

Section 4 Assessment

Have students work together to answer the questions. Tell them to note the location of the answers in the text.

Section Quiz

📋 **FORMAL ASSESSMENT**
Section Quiz, p. 239

Reteaching Activity

CLASS TIME: 20 MINUTES

Arrange small groups of students in the classroom to mimic the geographic locations of the countries discussed in this section. Tell each group which country they represent and have them explain who they are, who the prominent people in their country are, and what is currently going on in their country.

CLOSE ACTIVITY

CLASS TIME: 25 MINUTES

Predicting

Have students predict what will happen in the former Soviet bloc in the next ten years, basing their predictions on what has happened in the past decade. Tell them to write a series of imagined newspaper headlines that convey their predictions.

Eastern Europe Faces Problems

Compared with Yugoslavia, the nations of Eastern Europe were relatively stable in the 1990s and did not experience widespread violence. Nevertheless, countries like Poland faced ongoing challenges.

SPOTLIGHT ON

Rising Crime Rates in Poland
Ruling by fear, the Communist state held down crime rates. After communism fell, crime increased. In Poland, crime was on the rise in the 1990s. Many conditions made the situation worse.

- Criminals tried to make quick money in the open market—for example, by selling stolen goods.
- When Poland turned out the Communists, it replaced the police force with inexperienced officers.
- Police departments didn't have enough money to do their jobs.
- Many Poles ignored the legal system. For example, they paid ransoms for stolen cars instead of calling the police.

It remained to be seen whether rule by law would take root in Poland.

Poland Votes Out Walesa After becoming president in 1991, Lech Walesa tried to revive Poland's bankrupt economy. Like Boris Yeltsin, he adopted a strategy of shock therapy to move Poland toward a free market economy. As in Russia, inflation and unemployment shot up. By the mid-1990s, however, the economy was improving.

Nevertheless, many Poles remained unhappy with the pace of economic progress. In the elections of 1995, they turned Walesa out of office in favor of a former Communist, Aleksandr Kwasniewski (kfahs·N'YEHF·skee). Kwasniewski vowed to combine free market policies with greater social benefits. Despite his Communist background, it appeared that he was committed to democratic rule.

Czechoslovakia Breaks Up In Czechoslovakia, reformers also launched an economic program based on shock therapy. The program caused a sharp rise in unemployment. It especially hurt Slovakia, the republic occupying the eastern third of Czechoslovakia.

Unable to agree on economic policy, the country's two parts—Slovakia and the Czech Republic—drifted apart. In spite of President Havel's pleas for unity, a movement to split the nation gained support. Havel resigned because of this. Czechoslovakia split into two countries on January 1, 1993, just three years after the fall of communism. Havel was elected president of the Czech Republic.

The nations of the former Soviet bloc had made many gains. Even so, they continued to face serious obstacles to democracy. Resolving ethnic conflicts remained crucial, as did economic progress:

> **A VOICE FROM THE PAST**
> The clear lesson . . . is that opening up the political process without a corresponding opening up and success in the economy merely gives people more opportunity to gripe about more things. People can handle political processes. You can proclaim a free election and hold it relatively easily. You cannot propose economic success and obtain it easily.
> **U.S. SENATOR GEORGE MITCHELL,** quoted in "Neophyte Democracies Present a Challenge to U.S."

If the nations of Eastern Europe and the former Soviet Union can improve their standard of living, democracy might have a better chance to grow. In the meantime, economic reforms in Communist China sparked demands for democratic reforms.

THINK THROUGH HISTORY
D. Contrasting
Contrast the breakups of Yugoslavia and Czechoslovakia.
D. Answer
Yugoslavia's breakup turned into a violent and prolonged civil war; Czechoslovakia's was peaceful.

Section 4 Assessment

1. TERMS & NAMES
Identify
- Boris Yeltsin
- CIS
- "shock therapy"
- ethnic cleansing

2. TAKING NOTES
Use a chart like the one below to record the main reason or reasons that the Soviet Union, Yugoslavia, and Czechoslovakia each broke apart.

Former nations	Reasons for breakup
Soviet Union	
Yugoslavia	
Czechoslovakia	

3. ANALYZING CAUSES
Why did ethnic tension become such a severe problem in the Soviet Union and Yugoslavia in the early 1990s?

THINK ABOUT
- the role that past Communist leaders had played in holding those countries together
- the democratic reforms demanded by various ethnic groups
- how those demands affected national unity

4. ANALYZING THEMES
Revolution It has been said that Gorbachev's reforms led to a second Russian Revolution. What did this revolution overthrow?

THINK ABOUT
- changes in the Soviet government and in the political process
- who lost and who gained power

550 Chapter 19

ANSWERS

1. TERMS & NAMES
Boris Yeltsin, p. 546
CIS, p. 548
"shock therapy," p. 548
ethnic cleansing, p. 549

2. TAKING NOTES
Possible Responses:
Soviet Union—ethnic tensions, desire for self-rule by various republics, hard-liners' loss of control of people; Yugoslavia—ethnic tensions, loss of Tito's authority, Serbian aggression; Czechoslovakia—economic differences between regions

3. ANALYZING CAUSES
Possible Responses: In the past, Communist leaders had suppressed nationalism and demands for self-rule. With the spread of democratic reforms, many ethnic groups demanded self-rule. This broke apart the Soviet Union. In Yugoslavia, one group—the Serbs—tried to dominate others. This led to civil war.

4. ANALYZING THEMES
Possible Responses: The Soviet Union broke into 15 republics. Authoritarian rule was replaced by more democratic practices. Conservative Communists lost power, and the people gained power.

China Follows Its Own Path

TERMS & NAMES
- Zhou Enlai
- Deng Xiaoping
- Four Modernizations
- Tiananmen Square
- Hong Kong

MAIN IDEA

In recent years, China's government has experimented with capitalism but has rejected calls for democracy.

WHY IT MATTERS NOW

After the 1997 death of Chinese leader Deng Xiaoping, President Jiang Zemin seemed to be continuing those policies.

SETTING THE STAGE The trend toward democracy around the world also affected China to a limited degree. A political reform movement arose in the late 1980s. It built on economic reforms begun earlier in the decade. China's Communist government clamped down on the reformers, however, and maintained a firm grip on power.

Mao's Unexpected Legacy

After the Communists came to power in China in 1949, Mao Zedong set out to transform China. Mao believed that peasant equality, revolutionary spirit, and hard work were all that was needed to improve the Chinese economy. For example, intensive labor could make up for the lack of tractors on the huge agricultural cooperatives that the government had created.

However, lack of modern technology damaged Chinese efforts to increase agricultural and industrial output. In addition, Mao's policies stifled economic growth. He eliminated incentives for higher production. He tried to replace family life with life in the communes. These policies took away the peasants' motive to work for the good of themselves and their families.

Facing economic disaster, some Chinese Communists talked of modernizing the economy. Accusing them of "taking the capitalist road," Mao began the Cultural Revolution to cleanse China of anti-revolutionary influences. The

THINK THROUGH HISTORY
A. Recognizing Effects What was the ultimate result of Mao's radical Communist policies? Why?
A. Answer The destructiveness of the Cultural Revolution turned many Chinese people away from radical communism.

movement proved so destructive, however, that it caused many Chinese to distrust party leadership. Instead of saving radical communism, the Cultural Revolution turned many people against it. In the early 1970s, China entered another moderate period under **Zhou Enlai** (joh ehn·ly). Zhou had been premiere since 1949. During the Cultural Revolution, he had tried to restrain the radicals.

China and the West

Throughout the Cultural Revolution, China played almost no role in world affairs. In the early 1960s, China had split with the Soviet Union over the leadership of world communism. In addition, China displayed hostility toward the United States because of U.S. support for the government on Taiwan and memories of the Korean War.

China Opened Its Doors China's isolation worried Zhou. He began to send out signals that he was willing to form ties to the West. In 1971, Zhou startled the world by

Mao's Attempts to Change China

Mao's Programs	Program's Results
First Five-Year Plan 1953–1957	• Industry grew 15 percent a year. • Agricultural output grew very slowly.
Great Leap Forward 1958–1962	• China suffered economic disaster—industrial declines and food shortages. • Mao lost influence.
Cultural Revolution 1966–1976	• Mao regained influence by backing radicals. • Purges and conflicts among leaders created economic, social, and political chaos. • Moderates increasingly opposed radicals in Communist Party.

SKILLBUILDER: Interpreting Charts
1. *Which had more successful results, the first five-year plan or the Great Leap Forward? Explain.*
2. *Did conditions improve or grow worse during the Cultural Revolution? Explain.*

Struggles for Democracy **551**

Section 5 Overview

OBJECTIVES

1. To summarize Mao Zedong's rule.
2. To explain changes under Deng Xiaoping.
3. To describe the democracy movement in China.
4. To list China's challenges.

SKILLBUILDER
- Interpreting charts, p. 551

CRITICAL THINKING
- Recognizing effects, p. 551
- Analyzing causes, p. 552
- Contrasting, p. 553
- Drawing conclusions, p. 554
- Comparing, p. 554
- Making inferences, p. 555
- Supporting opinions, p. 555

FOCUS

5-Minute Warm-Up

▶ ***Identifying Main Ideas*** Answering the following questions will help students understand life in China.

1. Read Daily Life on page 553. Why did the soldiers accept such harsh training?

2. What was the training designed to do?

 WARM-UP TRANSPARENCY 19

OBJECTIVE 1 INSTRUCT

Mao's Unexpected Legacy

▶ **Key Ideas**
- China's economy suffers under Mao Zedong's rule.

 IN-DEPTH RESOURCES: UNIT 5
Guided Reading, p. 41

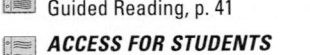 *ACCESS FOR STUDENTS ACQUIRING ENGLISH*
Guided Reading (Spanish), p. 209

OBJECTIVE 2 INSTRUCT

China and the West

▶ **Key Ideas**
- China opens to the West and begins to change.

Teacher's Edition **551**

Mao's Attempts to Change China

(See page 551.)

Interpreting the Chart Tell students to notice the increasing amount of political, social, and economic chaos caused by each succeeding plan. What political effects did the plans have on China? *Radicals took over for a while, then moderates came to have more power.*

Extension Activity Ask students to create a cause-and-effect chart about the programs. How did the failures of each program contribute to the failures of the next program? *Example: Agricultural shortages led to food shortages.*

SKILLBUILDER Answers
1. The first five-year plan—both industry and agriculture developed.
2. Conditions grew worse; there was economic, political, and social chaos.

HISTORYMAKERS
Deng Xiaoping

Tell students that Deng was ousted from politics twice and managed to fight his way back each time. Suggest that they read more about Deng's life and values.

 OBJECTIVE ③ INSTRUCT

Tiananmen Square

Key Ideas
- Economic success creates a demand for political change.
- A democracy movement arises, which the government suppresses.

ELECTRONIC LIBRARY OF PRIMARY SOURCES
"The Massacre in Tiananmen Square"

---

inviting an American table tennis team to tour China. It was the first visit by an American group to China since 1949.

The visit began a new era in Chinese-American relations. In 1971, the United States reversed its policy and endorsed UN membership for the People's Republic of China. The next year President Nixon made a state visit to China. He met with Mao and Zhou. The three leaders agreed to begin cultural exchanges and a limited amount of trade. In 1979, the United States and China established formal diplomatic relations.

Economic Reform Both Mao and Zhou died in 1976. Shortly afterward, moderates took control of the Communist Party. They jailed several of the radicals who had led the Cultural Revolution. By 1980, **Deng Xiaoping** (duhng show·pihng) had emerged as the most powerful leader in China. Like Mao and Zhou, Deng had survived the Long March. He was the last of the "old revolutionaries" who had ruled China since 1949.

Although a lifelong Communist, Deng boldly supported moderate economic policies. Unlike Mao, he was willing to use capitalist ideas to help China's economy. He embraced a set of goals known as the **Four Modernizations.** These called for progress in agriculture, industry, defense, and science and technology. Deng launched an ambitious program of economic reforms, which he called the "Second Revolution."

First, Deng eliminated Mao's unpopular communes and leased the land to individual farmers. The farmers paid rent by delivering a fixed quota of food to the government. They could then grow any crops they wished and sell them for a profit. Under this system, food production increased by 50 percent in the years 1978 to 1984.

Deng then extended his program to industry. The government permitted small private businesses to operate. It gave the managers of large state-owned industries more freedom to set production goals. Deng also welcomed some foreign technology and investment.

Deng's economic policies produced striking changes in Chinese life. As incomes increased, people began to buy appliances and televisions. Chinese youths now wore stylish clothes and listened to Western music. Gleaming hotels filled with foreign tourists symbolized China's new policy of openness.

Tiananmen Square

Deng's economic reforms produced a number of unexpected problems. As living standards improved, the gap between the rich and poor widened. Increasingly, the public believed that party officials took advantage of their positions by accepting bribes and enjoying privileges denied to others.

Furthermore, the new policies admitted not only Western investments and tourists but also Western political ideas. Increasing numbers of Chinese students studied abroad and learned about the West. Warned by hard-line officials that Communist values were at risk, Deng replied, "If you open the window, some flies naturally get in." In his view, the benefits of opening the economy exceeded the risks. Nevertheless, as Chinese students learned more about democracy, they began to question China's lack of political freedom.

Students Demand Democracy In 1989, students sparked a popular uprising that stunned China's leaders. Beginning in April of that year, more than 100,000 students occupied **Tiananmen** (tyahn·ahn·mehn) **Square.** This square is a huge public space in the heart of Beijing. The students mounted a protest for democracy by chanting, "Down with corruption!" "Down with dictatorship!" and "Long live democracy!"

HISTORY MAKERS

Deng Xiaoping
1904–1997

In his late teens, Deng Xiaoping became a Communist and a close associate of Mao Zedong and Zhou Enlai. In the 1960s, Deng embraced economic pragmatism—he was more interested in what produced results than in Communist theory. He summed up his views by saying, "It doesn't matter whether a cat is black or white, so long as it catches mice."

This flexible attitude caused Deng problems during the Cultural Revolution. Radicals removed him from his position and paraded him through the streets wearing humiliating labels.

Deng re-emerged in the 1970s, however, and became China's chief leader until his death in 1997. A key figure in world history, Deng would be remembered as the man who opened up China's economy while maintaining strict Communist rule.

Background
Table tennis is commonly called Ping-Pong after a brand of the game's equipment.

Background
The moderates jailed Mao's widow and three of her followers—known as the Gang of Four.

B. Answer Western businesses and tourists brought Western ideas into the country, and students went to school overseas for economic reasons but learned about democracy.
THINK THROUGH HISTORY
B. Analyzing Causes How did economic reform introduce new political ideas to China?

Task: Students will research the Tiananmen Square protest and write an eyewitness account.

Purpose: To understand more about events before, during, and after the protest.

Activity: Have students work in small groups to research the protest in Tiananmen Square. Have them write eyewitness accounts, as either participants or

observers, of specific events, such as the creation of the "Goddess of Democracy," the decision of students to remain in the square, or the army's attack on protesters. Students can read A Voice from the Past on page 553 for an example of an eyewitness account. Groups can read their accounts to the class.

 Building a Portfolio: Students can include a copy of their eyewitness account.

ALTERNATIVE ASSESSMENT BOOK
Standards for Evaluating a Cooperative Activity

Standards for Evaluation
Eyewitness accounts should . . .
- clearly describe the events chosen
- reveal the writers' feelings and observations
- demonstrate students' knowledge of the issues

The student protest won widespread popular support. When several thousand students began a hunger strike to highlight their cause, perhaps a million people poured into Tiananmen Square to support them. Many students now boldly called for Deng Xiaoping to resign.

Deng Orders a Crackdown Instead of considering political reform, Deng declared martial law. He ordered more than 250,000 troops to surround Beijing. One student recalled the mood at the time:

A VOICE FROM THE PAST
It would be a lie to say that we were not afraid, but we were mentally prepared and very determined. Some students could not believe that the army really would use deadly force. But most of all, we were motivated by a powerful sense of purpose. We believed that it would be worth sacrificing our lives for the sake of progress and democracy in China.

ANONYMOUS STUDENT, *San Francisco Examiner*

Although many students left the square after martial law was declared, about 3,000 chose to remain and continue their protest. The students revived their spirits by defiantly erecting a 33-foot statue that they named the "Goddess of Democracy." It resembled the American Statue of Liberty.

On June 4, 1989, the standoff came to an end. Thousands of heavily armed soldiers stormed Tiananmen Square. Tanks smashed through barricades and crushed the Goddess of Democracy. Soldiers sprayed gunfire into crowds of frightened students. They also attacked protesters elsewhere in Beijing. The assault killed hundreds and wounded thousands.

The attack on Tiananmen Square marked the beginning of a massive government campaign to stamp out protest. Police arrested an estimated 10,000 people. The state used the media to announce that reports of a massacre were untrue. Officials claimed that a small group of criminals had plotted against the government. After showing great restraint, officials said, the army was forced to crush a riot. Television news, however, had already broadcast the truth to the world.

China in the 1990s

The brutal repression of the pro-democracy movement left Deng firmly in control of China. During the final years of his life, Deng continued his program of economic reforms. By the mid-1990s, China's booming economy was producing extraordinary changes:

A VOICE FROM THE PAST
The country today is an endless series of jolting surprises. Streets are clogged with traffic. There is construction everywhere. Indoor malls with glittering new department stores surge with customers for whom shopping is rapidly becoming the recreational pastime of choice. At night, restaurants are packed with China's new urban middle class, raucously eating, drinking, and chain-smoking until the air inside turns gray.

ORVILLE SCHELL, "China—the End of an Era"

Although Deng moved out of the limelight in 1995, he remained China's unquestioned leader. In February 1997, after a long illness, Deng died. Communist Party General Secretary Jiang Zemin (jee·ahng zeh·meen) assumed the presidency.

China After Deng Many questions arose after Deng's death. What kind of leader would Jiang be? Would he be able to hold onto power and ensure political stability? A highly intelligent and educated man, Jiang had served as mayor of Shanghai. He was considered skilled, flexible, and practical. However, he had no military experience.

Struggles for Democracy **553**

Daily Life

Training the Chinese Army
Xiao Ye is a former Chinese soldier living in the United States. After Tiananmen Square, he explained how Chinese soldiers are trained to obey orders without complaint:

We usually developed bleeding blisters on our feet after a few days of . . . hiking. Our feet were a mass of soggy peeling flesh and blood, and the pain was almost unbearable. . . . We considered the physical challenge a means of tempering [hardening] ourselves for the sake of the Party. . . . No one wanted to look bad. . . .

And during the days in Tiananmen, once again the soldiers did not complain. They obediently drove forward, aimed, and opened fire on command. In light of their training, how could it have been otherwise?

History Through Art

Photojournalism

Tell students that early photojournalists, such as the Civil War photographer Mathew Brady, had only large-format stand-up cameras, which were bulky and hard to use. Brady could not take action pictures, only shots of stationary people, battlefields, and cities. His human subjects had to be posed and remain immobile while the photos were taken.

In the 1920s, the development of easy-to-handle miniature 35-millimeter cameras revolutionized the field, making it easier for photojournalists to capture people and events in action. Now, digital cameras, which produce images that can be computer enhanced and transmitted over telephone lines, allow photojournalists to snap dramatic, split-second action photos as events unfold.

MORE ABOUT. . .

Mao's Image

During Mao Zedong's lifetime, thousands of photos and paintings of his image were prominently displayed in public places and in private homes throughout China. Today his image is less common, but can still be found on tourist items such as T-shirts, key chains, and other mass-marketed products. None of these items would have been allowed in Mao's day.

Capturing Historical Moments

From the earliest days of photography, magazines and newspapers have used photographs to convey the news.

Photojournalists have to respond quickly to recognize the history-making moment and record it before the moment has passed. As the photographs on this page demonstrate, photojournalists have done much to capture the history of Communist China.

February 21, 1972
During his historic visit to China, President Richard Nixon raises a toast with Premier Zhou Enlai in a pledge of U.S.-Chinese friendship.

October 1, 1950
Workers, marching on the first anniversary of the founding of the People's Republic of China, carry posters to honor Mao Zedong.

June 5, 1989
A single Chinese man blocks tanks on their way to crush pro-democracy protests in Tiananmen Square. Bystanders pulled the man to safety.

Connect *to* History

Drawing Conclusions Which of these photographs seems to have been taken spontaneously when the photojournalist spotted an important historical moment? Which of these photographs seems to have been arranged ahead of time? Explain.

 SEE SKILLBUILDER HANDBOOK, PAGE 664

Connect *to* Today

Compare Look through newspapers or news magazines to find a news photograph that you find interesting. Bring it to class and explain how it compares with the photographs shown here in spontaneity, drama, and historical importance.

554 Chapter 19

Connect *to* History

Drawing Conclusions
The photo of the tanks is spontaneous because it is an action shot. The toast by Zhou Enlai and Richard Nixon seems prearranged because the leaders are posing for other diplomats and the press. The parade is probably prearranged. China was known for staging "spontaneous" demonstrations and parades. In the photo on this page, everyone is carrying the same image of Mao, which would suggest the parade had been organized by officials.

Connect *to* Today

Compare
The photographs that students bring should be news photos, not publicity shots or advertisements. Ask students to discuss the impact of the photos on public awareness of the events. Have them compare their photographs with those in the feature. Do their photos capture significant events in history or more fleeting moments? If there are people in their photos, what do the pictures show about their character?

Therefore, Jiang had few allies among the generals. He also faced challenges from rivals, including hard-line officials who favored a shift away from Deng's economic policies.

Other questions following Deng's death had to do with China's poor human rights record and relations with the United States. During the 1990s, the United States pressured China to release political prisoners and ensure basic rights for political opponents. China remained hostile to such pressure. Its government continued to repress the pro-democracy movement.

Nevertheless, the desire for freedom still ran through Chinese society. If China remained economically open but politically closed, tensions seemed bound to surface. As Chinese writer Liu Binyan observed in 1995, "The government Deng Xiaoping leaves behind will be the weakest in China since Communist rule began in 1949. . . . At the same time, the populace has become more difficult to rule than any other in Chinese history."

In late 1997, Jiang paid a state visit to the United States. During his visit, U.S. protesters demanded more democracy in China. Jiang admitted that China had made some mistakes but refused to promise that China's policies would change.

Transfer of Hong Kong Another major issue for China was the status of **Hong Kong.** Hong Kong was a thriving business center and British colony on the southeastern coast of China. On July 1, 1997, Great Britain handed Hong Kong over to China, ending 155 years of colonial rule.

As part of the negotiated transfer, China promised to respect Hong Kong's economic system and political liberties for 50 years. Many Hong Kong citizens worried about Chinese rule and feared the loss of their freedoms. Others, however, saw the transfer as a way to reconnect with their Chinese heritage.

The case of China demonstrates that the creation of democracy can be a slow, fitful, and incomplete process. Liberal reforms in one area, such as the economy, may not lead immediately to political reforms. Other nations, from Russia and Poland to Nigeria and Brazil, have found the path to democracy equally unpredictable. Even so, people around the world have a desire for more political freedom. As economic and social conditions improve—for example, as the middle class expands and educational opportunities grow—the prospects for democracy also may improve. In addition, as countries are increasingly linked through technology and trade, they will have more opportunity to influence each other politically. This too may promote democratic change.

In 1997, citizens of Hong Kong held their annual candlelight vigil to remember the massacre in Tiananmen Square. Many feared that the Chinese government would ban such memorials now that it controlled Hong Kong.

Section 5 Assessment

1. TERMS & NAMES
Identify
• Zhou Enlai
• Deng Xiaoping
• Four Modernizations
• Tiananmen Square
• Hong Kong

2. TAKING NOTES
Use a diagram like the one below to show the events leading up to the demonstration in Tiananmen Square and the events that followed it.

3. SUPPORTING OPINIONS
Judging from what you have read about the Chinese government, do you think Hong Kong will keep its freedoms under Chinese rule? Explain.

THINK ABOUT
• the economic reforms of Deng Xiaoping
• Tiananmen Square
• the Chinese government's promise to respect Hong Kong's liberties for 50 years

4. THEME ACTIVITY

Cultural Interaction Create a collage showing the different ways that contact with the West led to the call for democratic reform in China. Be sure to include pictures that symbolize all the different types of contact China had with the West.

Struggles for Democracy **555**

ANSWERS

1. TERMS & NAMES
Zhou Enlai, p. 551
Deng Xiaoping, p. 552
Four Modernizations, p. 552
Tiananmen Square, p. 552
Hong Kong, p. 555

2. TAKING NOTES
Possible Responses: China opens doors to U.S.; Deng Xiaoping begins Four Modernizations; Chinese buy Western goods and enjoy Western culture; Western tourists visit China; Chinese students study in West; **Tiananmen Square;** Chinese government massacres protesters; Chinese government represses pro-democracy movement.

3. SUPPORTING OPINIONS
Possible Responses: No—The Chinese government will try to apply its policy of allowing capitalism but repressing democracy in Hong Kong. Yes—The Chinese government will give Hong Kong special treatment, perhaps to keep its economy profitable or to avoid international criticism.

4. THEME ACTIVITY
Standards for Evaluation
Collages should meet the following criteria:
• Show ways that China had contact with the West.
• Illustrate effects of Western influence on Chinese society.

Chapter 19 Assessment

TERMS & NAMES

1. PRI, p. 534
2. apartheid, p. 539
3. Nelson Mandela, p. 539
4. Mikhail Gorbachev, p. 541
5. glasnost, p. 541
6. perestroika, p. 542
7. Lech Walesa, p. 542
8. Boris Yeltsin, p. 546
9. Deng Xiaoping, p. 552
10. Tiananmen Square, p. 552

REVIEW QUESTIONS

11. Free elections, citizen participation, majority rule, and constitutional government.

12. The military.

13. Ethnic conflict between the Igbo on one side and the Hausa-Fulani and Yoruba on the other led the Igbo region to secede. The government went to war to reunify the country.

14. Legalization of the ANC, holding of all-race (universal) elections, and writing of a new constitution and bill of rights.

15. Glasnost, perestroika, democratization, and foreign policy changes, such as pursuit of arms control and reduced interference in other countries.

16. Poland, Hungary, East Germany, Czechoslovakia, and Romania.

17. An attempt in 1991 by hard-line Communists to force Gorbachev to resign and to undo Gorbachev's reforms. It failed because the people would not go along with them.

18. The loss of Tito's leadership allowed ethnic conflicts to rise to the surface; when Serbia tried to dominate the other republics, several of them declared independence. The nation broke apart, and war resulted.

19. Zhou Enlai made overtures to the United States, and Deng Xiaoping initiated economic reforms.

20. It massacred demonstrators in Tiananmen Square, publicly lied about what had happened, and continued to repress the pro-democracy movement.

TERMS & NAMES

Briefly explain the importance of each of the following to the democratic movements that took place from 1945 to the present.

1. PRI	6. perestroika
2. apartheid	7. Lech Walesa
3. Nelson Mandela	8. Boris Yeltsin
4. Mikhail Gorbachev	9. Deng Xiaoping
5. glasnost	10. Tiananmen Square

Interact with History

On page 530, you considered what you might tell a foreign exchange student about how U.S. democracy works. Now that you've read the chapter, would your explanation be different? Would you add anything to what you said before? Would you change anything you said before?

REVIEW QUESTIONS

SECTION 1 (*pages 531–535*)
Patterns of Change: Democracy
Case Study: Latin American Democracies

11. Name four common democratic practices.

12. What group held up democratic progress in both Brazil and Argentina until the 1980s?

SECTION 2 (*pages 536–540*)
Democratic Challenges in African Nations

13. What brought about the civil war in Nigeria?

14. Name three significant steps toward democracy taken by South Africa in the 1990s.

SECTION 3 (*pages 541–545*)
Gorbachev Moves Toward Democracy

15. What were the main reforms promoted by Soviet leader Mikhail Gorbachev?

16. Which Eastern European nations overthrew Communist governments in 1989?

SECTION 4 (*pages 546–550*)
Collapse of the Soviet Union

17. What was the August Coup and how did it end?

18. What led to the breakup of Yugoslavia?

SECTION 5 (*pages 551–555*)
China Follows Its Own Path

19. What changes took place in China during the 1970s?

20. How did the Chinese government react to demands for democratic reform?

Visual Summary

15 Years of Democratic Struggles

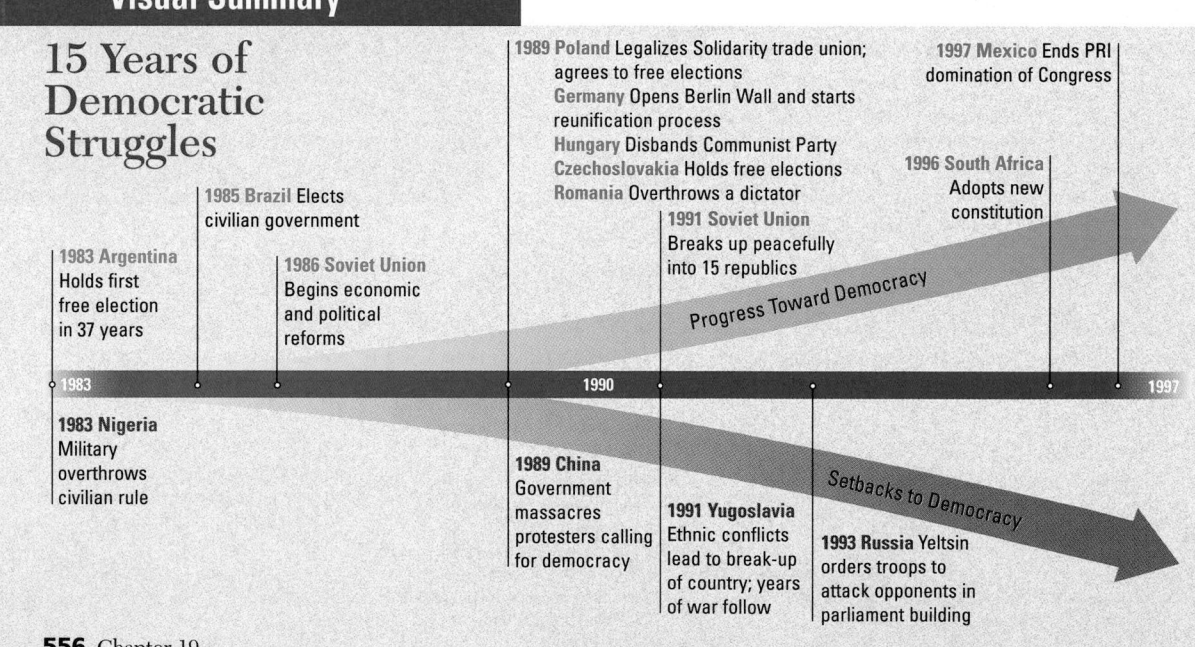

1989 Poland Legalizes Solidarity trade union; agrees to free elections
Germany Opens Berlin Wall and starts reunification process
Hungary Disbands Communist Party
Czechoslovakia Holds free elections
Romania Overthrows a dictator

1997 Mexico Ends PRI domination of Congress

1985 Brazil Elects civilian government

1983 Argentina Holds first free election in 37 years

1986 Soviet Union Begins economic and political reforms

1991 Soviet Union Breaks up peacefully into 15 republics

1996 South Africa Adopts new constitution

Progress Toward Democracy

1983   1990   1997

1983 Nigeria Military overthrows civilian rule

1989 China Government massacres protesters calling for democracy

1991 Yugoslavia Ethnic conflicts lead to break-up of country; years of war follow

1993 Russia Yeltsin orders troops to attack opponents in parliament building

Setbacks to Democracy

Interact with History

Ask students to list the remarks they would add, delete, or change. Students will probably add that building a stable democracy takes time and effort. Without key principles and institutions in place, it is easy for a democracy to be overthrown or torn apart by rival factions who ignore the law. Students may also have been surprised to learn how easily democracy can fall in the face of severe economic crises.

CRITICAL THINKING

1. ROADBLOCKS TO DEMOCRACY

THEME CULTURAL INTERACTION Name some examples from this chapter in which the negative impact of one culture on another blocked democratic progress.

2. DEMOCRATIC LEADERSHIP

Create a chart like the one below. List several leaders who you think helped their nations make democratic progress. For each leader, cite one example of an action that made a positive difference.

Leader	Nation	Positive Action

3. LESSONS OF DEMOCRACY

Think about the democratic movements you have studied in this chapter. Especially consider what conditions helped those movements succeed and what conditions caused difficulties for them. What do you think were the hardest challenges facing democratic movements?

4. ANALYZING PRIMARY SOURCES

The following excerpt comes from an article written about changes in the culture of Hong Kong in the months before it was returned to China. Read the paragraph and then answer the questions below it.

A VOICE FROM THE PAST
Whatever else you can say about the new Hong Kong, it will be more Chinese. Liu Heung-shing, the editor of the new Hong Kong magazine *The Chinese,* says that "for any meaningful art and culture to take off here, Hong Kong must find somewhere to anchor itself. To find that anchor, people will have to go north [to mainland China]." . . . Increasing numbers of Hong Kong's Cantonese speakers are studying mainland Mandarin. . . . At the same time that [Hong Kong] must resist China to retain Britain's legacy of rule of law, it knows that the most logical place for it to turn for commerce and culture is China.
ORVILLE SCHELL, "The Coming of Mao Zedong Chic"

- What is the main change that is taking place in Hong Kong's culture?
- What point of view might a business person have about this change?
- What point of view might a politician have about this change?

CHAPTER ACTIVITIES

1. LIVING HISTORY: Unit Portfolio Project

THEME ECONOMICS Your unit portfolio project focuses on economic changes within nations. For Chapter 19, you might use one of the following ideas to add to your portfolio.

- A government official has asked you for suggestions on how to move a Communist economy to a free market economy. Go through the chapter and compile a "Things to Do" list based on actions that other governments have taken.
- Create a poster with two contrasting lists: "Signs of a Healthy Economy" and "Signs of an Unhealthy Economy."
- Write an interview in which Deng Xiaoping discusses his economic reforms. Have him explain his goals for China.

2. CONNECT TO TODAY: Cooperative Learning

THEME REVOLUTION In this chapter, you read about how the democratic reforms initiated by Gorbachev led to an overturn of the Communist Soviet government. In effect, this was a second Russian Revolution.

Work with a team to create time lines of the first Russian Revolution in 1917 and the revolutionary events of 1985 to 1991. Then write a paragraph about the impact of the second revolution on Russia today.

INTERNET Using the Internet or a library, research Russian politics today. Is there still a Communist party? Is the Communist party still trying to undo the democratic reforms?

- Use this textbook, encyclopedias, or history books to find events for your time lines.
- Illustrate your time lines with photographs, drawings, or political cartoons.
- In your paragraph, evaluate how successful you think the second Russian Revolution was. Do you think the change will be long-lasting? Explain.

3. INTERPRETING A TIME LINE

Revisit the unit time line on pages 470–471. Use the Chapter 19 time line to learn what happened in Argentina in 1946.

FOCUS ON **POLITICAL CARTOONS**

Look carefully at this political cartoon, dated June 7, 1989.
- Do you recognize any world leaders in this cartoon? If so, who?
- What is the cartoon saying about the state of communism in Poland, China, and the Soviet Union?
- What is the cartoon's point of view—for or against communism? Explain.

Connect to History Judging from what you have read in the chapter, was the cartoon correct in its assessment of the state of communism? Explain your answer by citing specific events for each nation.

557

CHAPTER ACTIVITIES

1. LIVING HISTORY

Standards for Evaluation
"Things to Do" lists should meet the following criteria:

- Contain entries arranged in order of importance.
- Identify governments that have taken each suggested action.
- Explain each suggestion and its ranking.

Standards for Evaluation
Posters should meet the following criteria:

- Contain two distinguishable lists.
- Have related issues arranged in the same order.
- Include explanations of the choices made.

Standards for Evaluation
Interviews should meet the following criteria:

- Include questions by people from both inside and outside China.
- Reasonably reflect Deng Xiaoping's probable answers.
- Show a basic knowledge of events in the relevant period of Chinese history.

2. CONNECT TO TODAY: COOPERATIVE LEARNING

Standards for Evaluation
Time lines should meet the following criteria:

- Show only major events and dates.
- Include graphic information to illuminate specific events.
- Present personal opinions about the relative successes of the two revolutions.

3. INTERPRETING A TIME LINE

In 1946, Juan Perón, a former army officer, was elected president of Argentina. Once in office, he gradually assumed the powers of a dictator, quelling all opposition.

FOCUS ON **POLITICAL CARTOONS**

- Lech Walesa and Gorbachev.
- The cartoonist is saying that communism is dying in the USSR and Poland and is dead in China.
- Against—The artist depicts communism as dead or dying, and at least one leader is celebrating its demise.

Connect to History Students should justify their answers with examples from the text.

CRITICAL THINKING

1. ROADBLOCKS TO DEMOCRACY

Possible Responses: Legacy colonialism hindered democratic progress in Africa; ethnic clashes in Eastern Europe led to civil war; economic chaos delayed reforms.

2. DEMOCRATIC LEADERSHIP

Possible Responses: Raúl Alfonsín: Argentina—reformed democracy and economy; *Ken Saro-Wiwa: Nigeria*—fought injustice; *F. W. de Klerk: South Africa*—freed Mandela, helped end apartheid, agreed to open elections; *Nelson Mandela: South Africa*—protested apartheid; called for economic reform and reconciliation; *Mikhail Gorbachev: Soviet Union*—initiated reforms; *Lech Walesa: Poland*—led Solidarity; *Vaclav Havel: Czechoslovakia*—tried to prevent split of nation; *Boris Yeltsin: Russia*—criticized slow pace of reforms, led protest against coup.

3. LESSONS OF DEMOCRACY

Possible Responses: Colonial legacy, ethnic and racial conflict, oppressive governments, centrally controlled economies.

4. ANALYZING PRIMARY SOURCES

Possible responses: Hong Kong is turning to China for cultural inspiration. Business people may view China's markets as opportunities. Politicians may fear that China will curtail the city's freedoms.

	Key Ideas	COPY MASTERS	ASSESSMENT
SECTION 1 Science and Technology Shape Human Outlook *pp. 561–564*	*Advances in technology during the second half of the 20th century focus on the exploration of space and also on communications networks and medical and agricultural techniques that improve the quality of people's lives.*	*In-Depth Resources: Unit 8* • **Guided Reading,** p. 55 • **Primary Source:** from "Down to Earth," p. 62 • **Literature:** from "The Murderer," p. 66	*Section 1 Assessment,* p. 564 *Formal Assessment* • Section Quiz, p. 249 *Alternative Assessment Book* • Standards for Evaluating a Cooperative Activity
SECTION 2 Global Economic Development *pp. 565–571*	*As the global economy expands, the nations of the world are forced to adjust to new patterns of work and trade and to the necessity of maintaining economic growth while preserving the environment.*	*In-Depth Resources: Unit 8* • **Guided Reading,** p. 56 • **Skillbuilder Practice:** Analyzing Assumptions, p. 59 • **Geography Application:** Deforestation in Brazil, p. 60 • **Primary Source:** Recycling Symbol, p. 63 • **Literature:** "Paper," p. 66	*Section 2 Assessment,* p. 570 *Formal Assessment* • Section Quiz, p. 250 *Alternative Assessment Book* • Standards for Evaluating a Cooperative Activity
SECTION 3 Global Security Issues *pp. 572–576*	*Nations try to preserve peace and collective security and promote human rights but face many challenges, including ethnic and religious conflicts and the dislocation of peoples through migration.*	*In-Depth Resources: Unit 8* • **Guided Reading,** p. 57 • **Primary Source:** The Universal Declaration of Human Rights, p. 64 • **History Makers:** Kofi Annan, p. 69; Rigoberta Menchú, p. 70	*Section 3 Assessment,* p. 576 *Formal Assessment* • Section Quiz, p. 251 *Alternative Assessment Book* • Standards for Evaluating a Cooperative Activity
SECTION 4 Cultures Blend in a Global Age *pp. 577–581*	*Expanded communications technology brings peoples of the world closer together, creating conflict as they strive to preserve their uniqueness while respecting and living in harmony with their global neighbors.*	*In-Depth Resources: Unit 8* • **Guided Reading,** p. 58 • **Primary Source:** "Cupid's a Korean Computer, Making Wise Matches," p. 65 • **Connections Across Time and Cultures:** Progress and Change, p. 71	*Section 4 Assessment,* p. 581 *Formal Assessment* • Section Quiz, p. 252 *Alternative Assessment Book* • Standards for Evaluating a Cooperative Activity
CHAPTER RESOURCES	**Chapter Overview** *Advances in communications technology and increasing economic, cultural, and political interdependence give rise to a global community. People face growing responsibilities for maintaining the environment and working toward world peace.*	*Telescoping the Times* • Chapter Summary, pp. 81–83 *Planning for Block Schedules* *Case Studies* • **Case Study 9**—Japan and Mexico: Pluralistic Politics and Economic Growth, p. 114	*Chapter Assessment,* pp. 582–583 *Chapter Activities,* p. 583 *Formal Assessment* • Chapter Test, forms A and B, pp. 253–258 *Test Generator* *Alternative Assessment Book*

TECHNOLOGY

 Warm-Up Transparency 20

 Patterns of Interaction: Technology Transforms an Age

 INTERNET RESOURCES
www.mlworldhistory.com

 Warm-Up Transparency 20

 Geography Transparencies
• GT36 World Per Capita Income, 1990s

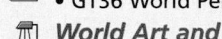 *World Art and Cultures Transparencies*
• AT79 *Time Goes By*

 Battles of the World
• The Gulf War

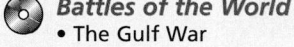 *Patterns of Interaction: Trade Connects the World*

 Electronic Library of Primary Sources
• "Tackling the Menace of Space Junk"

 Warm-Up Transparency 20

 Critical Thinking Transparencies
• CT36 Patterns of Refugee Movement

 Electronic Library of Primary Sources
• "The Making of a Terrorist"

 INTERNET RESOURCES
www.mlworldhistory.com

 Warm-Up Transparency 20

World Art and Cultures Transparencies
• AT80 *Technology* (Korean video sculpture)

Critical Thinking Transparencies
• CT72 Visual Summary

Electronic Library of Primary Sources
• "Un-American Ugly Americans"
• "Television Is Defying Borders"

Patterns of Interaction: Cultural Crossroads

INTERNET RESOURCES
www.mlworldhistory.com

 Chapter Summaries on Audiocassette in English and Spanish

INTERNET RESOURCES
www.mlworldhistory.com

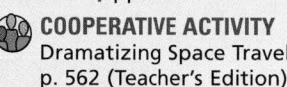 ## Block Scheduling (90 MINUTES)

Day 1
Section 1, pp. 561–564
 COOPERATIVE ACTIVITY
Dramatizing Space Travel, p. 562 (Teacher's Edition)
Section Assessment p. 564

Day 2
Section 2, pp. 565–571
COOPERATIVE ACTIVITY

Drafting a Trade Agreement, p. 568 (Teacher's Edition)
Section Assessment, p. 570

Day 3
Section 3, pp. 572–576
 COOPERATIVE ACTIVITY
Outlining a Nobel Prize Acceptance Speech, p. 574 (Teacher's Edition)
Section Assessment p. 576

Day 4
Section 4, pp. 577–581
COOPERATIVE ACTIVITY
Staging an International Literature Fair, p. 580 (Teacher's Edition)
Section Assessment, p. 581
Chapter Assessment, pp. 582–583

Yearly Pacing *Chapter 20 Total:* 4 days *Yearly Total:* 85 days

 Planning for Block Schedules

Customizing for Special Needs

Students Acquiring English

 Access for Students Acquiring English
• **Guided Reading** for Sections 1–4 (Spanish), pp. 216–219
• **Chapter Summary** (Spanish), pp. 213–215
• **Skillbuilder Practice** Analyzing Assumptions (Spanish), p. 220
• **Geography Application** Deforestation in Brazil (Spanish), p. 221

Spanish Reading Study Guide
• pp. 213–222

 Patterns of Interaction
Technology Transforms an Age; Trade Connects the World; Cultural Crossroads (Spanish tracks)

Less Proficient Readers

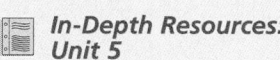 *In-Depth Resources: Unit 5*
• **Guided Reading** for Sections 1–4, pp. 55–58
• **Skillbuilder Practice** Analyzing Assumptions, p. 59
• **Geography Application** Deforestation in Brazil, p. 60

 Telescoping the Times
• Chapter Summary, pp. 81–83

 Reading Study Guide
• pp. 213–222

 Chapter Summaries on Audiocassette
in English and Spanish

Gifted and Talented Students

 In-Depth Resources: Unit 5
Primary Sources:
• from "Down to Earth," p. 62
• Recycling Symbol, p. 63
• The Universal Declaration of Human Rights, p. 64
• "Cupid's a Korean Computer, Making Wise Matches," p. 65

History Makers
• Kofi Annan, p. 69
• Rigoberta Manchú, p. 70

Connections to Literature READINGS FOR STUDENTS

 In-Depth Resources: Unit 5
Literature: "Paper," p. 66

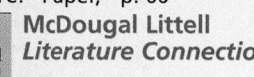 **McDougal Littell**
Literature Connections

• Foote, Horton
To Kill a Mockingbird (the screenplay) *(with related readings)*

Adapted from the Pulitzer Prize winning novel by Harper Lee, the story examines the results of ignorance and hate.

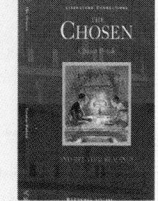

McDougal Littell
Literature Connections

• Potek, Chaim
The Chosen
(with related readings)

In this story, two teenage boys become best friends despite living in different worlds. Reuven, the narrator, slowly comes to understand Danny's sternly Hasidic world.

 = Pupil's Edition = Overhead Transparency = Software   = Video

 = Copy Master = CD-ROM = Audiocassette   = Internet

Global Interdependence, 1960–present

Accessing Prior Knowledge

- Ask students what picture comes to mind when they hear the phrase *global interdependence.* What does it imply about the peoples, languages, cultures, economies, and politics of the world?

Drawing Conclusions

- What do the pictures of the Arab man and the Huli children suggest about technology and the modern world?

- In what ways are the Tibetan women and the Brazilian Indians trying to influence the future of their world? What ways of the past do they cling to?

GEOGRAPHY CONNECTION

Ask students to examine the position of the continents on this world map.

- How does this presentation differ from a conventional map?

- What does it suggest about the relation of the world's nations and peoples?

CHAPTER
20
Global Interdependence, 1960–present

PREVIEWING THEMES

Science and Technology

Advances in science and technology have changed the lives of people around the globe. People today eat better, and live longer, healthier, and more comfortable lives. Improved communication and transportation have allowed goods and ideas to move rapidly. Science has even reached out to new horizons in space.

Cultural Interaction

New inventions and innovations have brought the nations of the world closer and exposed people to the ideas and habits of other cultures. Cultures are now blending ideas, customs, and habits. The people of the world have developed a greater sense of being part of a larger global culture.

Economics

Since World War II, nations have worked to expand trade and commerce in world markets. Changes in transportation and technology along with the establishing of multinational companies have blurred national boundaries and created a global market.

THE WORLD TODAY

Technology has reached into formerly isolated areas across the world to change ways of life. These two children of the **Huli tribe** of **Papua New Guinea** study a Polaroid picture.

AUSTRALIA
INDONES
PAPUA NEW GUINEA
PHILIPPINE
TAIWA
S. KOREA
N. KOREA
JAPAI
SOLOMON ISLANDS
NEW ZEALAND
PACIFIC OCEAN
FIJI
KIRIBATI
180°
120°E

Brazilian Indians ride a bus in **Rio de Janeiro, Brazil,** after a meeting during the Earth Summit in **1992.** The Indians discussed issues of the environment, hunger, and land disputes with the Brazilian government.

INTERNET CONNECTION

Visit us at **www.mlworldhistory.com** to learn more about global interdependence in the modern world.

558

GEOGRAPHY THEMES

Movement

In the modern world of air travel, the shortest route between places on different continents often involves flying over the North Pole. Ask students to locate the North Pole on the map. *The point in the Arctic Ocean where the lines of longitude converge.* Flights often follow one of the lines of longitude over the pole in what is called a great circle route. Have students trace great circle routes between various sets of points on different continents and compare them with routes that go around the globe. Encourage students to discuss how great circle routes might affect communication in the modern world.

Human–Environment Interaction

The proliferation of modern technology has drastically altered the way people think about and interact with their world. Causes and effects are no longer local and isolated, but act globally. Vastly increased emissions from automobiles and industry, for example, contribute to global warming. A 1997 monetary crisis in the Asian stock market sent the U.S. market plummeting. As technology continues to develop, it will bring new possibilities and opportunities, but also require the commitment of nations to protect the earth's environment.

Tibetan women demonstrate against human rights violations at the Forum on Women in **Huairou, China,** in September **1995.**

New technologies allow an Arab man in **Yemen** using a radio phone to conduct business or contact family and friends.

ADDITIONAL RESOURCES

Books for the Teacher

• Kaplan, Robert D. *The Ends of the Earth: A Journey at the Dawn of the 21st Century.* New York: Random, 1996. A pessimistic view of the future.

• Ostry, Sylvia, and Richard R. Nelson. *Techno-Nationalism and Techno-Globalism: Conflict and Cooperation.* Washington, D.C.: Brookings Institution, 1995.

• Rawlins, Gregory J. E. *Moths to the Flame: The Seductions of Computer Technology.* Cambridge: MIT P, 1996.

Books for the Student

• Markley, Oliver W., and Walter R. McCuan, eds. *America Beyond 2001: Opposing Viewpoints.* San Diego: Greenhaven, 1996.

• Yancey, Diane. *Life in War-Torn Bosnia.* San Diego: Lucent, 1996.

Videos

• *Exploring the Global Economy.* Social Studies School Service, 1994. 800-421-4246. The fundamental concepts that govern international trade.

• *The Technological Revolution/ Toward the Future.* Crystal Productions, 1989. 800-255-8629.

Software

• *Lines in the Sand: The Pursuit of Peace in the Middle East.* CD-ROM. Social Studies School Service, 1995. 800-421-4246.

• *Space: A Visual History.* CD-ROM. Queue, 1994. 800-232-2224.

HISTORY THROUGH ART

Clothing and Personal Adornment

Throughout history, clothing has provided not only protection from the elements, but also a way for people to decorate their bodies and present themselves as works of art. Even in the age of global interdependence, as these images attest, people adorn their bodies in ways that distinguish them from their global neighbors. The Brazilian Indians' headdresses and body paint, the Arab man's head covering and robe,

the Tibetan women's woven aprons, and the Papua New Guineans' face decoration not only identify these people, but also transmit a message about who they are and what they stand for.

Clothing also enables people to exhibit their feelings, such as mourning, and to elicit certain responses in others, such as "dressing for success." A person's mode of dress also places that person in time. Not only do styles of clothing change constantly, but the

materials they are made from reflect the resources and technologies at hand. In today's interdependent world, even an African's loincloth might be fashioned from polyester.

Interpreting the Art Ask students what the clothing of the people pictured here suggests about their geographical locations and ways of life.

Interact *with* History

This Interact with History feature motivates students by inviting them to take a broad view of world events. As they read the headlines of worldwide newspapers, students will consider not only the impact of these events on the people involved, but also the effects on their own and other people's lives.

Purpose
- To introduce students to the concept of a global community
- To give students a broad perspective on world events
- To help students appreciate the many ways in which the world's nations are interdependent

Teaching Strategy
Thinking Critically After students have imagined themselves in the situation described on this page, have them answer the key question and give reasons for their answers.

EXAMINING *the* ISSUES
Following are suggestions for addressing each bulleted question.

1 Remind students that the Common Market is an economic alliance formed in an attempt to eliminate trade barriers among the member nations.

2 Over several successive days, bring in the international section of a newspaper or play a radio news broadcast. Have students chart the news stories and discuss the effects of events in one part of the world on people in other parts.

3 Ask students to list foods, music, books, television shows, and web sites they've experienced in the past week. What international influences do they see?

Making Connections Ask students to discuss how people around the world might respond differently to growing global interdependence.

You are walking down a street of our nation's capital on a cloudy summer day. All of a sudden, the sky gets very dark and within minutes a heavy rain begins pouring down. You run for the closest shelter and find yourself at an international newsstand. As you wait for the rain to let up, you scan the headlines of dozens of newspapers from all over the world. They all focus on different events.

What impact do events in different countries have on your life?

Mir Cosmonauts Prepare for U.S. Crew Member

Southeast Asian Common Market Suggested

U.S., Israel, Palestinians to Work on Security

India Flash Floods Kill at Least 110

Brazil's Forests Fading Fastest, Tree Study Says

EXAMINING *the* ISSUES

- What evidence do the headlines give of economic interdependence in today's world?

- How do the headlines illustrate the political interdependence of different nations?

- What do the stories in the newspapers tell you about scientific and cultural interdependence among nations?

As a class, discuss these questions. Remember what you've learned about the recent history of nations in different regions of the world. Try to think of reasons why nations are becoming increasingly dependent on one another.

As you read this chapter, look for more examples of economic, political, and cultural interdependence among the nations of the world.

Follow-Up
A feature on the chapter assessment will ask students to reevaluate their responses to the situation presented on this page.

Science and Technology Shape Human Outlook

TERMS & NAMES
- Hubble Space Telescope
- Internet
- genetic engineering
- cloning
- green revolution

MAIN IDEA

Advances in technology after World War II led to increased global interaction and improved quality of life.

WHY IT MATTERS NOW

The lives of all people around the world are affected by advances in science and technology.

SETTING THE STAGE Beginning in the late 1950s, the United States and the Soviet Union competed in the exploration of space. The Soviets launched Earth's first artificial satellite, *Sputnik 1,* and put the first human in orbit around the planet. By the late 1960s, however, the United States had surpassed the Soviets. U.S. astronauts landed on the moon in 1969. The heavy emphasis on science and technology spilled over into developing products that improved the ways of life of human beings across the globe.

Probing the Solar System and Beyond

The space race of the 1950s, 1960s, and early 1970s was intensely competitive. Both the United States and the Soviet Union competed to reach the moon and beyond. Both nations developed manned and unmanned space programs. Although the space race was competitive, it carried the seeds of global cooperation. Orbiting spacecraft beamed back images of a small blue planet, Earth, floating like a jewel in the black void of space. People around the world who saw this view of Earth received a stirring reminder that though they lived in different countries, they all shared the planet. Eventually, space exploration became one of the world's first and most successful arenas for cooperation between U.S. and Soviet scientists.

Space Race Becomes Cooperative In 1972, more than 15 years before the end of the Cold War, the United States and the Soviet Union signed an agreement. Their goal was to work toward docking *Apollo* and *Soyuz* spacecraft in space. Not only did the American and Soviet staffs have to work out engineering problems, they also had to learn each other's language. On July 17, 1975, an American *Apollo* spacecraft docked with the Soviet *Soyuz 19* spacecraft 140 miles above Earth. As the astronauts opened the hatch connecting the space vehicles, TV viewers across the globe watched the crews from Earth's fiercest rival countries greet each other.

This first cooperative venture in space between the United States and the USSR was an isolated event. Over the next 15 years, American and Soviet space programs separately developed space shuttles. Unlike the *Apollo* spacecraft, these shuttles were reusable and could return to Earth under their own power. During the 1980s, shuttle missions put crews in orbit around Earth. The missions were designed to accomplish a variety of scientific and technological experiments. Colonel Frederick Gregory, a

Four U.S. astronauts and one Russian cosmonaut worked together in the Shuttle *Atlantis* cargo bay. They linked with the *Mir* space station.

Global Interdependence **561**

SECTION 1 RESOURCES

PRINT RESOURCES

 IN-DEPTH RESOURCES: UNIT 5
Guided Reading, p. 55
Primary Source: from "Down to Earth," p. 62
Literature: from "The Murderer," p. 66

 ACCESS FOR STUDENTS ACQUIRING ENGLISH
Guided Reading (Spanish), p. 216

 FORMAL ASSESSMENT
Section Quiz, p. 249

 ALTERNATIVE ASSESSMENT BOOK

TECHNOLOGY RESOURCES

VIDEO
Patterns of Interaction: Technology Transforms an Age

INTERNET www.mlworldhistory.com

Section 1 Overview

OBJECTIVES

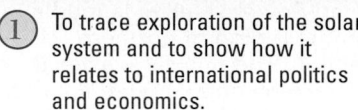 (1) To trace exploration of the solar system and to show how it relates to international politics and economics.

 (2) To identify the effects of expanding global communications in the late 20th century.

 (3) To list advances in health care, medicine, and agriculture, and to evaluate their effects.

CRITICAL THINKING
- Hypothesizing, p. 562
- Summarizing, pp. 563, 564
- Forming and supporting opinions, p. 564
- Analyzing themes, p. 564

FOCUS
5-Minute Warm-Up

Identifying Main Ideas
To spark students' interest in the far-reaching effects of science and technology, have them answer these questions.

- Read the Spotlight on Space Junk on page 562. What is space junk?
- What are some hazards it poses for both astronauts in space and people on Earth?

 WARM-UP TRANSPARENCY 20

OBJECTIVE (1) INSTRUCT

Probing the Solar System and Beyond

Key Ideas
- Exploration of space begins as a competition between the United States and the Soviet Union.
- By the 1980s, people from various countries cooperate in exploring the universe.
- Private companies become involved in scientific and commercial ventures in space.

 IN-DEPTH RESOURCES: UNIT 5
Guided Reading, p. 55
Primary Source: from "Down to Earth," p. 62

 ACCESS FOR STUDENTS ACQUIRING ENGLISH
Guided Reading (Spanish), p. 216

Spacelab 3 astronaut observed, "I think that science is the stuff that pays for itself on these missions. It's going to improve the quality of life down here [Earth]."

Beginning in the 1970s and increasing in the 1980s, people from different countries worked together to explore space. The Soviets were the first to send an international crew into space. In 1978, they invited Czech astronaut Vladimir Remek to orbit Earth in *Soyuz 28*. In the mid-1980s, the U.S. space agency invited people from Saudi Arabia, France, Germany, and Mexico to fly on the space shuttle.

Both the Soviets and the Americans had launched and lived in space stations since the early 1970s. Since 1986, the Soviet-launched *Mir* space station has been orbiting over 200 miles above Earth. In the mid-1990s, the Russians invited a number of U.S. astronauts to spend time on board *Mir*. Back on Earth, American and Russian scientists worked with scientists from 13 other nations to design and construct the first International Space Station.

Exploring the Universe Helping to study planets of the solar system, unmanned space probes such as *Voyager 2* sent dazzling pictures of Jupiter, Saturn, Uranus, and Neptune back to Earth. The Soviet *Venera* and *Vega* spacecraft and the U.S. *Magellan* spacecraft gathered in-depth information about Venus. In 1997, the U.S. space agency landed the *Pathfinder* probe on Mars. The public was fascinated with pictures sent back to Earth that included the activities of a mechanical rover named *Sojourner*.

In 1986, several nations, including Japan and the Soviet Union, sent spacecraft to study Halley's Comet as it swung by Earth. The U.S. space agency, NASA, and the European space agency, ESA, worked together to make and launch the **Hubble Space Telescope** in 1990. This advanced tool is today observing objects in the most remote regions of the universe.

Space Goes Commercial Meanwhile, private companies have become increasingly involved in space. One company has even contracted to take over much of the U.S. space shuttle program. Some companies launch rockets and satellites that help search for minerals and other resources on Earth. Satellites also follow the weather, aid long-distance learning programs, and even guide cars through cities. In the future, companies may use the zero-gravity environment of space to manufacture perfect crystals. They may eventually send solar collectors into orbit to help generate electricity for Earth. However, the most common commercial use of space today and in the near future will probably remain in the field of communications.

Expanding Global Communications

Since the 1960s, artificial satellites launched into orbit around Earth have aided worldwide communications. With satellite communication, the world was gradually transformed into a global village. Today, political and cultural events occurring in one part of the world often are witnessed live by people in other places. For example, in 1997, more than 2 billion television viewers across the world watched the funeral of Diana, the Princess of Wales. The linking of the globe through worldwide communications was made possible by the miniaturization of the computer.

Smaller, More Powerful Computers In the 1940s, when computers first came into use, they took up a huge room. The computer required fans or an elaborate air-conditioning system to cool the vacuum tubes that powered its operations. In the years since then, however, the circuitry that runs the computer had been miniaturized and made more powerful. This was due in part to the space program, where

---

equipment had to be downsized to fit in tiny space capsules. Silicon chips replaced the bulky vacuum tubes used earlier. Smaller than contact lenses, silicon chips hold millions of microscopic circuits.

Following this development, industries began to use computers and silicon chips to run assembly lines. A variety of consumer products such as microwave ovens, telephones, keyboard instruments, and cars today use computers and chips. Personal computers have become essential in most offices, and millions of people around the globe use personal computers in their homes.

Communications Networks Starting in the 1990s, businesses and individuals began using the Internet. The **Internet** is the voluntary linkage of computer networks around the world. It began in the late 1960s as a method of linking scientists so they could exchange information about research. Through telephone-line links, business and personal computers can be hooked up with computer networks. These networks allow users to communicate with people across the nation and around the world. In the period from 1993 to 1996, the use of the Internet increased by an estimated seven times.

Conducting business on the Internet has become a way of life for many. The Internet, along with fax machines, transmits information electronically to remote locations. Both paved the way for home offices and "telecommuting." Once again, as it has many times in the past, technology has changed how and where people work.

Transforming Human Life

Advances with computers and communications networks have transformed not only the ways people work but lifestyles as well. Technological progress in the sciences, medicine, and agriculture has changed the quality of the lives of millions of people.

Health and Medicine Before World War II, surgeons seldom performed operations on sensitive areas such as the eye, the inner ear, or the brain. Beginning in the 1950s, new technologies employed in advanced surgical techniques developed. More powerful microscopes and innovations such as the laser and ultrasound were among the improvements. For example, by the late 1970s, laser surgery to remove damaged lenses of the eye, such as lenses clouded with cataracts, was common. Such techniques made surgery safer and more accurate and improved patients' chances for quick recovery.

Advances in medical imaging also helped to improve health care. The use of CAT scans and MRI techniques gave doctors three-dimensional views of different organs or regions of the body. Using CAT scans and MRIs, doctors diagnose injuries, detect tumors, or collect other information needed to identify medical conditions.

In the 1980s, genetics, the study of heredity through research on genes, became a fast-growing field of science. Found in the cells of all organisms, genes are hereditary units that cause specific traits, such as eye color, in every living organism. Technology allowed scientists to isolate and examine individual genes that are responsible for different traits. Through **genetic engineering,** scientists were able to introduce new

---

SPOTLIGHT ON

The Human Genome Project
Human genetic material (DNA) contains approximately 50,000 to 100,000 genes. Mapping the thousands of genes contained in human DNA is the goal of the Human Genome Project.

The information led to the development of a new field of medicine called "molecular medicine." This field focuses on how genetic diseases develop and progress. It has resulted in early detection of disease. Eventually, it may lead to individualized treatment based on a person's genetic makeup.

Misuse of this information could drastically alter society. Therefore, a part of the project includes investigation of the ethical, legal, and social issues raised by genetic engineering.

genes into an organism to give that organism new traits. For example, with genetic engineering, scientists removed a gene from an Arctic fish and placed it in a plant. The resulting genetically engineered plant is better able to withstand frost.

Another aspect of genetic engineering is **cloning,** the creation of identical copies of DNA, the chemical chains of genes that determine heredity. Cloning actually allows scientists to reproduce both plants and animals that are identical to existing plants and animals. The applications of genetics research have led to many advances, especially in agriculture.

The Green Revolution In the 1950s, agricultural scientists around the world started a campaign known as the **green revolution.** It was an attempt to increase available food sources worldwide. Scientists promoted the use of fertilizers, pesticides, and high-yield, disease-resistant strains of a variety of crops. The green revolution helped avert famine in Asia and increased yields of crops in many different parts of the world.

However, the green revolution had its negative side, too. Fertilizers and pesticides are dangerous chemicals that cause cancer and pollute the environment. Also, the cost of the chemicals and the equipment to harvest more crops was far too expensive for an average peasant farmer. Consequently, owners of small farms received little benefit from the advances in agriculture. In some cases farmers were forced off the land by larger agricultural businesses.

Advances in genetics research have helped to fulfill some of the goals of the green revolution. In this new "gene revolution," resistance to pests was bred into plant strains, reducing the need for pesticides. Plants bred to tolerate poor soil conditions also reduced the need for fertilizers. The gene revolution involved some risks, including the accidental creation of disease-causing organisms. However, the revolution also brought great promises for increasing food production in a world with an expanding population.

Science and technology has changed the lives of millions of people. In many cases quality of life has improved. What people produce and even their jobs have changed. These changes have altered the economies of nations. Not only have nations become linked through communications networks but they are also linked in a global economic network, as you will see in Section 2.

THINK THROUGH HISTORY
C. Summarizing
What are some of the positive and negative effects of genetic engineering?
C. Possible Answers Positive—more food available, reduced need for fertilizer; negative—accidental creation of disease-causing organisms

---

Section 1 Assessment

1. TERMS & NAMES
Identify
- Hubble Space Telescope
- Internet
- genetic engineering
- cloning
- green revolution

2. TAKING NOTES
Copy the chart below and fill in information on ways science and technology has changed human life.

Science and Technology Changes Lives		
Communications	Health and Medicine	Green Revolution

Which of the three areas do you think has had the greatest global effect?

564 Chapter 20

3. FORMING AND SUPPORTING OPINIONS
What is your opinion about cloning? In your judgment, is there a limit to how far cloning should go? Support your opinion with reasons.

THINK ABOUT
- the Human Genome Project
- positive effects of cloning
- negative effects of cloning

4. ANALYZING THEMES
Science and Technology
Why do you think that space exploration became an arena for cooperation between the Soviet Union and the United States?

THINK ABOUT
- goals of space exploration
- technologies involved
- images of Earth from space

ANSWERS

1. TERMS & NAMES
Hubble Space Telescope, p. 562
Internet, p. 563
genetic engineering, p. 563
cloning, p. 564
green revolution, p. 564

2. TAKING NOTES
Possible Responses:

Communications: television contact across the globe, home offices and telecommuting; *Health and Medicine:* improved diagnoses and surgery; mapping and genetic engineering; *Green Revolution:* increased crop yields; decreased use of pesticides through plant genetics.

3. FORMING AND SUPPORTING OPINIONS
Possible Responses: Cloning has led to many advances in health and agriculture. It can be pushed too far; for example, creating dangerous biological weapons.

4. ANALYZING THEMES
Possible Responses: Both nations saw the advantages of sharing costs and information, pooling technologies, and increasing good will between their countries.

TERMS & NAMES
• developed nation
• developing nation
• global economy
• multinational corporation
• free trade
• Gulf War
• ozone layer
• sustainable development

MAIN IDEA

The economies of the world's nations are so tightly linked that the actions of one nation affect others.

WHY IT MATTERS NOW

Every individual is affected by the global economy and the environment.

Section 2 Overview

OBJECTIVES

(1) To discuss the effects of technology on the world economy.

(2) To explain the economic growth of Pacific Rim countries.

(3) To define the global economy.

(4) To identify challenges facing developing nations.

(5) To describe the environmental impact of development.

SKILLBUILDER
• Interpreting graphs, p. 566
• Interpreting maps: location, p. 568

CRITICAL THINKING
• Analyzing causes, p. 566
• Recognizing effects, pp. 566, 570
• Summarizing, pp. 567, 569
• Forming an opinion, p. 568
• Clarifying, p. 570
• Drawing conclusions, p. 571

SETTING THE STAGE At the end of World War II, much of Europe and Asia lay in ruins, with many of the major cities leveled by bombing. The devastation of the war was immense. However, within a decade, with U.S. aid, the economies of western European nations and Japan began expanding rapidly. Their growth continued for half a century, long after the United States ceased supplying aid.

Technology Revolutionizes the World's Economy

Advances in technology caused economic growth in both Asia and the Western world. The explosion in scientific knowledge prompted great progress that quickly led to new industries. A prime example was plastics. In the 1950s, a process to develop plastics at low pressures and low temperatures was perfected. Within a few years, industries made toys, cooking utensils, containers, and a host of other products easily and cheaply out of plastics. The plastics industry boomed. Other technological advances have also changed industrial processes, lowered costs, and increased the quality or the speed of production. For example, robotic arms on automobile assembly lines made possible the fast and safe manufacture of high-quality cars.

Information Industries Change Economies Technological advances in manufacturing reduced the need for factory workers. But in other areas of the economy new demands were emerging. Computerization and communications advances changed the processing of information. By the 1980s, people could transmit information quickly and cheaply. Information industries such as financial services, insurance, market research, and communications services boomed. Those industries depended on what Professor Peter Drucker called "knowledge workers."

Car production has changed a great deal since the production of pre–World War II cars. Today, car assembly plants using efficient robots have eliminated jobs once done by people.

FOCUS

5-Minute Warm-Up

▶ **Making Inferences**
To introduce students to the global economy, have them answer these questions.

• Look at the illustration on the bottom of page 567. Where is the car's engine made?

• What does the car suggest about the reliance of individual countries on each other?

WARM-UP TRANSPARENCY 20

OBJECTIVE (1) INSTRUCT

Technology Revolutionizes the World's Economy

▶ **Key Ideas**
• New technologies spur economic growth.

• A boom in service industries transforms world economies.

IN-DEPTH RESOURCES: UNIT 5
Guided Reading, p. 56

ACCESS FOR STUDENTS ACQUIRING ENGLISH
Guided Reading (Spanish), p. 217

SECTION 2 RESOURCES

PRINT RESOURCES

IN-DEPTH RESOURCES: UNIT 5
Guided Reading, p. 56
Skillbuilder Practice: Analyzing Assumptions, p. 59
Geography Application: Deforestation in Brazil, p. 60
Primary Source: Recycling Symbol, p. 63

ACCESS FOR STUDENTS ACQUIRING ENGLISH
Guided Reading (Spanish), p. 217
Skillbuilder Practice (Spanish), p. 220
Geography Application (Spanish), p. 221

FORMAL ASSESSMENT
Section Quiz, p. 250

TECHNOLOGY RESOURCES

GEOGRAPHY TRANSPARENCIES
GT36 World Per Capita Income, 1990s

WORLD ART AND CULTURES TRANSPARENCIES
AT79 *Time Goes By*

CD-ROM
Battles of the World: The Gulf War
Electronic Library of Primary Sources

VIDEO
Patterns of Interaction: Trade Connects the World

The Growth of Japan and the Pacific Rim

▶ **Key Ideas**

• Japan achieves rapid economic growth by adapting modern Western technologies.

• Education plays a key role in the economic development of Pacific Rim countries.

📃 **IN-DEPTH RESOURCES: UNIT 5**
Literature: "Paper," p. 66

History from Visuals

Growth in East Asia
Interpreting the Chart Make sure students understand that per capita gross domestic product (GDP) is the total value of the goods produced in a country divided by its population. Which country had the lowest per capita GDP in 1991? *South Korea.*

Extension Activity Suggest that interested students research current economic information on one of the Pacific Rim countries. Then have them photocopy the chart on this page and add their information to it.

SKILLBUILDER ANSWERS
1. Japan; $27,000
2. Hong Kong, Singapore

📰 *GEOGRAPHY TRANSPARENCIES*
GT36 World Per Capita Income, 1990s

MORE ABOUT . . .
The Pacific Rim

The video *Trade Connects the World: Silk Roads and the Pacific Rim* describes the flourishing economic development in the Pacific Rim and its impact on the rest of the world.

 PATTERNS OF INTERACTION
Trade Connects the World: Silk Roads and the Pacific Rim
Videocassette: Tape 1

A VOICE FROM THE PAST
By the end of this century knowledge workers [people whose jobs focus on working with information] will amount to a third or more of the work force in the United States. . . . The majority of knowledge workers will be paid at least as well as blue-collar workers ever were, or better. And the new jobs offer much greater opportunities. . . . The new jobs . . . require a habit of continuous learning.

PETER DRUCKER, *Managing a Time of Great Change*

The Effects of New Economies In the postwar era the expansion of the world's economies led to an increase in the production of goods and services so that many nations benefited. The economic base of some nations shifted. Manufacturing jobs began to move out of **developed nations**—those nations with the industrialization, transportation, and business facilities for advanced production of manufactured goods. The jobs moved to **developing nations,** that is, those in the process of becoming industrialized. Developing countries became prime locations for new manufacturing operations. Some economists believe these areas were chosen because they had many eager workers whose skills fit manufacturing-type jobs. Also, these workers would work for less money than those in developed nations. On the other hand, information industries that required better-educated workers multiplied in the economies of developed nations. The changes brought by technology changed the workplace of both developed and developing nations.

The Growth of Japan and the Pacific Rim

The Japanese began adopting modern technologies from Europe in the mid-1800s, during the Meiji era. After World War II, they continued to import and adapt the best of Western technology. For example, the Sony Corporation of Japan bought the rights to manufacture transistors, which are the basis for all electronic equipment, from an American company. Within 20 years, Sony had built a business empire based on the transistor. The company manufactured radios, stereo equipment, and televisions.

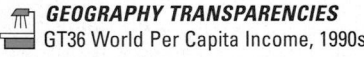

Pacific Rim Trade
As early as the 1700s, Europeans and Americans eagerly sought trade with nations on the Pacific Rim. When Commodore Matthew Perry of the United States opened Japan to trade, Pacific Rim trade began to develop quickly.

As Asian countries industrialized, trade with the region expanded. Although the Pacific Rim nations were once mainly markets for Western goods, they now produce and export great quantities of electronic products and other high quality goods.

Today, over 40 percent of United States foreign trade is with Pacific Rim nations. The state of California leads the nation in trade with these countries. About 25 percent of California's economy is tied to the Pacific Rim.

 VIDEO *Trade Connects the World: Silk Roads and the Pacific Rim*

The emphasis that the Japanese and other people from Asia's Pacific Rim have placed on education has made their work force knowledgeable, creative, and flexible. This helped the region enjoy amazing economic growth from the 1950s to the present. Japanese corporations produce high-quality cars, electronic goods, and ships. The success of Japanese corporations fueled the country's high economic growth rate of 10 percent per year from 1955 through 1970. In the 1990s, averaging between 3 and 4 percent annually, Japan's growth was above that of the United States.

Four places in the Pacific Rim—South Korea, Taiwan, Hong Kong, and Singapore—followed Japan's example. In the 1970s, they set out on programs of rapid industrialization designed to make their economies both modern and prosperous. South Korea became a major exporter of automobiles and of electronic goods. Hong Kong became a world financial center. These four newly industrialized countries recorded such impressive economic growth that they became known as the Four Tigers of Asia. In the 1990s, rapidly industrializing China and Malaysia began competing with the other nations of the Pacific Rim. With Japan, the Four Tigers, China, and Malaysia, the Pacific Rim became a key arena of world trade.

566 Chapter 20

EXPLORING PRIMARY SOURCES

A Voice from the Past Peter Drucker, an economics professor, has written many books on current economic trends. Share with students Drucker's additional thoughts on knowledge and learning.

"Knowledge can be acquired only through schooling. It is not tied to any country. It is portable. It can be created everywhere, fast and cheaply. Finally, it is by definition changing."

Encourage students to discuss whether or not they agree with Drucker's statements. What implications do these statements have for economic growth? for students' futures as members of the workforce?

CUSTOMIZING FOR SPECIAL NEEDS

Gifted and Talented Students Delving into the Pacific Rim
Ask students to choose a Pacific Rim country that intrigues them. Have them research the history of that country since World War II, focusing on political and cultural events that might help explain the country's explosive economic growth. When students finish their research, ask them to put together a bulletin board display about the country's history, showing political, cultural, and economic trends and suggesting interconnections among them. Have students use the bulletin board as the basis of an oral presentation to the class.

Growth in World Trade

Economies in different parts of the world have been linked for centuries through trade and through national policies, such as colonialism. However, a true global economy didn't take shape until the second half of the 1800s. The **global economy** includes all the financial interactions among people, businesses, and governments that cross international borders. In recent decades, several factors hastened growth in world trade. Huge cargo ships, the length of three football fields, could inexpensively carry enormous supplies of fuels and other goods from one part of the world to another. Telephone and computer linkages made global financial transactions quick and easy. In addition, multinational corporations developed around the world.

Multinational Corporations Companies that operate in a number of different countries are called **multinational corporations** or transnational corporations. U.S. companies such as Ford, IBM, and Exxon; European companies such as Nestlé and Volvo; and Japanese companies such as Honda and Mitsubishi all became multinational giants.

All of these companies have established manufacturing plants in many countries. They select spots where the raw materials or labor are cheapest. This enables them to produce components of their products on different continents. They ship the various components to another location to be assembled. This level of economic integration allows such companies to view the whole world as the market for their goods. Goods or services are distributed throughout the world as if there were no national boundaries.

Expanding Free Trade After World War II, many national leaders felt that economic cooperation among countries across the world would be key to peace and prosperity. The idea of **free trade,** which is the elimination of trade barriers such as tariffs among nations, began to gain acceptance. As early as 1947, nations began discussing ways to open trade. One such agreement was GATT—General Agreement on Tariffs and Trade. Over the years, a general lowering of protective tariffs and an expansion of free trade, region by region, has expanded the global marketplace. By 1995, the World Trade Organization was established to supervise free trade.

A European organization set up in 1951 promoted tariff-free trade among member countries. This experiment in economic cooperation was so successful that seven years later, a new organization, the European Economic Community (EEC), was formed. Over the next 40 years, most of the other western European countries joined the organization, which now is called the European Union (EU). The European Union began hammering out issues related to the introduction of a common currency and to integrating Eastern European nations as members.

Regional Trade Blocs Through this economic unification, Europe exerted a major force in the world economy. The economic success of the EU inspired countries in other regions to make trade agreements with each other. The North American Free Trade

THINK THROUGH HISTORY
C. Summarizing
What elements accelerated global trade?
C. Answer Better communication, transportation, financial resources, and multinational companies

Vocabulary
tariff: a tax on goods imported from another country.

Background
The first products to be tariff-free were iron and coal. This helped the countries develop their industries.

World Car

Same design used in cars sold in North and South America, Europe, and Asia, but sold under different company names

Instrument panels
Europe

Glass
China, Brazil, Argentina, Chile, or Poland

Frame
U.S.A.

Engine
Brazil, Mexico

Transmission
Europe

Seats
U.S.A.

Tires
Canada, Mexico, Argentina, or Brazil

Global Interdependence **567**

OBJECTIVE 3 INSTRUCT

Growth in World Trade

▶ *Key Ideas*
• The global economy grows rapidly with the acceleration of world trade.
• Multinational corporations help the global economy expand.
• Various international trade agreements spur economic growth.
• The success of the European Union inspires other regional trade agreements.

MORE ABOUT . . .
Politics and World Trade

Political influences are arguably as important as economic ones in promoting the growth of world trade. Policy changes in China, for example, have increased the world's workforce, spurred industrialization, and opened up vast new markets. Likewise, the breakup of the Soviet Union and the independence of the former Eastern bloc countries have injected new life into the world economy.

MORE ABOUT . . .
Multinational Corporations

The global economy includes about 37,000 multinational corporations, which control one-third of the world's wealth (excluding governmental assets). Because these corporations carry such weight in the global economy, some policy makers are pushing the World Trade Organization (WTO) to adopt regulatory guidelines to prevent monopolies, deter corruption, and promote occupational and environmental safety. The WTO could then grant accreditation to companies that uphold its standards.

TEACHING OPTION | **BLOCK SCHEDULING**
SKILLBUILDER MINI-LESSON: Analyzing Assumptions
CLASS TIME 20 MINUTES

Explaining the Skill People and governments make decisions and take action based on many factors, which may be complex and confusing even to the people involved. One of these factors is the assumption, or belief, that people take for granted as true. Examining the background, needs, and goals of a person or government can help historians understand the assumptions that lie behind historical decisions.

Applying the Skill: Multinational Corporations Ask students to analyze the assumptions that underlie the establishment of multinational corporations. Have them consider the following questions:
1. What needs or goals might motivate corporations to become multinational?
2. What do corporations gain from operating in worldwide markets?

3. What do consumers gain from buying products made by multinational corporations?
4. What problems might lack of national economic boundaries cause?

 IN-DEPTH RESOURCES: UNIT 5
Skillbuilder Practice: Analyzing Assumptions, p. 59

World Trading Blocs, 1997

History from Visuals

World Trading Blocs, 1997

Interpreting the Map Have students carefully examine the map key before looking at the map. Which countries are members of the Group of Seven?

Extension Activity Have students identify countries that are not members of any of the trading blocs included in the map. Ask them to research the politics and economics of one of these countries and hypothesize why it does not belong to a trading bloc.

SKILLBUILDER ANSWERS
1. Venezuela, Gabon, Nigeria, Libya, Algeria.
2. NAFTA, G-7

MORE ABOUT . . .
NAFTA

The assumptions underlying the formation of NAFTA are the same as those underlying the European Union: lowering or eliminating tariffs and other trade barriers should cause regional trade and economic growth to increase significantly. Some U.S. and Canadian citizens opposed the agreement, however, fearing that their countries would lose jobs to Mexico, where wages tend to be lower.

OBJECTIVE 4 INSTRUCT

Challenges Facing Less-Developed Nations

▶ **Key Ideas**
- A great chasm exists between life in developed and in less-developed nations.
- Some believe that developed nations should assist less developed nations.
- Long-term economic planning may help less-developed nations grow.

Map legend:

- 🛢 Organization of Petroleum Exporting Countries (OPEC)
- ☐ Asia-Pacific Economic Cooperation (APEC)
- G7 G-7 (Group of Seven)
- ☐ Andean Group
- Association of Southeast Asian Nations (ASEAN)
- Central American Common Market (CACM/MCCA)
- Council of Arab Economic Unity (CAEU)
- Caribbean Community and Common Market (CARICOM)
- Commonwealth of Independent States (CIS)
- European Free Trade Association (EFTA)
- European Union (EU)
- Southern Cone Common Market (MERCOSUR)
- North American Free Trade Agreement (NAFTA)
- Southern Africa Development Community (SADC)
- Central African Customs and Economic Union (UDEAC)

GEOGRAPHY SKILLBUILDER: Interpreting Maps
1. **Location** Which countries in OPEC are located outside of Southwest Asia?
2. **Location** To which world trade organizations does the United States belong?

Agreement (NAFTA), put into effect in 1994, called for the rapid elimination of tariffs and trade restrictions among Canada, the United States, and Mexico. This trade-barrier-free zone may eventually extend into other parts of Latin America, which already has its own free trade association, LAFTA. Organizations in Asia, Africa, and the South Pacific are also creating regional trade policies.

Multinational corporations, freer world trade, and regional trading blocs today tie nations together economically. Instead of two nations trading with each other exclusively, trade links many nations. Resources, work forces, and financial support for business and trade come together from many areas of the world. Just how closely linked international economies are was demonstrated in late 1997. In October of that year, the dramatic fall of the Hong Kong stock market caused a ripple effect in markets in Asia, Europe, and North America. Thus, economic and political conditions in one part of the world affect the economies of nations in other parts of the world.

Challenges Facing Less-Developed Nations

Less-developed nations wanting to expand their economies face many challenges. Many people in the less-developed nations live in grinding poverty. On average, people in these nations receive only one-twentieth the income of people in the developed nations. They may lack adequate shelter, a source of clean drinking water, or food for nourishment. Diseases weaken many, and health care is often unavailable. Such poverty can lead to political instability, which affects not only the nation but also the rest of the world.

THINK THROUGH HISTORY
D. Forming an Opinion Which of the elements of global trade do you think was most responsible for expanding world trade?
D. Possible Answer Free trade has helped to expand world trade.

568 Chapter 20

TEACHING OPTION **BLOCK SCHEDULING** | **COOPERATIVE ACTIVITY: Drafting a Trade Agreement** | **CLASS TIME 30 MINUTES**

Task: Students will research current trade agreements and then draft their own agreement.

Purpose: To enable students to experience the complexities of the world economy.

Activity: Divide students into three groups to research the existing trade agreements—GATT, NAFTA, and LAFTA. Have them share their information with the class. Have each group then choose either Asia, Africa, or the South Pacific and review the countries in those areas. Ask the groups to draft a trade agreement for their region using appropriate elements of existing agreements and make a presentation to the class.

 Building a Portfolio: Students might include their trade agreements in their portfolios.

📖 **ALTERNATIVE ASSESSMENT BOOK**
Standards for Evaluating a Cooperative Activity

Standards for Evaluation
Trade agreements should . . .

- be based on existing agreements
- take into account the special needs of the region
- present information clearly and concisely

THINK THROUGH HISTORY
E. Summarizing
What challenges do
developing nations
face in improving their
economies?
E. Answer
Overcoming poverty
and unstable political
conditions.

Many world leaders believe that the less-developed nations can ease the burden of poverty for their people only by economic development. Some economists have encouraged less-developed nations to assess their resources and to make long-term economic plans. Some also argue that developed nations need to assist the developing nations to climb out of poverty. A report issued by an international commission observed, "Peace, stability, and human justice around the globe depend on how well nations cooperate to help people in all lands share in the earth's resources and wealth."

Impacts of Economic Development

Global development has had a variety of effects, both positive and negative. It brought manufacturing jobs to developing nations. However, as industries moved out, it reduced manufacturing jobs and raised unemployment in developed nations. Global development had an even larger impact on the use of energy and other resources. Worldwide demand for these resources has led to both environmental and political problems.

Political Impacts Manufacturing requires the processing of raw materials; trade requires the transport of finished goods. These activities, essential for development, require the use of much energy. For the past 50 years, one of the main sources of energy used by developed and developing nations has been oil. For nations with little of this resource available in their own land, disruption of the distribution of oil or a large price increase causes economic and political problems. Nations possessing oil reserves have the power to affect economic and political situations in countries all over the world. For example, OPEC declared an oil embargo—a ban on trade—in the 1970s. This caused significant economic decline in developed nations during that decade.

In 1990, Iraq invaded Kuwait and threatened to stop the distribution of Kuwaiti oil. Fears began to mount that Iraq would also invade Saudi Arabia, another major source of oil, and cut off petroleum supplies to the world. When an international economic embargo failed to change Iraq's behavior, countries of the United Nations moved to wage war on Iraq. The war was known as the Persian Gulf War or **Gulf War.** The war served to point out how globally linked the economies of nations are.

Water is another important resource required for many manufacturing processes. It is also essential for agricultural irrigation. In many parts of the world, nations increasingly came into conflict over the use and maintenance of water resources. Poor quality water resources became one of many serious threats to the environment resulting from economic development.

Background
The Middle East
contains 62 percent
of all known oil
resources.

Environmental Impacts Economic development also threatens the environment. The burning of coal and oil as an energy source causes health-damaging air pollution and acid rain. It has led to global warming.

Background
Scientists have dis-
covered a hole in the
ozone layer in an area
above the continent of
Antarctica. Ozone in
this location has
dropped to 33 percent
of the 1975 amount.

The release of chemicals called chlorofluorocarbons (CFCs), used in refrigerators, air conditioners, and manufacturing processes, has destroyed ozone in the earth's upper atmosphere. The **ozone layer** is our main protection against the sun's damaging ultraviolet rays. With the increase in ultraviolet radiation reaching the earth's surface, the incidence of skin cancer continues to rise in many parts of the world. Increased ultraviolet radiation may damage populations of plants and plankton at the bases of the food chains, which sustain all life on Earth.

GlobalImpact

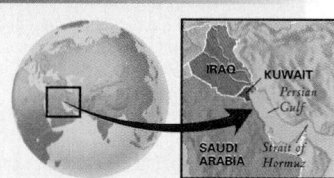

Allies Protect Oil Supplies

A perfect example of how the nations of the world are dependent on each other was the Gulf War. Iraq threatened to cut off supplies of oil from Kuwait and other parts of the Middle East. This threatened not only the U.S. and European nations but also Japan, which imports almost all of its oil, and other Asian and African countries. Nations worked together against Iraq to stop that threat.

The Gulf War, also known as "Operation Desert Storm," included 700,000 troops from 39 Allies and around 500,000 Iraqi troops. Within three months, the stubborn but out-gunned Iraqis accepted a cease-fire.

While the supplies of oil were made safe, the war resulted in great environmental damage. More than 465 million gallons of oil were dumped into the Persian Gulf.

Global Interdependence **569**

CRITICAL THINKING ACTIVITY
CLASS TIME: 10 MINUTES

Comparing and Contrasting
Ask students to complete a Venn diagram like the one below to help them understand the similarities and differences between developed and less-developed nations.

Developed nations | Both increasing global inter-dependence | Less-developed nations

OBJECTIVE 5 INSTRUCT

Impacts of Economic Development

▶ *Key Ideas*
• Economic growth has both positive and negative effects on politics and the environment.
• Political conflict often concerns the allocation and use of energy and water resources.
• Economic development has numerous harmful effects on the environment.
• Nations must decide how to meet economic needs while preserving the environment.

IN-DEPTH RESOURCES: UNIT 5
Geography Application: Deforestation in Brazil, p. 60

GlobalImpact
Allies Protect Oil Supplies

When Iraqi troops invaded Kuwait and headed toward Saudi Arabia, the world held its breath. If Iraq had managed to conquer both Kuwait and Saudi Arabia, it would have gained control of half the world's oil supplies. Have students discuss why this threat drew together countries from Africa to North America.

 BATTLES OF THE WORLD
The Gulf War

TEACHING OPTIONS

CONNECTIONS ACROSS THE CURRICULUM

Economics Ask students to research one or more of the various proposals that have been made in an attempt to solve the political and environmental problems that have accompanied rapid globalization and economic development. These problems include the overwhelming debt of developing nations and environmental pollution and destruction of habitats. Suggest that students investigate, for example, debt-for-nature deals and the establishment of pollution rights. Have them present their findings to the class.

MULTIPLE LEARNING STYLES

Kinesthetic Learners Ask students to choose a product such as an item of food or clothing, a piece of recreational or electronic equipment, or an appliance such as a refrigerator. Have them do research in the library or on the Internet to find out all the raw materials, including energy sources, needed to manufacture that product. Encourage them to make a display showing the raw materials and the process by which they are combined and transformed into a finished product. Suggest that students cut pictures from magazines or catalogs or make models to depict their products and collect actual samples of the raw materials, if possible, to include in their displays.

Teacher's Edition **569**

Daily Life
Recycling
The children above in Seoul, South Korea, are celebrating Earth Day by promoting recycling. People in many countries recycle paper, glass, metals, and plastics through community recycling programs. One of the most popular items to recycle is cans. Two-thirds of all aluminum cans used in the United States are recycled.

In Great Britain, the government has called for the expanded use of recycled paper. The goal for the near future is that newsprint be made of at least 40 percent recycled paper fibers. One new paper recycling plant may help Britain meet that ambitious goal. This recycling plant is so environmentally friendly that the water it releases from the paper recycling process is cleaner than the river into which the water is discharged.

Economic development has also often involved the deterioration of the land. Large-scale soil erosion is a worldwide problem due to damaging farming techniques. The habitat destruction that comes from land development has also caused the shrinking of numbers of wildlife around the world. In the 1990s the extinction rate of plants and animals is at least a hundred times greater than it ever has been in earth's history. This high extinction rate means that these animals can no longer serve as an economic resource. The loss of so many species also could endanger complex and life-sustaining processes that keep earth in balance.

"Sustainable Growth" Economists and scientists worked together to think of ways to reduce the negative effect development has on the environment. Their goal is to manage development so that growth can occur, but without destroying air, water and land resources. The concept is sometimes called "green growth." Economist Frances Cairncross suggests that completely reducing negative effects on the environment will not happen.

A VOICE FROM THE PAST
Many people hope that economic growth can be made environmentally benign [harmless]. It never truly can. Most economic activity involves using up energy and raw materials; this, in turn, creates waste that the planet has to absorb. Green growth is therefore a chimera [impossible idea]. But greener growth is possible.

FRANCES CAIRNCROSS, *Economic Growth and Sustainable Development*

Economic development has frequently led to huge environmental damage. Because of this, people around the world have come together at Earth Summits to try to formulate plans for sustainable development. **Sustainable development** involves two goals: meeting current economic needs, while ensuring the preservation of the environment and the conservation of resources for future generations. Making and putting into practice these plans has proved to be difficult. But meeting both goals is essential for the future of the human population on earth. Because economies of nations are tied to their political climates, such development plans will depend on the efforts of nations in both economic and political areas.

Section 2 Assessment

1. TERMS & NAMES
Identify
- developed nation
- developing nation
- global economy
- multinational corporation
- free trade
- Gulf War
- ozone layer
- sustainable development

2. TAKING NOTES
Using a diagram like the one below, list examples of forces that have shaped a global economy.

Forces that shape a global economy

3. RECOGNIZING EFFECTS
In what ways has technology changed the workplace of people across the world?

THINK ABOUT
- the kinds of industries people work in
- the location of the workplaces
- the speed at which work is done

4. THEME ACTIVITY
Economics Make a survey of the labels on class members' clothing and shoes. Look for the countries in which clothing or shoes were produced. List all the countries represented. On a world map, shade in each of the countries you listed. What does the information suggest to you about the global economy?

570 Chapter 20

Economics and the Environment

Is it possible to have economic development while protecting the environment at the same time? To answer this question, the concept of "sustainable development" was created and discussed at Earth Summits. Using this concept, economic development and environmental protection both are considered in producing a long-term development plan for a nation. Sustainable development, though, often involves making difficult choices and trade-offs. And it often highlights differences between developing and developed nations.

LETTER
José A. Lutzenberger

In the following letter written in 1991, the Environmental Secretary of Brazil, José A. Lutzenberger, asks the President of the United States, George Bush, to stop the clear-cutting (removal of all trees in one tract of land at a time) of America's ancient forest, saying it sets a bad example for the world.

Dear Mr. President:

. . . As an ecologist with a holistic view of the world, my concerns and the concerns of our Government go beyond Amazonia. So, we are also very much concerned with the fate of the last remaining old stands of temperate and boreal forests of North America in Alaska, British Columbia, Washington, Oregon and a few remains in California. . . .

At the present rate of clear-cutting practices for pulp and the export of logs, it will all be finished in about fifteen years. An irreparable loss for your country, a shame for Mankind and a very bad example for the Third World. How can we argue against the criminal devastation of tropical forests in Indochina, Malaysia, the Philippines, Indonesia, New Guinea and Africa, as well as here in South America? The powerful and rich U.S. can certainly afford to subsidize a few thousand jobs in a less destructive way.

POLITICAL CARTOON

In the beginning, God created Heaven and earth... ...and He created the seas...

...and then, God made Man... There goes the neighborhood.

EDITORIAL
Thomas L. Friedman

Thomas L. Friedman, a columnist, discusses the dilemma developing nations find themselves in when trying to consider both the economy and the environment.

Yes, the rich, developed northern nations, who've been polluting for years, have no right to lecture Indonesians, now that they're trying to develop too. Still, it is hard not to feel a sense of tragedy in the making, and those Indonesians who have reached an income and education level where they can afford to think about the environment share this sense of being overwhelmed by global capitalism. For a developing country like Indonesia, plugging into the global market often means a brutal ultimatum: Jobs or trees? You can't have both. This is globalization's dark side.

Connect *to* History

Drawing Conclusions What problems and tradeoffs do the demands of sustainable development create for developing nations and developed nations?

 SEE SKILLBUILDER HANDBOOK, PAGE 664.

Connect *to* Today

Researching Gather statistics on the ten fastest-growing national economies and the ten most environmentally degraded nations. Create a chart for each. Then, construct a third chart including information from both.

CD-ROM For another perspective on the environment, see World History: Electronic Library of Primary Sources.

Global Interdependence **571**

---

different **Perspectives**

Is Sustainable Development an Attainable Goal?
Discuss with students who the cartoonist holds responsible for the world's environmental problems. Then have students reread A Voice from the Past on page 570. How do they think Cairncross would respond to the ideas stated in each of the documents?

As students discuss these perspectives on economic development and the environment, have them consider whether or not sustainable development is attainable. Suggest that they find articles or editorials in newspapers or magazines that address these questions:
• What is the best way to help the economies of developing nations grow?
• How much does a nation's economy need to grow in order for the nation's people to prosper?
• Who has the right to use a nation's resources?
• Who is responsible for protecting the environment?
• Who is responsible for cleaning up or repairing environmental damage?

Make sure students understand that these questions are extremely complex and that the search for answers shapes the continuing debate on economics and the environment.

ELECTRONIC LIBRARY OF PRIMARY SOURCES
"Tackling the Menace of Space Junk"

Connect *to* History

Drawing Conclusions
Possible Responses:
Both—a choice of saving jobs or saving the environment, a loss of environmental resources as economic development continues; Developed nations—the responsibility to prevent environmental damage resulting from their extensive use of resources and to serve as a model for developing nations.

Connect *to* Today

Researching
Suggest that students consult sources such as almanacs, encyclopedias, and Internet references for current economic and environmental statistics.

Encourage students to gather data on each nation's economic growth and environmental degradation and to compile this information in their third chart.

(1) To identify security issues nations face and ways they pursue collective security.

(2) To cite examples of ongoing ethnic and religious conflicts, and explain how diversity can also lead to world peace.

(3) To describe how various organizations and movements have helped support human rights.

(4) To explain the increase in migration and discuss its worldwide effects.

CRITICAL THINKING

- Analyzing motives, p. 573
- Clarifying, p. 574
- Making Inferences, p. 575
- Analyzing causes, p. 576
- Identifying problems, p. 576
- Analyzing themes, p. 576

FOCUS
5-Minute Warm-Up

▶ **Identifying Main Ideas**
To introduce students to global security issues, have them answer these questions.

- Read the Spotlight on UN Peacekeepers on page 572. Where are UN peacekeeping forces sent?

- How have UN missions proved to be costly?

 WARM-UP TRANSPARENCY 20

OBJECTIVE (1) INSTRUCT

Nations Pursue Collective Security

▶ **Key Ideas**
- Nations seek collective security.
- The UN helps prevent aggression.
- Nations work to limit the spread of armaments.
- Terrorism threatens world security.

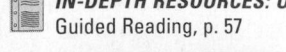 **IN-DEPTH RESOURCES: UNIT 5**
Guided Reading, p. 57

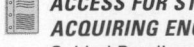 **ACCESS FOR STUDENTS ACQUIRING ENGLISH**
Guided Reading (Spanish), p. 218

TERMS & NAMES
- Nuclear Non-Proliferation Treaty
- proliferation
- terrorism
- fundamentalism
- Universal Declaration of Human Rights
- civil rights movement

MAIN IDEA

Since 1945, nations have used collective security efforts to solve problems.

WHY IT MATTERS NOW

Personal security of the people of the world is tied to security within and between nations.

SETTING THE STAGE World War II was one of history's most devastating conflicts. More than 55 million people died as a direct result of bombings, the Holocaust, combat, starvation, and disease. Near the end of the war, one of humankind's most destructive weapons, the atomic bomb killed more than 100,000 people in Hiroshima and Nagasaki in a matter of minutes. Perhaps because of those horrors, since 1945, powerful nations have repeatedly stepped back from the brink of destruction that could result from another all-out world conflict.

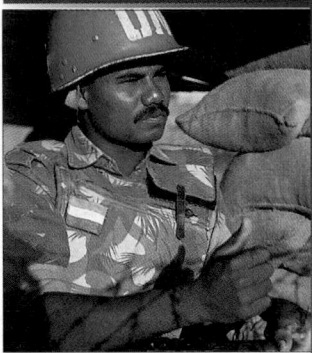

SPOTLIGHT ON

UN Peacekeepers

Soldiers in blue helmets, such as the one pictured above, have been sent on peacekeeping missions all over the world. They come from dozens of different nations, from Finland to Senegal, from Canada to Pakistan. As neutral soldiers they are sent to enforce peace in troubled areas.

Some missions have lasted for decades, such as the 40-year UN mission to monitor the cease-fire agreement between India and Pakistan. Other UN missions are brief. The 1962–1963 UN mission to New Guinea lasted for six months.

Some UN missions are successful in their goal of preventing the continuation of conflict, but others fail. Both kinds of missions have proved costly. More than 1,450 peacekeepers have died in the line of duty.

Nations Pursue Collective Security

In the decades since the end of World War II, the number of limited wars throughout the world increased. Such wars potentially threatened the economic, environmental, and personal security of people in all nations. So nations began to work together to pursue collective security.

Nations Unite and Take Action Many nations consider that having a strong army is important to their security. After World War II, nations banded together to make military alliances. They formed the North Atlantic Treaty Organization (NATO), the Southeast Asian Treaty Organization (SEATO), the Warsaw Pact, and others. The member nations of each of these alliances generally consider an attack on one of them to be an attack on them all. Thus, they each pledged military aid for their common defense.

In addition to military alliances to increase their security, world leaders have recognized that threats of war needed to be reduced. The United Nations (UN), an international agency established in 1945, works in a variety of ways toward increasing collective global security.

Peacekeeping Activities More than 180 nations send representatives to the UN, which has as one of its aims to promote world peace. The UN provides a public forum, private meeting places, and skilled mediators to help nations try to resolve conflicts at any stage of their development.

The UN also provides peacekeeping soldiers at the invitation of the warring parties. These forces try to prevent the outbreak of new fighting or to help enforce a cease-fire. The unarmed or lightly armed soldiers fire their weapons only in self-defense. The presence of neutral UN soldiers helps prevent aggression. In the late 20th century, the UN sent successful peacekeeping forces to such places as El Salvador in Central America, Kuwait in the Middle East, and Namibia in Africa. The UN, however, was only successful when the nations involved in a conflict maintained a commitment to working things out peacefully.

Background
A limited war is one in which only a few nations are involved and nuclear weapons are not used.

SECTION 3 RESOURCES

PRINT RESOURCES

 IN-DEPTH RESOURCES: UNIT 5
Guided Reading, p. 57
Primary Source: The Universal Declaration of Human Rights, p. 64
History Makers: Kofi Annan, p. 69; Rigoberta Menchú, p. 70

ACCESS FOR STUDENTS ACQUIRING ENGLISH
Guided Reading (Spanish), p. 218

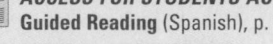 **FORMAL ASSESSMENT**
Section Quiz, p. 251

TECHNOLOGY RESOURCES

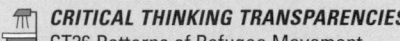 **CRITICAL THINKING TRANSPARENCIES**
CT36 Patterns of Refugee Movement

 CD-ROM
Electronic Library of Primary Sources

 INTERNET www.mlworldhistory.com

Controlling Weapons of Mass Destruction Just as nations banded together in the past five decades to try to prevent and contain conflicts, they also forged treaties to limit the manufacture, testing, and trade of weapons. The weapons of most concern are those that cause mass destruction. These include not only nuclear weapons but also chemical weapons, including poison gases and biological weapons that unleash deadly diseases.

In 1968, world nations gathered to work toward reducing their own arsenals of nuclear arms. Some signed a **Nuclear Non-Proliferation Treaty.** In this pact, nations both with and without nuclear power pledged to help prevent the **proliferation,** or spread, of nuclear weapons to other nations. In the 1970s, the United States and Russia signed the Strategic Arms Limitation Treaties. In the 1980s, both countries began to deactivate some of their nuclear weapons. However, at the beginning of the 1990s, ten nations still possessed nuclear weapons.

Many nations also signed treaties promising not to produce biological or chemical weapons. Because these weapons are fairly easy to produce and are so destructive, they are called the "poor countries' nuclear bomb." Use of these weapons is not limited to international situations. Sometimes terrorist groups use them to make their demands known.

Terrorism Threatens Security In March 1995, a Japanese cult member released nerve gas in a Tokyo subway, killing 12 people and injuring thousands. A month later, an American opposed to the power of the U.S. government planted a bomb near the Federal Building in Oklahoma City, Oklahoma, killing more than 160 people. Both tragedies are examples of **terrorism,** the use of force or threats to frighten people or governments to change policies. Terrorism is a tactic used by political or ideological groups to call attention to their demands and to gain major media coverage of their positions. The ease of international travel makes every nation vulnerable to attacks. Because terrorists cross national borders or escape to countries with governments friendly to their cause, terrorism is an international problem.

Two teenage terrorists hold hostages at the Japanese embassy in Lima, Peru. The terrorist group held hostages for over 100 days, in late 1996 and early 1997, before being forced out and killed by the Peruvian military.

THINK THROUGH HISTORY
A. Analyzing Motives Of what value would media coverage be to a terrorist group?
A. Possible Answer It allows them to tell thousands what their positions are on issues that concern them.

Ethnic and Religious Conflicts Disrupt Peace

Conflicts among people of different racial, national, religious, linguistic, or cultural groups are not new. Some ethnic or religious conflicts have roots that reach back for decades and, in some conflicts, for centuries. Such conflicts include the "troubles" between Catholics and Protestants in Northern Ireland and the hostilities between Palestinians and Jews in the Middle East.

Some ethnic conflicts have deep historic causes that simmered under the surface until recently. Examples from the 1990s include the Hutu-Tutsi rivalry in East Africa or the Serb-Bosnian-Croat disputes in the former nation of Yugoslavia. With the removal of authoritarian rule or colonial governments, sometimes these old problems flared into violent confrontations and wars. This created problems for the security of neighboring nations and caused many refugees to seek shelter in the nearby lands.

Religious Conflicts The growth of **fundamentalism**—a strict belief in the basic truths and practice of a particular faith—also contributed to conflict among different peoples. In some countries, fundamentalist groups have worked to gain control of a government in order to impose their ideas upon an entire nation. For example, in 1997, the Taleban movement in Afghanistan gained control of that country after a long civil war. The leaders immediately imposed strict Muslim law on the land. Many opposed the fundamentalist rule even though they also were Muslim.

Global Interdependence **573**

SPOTLIGHT ON
UN Peacekeepers

(See page 572.)

Have students investigate current conflicts around the world and learn what the United Nations has done or is doing to try to help ease the conflict. Students might give a brief newscast to share what they have learned and present daily or weekly updates on that conflict.

 IN-DEPTH RESOURCES: UNIT 5
History Makers: Kofi Annan, p. 69

MORE ABOUT . . .
Nuclear Weapons

The United States, Russia, Great Britain, France, China, and India have nuclear weapons, and it is likely that Pakistan and Israel also do. North Korea, Iran, and some countries of the former Soviet Union also may have weapons-producing capability.

 ELECTRONIC LIBRARY OF PRIMARY SOURCES
"The Making of a Terrorist"

OBJECTIVE ② INSTRUCT

Ethnic and Religious Conflicts Disrupt Peace

▶ *Key Ideas*
• Ethnic conflicts flare, especially in areas no longer ruled by outside forces.
• The growth of fundamentalism fuels religious conflicts.
• People of different religions and ethnic backgrounds must work together to promote peace.

TEACHING OPTIONS

CONNECTIONS ACROSS TIME AND PLACE

Ongoing Conflicts Dozens of ethnic and religious conflicts rage around the world every year. Have students make a chart like the one here listing some of these conflicts. Encourage them to include examples from each continent. Suggest that students research the historic roots of one of the conflicts and share what they learn with the class.

Country	People in Conflict
Chad	Zakawa and Gourane tribes
Sri Lanka	Hindu Tamils and Buddhist Sinhalese

CRITICAL THINKING TRANSPARENCIES
CT80, Horizontal Chart

CUSTOMIZING FOR SPECIAL NEEDS

Access for Students Acquiring English To help students identify roots and affixes, write *terrorism* and *terrorist,* and *fundamentalism* and *fundamentalist* on the board and divide them into root words and suffixes. Write the definitions of the suffixes *-ism* (action, process, or practice of) and *-ist* (one who performs an action). Then have students state the meanings of the

roots *terror* and *fundamental* or look them up in the dictionary. Have them combine the roots and suffixes and state the meanings of each of the four combined words. Encourage students to use a similar strategy to learn other words in this section, such as *nationalism* and *authoritarian*.

Teacher's Edition **573**

Ethnic and religious conflicts have often been characterized by terrible violence. People caught in these conflicts sometimes suffered torture or massacres of their whole towns or villages. An example of this is violence imposed on the Kurds, a nomadic group in southwest Asia. (See spotlight on Kurds.)

As violence escalates, communication between the conflicting groups shuts down. The Buddhist leader of Tibet, the Dalai Lama, argued that opening communication is the key to understanding differences and resolving conflicts.

A VOICE FROM THE PAST
The various religions must recognize their common responsibility. Therefore it is important that they live together and speak to each other in harmony. Certainly there is a great deal of difference between the religions. But if people openly approach each other wishing sincerely to exchange views and learn from each other they will discover that they are in agreement on many things. A large common basis, I am sure, could be found. The religions could devote this basis to the service of the world's positive development.

DALAI LAMA, quoted in *Global Trends: The World Almanac of Development and Peace*

While some have tried to find common ground through religion to ease conflict, others try to gain wide international guarantees of basic human rights.

Promoting Human Rights Worldwide

After the atrocities of the Holocaust in World War II, the newly formed United Nations resolved to work toward guaranteeing basic human rights for persons of all nations.

UN Issues a Declaration In 1948, to set human rights standards for all nations, the UN drew up and ratified the **Universal Declaration of Human Rights.** The declaration stated, "All human beings are born free and equal in dignity and rights. . . . Everyone has the right to life, liberty, and security of person." It further listed specific rights that all human beings should have. Later, in 1975, the Helsinki Accords addressed the issues of freedom of movement and freedom to publish and exchange information.

Both the declaration and the accords are nonbinding. But many people around the world became committed to ensuring that basic human rights are respected. The UN and other international nonprofit agencies, such as Amnesty International, work to track and publicize human rights violations. They also encourage people to work toward a world in which liberty and justice are available for all.

The American Civil Rights Movement The people of the United States made greater commitments to ensuring basic human rights, especially political rights, to its citizens through the civil rights movement. The **civil rights movement** was a grassroots effort by African Americans to fight discrimination and to make sure all citizens received their rights guaranteed by the U.S. Constitution. During the 1960s, the movement focused on eliminating legal segregation between African Americans and whites. Another goal was to fully empower African Americans with the right to vote and with equal public education.

During the 1950s and 1960s, thousands of Americans, both African Americans and others, organized groups and worked to change the conditions in the United States. One of the best-known leaders of the civil rights movement was Dr. Martin Luther King, Jr. Dr. King patterned his movement after Gandhi's in India, using nonviolent demonstrations to bring attention to serious injustices suffered by African Americans.

THINK THROUGH HISTORY
B. Clarifying How does the Dalai Lama think the world's religions could help world security?
B. Possible Answer They could facilitate discussions that would aid in bringing harmony to the relations between peoples.

Background
A nonbinding agreement means a nation does not suffer a penalty if it does not meet the terms of the declaration.

After King's assassination in 1968, people of all races and creeds continued to work to eliminate discrimination in employment, housing, and other key areas of life. The civil rights movement fueled the development of other equal rights movements by Native Americans, Hispanics, women, and people with disabilities.

Women's Status Improves
The women's rights movement grew along with the civil rights movement in the late 1950s and early 1960s. When women in Western nations entered the work force, they often met with discrimination in employment and salary. In non-Western countries, many women not only faced discrimination in jobs, they were denied access to education. In regions torn by war or ethnic conflict, they were often victims of violence and abuse. As women suffered, so also did their family members, especially children.

However, in the 1970s, with a heightened awareness of human rights, women in various parts of the world worked to improve their lives through changes in laws and government policies. In 1975, the United Nations held the first of several international conferences on women's status in the world. The fourth conference was held in Beijing, China, in 1995. It addressed such issues as preventing violence against women and empowering women to take leadership roles in politics and in business.

One of the most highly respected activists who attended the Beijing conference was the Albanian missionary Mother Teresa. She devoted her life to caring for the poor and sick. In 1979, Mother Teresa was awarded the Nobel Peace Prize for her efforts on behalf of the homeless on the streets of Calcutta, India. Although she died in 1997, her mission continues to reach more than 25 countries worldwide.

Global Movement of People

Migration is a worldwide phenomenon that has increased in size and scope. Each year poverty, war, drought, famine, and political violence affect millions of people. To escape these life-threatening problems, many people leave their homes and migrate to other countries. Wealthy people sometimes migrate as well. In the late 1980s, some businesspeople left Hong Kong, fearing that after the Chinese regained control of the island from the British in 1997, their rights and opportunities would be limited.

Global Interdependence **575**

THINK THROUGH HISTORY
C. Making Inferences How are civil rights and women's rights related?
C. Possible Answer Both are a part of fundamental human rights.

HISTORY MAKERS

Dr. Martin Luther King, Jr.
1929–1968
Nobel Peace Prize 1964

Dr. Martin Luther King, Jr.'s moving speeches and his commitment to active, nonviolent protest inspired people around the world. He urged them to work to end racial discrimination and toward obtaining full and equal rights for all. In his famous "I Have a Dream" speech, King urged his followers, *"Now* is the time to lift our nation from the quicksands of racial injustice to the solid rock of brotherhood."

King achieved many successes as he led a nationwide movement, organizing marches and sit-ins to demand equal justice before the law. In 1964 and 1965, the U.S. federal government passed laws protecting civil and voting rights.

During the civil rights struggles, Dr. King's home was dynamited and he and his family faced death threats. He was assassinated on April 4, 1968, in Memphis, Tennessee.

Rigoberta Menchú
1959–
Nobel Peace Prize 1992

Violence is no stranger to Guatemala's Rigoberta Menchú. Her brother was burned to death. Her father was killed by hand grenades while leading a peaceful sit-in. Her mother was kidnapped and killed by Guatemalan soldiers.

These wrongs against her family made Rigoberta Menchú more dedicated to preventing human rights abuses of her people, Maya Indians. Beginning in the late 1970s, she helped set up community organizations to speak for Indian rights. She organized marches and protests against unfair government actions.

Francis Sejersted, who presented the Nobel Prize, stated, "By maintaining a disarming humanity in a brutal world, Rigoberta Menchú appeals to the best in us. She stands as a uniquely potent symbol of a just struggle."

Faced with repeated death threats, Menchú now lives in Mexico.

HISTORY MAKERS
Dr. Martin Luther King, Jr.

In 1955, the American South was strictly segregated. Activists in Montgomery, Alabama, asked King, a young Baptist minister, to lead the African-American community in a boycott of the city bus system. King took up the challenge, beginning his leadership role in the civil rights movement. The Montgomery bus boycott ultimately was successful, though it lasted more than a year. Suggest that interested students research this boycott and other actions King led. Encourage them to make a time line of his contributions to civil rights.

Rigoberta Menchú

Rigoberta Menchú has been tireless in seeking to end discrimination and violent attacks against the Mayas. She has advocated a variety of protest methods, however, not just peaceful ones. For this reason, her receiving the Nobel Peace Prize has aroused some controversy. Suggest that students do more in-depth research on Menchú or King, either as a separate project or in conjunction with the Cooperative Activity on page 954.

 IN-DEPTH RESOURCES: UNIT 5
History Makers: Rigoberta Menchú, p. 70

OBJECTIVE 4 INSTRUCT

Global Movement of People

▶ *Key Ideas*
• Worldwide migration increases as people respond to harsh political, economic, or environmental conditions.
• Immigrants include people from every social class.
• Mass migration causes problems, but can also be a positive force for cultural understanding.

 CRITICAL THINKING TRANSPARENCIES
CT36 Patterns of Refugee Movement

TEACHING OPTIONS

CUSTOMIZING FOR SPECIAL NEEDS

Less Proficient Readers To help students understand the causes that led to an improvement in the status of women, suggest that they make a concept web such as this. Suggest that they summarize the information in each sentence as they read and enter it in the web. Students should add circles to their webs as necessary and draw lines to connect related concepts.

Women's status improves

 CRITICAL THINKING TRANSPARENCIES
CT78 Concept Web

MULTIPLE LEARNING STYLES

Interpersonal Learners Divide students into small groups and encourage them to discuss why people might come to the United States. Ask them to talk about conditions in countries they have visited or heard about, why people they know chose to migrate to the United States, and how those people have adjusted to life in this country. Ask students to indicate how these experiences reinforce or contradict the generalizations mentioned in the text, such as that people often feel pushed out of their homelands or pulled to better opportunities in other countries.

Teacher's Edition **575**

Section 3 Assessment

Have students work in pairs to answer question 1. Then have two pairs work together to answer question 2. Ask students to complete questions 3 and 4 as a class.

Section Quiz

FORMAL ASSESSMENT
Section Quiz, p. 251

Reteaching Activity

CLASS TIME: 15 MINUTES

List the phrases *collective security, ethnic conflicts, human rights,* and *global migration* on the board. Divide the class into four groups and assign each group to present the main ideas about one of these issues to the class. Then ask students to use their answer to question 3 as a basis for discussing how the four issues are interrelated.

CLASS TIME: 15 MINUTES

Ask students to stage a debate between the leaders of a developed nation with nuclear weapons and a developing nation. Have them address the benefits and drawbacks of nuclear nonproliferation. Ask the class to vote on the most persuasive ideas presented.

Push-Pull Factors Migration sometimes takes place because people feel pushed out of their homelands. Lack of food due to drought, natural disasters, and political oppression are examples of push factors. Between 1976 and 1996, the number of refugees—people who leave their country to move to another to find safety—grew from under 3 million to almost 20 million yearly.

Not only negative events push people to migrate. Most people have strong connections to their home countries and don't leave unless strong positive attractions pull them away. They hope for a better life for themselves and for their children, and thus migrate to developed nations. For example, hundreds of thousands of people migrate from Africa to Europe and from Latin America to the United States every year. Sometimes the poorest people migrate, but often educated middle-class people migrate.

Effects of Immigration Immigration has both negative and positive effects on the countries receiving new people. Countries generally receive two types of immigrants—political refugees and migrants who come for economic reasons. Although a person has the right to leave a country, the country receiving the migrant does not have to accept that person. The receiving country may have one policy about accepting refugees from political situations, and another about migrants coming for economic reasons. Because of the huge volume of people migrating from war-torn, famine-stricken, and politically unstable regions, millions of immigrants have no place to go. Crowded into refugee camps under squalid conditions, immigrants face a very uncertain future. The cost of supporting these camps may cause political problems and may raise issues of prejudice and discrimination.

On the positive side, immigrants are often a valuable addition to the country where they move. They help offset labor shortages in a variety of industries. They bring experiences and knowledge that can spur the economy. In addition, they contribute to the sharing, shaping, and blending of a newly enriched culture.

Cuban boat people plead for help from a helicopter about 50 miles from Key West, Florida. Some left Cuba because of political differences, while others were looking for a better economic future.

THINK THROUGH HISTORY
D. Analyzing Causes List the push and pull factors that cause people to migrate.
D. Possible Answers Push—natural disasters, political problems, lack of food. Pull—economic reasons, hope for a better life, political freedom.

Section ③ Assessment

1. TERMS & NAMES
Identify
• Nuclear Non-Proliferation Treaty
• proliferation
• terrorism
• fundamentalism
• Universal Declaration of Human Rights
• civil rights movement

2. TAKING NOTES
Using a chart like the one below, list collective methods employed by the nations of the world to increase world security. Give examples.

Method	Examples
1. Form military alliances	NATO, SEATO, Warsaw Pact
2.	
3.	

3. IDENTIFYING PROBLEMS
How are ethnic and religious conflicts related to problems of global security?

THINK ABOUT
• current conflicts
• political/ideological tactics of groups
• immigration

4. ANALYZING THEMES
Science and Technology In what ways have advances in science and technology increased threats to global security?

THINK ABOUT
• the destructive capability of one nuclear weapon
• the ability of less-powerful nations to produce biological or chemical weapons
• the ability to move easily across international borders

576 Chapter 20

ANSWERS

1. TERMS & NAMES
Nuclear Non-Proliferation Treaty, p. 573
proliferation, p. 573
terrorism, p. 573
fundamentalism, p. 573
Universal Declaration of Human Rights, p. 574
civil rights movement, p. 574

2. TAKING NOTES
Possible Responses: Reduce threats of war: UN formed
Promote world peace: UN peacekeeping missions
Control weapons: Nuclear Non-Proliferation Treaty; Strategic Arms Reduction Treaties

3. IDENTIFYING PROBLEMS
Possible Responses: People involved in ethnic and religious conflicts may use terrorist tactics to get attention. These conflicts often endanger the security of neighboring nations. Immigrants from troubled areas can present security problems to their host nations.

4. ANALYZING THEMES
Possible Responses: The technical ease of making biological or chemical weapons makes less-powerful nations able to be more aggressive and threaten security. Rapid transportation allows easy movement of terrorists or armies across international borders.

4 Cultures Blend in a Global Age

TERMS & NAMES
• popular culture
• materialism
• accommodation

MAIN IDEA

Technology has increased contact among the world's people, changing their cultures.

WHY IT MATTERS NOW

Globalization of culture has changed the ways people live, their perceptions, and their interactions.

SETTING THE STAGE Since the beginnings of civilization, people of every culture have blended ideas and ways of doing things from other cultures into their own culture. The same kind of cultural sharing and blending continues today. But it occurs at a much more rapid pace and among people at much wider distances than ever was common in the past.

The Sharing of Cultures Accelerates

The speed and breadth of today's cultural exchanges is due to advances in technology. Twentieth-century technologies allow people from all over the world to have increasing contact with one another. Such contacts promote widespread sharing of cultures.

Cultural elements that reflect a group's common background and changing interests are called popular culture. **Popular culture** involves music, sports, movies, clothing fashions, foods, and hobbies or leisure activities. Popular culture around the world incorporates features originating in many different lands. Of all the technologies that contribute to cultural sharing, television, movies, and other media have been the most powerful.

Television and Mass Media More people in the United States have televisions than telephones. In fact, 98 percent of American households have televisions. Eighty-eight percent of the homes have videocassette recorders (VCRs). In Europe, too, the vast majority of households include one or more televisions. The percentages are lower for developing nations. Nevertheless, in many of these countries, the television is a family's most cherished or most wished-for possession.

Television provides a window to the world through daily newscasts and documentaries. The speed at which information about other parts of the world is presented helps create an up-to-the-minute shared experience of global events. For example, in 1991, millions of television viewers across the world watched the waging of the Persian Gulf War. Wars, natural disasters, and political drama in faraway places become a part of everyday life.

Television and other mass media, including radio and movies, are among the world's most popular forms of entertainment. Popular programs not only entertain but also show how people live and what they value in other parts of the world. Mass media is the major way popular culture spreads to all parts of the globe.

A family in Afghanistan enjoys watching cartoons on the family TV.

Global Interdependence **577**

Section 4 Overview

OBJECTIVES

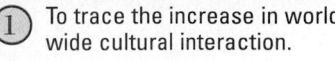 To trace the increase in world-wide cultural interaction.

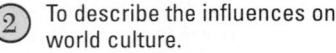 To describe the influences on world culture.

 To explain cultural bias and to explore possibilities for cultural understanding.

CRITICAL THINKING

• Recognizing effects, pp. 578, 581
• Summarizing, pp. 579, 580
• Making inferences, p. 579
• Analyzing issues, p. 581

FOCUS
5-Minute Warm-Up

Perceiving Effects
To help students understand global popular culture, have them answer these questions.

• Look at the Global Impact feature on pages 578 and 579. What types of music influenced the Beatles and the Rolling Stones?

• Which elements of American culture have been influenced by other cultures?

 WARM-UP TRANSPARENCY 20

OBJECTIVE ① INSTRUCT

The Sharing of Cultures Accelerates

▶ ***Key Ideas***
• Advanced technology connects people from all over the world.
• Television and other mass media help spread popular culture.
• Popular culture is now an international phenomenon.

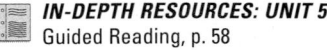 *IN-DEPTH RESOURCES: UNIT 5*
Guided Reading, p. 58

 ACCESS FOR STUDENTS ACQUIRING ENGLISH
Guided Reading (Spanish), p. 219

SECTION 4 RESOURCES

PRINT RESOURCES

IN-DEPTH RESOURCES: UNIT 5
Guided Reading, p. 58
Primary Source: "Cupid's a Korean Computer," p. 65

ACCESS FOR STUDENTS ACQUIRING ENGLISH
Guided Reading (Spanish), p. 219

FORMAL ASSESSMENT
Section Quiz, p. 252

ALTERNATIVE ASSESSMENT BOOK

TECHNOLOGY RESOURCES

WORLD ART AND CULTURES TRANSPARENCIES
AT80 *Technology* (Korean video sculpture)

CRITICAL THINKING TRANSPARENCIES
CT72 Visual Summary

CD-ROM
Electronic Library of Primary Sources

VIDEO
Patterns of Interaction: Cultural Crossroads

International Elements of Popular Culture The entertainment field, especially television, has a massive influence on popular culture. People from around the world are avid viewers of American TV programs. In India, *M°A°S°H* reruns are a huge hit. One U.S. business consultant conducted a meeting on cotton plantations in a remote part of northern China. The consultant said the 22 managers attending excused themselves at six o'clock in the evening and returned about an hour later. The American thought the farmers might have had other visitors or another important meeting to attend. When asked, they replied, "No. It was *Dallas* [a rerun of a famous 1980s evening soap opera] on television."

Broadcasts of international sporting events and the popularity of many team sports have found fans of soccer, cycling, and basketball all over the globe. Some figures from these sports attain worldwide fame. For example, a survey of teens in 44 countries of the world revealed that 93 percent recognized the Chicago Bulls logo. Broadcasts of the Olympics attract audiences of over 200 million from around the world.

Music is another aspect of popular culture that has become international. As the equipment for listening to music has become more portable, there are only a few places in the world that do not have access to music from other cultures. People from around the world dance to reggae bands from the Caribbean, chant rap lyrics from the United States, play air guitar to rowdy European bands, and enjoy the fast drumming of Afropop tunes. They might even sing to any of this music using a karaoke machine, which comes from Japan. Recording artists and groups often gain international fame.

Global Impact: Cultural Crossroads

Rock 'n' Roll

In the middle of the 1950s, a new style of music emerged on the American scene. It was called rock 'n' roll. The music explored social and political themes. Rock music, which seemed to adults to reflect a youth rebellion, soon became the dominant popular music for young people across the world. As the influence of rock music spread, international artists added their own traditions, instruments, and musical styles to the mix called rock.

"Rock and roll music, if you like it and you feel it, you just can't help but move to it. That's what happens to me, I can't help it."—Elvis

During the 1950s and 1960s, Elvis Presley was called the King of American Rock 'n' Roll.

578

Mick Jagger of the Rolling Stones was part of the "British Invasion." The "British Invasion" was a term for the innovations brought to rock by British bands. The enormously popular Beatles and the enduring Rolling Stones were heavily influenced by American rhythm & blues. For example, the Rolling Stones took their name from a song lyric done by American blues musician, writer, and performer Muddy Waters.

World Culture Blends Many Influences

Greater access to the ideas and customs of different cultures often results in cultural blending. As cultural ideas move with people among cultures, some beliefs and habits seem to have a greater effect than others. In the 20th century, ideas from the West have been very dominant in shaping cultures in many parts of the globe.

Westernizing Influences on Different Cultures
Western domination of the worldwide mass media helps explain the huge influence the West has on many different cultures today. However, heavy Western influence on the rest of the world's cultures is rooted in the 19th century. Western domination of areas all over the globe left behind a legacy of Western customs and ideas. Western languages are spoken throughout the world, mainly because of Europe's history of colonization in the Americas, Asia, and Africa.

Over the past 50 years, English has emerged as the premier international language. English is spoken by about 500 million people as their first or second language. Although more people speak Mandarin Chinese than English, English speakers are more widely distributed. English is the most common language used on the Internet and at international conferences. The language is used by scientists, diplomats, doctors, and businesspeople around the world. The widespread use of English is responsible, in part, for the emergence of a dynamic global culture.

Western influence can be seen in other aspects of popular culture. For example, blue jeans are the clothes of choice of most of the world's youth. Western business

Little Leaguers celebrate a win. Each year the League has a World Series. During the 1970s teams from Taiwan dominated the series.

Background
There are approximately 836 million Mandarin Chinese speakers.

The multicultural South African band Juluka blends sounds from traditional African instruments along with styles of American rock and sings in English and Zulu.

Patterns of Interaction

The spread of American culture, including sports, fashion, and fast food, has created an international culture recognizable in all corners of the globe. In some cases American culture is simply a powerful influence, as other societies blend American culture with local customs. Cultural blending is evident even in America's past. Symbols of American culture like baseball and hot dogs are themselves the result of cross-cultural influences.

VIDEO *Cultural Crossroads: The United States and the World*

Connect *to* History

Summarizing How have people in other parts of the world changed rock 'n' roll by adopting this American form of popular entertainment?

SEE SKILLBUILDER HANDBOOK, PAGE 650

Connect *to* Today

Making Inferences How have improvements in technology and global communications aided in the blending of musical styles?

Global Interdependence **579**

OBJECTIVE 2 INSTRUCT

World Culture Blends Many Influences

▶ **Key Ideas**
• Colonialism and the widespread use of Western languages lead to a strong Western influence on cultures around the world.
• Non-Western practices such as meditation influence the West.
• The arts, including painting, sculpture, and literature, become increasingly international.

 IN-DEPTH RESOURCES: UNIT 5
Primary Source: "Cupid's a Korean Computer, Making Wise Matches," p. 65

 ELECTRONIC LIBRARY OF PRIMARY SOURCES
"Un-American Ugly Americans"

Viewing the Video

Show *Cultural Crossroads: The United States and the World* to demonstrate how interaction among peoples can affect culture and everyday life.
• The first segment of the video looks at the impact of American popular culture—including music, movies, and food—on other parts of the world.
• The second segment explores the global origins of some "American" traditions, such as baseball and rock 'n' roll. Using the *Teacher's Resource Book* as a guide, have students think about the ways customs spread throughout the world. Discuss recent fads and fashions that have originated in one country and been spread to others. Enrich the lesson with the primary-source and visual-literacy activities included in the book.

 PATTERNS OF INTERACTION
Cultural Crossroads: The United States and the World
Videocassette: Tape 4

Connect *to* History	**Connect *to* Today**	
Summarizing **Possible Answer:** British bands built a unique rock style on the rhythms and sounds of American rhythm & blues. South African musicians melded traditional instruments and languages with American rock styles.	*Making Inferences* **Possible Answer:** Improvements in electronic equipment have given musicians increased versatility and the ability to simulate almost any sound. Modern	communications technology, such as satellite transmission, provides easy access to traditional instruments and modes of expression throughout the world.

suits are standard uniforms among many people. McDonald's hamburgers and Coca-Cola soft drinks can be purchased in many countries of the world. Mickey Mouse and other Disney characters are almost universally recognized. These examples of common dress, food, and entertainment figures all originated in the West and have been picked up and incorporated by other cultures. But Western influence also has an effect on ways of thinking. The Western mindset of placing a high value on acquiring material possessions—**materialism**—has been adopted by people of many different cultures.

Non-Western Influences Travel to the West Cultural ideas are not confined to moving only from the West to other lands. Non-Western cultures also influence people in Europe and the United States. From music and clothing styles, to ideas about art and architecture, to religious and ethical systems, non-Western ideas are incorporated into Western life. The non-Western mindset of placing value on meditation and contemplation has found a home in the West. The world's fastest-growing religion—Islam—comes from non-Western roots. Cultural blending of Western and non-Western elements opens communications channels for the exchange of ideas throughout the globe.

The Arts Become International Modern art, like popular culture, has become increasingly international. Advances in transportation and technology have facilitated the sharing of ideas about art and the sharing of actual works of art. Shows and museums throughout the world exhibit art of different styles and from different places. It became possible to see art from other cultures that had not previously been available to the public. For example, art from the Forbidden City in China or artifacts from Egyptian tombs can be viewed in museums in Europe and the Americas.

Literature, too, has become internationally appreciated. Well-known writers routinely have their works translated into dozens of languages, resulting in truly international audiences. The list of recent Nobel Prize winners in literature reflects a broad variety of writers' nationalities, including Nigerian, Egyptian, Mexican, West Indian, and Japanese.

THINK THROUGH HISTORY
B. Summarizing
Name three advances that allow a greater sharing of the arts.
B. Answer
Technology, improved transportation, widespread translations

Future Challenges and Hopes

As the differences between peoples lessen, some worry about losing their group identity. In some lands the leaders have taken measures to preserve the unique elements of their culture.

Cultural Clashes Fear of the loss of a unique identity as a people or nation may create conflict and clashes within groups. For example, in France in the late 1990s, a bureau of the French government was responsible for removing words from the French language that are believed to corrupt the language. A French official told members of the Higher Council of the French Language that keeping language from the excesses of foreign words was "an act of faith in the future of our country." In a similar vein, recently in the United States, debates raged over the question of making English the exclusive official language of the U.S. government. A poll showed that 73 percent of the population agreed with that position.

In other parts of the world, wearing certain kinds of clothing, such as short skirts or jeans, is forbidden because it represents an intrusion of other cultures. Elsewhere, mass media is strictly censored to keep unwanted ideas from entering the land.

Sometimes groups respond to the influence of other cultures by trying to return to traditional ways. Cultural practices and rites of passage may receive even more emphasis as a group tries to preserve its identity. In some countries, native groups take an active role in preserving the traditional ways of life. For example, tribal groups, such as the Maori in New

Background
Twenty-two states have enacted English-only laws.

Zealand, have revived ancestral customs rather than face cultural extinction. Many Maori cultural activities are conducted in a way that preserves Maori ways of thinking and behaving. In 1987, the Maori language was made an official language of New Zealand.

Even when a nation does not have serious concerns about the impact of other cultures, it may struggle with questions of accommodation. **Accommodation** is the level of acceptance of ideas from another culture. Charles Mann, a journalist, describes the feelings of uncertainty that questions of accommodation raise.

A Samburu warrior in Kenya uses a cellular phone to stay in contact with others in his group.

A VOICE FROM THE PAST
As human . . . patterns look more and more alike . . . that unique place becomes ever harder to find. Things feel scary; people hunker down. Some retreat into their dialects, others into their national clothes, others into religion or guns. Even as the world unifies, its constituent parts fragment.

CHARLES MANN, *The Material World: A Global Family Portrait*

Global Interdependence Despite the uncertainty accompanying global interdependence, economic, political, and environmental issues do bring all nations closer together. Nations have begun to recognize that they are dependent on other nations and deeply affected by the actions of others far away. As elements of everyday life and expressions of culture become more international in scope, people across the world gain a sense of oneness with people in other areas of the world. Responses to events such as flooding in Bangladesh were international in scope. Nations from around the world sent assistance. It was as if the flooding had happened in their own country.

Technology has changed the way people, businesses, and nations view the world. Restricting cultural change is now very unlikely except in a few isolated locations.

Throughout history, human beings have faced challenges to survive and to live better. In the 21st century, these challenges will be faced by people who are in increasing contact with one another. They have a greater stake in learning to live in harmony together and with the physical planet. As Dr. Martin Luther King, Jr., stated, "Our loyalties must transcend our race, our tribe, our class, and our nation; and this means we must develop a world perspective."

Section 4 Assessment

1. TERMS & NAMES
Identify
• popular culture
• materialism
• accommodation

2. TAKING NOTES
Draw a diagram like the one below and give details that illustrate the areas of popular culture that have become very international.

International popular culture

Which of the international popular culture aspects has the greatest effect on your life? Write a paragraph to explain why.

3. ANALYZING ISSUES
You have just immigrated to the United States. You are anxious to "fit in" in your new home but don't want to lose aspects of your former culture. What do you accept about the new culture and what do you retain of your birth culture?

THINK ABOUT
• elements of your birth culture you wish to maintain, adapt, or leave behind
• practical and day-to-day concerns
• feelings about your identity

4. THEME ACTIVITY
Cultural Interaction Look at the pictures in this section and those on the opening pages of this chapter. They show types of cultural blending. Study current newspapers and magazines to see if you can find examples similar to the pictures shown. Create a scrapbook of pictures you have found. Write a caption for each picture illustrating cultural blending.

Global Interdependence **581**

ANSWERS

Chapter 20 Assessment

TERMS & NAMES

1. genetic engineering, p. 563
2. green revolution, p. 564
3. global economy, p. 567
4. free trade, p. 567
5. Gulf War, p. 569
6. sustainable development, p. 570
7. terrorism, p. 573
8. fundamentalism, p. 573
9. civil rights movement, p. 574
10. popular culture, p. 577

REVIEW QUESTIONS

Answers may vary.

11. Satellites and computers link the globe in a worldwide communications network; they have made it possible for people to work in home offices, improved health diagnoses and treatment, and led to new and better food crops.

12. To increase the available food sources worldwide.

13. A developed nation has all the necessary facilities to produce and manufacture goods. A developing nation is a nation that may have natural and human resources but is still industrializing.

14. South Korea, Taiwan, Hong Kong, Singapore. They are all east Asian nations that grew rapidly after World War II and that have become major trading and economic centers affecting global markets.

15. The World Trade Organization was created to establish standards for and monitor world trade. It was an extension of the GATT agreements.

16. Banded together to form military alliances, supported the United Nations' peacekeeping efforts, controlled the spread of weapons through treaties.

17. Religious and ethnic strife underlie many recent wars and hostilities in the Middle East, Northern Ireland, and the former nation of Yugoslavia. Such conflicts often inspire terrorist activities and create huge numbers of immigrants and refugees.

18. The United Nations issued a Universal Declaration of Human Rights; the American civil rights movement arose to ensure that all citizens, including women and persons with disabilities, received basic rights guaranteed under the U.S. Constitution. In general, the status of women has improved worldwide.

TERMS & NAMES

Briefly explain the importance of each of the following to global interdependence from 1960 to the present.

1. genetic engineering
2. green revolution
3. global economy
4. free trade
5. Gulf War
6. sustainable development
7. terrorism
8. fundamentalism
9. civil rights movement
10. popular culture

Interact *with* History

After reading Chapter 20, do you believe events in other nations affect your life? Which kinds of events are more likely to affect you in a very personal way? Create a survey about global interdependence to ask students in your class or school. Consider asking questions about such things as clothing produced in places outside the United States, international phone calls, or travel to foreign countries.

REVIEW QUESTIONS

SECTION 1 *(pages 561–564)*
Science and Technology Shape Human Outlook

11. In what ways have science and technology changed the lives of people today?

12. What was the goal of the green revolution?

SECTION 2 *(pages 565–570)*
Global Economic Development

13. Explain the difference between a developed nation and a developing nation.

14. Who are the "Four Tigers," and what is significant about their development as major trading nations?

15. Why was the World Trade Organization founded?

SECTION 3 *(pages 572–576)*
Global Security Issues

16. What methods has the world community used to resolve conflicts since World War II?

17. How have religious and ethnic conflicts threatened global security?

18. Describe worldwide efforts to guarantee basic human rights.

SECTION 4 *(pages 577–581)*
Cultures Blend in a Global Age

19. Which technologies have had the most powerful impact on cultural sharing?

20. What explains why Western influences have had a major impact all over the world?

Visual Summary

Global Interdependence

Economics
- Service industries grow in developed nations.
- Free trade expands world markets.
- Environmental challenges continue.

Culture
- Mass media spreads many cultures.
- Pop culture becomes more international.
- Global interdependence awareness develops.

Science and Technology
- Space cooperation stretches horizons.
- Advanced communications allow wider contact.
- Inventions improve life and health.

Politics
- Nations take collective security actions.
- Human rights improve worldwide.
- Immigrants change cultures.

582 Chapter 20

19. TV, movies, the Internet, and other mass media.

20. Western domination and colonization in the 19th century had lasting effects. English continues to serve as an international language. Western popular culture has been widely accepted.

Interact *with* History

Students should recognize the effects of global events on their lives. They should describe the events that most affect them and explain what effect the events have had. For example, have the events changed the music students listen to, the food they eat, the clothes they wear? Or have events changed the way they think, see the world, or look at themselves? Encourage students to recognize the influence of global interdependence in their everyday lives.

CRITICAL THINKING

1. CHANGING LIVES

Using the cause-effect diagram below, show how advances in science and technology created changes in lifestyles.

Cause	Effect
Miniaturization of computer parts	→
Expanded global communication	→
Genetic research	→

2. INTERNATIONAL COOPERATION

THEME CULTURAL INTERACTION Reread the quote at the top of page 569 by the international commission. Do you agree or disagree with this statement? In what ways can developed nations assist developing nations?

3. THE GLOBAL INDIVIDUAL

In what ways are individual persons affected by the global economy and threats to the environment? Be specific.

4. ANALYZING PRIMARY SOURCES

The following passage was written by a German journalist as he reflected on the impact of American culture on the world. Read the passage and answer the questions below it.

> Imagine a roomful of 14-year-olds—from Germany, Japan, Israel, Russia and Argentina. Obviously, they would all be wearing Levi's and baseball caps. But how would they relate to one another? They would communicate in English, though haltingly and with heavy accents. About what? . . . They would debate the merits of Nike versus Converse, of Chameleon versus Netscape. Sure, they would not discuss Herman Melville or George Gershwin, but neither would they compare notes on Dante or Thomas Mann. The point is that they would talk about icons and images "made in the U.S.A."
>
> **JOSEF JOFFE**, in "America the Inescapable"

- Identify the aspects of popular culture mentioned by Mr. Joffe.
- Why would this group of teenagers communicate in English?
- How would these teenagers learn about American culture?

CHAPTER ACTIVITIES

1. LIVING HISTORY: Unit Portfolio Project

THEME ECONOMICS Your unit portfolio project focuses on how economic factors influence history. For Chapter 20, you might use one of the following ideas to add to your portfolio.

- Write a poem or song about the impact the global economy has on the environment.
- With a classmate create a map showing worldwide locations of manufacturing plants controlled by multinational corporations such as IBM, Ford, or Coca-Cola.
- Do some research to find out how the availability of jobs in the developed and developing countries influences the migration of people in various parts of the world. Construct graphs or charts to illustrate your findings.

2. CONNECT TO TODAY: Cooperative Learning

THEME SCIENCE AND TECHNOLOGY Science and technology continue to bring the world new ideas and inventions. These have resulted in greater global interaction and an improved quality of life.

Work with a team to create a 15-minute "special news segment" on the latest advances in science and technology and how they currently (or are expected to) affect everyday life.

 Using the Internet, magazines, or a local museum, research current products, new technologies, and new ideas.

- Divide your group so that each of the following categories has a representative: correspondents, scientists, corporate or government executives.
- Videotape or present the segment in class.

3. INTERPRETING A TIME LINE

Revisit the unit time line on pages 470–471. Look at the section that relates to Chapter 20. What events have occurred since the development of this time line that you think should be included to bring it up to date? Explain

FOCUS ON GRAPHS

Millions of people become refugees each year as the result of poverty, wars, political problems, and environmental disasters.

- Which area has had the largest increase in the number of refugees in the time period shown?
- In which years did Africa experience sharp increases in refugees?
- How many more total refugees were there in 1992 than in 1976?

Connect to History In which year did Europe experience a dramatic increase in refugees? What effect might this have on the nations of Europe?

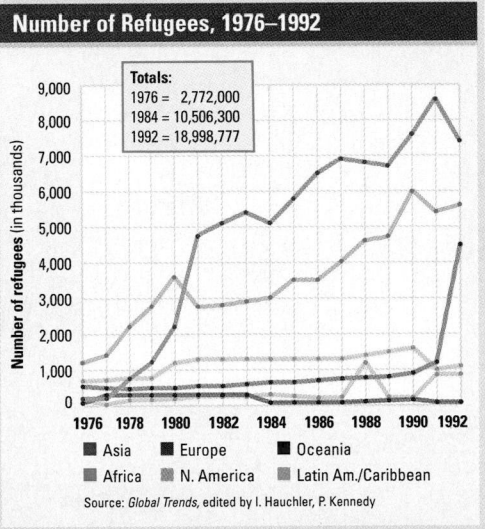

Number of Refugees, 1976–1992

Totals:
1976 = 2,772,000
1984 = 10,506,300
1992 = 18,998,777

■ Asia ■ Europe ■ Oceania
■ Africa ■ N. America ■ Latin Am./Caribbean

Source: *Global Trends*, edited by I. Hauchler, P. Kennedy

Global Interdependence **583**

CHAPTER ACTIVITIES

1. LIVING HISTORY

Standards for Evaluation
A poem or song should meet the following criteria:

- Clearly states an opinion about the effect of the global economy on the environment.
- Includes poetic and lyric elements such as rhythm, rhyme, and repetition.

Standards for Evaluation
A map should meet the following criteria:

- Focuses on one or more multinational companies.
- Includes a key that clearly identifies each company.
- Reflects each company's activity throughout the world.
- Includes a written explanation and summary of the data.

Standards for Evaluation
A graph or chart should meet the following criteria:

- Shows evidence of outside research.
- Identifies the countries chosen and the units used to report data on immigration and jobs.
- Organizes and presents information clearly.
- Includes a written interpretation of the graphic information.

2. CONNECT TO TODAY: COOPERATIVE LEARNING

Standards for Evaluation
A news segment should meet the following criteria:

- Focuses on one or two technological advances.
- Includes opinions about each advance from scientists, executives, and consumers to present a variety of responses.
- Is organized into a coherent videotaped or live presentation.

3. INTERPRETING A TIME LINE

Answers will vary, but should include technological, social, political, or ecological advances that have an impact on the world.

CRITICAL THINKING

1. CHANGING LIVES
Possible Responses: Miniaturization of computers led to information revolution in industry and home computers; expanded global communications equipment led to internationalization of culture; genetics research led to green revolution, genetic engineering, disease detection.

2. INTERNATIONAL COOPERATION
Agree—If a country does not have ample resources or wealth, political turmoil may affect the world economy. Disagree—The strongest will survive. Developed nations can help by ensuring that developing nations have access to resources and education, and by offering military, economic, and medical aid.

3. THE GLOBAL INDIVIDUAL
Possible Responses: Jobs and the cost of living are tied to the world economy; health depends on air, food, and water quality, which is affected by industrial pollution.

4. ANALYZING PRIMARY SOURCES
Clothing, language, communications technology; many students learn English as a second language; mass media such as TV, Internet, magazines, and movies have spread American culture.

FOCUS ON GRAPHS

- Asia; 1980; 1990
- 16,226,777 more refugees

CONNECT TO HISTORY 1992; The presence of these refugees might put extreme social and economic pressure on the countries in which they settled. The host countries would have to try to provide for the newcomers and integrate them into their societies.

Teacher's Edition **583**

Epilogue: Unresolved Problems of the Modern World

Accessing Prior Knowledge

• Ask students what they recall from Unit 5. What were the most important issues covered in that chapter?

• Based on the issues that were covered in Unit 5, have students predict what issues will be dealt with in the Epilogue. Have them debate whether the issues raised in Unit 5 will also be the most important issues the world will face in the 21st century.

Analyzing

• Ask a volunteer to read the quotation aloud. Engage students in a discussion of what they think Galsworthy meant with this quotation. Students can debate whether they think the quotation is true and talk about what they think about the future.

EPILOGUE

Unresolved Problems of the Modern World

"If you do not think about the future, you cannot have one."

John Galsworthy, 1928

The spread of weapons has contributed to warfare in many places around the world, including central Africa. This Red Cross worker in **Rwanda** walks between two columns of Hutu refugees fleeing war in **November 1996**.

GEOGRAPHY THEMES

Place

Have students read the caption about the Rwandan refugees. War and drought have contributed to the great misery faced by many of the people of this region. As students read the chapter, have them consider how the climate of central Africa has contributed to the problems of the people of this region.

Human/Environment Interaction

Ask students to read the information about the woman with the geese. Discuss what this farming practice shows about human interactions with the environment. Students might mention food production, soil depletion, and the elimination of agricultural pests. Let students talk about different ways people can produce more food. Students might address such issues as the use of fertilizers and pesticides, water quality, soil erosion, and conservation of resources.

ADDITIONAL RESOURCES

Books for the Teacher

• Commission on Global Governance. *Our Global Neighborhood.* Oxford: Oxford UP, 1995.

• Hauchler, Ingomar and Paul M. Kennedy. *Global Trends: The World Almanac of Development and Peace.* New York: Continuum, 1994.

• Weiss, John. *Economic Policy in Developing Countries.* London. Prentice Hall/Harvester Wheatsheaf, 1995.

Books for the Student

• Milbrath, Lester W. *Learning to Think Environmentally.* Albany: State U of New York P, 1996.

• Petersen, John L. *The Road to 2015.* Carte Madera, California: The Waite Group, 1994.

• Wiener, Brad and David Pescovitz. *Reality Check.* San Francisco: Hardwired, 1996.

HISTORY THROUGH ART

Technology and Art

Technology has always had a great impact on life and culture, including art. Almost all art forms have been changed in one way or another by new technologies. Literature became increasingly available after the invention of the printing press. Audio recordings and electronic amplification changed the way people listened to music as well as the way that music sounded.

Computer technology has been creating new directions for visual arts in the late 20th century. The background image on pages 584–585 is a computer-generated map. It shows the outlines of the earth's land masses in black. The areas where large numbers of people live are covered with white dots that look like stars. The denser the population, the closer the dots and the brighter the image. The stars in the oceans merely add to the impression of a starry night.

Interpreting the Art Ask students how this image makes them feel about their place on the earth. What impression does the stark black/white contrast give? Might computers be used to manipulate other images—such as any of the photographs in this Epilogue—to give them a stronger visual effect?

Interact *with* History

This Interact with History feature motivates students by challenging them to analyze the fears Americans had for the future in 1972 and to compare them to people's current hopes and fears for the future. Students should draw conclusions about the similarities and differences between people's views of the world in 1972 and today.

Purpose

- to give students a broad overview of worldwide issues
- to stimulate student thinking about the challenges of our modern world
- to motivate students to consider different solutions for current world problems

Teaching Strategy

Thinking Critically After students have completed their polls, have them make pie graphs to compare their results with those of other groups and with those presented on this page. Students should display their results and evaluate them as a class.

EXAMINING *the* ISSUES

Following are suggestions for addressing each bulleted question.

1 Direct students to look at the graph of people's fears as they start making a list of threats to world peace and stability. Then have them brainstorm to add any other possibilities to the list.

2 Have students define technology in their own words. Make a class list of ways that technology has been used to try to solve different global problems.

3 Ask students to make their own lists of organizations that are working to solve different problems facing the world.

Making Connections Ask students how they think people in different parts of the world might respond to the questions about their hopes and fears for the future. What fears might people in different regions have in common?

Interact *with* History

Much has been done in recent years to improve life for the people of the world. In spite of this progress, many unresolved problems remain. People around the world hope to solve these problems, but they also fear that many of the problems will continue to exist. In 1972, the Gallup organization took a poll to find out the hopes and fears that Americans had for the future. The charts below show the results of that poll. Now it is your turn to take a poll to find out the hopes and fears that people today have for the 21st century.

HOPES

End to drug abuse (4%)
End of pollution (3%)
World peace (31%)
International cooperation (4%)
To lead a useful life (4%)
Return to religion (5%)
Social justice (6%)
Safety from crime (6%)
Other (37%) includes improved economy, solutions to social problems, solutions to international problems

FEARS

Overpopulation (3%)
Threats by communist powers (3%)
Racial problems (3%)
Social injustice (4%)
Religious decline (5%)
Youth rebellion (2%)
War/Nuclear war (26%)
None (6%)
Pollution (6%)
Drug abuse (9%)
Crime (9%)
Other (24%) includes economic insecurity, persistent social problems, world problems

What hopes and fears do you have about the future?

EXAMINING *the* ISSUES

- What are some of the most serious threats to peace and well-being on the planet?

- How might technology be used to help solve some of the world's problems?

- What can organizations, governments, and individuals do to meet the challenges of modern life?

With a group of other students, make a list of questions to ask people about their hopes and fears for the future. After your group collects responses, tally the results and consider how they differ from those of the 1972 Gallup survey.

As you read this chapter, think about the issues raised in this survey and how they might be addressed most effectively.

Follow-Up

A feature on the Epilogue assessment will ask students to compare the results of their poll with the issues discussed in the Epilogue.

1 Technology Changes People's Lives

TERMS & NAMES
- mass media
- biotechnology
- genetic engineering

MAIN IDEA

The rapid emergence of new technologies holds promises as well as challenges for people around the world.

WHY IT MATTERS NOW

Technology has already affected communications and medicine and may help solve other problems.

SETTING THE STAGE For centuries, people have used science to find new ways to do things. But the pace of technological change has increased in the second half of the 20th century. For instance, the development of the silicon chip and other electronic circuits has paved the way for revolutions in electronics and computers. In addition, intensive research in the biological sciences has produced great advances in medicine and even the ability to clone living creatures.

A Revolution in Electronics

New forms of electronic circuits have made possible the production of powerful new machines, such as computers. Computers, along with advances in telecommunications, have greatly changed the way people handle information. They have done so by vastly increasing the speed at which information can be carried.

Background
One of the first computers was built in 1946. It was called ENIAC and weighed more than 30 tons. It was far less powerful than the average desktop computer of today.

The Influence of Computers The earliest and most basic use of computers was computing—figuring out math problems as one would with a pocket calculator. As electronic circuits have grown faster, computers have been able to solve problems ever more quickly. Powerful computers can make billions of computations every second.

The ability to compute quickly makes computers very helpful. They are used to guide rockets and satellites into space. Air traffic controllers use them to track airline traffic.

Computers Around the World

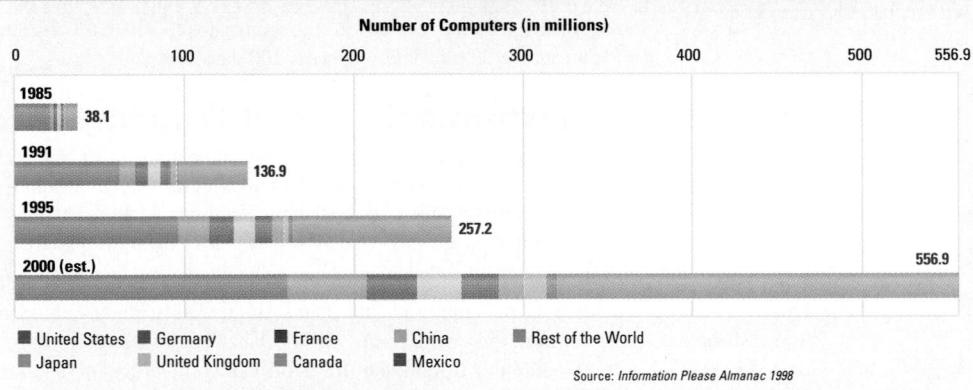

Number of Computers (in millions)

| 0 | 100 | 200 | 300 | 400 | 500 | 556.9 |

- 1985: 38.1
- 1991: 136.9
- 1995: 257.2
- 2000 (est.): 556.9

■ United States ■ Germany ■ France □ China ■ Rest of the World
■ Japan □ United Kingdom ■ Canada ■ Mexico

Source: *Information Please Almanac 1998*

SKILLBUILDER: Interpreting Graphs
1. *What percentage of the computers in the world in 1995 were in the United States?*
2. *What was expected to be the percentage of increase in the total number of computers from 1995 to 2000?*

Unresolved Problems of the Modern World **587**

Section 1 Overview

OBJECTIVES

1. To discuss how computers have spurred advances in many fields and allowed people to communicate more quickly.

2. To list ways that recent technologies have influenced the workplace and global economic issues.

3. To identify how the mass media have affected cultures around the world.

4. To describe how biotechnology has improved health but raised concerns about possible misuses.

SKILLBUILDER
- Interpreting graphs, p. 587

CRITICAL THINKING
- Clarifying, p. 588
- Hypothesizing, pp. 588, 590
- Recognizing effects, p. 589

FOCUS
5-Minute Warm-Up

Perceiving Effects
To introduce students to the idea of technological change, have them read Setting the Stage on page 587 and answer these questions.

1. How does the pace of technological change today compare with that of previous centuries?

2. What are some fields in which great technological advances have occurred?

 WARM-UP TRANSPARENCIES EPILOGUE

OBJECTIVE 1 INSTRUCT

A Revolution in Electronics

▶ *Key Ideas*
- Computers have become more powerful in recent years and are used in a variety of industries.
- People use fax machines, computers, and the Internet to move information around the world quickly.

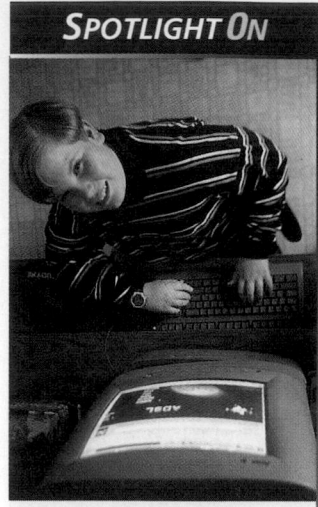

SPOTLIGHT ON

"Chat Room Savior" Sean Redden

On the afternoon of April 14, 1997, Sean Redden, a seventh-grader in Denton, Texas, received a startling message through the Internet: "Help me. I'm having trouble breathing," it read. "I can't get out of my chair." At first, Sean thought the message was a joke. When the pleas continued, though, Sean realized that the emergency was real.

In fact, the writer—Taija Laitinen, a 20-year-old student in Finland, 7,000 miles away—was having a seizure. Sean's mother phoned 911, and after a series of phone calls, Finnish rescue workers found Taija and rushed her to the hospital. Thanks to Sean and the Internet, Taija's life was saved.

Many automobiles use computers to control fuel gauges, engines, and even brakes. Banks and other businesses use computers to keep track of accounts and inventory.

New computers have ever greater capacities to "think." This ability is sometimes called artificial intelligence. In fact, in May 1997, an IBM-built computer named Deep Blue defeated world chess champion Garry Kasparov in a six-game chess match. Some people feared that computers might soon be smart enough to control humans. David Gelernter, a Yale University computer science professor, offered a different opinion:

A VOICE FROM THE PAST
Deep Blue is just a machine. It doesn't have a mind any more than a flowerpot has a mind. . . . It is an intellectual milestone, and its chief meaning is this: that human beings are champion machine builders. . . .

Machines will continue to make life easier, healthier, richer and more puzzling. And human beings will continue to care . . . about the same things they always have: about themselves, about one another and, many of them, about God. On those terms, machines have never made a difference. And they never will.

DAVID GELERNTER, *Time*

THINK THROUGH HISTORY
A. Clarifying Why does David Gelernter think machines will never control humans?

Information Spreads in New Ways Electronic technology has also had a great impact on how people communicate. People are increasing their use of cellular phones, fax machines, and computers—including the Internet—to move information instantly across the planet. As a result, people can conduct business—or just chat—very easily from great distances. These technologies have helped draw the world closer together.

The Internet has become one of the most exciting ways for people to communicate. People can use the Internet to find ever-increasing amounts of information. More and more businesses advertise and sell their goods on the Internet. Governments use the Internet to provide their citizens with more information than ever before. In addition, people around the world can use chat rooms and electronic mail, or e-mail, to send messages to one another. The result has been astounding growth in the popularity of the Internet. In 1993, there were only 50 Internet sites. By 1998, there were too many sites to accurately count, and Internet traffic was doubling every 100 days.

THINK THROUGH HISTORY
B. Hypothesizing How do you think the Internet will affect businesses in the 21st century?

Technology Transforms the World Economy

Electronic technology has led to enormous changes in the world economy. For instance, computer-driven robots now help to make many manufactured goods, such as automobiles. And modern telecommunications allow trade, banking, and financial transactions to be done electronically. Technological changes such as these have had both positive and negative effects on businesses and workers.

The Workplace Changes Rapid communications and data transmission have helped to transform workplaces around the world. Many white-collar workers now "telecommute," or do their jobs by computer from home. Investors can conduct business in any market in the world, from almost anywhere, by using telephones, fax machines, and computers. Television, radio, and the Internet can instantly give investors the news and information they need to conduct business. As a result, some professionals no longer need to live near business offices.

In manufacturing, robots perform more and more jobs that were once done by people. As a result, many companies have cut their workforces. In more technologically advanced economies, employment is shifting from blue-collar industries to high-tech industries. Many workers are being forced to improve their skills in order to keep their jobs because high-tech industries need workers with more technical skills.

Economic Domination High-tech workplaces are found mainly in industrialized countries, such as the United States, Japan, and the countries of western Europe. This technological imbalance has given rise to a new kind of economic imperialism in which the industrialized nations dominate less-developed countries.

Technology helps make the developed countries economically stronger than the less-developed countries. This economic strength gives the developed countries a great deal of control over economic aid and investment in less-developed countries. Technology also gives the developed nations better military equipment with which to influence the behavior of the less-developed countries.

The Mass Media Change Culture

The **mass media**—which include television, radio, movies, the music industry, and the popular press—are also expanding their influence with the growth of technology. As the mass media expand, their role in shaping people's views about the world also increases.

Television Transforms People's Lives Television is now found throughout the world, even in once isolated regions. Mass-produced television sets are now very affordable. In addition, satellites allow television signals to reach all parts of the world.

Television has spread to the extent that billions of people around the planet now watch sporting events such as the Olympics and the World Cup soccer championships. In addition, some 2 billion people worldwide viewed the funeral of Princess Diana of England on live television in 1997.

Popular Culture Spreads Because the media now reach around the world, they are able to spread images, ideas, and fashions from one country to another. Many of these ideas or trends travel from the developed world outward. But the mass media also bring cultural offerings from Africa, Asia, and Latin America to the richer nations. The increased familiarity in Europe and the United States with African music, Asian philosophy, and Latin American literature demonstrates the power of the mass media to promote a greater awareness of and mixing of different cultures. For instance, the English translation of *Como Agua Para Chocolate* (*Like Water for Chocolate*), the novel by Laura Esquivel, sold over two million copies in the United States.

Old Ways Abandoned As mass media spread new images, ideas, and fashions, however, they may cause deep changes in traditional cultures. Old ways may be lost. In some cases, people experience a loss of identity—a sense of their culture or what defines them as a people. Or they may find themselves in conflict over competing values.

Sometimes the challenge posed by new ideas can stimulate the desire to preserve traditions. Technology may even play a positive role in this process. In the Amazon region of Brazil, for example, some native Brazilians are using video cameras to document and preserve traditional ways of life.

The mass media have allowed many forms of popular music to spread around the world. For instance, Guitar Wolf, a Japanese rock band, played at a 1997 music festival in Austin, Texas.

589

Biotechnology Affects Health

▶ **Key Ideas**
- Biotechnology refers to scientific research to find new uses for cells, enzymes, and other biological materials.
- Biotechnology leads to many health improvements.
- Genetic engineering raises hopes for preventing diseases but causes fears about possible misuse.

CRITICAL THINKING ACTIVITY
CLASS TIME: 30 MINUTES

Forming and Supporting Opinions
Stage a debate on the issue of cloning animals. Divide students into small groups. Assign half of the groups to the pro-cloning side and the other half to the anti-cloning side. Have each group do research and then develop their position as clearly and concisely as possible. Select two groups, one from each side, to debate in front of the class. Allow more groups to debate, if time allows. For groups that do not debate, ask them what additional points they would make that were not made previously in the debate.

ASSESS & RETEACH

Section 1 Assessment
Ask students to work in small groups to answer the questions. Then discuss as a class the responses to question 3.

Reteaching Activity
CLASS TIME: 10 MINUTES

Ask volunteers to use the heads to summarize the main content of this section for the class.

CLOSE ACTIVITY

CLASS TIME: 10 MINUTES

Listing Effects
Write the following terms on the board: Computers; Internet; Biotechnology. For each term, have students discuss ways that new technologies related to these terms have directly affected their lives in the past week or month. Write students' answers on the board during the discussion.

Biotechnology Affects Health

Another area in which technology plays an important role is medical and biological research. **Biotechnology** refers to the scientific research performed on biological substances, such as enzymes or cells, in order to find new uses for such substances. These new technologies are having a tremendous impact on the health and welfare of millions of people.

Health Improvements Technological advances have led to the development of highly sophisticated machines to perform procedures such as MRIs, which help in the diagnosis of illnesses. The development of new drugs has helped to fight disease and infant mortality around the world. Researchers are also developing medicines that fight cancer by reducing the flow of blood to tumors.

Genetic Research Research in human genetics has led to important developments. For example, in 1997 genetic researchers discovered a gene that increases a person's risk for colon cancer. This knowledge may help scientists find ways to prevent this disease.

A controversial branch of genetic research is **genetic engineering.** This involves the changing of genes to create new types of living organisms. One example of genetic engineering is cloning. Cloning means creating a genetic copy of an organism. By 1997, scientists had successfully cloned animals, including a sheep in Scotland.

Critics fear that genetic technology could be abused. Some critics have suggested that genetic tests might lead some couples to try to create a super baby. Others fear that cloning might lead to the development of clone farms where scientists would raise clones to harvest organs for other people.

Genetic engineering provides just one example of the issues raised by modern technology. While new technologies raise hopes for the future, they also cause problems. Computer technology has changed workplaces around the world. Some workers have benefited greatly from this development, but other workers have been hurt by it. Biologists have unlocked many secrets about human genes, but some people fear that this technology may be put to dangerous uses. All of these issues confront people as they enter the 21st century.

Improvements in health care technology, such as MRI, allow doctors to diagnose illnesses more quickly and accurately than ever before.

Vocabulary
MRI: magnetic resonance imaging

Background
In 1990, the United States began the Human Genome Project to identify the 80,000 genes in human DNA and collect data on the three billion chemical bases that make up DNA.

Section **1** Assessment

1. TERMS & NAMES
Identify
- mass media
- biotechnology
- genetic engineering

2. TAKING NOTES
In a chart like the one below, list three technological innovations that have changed people's lives. Give an example that shows an effect that each device has had.

Innovation	Effect

3. HYPOTHESIZING
Which area of technology—electronics or biotechnology—do you think will have the greatest impact on life in the 21st century?

THINK ABOUT
- the Internet
- cloning

4. THEME ACTIVITY
Science and Technology
With a partner, use the library or the Internet to review the past year's issues of a leading science journal. Write a report on the most important technological advance that was made during the year.

THINK ABOUT
- what experts say about new technologies
- which technological advance is most likely to affect your life

ANSWERS

1. TERMS & NAMES
- mass media, p. 589
- biotechnology, p. 590
- genetic engineering, p. 590

2. TAKING NOTES
1. Innovation—satellite technology; Effect—2 billion people watched Princess Diana's funeral

2. Innovation—Internet; Effect—saved Taija Laitinen's life

3. Innovation—genetic engineering; Effect—cloning of a sheep in Scotland

3. HYPOTHESIZING
Possible Responses: Some students might say electronics, because all of the new gadgets change the ways people can work, play, and communicate. Others might say biotechnology, because things produced by genetic engineering might change the ways people eat and reproduce.

4. THEME ACTIVITY
Standards for Evaluation
The report should...

- tell which journals were reviewed
- describe the advance that was chosen as the most important
- explain why this advance was the most significant

2 Dangers to the Global Environment

TERMS & NAMES
- greenhouse effect
- CFCs
- sustainable development

MAIN IDEA

Technology and industrialization have created environmental challenges that affect the entire world.

WHY IT MATTERS NOW

Failure to solve environmental problems will threaten the health of the planet.

SETTING THE STAGE Technology and industrialization have helped to raise standards of living for many people. But they have also affected the global environment. At one time, the earth's natural resources seemed plentiful. That is no longer the case. For two centuries, industrialization has increased the demands for energy and natural resources. In addition, industry and technology have increased the amount of pollution on the planet. Pollution and the potential shortage of natural resources could have dire consequences for the environmental safety of people, wildlife, and plants throughout the world.

World Concern over the Environment

An important warning about the environment came from the American biologist Rachel Carson in 1962. In her book *Silent Spring*, Carson pointed to the dangers of pesticides—chemicals used to kill insects that threaten crops.

Carson argued that pesticides got into the plants, rivers, and streams where they were used. From there, pesticides threatened the health of any animals or people who ate those plants or drank any water contaminated with the chemicals.

Silent Spring fueled concern over the environment and contributed to the growth of environmentalism in the United States. In 1963, Congress passed the first Clean Air Act, designed to reduce air pollution. This law was followed by other legislation to promote clean water, reduce pesticide use, and protect endangered species.

People in other countries have also organized movements to protect their environments. In Nigeria, the Movement for the Survival of the Ogoni People (MOSOP) has fought to protect the Ogoni people from the pollution caused by oil production. In 1958, the Royal Dutch Shell company struck oil in the Ogoni lands in Nigeria. Since then, the company has extracted oil from the region worth about $30 billion. Critics charge that the region was polluted by more than 3,000 oil spills that occurred between 1976 and 1991.

Concerns About the Atmosphere

Two major areas of concern are the effects of industrial pollution on the earth's atmosphere and on its climate. Environmentalists are especially concerned about the **greenhouse effect**—also called global warming—and the destruction of the ozone layer.

The Greenhouse Effect Scientists use the term "greenhouse effect" to describe problems caused by industrial pollution. Much of this pollution comes in the form of gases, such as carbon dioxide.

THINK THROUGH HISTORY
A. Summarizing How has the discovery of oil affected the environment of Nigeria?
A. Answer It has been bad for the environment because there have been over 3,000 oil spills in the region since oil was discovered.

SPOTLIGHT ON

Kenya's Green Belt Movement

Wangari Maathai was the first woman in Kenya to earn a doctorate. She became a professor at the University of Nairobi. In the late 1970s, Maathai started Kenya's Green Belt Movement. The Green Belt Movement is composed mainly of women. It was founded to plant trees and prevent soil erosion. Since then, the movement has spread to a dozen African countries and has planted millions of trees.

Maathai later clashed with Kenyan officials over issues of economic development. As she put it, "You cannot fight for the environment without eventually getting into conflict with politicians."

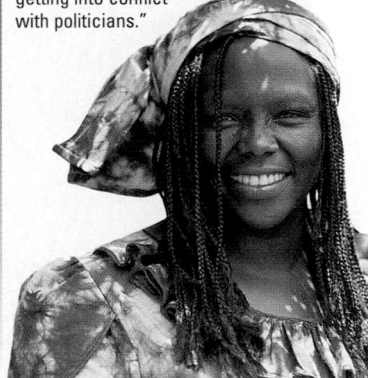

Unresolved Problems of the Modern World **591**

These gases—sometimes called greenhouse gases—are the exhaust from factories and automobiles. The gases create a kind of ceiling—like the roof of a greenhouse—that traps heat near the earth's surface. This buildup of heat near the earth's surface causes a gradual warming of the earth's atmosphere.

Not all scientists agree with the theory of the greenhouse effect. But tests do indicate that the earth's climate is slowly warming. If this trend continues, deserts will expand and crops will fail. The polar icecaps will melt and oceans will rise.

To combat this problem, the industrialized nations have called for limits on the release of greenhouse gases. In the past, developed nations were the worst polluters. But future limits would have the greatest effect on those countries that are trying to industrialize. So far, developing countries have resisted strict limits. They argue that they are being asked to carry too much of the burden for reducing greenhouse gases.

Destruction of the Ozone Layer Another major environmental issue concerns damage to the ozone layer. Ozone is a layer of gas in the atmosphere that absorbs cancer-causing radiation from space. Many scientists believe that the ozone layer is gradually being destroyed by **CFCs** (chlorofluorocarbons)—chemicals used in air conditioners and other products. In 1992, a huge hole in the ozone layer was discovered over Antarctica. Countries quickly moved to limit CFC emissions. But the problem is expected to get worse as the CFCs already in use continue to cause damage to the ozone layer.

Air Pollution Varies Lastly, air pollution also remains a serious problem. Many cities in Europe and the United States have taken steps to clean up the air. But air pollution is still severe in many parts of the world—especially Asia. The World Health Organization has pointed out that 13 of the world's 15 most-polluted cities are in Asia. In New Delhi, India, which ranks 4th on the most-polluted list, 7,500 people die every year from air pollution. Another 32,000 people die every year in six other Indian cities. According to Anil Aggarwal, a respected environmentalist in India, "If wrongs are not righted now, India may become the world's most polluted zone."

Meanwhile, South Korea, China, and Japan have begun talks to reduce the effects of pollution caused by China's rapid industrialization. And some Chinese cities are trying to reduce air pollution locally. For example, Shanghai has reportedly banned leaded gasoline and diesel fuel that cause heavy pollution.

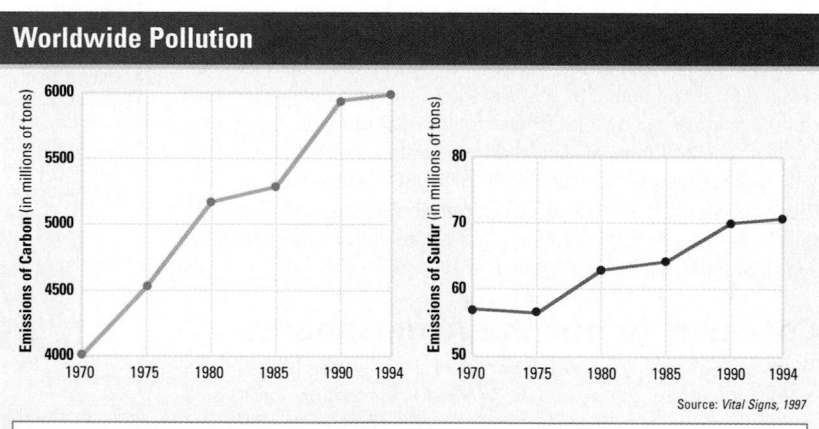

Worldwide Pollution

Source: *Vital Signs, 1997*

SKILLBUILDER: Interpreting Graphs
1. Which grew more quickly between 1985 and 1994, emissions of carbon or emissions of sulfur?
2. In which five-year period did sulfur emissions decrease?

592 Epilogue

Depletion of Natural Resources

Industrialization and population growth have also placed a severe strain on natural resources. Clean water, forests, and energy supplies all run the risk of becoming scarce.

Scarcity of Clean Water In the developing world, water pollution and scarcity of clean water are serious problems. One-fourth of the world's population has no access to clean water. Eighty percent of all illnesses in developing nations can be traced to inadequate supplies of fresh water.

In some parts of the world, nations share the water supplies in lakes and rivers. In southwest Asia, for example, Israel and Jordan share the Jordan River—an essential source of water for farming. Any nation that pollutes shared water or stops water from flowing into a neighboring country runs the risk of starting an international conflict. Many nations try to cooperate to make sure water supplies remain clean. In 1993, the United States and Mexico agreed to work together to improve their water and waste systems along the border.

The state of California in the United States has complex water issues. The state's large population and agricultural industry have put severe pressure on water resources. The problems worsened during a drought that lasted from 1987 to 1992. However, the state limited the negative effects of the drought by developing new ways to conserve and use water.

Destruction of Rain Forests Another critical resource issue is the destruction of tropical rain forests in such countries as Malaysia and Brazil. By 1990, the world had lost more than half its rain forests to logging or farming operations. It has been estimated that another 20 percent will be lost by the year 2000.

This loss could affect all people on the planet. The rain forests are home to as many as half of the world's species of plants and animals. Their extinction could upset the planet's environmental balance. As author Catherine Caufield has argued, the extinction of these plants and animals may have immense costs.

> **A VOICE FROM THE PAST**
> As man destroys the rain forests, millions of species of plants and animals, the vast majority of which are completely unknown to science, lose their habitats. Scientists have scarcely begun to ask how the human race might benefit from the products of the forest.
> Fewer than one percent of tropical forest species have been examined for their possible use to mankind.
> **CATHERINE CAUFIELD**, "Paradise Lost," *San Francisco Chronicle*

The rain forests also help to maintain water quality, recycle rainfall and oxygen into the atmosphere, and protect the soil. The burning of the rain forests, on the other hand, contributes to the greenhouse effect by reducing the number of trees, which absorb carbon dioxide.

In recent years, nations like Brazil have made efforts to slow the destruction of the rain forests. Success has been limited, however, by Brazil's desire to achieve economic development. As one American diplomat put it, "Environmental concerns are a luxury of the rich, and this is not a rich country. Brazilians are not going to just preserve the Amazon. They are going to develop it. The question is, how."

Many other developing nations face the same problem as Brazil. They need to achieve **sustainable development**—creating economic growth while preserving the environment.

The Kaiapo, a Brazilian Indian tribe, has organized protests to save the rain forests.

593

Energy Supplies Raise Concerns

▶ **Key Ideas**
- The use of some energy sources causes air pollution, soil erosion, and the production of hazardous wastes.
- Oil spills are a significant form of pollution caused by the use of oil as a fuel.
- In the future, people may develop technologies that may make renewable resources more efficient and less expensive.

ASSESS & RETEACH

Section 2 Assessment
After students respond to the items, have them form pairs to evaluate each other's responses. Students should note page references where answers can be found.

Reteaching Activity
CLASS TIME: 10 MINUTES

Discuss question 4 as a class. Ask students to cite information from the section to support their answers. Have the class formulate a group answer to the question.

CLOSE ACTIVITY

CLASS TIME: 15 MINUTES

Synthesizing
In their book *Healing the Planet,* scientists Anne and Paul Ehrlich state, "Achieving environmental security should be recognized as a top priority for all societies." Ask students to discuss whether they agree with the quotation.

Energy Supplies Raise Concern

Sustainable development depends on using energy sources wisely. All sources of energy can be defined as renewable or nonrenewable. Renewable energy sources, such as wind, water, and solar power, can be replenished. Non-renewable energy sources, such as oil and coal, cannot. Although nonrenewable sources are generally cheaper to use, supplies are limited. Also, their use typically causes environmental damage.

Problems Caused by Energy Use Eighty percent of the earth's energy supply now comes from nonrenewable sources, and most of this energy is consumed by the developed countries. Although these nations account for just 25 percent of the world's population, they use 75 percent of the energy consumed worldwide.

Using energy has many environmental effects. The burning of wood and coal emits greenhouse gases. Cutting down trees leads to soil erosion and the expansion of deserts in some areas. Nuclear power plants produce radioactive wastes that can remain hazardous for thousands of years.

The *Exxon Valdez* Oil Spill Oil spills are another example of energy-related pollution. Every year, several serious oil spills take place around the world. They foul water and shorelines and kill sea life. Although oil companies take precautions to prevent spills, spills appear to be an inevitable result of oil use.

The largest oil spill in U.S. history occurred in March 1989. The giant oil tanker *Exxon Valdez* hit a reef in Prince William Sound, off the coast of Alaska. The ship spilled 11 million gallons of crude oil into the sea. The environmental consequences were horrendous. But the federal government responded forcefully. It ordered a cleanup and forced Exxon to pay more than $5 billion in damages.

Solutions for the 21st Century Government action and improved technology may provide solutions to the world's environmental problems in the 21st century. Regulations, such as Shanghai's ban on leaded gasoline and diesel fuel, may help reduce pollution in many places in the near future. In the long run, however, improved technology might provide the best hope for a cleaner environment. More inexpensive ways to use renewable energy sources, such as wind and solar power, may reduce air pollution and the greenhouse effect. In any event, the nations of the world will need to agree on how to achieve sustainable development in the new millennium.

Oil slicks pose great dangers for the plants and wildlife along the world's shores. This bird was a victim of the 1989 *Exxon Valdez* oil spill in Prince William Sound.

THINK THROUGH HISTORY
D. Forming an Opinion Do you think nations should continue to use non-renewable energy sources instead of renewable ones?
D. Possible Answer Some students might say that nations should continue to use nonrenewable resources because they are less expensive. Other students might say that nations should use renewable resources because they are better for the environment.

Section **2** Assessment

1. TERMS & NAMES
Identify
- greenhouse effect
- CFCs
- sustainable development

2. TAKING NOTES
Use a web chart like the one below to take notes on the environmental problems that the world faces.

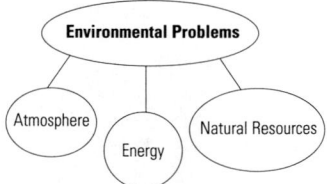

Environmental Problems

Atmosphere — Energy — Natural Resources

3. DRAWING CONCLUSIONS
How significant is the problem of a nation's access to clean water?

THINK ABOUT
- the size of the population with no clean water
- international disputes over water
- waterborne illnesses

4. ANALYZING PROBLEMS

Hypothesizing Why do you think the environmental problems of the earth have become more dangerous?

THINK ABOUT
- increases in population
- technological changes
- lack of worldwide environmental standards

594 Epilogue

ANSWERS

1. TERMS & NAMES
- greenhouse effect, p. 591
- CFCs, p. 592
- sustainable development, p. 593

2. TAKING NOTES
Possible Responses:
Atmosphere: greenhouse effect, ozone depletion, air pollution
Natural Resources: scarcity of clean water, destruction of rain forests
Energy: air pollution, nuclear waste

3. DRAWING CONCLUSIONS
Possible Responses: Clean water is a critical issue because one quarter of the world's population does not have access to clean water. Many citizens become ill from unclean water. International conflicts have resulted from disputes over access to water.

4. ANALYZING PROBLEMS
Possible Responses: A greater number of people will rely upon shrinking resources, creating even more stress on the environment. Technological demands for energy will place even greater demands on the sources of energy and possibly produce more problems as a result. Poor countries, in an effort to keep up with rich nations, may neglect the environment and produce great amounts of pollution.

3 Feeding a Growing Population

TERMS & NAMES
- overpopulation
- birth rates
- green revolution

MAIN IDEA	WHY IT MATTERS NOW
Population growth has put great pressure on the earth's resources, including the food supply.	Nations must find ways to support their growing human populations or else face famines.

SETTING THE STAGE As humanity faces the 21st century, two forces stand out as potential causes of famine—overpopulation and war. In the past two centuries, world population has grown from around 1 billion people to about 6 billion. This growth has put pressure on the environment's resources—including food, energy, and water. Some people worry that the rapid growth of the world's population will lead to **overpopulation.** Overpopulation occurs when there are too many people for the natural resources of an area to support. In some cases, governments enact policies that help push their people into famine. In other cases, wars and rebellions disrupt people's access to food leading to malnutrition and starvation.

Vocabulary
malnutrition: poor nutrition because of a bad diet or faulty digestion or use of foods

World Population Expands

Since 1950, the world's population has more than doubled, to about 6 billion people. **Birth rates**—the number of children born per 1,000 people—are now falling. Even so, the world's population is still growing by around 80 million people per year. According to reliable estimates, the world's population will increase to nearly 10 billion by 2050, an increase of 65 percent over the current population.

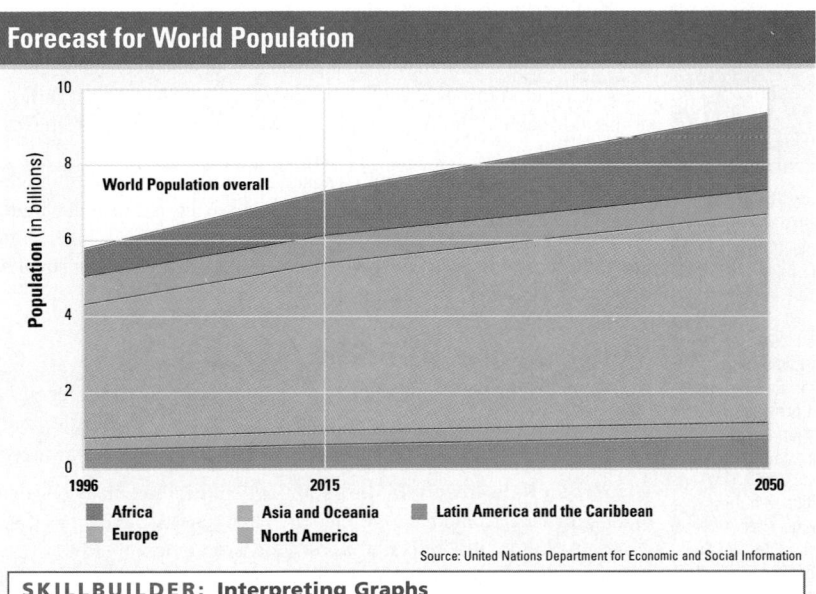

Forecast for World Population

World Population overall

Population (in billions)

Africa   Asia and Oceania   Latin America and the Caribbean
Europe   North America

Source: United Nations Department for Economic and Social Information

SKILLBUILDER: Interpreting Graphs
1. *Which part of the world has the greatest population?*
2. *Which continent is expected to have the fastest population growth between now and the year 2050?*

Gifted and Talented Students
Have students compile a world population atlas, tracing the population of the world and of specific regions from prehistoric times to today. Atlases can use line graphs, bar graphs, and charts to present information. Students should use this information to point out general trends and specific events that have caused significant population growth and decline. Have students make their atlas available to others as a reference.

Section 3 Overview

OBJECTIVES

(1) To define overpopulation and outline possible problems overpopulation may cause.

(2) To describe advances in food production, including the green revolution and the biorevolution.

(3) To discuss solutions to population problems, including improving economies, limiting population growth, and improving the status of women.

SKILLBUILDERS
- Interpreting graphs, pp. 595, 598

CRITICAL THINKING
- Summarizing, p. 596
- Recognizing effects, p. 596
- Forming an opinion, pp. 597, 598
- Making inferences, p. 598
- Analyzing themes, p. 598

FOCUS
5-Minute Warm-Up

▶ ***Making Inferences***
To introduce the idea of population growth, have students look at the graph on page 595 and answer these questions.

1. What was the world population in 1996? What is the projected population for 2050?

2. What kinds of problems do you think a large increase in world population could cause?

WARM-UP TRANSPARENCIES EPILOGUE

OBJECTIVE (1) INSTRUCT

World Population Expands

▶ ***Key Ideas***
- The world population is growing quickly.
- Rapid population growth can reduce the quality of life for people around the world.
- The risk of famine from natural causes increases with rapid population growth.
- Political instability often makes drought and famine conditions worse.

Forecast for World Population

(See page 595.)

Interpreting Graphs Have students use a ruler to measure population on the graph. Ask them how many people are represented by one-quarter inch. (one billion) What was the population of Asia and Oceania in 1996? What is the projected population for Asia and Oceania for 2050?

SKILLBUILDER Answers
1. Asia and Oceania
2. Africa

SPOTLIGHT*On*
Red Cross and UNICEF

Students may be familiar with the Red Cross because this international organization sponsors first-aid classes, swimming classes, and baby-sitting courses, among other things in many communities. They also may have heard of UNICEF, which focuses on health care and construction or improvement of educational facilities in developing nations. UNICEF also provides special emergency missions to help children caught in war, famine, or environmental disasters. Ask students to share experiences they have had with either organization.

OBJECTIVE ② INSTRUCT

Revolutions in Food Production

▶ **Key Ideas**

• The green revolution has contributed to increased crop yields in some parts of the world.

• New farming methods can cause problems such as a need for expensive chemicals and the abandonment of traditional farming methods.

• Genetic research has led to the development of new varieties of crops but may also present negative consequences.

Quality of Life Rapid population growth directly affects the quality of life on the planet. As more people try to live on a limited supply of natural resources, poverty rates rise and human health suffers. World Overpopulation Awareness, an organization that provides information about population issues, has painted a bleak picture of the problems that could result from overpopulation.

A VOICE FROM THE PAST

As our population grows, demands for resources increase, adding to pollution and waste. More energy is used, escalating the problems of global warming, acid rain, oil spills and nuclear waste. More land is required for agriculture, leading to deforestation and soil erosion. More homes, factories, and roads must be built, reducing agricultural land still further as well as habitat for other species, leading increasingly to their extinction.

WORLD POPULATION AWARENESS, "Things You Ought to Know About Population"

Supporters of population control believe that governments and organizations can establish policies to help slow population growth. Slower population growth could reduce food shortages in places such as Africa, where economic growth has been slow in recent years. In fact, some African nations face severe food shortages. Natural factors, such as the weather, and human actions, such as civil war, have caused these shortages.

Natural Causes of Famine In Africa, changes in the climate have played a major role in creating famine. During the 1950s and 1960s, rainfall was plentiful. The rain helped produce good crops and steady economic growth for many African nations. In 1968, however, drought began to weaken African agriculture. In the 1970s and 1980s, rainfall returned to typically low levels. In many areas, food supplies ran short. Ethiopia confronted severe famines in the 1980s and 1990s because of drought. Tens of thousands of Ethiopians died of starvation. Many others endured malnutrition and disease.

Government-Produced Famine In addition to droughts, wars have contributed to famine. The drought that hit Ethiopia in the early 1990s hit Somalia as well. But Somalia was also having a civil war that disrupted food production. Thousands of Somalis died of starvation. International organizations such as the Red Cross tried to send humanitarian aid to Somalia. But members of the warring factions demanded bribes from the aid organizations. As a result, little of the aid reached the starving masses. More than a million refugees fled the nation.

The reduction in food supply caused by drought and war created deep problems for many African nations. While agriculture declined, the prices for major African exports also fell. High African birth rates made these problems even worse. Food supplies were getting smaller while populations were getting larger.

Revolutions in Food Production

One response to the problem of rapid population growth has been to boost food production. Two important examples of this effort are the **green revolution** and the biorevolution.

The Green Revolution In the 1950s, agricultural scientists began to look for ways to increase crop yields. Their success, known as the green revolution, has helped to boost food production greatly.

Scientists focused their efforts on producing high-yield varieties of grain. Their first great success occurred in Mexico in the 1950s. An American-led team developed high-yield wheat plants. Thanks to these new plants, Mexican farmers doubled their wheat production.

SPOTLIGHT *On*

Red Cross and UNICEF

Two organizations that have played a crucial role in supplying food and other forms of aid to needy populations are UNICEF and the Red Cross.

UNICEF, the United Nations Children's Fund, was founded in 1946 to help children in Europe after World War II. Now, it provides food, medicine, and education funds to children in developing countries.

The Red Cross was first established in the 1800s to help war victims. Later it branched into peacetime service, including emergency food relief. The work of both of these organizations has been instrumental in helping to prevent starvation, disease, and hardship in many lands.

596 Epilogue

THINK THROUGH HISTORY
A. Summarizing
Name four problems caused by population growth.
A. Possible Answers pollution, global warming, acid rain, oil spills, soil erosion

THINK THROUGH HISTORY
B. Recognizing Effects How have droughts and wars affected African food supplies?
B. Possible Answer Droughts have reduced the amount of food that African farmers can grow. Wars have disrupted food production and distribution.

TEACHING OPTIONS   **EXPLORING PRIMARY SOURCES**   **CONNECTIONS ACROSS TIME AND PLACE**

Voices from the Past Ask a volunteer to read the World Population Awareness quotation aloud to the class. Let students work together to make a cause/effect diagram on the chalkboard to illustrate the interconnected problems that overpopulation could cause. Encourage students to brainstorm other possible effects and add them to their diagram as well.

Famine and War Famine has been a recurrent effect of wars, especially in this century. The civil war that spread in Russia after the Russian Revolution led to severe famine. The Balkan region was hit hard by famine during World War I. During World War II, famine spread across almost all of Europe. Encourage students to find out where famines are occurring today and to note the relationship between famine and war in these modern cases.

In the 1960s, another American-backed team helped to develop a hybrid rice plant in the Philippines. It allowed rice farmers to harvest up to four rice crops every year. Soon, Asian governments were funding their own scientists to develop other hybrid plants to meet the needs of people in their nations.

Unfortunately, the techniques of the green revolution often call for much irrigation, or watering, of crops. Because many African nations have limited water supplies, they have not been able to make full use of the new seeds. This severely limits the usefulness of these methods in much of Africa, where there is little water.

In addition, the new hybrid varieties of plants require chemicals, such as fertilizers, herbicides, and pesticides, to help them grow. This requirement has caused a number of problems. First, the chemicals are expensive. Peasants usually cannot afford them. Second, the use of such chemicals often clashes with age-old methods of farming. Third, these chemicals pose a threat to the environment.

The Biorevolution In addition to the methods of the green revolution, genetic research has played a growing role in agricultural science in recent years. In this approach, scientists alter plant genes to produce new plants that are more productive and more resistant to pests and disease.

This biorevolution, or gene revolution, has led to some important developments. For example, one American company has developed a genetically altered tomato that ripens more slowly than other tomatoes. This means that the altered tomatoes keep much of their flavor and freshness longer. Similar work is being tried with other kinds of produce.

But the biorevolution has raised some troubling issues. Critics fear that altering genes may accidentally create new disease-causing organisms. Another fear is that plants produced by altering genes may become diseased more easily. As with the green revolution, science offers great opportunities in the search for more food, but the results may also have negative consequences.

Other Solutions to Population Problems

Various approaches to limiting population growth have been proposed over the years. Three main strategies are to improve the economies of less-developed countries, to limit population growth, and to improve the status of women.

Improving Economies Many experts believe that the best way to tackle overpopulation is through economic development. When a country's economy improves, birth rates fall. They do so for two reasons. First, women become pregnant less frequently because more newborn children survive. More children survive because stronger economies provide better health care, nutrition, and child-care education for mothers. Second, when economies are strong, families do not need as many children to work to support the family and parents in their old age. The result is that strong economies lead to lower birth rates and slower population growth.

This typical Chinese family goes for a walk in 1985. China imposed a strict policy of one child per family in 1979.

Limiting Population Growth A second major strategy is to lower the rate at which the population is growing. In 1994, in Cairo, Egypt, the International Conference on Population and Development met for the third time. Delegates agreed on a plan to keep population growth to a minimum through the year 2050. The plan called for greater use of family planning,

Unresolved Problems of the Modern World **597**

Birth Rates and Literacy Rates in Oceania

Interpreting Graphs Explain that the bars to the left of the zero line tell the birth rate. Help students read the birth rate in Australia. (1.9 births per thousand) Point out that the percent of literate women is shown on the bars to the right of the zero line. Ask students to read the percentage of literate women in Australia from the graph. (99%)

Extension Activity Encourage students to use on-line sources or consult UNESCO publications to find the percent of literate women and the birth rate in other countries. Students can make their own graph that includes this information. Hold a class discussion on whether the generalizations they made about the original graph hold true for their new graphs.

SKILLBUILDER Answers

1. Vanuatu

2. The higher the literacy rate, the lower the birth rate; the lower the literacy rate, the higher the birth rate.

Section 3 Assessment

Have students answer the questions individually and then meet in small groups to discuss their answers.

Reteaching Activity

CLASS TIME: 15 MINUTES

To help review the main ideas of this section, ask groups of students to write a brief summary of the content under one headline. Have groups exchange their summaries with other groups.

CLASS TIME: 20 MINUTES

Making Judgments

Ask students to consider the different solutions presented to ease the problems of overpopulation. Have them discuss which solution they think would work the best and which they think would be most acceptable to people in different countries. Encourage them to talk about how they would try to implement this solution.

---

reductions in child mortality, and increased women's rights. Some delegates did not support all of this plan, but it passed anyway.

Some critics have pointed out problems in limiting population growth when it is carried out in extreme ways. A strict policy may reduce birth rates at the expense of personal freedom, or it may target specific groups that cannot defend their rights. For example, church leaders and some politicians in Peru have charged that a government program has forced poor Indian women to undergo sterilization, making them unable to have children. The critics have said that poor, uneducated women are lured into having the sterilization procedure by health workers who promise gifts for the families.

Improving Women's Status Most experts believe that protecting the rights of women is essential to reducing birth rates. For example, the birth rate for uneducated Peruvian women is 6.2. By contrast, the rate for Peruvian women with some college education is only 1.7. According to population experts like Dr. Nafis Sadik of the United Nations Population Fund, there is a close link between women's status in society and population growth. The greater the status of women, the lower the birth rates.

Improving conditions for women will be a crucial part of any effort to solve the world's population problem, but other actions will also need to be taken to reduce the threat of famine and food shortages. New technologies may provide a key to increasing food supplies. In addition, creating and protecting political stability around the world can help to ensure that people have access to food. The best way to conquer starvation, however, may be to improve the economies of developing nations.

THINK THROUGH HISTORY
D. Forming an Opinion Do you think governments should establish policies to reduce population growth?
D. Possible Answer Some students may say yes, because overpopulation will be a serious problem in the next century. Others may say no, because governments should not be so deeply involved in personal matters.

Background
Oceania is a term that refers to the thousands of islands in the Pacific Ocean.

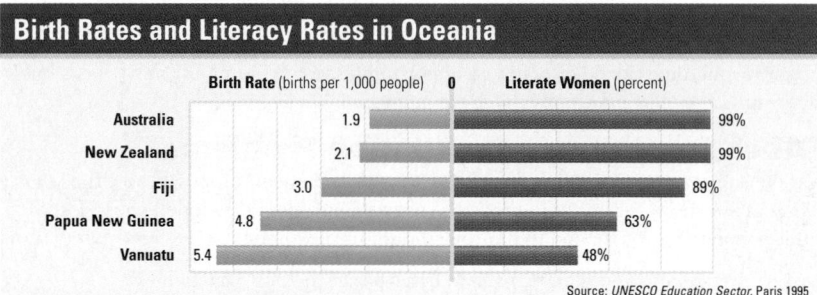

Birth Rates and Literacy Rates in Oceania

	Birth Rate (births per 1,000 people)	0	Literate Women (percent)
Australia	1.9		99%
New Zealand	2.1		99%
Fiji	3.0		89%
Papua New Guinea	4.8		63%
Vanuatu	5.4		48%

Source: *UNESCO Education Sector*, Paris 1995

SKILLBUILDER: Interpreting Graphs

1. *Which country has the highest birth rate?*
2. *What is the relationship between the literacy rates and the birth rates?*

Section 3 Assessment

1. TERMS & NAMES
Identify
• overpopulation
• birth rates
• green revolution

2. TAKING NOTES
In the chart below, compare and contrast the advantages and disadvantages of the green revolution and the biorevolution.

Green Revolution	Biorevolution
Positive Effects	Positive Effects
Negative Effects	Negative Effects

3. MAKING INFERENCES
How will improving women's rights have an impact on population problems?

THINK ABOUT
• women's status in society
• birth rates and literacy rates

4. ANALYZING THEMES
Identify and explain the different positions governments have taken on the issue of population growth.

THINK ABOUT
• economic development plans
• family planning
• the status of women

ANSWERS

1. TERMS & NAMES
• overpopulation, p. 595
• birth rates, p. 595
• green revolution, p. 596

2. TAKING NOTES
Possible Responses: Green Revolution—Positive: increased crop production

Negative: required too much water and expensive chemicals

Biorevolution—Positive: created more productive plants and plants resistant to disease and insects

Negative: potential creation of disease-causing organisms and plants with less resistance to disease

3. MAKING INFERENCES
Possible Responses: Giving a woman full rights in a society will improve her status. As women's status in society improves, the birth rate declines. Increasing women's education will improve their status and reduce birth rates.

4. ANALYZING THEMES
Possible Responses: Some nations have instituted family planning policies. Others have tried to improve their national economy in order to improve family well-being. Some organizations have tried to improve the status of women, which would lead to lower birth rates.

TERMS & NAMES
- less-developed countries (LDCs)
- investment capital
- World Bank
- International Monetary Fund (IMF)
- grassroots development

4 Economic Issues in the Developing World

MAIN IDEA

Developing nations face a set of economic challenges that must be resolved.

WHY IT MATTERS NOW

Sustainable economic development allows more people to lead productive lives and makes the world more stable.

SETTING THE STAGE The economies of the industrialized nations grew rapidly after World War II. However, **less-developed countries (LDCs)**—countries not fully industrialized—have faced many obstacles in their attempts at economic growth. Among other things, the LDCs have lacked financial resources and a strong infrastructure—the roads, airports, plumbing, and electrical systems necessary to a modern economy. Nevertheless, the industrialized nations have remained interested in the LDCs as sources of raw materials and as potential markets for goods. Indeed, the industrialized nations would like the economies of the LDCs to become strong and stable.

Economic Growth and International Aid

Most economists cite the following factors as necessary for economic development:

- **Investment capital** to pay for the construction of industries and infrastructure, such as roads and bridges.
- Technology to help companies and workers be as productive as they can be.
- Healthy and well-trained workers to help reduce waste and inefficiency.
- Qualified managers to help to make sure that workers and materials are used efficiently.

A serious problem that LDCs face is how to acquire these factors. Many people believe that imperialism and colonialism are the reasons that the LDCs have not industrialized. The imperial nations limited the economic growth of their colonies. In addition, the colonial governments robbed the colonized people of the chance to govern themselves. When most colonized regions gained their independence after World War II, they had underdeveloped economies and weak political traditions. These problems made it difficult for the LDCs to achieve stable economic growth. In recent years, however, more and more LDCs have been developing stable democratic governments. And the LDCs may now be able to cooperate with the industrialized nations to improve the LDCs' economies.

Industrialized nations have tried to work with the LDCs by providing aid through international organizations, such as the **World Bank** and the **International Monetary Fund (IMF).** The World Bank provides loans for large-scale development projects, such as dams. The IMF offers emergency loans to countries in financial crisis.

International agencies can play an important role in development, but they also have drawbacks. The World Bank, for example, might fund a project that it considers worthy, such as a large dam. But the project may do little to help the people of a country. The IMF has been criticized for setting harsh financial conditions for countries receiving IMF loans. For instance, the IMF might require a country to cut its government spending drastically.

SPOTLIGHT ON

The IMF Bailout of Indonesia

Indonesia was one of several East Asian nations that faced financial ruin in 1997. As the value of the Indonesian currency collapsed, foreign investors took their funds out of the country.

To blunt the crisis, the IMF offered $43 billion to bail out Indonesia. In return, the IMF forced Indonesia to close banks and cut budgets. Even so, the value of the Indonesian currency fell 80%. Looting and riots against high prices erupted. The unrest forced the Indonesian prime minister to resign from office.

Unresolved Problems of the Modern World **599**

A. Possible Answers Some students may say yes, because the money belongs to the nations that provide the aid. Others may say no, because the rich nations have no right to tell other nations what to do.

THINK THROUGH HISTORY
A. Forming an Opinion Should organizations providing economic aid have the right to place restrictions on the nations that receive aid?

Section 4 Overview

OBJECTIVES

1. To list the factors that aid economic growth in less-developed countries (LDCs).
2. To discuss different economic approaches to achieve economic growth in LDCs.
3. To compare the effects of free trade and protectionism on economic growth.

SKILLBUILDER

- Interpreting graphs, p. 600

CRITICAL THINKING

- Forming an opinion, pp. 599, 601
- Contrasting, p. 601
- Analyzing issues, p. 601
- Analyzing problems, p. 601

FOCUS

5-Minute Warm-Up

▶ **Making Generalizations**
To gauge students' prior knowledge about the world's economy, ask the following questions.

1. What does it mean for a country to be industrialized?
2. What does it mean for a country to be less developed economically?

 WARM-UP TRANSPARENCIES EPILOGUE

OBJECTIVE 1 INSTRUCT

Economic Growth and International Aid

▶ **Key Ideas**

- Economic growth requires investment capital, technology, well-trained workers, and qualified managers.
- Less-developed countries have difficulties achieving economic growth.
- Industrialized nations offer LDCs different forms of economic aid.

Latin American nations have had troubled relationships with international lenders. For instance, Brazil had repeatedly clashed with the IMF since the 1980s over economic policy and repayment schedules. By 1997, Brazil had worked out a repayment plan, but its debt level remained very high—$178 billion at the end of 1996.

Different Economic Approaches

Another source of economic growth for LDCs is investment by multinational corporations—companies that do business in many nations. These giant companies build factories in countries where the costs of labor and materials are low in order to increase their profits. Multinational companies often bring jobs, investment capital, and technology to nations that need them. Yet some of these companies have been criticized for exploiting workers and harming the environment in their host countries.

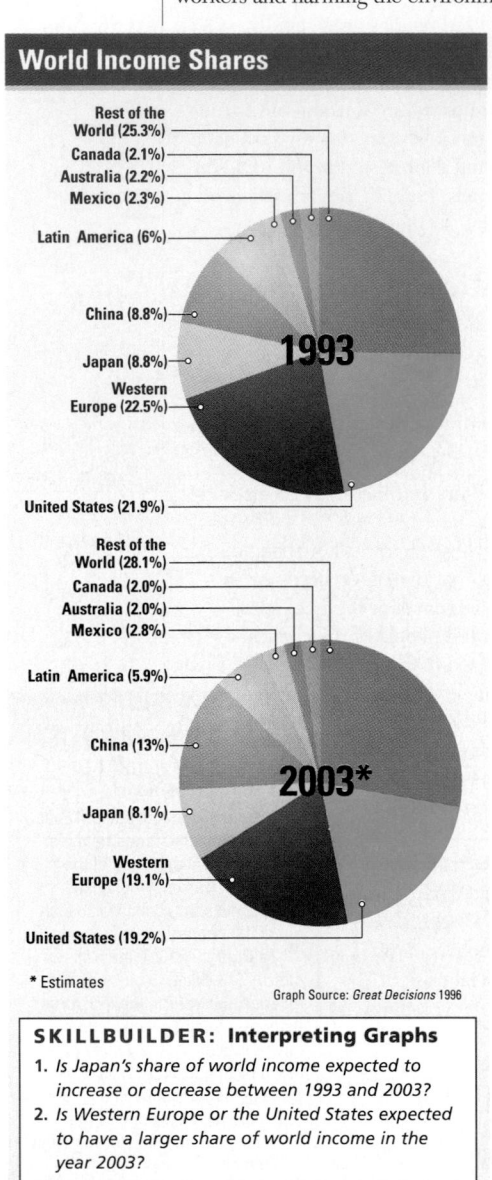

World Income Shares

1993
- Rest of the World (25.3%)
- Canada (2.1%)
- Australia (2.2%)
- Mexico (2.3%)
- Latin America (6%)
- China (8.8%)
- Japan (8.8%)
- Western Europe (22.5%)
- United States (21.9%)

2003*
- Rest of the World (28.1%)
- Canada (2.0%)
- Australia (2.0%)
- Mexico (2.8%)
- Latin America (5.9%)
- China (13%)
- Japan (8.1%)
- Western Europe (19.1%)
- United States (19.2%)

* Estimates

Graph Source: *Great Decisions* 1996

SKILLBUILDER: Interpreting Graphs
1. Is Japan's share of world income expected to increase or decrease between 1993 and 2003?
2. Is Western Europe or the United States expected to have a larger share of world income in the year 2003?

Multinational Corporations Most LDCs want multinational companies to invest in them because the multinationals do create jobs. Some LDCs offer multinational corporations favorable tax rates and work regulations. For instance, Nicaragua offers a package of benefits to multinational clothing firms that operate factories in Nicaragua. The package exempts the companies from having to pay income taxes for ten years and allows them to pay a minimum wage of 41 cents an hour.

Working conditions in many of these Nicaraguan *maquilas*, or factories, are poor. One woman who works at a factory operated by a Taiwanese-owned company complained about the strict rules. "We're not allowed to stand up [from our machines] and we're not allowed to talk, even if we're seated next to each other." Other workers have complained about forced overtime, timed bathroom breaks, unhealthy working conditions, and a lack of health care benefits.

On the whole, Nicaraguan *maquilas* are a mixed blessing for the country. The unemployment rate is high, and the *maquilas* provide jobs. But *maquilas* do little to contribute technology, capital, or infrastructure to the country.

Grassroots Development Another approach to economic development is **grassroots development.** Grassroots development calls for small-scale, community-based projects to help poor people lift themselves from poverty. Grassroots programs usually focus on helping individuals and communities to improve their lives. For example, U.S. Peace Corps workers have helped farmers in Paraguay improve their crops simply through crop rotation—planting different crops to keep the soil fertile. Grassroots development responds to community needs and can help raise standards of living while preserving local customs.

Another example of a grassroot development program is microcredit. Microcredit programs give

Vocabulary
grassroots: people or society at the local level instead of at the center of power

Vocabulary
microcredit: lending programs that give small loans to people

---

small loans—often less than $100—to individuals as seed money to enable them to begin small-scale businesses and lift themselves from poverty. Many organizations—including the World Bank and multinational corporations—run microcredit programs.

Julia Sairitupac, a single mother living in Sarita Colonia, Peru, has benefited from a microcredit program. She was having little success building a business selling fruit juice and *salchipapas*—hot dogs and french fries. In 1990, she received her first loan—between $100 and $200—and used it to buy some kitchen tools and a showcase. She is proud of the way her business has grown.

> **A VOICE FROM THE PAST**
> I feel that I have begun, for the first time, to leave poverty. . . . Although my work requires many sacrifices, I want to continue progressing and install my business in my own house, which, with the help of my children, we are already building bit by bit. My dream is to see it completely finished.
> **JULIA SAIRITUPAC,** "Borrower Success Stories"

No matter what approach is used, however, the development process is slow. And the gap between rich and poor nations remains large. Although the economic output of Asia and Africa grew during the 1980s, it still shrank as a percentage of total world output. In other words, the rich nations are getting more productive, while the poor nations are falling further behind.

Free Trade or Protectionism

Another key issue that developing countries face is whether to follow policies of protectionism or free trade. Protectionist policies protect local products and industries from competition. The most common way to limit competition is to place a tariff—or tax—on goods imported from other countries. Opponents of protectionism support a policy of free trade—trade between nations without protective tariffs. Free-trade supporters believe that free trade promotes commerce by making trade less expensive because it is not taxed.

Since the 1980s, many LDCs have embraced free trade under the terms established by the General Agreement on Tariffs and Trade (GATT). This agreement sets limits on tariffs and other barriers to trade. Meanwhile, regional trading blocs are taking shape to control and encourage trade in various regions of the world. For example, the North American Free Trade Agreement (NAFTA) has opened up trade between Canada, Mexico, and the United States. Regional trading blocs are now forming in Latin America, Africa, and Asia. These blocs may provide many LDCs with the support they need to strengthen their economies. The success of these trading blocs may be crucial not only to the economic growth of the developing countries but also to the countries' long-term stability.

Section 4 Assessment

1. TERMS & NAMES
Identify
• less-developed countries (LDCs)
• investment capital
• World Bank
• International Monetary Fund (IMF)
• grassroots development

2. TAKING NOTES
Create a web diagram showing the various solutions to creating economic growth.

Solutions to Economic Growth

Which of the solutions do you think is the one most LDCs will choose?

3. ANALYZING ISSUES
What are the advantages and disadvantages to grassroots development?
THINK ABOUT
• the requirements for economic growth
• the size of grassroots projects
• national pride

4. ANALYZING PROBLEMS
What factors must LDCs consider in making plans to develop their economies?
THINK ABOUT
• the requirements for economic growth
• international aid
• the impact of multinational corporations

Unresolved Problems of the Modern World **601**

Section 5
Overview

OBJECTIVES

1. To discuss reasons for the worldwide arms trade and how people are trying to restrict it.

2. To list weapons of mass destruction and identify the threats they pose to peace, security, and human survival.

3. To describe the increasing danger of global terrorism.

4. To explain the United Nations' role in securing peace.

SKILLBUILDER

• Interpreting maps, p. 603

CRITICAL THINKING

• Forming an opinion, pp. 602, 605
• Contrasting, p. 604
• Summarizing, p. 605
• Analyzing problems, p. 605

FOCUS
5-Minute Warm-Up

▶ **Clarifying**
To introduce the topic of war, weapons, and terrorism, have students read Setting the Stage and answer the following questions.

1. What are conventional weapons?

2. Define the term *terrorism*.

📖 **WARM-UP TRANSPARENCIES EPILOGUE**

OBJECTIVE ① INSTRUCT

Worldwide Arms Trade

▶ **Key Ideas**
• With the end of the Cold War, international arms dealers sell arms to warring parties around the world.

• An illegal market for arms contributes to weapons buildups in the world's trouble spots.

• Opponents of the arms trade protest against the sale of military equipment.

5 The Threat of Weapons and Terrorism

TERMS & NAMES
• conventional weapons
• terrorism
• weapons of mass destruction
• proliferation
• bioweapons

MAIN IDEA	WHY IT MATTERS NOW
War, terrorism, and weapons of mass destruction threaten the safety of people all over the world.	People can work against the dangers posed by war, terrorism, and weapons of mass destruction.

SETTING THE STAGE The wars of the 20th century have led to the development of new weapons, including nuclear missiles and powerful **conventional weapons.** Conventional weapons include all the standard weapons of war, such as tanks, planes, artillery, and rifles. So long as nations continue to use the threat of military force as a tool of foreign policy, armed conflicts will erupt. Wars, however, are not the only threat to international peace and security. The threat of **terrorism**—the use of violence against people or property to force changes in societies or governments—strikes fear in the hearts of many people. Nevertheless, many nations and organizations have been working together to reduce the threats of war and terrorism.

Worldwide Arms Trade

Many people hoped that the end of the Cold War would reduce the risk of armed conflict around the world. However, developments following the Cold War have introduced new threats. First, the collapse of the Soviet empire led to political instability in parts of the world the Soviets once controlled. Second, international arms dealers found they needed new markets for their weapons.

A brutal example of political instability following the collapse of the Soviet Union has been the disintegration of Yugoslavia. In 1991, the United Nations imposed an arms embargo on the former Yugoslavia to control the fighting there. Nonetheless, illegal weapons purchased from international arms dealers continued to flow into the region. The international market for conventional weapons helped fuel the Yugoslav war and is a serious concern to people interested in peace.

The Market for Weapons During the Cold War, the main suppliers of conventional arms were the United States, Western Europe, and the Soviet Union. These nations sold most of the weapons to developing nations. This government-sponsored trade has declined considerably since the mid-1980s, but it has not ceased.

For example, in 1994, arms manufacturers in the United Kingdom alone exported about $2.75 billion worth of arms. Two thirds of these exports went to developing countries. These arms dealers also took new orders that year valued at roughly $7.6 billion. In 1993–1994 arms trading employed up to 80,000 workers in the United Kingdom.

The growing illegal market for weapons is another alarming trend. Many of the weapons bought on the illegal market find their way to trouble spots around the world. These illegal weapons have frequently contributed to armed conflict in regions with political, ethnic, or religious tensions.

Two French soldiers work to disarm a land mine in Cambodia for the UN. Land mines are also a serious problem in other parts of the world, such as Korea and Yugoslavia, where warring armies have left them behind.

A. Possible Answer Arms dealers may be prolonging conflicts by continuing to supply weapons to the combatants.

THINK THROUGH HISTORY
A. Forming an Opinion What moral issues may arise from the sale of weapons?

Such sales can be enormously profitable for arms dealers. According to the Institute for Defense Analyses, Kintex, the state arms-export agency of Bulgaria, smuggled arms valued at $100 million into Croatia in the former Yugoslavia. When asked how he felt about these illegal sales, the General Director of Kintex said that he had "no idea where the weapons went, and anyway it's not my problem."

Protests Against Weapons Sales Some people are beginning to take action against international arms dealers. In Belgium, the Flemish Forum voor Vredesaktie (Forum for Peace Action) has organized nonviolent protests against the Armed Forces Communication and Electronics Association (AFCEA), which held its annual arms fair in Brussels, Belgium, in 1997. Protesters convinced Belgian customs officers to take all of the military equipment at the fair that year because the equipment was not properly licensed.

Demonstrations such as those led by the Forum voor Vredesaktie have a long way to go before they stop international arms deals. But opponents of the arms trade are determined not to abandon their fight.

Weapons of Mass Destruction

Weapons of mass destruction pose a different kind of threat to peace. Such weapons, which include nuclear armaments and biological and chemical weapons, have the potential to kill or injure large numbers of people at one time. Many of these tools of war are the products of sophisticated technologies. Even so, some are frighteningly easy to make and use.

The Threat of Nuclear Weapons The existence of nuclear weapons presents a threat to world peace—and even to human survival. Opponents of nuclear weapons have tried to prevent the **proliferation,** or spread, of such weapons.

Nuclear Weapons Around the World

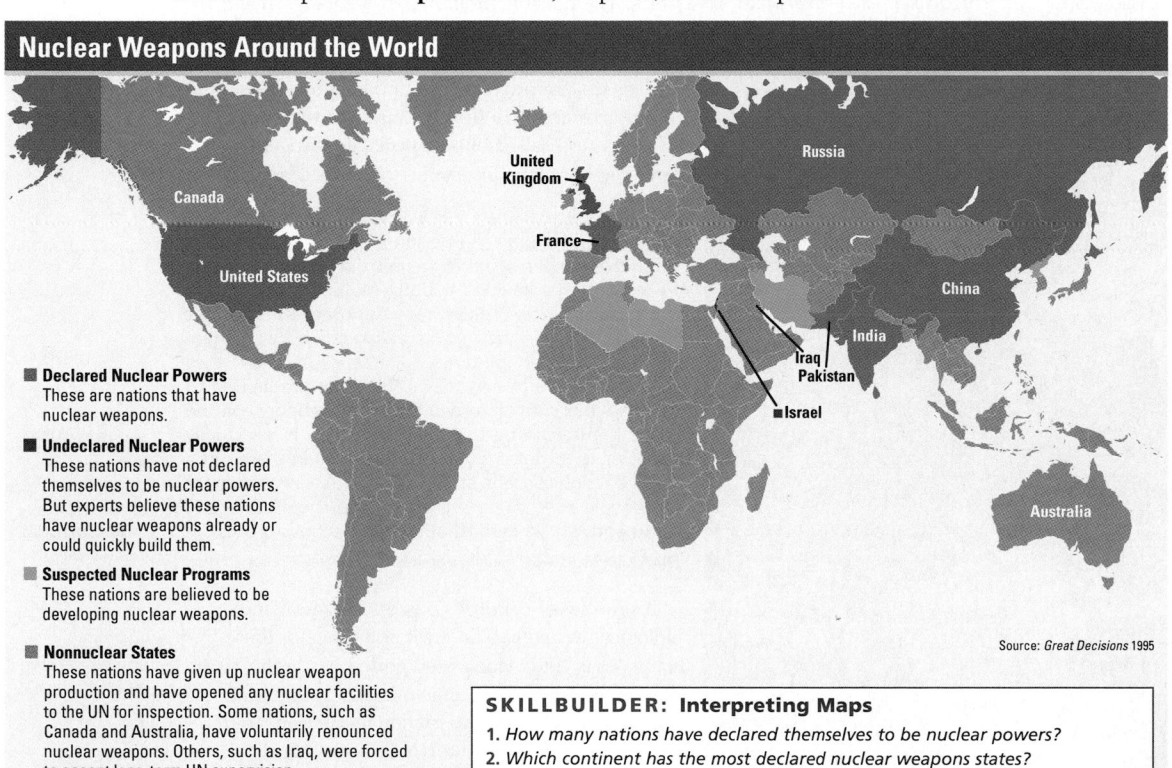

■ **Declared Nuclear Powers**
These are nations that have nuclear weapons.

■ **Undeclared Nuclear Powers**
These nations have not declared themselves to be nuclear powers. But experts believe these nations have nuclear weapons already or could quickly build them.

■ **Suspected Nuclear Programs**
These nations are believed to be developing nuclear weapons.

■ **Nonnuclear States**
These nations have given up nuclear weapon production and have opened any nuclear facilities to the UN for inspection. Some nations, such as Canada and Australia, have voluntarily renounced nuclear weapons. Others, such as Iraq, were forced to accept long-term UN supervision.

Source: *Great Decisions* 1995

SKILLBUILDER: Interpreting Maps
1. *How many nations have declared themselves to be nuclear powers?*
2. *Which continent has the most declared nuclear weapons states?*

Unresolved Problems of the Modern World **603**

▤ **CASE STUDY 6**—Ukraine and Yugoslavia: Resurgence of Nationalism, p. 72

OBJECTIVE ② INSTRUCT

Weapons of Mass Destruction

▶ *Key Ideas*
• Nuclear weapons threaten world peace and human survival.
• Many nations have signed the Treaty on Non-Proliferation of Nuclear Weapons (NPT).
• Because biological and chemical weapons are easy to make and hide, they pose threats to peace and security around the world.

History from Visuals

Nuclear Weapons Around the World
Interpreting Maps
Encourage students to read the key carefully. Ask a volunteer to define the listed categories of nations in his or her own words. Which category does China fall in? (declared nuclear power) Canada? (nonnuclear state)

SKILLBUILDER Answers
1. Seven
2. Asia

Task: Students will compile a fact book on nuclear arms.

Purpose: To learn more about nuclear weapons, their development, and the threats they pose.

Activity: Divide the class into small groups and assign each group a topic related to nuclear weapons. Possible topics include: science of fission bombs; science of fusion bombs; history of nuclear weapons development; history of civil defense; current state of nuclear weapons research; profiles of countries with nuclear capabilities; profiles of countries developing nuclear capabilities; efforts to limit nuclear weapons. Have students summarize their research in one to three pages, which may include diagrams, charts, and maps. Have an editorial board compile the class's work into a nuclear arms fact book.

📁 **Building a Portfolio:** Suggest that students include their research as well as a copy of the finished fact book in their portfolios.

A major step toward stopping nuclear proliferation was the Treaty on the Non-Proliferation of Nuclear Weapons (NPT). This treaty was passed by the United Nations General Assembly in 1968. It went into force in 1970 for a 25-year period. The treaty had three major provisions:

1. Nations that already possessed nuclear weapons pledged not to help more nations acquire nuclear weapons and pledged to work for universal nuclear disarmament.

2. Nations without nuclear weapons were prohibited from making or receiving nuclear weapons.

3. Nonnuclear nations promised to allow inspectors to make certain that these nations were not using nuclear materials to make weapons.

In 1995, 170 nations signed on to renew the NPT forever. Even so, India, a nation that has not signed the NPT, caused a great deal of international worry by testing nuclear bombs in May, 1998. Two weeks later, Pakistan tested nuclear devices, too. International leaders fear that the arms race between India and Pakistan could lead to nuclear war. The two nations have already fought three wars with conventional weapons since 1947.

Nuclear Weapons in the Former Soviet Union Despite the NPT, the problem of nuclear warheads in the nations of the former Soviet Union remains. Some of the former Soviet republics, especially Ukraine, wanted to keep the nuclear arsenals that they had inherited from the Soviet Union. In 1994, however, the United States convinced Ukraine to transfer its nuclear weapons to Russia. In exchange, the United States agreed to give Ukraine at least $175 million in financial assistance to dismantle and remove the weapons. Even so, fears remain that the nuclear arsenal of the former Soviet Union may find its way into the hands of terrorists.

Biological and Chemical Weapons The possible proliferation of biological and chemical weapons is also fueling concern. These weapons are relatively easy to produce and distribute, making them much more available than nuclear weapons to terrorists and less-developed countries. According to author Richard Preston, biological weapons, also called **bioweapons,** are especially troubling because they can be the most deadly.

Israeli citizens scour the wreckage following a bus bombing. Terrorist acts such as bus bombings strike fear in the hearts of many people.

A VOICE FROM THE PAST
A chemical weapon is a poison that kills upon contact with the skin. Bioweapons are microorganisms, bacteria or viruses, that invade the body, multiply inside it, and destroy it. Bioweapons can be used as strategic weapons. That is, they are incredibly powerful and dangerous. They can kill huge numbers of people if they are used properly, and their effects are not limited to one place or a small target. Chemical weapons, on the other hand, can be used only tactically. It is virtually impossible to put enough of a chemical in the air in a high enough concentration to wipe out a large number of people over a large territory. And chemicals aren't alive and can't spread through an infectious process.

RICHARD PRESTON, "The Bioweaponeers," *The New Yorker*

A number of countries possess chemical and biological weapons. The most noted one of these countries is Iraq, which used poison gas in the 1980s against the Kurds, an ethnic minority group that lives in Iraq. Despite international criticism, Iraq has resisted efforts by the UN to inspect Iraqi arms facilities.

Terrorism Strikes Globally

The threat of terrorism has spread to more and more places around the globe. Recent examples of terrorism include the bombing of the World Trade Center in New York in 1993 and the bombing of the Alfred P. Murrah Federal Building in Oklahoma City in 1995. In addition, the Tupac Amaru guerrillas in Peru took hostages in the Japanese embassy in 1997. Also in 1997, the Aum Shinrikyo cult in Japan released deadly sarin gas into the Tokyo subway system.

The Aum Shinrikyo attack highlighted the ways that weapons of mass destruction have worsened the threat that terrorism poses to international security. In addition, modern transportation allows terrorists to cross borders, commit terrorist acts, and escape to friendly nations with little difficulty.

Nations Join Forces to Ensure Peace

The UN plays a key role in international efforts to prevent war. Since World War II, the UN has sent 45 peacekeeping missions to various spots around the world. UN peace-keepers are recognizable by their distinctive blue helmets. These forces are made up of soldiers from different nations. The UN troops work to carry out peace agreements, monitor cease-fires, or put an end to fighting so that peace negotiations can go forward.

As of 1997, the UN had 16 peacekeeping forces around the world. Some, such as the mission in Israel and Palestine, have been in place for decades. Others, such as the mission in Liberia, have lasted only a few years. These UN missions, though, are not always successful. For example, UN efforts to end the fighting in the former Yugoslavia have been ineffective.

There is at least one encouraging sign for the future of UN peace-keeping. The end of the Cold War has produced greater cooperation between the United States and Russia. This has allowed the UN to play a larger role in international affairs than it could during the Cold War. Greater cooperation can only improve the prospects for peace in the 21st century.

United Nations "blue helmets" have been sent on peacekeeping missions to many trouble spots around the world— including Mogadishu, Somalia, where this soldier was on patrol.

C. Possible Answers Some students might say yes, because it is important to prevent wars in any way possible. Others might say no, because they do not want the UN telling people how to settle differences.

THINK THROUGH HISTORY
C. Forming an Opinion Should the UN play a military role in keeping the peace?

Section ⑤ Assessment

1. TERMS & NAMES
Identify
• conventional weapons
• terrorism
• weapons of mass destruction
• proliferation
• bioweapons

2. TAKING NOTES
Create a diagram like the one below to illustrate the sources of threats to international peace and security.

In your opinion, which of the threats to peace and security is the most dangerous?

3. SUMMARIZING
List ways in which people and nations of the world have attempted to control threats to the world's peace and security.

THINK ABOUT
• actions of the United Nations
• actions of individuals or groups

4. ANALYZING PROBLEMS
What reasons might nations have to retain or maintain a nuclear or bioweapons arsenal?

THINK ABOUT
• regions with political, ethnic, or religious tensions
• the rich nations versus the poor nations
• international political problems

Unresolved Problems of the Modern World **605**

ANSWERS

1. TERMS & NAMES
• conventional weapons, p. 602
• terrorism, p. 602
• weapons of mass destruction, p. 603
• proliferation, p. 603
• bioweapons, p. 604

2. TAKING NOTES
Possible Responses: worldwide arms trade; weapons of mass destruction; the spread of terrorism. Weapons of mass destruction are the most dangerous, because these can be used by terrorists.

3. SUMMARIZING
Possible Responses: UN peacekeeping forces have helped nations end fighting and carry out negotiations for peace. Individual groups and government bodies have worked on preventing the threat from weapons of mass destruction through treaties and education.

4. ANALYZING PROBLEMS
Possible Responses: Nations may want to keep such weapons for security. They could be used as a deterrent against an attack by another country or terrorists. Nuclear arsenals may also give a poor nation more power in a conflict against a rich nation.

Teacher's Edition 605

Section 6 Overview

OBJECTIVES

① To list human rights goals as described in the Universal Declaration of Human Rights.

② To cite examples of human rights violations throughout the world.

③ To explain why children are among the most vulnerable of the world's citizens.

④ To describe successes in human rights, such as women's rights.

CRITICAL THINKING

• Forming an opinion, pp. 606, 608
• Summarizing, p. 609
• Making inferences, p. 609
• Analyzing problems, p. 609

FOCUS

5-Minute Warm-Up

▶ **Making Inferences**

To introduce issues related to human rights, have students read the text under the headline Universal Human Rights and answer the following questions.

1. Which human rights listed in the Universal Declaration are listed in this section?

2. What human rights would you add to this list?

 WARM-UP TRANSPARENCIES EPILOGUE

OBJECTIVE ① INSTRUCT

Universal Human Rights

▶ **Key Ideas**

• The Universal Declaration of Human Rights was adopted by the UN in 1948.

• The declaration spells out the political rights that citizens of all nations should have and responsibilities governments have toward citizens and other governments.

 CASE STUDY 8—Argentina and South Africa: Authoritarianism to Democracy, p. 100

6 Defending Human Rights and Freedoms

MAIN IDEA	WHY IT MATTERS NOW
Human rights and freedoms have become a major international concern.	Protecting fundamental rights for all people is an important way to improve life in the 21st century.

SETTING THE STAGE Since the end of World War II, the international community—working through the United Nations and other organizations—has made human rights a primary concern in international affairs. The UN has passed several declarations setting standards for human rights and freedoms.

Universal Human Rights

The **Universal Declaration of Human Rights** was adopted by the United Nations in 1948. This declaration defines human rights goals for the world community. The preamble of the declaration lists several reasons why the declaration is necessary, including the need to promote friendly relations between nations. The declaration then reaffirms the world's "faith in fundamental human rights, in the dignity and worth of the human person and in the equal rights of men and women" in order to "promote social progress and better standards of life in larger freedom."

Article 1 of the declaration states, "All human beings are born free and equal in dignity and rights. They are endowed with reason and conscience and should act towards one another in a spirit of brotherhood." The declaration goes on to spell out the rights that all nations should seek to guarantee for their citizens.

With regard to people's political rights, the declaration states, "The will of the people shall be the basis of the authority of government" and that "everyone has the right to take part in the government of his country." The declaration also calls for free and

Possible Answers
Students will probably cite the rights to life, liberty, and the pursuit of happiness. They might also say people should have rights to political equality and economic opportunity.

THINK THROUGH HISTORY
A. Forming an Opinion What rights do you think all people should have?

Human Rights in the 20th Century

The Holocaust
American soldiers at Buchenwald at the end of World War II view the dead bodies of the Nazi death camp victims. Some 11 million people died in the Holocaust. In 1946, the Allies sentenced 12 Nazi leaders to death at the Nuremberg Trials for "crimes against humanity."

South African Apartheid
South Africa's white-dominated government imposed apartheid on black South Africans in 1948. Black South Africans resisted apartheid. In 1994, South Africa ended apartheid, and Nelson Mandela was elected president of the country.

606

TEACHING OPTIONS — MULTIPLE LEARNING STYLES

Visual Learners Have students make an illustrated time line of human rights abuses and victories in the 20th century based on information presented in the section and information students learn from reading the newspaper. Provide space for students to put their time line up on a classroom bulletin board.

CONNECTIONS ACROSS TIME & PLACE

War Crimes Genocide and heinous war crimes took place in World War II, but they also took place before World War II and still occur today. Encourage students to investigate how the world community responded to war crimes committed in Armenia during World War I, and in Europe, Southeast Asia, Africa, and Central America in more recent years.

fair elections. Finally, it calls for basic civil liberties such as freedom of speech and religion as well as freedom from political terror.

Various organizations, including UN agencies and independent groups such as Amnesty International and Americas Watch, observe whether countries are meeting human rights standards. These groups perform a valuable service by helping to improve conditions and even save lives.

Violations of Human Rights Continue

Despite the best efforts of human rights organizations, protecting human rights remains an uphill battle. Serious violations of fundamental rights continue to occur around the world. The violations result from a number of causes, including political dissent and racial or ethnic hatreds.

Political Dissent The fear of political dissent—the difference of opinion over political issues—is one of the most common causes of human rights violations. In many countries around the world, from El Salvador to Iran to the former Soviet Union, individuals and groups have been persecuted for holding political views that differ from those of the people in power.

There are many examples of political rights violations in the world. One nation that has been criticized for abuses is Nigeria. General Sani Abacha of Nigeria earned a reputation as a ruthless military dictator. Despite repeated statements that he intended to open up the Nigerian government and hold free elections, Abacha imprisoned his political opponents. Abacha took power in 1993 during the chaos that erupted after the results of the presidential election held that year were wiped out. Abacha refused to make public the results of that election. Among his prisoners was Moshood Abiola, a wealthy businessman who many believe won the 1993 election. Abacha died in June 1998. Observers hope that his successor will move the country toward democratic civilian rule.

Ethnic and Racial Conflicts In some countries, ethnic or racial hatreds lead to human rights abuses. For example, human rights groups have charged the fundamentalist Muslim military regime in Sudan of committing **genocide** against the Nuba, an agricultural people in southern Sudan. In addition, Christian groups have accused the

OBJECTIVE ② INSTRUCT

Violations of Human Rights Continue

▶ **Key Ideas**
- In many nations around the world, people who express views dissenting from those of a ruling government are subject to human rights abuses.
- Ethnic and racial conflicts sometimes lead to serious human rights abuses.
- Human rights violations also occur when people face religious persecution.

CRITICAL THINKING ACTIVITY
CLASS TIME: 10 MINUTES

Supporting Opinions
Discuss with students the reasons some governments fear political dissent. Then ask them how they would try to persuade a repressive government to allow dissent. Have students write letters supporting the rights of dissenters to the leader of a repressive regime. Have students read their letters aloud to the class.

The Mothers of the Disappeared
Three members of the Grandmothers of Plaza de Mayo—a group that works to have "disappeared" children returned to their parents—join in a demonstration in Buenos Aires, Argentina. Many of the "disappeared" children were taken into custody by Argentine security forces in the 1970s and 1980s. The group has helped locate more than 50 missing children.

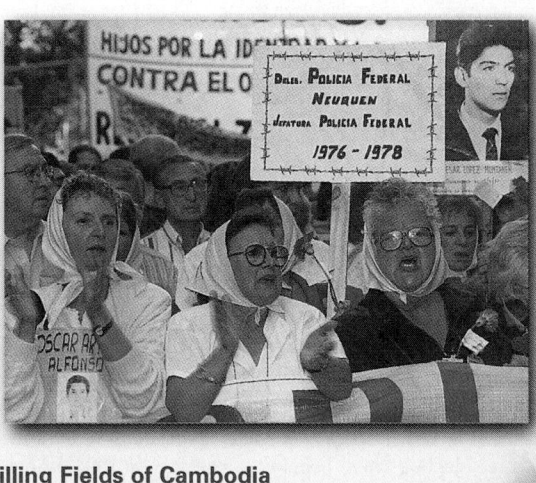

HIJOS POR LA IDENTIDAD CONTRA EL O...

Dr.n. POLICIA FEDERAL NEUQUEN Jefatura POLICIA FEDERAL 1976 - 1978

Kosovo, Serbia
Serbian police beat ethnic Albanians during 1998 riots in Pristina, the capital of the province of Kosovo in Serbia. Many of the majority Albanians want Kosovo to be free of Serbian rule.

The Killing Fields of Cambodia
A sign marks the spot of a mass grave in the Cambodian killing fields. One million Cambodians died in the 1970s at the hands of the Khmer Rouge, led by Pol Pot.

MASS GRAVE OF 166 VICTIMS WITHOUTH HEADS

607

TEACHING OPTION BLOCK SCHEDULING   COOPERATIVE ACTIVITY: Human Rights Watch   CLASS TIME 20 MINUTES

Task: Students will contact a human rights organization, such as Amnesty International, and find out about human rights abuses going on in a particular country.

Purpose: To give students concrete information about campaigns to promote human rights and prevent human rights abuses in specific countries or regions.

Activity: Ask students to contact an organization that promotes human rights, such as Amnesty International, to find out about human rights abuses in a particular country. Students can collect their information into a human rights watch booklet. Suggest that they periodically update the booklet with new information.

📁 ***Building a Portfolio:*** Students might include a photocopy of their group's booklet, along with updates to the booklet, in their portfolio.

📖 *ALTERNATE ASSESSMENT BOOK*
Standards for Evaluating a Cooperative Activity

Standards for Evaluation
Booklets should. . .

- present clear information about human rights abuses that are taking place in a country or region
- use reliable information from a respected international organization

Children at Risk

▶ **Key Ideas**
- Children run the highest risks of suffering human rights abuse.
- Lack of food, education, and health care are among the abuses suffered by children.
- More than 200 million children are working, often under terrible conditions, and have little chance for education or a normal childhood.

MORE ABOUT . . .
Craig Kielburger and Iqbal Masih

Craig Kielburger was inspired to begin his fight against child labor when he read about the murder of Iqbal Masih. Masih was a Pakistani boy who was sold into bondage by his parents to settle a debt. While in bondage, Masih was literally chained to a loom making carpets for many hours a day. He escaped and became active in the effort to liberate Pakistan's bonded children. Masih was awarded the 1994 Reebok Youth in Action Award for his work. In 1995 Masih was gunned down while riding his bicycle. Authorities have kept the circumstances of his murder a mystery.

Signs of Hope

▶ **Key Ideas**
- The advance of democracy in Eastern Europe and South Africa is an example of human rights success.
- Women's rights are expanding in many parts of the world.
- International trends show that democracy and human rights are growing.

Sudanese regime of persecuting Christians, who are a majority in southern Sudan.

In Rwanda, fighting between Hutus and Tutsis—the two main ethnic groups—has led to horrendous rights violations. In 1994, Hutus massacred up to 500,000 Tutsis in the worst case of genocide since the 1970s Khmer Rouge reign of terror in Cambodia.

Religious Persecution Human rights violations based on religious differences have also occurred. Such violations often have ethnic and political overtones. For example, Tibetans—under Chinese rule since 1950—have been persecuted by the Chinese for their Buddhist religion, their traditional culture, and their desire for political independence. Many Tibetan leaders remained imprisoned in China in the 1990s. And the Dalai Lama, the most important Tibetan religious leader, remained in exile.

Children at Risk

Children are the most vulnerable of the world's citizens. They are among those who run the highest risk of suffering human rights abuses. The abuses children suffer are mainly social and economic, and they occur primarily in less-developed countries. A lack of food, education, and health care is foremost among these abuses.

In addition, children in many parts of the world are forced to work long hours, often in dangerous conditions, for little or no pay. Craig Kielburger, a young child-labor activist in Canada, noted, "There are over 200 million children working in child servitude around the world. These children don't have a chance for education, to live a normal life, even a chance to play."

Craig Kielburger (left) visits with Khalid Khan (right) and another boy in 1996 in Islamabad, Pakistan. The 13-year-old Kielburger founded a group to protest child labor. Khan, who was 10, worked in an Islamabad car workshop.

The United Nations has played a leading role in trying to improve conditions for children around the world. In 1989, the UN adopted a document called the Convention on the Rights of the Child. Known as the Magna Carta for Children, this document established a framework for children's rights. It covers basic rights, such as health care and education, and calls for protection against the exploitation, abuse, and neglect of children. Similar goals were advanced in 1990 at the World Summit for Children, where world leaders adopted a 27-point program in favor of children's welfare.

Signs of Hope

The work of the international community is a positive sign in the struggle to advance human rights. Despite great obstacles, efforts to make human rights a priority are achieving some successes around the world.

Human Rights Successes The greatest human rights successes have come in the area of political rights and freedoms. In Europe, countries that were once part of the Soviet bloc, such as Poland, the Czech Republic, and Hungary, have opened up their political systems to allow for democratic elections and the free expression of ideas. There have been similar successes in South Africa, where the apartheid system of racial separation came to an end. Free elections were held in South Africa in 1994, bringing a multiracial government to power.

Women's Rights Addressed The past few decades have also seen major efforts to advance human rights for women. Throughout the world, women tend to be poorer

THINK THROUGH HISTORY
B. Forming an Opinion What responsibilities do nations have for protecting human rights in foreign countries?
B. Possible Answer Some students might say that nations should do everything they can to protect human rights wherever they are endangered. Other students might say that nations should not interfere with the internal affairs of other countries.

Less Proficient Readers Remind students that a topic sentence carries the main idea of a paragraph. Point out that the topic sentence can appear anywhere in the paragraph. Have students work in pairs to identify the topic sentences in the seven full paragraphs on this page. They should write information about the topic sentence in a chart like this.

¶ No.	Beginning of ¶	Middle of ¶	End of ¶
1			
2			
3			
4			
5			
6			
7			

Students Acquiring English Encourage students to use a variety of reading strategies to figure out difficult parts of the text. For example, they might look at the root and the suffix to try to figure out the meaning of the word *activist*. They might look up the term *Magna Carta* in the Glossary and then discuss why the Convention on the Rights of the Child is called the Magna Carta for Children. They might look up the word *exploitation* in a dictionary and then define *exploitation* in their own words.

than men and enjoy less access to social benefits such as education and health care. Conditions for women are especially poor in the less-developed countries. But even in the richer nations, women often have second-class status.

Beginning in the 1970s, international organizations began to address women's rights issues. In 1979, the UN adopted a measure called the Convention for the Elimination of All Forms of Discrimination Against Women. The convention was eventually signed by more than 100 nations. In 1995, the UN sponsored the Fourth Conference on Women, held in Beijing, China. Issues of women's leadership, property ownership, education, health, and population control were top priorities at the conference.

Human Rights in the 21st Century Progress in all areas of human rights is encouraging—but it is only a beginning. Much work must still be done before people in all countries of the world have the democratic rights and freedoms set forth in the Universal Declaration of Human Rights.

However, important trends in the world provide reasons to hope for continued progress on human rights. Rising levels of education are providing people with the skills to exercise their political rights and improve their lives. Modern communications networks are helping human rights organizations like Amnesty International to investigate and report on human rights abuses. In addition, today's mass media can make people instantly aware of abuses in almost any part of the world.

But perhaps the greatest reason for optimism regarding human rights arises from world history since 1989. In early 1989, millions of people in the Soviet Union, Eastern Europe, and South Africa lived under repressive governments that denied basic political rights, such as the right to vote in a multi-party election. Then, beginning with Poland later in 1989, one country after another threw off its old regime and turned to a democratic form of government. In 1989, the Berlin Wall fell, opening the way for the former East Germany to join with West Germany to form a unified—and democratic—Germany. The Soviet Union came to an end in 1991. In that same year, the republic of Russia had its first free presidential election. And in 1994, South Africa held its first universal elections, in which people of all races could vote.

These historic events transformed the world by extending human rights and democratic institutions to millions of people. They continue to inspire optimism that millions more can win their human and political rights while the new century is still young.

C. Answer Increased education, modern communications, and today's mass media help people get information to fight against human rights abuses.

THINK THROUGH HISTORY
C. Summarizing
What trends have raised hopes that progress will be made in protecting human rights?

Section **6** Assessment

1. TERMS & NAMES
Identify
• Universal Declaration of Human Rights
• genocide

2. TAKING NOTES
Using a chart like the one below, list the steps being taken to improve human rights.

Group	Examples of Improvement
Children	
Women	
Political Dissenters	

3. MAKING INFERENCES
What role can the mass media play in helping people understand human rights problems?

THINK ABOUT
• new developments in telecommunications
• recent cases of human rights abuses

4. ANALYZING PROBLEMS
What problems might arise when a government takes an official role in protecting human rights at home and abroad?

THINK ABOUT
• racial, ethnic, and religious prejudice
• the ability of governments to control their citizens

Unresolved Problems of the Modern Era **609**

ANSWERS

1. TERMS & NAMES
• Universal Declaration of Human Rights, p. 606
• genocide, p. 607

2. TAKING NOTES
Possible Answers: Children—UN adopted the Conventions on the Rights of Children; Women—UN adopted the

Convention for Elimination of All Forms of Discrimination Against Women and has held international conferences on women's issues; Political Dissenters—UN agencies and Amnesty International have worked to try to ensure that the Universal Declaration of Human Rights is upheld.

3. MAKING INFERENCES
Possible Response: Mass media can make the public aware of the violations and abuses to a group of people. It can bring more information to the general public very quickly.

4. ANALYZING PROBLEMS
Possible Response: Yes, certain groups of people such as the Kurds in Iraq might be denied protection. In some cases the government itself may violate the rights of its citizens, giving them no one to count on for protection. An example of this was apartheid in South Africa.

Epilogue Assessment

TERMS & NAMES

1. biotechnology, p. 590
2. genetic engineering, p. 590
3. greenhouse effect, p. 591
4. sustainable development, p. 593
5. overpopulation, p. 595
6. green revolution, p. 596
7. investment capital, p. 599
8. grassroots development, p. 600
9. bioweapons, p. 604
10. genocide, p. 607

REVIEW QUESTIONS

Answers will vary.

11. The use of computers has helped people improve many things such as automobiles and air traffic control. Telecommunications have also been improved and expanded.

12. New machines such as MRIs can improve the ways that doctors diagnose illnesses. New treatments can help cure people more effectively.

13. It contributes to the greenhouse effect, destroys the ozone layer, and can kill people in heavily polluted areas.

14. The rain forests maintain water quality, recycle rainfall and oxygen into the atmosphere, and protect the soil.

15. drought and war

16. These are international agencies that lend money to nations to help their economies grow and prevent financial crises.

17. Microcredit programs give small loans to people, usually in developing regions, so they can start businesses to lift them out of poverty.

18. 1. Nations that possess nuclear weapons pledge not to help other nations get them. 2. Nations without nuclear weapons are prohibited from acquiring them. 3. Nonnuclear nations promise to allow inspectors to verify that they do not have nuclear weapons.

19. Terrorist acts can happen almost anywhere, and terrorists are using more and more destructive weapons.

20. The UN adopted the Convention on the Rights of the Child in 1989. The UN also held a World Summit for Children in 1990.

EPILOGUE Assessment

TERMS & NAMES

Briefly explain the importance of each of the following terms and names to the unresolved problems that face the world in the 21st century.

1. biotechnology
2. genetic engineering
3. greenhouse effect
4. sustainable development
5. overpopulation
6. green revolution
7. investment capital
8. grassroots development
9. bioweapons
10. genocide

Interact *with* History

On page 586, you were asked to take a poll about the hopes and fears that people have for the future. Now that you have read about the unresolved problems in the world today, reexamine the results of your poll. How do the poll results differ from the issues raised in the Epilogue? How are they similar? Do you think the results accurately reflect the challenges and opportunities that face the world today? Discuss your conclusions with the students with whom you conducted the poll.

REVIEW QUESTIONS

SECTION 1 *(pages 587–590)*
Technology Changes People's Lives

11. Describe two ways in which the revolution in electronics has changed the world.
12. Name two ways in which technology can improve health care.

SECTION 2 *(pages 591–594)*
Dangers to the Global Environment

13. Discuss three effects of air pollution on the environment.
14. How do rain forests benefit the environment?

SECTION 3 *(pages 595–598)*
Feeding a Growing Population

15. Name two factors that have contributed to famine in Africa.

SECTION 4 *(pages 599–601)*
Economic Issues in the Developing World

16. What are the IMF and the World Bank?
17. What is microcredit?

SECTION 5 *(pages 602–605)*
The Threat of Weapons and Terrorism

18. What are the three major provisions of the NPT?
19. What makes terrorism frightening to so many people?

SECTION 6 *(pages 606–609)*
Defending Human Rights and Freedoms

20. How has the UN attempted to protect the rights of children?

Visual Summary

Technology Changes People's Lives
- The electronic revolution improves communications.
- Technological advances change businesses and workplaces.
- Mass media change culture.
- Biotechnological changes improve health care.

Economic Issues in the Developing World
- Investment capital, technology, good workers, and qualified managers are necessary for economic growth.
- International agencies and multinational corporations can help nations' economies grow.
- Free trade and protectionist policies offer different opportunities for economic development.

Dangers to the Global Environment
- Concern for the environment emerges around the world.
- Air pollution threatens the atmosphere and climate.
- Industry and population growth threaten to deplete natural resources.
- Energy use creates pollution and depletes resources.

UNRESOLVED PROBLEMS OF THE MODERN WORLD

The Threat of Weapons and Terrorism
- International arms sales can contribute to instability.
- Weapons of mass destruction and terrorism threaten international peace.
- Nations try to cooperate to maintain the peace.

Feeding a Growing Population
- World population will grow in the next century.
- Wars and droughts can cause famines.
- The green revolution and biorevolution increase food supplies.
- Organizations and nations try to reduce population growth.

Defending Human Rights and Freedoms
- The UN adopts the Universal Declaration of Human Rights.
- Human rights violations arise from political, ethnic, racial, and religious differences.
- Children are often victims of human rights abuses.
- Progress is made in the 1990s to expand democracy and human rights.

610 Epilogue

Interact *with* History

Students should make note of any hopes and concerns that arise in their polls that are different from the results of the 1972 Gallup Poll. They should also note anything in the Gallup Poll that is absent from their own polls. In addition, they should try to explain the differences.

CRITICAL THINKING

1. EVALUATING PROBLEMS

Which unresolved problem of the modern world do you think poses the most serious threat to humanity? Explain.

2. TECHNOLOGICAL SOLUTIONS

Using a problem-solution chart like the one below, show how technology can help solve two of the unresolved problems of the modern world.

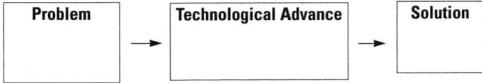

3. THE UN AND WORLD PROBLEMS

In what ways is the UN working to address the unresolved problems of the modern world? In your opinion, does the UN offer the best opportunity to solve these problems?

4. ANALYZING PRIMARY SOURCES

The Russian general Alexander Lebed has spoken about the dangers posed by nuclear weapons in the former Soviet Union. He has described a situation in which a rich dictator might pay nuclear scientists from the former Soviet Union to build nuclear devices. Read the paragraph and answer the questions below it.

> **A VOICE FROM THE PAST**
> The world will face a problem of nuclear terrorism and nuclear blackmail. . . . Then there would be a show nuclear explosion of one device that would level to the ground a large village somewhere, and then they can call Moscow, New York, Tokyo and demand any money. . . . There is a common principle . . . that nuclear charges can be dismantled by those who assembled them. Well, these [scientists] should be precisely the people who . . . should organize storage of the nuclear waste from those devices. These people must be gathered. Jobs must be given to these people. These people should be paid for loyalty—only then can we sleep calmly.
> **ALEXANDER LEBED,** testimony before Congress, March 19, 1998

- How realistic does Lebed's warning sound to you?
- What does he suggest should be done to prevent nuclear blackmail?
- What do you think should be done to prevent nuclear blackmail?

CHAPTER ACTIVITIES

1. EPILOGUE PORTFOLIO PROJECT

The Epilogue discusses several unresolved problems that face the world today. Choose one of the problems discussed in the Epilogue and complete one of the projects listed below to add to your portfolio.

- Create a poster that will convince people to take action about the unresolved problem you have chosen to focus on. Write a paragraph that explains what your poster says about the problem.
- Collect a scrapbook of news clippings from the last two weeks that relate to the unresolved problem you have chosen. Write an introduction that summarizes the articles and explains what can be done about the problem.
- Using the library or the Internet, research the problem you have chosen. After you have collected your information, write a letter to your congressional representative about what should be done to solve the problem you have chosen. Be sure to propose a specific solution.

2. CONNECT TO TODAY: Cooperative Learning

All of the unresolved problems discussed in the Epilogue have long histories. With a group of students, choose one of the six problems and create a multimedia presentation that explains the history of the problem you have chosen.

 Use the Internet, periodicals, and other library sources to research your presentation.

- Find historical, literary, musical, and visual materials that relate to your topic and collect them for a class presentation.
- Give your presentation to the rest of the class. Explain the history of the problem you chose, ending with the current situation.

FOCUS ON CHARTS

Consider which of the nations listed in the chart below appear to be prosperous and which do not.

- What characteristics do prosperous nations have in common?
- How are the infant mortality rate and gross national product (GNP) related?

Connect to History What historical information could help explain the low GNP in the nation of India?

COUNTRY	Infant Mortality Rate, 1992 (per 1,000 live births)	Life Expectancy at Birth, 1992 (years)	Illiteracy Rate, 1992 (percent)	Per capita GNP, 1992 (U.S. dollars)
India	88	60	52	310
Egypt	57	62	52	630
Ethiopia	168	49	greater than 60	110
Brazil	57	66	19	2,770
France	7	77	less than 5	22,300
United States	9	76	less than 5	23,120

Source: *The World Bank Atlas, 1994*

---

1. EPILOGUE PORTFOLIO PROJECT

Standards for Evaluation
The poster should meet the following criteria:

- Clearly represent the problem involved.
- Portray possible solutions to the problem.
- Communicate visually and verbally.

Standards for Evaluation
The scrapbook should meet the following criteria:

- Include as many relevant newspaper articles as possible.
- Include an accurate summary of the articles.
- Offer a clear explanation about what can be done to solve the problem.

Standards for Evaluation
The letter should meet the following criteria:

- Offer accurate statistics and data about the problem.
- Communicate the author's concerns in a clear and respectful manner.
- Tell the representative what the author wants done about the problem.

2. CONNECT TO TODAY: COOPERATIVE LEARNING

Standards for Evaluation
The presentation should meet these criteria:

- Provide a sound, basic history of the problem covered.
- Offer a good balance of elements from different media.
- Communicate visually and verbally.
- Be neat, colorful, and interesting.

FOCUS ON CHARTS

- Prosperous nations have high GNP and life expectancy rates and low infant mortality and illiteracy rates.
- A higher GNP seems to imply lower infant mortality. France and the United States slightly break that rule.

Connect to History *Possible Response:* India was a colony of Britain for many years. Some people believe that this imperial relationship has kept India from developing a stronger economy.

CRITICAL THINKING

1. EVALUATING PROBLEMS
Possible Responses: Some students might say protecting the environment, because pollution threatens the planet. Others might say weapons of mass destruction, because they can threaten lives.

2. TECHNOLOGICAL SOLUTIONS
Possible Response: Problem—greenhouse effect; Technological advance—development of renewable, non-polluting sources of energy; Solution—ability to use wind or solar power will reduce air pollution.

3. THE UN AND WORLD PROBLEMS
Possible Response: The UN offers humanitarian aid to reduce poverty and sends peacekeepers to stop wars. It also sponsors efforts to reduce population growth, protect children, and defend human rights. Some students might say the UN is the best way to get international cooperation. Others might say that nations should address their problems on their own.

4. ANALYZING PRIMARY SOURCES
Possible Responses: Students will probably think that Lebed's warning sounds realistic. Some students might suggest that the UN hire nuclear scientists to keep them from supplying dictators or terrorists with nuclear weapons.

A Global View

A Global View

Teaching Strategies

World Religions: A Global View presents an overview of some of the world's major religions in a contemporary context, showing religion as an enduring and vital part of our modern world. For historical information related to each religion, see the Chapter Connection references throughout.

These pages may be usefully presented at the beginning of a course to give students a sense of the contemporary practice of the religions before they study the religions' historical development. Or the pages for each religion may be presented as the religion is introduced in the text.

To students who wonder why Confucianism is distinguished from the "five major religions," you might explain that because of its strong emphasis on ethical activity in this world, Confucianism is considered by some to be a philosophy rather than a religion.

The Study of Religions

Encourage students to examine each religion on its own terms and not to judge it by the standards of other religions. You might explain to students that this approach may involve trying to deal in a nonbiased fashion with concepts that run counter to their own beliefs.

You may wish to ask the class to go beyond the study of the five major religions presented here. You might divide the class into groups and assign each group another religious tradition to study. Groups could then present the results of their research to the class.

Religion is defined as an organized system of beliefs, ceremonies, practices, and worship that center around one or more gods. Religion has had a significant impact on world history. Throughout the centuries, religion has guided the beliefs and actions of millions around the globe. It has brought people together. But it has also torn them apart.

Religion continues to be a dominant force throughout the world—affecting everything from what people wear to how they behave. There are thousands of religions in the world. The following pages concentrate on five major religions, as well as Confucianism. They examine some of the characteristics and rituals that make these religions similar as well as unique. They also present some of each religion's sects and denominations.

North America

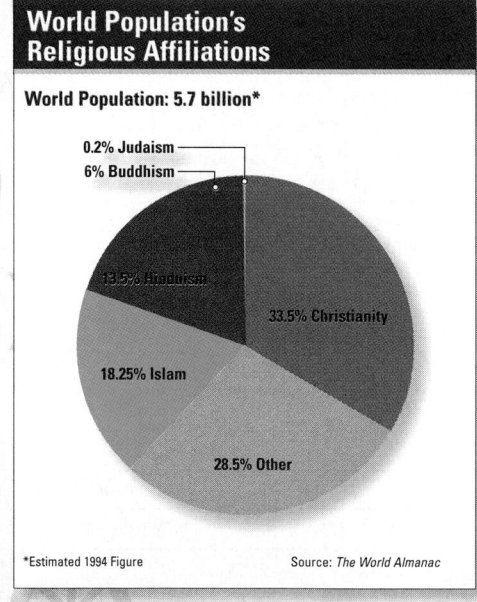

World Population's Religious Affiliations

World Population: 5.7 billion*

- 0.2% Judaism
- 6% Buddhism
- 13.5% Hinduism
- 18.25% Islam
- 33.5% Christianity
- 28.5% Other

*Estimated 1994 Figure Source: *The World Almanac*

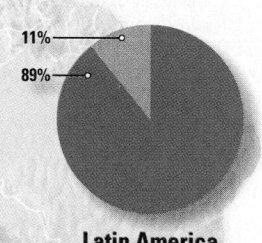

Latin America

Books Bowker, John. *World Religions: The Great Faiths Explored and Explained.* New York: DK Publishing, 1997. An amply illustrated overview of world religions, including ancient and native religions.

Clarke, Peter B., ed. *The World's Religions: Understanding the Living Faiths.* Pleasantville: Reader's Digest, 1993. Religions from historical and contemporary perspectives.

Osborne, Mary Pope. *One World, Many Religions: The Ways We Worship.* New York: Knopf, 1996. A discussion of seven major world religions, with bibliography.

Videos *Beliefs and Believers.* RMI Media Productions, 1992. Twenty-four one-hour videos dealing with myth, doctrine, ritual, and ethics in world religions.

Faith and Belief: Five Major World Religions. Knowledge Unlimited, 1992. Origins and beliefs of Hinduism, Buddhism, Judaism, Christianity, and Buddhism.

CD-ROM *Religions of the World.* Yorkshire International Thomson Multimedia, 1995. Worship, scriptures, artifacts, festivals, and sacred buildings of eight world religions. Over 1,000 graphics. Available from McDougal Littell.

You may wish to stress to your students that the percentages presented here are based on estimates of the numbers of people affiliated with the religions. The percentages are derived from official census figures, which may contain some inaccuracies because of flawed sampling methods and the political agendas of the reporting countries. The figures do, however, give a reasonable picture of the religious beliefs of the world's people, based on the best data available.

Some interested students may wish to investigate possible inaccuracies in current population estimates. Information might be obtained through a local library, a local census bureau office, or population sites on the World Wide Web.

"Officially Nonreligious"

In certain countries, such as Communist China and the former Soviet Union, the governments are or have been officially antireligious. As a result, the official counting of religious and nonreligious citizens may be biased in favor of the nonreligious, in an effort to demonstrate popular support for the government policy.

In addition, social pressures against religious observance in such countries often lead people to hide their true beliefs. Thus, the category "Officially Nonreligious" must be regarded skeptically.

 RELIGIONS OF THE WORLD CD-ROM
Overview

Europe
2.5%
15.5%
82%

Commonwealth of Independent States (Former USSR)
15%
19%
28%
38%

Israel
2%
2%
11%
85%

China*
1%
2%
6%
91%

Southwest Asia
2%
2%
96%

Africa
10%
41%
49%

India
1%
2%
3%
11%
83%

Southeast Asia
6%
9%
15%
28%
42%

Religious Affiliation

- ■ Christian
- ■ Muslim
- ■ Hindu
- ■ Buddhist
- ■ Jewish
- ■ Other
- ■ Officially Non-Religious*

*Communist China officially is atheist (a disbelief in the existence of God). Unofficially, the Chinese practice a number of belief systems, including Buddhism, Taoism, Confucianism, and a variety of folk religions.

World Religions **613**

Logical-Mathematical Learners
You might ask some students to convert the percentages for each religion to actual world population figures. (To do so, students must multiply 5.7 billion by the percentage for each religion.)
Answers: Christianity—1,909,500,000; Islam—1,040,250,000; Hinduism—769,500,000; Buddhism—342,000,000;

Judaism—11,400,000; Other—1,624,500,000

Ask students which of the two forms of the data is more meaningful to them and why. They might also discuss situations in which it is preferable to express data as percentages or as population numbers.

Mathematics You might ask students to create bar graphs showing the data presented in the pie charts, using the vertical axis to display percentages from 0% to 100% and the bars to represent each major religion, either in the world or in a specific region. These graphs may be plotted manually, on graph paper, or by means

of one of the many available computer graphing programs.

When students have created their bar graphs, ask them to compare the pie charts and the bar graphs as a means for displaying data. Have them describe what they think are the strong points of each format.

Buddhism

Sects

Buddhists are united in their respect for the Buddha and in their search for nirvana (enlightenment and liberation from suffering). But various groups understand the Buddha's message in somewhat different ways.

Theravada Buddhism is marked by an effort to stay as close as possible to the Buddha's recorded teachings. The Theravada ideal is the arhat, a saint who reaches nirvana alone. The arhat's pursuit of nirvana is carried out in a monastery, away from the world.

Mahayana Buddhism is more accepting of change and of the world. It considers reaching nirvana as an effort of all believers working together. The Mahayana ideal is the bodhisattva, who delays personal nirvana and returns to the world to help others attain nirvana.

A third Buddhist sect, known as Mantrayana Buddhism, gets its name from mantras—phrases recited over and over in prayer or meditation. Elements of Mantrayana practices can be found in both Theravada and Mahayana traditions.

Worship

The most common form of Buddhist worship is meditation (deep thought or reflection) before sacred images of the Buddha. Believers may meditate before shrines in their homes or in temples. They may offer gifts of food, flowers, or candles out of respect for or worship of the Buddha. (Some Buddhists consider the Buddha a god, though he himself did not.) Both in temples and at home, worshipers burn incense and light candles before images of the Buddha. The light of the candles recalls the light of Buddha's wisdom.

Buddhism

Buddhism has been a dominant religious, cultural, and social force throughout Asia. Today, most Buddhists live in Sri Lanka, East and Southeast Asia, and Japan.

The founder of Buddhism was Siddhartha Guatama, who lived in India from approximately 563 to 483 B.C. As a young man, Siddhartha achieved an understanding of the cause of suffering. From then on, he was known as the Buddha, meaning "the enlightened one."

Major Buddhist Sects

Mahayana
(the Wide Way)

Buddhism*

Theravada
(the Narrow Way)

Believed that many people could become Buddhas. The Mayahana ideal is the bodhisattva, who delays entering nirvana in order to return to the world and help others attain nirvana.

Held to the Buddha's stricter, original teachings.

*Buddhism consists of two major sects. A religious sect is a group within a religion that distinguishes itself by one or more unique beliefs.

Teachings

In his sermons, Siddhartha taught the four main ideas that he had understood in his enlightenment. He called those ideas the Four Noble Truths.

Worship

Statues of the Buddha, such as this one in Japan, appear in many forms and sizes throughout Asia. The Buddha preached that the key to happiness was detachment from all worldly goods and desires. This was achieved by following the Eightfold Path and the Middle Way, a life between earthly desires and extreme forms of self-denial.

First Noble Truth	Everything in life is suffering and sorrow.
Second Noble Truth	The cause of all suffering is people's selfish desire for the temporary pleasures of this world.
Third Noble Truth	The way to end all suffering is to end all desires.
Fourth Noble Truth	The way to overcome such desires and attain enlightenment is to follow the Noble Eightfold Path, which is called the Middle Way between desires and self-denial. Following this path could lead to nirvana, release from selfishness and pain. The Noble Eightfold Path is made up of the following:

Right views; Right livelihood;
Right aspirations; Right endeavor;
Right speech; Right mindfulness;
Right conduct; Right meditation.

ICONS, TEXTS & SYMBOLS

Wheel of the Law
The Buddha is said to have "set in motion the wheel of the dharma" during his first sermon. His teaching often is symbolized by a wheel.

CONNECTIONS ACROSS TIME AND PLACE

The Spread of Buddhism Two countries, India and China, have been largely responsible for the missionary work that has converted millions of Asians to Buddhism. The adoption of Theravada or Mahayana Buddhism by Asian countries has largely depended on whether they were introduced to Buddhism by missionaries from India or from China. Theravada missionaries from India made numerous converts in Sri Lanka, Burma, Laos, Thailand, and Cambodia. Chinese Mahayanists carried their form of Buddhism to Korea, Japan, and Tibet.

CONNECTIONS ACROSS TIME AND PLACE

Coming-of-Age Ceremonies In countries where Theravada Buddhism predominates, many boys and girls go through ceremonies in which they are recognized as adults. The ceremonies, intended for children between 8 and 12 years of age, temporarily initiate them as novice monks and nuns. Dressed as princes and princesses, like the Prince Gautama, the children walk in a procession to a monastery, along with musicians and guests. There, they remove their royal clothes and have their heads shaved—renouncing the world. Boys may stay with the monks for a day or for several years, depending on whether they want a monastic education.

Leadership

Those who dedicate their entire life to the teachings of the Buddha are known as Buddhist monks and nuns. In many Buddhist sects, monks are expected to lead a life of poverty, meditation, and study. Here, Buddhist monks in Thailand carry what are known as begging bowls. To learn humility, monks must beg for food and money. They are not allowed to speak to or notice their donors. Any communication with donors is believed to lessen the spirituality of the act.

Ritual

Women in Rangoon, Myanmar, sweep the ground so that monks can avoid stepping on and killing any insects. Many Buddhists believe in rebirth. Rebirth is the notion that human beings, after death, are reborn and continue to exist in one form or another. This also applies to animals, birds, fish, and insects. Buddhists believe that all living beings possess the potential for spiritual growth—and the possibility of rebirth as humans. Because of this, Buddhists take special care not to kill any living being.

The Three Cardinal Faults
This image depicts what Buddhists consider the three cardinal faults of humanity: greed (the pig); hatred (the snake); and delusion (the rooster).

Sacred Writings
This palm leaf is part of an 11th-century text called the *Perfection of Wisdom Sutra*, which contains some 8,000 verses. The text, written in Sanskrit, relates the life and teachings of the Buddha.

World Religions **615**

Leadership

There are significant religious and social differences in the leadership styles of Theravada and Mahayana Buddhism.

Theravada Buddhists try to follow the Buddha's own ideas on what an ideal society should be like. In his view, the king, the monks, and the laity (ordinary people) had important responsibilities to one another. For example, monks guided the spiritual development of the community. Laypeople, in return, had to provide support to the monks in the form of money and food.

Mahayana Buddhists tend to downplay Buddhism as a social force and concentrate more on its spiritual features. As a result, Mahayana clergy play a more limited political and social role than do Theravada monks.

Ritual

One of the most important symbols in Buddhist ritual and art is the lotus flower, which has acquired deep religious meaning over the centuries. The lotus flower takes root in mud but blossoms on the surface of tranquil water. Through the lotus, Buddhists are reminded that the spiritual life of a believer can blossom in enlightenment even though it is rooted in the impurity of the world and the heart.

References to the lotus occur in early Buddhist scriptures. As a result of the long tradition about the lotus, worshipers often offer lotus flowers at shrines and temples. Festival days, such as the Buddha's birthday (the day of the first full moon in May) provide special occasions for offering the lotus.

 RELIGIONS OF THE WORLD CD-ROM
Buddhism

TEACHING OPTION

CONNECTIONS ACROSS THE CURRICULUM

Zen Buddhism and the Arts Zen is a form of Mahayana Buddhism that developed in Japan around the 12th century. Zen is characterized by the directness of its teaching. It favors direct experience gained through rigorous sitting meditation (zazen) over philosophical speculation about the Buddha's message. Through this meditation, it is thought, a person can achieve sudden insight into reality, called satori, and ultimately nirvana. Zen teachers often use seemingly nonsensical questions, called koans.

Koans are intended to short-circuit the thinking process and bring students to satori. One famous koan is "What is the sound of one hand clapping?"

In the arts, Zen is most famous for its haiku poems and sand gardens. Haiku are short 17-syllable poems that are intended to capture the pure impression of a moment, unfiltered by thought. For example, this is how the 17th-century poet Matsuo Basho described a sensitive encounter with summer and the brevity of

life: "So soon to die, / and no sign of it is showing— / locust cry."

In a Zen sand garden, oddly shaped stones covered with moss are surrounded by sand raked in straight lines and curves. Such a garden shows the purity and simplicity in the heart of a true practitioner of Zen. Students may wish to bring in pictures of Zen sand gardens and show them to the class.

Christianity

Sects

There are many more Protestant groups than could have been mentioned on this page. Others include Congregationalist churches, the United Church of Christ, the Mennonites, the Quakers, the Seventh Day Adventists, the Christian Scientists, and the Jehovah's Witnesses. Each of the more than 250 Christian denominations has its own teachings, history, and organization.

Some Christians look sadly on the divisions in their religion, since such divisions contradict Jesus' wish "that they [Jesus' followers] may all be one." More recently, there has been a tendency to accept diversity—for example, in organizations such as the National Council of Churches.

Some students may wish to study and discuss with the rest of the class a Christian tradition of interest or importance to them.

Ritual

The Christian calendar contains important days (sometimes called feast days or holy days) that give a religious dimension to the year and recall important events in Christian history. In many traditions, the most important of these days are Christmas, Easter, and Pentecost (marking the descent of the Holy Spirit to inspire Jesus' closest followers, called the Apostles). Many Christians also observe religious seasons. For example, Advent and Lent are seasons of reflection and self-denial.

You may wish to ask students to pick an important day or season of the Christian calendar, study its rituals, and discuss them with the rest of the class. Photos or videos can enhance the discussion.

Christianity

Christianity is the largest religion in the world, with about 1.9 billion followers. It is based on the life and teachings of Jesus Christ. Most Christians are members of one of three major groups: Roman Catholic, Protestant, or Eastern Orthodox. Christianity teaches the existence of only one God. All Christians regard Jesus as the son of God. They believe that Jesus entered the world and died to save humanity from sin. Christians believe that they reach salvation by following the teachings of Jesus Christ.

Major Christian Sects

Eastern Orthodox • Roman Catholic

Christianity

AME • **Protestant** • Baptist

Lutheran • Methodist

Episcopal • Pentecostal

Mormon • Church of God

Presbyterian

*There are 30 Protestant denominations of over 400,000 members in each in the United States alone.

Chapter Connection
To learn about the Protestant and Catholic Reformations, see sections 3 and 4 of Chapter 1.

Ritual

Each year, hundreds of thousands of Christians from all over the world visit the Basilica of Guadalupe in northern Mexico City. The church is considered the holiest in Mexico. It is near the site where the Virgin Mary, believed to be the mother of Jesus Christ, is said to have appeared twice in 1531. Out of deep respect for Mary, some pilgrims approach the holy cathedral on their knees.

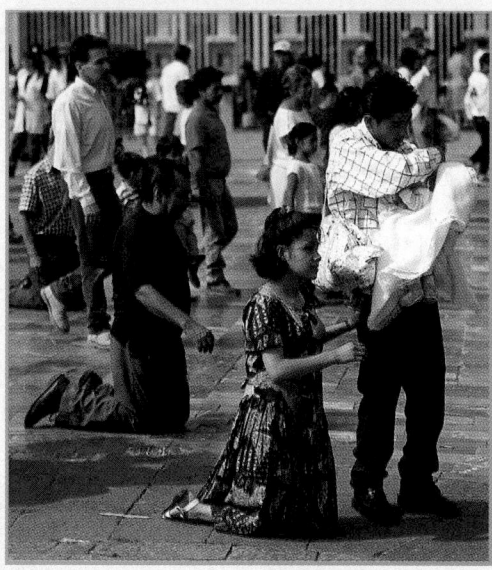

ICONS, TEXTS & SYMBOLS

The Cross
The cross, a symbol of the crucifixion of Jesus Christ, represents Jesus' love for humanity in dying for its sins.

TEACHING OPTIONS	CUSTOMIZING FOR SPECIAL NEEDS	EXPLORING PRIMARY SOURCES

Gifted and Talented Students: Comparing Water is essential to the Christian rite of baptism. It symbolizes the washing away of the sin that every human being is born with (Original Sin) and a birth into a new life.

Ask students to do research about the role of water in the ceremonies of a

non-Christian religion, such as Hinduism. Have them explain the function of water in that religion and compare it with water's role in Christian ceremonies, especially baptism. Students may go beyond world religions to other traditions (Native American, Polynesian, Australian Aborigine, Maori, Inuit, African, etc.).

And Jesus came and said to them, "All authority in heaven and on earth has been given to me. Go therefore and make disciples of all nations, . . . teaching them to obey everything that I have commanded you. And remember, I am with you always, to the end of the age." (Matthew 28:18–20)

These words of Jesus appear at the end of the Gospel of Matthew. The writer recorded them as Jesus' final advice to his followers. Ask students what effect these words may have had on the spread of Christianity as a world religion.

Worship

Christians worship in many different ways. Pictured here is a Protestant worship service in the United States. Most Protestant services share several basic features. The service includes praying, singing, reading from the Bible, and a sermon by a minister. The laity, or church members who are not ministers, participate extensively in the service. Some services include baptism and communion.

Leadership

In some Christian churches, the person who performs services in the local church is known as a priest. Shown here is a priest of the Ethiopian Christian Church holding a picture of the Virgin Mary with her infant, Jesus. These priests, like those in other Christian sects, perform such duties as presiding over the liturgy, as well as over marriages and funerals. Rules of behavior for priests differ throughout the Christian world. For example, priests with the Ethiopian Church may marry, while Roman Catholic priests may not.

The Bible
The Bible is the most sacred book of the Christian religion. It is divided into two major parts. The Old Testament focuses on Jewish history and religion. The New Testament describes the teachings of Jesus Christ.

A Cross of Palms
Palm Sunday marks the beginning of Holy Week in the Christian calendar. On this day, palms are distributed in remembrance of the palms laid before Jesus' feet as he entered Jerusalem days before his death.

World Religions **617**

Worship

Perhaps the most important rite of worship in Christianity is Holy Communion. This is a commemoration of Jesus' actions and words during his Last Supper with his disciples, when he identified bread and wine with his body and blood.

Christian denominations differ in their ideas about the meaning of Communion. In Eastern Orthodoxy, Roman Catholicism, and some Protestant denominations, the Communion service is viewed as an actual reenactment of Christ's sacrifice of his life for the human race. The bread and wine are considered to be in some sense Christ's actual body and blood.

Many Protestants, however, look upon Communion as a remembrance of Christ's death rather than a reenactment of it. These Protestants differ in their beliefs about the nature of the bread and wine.

Leadership

In most Christian churches, a group of clergy looks after the spiritual welfare of believers. They preside at worship services, baptize people, perform marriages, and preside at funerals.

Leaders of local Orthodox, Roman Catholic, and Episcopalian churches are called priests. These priests are granted special authority to administer the Christian sacraments.

In many Protestant groups, leaders of local churches are called ministers. A minister's calling and education give him or her the right to preside at worship. Nonetheless, Protestants tend to stress the equality of Christians, so the differences in the roles of the clergy and the people are less important than in other Christian groups. In fact, some Protestants—like the Quakers—have no ministers.

 RELIGIONS OF THE WORLD CD-ROM
Christianity

CONNECTIONS ACROSS TIME AND PLACE

Spread of Christianity Around the World Over the centuries, Christians have converted people throughout the world. Motivation for Christians' missionary work came from Jesus himself, who asked his followers to carry the faith to the whole world.

The first missionary efforts are recorded in the Acts of the Apostles and the letters of Saint Paul. Early missionaries spread throughout the Roman Empire. As Germanic peoples moved into the Empire,

Christians made efforts to convert them. Later, Byzantine missionaries worked in Eastern Europe among Slavic peoples. During the Middle Ages in the West, work continued among Vikings and Arabs.

The 16th century brought Catholics and Protestants to Africa, Asia, and the Americas. Besides religion, missionaries also brought education and Western ways of living. They also provided health care and some relief from poverty.

Students may wish to choose periods of history and study the work of prominent Christian missionaries, such as Saint Paul, Saints Cyril and Methodius, Albert Schweitzer, and Mother Teresa. They could examine the missionaries' methods and how those methods affected non-Christians. Students may discuss whether they agree or disagree with the missionaries' approaches.

WORLD RELIGIONS

Hinduism

Sects

Followers of Shaktism worship the supreme goddess of Hinduism, Shakti ("energy" or "force"). She may take on merciful aspects—such as Lakshmi, the partner of Vishnu—or destructive forms, such as Kali the Destroyer.

Hindus who follow Vaishnavism pay special devotion to Vishnu, the preserver.

Followers of Shaivism are devoted to the worship of Shiva, the destroyer. They seek to rid their souls of earthly bonds to attain "the nature of Shiva."

Reform Hinduism arose in the 19th century as a response to contact with Islam and the West. Reformers advocated strict monotheism, denounced statues and the caste system, and supported rights for women and Western forms of education.

Ritual

Hindus worship in both temples and at home—as individuals and families, not as congregations. A temple normally contains a principal shrine dedicated to an important god or goddess.

A temple usually also contains numerous other shrines, each devoted to a particular god. Individuals devoted to particular divinities perform their worship at those gods' altars. Hindus do not feel that they are worshiping the images of the gods; they believe that the gods themselves inhabit the images. Temples are also the scene of annual festivals celebrating highpoints in the lives of the gods.

At home, worship takes place around a family shrine, called a *puja*. The shrine is dedicated to a god or goddess that is part of the family tradition.

Hinduism

Hinduism, probably the world's oldest religion, is the major religion of India. It also has followers in Indonesia, as well as in parts of Africa, Europe, and the Western Hemisphere. Hinduism is a collection of religious beliefs that developed over thousands of years. Hindus worship several gods, which represent different forms of Brahman. Hinduism, like Buddhism, stresses that persons reach true enlightenment and happiness only after they free themselves from their earthly desires. Followers of Hinduism achieve this goal through worship, the attainment of knowledge, and a lifetime of virtuous acts.

The beliefs of Hinduism are contained in several different scriptures, including the *Vedas* and the *Bhagavad-Gita*. In the scriptures, the interconnectedness of all life is a basic concept. *Atman* is the word used for each living soul. Uniting all atmans is Brahman, the universal soul. When a person understands the relationship between atman and Brahman, that person achieves perfect understanding (*moksha*) and a release from life in this world.

However, this understanding does not usually come in one lifetime. By the process of reincarnation, an individual soul or spirit is born again and again until *moksha* is achieved. A soul's karma—good or bad deeds—follows from one reincarnation to another.

Major Hindu Sects

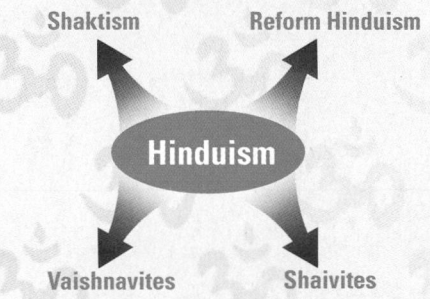

Shaktism   Reform Hinduism

Hinduism

Vaishnavites   Shaivites

Ritual

Each year, thousands of Hindus make a pilgrimage to India's Ganges River. The Ganges is considered a sacred site in the Hindu religion. Most Hindus come to bathe in the water, an act they believe will cleanse and purify them. The sick and disabled come in the belief that the holy water might cure their ailments. After most Hindus die, they are cremated. Some then have their ashes cast into the Ganges. According to traditional belief, this assures them an entry into Paradise.

ICONS, TEXTS & SYMBOLS

30

The Sacred Om
The sound *OM*, or *AUM*, represented here, is the most sacred syllable for Hindus. It often is used in prayers.

Om For many centuries, Hindus everywhere have revered the syllable *Om* as the most sacred of mantras. *Om* actually consists of three sounds (ah-oo-m). The sounds represent several groups of three that have special importance for Hindus. First of all, they represent the dimensions of earth, air, and heaven.

Next, they refer to the three most important Hindu gods: Brahma, Vishnu, and Shiva. Finally, the sounds symbolize the three collections of the Vedas: Rig, Sama, and Yajur.

Om is used in meditation, at the beginning and end of prayers, and at the beginning of sacred texts.

Linguistic Learners Over the centuries, Hinduism has coexisted comfortably with religions as diverse as Buddhism, Jainism, Islam, and Christianity. This fact points to an idea that is clearly expressed in Hindu tradition: that other religions are different paths to the same God.

Ramakrishna, a 19th-century Hindu

saint, stated, "God has made different religions to suit different aspirations, times, and countries. All doctrines are only so many paths; but a path is by no means God Himself." Hindu thinkers have taught that when the heart and mind are truly enlightened, an understanding of religions' essential unity will follow.

Leadership

Gurus, or spiritual teachers, like the one shown here, play a major role in spreading Hindu beliefs. These holy men are believed to have had the gods' words revealed to them. They interpret and provide insight into the religion. Gurus also travel to villages throughout the country and teach the ways of Hinduism to those villagers who cannot read.

Celebration

Each spring, Hindus in India celebrate the festival of Holi. This festival is a tribute to Shiva, one of the leading gods of Hinduism. Shiva is considered to be beyond good and evil. Hindus call him the Destroyer because he occasionally destroys the world in order to recreate it. The Holi festival honors Shiva with loud and colorful parades in some parts of India. In one of the more dramatic rituals, shown here, a throng gathers in a sacred temple in the village of Nandgaon. There, they are showered with colored powder and dyed water.

The Vedas

The Vedas are the oldest Hindu scriptures—and are older than the sacred writings of any other major religion. They contain prayers and hymns, as well as works of philosophy.

Brahma

This statue represents Brahma, creator of the universe. Brahma, Vishnu, and Shiva are the three main gods of Hinduism. Vishnu is the preserver of the universe, while Shiva is its destroyer.

619

Leadership

Spiritual leadership in the Hindu community is the responsibility of the Brahmin class. Because of good works performed in previous lives, Brahmins have earned a karma that entitles them to be born in the highest social class, or caste.

Brahmins take on the roles of priests, philosophers, artists, and teachers in Hindu society. They are responsible for performing sacrifices in temples and for the care of the shrines of the gods. Some of the priestly sacrifices can be traced back 3,000 years.

So much is expected of Hinduism's spiritual leaders that a Brahmin who has committed a crime receives a far more severe punishment than a Shudra (a member of the lowest caste) who has committed the same crime.

Celebration

Another joyous Hindu festival is Diwali, which marks the beginning of the Hindu new year. When it gets dark, believers light many small lamps. The lights serve to frighten away demons and welcome back the god Rama, who, tradition says, was driven out of his kingdom.

A celebration focused more on the family is the ceremony of the sacred thread. It is a coming-of-age ceremony for boys in the three highest of the four castes. Sometimes, it is celebrated the day before a boy marries. The boy's father drapes a sacred thread over his son's left shoulder and under his right arm. From that moment on, the boy will wear the thread as a symbol that he is "twice born," having been born first into the world and then into the religious life.

 RELIGIONS OF THE WORLD CD-ROM
Hinduism

Gifted and Talented Students: Pilgrimages

Pilgrimages are journeys to places that are considered to possess special spiritual power owing to their connection with gods, saints, or events of religious importance. By visiting these holy places, believers are thought to become more holy themselves.

During the more than 3,000 years of their religion's existence, the Hindus of India have set apart between 58,000 and 64,000 sites in their country as *tirthas,* or places of pilgrimage.

After the building of railroads in India, Hindus began taking 10-week "all-India pilgrimages." These take pilgrims to holy sites in the north, in the south, and on the eastern and western coasts of the country.

Interested students may wish to compare the traditions of pilgrimage in Hinduism and another religion (e.g., Buddhism, Christianity, Islam, or Judaism). In a report to the rest of the class, they could compare the two religions' ideas about who must or should go on pilgrimage, as well as the locations and histories of the religions' places of pilgrimage and the religious rituals associated with those places. Visuals of the places and the rituals might aid the discussion.

Islam

Sects

The split between Sunni and Shi'a Muslims arose from a dispute over who should succeed Muhammad as political leader of the Muslim community. Two theories emerged as to who should lead Muslims. The Sunni sect believed that any religious leader who had demonstrated a deep understanding of Muslim tradition had earned the right to leadership. In contrast, the Shi'a sect believed that only those directly related to the Prophet through Ali, Muhammad's cousin, could legitimately rule. Today, the Shi'a tradition is concentrated mainly in Iran, while Sunni Islam predominates in the rest of the Islamic world.

Celebration

The end of Ramadan fasting is celebrated by a major Islamic holiday called Eid al-Fitr. The celebration begins with a worship service that may be held in a mosque or a public place designed to hold a large number of people.

Later, the site of the celebration switches to the home. There, many festive foods that were not eaten during Ramadan, including sweets, are shared with family members and friends. The celebration may continue for three days or longer in Muslim countries. To help those less fortunate, many Muslims contribute money that allows the poor to share in the joy of the season.

The other great Islamic religious holiday, called Eid al-Adha, takes place in the last month of the Islamic calendar. Eid al-Adha commemorates the faithfulness of the prophet Abraham, who was willing to sacrifice his own son to obey God's command.

Islam

Islam is a religion based on the teachings of the prophet Muhammad (570–632). Followers of Islam, known as Muslims, live throughout the world. They are concentrated from Southwest to Central Asia, in parts of Africa, and in parts of Southeast Asia.

The main teachings of Islam are in the Qu'ran (KUR•an). The central belief of Islam is that there is only one God, called *Allah*. All other beliefs and practices follow from this teaching. Islam teaches that there is good and evil, and that each individual is responsible for the actions of his or her life. Muslim believers have to carry out five duties, called the Five Pillars of Islam.

The Five Pillars are:
- **Faith**—A believer must make the following statement of faith: "There is no God but Allah, and Muhammad is the Messenger of Allah."
- **Prayer**—Five times a day, Muslims face toward the holy city of Mecca to pray.
- **Alms**—Muslims must give alms, or money for the poor.
- **Fasting**—During the Islamic holy month of Ramadan, Muslims must fast.
- **Pilgrimage**—All Muslims perform the hajj, or pilgrimage to Mecca, once in a lifetime.

Major Islamic Sects

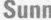

Believe that the first 4 caliphs who succeeded Muhammad were the rightful leaders of Islam.

Sunni

Islam

Shi'a

Believe that the leader of Islam must be a descendant of Ali, Muhammad's cousin and son-in-law.

Celebration

During the sacred month known as Ramadan, Muslims fast, or abstain from food and drink, from dawn to sunset. They do this as a sign of obedience, humility, and self-control. The fasting traditionally ends with eating a few dates and milk or water, followed by the sunset prayer. These foods accompany the other dishes that families, such as the one shown here, eat each night during the month.

The most important night of Ramadan is called the Night of Power (Laylat al-Qadr). This is believed to be the night the angel Gabriel, the messenger of God, first spoke to Muhammad.

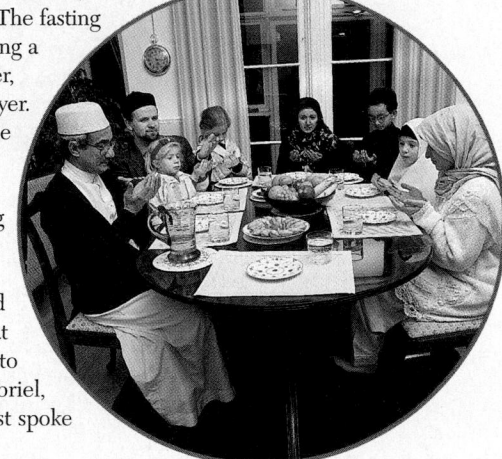

ICONS, TEXTS & SYMBOLS

Crescent Moon
The crescent moon has become a familiar symbol for Islam. It may be related to the new moon that begins each month in the Islamic lunar calendar, which orders religious life for Muslims.

Linguistic Learners Islam has no ordained clergy. Instead, scholars and spiritual leaders emerge after they have shown evidence of superior learning or judgment. Islamic scholars may specialize in one or several areas of religious knowledge and practice. An *alim* pursues in-depth studies of the Qur'an and the

recorded sayings of Muhammad, called *hadith*. A *faqih* decides cases and makes judgments based on guidance from the Qur'an and other Islamic traditions. A *hafiz* memorizes the Qur'an, while a *qari* specializes in chanting texts from Islam's sacred book.

You might ask some linguistic learners to organize these names and functions in a chart and explain them to the class.

Science: The Muslim Calendar Unlike the solar calendar used in the West, the Muslim calendar is lunar— that is, based on the phases of the moon. The lunar year is about 11 days shorter than the solar year. As a result, Muslim dates "jump backward" 11 days each year with respect to the dates of the Gregorian calendar used in the

West, so that during a period of 32.5 solar years, a Muslim date moves through all four seasons.

Students may wish to discuss what would happen if American holidays moved through the seasons. How might celebrations of a holiday like the Fourth of July be different in different seasons?

Worship

At least once in their lifetime, all Muslims who are physically and financially able, go on hajj, or pilgrimage, to the holy city of Mecca in Saudi Arabia. There, pilgrims perform several rites, or acts of worship. One rite, shown here, is walking seven times around the Ka'bah—the house of worship that Muslims face in prayer.

The climax of the hajj is the day when millions of believers stand at a place named Arafat. There, they ask forgiveness of God on the same spot where Muhammad gave a farewell sermon.

Ritual

Five times a day Muslims throughout the world face Mecca and pray to Allah. This prayer ritual, known as Salat, occurs at dawn, noon, late afternoon, sunset, and evening. Muslims recite these prayers at work, or school, or wherever they happen to be. Pictured here are Muslims praying at an intersection in Alexandria, Egypt.

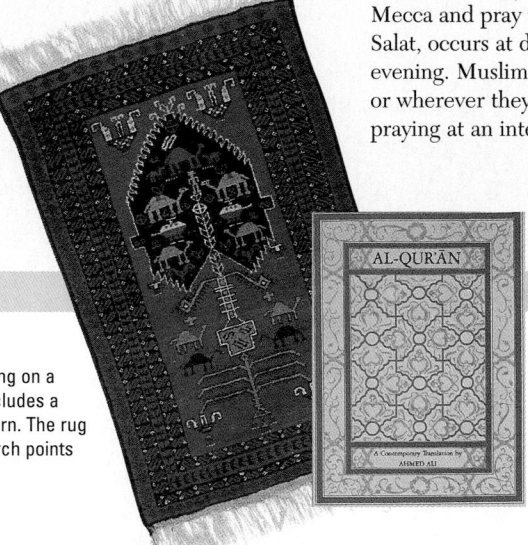

Prayer Rug
Muslims often pray by kneeling on a rug. The design of the rug includes a pointed or arch-shaped pattern. The rug must be placed so that the arch points toward Mecca.

The Qur'an
The Qur'an, the sacred book of Muslims, consists of verses grouped into 114 chapters, or suras. The book is the spiritual guide on matters of faith and practice for all Muslims. In addition, it contains teachings that guide Muslim daily life.

World Religions **621**

Worship

The basic ceremony of formal Islamic worship is called the *salah*. In areas that have a large enough Muslim population, the *salah* takes place in a mosque. Instead of containing chairs or pews, the worship space in a mosque is a large, often carpeted area that faces toward the Ka'bah in Mecca.

Muslim men and boys are required to participate in congregational worship on Friday at noon. Because of household duties, women and girls are exempt from this responsibility. At the beginning of a formal worship service, Muslims raise their hands up to their ears and declare "Allahu Akbar" ("God is greatest").

At each stage of the ceremony, worshipers stand, bow, and touch their foreheads to the ground twice. Verses from the Qur'an are read and prayers are said in Arabic. During the service, the congregation is led by an imam. The imam is not a priest but a worship leader chosen by the congregation.

Ritual

Muslims may eat all foods except those specifically forbidden (*haram*) by the Qur'an. Foods that are *haram* include pork, blood, and the meat of animals found dead, animals of prey, and animals slaughtered in the name of any god but Allah. When slaughtering meat, a Muslim butcher pronounces the name of Allah. This tradition arose to recognize God's generosity and his work as the Creator, and meat so blessed is said to be *halal*. Since both Jews and Christians worship the same God as Muslims, Islamic law allows Muslims to eat meat slaughtered by Jews or Christians.

 RELIGIONS OF THE WORLD CD-ROM
Islam

CONNECTIONS ACROSS TIME AND PLACE

The Other Scriptures of Islam Muslims regard the Qur'an—the final revelation from God to the Prophet Muhammad—as the last in a centuries-long series of revelations beginning with God's message to Abraham, founder of the Jewish people. As a result, Muslims accept certain scriptures revealed to Jewish and Christian prophets as inspired by God. The scriptures, other than the Qur'an, that Muslims accept as Allah's words are
• *Suhuf* ("Scrolls"), revealed to Abraham

• *Tawrah* ("Torah"), given to Moses
• *Zabur* ("Psalms"), received by David
• *Injeel* ("Gospel"), revealed to Jesus
Accepting these previous scriptures is an essential part of Islamic faith. For Muslims, the scriptures show how God gradually revealed religious truth to humans when they were ready to receive it. Muslims' acceptance of these scriptures also demonstrates their belief that Islam is the fulfillment of the religious tradition of Jews and Christians.

As a result, Muslims consider Jews and Christians "people of the Book," because they, like Muslims, received scriptures revealed by God. You might wish to ask students how this sense of kinship with Jews and Christians might help to explain the policy of religious tolerance practiced by Muslim rulers during their almost-800-year presence in Spain.

Teacher's Edition **621**

Sects

In the 19th century, Jews divided into three groups. The divisions were based on how closely believers followed the traditions recorded in the Torah and in commentaries on the Torah (the Talmud).

In Orthodox Judaism, believers follow traditional dietary (kosher) laws. During worship, Orthodox Jews pray in Hebrew—with men and women sitting apart. Orthodox men always cover their heads out of respect for God. Married women cover their heads with hats, scarves, or wigs.

Reform Judaism arose from efforts to adapt Judaism to life in the West. Reform Jews tend to select elements of tradition for observance and have changed some traditional practices—for example, allowing women to serve as rabbis.

Conservative Judaism represents an attempt to strike a balance between Orthodox and Reform Judaism. Conservatives balance tradition with the needs of the modern world.

Celebration

The Jewish year is marked by a series of holy days that remind Jews of their beliefs, history, and traditions.

Rosh Hashanah is a one- or two-day festival that marks the beginning of the new year in the Jewish calendar. Passover, or Pesach, lasts for seven or eight days and recalls the departure of the Jews from Egypt, where they had been enslaved.

Students may wish to read about and discuss other holy days or periods in the Jewish calendar—for example, Yom Kippur, Hanukkah, and Succoth.

Judaism

Judaism is the religion of the more than 13 million Jews throughout the world. Judaism was the first major religion to teach the existence of only one god. The basic laws and teachings of Judaism come from the Torah, the first five books of the Hebrew Bible. Judaism teaches that a person serves God by studying the Torah and living by its teachings.

According to the Bible, God gave laws of human conduct to the Hebrew leader Moses as he was leading the Jews out of slavery in Egypt in about 1300 or 1200 B.C. These laws are known as the Ten Commandments.

Prophets—religious teachers who interpreted the will of God—constantly urged the Jews to worship God and to live moral lives in accordance with God's laws. This emphasis on right conduct and the worship of one God is called ethical monotheism. It is a Hebrew idea that has deeply influenced Judaism, Christianity, and Islam.

Major Jewish Sects

Reform   Orthodox

Judaism

Conservative

Chapter Connection

For an examination of the impact that Judaism has had on the development of democratic ideas, see pages 12–13 of the Prologue: "The Rise of Democratic Ideas."

Celebration

Jews celebrate a number of holidays that honor their history as well as their God. Pictured here are Jews celebrating the holiday of Purim. Purim is a festival honoring the survival of the Jews who, in the fifth century B.C., were marked for death by their Persian rulers.

The story—found in the Book of Esther in the Hebrew Bible—describes how Esther, the Jewish queen of Persia, convinced the Persian king to spare her people. Jews celebrate Purim by sending food and gifts to friends, neighbors, and the poor. In addition, they dress in costumes and hold carnivals and dances.

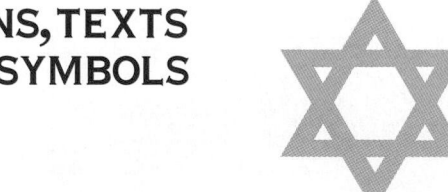

ICONS, TEXTS & SYMBOLS

The Star of David

The Star of David, also called the Shield of David, is the universal symbol of Judaism. The emblem refers to King David, who ruled the kingdom of Israel from about 1000–962 B.C.

Visual Learners Jewish art tends to be nonrepresentational. The law against "graven images" (statues) in the Book of Exodus (20) has discouraged the depiction of people and animals in religious art. Nevertheless, a number of European artworks depict events in Jewish history.

You could ask visually-oriented students to display artworks depicting various biblical events and to read to the class the corresponding passages in the Bible. Incidents of possible interest include the creation of the world, the sacrifice of Isaac, the finding of Moses in the bulrushes, the parting of the Red Sea, and David's battle with Goliath.

Contrasting The coming-of-age ceremonies in Judaism have parallels in other religious traditions. You might ask students to contrast the sacred-thread ceremony in Hinduism, the coming-of-age ceremonies in Buddhism, and the rite of confirmation in Christianity with Jewish traditions.

Books on world religions will provide students with material.

You might ask students to discuss what aspects of religious experience and of growing up are emphasized in each of the traditions. Ask them to point out similarities and differences among them.

Ritual

Some Jews follow strict dietary laws based on passages from the Hebrew Bible. These laws have established what is kosher, or acceptable, for Jews to eat. Kosher laws forbid the eating of animals considered unclean. These animals include pigs and shellfish.

The preparation of food is a significant part of kosher law. Animals must be killed in a certain way—a single cut across the neck made with a knife absent of nicks. This is intended to kill the animal as quickly and painlessly as possible. Before the meat is cooked, it must be drained of its blood.

There are additional kosher laws that determine everything from the preparation of food to what foods may not be eaten together. Shown here, a rabbi inspects a kitchen in the United States to ensure that it follows kosher guidelines.

Worship

Several women worship at the Western Wall—a place of prayer and pilgrimage held sacred to the Jewish people. The ancient structure formed the western wall of the courtyard of the Second Temple of Jerusalem. The Romans destroyed the temple in A.D. 70. The wall, which dates back to the second century B.C., measures about 160 feet long and about 60 feet high. Located in Jerusalem, it is also known as the Wailing Wall. This term was coined by European travelers who witnessed some Jews loudly mourning the destruction of the temple.

Yarmulke
Out of respect for God, Jewish men are not supposed to leave their head uncovered. Therefore, many Orthodox and Conservative Jews wear a skullcap known as a yarmulke, or kippah.

The Torah Scroll
During a synagogue service, the Torah scroll is lifted, while the congregation declares: "This is the Law which Moses set before the children of Israel."

Ritual

Significant events in the life of a Jew are marked by ritual.

One of the most important ceremonies in the life of a Jewish boy is that of his coming of age. At the age of 13, a boy accepts the full responsibilities of an adult in his religion and community. He becomes a bar mitzvah ("son of the commandments") by going through a bar mitzvah service in a synagogue. During the ceremony, he reads aloud from the Torah.

A girl can have a bat mitzvah ("daughter of the commandments") ceremony at the age of 12 or 13. The ritual recognizes her as a Jewish woman.

Some students may wish to study more deeply the traditions of coming of age and marriage in the Jewish faith. If possible, they should attend one or both of these services and discuss their experience with the class.

Worship

Jewish houses of worship are called synagogues (often *temples* in the Reform and Conservative traditions). A synagogue is usually built so that the congregation faces toward Jerusalem during worship. An ark, or cabinet, at the front of the synagogue contains the scroll of the Torah, the most sacred books of the Hebrew Bible. A lamp called the eternal light hangs before the ark, symbolizing the eternal presence of God.

A rabbi ("teacher") reads prayers and passages of the Bible during the service. He or she also delivers the sermon. During worship, the rabbi is assisted by a cantor (or musical leader) who chants prayers.

Playing recordings of Jewish sacred music might help students appreciate the Eastern origins and atmosphere of Jewish worship.

 RELIGIONS OF THE WORLD CD-ROM
Judaism

CONNECTIONS ACROSS THE CURRICULUM

Science, the Arts, Ideas In the 19th and 20th centuries, the magnitude of Jewish scientists', artists', and thinkers' influence on thought and creative expression in the Western world far exceeded the magnitude of the Jewish population. Karl Marx, Sigmund Freud, and Albert Einstein are just three examples of Jewish thinkers who permanently changed the course of thought in the West and the world.

Karl Marx created the theory of communism. Marx's ideas motivated others to rethink economic relations in the capitalist societies of Western Europe. Sigmund Freud founded the technique of psychoanalysis. His theory of the unconscious revealed a dimension of the mind that most people had never suspected. The theory of relativity formulated by the physicist Albert Einstein overturned the Newtonian view of the

universe that had dominated scientific thought in the West since the 1600s.

You might ask students to study and discuss in class great Jewish figures in the sciences and arts. A general history of the Jewish people should highlight such creative geniuses as Marc Chagall (painting), Milton Friedman (economics), Leonard Bernstein (music), and Saul Bellow (literature).

Confucianism

Golden Rule

Several religious thinkers and philosophers have formulated rules of conduct similar to Confucius' Golden Rule. The most famous is Jesus' statement in the Gospel of Matthew: "In everything, do to others what you would have them do to you."

The rule may be framed positively (Jesus' "Do to others . . .") or negatively (Confucius' "Do not do unto others . . ."). The moral content of the rule, however, remains essentially the same. It urges us to see other people as similar to ourselves—a moral breakthrough in the ancient world.

Some students may wish to discuss the implications of the positive and negative versions of the Golden Rule—for example, with regard to performing or avoiding actions and to seeing actions from one's own or another person's point of view.

Celebration

In celebrating Confucius' birthday, followers of the philosopher are also rejoicing in his 1,500 years of influence in Asia. Confucius was born about 551 B.C. in northeastern China. By the age of 3, he had lost his father; but his impoverished mother instilled a love of learning in him, and he eventually became a successful teacher.

One way Confucius tried to spread his ethical views in China was by holding government office. China's leaders, however, found his honesty and frankness to be impractical, even dangerous.

Despite his political setbacks, Confucius' reputation as a man of conscience and thought attracted many followers. Since then, his thoughts have influenced millions.

Confucianism

A look at the world's major religions would not be complete without an examination of Confucianism. With no clergy, or gods to worship, Confucianism is not considered a religion in the traditional sense. However, this ancient philosophy guides the actions and beliefs of millions of Chinese and other peoples of the East. Thus, it often is viewed as a major religion.

Confucianism is a way of life based on the teachings of the Chinese scholar, Confucius, who lived from about 551 to 479 B.C. It stresses social and civic responsibility. It also provides people with an ethical system to follow.

Confucius believed that a society could have social order, harmony, and good government if it was organized around five basic relationships. These were the relations between: 1) ruler and subject, 2) father and son, 3) husband and wife, 4) older brother and younger brother, and 5) friend and friend. A code of proper conduct regulated each of these relationships. For example, rulers should practice kindness and virtuous living. In return, subjects should be loyal and law-abiding.

Confucianism became the foundation for Chinese government and social order. In addition, the ideas of Confucius spread beyond China and influenced civilizations throughout East Asia. While East Asians declare themselves to be any one of a number of religions, many also claim to be Confucian.

Celebration

While scholars remain uncertain of Confucius' date of birth, people throughout East Asia celebrate it on September 28. In Taiwan, it is an official holiday, known as Teachers' Day (shown above). Aside from honoring Confucius, the holiday pays tribute to teachers, who play a significant role in Confucianism. Confucius himself was a teacher, and he believed that education was an important part of a fulfilled life. In Confucianism, teachers are highly regarded, and their authority is just below that of a father.

ICONS, TEXTS & SYMBOLS

The Yin–Yang
The yin–yang symbol represents opposite forces in the world working together. It symbolizes the social order and harmony that Confucianism stresses.

Tzu-kung [a disciple] asked about the true gentleman. The Master [Confucius] said, "He does not preach what he practices till he has practiced what he preaches. . . . A gentleman can see a question from all sides without bias. . . . A gentleman takes as much trouble to discover what is right as lesser men

take to discover what will pay."

These words of Confucius were recorded by his students in the *Analects*. To Confucius, the gentleman is the fully developed human being. The gentleman has important moral qualities. What moral qualities are emphasized in this passage? How does Confucius' view of the gentleman differ from modern notions?

Visual Learners Much traditional Chinese painting reflects Confucius' ideals of harmony and serenity, both in human interaction and in nature. In fact, Chinese landscape painting excels at showing human beings as elements of a serene world pattern. Such ideals are not exclusive to Confucianism in China. Buddhism and Taoism are also strong religious traditions in China, and they

also stress the calm order of the universe. Show students World Art and Cultures Transparencies AT25 (Court Ladies Preparing Newly Woven Silk) and AT60 (Sorting of Cocoons) to illustrate this point. You might also ask students to look in art books for illustrations of Chinese paintings that depict the tranquil world idealized by Chinese religion.

Ritual

A key aspect of Confucianism is respect for family members and elders. This helped promote the religious practice throughout East Asia of honoring ancestors. In homes such as the one in China shown here, residents build shrines to honor their deceased relatives. The family offers prayers and food at the shrine. Family members then eat the meal—believing the ancestors have already tasted it. The Chinese believe showing respect for ancestors will ensure continued cooperation and aid from their deceased relatives.

Worship

Confucius is said to have preached more about social order than religious matters. In spite of this, the Chinese scholar has become viewed by many as a god. By the sixth century A.D., every district in China had a temple dedicated to Confucius. Since then, millions of people have come to revere him as a spiritual leader. Here, children in Taiwan take part in a ceremony honoring Confucius.

The Analects
The earliest and most authentic record of Confucius' ideas was recorded by his students. Around 400 B.C., they compiled Confucius' words in a book called the *Analects*.

World Religions **625**

Ritual

Confucius' ethics emphasized earthly rather than heavenly matters. Nevertheless, Confucius approved of the rituals of traditional Chinese religion. These included sacrifices to the gods and to ancestors as well as ceremonies for foretelling the future.

While he did not express precise teachings about the supernatural, Confucius did believe in a heavenly force for good. He taught that the first requirement for living a fully human life was respect for the will of heaven. He is quoted as having said, "Heaven appointed me to teach my doctrines." A phrase often quoted from his writings is "He who offends the gods has no one to pray to."

Worship

Respect for Confucius has not been limited to Asians. Jesuit missionaries who arrived in China in the late 1500s came to believe that many of Confucius' teachings were really Christian. Some missionaries even wrestled with the question of whether Chinese converts to Christianity could continue to participate in Confucian ancestor worship. The missionaries admired Confucius so much that they translated his writings into Latin. By the early 1600s, Confucius was a widely read writer in the West.

Some Jesuits compared Confucius to Aristotle (whom they called the Philosopher) by calling him the Philosopher of the Chinese. His high moral standards and humanistic view of the world reminded them of the ideas of the Greek philosopher and the humanistic ideals of the Renaissance. By the early 18th century, however, the pope had put an end to the Jesuits' attempts to link Confucianism with Christianity.

 RELIGIONS OF THE WORLD CD-ROM
Confucianism

CONNECTIONS ACROSS TIME AND PLACE

The Chinese Examination System The teachings of Confucius inspired one of the major features of Chinese government: the examinations for civil servants. Written tests for government posts go back to the Han Dynasty (202 B.C.–A.D. 220). They reflected the Confucian respect for learning as a path to wisdom. Under the Tang Dynasty (618–907), the exams demanded a detailed knowledge of the literature of Confucianism, including the works believed to have been written by Confucius himself.

Passing the examinations became essential for social mobility. By long study, a poor man could move up to become rich and powerful. As a result, many who failed the examinations continued to take them even into old age. Despite its theoretical fairness, however, the system favored the children of the rich, who had the money and leisure to prepare for the exams.

In a concern for objectivity, the tests tended to emphasize dry fact over creativity. By the 19th century, a whole series of exams awaited those who wanted to rise in the civil service. The so-called final exam, given every three years, allowed only about 100 of several thousand candidates to pass. The hundred who succeeded would rise to the top of the imperial bureaucracy.

WORLD RELIGIONS

A Comparison Teaching Strategies

World Religions: A Comparison provides a useful summary of information concerning the five world religions and Confucianism presented in the *World Religions* feature of the Pupil's Edition. It provides in an accessible format essential information that can be supplemented by information in the textbook, by further reading, or by your knowledge or that of your students.

You might encourage the class to expand its understanding of the beliefs and values of each faith by further study. Stress that the digest of beliefs and values presented in the comparison chart is just a starting point and that each belief system can be the subject of in-depth research and study. The results of this study could provide valuable material for discussions and reports.

One important source for religious teachings is the holy book(s) of each faith. These books are listed in the chart, and they represent each religion's deepest expression of its teachings. Interested students may wish to read selections from these books.

You could ask the students what the texts seem to be saying about the religion(s) they have chosen to study. Some students may not be sure about what the texts are saying. This uncertainty can lead to a useful discussion about how students can better understand what they have read.

Stress that all these texts are to be treated with respect and that truly appreciating them may involve going beyond the views and opinions of our own culture. Drawing attention to culturally biased opinions expressed in class may help students understand this sometimes difficult concept.

A Comparison

	Buddhism	Christianity	Hinduism	Islam	Judaism	Confucianism
*Followers Worldwide	338 million	1.9 billion	764 million	1 billion	13.4 million	Not available
Name of Deity	The Buddha did not teach a personal deity	God	Three main Gods: Brahma, Vishnu, Shiva	God (Allah)	God (Yahweh)	Confucius (viewed by many as a god)
Founder	The Buddha	Jesus Christ	No one founder	Muhammad	Abraham	Confucius
Holy Book	No one book—sacred texts, including the *Perfection of Wisdom Sutra*	Bible	No one book—sacred texts, including the Vedas, the Puranas	Qur'an	Hebrew Bible, including the Torah	the *Analects*, the Five Classics
Leadership	Buddhist monks and nuns	Clergy (priests/ministers)	Guru, Holy Man, Brahman priest	No clergy	Rabbis	No Clergy
Basic Beliefs	•Persons achieve complete peace and happiness, known as nirvana, by eliminating their attachment to worldly things. •Nirvana is reached by following the Noble Eightfold Path: Right views; Right aspirations; Right speech; Right conduct; Right livelihood; Right endeavor; Right mindfulness; Right meditation.	•There is only one God, who watches over and cares for his people. •Jesus Christ was the son of God. He died to save humanity from sin. His death made eternal life possible for others. •Persons achieve salvation by following the teachings of Jesus.	•The soul never dies, but is continually reborn. •Persons achieve happiness and enlightenment after they free themselves from their earthly desires. •Freedom from earthly desires comes from a lifetime of worship, knowledge, and virtuous acts.	•Persons achieve salvation by following the Five Pillars of Islam and living a just life. These pillars are: faith; almsgiving, or charity to the poor; fasting, which Muslims perform during Ramadan; pilgrimage (to Mecca); and prayer.	•There is only one God, who watches over and cares for his people. •God loves and protects his people, but also holds people accountable for their sins and shortcomings. •Persons serve God by studying the Torah and living by its teachings.	•Social order, harmony, and good government should be based on strong family relationships. •Respect for parents and elders is important to a well-ordered society. •Education is important both to the welfare of the individual and to society.

*estimated 1994 figures

Assessment

REVIEW QUESTIONS

Buddhism

1. According to the Buddha, how does one achieve happiness and fulfillment?

Christianity

2. Why is Jesus Christ central to the Christian religion?

Hinduism

3. Explain the importance of the Ganges River in Hinduism.

Islam

4. What is the most important night of Ramadan? Why?

Judaism

5. Why do Jews consider the Western Wall to be sacred?

Confucianism

6. How has Confucianism's emphasis on familial respect affected religious worship in East Asia?

ANALYZING PRIMARY SOURCES

In her book, *A History of God*, Karen Armstrong explains why religion is such a powerful force in people's lives:

A VOICE FROM THE PAST

. . . Human beings are spiritual animals. Indeed, there is a case for arguing that *Homo sapiens* is also *Homo religiosus*. Men and women started to worship gods as soon as they became recognizably human; they created religions at the same time they created works of art. . . . These early faiths expressed the wonder and mystery that seem always to have been an essential component of the human experience of this beautiful yet terrifying world. Like art, religion has been an attempt to find meaning and value in life, despite the suffering that flesh is heir to.

- Based on information from the previous pages, how might religion give life meaning and value?
- Do you agree or disagree with Ms. Armstrong? Explain.

CRITICAL THINKING

1. COMPARING AND CONTRASTING

Using information from the text and chart, choose two religions and identify their similarities and differences in a Venn diagram like the one below.

2. COMMON THREADS

The previous pages reveal items and activities that play an important role in more than one religion. Determine what some are and explain how each is significant to different religions.

ACTIVITIES

1. LIVING HISTORY: Portfolio Project

Your portfolio project focuses on religious and ethical systems around the world. You may want to include one of the following activities in your portfolio.

- Imagine you are a newspaper reporter who has been granted entrance to a Buddhist monastery. Write a brief article describing what you think a day in the life of a Buddhist monk might be like.
- Write a persuasive speech in order to convince someone that Confucianism can be considered a religion.
- Write a dialogue between two people in which each explains the workings of one of the major religions to the other.

2. CONNECT TO TODAY: Cooperative Learning

As the previous pages explained, the world's major religions contain various sects. Sects are smaller groups within a religion. These groups hold one or more unique beliefs, which make them slightly different from other followers.

Working in small groups, find out what makes the major sects of a particular religion different. As a group, report your findings to the class.

Use the Internet and other sources to research the unique beliefs and practices of the major sects of a religion.

- Each group member should be responsible for one sect. He or she should write a brief report detailing the beliefs and practices that make that sect unique.
- The group should then present its findings to the class by having each group member read aloud his or her report.

Assessment

REVIEW QUESTIONS

1. **Buddhism** By detaching one's self from all worldly goods and desires—achieved by following the Eightfold Path and the Middle Way, a life between earthly desires and extreme forms of self-denial.

2. **Christianity** Christians believe Christ to be the son of God. They also believe that he died to save humanity from sin and that humans reach salvation by following Christ's teachings.

3. **Hinduism** The Ganges is considered a sacred site—Hindus believe that it has healing powers and that having their ashes cast into the river after death assures them entry into Paradise.

4. **Islam** The Night of Power, because it is believed to be the night the angel Gabriel first spoke to Muhammad.

5. **Judaism** The wall is held sacred to Jews because it is all that remains of the Second Temple of Jerusalem complex, destroyed around A.D. 70.

6. **Confucianism** Many families build shrines in their homes to honor their deceased relatives.

ANALYZING PRIMARY SOURCES

Possible Responses: Religion provides people with an ethical and spiritual path to follow; it adds order and structure to their life; it gives them hope for a better life; it provides them with a sense of community and belonging.
Students should state their opinion clearly and provide reasons for their opinion.

CHAPTER ACTIVITIES

1. LIVING HISTORY
Standards for Evaluation
An effective portfolio project should meet the following criteria:

- Shows an understanding of belief systems and/or ways of life that may not be the student's own
- Is carefully researched and thoughtfully written and presented
- Is clearly and effectively organized

2. CONNECT TO TODAY:
   COOPERATIVE LEARNING
Standards for Evaluation
Reports should meet the following criteria:

- Focuses on beliefs and practices that make a sect distinct
- Demonstrates an understanding of those beliefs and practices
- Is effectively organized and presented
- Shows thoughtful use of outside sources

CRITICAL THINKING

1. COMPARING AND CONTRASTING
Possible comparison: Buddhism and Hinduism—Similarities: both stress that the key to happiness is detachment from earthly goods and desires, both preach a type of reincarnation, neither has one Holy Book. Differences: Buddhism has a founder (Buddha), while Hinduism has no one founder; Buddhism rejects the notion of a deity, while Hinduism preaches several gods which represent different forms of the supreme being, Brahman.

2. COMMON THREADS
Possible answers: Food and drink—food is an important part of the Jewish religion, and it also plays a role in the Muslim celebration of Ramadan. The pilgrimage—the pilgrimage plays a key role in several religions: Muslims go on a hajj, or pilgrimage to Mecca; Hindus make a pilgrimage to the Ganges River; Jews travel to the Western Wall; and Christians make a pilgrimage to the Basilica of Guadelupe or other shrine.

MODERN WORLD HISTORY

PATTERNS OF INTERACTION

Reference Section

628

Atlas

The atlas contains a political map of the world and both political and physical maps of the continents.

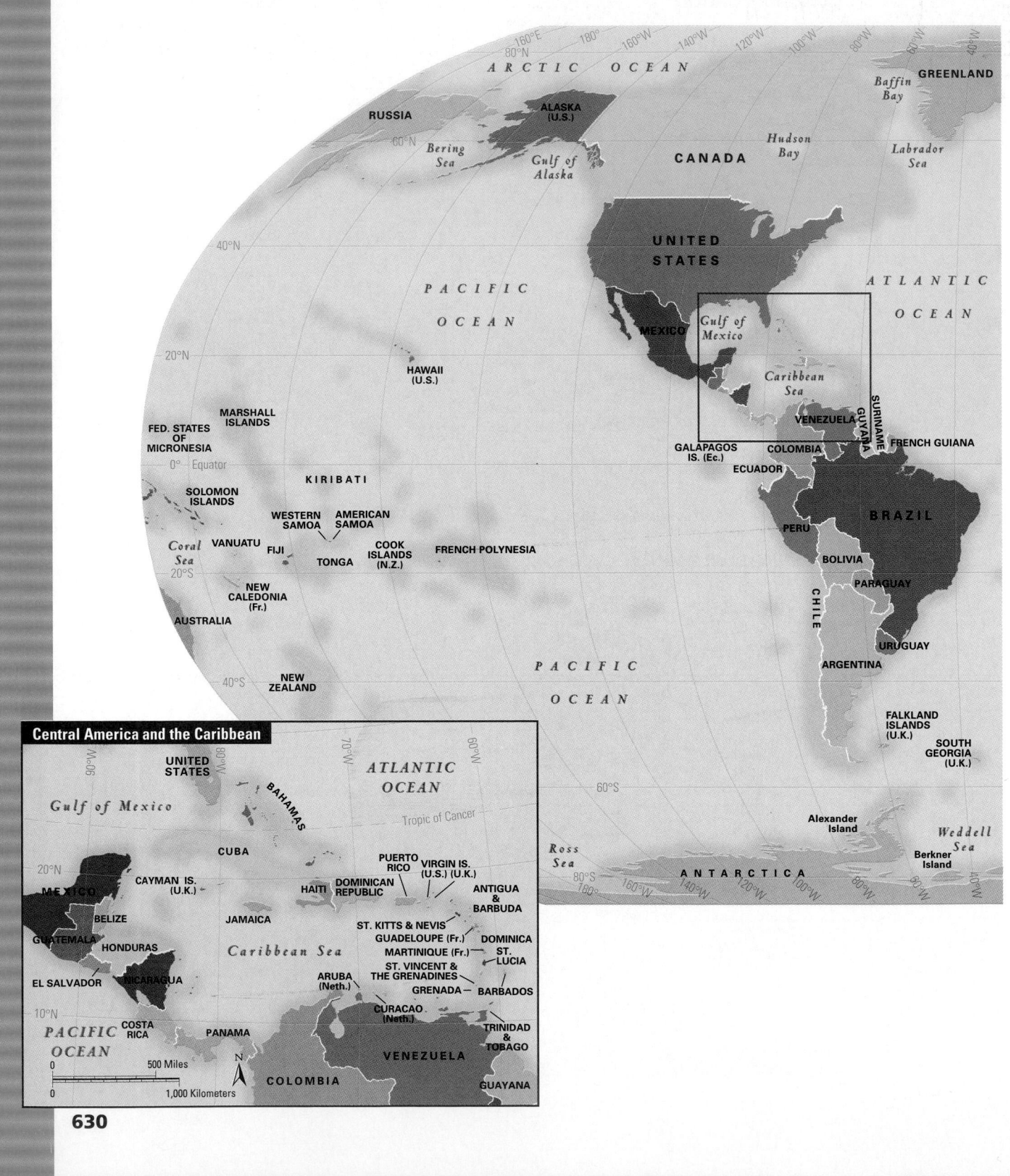

ARCTIC OCEAN

GREENLAND

Baffin Bay

RUSSIA

ALASKA (U.S.)

Bering Sea

Gulf of Alaska

CANADA

Hudson Bay

Labrador Sea

UNITED STATES

ATLANTIC OCEAN

PACIFIC OCEAN

MEXICO

Gulf of Mexico

Caribbean Sea

HAWAII (U.S.)

SURINAME

VENEZUELA

GUYANA

FRENCH GUIANA

MARSHALL ISLANDS

GALAPAGOS IS. (Ec.)

COLOMBIA

ECUADOR

FED. STATES OF MICRONESIA

Equator

KIRIBATI

BRAZIL

SOLOMON ISLANDS

PERU

WESTERN SAMOA

AMERICAN SAMOA

BOLIVIA

Coral Sea

VANUATU

FIJI

TONGA

COOK ISLANDS (N.Z.)

FRENCH POLYNESIA

PARAGUAY

CHILE

NEW CALEDONIA (Fr.)

AUSTRALIA

URUGUAY

PACIFIC OCEAN

ARGENTINA

NEW ZEALAND

FALKLAND ISLANDS (U.K.)

SOUTH GEORGIA (U.K.)

Ross Sea

Alexander Island

Weddell Sea

Berkner Island

ANTARCTICA

Central America and the Caribbean

UNITED STATES

Gulf of Mexico

BAHAMAS

ATLANTIC OCEAN

Tropic of Cancer

CUBA

PUERTO RICO

VIRGIN IS. (U.S.) (U.K.)

CAYMAN IS. (U.K.)

MEXICO

HAITI

DOMINICAN REPUBLIC

ANTIGUA & BARBUDA

BELIZE

JAMAICA

ST. KITTS & NEVIS

GUADELOUPE (Fr.)

DOMINICA

GUATEMALA

HONDURAS

Caribbean Sea

MARTINIQUE (Fr.)

ST. LUCIA

EL SALVADOR

NICARAGUA

ARUBA (Neth.)

ST. VINCENT & THE GRENADINES

GRENADA

BARBADOS

CURACAO (Neth.)

TRINIDAD & TOBAGO

COSTA RICA

PACIFIC OCEAN

PANAMA

VENEZUELA

COLOMBIA

GUAYANA

0   500 Miles

0   1,000 Kilometers

N

630

Europe

ATLANTIC OCEAN

NORWAY
SWEDEN
FINLAND

North Sea
Baltic Sea

IRELAND
DEN.
ESTONIA
LATVIA
LITH.

NETH.
UNITED KINGDOM
BELG.
LUX.
GERMANY
POLAND
BELARUS

RUSSIA

KAZAKHSTAN

CZECH REP.
SLVK.
UKRAINE

Bay of Biscay
SWITZ.
AUS.
HUNG.
MOLDOVA

FRANCE
SLVN.
CRO.
ROMANIA

Caspian Sea

PORTUGAL
ITALY
B.-H.
YUGO.
BULGARIA

Black Sea
GEORGIA

SPAIN
ALB.
MAC.

ARMENIA
AZERBAIJAN

Mediterranean Sea
GREECE
TURKEY

ALGERIA
TUNISIA
CYPRUS
SYRIA
IRAQ

500 Miles
1,000 Kilometers

ARCTIC OCEAN

Barents Sea

Norwegian Sea

ICELAND

RUSSIA

NORWAY
SWEDEN
FINLAND

IRELAND
UNITED KINGDOM
GERMANY
POLAND
BELARUS

FRANCE
UKRAINE

Caspian Sea

KAZAKHSTAN

MONGOLIA

AZORES (Port.)
PORTUGAL
SPAIN
ITALY
Black Sea
TURKEY
UZBEKISTAN
KYRGYZSTAN

TURKMENISTAN
TAJIKISTAN

NORTH KOREA
SOUTH KOREA
JAPAN

CHINA

CANARY IS. (Port.)
MOROCCO
Mediterranean Sea
LEBANON
SYRIA
IRAQ
IRAN
AFGHAN-ISTAN

WESTERN SAHARA
ALGERIA
LIBYA
EGYPT
ISRAEL
JORDAN
KUWAIT
PAKISTAN
NEPAL
BHUTAN

TAIWAN

PACIFIC OCEAN

MAURITANIA
MALI
NIGER
CHAD
QATAR
SAUDI ARABIA
U.A.E.
INDIA
MYANMAR
LAOS
VIETNAM

NO. MARIANA IS. (U.S.)

CAPE VERDE
NIGERIA
ERITREA
SUDAN
YEMEN
OMAN
Red Sea
Arabian Sea
BANGLA-DESH
THAILAND
CAMBODIA
South China Sea
PHILIPPINES

FED. STATES OF MICRONESIA

CEN. AFR. REP.
DJIBOUTI
ETHIOPIA
Bay of Bengal
BRUNEI
PALAU

CAMEROON
GABON
CONGO
UGANDA
SOMALIA
MALDIVES
SRI LANKA
MALAYSIA

Gulf of Guinea
RWANDA
KENYA
Sumatra
Borneo
Sulawesi
Equator
PAPUA NEW GUINEA

DEM. REP. OF THE CONGO
BURUNDI
TANZANIA
SEYCHELLES
INDONESIA
Java
New Guinea

ANGOLA
MALAWI
COMOROS
CHAGOS ARCH. (U.K.)

ZAMBIA
ZIMBABWE
MOZAMBIQUE
MADAGASCAR
MAURITIUS
INDIAN OCEAN

NAMIBIA
BOTSWANA
RÉUNION (Fr.)
AUSTRALIA

ATLANTIC OCEAN
SOUTH AFRICA
SWAZILAND
LESOTHO

KERGUÉLEN IS. (Fr.)

SO. SANDWICH ISLANDS (U.K.)

2,000 Miles
4,000 Kilometers

ANTARCTICA

West Africa

MAURITANIA
MALI
NIGER
CHAD

SENEGAL
GAMBIA
BURKINA FASO
BENIN
L. Chad

GUINEA
NIGERIA

GUINEA-BISSAU
CÔTE D'IVOIRE
GHANA
TOGO

SIERRA LEONE
LIBERIA
CAMEROON
CENTRAL AFRICAN REPUBLIC

ATLANTIC OCEAN
EQUATORIAL GUINEA
Gulf of Guinea
SÃO TOMÉ AND PRINCIPE
GABON
CONGO
DEM. REP. OF CONGO

CABINDA (Angola)

Equator

500 Miles
1,000 Kilometers

631

Africa Political

EUROPE

ASIA

ATLANTIC

OCEAN

SOUTHWEST
ASIA

Black Sea

Caspian Sea

Mediterranean Sea

MADEIRA
ISLANDS
(Port.)

Rabat • • Fes • Oran ✪ Algiers • Tunis ✪ Tripoli

Casablanca

TUNISIA

Benghazi • Alexandria • Cairo ✪

MOROCCO

CANARY
ISLANDS
(Sp.)

Las Palmas de
Gran Canaria

ALGERIA

LIBYA

EGYPT

Tropic of Cancer

Tropic of Cancer

• La'youn

WESTERN
SAHARA

Aswan •

Red Sea

Persian Gulf

MAURITANIA

CAPE
VERDE

• Nouakchott ✪

MALI

NIGER

CHAD

Port Sudan •

Gulf of Aden

Dakar • ✪
SENEGAL
Banjul • ✪— THE GAMBIA
Bissau ✪
GUINEA
BISSAU
GUINEA
Conakry ✪
Freetown ✪ SIERRA
LEONE
CÔTE
D'IVOIRE
Monrovia ✪ LIBERIA
Yamoussoukro ✪
Abidjan •

• Bamako ✪

Niamey ✪

BURKINA FASO
Ouagadougou ✪

• Kano

NIGERIA

Abuja ✪

GHANA
TOGO
BENIN
Lomé ✪ • Ibadan
Accra ✪ Porto-Novo ✪ • Lagos

N'Djamena •

Khartoum ✪

SUDAN

ERITREA
Asmara ✪

DJIBOUTI ✪ Djibouti •

Addis Ababa ✪

ETHIOPIA

SOMALIA

Mogadishu ✪

Equator

Equator

*Gulf of
Guinea*

CAMEROON
Douala • Yaounde ✪
Malabo ✪
EQUITORIAL
GUINEA
SÃO TOMÉ
& PRÍNCIPE
Libreville ✪ GABON

CENTRAL AFRICAN
REPUBLIC

Bangui ✪

Kisangani •

DEMOCRATIC
REPUBLIC
OF THE
CONGO

CONGO

UGANDA
Kampala ✪
RWANDA *L. Victoria*
Kigali ✪ • Mwanza
Bujumbura ✪
BURUNDI

KENYA
• Nakuru
Nairobi ✪

Mombasa •

INDIAN

OCEAN

Brazzaville ✪

Kinshasa ✪

Kananga •

• Mbuji-Mayi

Dodoma ✪

TANZANIA

Zanzibar •
Dar es Salaam •

Luanda ✪

ATLANTIC

OCEAN

Lobito •

Lubumbashi •

ANGOLA

Kitwe •
ZAMBIA
Lusaka ✪
Harare ✪
ZIMBABWE
Bulawayo •

Lilongwe ✪
Blantyre •

MALAWI
MOZAMBIQUE

Beira •

Moroni ✪ COMOROS

MAYOTTE
(France)

MADAGASCAR
Antananarivo ✪

Tropic of Capricorn

Tropic of Capricorn

NAMIBIA
Windhoek ✪

BOTSWANA

Gaborone ✪ Pretoria ✪
Johannesburg •
Mbabane ✪ SWAZILAND
Maseru ✪ LESOTHO

Maputo ✪

Durban •

SOUTH AFRICA

Cape Town ✪ • Port Elizabeth

Legend:
○ Capital cities
• Cities

Scale:
0   500   1,000 Miles
0   1,000   2,000 Kilometers

632

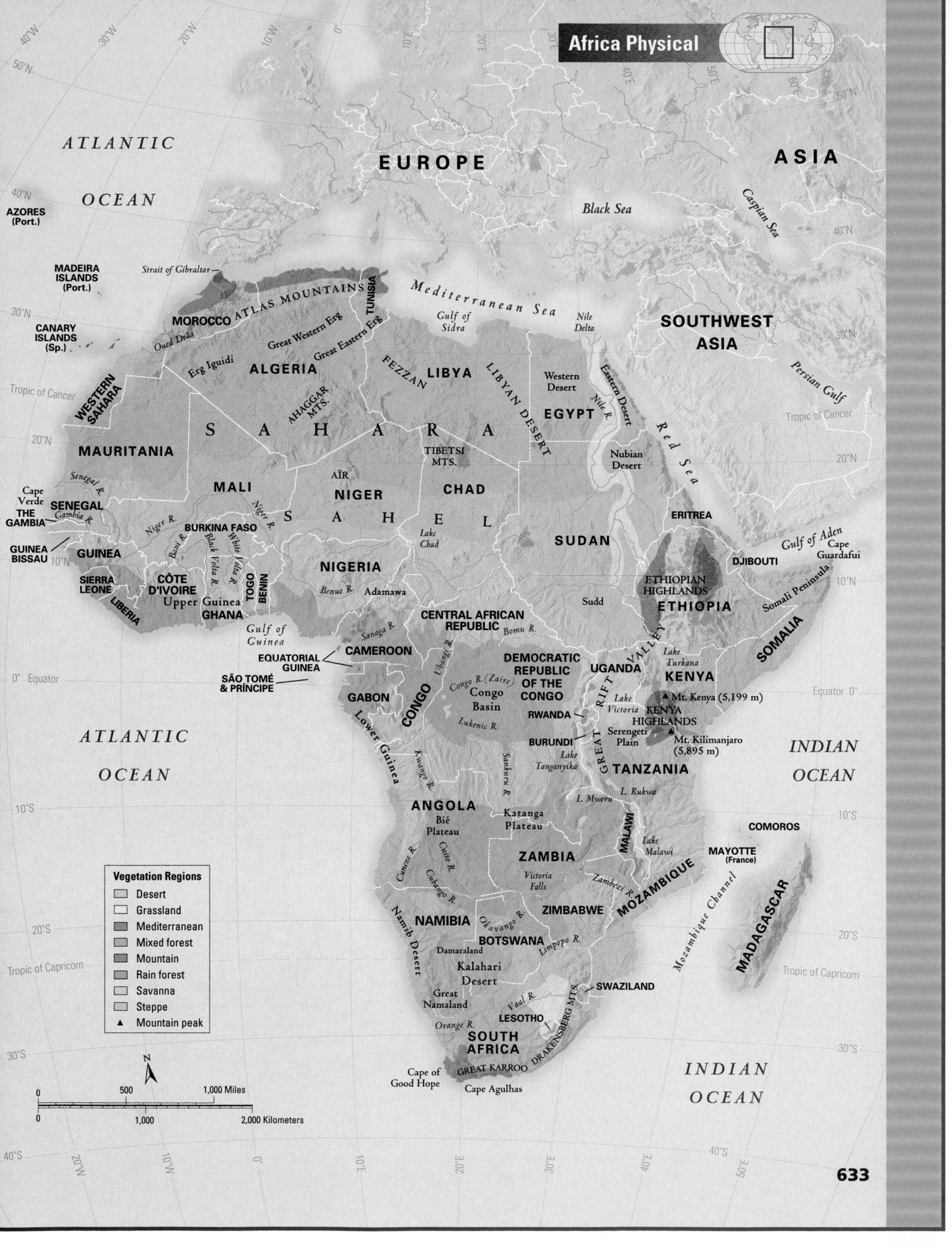

ATLANTIC
OCEAN

EUROPE

ASIA

AZORES
(Port.)

Black Sea

Caspian Sea

MADEIRA
ISLANDS
(Port.)

Strait of Gibraltar

Mediterranean Sea

SOUTHWEST
ASIA

CANARY
ISLANDS
(Sp.)

MOROCCO ATLAS MOUNTAINS

TUNISIA

Gulf of
Sidra

Nile
Delta

Persian Gulf

Oued Drâa

Great Western Erg

Great Eastern Erg

Tropic of Cancer

Erg Iguidi

ALGERIA

FEZZAN

LIBYA

LIBYAN DESERT

Western
Desert

Eastern Desert

Tropic of Cancer

WESTERN
SAHARA

AHAGGAR
MTS.

EGYPT

Nile R.

Red Sea

MAURITANIA

S   A   H   A   R   A

TIBETSI
MTS.

Nubian
Desert

Cape
Verde

Senegal R.

MALI

AÏR

NIGER

CHAD

SENEGAL
THE
GAMBIA

Gambia R.

Niger R.

S   A   H   E   L

SUDAN

ERITREA

Gulf of Aden
Cape
Guardafui

GUINEA
BISSAU

GUINEA

Bani R.

Black Volta R.

White Volta R.

BURKINA FASO

Niger R.

Lake
Chad

DJIBOUTI

SIERRA
LEONE

CÔTE
D'IVOIRE

TOGO

BENIN

NIGERIA

Benue R.

Adamawa

ETHIOPIAN
HIGHLANDS

LIBERIA

Upper

Guinea

GHANA

CENTRAL AFRICAN
REPUBLIC

Sudd

ETHIOPIA

Somali Peninsula

Gulf of
Guinea

Sanaga R.

Bomu R.

SOMALIA

Equator

CAMEROON

EQUATORIAL
GUINEA

SÃO TOMÉ
& PRÍNCIPE

Ubangi R.

DEMOCRATIC
REPUBLIC
OF THE
CONGO

UGANDA

Lake
Turkana

KENYA

Equator

GABON

CONGO

Congo R. (Zaire)

Congo
Basin

RWANDA

Lake
Victoria

KENYA
HIGHLANDS

Mt. Kenya (5,199 m)

Lukenie R.

BURUNDI

Serengeti
Plain

Mt. Kilimanjaro
(5,895 m)

INDIAN
OCEAN

Lower Guinea

Kwango R.

Sankuru R.

Lake
Tanganyika

TANZANIA

ATLANTIC

OCEAN

L. Rukwa

L. Mweru

ANGOLA

Bié
Plateau

Katanga
Plateau

MALAWI

Lake
Malawi

COMOROS

Cuanza R.

Cuito R.

ZAMBIA

MAYOTTE
(France)

Cubango R.

Victoria
Falls

Zambezi R.

MOZAMBIQUE

MADAGASCAR

NAMIBIA

Okavango R.

ZIMBABWE

Namib Desert

BOTSWANA

Limpopo R.

Mozambique Channel

Tropic of Capricorn

Damaraland

Kalahari
Desert

SWAZILAND

Tropic of Capricorn

Great
Namaland

Vaal R.

Orange R.

LESOTHO

DRAKENSBERG MTS.

SOUTH
AFRICA

GREAT KARROO

INDIAN

Cape of
Good Hope

Cape Agulhas

OCEAN

Vegetation Regions
- Desert
- Grassland
- Mediterranean
- Mixed forest
- Mountain
- Rain forest
- Savanna
- Steppe
- ▲ Mountain peak

N

0   500   1,000 Miles

0   1,000   2,000 Kilometers

633

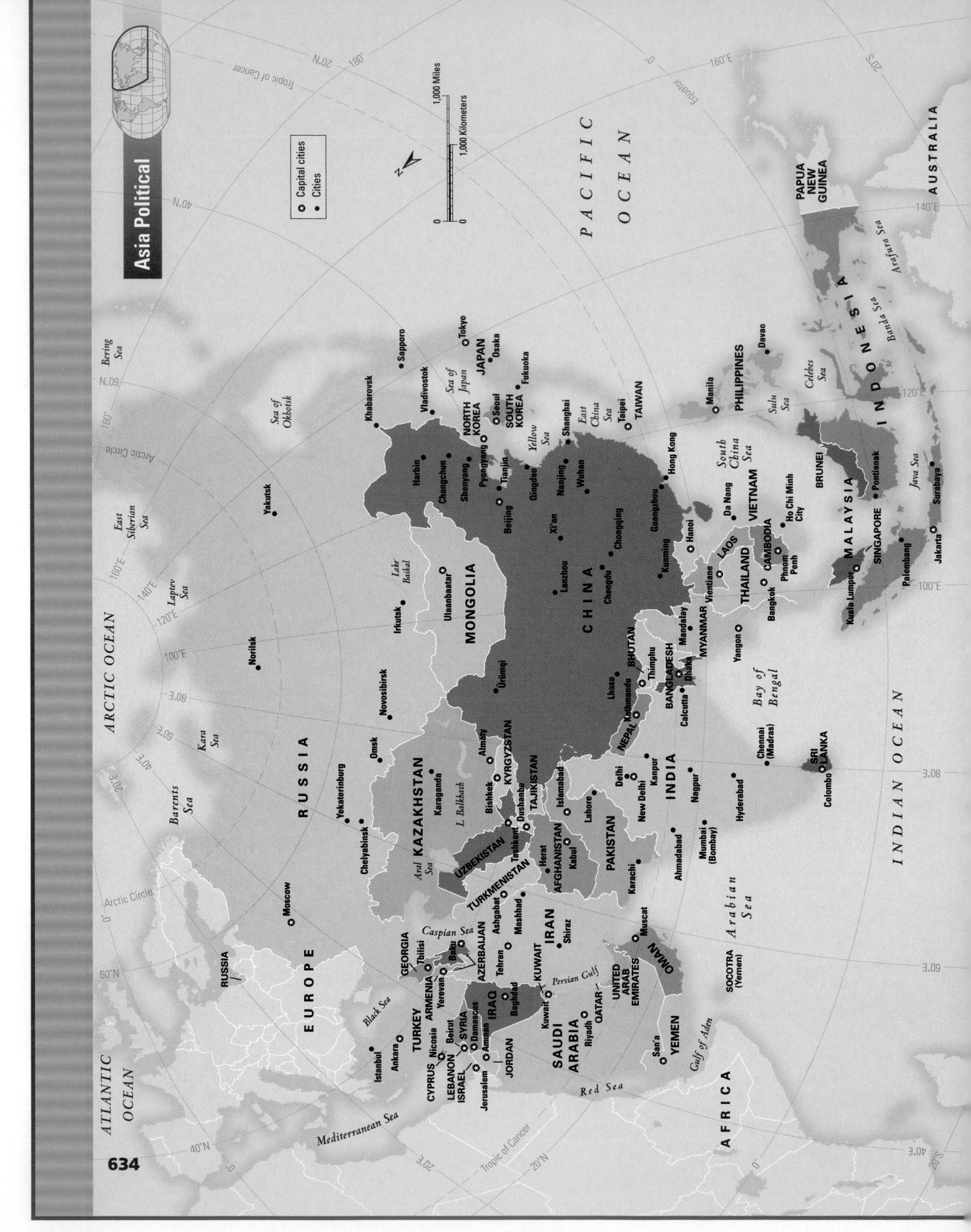

Capital cities
Cities

1,000 Miles
1,000 Kilometers

N

PACIFIC

OCEAN

AUSTRALIA

PAPUA
NEW
GUINEA

Arafura Sea

Banda Sea

INDONESIA

DAVAO

*Celebes
Sea*

*Sulu
Sea*

PHILIPPINES

Manila

140°E

120°E

Java Sea

Surabaya

Jakarta

Palembang

Pontianak

BRUNEI

MALAYSIA

SINGAPORE

Kuala Lumpur

100°E

*South
China
Sea*

Guangzhou

Hong Kong

Da Nang

VIETNAM

Ho Chi Minh
City

Hanoi

CAMBODIA

Phnom
Penh

Bangkok

THAILAND

Vientiane

LAOS

Mandalay

Yangon

MYANMAR

*Bering
Sea*

Tropic of Cancer

20°N

180°

0°

160°E

160°E

Sapporo

Vladivostok

Khabarovsk

*Sea of
Japan*

Tokyo

JAPAN

Osaka

Fukuoka

Seoul

NORTH
KOREA

SOUTH
KOREA

Pyongyang

Shenyang

Changchun

Harbin

Tianjin

Beijing

Qingdao

Shanghai

*Yellow
Sea*

*East
China
Sea*

Taipei

TAIWAN

Nanjing

Wuhan

Xi'an

CHINA

Chongqing

Chengdu

Lanzhou

Kunming

40°N

60°N

*East
Siberian
Sea*

Arctic Circle

Yakutsk

*Laptev
Sea*

120°E

140°E

Norilsk

*Lake
Baikal*

Irkutsk

Ulaanbaatar

MONGOLIA

Ürümqi

ARCTIC OCEAN

100°E

80°E

*Kara
Sea*

Novosibirsk

60°E

40°E

20°E

0°

*Barents
Sea*

RUSSIA

EUROPE

Omsk

Yekaterinburg

Chelyabinsk

KAZAKHSTAN

Karaganda

Almaty

*Aral
Sea*

L. Balkhash

Bishkek

Tashkent

KYRGYZSTAN

TAJIKISTAN

Dushanbe

UZBEKISTAN

TURKMENISTAN

Ashgabat

Herat

AFGHANISTAN

Kabul

Islamabad

PAKISTAN

Lahore

Karachi

Moscow

BHUTAN

Thimphu

NEPAL

Kathmandu

Lhasa

BANGLADESH

Dhaka

Calcutta

Delhi

New Delhi

Kanpur

INDIA

Nagpur

Ahmadabad

Mumbai
(Bombay)

Hyderabad

Chennai
(Madras)

SRI
LANKA

Colombo

*Bay of
Bengal*

*Arabian
Sea*

INDIAN OCEAN

80°E

60°E

Muscat

OMAN

UNITED
ARAB
EMIRATES

QATAR

SOCOTRA
(Yemen)

YEMEN

San'a

Gulf of Aden

Red Sea

AFRICA

40°E

20°N

Tropic of Cancer

40°N

Mediterranean Sea

Istanbul

Ankara

TURKEY

CYPRUS

Nicosia

Beirut

LEBANON

ISRAEL

Damascus

SYRIA

Amman

Jerusalem

JORDAN

IRAQ

Baghdad

Kuwait

KUWAIT

SAUDI
ARABIA

Riyadh

Tehran

IRAN

Shiraz

Mashhad

AZERBAIJAN

Baku

Caspian Sea

ARMENIA

Yerevan

GEORGIA

Tbilisi

RUSSIA

Black Sea

Persian Gulf

*ATLANTIC
OCEAN*

634

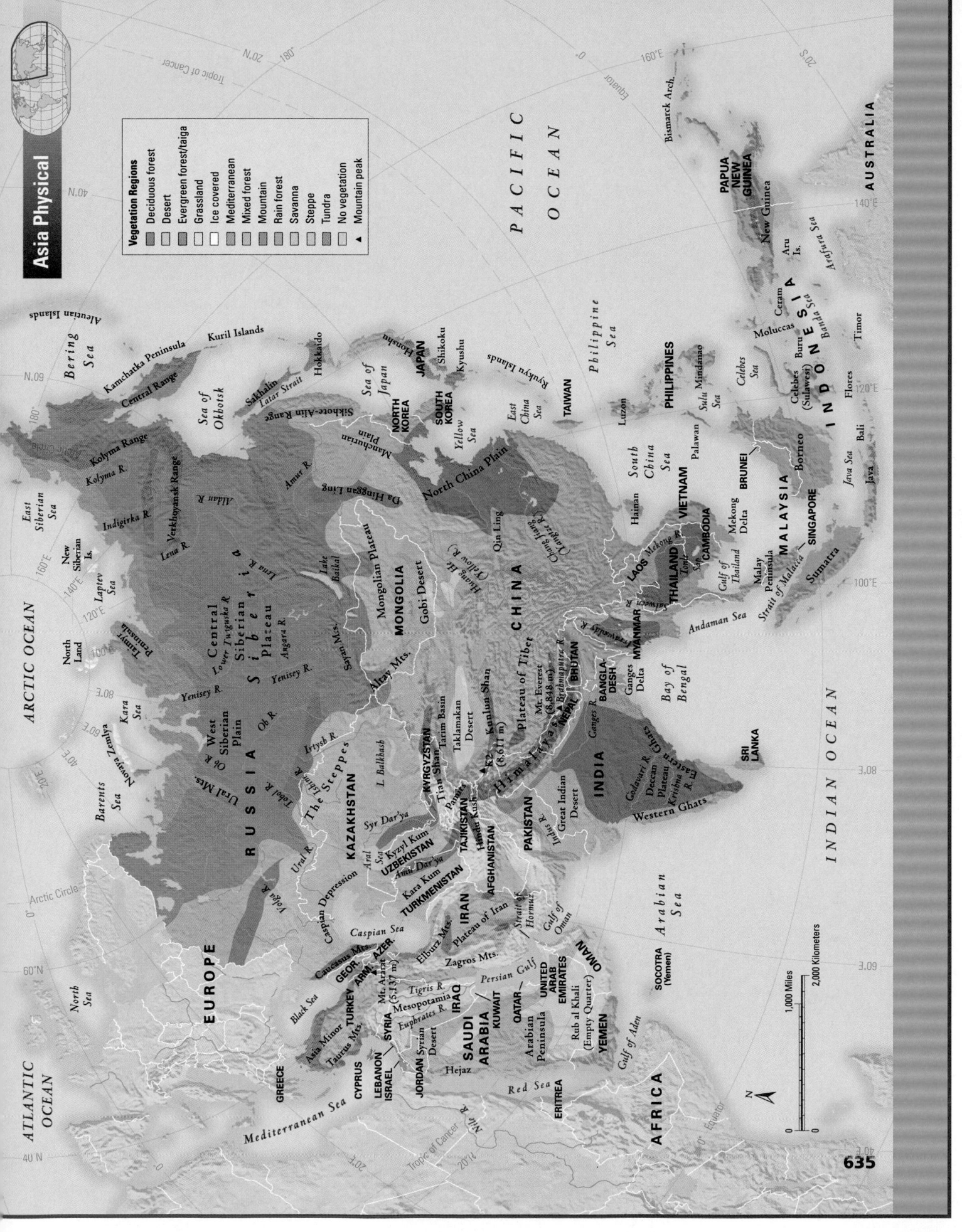

Asia Physical

Vegetation Regions
- Deciduous forest
- Desert
- Evergreen forest/taiga
- Grassland
- Ice covered
- Mediterranean
- Mixed forest
- Mountain
- Rain forest
- Savanna
- Steppe
- Tundra
- No vegetation
- ▲ Mountain peak

ARCTIC OCEAN

ATLANTIC OCEAN

PACIFIC OCEAN

INDIAN OCEAN

Aleutian Islands
Bering Sea
Kamchatka Peninsula
Central Range
Kolyma Range
Kolyma R.
Sea of Okhotsk
Kuril Islands
Sakhalin
Tatar Strait
Sikhote-Alin Range
Hokkaido
Sea of Japan
Honshu
JAPAN
Shikoku
Kyushu
Ryukyu Islands
Philippine Sea
East Siberian Sea
New Siberian Is.
Laptev Sea
Indigirka R.
Verkhoyansk Range
Lena R.
Aldan R.
Amur R.
Manchurian Plain
NORTH KOREA
SOUTH KOREA
Yellow Sea
East China Sea
TAIWAN
North Land
Taimyr Peninsula
Lower Tunguska R.
Central Siberian Plateau
Angara R.
Sayan Mts.
Da Hinggan Ling
North China Plain
Qin Ling
Luzon
PHILIPPINES
Mindanao
Celebes Sea
Bismarck Arch.
New Guinea
PAPUA NEW GUINEA
Yenisey R.
Lake Baikal
Mongolian Plateau
MONGOLIA
Gobi Desert
Huang He (Yellow R.)
CHINA
Chang Jiang (Yangtze R.)
South China Sea
Hainan
VIETNAM
LAOS
Mekong R.
Gulf of Tonkin
BRUNEI
Palawan
Sulu Sea
Borneo
Ceram
Buru
Moluccas
Celebes (Sulawesi)
INDONESIA
Ceram Sea
Banda Sea
Aru Is.
Arafura Sea
Timor
AUSTRALIA
Kara Sea
Novaya Zemlya
Yenisey R.
Ob R.
West Siberian Plain
Irtysh R.
Tobol R.
Ishim R.
The Steppes
RUSSIA
Ural Mts.
Altay Mts.
Tian Shan
Tarim Basin
Taklamakan Desert
Kunlun Shan
Plateau of Tibet
Mt. Everest (8,848 m)
Himalaya
BHUTAN
NEPAL
BANGLADESH
Ganges Delta
Bay of Bengal
Brahmaputra R.
Salween R.
Irrawaddy R.
MYANMAR
THAILAND
CAMBODIA
Mekong Delta
Gulf of Thailand
Malay Peninsula
Strait of Malacca
MALAYSIA
SINGAPORE
Sumatra
Java Sea
Java
Bali
Flores
North Sea
EUROPE
Barents Sea
Volga R.
Ural R.
Aral Sea
L. Balkhash
KAZAKHSTAN
Syr Dar'ya
Kyzyl Kum
UZBEKISTAN
Amu Dar'ya
Kara Kum
TURKMENISTAN
KYRGYZSTAN
TAJIKISTAN
Pamirs
Hindu Kush
AFGHANISTAN
PAKISTAN
Indus R.
Great Indian Desert
K2 (8,611 m)
INDIA
Godavari R.
Deccan Plateau
Eastern Ghats
Krishna R.
SRI LANKA
Western Ghats
Caspian Depression
Caspian Sea
Elburz Mts.
Plateau of Iran
IRAN
OMAN
Strait of Hormuz
Gulf of Oman
Arabian Sea
SOCOTRA (Yemen)
Black Sea
Caucasus Mts.
GEOR.
ARM.
AZER.
TURKEY
Mt. Ararat (5,137 m)
Zagros Mts.
Tigris R.
Euphrates R.
Mesopotamia
IRAQ
KUWAIT
QATAR
UNITED ARAB EMIRATES
Persian Gulf
Asia Minor
Taurus Mts.
CYPRUS
LEBANON
ISRAEL
SYRIA
Syrian Desert
JORDAN
SAUDI ARABIA
Arabian Peninsula
Rub al Khali (Empty Quarter)
YEMEN
Hejaz
Red Sea
Gulf of Aden
ERITREA
AFRICA
Nile R.
GREECE
Mediterranean Sea

Arctic Circle
Tropic of Cancer
Equator
Arctic Circle

N

1,000 Miles
2,000 Kilometers

635

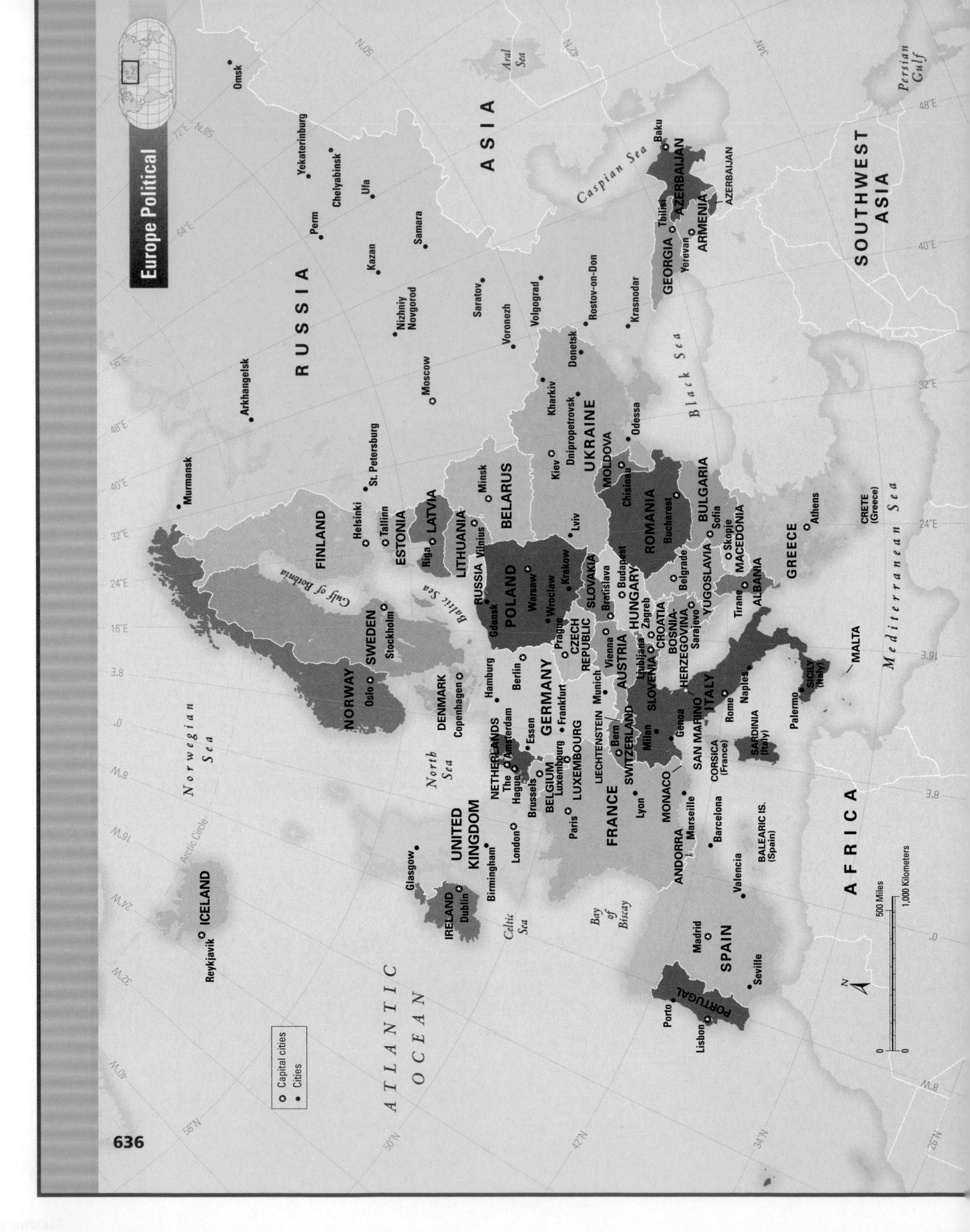

ATLANTIC OCEAN

ICELAND
Reykjavik ✪

Glasgow ●
UNITED KINGDOM
Birmingham ●
London ✪

IRELAND
Dublin ✪

Celtic Sea

Bay of Biscay

Norwegian Sea

Murmansk ●

NORWAY
Oslo ✪

SWEDEN
Stockholm ✪

Gulf of Bothnia

FINLAND
Helsinki ✪

Arkhangelsk ●

RUSSIA

Omsk ●

Yekaterinburg ●

Chelyabinsk ●
Ufa ●

Perm ●

ASIA

Kazan ●

Samara ●

Aral Sea

Persian Gulf

Nizhniy Novgorod ●

Moscow ✪

Saratov ●

Voronezh ●
Volgograd ●

Rostov-on-Don ●

Krasnodar ●

Caspian Sea

St. Petersburg ●

Tallinn ✪
ESTONIA

Riga ✪
LATVIA

LITHUANIA
Vilnius ✪

RUSSIA

Minsk ✪
BELARUS

Lviv ●
Kiev ✪

UKRAINE
Dnipropetrovsk ●

Kharkiv ●
Donetsk ●

Odessa ●

MOLDOVA
Chisinau ✪

Black Sea

GEORGIA
Tbilisi ✪

AZERBAIJAN
Baku ✪

ARMENIA
Yerevan ✪

AZERBAIJAN

SOUTHWEST ASIA

Gdansk ●
POLAND
Warsaw ✪
Wroclaw ●
Krakow ●

Hamburg ●
Berlin ✪
GERMANY
Frankfurt ●
Essen ●
Munich ●

DENMARK
Copenhagen ✪

NETHERLANDS
Amsterdam ✪
The Hague ✪
Brussels ✪
BELGIUM
LUXEMBOURG
Luxembourg ✪

Paris ✪
FRANCE
Lyon ●

LIECHTENSTEIN
SWITZERLAND
Bern ✪
MONACO

ANDORRA
Marseille ●
Barcelona ●

BALEARIC IS. (Spain)

Valencia ●

SPAIN
Madrid ✪
Seville ●

PORTUGAL
Porto ●
Lisbon ✪

Prague ✪
CZECH REPUBLIC
SLOVAKIA
Bratislava ✪
Vienna ✪
AUSTRIA
HUNGARY
Budapest ✪
Zagreb ✪
Ljubljana ✪
SLOVENIA
CROATIA
BOSNIA-HERZEGOVINA
Sarajevo ✪
Belgrade ✪
YUGOSLAVIA
Skopje ✪
MACEDONIA
Tirane ✪
ALBANIA

ROMANIA
Bucharest ✪

BULGARIA
Sofia ✪

GREECE
Athens ✪

CRETE (Greece)

Mediterranean Sea

Milan ●
Genoa ●
SAN MARINO
CORSICA (France)
ITALY
Rome ✪
Naples ●

SARDINIA (Italy)

Palermo ●
SICILY (Italy)

MALTA

AFRICA

N

Capital cities ✪
Cities ●

500 Miles
1,000 Kilometers

636

636 Atlas

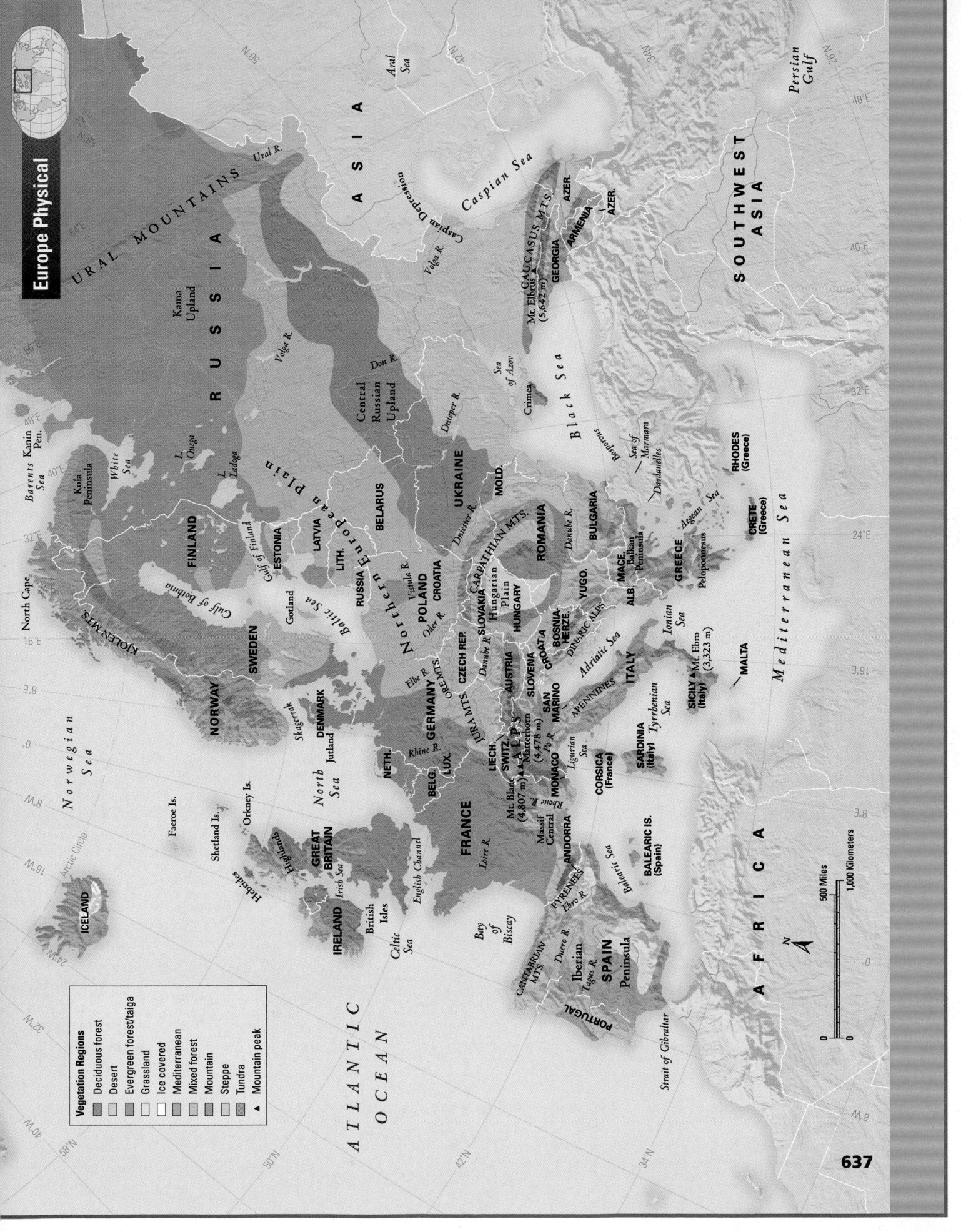

Europe Physical

Vegetation Regions
- Deciduous forest
- Desert
- Evergreen forest/taiga
- Grassland
- Ice covered
- Mediterranean
- Mixed forest
- Mountain
- Steppe
- Tundra
- ▲ Mountain peak

ASIA

URAL MOUNTAINS

RUSSIA

Kama Upland

Central Russian Upland

Caspian Depression

Aral Sea

Caspian Sea

Persian Gulf

SOUTHWEST ASIA

CAUCASUS MTS.

Mt. Elbrus (5,642 m)

GEORGIA

ARMENIA

AZER.

AZER.

Volga R.

Don R.

Dnieper R.

Sea of Azov

Crimea

Black Sea

Bosporus

Sea of Marmara

Dardanelles

RHODES (Greece)

CRETE (Greece)

Mediterranean Sea

Barents Sea

Kanin Pen.

White Sea

Kola Peninsula

L. Onega

L. Ladoga

Ural R.

FINLAND

Gulf of Finland

ESTONIA

LATVIA

LITH.

RUSSIA

BELARUS

UKRAINE

MOLD.

BULGARIA

ROMANIA

Danube R.

Dniester R.

Balkan Peninsula

Aegean Sea

MACE.

GREECE

Peloponnesus

ALB.

YUGO.

North Cape

KJÖLEN MTS.

SWEDEN

Gotland

Baltic Sea

Gulf of Bothnia

Northern European Plain

POLAND

Vistula R.

Oder R.

CZECH REP.

SLOVAKIA

Carpathian Mts.

Hungarian Plain

HUNGARY

CROATIA

BOSNIA HERZE.

DINARIC ALPS

Adriatic Sea

Ionian Sea

Tyrrhenian Sea

ITALY

SICILY (Italy)

Mt. Etna (3,323 m)

MALTA

NORWAY

Norwegian Sea

Skagerrak

DENMARK

Jutland

North Sea

NETH.

BELG.

LUX.

GERMANY

Elbe R.

ORE MTS.

JURA MTS.

Rhine R.

AUSTRIA

SLOVENIA

SAN MARINO

APENNINES

Danube R.

LIECH.

SWITZ.

ALPS

Mt. Blanc (4,807 m)

Matterhorn (4,478 m)

Po R.

MONACO

Ligurian Sea

CORSICA (France)

SARDINIA (Italy)

FRANCE

Loire R.

Rhône R.

Massif Central

ANDORRA

PYRENEES

Ebro R.

BALEARIC IS. (Spain)

Balearic Sea

AFRICA

Faeroe Is.

Shetland Is.

Orkney Is.

Hebrides

Highlands

GREAT BRITAIN

British Isles

IRELAND

Irish Sea

Celtic Sea

English Channel

Bay of Biscay

ICELAND

Arctic Circle

ATLANTIC OCEAN

CANTABRIAN MTS.

Duero R.

Tagus R.

Iberian Peninsula

SPAIN

PORTUGAL

Strait of Gibraltar

North Cape

500 Miles

1,000 Kilometers

637

ARCTIC OCEAN

North Pole

ASIA

EUROPE

Norwegian Sea

ELLESMERE ISLAND

GREENLAND

Beaufort Sea

Baffin Bay

Bering Strait

Bering Sea

ALASKA

Fairbanks•

•Anchorage

VICTORIA ISLAND

BAFFIN ISLAND

Nuuk•

Labrador Sea

Gulf of Alaska

Whitehorse•

Yellowknife•

Juneau•

Hudson Bay

CANADA

Happy Valley-Goose Bay

NEWFOUNDLAND

PACIFIC OCEAN

•Edmonton

Vancouver•

Calgary•

•Saskatoon

•Regina

•Winnipeg

Thunder Bay

Great Lakes

Québec•

Montréal•

MIQUELON I. (France)

Seattle•

Ottawa⊛

Halifax•

Portland•

•Billings

Toronto•

Boston•

Boise•

•Minneapolis

•Buffalo

Milwaukee•

Detroit•

New York•

Sacramento•

•Reno

•Salt Lake City

Omaha•

Chicago•

Cleveland•

Philadelphia•

San Francisco•

Denver•

Kansas City•

St. Louis•

Cincinnati•

Baltimore•

Washington⊛

Norfolk•

BERMUDA (U.K.)

Las Vegas•

UNITED STATES

Charlotte•

ATLANTIC OCEAN

Los Angeles•

Phoenix•

•Albuquerque

•Oklahoma City

San Diego•

Birmingham•

Atlanta•

Tijuana•

El Paso•

Dallas•

Ciudad Juárez•

Jacksonville•

Chihuahua•

San Antonio•

Houston•

New Orleans•

Tampa•

Miami•

BAHAMAS

Monterrey•

Gulf of California

Gulf of Mexico

Nassau⊛

VIRGIN IS. (U.S.) (U.K.)

Havana⊛

DOMINICAN REPUBLIC

San Juan

MEXICO

CUBA

PUERTO RICO (U.S.)

Guadalajara•

León•

Mérida•

Santiago de Cuba•

HAITI

Santo Domingo

LESSER ANTILLES

Veracruz•

CAYMAN IS. (U.K.)

Port-au-Prince⊛

México⊛

JAMAICA

Kingston⊛

TRINIDAD & TOBAGO

Acapulco•

Caribbean Sea

BELIZE

Belmopan⊛

GUATEMALA

HONDURAS

Guatemala⊛

Tegucigalpa⊛

San Salvador

NICARAGUA

EL SALVADOR

Managua⊛

Panamá•

COSTA RICA

San José⊛

PANAMA

SOUTH AMERICA

PACIFIC OCEAN

⊛ Capital cities

• Cities

N

0   1,000 Miles

0   2,000 Kilometers

0° Equator

Equator 0°

ASIA

ARCTIC OCEAN

North Pole

EUROPE

Norwegian Sea

Ellesmere Island

Queen Elizabeth Islands

Parry Islands

Devon I.

GREENLAND

Beaufort Sea

Banks I.

Boothia Pen.

Baffin Bay

Davis Strait

Victoria I.

Baffin Island

St. Lawrence I. Bering Strait

BROOKS RANGE

ALASKA

Yukon R.

Foxe Basin

Nunivak

Bering Sea

Mt. McKinley (6,194 m)

ALASKA RANGE

Great Bear Lake

Southampton I.

Hudson Strait

Ungava Pen.

Labrador Sea

Aleutian Islands

Kodiak I.

Gulf of Alaska

Mt. Logan (6,050 m)

COAST MOUNTAINS

MACKENZIE MTS.

Mackenzie R.

Great Slave Lake

Hudson Bay

James Bay

Newfoundland

Labrador

Alexander Archipelago

Yukon R.

L. Athabasca

Reindeer L.

Queen Charlotte Is.

Peace R.

ROCKY MOUNTAINS

Saskatchewan R.

CANADA

Canadian Shield

MIQUELON I. (France)

PACIFIC OCEAN

Vancouver I.

GREAT PLAINS

L. Winnipeg

Columbia R.

CASCADES

Snake R.

Great Basin

SIERRA NEVADA

Missouri R.

Platte R.

Colorado R.

Mt. Whitney (4,418 m)

Great Lakes

L. Superior

L. Michigan

L. Huron

L. Ontario

L. Erie

St. Lawrence R.

Nova Scotia

Cape Cod

Long Island

Central Lowland

Mississippi R.

Ohio R.

APPALACHIAN MTS.

Chesapeake Bay

BERMUDA (U.K.)

Arkansas R.

Ozark Plateau

Tennessee R.

Cape Hatteras

UNITED STATES

Canadian R.

Red R.

Colorado R.

Coastal Plain

ATLANTIC OCEAN

Baja California

SIERRA MADRE OCCIDENTAL

Rio Grande

SIERRA MADRE ORIENTAL

Gulf of California

Gulf of Mexico

BAHAMAS

Tropic of Cancer

VIRGIN IS. (U.S.) (U.K.)

DOMINICAN REPUBLIC

CUBA

HAITI

PUERTO RICO (U.S.)

Lesser Antilles

MEXICO

Mt. Orizaba (5,747 m)

Isthmus of Tehuantepec

Yucatan Peninsula

CAYMAN IS. (U.K.)

Greater Antilles

JAMAICA

Caribbean Sea

TRINIDAD & TOBAGO

BELIZE

HONDURAS

GUATEMALA

EL SALVADOR

NICARAGUA

L. Nicaragua

Orinoco R.

PACIFIC OCEAN

COSTA RICA

Isthmus of Panama

PANAMA

SOUTH AMERICA

Equator

Vegetation Regions

- Coniferous forest
- Deciduous forest
- Desert
- Grassland
- Mediterranean
- Mixed forest
- Mountain
- Rain forest
- Savanna
- Tundra
- Ice Cap
- ▲ Mountain peak

N

0   1,000 Miles

0   2,000 Kilometers

639

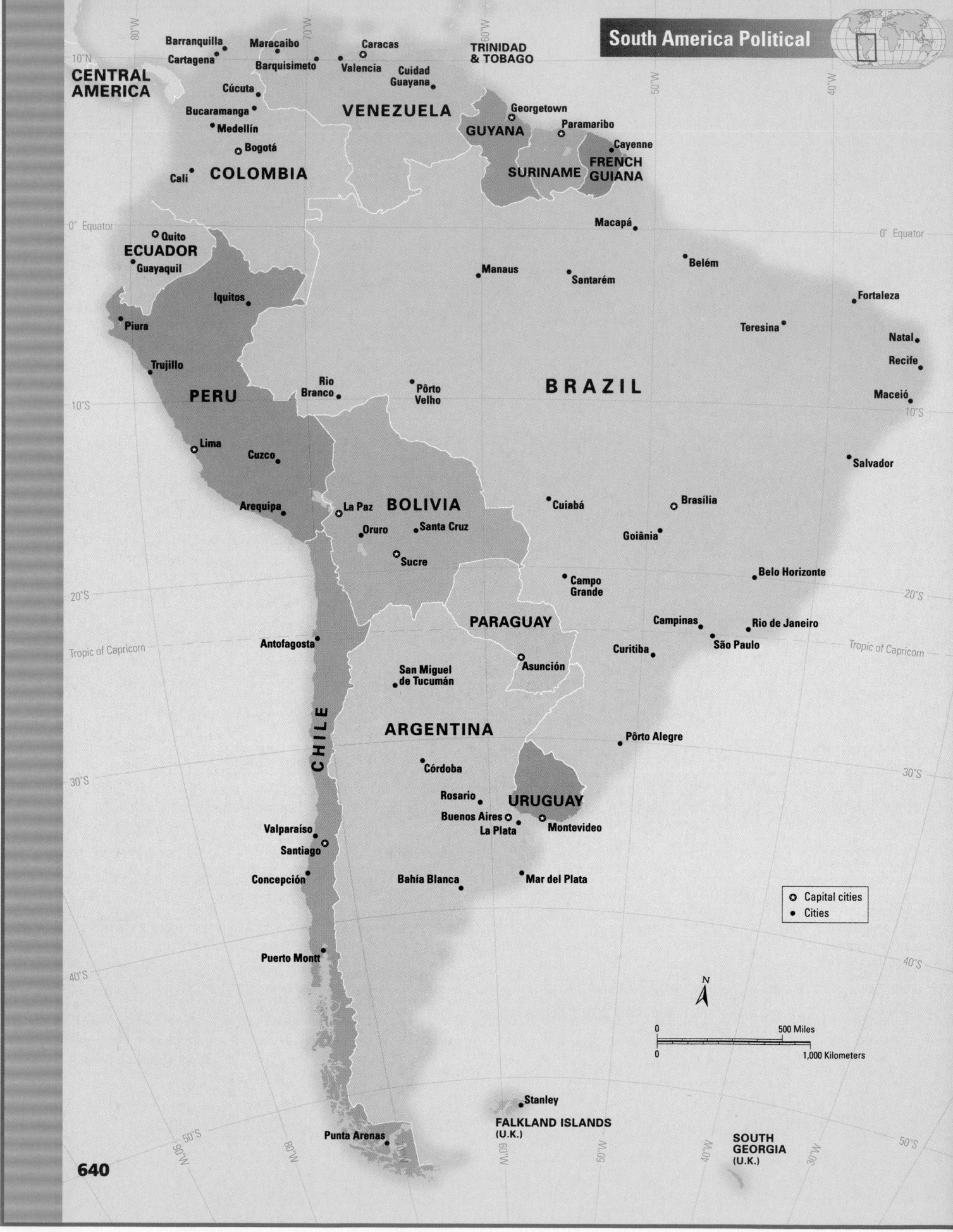

CENTRAL
AMERICA

Barranquilla
Cartagena
Maracaibo
Caracas
Barquisimeto
Valencia
Cuidad
Guayana
TRINIDAD
& TOBAGO

VENEZUELA

Cúcuta
Bucaramanga
Medellín
Bogotá
Cali
COLOMBIA

GUYANA
Georgetown
Paramaribo
SURINAME
Cayenne
FRENCH
GUIANA

0° Equator   0° Equator

Quito
ECUADOR
Guayaquil

Macapá

Iquitos

Manaus
Santarém
Belém

Piura

Fortaleza

Teresina
Natal
Recife

Trujillo

Rio
Branco
Pôrto
Velho
BRAZIL

Maceió

10°S   10°S

PERU

Lima
Cuzco

Salvador

Arequipa
La Paz
BOLIVIA
Cuiabá
Brasília

Oruro
Santa Cruz
Goiânia

Sucre

Belo Horizonte

20°S
Campo
Grande
20°S

PARAGUAY
Campinas
Rio de Janeiro
São Paulo

Antofagosta
Curitiba

Tropic of Capricorn   Tropic of Capricorn

San Miguel
de Tucumán
Asunción

CHILE

ARGENTINA
Pôrto Alegre

30°S
Córdoba
30°S

Rosario
URUGUAY

Valparaíso
Buenos Aires
La Plata
Montevideo

Santiago

Concepción
Bahía Blanca
Mar del Plata

◇ Capital cities
• Cities

Puerto Montt

40°S   40°S

N

0   500 Miles

0   1,000 Kilometers

Stanley

50°S   50°S

Punta Arenas
FALKLAND ISLANDS
(U.K.)
SOUTH
GEORGIA
(U.K.)

CENTRAL AMERICA

Cristóbal Colón
(5,775 m) ▲

Pt. Gallinas

Caribbean Sea

TRINIDAD & TOBAGO

ATLANTIC OCEAN

Gulf of Panamá

CORD. OCCIDENTAL

Cauca R.

CORD. DE MÉRIDA

Orinoco R.

VENEZUELA

Llanos

GUYANA

SURINAME

FRENCH GUIANA

CORD. CENTRAL

Magdalena R.

CORD. ORIENTAL

COLOMBIA

Orinoco R.

Guiana Highlands

Branco R.

C. San Francisco

0° Equator

0° Equator

ECUADOR

Gulf of Guayaquil

Putumayo R.

Japurá R.

Negro R.

Amazon

Marajó Island

Amazon R.

Pariñas Pt.

Marañón R.

Amazon R.

Basin

Madeira R.

Juruá R.

Purus R.

Tapajós R.

Xingu R.

Araguaia R.

Tocantins R.

Parnaíba R.

Cape São Roque

Mt. Huascarán
(6,768 m) ▲

PERU

10°S

São Francisco R.

BRAZIL

10°S

Ucayali R.

Guaporé R.

Mamoré R.

Mato Grosso Plateau

Brazilian

SERRA DO ESPINHAÇO

L. Titicaca

BOLIVIA

Highlands

L. Poopó

Pantanal

Atacama Desert

Paraguay R.

Gran Chaco

PARAGUAY

20°S

Cape São Tomé
Cape Frío

20°S

Tropic of Capricorn

Pilcomayo R.

Paraná R.

Campos

SERRA DO MAR

Tropic of Capricorn

PACIFIC OCEAN

Salado R.

Paraná R.

Entre Ríos

Uruguay R.

CHILE

ANDES

Pilcomayo R.

Patos Lagoon

Mt. Aconcagua
(6,960 m) ▲

Salado R.

URUGUAY

30°S

Pampas

Río de la Plata

ATLANTIC OCEAN

30°S

Colorado R.

ARGENTINA

Negro R.

San Matías Gulf

40°S

Chiloé I.

Chubut R.

Valdés Peninsula

40°S

Chonos Arch.

Patagonia

Gulf of San Jorge

Cape Tres Puntas

Wellington I.

Vegetation Regions
- Desert
- Grassland
- Mediterranean
- Mixed forest
- Mountain
- Rain forest
- Savanna
- Steppe
- Tundra
- ▲ Mountain peak

N

0   500   1,000 Miles

0   1,000   2,000 Kilometers

FALKLAND ISLANDS
(U.K.)

SOUTH GEORGIA
(U.K.)

50°S

Grande Bay

Strait of Magellan

Tierra del Fuego

Cape Horn

50°S

641

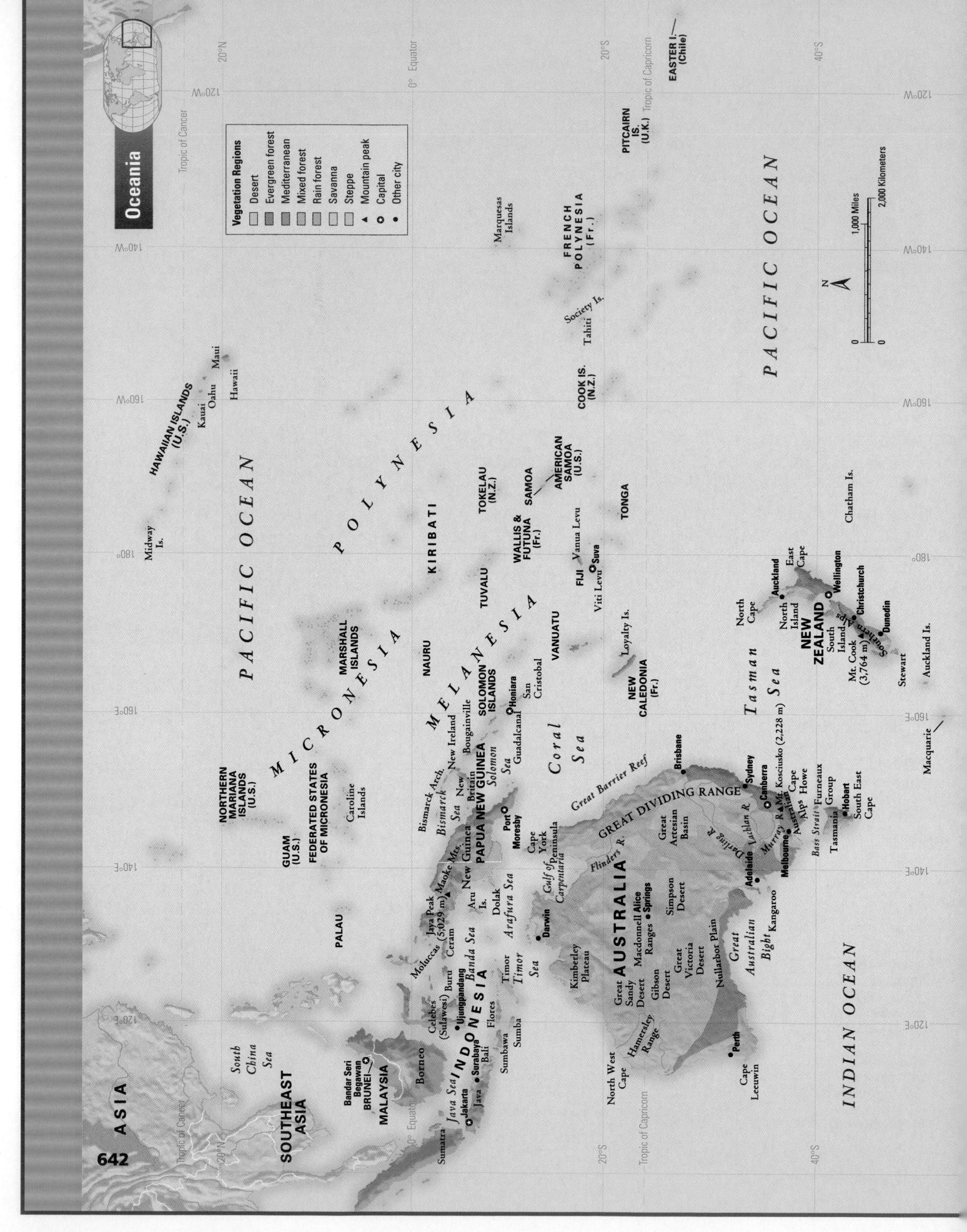

Oceania

Vegetation Regions
Desert
Evergreen forest
Mediterranean
Mixed forest
Rain forest
Savanna
Steppe
▲ Mountain peak
◎ Capital
● Other city

Tropic of Cancer

20°N

0° Equator

20°S

Tropic of Capricorn

EASTER I. (Chile)

PITCAIRN IS. (U.K.)

PACIFIC OCEAN

Marquesas Islands

FRENCH POLYNESIA (Fr.)

Society Is.

Tahiti

COOK IS. (N.Z.)

N

1,000 Miles
2,000 Kilometers

PACIFIC OCEAN

Midway Is.

HAWAIIAN ISLANDS (U.S.)
Kauai Oahu Maui
Hawaii

P O L Y N E S I A

KIRIBATI

TOKELAU (N.Z.)
SAMOA
AMERICAN SAMOA (U.S.)

WALLIS & FUTUNA (Fr.)
FIJI Vanua Levu
Viti Levu ● Suva

TONGA

NORTHERN MARIANA ISLANDS (U.S.)

GUAM (U.S.)

FEDERATED STATES OF MICRONESIA

Caroline Islands

M I C R O N E S I A

MARSHALL ISLANDS

NAURU

M E L A N E S I A

SOLOMON ISLANDS
● Honiara
San Cristobal

VANUATU

NEW CALEDONIA (Fr.)

Loyalty Is.

TUVALU

Guadalcanal

Bismarck Sea
New Ireland
New Britain
Bougainville
Solomon Sea

North Cape

Auckland ●

East Cape
North Island

NEW ZEALAND

● Wellington

South Island
Mt. Cook (3,764 m) ▲
Christchurch ●
Dunedin ●

Southern Alps

Stewart

Auckland Is.

Chatham Is.

Macquarie

160°E

PALAU

Bismarck Arch.
New Guinea
Maoke Mts.
PAPUA NEW GUINEA
Port ◎ Moresby

Jaya Peak (5,029 m) ▲
Aru Is.
Ceram
Moluccas
Celebes (Sulawesi)
Buru ● Ujungpandang
Banda Sea
Flores
Dolak
Arafura Sea
Timor
Timor Sea

Cape York

Gulf of Carpentaria

Cape York Peninsula

● Darwin

Kimberley Plateau

Great Barrier Reef

● Brisbane

GREAT DIVIDING RANGE

Great Artesian Basin

● Sydney
◎ Canberra
Mt. Kosciusko (2,228 m) ▲
Australian Alps
Cape Howe

A U S T R A L I A
Macdonnell Ranges ● Alice Springs

Simpson Desert

Great Sandy Desert

Hamersley Range

North West Cape

Gibson Desert

Great Victoria Desert

Great Australian Bight

Nullarbor Plain

Kangaroo

● Perth

Cape Leeuwin

Murray R.
Darling R.
Lachlan R.
Flinders R.
Adelaide ●
● Melbourne

Tasman Sea

Bass Strait
Furneaux Group
Tasmania
● Hobart
South East Cape

INDIAN OCEAN

South China Sea

A S I A

SOUTHEAST ASIA

MALAYSIA

BRUNEI ◎ Bandar Seri Begawan

Borneo

Sumatra

Java Sea
Jakarta ◎
Surabaya ●
Bali
Java

I N D O N E S I A

Sumbawa
Sumba

140°W
120°W
160°W
180°
160°E
140°E
120°E

40°S
20°S

642

642 Atlas

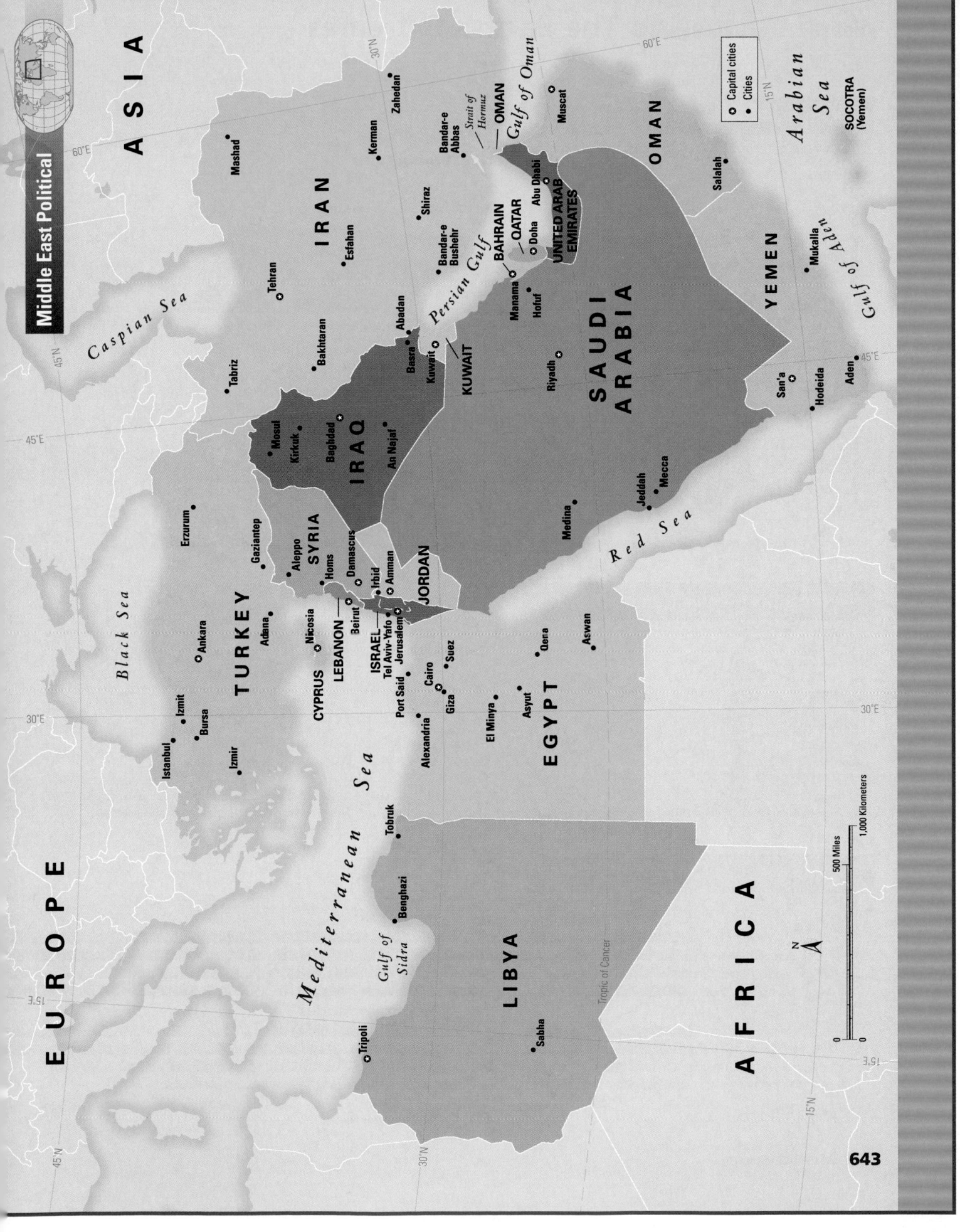

ASIA

EUROPE

AFRICA

Capital cities
• Cities

Caspian Sea

Black Sea

Mediterranean Sea

Gulf of Sidra

TURKEY

Istanbul
Izmit
Bursa
Izmir
Ankara
Adana
Erzurum
Gaziantep

CYPRUS
Nicosia

SYRIA
Aleppo
Homs
Damascus

LEBANON
Beirut

ISRAEL
Tel Aviv-Yafo
Jerusalem
Port Said

JORDAN
Irbid
Amman

EGYPT
Alexandria
Cairo
Giza
Suez
El Minya
Asyut
Qena
Aswan

LIBYA
Tripoli
Benghazi
Tobruk
Sabha

IRAN
Mashad
Tabriz
Tehran
Esfahan
Bakhtaran
Kerman
Shiraz
Zahedan

IRAQ
Mosul
Kirkuk
Baghdad
An Najaf
Basra
Abadan

KUWAIT
Kuwait

Bandar-e Abbas
Bandar-e Bushehr

BAHRAIN
Manama

QATAR
Doha

UNITED ARAB EMIRATES
Abu Dhabi

OMAN
Muscat
Salalah

SAUDI ARABIA
Riyadh
Hofuf
Medina
Mecca
Jeddah

YEMEN
San'a
Hodeida
Aden
Mukalla

SOCOTRA (Yemen)

Persian Gulf

Strait of Hormuz

Gulf of Oman

Arabian Sea

Gulf of Aden

Red Sea

Tropic of Cancer

30°N
45°N
15°N
30°E
45°E
60°E
15°E

500 Miles
1,000 Kilometers

N

643

Mini Almanac The Earth's Extremes

The High and The Low

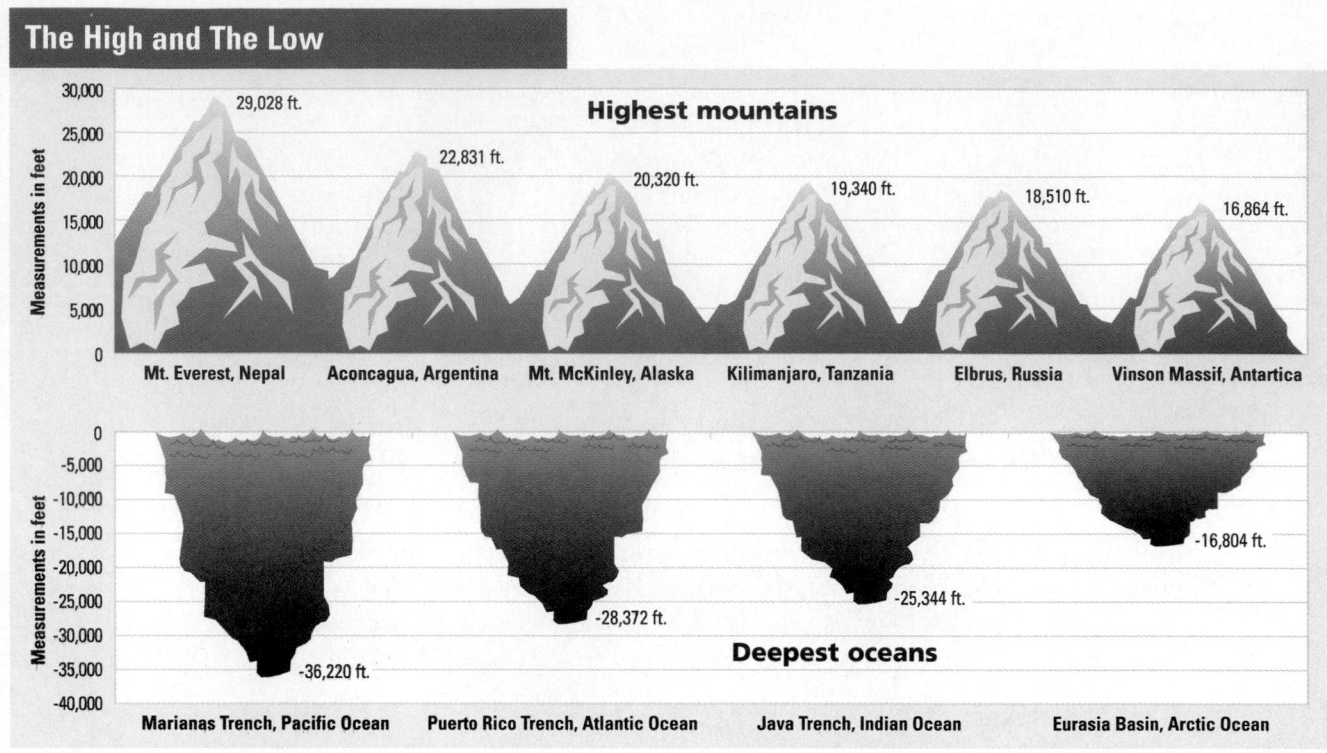

Highest mountains

Measurements in feet

- 29,028 ft. — Mt. Everest, Nepal
- 22,831 ft. — Aconcagua, Argentina
- 20,320 ft. — Mt. McKinley, Alaska
- 19,340 ft. — Kilimanjaro, Tanzania
- 18,510 ft. — Elbrus, Russia
- 16,864 ft. — Vinson Massif, Antartica

Deepest oceans

Measurements in feet

- -36,220 ft. — Marianas Trench, Pacific Ocean
- -28,372 ft. — Puerto Rico Trench, Atlantic Ocean
- -25,344 ft. — Java Trench, Indian Ocean
- -16,804 ft. — Eurasia Basin, Arctic Ocean

The Most Destructive Natural Disasters

Earthquakes

Death toll in thousands

- 830,000 — Shaanxi Province, China (1556)
- 36,000 — Netherlands Indies (1883)
- 85,000 — Messina, Sicily (1908)
- 200,000 — Gansu Province, China (1920)
- 25,000 — Mexico (1985)

The Longest

Rivers

- Nile, Africa
- Amazon, S. America
- Mississippi, N. America
- Chang Jiang (Yangtze), China

Mountain ranges

- Andes, S. America
- Rocky Mountains, N. America
- Himalayas, Central Asia — 2,400 mi.
- Trans-Antartic Mountains, Antartica — 2,200 mi.

500   1,000   1,500   2,000   2,500

Measurements in miles

The Wet and Dry

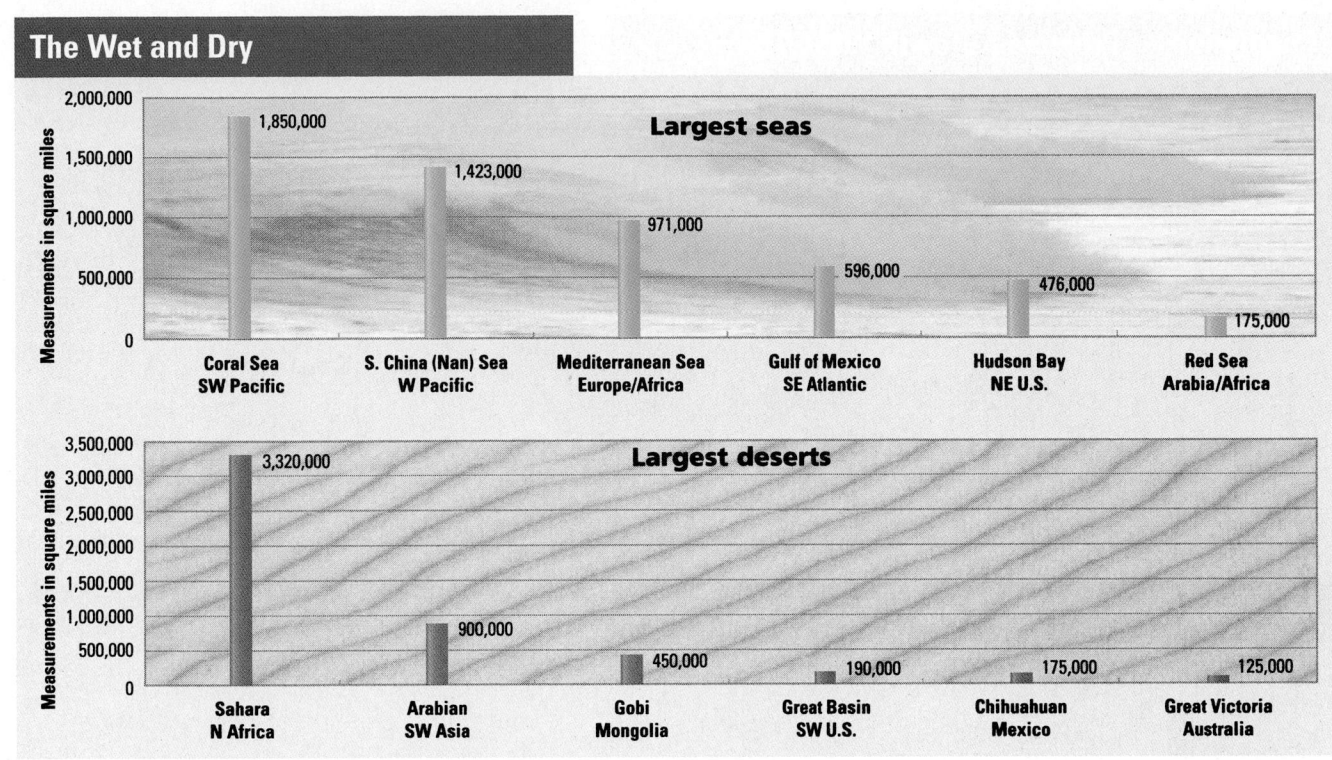

Largest seas
Measurements in square miles

- Coral Sea / SW Pacific: 1,850,000
- S. China (Nan) Sea / W Pacific: 1,423,000
- Mediterranean Sea / Europe/Africa: 971,000
- Gulf of Mexico / SE Atlantic: 596,000
- Hudson Bay / NE U.S.: 476,000
- Red Sea / Arabia/Africa: 175,000

Largest deserts
Measurements in square miles

- Sahara / N Africa: 3,320,000
- Arabian / SW Asia: 900,000
- Gobi / Mongolia: 450,000
- Great Basin / SW U.S.: 190,000
- Chihuahuan / Mexico: 175,000
- Great Victoria / Australia: 125,000

Storms and floods
Death toll in thousands

- Holland (1228): 100,000
- India (1864): 70,000
- Sankriku, Japan (1896): 27,000
- Hong Kong (1906): 10,000
- Pakistan (1970): 200,000
- Bangladesh (1991): 131,000

- 4,160 mi.
- 4,080 mi.
- 3,740 mi.
- 3,720 mi.
- 4,500 mi.
- 3,000 mi.

3,000   3,500   4,000   4,500   5,000   5,500

MINI ALMANAC **645**

Mini Almanac The Human Panorama

Population — Projected Growth 1995-2025

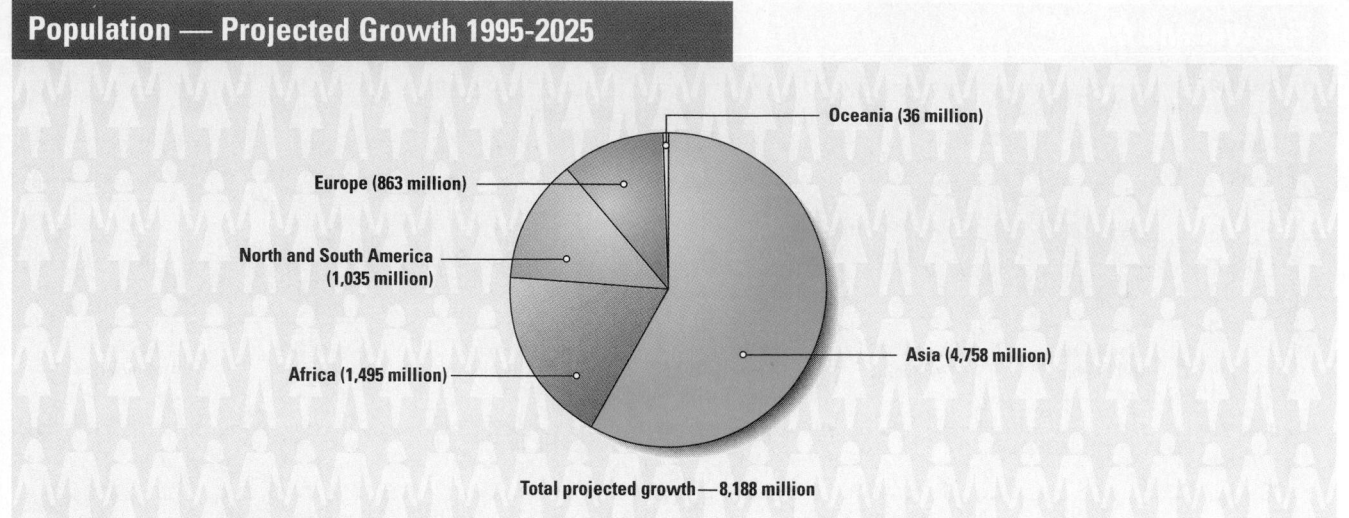

Oceania (36 million)

Europe (863 million)

North and South America
(1,035 million)

Africa (1,495 million)

Asia (4,758 million)

Total projected growth — 8,188 million

Communication — Most Widely Spoken Languages

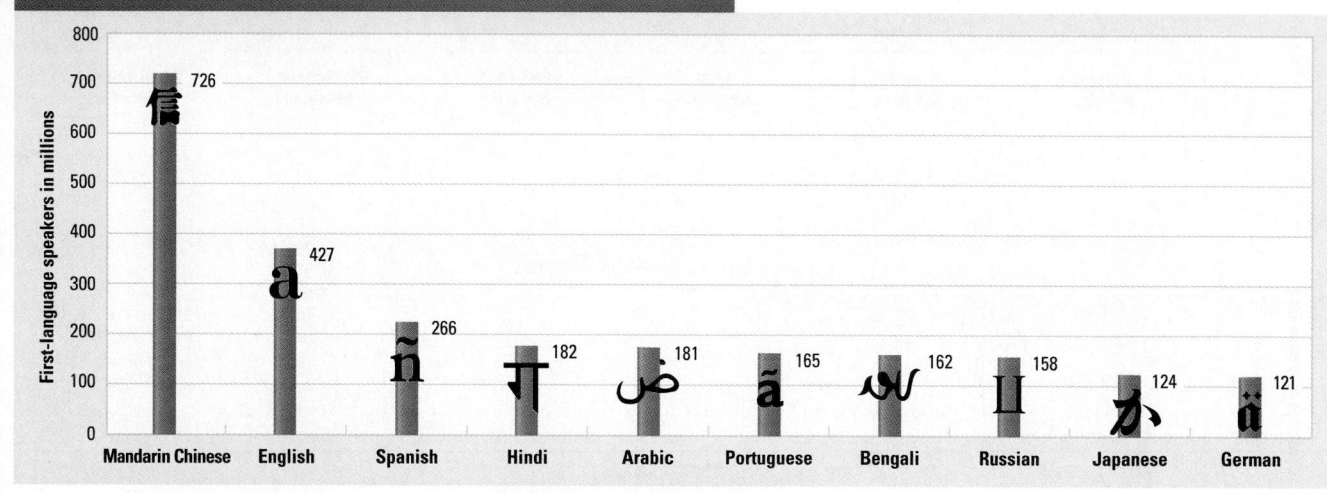

First-language speakers in millions

Language	Speakers
Mandarin Chinese	726
English	427
Spanish	266
Hindi	182
Arabic	181
Portuguese	165
Bengali	162
Russian	158
Japanese	124
German	121

Important Discoveries and Inventions

5000 B.C.

4400 B.C.
loom

4000 B.C.
cosmetics

3800 B.C.
wheel

3000 B.C.
plow

2000 B.C.
flush toilet

Technological Milestones

Longest bridges

Measurements in feet

- Humber Estuary, England — 4,626 ft.
- Verrazano Narrows, Brooklyn, NY, U.S. — 4,260 ft.
- Golden Gate, San Francisco, CA, U.S. — 4,200 ft.
- Minami Bisan-Seto, Japan — 3,609 ft.
- Bosporus I, Istanbul, Turkey — 3,576 ft.

0   1,000   2,000   3,000   4,000   5,000

Tallest structures

Measurements in feet

- KTHI-TV Mast, N. Dakota, U.S. — 2,063
- CN Tower, Canada — 1,822
- Ostankino Tower, Moscow, Russia — 1,762
- Petronas Twin Towers, Malaysia — 1,506

2,500
2,000
1,500
1,000
500
0

Life Expectancy

Worldwide Longevity

Measurements in years

100
80
60
40
20
0

Japan   United Kingdom   Burundi   Iraq   Mexico   China   Russia   Peru   South Africa   India   United States

■ Male   ■ Female

Changing life expectancy in the U.S. 1850-1996

Measurements in years

80
70
60
50
40
30

1850 1870 1890 1910 1930 1950 1970 1990 2010

■ Male   ■ Female

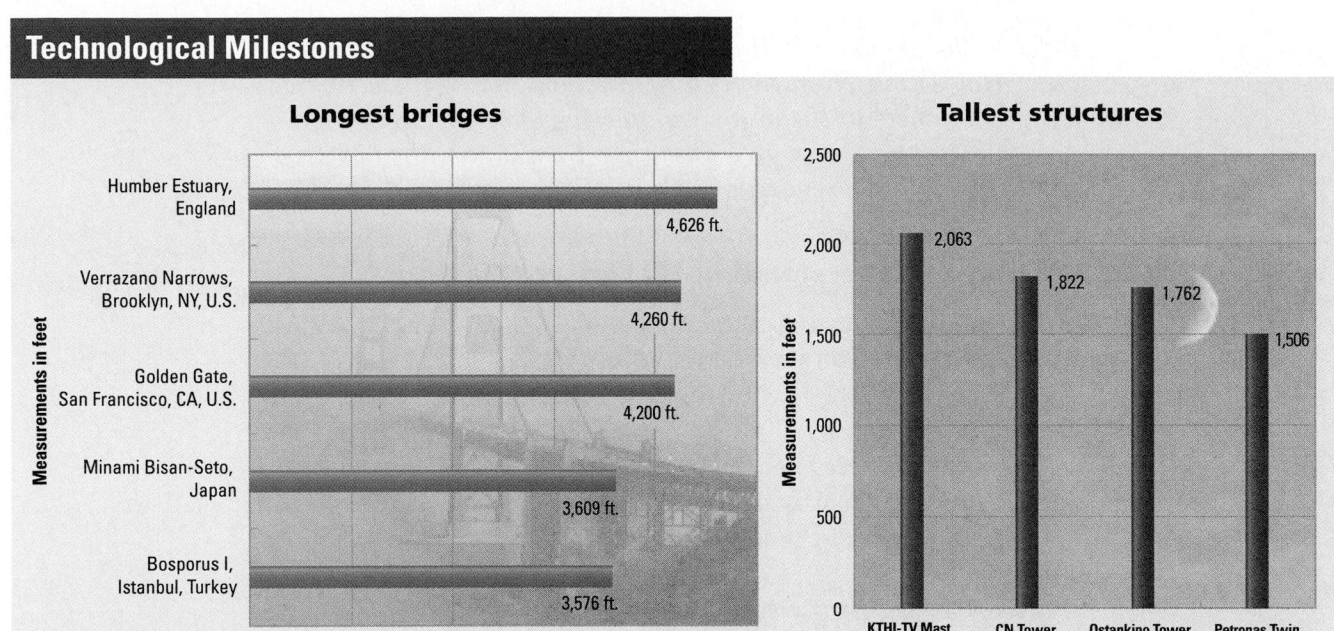

| 100 B.C. paper | 190 abacus | 600 windmill | 700 printing | 1475 rifle | 1590 microscope |

0

1600 to 2000

- 1608 telescope
- 1656 pendulum clock
- 1783 parachute
- 1842 anesthetics
- 1867 dynamite
- 1904 radar
- 1926 rocket
- 1975 home videotape systems

1600   1800   2000

- 1639 steam engine
- 1709 piano
- 1816 bicycle
- 1848 chewing gum
- 1876 telephone
- 1924 frozen food
- 1928 computer

Skillbuilder Handbook

Refer to the Skillbuilder Handbook when you need help in answering Think Through History questions, doing the activities entitled Connect to History, or answering questions in Section Assessments and Chapter Assessments. In addition, the handbook will help you answer questions about maps, charts, and graphs.

Section 1: Understanding Historical Readings

Section 2: Using Critical Thinking

Section 3: Exploring Historical Evidence

Section 1: Understanding Historical Readings

1.1 Following Chronological Order

Chronological order is the order in which events happen in time. Historians need to figure out the order in which things happened to get an accurate sense of the relationships among events. As you read history, figure out the sequence, or time order, of events.

UNDERSTANDING THE SKILL

Strategy: Look for time clues. The following paragraph is about the rulers of England after the death of Henry VIII. Notice how the time line that follows puts the events in chronological order.

HENRY'S CHILDREN RULE ENGLAND

| After | the death of Henry VIII in | 1547, | each of his three children eventually ruled. This created religious turmoil. Edward VI became king at age nine and ruled only six years. During his reign, the Protestants gained power. Edward's half-sister Mary | followed | him to the throne. She was a Catholic who returned the English Church to the rule of the pope. Mary had many Protestants killed. England's | next | ruler was Anne Boleyn's daughter, Elizabeth. After inheriting the throne in 1558, Elizabeth I returned her kingdom to Protestantism. In | 1559 | Parliament followed Elizabeth's request and set up a national church | much like the one under Henry VIII. |

Look for clue words about time. These are words like *first, initial, next, then, before, after, finally,* and *by that time.*

Use specific dates provided in the text.

Watch for references to previous historical events that are included in the background.

Strategy: Order events on a time line.

If the events are complex, make a time line of them. Write the dates below the line and the events above the line.

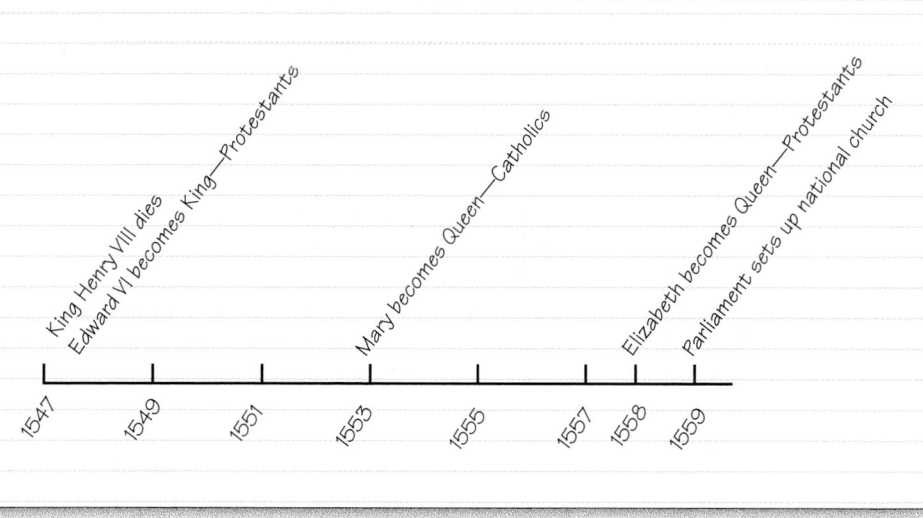

APPLYING THE SKILL

Make your own time line. Skim Chapter 19, Section 3, "Gorbachev Moves Toward Democracy," to find out about the spread of democracy in parts of Europe controlled by the Soviet Union. List the important dates and events. Start with the demonstrations in East Germany in October 1989, include events in Czechoslovakia and Romania, and end with reunification of Germany in October of 1990. Decide on a scale for your time line. Show the important dates below the line and write what happened on each date above the line.

SKILLBUILDER HANDBOOK **649**

1.2 Clarifying; Summarizing

Clarifying means making clear and fully understanding what you read. One way to do this is by asking yourself questions about the material. In your answers, restate in your own words what you have read.

Summarizing means condensing what you read into fewer words. You state only the main ideas and the most important details. In your own words, reduce the paragraph or section into a brief report of its general ideas.

UNDERSTANDING THE SKILL

Strategy: Understand and condense the text. The passage below tells about trade in West Africa between 300 and 1600. Following the description is a summary that condenses and also clarifies the key information.

> **WEST AFRICAN TRADE**
>
> The wealth of the savanna empires was based on trade in two precious commodities, gold and salt. The gold came from a forest region south of the savanna between the Niger and Senegal rivers. Working in utmost secrecy, miners dug gold from shafts as much as 100 feet deep or sifted it from fast-moving streams. Until about 1350, at least two thirds of the world's supply of gold came from West Africa.
>
> Although rich in gold, the savanna and forest areas lacked salt, a material essential to human life. In contrast, the Sahara contained abundant deposits of salt.
>
> Arab traders, eager to obtain West African gold, carried salt across the Sahara by camel caravan. After a long journey, they reached the market towns of the savanna. Meanwhile, the other traders brought gold north from the forest region. The two sets of merchants met in trading centers such as Timbuktu. Royal officials made sure that all traders weighed goods fairly and did business according to law.

Clarify: Look up words or concepts you don't know.

Summarize: Include key facts and statistics. Watch for numbers, dates, quantities, percentages, and facts.

Summarize: Look for topic sentences stating the main idea. These are often at the beginning of a section or paragraph. Restate each main idea briefly.

Clarify: Make sure you understand. Ask yourself questions and answer them. For example, who's carrying what?

Strategy: Clarify the main idea.

MAIN IDEA
Gold and salt were traded in West Africa.

Strategy: Write a summary.

Clarify and summarize: Write a summary to clarify your understanding of the main ideas.

SUMMARY
Trade in West Africa was based on gold from the south and salt from the north. Gold was mined in the forest regions. Two thirds of all the world's gold supply came from West Africa. Salt came from the desert. Arab traders met with African traders at trade centers such as Timbuktu.

APPLYING THE SKILL

Clarify and write your own summary. Turn to Chapter 14, pages 397–398, and read "Weapons of Totalitarianism." Note the main ideas. Look up any words you don't recognize. Then write a summary of the section. Condense the section in your own words.

1.3 Identifying Problems and Solutions

Identifying problems means finding and understanding the difficulties faced by a particular group of people at a certain time. Noticing how the people solved their problems is **identifying solutions.** Checking further to see how well those solutions worked is identifying outcomes.

UNDERSTANDING THE SKILL

Strategy: Look for problems and solutions. The passage below summarizes some economic problems facing Latin American nations during the early 20th century.

Look for implied problems. Problems may be suggested indirectly. This sentence suggests that a serious problem in Latin America was the uneven division of wealth.

Look for problems people face.

Look for solutions people tried to deal with each problem.

Check outcomes to the solutions. See how well the solutions worked. Sometimes the solution to one problem caused another problem.

LAND REFORM IN LATIN AMERICA

In Latin America, concentration of productive land in the hands of a few created extremes of wealth and poverty. Poor peasants had no choice but to work large estates owned by a few wealthy families. Landlords had no reason to invest in expensive farm machinery when labor was so cheap. Farming methods were inefficient and economic development was slow.

As Latin American nations began to modernize in the twentieth century, land ownership became a political issue. In response, a handful of countries began land reform programs. These programs divided large estates into smaller plots. Small plots of land were in turn distributed to farm families or granted to villages for communal farming. However, just turning over the land to the landless was not enough. Peasant farmers needed instruction, seeds, equipment, and credit. If the land and the people were to be productive, governments would have to provide assistance to the peasants.

Strategy: Make a chart.

Summarize the problems and solutions in a chart. Identify the problem or problems and the steps taken to solve them. Look for the short- and long-term effects of the solutions.

Problems	Solutions	Outcomes
A few wealthy people owned most of the land.	Land reform programs divided large estates into smaller plots.	Peasants were given land, and communal farms were set up.
Inefficient farming resulted in slow economic development.		
Peasants lacked equipment, resources, skills.	Governments would have to assist with loans and instruction.	Not stated.

APPLYING THE SKILL

Make your own chart. Turn to Chapter 15 and read "Europe After the War" on pages 421–423. Make a chart that lists the problems Germany faced after World War I. List the solutions that were tried and whatever outcomes are mentioned.

1.4 Analyzing Motives

Analyzing motives means examining the reasons why a person, group, or government takes a particular action. To understand those reasons, consider the needs, emotions, prior experiences, and goals of the person or group.

UNDERSTANDING THE SKILL

Strategy: Look for reasons why. On June 28, 1914, Serb terrorists assassinated Austria-Hungary's Archduke Franz Ferdinand and his wife when they visited Sarajevo, the capital of Bosnia. In the following passage, Borijove Jevtic, a Serb terrorist, explains why the assassination occurred. Before this passage, he explains that the terrorists had received a telegram stating that the Archduke would be visiting Sarajevo on June 28. The diagram that follows summarizes the motives of the terrorists for murdering the Archduke.

> THE ASSASSINATION OF THE ARCHDUKE
>
> How dared Franz Ferdinand, not only the representative of the oppressor but in his own person an arrogant tyrant, enter Sarajevo on that day? Such an entry was a studied insult.
>
> 28 June is a date engraved deeply in the heart of every Serb, so that the day has a name of its own. It is called the vidovnan. It is the day on which the old Serbian kingdom was conquered by the Turks at the battle of Amselfelde in 1389. It is also the day on which in the second Balkan War the Serbian arms took glorious revenge on the Turk for his old victory and for the years of enslavement.
>
> That was no day for Franz Ferdinand, the new oppressor, to venture to the very doors of Serbia for a display of the force of arms which kept us beneath his heel.
>
> Our decision was taken almost immediately. Death to the tyrant!

Look for motives based on basic needs and human emotions. Needs include food, shelter, safety, freedom. Emotions include fear, anger, pride, desire for revenge, patriotism, for example.

Look for motives based on past events or inspiring individuals.

Notice both positive and negative motives.

Strategy: Make a diagram.

Make a diagram that summarizes motives and actions. List the important action in the middle of the diagram. Then list motives in different categories around the action.

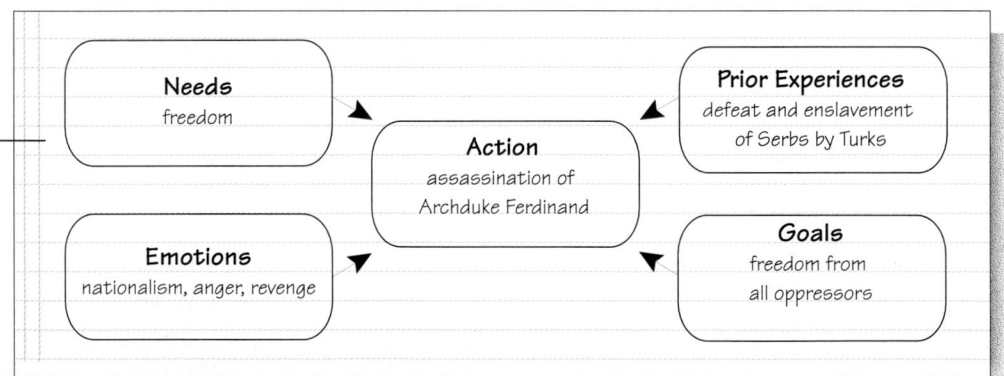

APPLYING THE SKILL

Make your own diagram. Turn to Chapter 11, Section 1, "Imperialists Divide Africa." Read the section and look for motives of European nations in acquiring lands in other parts of the world. Make a diagram like the one above showing the European nations' motives for taking the land.

1.5 Analyzing Causes; Recognizing Effects

Causes are the events, conditions, and other reasons that lead to an event. Causes happen before the event in time; they explain why it happened. **Effects** are the results or consequences of the event. One effect often becomes the cause of other effects, resulting in a chain of events. Causes and effects can be both short-term and long-term. Examining **cause-and-effect relationships** helps historians see how events are related and why they took place.

UNDERSTANDING THE SKILL

Strategy: Keep track of causes and effects as you read. The passage below describes events leading to the rise of feudalism in Japan. The diagram that follows summarizes the chain of causes and effects.

Effects: Look for results or consequences. Sometimes these are indicated by clue words such as *brought about, led to, as a result,* and *consequently.*

Notice that an effect may be the cause of another event. This begins a chain of causes and effects.

FEUDALISM COMES TO JAPAN

For most of the Heian period, the rich Fujiwara family held the real power in Japan. Members of this family held many influential posts. By about the middle of the eleventh century, the power of the central government and the Fujiwaras began to slip. This was due in part to court families' greater interest in luxury and artistic pursuits than in governing.

Since the central government was weak, ① large landowners living away from the capital set up private armies. As a result, ② the countryside became lawless and dangerous. Armed soldiers on horseback preyed on farmers and travelers, while pirates took control of the seas. ③ For safety, farmers and small landowners traded parts of their land to strong warlords in exchange for protection. Because the lords had more land, the lords gained more power. This marked the beginning of a feudal system of localized rule like that of ancient China and medieval Europe.

Causes: Look for clue words that show cause. These include *because, due to, since,* and *therefore.*

Look for multiple causes and multiple effects. The weakness of the central government caused the three effects shown here.

Strategy: Make a cause-and-effect diagram.

Summarize cause-and-effect relationships in a diagram. Starting with the first cause in a series, fill in the boxes until you reach the end result.

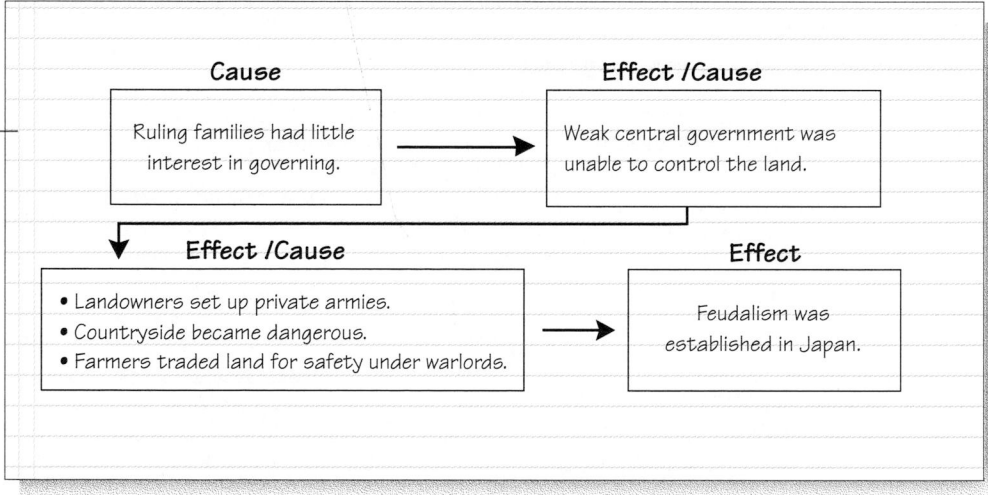

Cause
Ruling families had little interest in governing.

Effect /Cause
Weak central government was unable to control the land.

Effect /Cause
- Landowners set up private armies.
- Countryside became dangerous.
- Farmers traded land for safety under warlords.

Effect
Feudalism was established in Japan.

APPLYING THE SKILL

Make your own cause-and-effect diagram. Turn to Chapter 12, pages 350–351. Read "Juárez and *La Reforma*" and make notes about the causes and effects of Juárez's reform movement in Mexico. Make a diagram like the one shown above to summarize the information you find.

1.6 Comparing; Contrasting

Historians compare and contrast events, personalities, ideas, behaviors, beliefs, and institutions in order to understand them thoroughly. **Comparing** involves finding both similarities and differences between two or more things. **Contrasting** means examining only the differences between them.

UNDERSTANDING THE SKILL

Strategy: Look for similarities and differences. The following passage describes life in the ancient Greek city-states of Sparta and Athens. The Venn diagram below shows some of the similarities and differences between the two city-states.

Compare: Look for clue words indicating that two things are alike. Clue words include *all, both, like, as, likewise,* and *similarly.*

Contrast: Look for clue words that show how two things differ. Clue words include *unlike, by contrast, however, except, different,* and *on the other hand.*

SPARTA AND ATHENS

The Greek city-states developed separately but shared certain characteristics, including language and religion. Economically, all began as farming economies, and all except Sparta eventually moved to trade. Politically, all city-states, except for Sparta, evolved into early forms of democracies.

The leader in the movement to democracy was Athens. After a series of reforms, every Athenian citizen was considered equal before the law. However, as in the other Greek city-states, only about one fifth of the population were citizens. Slaves did much of the work, so Athenian citizens were free to create works of art, architecture, and literature, including drama.

By contrast, Sparta lived in constant fear of revolts by *helots*, people who were held in slave-like conditions to work the land. The city was set up as a military dictatorship, and Spartan men dedicated their lives to the military. In Sparta, duty, strength, and discipline were valued over beauty, individuality, and creativity. As a result, Spartans created little art, architecture, or literature.

Compare: Look for features that two subjects have in common. Here you learn that both Athens and Sparta started out as farming communities.

Contrast: Look for ways in which two things are different. Here you learn that Athens and Sparta had different values.

Strategy: Make a Venn diagram.

Compare and Contrast: Summarize similarities and differences in a Venn diagram. In the overlapping area, list characteristics shared by both subjects. Then, in one oval list the characteristics of one subject not shared by the other. In the other oval, list unshared characteristics of the second subject.

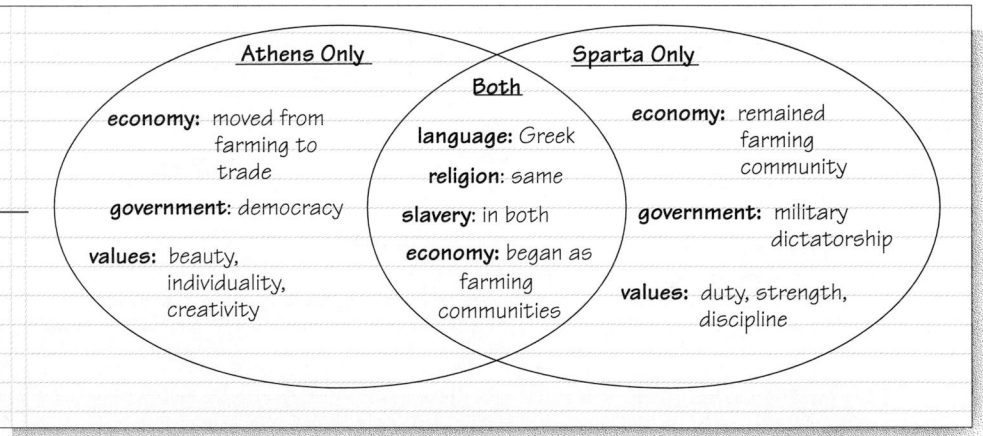

Athens Only — **economy:** moved from farming to trade; **government:** democracy; **values:** beauty, individuality, creativity

Both — **language:** Greek; **religion:** same; **slavery:** in both; **economy:** began as farming communities

Sparta Only — **economy:** remained farming community; **government:** military dictatorship; **values:** duty, strength, discipline

APPLYING THE SKILL

Make your own Venn diagram. Turn to Chapter 4, pages 113–114, and read the section called "Native American Reaction." Make a Venn diagram comparing and contrasting Dutch and English colonists' relations with Native Americans.

1.7 Distinguishing Fact from Opinion

Facts are events, dates, statistics, or statements that can be proved to be true. Facts can be checked for accuracy. **Opinions** are judgments, beliefs, and feelings of the writer or speaker.

UNDERSTANDING THE SKILL

Strategy: Find clues in the text. The following excerpt tells about the uprising of Jews in the Warsaw ghetto in 1943. The chart summarizes the facts and opinions.

THE WARSAW GHETTO UPRISING

With orders from Himmler to crush the Jews, the Nazis attacked on April 19, 1943, at the start of the holiday of Passover. Two thousand armed SS troops entered the ghetto, marching with tanks, rifles, machine guns, and trailers full of ammunition. The Jewish fighters were in position—in bunkers, in windows, on rooftops. They had rifles and handguns, hand grenades and bombs that they had made. And they let fly. . . .

Unbelievably, the Jews won the battle that day. The Germans were forced to retreat. . . . The Germans brought in more troops, and the fighting intensified. German pilots dropped bombs on the ghetto. . . .

On May 1, Goebbels [Nazi propaganda minister] wrote in his diary: "Of course this jest will probably not last long." He added a complaint. "But it shows what one can expect of the Jews if they have guns."

Goebbels' tone was mocking. But his forecast was inevitable—and correct. . . . Goebbels did not record in his diary, when the uprising was over, that the starving Jews of the ghetto, with their pathetic supply of arms, had held out against the German army for forty days, longer than Poland or France had held out.

Source: *A Nightmare in History*, by Miriam Chaikin. (New York: Clarion Books, 1987) pp. 77–78

Facts: Look for specific names, dates, statistics, and statements that can be proved. The first two paragraphs provide a factual account of the event.

Opinion: Look for assertions, claims, hypotheses, and judgments. Here Goebbels expresses his opinion of the uprising and of the Jews.

Opinion: Look for judgment words that the writer uses to describe the people and events. Judgment words are often adjectives that are used to arouse a reader's emotions.

Strategy: Make a chart.

FACTS	OPINIONS
On April 19, 1943, 2,000 armed SS troops attacked the Warsaw ghetto. Jewish fighters held out for 40 days.	*Goebbels:* The uprising was a jest, but showed the danger of letting Jews get hold of guns. *Author:* It is difficult to believe that Warsaw Jews with their pathetic supply of arms were able to defeat the powerful Nazis. The Jews showed greater courage and determination than did the Poles and French.

Divide facts and opinions in a chart. Summarize and separate the facts from the opinions expressed in a passage.

APPLYING THE SKILL

Make your own chart. Turn to Chapter 10, page 282, "Democratic Reform and Activism." Find the "Voice from the Past" from the Seneca Falls Convention. Make a chart in which you summarize the facts in your own words, and list the opinions and judgments stated. Look carefully at the language used in order to separate one from the other.

Section 2: Using Critical Thinking

2.1 Developing Historical Perspective

Developing **historical perspective** means understanding events and people in the context of their times. It means not judging the past by current values, but by taking into account the beliefs of the time.

UNDERSTANDING THE SKILL

Strategy: Look for values of the past. The following passage was written by Bartolomé de Las Casas, a Spanish missionary who defended the rights of Native Americans. It challenges an argument presented by a scholar named Sepúlveda, who held that the superior Spaniards had the right to enslave the Native Americans. Following the passage is a chart that summarizes the information from a historical perspective.

Identify the historical figure, the occasion, and the date.

Explain how people's actions and words reflected the attitudes, values, and passions of the era. Las Casas challenges prejudices about Native Americans that were widely held in Europe. His language emphasizes a favorable comparison between Native American and European societies.

IN DEFENSE OF THE INDIANS (1550)
BARTOLOMÉ DE LAS CASAS

Now if we shall have shown that among our Indians of the western and southern shores (granting that we call them barbarians and that they are barbarians) there are important kingdoms, large numbers of people who live settled lives in a society, great cities, kings, judges and laws, persons who engage in commerce, buying, selling, lending, and the other contracts of the law of nations, will it not stand proved that the Reverend Doctor Sepúlveda has spoken wrongly and viciously against peoples like these? . . . From the fact that the Indians are barbarians it does not necessarily follow that they are incapable of government and have to be ruled by others, except to be taught about the Catholic faith and to be admitted to the holy sacraments. They are not ignorant, inhuman, or bestial. Rather, long before they had heard the word Spaniard they had properly organized states, wisely ordered by excellent laws, religion, and custom. They cultivated friendship and, bound together in common fellowship, lived in populous cities in which they wisely administered the affairs of both peace and war justly and equitably, truly governed by laws that at very many points surpass ours, and could have won the admiration of the sages of Athens. . . .

Look for clues to the attitudes, customs, and values of people living at the time. As a Spanish missionary, Las Casas assumes that Europeans are more civilized than Native Americans and that Native Americans need to be converted to Catholicism.

Notice words, phrases, and settings that reflect the period. Las Casas speaks from a time when Europeans looked to classical Greece as a benchmark for civilization.

Use historical perspective to understand Las Casas's attitudes. In a chart, list key words, phrases, and details from the passage. In a short paragraph, summarize the basic values and attitudes of Las Casas.

Strategy: Write a summary.

Key Phrases	Las Casas's *In Defense of the Indians*
• barbarians • Catholic faith • not inhuman, ignorant, or bestial • properly organized states, wisely ordered • sages of Athens	Las Casas argues that Native Americans are not inhuman and do not deserve cruelty and slavery. Rather, they are fully capable of "coming up" to the level of Spanish civilization. Although he makes the statement that Native Americans are barbarians, his language and comparisons seem to suggest that he believes them to be highly civilized in many respects. At the same time, he believes in the importance of converting them to Catholicism.

APPLYING THE SKILL

Write your own summary. Turn to Chapter 8, page 245, and read the excerpt from Otto von Bismarck's speech to the German parliament. Read the passage using historical perspective. Then summarize your ideas in a chart like the one above.

Section 2: Using Critical Thinking

2.2 Formulating Historical Questions

Formulating historical questions is important as you examine primary sources—first-hand accounts, documents, letters, and other records of the past. As you analyze a source, ask questions about what it means and why it is significant. Then, when you are doing research, write questions that you want your research to answer. This step will help to guide your research and organize the information you collect.

UNDERSTANDING THE SKILL

Strategy: Question what you read. The Muslim scholar Ibn Battuta published an account of his journeys in Asia and Africa in the 1300s. Following is part of his description of China. After the passage is a web diagram that organizes historical questions about it.

Ask about the historical record itself. Who produced it? When was it produced?

Ask about the person who created the record. What judgments or opinions does the author express?

IBN BATTUTA IN CHINA, AROUND 1345

The Chinese themselves are infidels, who worship idols and burn their dead like the Hindus. . . . In every Chinese city there is a quarter for Muslims in which they live by themselves, and in which they have mosques both for the Friday services and for other religious purposes. The Muslims are honored and respected. The Chinese infidels eat the flesh of swine and dogs, and sell it in their markets. They are wealthy folk and well-to-do, but they make no display either in their food or their clothes. You will see one of their principal merchants, a man so rich that his wealth cannot be counted, wearing a coarse cotton tunic. But there is one thing that the Chinese take a pride in, that is gold and silver plate. Every one of them carries a stick, on which they lean in walking, and which they call "the third leg." Silk is very plentiful among them, because the silk-worm attaches itself to fruits and feeds on them without requiring much care. For that reason, it is so common as to be worn by even the very poorest there. Were it not for the merchants it would have no value at all, for a single piece of cotton cloth is sold in their country for the price of many pieces of silk.

Ask about the facts presented. Who were the main people? What did they do? What were they like?

Ask about the significance of the record. How would you interpret the information presented? How does it fit in with the history of this time and place? What more do you need to know to answer these questions?

Strategy: Make a web diagram.

Investigate a topic in more depth by asking questions. Ask a large question and then ask smaller questions that explore and develop from the larger question.

- What was the historical situation in China at this time?
- Why did Ibn Battuta go to China and who was the audience for his narrative?
- What was China like in the 1300s?
- How might Ibn Battuta's background have influenced his impressions?
- Do other sources agree with Ibn Battuta's description?

APPLYING THE SKILL

Make your own web diagram. Turn to the quotation by King Chulalongkorn in Chapter 11, page 328. Use a web diagram to write historical questions about the passage.

Section 2: Using Critical Thinking

2.3 Hypothesizing

Hypothesizing means developing a possible explanation for historical events. A hypothesis is an educated guess about what happened in the past or what might happen in the future. A hypothesis takes available information, links it to previous experience and knowledge, and comes up with a possible explanation, conclusion, or prediction.

UNDERSTANDING THE SKILL

Strategy: Find clues in the reading. In studying the Indus Valley civilization, historians do not yet know exactly what caused that culture to decline. They have, however, developed hypotheses about what happened to it. Read this passage and look at the steps that are shown for building a hypothesis. Following the passage is a chart that organizes the information.

> **MYSTERIOUS END TO INDUS VALLEY CULTURE**
>
> Around 1750 B.C., the quality of building in the Indus Valley cities declined. Gradually, the great cities fell into decay. What happened? Some historians think that the Indus River changed course, as it tended to do, so that its floods no longer fertilized the fields near the cities. Other scholars suggest that people wore out the valley's land. They overgrazed it, overfarmed it, and overcut its trees, brush, and grass.
>
> As the Indus Valley civilization neared its end, around 1500 B.C, a sudden catastrophe may have had a hand in the cities' downfall. Archaeologists have found a half-dozen groups of skeletons in the ruins of Mohenjo-Daro, seemingly never buried. Their presence suggests that the city, already weakened by its slow decline, may have been abandoned after a natural disaster or a devastating attack from human enemies. The Aryans, a nomadic people from north of the Hindu Kush mountains, swept into the Indus Valley at about this time. Whether they caused the collapse of the Indus Valley civilization or followed in its wake is not known.

Identify the event, pattern, or trend you want to explain.

Determine the facts you have about the situation. These facts support various hypotheses about what happened to the Indus Valley civilization.

Develop a hypothesis that might explain the event. Historians hypothesize that a combination of ecological change and sudden catastrophe caused the Indus Valley civilization to collapse.

Determine what additional information you need to test the hypothesis. You might refer to a book about India, for example, to learn more about the impact of the Aryan invasions.

Strategy: Make a chart.

Use a chart to summarize your hypothesis about events. Write down your hypothesis and the facts that support it. Then you can see what additional information you need to help prove or disprove it.

Hypothesis	Facts that support the hypothesis	Additional information needed
A combination of ecological change and sudden catastrophe caused the Indus Valley civilization to collapse	• Building quality declined • Indus River tended to change course • Unburied skeletons were found at Mohenjo-Daro • Aryan invasions occurred around same time	• What was Indus Valley culture like? • What were the geographical characteristics of the region? • How did overfarming tend to affect the environment? • What factors affected the decline of other ancient civilizations?

APPLYING THE SKILL

Make your own chart. Turn to Chapter 3, page 96, and read A Voice from the Past. Hypothesize what impact the introduction of firearms might have on Japan. Then read the surrounding text material. List facts that support your hypothesis and what additional information you might gather to help prove or disprove it.

658 SKILLBUILDER HANDBOOK

Section 2: Using Critical Thinking

2.4 Analyzing Issues

An issue is a matter of public concern or debate. Issues in history are usually economic, social, political, or moral. Historical issues are often more complicated than they first appear. **Analyzing an issue** means taking a controversy apart to find and describe the different points of view about the issue.

UNDERSTANDING THE SKILL

Strategy: Look for different sides of the issue. The following passage describes working conditions in English factories in the early 1800s. The cluster diagram that follows the passage helps you to analyze the issue of child labor.

Look for a central problem with its causes and effects.

CHILDREN AT WORK

Child labor was one of the most serious problems of the early Industrial Revolution. Children as young as 6 years worked exhausting jobs in factories and mines. Because wages were very low, many families in cities could not survive unless all their members, including children, worked.

In most factories, regular work hours were 6 in the morning to 6 in the evening, often with two "over-hours" until 8. It was common for 40 or more children to work together in one room—a room with little light or air. Those who lagged behind in their work were often beaten. Because safety was a low concern for many factory owners, accidents were common.

Look for facts and statistics. Factual information helps you understand the issue and evaluate the different sides or arguments.

In 1831, Parliament set up a committee to investigate abuses of child labor. Medical experts reported that long hours of factory work caused young children to become crippled or stunted in their growth. They recommended that children younger than age 14 should work no more than 8 hours. Factory owners responded that they needed children to work longer hours in order to be profitable. As one owner testified, reduced working hours for children would "much reduce the value of my mill and machinery, and consequently of . . . my manufacture." As a result of the committee's findings, Parliament passed the Factory Act of 1833. The act made it illegal to hire children under 9 years old, and it limited the working hours of older children.

Look for different sides to the issue. You need to consider all sides of an issue before deciding your position.

Strategy: Make a cluster diagram.

If an issue is complex, make a diagram. A diagram can help you analyze an issue.

Issue: Should Parliament restrict child labor?

Facts:
- Children as young as 6 years worked.
- Working hours were typically 12 hours a day, often with 2 hours overtime.
- Working conditions were dangerous, unhealthy, and inhumane.
- Factory work caused deformities in young children.

In favor of child labor:

Who: factory owners, some parents

Reasons: Shorter hours would reduce profits. Children's income essential for families.

Against child labor:

Who: medical examiners

Reasons: Children working in factories suffered permanent deformities.

APPLYING THE SKILL

Make your own cluster diagram. Chapter 18, page 506, describes the partition of India. Make a cluster diagram to analyze the issue and the positions of the people involved.

Section 2: Using Critical Thinking

2.5 Analyzing Assumptions and Biases

An **assumption** is a belief or an idea that is taken for granted. Some assumptions are based on evidence; some are based on feelings. Whether assumptions are clearly stated or just implied, you can usually figure out what they are.

Bias is a prejudiced point of view. Historical accounts that are biased tend to be one-sided and reflect the personal prejudices of the historian.

UNDERSTANDING THE SKILL

Strategy: Think about the writer as you read. The European explorer Amerigo Vespucci reached the coast of Brazil in 1502, on his second voyage to the Americas. Below are his impressions of the people he met.

> **Identify the author and information about him or her.** Does the author belong to a special-interest group, social class, political party, or movement that might promote a one-sided or slanted viewpoint on the subject?

> **Search for clues.** Are there words, phrases, statements, or images that might convey a positive or negative slant? What might these clues reveal about the author's bias?

AMERIGO VESPUCCI REPORTS ON THE PEOPLE OF BRAZIL

For twenty-seven days I ate and slept among them, and what I learned about them is as follows.

Having no laws and no religious faith, they live according to nature. They understand nothing of the immortality of the soul. There is no possession of private property among them, for everything is in common. They have no boundaries of kingdom or province. They have no king, nor do they obey anyone. Each one is his own master. There is no administration of justice, which is unnecessary to them, because in their code no one rules. . . .

They are also a warlike people and very cruel to their own kind. . . . That which made me . . . astonished at their wars and cruelty was that I could not understand from them why they made war upon each other, considering that they held no private property or sovereignty of empire and kingdoms and did not know any such thing as lust for possession, that is pillaging or a desire to rule, which appear to me to be the causes of wars and every disorderly act. When we requested them to state the cause, they did not know how to give any other cause than that this curse upon them began in ancient times and they sought to avenge the deaths of their forefathers.

> **Examine the evidence.** Is the information that the author presents consistent with other accounts? Is the behavior described consistent with human nature as you have observed it?

Strategy: Make a chart.

> **Make a chart of your analysis.** For each of the heads listed on the left side of the chart, summarize information presented in the passage.

Vespucci's impressions of the native peoples of Brazil	
author, date	Amerigo Vespucci, 1502
occasion	exploration of coast of Brazil on second voyage to Americas
tone	judging, negative, superior
assumptions	Since the native people do not live in organized states and have no private property, they have no system of authority, laws, or moral principles. They have no apparent religious beliefs. They are warlike and cruel and seem to make war on one another for no reason.
bias	The author's comments about the soul seem to show a bias towards his own religious beliefs. He also reveals a prejudice that European customs and practices are superior to all others.

APPLYING THE SKILL

Make your own chart. Look at the quotation by the Qing emperor Kangxi in "A Voice from the Past" in Chapter 3, page 99. Summarize the underlying assumptions and biases using a chart like the one shown.

660 SKILLBUILDER HANDBOOK

2.6 Evaluating Decisions and Courses of Action

Evaluating decisions means making judgments about the decisions that historical figures made. Historians evaluate decisions on the basis of their moral implications and their costs and benefits from different points of view.

Evaluating various courses of action means carefully judging the choices that historical figures had to make. By doing this, you can better understand why they made some of the decisions they did.

UNDERSTANDING THE SKILL

Strategy: Look for choices and reasons. The following passage describes the decisions U.S. President John Kennedy had to make when he learned of Soviet missile bases in Cuba. As you read it, think of the alternative responses he could have made at each turn of events. Following the passage is a chart that organizes information about the Cuban missile crisis.

THE CUBAN MISSILE CRISIS

During the summer of 1962, the flow of Soviet weapons into Cuba—including nuclear missiles—greatly increased. President Kennedy responded cautiously at first, issuing a warning that the United States would not tolerate the presence of offensive nuclear weapons in Cuba. Then, on October 16, photographs taken by American U-2 planes showed the president that the Soviets were secretly building missile bases on Cuba. Some of the missiles, armed and ready to fire, could reach U.S. cities in minutes.

On the evening of October 22, the president made public the evidence of missiles and stated his ultimatum: any missile attack from Cuba would trigger an all-out attack on the Soviet Union. Soviet ships continued to head toward the island, while the U.S. navy prepared to stop them and U.S. invasion troops massed in Florida. To avoid confrontation, the Soviet ships suddenly halted. Soviet Premier Nikita Khrushchev offered to remove the missiles from Cuba in exchange for a pledge not to invade the island. Kennedy agreed, and the crisis ended.

Some people criticized Kennedy for practicing brinkmanship, when private talks might have resolved the crisis without the threat of nuclear war. Others believed he had been too soft and had passed up a chance to invade Cuba and oust its Communist leader, Fidel Castro.

Look at decisions made by individuals or by groups. Notice the decisions Kennedy made in response to Soviet actions.

Analyze a decision in terms of the choices that were possible. Both Kennedy and Khrushchev faced the same choice. Either could carry out the threat, or either could back down quietly and negotiate.

Look at the outcome of the decisions.

Strategy: Make a chart.

Make a simple chart of your analysis. The problem was that Soviet nuclear missiles were being shipped to Cuba. The decision to be made was how the United States should respond.

Kennedy's choices	pros	cons	your evaluation
Publicly confront Khrushchev with navy and prepare for war.	Show Khrushchev and world the power and strong will of the U.S.; force him to back off.	Nuclear war could occur.	In your opinion, which was the better choice? Why?
Say nothing to U.S. public and negotiate quietly.	Avoid frightening U.S. citizens and avoid threat of nuclear war.	The U.S. would look weak publicly; Khrushchev could carry out plan.	

APPLYING THE SKILL

Make a chart. Chapter 15, page 435, describes the decisions British and French leaders made when Hitler took over the Sudetenland in Czechoslovakia just before World War II. Make a chart like the one shown to summarize the pros and cons of their choice of appeasement and evaluate their decision yourself.

SKILLBUILDER HANDBOOK **661**

2.7 Forming and Supporting Opinions

Historians do more than reconstruct facts about the past. They also **form opinions** about the information they encounter. Historians form opinions as they interpret the past and judge the significance of historical events and people. They **support their opinions** with logical thinking, facts, examples, quotes, and references to events.

UNDERSTANDING THE SKILL

Strategy: Find arguments to support your opinion. In the following passage, journalist Paul Gray summarizes differing opinions about the significance and impact of Columbus's voyages. As you read, develop your own opinion about the issue.

> ### HOW SHOULD HISTORY VIEW THE LEGACY OF COLUMBUS?
>
> In one version of the story, Columbus and the Europeans who followed him brought civilization to two immense, sparsely populated continents, in the process fundamentally enriching and altering the Old World from which they had themselves come.
>
> Among other things, Columbus' journey was the first step in a long process that eventually produced the United States of America, a daring experiment in democracy that in turn became a symbol and a haven of individual liberty for people throughout the world. But the revolution that began with his voyages was far greater than that. It altered science, geography, philosophy, agriculture, law, religion, ethics, government—the sum, in other words, of what passed at the time as Western culture.
>
> Increasingly, however, there is a counterchorus, an opposing rendition of the same events that deems Columbus' first footfall in the New World to be fatal to the world he invaded, and even to the rest of the globe. The indigenous peoples and their cultures were doomed by European arrogance, brutality, and infectious diseases. Columbus' gift was slavery to those who greeted him; his arrival set in motion the ruthless destruction, continuing at this very moment, of the natural world he entered. Genocide, ecocide, exploitation . . . are deemed to be a form of Eurocentric theft of history from [the Native Americans].

Decide what you think about a subject after reading all the information available to you. After reading this passage, you might decide that Columbus's legacy was primarily one of genocide, cruelty, and slavery. On the other hand, you might believe that, despite the negatives, his voyages produced many long-term benefits.

Consider the opinions and interpretations of historians and other experts. Weigh their arguments as you form your own opinion.

Support your opinion with facts, quotes, and examples, including references to similar events from other historical eras.

Strategy: Make a chart.

Summarize your opinion and supporting information in a chart. Write an opinion and then list facts, examples, interpretations, or other information that support it.

Opinion: Voyages of Columbus brought more bad than good to the Americas	
Facts:	**Historical interpretations:**
• Europeans replaced existing cultures with their own	• Europeans were arrogant and brutal
• European diseases killed many Native Americans	• Columbus's arrival set in motion ruthless destruction of environment
• Columbus enslaved Native Americans	• Through conquest and exploitation, Europeans "stole" Native Americans' history and culture

APPLYING THE SKILL

Strategy: Make your own chart. Look at the Different Perspectives on Economics and the Environment in Chapter 20, page 571. Read the selections and form your own opinion about the concept of sustainable development. Summarize your supporting data in a chart like the one shown.

662 SKILLBUILDER HANDBOOK

2.8 Making Inferences

Inferences are ideas and meanings not stated in the material. **Making inferences** means reading between the lines to extend the information provided. Your inferences are based on careful study of what is stated in the passage as well as your own common sense and previous knowledge.

UNDERSTANDING THE SKILL

Strategy: Develop inferences from the facts. This passage describes the Nok culture of West Africa. Following the passage is a diagram that organizes the facts and ideas that lead to inferences.

Read the stated facts and ideas.

Use your knowledge, logic, and common sense to draw conclusions. You could infer from these statements that the Nok were a settled people with advanced technology and a rich culture.

THE NOK CULTURE

The earliest known culture of West Africa was that of the Nok people. They lived in what is now Nigeria between 900 B.C. and A.D. 200. Their name came from the village where the first artifacts from their culture were discovered by archaeologists. The Nok were farmers. They were also the first West African people known to smelt iron. The Nok began making iron around 500 B.C., using it to make tools for farming and weapons for hunting. These iron implements lasted longer than wood or stone and vastly improved the lives of the Nok.

Nok artifacts have been found in an area stretching for 300 miles between the Niger and Benue rivers. Many are sculptures made of terra cotta, a reddish-brown clay. Carved in great artistic detail, some depict the heads of animals such as elephants and others depict human heads. The features of some of the heads reveal a great deal about their history. One of the human heads, for example, shows an elaborate hairdo arranged in six buns, a style that is still worn by some people in Nigeria today. This similarity suggests that the Nok may have been the ancestors of modern-day Africans.

Consider what you already know that could apply. Your knowledge of history might lead you to infer the kinds of improvements in life brought about by better farming tools.

Recognize inferences that are already made. Phrases like "the evidence suggests" or "historians believe" indicate inferences and conclusions experts have made from historical records.

Strategy: Make a diagram.

Summarize the facts and inferences you make in a diagram.

Stated Facts and Ideas	Inferences
• iron farming tools • iron harder than wood • tools improved life	iron tools improved agriculture and contributed to cultural development
• Nok artifacts found in 300 mile radius	Nok culture spread across this area
• heads carved in great artistic detail	Nok were skilled potters and sculptors
• sculptures included elephant heads	elephants played a role in people's lives

APPLYING THE SKILL

Make your own diagram. Read the passage that describes Czar Peter's policy to westernize Russia in Chapter 5 on page 153. Using a chart like the one above, make inferences from the poem about its author, its subject, and the culture it comes

Section 2: Using Critical Thinking

2.9 Drawing Conclusions

Drawing conclusions means analyzing what you have read and forming an opinion about its meaning. To draw conclusions, you look closely at the facts, combine them with inferences you make, and then use your own common sense and experience to decide what the facts mean.

UNDERSTANDING THE SKILL

Strategy: Combine information to draw conclusions. The passage below presents information about the reunification of East and West Germany in 1990. The diagram that follows shows how to organize the information to draw conclusions.

GERMANY IS REUNIFIED

On October 3, 1990, Germany once again became a single nation. After more than 40 years of Communist rule, most East Germans celebrated their new political freedoms. Families that had been separated for years could now visit whenever they chose.

Economically, the newly united Germany faced serious problems. More than 40 years of Communist rule had left East Germany in ruins. Its transportation and telephone systems had not been modernized since World War II. State-run industries in East Germany had to be turned over to private control and operate under free-market rules. However, many produced shoddy goods that could not compete in the global market.

Rebuilding eastern Germany's bankrupt economy was going to be a difficult, costly process. Some experts estimated the price tag for reunification could reach $200 billion. In the short-term, the government had to provide unemployment benefits to some 1.4 million workers from the east who found themselves out of work.

In spite of these problems, Germans had reasons to be optimistic. Unlike other Eastern European countries, who had to transform their Communist economies by their own means, East Germany had the help of a strong West Germany. Many Germans may have shared the outlook expressed by one worker: "Maybe things won't be rosy at first, but the future will be better."

Read carefully to understand all the facts. Fact: Reunification brought social and political freedoms to East Germans.

Read between the lines to make inferences. Inference: After a market economy was introduced, many industries in eastern Germany failed, which put people out of work.

Use the facts to make an inference. Inference: Reunification put a strain on government resources.

Ask questions of the material. What are the long-term economic prospects for eastern Germany? Conclusion: Although it faced challenges, it seemed to have a greater chance for success than other former Communist countries.

Strategy: Make a diagram.

Summarize the facts, inferences, and your conclusion in a diagram.

Facts	Inferences	Conclusion About Passage
East Germans gained freedoms.	East Germans welcomed the end of Communist rule.	Although eastern Germany was in bad shape at the time of reunification, it had the advantage of the strength of western Germany as it made the transition to democracy and capitalism.
Transportation and telephone systems were outmoded.	Rebuilding took time.	
State-run industries produced shoddy goods.	Industries couldn't compete in free-market economy.	
Unemployment skyrocketed.	Reunification put a great financial burden on Germany.	
Cost for reunification could be $200 billion.		

APPLYING THE SKILL

Strategy: Make a diagram. Look at Chapter 7, pages 194–195, on forces that led to revolution in France. As you read, draw conclusions based on the facts. Use a diagram like the one above to organize facts, inferences, and conclusions about the passage.

664 SKILLBUILDER HANDBOOK

Section 2: Using Critical Thinking

2.10 Synthesizing

Synthesizing is the skill historians use in developing interpretations of the past. Like detective work, synthesizing involves putting together clues, information, and ideas to form an overall picture of a historical event.

UNDERSTANDING THE SKILL

Strategy: Build an interpretation as you read. The following passage describes the first settlement of North and Central America. The call-outs indicate the different kinds of information that lead to a synthesis—an overall picture of Native American life.

Read carefully to understand the facts. Facts such as these enable you to base your interpretations on physical evidence.

Bring together the information you have about a subject. This interpretation brings together different kinds of information to arrive at a new understanding of the subject.

Look for explanations that link the facts together. This statement is based on the evidence provided by baskets, bows and arrows, and nets, which are mentioned in the sentences that follow.

Consider what you already know that could apply. Your general knowledge will probably lead you to accept this statement as reasonable.

THE FIRST AMERICANS

From the discovery of chiseled arrowheads and charred bones at ancient sites, it appears that the earliest Americans lived as big game hunters. The woolly mammoth, their largest prey, provided them with food, clothing, and bones for constructing tools and shelters. People gradually shifted to hunting small game and gathering available plants. They created baskets to collect nuts, wild rice, chokeberries, gooseberries, and currants. Later they invented bows and arrows to hunt small game such as jackrabbits and deer. They wove nets to fish the streams and lakes.

Between 10,000 and 15,000 years ago, a revolution took place in what is now central Mexico. People began to raise plants as food. Maize may have been the first domesticated plant, with pumpkins, peppers, beans, and potatoes following. Agriculture spread to other regions.

The rise of agriculture brought about tremendous changes to the Americas. Agriculture made it possible for people to remain in one place. It also enabled them to accumulate and store surplus food. As their surplus increased, people had the time to develop skills and more complex ideas about the world. From this agricultural base rose larger, more stable societies and increasingly complex societies.

Strategy: Make a cluster diagram.

Summarize your synthesis in a diagram. Use a cluster diagram to organize the facts, opinions, examples, and interpretations that you have brought together to form a synthesis.

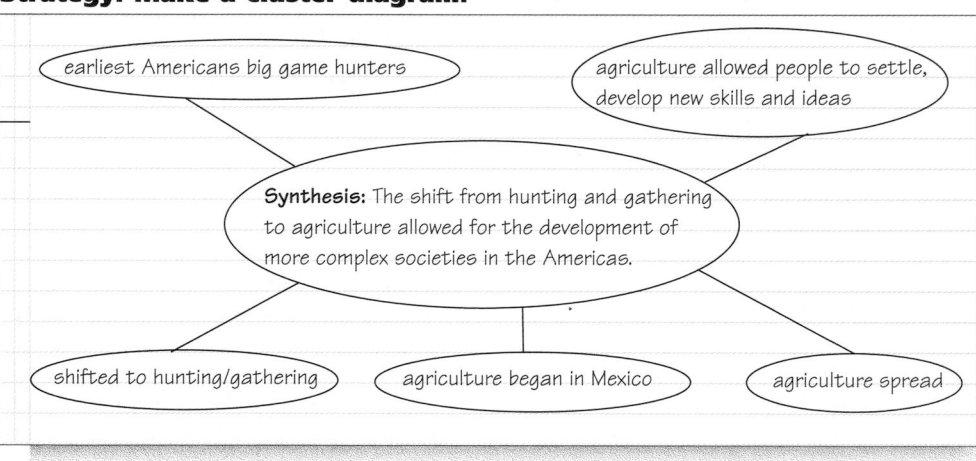

APPLYING THE SKILL

Make your own cluster diagram. In Chapter 1 on pages 48–49, the beginnings of the Protestant Reformation are discussed. Read the passage and look for information to support a synthesis about its fundamental causes.

3.1 Primary and Secondary Sources

Primary sources are written or created by people who lived during a historical event. The writers might have been participants or observers. Primary sources include letters, diaries, journals, speeches, newspaper articles, magazine articles, eye-witness accounts, and autobiographies.

Secondary sources are derived from primary sources by people who were not present at the original event. They are written after the event. They often combine information from a number of different accounts. Secondary sources include history books, historical essays, and biographies.

UNDERSTANDING THE SKILL

Strategy: Evaluate the information in each type of source. This passage describes political reforms made by Pericles, who led Athens from 461 to 429 B.C. It is mainly a secondary source, but it includes a primary source in the form of a speech.

Secondary source: Look for information collected from several sources. Here the writer presents an overall picture of the reforms made by Pericles and the reasons for them.

Secondary source: Look for analysis and interpretation. A secondary source provides details and perspective that are missing in a primary source. It also provides context for the secondary source.

Primary source: Identify the author and evaluate his or her credentials. How is the speaker connected to the event? Here, this speaker is Pericles himself.

Primary source: Analyze the source using historical perspective. Read the source for factual information while also noting the speaker's opinions, biases, assumptions, and point of view.

STRONGER DEMOCRACY IN ATHENS

To strengthen democracy, Pericles increased the number of public officials who were paid salaries. Before, only wealthier citizens could afford to hold public office because most positions were unpaid. Now even the poorest could serve if elected or chosen by lot. This reform made Athens one of the most democratic governments in history. However, political rights were still limited to those with citizenship status—a minority of Athens' total population.

The introduction of direct democracy was an important legacy of Periclean Athens. Few other city-states practiced this style of government. In Athens, male citizens who served in the assembly established all the important policies that affected the polis. In a famous "Funeral Oration" for soldiers killed in the Peloponnesian War, Pericles expressed his great pride in Athenian democracy:

Our constitution is called a democracy because power is in the hands not of a minority but of the whole people. When it is a question of settling private disputes, everyone is equal before the law; when it is a question of putting one person before another in positions of public responsibility, what counts is not membership of a particular class, but the actual ability which the man possesses. No one, as long as he has it in him to be of service to the state, is kept in political obscurity because of poverty.

Strategy: Make a chart.

Summarize information from primary and secondary sources on a chart.

Primary Source	Secondary Source
Author: Pericles	Author: world history textbook
Qualifications: main figure in the events described	Qualifications: had access to multiple accounts of event
Information: describes his view of Athenian democracy—power in the hands of "the whole people"	Information: puts events in historical perspective—Athens one of most democratic governments in history but limited rights to citizens

APPLYING THE SKILL

Make your own chart. Read the passage "Mehmet II Conquers Constantinople" in Chapter 2, pages 64–65, which includes a quote from the Muslim historian Oruc. Make a chart in which you summarize information from the primary and secondary sources.

666 SKILLBUILDER HANDBOOK

Section 3: Exploring Historical Evidence

3.2 Visual, Audio, Multimedia Sources

In addition to written accounts, historians use many kinds of **visual sources.** These include paintings, photographs, political cartoons, and advertisements. Visual sources are rich with historical details and sometimes reflect the mood and trends of an era better than words can.

Spoken language has always been a primary means of passing on human history. **Audio sources,** such as recorded speeches, interviews, press conferences, and radio programs, continue the oral tradition today.

Movies, CD-ROMs, television, and computer software are the newest kind of historical sources, called **multimedia sources.**

UNDERSTANDING THE SKILL

Strategy: Examine the source carefully. Below are two portraits from the late 1700s, one of Marie Antoinette, the queen of France, and one of a woman who sells vegetables at the market. The chart that follows summarizes historical information gained from interpreting and comparing the two paintings.

A Woman of the Revolution [*La maraîchère*] (1795), Jacques Louis David

Marie Antoinette, Jacques Gautier d'Agoty

Identify the subject and source.

Identify important visual details. Look at the faces, poses, clothing, hairstyles, and other elements.

Make inferences from the visual details. Marie Antoinette's rich clothing and her hand on the globe symbolize her wealth and power. The contrast between the common woman's ordinary clothing and her defiant pose suggests a different attitude about power.

Use comparisons, information from other sources, and your own knowledge to give support to your interpretation. Royalty usually had their portraits painted in heroic poses. Ordinary people were not usually the subjects of such portraits. David's choice of subject and pose suggests that he sees the common people as the true heroes of France.

Strategy: Make a chart.

Summarize your interpretation in a simple chart.

Subject	Visual Details	Inferences	Message
Common woman	Face is worn and clothing is plain, but her head is held high and she wears the red scarf of revolution	Has worked hard for little in life, but strong, proud, and defiant	Although the details are strikingly different, the two paintings convey similar characteristics about their subjects.
Marie Antoinette	Richly dressed and made up; strikes an imperial pose	Lives life of comfort and power; proud, strong, and defiant	

APPLYING THE SKILL

Make your own chart. Turn to the photograph of a British man and his servants in Chapter 11, page 703. Use a chart like the one above to analyze and interpret the photograph.

SKILLBUILDER HANDBOOK **667**

3.3 Interpreting Maps

Maps are representations of features on the earth's surface. Historians use maps to locate historical events, to show how geography has influenced history, and to illustrate human interaction with the environment.

Different kinds of maps are used for specific purposes.

Political maps show political units, from countries, states, and provinces, to counties, districts, and towns. Each area is shaded a different color.

Physical maps show mountains, hills, plains, rivers, lakes, and oceans. They may use contour lines to indicate elevations on land and depths under water.

Historical maps illustrate such things as economic activity, political alliances, land claims, battles, population density, and changes over time.

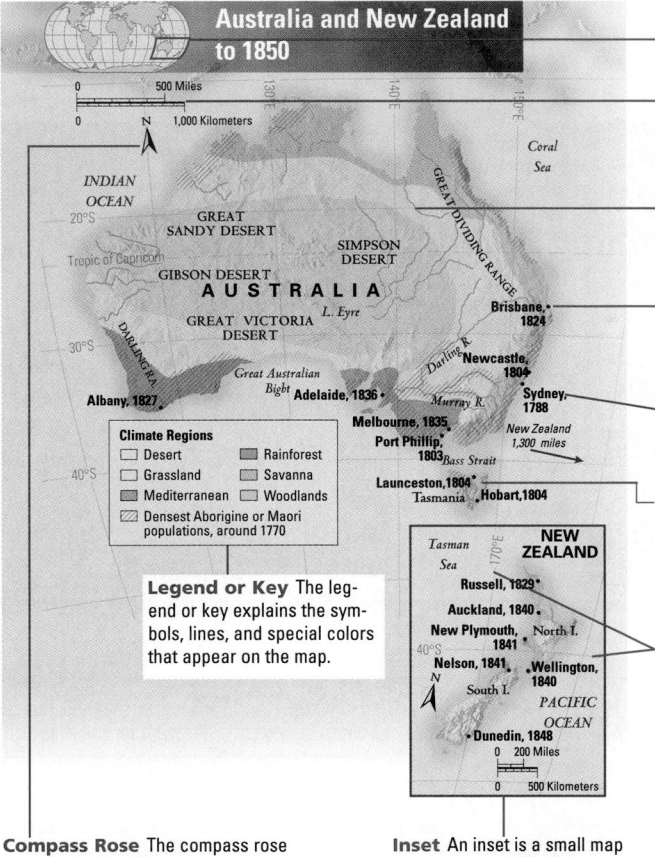

Locator A locator map shows which part of the world the map subject area covers.

Scale The scale shows the ratio between a unit of length on the map and a unit of distance on the earth. The maps in this book usually show the scale in miles and kilometers.

Lines Lines indicate rivers and other waterways, political boundaries, roads, and routes of exploration or migration.

Symbols Locations of cities and towns often appear as dots. A capital city is often shown as a star or as a dot with a circle around it. Picture symbols might be used to indicate an area's products, resources, and special features.

Labels Key places such as cities, bodies of water, and landforms are labeled. Key dates, such as those for the founding of cities, may also be labeled.

Colors Maps use colors and shading for various purposes. On physical maps, color may be used to indicate different physical regions or altitudes. On political maps, color can distinguish different political units. On specialty maps, color can show variable features such as population density, languages, or culture areas.

Lines of Latitude and Longitude Lines of latitude and longitude appear on maps to indicate the absolute location of the area shown.
• Lines of latitude show distance measured in degrees north or south of the equator.
• Lines of longitude show distance measured in degrees east or west of the prime meridian, which runs through Greenwich, England.

Legend or Key The legend or key explains the symbols, lines, and special colors that appear on the map.

Compass Rose The compass rose is a feature indicating the map's orientation on the globe. It may show all four cardinal directions (N, S, E, W) or just indicate north.

Inset An inset is a small map that appears within a larger map. It often shows an area of the larger map in greater detail. Inset maps may also show a different area that is in some way related to the area shown on the larger map.

Strategy: Read all the elements of the map. The historical maps below show European landholdings in North America in 1754 and after 1763. Together they show changes over time.

Europeans in N. America, 1754

UNCLAIMED

Arctic Circle

Hudson Bay

Lake Winnipeg

Quebec

ACADIA

NEW-FOUNDLAND

Boston

New York

Great Salt L.

Colorado R.

Missouri R.

Great Lakes

St. Lawrence R.

Ohio R.

ATLANTIC OCEAN

Santa Fe

New Orleans

St. Augustine

FLORIDA

Mississippi R.

Rio Grande

Gulf of Mexico

Tropic of Cancer

20°N

N

0 500 Miles
0 1,000 Kilometers

Mexico City

Caribbean Sea

CUBA

JAMAICA

HAITI

Santo Domingo

Legend:
☐ Disputed
☐ English
☐ French
☐ Spanish

Holdings after 1763

Look at the map's title to learn the subject and purpose of the map. What area does the map cover? What does the map tell you about the area? Here the maps show North America in 1754 and after 1763 with the purpose of comparing European claims at two different times.

UNCLAIMED

Arctic Circle

Hudson Bay

Lake Winnipeg

Quebec

Boston

New York

ST-PIERRE AND MIQUELON

Great Salt L.

Colorado R.

Missouri R.

Great Lakes

St. Lawrence R.

Ohio R.

ORIGINAL 13 COLONIES

ATLANTIC OCEAN

Charleston

40°N

Mississippi R.

Rio Grande

Gulf of Mexico

Tropic of Cancer

20°N

N

0 500 Miles
0 1,000 Kilometers

Mexico City

Caribbea[n]

CUBA

JAMAICA

HAITI

Legend:
☐ English
☐ French
☐ Russian
☐ Spanish

Read the legend. The legend tells you what the symbols and colors on the map mean.

Look at the scale and compass. The scale shows you how many miles or kilometers are represented. Here the scale is 500 actual miles to approximately 5/8 inch on the map. The compass shows you which direction on the map is north.

Find where the map area is located on the earth. These maps show a large area from the Arctic Circle to below latitude 20°N and 50° to 120°W.

Strategy: Make a chart.

Relate the map to the five geographic themes by making a chart. The five themes are described on pages xxxii–xxxiii.

Location	Place	Region	Movement	Human/ Environment Interaction
Large area from Arctic Circle to below 20° N, and 50° to 120° W	North American continent	Western Hemisphere	Between 1754 and 1763, land claimed by France was largely taken over by the other two colonialist powers. Spain expanded its territories northward, while Britain took control of almost the entire eastern half of the continent.	Europeans carved out political units in the continent, which already had inhabitants. The land they claimed covered vast areas, with waterways and large mountain ranges to cross.

Make your own chart. Turn to Chapter 14, page 393, and study the map titled "Russian Revolution and Civil War, 1905–1922." Make a chart like the one shown above in which you summarize what the map tells you according to the five geography themes.

SKILLBUILDER HANDBOOK **669**

Section 3: Exploring Historical Evidence

3.4 Interpreting Charts

Charts are visual presentations of materials. Historians use charts to organize, simplify, and summarize information in a way that makes it more meaningful or easier to remember. Several kinds of charts are commonly used.

Simple charts are used to summarize information or to make comparisons.

Tables are used to organize statistics and other types of information into columns and rows for easy reference.

Diagrams provide visual clues to the meaning of the information they contain. Venn diagrams are used for comparisons. Web diagrams are used to organize supporting information around a central topic. Illustrated diagrams or diagrams that combine different levels of information are sometimes called **infographics.**

UNDERSTANDING THE SKILL

Strategy: Study all the elements of the chart. The infographic below conveys a great deal of information about the three estates, or classes, that existed in 18th-century France. The infographic visually combines a political cartoon, a bulleted chart, a pie graph, and a bar graph.

Read the title.

The Three Estates

■ **First Estate**
• made up of clergy of Roman Catholic Church
• scorned Enlightenment ideas

■ **Second Estate**
• made up of rich nobles
• held highest offices in government
• disagreed about Enlightenment ideas

■ **Third Estate**
• included bourgeoisie, urban lower class, and peasant farmers
• had no power to influence government
• embraced Enlightenment ideas

Identify the symbols and colors and what they represent. Here, three colors are used consistently in the infographic to represent the three estates.

Population of France, 1787

98% (Third Estate)

less than 1% (First Estate)

2% (Second Estate)

Percent of Income Paid in Taxes

2% (First Estate)

0% (Second Estate)

50% (Third Estate)

0%   20%   40%   60%   80%   100%

Survey each of the elements of the infographic and study the information presented. The political cartoon visually represents the power of the First and Second Estates over the Third Estate. The bulleted chart gives details about the estates. The two graphs give statistics about population and taxes.

Look for the main idea. Make connections among the types of information presented. The infographic shows that the Third Estate made up the vast majority of France's population but had no political power and paid high taxes. The First and Second Estates guarded their power.

Strategy: Write a summary.

Write a paragraph to summarize what you learned from the chart.

In 1787, French society was unevenly divided into three estates. Almost all the people, from the bourgeoisie to the peasants, belonged to the Third Estate. They had no political power, paid high taxes, and supported Enlightenment ideas. The First Estate, made up of the clergy, and the Second Estate, made up of rich nobles, held the power and the wealth. Both opposed change, generally rejected Enlightenment ideas, and took advantage of the Third Estate.

APPLYING THE SKILL

Write your own summary. Turn to Chapter 3, page 95, and look at the chart titled "Japanese Society." Study the chart and write a paragraph in which you summarize what you learn from it.

670 SKILLBUILDER HANDBOOK

Section 3: Exploring Historical Evidence

3.5 Interpreting Graphs

Graphs show statistical information in a visual manner. Historians use graphs to show comparative amounts, ratios, economic trends, and changes over time.

Line graphs are good for showing changes over time, or trends. Usually, the horizontal axis shows a unit of time, such as years or months, and the vertical axis shows numbers or quantities.

Pie graphs are useful for showing relative proportions. The circle represents the whole, such as the entire population, and the slices represent the different groups that make up the whole.

Bar graphs compare numbers or sets of numbers. The length of each bar indicates a quantity. With bar graphs, it is easy to see at a glance how different categories compare.

UNDERSTANDING THE SKILL

Strategy: Study all the elements of the graph. The line graphs below show average global temperatures and world population figures over a period of 25,000 years.

Read the title to identify the main idea of the graph. When two subjects are shown, look for a relationship between them. This set of graphs shows that the agricultural revolution had links to both global temperature and population.

Read the vertical axis. The temperature graph shows degrees Fahrenheit. The other shows population in millions, so that 125 indicates 125,000,000.

Summarize the information shown in each part of the graph. What trends or changes are shown in each line graph?

Look at the legend to understand what colors and certain marks stand for.

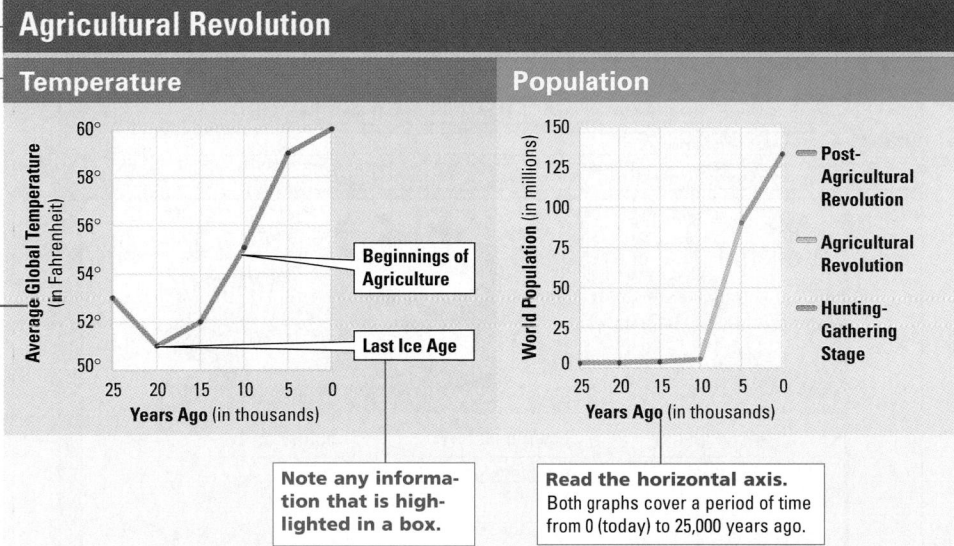

Note any information that is highlighted in a box.

Read the horizontal axis. Both graphs cover a period of time from 0 (today) to 25,000 years ago.

Strategy: Write a summary.

Write a paragraph to summarize what you learned from the graphs.

Some 20,000 years ago, after the last Ice Age, temperatures started to rise worldwide. This steady rise in average temperature from 51° to 55° made possible the beginnings of agriculture. As a result of the agricultural revolution, world population grew from about 2 million to about 130 million over a period of 10,000 years.

APPLYING THE SKILL

Write your own summary Turn to Chapter 15, page 425, and look at the graph "Unemployment in Germany and Great Britain." Study the graph and write a paragraph in which you summarize what you learn from it.

Section 3: Exploring Historical Evidence

3.6 Using the Internet

The **Internet** is a network of computers associated with universities, libraries, news organizations, government agencies, businesses, and private individuals worldwide. Each location on the Internet has a **home page** with its own address, or **URL.**

With a computer connected to the Internet, you can reach the home pages of many organizations and services. You might view your library's home page to find the call number of a book or visit an on-line magazine to read an article. On some sites you can view documents, photographs, and even moving pictures with sound.

The international collection of home pages, known as the **World Wide Web**, is a good source of up-to-the minute information about current events as well as in-depth research on historical subjects. This textbook contains many suggestions for navigating the World Wide Web. Begin by entering **www.mlworldhistory.com** to access the home page for McDougal Littell World History.

UNDERSTANDING THE SKILL

Strategy: Explore the elements on the screen. The computer screen below shows the home page of the history area at PBS, the public television service in Washington, D.C.

Go directly to a Web page. If you know the address of a particular Web page, type the address in the box at the top of the screen and press ENTER (or RETURN). After a few seconds, the Web page will appear on your screen.

Explore the links. Click on any one of the images or topics to find out more about a specific subject. These links take you to another page at this Web site. Some pages include links to related information that can be found at other places on the Internet.

Learn more about the page. Scan the page to learn the types of information contained at this site. This site has information about PBS history programs as well as other historical information and special features.

Explore the features of the page. This page has a feature that lets you find out what happened in history on any given day of the year.

PBS History screen shot courtesy of PBS ONLINE®.

APPLYING THE SKILL

Do your own Internet research. Turn to Chapter 18, Section 4, "Conflicts in the Middle East." Read the section and make a list of topics you would like to research. If you have a computer with Internet access, go to the McDougal Littell World History home page **www.mlworldhistory.com**. Click on "General World History Links" and then click on "Perspectives on the Present" to begin your search.

672 SKILLBUILDER HANDBOOK

Glossary

The Glossary is an alphabetical listing of many of the key terms from the chapters, along with their meanings. The definitions listed in the Glossary are the ones that apply to the way the words are used in this textbook. The Glossary gives the part of speech of each word. The following abbreviations are used:

adj. adjective   *n.* noun   *v.* verb

Pronunciation Key

Some of the words in this book are followed by respellings that show how the words are pronounced. The following key will help you understand what sounds are represented by the letters used in the respellings.

Symbol	Examples	Symbol	Examples
a	**a**pple [AP·uhl], **ca**tch [kach]	oh	r**oa**d, [rohd], kn**ow** [noh]
ah	b**a**rn [bahrn], p**o**t [paht]	oo	sch**oo**l [skool], gl**ue** [gloo]
air	b**ea**r [bair], d**a**re [dair]	ow	**ou**t [owt], c**ow** [kow]
aw	b**ou**ght [bawt], h**o**rse [hawrs]	oy	c**oi**n [koyn], b**oy**s [boyz]
ay	**a**pe [ayp], m**ai**l [mayl]	p	**p**ig [pihg], to**p** [tahp]
b	**b**ell [behl], ta**b**le [TAY·buhl]	r	**r**ose [rohz], sta**r** [stahr]
ch	**ch**ain [chayn], di**tch** [dihch]	s	**s**oap [sohp], i**c**y [EYE·see]
d	**d**og [dawg], raine**d** [raynd]	sh	**sh**are [shair], na**ti**on [NAY·shuhn]
ee	**e**ven [EE·vuhn], m**ea**l [meel]	t	**t**ired [tyrd], boa**t** [boht]
eh	**e**gg [ehg], t**e**n [tehn]	th	**th**in [thihn], mo**th**er [MUH·thuhr]
eye	**i**ron [EYE·uhrn]	u	p**u**ll [pul], l**oo**k [luk]
f	**f**all [fawl], lau**gh** [laf]	uh	b**u**mp [buhmp], aw**a**ke [uh·WAYK],
g	**g**old [gohld], bi**g** [bihg]		h**a**ppen [HAP·uhn], penc**i**l [PEHN·suhl],
h	**h**ot [haht], ex**h**ale [ehks·HAYL]		p**i**lot [PY·luht]
hw	**wh**ite [hwyt]	ur	**ea**rth [urth], b**i**rd [burd], w**o**rm [wurm]
ih	**i**nto [IHN·too], s**i**ck [sihk]	v	**v**ase [vays], lo**v**e [luhv]
j	**j**ar [jahr], ba**dg**e [baj]	w	**w**eb [wehb], t**w**in [twihn]
k	**c**at [kat], lu**ck** [luhk]	y	As a consonant: **y**ard [yahrd], m**u**le [myool]
l	**l**oad [lohd], ba**ll** [bawl]		As a vowel: **i**ce [ys], tr**ie**d [tryd], s**igh** [sy]
m	**m**ake [mayk], ge**m** [jehm]	z	**z**one [zohn], rea**s**on [REE·zuhn]
n	**n**ight [nyt], wi**n** [wihn]	zh	trea**s**ure [TREHZH·uhr], gara**ge** [guh·RAHZH]
ng	so**ng** [sawng], a**ng**er [ANG·guhr]		

Syllables that are stressed when the words are spoken appear in CAPITAL LETTERS in the respellings. For example, the respelling of *patterns* (PAT·uhrnz) shows that the first syllable of the word is stressed.

Syllables that appear in SMALL CAPITAL LETTERS are also stressed, but not as strongly as those that appear in capital letters. For example, the respelling of *interaction* (IHN·tuhr·AK·shuhn) shows that the third syllable receives the main stress and the first syllable receives a secondary stress.

A

Aborigine [AB·uh·RIHJ·uh·nee] *n.* a member of any of the native peoples of Australia. (p. 285)

absolute monarch [MAHN·uhrk] *n.* a king or queen who has unlimited power and seeks to control all aspects of society. (p. 137)

accommodation [uh·KAHM·uh·DAY·shuhn] *n.* an acceptance of the ideas and customs of other cultures. (p. 201)

Allies [uh·LYZ] *n.* in World War I, the nations of Great Britain, France, and Russia, along with the other nations that fought on their side; also, the group of nations—including Great Britain, the Soviet Union, and the United States—that opposed the Axis Powers in World War II. (p. 368)

American Revolution *n.* the American struggle for independence from Britain that began on April 19, 1775 and ended in 1781 with an American victory. (p. 24)

Anabaptist [AN·uh·BAP·tihst] *n.* in the Reformation, a member of a Protestant group who believed that only adults should be baptized and that church and state should be separate. (p. 54)

Anglican [ANG·glih·kuhn] *adj.* relating to the Church of England. (p. 52)

annexation [AN·ihk·SAY·shuhn] *n.* the adding of a region to the territory of an existing political unit. (pp. 329, 343)

annul [uh·NUHL] *v.* to cancel or put an end to. (p. 51)

anti-Semitism [AN·tee·SEHM·ih·TIHZ·uhm] *n.* prejudice against Jews. (p. 283)

apartheid [uh·PAHRT·HYT] *n.* a South African policy of complete legal separation of the races, including the banning of all social contacts between blacks and whites. (p. 539)

appeasement *n.* the making of concessions to an aggressor in order to avoid war. (p. 433)

aristocracy [AR·ih·STAHK·ruh·see] *n.* a government in which power is in the hands of a hereditary ruling class or nobility. (p. 5)

armistice [AHR·mih·stihs] *n.* an agreement to stop fighting. (p. 377)

Aryans [AIR·ee·uhnz] *n.* **1.** an Indo-European people who, about 1500 B.C., began to migrate into the Indian subcontinent (p. 59). **2.** to the Nazis, the Germanic peoples who formed a "master race." (p. 451)

assembly line *n.* in a factory, an arrangement in which a product is moved from worker to worker, with each per-

GLOSSARY **673**

son performing a single task in its manufacture. (p. 294)

Atlantic Charter *n.* a declaration of principles issued in August 1941 by British prime minister Winston Churchill and U.S. president Franklin Roosevelt, on which the Allied peace plan at the end of World War II was based. (p. 446)

Atlantic slave trade *n.* the buying, transporting, and selling of Africans for work in the Americas. (p. 116)

Axis Powers *n.* in World War II, the nations of Germany, Italy, and Japan, which had formed an alliance in 1936. (p. 433)

B

balance of power *n.* a political situation in which no one nation is powerful enough to pose a threat to others. (p. 213)

Balfour Declaration *n.* a statement that the British government supported the establishment of a Jewish national homeland in Palestine, made in a 1917 letter by British foreign secretary Sir Arthur Balfour. (p. 521)

Balkans [BAWL·kuhnz] *n.* the region of southeastern Europe now occupied by Greece, Albania, Bulgaria, Romania, the European part of Turkey, and the former republics of Yugoslavia. (p. 229)

baroque [buh·ROHK] *adj.* relating to a grand, ornate style that characterized European painting, music, and architecture in the 1600s and early 1700s. (p. 179)

Battle of Britain *n.* a series of battles between German and British air forces, fought over Britain in 1940–1941. (p. 444)

Battle of Guadalcanal [GWAHD·uhl·kuh·NAL] *n.* a 1942–1943 battle of World War II, in which Allied troops drove Japanese forces from the Pacific island of Guadalcanal. (p. 450)

Battle of Midway *n.* a 1941 sea and air battle of World War II, in which American forces defeated Japanese forces in the central Pacific. (p. 449)

Battle of Stalingrad [STAH·lihn·GRAD] *n.* a 1942–1943 battle of World War II, in which German forces were defeated in their attempt to capture the city of Stalingrad in the Soviet Union. (p. 456)

Battle of the Bulge *n.* a 1944–1945 battle in which Allied forces turned back the last major German offensive of World War II. (p. 459)

Battle of Trafalgar [truh·FAL·guhr] *n.* an 1805 naval battle in which Napoleon's forces were defeated by a British fleet under the command of Horatio Nelson. (p. 207)

Berlin Conference of 1884–85 *n.* a meeting at which representatives of European nations agreed upon rules for the European colonization of Africa. (p. 307)

bilateral aid *n.* money and resources provided directly from one government to another. (p. 600)

Bill of Rights *n.* the first ten amendments to the U.S. Constitution, which protect citizens' basic rights and freedoms. (p. 187)

biotechnology *n.* the scientific research performed on biological substances like enzymes or cells in order to find new uses for such substances. (p. 590)

bio-weapons *n.* living organisms such as anthrax used to kill or injure large numbers of people at once. (p. 605)

birth rates *n.* the number of children born per woman. (p. 595)

blitzkrieg [BLIHTS·kreeg] *n.* "lightning war"—a form of warfare in which surprise attacks with fast-moving airplanes are followed by massive attacks with infantry forces. (p. 442)

blockade [blah·KAYD] *n.* the use of troops or ships to prevent commercial traffic from entering or leaving a city or region. (p. 209)

Boer [bohr] *n.* a Dutch colonist in South Africa. (p. 309)

Boer War *n.* a conflict, lasting from 1899 to 1902, in which the Boers and the British fought for control of territory in South Africa. (p. 309)

Bolsheviks [BOHL·shuh·VIHKS] *n.* a group of revolutionary Russian Marxists who took control of Russia's government in November 1917. (p. 390)

Boxer Rebellion *n.* a 1900 rebellion in China, aimed at ending foreign influence in the country. (p. 339)

boyars [boh·YAHRZ] *n.* landowning nobles of Russia. (p. 151)

brinkmanship *n.* a policy of threatening to go to war in response to any enemy aggression. (p. 480)

Buddhism [BOO·DIHZ·ahm] *n.* a religion by Siddhartha Guatama (the Buddha) around 527 B.C. The goal of Buddhism is to achieve perfect spiritual enlightenment. (p. 614)

C

cabinet *n.* a group of advisers or ministers chosen by the head of a country to help make government decisions. (p. 159)

Calvinism [KAL·vih·NIHZ·uhm] *n.* a body of religious teachings based on the ideas of the reformer John Calvin. (p. 53)

Camp David Accords *n.* the first signed agreement between Israel and an Arab country, in which Egyptian president Anwar Sadat recognized Israel as a legitimate state and Israeli prime minister Menachem Begin agreed to return the Sinai Peninsula to Egypt. (p. 523)

capitalism *n.* an economic system based on private ownership and on the investment of money in business ventures in order to make a profit. (pp. 122, 267)

Catholic Reformation [REHF·uhr·MAY·shuhn] *n.* a 16th-century movement in which the Roman Catholic Church sought to reform itself in response to the Protestant Reformation. (p. 55)

caudillo [kaw·DEEL·yoh] *n.* a military dictator of a Latin American country. (p. 344)

Central Powers *n.* in World War I, the nations of Germany and Austria-Hungary, along with the other nations that fought on their side. (p. 368)

CFCs *n.* (chlorofluorocarbons)—chemicals used in air conditioners and other products. (p. 593)

Chartist movement *n.* a 19th-century British movement in which members of the working class demanded reforms in Parliament and in elections, including suffrage for all men. (p. 280)

checks and balances *n.* measures designed to prevent any one branch of government from dominating the others. (pp. 186–187)

Christianity *n.* the monotheistic religion based on the life and teachings of Jesus begun in the first century A.D. (p. 13)

CIS *n.* the Commonwealth of Independent States—a loose association of former Soviet republics that was formed after the breakup of the Soviet Union. (p.548)

citizen *n.* a native of a state or nation with certain rights and privileges. (p. 5)

civil disobedience *n.* a deliberate and public refusal to obey a law considered unjust. (p. 406)

civil rights movement *n.* a grassroots effort to fight discrimination in the United States and to make sure that all U.S. citizens receive the rights guaranteed by the Constitution. (p. 574)

cloning [KLOH·nihng] *n.* the creation of plants or animals that are genetically identical to an existing plant or animal. (p. 564)

coalition [KOH·uh·LIHSH·uhn] **government** *n.* a government controlled by a temporary alliance of several political parties. (p. 421)

Cold War *n.* the state of diplomatic hostility between the United States and the Soviet Union in the decades following World War II. (p. 479)

collective bargaining *n.* negotiations between workers and their employers. (p. 270)

collective farm *n.* a large government-controlled farm formed by combining many small farms. (p. 397)

colony *n.* a land controlled by a distant nation. (p. 104)

Columbian Exchange *n.* the global transfer of plants, animals, and diseases that occurred during the European colonization of the Americas. (p. 120)

command economy *n.* an economic system in which the government makes all economic decisions. (p. 396)

Commercial Revolution *n.* the expansion of trade and business that transformed European economies during the 16th and 17th centuries. (p. 120)

Committee of Public Safety *n.* a committee established during the French Revolution to identify "enemies of the republic." (p. 202)

common law *n.* the body of English law that reflected customs and principles established over time rather than the will of a ruler or lawmaker. (p. 17)

commune [KAHM·YOON] *n.* in Communist China, a collective farm on which a great number of people work and live together. (p. 384)

communism *n.* an economic system in which all means of production—land, mines, factories, railroads, and businesses—are owned by the people, private property does not exist, and all goods and services are shared equally. (p. 269)

Concert [KAHN·surt] **of Europe** *n.* a series of alliances among European nations in the 19th century, devised by Prince Klemens von Metternich to prevent the outbreak of revolutions. (p. 215)

concordat [kuhn·KAWR·dat] *n.* a formal agreement—especially one between the pope and a government, dealing with the control of church affairs. (p. 206)

Confucianism [kahn·FYOO·shan·IHZ·ahm] *n.* a way of life based on the teachings of the Chinese scholar, Confucius. (p. 624)

Congress of Vienna [vee·EHN·uh] *n.* a series of meetings in 1814–1815, during which the European leaders sought to establish long-lasting peace and security after the defeat of Napoleon. (p. 213)

Congress Party *n.* a major national political party in India—also known as the Indian National Congress. (p. 506)

conquistadors [kahng·KEE·stuh·DAWRZ] *n.* the Spanish soldiers, explorers, and fortune hunters who took part in the conquest of the Americas in the 16th century. (p. 105)

conservatives *n.* in the first half of the 19th century, those Europeans—mainly wealthy landowners and nobles—who wanted to preserve the traditional monarchies of Europe. (p. 229)

constitutional monarchy [MAHN·uhr·kee] *n.* a monarchy in which the ruler's power is limited by law. (p.159)

containment *n.* a U.S. foreign policy adopted by President Harry Truman in the late 1940s, in which the United States tried to stop the spread of communism by creating alliances and helping weak countries to resist Soviet advances. (p. 477)

Continental System *n.* Napoleon's policy of preventing trade between Great Britain and continental Europe, intended to destroy Great Britain's economy. (p. 209)

conventional weapons *n.* all the standard weapons of war, such as tanks, planes, artillery, and rifles. (p. 602)

corporation *n.* a business owned by stockholders who share in its profits but are not personally responsible for its debts. (p. 265)

Council of Trent *n.* a meeting of Roman Catholic leaders, called by Pope Paul III to rule on doctrines criticized by the Protestant reformers. (p. 56)

coup d'état [KOO day·TAH] *n.* a sudden seizure of political power in a nation. (p. 205)

creoles [KREE·OHLZ] *n.* in Spanish colonial society, colonists who were born in Latin America to Spanish parents. (p. 224)

Crimean [kry·MEE·uhn] **War** *n.* a conflict, lasting from 1853 to 1856, in which the Ottoman Empire, with the aid of Britain and France, halted Russian expansion in the region of the Black Sea. (p. 318)

crop rotation *n.* the system of growing a different crop in a field each year to preserve the fertility of the land. (p. 253)

Cultural Revolution *n.* a 1966–1976 uprising in China, led by the Red Guards, with the goal of establishing a society of peasants and workers in which all were equal. (p. 485)

D

daimyo [DY·mee·OH] *n.* a Japanese feudal lord who commanded a private army of samurai. (p. 94)

D-Day *n.* June 6, 1944—the day on which the Allies began their invasion of the European mainland during World War II. (p. 458)

Declaration of Independence *n.* a statement of the reasons for the American colonies' break with Britain, approved by the Second Continental Congress in 1776. (p. 184)

Declaration of the Rights of Man *n.* a statement of revolutionary ideals adopted by France's National Assembly in 1789. (p. 197)

demilitarization [dee·MIHL·ih·tuhr·ih·ZAY·shuhn] *n.* a reduction in a country's ability to wage war, achieved by disbanding its armed forces and prohibiting it from acquiring weapons. (p. 464)

democracy *n.* a government controlled by its citizens, either directly or through representatives. (p. 5)

destalinization [dee·STAH·lih·nih·ZAY·shuhn] *n.* Nikita Khrushchev's policy of eliminating all memory of Joseph Stalin and his programs in the Soviet Union. (p. 496)

détente [day·TAHNT] *n.* a policy of reducing Cold War tensions that was adopted by the United States during the presidency of Richard Nixon. (p. 498)

developed nation *n.* a nation with all the facilities needed for the advanced production of manufactured goods. (p. 566)

developing nation *n.* a nation in which the process of industrialization is not yet complete. (p. 566)

devshirme [dehv·SHEER·meh] *n.* in the Ottoman Empire, the policy of taking children from conquered Christian peoples to be trained as Muslim soldiers. (p. 66)

direct democracy *n.* a government in which citizens rule directly rather than through representatives. (p. 7)

dissident [DIHS·ih·duhnt] *n.* an opponent of a government's policies or actions. (p. 538)

divine right *n.* the idea that monarchs are God's representatives on earth and are therefore answerable only to God. (p. 137)

dominion *n.* in the British Empire, a nation (such as Canada) allowed to govern its own domestic affairs. (p. 285)

domino theory *n.* the idea that if a nation falls under Communist control, nearby nations will also fall under Communist control. (p. 38)

Dreyfus [DRY·fuhs] **affair** *n.* a controversy in France in the 1890s, centering on the trial and imprisonment of a Jewish army officer, Captain Alfred Dreyfus, who had been falsely accused of selling military secrets to Germany. (p. 283)

due process of law *n.* administration of the law by proceeding according to established legal principles that protect individual rights. (p. 18)

Duma [DOO·muh] *n.* a Russian national parliament formed in the early years of the 20th century. (p. 391)

Dutch East India Company *n.* a company founded by the Dutch in the early 17th century to establish and direct trade throughout Asia. (p. 88)

dynasty [DY·nuh·stee] *n.* a series of rulers from a single family. (p. 89)

E

Eastern Front *n.* in World War I, the region along the German-Russian border where Russians and Serbs battled Germans, Austrians, and Turks. (p. 370)

Edict of Nantes [EE·DIHKT uhv NAHNT] *n.* a 1598 declaration in which the French king Henry IV promised that Protestants could live in peace in France and could set up houses of worship in some French cities. (p. 138)

Emancipation Proclamation [ih·MAN·suh·PAY·shuhn PRAHK·luh·MAY·shuhn] *n.* a declaration issued by U.S. president Abraham Lincoln in 1862, stating that all slaves in the Confederate states were free. (p. 291)

émigrés [EHM·ih·CRAYZ] *n.* people who leave their native country for political reasons, like the nobles and others who fled France during the peasant uprisings of the French Revolution. (p. 199)

enclosure *n.* one of the fenced-in or hedged-in fields created by wealthy British landowners on land that was formerly worked by village farmers. (p. 253)

encomienda [ehng·kaw·MYEHN·dah] *n.* a grant of land made by Spain to a settler in the Americas, including the right to use Native Americans as laborers on it. (p. 106)

English Civil War *n.* a conflict, lasting from 1642 to 1649, in which Puritan supporters of Parliament battled supporters of England's monarchy. (p. 157)

enlightened despot [DEHS·puht] *n.* one of the 18th-century European monarchs who were inspired by Enlightenment ideas to rule justly and respect the rights of their subjects. (p. 181)

Enlightenment *n.* an 18th-century European movement in which thinkers attempted to apply the principles of reason and the scientific method to all aspects of society. (p. 171)

entrepreneur [AHN·truh·pruh·NUR] *n.* a person who organizes, manages, and takes on the risks of a business. (p. 256)

estate [ih·STAYT] *n.* one of the three social classes in France before the French Revolution—the First Estate consisting of the clergy; the Second Estate, of the nobility; and the Third Estate, of the rest of the population. (p. 193)

Estates-General [ih·STAYTS·JEHN·uhr·uhl] *n.* an assembly of representatives from all three of the estates, or social classes, in France. (p. 195)

ethnic cleansing *n.* a policy of murder and other acts of brutality by which Serbs hoped to eliminate Bosnia's Muslim population after the breakup of Yugoslavia. (p. 549)

existentialism [EHG·zih·STEHN·shuh·LIHZ·uhm] *n.* a philosophy based on the idea that people give meaning to their lives through their choices and actions. (p. 416)

extraterritorial [EHK·struh·TEHR·ih·TAWR·ee·uhl] **rights** *n.* an exemption of foreign residents from the laws of a country. (p. 336)

F

factors of production *n.* the resources—including land, labor, and capital—that are needed to produce goods and services. (p. 254)

factory *n.* a large building in which machinery is used to manufacture goods. (p. 255)

fascism [FASH·IHZ·uhm] *n.* a political movement that promotes an extreme form of nationalism, a denial of individual rights, and a dictatorial one-party rule. (p. 427)

favorable balance of trade *n.* an economic situation in which a country exports more than it imports—that is, sells more goods abroad than it buys from abroad. (p. 122)

federal system *n.* a system of government in which power is divided between a central authority and a number of individual states. (pp. 187, 537)

feudalism [FYOOD·uhl·IHZ·uhm] *n.* a political system in which nobles are granted the use of lands that legally belong to their king, in exchange for their loyalty, military service, and protection of the people who live on the land. (p. 17)

Final Solution *n.* Hitler's program of systematically killing the entire Jewish people. (p. 453)

FLN *n.* the National Liberation Front—an Algerian group that waged a guerrilla struggle for independence from France. (p. 519)

Four Modernizations *n.* a set of goals adopted by the Chinese leader Deng Xiaoping in the late 20th century, involving progress in agriculture, industry, defense, and science and technology. (p. 552)

Fourteen Points *n.* a series of proposals in which U.S. president Woodrow Wilson outlined a plan for achieving a lasting peace after World War I. (p. 380)

free trade *n.* commerce between nations without economic restrictions or barriers (such as tariffs). (p. 567)

French and Indian War *n.* a conflict between Britain and France for control of territory in North America, lasting from 1754 to 1763. (p. 113)

French Revolution *n.* the French war for democracy that began in 1789 and ended with the overthrow of the monarchy. (p. 25)

fundamentalism [FUHN·duh·MEHN·tuhl·IHZ·uhm] *n.* a strict belief in the basic truths and practices of a particular religion. (p. 573)

G

genetic [juh·NEHT·ihk] **engineering** *n.* the transferring of genes from one living thing to another in order to produce an organism with new traits. (p. 564)

genocide [JEHN·uh·SYD] *n.* the systematic killing of a entire people. (p. 453)

geopolitics [JEE·oh·PAHL·ih·tihks] *n.* a foreign policy based on a consideration of the strategic locations or products of other lands. (p. 318)

ghazi [GAH·zee] *n.* a warrior for Islam. (p. 63)

ghettos [GEHT·ohz] *n.* city neighborhoods in which European Jews were forced to live. (p. 452)

glasnost [GLAHS·nuhst] *n.* a Soviet policy of openness to the free flow of ideas and information, introduced in 1985 by Mikhail Gorbachev. (p. 541)

global economy *n.* all the financial interactions—involving people, businesses, and governments—that cross international boundaries. (p. 567)

Glorious Revolution *n.* the bloodless overthrow of the English king James II and his replacement by William and Mary. (p. 159)

government *n.* a political system for exercising authority. (p. 5)

grassroots development *n.* a program focused on helping individuals and communities use basic methods to improve their lives. (p. 600)

Great Depression *n.* the severe economic slump that followed the collapse of the U.S. stock market in 1929. (p. 424)

Great Fear *n.* a wave of senseless panic that spread through the French countryside after the storming of the Bastille in 1789. (p. 196)

Great Purge *n.* a campaign of terror in the Soviet Union during the 1930s, in which Joseph Stalin sought to eliminate all Communist Party members and other citizens who threatened his power. (p. 397)

Great Trek *n.* a migration of Dutch colonists out of British-controlled territory in South Africa during the 1830s. (p. 309)

green revolution *n.* a 20th-century attempt to increase food resources worldwide, involving the use of fertilizers and pesticides and the development of disease-resistant crops. (p. 564)

greenhouse effect *n.* problems caused by emissions of carbon dioxide and other gases, also called global warming. (p. 592)

guerrilla [guh·RIHL·uh] *n.* a member of a loosely organized fighting force that makes surprise attacks on enemy troops occupying his or her country. (p. 210)

guillotine [GIHL·uh·TEEN] *n.* a machine for beheading people, used as a means of execution during the French Revolution. (p. 200)

Gulf War *n.* a 1991 conflict in which UN forces defeated Iraqi forces that had invaded Kuwait and threatened to invade Saudi Arabia. (p. 569)

Gutenberg [GOOT·uhn·BURG] **Bible** *n.* the first full-sized book printed with movable type and a printing press. (p. 46)

H

habeas corpus [HAY·bee·uhs KAWR·puhs] *n.* a document requiring that a prisoner be brought before a court or judge so that it can be decided whether his or her imprisonment is legal. (p. 158)

haiku [HY·koo] *n.* a Japanese form of poetry, consisting of three unrhymed lines of five, seven, and five syllables. (p. 96)

heliocentric [HEE·lee·oh·SEHN·trihk] **theory** *n.* the idea that the earth and the other planets revolve around the sun. (p. 166)

Hinduism [HIHN·doo·IHZ·ahm] *n.* a religion that began in India. The teachings of Hindu include a belief in reincarnation and belief in the interconnectedness of all life. (p. 618)

Holocaust [HAHL·uh·KAWST] *n.* a mass slaughter of Jews and other civilians, carried out by the Nazi government of Germany before and during World War II. (p. 451)

Holy Alliance *n.* a league of European nations formed by the leaders of Russia, Austria, and Prussia after the Congress of Vienna. (p. 215)

home rule *n.* a control over internal matters granted to the residents of a region by a ruling government. (p. 288)

Hubble Space Telescope *n.* a powerful telescope put into orbit around the earth by NASA and the European Space Agency in 1990. (p. 562)

humanism [HYOO·muh·NIHZ·uhm] *n.* a Renaissance intellectual movement in which thinkers studied classical texts and focused on human potential and achievements. (p. 38)

Hundred Days *n.* the brief period during 1815 when Napoleon made his last bid for power, deposing the French king and again becoming emperor of France. (p. 212)

I

imperialism [ihm·PEER·ee·uh·LIHZ·uhm] *n.* a policy in which a strong nation seeks to dominate other countries politically, economically, or socially. (p. 306)

impressionism [ihm·PREHSH·uh·NIHZ·uhm] *n.* a movement in 19th-century painting, in which artists reacted against realism by seeking to convey their impressions of subjects or moments in time. (p. 243)

indulgence [ihn·DUHL·juhns] *n.* a pardon releasing a person from punishments due for a sin. (p. 49)

industrialization [ihn·DUHS·tree·uh·lih·ZAY·shuhn] *n.* the development of industries for the machine production of goods. (p. 254)

Industrial Revolution *n.* the shift, beginning in England during the 18th century, from making goods by hand to making them by machine. (p. 253)

intendant [ihn·TEHN·duhnt] *n.* a French government official appointed by the monarch to collect taxes and administer justice. (p. 140)

International Monetary Fund *n.* a multinational organization that offers emergency loans to countries in financial crisis. (p. 600)

Internet *n.* a linkage of computer networks that allows people around the world to exchange information and communicate with one another. (p. 563)

investment capital *n.* the funds needed for economic growth to build industries and to build an infrastructure, such as roads and bridges. (p. 599)

iron curtain *n.* during the Cold War, the boundary separating the Communist nations of Eastern Europe from the mostly democratic nations of Western Europe. (p. 477)

Islam [ihs·LAHM] *n.* a monotheistic religion that developed in Arabia in the seventh century A.D. (p. 234)

isolationism *n.* a policy of avoiding political or military involvement with other countries. (p. 434)

J

janissary [JAN·ih·SEHR·ee] *n.* a member of an elite force of soldiers in the Ottoman Empire. (p. 66)

jazz *n.* a 20th-century style of popular music developed mainly by African-American musicians. (p. 417)

Jesuits [JEHZH·oo·ihts] *n.* members of the Society of Jesus, a Roman Catholic religious order founded by Ignatius of Loyola. (p. 55)

"jewel in the crown" *n.* the British colony of India—so called because of its importance in the British Empire, both as a supplier of raw materials and as a market for British trade goods. (p. 321)

joint-stock company *n.* a business in which investors pool their wealth for a common purpose, then share the profits. (p. 122)

Judaism [JOO·dee·IHZ·ehm] *n.* the monotheistic religion of the Hebrews founded by Abraham around 2000 B.C. (p. 12)

K

kabuki [kuh·BOO·kee] *n.* a type of Japanese drama in which music, dance, and mime are used to present stories. (p. 96)

kaiser [KY·zuhr] *n.* a German emperor (from the Roman title *Caesar*). (p. 238)

kamikaze [KAH·mih·KAH·zee] *n.* during World War II, Japanese suicide pilots trained to sink Allied ships by crashing bomb-filled planes into them. (p. 461)

Khmer Rouge [roozh] *n.* a group of Communist rebels who seized power in Cambodia in 1975. (p. 490)

Kristallnacht [krih·STAHL·NAHKT] *n.* "Night of Broken Glass"—the night of November 9, 1838, on which Nazi storm troopers attacked Jewish homes, businesses, and synagogues throughout Germany. (p. 451)

kulak [koo·LAK] *n.* a member of a class of wealthy Russian peasants. (p. 397)

Kuomintang [KWOH·mihn·TANG] *n.* the Chinese Nationalist Party, formed after the fall of the Qing Dynasty in 1912. (p. 401)

L

laissez faire [LEHS·ay·FAIR] *n.* the idea that government should not interfere with or regulate industries and businesses. (p. 267)

land reform *n.* a redistribution of farmland by breaking up large estates and giving the resulting smaller farms to peasants. (p. 532)

La Reforma [lah reh·FAWR·mah] *n.* a liberal reform movement in 19th-century Mexico, founded by Benito Juárez. (p. 350)

League of Nations *n.* an international association formed after World War I with the goal of keeping peace among nations. (p. 381)

lebensraum [LAY·buhns·ROWM] *n.* "living space"—the additional territory that, according to Adolf Hitler, Germany needed because it was overcrowded. (p. 429)

Legislative [LEHJ·ih·SLAY·tihv] **Assembly** *n.* a French congress with the power to create laws and approve declarations of war, established by the Constitution of 1791. (p. 198)

legitimacy [luh·JIHT·uh·muh·see] *n.* the hereditary right of a monarch to rule. (p. 214)

less developed countries *n.* (LDCs)—countries that are not fully industrialized. (p. 599)

liberals *n.* in the first half of the 19th century, those Europeans—mainly middle-class business leaders and merchants—who wanted to give more political power to elected parliaments. (p. 229)

Long March *n.* a 6,000-mile journey made in 1934–1935 by Chinese Communists fleeing from Jiang Jieshi's Nationalist forces. (p. 404)

Lutheran [LOO·thuhr·uhn] *n.* a member of a Protestant church founded on the teachings of Martin Luther. (p. 50)

lycée [lee·SAY] *n.* a government-run public school in France. (p. 205)

M

Magna Carta [MAG·nuh KAHR·tuh] *n.* "Great Charter"—a document guaranteeing basic political rights in England, drawn up by nobles and approved by King John in A.D. 1215. (p. 17)

Manchus [MAN·chooz] *n.* a people, native to Manchuria, who ruled China during the Qing Dynasty (1644–1912). (p. 91)

manifest destiny *n.* the idea, popular among mid-19th-century Americans, that it was the right and the duty of the United States to rule North America from the Atlantic Ocean to the Pacific Ocean. (p. 290)

Maori [MOW·ree] *n.* a member of a Polynesian people who settled in New Zealand around A.D. 800. (p. 285)

Marshall Plan *n.* a U.S. program of economic aid to European countries to help them rebuild after World War II. (p. 478)

martial [MAHR·shuhl] **law** *n.* a temporary rule by military authorities over a civilian population, usually imposed in times of war or civil unrest. (p. 537)

mass culture *n.* the production of works of art and entertainment designed to appeal to a large audience. (p. 294)

mass media *n.* public communications including television, radio, movies, the music industry, and the popular press. (p. 590)

materialism *n.* a placing of high value on acquiring material possessions. (p. 580)

Mau Mau [MOW MOW] *n.* a secret society of Kikuyu tribesmen that attempted to drive British settlers out of Kenya in the mid-20th century. (p. 517)

May Fourth Movement *n.* a national protest in China in 1919, in which people demonstrated against the Treaty of Versailles and foreign interference. (p. 402)

Meiji [MAY·JEE] **era** *n.* the period of Japanese history from 1867 to 1912, during which the country was ruled by Emperor Mutsuhito. (p. 341)

Mein Kampf [MYN KAHMPF] *n.* "My Struggle"—a book written by Adolf Hitler during his imprisonment in 1923–1924, in which he set forth his beliefs and his goals for Germany. (p. 429)

mercantilism [MUR·kuhn·tee·LIHZ·uhm] *n.* an economic policy under which nations sought to increase their wealth and power by obtaining large amounts of gold and silver and by selling more goods than they bought. (p. 122)

mestizo [mehs·TEE·zoh] *adj.* of mixed Spanish and Native American ancestry. (p. 106)

middle class *n.* a social class made up of skilled workers, professionals, businesspeople, and wealthy farmers. (p. 259)

middle passage *n.* the voyage that brought captured Africans to the West Indies, and later to North and South America, to be sold as slaves—so called because it was considered the middle leg of the triangular trade. (p. 117)

militarism [MIHL·ih·tuh·RIHZ·uhm] *n.* a policy of glorifying military power and keeping a standing army always prepared for war. (p. 364)

Ming Dynasty *n.* a Chinese dynasty that ruled from 1368 to 1644. (p. 89)

monarchy [MAHN·uhr·kee] *n.* a government in which power is in the hands of a single person. (p. 7)

Model Parliament [PAHR·luh·muhnt] *n.* the gathering of lords, knights, and burgesses first called by King Edward I in 1295 that voted on taxes and reforms. The Model Parliament established a standard for later Parliaments. (p. 18)

Monroe Doctrine *n.* a U.S. policy of opposition to European interference in Latin America, announced by President James Monroe in 1823. (p. 346)

Mughal [MOO·guhl] *n.* one of the nomads who invaded the Indian subcontinent in the 16th century and established a powerful empire there. (p. 71)

mulattos [mu·LAT·ohz] *n.* persons of mixed European and African ancestry. (p. 224)

multilateral aid *n.* money and resources provided by an organization with many members. (p. 600)

multinational corporation *n.* a company that operates in a number of different countries. (p. 567)

Munich [MYOO·nihk] **Conference** *n.* a 1938 meeting of representatives from Britain, France, Italy, and Germany, at which Britain and France agreed to allow Nazi Germany to annex part of Czechoslovakia in return for Adolf Hitler's pledge to respect Czechoslovakia's new borders. (p. 435)

Muslim League *n.* an organization formed in 1906 to protect the interests of India's Muslims, which later proposed that India be divided into separate Muslim and Hindu nations. (p. 506)

N

Napoleonic [nuh·POH·lee·AHN·ihk] **Code** *n.* a comprehensive and uniform system of laws established for France by Napoleon. (p. 206)

National Assembly *n.* a French congress established by representatives of the Third Estate on June 17, 1789, to enact laws and reforms in the name of the French people. (p. 195)

nationalism *n.* the belief that people should be loyal mainly to their nation—that is, to the people with whom they share a culture and history—rather than to a king or empire. (p. 229)

nation-state *n.* an independent nation of people having a common culture and identity. (p. 229)

NATO [NAY·toh] *n.* the North Atlantic Treaty Organization—a defensive military alliance formed in 1949 by ten Western European nations, the United States, and Canada. (p. 479)

natural laws *n.* patterns and explanations of the world discovered through reason and intelligence; used by the Greeks in place of superstition and traditional explanations of the world. (p. 7)

natural rights *n.* the rights that all people are born with—according to John Locke, the rights of life, liberty, and property. (p. 171)

Nazism [NAHT·SIHZ·uhm] *n.* the fascist policies of the National Socialist German Workers' party, based on totalitarianism, a belief in racial superiority, and state control of industry. (p. 428)

Negritude [NEE·grih·TOOD] **movement** *n.* a movement in which French-speaking Africans and West Indians celebrated their heritage of traditional African culture and values. (p. 516)

neoclassical [NEE·oh·KLAS·ih·kuhl] *adj.* relating to a simple, elegant style (based on ideas and themes from ancient Greece and Rome) that characterized the arts in Europe during the late 1700s. (p. 179)

New Deal *n.* U.S. president Franklin Roosevelt's economic reform program designed to solve the problems created by the Great Depression. (p. 426)

nonaggression [NAHN·uh·GREHSH·uhn] **pact** *n.* an

agreement in which nations promise not to attack one another. (p. 441)

nonaligned nations *n.* the independent countries that remained neutral in the Cold War competition between the United States and the Soviet Union. (p. 491)

non-renewable energy n. forms of energy that can not be replaced such as oil and coal (p. 594)

Nuclear Non-Proliferation [NOO·klee·uhr NAHN·pruh·LIHF·uh·RAY·shuhn] **Treaty** *n.* a 1968 agreement intended to reduce the spread of nuclear weapons. (p. 573)

Nuremberg [NUR·uhm·BURG] **Trials** *n.* a series of court proceedings held in Nuremberg, Germany, after World War II, in which Nazi leaders were tried for aggression, violations of the rules of war, and crimes against humanity. (p. 463)

O

Old Regime [ray·ZHEEM] *n.* the political and social system that existed in France before the French Revolution. (p. 193)

Open Door Policy *n.* a policy, proposed by the United States in 1899, under which all nations would have equal opportunities to trade in China. (p. 338)

Opium War *n.* a conflict between Britain and China, lasting from 1839 to 1842, over Britain's opium trade in China. (p. 336)

ozone layer *n.* a layer of the earth's upper atmosphere, which protects living things from the sun's damaging ultraviolet rays. (p. 569)

P

Pacific Rim *n.* the lands surrounding the Pacific Ocean—especially those in Asia. (p. 326)

Panama Canal *n.* a manmade waterway connecting the Atlantic and Pacific oceans, built in Panama by the United States and opened in 1914. (p. 347)

parliament [PAHR·luh·muhnt] *n.* a body of representatives that makes laws for a nation. (p. 354)

partition *n.* a division into parts, like the 1947 division of the British colony of India into the two nations of India and Pakistan. (p. 506)

paternalism [puh·TUR·nuh·LIHZ·uhm] *n.* a policy of treating subject people as if they were children, providing for their needs but not giving them rights. (p. 311)

patron [PAY·truhn] *n.* a person who supports artists, especially financially. (p. 38)

Peace of Augsburg [AWGZ·BURG] *n.* a 1555 agreement declaring that the religion of each German state would be decided by its ruler. (p. 50)

penal [PEE·nuhl] **colony** *n.* a colony to which convicts are sent as an alternative to prison. (p. 285)

peninsulares [peh·neen·soo·LAH·rehs] *n.* in Spanish colonial society, colonists who were born in Spain. (p. 224)

Peninsular [puh·NIHN·syuh·luhr] **War** *n.* a conflict, lasting from 1808 to 1813, in which Spanish rebels, with the aid of British forces, fought to drive Napoleon's French troops out of Spain. (p. 210)

perestroika [PEHR·ih·STROY·kuh] *n.* a restructuring of the Soviet economy to permit more local decision-making, begun by Mikhail Gorbachev in 1985. (p. 542)

perspective [puhr·SPEHK·tihv] *n.* an artistic technique that creates the appearance of three dimensions on a flat surface. (p. 39)

philosophe [FIHL·uh·SAHF] *n.* one of a group of social thinkers in France during the Enlightenment. (p. 172)

philosophers *n.* thinkers who use logic and reason to investigate the nature of the universe, human society, and morality. (p. 7)

Pilgrims *n.* a group of people who, in 1620, founded the colony of Plymouth in Massachusetts to escape religious persecution in England. (p. 111)

plebiscite [PLEHB·ih·SYT] *n.* a direct vote in which a country's people have the opportunity to approve or reject a proposal. (p. 205)

PLO *n.* the Palestine Liberation Organization—an organization dedicated to the establishment of an independent state for Palestinians in the Middle East. (p. 525)

pogrom [puh·GRAHM] *n.* one of the organized campaigns of violence against Jewish communities in late-19th-century Russia. (p. 389)

Politburo [PAHL·iht·BYOOR·oh] *n.* the ruling committee of the Communist Party in the Soviet Union. (p. 541)

popular culture *n.* the cultural elements—sports, music, movies, clothing, and so forth—that reflect a group's common background and changing interests. (p. 577)

predestination [pree·DEHS·tuh·NAY·shuhn] *n.* the doctrine that God has decided all things beforehand, including which people will be eternally saved. (p. 53)

Presbyterian [PREHZ·bih·TEER·ee·uhn] *n.* a member of a Protestant church governed by elders (presbyters) and founded on the teachings of John Knox. (p. 53)

PRI *n.* the Institutional Revolutionary Party—the main political party of Mexico. (p. 534)

printing press *n.* a machine for reproducing written material by pressing paper against arrangements of inked type. (p. 46)

proliferation [pruh·LIHF·uh·RAY·shuhn] *n.* a growth or spread—especially the spread of nuclear weapons to nations that do not currently have them. (p. 573)

propaganda [PRAHP·uh·GAN·duh] *n.* information or material spread to advance a cause or to damage an opponent's cause. (p. 376)

prophet [prahf·iht] *n.* a spiritually inspired leader or teacher believed to be a messenger from God. (p. 13)

Protestant [PRAHT·ih·stuhnt] *n.* a member of a Christian church founded on the principles of the Reformation. (p. 50)

provisional government *n.* a temporary government. (p. 392)

psychology [sy·KAHL·uh·jee] *n.* the study of the human mind and human behavior. (p. 299)

Puritans *n.* a group of people who sought freedom from religious persecution in England by founding a colony at Massachusetts Bay in the early 1600s. (p. 111)

Q

Qing [chihng] **Dynasty** *n.* China's last dynasty, which ruled from 1644 to 1912. (p. 91)

R

racism [RAY·SIHZ·uhm] *n.* the belief that one race is superior to others. (p. 306)

radicals *n.* in the first half of the 19th century, those Europeans who favored drastic change to extend democracy to all people. (p. 229)

radioactivity *n.* a form of energy released as atoms decay. (p. 298)

Raj [rahj] *n.* the British-controlled portions of India in the years 1757–1947. (p. 324)

rationing [RASH·uh·nihng] *n.* the limiting of the amounts of goods people can buy—often imposed by governments during wartime, when goods are in short supply. (p. 375)

realism *n.* a 19th-century artistic movement in which writers and painters sought to show life as it is rather than life as it should be. (p. 241)

realpolitik [ray·AHL·POH·lih·TEEK] *n.* "the politics of reality"—the practice of tough power politics without room for idealism. (p. 237)

recession *n.* a slowdown in a nation's economy. (p. 533)

Red Guards *n.* militia units formed by young Chinese people in 1966 in response to Mao Zedong's call for a social and cultural revolution. (p. 485)

Red Shirts *n.* the followers of the 19th-century Italian nationalist leader Giuseppe Garibaldi. (p. 236)

Reformation [REHF·uhr·MAY·shuhn] *n.* a 16th-century movement for religious reform, leading to the founding of Christian churches that rejected the pope's authority. (p. 49)

Reign [rayn] **of Terror** *n.* the period, from mid-1793 to mid-1794, when Maximilien Robespierre ruled France nearly as a dictator and thousands of political figures and ordinary citizens were executed. (p. 202)

Renaissance [REHN·ih·SAHNS] *n.* a period of European history, lasting from about 1300 to 1600, during which renewed interest in classical culture led to far-reaching changes in art, learning, and views of the world. (p. 37)

renewable energy *n.* forms of energy that can be replaced such as wind, water, and solar power, can be replenished. (p. 594)

representative government *n.* a government in which citizens elect representatives to make laws and policies for them. (p. 25)

republic *n.* a form of government in which power is in the hands of representatives and leaders are elected by the people. (p. 8)

Restoration [REHS·tuh·RAY·shuhn] *n.* the period of Charles II's rule over England, after the collapse of Oliver Cromwell's government. (p. 158)

reunification [ree·YOO·nuh·fih·KAY·shuhn] *n.* a bringing together again of things that have been separated, like the reuniting of East Germany and West Germany in 1990. (p. 544)

Roman Catholic Church *n.* the Christian church that developed in 1054 A.D. (p. 14)

romanticism [roh·MAN·tih·SIHZ·uhm] *n.* an early-19th-century movement in art and thought, which focused on emotion and nature rather than reason and society. (p. 239)

Roosevelt Corollary [ROH·zuh·VEHLT KAWR·uh·lehr·ee] *n.* President Theodore Roosevelt's 1904 extension of the Monroe Doctrine, in which he declared that the United States had the right to exercise "police power" throughout the Western Hemisphere. (p. 347)

Russo-Japanese War *n.* a 1904–1905 conflict between Russia and Japan, sparked by the two countries' efforts to dominate Manchuria and Korea. (p. 343)

S

Safavid [suh·FAH·VIHD] *n.* a member of a Shi'a Muslim dynasty that built an empire in Persia in the 16th–18th centuries. (p. 69)

salon [suh·LAHN] *n.* a social gathering of intellectuals and artists, like those held in the homes of wealthy women in Paris and other European cities during the Enlightenment. (p. 178)

SALT *n.* the Strategic Arms Limitation Talks—a series of meetings in the 1970s, in which leaders of the United States and the Soviet Union agreed to limit their nations' stocks of nuclear weapons. (p. 499)

sans-culottes [SANS·kyoo·LAHTS] *n.* in the French Revolution, a radical group made up of Parisian wage-earners and small shopkeepers who wanted a greater voice in government, lower prices, and an end of food shortages. (p. 199)

Schlieffen [SHLEE·fuhn] **Plan** *n.* Germany's military plan at the outbreak of World War I, according to which German troops would rapidly defeat France and then move east to attack Russia. (p. 367)

scientific method *n.* a logical procedure for gathering information about the natural world, in which experimentation and observation are used to test hypotheses. (p. 167)

Scientific Revolution *n.* a major change in European thought, starting in the mid-1500s, in which the study of the natural world began to be characterized by careful observation and the questioning of accepted beliefs. (p. 165)

scorched-earth policy *n.* the practice of burning crops and killing livestock during wartime so that the enemy cannot live off the land. (p. 210)

secede [sih·SEED] *v.* to withdraw formally from an association or alliance. (p. 290)

secular [SEHK·yuh·luhr] *adj.* concerned with worldly rather than spiritual matters. (p. 38)

segregation [SEHG·rih·GAY·shuhn] *n.* the legal or social separation of people of different races. (p. 292)

self-determination [SEHLF·dih·TUR·muh·NAY·shuhn] *n.* the freedom of a people to decide under what form of government they wish to live. (p. 380)

senate *n.* in ancient Rome, the supreme governing body, originally made up only of aristocrats. (p. 9)

separation of powers *n.* the assignment of executive, legislative, and judicial powers to different groups of officials in a government. (p. 173)

sepoy [SEE·POY] *n.* an Indian soldier serving under British command. (p. 321)

Sepoy Mutiny [MYOOT·uh·nee] *n.* an 1857 rebellion of Hindu and Muslim soldiers against the British in India. (p. 323)

Seven Years' War *n.* a conflict in Europe, North America, and India, lasting from 1756 to 1763, in which the forces of Britain and Prussia battled those of Austria, France, Russia, and other countries. (p. 150)

"shock therapy" *n.* an economic program implemented in Russia by Boris Yeltsin in the 1990s, involving an abrupt shift from a command economy to a free-market economy. (p. 548)

Sikh [seek] *n.* a member of a nonviolent religious group whose beliefs blend elements of Buddhism, Hinduism, and Sufism. (p. 74)

Six-Day War *n.* a brief 1967 conflict between Israel and several Arab states, during which Israel took control of Jerusalem, the Sinai Peninsula, the Golan Heights, and the West Bank. (p. 523)

skepticism [SKEHP·tih·SIHZ·uhm] *n.* a philosophy based on the idea that nothing can be known for certain. (p. 139)

social contract *n.* the agreement by which people define and limit their individual rights, thus creating an organized society or government. (p. 171)

Social Darwinism [DAHR·wih·NIHZ·uhm] *n.* the application of Charles Darwin's ideas about evolution and "survival of the fittest" to human societies—particularly as justification for imperialist expansion. (p. 306)

socialism *n.* an economic system in which the factors of production are owned by the public and operate for the welfare of all. (p. 268)

socialist realism *n.* a style of art in which Communist values and life under communism are glorified. (p. 398)

Solidarity [SAHL·ih·DAR·ih·tee] *n.* a Polish labor union that during the 1980s became the main force of opposition to Communist rule in Poland. (p. 542)

soviet [SOH·vee·EHT] *n.* one of the local representative councils formed in Russia after the downfall of Czar Nicholas II. (p. 392)

Spanish-American War *n.* an 1898 conflict between the United States and Spain, in which the United States supported Cubans' fight for independence. (p. 346)

sphere of influence *n.* a foreign region in which a nation has control over trade and other economic activities. (p. 338)

standard of living *n.* the quality of life of a person or a population, as indicated by the goods, services, and luxuries available to the person or people. (p. 532)

Star Wars *n.* a program to protect the United States against attack by enemy missiles, proposed in 1983 by President Ronald Reagan but never implemented—formally known as the Strategic Defense Initiative. (p. 499)

strike *v.* to refuse to work in order to force an employer to meet certain demands. (p. 270)

Suez [soo·EHZ] **Canal** *n.* a manmade waterway connecting the Red Sea and the Mediterranean Sea, which was opened in 1869. (p. 319)

Suez Crisis *n.* an international crisis that occurred after Egypt seized control of the Suez Canal in 1956, when Israel, with the support of Britain and France, took the canal by force but withdrew under pressure from the United States and the Soviet Union. (p. 522)

suffrage [SUHF·rihj] *n.* the right to vote. (p. 279)

surrealism [suh·REE·uh·LIHZ·uhm] *n.* a 20th-century artistic movement that focuses on the workings of the unconscious mind. (p. 417)

sustainable development *n.* economic development that meets people's needs but preserves the environment and conserves resources for future generations. (p. 570)

T

Taiping [ty·pihng] **Rebellion** *n.* a mid-19th century rebellion against the Qing Dynasty in China, led by Hong Xiuquan. (p. 337)

Taj Mahal [TAHZH muh·HAHL] *n.* a beautiful tomb in Agra, India, built by the Mughal emperor Shah Jahan for his wife Mumtaz Mahal. (p. 74)

Ten Commandments *n.* the written law code, followed by Jews and Christians, given by God to Moses around 1200 B.C. (p. 13).

Tennis Court Oath *n.* a pledge made by the members of France's National Assembly in 1789, in which they vowed to continue meeting until they had drawn up a new constitution. (p. 196)

terrorism *n.* the use of force or threats to frighten people or governments to change their policies. (p. 193)

theocracy [thee·AHK·ruh·see] *n.* a government controlled by religious leaders. (p. 53)

theory of evolution *n.* the idea, proposed by Charles Darwin in 1859, that species of plants and animals arise by means of a process of natural selection. (p. 298)

theory of relativity [REHL·uh·TIHV·ih·tee] *n.* Albert Einstein's ideas about the interrelationships between time and space and between energy and matter. (p. 415)

Third Reich [ryk] *n.* the Third German Empire, established by Adolf Hitler in the 1930s. (p. 434)

Third Republic *n.* the republic that was established in France after the downfall of Napoleon III and ended with the German occupation of France during World War II. (p. 283)

Third World *n.* during the Cold War, the developing nations not allied with either the United States or the Soviet Union. (p. 491)

Thirty Years' War *n.* a European conflict over religion, over territory, and for power among ruling families, lasting from 1618 to 1648. (p. 146)

Tiananmen [tyahn·ahn·mehn] **Square** *n.* a huge public space in Beijing, China—in 1989, the site of a student uprising in support of democratic reforms. (p. 552)

Tokugawa Shogunate [TOH·koo·GAH·wah SHOH·guh·niht] *n.* a dynasty of shoguns that ruled a unified Japan from 1603 to 1867. (p. 95)

totalitarianism [toh·TAL·ih·TAIR·ee·uh·NIHZ·uhm] *n.* government control over every aspect of public and private life. (p. 395)

total war *n.* a conflict in which the participating countries devote all their resources to the war effort. (p. 375)

Trans-Siberian [TRANS·sy·BEER·ee·uhn] **Railway** *n.* a rail line built between 1891 and 1904 to connect European Russia with Russian ports on the Pacific Ocean. (p. 390)

Treaty of Kanagawa [kah·NAH·gah·wah] *n.* an 1854 agreement between the United States and Japan, which opened two Japanese ports to U.S. ships and allowed the United States to set up an embassy in Japan. (p. 340)

Treaty of Tordesillas [TAWR·day·SEEL·yahs] *n.* a 1494 agreement between Portugal and Spain, declaring that newly discovered lands to the west of an imaginary line in the Atlantic Ocean would belong to Spain and newly discovered lands to the east of the line would belong to Portugal. (p. 86)

Treaty of Versailles [vuhr·SY] *n.* the peace treaty signed by Germany and the Allied powers after World War I. (p. 381)

trench warfare *n.* a form of warfare in which opposing armies fight each other from trenches dug in the battlefield. (p. 369)

triangular trade *n.* the transatlantic trading network along which slaves and other goods were carried between Africa, England, Europe, the West Indies, and the colonies in North America. (p. 117)

Triple Alliance *n.* a military alliance between Germany, Austria-Hungary, and Italy in the years preceding World War I. (p. 364)

Triple Entente [ahn·TAHNT] *n.* a military alliance between Great Britain, France, and Russia in the years preceding World War I. (p. 365)

Truman Doctrine *n.* a U.S. policy of giving economic and military aid to free nations threatened by internal or external opponents, announced by President Harry Truman in 1947. (p. 478)

union *n.* an association of workers, formed to bargain for better working conditions and higher wages. (p. 270)

United Nations *n.* an international peacekeeping organization founded in 1945 to provide security to the nations of the world. (p. 475)

Universal Declaration of Human Rights *n.* a 1948 statement in which the United Nations declared that all human beings have rights to life, liberty, and security. (p. 574)

unrestricted submarine warfare *n.* the use of submarines to sink without warning any ship (including neutral ships and unarmed passenger liners) found in an enemy's waters. (p. 374)

urbanization [UR·buh·nih·ZAY·shuhn] *n.* the growth of cities and the migration of people into them. (p. 258)

U.S. Civil War *n.* a conflict between Northern and Southern states of the United States over the issue of slavery, lasting from 1861 to 1865. (p. 291)

utilitarianism [yoo·TIHL·ih·TAIR·ee·uh·NIHZ·uhm] *n.* the theory, proposed by Jeremy Bentham in the late 1700s, that government actions are useful only if they promote the greatest good for the greatest number of people. (p. 268)

Utopia [yoo·TOH·pee·uh] *n.* an imaginary land described by Thomas More in his book *Utopia*—hence, an ideal place. (p. 45)

U-2 incident *n.* the shooting down of a U.S. spy plane and capture of its pilot by the Soviet Union in 1960. (p. 480)

vernacular [vuhr·NAK·yuh·luhr] *n.* the everyday language of people in a region or country. (p. 41)

Vietcong [vee·EHT·KAHNG] *n.* a group of Communist guerrillas who, with the help of North Vietnam, fought against the South Vietnamese government in the Vietnam War. (p. 488)

Vietnamization [vee·EHT·nuh·mih·ZAY·shuhn] *n.* President Richard Nixon's strategy for ending U.S. involvement in the Vietnam War, involving a gradual withdrawal of American troops and replacement of them with South Vietnamese forces. (p. 489)

War of the Spanish Succession *n.* a conflict, lasting from 1701 to 1713, in which a number of European states fought to prevent the Bourbon family from controlling Spain as well as France. (p. 143)

Warsaw Pact *n.* a military alliance formed in 1955 by the Soviet Union and seven Eastern European countries. (p. 479)

weapons of mass destruction *n.* weapons that have the potential to kill or injure large numbers of people at once including nuclear armaments, and biological and chemical weapons. (p. 604)

Weimar [WY·MAHR] **Republic** *n.* the republic that was established in Germany in 1919 and ended in 1933. (p. 422)

Western Front *n.* in World War I, the region of northern France where the forces of the Allies and the Central Powers battled each other. (p. 368)

westernization *n.* an adoption of the social, political, or economic institutions of Western—especially European or American—countries. (p. 153)

World Bank *n.* a multinational organization that provides loans for large-scale development projects. (p. 600)

Zionism [ZY·uh·NIHZ·uhm] *n.* a movement founded in the 1890s to promote the establishment of a Jewish homeland in Palestine. (p. 283)

Spanish Glossary

A

Aborigine [aborigen] *s.* miembro de cualquiera de los pueblos nativos de Australia. (pág. 285)

absolute monarch [monarca absoluto] *s.* rey o reina que tiene poder ilimitado y que procura controlar todos los aspectos de la sociedad. (pág. 137)

absolute ruler [gobernante absoluto] *s.* gobernante que ejerce todo el poder. (pág. 5)

accommodation [acomodación] *s.* aceptación de las ideas y constumbres de otras culturas. (pág. 581)

Allies [Aliados] *s.* durante la I Guerra Mundial, las naciones de Gran Bretaña, Francia y Rusia, junto con otras que lucharon a su lado; también, el grupo de naciones —entre ellas Gran Bretaña, la Unión Soviética y Estados Unidos— opuestas a las Potencias del Eje en la II Guerra Mundial. (pág. 368)

American Revolution [Revolución Norteamericana] *s.* lucha de independencia de las colonias inglesas en Norteamérica; empezó el 19 de abril de 1775 y terminó en victoria en 1781. (pág. 24)

Anabaptist [anabaptista] *s.* en la Reforma, miembro de un grupo protestante que enseñaba que sólo los adultos podían ser bautizados, y que la Iglesia y el Estado debían estar separados. (pág. 54)

Anglican [anglicano] *adj.* relacionado con la Iglesia de Inglaterra. (pág. 52)

annexation [anexión] *s.* añadir una región al territorio de una unidad política existente. (págs. 329, 343)

annul [anular] *v.* cancelar o suspender. (pág. 51)

anti-Semitism [antisemitismo] *s.* prejuicio contra los judíos. (pág. 283)

apartheid *s.* política de Sudáfrica de separación total y legalizada de las razas; prohibía todo contacto social entre negros y blancos. (pág. 539)

appeasement [apaciguamiento] *s.* otorgar concesiones a un agresor a fin de evitar la guerra. (pág. 433)

aristocracy [aristocracia] *s.* gobierno en que el poder está en manos de una clase dominante hereditaria o nobleza. (pág. 5)

armistice [armisticio] *s.* acuerdo de suspender combates. (pág. 377)

Aryans [arios] *s.* **1.** pueblo indoeuropeo que, hacia 1500 a.C., comenzó a emigrar al subcontinente de India. (pág. 59). **2.** para los nazis, los pueblos germanos que formaban una "raza maestra". (pág. 451)

assembly line [línea de montaje] *s.* en una fábrica, correa que lleva un producto de un trabajador a otro, cada uno de los cuales desempeña una sola tarea. (pág. 294)

assimilation [asimilación] *s.* política de una nación de obligar o alentar a un pueblo subyugado a adoptar sus instituciones y costumbres. (pág. 311)

Atlantic Charter [Carta del Atlántico] *s.* declaración de principios emitida en agosto de 1941 por el primer ministro británico Winston Churchill y el presidente de E.U.A. Franklin Roosevelt, en la cual se basó el plan de paz de los Aliados al final de la II Guerra Mundial. (pág. 446)

Atlantic slave trade [trata de esclavos del Atlántico] *s.* compra, transporte y venta de africanos para trabajar en las Américas. (pág. 116)

Axis Powers [Potencias del Eje] *s.* en la II Guerra Mundial, las naciones de Alemania, Italia y Japón, que formaron una alianza en 1936. (pág. 433)

B

balance of power [equilibrio de poder] *s.* situación política en que ninguna nación tiene suficiente poder para ser una amenaza para las demás. (pág. 213)

Balfour Declaration [Declaración de Balfour] *s.* declaración de que el gobierno de Gran Bretaña apoyaba el establecimiento de una patria nacional judía en Palestina, expresada en una carta de 1917 del secretario de relaciones exteriores, Sir Arthur Balfour. (pág. 521)

Balkans [Balcanes] *s.* región del sureste de Europa ocupada actualmente por Grecia, Albania, Bulgaria, Rumania, la parte eureopea de Turquía y las antiguas repúblicas de Yugoslavia. (pág. 229)

baroque [barroco] *s.* estilo grandioso y ornamentado del arte, la música y la arquitectura a fines del siglo 17 y principios del 18. (pág. 179)

Battle of Britain [Batalla Británica] *s.* batallas entre las fuerzas aéreas de Alemania y Gran Bretaña que se libraron sobre el territorio británico entre 1940–1941. (pág. 444)

Battle of Guadalcanal [Batalla de Guadalcanal] *s.* batalla de la II Guerra Mundial ocurrida en 1942–1943 en que las fuerzas aliadas expulsaron a las fuerzas japonesas de la isla de Guadalcanal en el Pacífico. (pág. 450)

Battle of Midway [Batalla del Midway] *s.* batalla aérea y naval de la II Guerra Mundial librada en 1941 en que las fuerzas estadounidenses derrotaron a las japonesas en el Pacífico central. (pág. 449)

Battle of Stalingrad [Batalla de Stalingrado] *s.* batalla de la II Guerra Mundial ocurrida en 1942–1943 en que las fuerzas alemanas perdieron y no lograron capturar la ciudad de Stalingrado en la Unión Soviética. (pág. 456)

Battle of the Bulge [Batalla del Bolsón] *s.* batalla de 1944–45 en que las fuerzas aliadas repulsaron la última ofensiva alemana de envergadura en la II Guerra Mundial. (pág. 459)

Battle of Trafalgar [Batalla de Trafalgar] *s.* batalla naval de 1805 en que las fuerzas de Napoleón fueron derrotadas por una flota inglesa al mando de Horacio Nelson. (pág. 207)

Berlin Conference of 1884–85 [Conferencia de Berlín de 1884] *s.* reunión en la cual representantes de las naciones europeas acordaron reglas para la colonización europea de África. (pág. 307)

bilateral aid [ayuda bilateral] *s.* dinero y recursos que ofrece directamente un gobierno a otro. (pág. 600)

Bill of Rights [Carta de Derechos] *s.* primeras diez enmiendas a la Constitución de E.U.A., que protegen los derechos y libertades básicos de los ciudadanos. (pág. 187)

biotechnology [biotecnología] *s.* investigación científica con sustancias biológicas, como enzimas o células, que busca nuevas aplicaciones. (pág. 590)

bio-weapons [armas biológicas] *s.* organismos vivos, como el ántrax, que se usan para matar o herir a mucha gente de una vez (pág. 605)

birth rate [tasa de nacimiento] *s.* número de niños nacidos por mujer. (pág. 595)

blitzkrieg *s.* "guerra relámpago"; táctica bélica de ataque sorpresa con aviones rápidos, seguidos de numerosas fuerzas de infantería. (pág. 442)

blockade [bloqueo] *s.*desplazamiento de tropas o barcos para impedir para evitar la entrada o salida de todo tráfico comercial a una ciudad o región. (pág. 209)

Boer [bóer] *s.*colono holandés que se estableció en Sudáfrica. (pág. 309)

Boer War [Guerra de los Bóers] *s.*conflicto de 1899 a 1902 entre los bóers y los británicos por el control de territorio en Sudáfrica. (pág. 309)

Bolsheviks [bolcheviques] *s.*grupo de marxistas revolucionarios rusos que tomó el control del gobierno ruso en noviembre de 1917. (pág. 390)

Boxer Rebellion [Rebelión de los Bóxers] *s.*rebelión de 1900 en China contra la influencia extranjera en el país. (pág. 339)

boyars [boyardos] *s.*nobles terratenientes de Rusia. (pág. 151)

brinkmanship [política arriesgada] *s.*política de amenazar con lanzarse a la guerra en respuesta a una agresión enemiga. (pág. 480)

Buddhism [budismo] *s.*religión iniciada por Siddharta Gautama (Buda) aproximadamente en 527 a.C; busca alcanzar la iluminación espiritual perfecta. (pág. 614)

C

cabinet [gabinete] *s.*grupo de asesores o ministros escogidos por el jefe de gobierno de un país para que participen en la toma de decisiones del gobierno. (pág. 159)

Calvinism [calvinismo] *s.*conjunto de enseñanzas religiosas basadas en las ideas del reformador Juan Calvino. (pág. 53)

Camp David Accords [Acuerdos de Camp David] *s.*primer tratado firmado entre Israel y un país árabe, en que el presidente Anwar Sadat de Egipto reconoció el derecho a existir de Israel y el primer ministro israelí Menachem Begin acordó devolver la península del Sinaí a Egipto. (pág. 523)

capitalism [capitalismo] *s.*sistema económico basado en la propiedad privada y en la inversión de dinero en empresas comerciales con el objetivo de obtener ganancias. (págs. 122, 267)

Catholic Reformation [Contrarreforma] *s.*movimiento del siglo 16 en el que la Iglesia Católica intentó reformarse en respuesta a la Reforma protestante. (pág. 55)

caudillo *s.*dictador militar de un país latinoamericano. (pág. 344)

Central Powers [Potencias Centrales] *s.*en la I Guerra Mundial, las naciones de Alemania y Austro-Hungría, y las demás que lucharon a su lado. (pág. 368)

CFCs [clorofluorocarbonos] *s.*químicos que se usan en equipos de aire acondicionado y otros productos. (pág. 593)

Chartist movement [movimiento cartista] *s.*movimiento de reforma inglés del siglo 19 en que miembros de la clase trabajadora pidieron reformas en el Parlamento y en las elecciones, como el voto para todos los hombres. (pág. 280)

checks and balances [control y compensación de poderes] *s.*medidas para evitar que una rama del gobierno domine sobre las otras. (págs. 186–187)

Christianity [cristianismo] *s.*religión monoteísta basada en la vida y las enseñanzas de Jesús, que empezó en el siglo 1 d.C. (pág. 13)

CIS [CEI] *s.*Comunidad de Estados Independientes: asociación de los antiguos territorios soviéticos formada cuando la Unión Soviética se desmembró. (pág. 548)

citizen [ciudadano] *s.*nacido en un estado o nación, lo que le concede ciertos derechos y privilegios. (pág. 25)

civil disobedience [desobediencia civil] *s.*negativa pública y deliberada a obedecer una ley considerada injusta. (pág. 406)

civil rights movement [movimiento de derechos civiles] *s.*lucha popular en Estados Unidos contra la discriminación y por lograr que todos los ciudadanos reciban los derechos garantizados en la Constitución. (pág. 574)

cloning [clonación] *s.*creación de plantas o animales genéticamente idénticos a plantas o animales existentes. (pág. 564)

coalition government [gobierno de coalición] *s.*gobierno controlado por una alianza temporal de varios partidos políticos. (pág. 421)

Cold War [Guerra Fría] *s.*estado de hostilidad diplomática entre Estados Unidos y la Unión Soviética en las décadas siguientes a la II Guerra Mundial. (pág. 479)

collective bargaining [contrato colectivo] *s.*negociaciones entre trabajadores y patrones. (pág. 270)

collective farm [granja colectiva] *s.*granja controlada por el gobierno, formada mediante la unión de muchas pequeñas granjas. (pág. 397)

colony [colonia] *s.*tierra controlada por una nación distante. (pág. 104)

Columbian Exchange [trasferencia colombina] *s.*trasferencia mundial de plantas, animales y enfermedades durante la colonización europea de América. (pág. 120)

command economy [economía de mando] *s.*sistema económico en el que el gobierno toma todas las decisiones económicas. (pág. 396)

Commercial Revolution [Revolución Comercial] *s.*expansión del comercio y los negocios que transformó las economías europeas en los siglos 16 y 17. (pág. 120)

Committee of Public Safety [Comité de Seguridad Pública] *s.*comité establecido durante la Revolución Francesa para identificar a los "enemigos del pueblo". (pág. 202)

common law [derecho tácito] *s.*conjunto de leyes inglesas establecidas a lo largo del tiempo por la costumbre y los principios, no por la voluntad de un gobernante o legislador. (pág. 18)

commune [comuna] *s.*en la China comunista, granja colectiva en la que mucha gente trabaja y vive junta. (pág. 484)

communism [comunismo] *s.*sistema económico en el que todos los medios de producción —tierras, minas, fábricas, ferrocarriles y negocios— son propiedad del pueblo, en que no existe la propiedad privada, y en que todos los productos y servicios se comparten por igual. (pág. 269)

Concert of Europe [Concierto de Europa] *s.*serie de alianzas entre naciones europeas en el siglo 19, ideadas por el príncipe Klemens von Metternich para impedir revoluciones. (pág. 215)

concordat [concordato] *s.*acuerdo firmado entre Napoleón y el Papa para establecer una nueva relación entre la Iglesia y el Estado. (pág. 206)

Confucianism [confucianismo] *s.*modo de vida basado en las enseñanzas de Confucio, un erudito chino. (pág. 624)

Congress of Vienna [Congreso de Viena] *s.*serie de reuniones en 1814–1815 en que los líderes europeos trataron de establecer una paz duradera después de la derrota de Napoléon. (pág. 213)

Congress Party [Partido dcsl Congreso] *s.*importante partido político de India; también se le conoce como el

Congreso Nacional de India. (pág. 506)

conquistadors [conquistadores] *s.*soldados, exploradores y aventureros españoles que participaron en la conquista de América en el siglo 16. (pág. 105)

conservatives [conservadores] *s.*en la primera mitad del siglo 19, los europeos —principalmente los terratenientes y nobles acaudalados— que querían preservar las monarquías tradicionales. (pág. 229)

constitutional monarchy [monarquía constitucional] *s.*monarquía en que el poder del gobernante está limitado por la ley. (pág. 159)

containment [contención] *s.*política exterior estadounidense adoptada por el presidente Harry Truman a fines de la década de 1940 para impedir la expansión del comunismo creando alianzas con países débiles y ayudándolos a contener los avances soviéticos. (pág. 477)

Continental System [Sistema Continental] *s.*política de Napoleón de impedir el comercio de Gran Bretaña con la Europa continental para destruir la economía británica. (pág. 209)

conventional weapons [armas convencionales] *s.*armas usuales de la guerra, como tanques, aviones, artillería y rifles. (pág. 602)

corporation [corporación] *s.*empresa de accionistas que comparten las ganancias pero que no son personalmente responsables de sus deudas. (pág. 265)

Council of Trent [Concilio de Trento] *s.*reunión de líderes de la Iglesia Católica Romana, convocada por el papa Pablo III, para fallar sobre varias doctrinas criticadas por los reformadores protestantes. (pág. 56)

coup d'etat [golpe de Estado] *s.*toma repentina del poder político de una nación. (pág. 205)

creoles [criollos] *s.*en la sociedad española colonial, los colonos nacidos en Latinoamérica de padres españoles. (pág. 224)

Crimean War [Guerra de Crimea] *s.*conflicto de 1853 a 1856, en el cual el imperio otomano, con ayuda de Gran Bretaña y Francia, frenó la expansión rusa en la región del mar Negro. (pág. 318)

crop rotation [rotación de cultivos] *s.*sistema que cultiva distintos productos en un campo cada año para conservar la fertilidad de la tierra. (pág. 253)

Cultural Revolution [Revolución Cultural] *s.*levantamiento de 1966–1976 en China, encabezado por los Guardias Rojos de Mao Tsetung, con el propósito de establecer una sociedad de campesinos y trabajadores donde todos fueran iguales. (pág. 485)

D

daimyo *s.*señor feudal de Japón que comandaba un ejército privado de samurais. (pág. 94)

D-Day [Día D] *s.*6 de junio de 1944; día elegido para la invasión aliada de Europa continental durante la II Guerra Mundial. (pág. 458)

Declaration of Independence [Declaración de Independencia] *s.*declaración de las razones de la ruptura de las colonias americanas con Gran Bretaña, aprobada por el Segundo Congreso Continental. (pág. 184)

Declaration of the Rights of Man [Declaración de los Derechos del Hombre] *s.*declaración de ideales revolucionarios adoptada por la Asamblea Nacional Francesa en 1789. (pág. 197)

demilitarization [desmilitarización] *s.*reducción de la capacidad bélica de un país que se logra desbandando sus fuerzas armadas y prohibiéndole que adquiera

armas. (pág. 464)

democracy [democracia] *s.*gobierno controlado por sus ciudadanos, bien sea directa o indirectamente, por medio de sus representantes. (pág. 5)

destalinization [desestalinización] *s.*política de Nikita Khrushchev para borrar a José Stalin y sus programas de la memoria de la Unión Soviética. (pág. 496)

détente *s.*política de reducir las tensiones de la Guerra Fría, adoptada por Estados Unidos durante la presidencia de Richard Nixon. (pág. 498)

developed nation [país desarrollado] *s.*nación con las instalaciones necesarias para la producción avanzada de productos manufacturados. (pág. 566)

developing nation [país en desarrollo] *s.*nación en vías de industrialización. (pág. 566)

devshirme *s.*en el imperio otomano, política de llevarse a los niños de los pueblos cristianos conquistados para entrenarlos como soldados musulmanes. (pág. 66)

direct democracy [democracia directa] *s.*gobierno en el cual los ciudadanos gobiernan directamente, no a través de sus representantes. (pág. 7)

dissident [disidente] *s.*opositor a la política oficial de un gobierno. (pág. 538)

divine right [derecho divino] *s.*noción de que los monarcas son representantes de Dios en la Tierra y, por lo tanto, sólo le deben responder a él. (pág. 137)

dominion [dominio] *s.*en el imperio británico, una nación (como Canadá) a la que se permitía gobernar sus asuntos internos. (pág. 285)

domino theory [teoría del dominó] *s.*noción de que si una nación cae bajo control comunista, los países vecinos también lo harán. (pág. 488)

Dreyfus affair [caso Dreyfus] *s.*controversia surgida en Francia en la década de 1890 por el juicio y encarcelamiento del capitán Alfred Dreyfus, oficial judío falsamente acusado de vender secretos militares a Alemania. (pág. 283)

due process of law [proceso legal establecido] *s.*administración del derecho conforme a principios legales establecidos para proteger los derechos del individuo. (pág. 18)

Duma *s.*parlamento nacional ruso formado a principios del siglo 20. (pág. 391)

Dutch East India Company [Compañía Holandesa de las Indias Orientales] *s.*empresa fundada por holandeses a principios del siglo 17 para establecer y dirigir comercio por todo Asia. (pág. 88)

E

Eastern Front [Frente Oriental] *s.*en la I Guerra Mundial, región a lo largo de la frontera ruso-alemana donde rusos y servios pelearon contra alemanes, austriacos y turcos. (pág. 370)

Edict of Nantes [Edicto de Nantes] *s.*declaración en que el rey francés Enrique IV prometió que los protestantes podían vivir en paz en Francia y tener centros de veneración en algunas ciudades. (pág. 138)

Emancipation Proclamation [Proclama de Emancipación] *s.*declaración emitida por el presidente Abraham Lincoln en 1862, asentando la libertad de todos los esclavos de los estados confederados. (pág. 291)

émigrés *s.*quienes abandonan su país de origen por razones políticas, como los nobles y otros que huyeron de Francia durante los levantamientos campesinos de la Revolución Francesa. (pág. 199)

enclosure [cercado] *s.*uno de los campos rodeados de

cercas o de arbustos que crearon terratenientes británicos ricos en tierras que antes trabajaban los campesinos. (pág. 253)

encomienda *s.*tierras otorgadas por España a un colonizador de América, con el derecho de hacer trabajar a los amerindios que vivían en ellas. (pág. 106)

English Civil War [Guerra Civil Inglesa] *s.*conflicto de 1642 a 1649 en que los seguidores puritanos del Parlamento lucharon contra los defensores de la monarquía de Inglaterra. (pág. 157)

enlightened despot [déspota ilustrado] *s.*uno de los monarcas europeos del siglo 18 inspirados por las ideas de la Ilustración a gobernar con justicia y respeto a los derechos de sus súbditos. (pág. 181)

Enlightenment [Ilustración] *s.*movimiento del siglo 18 en Europa que trató de aplicar los principios de la razón y el método científico a todos los aspectos de la sociedad. (pág. 171)

entrepreneur [empresario] *s.*persona que organiza, administra y asume los riesgos de un negocio. (pág. 256)

estate [estado] *s.*una de las tres clases sociales existentes en Francia antes de la Revolución Francesa; el primer estado era el de la clerecía; el segundo era el de la nobleza; y el tercero era del resto de la población. (pág. 193)

Estates-General [Estados Generales] *s.*asamblea de representantes de los tres estados, o clases sociales, de Francia. (pág. 195)

ethnic cleansing [limpia étnica] *s.*política de asesinatos y otros actos de brutalidad con que los servios quisieron eliminar la población musulmana de Bosnia después de la división de Yugoslavia. (pág. 549)

existentialism [existencialismo] *s.*filosofía basada en la idea de que el ser humano da significado a su vida con sus decisiones y acciones. (pág. 416)

extraterritorial rights [derechos extraterritoriales] *s.*exención a los extranjeros de las leyes de un país. (pág. 336)

F

factors of production [factores de producción] *s.*recursos —como tierra, mano de obra y capital— necesarios para producir bienes y servicios. (pág. 254)

factory [fábrica] *s.*construcción amplia en que se manufacturan productos con maquinaria. (pág. 255)

fascism [fascismo] *s.*movimiento político que postula una forma extrema de nacionalismo, la supresión de los derechos individuales y un régimen dictatorial de un solo partido. (pág. 427)

favorable balance of trade [balanza comercial favorable] *s.*situación económica en la cual un país exporta más de lo que importa, es decir, que vende más productos de los que compra en el extranjero. (pág. 122)

federal system [sistema federal] *s.*sistema de gobierno en el que el poder se divide entre una autoridad central y varios estados. (págs. 187, 537)

feudalism [feudalismo] *s.*sistema político en el cual a los nobles se les otorga el uso de tierras de propiedad del rey, a cambio de lealtad, servicio militar y protección de sus habitantes. (pág. 17)

Final Solution [solución final] *s.*programa de Hitler de asesinar sistemáticamente a todo el pueblo judío. (pág. 453)

FLN *s.*Frente de Liberación Nacional: grupo de Argelia que libró una lucha de guerrillas buscando independizarse de Francia. (pág. 519)

Four Modernizations [cuatro modernizaciones] *s.*serie de objetivos adoptados por el líder chino Deng Xiaoping a finales del siglo 20 con miras al progreso en agricultura, industria, defensa, y ciencia y tecnología. (pág. 552)

Fourteen Points [los catorce puntos] *s.*serie de propuestas en que el presidente estadounidense Woodrow Wilson esbozó un plan para alcanzar una paz duradera después de la I Guerra Mundial. (pág. 380)

free trade [libre comercio] *s.*comercio entre naciones sin restricciones o barreras económicas (tales como aranceles). (pág. 567)

French and Indian War [Guerra contra Franceses e Indígenas] *s.*conflicto entre Gran Bretaña y Francia por control de territorio en Norteamérica, de 1754 a 1763. (pág. 113)

French Revolution [Revolución Francesa] *s.*guerra por la democracia que empezó en 1789 y terminó con la caída de la monarquía. (pág. 25)

fundamentalism [fundamentalismo] *s.*creencia estricta en las verdades básicas y en las prácticas de una religión. (pág. 573)

G

genetic engineering [ingeniería genética] *s.*transferencia de genes de un organismo a otro para producir un organismo con nuevos rasgos. (pág. 564)

genocide [genocidio] *s.*matanza sistemática de todo un pueblo. (pág. 453)

geopolitics [geopolítica] *s.*política exterior basada en una consideración de la ubicación estratégica o de los productos de otras tierras. (pág. 318)

ghazi *s.*guerrero del islam. (pág. 63)

ghettos *s.*barrios en que tenían que vivir los judíos europeos. (pág. 452)

glasnost *s.*política soviética de "apertura" a la libre circulación de ideas e información introducida en 1985 por Mijail Gorbachev. (pág 541)

global economy [economía global] *s.*todas las interacciones financieras —entre individuos, empresas y gobiernos— que rebasan fronteras internacionales. (pág. 567)

Glorious Revolution [Revolución Gloriosa] *s.*derrocamiento incruento del rey Jacobo II de Inglaterra, quien fue reemplazado por Guillermo y María. (pág. 159)

government [gobierno] *s.*sistema político para el ejercicio de la autoridad. (pág. 5)

grassroots development [desarrollo de base] *s.*programa que ayuda a los individuos y las comunidades a usar métodos básicos para mejorar la vida. (pág. 600)

Great Depression [Gran Depresión] *s.*crisis económica aguda que siguió a la caída del mercado de valores en 1929. (pág. 424)

Great Fear [Gran Miedo] *s.*ola de temor insensato que se extendió por las provincias francesas después de la toma de la Bastilla en 1789. (pág. 196)

Great Purge [Gran Purga] *s.*campaña de terror en la Unión Soviética durante la década de 1930, en la cual José Stalin trató de eliminar a todos los miembros del Partido Comunista y ciudadanos que amenazaban su poder. (pág. 397)

Great Trek [Gran Jornada] *s.*salida de colonos holandeses de territorio controlado por los británicos en Sudáfrica durante la década de 1830. (pág. 309)

green revolution [revolución verde] *s.*esfuerzo en el siglo 20 de aumentar los alimentos en el mundo entero, a través del uso de fertilizantes y pesticidas, y de la creación de cultivos resistentes a enfermedades. (pág. 564)

greenhouse effect [efecto invernadero] *s.*problemas causados por la emisión de dióxido de carbono y otros gases; también se llama calentamiento global. (pág. 592)

guerrilla [guerrillero] *s.*miembro de una unidad de combate informal que ataca por sorpresa las tropas enemigas que ocupan su país. (pág. 210)

guillotine [guillotina] *s.*máquina para decapitar con que se hicieron ejecuciones durante la Revolución Francesa. (pág. 200)

Gulf War [Guerra del Golfo] *s.*conflicto de 1991 en que fuerzas de la ONU derrotaron las fuerzas de Iraq que invadieron a Kuwait y amenazaban invadir a Arabia Saudita. (pág. 569)

Gutenberg Bible [Biblia de Gutenberg] *s.*primer libro completo impreso con tipos móviles y prensa de imprenta. (pág. 46)

H

habeas corpus *s.*documento que requiere que un detenido comparezca ante un tribunal o juez para que se determine si su detención es legal. (pág. 158)

haiku *s.*poema japonés que tiene tres versos no rimados de cinco, siete y cinco sílabas. (pág. 96)

heliocentric theory [teoría heliocéntrica] *s.*idea de que la Tierra y los otros planetas giran en torno al Sol. (pág. 166)

Hinduism [hinduismo] *s.*religión que empezó en India; predica la reencarnación y la interconexión de todos los seres vivos. (pág. 618)

Holocaust [Holocausto] *s.*matanza en masa de judíos y otros civiles, ejecutada por el gobierno de la Alemania nazi, antes y durante la II Guerra Mundial. (pág. 451)

Holy Alliance [Alianza Sagrada] *s.*liga de naciones europeas formada por los dirigentes de Rusia, Austria y Prusia después del Congreso de Viena. (pág. 215)

home rule [autogobierno] *s.*control sobre asuntos internos que da el gobierno a los residentes de una región. (pág. 288)

Hubble Space Telescope [telescopio espacial Hubble] *s.*potente telescopio puesto en órbita alrededor de la Tierra por NASA y la Agencia Europea del Espacio (AEE) en 1990. (pág. 562)

humanism [humanismo] *s.*movimiento intelectual del Renacimiento que estudió los textos clásicos y se enfocó en el potencial y los logros humanos. (pág. 38)

Hundred Days [Cien Días] *s.*corto período de 1815 en que Napoleón hizo su último intento de recuperar el poder, depuso al rey francés y de nuevo se proclamó emperador de Francia. (pág. 212)

I

imperialism [imperialismo] *s.*política en que una nación fuerte buscar dominar la vida política, económica y social de otros países. (pág. 306)

impressionism [impresionismo] *s.*movimiento de la pintura del siglo 19 en reacción al realismo, que buscaba dar impresiones personales de sujetos o momentos. (pág. 243)

indulgence [indulgencia] *s.*perdón que libera al pecador de la penitencia por un pecado. (pág. 49)

industrialization [industrialización] *s.*desarrollo de industrias para la producción con máquinas. (pág. 254)

Industrial Revolution [Revolución Industrial] *s.*cambio, que comenzó en Inglaterra durante el siglo 18, de la producción manual a la producción con máquinas. (pág. 253)

intendant [intendente] *s.*funcionario del gobierno francés nombrado por el monarca para recaudar impuestos e impartir justicia. (pág. 140)

International Monetary Fund [Fondo Monetario Internacional] *s.*organización multinacional que ofrece préstamos de emergencia a países en crisis financieras. (pág. 600)

Internet *s.*vinculación de redes de computadora que permite a gente de todo el mundo comunicarse e intercambiar información. (pág. 563)

investment capital [capital de inversión] *s.*fondos necesarios para el crecimiento económico a fin de construir industrias e infraestructura, como carreteras y puentes. (pág. 599)

iron curtain [cortina de hierro] *s.*durante la Guerra Fría, división que separaba las naciones comunistas de Europa oriental de las naciones democráticas de Europa occidental. (pág. 477)

Islam [islam] *s.*religión monoteísta que se desarrolló en Arabia en el siglo 7 d.C. (pág. 234)

isolationism [aislacionismo] *s.*política de evitar lazos políticos o militares con otros países. (pág. 434)

J

janissary [janísero] *s.*miembro de una fuerza élite de soldados del imperio otomano. (pág. 86)

jazz *s.*estilo de música popular del siglo 20 concebido principalmente por músicos afroamericanos. (pág. 417)

Jesuits [jesuitas] *s.*miembros de la Sociedad de Jesús, orden católica romana fundada por Ignacio de Loyola. (pág. 55)

"jewel in the crown" ["joya de la corona"] *s.*colonia británica de India, así llamada por su importancia para el imperio británico, tanto como proveedor de materia prima como mercado para sus productos. (pág. 321)

joint-stock company [sociedad de capitales] *s.*negocio en el que los inversionistas reúnen capital para un propósito común y después comparten las ganancias. (pág. 122)

Judaism [judaísmo] *s.*religión monoteísta de los hebreos, creada por Abraham alrededor del año 2000 a.C. (pág. 12)

K

kabuki *s.*forma de teatro japonés en que se representa una historia con música, danza y mímica. (pág. 96)

kaiser *s.*emperador alemán (del título romano *Caesar*). (pág. 238)

kamikaze *s.*durante la II Guerra Mundial, pilotos suicidas japoneses entrenados para hundir barcos de los Aliados lanzándose sobre ellos con aviones llenos de bombas. (pág. 461)

Khmer Rouge *s.*grupo de rebeldes comunistas que tomaron el poder en Camboya en 1975. (pág. 490)

Kristallnacht *s.*"Noche de cristales rotos": noche del 9 de noviembre de 1938, en que milicianos nazis atacaron hogares, negocios y sinagogas judíos en toda Alemania. (pág. 451)

kulak *s.*miembro de una clase de campesinos ricos en Rusia. (pág. 397)

Kuomintang *s.*Partido Nacionalista de China, formado después de la caída de la dinastía Qing en 1912. (pág. 401)

laissez faire s.idea de que el gobierno no debe regular ni interferir en las industrias y empresas. (pág. 267)

land reform [reforma agraria] s.redistribución de tierras agrícolas con división de grandes latifundios y reparto de fincas a campesinos. (pág. 532)

La Reforma s.movimiento de reforma liberal en el siglo 19 en México fundado por Benito Juárez. (pág. 350)

League of Nations [Liga de las Naciones] s.organización internacional formada después de la I Guerra Mundial cuyo propósito era mantener la paz entre las naciones. (pág. 381)

lebensraum s."espacio vital": territorio adicional que, según Adolfo Hitler, Alemania necesitaba porque estaba sobrepoblada. (pág. 429)

Legislative Assembly [Asamblea Legislativa] s.congreso creado por la Constitución francesa de 1791, con poder para emitir leyes y aprobar declaraciones de guerra. (pág. 198)

legitimacy [legitimidad] s.derecho hereditario de un monarca a gobernar. (pág. 214)

less developed countries [países menos desarrollados] s. países que no están completamente industrializados. (pág. 599)

liberals [liberales] s.en la primera mitad del siglo 19, europeos —principalmente empresarios y comerciantes de clase media— que deseaban darle más poder político a los parlamentos elegidos. (pág. 229)

Long March [Larga Marcha] s.viaje de 6,000 millas que realizaron en 1934–35 las fuerzas comunistas de China para escapar de las fuerzas nacionalistas de Jiang Jieshi. (pág. 404)

Lutheran [luterano] s.miembro de una iglesia protestante basada en las enseñanzas de Martín Lutero. (pág. 50)

lycée [liceo] s.escuela pública en Francia. (pág. 205)

Magna Carta [Carta Magna] s."Gran Carta": documento de Inglaterra que garantiza derechos políticos elementales, elaborado por nobles ingleses y aprobado por el rey Juan en 1215 d.C. (pág. 17)

Manchus [manchú] s.pueblo originario de Manchuria que gobernó en China durante la dinastía Qing (1644–1912). (pág. 91)

manifest destiny [destino manifiesto] s.idea popular en el siglo 19 en Estados Unidos de que era su derecho y obligación regir Norteamérica, desde el océano Atlántico hasta el Pacífico. (pág. 290)

Maori [maorí] s.miembro de un pueblo polinesio establecido en Nueva Zelanda hacia 800 d.C. (pág. 285)

Marshall Plan [Plan Marshall] programa estadounidense de ayuda económica a países europeos para su reconstrucción después de la II Guerra Mundial. (pág. 478)

martial law [ley marcial] s.gobierno militar temporal impuesto a la población civil, normalmente en época de guerra o de trastornos civiles. (pág. 537)

mass culture [cultura de masas] s.producción de obras de arte y diversión concebidas con el fin de atraer a un amplio público. (pág. 294)

mass media [medios informativos] s.medios de comunicación pública, como televisión, radio, cine, música y la prensa popular. (pág. 590)

materialism [materialismo] s.alto interés en la adquisición de posesiones materiales. (pág. 580)

Mau Mau [Mau-mau] s.sociedad secreta de miembros de la tribu kikuyu que trataron de expulsar a los británicos de Kenia a mediados del siglo 20. (pág. 517)

May Fourth Movement [Movimiento del 4 de Mayo] s.protesta nacional china en 1919 con manifestaciones contra el Tratado de Versalles y la interferencia extranjera. (pág. 402)

Meiji era [era Meiji] s.período de la historia japonesa entre 1867 y 1912, cuando gobernó el emperador Mutshito. (pág. 341)

Mein Kampf [Mi lucha] s.libro escrito por Adolfo Hitler en prisión (1923–1924), en el cual expone sus creencias y sus ideales para Alemania. (pág. 429)

mercantilism [mercantilismo] s.política económica de aumentar la riqueza y poder de una nación obteniendo grandes cantidades de oro y plata, y vendiendo más bienes de los que se compran. (pág. 122)

mestizo s.mezcla de español y amerindio. (pág. 106)

middle class [clase media] s.clase social formada por trabajadores especializados, profesionales, comerciantes y granjeros acaudalados. (pág. 259)

middle passage [travesía intermedia] s.viaje que trajo a africanos capturados al Caribe y, posteriormente, a América del Norte y del Sur, para venderlos como esclavos; recibió este nombre porque era considerada la porción media del triángulo comercial trasatlántico. (pág. 117)

militarism [militarismo] s.política de glorificar el poder militar y de mantener un ejército permanente, siempre preparado para luchar. (pág. 364)

Ming Dynasty [dinastía Ming] s.dinastía que reinó en China desde 1368 hasta 1644. (pág. 89)

Model Parliament [Parlamento Modelo] s.reunión de lores, caballeros y burgueses convocada por el rey Edward I en 1295 para dar su voto sobre impuestos y reformas. Sentó una norma para los parlamentos futuros (pág. 18)

monarchy [monarquía] s.gobierno en que el poder está en manos de una sola persona. (pág. 7)

Monroe Doctrine [doctrina Monroe] s.política estadounidense de oposición a la interferencia europea en Latinoamérica, anunciada por el presidente James Monroe en 1823. (pág. 346)

Mughal [mogol] s.uno de los nómadas que invadieron el subcontinente de India en el siglo 16 y establecieron un poderoso imperio. (pág. 71)

mulattos [mulatos] s.personas de ascendencia europea y africana. (pág. 224)

multilateral aid [ayuda multilateral] s.dinero y recursos que ofrece una organización de muchos miembros. (pág. 600)

multinational corporation [corporación trasnacional] s.empresa que opera en numerosos países. (pág. 567)

Munich Conference [Conferencia de Munich] s.reunión en 1938 de Inglaterra, Francia, Italia y Alemania, en la cual Gran Bretaña y Francia aceptaron que la Alemania nazi anexara parte de Checoslovaquia, a cambio de la promesa de Adolfo Hitler de respetar las nuevas fronteras checas. (pág. 435)

Muslim League [Liga Musulmana] s.organización formada en 1906 para proteger los intereses de los musulmanes de India; más adelante propuso la división del país en una nación hindú y una nación musulmana. (pág. 506)

Napoleonic Code [código napoleónico] s.sistema extenso y uniforme de leyes establecido para Francia por Napoleón. (pág. 206)

National Assembly [Asamblea Nacional] s.congreso

francés establecido el 17 de junio de 1789 por representantes del Tercer Estado para promulgar leyes y reformas en nombre del pueblo. (pág. 195)

nationalism [nacionalismo] *s.*creencia de que la principal lealtad del pueblo debe ser a su nación —es decir, a la gente con quien comparte historia y cultura— y no al rey o al imperio. (pág. 229)

nation-state [nación Estado] *s.*nación independiente de gente que tiene una cultura e identidad común. (pág. 229)

NATO [OTAN] *s.*Organización del Tratado del Atlántico Norte: alianza militar defensiva formada en 1949 por diez naciones de Europa occidental, Estados Unidos y Canadá. (pág. 479)

natural laws [leyes naturales] *s.*patrones y explicaciones del mundo a los que se llega por medio de la razón y la inteligencia; propuestos por los griegos en lugar de la superstición y las explicaciones tradicionales del mundo. (pág. 7)

natural rights [derechos naturales] *s.*derechos con los que nacen todos los individuos, conforme a John Locke: vida, libertad y propiedad. (pág. 171)

Nazism [nazismo] *s.*políticas fascistas del Partido Nacional socialista de los Trabajadores de Alemania, basadas en el totalitarismo, la creencia en superioridad racial y el control estatal de la industria. (pág. 428)

Negritude movement [movimiento de negritud] *s.*movimiento de africanos de lengua francesa que celebra el legado de la cultura tradicional africana y sus valores. (pág. 516)

neoclassical [neoclásico] *adj.* relacionado con un estilo sencillo y elegante (inspirado en ideas y temas de la antigua Grecia y Roma) que caracterizó las artes en Europa a fines del siglo 18. (pág. 179)

New Deal *s.*programa de reformas económicas del presidente Franklin D. Roosevelt ideado para solucionar los problemas creados por la Gran Depresión. (pág. 426)

nonaggression pact [pacto de no agresión] *s.*acuerdo en que dos o más naciones prometen no atacarse. (pág. 441)

nonaligned nations [países no alineados] *s.*naciones independientes que permanecieron neutrales durante la Guerra Fría entre Estados Unidos y la Unión Soviética. (pág. 491)

non-renewable energy [energía renovable] *s.*formas de energía que provienen de fuentes que se pueden usar repetidamente, como el viento, el agua y el Sol. (pág. 594)

Nuclear Non-Proliferation Treaty [Tratado de No Proliferación Nuclear] *s.*acuerdo de 1968 ideado para reducir la diseminación de las armas nucleares. (pág. 573)

Nuremberg Trials [juicios de Nuremberg] *s.*serie de juicios realizados en Nuremberg, Alemania, tras la II Guerra Mundial a líderes nazis por agresión, violación a las leyes de guerra y crímenes contra la humanidad. (pág. 463)

O

Old Regime [antiguo régimen] *s.*sistema político y social que existía en Francia antes de la Revolución Francesa. (pág. 193)

Open Door Policy [política de puertas abiertas] *s.*política propuesta por E.U.A. en 1899, que postulaba que todas las naciones tuvieran las mismas oportunidades de comerciar con China. (pág. 338)

Opium War [Guerra del Opio] *s.*conflicto entre Inglaterra y China, de 1830 a 1842, por el comercio inglés de opio en China. (pág. 336)

ozone layer [capa de ozono] *s.*capa de la atmósfera superior de la Tierra que protege a los seres vivos de los rayos ultravioleta de la luz solar. (pág. 569)

P

Pacific Rim [Cuenca del Pacífico] *s.*tierras que bordean el océano Pacífico, especialmente las de Asia. (pág. 326)

Panama Canal [canal de Panamá] *s.*vía marítima que une al océano Atlántico con el Pacífico, construida en Panamá por Estados Unidos y terminada en 1914. (pág. 347)

parliament [parlamento] *s.*cuerpo de representantes que promulga las leyes de una nación. (pág. 354)

partition [partición] *s.*división en partes, como la división en 1947 de la colonia británica de India en dos naciones: India y Paquistán. (pág. 506)

paternalism [paternalismo] *s.*política de tratar a los gobernados como si fueran niños, atendiendo a sus necesidades pero sin darles derechos. (pág. 311)

patron [mecenas] *s.*persona que apoya a los artistas, especialmente, en el aspecto financiero. (pág. 38)

Peace of Augsburg [Paz de Augsburgo] *s.*acuerdo realizado en 1555 que declaró que la religión de cada Estado alemán sería decidida por su gobernante. (pág. 50)

penal colony [colonia penal] *s.*colonia a donde se mandan convictos como alternativa a una prisión. (pág. 665)

peninsulares *s.*en la sociedad española colonial, colonos nacidos en España. (pág. 224)

Peninsular War [Guerra Peninsular] *s.*conflicto de 1808–1813 en que los rebeldes españoles lucharon con la ayuda de Gran Bretaña para expulsar de España las tropas de Napoleón. (pág. 210)

perestroika *s.*reestructuración de la economía soviética para permitir mayor poder de decisión local, iniciada por Mijail Gorbachev en 1985. (pág. 542)

perspective [perspectiva] *s.*técnica artística que crea la apariencia de tres dimensiones en una superficie plana. (pág. 39)

philosophe *s.*miembro de un grupo de pensadores sociales de la Ilustración en Francia. (pág. 172)

philosophers [filósofos] *s.*pensadores que investigan la naturaleza del universo, la sociedad humana y la moral a través de la lógica y la razón. (pág. 7)

Pilgrims [peregrinos] *s.*grupo que en 1620 fundó la colonia de Plymouth en Massachusetts para escapar de persecución religiosa en Inglaterra. (pág. 111)

plebiscite [plebiscito] *s.*voto directo mediante el cual la población de un país tiene la oportunidad de aceptar o rechazar una propuesta. (pág. 205)

PLO [OLP] *s.*Organización de Liberación Palestina: organización dedicada a establecer un Estado independiente para los palestinos en el Medio Oriente. (pág. 525)

pogrom *s.*campaña organizada de violencia contra las comunidades judías en Rusia a finales del siglo 19. (pág. 389)

Politburo [Politburó] *s.*comité dirigente del Partido Comunista en la Unión Soviética. (pág. 541)

popular culture [cultura popular] *s.*elementos culturales —deportes, música, cine, ropa, etc.— que muestran los antecedentes comunes de un grupo y sus intereses cambiantes. (pág. 577)

predestination [predestinación] *s.*doctrina que postula que Dios ha decidido todo de antemano, incluso quiénes obtendrán la salvación eterna. (pág. 53)

Presbyterian [presbiteriano] *s.* miembro de una iglesia protestante gobernada por presbíteros conforme a las enseñanzas de John Knox. (pág. 53)

PRI *s.* Partido Revolucionario Institucional: principal partido político en México. (pág. 534)

printing press [prensa de imprenta] *s.* máquina para reproducir material escrito oprimiendo papel contra una bandeja de tipos móviles entintados. (pág. 46)

proliferation [proliferación] *s.* crecimiento o expansión, especialmente la expansión de armas nucleares a naciones que actualmente no las tienen. (pág. 573)

propaganda *s.* información o material distribuido para apoyar una causa o socavar una causa opuesta. (pág. 376)

prophet [profeta] *s.* líder o director espiritual, considerado mensajero de Dios. (pág. 13)

Protestant [protestante] *s.* miembro de una iglesia cristiana fundada de acuerdo a los principios de la Reforma. (pág. 50)

provisional government [gobierno provisional] *s.* gobierno temporal. (pág. 392)

psychology [psicología] *s.* estudio de la mente y la conducta humanas. (pág. 299)

Puritans [puritanos] *s.* grupo que, para liberarse de la persecución religiosa en Inglaterra, fundó una colonia en la bahía de Massachusetts a principios del siglo 17. (pág. 111)

Q

Qing Dynasty [dinastía Qing] *s.* última dinastía china; reinó de 1644 a 1912. (pág. 91)

R

racism [racismo] *s.* creencia de que una raza es superior a otras. (pág. 306)

radicals [radicales] *s.* en la primera mitad del siglo 19, los europeos a favor de cambios drásticos para extender la democracia a toda la población. (pág. 229)

radioactivity [radioactividad] *s.* forma de energía liberada mediante la descomposición de átomos. (pág. 298)

Raj *s.* porciones de India controladas por Gran Bretaña de 1757 a 1947. (pág. 324)

rationing [racionamiento] *s.* limitación de la cantidad de bienes que la población puede comprar, generalmente impuesta por un gobierno durante una guerra debido a escasez. (pág. 375)

realism [realismo] *s.* movimiento artístico del siglo 19 en que los escritores y pintores trataron de mostrar la vida como es, no como debiera ser. (pág. 241)

realpolitik *s.* "política de la realidad"; posición política dura que no da lugar al idealismo. (pág. 237)

recession [recesión] *s.* descenso de la economía de una nación. (pág. 533)

Red Guards [Guardias Rojos] *s.* unidades de milicianos formadas por jóvenes chinos en 1966 en respuesta al llamado de Mao Zedong a llevar a cabo una revolución social y cultural. (pág. 485)

Red Shirts [Camisas Rojas] *s.* seguidores del líder nacionalista italiano del siglo 19 Giuseppe Garibaldi. (pág. 236)

Reformation [Reforma] *s.* movimiento del siglo 16 para realizar cambios religiosos que llevó a la fundación de iglesias cristianas que rechazaron la autoridad del Papa. (pág. 49)

Reign of Terror [Régimen del Terror] *s.* período entre 1793–1794 en que Maximilien Robespierre gobernó a Francia casi como dictador, durante el cual fueron ejecutados miles de personajes políticos y de ciudadanos comunes. (pág. 202)

Renaissance [Renacimiento] *s.* período de la historia europea de aproximadamente 1300 a 1600, durante el cual renació un interés en la cultura clásica que generó importantes cambios en el arte, la educación y la visión del mundo. (pág. 37)

renewable energy [energía renovable] *s.* formas de energía que provienen de fuentes que se pueden usar repetidamente, como el viento, el agua y el Sol. (pág. 594)

representative government [gobierno representativo] *s.* gobierno en que los ciudadanos eligen representantes para formular leyes y políticas en su nombre. (pág. 25)

republic [república] *s.* forma de gobierno en que el poder está en manos de representantes y líderes elegidos por los ciudadanos. (pág. 8)

Restoration [Restauración] *s.* en Inglaterra, período del reinado de Carlos II, después del colapso del gobierno de Oliver Cromwell. (pág. 158)

reunification [reunificación] *s.* proceso de unir dos elementos que estaban separados, como la reunificación de Alemania oriental y Alemania occidental en 1990. (pág. 544)

Roman Catholic Church [Iglesia Católica Romana] *s.* iglesia cristiana que se fundó el año 1054 d.C. (pág. 14)

romanticism [romanticismo] *s.* movimiento de principios del siglo 19 en el arte y las ideas que recalca la emoción y la naturaleza, más que la razón y la sociedad. (pág. 239)

Roosevelt Corollary [corolario Roosevelt] *s.* ampliación de la doctrina Monroe, emitida por el presidente Theodore Roosevelt en 1904, en que declaró que Estados Unidos tenía el derecho de ejercer "poderes policiales" en el hemisferio occidental. (pág. 347)

Russo-Japanese War [Guerra Ruso-Japonesa] *s.* conflicto de 1904–1905 entre Rusia y Japón, causada por el interés de los dos países de dominar Manchuria y Corea. (pág. 343)

S

Safavid [safávido] *s.* miembro de una dinastía musulmana shi'a que construyó un imperio en Persia del siglo 16 al 18. (pág. 69)

salon [salón] *s.* reunión social de intelectuales y artistas, como las que celebraban en sus hogares señoras acaudaladas de París y otras ciudades europeas durante la Ilustración. (pág. 178)

SALT *s.* Conversaciones para la Limitación de Armas Estratégicas: serie de reuniones durante la década de 1970 en que líderes de Estados Unidos y la Unión Soviética acordaron limitar el número de armas nucleares de sus países. (pág. 499)

sans-culottes *s.* en la Revolución Francesa, grupo político radical de parisienses asalariados y pequeños comerciantes que anhelaban más voz en el gobierno, bajas de precios y fin a la escasez de alimentos. (pág. 199)

Schlieffen Plan [Plan Schlieffen] *s.* plan militar alemán al comienzo de la I Guerra Mundial, que preveía que Alemania derrotaría rápidamente a Francia y después atacaría a Rusia en el este. (pág. 367)

scientific method [método científico] *s.* procedimiento lógico para reunir información sobre el mundo natural, en que se usa experimentación y observación para poner a prueba hipótesis. (pág. 167)

Scientific Revolution [Revolución Científica] *s.* profundo cambio en el pensamiento europeo que comenzó a mediados del siglo 16, en que el estudio del mundo natural se caracterizó por cuidadosa observación y cuestionamiento de teorías aceptadas. (pág. 165)

scorched-earth policy [política de arrasamiento de campos] *s.* práctica de quemar campos de cultivo y de matar ganado durante la guerra para que el enemigo no pueda vivir de las tierras. (pág. 210)

secede [seceder] *v.* retirarse formalmente de una asociación o alianza. (pág. 290)

secular *adj.* relacionado con lo mundano más que con los asuntos espirituales. (pág. 38)

segregation [segregación] *s.* separación legal o social de gente de diferentes razas. (pág. 292)

self-determination [autodeterminación] *s.* libertad de un pueblo para decidir libremente la forma de gobierno que desea. (pág. 380)

senate [senado] *s.* en la antigua Roma, organismo supremo de gobierno formado inicialmente sólo por aristócratas. (pág. 9)

separation of powers [separación de poderes] *s.* división de poderes del gobierno en ejecutivo, legislativo y judicial. (pág. 173)

sepoy [cipayo] *s.* soldado hindú bajo el mando británico. (pág. 321)

Sepoy Mutiny [Motín de Cipayos] *s.* rebelión de 1857 de soldados hindúes y musulmanes contra los británicos en India. (pág. 323)

Seven Years' War [Guerra de los Siete Años] *s.* conflicto en Europa, Norteamérica e India de 1756 a 1763, en que las fuerzas de Inglaterra y Prusia lucharon con las de Austria, Francia, Rusia y otros países. (pág. 150)

"shock therapy" [terapia de shock] *s.* programa económico implementado en Rusia por Boris Yeltsin en la década de 1990, que implicó un cambio abrupto de una economía de mando a una economía de mercado libre. (pág. 548)

Sikh [sikh] *s.* miembro de un grupo religioso no violento cuyas creencias combinaban elementos del budismo, el hinduismo y el sufismo. (pág. 74)

Six-Day War [Guerra de los Seis Días] *s.* breve conflicto en 1967 entre Israel y varios países árabes, durante el cual Israel se apoderó de Jerusalén, la península del Sinaí, la meseta de Golán y Cisjordania. (pág. 523)

skepticism [escepticismo] *s.* filosofía basada en la noción de que nada puede saberse con certeza. (pág. 139)

social contract [contrato social] *s.* acuerdo mediante el cual el pueblo define y limita sus derechos individuales, creando así una sociedad o gobierno organizados. (pág. 171)

Social Darwinism [darvinismo social] *s.* aplicación de las teorías de Charles Darwin sobre la evolución y la "sobrevivencia del más apto" a las sociedades humanas, particularmente como justificación para la expansión imperialista. (pág. 306)

socialism [socialismo] *s.* sistema económico en el cual los factores de producción son propiedad del pueblo y se administran para el bienestar de todos. (pág. 268)

socialist realism [realismo socialista] *s.* estilo artístico que exalta los valores comunistas y la vida bajo el comunismo. (pág. 398)

Solidarity [Solidaridad] *s.* sindicato polaco de trabajadores que presentó la principal fuerza de oposición al gobierno comunista en Polonia en la década de 1980. (pág. 542)

soviet *s.* consejo local de representantes formado en Rusia después de la caída del zar Nicolás II. (pág. 392)

Spanish-American War [Guerra Hispano-Americana] *s.* conflicto de 1898 entre Estados Unidos y España, en que Estados Unidos apoyó la lucha de independencia cubana. (pág. 346)

sphere of influence [esfera de influencia] *s.* región extranjera en que una nación controla el comercio y otras actividades económicas. (pág. 338)

standard of living [nivel de vida] *s.* calidad de la vida de una persona o población que se mide conforme a los bienes, servicios y lujos que tiene a su disposición. (pág. 532)

Star Wars [Guerra de las Galaxias] *s.* programa para proteger a Estados Unidos de un ataque de misiles enemigos, propuesto en 1983 por el presidente Ronald Reagan pero nunca implementado; su nombre oficial es Iniciativa de Defensa Estratégica. (pág. 499)

strike [huelga] *s.* paro de trabajo para obligar al patrón a acceder a ciertas demandas. (pág. 270)

Suez Canal [canal de Suez] *s.* canal marítimo que une al mar Rojo y al golfo de Suez con el mar Mediterráneo, cuya construcción terminó en 1869. (pág. 319)

Suez Crisis [Crisis de Suez] *s.* crisis internacional ocurrida en 1956 cuando Egipto nacionalizó el canal de Suez e Israel (con ayuda de Gran Bretaña y Francia) tomó el canal por la fuerza, pero se retiró bajo presión de Estados Unidos y la Unión Soviética. (pág. 522)

suffrage [sufragio] *s.* derecho al voto. (pág. 279)

surrealism [surrealismo] *s.* movimiento artístico del siglo 20 que se concentra en el inconsciente. (pág. 417)

sustainable development [crecimiento sostenido] *s.* desarrollo económico que satisface las necesidades de la población pero preserva el entorno y conserva recursos para futuras generaciones. (pág. 570)

T

Taiping Rebellion [Rebelión Taiping] *s.* rebelión a mediados del siglo 19 contra la dinastía Qing en China, encabezada por Hong Xiuquan. (pág. 337)

Taj Mahal *s.* bella tumba en Agra, India, construida por el emperador mogol Shah Jahan para su esposa Mumtaz Mahal. (pág. 74)

Ten Commandments [Diez Mandamientos] *s.* código escrito de leyes, respetado por judíos y cristianos, que Moisés recibió de Dios aproximadamente en 1200 A.C. (pág. 13)

Tennis Court Oath [Juramento de la Cancha de Tenis] *s.* promesa hecha por los miembros de la Asamblea Nacional de Francia en 1789 de permanecer reunidos hasta que elaboraran una nueva constitución. (pág. 196)

terrorism [terrorismo] *s.* uso de la fuerza o de amenazas para presionar a personas o gobiernos a que cambien sus políticas. (pág. 573)

theocracy [teocracia] *s.* gobierno controlado por líderes religiosos. (pág. 53)

theory of evolution [teoría de la evolución] *s.* concepto propuesto por Charles Darwin en 1859 de que las especies de plantas y animales surgen debido a un proceso de selección natural. (pág. 298)

theory of relativity [teoría de la relatividad] *s.* ideas de Albert Einstein acerca de la interrelación entre el tiempo y el espacio, y entre la energía y la materia. (pág. 415)

Third Reich [Tercer Reich] *s.* Tercer Imperio Alemán establecido por Adolfo Hitler en la década de 1930. (pág. 434)

Third Republic [Tercera República] *s.* república establecida en Francia después de la caída de Napoleón III;

acabó con la ocupación alemana de Francia durante la II Guerra Mundial. (pág. 283)

Third World [Tercer Mundo] *s.*durante la Guerra Fría, naciones que no se aliaron ni con Estados Unidos ni con la Unión Soviética. (pág. 491).

Thirty Years' War [Guerra de los Treinta Años] *s.*conflicto europeo de 1618 a 1648 por cuestiones religiosas, territoriales y de poder entre familias reinantes. (pág. 146)

Tiananmen Square [Plaza Tiananmen] *s.*plaza pública en Beijing, China; sede en 1989 de un enorme levantamiento estudiantil en favor de reformas democráticas. (pág. 552)

Tokugawa Shogunate [shogunato Tokugawa] *s.*dinastía de shogúns que gobernó un Japón unificado de 1603 a 1867. (pág. 95)

totalitarianism [totalitarismo] *s.*gobierno que controla todo aspecto de la vida pública y privada. (pág. 395)

total war [guerra total] *s.*conflicto en el que los países participantes dedican todos sus recursos a la guerra. (pág. 375)

Trans-Siberian Railway [Ferrocarril Transiberiano] *s.*vía de ferrocarril construida en Rusia entre 1891 y 1904 para conectar puertos rusos con el océano Pacífico. (pág. 390)

Treaty of Kanagawa [Tratado de Kanagawa] *s.*acuerdo de 1854 entre Estados Unidos y Japón, que abrió dos puertos japoneses a los barcos de Estados Unidos y le permitió abrir una embajada en Japón. (pág. 340)

Treaty of Tordesillas [Tratado de Tordesillas] *s.*acuerdo de 1494 entre Portugal y España que estableció que las tierras descubiertas al oeste de una línea imaginaria en el océano Atlántico pertenecerían a España y las tierras al este pertenecerían a Portugal. (pág. 86)

Treaty of Versailles [Tratado de Versalles] *s.*acuerdo de paz firmado por Alemania y los Aliados después de la I Guerra Mundial. (pág. 381)

trench warfare [guerra de trincheras] *s.*forma de guerra en la que dos ejércitos contrincantes luchan detrás de trincheras cavadas en el campo de batalla. (pág. 369)

triangular trade [triángulo comercial] *s.*red comercial trasatlántica que transportaba esclavos y productos entre África, Inglaterra, Europa continental, el Caribe y las colonias de Norteamérica. (pág. 117)

Triple Alliance [Triple Alianza] *s.* alianza militar establecida entre Alemania, Austro-Hungría e Italia antes de la I Guerra Mundial. (pág. 364)

Triple Entente [Triple Entente] *s.*alianza militar entre Gran Bretaña, Francia y Rusia establecida antes de la I Guerra Mundial. (pág. 365)

Truman Doctrine [Doctrina Truman] *s.*política estadounidense de dar ayuda económica y militar a las naciones libres amenazadas por oponentes internos o externos, anunciada por el presidente Harry Truman en 1947. (pág. 478)

U

union [sindicato] *s.*asociación de trabajadores formada para negociar mejores salarios y condiciones de trabajo. (pág. 270)

United Nations [Organización de las Naciones Unidas (ONU)] *s.*organización internacional fundada en 1945 con el propósito de ofrecer seguridad a las naciones del mundo. (pág. 475)

Universal Declaration of Human Rights [Declaración Universal de Derechos Humanos] *s.*declaración en que la ONU proclamó en 1948 que todos los seres humanos tienen derecho a la vida, la libertad y la seguridad. (pág. 574)

unrestricted submarine warfare [guerra submarina irrestricta] *s.*uso de submarinos para hundir sin alerta previa cualquier barco (incluso barcos neutrales y de pasajeros sin armamento) que se encuentre en aguas enemigas. (pág. 374)

urbanization [urbanización] *s.*crecimiento de ciudades y migración hacia ellas. (pág. 258)

U.S. Civil War [Guerra Civil de E.U.A.] *s.*conflicto entre los estados del Norte y el Sur de Estados Unidos desde 1861 a 1865, sobre el asunto de la esclavitud. (pág. 291)

utilitarianism [utilitarismo] *s.*teoría, propuesta por Jeremy Bentham a fines del siglo 18, de que las acciones del gobierno sólo son útiles si promueven el mayor bien para el mayor número de personas. (pág. 268)

Utopia [Utopía] *s.*tierra imaginaria descrita por Tomás Moro en su libro del mismo nombre; lugar ideal. (pág. 45)

U-2 incident [incidente del U-2] *s.*derribamiento en 1960 de un avión estadounidense de espionaje y captura de su piloto por la Unión Soviética. (pág. 480)

V

vernacular *s.*lenguaje común y corriente de la gente de una región o país. (pág. 41)

Vietcong *s.*grupo de guerrilleros comunistas que, con la ayuda de Vietnam del Norte, pelearon contra el gobierno de Vietnam del Sur durante la Guerra de Vietnam. (pág. 488)

Vietnamization [vietnamización] *s.*estrategia del presidente de E.U.A. Richard Nixon para terminar con la participación en la Guerra de Vietnam, mediante el retiro gradual de tropas estadounidenses y su reemplazo con fuerzas survietnamitas. (pág. 489)

W

War of the Spanish Succession [Guerra de Sucesión Española] *s.*conflicto de 1701 a 1713 en que varios Estados europeos lucharon para impedir que la familia Borbón controlara a España, como a Francia. (pág. 143)

Warsaw Pact [Pacto de Varsovia] *s.*alianza militar formada en 1955 por la Unión Soviética y siete países de Europa oriental. (pág. 479)

weapons of mass destruction [armas de destrucción masiva] *s.*armas que tienen el potencial de matar o herir a gran cantidad de personas de una vez, como las armas nucleares, biológicas y químicas. (pág. 604)

Weimar Republic [República de Weimar] *s.*república establecida en Alemania en 1919 que acabó en 1933. (pág. 422)

Western Front [Frente Occidental] *s.*en la I Guerra Mundial, región del norte de Francia donde peleaban las fuerzas de los Aliados y de las Potencias Centrales. (pág. 368)

westernization [occidentalización] *s.*adopción de las instituciones sociales, políticas o económicas del Occidente, especialmente de Europa o Estados Unidos. (pág. 153)

World Bank [Banco Mundial] *s.*organización multinacional que ofrece préstamos para proyectos de desarrollo de gran escala. (pág. 600)

Z

Zionism [sionismo] *s.*movimiento fundado en la década de 1890 para promover el establecimiento de una patria judía en Palestina. (pág. 283)

Index

An *i* preceding a page reference in italics indicates that there is an illustration, and usually text information as well, on that page. An *m* or a *c* preceding an italic page reference indicates a map or a chart, as well as text information on that page.

chemistry, 170
Chiapas, 534
child labor, *c 262*, 271, 390
children
  in the Enlightenment, 176
  in the Industrial Revolution, *c 262*, 271,
    273
  slavery of, 66
  in South African constitution, 540
Chile, 492
China, *m 404, c 483. See also* names of
    dynasties.
  in the 1990s, 553–555
  army, 553
  Boxer Rebellion, 339
  Boxers of, 333
  civil war in, 403–404, 482–483
  communes, 484
  communism in, 402–404, *c 483*, 497–498,
    i 554
  Cultural Revolution, 485, 551
  early modern, *c 92*
  expansion of, 483–484
  fight for democracy, 528
  "Great Leap Forward," 484, 551
  and Hong Kong, transfer to China, 555
  isolationism in, 81, 89–93, *c 98*, 335,
    c 354, 551–552
  Japanese invasion of, *m 413*, 432
  last emperor (Puyi), *i 387*
  Long March, 404
  Mao Zedong, 402, 482
  May Fourth movement in, 402, 411
  nationalists in, 401, 482, *c 483*
  Opium War, 336–337
  peasants, 403
  People's Republic of China (Mainland
    China), 483
  Red Guards, 485
  reform in, 337–339, 551–555
  revolution in, 401–404
  Soviet split with, 497–498
  Taiwan, 483
  Tiananmen Square, 4, *i 4*, 552–553
  Tibet, 483
  and World War I, 402
  and World War II, 482
Christian humanists, 45
Christianity, *c 612–613*, 616–617, *c 626*
    See also Church; Crusades; Roman
    Catholic Church.
  in European expansion, 83–84
  in Holocaust, 454
  in Japan, 97
  Jesus and, 13
  legacy of, 14
  rise of, 13–14
  in Roman empire, 14
  sects, 616
  and science, 165
  spread of, 14, *m 14*, 83
church. *See also* Roman Catholic Church.
  Russian Orthodox, 153, 398
Churchill, Winston, 443, *i 444*, 446, 455
  on appeasement, 435
  "Iron Curtain" speech, 477
  at Yalta Conference, *i 475*
CIA, 491
CIS, 548. *See* Commonwealth of
    Independent States.
cities
  and absolute monarchy, 137
  growth of, *c 275*

citizens, 181–182
  role in democracy, *c 531*
  in United States, 291
city-state(s)
  Northern Italian, 37
civic duty. *See* citizens.
civil disobedience, 406–407
  in Israel, 525
Civilian Conservation Corps, 426
civil rights, 457, 574–575
  under dictatorship, 430
civil war(s)
  American, 271, 290, *m 291*
  in Angola, 520
  in China, 403–404, 482–483
  English, *m 157–158*
  in Japan, 94
  in Lebanon, 525
  Mexican, 332
  in Nicaragua, 493
  in Nigeria, 537–538
  Russian, *m 393*
  Saint Domingue, 206
  Spanish, 433–434
Cixi (Chinese dowager empress), 337–339,
    i 341
Cleisthenes, 6
Clemenceau, Georges, *i 380*
cloning, 564, *i 588*
clothing, *i 144–145*
coalition, 200
coalition government, 421
Code of Justinian, 9
Colbert, Jean Baptiste, 140
Cold War, *m 472–473, m 477*, 479, *i 480*,
    491–501, *m 501*
  aftermath of, 602
  in Angola, 520
  brinkmanship, 480
  China in, 483–484
  end of, 496–499
  hot spots in, *m 493*
  Internet, 588
  NATO, 479
  nonaligned nations, 491
  nuclear threat, 479–480, 498–499, *m 501*
  revolutions during, 472
  strategies, 491
  and Third World, 491
  time line, *c 500*
  U-2 incident, 480
  Warsaw Pact, 479
collective bargaining, 270
collective farms, 397
colonialism, *c 124. See also* colonies,
    imperialism.
  British, 111–113, 505
  and capitalism, 120–123
  cultural influence of, 105
  economics of, 100
  effects of, *c 124*, 166, 532, 536, 538–539
  of France, 110–112
  in Latin America (1800 and 1830),
    m 228
  impact on Native Americans of, 106–108
  of Netherlands, 111–112
  of Portugal, 107
  and slavery, 107, 115–116
  of southeast Asia, 326–329
  of Spain, 103–109
  after World War I, 382
  after World War II, 491
colonies, 104. *See also* colonialism.

of Belgium Congo, 306
British, 111–*m 113*, 183–185, 276, *i 277*,
    m 331
Dutch, 515
European (1470–1534), *m 302–m 303*
independence of British, 514
revolt in French, 223–224
self-rule of, 505–520
Columbian Exchange, 120–123
Columbus, Christopher, 86, *i 100*,
    i 103–104, 584
  legacy of, 109
  native resistance to, 108
command economy, 396
Commercial Revolution, 120–123
Committee of Public Safety, 202
commonwealth, 157
  of Australia, 286
Commonwealth of Independent States
    (CIS), 548
communes, 484
communications
  global, 562–563, 565–566
communism, 269, *c 270*, 394, 395, *c 437.*
    See also Cold War.
  in Cambodia, 490
  in China, 402–404, 482–485, 497–499
  and democratic reforms, 528
  domino theory of, 488
  in eastern Europe, 476–479, 496–497
  economic effects of, 544, 548, 550, 551
  fall of, 543–550
  and fascism, 427
  historic origins of, 269–270, 389–394
  in Latin America, 492–493
  in Middle East, 495
  Politburo of, 541
  in Russia, 395–400
  in Southeast Asia, 486–490
  spread of, 463, *c 476–477*, 482–485,
    487–490, 492, *m 493*
compass, 85
computers, 562–563, 587
  Internet, 588
concordat, 206
Confucianism, *c 613*, 624–625, *c 626*
  and agriculture, 90, 95
  and commerce, 90, 95
  in Japan, 95
  values of, 89
Congo, 518–519
Congress of Vienna, 191, 213–216, *c 218*
Congress Party, 405, 506
conquistadors, 105
Conservatives, 198, 229
Constantinople, *m 60*
  fall of, *i 60*
  Ottoman defeat of, 64–65
Constitution
  first, 157
  of Japan, post-World War II, 464
  Korean, 487
  Mexican, *c 353*
  Russian, 394
  South African, 540
  United States, 173, *c 186*, 291
constitutional monarchy, 20–21, 391. *See*
    also monarchy.
containment, 477
  in South Korea, 486
  in Vietnam, 488
Continental System, 209
Contras, *i 472*, 493

Copernicus, Nicolaus, 166
Coronado, Francisco Vasquez de, 107
corporation, 265
    multinational, 599–601
Cortés, Hernando, *i 105*, 106
cotton
    consumption in Britain, *c 256*
    in India, 322–323
    in United States, 290
cotton gin, 256
Council of Trent, 56
coup, 515
coup d'état, 205
Creoles, 210, 224–225
criminal justice, 174
Croatia, 548, *m 549*
Cromwell, Oliver, 20, *i 130*, 157, 158
Cuba
    Batista, 492
    Bay of Pigs, 492
    Castro, Fidel, 492
    independence of, 346
    migrations from, *i 576*
    revolution, 492
Cuban missile crisis, 492, 498
cultural blending. *See also* global culture.
    in the Americas, 100
    in Safavid Empire, *c 68–m 70*
    in world, 577–581
cultural identity, 233, 532, 580
Cultural Revolution (China), 485
culture(s). *See also* Africa; Americas; China;
    India; Japan
    mass, *i 296–i 297*
    and nationalism, *c 233*
    popular, 577, 578
Curie, Marie, *i 298*
Cyrillic alphabet, 273
czar, 278. *See also* individual names of czars.
Czechoslovakia
    in 1990s, 550
    democracy in, 430, 434, 544–545
    falls to Hitler, 434–435
    reforms, 544–545
    Soviet invasion of, *i 497*

D

Dada movement, 417
daimyo, 94
Dalai Lama, 483–484, 574, 608
Dali, Salvador, *i 417*
Danzig, 435
Darius (Persian King), 6
Darwin, Charles, *i 298*, 299
David, Jacques Louis, 191, 195
Dawes, Charles, 422
D-Day Invasion (World War II), 458
Decameron (Boccaccio), 42
Declaration of Independence, 25
    Locke's influence on, *c 174*, 184
    and slavery, 271
Declaration of the Rights of Man, 25–26,
    c 174, 197
De Gaulle, Charles, 443, 519
de Klerk, F. W., 539, *i 540*
Delian League, 6
demilitarization, 464
democracy, 220, *c 531*, 532. *See also* demo-
    cratic reforms; government; demo-
    cratic–republican government.
    1945–present, 528–557

in ancient Greece, 5–7
in ancient Rome, 8–9
in Cambodia, 490
in China, 404
Congress of Vienna and, 213
democratic revolutions, 24–26
direct, 7, 174, 531
Enlightenment and, 22–24
in France, 26
and French Revolution, 215–216
in Great Britain, 17–21, 279–282
in India, 507
indirect, 531–534
in industrialized countries, 272
in Japan, 431
in Latin America, 531–534
loss of confidence in, 427
modern struggles for, 27
monarchy and, *c 160*
separation of powers and, 23–24
in South Korea, 487
struggles, *c 556*
time line of, *c 300*
United Nations and, 26–27
in United States, *c 159*
Western (1520), *m 276*
post-World War I, 412, 421–422
democratic reforms, 271, 279–280,
    c 531–532
    in England, 279–280
    of French Revolution, 197, 205, 213, 217
    in Industrial Revolution, 266
    in Japan, 464
    in modern world, 528–550, 552–553,
        c 556, 587
    in revolutionary China, 401–402
Deng Xiaoping, *i 552*, 553
    Four Modernizations, 552
Depression, the, 423–426, *c 436*
    causes of, 421–425, *c 437*
    effects of, 425–426, *c 437*
    and fascism, 427–430, 434–435, *c 437*
    global effects, 424–425
    in Japan, 431–432
    and Nazism, 429
    recovery, 426
    responses to, 425, 426
    Roosevelt, Franklin D., 426
    unemployment during, *i 412*, *c 425*
    in United States, 423, 424
Descartes, René, 138, 168
deserts, world's largest, *c 645*
destalinization, 496
détente, 498–499
developed nations, 566
developing nations, 491, 566, 599–601
devshirme, 66
Dias, Bartolomeu, 84
Díaz, Porfirio, 352
dictators, 396, 401. *See also* fascism; Nazism;
    and individual names of dictators.
    in Argentina, 429, 535
    in Brazil, 532–533
    in Cuba, 492
    in France, 202
    in Germany, 429
    in Nicaragua, 493
    in North Korea, 487
    in Russia, 395, 397
    in Spain, 434
    pre-World War II, 430
Diderot, Denis, 178–179
Diem, Ngo Dinh, 488

disease, 486, 106, 107, 113–114. *See also*
    bubonic plague.
    of Aborigines, 287
    cholera, 281
    germ theory of, 295
    during Industrial Revolution, 259
    inoculation against, 170
    of Maoris, 287
    in North America, 113–114
    small pox, 114
    in World War I, 375
    after World War II, 463
dissidents, 538
divine right, 19, 137, 151
DNA, 564
dominion, 285
domino theory, 488
Don Quixote, 134
drama. *See also* art.
    Greek, *i 6*
    Chinese, 93
    in French Revolution, *i 197*
    Japanese, 95–96
Dresden, 459
Dreyfus affair, 283
Drucker, Peter, 565–566
Dubĉek, Alexander, *i 497*
Duma, 391
Dutch. *See also* Netherlands.
    colonies, 111–112
    East India Company, 88
    in Southeast Asia, 326–327
dynasties, *See also* empires.
    Han, *c 79*
    Ming, 89–90, 92
    Qing, 91–93

E

East Africa, *See also* Africa.
    cultural blending in, *c 68*
East Asia, *See also* empire(s).
    growth in, *c 566*
Eastern Europe
    in 1990s, 550
Eastern Front
    in World War I, 370–371
    in World War II, 444–446
Eastern Orthodox Church, 616
East Germany, 543. *See also* Germany.
    Berlin Wall, 543
economics, 267–271, 408
    capitalism, 120–123, 267, *c 270*
    colonialism, 100
    communism, 269, *c 270*
    environmental impact of, 569–571
    factors of production, 254
    Gross Domestic Product, *c 515*, *c 586*
    of industrialization, 254
    laissez faire, 267
    Marxism, 268–269
    socialism, 268–269, 425–426
economy. *See also* economics.
    command, 396
    of developing world, 599–601
    global, 565–571, *c 582*, 599–601
    grassroots development, 600
    multinational corporations and, 599–600
    recession, 533
    reform of Russian, 548
    Soviet, *c 397*
    technology's effect on, 565–566
Edict of Nantes, 138

Leningrad, 445, 456
Leonardo da Vinci, *i 41*, 43, 59
Leviathan (Hobbes), 22
Liberals, 229
liberation theology, 533
libraries
    of Akbar, 72
life expectancy, *c 647*
Liliuokalani (Hawaiian queen), *i 329*
Lincoln, Abraham, 232, 290, *i 291*
Lindbergh, Charles, *i 412*, 418, 419
Lister, Joseph, 295
literature. *See also* writers.
    of early China, 93
    of the Enlightenment, 177, 179–181
    essay, 138
    French, 142
    Greek influence on, 34
    of Harlem Renaissance, 516
    Hindu, 73
    of Industrial Revolution, 259
    Japanese, 96
    movements, 239–243
    Nazi, 430
    in Ottoman Empire, 67
    political, 283
    Realism in, 241
    Renaissance, 41–42, 45–46
    Roman influence on, 34
    Romanticism and, 239–240
    Spanish, 134
    war's influence on, 416
    World War I's effect on, 383, 416
Lithuania, 382, 441, 442, 546
Lloyd George, David, 380
Locke, John, 22–23, *i 22*, 171–172, *c 174*,
    184, *c 186*
London
    fire, 158
    German bombing of, 444
Long March, *m 404*
Lost Generation, 416
Louis XIII (French king), 138–138
Louis XIV (French king), 25, 74, 110, 137,
    138–143, *i 144*, 231
Louis XV (French king), 25
Louis XVI (French king), 25, 185, *i 193*,
    194–196, 199, 214
Louis XVIII (French king), 211–212, 214,
    215
Louisiana, 110
    Purchase, 276, *m 289*
    Territory, 206–207
Luther, Martin, 15, *i 49–50*, 57. *See also*
    Reformation.
    excommunication, 49
    95 Theses, 49
Lutherans, 50, 146
lycée, 205

MacArthur, General Douglas, 449, *i 450*,
    459–461, *i 464*, 486
Macedonia, 7, *m 549*
Machiavelli, Niccolo, 42
Madero, Francisco, 352
Madison, James, 25, *i 25*
Magellan, Ferdinand, 87, 104–105
Magna Carta, 17–18, *i 17*
Malaysia, 514
Malthus, Thomas, 267, 268
Manchester, 258–262

Manchuria
    invasion by Japan of, *i 431–432*, 447–448
Manchus, 91–93
Mandela, Nelson, 539, *i 540*
manifest destiny, 290
Maoris, 285, 287
Mao Zedong, 269, *i 388*, 396, *i 402–404*,
    i 410, 432, 482, *i 484*, 551, *i 554*
    Marxist socialism, 484
    reforms, *c 551*
maps
    by Bartolomeu Dias (1110), *i 99*
Marat, Jean Paul, 200, 202, 203
Marconi, Guglielmo, 293
Marcos, Ferdinand, 513
Maria Theresa (empress), *i 149–150*
Marie Antoinette (queen), 25, *i 190*, *i 195*,
    202
Marshall Plan, *c 478*
Martí, José, *i 346*
martial law, 537
Marx, Karl, *i 269*, 270, 390
Marxism, *c 270*
massacre at Amritsar, 406, 505
mass culture, 294
materialism, 580
mathematics,
    Muslim, 165
    in Scientific Revolution, 168
Mau Mau rebellion, 517
Maya Indians, 534
Mayan Civilization
    modern, 534
Mazarin, Cardinal, 138–140, 146
Mazzini, Giuseppe, 235
Medici family, 37, 38
medicine
    of 1500s, *i 163*
    genetics, 563
    germ theory in, 295
    Lister, Joseph, 295
    modern advances in, 563
    molecular medicine, 564
    Nazi, 453
    Pasteur, Louis, 295
    quinine, 307
    in Scientific Revolution, 169–170
Mehmet II (Mehmet the Conquerer,
    Byzantine emperor), 64
Meiji era, 341
Mein Kampf (Hitler), 429
Meir, Golda, *i 522*, 523
Menchu, Rigoberta, *i 575*
Menelik II (Ethiopian emperor), *i 303*, 314
mercantilism, 122–123, 130, 140
mercenary, 196
Mesoamerican Civilizations. *See* Aztec,
    Mayan civilizations.
mestizo, 106
Metacom (King Philip), 114
Metternich, Klemens von, *i 213*
Mexico, *c 354*
    Basilica of Guadalupe, 616
    Chiapas, 534
    civil war in, 332, 352–353
    cultural blending in, *c 68*
    democracy in, 533–534
    independence of, 227
    oil in, 534
    political upheaval in, 533–534
    PRI (Institutional Revolutionary Party),
        534
    revolution in, 349–354

Michelangelo, 39, *i 40*
microscope, *i 168*
middle class
    in 1990s China, 553
    African, 516
    in Canadian colonies, 284–285
    and capitalism, 148
    in democracy, 532
    and democratic reforms, 276, 279
    during Enlightenment, 179
    during Industrial Revolution, 259
    Dutch, 135
    Italian, 235
    Marx and Engels on, 269
    and monarchy, 137
    in Nazi Germany, 428
    rise of, *c 160*, 266
    role in government, 220
Middle East, 494, 495, 521–525, *m 523*,
    m 643
middle passage, 117
migrations
    effect of colonization on, 120
    effects of large-scale, 575–576, *c 583*
    and Great Famine, 288
    of Jews to Palestine, 521
    migrants, 576
    political refugees, 576
militarism
    in World War I, 364
Mill, John Stuart, 268
Mines Act, 271
Ming Dynasty, 89–90, 92
missionaries
    Catholic, 110
    Christian, 90, 96–97, 107
    in colonies, 307
    and imperialism, *c 330*
    Jesuit, 55
mita, 409
Mobutu, Colonel Joseph (later, Mobutu
    Sese Seko), 518
moderates, 198
Molière, 142
monarchs
    absolute (1500–1800), *m 130–161*, 199
    European, *i 160*, *m 161*
monarchy, 7, 19, 171, 181–182. *See also*
    Kings.
    after Napoleon, 214
    clothing and, *i 144–i 145*
    constitutional, 159, 214, 279, 391
    divine right and, 19
    and Enlightenment, 181–182
    limited, 198, 200
    modern, *m 161*
Monghut (Siamese king), *i 328*
Mongols
    decline of, 89
monotheism, 12, 13. *See also* ethical
    monotheism; polytheism.
Monroe Doctrine, 346
Montesquieu, Baron de, 23, 25, *i 173*
Montezuma II (Aztec ruler), *i 105*
Montgomery, General Bernard, 455
More, Thomas, 45, 48
Morelos, Padre Jose, *i 227*
Moscow. *See also* Russia.
Mother Theresa, 575
Mott, Lucretia, 282
Mountbatten, Lord Louis, 506
mountains, world's highest, *c 644*
movies, 295, *i 296*, 420

of China, 337
during agricultural revolution, 254
economists on, 267
effect of industrialization on, 258
effect of trade on, 120
in empires, *c 79*
Israel's Jewish, *c 524*
projected growth (1995–2025), *c 646*
population growth, 593
birth rates and, 595
development first policy and, 597
famine/food supply and, 253, 596
forecast for, *c 595*
quality of life and, 596
limiting, 597–598
literacy rates and, *c 598*
women's status and, 598
Portugal
Angolan colony of, 520
Asian trade with, *c 98*
colonies of, 107, 227–228
in European expansion, 84–87
influence in Africa, 84–87
Japanese trade with, 96
North American slaves of, 107
slave trade of, 115–116
trade with India, 77
poverty
in Brazil, 532
predestination, 53
Presbyterians, 53–54
PRI (Institutional Revolutionary Party in Mexico), 534
priests
political activism of, 107–108
prime minister, 159
The Prince (Machiavelli), 42
printing, 46–47
in China, 46
Gutenberg, 46
and Renaissance ideas, 46, 47
printing press, 46
prison reform, 272
production, factors of, 254
proletariat, 269
proliferation, 573
propaganda, *i 367*
Allied, 457
totalitarian, 398, *i 399*
in World War I, 376
in World War II, *i 441*
prophets, 13
Protestantism, 15–16, 50–52, 616, 617
Calvin's influence on, 53
in Spanish Netherlands, 135
Protestants, 15–16, 50, 146
Protestant Union, 146
provisional government, 392
Prussia, 149
alliances of, 364
during the Enlightenment, 181
rise of, 149–150, 236–238
psychology, 299, 415
Freud, Sigmund, 299, 415
Pavlov, Ivan, 299
Ptolemy, 165
public works projects, 426
purge, 397
Puritans, 19, 20
in English Civil War, 157–158
in "New England," 111
victory over Metacom, 114

Q

Qian-long, 91–92
Qing Dynasty, 91–93, 336
Queen. *See* individual names.
Queen of Sheba, 432
Qur'an, 11

R

Rabelais, François, 45
Rabin, Yitzhak, 525
racism, 306, 307
in India, 323
and Social Darwinism, 299, 306
radar, 444
Radicals, 198, 229
radio, 420
BBC, 420
KDKA, 420
Nazi, 430
radioactivity, 298
railroads, 250
and Indian economy, 322
in Industrial Revolution, 256–257, 264–265
U.S., 292
Raj, 324
Raphael, *i 34, i 41*
Rasputin, 391
rationing, 375
Reagan, Ronald, 499
INF Treaty, 542
Strategic Defense Initiative, 499
realism, 241, *i 242*
realpolitik, 237
recession, 533
Reconquista, 106, 133
reconstruction, 292
recycling, 570
Red Guards, 485
Red Shirts, 236
Reformation, 15–16, 34, 48–58
and absolute monarchy, 137
Catholic, 55–56
causes of, 48–49, *c 58*
characteristics of, 49, 53–54, 56
effects of, 50–52, 56, *c 58*, 130
indulgences, 49
Luther, Martin, 15, 49
Peasant's Revolt, 50
Protestants, 15
values in, 49–50, 53–54, 56
women in, 54
Reformation Parliament, 51
refugees, statistics (1976–1992), *c 583*
Reign of Terror, 26, *c 201–203*, *c 218*
relativity, theory of, 415
religion, 612–626. *See also* Buddhism; Christianity; Hinduism; Islam; Judaism
effect of printing press on, 47
in Europe (1180), *m 54*
and nationalism, *c 233*
reformers, 48, 51, 53, 54, 55
world, 612–626, *c 612–613*, *c 626*
religious beliefs. *See also* religion; sacrifice.
effects of science on, 166
fundamentalism, 573
religious conflict, 573–574
religious persecution. *See also* Christianity; Holocaust; Inquisition.
in Japan, 97

of Muslims, 549
in Spanish colonies, 108
under Stalin, 398
religious rituals. *See also* burial rites; sacrifice.
religious symbolism, *i 614–625*
religious tolerance, *c 174*
in Austria, 181
in Edict of Nantes, 138
and French Revolution, *c 205*
limited, 158
in Mughal Empire, 73
in Netherlands, 135–136
in Ottoman Empire, 66–67
Rembrandt van Rijn, 136, 163
Renaissance, 15–16, 22, 37. *See also* Northern Renaissance.
art, *i 36, i 39–i 41*
British, 45–47
causes of, 34, 37, 43, 46–47, *c 58*
characteristics of, 15, 38–42, 44–47, *c 58*
Chinese, 37
effects of, 47, 83
European, 34–47, *c 58*
Flanders, 44–45
Greek influence on, *i 34*
humanism, 38
individualism and, 15, 22
Italian, 37–42
Leonardo da Vinci, 41
literature, 41
Michelangelo, 40
Northern, 43–47
Petrarch, 42
Raphael, 41
Russia during the, 152
themes of, 37
values of, 36–39
women in, 39
"Renaissance men," 38–39
republic, 8
China, 401
French, 26, 282–283
Roman, 8
U.S., 24–25, 185–186
The Republic (Plato), 7
Restoration, 20, 158
reunification, 544
Revolution(s) *c 585*
agricultural, 253–254
American, 162, 183–189, *c 188*
Bolshevik, 392–393
Chinese, 401–404
Commercial, 120–123
Cuban, 492
Cultural (Chinese), 485–486
democratic, 528
English, 156–159
and Enlightenment, *i 188*
failed, 230–231
French, 174, 187, 190–219, *c 205*
Glorious, 159
in Haiti, 223
ideas and, 226
Indian, 405–407
Industrial, *m 250–275*
Latin American, 210, 215, *c 218*, 222–229
leaders of, *c 410*
Mexican, 349–354
nationalist, *c 244, m 220–245*
of 1989, 27
role of Enlightenment on, 175, 184, *c 188*

ACKNOWLEDGMENTS

Text Acknowledgments

Title Page: Quotation from *A History of Civilizations* by Fernand Braudel, translated by Richard Mayne. Copyright © 1987 by Les Editions Arthaud; English translation copyright © 1994 by Richard Mayne. Used by permission of Penguin, a division of Penguin Books USA Inc.

Chapter 3, page 476: Haiku poem, from *Matsuo Basho,* translated by Makoto Veda. By permission of Makoto Veda.

Chapter 13, page 763: Excerpt from *You Will Hear Thunder, Akhmatova,* Poems, translated by D. M. Thomas, Martin Secker & Warburg, publisher. By permission of Random House UK Limited.

Chapter 19, page 937: Excerpts from "The Coming of Mao Zedong Chic," from Newsweek, May 19, 1997, Newsweek, Inc. All rights reserved. Reprinted by permission.

Backcover: Extract from *Millennium: A History of the Last Thousand Years* by Felipe Fernández-Armesto. Copyright © Felipe Fernández-Armesto 1995. Published by Bantam Press, a Division of Transworld Publishers Ltd. All rights reserved.

McDougal Littell Inc. has made every effort to locate the copyright holders for selections used in this book and to make full acknowledgment for their use. Omissions brought to our attention will be corrected in a subsequent edition.

Art and Photography Credits

COVER

front *background* Photo by Neil Beer. Copyright © 1997 PhotoDisc, Inc.; *insets, top to bottom* Corbis-Bettmann; Copyright © Jack Hollingsworth; Copyright © Culver Pictures; Hermitage, Leningrad/Scala/Art Resource, New York; Copyright © 1992 Carl Scofield/Index Stock Photography, Inc.; Copyright © Index Stock Photography, Inc.; **back** *top* Copyright © Culver Pictures; *center* Glasgow City Art Museum & Galleries, Scotland/Bridgeman Art Library, London/SuperStock; *bottom* Copyright © SuperStock.

FRONT MATTER

title spread *background* Photo by Neil Beer. Copyright © 1997 PhotoDisc, Inc.; *top row, left to right* Corbis-Bettmann; Copyright © Jack Hollingsworth; Copyright © Culver Pictures; Copyright © Culver Pictures; Glasgow City Art Museum & Galleries, Scotland/Bridgeman Art Library, London/SuperStock; *second row, left to right* Hermitage, Leningrad/Scala/Art Resource, New York; Copyright © 1992 Carl Scofield/Index Stock Photography, Inc.; Copyright © SuperStock; *bottom* Copyright © Index Stock Photography, Inc.; **viii** *left* Detail of *Patrick Henry Before the Virginia House of Burgesses* (1851), Peter F. Rothermel. Red Hill, The Patrick Henry National Memorial, Brookneal, Virginia; *right* Copyright © SuperStock; **ix** *top* Portrait of Elizabeth I (1588), George Gower. By courtesy of The National Portrait Gallery, London; *center, Shah Jahan Holding a Turban Jewel* (1617), Abu al-Hasan. Victoria & Albert Museum, London/Art Resource, New York; *bottom, Christopher Columbus,* attributed to Pedro Berruguete. Copyright © Giuliana Traverso/Grazia Neri; **x** *top* Detail of *Louis XIV, King of France,* Hyacinthe Rigaud. Louvre, Paris/Scala/Art Resource, New York; *center* Two of Galileo's telescopes. The Granger Collection, New York; *bottom* Painting of Simón Bolívar and Antonio José de Sucre. Mary Evans Picture Library, London; **xi** *top* View of Sheffield, England, 1879. The Granger Collection, New York; *center* Queen Victoria. Copyright © 1994 Archive Photos/PNI; *bottom, The Siege of the Alamo* (19th-century engraving). The Granger Collection, New York; **xii** *top* British soldiers in World War I. Popperfoto; *center* Mohandas K. Gandhi. Corbis; *bottom* Ships afire at Pearl Harbor. UPI/Corbis-Bettmann; **xiii** *top* Fidel Castro and Nikita Khrushchev. Copyright © 1961 Seymour Raskin/Magnum Photos; *center* Nelson Mandela and F. W. de Klerk. Copyright © Mark Peters/Sipa Press; *bottom* Cuban refugees. Copyright © Hans Deryk/AP/Wide World Photos; **xiv** *left* Copyright © Orion Press/Pacific Stock; *right* Copyright © Rene Sheret/Tony Stone Images; **xvi** *background right* U.S. Air Force; *foreground right* UPI/Corbis-Bettmann; **xix** *top left* Copyright © Ron Levy/Gamma-Liaison; *bottom left* Copyright © Charles Loviny/Gamma-Liaison; *right* Copyright © Ahn Young-joon/AP/Wide World Photos; **xx** The Granger Collection, New York; **xxiii** Tony Auth, *Philadelphia Inquirer.* Copyright © 1989. Reprinted with permission of Universal Press Syndicate. All rights reserved; **xxiv** *left* Palace Museum, Beijing; *right* The Granger Collection, New York; **xxv** Copyright © Black Star; **xxvi** *top* Copyright © Jeff Widener/AP/Wide World Photos; *bottom* The Granger Collection, New York; **xxvii** *bottom right* Corbis; *top left* Copyright © Chad Ehlers/Tony Stone Images; **xxviii–xxix** Copyright © Pacific Stock/Orion Press; **xxix** FPG International; **xxxii** Copyright © Stephen Alvarez/National Geographic Image Collection; **xxxiii** *top* Copyright © Kenneth Garrett; *center* Flying machine sketch from Codex Atlanticus, Leonardo da Vinci. Biblioteca Ambrosiana, Milan, Italy/Art Resource, New York; *bottom* Copyright © Warren Morgan/Westlight.

PROLOGUE

xxxvi–1 Copyright © Denis Farrell/AP/Wide World Photos; **2** *Washington Addressing the Constitutional Convention* (1856), Junius Brutus Stearns. Oil on canvas, 95.2 cm × 137.1 cm. Virginia Museum of Fine Arts, Richmond. Gift of Edgar William and Bernice Chrysler Garbisch. Photo by Ron Jennings. Copyright © 2000 Virginia Museum of Fine Arts; **3** *top* Copyright © Glen Allison/Tony Stone Images; *center* American School of Classical Studies at Athens, Agora excavations; *bottom* The Emir of Katsina's morning greeting ceremony, Nigeria. Hausa peoples, Nigeria. Photograph by Eliot Elisofon, 1959. Slide No. T HSA 1 (16275). Eliot Elisofon Photographic Archives, National Museum of African Art; **4** Copyright © Jeff Widener/AP/Wide World Photos; **5** Uffizi, Florence, Italy/Art Resource, New York; **6** Photo by Nobby

Clark; **8** The Granger Collection, New York; **9** Bibliothèque Nationale, Paris; **10** *center left, bottom right, bottom left* American School of Classical Studies at Athens, Agora excavations; **11** *top to bottom* The Granger Collection, New York; National Palace Museum, Taipei, Taiwan; Stock Montage, Inc.; Copyright © R. Sheridan/Ancient Art & Architecture Collection; **12** The Granger Collection, New York; **15** The Granger Collection, New York; **17** Department of the Environment, London/Bridgeman Art Library, New York; **18** The Granger Collection, New York; **21** Ashmolean Museum, Oxford, U.K.; **22** The Granger Collection, New York; **25** The Granger Collection, New York; **26** The Granger Collection, New York; **28** Copyright © Jeff Widener/AP/Wide World Photos.

UNIT ONE

30–31 Copyright © SuperStock; **32** *top* Detail of portrait of Timur the Lame. Uffizi, Florence, Italy/SEF/Art Resource, New York; *bottom* Building in the Forbidden City, Beijing, China. Copyright © Bob Handelman/Tony Stone Images; **33** *top* Portrait of Elizabeth I (1588), George Gower. By courtesy of The National Portrait Gallery, London; *bottom* Engraving of Native Americans attacking a Massachusetts village during King Philip's War. The Granger Collection, New York.

Chapter 1

34 *top* By courtesy of the National Portrait Gallery, London; *bottom, The School of Athens* (1508), Raphael. Stanza della Segnatura, Vatican Palace, Vatican State/Scala/Art Resource, New York; **35** Detail of *The Gates of Paradise,* Lorenzo Ghiberti. Baptistery, Florence, Italy/Scala/Art Resource, New York; **36** *The Madonna of Chancellor Rolin* (about 1434), Jan van Eyck. Louvre, Paris/Scala/Art Resource, New York; **38** *Lorenzo de'Medici* (15th–16th century), unknown artist. Painted terra cotta, 65.8 cm × 59.1 cm x 32.7 cm. National Gallery of Art, Washington, D.C., Samuel H. Kress Collection. Photograph by Philip A. Charles; **39** *top* The Granger Collection, New York; *bottom, Marriage of the Virgin* (1504), Raphael. Brera, Milan, Italy/Scala/Art Resource, New York; **40** *top right* Sistine Chapel, Vatican State/Scala/Art Resource, New York; *center left* Scala/Art Resource, New York; *bottom center, David,* Michelangelo. Accademia, Florence, Italy/Scala/Art Resource, New York; **41** *left* Self-portrait by Leonardo da Vinci. Biblioteca Reale, Turin, Italy/Scala/Art Resource, New York; *right* Detail of *The School of Athens* (1508), Raphael. Stanza della Segnatura, Vatican Palace, Vatican State/Scala/Art Resource, New York; **42** Palazzo Vecchio, Florence, Italy/Scala/Art Resource, New York; **43** *The Adoration of the Trinity* (1511), Albrecht Dürer. Oil on poplar wood, 135 cm × 123.4 cm. Kunsthistorisches Museum, Gemäldegalerie, Vienna, Austria/Erich Lessing/Art Resource, New York; **44** *Peasant Wedding* (1568), Peter Brueghel the Elder. Kunsthistorisches Museum, Vienna, Austria/Saskia/Art Resource, New York; **45** Corbis; **46** Copyright © 1990 Warner Bros., Inc./Photofest; **47** *left, right* The Granger Collection, New York; **48** *Girolamo Savonarola* (early 16th century), Alessandro Bonvicino. E.T. Archive, London; **49** *Portrait of Martin Luther* (1529), Lucas Cranach the Elder. Museo Poldi Pezzoli, Milan, Italy/Bridgeman Art Library, London; **50** The Granger Collection, New York; **51** Corbis; **52** Portrait of Elizabeth I (1588), George Gower. By courtesy of The National Portrait Gallery, London; **53** Bibliothèque Publique et Universitaire, Geneva, Switzerland/Erich Lessing/Art Resource, New York; **54** Musée Condé, Chantilly, France/Giraudon/Art Resource, New York; **56** Louvre, Paris/Giraudon/Bridgeman Art Library, London; **57** Detail of *Portrait of Martin Luther* (1529), Lucas Cranach the Elder. Museo Poldi Pezzoli, Milan, Italy/Bridgeman Art Library, London; **58** Detail of *The Madonna of Chancellor Rolin* (about 1434), Jan van Eyck. Louvre, Paris/Scala/Art Resource, New York.

Chapter 2

60 *First Attack on Constantinople by the Turks* in 1453, Jacopo Palma Giovane. Oil on canvas. Palazzo Ducale, Venice, Italy/Erich Lessing/Art Resource, New York; **61** *top* SEF/Art Resource, New York; bottom Victoria & Albert Museum, London/Art Resource, New York; **62** *The Enthroning of Mehmet II.* MS H. 1523, p. 153b. Topkapi Palace Museum, Istanbul, Turkey. Photo copyright © Sonia Halliday Photographs; **63** Topkapi Palace Museum, Istanbul, Turkey. Photo copyright © Sonia Halliday and Laura Lushington; **64** Uffizi, Florence, Italy/SEF/Art Resource, New York; **66** The Granger Collection, New York; **67** Archives Nationales, Paris/Giraudon/Art Resource, New York; **72** MS Add. Or. 1039. Courtesy of the British Library; **73** Victoria & Albert Museum, London/Art Resource, New York; **74** Copyright © M. Khursheed/AP/Wide World Photos; **75** Copyright © Alvaro de Leiva/Liaison International; **76** *bottom left* Copyright © R. Sheridan/Ancient Art & Architecture Collection; *center* Copyright © Norbert Wu; *top right* Victoria & Albert Museum, London/Art Resource, New York; **77** Copyright © British Museum.

Chapter 3

80 By courtesy of the Bibliothèque Nationale, Paris; **81** *top left* The Granger Collection, New York; *inset left* Woodcut of Zheng He from *The Western Sea Cruises of Eunuch San Bao* by Luo Moudeng, 1597; *bottom right* Rijksmuseum, Amsterdam, The Netherlands; **82** The Granger Collection, New York; **83** Globe by Martin Behaim (about 1492). Bibliothèque Nationale, Paris/Giraudon/Art Resource, New York; *84* The Granger Collection, New York; **85** *bottom left, center* Copyright © National Maritime Museum, London; *top right* Museo Naval, Madrid, Spain; **86** Copyright © National Maritime Museum, London; **89** Musée Guimet, Paris/Giraudon/Art Resource, New York; **90** Copyright © Bob Handelman/Tony Stone Images; **91** Palace Museum, Beijing, China; **92** Palace Museum, Beijing, China/Wan-go Weng, Inc.; **93** Copyright © British Museum; **94** Victoria & Albert Museum, London/Art Resource, New York; **96** Bruce Coleman, Inc.; **98** Copyright © National Maritime Museum, London; **99** The Granger Collection, New York.

Chapter 4

100 *top* The Granger Collection, New York; *bottom* Fotomas Index, Kent, England; **101** 1786 C. 9, Pl. IV. By permission of the British Library; **102** Courtesy Department of Library Services, American Museum of Natural History (Neg. #329243). Photo by Logan; **103** Copyright © Giuliana Traverso/Grazia Neri; **105** *left, right* The Granger Collection, New York; **107** The Granger Collection, New York; **108** The John Carter Brown Library at Brown University, Providence, Rhode Island; **109** *left* Copyright © Karsh, Ottawa/Woodfin Camp & Associates; *center* The Granger Collection, New York; *right, Newsweek*/Chris Kleponis. Copyright © 1991, Newsweek, Inc. All rights reserved. Reprinted by permission; **111** The

Art and Photography Credits (Cont.)

Babcock. Courtesy, Museum of Fine Arts, Boston.

Chapter 7

190 *top, Portrait of Marie Antoinette,* Jean Baptiste Augustin. Aquarelle on ivory. National Museum of Art, Bucharest, Romania. Copyright © Gérard Blot/Photo RMN; *bottom* Copyright © Labat JM/Explorer, Paris; **191** *top* Mary Evans Picture Library, London; *bottom* Château de Malmaison, Rueil-Malmaison, France/Giraudon/Art Resource, New York; **192** Musée Carnavalet, Paris/Jean-Loup Charmet; **193** *Portrait of Louis XVI,* Antoine François Callet. Versailles and Trianon, France. Copyright © Photo RMN; **194** *Taille: impots et corvées* (late-18th-century engraving). Musée de la Ville de Paris, Musée Carnavalet, Paris/Giraudon/Art Resource, New York; **195** *left, La maraîchère* [Woman of the French Revolution], Jacques Louis David. Musée des Beaux-Arts, Lyon, France/Giraudon/Art Resource, New York; *right, Marie Antoinette,* Jacques Gautier d'Agoty. Château, Versailles, France/Giraudon/Art Resource, New York; **197** Musée de la Ville de Paris, Musée Carnavalet, Paris/Giraudon/Art Resource, New York; **199** *Attaque du palais des Tuileries, le 20 juin 1792: les émeutiers envahissent le palais en présence du roi et de la reine* [Attack on the Tuileries Palace, June 20, 1792: The rioters overrun the palace in the presence of the king and queen], Jean Baptiste Verité. Hand-colored engraving. Versailles and Trianon, France. Copyright © Photo RMN; **200** Musée de la Ville de Paris, Musée Carnavalet, Paris/Giraudon/Art Resource, New York; **201** Illustration by Patrick Whelan; **202** Musée Carnavalet, Paris/Bulloz; **203** Musées Royaux des Beaux-Arts, Brussels, Belgium/Giraudon/Art Resource, New York; **204** Photo by Soalhat/Sipa Press, New York; **206** Musée de l'Armée, Paris/Giraudon/Art Resource, New York; **209** Fotomas Index, Kent, England; **212** Musée de l'Armée, Paris/Giraudon/Art Resource, New York; **213** The Bettmann Archive; **214** *Detail of Masked Ball in the Redoutensaal on Occasion of the Congress of Vienna with Performance of Beethoven's Seventh Symphony and His Composition "Wellington's Victory in the Battle of Vittoria"* (around 1815), Carl Schuetz. Color print. Historisches Museum der Stadt Wien, Austria/Erich Lessing/Art Resource, New York; *inset left* Mary Evans Picture Library, London; **217** *left* Musée des Beaux-Arts, Lille, France/Giraudon/Art Resource, New York; *right* Victoria & Albert Museum, London/Art Resource, New York; **218** *far left center* Parisian sans-culotte (18th century), unknown artist. Musée de la Ville de Paris, Musée Carnavalet, Paris/Giraudon/Art Resource, New York; *left center* Model of a guillotine. Musée de la Ville de Paris, Musée Carnavalet, Paris/Giraudon/Art Resource, New York; *bottom* Musée Carnavalet, Paris/Jean-Loup Charmet.

Chapter 8

220 The Granger Collection, New York; **221** *bottom left* Copyright © 1986 R. van Butselle/Image Bank; *top right, Incontro di Teano* [Encounter at the Teano Bridge], Cesare Maccari. Palazzo Pubblico, Siena, Italy/Scala/Art Resource, New York; **222** *center left, bottom left, center, center right* Courtesy of the Flag Institute; **223** Copyright © 1991 Kathleen Marie Rohr/DDB Stock Photo; **224** The Granger Collection, New York; **225** The Granger Collection, New York; **226** *bottom left* Copyright © D. Donne Bryant; *top right* Corbis-Bettmann; **227** The Granger Collection, New York; **229** Arc de Triomphe de l'Etoile, Paris/Giraudon/Art Resource, New York; **230** *top* Historical and Ethnological Museum of Greece; *center right, George Gordon Byron,* 6th Baron Byron (1813), Thomas Phillips. By courtesy of the National Portrait Gallery, London; **231** The Granger Collection, New York; **232** Victoria & Albert Museum, London/Art Resource, New York; **234** E.T. Archive, London; **236** The Granger Collection, New York; **238** The Granger Collection, New York; **239** Illustration by Arthur Rackham from *Little Brother and Little Sister* by Jakob and Wilhelm Grimm. University of Louisville, Special Collections; **240** Copyright © Photofest; **241** Beethoven House, Bonn, Germany/Erich Lessing/Art Resource, New York; **242** *top left, The Winnowers* (1855), Gustave Courbet. Oil on canvas, 131 cm × 167 cm. Musée des Beaux-Arts, Nantes, France/Giraudon/Art Resource, New York; *bottom left, Coquelicots, environs d'Argenteuil* [Poppy field at Argenteuil] (1873), Claude Monet. Oil on canvas, 50 cm × 65 cm. Musée d'Orsay, Paris. Photo copyright © Photo RMN-ADAGP; *top right, Mondaufgang am Meer* [Moonrise over the sea] (1822), Caspar David Friedrich. Oil on canvas, 55 cm × 71 cm. Staatliche Museen zu Berlin/Preussischer Kulturbesitz Nationalgalerie; **243** *Ships at Low Tide* (about 1844), William Henry Fox Talbot. Salted paper print from calotype negative, 16.5 cm × 21.6 cm. National Museum of American History, Smithsonian Institution, Division of Photographic History; **244** Courtesy of the Flag Institute; **245** Copyright © Stock Montage, Inc.

UNIT THREE

246–247 Copyright © Peabody Essex Museum. Photo by Jeffrey Dykes; **248** *top* Detail of *Kansas Pioneers* (1920), George Melville Stone. Oil on canvas, 72″ × 120″. Kansas State Historical Society, Topeka. Photo courtesy of the State of Kansas; *bottom* Tea being loaded onto elephants at the Lipton Plantation, India. E.T. Archive, London; **249** *top, Vor dem Streik* [Before the strike], after a painting by Michael Munkacsy. Bildarchiv Preussischer Kulturbesitz, Berlin; *bottom* 19th-century Japanese woman. Mary Evans Picture Library, London.

Chapter 9

251 *left* Detail of *Vor dem Streik* [Before the strike], after a painting by Michael Munkacsy. Bildarchiv Preussischer Kulturbesitz, Berlin; *right* Weidenfeld & Nicolson Archives; **252** Illustration by Patrick Whelan; **254** *left, right* The Granger Collection, New York; **254–255** The Granger Collection, New York; **257** The Granger Collection, New York; **258** The Granger Collection, New York; **259** The Granger Collection, New York; **261** The Granger Collection, New York; **263** The Granger Collection, New York; **265** *Das Eisenwalzwerk: Moderne Zyklopen* [The rolling mill: a modern behemoth] (1875), Adolph von Menzel. Staatliche Museen zu Berlin/Preussischer Kulturbesitz, Nationalgalerie; *267* The Granger Collection, New York; **268** Copyright © The College Shop, University College, London; **269** The Granger Collection, New York; **270** *left, right* The Granger Collection, New York; **271** Mansell Collection/Time, Inc.; **272** Jane Addams Memorial Collection, Special Collections, The University Library, The University of Illinois at Chicago; **273** *center* U.S. Steel; *right* Karl Marx Museum, Trier, Germany/E.T. Archive, London; **274** Illustration by Patrick Whelan.

Art and Photography Credits (Cont.)

Chapter 10

276 Kansas State Historical Society, Topeka. Photo courtesy of the State of Kansas; **277** *bottom left* Lauros-Giraudon/Art Resource, New York; *top right* Mary Evans Picture Library, London; **278** *bottom left, center* The Granger Collection, New York; *top right* Corbis-Bettmann; **279** National Portrait Gallery, London; **280** *top* Copyright © SuperStock; *bottom* Detail of *Queen Victoria* (1838), Sir George Hayter. National Portrait Gallery, London; **281** *center left* Photo by Sharon Hoogstraten; *top right* Corbis; *center right, The Railway Station* (1862), William Powell Frith. Royal Holloway and Bedford New College, Surrey, England/Bridgeman Art Library, London; **283** *Une rue de Paris en mai* 1871, ou *La Commune* [A Paris street in May 1871; or, The commune] (1903–1905), Maximilien Luce. Oil on canvas, 150 cm × 225 cm. Musée d'Orsay, Paris/Erich Lessing/Art Resource, New York; **284** Copyright © 1993 Brian Stablyk/Tony Stone Images; **287** Copyright © Hawaii State Archives/Pacific Stock; **288** Photograph reproduced with the kind permission of the Trustees of the Ulster Museum, Belfast, Northern Ireland; **291** *top* Copyright © Hulton Getty Picture Collection; bottom Library of Congress; **294** *La chaîne Simpson* (1896), Henri de Toulouse-Lautrec. Poster. Musée Toulouse-Lautrec, Albi, France/Giraudon/Art Resource, New York; **295** Copyright © Hulton Getty Picture Collection/Tony Stone Images; **296** *center left, bottom left* Photofest; *bottom center, bottom right* Copyright © 1994 Archive Photos/PNI; **297** *top left* Copyright © 1988 Itar-Tass/PNI; *center left* Corbis; *bottom left* Copyright © 1994 Archive Photos/PNI; *top right* Copyright © 1979 New China Pictures/Eastfoto/PNI; **298** *top* Corbis-Bettmann; bottom Corbis; **300** Corbis-Bettmann; **301** By permission of the British Library.

Chapter 11

302 Copyright © Werner Forman/Corbis; **303** *top left* Copyright © 1994 Archive Photos/PNI; *bottom right* Copyright © Culver Pictures; **304** *top left* The Granger Collection, New York; *center left* Copyright © Hulton Getty Picture Collection/Tony Stone Images; *bottom left* Crown copyright is reproduced with the permission of the Controller of Her Majesty's Stationery Office; *right* Photo by Sharon Hoogstraten; 305 Copyright © British Museum; **306** The Granger Collection, New York; **312** *bottom left* Photo by Sharon Hoogstraten; *top right* Dave Houser/Corbis; **316** Copyright © Culver Pictures; **318** The Granger Collection, New York; **321** E.T. Archive, London; **323** Copyright © Hulton Getty Picture Collection/Tony Stone Images; **324** The Granger Collection, New York; **325** Mary Evans Picture Library, London; **326** Jack Fields/Corbis; **327** Copyright © 1989 Jose Azel/PNI; **328** Corbis-Bettmann; **329** UPI/Corbis-Bettmann.

Chapter 12

332 Photograph from *Historia gráfica de la Revolución mexicana, 1900–1960* by Gustavo Casasola, ed. commemorativa. Copyright © 1960 Editorial F. Trillas, Mexico City; **333** *top* Snark International, Paris/Art Resource, New York; bottom Carl H. Boehringer Collection/Laurie Platt Winfrey, Inc., New York; **334** Peabody Museum, Salem, Massachusetts/Werner Forman Archive/Art Resource, New York; **335** Laurie Platt Winfrey, Inc.; **336** Copyright © 1989 Jan Halaska/Tony Stone Images/PNI; **339** The Granger Collection, New York; **340** Mary Evans Picture Library, London; **341** *left, right* The Granger Collection, New York; **343** Mary Evans Picture Library, London; **344** Copyright © Loren McIntyre; **346** The Granger Collection, New York; **347** Copyright © Culver Pictures; **348** *bottom left* Copyright © John Lopinot/Black Star; *center, top right* The Granger Collection, New York; **349** The Granger Collection, New York; **351** *top* Detail of fresco at University of Guadalajara, Mexico (1936–1939), José Clemente Orozco; *bottom* The Granger Collection, New York; 352 Copyright © 1994 Archive Photos/PNI.

UNIT FOUR

356–357 Imperial War Museum, London; **358** Nazi Party parade in Nuremberg, Germany, 1933. Copyright © Hulton Getty Picture Collection/Tony Stone Images; **359** *top* German machine-gun team in World War I. Copyright © Imperial War Museum/Archive Photos; bottom Mohandas K. Gandhi. Corbis.

Chapter 13

360 The Granger Collection, New York; **361** *top* Copyright © Imperial War Museum/Archive Photos; *bottom, Signing of the Treaty of Versailles* (1919), John Christen Johansen. National Portrait Gallery, Smithsonian Institution, Washington, D.C./Art Resource, New York; **362** The Granger Collection, New York; **363** Copyright © Hulton Getty Picture Collection/Tony Stone Images; **364** The Granger Collection, New York; **367** The Granger Collection, New York; **369** Copyright © Archive Photos/Express Newspapers; **370** *left* Popperfoto; *right* The Granger Collection, New York; **371** *left* Copyright © Archive Photos/Express Newspapers; *right* Copyright © Archive Photos; **372** *top* National Air and Space Museum, Smithsonian Institution, Washington, D.C.; *center* Aero Publishers/McGraw Hill; *bottom* Courtesy of United Airlines; **373** Copyright © Imperial War Museum/Archive Photos; **376** Roger-Viollet; **377** Copyright © Archive Photos; **378** *center* Copyright © Archive Photos; *bottom* Copyright © Ullstein Bilderdienst, Berlin; **379** *top left* Copyright © Rolf Adlercreutz/Gamma-Liaison; *top right background* Photograph copyright © Anne and Henri Stierlin; *top right foreground* Detail of Trajan's Column. Scala/Art Resource, New York; *center* Sovfoto/Eastfoto; *bottom left* Copyright © Hulton Getty Picture Collection/Tony Stone Images; **380** Copyright © Hulton Getty Picture Collection/Tony Stone Images; **384** The Granger Collection, New York.

Chapter 14

387 *top* Copyright © Vladimirov/Tass; bottom Copyright © Hulton Getty Picture Collection; **388** *left* Corbis; right UPI/Corbis-Bettmann; **389** Copyright © 1995 Elena & Walter Borowski Collection/PNI; **390** Armory Museum, Kremlin, Moscow/Bridgeman Art Library, London; **391** Copyright © Hulton Getty Picture Collection/Tony Stone Images; **392** FPG International; **393** Itar-Tass/Sovfoto; **394** Copyright © 1994 Archive Photos/PNI; **395** Sovfoto; **396** Itar-Tass/Sovfoto/PNI; **398** Photo by Sharon Hoogstraten; **399** *top left, top right* Sovfoto/Eastfoto; *bottom center* AKG Photo; **400** David King Collection; **401** Copyright © 1994 Archive Photos/AFP/PNI; **402** *top* Photo by Sidney D. Gamble; *bottom* AP/Wide World Photos; **403** David King Collection; **405** Imperial War Museum, London; **406** Corbis; **407** Copyright © Mansell Collection/Time, Inc.; **410** *left to right* Copyright © 1994 Archive Photos/PNI; Sovfoto; Copyright © 1994 Archive Photos/AFP/PNI; UPI/Corbis-Bettmann; Corbis; Copyright © Hulton Getty Picture

714 Acknowledgments

Collection/Tony Stone Images.

Chapter 15

412 Copyright © The Dorothea Lange Collection, The Oakland Museum of California, The City of Oakland. Gift of Paul S. Taylor; **412–413** Richard Nowitz/Corbis; **413** *bottom* Copyright © Hulton Getty Picture Collection/Tony Stone Images; **414** *bottom* Copyright © 1995 Chicago Historical Society/PNI; **415** The Granger Collection, New York; **416** The Granger Collection, New York; **417** *The Persistence of Memory (Persistance de la mémoire)* (1931), Salvador Dali. Oil on canvas, 9 1/2″ × 13″. The Museum of Modern Art, New York. Given anonymously. Photograph copyright © 1999 The Museum of Modern Art, New York; **418** *top* Copyright © 1995 Elena & Walter Borowski/PNI; *bottom* Copyright © Ullstein Bilderdienst, Berlin; **419** *top left background* The Granger Collection, New York; *top left foreground* Penguin/Corbis-Bettmann; *bottom left* Hulton-Deutsch Collection/Corbis; *center right* Corbis-Bettmann; **420** Copyright © 1994 Archive Photos/PNI; **421** The National Archives/Corbis; **422** UPI/Corbis-Bettmann; **424** Corbis-Bettmann; **426** Library of Congress; **427** Copyright © Hulton Getty Picture Collection/Tony Stone Images; **428** *center left* Copyright © Hulton Getty Picture Collection/Tony Stone Images; *bottom center* Copyright © 1995 Archive Photos/PNI; **430** Copyright © Hulton Getty Picture Collection/Tony Stone Images; **431** Copyright © Hulton Getty Picture Collection/Tony Stone Images; **432** Copyright © Hulton Getty Picture Collection/Tony Stone Images; **434** The Granger Collection, New York.

Chapter 16

438 National Archives, courtesy of USHMM Photo Archives; **439** *top* National Archives/U.S. Coast Guard; *bottom* UPI/Corbis-Bettmann; **440** Copyright © Imperial War Museum/Archive Photos; **441** Copyright © Tallandier/Archive France/Archive Photos; **443** Copyright © Archive Photos; **444** The Granger Collection, New York; **445** Itar-Tass/Sovfoto; **446** U.S. Naval Historical Center; **447** UPI/Corbis-Bettmann; **449** W. Eugene Smith/Life magazine. Copyright © 1945 Time, Inc.; **450** Copyright © 1994 Archive Photos/PNI; **451** Eastfoto; **452** *bottom background* Reuters/Corbis-Bettmann; *bottom foreground* Yad Vashem Photo Archives, courtesy of USHMM Photo Archives; **453** UPI/Corbis-Bettmann; **454** Courtesy of the Spertus Museum, Chicago; **455** AP/Wide World Photos; **456** UPI/Corbis-Bettmann; **457** Library of Congress; **458** National Portrait Gallery, Smithsonian Institution, Washington, D.C./Art Resource, New York; **460** *center left background* U.S. Air Force; *center left foreground* UPI/Corbis-Bettmann; *top right* AP/Wide World Photos; *bottom* Photo of aftermath of bombing of Nagasaki, August 10, 1945, by Yosuke Yamahata. Photo restoration by TX Unlimited, San Francisco; **462** William Vandivert/Life magazine. Copyright © Time, Inc.; **464** AP/Wide World Photos; **466** Copyright © Imperial War Museum/Archive Photos.

UNIT FIVE

468–469 Copyright © Bernstein/FSP/Gamma-Liaison; **470** Afghan family watching TV in their tent. Copyright © 1985 Steve McCurry/Magnum Photos/PNI; **471** *top* Chinese youths celebrating Nikita Khrushchev's visit to Beijing. Copyright © Brian Brake/Photo Researchers, Inc.; *bottom* Nelson Mandela and F. W. de Klerk. Copyright © Mark Peters/Sipa Press.

Chapter 17

472 *top* Bruce Shanks in the Buffalo Evening News (7/31/72); *bottom* Copyright © 1978 Susan Meiselas/Magnum Photos; **473** *top* Copyright © Brian Brake/Photo Researchers, Inc.; *bottom* UPI/Corbis-Bettmann; **474** *bottom* Jeremy Horner/Corbis; *inset* Copyright © Gamma-Liaison; **475** AP/Wide World Photos; **479** UPI/Corbis-Bettmann; **480** Copyright © Earl Young/Archive Photos; **481** *top left* Tass/Sovfoto; *top right, bottom left* NASA; **482** Copyright © 1997 ABC; **484** The Granger Collection, New York; **485** UPI/Corbis-Bettmann; **486** Copyright © Archive Photos; **488** Copyright © 1967 Charles Bonnay/Black Star/PNI; **490** Chris Rainier/Corbis; **491** Art Rickerby/Life magazine. Copyright © Time, Inc.; **492** Copyright © 1961 Seymour Raskin/Magnum Photos; **494** *top, bottom* Copyright © Alain Mingam/Gamma-Liaison; **496** Copyright © 1991 Deborah Copaken/Contact Press Images/PNI; **497** *left* Copyright © 1994 Sovfoto/PNI; *center, right* AP/Wide World Photos; **498** Copyright © Szabo/Rothco; **499** UPI/Corbis-Bettmann; **500** Jeremy Horner/Corbis.

Chapter 18

502 *top* Copyright © Popperfoto/Archive Photos; *bottom* Copyright © Hulton Getty Picture Collection/Tony Stone Images; **503** *top* Courtesy of Nehru Memorial Museum, New Delhi, India; *bottom* Copyright © Alberto Garcia/Gamma-Liaison; **504** UPI/Corbis-Bettmann; **505** Copyright © Black Star; **506** Copyright © Archive Photos; **508** *top center* Copyright © 1979 Romano Cagnoni/Black Star; *top right, bottom right* Copyright © Gamma-Liaison; *bottom left* Margaret Bourke-White/*Life* magazine. Copyright © Time, Inc.; *bottom center* Copyright © 1968 Fred Mayer/Magnum Photos; **509** Copyright © Nokelsberg/Liaison; **510** *center left* Robyn Beeche with permission of Conran Octopus; *bottom right* Copyright © J. C. Carton/Bruce Coleman, Inc.; **511** *top to bottom* Copyright © Siegfried Tauquer/Leo de Wys, Inc.; Copyright © Black Star; Copyright © 1987 James Nachtwey/Magnum Photos; Photograph by Marilyn Silverstone; **514** Copyright © 1995 Yamamoto Munesuke/Black Star; **516** Copyright © 1984 P. Jordan/Gamma-Liaison; **517** Copyright © Black Star; **519** Copyright © Laurent Rebours/AP/Wide World Photos; **521** *top, bottom* The Granger Collection, New York; **522** Copyright © Gamma; **524** *left* AP/Wide World Photos; *right* United Press International; **525** AP/Wide World Photos; **526** UPI/Corbis-Bettmann.

Chapter 19

528 AP/Wide World Photos; **529** *bottom left* Copyright © Lee/Archive Photos; **top right** Copyright © 1988 Carlos Humberto TDC/Contact Press Images/PNI; **530** Copyright © 1989 Alon Reininger/Contact Press Images/PNI; *inset* Reuters/Corbis-Bettmann; **533** Corbis; **534** Copyright © Scott Sady/AP/Wide World Photos; **535** AP/Wide World Photos; **536** AP/Wide World Photos; **537** Copyright © Archive Photos; **539** Copyright © J. R. Holland/SuperStock/PNI; **540** Copyright © Mark Peters/Sipa Press; **541** Copyright © 1991 Peter Turnley/Black Star/PNI; **542** Sovfoto; **543** Copyright © 1985 W. Laski/Black Star/PNI; **544** Andreas Altwein Archiv/dpa; **545** AP/Wide World Photos; **546** Copyright © 1993 Peter Turnley/Newsweek/Black Star/PNI; **547** Copyright © 1992 Alexandra Avakian/Contact Press Images/PNI;

Art and Photography Credits (Cont.)

549 Copyright © Rikard Larma/AP/Wide World Photos; **552** New China Pictures/Eastfoto; **553** AP/Wide World Photos; **554** *top* Eastfoto; *center* Dominis/*Life* magazine. Copyright © Time, Inc.; *bottom* Copyright © Jeff Widener/AP/Wide World Photos; **555** Copyright © Vincent Yu/AP/Wide World Photos; **556** Copyright © 1989 Alon Reininger/Contact Press Images/PNI; **557** Tony Auth, *Philadelphia Inquirer.* Copyright © 1989. Reprinted with permission of Universal Press Syndicate. All rights reserved.

Chapter 20

558 *top* Copyright © Kevin Schafer/Tony Stone Images; *bottom* AP/Wide World Photos; **559** *top* Agence France Presse/Corbis-Bettmann; *bottom* Copyright © Gary John Norman/Tony Stone Images; **560** Copyright © Imtek Imagineering/Masterfile; **561** NASA; **563** Courtesy of National Center for Supercomputing Applications, University of Illinois, Urbana; **564** Copyright © 1994 Dan McCoy/R. Landridge/Rainbow/UCSF/PNI; **565** *left* Copyright © 1995 Culver Pictures/PNI; *right* Copyright © Kevin Horan/PNI; **567** Copyright © 1997 Ron Kimball; **570** Copyright © Ahn Young-joon/AP/Wide World Photos; **571** Copyright © Jim Morin. Reprinted with special permission of King Features Syndicate, Inc.; **572** Copyright © Scott Daniel Peterson/Gamma-Liaison; **573** Copyright © Reuters/Zoraida Diaz/Archive Photos; **575** *left* Howard Sochurek/*Life* magazine. Copyright © Time, Inc.; *right* Copyright © 1992 Richard Falco/PNI; **576** Copyright © Hans Deryk/AP/Wide World Photos; **577** Copyright © Steve McCurry/Magnum Photos/PNI; **578** *left* Copyright © Archive Photos/PNI; *right* Copyright © Dominique Berretty/Black Star/PNI; 579 top right Copyright © 1991 Robert Holmes/PNI; *bottom center* Copyright © Jason Lauré; **581** Copyright © 1995 Sally Wiener Grotta/The Stock Market.

EPILOGUE

584 Copyright © Laurent Rebours/AP/Wide World Photos; **584–585** *background* Copyright © Imtek Imagineering/Masterfile; **585** *top* Copyright © Matt Bradley/Heifer Project International; *bottom* Copyright © Hidajet Delic/AP/Wide World Photos; **586** Copyright © Bob Daemmrich/Stock Boston/PNI; **587** Copyright © Karen Stallwood, *Dallas Morning News*/AP/Wide World Photos; **589** Copyright © Sung Park, *Austin American-Statesman*/AP/Wide World Photos; **590** Copyright © Dan McCoy/Rainbow; **591** Copyright © Ron Dirito/Sygma; **592** Copyright © 1985 Abbas/Magnum Photos; **593** Reuters/Corbis-Bettmann; **594** Copyright © Ron Levy/Gamma-Liaison; **596** Copyright © Jean-Michel Turpin/Gamma-Liaison; **597** Copyright © 1985 Rene Burri/Magnum Photos; **602** Copyright © Charles Loviny/Gamma-Liaison; **604** Copyright © Will Yurman/Gamma-Liaison; **605** Copyright © L. Gilbert/Sygma; **606** *left, right* AP/Wide World Photos; **607** *left* Copyright © 1992 P. J. Griffiths/Magnum Photos; *center* Copyright © Daniel Muzio/AP/Wide World Photos; *right* Copyright © Srdjan Ilic/AP/Wide World Photos; **608** Reuters/Muzammil Pasha/Archive Photos.

WORLD RELIGIONS

614 Copyright © SuperStock; **615** *top left* Copyright © David Hanson/Tony Stone Images; *bottom left* Oriental Museum, Durham University, England/Bridgeman Art Library, London; *top right* The Hutchison Library; *bottom right* MS Sansk 87r. Copyright © Bodleian Library, Oxford, U.K.; **616** Copyright © Rene Sheret/Tony Stone Images; **617** *top left* Copyright © 1990 Gabe Palmer/The Stock Market; *bottom left* Riverside Book and Bible House, Iowa Falls, Iowa. Style No. 220DN. Photo by Sharon Hoogstraten; *center right* Copyright © Haroldo de Faria Castro/FPG International; **618** Copyright © George Hunter/Tony Stone Images; **619** *top left* Copyright © Anthony Cassidy/Tony Stone Images; *center* Robyn Beeche with permission of Conran Octopus; *bottom left* Copyright © Bipinchandra Mistry; *bottom right* National Museum of India, New Delhi; **620** Copyright © Peter Sanders; **621** *top left* Copyright © Nabeel Turner/Tony Stone Images; *center right* Copyright © Carlos Freire/The Hutchison Library; *bottom left* From *Traditional Textiles of Central Asia* by Janet Harvey. Copyright © 1996 Thames and Hudson Ltd., London. Reproduced by permission of the publishers; *bottom right* By permission of Princeton University Press. Photo by Sharon Hoogstraten; **622** Copyright © Zev Radovan; **623** *center left* Copyright © 1989 Joseph Nettis/Stock Boston; *bottom left* Copyright © Impact Photos; *top right* Copyright © Paul Chesley/Tony Stone Images; *bottom right* Copyright © Zev Radovan; **625** *top left* Copyright © Keren Su/Pacific Stock; *center* Copyright © Orion Press/Pacific Stock; *bottom left* From *The Analects of Confucius,* edited by Chichung Huang. Copyright © 1997 by Chichung Huang. Used by permission of Oxford University Press, Inc.

MINI ALMANAC

644 *graph background (earthquakes)* Image copyright © 1997 PhotoDisc, Inc.; **645** *graph backgrounds (seas, deserts, storms and floods)* Images copyright © 1997 PhotoDisc, Inc.; **647** *graph backgrounds (bridges, structures)* Copyright © Sense Interactive Multimedia.

SKILLBUILDER HANDBOOK

667 *left, La maraîchère* [Woman of the French Revolution], Jacques Louis David. Musée des Beaux-Arts, Lyon, France/Giraudon/Art Resource, New York; *right, Marie Antoinette,* Jacques Gautier d'Agoty. Château, Versailles, France/Giraudon/Art Resource, New York; **670** *Taille: impots et corvées* (late-18th-century engraving). Musée de la Ville de Paris, Musée Carnavalet, Paris/Giraudon/Art Resource, New York; **672** *frame* Netscape Communications Corporation has not authorized, sponsored, or endorsed, or approved this publication and is not responsible for its content. Netscape and the Netscape Communications corporate logos are trademarks and trade names of Netscape Communications Corporation. All other product names and/or logos are trademarks of their respective owners.